THE NEW INTERNATIONAL
GREEK TESTAMENT COMMENTARY

Editors
I. Howard Marshall
and
Donald A. Hagner

THE SECOND EPISTLE TO THE
CORINTHIANS

The Second Epistle to the
CORINTHIANS

A Commentary on the
Greek Text

by

MURRAY J. HARRIS

WILLIAM B. EERDMANS PUBLISHING COMPANY
GRAND RAPIDS, MICHIGAN

PATERNOSTER
MILTON KEYNES

Published jointly 2005
in the United States of America by
Wm. B. Eerdmans Publishing Co.
255 Jefferson Ave. S.E., Grand Rapids, Michigan 49503
www.eerdmans.com
and in the U.K. by
Paternoster Press
an imprint of Authentic Media
9 Holdom Avenue, Bletchley, Milton Keynes, Bucks., MK1 1QR, UK
www.authenticmedia.co.uk

Printed in the United States of America

10 09 08 07 06 05   7 6 5 4 3 2 1

Library of Congress Cataloging-in-Publication Data

Eerdmans ISBN 0-8028-2393-3

British Library Cataloguing in Publication Data

A library record for this book is available from the British Library.
Paternoster ISBN 0-85364-580-9

*Me fateri non pudet multo
obscuriorem esse hanc epistulam
quam multas alias*

J. S. Semler

In grateful memory of
KENNETH S. KANTZER
mentor, colleague, friend

Contents

COMMENTARY

CONTENTS

Foreword

Although there have been many series of commentaries on the English text of the New Testament in recent years, very few attempts have been made to cater particularly to the needs of students of the Greek text. The present initiative to fill this gap by the publication of the New International Greek Testament Commentary is very largely due to the vision of W. Ward Gasque, who was one of the original editors of the series. At a time when the study of Greek is being curtailed in many schools of theology, we hope that the NIGTC will demonstrate the continuing value of studying the Greek New Testament and will be an impetus in the revival of such study.

The volumes of the NIGTC are for students who want something less technical than a full-scale critical commentary. At the same time, the commentaries are intended to interact with modern scholarship and to make their own scholarly contribution to the study of the New Testament. The wealth of detailed study of the New Testament in articles and monographs continues without interruption, and the series is meant to harvest the results of this research in an easily accessible form. The commentaries include, therefore, extensive bibliographies and attempt to treat all important problems of history, exegesis, and interpretation that arise from the New Testament text.

One of the gains of recent scholarship has been the recognition of the primarily theological character of the books of the New Testament. The volumes of the NIGTC attempt to provide a theological understanding of the text, based on historical-critical-linguistic exegesis. It is not their primary aim to apply and expound the text for modern readers, although it is hoped that the exegesis will give some indication of the way in which the text should be expounded.

Within the limits set by the use of the English language, the series aims to be international in character, though the contributors have been chosen not primarily in order to achieve a spread between different countries but above all because of their specialized qualifications for their particular tasks.

The supreme aim of this series is to serve those who are engaged in the ministry of the Word of God and thus to glorify God's name. Our prayer is that it may be found helpful in this task.

I. HOWARD MARSHALL
DONALD A. HAGNER

Preface

New series of commentaries on the New Testament, not to speak of individual commentaries, are now appearing at such a rate that it has become incumbent on authors to indicate in what ways they believe their commentaries make a distinctive contribution to New Testament studies. What follows is my own understanding of the distinctives of the present work. Whether they in any sense constitute strengths is for others to decide.

1. It is not often that someone has the opportunity to write two commentaries on the same New Testament book. But, strangely, there are several examples of this with regard to 2 Corinthians. We have the work of C. F. Georg Heinrici (1883 and 1887), James Denney (1894, 1903), Alfred Plummer (1903 and 1915), Adolf Schlatter (1909 and 1934), Margaret E. Thrall (1965 and 1994/2000), Maurice Carrez (1983, 1985, and 1986), and Paul W. Barnett (1988 and 1997). In my case, it has been interesting to compare what I wrote in 1976 for the *Expositor's Bible Commentary* with the conclusions reached about twenty-five years later as a result of even closer examination of the Greek text. In general, my conclusions in broad matters of criticism and exegesis have remained unchanged, although in many points of exegetical detail there are differences between the two commentaries. I am now inclined to defend the integrity of the canonical 2 Corinthians with even more confidence and have been interested to observe how many commentators during the last seven or eight years have come to a similar conclusion about the letter's integrity (Witherington, Belleville, Kistemaker, Barnett, Scott, Lambrecht, Garland, Hafemann). What is offered here, then, is a defense of the integrity of 2 Corinthians in the context of a detailed exegesis of the Greek text.

2. One of the aims of the New International Greek Testament Commentary series is "to cater particularly to the needs of students of the Greek text" (from the Editors' Foreword). This being so, no apology is needed for the close attention I give to matters of grammar, syntax, and textual criticism. So often these are the issues that cause most frustration to those who are grappling with the Greek text. It is an insidious temptation for commentators to hurry on past grammatical or syntactical questions to "more substantial" issues of history or theology, content simply to give references to the "authorities" without patiently analyzing the competing exegetical options. I have endeavored resolutely to resist that temptation. We must never forget the time-honored dictum

that at root Christian theology is grammar applied to the biblical text; Scripture cannot be understood theologically unless it has first been understood grammatically. As for textual criticism, I have commented on all the variants given in the twenty-seventh edition of the Nestle-Aland Greek text, seeking, where appropriate, to give the reasoning behind the readings I prefer.

In keeping with the aims of the series, I have not treated the history of the interpretation (or "the history of the effect" or "textual posthistory") of 2 Corinthians or of various verses or passages that have been influential down through the Christian centuries. Other commentators and authors of specific studies have attempted that daunting task. But it should be noted that we now have accessible in convenient and handsome form volume VII (edited by Gerald Bray; Downers Grove: InterVarsity, 1999) of the *Ancient Christian Commentary on Scripture* (general editor, Thomas C. Oden), which provides a selection of exegetical and theological comments on 1 and 2 Corinthians (arranged by verse) from early Christian writers spanning the period from the end of the New Testament era down to A.D. 750.

3. People in the English-speaking world have an extraordinarily rich heritage in the English translations of the New Testament. I have sought to expose the reader to some of the older versions without ignoring the standard modern translations. Each translation has its distinctive features, and no one translation captures 100% of the text's meaning all of the time. If each captures, say 95%, it is a *distinctive* 95% that is captured, so perhaps there is, after all, room for the plethora of English versions that form our heritage. Some of the older translations — I am thinking especially of the precise renderings of the committee that produced *The Twentieth Century New Testament* (1904) and the individual sparkle of the classicist R. F. Weymouth (1903), the polymath J. Moffatt (1913), and the papyrologist E. J. Goodspeed (1923) — deserve more attention than they commonly receive. In many ways Moffatt and Goodspeed anticipated the linguistic approach of *The Good News Bible* (1966).

A neglected aspect of the history of the English Bible is paraphrases that are based on the Greek text. (I am not referring to works such as *The Living Bible* that are paraphrases of an English translation.) Often the quickest way to determine how commentators construe a particular phrase or verse is to read their paraphrase, which will immediately indicate, for example, how a genitive or an aorist is understood. What is more, the flow of an author's argument is often best portrayed by means of a paraphrase. Suffice it to say that I have benefited from consulting, in particular, *An Expanded Paraphrase of the Epistles of Paul* (Exeter: Paternoster, 1965) by F. F. Bruce and the paraphrase found in A. Plummer's ICC commentary at the beginning of each of his sections. But the paraphrases of Stanley, Isaacs, Wand, and Phillips are also always worth reading. So, in addition to giving a translation of the text, section by section, I offer (in an Appendix) my own paraphrase as a convenient and quick way for the reader to discover how I have understood a verse or passage and the flow of Paul's argument. Following Bruce's lead, I refer to my effort as an "expanded paraphrase" because as well as spelling out certain nuances of the Greek text it-self, I have sometimes supplied words or phrases that, while not representing anything in the Greek text, are implied by the text or are necessary or helpful for understanding Paul's movement of thought.

4. The suggested "Chronology of the Relations of Paul, Timothy, and Ti-tus with the Corinthian Church" (Introduction C) aims to provide a useful "time line," a documented and dated sequence of events that will enable the reader to see at a glance my position on various issues of criticism and dating.

5. The reader will notice that disproportionate space has been given to the exegesis of 1:8-11 and 5:1-10. 5:1-10 and 5:16-21 are among the most theologi-cally important sections of 2 Corinthians, one passage dealing with the signifi-cance of the death of the Christian, the other with the nature and consequences of the death of Christ. 5:1-10 is probably the most contested section of the let-ter. As it happens, it was the focus of my 1970 doctoral thesis at the University of Manchester, in which I explored the close relation of 1:8-11 and 5:1-10 in some detail. More recently A. E. Harvey has argued (in *Renewal through Suf-fering* [Edinburgh: Clark, 1996]) for a correlation between this Asian crisis (1:8-11) and Paul's view of the positive value of suffering, especially as seen in 2 Corinthians 4–5. The one excursus in my commentary deals with Paul's expe-rience in Asia and needs to be read in conjunction with the exegesis of 5:1-10. This experience turned out, I believe, to be influential in Paul's life in that it compelled him to give up his persistent self-reliance (1:9) and in his theological outlook in that it forced him to surrender his expectation, although not his hope, of being alive at the parousia of Christ and prompted him to formulate his view of the significance of physical death for the believer (5:1-10). Also, this dra-matic encounter with death in Asia may account for the apostle's unparalleled preoccupation in 2 Corinthians with his own physical state and with dying and death.

In the view of the author, then, these are the five distinctive features of the present commentary. On more specific matters, when referring to Bauer-Arndt-Gingrich-Danker (BAGD) I have used the 1979 second English edition because most readers of the commentary will have been using the second edi-tion and not all will have access to the third edition (2000) and also because the writing of the commentary was too far advanced when the new edition ap-peared to change multitudes of page numbers and quadrant indicators. Refer-ences to BAGD and to Moulton-Milligan's *Vocabulary* (but not to the Liddell-Scott-Jones *Lexicon*) are given by page number and quadrant on the page, *a* in-dicating the upper half and *b* the lower half of the left-hand column, and *c* and *d* the upper and lower halves of the right-hand column. When references to these two authorities are given, the verse under consideration is actually cited there as an instance of the particular meaning or construction. Otherwise, the word and section are referred to (e.g., BAGD 287 s.v. [ἐπί] II.1.b.d.). The abbreviation cf. indicates that a similar but not identical point is made or translation given by the authority cited. I have chosen to supply references to the Blass-Debrunner-

Funk *Grammar* (1961) rather than to the new German edition of Blass-Debrunner-Rehkopf (1984[16]), given the likely readership of this commentary. Some may wonder why references are given to M. Zerwick's *Analysis Philologica Novi Testamenti Graeci* (Rome: Pontifical Biblical Institute, 1966[3]) when a translation is available (M. Zerwick and H. Grosvenor, *A Grammatical Analysis of the Greek New Testament* [Rome: Pontifical Biblical Institute, 1988[3]]). In fact, the Latin original contains material not appearing in the English translation and sometimes differing from it. Translations of ancient sources and of excerpts from commentaries or works in languages other than English are mine.

For considerations of length I decided not to deal with the history and archaeology of Roman Corinth, given the ready availability of fine treatments of these topics.[1]

Bibliographies on 2 Corinthians may be found in R. Bieringer and J. Lambrecht, *Studies in 2 Corinthians,* BETL 112 (Leuven: Leuven University, 1994) 3-66 (by R. Bieringer), up to 1992-93, and in W. E. Mills, *2 Corinthians,* Bibliographies for Biblical Research, New Testament Series 8 (Lewiston/Queenstown/Lampeter: Mellen Biblical, 1977), up to 1996-97.

MURRAY J. HARRIS
March 2003

---

1. See, e.g., J. R. Wiseman, "Corinth and Rome I: 228 B.C.–A.D. 267," in *ANRW* II.7/1, 438-548; J. R. Wiseman, *The Land of the Ancient Corinthians,* Studies in the Mediterranean Archaeology 50 (Göteborg: Åströms, 1978); D. Engels, *Roman Corinth: An Alternative Model for the Classical City* (Chicago: University of Chicago, 1990); J. Murphy-O'Connor, *St. Paul's Corinth: Texts and Archaeology* (Wilmington: Glazier, 1983); and on the social setting of first-century Corinth, T. B. Savage, *Power through Weakness: Paul's Understanding of the Christian Ministry in 2 Corinthians* (Cambridge: Cambridge University, 1996) 19-53.

Acknowledgments

Numbers of my students in the United States have helped me at various stages with typing or with bibliographical or translational data — David Burdett, Jay Phelan, Bob Flayhart, Paul Winters, Steve Dutton, Jon Gutierrez, Dana Anderson, Paul Cheung, Sam Lamerson, Don Aguilo, Steve Chang, David Jones, Jae Noh, Jim Sweeney, Michael Van Laningham, Andrew Emmert, and David Miller. More recently, here in New Zealand, Mrs. Bev Heydenrych, Ms. Frankie Dean, and Mrs. Keren Brewerton have rendered sterling service in typing the second half of the commentary and changes in the first half. To each of these kind friends my warm thanks. Also, I am grateful to the trustees of the Longview, Lichfield, and Hillview Trusts for grants toward typing costs.

Permission was kindly given by Dr. Stanley N. Gundry of Zondervan Publishing House to reproduce (with some minor changes) the Outline of the Epistle and to use other material found in the author's earlier commentary on 2 Corinthians in *The Expositor's Bible Commentary,* volume 10, ed. F. E. Gaebelein (Grand Rapids: Zondervan, 1976) 299-406. Also, Dr. Bruce W. Winter, editor of the *Tyndale Bulletin,* graciously gave permission for the use in an excursus of parts of my article "2 Corinthians 5:1-10: Watershed in Paul's Eschatology?" *TynB* 22 (1971) 32-57. In the "Summary of the Theology of 2 Corinthians" (Introduction, E.) I have used, with permission, some material first published in my article on "2 Corinthians" in the *New Dictionary of Biblical Theology,* ed. T. D. Alexander and B. S. Rosner (Downers Grove: InterVarsity, 2000) 306-11.

For over two decades my appreciation of the apostle Paul was enriched by the comments and questions of students at Trinity Evangelical Divinity School in my classes on the Corinthian correspondence and the Greek text of 2 Corinthians. Nor can I ever forget the kindness of Dr. Kenneth S. Kantzer, formerly Academic Dean of that Divinity School, who recognized some potential in a young Kiwi teacher from "Down Under" and encouraged and challenged me over many years. I am pleased that I was able to give him a copy of these acknowledgements before his final illness and death, for to him this commentary is dedicated.

To the two editors of the series, Professors I. Howard Marshall and Donald A. Hagner, I express my gratitude for their careful reading of the typescript, their helpful suggestions, and their constant encouragement. The series editor at Eerdmans, Dr. John W. Simpson, Jr., has again demonstrated his technical expertise by guiding yet another sizeable manuscript through the production process.

To my wife, Jennifer, I am indebted for her gracious and unfailing support during this apparently interminable project and for her help in preparing the indexes.

Abbreviations

AB	Anchor Bible
ABD	*The Anchor Bible Dictionary,* ed. D. N. Freedman (6 vols.; New York: Doubleday, 1992)
ABR	*Australian Biblical Review*
ACNT	Augsburg Commentaries on the New Testament
AGJU	Arbeiten zur Geschichte des antiken Judentums und des Urchristentums
AJA	*American Journal of Archaeology*
AJP	*American Journal of Philology*
AJT	*American Journal of Theology*
AnBib	Analecta Biblica
ANRW	*Aufstieg und Niedergang der römischen Welt,* ed. H. Temporini and W. Haase (Berlin)
ARSHLL	Acta Reg. Societatis Humaniorum Litterarum Ludensis
ASNU	Acta seminarii neotestamentici upsaliensis
AsSeign	*Assemblées du Seigneur*
ASV	American Standard Version
ATANT	Abhandlungen zur Theologie des Alten und Neuen Testaments
ATR	*Anglican Theological Review*
AUSS	*Andrews University Seminary Studies*
BA	*Biblical Archaeologist*
BAGD	W. Bauer, *A Greek-English Lexicon of the New Testament and Other Early Christian Literature,* ed. W. F. Arndt, F. W. Gingrich, and F. W. Danker (Chicago: University of Chicago, 1979)
BAR	*Biblical Archaeologist Review*
BBB	Bonner biblische Beiträge
BBR	*Bulletin of Biblical Research*
BDB	F. Brown, S. R. Driver, and C. A. Briggs, *A Hebrew and English Lexicon of the Old Testament* (Oxford: Clarendon, 1953)
BDF	F. Blass, A. Debrunner, and R. W. Funk, *A Greek Grammar of the New Testament* (Chicago: University of Chicago, 1961)
BDR	F. Blass and A. Debrunner, *Grammatik des Neutestamentlichen Griechisch,* ed. F. Rehkopf (Göttingen: Vandenhoeck und Ruprecht, 1984[16])
BET	Beiträge zur evangelischen Theologie
BETL	Bibliotheca Ephemeridum Theologicarum Lovaniensium
BFCT	Beiträge zur Förderung christlicher Theologie
BGBE	*Beiträge zur Geschichte der biblischen Exegese*

BGU	*Berliner Griechische Urkunden*
BHT	Beiträge zur historischen Theologie
Bib	*Biblica*
BibLeb	*Bibel und Leben*
BibS(N)	Biblische Studien (Neukirchen)
BJRL	*Bulletin of the John Rylands Library*
BJRUL	*Bulletin of the John Rylands University Library*
BK	*Bibel und Kirche*
BLE	*Bulletin de littérature ecclésiastique*
BNTC	Black's New Testament Commentary
BR	*Biblical Research*
BRev	*Bible Review*
BS	Biblische Studien
BSac	*Bibliotheca Sacra*
BT	*Bible Translator*
BTB	*Biblical Theology Bulletin*
BTS	*Bible et terre sainte*
BU	Biblische Untersuchungen
BZ	*Biblische Zeitschrift*
BZNW	Beihefte zur *ZNW*
CAH	*Cambridge Ancient History*
CBQ	*Catholic Biblical Quarterly*
CBQMS	Catholic Biblical Quarterly Monograph Studies
CEV	Contemporary English Version
CGT	Cambridge Greek Testament
CGTC	*Cambridge Greek Testament Commentary*
ChicStud	*Chicago Studies*
CIG	*Corpus Inscriptione Graecarum*
CJ	*Concordia Journal*
ClerRev	*Clergy Review*
CNT	Commentaire du Nouveau Testament
ConJ	*Coniectanea*
ConNT	Coniectanea Neotestamentica
CRBS	*Currents in Research: Biblical Studies*
CrQ	*Crozier Quarterly*
CTM	*Concordia Theological Monthly*
CTR	*Criswell Theological Review*
CurTM	*Currents in Theology and Mission*
DPL	*Dictionary of Paul and His Letters,* ed. G. F. Hawthorne et al. (Downers Grove/Leicester: InterVarsity, 1993)
DSS	Dead Sea Scrolls
EB	*Encyclopaedia Biblica,* ed. T. K. Cheyne and J. S. Black (4 vols.; London: Macmillan, 1899-1903)
Ébib	Études bibliques
EDNT	*Exegetical Dictionary of the New Testament,* ed. H. Balz and G. Schneider (3 vols.; Grand Rapids: Eerdmans, 1990-93)
EGGNT	Exegetical Guide to the Greek New Testament

EGT	W. R. Nicoll (ed.), *The Expositor's Greek Testament,* 5 vols. (reprinted Grand Rapids: Eerdmans, 1970 [= 1907-10 original])
EQ	*Evangelical Quarterly*
ETL	*Ephemerides Theologicae Lovanienses*
ETR	*Études théologiques et religieuses*
ETr	English translation
EvT	*Evangelische Theologie*
EVV	English Versions
Exp	*Expositor*
ExpT	*Expository Times*
FN	*Filologia Neotestamentaria*
FRLANT	Forschungen zur Religion und Literatur des Alten und Neuen Testaments
FS	Festschrift
FZB	Forschung zur Bibel
GNB	Good News Bible
GNS	*Good News Studies*
GTA	Göttinger theologischer Arbeiten
GTJ	*Grace Theological Journal*
GTS	Grundriss des Theologiestudiums
GuL	*Geist und Leben*
HBT	*Horizons in Biblical Theology*
HDB	*A Dictionary of the Bible,* ed. J. Hastings (5 vols.; Edinburgh: Clark, 1899-1904)
Herm	*Hermanthena*
HM	Hallische Monographien
HNT	Handbuch zum Neuen Testament
HNTC	Harper's New Testament Commentaries
HTR	*Harvard Theological Review*
HUT	Hermeneutische Untersuchungen zur Theologie
IB	*Interpreter's Bible*
IBS	*Irish Biblical Studies*
ICC	International Critical Commentary
IDB	*Interpreter's Dictionary of the Bible,* ed. G. A. Buttrick (5 vols.; Nashville: Abingdon, 1962-76)
Int	*Interpretation*
ISBE[2]	G. W. Bromiley et al. (eds.), *The International Standard Bible Encyclopedia* (4 vols., 2nd ed.; Grand Rapids: Eerdmans, 1979-88)
ITQ	*Irish Theological Quarterly*
JAC	*Jahrbuch für Antike und Christentum*
JAOS	*Journal of the American Oriental Society*
JB	Jerusalem Bible
JBL	*Journal of Biblical Literature*
JBR	*Journal of Bible and Religion*
JETS	*Journal of the Evangelical Theological Society*
JJS	*Journal of Jewish Studies*
JPT	*Journal of Pentecostal Theology*
JR	*Journal of Religion*

JSNT	*Journal for the Study of the New Testament*
JSNTSS	*JSNT* Supplement Series
JSOT	*Journal for the Study of the Old Testament*
JSS	*Journal of Semitic Studies*
JTS	*Journal of Theological Studies*
KD	*Kerygma und Dogma*
KEK	Kritisch-exegetischer Kommentar über das Neue Testament
KJV	King James Version (= Authorized Version)
KNT	Kommentar zum Neuen Testament
κτλ.	καὶ τὰ λοιπά (and the rest)
LEH	J. Lust, E. Eynikel, and K. Hauspie, *A Greek-English Lexicon of the Septuagint* (2 vols.; Stuttgart: Deutsche Bibelgesellschaft, 1992, 1996)
LingB	*Linguistica Biblica*
LouvStud	*Louvain Studies*
LQ	*Lutheran Quarterly*
LSJ	H. G. Liddell and R. Scott, *A Greek-English Lexicon,* rev. H. S. Jones (Oxford: Clarendon, 1940^9; with supplement, 1968)
LXX	Septuagint
mg	margin
MM	J. H. Moulton and G. Milligan, *The Vocabulary of the Greek Testament* (London: Hodder, 1930; reprinted Grand Rapids: Eerdmans, 1972)
MNTC	Moffatt New Testament Commentary
MS(S)	Manuscript(s)
MT	Masoretic text
n(n).	note(s)
NA	*Novum Testamentum Graece,* ed. Eberhard Nestle, Erwin Nestle, Kurt Aland, and Barbara Aland (various editions; London: United Bible Societies)
NAB^1	New American Bible
NAB^2	New American Bible: Revised New Testament
NAC	New American Commentary
NASB	New American Standard Bible
NBD	*New Bible Dictionary,* ed. J. D. Douglas et al. (Leicester: Inter-Varsity/ Wheaton: Tyndale, 1982^2)
NCB(C)	New Century Bible (Commentary)
NEASB	*Near Eastern Archaeological Society Bulletin*
NEB	New English Bible
Neot	*Neotestamentica*
NewB	*New Blackfriars*
NICNT	New International Commentary on the New Testament
NIDNTT	C. Brown (ed.), *The New International Dictionary of New Testament Theology* (3 vols.; Grand Rapids: Zondervan/Exeter: Paternoster, 1975-78)
NIGTC	New International Greek Testament Commentary
NIV	New International Version
NJB	New Jerusalem Bible
NKZ	*Neue kirchliche Zeitschrift*
NLT	New Living Translation of the Bible

NovT	*Novum Testamentum*
NovTSup	*NovT* Supplements
NRSV	New Revised Standard Version
NRT	*Nouvelle revue théologique*
NT	New Testament
NTA	*New Testament Abstracts*
NTAbh	Neutestamentliche Abhandlungen
NTD	Das Neue Testament Deutsch
NTOA	Novum Testamentum et Orbis Antiquus
NTS	*New Testament Studies*
NTTS	New Testament Tools and Studies
Numen	*Numen: International Review for the History of Religion*
OCD	N. G. L. Hammond and H. H. Scullard (eds.), *Oxford Classical Dictionary* (Oxford: Clarendon, 1970)
OGIS	*Orientis Graeci Inscriptiones Selectae,* ed. W. Dittenberger (3 vols.; 1903, 1905)
OT	Old Testament
OTP	*Old Testament Pseudepigrapha,* ed. J. H. Charlesworth, 2 vols. (New York: Doubleday, 1983)
PGL	*Patristic Greek Lexicon,* ed. G. W. H. Lampe (Oxford: Clarendon, 1961)
PIBA	*Proceedings of the Irish Biblical Association*
P. Oxy.	Oxyrhynchus Papyrus/Papyri
PTMS	Pittsburgh Theological Monograph Series
PTR	*Princeton Theological Review*
RB	*Revue biblique*
REB	Revised English Bible (1990)
RechBib	*Recherches bibliques*
RestQ	*Restoration Quarterly*
RevExp	*Review and Expositor*
RevQ	*Revue de Qumran*
RevScRel	*Revue de sciences religieuses*
RGG	*Religion in Geschichte und Gegenwart*
RHPR	*Revue d'histoire et de philosophie religieuses*
RivB	*Revista biblica*
RNT	Regensburger Neues Testament
RSPT	*Revue des sciences philosophiques et théologiques*
RSR	*Recherches de science religieuse*
RSV	Revised Standard Version
RTP	*Revue de théologie et de philosophie*
RTR	*Reformed Theological Review*
RV	Revised Version
SANT	Studien zum Alten und Neuen Testament
SB	H. L. Strack and P. Billerbeck, *Kommentar zum Neuen Testament aus Talmud und Midrasch* (4 vols.; Munich: Beck, 1922-28)
SBL	Society of Biblical Literature
SBLDS	Society of Biblical Literature Dissertation Series
SBLSBS	Society of Biblical Literature Sources for Biblical Study
SBT	Studies in Biblical Theology

ScEs	*Science et esprit*
SCHNT	Studia ad corpus hellenisticum Novi Testamenti
SciEccl	*Sciences ecclésiastiques*
SD	Studies and Documents
SE	*Studia Evangelica*
SEÅSup	Svensk exegetisk årsbok Supplements
SJT	*Scottish Journal of Theology*
SNT	Studien zum Neuen Testament
SNTSMS	Society for New Testament Studies Monograph Series
SNTU	Studien zum Neuen Testament und seiner Umwelt
SO	*Symbolae Osloenses*
SP	Sacra pagina
ST	*Studia Theologica*
StBibT	*Studia Biblica et Theologica*
SUNT	Studien zur Umwelt des Neuen Testaments
s.v.	*sub voce* (under the word)
SWJT	*Southwestern Journal of Theology*
TANZ	Texte und Arbeiten zum neutestamentlichen Zeitalter
TBC	Torch Bible Commentaries
TBl	*Theologische Blätter*
TBü	Theologische Bücherei
TCNT	Twentieth Century New Testament (1904)
TDNT	G. Kittel and G. Friedrich (eds.), *Theological Dictionary of the New Testament* (10 vols.; Grand Rapids: Eerdmans, 1964-76)
TDOT	G. J. Botterweck and H. Ringgren (eds.), *Theological Dictionary of the Old Testament* (14 vols. to date; Grand Rapids: Eerdmans, 1974-2004)
TF	*Theologische Forschung*
Th	*Theologica*
ThBeitr	*Theologische Beiträge*
Them	*Themelios*
Theol	*Theology*
THKNT	Theologische Handkommentar zum Neuen Testament
TLZ	*Theologische Literaturzeitung*
TPQ	*Theologisch-Praktische Quartalschrift*
TQ	*Theologische Quartalschrift*
TR	Received Text
TrinJ	*Trinity Journal*
TS	*Theological Studies*
TSK	*Theologische Studien und Kritiken*
TThQ	*Tübinger theologische Quartalschrift*
TToday	*Theology Today*
TU	Texte und Untersuchungen
TynB	*Tyndale Bulletin*
TZ	*Theologische Zeitschrift*
UBS	*The Greek New Testament,* ed. K. Aland et al. (New York/London: United Bible Societies, 1966[1], 1968[2], 1975[3], 1993[4])
UNT	Untersuchungen zum Neuen Testament
US	*Una Sancta*

ABBREVIATIONS

UUÅ	Uppsala Universitetsårskrift
VD	Verbum domini
v.l.	*varia lectio* (variant reading)
VoxEv	*Vox Evangelica*
WBC	Word Biblical Commentary
WC	Westminster Commentary
WH	B. F. Westcott and F. J. A. Hort, *The New Testament in the Original Greek,* vol. 1: *Text;* vol. 2: *Introduction, Appendix* (London: Macmillan, 1881)
WMANT	Wissenschaftliche Monographien zum Alten und Neuen Testament
WTJ	*Westminster Theological Journal*
WUNT	Wissenschaftliche Untersuchungen zum Neuen Testament
ZAW	*Zeitschrift für die alttestamentliche Wissenschaft*
ZKT	*Zeitschrift für katholische Theologie*
ZNW	*Zeitschrift für die neutestamentliche Wissenschaft*
ZPEB	M. C. Tenney and S. Barabas (eds.), *The Zondervan Pictorial Encyclopedia of the Bible* (5 vols.; Grand Rapids: Zondervan, 1975)
ZST	*Zeitschrift für systematische Theologie*
ZTK	*Zeitschrift für Theologie und Kirche*
ZWB	Zürcher Werkkommentare zur Bibel
ZWT	*Zeitschrift für wissenschaftliche Theologie*

Bibliography

Adams

E. Adams, *Constructing the World: A Study in Paul's Cosmological Language.* Edinburgh: Clark, 2000.

Aejmelaeus

L. Aejmelaeus, *Streit und Versöhnung. Das Problem der Zusammensetzung des 2. Korintherbriefes.* Helsinki: Finnish Exegetical Society, 1987.

Ahern

B. M. Ahern, "The Indwelling Spirit, Pledge of Our Inheritance (Eph. 1:14)," *CBQ* 9 (1947) 179-89.

Alexander

W. M. Alexander, "St. Paul's Infirmity," *ExpT* 10 (1904) 469-73, 545-48.

Alford

H. Alford, "ΠΡΟΣ ΚΟΡΙΝΘΙΟΥΣ Β.," in Alford's *Greek Testament: An Exegetical and Critical Commentary,* II. Grand Rapids: Guardian, 1976 reprint of 1877[7], pp. 627-723.

Allen

L. C. Allen, *Psalms 101–50.* WBC 21. Waco: Word, 1983.

Allo

E. B. Allo, *Saint Paul: seconde épître aux Corinthiens.* ÉBib. Paris: Gabalda, 1937 (the second edition of 1956 is merely a reprint of the first edition).

Allo, *Première épître*

E. B. Allo, *Saint Paul: première épître aux Corinthiens.* ÉBib. Paris: Gabalda, 1934.

Amador

J. D. H. Amador, "Revisiting 2 Corinthians: Rhetoric and the Case for Unity," *NTS* 46 (2000) 92-111.

Amstutz

J. Amstutz, ΆΠΛΟΤΗΣ. *Eine begriffsgeschichtliche Studie zum jüdisch-christlichen Griechisch.* Theophaneia 19. Bonn: Hanstein, 1968.

Andersen FS

Perspectives on Language and Text: Essays and Poems in Honor of Francis I. Andersen's Sixtieth Birthday. Ed. E. W. Conrad and E. G. Newing. Winona Lake: Eisenbrauns, 1987.

Andrews

S. B. Andrews, "Too Weak Not to Lead: The Form and Function of 2 Cor 11.23b-33," *NTS* 41 (1994-95) 263-76.

Andriessen

P. Andriessen, "L'impuissance de Paul en face de l'ange de Satan," *NRT* 81 (1959) 462-68.

Arai

S. Arai, "Zur Definition der Gnosis in Rücksicht auf die Frage nach ihrem Ursprung," in *The Origins of Gnosticism: Colloquium of Messina 13-18 April 1966. Text and Discussions.* Ed. U. Bianchi. Leiden: Brill, 1967, pp. 181-87.

Arai, "Gegner"

S. Arai, "Die Gegner des Paulus im 1. Korintherbrief und das Problem der Gnosis," *NTS* 19 (1972-73) 430-37.

Ascough

R. S. Ascough, "The Completion of a Religious Duty: The Background of 2 Cor 8.1-15," *NTS* 42 (1995-96) 584-99.

Aus

R. D. Aus, "Paul's Travel Plans to Spain and the 'Full Number of the Gentiles' of Rom. XI 25," *NovT* 21 (1979) 232-62.

Bachmann

P. Bachmann, *Der zweite Brief des Paulus an die Korinther.* Leipzig: Scholl, 1909 (later editions unavailable).

Badenas

R. Badenas, *Christ the End of the Law: Romans 10.4 in Pauline Perspective.* JSNTSS 10. Sheffield: JSOT, 1985.

Bahr

G. J. Bahr, "The Subscriptions in the Pauline Letters," *JBL* 87 (1968) 27-41.

Baillie

J. Baillie, *And the Life Everlasting.* London: Oxford University Press, 1934.

Bain

J. A. Bain, "2 Cor. iv.3-4," *ExpT* 18 (1906-07) 380.

Baird

W. Baird, "Visions, Revelation, and Ministry: Reflections on 2 Cor 12:1-5 and Gal 1:11-17," *JBL* 104 (1985) 651-62.

Baird, "Letters"

W. R. Baird, "Letters of Recommendation: A Study of II Cor. 3:1-3," *JBL* 80 (1961) 166-72.

Baker

W. R. Baker, "Did the Glory of Moses' Face Fade? A Reexamination of καταργέω in 2 Corinthians 3:7-18," *BBR* 10 (2000) 1-15.

Balch
> D. L. Balch, "Backgrounds of I Cor. VII: Sayings of the Lord in Q; Moses as an Ascetic ΘΕΙΟΣ ΑΝΗΡ in II Cor. III," *NTS* 18 (1971-72) 351-64.

Bammel FS
> *Suffering and Martyrdom in the New Testament.* Ed. W. Horbury and B. McNeil. Cambridge: Cambridge University Press, 1981.

Banks
> R. Banks, *Paul's Idea of Community: The Early House Churches in Their Historical Setting.* Grand Rapids: Eerdmans/Exeter: Paternoster, 1980.

Banks, "Walking"
> R. Banks, "'Walking' as a Metaphor of the Christian Life: The Origins of a Significant Pauline Usage," in *Andersen FS* 303-13.

Barclay
> W. Barclay, Translation in *The Daily Study Bible: The Letters to the Corinthians.* 2nd edition; Philadelphia: Westminster, 1975.

Barclay, *Flesh*
> W. Barclay, *Flesh and Spirit: An Examination of Galatians 5:19-23.* Nashville: Abingdon, 1962.

J. M. G. Barclay
> J. M. G. Barclay, "Mirror-Reading a Polemical Letter: Galatians as a Test Case," *JSNT* 31 (1987) 73-93.

Barnett
> P. Barnett, *The Second Epistle to the Corinthians.* Grand Rapids: Eerdmans, 1997.

Barnett, *Message*
> P. Barnett, *The Message of 2 Corinthians.* Leicester: Inter-Varsity, 1988.

Barnett, "Opposition"
> P. Barnett, "Opposition in Corinth," *JSNT* 22 (1984) 3-17.

A. E. Barnett
> A. E. Barnett, *Paul Becomes a Literary Influence.* Chicago: University of Chicago, 1941.

Barré
> M. L. Barré, "Paul as 'Eschatologic Person': A New Look at 2 Cor 11:29," *CBQ* 37 (1975) 500-26.

Barré, "Qumran"
> M. L. Barré, "Qumran and the 'Weakness' of Paul," *CBQ* 42 (1980) 216-27.

Barrett FS
> *Paul and Paulinism: Essays in Honour of C. K. Barrett.* Ed. M. D. Hooker and S. G. Wilson. London: SPCK, 1982.

Barrett
> C. K. Barrett, *A Commentary on the Second Epistle to the Corinthians.* New York: Harper/London: Black, 1973.

Barrett, *Adam*
C. K. Barrett, *From First Adam to Last: A Study in Pauline Theology.* London: Black, 1962.

Barrett, "Boasting"
C. K. Barrett, "Boasting (καυχᾶσθαι, κτλ.) in the Pauline Epistles," in Vanhoye (ed.) 363-68.

Barrett, "Cephas"
C. K. Barrett, "Cephas and Corinth," in *Michel FS* 1-12.

Barrett, "Christianity"
C. K. Barrett, "Christianity at Corinth," *BJRL* 46 (1964) 269-97. Reprinted in his *Essays* 1-27.

Barrett, "Council"
C. K. Barrett, "Apostles in Council and in Conflict," *ABR* 31 (1983) 14-32.

Barrett, "Eschatology"
C. K. Barrett, "New Testament Eschatology I: Jewish and Pauline Eschatology," *SJT* 6 (1953) 136-55.

Barrett, *Essays*
C. K. Barrett, *Essays on Paul.* Philadelphia: Westminster/London: SPCK, 1982.

Barrett, *1 Corinthians*
C. K. Barrett, *A Commentary on the First Epistle to the Corinthians.* HNTC. New York: Harper/London: Black, 1968.

Barrett, "Idols"
C. K. Barrett, "Things Sacrificed to Idols," *NTS* 11 (1964-65) 138-53.

Barrett, "Opponents"
C. K. Barrett, "Paul's Opponents in II Corinthians," *NTS* 17 (1970-71) 233-54. Reprinted in his *Essays* 60-86.

Barrett, *Paul*
C. K. Barrett, *Paul: An Introduction to His Thought.* Louisville: Westminster, 1994.

Barrett, "'Pillar' Apostles"
C. K. Barrett, "Paul and the 'Pillar' Apostles," in *de Zwaan FS* 1-19.

Barrett, "2 Cor. 11:13"
C. K. Barrett, "ΨΕΥΔΑΠΟΣΤΟΛΟΙ (2 Cor 11,13)," in *Rigaux FS* 377-96. Reprinted in his *Essays* 87-107.

Barrett, "2 Cor. 7:12"
C. K. Barrett, "Ὁ ΑΔΙΚΗΣΑΣ (2 Cor 7,12)," in *Stählin FS* 149-57. Reprinted in his *Essays* 108-17.

Barrett, "Shaliaḥ"
C. K. Barrett, "*Shaliaḥ* and Apostle," in *Daube FS* 88-102.

Barrett, *Signs*
C. K. Barrett, *The Signs of an Apostle.* London: Epworth, 1970/Philadelphia: Fortress, 1972.

Barrett, "Titus"
C. K. Barrett, "Titus," in *M. Black FS* (1) 1-14. Reprinted in his *Essays* 118-31.

Barth
M. Barth, *Ephesians.* 2 vols. AB 34. Garden City: Doubleday, 1974.

G. Barth
G. Barth, "Die Eignung des Verkündigers in 2 Kor 2,14–3,6," in *Bornkamm FS* 257-70.

Barton
S. C. Barton, "Paul's Sense of Place: An Anthropological Approach to Community Formation in Corinth," *NTS* 32 (1985-86) 225-46.

Bash
A. Bash, *Ambassadors for Christ.* WUNT 2/92. Tübingen: Mohr, 1997.

Bates
W. H. Bates, "The Integrity of II Corinthians," *NTS* 12 (1965-66) 56-69.

Batey
R. Batey, *New Testament Nuptial Imagery.* Leiden: Brill, 1971.

Batey, "Image"
R. Batey, "Paul's Bride Image: A Symbol of Realistic 'Eschatology,'" *Int* 17 (1963) 176-82.

Batey, "Interaction"
R. Batey, "Paul's Interaction with the Corinthians," *JBL* 84 (1966) 139-46.

Bauckham
R. J. Bauckham, "Weakness — Paul's and Ours," *Them* 7 (1982) 4-6.

Bauer
K. A. Bauer, *Leiblichkeit — das Ende aller Werke Gottes.* Gütersloh: Mohn, 1971.

Baumert
N. Baumert, *Täglich Sterben und Auferstehen. Der Literalsinn von 2 Kor 4,12–5,10.* SANT 34. Munich: Kösel, 1973.

Baumgarten
J. Baumgarten, *Paulus und die Apokalyptik. Die Auslegung apokalyptischer Überlieferung in den echten Paulusbriefen.* WMANT 44. Neukirchen-Vluyn: Neukirchener, 1975.

Baur
F. C. Baur, *Paul: His Life and Work.* 2 vols. ETr. London: Williams, 1875-76.

Beale
G. K. Beale, "The Old Testament Background of Reconciliation in 2 Corinthians 5–7 and Its Bearing on the Literary Problem of 2 Corinthians 6.14–7.1," *NTS* 35 (1989-90) 550-81.

Bean
G. E. Bean, *Aegean Turkey: An Archaeological Guide* (London: Benn, 1966).

Beare FS
    From Jesus to Paul: Studies in Honour of Francis Wright Beare. Ed. P. Richardson and J. C. Hurd. Waterloo: Wilfrid Laurier University, 1984.

Beasley-Murray FS
    Eschatology and the New Testament: Essays in Honor of George Raymond Beasley-Murray. Ed. W. H. Gloer. Peabody: Hendrickson, 1989.

Becker
    J. Becker, *Paul: Apostle to the Gentiles.* ETr. Louisville: Westminster, 1993.

Beet
    J. A. Beet, *II Corinthians.* London: Hodder, 1882.

Belleville
    L. L. Belleville, *2 Corinthians.* Downers Grove/Leicester: InterVarsity, 1996.

Belleville, "Discipleship"
    L. L. Belleville, "'Imitate Me, Just as I Imitate Christ': Discipleship in the Corinthian Correspondence," in *Patterns of Discipleship in the New Testament.* Ed. R. N. Longenecker. Grand Rapids: Eerdmans, 1996, pp. 120-42.

Belleville, "Gospel"
    L. L. Belleville, "Gospel and Kerygma in 2 Corinthians," in *Longenecker FS* 134-64.

Belleville, "Letter"
    L. L. Belleville, "A Letter of Apologetic Self-Commendation: 2 Cor. 1:8–7:16," *NovT* 31 (1989) 142-63.

Belleville, "Polemic"
    L. L. Belleville, "Paul's Polemic and the Theology of the Spirit in Second Corinthians," *CBQ* 58 (1996) 281-304.

Belleville, *Reflections*
    L. L. Belleville, *Reflections of Glory: Paul's Polemical Use of the Moses–Doxa Tradition in 2 Corinthians 3.1-18.* JSNTSS 52. Sheffield: Sheffield Academic, 1991.

Belleville, "Tradition"
    L. L. Belleville, "Tradition or Creation? Paul's Use of the Exodus 34 Tradition in 2 Corinthians 3.7-18," in Evans and Sanders 165-86.

Belser
    J. E. Belser, *Der zweite Brief des Apostels Paulus an die Korinther.* Freiburg: Herder, 1910.

Bengel
    J. A. Bengel, *Gnomon of the New Testament* III: *Romans, I and II Corinthians.* ETr. Edinburgh: Clark, 1863.

Benoit
    P. Benoit, "Qumrân et le Nouveau Testament," *NTS* 7 (1960-61) 276-96.

Berger

K. Berger, "Die impliziten Gegner. Zur Methode des Erschliessens von 'Gegnern' in neutestamentlichen Texten," in *Bornkamm FS* 373-400.

Berger, "Almosen"

K. Berger, "Almosen für Israel. Zum historischen Kontext der paulinischen Kollekte," *NTS* 23 (1976-77) 180-204.

Berger, "Apostelbrief"

K. Berger, "Apostelbrief und apostolische Rede. Zum Formular frühchristlicher Briefe," *ZNW* 65 (1974) 190-231.

Berkeley

The Holy Bible: The Berkeley Version in Modern English (G. Verkuyl translator of New Testament). Grand Rapids: Zondervan, 1959³.

Bernard

J. H. Bernard, "The Second Epistle to the Corinthians," in *EGT* 3.1-119.

Berry

R. Berry, "Death and Life in Christ: The Meaning of 2 Corinthians 5.1-10," in *SJT* 14 (1961) 60-76.

Best

E. Best, *Second Corinthians*. Atlanta: John Knox, 1987.

Best, *Body*

E. Best, *One Body in Christ*. London: SPCK, 1955.

Betz

H. D. Betz, *2 Corinthians 8 and 9: A Commentary on Two Administrative Letters of the Apostle Paul*. Ed. G. W. MacRae. Philadelphia: Fortress, 1985.

Betz, *Aufsätze*

H. D. Betz, *Gesammelte Aufsätze III. Paulinische Studien*. Tübingen: Mohr, 1994.

Betz, "Christus-Aretalogie"

H. D. Betz, "Eine Christus-Aretalogie bei Paulus (2 Kor 12,7-10)," *ZTK* 66 (1969) 288-305. Reprinted in his *Aufsätze* 1-19.

Betz, "Corinthians"

H. D. Betz, "Corinthians, Second Epistle to the," *ABD* 1.1148-54.

Betz, "De laude"

H. D. Betz, "De laude ipsius (Moralia 539A-547F)," in *Plutarch's Ethical Writings and Early Christian Literature*. Ed. H. D. Betz. Leiden: Brill, 1978, pp. 367-93.

Betz, "Fragment"

H. D. Betz, "2 Cor 6:14–7:1: An Anti-Pauline Fragment?" *JBL* 92 (1973) 88-108. Reprinted in his *Aufsätze* 20-45.

Betz, *Galatians*

H. D. Betz, *Galatians*. Hermeneia. Philadelphia: Fortress, 1979.

Betz, *Paulus*

H. D. Betz, *Der Apostel Paulus und die sokratische Tradition. Eine exegetische Untersuchung zu seiner "Apologie" 2 Korinther 10–13.* BHT 45. Tübingen: Mohr, 1972. Summarized in *Paul's Apology 2 Cor 10–13 and the Socratic Tradition.* Berkeley: Center for Hermeneutical Studies, 1970.

Betz, "Problem"

H. D. Betz, "The Problem of Rhetoric and Theology according to the Apostle Paul," in Vanhoye (ed.) 16-48.

O. Betz

O. Betz, "Fleischliche und 'geistliche' Christuserkenntnis nach 2. Korinther 5,16," *ThBeitr* 14 (1983) 167-79.

Beyschlag

W. Beyschlag, *New Testament Theology II.* ETr. Edinburgh: Clark, 1899².

Bieder

W. Bieder, "Paulus und seine Gegner in Korinth," *TZ* 17 (1961) 319-33.

Bieler

L. Bieler, *ΘΕΙΟΣ ΑΝΗΡ Das Bild des "Göttlichen Menschen" in Spätantike und Frühchristentum.* 2 vols. Vienna: Höfels, 1935.

Bieringer

R. Bieringer, *"Lasst euch mit Gott versöhnen." Eine exegetische Untersuchungen zu 2 Kor 5,14-21 in seinem Kontext.* Unpublished doctoral dissertation, Catholic University of Leuven, 1986 (known through Lambrecht, "Reading" 161 n. 1).

Bieringer, "Bibliography"

R. Bieringer, "Bibliography," in Bieringer and Lambrecht 3-66.

Bieringer, "Diakonia"

R. Bieringer, "Paul's Understanding of Diakonia in 2 Corinthians 5,18," in Bieringer and Lambrecht 413-28.

Bieringer, "Einheit"

R. Bieringer, "Der 2. Korintherbrief als ursprüngliche Einheit. Ein Forschungsüberblick," in Bieringer and Lambrecht 107-30.

Bieringer, "Einheitlichkeit"

R. Bieringer, "Plädoyer für die Einheitlichkeit des 2. Korintherbriefes. Literarkritische und inhaltliche Argumente," in Bieringer and Lambrecht 131-79.

Bieringer, "Gegner"

R. Bieringer, "Die Gegner des Paulus im 2. Korintherbrief," in Bieringer and Lambrecht 181-221.

Bieringer, "Jealousy"

R. Bieringer, "Paul's Divine Jealousy: The Apostle and His Communities in Relationship," *LouvStud* 17 (1992) 197-231. Reprinted in Bieringer and Lambrecht 223-53.

Bieringer, "Kontext"
R. Bieringer, "2 Korinther 6,14–7,1 im Kontext des 2. Korintherbriefes. Forschungsüberblick und Versuch eines eigenen Zugangs," in Bieringer and Lambrecht 551-70.

Bieringer, "Liebe"
R. Bieringer, "Die Liebe des Paulus zur Gemeinde in Korinth. Eine interpretation von 2 Korinther 6,11," *StudNTUmwelt* 23 (1998) 193-213.

Bieringer, "Sünde"
R. Bieringer, "Sünde und Gerechtigkeit Gottes in 2 Korinther 5,21," in Bieringer and Lambrecht 462-514.

Bieringer, "Teilungshypothesen"
R. Bieringer, "Teilungshypothesen zum 2. Korintherbrief. Ein Forschungsüberblick," in Bieringer and Lambrecht 67-105.

Bieringer, "Versöhnung"
R. Bieringer, "2 Kor 5,19a und die Versöhnung der Welt," *ETL* 63 (1987) 295-326. Reprinted in Bieringer and Lambrecht 429-59.

Bieringer (ed.)
R. Bieringer (ed.), *The Corinthian Correspondence.* Leuven: Leuven University, 1996.

Bieringer and Lambrecht
R. Bieringer and J. Lambrecht, *Studies on 2 Corinthians.* BETL 112. Leuven: Leuven University, 1994.

Bietenhard
H. Bietenhard, *Die himmlische Welt im Urchristentum und Spätjudentum.* WUNT 2. Tübingen: Mohr, 1951.

Binder
H. Binder, "Die angebliche Krankheit des Paulus," *TZ* 32 (1976) 1-13.

Bishop
E. F. F. Bishop, "Does Aretas Belong in 2 Corinthians or Galatians?" *ExpT* 64 (1953) 188-89.

Bishop, "Famine"
E. F. F. Bishop, "'In Famine and Drought,'" *EvQ* 38 (1966) 169-71.

Bishop, "Nights"
E. F. F. Bishop, "The 'Why' of Sleepless Nights," *EvQ* 37 (1965) 29-31.

Bjerkelund
C. J. Bjerkelund, *Parakalô. Form, Funktion und Sinn der parakalô-Sätze in den paulinischen Briefen.* Bibliotheca Theologica Norvegica, 1. Oslo: Universitetsforlaget, 1967.

Black
D. A. Black, *Paul, Apostle of Weakness.* New York: Lang, 1984.

Black, "Weakness"
D. A. Black, *Paulus Infirmus:* The Pauline Concept of Weakness," *GTJ* 5 (1984) 77-93.

M. Black FS (1)
Neotestamentica et Semitica: Studies in Honour of Matthew Black. Ed. E. E. Ellis and M. Wilcox. Edinburgh: Clark, 1969.

M. Black FS (2)
Text and Interpretation: Studies in the New Testament Presented to Matthew Black. Ed. E. Best and R. McL. Wilson. Cambridge: Cambridge University Press, 1979.

Blank
J. Blank, *Paulus und Jesus. Eine theologische Grundlegung.* SANT 18. Munich: Kösel, 1968.

Blass
F. Blass, *Grammar of New Testament Greek.* London: Macmillan, 1898.

Blomberg
C. L. Blomberg, "The Structure of 2 Corinthians 1–7," *CTR* 4 (1989) 3-20.

Böttrich
C. Böttrich, "2 Kor 11,1 als Programmwort der 'Narrenrede,'" *ZNW* 88 (1997) 135-39.

Bonnard
P. Bonnard, "Faiblesse et puissance du chrétien selon St. Paul," *ETR* 33 (1958) 61-82.

Bonnard, "Création"
P. Bonnard, "Création et nouvelle création," *Foi et Vie* 58 (1959) 19-32.

Bonneau
G. Bonneau, "La vie, à la mort. Le conflit à Corinthe et ses enjeux théologiques en 2 Co 2,14–7,4," *ScEs* 51 (1999) 351-66.

Bonsirven
J. Bonsirven, *Exégèse rabbinique et exégèse paulinienne.* Bibliothèque de théologie historique. Paris: Beauchesne, 1939.

Bonsirven, *Textes*
J. Bonsirven, *Textes rabbiniques des deux premiers siècles chrétiens.* Rome: Pontifical Biblical Institute, 1955.

Boobyer
G. H. Boobyer, *"Thanksgiving" and the "Glory of God" in Paul.* Borna-Leipzig: Noske, 1929.

Bornkamm FS
Kirche. Ed. D. Lührmann and G. Strecker. Tübingen: Mohr, 1980.

Bornkamm
G. Bornkamm, *Die Vorgeschichte des sogenannten zweiten Korintherbriefes.*

SAH Phil.-hist. Klasse. Heidelberg: Winter, 1961. Reprinted in his *Aufsätze* 162-94.

Bornkamm, *Aufsätze*
G. Bornkamm, *Gesammelte Aufsätze,* IV. BET 53. Munich: Evangelischer, 1971.

Bornkamm, *Guide*
G. Bornkamm, *The New Testament: A Guide to Its Writings.* ETr. Philadelphia: Fortress, 1973/London: SPCK, 1974.

Bornkamm, "History"
G. Bornkamm, "The History of the Origin of the So-Called Second Letter to the Corinthians," in *The Authority and Integrity of the New Testament.* By K. Aland, et al. London: SPCK, 1965, pp. 73-81 (from *NTS* 8 [1962] 258-64). This is a partial ETr of the preceding work.

Bornkamm, *Paul*
G. Bornkamm, *Paul.* ETr. New York: Harper, 1971.

Borse
U. Borse, "Zur Todes- und Jenseitserwartung Pauli nach 2 Kor 5,1-10," *BibLeb* 13 (1972) 129-38.

Bosch
J. S. Bosch, *"Gloriarse" segun san Pablo. Sentido y teologia de καυχάομαι.* AnBib 40. Rome: Pontifical Biblical Institute, 1970.

Bosenius
B. Bosenius, *Die Abwesenheit des Apostels als theologisches Programm. Der zweite Korintherbrief als Beispiel für die Brieflichkeit der paulinischen Theologie.* TANZ 11. Tübingen/Basel: Francke, 1994.

Bousset
W. Bousset, "Der zweite Brief an die Korinther," in *Die Schriften des Neuen Testaments,* II. Ed. J. Weiss. Göttingen: Vandenhoeck und Ruprecht, 1907, 141-90 (in Part I).

Bousset, *Kyrios*
W. Bousset, *Kyrios Christos: A History of the Belief in Christ from the Beginnings of Christianity to Irenaeus.* ETr. Nashville: Abingdon, 1970.

Bouttier
M. Bouttier, *En Christ. Étude d'exégèse et de théologie pauliniennes.* 1962.

Bowersock
G. W. Bowersock, *Roman Arabia.* Cambridge: Harvard University, 1983.

Bowersock, *Sophists*
G. W. Bowersock, *Greek Sophists in the Roman Empire.* Oxford: Clarendon, 1969.

Bowker
J. W. Bowker, "'Merkabah' Visions and the Visions of Paul," *JSS* 16 (1971) 157-73.

Bowman Thurston
> B. Bowman Thurston, "2 Corinthians 2:14-16a: Christ's Incense," *RestQ* 29 (1987) 65-69.

Brady FS
> *Studies Honoring Ignatius Charles Brady, Friar Minor.* Franciscan Institute Publications. Theology Series 6. Ed. R. S. Almagno and C. L. Harkins. St. Bonaventure: Franciscan Institute, 1976.

Brandenburger
> E. Brandenburger, *Fleisch und Geist. Paulus und die dualistische Weisheit.* WMANT 29. Neukirchen-Vluyn: Neukirchener, 1968.

Branick
> V. P. Branick, "The Sinful Flesh of the Son of God (Rom. 8:3): A Key Image of Pauline Theology," *CBQ* 47 (1985) 246-62.

Bratcher
> R. G. Bratcher, *A Translator's Guide to Paul's Second Letter to the Corinthians.* New York: United Bible Societies, 1983.

Brauch
> M. T. Brauch, *Hard Sayings of Paul.* Downers Grove: InterVarsity, 1989.

Brauch, "Perspectives"
> M. T. Brauch, "Perspectives in 'God's Righteousness' in Recent German Discussion," in E. P. Sanders 523-42.

Braun FS
> *Neues Testament und christliche Existenz. Festschrift für Herbert Braun.* Ed. H. D. Betz and L. Schottroff. Tübingen: Mohr, 1973.

Braun
> H. Braun, *Qumran und das Neue Testament.* 2 vols. Tübingen: Mohr, 1966.

Breytenbach
> C. Breytenbach, *Versöhnung. Eine Studie zur paulinischen Soteriologie.* WMANT 60. Neukirchen-Vluyn: Neukirchener, 1989.

Breytenbach, "Bemerkungen"
> C. Breytenbach, "Versöhnung, Stellvertretung und Sühne. Semantische und traditionsgeschichtliche Bemerkungen am Beispiel der paulinischen Briefe," *NTS* 39 (1993-94) 59-79.

Breytenbach, "Proclamation"
> C. Breytenbach, "Paul's Proclamation and God's 'Thriambos' (Notes on 2 Corinthians 2:14-16b)," *Neot* 24 (1990) 257-71.

Brillet
> G. Brillet, "Voici les jours de salut (2 Cor. 6:10)," *AsSeign* 26 (1962) 21-36.

Bring
> R. Bring, *Christus und das Gesetz. Die Bedeutung des Gesetzes des Alten Testaments nach Paulus und seine Glauben an Christus.* Leiden: Brill, 1969.

Brown
P. C. Brown, "What Is the Meaning of 'Examine Yourselves' in 2 Corinthians 13:5?" *BSac* 154 (1997) 175-88.

***Bruce FS* (1)**
Apostolic History and the Gospel: Biblical and Historical Essays Presented to F. F. Bruce. Ed. W. W. Gasque and R. P. Martin. Exeter: Paternoster/Grand Rapids: Eerdmans, 1970.

***Bruce FS* (2)**
Pauline Studies: Essays Presented to Professor F. F. Bruce. Ed. D. A. Hagner and M. J. Harris. Grand Rapids: Eerdmans/Exeter: Paternoster, 1980.

Bruce
F. F. Bruce, *1 and 2 Corinthians.* NCB. Grand Rapids: Eerdmans/London: Marshall, 1971.

Bruce, *Acts*
F. F. Bruce, *The Acts of the Apostles: Greek Text with Introduction and Commentary.* Grand Rapids: Eerdmans/Leicester: Apollos, 1990^3.

Bruce, *Converts*
F. F. Bruce, *Paul and His Converts.* New York: Abingdon, 1962.

Bruce, *Galatians*
F. F. Bruce, *The Epistle of Paul to the Galatians.* NIGTC. Grand Rapids: Eerdmans/Exeter: Paternoster, 1982.

Bruce, *History*
F. F. Bruce, *New Testament History.* New York: Doubleday/London: Nelson, 1969.

Bruce, "Immortality"
F. F. Bruce, "Paul on Immortality," *SJT* 24 (1971) 457-74.

Bruce, "Jerusalem"
F. F. Bruce, "Paul and Jerusalem," *TynB* 19 (1968) 3-25.

Bruce, "Macedonia"
F. F. Bruce, "St. Paul in Macedonia," *BJRUL* 61 (1978-79) 337-54.

Bruce, *Mind*
F. F. Bruce, *A Mind for What Matters: Collected Essays of F. F. Bruce.* Grand Rapids: Eerdmans, 1990.

Bruce, "Mystic"
F. F. Bruce, "Was Paul a Mystic?" *RTR* 34 (1975) 66-75.

Bruce, *Paraphrase*
F. F. Bruce, *An Expanded Paraphrase of the Epistles of Paul.* Exeter: Paternoster, 1965.

Bruce, *Paul*
F. F. Bruce, *Paul, Apostle of the Heart Set Free.* Grand Rapids: Eerdmans, 1977. UK title *Paul, Apostle of the Free Spirit.* Exeter: Paternoster, 1977.

Bruce, *Romans*

F. F. Bruce, *The Epistle of Paul to the Romans.* Grand Rapids: Eerdmans, 1963.

Bruce, *Thessalonians*

F. F. Bruce, *1 and 2 Thessalonians.* WBC 45. Waco: Word, 1982.

Brun

L. Brun, "Zur Auslegung von 2 Cor. 5 1-10," *ZNW* 28 (1929) 207-29.

Buchanan

G. W. Buchanan, "Jesus and the Upper Class," *NovT* 7 (1964) 195-209.

Buck

C. H. Buck, Jr., "The Collection for the Saints," *HTR* 43 (1950) 1-29.

Buck and Taylor

C. H. Buck, Jr., and G. Taylor, *Saint Paul: A Study of the Development of His Thought.* New York: Scribner, 1969.

Bullinger

E. W. Bullinger, *Figures of Speech Used in the Bible.* Grand Rapids: Baker, 1968 reprint of 1898 original.

***Bultmann FS* (1)**

Neutestamentliche Studien für Rudolf Bultmann. Ed. W. Eltester. BZNW 21. Berlin: Töpelmann, 1954.

***Bultmann FS* (2)**

The Future of Our Religious Past. ETr. Ed. J. M. Robinson. London: SCM, 1971.

Bultmann

R. Bultmann, *The Second Letter to the Corinthians.* ETr. Minneapolis: Augsburg, 1985.

Bultmann, "DIKAIOSYNĒ"

R. Bultmann, "DIKAIOSYNĒ THEOU," *JBL* 83 (1964) 12-16.

Bultmann, *Existence*

R. Bultmann, *Existence and Faith: Shorter Writings of Rudolf Bultmann.* ETr. New York: Meridian, 1960.

Bultmann, *Probleme*

R. Bultmann, *Exegetische Probleme des zweiten Korintherbriefes.* SEÅSup 9. Uppsala: Wretmans, 1947. Reprinted Darmstadt: Wissenschaftliche Buch- gesellschaft, 1963.

Bultmann, *Stil*

R. Bultmann, *Der Stil der paulinischen Predigt und die kynisch-stoische Dia- tribe.* FRLANT 13. Göttingen: Vandenhoeck und Ruprecht, 1910 (reprinted 1984).

Bultmann, *Theology*

R. Bultmann, *Theology of the New Testament,* Vol. I. ETr. New York: Scribner's, 1951/London: SCM, 1952. Vol. II. ETr. New York: Scribner/London: SCM, 1955.

Burchard

C. Burchard, *Der dreizehnte Zeuge. Traditions- und kompositionsgeschichtliche Untersuchungen zu Lukas' Darstellung der Frühzeit des Paulus.* FRLANT 103. Göttingen: Vandenhoeck und Ruprecht, 1979.

Burdick

D. W. Burdick, "Οἶδα and Γινώσκω in the Pauline Epistles," in Longenecker and Tenney 344-56.

Burdick, "Troad"

D. W. Burdick, "With Paul in the Troad," *NEASB* n.s. 12 (1978) 31-65.

Burke

T. J. Burke, "Pauline Paternity in 1 Thessalonians," *TynB* 51 (2000) 59-80.

Burton

E. de W. Burton, *Syntax of the Moods and Tenses in New Testament Greek.* Edinburgh: Clark, 1898[3].

Burton, *Galatians*

E. de W. Burton, *A Critical and Exegetical Commentary on the Epistle to the Galatians.* ICC. Edinburgh: Clark, 1921.

Burton, *Spirit*

E. de W. Burton, *Spirit, Soul, and Flesh.* Chicago: University of Chicago, 1918.

Burton, *Studies*

E. de W. Burton, *New Testament Word Studies.* Chicago: University of Chicago, 1927.

Buttmann

A. Buttmann, *A Grammar of the New Testament Greek.* Andover: Draper, 1873.

Caird FS

The Glory of Christ in the New Testament: Studies in Christology in Memory of George Bradford Caird. Ed. L. D. Hurst and N. T. Wright. New York: Oxford University Press/Oxford: Clarendon, 1987.

Caird

G. B. Caird, *New Testament Theology.* Completed and ed. by L. D. Hurst. Oxford: Clarendon, 1994.

Caird, *Language*

G. B. Caird, *The Language and Imagery of the Bible.* Philadelphia: Westminster, 1980.

Calvin

J. Calvin, *The Second Epistle of Paul the Apostle to the Corinthians and the Epistles to Timothy, Titus, and Philemon.* ETr. Calvin's New Testament Commentaries 10. Grand Rapids: Eerdmans/Edinburgh: Oliver and Boyd, 1964 (= 1547).

Cambier

J. Cambier, "The Second Epistle to the Corinthians," in *Introduction to the New Testament.* Ed. A. Robert and A. Feuillet. New York: Desclée, 1965, pp. 433-46.

xl

Cambier "Connaissance"

J. Cambier, "Connaissance charnelle et spirituelle du Christ dans 2 Co 5,16," in *Littérature et théologie pauliniennes*. Ed. A. Descamps. RechBib 5. Louvain: Desclée de Brouwer, 1960, pp. 72-92.

Cambier, "Critère"

J. Cambier, "Le critère paulinien de l'apostolat en 2 Cor. 12, 6s," *Bib* 43 (1962) 481-518.

Cambier, "Lecture"

J. Cambier, "Une lecture de 2 Cor 12,6-7a. Essai d'interprétation nouvelle," in *Congressus* 2.475-85.

Cambier, "Liberté"

J. Cambier, "La liberté chrétienne selon saint Paul," in *SE* II (= TU 87). Ed. F. L. Cross. Berlin: Akademie, 1964, pp. 315-53.

Campbell

J. Y. Campbell, "KOINΩNIA and Its Cognates in the New Testament," *JBL* 51 (1932) 352-80. (Reprinted in his *Three New Testament Studies*. Leiden: Brill, 1965, pp. 1-28).

Capes

D. B. Capes, *Old Testament Yahweh Texts in Paul's Christology*. WUNT 2/47. Tübingen: Mohr, 1992.

Caragounis

C. C. Caragounis, "ὀψώνιον: A Reconsideration of Its Meaning," *NovT* 16 (1974) 35-57.

Carmignac

J. Carmignac, "II Corinthiens iii.6, 14 et le début de la formulation du Nouveau Testament," *NTS* 24 (1977-78) 384-86.

Carrez

M. Carrez, *La deuxième Épître de Saint Paul aux Corinthiens*. CNT 2/8. Geneva: Labor et Fides, 1986.

Carrez, "ΙΚΑΝΟΤΗΣ"

M. Carrez, "ΙΚΑΝΟΤΗΣ: 2 Co 2,14-17," in Lorenzi (ed.) 79-95.

Carrez, "Le 'Nous'"

M. Carrez, "Le 'Nous' en 2 Corinthiens," *NTS* 26 (1979-80) 474-86.

Carrez, "Odeur"

M. Carrez, "Odeur de mort, Odeur de vie (à propos de 2 Co 2,16)," *RHPR* 64 (1984) 135-42.

Carrez, "Réalité"

M. Carrez, "Réalité christologique et référence apostolique de l'apôtre Paul en présence d'une église divisée (2 Co 10–13)," in Vanhoye (ed.) 163-83.

Carrez, *Souffrance*

M. Carrez, *De la souffrance à la gloire. De la ΔΟΞΑ dans la pensée paulinienne*. Neuchâtel: Delachaux et Niestlé, 1974.

Carson

D. A. Carson, *From Triumphalism to Maturity: An Exposition of 2 Corinthians 10–13.* Grand Rapids: Baker, 1984.

Cassidy

R. Cassidy, "Paul's Attitude to Death in II Corinthians 5:1-10," *EvQ* 43 (1971) 210-17.

Cassirer

H. W. Cassirer, *God's New Covenant: A New Testament Translation.* Grand Rapids: Eerdmans, 1989.

Casson

L. Casson, *Travel in the Ancient World.* London: Allen, 1974.

Cerfaux

L. Cerfaux, *Christ in the Theology of St. Paul.* ETr. New York: Herder/London: Nelson, 1959.

Cerfaux, *Christian*

L. Cerfaux, *The Christian in the Theology of St. Paul.* ETr. London: Chapman, 1967.

Cerfaux, *Church*

L. Cerfaux, *The Church in the Theology of St. Paul.* ETr. New York: Herder/London: Nelson, 1959.

Chambers

T. W. Chambers, Supplementary notes in H. A. W. Meyer, *Critical and Exegetical Hand-Book to the Epistles to the Corinthians.* ETr. New York: Funk and Wagnalls, 1884.

Champion

L. G. Champion, *Benedictions and Doxologies in the Epistles of Paul.* Oxford: Kemp Hall, 1934.

Charles

R. H. Charles, *Eschatology: The Doctrine of a Future Life in Israel, Judaism and Christianity.* New York: Schocken, 1963 (= 1913).

Charlesworth

J. H. Charlesworth (ed.), *The Old Testament Pseudepigrapha,* 2 vols. London: Darton, Longman and Todd/New York: Doubleday, 1983.

Chevallier

M. A. Chevallier, "L'argumentation de Paul dans II Corinthiens 10 à 13," *RHPR* 70 (1990) 3-15.

Childs

B. S. Childs, *The New Testament as Canon: An Introduction.* Philadelphia: Fortress, 1985.

Childs, *Exodus*

B. S. Childs, *The Book of Exodus: A Critical Theological Commentary.* The Old Testament Library. Philadelphia: Westminster, 1974.

Chilton

B. D. Chilton, "Galatians 6^{15}: A Call to Freedom before God," *ExpT* 89 (1977-78) 311-13.

Chow

J. K. Chow, *Patronage and Power: A Study of Social Networks in Corinth.* JSNTSS 75. Sheffield: Sheffield Academic, 1992.

Clark FS

Studies in the History and Text of the New Testament. Ed. B. L. Daniels and M. J. Suggs. SD 29. Salt Lake City: University of Utah/Grand Rapids: Eerdmans, 1967.

Clark

K. W. Clark, "The Meaning of [KATA] KYPIEYEIN," in *Kilpatrick FS* 100-105.

Clark, "ἐνεργέω"

K. W. Clark, "The Meaning of ἐνεργέω and καταργέω in the New Testament," *JBL* 54 (1935) 93-101.

G. Clark

G. Clark, "The Social Status of Paul," *ExpT* 96 (1985) 110-11.

Clarke

A. D. Clarke, "'Refresh the Hearts of the Saints': A Unique Pauline Context?" *TynB* 47 (1996) 277-300.

Classen

C. J. Classen, "St Paul's Epistles and Ancient Greek and Roman Rhetoric," in Porter and Olbricht 265-91.

Clavier

H. Clavier, "La santé de l'apôtre Paul," in *de Zwaan FS* 66-82.

Clavier, "Remarques"

H. Clavier, "Brèves remarques sur la notion de σῶμα πνευματικόν," in *Dodd FS* 342-62.

Clemen

C. Clemen, *Paulus, sein Leben und Wirken,* 2 vols. Giessen: Töpelmann, 1904.

Clemen, *Einheitlichkeit*

C. Clemen, *Die Einheitlichkeit der paulinischen Briefe.* Göttingen: Vandenhoeck und Ruprecht, 1894.

Clements

R. E. Clements, *God and Temple.* Oxford: Blackwell, 1965.

Cobb

W. H. Cobb, "Αἰώνιος II. Cor. iv.17 and v.1," *JBL* 3 (June and December 1883) 61.

Cohen

B. Cohen, "Note on Letter and Spirit in the New Testament," *HTR* 47 (1954) 197-203.

Collange

J. F. Collange, *Enigmes de la deuxième épître de Paul aux Corinthiens. Étude exégétique de 2 Cor. 2:14–7:4.* SNTSMS 18. Cambridge: Cambridge University Press, 1972.

Collins

J. N. Collins, *DIAKONIA: Reinterpreting the Ancient Sources.* New York: Oxford University Press, 1990.

Collins, "Envoys"

J. N. Collins, "Georgi's 'Envoys' in 2 Cor 11:23," *JBL* 93 (1974) 88-96.

Collins, "Role"

J. N. Collins, "The Mediatorial Aspect of Paul's Role as *Diakonos*," *ABR* 40 (1992) 34-44.

J. J. Collins

J. J. Collins, "Chiasmus, the 'ABA' Pattern and the Text of Paul," in *Congressus* 2.575-83.

Congressus

Studiorum Paulinorum Congressus Internationalis Catholicus 1961. 2 vols. AnBib 17-18. Rome: Pontifical Biblical Institute, 1963.

Conybeare and Howson

W. J. Conybeare and J. S. Howson, *The Life and Epistles of St. Paul.* New York: Longmans, 1898.

Conzelmann FS

Jesus Christus in Historie und Theologie. Ed. G. Strecker. Tübingen: Mohr, 1975.

Conzelmann

H. Conzelmann, *I Corinthians.* ETr. Hermeneia. Philadelphia: Fortress, 1975.

Cook

J. M. Cook, *The Troad: An Archaeological and Topographical Study.* Oxford: Clarendon, 1973.

Cooper

J. W. Cooper, *Body, Soul, and Life Everlasting.* Grand Rapids: Eerdmans, 1989.

Corley (ed.)

B. Corley (ed.), *Colloquy on New Testament Studies.* Macon: Mercer University Press, 1983.

Craddock

F. B. Craddock, "The Poverty of Christ: An Investigation of II Corinthians 8:9," *Int* 22 (1968) 158-70.

Crafton

J. A. Crafton, *The Agency of the Apostle: A Dramatistic Analysis of Paul's Responses to Conflict in 2 Corinthians.* JSNTSS 51. Sheffield: Sheffield Academic, 1991.

Craig

W. L. Craig, "Paul's Dilemma in 2 Corinthians 5:1-10: A 'Catch-22'?" *NTS* 34 (1987-88) 145-47.

Cranfield

C. E. B. Cranfield, *A Critical and Exegetical Commentary on the Epistle to the Romans*. 2 vols. ICC. Edinburgh: Clark, 1975, 1979.

Cranfield, *Bible*

C. E. B. Cranfield, *The Bible and the Christian Life*. Edinburgh: Clark, 1985.

Cranfield, "Changes"

C. E. B. Cranfield, "Changes of Person and Number in Paul's Epistles," in *Barrett FS* 280-89. Reprinted in Cranfield, *Bible* 215-28.

Cranfield, "Law"

C. E. B. Cranfield, "St. Paul and the Law," in *New Testament Issues,* ed. R. Batey (London: SCM, 1970) 148-72 (= *SJT* 17 [1964] 43-68).

Cranfield, "Minister"

C. E. B. Cranfield, "Minister and Congregation in the Light of II Corinthians 4:5-7: An Exposition," *Int* 19 (1965) 163-67.

Cranford

L. Cranford, "A New Look at 2 Corinthians 5:1-10," *SWJT* 19 (1976) 95-100.

***Cullmann FS* (1)**

Neotestamentica et Patristica. Eine Freundesgabe . . . überreicht. Ed. W. C. van Unnik. NovTSup 6. Leiden: Brill, 1962.

***Cullmann FS* (2)**

Neues Testament und Geschichte. Historisches Geschehen und Deutung im Neuen Testament, Ed. H. Baltensweiler and B. Reicke. Zurich: Theologischer, 1972.

Cullmann

O. Cullmann, *Peter: Disciple, Apostle, Martyr.* London: SCM, 1962.

Cullmann, *Church*

O. Cullmann, *The Early Church*. Ed. A. J. B. Higgins. London: SCM, 1956.

Cullmann, *Immortality*

O. Cullmann, *Immortality of the Soul or Resurrection of the Dead? The Witness of the New Testament*. ETr. London: Epworth, 1958.

Cullmann, *Retour*

O. Cullmann, *Le retour du Christ. Espérance de l'Église selon le Nouveau Testament*. Neuchâtel: Delachaux et Niestlé, 1945².

Cullmann, *Salvation*

O. Cullmann, *Salvation as History*. ETr. London: SCM, 1967.

Cullmann, *Time*

O. Cullmann, *Christ and Time*. ETr. London: SCM, 1962².

Cuming

G. J. Cuming, "Service-Endings in the Epistles," *NTS* 22 (1975-76) 110-13.

Dahl FS
God's Christ and His People: Studies in Honour of Nils Alstrup Dahl. Ed.
J. Jervell and W. A. Meeks. Oslo: Universitets, 1977.

Dahl
N. A. Dahl, Studies in Paul. Minneapolis: Augsburg, 1977.

Dahl, "Corinth"
N. A. Dahl, "Paul and the Church at Corinth according to 1 Corinthians 1:10–
4:21," in J. Knox FS 313-35. Reprinted in his Studies 44-66.

Dahl, "Fragment"
N. A. Dahl, "A Fragment and Its Context: 2 Corinthians 6:14–7:1," in Dahl FS
62-69.

Dahood
M. J. Dahood, Psalms III: 101–150. AB 17A. Garden City: Doubleday, 1970.

Dahood, "Quotations"
M. J. Dahood, "Two Pauline Quotations from the Old Testament," CBQ 17
(1955) 19-24.

Dalton
W. J. Dalton, "Is the Old Covenant Abrogated (2 Cor 3.14)?" ABR 35 (1987)
88-94.

Daniel
C. Daniel, "Une mention paulinienne des Esséniens de Qumrân," RevQ 5 (1966)
553-67.

Danker
F. W. Danker, II Corinthians. ACNT. Minneapolis: Augsburg, 1989.

Danker, Benefactor
F. W. Danker, Benefactor: Epigraphic Study of a Graeco-Roman and New Testament Semantic Field. St. Louis: Clayton, 1982.

Danker, "Consolation"
F. W. Danker, "Consolation in 2 Cor. 5:1-10," CTM (1968) 552-56.

Danker, "Debt"
F. W. Danker, "Paul's Debt to the De Corona of Demosthenes: A Study of Rhetorical Techniques in Second Corinthians," in Kennedy FS 262-80.

Danker, "Reciprocity"
F. W. Danker, "Bridging St. Paul and the Apostolic Fathers: A Study in Reciprocity," CurTM 15 (1988) 84-94.

Danker, "Review"
Review of R. P. Martin, 2 Corinthians in JBL 107 (1988) 550-53.

Danker, "Romans 5:12"
F. W. Danker, "Romans 5:12: Sin under Law," NTS 14 (1967-68) 424-39.

Daube FS
Donum Gentilicium: New Testament Studies in Honour of David Daube. Ed.
C. K. Barrett, E. Bammel, and W. D. Davies. Oxford: Clarendon, 1978.

Dautzenberg
G. Dautzenberg, "Der zweite Korintherbrief als Briefsammlung. Zur Frage der literarischen Einheitlichkeit und des theologischen Gefüges von 2 Kor 1–8," in *ANRW* II.25.4, 3045-66.

Dautzenberg, "Glaube"
G. J. Dautzenberg, "'Glaube' oder 'Hoffnung' in 2 Kor 4,13–5,10," in Lorenzi (ed.), *Diakonia* 75-104.

Dautzenberg, "Überlegungen"
G. J. Dautzenberg, "Überlegungen zur Exegese und Theologie von 2 Kor 4,1-6," *Bib* 82 (2001) 325-44.

Davids
P. H. Davids, *The First Epistle of Peter.* NICNT. Grand Rapids: Eerdmans, 1990.

Davies
W. D. Davies, *Paul and Rabbinic Judaism.* Philadelphia: Fortress, 1980[4].

Davies, "Flesh"
W. D. Davies, "Paul and the Dead Sea Scrolls: Flesh and Spirit," in *The Scrolls and the New Testament.* Ed. K. Stendahl. New York: Harper, 1957, pp. 157-82.

Davies, *Gospel*
W. D. Davies, *The Gospel and the Land: Early Christianity and the Jewish Territorial Doctrine.* Berkeley: University of California, 1974.

Davies, "Israel"
W. D. Davies, "Paul and the People of Israel," *NTS* 24 (1977) 4-39.

Davies, *Studies*
W. D. Davies, *Jewish and Pauline Studies.* Philadelphia: Fortress, 1984.

S. Davies
S. Davies, "Remarks on the Second Epistle to the Corinthians 4:3, 4," *BSac* 25 (1868) 23-30.

Dean
J. T. Dean, *Saint Paul and Corinth.* London: Lutterworth, 1947.

Dean, "Digression"
J. T. Dean, "The Great Digression: 2 Corinthians 2:14–7:4," *ExpT* 50 (1938-39) 86-89.

de Boor
W. de Boor, *Der zweite Brief des Paulus an die Korinther.* Wüppertal: Brockhaus, 1977[3].

Deichgräber
R. Deichgräber, *Der Gotteshymnus und Christushymnus in der frühen Christenheit. Untersuchungen zu Form, Sprache und Stil der frühchristlichen Hymnen.* SUNT 5. Göttingen: Vandenhoeck und Ruprecht, 1967.

Deissmann FS
Festgabe für Adolf Deissmann zum 60. Geburtstag. Tübingen: Mohr, 1927.

Deissmann

G. A. Deissmann, *Bible Studies*. ETr. Edinburgh: Clark, 1903².

Deissmann, *Light*

G. A. Deissmann, *Light from the Ancient East*. ETr. New York: Doran/London: Hodder, 1927².

Deissner

K. Deissner, *Auferstehungshoffnung und Pneumagedanke bei Paulus*. Leipzig: Deichert, 1912.

De Jong

M. de Jong, *Paulus struikelblok of toetssteen. Een studie van 2 Korintiërs 2:12–4:6 als bijdrage in het gesprek met Israël*. Kampen: Mondiss, 1989.

de la Potterie

I. de la Potterie, "L'onction du chrétien par la foi," *Bib* 40 (1959) 12-69.

Delatte

P. Delatte, *Les Épîtres de saint Paul replacées dans le milieu historique des Actes des Apôtres. I*. Tours: Mame, 1938.

Delcor

M. Delcor, "The Courts of the Church of Corinth and the Courts of Qumran," in Murphy-O'Connor (ed.) 69-84.

de Lorenzi (ed.)

L. de Lorenzi (ed.), *Paolo. Ministro del Nuovo Testamento* (2 Co 2,14–4,6). Benedictina 9. Rome: Benedictina, 1987.

de Lorenzi (ed.), *Diakonia*

L. de Lorenzi (ed.), *The Diakonia of the Spirit* (2 Co 4:7–7:4). Benedictina 10. Rome: Benedictina, 1989.

Déman

P. Déman, "Moïse et la loi dans la pensée de St Paul," in *Moïse, l'homme de l'alliance*. Paris: Gabalda, 1955, pp. 189-242.

Demke

C. Demke, "Zur Auslegung von 2. Korinther 5,1-10," *EvT* 29 (1969) 589-602.

Denis

A.-M. Denis, "La fonction apostolique et la liturgie spirituelle en Esprit. Étude thématique des métaphores pauliniennes du culte nouveau," *RSPT* 42 (1958) 401-36, 617-56.

Denney

J. Denney, *The Second Epistle to the Corinthians*. The Expositor's Bible. London: Hodder/New York: Armstrong, 1894. Reprint Grand Rapids: Eerdmans, 1943.

Denney, *Death*

J. Denney, *The Death of Christ*. London: Tyndale, 1951.

de Oliveira

A. de Oliveira, *Die Diakonie der Gerechtigkeit und der Versöhnung in der*

Apologie des 2. Korintherbriefes. Analyse und Auslegung von 2 Kor 2,14–4,6; 5,11–6,10. NTAbh n.s. 21. Münster: Aschendorff, 1990.

Depasse-Livet

J. Depasse-Livet, "L'existence chrétienne. Participation à la vie trinitaire, 2 Cor 13,11-13," *AsSeign* 31 (1973) 10-13.

Derrett

J. D. M. Derrett, "2 Cor 6,14ff. a Midrash on Dt 22,10," *Bib* 59 (1978) 231-50.

Derrett, "Ναί"

J. D. M. Derrett, "Ναί (2 Cor 1:19-20)," *FN* 4 (1991) 205-9.

deSilva

D. A. deSilva, *The Credentials of an Apostle: Paul's Gospel in 2 Corinthians 1–7.* N. Richland Hills: Bibal, 1998.

deSilva, "Decision"

D. A. deSilva, "Recasting the Moment of Decision: 2 Corinthians 6:14–7:1 in Its Literary Context," *AUSS* 31 (1993) 3-16.

deSilva, "Integrity"

D. A. deSilva, "Measuring Penultimate against Ultimate Reality: An Investigation of the Integrity and Argumentation of 2 Corinthians," *JSNT* 52 (1993) 41-70.

de Surgy

Surgy, P. de, "Le ministère apostolique de la nouvelle alliance. 2 Co 3,1b-6," *AsSeign* 39 (1972) 36-43.

De Wette

W. M. L. de Wette, *Kurze Eklärung der Briefe an die Corinther.* Leipzig: Hirzel, 1855[3].

De Zwaan FS

Studia Paulina in honorem Johannis de Zwaan septuagenarii. Ed. J. N. Sevenster and W. C. van Unnik. Haarlem: Bohn, 1953.

Dibelius

M. Dibelius, *A Fresh Approach to the New Testament and Early Christian Literature.* New York: Scribner, 1936.

Dibelius, *Botschaft*

M. Dibelius, *Botschaft und Geschichte. Gesammelte Aufsätze II.* Ed. G. Bornkamm. Tübingen: Mohr, 1956.

Dibelius, *Geisterwelt*

M. Dibelius, *Die Geisterwelt im Glauben des Paulus.* Göttingen: Vandenhoeck und Ruprecht, 1909.

Dibelius, *Paul*

M. Dibelius, *Paul.* Ed. and completed by W. G. Kümmel. London: Longmans, 1953.

DiCicco
M. DiCicco, *Paul's Use of Ethos, Pathos, and Logos in 2 Corinthians 10–13*. Macon: Mellen Biblical, 1994.

Didier
G. Didier, *Désintéressement du chrétien. La rétribution dans la morale de Saint Paul.* Aubier: Montaigne, 1955.

Di Marco
A. S. Di Marco, "ΚΟΙΝΩΝΙΑ ΠΝΕΥΜΑΤΟΣ (2 Cor 13,13; Flp 2,1) — ΠΝΕΥΜΑ ΚΟΙΝΩΝΙΑΣ. Circolarità e ambivalenza linguistica e filologica," *FN* 1 (1988) 63-75.

Di Marco "Rhetoric"
A. S. Di Marco, "Rhetoric and Hermeneutic — On a Rhetorical Pattern: Chiasmus and Circularity," in Porter and Olbricht 479-91.

Dinkler
E. Dinkler, *Signum Crucis. Aufsätze zum Neuen Testament und zur christlichen Archäologie.* Tübingen: Mohr, 1967.

Dinkler, "Korintherbriefe"
E. Dinkler, "Korintherbriefe," *RGG* 4 (1960³) 17-23.

Dinkler, "Taufterminologie"
E. Dinkler, "Die Taufterminologie in 2 Kor. i 21f.," in *Cullmann FS* 173-91. Reprinted in Dinkler 99-117.

Dinkler, "Verkündigung"
E. Dinkler, "Die Verkündigung als eschatologisch-sakramentales Geschehen. Auslegung von 2 Kor 5,14–6,2," in *Schlier FS* 169-89.

Dobbeler
A. von Dobbeler, *Glaube als Teilhabe. Historische und semantische Grundlagen der paulinischen Theologie und Ekklesiologie des Glaubens.* WUNT 2.22. Tübingen: Mohr, 1987.

Dockx
S. Dockx, "Chronologie paulinienne de l'année de la grande collecte," *RB* 81 (1974) 183-95.

Dodd FS
The Background of the New Testament and Its Eschatology: In Honour of Charles Harold Dodd. Ed. W. D. Davies and D. Daube. Cambridge: Cambridge University Press, 1956.

Dodd
C. H. Dodd, *New Testament Studies.* New York: Scribner, 1954/Manchester: Manchester University Press, 1953.

Dodd, "Problems"
C. H. Dodd, "New Testament Translation Problems," *BT* 28 (1977) 101-16.

Dodd, Romans
C. H. Dodd, *The Epistle of Paul to the Romans.* London: Hodder and Stoughton, 1932.

Doignon

J. Doignon, "Le libellé singulier de II Corinthiens 3.18 chez Hilaire de Poitiers: Essai d'explication," *NTS* 26 (1978-79) 118-26.

Donfried

K. P. Donfried, *The Setting of Second Clement in Early Christianity.* NovTSup 38. Leiden: Brill, 1974.

Doty

W. G. Doty, *Letters in Primitive Christianity.* Philadelphia: Fortress, 1973.

Doughty

D. J. Doughty, "The Presence and Future of Salvation at Corinth," *ZNW* 66 (1975) 61-90.

Drane

J. W. Drane, *Paul: Libertine or Legalist? A Study in the Theology of the Major Pauline Epistles.* London: SPCK, 1975.

Drescher

R. Drescher, "Der zweite Korintherbrief und die Vorgänge in Korinth seit Abfassung des ersten Korintherbriefs," *TSK* 70 (1897) 43-111.

Duff

P. B. Duff, "The Mind of the Redactor: 2 Cor. 6:14–7:1 in Its Secondary Context," *NovT* 35 (1993) 160-80.

Duff, "Metaphor"

P. B. Duff, "Metaphor, Motif, and Meaning: The Rhetorical Strategy behind the Image 'Led in Triumph' in 2 Corinthians 2:14," *CBQ* 53 (1991) 79-92.

Duff, "Transformation"

P. B. Duff, "The Transformation of the Spectator: Power, Perception, and the Day of Salvation," in *SBL Seminar Papers, Annual Meeting 1987,* ed. K. H. Richards (Atlanta: Scholars, 1987) 233-43.

Dugandzic

I. Dugandzic, *Das "Ja" Gottes in Christus.* FZB 26. Würzburg: Echter, 1977.

Dumbrell

W. J. Dumbrell, "Paul's Use of Exodus 34 in 2 Corinthians 3," in *D. B. Knox FS* 179-94.

Duncan

G. S. Duncan, *St. Paul's Ephesian Ministry.* London: Hodder, 1929/New York: Scribner, 1930.

Duncan, "Ephesus"

G. S. Duncan, "Important Hypotheses Reconsidered VI: Were Paul's Imprisonment Epistles Written from Ephesus?" *ExpT* 67 (1955-56) 163-66.

Duncan, "Ministry"

G. S. Duncan, "Paul's Ministry in Asia — The Last Phase," *NTS 3* (1956-57) 211-18.

Duncan, "Table"
G. S. Duncan, "Chronological Table to Illustrate Paul's Ministry in Asia," *NTS* 5 (1958-59) 43-45.

Dunn
J. D. G. Dunn, *The Unity and Diversity of the New Testament.* Philadelphia: Westminster/London: SCM, 1977.

Dunn, "Antioch"
J. D. G. Dunn, "The Incident at Antioch," *JSNT* 18 (1983) 3-57.

Dunn, *Baptism*
J. D. G. Dunn, *Baptism in the Holy Spirit.* SBT 2/15. London: SCM, 1970.

Dunn, *Christology*
J. D. G. Dunn, *Christology in the Making: A New Testament Enquiry in the Origins of the Doctrine of the Incarnation.* London: SCM, 1980.

Dunn, "Death"
J. D. G. Dunn, "Paul's Understanding of the Death of Jesus," in *Morris FS* 125-41.

Dunn, *Jesus*
J. D. G. Dunn, *Jesus and the Spirit.* Philadelphia: Westminster/London: SCM, 1975.

Dunn, "Lord"
J. D. G. Dunn, "2 Corinthians III.17 — 'The Lord is the Spirit,'" *JTS* n.s. 21 (1970) 309-20.

Dunn, *Romans*
J. D. G. Dunn, *Romans 1–8, 9–16* (2 vols.). Dallas: Word, 1988.

Dunn, *Theology*
J. D. G. Dunn, *The Theology of Paul the Apostle.* Grand Rapids/Cambridge: Eerdmans, 1998.

Dupont
J. Dupont, *Gnosis. La connaissance religieuse dans les épîtres de Saint Paul.* Paris: Gabalda, 1949.

Dupont, "Chrétien"
J. Dupont, "Le Chrétien, miroir de la gloire divine d'après 2 Cor. 3:18," *RB* 56 (1949) 392-411.

Dupont, "Christ"
J. Dupont, "Pour vous le Christ s'est fait pauvre (2 Cor. 8:7, 9, 13-15)," *AsSeign* 44 (1969) 32-37.

Dupont, *Réconciliation*
J. Dupont, *La réconciliation dans la théologie de saint Paul.* Louvain: Université de Louvain, 1953.

Dupont, *Union*
J. Dupont, *ΣΥΝ ΧΡΙΣΤΩΙ. L'union avec le Christ suivant Saint Paul.* Paris: Desclée de Brouwer, 1952.

Durham

J. I. Durham, *Exodus*. WBC. Waco: Word, 1987.

Eastman

B. Eastman, *The Significance of Grace in the Letters of Paul*. New York: Lang, 1999.

Ebner

M. Ebner, *Leidenlisten und Apostelbrief. Untersuchungen zu Form, Motivik und Funktion der Peristasenkataloge bei Paulus*. FZB 66. Würzburg: Echter, 1991.

Eckstein

H.-J. Eckstein, *Der Begriff Syneidesis bei Paulus*. WUNT 2/10. Tübingen: Mohr, 1983.

Egan

R. B. Egan, "Lexical Evidence on Two Pauline Passages," *NovT* 19 (1977) 34-62.

Ellingworth

P. Ellingworth, " 'We' and 'I' in 2 Corinthians: A Question," *BT* 34 (1983) 246.

Ellingworth, "Grammar"

P. Ellingworth, "Grammar, Meaning, and Verse Divisions in 2 Cor 11.16-29," *BT* 43 (1992) 245-46.

Ellingworth, "2 Cor. 5:21"

P. Ellingworth, " 'For Our Sake God Made Him Share Our Sin'? (2 Corinthians 5.21, GNB)," *BT* 38 (1987) 237-41.

Ellis FS

Tradition and Interpretation in the New Testament: Essays in Honor of E. Earle Ellis. Ed. G. F. Hawthorne and O. Betz. Grand Rapids: Eerdmans/Tübingen: Mohr, 1987.

Ellis

E. E. Ellis, *Paul's Use of the Old Testament*. Edinburgh: Oliver and Boyd, 1957.

Ellis, "Co-Workers"

E. E. Ellis, "Paul and His Co-Workers," *NTS* 17 (1970-71) 437-52. (Reprinted in *Prophecy* 3-22).

Ellis, "Eschatology"

E. E. Ellis, "II Corinthians v.1-10 in Pauline Eschatology," *NTS* 6 (1959-60) 211-24.

Ellis, "Gifts"

E. E. Ellis, " 'Spiritual' Gifts in the Pauline Community," *NTS* 20 (1973-74) 128-44.

Ellis, *Interpreters*

E. E. Ellis, *Paul and His Recent Interpreters*. Grand Rapids: Eerdmans, 1961.

Ellis, *Ministry*

E. E. Ellis, *Pauline Theology: Ministry and Society*. Grand Rapids: Eerdmans, 1989.

Ellis, "Note"
E. E. Ellis, "A Note on Pauline Hermeneutics," *NTS* 2 (1955-56) 127-33.

Ellis, "Opponents"
E. E. Ellis, "Paul and His Opponents: Trends in the Research," in *Smith FS* 264-98. (Reprinted in *Prophecy* 80-128).

Ellis, *Prophecy*
E. E. Ellis, *Prophecy and Hermeneutic in Early Christianity: New Testament Essays.* Tübingen: Mohr/Grand Rapids: Eerdmans, 1978.

W. Ellis
W. Ellis, "Some Problems in the Corinthian Letters," *ABR* 14 (1966) 35.

Eltester
F. W. Eltester, *Eikon im Neuen Testament.* BZNW 23. Giessen: Töpelmann, 1958.

Erlemann
K. Erlemann, "Der Geist als ἀρραβών (2 Kor 5,5) im Kontext der paulinischen Eschatologie," *ZNW* 83 (1992) 202-23.

Evans and Sanders
C. A. Evans and J. A. Sanders (eds.), *Paul and the Scriptures of Israel.* JSNTSS 83. Sheffield: JSOT, 1993.

Evans
E. Evans, *The Epistles of Paul the Apostle to the Corinthians.* The Clarendon Bible 13. Oxford: Clarendon, 1930.

T. S. Evans
T. S. Evans, "Critical Remarks on the Translations of the Revised Version," *Exp,* 2nd series, 3 (1882) 161-77.

Fahy
T. Fahy, "St. Paul's 'Boasting' and 'Weakness,'" *ITQ* 31 (1964) 214-27.

Fallon
F. T. Fallon, *2 Corinthians.* Wilmington: Glazier, 1980.

Fallon, "Sufficiency"
F. T. Fallon, "Self's Sufficiency or God's Sufficiency: 2 Corinthians 2:16," *HTR* 76 (1983) 369-74.

Fanning
B. M. Fanning, *Verbal Aspect in New Testament Greek.* Oxford: Clarendon, 1990.

Fascher
E. Fascher, "Die Korintherbriefe und die Gnosis," in *Gnosis und Neues Testament.* Ed. K. W. Tröger. Gütersloh: Mohn, 1973, pp. 281-91.

Fascher, "Beobachtungen"
E. Fascher, "Theologische Beobachtungen zu δεῖ," in *Bultmann FS* (1) 248-54.

Fatehi
M. Fatehi, *The Spirit's Relation to the Risen Lord in Paul: An Examination of Its Christological Implications.* WUNT 2/128. Tübingen: Mohr, 2000.

Faw

C. E. Faw, "Death and Resurrection in Paul's Letters," *JBR* 27 (1959) 291-98.

Fee

G. D. Fee, *The First Epistle to the Corinthians*. NICNT. Grand Rapids: Eerd-mans/London: Marshall, 1987.

Fee, "Chronology"

G. D. Fee, "ΧΑΡΙΣ in II Corinthians 1.15: Apostolic Parousia and Paul-Corinth Chronology," *NTS* 24 (1977-78) 533-38.

Fee, "Food"

G. D. Fee, "II Corinthians VI.14–VII.1 and Food Offered to Idols," *NTS* 23 (1976-77) 140-61.

Fee, "Gospel"

G. D. Fee, "'Another Gospel Which You Did Not Embrace': 2 Corinthians 11.4 and the Theology of 1 and 2 Corinthians," in *Longenecker FS* 111-33.

Fee, "Interpretation"

G. D. Fee, "Εἰδωλόθυτα Once Again: An Interpretation of I Corinthians 8–10," *Bib* 61 (1980) 172-97.

Fee, *Presence*

G. D. Fee, *God's Empowering Presence: The Holy Spirit in the Letters of Paul.* Peabody: Hendrickson, 1994.

Fenner

F. Fenner, *Die Krankheit im Neuen Testament. Eine religions- und medizin-geschichtliche Untersuchung.* UNT 18. Leipzig: Hinrichs, 1930.

Feuillet

A. Feuillet, *Le Christ sagesse de Dieu d'après les épîtres pauliniennes.* Ébib. Paris: Gabalda, 1966.

Feuillet, "Christ-Image"

A. Feuillet, "The Christ-Image of God according to St. Paul (2 Cor. 4:4)," *Bible Today* 1 (1965) 1409-14.

Feuillet, *Christologie*

A. Feuillet, *Christologie paulinienne et tradition biblique.* Paris: Cerf, 1972.

Feuillet, "Demeure"

A. Feuillet, "La demeure céleste et la destinée des chrétiens. Exégèse de 2 Co 5,1-10 et contribution à l'étude des fondements de l'eschatologie paulinienne," *RSR* 44 (1956) 161-92, 360-402.

Feuillet, "Mort"

A. Feuillet, "Mort du Christ et mort du chrétien d'après les épîtres pauliniennes," *RB* 66 (1954) 481-513.

Field

F. Field, *Notes on the Translation of the New Testament.* Cambridge: Cambridge University Press, 1879.

Filson

F. V. Filson, "The Second Epistle to the Corinthians," in *IB* 10. New York: Abingdon, 1953, pp. 265-425.

Filson, *Recompense*

F. V. Filson, *St. Paul's Conception of Recompense*. Leipzig: Hinrichs, 1931.

Findlay

G. G. Findlay, *The Epistles of Paul the Apostle: A Sketch of Their Origin and Contents*. London: Kelly, 1895.

Findlay, "Paul"

G. G. Findlay, "Paul the Apostle," in *HDB* 3.696-731.

Finegan

J. Finegan, *Light from the Ancient Past*. Princeton: Princeton University, 1946.

Finegan, *Chronology*

J. Finegan, *Handbook of Biblical Chronology*. Princeton: Princeton University, 1964.

Fitzgerald

J. T. Fitzgerald, *Cracks in an Earthen Vessel: An Examination of the Catalogues of Hardship in the Corinthian Correspondence*. SBLDS 99. Atlanta: Scholars, 1988.

Fitzmyer

J. A. Fitzmyer, *Essays on the Semitic Background of the New Testament*. SBLSBS 5. Missoula: Scholars, 1974/London: Chapman, 1971.

Fitzmyer, "Glory"

J. A. Fitzmyer, "Glory Reflected on the Face of Christ (2 Cor 3:7–4:6) and a Palestinian Jewish Motif," *TS* 42 (1981) 630-44. Reprinted in his *According to Paul: Studies in the Theology of the Apostle* 64-79. New York: Paulist, 1993.

Fitzmyer, "Qumrân"

J. A. Fitzmyer, "Qumrân and the Interpolated Paragraph in 2 Cor 6,14–7,1," *CBQ* 23 (1961) 271-80. (Reprinted in Fitzmyer 205-17).

Fitzmyer, "Reconciliation"

J. A. Fitzmyer, "Reconciliation in Pauline Theology," in his *To Advance the Gospel: New Testament Studies*. New York: Crossroad, 1981, pp. 162-85 (originally published in *McKenzie FS* 155-77).

Forbes

C. Forbes, "Comparison, Self-Praise and Irony: Paul's Boasting and the Conventions of Hellenistic Rhetoric," *NTS* 32 (1986) 1-30.

Forbes, "Opponents"

C. Forbes, "Paul's Opponents in Corinth," *Buried History* 19 (1983) 19-23.

Forbes, "Paul"

C. Forbes, "'Unaccustomed as I Am': St. Paul the Public Speaker in Corinth," *Buried History* 19 (1983) 11-16.

Fortna

R. T. Fortna, *The Gospel of Signs*. Cambridge: Cambridge University Press, 1970.

Fowl

S. E. Fowl, *The Story of Christ in the Ethics of Paul: An Analysis of the Function of the Hymnic Material in the Pauline Corpus*. JSNTSS 36. Sheffield: JSOT, 1990.

Fraser

J. W. Fraser, *Jesus and Paul: Paul as Interpreter of Jesus from Harnack to Kümmel*. Appleford: Marcham Manor, 1974.

Fraser, "Knowledge"

J. W. Fraser, "Paul's Knowledge of Jesus: II Corinthians V.16 Once More," *NTS* 17 (1970-71) 293-313.

Freundorfer

J. Freundorfer, *Erbsünde und Erbtod beim Apostel Paulus*. NTAbh 13,1-2. Münster: Aschendorff, 1927.

Fridrichsen

A. Fridrichsen, "Zum Stil des paulinischen Peristasenkatalogs. 2 Cor. 11,23ff.," *SO* 7 (1928) 25-29.

Fridrichsen, "Apostle"

A. Fridrichsen, "The Apostle and His Message," *UUÅ* 3 (1947) 1-23.

Fridrichsen, "Nachtrag"

A. Fridrichsen, "Peristasenkatalog und res gestae. Nachtrag zu 2 Cor. 11,23ff.," *SO* 8 (1929) 78-82.

Fridrichsen, "Stilparallele"

A. Fridrichsen, "Zum Thema 'Paulus und die Stoa.' Eine stoische Stilparallele zu 2 Kor. 4:8f.," *ConNT* 9 (1944) 27-31.

Friedrich

G. Friedrich, *Amt und Lebensführung. Eine Auslegung von 2 Kor. 6,1-10*. BibS(N) 39. Neukirchen-Vluyn: Neukirchener, 1963.

Friedrich, "Briefpräskript"

G. Friedrich, "Lohmeyers These über das paulinische Briefpräskript kritisch beleuchtet," *TLZ* 81 (1956) 343-46.

Friedrich, "Gegner"

G. Friedrich, "Die Gegner des Paulus im 2. Korintherbrief," in *Michel FS* 181-215.

Friesen

I. I. Friesen, *The Glory of the Ministry of Jesus Christ Illustrated by a Study of 2 Cor. 2:14–3:18*. Basel: Reinhardt, 1971.

Fry

E. Fry, "Translating 'glory' in the New Testament," *BT* 27 (1976) 422-27.

Fuchs

E. Fuchs, "La faiblesse, gloire de l'apostolat selon Paul. Étude sur 2 Corinthiens 10–13," *ETR* 55 (1980) 231-53.

Fürst

W. Fürst, "2. Korinther 5,11-21. Auslegung und Meditation," *EvT* 28 (1968) 221-38.

Fuller

R. H. Fuller, *A Critical Introduction to the New Testament.* London: Duckworth, 1966.

Fung

R. Y.-K. Fung, "Justification by Faith in 1 and 2 Corinthians," in *Bruce FS* (2) 246-61.

Fung, *Galatians*

R. Y.-K. Fung, *The Epistle to the Galatians.* Grand Rapids: Eerdmans, 1988.

Funk

R. W. Funk, "The Apostolic *Parousia:* Form and Significance," in *J. Knox FS* 249-68.

Furnish

V. P. Furnish, *II Corinthians.* AB 32A. Garden City: Doubleday, 1984.

Furnish, "Corinth"

V. P. Furnish, "Corinth in Paul's Time: What Can Archaeology Tell Us?" *BAR* 15 (1988) 14-27.

Furnish, "Fellow-Workers"

V. P. Furnish, "Fellow-Workers in God's Service," *JBL* 80 (1961) 364-70.

Furnish, *Love*

V. P. Furnish, *The Love Command in the New Testament.* Nashville: Abingdon, 1972.

Furnish, "Reconciliation"

V. P. Furnish, "The Ministry of Reconciliation," *CurTM* 4 (1977) 204-18.

Furnish, *Theology*

V. P. Furnish, *Theology and Ethics in Paul.* Nashville: Abingdon, 1968.

Gärtner

B. Gärtner, *The Temple and the Community in Qumran and the New Testament: A Comparative Study in the Temple Symbolism of the Qumran Texts and the New Testament.* SNTSMS 1. Cambridge: Cambridge University Press, 1965.

Gaffin

R. B. Gaffin, *The Centrality of the Resurrection: A Study in Paul's Soteriology.* Grand Rapids: Baker, 1978.

Gager

J. G. Gager, Jr., "Functional Diversity in Paul's Use of End-Time Language," *JBL* 89 (1970) 325-37.

Gale

H. M. Gale, *The Use of Analogy in the Letters of Paul.* Philadelphia: Westminster, 1964.

Galletto

P. Galletto, "Dominus autem spiritus est, II Cor. 3,17," *RivB* 5 (1957) 245-81.

Gapp

K. S. Gapp, "The Universal Famine under Claudius," *HTR* 28 (1935) 258-65.

Garland

D. E. Garland, *2 Corinthians.* NAC 29. Nashville: Broadman, 1999.

Garland, "Authority"

D. E. Garland, "Paul's Apostolic Authority: The Power of Christ Sustaining Weakness," *RevExp* 86 (1989) 371-89.

Garland, "Sufficiency"

D. E. Garland, "The Sufficiency of Paul, Minister of the New Covenant," *CTR* 4 (1989) 21-37.

Garrett

S. R. Garrett, "Paul's Thorn and Cultural Models of Affliction," in *The Social World of the First Christians: Essays in Honor of Wayne A. Meeks,* ed. L. M. White and O. L. Yarbrough, Minneapolis: Fortress, 1995, pp. 82-99.

Gaston

L. Gaston, *Paul and the Torah.* Vancouver: University of British Columbia, 1987.

Genths

P. Genths, "Der Begriff des *kauchema* bei Paulus," *NKZ* 38 (1927) 501-21.

George

A. R. George, *Communion with God in the New Testament.* London: Epworth, 1953.

Georgi FS

Religious Propaganda and Missionary Competition in the New Testament: Essays Honoring Dieter Georgi. Ed. L. Bormann, K. Del Tredici, and A. Standhartinger. Leiden: Brill, 1994.

Georgi

D. Georgi, *Remembering the Poor: The History of Paul's Collection for Jerusalem.* ETr. Nashville: Abingdon, 1992.

Georgi, *Opponents*

D. Georgi, *The Opponents of Paul in Second Corinthians.* ETr. Philadelphia: Fortress, 1985.

Georgi, "2 Corinthians"

D. Georgi, "Corinthians, Second Letter to the," *IDB* 5.183-86.

Giblin

C. H. Giblin, *In Hope of God's Glory: Pauline Theological Perspectives.* New York: Herder, 1970.

Giglioli

A. Giglioli, "Il Signore è lo Spirito," *RivB* 20 (1972) 263-76.

Gilchrist

J. M. Gilchrist, "Paul and the Corinthians — The Sequence of Letters and Visits," *JSNT* 34 (1988) 47-69.

Gillman

J. Gillman, "A Thematic Comparison: 1 Cor 15:50-57 and 2 Cor 5:1-5," *JBL* 107 (1988) 439-54.

Glasson

T. F. Glasson, "Theophany and Parousia," *NTS* 34 (1988-89) 259-70.

Gleason

R. C. Gleason, "Paul's Covenantal Contrasts in 2 Corinthians 3:1-11," *BSac* 154 (1997) 61-79.

Gloer

W. H. Gloer, *An Exegetical and Theological Study of Paul's Understanding of New Creation and Reconciliation in 2 Cor. 5:14-21*. Lewiston: Mellen Biblical, 1996.

Gnilka

J. Gnilka, "2 Cor 6:14–7:1 in the Light of the Qumran Texts and the Testaments of the Twelve Patriarchs," in Murphy-O'Connor (ed.) 48-68. ETr of an article first appearing in *Schmid FS* 86-99.

Godet

F. Godet, *Commentary on St. Paul's First Epistle to the Corinthians,* Vol. 1. ETr. Edinburgh: Clark, 1893.

G. E. Godet

G. E. Godet, *La Seconde Épître aux Corinthiens.* Neuchâtel: Attinger, 1914.

Goddard and Cummins

A. J. Goddard and S. A. Cummins, "Ill or Ill-Treated? Conflict and Persecution as the Context of Paul's Original Ministry in Galatia (Galatians 4:12-20)," *JSNT* 52 (1993) 93-126.

Göttsberger

J. Göttsberger, "Die Hülle des Moses nach Ex 34 und 2 Kor 3," *BZ* 16 (1922) 1-17.

Goguel

M. Goguel, "Le caractère, à la fois actuel et futur, du salut dans la théologie paulinienne," in *Dodd FS* 322-41.

Goguel, *Introduction*

M. Goguel, *Introduction au Nouveau Testament* IV/2: *Les épîtres pauliniennes*. Paris: Leroux, 1926.

Goguel, *Jugement*

M. Goguel, *Le jugement dans le Nouveau Testament*. Bulletin de la faculté libre de théologie protestante de Paris. Paris, 1943.

Gollwitzer

H. Gollwitzer, " 'Hinfort nicht mehr.' Predigt über 2 Kor 5,15 . . . ," *EvT* 14 (1954) 1-6.

Goodspeed

E. J. Goodspeed, *The New Testament: An American Translation.* Chicago: University of Chicago, 1923.

Goodspeed, *Introduction*

E. J. Goodspeed, *An Introduction to the New Testament.* Chicago: University of Chicago, 1937.

Goodspeed, *Problems*

E. J. Goodspeed, *Problems of New Testament Translation.* Chicago: University of Chicago, 1945.

Goppelt

L. Goppelt, *Theology of the New Testament.* 2 vols. ETr. Ed. J. Roloff. Grand Rapids: Eerdmans, 1981.

Goppelt, *Christologie*

L. Goppelt, *Christologie und Ethik.* Göttingen: Vandenhoeck und Ruprecht, 1968.

Goudge

H. L. Goudge, *The Second Epistle to the Corinthians.* WC. London: Methuen, 1927.

Goulder

M. D. Goulder, "2 Cor. 6:14–7:1 as an Integral Part of 2 Corinthians," *NovT* 36 (1994) 47-57.

Goulder, *Mission*

M. D. Goulder, *Paul and the Competing Mission in Corinth.* Peabody: Hendrickson, 2001.

Gräbe

P. J. Gräbe, "The All-Surpassing Power of God through the Holy Spirit in the Midst of Our Broken Earthly existence: Perspectives on Paul's Use of δύναμις in 2 Corinthians," *Neot* 28 (1994) 147-56.

Grabner-Haider

A. Grabner-Haider, *Paraklese und Eschatologie bei Paulus. Mensch und Welt im Anspruch der Zukunft Gottes.* NTAbh n.F. 4. Münster: Aschendorff, 1968.

Grässer

E. Grässer, "Paulus, der Apostel des Neuen Bundes (2 Kor 2,14–4,6), in Lorenzi (ed.) 7-43.

Grant

F. C. Grant, *The Economic Background of the Gospels.* New York: Russell, 1973 (= 1926).

Grant FS

Early Christian Literature and the Classical Intellectual Tradition: In honorem

Robert M. Grant. Ed. W. R. Schoedel and R. L. Wilken. *Théologie Historique*
54. Paris: Beauchesne, 1979.

R. M. Grant

R. M. Grant, *A Historical Introduction to the New Testament.* New York: Harper
and Row/London: Collins, 1963.

R. M. Grant, *Letter*

R. M. Grant, *The Letter and the Spirit.* New York: Macmillan, 1957.

Grayston

K. Grayston, *Dying, We Live: A New Enquiry into the Death of Christ in the New
Testament.* New York: Oxford University Press, 1990.

Grech

P. Grech, "2 Corinthians 3,17 and the Pauline Doctrine of Conversion to the Holy
Spirit," *CBQ* 17 (1955) 420-37.

Greenwood

D. Greenwood, "The Lord Is the Spirit: Some Considerations of 2 Cor 3:17,"
CBQ 34 (1972) 467-72.

Grelot

P. Grelot, "Note sur 2 Corinthiens 3.14," *NTS* 33 (1986-87) 135-44.

Griffiths

D. R. Griffiths, "'The Lord is the Spirit' (2 Corinthians iii.17, 18)," *ExpT* 55
(1943-44) 81-83.

Grindheim

S. Grindheim, "The Law Kills but the Gospel Gives Life: The Letter-Spirit Dualism in 2 Corinthians 3.5-18," *JSNT* 84 (2001) 97-115.

Grosheide

F. W. Grosheide, "Enkele opmerkingen over 2 Kor. 5:1-4," in *Theologische
Studiën* 27 (1909) 253-88.

Gundry

R. H. Gundry, Sōma *in Biblical Theology with Emphasis on Pauline Anthropology.* SNTSMS 29. Cambridge: Cambridge University Press, 1976.

Gundry Volf

J. M. Gundry Volf, *Paul and Perseverance: Staying In and Falling Away.* WUNT
2.37. Tübingen: Mohr, 1990.

Guntermann

F. Guntermann, *Die Eschatologie des Hl. Paulus.* NTAbh 13. 4/5. Münster:
Aschendorff, 1932.

Gunther

J. J. Gunther, *St. Paul's Opponents and Their Background: A Study of Apocalyptic and Jewish Sectarian Teachings.* NovTSup 35. Leiden: Brill, 1973.

Gunther, *Paul*

J. J. Gunther, *Paul: Messenger and Exile.* Valley Forge: Judson, 1972.

Guthrie

D. Guthrie, *New Testament Theology.* Downers Grove/Leicester: InterVarsity, 1981.

Guthrie, *Introduction*

D. Guthrie, *New Testament Introduction.* Downers Grove/Leicester: InterVarsity, 1970³.

Gutierrez

P. Gutierrez, *La paternité spirituelle selon saint Paul.* Ébib. Paris: Gabalda, 1968.

Güttgemanns

E. Güttgemanns, *Der leidende Apostel und sein Herr. Studien zur paulinischen Christologie.* FRLANT 90. Göttingen: Vandenhoeck und Ruprecht, 1966.

Hadidian

D. Y. Hadidian, "A Case in Study: 2 Cor. 5:16," in *Miller FS* 107-25.

Haenchen FS

Apophoreta. Festschrift für Ernst Haenchen zu seinem 70. Geburtstag. BZNW 30. Berlin: Töpelmann, 1964.

Haenchen

E. Haenchen, *The Acts of the Apostles.* ETr. Philadelphia: Westminster, 1971.

Hafemann

S. J. Hafemann, *2 Corinthians.* The NIV Application Commentary. Grand Rapids: Zondervan, 2000.

Hafemann, "Argument"

S. J. Hafemann, "Paul's Argument from the Old Testament and Christology in 2 Cor 1–9. The Salvation-History/Restoration Structure of Paul's Apologetic," in Bieringer (ed.) 277-303.

Hafemann, "Comfort"

S. J. Hafemann, "The Comfort and Power of the Gospel: The Argument of 2 Corinthians 1–3," *RevExp* 86 (1989) 325-44.

Hafemann, *Defense*

S. J. Hafemann, *Suffering and Ministry in the Spirit: Paul's Defense of His Ministry in 2 Corinthians 2:14–3:3.* Grand Rapids: Eerdmans, 1990/Carlisle: Paternoster, 2000.

Hafemann, "Glory"

S. J. Hafemann, "The Glory and Veil of Moses in 2 Cor 3:7-14: An Example of Paul's Contextual Exegesis of the OT — A Proposal," *HBT* 14 (1992) 31-49.

Hafemann, "Legitimacy"

S. J. Hafemann, "'Self-Commendation' and Apostolic Legitimacy in 2 Corinthians: A Pauline Dialectic?" *NTS* 36 (1990-91) 66-88.

Hafemann, *Moses*

S. J. Hafemann, *Paul, Moses and the History of Israel: The Letter/Spirit Contrast and the Argument from Scripture in 2 Corinthians 3.* Tübingen: Mohr, 1995.

Hafemann, "Old Testament"

S. J. Hafemann, "Paul's Use of the Old Testament in 2 Corinthians," *Int* 52 (1998) 246-57.

Hafemann, *Spirit*

S. J. Hafemann, *Suffering and the Spirit: An Exegetical Study of II Cor. 2:14–3:3 within the Context of the Corinthian Correspondence.* WUNT 2/19. Tübingen: Mohr, 1986.

Hafemann, "Weakness"

S. J. Hafemann, "'Because of Weakness' (Galatians 4:13): The Role of Suffering in the Mission of Paul," in *O'Brien FS* 131-46.

Hagner

D. A. Hagner, *The Use of the Old and New Testaments in Clement of Rome.* NovTSup 34. Leiden: Brill, 1973.

Hahn

F. Hahn, "Das Ja des Paulus und das Ja Gottes. Bemerkungen zu 2 Kor 1,12–2,1," in *Braun FS* 229-39.

Hahn, "Tag"

F. Hahn, "'Siehe, jetzt ist der Tag des Heils.' Neuschöpfung und Versöhnung nach 2. Korinther 5,14–6,2," *EvT* 33 (1973) 244-53.

Hainz

J. Hainz, *Ekklesia. Strukturen paulinischer Gemeinde-Theologie und Gemeinde-Ordnung.* Regensburg: Pustet, 1972.

Hainz, *Koinonia*

J. Hainz, *KOINONIA. "Kirche" als Gemeinschaft bei Paulus.* BU 16. Regensburg: Pustet, 1982.

Hainz, "Paulus"

J. Hainz, "KOINΩNIA bei Paulus," in *Georgi FS* 375-91.

Hall

D. R. Hall, "Pauline Church Discipline," *TynB* 20 (1969) 3-26.

Hall, "Famine"

D. R. Hall, "St. Paul and Famine Relief: A Study in Galatians 2[10]," *ExpT* 82 (1970-71) 309-11.

Halmel

A. Halmel, *Der zweite Korintherbrief des Apostels Paulus. Geschichte und literarkritische Untersuchungen.* Halle: Niemeyer, 1904.

Halperin

D. L. Halperin, "Heavenly Ascension in Ancient Judaism: The Nature of the Experience," in *SBL 1987 Seminar Papers,* ed. K. H. Richards. Atlanta: Scholars, 1987, pp. 218-32.

Hamerton-Kelly

R. G. Hamerton-Kelly, *Pre-Existence, Wisdom, and the Son of Man.* SNTSMS 21. Cambridge: Cambridge University Press, 1973.

Hanhart

K. Hanhart, *The Intermediate State in the New Testament.* Franeker: Wever, 1966.

Hanhart, "Hope"

K. Hanhart, "Paul's Hope in the Face of Death," *JBL* 88 (1969) 445-57.

Hansen

M. Hansen, *Om Trosbegrebet hos Paulus.* Copenhagen: Gyldendal, 1937.

G. W. Hansen

G. W. Hansen, *Abraham in Galatians: Epistolary and Rhetorical Contexts.* JSNTSS 29. Sheffield: JSOT, 1989.

Hanson FS

Scripture: Meaning and Method: Essays Presented to Anthony Tyrrell Hanson for His Seventieth Birthday. Ed. B. P. Thompson. Hull: Hull University, 1987.

Hanson

A. T. Hanson, *Studies in Paul's Technique and Theology.* Grand Rapids: Eerdmans/London: SPCK, 1974.

Hanson, *Christ*

A. T. Hanson, *Jesus Christ in the Old Testament.* London: SPCK, 1965.

Hanson, *Image*

A. T. Hanson, *The Image of the Invisible God.* London: SCM, 1982.

Hanson, "Midrash"

A. T. Hanson, "The Midrash in II Corinthians 3: A Reconsideration," *JSNT* 9 (1980) 2-23.

Hanson, *Ministry*

A. T. Hanson, *The Pioneer Ministry.* London: SCM, 1961.

Hanson, *Paradox*

A. T. Hanson, *The Paradox of the Cross in the Thought of St. Paul.* JSNTSS 17. Sheffield: JSOT, 1987.

R. P. C. Hanson

R. P. C. Hanson, *2 Corinthians.* TBC. London: SCM, 1967.

Harada

M. Harada, "Paul's Weakness: A Study in Pauline Polemics (II Corinthians 10–13)." Unpublished Ph.D. dissertation, Boston University, 1968.

Harding

M. Harding, "The Classical Rhetoric of Praise and the New Testament," *RTR* 45 (1986) 73-82.

Harding, "Historicity"

M. Harding, "On the Historicity of Acts: Comparing Acts 9.23-5 with 2 Corinthians 11.32-3," *NTS* 39 (1993) 518-38.

Härle

W. Härle, "'Christus factus est peccatum metaphorice.' Zur Heilsbedeutung des Kreuzestodes Jesu Christi," *NZSTRP* 36 (1994) 302-15.

Harman

A. M. Harman, "Aspects of Paul's Use of the Psalms," *WTJ* 32 (1969) 1-23.

Harris

M. J. Harris, *Raised Immortal: Resurrection and Immortality in the New Testament*. Grand Rapids: Eerdmans, 1985/London: Marshall, 1983.

Harris, *Colossians*

M. J. Harris, *Colossians and Philemon*. EGGNT. Grand Rapids: Eerdmans, 1991.

Harris, "Death"

M. J. Harris, "Paul's View of Death in 2 Corinthians 5:1-10," in Longenecker and Tenney 317-28.

Harris, *Grave*

M. J. Harris, *From Grave to Glory: Resurrection in the New Testament*. Grand Rapids: Zondervan, 1990.

Harris, *Jesus*

M. J. Harris, *Jesus as God: The New Testament Use of* Theos *in Reference to Jesus*. Grand Rapids: Baker, 1992.

Harris, "Prepositions"

M. J. Harris, "Prepositions and Theology in the Greek New Testament," in *NIDNTT* 3.1171-1215.

Harris, "Resurrection"

M. J. Harris, "Resurrection and Immortality: Eight Theses," *Them* 1 (1976) 50-55.

Harris, "2 Corinthians"

M. J. Harris, "2 Corinthians," in *The Expositor's Bible Commentary*. Ed. F. E. Gaebelein. Vol. 10. Grand Rapids: Zondervan, 1976, pp. 299-406.

Harris, *Slave*

M. J. Harris, *Slave of Christ: A New Testament Metaphor for Total Devotion to Christ*. Leicester: Apollos, 1999/Downers Grove: InterVarsity, 2001.

Harris, "Watershed"

M. J. Harris, "2 Corinthians 5:1-10: Watershed in Paul's Eschatology?" *TynB* 22 (1971) 32-57.

J. R. Harris

J. R. Harris, "Enoch and 2 Corinthians," *ExpT* 33 (1921-22) 423-24.

Harrison

J. Harrison, "Paul's House Churches and the Cultic Associations," *RTR* 47 (1988) 31-47.

Harrison, *Grace*

J. Harrison, *Paul's Language of Grace (χάρις) in Its Graeco-Roman Context*. Tübingen, Mohr, 2000.

Harrisville

R. A. Harrisville, *The Concept of Newness (καινότης) in the New Testament*. Minneapolis: Fortress, 1960.

Harrisville, "Newness"

R. A. Harrisville, "The Concept of Newness in the NT," *JBL* 74 (1955) 69-79.

Harvey

A. E. Harvey, *Renewal through Suffering: A Study of 2 Corinthians.* Edinburgh: Clark, 1996.

Harvey, "Aspects"

A. E. Harvey, "Forty Strokes Save One: Social Aspects of Judaizing and Apostasy," in *Alternative Approaches to New Testament Study.* Ed. A. E. Harvey. London: SCM, 1985, pp. 79-96.

J. D. Harvey

J. D. Harvey, *Listening to the Text: Oral Patterning in Paul's Letters.* Grand Rapids: Baker/Leicester: Apollos, 1998.

Hatch

W. H. P. Hatch, *The Pauline Idea of Faith in Its Relation to Jewish and Hellenistic Religion.* Cambridge: Harvard University Press, 1917.

Haulotte

E. Haulotte, *La symbolique du vêtement selon la Bible.* Paris: Aubier, 1966.

Hausrath

A. Hausrath, *Der Vier-Capitelbrief des Paulus an die Korinther.* Heidelberg: Bassermann, 1870.

Hay

D. M. Hay (ed.), *Pauline Theology Volume II: 1 and 2 Corinthians.* Minneapolis: Fortress, 1993.

Hay, "Shaping"

D. M. Hay, "The Shaping of Theology in 2 Corinthians: Convictions, Doubts, and Warrants," in Hay 135-55.

Hays

R. B. Hays, *Echoes of Scripture in the Letters of Paul.* New Haven: Yale University, 1989.

Heckel

U. Heckel, *Kraft in Schwachheit. Untersuchungen zu 2. Kor 10–13.* WUNT 2/56. Tübingen: Mohr, 1993.

Heckel, "Dorn"

U. Heckel, "Der Dorn im Fleisch. Die Krankheit des Paulus in 2 Kor 12,7 und Gal 4,13f.," *ZNW* 84 (1993) 65-92.

T. K. Heckel

T. K. Heckel, *Der Innere Mensch. Die paulinische Verarbeitung eines platonischen Motivs.* WUNT 2/53. Tübingen: Mohr, 1993.

Heiny

S. B. Heiny, "2 Corinthians 2:14–4:6: The Motive for a Metaphor," in *SBL 1987 Seminar Papers.* Ed. K. H. Richards. Atlanta: Scholars, 1987, pp. 1-22.

Helbing

    R. Helbing, *Die Kasussyntax der Verba bei den Septuaginta.* Göttingen: Vandenhoeck und Ruprecht, 1928.

Hemer

    C. J. Hemer, "A Note on 2 Corinthians 1:9," *TynB* 23 (1972) 103-7.

Hemer, "Chronology"

    C. J. Hemer, "Observations on Pauline Chronology," in *Bruce FS* (2) 3-18.

Hemer, "Troas"

    C. J. Hemer, "Alexandria Troas," *TynB* 26 (1975) 79-112.

Hennecke and Schneemelcher

    E. Hennecke, *New Testament Apocrypha.* Volume Two, ed. W. Schneemelcher. ETr. London: SCM, 1974.

Heinrici FS

Neutestamentliche Studien für Georg Heinrici. UNT 6. Leipzig: Hinrichs, 1914.

Heinrici

    C. F. G. Heinrici, *Der zweite Brief an die Korinther.* KEK 6. Göttingen: Vandenhoeck und Ruprecht, 1900[8].

Héring

    J. Héring, *The Second Epistle of Saint Paul to the Corinthians.* ETr. London: Epworth, 1967.

Héring, *Royaume*

    J. Héring, *Le Royaume de Dieu et sa Venue.* Paris: Alcan, 1937.

Hermann

    I. Hermann, *KYRIOS und PNEUMA. Studien zur Christologie der paulinischen Hauptbriefe.* SANT 2. Munich: Kösel, 1961.

Hester

    D. A. Hester, "The Unity of 2 Corinthians: A Test Case for a Re-Discovered and Re-Invented Rhetoric," *Neot* 33 (1999) 411-32.

J. D. Hester

    J. D. Hester, *Paul's Concept of Inheritance.* SJT Occasional Papers, 14. Edinburgh: Clark, 1968.

Hettlinger

    R. F. Hettlinger, "2 Corinthians 5.1-10," *SJT* 10 (1957) 174-94.

Hickling

    C. J. A. Hickling, "The Sequence of Thought in II Corinthians, Chapter Three," *NTS* 21 (1974-75) 380-95.

Hickling, "Exodus"

    C. J. A. Hickling, "Paul's Use of Exodus in the Corinthian Correspondence," in Bieringer (ed.) 367-76.

Hickling, "Source"

    C. J. A. Hickling, "Is the Second Epistle to the Corinthians a Source for Early Church History?" *ZNW* 66 (1975) 284-87.

Hill

D. Hill, *Greek Words and Hebrew Meanings.* Cambridge: Cambridge University Press, 1967.

A. E. Hill

A. E. Hill, "The Temple of Asclepius: An Alternative Source for Paul's Body Theology?" *JBL* 99 (1980) 437-39.

E. Hill

E. Hill, "The Construction of Three Passages from St. Paul: Romans 8:20-21, 2 Corinthians 1:20, 2 Corinthians 3:10," *CBQ* 23 (1961) 296-301.

Himmelfarb

M. Himmelfarb, *Ascent to Heaven in Jewish and Christian Apocalypses.* New York: Oxford University Press, 1993.

Hoad

J. Hoad, "Some New Testament References to Isaiah 53," *ExpT* 68 (1957) 254-55.

Hoch

C. B. Hoch, Jr., *All Things New: The Significance of Newness for Biblical Theology.* Grand Rapids: Baker, 1995.

Hock

R. F. Hock, *The Social Context of Paul's Ministry: Tentmaking and Apostleship.* Philadelphia: Fortress, 1980.

Hock, "Tentmaking"

R. F. Hock, "Paul's Tentmaking and the Problem of His Social Class," *JBL* 97 (1978) 555-64.

Hock, "Workshop"

R. F. Hock, "The Workshop as a Social Setting for Paul's Missionary Preaching," *CBQ* 41 (1979) 438-50.

Hodge

C. Hodge, *A Commentary on the Second Epistle to the Corinthians.* London: Banner of Truth Trust, 1959 reprint of 1891 ed.

Hodgson

R. Hodgson, "Paul the Apostle and First Century Tribulation Lists," *ZNW* 74 (1983) 59-80.

Höistad

R. Höistad, "Eine hellenistische Parallele zu 2. Kor 6,3ff.," *ConNT* 9 (1944) 22-27.

Hoffmann

P. Hoffmann, *Die Toten in Christus.* Münster: Aschendorff, 1966².

Hofius

O. Hofius, *Paulusstudien.* WUNT 51. Tübingen: Mohr, 1989.

Hofius, "Erwägungen"

O. Hofius, "Erwägungen zur Gestalt und Herkunft des paulinischen Versöhnungsgedankens," *ZTK* 77 (1980) 186-99. Reprinted in his *Paulusstudien* 1-14.

Hofius, "Gesetz"
O. Hofius, "Gesetz und Evangelium nach 2 Korinther 3," in *Paulusstudien* 75-120.

Hofius, "Gott"
O. Hofius, "'Der Gott allen Trostes.' Παράκλησις und παρακαλεῖν in 2 Kor 1,3-7," *ThBeitr* 14 (1983) 217-27. Reprinted in his *Paulusstudien* 224-54.

Hofius, "2 Kor 5,19"
O. Hofius, "'Gott hat unter uns aufgerichtet das Wort von der Versöhnung' (2 Kor 5,19)," *ZNW* 71 (1980) 3-20. Reprinted in his *Paulusstudien* 15-32.

Holl
K. Holl, "Der Kirchenbegriff des Paulus in seinem Verhältnis zu dem der Urgemeinde," in his *Gesammelte Aufsätze zur Kirchengeschichte, II: Der Osten.* Tübingen: Mohr, 1928, pp. 44-67.

Holladay
C. R. Holladay, Theios Anēr *in Hellenistic-Judaism: A Critique of the Use of This Category in New Testament Christology.* SBLDS 40. Missoula: Scholars, 1977.

Holland
G. Holland, "Speaking Like a Fool: Irony in 2 Corinthians 10–13," in Porter and Olbricht 250-64.

Holleman
J. Holleman, *Resurrection and Parousia: A Traditio-Historical Study of Paul's Eschatology in 1 Corinthians 15.* Leiden: Brill, 1996.

Holloway
J. O. Holloway III, *ΠΕΡΙΠΑΤΕΩ as a Thematic Marker for Pauline Ethics.* San Francisco: Mellen Research University, 1992.

Holmberg
B. Holmberg, *Paul and Power: The Structure of Authority in the Primitive Church as Reflected in the Pauline Epistles.* Lund: Gleerup, 1978/Philadelphia: Fortress, 1980.

Holsten
C. Holsten, "Zur Erklärung von 2 Kor 11,4-6," *ZWT* 16 (1873) 1-56.

Hooker
M. D. Hooker, "Interchange in Christ," *JTS* n.s. 22 (1971) 349-61.

Hooker, *Adam*
M. D. Hooker, *From Adam to Christ: Essays on Paul.* Cambridge: Cambridge University Press, 1990.

Hooker, "Ethics"
M. D. Hooker, "Interchange in Christ and Ethics," *JSNT* 25 (1985) 3-17.

Hooker, "Scripture"

M. D. Hooker, "Beyond the Things That Are Written? St. Paul's Use of Scripture," *NTS* 27 (1980-81) 295-309. Reprinted in Hooker, *Adam* 139-54.

Hooker, "Suffering"

M. D. Hooker, "Interchange and Suffering," in *Bammel FS* 70-83.

Höpfl

H. Höpfl, "2 Cor iv.3, 4," *ExpT* 18 (1906-07) 428.

Horrell

D. G. Horrell, *The Social Ethos of the Corinthian Correspondence: Interests and Ideology from 1 Corinthians to 1 Clement.* Edinburgh: Clark, 1996.

Horsley

G. H. R. Horsley, *New Documents Illustrating Early Christianity: A Review of the Greek Inscriptions and Papyri Published in 1976* (Vol. 1). North Ryde: Macquarie University, 1981. *New Documents . . . Published in 1977* (Vol. 2), 1982. *New Documents . . . Published in 1978* (Vol. 3), 1983. *New Documents . . . Published in 1979* (Vol. 4), 1987. Cited by vol. and page.

Hort

F. J. A. Hort, "A Note by the Late Dr Hort on the Words κόφινος, σπυρίς, σαργάνη," *JTS* 10 (1909) 567-71.

Hotze

G. Hotze, *Paradoxien bei Paulus. Untersuchungen zu einer elementaren Denkform in seiner Theologie.* NTAbh n.F. 33. Münster: Aschendorff, 1997.

Howell

D. N. Howell, Jr., "The Center of Pauline Theology," *BSac* 151 (1994) 50-70.

Hubbard

M. V. Hubbard, *New Creation in Paul's Letters and Thought.* SNTS 119. Cambridge: Cambridge University Press, 2002.

Hübner

H. Hübner, *Law in Paul's Thought.* ETr. Edinburgh: Clark, 1984.

Hugedé

N. Hugedé, *La métaphore du miroir dans les épîtres de S. Paul aux Corinthiens.* Neuchâtel: Delachaux et Niestlé, 1957.

Hugedé, *Paul*

N. Hugedé, *St. Paul et la culture grecque.* Paris: Librairie Protestante, 1966.

Hughes

P. E. Hughes, *Paul's Second Epistle to the Corinthians.* NICNT. Grand Rapids: Eerdmans/London: Marshall, 1962.

F. W. Hughes

F. W. Hughes, "The Rhetoric of Reconciliation: 2 Corinthians 1.1–2.13 and 7.5–8.24," in *Kennedy FS* 246-61.

Hunt

E. W. Hunt, *Portrait of Paul.* London: Mowbrays, 1968.

Hunter
A. M. Hunter, *Paul and His Predecessors*. London: SCM, 1961.

Hunzinger
C. H. Hunzinger, "Die Hoffnung angesichts des Todes im Wandel der paulinischen Aussagen," in *Thielicke FS* 69-89.

Huppenbauer
H. W. Huppenbauer, "Belial in den Qumrantexten," *TZ* 15 (1959) 81-89.

Hurd
J. C. Hurd, Jr., *The Origin of I Corinthians*. New York: Seabury, 1965.

Hurtado
L. W. Hurtado, "The Jerusalem Collection and the Book of Galatians," *JSNT* 5 (1979) 46-62.

Hyldahl
N. Hyldahl, *Die paulinische Chronologie*. Acta Theologica Danica 19. Leiden: Brill, 1986.

Hyldahl, "Einheit"
N. Hyldahl, "Die Frage nach der literarischen Einheit des Zweiten Korintherbriefes," *ZNW* 64 (1973) 289-306.

Iori
R. Iori, "Uso e significato di ΙΣΟΤΗΣ in 2 Cor 8,13-14," *RivB* 36 (1988) 425-38.

Isaacs
W. H. Isaacs, *The Second Epistle of Paul to the Corinthians: A Study in Translations and an Interpretation*. London: Oxford University Press, 1921.

M. E. Isaacs
M. E. Isaacs, *The Concept of Spirit*. HM 1. London: Heythrop, 1976.

Jeremias FS
Der Ruf Jesu und die Antwort der Gemeinde. Ed. E. Lohse, et al. Göttingen: Vandenhoeck und Ruprecht, 1970.

Jeremias
J. Jeremias, "Flesh and Blood Cannot Inherit the Kingdom of God," *NTS* 2 (1955-56) 151-59.

Jeremias, *Abba*
J. Jeremias, *Abba. Studien zur neutestamentlichen Theologie und Zeitgeschichte*. Göttingen: Vandenhoeck und Ruprecht, 1966.

Jeremias, *Jerusalem*
J. Jeremias, *Jerusalem in the Time of Jesus*. ETr. London: SCM, 1969.

Jeremias, *Prayers*
J. Jeremias, *The Prayers of Jesus*. Naperville: Allenson, 1967.

Jervell
J. Jervell, *Imago Dei. Gen 1,26f. im Spätjudentum, in der Gnosis und in den paulinischen Briefen*. FRLANT 76. Göttingen: Vandenhoeck und Ruprecht, 1960.

Jervell, "Charismatiker"
J. Jervell, "Der schwache Charismatiker," in *Käsemann FS* 185-98.

Jervell, *Paul*
J. Jervell, *The Unknown Paul.* ETr. Minneapolis: Augsburg, 1984.

Jewett
R. Jewett, *Paul's Anthropological Terms: A Study of Their Use in Conflict Settings.* AGJU 10. Leiden: Brill, 1972

Jewett, "Agitators"
R. Jewett, "The Agitators and the Galatian Congregation," *NTS* 17 (1970-71) 198-212.

Jewett, *Chronology*
R. Jewett, *A Chronology of Paul's Life.* Philadelphia: Fortress, 1979.

Jewett, *Correspondence*
R. Jewett, *The Thessalonian Correspondence.* Philadelphia: Fortress, 1986.

John
M. P. John, "The Jealousy of God — 2 Cor 11:2," *BT* 30 (1979) 447-48.

Johnson
S. E. Johnson, "A New Analysis of Second Corinthians," *ATR* 47 (1965) 436-45.

Johnston
G. Johnston, "2 Corinthians xiii.8," *ExpT* 5 (1893-94) 68-69.

Jones
P. R. Jones, "The Apostle Paul: A Second Moses according to II Corinthians 2:14–4:7." Unpublished Ph.D. dissertation, Princeton Theological Seminary, 1973.

Jones, "Moses"
P. R. Jones, "The Apostle Paul: Second Moses to the New Covenant Community," in *God's Inerrant Word.* Ed. J. W. Montgomery. Minneapolis: Bethany, 1974, pp. 219-41.

F. S. Jones
F. S. Jones, *"Freiheit" in den Briefen des Apostels Paulus. Eine historische, exegetische und religionsgeschichtliche Studie.* GTA 34. Göttingen: Vandenhoeck und Ruprecht, 1987.

Joubert
S. J. Joubert, *Paul as Benefactor: Reciprocity, Strategy and Theological Reflection in Paul's Collection.* WUNT 2/124. Tübingen: Mohr, 2000.

Joubert, "Rhetoric"
S. J. Joubert, "Behind the Mask of Rhetoric: 2 Corinthians 8 and the Intra-Textual Relation between Paul and the Corinthians," *Neot* 26 (1992) 101-12.

Judge
E. A. Judge, "Paul's Boasting in Relation to Contemporary Professional Practice," *ABR* 16 (1968) 37-50.

Judge, "Conflict"
E. A. Judge, "The Conflict of Educational Aims in N.T. Thought," *Journal of Christian Education* 9 (1966) 32-45.

Judge, "Conformity"
E. A. Judge, "Cultural Conformity and Innovation in Paul: Clues from Contemporary Documents," *TynB* 35 (1984) 3-24.

Judge "κανών"
E. A. Judge, "The Regional κανών for Requisitioned Transport," in Horsley 1.36-45.

Jülicher FS
Festgabe für Adolf Jülicher zum 70. Geburtstag. Tübingen: Mohr, 1927.

Jülicher
A. Jülicher, *An Introduction to the New Testament.* ETr. New York: Putnam, 1904.

Kabisch
R. Kabisch, *Die Eschatologie des Paulus in ihren Zusammenhängen mit dem Grundbegriff des Paulinismus.* Göttingen: Vandenhoeck und Ruprecht, 1893.

Kamlah
E. Kamlah, *Die Form der katalogischen Paränese im Neuen Testament.* WUNT 7. Tübingen: Mohr, 1964.

Kamlah, "Buchstabe"
E. Kamlah, "Buchstabe und Geist. Die Bedeutung dieser Antithese für die alttestamentliche Exegese des Apostels Paulus," *EvT* 14 (1954) 276-82.

Kamlah, "Paulus"
E. Kamlah, "Wie beurteilt Paulus sein Leiden? Ein Beitrag zur Untersuchung seiner Denkstruktur," *ZNW* 54 (1964) 217-32.

Kantzer
R. F. Kantzer, "Titus and Corinth," *Trinity Studies (= TrinJ)* 2 (1972) 84-97.

Käsemann FS
Rechtfertigung. Ed. J. Friedrich, et al. Tübingen: Mohr/Göttingen: Vandenhoeck und Ruprecht, 1976.

Käsemann
E. Käsemann, *Die Legitimität des Apostels. Eine Untersuchung zu II Korinther 10–13.* Darmstadt: Wissenschaftliche Buchgesellschaft, 1956. Reprinted from *ZNW* 41 (1942) 33-71.

Käsemann, *Leib*
E. Käsemann, *Leib und Leib Christi. Eine Untersuchung zur paulinischen Begrifflichkeit.* Tübingen: Mohr, 1933.

Käsemann, *Perspectives*
E. Käsemann, *Perspectives on Paul.* ETr. Philadelphia: Fortress, 1971.

Käsemann, *Questions*

E. Käsemann, *New Testament Questions of Today.* ETr. Philadelphia: Fortress/ London: SCM, 1969.

Käsemann, "Reconciliation"

E. Käsemann, "Some Thoughts on the Theme 'The Doctrine of Reconciliation in the New Testament,'" in *Bultmann FS* (2) 49-64.

Käsemann, *Romans*

E. Käsemann, *Commentary on Romans.* ETr. Grand Rapids: Eerdmans/London: SCM, 1980.

Keck FS

The Future of Christology: Essays in Honor of Leander E. Keck. Ed. A. J. Malherbe and W. G. Meeks. Minneapolis: Fortress, 1993.

Keck

L. E. Keck, "The Poor among the Saints in the New Testament," *ZNW* 56 (1965) 100-129.

Keck, "Christianity"

L. E. Keck, "The Poor among the Saints in Jewish Christianity and Qumran," *ZNW* 57 (1966) 54-78.

Kee

D. Kee, "Who Were the Super-Apostles of 2 Corinthians 10–13?" *RestQ* 23 (1980) 65-76.

Kennedy

J. H. Kennedy, *The Second and Third Epistles of St. Paul to the Corinthians.* London: Methuen, 1900.

Kennedy, "Epistles"

J. H. Kennedy, "Are the [sic] two epistles in 2 Corinthians?" *Exp,* 5th series, 6 (1897) 231-38, 285-304.

Kennedy, "Problem"

J. H. Kennedy, "The Problem of Second Corinthians," in *Herm* 12 (1902-03) 340-67.

G. A. Kennedy FS

Persuasive Artistry: Studies in New Testament Rhetoric in Honor of George A. Kennedy. Ed. D. F. Watson. JSNTSS 50. Sheffield: JSOT, 1991.

G. A. Kennedy

G. A. Kennedy, *Classical Rhetoric and Its Christian and Secular Tradition from Ancient to Modern Times.* London: Croom Helm, 1980.

G. A. Kennedy, *Interpretation*

G. A. Kennedy, *New Testament Interpretation through Rhetorical Criticism.* Chapel Hill/London: University of North Carolina, 1984.

H. A. A. Kennedy

H. A. A. Kennedy, *St. Paul's Conceptions of the Last Things.* London: Hodder, 1904^2.

H. A. A. Kennedy, "Weakness"

H. A. A. Kennedy, "'Weakness and Power': 2 Corinthians XIII.3, 4," *ExpT* 13 (1901-02) 349-50.

Kent

H. A. Kent, "The Glory of Christian Ministry: An Analysis of 2 Corinthians 2:14–4:18," *GTJ* 2 (1981) 171-89.

Ker

R. E. Ker, "Fear or Love? A Textual Note," *ExpT* 72 (1960-61) 195-96.

Kerr

A. J. Kerr, "APPABΩN," *JTS* n.s. 39 (1988) 92-97.

Kertelge

K. Kertelge, *"Rechtfertigung" bei Paulus. Studien zur Struktur und zum Bedeutungsgehalt des paulinischen Rechtfertigungsbegriffs.* NTAbh n.F. 3. Münster: Aschendorff, 1967.

Keyes

C. W. Keyes, "The Greek Letter of Introduction," *AJP* 56 (1935) 28-44.

Kilpatrick FS

Studies in New Testament Language and Text. Ed. J. K. Elliott. NovTSup 44. Leiden: Brill, 1976.

Kim

S. Kim, *The Origin of Paul's Gospel.* WUNT 2/4. Tübingen: Mohr, 1981/Grand Rapids: Eerdmans, 1982.

Kim, "Reconciliation"

S. Kim, "2 Cor. 5:11-21 and the Origin of Paul's Concept of 'Reconciliation,'" *NovT* 39 (1997) 360-84.

C. H. Kim

C. H. Kim, *Form and Structure of the Familiar Letter of Recommendation.* SBLDS 4. Missoula: Scholars, 1972.

Kinsey

A. B. Kinsey, "The Triumph-Joy," *ExpT* 21 (1909-10) 282-83.

Kirk

J. A. Kirk, "Apostleship since Rengstorf: Towards a Synthesis," *NTS* 21 (1974-75) 249-64.

Kistemaker

S. J. Kistemaker, *Exposition of the Second Epistle to the Corinthians.* New Testament Commentary. Grand Rapids: Baker, 1997.

Kitzberger

I. Kitzberger, *Bau der Gemeinde. Das paulinische Wortfeld* οἰκοδομή/(ἐπ)-οικοδομεῖν. FZB 53. Würzburg: Echter, 1986.

Klassen

W. Klassen, "The Sacred Kiss in the New Testament: An Example of Social Boundary Lines," *NTS* 39 (1993) 122-35.

Klauck

H. J. Klauck, *2 Korintherbrief.* KNT 8. Würzburg: Echter, 1986.

Klauck, "Erleuchtung"

H. J. Klauck, "Erleuchtung und Verkündigung. Auslegungsskizze zu 2 Kor 4,1-6," in Lorenzi (ed.) 267-97.

Klauck, *Gemeinde*

H. J. Klauck, *Gemeinde — Amt — Sakrament. Neutestamentliche Perspektiven.* Würzburg: Echter, 1989.

Klauck, "Himmelfahrt"

H. J. Klauck, "Die Himmelfahrt des Paulus (2 Kor 12.2-4) in der koptischen Paulusapokalypse aus Nag Hammadi (NHC V/2)," *SNTU* 10 (1985) 151-90.

Klausner

J. Klausner, *From Jesus to Paul.* London: Allen and Unwin, 1943.

Klein

G. Klein, *Die zwölf Apostel. Ursprung und Gehalt einer Idee.* FRLANT n.F. 59. Göttingen: Vandenhoeck und Ruprecht, 1961.

Klein, "Naherwartung"

G. Klein, "Apokalyptische Naherwartung bei Paulus," in *Braun FS* 241-62.

Kleinknecht

K. T. Kleinknecht, *Der leidende Gerechtfertigte.* WUNT 2/13. Tübingen: Mohr, 1984.

Klinzing

G. Klinzing, *Die Umdeutung des Kultus in der Qumrangemeinde und im Neuen Testament.* SUNT 7. Göttingen: Vandenhoeck und Ruprecht, 1971.

Knauf

E. A. Knauf, "Zum Ethnarchen des Aretas 2 Kor 11:32," *ZNW* 74 (1983) 145-47.

D. B. Knox FS

God Who Is Rich in Mercy. Ed. P. T. O'Brien and D. G. Peterson. Grand Rapids: Baker, 1986.

J. Knox FS

Christian History and Interpretation: Studies Presented to John Knox. Ed. W. R. Farmer, C. F. D. Moule, and R. R. Niebuhr. Cambridge: Cambridge University Press, 1967.

Knox

J. Knox, *Chapters in a Life of Paul.* New York: Abingdon, 1950/London: Black, 1954.

Knox, "2 Corinthians"

J. Knox, "2 Corinthians and the Pauline Corpus," *JBL* 55 (1936) 145-53.

R. A. Knox

R. A. Knox, *A New Testament Commentary for English Readers* II: *The Acts of the Apostles, St. Paul's Letters to the Churches.* New York: Sheed and Ward, 1954.

W. L. Knox

W. L. Knox, *St. Paul and the Church of the Gentiles.* Cambridge: Cambridge University Press, 1939.

W. L. Knox, *Jerusalem*

W. L. Knox, *St. Paul and the Church of Jerusalem.* Cambridge: Cambridge University Press, 1925.

Koch

D. A. Koch, "Abraham und Mose im Streit der Meinungen. Beobachtungen und Hypothesen zur Debatte zwischen Paulus und seinen Gegnern in 2 Kor 11,22-23 und 3,7-18," in Bieringer (ed.) 305-24.

Koch, *Schrift*

D. A. Koch, *Die Schrift als Zeuge des Evangeliums. Untersuchungen zur Verwendung und zum Verständnis der Schrift bei Paulus.* Tübingen: Mohr, 1986.

Koester

H. Koester, *Introduction to the New Testament.* 2 vols. Philadelphia: Fortress, 1982.

C. R. Koester

C. R. Koester, *The Dwelling of God: The Tabernacle in the Old Testament, Intertestamental Jewish Literature, and the New Testament.* CBQMS 22. Washington: Catholic Biblical Association, 1989.

W. Koester

W. Koester, *Die Idee der Kirche beim Apostel Paulus.* Münster, 1928.

Kolenkow

A. B. Kolenkow, "Paul and His Opponents in 2 Cor 10–13: THEIOI ANDRES and Spiritual Guides," in *Georgi FS* 351-74.

Koperski

V. Koperski, "Knowledge of Christ and Knowledge of God in the Corinthian Correspondence," in Bieringer (ed.) 377-96.

Köstenberger

A. J. Köstenberger, " 'We Plead on Christ's Behalf: "Be Reconciled to God," ' " *BT* 48 (1997) 328-31.

Kraftchick

S. J. Kraftchick, "Death in Us, Life in You: The Apostolic Medium," in *Society of Biblical Literature 1991 Seminar Papers,* pp. 618-37. Ed. E. H. Lovering, Jr. Atlanta, Scholars, 1991. (Reprinted in Hay [ed.] 69-77).

Kramer

W. Kramer, *Christ, Lord, Son of God.* ETr. SBT 5. London: SCM, 1966.

Kreitzer

L. J. Kreitzer, *2 Corinthians.* Sheffield: Sheffield Academic, 1996.

Kreitzer, *Jesus*

L. J. Kreitzer, *Jesus and God in Paul's Eschatology.* JSNTSS 19. Sheffield: JSOT, 1987.

Kremendahl

D. Kremendahl, *Die Botschaft der Form. Zum Verhaltnis von antiker Epistolographie und Rhetorik im Galaterbrief.* NTOA 46. Fribourg: Editions Universitaires, 2000.

Kremer

J. Kremer, " 'Denn der Buchstabe tötet, der Geist aber macht lebendig.' Methodologische und hermeneutische Erwägungen zu 2 Kor 3,6b," in *Zimmermann FS* 219-50.

Krenkel

M. Krenkel, *Beiträge zur Aufhellung der Geschichte und der Briefe des Apostels Paulus.* Braunschweig: Schwetschke, 1895².

Kruse

C. G. Kruse, *The Second Epistle of Paul to the Corinthians.* TNTC. Grand Rapids: Eerdmans/Leicester: Inter-Varsity, 1987.

Kruse, *Ministry*

C. G. Kruse, *New Testament Foundations of Ministry.* London: Marshall, 1983.

Kruse, "Offender"

C. G. Kruse, "The Offender and the Offence in 2 Corinthians 2:5 and 7:12," *EvQ* 60 (1988) 129-39.

Kruse, "Opposition"

C. G. Kruse, "The Relationship between the Opposition to Paul Reflected in 2 Corinthians 1–7 and 10–13," *EvQ* 61 (1989) 195-202.

Kruse, *Paul*

C. G. Kruse, *Paul, the Law and Justification.* Leicester: Apollos, 1996.

Kühl

E. Kühl, *Über 2 Korinther 5:1-10. Ein Beitrag zur Frage nach dem Hellenismus bei Paulus.* Königsberg: Koch, 1904.

Kuhn

K. G. Kuhn, "Les rouleaux de guerre de Qumrân," *RB* 61 (1954) 193-205.

Kuhn, "Schriftrollen"

K. G. Kuhn, "Die Schriftrollen vom Toten Meer," *EvT* 11 (1951) 72-75.

Kümmel

W. G. Kümmel, Supplementary notes in H. Lietzmann, *An die Korinther* I, II. HNT 9. Tübingen: Mohr, 1949, pp. 165-214.

Kümmel, *Introduction*

W. G. Kümmel, *Introduction to the New Testament.* ETr. Nashville: Abingdon/London: SCM, 1975².

Kümmel, *Man*

W. G. Kümmel, *Man in the New Testament.* ETr. London: SCM, 1963.

Kümmel, *Problems*

W. G. Kümmel, *The New Testament: The History of the Investigation of Its Problems.* ETr. Nashville: Abingdon, 1972.

Kuss

O. Kuss, *Paulusbriefe. I: Die Briefe an die Römer, Korinther und Galater.* RNT 6/
1. Regensburg: Pustet, 1940.

Ladd FS

Unity and Diversity in New Testament Theology. Ed. R. A. Guelich. Grand
Rapids: Eerdmans, 1978.

Ladd

G. E. Ladd, *A Theology of the New Testament.* Revised by D. A. Hagner. Grand
Rapids: Eerdmans, 1993.

Lake

K. Lake, *The Earlier Epistles of St Paul.* London: Rivington, 1927.

Lambrecht

J. Lambrecht, *Second Corinthians.* SP 8. Collegeville: Liturgical, 1999.

Lambrecht, "Appeal"

J. Lambrecht, "Paul's Appeal and the Obedience to Christ: The Line of Thought
in 2 Corinthians 10,1-6," *Bib* 77 (1996) 398-416.

Lambrecht, "Boasting"

J. Lambrecht, "Paul's Boasting about the Corinthians: A Study of 2 Corinthians
8:24–9:5," *NovT* 40 (1998) 352-68.

Lambrecht, "Context"

J. Lambrecht, "The Fool's Speech and Its Context: Paul's Particular Way of Arguing in 2 Cor 10–13," *Bib* 82 (2001) 305-24.

Lambrecht, "Fragment"

J. Lambrecht, "The Fragment 2 Cor vi 14–vii 1: A Plea for Its Authenticity," in
Miscellanea Neotestamentica, vol. 2. Ed. T. Baarda, A. F. J. Klijn, and W. C.
van Unnik. NovTSup 47. Leiden: Brill, 1978, pp. 143-61. Reprinted in
Bieringer and Lambrecht 531-49.

Lambrecht, "Nekrosis"

J. Lambrecht, "The Nekrosis of Jesus: Ministry and Suffering in 2 Cor 4,7-15,"
BETL 73 (1986) 120-43. Reprinted in Bieringer and Lambrecht 309-33.

Lambrecht, "Notes"

J. Lambrecht, "Philological and Exegetical Notes on 2 Cor 13,4," *Bijdragen* 46
(1985) 261-69. Reprinted in Bieringer and Lambrecht 589-98.

Lambrecht, "Outlook"

J. Lambrecht, "The Eschatological Outlook in 2 Corinthians 4,7-15," in Bieringer
and Lambrecht 335-49.

Lambrecht, "Reading"

J. Lambrecht, "'Reconcile Yourselves . . .': A Reading of 2 Cor 5,11-21,"
Benedictina 10 (1989) 161-209. Reprinted in Bieringer and Lambrecht
363-412.

Lambrecht, "2 Cor. 7:3"

J. Lambrecht, "To Die Together and to Live Together: A Study of 2 Corinthians
7,3," in Bieringer and Lambrecht 571-87.

Lambrecht, "Self-Commendation"

J. Lambrecht, "Dangerous Boasting: Paul's Self-Commendation in 2 Corinthians 10–13," in Bieringer (ed.) 325-46.

Lambrecht, "Strength"

J. Lambrecht, "'Strength in Weakness': A Reply to Scott B. Andrews' Exegesis of 2 Cor 11.23b-33," *NTS* 43 (1997) 285-90.

Lambrecht, "Structure"

J. Lambrecht, "Structure and Line of Thought in 2 Cor 2,14–4,6" *Bib* 64 (1983) 344-80. Reprinted in Bieringer and Lambrecht 257-94.

Lambrecht, "Time"

J. Lambrecht, "The Favourable Time: A Study of 2 Corinthians 6,2a in Its Context," in Bieringer and Lambrecht 515-29.

Lambrecht, "Transformation"

J. Lambrecht, "Transformation in 2 Cor 3,18," *Bib* 64 (1983) 243-54. Reprinted in Bieringer and Lambrecht 295-307.

Lambrecht, "Vie"

J. Lambrecht, "La vie engloutit ce qui est mortel. Commentaire de 2 Corinthiens 5,4c," in Bieringer and Lambrecht 351-61.

Lampe

G. W. H. Lampe, "Church Discipline and the Interpretation of the Epistles to the Corinthians," in *J. Knox FS* 337-61.

Lampe, *Seal*

G. W. H. Lampe, *The Seal of the Spirit: A Study in the Doctrine of Baptism and Confirmation in the New Testament and the Fathers.* London: Longmans, 1951.

Lane

W. L. Lane, "Covenant: The Key to Paul's Conflict with Corinth," *TynB* 33 (1982) 3-30.

Lang

F. Lang, *Die Briefe an die Korinther.* NTD 7. Göttingen: Vandenhoeck und Ruprecht, 1986.

F. G. Lang

F. G. Lang, *2. Korinther 5,1-10 in der neueren Forschung.* BGBE 16. Tübingen: Mohr, 1973.

Larsson

E. Larsson, *Christus als Vorbild. Eine Untersuchung zu den paulinischen Tauf und Eikontexten.* ASNU 23. Uppsala: Gleerup, 1962.

Lattey

C. Lattey, "Λαμβάνειν in 2 Cor. xi.20," *JTS* 44 (1943) 148.

Leaf

W. Leaf, *Strabo on the Troad Book XIII, Cap. 1.* Cambridge: Cambridge University Press, 1923.

Leary

T. J. Leary, "'A Thorn in the Flesh' — 2 Corinthians 12:7," *JTS* n.s. 43 (1992) 520-22.

Le Déaut

R. Le Déaut, "Traditions targumiques dans le corpus paulinien? (Hebr 11,4 et 12,24; Gal 4,29-30; II Cor 3,16)," *Bib* 42 (1961) 28-48.

Leivestad

R. Leivestad, "'The Meekness and Gentleness of Christ' II Cor. X.1," *NTS* 12 (1965-66) 156-64.

Lenski

R. C. H. Lenski, *The Interpretation of St. Paul's First and Second Epistles to the Corinthians.* Minneapolis: Augsburg, 1963 reprint of 1937 ed.

Lewis

J. P. Lewis (ed.), *Interpreting 2 Corinthians 5:14-21: An Exercise in Hermeneutics.* Lewiston: Mellen, 1984.

Lietzmann

H. Lietzmann, *An die Korinther 1/2.* With supplementary notes (pp. 165-214) by W. G. Kümmel. HNT 9. Tübingen: Mohr, 1949.

Lieu

J. M. Lieu, "'Grace to You and Peace': The Apostolic Greeting," *BJRL* 68 (1985) 161-78.

Lightfoot

J. B. Lightfoot, *Biblical Essays.* New York/London: Macmillan, 1893.

Lightfoot, *Galatians*

J. B. Lightfoot, *St. Paul's Epistle to the Galatians.* London: Macmillan, 1880[6].

Lightfoot, *Notes*

J. B. Lightfoot, *Notes on the Epistles of St. Paul.* London: Macmillan, 1895 (reprinted Grand Rapids: Baker, 1957).

Lillie

W. Lillie, "An Approach to II Corinthians 5.1-10," *SJT* 30 (1977) 59-70.

Lincoln

A. T. Lincoln, *Paradise Now and Not Yet.* SNTSMS 43. Cambridge: Cambridge University Press, 1981.

Lincoln, "Paul"

A. T. Lincoln, "Paul the Visionary: The Setting and Significance of the Rapture to Paradise in II Corinthians XII.1-10," *NTS* 25 (1978-79) 204-20.

Lindars

B. Lindars, *New Testament Apologetic: The Doctrinal Significance of the Old Testament Quotations.* Philadelphia: Westminster/London: SCM, 1961.

Lindars, "Eschatology"

B. Lindars, "The Sound of the Trumpet: Paul and Eschatology," *BJRL* 67 (1985) 766-82.

Ljungman

H. Ljungman, *PISTIS: A Study of Its Presuppositions and Its Meaning in Pauline Use.* ARSHLL 64. Lund: Gleerup, 1964.

Lohse

E. Lohse, *The Formation of the New Testament.* ETr. Nashville: Abingdon, 1981.

Lohse, *Verteidigung*

E. Lohse, *Verteidigung und Begründung des apostolischen Amtes* (2 Kor 10–13). Benedictina 11. Rome: Abbazia San Paolo fuori le mura, 1992.

Lohse, "Amt"

E. Lohse, "Das Amt, das die Versöhnung predigt," in *Käsemann FS* 339-49.

Longenecker FS

Gospel in Paul: Studies on Corinthians, Galatians and Romans for Richard N. Longenecker. Ed. L. A. Jervis and P. Richardson. JSNTSS 108. Sheffield: Sheffield Academic, 1994.

Longenecker

R. N. Longenecker, *Paul: Apostle of Liberty.* New York/London: Harper, 1964.

Longenecker and Tenney

R. N. Longenecker and M. C. Tenney (ed.), *New Dimensions in New Testament Study.* Grand Rapids: Zondervan, 1974.

Loubser

J. A. Loubser, "A New Look at Paradox and Irony in 2 Corinthians 10–13," *Neot* 26 (1992) 507-21.

Louw and Nida

J. P. Louw and E. A. Nida (eds.), *Greek-English Lexicon of the New Testament Based on Semantic Domains* I: *Introduction and Domains.* New York: United Bible Societies, 1988.

Lowe

J. Lowe, "An Examination of Attempts to Detect Developments in St. Paul's Theology," *JTS* 42 (1941) 129-42.

Lowrie

S. T. Lowrie, "An Exegesis of 2 Corinthians 5:1-5," *PTR* 1 (1903) 51-61.

Lüdemann

G. Lüdemann, *Paul, Apostle to the Gentiles: Studies in Chronology.* ETr. Minneapolis: Fortress/London: SCM, 1984.

Lüdemann, *Opposition*

G. Lüdemann, *Opposition to Paul in Jewish Christianity.* Philadelphia: Fortress, 1989.

Lührmann

D. Lührmann, *Das Offenbarungsverständnis bei Paulus und in paulinischen Gemeinden.* WMANT 16. Neukirchen-Vluyn: Neukirchener, 1965.

Lührmann, "Rechtfertigung"

D. Lührmann, "Rechtfertigung und Versöhnung," *ZTK* 67 (1970) 437-52.

Lütgert

W. Lütgert, *Freiheitspredigt und Schwarmgeister in Korinth.* BFCT 12/3. Gütersloh, 1908.

Luz

U. Luz, *Das Geschichtsverständnis des Paulus.* BZET 49. Munich: Kaiser, 1968.

Luz, "Bund"

U. Luz, "Der alte und der neue Bund bei Paulus und im Hebräerbrief," *EvT* 27 (1967) 318-36.

Lyonnet

S. Lyonnet, "Le sens de ἐφ' ᾧ en Rom. 5:12 et l'exégèse des Pères grecs," *Bib* 36 (1955) 436-56.

Lyonnet and Sabourin

S. Lyonnet and L. Sabourin, *Sin, Redemption and Sacrifice: A Biblical and Patristic Study.* Rome: Pontifical Biblical Institute, 1970.

MacDonald

M. Y. MacDonald, *The Pauline Churches: A Socio-Historical Study of Institutionalization in the Pauline and Deutero-Pauline Writings.* SNTSMS 60. Cambridge: Cambridge University Press, 1988.

Machalet

C. Machalet, "Paulus und seine Gegner. Eine Untersuchung zu den Korintherbriefen," *Theokratia* 2 (1970-72) 183-203.

Mackintosh

R. Mackintosh, "The Four Perplexing Chapters (2 Cor 10–13)," *Exp,* 7th series, 6 (1908) 336-44.

Mackintosh, "Visit"

R. Mackintosh, "The Brief Visit to Corinth," *Exp,* 7th series, 6 (1908) 226-34.

MacRae

G. W. MacRae, "Anti-Dualist Polemic in 2 Cor 4:6?" in *SE* IV/1: *The New Testament Scriptures.* Ed. F. L. Cross. TU 102. Berlin: Akademie, 1968, pp. 420-31.

MacRory

J. MacRory, *The Epistles of St. Paul to the Corinthians.* Dublin: Gill, 1935.

Madros

P. Madros, *The Pride and Humility of Saint Paul in His Second Letter to the Corinthians.* ETr. Jerusalem: Franciscan, 1986.

Maleparampil

J. Maleparampil, *The "Trinitarian" Formulae in St. Paul: An Exegetical Investigation into the Meaning and Function of Those Pauline Sayings Which Compositely Make Mention of God, Christ and the Holy Spirit.* Frankfurt am Main/New York: Lang, 1998.

Malherbe

A. J. Malherbe, *Ancient Epistolary Theorists.* Atlanta: Scholars, 1988.

Malherbe, "Contribution"
A. J. Malherbe, "The Corinthian Contribution," *RestQ* 3 (1959) 221-33.

Malherbe, "Paul"
A. J. Malherbe, "Antisthenes and Odysseus, and Paul at War," *HTR* 76 (1983) 143-73.

Manson FS
New Testament Essays: Studies in Memory of Thomas Walter Manson. Ed. A. J. B. Higgins. Manchester: Manchester University, 1959.

Manson
T. W. Manson, *Studies in the Gospels and Epistles.* Philadelphia: Westminster/ Manchester: Manchester University, 1962.

Manson, "ΙΛΑΣΤΗΡΙΟΝ"
T. W. Manson, "ΙΛΑΣΤΗΡΙΟΝ," *JTS* 46 (1945) 1-10.

Manson, "Suggestions"
T. W. Manson, "2 Cor. 2,14-17: Suggestions towards an Exegesis," in *de Zwaan FS* 155-62.

Marguerat
D. Marguerat, "2 Corinthiens 10–13: Paul et l'expérience de Dieu," *ETR* 63 (1988) 497-519.

Marrow
S. B. Marrow, "*Parrhesia* and the New Testament," *CBQ* 44 (1982) 431-46.

Marshall
P. Marshall, *Enmity in Corinth: Social Conventions in Paul's Relations with the Corinthians.* WUNT 2/23. Tübingen: Mohr, 1987.

Marshall, "Hybrists"
P. Marshall, "Hybrists Not Gnostics in Corinth," in *SBL 1984 Seminar Papers.* Ed. K. H. Richards. Chico: Scholars, 1984, pp. 275-87.

Marshall, "Invective"
P. Marshall, "Invective: Paul and His Enemies in Corinth," in *Andersen FS* 359-73.

Marshall, "Metaphor"
P. Marshall, "A Metaphor of Social Shame: ΘΡΙΑΜΒΕΥΕΙΝ in 2 Cor. 2:14," *NovT* 25 (1983) 302-17.

I. H. Marshall
I. H. Marshall, "The Meaning of 'Reconciliation,'" in *Ladd FS* 117-32.

I. H. Marshall, "Ekklesia"
I. H. Marshall, "New Wine in Old Wine Skins V: The Biblical Use of the Word 'Ekklesia,'" *ExpT* 84 (1972-73) 359-64.

I. H. Marshall, *Power*
I. H. Marshall, *Kept by the Power of God: A Study of Perseverance and Falling Away.* London: Epworth, 1969.

Martin FS

Worship, Theology and Ministry in the Early Church: Essays in Honor of Ralph P. Martin. Ed. M. J. Wilkins and T. Paige. Sheffield: JSOT, 1992.

Martin

R. P. Martin, *2 Corinthians.* WBC 40. Waco: Word, 1986.

Martin, *Carmen*

R. P. Martin, *Carmen Christi: Philippians ii.5-11 in Recent Interpretation and in the Setting of Early Christian Worship.* Cambridge: Cambridge University Press, 1967.

Martin, *Foundations*

R. P. Martin, *New Testament Foundations,* vol. 2. Grand Rapids: Eerdmans/ Exeter: Paternoster, 1978.

Martin, "Opponents"

R. P. Martin, "The Opponents of Paul in 2 Corinthians: An Old Issue Revisited," in *Ellis FS* 279-87.

Martin, *Reconciliation*

R. P. Martin, *Reconciliation: A Study of Paul's Theology.* Atlanta: John Knox/ London: Marshall, 1981.

Martin, "Setting"

R. P. Martin, "The Setting of 2 Corinthians," *TynB* 37 (1986) 3-19.

Martin, "Spirit"

R. P. Martin, "The Spirit in 2 Corinthians in Light of the 'Fellowship of the Holy Spirit' in 2 Corinthians 13:14," in *Beasley-Murray FS* 113-28.

Martin, "Theology"

R. P. Martin, "Theology and Mission in 2 Corinthians," in *O'Brien FS* 63-82.

D. B. Martin

D. B. Martin, *The Corinthian Body.* New Haven: Yale University, 1995.

Martyn

J. L. Martyn, "Epistemology at the Turn of the Ages: 2 Corinthians 5:16," in *J. Knox FS* 269-87.

Marxsen

W. Marxsen, *Introduction to the New Testament.* ETr. Philadelphia: Fortress/Oxford: Blackwell, 1968.

Massie

J. Massie, *I and II Corinthians.* Edinburgh: Jack, 1902.

Masson

C. Masson, "Immortalité de l'âme ou résurrection des morts? Réflexions critiques sur une étude récente," *RTP* 8 (1958) 250-67.

Masson, "Note"

C. Masson, "A propos de Act. 9.19b-25. Note sur l'utilisation de Gal. et de 2 Cor. par l'auteur des Acts," *TZ* 18 (1962) 161-66.

Mattern

L. Mattern, *Das Verständnis des Gerichtes bei Paulus.* ATANT 47. Zurich: Zwingli, 1966.

McCant

J. W. McCant, *2 Corinthians.* Sheffield: Sheffield Academic, 1999.

McCant, "Thorn"

J. W. McCant, "Paul's Thorn of Rejected Apostleship," *NTS* 34 (1987-88) 550-72.

McClelland

S. E. McClelland, "'Super-Apostles, Servants of Christ, Servants of Satan': A Response," *JSNT* 14 (1982) 82-87.

McDermott

J. M. McDermott, "The Biblical Doctrine of KOINΩNIA," *BZ* n.F. 19 (1975) 64-77, 219-33.

McDonald

J. I. H. McDonald, "Paul and the Preaching Ministry: A Reconsideration of 2 Cor. 2:14-17 in Its Context," *JSNT* 17 (1983) 35-50.

McKay

K. L. McKay, *A New Syntax of the Verb in New Testament Greek: An Aspectual Approach.* New York: Lang, 1994.

McKay, "Observations"

K. L. McKay, "Observations on the Epistolary Aorist in 2 Corinthians," *NovT* 37 (1995) 154-58.

McKay, "Syntax"

K. L. McKay, "Syntax in Exegesis," *TynB* 23 (1972) 39-57.

McKay, "Time"

K. L. McKay, "Time and Aspect in New Testament Greek," *NovT* 34 (1992) 209-28.

McKelvey

R. J. McKelvey, *The New Temple.* Oxford: Clarendon, 1969.

McKenzie FS

No Famine in the Land. Ed. J. Flanagan and A. Robinson. Missoula: Scholars, 1975.

McKnight

S. McKnight, *A Light among the Gentiles: Jewish Missionary Activity in the Second Temple Period.* Minneapolis: Fortress, 1991.

McNamara

M. McNamara, *The New Testament and the Palestinian Targum to the Pentateuch.* AnBib 27. Rome: Pontifical Biblical Institute, 1966.

McNamara, "Midrash"

M. McNamara, "Midrash, Culture Medium and Development of Doctrine: Some Facts in Quest of a Terminology," *PIBA* 2 (1988) 67-87.

McNamara, *Paraphrases*

M. McNamara, *Targum and Testament Aramaic Paraphrases of the Hebrew Bible: A Light on the New Testament.* Grand Rapids: Eerdmans, 1972.

McNeile

A. H. McNeile, *Introduction to the New Testament.* Oxford: Clarendon, 1953².

Mealand

D. L. Mealand, "'As Having Nothing, and Yet Possessing Everything,' 2 Kor 6:10c," *ZNW* 67 (1976) 277-79.

Meeks

W. A. Meeks, *The First Urban Christians.* New Haven/London: Yale University, 1983.

Meeks, "Moses"

W. A. Meeks, "Moses as God and King," in *Religions in Antiquity: Essays in Memory of Erwin Ramsdell Goodenough.* Ed. J. Neusner. NumenSup 14. Leiden: Brill, 1970, pp. 354-71.

Meeks, *Prophet-King*

W. A. Meeks, *The Prophet-King: Moses Traditions and the Johannine Christology.* NovTSup 14. Leiden: Brill, 1967.

Mell

U. Mell, *Neue Schöpfung. Eine traditionsgeschichtliche und exegetische Studie zu einem soteriologischen Grundsatz paulinischer Theologie.* BZNW 56. Berlin: Töpelmann, 1989.

Menoud

P. H. Menoud, *Le sort des trépassés d'après le Nouveau Testament.* Neuchâtel: Delachaux, 1966².

Menoud, "Thorn"

P. H. Menoud, "The Thorn in the Flesh and Satan's Angel (2 Cor. 12:7)," in *Jesus Christ and the Faith: A Collection of Studies.* PTMS 18. Pittsburgh: Pickwick, 1978, pp. 19-30. ETr of "L'écharde et l'ange Satanique (2 Cor. 12,7)," in *de Zwaan FS* 163-71.

Menzies

A. Menzies, *The Second Epistle of the Apostle Paul to the Corinthians.* London: Macmillan, 1912.

Menzies, "Integrity"

A. Menzies, "The Integrity of II. Corinthians," *Exp,* 8th series, 6 (1913) 370-73.

Metzger FS

New Testament Textual Criticism: Its Significance for Exegesis. Essays in Honor of Bruce M. Metzger. Ed. E. J. Epp and G. D. Fee. Oxford: Clarendon, 1981.

Metzger

B. M. Metzger, *A Textual Commentary on the Greek New Testament.* Second edition. New York: United Bible Societies, 1994.

Metzger, *Canon*

B. M. Metzger, *The Canon of the New Testament.* Oxford: Clarendon, 1987.

Metzger (1971)
B. M. Metzger, *A Textual Commentary on the Greek New Testament.* New York/ London: United Bible Societies, 1971.

Metzger, *Text*
B. M. Metzger, *The Text of the New Testament.* New York: Oxford University Press, 1968².

Meurer
S. Meurer, *Das Recht im Dienst der Versöhnung und des Friedens.* Zurich: Theologischer Verlag, 1972.

Meyer
H. A. W. Meyer, *Critical and Exegetical Hand-Book to the Epistles to the Corinthians.* ETr. With supplementary notes by T. W. Chambers. New York: Funk and Wagnalls, 1884.

B. F. Meyer
B. F. Meyer, "Did Paul's View of the Resurrection of the Dead Undergo Development?" *TS* 47 (1986) 363-87.

Michaelis
W. Michaelis, *Einleitung in das Neue Testament.* Bern: Haller, 1961³.

Michel FS
Abraham unser Vater. Juden und Christen im Gespräch über die Bibel. Ed. O. Betz, M. Hengel, and P. Schmidt. AGJU 5. Leiden: Brill, 1963.

Michel
O. Michel, "'Erkennen dem Fleisch nach' (II Kor. 5,16)," *EvT* 14 (1954) 22-29.

Miller FS
From Faith to Faith. Ed. D. Y. Hadidian. PTMS 23. Pittsburgh: Pickwick, 1979.

Minear
P. S. Minear, *Images of the Church in the New Testament.* Philadelphia: Westminster, 1960.

Minear, "Dying"
P. S. Minear, "Some Pauline Thoughts on Dying: A Study of 2 Corinthians," in *Miller FS* 91-106.

Mitchell
M. M. Mitchell, *Paul and the Rhetoric of Reconciliation: An Exegetical Investigation of the Language and Composition of 1 Corinthians.* Louisville: Westminster, 1992.

Mitchell, "Envoys"
M. M. Mitchell, "New Testament Envoys in the Context of Greco-Roman Diplomatic and Epistolary Conventions: The Example of Timothy and Titus," *JBL* 111 (1992) 641-62.

Mitchell, "Perspective"
M. M. Mitchell, "A Patristic Perspective on Pauline περιαυτολογία," *NTS* 47 (2001) 354-71.

Mitchell, "Shorthand"
M. M. Mitchell, "Rhetorical Shorthand in Pauline Argumentation: The Functions of the 'Gospel' in the Corinthian Correspondence," in *Longenecker FS* 63-88.

Mitton
C. L. Mitton, "Paul's Certainties. V. The Gift of the Spirit and Life beyond Death — 2 Corinthians v.1-5," *ExpT* 69 (1957-58) 260-63.

Moberly
R. W. L. Moberly, *At the Mountain of God: Story and Theology in Exodus 32–34.* Sheffield: JSOT, 1983.

Moffatt
J. Moffatt, *The Moffatt Translation of the Bible.* London: Hodder, 1935[2].

Moffatt, "Corinthians"
J. Moffatt, "2 Corinthians vi.14–vii.1," *ExpT* 20 (1908-09) 428-29.

Moffatt, *Introduction*
J. Moffatt, *An Introduction to the Literature of the New Testament.* Edinburgh: Clark, 1918[3].

Moncure
J. Moncure, "II Corinthians 7:8-10," *RevExp* 16 (1919) 476-77.

Montgomery
The New Testament in Modern English: Centenary Translation. Translated by H. B. Montgomery. Philadelphia: Judson, 1929.

Moore
A. L. Moore, *The Parousia in the New Testament.* Leiden: Brill, 1966.

G. F. Moore
G. F. Moore, *Judaism in the First Centuries of the Christian Era: The Age of the Tannaim.* 3 vols. Cambridge: Harvard University Press, 1927, 1930.

G. F. Moore, "Savour"
G. F. Moore, "Conjectanea Talmudica: 2 Corinthians 2:14-16. The Savour of Life or of Death," *JAOS* 26 (1906) 329-30.

Morgan-Wynne
J. E. Morgan-Wynne, "2 Corinthians VIII.18f. and the Question of a *Traditionsgrundlage* for Acts," *JTS* n.s. 30 (1979) 172-73.

Morray-Jones
C. R. A. Morray-Jones, "Paradise Revisited (2 Cor 12:1-12): The Jewish Mystical Background of Paul's Apostolate. Part 2: Paul's Heavenly Ascent and Its Significance," *HTR* 86 (1993) 177-217, 265-92.

Morrice
W. G. Morrice, *Joy in the New Testament.* Grand Rapids: Eerdmans, 1985.

Morrice, "Hina"
W. G. Morrice, "The Imperatival *hina*," *BT* 23 (1972) 326-30.

Morris FS
Reconciliation and Hope: New Testament Essays on Atonement and Eschatology

Presented to L. L. Morris. Ed. R. Banks. Exeter: Paternoster/Grand Rapids: Eerdmans, 1974.

Morris
L. Morris, *The Apostolic Preaching of the Cross.* London: Tyndale, 1955.

Morton
A. Q. Morton, "Dislocations in 1 and 2 Corinthians," *ExpT* 78 (1966-67) 119.

Mott
S. C. Mott, "The Power of Giving and Receiving: Reciprocity in Hellenistic Benevolence," in *Tenney FS* 60-72.

Mott, *Ethics*
S. C. Mott, *Biblical Ethics and Social Change.* Oxford: Oxford University Press, 1982.

Moule FS
Christ and Spirit in the New Testament: Studies in Honour of Charles Francis Digby Moule. Ed. B. Lindars and S. S. Smalley. Cambridge: Cambridge University Press, 1973.

Moule
C. F. D. Moule, *An Idiom Book of New Testament Greek.* Cambridge: Cambridge University Press, 1960^2.

Moule, *Birth*
C. F. D. Moule, *The Birth of the New Testament.* London: Black, 1962.

Moule, "Dualism"
C. F. D. Moule, "St. Paul and Dualism: The Pauline Conception of Resurrection," *NTS* 12 (1965-66) 106-23. Reprinted in his *Essays* 200-221.

Moule, *Essays*
C. F. D. Moule, *Essays in New Testament Interpretation.* Cambridge: Cambridge University Press, 1982.

Moule, "Influence"
C. F. D. Moule, "The Influence of Circumstances on the Use of Eschatological Terms," *JTS* n.s. 15 (1964) 1-15. Reprinted in his *Essays* 184-99.

Moule, "Peculiarities"
C. F. D. Moule, "Peculiarities in the Language of II Corinthians," in Moule, *Essays* 158-61.

Moule, "2 Cor. 3:18b"
C. F. D. Moule, "2 Cor 3:18b," in *Cullmann FS* (2) 231-38. Reprinted in Moule, *Essays* 227-34.

H. C. G. Moule
H. C. G. Moule, *The Second Epistle to the Corinthians.* Ed. by A. W. H. Moule. London: Pickering and Inglis, 1962/Fort Washington: Christian Literature Crusade, 1976.

Moulton

J. H. Moulton, *A Grammar of New Testament Greek* I: *Prolegomena.* Edinburgh: Clark, 1908³.

Moulton and Howard

J. H. Moulton and W. F. Howard, *A Grammar of New Testament Greek* II: *Accidence and Word-Formation.* Edinburgh: Clark, 1919, 1929.

Mozley

J. F. Mozley, "2 Corinthians xi.12," *ExpT* 42 (1930-31) 212-14.

Muellensiefen

W. Muellensiefen, "Satan der θεὸς τοῦ αἰῶνος τούτου, 2 Kor. 4:4?" *TSK* 95 (1923-24) 295-98.

Mullins

T. Y. Mullins, "Paul's Thorn in the Flesh," *JBL* 76 (1957) 299-303.

Mullins, "Ascription"

T. Y. Mullins, "Ascription as a Literary Form," *NTS* 19 (1973) 194-205.

Mullins, "Disclosure"

T. Y. Mullins, "Disclosure: A Literary Form in the New Testament," *NovT* 7 (1964) 44-50.

Mullins, "Formulas"

T. Y. Mullins, "Formulas in New Testament Epistles," *JBL* 91 (1972) 380-90.

Mullins, "Petition"

T. Y. Mullins, "Petition as a Literary Form," *NovT* 5 (1962) 46-54.

Mullins, "Visit Talk"

T. Y. Mullins, "Visit Talk in New Testament Letters," *CBQ* 35 (1973) 350-58.

Munck

J. Munck, *Paul and the Salvation of Mankind.* ETr. Richmond: John Knox/London: SCM, 1959.

Munck, "Paul"

J. Munck, "Paul, the Apostles, and the Twelve," *ST* 3 (1949) 96-110.

Mundle

W. Mundle, "Das Problem des Zwischenzustandes in dem Abschnitt 2 Kor. 5 1-10," in *Jülicher FS* 93-109.

Munro

W. Munro, *Authority in Paul and Peter.* SNTSMS 45. Cambridge: Cambridge University Press, 1983.

Muraoka

T. Muraoka, "The Use of ΩΣ in the Greek Bible," *NovT* 7 (1964) 51-72.

Murphy-O'Connor (ed.)

J. Murphy-O'Connor (ed.), *Paul and Qumran: Studies in New Testament Exegesis.* Chicago: Priory/London: Chapman, 1968.

Murphy-O'Connor

J. Murphy-O'Connor, *The Theology of the Second Letter to the Corinthians.* Cambridge: Cambridge University Press, 1991.

Murphy-O'Connor, "Arabia"

J. Murphy-O'Connor, "Paul in Arabia," *CBQ* 55 (1993) 732-37.

Murphy-O'Connor, "Co-Authorship"

J. Murphy-O'Connor, "Co-Authorship in the Corinthian Correspondence," *RB* 100 (1993) 562-79.

Murphy-O'Connor, "Context"

J. Murphy-O'Connor, "Relating 2 Corinthians 6.14–7.1 to Its Context," *NTS* 33 (1986-87) 272-75.

Murphy-O'Connor, *Corinth*

J. Murphy-O'Connor, *St. Paul's Corinth: Texts and Archaeology.* Good News Studies 6. Wilmington: Glazier, 1983.

Murphy-O'Connor, "Corinth"

J. Murphy-O'Connor, "The Corinth St. Paul Saw," *BA* 47 (1984) 147-59.

Murphy-O'Connor, "Date"

J. Murphy-O'Connor, "The Date of 2 Corinthians 10–13," *ABR* 39 (1991) 31-43.

Murphy-O'Connor, "Faith"

J. Murphy-O'Connor, "Faith and Resurrection in 2 Cor. 4:13-14," *RB* 95 (1988) 543-50.

Murphy-O'Connor, "Jesus"

J. Murphy-O'Connor, "Another Jesus (2 Cor 11:4)," *RB* 97 (1990) 238-51.

Murphy-O'Connor, "Judaizers"

J. Murphy-O'Connor, "*Pneumatikoi* and Judaizers in 2 Cor 2:14–4:6," *ABR* 34 (1986) 42-58.

Murphy-O'Connor, *Letter-Writer*

J. Murphy-O'Connor, *Paul the Letter-Writer: His World, His Options, His Skills.* GNS 41. Collegeville: Liturgical, 1995.

Murphy-O'Connor, "Macedonia"

J. Murphy-O'Connor, "Paul and Macedonia: The Connection between 2 Corinthians 2.13 and 2.14," *JSNT* 25 (1985) 99-103.

Murphy-O'Connor, "Ministry"

J. Murphy-O'Connor, "A Ministry beyond the Letter (2 Cor 3:1-6)," in Lorenzi (ed.) 105-29.

Murphy-O'Connor, *Paul*

J. Murphy-O'Connor, *Paul: A Critical Life.* Oxford: Clarendon, 1996.

Murphy-O'Connor, "Philo"

J. Murphy-O'Connor, "Philo and 2 Cor 6:14–7:1," *RB* 95 (1988) 55-69. Reprinted in Lorenzi (ed.), *Diakonia* 133-46.

Murphy-O'Connor, "Road"
J. Murphy-O'Connor, "On the Road and on the Sea with St. Paul: Traveling Conditions in the First Century," *BRev* 1 (1985) 38-47.

Murphy-O'Connor, "2 Corinthians"
J. Murphy-O'Connor, "*Pneumatikoi* in 2 Corinthians," *PIBA* 11 (1988) 59-66.

Murphy-O'Connor, "2 Cor. 5:6b"
J. Murphy-O'Connor, "'Being at Home in the Body We Are in Exile from the Lord' (2 Cor 5:6b)," *RB* 93 (1986) 214-21.

Murray
R. Murray, "On Commending Authority," *Month* 6 (1973) 89-92.

J. Murray
J. Murray, *Redemption — Accomplished and Applied.* Grand Rapids: Eerdmans, 1955.

Mussies
G. Mussies, *Dio Chrysostom and the New Testament.* SCHNT 2. Leiden: Brill, 1972.

Nägeli
T. Nägeli, *Der Wortschatz des Apostels Paulus.* Göttingen: Vandenhoeck und Ruprecht, 1905.

Neumann
M. Neumann, "Ministry, Weakness, and Spirit in II Corinthians," *ClerRev* 59 (1974) 647-60.

Newman
C. C. Newman, *Paul's Glory-Christology: Tradition and Rhetoric.* Leiden: Brill, 1991.

Newton
M. Newton, *The Concept of Purity at Qumran and in the Letters of Paul.* SNTSMS 53. Cambridge: Cambridge University Press, 1985.

Nickle
K. F. Nickle, *The Collection: A Study in Paul's Strategy.* SBT 48. Naperville: Allenson/London: SCM, 1966.

Nielsen
H. K. Nielsen, "Paulus' Verwendung des Begriffes *Dynamis.* Eine Replik zur Kreuzestheologie," in *Die Paulinische Literatur und Theologie.* Teologiske Studier 7. Ed. S. Pedersen. Åarhus: Aros/Göttingen: Vandenhoeck und Ruprecht, 1980, pp. 137-58.

Nisbet
P. Nisbet, "The Thorn in the Flesh," *ExpT* 80 (1969) 126.

Nisius
J. B. Nisius, "Zur Erklärung von 2 Kor. 3,16ff.," *ZKT* 30 (1916) 617-75.

Noack

B. Noack, Satanás *und* Sotería. *Untersuchungen zur neutestamentliche Dämonologie.* Copenhagen: Gads, 1948.

Noack, "Note"

B. Noack, "A Note on 2 Cor. iv.15," *ST* 17 (1963) 129-32

O'Brien FS

The Gospel to the Nations: Perspectives on Paul's Mission. Ed. P. Bolt and M. Thompson. Leicester: Apollos, 2000.

O'Brien

P. T. O'Brien, *Introductory Thanksgivings in the Letters of Paul.* NovTSup 49. Leiden: Brill, 1977.

O'Brien, *Colossians*

P. T. O'Brien, *Colossians, Philemon.* WBC 44. Waco: Word, 1982.

O'Brien, "Gospel"

P. T. O'Brien, "Thanksgiving and the Gospel of Paul," *NTS* 21 (1974-75) 144-55.

O'Brien, *Mission*

P. T. O'Brien, *Gospel and Mission in the Writings of Paul: An Exegetical and Theological Analysis.* Grand Rapids: Baker/Carlisle: Paternoster, 1995.

O'Brien, *Philippians*

P. T. O'Brien, *The Epistle to the Philippians.* Grand Rapids: Eerdmans, 1991.

O'Brien, "Structure"

P. T. O'Brien, "Thanksgiving within the Structure of Pauline Theology," in *Bruce FS* (2) 50-66.

O'Collins

G. G. O'Collins, "Power Made Perfect in Weakness: 2 Cor 12:9-10," *CBQ* 33 (1971) 528-37.

Ogg

G. Ogg, *The Chronology of the Life of Paul.* London: Epworth, 1968 = *Odyssey of Paul.* Old Tappan: Revell, 1968.

Olivier

F. Olivier, "ΣΥΝΑΠΟΘΝΗΙΣΚΩ. D'un article de lexique à Saint Paul, 2 Cor. 7:3," *RTP* 17 (1929) 103-33.

Olley

J. W. Olley, "A Precursor of the NRSV? 'Sons and Daughters' in 2 Cor 6.18," *NTS* 44 (1998-99) 204-12.

Ollrog

W. H. Ollrog, *Paulus und seiner Mitarbeiter.* WMANT 50. Neukirchen-Vluyn: Neukirchener, 1979.

Olshausen

H. Olshausen, *Biblical Commentary on St Paul's First and Second Epistles to the Corinthians.* ETr. Edinburgh: Clark, 1851.

Olson

S. N. Olson, "Epistolary Uses of Expressions of Self-Confidence," *JBL* 103 (1984) 585-97.

Olson, "Confidence"

S. N. Olson, "Pauline Expressions of Confidence in His Addressees," *CBQ* 47 (1985) 282-95.

O'Mahony

K. J. O'Mahony, *Pauline Persuasion: A Sounding in 2 Corinthians 8–9.* JSNTSS 199. Sheffield: Sheffield Academic, 2000.

O'Mahony, "Rhetoric"

K. J. O'Mahony, "The Rhetoric of Benefaction," *PIBA* 22 (1999) 9-40.

O'Neill

J. O'Neill, "The Absence of the 'in Christ' Theology in 2 Corinthians 5," *ABR* 35 (1987) 99-106.

Oostendorp

D. W. Oostendorp, *Another Jesus: A Gospel of Jewish-Christian Superiority in II Corinthians.* Kampen: Kok, 1967.

Oropeza

B. J. Oropeza, *Paul and Apostasy: Eschatology, Perseverance, and Falling Away in the Corinthian Congregation.* WUNT 2. Tübingen: Mohr, 2000.

Ortlund

R. C. Ortlund, Jr., *God's Unfaithful Wife: A Biblical Theology of Spiritual Adultery.* Downers Grove: InterVarsity, 1999.

Osborne

R. E. Osborne, "St. Paul's Silent Years," *JBL* 84 (1965) 59-65.

Osei-Bonsu

J. Osei-Bonsu, "Does 2 Cor. 5:1-10 Teach the Reception of the Resurrection Body at the Moment of Death?" *JSNT* 28 (1986) 81-101.

Osei-Bonsu, "Dualism"

J. Osei-Bonsu, "Anthropological Dualism in the New Testament," *SJT* 40 (1987) 571-90.

Osei-Bonsu, "State"

J. Osei-Bonsu, "The Intermediate State in the New Testament," *SJT* 44 (1991) 169-94.

Oster

R. E. Oster, "Use, Misuse and Neglect of Archaeological Evidence in Some Modern Works on 1 Corinthians (1 Cor 7,1-5; 8,10; 11,2-16; 12,14-26)," *ZNW* 83 (1992) 52-73.

Osty

E. Osty, *Les épîtres de saint Paul aux Corinthiens.* Paris: Cerf, 1959³.

Otis

W. S. C. Otis, "Exposition of 2 Cor. V.14," *BSac* 27 (1870) 545-64.

Pagels

E. H. Pagels, *The Gnostic Paul: Gnostic Exegesis of the Pauline Letters.* Philadelphia: Fortress, 1975.

Painter

J. Painter, "Paul and the *Pneumatikoi* at Corinth," in *Barrett FS* 237-50.

Pamment

M. Pamment, "Raised a Spiritual Body: Bodily Resurrection according to Paul," *NewB* 66 (1985) 372-88.

Panagopoulos

J. Panagopoulos, "'Diakonia tes katallages' (2 Kor 5,18). Eine orthodoxe Studie zur exegetischen und dogmatischen Problematik des Amtes," *US* 20 (1965) 126-51.

Panikulam

G. Panikulam, *Koinonia in the New Testament: A Dynamic Expression of Christian Life.* AnBib 85. Rome: Pontifical Biblical Institute, 1979.

Park

D. M. Park, "Paul's ΣΚΟΛΟΨ ΤΗ ΣΑΡΚΙ: Thorn or Stake? (2 Cor. xii.7)," *NovT* 22 (1980) 179-83.

Parsons

M. Parsons, "The New Creation," *ExpT* 99 (1987) 3-4.

Pate

C. M. Pate, *Adam Christology as the Exegetical and Theological Substructure of 2 Corinthians 4:7–5:21.* Lanham: University Press of America, 1991.

Pate, *Glory*

C. M. Pate, *The Glory of Adam and the Afflictions of the Righteous: Pauline Suffering in Context.* Lampeter/Lewiston: Mellen Biblical, 1993.

Patte

D. Patte, "A Structural Exegesis of 2 Corinthians 2:14–7:4 with Special Attention on 2:14–3:6 and 6:11–7:4," in *SBL Seminar Papers. Annual Meeting 1987.* Ed. K. H. Richards. Atlanta: Scholars, 1987, pp. 23-49.

Peake

A. S. Peake, *The Quintessence of Paulinism.* Manchester: Manchester University Press, 1918.

Peel

M. L. Peel, *The Epistle to Rheginus: A Valentinian Letter on the Resurrection.* London: SCM, 1969.

Penna

R. Penna, *Paul the Apostle: Wisdom and Folly of the Cross.* ETr. Collegeville: Liturgical, 1996.

Percy

E. Percy, *Der Leib Christi (Σῶμα Χριστοῦ).* Lund: Gleerup, 1942.

Perkins

P. Perkins, *Gnosticism and the New Testament*. Minneapolis: Fortress, 1993.

Perriman

A. C. Perriman, "Between Troas and Macedonia: 2 Cor 2:13-14," *ExpT* 101 (1989-90) 39-41.

Perriman, "Parousia"

A. C. Perriman, "Paul and the Parousia: 1 Corinthians 15.50-57 and 2 Corinthians 5.1-5," *NTS* 35 (1989-90) 512-21.

Perrin

N. Perrin, *The New Testament: An Introduction*. New York: Jovanovich, 1982².

Perrin, "Passion"

N. Perrin, "The Use of (παρα)δίδοναι in Connection with the Passion of Jesus in the New Testament," in *Jeremias FS* 204-12.

Pesch

R. Pesch, *Paulus kämpft um sein Apostolat. Drei weitere Briefe an die Gemeinde Gottes in Korinth. Paulus-neugesehen*. Freiburg: Herder, 1987.

Peterman

G. W. Peterman, *Paul's Gift from Philippi: Conventions of Gift-Exchange and Christian Giving*. Cambridge: Cambridge University Press, 1997.

Peterman, "Contribution"

G. W. Peterman, "Romans 15.26: Make a Contribution or Establish Fellowship?" *NTS* 40 (1993-94) 457-63.

Peterson

B. K. Peterson, *Eloquence and the Proclamation of the Gospel in Corinth*. SBLDS 163. Atlanta: Scholars, 1998.

Peterson, "Conquest"

B. K. Peterson, "Conquest, Control, and the Cross: Paul's Self-Portrayal in 2 Corinthians 10–13," *Int* 52 (1998) 258-70.

Pherigo

L. P. Pherigo, "Paul and the Corinthian Church," *JBL* 68 (1949) 341-50.

Phillips

J. B. Phillips, *The New Testament in Modern English*. London: Bles/Collins, 1958.

Pickett

R. Pickett, *The Cross in Corinth: The Social Significance of the Death of Jesus*. JSNTSS 143. Sheffield: Sheffield Academic, 1997.

Pierce

C. A. Pierce, *Conscience in the New Testament*. SBT 15. London: SCM, 1955.

Plank

K. A. Plank, *Paul and the Irony of Affliction*. Atlanta: Scholars, 1987.

Plevnik
J. Plevnik, "The Destination of the Apostle and of the Faithful: Second Corinthians 4:13b-14 and First Thessalonians 4:14," *CBQ* 62 (2000) 83-95.

Plummer
A. Plummer, *A Critical and Exegetical Commentary on the Second Epistle of St. Paul to the Corinthians.* ICC. Edinburgh: Clark, 1915.

Plummer (CGT)
A. Plummer, *The Second Epistle of Paul the Apostle to the Corinthians.* CGT. Cambridge: Cambridge University Press, 1903.

Pollard
T. E. Pollard, "Martyrdom and Resurrection in the New Testament," *BJRL* 55 (1972-73) 240-51.

Pope
R. M. Pope, "Studies in Pauline Vocabulary 1: Of the Triumph-Joy," *ExpT* 21 (1909-10) 19-21.

Popkes
W. Popkes, *Christus Traditus. Eine Untersuchung zum Begriff der Dahingabe im Neuen Testament.* ATANT 49. Zurich: Zwingli, 1967.

Porter
S. E. Porter, *Verbal Aspect in the Greek of the New Testament with Reference to Tense and Mood.* New York: Lang, 1989.

Porter, "Justification"
S. E. Porter, "The Theoretical Justification for Application of Rhetorical Categories to Pauline Epistolary Literature," in Porter and Olbricht 100-122.

Porter, "Καταλλάσσω"
S. E. Porter, *Καταλλάσσω in Ancient Greek Literature, with Reference to the Pauline Writings.* Cordoba: El Almendro, 1994.

Porter and Olbricht
S. E. Porter and T. H. Olbricht (eds.), *Rhetoric and the New Testament: Essays from the 1992 Heidelberg Conference.* JSNTSS 90. Sheffield: JSOT, 1993.

Prat
F. Prat, *The Theology of St. Paul.* 2 vols. ETr. Westminster: Newman, 1926-27.

Prat, "Triomphe"
F. Prat, "Le triomphe du Christ sur les principautés et les puissances (Col 2:15)," *RSR* 3 (1912) 201-29.

Pratscher
W. Pratscher, "Der Verzicht des Paulus auf finanziellen Unterhalt durch seine Gemeinden. Ein Aspekt seiner Missionsweise," *NTS* 25 (1979) 284-98.

Preisker
H. Preisker, "Zur Komposition des zweiten Korintherbriefes," *TBl* 5 (1926) 154-57.

Price
J. L. Price, *Interpreting the New Testament.* New York: Holt, 1961.

Price, "Aspects"
J. L. Price, "Aspects of Paul's Theology and Their Bearing on Literary Problems of Second Corinthians," in *Clark FS* 95-106.

R. M. Price
R. M. Price, "Punished in Paradise (an Exegetical Theory on II Corinthians 12:1-10)," *JSNT* 7 (1980) 33-40.

Proudfoot
C. M. Proudfoot, "Imitation or Realistic Participation? A Study of Paul's Concept of Suffering with Christ," *Int* 17 (1963) 140-60.

Provence
T. E. Provence, "'Who Is Sufficient for These Things?' An Exegesis of 2 Corinthians ii 15–iii 18," *NovT* 24 (1982) 54-81.

Prümm
K. Prümm, *Diakonia Pneumatos. Der zweite Korintherbrief als Zugang zur apostolischen Botschaft. Auslegung und Theologie.* Rome: Freiburg/Wien: Herder. I: *Theologische Auslegung des zweiten Korintherbriefes* (1967). II: *Theologie des zweiten Korintherbriefes.* 1: Apostolat und christliche Wirklichkeit; Theologie des ersten Briefteils *(Kap. 1–7)* (1960). 2: *Das christliche Wert. Die apostolische Macht; Theologie des 2. und 3. Briefteils (Kap. 8–13). Quellenfragen. Auswertung und Religionsgeschichtliche Sicherung* (1962).

Prümm, "Auslegung"
K. Prümm, "Die katholische Auslegung von 2 Kor. 3,17a in den letzten vier Jahrzehnten nach ihren Hauptrichtungen," *Bib* 31 (1950) 316-45, 459-82.

Prümm, "Offenbarung"
K. Prümm, "Phänomenologie der Offenbarung laut 2 Kor," *Bib* 43 (1962) 396-416.

Prümm, "2 Kor. 3"
K. Prümm, "Röm. 1–11 und 2 Kor. 3," *Bib* 31 (1950) 164-203.

Prümm, "Vergleich"
K. Prümm, "Gal. und 2 Kor. — Ein lehrgehaltliche Vergleich," *Bib* 31 (1950) 27-72.

Rackham
R. B. Rackham, *The Acts of the Apostles.* London: Methuen, 1909[4].

Räisänen
H. Räisänen, *Paul and the Law.* ETr. Tübingen: Mohr, 1983.

Ramsay
W. M. Ramsay, *St. Paul the Traveller and Roman Citizen.* London: Hodder and Stoughton, 1896.

Ramsay, "Corinthians"
W. M. Ramsay, "Historical Commentary on the Epistles to the Corinthians," *Exp,* 6th series, 3 (1901) 220-40, 343-60.

Ramsay, "Roads"
W. M. Ramsay, "Roads and Travel (in the NT)," in *HDB* 5.375-402.

Ramsay, "Words"
W. M. Ramsay, "The Words in Acts Denoting Missionary Travel," *Exp,* 5th series, 1 (1895) 385-99.

Rauer
M. Rauer, *Die "Schwachen" in Korinth und Rom nach den Paulusbriefen.* BS 21/2-3. Freiburg: Herder, 1923.

Rebell
W. Rebell, *Christologie und Existenz bei Paulus. Eine Auslegung von 2. Kor 5,14-21.* Stuttgart: Calwer, 1992.

Reed
J. T. Reed, "Using Ancient Rhetorical Categories to Interpret Paul's Letters: A Question of Genre," in Porter and Olbricht 292-324.

Regard
P. F. Regard, *Contribution à l'étude des prépositions dans la langue du Nouveau Testament.* Paris: Gabalda, 1919.

Reicke FS
The New Testament Age. Ed. D. A. Brownell, W. C. Weinrich, and J. Brownell. Leiden: Brill, 1983.

Reicke
B. Reicke, *The New Testament Era.* ETr. London: Black, 1968.

Reicke, *Diakonie*
B. Reicke, *Diakonie, Festfreude und Zelos.* Uppsala: Lundequistska bokhandeln, 1951.

Reicke, "Reward"
B. Reicke, "The New Testament Conception of Reward," in *Aux sources de la tradition chrétienne: Mélanges offerts à M. Maurice Goguel.* Paris: Gabalda, 1950, pp. 195-206.

Reimherr
O. Reimherr, "2 Corinthians and the Problem of Easter Faith," in *Stamm FS* 106-17.

Reitzenstein
R. Reitzenstein, *The Hellenistic Mystery-Religions: Their Basic Ideas and Significance.* ETr. Pittsburgh: Pickwick, 1978.

Rendall
G. H. Rendall, *The Epistles of St. Paul to the Corinthians.* London: Macmillan, 1909.

Rengstorf FS
Theocratia. Jahrbuch des Institutum Judaicum II. *Festschrift für K. H. Rengstorf zum 70. Geburtstag.* Ed. W. Dietrich, et al. Leiden: Brill, 1973.

Rensberger
> D. Rensberger, "2 Corinthians 6:14–7:1 — A Fresh Examination," *SBT* 8 (1978) 25-49.

Renwick
> D. A. Renwick, *Paul, the Temple, and the Presence of God.* Atlanta: Scholars, 1991.

Reumann
> J. Reumann, *"Righteousness" in the New Testament.* Philadelphia: Fortress, 1982.

Reumann, "Irony"
> J. H. P. Reumann, "St. Paul's Use of Irony," *LQ* 7 (1955) 140-45.

Rex
> H. H. Rex, "Immortality of the Soul, or Resurrection of the Dead, or What?" *RTR* 17 (1958) 73-82.

Rey
> B. Rey, *Créés dans le Christ Jésus. La création nouvelle selon St Paul.* Paris: Gabalda, 1966.

Rey, "Homme"
> B. Rey, "L'homme nouveau d'après Saint Paul," *RSPT* 49 (1965) 161-95.

Richard
> E. Richard, "Polemics, Old Testament, and Theology: A Study of II Cor. III,1–IV,6," *RB* 88 (1981) 340-67.

Richards
> E. R. Richards, *The Secretary in the Letters of Paul.* WUNT 2/42. Tübingen: Mohr, 1991.

Richardson
> A. Richardson, *An Introduction to the Theology of the New Testament.* London: SCM, 1958.

P. Richardson
> P. Richardson, "Spirit and Letter: A Foundation for Hermeneutics," *EvQ* 45 (1973) 208-18.

Ridderbos
> H. Ridderbos, *Paul: An Outline of His Theology.* ETr. Grand Rapids: Eerdmans, 1975.

Riddle
> D. W. Riddle, *Paul: Man of Conflict.* Nashville: Cokesbury, 1940.

Riddle and Hutson
> D. W. Riddle and H. H. Hutson, *New Testament Life and Literature.* Chicago: University of Chicago, 1946.

Rieger
> J. Rieger, "Siegel und Angeld," *BibLeb* 7 (1966) 158-61.

Riesner

R. Riesner, *Paul's Early Period: Chronology, Mission Strategy, Theology.* ETr. Grand Rapids: Eerdmans, 1994.

Rigaux FS

Mélanges Bibliques en hommage au R. P. Béda Rigaux. Ed. A. Descamps and A. de Halleux. Gembloux: Duculot, 1970.

Rigaux

B. Rigaux, *The Letters of St. Paul: Modern Studies.* ETr. Chicago: Franciscan Herald, 1968.

Rigaux, *Thessaloniciens*

B. Rigaux, *Les épîtres aux Thessaloniciens.* Paris: Gabalda, 1956.

Rissi

M. Rissi, *Studien zum zweiten Korintherbrief. Der alte Bund — Der Prediger — Der Tod.* ATANT 56. Zurich: Zwingli, 1969.

Robertson

A. T. Robertson, *A Grammar of the Greek New Testament in the Light of Historical Research.* Nashville: Broadman, 1934[4].

Robertson, *Glory*

A. T. Robertson, *The Glory of the Ministry.* New York: Revell, 1911.

Robertson, *Pictures*

A. T. Robertson, "Second Corinthians," in his *Word Pictures in the New Testament* IV: *The Epistles of Paul.* Nashville: Broadman, 1931, pp. 205-71.

A. Robertson

A. Robertson, "Corinthians, Second Epistle to the," *HDB* I, 491-98.

Robertson and Plummer

A. Robertson and A. Plummer, *A Critical and Exegetical Commentary on the First Epistle of St. Paul to the Corinthians.* ICC. Edinburgh: Clark, 1914[2].

Robinson

J. A. T. Robinson, *The Body: A Study in Pauline Theology.* SBT 5. London: SCM, 1952.

Robinson, *Redating*

J. A. T. Robinson, *Redating the New Testament.* Philadelphia: Westminster/London: SCM, 1976.

J. M. Robinson

J. M. Robinson, "Die Hodayot-Formel in Gebet und Hymnus des Frühchristentums," in *Haenchen FS* 194-235.

J. M. Robinson "Trajectory"

J. M. Robinson, "The Johannine Trajectory," in *Trajectories through Early Christianity.* Ed. J. M. Robinson and H. Koester. Philadelphia: Fortress, 1971, pp. 232-68.

J. M. Robinson, "Kerygma"
  J. M. Robinson, "Kerygma and History in the New Testament," in *The Bible in Modern Scholarship*. Ed. J. P. Hyatt. Nashville: Abingdon, 1965, pp. 114-50.

Roetzel
  C. J. Roetzel, *Judgment in the Community: A Study of the Relationship between Eschatology and Ecclesiology in Paul*. NovTSup. Leiden: Brill, 1972.

Rolland
  P. Rolland, "La structure littéraire de la Deuxième Épître aux Corinthiens," *Bib* 71 (1990) 73-84.

Roller
  O. Roller, *Das Formular der paulinischen Briefe. Ein Beitrag zur Lehre vom antiken Briefe*. Stuttgart: Kohlhammer, 1933.

Romaniuk
  K. Romaniuk, *L'amour du Père et du Fils dans la sotériologie de saint Paul*. AnBib 15A. Rome: Pontifical Biblical Institute, 1974².

Romaniuk, "Origine"
  K. Romaniuk, "L'origine des formules pauliniennes 'le Christ s'est livré pour nous,'" *NovT* 5 (1962) 55-76.

Romaniuk, "Résurrection"
  K. Romaniuk, "Résurrection existentielle ou eschatologique en 2 Co 4,13-14?" *BZ* 34 (1990) 248-52.

Rosenmüller
  G. Rosenmüller, *Scholia in Novum Testamentum. Tomus IV.* Norimbergae, 1806.

Ross
  A. Ross, "The Grace of Our Lord Jesus Christ," *EvQ* 13 (1941) 219-25.

G. A. J. Ross
  G. A. J. Ross, "The Epistle of the Torn Heart," *Exp,* 8th series, 25 (1923) 130-33.

Rostron
  S. N. Rostron, *The Christology of St. Paul*. New York: Revell, 1912.

Rowland
  C. Rowland, *The Open Heaven: A Study of Apocalyptic in Judaism and Early Christianity*. London: SPCK, 1982.

Rowland, *Origins*
  C. Rowland, *Christian Origins: From Messianic Movement to Christian Religion*. Minneapolis: Augsburg/London: SPCK, 1985.

Rüger
  H. P. Rüger, "Hieronymous, die Rabbinen und Paulus. Zur Vorgeschichte des Begriffspaars 'innerer und äusserer Mensch,'" *ZNW* 68 (1977) 132-37.

Saake
  H. Saake, "Paulus als Ekstatiker. Pneumatologische Beobachtungen zu 2 Kor 12,1-10," *Bib* 53 (1972) 404-10. (Also in *NovT* 15 [1973] 153-60).

Sabourin

L. Sabourin, "Note sur 2 Cor. 5,21. Le Christ fait 'peché,'" *SciEccl* 11 (1959) 419-24.

Safrai and Stern

The Jewish People in the First Century. 2 vols. Ed. S. Safrai and M. Stern in co-operation with D. Flusser and W. C. van Unnik. Philadelphia: Fortress, 1974-76.

Salom

A. P. Salom, "The Imperatival Use of *hina* in the New Testament," *ABR* 6 (1958) 124-41.

Sampley

J. P. Sampley, "2 Corinthians," in *The New Interpreter's Bible* XI: *The Second Letter to the Corinthians; the Letter to the Galatians; the Letter to the Ephesians; the Letter to the Philippians; the Letter to the Colossians; the First and Second Letters to the Thessalonians; the First and Second Letters to Timothy and the Letter to Titus; the Letter to Philemon.* Ed. L. E. Keck, et al. Nashville: Abingdon, 2000, pp. 3-180.

Sampley, "Opponents"

J. P. Sampley, "Paul, His Opponents in 2 Corinthians 10–13, and the Rhetorical Handbooks," in J. Neusner, et al. (eds.), *The Social World of Formative Christianity and Judaism: In Tribute to Howard Clark Kee.* Philadelphia: Fortress, 1988, pp. 162-77.

Sampley, *Partnership*

J. P. Sampley, *Pauline Partnership in Christ: Christian Community and Commitment in Light of Roman Law.* Philadelphia: Fortress, 1980.

Sampley, "Societas"

J. P. Sampley, "Societas Christi: Roman Law and Paul's Conception of the Christian Community," in *Dahl FS* 158-74.

Sánchez Bosch

J. Sánchez Bosch, *"Gloriarse" según San Pablo. Sentido y teología de kaucha-omai.* AnBib 40. Rome: Pontifical Biblical Institute, 1970.

Sand

A. Sand, *Der Begriff "Fleisch" in den paulinischen Hauptbriefen.* BU 2 Regensburg: Pustet, 1967.

Sanday

W. Sanday, "Corinthians, Epistles to the," *EB* 1.899-907.

Sanday and Headlam

W. Sanday and A. C. Headlam, *A Critical and Exegetical Commentary on the Epistle to the Romans.* ICC. Edinburgh: Clark, 1902⁵.

Sanders

J. T. Sanders, "The Transition from Opening Epistolary Thanksgiving to Body in the Letters of the Pauline Corpus," *JBL* 81 (1962) 348-62.

E. P. Sanders

E. P. Sanders, *Paul and Palestinian Judaism: A Comparison of Patterns of Religion.* Philadelphia: Fortress/London: SCM, 1977.

Sandnes

K. O. Sandnes, *Paul — One of the Prophets? A Contribution to the Apostle's Self-Understanding.* WUNT 2/43. Tübingen: Mohr, 1991.

Särkiö

R. Särkiö, "Die Versöhnung mit Gott — und mit Paulus. Zur Bedeutung der Gemeindesituation in Korinth für 2 Kor 5.14-21," *ST* 52 (1998) 29-42.

Sass

G. Sass, *Der paulinische Apostelbegriff. Eine theologisch-exegetische Untersuchung.* Fürstenfeldbruck: Sighart, 1938.

Sass, "Bedeutung"

G. Sass, "Zur Bedeutung von δοῦλος bei Paulus," *ZNW* 40 (1941) 24-32.

Sass, "Waffen"

G. Sass, "Noch einmal 2 Kor 6,14–7,1. Literarkritische Waffen gegen einen 'unpaulinischen' Paulus?" *ZNW* 84 (1993) 36-64.

Savage

T. B. Savage, *Power through Weakness: Paul's Understanding of the Christian Ministry in 2 Corinthians.* SNTSMS 86. Cambridge: Cambridge University Press, 1996.

Schäfer

P. Schäfer, "New Testament and Hekhalot Literature: The Journey into Heaven in Paul and in Merkavah Mysticism," *JJS* 35 (1984) 19-35.

Scharlemann

M. H. Scharlemann, "Of Surpassing Splendor: An Exegetical Study of 2 Corinthians 3:4-18," *ConJ* 4 (1978) 108-17.

Schatzmann

S. S. Schatzmann, *A Pauline Theology of Charismata.* Peabody: Hendrickson, 1987.

Schauf

W. Schauf, *Sarx. Der Begriff "Fleisch" beim Apostel Paulus unter besonderer Berücksichtigung seiner Erlösungslehre.* NTAbh 11. 1-2. Münster: Aschendorff, 1924.

Schelkle

K. H. Schelkle, *The Second Epistle to the Corinthians.* ETr. New York: Herder/London: Burns, 1969. (Reprinted New York: Crossroad, 1981).

Schenke and Fischer

H. M. Schenke and K. M. Fischer, *Einleitung in die Schriften des Neuen Testament* I: *Die Briefe des Paulus und die Schriften des Paulinismus.* Berlin: Evangelische Verlagsanstalt, 1978.

Schildenberger

J. Schildenberger, "2 Kor 3,17a. 'Der Herr aber ist der Geist,'" im Zusammenhang des Textes und der Theologie des hl. Paulus," in *Congressus* 1.451-60.

Schlatter

A. Schlatter, *Paulus, der Bote Jesu. Eine Deutung seiner Briefe an die Korinther.* Stuttgart: Calwer, 1956².

Schlier FS

Die Zeit Jesu. Ed. G. Bornkamm and K. Rahner. Freiburg: Herder, 1970.

Schmid FS

Neutestamentliche Aufsätze. Ed. J. Blinzler, et al. Regensburg: Pustet, 1963.

Schmid

J. Schmid, *Zeit und Ort der paulinischen Gefangenschaftsbriefe.* Freiburg: Herder, 1931.

Schmiedel

P. W. Schmiedel, *Hand-Commentar zum Neuen Testament,* vol. 2. Freiburg: Mohr, 1892².

Schmithals

W. Schmithals, *Gnosticism in Corinth: An Investigation of the Letters to the Corinthians.* ETr. Nashville: Abingdon, 1971.

Schmithals, "Abfassung"

W. Schmithals, "Zur Abfassung und altesten Sammlung des paulinischen Hauptbriefe," *ZNW* 51 (1960) 225-45.

Schmithals, *Apostle*

W. Schmithals, *The Office of Apostle in the Early Church.* ETr. Nashville: Abingdon, 1969.

Schmithals, *Gnostics*

W. Schmithals, *Paul and the Gnostics.* ETr. Nashville: Abingdon, 1972.

Schmithals, "Korintherbriefe"

W. Schmithals, "Die Korintherbriefe als Briefsammlung," *ZNW* 64 (1973) 263-88.

Schmithals *Briefe*

W. Schmithals, *Die Briefe des Paulus in ihrer ursprünglichen Form.* ZWB. Zurich: Theologischer, 1984.

Schnackenburg FS

Neues Testament und Kirche. Festschrift für Rudolf Schnackenburg. Ed. J. Gnilka. Freiburg: Herder, 1974.

Schnackenburg

R. Schnackenburg, *The Moral Teaching of the New Testament.* ETr. New York: Herder, 1968.

Schneider

B. Schneider, *Dominus autem Spiritus est (2 Cor. 3:17a). Ο ΔΕ ΚΥΡΙΟΣ ΠΝΕΥΜΑ ΕΣΤΙΝ. Studium exegeticum.* Rome: Officium Libri Catholici, 1951.

Schneider, "Antithesis"

B. Schneider, "The Meaning of St. Paul's Antithesis 'the Letter and the Spirit,'"
CBQ 15 (1953) 163-207.

Schneider, "II Cor. 13:13"

B. Schneider, "HE KOINONIA TOU HAGIOU PNEUMATOS (II Cor. 13,13),"
in *Brady FS* 421-47.

N. Schneider

N. Schneider, *Die rhetorische Eigenart der paulinischen.* HUT 11. Tübingen:
Mohr, 1970.

Schnider and Stenger

F. Schnider and W. Stenger, *Studien zum Neutestamentlichen Briefformular.*
Leiden: Brill, 1987.

Schniewind

J. Schniewind, "Die Leugner der Auferstehung in Korinth," in *Nachgelassene
Reden und Aufsätze.* Ed. E. Kähler. Berlin: Töpelmann, 1952, pp. 110-39.

Schoeps

H. J. Schoeps, *Paul: The Theology of the Apostle in the Light of Jewish Religious
History.* ETr. Philadelphia: Westminster, 1961.

Scholem

G. G. Scholem, *Jewish Gnosticism, Merkabah Mysticism, and Talmudic Tradition.* New York: Jewish Theological Seminary, 1965[2].

Scholtissek

K. Scholtissek, "'Ihr seid ein Brief Christi' (2 Kor 3,3). Zur einer ekklesio-
logischen Metapher bei Paulus," *BZ* 44 (2000) 183-205.

Schrage

W. Schrage, "Leid, Kreuz und Eschaton. Die Peristasenkataloge als Merkmale
paulinischer *theologia crucis* und Eschatologie," *EvT* 34 (1974) 141-75.

Schrage, "Ekklesia"

W. Schrage, "'Ekklesia' und 'Synagoge' — zum Ursprung des urchristlichen
Kirchenbegriffs," *ZTK* 60 (1963) 178-202.

Schreiner

J. Schreiner, "Jeremia 9,22.23 als Hintergrund des paulinischen Sich-Rühmens,"
in *Schnackenburg FS* 530-42.

T. R. Schreiner

T. R. Schreiner, *The Law and Its Fulfillment: A Pauline Theology of Law.* Grand
Rapids: Baker, 1993.

Schröter

J. Schröter, *Der versöhnte Versöhner. Paulus als unentbehrlicher Mittler im
Heilsvorgang zwischen Gott und Gemeinde nach 2 Kor 2.14–7.4.* TANZ 10.
Tübingen: Francke, 1993.

Schubert

P. Schubert, *Form and Function of the Pauline Thanksgivings.* BZNW 20. Berlin:
Töpelmann, 1939.

Schulz

S. Schulz, "Die Decke des Moses. Untersuchungen zu einer vorpaulinischen Überlieferung in II Cor. 3.7-18," *ZNW* 49 (1958) 1-30.

Schürer

E. Schürer, *The History of the Jewish People in the Age of Jesus Christ (175 B.C.– A.D. 135),* vol. I. Revised and ed. by G. Vermes and F. Miller. Edinburgh: Clark, 1973.

Schütz

J. H. Schütz, *Paul and the Anatomy of Apostolic Authority.* SNTSMS 26. Cambridge: Cambridge University Press, 1975.

Schwantes

H. Schwantes, *Schöpfung der Endzeit. Beitrag zum Verständnis der Auferweckung bei Paulus.* Stuttgart, 1963.

Schweitzer

A. Schweitzer, *The Mysticism of Paul the Apostle.* ETr. London: Black, 1931.

Schweizer FS

Die Mitte des Neuen Testament. Ed. U. Luz and H. Weder. Göttingen: Vandenhoeck und Ruprecht, 1983.

Schweizer

E. Schweizer, *Lordship and Discipleship.* SBT 28. London: SCM, 1960.

Schweizer, "Dying"

E. Schweizer, "Dying and Rising with Christ," *NTS* 14 (1967-68) 1-11.

Schweizer, "Herkunft"

E. Schweizer, "Zur Herkunft der Präexistenzvorstellung bei Paulus," *EvT* 19 (1959) 65-70.

Schweizer, *Order*

E. Schweizer, *Church Order in the New Testament.* ETr. SBT 32. London: SCM, 1961.

C. A. A. Scott

C. A. A. Scott, *Footnotes to St. Paul.* Cambridge: Cambridge University Press, 1935.

Scott

J. M. Scott, *2 Corinthians.* Peabody: Hendrickson/Carlisle: Paternoster, 1998.

Scott, *Adoption*

J. M. Scott, *Adoption as Sons of God: An Exegetical Investigation into the Background of ΥΙΟΘΕΣΙΑ in the Pauline Corpus.* WUNT 2/48. Tübingen: Mohr, 1992.

Scott, *Nations*

J. M. Scott, *Paul and the Nations: The Old Testament and Jewish Background of Paul's Mission to the Nations with Special Reference to the Destination of Galatians.* Tübingen: Mohr, 1995.

Scott, "Scripture"

J. M. Scott, "The Use of Scripture in 2 Corinthians 6.16c-18 and Paul's Restoration Theology," *JSNT* 56 (1994) 73-99.

Scott, "Triumph"

J. M. Scott, "The Triumph of God in 2 Cor 2.14: Additional Evidence of Merkabah Mysticism in Paul," *NTS* 42 (1996) 260-81.

Seesemann

H. Seesemann, *Der Begriff KOINONIA im Neuen Testament.* BZNW 14. Giessen: Töpelmann, 1933.

Segal

A. F. Segal, *Paul the Convert: The Apostolate and Apostasy of Saul the Pharisee.* New Haven: Yale University, 1990.

Segal, "Ascent"

A. F. Segal, "Heavenly Ascent in Hellenistic Judaism, Early Christianity and Their Environment," in *ANRW* II.23/2 (1980) 1333-94.

Segal, "Ecstasy"

A. F. Segal, "Paul and Ecstasy," *SBL 1986 Seminar Papers Series.* Ed. K. H. Richards. Atlanta: Scholars, 1986, pp. 555-80.

Segalla

G. Segalla, "Coerenza linguistica ed unità letteraria della 2 Corinzi," *Teologia* 13 (1988) 149-66.

Segalla, "Struttura"

G. Segalla, "Struttura letteraria e unità della 2 Corinzi," *Teologia* 13 (1988) 189-218.

Seidensticker

P. Seidensticker, "St. Paul and Poverty," in *Gospel Poverty: Essays in Biblical Theology.* ETr. Chicago: Franciscan Herald, 1977, pp. 81-120.

Seifrid

M. A. Seifrid, *Christ, Our Righteousness: Paul's Theology of Justification.* Leicester: Apollos, 2000.

Selwyn

E. G. Selwyn, *The First Epistle of St. Peter.* London: Macmillan, 1946.

Semler

J. S. Semler, *Paraphrasis II epistolae ad Corinthios.* Halle, 1776.

Sevenster

J. N. Sevenster, "Some Remarks on the ΓΥΜΝΟΣ in II Cor. V.3," in *de Zwaan FS* 202-14.

Sevenster, "Bemerkungen"

J. N. Sevenster, "Einige Bemerkungen über den 'Zwischenzustand' bei Paulus," *NTS* 1 (1954-55) 291-96.

Shead

A. G. Shead, "The New Covenant and Pauline Hermeneutics," in *O'Brien FS* 33-49.

Shedd

R. P. Shedd, *Man in Community.* Grand Rapids: Eerdmans, 1958.

Sherwin-White

A. N. Sherwin-White, *Roman Society and Roman Law in the New Testament.* Oxford: Clarendon, 1963.

Siber

P. Siber, *Mit Christus Leben. Eine Studie zur paulinischen Auferstehungshoffnung.* Zurich: Theologischer Verlag, 1971.

Sickenberger

J. Sickenberger, *Die beiden Briefe des heiligen Paulus an die Korinther und sein Brief an die Römer.* Die Heilige Schrift des Neuen Testaments V. Bonn: Hanstein, 1921².

Siegert

F. Siegert, *Argumentation bei Paulus gezeigt an Röm 9–11.* Tübingen: Mohr, 1985.

Silva

M. Silva, "The Pauline Style as Lexical Choice: ΓΙΝΩΣΚΕΙΝ and Related Verbs," in *Bruce FS* (2) 184-207.

Simon FS

Mélanges offerts à Marcel Simon: Paganisme, Judaïsme, Christianisme. Ed. A. Benoit, M. Philonenko, and C. Vogel. Paris: De Boccard, 1978.

Sjöberg

E. Sjöberg, "Wiedergeburt und Neuschöpfung im palästinischen Judentum," *ST* 4 (1951-52) 44-85.

Skeat

T. C. Skeat, "Early Christian Book Production: Papyri and Manuscripts," in *Cambridge History of the Bible,* vol. 2. Ed. G. W. H. Lampe. Cambridge: Cambridge University Press, 1969, pp. 54-79.

Smith

D. Smith, *The Life and Letters of St. Paul.* London: Hodder, 1921.

M. Smith FS

Christianity, Judaism and Other Greco-Roman Cults: Studies for Morton Smith. Ed. J. Neusner. Leiden: Brill, 1975.

N. G. Smith

N. G. Smith, "The Thorn That Stayed. An Exposition of II Corinthians 12:7-9," *Int* 13 (1959) 409-16.

Smyth

H. W. Smyth, *Greek Grammar.* Revised by G. M. Messing. Cambridge: Harvard University Press, 1956.

K. Smyth

K. Smyth, "Heavenly Man and Son of Man in St. Paul," in *Congressus* 1.219-30.

Sophocles

E. A. Sophocles, *Greek Lexicon of the Roman and Byzantine Periods (from B.C. 146 to A.D. 1100)*. 2 vols. New York: Ungar, 1887.

Souček

J. B. Souček, "Wir erkennen Christus nicht mehr nach dem Fleisch," *EvT* 19 (1959) 300-314.

Souter

A. Souter, "A Suggested Relationship between Titus and Luke," *ExpT* 18 (1906-07) 285.

Souter, "Relationship"

A. Souter, "The Relationship between Titus and Luke," *ExpT* 18 (1906-07) 335-36.

South

J. T. South, *Disciplinary Practice in Pauline Texts*. Lewiston: Mellen Biblical, 1992.

Sparks

H. F. D. Sparks, *The Formation of the New Testament*. London: SCM, 1952.

Spencer

A. B. Spencer, *Paul's Literary Style: A Stylistic and Historical Comparison of II Corinthians 11:16–12:13, Romans 8:9-39, and Philippians 3:2–4:13*. Jackson: Evangelical Theological Society, 1984.

Spencer, "Irony"

A. B. Spencer, "The Wise Fool (and the Foolish Wise): A Study of Irony in Paul," *NovT* 23 (1981) 349-60.

Spicq

C. Spicq, *Theological Lexicon of the New Testament*. ETr and ed. J. D. Ernest. 3 vols. Peabody: Hendrickson, 1994.

Spicq, *Agape*

C. Spicq, *Agape in the New Testament* II. ETr. St. Louis: Herder, 1965.

Spicq, "Ἐπιποθεῖν"

C. Spicq, "Ἐπιποθεῖν, désirer ou chérir?" *RB* 64 (1957) 184-95.

Spicq, "Image"

C. Spicq, "L'image sportive de 2 Corinthiens 4,7-9," *ETL* 13 (1937) 202-29.

Spittler

R. P. Spittler, "The Limits of Ecstasy: An Exegesis of 2 Corinthians 12:1-10," in *Tenney FS* 259-66.

Spörlein

B. Spörlein, *Die Leugnung der Auferstehung*. Regensburg: Pustet, 1971.

Stacey

W. D. Stacey, *The Pauline View of Man*. London: Macmillan, 1956.

Stachowiak
L. R. Stachowiak, "Die Antithese Licht-Finsternis — ein Thema der paulinischen Paränese," *TQ* 143 (1963) 385-421.

Stagg
F. Stagg, *New Testament Theology.* Nashville: Broadman, 1962.

Stählin FS
Verborum Veritas. Festschrift für Gustav Stählin. Ed. O. Böcher and K. Haacker. Wuppertal: Brockhaus, 1970.

Stählin
G. Stählin, "'Um mitzusterben und mitzuleben.' Bemerkungen zu 2 Kor 7,3," in *Braun FS* 503-21.

Stählin, "Gebrauch"
G. Stählin, "Zum Gebrauch von Beteuerungsformeln im Neuen Testament," *NovT* 5 (1962) 115-43.

Stalder
Stalder, K., *Das Werk des Geistes in der Heiligung bei Paulus.* Zurich: EVZ, 1962.

Stamm FS
Search the Scriptures: New Testament Studies in Honor of Raymond T. Stamm. Ed. J. M. Myers, O. Reimherr, and H. N. Bream. GTS 3. Leiden: Brill, 1969.

Stange
E. Stange, "Diktierpausen in den Paulusbriefen," *ZNW* 18 (1917-18) 109-17.

Stanley
C. D. Stanley, *Paul and the Language of Scripture: Citation Technique in the Pauline Epistles and Contemporary Literature.* SNTSMS 74. Cambridge: Cambridge University Press, 1992.

A. P. Stanley
A. P. Stanley, *The Epistles of St. Paul to the Corinthians.* Vol. II. London: Murray, 1855.

D. M. Stanley
D. M. Stanley, *Christ's Resurrection in Pauline Soteriology.* AnBib 13. Rome: Pontifical Biblical Institute, 1961.

D. M. Stanley, *Boasting*
D. M. Stanley, *Boasting in the Lord: The Phenomenon of Prayer in Saint Paul.* New York: Paulist, 1973.

Stanton
G. N. Stanton, *Jesus of Nazareth in New Testament Preaching.* SNTSMS 27. Cambridge: Cambridge University Press, 1974.

Starcky
J. Starcky, "The Nabateans: A Historical Sketch," *BA* 18 (1955) 84-106.

Stegemann

E. Stegemann, "Der Neue Bund im Alten. Zum Schriftverständnis des Paulus in II Kor 3," *TZ* 42 (1986) 97-114.

Steinmann

A. Steinmann, *Aretas IV. König der Nabatäer. Eine historisch-exegetische Studie zu 2 Kor 11,32f.* Freiburg: Herder, 1909.

Stephenson

A. M. G. Stephenson, "A Defense of the Integrity of 2 Corinthians," in *The Authorship and Integrity of the New Testament* by K. Aland, et al. SPCK Theological Collections 4. London: SPCK, 1965, pp. 82-97.

Stephenson, "Theories"

A. M. G. Stephenson, "Partition Theories on II Corinthians," in *SE* II/I: *The New Testament Scriptures* (= TU 87). Berlin: Akademie, 1964, pp. 639-46.

Stevens

G. B. Stevens, *The Theology of the New Testament.* Edinburgh: Clark, 1911.

Stevens, *Pauline Theology*

G. B. Stevens, *The Pauline Theology.* New York: Scribner, 1892.

Stewart-Sykes

A. Stewart-Sykes, "Ancient Editors and Copyists and Modern Partition Theories: The Case of the Corinthian Correspondence," *JSNT* 61 (1996) 53-64.

Stirewalt

M. L. Stirewalt, "Paul's Evaluation of Letter-Writing," in *Stamm FS* 186-90.

Stockhausen

C. K. Stockhausen, *Moses' Veil and the Glory of the New Covenant.* AB 116. Rome: Pontifical Biblical Institute, 1989.

Stockhausen, "2 Corinthians 3"

C. K. Stockhausen, "2 Corinthians 3 and the Principles of Pauline Exegesis," in Evans and Sanders 143-64.

Stöger

A. Stöger, "Die paulinische Versöhnungstheologie," *TPQ* 122 (1974) 118-31.

Story

C. I. K. Story, "The Nature of Paul's Stewardship with Special Reference to I and II Corinthians," *EvQ* 48 (1976) 212-29.

Stowers

S. K. Stowers, "Περὶ μὲν γάρ and the Integrity of 2 Cor. 8 and 9," *NovT* 32 (1990) 340-48.

Strachan

R. H. Strachan, *The Second Epistle of Paul to the Corinthians.* MNTC 7/2. New York: Harper/London: Hodder, 1935.

Strange

J. F. Strange, "2 Corinthians 10:13-16 Illuminated by a Recently Published Inscription," *BA* 46 (1983) 167-68.

Strecker

G. Strecker, "Die Legitimität des paulinischen Apostolates nach 2 Korinther 10–13," *NTS* 38 (1992) 566-86.

Stuhlmacher

P. Stuhlmacher, *Gerechtigkeit Gottes bei Paulus.* FRLANT 87. Göttingen: Vandenhoeck und Ruprecht, 1966².

Stuhlmacher, *Evangelium*

P. Stuhlmacher, *Das paulinische Evangelium* I: *Vorgeschichte.* FRLANT 95. Göttingen: Vandenhoeck und Ruprecht, 1968.

Stuhlmacher, *Reconciliation*

P. Stuhlmacher, *Reconciliation, Law, and Righteousness: Essays in Biblical Theology.* Philadelphia: Fortress, 1986.

Stuhlmacher, "Erwägungen"

P. Stuhlmacher, "Erwägungen zum ontologischen Charakter der καινὴ κτίσις bei Paulus," *EvT* 27 (1967) 1-35.

Suhl

A. Suhl, *Paulus und seine Briefe. Ein Beitrag zur paulinischen Chronologie.* SNT 11. Gütersloh: Gütersloher, 1975.

Sumney

J. L. Sumney, *Identifying Paul's Opponents: The Question of Method in 2 Corinthians.* JSNTSS 40. Sheffield: Sheffield Academic, 1990.

Sumney, "Weakness"

J. L. Sumney, "Paul's 'Weakness': An Integral Part of His Conception of Apostleship," *JSNT* 52 (1993) 71-91.

Sumney *Servants*

J. L. Sumney, *"Servants of Satan," "False Brothers" and Other Opponents of Paul.* JSNTSS 188. Sheffield: Sheffield Academic, 1999.

Sundermann

H. G. Sundermann, *Der schwache Apostel und die Kraft der Rede: Eine rhetorische Analysis von 2 Kor 10–13.* Europäische Hochschulschriften XXIII 575. Frankfurt, 1996.

Sweet

J. P. M. Sweet, "A House Not Made with Hands," in *Templum Amicitiae: Essays on the Second Temple Presented to Ernst Bammel.* Ed. W. Horbury. JSNTSS 48. Sheffield: JSOT, 1991, pp. 368-90.

Swete

H. B. Swete, *The Life of the World to Come.* London: Macmillan, 1930.

Sylvia

M. Sylvia, "2 Corinthians 12,1-5 and the Recent Discussion on 'Height and Depth,'" in *SE* IV/1 (= TU 102). Berlin: Akademie, 1968, pp. 462-72.

Tabor

J. D. Tabor, *Things Unutterable: Paul's Ascent to Paradise in Its Greco-Roman,*

Judaic, and Early Christian Contexts. New York: University Press of America, 1986.

Talbert
C. H. Talbert, *Reading Corinthians: A Literary and Theological Commentary on 1 and 2 Corinthians*. New York: Crossroad, 1987.

Tannehill
R. C. Tannehill, *Dying and Rising with Christ: A Study in Pauline Theology*. BZNW 32. Berlin: Töpelmann, 1967.

Tasker
R. V. G. Tasker, *The Second Epistle to the Corinthians*. TNTC 8. Grand Rapids: Eerdmans/London: Tyndale, 1958.

Tasker, "Unity"
R. V. G. Tasker, "The Unity of 2 Corinthians," *ExpT* 47 (1935-36) 55-58.

Taylor
J. Taylor, "The Ethnarch of King Aretas at Damascus: A Note on 2 Cor 11,32-33," *RB* 99 (1992) 719-28.

Tenney FS
Current Issues in Biblical and Patristic Interpretation: Studies in Honor of Merrill C. Tenney. Ed. G. F. Hawthorne. Grand Rapids: Eerdmans, 1975.

Thackeray
H. St.-J. Thackeray, *The Relation of St. Paul to Contemporary Jewish Thought*. London: Macmillan, 1900.

Theissen
G. Theissen, *The Social Setting of Pauline Christianity: Essays on Corinth*. ETr. Philadelphia: Fortress, 1982.

Theissen, *Aspects*
G. Theissen, *Psychological Aspects of Pauline Theology*. ETr. Philadelphia: Fortress/Edinburgh: Clark, 1987.

Theobald
M. Theobald, *Die überströmende Gnade. Studien zu einem paulinischen Motivfeld*. Würzburg: Echter, 1982.

Therrien
G. Therrien, *Le Discernement dans les écrits pauliniens*. Ébib. Paris: Gabalda, 1973.

Thielicke FS
Leben angesichts des Todes. Beiträge zum theologischen Problem des Todes. Ed. B. Lohse and H. P. Schmidt. Tübingen: Mohr, 1968.

Thielman
F. Thielman, *Paul and the Law*. Downers Grove: InterVarsity, 1994.

Thierry
J. J. Thierry, "Der Dorn im Fleische (2 Kor. xii 7-9)," *NovT* 5 (1962) 301-10.

Thiselton

A. C. Thiselton, *The First Epistle to the Corinthians*. NIGTC. Grand Rapids: Eerdmans/Carlisle: Paternoster, 2000.

Thiselton, "Eschatology"

A. C. Thiselton, "Realized Eschatology at Corinth," *NTS* 24 (1977-78) 510-26.

Thomas

J. C. Thomas, "'An Angel from Satan': Paul's Thorn in the Flesh (2 Corinthians 12.7-10)," *JPT* 9 (1996) 39-52.

Thornton

T. Thornton, "Satan — God's Agent for Punishing," *ExpT* 83 (1972) 151-52.

Thraede

K. Thraede, "Ursprünge und Formen des 'Heiligen Kusses' im frühen Christentum," *JAC* 11/12 (1968-69) 124-80.

Thrall

M. E. Thrall, *The Second Epistle to the Corinthians* I: *Introduction and Commentary on II Corinthians I–VII*. Edinburgh: Clark, 1994. II: *Commentary on II Corinthians VIII–XIII*. Edinburgh: Clark, 2000.

Thrall, "Christ"

M. E. Thrall, "Christ Crucified or Second Adam? A Christological Debate between Paul and the Corinthians," in *Moule FS* 143-56.

Thrall, "Conversion"

M. E. Thrall, "Conversion to the Lord: The Interpretation of Exodus 34 in II Cor. 3:14b-18," in Lorenzi (ed.) 197-218.

Thrall, *First Letter*

M. E. Thrall, *The First and Second Letter of Paul to the Corinthians*. The Cambridge Bible Commentary. Cambridge: Cambridge University Press, 1965.

Thrall, "Journey"

M. E. Thrall, "Paul's Journey to Paradise: Some Exegetical Issues in 2 Cor 12,2-4," in Bieringer (ed.) 347-63.

Thrall, "Offender"

M. E. Thrall, "The Offender and the Offence: A Problem of Detection in 2 Corinthians," in *Hanson FS* 65-78.

Thrall, *Particles*

M. E. Thrall, *Greek Particles in the New Testament*. NTTS 3. Leiden: Brill, 1962.

Thrall, "Problem"

M. E. Thrall, "The Problem of II Cor. vi.14–vii.1 in Some Recent Discussion," *NTS* 24 (1977-78) 132-48.

Thrall, "Salvation"

M. E. Thrall, "Salvation Proclaimed V: 2 Corinthians 5:18-21: Reconciliation with God," *ExpT* 93 (1981-82) 227-32.

Thrall, "2 Cor. 1:12"
M. E. Thrall, "2 Corinthians 1:2 [sic]: AΓIOTHTI [sic] or AΠΛOTHTI?" in *Kilpatrick FS* 366-72.

Thrall, "2 Corinthians 5:3"
M. E. Thrall, "'Putting On' or 'Stripping Off' in 2 Corinthians 5:3," in *Metzger FS,* pp. 221-37.

Thrall, "Super-Apostles"
M. E. Thrall, "Super-Apostles, Servants of Christ, and Servants of Satan," *JSNT* 6 (1980) 42-57.

Thrall, "ΣΥΝΕΙΔΗΣΙΣ"
M. E. Thrall, "The Pauline Use of ΣΥΝΕΙΔΗΣΙΣ," *NTS* 14 (1967-68) 118-25.

Thrall, "Thanksgiving"
M. E. Thrall, "A Second Thanksgiving Period in II Corinthians," *JSNT* 16 (1982) 101-24.

Thüsing
W. Thüsing, *Gott und Christus in der paulinischen Soteriologie* I: *Per Christum in Deum. Das Verhältnis der Christozentrik zur Theozentrik.* NTAbh n.F. 1/1. Münster: Aschendorff, 1986³.

Thüsing, "Christologie"
W. Thüsing, "Rechtfertigungsgedanke und Christologie in den Korintherbriefen," in *Schnackenburg FS* 301-24.

Thuruthumaly
J. Thuruthumaly, *Blessing in St. Paul.* Alwaye, Kerala: Pontifical Institute of Theology and Philosophy, 1981.

Thyen
H. Thyen, *Studien zur Sündenvergebung im Neuen Testament und seinen alttestamentlichen und jüdischen Voraussetzungen.* FRLANT 96. Göttingen: Vandenhoeck und Ruprecht, 1970.

Towner
P. Towner, "Gnosis and Realised Eschatology in Ephesus (of the Pastoral Epistles) and the Corinthian Enthusiasm," *JSNT* 31 (1987) 95-124.

Travis
S. H. Travis, "Paul's Boasting in 2 Corinthians 10–12," in *SE* VI. (= TU 112). Ed. E. A. Livingstone. Berlin: Akademie, 1973, pp. 527-32.

Trench
R. C. Trench, *Synonyms of the New Testament.* Grand Rapids: Eerdmans, 1953 reprint of 1876 edition.

Trobisch
D. Trobisch, *Paul's Letter Collection: Tracing the Origins.* Minneapolis: Augsburg Fortress, 1994.

Trocmé
E. Trocmé, "Le rempart de Damas. Un faux pas de Paul?" *RHPR* 69 (1989) 475-79.

Turner

N. Turner, *A Grammar of New Testament Greek* III: *Syntax.* Edinburgh: Clark, 1963.

Turner, *Insights*

N. Turner, *Grammatical Insights into the New Testament.* Edinburgh: Clark, 1965.

Turner, *Style*

N. Turner, *A Grammar of New Testament Greek* IV: *Style.* Edinburgh: Clark, 1976.

Turner, *Words*

N. Turner, *Christian Words.* Edinburgh: Clark, 1981.

D. L. Turner

D. L. Turner, "Paul and the Ministry of Reconciliation in 2 Cor. 5:11–6:2," *CTR* 4 (1989) 77-95.

H. E. W. Turner

H. E. W. Turner, *The Pattern of Christian Truth.* London: Mowbray, 1954.

Uddin

M. Uddin, "Paul, the Devil and 'Unbelief' in Israel (with Particular Reference to 2 Corinthians 3–4 and Romans 9–11)," *TynB* 50 (1999) 265-80.

Ulonska

H. Ulonska, "Die Doxa des Mose. Zum Problem des Alten Testaments in 2. Kor. 3,1-16," *EvT* 26 (1966) 378-88.

Vanhoye (ed.)

L'Apôtre Paul. Personnalité, style et conception du ministère. Ed. A. Vanhoye. BETL 73. Leuven: Leuven University, 1986.

Vanhoye

A. Vanhoye, "L'interpretation d'Ex 34 en 2 Co 3,7-14," in Lorenzi (ed.) 159-80.

van Unnik

Sparsa Collecta: The Collected Essays of W. C. van Unnik. Part I. NovTSup 29. Leiden: Brill, 1973. *Part II.* NovTSup 30. Leiden: Brill, 1980.

van Unnik, "Background"

W. C. van Unnik, "The Semitic Background of παρρησία in the New Testament," in *Sparsa* II.290-306.

van Unnik, "Conception"

W. C. van Unnik, "La conception paulinienne de la nouvelle alliance," in *Littérature et théologie pauliniennes,* by A. Descamps, et al. Louvain: Desclée de Brouwer, 1960 = *RechBib* 5 (1960) 109-26. (Reprinted in *Sparsa* I. 174-93).

van Unnik, "Face"

W. C. van Unnik, "'With Unveiled Face,' an Exegesis of 2 Corinthians iii 12-18," *NovT* 6 (1963) 153-69. (Reprinted in *Sparsa* I.194-210).

van Unnik, "Freedom"
>   W. C. van Unnik, "The Christian's Freedom of Speech in the New Testament,"
>   *BJRL* 44 (1962) 466-88.

van Unnik, "Reisepläne"
>   W. C. van Unnik, "Reisepläne und Amen-sagen. Zusammenhang und Gedanken-
>   folge in 2. Korinther i 15-25," in *de Zwaan FS* 215-34. (Reprinted in Unnik,
>   *Sparsa* I.144-59).

van Vliet
>   H. van Vliet, *No Single Testimony: A Study on the Adopting of the Law of Deut.
>   19:15 par. into the New Testament.* Studia Theologica Rheno-Traiectina 4.
>   Utrecht: Kemink and Zoon, 1958.

Verbrugge
>   V. D. Verbrugge, *Paul's Style of Church Leadership Illustrated by His Instruc-
>   tions to the Corinthians on the Collection.* San Francisco: Mellen Research
>   University, 1992.

Verhoef
>   E. Verhoef, "The Senders of the Letters to the Corinthians and the Use of 'I' and
>   'We,'" in Bieringer (ed.) 417-25.

Versnel
>   H. S. Versnel, Triumphus: *An Inquiry into the Origin, Development, and Mean-
>   ing of the Roman Triumph.* Leiden: Brill, 1970.

Vielhauer
>   P. Vielhauer, "Oikodome. Das Bild vom Bau in der christlichen Literatur vom
>   Neuen Testament bis Clemens Alexandrinus," pp. 1-168 in *Oikodome.
>   Aufsätze zum Neuen Testament, 1.* Ed. G. Klein. TBü 65. Munich: Kaiser,
>   1979.

Vielhauer, *Geschichte*
>   P. Vielhauer, *Geschichte der urchristlichen Literatur.* New York: de Gruyter,
>   1975.

Vincent
>   M. R. Vincent, "The Second Epistle to the Corinthians," in *Word Studies in the
>   New Testament* II. Florida: MacDonald, n.d. (reprint), pp. 808-44.

Vögtle
>   A. Vögtle, *Die Tugend- und Lasterkataloge im Neuen Testament.* NTAbh 16, 4/5.
>   Münster: Aschendorff, 1936.

Vollenweider
>   S. Vollenweider, *Freiheit als neue Schöpfung. Eine Untersuchung zur Eleutheria
>   bei Paulus und in seiner Umwelt.* FRLANT 147. Göttingen: Vandenhoeck
>   und Ruprecht, 1989.

von Allmen
>   D. von Allmen, "Réconciliation du monde et christologie cosmique, de II Cor.
>   5:14-21 à Col. 1:15-23," *RHPR* 48 (1968) 32-45.

von der Osten-Sacken

P. von der Osten-Sacken, *Gott und Belial. Traditionsgeschichtliche Untersuchungen zum Dualismus in den Texten aus Qumran.* SUNT 6. Göttingen: Vandenhoeck und Ruprecht, 1969.

von der Osten-Sacken, *Evangelium*

P. von der Osten-Sacken, *Evangelium und Tora. Aufsätze zu Paulus.* TBü 77. Munich: Kaiser, 1987.

von der Osten-Sacken, "Geist"

P. von der Osten-Sacken, "Geist im Buchstaben. Vom Glanz des Mose und des Paulus," *EvT* 41 (1981) 230-35 (reprinted in his *Evangelium* 150-55).

von der Osten-Sacken, *Heiligkeit*

P. von der Osten-Sacken, *Die Heiligkeit der Tora: Studien zum Gesetz bei Paulus.* Munich: Kaiser, 1989.

von Dobschütz

E. von Dobschütz, "Zwei- und dreiliedrige Formeln. Ein Beitrag zur Vorgeschichte der Trinitätsformel," *JBL* 50 (1931) 117-47.

von Loewenich

W. von Loewenich, *Paul: His Life and Work.* Edinburgh: Oliver and Boyd, 1960.

Vos

G. Vos, *The Pauline Eschatology.* Grand Rapids: Eerdmans, 1961 reprint of 1930 edition.

J. S. Vos

J. S. Vos, *Traditionsgeschichtliche Untersuchungen zur paulinischen Pneumatologie.* TBü 47. Assen: Van Gorcum, 1973.

Wagner

G. Wagner, "Le tabernacle et la vie 'en Christ.' Exégèse de 2 Corinthiens 5:1 à 10," *RHPR* 41 (1961) 379-93. ETr in *IBS* 3 (1981) 145-65.

Wainwright

A. W. Wainwright, *The Trinity in the New Testament.* London: SPCK, 1962.

Walker

W. O. Walker, Jr., "The Burden of Proof in Identifying Interpolations in the Pauline Letters," *NTS* 33 (1987) 610-18.

Walker, "Structure"

W. O. Walker, Jr., "2 Cor 6.14–7.1 and the Chiastic Structure of 6.11-13; 7.2-3," *NTS* 48 (2002) 142-44.

Walter

N. Walter, "Hellenistische Eschatologie bei Paulus? Zu 2 Kor 5,1-10," *TQ* 176 (1996) 53-64.

Wand

J. W. C. Wand, *The New Testament Letters Prefaced and Paraphrased.* London/ New York: Oxford University Press, 1946.

Warfield
B. B. Warfield, "Some Difficult Passages in the First Chapter of 2 Corinthians," *Journal of the Exegetical Society* (= *JBL*) 6 (1886) 27-39.

Watson
N. M. Watson, *The Second Epistle to the Corinthians*. London: Epworth, 1993.

Watson, "2 Cor 1,9b"
N. M. Watson, ". . . 'To Make Us Rely Not on Ourselves but on God Who Raises the Dead' — 2 Cor 1,9b as the Heart of Paul's Theology," in *Schweizer FS* 384-98.

D. F. Watson
D. F. Watson, "Rhetorical Criticism of the Pauline Epistles since 1975," *CRBS* 3 (1995) 219-48.

F. Watson
F. Watson, "2 Cor. x–xiii and Paul's Painful Visit to the Corinthians," *JTS* 35 (1984) 324-46.

Webb
W. J. Webb, *Returning Home: New Covenant and Second Exodus as the Context for 2 Corinthians 6.14–7.1*. JSNTSS 85. Sheffield: JSOT, 1993.

Webb, "Unbelievers"
W. J. Webb, "Unequally Yoked with Unbelievers, Part 1: Who Are the Unbelievers (ἄπιστοι) in 2 Corinthians 6:14?" *BSac* 149 (1992) 27-44.

Webb, "Yoke"
W. J. Webb, "Unequally Yoked with Unbelievers, Part 2: What Is the Unequal Yoke (ἑτεροζυγοῦντες) in 2 Corinthians 6:14?" *BSac* 149 (1992) 162-79.

Wedderburn (ed.)
Paul and Jesus. Collected Essays. Ed. A. J. M. Wedderburn. JSNTSS 37. Sheffield: JSOT, 1989.

Wedderburn
A. J. M. Wedderburn, *Baptism and Resurrection: Studies in Pauline Theology against Its Greco-Roman Background*. WUNT 44. Tübingen: Mohr, 1987.

Wedderburn, "Observations"
A. J. M. Wedderburn, "Some Observations on Paul's Use of the Phrases 'in Christ' and 'with Christ,'" *JSNT* 25 (1985) 83-97.

Weher
U. Weher, "Erklärung von 2 Kor 10:1-6," *BZ* 1 (1903) 64-78.

Weima
J. A. D. Weima, *Neglected Endings: The Significance of the Pauline Letter Closings*. JSNTSS 101. Sheffield: Sheffield Academic, 1994.

Weinel
H. Weinel, *St. Paul: The Man and His Work*. ETr. Ed. W. D. Morrison. London: Williams and Norgate, 1906.

Weiss

J. Weiss, *Der erste Korintherbrief.* KEK 5. Göttingen: Vandenhoeck und Ruprecht, 1910².

Weiss, *Christianity*

J. Weiss, *Earliest Christianity.* 2 vols. ETr. New York: Harper, 1959 ed. of 1937 translation.

Weiss, *Paul*

J. Weiss, *Paul and Jesus.* ETr. New York: Harper, 1909.

B. Weiss

B. Weiss, *Biblical Theology of the New Testament.* ETr. Edinburgh: Clark, 1893.

Welborn

L. L. Welborn, *Politics and Rhetoric in the Corinthian Epistles.* Macon: Mercer University Press, 1997.

Welborn, "Emotions"

L. L. Welborn, "Paul's Appeal to the Emotions in 2 Corinthians 1.1–2.13; 7.5-16," *JSNT* 82 (2001) 31-60.

Welborn, "Identification"

L. L. Welborn, "The Identification of 2 Corinthians 10–13 with the 'Letter of Tears,'" *NovT* 37 (1995) 138-53.

Welborn, "Runaway"

L. L. Welborn, "The Runaway Paul," *HTR* 92 (1999) 115-63.

Welborn, "Theories"

L. L. Welborn, "Like Broken Pieces of a Ring: 2 Cor 1.1–2.13; 7.5-16 and Ancient Theories of Literary Unity," *NTS* 42 (1996) 559-83.

Welborn, "Tirocinium"

L. L. Welborn, "Primum tirocinium Pauli (2 Cor 11,32-33)," *BZ* n.F. 43 (1999) 49-71.

Wendland

H. D. Wendland, *Die Briefe an die Korinther.* NTD 7. Göttingen: Vandenhoeck und Ruprecht, 1968¹².

Wengst

K. Wengst, *Christologische Formeln und Lieder des Urchristentums.* SNT 7. Gütersloh: Gütersloher, 1972.

Wenham

D. Wenham, "2 Corinthians 1:17, 18: Echo of a Dominical Logion," *NovT* 28 (1986) 271-79.

Wenham, "Last Day"

D. Wenham, "Being 'Found' on the Last Day: New Light on 2 Peter 3.10 and 2 Corinthians 5.3," *NTS* 33 (1987) 477-79.

Westerholm

S. Westerholm, *Israel's Law and the Church's Faith: Paul and His Recent Interpreters.* Grand Rapids: Eerdmans, 1988.

Weymouth

R. F. Weymouth, *The New Testament in Modern Speech.* Boston: Pilgrim/London: Clarke, 1909³ (edited and partly revised by E. Hampden-Cook).

White

N. J. D. White, "Are There Two Epistles in 2 Corinthians? A Reply," *Exp,* 5th series, 7 (1898) 113-23.

White, "Visits"

N. J. D. White, "The Visits of St. Paul to Corinth," *Herm* 12 (1903) 79-89.

J. L. White

J. L. White, *The Form and Function of the Body of the Greek Letter: A Study of the Letter-Body in Non-Literary Papyri and in Paul the Apostle.* SBLDS 2. Missoula: Scholars, 1972.

J. L. White, "Formulae"

J. L. White, "Introductory Formulae in the Body of the Pauline Letter," *JBL* 90 (1971) 91-97.

Whiteley

D. E. H. Whiteley, *The Theology of St. Paul.* Philadelphia: Fortress/Oxford: Blackwell, 1964.

Wibbing

S. Wibbing, *Die Tugend- und Lasterkataloge im Neuen Testament.* BZNW 25. Berlin: Töpelmann, 1959.

Wikenhauser

A. Wikenhauser, *New Testament Introduction.* ETr. New York: Herder, 1958.

Wilckens

U. Wilckens, *Weisheit und Torheit.* BHT 26. Tübingen: Mohr, 1959.

Wiles

G. P. Wiles, *Paul's Intercessory Prayers: The Significance of the Intercessory Prayer Passages in the Letters of Paul.* SNTSMS 24. Cambridge: Cambridge University Press, 1974.

Williams

C. B. Williams, *The New Testament: A Translation in the Language of the People.* Chicago: Moody, 1950 (= 1937 edition).

D. J. Williams

D. J. Williams, *Paul's Metaphors: Their Context and Character.* Peabody: Hendrickson, 1999.

Williamson

L. Williamson, Jr., "Led in Triumph: Paul's Use of *Thriambeuō*," *Int* 22 (1968) 317-32.

Willis

W. L. Willis, *Idol Meat in Corinth: The Pauline Argument in 1 Corinthians 8 and 10.* SBLDS 68. Chico: Scholars, 1985.

Wilson

R. McL. Wilson, *Gnosis and the New Testament.* Oxford: Blackwell, 1968.

Wilson, "Corinth"

R. McL. Wilson, "Gnosis at Corinth," in *Barrett FS* 102-14.

Wilson, "Corinthians"

R. McL. Wilson, "How Gnostic Were the Corinthians?" *NTS* 19 (1972-73) 65-74.

Wilson, *Philip*

R. McL. Wilson, *The Gospel of Philip.* London: Mowbray, 1962.

Wilson, *Problem*

R. McL. Wilson, *The Gnostic Problem.* London: Mowbray, 1958.

J. H. Wilson

J. H. Wilson, "The Corinthians Who Say There Is No Resurrection of the Dead," *ZNW* 59 (1968) 90-107.

W. E. Wilson

W. E. Wilson, "The Development of Paul's Doctrine of Dying and Rising Again with Christ," *ExpT* 42 (1930-31) 562-65.

Wimmer

A. Wimmer, "Trostworte des Apostels Paulus an Hinterbliebene in Thessalonich (1 Th. 4,13-17)," *Bib* 36 (1955) 273-86.

Windisch

H. Windisch, *Der zweite Korintherbrief.* MeyerK 6. Göttingen: Vandenhoeck und Ruprecht, 1924.

Winer

G. B. Winer, *A Grammar of the Idiom of the New Testament.* ETr. Andover: Draper/London: Trübner, 1872[7].

Winter

B. W. Winter, *Philo and Paul among the Sophists.* Cambridge: Cambridge University Press, 1997.

Winter, *Corinth*

B. W. Winter, *After Paul Left Corinth: The Influence of Secular Ethics and Social Change.* Grand Rapids: Eerdmans, 2001.

Winter, "Paul"

B. W. Winter, "Is Paul among the Sophists?" *RTR* 53 (1994) 28-38.

Winter, "Pluralism"

B. W. Winter, "Theological and Ethical Responses to Religious Pluralism — 1 Corinthians 8–10," *TynB* 41 (1990) 209-26.

Winter, "Responses"

B. W. Winter, "Secular and Christian Responses to Corinthian Famines," *TynB* 40 (1989) 86-106.

Wiseman

J. R. Wiseman, "Corinth and Rome I: 228 B.C.–A.D. 267," in *Aufstieg* II. 7/1, 438-548.

Wiseman, *Land*
J. R. Wiseman, *The Land of the Ancient Corinthians.* Studies in the Mediterranean Archaeology 50. Göteborg: Åströms, 1978.

Witherington
B. Witherington III, *Conflict and Community in Corinth: A Socio-Rhetorical Commentary on 1 and 2 Corinthians.* Grand Rapids: Eerdmans/Carlisle: Paternoster, 1995.

Witherington, *Jesus*
B. Witherington III, *Jesus, Paul and the End of the World: A Comparative Study in New Testament Eschatology.* Downers Grove: InterVarsity, 1992.

Witherington, *Narrative Thought*
B. Witherington III, *Paul's Narrative Thought World: The Tapestry of Tragedy and Triumph.* Louisville: Westminster, 1994.

Wolff
C. Wolff, *Der zweite Brief des Paulus an die Korinther.* THKNT 8. Berlin: Evangelische Verlagsanstalt, 1989.

Wolff, "Humility.
C. Wolff, "Humility and Self-Denial in Jesus' Life and Message and in the Apostolic Existence of Paul," in Wedderburn (ed.) 145-60.

Wolff, "Knowledge"
C. Wolff, "True Apostolic Knowledge of Christ: Exegetical Reflections on 2 Corinthians 5.14ff.," in Wedderburn (ed.) 81-98.

Wong
K. H. Wong, *Boasting and Foolishness: A Study of 2 Cor 10,12-18 and 11,1a.* Hong Kong: Alliance Bible Seminary, 1998.

Wong, "Lord"
K. H. Wong, "'Lord' in 2 Corinthians 10.17," *LouvStud* 17 (1992) 243-53.

E. Wong
E. Wong, "The Lord is the Spirit (2 Cor 3,17a)," *ETL* 61 (1985) 48-72.

Wonneberger
R. Wonneberger, "Der Beitrag der generativen Syntax zur Exegese. Ein Beispiel (2. Kor 5,2f) und neuen Thesen," *Bijdragen* 36 (1975) 312-17.

Wood
J. E. Wood, "Death at Work in Paul," *EvQ* 54 (1982) 151-55.

C. T. Woods
C. T. Woods, *The Life, Letters and Religion of St. Paul.* Edinburgh: Clark, 1925.

Wright
N. T. Wright, "Reflected Glory: 2 Corinthians 3:18," in *Caird FS* 139-49. Revised form in *The Climax of the Covenant: Christ and the Law in Pauline Theology.* Edinburgh: Clark, 1991, pp. 175-92.

Wright, "Righteousness"
N. T. Wright, "On Becoming the Righteousness of God: 2 Corinthians 5:21," in Hay (ed.) 200-208.

Wuellner
W. H. Wuellner, "Greek Rhetoric and Pauline Argumentation," in *Grant FS* 177-88.

Yamauchi
E. M. Yamauchi, *Pre-Christian Gnosticism: A Survey of the Proposed Evidences.* Grand Rapids: Eerdmans, 1973.

Yamauchi, "Debate"
E. Yamauchi, "Pre-Christian Gnosticism, the New Testament and Nag Hammadi in Recent Debate," *Them* 10 (1984) 22-27.

Yates
R. J. Yates, "Paul's Affliction in Asia: 2 Corinthians 1:8," *EvQ* 53 (1981) 241-45.

Yates, "State"
R. J. Yates, "Immediate or Intermediate? The State of the Believer upon Death," *Churchman* 101 (1987) 310-22.

Yinger
K. L. Yinger, *Paul, Judaism, and Judgment according to Deeds.* SNTSMS 105. Cambridge: Cambridge University Press, 1999.

Young
F. M. Young, "Note on 2 Corinthians 1.17b," *JTS* n.s. 37 (1986) 404-15.

B. H. Young
B. H. Young, "The Ascension Motif of 2 Corinthians 12 in Jewish, Christian and Gnostic Texts," *GTJ* 9 (1988) 73-103.

Young and Ford
F. Young and D. F. Ford, *Meaning and Truth in 2 Corinthians.* Grand Rapids: Eerdmans/London: SPCK, 1987.

Zahn
T. Zahn, *Introduction to the New Testament.* ETr. Vol. 1. Minneapolis: Klock, 1977 reprint of 1909 edition.

Zeilinger
F. Zeilinger, "Die Echtheit von 2 Cor 6:14–7:1," *JBL* 112 (1993) 71-80.

Zerwick
M. Zerwick, *Biblical Greek.* ETr. Rome: Pontifical Biblical Institute, 1963.

Zerwick, *Analysis*
M. Zerwick, *Analysis Philologica Novi Testamenti Graeci.* Rome: Pontifical Biblical Institute, 1966[3]. (This original contains material not found in the English edition [= Zerwick and Grosvenor]).

Zerwick and Grosvenor
M. Zerwick and M. Grosvenor, *A Grammatical Analysis of the Greek New Testa-*

ment. Rome: Pontifical Biblical Institute, 1974 (vol. 1: Gospels-Acts), 1979 (vol. 2: Epistles-Apocalypse).

Ziesler

J. A. Ziesler, *The Meaning of Righteousness in Paul.* SNTSMS 20. Cambridge: Cambridge University Press, 1972.

Ziesler, *Christianity*

J. A. Ziesler, *Pauline Christianity.* Oxford: Oxford University Press, 1983.

Zimmermann FS

Begegnung mit dem Wort. Ed. J. Zmijewski and E. Nellesen. BBB 53. Bonn: Hanstein, 1980.

Zimmermann

H. Zimmermann, *Untersuchungen zur Geschichte der altlateinischen Überlieferung des zweiten Korintherbriefes.* Bonn: Hanstein, 1960.

Zmijewski

J. Zmijewski, *Der Stil der paulinischen "Narrenrede." Analyse der Sprachgestaltung in 2 Kor 11,1–12,10 als Beitrag zur Methodik von Stiluntersuchungen neutestamentlicher Texte.* BBB 52. Köln: Hanstein, 1978.

Zmijewski, "Kontextbezug"

J. Zmijewski, "Kontextbezug und Deutung von 2 Kor 12,7a. Stilistische und Strukturale Erwägungen zur Lösung eines alten Problems," *BZ* n.F. 21 (1977) 265-72. Reprinted in J. Zmijewski, *Das Neue Testament — Quelle christlicher Theologie und Glaubenspraxis.* Stuttgart: Katholisches Bibelwerk, 1986.

Zorell

F. Zorell, " 'Deus huius saeculi' (2 Cor. 4.4)," *VD* 8 (1928) 54-57.

Zorn

R. O. Zorn, "II Corinthians 5:1-10: Individual Eschatology or Corporate Solidarity, Which," *RTR* 47 (1988) 93-104.

Zuntz

G. Zuntz, *The Text of the Epistles: A Disquisition upon the* Corpus Paulinum. London: Oxford University Press, 1953.

INTRODUCTION

Every Pauline letter arose, at least in part, from pastoral needs. But among Paul's extant letters none is more closely tied to the vagaries of historical circumstance than 2 Corinthians. There is therefore all the more reason to examine carefully the circumstances that gave rise to this letter and formulate the critical assumptions, both literary and historical, on which its exegesis will proceed. Four literary and five historical problems demand consideration and the positing of such solutions as will enable a consistent interpretation of the whole canonical letter.

A. LITERARY ISSUES

1. Authorship and Attestation of 2 Corinthians

a. Authorship

One of the areas in which there is a consensus among NT scholars is that Paul was the author of 2 Corinthians, along with the other three letters, viz. Galatians, 1 Corinthians, and Romans, which make up the "chief epistles" *(Hauptbriefe),* as Baur called them.[1] On the one hand, 2 Corinthians contains examples of all the characteristically Pauline stylistic devices, such as antithetic parallelism, chiasmus, paradox, anacolutha, ellipsis, and litotes;[2] it reflects that delicate blend of generous encouragement, gentle expostulation, and (if necessary) stern rebuke that was typical of Paul when he addressed his spiritual chil-

---

1. Baur 1.246; 2.18-21, 35-42. For Baur, these four major epistles constitute the "first class" of Paul's letters, the *homologoumena,* whose authenticity has never been seriously doubted, with Philippians, 1 Thessalonians, and Philemon forming the "second class," the *antilegomena,* whose genuineness has with good reason been questioned, while the Pastoral Epistles belong to a "third class" whose inauthenticity is highly probable (1.246-47).
2. Speaking of Paul's style in all four "chief epistles," Sanday and Headlam (lv) observe that "there is a rush of words, rising repeatedly to passages of splendid eloquence; but the eloquence is spontaneous, the outcome of strongly moved feeling; there is nothing about it of labored oratory. The language is rapid, terse, incisive; the argument is conducted by a quick cut and thrust of dialectic; it reminds us of a fencer with his eye always on his antagonist."

dren; and it witnesses to most of the distinctively Pauline doctrines, such as jus-tification by grace through faith, the Christian life as being lived "in Christ" and by the Spirit, and Christian suffering as a sharing in Christ's suffering. On the other hand, this letter can scarcely be explained as the work of a forger or a dis-ciple writing in Paul's name, for no such author would have tantalized his read-ers with so many cryptic allusions to shadowy persons and disturbing events or have made imprecision such a virtue as when he describes Paul's devastating experience in Asia (1:8-10) or his startling ascent into paradise and its after-math (12:1-10). Moreover, a pious imitator would be unlikely to portray Paul as an apostle in danger of losing his authority at Corinth or an apostle struggling to preserve the Corinthians from apostasy.

b. Attestation

Writing in A.D. 95 or 96, Clement of Rome clearly alludes to 1 Cor. 1:11-13 when he directs the Corinthians (47:1): "Take up the letter of the blessed apos-tle Paul. What did he first write to you at the beginning of the gospel? In very truth he gave you directions in the Spirit with regard to himself and Cephas and Apollos, because even then you had created party divisions." Moreover, *1 Clement* contains several other indisputable allusions to 1 Corinthians (see A. E. Barnett 88-104; Hagner 196-209). But conclusive evidence is lacking that our canonical 2 Corinthians was known to Clement and the church of Rome in the mid-90s of the first century.[3] Not only does Clement refer (in the quotation above) to a single letter (τὴν ἐπιστολήν) of Paul; he nowhere clearly alludes to 2 Corinthians.[4] To conclude that Clement probably did not know 2 Corinthians involves a legitimate use of the argument from silence, for there are not a few passages in 2 Corinthians (e.g., 11:2-3; 12:20; 13:5, 9b) that would have been

---

3. So Hagner 212, who nevertheless concludes that there "remains a strong possibility that Clement knew and alluded to 2 Corinthians" (213). It would seem that only Romans and 1 Corin-thians were certainly known to Clement (thus Hagner 237).

4. Appeal is sometimes made to the following alleged allusions to 2 Corinthians in *1 Clem-ent:*

2 Corinthians	*1 Clement*
1:5	2:1
3:3	2:8
3:18	36:2
8:9	16:2
9:8	2:7
9:12	38:2
10:3-4	37:1
10:13-16	1:3; 41:1
10:17	13:1
10:18	30:6
11:23-27	5:5-6.

directly relevant to Clement's concerns (e.g., at *1 Clement* 5:6) as he sought to combat the Corinthian pneumatics of the 90s who had tried to supplant the presbyters (see, e.g., 13:1; 38:1-2; 48:5-6). Since the situation Clement faced at Corinth related more directly to opposition to authority than to mere party-strife, 2 Corinthians would have been more apposite to cite than 1 Corinthians.

Similarly, although there are frequent echoes of 1 Corinthians in the letters of Ignatius of Antioch, written early in the second century, unambiguous reminiscences of 2 Corinthians are lacking.[5] But when we examine the epistle to the Philippians written in the mid-second century by Polycarp of Smyrna, we find three or four clearer allusions to 2 Corinthians (2 Cor. 3:2 in *Philippians* 11:3; 2 Cor. 4:14 in *Philippians* 2:2; 2 Cor. 5:10 in *Philippians* 6:2; and possibly 2 Cor. 6:7 in *Philippians* 4:1 and 2 Cor. 8:21 in *Philippians* 6:1). Writing toward the end of the second century, Irenaeus of Lyons not only often quotes from 2 Corinthians but actually names the epistle: *apostolus ait in epistola secunda ad Corinthios* (*Adversus Haereses* 4.28.3); *in secunda [epistola] quae est ad Corinthios dicens* (5.3.1). Also, the anonymous *Letter to Diognetus* 5:8 (late second century?) reflects a knowledge of 2 Cor. 6:8-10; 10:3. In his Περὶ Τὰ Ἀναστάσεως Νεκρῶν 18 (ca. 180) Athenagoras of Athens cites a portion of 2 Cor. 5:10. At a slightly later time Clement of Alexandria (*floruit* 200-215), Tertullian of Carthage (*floruit* 195-220), and Cyprian of Carthage (*floruit* 246-58) frequently cite 2 Corinthians. Finally, 2 Corinthians finds a place in Marcion's canon (ca. 150) and in the Muratorian Canon (late second century).[6]

To judge by the extant attestation of 2 Corinthians, we may conclude that this epistle became widely known throughout the early church only during the second half of the second century.

2. The "Severe Letter"

That Paul wrote and sent a "severe letter" to the Corinthians at some time after his founding visit is clear from 2 Cor. 1:23–2:11 and 7:5-16. In the former passage there is a threefold use of ἔγραψα (2:3-4, 9; also 7:12), while in the latter passage we find a twofold reference to an ἐπιστολή that caused the Corinthians pain (7:8). It is not the historicity of this "severe letter" (sometimes called the "letter of tears" [*Tränenbrief*] or "sorrowful/painful letter") but its identity that raises critical problems. But before we evaluate the proposed identifications of the letter, we shall summarize what may be known of its purpose and effect. Its contents must be inferred from scanty data: on an inductive approach the only

5. But see the discussion of A. E. Barnett 155-56 (on 2 Cor. 6:16: *Ephesians* 15:3), 162-63 (on 2 Cor. 1:12; 11:9-10; 12:16: *Philippians* 6:3), 168 (2 Cor. 13:13: *Magnesians* 13:1; 2 Cor. 10:12-13: *Trallians* 4:1; 2 Cor. 4:14: *Trallians* 9:2), 169 (2 Cor. 5:20: *Philippians* 10:1), who concludes that Ignatius "may . . . have known II Corinthians" (170).

6. On these two canons, see Metzger, *Canon* 90-99 (Marcion's), 191-201, 305-7 (the Muratorian).

parts of the letter that may be regarded as incontestable are Paul's assurance to the Corinthians of his intense love for them (2:4) and his demand that they take disciplinary action against a certain offender as evidence of their total obedience to him (2:6, 9).[7]

a. Its Purpose

The general aim of the "severe letter" was to arouse the Corinthian church to discipline ὁ ἀδικήσας, "the one who did the wrong," and thus vindicate the ὁ ἀδικηθείς, "the one who suffered the wrong" (2 Cor. 2:6, 9; 7:12).[8] But 2 Corinthians contains four additional statements of Paul's purpose in writing:

1. to spare the Corinthians (1:23–2:2, 4) and himself (2:3) another painful visit,
2. to demonstrate his affection for the Corinthians (2:4),
3. to put to the test the Corinthians' obedience to apostolic authority (either as vested in himself or as embodied in certain principles) (2:9), and
4. to make the Corinthians aware, in God's sight, of their genuine concern and real affection for him as their spiritual father (7:12; cf. 1 Cor. 4:15). This last purpose Paul states as his principal objective.

b. Its Effect

(1) On the Corinthians

The Corinthians as a whole had felt concern (σπουδή, 7:11), remorse (ὀδυρμός, 7:7), and even apprehension (φόβος, 7:11, 15) over their behavior during the "painful visit." They had longed to see Paul in person (ἐπιπόθησις, 7:7, 11) to assure him of their change of attitude (μετάνοια, 7:9-10) and of their desire to exculpate themselves (ἀπολογία, 7:11), and they had been zealous (ζῆλος, 7:7, 11) to avoid further complicity and to requite the offender (ἐκδίκησις, 7:11), whose scandalous action had now provoked their indignation (ἀγανάκτησις, 7:11). By the decision of the majority (οἱ πλείονες, 2:6), some penalty was inflicted on "the guilty party" (7:12), but whether publicly or privately, whether by reprimand or by exclusion, is not known. In opposition to a minority contrary view, Paul exhorted the Corinthians to accept his judgment that the penalty already imposed was sufficient retribution: ὁ ἀδικήσας would be rescued

---

7. The letter may also have accredited its bearer, Titus, as Paul's agent in the matter (cf. 2 Cor. 7:13-15).

8. Although 7:12 appears to express two rejected causes (οὐχ ἕνεκεν τοῦ ἀδικήσαντος, οὐδὲ ἕνεκεν τοῦ ἀδικηθέντος) alongside a sole purpose (ἀλλ' ἕνεκεν κτλ.) for the "severe letter," in reality the rejected causes form subsidiary objectives (see on 7:12).

from inordinate grief and his reformation completed only if they forgave him and reaffirmed their love for him, thereby affording further evidence of their repentance and obedience (2:6-9).

(2) On Paul

After Paul had learned from Titus the Corinthian response to the letter, his initial reaction was to regret (μετεμελόμην, 7:8) that he had actually caused them such pain (cf. 2:2, 4; 7:8-9), although that pain had been only temporary (πρὸς ὥραν, 7:8). Upon reflection, however, his opinion had altered so that at the time of writing he could say, "I do not regret it" (οὐ μεταμέλομαι, 7:8), for the infliction of λύπη, though unavoidable, had proved remedial; in fact their "grief" had been in accordance with God's will (κατὰ θεόν, three times in 7:9-11) and had prevented the letter from causing them any permanent injury (7:9b). In addition, Paul felt relief that his boasting about the Corinthians to Titus had not proved unfounded (7:13-14), just as Titus himself had previously felt relieved that his misgivings about his mission to Corinth had proved unfounded (7:7, 13, 15).

c. Its Identification

Theoretically, there are six possible identifications of the "severe letter": (1) an unattested letter written before the "previous letter" or before 1 Corinthians, (2) the "previous letter" (cf. 1 Cor. 5:9, 11), (3) 1 Corinthians, (4) a letter, no longer extant, written between 1 and 2 Corinthians, (5) a letter, partially preserved in 2 Corinthians 10–13, that preceded the writing of 2 Corinthians 1–9, or (6) 2 Corinthians. The first, second, and sixth of these identifications are too improbable to warrant consideration.[9] This leaves us with three possibilities.

(1) 1 Corinthians

This time-honored identification rests on three principal grounds.

First, when the nature and extent of the Corinthian disorders are recalled — the rampant spirit of divisiveness, carnality, self-complacency, litigiousness, and libertinism, together with the condoning of incest and the profanation of the Lord's Supper — the apostle's description, *ex hypothesi,* of 1 Corinthians or at least parts of it as having been written "in great distress and anguish of heart and with many tears" (2 Cor. 2:4; cf. Phil. 3:18; Acts 20:19, 31) and as causing him temporary regret and them temporary grief (2 Cor. 7:8), seems not inappropriate.[10]

---

9. For the difficulties in such identifications see Lake 154; Hurd 55-56.

10. "In the phrase 'the Painful Letter,'" claims Bernard (14), "there is, in fact, a latent fallacy. The language of 2 Cor. ii.4, vii.8, would be sufficiently accounted for if *any* part of the letter to

Second, there is a certain congruity in interpreting one difficult passage (2 Cor. 2:5-11; cf. 7:12) by reference to an earlier extant letter to the same church, a letter in which we find a paragraph (1 Cor. 5:1-8) bearing at least a superficial resemblance to the *crux interpretum* in question. In each case there are a single guilty party (1 Cor. 5:1-2, 4-5, 13; 2 Cor. 2:5-8), who is identified as ὁ τοιοῦτος (1 Cor. 5:5; 2 Cor. 2:6-7) or τις (1 Cor. 5:1; 2 Cor. 2:5), an exercise of church discipline (1 Cor. 5:3-5, 13; 2 Cor. 2:6), an appeal to the name or presence of Christ (1 Cor. 5:4; 2 Cor. 2:10), and the involvement of Satan (1 Cor. 5:5; 2 Cor. 2:11).

Third, the equation of ὁ ἀδικήσας (2 Cor. 7:12) = τις (2:5) = ὁ τοιοῦτος (2:6-7) with τις (1 Cor. 5:1) = ὁ τοιοῦτος (5:5), and of ὁ ἀδικηθείς of 2 Cor. 7:12 with ὁ πατήρ of 1 Cor. 5:1 need not compound exegetical problems, provided the exegete remembers "the fact that unrelenting severity is not a Christian virtue" (Bernard 14) and that "St. Paul had never meant to convey (although the Corinthians had misunderstood his counsel) that the ban [of excommunication] could not be taken off by the same authority which had imposed it, if evidence of penitence were forthcoming" (Bernard 14-15). In this case, "binding" was replaced by "loosing" (cf. Matt. 18:18).[11]

Although it is not a view commonly held today, this identification of the "sorrowful letter" with 1 Corinthians should certainly not be dismissed as unworthy of serious consideration (as Moffatt, *Introduction* 122 n. 2 and Plummer xxviii tend to do). An impressive array of scholars from Chrysostom and Theodoret down to Meyer (443), Lightfoot (*Notes* 202-4), Hughes (54-58, 270-71), Lampe (353-54), and Hyldahl ("Einheit" 299-302) endorse this view. Nevertheless, there are several compelling reasons for abandoning it (see also Furnish 164-66; Thrall 57-61).

(a) 2 Cor. 2:6 and 7:12 suggest that the "letter of tears" as a whole dealt primarily with ὁ ἀδικήσας and the need for his punishment, which is patently not the case with 1 Corinthians, in which a wide range of issues is discussed, with divisiveness, not immorality, the first addressed.

(b) 1 Corinthians does not seem to have been written in the place of a second painful visit (see, on the contrary, 1 Cor. 4:18-19; 11:34; 16:2-3, 5-7), as is demanded by 2 Cor. 1:23; 2:1, 3.

(c) In 2 Cor. 2:10a Paul offers his personal forgiveness to the individual (ᾧ = ὁ ἀδικήσας), whom the Corinthians also are to forgive (2:7). But the apostle would scarcely have regarded a man's illicit relations with his stepmother as a personal injury inflicted on himself and requiring his forgiveness, even if such action constituted a repudiation of his teaching. On the other hand, if the offense alluded to in 2 Cor. 2:5-10 and 7:12 was an act of public effrontery

---

which he refers seemed to St. Paul (for the moment) to be unduly severe, or if *any* section of it had caused unexpected grief to the Corinthians."

11. As a consequence of this identification of ἡ ἐπιτιμία (2 Cor. 2:6) with (τὸ) παραδοῦναι τῷ Σατανᾷ (1 Cor. 5:5) 2 Cor. 2:7 comes to mean "replace discipline with forgiveness and comfort" (note τοὐναντίον μᾶλλον).

against Paul himself or against his acknowledged or delegated representative by some vocal spokesman of an anti-Pauline clique (see the commentary on 2:5-10), Paul's offer of forgiveness becomes explicable.

(d) If, in fact, ὁ ἀδικήσας ("the guilty party," 2 Cor. 7:12) is ὁ τοιοῦτος ("this individual," 1 Cor. 5:5), the case of incest becomes more heinous than 1 Corinthians 5 would suggest. On this view, the incestuous son was not "living with" (ἔχειν, 1 Cor. 5:1) his widowed stepmother (as is probably the true explanation) but with his stepmother while his father (ὁ ἀδικηθείς) was still alive (and living with her?). Paul would not have referred to a dead man as "the aggrieved party." Surely such an offense, more properly described as μοιχεία than as πορνεία (1 Cor. 5:1), would have scandalized even the πεφυσιωμένοι (5:2) at Corinth and impelled them to seek some form of redress for the father if not punishment for the son.

(e) In 1 Corinthians 5 there is no reference, as might be expected on the 1 Corinthians 5 = 2 Corinthians 2 equation, to disciplinary action as evidence of obedience (cf. 2 Cor. 2:9) but only to its absence as an indication of infection (1 Cor. 5:6-7).

(f) Any solution to the disputed question of the aptness of 2 Cor. 2:4 as a description of parts or the whole of 1 Corinthians is necessarily inconclusive since it rests on subjective impressions gained from examining ambiguous evidence.[12]

(2) A Letter Incorporating 2 Corinthians 10–13

Although the view is far less popular than it once was, a considerable number of commentators believe that 2 Corinthians 10–13 was written before chs. 1–9 and that chs. 10–13 form the principal part of the "sorrowful letter" (A. Hausrath's theory). The various difficulties to which this thesis gives rise will be discussed below (B.3.e.[2]).

(3) A Lost "Intermediate Letter"

Scholars who reject these two identifications of the "sorrowful letter" (1 Corinthians, 2 Corinthians 10–13) are compelled to assume that the letter is no longer extant. Such scholars include those who identify the bulk of 2 Corinthians with a fifth letter Paul wrote to Corinth after sending 2 Corinthians 1–9 (the Semler hypothesis) and those who defend the integrity of 2 Corinthians.

But, it may be fairly asked, why was this "severe letter" not preserved when the equally severe chs. 10–13 of 2 Corinthians were preserved and 1 Corinthians 5 contains a call for the exercise of church discipline against an erring member such as the "severe letter" must have contained?

12. One may compare, for example, the comments of Kennedy 63-66; "Epistles" 295, or Moffatt, *Introduction* 119 with those of White 122 or Zahn 330-31.

Not all of Paul's letters to churches have survived; 1 Cor. 5:9, 11 and Col. 4:16 establish this point.[13] Indeed, we may safely assume that the majority of his letters to churches or individuals have not been preserved (cf. 2 Thess. 3:17; 2 Pet. 3:15-16). Apart from some unknown mishap that may conceivably account for the non-preservation of this letter, we may propose several other reasons. Unlike 1 Corinthians 5, which is merely part of a much longer letter, and unlike 2 Corinthians 10–13, which forms a continuation of chs. 1–9 (assuming the unity of our epistle), the "severe letter" may have been a very brief and intensely personal missive, simply calling for the discipline of the "guilty party." Now it is true that the letter to Philemon also is both very brief and intensely personal and yet has survived. But the difference is that the "severe letter" may have lacked any content of universal interest or applicability but rather focused on a specific, unedifying chapter in the history of the Corinthian church that reflected poorly on that church and was an embarrassment to its spiritual father. There may have been, on the one hand, every reason to suppress or destroy the letter or simply to let it disappear, and, on the other, no reason to preserve it.

3. The Integrity of 2 Corinthians

We have seen that the Pauline authorship of 2 Corinthians is a virtually universal assumption among NT scholars (see 1.a above). But when we turn to investigate the integrity, as opposed to the authenticity, of this letter, we are confronted with a complex array of data in the text, and, perhaps not surprisingly, with a bewildering variety of partition hypotheses.

A brief descriptive survey of the most influential or noteworthy theories which propose that our canonical 2 Corinthians is composed of more than two separate letters or of several dislocated parts will indicate the main areas of dispute.

a. Complex Partition or Dislocation Theories

Almost all twentieth-century hypotheses regarding the original letters or fragments that now form 2 Corinthians are based on nineteenth-century antecedents. Here we shall deal only with the main theories put forward in the twentieth century.[14]

In his commentary published in 1904 A. Halmel identified *three* letters:

---

13. On the apocryphal "Letter to the Laodiceans," see Schneemelcher in Hennecke and Schneemelcher 2.128-32.

14. For a convenient summary of nineteenth-century hypotheses, see Moffatt, *Introduction* 108-11, 116-30.

8

Letter A: 1:1-2; 1:8–2:13; 7:5–8:24; 13:13
Letter B: 10:1–13:10
Letter C: 1:3-7; 2:14–7:4; 9:1-15; 13:11-12

The third of these, said Halmel, incorporated several interpolations (3:12-18; 4:3-4, 6; 6:14–7:1).

Both in his major commentary on 1 Corinthians (1910) and in his two-volume *Urchristentum* (1914-1917; ETr *Earliest Christianity*), J. Weiss allocated the material in 2 Corinthians to *four* different letters:

Letter A (referred to in 1 Cor. 5:9), which included 6:14–7:1
A letter of commendation (8:1-24) sent with Titus and the two brothers,
    written between letters B^1 and B^2
Letter C: 2:14–6:13; 7:2-4; 10:1–13:13
Letter D: 1:1–2:13; 7:5-16; 9:1-15

Material in 1 Corinthians is found in letters A, B^1, and B^2 (see Weiss, *Christianity* 1.323-57, especially 356-57). Weiss's influence may be traced in the similar reconstructions of J. T. Dean (11-14, 40-94), R. Bultmann (17-18, 52, 179-80, 256; *Probleme* 14 n. 16 = *Exegetica* 307 n. 17), E. Dinkler ("Korintherbriefe" 18, 22-23), and P. Vielhauer (*Geschichte* 150-55), especially in their linking of 2:14–7:4 (omitting 6:14–7:1) with the final four chapters as constituting the whole or the larger part of the "interim/tearful letter."

Undoubtedly the most influential partition hypothesis proposed in the twentieth century was that of G. Bornkamm (*Aufsätze* 162-94; "History"; *Paul* 74-77, 244-46; *Guide* 100-103). He isolates *five* letters in 2 Corinthians, in addition to two (A and B) in 1 Corinthians.

Letter C (letter of defense): 2:14–6:13; 7:2-4
Letter D (letter of tears): 10:1–13:10
Letter E (letter of reconciliation): 1:1–2:13; 7:5-16
Letter F: 8:1-24, a letter of commendation for Titus and the two brothers,
    whose relationship to the rest of Paul's correspondence with Cor-
    inth cannot be finally determined, although it could be an appendix
    to the letter of reconciliation.
Letter G: 9:1-15, a letter concerning arrangements for the collection.

A redactor added 6:14–7:1, a non-Pauline fragment, to letter C, and the exhortation, greeting, and benediction of 13:11-13 to letter E. Bornkamm's reconstruction has been followed, sometimes with minor alterations (such as the inclusion of ch. 8 [thus Lohse] or chs. 8 and 9 [thus Fuller and Becker] in the letter of reconciliation), by D. Georgi (75-79; *Opponents* 9-18; "2 Corinthians" 184), R. H. Fuller (48-49), H. D. Wendland (7-11), W. Marxsen (77-82), E. Lohse (72-73), N. Perrin (104-5), H. Koester (1.53-54; 2.126-30), F. T.

Fallon (6-7), H. D. Betz (142-43; "Corinthians" 1149-50; "Problem" 40-46), M. Carrez (16-18), J. A. Crafton (49-53), J. Becker (216-21), and M. M. Mitchell (75-76). Bornkamm's proposal has proved persuasive to many partly because he paid special attention to the reconstruction of Paul's dealings with the Corinthians and endeavored to trace the stages by which the original five letters were combined to form the canonical 2 Corinthians.

Finally, there is the view of W. Schmithals (1984),[15] who finds portions of 2 Corinthians in seven (*) of thirteen pieces written by Paul to the Corinthian church (*Briefe* 19-85):

  A: 1 Cor. 11:2, 17-34
  B: 1 Cor. 9:24–10:22; 6:12-20
*C: 1 Cor. 6:1-11; 2 Cor. 6:14–7:1
  D: 1 Cor. 15:1-58; 16:13-24
  E (letter of response): 1 Cor. 11:3-16; 7:1–8:13; 9:19-22; 10:23–11:1; 12:1-31a; 14:1b-40; 12:31b–13:13; 16:1-12
  F: 1 Cor. 1:1–3:23; 4:14-21
  G: 1 Cor. 5:1-13
*H: 1 Cor. 4:1-5; 9:1b-18; 2 Cor. 6:3-13; 7:2-4a
*J: 2 Cor. 4:2-14
*K: 1 Cor. 4:7-13; 2 Cor. 2:14–3:18; 4:16–6:2; Rom. 13:12b-14
*L: (letter of tears): 2 Cor. 10:1–13:13
*M: (collection letter): 2 Cor. 8:1-24a
*N: (joyful letter): 2 Cor. 1:1–2:13; 7:5-7, 4b, 8-16; 9:1-15; Rom. 5:1b-10.

Whether or not these complex partition theories are valid will become apparent in the following discussion of the four passages that have become the focus of dispute: 2:14–7:4; 6:14–7:1; 8:1–9:15; 10:1–13:13. Only two comments are needed at this point. First, it is no argument against these partition hypotheses that their proponents do not agree in detail; at most we might say their disagreement shows that the arguments for dissection on which they rely fall short of demonstration. The best hypothesis is not necessarily the simplest — in this case one which posits the fewest partitions or else the integrity of the book — but rather that hypothesis which best accommodates all the evidence. Second, with this said, it remains true, in the absence of any MS tradition witnessing to textual dislocation, that the more intricate a partition theory, the more pressing and demanding the task of re-creating the possible circumstances in which 2 Corinthians as we know it was constructed from disparate letters or epistolary fragments.[16]

15. In an earlier reconstruction (1955; Schmithals 90-113, especially 100 n. 30), repeated without change in 1960 ("Abfassung") and 1965 (*Gnostics* 245-53), Schmithals posited only six different letters to Corinth, with sections of 2 Corinthians appearing in five of these. But in a more recent analysis (1973) he isolated parts of 2 Corinthians in six of nine letters written to Corinth ("Korintherbriefe," especially 288 n. 70).

16. See the salutary cautionary remarks about complex partition theories and ancient scribal

b. 2 Corinthians 2:14–7:4

In three of the four reconstructions outlined above, those of Halmel, Weiss, and Bornkamm, 2:14–7:4 (omitting 6:14–7:1) is identified as an independent unit forming part or the whole of a separate letter of Paul to Corinth. Three reasons are commonly given.

(1) The internal literary unity of 2:14–7:4 seems beyond doubt. Kleinknecht (250-54) points to major themes that recur throughout these chapters (such as ministry, capability, commendation, revelation, and the death-life antithesis), while McDonald (43-48) finds in 2:14-17 a thematic statement for a sermonic discourse running from 2:14 to 7:1[17] that is marked by an abundance of homiletic features such as rhetorical questions simulating debate with the audience, a polemical tone, and an inconsistent use of images; use of Christian *pesher* (in ch. 3), "the handmaid of the preaching ministry" (45); and a formal structure that accords with the criteria for a discourse as set out by the rhetorical tradition of the ancient world and that reflects the scriptural homily of the synagogue. The overall thematic unity of 2:14–7:4 is recognized on all sides: "the apostolic office" (Bultmann 61; Schelkle, xviii, 39 [regarding 2:14–6:10]), "the apostolic ministry" (Bruce 175, 187 [regarding 2:14–7:1]; similarly Martin, xxxvii, 43 [regarding 2:14–7:16]), "an apology for his apostolic office" (Kümmel, *Introduction* 291), "a rationale of his [Paul's] apostolic mission" (McDonald 43 [regarding 2:14–7:1]).

It is one thing to infer from the structural and thematic coherence of 2:14–7:4 that this section of 2 Corinthians forms a complete argument or a self-contained literary unity; it is quite another to claim this datum as evidence or confirmation that we are here dealing with an independent letter, the "letter of defense" written before the "letter of tears" (Bornkamm and others), or an independent fragment of a letter, part of the "intermediate/tearful letter" (Weiss and others; see above, A.3[a]).[18] Such coherence comports as well with a theory of digression as with a hypothesis of independence. That is, 2:14–7:4 could as easily be an extended digression that forms a thematic unit as an independent letter with a unified theme, particularly since the sections on either side of

---

practice in Stewart-Sykes 53-64. For a summary and penetrating critique of partition theories before 1900, see Heinrici 5-32.

17. That 2:14-17 enunciates the theme of 2:14–7:4 and summarizes Paul's argument in this section is argued in exegetical detail by Collange (21-41, 318-19).

18. Collange goes one step further and proposes (301, 317, 319, 325), on the basis of an examination of the transitions of thought in 6:1–7:4, that 2:14–7:4 existed in two editions, addressed to two different groups: (1) 2:14–6:13, addressed to the Corinthians (6:11) as children (6:13), ended with a summary of the marks of a true apostle (6:3-10) and a warm appeal to Paul's readers to respond affectionately to his openness (6:11-13)(and perhaps ch. 8); (2) 2:14–6:2 + 6:14–7:4, addressed to a group (possibly the Achaeans of 1:1) more directly linked with the "false apostles," concluded with a polemical fragment from a Jewish-Christian document (6:14–7:1) and a somewhat less affectionate appeal (7:2-4) (and, just possibly, ch. 9).

2:14–7:4, namely 1:1–2:13 and 7:5-16, may be said to discuss Paul's exercise of "the apostolic office."

(2) There are abrupt transitions of thought after 2:13 and 7:4, and a smooth transition from 2:13 to 7:5 is formed if 2:14–7:4 is left out. It is a common feature of all the reconstructions listed above that 7:5 follows directly on 2:13 within a single letter.

After mentioning his arrival in Troas to preach the gospel, his restlessness of spirit because Titus failed to arrive, and his departure for Macedonia in spite of remarkable preaching opportunities in Troas (2:13), Paul bursts into praise to God for God's incessant triumph in making himself known far and wide (2:14).

Plausible explanations may be given, however, to account for this dramatic apostrophe. First, after writing (or, rather, dictating) 2:13, Paul vividly recollects the immense relief from anxiety about the Corinthians and Titus that he experienced when Titus finally arrived in Macedonia with the welcome news of the positive Corinthian reaction to the "letter of tears" (7:5-16).[19] He traces this relief to the gracious intervention of God at a time of unalleviated distress (see the commentary at 2:12-13). Or, second, 2:14 contrasts (note the adversative δέ) the weakness of man, evidenced in Paul's failure to grasp divinely provided evangelistic opportunities in one place (2:12-13), with the power of God demonstrated in the spread of the gospel "in every place." Paul found occasion for praise in the changeless truth that divine strength finds its full scope and comes to its full strength in human weakness (cf. 12:9). Manson paraphrases 2:14 thus: "But we must be thankful to God, who does not leave us a prey to our cares and anxieties but carries us along in the victorious progress of the Messianic triumph, which is sweeping through the world" ("Suggestions" 161).

No less pronounced is the change of tone from 7:4 to 7:5. Having just declared that he cannot contain himself for happiness (7:4c), Paul proceeds to recount his physical restlessness in Macedonia, with "conflicts without, anxieties within" (TCNT).

But we should not overlook the fact that, as well as speaking of frankness, boasting, comfort, and joy, 7:4 ends with the phrase "in the midst of all these trials of mine" (Knox) (ἐπὶ πάσῃ τῇ θλίψει ἡμῶν). Indeed, the themes of 7:4, especially comfort and joy in the midst of affliction (7:4b), are continued in 7:5-16, which, significantly, is introduced by the explanatory καὶ γάρ, "for in fact" (cf. 3:10) (but see per contra Welborn, "Theories" 559-83, especially 578-83).

19. If it be objected that only in 7:5-16 is there any indication of Paul's having received relief in Macedonia, we may observe that 2:5-11 witnesses to that relief, that Paul's readers already knew of the reassurance about Corinth that Paul must have gained when he met Titus (Barrett 97), and that the excited, passionate outburst of 2:14 itself implies that relief was obtained (cf. Menzies 17). But see Thrall, "Thanksgiving" 103, who argues (118-19) that 2:14-17 looks forward, not back, the only general link with 2:12 being the theme of evangelization. For the view that the cause of Paul's praise in 2:14-16a is his apostolic affliction, God's "leading him (as a prisoner) to death" (θριαμβεύειν, 2:14), see Hafemann, Spirit 10-86; Defense 7-83.

7:4	7:5-16
καύχησις	κεκαύχημαι . . . καύχησις (v. 14)
παρακλήσει	ὁ παρακαλῶν . . . παρεκάλεσεν (v. 6)
	παρακλήσει . . . παρεκλήθη (v. 7)
	παρακεκλήμεθα . . . παρακλήσει (v. 13)
χαρᾷ	χαρῆναι (v. 7)
	χαίρω (v. 9)
	ἐχάρημεν . . . χαρᾷ (v. 13)
	χαίρω (v. 16)
θλίψει	θλιβόμενοι (v. 5)

Citing some of these verbal correspondences, Lietzmann (131) aptly comments that "here exceptional difficulties confront the 'interpolation hypotheses' that want to attach 7:5 to 2:13." On the other hand, Bultmann appeals to such correspondences as evidence of the skill of the redactor, who also added the γάρ (52, 179). But such arbitrary explanations of data place the defenders of the integrity of any document in an impossible situation: *prima facie* evidence of textual coherence could always be claimed as pointing to the skillful artistry of a redactor, and the defense then reaches a stalemate, for the activity of the redactor can, in the nature of the case, be neither finally proved nor disproved. And if the putative "seams" of the redactional process are clumsy or obvious, this points (it is claimed) to a redactor who lacks literary sensitivity, while unobtrusive or smooth "seams" reflect the work of a sophisticated redactor.

With regard to the alleged smoothness of the text if 7:5 in fact originally followed directly on 2:13, we may observe that for all the obvious similarities between the two verses, there are important differences, namely the change from πνεῦμα to σάρξ and from singular to plural.

2:13a	οὐκ	ἔσχηκα	ἄνεσιν	τῷ πνεύματί	μου
7:5b	οὐδεμίαν	ἔσχηκεν	ἄνεσιν	ἡ σὰρξ	ἡμῶν

2:13b	ἀλλὰ . . .	ἐξῆλθον	εἰς Μακεδονίαν
7:5a	καὶ γὰρ	ἐλθόντων ἡμῶν	εἰς Μακεδονίαν

The issue here is this: Are the differences as well as the similarities best accounted for by the theory of editorial activity or by a hypothesis of authorial digression? J. M. Robinson observes that redactors usually add a resumptive comment that repeats an earlier statement (as at 7:5 after 2:13) to mark the end of an insertion (J. M. Robinson, "Trajectory" 244-45). Such a "resumptive repetition" may explain the similarities between the two verses, but should we attribute the crucial differences to a sophisticated redactor who wished to cover his traces by creating the impression that the author was actually aware of the "insertion" of 2:14–7:4? It seems far less difficult to assume that Paul himself is aware of having indulged in a massive digression, and so resumes his travel

narrative without concern for verbal identity, in fact adding two new points —
his ἄνεσις ("restlessness") was felt in Macedonia as well as in Troas (2:12-13);
so far from finding Titus immediately on arrival in Macedonia (as 2:12-13
might lead us to expect), Paul experienced "conflicts" and "anxieties" there. If
the digression forms "an apology for his apostolic office," what precedes (1:1–
2:13) and follows (7:5-16) deals with the exercise of that office, so that at 7:5 he
merely takes up again his overall theme in 1–7, that is, the defense of his apostolic ministry.

Most scholars who hold to the integrity of 2 Corinthians 1–7 describe
2:14 (or 3:1)–7:4 as a "digression,"[20] not in the sense that at 2:14 Paul departs
from his central theme, but in the sense that here he leaves the immediate topic
of his personal travel narrative (Troas to Macedonia, 2:12-13), only to resume it
at 7:5.

(3) Thanksgiving is found at the beginning of almost all Paul's letters,
and 2:14 makes a suitable beginning for a letter (Collange 23, 40, 319). This
corroborative argument is not without difficulty. The other five Pauline uses of
τῷ (δὲ) θεῷ χάρις or χάρις (δὲ) τῷ θεῷ stand at the end (Rom. 7:25; 1 Cor.
15:57; 2 Cor. 9:15) or in the center (Rom. 6:17) of Paul's argument, and only
once (2 Cor. 8:16) at the beginning of a new section, but never at the beginning
of a letter. Moreover, as Collange himself admits (23), it is always the cognate
verb εὐχαριστέω rather than the substantive χάρις that Paul uses to introduce his
thanksgiving to God at the outset of his letters.

We propose that at 2:14 τῷ δὲ θεῷ χάρις is an apostrophe signaling a digression. The mention of Titus and Macedonia in 2:13 reminded Paul of their
ultimate reunion there (7:6-7) and prompted a brief doxology (2:14; cf. 8:16),
for he perceived a divine vindication of his apostleship in the positive Corinthian reaction to the "severe letter" as reported by Titus in Macedonia. Thus begins "the great digression" (2:14–7:4) which, as Paul's apology for the apostolic ministry, is the heart of chs. 1–7.

c. 2 Corinthians 6:14–7:1

By one of those strange coincidences of literary criticism, two Scottish biblical
scholars of a past generation who represented very different critical perspectives concurred in their (presumably independent) use of a simile to describe
the apparently incongruous position of 6:14–7:1 in the flow of Paul's argument
in 2 Corinthians. Writing in 1894, James Denney declared that in its present position this passage "jolts the mind as a stone on the road does a carriage wheel"
(775), yet he vigorously defended the integrity of the passage (775-78). Some
seventeen years later, in his famous *Introduction,* James Moffatt expressed the

20. E.g., Bengel 3.361; Plummer (CGT) 51; (ICC) 67; Lietzmann 131; Tasker 29; Hughes
77; Schelkle 39; Bruce 171; Hyldahl, "Einheit" 289, 293.

opinion that "in its present situation it looks like an erratic boulder" (125) and argued that it was probably a fragment of Paul's "previous letter" (1 Cor. 5:9) (109, 125; similarly "Corinthians" 428-29). Although discussion of the issues surrounding the authenticity of this passage has continued since then, interest was quickened with the publication of the DSS so that the last forty years has seen a spate of articles on the topic. It is of interest to note that whereas the most influential studies of the 1960s[21] (J. A. Fitzmyer, 1961 [in *CBQ*]; J. Gnilka, 1963 [ETr 1968]; N. A. Dahl in a paper delivered in 1969 and published in 1977) viewed the paragraph as a non-Pauline interpolation reflecting "Christianized" Essene theology, the most recent specialist studies of the passage, with few exceptions,[22] have defended not only its Pauline authorship but also its integrity in the context (Fee, "Food"; Thrall, "Problem"; Derrett; Lambrecht, "Fragment"; Murphy-O'Connor, "Context" and "Philo"; Beale; Sass, "Waffen"; Zeilinger; deSilva, "Integrity"; Webb; Goulder; Scott, "Scripture"; Bieringer, "Kontext").[23]

In our treatment of the issues we shall examine first the allegedly non-Pauline features of the paragraph, then its supposed Pauline characteristics, in the first case also stating the explanations that have been proposed to account for the data.

(1) "Non-Pauline" Features

The passage is self-contained and lacks any specific connection with Corinthian problems. Although the independent character of the paragraph is beyond dispute — it reads as a timeless ethical homily, calling for holiness of life — this in itself does not prove either that it is misplaced or that it is non-Pauline, for it is quite conceivable that Paul himself could be quoting such a homily, whether of his own composition or not, or even indulging in a sustained rhetorical flourish. True, there are no concrete details that link the passage with specific Corinthian problems, but what is not specific is not therefore irrelevant. Indeed, the more general Paul's plea for Christian distinctiveness, the wider its

---

21. For an overview of the history of interpretation from the Reformation to the present, see Webb 16-30; also Bieringer, "Kontext" 551-60 and the comprehensive chart on p. 559.

22. E.g., Betz ("Fragment" [1973]; cf. his *Galatians* 329-30), who believes that the redactor of the Pauline corpus, "for reasons unknown to us" (108), incorporated in the Pauline letters this fragment whose anti-Pauline stance reflects the theology of Paul's Galatian opponents; Rensberger (1978), who concludes that the passage is "an exhortation composed by a Christian of sectarian or 'Essene' background, 'Paulinized' and used by the Apostle to urge his readers to avoid his opponents" (= the ἄπιστοι of 6:14) (41). Walker ("Structure" [2002]) does not address the question of authorship but proposes that the passage is "a later insertion" on the basis of the presence of chiasmus if 7:2-3 originally followed 6:11-13 (143-44).

23. Although Dahl holds firmly to the non-Pauline origin of the paragraph and tends to favor the theory of interpolation, his concluding sentence seems to anticipate in part the present trend: "The possibility that the apostle himself incorporated the fragment may after all have to be reconsidered" ("Fragment" 69).

relevance to a range of Corinthian practices that amounted to compromise with heathendom.

The passage interrupts the flow of thought from 6:13 to 7:2. If 6:14–7:1 is omitted, 7:2 follows naturally after 6:13. It is incontestable that the transitions from 6:13 to 6:14 and from 7:1 to 7:2 are abrupt. In one case, after his passionate appeal to the Corinthians to open their hearts wide to him as a matter of fair exchange for his generous fatherly affection (6:13), Paul suddenly issues the blunt command, "Keep out of all incongruous ties with unbelievers" (6:14a, Moffatt). In the other case, directly after his call for self-purification and total consecration to God (7:1), he repeats his plea to the Corinthians for their openheartedness in their dealings with him (7:2a).

These are the close verbal and conceptual similarities between 6:11-13 and 7:2-4:

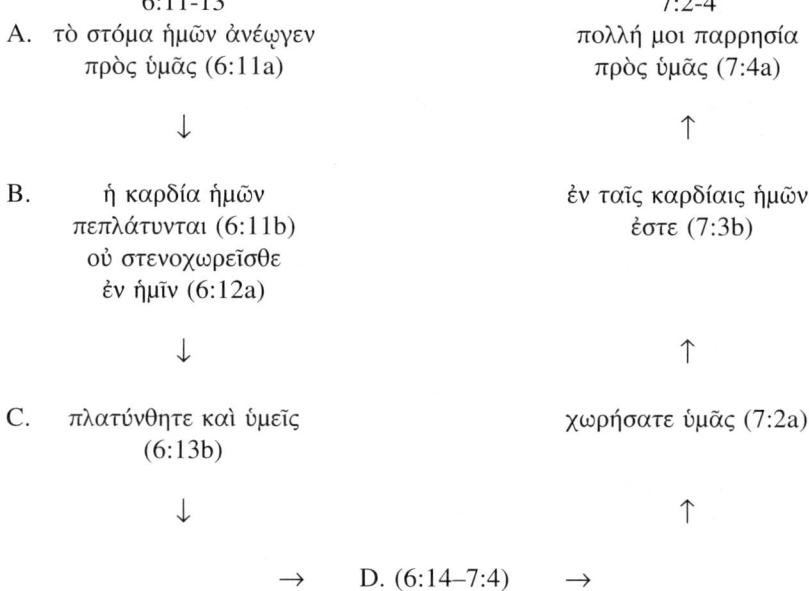

	6:11-13	7:2-4
A.	τὸ στόμα ἡμῶν ἀνέῳγεν πρὸς ὑμᾶς (6:11a)	πολλή μοι παρρησία πρὸς ὑμᾶς (7:4a)
	↓	↑
B.	ἡ καρδία ἡμῶν πεπλάτυνται (6:11b) οὐ στενοχωρεῖσθε ἐν ἡμῖν (6:12a)	ἐν ταῖς καρδίαις ἡμῶν ἐστε (7:3b)
	↓	↑
C.	πλατύνθητε καὶ ὑμεῖς (6:13b)	χωρήσατε ὑμᾶς (7:2a)
	↓	↑

→   D. (6:14–7:4)   →

Two overlapping literary techniques are in evidence here: *inclusio,* or cyclic (or ring) composition, A¹ (6:11-13), B (6:14–7:1), A² (7:2-4), where A² repeats the themes of A¹,[24] and *chiasmus,* the arrows in the chart pointing to the presence

24. This has been observed by Lambrecht (147) and Talbert (xv). Citing examples of *inclusio* in 1 Cor. 12:31 and 14:1; 2 Cor. 11:1 and 16; and Josephus, *Antiquities* 18.5.2 §§116, 119, as well as in 2 Cor. 6:11-13 and 7:2, Talbert observes that whereas in a literary culture the beginning and ending of a thought unit "are designated by paragraphs, chapters, subheadings, or even enumeration, in an oral culture the signals had to be heard. It was customary to repeat key words, phrases, and ideas at the start and finish of a thought unit to indicate its boundaries. . . . Sometimes the beginning and end of an excursus were so similar that modern scholars have contended that, if

of this ABCDCBA pattern. Is it easier to attribute these rhetorical devices to the conscious artistry of an editor or to assume that in 7:2-4, conscious of having indulged in a brief digression or excursus or exhortation, Paul has resumed and expanded on his emotional appeal for frankness of speech (6:11a) and openness of heart (6:11b-13), simply treating these matters in inverse order? In any case, we would expect the editorial work of a redactor to be less extensive and to involve merely the insertion of χωρήσατε ὑμᾶς in 7:2a to resume the πλατύνθητε καὶ ὑμεῖς in 6:13b. But does not προείρηκα . . . ἐστε (7:3) look back specifically to 6:11b?

The passage contains an accumulation of hapax legomena: *four words occur nowhere else in the Greek Bible (ἑτεροζυγέω, συμφώνησις, συγκατάθεσις, Βελιάρ), while another two*[25] *are NT* hapaxes *(μετοχή, μολυσμός).* At first sight these data may seem to weigh heavily against the authenticity of the paragraph, but several considerations considerably lessen their weight. First, as Fee points out, five of these *hapaxes* occur in "a burst of rhetoric" (6:14-16a), and it is characteristic of Pauline rhetoric to have a "sudden influx of *hapax legomena.*"[26] Second, Pauline rhetoric apart, the more incidence of *hapax legomena* in a passage, even in relatively great numbers, does not in itself prove non-Pauline authorship. Smith lists 160 Pauline *hapaxes* in 2 Corinthians (excluding OT quotations), of which 84 are also NT *hapaxes* (685-87). In the 257 verses of 2 Corinthians there is, on average, one Pauline *hapax* per 1.6 verses, and one NT *hapax* every three verses. That is, the incidence of six Pauline *hapaxes* in six verses (6:14–7:1) is not particularly remarkable, especially when one considers that three of them (συμφώνησις, συγκατάθεσις, and μετοχή) are merely variant ways of expressing substantively the idea of association that is implicit in ἑτεροζυγοῦντες (cf. Allo 190). Third, cognates of four of these six Pauline *hapaxes* occur elsewhere in the Pauline letters: μετέχω (five uses, e.g., 1 Cor. 10:21), μολύνω (1 Cor. 8:7), σύζυγος (Phil. 4:3), and σύμφωνος (1 Cor. 7:5).[27] As for the other two *hapaxes*, συγκατάθεσις (6:16) is a stylistic variant of κοινωνία (6:14), used for rhetorical purposes, while Βελιάρ was a common name for the prince of evil in Jewish and Jewish-Christian eschatology at the beginning of the Christian era.

Certain Pauline terms (δικαιοσύνη, 6:14; πιστός, 6:15; σάρξ and πνεῦμα, 7:1) are used in non-Pauline senses, and two phrases in 7:1 (καθαρίσωμεν ἑαυτοὺς ἀπὸ παντὸς μολυσμοῦ σαρκὸς καὶ πνεύματος and ἐπιτελοῦντες ἁγιωσύνην)

---

the excursus were taken out, the two edges would join naturally; hence the excursus is an interpolation. This is an improper inference" (xv).

25. This excludes ἐμπεριπατέω (6:16) and εἰσδέχομαι (6:17), which occur in quotations from the LXX; and παντοκράτωρ (6:18), a Pauline *hapax legomenon* (found nine times in Revelation), which is also in an OT citation.

26. "Food" 144. Fee cites two comparable examples from the Corinthian letters — 1 Cor. 4:7-13 (six NT *hapaxes* and two Pauline *hapaxes*) and 2 Cor. 6:3-10 (four NT *hapaxes* and one Pauline *hapax*).

27. For further details, see Fee, "Food" 145.

are unique in Paul. In general, we may urge that no literary critic should disallow a writer occasional uses of words or expressions that do not conform to his or her normal usage; otherwise linguistic or conceptual *hapax legomena* would be excluded *a priori* from every writer. But to deal with these specific cases, δικαιοσύνη bears a "moral" sense, "the practice of piety," "uprightness of (human) behavior," in Rom. 6:13; 14:17; 2 Cor. 6:7; 9:9; 11:15, as well as here in 6:14, although more often it has a forensic sense in Paul. πιστός elsewhere in Paul usually is an adjective meaning "faithful," "reliable," but the present substantival use ("believer") is found in the Pastorals (e.g., 1 Tim. 4:10, 12; 5:16; 6:2b) and οἱ ἄπιστοι is Paul's regular term for "unbelievers" (e.g., 1 Cor. 6:6; 10:27; 2 Cor. 4:4).[28] It is true that when Paul uses σάρξ and πνεῦμα together, they are generally opposed, not merely conjoined (as here). But all Paul's anthropological terms are fluid in use (see Jewett, *passim*) so that although the theological antithesis "flesh-spirit" is common in Paul (e.g., Rom. 8:4-5, 7-9, 12-13; Gal. 5:16-24), a popular use of these two terms is sometimes found in which either term may denote the whole person, the self (cf. 2 Cor. 2:13 [πνεῦμα] and 7:5 [σάρξ]), or, as here in 7:1, σάρξ denotes the outward, and πνεῦμα the inward, aspects of the whole person.[29] Paul is calling for the total purity of the person, both inwardly and outwardly. Although the parallel in 1 Thess. 5:23 shows that sanctification is the work of God,[30] passages such as 1 Cor. 6:18; 7:34; 10:8, 14 emphasize the human responsibility in this cooperative process, so that the unabashed synergism reflected in "Let us purify ourselves from everything that defiles body or spirit and complete our consecration" should not be declared an un-Pauline sentiment, particularly since ἁγιωσύνη is an exclusively Pauline word in the NT (Rom. 1:4; 2 Cor. 7:1; 1 Thess. 3:13).

Paul's citation formulas in 6:16, 17, 18 are unique, and the OT passages cited in 6:16-18 are not referred to elsewhere in his letters. Καθὼς γέγραπται is Paul's favorite introductory formula when quoting the OT, but many variations of this precise formula occur.[31] When the verb λέγειν is used, the subject is sometimes ἡ γραφή (Rom. 4:3; 9:17; 10:11; 11:2; Gal. 4:30; 1 Tim. 5:18), sometimes the particular human author (Rom. 4:7; 9:29; 10:5, 16, 19-20; 11:9; 15:12; 1 Cor. 9:9; cf. Rom. 9:27), sometimes ὁ νόμος (Rom. 7:7; cf. 1 Cor. 14:21; Gal. 5:14), but often the subject is unexpressed, the implication being that (ὁ) κύριος or (ὁ) θεός (Rom. 9:15, 25; 10:21; 1 Cor. 6:16; 2 Cor. 6:2; Gal.

28. The use of the expressions οἱ ἐκ πίστεως ("people of faith," "believers") and τῷ πιστῷ Ἀβραάμ ("believing Abraham") in Gal. 3:9 shows how easily πιστός passed from being adjectival ("believing") to being substantival ("believer" = ὁ ἐκ πίστεως).

29. Cf. Hughes 259; Barrett 202. Burton classifies σάρξ in 2 Cor. 7:1 as denoting "the whole material part of a living being" (*Spirit* 184; *Galatians* 492), and πνεῦμα as denoting "the seat of emotion and will" (*Spirit* 179; *Galatians* 490).

30. Ἁγιάσαι in 1 Thess. 5:23 is a constative aorist (optative), depicting the whole process of divine sanctification comprehensively as a single entity.

31. Viz. καθάπερ γέγραπται (Rom. 3:4; 9:13; 10:15; 11:8), οὕτως . . . γέγραπται (1 Cor. 15:45), ὥσπερ γέγραπται (1 Cor. 10:7), with ὅτι preceding (Gal. 3:13) or following (Rom. 3:10) γέγραπται, γέγραπται γάρ (Rom. 12:19; 14:11; 1 Cor. 1:19; 3:19; Gal. 3:10; 4:27).

18

3:16) is the subject. λέγει κύριος is found with quotations in Rom. 12:19; 14:11; 1 Cor. 14:21 as well as in 2 Cor. 6:17b, 18c. καθὼς εἶπεν ὁ θεὸς ὅτι (6:16) is distinctive, but simply combines features of other Pauline introductory formulas and is therefore no more remarkable than ἐν γὰρ τῷ Μωϋσέως νόμῳ γέγραπται (1 Cor. 9:9) or ὁ λόγος ὁ γεγραμμένος (1 Cor. 15:54) or καθάπερ καὶ Δαυὶδ λέγει (Rom. 4:7).

Three principal OT passages are cited in 6:16-18, and each is associated with (rather than introduced by) an introductory formula:

6:16	καθὼς εἶπεν ὁ θεὸς ὅτι	Lev. 26:11-12 (and Ezek. 37:27)
6:17	λέγει κύριος	Isa. 52:11 (and Ezek. 20:34)
6:18	λέγει κύριος παντοκράτωρ	2 Sam. 7:14 (and Isa. 43:6; 2 Sam. 7:8)

That Paul cites or alludes to these OT passages nowhere else is inconclusive evidence regarding Pauline authorship, because the same thing occurs in other comparable chains of scriptural texts in the Pauline corpus (e.g., Rom. 3:10-18; 9:25-29; 10:18-21; 15:9-12).

There are striking affinities between 6:14–7:1 and Qumran terminology and theology. Benoit characterized this passage as "a kind of meteorite fallen from the sky of Qumran into a Pauline letter" (279). In an influential article published in 1961 J. A. Fitzmyer identified five elements in the passage "which suggest Qumran contacts or the reworking of Qumran ideas" ("Qumran" 208):

The triple dualism of uprightness and iniquity (6:14a),[32] light and darkness (6:14b),[33] Christ and Beliar (6:15a);[34]

opposition to idols (6:16);[35]

the concept of the temple of God (6:16);[36]

separation from all impurity (6:17; 7:1);[37] and

the concatenation of OT texts (6:16-18).[38]

32. Cf. 1QH 14:15-16; 16:10-11; 1QS 5:1-4; CD 20:20-21. These and the following references are cited by Fitzmyer, "Qumran" 208-16 and Gnilka 61-66. See also Braun 201-4; Klinzing 172-82.

33. Cf. 1QS 1:9-11; 3:3, 13, 19-20, 24-25; 1QM 1:1, 3, 9, 11, 13; 13:5-6, 9, 15-16; 1QH 12:6; 4QFlor 1:9 (Fitzmyer, "Qumran" 209, who observes that the "light-darkness" figure is employed neither in the OT nor in rabbinic literature to express the two classes of mankind).

34. The "God/Lord–Belial/Beliar" antithesis is found not only at Qumran (e.g., 1QM 13:1-4, 11-12), but also in several Jewish intertestamental texts such as *Jubilees* (1:20) and the *Testaments of the Twelve Patriarchs* (*Simeon* 5:3; *Levi* 19:1; *Issachar* 6:1; *Naphtali* 2:6; *Joseph* 20:2). See Fitzmyer, "Qumran" 212; Gnilka 54-55, 66.

35. Cf. 1QS 2:11, 16-17; 4:5; 1QH 4:19.

36. Cf. 1QS 5:6; 8:4-6, 8-9; 9:5-7; 11:8; 4QFlor 1:6.

37. Cf. 1QS 4:5, 10; 5:13-20; 9:8-9; 1QM 13:5; CD 6:17; 7:3; 9:21; 10:10-12; 11:19-21; 12:19. Gnilka expresses this concept more generally: "separation from a godless environment" (61).

38. Cf. 4QTest, on which see Fitzmyer 59-89.

These affinities are both clear and striking.[39] But the essential question is this: Are they common only to this paragraph and Qumran, or are they motifs that are found in other NT writers and elsewhere in the Pauline corpus? The latter alternative can be shown to be true:

dualism of
- righteousness and iniquity (e.g., Rom. 6:13, 16, 19; Matt. 13:49; 1 Pet. 2:24; 3:18)
- light and darkness (e.g., Rom. 13:12; 1 Thess. 5:4-5; John 3:19-20; 12:35-36; 1 Pet. 2:9)
- Christ and Satan (e.g., 1 Cor. 5:4-5; Matt. 16:23; Rev. 12:9-10)

opposition to idolatry (e.g., 1 Cor. 10:7, 14-22; Gal. 5:19-20; 1 Pet. 4:3; 1 John 5:21)

the community as God's temple (e.g., 1 Cor. 3:16-17; Eph. 2:21-22; cf. 1 Pet. 2:5; Rev. 3:12; 7:15; 21:3)

separation from evil and from godlessness (e.g., 1 Cor. 6:1-6, 15-18; 10:8; Heb. 3:12; 3 John 11)

a catena of OT texts (e.g., Rom. 3:10-18; 15:9-12; 1 Pet. 2:6-8)

The affinities that have been adduced are, therefore, not restricted to Qumran and the paragraph under consideration, but are motifs in evidence throughout the NT, particularly in Paul.[40]

The paragraph betrays an uncompromising exclusivism that is levitical or pharisaic in nature and incompatible with Paul, the champion of Christian liberty. The five imperatives found in 6:14–7:1 certainly call for separation — both from contaminating evil (ἀκαθάρτου μὴ ἅπτεσθε, 6:17b; καθαρίσωμεν ἑαυτοὺς ἀπὸ παντὸς μολυσμοῦ κτλ., 7:1) and from unbelievers (μὴ γίνεσθε ἑτεροζυγοῦντες ἀπίστοις, 6:14a; ἐξέλθατε ἐκ μέσου αὐτῶν καὶ ἀφορίσθητε, 6:17a). Of these five injunctions, the first two are absolute ("Renounce all association with evil wherever it is found and in whatever form"), but the other three are relative ("Avoid any personal relationships that would compromise your profession of faith in Christ"). That Paul is not calling for a complete severance of ties with unbelievers is clear from 1 Cor. 5:10 — a thoroughgoing isolationism would demand one's departure from the world! Moreover, he has

---

39. Accordingly Fitzmyer (1961) describes the fragment as "a Christian reworking of an Essene paragraph which has been introduced into the Pauline letter" and which should be regarded as "a non-Pauline interpolation" ("Qumran" 217), Gnilka regards it as "a Christian exhortation in the Essene tradition, whose author is not Paul, but some unknown Christian" (66), and Dahl concludes that it is "a slightly Christianized piece of Qumran theology" (63), "a fragment of non-Pauline origin" (64; but cf. 69) "reworked in a Pauline style" (63 n. 3).

40. It is only in Paul, among NT authors, that we find the church explicitly referred to as the temple of God. Murphy-O'Connor has argued that the language and ideas of 2 Cor. 6:14–7:1 are best paralleled, not from the Dead Sea Scrolls, but in the Hellenistic Judaism represented by Philo ("Philo" 137-40).

already encouraged the Christian partner in a "mixed marriage" to maintain the union unless the unbelieving partner (ὁ ἄπιστος) sought a separation (1 Cor. 7:12-16), and he envisaged situations in which Corinthian Christians would gladly accept invitations to meals in the homes of unbelievers (οἱ ἄπιστοι, 1 Cor. 10:27) and in which outsiders or unbelievers (ἰδιῶται ἤ ἄπιστοι) would enter the Corinthian assembly (1 Cor. 14:23-24). What Paul is directing the Corinthians to repudiate is any association with unbelievers that amounts to a compromise with paganism such as attendance at a feast held in a pagan temple (1 Cor. 8:10; 10:14-22) or entering into marriage with an unbeliever (cf. 1 Cor. 7:39). To enjoy the company of unbelievers in their own homes or to welcome them to gatherings of Christians would in no sense involve unacceptable compromise. Only with regard to the world's value-system and outlook and the doing of evil was Paul a rigorous separatist.[41] And unlike the Qumran covenanters, Paul was preoccupied only with moral, not physical, defilement.

Those who argue that this paragraph is non-Pauline generally explain its presence in 2 Corinthians by proposing that it was interpolated by a later redactor.[42] But some, although viewing the passage as non-Pauline in origin, believe that Paul himself incorporated it in the letter.[43] Of these two explanations, the latter avoids the objections that may be raised against any interpolation hypothesis that postulates editorial activity after Paul composed the letter. These objections will be discussed below.

(2) Pauline Features

In examining the purportedly non-Pauline characteristics of this paragraph, we had occasion to mention several features that are, in fact, found elsewhere in 2 Corinthians or in other Pauline letters:

> When Paul indulges in rhetorical flourishes, there tends to be a high incidence of *hapax legomena*.
> The distinctive meaning of δικαιοσύνη and πιστός and the special sense of the σάρξ-πνεῦμα conjunction reflected in the paragraph are not without Pauline parallels.
> The antitheses of uprightness and iniquity, light and darkness, Christ and Satan; the call for separation from evil in general and from idolatry

---

41. This distinction between absolute and relative separation shows (*pace* Furnish 376) that the injunctions of 6:14–7:1 need not be viewed as inconsistent with Pauline teaching elsewhere. Such a distinction also renders unnecessary the suggestion of Thrall ("Problem" 147-48) that the injunctions of 6:17 advocating separation, which somewhat outstripped Paul's own view, were retained because they were already part of an existing catena of scriptural allusions (6:16b-18).

42. E.g., Bornkamm, *Paul* 246; Fitzmyer 217; Gnilka 67; Georgi, "2 Corinthians" 183-84.

43. E.g., Furnish (383, following Klinzing 179-82) concludes that "one might speak of a Pauline interpolation of non-Pauline material, perhaps drawn from Christian baptismal parenesis."

in particular; the idea of Christian believers as constituting God's temple; the chain of OT texts; the distinction between an absolute separation from any form of evil and a qualified or relative separation from evil persons — all these features are Pauline in nature.

To these we may now add the following features which also argue for Pauline authorship.

There are significant verbal and conceptual links between 6:14–7:1 and what precedes. Thrall[44] has drawn attention to a threefold connection with 4:3-6, a passage which refers to the blinded minds of the ἄπιστοι and to Satan, "the god of this age," and which implies that unbelievers are in a state of darkness. She also notes the use of δικαιοσύνη in 5:21 and 6:14 and the ideas of relationship to God in 5:18-20 and 6:16-18, acceptance by God in 6:2 (δεκτῷ) and 6:17 (εἰσδέξομαι), and the fear of God as motivation for conduct in 5:11 and 7:1.[45]

The whole pericope is structured around the typically Pauline "indicative-imperative" dialectic:[46]

- Μὴ γίνεσθε . . . γάρ (6:14). The first element in each of the five consecutive questions in 6:14b-16a implies the presence of salvation (the "indicative").
- Ναὸς θεοῦ ἐσμεν ζῶντος· καθὼς . . . διὸ ἐξέλθατε κτλ. (6:16b-17).
- . . . οὖν ἔχοντες ("so then . . . since we have") . . . καθαρίσωμεν κτλ.

The paragraph incorporates several words, phrases, or constructions that are common in Paul's letters: μὴ γίνεσθε (Rom. 12:16; 1 Cor. 7:23; 10:7; 14:20; Eph. 5:7, 17), ἄπιστος (eleven instances in 1 Corinthians; 2 Cor. 4:4), θεὸς ζῶν (Rom. 9:26; 2 Cor. 3:3; 1 Thess. 1:9), the causal participle ἔχοντες (Rom. 8:23; 2 Cor. 3:12; 4:1, 13), the vocative ἀγαπητοί (μου) (Rom. 12:19; 1 Cor. 10:14; 2 Cor. 12:19; Phil. 2:12; 4:1), ἐπιτελέω (seven Pauline uses, four in 2 Corinthians). Moreover, the term ἁγιωσύνη is found only in Paul (Rom. 1:4; 1 Thess. 3:13).

(3) An Interpolation?

Even scholars who are convinced of the Pauline character of the passage do not agree on whether its present position in 2 Corinthians is the work of Paul. For instance, Strachan claimed that "any connexion of thought with what precedes

---

44. "Problem" 145, developing the suggestions of Schlatter 576.
45. "Problem" 145.
46. Lambrecht ("Fragment" 159) comments on this tension, particularly in relation to 6:16b-18.

and what follows is unrecognizable" (xv) and so proposed that 6:14–7:1 may well be a fragment of the "previous letter" mentioned in 1 Cor. 5:9 (xv, 3-4).[47] Any such view assumes that the paragraph has been interpolated by a redactor or copyist. How probable is it that this fragment of 111 words, be it Pauline, non-Pauline, or anti-Pauline in origin, was inserted into the text by someone other than Paul?

On occasion the textual tradition makes it clear that a verse or passage has been inserted into the text (e.g., John 5:3b-4; 7:53–8:11; Acts 8:37). But when textual evidence is lacking,[48] what are the criteria for identifying interpolations? There are three or perhaps four: (1) the presence of ideas alien to the author, (2) evidence of stylistic preferences or linguistic usage uncharacteristic of the author, and (3) dissonance with the immediate context.[49] In her discussion of this issue, Munro (24) proposes a further criterion that might sometimes apply, that of (4) literary dependence, that is, when an alleged interpolation draws on or coheres with some other piece of writing. Her overall conclusion is sound: "The judgment as to whether any passage is interpolated depends on a variety of factors and depends on no one infallible criterion. It is a matter of taking into account the cumulative effect of converging lines of evidence" (24-25). Also, once it has been established that an interpolation is probable, an adequate explanation must be given of how the interpolation found its way into the text.[50]

---

47. Such a proposal was earlier made by Moffatt (*Introduction* 109, 125) and has more recently been defended by Hurd (235-37) and Newton (110-11). On the opposite side, it is the central thesis of Webb in his monograph on 6:14–7:1 (14, 144-45, 157-58, 175-76) that new covenant and exilic return traditions may be traced throughout 2:14–7:4, so that 6:14–7:1 with its exilic return theology is completely consonant with the wider context (what Webb calls "contextual integration" [14, 27-28, 30]). As a servant of the new covenant (3:6), as identified with the *'ebed Yahweh,* Paul stands between God and the Corinthians, insisting that "now" is the time for their homecoming (6:1-2) and calling them to a second exodus ("Come out from . . .") (158, 182). "Through skillful use of return traditions, both inside and outside the fragment, Paul effectively parallels the Corinthians' need to return to him as apostle with their need to return to God" (158). The monograph's longer title is *Coming Out of Babylon and Returning Home* (14, 215). Given 6:17, there can be no strong objection to Webb's insistence that the "come out from" theme is central to the fragment — "out of Egypt . . . out of Babylon . . . out of Corinth" (214) — but the "returning home" motif is merely implicit. Paul nowhere suggests that after leaving "idolatry" they are returning to any specific point such as "home," far less that he himself represents "home" (*pace* 158, 178), although Webb does argue that the reception (implied in εἰσδέξομαι, 6:16) takes place "in communal worship, but with strong salvific implications" (48). Other recent writers who have stressed the covenantal and/or second exodus–restoration motifs in 6:14–7:1 include Lane 22-25; Beale 569-78; Scott 151-58; "Scripture" 73-99.

48. The absence of any textual evidence for the omission of 6:14–7:1 is no argument against it being an interpolation, for the putative editorial work by a redactor would predate the earliest textual witness.

49. These three correspond to the three criteria (ideological, stylistic, contextual) used by Fortna (15-21) to distinguish a source from later redaction in the Fourth Gospel.

50. Walker observes rightly that the burden of proof rests with any argument that a *particular passage* in the Pauline letters is an interpolation (610). But, claiming that both literary-critical considerations (the Pauline corpus represents an edited Paul as well as an expanded and abbreviated

In applying these criteria the commentator must proceed with caution. There is, first of all, the danger of circular reasoning: in determining whether or not certain ideas and various features of style or vocabulary are characteristic of a writer, one must have a yardstick by which to measure these matters, yet that yardstick itself is formed by examining these very features in other documents assumed to be authentic. Second, to the extent that Paul's manner of thinking may be described as paradoxical, the appearance of apparent inconsistencies in his writing should not be treated as evidence of inauthenticity. Third, every writer must be allowed the luxury of *hapax* (or *dis* or *tris*) *legomena* in the realm of ideas, style, and vocabulary. Fourth, there can be no denying the tendency of Paul to digress,[51] a literary feature that is totally consonant with his dictation of letters and his homiletical style. Fifth, a change in a writer's purpose or subject matter may affect his or her vocabulary and style. Finally, neither the presence of stylistic or linguistic distinctives nor the inner coherence of an alleged interpolation is proof of later insertion, for a writer may merely be using or adapting existing material of his own or another's composition.[52]

How do all these considerations apply to 6:14–7:1? With regard to the four criteria for determining possible interpolations that were mentioned above, we have observed that so far from containing ideas, "stylistic preferences," and "linguistic usage" foreign to Paul (criteria 1 and 2), the paragraph contains many Pauline themes and evidences several words, phrases, and constructions that often occur in Paul's letters. Granted, these six verses are self-contained and begin with an abrupt transition of thought, but their consonance with the immediate and wider context (cf. criterion 3) can be clearly demonstrated. We should not overlook the fact that the problem of the abrupt disjuncture at 6:14 remains, whether Paul is the writer or a later redactor is the editor. Indeed, we might argue that it is more appropriate to suppose that Paul himself, known for his propensity to digress as he dictated his letters, has abruptly digressed at 6:14 than that some unknown editor, devoid of literary sensibilities, has awkwardly

---

Paul) and text-critical considerations (the surviving text of Paul's letters tells us nothing about the state of the Pauline literature before the third century) support the *a priori* assumption that Paul's letters as they have been preserved do in fact contain interpolations, he argues in addition that the burden of proof also lies with any a priori argument that a *particular letter* within the Pauline corpus contains no interpolations (611-15). It is difficult, however, to perceive the value of this latter observation, for whether or not a particular *letter* contains interpolations can be determined only by examining particular *passages* claimed to be interpolations. That a particular letter contains no interpolations cannot, in the nature of the case, be argued a priori.

51. E.g., the brief digressions found in 1 Cor. 1:16; 7:11a; 10:28-29a; 11:8-9, 11-12 are appropriately marked by parentheses in the RSV.

52. The unanimity of scholars regarding the extent of the supposed interpolation (namely, 6:14–7:1) is not evidence in support of the interpolation hypothesis, although it is interesting to note that elsewhere in the Pauline corpus efforts that have been made to identify interpolations have usually led to mutually contradictory conclusions. For instance, see the illuminating discussion by Jewett (*Correspondence* 42-46) of interpolation hypotheses regarding the Thessalonian letters put forward by K. G. Eckart, E. Refshauge, C. Demke, and W. Munro.

interpolated the passage at this point in Paul's letter.[53] While there are unmistakable affinities between these verses and some Qumran texts, no "literary dependence" (criterion 4) in the sense of the borrowing of ideas or terminology can be established, as we have seen. Moreover, each of the objections to Pauline authorship can be satisfactorily answered, although it is true that the clustering of *hapax legomena* and of unusual uses of Pauline words and phrases constitutes a powerful argument against Pauline authorship.

We conclude that, notwithstanding the *prima facie* non-Pauline features of the paragraph, its incontestable Pauline characteristics and the very presence of the paragraph in a genuine Pauline letter and in such an expected place suggest that it stems *in toto* from Paul's own hand. Perhaps Paul had composed it at an earlier time, under Essene influence,[54] and now incorporated it, possibly after a pause in dictation,[55] as a digressive appeal[56] to the Corinthians to sever all their ties with paganism[57] and thereby become fully reconciled to their father in the faith, whose gospel of reconciliation they had embraced (cf. 5:18-20).

d. 2 Corinthians 8–9

When we survey scholarly opinion about the integrity of chs. 8 and 9, again we are confronted by a bewildering array of views,[58] which may be conveniently summarized as follows.

53. It is even more difficult to assume, with R. P. C. Hanson (19-20), that the fragment was fortuitously inserted at the point where it happened to be rolled up with 2 Corinthians 1–9 (similarly Rissi 79-80). For an attempt to explain the motivation of a "redactor" (probably a later editor but possibly Paul himself) in inserting the fragment between 6:13 and 7:2, see Duff 160-80. See further the telling comments of Allo (191) and Fee ("Food" 142-43) regarding the theory of interpolation.

54. But Kuhn (203 n. 2) and Martin (195) have proposed that Paul has remodeled a text of Essene origin.

55. "A long dictation pause" was postulated by Lietzmann (129). Martin goes one step further in suggesting that during this intermission in dictation Paul may have "encountered a tract from, or one resembling something from, the Qumran community's library" and reworked it before inserting it into his letter after 6:13 (xliv).

56. Similarly Plummer 205-6; Tasker 30, 102; Bruce 170-71, 214; Barrett 194. Thrall identifies the digression as 6:3-13 (similarly Kümmel 206), with 6:14 resuming 6:2 and introducing "the exhortation which logically should have followed immediately" ("Problem" 144). Martin views 6:14–7:1 as an "inserted appeal" but not as a digression; rather, it enforces Paul's call for reconciliation begun in 5:20 and completed in 7:3-4. (xxxviii, xliv, 195; but cf. his earlier *Foundations* 2.183).

57. Precisely what constituted the Corinthians' inconsistent ties with heathendom and the way in which Paul expected them to terminate these associations are not known to us. For some tentative proposals, however, see the commentary on 6:14. Not inappropriately, Lambrecht characterizes the passage as "a piece of 'common' parenesis meant for Christians who live in the midst of manifold dangers in a gentile world" ("Fragment" 160).

58. On the history of the interpretation of 2 Corinthians 8 and 9, see Betz 3-35. According to Betz himself, ch. 8 forms the body of a letter of mixed rhetorical genre addressed to the church in Corinth, vv. 1-15 being advisory or deliberative and vv. 16-23 administrative or juridical, while ch. 9 is the body of an advisory letter to other Achaian Christians. What is lacking in each case are the

(1) Partition Theories

It is held by some scholars that chs. 8 and 9 were originally separate letters or fragments of separate letters, divorced from the rest of the extant Corinthian correspondence, and that ch. 8 was written before ch. 9 (H. Windisch 242-43, 268-71, 286-89; G. Bornkamm, *Paul* 245-46; H. D. Wendland 8-9, 167, 218, 222-23; D. Georgi 75-79; "Second Corinthians" 184; H. Koester 53-54; H. D. Betz, *passim,* especially 142-43; M. Carrez 17-18, 189). They usually argue that ch. 8 was a letter addressed to the Corinthian church alone, with ch. 9 written to Christians of Achaia (cf. 9:2) other than those in Corinth.

Sometimes other parts of 2 Corinthians are associated with either of these two chapters:

an "intermediate letter" containing 2:14–7:4 (except 6:14–7:1); chs. 10–13; and ch. 9, followed by Paul's last letter to Corinth, containing 1:1–2:13; 7:5-16; and ch. 8 (Bultmann 18, 256; but cf. *Probleme* 14 n. 6)

the "letter of tears" containing chs. 10–13; 2:14–7:4 (except 6:14–7:1); ch. 9; and 13:11-13, followed by the "letter of reconciliation" containing 1:1–2:13; 7:5-16; and ch. 8 (Dinkler, "Korintherbriefe" 18)

an "apologetic letter" containing 2:14–7:4 (except 6:14–7:1) and ch. 9, the "letter of tears" containing chs. 10–13, and the "letter of reconciliation" containing 1:1–2:13; 7:5-16; and ch. 8 (Schenke and Fischer 1.108-23).

ch. 8 as one letter, and ch. 9 with 1:1–2:13 and 7:5-16 constituting the "letter of reconciliation" (Weiss, *Christianity* 1.356-57; Schmithals, *Briefe* 77-85[59] [ch. 8 earlier than ch. 9]; Vielhauer, *Geschichte* 153 [the two letters written at the same time][60]).

ch. 9 as one letter, and ch. 8 linked with chs. 1–7 (Semler, *praefatio* to his *Paraphrasis II*; Goguel, *Introduction* 2.85-86 [without 6:14–7:1]; Nickle 17 and n. 17, 22 and n. 36; Héring xiii-xiv, 65; Thrall 36-43) or with the "letter of reconciliation," that is, 1:1–2:13; 7:5-16 (Dean 13, 57-59; Bornkamm 186-87;[61] Suhl 260-63; E. Lohse 72-73[62]).

Other scholars regard chs. 8 and 9 as part of the same letter to Corinth along with 13:11-13 (Schmiedel 226-27), with 1:1–2:13 and 7:5-16, that is, the

epistolary prescripts and postscripts (129-40). But, as Stowers points out in a review of Betz's work (*JBL* 106 [1987] 728), Betz does not produce any ancient analogies for the putative editorial fusion of two independent letters into a new work (the canonical 2 Corinthians).

59. According to Schmithals the "joyful letter" (= the letter of reconciliation) incorporated 2 Cor. 1:1–2:13; 7:5-7, 4b, 8-16; 9:1-15; Rom. 5:1b-10.

60. Vielhauer associates ch. 9 with the letter of reconciliation only tentatively.

61. For Bornkamm ch. 9 definitely is a separate letter, and ch. 8 may be.

62. Dean and Lohse add 13:11-13/14 to the "letter of reconciliation."

"letter of reconciliation" (Fuller 48-49), with chs. 1–7 (excluding 6:14–7:1) and 13:11-13 (Clemen 1.75-85), or with chs. 1–7, with or without chs. 10–13 (most commentators).

(2) The Two Chapters Belong Together

A careful examination of these two chapters reveals a network of specific links between them. Μέν in 9:1 points forward to the adversative δέ in 9:3 ("although . . . still . . .") so that 9:1-3 (or 9:1-4) forms a single thought-unit. Γάρ in 9:1, on the other hand, points back to 8:24 and introduces the reason for Paul's request there that the Corinthians show by their ready response to the three-man delegation that his boasting about their responsiveness has been justified: "for (γάρ) although (μέν) . . . it is superfluous for me to be writing to you like this (since [γάρ] I know your eager willingness which I am boasting about . . .), yet (δέ) I am sending (ἔπεμψα) the brothers precisely so that our expressed pride about you should not prove to be unwarranted in this particular regard" (9:1-3a). That is, this explanatory γάρ links ἡμῶν [ἡ] καύχησις ὑπὲρ ὑμῶν (8:24) with both τὴν προθυμίαν ὑμῶν ἣν ὑπὲρ ὑμῶν καυχῶμαι (9:2) and τὸ καύχημα ἡμῶν τὸ ὑπὲρ ὑμῶν (9:3). If 9:1 were in fact the beginning of an independent letter, we would have expected περὶ δέ ("now concerning"), which regularly introduces a new topic (as in 1 Cor. 7:1, 25; 8:1; 12:1; 16:1, 12). The article τῆς before διακονίας may well be anaphoric ("this service," NIV), especially since τῆς διακονίας τῆς εἰς τοὺς ἁγίους (9:1a) is resumptive of the identical expression in 8:4b.[63] Moreover, the present infinitive (τὸ) γράφειν suggests the meaning "continuing to write" or "to be writing (like this)." Then again, the unqualified reference to τοὺς ἀδελφούς (9:3, 5) presupposes some prior identification of these brothers, which is supplied by 8:6, 16-23. For other verbal links between the two chapters, see Carrez 190 (referring to the work of Rolland 76-77).

The objections that have been brought against these two chapters originating together may all be satisfactorily answered. First, it is no evidence of the independence of the two chapters that 8:20 and 9:3-5 state differing purposes for the sending of the brothers (*pace* Windisch 271-72). The purposes are not mutually exclusive but complementary. In 8:18-20 Paul declares that the appointment by the churches of the renowned brother as Titus's traveling companion and his dispatch of him with Titus were aimed at guarding against any criticism of his own handling of this charitable fund. In 9:3-5 Paul affirms that "the brothers" (presumably referring to Titus and the two anonymous envoys of the churches) were being sent to the Corinthians to show that his boasting about their willingness to contribute was fully justified (9:3), to avoid the personal embarrassment of finding them unprepared (9:4), and to ensure that arrangements for the gift were completed before his own arrival (9:5).

---

63. It is not impossible that a dictation pause occurred between the writing of the two chapters (thus Bruce [225] followed by Martin [xliii]).

Second, it has been argued that because "Achaia" is found in ch. 9 but not in ch. 8 and because 1:1 distinguishes between believers in Corinth and "all God's people who are in the whole of Achaia," ch. 9 is a circular letter addressed to churches in the province of Achaia other than at Corinth while the addressees in ch. 8 are the Corinthian Christians (Windisch 288; Georgi 77-78; similarly Betz 91-93, 139-40; Carrez 17-18, 189). But there is no need to exclude Corinth from the reference to Achaia. After all, Corinth was the capital of this province, and unlike 1:1, where the use of both "Corinth" and "Achaia" suggests that "Achaia" excludes Corinth, 9:2 mentions only Achaia and ch. 8 mentions neither. Our options seem to be that in 9:2 "Achaia" refers *either* to all the Christians scattered throughout the province of Achaia, including the numerically preponderant Corinthians, that is, both groups addressed in 1:1,[64] *or,* more probably, to the Corinthians alone.[65]

Third, for some commentators (e.g., Bultmann 256) the content of Paul's appeals is consistent only if the two letters are independent. In 8:1-5 Paul appeals to Macedonian generosity as a model for the Corinthians to follow, but in 9:2 Achaia forms the pattern for the Macedonians to follow. But this alleged inconsistency or circularity of argument is more apparent than real. Paul appeals to the Corinthians' preparedness of intention and their eagerness in initiating the collection (8:6, 10-11) as a good example in his effort to have the Macedonians advance their own contribution (9:2). Thus it was the Corinthians' ζῆλος (9:2), not their ἐπιτελέσαι (8:11), which stirred up the majority of the Macedonians. On the other side, because, by the time of writing, the Macedonians had almost brought to a successful completion what they had enthusiastically begun under the stimulus of the Corinthian example, their exemplary action was a natural ground for Paul's appeal to the Corinthians to complete their offering (8:6, 11) in order that his initial boasting about their readiness to contribute might not prove unfounded when any Macedonians arrived (9:2-4).

Fourth, Dean believes that ch. 9 breathes a different atmosphere than ch. 8. Whereas in ch. 8 Paul "trusts to the impulse of the joy of reconciliation to stimulate them [the Corinthians]" (93) and appeals to lofty motives, in ch. 9 a certain anxiety and urgency is in evidence and Paul appeals to self-interest (93-94). But this contrast in tone is overdrawn. Urgency is evident in 8:6-7, 10-11, 24, and in 9:8-14 Paul confidently expects a positive and cheerful response. Appeal to exalted motives may be seen in 9:11b-13, 15 and an appeal to "self-interest" in 8:14-15.

---

64. "He purposely includes Christians outside Corinth, perhaps to avoid exaggeration" (Plummer 254).

65. Thus Suhl 263 n. 28. "Paul flatters the Corinthians by this virtual identification of the province with their own city" (Tasker 123).

(3) The Two Chapters Belong with Chapters 1–7

Few will doubt that the transition from chs. 1–7 to ch. 8 is to a large extent a move from apologetic to exhortation. The change of tone — from relief and almost excessive exuberance regarding the recent past to somewhat embarrassed admonition concerning the immediate future — may be readily accounted for by the change of subject and purpose. After seeking to explain his pastoral conduct and defend his apostolic ministry (chs. 1–7), Paul takes up the challenge of reviving the flagging collection at Corinth (chs. 8–9). His reconciliation with the Corinthians affords the secure base from which to launch his appeal. It is psychologically probable that he would encourage the Corinthians to follow through on their initial enthusiasm for the project only when he was assured that he had regained their confidence on a personal level (cf. 7:4, 16).

This leads us to conclude that once it is agreed that chs. 8 and 9 belong together, there is no difficulty in viewing them as a natural addition to chs. 1–7, given the apostle's desire to have the Corinthians revive and complete their relief aid for Jerusalem. Few scholars who hold to the integrity of 8–9 divorce these chapters from 1–7[66] (or parts of 1–7).[67]

e. 2 Corinthians 10–13

The following discussion will assume, for the reasons rehearsed above (3.b-d), that 2 Corinthians 1–9 is a unity and will argue for the integrity of the whole letter.

(1) Reasons for Separating 10–13 from 1–9

Four main reasons are commonly brought forward for regarding chs. 1–9 and 10–13 as originally separate compositions dispatched by Paul to the Corinthian church at different periods of his ministry. This "four-chapter hypothesis" proposes that chs. 10–13 were written and sent either before or after chs. 1–9.

(a) There is a dramatic change of tone at 10:1 which is unexpected and unannounced. Patent relief, unbridled joy, and gentle appeal are succeeded by scathing remonstrance, biting irony (or, some would say, sarcasm), and impetuous self-defense. After the weather has improved, the storm breaks! A change in the opposite direction — from restless frustration to contented relief, from crushing severity to peaceful geniality — would present considerably less difficulty from the point of view of pastoral technique (cf. Osty 84). As Plummer expresses it (xxix), "The change is not only surprising in its intensity, it is in the wrong direction."

Within Paul's letters there is not infrequently found an abrupt change in

---

66. Schmiedel is an exception.
67. See the view of Fuller mentioned above.

tone (e.g., Rom. 9:1-2 after 8:31-39; Rom. 16:17-20 between 16:16 and 16:21; 1 Cor. 1:10-13 after 1:4-9; Gal. 5:2 after 5:1; Phil. 3:2 after 3:1), so a shift in mood is no conclusive indication of dislocation. Nor should we overdraw the alteration of temper at 10:1, for chs. 1–7 contain polemic (2:17; 3:1-6; 4:2; 5:12-13; 6:14-16a), so much so that several scholars (e.g., Weiss, Dean, Bultmann, Dinkler, Vielhauer) actually include 2:14–7:4, without 6:14–7:1 and with chs. 10–13, in the "stern letter," while the literary critic R. A. Knox (175) declares that apart from chs. 7–9, which "breathe a spirit of confidence and approval, . . . *all* the rest of the epistle is disappointment and expostulation." W. Ellis (35) argued that 2 Corinthians is polemical in tone, with 10:1 marking an intensification of degree, not a variation of kind. Moreover, chs. 10–13 are not unalleviated invective or a sustained philippic. Not only are there some tender expressions of affection (e.g., 11:2-3; 12:14-15a; 13:7); the sensitive reader may also detect a certain "playful strain" (Tasker 32) in these chapters, as when Paul boasts "as a fool" (11:16-18) or asks to be forgiven for the "fault" of not being a financial parasite (12:13) or describes his ascent into paradise in the third person (12:2-5) or cites the Corinthian charge that he had caught them by being "a crafty knave" (πανοῦργος, 12:16).

Attempts to account for the change of mood at 10:1 vary greatly in the conviction they carry. Not altogether persuasive are appeals to such factors as an intervening sleepless night,[68] with irritability then channeled into vindictiveness; the vagaries of Paul's temperament,[69] coupled with an Oriental fondness for verbal extravagance; the suppression of deep feelings throughout chs. 1–9, which then erupt at 10:1;[70] doubts in Paul's mind over the genuineness of the Corinthians' repentance;[71] Paul acting as his own amanuensis beginning at 10:1;[72] Paul first consolidating his apostolic authority (chs. 1–7) and then exercising it (chs. 10–13);[73] a change of audience, so that Paul is addressing in chs. 10–13 not the whole community but intruders from Palestine and their Corinthian partisans;[74] Paul intentionally reserving his criticism until after commendation[75] so as to guarantee a hearing for his reproof; in rhetorical style Paul reserving the most controversial matters until the end and concluding the letter with a recapitulation of previous topics and a powerful emotional appeal for change in his hearers.[76] The most convincing explanation, which in the na-

---

68. Lietzmann 139.

69. Sanday 906 (Paul "was one whose mind responded with singular quickness to every gust of passing emotion"); Goudge li ("As with the great mystics, 'joy unspeakable' may soon be followed by 'the dark night of the soul,' and all the more if the 'thorn in the flesh' has once more laid him [Paul] low").

70. Menzies xxxvi, xl, xlii; "Integrity" 370-73.

71. A tentative suggestion made by Guthrie, *Introduction* 433.

72. Dibelius 157; cf. 144; Bates 66-67; Richards 180-81, 190.

73. Cf. Goudge lvii-lviii.

74. Wikenhauser 397-98; followed by Rigaux 111.

75. Jülicher 100-102; Hughes xxiii-xxiv.

76. Barnett 18, 450 n. 1, 452, followed by Garland 420.

ture of the case cannot be verified, is that after 9:15 there was a "dictation pause" of indeterminate length[77] during which time the disturbing news reached Paul that the situation at Corinth had markedly deteriorated, so that he deemed it necessary to add a detailed vindication of his apostolic authority and dire warnings concerning his forthcoming visit.[78]

A common response to this latter explanation is that chs. 10–13 give no indication that Paul did receive recent news about deteriorating conditions at Corinth. It is true that Paul sometimes indicates the source of his information (e.g., "Chloe's people," 1 Cor. 1:11), but was it imperative that he always name his source or mention his dependence on an oral report (as in 1 Cor. 5:1: ἀκούεται, "it is reported")? The more sensitive and embarrassing the issue *and* the more directly it involved Paul himself the less likely he would have been to specify his source (e.g., Gal. 1:6-9). On the other hand, if a report was positive and reflected well on the persons involved, he did not hesitate to mention who had carried the good news to him (e.g., 1 Thess. 3:6). In the case of 2 Corinthians 10–13, perhaps Paul may have chosen not to disclose the source of his recently acquired knowledge of the specific charges leveled against him because the news was negative and related directly to himself and may have been brought by a Corinthian whose standing at Corinth he would not want to jeopardize.

(b) An abrupt transition at 10:1 to what is almost unalleviated remonstrance would have merely served to renew Paul's earlier suspense concerning the Corinthian response to harsh words and to jeopardize both his rapprochement with the Corinthians and the progress of the collection.[79]

The potency of this argument depends on one's assessment of the emotional relationship between chs. 10–13 and 1–7. If chs. 1–7 are marked principally by "tenderness" and chs. 10–13 by "biting sarcasms and lashing reproofs,"[80] the argument is powerful; but to the extent that chs. 1–7 contain an admixture of quiet assurance (e.g., 1:13-14; 7:4, 16) and pointed admonition (e.g., 6:1, 14-16; 7:1) and that chs. 10–13 reflect both stern rebuke (e.g., 10:2; 12:20-21) and affectionate pleading (e.g., 11:1; 13:5, 11), the argument forfeits its potency. In addition, we should not overlook the fact that chs. 1–9 contain not a few indications that reconciliation with the Corinthians had been only partially achieved by the "severe letter," so that distrust of the apostle persisted:[81] they called into question Paul's straightforwardness in action (1:15-18) and

---

77. Stange 113; Michaelis 179.

78. This seems a more satisfactory explanation of the change of tone at 10:1 than the assumption that in his report to Paul (cf. 7:7-15) Titus had unwittingly misrepresented the state of affairs at Corinth or had been unduly optimistic about Corinthian attitudes toward Paul, so that Paul's assessment of the situation changed dramatically (at some point after he had written chs. 1–9) when the actual facts became known.

79. Plummer xxx, xxxv, 67.

80. Plummer (CGT) xxxvi.

81. Cf. Price 100.

writing (1:13), they suspected his motives (2:17; 4:2), they questioned his credentials (3:1; 6:8) and his sanity (5:13), and they continued to flirt with paganism (6:14–7:1) and so felt a general uneasiness in their relations with him (6:11-13; 7:2). True, if 2 Corinthians was sent as a single letter, chs. 10–13 would have led to renewed suspense concerning his converts' reaction to stern words, but a pastor who experienced a "daily burden of anxiety" for all his churches (11:28) would not shrink from such a renewal of tension if it was necessary, irrespective of the dangers and unpleasantness involved. Nor should we fail to distinguish the situation reflected in chs. 10–13 from the circumstances behind the "severe letter." That letter had sought to combat *actual* defection at Corinth; now there was a *danger* of renewed defection. That letter had been written in place of a visit (2:1, 3-4); 10–13 was penned to prepare for a visit (12:20-21; 13:1-2, 10). It was not a case of "suspense" for identical reasons.

(c) Chs. 1–9 give no intimation of an *imminent* visit such as that promised or threatened in 12:14 and 13:1.[82]

It is true that where the intimation of a visit — whether immediate or distant — might have been expected, namely in 1:15–2:4, no such reference is made. But there Paul is explaining and justifying his previous travel movements in the face of charges of fickleness and haughtiness, rather than announcing his future travel plans. If we accept that chs. 1–7 are principally apologetic in tone as Paul explains his recent conduct and describes his apostolic ministry, we should not be surprised that his specific plans for future travel are not mentioned.

In chs. 8–9, on the other hand, he is exhorting and instructing the Corinthians with regard to the collection precisely in light of his intended visit. "I sent (ἔγραψα) the brothers . . . in order that you may be ready, as I said you would be, lest, if any Macedonians come (ἐὰν ἔλθωσιν) with me and find you not yet ready, we be ashamed — to say nothing about you — of having been so confident" (9:3-4). But was the visit imminent? It would be improper to press the repeated προ- ("in advance") in 9:5 (the first two occurrences) into signifying an impending visit. But, along with vv. 3-4, v. 5 could certainly be understood as referring to a visit in the near future (similarly Horrell 303; also Murphy-O'Connor, *Paul* 30, 316, in reference to 9:4), especially if ἡγησάμην (v. 5) is not an epistolary aorist but a preterit aorist, for in that case at the time of writing Titus and the two brothers were about to leave for Corinth to help to complete the collection in advance of Paul's arrival. "So I have thought it necessary to urge the brothers to go on to you *ahead of me* and to organize *in advance* your gift of blessing, previously promised, so that it may thus be ready as indeed a gift of blessing and not as a gift that reflects avarice" (9:5).

(d) "While the first person plural predominates in chaps. 1–9, the first person singular predominates in chaps. 10–13 (emphatically introduced in 10:1). While alternation between the first person singular and plural is common

---

82. Cf. Furnish 31.

in Paul's letters . . . the kind of shift apparent here in 2 Cor occurs in no other Pauline letter" (Furnish 32; cf. 43-44, 47).

This argument would be more potent if Paul had *rarely* used the plural in chs. 10–13, but in fact it occurs some thirty-five times in finite verbs and pronouns (not counting participles),[83] on three separate occasions in a sustained fashion: 10:2b-7 (four uses), 10:11-18 (ten uses), and 13:6b-9 (twelve uses). Given the distinctively individual nature of most of the issues discussed in chs. 10–13, it is not surprising that the singular predominates. In the letter to Philemon (v. 1), Timothy is associated with Paul as co-author (cf. 2 Cor. 1:1), yet the first person singular is found throughout, apart from the salutation (vv. 1-3) and one generic plural (v. 6). That is, the more personally Paul is involved in the subject matter in question, the higher the incidence of first person singulars. Like Philemon, 2 Corinthians 10–13 is intensely personal, as the opening phrase of ch. 10 (αὐτὸς δὲ ἐγὼ Παῦλος) clearly indicates.

Subsidiary reasons are sometimes given for the separation of chs. 10–13 from chs. 1–9, but each is decidedly inconclusive. First, some have discerned a different attitude toward self-commendation in the two parts, the καυχ- root (καυχᾶσθαι, καύχησις, and καύχημα) denoting "boasting" in a complimentary sense in chs. 1–9 but in an apologetic or vindicative sense in chs. 10–13.[84] But this conclusion oversimplifies the data. καυχᾶσθαι in 5:12 is undoubtedly apologetic in sense, while καύχησις in 11:10 and καυχᾶσθαι in 10:17 are complimentary and positive in meaning. And cannot "apologetic" uses of καυχᾶσθαι such as in 11:30; 12:1, 5 (twice), 6, 9 be classified also as "complimentary"? Are these two categories necessarily mutually exclusive?

Second, in a related issue, certain statements in chs. 10–13 (e.g., 10:7; 11:5-6, 16-18, 21b-29; 12:1, 11-12) appear to violate Paul's refusal in chs. 1–9 to resort to self-commendation (3:1; 5:12).[85] But the occurrence of 6:4-10 within chs. 1–9 and of 10:15-18 within chs. 10–13 betrays the insecure foundation of the argument and suggests rather that we should maintain a distinction between self-commendation that does not and indeed cannot appeal to solid evidence but is directed toward purely personal gain, and self-commendation or "boasting in the Lord" by the servant of God that seeks to validate a God-given status by invoking the testimony of the past regarding God's action in and through his servant and that promotes God's glory.

Third, Kennedy (136) observes that if chs. 1–9 were in fact a separate letter, it would end naturally and appropriately, as does 1 Corinthians, with instructions regarding the collection. This observation is suggestive but hardly decisive.

---

83. This excludes 12:18b, which clearly refers to Paul and Titus.

84. E.g., Kennedy 88-90; "Problem" 343; Hanson 15. On this view, see the comments of Bernard 26; Young and Ford 13-14.

85. See the discussion of Kennedy 88-89, 132-34.

(2) The Four-Chapter Hypothesis

These reasons for holding that chs. 1–9 and chs. 10–13 belong to different historical situations form the foundation of the so-called "four-chapter hypothesis." On this foundation, *two different superstructures* have been erected. Some scholars hold that chs. 10–13 were written earlier than chs. 1–9 and form part of the "severe letter" (see 2.c.[2] above). Paul's Corinthian correspondence would then consist of:

1. the "previous letter" referred to in 1 Cor. 5:9,
2. 1 Corinthians,
3. the "severe letter," of which 2 Corinthians 10–13 forms a part, and
4. 2 Corinthians 1–9.

This reconstruction we shall call the Hausrath hypothesis, since it was A. Hausrath who in 1870 first set forth this view systematically. The classic defense of this hypothesis was given by Kennedy (1900). Rendall (1909) sought to assess the truth of Kennedy's theory and concluded that it "emerges triumphantly" (*Epistles* 3-5, 86-87). Other twentieth-century proponents include Moffatt (1901), Plummer (1903, 1915), Lake (1911), Goguel (1926), Strachan (1935), Manson (1942), Sparks (1952), Filson (1953), Dodd (1953), Hanson (1954), Nickle (1966), Buck and Taylor (1969), Gunther (1973), Watson (1984), Klauck (1986), Aejmelaeus (1987), Talbert (1987), Rolland (1990), Welborn (1995, 1997), Horrell (1996), and Peterson (1997, 1998).

Others maintain that chs. 10–13 were penned later than chs. 1–9 and form part of a fifth letter that Paul wrote to Corinth. The sequence of letters on this view is (usually) thought to be:

1. the "previous letter" (1 Cor. 5:9),
2. 1 Corinthians,
3. the "severe letter,"
4. 2 Corinthians 1–9, and
5. 2 Corinthians 10–13.

The name of J. S. Semler is usually attached to this hypothesis since he was its first proponent (in 1776) (although he regarded ch. 9 as originally independent of chs. 1–8). Supporters of this view have included Bruston (1917), Windisch (1924, the classic defense of an earlier period), Pherigo (1949), Munck (1954), Osty (1959), Barrett (1964, 1973), Batey (1965), Bruce (1968, 1971), Furnish (1984), Martin, (1986, 2000), Best (1987), Kruse (1987, 1989, 1996), Gilchrist (1988), Sumney (1990, 1999), Murphy-O'Connor (1991, 1996), Watson (1993), deSilva (1993), Thrall (1994, 2000 — the classic recent defense), Savage (1996), and Sampley (2000).

According to the Hausrath hypothesis, the "superstructure" consists of two basic claims. First, it is argued that several passages in chs. 1–9 contain intentional allusions to previous statements in chs. 10–13:[86]

10:1	I am confident against you (θαρρῶ εἰς ὑμᾶς)	7:16	I am completely (ἐν παντί) confident in you (θαρρῶ ἐν ὑμῖν)
10:2	With the confidence (πεποιθήσει) which I expect to have to show	8:22	Because of his great confidence (πεποιθήσει) in you
10:6	We are prepared to punish every act of disobedience, once your obedience (ὑπακοή) is complete	2:9	The reason I wrote was to see if you would stand the test, to see if you were totally obedient (ὑπήκοοι)
10:8	Even if I boast somewhat too much	3:1	Are we beginning to commend ourselves again? (cf. 5:12a)
10:13	We will not boast beyond proper limits		
11:11	Because I do not love (ἀγαπῶ) you? God knows I do!	2:4	I wrote . . . to let you know how intense (περισσοτέρως) is my love (ἀγάπην) for you
12:15	If I love (ἀγαπῶ) you so intensely (περισσοτέρως), am I to be loved (ἀγαπῶμαι) the less?		
12:16	Crafty fellow (πανοῦργος) that I am, I trapped you by trickery	4:2	We do not use crafty techniques (πανουργίᾳ)
12:17	Did I exploit (ἐπλεονέκτησα) you?	7:2	We have exploited (ἐπλεονεκτήσαμεν) no one
13:2	When I return (ἐὰν ἔλθω εἰς τὸ πάλιν) I will not spare (φείσομαι) them	1:23	It was in order to spare (φειδόμενος) you that I did not return (οὐκέτι ἦλθον)
13:10	The reason I am writing (γράφω) this when I am absent is that when I am present with you I may not have to be harsh	2:3	I wrote (ἔγραψα) as I did so that when I came I might not be pained

86. See, e.g., Kennedy 79-92; Plummer (CGT) xxxvii-xxxix; (ICC) xxxi-xxxii. Goodspeed finds in 2 Corinthians 1–7 a calm review of the misunderstandings that had come into prominence during the previous heated controversy (chs. 10–13) (*Introduction* 64-65).

If only one or two sets of verbal parallels which show an appropriate reversal of mood and contrast of tense could be discerned on examination, the correspondences might be explained as simply coincidental. The potency of the case, however, lies in the cumulative effect of a series of striking correspondences. Yet it may be fairly asserted that these cases of parallelism support, but do not demand, the identification of chs. 10–13 with the "severe letter."

But each of the alleged allusions may be equally well interpreted on the assumption that chs. 10–13 followed chs. 1–9. For example, 1:23 and 2:3 may together explain that, having canceled his promised return visit to Corinth (1:15) because of his wish to avoid a second painful encounter, Paul wrote a letter instead, while 13:2, 10 may together announce a visit which could prove painful for any who sympathized with the Corinthian dissidents. Moreover, Buck (5) points out that 1:23; 2:3; 2:9 — passages adduced by Kennedy (ix-x, 79-86) as the primary "proofs of identification" — might just as appropriately allude to 1 Cor. 4:18-19; 4:21; and 4:14 respectively. Moreover, sometimes the similarity between the two passages adduced seems merely verbal (8:22 and 10:2); sometimes the validity of the correspondence is undermined by a close examination of the context (2:9 and 10:6; 4:2 and 12:16; 3:1 and 10:8, 13), or by recalling the slanderous accusations of Paul's opponents (7:16 and 10:1; 8:22 and 10:2; 4:2 and 12:16; 7:2 and 12:17; 2:4 and 11:11; 12:15). Again, can it be established on the basis of verbal correlation that Paul remembered the phrasing of the "severe letter" (or reread its contents?) and made intentional allusions to previous statements, allusions which he expected the Corinthians to recognize as indications of their changed relationship with him? Even if the interval between the "severe letter" and the letter of reconciliation had been only several weeks, it is difficult to believe that the Corinthians would appreciate much more than the joyous *fact* of reconciliation with Paul. Time would probably have dulled all but the memory of the *impression* caused by the letter, and severe letters are not usually reread, far less studied. Other considerations apart, verbal allusions would be more potent (at least for the hearers, as opposed to the writer) within the context of a single letter read in its entirety to a church on a single occasion. But this is not to suggest that the situation should be reversed, so that if the letter is seen as a unit, the passages from chs. 10–13 cited above actually allude to those in chs. 1–9, although Batey ("Interaction" 145) believes that in several passages in chs. 10–13 Paul is intentionally retracting or modifying earlier expressions of confidence (compare 10:8; 11:16-18, 30 with 1:12; 7:4, 16 and 10:1-2 with 1:15; 7:16).

The second reason for the equation of chs. 10–13 with the "severe letter" revolves about the implications of the expression τὰ ὑπερέκεινα ὑμῶν ("lands beyond you") in 10:16. In all probability Paul is speaking of his desire to preach in Italy and Spain (see Rom. 15:24, 28). Therefore it is urged that the phrase is geographically accurate only if Paul is writing from Ephesus, the city from which Paul wrote the "severe letter." This argument, which is at most corroborative rather than conclusive, is robbed of its slender validity if in 10:16 Paul is contemplating in general terms the future westward orientation of his mission-ary enterprise, which began in Syria-Cilicia-Arabia. That is, should a *third* point of reference (in addition to Corinth and Italy-Spain) be required by τὰ ὑπερέκεινα, it may be the place where Paul's mission work began[87] (which would result in an even straighter geographical line!) and not the city from which he was writing (whether Ephesus or Philippi).[88]

Further objections can be raised against the identification of chs. 10–13 with the "severe letter." First, there is the silence of chs. 10–13 concerning the one indisputable fact about the content of the "severe letter" — Paul's demand for the punishment of ὁ ἀδικήσας as an indication of the Corinthians' obedience (2 Cor. 2:5-9). Attempts to meet this objection fail to convince: the demand was found in the lost beginning of the letter[89] (a rather precarious appeal to "the ar-gument from silence"!); when this "tearful letter" was published, the demand was intentionally omitted presumably because the offender was now repentant and had been reinstated in the church or because the matter had already been mentioned as being settled (2:5-11; 7:7-13);[90] 10:1-11 contains Paul's threat to punish any members of the Corinthian congregation who oppose him, so that nothing has been lost from the "severe letter" (except the opening greeting and possibly the ending).[91]

2:4 describes the "severe letter" as "stemming from (ἐκ) much affliction and anguish of heart" and as written "amid (διά) many tears." Is this an appropri-ate description of chs. 10–13 as a whole, with its mixture of vigorous self-defense, "playing the fool," taunting irony, and stern warnings? 12:21 and 13:10 suggest that in Paul's mind funereal mourning (πένθος; cf. πενθήσω, 12:21) that involved anguish and tears would be the consequence of a "tearing down" (καθαίρεσις) in which he had not yet engaged and which he hoped to avoid.

The "severe letter" *replaced* a promised return (= third) visit that would have proved painful (1:15, 23; 2:1), but chs. 10–13 *promise* an imminent third visit that might prove painful (12:14, 21; 13:1-2). Also, chs. 1–9 betray no knowl-edge of a previous and recent encounter between Paul and the group of foreign in-truders at Corinth, but refer only to a single erring member of the church.[92] And

---

87. An alternative explanation is offered by Goudge (xlviii): in "the natural order of the cit-ies of the Empire," irrespective of the place of writing, Rome would always be beyond Corinth, just as Corinth was always beyond Ephesus.

88. Cf. Allo lvii.

89. Plummer mentions this as a possibility ([CGT] xlii; [ICC] xxxiv).

90. Marxsen (80) entertains this latter view as an option.

91. F. Watson 342-46, who observes that the references to τις ("someone") in 10:7 and ὁ τοιοῦτος ("such a person") in 10:11 correspond exactly to τις in 2:5 and τῷ τοιούτῳ in 2:6. For a cri-tique of Watson's defense of the identification of chs. 10–13 with the "severe letter," see Murphy-O'Connor, "Date" 32-38.

92. Cf. Buck 7-8; Munck 171. Anticipating this objection, Bornkamm ("History" 75) pro-poses that by the time Paul wrote the "letter of reconciliation" the wandering prophets either had long since departed from the Corinthian congregation or had lost their sway over the church. See also F. Watson 340-42.

finally, chs. 1–9 lack any description of the church's reaction to Paul's attack against the "false apostles" (11:13-15), although one would expect some account of this matter in 2:3-11 or 7:8-11, where Paul reviews in detail the Corinthian response to his "severe letter."

The Semler hypothesis gained increasing scholarly support as a viable alternative to Hausrath's theory as the twentieth century proceeded. It shares with the Hausrath hypothesis a common foundation of reasons for separating chs. 10–13 from chs. 1–9: the change of tone at 10:1, the possibility of chs. 10–13 jeopardizing both the reconciliation spoken of in the earlier chapters and the success of the collection, the lack in chs. 1–9 of any hint of an imminent visit to Corinth, and the predominance of the first person plural in chs. 1–9 and the first person singular in chs. 10–13. We have seen that this foundation is decidedly insecure. Two arguments given for the superstructure of the Semler hypothesis call for attention.

(a) While we may safely presume that in both sections of 2 Corinthians (chs. 1–9 and 10–13) the interlopers who foment resistance to Paul at Corinth are identical,[93] the anti-Paulinism reflected in chs. 10–13 is so much more pronounced than that in chs. 1–9 that a different *and subsequent* situation in the Corinthian church must be presupposed.[94]

We concur that the opposition to Paul portrayed in chs. 1–9 is more naturally interpreted as a foreshadowing, than as the aftermath, of the anti-Paulinism which gave rise to chs. 10–13. In the first nine chapters of 2 Corinthians, Paul's adversaries are content to make calumnious innuendoes against Paul — his person, status, and activity — through their spokesmen or accomplices at Corinth, without specifically proposing an alternative gospel: their polemic is negative, destructive, and indirect. In chs. 10–13, on the other hand, the opposition to Paul has emerged from the shadows into the full light of day. The adversaries, now termed ψευδαπόστολοι, ἐργάται δόλιοι, and διάκονοι Σατανᾶ (11:13-15) rather than merely ἄπιστοι (4:4), continue their systematic disparagement of Paul but their imperious calumny now involves a brazen calling into question of Paul's apostolic credentials and even personal faith. In the second phase of anti-Paulinism at Corinth, the intruding impostors, having already gained a foothold in the congregation through their introductory letters, themselves resort to the same kind of self-commendation of which they have earlier accused Paul (10:7, 12, 18; 11:15, 18, 21-23) and propose for Corinthian acceptance what Paul describes as an ἄλλος Ἰησοῦς, πνεῦμα ἕτερον, and εὐαγγέλιον ἕτερον (11:4). Paul's calumniators have not only intensified their denigration of the apostle but have also supplemented their negative criticism by positive proposal.

But all that these data demand is the supposition that some unspecified interval of time elapsed between the writing of chs. 1–9 and chs. 10–13 that al-

---

93. Thus Allo lii; Georgi, *Opponents* 229-30 (Georgi is comparing 2:14–7:4 with chs. 10–13); Sumney 181-84; *Servants* 130-31. See further below, A.4.

94. Cf. Furnish 45.

lowed for the deterioration of the situation at Corinth. "A different and subsequent situation" yes, but two distinct letters not necessarily. We shall develop this latter point below (B.3.e.[3]), when we attempt a positive defense of the letter's integrity.

(b) An identical visit of Titus to Corinth is mentioned in 8:17-18, 22 as a future event but in 12:18 as a past event.

The two problems which clamor for a solution in these passages are whether the relevant aorists (ἐξῆλθεν, 8:17; συνεπέμψαμεν, 8:18, 22; παρεκάλεσα, συναπέστειλα, 12:18) are epistolary and whether they refer to the same visit of Titus. Several solutions emerge.

(i) If all four aorists are epistolary, one mission of Titus is referred to — the completion of the collection — but it was still future at the time of writing.[95]

(ii) If the aorists are all regarded as preterit and therefore non-epistolary, once again the visit of Titus mentioned in ch. 12 is not to be distinguished from that of ch. 8. In this case, however, the mission to bring the collection to completion was already in progress when Paul was writing — hence the ἀπέσταλκα of 12:17.[96]

(iii) If in 8:17-18, 22 the aorists are preterit and in 12:18 epistolary, and if chs. 10–13 are part of the "severe letter," then one and the same visit of Titus could be mentioned in chs. 8 and 12, its purpose being to commence, organize, or complete the collection. But if chs. 10–13 were penned at the same time as or after chs. 1–9, the two missions cannot be the same.

(iv) If the aorists of ch. 8 are epistolary and those of ch. 12 preterit, then in chs. 8 Titus's task was to complete the collection at Corinth, but in ch. 12 his mission may have been (a) to initiate the Corinthian contribution (8:6a) when or after 1 Corinthians was delivered,[97] (b) to deliver the "sorrowful letter,"[98] or (c) to complete the collection (8:6b, 10-11, 17-18, 22).[99]

The exit from this maze of conflicting possibilities is marked by two signposts. First, that the aorists of 12:18a are not epistolary seems demonstrated by the subsequent verbs (in 12:18b) in the same tense (ἐπλεονέκτησεν [cf. 12:17b], περιεπατήσαμεν), which could hardly be translated as epistolary or gnomic aorists. Even if the perfect ἀπέσταλκα in 12:17 refers to both past *and* present "sendings" (thus Hughes 468), the four aorists in 12:18 constitute an appeal to past practice: "I urged Titus to visit you, and with him I sent the

---

95. E.g., Menzies 62, 98-99; Duncan 248 n. 1; Tasker 118-20.

96. E.g., Allo 222-28, 328-32, who argues that after ch. 7 had been written the three-man delegation departed for Corinth.

97. E.g., Lietzmann 159; Hughes 466, 468; Thrall 854. The majority of scholars who may be classified under (iv) and who identify chs. 10–13 with the major part of the "severe letter" also adopt this alternative, since 12:18 could not then allude to the future visit of the *(ex hypothesi)* subsequently written 8:17-18 nor could it naturally refer to Titus's visit as the bearer of the "severe letter." See, e.g., Plummer (CGT) 212-13; (ICC) 364-65; Goguel, *Introduction* 67; R. P. C. Hanson 90; F. Watson 332-35; but cf. Kennedy xxix-xxv, 116-20.

98. E.g., Lightfoot 281 and n. 1; Bernard 8-9, 12, 88, 114.

99. E.g., Bruce 168-69, 251; Barrett 325; "Titus" 12; Furnish 38, 559.

brother whom you know. Titus did not exploit you, did he? Did not both of us exhibit the same spirit?" Second, 8:17-18, 22 most naturally refer to an imminent visit to Corinth by three delegates, two of whom are not named because all three would personally deliver the epistle in which they are mentioned as their credentials from Paul. On this the majority of commentators are agreed.

These two observations, if valid, exclude each of the alternatives listed above except (iv), but does 12:18 refer to (a) the initiation of the collection, (b) the delivering of the "severe letter," or (c), as in the Semler hypothesis, the completion of the collection? The difficulty with the third option is that whereas ch. 8 refers to two brothers who accompany Titus (8:18, 22), 12:18 refers to only one. The ἀδελφός of 12:18 is usually equated with the ἀδελφός of 8:22 (e.g., Lietzmann 136, 159) rather than that of 8:18, since the former was Paul's personal envoy (τὸν ἀδελφὸν ἡμῶν) while the latter was the appointed representative of "the churches" (cf. Nickle 17-22). This explains, it is claimed, why 12:18 mentions only one traveling companion of Titus. But the tenuous nature of this reasoning becomes apparent when Stephenson draws attention to the simple τὸν ἀδελφόν in both 12:18 and 8:18 and astutely claims that only the delegate of the *churches* (8:18) could properly witness to Titus's, and therefore Paul's, honesty ("Theories" 641-42, 645). In any case, as Watson observes (333), "both brothers are 'sent' by Paul [8:18, 22], as was the 'brother' of xii. 18, and so neither can be regarded as independent of him." This patent ambiguity of τὸν ἀδελφόν in 12:18, given the certain Corinthian knowledge that two envoys accompanied Titus to complete the collection, leads one to suppose that this verse in fact alludes to Titus's initiation of the collection (8:6a), to his delivery of the "sorrowful letter," *or* to both of these visits. On both occasions Titus and his colleague ("the brother whom you know") were dealing with delicate financial or pastoral matters which might easily have prompted accusations of fraud or exploitation.

We therefore conclude that 8:17-18, 22 and 12:18 are not alluding to an identical visit of Titus to Corinth, so that this second argument in favor of the Semler hypothesis, like the first, is deprived of its validity.

Defenders of the epistle's integrity sometimes bring forward two difficulties with the Hausrath and Semler hypotheses, which in reality are invalid objections.[100]

One alleged problem is that those who embrace a partition theory regarding 2 Corinthians are obliged to reconstruct probable or at least possible historical circumstances in which separate letters (chs. 1–9 and 10–13) might have been combined and to suggest adequate motives for such collation of documents. Two typical reconstructions may be mentioned.

100. It is no argument against the Semler hypothesis that the last glimpse (on this view) of the church at Corinth which Paul bequeathed to posterity (2 Corinthians 10–13) was of a community partially at odds with its founder. The bishop of Rome's remonstrance with the church at Corinth forty years later (*1 Clement,* ca. A.D. 96) shows that the most appealing view of the Corinthians need not be the most accurate one.

Kennedy (153-62) observes that about A.D. 95 the church of Corinth received a letter from Clement of Rome *(1 Clement)* and a visit from representatives of the Roman church, Claudius Ephebus and Valerius Bito, who were to report the outcome of the letter. In *1 Clement* 47:1 the Corinthians are exhorted to "take up the epistle [τὴν ἐπιστολήν, referring to 1 Corinthians] of the blessed apostle Paul." This appeal, Kennedy suggests, may have prompted some member of the Corinthian church to draw the visitors' attention to two mutilated letters from Paul that had never been circulated, the longer manuscript (2 Corinthians 1–9) lacking a conclusion and apostolic signature, the shorter one (chs. 10–13) lacking the traditional initial salutation.[101] These representatives from Rome may then have joined these two mutilated manuscripts together to form a single Pauline letter with the customary beginning and conclusion, the appropriateness of this action being confirmed by the fact that at first glance both parts spoke of the apostle's approaching visit to Corinth. Two copies of the restored letter were made, one for Rome and one for Corinth.[102] Furnish (41) mentions the possibility that because their authority was being threatened (see, e.g., *1 Clement* 3:3; 44:1-6; 47:5-6; 54:1-2), the Corinthian presbyters edited two letters or parts of two letters that existed in the church's archives and that dealt with Paul's response to similar threats so that they might be used in quelling the current insurgency in the church.[103]

In the nature of the case, such conjectures merely indicate that the proposed reconstruction of events is at least not impossible and at most highly probable. Conclusiveness is ruled out, as also should be the rejection of such attempts to re-create the stages by which 2 Corinthians reached publication on the *a priori* ground that all such reconstructions are conjectural.[104]

Another imagined difficulty confronting either form of the "four-chapter hypothesis" is that the textual tradition witnesses unanimously to the integrity of 2 Corinthians. No manuscript or version or patristic citation affords any evidence that 2 Corinthians ever circulated in a form other than the canonical shape in which we know it. Now while it is true that the case for the dissection of the epistle rests upon a subjective assessment of *internal* evidence, this fact, in itself, is no argument in favor of the epistle's integrity, since there are reasons for believing that the *external* evidence of an unambiguous textual tradi-

101. That ancient letters were sometimes preserved without their beginnings or endings is clear (see Vielhauer, *Geschichte* 154-55).

102. Because of its detailed reconstruction of events, Kennedy's thesis has an advantage over the bald suggestion that some editor simply found two separate letters of Paul and removed the end of one and the beginning of the other prior to publication, or, finding one letter incomplete, attached it to a complete Pauline letter through the deletion of either an introduction or a conclusion.

103. For a more complex reconstruction that corresponds to his more complex partition theory, see Bornkamm, *Aufsätze* 179-94; and, more briefly, "History" 77-80.

104. Trobisch has recently argued that Paul himself combined his seven original letters to the Corinthians into our canonical 1 and 2 Corinthians, which, along with Romans 1–15 and Galatians, formed a four-letter "authorized recension" intended for the Ephesian church, with Romans 16 being a covering letter (55-96).

tion is itself inconclusive.[105] (i) The canonical 2 Corinthians need not have circulated in its putative two parts before editorial combination took place; therefore only the autographs of chs. 1–9 and chs. 10–13 need have been originally distinct. (ii) The circumstances of the alleged collation would presumably not become widely known outside Corinth but would rather be rapidly forgotten or immediately ignored even there, since such editorial work was purely scribal (not revisionary) and had been undertaken at the instigation of church leaders. There is accordingly no need to expect that the combination of originally separate letters should be reflected in any manuscript, version, or Father.

(3) 2 Corinthians as a Unity (Traditional Hypothesis)

We have discovered difficulties both with the Hausrath hypothesis (chs. 10–13 precede chs. 1–9 as part of a separate letter) and with the Semler hypothesis (chs. 10–13 follow chs. 1–9 as [part of] a separate letter). This prepares the way for an examination of the hypothesis that chs. 1–13 constitute a single document. Twentieth-century *commentators* who espoused this view[106] include Bernard (1903) 19-28; Lietzmann (1909) 139-40; Bachmann (1909) 3; Menzies (1912) xxxiv-xlii; Goudge (1927) xxxii-lvii; Schlatter (1934) 53-55 (in second ed., 1956); Allo (1936) l-lvi; Tasker (1958) 23-35; Hughes (1962) xxi-xxxv; de Boor (1972) 17, 196-97; Harris (1976) 303-6; Danker (1989) 18-20, 147 (tentatively); Wolff (1989) 1-3; Witherington (1995) 328-39; Belleville (1996) 23-33, 247-50; Kistemaker (1997) 14-15; Barnett (1997) 15-24, 450-56; Scott (1998) 4-7, 200; Lambrecht (1999) 7-9, 158-59; Garland (1999), 33-44; McCant (1999) 20-23, 101-2; and, more recently, Hafemann (2000) 31-33. Other twentieth-century supporters of the integrity of 2 Corinthians include: Jülicher (1900) 96-102; Michaelis (1946) 176-82 (in third ed., 1961); Wikenhauser (1958) 396-98; Munck (1959) 168-71; von Loewenich (1960) 121, 123; Guthrie (1961), *Introduction* 430-37 (in third ed., 1970); Price (1961) 370-72, 385; "Aspects" (1967) 95-106; Kümmel (1963), *Introduction* 287-93 (in second ed., 1975); Stephenson, "Theories" (1964) 639-46; "Integrity" (1965) 82-97; Bates (1965) 56-69; Prümm (1967) 1.404 n. 1, 547-62; Bahr (1968) 37-38; Hyldahl, "Einheit" (1973) 289-306; *Chronologie* 32-42; Dahl (1977) 38-39;[107] Black (1984) 88-91; Childs (1985) 286-89; Segalla (1988) 149-66; "Struttura" 189-218; and, more recently, Goulder, *Mission* (2001) 241-48.

What is of special interest is the recent trend toward defense of the unity of the epistle from the viewpoint of ancient rhetoric. In 1987 F. M. Young (in

---

105. *Pace* Tasker, "Unity" 58: "It is bad scholarship to resort to partition theories in the total absence of external evidence, merely because we do not think it is psychologically probable that St. Paul would have written 2 Co. as it has come down to us."

106. For earlier proponents, see Clemen, *Einheitlichkeit* 19-68.

107. Dahl tends to favor the view that 6:14–7:1 is an interpolated non-Pauline paragraph (64, 69).

Young and Ford) proposed that 2 Corinthians as a whole is a self-consciously conceived apologetic letter in keeping with the rhetorical conventions of the Greco-Roman culture of Paul's time (28, 37-38, 43-44). Chs. 10–13 simply form "the emotional peroration [*peroratio*] recapitulating the proofs and arguments laid out in the body of the epistle" (39; similarly Barnett 18, 452). The dramatic change of tone at 10:1 may be paralleled by a comparable shift in tone from gentle remonstration to passionate appeal in the *Second Epistle* of Demosthenes (37; but see Thrall 11-12 against the relevance of this parallel). Then in 1989 in his commentary on 2 Corinthians and again in a 1991 article ("Debt") F. W. Danker examines rhetorical techniques that are common to 2 Corinthians and Demosthenes' oration and concludes that 2 Corinthians 10–13 "are an appropriate rhetorical climax to Paul's application of the reciprocity paradigm that appears in chs. 1–9" ("Debt" 280). More recently still (1995), B. Witherington maintains that "2 Corinthians taken as a compositional whole is an example of forensic or judicial rhetoric" (333; cf. 28, 41 n. 140), although he views 6:14–7:1 as a deliberative digression and chs. 8–9 as having a deliberative form that subserves the overall forensic purpose (28). In his defense of the letter's unity, he accounts for the shift in tone at 10:1 by Paul's change of approach to "counterattack by means of a rhetorical *synkrisis,* and this will include *pathos,* an appeal to the stronger emotions" (338). The parallel Witherington finds convincing is the alteration of syntax, style, and pathos evident in Galatians 5–6 in comparison with Galatians 1–4 (338 n. 32). Finally, in 1999 D. A. Hester (411-32) and in 2000 J. D. H. Amador (92-111) sought to demonstrate the complex integrity of 2 Corinthians by appealing to rhetorical considerations. For comments on the rhetorical analysis of 2 Corinthians, see D.1. below.

In the light of all these recent developments, Betz's comment, made in 1992 or before ("Corinthians" 1149), that "few scholars continue to defend the unity of 2 Corinthians" certainly now needs modification, as does Martin's claim, made in 2000 ("Theology" 66), that the view that chs. 10–13 form a letter subsequent to chs. 1–7 (with or without 6:14–7:1 and chs. 8 and 9) represents "the emerging consensus."

Many of the objections to the unity of 2 Corinthians have been discussed — and found to be either inconclusive or insubstantial — in our treatment of alternative solutions to the integrity of 2 Corinthians. As we sought to answer these objections, we discovered that plausible reasons may be suggested for the notable alteration of mood at 10:1, that dramatic shifts in mood are found elsewhere in Paul's epistles, that chs. 10–13 are not unalleviated invective, that the higher incidence of first person plurals in these chapters may be explained by their intensely personal and distinctively individual nature, that if an interval is assumed between the writing of chs. 1–9 and chs. 10–13 during which news reached Paul of further challenges to his authority at Corinth, the more pronounced anti-Paulinism reflected in 10–13 is explicable, that 12:18a may as easily allude to 8:6a or to Titus's delivery of the "severe letter" as to 8:17-18,

22. We also saw that the close verbal parallelism between certain passages in chs. 10–13 and others in chs. 1–9 is as readily explicable on the hypothesis of the unity of 2 Corinthians as on the hypothesis of the priority of chs. 10–13 over chs. 1–9.

Attention may now be given to four *additional* considerations that support the traditional view.

(a) The whole letter is concerned with Paul's visits to Corinth — actual visits, planned visits not carried out as planned, and an imminent visit. Eleven of the sixteen uses of ἔρχομαι in 2 Corinthians relate to these visits,[108] as do all five uses of πάρειμι.

Visit	Route	ἔρχομαι	πάρειμι
1. Actual: founding/ evangelistic	Athens–Corinth (Acts 18:1-18)	(1 Cor. 2:1)	11:9
2. Planned, but not carried out	Ephesus–Macedonia– Corinth (plan A)	(1 Cor. 16:2, 5)	
3. Actual: "painful"/ brief/intermediate	Ephesus–Corinth– Ephesus (cf. Acts 19:11)	2:1; 12:21	13:2
4. Planned, but not carried out	Corinth–Macedonia– Corinth (plan B)	1:15, 16, 23; 2:3	
5. Imminent: collec- tion/final	Macedonia–Corinth (Acts 20:2-3)	9:3-5; 12:14, 20, 21; 13:1, 2	10:2, 11; 13:10

When Paul wrote 2 Corinthians, he had already visited Corinth twice, and on two other occasions his plans to travel to Corinth had been altered. But the majority of his references to visiting Corinth relate to his forthcoming visit (5. in the chart above).

All of the content of the letter can be related to a single, coordinating purpose in writing — to prepare for this imminent visit by seeking to remove present or potential obstacles that could prevent the visit from being pleasant,[109] specifically

---

108. Of the other five uses of ἔρχομαι, two relate to Paul's travel elsewhere (2:12; 7:5), two relate to the coming of other persons to Corinth (11:4, 9), and one is metaphorical (12:1).

109. With this compare the similar observation of Prat (1.499; cf. 1.144 and Scott 5): "The unity of the Epistle is seen in the plan pursued by the Apostle — to prepare for his arrival in Corinth by removing the difficulties which prevent his immediate return. These obstacles are of three kinds — *the doubtful feelings* of the Corinthians towards him, *the affair of the collection,* still in suspense, *the actions of his enemies.*" In his article, "Visit Talk in New Testament Letters," Mullins argues (against Funk, "Parousia") that references to visits in Paul's letters constitute a theme rather than adhering to a formal structure ("Visit Talk" 350-54).

by informing the Corinthians of Paul's recent encounter with death and experience of God's comfort and then soliciting their prayer for his future deliverance (1:3-11),

by reviewing and explaining his recent conduct as a traveling pastor against the accusations of his Corinthian detractors, in particular encouraging the reinstatement of the penitent wrongdoer and expressing his consummate relief and delight at the Corinthians' positive response to his "severe letter" (1:12–2:13; 7:5-16),

by describing the true nature and high calling of the apostolic ministry (2:14–6:13; 7:2-4) and insisting on the Corinthian Christians' separation from all idolatrous associations (6:14–7:1),

by encouraging their completion of their promised contribution to "the collection for the poor" prior to his arrival in Corinth (8:1–9:15),[110]

by defending his apostolic authority against the claims of rival apostles at Corinth (10:1–12:13), and

by emphasizing their need for self-examination, repentance, and mending their ways (12:14–13:10).

What Paul regarded as obstacles to an enjoyable visit that would bring mutual spiritual refreshment (cf. 7:13b; Rom. 15:32) is reflected in his use of (φοβοῦμαι) μή πως and ἵνα μή. He was concerned "lest" his repeated and confident boast to the Macedonians about the Corinthians' "eagerness to help" and their expected "readiness" on his arrival should prove hollow (9:2-3, ἵνα μή). He was apprehensive that both he and the Corinthians would be embarrassed before the Macedonian visitors if they failed to revive the flagging "collection for the poor" before his arrival with the delegates (9:4, μή πως). He was fearful that the Corinthians might deviate in their thoughts from a single-hearted and untainted fidelity to Christ (11:3, φοβοῦμαι . . . μή πως). Also, he was afraid that there would be mutual disappointed hopes on his arrival at Corinth, that he would find sins of attitude and tongue, along with general disorder and disharmony, that God had renewed humiliation in store for him in his dealings with the Corinthians, and that he would have to mourn over the failure of many Corinthians to repent of their persistent sensuality (12:20-21, φοβοῦμαι . . . μή πως . . . μή πως . . . μή . . .). Finally he wished to avoid having to act severely in the exercise of his apostolic authority (13:10, ἵνα . . . μή).

It is our contention that this consonance in *all* the content of the letter and a *single,* unifying purpose argues for the unity of the letter. There is, of course, the danger here of circular reasoning, for the purpose of the letter may be deduced only from its content.

---

110. Since 9:4 specifically links the collection with his promised visit, it is unnecessary to assert with Price (*New Testament* 385) that "after writing his counsel concerning the offering, Paul's thoughts *reverted* to his chief purpose of the letter, the preparation of the church for a third visit" (italics added).

45

(b) This leads to a second argument in favor of the integrity of 2 Corinthians — its unified character as an *apologia*. It is such a time-honored tradition among commentators to stress the diversity of theme in 2 Corinthians by characterizing chs. 1–7 as apologetic, chs. 8–9 as hortatory, and chs. 10–13 as polemical[111] that it is easy to overlook the facts that (i) all three elements are present in each section of the letter, and (ii) basically the whole letter forms an *apologia*.

(i) The chart that follows demonstrates the presence of apology, exhortation, and polemic in each of the three sections of the letter.[112]

	1-7	8-9	10–13
Apologetic	*passim,* especially 1:12–2:4; 3:7-18; 4:7-15; 5:11-13; 6:3-10; 7:2, 8-9	8:1-5, 13-15; 9:1-2, 6, 8-14	10:3-4, 7-10, 13-18; 11:1-2, 5-12, 16-21a; 11:30–12:19; 13:6
Hortatory	1:11; 2:7-9; 6:1-2, 13-14, 17; 7:1-2a	*passim,* especially 8:7-8, 10-11, 24; 9:3-5, 7	10:1-2; 11:3; 13:5, 7, 9-12
Polemical	2:17; 3:1-6; 4:2; 5:12-13; 6:14-16a	8:20-21	*passim,* especially 10:5-6, 11-12; 11:4, 13-15, 21b-27; 12:20-21; 13:1-4

(ii) A wide range of interpreters recognize that 2 Corinthians as a whole is essentially an *apologia*,[113] a defense of the apostolic and pastoral ministry in general and of Paul's apostolic authority in particular. Typical stylistic features of a substantial apologetic letter of a religious nature are present throughout 2 Corinthians:[114]

111. E.g., Prat 1.500-504.

112. Jülicher (88) comments that "apart from its [hortatory] business discussions it [2 Corinthians] is entirely occupied with self-defense and controversy." Regarding 2:14–3:6, Lambrecht observes that "the tone of the passage is at the same time apologetic (an apology directed towards the Corinthian Christians) and polemic (a counter-attack against the intruders and opponents)" ("Structure" 347). Or again, Dahl avers that 6:14–7:1 anticipates chs. 10–13 (*Studies* 68-69).

113. E.g., "a defense of his apostolate" (Cambier 436), "a vindication of his apostleship" (Hughes 2), "an *apologia in absentia* for Paul's style of mission" (Young and Ford 27; cf. 44). It is interesting that in his analysis of 2 Corinthians Martin, who holds that chs. 10–13 are a letter written after 1–9, describes 2:14–7:4 as "First defense of the apostolic ministry" and 10:1–13:10 as "Polemical argument and defense" (xxxvi).

114. The letter of apology is eighteenth among the twenty-one "Epistolary Types" (τύποι ἐπιστολικοί) listed in a work of that name attributed to Demetrius of Phalerum. See further Malherbe, *Ancient Epistolary Theorists*. In speaking of 2 Corinthians as an "apologetic letter," I am not suggesting that Paul is consciously following contemporary rhetorical conventions (*pace*

rhetorical questions that appeal to logic (2:2; 3:8; 12:15), experience (1:17 twice; 11:7, 11, 22 three times, 23, 29 twice; 12:13, 17, 18 three times; 13:5c), common sense (3:1 twice; 12:19), conscience (11:7; cf. 4:2; 5:11), and spiritual awareness (2:16; 6:14 twice, 15 twice, 16; 13:5),

exclamatory statements (3:9, 11; 4:12; 5:17; 6:13; 7:11; 9:15; 10:1; 11:4, 11, 19, 21; 12:11, 13c, 16b; 13:5d), and

invocation of or appeal to God or Christ as witness to Paul's integrity or honesty or to the truth of an affirmation (1:18, 23; 2:17; 11:10-11, 31; 12:19).

It requires no demonstration that chs. 1–7 are primarily apologetic in thrust; there is scholarly unanimity on this point. Chs. 8–9 are not merely Paul's exhortation to complete the collection but also an apology for his appeal to the Corinthians to give generously (8:1-5, 13-15; 9:1-2, 6, 8-14). Then, given the fact that the remonstrance of chs. 10–13 is tempered by irony, parody, and mischievous teasing, the polemic of these chapters can also be viewed as apology, especially since in dealing with theological opponents, as in military strategy, attack is often the best form of defense. Not infrequently, therefore, it is difficult to decide whether certain passages are offensive or defensive; in addition, polemic may take the form of self-vindication (e.g., 10:8). And toward the end of his "polemic" Paul asks in 12:19, "Have you been thinking all this time that we are defending ourselves (ἀπολογούμεθα) before you?" Although the adverb πάλαι ("all along") in this verse need not refer to more than 10:1–12:18, it may well allude in general terms to everything that has been said from 1:1 onward, since 1:12–2:13 constitutes a prolonged defense of Paul's recent conduct (see the outline of the letter in the Table of Contents above). We suggest that what Paul wrote in 1 Cor. 9:3 about his defense of his apostolic rights in vv. 4-12a could equally well be applied to 2 Corinthians as a whole: ἡ ἐμὴ ἀπολογία τοῖς ἐμὲ ἀνακρίνουσίν ἐστιν αὕτη, "This is my defense against those who question me (= my authority)."

(c) Several expressions in chs. 10–13 presuppose comparable statements in chs. 1–9 or derive their relevance and potency from being verbal echoes of passages in chs. 1–9.

11:15	3:9
διάκονοι δικαιοσύνης	ἡ διακονία τῆς δικαιοσύνης

One of Paul's accusations against his opponents is that they masquerade as "ministers of righteousness" (11:15). This distinctive phrase, a *hapax legomenon* in the Greek Bible, would have become luminous for the Corinthians only when they recalled that Paul had already described the new covenant

Barnett 17-18) so that we may clearly identify within 2 Corinthians an introduction *(exordium)*, a statement of facts *(narratio)*, a proof *(probatio)*, and a conclusion *(peroratio)*. See below, D.1.

and its gospel as "the ministry of righteousness," "the administration that brings righteousness."

12:19   2:17

κατέναντι θεοῦ ἐν Χριστῷ λαλοῦμεν = κατέναντι θεοῦ ἐν Χριστῷ λαλοῦμεν

There are no other instances of this stylized phrase in the Pauline corpus (although κατέναντι is used in Rom. 4:17). In each use in 2 Corinthians Paul is appealing to the fact of his divine dependence and responsibility ("we speak before God") and his divine authority and power ("we speak in Christ"). Witherington believes that the close connection between these two verses "argues for the unity of the discourse" (335 n. 27).

10:2   1:17

. . . τολμῆσαι ἐπί τινας τοὺς   ἃ βουλεύομαι *κατὰ σάρκα*

λογιζομένους ἡμᾶς ὡς *κατὰ σάρκα*   βουλεύομαι;

περιπατοῦντας (similarly 10:3)

Behind these two instances of Paul's remonstrance is the same accusation, namely that he was acting "from worldly motives" (κατὰ σάρκα) or "merely as a worldling."

12:14   6:13

οὐ γὰρ ζητῶ τὰ ὑμῶν ἀλλὰ ὑμᾶς,   ὡς *τέκνοις* λέγω

οὐ γὰρ ὀφείλει *τὰ τέκνα* τοῖς

γονεῦσιν θησαυρίζειν, ἀλλὰ οἱ

γονεῖς *τοῖς τέκνοις*

Having reminded the Corinthians of his father-children relationship to them (6:13), Paul can refer to the obligations of parenthood (12:14).

12:11   3:2

ἐγὼ γὰρ ὤφειλον ὑφ' ὑμῶν   ἡ [*συστατικὴ*] ἐπιστολὴ ἡμῶν ὑμεῖς

συνίστασθαι   ἐστε (cf. 3:1)

One compelling reason that Paul ought to have been commended by the Corinthians (12:11) was that they themselves were his letter of commendation (3:2).

12:16   4:2

ὑπάρχων *πανοῦργος δόλῳ* ὑμᾶς ἔλαβον   μὴ περιπατοῦντες ἐν *πανουργίᾳ* μηδὲ

                                 δολοῦντες τὸν λόγον τοῦ θεοῦ

Both passages reflect an identical charge leveled against Paul by his opponents, namely that he was "a crafty fellow" (πανοῦργος) guilty of dishonest manipulation (δόλος) by peddling the word of God for monetary gain (cf. 2:17).

One could argue that these correspondences indicate only that chs. 10–13

48

were written after chs. 1–9 and that they do not necessarily support the integrity of the letter. But it is the *ex hypothesi* recentness of the earlier statements that makes the verbal echoes precise and potent. If the Corinthians had received chs. 1–9 and 10–13 as separate letters, the likelihood that chs. 10–13 contains intended verbal allusions to chs. 1–9 is slender, for the readers or hearers would have been unlikely to recognize such allusions, given the passage of time. On the other hand, if 2 Corinthians was received in the form in which we now have it, with chs. 1–9 and 10–13 together, Paul might well have indulged in verbal reminiscences to reinforce points he was making in chs. 10–13.[115]

(d) Our fourth and final consideration is this. The fewer the unprovable assumptions that a hypothesis makes or requires, the stronger that hypothesis. The view that 2 Corinthians is a unity does not need to assume, as do the Hausrath and Semler hypotheses,

> that two independent Pauline letters to Corinth (chs. 1–9, chs. 10–13) were preserved,
>
> that at some date between A.D. 90 and 96 (the probable period of the formation and publication of the Pauline corpus), some redactor who had access to these two separate letters decided, for reasons that we can only surmise, to issue them in Paul's name as a single letter,[116]
>
> that *either* the end of chs. 1–9 and the beginning of chs. 10–13 had been mutilated, *or* the editor excised the customary Pauline greetings and benediction at the end of chs. 1–9 along with the customary apostolic salutation at the beginning of chs. 10–13, *or* there was some mutilation and some editorial work to produce our chs. 1–13,[117] and

115. Examples of close linguistic or thematic continuity between chs. 1–9 and chs. 10–13 such as those noted by Barnett (19-21, 451) and Garland (44, 419-20) may strongly suggest the unity of the letter, but they are far from conclusive evidence. The same must be said of Segalla's comprehensive and creative work in this area. Arguing that the historical-critical method must be supplemented and checked by a linguistic-structural approach to texts, Segalla mounts a two-pronged defense of the unity of 2 Corinthians (149-66 and "Struttura"). First, he isolates fifteen terms or expressions that are common to chs. 1–9 and 10–13 and groups them under three headings: references to Paul's opponents (τις, τινές, e.g., 3:1 and 10:2; [οἱ] πολλοί, 2:17 and 11:18), expressions of confidence regarding the Corinthian community (θαρρέω, e.g., 7:16 and 10:2; καυχ-words, e.g., 7:14 and 10:8; πεποίθησις, e.g., 3:4 and 10:2; περισσ- root, e.g., 1:12 and 10:15), and apologetic language (ἀλήθεια, e.g., 4:2 and 13:8; ἀπολογία, 7:11 and cf. 12:19; διακον- words, e.g., 3:6 and 11:23; δοκιμ- words, 2:9 and 13:3; κατὰ σάρκα, e.g., 1:17 and 11:18; κόπος, e.g., 6:5 and 11:27; πλεονεκτέω, e.g., 2:11 and 12:18; συνιστάνω, e.g., 4:2 and 10:12; φείδομαι, e.g., 1:23 and 13:2). Second, he analyzes the literary structure of the whole letter and finds a chiastic pattern (see below, D.2.). Segalla's linguistic argument is powerful in its own right and is not materially strengthened by this additional appeal to a purported chiastic structure.

116. But for Trobisch's view, see above n. 104.

117. G. A. Kennedy suggests that when other churches requested copies of Paul's letters to the Corinthians (which were probably kept together in a papyrus roll box), the material now found in 2 Corinthians was copied on to a single papyrus with the end of chs. 1–7, the salutation and end of chs. 8–9, and the salutation of chs. 10–13 omitted (*Interpretation* 92).

that the letter known to us as 2 Corinthians was issued for wider circulation precisely in the form in which we know it, which would explain the absence of any textual evidence witnessing to this editorial process.

If, then, the cumulative effect of these observations is to render probable the unity of 2 Corinthians, are we obliged to maintain that the letter was written on a single occasion, at one sitting? Not at all. We need hold only that the work was regarded by its author as a single composition and was dispatched to its addressees as a single missive.[118] Indeed, given the unpredictable yet relentless demands and pressures of Paul's pastoral ministry (2 Cor. 11:28), it is antecedently probable that each of Paul's letters, apart from Philemon, was written over a considerable period of time, perhaps days or even weeks or months, and was then sent to the addressees when weather permitted travel and a trusted deputy was available to deliver it and, if necessary, to explain and reinforce its contents, and perhaps to report back to Paul on the church's reaction. With regard to all the longer letters, we should not think merely of dictation pauses[119] — which Betz (31) has dubbed "the cure-all of traditionalists" — but also of stages of composition. In an illuminating discussion of the circumstances surrounding the writing and sending of Paul's letters, Ramsay proposed that "considerable intervals elapsed between the composition of the parts" of 2 Corinthians, "intervals of thought and meditation."[120] In a similar vein, Rackham (371) observes that our epistle "seems to have been written from time to time, like a diary," while H. C. G. Moule (xix, xxviii) makes the specific suggestion that Paul composed 2 Corinthians in sections, beginning the letter at Philippi and continuing it as he traveled to Thessalonica.

It is certainly tempting to associate the three sections of 2 Corinthians with three distinct times and places. Chs. 1–7 might have been written in Philippi, shortly after Titus's arrival from Troas (summer A.D. 56; cf. 2:12-13; 7:5-6), chs. 8–9 while Paul was traveling west along the Egnatian Way and organizing the collection (late the same summer; note present tense καυχῶμαι and the general term Μακεδόσιν [as distinct from Φιλιππησίοις] in 9:2; cf. 8:1), and chs. 10–13 from Berea shortly before his projected visit to Corinth (fall 56). But such reconstructions are purely hypothetical, although καυχῶμαι Μακεδό-

118. What this view and the "four-chapter" hypothesis of Semler have in common is the conviction that chs. 10–13 were written at an interval of indeterminate length after chs. 1–9. (Bruce, for example, speaks of "a few weeks," 172.) Where they differ is that the integrity hypothesis alleges that these two sections were sent at the same time as part of a single letter. Danker, too, believes that it is probable that chs. 10–13 were written after fresh news about Corinth had reached Paul and that 2 Corinthians in its present canonical form was not written at one sitting (17-18, 147), but he suggests that the "overall argumentative consistency" of the letter may be ultimately traced to the work of later editors (19; cf. 147).

119. See Stange 109-17, especially 113; Michaelis (1946 edition) 178-79.

120. "Corinthians" 220 and n. 1; similarly Allo 223; Price 385.

50

σιν in 9:2 is significant. What remains perfectly feasible is that, though sent as a single letter, 2 Corinthians was composed in stages, not at a single sitting.[121]

Our overall conclusion is that with respect to the three principal hypotheses concerning the relation of chs. 10–13 to chs. 1–9, there are fewer difficulties with the hypothesis of the letter's integrity than with either the Hausrath or the Semler hypothesis. But with this said, the caveat entered by Moffatt remains valid: "On any hypothesis there is a residuum of obscurity owing to the extremely intricate and subtle character of the relations between Paul and the Corinthian church" (*Introduction* 123).

4. The Occasion, Purpose, and Outcome of 2 Corinthians

The chronology of Paul's relations with the Corinthian church outlined below (Introduction, C.) suggests that the circumstances prompting Paul to send 2 Corinthians were twofold: the arrival of his pastoral assistant Titus, who brought welcome news of the favorable response of the majority of the Corinthians to the "severe letter" (7:6-16), and the arrival of fresh, disturbing news concerning Corinth. A considerable interval between the arrival of Titus and the sending of 2 Corinthians seems indicated by 7:8 (see the commentary there).

Any treatment of the purpose of 2 Corinthians must presuppose some solution to the issue of the integrity of the letter. Here the assumption is that although the canonical letter was composed in stages, it was regarded by Paul as a single piece of correspondence and was sent to the believers in Corinth as a single composition.

In 12:19 Paul states "Everything (τὰ . . . πάντα), dear friends, is for your upbuilding (ὑπὲρ τῆς ὑμῶν οἰκοδομῆς)." The "everything" includes all that Paul said and did in his relationship with the Corinthians, but the primary reference is to all he was writing in the present letter. ὑπέρ here means "with a view to achieving," so we may deduce that the apostle's *general purpose* in writing was to promote his converts' οἰκοδομή (cf. 10:8; 13:10), that is, to strengthen and stabilize their individual and corporate faith and to promote their advance and maturation in the Christian life. This deduction is supported by Paul's statement in 13:9 that he was praying for their "restoration" (κατάρτισις), their return to proper relations with God, with himself, and with one another, which all are aspects of their progress in appropriate Christian living (οἰκοδομή). Such a prayer presumably corresponds to his aim in writing. Similarly, his prayer-report in

---

121. Similarly, one may surmise that there were three stages in the composition of 1 Corinthians. Chs. 1–4 express Paul's reaction to an oral report from members of Chloe's household (1 Cor. 1:11) regarding bickering, cliques, and the partisan spirit in the Corinthian church. Chs. 5–6 contain Paul's reaction to an oral report given by the church's representatives Stephanas, Fortunatus, and Achaicus (1 Cor. 16:17) regarding immorality and lawsuits among church members. Finally, in chs. 7–16 we have Paul's replies to questions contained in a letter from the church at Corinth brought by these three men.

13:7 must reflect his purpose: he was asking God that they would reject all wrongdoing (κακόν) and espouse right conduct (τὸ καλόν).

If the letter was written in stages during Paul's ministry in Macedonia (see above, A.3.e.[3]), it is not surprising that the three main divisions of the canonical letter (chs. 1–7, 8–9, and 10–13) should have different although complementary *specific purposes.* In chs. 1–7 Paul seeks to express his great relief and delight at the Corinthians' positive response to his "severe letter," which had been delivered and reinforced by Titus (2:6, 9, 12-14; 7:5-16). In chs. 8–9 he aims to exhort the Corinthians to complete their promised collection for the saints at Jerusalem before his arrival on the next visit (8:6-7, 10-11; 9:3-5). Finally, in the last four chapters (10–13) his intent is (a) to help them recognize the proper criteria for distinguishing among rival apostles (10:1-5, 7, 12-18; 11:7-15, 22-30; 12:6, 9-10, 12, 14-15; 13:3-4, 10) and thus become convinced of the genuineness of his own apostleship (10:7-8, 14-15; 11:2, 5-6; 12:11-12; 13:6-7, 10) and (b) to encourage then to engage in self-examination with a view to mending their ways (12:2-21; 13:2, 5, 7, 9, 11). In a nutshell he is saying first "I rejoice over you and have complete confidence in you" (cf. 7:4, 16), then "I urge you to finish what you have commendably begun" (cf. 8:10-11), and lastly "I am about to come, so get ready" (cf. 12:14; 13:1, 11). Each major section of the letter prepares for the next. Once Paul had reestablished a favorable relationship with his converts (reflected in chs. 1–7), he could confidently appeal to them to complete the collection project before his arrival (chs. 8–9). Then, having mentioned his coming (in 9:4), he could announce its imminence and indicate how they should prepare for it (chs. 10–13).

In addition to the three primary specific purposes outlined above, we may infer several secondary specific purposes. Paul wanted

> to inform the Corinthians of the severity of his affliction in Asia and solicit their prayer for future deliverance from similar trouble (1:8-11),
>
> to answer the charge that he had acted insincerely, and with disregard for promises made, in altering his travel plans (1:12–2:4),
>
> to encourage them to end the punishment of the repentant wrongdoer and reaffirm their love for him (2:5-11),
>
> to describe the true nature and high calling of the Christian ministry (2:14–7:4),
>
> to have the Corinthians renew their pride in him (1:14, 5:12) and reciprocate his warm love for them (2:4; 6:11-13; 11:11; 12:15), and
>
> to highlight their need to make a decisive break with all idolatrous associations and pursue personal holiness (6:14–7:1).

These specific purposes in writing, whether regarded as primary or secondary in significance, all serve, we suggest, one overriding purpose. Paul is seeking to prepare the way for an enjoyable third visit to Corinth by removing any obstacles that might prevent that visit from being pleasing and beneficial to all. That Paul always hoped his visits to his converts would be free of distress, enjoyable, and mutually beneficial is clear from 2:3 and Rom. 1:11-12. How all the material in the letter relates to this single purpose has been shown above (in the discussion of the unity of the letter, A.3.e.[4]). For their part, if the Corinthians engaged in self-examination that led to repentance (6:14–7:1; 12:20-21; 13:2, 5), Paul would be spared the pain of having to exercise discipline (13:2, 7, 9-10) and suffer another "painful visit" like his second visit (2:1). If, by the time he arrived in Corinth, they had finally repudiated the rival apostles, had fully endorsed their apostle and his gospel, and had completed their offering for Jerusalem with generous gifts, the reunion would be pleasurable and free of embarrassment. Paul's wish was that the wholehearted welcome the Corinthians had accorded Titus on his visit with the "severe letter" should now also be given to the apostle himself on his forthcoming visit. Titus had been greatly relieved and refreshed in spirit by the welcome they had all given him (7:13). They all had shown him ready obedience in receiving him with fear and trembling, knowing they were accountable to God for their conduct (7:15). If Paul was accepted in a similar way, the visit would prove peaceful, joyful, and profitable for one and all.

This overarching specific purpose is wholly compatible with the general purpose suggested above. If the letter sought to pave the way for a trouble-free and mutually advantageous visit, that visit, if successful, would promote the Corinthians' upbuilding as their Christian life was enriched.

In this matter of purpose and how it was achieved, there is a remarkable similarity between 2 Corinthians and Romans, a letter written about four or five months later (early A.D. 57). Paul sent both letters to prepare Christians for a forthcoming visit (2 Cor. 9:4; 10:2; 12:14, 20-21; 13:1-2, 10; Rom. 1:10-13, 15; 15:22-24, 28-29, 32). In each case the principal ingredient in that preparation is an *apologia* — in 2 Corinthians, an *apologia* for his apostolic conduct and ministry (chs. 1–7) and his apostolic authority (chs. 10–13); in Romans, an *apologia* for his gospel (1:16b–15:13). Such a defense served to remove possible obstacles to an enjoyable visit (see A.3.e.[3] above for 2 Corinthians; Rom. 15:24b, 32).[122]

Was 2 Corinthians successful where 1 Corinthians had been only partially so? Apparently it was, because Paul made the promised visit (Acts 20:2-3) and during this three-month stay in "Greece" (primarily Corinth, in the winter of 56-57) he wrote or completed his letter to the Romans. This letter seems to betray some apprehension for the future (15:30-31) but none for the present, and Paul would hardly have contemplated implementing his long-standing desire to visit Rome (Rom. 1:10-11, 13, 15; 15:22-24, 28-29, 32; cf. Acts 19:21) and to prosecute pioneer evangelism in the west (Rom. 15:20-21, 23-24, 28) if the congregation in the city from which he was writing was not

122. Cranfield suggests that one aim of Paul's apology in Rom. 1:16b–15:13 was "clearing away some misunderstandings and suspicions against himself among the Jewish Christians in Rome" (818; cf. 823 n. 3). There are, of course, many differences between the two apologies, one of the most important that Paul had already visited Corinth and so was personally known to the recipients of this *apologia*.

only harboring his opponents but was also so opposed to him (2 Cor. 11:4, 20) that they were actually being seduced from a sincere and pure devotion to Christ (cf. 11:3). Also, the use of ηὐδόκησαν in Rom. 15:26-27 with reference to the spirit which prevailed among the Corinthians (and their neighbors [= Ἀχαΐα; cf. 2 Cor. 1:1; 9:2; 10:11] together with the Macedonians) in making their contribution to the collection would scarcely have been appropriate unless the church in Corinth were in harmony with the promoter of that collection. Moreover, the very preservation of 2 Corinthians is evidence that Paul's contest with his adversaries turned out successfully (cf. Windisch 432). But it is sadly true that when Clement of Rome wrote to the church at Corinth in 96 he had to rebuke the same internal strife (*1 Clement* 46:5-7; 47:3-4) and rebellion against authority (44:3, 6; 54:1-2; 57:2) that had plagued the church forty years earlier.

B. HISTORICAL ISSUES

1. The "Painful Visit"

a. Its Historicity

Although the historicity of a visit by Paul to Corinth between his founding visit (Acts 18:1-17) and the visit recorded in Acts 20:2-3 has sometimes been challenged — often on the ground of the ambiguity of the evidence and the silence of Acts[123] — there are at least three reasons why an "intermediate visit" which was unpleasant for both the visitor and those visited should be postulated.

(1) There is the "antecedent probability" that during his three-year residence in Ephesus (Acts 20:18, 31) Paul undertook the one-week voyage from Ephesus to Corinth in order to revisit the Corinthian church.[124]

(2) There are three references in 2 Corinthians which are most naturally understood as referring to two actual visits prior to the composition of this letter:

(a) Ἰδοὺ τρίτον τοῦτο ἑτοίμως ἔχω ἐλθεῖν πρὸς ὑμᾶς (12:14)
(b) Τρίτον τοῦτο ἔρχομαι πρὸς ὑμᾶς (13:1)
(c) Προείρηκα καὶ προλέγω, ὡς παρὼν τὸ δεύτερον καὶ ἀπὼν νῦν, τοῖς προημαρτηκόσιν καὶ τοῖς λοιποῖς πᾶσιν, ὅτι ἐὰν ἔλθω εἰς τὸ πάλιν οὐ φείσομαι (13:2)

While all agree that the third anticipated visit is a personal visit, there is disagreement as to the nature of these two previous "comings," whether Paul

123. E.g., Heinrici 7-9, 44-45, 382-83, 390, 393-94, 396-97; White, "Visits" 79-89; Dockx 191-93; Hyldahl 102-6, 121-22; "Einheit" 299-306.
124. Robertson and Plummer xxii. The probability that the "sorrowful visit" was unpremeditated need not detract from this argument: the likelihood of a visit, not its timing, is the point being made.

speaks of coming in person or by letter or planning to come but not carrying out that plan. They could be reckoned as

> two "epistolary" comings (previous letter and 1 Corinthians, or 1 Corinthians and 2 Corinthians 1–9),
> one personal and one "epistolary" visit (Acts 18:1 and 1 Corinthians),
> a *willingness* to come on two previous occasions,
> two earlier *intentions* or *decisions* to come which were never fulfilled,
> *preparations* made on two previous occasions for visits which did not eventuate,
> one actual and one intended visit (Acts 18:1 and 2 Cor. 1:15-16, 23) (Dockx 193), or
> two previous actual visits (Acts 18:1 and the painful visit).[125]

Although some slight textual and grammatical ambiguities exist in 12:14 and 13:1,[126] all contextual considerations favor the last proposal, that these verses refer to two actual visits by Paul to Corinth. It would have been inept for Paul to reckon one or two letters as visits when his imminent third visit was decidedly personal.[127] Moreover, the sense of ἑτοίμως ἔχω ἐλθεῖν πρὸς ὑμᾶς in 12:14 is shown by the futuristic present ἔρχομαι in 13:1 to be "I am about to come to you (this third time)," rather than simply "I am now ready and willing (as on two previous occasions) to come to you": a definite visit, not the mere willingness or preparation for a visit, is in mind. In any case, in one instance at least (Acts 18:1) Paul's decision and preparation had actually issued in a visit. If Paul had actually visited only once and had merely intended or prepared to visit on another occasion, he would have said "I am ready to visit you for the second time (δεύτερον τοῦτο)." And for Paul to have appealed to his intentions, willingness, or preparations to come to the Corinthians, which had failed to result in a visit, would have been to lay himself open to a just charge of fickleness (cf. ἐλαφρία, 2 Cor. 1:17; see Windisch 398-99). As Strachan (64) expresses the point: Paul was "surely too experienced an apologist to bring forward such a weak argument as that he had three times made up his mind to come, had changed it twice, and now threatened actually to arrive." See further the commentary at 12:14.

125. Gilchrist identifies the two visits as the "painful visit" and a visit between the writing of chs. 1–9 and chs. 10–13 (47, 52-53, 63-64).

126. In 12:14 the omission of τοῦτο after τρίτον (K L P 614 629 945 1241 *pm* b) or the reversal of their order to conform with the usual practice (D E cop arm) does not alter the sense. In 13:1, ℵ³ A it eth Augustine introduce ἰδού from 12:14, while ἑτοίμως ἔχω ἐλθεῖν is the reading of A vg^ms. τρίτον τοῦτο in 12:14 may be construed either with ἑτοίμως ἔχω or with ἐλθεῖν; the word order does not prejudice the second alternative (cf. Acts 21:13).

127. Such confusion of the "epistolary visits" with personal visits involves White ("Visits") in an unresolved dilemma: if the first visit is Acts 18:1 (87), and the second 2 Corinthians (89), why is 1 Corinthians (or the "previous letter") not reckoned by Paul as constituting a visit?

In the complex sentence in 13:2 Paul reiterates (καὶ προλέγω . . . ἀπὼν νῦν) a warning (ὅτι κτλ.) he had already given (προείρηκα) to two parties (τοῖς προημαρτηκόσιν καὶ τοῖς λοιποῖς πᾶσιν) when he was present on a second visit. In the key phrase, ὡς παρὼν τὸ δεύτερον, the conjunction ὡς should be rendered "as" (anticipating its correlative καί [= οὕτως]), not "as if" [= καίπερ]). The translation "as if I were present a second time, although I am now absent" (cf. KJV, RV^mg) fails to reflect the symmetry of the sentence, overlooks the temporal sense of ὡς παρὼν . . . καὶ ἀπὼν νῦν ("as when I was present . . . so now when I am absent"), and makes καὶ ἀπὼν νῦν pleonastic and the article before δεύτερον nugatory.

(3) 2 Corinthians twice alludes to a visit that occurred before the time of writing and that was characterized by λύπη.

(a) Ἔκρινα γὰρ ἐμαυτῷ τοῦτο τὸ μὴ πάλιν ἐν λύπῃ πρὸς ὑμᾶς ἐλθεῖν (2:1).

At some indefinite time after returning to Ephesus from the painful visit (and thus canceling plan B),[128] Paul heard about some serious action against him or one of his representatives taken by "the wrongdoer" at Corinth. Apparently his immediate reaction was to plan yet another visit, but in order to avoid a second sorrowful encounter (πάλιν ἐν λύπῃ) he refrained from visiting Corinth in person but sent a letter (1:23; 2:3). It is highly unlikely that this *previous* visit ἐν λύπῃ is to be equated with any of the three following visits.

Paul's initial visit (Acts 18:1-18), which was ἐν ἀσθενείᾳ καὶ ἐν φόβῳ καὶ ἐν τρόμῳ πολλῷ (1 Cor. 2:3). No one will contest that, to some extent, all Paul's missionary labors were ἐν λύπῃ, in the sense of "attended by (intermittent) pain," whether physical (e.g., 2 Cor. 4:10-12; 6:4-5, 9) or spiritual (e.g., 2 Cor. 6:8, 10; 11:28). But 2 Cor. 1:23-24 and 2:2 (which may be paraphrased "Who can gladden me if I have made the source of my gladness sad?" cf. 1:24) seem to restrict the variety of λύπη indicated in 2:1 *primarily* to pain inflicted by Paul on the Corinthians for their benefit. That is, in 2:1, as opposed to 2:3, Paul is not thinking *primarily* of sorrow experienced by himself at the hands of either the Corinthians or the Jews of Corinth. It is inconceivable that Paul would sum up his founding visit as his imposition of λύπη on the Corinthians (or even as being painful *to* him, in spite of the opposition he encountered at that time — Acts 18:6, 9-10, 12-17).

A visit that occurred after the founding visit but before 1 Corinthians was written. The difficulties with identifying this visit with the one of 2 Cor. 2:1 are twofold. First, 1 Corinthians contains no reference to an earlier visit that proved painful. Second, 1 Corinthians mentions only one prior visit (1 Cor. 2:1-4; 11:2; 15:1, 3), although a second is intended (1 Cor. 4:18-19; 11:34; 16:2-3, 5-7).

1 Corinthians itself, reckoned as a sorrowful visit (cf. 2:4). Against such an identification is the fact that all the other twenty-four uses of ἔρχομαι πρός in the Pauline corpus refer to a visit in person.

128. See B.2 for a discussion of Paul's itinerary.

(b) [Φοβοῦμαι . . .] μὴ πάλιν ἐλθόντος μου ταπεινώσῃ με ὁ θεός μου πρὸς ὑμᾶς καὶ πενθήσω πολλοὺς τῶν προημαρτηκότων καὶ μὴ μετανοησάντων ἐπὶ τῇ ἀκαθαρσίᾳ καὶ πορνείᾳ καὶ ἀσελγείᾳ ᾗ ἔπραξαν (12:21).

What was the content of Paul's fear? A mere return to Corinth? A return that might lead to his humiliation? Or a ταπείνωσις on his arrival, comparable to a previous painful experience? It appears preferable to construe πάλιν with ἐλθόντος μου ταπεινώσῃ με ὁ θεός μου πρὸς ὑμᾶς[129] ("I fear lest again after my arrival my God should humiliate me in my relations with you") or simply with ταπεινώσῃ[130] ("lest my God should once more humble me") rather than with ἐλθόντος μου alone ("when I return"; cf. KJV, RV, NEB),[131] in the light of Paul's use of ἔρχομαι without πάλιν for "return" in the previous verse (as frequently elsewhere[132]), the emphatic position of πάλιν in v. 21, and the immediate context, in which not the return itself (as if Paul had written μὴ πάλιν ἐλθών in v. 20) but conditions upon Paul's arrival are emphasized. As in 13:2, the prefix in προημαρτηκότες alludes, like πάλιν (12:21), to an earlier humiliating visit when certain persons who had been leading immoral lives prior to and during that visit refused to heed Paul's warning at that time and repent (μὴ μετανοησάντων).

With reference to the hypothesis of a "sorrowful visit" to Corinth by Paul, it has now been established that a visit during Paul's Ephesian ministry was probable, that there was an actual visit subsequent to his founding visit yet before the writing of 2 Corinthians, and that this second visit was painful.

b. Its Time

As to the time of the "painful visit," the four major possibilities are:

(1) after the founding visit and before the "previous letter,"
(2) after the "previous letter" and before 1 Corinthians,
(3) after 1 Corinthians and before the "severe letter," or
(4) after the "severe letter" and before 2 Corinthians.

The last suggestion may readily be dismissed since in 2 Corinthians 1–9 Paul is dependent on Titus for his information concerning the church at Corinth, and from the day that Titus departed with the "sorrowful letter" until the reunion of Paul and Titus in Macedonia, Paul experienced the frustrations and anxiety of a person dealing with a troublesome situation through a representative. Damaging to the second hypothesis is the silence of 1 Corinthians with respect to the

129. E.g., Meyer 693; Plummer (CGT) 217.
130. E.g., Bernard 115; Hughes 472 and n. 166.
131. The RSV retains the ambiguity of the original: "I fear that when I come again my God may humble me before you." The NRSV inserts a comma after "again."
132. E.g., 2 Cor. 1:15, 23; 2:3; 12:20.

visit.[133] Only one previous visit is presupposed in that epistle,[134] although a second visit is foreshadowed.[135] Again, why would painful memories be revived in 2 Corinthians after being ignored or forgotten in 1 Corinthians? Moreover, the uneasy tension and challenge to apostolic authority presupposed by the painful visit are not reflected in 1 Corinthians. For some, the only exit from this dilemma caused by the silence of 1 Corinthians is to assume (on view [1]) that because the "previous letter" had dealt exhaustively with the sources and circumstances of the λύπη, the whole episode was thereafter treated as closed.[136] While this possibility cannot be excluded (the "previous letter," no longer extant, not being open to examination), it seems preferable to adopt the third dating for the "sorrowful visit" (so also Thrall 74; cf. 53-56) on the twofold ground of the silence of 1 Corinthians and the allusions in 2 Corinthians to such a visit, matters which have already been discussed.

c. Its Occasion, Purpose, and Outcome

On these matters little may be said which is not merely inferential. At some stage after the receipt of 1 Corinthians at Corinth, conditions within the church there deteriorated. Possibly there was a cleavage over the implementing of Paul's injunction in 1 Cor. 5:2, 5, 13 concerning the incestuous man. Perhaps an ultra-loyal group of Paulinists (cf. 1 Cor. 1:12; 2 Cor. 2:6-7) confronted the influential anti-Pauline clique of intruders from Palestine and their Corinthian adherents in a bid for control of the uncommitted and vacillating majority, which was acquiescing in the status quo and was unwilling to follow either minority in making an issue of a matter of private morals. If Timothy was present[137] but unable, as a timid νεανίας (cf. 1 Tim. 4:12), to arrest the undermining of Paul's influence and the decline of Corinthian Christian morals, his report to Paul in Ephesus of his worst fears (cf. 1 Cor. 16:10) about the organized opposition may have induced Paul to hurry to Corinth to reinforce the effect of 1 Corinthians and prevent the igniting of the flammable material already kindled by the Judaizing missionaries from Judea.[138]

133. The hypothesis (advanced by Conybeare in Conybeare and Howson 377; Bernard 5 n. 2) that ἄρτι ἐν παρόδῳ in 1 Cor. 16:7 implies a previous brief visit would be more convincing if Paul had written πάλιν ἐν παρόδῳ. ἄρτι means "just now" in contrast to the future (after Pentecost), not the past. Paul is saying that if he were to visit the Corinthians immediately after writing (as opposed to after Pentecost, as he planned), there would be time only for a flying visit (ἐν παρόδῳ). The postponement of his arrival made possible a longer visit.

134. E.g., 1 Cor. 2:1-5; 3:1-3, 6, 10; 11:12, 23.

135. 1 Cor. 4:18-19, 21; 11:34; 16:2-3, 5-7.

136. Thus Alford 2.54; Zahn 272 n. 14; Lightfoot 275; Bernard 46; Hughes 32, 462.

137. Findlay (711) proposes that Timothy may have been ὁ ἀδικηθείς (2 Cor. 7:12) as a consequence of his taking the initiative in the discipline of the incestuous man. On Timothy's movements, see below, C.

138. This metaphor is used by Strachan 69.

Little is known about what happened during the visit. Certainly Paul would have explained the reasons for the change in his travel plans (see the commentary on 1:15-17), for the Corinthians were expecting him to arrive from Macedonia (cf. 1 Cor. 16:5-6), not from Ephesus. Apparently he rebuked those guilty of immorality ("those who sinned earlier," 2 Cor. 12:21; 13:2), but refrained from exercising summary discipline, choosing rather to issue a warning: "If I come again, I will not spare you" (cf. 2 Cor. 13:2). Also, he seems to have been humiliated by the Corinthians' failure to champion his cause against the false apostles (cf. 2 Cor. 12:21). It is unlikely that the visit became "painful" because Paul was affronted by an intruder or by a native Corinthian (cf. 2 Cor. 2:5-11; 7:12).[139] He was not a man who would retreat before opposition only to resort to a letter and the intervention of his delegate Titus to gain what he himself had failed to achieve.[140] (See the discussion of the nature and time of the offense against Paul in the commentary on 2:5.)

The sequel of this brief visit was that Paul or his representative was personally insulted by some individual at Corinth in an open act of defiance by which all the Corinthian Christians were to some extent pained — if not at the actual time, at least later on (2 Cor. 2:5-11; 7:12). So Paul sent Titus to Corinth after considerable persuasion (7:14) as his personal envoy to deliver the "severe letter" and revive the flagging collection (8:6a).

2. Paul's Itinerary during and Immediately after His Ephesian Ministry

In 1 Cor. 16:2-8 and 2 Cor. 1:15-16 we find the outlines of two itineraries. In the earlier letter Paul intimates his intention (hereafter called Plan A) of leaving Ephesus after Pentecost and visiting the Corinthians, possibly for a period of about three months (probably the winter of 55-56) after a preaching tour while passing through Macedonia. Thereafter his plans were indefinite. As far as the Palestinian relief fund was concerned, he would either dispatch the Corinthian delegates to Jerusalem with commendatory letters from their church,[141] or,

---

139. But many (e.g., Kruse 22, 41; "Offender"; "Opposition"; Lüdemann 94; *Opposition* 81; Garland 27) believe that an offense against Paul took place during this "intermediate" visit. According to Kruse, it was the incestuous man against whom Paul had demanded disciplinary action (1 Cor. 5:1-13) who committed a second offense by mounting a bitter personal attack on Paul (41-43).

140. Similarly Mackintosh, "Visit" 226; Allo ix, xii, 55, 62, 76; Schmithals 104. Paul was "not the man to have retreated before a personal attack, shooting Parthian arrows by letters from a distance; such a defeat would have been irreparable" (Findlay 711). Also, 2 Cor. 10:2 loses its pungency if Paul withdrew defeated, but if he was attacked in his absence, his words are explicable and potent. Moreover, it is difficult to see on what grounds Paul could, in advance, have reassured Titus, the bearer of a letter, of the Corinthian reaction to that letter (2 Cor. 7:13-15) if he, the founder of the church, had recently been publicly humiliated (cf. Mackintosh, "Visit" 228).

141. This view construes δι' ἐπιστολῶν with δοκιμάσητε in 1 Cor. 16:3 (cf. RSV, "those whom you accredit by letter"; Nickle 15 n. 12).

should it seem appropriate or propitious at the time, he himself would escort the delegates. On the other hand, 2 Corinthians presents Paul's design[142] (hereafter Plan B) to cross from Ephesus[143] to Corinth to give the Corinthians the pleasure of a visit both before[144] and after his transit through Macedonia.[145] After this return visit to Corinth[146] he would proceed to Judea. In summary form:

PLAN A: Ephesus — Macedonia — Corinth — Jerusalem (possibly)
PLAN B: Ephesus — Corinth — Macedonia — Corinth — Judea (definitely).

Whereas the content of these two plans is relatively free from ambiguity,[147] the extent of their fulfillment and the order of their occurrence are matters of dispute: Plan B, for example, could represent Paul's original intention and have been known by the Corinthians when they heard of Plan A; again, neither Plan A nor Plan B may describe the route Paul actually followed. These areas of uncertainty must now be investigated.

Probably the most detailed and certainly the most fascinating examination of Paul's movements during his residence in Ephesus ever published is G. S. Duncan's *St. Paul's Ephesian Ministry* (1929). Postulating the priority of Plan B in the intention of Paul, Duncan (171) appeals to ἄρτι in 1 Cor. 16:7 as an indication of such an earlier plan, which, unlike his present plan in that

142. ἐβουλόμην (1:15) signifies not "I would have liked" (as in Phlm. 13) or "I should like" (as in Acts 25:22) but "I was actually intending" (almost the equivalent of ἠθέλησα), implying not simply the entertaining of a vague desire but the formation of a specific plan (cf. 2 Cor. 2:1, ἔκρινα). BAGD (146b) classifies 1:15 under the general category, "of decisions of the will after previous deliberation" (the other category is "of the pers[on] desiring someth[ing]").

143. That Paul was at Ephesus at the time is an inference from the fact that he was writing from Macedonia (cf. Acts 20:1b-2; 2 Cor. 9:2) after spending over three years at Ephesus (Acts 19:1–20:1a, 31). Note also 2 Cor. 1:8.

144. πρότερον (1:15) is to be construed with πρὸς ὑμᾶς ἐλθεῖν ("to visit you first") rather than with ἐβουλόμην ("it was originally my intent").

145. Since an apostolic visit might be both a means of χάρις ("spiritual benefit," Rom. 1:11; 15:29) or a source of χαρά ("personal pleasure," Phil. 1:25), the sense is not materially altered whether χαράν or χάριν be read. See the textual note on 1:15 in the Commentary.

146. The second part of the δευτέρα χάρις of 1:15 was Paul's formerly *intended* third visit to Corinth on his return from Macedonia, not the second actual visit, or the third projected visit (12:14; 13:1, where the point of orientation is the time of writing [ἑτοίμως ἔχω and ἔρχομαι], not some superseded intention of the past [ἐβουλόμην]).

147. On such possible ambiguities, the following comments may be made: διέρχομαι at the end of 1 Cor. 16:5 is a futuristic present ("it is my intention to pass through") and points to a definite plan, not present activity. Both uses of the verb in that verse are preceded by Μακεδονίαν, the accusative of the district traversed and probably point to "transit with preaching," whereas in 2 Cor. 1:16 διελθεῖν εἰς Μακεδονίαν means "to pass on into Macedonia (without preaching en route)" (cf. Acts 18:27, "to cross over [sea] into"). See the discussions of Moffatt, *Introduction* 95; Duncan 167 n. 1; and especially Ramsay 72, 384; "Words" 385-99. In 1 Cor. 16:7, ἄρτι should be taken to mean "just now" in contrast to the future (after Pentecost), not the past, since Paul wrote neither ἄρτι γὰρ οὐ θέλω nor πάλιν ἐν παρόδῳ.

verse, limited his residence in Corinth to a relatively brief period (since he was en route to Macedonia). Moreover, ἐβουλόμην πρότερον (2 Cor. 1:15) "indicates that before formulating (as in 1 Cor. xvi.) the plan which he had ultimately adopted (i.e., on the occasion of the "sorrowful visit")[148] the apostle *had intended* to pay them the double compliment, and give himself the double joy of visiting the Corinthians on his way both to and from Macedonia" (172). This intention, although unfulfilled, would have acquitted Paul of the specific charge the Corinthians had urged against him — that of ἐλαφρία, not "'fickleness' manifested in a change of purpose, but 'light-heartedness,' 'lack of interest,' manifested in his neglect of Corinth (in favour of Macedonia)" (173). In 2 Corinthians 1, therefore, Paul is not anticipating and defending himself against possible criticism but replying to actual reproaches. 1 Corinthians 16, on the other hand, is apologetic in tone because Paul's plan to proceed to Macedonia first disappointed Corinthian hopes of a visit before and after the Macedonian visit (2 Corinthians 1) (171-72, 174, 178 with n. 1).

On this reading of the evidence, Plan B, if known to the Corinthians, must have been explained to them either in the "previous letter," during a second visit prior to 1 Corinthians, or by Timothy. Moreover, its modification must have either preceded the writing of 1 Corinthians (the usual view) or occurred during the composition of that letter. In support of the latter alternative, A. P. Stanley (28) points to a tacit allusion to Plan B in 1 Cor. 4:19 (ἐλεύσομαι δὲ ταχέως πρὸς ὑμᾶς; cf. οὐ . . . ἐν παρόδῳ, 16:7). This is not incompatible with the announcement of Plan A in ch. 16 on the assumption, which is probable, that that epistle was composed in stages. Finally, proponents of this view that Plan B preceded Plan A[149] propose a variety of motives for Paul's partial alteration of his itinerary (the omission of a visit to Corinth ἐν παρόδῳ, "en route" to Macedonia): the receipt of disturbing news from members of the household of Chloe (1 Cor. 1:11) and of a letter from Corinth sent with envoys (16:17), which suggested that a written response rather than a personal visit would be appropriate; Paul's wish to spare the Corinthians (2 Cor. 1:23); the recognition that a hasty visit (or even two such visits) would do less than justice to the Corinthians and therefore might be misinterpreted; and continuing unique opportunities for ministry in Ephesus (1 Cor. 16:9).

Such a reconstruction of events has not gone unchallenged since it leaves unanswered a number of pressing questions. In the first place, *pace* Duncan,

---

148. Duncan (165-83, 298-99) conceived of Paul's actual movements during his Asian ministry as follows: Ephesus — Troas (en route to Macedonia) — Corinth (sorrowful visit) — Miletus — Ephesus — Lycus valley (third crisis at Laodicea?) — Ephesus — Troas (2 Cor. 2:12) — Macedonia — Illyricum — Nicopolis — Corinth. The only significant difference in his reconstruction in 1957 ("Ministry," "Table") was his suggestion that Paul did not twice leave Ephesus for Troas: the painful visit to Corinth interrupted Paul's Asian ministry so that he probably left from and returned to Ephesus.

149. Proponents include Meyer 397, 427; A. P. Stanley 27-28; Denney 719-20; Ramsay 275; White, "Visits" 86-87; Strachan 66-67; Hughes 32-33.

can 1 Cor. 16:5-9 really be understood as an *apologia* for altered plans in the face of malicious Corinthian misinterpretation? Second, what circumstances impelled Paul to become uncertain *(ex hypothesi)* of his own going to Jerusalem? If he had become increasingly aware of the difficulties involved in the expeditious completion of the collection so that he felt "less certain that the amount collected would make it worth his while to go in person" (thus Duncan 175),[150] would not these circumstances have strengthened rather than undermined his determination (cf. 1 Cor. 16:8-9) to fulfill his "resolve in the Spirit" (Acts 19:21), that is, to go to Jerusalem? Indeed, Kennedy argues (20-32) that Acts 19:21 reflects "a mental crisis" which converted Paul's uncertainty concerning his going to Jerusalem (1 Cor. 16:3-4, 6) into "intense feeling and immovable resolve" (32; see Rom. 15:25, 28, 30-32; 2 Cor. 1:16; 8:19). Third, if Plan A superseded Plan B before or during the composition of 1 Corinthians and Plan B was already known to the Corinthians, why did Paul not *explicitly* retract Plan B, or part of it, in 1 Corinthians 16? Fourth, in his defence in 2 Corinthians 1, why did Paul not appeal to his clear statement of intention in 1 Cor. 16:5 (A. Robertson 493)?

It now remains to examine the other alternative, namely that Plan B succeeded Plan A. If Plan A in fact discloses Paul's original intention, Plan B, presumably made after the writing of 1 Corinthians, introduces two modifications of that previous itinerary: Paul now planned to visit Corinth twice — before as well as after his activity in Macedonia (which remained definite) — and his intention to travel to Judea with the collection was now settled.[151] Whether the Corinthians were aware of Plan B before hearing of its abandonment in 2 Corinthians is contested. Kennedy (xxv, 36) and Plummer (CGT, xviii, 34), for example, vigorously deny such awareness. But there is reason to believe that on the intermediate visit of Paul to Corinth, the Corinthians were informed of the second travel plan.[152] This supposition may be shown to be feasible by a tentative outline of events.

Sometime after sending 1 Corinthians and as a result of hearing discour-

---

150. Alternatively, Duncan proposes that in 2 Corinthians 1 Paul "has invested his earlier intention with a definiteness which did not always belong to it" (175), surely a gratuitous assumption on Duncan's part.

151. This latter point has been contested by Zahn (268 n. 7), who, apparently overlooking the ἐάν and κἀμέ of 1 Cor. 16:4a, points to σὺν ἐμοὶ πορεύσονται — not σὺν αὐτοῖς πορεύσομαι — in v. 4b as evidence that the issue was merely whether or not Paul would travel in the company of the Corinthian delegates. The reason for the first modification of Paul's itinerary, suggests Manson (212), was Paul's wish to reinforce the appeal of 1 Corinthians and to check the inroads of the Cephas party, and the reason for the second modification was the need to prevent all such intrusion (or, we may suggest, at least to clarify the implications of the Gal. 2:1-10 concordat; cf. 2 Cor. 10:13-18).

152. It is *a priori* unlikely that the "severe letter" contained any rationale for Paul's travel plans: exercise of authority rather than self-defense would have characterized that document. The considerable treatment of Paul's itinerary at the commencement of 2 Corinthians confirms this supposition.

aging news of the deteriorating state of affairs at Corinth, Paul decided (Plan A) to postpone his journey to Macedonia and to visit Corinth before proceeding to Macedonia and then back to Corinth as originally planned. On his arrival at Corinth from Ephesus — not from Macedonia, as 1 Cor. 16:5 would have led the Corinthians to expect — and on being asked the state of the churches in Macedonia, Paul replied that he now intended, after the present visit, to engage in ministry in Macedonia before returning to Corinth and setting out for Judea (Plan B). At this time, then, the Corinthians learned not only that Plan A had been discarded but also that Paul had conceived of Plan B, which favored them with a double benefit, before his departure from Ephesus.[153] The unknown events of the "painful visit" then occurred. By Paul's departure for Ephesus — not Macedonia — after the visit,[154] or at least by the time of the receipt of the subsequent "severe letter" from Ephesus, the Corinthians became aware of the annulment of Plan B. On his final visit to Corinth (probably the winter of 56-57) Paul traveled from Ephesus via Macedonia (Acts 20:1-2; 2 Cor. 2:12-13; 7:5), which in the event was the first part of Plan A!

If the foregoing reconstruction of events is accurate in its broad outline, we may conclude that Plan B followed and superseded Plan A. The apostle's "sorrowful visit" caused an interruption in his Asian ministry (since he set out from and returned to Ephesus) and the disruption of both his travel plans. Just as Plan A was nullified by Paul's crossing from Ephesus to Corinth on the "painful visit," so Plan B was annulled by his return to Ephesus after that visit. In both cases, a Macedonian visit was postponed. It may be said that after the "sorrowful visit" Paul reverted to Plan A.[155] Consequently 2 Cor. 1:15–2:1 does not offer justification for merely *one* change of itinerary, but rather contains

---

153. On this view ἐβουλόμην (1:15) points to a specific intention formed in Ephesus and announced in Corinth on Paul's arrival on what was to become the "painful visit." But Furnish has Paul making his decision to adopt Plan B at Corinth on the "painful visit" (55, 143-44).

154. Precisely why Paul should have returned to Ephesus (as also Lüdemann 99; *Opposition* 81) is not known, although the presence there of Titus, who was later to become the bearer of the "severe letter" and Paul's personal ambassador to Corinth in place of Timothy, would be sufficient reason. Paul's recent residence in Ephesus and its proximity to Corinth would also be contributory factors.

But *that* Paul returned to Ephesus is contested. For example, Manson (212-14) has alleged that after the "sorrowful visit" Paul adhered to Plan B by proceeding to Macedonia: Ephesus — Corinth (sorrowful visit) — Macedonia (2 Cor. 1:16) — Troad (2:12) — Macedonia (7:5) — Corinth (1:16). On this view Titus would have been sent to Corinth from Macedonia with instructions to meet Paul in Troas, the scene of Paul's next missionary campaign. But 2:12-13 seems to imply that on his *arrival* at Troas (or in the Troad), Paul expected to find Titus. Alternatively, if Paul remained in Macedonia and Titus was to sail back from Corinth to Neapolis, how is Paul's expectance of meeting Titus in Troas to be accounted for? On the other hand, Massie (67) and Bruce (164) propose that from Corinth Paul went to Macedonia (in accord with the first part of Plan B) and then back to Ephesus (in disregard of the second part of Plan B).

155. But even Plan A was not carried out in detail, for whereas in 1 Cor. 16:3-4 Paul envisages travel directly from Corinth to Jerusalem, his actual route was via Macedonia and Troas (Acts 20:3-12).

Paul's defense against the Corinthian indictment of capricious vacillation (1:17) and insensitive domineering (1:24) — the accusation, that is, that he had twice capriciously altered his itinerary after the manner of a mere worldling who was devoid of the Spirit and therefore lacked two authenticating signs of true apostleship: reliability in keeping promises and consistency in nurturing converts.

3. Place of Composition and Date of Sending of 1 and 2 Corinthians

a. 1 Corinthians

From 1 Cor. 16:8-9 we learn that at the time of writing Paul was planning to remain in Ephesus until the following Pentecost in order to take full advantage of unique evangelistic opportunities. Like 2 Corinthians, the first canonical letter to Corinth was probably written in stages over a period of time (see above, A.3.e.iv). But we need not conclude that only ch. 16 of 1 Corinthians was written in Ephesus, for Paul spent some three continuous years in that city (Acts 20:18, 31). The residence in Ephesus that Luke mentions in Acts 18:19-21 is too brief to accommodate the writing of 1 Corinthians, because Luke informs us that Paul declined to prolong that visit (Acts 18:20) whereas in 1 Cor. 16:8 Paul's plan is to "stay on in Ephesus until Pentecost." Accordingly we must locate 1 Corinthians during the period covered by Paul's next sojourn in Ephesus, namely Acts 19:1–20:1, probably fall 52–spring 56.[156] Not only this reference to a coming Pentecost (perhaps one or two months away) but the possible allusions to an imminent paschal celebration in 1 Cor. 5:7-8 and to the presentation of firstfruits in 1 Cor. 15:20 suggest that the letter was written during the spring. The year was probably 55, after the "two years" of Acts 19:10 and during the events outlined in Acts 19:11-20.[157] At any rate, we ought to place 1 Corinthians before Acts 19:21 ("After these events Paul resolved in the Spirit to pass through Macedonia and Achaia and then go to Je-

156. τριετίαν in Acts 20:31 is clearly a round number. Significantly D adds τριετίαν ἢ καὶ πλεῖον ("for three years or even more") in Acts 20:18. See the chronology below (C). One most significant point of orientation for the chronology of Paul's ministry is Luke's reference in Acts 18:12 to Gallio's proconsulship of Achaia (ca. July 1, 51 to July 1, 52; see Jewett, *Chronology* 38-40; Ogg 104-11 [May 51–May 52]). If we follow Luke's order of events, namely eighteen months (Acts 18:11) — Gallio episode (vv. 12-17) — "many more days" (v. 18), we may tentatively date Paul's stay in Corinth as fall 50 to spring 52, with his Ephesian residence of Acts 19:1–20:1 beginning several months later (fall 52; see Bruce, *Acts* 93; Hemer, "Chronology" 8 ["from autumn 50 to early summer 52"]).

157. In 55 Passover fell on April 1 and Pentecost on May 25 (so Jewett, *Chronology* 48, following D. Plooij's calculations of Nisan 1 [*De Chronologie van het Leven van Paulus,* Leiden, Brill, 1918, 85]). A date of spring 55 for 1 Corinthians is also accepted by Bruce (*Acts* 93), Conzelmann (4 n. 31), Robinson (*Redating* 48, 54, 352), and Jewett (*Chronology* 104).

rusalem"), since in 1 Cor. 16:3-4, 6 Paul is unsure whether or not he will travel to Jerusalem.[158]

b. 2 Corinthians

Several references within 2 Corinthians suggest that Paul was in the province of Macedonia when writing (see 2:13; 7:5; 8:1; 9:2-4). Of special significance is present tense καυχῶμαι in 9:2, "I have been boasting about it [namely your eagerness to help] to the Macedonians" (NIV). Such a provenance is confirmed by those MSS (e.g., B^c K L P) that note in the subscription to the epistle that it was written "from Philippi" (see Textual Note d. on 13:13). Also, in 11:9 "Macedonia" probably signifies primarily Philippi (see Phil. 4:15). But of course it is not impossible that Paul was at Thessalonica or Berea (also Macedonian cities), since 2 Cor. 8:1 and 9:2 speak of the churches and people of Macedonia, not simply of the Philippians.

Any suggested dates for 2 Corinthians must assume either a partition theory or the letter's integrity. For the reasons given above (A.3), we shall assume that although the letter was composed in stages, it forms an integral whole and was sent as a single missive.

Acts 20:6 relates that Paul left Philippi for Jerusalem in the spring ("after the days of Unleavened Bread").[159] Previously, three winter months had been spent in Corinth (Acts 20:2b, 3a),[160] where Paul arrived from Macedonia. Intimations of a forthcoming visit to Corinth found in 2 Cor. 12:14; 13:1 suggest that the letter was written shortly before that winter. But was it the fall of 55 or 56? Either the two canonical Corinthian epistles belong to the same year, 1 Corinthians being written in the spring and 2 Corinthians in the fall of 55, or a period of eighteen or more months separated the two letters. The former view appears to be confirmed by the correspondence between the travel plans of 1 Cor. 16:5-8 (Ephesus — Macedonia — Corinth, possibly for the winter [beginning in the year of writing]) and the synopsis of Paul's movements recorded in Acts 20:1-3 (Ephesus — Macedonia — Greece). On this interpretation approximately six months intervened between 1 and 2 Corinthians[161] and the χειμών of 1 Cor. 16:6 corresponds to the μῆναι τρεῖς of Acts 20:3. But it must be observed that 1 Corinthians 16 re-

158. But Robinson (*Redating* 48) notes the tentativeness of Paul's plans in 1 Cor. 16:3-4, 6-7 "which suggests that in Acts 19.21f. Luke is summarizing in the light of subsequent events." Accordingly he seems to place the writing of 1 Corinthians (spring A.D. 55) during Paul's continued stay in Asia (Acts 19:22b) which ended in the early summer of 55 (*Redating* 47).

159. By a succession of scholars (Ramsay, Plooij, Jewett — see Jewett, *Chronology* 49-50) the date of Paul's departure has been reckoned to be Friday, April 15, 57. But such precision is impossible, given the ambiguity of the data in Acts 20:6 (see Bruce, *Acts* 424; Riesner 218-19, 321).

160. But Pherigo (347-48) takes Ἑλλάς ("Greece") in Acts 20:2 to mean Athens.

161. A six-month interval is proposed by Lake 139-44; Kümmel, *Introduction* 293; Hughes 33; Guthrie, *Introduction* 442-43 ("about seven months").

cords an intention for the future, not a description of the past, and we have argued above (B.2) that the tentative plans of 1 Corinthians 16 were in fact superseded by those recorded in 2 Cor. 1:15-16. Consequently the χειμών need not harmonize with the μῆναι τρεῖς. Nor does the phrase ἀπὸ πέρυσι in 2 Cor. 8:10; 9:2 necessarily point to a six-month interval, since it means "last year" and so is consonant with a period of either under or over one year, and it is uncertain by which calendar Paul was reckoning (see the commentary on 8:10 and 9:2).

There are two positive pointers to an eighteen-month interval. First, it is generally agreed that if Paul conducted a mission in the Roman province of Illyricum (as Rom. 15:19 may suggest), it must have occurred after his Ephesian residence (Acts 19) on his third "missionary journey" and before his arrival in Greece (Acts 20:2b);[162] it would be covered by Luke's condensed statement διελθὼν δὲ τὰ μέρη ἐκεῖνα καὶ παρακαλέσας αὐτοὺς λόγῳ πολλῷ (Acts 20:2a). This is relevant to the issue at hand, for 1 Corinthians must be dated *during* Paul's Ephesian residence and 2 Corinthians (written from Macedonia) was sent *shortly* if not immediately *before* Paul's sojourn in Greece (note 2 Cor. 12:14; 13:1). But what is the likelihood of an Illyrian mission? In Rom. 15:19 Paul states that he has fully preached the gospel of Christ ἀπὸ Ἰερουσαλὴμ καὶ κύκλῳ μέχρι τοῦ Ἰλλυρικοῦ. Just as Jerusalem is the included *terminus a quo* (geographically, not temporally) in the southeast, so Illyricum is probably an included *terminus ad quem* in the northwest at the opposite end of the κύκλος. The latter term seems consonant rather with the idea of a district incorporated within the arc of a circle than with the conception of an area lying beyond a circular boundary line: "from Jerusalem and [thence] in a circuit as far as Illyricum." Again, if Illyricum denoted merely the frontier beyond which Paul had not traveled or preached, he could only with difficulty be exonerated from his own implied indictment in Rom. 15:18. And the reference to τὸ Ἰλλυρικόν in v. 19, however interpreted, seems to necessitate its inclusion in the τὰ κλίματα ταῦτα of v. 23 which, Paul declares, no longer afforded scope for pioneer activity. Such evangelistic endeavor need not have been prolonged, but Paul's word πεπληρωκέναι ("fully preached"), while not implying exhaustiveness, certainly suggests a presentation of the gospel that was not superficial. Travel to and from Illyricum, as well as preaching there, would have taken at least one or two months.

The second pointer to an eighteen-month interval is the difficulty, if not impossibility, of fitting into a six-month period all the travel and events that took place between the sending of the two epistles, that is (see C below), Timothy's return to Ephesus from Corinth, Titus's visit to initiate the collection, the advent and activity of intruders from Palestine and the gradual deterioration of the church's relations with Paul, Paul's "painful visit," followed sometime later

162. So also Dodd, *Romans* xxiv, 228; Jewett, *Chronology* 104 and the chart on p. 161; and especially Bruce, *History* 335-36; "Macedonia" 353-54, where he suggests that Paul may have visited Latin-speaking Illyricum at this time in order to familiarize himself with the sound of Latin and perhaps to give himself an opportunity to speak it in preparation for his projected ministry in Spain (Rom. 15:24, 28), where Latin was the language of administration and culture.

by the ἀδικία of 2 Cor. 7:12, Titus's visit with the "severe letter," Paul's (curtailed) evangelism in and around Troas and his "affliction in Asia," his pastoral activity in Macedonia while awaiting Titus's arrival, and further pastoral and evangelistic work in Macedonia and probably Illyricum.

We conclude that about eighteen months elapsed between the two letters[163] and that 1 Corinthians was sent in the spring of 55 and 2 Corinthians in the fall of 56.[164]

4. Paul's Opponents in 2 Corinthians

a. Methodology

The literature on this topic is immense and the variety of views bewildering. Useful discussions of the history of research may be found in Schmithals (117-24), Georgi (1-9), Friedrich (192-96), Machalet (183-90), and Bieringer and Lambrecht (192-221); and on Paul's opponents in general, Gunther (1-16), Ellis (*Prophecy* 80-115), Lüdemann, *Opposition,* and Sumney, *Servants.* One reason for the great diversity of opinion is lack of agreement regarding the criteria that may be used to determine from Paul's letters what his opponents at any given time were saying and doing.[165] In the absence of his opponents' writings, what checks should be applied in our search for reliable data that will prevent our imagining that behind every positive assertion Paul makes is an antithetical view that he is rebutting? We suggest that there are several specific criteria that are relevant to 2 Corinthians and that enable us to proceed with some confidence, although the subjective element in applying the criteria can never be eliminated. But it should be stressed that not all the examples in 2 Corinthians of the criteria listed below have been included in this classification. Only when the context is clearly polemical or vigorously apologetic is an allusion found to Paul's antagonists. As a result, we have resisted the temptation to engage in "mirror reading" and so find in 2 Cor. 3:12-18, for example, sustained polemic against an inflated view of Moses purportedly held by Paul's opponents. On the limitations and dangers of "mirror reading" as a technique for discovering the views or conduct of Paul's opponents, see J. M. G. Barclay 73-93.

---

163. So also Jülicher 95; Massie 68. Allo argues for a two-year interval (lvii–lx, 218-19). Thrall's chronology is as follows (77): 1 Corinthians written in April 55, 2 Corinthians 1–8 in late March 56, 2 Corinthians 9 in June-July 56, and 2 Corinthians 10–13 in August-September 56.

164. If 2 Corinthians 10–13, as a separate letter, belongs to a later period than chs. 1–9, these last four chapters will date from the fall of 56, while the first nine may have been sent at any time between the fall of 55 and early fall 56. This date of fall 56 for all of 2 Corinthians or chs. 10–13 is held, *inter alios,* by Robinson, *Redating* 50-51, 54-55.

165. For an analysis of the methodological problems involved in determining the presence and views of "opponents" in NT texts, see Berger 373-400; G. W. Hansen 167-70; and especially Sumney 75-120 and, more briefly, *Servants* 20-32.

citation of a view, with a verb of saying expressed (10:10) or implied (10:2),

direct allusion to specific views (5:12b; 10:7; 11:4-5, 12a; 13:3) or conduct (2:17; 3:1; 10:8a, 9, 12; 11:13, 15, 18, 20, 21b; 12:17-18),

the οὐ(κ)/μὴ . . . ἀλλά/δέ antithesis[166] in an apologetic or polemical context (1:12-13, 19; 2:4, 17; 4:5; 5:4; 8:13; 10:[8], 13; 12:14; [13:10]),[167]

the combination οὐχ ὅτι (1:24; 3:5) or the negative particle followed by a catchword or catchphrase: 1:18 (οὐκ ἔστιν Ναὶ καὶ Οὔ, cf. 1:19); 5:3 (οὐ γυμνοί), 7 (οὐ διὰ εἴδους); 10:3 (οὐ κατὰ σάρκα), 4 (οὐ σαρκικά), 14 (οὐ . . . ὑπερεκτείνομεν), 15 (οὐκ εἰς τὰ ἄμετρα, cf. 10:13), 16 (οὐκ ἐν ἀλλοτρίῳ κανόνι), 18 (οὐ . . . ὁ ἑαυτὸν συνιστάνων); 11:6 (οὐ τῇ γνώσει), 9 (οὐ κατενάρκησα οὐθενός, cf. 12:13-14, 16); 13:6 (οὐκ ἐσμὲν ἀδόκιμοι); note also the thrice-repeated οὐδένα in 7:2,

rhetorical questions (1:17 twice; 11:7, 11, 22 three times, 23; 12:13, 17),

concessive εἰ καί (4:3; 11:6),

sentiments obviously foreign to Paul's thought (12:1) or inappropriate from Paul's pen (4:2a; 5:13a; 10:1b; 12:16b; 13:5-6),

words used in unique senses or contexts (ἁμαρτία, 11:7; ἀδικία, 12:13),

specialized terms or expressions relevant to Paul's *apologia* or polemic: πλάνος (6:8), λογισμοί (10:5 [or 4]), οἱ ὑπερλίαν ἀπόστολοι (11:5; 12:11), ἄφρονες (11:19), τὰ σημεῖα τοῦ ἀποστόλου (12:12), and

references that accord with charges or countercharges established on other grounds: 11:3 (deceit and cunning, cf. 4:2), 10 (boasting of financial independence, cf. 11:12).

As we correlate these data and build up a composite sketch of the views and conduct of Paul's adversaries at Corinth at the time represented by 2 Corinthians (on the assumption of its unity), several precautionary notes must be sounded. It is impossible to distinguish clearly between the views of native Corinthians and the teaching of the rival apostles, for many of the Corinthians seem to have adopted some of the ideas or attitudes of these intruders (11:4). Nor can we confidently align the aberrant views mentioned by Paul with the positions of any one of the three or four groups referred to in 1 Cor. 1:12. Again, we should not discount

---

166. This criterion excludes, of course, the expression οὐ μόνον . . . ἀλλὰ καί (7:7; 8:10, 19, 21; 9:12), which is conjunctive, not antithetical. But it includes instances where οὐ(κ) stands in the second place (X not Y: 10:8 and 13:10, εἰς οἰκοδομὴν καὶ οὐκ εἰς καθαίρεσιν).

167. Since the "not . . . but" antithesis is a natural and therefore common mode of expression, it often signifies a simple contrast where the negative is merely a foil for the positive (3:3 twice, 6; 4:18; 6:12; 8:5, 8; 10:18; 12:14c; 13:3, 8), and sometimes it anticipates *future* objections (5:12a) or misunderstandings (7:9; 13:7) rather than answering past objections or correcting past misunderstandings. On occasion this antithesis is "Semitic," signifying "not so much A as B" rather than "not A but B" (see Zerwick §445), as in 2:5; 7:12; 13:7, where there is no repudiation of the affirmation contained in the οὐ phrase.

the possibility that, as a skilled polemicist and sensitive pastor, Paul may have gone beyond the actual views of his opponents and rebutted logical developments from their thought or may have anticipated and answered possible objections to his own teaching or conduct (2:2, 4; 6:3a; 11:16a; 12:6, 19). Moreover, there is no need to imagine that the opposition to Paul at Corinth was large in number or uniform in outlook.[168] When he uses the singular τις (10:7; 11:20 five times; 11:21b) or ὁ τοιοῦτος (10:11), we need not assume a single opponent, since these could be generic singulars.[169] Similarly, the plurals τινες (3:1; 10:2, 12) and οἱ τοιοῦτοι (11:13) need not imply a large, unified group. We should also remember that although we are attempting to identify the teaching of Paul's rivals at Corinth, the differences between Paul and them were not merely theological but also social and cultural (see Theissen 40-54). Finally, it is sometimes unclear whether Paul is responding to an accusation made against him or is himself leveling an accusation against his antagonists (e.g., 4:5, οὐ γὰρ ἑαυτοὺς κηρύσσομεν).

b. Their View of Paul

With these basic criteria stated and certain precautions noted, we may now attempt to summarize *the charges made against Paul by his opponents*. They may be conveniently grouped under five headings.

(1) His Letters

He carried no letter of commendation to Corinth or from Corinth that might validate his apostolic credentials (3:1-3). On the other hand, when he himself chose to write letters, he exhibited a worldly shrewdness, for his real meaning lay below the surface or "between the lines," so that a straightforward reading of his letters was unproductive (1:12b-13). What was more, he used his weighty and forceful letters to frighten his converts and stun them into submission (10:9-10).

(2) His Pastoral Conduct and Ability

In his dealings with the Corinthians he had acted shamelessly[170] and insincerely (1:12), lording it over his converts (1:24; cf. 10:8a). His vaunted authority had

---

168. Marshall has argued that in choosing not to name his opponents Paul was following an ancient rhetorical custom designed to denigrate one's enemies by denying them the status attached to a name (341-48, and more briefly in his "Invective" 366-67). This is possible, but more often than not we can attribute Paul's choice to his pastoral tact (e.g., in 2 Cor. 2:5-11).

169. The phrase οὐ . . . ὡς οἱ πολλοί ("unlike many") in 2:17 may refer not only to Paul's adversaries at Corinth but also to any pseudo-missionaries who dispensed God's word for personal gain (cf. 1 Pet. 5:2).

170. This assumes that ἁγιότητι is the right reading in 1:12 (see textual note a. in the Commentary at that verse). If ἁπλότητι be preferred, the implied charge would be one of deviousness.

been used negatively to tear down (7:3a; 10:8b; 13:10), so that the Corinthians felt hemmed in and restricted in their spiritual development (6:12). He was inferior in knowledge (11:6) and an amateur in eloquence, his abilities as a public speaker amounting to nothing (10:10; 11:6). Also, the content of his message was unclear; his gospel was veiled (4:3).

(3) His Financial Independence

He had always obstinately refused to accept remuneration from the Corinthians (11:7, 9; 12:13), an insult (ἁμαρτία, 11:7; ἀδικία, 12:13) which indicated that he lacked genuine love for them (11:11; cf. 12:15) and was a counterfeit apostle (12:12-13[171]). Yet he exploited the willingness of the Corinthian church to support him by having his agents organize a collection, ostensibly for Jerusalem but at least in part for himself (12:17-18). In so doing he had unscrupulously taken advantage of the Corinthians and wronged them (7:2; 12:16).

(4) His Apostleship

He lacked the genuine marks of an apostle (12:12), and in the absence of evidence that Christ was using Paul as his spokesman to the Corinthians (13:3a), it was clear that he was an imposter (6:8), a false apostle (11:13), and inferior to the Twelve (11:5; 12:11).[172] Whether he really belonged to Christ (10:7) and was holding to the faith (13:5-6) was open to question.

(5) His Character

Although his letters, sent from a safe distance, were solemn and portentous, in person he was unimpressive and ineffective. Meekly deferential when face to face, he was fiercely combative when out of sight (10:1, 10; cf. 11:21a; 13:3-4). In his financial dealings with the Corinthians, he had shown himself to be a crafty fellow, preying on them through tricks (12:16-17). His word was unreliable, for his plans were made and changed impulsively so that his "Yes" became "No" and his "No" turned out to be "Yes." He was a fickle vacillator who acted like a worldling (1:17-19; 10:2). And on occasion he seemed to be "out of his mind" (5:13).[173]

---

171. The close association of these two verses (note γάρ in 12:13) indicates the link that was made between financial independence and imagined non-apostolicity.

172. On this latter point, see below, B.4.d.

173. Goudge (xli-xlii) has acutely observed that

S. Paul's opponents understood what scholars in their studies do not always understand, that for the vast majority of mankind the acceptance of truth primarily rests upon the trust which they repose in the character and competence of their teachers, and not upon understanding of the intellectual grounds upon which their teachers base what they say. "Abide thou in the

Now we may turn to *the characteristics of his opponents' teaching, claims, conduct, and character* as described by Paul.[174]

c. Paul's View of Them

(1) Their Teaching and Claims

Paul accuses them of peddling an adulterated word of God (2:17) and of falsifying that word by craftiness (4:2). So dishonest was their manipulation of the message that theirs was in fact a "different gospel" that proclaimed another Jesus and offered an alien spirit (11:4). Because they had accepted this false gospel so readily, the Corinthians had been seduced from their undivided allegiance to Christ (11:3). This rival gospel had corrupted their thoughts.

For their part, Paul's rivals claimed to be the true servants of Christ (10:7; 11:23), apostles of Christ (11:13), and servants of righteousness (11:15). Given Paul's total repudiation of this "different gospel" (cf. Gal. 1:8-9), we may assume that the "righteousness" they sought to preach and administer involved adherence to the Mosaic law (cf. 3:1-18) as the means of admission into the church or of enjoying the benefits of salvation. They seem to have treasured their pure pedigree as Hebrews, Israelites, and descendants of Abraham (11:22). Since they were Ἑβραῖοι (11:22) rather than Ἑλληνισταί (cf. Acts 6:1), their Palestinian origin must have been a special source of pride to them, perhaps because they had known Jesus personally (cf. 5:16) and sought to claim some link, however tenuous, with the Jerusalem church and its leadership. The letters of commendation that they brought to Corinth with them (ὥς τινες, 3:1) presumably highlighted these Palestinian associations. Not surprisingly, then, they had a lofty view of the Twelve in Jerusalem — a view that Paul parodies with the coinage οἱ ὑπερλίαν ἀπόστολοι, "these (= your) 'superlative' apostles" (11:5; 12:11).

(2) Their Conduct and Character

Paul charges these interlopers from Palestine with misguided self-appraisal. They estimated their merits by measuring themselves against standards that they themselves had determined (10:12). Such a procedure was sheer folly (οὐ

---

things which thou hast learned and hast been assured of, knowing of whom thou hast learned them" (2 Tim. iii.14). The great battles are won not so much by doctrines as by personalities, though no doubt it is the doctrine which forms the personality identified with it, and judgment upon the one involves judgment upon the other. Arius, e.g., was defeated by S. Athanasius, as the Pharisaic teachers by S. Paul, not so much by argument, as by greater suffering and nobler action. Thus the most effective method of undermining S. Paul's teaching was to attack his character, and to deny the reality of his apostleship.

174. Compare the list of nine characteristics given by Carrez, "Réalité" 164-74.

συνιᾶσιν, 10:12). They were, in fact, "fools" (ἄφρονες) whom the Corinthians were benignly tolerating (11:19). They prided themselves on appearances rather than character, on externals rather than inward realities (5:12), placing high value on conceited sophistry (10:5), polished eloquence (10:10; 11:6), and visions and revelations (12:1). Associated with this pride was their persistent self-commendation (10:12, 18) and their boasting about credentials (11:21b-23a) and achievements (10:13-17; 11:12). Not only had they trespassed on Paul's distinctive "province" at Corinth (10:13). They were boasting of Paul's own exploits at Corinth as though they were their own achievements (10:13, 15-16). Their very presence in Corinth was a case of "overextension" (10:14).

With regard to remuneration, they had evidently availed themselves of the Corinthians' offer of support — perhaps to prove their claim to apostolic status (cf. 1 Cor. 9:14) — and had thereby forfeited their ability to claim, as Paul did, that pastoral services were rendered free of charge (11:7, 9, 12). This undeniable difference in mode of operation seems to have embarrassed and irritated Paul's antagonists (11:10, 12), for they had apparently become a financial burden on the church (12:13-14, 16). Being unable to force Paul to surrender his financial independence (11:10, 12; 12:14; cf. 1 Cor. 9:12b-18), they sought to convert his stubborn refusal to exercise his right to "live by the gospel" (1 Cor. 9:14) — one sign of a genuine apostle — into a "sin" (11:7) or a "wrong" (12:13).

Perhaps Paul's most damning criticism of his antagonists is the charge that they were masters of deceit. Like fraudulent merchants (2:17), they had acted with unscrupulous cunning (4:2) and crafty deceit (11:3). Counterfeit apostles as they were, they masqueraded as Christ's apostles (11:13). Although in reality they were commissioned by Satan and executed his plans, they tried to pass themselves off as emissaries of righteousness (11:15a). Their doom would be a fitting climax to their nefarious deeds (11:15b).

Paul's dual approach to the ψευδαπόστολοι is indisputable. On the one hand, he vigorously lambasts them (11:13, 15), yet he takes their charges seriously and seeks to show that they are groundless (10:2-5, 9-11). He compares himself to his opponents (11:23-29), yet repudiates all such comparison (10:12; cf. Käsemann 41-48). This dialectic is occasioned not by the fact that behind the intruders lay the authority of the Twelve (as Käsemann alleges), nor by uncertainty on Paul's part whether some of the Jerusalem apostles might be included among his adversaries (as Thrall, "Super-Apostles" 49, 55 believes), but by the fact that the Corinthians had been duped into heeding and perhaps believing the false charges against Paul. He therefore felt obliged to respond to the accusations for the sake of the immature Corinthians at the same time as he exposed the accusers' character and mission as the minions of Satan masquerading as the deputies of Christ.

As we have delineated all these charges and countercharges, it all comes down to this. Paul's opponents regarded themselves as ἀπόστολοι Χριστοῦ

(11:13) and Paul as a πλάνος, an imposter (6:8).[175] Paul viewed himself as an ἀπόστολος Χριστοῦ Ἰησοῦ (1:1) and his rivals as ψευδαπόστολοι (11:13). The Corinthians were faced with rival apostolates. There can be no doubt that the primary and immediate aim of Paul's rivals was to undermine and destroy his reputation and apostolic authority and thus subvert his gospel. What they taught and did was calculated to bring about Paul's downfall, at least at Corinth, and to establish their own credentials as authentic servants of Christ. If they entertained wider plans, they may have wished to impose a Christianized form of Jewish doctrine and practice on believers everywhere.

Thus far we have been proceeding with a fair degree of confidence. But as we approach these next two issues — the relation of the rival apostles to the church of Jerusalem and the matter of their identity — the data are so ambiguous that the most appropriate way to proceed is to try to classify and evaluate some of the scholarly interaction with these data.

d. Their Relation to Jerusalem

On all sides it is agreed that at least part of the opposition to Paul at Corinth at the time of 2 Corinthians originated outside Greece. Certain persons had illegitimately invaded Paul's "assigned area" (κανών) at Corinth and were making improper claims for themselves on the basis of Paul's pastoral work there (10:13-15). Preaching a "different Jesus" and a "different gospel" (11:4), they had descended on the unsuspecting Corinthians with letters of introduction from persons or churches outside Corinth (3:1).

But by no means do all scholars concur that these intruders had any relation to the mother church in Jerusalem. Munck, for example, sees the "adversaries" as Jewish Christians, "either emissaries of other churches or missionaries sent by Christ" (185), whose time of arrival at Corinth — just when Paul thought his authority was once again recognized by the Corinthians — rather than any false doctrine they brought unsettled Paul, who believed they would tempt the Corinthians to apostatize (184-87). In his full-scale treatment of *The Opponents of Paul in Second Corinthians,* Georgi argues that they were Jewish Christian missionary propagandists or migrant preachers whose "spiritual origin was in the world of Hellenistic-Jewish Apologetics" (248; cf. 422-34). They were not official inspectors from Jerusalem or representatives of any institution, and their letters of accreditation came not from Jerusalem but from Corinth itself (244-45).[176]

---

175. With this compare the earlier characterization of Paul by his Corinthian detractors as an ἔκτρωμα, "an 'abortion' of an apostle, implying that he was as much an ugly parody of a true apostle as an abortion is of a healthy infant born at the proper time" (Bruce 142). Indeed, Schoeps finds in this accusation that Paul was an ἔκτρωμα, "immature and abortive, no genuine apostle" (81), "the real keynote of the whole Judaizing polemic" (82).

176. Georgi confines his investigation to 2:14–7:4 (without 6:14–7:1) and 10:1–13:13 for

73

But it is difficult to see how any group of missionaries active outside Judea before A.D. 66 (the outbreak of the Jewish revolt against Rome) who claimed to be preaching the Christian gospel could be without some connection with at least some figures within the Jerusalem church, whether that relation was formal, informal, *or merely purported.* Following the lead of Baur, who believed that the ψευδαπόστολοι were probably the disciples and emissaries of the Twelve in Jerusalem (1.253, 256, 277), Käsemann (45-48) identified these "false apostles" as envoys from the Jerusalem church but distinguished them from the ὑπερλίαν ἀπόστολοι, the original apostles,[177] whose authority was being shrewdly exploited by these delegates at Paul's expense. By referring to the Twelve or the "pillars" (James, Cephas, and John, Gal. 2:9) by the partially ironic expression, "superlative apostles," Paul was, at one and the same time, recognizing a certain preeminence that attached to the primitive apostles and yet maintaining a total aloofness from all the false inferences his opponents drew from their association with Jerusalem that had been expressed in their letters of commendation. In a similar way, Barrett regards the "false apostles" as Judaizing Jews, envoys of the Jerusalem church and of the three "pillars" or the Twelve in particular, but he also suggests that these "unsatisfactory agents" were in fact misrepresenting their principals, the "super-apostles."[178] Like Käsemann and Barrett, Martin distinguishes the ψευδαπόστολοι from the ὑπερλίαν ἀπόστολοι, a "slightly derogatory" reference to the "pillars" ("Opponents" 286); however, he proposes that these intruding "false apostles" were acting *ultra vires* even in coming to Corinth ("Opponents" 285), so that they were "possibly a group of self-appointed emissaries" (427).[179] In this latter suggestion Martin is following a proposal made in my 1976 commentary (313), which we may now develop in greater detail. Three affirmations about Paul's adversaries at the time of 2 Corinthians may be made and defended.

(1) They were Jews from Judea.

In 2 Cor. 11:22 Paul begins his distasteful task of foolish boasting (cf. 11:16). He assures the Corinthians that no bold claim of his rivals would go unmatched (11:21b). The first three claims establish their Jewishness — by descent, citizenship, and heritage. "Are they Ἑβραῖοι? So am I. Are they Ἰσραηλῖται? So am I. Are they σπέρμα Ἀβραάμ? So am I." Neither "Israelites" nor "seed of Abraham" proves that the adversaries were from Palestine, but "Hebrews" here probably denotes "a Jew of Palestinian descent" (W. Gutbrod, *TDNT* 3.390).

---

critical reasons which he discusses (*Opponents* 9-14), but his subsequent reflections (in his Epilogue of 1986) on the "Widening of the Textual Base" (*Opponents* 338-44) should be noted.

177. Baur (1.277) had regarded the ὑπερλίαν ἀπόστολοι as either the ψευδαπόστολοι or the three στῦλοι of Gal. 2:9.

178. Barrett 30-32, 276; "Christianity" 294-96; *Signs* 37-40; "Opponents" 252-53.

179. Martin ("Opponents" 286) speaks of these intruders as being from "the Antiochian hellenistic faction" (on which see his "Setting" 8-14).

74

The Palestinian provenance of Paul's opponents would be confirmed if they prided themselves on having a personal knowledge of the earthly Jesus (cf. 2 Cor. 5:16).

(2) They were independent agents, but
(3) they claimed to have the support of the Twelve in Jerusalem.

We must seek to substantiate the implied distinction between the "false apostles" and the "superlative apostles."

First, although Paul compares himself with both groups, in the former case the comparison is confident and positive ("so am I . . . I am a better one . . . far greater . . . far more . . . ," 11:22-23), whereas in the latter case it is mild and negative ("I am in no way inferior," 11:5; 12:11). Would Paul simultaneously claim to be "far superior" and "not in the least inferior" to one and the same group (cf. Käsemann 42)? In 1 Cor. 15:8-9 (cf. Gal. 2:6) Paul lays claim to parity of status with the original apostles in regard to apostleship, which correlates with "not in the least inferior."

Second, Paul's attitude toward the two groups seems vastly different. So far from according the intruders the status of ἀπόστολοι, he entitles them ψευδαπόστολοι, pretenders to apostleship, a term pregnant with OT connotations of deceit and doom. Though claiming to be Christ's apostles and servants (11:13, 23), they were in reality Satan's minions, whose destiny would be in accordance with their deeds (11:15). The other group, however, are ἀπόστολοι, genuine apostles, even if some people were elevating them above Paul to such a degree that they were being solemnly referred to as οἱ ὑπερλίαν ἀπόστολοι, "the super-extra apostles" (a rendering of Plummer [CGT] 208), or could be playfully given this title. Whereas the false apostles are precisely described (11:13, 15), the two references to the "ultra-apostles" (Lake's translation, 230) are mere allusions, each affording a ground (γάρ) for preceding statements (11:5; 12:11). This distinction between "false apostles" and "apostles," and between frontal attack and incidental allusion, corresponds to the ambiguity of Paul's situation in Corinth: he must smite the intruders but deal gently with the original apostles.

If, then, we ought to distinguish the ὑπερλίαν ἀπόστολοι from the ψευδαπόστολοι (see also the commentary at 11:5),[180] what was the genesis of the former expression? If it is closely associated with Gal. 2:9, these "superlative apostles" are the three "pillars," James (the brother of Jesus), Peter, and John; thus Martin 427, who renders οἱ ὑπερλίαν ἀπόστολοι by "the highest ranking apostles" (327, 425). This translation seems to imply a distinct group within the apostolic band, namely the Three. Even if Barrett is right in contending that "in course of time the Twelve tended to drop out of the picture, leaving

---

180. For a discussion of the difficulties of this view, see Furnish (503-5), Carson (25-27), and especially Thrall (671-76), all of whom, along with the majority of commentators, equate "the superlative apostles" with the "false apostles."

the direction of affairs in Jerusalem to the three 'pillars' " (*Signs* 39), we need not assume that the titular significance of "the Twelve" (οἱ δώδεκα) disappeared with any waning of their corporate influence (cf. Acts 6:2; 1 Cor. 15:5). We suggest that the phrase οἱ ὑπερλίαν ἀπόστολοι, rather than pointing to a subgroup within the Twelve, refers to all the original apostles, *regarded as* in some way superior (ὑπερλίαν) to other actual or would-be apostles. It is not a derogatory description of the Twelve coined by Paul, nor is he parodying a Corinthian view of the ψευδαπόστολοι. It is either the description of the Twelve regularly used by Paul's opponents as they compared his claim to be an ἀπόστολος Χριστοῦ Ἰησοῦ (1 Cor. 1:1; 2 Cor. 1:1) or ὁ ἐλάχιστος τῶν ἀποστόλων (1 Cor. 15:9) with the actual and superior status of the Twelve, or, more probably, the apostle's ironic description of the exalted view of the Twelve held by the "false apostles."[181]

Our suggestion, then, is that these Palestinian interlopers were, without justification, simply appealing to the Twelve in their effort to win over the Corinthians to their distinctive form of "Christian" doctrine and practice. They were not deputies of the Twelve or the Three who exceeded their delegated powers or misrepresented their principals.[182] It is exceedingly difficult to envisage Paul's branding his rivals as "sham apostles whose work is fraudulent" (11:13) and as "Satan's agents" (11:15) if in fact they could document some official link with the Twelve or the Three. It is impossible to say with any degree of confidence who wrote their letters of commendation (3:1), but these testimonials might have emanated from any of "the churches of Christ in Judea" (Gal. 1:22) or from representatives of the Pharisaic wing of the Jerusalem church, those Judaizers who regarded the scrupulous observance of the Mosaic Law as essential for salvation (Acts 15:5).[183]

---

181. Cf. Bruce 237: the designation is probably "Paul's way of summing up his opponents' portrayal of the Jerusalem leaders," with the "pillars" perhaps primarily in view. This identification is strengthened if the article in οἱ ὑπερλίαν ἀπόστολοι is taken as anaphoric or emphatically demonstrative: "those exalted apostles of yours" (cf. Hanson, *Ministry* 92). Thrall argues that although οἱ ὑπερλίαν ἀπόστολοι refers to the original Jerusalem apostles, Paul applies it to the intruders because they claimed to be ἀπόστολοι sent from Jerusalem and because it was (for Paul) conceivable, in the absence of precise news from Corinth (via Titus), that some of the original apostles might be numbered among these visiting missionaries ("Super-Apostles" 42, 48-49, 55; cf. her commentary 671-76). She rightly discerns the difficulty with this view when she maintains that in 11:13-15 Paul momentarily repudiates the possibility, entertained in 11:18-23, that some of the Jerusalem apostles were among his opponents ("Super-Apostles" 50).

182. We prefer to describe these interlopers as "self-appointed agents" carrying out their own mission. We may distinguish such "agents" from those sent to investigate, "inspectors" (e.g., Peter and John, Acts 8:14-25), from individuals who carry a message, "envoys" or "emissaries" (e.g., "certain men from James," Gal. 2:12), from persons sent to represent others, "delegates" or "deputies" (e.g., the two companions of Titus, 2 Cor. 8:23), and from persons dispatched to proselytize, "missionaries" (e.g., Philip, Acts 8:26).

183. Schoeps argues that Paul's adversaries were "emissaries of the Jerusalem church," authorized by letters from "leaders of the Jerusalem Judaistic group, who were the real ancestors of the Ebionites" (75). "These Corinthian intruders would never have been able to undermine Paul's

A historical precedent for such a purported relation to Jerusalem authorities may be found in the case mentioned in the letter promulgated after the Jerusalem council. "We have heard that some of our people (τινὲς ἐξ ἡμῶν) have disturbed you by their arguments, unsettling your minds, although they were not authorized by us (οἷς οὐ διεστειλάμεθα)" (Acts 15:24). What follows in the letter (Acts 15:25-27) is designed to reassure the addressees that, unlike their predecessors, the bearers of the letter, Judas and Silas, come with explicit and full accreditation from the apostles and elders of the Jerusalem church. If, as seems probable, the τινὲς ἐξ ἡμῶν of Acts 15:24 are to be equated with the τινὲς (κατελθόντες) ἀπὸ τῆς Ἰουδαίας of Acts 15:1 (and the ψευδάδελφοι of Gal. 2:4),[184] then we have an instance of self-appointed Jewish agents from Judea who were carrying their message beyond Judea and were claiming some relation to the Jerusalem leadership.[185]

e. Their Identity

There have always been scholars who have traced all the opposition to Paul reflected in his letters to a single source. Three modern proponents of this position may be mentioned.

In his two books *Gnosticism in Corinth* and *Paul and the Gnostics,* Schmithals argues vigorously for "the unity of the battlefront" in the Pauline epistles composed during the so-called third missionary journey: Paul confronted missionary representatives of a Jewish or Jewish-Christian Gnosticism, "a *Gnosticism* in the setting of Judaism or of Jewish Christianity with certain influences from the setting which did not alter the Gnostic substance" (294 n. 17; cf. *Gnostics* 62-64, 117-18, and especially 242-45). It was in Mesopotamia, the homeland of true Gnosticism and the second home of Judaism, that Jewish Gnosticism arose and flourished before migrating to the Mediterranean, where it was absorbed into Christian Gnosticism and other forms of Gnosticism (25-36, 295-96).[186]

---

prestige had they not been able to appeal to a real authority, indisputable in Christian eyes, namely that of the mother church" (76).

184. But the τινὲς ἀπὸ Ἰακώβου of Gal. 2:12 are almost certainly a different group, for they brought to Peter at Antioch an urgent warning ("Avoid fraternizing with Gentiles!"), whereas those "from Judea" brought to Gentile believers in Antioch an ultimatum ("Unless you are circumcised and keep the law of Moses, you cannot be saved"; cf. Acts 15:1, 5).

185. The latter point seems to be implied by οἷς οὐ διεστειλάμεθα (Acts 15:24), which means not "although we gave them no such instructions" but "although we gave them no instructions at all" or "although they had received no authorization from us." The need for the apostles and elders in Jerusalem to defend themselves by dissociating themselves from the cause espoused by the τινές suggests that these agents from Judea had been invoking the support of the leaders in Jerusalem.

186. On the debated question of the definition of Gnosticism and its existence in the pre-Christian era and the first century see Arai; Wilson, *Gnosis, Problem,* "Corinthians," and "Corinth;" and Yamauchi, *Gnosticism,* "Debate."

Gunther chooses seven broad themes — Judaic legalism, asceticism, sacerdotal separation, angelology, messianism and pneumatology, apocalyptic-mystic Gnosticism, and apostolic authority — and examines the polemical sections of Paul's letters[187] and of literature that emanates from the Pauline circle for evidence of these themes, which is then compared with corresponding data ("parallels") from apocalyptic and Jewish sectarian literature. He summarizes his findings thus: "Paul's literary adversaries were believers whose background was a mystic-apocalyptic, ascetic, non-conformist, syncretistic Judaism more akin to Essenism than to any other well-known 'school' or holiness sect" (315). More briefly he states this conclusion in his foreword: the substance of the beliefs and practices of Paul's opponents should be seen "as being akin to contemporary esoteric Palestinian Judaism, qualified by the teachings of Jesus."

Finally, according to Ellis, early Christianity was composed of two groups, Hebrews and Hellenists. The Hebrews, not to be distinguished from "those of the circumcision" or "the circumcision party," were Jewish Christians (and/or Jews) who had a strict attitude toward Jewish law and customs and exhibited ascetic tendencies. On the other hand, the Hellenists, who included Paul and most of his co-workers in their number, were marked by a more liberal attitude toward the ritual law and showed some gnosticizing-libertine tendencies. The tension between these two groups was apparent in the Jerusalem church (Acts 6:1) before the Gentile question arose and was reflected in a two-pronged diaspora mission, Hellenist *and* Hebrew, although Col. 4:11 shows that some ritually strict Hebrews cooperated with Paul as they pursued their distinctive missions. But other Hebrews from within the Jerusalem church were factious and spearheaded opposition to the Hellenist missions, including Paul's mission. Active from Syria to Rome, these adversaries sometimes operated as a counter-mission and sometimes merely as an infiltrating influence. Wherever we find opposition to Paul reflected in his letters, it stems from this single integrated group of "pneumatics" who, like Paul and his co-workers, laid claim to "pneumatic" experiences such as discernment into the meaning of Scripture, inspired speech, visions, and revelation (*Prophecy* xiv-xv, 101-28).

So multifarious were the forms of anti-Paulinism in the early church that most scholars regard it as antecedently improbable that the opposition everywhere was, for instance, Gnostic (Schmithals) or pneumatic (Ellis). And Gunther's description of Paul's antagonists as everywhere "syncretists, gnostics and pneumatics in the same sense that the terms are applicable to the Essenes or Qumranians" (317) is so generalized that they are effectively reduced to faceless entities.

If we now restrict our attention to the Corinthian letters, again we discover that some argue for identity of opponent at each stage of Paul's relation to the church at Corinth as reflected in 1 and 2 Corinthians. To mention two schol-

187. Namely, in the chronological order proposed by Gunther (16): Galatians, 2 Corinthians, Phil. 3:1b-19, Rom. 16:1-27, Colossians.

ars whose research is separated by a century, Godet identifies Paul's rivals as intruding proto-gnostics, forerunners of the fully developed Gnosticism of the second and third centuries (74-79), while Marshall depicts them as principally Corinthian "hybrists," educated Hellenists of high social status who contemptuously denigrated Paul, using traditional forms of invective (364-80, 403-4; "Hybrists"; "Invective").[188] For our later discussion it is significant to note that whereas Godet locates the continuity of opposition in persons outside the Corinthian congregation, Marshall finds the continuity in a sector of the church itself.[189]

But there is a fair degree of unanimity that we should distinguish 2 Corinthians from 1 Corinthians with respect to the nature of the opposition Paul faced (but see Winter, *Philo* 234-35 and *passim*). In spite of a superficial resemblance between ἐγὼ δὲ Χριστοῦ (1 Cor. 1:12) and Χριστοῦ εἶναι (2 Cor. 10:7) in that both are claims to belong to Christ which Paul reports, the situation he confronts has significantly changed in the interval between the letters. "Whereas 1 Cor. i.12 deals with native inhabitants of the Corinthian Church, 2 Cor. x–xiii is directed against strangers who intrude themselves into the Church from without" (Barrett, "Christianity" 287; similarly Windisch 25-26). Those scholars who hold to a partition theory of 2 Corinthians in one form or another rarely distinguish the opposition in chs. 10–13 from that encountered in chs. 1–9 (or 1–7 or 2:14–7:4), though they often argue that the gravity of the situation at Corinth has altered (e.g., Georgi 13-14).

Writing in 1973, Gunther isolated some thirteen identifications of Paul's opponents in 2 Corinthians that had been proposed in the previous 150 years, adding the names of some proponents of these views (1):

> wandering Jewish preachers taking over the Gnostic pneumatic opposition of 1 Corinthians (Windisch)
> the same Jewish Christian Gnostics opposed in 1 Corinthians (Bultmann, Schmithals, Dinkler, Wilckens, Güttgemanns)
> pneumatic-libertine Gnostics (Lütgert, Schlatter)
> Gnostics (Bousset, Reitzenstein, Schniewind)
> Alexandrian syncretistic, antinomian pneumatics (Lake)

---

188. Marshall believes that an alliance was formed between these Corinthian "hybrists" and the rival apostles (263-65). Negotiations between the two groups began before 1 Corinthians was written (265) and by the time of 2 Corinthians (which is viewed as a unity) the enmity between Paul and this alliance had reached a peak ("Hybrists" 286-87).

189. A detailed defense of the view that in both 1 and 2 Corinthians Paul is dealing with the same opponents is found in Hall (3-14; see also Lüdemann, *Opposition* 94), who identifies some nine themes common to Paul's discussion of his opponents in the two letters: apostleship, payment, the signs of an apostle, boasting, eloquence, Gnostic dualism, spirituality, Jewish birth, and apostolic qualifications. But Paul's approach differs. Because, in 1 Corinthians, Paul is in danger of losing his influence at Corinth, his approach is indirect and conciliatory, but in 2 Corinthians 10–13 he dares to launch a frontal attack against his opponents because news has reached him through Titus of the Corinthian reconciliation (21-22).

Jewish-pagan-Christian Gnostics (Allo)
Hellenistic Jewish Christians (Menzies, Bornkamm, Georgi, Betz)[190]
Non-Judaizing Jewish Christians (McGiffert)
Palestinian Jewish Christian Gnostics (Kümmel, Gilmour)
Jewish Christian syncretists with Gnostic elements (Marxsen)
Jerusalem Judaizers (Baur, Klöpper, Holtzmann, Hausrath, Holsten, Schmiedel, Hort, Manson, Käsemann, Schoeps, Barrett)[191]
Palestinian Jews — not Judaizers in the Galatian sense (Bruce)
Judaizers (Jervell, Prümm, Oostendorp, Bandstra)
Judaizers and pneumatic Gnostics (Lietzmann, Wikenhauser)

To these proposals we may now add:

Conservative Hebrew pneumatics from Jerusalem (Ellis, *Prophecy* 115)[192]
Jewish-Christian nationalists representing the Judaizing wing of Palestinian Christianity (Forbes 15; "Opponents" 22)
Educated Hellenists who were "hybrists" (Marshall, "Hybrists" 283-87)
Hellenistic Jews propagating "spiritual gnosticism" (Kee 69)
pneumatics who required and emphasized manifestations of the Spirit in apostles (Sumney 147, 177-79, 190; *Servants* 101, 29)
pneumatic Jewish Christians with an interest in *sophia* (Witherington 346 n. 49)

Because some of the categories in Gunther's list overlap, we may reduce all this to four principal identifications: Hellenistic Jewish propagandists, pneumatics, Gnostics, and Judaizers.

My own solution to this complex problem may be summed up in two proposals, which may be stated and then defended.

(1) *Throughout his ministry at Corinth and therefore at the time of both 1 and 2 Corinthians, Paul encountered opposition from a sector of the Corinthian church that may be termed "proto-gnostic" in their denial of a future bodily resurrection, their libertinism or asceticism in morals, and their pride in γνῶσις.*[193]

---

190. So also Friedrich ("Gegner" 181-215), Furnish (48-54), Koester (127), and F. Lang (359).

191. So also Lüdemann (*Opposition* 94-97) and Barnett (34-35, 35 n. 141, 162; "Opposition"), who argues that Paul's opponents were "on a Judaizing mission to bring the Gentile Corinthians under obligation to the written Mosaic code"("Opponents of Paul," in *DPL* 649).

192. Ellis defines "pneumatics" as "persons with charisms of inspired speech and discernment" ("Opponents" 287 [= *Prophecy* 104]; cf. his "Gifts" 128-44).

193. In this context we must distinguish "opponents" from recalcitrant church members. When visitors infiltrate a church with a view to undermining the leadership, they are clearly "opponents." But this term may also be appropriately applied to any segment of a Pauline church that on a long-term and principial basis rejected apostolic doctrine or practice.

From 1 Cor. 15:12 we learn that an influential group within the Corinthian church (ἐν ὑμῖν τινες) was propagating (λέγουσιν) the belief "that there is no resurrection of the dead." There is, however, no scholarly unanimity concerning the precise nature of their denial (see Thiselton 1172-76, 1216). This vocal minority may have asserted that the concept of the resurrection is superfluous, since the soul perishes with the body; that resurrection is impossible, since only the soul survives death and is immortal; or that the resurrection is past, since at baptism Christians are spiritually raised with Christ to "walk in newness of life" (cf. Rom. 6:4).[194] Paul's argument in 1 Corinthians 15 could be read as an apt response to any one of these assertions. Certainly we should not dismiss the possibility that the Corinthian "anti-resurrectionists" were a group of proud rationalists or mystical enthusiasts who were promulgating the doctrine of the immortality of the soul and arguing that resurrection was impossible or inconceivable. But, since at least some of the Corinthians believed that the Age to Come had already fully arrived (1 Cor. 4:8; cf. Phil. 3:11-12; 2 Tim. 2:17-18), it seems more probable that the deniers of the resurrection at Corinth asserted that the only resurrection — the spiritual — was accomplished at baptism and therefore lay in the past.[195] While the motives behind this Corinthian denial of a future resurrection cannot be precisely determined, it is unlikely that ultra-spiritualists were simply pressing Paul's doctrine of baptismal resurrection to its logical conclusions or merely ignoring its futuristic implications, since this doctrinal formulation itself appears only in epistles written after the Corinthian correspondence. More probably the defense of the ἤδη principle, or resurrection as a *fait accompli,* arose from the desire of these Corinthians to maintain a facade of orthodoxy (namely the doctrine of baptismal resurrection) while propounding their aberrant view that the Christian hope consisted primarily of emancipation from corporeal defilement.

An indication of the persistent influence of this view at Corinth may be found in 2 Cor. 5:2-4. Whereas in 1 Cor. 15:53-54 Paul spoke twice of "putting on immortality," in his second letter he seems deliberately to be avoiding that earlier phrase (even though a mixed metaphor results in 2 Cor. 5:2!), and has substituted the verb "put on *over*" for "put on" to stress the continuity between the inner person being renewed each day (2 Cor. 4:16) and the resurrection body to be gained after death. Even in 5:4 where "immortality" would neatly match "mortality," the term is avoided and the more positive word "life" is used. Could it be that the τινές of 1 Cor. 15:12 had maliciously understood the innocent clause "put on immortality" to imply that disembodied immortality formed the

---

194. This minority believed that the concept of the resurrection was superfluous, according to Doughty (75). According to Lietzmann (79) and Wilson (53), this group argued that resurrection is impossible. Schniewind (110-39), Käsemann (125-26), Kümmel (192-93), J. H. Wilson (90-107), and, with some qualifications, Thiselton ("Eschatology" 510-26) hold that these dissidents regarded resurrection as a *fait accompli.*

195. On the matter of "realized eschatology" at Corinth, see Thiselton 357-65; "Eschatology" 510-26; Towner 95-124.

content of the Christian hope? In keeping with this, 2 Cor. 5:3 might be paraphrased this way: "My assumption, to be sure, is that once this investiture has taken place, we shall not find ourselves to be disembodied — as some of you wish!" Similarly 5:4 may be rendered, "For it is a fact that as long as we are tent-dwellers we sigh with a sense of oppression because — so far from wishing to become disembodied — we desire to put on [our heavenly dwelling] over [our earthly]." Paul here uses his favorite οὐ(κ) . . . ἀλλά antithesis (literally, "we sigh . . . because we do *not* wish to strip off *but* to put on over"), which, as we have seen, not infrequently contains an explicit or implicit yet clear reference to some well-known conception of which he expresses disapproval.[196] That is, in the parenthesis of 5:3 and the "put off–put on" antithesis of 5:4 we probably have Paul's rebuttal of an aberrant view of the hereafter entertained by some Corinthians who appear to have accepted the idea of a spiritual resurrection as signified in baptism but refused to accept the idea of a future bodily resurrection. Those who were the targets of a frontal assault in 1 Cor. 15:12-57 have become, we suggest, the objects of an incidental attack in 2 Cor. 5:2-4.

In addition, both Corinthian epistles testify to the presence of libertines in the church. Even if 1 Cor. 6:9-10 is similar to contemporary pagan or Jewish lists of vices to be avoided and although Paul can affirm that "some of you (Corinthians) once belonged to these classes of people" (v. 11), he is warning some or all the Christians at Corinth to stop imagining (cf. μὴ πλανᾶσθε, v. 19) that they can continue practicing these sins yet inherit the kingdom of God. He immediately proceeds to cite two or perhaps three libertarian slogans used at Corinth, as he inveighs against sexual license (vv. 12-20): "everything is permissible for me" (6:12; cf. 10:23); "food is for the stomach and the stomach for food" (6:13a), from which some Corinthians apparently inferred that the satisfaction of other physical appetites, such as the sexual drive, was equally inevitable and desirable, that "the body is . . . meant for sexual immorality" (cf. 6:13b). Behind the Corinthian failure to discipline the man guilty of incest (1 Cor. 5:1-2) lay just such a permissive attitude toward sexuality. The few had infected the many: "Don't you realize that a little leaven (μικρὰ ζύμη) ferments the whole batch of dough?" (5:6).

In spite of Paul's injunctions, encapsulated in 1 Cor. 6:18 ("Flee from immorality"), it seems that sexual permissiveness persisted among some of the Corinthian Christians. As he anticipated his third visit to Corinth, Paul feared that on arrival he might have to mourn over "many" (πολλοί) who have sinned previously and have not yet repented of "their filthy, immoral, licentious behavior" (2 Cor. 12:21, Wand). It was especially to these persons who were given

---

196. On this view, what Paul is repudiating in v. 4 is the notion that "stripping off," that is, becoming disembodied, leads to an ideal state of somatic nakedness. Certainly it is apparent that γυμνός in v. 3 is intimately connected with ἐκδύσασθαι in v. 4, one referring to the state of nakedness, the other to entrance upon that state. Moreover, both words are linked with the negative (οὐ) as well as with their opposite ("assuming that, when we have *put it on,* we shall find ourselves *not* naked"; "we do *not* wish to strip off but to *put it on as an overgarment*").

over to sensuality, but also to all the Corinthians, that Paul issued the directive, unique in its comprehensiveness, "Let us cleanse ourselves from everything that can defile flesh or spirit" (2 Cor. 7:1).

Thus far we have discussed two features of the belief and behavior of Paul's Corinthian adversaries that are common to both epistles: spiritualized eschatology and libertinism. This might encourage us to speak of his internal opponents as pneumatic libertines, or even more generally as educated freethinking natives of Corinth.[197] But there are two further characteristics of these opponents, evident only in 1 Corinthians, that lead us to prefer the label "precursors of Gnosticism" or more simply "proto-gnostics."[198] One was their claim to have distinctive γνῶσις; the other, their advocacy of asceticism. As it happens, both of these characteristics were summed up in slogans that we may reconstruct from Paul's reply.

From 1 Cor. 8:1-13 it appears that a particular clique at Corinth, laying claim to true knowledge about the nature of idols, were scandalizing those who lacked such knowledge ("the weak") by accepting invitations to meals in heathen temples and eating food that had been offered to idols. Vv. 1 and 4 probably contain their claim, which Paul may have reproduced from the letter from Corinth brought to him at Ephesus. "Concerning food offered to idols, all of us possess knowledge: an idol has no existence in the real world and there is no God but one." Although Paul agrees (οἴδαμεν ὅτι, vv. 1, 4) that the gods of idolatry have no objective existence, he recognizes that for the worshiper these gods have a subjective reality, so that some of the Corinthians who had been immersed in idolatry before their conversion continued to regard food which had been offered to idols as real sacrifice to real gods (v. 7). Those with robust consciences must not bring ruin on those with weak consciences (vv. 9–13). Paul's point is that within the Christian community the possession of γνῶσις concerning εἰδωλόθυτα afforded a basis, not for scornful discrimination against "the weak," but for considerate understanding of "believers for whom Christ died" (v. 11). Such discrimination on the basis of γνῶσις is not unlike that of those second- and third-century Gnostics who distinguished average, common

197. H. E. W. Turner, for example, finds behind 1 Cor. 15:12b "a protest against the Hebrew doctrine of the Resurrection of the Body in the interests of the Greek theory of the Immortality of the Soul" (10), and wryly observes that "a strict sexual morality does not usually characterize the life of a great port. Immorality may as easily be 'unprincipled' as 'principled' " (69). On the relation between the hedonistic lifestyle of some of the Corinthian Christians and belief in the immortality of the soul, see Winter 76-109.

198. This argument presupposes that in the case of the church at Corinth it is methodologically preferable to attempt to explain how various beliefs and patterns of behavior may be predicated of a single group than to multiply entities and posit several vying minorities in the church, especially if the size of the whole congregation was fewer than fifty (see Banks 41-42) and if Dahl is correct in his contention ("Corinth" 322) that within the congregation itself there were not four "parties," as 1 Cor. 1:12 might suggest at first glance, but only two, a pro-Pauline group whose slogan was "I belong to Paul" and an anti-Pauline consensus whose party cries were really declarations of independence from Paul.

Christians ("the many," σαρκικοί or ὑλικοί) who were characterized by unreasoning faith from the initiated, privileged Christians (the few, τέλειοι or πνευματικοί) who possessed the distinctive γνῶσις of self and of the hidden mysteries of the universe (cf. Wilson, *Problem* 72-73, 90 n. 59).

The transition from 1 Cor. 6:12-20 to ch. 7 illustrates the fact that Paul was obliged to wage warfare on two fronts — against libertines and against ascetics (Bruce 66). As he begins to answer the questions raised in the Corinthians' letter (note περὶ δέ in 1 Cor. 7:1, 25; 8:1; 12:1; 16:1,12), Paul first cites the watchword of these ascetics: "It is appropriate for a man not to have any sexual relations with a woman" (1 Cor. 7:1). Applying this principle to various groups within the church, the ascetics apparently urged married persons to remain celibate (7:2-6 is Paul's response) or preferably to dissolve their marriages (cf. 7:10-16, 27a); the unmarried, including widows, should remain single (cf. 7:7-9, 25-35, 39-40); and engaged couples should not marry (cf. 7:36-38).

Now it may seem strange that one and the same group could include both libertines and ascetics, but here too a "proto-gnostic" hypothesis may prove helpful. One cardinal doctrine of developed Gnosticism, which arose from an emphasis on the transcendence of God, concerned the utter vileness of the material world. The assertion that the material body was defiled and its corollary that bodily actions were completely indifferent gave rise not only to abstinence from all fleshly gratification but also to the unembarrassed fulfillment of all natural appetites. From the same premiss two radically different ethical codes were derived, one advocating asceticism, the other, libertinism. These two codes of conduct solidified in two later Gnostic groups, the Encratites and the Carpocratians (respectively).

To speak of incipient Gnosticism or of "proto-gnostics" at Corinth is not to imply that a lineal connection may be traced between alleged antecedents of Gnosticism at Corinth and any one of the second-century classical systems, but rather to suggest that certain gnosticizing tendencies were in evidence within one sector of the Corinthian church which were symptomatic of mature Gnosticism in one or another of its forms, namely denial of future bodily resurrection,[199] vaunting of γνῶσις, libertinism, and asceticism. If we are to find continuity in the opposition to Paul from 1 Corinthians to 2 Corinthians, it is not to be located in missionary intruders, nor in the Cephas party (as Barrett, "Chris-

---

199. See Pagels 81-86 and references there. That not all Gnostic thought adhered to the purely spiritual character of the resurrection is shown, for example, by the *Epistle to Rheginus* (see Peel 145-49) and the *Gospel of Philip*. Wilson (*Philip* 88-89; cf. *Gnosis* 74-75) points out that in *Philip* 104:26-34 the author may be attacking those who would uphold *simply* a resurrection of the flesh ("those who bear the flesh [it is they who are] naked"), while in 105:9-15 the Greek doctrine that only the soul is immortal ("you say that the flesh will not rise") is possibly being contested, with a view to defending the position that a fleshly resurrection is a necessary prelude to a fleshly stripping and then a clothing in a heavenly garment (cf. 114:4-7: "Be not fearful of the flesh, nor love it. If you fear before it, it will become master over you. If you love it, it will swallow and paralyze you").

tianity" 297 holds) or the Christ party (as Allo, *Première épître* 86-87), but in a "proto-gnostic" segment of the church which it is impossible to align with any of the watchwords or parties mentioned in 1 Cor. 1:12.[200]

(2) *When he wrote 2 Corinthians, Paul was in conflict with a group of Palestinian intruders who had infiltrated the Corinthian church after 1 Corinthians had been received there and who, although claiming to be Christian, were in reality "Judaizers."*

That his antagonists purported to be Christian is evident from several passages: "If anyone is confident in his own mind (ἑαυτῷ) that he belongs to Christ . . ." (2 Cor. 10:7), "masquerading as apostles of Christ" (11:13), "Are they Christ's servants?" (11:23). However, the form in which Paul expresses these claims indicates that he repudiates or at least demurs at such claims. When he asks the rhetorical question "Are they Christ's servants?" (11:23) and answers it with "I am more one than they," he interposes the observation "I am out of my senses in saying this," which may well apply to what precedes as much as to what follows. In this case he would be arguing *e concessis.* Alternatively, the sense may be "Do they claim to be/do you hold them to be servants of Christ?" Unlike the first three rhetorical questions in 11:22-23, which relate to matters of incontestable fact, this fourth question may introduce the dimension of personal estimation. Either way, 11:23 affords no evidence that would contradict Paul's blanket condemnation of the rival apostles in 11:13-15.

In reference to the view that Paul's opponents were "Judaizers," Lake delivers what he takes to be the *coup de grâce:* "The great objection to it can be stated in one sentence, — there is from the beginning to the end of the Epistles to the Corinthians not the faintest trace of any controversy as to that insistence on circumcision and on the Law, which we recognize as cardinal in those to the Galatians and Romans" (222; similarly Lütgert 41-47). Indeed. But Lake recognizes that it is a matter of what is meant by "Judaizer" (225-26). If a Judaizer is defined as one who insists on circumcision as a prerequisite for salvation (cf. Acts 15:1), Paul's antagonists were not Judaizers, for 2 Corinthians lacks any trace of a dispute over circumcision. But if a Judaizer is one who tries to impose Jewish practices upon Gentiles as conditions either for salvation or for the enjoyment of Christian fellowship, then the opposition to Paul may appropriately be labeled Judaizing. There is good reason, therefore, to pause before identifying the ψευδαδελφοί of Gal. 2:4, who insisted on circumcision (Gal. 5:2-3, 12; 6:12-13), calendrical observances (4:10), and law-keeping (2:16; 5:4), with the ψευδαπόστολοι of 2 Cor. 11:13. Both may be termed "Judaizers," but they differed in modus operandi.[201]

---

200. But J. M. Robinson claims that "we may assume that the arrival of 1 Corinthians in Corinth collapsed the radical, gnosticizing left wing of the congregation which was perhaps the Apollos party" ("Kerygma" 140). A position similar to that espoused in the text is found in Drane 100-106.

201. It is the view of Bruce that "the earlier form of judaizing activity in Paul's mission field, which invoked the name of James and insisted on circumcision, gave way to a later form,

This alteration of tactic is most easily explained if we date Galatians before the Apostolic Council of Acts 15 (a date which is in any case preferable on other grounds[202]). That Jerusalem Council of A.D. 49 had settled, at least for the time being, the matter of the role of circumcision in Christian salvation by rejecting this Jewish rite as a means of obtaining and maintaining membership among the newly constituted people of God (Acts 15:19).[203] Those Judaizers who had made the demand for circumcision the central plank of their Judaizing platform in Galatia were replaced by others who surrendered this demand, along with any insistence on calendrical observances, in their Judaizing efforts in Corinth in the mid-fifties. Even if these missionary propagandists shared with their predecessors the ultimate goal of bringing all Gentile churches into submission to the mother church in Jerusalem, their tactics were different as a result of the principal decision of the Council.[204] Perhaps the focus of their attention now was the codicil of the Jerusalem Decree, especially its food regulations (Acts 15:20, 29; 21:25).[205] But it is not inappropriate to speak in more general terms of the opponents' attempt to reproduce Jerusalem in Corinth or to claim Corinth for Jerusalem by instilling Palestinian thought and practice in the Corinthian believers, and in particular a general adherence to the Mosaic Law.

We may bring this discussion to a close by relating (1) and (2), and therefore suggesting that at the time he wrote 2 Corinthians Paul faced two sets of opponents, Corinthian "proto-gnostics" and Palestinian "Judaizers." Since both groups had a virulent antipathy to aspects of Pauline teaching and to Paul himself, it would have been strange if they had not closed ranks in their common opposition to the apostle and formed a temporary, if uneasy, alliance.[206]

---

which invoked rather the name of Peter and did not insist on circumcision. The former is reflected in Galatians, the latter in the Corinthian correspondence" ("Jerusalem" 12-13; cf. 14-15).

202. See Fung, *Galatians* 9-28 and the literature cited there.

203. The demand for circumcision was not always part of Jewish missionary efforts in the first century (cf. Josephus, *Antiquities* 20.38-48; Lüdemann, *Opposition* 95-96). In his thorough discussion of Jewish missionary activity during the Second Temple period, McKnight concludes that there is no evidence that prompts the conclusion that Judaism was a "missionary religion" in the sense of aggressive attempts to convert Gentiles or exhibition of self-identity (117). He emphasizes the absence of firm data regarding initiatory requirements imposed on converts to Judaism during the first century A.D.: "Different Jews had different requirements at different periods in history" (78). So while in many cases circumcision, and in some cases baptism and/or sacrifice, might have been required, the principal obligations for the proselyte were repentance from sin and idolatry and joining Jews in the worship of the one true God and in obedience to the law (78-89).

204. It is theoretically possible, but unlikely, that Paul's adversaries at Corinth were the same as those he faced in Galatia but had chosen no longer to include circumcision in their Judaizing demands or, for reasons unknown to us, had suppressed this requirement at Corinth.

205. So Barrett, "Idols"; Bruce, "Jerusalem" 14, 16; Barnett, "Opposition." There is no evidence in the Corinthian epistles of Paul's own effort to enforce at Corinth the supplementary addition to the decree (cf. Acts 15:41; 16:4; *pace* Barnett, "Opposition") or that he regarded it as permanently and universally binding on Christians.

206. This proposal of an "alliance of convenience" between two *distinct* groups, legalistic Judaizers and libertine "proto-gnostics," overcomes the difficulty with Ellis's view that the opponents were strict, conservative Jews of an Essene type who *nevertheless* themselves shared the lib-

Our overall conclusion is this. Paul's opponents were probably Jews from Judea — perhaps Jerusalem — who came to Corinth as self-appointed agents of a Judaizing program. They claimed to be Christian, illegitimately invoked the authority of the Twelve, and found common cause with a group of Corinthian "proto-Gnostics" in their attempt to undermine Paul and his apostolic work.

5. Paul's Collection for Jerusalem

No clearer evidence exists of Paul's commitment to social service and his abilities as a skilled strategist than the "collection for the poor" to which he devoted a considerable part of his time and energy during A.D. 52-57. Of the three passages in which he discusses this collection (Rom. 15:25-32; 1 Cor. 16:1-4; 2 Corinthians 8–9), by far the longest is in 2 Corinthians (some 39 verses). We have already reviewed the various partition theories involving 2 Corinthians 8–9 (see A.3.d. above) and reached the conclusion that the objections that have been raised against the integrity of these two chapters are less potent than the evidence for their belonging together and their coherence with chs. 1–7. Their integrity within 2 Corinthians as a whole (see A.3.e.[3]) will therefore be assumed in the discussion that follows.

In referring to this collection Paul uses several designations. The fullest is found in Rom. 15:26, (κοινωνία . . .) εἰς τοὺς πτωχοὺς τῶν ἁγίων[207] τῶν ἐν Ἰερουσαλήμ, "(contribution) for the poor among God's people in Jerusalem." Other descriptions seem to be abbreviations or modifications of this: ἡ διακονία ἡ εἰς τοὺς ἁγίους (2 Cor. 8:4; 9:1; cf. Rom. 15:25; 2 Cor. 9:12, "the relief aid/ contribution/service for God's people"), which may have been the official name for the whole enterprise (so Betz 46, 90), ἡ λογεία ἡ εἰς τοὺς ἁγίους (1 Cor. 16:1, "the collection for God's people"), ἡ διακονία μου ἡ εἰς Ἰερουσαλήμ (Rom. 15:31, "my service for Jerusalem"), ἡ χάρις ὑμῶν εἰς Ἰερουσαλήμ (1 Cor.

---

ertine sentiments of some of the Corinthians (*Prophecy* 104, 115), or with Hughes's description of the rival apostles as *both* "judaizers" *and* "libertines" (357). And it is of interest to note that Jewett claims to have discovered a similar alliance or alignment of agitators from outside the church and "pneumatic libertines" from within the church in the case of the Galatian congregation ("Agitators"). For Marshall's suggestion of an alliance between Corinthian "hybrists" and Paul's rival apostles, see n. 188 above. In a similar way Murphy-O'Connor (12-15; cf. "Judaizers," "2 Corinthians," and *Paul* 302-4) perceives an alliance between the Corinthian "Spirit-people" (*pneumatikoi;* cf. 1 Cor. 2:15), who were influenced by Philonism through Apollos and alienated by 1 Corinthians, and the intruding Judaizers who came from the conservative Jerusalem church. These two groups of opponents found "tenuous common ground" in the figure of Moses. "The Judaizers revered him as the Law-giver, while the Spirit-people probably saw him as the perfect wise man who embodied all the Hellenistic virtues" (15). Then again, according to Kee, it was a reconstituted "Christ party," composed of Christians with Gnostic tendencies, that formed the nucleus around which Paul's adversaries — Hellenistic Jews propagating "spiritual gnosticism" (69) — built up their opposition (74).

207. For a discussion of the meaning of this genitive, see below under 5.b.

16:3, "your gift for Jerusalem"). From these data, we can see that either "Jerusalem" or "God's people" (οἱ ἅγιοι) serve as abbreviations for the destination of the collection, "the poor among God's people in Jerusalem.'

a. The Need at Jerusalem

Whether the collection was actually delivered to Jerusalem in A.D. 55 (Jeremias, *Abba* 237-38) or, as seems more probable, in A.D. 57 (Jewett, *Chronology* 101), there are numerous indications that there had been a persistent need for economic relief for impoverished members of the Jerusalem church since its inception.

(1) The constant influx of Jewish converts (Acts 2:41, 47; 4:4; 6:7; 9:31; 21:20) put continual pressure on the resources of the church as it sought to care for those who were ostracized socially and economically as a result of their conversion (cf. Acts 8:1; 9:1-2; cf. Duncan 259-60). Also, there was a considerable number of needy widows in the church (Acts 6:1; cf. Mark 12:42; Luke 21:1-4).

(2) On two occasions Luke refers to the voluntary sharing of proceeds from the sale of goods and property (Acts 2:44-45; 4:34-35). This was no luxurious "experiment in communism" or reckless liquidation of capital assets, but an economic necessity to ensure corporate survival.[208] But in the long run this communal sharing undoubtedly would have aggravated — though it did not cause (*contra* Dodd, *Romans* 230) — the poverty that had become endemic.

(3) Throughout the principate of Claudius (A.D. 41-54) there were droughts and famines (Suetonius, *Claudius* 18.2; see Bruce, *Acts* 276), the most severe and widespread spanning the years 45-47 (cf. Acts 11:28). This famine would have been prolonged and aggravated by the sabbatical year, beginning fall 47, when land had to lie fallow (Jeremias, *Jerusalem* 143; *Abba* 235 n. 15). Gapp rightly observes (261) that famine is always a class famine, affecting the poor before and more than the rich. "While all classes of society suffered serious economic discomfort during a shortage of grain, the actual hunger and starvation were restricted to the lower classes" (261), from which Christians (at least in Jerusalem) largely came.

(4) Living in Jerusalem was expensive in the first century. The city's unfavorable geographical and commercial position meant that water was always in short supply, raw materials scarce, and food prices inflated.[209] At the gates of Jerusalem custom duties were levied on agricultural produce for sale in the city (M. Stern in Safrai and Stern 333). Fruit purchased in Jerusalem cost three to

---

208. The succession of iterative imperfects (ἐπίπρασκον . . . διεμέριζον, Acts 2:45; ὑπῆρχον . . . ἔφερον . . . ἐτίθουν . . . διεδίδετο, Acts 4:34-35) suggests that although a common fund had doubtless been created, it was supplemented at intervals to meet needs as they arose.

209. But for an indication of the intense economic activity in Jerusalem during the first century, see S. Applebaum in Safrai and Stern 683-84.

six times its price in the country (Jeremias, *Jerusalem* 121). When a harvest failed, the normal prices — already inflated — could multiply up to sixteen times (*Jerusalem* 122-23). And Josephus mentions a house tax that was levied in Jerusalem (*Antiquities* 19.299).

(5) As the mother church of Christendom, the Jerusalem church was obliged to support a proportionately large number of teachers (cf. Acts 6:4; 1 Cor. 9:4-6) and probably to provide hospitality for frequent Christian visitors to the holy city (cf. Rom. 12:13; Heb. 13:2; 1 Pet. 4:9).

(6) Palestinian Jews were subject to a crippling twofold taxation — civil (Roman) and religious (Jewish) — which, in the time of Jesus, may have been between thirty and forty percent of total income (see Grant 87-105). During the reign of Tiberius (A.D. 14-37) Judea became overwhelmed by its tax burden and requested imperial relief (Tacitus, *Annals* 2.42).

b. "The Poor" in Jerusalem

There are two Pauline passages where "the poor" (οἱ πτωχοί) at Jerusalem are mentioned in connection with monetary aid — Gal. 2:10 and Rom. 15:26.

Gal. 2:1-10 recounts a visit that Paul and Barnabas paid to Jerusalem during which they received from the three "pillars," James, Cephas, and John, not only recognition of their role as missionaries to the Gentiles but also a single urgent request: "All they asked was that we should go on remembering (ἵνα μνημονεύωμεν) the poor — which in fact, was the very thing I had shown my eagerness (ἐσπούδασα) to do" (Gal. 2:10).[210] If we equate this visit with the famine relief visit of Acts 11:30; 12:25 (see Fung, *Galatians* 10-28), Paul is not referring in v. 10b to his diligence *after* the visit in complying with the request to remember the poor but to the fact that he had *already* taken the initiative in this matter by helping to organize and deliver to Jerusalem the Antiochene famine relief; he was no puppet of the Twelve or the Three. This interpretation — certainly a contested one[211] — accords well with the central thrust of Galatians 1–2, where Paul emphasizes, not his dependence on Jerusalem as would be evidenced by obedience to a demand ("Remember the poor — and I did"), but his independence of the Jerusalem apostles especially with respect to his receipt of the gospel and his calling to proclaim it (1:1, 11-12, 15-19; 2:6-9).

But who were "the poor" to whom the "pillars" referred? It is certainly

---

210. For a discussion of the translation of this verse, and in particular the two verbs noted, see Hall, "Famine" 310; Bruce, *Paul* 156, who renders the verse, " 'Only,' said they, 'please continue to remember the poor'; and in fact I had made a special point of attending to this very matter."

211. Knox, for example, regards ἐσπούδασα as a reference to the "unique undertaking" of the major collection for the saints that Paul began after the conference of Gal. 2:1-10 (57-58). Or again, according to Georgi (41-42), μνημονεύωμεν envisages that Gentile believers should constantly bear in mind the importance and achievements of the Jerusalem church and express this attitude in due recognition, gratitude, and intercession, and also in financial aid.

tempting to regard οἱ πτωχοί here as a technical term for Jerusalem Christians as a whole (thus Georgi 33-34), given the fact that at an earlier time the Qumranites called themselves *hā'ebyônîm*, "the poor," and at a later time Jewish Christians who claimed to be successors of the Jerusalem church were called Ebionites (from *'ebyônîm*, "poor ones"). But there is no firm connection between οἱ πτωχοί of Jerusalem and the second-century Ebionites,[212] and although Luke uses some nineteen different designations for Christians in Acts, never do we find "the poor" used in reference to any group of Christians.[213] In addition, if οἱ πτωχοί were a familiar title for the *whole* Jerusalem church, we would have expected Gal. 2:10 to read αὐτῶν τῶν πτωχῶν: "(only they requested us to remember) them, the poor." There is thus no reason to depart from the common, literal sense of οἱ πτωχοί, particularly since it stands without a qualification such as τῷ πνεύματι (cf. Matt. 5:3).

In Rom. 15:22-29 Paul intimates his intention to visit Jerusalem with his relief aid for the believers before continuing on to Rome and Spain. This intended journey to Jerusalem may be identified with the projected departure for Syria mentioned in Acts 20:3 (cf. 21:3, 15) if Romans was written from Corinth (Acts 20:2-3). Paul states in v. 26 that the destination of the offering is οἱ πτωχοὶ τῶν ἁγίων τῶν ἐν Ἰερουσαλήμ. The key issue here is whether this expression means "the poor *who are* the saints at Jerusalem" (τῶν ἁγίων being an epexegetic genitive; thus K. Holl, 60) or "the poor *among* God's people at Jerusalem" (NEB, REB,[214] τῶν ἁγίων being a partitive genitive). In other words, is the "poverty" referred to spiritual or economic?

In an influential essay written in 1928, Holl maintained (58-60) that "the poor" are not to be distinguished from "the saints," the two titles being familiar and virtually synonymous self-designations of Jerusalem Christians, "the poor in spirit" (Matt. 5:3) and "the saints" par excellence.[215] He was unwilling to concede that when οἱ ἅγιοι is used in connection with the collection (e.g., Rom. 15:25; 2 Cor. 8:4; 9:1), it is an abbreviation of οἱ πτωχοὶ τῶν ἁγίων. With this longer description, then, Paul is speaking in a veiled manner because he is embarrassed to be involved in a collection that was in fact a tax imposed by and destined for the Jerusalem church as a whole (60). Against Holl we would urge that the most natural way to understand τῶν ἁγίων here is as a partitive genitive (thus also BAGD 728b), οἱ ἅγιοι ἐν Ἰερουσαλήμ denoting the whole church in Jerusalem,[216] of which οἱ πτωχοί formed a part of an undisclosed size (so also Becker 259). Holl's view would conform better with οἱ πτωχοὶ οἱ ἅγιοι or οἱ

212. Keck, "Christianity" 55-66; Lüdemann 127 n. 119.

213. See Keck 103-8, who rightly argues that this silence is significant.

214. Similarly Moffatt, Goodspeed, RSV, NASB, GNB, NIV, NRSV.

215. The most detailed critique of Holl's essay is that of Keck 100-29. Keck observes that interest in Holl's theory was revived by the Qumran discoveries (102).

216. Cerfaux argues that in the context of the collection οἱ ἅγιοι may refer to the whole of the original Christian community in Jerusalem but that the term denotes in particular the leaders of the church — the apostles and the elders, or the three "pillars" (*Church* 130-40).

ἄγιοι οἱ πτωχοί or οἱ πτωχοὶ ἄγιοι. Other references to the collection support the view that οἱ πτωχοί in Rom. 15:26 is simply a sociological term, denoting those who are financially poor.[217]

Against the backdrop of the quotation of Exod. 16:18 (the gathering of manna) in 2 Cor. 8:15, the περίσσευμα-ὑστέρημα antithesis of 8:14 must refer to economic plenty and want. 2 Cor. 9:12 shows that the immediate function of the collection was to supply "the (physical) necessities of the saints" (τὰ ὑστερήματα τῶν ἁγίων). Also, since Paul's speech to the Ephesian elders was delivered en route to Jerusalem with the collection, it seems natural to hear an allusion to the poor in Jerusalem when he speaks of the necessity of helping the weak (δεῖ ἀντιλαμβάνεσθαι τῶν ἀσθενούντων, Acts 20:35), the economically depressed.

We conclude that in both Gal. 2:10 and Rom. 15:26 οἱ πτωχοί is not a title denoting all the Jerusalem Christians but a description of a group within the Jerusalem church who had urgent material needs.[218]

c. The Contributors

On the basis of information gleaned from Acts and the Pauline epistles we may assume that contributors to the "offering for the saints" came from Pauline churches in four Roman provinces — Macedonia, Galatia, Asia, and Achaia.

For reasons that are not immediately apparent, Acts makes no explicit reference to the collection,[219] but there are probable allusions in 20:4; 21:17, 20; 24:17. In 20:4 Luke inserts the names of seven traveling companions of Paul as

217. So also, *inter alios,* Munck 288; Bruce, *Galatians* 126; Lüdemann 79.

218. To the objection that because αὐτῶν in Rom. 15:27 (twice) clearly refers to all Jerusalem Christians, τοὺς πτωχούς in 15:26 must then have a similar reference, we reply that αὐτῶν and also αὐτοῖς (15:27) may look back to τῶν ἁγίων in 15:26 and that material aid that benefited the indigent members of the church benefited all. Certainly 15:27 envisages the whole Jerusalem community as the mother church and therefore the source of spiritual blessings and is not alluding simply to the impoverished members of the church.

We have been assuming that the expressions "at Jerusalem" (Rom. 15:26) and "to Jerusalem" (Rom. 15:25) indicate that the recipients of relief all lived in Jerusalem. But it is possible that just as the earlier relief aid met needs both in Jerusalem and elsewhere in Judea (Acts 11:29), so the "great collection" was designed not only for poor Jerusalemites within the church but also other indigent believers in Judea; 2 Cor. 9:13 adds καὶ εἰς πάντας after τῆς κοινωνίας εἰς αὐτούς (see the Commentary there).

219. Holmberg suggests that the arrest of Paul shortly after his arrival in Jerusalem (Acts 21:15-33) "must have caused a storm of antipathy to break out against all Christians in Jerusalem and will in all likelihood have discredited 'his' Collection in their eyes." With the collection, then, "being something of a missionary and diplomatic catastrophe," the author of Acts deemed it best to pass over it "in merciful silence" (43; on the receipt of the collection in Jerusalem, see below, 5.e). More satisfactory is the proposal that Luke wished to avoid unnecessarily compromising the reputation of Paul and Christianity in the eyes of Roman authorities by explicitly distinguishing between the half-shekel Temple tax, which was collected and delivered with Roman approval, and the "alms and offerings" (Acts 24:17) that Paul was bringing to Jewish members of the new Israel (cf. Nickle 88 and n. 110, 148-51).

he sets sail from Greece (= Corinth) for Syria and Jerusalem (vv. 3, 16). There is general agreement that Romans was written during the three months Paul spent in Corinth (Acts 20:2-3; note the references to Gaius in Rom. 16:23 and 1 Cor. 1:14). Consequently we may equate this intended Jerusalem visit mentioned by Luke with the imminent collection visit to Jerusalem mentioned by Paul in Rom. 15:25: "At present . . . I am going to Jerusalem with aid for God's people." These seven companions of Paul, then, are traveling to Jerusalem on the collection visit. Since Luke has neatly grouped the seven according to Roman province — Sopater of Berea and Aristarchus and Secundus of Thessalonica representing Macedonia, Gaius of Derbe[220] and Timothy (of Lystra; cf. Acts 16:1-2) representing Galatia, Tychicus and Trophimus representing Asia — and we know from 1 Cor. 16:3 and 2 Cor. 8:23 that certain churches had appointed delegates in connection with the collection — we may confidently infer that these seven men were representatives of churches from Macedonia, Galatia, and Asia.[221]

That the Macedonians participated in the project is clear from Rom. 15:26: "Macedonia and Achaia have been pleased (εὐδόκησαν) to make some contribution for the poor among God's people at Jerusalem." Since the verse affords the reason (γάρ) for Paul's readiness to go to Jerusalem with aid (15:25), εὐδόκησαν means "were delighted" (Williams) or "have seen fit" (Bruce, *Paraphrase* 237), rather than "have determined" (Goodspeed) or "have resolved" (cf. BAGD 319b).[222] References to the generous giving of the Macedonians in 2 Cor. 8:1-5 (cf. 9:2) confirm the fact of their participation.

Because no mention is made of Galatia in Rom. 15:26 or in 2 Corinthians 8–9, some have surmised that the Galatians failed to contribute,[223] although it is clear from 1 Cor. 16:1 that directions about organizing the contribution had been received in the churches of Galatia.[224] Nor is reference made to Asia in either of these passages. But even a twofold silence should not be converted into an affirmation: simply from the absence of any reference to Galatia and Asia in Romans 15 and 2 Corinthians 8–9 we may not infer that Christians in these two

220. On the textual problem here — D* reads Δουβ(έ)ριος and Acts 19:29 says that (this?) Gaius was a Macedonian — see Metzger 421-22; Bruce, *Acts* 423-24.

221. There may have been other delegates (such as Luke from Philippi; cf. Acts 20:6 — thus Munck 294) picked up as the party moved from the starting point at Corinth on to Jerusalem. See further Ollrog 52-58.

222. See, *per contra,* Buck 10; Suhl 266. In Rom. 15:28 ἐπιτελέσας and σφραγισάμενος both refer to the delivery of the collection, for τοῦτο (ἐπιτελέσας) looks back to the Gentile service (15:27b) to Jerusalem, not to the completion of the collection in Macedonia and Achaia: "But when I have fulfilled this duty, and set the final seal upon this tangible fruit of the Gentile mission, I will set out for Spain, and visit you on the way there" (Bruce, *Paraphrase* 237).

223. E.g., Sampley, *Partnership* 83; and especially Lüdemann 86-87 ("we are able to conclude with a degree of probability approaching certainty that the collection was overthrown [in Galatia] in connection with the adversaries' opposition to Paul," 87). More cautiously, Hurtado 50.

224. These instructions were presumably given by Paul in person when he traveled through Galatic Lycaonia (Lystra, Derbe) and Galatic Phrygia (Iconium and Antioch) (Acts 18:23) on his way from Jerusalem to Ephesus (Acts 18:22; 19:1) in the summer of 52 (cf. Bruce, *Paul* 319).

provinces did not contribute, especially since delegates from Asia (Tychicus and Trophimus) and Galatia (Gaius and Timothy) are actually mentioned in Acts 20:4. Dunn (*Romans* 875) suggests that in Rom. 15:26 Paul simply mentions the two regions (Macedonia and Achaia) nearest to his addressees or the two areas on which he had concentrated his attention.

When Paul gives his converts in Corinth specific instructions about how they should organize their contribution (1 Cor. 16:1-2), his use of περὶ δέ and the articular λογεία suggests not only that they already knew of the project and had agreed to participate but also that they had requested information and directions about it in their earlier letter to Paul (see Lüdemann 81). They may have been first informed about the collection by Paul's "previous letter" (referred to in 1 Cor. 5:9, 11 and written perhaps in A.D. 53) or by one of his deputies or by news from the Galatian churches (cf. 1 Cor. 16:1). Whether the Corinthians acted on these instructions is uncertain. But in all probability any progress made on the collection was soon halted, particularly as the result of Paul's painful "intermediate visit," the unfortunate incident alluded to in 2 Cor. 2:5-11; 7:12 and its aftermath, and the malevolent influence of the intruders from Palestine, who at least for a period gained their support from some Corinthian sympathizers (cf. 2 Cor. 11:7-12, 20). But when Paul sent Titus to deliver and reinforce the effect of the "letter of tears," he probably enjoined him to attempt to revive the flagging collection if the church responded favorably to the letter (cf. 2 Cor. 8:6a). In 2 Corinthians 8–9, with firm evidence from Titus of the Corinthians' loyalty to him (7:6-16), Paul discusses the project again and presses for its early completion.

Were Paul's appeals to the Corinthians in these two chapters successful? We have seen from Rom. 15:26 (written from Corinth on his third visit; cf. 2 Cor. 12:14; 13:1; Acts 20:2-3) that Christians from Achaia saw fit to contribute. Also, is it likely that Clement, writing about A.D. 96, would have complimented the Corinthians for "giving more gladly than receiving" (ἥδιον διδόντες ἢ λαμβάνοντες (*1 Clement* 2:1, alluding to the saying of Jesus cited in Acts 20:35), if in fact the church had earlier failed to contribute to Paul's collection in spite of his urgent appeals? Evidently in the five or so months between the writing of 2 Corinthians (fall 56) and Romans (early 57), the believers at Corinth had responded to Paul's urging. But why, then, does Acts 20:4 make no reference to a delegate or delegates from Achaia? It is unlikely that Paul himself was their appointed delegate, for one purpose in having delegates was to forestall any accusation that he was fostering the collection for his own financial gain (2 Cor. 8:18-21). No more likely is the suggestion that because Paul refers to the Macedonian and Achaean contribution as κοινωνίαν τινά ("*some* contribution," Rom. 15:26), it was too small to merit a delegate.[225] Given his close as-

225. The indefinite adjective τινά should not be interpreted here as a derogatory reference to the size of the offering. It simply denotes an indefinite yet not therefore insignificant quantity (cf. BAGD 820 s.v. τὶς 2.c).

sociation with Corinth and its collection (see C. below), Titus may have served as the Corinthian representative, but for some reason that may only be guessed at[226] he is nowhere mentioned in Acts. But it is possible that the Corinthian gift was sent independently of Paul (thus Malherbe, "Collection" 223 n. 12). If we assume that the list of delegates in Acts 20:4 is partial (Koester 2.143), we may appeal to 1 Cor. 16:3 ("those whom you approve, I shall send with letters of introduction to convey your gift to Jerusalem") and argue that Corinth was not without its delegates (cf. Nickle 69).

d. Its Significance for Paul

Another distinctive feature of Holl's 1928 essay was his proposal that as the mother church, composed of "the poor" = "the saints," the Jerusalem church believed it had the right to impose a tax on Gentile congregations by which these "second-class half-citizen" Gentiles would acknowledge the primacy and supervision of the Jerusalem church and their own indebtedness to Jerusalem. Holl speaks of both "a certain right of taxation" (*ein gewisses Besteuerungsrecht,* 62) and "certain legal claims" (*gewisse Rechtsforderungen,* 60).

But was the collection viewed by the Jerusalem church as a church tax analogous to the Temple tax, as Holl maintains?

Any attempt to extrapolate from innocuous Pauline terms or statements information about the views of the collection entertained by those in Jerusalem is a hazardous procedure. For example, the *dis legomenon* λογεία (1 Cor. 16:1-2) may mean "tax" in an administrative setting such as a taxation roll (see Deissmann 143), just as ὀφείλω and ὀφειλέτης (Rom. 15:27) can be used of financial and therefore legal indebtedness (e.g., Matt. 18:23-35 *passim*), but in a religious context such as Paul's letters there is no justification for disallowing the more general meaning of "collection" for λογεία (thus BAGD 475d; G. Kittel, *TDNT* 4.282-83) and the idea of moral or spiritual indebtedness for the ὀφειλ- root. Perhaps Paul avoids using the terms ὀφειλή and ὀφείλημα (both of which mean "debt," not "indebtedness" = ὀφείλεια) and φόρος ("tax, tribute") in reference to the collection precisely because they could be so easily misunderstood as suggesting a formal, financial obligation and therefore a Jerusalemite levy.[227] As it is, Paul's synonyms for the "collection" are drawn from religious rather than legal vocabulary: χάρις (1 Cor. 16:3; 2 Cor. 8:6-7, 19), κοινωνία (Rom. 15:26; 2 Cor. 9:13), διακονία (Rom. 15:31; 2 Cor. 8:4; 9:1, 13), εὐλογία (2 Cor. 9:5, twice), λειτουργία (2 Cor. 9:12).[228]

226. See Kantzer (97) for three suggested reasons.
227. In Rom. 13:7, τὰς ὀφειλάς is defined by τὸν φόρον ("tax[es]"; cf. φόρους, Rom. 13:6) and τὸ τέλος ("revenue") as well as by τὸν φόβον and τὴν τιμήν, and in Rom. 4:4 ὀφείλημα is associated with ὁ μισθός ("wages").
228. But see *per contra* Stuhlmacher, *Evangelium* 103-4.

Also, if the collection was in fact a formal tax levied on all Gentile congregations, then (1) Paul's emphasis on the voluntary nature of the contributions (in spite of his not inconsiderable pastoral pressure!) (2 Cor. 8:8, 10; 9:5, 7) would seem duplicitous; (2) the Macedonians, who volunteered to participate (2 Cor. 8:4), would be liable (Munck 292 n. 1); and (3) Paul's uncertainty about the reception of the offering (Rom. 15:31) would be unexplainable (Barrett, *1 Corinthians* 386).

The Temple tax was a contribution of a half-shekel (= two Roman dinars) paid annually by every adult male Jew for the maintenance of the Temple in Jerusalem and in particular the offering of the daily public sacrifices for the Jewish nation (cf. Matt. 17:24-27).[229] Nickle has drawn attention to eight parallels between this tax and Paul's collection (87-89):

> Jerusalem was the destination (cf. Rom. 15:25),
>
> Pentecost was a significant date for the delivery (cf. Acts 20:16),
>
> delegates were appointed from each local community to accompany the funds to Jerusalem (cf. 1 Cor. 16:3),
>
> central gathering points were established for both funds and delegates (cf. Acts 20:2-4),
>
> use was made of the special protection for the undertaking afforded by Roman legislation (cf. Acts 24:17),
>
> encouragement was given for the regular setting aside of money for the contribution (cf. 1 Cor. 16:2),
>
> special precautions were taken so that persons involved in handling the funds should be above reproach (cf. 2 Cor. 8:20-21), and
>
> the contributions were a tangible sign of solidarity and unity (cf. Rom. 15:27).

These similarities make it virtually incontestable that Paul borrowed certain organizational elements from the Temple tax (Nickle 99).[230] But several basic differences between the tax and the collection suggest that we should look for the impulse behind Paul's project in another quarter. Whereas the Temple tax was a compulsory tax of a specific amount levied on every Jewish male aged twenty or older[231] and paid once a year but delivered to Jerusalem three times a year, primarily for the offering of daily sacrifices in the Temple, Paul's collection

---

229. See further S. Safrai in Safrai and Stern 188-92, 880-81.

230. Nickle suggests further that Paul was prompted to borrow all these organizational features because the sense of identity with cultic Judaism that was symbolized for dispersed Jews in the Temple tax corresponded precisely with Paul's hope that the collection would strengthen the unity of the church (89, 99).

231. Exod. 30:14-15; Mishnah *Shekalim* 1.3; Josephus, *Antiquities* 3.196. Contributions from Samaritans and Gentiles were not permitted (*Shekalim* 1.5). Women were under no obligation to contribute but often did so.

was a single project[232] involving voluntary gifts of varying amounts,[233] contributed by Jew and Gentile, young and old, male and female,[234] at different times in different places, basically for the relief of the material needs of certain individuals within the Jerusalem church.

Holmberg offers a modification of Holl's view. Although he rejects the idea that the task of collecting money for Jerusalem was viewed there as a formal, legal obligation, he alleges that at the Apostolic Council of 48 or 49 (Acts 15 = Galatians 2 on his view) the Jerusalem leaders not only recognized Paul's apostolic office but also assigned him the task of organizing a collection that would illustrate the primacy of the Jerusalem church (35-56). "Thus he is at one and the same time defined as an Apostle of Christ (preaching the gospel to the Gentiles) and an apostle of the Jerusalem church (with the task of collecting money from the Gentiles to manifest their solidarity with the center of the Church: Jerusalem)" (54).

But is it really probable that the Jerusalem church actually assigned Paul this task and regarded it as "a solemn and binding obligation . . . a "duty" that documented its spiritual supremacy" (Holmberg 41)? This issue brings us back to Gal. 2:10. Holmberg's reconstruction assumes that this verse describes Paul's obedience to a directive that reflects Jerusalem's supremacy: μόνον τῶν πτωχῶν ἵνα μνημονεύωμεν, ὃ καὶ ἐσπούδασα αὐτὸ τοῦτο ποιῆσαι. Interestingly, no verb of commanding or asking is expressed. The ἵνα could be imperatival in indirect speech (BAGD 378b; Moule 144), "we must remember" (Turner 95) or "we were to remember," or could be dependent on the idea of agreement implied in δεξιὰς ἔδωκεν, "provided only that we should remember the poor" (Burton, *Galatians* 99). Alternatively we might supply a verb such as ᾔτησαν (cf. Col. 1:9), "they requested," or ἐθέλησαν (cf. John 17:24), "they expressed the wish," before the ἵνα clause, which would then supply the content of the request or wish. If James, Cephas, and John were issuing a directive, the absence of a strong introductory verb such as ἐπέταξαν or διεστείλαντο is surprising. As it is, the immediate context, and in particular the expression δεξιὰς δοῦναι κοινωνίας (Gal. 2:9), point to a "gentlemen's agreement" or an amicable compact, with κοινωνία stressing mutuality and joint participation in the task of evangelism. This same idea of κοινωνία figures prominently in Rom. 15:26-27; for Paul the collection was a sign of fellowship, not a documentation of pri-

---

232. This is indicated by several features: the project began at different times in different places (perhaps 52 in Galatia and 53 or 54 in Corinth — see above, B.5.c.) and spanned a period of five or six years (52-57); there was no set delivery date, although Paul hoped that his arrival in Jerusalem would coincide with Pentecost (Acts 20:16); he found it necessary to be flexible in his plans concerning the collection because of the unexpected plea of the Macedonians to be permitted to participate (2 Cor. 8:4), the dilatoriness of the Corinthians in bringing their contribution to completion (2 Cor. 8:6-7, 10-11; 9:3-5), and the plot on his life as he was about to depart for Jerusalem with the delegates (Acts 20:3).

233. Cf. 1 Cor. 16:2; 2 Cor. 8:12.

234. Note ἕκαστος ὑμῶν in 1 Cor. 16:2.

macy. What is more, we have already observed that the principal thrust of Galatians 1–2 is not "Jerusalem lays down stipulations, I obey," but rather "While my apostolic ministry has not been exercised independently of Jerusalem, I am not dependent on any human authority for my apostolic calling or my message." When the three "pillars" spoke to Paul about "remembering the poor," they were not levying a tax (as Holl 62) or imposing a requirement (as Sampley, *Partnership* 82; Holmberg 39-41), but simply making a request: "'Only,' they said, 'please go on remembering the poor'" (Bruce, *Paraphrase* 23; cf. his *Galatians* 126-27).

Thus far we have argued that in organizing the collection Paul was not motivated by a desire to find a Christian substitute for the Temple tax levied on Jews or by a sense of obligation to obey a directive from the Jerusalem leaders. Now, positively, we may suggest why the collection was so significant for Paul, or, in other words, his motives and aims in the whole enterprise. These suggestions may be conveniently grouped under three broad headings — historical, theological, and pastoral. It is probably true that any enterprise undertaken by an individual which demands concentrated effort over a prolonged period is entered into with a variety of motives. So it was, we suggest, with Paul and the collection. He was acting from multiple motives, and with various aims in view, corresponding to his several roles as evangelist, pastor, theologian, and strategist. How seriously he viewed the project may be gauged from the fact that he was willing to risk his life to ensure its success (Rom. 15:31a; cf. Acts 20:3, 24).

(1) Historical

(a) At every stage the collection was a visible sign of Paul's fulfillment of a promise. Now it is true that Gal. 2:10 does not explicitly indicate Paul's response to the leaders' request,[235] but his comment that he had already made a point of "remembering the poor" clearly implies his intention, undoubtedly expressed in a promise, to continue this course of action.

(b) The completion of the collection and its delivery to Jerusalem marked the culmination of Paul's ministry in the eastern Mediterranean, for he now planned to turn westward, first visiting the Christians in Rome who he hoped would form a support base for pioneer evangelism in Spain (Rom. 15:23-29). With the end of the collection project came a geographical turning point in Paul's work (note the repeated νυνὶ δέ, "but now," in Rom. 15:23, 25). But the collection was also climactic in the sense that when Paul took to Jerusalem a representative group of his Gentile converts — the collection delegates would have been predominantly Gentile — he was rendering account of his stewardship as apostle to the Gentiles. As a part of his "priestly service relating to the gospel of God" he would present to God these Gentile believers as an

---

235. That is, unless ἐσπούδασα refers to Paul's diligence subsequent to the conference (so Burton, *Galatians* 100; see above, B.5.b.).

offering[236] which he hoped would be "acceptable [to God], sanctified as it is by the Holy Spirit" (Rom. 15:16; cf. Isa. 66:20).[237]

(c) It is not improbable that one of Paul's subsidiary or even unconscious motives in the collection project was to compensate for his earlier persecution of the Jerusalem church. Although his violent repression of Christians extended beyond the frontiers of Israel (Acts 9:2; 26:11), his "murderous threats against the Lord's disciples" (Acts 9:1) focused on Jerusalem. Before Herod Agrippa II he confessed that in his "frantic fury" he had imprisoned or punished many Jerusalem believers, had cast his vote in favor of their condemnation and death, and had tried to make them recant by blaspheming Christ (Acts 26:10-11). Sustained effort in arranging for the relief of the poor in the mother church must have helped to alleviate Paul's acute embarrassment at having been such a vigorous and persistent persecutor (cf. 1 Cor. 15:9; Gal. 1:13).

(2) Theological

(a) First and foremost, the collection was seen as an act of brotherly love (2 Cor. 8:8, 24) that would help to effect equality of provision of the necessities of life (8:13-15; 9:12), bring honor to Christ (8:19) and God (9:13), and demonstrate Paul's readiness to help (8:19). Keck (127) is right in recognizing that "the offering was basically a relief-mission." For Paul, interchurch social concern operated on the same principle as intrachurch charity, that is, the need to demonstrate the interdependence of members of the body of Christ (1 Cor. 12:25-26) by sharing resources (Rom. 12:13).

(b) That Paul did not view the collection merely as a means of relieving poverty is evident from the fact that other churches, notably the Macedonians (2 Cor. 8:1-2), suffered from poverty. Being essentially a gift from Gentile believers to Jewish believers, the collection effectively symbolized both the eradication of "the hostile dividing wall" that separated Gentile from Jew and their resulting unity in Christ (Eph. 2:11-22). Gentiles voluntarily support Jews, who in turn graciously accept benevolence.

(c) Did Paul believe that the collection had a distinctive function in relation to the eschaton? Munck has argued (299-305; cf. 51-52) that in Paul's mind the conversion of Israel was linked to the success of the collection project. When Paul arrived in Jerusalem with "the fullness of the Gentiles" (Rom. 11:25), a representative group of believing Gentiles bearing gifts, OT prophecies would be fulfilled which predicted that in the end times nations along with their wealth would flow into Jerusalem (Isa. 2:2-3; 60:5-6; Mic. 4:1-2). This would provoke the Jewish nation to jealousy (Deut. 32:21, cited in Rom. 10:19) and thus prompt

236. In the phrase ἡ προσφορὰ τῶν ἐθνῶν (Rom. 15:16), the genitive is either objective or epexegetic, but not subjective (referring to the monetary offering given by the Gentiles). So also Bruce, "Jerusalem" 23 (cf. his *Paul* 323).

237. But for the view that the προσφορά was offered to God by Christ, see Cranfield 756-57; or to Christ by Paul (cf. 2 Cor. 11:2), see Aus 237 and n. 20, 261-62.

their conversion to Christ (Rom. 11:13-15, 25-26).[238] "The fullness of the Gentiles will bring with it the salvation of all Israel" (301).

This thesis is made improbable by several considerations: (1) Paul recognized that Jewish machinations in Jerusalem might bring about his death (Rom. 15:31); (2) there is no reference to the role of the collection and its delivery to Jerusalem as an "eschatological provocation" in either Romans 9–11 or 2 Corinthians 8–9;[239] (3) it is difficult to believe that Paul's geographical knowledge was so circumscribed that he could envisage the collection as demonstrating the completion of evangelism in the East[240] or the delegates as fully representative Gentiles; and (4) if Paul hoped that after the delivery of the completed collection he would visit Rome and then engage in evangelism in Spain (Rom. 15:28), any close temporal association between his presentation of the Gentiles and their offering to Jewish Christians in Jerusalem and the arrival of the eschaton would seem to be compromised.[241]

(3) Pastoral

(a) Paul was a strategist as well as a theologian. He envisaged the collection as not only demonstrating but also cementing Jewish-Gentile unity. At every stage of his career Paul was concerned to maintain unity within each local community of Christians (e.g., 1 Cor. 1:10; Phil. 2:2; Eph. 4:3). But he was equally committed to preserving unity among churches, and in particular between the predominantly Gentile congregations outside Judea and the Jewish mother church of Jerusalem. Just as Gentile converts living in Greco-Roman cities were predisposed to view Jewish Christians in far-off Palestine as rigid conservatives to whom they owed nothing, so believers in Jerusalem and Judea were reluctant to regard Gentile Christians as fully accredited citizens of the new Israel. If, however, Gentile believers gave generously to the offering for the poor and Jewish Christians received it graciously, the sense of unity would be enhanced.

238. In their studies of the collection, both Georgi (*Collection* 99-102) and Nickle (129-43) have embraced and developed Munck's general thesis. As an eschatological sign for unbelieving Jews, intended to provoke them to jealousy and then receipt of their Messiah, "Paul's project was a crashing failure" (Nickle 155; similarly Georgi, *Collection* 125-27).

239. Nickle's effort to address this difficulty cannot be deemed successful (137-38, 140-41).

240. Cf. Cranfield 766-68, who rightly recognizes that μηκέτι τόπον ἔχων (Rom. 15:23; cf. 15:19b) means only that Paul's distinctive work as a pioneer evangelist had been completed in the region "from Jerusalem and round even to Illyricum."

241. Munck is acutely aware of this problem for his thesis and so is forced to argue that there are two stages (east and west) in the coming of "the fullness of the Gentiles" (301) and that "all eschatological points of time are uncertain" (304). For the bold hypothesis that for Paul "Spain" was the "Tarshish" of Isa. 66:19 and the "end of the earth," and that "the full number of the Gentiles" (Rom. 11:25; cf. Isa. 60:5; Jer. 3:14) would "come in" only when Paul came to Jerusalem with Christians from Spain as a part of his collection project, see Aus: "Paul firmly believed when he wrote Romans that his collection enterprise would be completed during his own lifetime and primarily through his own efforts. Then the Messiah would come (again)" (261).

That increased unity was Paul's hope in arranging the collection is clear from the fact that he feared that the outcome might be disunity. He urged the Roman Christians to join him in praying that he might be rescued from unbelieving Jews in Judea and that the service he had undertaken for Jerusalem might be favorably received by the saints (Rom. 15:31). Paul's fear was that if his own life was threatened by Jewish unbelievers during his forthcoming visit,[242] Jerusalem Christians might feel compelled to refuse the collection, lest, by accepting it, they provoke a fresh wave of persecution or compromise their efforts to win fellow Jews to Christ.[243]

(b) But in addition to being "a clamp *(Klammer)* for the unity of the Church," as Berger (199) expresses it picturesquely, the collection dramatized in material terms the spiritual indebtedness of Gentile believers to the church in Jerusalem. Paul insisted that "they [Gentile believers] are in debt to them ["the saints at Jerusalem," Rom. 15:26[244]], for if the Gentiles have gained a share in their spiritual blessings, they certainly ought (ὀφείλουσιν καί) to be of service to them with regard to material goods" (Rom. 15:27). If Jesus could say that "it is from the Jews that salvation comes" (John 4:22, NEB), Paul affirms, in effect, that "it was ultimately from Jerusalem that the good news reached you Gentiles."[245] So then, just as it is proper and needful for children to honor parents, so it was appropriate and necessary for daughter churches to support the mother church, and this, not as a sign of inferiority but rather of family loyalty.

(c) Malherbe perceptively comments ("Contribution" 225 n. 18) that Paul hoped that Corinthian participation in a common cause would engender unity at Corinth as well as bonding Gentile churches to the Jerusalem church.

e. The Response in Jerusalem

Some scholars argue that the best explanation of Luke's failure to mention the collection in explicit terms is that the Jerusalem church refused to accept it.[246]

---

242. That Paul had good reason to fear for his own safety is evident from Acts 20:3, 22-25; 21:11; 23:12-31. Perhaps some Jews, especially Zealots, hearing of this collection organized by an apostate Jew, regarded it as being in competition with the half-shekel Temple tax and therefore as a repudiation of the Temple (cf. the comparable situation of Stephen in Acts 6:13-14; 7:47-48, 57-58).

243. We are justified in thus associating the two parts of Paul's prayer request, for they stand under a single ἵνα (of content).

244. With regard to the referent of αὐτῶν, see above, n. 218.

245. Paul seems to have in mind a spiritual indebtedness that is historical rather than ongoing, for he wrote that "the Gentiles have gained a share" (ἐκοινώνησαν), not "continue to share" (κοινωνοῦσιν). This makes dubious Cerfaux's suggestion (*Church* 136) that "Paul considers the collection rather in the nature of a *do ut des* contract. The gentiles give material alms, while the *hagioi* supply spiritual benefits."

246. E.g., Haenchen 614; Dunn 256-57; *Romans* 880. Both these scholars suggest that the Jerusalem leaders offered to accept the collection once Paul had proved to all that he was not antinomian by paying the expenses of the four poor Nazarites (Acts 21:21-24). "The purification to

Neither part of Paul's prayer in Rom. 15:31 was answered as he had hoped: he was not delivered from unbelievers in Judea (cf. Acts 21:11, 27-36) and his service for Jerusalem (the collection) was not favorably received.

What happened after Paul's arrival in Jerusalem and that ultimately led to his journey to Rome shows that "unbelievers in Judea" with the help of "Jews from Asia" (Acts 21:27) were successful in engineering his arrest and prolonged custody, but Paul's prayer was answered in that his life was preserved from the murderous intent of the Jerusalem crowd (Acts 21:30-36) and the planned ambush of the forty or so conspiratorial assassins (Acts 23:12-31). We suggest that the second part of his prayer also received a positive answer. Οἱ ἀδελφοί in Acts 21:17 is ambiguous, for it could refer back to Mnason and other unnamed persons (Acts 21:16) or forward, anticipating the reference in v. 18 to James and the elders, with v. 17 describing an unofficial, informal welcome and v. 18 the official reception of Paul and the delegates on the following day. Because v. 17 repeats εἰς Ἱεροσόλυμα from v. 15, it is probable that v. 17 stands as the introduction to a new paragraph (vv. 17-26), with the result that οἱ ἀδελφοί is prospective. In any case, v. 16 refers to only one ἀδελφός in Jerusalem (Mnason). See also the commentary at 9:14. We conclude that it was the Jerusalem leadership who "warmly welcomed" the collection delegation — and therefore the collection itself. This is confirmed by v. 20: "they glorified God" on hearing the itemized account (καθ' ἓν ἕκαστον) of what God had done among the Gentiles through Paul's ministry (διὰ τῆς διακονίας αὐτοῦ), a detailed description that must have included reference to his διακονία (Rom. 15:31; cf. 2 Cor. 8:4; 9:1, 13) with regard to the collection. There is also a significant correlation between Luke's ἐδόξαζον τὸν θεόν here and Paul's δοξάζοντες τὸν θεόν ("people will give glory to God") in 2 Cor. 9:13, both expressions referring to the recipients' response (projected or actual) to the collection.

C. CHRONOLOGY OF THE RELATIONS OF PAUL, TIMOTHY, AND TITUS WITH THE CORINTHIAN CHURCH

The following reconstruction of the complex relations between Paul, his associates, and the church at Corinth reflects all of the foregoing discussion as well as furnishing a brief statement of the critical presuppositions on which the commentary proper rests. In the footnotes is found an abbreviated defense of some of the controversial aspects of the reconstruction.

---

which Paul had to submit in order to participate in the absolution of the four Nazarites held him fast in Jerusalem for a week, and compelled him on the third and seventh days to seek out the 'holy place.' On the second visit [Acts 21:27] — immediately before the happy outcome — catastrophe struck" (Haenchen 614). "The plan [of James] went very badly wrong and in the ensuing confrontation and crisis Paul seems hardly to have been supported, let alone his collection accepted by the local Christians" (Dunn 257).

Events	*References*	*Date*
1. At the end of his "second missionary journey," after arrival from Athens, Paul spends eighteen months at Corinth.	Acts 18:1-8	fall 50–spring 52
2. During that time Silas and Timothy[247] arrive from Macedonia.	Acts 18:5	
3. Paul has his hearing before Gallio.	Acts 18:12-17	summer or fall 51
4. Paul proceeds from Corinth to Ephesus, where Aquila and Priscilla remain.	Acts 18:18-19	spring 52
5. During Paul's absence in Judea, Syria, Galatic Lycaonia, and Phrygia and for an indefinite time thereafter, Apollos preaches in Ephesus and Corinth before returning to Ephesus.	Acts 18:22-23; 18:24–19:1; 1 Cor. 1:12; 3:4-6; 16:12	spring-summer 52
6. Paul resides in Ephesus.	Acts 19:1–20:1	fall 52–spring 56[248]
7. Paul dispatches the "previous letter" (not extant and bearer unknown).	1 Cor. 5:9-11	
8. Timothy is sent to Macedonia (to initiate the collection?) and Corinth.	Acts 19:22; 1 Cor. 4:17; 16:10	early 55
9. Paul receives news of bickering and cliques at Corinth from οἱ Χλόης, and rebukes the Corinthian partisan spirit in 1 Corinthians 1–4.	1 Cor. 1:11	

247. Any attempt to plot Timothy's movements during the period covered by Acts 18–19 must remain conjectural. The following outline is one of several possible reconstructions:

- Macedonia to Corinth (Acts 18:5),
- Corinth to Ephesus (since 1 Cor. 4:17 speaks of the dispatch of Timothy, presumably from the place of writing — Ephesus),
- Ephesus to Macedonia and then Corinth (ἔπεμψα in 1 Cor. 4:17 is more probably epistolary than preterit [cf. 2 Cor. 8:18; 9:3; Eph. 6:22; Phil. 2:28; Col. 4:8], while ἐάν in 1 Cor. 16:10 is less likely to mean "if" than "when" [RSV]; Paul expected 1 Corinthians to arrive at Corinth before Timothy [1 Cor. 16:10]),
- Corinth to Ephesus (Paul anticipated that Timothy would return from Corinth before he himself left Ephesus [1 Cor. 16:11]; Timothy's lack of success in Corinth [cf. 1 Cor. 16:10-11] may account for the silence of 2 Corinthians concerning his mission and illuminate Paul's reference to him in the greeting [2 Cor. 1:1]), and
- Ephesus to Macedonia (2 Cor. 1:1).

248. D reads τριετίαν ἢ καὶ πλεῖον ("for three years or even more") in Acts 20:18.

10. An official delegation (Stephanas, Fortunatus, and Achaicus) arrives from Corinth with a letter (to which Paul replies in 1 Corinthians 7–16), confirms the report of οἱ Χλόης, and conveys further disquieting news about immorality, litigiousness, and licentiousness in the church (which Paul reproves in 1 Corinthians 5–6).

1 Cor. 16:17; 7:1a; 11:18

11. 1 Corinthians is delivered to Corinth, presumably by the delegation.

1 Cor. 16:12a   spring 55

12. Titus[249] visits Corinth to initiate the collection by implementing the directions of 1 Cor. 16:2.

2 Cor. 8:6a

13. In spite of Paul's letter and the efforts of Timothy and Titus, and possibly because of the advent of Judaizing intruders from Palestine, conditions in the church at Corinth deteriorate, necessitating Paul's "painful visit" (Ephesus — Corinth — Ephesus).

2 Cor. 11:4, 22;   summer or
2:1; 12:21; 13:2   fall 55

14. At some time after this visit, Paul (or his representative) is openly insulted at Corinth by a spokesman of an anti-Pauline faction.

2 Cor. 2:5-8, 10; 7:12

---

249. It would seem that Titus was sent to Corinth as Paul's representative on three occasions:

- after the receipt of 1 Corinthians at Corinth, to help to initiate the collection by implementing the directions of 1 Cor. 16:2 (2 Cor. 8:6a [cf. 8:10; 9:2; 12:18], where the first καί alludes to the commencement of the contribution, and the second to the successful outcome of the "severe letter"; the belief that Titus and ὁ ἀδελφός were the bearers of 1 Corinthians [e.g., Strachan xxxix] rests on a somewhat precarious identification of 2 Cor. 12:18a with 2 Cor. 8:6a and 1 Cor. 16:11b, 12a),
- after Paul's "painful visit," to deliver and reinforce the effect of the "severe letter" (since it is probable that the person who witnessed the outcome of the letter [2 Cor. 7:6-15] also delivered it, *pace* Furnish 397) and perhaps to revive the flagging collection (the resuscitation of the collection would have been conditional upon a favorable response by the Corinthians to Paul's letter), and
- some time after his reunion with Paul in Macedonia, to deliver 2 Corinthians and to help to bring the collection to completion (2 Cor. 8:6b, 16-17, 23-24), in the company of the two delegates of the Macedonian churches (8:18, 23; 9:3).

On this complex issue of Titus's visits to Corinth, see Lightfoot 273-84; Kennedy 115-25; Lake 146, 164-69; Allo 74-76, 204-10, 330-32; Barrett, "Titus" 1-14; Ollrog 33-37; Kantzer 91-97; F. Watson 333-35; Hyldahl 88-102.

15. Titus is sent from Ephesus to Corinth with the "severe letter" (not extant),[250] with instructions to promote the collection if the letter proves successful and to meet Paul in Troas, or, failing that, in Macedonia (= Philippi[251]).	2 Cor. 2:3-4, 6, 9; 7:8, 12; 2:12-13; 7:5-6	spring 56
16. Paul leaves Ephesus shortly after the Demetrius riot, begins evangelism in Troas, but then suffers his "affliction in Asia."[252]	Acts 19:23– 20:1; 2 Cor. 2:12-13; 1:8-11	spring 56
17. Paul travels on to Macedonia and engages in pastoral activity[253] while organizing the collection in the Macedonian churches[254] and awaiting the arrival of Titus from Corinth.	2 Cor. 2:13; 7:5; Acts 20:2; 2 Cor. 8:1-4; 9:2	spring– summer 56
18. Titus arrives in Macedonia (? = Thessalonica or Berea[255]) from Corinth with his welcome report of the Corinthians' responsiveness to the "severe letter."	2 Cor. 7:5-16	summer 56
19. Paul begins to write 2 Corinthians 1–9 as he undertakes further pastoral and evangelistic work in Macedonia and probably in Illyricum.[256]	Rom. 15:19-21	

250. On the identity of the "severe letter," see above, B.2.c.

251. That Macedonia means Philippi in 2 Cor. 2:13; 7:5 is suggested by two facts: (1) Neapolis, where Paul would arrive on a sea voyage from Troas, was the port of Philippi; (2) in 2 Cor. 11:9 "Macedonia" probably alludes to Philippi (cf. Phil. 4:15).

252. The evidence supporting this conclusion is set out in the excursus below at 1:11.

253. τὰ μέρη ἐκεῖνα in Acts 20:2 certainly refers to Macedonia (see Acts 20:1), and may also include Troas and Illyricum. In Acts 20:2; 1 Cor. 16:5 (twice), διέρχεσθαι followed by the accusative of the district traversed with no preposition probably signifies "transit with preaching" (cf. Acts 13:6; 14:24; 15:3, 41; 16:6; 18:23; 19:1, 21; 20:25 [no accusative]) — see Ramsay, "Words" 385-99.

254. Even if Timothy had introduced the collection scheme in Macedonia (cf. Acts 19:22), only the arrival of Paul saw its real advancement (Duncan 238-39).

255. Thessalonica or Berea is perhaps more probable than Philippi since 2 Cor. 8:1 and 9:2 speak of the churches and people of Macedonia (not simply of the Philippians) and Paul would be traveling west along the Via Egnatia and south to Berea (cf. Alford 2.59-60; but see Conybeare in Conybeare and Howson 436 nn. 2, 4; Bachmann 322-23).

256. For a discussion of the issues surrounding this mission in Illyricum, see above, p. 66. Items 18-19 and 21 of this chronology represent a modification of my earlier view ("2 Corinthians" 302-3) that Paul wrote all of 2 Corinthians sometime after Titus's arrival and also after "pioneer evangelism along the Egnatian Road and probably in Illyricum" (303). My altered view, arrived at independently, is essentially the same as the proposal of Carson (13-14).

20. Meanwhile, the foreign agitators in Corinth continue to undermine Paul's authority there.

2 Corinthians 10–13

21. On returning to Macedonia and hearing of fresh problems at Corinth, Paul pens 2 Corinthians 10–13 and sends the whole letter to Corinth with Titus and his two colleagues.

2 Cor. 8:17-18, 22

fall 56

22. Paul spends three months in Greece (= primarily Corinth) during which he writes Romans.

Acts 20:2b-3a; Rom. 15:25-28; 16:23 (cf. 1 Cor. 1:14)

winter 56-57,[257] early 57

23. Paul departs for Jerusalem, accompanied by delegates of the churches, in order to deliver the "collection for the poor."

Acts 20:3b-4; 21:17; 24:17

spring 57

D. ANALYSES OF 2 CORINTHIANS

Analyses or outlines of 2 Corinthians fall into three main categories.[258]

1. Analysis by Rhetorical Form

Especially in the last thirty years great interest has been taken in the rhetorical criticism of the NT[259] and of Paul's letters in particular,[260] with 2 Corinthians

257. "The sea was closed from 10 November to 10 March; but perfectly safe navigation was only between 26 May and 14 September, while there were two doubtful periods 11 Mar.–26 May, and 15 Sept.–10 Nov., when merchants might risk sailing, but fleets of war vessels were loath to do so" (Ramsay, "Roads" 376, citing Vegetius, *De Re Militari* 4.39; 5.9). What was general practice at sea probably applied on land also ("Roads" 377), but Ramsay admits the possibility of coasting voyages even in winter (*Paul* 283-85). See further Jewett, *Chronology* 56-57. "The reason for the closure of the sea lanes was not only storms, but also the reduced visibility of the sun and stars (which were essential for navigation) due to persistent cloud cover in these months (cf. Acts 27.20)" (A. L. Connolly, in Horsley 4.113).

258. Martin (xxxv-xxxviii) has both an "analysis" and an "outline."

259. For bibliographical data, see D. F. Watson and A. J. Hauser, *Rhetorical Criticism of the Bible: A Comprehensive Bibliography with Notes on History and Method* (Leiden: Brill, 1994); more briefly, D. F. Watson, "The New Testament and Greco-Roman Rhetoric: A Bibliography," *JETS* 31 (1988) 465-72, and more recently, C. J. Classen, *Rhetorical Criticism of the New Testament* (Tübingen: Mohr, 2000). Useful brief analyses of the rhetorical approach to biblical texts may be found in R. Meynet, "Histoire de 'l'analyse rhétorique' en exégèse biblique," in *Rhetorica* 8 (1990) 291-312; Peterson 9-38; and O'Mahony 15-24.

260. See D. F. Watson, "Rhetorical Criticism of the Pauline Epistles since 1975," *CRBS* 3 (1995) 219-48; R. D. Anderson, Jr., *Ancient Rhetorical Theory and Paul* (Kampen: Kok Pharos, 1996).

figuring prominently.[261] In classical times there were three main types of rhetoric (Aristotle, *Rhetoric* 1.3.1-9): *forensic* or judicial rhetoric, the most common type of rhetoric, aimed at accusing or defending someone with regard to past events; *deliberative* rhetoric, which sought to persuade or dissuade the audience regarding future action; and *epideictic* or demonstrative rhetoric, concerned with assigning praise or blame to someone with respect to present actions. In these three categories the primary appeal is (respectively) to justice ("Did he do this or not?"), expediency ("Is this course of action more beneficial or is that?"), and to praiseworthiness ("Should this be praised or blamed?").

According to the classical rhetorical handbooks, a forensic or judicial speech has six parts:[262]

1. *exordium* (introduction), which establishes the speaker's (or writer's) good moral character (ἦθος) and seeks to ensure the audience's receptivity,
2. *narratio* (narration), which states the agreed facts of the case,
3. *propositio* (proposition), which sets out the basic facts to be proved true or false and areas of agreement or disagreement with the opponent,
4. *probatio* or *argumentatio* (proof), which gives the reasoning (λόγος) in support of the speaker's case,
5. *refutatio* (refutation), which disproves or impairs the opponent's arguments, and
6. *peroratio* (conclusion), which sums up the case and seeks to arouse the audience's sympathetic emotions (πάθος).[263]

Sometimes in theory these six elements were reduced to four or five by including the *propositio* within the *narratio* and/or the *refutatio* within the *probatio*. But in actual practice speeches would commonly omit one or more of the basic elements, however calculated.

Examples of a literary analysis of parts or the whole of 2 Corinthians in the light of rhetorical criticism may now be given.[264]

---

261. Note the following (full titles in the bibliography): Betz, *2 Corinthians 8 and 9; Apology;* Crafton, *Agency;* DiCicco, *Ethos;* Forbes, "Comparison"; Heiny, "Metaphor"; Holland, "Irony"; F. W. Hughes, "Rhetoric"; Judge, "Boasting"; Loubser, "Paradox"; Marguerat, "Paul"; Marshall, "Invective"; Mitchell, "Shorthand"; de Oliveira, *Diakonie;* Plank, *Paul;* Sampley, "Opponents"; Spencer, *Style;* Sundermann, *Apostel;* Travis, "Boasting"; Welborn, *Politics;* Witherington, *Conflict;* Zmijewski, *Stil.* Brief notes on the work of Betz, Crafton, Holland, Hughes, Loubser, Marguerat, Sampley, and Zmijewski are found in Watson, "Criticism" 230-32 (see previous note).

262. Cf. G. A. Kennedy 129-60; P. Dixon, *Rhetoric* (London: Methuen, 1971) 22-23; O'Mahony 40-48.

263. On these three techniques of persuasion, ἦθος, λόγος, and πάθος (cf. Aristotle, *Rhetoric* 1.2) see DiCicco.

264. On steps to be followed in the practice of rhetorical criticism, see G. A. Kennedy, *Interpretation* 33-38; on general principles or "mandates" to be followed, Mitchell 6-17 (on which see Classen 291 n. 78).

2 Corinthians as a compositional whole of forensic rhetoric
    (Witherington viii-ix, 335-36):
    Epistolary prescript (1:1-2)
    Epistolary thanksgiving and *exordium* (1:3-7)
    Narratio (1:8–2:16)[265]
    Propositio (2:17)
    Probatio (refutatio) (3:1–13:4)
        Argument I (3:1–6:13)
        Argument II: Digression (*egressio*) (6:14–7:1)
        Argument III (with *amplificatio*) (7:2-16)
        Argument IV (8:1–9:15)
        Argument V (10:1–13:4)
    Peroratio (13:5-10)
    Closing epistolary greetings and remarks (13:11-13)

2 Corinthians 1–7 as a rhetorical unit of forensic rhetoric
    (Kennedy, *Interpretation* 87-91):
    Salutation (1:1-2)
    Proem (= *exordium*) (1:3-7)
    Narratio (1:8–2:13)
    Propositio (2:14-17 and 3:1-3 — the Corinthians as "character wit-
        nesses")
    Probatio (3:4–6:13) (6:14–7:1 apparently an interpolation)
    Peroratio (7:2-16)

2 Corinthians 8–9 as two independent letters showing rhetorical cohesion
    (Betz 38-41, 88-90):
    Ch. 8
    Epistolary prescript (omitted)
    Exordium (8:1-5)
    Narratio (8:6)
    Propositio (8:7-8)
    Probatio (8:9-15)
        Commendation of the delegates (8:16-22)
        Authorization of the delegates (8:23)
    Peroratio (8:24)
    Epistolary postscript (omitted)[266]
    Ch. 9
    Epistolary prescript (omitted)

265. But on p. 335 n. 27, 2:14-16 is seen as a transition to the *propositio*.
266. The success of Betz's rhetorical analysis of 2 Corinthians 8 is questioned by Thrall 37-38, and also by F. W. Hughes 258 n. 1, who himself attempts to demonstrate the thematic unity and rhetorical coherence of 1:1–2:13; 7:5–8:24.

Exordium (9:1-2)
Narratio (9:3-5a)
Propositio (9:5b-c)
Probatio (9:6-14)
Peroratio (9:15)
Epistolary postscript (omitted)[267]

2 Corinthians 10–13 as a rhetorical unit (Peterson 75-139, 162):
    Exordium (10:1-6)
    Propositio (10:7-11)
    Narratio (10:12-18)
    Probatio (11:1–12:18)
    Peroratio (12:19–13:10)

2 Corinthians 10–13 as a rhetorical unit (Sundermann 45):
    Exordium (10:1-11)
    Narratio and *Propositio* (10:12-18)
    Argumentatio (11:1–12:18)
    Refutatio (11:1-15)
    Probatio (11:16–12:18)[268]
    Transitus (transition)(12:19-21)
    Peroratio (13:1-10)

Several general observations may be made regarding the application of rhetorical criticism to Paul's letters and to 2 Corinthians in particular. First, we must remember that knowledge of rhetorical skills was common coin among educated people in the first century A.D. As G. A. Kennedy expresses it, "Even if he [Paul] had not studied in a Greek school, there were many handbooks of rhetoric in common circulation which he could have seen. He and the evangelists as well would, indeed, have been hard put to escape an awareness of rhetoric as practiced in the culture around them, for the rhetorical theory of the schools found its immediate application in almost every form of oral and written communication" (*Interpretation* 10; cf. 19). True, Paul eschews reliance on rhetorical skills in declaring the gospel to unbelievers (1 Cor. 2:1-5), but he makes use of a wide range of rhetorical techniques as he engages in his pastoral task of bringing his converts to spiritual maturity (see Siegert 181-241). More particularly, Luke's summary of Paul's defense in the court of Felix against the charges brought by the Sanhedrin's legal consultant and professional forensic rhetorician, Tertullus (Acts 24:1-21), affords evidence of Paul's knowledge of

267. For rhetorical analysis of 2 Corinthians 8–9 seen as a unity, see G. A. Kennedy, *Interpretation* 91-92; O'Mahony 105-63. O'Mahony also provides a history of rhetorical readings of chs. 8–9 (49-77) and a critique of Betz's rhetorical analysis of these chapters (164-74).

268. Sundermann believes that both the *refutatio* and the *probatio* have four parts: *exordium, propositio, argumentatio,* and *peroratio.*

the basic stages in forensic rhetoric (see Winter, *Philo* 238-39 and references at 238 n. 23).

But second, some of the hallmarks of ὁ συζητητὴς τοῦ αἰῶνος τούτου (1 Cor. 1:20), "the debater of this age," the virtuoso rhetorician, would have been anathema to Paul. He repudiated ornamental rhetoric that was designed to impress an audience and win their plaudits (1 Cor. 2:1, 4). For him, form was always secondary to content; style was invariably the servant of substance, never its master and never an end in itself. Nevertheless, his letters show that he believed that truth was well served if it was presented attractively and persuasively. Again, for the rhetorician, but not for Paul, truth was inconsequential but presentation all-important. Also, Paul would have rejected psychological manipulation by arousing of emotions (πάθος), preferring a rational appeal to Scripture or to Christian truth that he believed the Spirit would use to alter attitudes and conduct.

Third, even if we grant that Paul was aware of the classical stages of rhetorical argument and could use that knowledge to advantage when faced with serious charges before a Roman court, it is far from obvious that in a situation of his own making — writing letters to friends — he would have consciously developed his argumentation in accordance with the successive divisions of forensic or deliberative or epideictic rhetoric.[269] His letters are not transcripts of formal speeches[270] on a single topic delivered to a live audience but discourses for absent friends on a variety of topics, first given orally to an amanuensis and having all the marks of informality that attach to dictation. But if this is the case, how are we to account for the signs of rhetoric that scholars have discovered in his letters? Any document of the length of 2 Corinthians (or chs. 1–7 or 10–13) that is (1) written by a highly educated person, (2) apologetic in character, (3) logical in presentation, and (4) aimed at winning over an audience and influencing their way of thinking and acting is likely to display the basic ingredients of forensic, deliberative, or epideictic rhetoric — but not necessarily in a recognizable or schematic sequence. Obviously such a document would have some kind of introduction and conclusion. Would there not also be a "narration" of the facts or events under discussion? And might it not state and defend more than one "proposition" and therefore have more than one "proof" and "refutation"? A document with those characteristics would naturally include appeals to character (ἦθος), to reason (λόγος), and to emo-

---

269. On the relation between rhetoric and epistolography see Classen 265-91; Reed 292-324; Porter, "Justification" 100-122, especially 100-102, and with reference to Galatians, Kremendahl. Reed notes that the three basic parts of a letter have a certain functional but not formal similarity with the four principal elements of rhetorical arrangement: the letter opening corresponds to the *exordium*, the body contains at least the *narratio* and *confirmatio (= probatio),* while the letter closing corresponds to the *conclusio (= peroratio)* (306-8). Paul "enmeshed various forms of epistolary and rhetorical traditions into his letters" (314).

270. But the letter may be regarded as speech in a written form (Cicero, *Atticus* 8.14.1, Seneca, *Epistle* 75.1).

tion (πάθος). Moreover, Paul's letters were written to be heard, that is, to be read aloud not read silently. They were aimed at the ear, not the eye. So it is not surprising that there are rhetorical flourishes, whether they be produced consciously or instinctively.

Fourth, the practice of rhetorical criticism seems to be more of an art than a science, with the highly subjective nature of the enterprise reflected in the wide divergence between the findings of the practitioners. With respect to the two analyses of 2 Corinthians 10–13 given above, the only division on which Peterson and Sundermann agree is 11:1–12:18, which Peterson calls the *probatio,* whereas Sundermann discerns the *probatio* within that passage (11:16–12:18). In addition, they disagree on the central issue of identifying the *propositio,* the basic issue to be proved. It would appear that as rhetorical criticism is practiced, the focus of attention can all too easily become the relationship of the text to extraneous classical rhetorical norms, and, on the assumption that Paul is following these norms, the explanation for any deviations: in Peterson's case, why the *propositio* precedes the *narratio;* in Sundermann's case, why the *probatio* follows the *refutatio.* And is it not true that to a considerable extent what one discovers in a text is determined by what one looks for? For instance, it is fascinating to note that exactly the same verses that Garland (422-23) sees as the outer elements of his chiasmus in chs. 10–13 (i.e., 10:1-11 [A] and 13:1-10 [A¹]), Sundermann (47) views as (respectively) the *exordium* and *peroratio.*

In my exegesis of the text I shall not be interacting in detail with the various proposed rhetorical analyses. Thrall has assessed the contributions of Betz, Sundermann, and DiCicco in the context of her exegesis (and also in Excursus XVI, pp. 922-25).

2. Analysis by Chiastic Structure

The English literary term "chiasmus" or "chiasm" derives from the Greek word χιασμός (cf. the Greek letter X) which means *"placing crosswise, diagonal arrangement,* esp[ecially] of the clauses of a period, so that the 1st corresponds with the 4th, and the 2nd with the third" (LSJ 1991. 1. s.v.). But the term is also used more loosely to describe concentric structure or "concentric symmetry" (Rolland 73) involving longer passages or even entire books.

Four recent attempts to discern chiasmus within 2 Corinthians may be mentioned.[271]

---

271. On chiasmus in Paul and the NT see N. W. Lund, *Chiasmus in the New Testament* (Chapel Hill: University of North Carolina, 1942); idem, "The Presence of Chiasmus in the New Testament," *JR* 10 (1930) 74-93; J. Jeremias, "Chiasmus in den Paulusbriefen," *ZNW* 49 (1958) 145-56; J. J. Collins; D. Clark, "Criteria for Identifying Chiasm," *LingB* 35 (1975) 63-72; J. W. Welch, "Chiasmus in the New Testament," in *Chiasmus in Antiquity: Structures, Analyses, Exe-*

2 Corinthians as a whole (Segalla, "Struttura" 217 [189-218 for full details]):

A. *Prologo* (1:1-11): 1,2–3.7/13,11-13
   B. *Apologia della gloria di Paolo* 1,12–7,16):
      a. Apologia di Paolo e Tito (1,12–2,13)
      b. Apologia polemica del ministero di Paolo (2,14–4,6)
      c. Escatologia presente e futura (4,7–5,10)
      b′. Apologia critica del ministero di Paolo (5,11–7,3)
      a′. Apologia di Paolo e Tito (7,4-16)

      C. *La grazia della colletta* (8,1–9,15):
         a. La colletta: una grazia, una *diakonia,* un sopperire alla "indigenza dei santi" (8,1-15)
         b. Missione di Tito e dei fratelli (8,16-24)
         b′. Missione dei "fratelli" all' Acaia (9,1-5)
         a′. La colletta: una grazia, una *diakonia,* e un sopperire alla "indigenza dei santi" (9,6-15)

   B′. *L'apologia dell'autorità apostolica di Paolo* (10,1–13,10):
      a. L'autorità di Paolo, difesa "per l'edificazione della comunità" (10,1-11)
      b. Apologia del ministero di Paolo contro gli "intrusi" (10,12-18)
      c. Il discorso da stolto (11,1–12,10):
         polemico contro i "superapostoli" (11,1-21a)
         apologetico in favore del "ministro di Cristo" (11,21b–12,10)
      b′. Apologia dell'apostolo nei confronti della communità di Corinto (12,11-18).
      a′. L'autorità di Paolo, esercitata nei moniti conclusivi, "per la edificazione" (12, 19–13,10).
A′. Conclusione con saluti ed auguri, che si richiamano al prologo (13,11-13 e 1,2–3.7).

While one of the chiastic patterns that are based on conceptual parallelism emerges naturally from the text (the abb′a′ within C.), the others appear rather forced, and if it is true that "the climax of a chiasmus is its center" (Blomberg

gesis, ed. J. W. Welch (Hildesheim: Gerstenberg, 1981), 213-90; J. Breck, "Biblical Chiasmus: Exploring Structure for Meaning," *BTB* 17 (1978) 70-74; C. L. Blomberg; J. D. Harvey 98-100, 283, 287, who finds seven additional "categories of oral patterning" in Paul's letters (283-92). On chiasmus in recent NT study see S. E. Porter and J. T. Reed, "Philippians as a Macro-Chiasm and Its Exegetical Significance," *NTS* 44 (1998) 213-21 (= Part I); and the bibliography in Di Marco, "Rhetoric" 488-91. Di Marco restricts chiasmus proper to an A-B-C-B′-A′ or A-B-B′-A′ sequence (479) but even allows what he calls *"implicit* chiasmus" ("when we assert something in one direction, perhaps the inverse direction is implicit") and "chiasmus *in distance*" (e.g., ἐπαγγελία πνεύματος in Acts 2:23 and πνεῦμα ἐπαγγελίας in Gal. 3:14) (485).

15), chs. 8–9, which are item C. in Segalla's ABCB′A′ chiasm, form the climax of 2 Corinthians — an unlikely honor indeed.

Blomberg usefully isolates a set of nine "criteria for detecting extended chiasmus" (4-7) and argues (9-15) that they are all satisfied in his chiastic outline of 1:12–7:16.

2 Cor. 1:12–7:16 (Blomberg 8-9; see also Rolland 77-78, 83):

A
1:12-22 — the Corinthians can rightfully boast in Paul

A′
7:13b-16 — Paul can rightfully boast in the Corinthians

B
1:23–2:11 — grief and comfort over the painful letter; hope for forgiving the offender

B′
7:8-13a — grief and comfort over the painful letter; joy after forgiving the offender

C
2:12-13 — looking for Titus in Macedonia

C′
7:5-7 — finding Titus in Macedonia

D
2:14–4:6 — a series of contrasts — belief vs. unbelief, centered on Christians as the letters of the living God, in glory being transformed into his image

D′
6:11–7:4 — a series of contrasts — belief vs. unbelief, centered on Christians as the temple of the living God, in light being transformed into his holiness

   a 2:14-16a — death vs. life

   b 2:16b–3:3 — false vs. true approaches to ministry

   c 3:4-18 — old covenant vs. new

   b′ 4:1-2 — false vs. true approaches to ministry

   a′ 4:3-6 — darkness vs. light

   a 6:11-13 — widen your hearts

   b 6:14–7:1 — separate yourselves from uncleanness

   a′ 7:2-4 — open your hearts

E
4:7–5:10 — surviving and triumphing despite every hardship (see especially vv. 8-10)

E′
6:1-10 — surviving and triumphing despite every hardship (see especially vv. 8b-10)

            F
            5:11-21 — the theological climax: the ministry of reconciliation

This ingenious analysis highlights instances of undoubted parallelism (e.g., C and C') and simple chiasmus (e.g., aba' in 6:11–7:4), but some of the proposed correspondences seem artificial (e.g., E and E') and it is far from clear that 5:11-21, as the climax of the chiasmus, contains "the central point which Paul was trying to make" (15), even if it is true that this passage "provides the theological basis which alone can make possible the practical and pastoral solution" to the conflicts at Corinth (16).[272]

2 Corinthians 10–13 (Chevallier 3-15; cf. Rolland 74-75, 84):

A. 10:1-18 Pastoral introduction:
   a. 10:1-11
   b. 10:12-18

   B. 11:1-21a Prologue to the fool's speech
   C. 11:21b–12:10 Fool's speech
   B'. 12:11-18 Epilogue to the fool's speech

A'. 12:19–13:10 Pastoral conclusion
   b'. 12:19-21
   a'. 13:1-10

2 Corinthians 10–13 (Garland 422-23, cf. 558)

A. 10:1-11 Warning that Paul can be as bold to punish disobedience when present as he is in his letters [set off by inclusion with the idea "when present," "when absent," and the verb *logizomai* (10:2, 11), and the inconsistency between his letters and his presence (10:1b; and 10:10)]
   B. 10:12-18 Self-Commendation and God's Commendation [set off by inclusion with the verb commend, *synistemi* (10:12, 18)]
      C. 11:1:1-21a Bearing with Foolishness [set off by inclusion with the verb "bearing," *anechomai* (11:1, 4, 19, 20)]
      C'. 11:21b–12:13 Paul's Foolish Boasts [set off by inclusion by his declaration that he is speaking as a fool (11:21; 12:11)]
   B'. 12:14-21 Paul's Return to Corinth [set off by inclusion with his reference to coming to them again (12:14, 21)]
A'. 13:1-10 Warning that he may have to be severe in his use of authority [marking an inclusion with 10:1-11 with the reference to being absent and present (10:1-2; 13:10) and the authority the Lord gave to him for building up and not tearing down (10:8; 13:10)].

---

272. Bonneau proposes a concentric structure for 2:14–7:4 ("Corinthians C" on his analysis): A — 2:14-17 (introduction); B — 3:1–4:4 (Paul's defense); C — 4:5–6:2 (theological argument in two stages); B[1] — 6:3-13 (Paul's defense); A[1] — 6:14–7:4 (exhortations) (351-66).

What Chevallier and Garland (and Segalla) agree on is the centrality of the "fool's speech" in chs. 10–13, whether the speech runs from 11:21b to 12:10 (so Segalla and Chevallier) or to 12:13 (so Garland). Garland's appeal to multiple instances of "inclusion" strengthens his proposal, although his case would have been even stronger if there had been instances of verbal (as well as conceptual) "inclusion" in 11:21b–12:13 (= C′) and 12:14-21 (= B′), as in A, B, and C. He could also have mentioned the instance of verbal "inclusion" in 13:1-10 (= A′), namely the "present-absent" antithesis in 13:1 and 10. And Garland's analysis has another advantage over Chevallier's in that there is a general correspondence between the matching pairs (A-A′, B-B′, C-C′) with regard to length.

3. Analysis by Content (and Epistolary Form)

Furnish analyzes 2 Corinthians 1–9 (his "Letter B″") by both epistolary form and content (43; see xi-xii for full details):

  I. letter opening 1:1-11
    A. address 1:1-2
    B. blessing 1:3-11
 II. letter body 1:12–9:15
    A. assurances of concern 1:12–2:13
    B. comments on apostolic service 2:14–5:19
    C. appeals 5:20–9:15

Compare Schelkle xvii-xx and Hafemann 37-39 for similar analyses of the whole letter.

The majority of commentators analyze the canonical 2 Corinthians according to content alone and find three clearly discernible sections, chs. 1–7, 8–9, and 10–13. The present commentary is based on such an analysis (see Contents).

E. SUMMARY OF THE THEOLOGY OF 2 CORINTHIANS

In its essence Paul's theology was contained in his Damascus encounter with the risen Lord, but its particular expressions were prompted by his pastoral experience. That is, while the boundaries of his spiritual horizons were marked out at his conversion, his subsequent reflection on that experience and the compulsive effect of pastoral circumstances influenced the expression of his theology. At the time of 2 Corinthians the circumstances that stimulated his theological thinking included in particular his devastating encounter with death in Asia as an instance of his perpetual trials, the discipline of the "wrongdoer" by the Corinthian congregation, the Corinthians' favorable response to the mission of Titus when he brought them the "severe letter," the suspension at Corinth of the relief operation Paul was organizing for destitute believers in the Jerusalem church, and the arrival and malevolent influence of the Palestinian intruders with their rival claim to true apostleship, their illegitimate boasting, and their preaching of a false gospel. Although the issues dealt with in this letter were triggered by various situations in the church at Corinth, the letter is also addressed to "all God's people who are in the whole of Achaia" (1:1). The apostle assumes the distribution of the letter and the relevance to other believers of his theological response to issues that were unique to Corinth.

Because all of Paul's letters are occasional, none touches on all the aspects of his theology. The distinctive emphases of the theology of 2 Corinthians may be gathered up under the following general headings. We presuppose the exegesis of the relevant texts.

1. The Godhead

Paul makes several timeless affirmations about the character and actions of *God the Father,* often by the use of the present tense or a descriptive genitive. He is the one who is a source of grace (1:2; 8:1; 9:14), purity and sincerity (1:12), who shows mercy and gives comfort (1:3-4; 7:6), who raises the dead (1:9), who acts as an impeccable witness (1:18; 11:31), who strengthens believers in their faith in Christ and faithfulness to Christ (1:21), who is ever-living (3:3), who no longer debits people's offenses to their account (5:19), who loves the person who gives generously (9:7), who is able to shower people with every kind of blessing (9:8), who produces seed for people to sow and thus bread for them to eat (9:10), who is both the God and the Father of the Lord Jesus (1:3; 11:31), who is entitled to eternal praise (11:31), who knows the details of human experience (12:2-3), and who is marked by love and peace as both his attributes and his gifts (13:11; cf. 1:2). Also, Paul credits God with specific acts (in this case indicated by the aorist tense), all of them associated with God's saving sovereignty. He rescued Paul from the jaws of death in Asia (1:10), he has commissioned believers to divine service (1:21b), he has sealed believers by giving them his Spirit as a down payment and pledge (1:22; 5:5), he made Paul and his colleagues his agents in promulgating the new covenant (3:6), he shone into Paul's heart and the hearts of all believers with the light of the gospel (4:6), he raised the Lord Jesus from the dead (4:14), he entrusted Christian evangelists with the task of announcing reconciliation through Christ (5:18-19), he caused Christ to be "sin" for the sake of sinners (5:21), he inspired Titus with a zeal for the Corinthians' welfare (8:16), he conferred apostolic authority on Paul (10:8; 13:10; cf. 1:1), and he allotted to Paul a mission assignment that included Corinth (10:13-15).

The Lord Jesus Christ and God the Father jointly form a single source of grace and peace (1:2); Christ's deity is clearly implied. Through his pre-incarnate choice Christ exchanged the richness of heavenly existence for the relative poverty of earthly life (8:9). During his life on earth he showed meekness and forbearance (10:1). His death, which inaugurated the new era, the day of salvation (5:15-17; 6:2), was for the benefit of all people without distinction (5:14-15). God was present and active in Christ; this was shown preeminently in God's reconciling humankind to himself through Christ (5:19). Christ was totally devoid of sin, yet on God's initiative he became "sin" on behalf of humans and in their place, being the object of God's wrath and so estranged from him, so that by being in Christ believers might become righteous in God's sight (5:21). Christ died so that those who enjoy new life through him should live wholly for him and not for themselves (5:15). From one viewpoint he was crucified because of his "weakness" in obeying God and in not retaliating, but he now lives a permanent resurrection life that is sustained by God's power (13:4). All God's promises find their "yes" of fulfillment in him (1:19-20), and he is the content of Christian preaching (1:19; 9:13; 10:14) as the risen and glorified Lord (4:5). Believers are "in Christ" (2:17; 5:17; 12:2, 19; 13:5) in the sense of being in personal union with the risen Christ and in the body of Christ. He is the one and only husband of his bride, the church (11:2). When unbelievers come to be "in Christ," a veil of ignorance or misapprehension is lifted from their hearts (3:14-15; 4:3-4), and God performs a new act of creation in making them altogether new persons (5:17). It is "through Christ" that Christian worship ascends to God (1:20) and that Paul had confidence before God that he was God's agent in Corinth (3:4; cf. 2:7; 3:2-3). Paul was administering the collection project "for (= "to promote") the glory of the Lord (Jesus)" (8:19). And it was the risen Lord (Jesus) who had given Paul a special revelation fourteen years earlier (12:1; cf. 12:2-4).

The *Spirit* is given to believers as God's down payment on their inheritance and as a pledge of the resurrection (1:22; 5:5; cf. 11:4). As "the Spirit of the living God" (3:3), he is the means by which Christ wrote the letter of commendation that is the Corinthians; whereas ink is erasable, the person and work of the Spirit are imperishable (3:2-3). Regarded as external commandments, the written Law is lifeless, but the Spirit is life-giving, for he indwells believers and revitalizes them (3:6; cf. 3:18). The new covenant era is a period characterized not only by extraordinary divine glory but also and especially by the Spirit's presence and activity within and among God's people (3:6-11) — people turn to the Spirit (3:16-17a), gain freedom through the Spirit (3:17b), and are transformed by the Spirit (3:18). "Where the Spirit of the Lord is, there is freedom" (3:17); negatively, freedom from hardheartedness and from ignorance about Christ, and positively, freedom to see Yahweh's glory uninterruptedly and freedom of access into God's presence without fear (3:13-18).

Paul's parting benediction (13:14) is the most developed *trinitarian affirmation* in the NT. His desire is that all his addressees may always be fortified by the grace given by Christ and the love that stems from God, and may continue to enjoy a common participation in the Spirit's life and power that results in enriched fellowship among believers. Relations among the members of the Trinity are not in view here. The unusual order of Son-Father-Spirit points to the chronological order of believers' experience of the Godhead: in coming to Christ we encounter God, who then gives us his Spirit.

2. Salvation

The expression the "old covenant" (3:14) may be a Pauline coinage, a natural deduction from Jeremiah's "new covenant" (Jer. 31:31, LXX 38:31) and from the eucharistic tradition of the cup as "the new covenant" ratified by Christ's blood (1 Cor. 11:25). Behind 2 Cor. 3:7-18 lies the account in Exod. 34:29-35 of the interaction between Moses and the Israelites after Moses had received on Mount Sinai the two tablets of the Law for a second time. 2 Cor. 3:7-11 is a commentary on Exod. 34:29-30 and basically a comparison of *the two covenants* that establishes the surpassing glory of the new covenant. Both covenants are glorious (3:7-8), but the new is far more glorious (3:9-11). The old was engraved on stone tablets (3:3, 7), the new is written on hearts-of-flesh tablets (3:3). One was a death-dealing written code, the other involves a life-giving Spirit (3:6). The era of the old covenant was a dispensation of death (3:7) and condemnation (3:9), a fading order (3:7,11), whereas the era of the new covenant is a dispensation of the Spirit (3:8) and of righteousness (3:9), a permanent order (3:11). The second paragraph, 3:12-18, is an allusive homily based on Exod. 34:33-35, the account of Moses' regular encounters with Yahweh in the "tent of meeting" before speaking with the Israelites. In 3:18 Paul states or implies certain contrasts that illustrate the superiority of the new covenant. Under this new economy, not one person alone but all believers see and then reflect the glory of the Lord; unlike the Jews, who still read the law with veiled hearts, Christians, with unveiled faces, see the glory of Yahweh, which is Christ, in the mirror of the gospel; glory is displayed inwardly in the character, not outwardly on the face; and so far from waxing and waning, the glory progressively increases until the believer acquires through resurrection a "glorious body" comparable to Christ's (Phil. 3:21).

In the work of *reconciliation* God is both the initiator and the goal, Christ was God's agent, the beneficiaries are primarily humans, and although reconciliation is an accomplished fact it is also an ongoing process, for humans must embrace it by responding to "the message of reconciliation" and thus becoming reconciled to God (5:18-21). The *conversion* of unbelievers occurs when God shines into their hearts with spiritual illumination (4:6), when he graciously answers their cry for help and salvation (6:2), when they turn to the Spirit and respond to his overtures concerning Christ (3:14-16). It involves gaining a new view of Christ — he is God's promised Messiah — and consequently a new

117

view of other people, who are now seen in their relation to Christ and in the light of the cross (5:16). The converted person enjoys a new relationship with Christ and his people (5:17a); the old state of affairs has entirely disappeared and a brand new order has come to stay (5:17b).

We suggest that the unifying theme or center of Paul's theology is "God the Father's salvation through Christ," that is, God the Father's provision, through the death of Christ, of a way for humans to be reconciled to himself and to lead lives that are pleasing to him. This implies that Paul's theology is primarily patrocentric, soteriological, and christological. 5:19a encapsulates this coordinating motif in Pauline thought: "God was in Christ, reconciling the world (of humans) to himself."

3. The Gospel

At its heart the gospel is "the message of reconciliation" (5:19c), namely that reconciliation to God has been achieved by the work of Christ (5:18-19a) so that forgiveness of sins is granted (5:19b) and a right standing before God is imparted (5:21) to those who become reconciled to God (5:20b). Although the gospel is an indescribably valuable treasure whose all-surpassing power derives from God, God has entrusted its spread to "earthenware jars," people who in themselves are frail and relatively insignificant (4:7). Yet proclaimers of the good news (4:5) are privileged and willing captives in God's triumphal procession, for as they diffuse the fragrant knowledge of Christ they are an aroma of Christ that brings God pleasure (2:14-15). The function of evangelists is threefold: they are trustees of a message (5:19c), ambassadors for Christ, and advocates for God (5:20). From one perspective evangelism is "trying to persuade people" (5:11) of the truth of the gospel. Paul's motivation for his evangelistic effort was, in part, "the fear of the Lord" (5:11), that is, the sobering awareness of ultimate accountability to the Lord Christ (5:10). But other impulses for proclaiming the good news were the honor of God (5:13) and the love of Christ (5:14). Pioneer evangelism in a particular area brings the right and privilege of pastoral ministry in that area (10:13-15).

4. The Church

Local Christian congregations are real and representative expressions of the worldwide and yet heavenly community which is the church of God: "the church of God as it is found in Corinth" (1:1). As the betrothed bride of the heavenly bridegroom, Christ, the church is called to retain virgin purity until her presentation to him at his parousia (11:2-3).

At some stage after 1 Corinthians had been received at Corinth, Paul or one of his representatives was apparently verbally insulted by someone in the

Corinthian church. The precise nature of the offense is not known, but it clearly involved Paul since he offers his personal forgiveness (2:10). At first the congregation had not rallied to Paul's defense, but, stung by the "severe letter" that called for the punishment of the wrongdoer, the majority inflicted some unspecified penalty on the man. Now Paul calls for the termination of the penalty and the reaffirmation of love toward the man (2:8). For offenses serious enough to warrant corporate church discipline (such as overt immorality not repented of [1 Cor. 5:1-11], false teaching actively propagated [Rom. 16:17], or divisiveness [Tit. 3:10]), there appear to be five stages in the whole process, stages that are not only necessary but should occur in a fixed order: (1) the wrongdoing (2:5), which implies an offending party (7:12) and sometimes an offended party (7:12), (2) the punishment (2:6), which is inflicted by "the majority," (3) the pain or sorrow suffered by the wrongdoer (2:5, 7) and in a different sense by the whole congregation (2:5), (4) repentance (implied in 2:6), which is the outcome of "godly sorrow" (cf. 7:9-10), and (5) forgiveness (2:7, 10) and restoration (2:8), which are granted by congregation as well as by the offended party. All this implies that church discipline is not simply retributive but also remedial, aiming at producing repentance (7:9), and that it is effective only when it is supported and reinforced by the congregation as a whole (10:6).

As Paul anticipates his next (third) visit to Corinth (12:14; 13:1), he sees no conflict between the expression of tender affection (11:11; 12:15, 19) and the threat of uncompromising discipline (10:2; 13:2, 10). Love is an essential aspect of "upbuilding" (12:19); discipline is sometimes a necessary aspect, as when there is no repentance for wrongdoing (cf. 12:21; 13:2). "Destruction" must sometimes precede "upbuilding" (cf. 10:8; 13:10).

Paul encourages the Corinthian believers to exchange the Christian kiss (13:12; cf. 1 Pet. 5:14) as an expression of love, reconciliation, and fellowship in Christ.

5. Apostleship

To judge by Paul's response to his opponents, they sought to validate their claim to be genuine apostles of Christ (cf. 11:13) or "servants of Christ" (11:23) in a distinctive sense (10:7) by their ecstatic experiences such as visions and revelations (cf. 12:1), their acceptance of financial support from (at least some of) the Corinthians (11:12, 20), their pedigree and their achievements in ministry (11:22-23), their personal bearing and powerful eloquence (cf. 10:10; 11:6, 20), and their accomplishments at Corinth (cf. 10:13-15; 11:20). Throughout the epistle but especially in chs. 10–13 Paul is providing the Corinthians with alternative criteria for assessing true apostleship by which they will be able to recognize the falsity of his rivals' claims and the validity of his own.

For Paul, what validated apostleship was not the parading of one's spiritual experiences, one's personal value and qualifications, one's eloquence and exploits, but declaration of an unadulterated gospel (1:19; 2:17; 5:20; 11:4, 10), God-given evangelistic success shown in the transformed lives of converts (3:2-3), enduring of sufferings for Christ with the utmost endurance (4:8-9; 6:4-5, 8-9; 11:23-27; 12:10, 12), sincerity and openness of speech and conduct (1:12-13; 2:17; 4:2; 5:11; 6:11; 11:6; 12:6), God's working of miracles ("signs, marvels, and powerful deeds") during one's service (12:12), adherence to the territorial assignment allotted by God (10:13-16), and, above all, humble, slave-like service (1:24; 4:5) for the upbuilding or "elevation" of others (10:8; 11:7-8; 12:19; 13:10). In this latter regard Christ's own career was the pattern for Paul's ministry. But whereas Christ's death because of "weakness" was followed by resurrection life and power (13:4a), Paul experienced the powerful life of the risen Christ at the same time that he shared the "weakness" of Christ's Passion (4:10-11; 13:4b).

6. Christian Ministry

Throughout the letter but particularly in the last four chapters we may discern Paul's theology of pastoral service as he exhibits the characteristics of a spiritual father (1 Cor. 4:14-16) who has been entrusted by God with the care of his children.

a. Adaptability

As Paul sought to get his "children" to open their hearts wide to him (6:13) and to close their hearts against his adversaries, he used a delicate blend of meekness (10:1; 13:10) and boldness (10:2, 11; 11:13). Because the immature Corinthians were dazzled by the pompous boasting of the Judaizers about their credentials and achievements, he was forced to indulge in boasting as they did (10:8; 11:1, 16-18, 21-27; 12:1, 11), although he chose to boast in matters that showed his weakness (11:30), namely his humiliating nocturnal escape from Damascus (11:31-33) and his debilitating "thorn in the flesh" (12:7). He uses biting irony (11:4, 19-21; 12:11, 13) that stops short of sarcasm. He shows sensitivity to the requirements of a situation, in addressing the psychological needs of the repentant wrongdoer (2:6-8), and in refusing to forgo his financial independence of his converts (11:7-12).

b. Jealousy

Paul was jealous for the Corinthians' undivided loyalty to Christ during the period between their betrothal to Christ (= their conversion) and their presentation to Christ, their heavenly bridegroom (= their glorification; 11:2-3). Paul pictures himself as the father of the bride, whose aim was to preserve her virginity, her "sincere and pure devotion to Christ" (11:3), until her marriage. Such jealousy reflects God's jealousy for the protection of his name and his people (11:2).

c. Devotion

Indicative of Paul's paternal devotion to his children was the "daily pressure" of his anxious concern for all his churches (11:28) as he sympathized with their weakness in faith, conduct, and conscience (11:29; cf. 1 Cor. 8:7-13; 9:22; 12:26). In this "anxious concern" Paul was not violating Jesus' teaching about anxiety (Matt. 6:25-34) since he was, in fact, seeking first the kingdom of God and grappling with present, not future, problems and was free of anxiety about relatively trivial matters such as food and clothing (see 11:27).

d. Affection

Like parents who work hard and save up for their children (12:14), Paul was willing "to spend and be spent" for the benefit of his spiritual children (12:15). Neither property nor energies would be spared in his endeavor to win their devotion to Christ. When he asks, "Am I to be loved the less because I love you the more [that is, so intensely]?" (12:15), he is seeking an appropriate response of filial love to his own paternal affection (cf. 6:11-13; 11:11).

e. Fear

As he contemplated his forthcoming third visit (12:14), Paul was fearful that the visit might lead to mutual embarrassment (12:20), that sin might continue to be rampant in the church (12:20), and that he might again be humiliated and grieved because of certain unrepentant Corinthians (12:21). These fears induced Paul to issue a warning of impending discipline (13:1-4) and a plea for self-examination (13:5-10). In each case he reverts to the theme of "strength in weakness." As a result of being "in Christ," Paul shared the weakness of his Lord, but as a consequence of his fellowship "with" Christ, Paul shared in the power of the risen Christ (13:4b), which would be shown, if necessary, in his "not sparing" any erring Corinthians (13:2-3). But if the Corinthians were "strong" in Christ, giving evidence of robust and mature Christian character, Paul would be able to come to them in the "weakness" of a "gentle spirit" (1 Cor. 4:21), a situation which would make him rejoice (13:9).

These are not the only aspects of Paul's pastoral conduct that Christian workers may profitably follow. They should depend on divine weapons for the demolition of the strongholds and bastions of argumentation that oppose the knowledge of God given in the gospel of Christ (10:4-5), they cannot justifiably lay claim to credit or honor for success in ministry, since God alone provides the adequacy for service (3:5-6), they must avoid putting any obstacle in the way of the gospel (6:3) but endeavor so to live and work that in every regard their conduct may be commendable (6:4), they must repudiate the deceitful manipulation of their charges (4:2; 7:2; 11:20; 12:16-18) and any interest in their possessions or money (12:14), they should seek to do what is right and honorable in the eyes of humans as well as in God's eyes (8:21), they are never to forget the triumphs of God's grace (7:4) even when pastoral problems persist (chs. 8–13), and they are constantly to be aware of accountability to God or Christ (2:17; 5:10-11; 12:19).

7. The Christian Life

If *sorrow or pain* is borne "in a godly way" or "as God intended," it will not be harmful but will produce spiritual benefit such as a repentance that leads to spiritual vitality and eternal life and that leaves no room for regret (7:9-10).

In 6:14–7:1 Paul issues a clarion call to *holiness of life*. He directs the Corinthians to avoid getting into a "double harness" with unbelievers (6:14a), that is, to sever all close attachments with non-Christians (such as membership in local pagan cults) that would compromise their professed loyalty to Christ or jeopardize the consistency of their Christian witness. This is not an injunction against all association with unbelievers (see 1 Cor. 5:9-10; 7:12-16; 10:27). However, Christianity and heathenism (especially idolatry) are incompatible, as Paul shows by five rhetorical questions (6:14b-16a). Such discerning separation from the world (6:17) leads to fellowship with God and his people. If Christians corporately are the temple of the living God (6:16), individually they are the sons and daughters of a Father who is the Lord Almighty (6:18). The privilege of being a dwelling place of God (6:16) and the benefits of compliance with the divine will (6:17-18) Paul calls "promises," which motivate believers to avoid every source of possible defilement and bring their consecration to completion by having a reverential awe before God (7:1). Living for the honor of Christ (5:15) involves not only separation from outward evil (6:17) and inward defilement (7:1) but also fellowship with the living God and with those in his family (6:16, 18).

Christian existence is often marked by *paradox:* divine comfort in the midst of human affliction (1:3-4; 7:5-6), divine strength in the midst of human weakness (4:8-9; 7:4; 12:7, 9-10), life in the midst of death (4:10-12; 5:4; 6:9), spiritual rejuvenation in the midst of physical debilitation (4:16), joy in the midst of sorrow (6:10), and generosity in the midst of poverty (6:10; 8:2).

8. Suffering

This letter contains two lengthy lists of Paul's apostolic sufferings (6:4-10; 11:23-29), but his theology of Christian suffering is most apparent in 1:3-11. He had recently experienced some unspecified affliction in the province of Asia that caused him to be so utterly and unbearably crushed that he was forced to renounce all hope of survival (1:8). But God had graciously intervened to deliver him and would do so again, provided the Corinthians cooperated in prayer (1:10-11). Several principles emerge from Paul's discussion: (1) Suffering patiently endured deepens our appreciation of God's character, in particular his limitless compassion and never-failing comfort (1:3-4). (2) Suffering drives us to trust God alone. Paul's desperate plight had undermined his self-reliance and compelled his total dependence on a God who raises the dead and therefore can rescue the dying from the grip of death (1:9). (3) Suffering brings identification with Christ. Paul could identify his sufferings as "the sufferings of Christ" (1:5) probably because they befell him as "a person in Christ" (12:2) who was engaged in the service of Christ (4:11). They were *Christ's* sufferings because they contributed to the fulfillment of the suffering destined for the body of Christ (Acts 14:22; Col. 1:24) or because Christ continued to identify himself with his afflicted church (Acts 9:4-5). (4) The experience of God's comfort (his help, consolation, and encouragement) in our suffering qualifies, equips, and obliges us to comfort others undergoing any type of suffering (1:4, 6). The apostle's thought seems to imply four stages: Paul's own sufferings (= Christ's sufferings) (1:4), his experience of God's comfort mediated through Christ (1:5), the Corinthians' sufferings, and their experience of God's comfort mediated through Paul (1:6-7). (5) Suffering is not forever. In comparison with the weighty and eternal glory that is produced by suffering patiently endured, suffering is relatively insignificant and momentary (4:17). Glory follows suffering.

9. Stewardship

In the years 52-57 a large portion of Paul's time and energies were devoted to arranging a collection among his Gentile churches for "the poor among the saints in Jerusalem" (Rom. 15:26). He regarded this collection as an act of fraternal love (Gal. 6:10) that expressed the interdependence of the members of the body of Christ (1 Cor. 12:25-26), that symbolized the unity of Jew and Gentile in Christ (Eph. 2:11-22), and that dramatized for Gentile believers in material terms their spiritual indebtedness to the mother church in Jerusalem (Rom. 15:19, 27).

As Paul encourages the Corinthians to finalize their contribution to the collection, he appeals to a variety of motives designed to prompt their generous giving (8:1-15). There is the example of other believers (8:1-5, 8), their own promising start and desire for spiritual excellence (8:6-7), and the supreme example of Christ himself, who showed eagerness and generosity in giving as demonstration of his love (8:8-9). Christ "became poor" by the act of incarnation that followed his pre-incarnate renunciation of his "wealth," the glory of heavenly existence (cf. Phil. 2:6-8). Paul then shows that Christian stewardship does not aim at an exchange of financial burdens so that the rich become poor and the poor rich, but rather at an equal sharing of burdens that will lead to an equal supply of the necessities of life (8:13). Moreover, voluntary mutual sacrifice maintains that equality of supply (8:14), an equality which was enforced when God miraculously provided manna to the Israelites in the wilderness (8:15, citing Exod. 16:18).

Having spoken of the need for generosity (8:1-15), Paul illustrates the twofold result of generosity (9:6-15). First, "cheerful givers" who sow generously will also reap generously in God's provision of both spiritual grace and material prosperity ("all grace"), which will permit them constantly to dispense spiritual and material benefits to others (9:6-11a). Second, because generous giving is an evidence of God's grace (9:14; cf. 8:1-4), it prompts "many expressions of thanks to God" (9:11b-13).

2 Corinthians 8 and 9 highlight several characteristics of genuine Christian stewardship. It is voluntary, not enforced (8:3; 9:5, 7), generous, not parsimonious (8:2; 9:6, 13), enthusiastic, not grudging (8:4, 11-12; 9:7), deliberate, not haphazard (9:7), and sensible, not reckless (8:11-15).

10. Satan

There are six incidental but significant references to the work of the devil. He seeks to outwit and defraud believers (2:11) by overwhelming them with excessive sorrow after their wrongdoing (cf. 2:7) or by encouraging an unforgiving spirit (cf. 2:6, 8). As the ruler of the present age, he blinds the understanding of unbelievers to prevent their belief in the gospel (4:4). His purposes are diametrically opposed to Christ's (6:15). In keeping with his cunning deceit of Eve, he tries to lead believers astray from wholehearted devotion to Christ (11:3). He himself masquerades as an angel of light, and correspondingly his minions masquerade as agents of righteousness (11:14-15). On occasion, by divine permission, he uses a "thorn" to batter believers with suffering (12:7).

11. Eschatology

Paul's disconcerting encounter with death (1:8-11), his incessant suffering (11:23-29), and his progressive physical debility (4:16) prompted him to reflect as never before on the nature of death for the Christian. Negatively, death means the destruction of the earthly tent-dwelling (5:1), the loss of both physical corporeality (we are no longer "in the flesh") and earthly corporateness (we are no longer "in Adam," although we remain "in Christ"; 1 Cor. 15:18; 1 Thess. 4:16). Positively, death brings departure from mortal embodiment to the presence of the Lord (2 Cor. 5:8; cf. Phil. 1:23). A departure implies a destination as well as an evacuation, a "to" as well as a "from." At death, the believer is not left homeless but experiences a change of residence. Earthly embodiment means spatial distance or exile from the immediate presence of the Lord (5:6), since the Christian pilgrimage is through the realm of faith, not the realm of sight (5:7). But the same moment of death that marks the dismantling of the transitory tent of the physical body also marks the entrance upon permanent residence "with the Lord" (5:8) and therefore the enjoyment of active and mutual fellowship with him.

Although the terms "raise" and "resurrection" are not found in 5:1-10 (but see 4:14), it is clear that when Paul is indicating the sources of divine comfort that are afforded the believer who faces the possibility of death, there is not only the assurance that death brings enriched communion with Christ (5:7-8) but also the certainty of a future possession of a "spiritual body" (5:1; cf. 1 Cor. 15:44) and the knowledge that the indwelling Spirit is God's pledge of a resurrection transformation (5:4-5). This splendid hope (5:1-8), along with accountability to Christ (5:10), prompt the believer to seek the Master's constant approval (5:9).

From Paul's account of his heavenly ascent (12:2-4) we learn that although the final destiny of believers is not disembodiment but reembodiment, sentient experience in a temporary disembodied state is possible, and that "the third heaven" and "paradise" are closely related, with paradise, the dwelling-place of the righteous dead, perhaps to be located within the "third (= highest) heaven," the abode of God.

COMMENTARY

I. PAUL'S EXPLANATION OF HIS CONDUCT AND APOSTOLIC MINISTRY (2 CORINTHIANS 1–7)

A. Introduction (1:1-11)

1. Salutation (1:1-2)

Paul and Timothy give Christian greetings to the Corinthian believers and other Christians throughout Achaia.

1:1*Paul, an apostle of Christ Jesus[a] by the will of God, and Timothy our brother, to the church of God that is in Corinth, together with all God's people who are in the whole of Achaia. 2Grace and peace to you from God our Father and the Lord Jesus Christ.*

TEXTUAL NOTE

a. A D G K L Ψ most minuscules it[d, g, r] vg syr[p] cop[bo] goth arm eth read Ἰησοῦ Χριστοῦ, but Χριστοῦ Ἰησοῦ is the order found in the important proto-Alexandrian witnesses p[46] ℵ B (see Metzger 505) and is to be preferred.

Paul follows the normal practice of Greco-Roman letter writing by beginning his letters with the stereotyped formula: "A (sender) to B (addressee), greetings!" An example of this formula is found in Acts 23:26: "Claudius Lysias, to his Excellency, the Governor Felix, greetings!" (Κλαύσιος Δυσίας τῷ κρατίστῳ ἡγεμόνι Φήλικι χαίρειν.[1] But Paul expands this basic pattern by adding a self-designation, by mentioning an associate, by describing the recipients, and by substituting χάρις ("grace") for χαίρειν ("greetings!") and combining it with the traditional Hebrew greeting (*šālôm* = εἰρήνη, "peace").[2]

---

1. χαίρειν ("greetings!") is an imperatival use of the infinitive (cf. Acts 15:23; Jas. 1:1), although sometimes an actual imperative form replaces the infinitive, e.g., χαῖρε, κύριέ μου Ἀπίων, "Greetings, my lord Apion," P. Oxy. XIV.1664[1], cited by MM 682b).
2. Cf. Doty 29-30; Schnider and Stenger 3-41, especially the charts on 5-6 and 16-17 (in relation to v. 1).

1:1 Παῦλος. In Acts 13:9 Luke refers to Paul as Σαῦλος δέ, ὁ καὶ Παῦλος, "Saul, who is also [known as] Paul." Σαῦλος, the Greek form of the Hebrew šā'ûl ("asked [of God]"), transliterated Σαούλ, was Paul's Jewish birth name (like King Saul, he belonged to the tribe of Benjamin, Phil. 3:5), while Παῦλος was his Greco-Roman name and his *cognomen* (Lat. *Paullus*) as a Roman citizen. Jews who adopted Greek names generally assumed names similar in sound to their original Hebrew or Aramaic names; thus Σαῦλος became Παῦλος and Σιλᾶς became Σιλουανός.[3]

ἀπόστολος Χριστοῦ Ἰησοῦ. In epistolary salutations proper names (here Παῦλος and Τιμόθεος) are generally anarthrous. On the other hand, nouns that are added to anarthrous proper names by way of qualification are generally articular (e.g., Col. 4:10-11, 14). Presumably ἀπόστολος is anarthrous here because Paul did not claim to be "the one and only apostle" of Christ or "the apostle *par excellence*" (cf. 1 Cor. 15:8-9; 1 Tim. 1:12-15), only "an apostle of Christ Jesus." Χριστοῦ Ἰησοῦ may express agency ("sent/commissioned by Christ Jesus," subjective genitive) as well as possession ("belonging to Christ Jesus," possessive genitive).

Apart from 1 and 2 Thessalonians, Philippians, and Philemon, Paul always begins his letters with a reference to his apostleship. Such a reminder to his addressees was never more needed than at Corinth and never more timely than when serious doubts about his apostolicity were being sown in the fertile soil of the Corinthians' minds by the interlopers from Judea (2 Cor. 11:4-5, 12-13; 12:11-12). Now it is true that the term ἀπόστολος appears only five other times in 2 Corinthians (8:23; 11:5, 13; 12:11-12) and never in direct reference to Paul himself, but the heart of 2 Corinthians 1–7 is Paul's description of the apostolic ministry (2:14–7:4), while chs. 10–13 are essentially his defense of his apostolic authority.[4]

Paul uses the term ἀπόστολος ("one who is sent"; cf. John 13:16) in three basic senses: (1) in a general, nontechnical sense, of an emissary, delegate, representative, or messenger commissioned by people for a specific, temporary task (8:23, of Titus's two companions; Phil. 2:25, of Epaphroditus); (2) in a semitechnical sense, of a Christian with a particular, permanent commission from Christ or the local church (Rom. 16:7, of Andronicus and Junia[s]; 1 Cor. 9:5-6, of Barnabas, by implication [cf. Acts 14:4, 14]; 1 Cor. 15:7 and Gal. 1:19, of James, the brother of Jesus; and possibly 1 Cor. 4:9, of Apollos, by implication from 1 Cor. 4:6; and 1 Thess. 2:7, of Silas); (3) in a technical sense, of the Twelve (1 Cor. 15:5, 7; Gal. 1:17; cf. Luke 6:13) and of himself (1 Cor. 9:1; 15:9) as commissioned directly by Christ for permanent and distinctive leadership in the universal church. With regard to apostolic status, Paul recognized no distinction between himself and the Twelve (1 Cor. 9:1, 5; 15:8-10; 2 Cor. 11:5; 12:11; Gal. 2:6). For Paul's view of the qualifications for apostleship (in sense [3]), see 12:12.

---

3. Cf. Deissmann 314-15.
4. See the Introduction, D.3.

Investigating the relationship between the Jewish *šālîaḥ* ("envoy," "agent") and the Christian ἀπόστολος, Barrett ("Shaliah?" 99-100) suggests that the Greek noun was already current in the first century among some Hellenistic Jews as an established rendering of *šālîaḥ* and that the most plausible origin of the primitive Christian apostolate is to be found in Hellenistic-Jewish circles, not on Gnostic soil.[5] According to Barrett, whereas the Jerusalem church viewed the ἀπόστολος as exercising principally an administrative and organizational role, Paul saw the ἀπόστολος as first and foremost a missionary, although the two roles were not mutually exclusive ("Shaliah?" 100-101) This latter suggestion is attractive and seems antecedently probable, but beyond this the data are too meager and insufficiently precise to establish any competing "theologies of apostleship" within the NT period.[6]

When the two nouns Ἰησοῦς and Χριστός were first conjoined by Christians, (ὁ) Χριστός was a title added to the name Ἰησοῦς, "Jesus the Messiah" (Ἰησοῦς [ὁ] Χριστός) or "the Messiah Jesus" [ὁ] Χριστὸς Ἰησοῦς). But the original titular significance of Χριστός was rapidly lost, so that it became a proper name and the two words together, in either order, formed a single name.[7] That is not to say that ὁ Χριστός never means "the Messiah"; Rom. 9:5 and probably Col. 2:6 contain instances where the term is titular. In genitive constructions and after the preposition ἐν Paul generally places Χριστός before Ἰησοῦς; in the present case we have ἀπόστολος Χριστοῦ Ἰησοῦ.[8] Against Käsemann (27) and Klein (55, 57 n. 244), who propose that the phrase "apostle of Christ (Jesus)" was coined by Paul's opponents (cf. 11:13), Kramer argues that although the concept of the apostle as a special church official was current before Paul's time, it was Paul himself who linked the term "apostle" with the title "Christ."[9]

διὰ θελήματος θεοῦ. Against his opponents, who apparently arrogated to

5. As Schmithals argues (*Apostle* 96-230).

6. Cf. Kirk 262. On apostles and apostleship in the NT, see in particular Burton, *Galatians* 363-84; H. von Campenhausen, "Der urchristliche Apostelbegriff," *ST* 1 (1948) 96-130; A. C. Clark, "Apostleship: Evidence from the New Testament and Early Christian Literature," *VoxEv* 19 (1989) 49-82; R. W. Herron, "The Origin of the New Testament Apostolate," *WTJ* 45 (1983) 101-31; G. Klein, *Die zwölf Apostel. Ursprung und Gehalt einer Idee* (Göttingen: Vandenhoeck und Ruprecht, 1961); K. H. Rengstorf, *TDNT* 1.407-47, which is updated by J. A. Kirk, "Apostleship since Rengstorf: Towards a Synthesis," *NTS* 21 (1974-75) 249-64; and "Essay II: Paul the Apostle," in Thrall 946-65.

7. Cf. Kramer 203-14.

8. The reason for the reversal of the more common word order of Ἰησοῦς Χριστός, which corresponds to the Aramaic *yᵉšua' mᵉšîḥā*, may be grammatical. The genitive and dative cases of Ἰησοῦς are identical, namely Ἰησοῦ, but with Χριστός these cases are distinct, namely Χριστοῦ and Χριστῷ. If Χριστός was placed first, ambiguity was immediately obviated. Special theological significance should not therefore be read into Paul's oscillation from "Jesus Christ" to "Christ Jesus." Cf. Kramer 206. The alternative explanation of the word order in 1:1 is to regard Χριστὸς Ἰησοῦς as a merely stylistic variation of an original Ἰησοῦς Χριστός or (following Sanday and Headlam 4) as the later developed form where Χριστός no longer has the titular overtones that attach to it in the expression Ἰησοῦς Χριστός. See further Thrall 81-82.

9. Kramer 59-61, especially nn. 168, 177.

themselves the title "apostles" (11:13), Paul boldly states, without embarrassment or self-assertiveness, that he was chosen and commissioned to be an apostle of Christ Jesus through the express will of God (διά denoting "efficient cause," BAGD 180b, c). As he asserts in Gal. 1:1, his apostolic calling neither originated in human appointment (ἀπόστολος οὐκ ἀπ' ἀνθρώπων) nor was mediated by human agency (οὐδὲ δι' ἀνθρώπου) but came by commission from Jesus Christ and God the Father (ἀλλὰ διὰ Ἰησοῦ Χριστοῦ καὶ θεοῦ πατρός). With its single preposition (διά), the latter Greek phrase shows that Paul believed that Christ and God had jointly commissioned him.[10]

καὶ Τιμόθεος ὁ ἀδελφός. Timothy, a native of Lystra (Acts 16:1), was converted probably on Paul's first "missionary journey" (ca. A.D. 47-48), which included two visits to Lystra (Acts 14:6-20a, 21b-23). Timothy's spiritual growth was rapid, his Christian character exemplary, and his Christian service effective, for by about A.D. 50 he had gained a good reputation (ἐμαρτυρεῖτο) among the Christians at Iconium as well as at Lystra (Acts 16:2).[11]

ἀδελφός may indicate no more than "membership in the church"[12] and thus mean "fellow Christian," with the article denoting relationship, "our brother" (Goodspeed) or, pointing to a person well known to the addressees, "the brother you all know" (Barclay). This traditional Christian term for a fellow believer became indelibly impressed on Paul's mind when Ananias, one of the Damascene believers against whom he was making murderous threats (Acts 9:1-2), greeted him with the reassuring words, Σαοὺλ ἀδελφέ, "Brother Saul" (Acts 9:17). But the sense of ἀδελφός here could also be "coworker,"[13] although συνεργός more regularly has that meaning.[14] Both ideas are combined in the paraphrase of H. C. G. Moule (1): "the fellow-Christian and fellow-worker known to all." There is no need to maintain a third person reference, "his brother Christian,"[15] since even the standard "A to B" formula sometimes includes first person pronouns.[16]

Ollrog (93-96) distinguishes three categories of Paul's coworkers: (1) the small, inner circle consisting of Barnabas, Silvanus, and Timothy; (2) the independent missionaries whom Paul regarded as coworkers, including Apollos, Prisca and Aquila, and, in a certain sense, Titus; (3) church envoys who worked with Paul in their own communities, for example, Epaphras and Epaphroditus.

It was not uncommon for Paul to name some associate in the address (the exceptions are Romans, Galatians, Ephesians, and the Pastorals). Timothy's name appears in the salutations of 1 Thessalonians (1:1) and 2 Thessalonians (1:1) after "Paul and Silvanus." In the salutations of 2 Corinthians (1:1),

10. Cf. Χριστοῦ Ἰησοῦ as subjective genitive in 1:1, "sent/commissioned by Christ Jesus."
11. See further, Ollrog 20-23.
12. BAGD 16b; cf. Deissmann 87-88; MM 8-9; Turner, *Words* 56.
13. Cf. Ellis, "Co-Workers"; NEB and REB have "our colleague."
14. E.g., Rom. 16:21, of Timothy; 1 Thess. 3:2 conjoins ἀδελφός and συνεργός.
15. Barrett 53; similarly Wand and NAB[1].
16. Gal. 1:2; 2 Thess. 1:1; 1 Tim. 1:1; Phlm. 1-2.

Colossians (1:1), Philemon (1), and Philippians (1:1) he alone is mentioned with Paul. Whatever reasons might be suggested for the inclusion of Timothy's name in the other salutations,[17] in the case of 2 Corinthians there are at least four possibilities — that Timothy was the scribe, the bearer, the joint author, or the co-sender of 2 Corinthians. (1) It is not impossible that Timothy was Paul's amanuensis; against this, however, we should observe that stylistically 2 Corinthians does not belong with the other five letters which name Timothy in the salutation, but rather with Galatians, 1 Corinthians, and Romans, which together make up F. C. Baur's "chief epistles" *(Hauptbriefe),* and that in the one place where Paul does name his amanuensis (Rom. 16:22, Tertius), the scribe's name is not found in the salutation.[18] (2) Evidence is lacking that Timothy was the bearer of 2 Corinthians, for when Paul entrusts a coworker with the responsibility of delivering a letter and reinforcing its impact, he names the bearer at the end of the letter, not in the salutation.[19] (3) That Timothy is not a coauthor and 2 Corinthians not a joint production is clear from the expression δι' ἐμοῦ καὶ Σιλουανοῦ καὶ Τιμοθέου in 1:19 and the oscillation throughout the letter between the first person singular and the first person plural.[20] (4) Co-senders named in Paul's letters seem always to be well known to the addressees: for example, Silvanus/Silas (1 Thess. 1:1; 2 Thess. 1:1) was known at Thessalonica (Acts 17:4, 10a; 18:5a), and Timothy (Phil. 1:1) at Philippi (Acts 16:3, 11-12; Phil. 2:22). Timothy had been associated with Paul and Silvanus in the founding of the Corinthian church (2 Cor. 1:19; cf. Acts 18:5). Subsequently Paul sent him back to Corinth,[21] in all likelihood to try to arrest the undermining of Paul's influence in the church. Since, then, Timothy was no stranger to the Corinthians, Paul's mention of him in the salutation assured them of this young man's ongoing pastoral concern for them as well as showing his identification with Paul in all the teaching and admonitions contained in the letter.

Apart from these general reasons for the mention of Timothy that might apply, *mutatis mutandis,* to any co-sender named by Paul in a letter, there may be a specific reason that reflects Timothy's recent dealings with the Corinthians. In the Introduction we sought to establish that Timothy paid a second visit

17. Bruce *(Paraphrase* 10) raises the possibility that in these other letters (i.e., excluding 2 Corinthians) Timothy may have acted as Paul's scribe, being allowed to exercise "considerable stylistic discretion." On the role of the scribe in the composition of Paul's letters, see E. R. Richards, *The Secretary in the Letters of Paul* (Tübingen: Mohr, 1991), and R. N. Longenecker, "Ancient Amanuenses and the Pauline Epistles," in Longenecker and Tenney 281-97.

18. Compare 1 Pet. 1:1 with 5:12.

19. Eph. 6:21-22 and Col. 4:7-8, of Tychicus. Cf. Richards 47 n. 138.

20. E.g., 1:13-18, 21-24; 2:12-14. But see Murphy-O'Connor ("Co-Authorship" 570-79), who, noting that the "we" sections total 72% of 2 Corinthians 1–9 and the "I" sections only 28% (573), argues that Paul invoked the aid of Timothy in composing chs. 1–9, notably in the section on the apostolate (2:14–7:2). Similarly Murphy-O'Connor's *Paul* (309), where the percentages are given as 74% and 26%.

21. See 1 Cor. 4:17, where the aorist ἔπεμψα is more probably epistolary than preterit; 1 Cor. 16:10, where ἐάν may be temporal ("when") rather than conditional ("if").

to Corinth after the founding visit and the delivery of 1 Corinthians; that he was Paul's principal agent in Corinth at that time; that, as ὁ ἀδικηθείς (2 Cor. 7:12), he suffered some rebuff at Corinth after Paul's "painful visit"; and that by the time Paul wrote the "severe letter" Titus had become his chief envoy at Corinth.[22] If there is truth in these inferences from the data, Paul's reference to Timothy in 1:1 may be intended to reinstate this νεανίας (cf. 1 Tim. 4:12), who was naturally timid (2 Tim. 1:7; 2:1; cf. 1 Cor. 16:10) in the eyes of the Corinthians. 2 Corinthians was the first communication of Paul with Corinth since he called for the discipline of ὁ ἀδικήσας in the "severe letter."[23]

τῇ ἐκκλησίᾳ τοῦ θεοῦ τῇ οὔσῃ ἐν Κορίνθῳ. In the Greek city-state, ἐκκλησία denoted "a summoned assembly" (from ἐκ-καλέω) of all citizens called out to carry on legislative or judicial business. In the Greek Pentateuch συναγωγή generally renders both qāhāl ("assembly," the people of Israel convened in assembly) and 'edâ ("congregation," the people of Israel constituting a national entity). Elsewhere in the LXX ἐκκλησία regularly translates qāhāl and συναγωγή generally renders 'edâ (and sometimes qāhāl). On the Jewish preference for συναγωγή to denote a local congregation and the Christian preference for ἐκκλησία, E. de W. Burton makes the perceptive observation that

> the common use of ἐκκλησία in the Greek-speaking world to designate a civil assembly (cf. Acts 19:39) led the Jews as they spread through that world and established their local congregations to prefer what had previously been the less used term, συναγωγή. On the other hand, when, in the same regions in which these Jewish συναγωγαί existed, the Christians established their own assemblies they, finding it more necessary to distinguish these from the Jewish congregations than from the civil assemblies, with which they were much less likely to be confused, chose the term ἐκκλησία, which the Jews had discarded.[24]

The possessive genitive τοῦ θεοῦ distinguishes the Christian ἐκκλησία from secular political assembles: the church belongs to God, having been brought into existence by him and being sustained by his power.

The uses of ἐκκλησία in the Pauline corpus fall into three principal categories:

> a local sense, in reference to individual Christian congregations that can be identified and distinguished from similar assemblies by geographical reference, for example, "the church of the Thessalonians" (1 Thess. 1:1; 2 Thess. 1:1), "the churches of Galatia" (Gal. 1:2; 1 Cor. 16:1), "Nympha and the church in her home" (Col. 4:15); sometimes this usage is abbreviated to "the church";[25]

22. Introduction, B.1(c), C.
23. Similarly Martin (2), following Strachan (40); but see *per contra* Furnish 105.
24. *Galatians* 419. Cf. Schrage, "Ekklesia" 178-202.
25. E.g., 1 Cor. 11:18; 1 Tim. 5:16.

a generic sense, in reference to one, universal church consisting of all Christians worldwide or the whole body of believers on earth or in heaven; or in reference to a heavenly community with localized, earthly manifestations — "the church of God"[26] or simply "the church";[27]

a combination of the generic and local senses — e.g., "the church of God that is at Corinth" (1 Cor. 1:2; 2 Cor. 1:1; cf. 1 Thess. 1:1), that is, the local representatives at Corinth of God's universal church and/ or of the heavenly congregation. The plural, "the churches of God in Christ Jesus that are in Judea" (1 Thess. 2:14), "the churches of Christ" (Rom. 16:16), "all the churches of the Gentiles" (Rom. 16:4), or the virtual plural, "in every church" (1 Cor. 4:17), "no church . . . except you only" (Phil. 4:15), is a variation of (1); thus 1 Thess. 2:14 ("the churches of God in Christ Jesus that are in Judea") refers to the Judean local churches that belong to God.

In 2 Cor. 1:1, then, ἡ ἐκκλησία τοῦ θεοῦ τῇ οὔσῃ ἐν Κορίνθῳ refers, not to "the Corinthian church that belongs to God" or the Corinthian congregation as a mere part of God's invisible, universal church, but to that worldwide and yet heavenly community which is the church of God as it finds real and representative expression in the local congregation of believers at Corinth, "the church of God as it is found in Corinth." Perceptive Corinthians could draw two inferences from this expression: first, as a visible manifestation of a single, undivided community, the Corinthians should be marked by unity in thought and practice (cf. 1 Cor. 1:10; Eph. 4:3); second, as one local representation of a universal community, the Corinthians should never imagine that they alone constituted the whole church of God and were above general Christian tradition (cf. 1 Cor. 11:2, 16; 14:36).[28]

σὺν τοῖς ἁγίοις πᾶσιν τοῖς οὖσιν ἐν ὅλῃ τῇ Ἀχαΐᾳ. In classical and pre-Roman times Achaia signified the Peloponnese north of Arcadia,[29] although in Homer οἱ Ἀχαιοί often refers to Greeks in general. But in 27 B.C., under Augustus, Achaia became an independent senatorial province governed by a proconsul (ἀνθύπατος; cf. Acts 18:12) and included all of ancient Greece (probably without Thessaly).[30] As a Roman citizen Paul probably used Ἀχαΐα in this provincial sense.[31] ἐν ὅλῃ τῇ Ἀχαΐᾳ refers to the same geographical and political area as (ἐν) τοῖς κλίμασιν τῆς Ἀχαΐας (11:10).

---

26. E.g., 1 Cor. 10:32; 11:22; 12:28.

27. E.g., Eph. 1:22; 3:10; 5:25, 32; Col. 1:18, 24. Even in 1 Cor. 15:9; Gal. 1:13; Phil. 3:6 "the church (of God)" need not be restricted to the Jerusalem church.

28. On Paul's view of the ἐκκλησία, see in particular Banks; Best, *Body;* Cerfaux, *Church;* Hainz; and more briefly Burton, *Galatians* 417-20; O'Brien, *Colossians* 57-61; Thrall 89-93.

29. See the map in *CAH* 11.557.

30. Strabo 17.840.

31. *Pace* Barrett 56; Furnish 106. Ἑλλάς, "Greece" (Acts 20:2), a NT *hapax legomenon,* was

If, then, "Achaia" denotes the Roman province of that name, "all God's people who are in the whole of Achaia" will include believers at Corinth's eastern port of Cenchreae, such as Phoebe (Rom. 16:1), and those at Athens, such as Dionysius the Areopagite and Damaris (Acts 17:34). Precisely where other Christians resided "in the regions of Achaia" (11:10) is not known, and apart from Corinth and Cenchreae, we have no evidence of churches in Achaia. But Luke's allusion to οἱ μαθηταί in Achaia (Acts 18:27a), while having primary reference to the Corinthian Christians (Acts 18:27b-28; 19:1; cf. 1 Cor. 3:5-6), may have included believers throughout Achaia. Certainly the combination of πᾶσιν and ὅλῃ[32] suggests that a substantial number of Achaian believers resided outside Corinth and its environs. On the other hand, this is not to imply that 2 Corinthians was a circular letter, as Héring (1) proposes. All that we need to assume is that Christians outside Corinth would have access to Paul's letter through their informal or regular contact with the church of Corinth. From the content of the letter there can be no doubt that the Corinthian believers are the main addressees, but perhaps the joint address explains the absence of personal greetings in ch. 13.

The verbal distinction Paul makes between "the church of God at Corinth" and "all the saints throughout Achaia" should not be pressed, of course, to suggest that he did not reckon the Corinthians among οἱ ἅγιοι; the preposition σύν ("together with," "including") points to inclusiveness, not exclusiveness. Paul's two categories are not mutually exclusive: the Corinthians were also οἱ ἅγιοι, and "God's people in the whole of Achaia," along with the Corinthians, formed ἡ ἐκκλησία τοῦ θεοῦ ἡ οὖσα ἐν τῇ Ἀχαΐᾳ (as Paul would have expressed it).

For Paul οἱ ἅγιοι are all believers in Christ who, as God's chosen ones (Col. 3:12), are set apart by God for his service and therefore are to be separated from evil (cf. Exod. 19:5-6; Lev. 11:44-45). This elect community of the end times, the church, is "the true circumcision" (Phil. 3:3) and "Abraham's offspring" (Gal. 3:29), being composed of both believing Jews (the "remnant chosen by grace," Rom. 11:5) and believing Gentiles (Rom. 4:11-12; 9:24; 1 Cor. 1:24). Since the notions of divine election, divine possession, community, separation, and holiness attach to the expression οἱ ἅγιοι as a result of LXX usage,[33] it is impossible adequately to render the term in English. In their renderings of this word in v. 1 most EVV focus on one of two aspects: (1) holiness, "the saints" (RV, RSV,

---

a popular synonym for this Roman provincial name of Ἀχαΐα. It is not surprising that Achaia and Macedonia are sometimes closely associated in the NT (Acts 19:21; Rom. 15:26; 1 Thess. 1:8) because from 146 B.C., when the Romans under Lucius Mummius crushed the Achaian confederacy, of which Corinth was a leading member, and annexed Macedonia as a Roman province, down to 27 B.C., when it was organized as a separate Roman province, Achaia was treated administratively as part of Macedonia. Furthermore, from A.D. 15-44 Achaia and Macedonia were combined with Moesia as a single imperial province under the legate of Moesia (Tacitus, *Annales* 1.76.4; 80.1).

32. Cf. the same combination in 1 Thess. 4:10, εἰς πάντας τοὺς ἀδελφοὺς τοὺς ἐν ὅλῃ τῇ Μακεδονίᾳ.

33. In the LXX ἅγιος and ἁγιάζειν regularly represent the Hebrew root *qdš*. See O. Procksch, *TDNT* 1.89-96.

NASB, JB, NRSV), "the holy ones" (NAB[2]), "the holy people" (Thrall 78), or (2) divine possession, "God's people" (Weymouth, Goodspeed, Williams, GNB, REB), "Christ's People" (TCNT), "the Lord's people" (Isaacs). The renderings "God's holy people" (NJB), "God's dedicated people" (Barclay), "and those . . . who are consecrated to God" (Cassirer) combine these two aspects.

1:2 χάρις ὑμῖν καὶ εἰρήνη. These nouns lack the article because they occur in a common, stereotyped expression and because abstract nouns are generally anarthrous when they express a quality without particular reference to specific, concrete expressions of that quality.[34] A singular verb such as εἴη or ἔστω (BDF §128[5]) or πληθυνθείη[35] may be understood.

Paul's wish for the Corinthians in effect constitutes a prayer for them: "May grace and peace be yours from God . . ." = "[I pray that] God . . . may grant you grace and peace." ὑμῖν belongs with both χάρις and εἰρήνη: "grace and peace to you." εἰρήνη may well be related to χάρις as result to cause, "and the peace which this favour brings" (Plummer 1), but scarcely by hendiadys ("the gift of peace").

While the combination "mercy and peace" is found in an epistolary greeting in the Syriac *Apocalypse of Baruch* (*2 Baruch* 78:2), a Jewish document of the early second century A.D., it is doubtful whether "grace and peace" was a common Jewish epistolary salutation a century earlier. But even if the *form* of Paul's opening epistolary benediction is conventional and is ultimately based on Near Eastern epistolary traditions,[36] the *content* of these salutations is distinctly Christian in two regards. First, Paul modifies the traditional χαίρειν ("greetings") or πολλὰ/πλεῖστα χαίρειν ("warm greetings") of Hellenistic letters (cf. Acts 15:23; 23:26; Jas. 1:1) by substituting the cognate term χάρις, which for Paul sums up God's unsought and unmerited favor in Christ which is sufficient for every need, and combines it with the customary Jewish greeting *šālôm* (e.g., 2 Sam. 18:28; Greek εἰρήνη), which for Paul denotes not simply a fully rounded well-being (physical, emotional, mental, spiritual) but the spiritual tranquility or serenity of spirit that comes to the believer from God (Phil. 4:7) as a result of having peace with God (Rom. 5:1). Second, Paul identifies the source of this spiritual blessing as Jesus Christ as well as God the Father (see below for further discussion of this point).

ἀπὸ θεοῦ πατρὸς ἡμῶν καὶ κυρίου Ἰησοῦ Χριστοῦ. Several syntactical observations should be made about this important phrase.

1. ἀπὸ θεοῦ κτλ. belongs to both χάρις and εἰρήνη, rather than to εἰρήνη alone (as though ἀπὸ θεοῦ κτλ. balanced ὑμῖν). ἀπό, "that comes from," points to the originator of action (BAGD 88a, b).

2. While it is grammatically possible that both ἡμῶν and κυρίου Ἰησοῦ

---

34. Cf. BDF §258; Turner 176-77; and especially Zerwick §§176-79.

35. As in 1 Pet. 1:2; 2 Pet 1:2; and also Jude 2, where three coordinate subjects are followed by a singular verb.

36. As Friedrich ("Briefpräskript" 343-46) proposes.

Χριστοῦ are dependent on πατρός (". . . the Father of us and of the Lord Jesus Christ"; cf. 1:3), such an understanding seems excluded by: (1) the parallel construction in 2 Thess. 1:1 (ἐν θεῷ πατρὶ ἡμῶν καὶ κυρίῳ Ἰησοῦ Χριστῷ), where the ambiguity of successive genitives is not present; (2) the unambiguous coordination (by καί) of "God the/our Father" and "(the Lord) Jesus Christ" in 1 Cor. 8:6; Gal. 1:1; 1 Thess. 1:1; 3:11; (3) the parallel passages in 1 Tim. 1:2; 2 Tim. 1:2; Tit. 1:4, which place ἡμῶν after the reference to Christ and thus make it imperative to coordinate κυρίου Ἰησοῦ Χριστοῦ with θεοῦ πατρός; (4) the probability that if the Lord Jesus Christ and believers were thus associated (and there is no explicit Pauline parallel), the order in which they were mentioned would be reversed, viz. θεοῦ πατρὸς κυρίου Ἰησοῦ Χριστοῦ καὶ ἡμῶν;[37] and (5) v. 3, which speaks unambiguously of God as the "Father of our Lord Jesus Christ"; it would be a tautology uncharacteristic of Paul for v. 2 to make virtually the same affirmation.

3. If, as seems likely, the phrase πατρὸς ἡμῶν is an allusion to the divine address in the Lord's Prayer (πάτερ ἡμῶν, Matt. 6:9), ἡμῶν probably modifies πατρός alone, and not θεοῦ also, so that πατρός is in epexegetic apposition to θεοῦ ("God, our Father," TCNT; "God our Father," most EVV).

4. If, then, "the Lord Jesus Christ" is coordinate with "God our Father," what is the significance of the fact that the preposition ἀπό is not repeated before κυρίου? When ἀπό is used of persons, the repetition of the preposition would serve to highlight the distinctiveness and duality of the sources (Rev. 1:4-5; cf. 2 John 3); conversely, a single preposition stresses the unity and singularity of the source (although not the identity of the persons, as if καί were epexegetic). God the Father and the Lord Jesus Christ jointly form a single source of divine grace and peace. "They sustain a single relation (not two diverse relations)[38] to the grace and peace that come to believers."[39] But quite apart from the theological implications of a single preposition, the deity of Christ is here implicitly affirmed, for a monotheistic Jew would never juxtapose a mere human being with God as a comparable fount of spiritual blessing; equality bespeaks deity.

5. Finally, we should note the precise structural balance of this salutation.

Χάρις ὑμῖν καὶ εἰρήνη
ἀπὸ θεοῦ πατρὸς ἡμῶν
καὶ κυρίου Ἰησοῦ Χριστοῦ.

---

37. For the expression "God the Father [or "the God and Father"] of our/the Lord Jesus (Christ)," see Rom. 15:6; 2 Cor. 1:3; 11:31; Eph. 1:3; Col. 1:3.

38. Such as source and channel, as Barrett (*1 Corinthians* 35) proposes.

39. Harris, "Prepositions" 1178. It is these considerations that render improbable the view of Weima (90, 100), who argues on the basis of the "grace benediction" (at the end of Paul's letters) where Christ is always the divine source, and the "peace benediction" where God is typically (but cf. 2 Thess. 3:16) the divine source, that 1:2 forms a chiasm (ABB′A′) so that χάρις comes from the Lord Jesus Christ and εἰρήνη comes from God the Father.

There are four words in each line, and each line has three points of reference (excluding καὶ . . . ἀπὸ . . . καί).[40] There is no reason to doubt that Paul himself was the creator of this epistolary benediction,[41] which stands in a similar but not identical form at the beginning of each of his letters.[42]

Bibliography

D. E. Aune, "Opening Formulas," in his *The New Testament in Its Literary Environment* (Philadelphia: Westminster/Cambridge: Clarke, 1987) 184-86 • Berger, "Apostelbrief" • Deissmann • G. Delling, "Zusammengesetzte Gottes- und Christusbezeichnungen in den Paulusbriefen," in *Holtz FS* 65-71 • Doty • W. G. Doty, "The Classification of Epistolary Literature," *CBQ* 31 (1969) 183-99 • Eastman • Ellis, "Co-Workers" • Friedrich, "Briefpräskript" • W. Grundmann, "Paulus, aus dem Volke Israel, Apostel der Völker," *NovT* 4 (1960) 269-91 • Hainz • R. Jewett, "The Form and Function of the Homiletic Benediction," *ATR* 51 (1969) 18-34 • C. H. Kim • Kramer • D. H. Liebert, "The 'Apostolic Form of Writing' Group Letters before and after 1 Corinthians," in Bieringer (ed.) 433-40 • Lieu • E. Lohmeyer, "Probleme paulinischer Theologie. I: Briefliche Grussüberschriften," *ZNW* 26 (1927) 158-73 • R. N. Longenecker, "On the Form, Function, and Authority of the New Testament Letters," in *Scripture and Truth,* ed. D. A. Carson and J. D. Woodbridge (Grand Rapids: Zondervan, 1983) 101-14 • M. R. P. McGuire, "Letters and Letter Carriers in Ancient Antiquity," *Classical World* 53 (1960) 148-99 • T. Y. Mullins, "Benediction as a NT Form," *AUSS* 15 (1977) 59-64 • Murphy-O'Connor, "Co-Authorship" • Ollrog • V. Perkin, "Some Comments on the Pauline Prescripts," *IBS* 8 (1986) 92-99 • M. Prior, *Paul the Letter Writer and the Second Letter to Timothy* (Sheffield: JSOT, 1989) • Richards • Roller • Schnider and Stenger 3-41 • Schrage, "Ekklesia" • S. K. Stowers, *Letter Writing in Greco-Roman Antiquity* (Philadelphia: Westminster, 1986)

2. A Doxology Celebrating Divine Comfort (1:3-7)

Paul ascribes praise to God for his constant encouragement in the midst of a variety of distressing circumstances which he identifies as "Christ's sufferings." He recognizes that the purpose of his ongoing experience of divine comfort was to equip him to be an agent of God's bountiful comfort and encouragement to those facing any kind of distress. The Corinthians therefore stand to gain from Paul's affliction and subsequent comfort as they themselves patiently face comparable suffering.

3*Blessed be the God and Father of our Lord Jesus Christ, the compassionate Father and the God who always gives comfort.* 4*For he comforts us in all our distress,*

---

40. Cf. Kramer 154, who also observes that a ἡμῶν qualifying κυρίου is omitted "for purely stylistic reasons."

41. Similarly Lieu 167-70, 178.

42. See the comparative chart of "Early Christian Letter Greetings" in Lieu 171.

so that we may be able to comfort those in any kind of distress by means of that same comfort which we ourselves^a receive from God. 5For just as Christ's sufferings overflow into our lives, so also through Christ the comfort we receive is overflowing. 6So whether we are suffering distress, it is to achieve your comfort^b and salvation; or whether we are receiving comfort, it is to achieve your comfort,^c which brings about your patient endurance of the same sufferings that we ourselves endure. 7Our hope for you is firmly established, because we know that just as you share in Christ's sufferings, so too you will share in God's comfort.

TEXTUAL NOTES

a. D* F G lat add καί before αὐτοί, "(we) ourselves *also*," which would serve to emphasize the correspondence between Paul's experience of divine consolation and that of the Corinthians.

b, c. This rendering of v. 6a, which includes the key terms in this textual problem, παρακλήσεως καὶ σωτηρίας . . . παρακλήσεως, reflects the reading of (p⁴⁶) ℵ A C P Ψ 0243 104 436 1739 1877 1881 it^{r1}, z vg^{ww} syr^p cop^{sa, bo} eth Ambrosiaster Ephraem Jerome Antiochus, a reading which is to be preferred (so also UBS¹⁻⁴, NA²⁷), given its difficulties with the awkward repetition of ὑπὲρ τῆς ὑμῶν παρακλήσεως, its wide geographical distribution, and its presence in proto-Alexandrian and Western texts. A scribal error of eye, caused by homoeoteleuton (παρακλήσεως . . . παρακλήσεως), led to the accidental omission of καὶ σωτηρίας . . . παρακλήσεως, as seen in 81 104 630, but the words were subsequently reinserted after ὑπὲρ ὑμῶν in v. 7 with καὶ σωτηρίας placed at the end of the phrase to permit good sense (thus B [33]). The last stage of this process, where καὶ σωτηρίας is found after the first παρακλήσεως as well as after the second, is represented by D (G) (K) 0209 326 1241 1984 2492 2495 *Byz Lect* it^{ar, d, e, f, g} (syr^h) goth Chrysostom Theodoret John-Damascus. See UBS⁴ 610-11 for other variants.

Paul generally follows his epistolary salutations with an expression of thanksgiving for the divine grace evident in the lives of his addressees (e.g., 1 Cor. 1:4-9) and a summary of his prayer requests for them (e.g., Phil. 1:3-11; Col. 1:3-12). In 2 Corinthians, however, he offers praise to God for consoling and comforting himself, while in v. 11 he solicits his converts' prayer for himself.[1] How are we to account for this reversal of his uniform practice? Paul himself supplies the answer in 1:8-11. Relatively recently he had suffered such a crushing θλῖψις in Asia that he had been forced to renounce all hope of survival. Only direct divine intervention, God's παράκλησις ἐν θλίψει, had rescued him from the jaws of a fearful death. Add to this his "daily burden of anxiety about all the congregations" (11:28), his recent restlessness of spirit (2:13) and body (7:5) as he agonized over the "severe letter" and its possible effects at Corinth, and the combination of "conflicts without, anxieties within" (7:5, TCNT) that

---

1. "This introductory blessing [1:3-11] represents . . . a curiously inverted form of the usual Pauline thanksgiving period: The *eucharistō*-clause concludes rather than opens the paragraph, and it has reference to the hoped-for thanksgivings of the addressees rather than the present thanksgiving of Paul himself" (Furnish 116; cf. Schubert 8, 50; Sanders 360-61; Wiles 227-29).

prompted his state of depression in Macedonia (ταπεινούς, 7:6; see notes there), and we can readily appreciate why he speaks of "all my trouble" ([ἐπὶ] πάσῃ τῇ θλίψει ἡμῶν, 1:4). But just as God had graciously intervened on his behalf in Asia, so also in Macedonia: God comforted him in his distress by the safe arrival of Titus with news of the favorable Corinthian reaction to the "severe letter" (7:6-7). Apparently, then, the dramatic and unparalleled nature of Paul's recent experiences prompted an atypical preoccupation with his own circumstances, with his recurring θλῖψις and God's repeated παράκλησις. So it is that this introductory paragraph clearly sounds out the principal theme of chs. 1–7, "comfort in the midst of affliction" (παράκλησις ἐν θλίψει).[2] The παράκλησις ("comfort") root occurs no fewer than ten times in vv. 3-7, the θλῖψις ("trouble," "affliction," "distress") root three times, and the πάθημα ("suffering") root four times.

Throughout this paragraph, when Paul is using the first person of verbs and pronouns he invariably employs the plural.[3] Does this indicate that he is referring to others in addition to himself, or is he referring to himself alone so that the plural is to be explained as epistolary?

Where we find a first person plural pronoun or verb in Paul's letters, the referent or referents may be: (1) a plural subject made clear in the context (e.g., 2 Cor. 1:19), (2) Paul and his addressees (e.g., Rom. 16:1), (3) Paul and his coworkers mentioned in the salutation (e.g., 1 Thess. 1:5), (4) Paul and his fellow apostles (e.g., 1 Cor. 15:11), (5) Paul and his fellow Jews (e.g., Rom. 3:5), (6) Paul himself (e.g., Rom. 3:8), (7) all believers (e.g., 2 Cor. 10:3), or (8) all people, humankind in general (e.g., 1 Cor. 15:32).[4] It seems incontestable that Paul sometimes used the epistolary plural. For instance, in the example cited above (Rom. 3:8, under [6]), ἡμᾶς in the expression καθώς φασίν τινες ἡμᾶς λέγειν certainly refers to Paul alone, for the slander of which he is being accused is specific ("Let us do evil that good may come!") and his letter to the Romans names no coauthors. Or again, that Paul on occasion can oscil-

2. Cf. Murphy-O'Connor, *Paul* 310: "Paul's unusual focus on his own experience prefigures the major theological theme of the letter, namely, that suffering and weakness, not power and eloquence, are the distinctive signs of the true apostle."

3. Pronouns — ἡμῶν (vv. 3, 4, 5, 7), ἡμᾶς (vv. 4 twice, 5), ἡμεῖς (v. 6); verbs — παρακαλούμεθα (vv. 4, 6), θλιβόμεθα (v. 6), πάσχομεν (v. 6), εἰδότες (v. 7).

4. On the issue of the epistolary plural in Paul, the classic study is that of K. Dick, *Der schriftstellerische Plural bei Paulus* (Halle: Niemeyer, 1900). More recent general discussions are found in E. von Dobschütz, "Wir und Ich bei Paulus," *ZST* 10 (1993) 251-77; Prümm 2.1, 31-35; Roller 169-87; E. Stauffer, *TDNT* 2.356-62; Baumert 23-36; Thrall 105-7. For special reference to the Corinthian correspondence, see Murphy-O'Connor, "Co-Authorship" 562-79; "Letter-Writer" 24-31; E. Verhoef, "The Senders of the Letters to the Corinthians and the Use of 'I' and 'We'," in Bieringer (ed.) 417-25; and with reference to 2 Corinthians alone, Carrez, "Le 'Nous'" 474-86; and, more briefly, Sampley 19-20. Also, there are useful discussions scattered throughout Barnett's commentary (see, e.g., 58 and n. 7, 134 n. 4, 140 n. 6, 359 and n. 4, 361). Carrez isolates four uses of "we" in 2 Corinthians, each of which includes Paul: (1) all the members of the Christian community; (2) Paul's collaborators who were not apostles; (3) apostles; and (4) Paul himself (= the epistolary plural) (474-86).

late from singular to plural or from plural to singular, apparently without intending a distinction, seems clear from 2 Cor. 1:13-14; 5:11-12; 7:2-7; 10:1-2; 13:6-10. Of special significance is the close parallelism between 2 Cor. 2:13 and 7:5, passages that describe a restlessness (ἄνεσις) that was exclusively Paul's:

2:13		ἔσχηκα ἄνεσιν τῷ πνεύματί	μου	
7:5	οὐδεμίαν ἔσχηκεν ἄνεσιν ἡ σὰρξ		ἡμῶν	

We conclude that in Paul's letters just as the use of the singular *may* be generic or "historically paradigmatic"[5] (as in Rom. 7:7-25), so the use of the plural *may* be epistolary. Only the context can determine whether or not this is the case in a particular passage.

For several reasons 2 Cor. 1:4-7 appears to afford an instance of the sustained use of the epistolary plural.[6]

1. The immediate historical background to Paul's theological reflections in 1:4-7 is to be found in his recent experiences in Asia (1:8-11)[7] and in Troas and Macedonia (2:12-13; 7:5-6).[8]
2. Paul's description of the encounter with death in Asia (1:8-11) is most naturally read as a transcript of his own personal experience. Is it really conceivable that, whatever the precise nature of this θλῖψις, Paul *and others* simultaneously (a) were "utterly, unbearably crushed" (1:8, RSV), (b) despaired of life (1:8), (c) received a suspended death sentence (1:9), and (d) had their self-reliance shattered (1:9)?
3. In 2:12-13 the singular is used. Describing the same events in Paul's life, 7:5-6 uses the plural, which must therefore refer to Paul alone.

The movement of Paul's thought in 1:4-7 is not immediately obvious. In simplified form, it would seem to run this way:

v. 4   God comforts me when I suffer so that I can comfort others who suffer,

v. 5   (for in fact my experience of God's comfort is as abundant as my experience of Christ's sufferings).

5. E. Stauffer, *TDNT* 2.358.

6. Since in 1:4 Paul enunciates a Christian principle of universal application, derived from his reflection on his own particular experience, we may say that whereas in 1:5-7 he is speaking exclusively of himself, in 1:4 he is speaking primarily of himself. In 1:3 ἡμῶν clearly denotes all believers.

7. The γάρ of 1:8 indicates that 1:8-11 is an instance of παράκλησις ἐν θλίψει, a theme enunciated in 1:4-7.

8. It is the identical description of God as ὁ παρακαλῶν in 1:4 and 7:6 that links 1:4-7 with 7:5-6.

v. 6   So then, my suffering ultimately leads to your comfort as you patiently endure comparable suffering.

v. 7   That is, as you experience suffering, you will also experience God's comfort brought to you by me.

1:3   εὐλογητὸς ὁ θεὸς καὶ πατὴρ τοῦ κυρίου ἡμῶν Ἰησοῦ Χριστοῦ. "Blessed be the God and Father of our Lord Jesus Christ." εὐλογητός is a verbal adjective corresponding to the Hebrew *bārûk,* Aramaic *b^erîk,* "blessed."[9] It introduces what may be called either a "eulogy" or a "doxology." O'Brien speaks of 2 Cor. 1:3-4, Eph. 1:3ff., and 1 Pet. 1:3ff. as "introductory eulogies," distinguishing between "doxologies, in which δόξα or synonyms such as τιμή, κράτος, etc. appear, and eulogies (= *berakoth*) in which εὐλογητός occurs."[10] On the other hand, if we define a doxology as a formal ascription of praise, honor, glory, or blessing to God or Christ, 2 Cor. 1:3 may be included within this category.[11]

NT doxologies are of two types. There is the volitive doxology in which a wish is expressed, with an implied optative (such as εἴη or γένοιτο: "may he be") or imperative (such as ἔστω/ἤτω: "let him be"). Accordingly, most EVV render 1:3 by "Blessed be . . ."[12] or "Praise be to. . . ."[13] Then there is the descriptive doxology in which an affirmation is made, with an indicative form such as ἐστίν ("he is") or a participial form such as ὁ ὤν ("[he] who is") expressed or implied; thus "Blessed is. . . ."[14] Whether εὐλογητὸς ὁ θεός expresses a wish that God be praised or affirms that God is worthy of praise, the very wish or affirmation amounts to praise or thanksgiving. That is, doxology is an indirect expression of gratitude.[15]

It is the addition of the phrase "the Father of our Lord Jesus Christ" which converts the regular synagogue blessing ("Blessed be God") into a dis-

9. On blessing in the OT, see C. W. Mitchell, *The Meaning of BRK: 'To Bless' in the Old Testament* (Atlanta: Scholars, 1987). On blessing in the NT, see H. W. Beyer, *TDNT* 2.754-65; W. Schenk, *Der Segen im Neuen Testament* (Berlin: Evangelische Verlagsanstalt, 1967).

10. O'Brien 236 n. 19; cf. Deichgräber 64-87. Similarly Mullins, "Ascription" 195, 201-3, who isolates three types of "ascription" in the LXX and NT — woes, beatitudes, and eulogies — with the four formal eulogies or "didactic ascriptions" in the NT being Luke 1:68; 2 Cor. 1:3; Eph. 1:3; 1 Pet. 1:3.

11. 2 Cor. 1:3 is classified as a doxology in BDF §128(5).

12. So most EVV.

13. NEB, NIV, REB, Cassirer.

14. Barrett 56; Furnish 108; Young and Ford 262; TCNT.

15. Cf. O'Brien 237-39, who also observes "that although either the εὐχαριστέω- or εὐλογητός- formulas could have been used of thanksgiving or praise to God for blessings *either* to others *or* for oneself, Paul, in the introductions of his letters, uses εὐχαριστέω consistently of *Fürdank* for God's work in the lives of the addressees, and εὐλογητός for blessings in which he himself participated. . . . Apparently for Paul it seemed more fitting to use the term with a Greek background (εὐχαριστέω) when referring to graces, etc., given to others, particularly Gentiles; while the formula with a Jewish background (εὐλογητὸς κτλ.) was more apt when he himself came within the circle of blessing" (239) For a distinctive use of εὐχαριστέω, see 1:11. For a chart that exhibits the syntactical units of the εὐχαριστέω period in Paul's thanksgivings, see Schubert 54-55.

tinctively Christian doxology, for while God is called "the merciful and compassionate Father" in the synagogue liturgy,[16] only in Christianity is he called the Father of an identified Messiah. The single article joining θεός and πατήρ indicates that only one person is being spoken of, not two: The "Father" is indistinguishable from "God."[17] But then the question is: Does the dependent genitive of possession or relationship (τοῦ κυρίου . . . Ἰησοῦ Χριστοῦ) qualify only πατήρ ("Blessed is God, the Father of our Lord Jesus Christ"),[18] or both θεός and πατήρ ("Blessed be the God and Father of our Lord Jesus Christ"[19])? In the former case the implication is that the supreme God of the OT is none other than the Father of the Son whom he sent into the world to achieve redemption (Gal. 4:4-5).[20] In the latter case, the point is that Christ stands in a dual relation to ὁ θεός: God is not only his "Father" but also his "God." With the majority of EVV we prefer this latter view on the ground that θεός and πατήρ, while linked by a single article that equates the two, are separated by καί (here meaning "and"),[21] which suggests a duality of relation.[22] See also the commentary at 11:31 where a comparable statement occurs.

ὁ πατὴρ τῶν οἰκτιρμῶν καὶ θεὸς πάσης παρακλήσεως. "The compassionate Father and the God who always gives comfort." After speaking of ὁ θεὸς καὶ πατήρ, Paul now reverses the order, ὁ πατὴρ . . . καὶ θεός, thus creating chiasmus (ABBA). As before, the single article equates "the Father" and "God." τῶν οἰκτιρμῶν is a qualitative genitive, "characterized by compassion." The plural may be explained as generalizing, as reflecting the Hebrew plural (raḥᵃmîm, "compassion"),[23] or as alluding to concrete instances of mercy (cf. BDF §142) or successive acts of pity. One characteristic of the divine fatherhood is tender mercy, a gracious and gentle compassion toward his children in their creatureliness and sinfulness. "Because of the LORD's great love we are not cut off, for his compassions never come to an end" (Lam. 3:22).

πάσης παρακλήσεως, like οἰκτιρμῶν, is a descriptive or qualitative genitive, "characterized by comfort of every kind."[24] πάσης may have a temporal

16. In the prayer ʾAhabah Rabbah.

17. On this grammatical point, see Harris, Jesus 307-9.

18. Thus Barrett 56; Furnish 108; NAB[1] ("Praised be . . ."); also G. Schrenk, TDNT 5.1008.

19. Thus RV, Moffatt, Goodspeed, RSV, NASB, JB, Barclay, NJB, NAB[2], NRSV; similarly TCNT, Weymouth, NEB, GNB, NIV, REB, Cassirer.

20. "The apostle is . . . stressing the divine glory when he uses θεός and the revelation in Christ when he speaks of the 'Father of the Kurios'" (G. Schrenk, TDNT 5.1008).

21. But BAGD (391d) gives καί an adjunctive sense: "God, who is also the Father." Cf Prümm's rendering, "Praise be to God [who is at the same time (zugleich)] Father of our Lord Jesus Christ" (8).

22. Paul did not write ὁ θεὸς πατὴρ τοῦ κυρίου Ἰησοῦ Χριστοῦ or ὁ θεὸς ὁ (καὶ) πατὴρ τοῦ κυρίου Ἰησοῦ Χριστοῦ.

23. See SB 3.494. In the NT the singular of οἰκτιρμός is found only in Col. 3:12: σπλάγχνα οἰκτιρμοῦ, "heartfelt compassion."

24. A qualitative genitive, sometimes known as a Hebrew or Semitic genitive, is sometimes difficult to distinguish from an objective genitive: a God who is characterized by his giving comfort of every kind is clearly also a God who creates or supplies comfort. Cf. Windisch 38.

connotation, "ever ready to console" (TCNT), "whose consolation never fails us!" (NEB, REB); it may also denote the comprehensiveness of God's compassion, "who gives every possible encouragement" (NJB). In accordance with his limitless compassion (cf. Ps. 145:9; Mic. 7:19), God provides his people with never-failing comfort of every variety (cf. Isa. 40:1; 51:3, 12; 66:13). With regard to his own situation, Paul undoubtedly has in mind his devastating affliction in Asia (1:8-10) and his debilitating depression in Troas and Macedonia (2:12-13; 7:5-6). In each case he was delivered by his all-merciful heavenly Father and experienced the all-embracing comfort of God.

In this introductory doxology, then, the apostle highlights the two aspects of God's character that he had come to value in deeper measure as a result of his personal need and the divine response. To experience God's comfort is to have one's appreciation of God's character enhanced.

1:4 ὁ παρακαλῶν ἡμᾶς ἐπὶ πάσῃ τῇ θλίψει ἡμῶν εἰς τὸ δύνασθαι ἡμᾶς παρακαλεῖν τοὺς ἐν πάσῃ θλίψει. "For he comforts us in[25] all our distress, so that we may be able to comfort those in any kind of distress." παράκλησις is the controlling concept in vv. 3-7, where this word group occurs ten times. In NT usage the term has three basic meanings: encouragement/exhortation, appeal/request, and comfort/consolation.[26] Throughout 2 Corinthians the "comfort" Paul is depicting is a consolatory strengthening[27] in the face of adversity that affords spiritual refreshment. It is much more than verbal solace or an expression of sympathy. While its source is always God, this comfort sometimes is mediated by fellow believers (e.g., 7:6-7, 13). The articular participle ὁ παρακαλῶν, found also at 7:6, is gnomic or timeless, "who always comforts," "whose nature it is to comfort," and has causal overtones, following, as it does, directly on πάσης παρακλήσεως (v. 3). "Blessed be . . . the God of all comfort, for he constantly comforts us." The divine purpose in granting such strengthening aid during suffering is to enable the sufferer to administer comfort to others: εἰς here is telic, "to the end that" (Barrett 56), "so that (we may be able)" (RSV, NRSV), although an ecbatic meaning is certainly possible, "and thus (enables us)" (NAB[1]), "so that (we are able)" (NJB).[28]

---

25. After παρακαλεῖν, the preposition ἐπί may be referential, "with regard to" (BAGD 617c), or temporal, "at the time of" (cf. BAGD 287d, 288a), "in (the midst of)," "during." If we prefer the temporal sense, ἐπί is indistinguishable from ἐν in the phrase ἐν πάσῃ θλίψει.

26. BAGD 618a, b. See also O. Schmitz and G. Stählin, *TDNT* 5.773-99; J. Thomas, *EDNT* 3.23-27; Turner, *Words* 73-78.

27. It is of interest that the English word "comfort" ultimately derives from the late Latin verb *confortare,* "to strengthen greatly," by way of the Old French *conforter,* "to strengthen." But Hofius ("Gott" 217-27) emphasizes the OT background to the terms παράκλησις and παρακαλέω, words that in the LXX denote God's actual intervention to deliver his people from affliction. So, for example, the promise of Isa. 51:12, "I, even I, am the One who comforts (ὁ παρακαλῶν) you," is the divine answer to the human plea for rescue, "Awake, awake! Clothe yourself with strength, O arm of Yahweh!" (Isa. 51:9).

28. Zerwick and Grosvenor regard εἰς τὸ κτλ. . . . as "hovering between final and consec[utive] sense" (534); cf. BDF §402 (2); A. Oepke, *TDNT* 2.430.

A careful distinction should be drawn between the articular expression ἐπὶ πάσῃ τῇ θλίψει ἡμῶν and the anarthrous phrase ἐν πάσῃ θλίψει. Paul's experience of God's support in the midst of *all* the tribulation[29] he *actually encountered* (articular πᾶς) enabled him to become a channel for God's support to those who found themselves in *any type of* distress (anarthrous πᾶς).[30] The apostle regarded his suffering and the experience of divine comfort it prompted not merely as beneficial in his own spiritual life, driving him to trust solely in God (1:19; cf. 12:7), but also as directly benefiting the fellow believers he ministered to: "God, who is always ready to comfort [v. 3b], comforts us . . . so that we can comfort." εἰς τὸ δύνασθαι ἡμᾶς παρακαλεῖν does not imply that Paul himself was the source of comfort. Rather, the spiritual principle he is enunciating is that Christians' experience of God's help, consolation, and encouragement in the midst of all life's afflictions constantly qualifies and empowers them to communicate the divine "comfort" to others who face troubles of any variety.[31]

It is God, not the apostle, from whom all help and succor comes. With regard to the spiritual commodity of παράκλησις, Paul was simply the "middle man" between producer and consumers. This notion of Paul's mediation becomes explicit in the next phrase.

διὰ τῆς παρακλήσεως ἧς[32] παρακαλούμεθα αὐτοὶ ὑπὸ τοῦ θεοῦ. "By means of that same comfort which we ourselves receive from God." As God's agent, Paul applied to his converts' needs precisely the same remedy as God was in the habit of applying to him, namely the encouragement, consolation, and strengthening that are denoted by παράκλησις. Although διά here could denote the ground or basis for Paul's παρακαλεῖν ("because of," NJB),[33] it more probably bears an instrumental sense, "through" (RV), "with" (TCNT, NIV), "by using."[34] Present tense παρακαλούμεθα highlights the constancy and even

29. In nonbiblical Greek θλῖψις refers literally to "pressure" or "crushing" or metaphorically to "oppression," the cognate verb θλίβω meaning "exert pressure, compress." In the NT θλῖψις refers to adverse outward circumstances, "tribulation, trial, hardship, trouble" or the resulting inward state of mind, "distress, anxiety." See further H. Schlier, *TDNT* 3.139-48; J.Kremer, *EDNT* 2.151-53 and literature cited there.

30. See the discussion of this grammatical issue in BDF §275(3); Robertson 772; Turner 200; Zerwick §188; B. Reicke, *TDNT* 5.887-89.

31. Bultmann observes that the two present tenses ὁ παρακαλῶν and παρακαλούμεθα in v. 4 indicate that Paul converts his actual experience into a principle (23 n. 3). Yet in the form in which Paul states the principle, it is distinctively Christian, so that Windisch's two parallels (Epictetus, *Dissertationes* 3.23.8 and Seneca, *Ad Polybium de Consolatione* 15.5) illustrate merely the general principle that "only he can render help to someone else in his distress who himself has experienced a similar affliction" (39).

32. This is an instance of the attraction of the relative pronoun from the dative of means (ᾗ) that might otherwise have been expected into the case of its antecedent (παρακλήσεως, genitive). See BDF §294(2). Such attraction from dative to genitive is not as common as from accusative to a preceding genitive (as in 1:6; 10:8, 13) or dative. Cf. BAGD 584a.

33. For such a sense of διά with the genitive, see BAGD 180d-181a.

34. Note Plummer's paraphrase (6), "by using the same way of comforting that God uses with us."

the predictability of God's comfort: παράκλησις follows θλῖψις as surely as day follows night; *ubi θλῖψις, ibi παράκλησις.* This theme of παράκλησις ἐν θλίψει is never far from Paul's thought in chs. 1–7. Alongside these emphases on the constant availability of God's comfort and Paul's role as mediator is a stress on God as the source of comfort (cf. 1:3): ὑπὸ τοῦ θεοῦ is emphatic by position, "by none other than God himself."[35]

1:5 ὅτι καθὼς περισσεύει τὰ παθήματα τοῦ Χριστοῦ εἰς ἡμᾶς οὕτως διὰ τοῦ Χριστοῦ περισσεύει καὶ ἡ παράκλησις ἡμῶν. "For just as Christ's sufferings overflow into our lives, so also through Christ the comfort we receive is overflowing." Given the presence of correlatives καθὼς . . . οὕτως (. . . καί) it is not surprising that there are two cases of parallelism in this verse, περισσεύει τὰ παθήματα . . . περισσεύει . . . ἡ παράκλησις and εἰς ἡμᾶς . . . ἡμῶν.[36] We might have expected Paul, with his love of precise parallelism, to write καθὼς περισσεύει τὰ παθήματα τοῦ Χριστοῦ, οὕτως καὶ περισσεύει ἡ παράκλησις *τοῦ Χριστοῦ εἰς ἡμᾶς.* However, it was God the Father, not Christ, who was the source of comfort (see v. 3), and Paul proceeds to show in v. 6 that the comfort he experienced (ἡμῶν, "we have/receive," v. 5) overflowed into the *Corinthians'* lives, not merely his own.[37]

This verse specifies the reason (ὅτι) that suffering or the experience of trouble equipped Paul (δύνασθαι) to mediate God's comfort. Whenever Christ's sufferings were multiplied in Paul's life, God's comfort was correspondingly multiplied through the ministry of Christ.[38] Paul discerned a divinely ordered correspondence (καθὼς . . . οὕτως . . . καί, "just as . . . to precisely the same extent")[39] between the intensity of his suffering and the adequacy of God's comfort. It was precisely because the divine comfort always matched his apostolic suffering (v. 5) that Paul was enabled to mediate that comfort to others (v. 4). If v. 4 enunciates a universal Christian principle that is applicable to Paul as to all believers, v. 5 grounds that principle in specific Pauline experience as a prelude to v. 6 with its unambiguous distinction between Corinthian and Pauline experience.

But to what does τὰ παθήματα τοῦ Χριστοῦ refer?[40] Certainly not the

---

35. Although ὁ θεός is the subject of the Greek sentence that includes vv. 3 and 4, Paul writes ὑπὸ τοῦ θεοῦ, not ὑπ᾽ αὐτοῦ.

36. Chiasmus may be discerned in the sequence περισσεύει . . . τοῦ Χριστοῦ . . . τοῦ Χριστοῦ περισσεύει.

37. Barrett renders v. 5b by "our comforting also overflows *to you*" (italics mine).

38. Given the prominent position of διὰ τοῦ Χριστοῦ in v. 5b, it should perhaps be construed with both παράκλησις and περισσεύει. God's comfort to Paul was mediated through Christ and its overflow into the lives of others was also accomplished by Christ. That is, Christ was the channel for both the comforting and the overflowing.

39. These correlatives here express correspondence ("Y corresponds to X") rather than a mere comparison ("Y is like X").

40. See the discussions of this matter in Bultmann 23-24; Güttgemanns 323-28; Rissi 54-56; Tannehill 91-93; B. M. Ahern, " 'The Fellowship of His Sufferings' (Phil 3,10) — A Study of St. Paul's Doctrine on Christian Suffering," *CBQ* 22 (1960) 1-32; C. M. Proudfoot, "Imitation or Realistic Participation? A Study of Paul's Concept of 'Suffering with Christ'," *Int* 17 (1963) 140-60; W. Michaelis, *TDNT* 5.931-32; and especially the review in Thrall 107-10.

atoning sacrifice of Christ, which Paul regarded as a completed event (Rom. 5:8-10) that need not and could not be repeated: "the death that he died was a death in relation to sin, once and for all" (Rom. 6:10). The genitive τοῦ Χριστοῦ need not be possessive, "the sufferings personally experienced by Christ,"[41] nor need this articular expression be titular, "the afflictions (or "woes") of the Messiah." Rather, the reference is to the person of Christ conceived of as the head and epitome of the messianic community, and the genitive is relational, "the sufferings associated with Christ," or possibly subjective (as Rissi 55-56), "the sufferings imposed (on his followers) by Christ" (cf. Acts 9:15-16). The main support for such a view comes from the close parallel in Col. 1:24, where Paul affirms that in his own person he is filling up what is still lacking (ἀνταναπληρῶ τὰ ὑστερήματα) with regard to "the afflictions of Christ" (αἱ θλίψεις τοῦ Χριστοῦ). In both verses ὁ Χριστός seems to bear a corporate as well as a personal sense: Christ, the suffering Son of Man, wholly identifies himself with the messianic community of the last days (cf. Acts 9:4-5, 16), to whom God has apportioned a quota of sufferings (cf. Acts 14:22). Consequently any suffering endured by the followers of Christ for the sake of Christ (cf. 4:11) (that is, suffering experienced while engaged in his service and for the benefit of his church) constituted a part of "Christ's sufferings" (cf. Rom. 8:17). For Paul, "the sufferings of Christ" perhaps differed from human suffering in general, not by their nature but by the person of the sufferer and the purpose of the suffering: τὰ παθήματα τοῦ Χριστοῦ befell the person "in Christ" (5:17; 12:2) who was living "for Christ" (cf. 5:15).[42] So then, Paul could simultaneously declare that he himself shared abundantly in Christ's sufferings (v. 5) *and* that the Corinthians also were participants in that suffering (v. 7).

These sufferings "in" and "for" Christ apparently included both physical afflictions and psychological or spiritual suffering. An obvious example of Paul's physical suffering would be his stoning at Lystra (Acts 14:19; cf. Gal. 6:17), which arose from Jewish agitation, while the daily pressure of his anxious concern for all the churches (2 Cor. 11:28) illustrates his spiritual suffering for Christ's sake. That some of his experiences involved both external and internal affliction is clear from his ordeal in Macedonia (ἐν παντὶ θλιβόμενοι), which caused both ἄνεσις of σάρξ and inward φόβοι (7:5). In addition, the case of Epaphroditus suggests that Paul may have included illness that was a direct consequence of engaging in the work of Christ within "the sufferings of Christ."[43] Paul describes this illness (ἠσθένησεν, Phil. 2:26-27) of Epaphro-

---

41. Proudfoot regards τὰ παθήματα τοῦ Χριστοῦ as Christians' actual sharing in the historical sufferings of Jesus, for by baptism and through the Spirit believers entered into a "realistic" spiritual bond with the risen Christ and with one another in the body of Christ (144-47, 160).

42. Similarly Zerwick §38.

43. *Pace* Davids, who, in an excursus on "Suffering in 1 Peter and the New Testament" in his commentary on 1 Peter (30-44), argues that "in the NT suffering is persecution and does not appear to include illness" (40).

ditus that "very nearly proved fatal" (Phil. 2:27, TCNT) as a brush with death that resulted from his devotion to Christ's work (διὰ τὸ ἔργον Χριστοῦ, Phil. 2:30) in helping to meet Paul's needs as an envoy of the Philippian church (Phil. 2:25, 30). But with this said, one must allow that afflictions, whether physical or spiritual, that arise as a result of bearing Christ's name (cf. 1 Pet. 4:12-14) or testifying to the gospel are the principal referent in τὰ παθήματα τοῦ Χριστοῦ.

1:6 At this point, for the first time in this paragraph, the distinction between Paul's experience and that of the Corinthians becomes explicit. If the four gnomic presents of 1:4[44] point to universal Christian experience with particular relevance to Paul himself, in 1:5 the spotlight falls on the apostle alone, for he implies that the comfort he receives from God overflows into the lives of the Corinthians. He suffers, they benefit (cf. 4:12).

εἴτε δὲ θλιβόμεθα, ὑπὲρ τῆς ὑμῶν παρακλήσεως καὶ σωτηρίας· εἴτε παρακαλούμεθα, ὑπὲρ τῆς ὑμῶν παρακλήσεως. "So whether we are suffering distress, it is to achieve your comfort and salvation; or whether we are receiving comfort, it is to achieve your comfort." δέ draws an inference ("so then") from v. 5: "whether it is a case of our παθήματα or our παράκλησις, you Corinthians stand to gain." The combination εἴτε . . . εἴτε does not introduce mutually exclusive alternatives but rather successive experiences, θλιβόμεθα corresponding to τὰ παθήματα . . . εἰς ἡμᾶς, and παρακαλούμεθα corresponding to ἡ παράκλησις ἡμῶν. ὑπέρ denotes a purpose to be achieved or an advantage to be gained.[45] The Corinthians are the beneficiaries, the repeated and emphatic ὑμῶν being an objective genitive.[46] The two presents, θλιβόμεθα and παρακαλούμεθα, describe repeated experiences that establish gnomic truths. Each may be classified as a "theological passive," with God as the implied agent, but in the former case the agency was indirect[47] whereas in the latter case it was direct. Standing under a single preposition and article (ὑπὲρ τῆς), σωτηρίας further defines the nature of the παράκλησις. The comfort that the Corinthians would enjoy as a consequence of Paul's experience of affliction and comfort would be general spiritual well-being, "spiritual safety, health, and joy in your renewed experience of God's grace" (H. C. G. Moule 3).

There are four distinct stages in the progression of Paul's thought in vv. 4-6:

1. Paul's θλίψεις (vv. 4, 6) or παθήματα (vv. 5, 6),
2. God's παράκλησις (vv. 3-6) given to Paul through Christ (v. 5),
3. the Corinthians' θλίψεις (v. 4) or παθήματα (v. 6), and

44. ὁ παρακαλῶν . . . τὸ δύνασθαι . . . παρακαλεῖν . . . παρακαλούμεθα.
45. Cf. BDF §231(2); Robertson 632 ("with a view to"; also Moule 65).
46. BDF §284(2); Robertson 685. In Paul ὑμῶν is emphatic in the attributive position.
47. That Paul could discern divine providence operating even through suffering created by others is illustrated by his depiction of his σκόλοψ τῇ σαρκί not only as ἄγγελος Σατανᾶ but also as given by God (ἐδόθη μοι, 12:7).

4. God's παράκλησις (vv. 4, 6 twice) given to the Corinthians through Paul (v. 6).

In the first part of v. 6, εἴτε . . . σωτηρίας moves from 1. to 4., with 2. and 3. assumed. On the other hand, εἴτε . . . παρακλήσεως moves from 2. to 4., with 1. and 3. assumed.

(ὑπὲρ τῆς ὑμῶν παρακλήσεως) τῆς ἐνεργουμένης ἐν ὑπομονῇ τῶν αὐτῶν παθημάτων ὧν[48] καὶ ἡμεῖς πάσχομεν. "(It is to achieve your comfort) which brings about your patient endurance of the same sufferings that we ourselves endure." As an intransitive verb ἐνεργέω means "be effective," "exert (one's) force." The articular participle τῆς ἐνεργουμένης is equivalent to a relative clause (ἣ ἐνεργεῖται). If this participle is construed as a passive,[49] the sense will be "which is produced" or "which is made effective," with one element ("within you") and perhaps a second ("by God") implied. A full rendering would then be "which God produces within you."[50] With this passive sense of the participle, ἐν ὑπομονῇ could be instrumental ("[a comfort] produced within you by your patient fortitude," Montgomery; similarly Weymouth), where ὑπομονή is the cause and παράκλησις the effect,[51] or temporal ("[encouragement] which [God] produces as you remain steadfast").[52] Alternatively, if ἐνεργουμένης is middle, Paul's meaning will be "which becomes effective" or "which energizes (you)." Then the phrase ἐν ὑπομονῇ may be either local in import ("[your comforting], which takes effect in your endurance")[53] or temporal ("[your comfort], which is effective as it nerves you to endure," Moffatt), where παράκλησις is the cause and ὑπομονή is the effect. τῶν αὐτῶν παθημάτων (objective genitive) refers to the Corinthians' sufferings that were the same (τῶν αὐτῶν) as Paul's because they too formed part of "the sufferings of Christ" (v. 5), sufferings endured in union with Christ and for the sake of Christ, not because they were identical with Paul's afflictions in nature;[54] they were generically, not actually, "the same." For example, it is clear from 1:8 that it was Paul, not the Corinthians, who experienced a θλῖψις in Asia. Moreover, 1:4 has al-

48. This is a further example (see 1:4 and note) of the attraction of the relative (here ἅ) into the case of its antecedent.

49. For a defense of this passive meaning of ἐνεργεῖσθαι here, see Clark's article, "The Meaning of ἐνεργέω and καταργέω in the New Testament," *JBL* 54 (1935) 93-101.

50. Construing the articular participle as causal, Plummer paraphrases thus: "for God makes it effective to you" (6).

51. Cassirer represents a variation of this: "(that comfort) which is brought to fruition by your patient endurance."

52. Martin 6; similarly Goodspeed.

53. Barrett 57; similarly BAGD 265b, c; NASB. This notion of "takes effect in (producing)" prompts the rendering, "encouragement that produces endurance" (Young and Ford 262; similarly NIV and the rendering proposed in the text).

54. Cf. W. Michaelis, *TDNT* 5.931. Thrall suggests (113) that the Corinthians may have been experiencing a form of Jewish opposition less intense than the hostility Paul himself had encountered in Corinth (Acts 18:5-17).

ready distinguished different varieties of θλίψεις by the carefully worded phrases ἐπὶ πάσῃ τῇ θλίψει . . . ἐν πάσῃ θλίψει (see above). The three present tenses in v. 6 (θλιβόμεθα . . . παρακαλούμεθα . . . πάσχομεν) may be durative in a sense, describing continuous suffering and comfort, or iterative, denoting intermittent experiences of suffering and comfort.

The overall sense of v. 6 may be expressed thus: Paul's suffering of affliction and endurance of trial ultimately benefited the Corinthians in that he was thereby equipped to administer divine encouragement to them when they were afflicted and to ensure their preservation and spiritual well-being when they underwent trial (cf. Eph. 3:13; 2 Tim. 2:10). The apostle then makes explicit what he has assumed (in v. 6a) in arguing from *his* experience of suffering to *their* experience of comfort and deliverance, that is, his own receipt of divine comfort in the midst of affliction ("if we are comforted"). Whether he suffered affliction or received comfort, the advantage remained the same for the Corinthians (cf. 4:8-12, 15). They too would know an inner revitalization, an infusion of divine strength that would enable them to endure patiently the same type of trial that confronted Paul (cf. 1 Pet. 5:9).

1:7 καὶ ἡ ἐλπὶς ἡμῶν βεβαία ὑπὲρ ὑμῶν. "Our hope for you is firmly established." The content of the hope that Paul cherished with regard to (ὑπέρ)[55] the Corinthians is not defined by the following εἰδότες, which is causal in meaning ("because we know"), but must be determined by the context.[56] His confident expectation was that in the midst of their various ongoing παθήματα, the Corinthians would show patient fortitude (ὑπομονή, 1:6; cf. 1 Thess. 1:3) and be preserved spiritually intact (σωτηρία, 1:6), and that he would be proud of them on the day of the Lord Jesus (1:14; cf. 1 Thess. 2:19) as he presented them before God "mature in Christ" (Col. 1:28). The apostle describes this hope of his as "unwavering" or "well founded" (βεβαία).

εἰδότες ὅτι ὡς κοινωνοί[57] ἐστε τῶν παθημάτων, οὕτως καὶ τῆς παρακλήσεως. "Because we know that just as you share in Christ's sufferings, so too you will share[58] in God's comfort." WH 1.403 places a comma after πάσχομεν at the end of 1:6 and a period after ὑμῶν, with εἰδότες beginning a new sentence. This alternative punctuation has the advantage of relieving the grammatical tension of the genitive ἡμῶν and the nominative εἰδότες referring to the same person(s), but since an imperatival participle ("know that . . .") or a participle functioning as a finite verb ("you/we know") is not common in Paul, it

---

55. Not infrequently in Hellenistic Greek, as in the LXX under the influence of the Hebrew preposition 'al (BDB 754), ὑπέρ means "concerning" or "with reference to," sharing common territory with περί. See BAGD 839b; H. Riesenfeld, *TDNT* 8.514 and n. 37.

56. When Paul explicitly defines the nature of his ἐλπίς, he regularly uses an objective genitive (Gal. 5:5; Col. 1:27; 1 Thess. 5:8; Tit. 1:2; 3:7) or occasionally a ὅτι clause (Phil. 1:20) or the accusative and infinitive construction (2 Cor. 10:15).

57. On the term κοινωνός, see Seesemann 3-23.

58. Whether κοινωνοί ἐστε ("you share") or κοινωνοὶ ἔσεσθε ("you will share," "you will be partners") be supplied with οὕτως καί, the sense is gnomic.

seems preferable to regard εἰδότες as a *constructio ad sensum* ("construction according to the sense") and as specifying the reason for the "firmly grounded" character (βεβαία) of Paul's ἐλπίς.[59] ὡς is correlative with οὕτως καί, "just as . . . so too," "just as surely as . . . just so surely" (Goodspeed). The articles in the expressions τῶν παθημάτων and τῆς παρακλήσεως may be generic ("sufferings," "comfort"), but are probably anaphoric ("these sufferings," "this comfort"). When we ask to what "these" and "this" refer, the answer usually given is *Paul's* sufferings and comfort.[60] That is, Paul is affirming that a Corinthian partnership in his sufferings guarantees partnership in the comfort he enjoys; if they suffer as he does, they will also receive comfort just as he does. But the preceding expressions τὰ παθήματα τοῦ Χριστοῦ (1:5) and παρακαλούμεθα αὐτοὶ ὑπὸ τοῦ θεοῦ (1:4) make it more likely that Paul is alluding to *Christ's* sufferings and *God's* comfort.[61] On this view, in 1:7 Paul is declaring that given his settled conviction (εἰδότες) that sharing in Christ's sufferings involved participation in God's comfort in the midst of that suffering, his hope that the Corinthians would be triumphant in their time of trial was securely grounded. But 1:6 shows that it was not simply a matter of Corinthian suffering followed automatically and directly by divine comfort, but rather of Paul's mediating God's comfort to the Corinthians in their suffering.[62]

Bibliography

Bjerkelund 141-55 • Deichgräber 64-87 • Hainz, *Koinonia* 99-102 • Hofius, "Gott" • F. W. Hughes • Kleinknecht • C. W. Mitchell, *The Meaning of BRK "To Bless" in the Old Testament* (Atlanta: Scholars, 1987) • O'Brien 233-58 • O'Brien, "Structure" 50-56 • O'Brien, "Gospel" • Rissi 53-56 • J. M. Robinson • Sanders • Schnider and Stenger 42-49 • Schubert 46-50 • D. M. Stanley, *Boasting* 93-96 • Tannehill 90-98 • Warfield • C. Westermann, *Blessing in the Bible and the Life of the Church* (Philadelphia: Fortress, 1978) • J. L. White • Wiles 226-29, 271-76

3. Deliverance from Affliction (1:8-11)

As a primary illustration of his theme ("comfort in affliction") Paul now informs the Corinthians of the dire nature of his recent brush with death in the province of Asia, an experience so devastating that only through God's direct intervention was his life spared. The outcome was the surrender of his self-dependence and the realization that further encounters with death awaited him.

---

59. Thus most commentators and EVV.

60. Thus "our . . . our" (TCNT, RSV, JB, NIV, NRSV) or "my . . . my" (Goodspeed, Williams).

61. NEB approximates to this sense: "if you have part in the suffering, you have part also in the divine consolation."

62. Cf. Hainz, *Koinonia* 99-102; Prümm 1.17-18.

But if the Corinthians were faithful in their intercession for him, he would continue to enjoy deliverance from death's clutches.

Many of the issues that arise from this passage are dealt with in an excursus below: "Paul's Affliction in Asia (2 Cor. 1:8-11): The Personal Background to 2 Corinthians." These issues include:

when the θλῖψις occurred (A.2. in the excursus),
evidence that Paul regarded this experience as unique (A.4.),
proposed identifications of the θλῖψις (B.),
evidence that the θλῖψις was a severe recurrent illness (B.5.),
Paul's circumstances when the θλῖψις occurred (C.), and
the influence of the θλῖψις on Paul's life and thought (D.).

8Now about[a] the affliction that overtook[b] us in Asia, we do not want[c] you to be unaware, brothers and sisters, that we were excessively weighed down, beyond our strength, so that we despaired even of survival. 9Indeed, we ourselves feel we received within our own selves a verdict of death. This was intended to make us rely no longer on ourselves but on the God who raises[d] the dead. 10He rescued us from such gigantic encounters with death,[e] and he will deliver[f] us — at least we have set our hope on him that[g] he will continue to deliver us 11provided you, for your part, join in helping us by your prayer for us, so that many people[h] may give God thanks regarding us[i] for his gracious favor granted us through the prayers of many.

TEXTUAL NOTES

a. Elsewhere in Paul the standard formula οὐ θέλω/θέλομεν ὑμᾶς ἀγνοεῖν is followed by περί (1 Cor. 12:1; 1 Thess. 4:13) (as well as by ὅτι or the accusative). Accordingly, ὑπέρ, read by proto-Alexandrian (p⁴⁶ᵛⁱᵈ B) and other witnesses (Ψ 0121 0243 1739 1881 𝔐), is to be preferred over περί (ℵ A C D F G P 0209 33 81 104 365 1175 1505 pc) as the more difficult reading. On this disclosure formula, see Mullins, "Disclosure" 44-50.

b. The simple τῆς γενομένης is read by almost all the earliest Greek mss., including ℵ* A B C D*, but ἡμῖν is added after γενομένης by ℵ² D¹ 0209 𝔐 syr cop. This latter reading accords with the sense ("that happened to us") but is clearly secondary (cf. 1 Pet. 4:12), having relatively weak external attestation and being redundant after the preceding ἡμῶν.

c. The singular θέλω, read by K pc bo (perhaps under the influence of Rom. 1:13; 11:25; 1 Cor. 10:1; 12:1), removes the ambiguity of θέλομεν, which could refer to Paul and others or, as an epistolary plural, to Paul alone. See the note on 1:8 and the introduction to 1:3-7.

d. The vast majority of witnesses read τῷ ἐγείροντι, a "timeless present participle expressing a permanent attribute" (Plummer 18), but p⁴⁶, the later Alexandrian MSS 326 1881, along with 365 614 1881 pc vgᵐˢ boᵐˢ, have τῷ ἐγείραντι, which could be a gnomic aorist ("who raises") but probably is preterit ("who raised"), referring either to the resurrection of Christ (with τοὺς νεκρούς as a generalizing plural) or to the deliverance of Paul from virtual death.

e. This reflects the plurals τηλικούτων θανάτων read by p⁴⁶ 81 630 1739 *pc* it^(a, e) syr^(p, h) goth Origen^(gr, lat) Ambrosiaster Ephraem Jerome Theodoret. This reading is defended by Zuntz as being consonant with "genuine Pauline diction" (cf. 6:4-5, 9; 11:23) and because "the singular [τηλικούτου θανάτου] clearly arose from the pedantic idea that no one could risk more than one death" (104; cf. 77, 197 n. 1; so also Kümmel 197; UBS^(1, 2), with a "D" rating; A. Wikgren [in Metzger 506], who notes "it is the harder reading, that of the oldest Greek witnesses and of most Old Latin manuscripts"). However, a majority of the UBS³ ^(and 4) committees preferred (with a "D" [= high doubt] rating in UBS³ and a "B" [= almost certain] rating in UBS⁴!) the singular reading because of the strength of the external evidence (א A B C D^(gr) G^(gr) K P Ψ 33 614 1739* *Byz Lect* cop^(sa, bo) arm Clement *al*) and because the plural could have arisen from a scribal desire to elevate the intensity of an account in which Paul himself mentions more than one deliverance (ἐρρύσατο . . . καὶ ῥύσεται). If we prefer the plural, the reference will be to gigantic encounters with death rather than merely exposure to the danger or risk of death (as in 1 Cor. 15:31), "such terrible dangers of death" (GNB), although Turner suggests that θάνατοι in 1:10; 11:23 "may imply ways of dying, i.e. *deadly perils*" (28; cf. minuscule 629, τηλικούτου κινδύνου, and many witnesses of the Old Latin tradition, *tantis periculis*).

f. Reading καὶ ῥύσεται (p⁴⁶ B C P 0209^(vid) 33 81 365 1175 *pc* it^g vg^(st) cop arm Euthalius John-Damascus). To some scribe(s) these words appeared redundant because the same verbal form ῥύσεται follows six words later; accordingly they are omitted in A D* Ψ it^(ar, d, e) syr^p eth^(pp) Chrysostom Pelagius. Other witnesses read the present tense καὶ ῥύεται (D^c F G^(gr) K 0121 0243 104 326 614 1739 1881 𝔐 syr^h *al*), a patently secondary reading (*pace* Allo 13) in that it removes the apparently tautologous καὶ ῥύσεται and creates a past-present-future pattern (ἐρρύσατο . . . καὶ ῥύεται . . . καὶ ἔτι ῥύσεται).

g. ὅτι καὶ ἔτι, read by א A C D^c K P Ψ 33 81 326 𝔐 it^(dem, f, x, z) vg cop^(sa, bo), should be preferred as the most difficult reading (as in UBS^(3, 4), with ὅτι bracketed). Some scribes omitted ὅτι to produce καὶ ἔτι (p⁴⁶ B D^(gr*) 0121 0243 1739 1881 *pc*) (see Zuntz 196 and n. 4 and UBS^(1, 2)), others omitted ἔτι to produce καὶ ὅτι (F G it^g and some Fathers) or ὅτι καί (D^b 104 it^(ar, d, e) syr^h), and yet others omitted καί or καὶ ἔτι. In 1:9 Zuntz reads ὃς ἐκ τηλικούτων θανάτων ἐρρύσατο ἡμᾶς. εἰς ὃν ἠλπίκαμεν. καὶ ἔτι ῥύσεται κτλ. (197 n. 1).

h. Reading ἐκ πολλῶν προσώπων with the great majority of witnesses. However, p⁴⁶ F G Ψ 0121 0243 6 1739 1881 *pc* it^(a, b) read ἐν πολλῷ προσώπῳ, which, construed as a generic singular, would mean "among (= by) many people." Héring is inclined to prefer the reading ἐν προσώπῳ πολλῶν (365 1175 *pc* it^r Ambrosiaster), "in the presence of many people": "we must assume that the many people present, not all of whom could make verbal contribution to this volume of prayer, must have united themselves inwardly to the prayers and given them, so to speak, more resonance" (7, but see his n. 27).

i. Both ἡμῶν and ὑμῶν are supported by witnesses in the Alexandrian, Western, and Byzantine textual families, but ὑμῶν probably arose to avoid the seemingly repetitive εἰς ἡμᾶς . . . ὑπὲρ ἡμῶν or as a result of an itacistic error in copying. As in 1:8; 8:23; 12:8 (and elsewhere) ὑπέρ here probably means "regarding, concerning."

1:8 Οὐ γὰρ θέλομεν ὑμᾶς ἀγνοεῖν, ἀδελφοί, ὑπὲρ τῆς θλίψεως ἡμῶν τῆς γενομένης ἐν τῇ Ἀσίᾳ ὅτι. . . . "Now¹ about the affliction that overtook us in

---

1. For γάρ as a conjunction marking a transition, see BAGD 152c. Cf. Cassirer, "Now"; Martin 12, "then."

Asia, we do not want you to be unaware, brothers and sisters, that. . . ." In the Pauline corpus, ἀγνοεῖν is sometimes used absolutely,[2] sometimes it is followed by the accusative[3] or by ὅτι[4] and twice by περί,[5] but it is never elsewhere qualified by ὑπέρ. In addition, there is no instance where ἀγνοεῖν is modified by two qualifiers such as ὑπέρ and ὅτι. These considerations suggest that the ὑπέρ clause ("about," "concerning")[6] modifies the whole sentence and that only the ὅτι clause defines the content of ἀγνοεῖν (see the suggested translation).[7] As he makes his warmhearted appeal to the Corinthians' sympathetic understanding (ἀδελφοί),[8] Paul desires that they should become aware of the devastating character of his experience in Asia; the absence of detail concerning its precise nature (merely ἡ θλῖψις ἡμῶν) and its exact location (merely ἐν τῇ Ἀσίᾳ) suggest that the Corinthians lacked information about the severity of the particular incident or sequence of events although they had knowledge of its occurrence. The apostle now focuses on the inward aspects of the event that demonstrate its dramatic nature and effect.[9]

2. 1 Cor. 14:28; 2 Cor. 6:9; Gal. 1:22; 1 Tim. 1:13.

3. Rom. 10:3; 11:25; 2 Cor. 2:11.

4. Rom. 1:13; 2:4; 6:3; 7:1; 1 Cor. 10:1.

5. 1 Cor. 12:1; 1 Thess. 4:13.

6. ὑπέρ has this meaning also in 1:7; 5:12; 7:4, 14; 8:23-24; 9:3; 12:5 (twice), 8; and probably 1:11.

7. Cf. Weymouth: "For as for our troubles which came upon us in the province in Asia, we would have you know, brethren, that we were exceedingly weighed down."

8. Plummer makes the interesting observation that whereas the phrase θέλω ὑμᾶς εἰδέναι (1 Cor. 11:3; Col. 2:1) is not followed by ἀδελφοί, the formula οὐ θέλω/θέλομεν ὑμᾶς ἀγνοεῖν (1 Cor. 10:1; 12:1; Rom. 1:13; 11:25; 1 Thess. 4:13) always has this tender address. Whereas ἀδελφοί ("brothers and sisters," NRSV, NIV [1995]) is often used as a term of address in 1 Corinthians (20 times), this use is comparatively rare in 2 Corinthians (only at 1:8; 8:1; 13:11). As Barnett comments (83 n. 9), in keeping with the strained relationship between Paul and the Corinthians, the emphasis in 2 Corinthians is rather on Paul's paternal and authoritative role (see 6:13; 10:8; 11:2; 12:14; 13:10).

9. Cf. Schlatter 466, and Welborn ("Emotions" 41) who observes that "the extraordinary power of this brief narrative is a result of the combination of extreme reticence in the description of the external data of the experience with intimate disclosure of the subjective, emotional state that it produced." Focusing on a neglected aspect in the rhetorical analysis of Paul's letters, Welborn ("Emotions" 31-60) analyzes the appeals to certain emotions found in the portions of 2 Corinthians that exhibit the style of the "conciliatory" type of letter, viz. 1:1–2:13 and 7:5-16 (in isolating these sections on this basis Welborn follows Windisch 8). Those emotions are pity (ἔλεος), anger (ὀργή), and zeal (ζῆλος), πάθη that the ancient rhetorical theorists thought could be appropriately appealed to in "conciliatory" speech or writing. Welborn argues that Paul not only seeks to arouse these emotions in the Corinthians but also endeavors to transform these feelings into Christ-like passions — "pity into hope (1.3-11, esp. 1.7, 10), anger into love (2.5-11, esp. 2.8, 10), and zeal into confidence (7.5-16, esp. 7.13-16" (59). With respect to 1:8-11, Welborn believes (41-43) that the aspects of this "lament" that are designed to evoke pity include Paul's portrayal of his affliction as an experience of death (cf. Aristotle, *Rhetorica* 2.8.9, 16), the disclosure formula in 1:8a which depicts the incident as recent (cf. Aristotle, *Rhetica* 2.8.14), the use of the term ἀδελφοί (cf. Aristotle, *Rhetica* 2.18.3), his silence about what actually happened (cf. Demetrius, *De Elocutione* 44, 103, 253, 264), and the focus on the psychological effect of the experience (cf. Aristotle, *Rhetica* 2.8.14-16) and his

ἐν τῇ Ἀσίᾳ, like εἰς τὴν Ἀσίαν (Acts 19:22), in all probability refers to some part of the province of Asia other than Ephesus;[10] otherwise ἐν Ἐφέσῳ (cf. 1 Cor. 15:32; 16:8) would doubtless have been used, all the more so since Paul was now writing from Macedonia, not Ephesus.[11] In the excursus below it is proposed that the θλῖψις was an unnerving drastic illness that struck Paul while he was at Troas (cf. 2:12-13).[12]

ὅτι καθ' ὑπερβολὴν ὑπὲρ δύναμιν ἐβαρήθημεν, ὥστε ἐξαπορηθῆναι ἡμᾶς καὶ τοῦ ζῆν. ". . . that we were excessively weighed down, beyond our strength, so that we despaired even of survival." The extraordinary nature of the burden (ἐβαρήθημεν) imposed on Paul by the θλῖψις is conveyed by two prepositional phrases whose juxtaposition and repetition of ὑπέρ ("beyond") accentuate the unique oppressiveness of the experience. The burden was both "beyond measure" (καθ' ὑπερβολήν) and "beyond [Paul's] ability [to endure]" (ὑπὲρ δύναμιν), "we were . . . utterly, unbearably crushed" (RSV, NRSV); or, if the two phrases are combined, "we were burdened altogether beyond our strength" (BAGD 133c). The ὥστε clause explains the result of being "utterly and unendurably crushed" (Goodspeed). The colorful compound verb ἐξαπορέομαι means "be in extreme difficulty or doubt." Its components point to the total (ἐξ-) unavailability (-α-) of an exit (πόρος, "passage") from oppressive circumstances, a situation prompting not so much acute embarrassment as unnerving despair.[13] καὶ τοῦ ζῆν defines the content of Paul's despair: "even of living," "for our lives,"[14] with the articular infinitive being epexegetic of ἐξαπορηθῆναι[15] and καί being ascensive. By the severity of the θλῖψις Paul had

---

sense of helplessness (cf. Cicero, *De Inventione* 1.55.109). But it is unnecessary to follow Welborn (43-44) in alleging that Paul indulges in exaggeration (in the phrases καθ' ὑπερβολὴν ὑπὲρ δύναμιν [v. 8] and τὸ ἀπόκριμα τοῦ θανάτου [v. 9] and in the terms ἐξαπορέομαι [v. 8] and τηλικοῦτος [v. 10]) as a technique to arouse the emotions.

10. Thus Duncan ("Ministry" 212; cf. his book *Ministry* 67, 136, 193-95, 197-99), who suggests that the reference is to the Lycus Valley, possibly Laodicea.

11. But it is not impossible that ἐν τῇ Ἀσίᾳ means Ephesus and its environs (cf. Acts 16:6; 19:10), or implies (cf. Schmid 51 n. 1) that temporally the θλῖψις was not restricted to Paul's actual sojourn in Ephesus.

12. Troas was part of Mysia, the northwestern section of Roman proconsular Asia, and could therefore be referred to by the phrase ἐν τῇ Ἀσίᾳ. When Zahn asserts that "it necessarily follows from ἐλθὼν δὲ εἰς τὴν Τρῳάδα [2:12] that in 1:8 it is not Troas that is meant, but either Ephesus or some point between Ephesus and Troas" (1.318 n. 4), he overlooks the fact that Paul's mention of localities in 2 Corinthians 1–7 is not bound by any geographical progression such as Ephesus (1:8) — Troas (2:12) — Macedonia (7:5). Cf. 2 Cor. 1:16. It might be noted here that news of a θλῖψις at Troas might easily have reached Corinth before Paul sent 2 Corinthians or 2 Corinthians 1–9 since he seems to have engaged in pastoral activity in Macedonia for some months before Titus arrived (cf. 2 Cor. 7:5) (see the chronological chart, Introduction, C).

13. Moulton cites the use of this verb in 4:8 as an instance of the "perfectivising" function of a preposition, "where perfective ἐξ shows the ἀπορία in its final result of despair" (237; cf. 111-12).

14. Zerwick and Grosvenor 534.

15. But some explain τοῦ ζῆν as a genitive of separation (an "ablatival genitive") after a verb of despairing (e.g., Robertson 518, 765; Burton 401).

been forced to surrender even the prospect of surviving this encounter with death.

Bernard (40) emphasizes how remarkable are the expressions ὑπὲρ δύναμιν and ἐξαπορηθῆναι in the light of Phil. 4:13 (πάντα ἰσχύω ἐν τῷ ἐν δυναμοῦντί με) and 2 Cor. 4:8 (ἀπορούμενοι ἀλλ᾽ οὐκ ἐξαπορούμενοι). To these two verses we could well add 1 Cor. 10:13: the trial he faced in Asia *was* in fact beyond "what a person can bear" (ἀνθρώπινος), "beyond powers of endurance" (ὑπὲρ ὃ δύνασθε), and at one stage there was no "way of escape enabling a person to endure it" (τὴν ἔκβασιν τοῦ δύνασθαι ὑπενεγκεῖν).

1:9 ἀλλὰ αὐτοὶ ἐν ἑαυτοῖς τὸ ἀπόκριμα τοῦ θανάτου ἐσχήκαμεν. "Indeed, we ourselves feel we received within our own selves a verdict of death." Here ἀλλά is "rhetorically ascensive"[16]: not only was Paul intolerably crushed and despairing of life, "but even. . . ." αὐτοὶ ἐν ἑαυτοῖς (= ἐν ἡμῖν αὐτοῖς[17]) is strongly emphatic, "we ourselves, within our very persons," or, as an epistolary plural, "I myself, within my very self." The majority of EVV and many commentators render τὸ ἀπόκριμα τοῦ θανάτου by "sentence of death" or "death sentence."[18] There is no doubt that τοῦ θανάτου is an epexegetic genitive; the ἀπόκριμα was "death." But there seems to be no contemporary instance where ἀπόκριμα, a *hapax legomenon* in biblical Greek, refers to a judicial sentence. Rather, as Hemer has demonstrated, the word "became a technical term for an official decision in answer to the petition of an embassy."[19] Related to ἀποκρίνομαι, this term means "answer" (RV) or "response" (cf. *responsum mortis,* Vulgate) or "verdict" (Barclay) in a non-legal sense, but only the context indicates whether the "verdict" is favorable or unfavorable. It is true that Paul does not specify the author of the decision (τοῦ θανάτου is not a subjective genitive),[20] but since it was a decision or verdict that Paul actually *received* (ἐσχήκαμεν), we must assume that there was a source other than Paul himself.[21] But only God could give a response, or announce a verdict, of "Death!"[22]

---

16. For this category, see BAGD 38d.

17. See Zerwick §209, and on αὐτοί, BDF §283(4).

18. E.g., RSV, NEB, NASB, NIV, REB, NRSV; Barrett 57; Furnish 108; Martin 12. Chrysostom gives κρίσις ("sentence") as well as ψῆφος ("resolution, decree") and προσδοκία ("expectation") as synonyms for ἀπόκριμα (*PGL* s.v. ἀπόκριμα). Sophocles (1.221) gives "sentence, condemnation" as the meaning in 2 Cor. 1:9.

19. Hemer 103-6 (quotation from p. 104), who notes the "embassy theme" in 2 Cor. 5:20 (πρεσβεύομεν).

20. F. Büchsel, *TDNT* 3.946.

21. But some have suggested that Paul engaged in self-questioning. "Why, looking into ourselves, we could find but one answer: that death must come" (Cassirer). Plummer, on the other hand, proposes a divine-human conjunction at this point: "Indeed, when we asked within ourselves, whether it was to be life or death for us, our own presentiment said 'Death', a presentiment which God sent . . ." (6; cf. Windisch 46-47).

22. The combination of ἐν ἑαυτοῖς with ἐσχήκαμεν does not introduce any notion of uncertainty about the receipt or the verdict, as the comment of Louw and Nida suggests: "No actual official decision had been made, but in view of all of the difficulties which Paul and his colleagues had

If this, then, is the meaning of ἀπόκριμα, the issue becomes: What was Paul's implied request that could have prompted the divine verdict of "Death!"? It could not be "Shall I die as a result of this present experience?" for Paul did not die there and then, but rather was rescued from death by God. But it may have been "Will I experience death before Christ returns or live until the advent?"[23] God's response to Paul's petition was "You will die." Even if it is illegitimate to try to reconstruct Paul's petition from God's verdict, we must reckon with the fact that the response was "Death," *yet* Paul did not die at that time, and he expected that God would deliver him from comparable brushes with death. So the divine verdict must have signified something like, "Not death now, but ultimately death from a similar θλῖψις."

It is certainly possible to follow Moulton who (very tentatively) regards ἐσχήκαμεν here, as well as ἔσχηκα in 2:13 and ἔσχηκεν in 7:5, as aoristic perfects, such usage being perhaps a mannerism or idiosyncrasy that Paul dropped before writing (. . . Ἰησοῦ Χριστοῦ), δι᾽ οὗ καὶ τὴν προσαγωγὴν ἐσχήκαμεν in Rom. 5:2, where ἐσχήκαμεν cannot mean "we possessed."[24] In 2:13 and 7:5 these perfects are probably aoristic,[25] since by the time of writing relief had come to Paul through the arrival of Titus. But in 1:9, although ἐσχήκαμεν is preceded by γενομένης . . . ἐβαρήθημεν . . . ἐξαπορηθῆναι (1:8), it is followed by ἵνα μὴ πεποιθότες ὦμεν κτλ.: perhaps in this case ἐσχήκαμεν implies both ἔσχομεν ("we received") and ἔχομεν ("we [still] possess").[26] That is, the divine verdict of "Death" remained unaltered and kept ringing in his ears: "we received and still have the verdict, 'You will die!'"[27] There is little ground for rendering ἐσχήκαμεν as "we have accepted,"[28] as if Paul had written ἐλάβομεν or εἰλήφαμεν, and no basis for believing that Paul is saying that he had accepted or become reconciled to a pre-parousia death or the possibility of a premature

---

suffered, it seemed as though such an official decision had been rendered" (§56.26). Cf. the rendering of Furnish (108) and Martin (12), "it seemed to us that we had received," and the claim by F. Büchsel that "by human judgment Paul could only reckon that his position was like that of a man condemned to death who had made a petition for mercy and received the answer that he must die" (*TDNT* 3.946).

23. Cf. Hemer: "It may well have been that a critical experience of the closeness of physical death occasioned the prayer and a consequent assurance of and resignation to a new understanding of the divine purpose for a continuing present ministry terminating in death before the Parousia" (106-7 n. 16).

24. Moulton 145, 238, 248. Burton (§80) and Turner (70) also take these three uses of ἔσχηκα in 2 Corinthians as aoristic. It could be argued that since the aorist form ἔσχον usually means "I acquired," only the perfect meant "I possessed," "I had" = "I was in the possession of," in an aoristic sense (cf. Moulton, 145). On the other hand, BDF §343 (2) regards the perfects in 1:9 and 7:5 as "correct perfects."

25. ἔσχεν is read in 7:5 by p[46] B F G K.

26. Similarly in Rom. 5:2 ἐσχήκαμεν means "we have obtained" (RSV), implying both ἔσχομεν ("we obtained") and ἔχομεν ("we enjoy possession of," "we have"). Cf. McKay, who renders ἔσχηκα by "having got I continue to have" ("Syntax" 48).

27. Cf. Weymouth, "we had, as we still have, the sentence of death."

28. Young and Ford 262 and cf. NAB[2] ("we had accepted").

ending to his apostolic mission.[29] A simple receipt and its effects are expressed by ἐσχήκαμεν, not a final acceptance of a verdict after a period of resistance.

ἵνα μὴ πεποιθότες ὦμεν ἐφ' ἑαυτοῖς ἀλλ' ἐπὶ τῷ θεῷ τῷ ἐγείροντι τοὺς νεκρούς. "This was intended to make us rely no longer on ourselves but on the God who raises the dead." πεποιθότες ὦμεν is a periphrastic perfect subjunctive after ἵνα. The perfect tense of the transitive verb πείθω is intransitive and has a present meaning: "I trust in, put my confidence in." In a sense, therefore, this periphrastic form is composed of two durative presents: "continue to be relying." The negated purpose (ἵνα μή), "so that we may not trust in ourselves," was not inserted by Paul merely as a foil for the following positive statement of purpose (ἀλλ' [ἵνα πεποιθότες ὦμεν] ἐπὶ κτλ.). Apparently, self-reliance had sometimes or even often marked his experience as a Christian. The devastating θλῖψις had the purpose — and the effect — of undermining Paul's dependence on his own resources.[30] So, although ἵνα μηκέτι is not used (as in 5:15; Eph. 4:14), the sense of μή in conjunction with this periphrastic perfect is "no longer" or "no more":[31] "so that we would no longer be reliant on ourselves." Paul's earlier partial self-reliance on his own strength or charisma or education was now a thing of the past.[32] It is quite possible that Paul is here alluding to the confident appeal he had made in 1 Cor. 15:31, "Not a day but I am at death's door! I swear it by my pride in you, brothers, through Christ Jesus our Lord" (Moffatt). In the aftermath of his affliction Paul reposed his trust and hope only in God. He had learned the spiritual lesson that for the Christian self-reliance not only is inadequate to meet the demands of a life that is pleasing to the Lord (cf. 5:9; Col. 1:10) but also constitutes an affront to God on whom we are totally dependent for our physical and spiritual well-being.[33]

The atemporal present participle τῷ ἐγείροντι describes a permanent characteristic of God. One typical and distinctive feature of God's action is his raising of dead persons (cf. Rom. 4:17). Paul is reproducing, without any explicit Christian addition, a common Semitic description of God, found notably in the second prayer of the "Eighteen Benedictions," which were recited two or three times each day in synagogue worship.[34] Why did Paul choose to use this

29. *Pace* Héring 5.

30. That ἵνα in 1:9 introduces a purpose which was actually effected is evident from the subsequent εἰς ὃν ἠλπίκαμεν.

31. Similarly Lietzmann 100; Martin 12; Barrett 57, 65 ("the perfect subjunctive, πεποιθότες ὦμεν, with the negative, suggests the discontinuance of an existing condition").

32. There is a similar movement of thought in Phil. 3:4-9, from confidence in the flesh to total reliance on God.

33. Watson finds in 2 Cor. 1:9b summed up "with unequalled clarity" the "heart" (rather than the "center") of Paul's theology, reflecting as it does his central conviction that "salvation is of the Lord" (cf. Jon. 2:9, KJV) and providing "coinherence" to the various aspects of Paul's thought ("2 Cor. 1,9b" 386-95).

34. See SB 3.212; 4.208-49; S. Safrai in Safrai and Stern 2.801, 916. It is possible that Paul recognized a distinctively Christian dimension in the description "(God) who raises the dead," namely God's raising of believers to new spiritual life after spiritual death (Eph. 2:1, 5-6; Col. 2:12;

157

particular description of God when he himself did not die as a result of the θλῖψις? He apparently viewed his deliverance from the θλῖψις as a veritable resurrection from the dead brought about by God, because he assumed that his death at that time was inevitable; he was as good as dead (cf. Rom. 4:19). Or he may be arguing *a fortiori*: if God can raise the dead, all the more can he rescue the dying from the grip of death. On this latter view οἱ νεκροί is equivalent to οἱ μέχρι θανάτου ἐγγίζοντες (cf. Phil. 2:27, 30).

1:10 ὃς ἐκ τηλικούτων θανάτων ἐρρύσατο ἡμᾶς, "He rescued us from such gigantic encounters with death." Textual critics are divided over whether θανάτων or (τηλικούτου) θανάτου is to be read. If the plural is preferred (see textual note e. above), θάνατοι will signify "ways of dying, i.e. *deadly perils*" (Turner 28) or "dangers to life" (Zerwick, *Analysis* 391) or "encounters with death." If θανάτου be regarded as original, this word will betoken "danger of death," as in Job 5:20 (LXX).[35] All four NT uses of the correlative demonstrative τηλικοῦτος[36] are anarthrous and refer to size (Robertson 710); thus, "so great a peril of death" (BAGD 814c), or, with θανάτων, "such immense mortal perils" (Thrall 78) or "such gigantic encounters with death." ἐκ points to an emancipation from the actual clutches of mortal danger, an emergence from within the realm of deadly perils, rather than a simple deliverance from proximity to death (ἀπό).[37] Also, by using ἐκ, not ἀπό, Paul seems to stop short of personifying death, since after ῥύεσθαι he usually uses ἐκ of things and ἀπό of persons.[38]

καὶ ῥύσεται, εἰς ὃν ἠλπίκαμεν ὅτι καὶ ἔτι ῥύσεται. "And he will deliver us — at least we have set our hope on him that he will continue to deliver us." The repeated future ῥύσεται, with the earlier ἐκ θανάτου/θανάτων ἡμᾶς understood, implies that Paul expected to confront comparable θλίψεις in the future. If so, it is highly improbable that the second and third instances of ῥύεσθαι in this verse point to deliverance from spiritual, eternal death, that is, to the general resurrection of the righteous.[39] The perfect ἠλπίκαμεν does not advert to a more settled or secure hope than would ἐλπίζομεν,[40] but rather depicts an ongoing state, a

---

3:1). For Paul these two resurrections, the spiritual and the somatic, were directly related, because spiritual resurrection not only precedes but also guarantees bodily resurrection (see Harris 101-7).

35. Cf. BAGD 351b.

36. The other three uses are Heb. 2:3; Jas. 3:4; Rev. 16:18.

37. In 1:10a ῥύεσθαι ἐκ τοῦ θανάτου "does not mean 'preserve from death' in general, but 'rescue from a(n actual) situation in which death was threatened'" (BAGD xxvii). BAGD cites Aristoxenus (300 B.C.), fragment 113: ῥύεσθαι καὶ ἐρύεσθαι διαφορὰν ἔχει πρὸς ἄλληλα. — τὸ μὲν γὰρ ῥύεσθαι ἐκ θανάτου ἕλκειν, τὸ δὲ ἐρύεσθαι φυλάττειν ("ῥύεσθαι and ἐρύεσθαι may be distinguished from one another. For whereas ῥύεσθαι means to rescue from [actual] death, ἐρύεσθαι means to protect from [the danger of] death").

38. On this latter point see Rigaux, *Thessaloniciens* 396.

39. *Pace* D. M. Stanley 130.

40. As Furnish 108, 114, "we firmly set our hope." Burton classifies 1:10 as an intensive perfect, representing an emphatic present tense. Similarly, "πέποιθα practically expresses the thought of πείθομαι intensified. Πεπίστευκα is also clearly a stronger way of saying πιστεύω" (§77).

present condition, that results from an implied entrance upon that state:[41] "we placed our hope in God and consequently we now hope in him." Twice in the Pastorals the perfect of ἐλπίζω is followed by ἐπί (ἐπὶ θεῷ ζῶντι, 1 Tim. 4:10; ἐπὶ θεόν, 1 Tim. 5:5), the prepositional phrase denoting the basis of the hope. Here εἰς ὅν points to the object of Paul's hope — "the Father who is ever compassionate" (1:3) and "who raises the dead" (1:9).

The content of this hope that is focused on God is introduced by ὅτι: "that he will deliver [us from comparable deaths] yet again (καὶ ἔτι)." Because εἰς ὅν κτλ. follows ῥύσεται asyndetically and repeats ῥύσεται with the qualification "we have fixed our hope on him," we probably have here a case of epidiorthosis, the correction of a previous expression or impression.[42] Paul qualifies his bold assertion, "and he will deliver us," by immediately adding, "(at least) on him we have placed our reliance that he will continue to deliver us."[43] He could not presume on the gracious intervention of God whenever the θλῖψις struck;[44] no human being has access to the divine counsels. This general lesson Paul had already well learned, for his σκόλοψ had remained in spite of his three urgent requests that this "messenger of Satan" be removed (12:7-8). Were it not for this uncertainty about future divine intervention, it could be argued that the remarkable escape from death recounted in this passage strengthened rather than diminished Paul's expectation of being alive at the advent. It is instructive to compare this whole episode with the Lukan account in Acts 27 of the events leading up to Paul's shipwreck.[45] When all hope of being saved had been abandoned (27:20), *on the ground of a divine revelation* (27:22-25) Paul assured his shipmates that there would be no loss of life (cf. 27:9-10). In the case of Paul's Asian experience, not only had he not received an assurance about future deliverance, but the divine verdict in response to his inquiry about survival until the advent had been "Death," "You will die!" (see 1:9). Yet Paul did not know whether his future span of life would be brief or long, so it was appropriate to trust God for future deliverance from recurring θλίψεις without presuming on the divine grace. As he expresses it in Phil. 1:25, he believed that his preservation from death would promote the progress and joy of his converts.[46] To hope for preservation was natural,

41. Similarly Fanning 138-39, 292-93, who observes that, in a sense, the perfect of a stative verb "combines the meaning of the aorist and the present together in one form, denoting the ingressive sense of the aorist and the stative meaning of the present" (292). Cf. BDF §341.

42. Cf. 1 Cor. 7:10; 15:10; 2 Cor. 12:11a.

43. The sense of *continuous* deliverance arises from the linear future ῥύσεται in conjunction with καὶ ἔτι.

44. "His bold declaration of future deliverance must become a more modest statement of prayerful hope, based in God and conditional on the prayers of the Corinthians, in a situation that will remain difficult and dangerous" (Wiles 273).

45. See in particular Acts 27:9-10, 20-26, 31, 33-38.

46. There is a significant difference, however, between Phil. 1:19-26 and 2 Cor. 1:9-10. In the former passage, although Paul realized that death or life, execution or release, could be his experience in the immediate and uncertain future (Phil. 1:20), in 1:25-26, perhaps optimistically, he expresses an assurance (οἶδα) of the successful outcome of his trial and therefore the preservation

especially for one whose ancestors had hoped in God and experienced deliverance.[47] Actual preservation from death would give rise to thanksgiving to God, a thought to which Paul now turns.

1:11 συνυπουργούντων καὶ ὑμῶν ὑπὲρ ἡμῶν τῇ δεήσει. "Provided you, for your part, join in helping us by your prayer for us." The verb συνυπουργέω is composed of two elements, ὑπουργέω ("assist") and σύν ("in conjunction with"), means "I join in rendering help," "I cooperate with," and is virtually synonymous with συλλαμβάνομαι, "I come to the aid of," "I assist" (cf. Luke 5:7). Paul does not specify the party who is helped, but it is unlikely to be God since he is addressed in the δέησις, or the Corinthians since in that case ἐν ἑαυτοῖς might have been added.[48] Pointing to the close parallel in Rom. 15:30 ("I appeal to you . . . to strive together with me [συναγωνίσασθαί μοι] in your prayers to God on my behalf"), Bultmann aptly comments that "the συνυπουργεῖν here corresponds to the συναγωνίσασθαι there; the συν- thus means, together with me"(29). The genitive absolute συνυπουργούντων could be temporal ("while you join in helping us"[49]), with the Corinthian cooperation in prayer assumed, or even modal ("through your cooperation with us") or causal ("because you are helping me," Williams), but in keeping with Paul's regular requests to his addressees for their prayers, this construction probably bears a conditional sense ("provided you join in helping us").[50] Divine deliverance, when it occurs, is always an undeserved blessing (χάρισμα), but in some mysterious way it is intimately related to human intercession (cf. Phil. 1:19; Phlm. 22). Here Paul is indirectly requesting cooperation (σύν-) on the part of the Corinthians (καί) in petitioning God for deliverance whenever θλίψεις occur. Prayer is cooperative work (Rom. 15:30; Col. 2:1; 4:12-13), expressive of the interdependence of the members of Christ's body (1 Cor. 12:25-26). If δέησις is not simply a synonym for προσευχή, it points to a specific request for Paul's deliverance rather than general intercession for Paul's well-being. τῇ δεήσει is an instrumental dative, with the article denoting possession, "by your prayer."

ἵνα ἐκ πολλῶν προσώπων τὸ εἰς ἡμᾶς χάρισμα διὰ πολλῶν εὐχαριστηθῇ ὑπὲρ ἡμῶν. "So that many people may give God thanks regarding us for his gracious favor granted us through the prayers of many." At first glance this complex clause may seem somewhat clumsy, with its apparent repetition (ἐκ πολλῶν προσώπων — διὰ πολλῶν, and εἰς ἡμᾶς — ὑπὲρ ἡμῶν).[51] But *prima*

---

of his life (cf. 2 Tim. 4:18), which he grounds (τοῦτο πεποιθώς) objectively on the pastoral needs of the Philippian church (1:24). 2 Corinthians 1, on the other hand, expresses an eager hope rather than a settled conviction regarding future deliverance.

47. See especially Ps. 21:5 (LXX): ἐπὶ σοὶ ἤλπισαν οἱ πατέρες ἡμῶν, ἤλπισαν, καὶ ἐρρύσω αὐτούς, "Our ancestors put their hope in you; they hoped (in you) and you rescued them."

48. But cf. Hughes 23 n. 20.

49. BAGD 793d; similarly TCNT, Weymouth, Berkeley, NIV, NRSV, REB.

50. Similarly NEB; Wiles 273 n. 6. Wolff rightly notes (19 n. 13) that συνυπουργούντων bears a future sense, being a present participle that expresses action that is contemporaneous with the (future) main verb ῥύσεται.

51. Cf. Lietzmann 101. Note Furnish's awkward rendering: "so that from many people

facie[34] difficulties disappear if διὰ πολλῶν is construed not with the word that follows (εὐχαριστηθῇ) but with the phrase that precedes (τὸ εἰς ἡμᾶς χάρισμα). As Moule (108) notes, τὸ διὰ πολλῶν might in that case have been expected if the dictates of strict grammar were followed. But a prepositional phrase that modifies a preceding articular substantive is not always articular in NT Greek.[52]

ἵνα . . . εὐχαριστηθῇ describes the purpose of the Corinthians' assistance in prayer, although, given the relative frequency of an ecbatic ἵνα in Paul (e.g., 1:17), it is quite possible that the clause defines a result.[53] In the active voice εὐχαριστέω *may* be accompanied by the accusative of the thing and the dative of the person (τινί τι, "[I thank] someone for something").[54] In the passive, that accusative may become the subject.[55] In the present instance, the active would be τῷ θεῷ τὸ χάρισμα εὐχαριστῶ, "I give thanks to God for his gracious gift." The corresponding passive would be τῷ θεῷ τὸ χάρισμα εὐχαριστήθη, "thanksgiving was given to God for his gracious gift," where τὸ χάρισμα is in fact the subject of the verb.[56] τῷ θεῷ is implied.

The source or agent (ἐκ) of the thanksgiving is expressed by ἐκ πολλῶν προσώπων. There are three basic ways of understanding this phrase:

"from many Godward-turned faces" (Berkeley), that is, faces turned upward to heaven in prayer;[57]

"from many lips" (Weymouth, Montgomery), "by the mouth of a multitude of persons" (Cassirer), "from many tongues" (Conybeare in Conybeare and Howson 441), where πρόσωπα ("faces") stands for lips or mouths or tongues (whole for the part); or

"from many people" (Furnish 108; Martin 12), "by many persons,"[58] where πρόσωπα stands for "people" or "persons" (part for the whole).[59]

---

thanks may be rendered on our behalf, through many, for the gracious benefit . . ." (108). He construes διὰ πολλῶν as masculine, "through many people," and as duplicating in effect the earlier expression, "from many people," "thereby re-emphasizing the multitude of thanksgivings Paul has in mind. . . . It must be conceded, however, that there is no completely satisfactory way to unscramble the syntax of this verse" (115).

52. E.g., τῆς κοινωνίας εἰς αὐτοὺς καὶ εἰς πάντας (9:13) and the several other Pauline examples cited by Robertson 783.

53. As in TCNT, GNB, NIV.

54. See BAGD 328b; Robertson 474. But the more common construction is τινὶ ἐπί τινι εὐχαριστῶ.

55. BDF §312(2); cf. Windisch 51.

56. There seems to be no biblical parallel for this usage of εὐχαριστέω; but see Justin, *Apology* 65:5; 66:2 (cited by Schubert [49] who explains εὐχαριστηθῇ as the passive of the active εὐχαριστεῖν ἐπί τινι, "to thank for something" 47-49).

57. Similarly Plummer 6 ("from many uplifted faces").

58. BAGD 328c, 721d (but cf. 235b); Zerwick and Grosvenor 535. Cf. Thrall 78: "by the agency of many figures" (= intercessors, 125 and nn. 325-26).

59. Zerwick remarks that if πρόσωπα here means "persons," ἐκ should be taken as equivalent to ὑπό, as sometimes in Hellenistic Greek (*Analysis* 392; cf. his *Biblical Greek* §87-90).

The gracious gift or favor (χάρισμα) that would prompt thanksgiving to God could be considered in a general sense to be God's answering of Corinthian prayer, but this would make εἰς ἡμᾶς awkward. More probably, the χάρισμα is the boon granted to Paul (εἰς ἡμᾶς) of future "deliverance" (NEB)[60] from death, not mere protection from danger, that would result from Corinthian cooperation in prayer. Paul's movement of thought in vv. 10-11 seems to be this: "I am hopeful that God will deliver me from any future θλῖψις, but any such future deliverance is in part dependent on your prayer for me. If, then, you pray and God intervenes again, thanksgiving will arise to him for his gracious deliverance of me from death."[61] Such a blessing would come διὰ πολλῶν. If πολλῶν is neuter, the meaning will be, "through many prayers," or "in answer to many prayers";[62] if masculine, "through the prayers of many" (NAB[2]), or "through the help of many people."[63] We have seen that there is no grammatical objection to construing διὰ πολλῶν with τὸ . . . χάρισμα. But if πολλῶν is masculine and this prepositional phrase (διὰ πολλῶν) is linked to εὐχαριστηθῇ, an awkward redundancy results, with the ἐκ and διά phrases specifying the same agents.[64] The difficulty is scarcely removed by treating πολλῶν as neuter, "by many people . . . through many prayers." So the most satisfactory solution — one free of awkwardness — is to take ἐκ πολλῶν προσώπων with εὐχαριστηθῇ and διὰ πολλῶν with τὸ . . . χάρισμα (as in the translation proposed above). On this understanding, an alternative way Paul might have expressed the same sentiments would have been . . . ἵνα πολλοὶ ἐπὶ τῷ χαρίσματι τῷ εἰς ἡμᾶς διὰ τῶν προσευχῶν πολλῶν τῷ θεῷ εὐχαριστήσωσιν περὶ ἡμῶν. We need not identify the "many" who render thanks totally with the "many" who intercede for Paul's deliverance, but presumably the overlap would be considerable. And unlike οἱ πλείονες in 2 Cor. 2:6, πολλοί in the phrase διὰ πολλῶν need not imply a dissident "few."

To summarize the overall meaning of 1:8-11:[65] Before his affliction in Asia, Paul had reckoned himself to be an apostle exhibited by God to both angels and men ὡς ἐπιθανάτιος (1 Cor. 4:9), "*like* a man condemned to death."

60. So also Bultmann 30; Wiles 274, 275 n. 4 ("continued rescue in the future"); O'Brien 253 and n. 124.

61. A threefold movement is envisaged: Corinthian prayer for Paul's deliverance; God's deliverance of Paul; Corinthian thanksgiving for this deliverance. Cf. Bratcher, 12. This makes it highly unlikely that the χάρισμα is a *past* deliverance, as Schatzmann (48-49) and Carrez (53) propose. On the other hand, Furnish seems to overtranslate: "the gracious benefit which shall have been bestowed on us" (108).

62. Thus TCNT, Goodspeed, RSV. In Phlm. 22 διὰ τῶν προσευχῶν ὑμῶν has the sense, "in answer to your prayers."

63. Martin 12; cf. Barrett 57, "through the agency of many."

64. Cf. BAGD 180d: "διὰ πολλῶν resumes ἐκ πολλῶν προσώπων." Barclay's distinction between the prepositions ἐκ and διά relieves the problem only slightly: "from many faces and through many people."

65. The epistolary, didactic, and hortatory functions of 1:3-11 are usefully discussed by O'Brien 254-56.

Now, as a result of this incapacitating θλῖψις, he was not only forced to renounce self-reliance in favor of total God-reliance; he actually *was* an ἐπιθανάτιος, a man under a death verdict from which, humanly speaking, there was no reprieve. Divine intervention in Asia had enabled him to retreat from the portals of death to the land of the living. But because he realized that similar encounters with death lay ahead of him as an ἐπιθανάτιος, and that he could not presume on God's intervention, he requested the Corinthians' assistance by their prayer for his future deliverance from the clutches of death. If they prayed and God graciously intervened once again, many would be prompted to offer prayers of thanksgiving to God.[66]

This paragraph illustrates vividly a theme Paul has already enunciated in 1:3-4 — divine comfort experienced in the midst of human affliction — but also anticipates a motif that will dominate chs. 10–13, divine strength displayed in the midst of human weakness.[67] So 1:8-11 not only explains Paul's remarkable preoccupation with death throughout 2 Corinthians[68] but also unmistakably sounds two dominant notes heard throughout the letter.

Bibliography

Alexander • Baumert 111-12, 409 • Belleville, "Letter" • Deissmann 257 • Dodd 67-68, 80-81 • Duncan 130-32 • Harvey 1-34 • Heckel 261-65 • Hemer • Hoffmann 234, 247, 328-29, 344 • Kreitzer 93-95 • Mullins, "Disclosure" • O'Brien 248-58 • Rissi 56-58 • Sanders • Schnider and Stenger 46-50 • D. M. Stanley 75-77, 129-31 • D. M. Stanley, *Boasting* 69-72 • Warfield 30-35 • J. L. White • J. L. White, "Formulae" • Wiles 271-76 • W. E. Wilson • Yates • N. M. Young, "'. . . To Make Us Rely Not on Ourselves but on God Who Raises the Dead.' 2 Cor 1,9b as the Heart of Paul's Theology," in *Schweizer FS* 384-98

---

66. In discussing v. 3 we noted how Paul has departed in 1:3-11 from his customary practice of following his salutation with thanksgiving for his addressees. Even when he finally comes in v. 11 to use the verb εὐχαριστέω, there are significant divergences from his normal pattern.

   (1) It is the Corinthians, not Paul, who give thanks to God.
   (2) Their thanksgiving would be for a future blessing that Paul would experience, whereas ordinarily he gives thanks for evidence of God's past and present blessing in his converts' lives.
   (3) εὐχαριστέω is used in the passive voice, not the active. Cf. Schubert 50, 183-84.

67. But cf. O'Brien: "The tone, language and themes of 1:3-11 do not point forward to chaps. 10-13" (256 n. 133). This may be true of tone and language, but not of theme. See further, Introduction, A.3.e.(3).

68. On this see the Excursus which follows, especially D.1.

EXCURSUS: PAUL'S AFFLICTION IN ASIA (2 COR. 1:8-11): THE PERSONAL BACKGROUND TO 2 CORINTHIANS

Paul's Description of the θλῖψις

What is initially striking about 2 Cor. 1:8-11 is the absence of specific details about the precise nature of the θλῖψις. How did it come about? How long did it last? Were other people involved, either as causing the θλῖψις or as experiencing it with Paul? Did it cause physical as well as psychological pain? In his description Paul focuses on the subjective effects of the experience. What we may deduce from 1:8-11 regarding this affliction can be summarized thus.

It Occurred in the Province of Asia.

Given Paul's use of ἐν Ἐφέσῳ in 1 Cor. 15:32; 16:8; 1 Tim. 1:3; 2 Tim. 1:18, it would be strange that an experience which centered on Ephesus should be depicted vaguely as being ἐν τῇ Ἀσίᾳ. In the other four NT uses of this latter phrase, it is unlikely or impossible that we should identify "in Asia" as "in Ephesus."[1] Indeed, in three other passages the city of Ephesus within Asia seems to be distinguished from the whole province.[2] This leads us to suppose that in 1:8 ἐν τῇ Ἀσίᾳ refers principally, if not exclusively, to some part of proconsular Asia other than the leading city of Ephesus.

It Occurred between the Writing of 1 and 2 Corinthians.

Paul's θλῖψις must not have occurred prior to the writing of 1 Corinthians, for otherwise we would expect him to have alluded to it, if not described it, in that letter, given its profound effect on his whole spiritual outlook (2 Cor. 1:9).[3] If, then, the *terminus a quo* is perhaps the spring of 55, the *terminus ad quem* is possibly the summer or fall of 56 when 2 Corinthians 1 was penned, or, more precisely, an earlier time when Paul crossed from Troas into Macedonia (2:12-13; 7:5), for the incident took place "in Asia." Scholars who specify the *terminus a quo* more closely place the event after the "sorrowful visit"[4] or after the "severe letter."[5] If we are right in inferring from ἐν τῇ Ἀσίᾳ that the incident occurred somewhere in the province of Asia other than Ephesus, it

1. Acts 16:6; 20:16; 2 Tim. 1:15; Rev. 1:4. It is possible that in Acts 20:16 "Ephesus" stands for "Asia" by synecdoche.
2. Acts 19:26; 2 Tim. 1:15 compared with 1:18; Rev. 1:4 compared with 1:11.
3. This may be safely called a "scholarly consensus" among both commentators and general writers on Paul.
4. E.g., Duncan 131-36, 140, 298; "Table" 43.
5. E.g., Strachan xl, 68 and n. 2; Lüdemann 133 n. 174.

seems more probable that it occurred after Paul's departure from Ephesus in the wake of the Demetrius riot than during his Ephesian ministry.[6] The θλῖψις would then postdate not only 1 Corinthians but also the "painful visit" and the "letter of tears."

It Had a Devastating Effect on Paul.

The θλῖψις proved so devastating and overwhelming that Paul was forced to renounce all hope of survival (1:8); he felt as if he had had a verdict of "Death" pronounced over his head (1:9). But in the wake of this experience which was tantamount to death there followed a further experience which was tantamount to resurrection (1:10). All this had the effect of undermining Paul's self-confidence and self-reliance and compelling his utter dependence on a God who raises the dead (1:9; cf. Rom. 4:17) and therefore also rescues the dying (such as Paul in Asia) from the danger of death (cf. Phil. 2:27, 30).

It Was Unique in Paul's Experience.

Although statements such as καθ' ἡμέραν ἀποθνῄσκω, "not a day but I am at death's door" (1 Cor. 15:31, Moffatt) and ἐν θανάτοις πολλάκις (2 Cor. 11:23) cannot be dismissed as rhetorical exaggeration, there is an important difference between constant exposure to death and an actual confrontation with death, whatever be said concerning the stoning at Lystra (Acts 14:19). Indications that Paul himself viewed this episode as unparalleled in his experience include the following.

As he begins 2 Corinthians, he departs from his usual custom in his letters to churches of recording his thanksgiving to God for the spiritual welfare of the addressees (Galatians is the other exception) and instead describes his own situation and welfare and requests his addressees' intercession for him (1:3-11). This unique epistolary exordium calls for a unique explanation — which Paul himself furnishes in 1:8-10.

The effect of the double ὑπέρ in 1:8 is dramatic: καθ' ὑπερβολὴν ὑπὲρ δύναμιν, "beyond measure, beyond my capability [to cope with]." This self-confession is unparalleled, especially when seen against the background of Paul's confident assertion that "nothing is beyond my power in the strength of him who makes me strong!" (Phil. 4:13, TCNT).

In the light of ἀπορούμενοι ἀλλ' οὐκ ἐξαπορούμενοι (4:8), "despairing, but not utterly desperate" (Furnish 252), Paul's frank admission, ὥστε

---

6. From Col. 1:7; 2:1; 4:12-13, we may legitimately deduce that it was Epaphras, not Paul, who engaged in pioneer evangelism or pastoral work in the Lycus Valley during the apostle's residence in Ephesus. See the Textual Notes on 1:10.

ἐξαπορηθῆναι ἡμᾶς καὶ τοῦ ζῆν (1:8), "we utterly despaired even of remaining alive," is singular. If, as Héring observes (5), ἐξαπορηθῆναι denotes "a kind of paroxysm of anguish which banishes all hope," this word is extraordinary on the lips of the "apostle of hope."

Finally, Paul had previously brought consolation to others who grieved for their dead (e.g., 1 Thess. 4:13, 18); now he himself received consolation during a personal encounter with death. παρακαλεῖτε ἀλλήλους ἐν τοῖς λόγοις τούτοις (1 Thess. 4:18) has become παρακαλούμεθα αὐτοὶ ὑπὸ τοῦ θεοῦ (2 Cor. 1:4).

Yet Paul Expected Similar Afflictions in the Future.

Whether καὶ ῥύεται or καὶ ῥύσεται be read in 1:10 or the phrase be regarded as a scribal interpolation, the following ῥύσεται in the same verse shows that Paul anticipated further experiences of the same or a similar type, although he hoped that, with Corinthian cooperation by prayer, God would again mercifully grant him the blessing of deliverance and comfort (1:3-4, 10-11). This being so, ἐσχήκαμεν (1:9) may not be an aoristic perfect ("we had") but is probably perfective in sense ("we have come to have") and, like τὸ ἀπόκριμα τοῦ θανάτου (1:9) and possibly ἐκ τηλικούτων θανάτων (1:10), may therefore imply Paul's continual exposure to a particular danger or its consequences (cf. 4:10-12, 16; 6:9).

Proposed Identifications of the θλῖψις

Commentators have not been reluctant to attempt to identify Paul's θλῖψις, but, equally, all are willing to concede that no proposal can claim more than conjectural status. A review and brief assessment of the principal identifications may be undertaken before a more detailed defense is given of one of the options.[7]

A Literal "Fighting with Beasts" in Ephesus (1 Cor. 15:32)

From the time of Tertullian onward, 2 Cor. 1:8-11 has been interpreted by some in terms of 1 Cor. 15:32: εἰ κατὰ ἄνθρωπον ἐθηριομάχησα ἐν Ἐφέσῳ, τί μοι τὸ

---

7. Two highly improbable identifications may be mentioned. If the affliction was the Corinthian revolt against Paul's authority and the danger he confronted was "death from a broken heart" (Dean 12, 44-47), his request for cooperation by prayer (2 Cor. 1:11) would be singularly inappropriate since the addressees (on this view) were responsible for the state of affairs that necessitated that prayer, and, moreover, he would hardly envisage a repetition (cf. 2 Cor. 1:10) of such a defection, whether at Corinth or elsewhere. If, on the other hand, the affliction was "the imminent peril of drowning" (cf. 2 Cor. 11:25) (the preference of Denney 725), one may justifiably ask why Paul describes it as having occurred ἐν τῇ Ἀσίᾳ as opposed to using an expression such as ἐν τῷ κατὰ τὴν Ἀσίαν τόπῳ ("at a spot along the coast of Asia"; cf. Acts 27:2).

ὄφελος; On this view, through God's intervention Paul was literally "saved from the mouth of the lion" (an expression found in 2 Tim. 4:17).[8]

The following three considerations make it virtually impossible to believe that Paul actually underwent the beast-fight in the stadium at Ephesus. First, it is remarkable that no specific or unequivocal record of the event and Paul's miraculous deliverance is found in Acts, in 1 Cor. 4:9-13; 2 Cor. 6:4-10; 11:23-27, or in *1 Clement* 5. In the second place, even if Paul, a Roman citizen, had been thrown *ad bestias* and had survived and been released, the consequent loss of citizenship would have precluded his later appeals to citizens' privileges (see Acts 22:25; 23:27; 25:11).[9] Thirdly, and most important of all, it now seems probable that the stadium at Ephesus was not used for beast-fighting in the first two centuries A.D. since the circular enclosed area at the east end, which evidently served as a substitute for an amphitheater and was not part of the original stadium, cannot be dated earlier than the third century (Bean 170-71).

Opposition to Paul at Ephesus

If the reference to "fighting with beasts" (1 Cor. 15:32) is interpreted figuratively of violent human opposition at Ephesus, or if appeal is made to 1 Cor. 16:8-9, where Paul refers to ἀντικείμενοι πολλοί at Ephesus, Paul's θλῖψις may be identified as exposure to extraordinary danger from his opponents in Ephesus.[10] Yates proposes that Paul's "deadly peril" may have been legal charges brought against him by Ephesian Jews, possibly in the wake of the assassination of M. Junius Silanus, proconsul of Asia, in A.D. 54 — charges that involved the death penalty.[11]

These identifications encounter several difficulties. First, ἐν τῇ Ἀσίᾳ is treated as identical to ἐν Ἐφέσῳ (on which we see above, A.1.) Second, the intensity and the vividness of Paul's language in 1:8-11 suggest that the θλῖψις occurred in the recent past, not two or more years previously. Third, Jewish opposition was nothing novel in Paul's experience, even if it was at times more acute in Ephesus. At Lystra, where Jews from Antioch and Iconium had incited the people to stone Paul, he himself warned the believers that they could not enter the kingdom of God without undergoing many trials (Acts 14:19, 21-22). The uniqueness of Paul's θλῖψις (see above, A.4.) is compromised by this identification. Fourth, regarding Yates's view, would Paul expect repeated capital sentences (see A.5. above), as opposed to merely continuing Jewish opposition?

8. Tertullian, *De Resurrectione Carnis* 48.12; and in recent times, *inter alios,* Warfield 30-35, who finds the link with resurrection in each passage (viz. 1 Corinthians 15 *passim* and 2 Cor. 1:9) significant; Riddle 114, 117-18.

9. See *Digesta Iustiniani* XXVIII.1.8.4.

10. So, e.g., Bengel (3.332), who equates 1 Cor. 15:32 with both Acts 19:29-30 and 2 Cor. 1:8.

11. Yates 241-45 (following Bruce, *Paul* 295-98).

Imprisonment in Asia, or More Specifically in Ephesus

In 1929 in his influential volume *St. Paul's Ephesian Ministry,* G. S. Duncan proposed that during his ministry in Asia Paul suffered three "imprisonments."[12] The first, associated with the crisis of 1 Cor. 15:32 and the writing of Philippians, occurred in Ephesus; the second, also in Ephesus but less serious in nature, took place after the Demetrius riot and was when Philemon and Colossians were written;[13] the third, reflected in 2 Tim. 4:16-18 and 2 Cor. 1:8, probably occurred in the Lycus Valley, possibly in Laodicea.[14] More recently, however, Duncan contended that this third crisis or ordeal consisted of Paul's suffering the "thirty-nine stripes" (2 Cor. 11:24) after being arraigned before a local Jewish ecclesiastical court.[15] This equating of 2 Cor. 1:8-11 and 2 Tim. 4:16-18, supported by two superficial resemblances between the passages,[16] presupposes the validity of Duncan's assertion that of the many personal passages in the Pastorals (particularly in 2 Timothy and Titus) which are genuine Pauline compositions, the majority have their historical setting in the period of the third "missionary journey." While the infliction of the Jewish "thirty-nine stripes" might have brought Paul within the shadow of death (2 Cor. 1:8-9), it is more difficult to imagine this as the background of 2 Tim. 4:16-18, where there is no indication of physical danger or suffering before the deliverance "from the lion's mouth." Apart from Duncan's particular theory, the association of 2 Cor. 1:8-11 with the circumstances of an imprisonment in Ephesus[17] cannot be deemed impossible, provided the imprisonment occurred at the end of Paul's sojourn in and around that city (? fall 52-spring 56).

But whether Paul suffered an Ephesian imprisonment remains an open question, and the legitimacy of the equation "in Asia" = "in Ephesus" is at least suspect. Moreover, if the θλῖψις was unique, this proposal founders on Paul's af-

---

12. Duncan 140-43, 195, 288-93, 298-99. For Duncan, an "imprisonment" implied not rigorous confinement, but an outbreak of hostility followed by *libera custodia* — protective custody under police supervision (7, 109, 141).

13. One of the modifications Duncan later made of his original reconstruction of the historical background of Paul's ministry in Asia was to dissociate the Philemon imprisonment from the Demetrius riot by dating this Ephesian uproar in the spring of A.D. 56, shortly before Paul left Ephesus for Troas and about a year after the period of detention when Paul wrote Philemon and Colossians ("Table" 43-44).

14. Duncan held that αὐτὸς ἐπέσχεν χρόνον εἰς τὴν Ἀσίαν (Acts 19:22) covered the reference to 2 Cor. 1:8-11 ("Ephesus" 165).

15. "Foiled in their efforts to secure his condemnation before a Roman governor (at the time when Philippians was written), the Jews of Asia . . . now saw their opportunity in a remote part of the province to take the law into their own hands" ("Ministry" 215). The *personalia* of 2 Tim. 4:10-12 arose, it is claimed ("Ministry" 218), from this "sudden and unexpected emergency."

16. These are the notions of rescue from peril in the recent past and of hope or assurance of future preservation through divine intervention (cf. Duncan 194 n. 1).

17. Thus, e.g., Dibelius, *Paul* 81; Furnish 42, 123, who places Philippians (or at least Philippians 1–2) during this imprisonment, discovering some five correspondences between 2 Corinthians 1–2 and Philippians 1–2.

firmation at the time of 2 Corinthians that he had undergone multiple imprison-ments (ἐν φυλακαῖς περισσοτέρως, 2 Cor. 11:23). And, if Philippians 1 was penned during this period, it is difficult to square Paul's positive attitude toward his imprisonment in Phil. 1:12-14, 19-20 with the indications of trauma and in-ability to cope in 2 Cor. 1:8-9.

The Demetrius Riot

Not infrequently Paul is thought to be alluding, in 2 Cor. 1:8-11, to the riot at Ephesus instigated by Demetrius the silversmith (Acts 19:23-41).[18] Several considerations, however, militate against this identification, which was popular among the older commentators. First, the Lukan account offers no suggestion that Paul himself was in grave danger before, during, or after the tumult,[19] nor does it even hint that he was miraculously delivered from a deadly peril[20] which had already left its mark on him[21] and which he wished to avoid. Although Luke does not explicitly state that Paul refrained from hastening to the theater, this seems clearly implied in 19:31. Only the timely intervention of his friends, reinforced by some of the Asiarchs, prevented Paul from fulfilling his wish of mixing with the infuriated crowd and addressing the riotous assembly (19:30-31). Second, while 2 Cor. 1:8 alludes to an isolated event or events in the past, equally clearly vv. 9 and 10 point to probable recurrences of the same or a similar θλῖψις in the future, which makes the proposed identification un-likely. And third, on this view, as on others, ἐν Ἐφέσῳ might have been ex-pected in place of ἐν τῇ Ἀσίᾳ, especially since, to judge from the record in Acts, the riot itself (cf. 19:26-27) affected no parts of proconsular Asia other than Ephesus.

Perhaps because of the difficulties of the simple equation 2 Cor. 1:8-11 = Acts 19:23-41, several commentators have been prompted to entertain the pos-sibility that 2 Corinthians 1 is describing some unsuccessful attempt by the

18. E.g., Bachmann 37-38; Ramsay 280, 283-84; W. L. Knox, *Jerusalem* 340 n. 18; Kruse 69.

19. But it is not impossible that the mob of infuriated artisans made an unsuccessful bid to lynch Paul on the way to the theater. Howson (in Conybeare and Howson 430 n. 9; similarly Schmiedel 212) discerns in such an episode the background of Rom. 16:3-4: "perhaps the house of Aquila and Priscilla may have been a Christian home to the Apostle at Ephesus, like Jason's house at Thessalonica"; cf. Acts 17:5, 7; 18:26; 1 Cor. 16:19 (where D* F G it vg^{cl} add παρ' οἷς καὶ ξενίζομαι).

20. But Ramsay contends that Luke regularly omits or tones down the sufferings or dangers Paul encountered (94, 279-80; similarly Ogg 135-36).

21. Admittedly, Paul may have been profoundly disturbed by the prospect of a repetition of his experience at Lystra (Acts 14:19), by the threat of death by mob violence, in spite of the fact that such danger arose from the success of the gospel. But 2 Cor. 1:8-10 speaks of deliverance from an appalling peril which Paul was actually experiencing and not simply from an imminent danger by which he was merely threatened.

populace, after the Ephesian uproar, to lynch the apostle,[22] or, alternatively, that Paul here refers to a particular persecution encountered in and around Ephesus or in Asia (cf. Acts 20:19; 1 Cor. 16:9) shortly before his departure for Troas.[23] These proposals are free of virtually all the objections levelled against the association of 2 Corinthians 1 and Acts 19 and can perhaps claim in their favor the evidence of 2 Cor. 1:5, interpreted as meaning that the persecution which was once Christ's was now Paul's in abundant measure (cf. 2 Cor. 4:9).

A Severe Illness

It can scarcely be denied that the description of Paul's affliction in 2 Cor. 1:8-11 aptly portrays, or at least is consonant with, a prostrating attack of a recurrent malady. A painful, death-threatening illness would certainly seem to the sufferer to be an intolerable burden (ὑπὲρ δύναμιν ἐβαρήθημεν) that expelled all hope of survival (1:8). In Jewish thought sickness was often regarded as death, and healing or recovery was depicted as a virtual return to life. For example, in 2 Kgs. 5:7 ("Can I kill and bring back to life?") "kill" means "inflict illness" and "bring back to life" carries the sense "heal of an ailment." Or again, after his recovery from illness, King Hezekiah says to Yahweh, "You restored me to health and let me live" (Isa. 38:16). In Hos. 6:1-2 the healing of the nation after its "injury" or "burial" in exile is depicted as restoration to life. As a result of his θλῖψις Paul saw himself as νεκρός, God's ἀπόκριμα as θάνατος, and his recovery as ἔγερσις (2 Cor. 1:9).[24] Furthermore, in conjunction with the unique turn of phrase τὸ ἀπόκριμα τοῦ θανάτου, the expression ἐν ἑαυτοῖς (1:9) seems to mean more than "in our estimation" or "in our consciousness"; rather, "within ourselves"[25] or "within our own selves"[26] seems a more appropriate rendering. 4:12 expresses a similar sentiment: "death is operative in our person," where θάνατος is more than the universal phenomenon of the διαφθορά of the ὁ ἔξω ἄνθρωπος (4:16).

If v. 10 alludes to Job 33:30a LXX, which reads ἀλλ᾽ ἐρρύσατο τὴν ψυχήν μου ἐκ θανάτου (cf. Job 33:22 LXX), Paul may have recognized a general correspondence between Job's physical plight (see Job 2:7) and his own. In Job 33:12-22 Elihu seeks to rebut Job's claim that God considers him an enemy (33:10). He observes that through dreams and visions or through the chastening of illness God speaks to people "to turn them from wrongdoing and to keep them from pride" (33:17). This latter phrase (the LXX has only τὸ δὲ σῶμα αὐτοῦ ἀπὸ πτώματος ἐρρύσατο) may be reflected in Paul's testimony that the

22. See, e.g., Windisch 45; Strachan 52.
23. See, e.g., Heinrici 65; Plummer 16, 19; Schmid 50.
24. "Paul intentionally uses the term θάνατος [in 1:10] instead of 'danger of death', since he already regarded himself as νεκρός" (Lietzmann 101).
25. NASB, NAB²; Barrett 57.
26. Weymouth, NJB; similarly Williams.

purpose of his θλῖψις with its attendant death-warrant was that he might not rely on himself but on God (2 Cor. 1:9).

That this malady was recurrent (or its effects chronic), that Paul's exposure to a particular mortal peril was not simply an event of the past but an ever-present reality, seems indicated by the present tenses of 1:4-6 (constant comfort corresponds to constant affliction), the perfective implications of ἐσχήκαμεν (see the commentary at 1:9), the twice-repeated ῥύσεται in 1:10, and perhaps the plural phrase (if it is the correct reading) ἐκ τηλικούτων θανάτων (1:10).

This theory, like all others, is not susceptible of proof,[27] but it has not lacked for proponents.[28] Its most enterprising advocate is W. M. Alexander, who, on the basis of τρὶς τὸν κύριον παρεκάλεσα in 2 Cor. 12:8, alleges that Paul suffered three assaults from his σκόλοψ τῇ σαρκί (2 Cor. 12:7). The first occurred in Cilicia in about 42 or 43, that is, fourteen years before 2 Corinthians was written (cf. 2 Cor. 12:2), the second in Pisidian Antioch (cf. Acts 13:13-14; Gal. 4:13) in 47, and the third and most severe in Troas (2 Cor. 1:8) in 56 or 57.[29]

Several observations support Alexander's theory. That the σκόλοψ τῇ σαρκί of 2 Cor. 12:7, the ἀσθένεια τῆς σαρκός of Gal. 4:13, and the θλῖψις ἡ ἐν τῇ Ἀσίᾳ of 2 Cor. 1:8 are to be associated seems highly probable.[30] And τρίς in 2 Cor. 12:8, rather than standing for πολλάκις or signifying "three times in succession on one occasion," may well point to three distinct occasions, after an assault of his malady, when Paul's prayers for the removal of the harassing ἄγγελος Σατανᾶ were especially urgent. Alexander's view supplies an adequate reason for the cessation of Paul's preaching in Troas (see 2 Cor. 2:12-13), and a contributing factor to Paul's restlessness of πνεῦμα and σάρξ in both Troas and Macedonia (2:13-14; 7:5) could well have been a prostrating attack of the σκόλοψ at Troas.

---

27. Four ostensible difficulties attend the view that the θλῖψις was an illness experienced only by Paul. (1) The plural is used throughout 1:8-11, which, if not an epistolary plural, must refer to more than one person. In response, see the introduction to 1:3-7. *Per contra* see Zahn 1.307, 316-18. (2) At first glance 1:6 appears to suggest that the Corinthians were currently experiencing exactly the same sufferings as Paul. For a reply, see the commentary at 1:6. (3) Would Paul have reckoned illness among "the sufferings of Christ" (an objection raised by Schmid 47, and others)? On this, see the discussion of τὰ παθήματα τοῦ Χριστοῦ at 1:5. Attention should also be given to the distinction between πᾶσα ἡ θλῖψις ἡμῶν (1:4; 7:4) and ἡ θλῖψις ἡμῶν ἡ γενομένη ἐν τῇ Ἀσίᾳ (1:8). It was not his Asian affliction in particular but all his afflictions in general, whatever their precise nature, which Paul counted among "the sufferings of Christ." (4) θλῖψις is not the normal term for an illness (Garland 76). But 7:5, where θλιβόμενοι includes ἔσωθεν φόβοι, suggests that in Paul's thought θλῖψις may refer to an inward state of affairs.

28. *Inter alios,* Alford 2.595-96; Lightfoot, *Galatians* 186; Findlay 94-98; "Paul" 711; Bernard 40-41; C. T. Wood 160; Allo 11-19; cf. 311, 320-21; Dodd 68 (Paul was "a man of generally sound constitution and great resistant and recuperative powers, but suffering from some physical disability which from time to time checked his efficiency and hindered his work"), 81; Clavier 77 n. 2; D. M. Stanley, *Boasting* 71 ("some incurable malady, which had at one point almost killed him"), 72 ("the fatal malady"); Harvey 20-21.

29. Alexander 469-73, 545-48.

30. Lightfoot, *Galatians* 186, 190; Allo 312; Dodd 67-68.

Before discovering Alexander's article, I had developed a similar theory, using the same basic data — the association of the θλῖψις of 2 Cor. 1:8 with the σκόλοψ of 2 Cor. 12:7, the use of τρίς in 2 Cor. 12:8, the reference to "fourteen years ago" in 2 Cor. 12:2, and Paul's remarkable suspension of preaching at both Perga (Acts 13:13-14) and Troas (2 Cor. 2:12-13). The one material difference between our proposals is my suggestion that the second of the three onsets of his malady was not an attack of Malta fever in Pisidian Antioch, as Alexander hypothesized,[31] but a severe occurrence at Perga of his chronic affliction which prevented or curtailed his intended evangelization in the province of Pamphylia and prompted his passage inland to Pisidian Antioch where he suffered a relapse of his malady (cf. Gal. 4:13-14).[32] On my hypothesis, then, the three attacks of Paul's σκόλοψ τῇ σαρκί were in Cilicia about 43 (fourteen years, by inclusive reckoning, before the writing of 2 Corinthians 12 in 56), in Perga (Acts 13:13-14) about 47, and in Troas (2 Cor. 1:8; 2:12; cf. 7:5), perhaps in the spring of 56, the most severe attack. The second and third of these illnesses would have several features in common: the attack frustrated a program of preaching that had been either commenced or planned and was followed by a convalescence that enabled Paul to undertake a journey of approximately one hundred miles (Perga to Pisidian Antioch, Troas to Philippi) and then a relapse when Paul was with sympathetic friends (the Galatians, the Philippians). Furthermore, Paul was careful to rectify at a later time the curtailment or abandonment of preaching activity in Perga and Troas (see Acts 14:25; 20:6-12).

Paul's Circumstances When the θλῖψις Occurred

In general terms, and apart from the particular hypothesis I have been seeking to defend, we have seen that the θλῖψις occurred between the writing of 1 Corinthians and Paul's departure for Macedonia from Troas.[33] In terms of Luke's historical framework in Acts, it fell between Acts 19:21 and 20:1,[34] that is, toward the end of or probably after Paul's two-year residence in Ephesus mentioned in Acts 19:10. It will therefore be appropriate to sketch Paul's circumstances at this period of his ministry so that we can appreciate the potent psychological factors that intensified the effect of the θλῖψις on Paul.[35]

31. Alexander contends that Paul suffered an attack in Antioch of a disease contracted in the lowlands of Pamphylia: the brevity of the sojourn in Perga (Acts 13:13-14) is attributed to the prevalence of an epidemic of Malta fever, and the eight-day journey from Perga to Antioch is compared with the ten-day period of incubation of that disease (545-46).

32. On Paul at Perga, see Ramsay 90-94.

33. See above, A.2.

34. We may infer from a comparison of 1 Cor. 16:3-4 (where Paul is unsure whether he will accompany the delegates going to Jerusalem with the collection) and Acts 19:21 (where he has resolved to go to Jerusalem) that the writing of 1 Corinthians took place before the time represented by Acts 19:21, but after a considerable period had been spent in Ephesus (cf. 1 Cor. 16:8-9).

35. This is altogether different from claiming that the severity of Paul's anguish concerning

To judge from numerous allusions in both 1 Corinthians and Acts,[36] Paul's sojourn in and around Ephesus was characterized not only by plentiful evangelistic opportunities but also by widespread opposition owing to his conspicuous success. Whether or not the Demetrius riot (Acts 19:23-41) actually precipitated his withdrawal from Ephesus, it must have formed the climax of the hostility directed against Paul by the devotees of Artemis, not to speak of opposition from Jews which Paul encountered in the city (Acts 20:19).

But even more disturbing for Paul than the situation which necessitated his premature exit from Ephesus was the crisis which had arisen at Corinth. The period after 1 Corinthians arrived in Corinth had been marked by a rapid deterioration of conditions in the church there. Rival minorities, pro- and anti-Pauline, were vying in an effort to win the support of the majority. Behind the anti-Paulinists stood a group of Judaizing interlopers from Palestine who were intent on undermining and usurping the authority of Paul in Corinth.

Such were Paul's circumstances toward the end of his Ephesian ministry — burgeoning opposition in Ephesus and an ever-worsening state of affairs in the church at Corinth. If we are right in suggesting that Paul's affliction befell him in Troas, sometime after his "painful visit" and the sending of the "sorrowful letter,"[37] we may delineate his situation in considerably more detail.

An indication of the intensity of Paul's anxiety at this time is afforded by three observations.[38] (1) In a manner quite uncharacteristic of a missionary who had recently asserted ἀνάγκη γάρ μοι ἐπίκειται· οὐαὶ γάρ μοί ἐστιν ἐὰν μὴ εὐαγγελίσωμαι (1 Cor. 9:16), Paul curtailed his evangelistic activity in Troas in spite of continuing preaching opportunities signally granted him in that city. This remarkable cessation of evangelism was occasioned by Paul's concern about the non-arrival of Titus with news of Corinth (2 Cor. 2:12-13) and possibly by an illness (= the θλῖψις). That Paul was somewhat embarrassed by his premature departure may be indicated by his particular mention of the reluctant farewell (ἀποταξάμενος αὐτοῖς [2 Cor. 2:13], the verb being a *hapax legomenon* in Paul). (2) Paul described his own state of mind on arrival in Macedonia (= Philippi) — as earlier in Troas and probably Ephesus — as one of despondency and depression (ταπεινός, 2 Cor. 7:5-6). He was not simply harassed by outward opposition (ἔξωθεν μάχαι); he was also perturbed by inward forebodings (ἔσωθεν φόβοι). Would his labor at Corinth prove in vain and his Jewish detractors finally prevail? Would his change of tactics — from personal intervention as on the "painful visit" to a vigorous epistolary assertion of au-

---

his estrangement from his Corinthian converts actually induced some form of sickness, implying that without this anxiety no illness, or at least only a milder form of it, would have occurred. Certainly, apprehension, however intense, is in itself an inadequate explanation of the language of 2 Corinthians 1 (*pace* Bean 12, 44-47).

36. 1 Cor. 4:9-13; 15:30-32; 16:9; Acts 20:18-21, 25, 31; cf. 2 Cor. 4:8-9.

37. See above, A.2 and B.1.

38. "It is at this point of his life more than at any other that he reveals to us his inner history" (E. Hatch, "Paul," in *EB* 3, col. 3616).

thority — in fact achieve the desired effect? Would his boasting to Titus of the Corinthians' responsiveness (2 Cor. 7:14) really prove justified? And would Titus, who had embarked on this delicate mission reluctantly and apprehensively (cf. 2 Cor. 7:7, 13, 15), actually be successful where (probably) Timothy had failed? (3) The sense of joyous relief evident in 2 Corinthians 1–7 is an accurate index of Paul's fretful tension until he was reunited with Titus and heard news of the favorable Corinthian response to the "letter of tears."

The Influence of the θλῖψις

An assessment of the influence of the θλῖψις on Paul's life and thought does not depend for its validity on a particular identification of the nature and time of the θλῖψις. The apostle's description of its subjective effects in 1:8-10 affords a more than adequate basis for relating the incident to the theology of 2 Corinthians.

It is clear from 2 Cor. 1:9 that the area of Christian experience most affected by the θλῖψις was his awareness of dependence on God. The affliction compelled him to abandon self-reliance and to entrust his life to the power of God. On the anvil of experience there had been forged a new regulative motto for his Christian life: ἡ ἱκανότης ἡμῶν ἐκ τοῦ θεοῦ, "our competency comes from God" (2 Cor. 3:5).[39]

But his thought as well as his experience was molded by the θλῖψις. The exegesis of 1:8-10 above and the remarks above under "A. Paul's Description of the θλῖψις" have shown that the apostle's "affliction in Asia" was essentially an encounter with death. If this dramatic confrontation was unique in his experience (see A.3.-4. above), it should occasion no surprise that the two areas of his thought most influenced were his understanding of the significance of physical death and his understanding of his own relation to the parousia.[40]

---

39. For further details, see the commentary at 1:9.

40. To the influence of Paul's Asian θλῖψις there have been traced other developments than those outlined in this Excursus. For example, behind 2 Cor. 1:8-10 W. E. Wilson (562-65) sees the arrest and imprisonment of Paul and his vivid expectation of death. "In this terrible experience the presence of Christ had been so strongly with him that he felt himself to be going through the very Passion itself, and then, as despair was turned into joy through release, his experience of return to life seemed like being raised with Christ" (564). From this one specific experience of "mortal distress and vital succor" arose Paul's doctrine of dying and rising again with Christ which, absent from 1 Corinthians, appears in 2 Corinthians yet in a less developed form than in Romans 6 and Colossians 2–3. 2 Cor. 5:14 ("We have reached this conviction, that one died for all, therefore all died") establishes the link between Paul's unique experience of deadly affliction and divine aid on the one hand, and on the other, "the calm assumption of Rom. 6 and Col. 2, that every Christian is united with Christ in death and resurrection" (564-65). With this theory, the validity of which depends on the late dating of Galatians, may be compared the proposal of Faw that "it was precisely at the period in his life when he gave up his expectation of being alive at the *Parousia* and accepted physical death as a part of his own future [2 Cor. 1:8-10] that Paul began to use the metaphor of death and resurrection to explain the various aspects of present religious experience" (296). But unlike Wilson (564) who finds the notion of resurrection in the divine deliverance Paul received (2 Cor.

The Nature and Consequences of the Believer's Physical Death

Allo maintained that "this epistle, so original from so many points of view, in several passages takes on a distinctive tone, a very special color, from the fact that Paul seems much more preoccupied here than elsewhere with his own uncertain physical state and with the idea of death" (18). So not without reason does Weinel observe that throughout 2 Corinthians can be heard "the rustling of the wings of the angel of death."[41] Nowhere is this rustling more strident than in 5:1-10, which deals with Christian confidence in the face of death.[42]

The Nature of Physical Death[43]

In 5:1a death is portrayed as *the destruction of a tent-dwelling*, the κατάλυσις of an οἰκία τοῦ σκήνους. Since the σκῆνος-concept remains in or near the foreground of Paul's thought throughout the passage (vv. 2, 4, 6-7), it may be that the καταλυθῆναι of v. 1 signifies the dismantling of a tent rather than simply the demolition of a building. If, however, ἐὰν ... καταλυθῇ refers generally both to the metaphors οἰκία and σκῆνος and to the σῶμα as the object signified, the κατάλυσις would merely denote "destruction" — whether of house, tent, or

---

1:10), Faw (297) associates the resurrection concept with Paul's release from anxiety in Macedonia when Titus arrived with news of the Corinthian repentance. More recently, Harvey has argued that the θλῖψις was a severe illness of some kind (20-21) which had several consequences. Economically, Paul would have been incapacitated for work and so his financial independence would be compromised (21-22). Socially, he would have received rebuffs and lost credibility, since illness was commonly seen as a consequence of wrongdoing (cf. Ps. 38:10-11) (22-23, 28). Personally, a critical illness would have prompted a loss of self-confidence, for a premature death would jeopardize his calling to preach the gospel throughout the Gentile world and frustrate his expectation of being alive at the parousia (23-28). Theologically, Paul's near-death experience in Asia radically affected his concept of suffering (1, 31, 63, 113, 118). "The way in which Paul had come to find a meaning in suffering after his experience of nearly dying was in the 'renewal' of the 'inner man'" (116). In and through the θλῖψις Paul discovered "a solidarity with Christ in *his* sufferings [cf. 1:5] and an interior renewal in counterpoint to the battering of his outward person [cf. 4:16] which meant that there was now no suffering beyond the reach of the 'consolation' offered by God through Christ" (118).

41. Weinel 379. See in particular 1:8-10; 4:10-12, 16; 5:1; 6:9; 11:23.

42. Being part of Paul's defense of the apostolic office (2 Cor. 2:14–6:10), 2 Cor. 5:1-10 has primary reference to the apostle himself (note especially φιλοτιμούμεθα in 5:9). Yet since the acquisition of a spiritual body (5:1), longing for inheritance (5:2), tent-dwelling (5:4), receipt of the Spirit (5:5), walking in the realm of faith (5:7), dwelling with Christ (5:8), and accountability to him (5:10) were not exclusively Pauline experiences or prerogatives, the whole passage was clearly applicable to the Corinthians and to Christians in general (cf. 2 Tim. 4:8). Paul's own experience was a paradigm of that of the ἄνθρωπος ἐν Χριστῷ. It is therefore assumed in this discussion that what Paul affirms in 5:1-10 concerning his own physical death is equally true of all Christians. But for the view that Paul regarded a martyr's death as bringing distinctive benefits, see Schweitzer 135-37; Pollard 240-51.

43. Elsewhere Paul speaks also of *spiritual death,* the alienation from God experienced by human beings and the hostility to God that is evident in their sin (Rom. 7:9, 24; Eph. 2:1-3; Col. 1:21), and of *death to sin,* that repudiation of sinful desires or unresponsiveness to the appeal and power of sin that marks ideal Christian experience (Rom. 6:6-7, 11-13; Col. 3:5).

body. Paul describes the οἰκία that is destroyed by death as ἐπίγειος. That is, death involves the loss not only of physical corporeality but also of earthly corporateness. These two losses are, of course, interrelated, for since death deprives people of the σῶμα ψυχικόν, the organ of their relationship with other human beings, it also involves the forfeiture of "psychical" corporateness. But although at death Christians cease to be ἐν σαρκί, they do not cease to be ἐν Χριστῷ.

Paul's second description of the nature of death is this: it is *departure from mortal embodiment,* an ἐκδημία from a σῶμα (5:8a). Structurally, v. 8 is in antithetic parallelism with v. 6. The basic contrast is not between two modes of human existence (ἐν τῷ σώματι and ἐκ τοῦ σώματος) or two possible relationships with ὁ κύριος (ἀπὸ τοῦ κυρίου and πρὸς τὸν κύριον) but between successive spheres of Christian residence (ἐν τῷ σώματι and πρὸς τὸν κύριον). Residence in the body (v. 6a) implies absence from the Lord's immediate presence, while residence with the Lord (v. 8b) implies absence from mortal corporeality.

On the basis of this realization, Paul expresses his preference (εὐδοκοῦμεν μᾶλλον, v. 8) to leave earthly existence behind in order to participate exclusively in the heavenly life. Basically, the object of his preference was positive, not negative: residence with the Lord, not emancipation from corporeality as such. He did not share the Orphic sentiment, σῶμα σῆμα ("the body is a tomb"), but envisaged the Christian *summum bonum* in terms of the possession of a spiritual corporeality perfectly suited to the ecology of heaven.

The Consequences of Death

2 Cor. 5:1-10 specifies at least three consequences of the believer's death, but commentators differ on whether each consequence is experienced at the moment of death or only at the second advent.

Possession of a building from God (5:1b). Paul expresses the first result of the advent of death in the phrase οἰκοδομὴν ἐκ θεοῦ ἔχειν. This building provided by God and possessed by the believer is almost certainly the believer's resurrection body.[44] Since the ἐπίγειος οἰκία of 5:1a cannot be distinguished from the physical body referred to in 4:10-11, 16, it is likely that the parallel expression in 5:1b, οἰκοδομὴν ἐκ θεοῦ, refers to another type of personal embodiment, the σῶμα πνευματικόν (1 Cor. 15:44), especially since the fourfold description of the οἰκοδομή in 5:1b corresponds precisely to four characteristics of the celestial body mentioned in 1 Corinthians 15: both are "from God" (1 Cor. 15:38), spiritual (1 Cor. 15:44, 46), indestructible (1 Cor. 15:42, 52-54), and heavenly (1 Cor. 15:40, 48-49).

Dwelling in the presence of the Lord (5:8b). After the ἐκδημία, which occurred at death, Paul foresaw an ἐνδημῆσαι (and by implication an ἐνδημεῖν)

---

44. See the discussion of the options in the commentary on 5:1.

πρὸς τὸν κύριον (5:8b), which forms the second outcome of death depicted in 2 Corinthians 5. Just as no rigid temporal distinction can be drawn between the κατάλυσις of v. 1 and the ἐκδημία of v. 8, so it seems unnatural to imagine that a period of time, whether brief or prolonged, intervenes between the ἐκδημῆσαι of v. 8a and the ἐνδημῆσαι of v. 8b. Two contextual observations confirm that dwelling in the Lord's presence is the believer's experience immediately after his death. First, v. 6 states that residence in a physical body is contemporaneous with absence from the immediate presence of the Lord, clearly implying that when the former ceases, so also does the latter. What v. 6 implies, v. 8 states positively. Secondly, in v. 7 walking διὰ πίστεως and walking διὰ εἴδους are presented as opposites, with no interval posited between the end of the one and the beginning of the other. To cease walking in the realm of faith was to commence that life in the realm of sight, which v. 8b defines as ἐνδημεῖν πρὸς τὸν κύριον and Phil. 1:23 as σὺν Χριστῷ εἶναι. While Paul saw death as the end of earthly life, it meant the enrichment, not the negation, of life itself. Death allows ἐν Χριστῷ corporeality to achieve its goal in consummated σὺν Χριστῷ fellowship. Death may terminate the pilgrimage of faith, but it inaugurates the beatific *visio Christi*.

Appearance before Christ's tribunal (5:10). The purpose of this compulsory appearance in the court of heaven (τὸ φανερωθῆναι ἔμπροσθεν τοῦ βήματος τοῦ Χριστοῦ) is individual and just recompense, exact requital for actions, whether good or bad, performed by means of the earthly body and therefore during life on earth.

As Paul describes physical death in 2 Cor. 5:1-10, we should carefully distinguish what death *is* from what death immediately or eventually *brings*. By its nature, death is negative, being a κατάλυσις and an ἐκδημία, a destruction and a departure. In its results, death is positive, leading to an ἔχειν, an ἐνδημεῖν, and an φανερωθῆναι, a possession, a residence, and an appearance. On the essential ingredients of the Christian view of physical death, see the discussion of the end of the commentary on 5:8.

Paul's Relation to the Parousia

"For we know," Paul writes in 2 Cor. 5:1, "that if our earthly tent-dwelling is destroyed, we have a building provided by God, a permanent heavenly house not built by human hands." The protasis of this sentence, ἐὰν . . . καταλυθῇ, should not be treated as concessive ("even if . . ."), not only because such a meaning of a simple ἐὰν is unparalleled, but also because so far from there being any indication in the context that Paul is merely envisaging his death as a remote and almost hypothetical possibility, 2 Cor. 4:10-12, 14, 16 points to the apostle's awareness that at any time in the near future the ἐνέργεια τοῦ θανάτου (2 Cor. 4:12) could reach its climax in his actual death. Also, since Paul believed in the universality of death, the protasis cannot mean simply "if I die," but only "if I die

(before the parousia)" or "when(ever) I die."[45] That is, at the time of the composition of 2 Corinthians (or at least of chs. 1–9), his pre-parousia decease seemed
to him more probable than his survival until the advent. In particular, 2 Cor. 4:14
apparently presupposes that his περιφέρειν of the νέκρωσις of Jesus (2 Cor. 4:10)
and the ἐνέργεια τοῦ θανάτου within him (2 Cor. 4:12) would ultimately issue in
his death, but just as the preservation of his life amid apostolic tribulation witnessed to the resurrection power of Jesus (2 Cor. 4:8-11; cf. Phil. 3:10), so his
preservation in death through a resurrection like Christ's (cf. σὺν Ἰησοῦ, 2 Cor.
4:14) would testify to God's transcendent power (vv. 7, 14). Although the distinction between ἡμεῖς and ὑμεῖς in 4:12, 14 (cf. 1:14) need not imply that Paul
expected that the Corinthians, unlike himself, would be spared death before the
parousia, it certainly suggests that he was reckoning himself among those destined to be raised as well as transformed.

There is compelling evidence, on the other hand, that before the time of
2 Corinthians, Paul reckoned on the probability of his own survival until the advent.[46] In 1 Thessalonians 4, in the course of his reply to Thessalonian Christians who were grieving over the pre-advent death of fellow believers who, they
feared, had thereby forfeited the right to share in the parousial glory of Christ,
Paul twice uses the expression ἡμεῖς οἱ ζῶντες οἱ περιλειπόμενοι (εἰς τὴν
παρουσίαν τοῦ κυρίου) (vv. 15, 17). It cannot be claimed that, because neither
writer(s) nor addressees had already died, ἡμεῖς was an inevitable designation,
for subsequently Paul classed himself with the dead (see 1 Cor. 6:14; 2 Cor.
4:14; Phil. 3:11). Nor need the use of ἡμεῖς imply that Paul believed in a fixity
within the two designated groups (οἱ ζῶντες and οἱ νεκροί) since presumably he
was not merely comforting the Thessalonians concerning the past but also reassuring them for the future: they were to cease mourning (ἵνα μὴ λυπῆσθε,
1 Thess. 4:13) for those of their numbers who had died and never recommence
mourning should others die (cf. οἱ κοιμώμενοι, v. 13; 5:10). Yet 1 Thess. 4:15
provides more than a general and impersonal statement of the two categories of
Christians at the advent.[47] οἱ ζῶντες are identified, not merely as "those alive at
the coming of the Lord" (as if Paul had written simply οἱ ζῶντες ἐν τῇ παρουσίᾳ
τοῦ κυρίου), but as "we who shall continue living until (εἰς)[48] the Lord's ad-

45. See the commentary on 5:1.

46. For the purposes of this discussion, it is assumed that 1 Corinthians 15 was penned after
1 Thessalonians 4 and before 2 Corinthians 5 and that the date of Philippians is subsequent to the
second Corinthian epistle. No scholar known to the present writer (except Schmithals, *Gnostics*
245-46) accepts the authenticity of these three epistles, but rejects the sequence 1 Thessalonians 4–
1 Corinthians 15–2 Corinthians 5. Particularly when the Roman provenance and therefore late dating of Philippians are assumed, the implications of a Ephesian dating immediately before or after
1 Corinthians should not be ignored. See below (n. 55) and also Hoffmann 323-29.

47. *Pace* Moore 110.

48. εἰς τὴν παρουσίαν (τοῦ κυρίου), which should be construed with οἱ περιλειπόμενοι and
not (as Wimmer 275-76, 285) with οὐ μὴ φθάσωμεν, is not simply the equivalent of ἐν τῇ παρουσίᾳ
(cf. 1 Thess. 2:19; 3:13; 5:23; 1 Cor. 15:23) but specifies the temporal limit (εἰς) of περιλείπεσθαι.
"Paul is not prone to confuse εἰς and ἐν" (Turner 256).

vent." The asyndetic οἱ περιλειπόμενοι is epexegetic, further describing the ἡμεῖς οἱ ζῶντες: "we who are now[49] alive, [namely those] who are destined to survive until the parousia."

The interpretation of 1 Cor. 15:51 bristles with problems. The original text, it seems, read ἰδοὺ μυστήριον ὑμῖν λέγω. πάντες οὐ κοιμηθησόμεθα, πάντες δὲ ἀλλαγησόμεθα.[50] But does the enigmatic phrase πάντες οὐ κοιμηθησόμεθα, which, to judge by the textual variants, caused considerable difficulty to the scribes, signify universal survival until the parousia, universal escape from death at the parousia, majority survival until the parousia, minority survival until the parousia, or the survival of at least some Christians until the parousia? If, as the majority of grammarians believe,[51] πάντες οὐ is equivalent to οὐ πάντες, the first two views are excluded. Again, on the last interpretation ("[Christians such as] we shall not all fall asleep") it is difficult adequately to explain why Paul did not write πάντες οὐ κοιμηθήσονται or simply οἱ ζῶντες ἀλλαγήσονται. The viable alternatives, then, are: (1) "*not* all of us [presently alive] shall fall asleep," that is, while some of us may die, most of us will not, and (2) "we shall not, *all* of us [presently alive], fall asleep," that is, while most of us will die, some of us will not. Two observations favor the latter view (minority survival until the parousia): in a negative sentence, πάντες may stand for τινές; in writing πάντες οὐ, and not, as logic might have demanded, οὐ πάντες, Paul probably intended the emphasis to be placed on πάντες (note the πάντες . . . πάντες parallelism), rather than on the negative.

For the exegesis of the concluding clause of 1 Cor. 15:51 (πάντες δὲ ἀλλαγησόμεθα), the most secure point of orientation is undoubtedly the parallel expression ἡμεῖς ἀλλαγησόμεθα in v. 52, where ἡμεῖς and οἱ νεκροί are contrasted. Thus the "we shall be changed" of v. 52 would indicate that the "we shall all be changed" of v. 51 refers to the universal transformation of Christians alive at the parousia, rather than to the transformation of all Christians, survivors and deceased, at the parousia. On this showing, the essence of the μυστήριον was not that a transformation of both the living and the dead was to occur immediately at the parousia,[52] but rather that those Christians who did not, by a pre-parousia death, qualify for the transformation which was the prerequisite for the inheritance of the kingdom (1 Cor. 15:36, 50), nevertheless would all, without exception, undergo the required transformation at the parousia.

"While we who are now alive shall not *all* fall asleep, *all* of us who survive until the parousia will be changed." πάντες οὐ κοιμηθησόμεθα shows that

---

49. While Prat (1.76 n. 1) claims that ἁρπαγησόμεθα in 1 Thess. 4:17 gives to both ἡμεῖς οἱ ζῶντες *(nos viventes)* and (ἡμεῖς) οἱ περιλειπόμενοι *(nos superstites)* its future connotation, Rigaux *(Thessaloniciens* 540) comments, "We willingly admit that the present tenses ought to be understood as such and not as 'those who will be alive at the parousia'."

50. See Metzger 502.

51. See, e.g., BDF §433(2); Turner 287.

52. As Jeremias (159) proposes.

Paul now regarded survival until the parousia — and not, as in 1 Thessalonians 4, death before the parousia — as an exceptional experience among Christians in general,[53] while πάντες δὲ ἀλλαγησόμεθα, when compared with ἡμεῖς ἀλλαγησόμεθα in v. 52, indicates that he could still classify himself with those who would remain alive until the advent.

But even when Paul could reckon on his survival until the parousia, along with a majority (as in 1 Thess. 4:15, 17) or a minority (as in 1 Cor. 15:51-52) of Christians, he did not discount the possibility of his being "poured out as a libation." In 1 Thess. 5:9-10 he speaks of "our Lord Jesus Christ who died for us, so that whether we are awake or asleep we may live with him" (NRSV). In spite of the potent arguments that may be adduced in favor of the view that γρηγορεῖν and καθεύδειν here allude, possibly in a proverbial expression, to being awake and being asleep (in a physical sense), the context of 1 Thess. 4:13–5:11 supports the traditional exegesis in which γρηγορεῖν and καθεύδειν specify, in the manner of οἱ ζῶντες οἱ περιλειπόμενοι and οἱ κοιμηθέντες (= οἱ νεκροί) in 1 Thess. 4:13-17, the two categories of believers at the parousia.[54] But here, be it noted, Paul is simply stating alternative possibilities (εἴτε γρηγορῶμεν εἴτε καθεύδωμεν), not expressing his personal expectancy (as in 1 Thessalonians 4 and 1 Corinthians 15) or reckoning with the implications of a distinct probability (as in 2 Corinthians 5). Again, with its assertion "God raised the Lord and will raise us up in turn by his power," 1 Cor. 6:14 is equally clear evidence that Paul always perceived that pre-parousia death was not impossible for himself or any Christian. In this matter of Paul's "life expectancy" it is appropriate only to speak of possibilities or probabilities, never of certainties.

2 Corinthians 5, therefore, marks a decisive turning point in the apostle's estimate of his own relation to the parousia.[55] No longer is his pre-advent decease a possibility more hypothetical than real. For the first time — to judge by the extant Pauline epistles — he has begun to reckon with the implications of that possibility, a possibility which had ceased to be a distant reality by becoming a probability.[56]

Moreover, evidence is not lacking to suggest that after the turning point represented by 2 Corinthians, Paul continued to regard his survival until the

53. Thus also Dodd 110; Barrett, "Eschatology" 143; *1 Corinthians* 380.

54. Thus, e.g., Guntermann 50, 283, 290.

55. If, however, Philippians is dated before 2 Corinthians, the significance of 2 Corinthians 5 would be eclipsed since Phil. 1:19-26; 3:11 shows Paul seriously reckoning with the possibility of a pre-advent decease.

56. It should be observed that to assert that Paul has now come to realize that he will probably die before the parousia does not necessarily imply that he has recognized "the necessity to reconcile himself to death as a physical event" (Davies 319) or "has ceased rebelling against the idea of his premature death" (Héring 5, who renders 2 Cor. 1:9a, "But in our innermost heart we have accepted the sentence of death"; cf. Kümmel 197). The new realization accorded Paul need not be thought of as ending any supposed period of resistance to the reality of his own death. 2 Cor. 1:8-10 does not describe so much the termination of a struggle as submission to the will of the One whose ways are inscrutable (cf. Rom. 11:33).

advent as less probable than his death. Rom. 6:5, with its assurance that Christians are destined to experience a resurrection ἐκ νεκρῶν comparable to Christ's, seems to presuppose that Paul was anticipating a pre-parousia death for himself and his readers. Again, in itself the argument of Romans 11 does not necessitate a prolonged interval before the parousia and the prior intervention of Paul's death, but as Dodd comments, "The forecast of history in chap. xi is hardly framed for a period of a few months or years."[57] The testimony of Phil. 1:19-26 on this point is indecisive. Here, reckoning with the possibility of his experiencing a martyr's death in the near future (cf. Phil. 2:23-24), Paul expresses his earnest wish that he might glorify Christ whether by living or by dying (v. 20). Subjectively, his desire tended to be that the glorification of Christ should be accomplished by his death, since that also effected his departure to Christ's presence. But although, in actual fact, either alternative — death or life, execution or release — could be his experience in the immediate and uncertain future, in vv. 25-26 (and possibly v. 19; cf. 2:24), perhaps optimistically, he expresses an assurance (οἶδα) of the successful outcome of his trial and therefore the preservation of his life, which he grounds (τοῦτο πεποιθώς, v. 25) objectively on the pastoral needs of the Philippian church (v. 24). Phil. 3:11 seems more conclusive, however. The element of doubt inseparable from εἴ πως testifies to Paul's self-distrust and modesty of hope, not to any uncertainty of his own salvation and certainly not to the improbability of his dying before the advent. Compared with 1 Cor. 6:14 ("God will raise us"), this verse states Paul's resurrection hope personally (". . . that if possible I may attain the resurrection from the dead"), the apostle apparently assuming that he himself would enter the heavenly commonwealth after first dying. Here is no general "whether we are awake or asleep" (1 Thess. 5:10) but a personal statement which proposes no alternatives. Paul's death, whether by martyrdom or not, would consummate his participation in Christ's sufferings during his life (cf. Phil. 3:10).

When we turn to the Pastoral Epistles, the overall situation is no different. References to "later times" (ἐν ὑστέροις καιροῖς, 1 Tim. 4:1) or "the last days" (ἐν ἐσχάταις ἡμέραις, 2 Tim. 3:1) do not imply the temporal proximity of the parousia but describe the whole period between the two advents of Christ ("the last days") or an indefinite period prior to the second advent ("later times"). The appearing of the Lord Jesus Christ will occur simply "at the proper time," "in due time" (καιροῖς ἰδίοις, 1 Tim. 6:15). Whatever the interval (one to two years?) between the writing of these letters, when Paul pens 2 Timothy he knows that his death is imminent — yet assumes his ultimate participation in the Day of the Lord (2 Tim. 4:6, 8).

On no reading of the evidence can it be claimed that the theology of death reflected in 2 Corinthians 5 rendered superfluous the notion of the future parousia. In each of his epistles written after 2 Corinthians (except for the brief

57. Dodd, *Romans* 209.

letter to Philemon) Paul's eager longing for the day of Christ finds expression.[58] Paul's advent hope never receded, as is frequently asserted,[59] from the foreground to the background of his thought.

We may now sum up this discussion of the influence of Paul's Asian θλῖψις. By his own confession it caused him to surrender his self-reliance before God's infinitely greater power (2 Cor. 1:9). It is also probable that as a consequence of recognizing that any future θλῖψις comparable to that from which he had just been delivered could bring him death (cf. 2 Cor. 5:1), he was forced to relinquish his expectation (although not this hope) of surviving until the parousia and to consider as never before the significance of death for the Christian believer.[60]

B. Paul's Conduct Defended (1:12–2:13)

Evidently Paul's conduct as a pastor had recently come under the careful scrutiny of the Corinthians, friends and foes alike. Charged by some Corinthians with being fickle, insensitive, and domineering, Paul was obliged to rally to his own defense. He asserts that so far from indicating capriciousness or overlordship, his recent relations with the church at Corinth had demonstrated his pastoral concern and fatherly love. Any apparent indications to the contrary, such as changes of travel plans, a stern letter, or a call for church discipline, should be seen in this light.

1. Characteristics of His Conduct (1:12-14)

Before he defends himself against the specific charges of vacillation and domineering brought by his opponents (1:15–2:11), Paul deals with two more general accusations: that he had acted shamelessly, insincerely, and with worldly shrewdness in his relations with the Corinthians (cf. 1:12) and that in his letters he had been evasive by writing one thing but meaning or intending another (cf.

---

58. See, in probable order of the time of writing, 2 Cor. 1:14; Rom. 2:5, 16; 13:12-13; Col. 3:4; Eph. 4:30; Phil. 1:6, 10; 2:16; 1 Tim. 6:14-15; Tit. 2:13; 2 Tim. 1:12, 18; 4:1, 8.

59. See, e.g., Hunter 149.

60. It is sometimes objected that personal experience could never have granted Paul insights which his pastoral concern had failed to prompt. "Can any one who knows the kind of man Paul was deliberately suggest that fear and self-pity conferred on him an enlargement of spiritual vision which no sympathy for bereaved disciples, and no sense of fellowship with those who had fallen asleep in Jesus, availed to bestow?" (Denney 761; similarly Berry 61). However, that a shattering encounter with death should cause Paul to ponder more deeply than before on death and the *post mortem* state of the believer, and that such reflection should, under God, deepen his eschatological insight cannot be dismissed as improbable, especially since previously the state of believers after death had not become a pressing, personal issue for him (cf. Dupont, *Union* 170 n. 1, 186) as he was expecting to be found among believers who survived to witness the parousia.

1:13a). These baseless charges Paul answers in the only way possible for him — by appealing to the testimony of his own conscience (1:12) and the Corinthians' knowledge of his conduct (1:13b-14).

Given the close verbal and conceptual links between 1:3-7 and 1:8-11, those two paragraphs should be taken together, with 1:12 commencing the main body of the letter.[1]

12*Now our boast is this — the witness borne by our conscience, that we have conducted ourselves in the world, and especially in our relations with you, in godly holiness[a] and sincerity, not[b] with worldly[c] wisdom but relying on God's grace.* 13a*For we do not write anything different from what[d] you read or[e] indeed understand.* 13b-14*And I hope that just as you have understood us partially, so you will indeed come to understand fully that you can be proud of us, just as we in turn shall be proud of you on the Day of our[f] Lord Jesus.*

TEXTUAL NOTES

a. Reading ἁγιότητι ("holiness"), with Hughes, 25-26 n. 2, and Thrall "2 Cor. 1:12." ἁπλότητι ("simplicity," "integrity") is preferred by O. Procksch, *TDNT* 1.114; Schlatter 471-73; Amstutz, 49-50; Eckstein 193 n. 65; and UBS[1, 2, 3] with a "D" rating (= "a very high degree of doubt concerning the reading selected for the text") and UBS[4] with a "B" rating (= "the text is almost certain"!). The issue is delicately balanced. Transcriptional probabilities prove indecisive, for scribal confusion could operate in either direction (ΑΠΛΟΤΗΤΙ → ΑΠΟΤΗΤΙ → ΑΓΙΟΤΗΤΙ, or ΑΓΙΟΤΗΤΙ → ΑΠΟΤΗΤΙ → ΑΠΛΟΤΗΤΙ). The main arguments in favor of ἁπλότητι may be summarized thus. (1) This reading has wide geographical support: secondary Alexandrian (104), Western (D F G it), and Byzantine (424* *Byz Lect*). (2) A reference to "simplicity" rather than "holiness" affords the necessary contrast with the following ἐν σοφίᾳ σαρκικῇ and the allusion to duplicity in v. 13 (but see Thrall, "2 Cor. 1:12" 370-72). (3) There are four other uses of ἁπλότης in 2 Corinthians (8:2; 9:11, 13; 11:3; cf. Rom. 12:8; Eph. 6:5; Col. 3:22) (but see Thrall, "2 Cor. 1:12" 368-70). (4) "Since ἁγιότης denotes a state, but εἰλικρινία (as sincerity) a disposition (1 C. 5:8; 2 C. 2:17) never elsewhere ascribed to God (cf. Phil. 1:10; 2 Pt. 3:1), the well-attested reading [ἁγιότητι] is questionable" (O. Procksch, *TDNT* 1.114). Supporting ἁγιότητι are the following considerations. (1) This reading enjoys proto-Alexandrian (p[46] ℵ* B 1739) and later Alexandrian (A C Ψ 0243 33 81 1175 1881) support, as well as some representation in the Western (it[r]) and Byzantine (K) textual families. (2) ἁγιότης is a *hapax legomenon* in Paul (cf. the seven Pauline uses of ἁπλότης) and therefore *lectio difficilior*. (3) In using ἁγιότης ("moral purity") Paul may be defending himself against the accusation of corrupt practice with regard to the collection (cf. 2 Cor. 2:16; 4:2) (Thrall, "2 Cor. 1:12" 371-72).

b. Some early MSS (ℵ A C) omit καί, perhaps to draw attention by asyndeton to the parallelism between the ἐν phrases, but the conjunction should be retained (p[46] B 1739) as the more difficult reading, although it need not be reflected in translation.

1. So also Furnish 112. But against the prevailing view that the body of the letter begins at 1:12 after the thanksgiving formula of 1:11, Belleville argues that the disclosure formula of 1:8 marks the beginning of the letter's body ("Letter" 145-49).

c. Two ninth-century Western uncials (F G) substitute σαρκίνῃ for σαρκικῇ. Although σάρκινος can mean "made of flesh," both adjectives here mean "belonging to the realm of the flesh" (see BAGD 743a).

d. The cumbersome combination ἀλλ' ἢ ἅ, read by ℵ B C Ψ *al*, prompted some scribe(s) to drop ἀλλά (F G), some to omit ἢ (p⁴⁶ 33 *pc* syr), and some ἅ (D* 1739 *pc*), while Codex Alexandrinus omits ἢ ἅ.

e. p⁴⁶ B 104 *pc* bo^ms omit ἢ καὶ ἐπιγινώσκετε, probably through *homoioteleuton*, but possibly because this phrase was regarded as tautologous.

f. Although there is early and wide support for τοῦ κυρίου (preferred by UBS[1, 2] with a "C" rating), the longer reading τοῦ κυρίου ἡμῶν (UBS[3, 4], with ἡμῶν bracketed and a "C" rating given) is slightly superior, given the strength of the external evidence (including ℵ B 0243 33 81 104 1175 1739 1881 [all Alexandrian] and F G it [Western]) and the rarity of the formula "our Lord Jesus."

1:12 Ἡ γὰρ καύχησις ἡμῶν αὕτη ἐστίν, τὸ μαρτύριον τῆς συνειδήσεως ἡμῶν. "Now our boast is this — the witness borne by our conscience. . . ." It is possible that γάρ introduces the basis of Paul's confidence in the Corinthians' cooperation in prayer (1:11),[2] but more probably this conjunction functions here as a loose connective, equivalent to δέ ("now").[3] If there be a distinction between the καύχησις of v. 12 and the καύχημα of v. 14 (which together form an *inclusio*), the former word will denote the act of boasting and the latter the ground or content of boasting, reflecting the general distinction between -σις and -μα substantival endings.[4] However, such a distinction seems inapplicable here, for καύχησις in v. 12 signifies the ground or basis for boasting ("the reason for our exultation," Berkeley),[5] or, better, the content or object of boasting ("what we boast about[6]/are proud of").[7] Following the prospective αὕτη, the phrase τὸ μαρτύριον τῆς συνειδήσεως ἡμῶν defines what Paul is proud of,[8] "the testimony that our conscience gives" (BAGD 494a), or simply, "what my conscience tells me" (Goodspeed).[9] Sometimes an objective genitive follows μαρτύριον and refers, for example, to testimony about the resurrection (Acts 4:33) or Christ (1 Cor. 1:6), but here the genitive τῆς συνειδήσεως is subjective.

Behind the term συνείδησις lies the verbal expression σύν-οιδα ἐμαυτῷ, literally, "I know with myself," and thus "I am conscious." When the information imparted to oneself falls within the ethical realm, συνείδησις denotes not merely

---

2. It is unnecessary, with R. Bultmann (*TDNT* 3.651 n. 45), to regard v. 12 with its reference to καύχησις as Paul's response to an anticipated misunderstanding of v. 11, namely that his claim that the Corinthians had a duty to thank God for τὸ εἰς ἡμᾶς χάρισμα amounted to boasting.

3. For this usage, see BAGD 152c; Zerwick §473.

4. On this latter point, see BDF §109 (2, 4).

5. Similarly Zerwick and Grosvenor 535 ("reason for boasting").

6. So Louw and Nida §33.371.

7. So also BAGD 426b. Elsewhere in 2 Corinthians καύχησις refers to the act of boasting (7:4, 14; 8:24; 11:10, 17).

8. This relation may be indicated by a dash (Barclay), a colon (Barrett 68), or the word "namely" (NJB).

9. Cf. Rom. 9:1, συμμαρτυρούσης μοι τῆς συνειδήσεώς μου (similarly Rom. 2:15).

"awareness" or "consciousness" but "moral consciousness" or "conscience" or "self-awareness before God." Twenty of the thirty NT uses of the word are Pauline, and it is probable that it entered Paul's vocabulary — and Christian vocabulary — not from Hellenistic popular philosophy but as a result of the Corinthian dispute about εἰδωλόθυτα.[10] Plummer defines the term as "reflexion on the value of the actions which we are conscious of doing" (24), while Furnish describes the general Pauline meaning, apart from the distinctive use in 1 Corinthians in reference to "food offered to idols," as "the human faculty of critical self-evaluation" (127). Crucial in this self-evaluation is awareness of divine norms (cf. 1 Pet. 2:19), whether the Mosaic Law in the case of Jews, or "what the Law requires," which is written on the hearts of Gentiles (Rom. 2:12-15).

ὅτι ἐν ἁγιότητι καὶ εἰλικρινείᾳ τοῦ θεοῦ, καὶ οὐκ ἐν σοφίᾳ σαρκικῇ ἀλλ' ἐν χάριτι θεοῦ, ἀνεστράφημεν ἐν τῷ κόσμῳ, περισσοτέρως δὲ πρὸς ὑμᾶς. "That we have conducted ourselves in the world, and especially in our relations with you, in godly holiness and sincerity, not with worldly wisdom but relying on God's grace." Just as in the first part of this verse, where τὸ μαρτύριον κτλ. defines ἡ καύχησις ἡμῶν, so here this ὅτι clause defines μαρτύριον.[11] Reasons for preferring the reading ἁγιότητι ("holiness") have been given in textual note a. above. But if ἁπλότητι is preferred, Paul would be appealing to the "simplicity" of his conduct, his "singleness of purpose" (Isaacs) or "single-minded commitment,"[12] the absence of any duplicity or deviousness on his part. Closely associated (note the single preposition) with Paul's moral purity was his absolute transparency (εἰλικρίνεια). This latter word is derived from εἴλη ("the sun's heat") and κρίνω ("I judge"), denoting the state of something which has survived the searching and searing light of the sun, "judged by the sun's splendor/heat"; thus "sincerity," "ingenuousness." Both "holiness" and "sincerity" are qualified by τοῦ θεοῦ, a genitive that may be construed in three ways, although the third option seems preferable: (1) objective,[13] "before God," "in the sight of God," equivalent to κατέναντι θεοῦ (2:17; 12:19) or ἐνώπιον τοῦ θεοῦ (4:2; 7:12); (2) subjective, "God-given" (Plummer 25), "inspired by God" (TCNT); (3) adjectival, "godly," "like that of God" (Martin 18). Although ἐν could denote attendant circumstances ("[our conduct was] marked by"), more probably it is either instrumental, depicting the impelling force or governing principles behind Paul's pastoral ministry ("[our conduct was] guided by," Cassirer; "prompted by," NAB[1]; "governed by," NEB) or local, describing the sphere in which Paul operated ("we have conducted ourselves in . . .").

10. Note the use of συνείδησις in 1 Cor. 8:7, 10, 12; 10:25, 27, 28, 29 (twice). For literature on this term, see G. Lüdemann, *EDNT* 3.301, supplemented by Fee 380 n. 24.

11. It is not impossible that ὅτι κτλ. defines ἡ . . . καύχησις . . . αὕτη, with τὸ μαρτύριον κτλ. being parenthetical ("The only boast we make is this — and it is backed by the witness of our conscience — that . . . ," Barclay), but the Greek word order makes this unlikely; also, in that case a genitive absolute construction might have been expected, as in Rom. 2:15; 9:1.

12. Young and Ford 262-63.

13. Thus Williams, Bruce (*Paraphrase* 127), and Eckstein 194.

In the second word-pair of this verse, σοφία-χάρις, a stark contrast (οὐκ . . . ἀλλά) is drawn between "worldly shrewdness" (Goodspeed) or "human cleverness" (ἐν σοφίᾳ σαρκικῇ) and "divine grace" (Berkeley) or "God's grace" (ἐν χάριτι θεοῦ). With the former ἐν is modal, "with worldly wisdom"; with the latter, instrumental, "but relying on God's gracious help." In general, the adjective σαρκικός denotes what belongs exclusively to the natural order ("human," "worldly"). But because σάρξ is the seat of sin (Rom. 7:17-18, 23, 25), in Paul's usage σαρκικός sometimes gains the pejorative sense of "guided by sinful passions" (1 Cor. 3:3 twice). Here it imparts to σοφία the negative connotation of "cunning" or "shrewdness."

Of the three principal NT verbs referring to general human behavior, περιπατέω ("walk") and πορεύομαι ("live") reflect Hebrew usage *(hālak),* while ἀναστρέφομαι ("behave") is a natural Greek idiom.[14] As a constative aorist, ἀνεστράφημεν looks back over the entirety of Paul's life as a Christian in a single, comprehensive glance. ἐν τῷ κοσμῷ means "in the world" in the sense of "among my fellow human beings" or simply "among people." Whether περισσοτέρως is a comparative adverb meaning "even more," or is equivalent to an elative superlative, "above all," "most of all,"[15] "especially" (NIV), there is no contrast between Paul's conduct "in the (outside) world" and his behavior toward the Corinthians. Rather, πρὸς ὑμᾶς ("in our dealings with you") specifies one group within the category of "people" (κόσμος), so that περισσοτέρως δέ means "and especially," not "but particularly." Certainly the apostle is not suggesting that he operated on different principles of conduct depending on his observers, being scrupulous in his relations with believers and less scrupulous before unbelievers. It was because Paul had poured his energy into his pastoral work at Corinth over a prolonged period (Acts 18:11, 18) that the Corinthians had more opportunity than others to observe the integrity of his conduct and way of life. So it is that Paul's appeal to his own conscience in this verse indirectly becomes an appeal to the Corinthians' conscience.

There are occasions when Christians, confronted by groundless accusations of impropriety of conduct, are justified in appealing to their motives for acting in a particular way. An unjustifiable stigma that may have become attached to a certain course of action may sometimes be removed by a frank appeal to one's clear conscience over the behavior in question.

1:13a οὐ γὰρ ἄλλα γράφομεν ὑμῖν ἀλλ᾽ ἢ ἃ ἀναγινώσκετε ἢ καὶ ἐπιγινώσκετε. "For we do not write anything different from what you read or indeed understand." Paul has just affirmed that his actions have always been impelled by God's grace, not marked by scheming calculation. He now affords evidence (γάρ) for this affirmation.[16] In none of his previous correspondence — the "previous letter," 1 Corinthians, or the "severe let-

14. See Deissmann 88, 194; MM 38.
15. As Zerwick, *Analysis* 392.
16. Barrett (68, 73) links the γάρ specifically with εἰλικρίνεια: "Sincerity — yes, for . . . ."

ter" (see the Introduction, C.) — had his meaning become apparent only by "reading between the lines." Rather, his meaning, which always lay right on the surface, could be fully understood simply by reading; there were no hidden meanings. What prompted this Pauline defense may have been a general accusation that his letters were filled with obscurities that cloaked his true motives (cf. 2 Pet. 3:16), or the more specific charge that his letters were difficult to interpret because what he really meant was sometimes precisely the opposite of what he actually said — his ναί was sometimes οὔ and his οὔ sometimes ναί (cf. 1:17).

If γράφομεν is linear in sense and refers to the present letter, the meaning will be: "We are writing to you nothing different from what we have written before" (Weymouth).[17] But if, as is probable, γράφομεν is gnomic ("in our writing," NJB) and refers to all Paul's earlier correspondence with the Corinthians, the sense is: "We never write anything to you other than what . . ." (TCNT). In the combination ἀλλ' ἤ ("other than," "except" [= εἰ μή]),[18] ἀλλά looks back to οὐ ("not . . . but") and ἤ looks back to ἄλλα ("other things . . . than").[19] It is not possible to represent in translation Paul's paronomasia in ἀναγινώσκετε . . . ἐπιγινώσκετε ("read . . . understand");[20] "apprehend . . . comprehend" seems to be the closest approximation possible in English. Because ἀναγινώσκω regularly means simply "read" in Paul's diction,[21] it is unnecessary to attach the sense of "in public" (TCNT) or "aloud" (Montgomery) or "openly" (Conybeare)[22] to the prefix ἀνα-. Paul's letters were "read aloud" *to* all the believers in particular localities (cf. πᾶσιν τοῖς ἀδελφοῖς, 1 Thess. 5:27) but not "read aloud" *by* them all. At most, ἀναγινώσκετε signifies "you hear read."[23] There is therefore no need to follow Conybeare in surmising that Paul "had been suspected of writing privately to some individuals in the church, in a different strain from that of his public letters to them."[24]

1:13b-14 ἐλπίζω δὲ ὅτι ἕως τέλους ἐπιγνώσεσθε, καθὼς καὶ ἐπέγνωτε ἡμᾶς ἀπὸ μέρους, ὅτι καύχημα ὑμῶν ἐσμεν καθάπερ καὶ ὑμεῖς ἡμῶν ἐν τῇ ἡμέρᾳ τοῦ κυρίου [ἡμῶν] Ἰησοῦ. "And I hope that just as you have understood us partially, so you will indeed come to understand fully that you can be proud of us, just as we in turn shall be proud of you on the Day of our Lord Jesus." Paul's transition from the plural (1:1-13a) to the singular (ἐλπίζω) at this point (cf.

17. The construction with γράφω is τινί τι (see BAGD 167a), here represented by ἄλλα . . . ὑμῖν.

18. BAGD 38a; BDF §448(8).

19. Cf. Zerwick, *Analysis* 392. Robertson speaks of "a sort of pleonastic use of ἀλλά" (1187).

20. Other instances of paronomasia in the Corinthian letters include 1 Cor. 2:13-14; 7:31; 9:17; 11:31; 12:2; 2 Cor. 3:2; 4:8; 8:22; 9:8; 10:12.

21. 2 Cor. 3:2, 15; Eph. 3:4; Col. 4:16 (three times); 1 Thess. 5:27.

22. In Conybeare and Howson 442.

23. But Kennedy argues at some length (52-60) that ἀναγινώσκω here retains its ancient meaning of "admit" or "acknowledge."

24. In Conybeare and Howson 441-42 n. 6.

1:15-17, 23; 2:1-13) perhaps was prompted by the intensity of his hope for the Corinthians' maturation from partial to full understanding.[25] Just as in 1:12 where a ὅτι clause defines τὸ μαρτύριον, so here ὅτι ἕως κτλ. describes the content of Paul's ἐλπίς, namely that the Corinthians would reach the full assurance that he could give them as much cause for pride at the present time as they would give him cause for pride on the great Day when the Lord Jesus returned.

This understanding presupposes several exegetical conclusions:

In conjunction with ἀπὸ μέρους ("partially"), the phrase ἕως τέλους means "fully,"[26] not "to the end" (of the age/of your lives).[27]

The second ὅτι clause, viz. ὅτι καύχημα κτλ., defines the content of the understanding that Paul hopes the Corinthians will gain (ἐλπίζω . . . ὅτι . . . ἐπιγνώσεσθε . . . ὅτι . . .).[28]

The comparison expressed by καθὼς καί involves three elements: the time of the knowledge — past understanding (ἐπέγνωτε) versus future understanding (ἐπιγνώσεσθε), the content of the knowledge — a person, Paul, his actions, aspirations, and motives (ἡμᾶς)[29] versus a certain item of knowledge (ὅτι καύχημα ὑμῶν ἐσμεν), and the extent of the knowledge — partial (ἀπὸ μέρους) versus complete (ἕως τέλους). That is, a past and partial understanding of Paul is contrasted with a future and complete understanding of a fact.

ἐπιγνώσεσθε is a punctiliar rather than a linear future: "you will come to understand (fully)," rather than "you will continue to recognize (to the end)." Also, ἐπέγνωτε is a constative aorist, portraying the totality of the Corinthians' previous partial recognition of Paul.

ἀπὸ μέρους refers to partial acknowledgment or understanding, rather than implying that a few of the Corinthians (perhaps the Pauline clique, 1 Cor. 1:12; 3:4) already understood Paul accurately, as if ἀπὸ μέρους = ἐν ὑμῖν τινες.[30]

---

25. On ἐλπίς and ἐλπίζω in secular and Biblical Greek, see Turner, *Words* 213-15.

26. So, e.g., Lietzmann 101-2; Allo 23 ("jusqu'à la pleine mesure"); Bultmann 33, 36 n. 11; Furnish 126, 128 ("completely"); Carrez 54.

27. So, e.g., Plummer 27; Windisch 58.

28. So also Zerwick and Grosvenor 535. It is possible that ὅτι καύχημα κτλ. states the basis of Paul's hope for deeper Corinthian understanding (v. 13b), or the reason for their earlier acknowledgment of him (v. 14a) (ὅτι = "because"), or states the content of the Corinthians' present understanding (ἐπιγινώσκετε, v. 13a) or past understanding (ἐπέγνωτε, v. 14a) (ὅτι = "that"). See the discussion in Windisch 58.

29. Moffatt takes ἡμᾶς in the sense "the meaning of my life (, namely that I am your source of pride)," as opposed to "the full meaning of my letters." On the other hand, Barclay finds in ἡμᾶς a reference to the "deepest meanings and significances" of what Paul had previously written to the Corinthian congregation. Those who omit ἡμᾶς in translation (e.g., RSV [but cf. NRSV]; Barrett 69) construe ὅτι καύχημα κτλ. with both ἐπιγνώσεσθε (v. 13b) and ἐπέγνωτε (v. 14a), so that ἡμᾶς means virtually "this fact about us (, namely that . . .)."

30. But cf. Conybeare in Conybeare and Howson 442, and Goodspeed, "some of you"; Weymouth, "some few of you."

The comparison expressed by καθάπερ καί (a stylistic variation of καθὼς καί, v. 14a)[31] is twofold: the time of the (justifiable) pride — the present (ἐσμεν) — versus the future (ὑμεῖς [ἔσεσθε] . . . ἐν τῇ ἡμέρᾳ),[32] and the content of the pride or boasting — Corinthian pride in Paul (καύχημα ὑμῶν ἐσμεν) versus Paul's pride in the Corinthians (ὑμεῖς [καύχημα] ἡμῶν [ἔσεσθε]). That is, the Corinthians' cause for pride at the present time (Paul) is contrasted with Paul's ground for boasting at the parousia (the Corinthians).

"The Day of our Lord Jesus" refers, as regularly in Paul, to the time of divine judgment when the glory of Christ will be manifested.[33]

Paul is hopeful that the Corinthians will soon come to recognize that there are already totally adequate reasons for them to feel proud of him — such as their awareness of his devoted spiritual fatherhood (cf. 1 Cor. 4:14-15) or their knowledge of his skilled service as a master builder (cf. 1 Cor. 3:9-10). He reverts to this theme in 5:11-12 where he expresses the hope that his converts at Corinth will reach a proper understanding of his apostolic status and conduct: "What we are is plain to God, and I hope it is also plain to your conscience . . . we are giving you cause for pride in us." Some significant progress has already been made toward this right evaluation of Paul, for through the report that Titus has given of the church's response to the severe letter (7:6-16), Paul recognizes that the Corinthians have understood the intentions behind his conduct (= ἡμᾶς) in some measure (ἀπὸ μέρους). This justifies his hope for their complete understanding (ἕως τέλους ἐπιγνώσεσθε).

Bibliography

Amstutz • Bultmann, *Theology* 1.211-20 • M. Carrez, "La confiance en l'homme et la confiance en soi selon l'apôtre Paul (καυχάομαι)," *RHPR* 44 (1964) 191-99 • Eckstein 179-98 • E. Fuchs, "Gloire de Dieu, gloire de l'homme. Essai sur les termes kauchasthai, kauchèma, kauchèsis, dans la Septante," *RTP* 27 (1977) 321-32 • Hahn • Jewett 402-46, 458-60 • D. E. Marietta, "Conscience in Greek Stoicism," *Numen* 17 (1970) 176-87 • Olson • Pierce • Schnackenburg 287-96 • Schütz 233-38 • Thrall, "ΣΥΝΕΙΔΗΣΙΣ" • Thrall, "2 Cor. 1:12" 366-72 • Turner, *Words* 138-39, 402, 416-17

---

31. In each element of the καθὼς καί comparison (vv. 13b-14a), the same persons are involved (ἐπιγνώσεσθε . . . ἐπέγνωτε) so that καί probably means "indeed"; but in the καθάπερ καί comparison the movement of thought is from ἐσμεν to ὑμεῖς so that καί here will bear the sense "in turn" or "also" or "correspondingly."

32. There is no reason to treat ἐσμεν as a futuristic present ("we shall be," NAB[1]), but since the Day of Christ lay in the future, ἔσεσθε (not ἐστέ) should be supplied with ὑμεῖς.

33. Cf. 1 Cor. 1:7-8; 3:13; 5:5; Phil. 1:6, 10; 2:16; 1 Thess. 5:2, 4; 2 Thess. 1:10; 2:2. It is not impossible that ἐν means "in the light of" (so Warfield 35; Martin 18), but a temporal sense ("on the Day") seems preferable.

2. Charge of Fickleness Answered (1:15-22)

From 7:6-16 we learn that the Corinthian response to the "severe letter" delivered by Titus was favorable.[1] As Titus provided Paul with a detailed account of recent proceedings in the church at Corinth, it was clear that the congregation had been greatly embarrassed by their failure to support and defend Paul (7:7-8) and that their pain had induced them to repent (7:9). By acting against the guilty party in the affair that led to the "severe letter," the Corinthians had put themselves in the right (7:11). However, it seems that Paul also discovered from Titus that there were lingering questions in the church, perhaps generated by the anti-Pauline clique, about the apostle's dependability, his being a man of his word. Paul knew that he had altered his announced travel plans that involved the Corinthians and now knew that some of them had used these changes of plan as a basis for an informal charge of "fickleness" (ἡ ἐλαφρία, 1:17). Paul's response to this stinging accusation is, in essence, a classic instance of argument from the greater to the lesser: "If I was true and faithful in proclaiming to you Corinthians the magnificent message of a true and faithful God, a message that focuses on the Son of God who is God's 'Yes' of fulfillment with regard to all his promises, is it likely that I am capricious and untrustworthy in the relatively insignificant matter of making and executing plans?" A powerful argument indeed!

15Because I was so confident of this, I was intending to visit you first[a] so that you might gain[b] a second benefit;[c] 16that is, I was intending to visit you on my way[d] to Macedonia and again on my return from Macedonia and to be helped forward by you[e] on my way to Judea. 17Well, did I really show fickleness when I wanted[f] to do this? Or the decisions that I make — do I make them impulsively, so that with me it is first "Yes, yes," and then "No, no"?[g] 18Now God is my true witness that the language we use in addressing you[h] is[i] not "Yes" and "No." 19For the Son of God, Jesus Christ,[j] whom we proclaimed among you, I and Silvanus and Timothy, did not prove to be both "Yes" and "No"; on the contrary, in him God's "Yes" has taken effect. 20I mean that God's promises, however many they may be, have their "Yes" in him. For this reason it is through Christ[k] also that our "Amen" ascends to God for his glory through us.[l] 21Now the one who is confirming us as well as you[m] in our union with Christ, and who anointed us, is God himself. 22He[n] also sealed us by putting the Spirit in our hearts as a down payment and pledge.

TEXTUAL NOTES

a. The Greek-Latin (Western) bilinguals D F G, the minuscules 365 629 and a few others, along with all Latin manuscripts, read πρότερον ἐλθεῖν πρὸς ὑμᾶς, while ℵ* omits πρότερον (cf. BDF §62) and Ψ and 𝕸 have ἐλθεῖν πρὸς ὑμᾶς τὸ πρότερον (K has

---

1. See the commentary on 7:6-16 and the Introduction, C.

δεύτερον; cf. 13:2). But these variations of the NA²⁶/UBS¹⁻⁴ text, πρότερον πρὸς ὑμᾶς ἐλθεῖν (read by the proto-Alexandrian witnesses 𝔭⁴⁶ᵛⁱᵈ B 1739 and the later Alexandrian manuscripts C 0243 33 81 104 1175 1881), probably arose from the ambiguous meaning of πρότερον: "originally" if construed with ἐβουλόμην, "first of all" if taken with ἐλθεῖν. See the commentary on 1:15.

b. The Western manuscripts D F G, along with Ψ and 𝔐, read the present subjunctive ἔχητε ("have" = "experience") in place of the preferred aorist subjunctive σχῆτε ("come to have" = "get," "gain"). An error of eye may explain how ς or Σ became E.

c. The reading χάριν (NA²⁷/UBS⁴, with a "B" rating = "almost certain") is to be preferred over χαράν for several reasons: (1) it has stronger and wider external attestation (proto-Alexandrian: א* 1739; later Alexandrian: A C Ψ 0243 33 1881; Western: D F G it; Byzantine: Byz Lect; cf. in favor of χαράν, proto-Alexandrian: B; later Alexandrian: 81 104 1175 copᵇᵒ; Byzantine: L); (2) it is the more difficult reading, since χαρά may here bear its usual sense of "joy" or "pleasure," whereas χάρις is unlikely to carry its common Pauline sense of "grace (conferred by God)"; (3) the variant χαράν may have arisen under the influence of 1:24 (συνεργοί ἐσμεν τῆς χαρᾶς ὑμῶν) or 2:3 (ἡ ἐμὴ χαρὰ πάντων ὑμῶν ἐστιν). For the meaning of χάρις here, see the commentary. However, χαράν is preferred by WH 2.404; Warfield 35-36, 38; and Plummer 32 ("As in 3 Jn. 4, a copyist may have substituted [for χαράν] a more spiritual word [viz. χάριν]").

d. A D* F G P 365 pc itᵇ· ʳ have ἀπελθεῖν ("I was intending to go off to Macedonia by way of you") in place of διελθεῖν; cf. ἀπέρχομαι διά in Rom. 15:28.

e. Instead of ὑφ' ὑμῶν, 𝔭⁴⁶ D F G 614 1175 pc read ἀφ' ὑμῶν. It is the difference between being "helped forward by (ὑπό) you" and being "sent on our way from (ἀπό) you to Judea."

f. In order to bring βουλόμενος (read by 𝔭⁴⁶ א A B C F G P Ψ 0243 6 33 81 104 1175 1739 2464 al it vg co) in v. 17a into line with βουλεύομαι (twice) in v. 17b, D Ψ 1881 𝔐 itᵃ· ᵇ Ambrosiaster read βουλευόμενος ("when I was planning").

g. Because the double ναί and the double οὔ appeared to some scribe(s) to be pleonastic, 𝔭⁴⁶ 0243 6 424ᶜ 1739 pc it vg Or¹⁷³⁹ᵐᵍ Pelagius omit the second ναί and οὔ, reading τὸ ναὶ καὶ τὸ οὔ ("'yes' and 'no'"). Being the less difficult reading and one that probably arose from assimilation to ναὶ καὶ οὔ, which is found in both v. 18 and v. 19, this variant is to be rejected as secondary, although Héring (10), defending this shorter text, alleges that the repeated ναὶ ναί and οὔ οὔ may be a scribal harmonization with Matt. 5:37 (ἔστω δὲ ὁ λόγος ὑμῶν ναὶ ναί, οὔ οὔ; so also Kümmel [197] who adds, rightly, that Nissen's suggestion that μή should be interpolated after ἵνα is unnecessary). The conjecture of Schmiedel, ἵνα ᾖ παρ' ἐμοὶ τὸ ναὶ οὔ, καὶ τὸ οὔ ναί, "so that my Yes means a No, and my No a Yes," certainly accords with the context and eases the difficulty of the repetition, but is devoid of textual support. No more convincing is the proposal of Hahn (234-37) that the text originally read ἵνα ᾖ παρ' ἐμοὶ τὸ ναὶ ναὶ καὶ οὔ, "so that my 'Yes' was (simultaneously) 'Yes' and 'No'."

h. 𝔭⁴⁶ D* omit the article ὁ before πρὸς ὑμᾶς, although "correct" Greek requires that qualifying prepositional phrases be articular.

i. Some secondary witnesses (א² D² Ψ 𝔐 itᵇ syr) have οὐκ ἐγένετο in place of οὐκ ἔστιν, probably because ὁ λόγος ἡμῶν was taken to be referring to Paul's previous preaching to the Corinthians and in order to create precise parallelism with v. 19.

j. Some fourth- or fifth-century uncials (א* A C) (also 0223 2464 pc) invert the word order to Χριστὸς Ἰησοῦς, while "the queen of the cursives" (33) has simply Ἰησοῦς.

k. Perhaps because of uncertainty about the logical link between v. 20a and v. 20b, p⁴⁶ D* itᵇ omit διό. D² 𝕸 syrʰ Ambrosiaster do the same, but also substitute ἐν αὐτῷ for δι' αὐτοῦ, undoubtedly to remove the ambiguity caused by two διά + genitive phrases in one sentence. But the vast majority of witnesses support the reading διὸ καὶ δι' αὐτοῦ.

l. F G add καὶ τιμήν to πρὸς δόξαν, "for his glory and honor" (cf. Rom. 2:7, 10; Heb. 2:7, 9; 1 Pet. 1:7; Rev. 4:9; 5:13; 7:12; 21:26).

m. C 104 630 *pc* syrʰ invert the order, reading ὑμᾶς σὺν ἡμῖν, "you as well as us."

n. In order to create the pattern of one article modifying four participles (βεβαιῶν . . . καὶ χρίσας . . . καὶ σφραγισάμενος . . . καὶ δούς), many significant witnesses (ℵ* A C* K P Ψ 33 81 365 630 1881*ᵛⁱᵈ 2464 *al* itʳ) omit the article with σφραγισάμενος. The more difficult and therefore preferable reading, ὁ καὶ σφραγισάμενος, is represented by p⁴⁶ ℵ² B C³ D (F G read καὶ ὁ) 0243 0285 1739 1881ᶜ 𝕸 vgᶜˡ Ambrosiaster.

1:15 καὶ ταύτῃ τῇ πεποιθήσει ἐβουλόμην πρότερον πρὸς ὑμᾶς ἐλθεῖν, ἵνα δευτέραν χάριν σχῆτε. "Because I was so confident of this, I was intending to visit you first so that you might gain a second benefit." πεποίθησις, "confidence," "trust," a word of later Greek rejected by the Atticists, was formed from πέποιθα (the perfect of πείθω, "persuade"). ταύτῃ τῇ πεποιθήσει is a dative of cause ("on account of this confidence") which is closely related to the more common instrumental dative.[2] What Paul was confident about was his expressed hope that the Corinthians would fully recognize that he himself, as their spiritual father, was in fact a worthy ground for their pride, just as they would be his ground for boasting at the parousia (1:13-14). So, "encouraged by this conviction" (Isaacs) or "relying on this" (Moffatt), Paul entertained the desire and had a plan formulated (ἐβουλόμην) to visit the Corinthians before going anywhere else. Given the fact that adverbs generally follow the verbs they modify,[3] πρότερον ("earlier," "beforehand") may be construed with ἐβουλόμην to give the meaning "I originally intended," "my original plan."[4] But since the next verse (1:16) indicates that Paul was intending to visit the Corinthians twice, once en route to Macedonia and again on his return from Macedonia, πρότερον must anticipate the πάλιν of v. 16 as well as the δευτέραν of v. 15 and refer to the former of two intended visits; thus it means "first of all" (NEB, REB).[5]

ἵνα δευτέραν χάριν σχῆτε. "So that you might gain a second benefit." This specifies the purpose (ἵνα) of Paul's intent to visit Corinth first. σχῆτε, being the aorist of the stative verb ἔχω, is ingressive (or inceptive) in sense, "come to have," thus "obtain," "acquire," "receive."[6] χάρις is a central term in Paul's

2. Cf. BDF §§195-96.
3. BDF §474(2); Turner 227-28.
4. Cf. NEB mg, GNB, Barclay ("I previously planned"); Robertson 919; *Pictures* 212.
5. The two main textual variants involving πρότερον, viz. πρότερον ἐλθεῖν πρὸς ὑμᾶς and ἐλθεῖν πρὸς ὑμᾶς τὸ πρότερον, reflect this understanding (see Textual Note a.).
6. "The present stem [of ἔχω] is regularly durative, 'to hold,' while ἔσχον is a point word, 'I received': thus ἔσχον παρά or ἀπὸ σοῦ is the normal expression in a papyrus receipt" (Moulton 110; cf. Fanning 393-94).

theological vocabulary, comparable to the centrality of *abba* in Jesus' message. For Paul it usually denotes God's unsought and unmerited benevolence, but sometimes it is Paul's shorthand for the sum total of God's blessings afforded in Christ. Here in 1:16 it obviously has a more specialized sense, as the epithet δευτέραν indicates.[7] Some would associate χάρις here with the expression χάρισμα πνευματικόν in Rom. 1:11 (cf. Rom. 15:29). Certainly all would agree that the concept of a "second spiritual gift" introduces a quantitative notion and a specificity (δευτέραν) that ill accords with Paul's view of the χαρίσματα,[8] but even to understand χάριν as the operation of God's grace and δευτέραν as meaning "for the second time"[9] or "on a second occasion"[10] (= τὸ δεύτερον; cf. 13:2) seems unwarranted. It is appropriate to render χάριν by "kindness"[11] or "opportunity for kindness,"[12] or even "proof of (my) goodwill"[13] or "evidence of friendliness."[14] But the comprehensive term "benefit" perhaps best catches the multiple nuances of χάρις here,[15] and with δευτέραν and in the context of v. 16 the sense is "the benefit of a double visit" (NEB, REB). Since an apostolic visit might be both a means of χάρις ("spiritual benefit"; cf. Rom. 1:11; 15:29) and a source of χαρά ("personal pleasure"; cf. Phil. 1:25), the sense is not materially altered whether χάριν or χαράν be read, although the former may be preferred as the more difficult reading.[16]

1:16 καὶ δι' ὑμῶν διελθεῖν εἰς Μακεδονίαν, καὶ πάλιν ἀπὸ Μακεδονίας ἐλθεῖν πρὸς ὑμᾶς καὶ ὑφ' ὑμῶν προπεμφθῆναι εἰς τὴν Ἰουδαίαν. "(That is, I was intending) to visit you on my way to Macedonia and again on my return from Macedonia and to be helped forward by you on my way to Judea." When, in v. 15, Paul assures the Corinthians that he was intending to visit them *first,* so that they might receive a *second* benefit, he apparently realizes that he is only implying that

7. But see de Boor 41 and n. 52; NAB[1], "a double grace."
8. Note that Rom. 1:11 merely has τι χάρισμα . . . πνευματικόν.
9. E.g., Lietzmann 102; Wendland 170-71.
10. E.g., Klauck 23-24.
11. Barrett 69, 74. On χάρις = "favor" in the papyri, see MM 684.
12. Fee, "Chronology" 534, 537 (followed by Martin [22, 24-25], who takes δευτέρα χάρις as "a second opportunity to do a favor") departs from traditional views and takes the δευτέρα χάρις to refer, not to any benefit or favor that Paul's double visit might bring to the Corinthians, but to the double opportunity they would have, as a result of his two passing visits, to experience God's grace as they assisted his ministry and sent him on his way (προπεμφθῆναι) in connection with the collection for the saints in Jerusalem, first to Macedonia and later to Judea. For a succinct critique of Fee's proposal, see Furnish 142.
13. BAGD 877d.
14. *Freundlichkeitserweis* (a translation mentioned by de Boor 41 n. 52). Cf. Allo's renderings, "mark of high regard" *(marque de considération)* and "mark of deference" *(égards;* 25).
15. So Conybeare in Conybeare and Howson 442; RV; Furnish 132-33; "benefit" as a verb, JB, NIV, NJB.
16. See further Textual Note c. If δευτέραν χαράν is read or χάρις is treated as equivalent to χαρά (as Chrysostom [*Homiliae 3 in Epistulam ii ad Corinthios*] proposes), the meaning will be "a double pleasure" (Goodspeed, Montgomery, RSV; Young and Ford 263), "a double delight" (Moffatt, Williams), or "a twofold joy" (Cassirer; similarly Bruce, *Paraphrase* 127).

he will visit them twice; there is a latent ambiguity in what he has said. So in v. 16 he proceeds to make that implication explicit; καί is therefore epexegetic, "that is," "namely" (NAB²). Syntactically, the four coordinated aorist infinitives in vv. 15-16 are all dependent on ἐβουλόμην ("it was my intent"): ἐβουλόμην . . . ἐλθεῖν . . . καὶ . . . διελθεῖν . . . καὶ . . . ἐλθεῖν . . . καὶ . . . προπεμφθῆναι. The combination δι' ὑμῶν διελθεῖν does not mean "to go past without visiting you," but "to visit you en route" or "to go on by way of you" (Barrett 69); an actual visit is implied, not excluded. The particular prepositions used in the sequence πρὸς ὑμᾶς . . . εἰς Μακεδονίαν . . . πρὸς ὑμᾶς . . . εἰς τὴν Ἰουδαίαν in vv. 15-16 illustrate the general rule in NT Greek that in expressing the idea of direction, πρός is used with personal objects and εἰς with impersonal (Turner 257).

Ἰουδαίαν is articular because names of countries regularly take the article when they are derived from adjectives (here Ἰουδαῖος) (BDF §261[4]); that is, τὴν Ἰουδαίαν stands for τὴν Ἰουδαίαν γῆν/χώραν. Here, "Judea" refers not to the whole of Palestine[17] but to "the southern part of Palestine in contrast to Samaria, Galilee, Peraea and Idumea" (BAGD 379a) with special reference to Jerusalem,[18] the destination of the collection for the poor believers (Rom. 15:25-26; 1 Cor. 16:3-4). The verb προπέμπω means "escort" in Acts 20:38; 21:5, but in its other seven NT uses (including this verse) the sense is "help forward," "equip for a journey."[19] It may be rendered "see off," "send off," or "send on one's way," only if this implies that the sender not only says farewell but also provides food or money and perhaps traveling companions or a means of travel. As Zerwick aptly summarizes the connotation of this picturesque verb: "send off by equipping a person who is setting out on a journey with the things necessary for that journey" (*Analysis* 392). If, at the time represented by ἐβουλόμην, Paul planned to take Corinthian delegates with him to Jerusalem on his collection visit, there is no clear evidence that this plan was actually carried out, for the list of provincial delegates given in Acts 20:4 makes no mention of representatives from Greece, although Paul's later comment in Rom. 15:26 indicates that Achaia had in fact made a contribution to the collection.[20]

Paul's travel plans as outlined in 1:15-16 and 1 Cor. 16:2-8 are discussed in detail in the Introduction (B.2: "Paul's Itinerary during and Immediately after His Ephesian Ministry"; see also C.). Here we shall simply summarize our principal findings.

1. The Corinthian letters outline two projected itineraries. In Plan A (1 Cor. 16:2-8) the route was: Ephesus (the place of writing) — Macedonia — Corinth — Jerusalem (possibly). Plan B (2 Cor. 1:15-16) was: Ephesus — Corinth — Macedonia — Corinth — Judea (definitely).

17. W. Gutbrod, *TDNT* 3.382.
18. For the virtual equation ἡ Ἰουδαία = Jerusalem see Acts 12:19; 15:1; 28:21; Rom. 15:31.
19. Acts 15:3; Rom. 15:24; 1 Cor. 16:6, 11; 2 Cor. 1:16; Tit. 3:13; 3 John 6.
20. See further, Introduction, B.5.c.

2. In spite of efforts — especially those of Duncan — to establish the priority of Plan B, we may safely assume that Plan B succeeded Plan A. On this view, Plan B introduced two modifications of Plan A: Paul now intended to pay two visits to Corinth, before and after visiting Macedonia;[21] he would definitely travel to Judea/Jerusalem with the collection.
3. Plan B, formed in Ephesus, was announced at Corinth when Paul arrived on the "painful visit."
4. Paul's actual itinerary was: Ephesus — Corinth (= the "painful visit") — Ephesus (where the Demetrius riot [Acts 19:23-41] occurred) — Troas (2 Cor. 2:12-13) — Macedonia (2 Cor. 2:13; 7:5, Macedonia being the place from which 2 Corinthians was written [Acts 20:1b-2a]) — Corinth (Acts 20:2b-3a).
5. This reconstruction of Paul's planned and actual travel prior to the time when 2 Corinthians was written may be set out diagrammatically as follows.

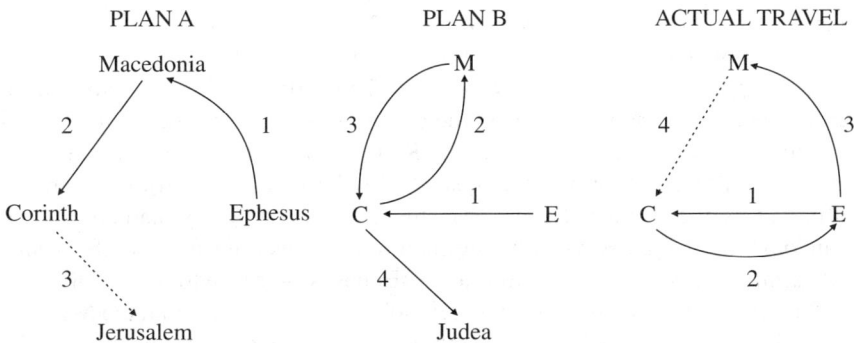

6. If this reconstruction is valid, we may say that neither Plan A nor Plan B was carried out as intended. Plan A was nullified when Paul crossed from Ephesus to Corinth on the "painful visit," and Plan B was nullified when he returned to Ephesus after that visit. Then he readopted Plan A, traveling from Ephesus to Macedonia to Corinth. That is, to Plan A Paul had said "Yes-No-Yes"; to Plan B, "Yes-No." Here was ample ammunition for his detractors' attack!

1:17 τοῦτο οὖν βουλόμενος μήτι ἄρα τῇ ἐλαφρίᾳ ἐχρησάμην; "Well (οὖν), did I really show fickleness when I wanted to do this?" As opposed to the generalized ἃ βουλεύομαι in v. 17b, τοῦτο . . . βουλόμενος . . . ἐχρησάμην is spe-

21. If some of the Corinthians harbored a certain jealousy of the Macedonian believers born of Paul's willingness to accept financial support from those Christians (2 Cor. 11:9; Phil. 4:15-16) yet his adamant refusal to receive monetary gifts from Corinth (1 Cor. 9:3-18; 2 Cor. 11:7-11; 12:14-16), the apostle's planned double visit to Corinth would have served to allay any suspicions of partiality.

cific: Paul did not write τὰ τοιαῦτα . . . βουλόμενος . . . χρῶμαι, "when I plan such things, do I show . . . ?" τοῦτο refers either to Paul's intent to visit the Corinthians twice (v. 16) or to the revised itinerary as a whole (= Plan B) (vv. 15-16). The combination of the particles μήτι ἄρα introduces a rhetorical question that expects a firm negative answer: "Surely not!"[22]

ἐλαφρία is a *hapax legomenon* in the Greek Bible and is not found in Greek writers before the Christian era. The word means "fickleness," referring to levity of character or to "behavior characterized by caprice and instability,"[23] although here the reference may be to both character and behavior or perhaps to behavior as reflecting character. When followed by the dative of the characteristic shown, χράομαι ("use") means "act" or "proceed" (BAGD 884d), so that τῇ ἐλαφρίᾳ χρᾶσθαι means "to act irresponsibly[24]/insincerely,"[25] "to show fickleness,"[26] or "to act with fickle intention."[27] On the grammatical principle that an articular abstract noun calls for special attention,[28] we may propose that ἐλαφρία is articular because Paul is alluding to a charge that had been leveled against him by certain Corinthians,[29] probably as a result of his rejection of Plan A (1 Cor. 16:2-8) in favor of Plan B (2 Cor. 1:15-16).

ἢ ἃ βουλεύομαι κατὰ σάρκα βουλεύομαι . . . ; "Or the decisions that I make — do I make them impulsively . . . ?" The particle ἤ does not introduce a generalized restatement of the first rhetorical question, as though v. 17b stood in synonymous parallelism with v. 17a. Rather, it introduces an additional and more general accusation made against Paul (μήτι is understood), one perhaps prompted by the further alterations to his projected itinerary, namely (1) the abandonment of Plan B when he returned to Ephesus after the "painful visit," and (2) his reversion after this to Plan A (Ephesus — Macedonia, 1 Cor. 16:5, 8). With regard to (2), given the general mobility of people around the Mediterranean in the first century, it is perfectly feasible to imagine that news of Paul's departure from Ephesus (spring 56) and his arrival and ministry in Macedonia (spring-summer 56) reached Corinth before he wrote 2 Corinthians 1 (late summer 56?).[30] Even if the Corinthians were unaware of Paul's readoption of Plan A, he himself would realize that upon receipt of the present letter — written from Macedonia — the believers at Corinth would see that Plan B had now been abandoned in favor of Plan A, further reinforcement of the charges of vacillation and impulsive decision-making.

22. ἄρα as an illative interrogative particle (Robertson 1176) is not be confused with the inferential ἄρα (BDF §440[2]).

23. Louw and Nida §88.99.

24. Cf. Zerwick and Grosvenor 536; Furnish 132.

25. Cf. NAB[1].

26. Cf. Cassirer: "was it levity of mind which I displayed . . . ?"

27. Cf. Barclay.

28. See Zerwick §§176, 179.

29. So also, among others, Menzies 10; Windisch 64; Tasker 47; Bultmann 39.

30. For this chronology, see the Introduction, C. (16-19).

It is impossible to be confident about the precise meaning of κατὰ σάρκα here, although it must belong to the second βουλεύομαι. If the phrase looks back to τῇ ἐλαφρίᾳ (v. 17a), it will mean "whimsically" or "impulsively." If it alludes to ἐν σοφίᾳ σαρκικῇ (v. 12), it could mean "like an unprincipled worldling" or "as one unenlightened by the Spirit" (cf. 10:2).[31] If it anticipates ἵνα ᾖ κτλ. (see below) which immediately follows, the sense may be "according to the mood of the moment"[32] or perhaps "opportunistically" (Furnish 132). Or if the expression looks forward to the charge of domineering (v. 24), it may mean "on the basis of self-interest" or "for personal advantage." However we construe this phrase, it is part of a rhetorical question (with μήτι understood from the previous sentence) by which Paul firmly rejects the supposition or charge of a κατὰ σάρκα βουλεύεσθαι.

ἵνα ᾖ παρ' ἐμοὶ τὸ Ναὶ ναὶ καὶ τὸ Οὒ οὔ; "So that with me it is first 'Yes, yes', and then 'No, no'?" In spite of some energetic efforts to construe ἵνα in its usual telic sense[33] or in an epexegetic sense,[34] it is preferable, after the rhetorical question [μήτι] κατὰ σάρκα βουλεύομαι, to regard it as ecbatic or consecutive:[35] "Surely I don't make my decisions whimsically, with the result that . . . ?" Because this outcome is repudiated by Paul by means of the implied μήτι, it may be classified as a conceived rather than actual result.[36]

The distinctive word order, with ᾖ παρ' ἐμοί occurring immediately after ἵνα rather than (as one might expect) παρ' ἐμοὶ ᾖ at the end of the clause, is taken by Young to indicate that Paul is stressing that his wishes and his decision-making, the whole issue of "yes" and "no," do not in fact depend on himself (ᾖ παρ' ἐμοί) but on God. The responsibility for the change of plans rested on God, not Paul, so that the succeeding argument focuses not on Paul's reliability as such but on God's reliability. As Young renders v. 17, "Or do I make plans at the human level so that yes being yes and no being no rests in my hands?"[37] An alternative explanation of this word order is that Paul is isolating the Corinthian charge: "the 'Yes-yes' and the 'No-no' I am accused of saying," with the repeated anaphoric τό clarifying the allusion to this charge.

The idiom ἔστιν τι παρά τινι means simply "something is in/with some-

---

31. Cf. E. Schweizer, *TDNT* 7.131: "βουλεύεσθαι κατὰ σάρκα in 2 C. 1:17 is a planning which takes note only of human and earthly circumstances and not the Lord's will."

32. Bruce, *Paraphrase* 127.

33. Winer 460; Moulton 210 ("Paul is disclaiming the mundane virtue of unsettled convictions, which *aims* at saying yes and no in one breath").

34. E.g., Young 405: "The natural assumption is that the ἵνα-clause explains κατὰ σάρκα βουλεύεσθαι."

35. So also BDF §391(5); Zerwick §352; BAGD 378a.

36. Burton §218.

37. Young 407-13 (the quotation is from p. 415). Similarly Young and Ford 18, 35, 100-103, 263. Young 409 cites, with cautious approval, the generalization of W. R. Roberts (*Dionysius of Halicarnassus on Literary Composition* [London: Macmillan, 1910] 18 n. 3) that "in the matter of emphasis, Greek sentences are usually constructed on a diminuendo, English sentences on a crescendo principle."

one" (BAGD 610d), so that παρ' ἐμοί does not need to signify "in my hands" or "in my power"; the rendering "in my case" or simply "with me" is adequate. Why are ναί and οὔ doubled? It could reflect an Aramaic idiom and so mean "constantly Yes" and "constantly No";[38] or the second and anarthrous ναί and οὔ could be predicative (as in Jas. 5:12), "yes being yes and no being no."[39] But probably the doubling is merely emphatic, strengthening or confirming the simple ναί and οὔ, as in the comparable phrase ἀμὴν ἀμήν.[40] "The *duplication* of the ναί and οὔ strengthens the picture of the untrustworthy man who affirms just as fervently as he afterwards denies" (Meyer 429).

How is 2 Cor. 1:17 related to Matt. 5:37 and Jas. 5:12? The similarities are striking.

Matt. 5:37		ἔστω δὲ ὁ λόγος	ὑμῶν	ναὶ ναί,	οὒ οὔ
Jas. 5:12		ἤτω δὲ	ὑμῶν τὸ ναὶ ναὶ καὶ τὸ	οὒ οὔ
2 Cor. 1:17	ἵνα ᾖ	παρ'	ἐμοὶ τὸ ναὶ ναὶ καὶ τὸ	οὒ οὔ

Wenham proposes that lying behind these three texts is a dominical logion, perhaps ἔστω δὲ ὁ λόγος ὑμῶν τὸ Ναὶ ναὶ καὶ τὸ Οὒ οὔ, which has been variously used by each writer (271-72). He argues convincingly that in 2 Cor. 1:17-18 Paul is picking up not Jesus' saying as such, but these well-known words as used by his Corinthian opponents when they accused him of prevarication. They were using Jesus' words against Paul: whereas Jesus called for honest, oath-free speech, Paul was a two-faced vacillator, in effect distorting Jesus' words to justify his saying both "Yes, yes" *and* "No, no" (274-76).

From the apostle's defense of his conduct, we may therefore deduce that his detractors at Corinth alleged that he made his plans on mere impulse like a worldly man, according to the mood of the moment, so that he could say "Yes, yes" one day and "No, no" the next day to various travel plans, with the result that he actually seemed to be saying both "Yes" and "No" in the same breath.[41]

1:18 πιστὸς δὲ ὁ θεὸς ὅτι ὁ λόγος ἡμῶν ὁ πρὸς ὑμᾶς οὐκ ἔστιν Ναὶ καὶ Οὔ. "Now God is my true witness that the language we use in addressing you is not 'Yes' and 'No'." This sentence is transitional (δέ, "now"), for as Paul develops his defense, he moves from particular accusations (v. 17) to general theological truths that are relevant to the issues at hand (vv. 18-22) before returning to answer further accusations (vv. 23-24). It is also noteworthy that several of the crucial Greek terms in vv. 17-24 represent various forms of the Semitic root '-m-n: πιστός (v. 18) = ne'ʾmān, "faithful"; ναί (vv. 17-20) or ἀμήν (v. 20) = 'āmēn, "yes," "surely!"; βεβαιῶν (v. 21) = ma'ᵃmîn, "confirming"; πίστις (v. 24)

---

38. Van Unnik, "Reisepläne" 219.

39. Young 407-8.

40. So also BAGD 590a; cf. SB 1.336.

41. Plummer paraphrases v. 17b thus: "Do I follow mere whims, that there should be in my life a perpetual variation, — a decision today, an alteration to-morrow, refusal following on consent?" (CGT 35).

= *ᵉmûnâ*, "faith." It is possible that Paul's train of thought was influenced by these word associations — a case of Semitic thoughts being clothed in Greek words — but these associations would not have been recognized by the predominantly Gentile congregation at Corinth.⁴²

The confessional formula πιστός [ἐστιν] ὁ θεός or its equivalent is found elsewhere in Paul,⁴³ but always in conjunction with some form of the relative pronoun ὅς ("God is faithful, who . . ."), never with ὅτι. This combination πιστὸς . . . ὅτι indicates the presence of an oath:⁴⁴ "I swear by God's truth" (JB), "as surely as God is trustworthy" (NJB), or "God is my true witness that. . . ." In this same context of the discussion of altered travel plans, Paul gives a full oath formula: ἐγὼ δὲ μάρτυρα τὸν θεὸν ἐπικαλοῦμαι ἐπὶ τὴν ἐμὴν ψυχήν, ὅτι . . . (v. 23). Accordingly, in the abbreviated formula of v. 18, God's function as a μάρτυς is clearly implied, and what God guarantees as true is defined by the ὅτι clause.⁴⁵

Because Paul uses the present tense, οὐκ ἔστιν, "is not (now, and has never been)," and not the imperfect (οὐκ ἦν), the meaning of ὁ λόγος cannot be restricted to the initial proclamation of the gospel at Corinth (cf. v. 19) but presumably includes not only the preaching and teaching of Paul and others at Corinth but also Paul's letters to the Corinthians — that is, all his spoken and written words, his language, not simply "the word of the gospel." ὁ πρὸς ὑμᾶς, qualifying ὁ λόγος ἡμῶν, means "(the language we use) in addressing you." From v. 19 we learn that ἡμῶν includes Silvanus and Timothy, although, as far as we know, neither of these associates of Paul ever wrote a letter to the Corinthians.

"The language by which we communicate with you is not 'Yes' and 'No'." That is, Paul's words did not amount to saying "Yes" and "No" *in quick succession* or *at the same time.*⁴⁶ When he first preached at Corinth, he did not speak of Christ as both the fulfillment and the negation of God's promises or proclaim two contradictory ways of getting right with God. How, then, in the far less significant matter of formulating travel plans could he be guilty of ambiguity or levity or indecision? In this verse Paul is solemnly attesting to the

42. See further van Unnik, "Reisepläne" 215-34.

43. 1 Cor. 1:9; 10:13; 1 Thess. 5:24 (πιστὸς ὁ καλῶν ὑμᾶς); 2 Thess. 3:3 (πιστὸς δέ ἐστιν ὁ κύριος).

44. Cf. μάρτυς ὅτι (2 Cor. 1:23); ἀλήθεια ὅτι (2 Cor. 11:10); ζῶ ἐγώ, ὅτι (Rom. 14:11, citing Isa. 45:23, which reads κατ' ἐμαυτοῦ ὀμνύω in the LXX); ἰδοὺ ἐνώπιον θεοῦ ὅτι (Gal. 1:20); ὀμνύω ὅτι (Rev. 10:6) — cited by Robertson 1034. But Plummer (35) takes ὅτι here to mean "in that," citing John 2:18; 9:17.

45. Cf. Cassirer ("The faithful God warrants it that . . ."); Carrez 56 ("Dieu en est garant: . . .").

46. That some such phrase needs to be supplied in v. 17 or 18 to arrive at Paul's meaning is recognized by most commentators and translators — e.g., with regard to v. 18, Lietzmann 102 ("at the same time"); Furnish, 132 ("both yes and no"); Conybeare in Conybeare and Howson 442 ("no [deceitful] mixture of yea and nay"; similarly REB); Weymouth ("now 'Yes' and now 'No' "); NEB ("not an ambiguous blend of Yes and No"); Barclay ("does not vacillate between yes and no"; similarly TCNT); NAB¹ (" 'yes' one minute and 'no' the next"); Cassirer (" 'Yes' first, and then 'No' ").

fact that in all his spoken and written dealings with the Corinthians he has never been guilty of verbal equivocation or duplicity, intending one thing but saying another (cf. 1:13), announcing opposites simultaneously, or vacillating between a "Yes" and a "No."

1:19 ὁ τοῦ θεοῦ γὰρ υἱὸς Ἰησοῦς Χριστὸς ὁ ἐν ὑμῖν δι᾽ ἡμῶν κηρυχθείς, δι᾽ ἐμοῦ καὶ Σιλουανοῦ καὶ Τιμοθέου. "For the Son of God, Jesus Christ, whom we proclaimed among you, I and Silvanus and Timothy." γάρ usually stands second in its phrase (as in v. 20), sometimes third (e.g., Mark 1:38), but rarely fourth (as here). Its exceptional position serves to emphasize τοῦ θεοῦ (BDF §475[2]): Jesus Christ is the Son of none other than this faithful God whose witness is true (v. 18a). Only here and in Gal. 2:20; Eph. 4:13 do we find in Paul the full articular form, ὁ υἱὸς τοῦ θεοῦ. But in content this full form is indistinguishable from the anarthrous υἱὸς θεοῦ (Rom. 1:4) and the ubiquitous (ὁ) υἱὸς αὐτοῦ.[47] Even when Jesus is termed merely ὁ υἱός (1 Cor. 15:28), it remains evident that God is his Father and that his sonship is exclusive in the sense of being unique;[48] never does Paul refer to an individual Christian as ὁ υἱός,[49] although Christians corporately are (οἱ) υἱοὶ (τοῦ) θεοῦ (e.g., Rom. 8:14, 19).

We might have expected Paul to write ὁ . . . ὑφ᾽ ἡμῶν κηρυχθείς. His choice of διά rather than ὑπό highlights the intermediary or secondary role of the preacher, just as Rom. 10:14-17 focuses on the indispensable or primary role of the preacher. Paul proceeds to define the ἡμῶν. Certainly the reminder that the gospel was first proclaimed at Corinth by Silvanus, Timothy, and himself (cf. Acts 18:5) would have reawakened many memories among the Corinthians and may possibly have been designed to prompt a renewal of their "first love" (cf. Rev. 2:4-5): Paul could be saying, in effect, "Remember what you received and heard" (Rev. 3:3).[50] Or the mention of the three could correspond to the need for two or three witnesses to validate judicial testimony according to Deut. 19:15,[51] especially since Paul cites this OT passage in 13:1. If so, as Carrez observes, the two or three witnesses needed to establish facts that will bring about a legal conviction have become the three witnesses to God's salvation (60). In addition, Paul is undoubtedly contrasting the plurality of the messengers with the singularity of the message: three messengers yet one message, namely Jesus Christ presented as crucified (1 Cor. 2:2; 15:3) and as Lord (2 Cor. 4:5). That is, Paul is hinting at what is explicitly affirmed in 1 Cor. 15:11, the unity of early church preaching.

Σιλουανός reflects the Latinized form (Silvanus) of the name šeʾîlāʾ (Greek Σίλας or Σιλᾶς), the Aramaic form of the Hebrew name šāʾûl, "Saul."

---

47. Rom. 1:3, 9; 5:10; (8:3); 8:29, (32); 1 Cor. 1:9; Gal. 1:16; 4:4; (Col. 1:13); 1 Thess. 1:10.

48. See further Deissmann 166-67; Cerfaux 439-60; Kramer 183-89.

49. But note the anarthrous υἱός in Gal. 4:7.

50. Paul does not mention Apollos, who was deeply involved in ministry at Corinth (Acts 18:27–19:1; 1 Cor. 1:12; 3:4-6, 22; 4:6), presumably because Apollos had not been present during the initial eighteen-month evangelization of Corinth (Acts 18:11, fall 50–spring 52).

51. Cf. Num. 35:30; Deut. 17:6.

There is no reason to distinguish this Silvanus from the Silas of Acts. He was a Roman citizen (Acts 16:37), a trusted leader of the Jerusalem church (Acts 15:22, 27) who exercised the gift of prophecy (Acts 15:32 and possibly 16:6), and Paul's chosen companion on his second "missionary journey" (Acts 15:40).[52] On Timothy, see 1:1. In Rom. 16:21 Paul calls Timothy a συνεργός, a colleague in the missionary enterprise which focused on the proclamation of Christ (ὁ . . . κηρυχθείς, 1:19).

The movements of Silvanus and Timothy immediately prior to their arrival in Corinth (Acts 18:5) seem to have been as follows:

1. Paul left them in Berea (Acts 17:10, 14) and went on to Athens, where he gave instructions for them to join him (Acts 17:15).
2. Timothy and perhaps Silas went to Athens (cf. 1 Thess. 3:1-2).
3. Timothy journeyed north to Thessalonica (1 Thess. 3:2) and Silas to Macedonia (? = Philippi) (cf. Acts 18:5).
4. Paul proceeded from Athens to Corinth (Acts 18:1) where he was later rejoined by Silas and Timothy (Acts 18:5), who brought a monetary gift from the Macedonians (2 Cor. 11:9) — probably the Philippians (cf. Phil. 4:15-16) — which enabled Paul to devote himself exclusively to preaching.[53] Since they also brought Paul welcome news of the Macedonians' steadfast faith in the midst of suffering,[54] he was prompted to write 1 Thessalonians, which (like 2 Thessalonians) begins with "Paul, Silvanus, and Timothy" (1 Thess. 1:1).[55]

οὐκ ἐγένετο Ναὶ καὶ Οὔ, ἀλλὰ Ναὶ ἐν αὐτῷ γέγονεν. "(The Son of God . . .) did not prove to be both 'Yes' and 'No'; on the contrary, in him God's 'Yes' has taken effect." Although Paul has not yet mentioned God's promises (cf. v. 20), it is clear from γάρ in v. 20 that he already has those promises in mind here in v. 19. His point is that the life of Jesus Christ did not turn out to be (οὐ ἐγένετο) an ambiguous blend of affirmation and denial with regard to God's promises. Observers of Christ's life found in him no vacillation between a "Yes" and a "No" to God; his life was free of self-contradiction. On the contrary (ἀλλά), that is, positively stated, God's "Yes," which is unambiguous, sure, and final, has come into permanent effect (γέγονεν) in Christ's person and ministry (ἐν αὐτῷ). That the "Yes" is God's is clear from θεοῦ in v. 20.[56] The

52. See further Ollrog 19-20.
53. συνείχετο (Acts 18:5) may be an inceptive imperfect: "(Paul) began to devote himself entirely (to preaching)." See also the commentary at 11:9.
54. 1 Thess. 1:3; 2:14; 3:4, 6-7.
55. The correlation between Luke's testimony (Acts 18:5) and Paul's (2 Cor. 1:19) regarding the simultaneous involvement of Paul, Silvanus, and Timothy in ministry at Corinth is one of W. Paley's noteworthy "undesigned coincidences" between Acts and the Pauline epistles (*Horae Paulinae* [London: Religious Tract Society, 1849], 1-8, 56, 175-77). See the commentary at 11:9.
56. "In 2 C. 1:19f. the correspondence between the ἐπαγγελίαι θεοῦ and the ναί is so plain

distinction between ἐγένετο ("proved to be") and γέγονεν ("has taken effect") should not be overlooked.[57] The aorist ἐγένετο envisages Christ's incarnate life as a whole; the perfect γέγονεν focuses on the permanence of the enactment of God's "Yes" in Christ, implying both ἐγένετο and ἐστίν.[58]

How, then, is v. 19 related to v. 18? V. 19 presents principial evidence (cf. γάρ) of Paul's claim in v. 18, which was validated by God himself, that his verbal dealings with the Corinthians were never characterized by a blend of a reassuring "Yes" and a disconcerting "No." The evidence? The divine Son, Jesus Christ, whom Paul and his colleagues faithfully preached at Corinth, was no prevaricator, blending "Yes" and "No" in life or speech. On the contrary, he was and is God's incarnate "Yes."

1:20 ὅσαι γὰρ ἐπαγγελίαι θεοῦ, ἐν αὐτῷ τὸ Ναί. "I mean (γάρ) that God's promises, however many they may be (ὅσαι), have their 'Yes' in him." Paul now explains why it is true that God's definitive "Yes" has been pronounced in Christ, why Christ is not simultaneously a "Yes" and a "No" but only a "Yes." ὅσαι ("as many as") refers to an indeterminate number of OT promises regarding the new age that God gave (θεοῦ, subjective genitive[59]).[60] A similar generic use of ἐπαγγελίαι is found in Rom. 9:4; 15:8. If ἐστίν is supplied with ἐν αὐτῷ τὸ Ναί, the meaning will be "in him is the 'Yes'" (Thüsing 178), or "in Christ is the Yes that fulfils them" (TCNT). On this general view, the initial phrase ὅσαι κτλ. is a "hanging nominative," standing in the place of πάσαις ταῖς ἐπαγγελίαις τοῦ θεοῦ, ὅσαι γὰρ εἰσίν, γέγονεν ἐν αὐτῷ τὸ ναί,[61] "with regard to all God's promises, however many they are, the 'Yes' has come into effect in him." But it is equally appropriate to supply εἰσίν or ἔχουσιν in reference to ἐπαγγελίαι: "they are 'Yes' in him," or "they have their confirmation in him," in which case there is no *nominativus pendens*. Whatever verb we supply, the sense remains basically the same: God's promises all find their "Yes" of fulfillment in Christ; he forms the climax and summation of the divine self-revelation. Derrett is undoubtedly correct in saying that "no Greek speaker will say Ναί in response to a promise. Ναί is an answer to a proposition, to a question, to an order, and to an obligation" (206). But here Paul is envisaging the fulfillment of a set of promises, not a response to a particular promise, so that the notion of a Ναί that confirms and fulfills is perfectly feasible.

διὸ καὶ δι' αὐτοῦ τὸ Ἀμὴν τῷ θεῷ πρὸς δόξαν δι' ἡμῶν. "For this reason it

---

that one can speak of the ναί as a ναὶ θεοῦ, the more so as the continuation (linked by διό) summons to ἀμὴν τῷ θεῷ πρὸς δόξαν in virtue of this 'yes' of God enacted in Christ" (G. Kittel, *TDNT* 4.125).

57. Cf. a similar significant move from the aorist to the perfect of the same verb (κτίζω) in Col. 1:16: "(all things) were once created (ἐκτίσθη) . . . were created and now exist (ἔκτισται)."

58. NEB renders ἀλλὰ κτλ. in v. 20 by "With him it was, and is, Yes." Cf. Hughes 35 n. 15: "In Him yes was and continues to be a reality." But Bultmann defines γέγονεν more explicitly: "ἐγένετο is used of his mission, γέγονεν of his presence in the kerygma, or in the community" (40).

59. As also in Rom. 4:20; Gal. 3:21 (BAGD 280c).

60. Although the point is incapable of demonstration, Carrez suggests that Paul has in mind not only OT promises but also the old covenant itself as expressive of all the promises (60).

61. Bultmann (40), citing BDF §466(2).

is through Christ also that our 'Amen' ascends to God for his glory through us."
καί may strengthen διό, "so indeed," or qualify δι' αὐτοῦ, "through him too."[62]
Either way, διό states an evident inference: if divine promises, whatever their
number, are realized in and through Christ (v. 20a), the worship of God through
Christ is a natural corollary.

After διὸ καί, the sentence bristles with exegetical ambiguities. (1) Do δι'
αὐτοῦ and δι' ἡμῶν both depend on τὸ Ἀμήν, as Furnish maintains ("through
him as well as through us the 'Amen' glorifies God")?[63] E. Hill has proposed,
with considerable hesitation, that Paul's word order suggests that δι' αὐτοῦ belongs to τὸ Ἀμήν and δι' ἡμῶν with πρὸς δόξαν. This produces the following
sense: "Therefore it is also through him that the Amen goes to God at the glorification (of God) by us/at the doxology (which is offered) through us" (298).
Recognizing the difficulty of rendering δόξα by "glorification" or "doxology,"
Hill makes the alternative suggestion that πρὸς δόξαν δι' ἡμῶν may mean
"when we give glory (to God)" (299). But the problem with each of these proposals is that in NT Greek, πρός with the accusative expresses temporal proximity or extent but never temporal location ("time at which").[64] We suggest that
δι' αὐτοῦ belongs with τὸ Ἀμήν and that δι' ἡμῶν stands at the end of this elliptical sentence because it qualifies both τὸ Ἀμήν ("the Amen uttered by us" = "our
Amen") and πρὸς δόξαν ("for [God's] glory through us"). Alternatively, if both
διά phrases are construed with τὸ Ἀμήν alone, δι' αὐτοῦ may denote the ground
of Christians' access to God in worship (cf. Rom. 5:2; Eph. 2:18),[65] and δι'
ἡμῶν the means or agency[66] or the source[67] of that worship.

(2) Is this Ἀμήν a liturgical response to divine action or truth, or is it the
conclusion of a prayer?[68] Christian doxologies and prayers regularly end with
ἀμήν, expressing the individual's or the community's agreement with the sentiments expressed[69] or, more commonly, the desire that the wishes expressed
would be fulfilled.[70] But the immediate context in 2 Corinthians 1 — the six
uses of ναί — points rather to worship in general (cf. 1 Cor. 14:16) than prayer
in particular as the background of the present usage. The close relation between

---

62. If ἐν were taken as causal in the phrase ἐν αὐτῷ τὸ Ναί (so Zerwick, *Analysis* 536), this
latter option would gain strength.

63. Furnish 132, 136. Cf. Thüsing, 180: "This Amen for God's glorification . . . Christ pronounces through Christians; but also Christians pronounce it 'through Christ.' "

64. See BAGD 710a.

65. But it is also possible that δι' αὐτοῦ signifies "in Christ's name" (cf. Eph. 5:20), "by
Christ" ("of the originator of an action," BAGD 180d), or "through Christ's being the 'Yes' to
God's promises."

66. Bultmann 37 ("That is why we utter the Amen through him"); Barrett 69 ("It is through
him too that the Amen to God, to his glory, is pronounced by us").

67. Zerwick and Grosvenor 536 ("through him also the Amen from us to God for his
glory").

68. On the use of *'āmēn* in the OT and Judaism, see H. Schlier, *TDNT* 1.335-36.

69. E.g., Rom. 1:25; 9:5. Cf. Deut. 27:14-26.

70. E.g., Rom. 15:33; Gal. 6:18.

ναί and ἀμήν is also evident in Rev. 1:7 (ναί, ἀμήν) and 22:20 (ναί, ἔρχομαι ταχύ. Ἀμήν, ἔρχου κύριε Ἰησοῦ). Here in v. 20, Ἀμήν is the community's response to God's Ναί. In Christ, God says "Yes." Through Christ the church says "Amen" to God's "Yes." To express the point more formally, the asseverative particle ἀμήν is the church's liturgical response to God, indicating whole-hearted concurrence with the truth that all of God's promises stand fulfilled in Christ.[71] If ἀμήν in Rev. 22:20 witnesses to the Christian community's adoring recognition of the fact of Christ's promise ("Surely I am coming soon"), here it points to their worshipful acknowledgment of the fulfillment of God's promises in the person and work of Christ.

(3) Is τῷ θεῷ to be construed with πρὸς δόξαν or with τὸ Ἀμήν? Since Paul expresses the thought "for the glory of God" with εἰς δόξαν θεοῦ in 1 Cor. 10:31 and Phil. 2:11, it seems unlikely that here the dative θεῷ would replace θεοῦ and the natural word order would be reversed,[72] whereas τὸ Ἀμήν τῷ θεῷ, if construed together, is a natural sequence of words.

(4) What verb is to be supplied with τὸ Ἀμήν? If we assume that τῷ θεῷ qualifies τὸ Ἀμήν (3. above), we might supply λέγεται[73] or κράζεται[74] or προσφέρεται or simply ἐστίν.[75] But the volitive εἴη would be inappropriate in the midst of a series of affirmations (vv. 18-22).[76]

(5) Does δι' ἡμῶν refer only to Paul and his colleagues or to the Christian community at large? It is true that both vv. 19 and 21 distinguish between ἡμεῖς and ὑμεῖς, but there is the significant difference that in v. 19 "we" is opposed to "you" (preachers as opposed to hearers), whereas in v. 21 "we" and "you" are associated on an equal footing, so that v. 20, with its reference to the liturgical acclamation "Amen" used by all believers (ἡμεῖς), represents a transition from ἡμεῖς as Christian preachers (v. 19) to ἡμεῖς as all Christians (vv. 21b, 22 twice). On this view, the phrase σὺν ὑμῖν after ἡμᾶς in v. 21 ensures that in vv. 21b-22 ἡμεῖς is no longer understood (as in v. 19) in an exclusive sense.

How does v. 20 contribute to the flow of Paul's argument? When, in their corporate worship offered to God through Christ, the Corinthians and all believers joyfully uttered their "Yes" or "Amen," they were concurring that Christ fulfilled all of God's promises. But this was also the essence of Paul's own preaching at Corinth (v. 19). That is, the Corinthians' "Amen" to the gospel declaration itself validated the apostolic preaching (cf. 1 Cor. 1:6; 2 Cor. 3:2-3). With his reliability in this weighty matter thus confirmed by the Corinthians themselves, was it likely that Paul would act in a worldly manner in relatively

---

71. In Rev. 3:14 Christ himself is ὁ Ἀμήν in that he was and is the faithful and true witness to God.

72. *Pace* KJV, RV, RSV, NRSV: "(un)to the glory of God." Also BAGD 46a, 710b; Thrall 128.

73. Cf. BAGD 46a.

74. Cf. Zerwick, *Analysis* 393 ("scl in liturgia acclamatur").

75. Cf. Thrall 128 ("Therefore also through him there is the Amen to God").

76. Cf. TCNT: "Therefore, through Christ again, let the 'Amen' rise."

trivial affairs such as travel plans? How could they distrust the apostle who himself had taught them to affirm the trustworthiness of God by repeating the "Amen"? This is a potent *a fortiori* argument.

1:21 ὁ δὲ βεβαιῶν ἡμᾶς σὺν ὑμῖν εἰς Χριστὸν καὶ χρίσας ἡμᾶς θεός. "Now the one who is confirming us as well as you in our union with Christ, and who anointed us, is God himself." Deissmann has demonstrated that the word group βεβαιόω ("confirm," "establish," "make secure/good"), βέβαιος ("sure"), βεβαίωσις ("confirmation") was common juristic terminology in the pre-Christian and early Christian eras to express legally guaranteed security. For instance, βεβαίωσις denoted the seller's obligation to guarantee to defend the validity of a sale against any possible third-party claims.[77] If such legal connotations are present in Paul's mind, he is affirming here that God has placed himself in an indisputable and irreversible relation to believers.[78] God is constantly engaged (βεβαιῶν, present participle) in strengthening or confirming believers in their relationship to Christ (εἰς Χριστόν). On linguistic grounds it is preferable to classify εἰς as referential ("with respect/reference to"),[79] rather than taking εἰς Χριστόν as equivalent to ἐν Χριστῷ,[80] since, although εἰς and ἐν share some common territory in Hellenistic Greek, Paul is not prone to confuse them.[81] But either way, the resulting sense of εἰς Χριστόν is "in our union with Christ."[82] Both believers' faith in Christ and their faithfulness to Christ are continuously confirmed and strengthened by God.

Just as the use of the legal and commercial term βεβαιοῦν probably prompted Paul to use two further terms drawn from this milieu (σφραγίζειν and ἀρραβών, v. 22), so also Χριστός, "the Anointed One," may have suggested the use of χρίειν, "anoint." However it arose, the paronomasia is unambiguous. In the LXX χρίω regularly refers to the anointing of the head with oil as a symbol of consecration to a royal or priestly office. For example, Saul, David, and Solomon are anointed as kings[83] and Aaron and his sons as priests.[84] But a comparison of Zech. 4:6 ("'Not by might nor by power, but by my Spirit,' says the LORD Almighty") and Zech. 4:14, which calls Zerubbabel and Joshua "sons of

77. Deissmann 104-9; cf. MM 107-8.

78. But H. Schlier proposes that Paul may have "found himself forced by the legal term ἀρραβών [v. 22] to use βεβαιοῦν instead of στηρίζειν, so that in this indirect way we have the intrusion of a legal character even in recollection of the sacrament [of baptism]" (*TDNT* 1.603).

79. See BAGD 230a for this use.

80. So BAGD 138c; RSV, NAB[1, 2], NRSV; Furnish 132 (but cf. 137).

81. On this latter point, see Harris, "Prepositions" 1185-86.

82. Others find the idea of direction or goal in εἰς: Conybeare in Conybeare and Howson 442 ("God is He who keeps both us and you stedfast [*sic*] to His anointed"); Barrett 69 ("He who guarantees us, along with you, for Christ"; the commercial metaphor in βεβαιοῦν explains the εἰς: "we are, as it were, 'entered to Christ's account,'" 79); Klauck 26 ("God, who strengthens us and you in faithfulness to Christ").

83. E.g., 1 Kgdms. 10:1; 16:13; 3 Kgdms. 1:39.

84. E.g., Exod. 28:41, where the link between anointing (χρίσεις) and consecration (ἁγιάσεις) is explicit (similarly Exod. 30:30).

oil," shows that the idea of a metaphorical anointing with the Spirit for a God-given task is not foreign to the OT. Acts 10:38 says that God "anointed Jesus of Nazareth with the Holy Spirit and with power" (cf. Luke 4:18; Acts 4:27), presumably referring to God's bestowal of the Spirit on Jesus at his baptism (Luke 3:21-22). If Paul reflects this Lukan tradition that associates "anointing" with receipt of the Spirit, χρίσας ἡμᾶς will denote God's giving of his Spirit to believers.[85] The difficulty with this interpretation is that v. 22 would then be redundant and we might have expected v. 21 to read χρίσας ἡμᾶς πνεύματι ἁγίῳ (cf. Acts 10:38). Accordingly, Thrall develops a suggestion of Chrysostom and proposes that Paul is describing believers as themselves "christed" (at the time of their baptism) for a future share in the royal privileges of the messianic kingdom.[86] Perhaps the most straightforward solution is to regard this "anointing" of believers against its OT background as simply "consecration to divine service." In OT times it was consecration to royal or priestly or (apparently exceptionally, 1 Kgs. 19:16) prophetic service; in NT times it was consecration to the divine service of doing God's will (cf. Isa. 61:1-2a, cited in Luke 4:18-19; and Matt. 12:50; John 4:34; 6:38; Heb. 10:7; 1 John 2:17). Implied in such commissioning for service[87] is the receipt of those special gifts necessary for the appointed tasks.[88]

There is no need to follow Denney when he asserts that "by including the Corinthians with himself in the first clause [cf. v. 21], he [Paul] virtually excludes them in the second," so that χρίσας ἡμᾶς refers to the consecration of Paul and others to the apostolic or evangelistic ministry (730). Rather, σὺν ὑμῖν after ἡμᾶς alerts the readers that in the further two uses of ἡμεῖς in this sentence, the pronoun refers not to Paul alone (as in v. 18) or to Paul and his colleagues (as in v. 19) but to Paul and the Corinthians as typical of all believers (as in the transitional v. 20). And just as "anointing" is a universal Christian privilege (1 John 2:20, 27), so too are "sealing" and receipt of the Spirit (v. 22).[89] The position of θεός shows not only that it is predicative but also that it is emphatic (as in 2 Cor. 5:5):[90] "the one who . . . is God himself." NEB and REB catch this emphasis by rendering "it is God also who. . . ." The one-time consecration of be-

---

85. In rejecting any allusion to water baptism or confirmation in 2 Cor. 1:21-22 Dunn argues that "the proper interpretation is of the experience of the Spirit in conversion-initiation," that is, Spirit-baptism (*Baptism* 131-34).

86. Thrall 154-55, citing Rom. 5:17; 1 Cor. 4:8; Dan. 7:22, 27.

87. Whereas the RSV has "God . . . has commissioned us," the NRSV has "God has anointed us."

88. Zerwick observes that χρίω "connotes consecration to the performance of a particular task and the provision of the gifts necessary for carrying out such a task" (*Analysis* 393).

89. But Hughes refers the anointing, sealing, and receipt of the Spirit specifically to Paul, as part of the apostle's effort to convince the Corinthians that their charges of fickleness are totally groundless, although "Paul's outlook [in vv. 21-22] is in no way exclusive or self-centred" (43).

90. It would be decidedly awkward to take θεός as being in apposition to ὁ βεβαιῶν, with v. 22 forming the predicate. The other NT instances of a predicative θεός with εἶναι unexpressed are 1 Cor. 8:4, 6; 2 Cor. 5:5; Eph. 4:6; 1 Tim. 2:5a; Heb. 3:4; Rev. 21:3b (Harris, *Jesus* 34-35).

lievers to the performance of the divine will as well as the constant strengthening of believers in their union with Christ are the prerogative, responsibility, and achievement of God alone.

1:22 ὁ καὶ σφραγισάμενος ἡμᾶς καὶ δοὺς τὸν ἀρραβῶνα τοῦ πνεύματος ἐν ταῖς καρδίαις ἡμῶν. "He also sealed us by putting the Spirit in our hearts as a down payment and pledge." Like βεβαιοῦν (v. 21), σφραγίζεσθαι and ἀρραβών are commercial terms. σφραγίζομαι, in the middle voice, means "I mark with a seal (σφραγίς), thus indicating that something or someone belongs to me." Although this idea of (1) *ownership* is primary,[91] two further ideas attach to the word: (2) *authentication,* in that a person's seal was the guarantee that the goods in question were exactly what they were described to be, both in nature and in quantity,[92] and (3) *security,* in that with the seal owners pledged themselves to protect the thing so identified, thus preventing any tampering with the goods while in transit. If these three concepts are implied when Paul says that God has "sealed" believers, he means that God (1) has "branded" believers as his property, (2) has attested the reality of their status in Christ, and (3) has guaranteed their "protection in transit" as his permanent and inviolable possession.[93] There is no justification for finding the background of Paul's usage in the mystery religions or in rabbinic descriptions of circumcision or in a putative early Christian baptismal liturgy or hymn.

ἀρραβών had two basic meanings in Greek commercial usage. It was the first installment of a purchase, a *down payment* or deposit that required further payments but gave a legal claim to the goods in question. Sometimes this partial payment was a sizeable portion of the total, but on other occasions it was merely a token deposit. In its other sense, ἀρραβών denoted a *pledge* or guarantee that differed in kind from the actual payment but rendered it obligatory. The classic instance of this latter sense is Gen. 38:17-20, where Judah gives Tamar his seal, cord, and staff as a pledge (*'ērābôn,* LXX ἀρραβών) of his payment of a young goat.

Here many commentators prefer the former meaning, pointing to a parallel thought in Rom. 8:23, where Paul speaks of "the firstfruits (ἀπαρχή) of the Spirit." However, because that phrase may simply refer to "the first fruits *brought by* the Spirit" (that is, the spirit of sonship, to be consummated in adoptive sonship, Rom. 8:14-16, 23), we need not insist on the meaning "down payment" for ἀρραβών in 2 Cor. 1:22. But perhaps neither meaning of ἀρραβών should be excluded, for the deposit is also the guarantee.[94] Barclay has "first instalment and pledge" and the NIV "a deposit, guaranteeing what is to come."

91. Cf. NIV: "God . . . set his seal of ownership on us."

92. Cf. Deissmann 239.

93. Zerwick defines σφραγίζομαι as "I make secure with a seal" (*Analysis* 393). This protective aspect of sealing is highlighted by Gundry Volf 31-32.

94. For the view that ἀρραβών bears a twofold sense (a pledge-guarantee, making final payment an obligation, and a part payment, bringing the creditor a portion of the final payment), see Ahern 178-89; similarly Mitton 262-63; Ladd 409.

Clearly not all the commercial nuances of the word may be pressed, for salvation is no process of reciprocal bargaining ratified by a contractually binding agreement but is the result of the grace of God, who bestows his Spirit on believers as an unsolicited gift. We may also be sure that Paul did not regard the Spirit as a returnable pledge, as with Judah and Tamar,[95] or as a mere advance sample and therefore an inferior part of the Christian's inheritance.

As in 5:5, τοῦ πνεύματος is clearly an epexegetic genitive after τὸν ἀρραβῶνα,[96] "a down payment and pledge consisting of the Spirit" = "the Spirit as a down payment and pledge." But that of which the Spirit is an ἀρραβών is not immediately apparent. Nor does the term ἀρραβών in itself yield the vital clue, for while it is true that ἀρραβών alludes to some future completion of an agreement, the nature of that "contract" remains unspecified. In Eph. 1:14, however, τῆς κληρονομίας ἡμῶν follows and defines ἀρραβών. The Spirit promised by God is himself God's promise of the Christian's future inheritance,[97] which for Paul included the redemption of the body (Rom. 8:17, 23) and conformity to the image of Christ (Rom. 8:29; 1 Cor. 15:49). As long as, but only as long as, that heritage of glory remains unpossessed and an object of hope (note "until the day . . . ," Eph. 1:14), the Spirit functions as its deposit and guarantee. Inseparable from the notion of ἀρραβών is the threefold idea of the redeeming of a promise by the donor of the pledge (cf. Eph. 1:13-14), the realization of a hope by the recipient of the pledge (cf. Rom. 5:5; 8:24-25; 2 Cor. 4:17-18; 5:7), and the acquisition of an inheritance by an heir (cf. Rom. 8:17, 23; 2 Cor. 5:1; Eph. 1:14).

The use of ἐν after δούς need not be taken as an instance of ἐν = εἰς (so BDF §218) (although we find διδόναι εἰς τὰς καρδίας in Rev. 17:17); rather, ἐν is pregnant, presupposing εἰς, as also in 8:16. The emphasis is not on the direction of the giving but on the final location of the gift: "(God) has put the Spirit in our hearts."[98]

What is the relation among the four participles in vv. 21-22 (ὁ . . . βεβαιῶν . . . καὶ χρίσας . . . ὁ καὶ σφραγισάμενος . . . καὶ δούς)? Dinkler associates all four terms with baptism and the Spirit. βεβαιῶν depicts the baptismal event in its total effect, with the following three aorist participles describing

95. This point obviates Kerr's objection to the rendering "pledge" and to Genesis 38 as a background ("The Holy Spirit is not something which will be reclaimed by God the Father at a later date," 94; cf. 96). Kerr, who prefers the rendering "first instalment," argues that contracts for the hire of services are a more likely possible source of Paul's metaphor than contracts of sale.

96. Robertson 498; Turner 214; Hermann 33; E. Schweizer, *TDNT* 6.422 n. 595.

97. Cf. TCNT: "a pledge of future blessings"; Williams, "a first installment of future rewards"; Conybeare in Conybeare and Howson 443, "the earnest of His promises"; Barrett 69, "the first instalment of our full blessedness"; Cassirer, "the pledge of what is to be"; Dinkler 188, "eschatological σωτηρία with full entrance upon κληρονομία"; Klauck 26, "the first part of promised salvation." On Paul's concept of inheritance, see Hester, especially 96-97.

98. The heart is here "the dwelling-place of heavenly powers and beings" (BAGD 404b), "the one centre in man to which God turns, in which the religious life is rooted, which determines moral conduct" (J. Behm, *TDNT* 3.612).

successive stages and particular themes in the administration of the rite: χρίσας refers to the pouring of water over the head, σφραγισάμενος denotes the legal assignment of believers into Christ's name, and δούς, the gift of the Spirit as the pledge of salvation in fulfillment of the anointing and sealing.[99] According to Bultmann, σφραγισάμενος and δούς explain the two preceding participles, "perhaps as visible signs of the invisible βεβαιοῦν and χρίειν" (42). In the view of de la Potterie, βεβαιῶν alludes to confirmation in the Christian faith, especially in the teaching about the gospel that the Corinthians had received (v. 19). χρίσας denotes God's action in producing faith in the hearers of the gospel, while δούς explicates σφραγισάμενος and refers to the gift of the Spirit conferred and received in the actual act of baptism (14-30). Another representative position is that of Grundmann, who links the three aorists with God's action in baptism which aims at and leads to his ongoing work of confirmation (βεβαιῶν) in those who are baptized. χρίσας is defined by the following two participles: God's appropriation of believers to Christ (χρίσας) is sealed by baptism (σφραγισάμενος) and becomes efficacious through the gift of the Spirit (δούς).[100]

In determining the relationship of these participles, careful attention must be given to the structure of the sentence. βεβαιῶν and χρίσας are linked by a single article and an identical predicate (θεός), but are distinguishable from one another by tense (present — aorist) and from the following two participles by the repeated ὁ (v. 22). On the other hand, σφραγισάμενος and δούς are bound together by a single article, by tense (aorist), and by an explicative καί.[101] The first καί in v. 22 should not be construed with the second, as if the meaning were "both . . . and"; rather, it links the two aorist participles of v. 22 with χρίσας in v. 21. All this suggests that God's constant strengthening of believers (βεβαιῶν) should be distinguished from his prior consecration of them to divine service (χρίσας) and that this commissioning to service is associated with, but distinguishable from, God's sealing of believers at the time of their initiation into Christ, through his gift of the Spirit to them. To put it another way, God's unrepeatable action at the time of the believer's conversion and baptism — "anointing" and "sealing" by "giving" the Spirit — is followed by his ongoing action throughout the believer's life, "confirmation."

None of the four participles unambiguously refers to baptism; given its present tense, βεβαιῶν almost certainly does not contain such a reference. Of the three aorist participles, only σφραγισάμενος could be so construed; an association between sealing and Christian baptism is undeniable in the second half

---

99. "Taufterminologie" 103-15.

100. W. Grundmann, *TDNT* 9.555-56.

101. That δοὺς κτλ. may be explicative of σφραγισάμενος is recognized, *inter alios,* by Zerwick, *Analysis* 393 ("coordination [καὶ δούς] in the place of subordination"); de la Potterie 22. (Chrysostom regarded δοὺς κτλ. as defining the sealing *and* the anointing [cited by Héring 12 n. 48].) On this view, the sealing and the giving are not two actions but one; it is by his gift of the Spirit as an ἀρραβών that God seals believers at their regeneration.

of the second century.[102] Yet because the rite of water baptism was inextricably associated with conversion in early Christian thought and practice, references to the receipt of the Spirit (δούς), divine ownership and protection (σφραγι-σάμενος), and commissioning and endowment for service (χρίσας) would have been naturally evocative of baptism.[103]

Another noteworthy feature of vv. 21-22 is the trinitarian reference. God gave believers his Spirit and now confirms them in their union with Christ. Or, more broadly, in vv. 18-22 God (the Father) is the faithful witness, Christ is the fulfillment of God's promises, and the Spirit is God's pledge of inheritance. The biblical roots of the church's doctrine of the Trinity may be found in such embryonic formulations, along with affirmations or implications of the Son's deity and the Spirit's divinity and what R. R. Williams calls "overlapping binitarianisms."[104]

As we look back over vv. 15-22, we can see that in defending himself against the charge of levity (v. 17a), Paul has appealed to the fact that he makes decisions as a man in Christ, one who acts κατὰ πνεῦμα ("by the Spirit" or "in a spiritual manner," a phrase implied in the argument), not κατὰ σάρκα ("in a worldly manner," v. 17b); to the trustworthiness and faithfulness of God whose sure word he preaches (v. 18); to the unambiguous and positive nature of the message he proclaimed — Jesus Christ, the Son of God (v. 19); and to the validation of that sure proclamation in the Corinthian use of the liturgical response "Amen" (v. 20). Finally (vv. 21, 22), Paul points to the constant activity of God in producing stability in Paul *and* the Corinthians — those who have been brought into intimate and dynamic relation with Christ, who is God's secure and permanent "Yes."

Bibliography

Belleville, "Polemic" 283-86 • Bosenius 7-43 • G. Delling, *Die Taufe im Neuen Testament* (Berlin: Evangelische Verlagsanstalt, 1963) 105-7 • Derrett, "Ναί" • Dinkler, "Taufterminologie" 173-91 (= Dinkler 99-117) • Dugandzic 20-56 • Dunn, *Baptism* 131-34 • Fee, "Chronology" • Furnish, "Fellow-Workers" • Gundry Volf 27-33 • Hahn • F. Hahn, "Ist das textkritische Problem von 2 Kor 1,17 lösbar?" in *Studien zum Text und zur Ethik des Neuen Testaments (FS for H. Greeven)* (Berlin: de Gruyter, 1989) 158-65 • W. Heitmüller, "Sphragis," in *Heinrici FS* 40-59 • E. Hill • Kerr • Maleparampil 51-78 • W. Michaelis, "Zeichen, Siegel, Kreuz," *TZ* 12 (1956) 505-25 • Panikulam 59-63 • de la Potterie • Rieger • Thrall, "Christ" 143-50 • Thüsing 178-81 • M. Trimaille and M. Coune, "Les Apôtres, envoyés authentiques du Dieu fidèle (2 Co 1,18-22)," *AsSeign*

102. See Thrall 157-58.
103. *Pace* Dunn, *Baptism* 131-34.
104. See Maleparampil 51-78, and more generally A. W. Wainwright, *The Trinity in the New Testament* (London: SPCK, 1962) 53-267, and R. R. Williams, "Overlapping Binitarianisms in the New Testament," pp. 30-36 in *Studia Evangelica*, 5.2: *The New Testament Message*, ed. by F. L. Cross (Berlin: Akademie, 1968).

38 (1970) 42-50 • van Unnik, "Reisepläne" • Welborn 133-84 • L. L. Welborn, "The Dangerous Double Affirmation: Character and Truth in 2 Cor 1,17," *ZNW* 86 (1995) 34-52 • Wenham • Young

3. A Canceled Painful Visit (1:23–2:4)

Allied to the charge that Paul had arbitrarily altered his travel plans regarding Corinth according to his personal whims and the mood of the moment, there was in all probability the accusation that by making these arbitrary changes he had shown himself to be a spiritual dictator who tried to dominate his converts and dictate the terms of their faith and who did not hesitate to cause them pain.

23*Now, for myself, I call on God as a witness to this, and my life shall answer for it: it was to spare you that I refrained from coming[a] to Corinth.* 24*Not that we are lording it over you with regard to your faith. On the contrary, we are working with you to promote your joy, for you stand firm in your faith.* 2:1*So[b] in my own mind I came to a decision, which was this: not to pay you another painful visit.* 2*For if I cause you pain, who then is there[c] to cheer me except the very people who are being pained by me?* 3*In addition,[d] I wrote as I did[e] so that I would not have to come and be[f] pained[g] at the hands of those who ought to have made me rejoice. I am confident with regard to all of you that my joy means the joy of you all.* 4*For it was out of deep distress and anguish of heart and with many tears that I wrote to you. My aim was not to cause you pain but to let you know the love, the very intense love, I have for you.*

TEXTUAL NOTES

a. In the place of οὐκέτι ἦλθον, "I no longer came," "I refrained from coming" (Bultmann 37), some witnesses (F G 1175 1881 2495 *pc* it syr^p Ambrosiaster) read οὐκ ἦλθον, "I did not come."

b. Failing to discern any clear causal link between 2:1 and 1:24, some scribe(s) replaced γάρ with δέ (ℵ A C D^b, c [D^gr* τε] F G Ψ 081 *Byz Lect* and most of the Latin tradition). γάρ may be regarded as original, being the more difficult reading and having the support of both proto-Alexandrian (p^46 B 1739) and later Alexandrian (0243 33 1175 1881) manuscripts as well as a range of versional evidence (it^r syr^h, pal cop^samss, bo). For different reasons for preferring γάρ, see Metzger 508.

c. Since ἐστίν is frequently omitted in questions (BDF §127[3]), the reading τίς ὁ εὐφραίνων (ℵ* A B C 81 *pc*) is to be preferred over τίς ἐστιν ὁ εὐφραίνων (ℵ² D F G Ψ 081 0243 *Byz*).

d. In place of the simple καί some witnesses (33 81 365 1175 *pc* syr^h** sa) read the common Pauline combination καὶ γάρ, perhaps being influenced by the occurrence of γάρ in the previous two verses.

e. Representatives of both the proto-Alexandrian (p^46 ℵ* B 1739) and the later Alexandrian (A C* 0243 33 1175) text-types read ἔγραψα τοῦτο αὐτό, which is clearly the superior reading. Some MSS omit αὐτό (A 81* 1881 *pc;* 630 has a simple ἔγραψα), while other witnesses add ὑμῖν after ἔγραψα (ℵ² C³ 𝔐 syr), perhaps to remove any ambiguity about the recipients of the earlier letter (cf. v. 4), or reverse the word order, reading τοῦτο αὐτὸ ἔγραψα ὑμῖν (D F G 629 it vg^ww).

f. Although the present subjunctive ἔχω has support from the Alexandrian (C), Western (D F G), and Byzantine (𝔐) text-types, the aorist subjunctive σχῶ, found in the primary Alexandrian witnesses (𝔭⁴⁶ ℵ* B 1739) and elsewhere (A P Ψ 081 0243 6 33 81 365 630 1175 1881 2464 2495 *pc*), is the preferred reading on the basis of this superior external evidence.

g. The longer reading λύπην ἐπὶ λύπην, "sorrow upon sorrow," "multiplied pain," though widely attested (D F G Ψ 0243 81 104 365 629 [1175] 1739 1881 *pc* lat syr^h**), may have arisen from the close parallel in Phil. 2:27 (ἵνα μὴ λύπην ἐπὶ λύπην σχῶ).

1:23 Ἐγὼ δὲ μάρτυρα τὸν θεὸν ἐπικαλοῦμαι ἐπὶ τὴν ἐμὴν ψυχήν. "Now, for myself, I call on God as a witness to this, and my life shall answer for it." With the resumptive δέ and the emphatic ἐγώ ("I, for my own part") Paul returns to the matter of altered travel plans discussed in 1:15-17. In a formal oath he solemnly invokes God as both his witness (μάρτυρα) and his judge (ἐπὶ τὴν ἐμὴν ψυχήν). In the middle voice ἐπικαλέομαί τινα means "I appeal to someone in my favor." Elsewhere Paul uses a different oath formula: "God is my witness," where ὁ θεός is nominative (Rom. 1:9; Phil. 1:8; 1 Thess. 2:5; cf. 2:10). Here Paul conforms to normal Greek usage where the particular god or gods invoked are in the accusative case.[1] The article with θεόν is anaphoric — "*this* faithful, unchanging God who is committed to strengthening us" (cf. 1:18, 20-21). As a μάρτυς invoked by a human being, God is the one who not only knows all human actions but also perceives all human motives. In the absence of human witnesses who could vouch for his motivation in making or changing his travel plans, Paul appeals to the irrefutable knowledge of God.[2]

ἐπὶ τὴν ἐμὴν ψυχήν is a Hebraism ('al-napšî) meaning "against my soul" (= "against me," RSV, NRSV[3]) or "on my own life"[4] (= "with my life as the forfeit," or "I stake my life on it," NEB). So sure is Paul of his own truthfulness at this point that he can say, in effect, "Let God destroy me if I am lying."[5] By implication, God is presented here as the judge or divine assessor to whom all persons are ultimately accountable.[6] The destruction Paul has in mind could be the loss of spiritual life (that is, the forfeiture of salvation; cf. Rom. 9:3)[7] but is

---

1. See examples in Windisch (74) and (especially for the papyri) Spicq (2.43-46), who renders 1:23, "As for me, I take God as my witness" (2.44).

2. Cf. H. Strathmann, *TDNT* 4.491.

3. So also K. L. Schmidt, *TDNT* 3.497.

4. ἐμήν here may be reflexive (Turner 191).

5. But Lietzmann (104) proposes "He ought to (*er soll*) punish me if I lie."

6. Cf. Stählin, "Gebrauch" 134. E. Schweizer views ψυχή in 1:23 as "the self that is aware of being responsible to God" (*TDNT* 9.649).

7. BAGD 893d: "If he is lying he will forfeit his salvation"; cf. Conybeare in Conybeare and Howson (443): "as my soul shall answer for it."

more probably the loss of physical life. Either way, that Paul expresses here a formal oath and invokes a formal curse indicates the seriousness of the charges leveled against him:[8] his own integrity as a minister of the gospel, and also, ultimately, the integrity of the gospel itself, were at stake.

ὅτι φειδόμενος ὑμῶν οὐκέτι ἦλθον εἰς Κόρινθον. "It was to spare you that I refrained from coming to Corinth." ὅτι introduces the content of the asseveration to which God is a true and faithful witness (cf. 1:18; Jer. 42:5). Although the present participle φειδόμενος could be causal ("because I was sparing you"),[9] it is more naturally taken as telic ("in order to spare you," NIV).[10] But two questions remain. Of what were the Corinthians spared? And how were they spared? οὐκέτι ἦλθον, which should be carefully distinguished from both οὐκέτι ἔρχομαι ("I am [now] no longer coming") and οὔπω ἦλθον ("I have as yet not gone"[11]), implies the abandonment of a previous intention or plan to visit Corinth. The phrase must be interpreted in conjunction with 2:1 ("So . . . I came to a decision, which was this: not to pay you another painful visit"). What Paul canceled — not merely postponed[12] — was a return visit to Corinth that would have proved painful to both himself and the Corinthians, for it would have involved *not* sparing the Corinthians additional pain; if he had paid the visit, he would have come ἐν ῥάβδῳ, "rod in hand" (1 Cor. 4:21). But instead of another personal visit that would have proved mutually painful, he resolved to pay the Corinthians an "epistolary visit" (2:3, 4; 7:8, 12). See further on 2:1 and the Introduction (B.1-2).

1:24 οὐχ ὅτι κυριεύομεν ὑμῶν τῆς πίστεως. "Not that we are lording it over you with regard to your faith." When Paul spoke of "sparing" the Corinthians (φειδόμενος, 1:23), he implied that, if circumstances had been different, he might have found it necessary to cause them pain; the power to spare someone pain implies the power to inflict pain. He therefore proceeds in 1:24, which is parenthetical, to reject any possible inference that he was some tyrannical overlord, seeking to intimidate and domineer in matters of faith and conduct. This verse, then, may be seen as an instance of *epanorthosis* (sometimes termed *epidiorthosis*), the correction of a previous expression to forestall misunderstanding,[13] although it could also be Paul's response to an actual Corinthian charge against him or even an allusion to the domineering tactics of his opponents (see 11:20).

---

8. Jesus' apparently absolute prohibition of oath-taking (Matt. 5:33-37; cf. Jas. 5:12) should probably be seen as a rejection of verbal casuistry that compromises or destroys straightforward honesty in speech.

9. Cf. BAGD 588d; BDF §397(3).

10. Robertson, *Pictures* 214; Lietzmann 104: "(only) out of consideration for you" (so also REB); Wolff 38: "(only) because I (wanted) to spare you."

11. This is how Louw and Nida (§22:28) render οὐκέτι ἦλθον.

12. Cf. TCNT: "It was to spare you that I deferred my visit to Corinth." REB catches the right sense with "I did not after all come to Corinth."

13. Thus Robertson 1429; *Pictures* 214; W. Foerster, *TDNT* 3.1097. Other instances of epanorthosis involving οὐχ ὅτι are found in 2 Cor. 3:5; Phil. 4:11, 17; 2 Thess. 3:9.

οὐχ ὅτι (cf. 3:5) is elliptical for either ἔστιν οὐχ ὅτι[14] ("It is not that . . ." = "not as if") or οὐ λέγω ὅτι[15] ("I am not saying that . . ."), rather than οὐ λέγω τοῦτο ὅτι ("I am not saying this because . . .").[16] Examining the use of (κατα)κυριεύειν from the LXX to Byzantine Greek, Clark argues vigorously that this verb has no connotation of arrogance or oppression but means simply "to exercise lordship over," that is, "to be lord over" rather than "to lord it over" (100-105). But here it seems difficult to deny that a contrast is being drawn between domineering over people (ὑμῶν) and cooperating with people (συνεργοί). Such a pejorative nuance of (κατα)κυριεύειν is found also in Gen. 3:16; Mark 10:42; Acts 19:16; and 1 Pet. 5:3.[17] Since this verb is followed by the genitive of the person in NT usage,[18] it is better to construe ὑμῶν directly with κυριεύομεν, "(not that) we lord it over you," with τῆς πίστεως as a genitive of reference ("with regard to your faith"),[19] rather than taking τῆς πίστεως as the genitive object of κυριεύομεν, with the preceding ὑμῶν as possessive, "(not that) we exercise control over your faith."[20] But either way, the sense is the same: faith recognizes no human master or director. As the champion of freedom in Christ, Paul repudiated any hierarchical despotism or spiritual imperialism. The believer, set free from enslavement to sin (Rom. 6:14, 17-18), submits only to enslavement to God (Rom. 6:22) or to Christ (Rom. 14:9; 1 Cor. 7:22), the only legitimate κύριος τῆς πίστεως, not to any person (1 Cor. 7:23) or thing (1 Cor. 6:12).

ἀλλὰ συνεργοί ἐσμεν τῆς χαρᾶς ὑμῶν. "On the contrary, we are working with you to promote your joy." The οὐ(κ) . . . ἀλλά antithesis contrasts domination (κυριεύομεν) with cooperation (συνεργοί).[21] So far from being an overlord who graciously deigns to spare his subjects, Paul is a spiritual father (1 Cor. 4:15) who is committed to working with his children to consummate their joy in the faith (Rom. 15:13; Phil. 1:25). The proper sphere of pastoral activity is the creation of χαρά, not the imposition of λύπη. This χαρά/χαίρω — λύπη/λυπέω antithesis is of importance in 1:23–2:4. Because 1:23 and 2:1 are couched in the first person singular, κυριεύομεν and ἐσμέν in the intervening 1:24 probably refer (as epistolary plurals) to Paul alone. If this is so, the συν- in συνεργοί points not to Silvanus and Timothy (1:19) but either to God (cf. 1 Cor. 3:9) or, more probably, to the Corinthians themselves.

τῇ γὰρ πίστει ἑστήκατε. "For you stand firm in your faith." If the conjunc-

---

14. Turner 303.
15. BAGD 589a.
16. Zerwick (*Analysis* 393) renders οὐχ ὅτι as "not because" or "not as if."
17. Spicq 2.352, who observes that "this nuance of despotism, constraint, or tyranny is found again in 2 Cor. 1:24 — 'It is not that we hold dictatorial power over your faith, but we cooperate for your joy.'"
18. Luke 22:25; Rom. 6:9, 14; 7:1; 14:9; cf. 1 Tim. 6:15.
19. So also Plummer 45; Furnish 139.
20. Thus Thrall 161 n. 227.
21. On the term συνεργός in Paul, see Ollrog 63-72, 91-92.

tion γάρ looks back to οὐχ ὅτι κυριεύομεν, Paul is saying "It is neither necessary nor possible to have control over your faith, because (γάρ) you have a firm standing of your own in the faith." Alternatively, if γάρ explains συνεργοί ἐσμεν, the sense will be: "My concern is with deepening your joy, not prompting your faith, for (γάρ) with regard to/in faith, you stand firm." τῇ πίστει would then be either locative ("in [the/your] faith") or referential ("with regard to faith"), specifying the sphere in which the Corinthians were standing firm (cf. 1 Cor. 16:13).[22] ἡ πίστις here could refer to personal trust (fides qua creditur) or, less probably, to "the faith," transmitted apostolic teaching (fides quae creditur).[23]

2:1 ἔκρινα γὰρ ἐμαυτῷ τοῦτο, τὸ μὴ πάλιν ἐν λύπῃ πρὸς ὑμᾶς ἐλθεῖν. "So in my own mind I came to a decision, which was this — not to pay you another painful visit." If 1:24 is parenthetical (see above), γάρ may introduce a statement that explains why Paul chose to spare the Corinthians (1:23). Significantly, τὸ μὴ . . . ἐλθεῖν corresponds to οὐκέτι ἦλθον (1:23) and πρὸς ὑμᾶς to εἰς Κόρινθον. But even with such conceptual links with 1:23, γάρ could function as a more general connective ("so").[24] The aorist ἔκρινα ("I determined/resolved"; cf. 1 Cor. 2:2) stands in sharp contrast with the imperfect ἐβουλόμην ("I was intending") of 1:15. ἐμαυτῷ may be equivalent to the ethical dative (= μοι "for me"; Carrez 64), but should probably be classified as a dative of advantage (Robertson 539; Turner 238) that here emphasizes the personal character of Paul's resolve "for myself," "in my own mind." The negated articular infinitive (τὸ μὴ . . . ἐλθεῖν) is in opposition to the accusative τοῦτο[25] and specifies the content of the decision Paul reached. In itself the phrase ἐν λύπῃ, "with pain" (ἐν of attendant circumstances), does not indicate whether the pain would be mutual,[26] but in the light of 1:23-24 and 2:2 it would seem that the anticipated λύπη of 2:1 was primarily pain inflicted by Paul on the Corinthians. Indeed, Meyer paraphrases ἐν λύπῃ, *"bringing affliction with me, i.e., afflicting you"* (440), and Héring (14) observes that ἐλθεῖν ἐν reflects the Aramaic *ʾⁱtā' bᵉ*, "cause," "bring" (cf. 1 Cor. 4:21; Rom. 15:29, 32). The order πάλιν ἐν λύπῃ — not τὸ μὴ . . . πάλιν ἐλθεῖν[27] — indicates that the apostle decided against a visit to Corinth "again with pain," not against a "coming again" to Corinth which

22. Some, however, construe τῇ πίστει as instrumental (cf. Rom. 11:20), indicating that Christian existence or *bene esse* (ἑστάναι) is always "by/through faith" (e.g., Barrett 82; Zerwick and Grosvenor 536; TCNT).

23. Thus: "in faith" (BAGD 382d), "in the faith" (cf. 1 Cor. 15:1) (Moffatt, NEB, JB); if the article is possessive, "in the matter of your faith" (Weymouth); if anaphoric, "by that faith" (REB).

24. Cf. BAGD 152c.

25. BDF §399(3); Burton §395; Robertson 401, 700, 1059. A similar construction is found in Rom. 14:13.

26. The mutuality of the pain is proposed by Zerwick and Grosvenor 537; Young and Ford 263.

27. The reading ἐλθεῖν ἐν λύπῃ in the TR is probably an intentional rearrangement of the word order by a scribe intent on harmonizing Paul with Acts (which mentions no visit of Paul to Corinth ἐν λύπῃ).

would prove painful. A previous painful visit is implied, a view espoused by the overwhelming majority of modern scholars.[28] Not only word order but personal factors support this dominant view. If Paul had visited Corinth only once before penning these words, he would here be confessing that he chose to avoid a pastoral situation that involved confrontation and that might or would prove painful, a confession scarcely consistent with the threat of 1 Cor. 4:21 (ἐν ῥάβδῳ ἔλθω;) or the affirmation of 2 Cor. 12:15 that he would gladly spend himself and be spent for the Corinthians' sake.

If, then, πάλιν ἐν λύπῃ implies an earlier painful visit, can we identify when it occurred? In the Introduction (B.1) I have identified and evaluated four options: the founding visit; a visit after the founding visit but prior to 1 Corinthians; 1 Corinthians, regarded as an "epistolary visit"; and a visit not mentioned in Acts which occurred between the writing of 1 Corinthians [where only the founding visit is referred to — see 1 Cor. 2:1-3; 11:2; 15:3] and the dispatch of the "severe letter." I gave reasons for preferring the fourth option. More importantly at this point, can we identify the projected second painful visit that Paul declined to make? If we assume that the initial ἐλθεῖν ἐν λύπῃ is not the founding visit (see the Introduction, B.1.a.), the second visit ἐν λύπῃ cannot be the visit mentioned in 1 Cor. 16:2, 5-6, for that was to be a second, not a third, visit; or the second leg of the double visit mentioned in 2 Cor. 1:15-16, for when Paul made his decision (ἔκρινα) he had reason to believe that the projected (third) visit would be painful, not beneficial (cf. δευτέραν χάριν, 1:15).[29]

We may therefore propose that at some stage after he had returned to Ephesus from the painful visit, Paul heard of the open defiance at Corinth of ὁ ἀδικήσας (7:12; cf. 2:6-8). He found himself in the proverbial cleft stick. If he refrained from any response, his silence would be seen by his opponents as a vindication of their position and his influence at Corinth would wane still further, if not totally collapse, as the prestige of his opponents soared. If, on the other hand, he revisited the Corinthians in person, he risked a second painful visit that would be unpleasant to all parties and possibly a confirmation in the eyes of the Corinthians of his opponents' assertion that he was puny, unimpressive weakling when face-to-face (10:1, 10b). Alternatively, if he wrote a stinging letter, calling for the punishment of the wrongdoer, he might lend further credence to his opponents' insistence that he was a powerful leader only at a distance (10:1, 10a) and a person given to self-commendation (3:1; 5:12). Apparently, after Paul heard of the defiance, his initial reaction was to plan another visit (οὐκέτι ἦλθον alludes to the

28. There remains difference of opinion, however, concerning the time of this visit (see the Introduction, B.1.b.).

29. The difficulty with equating the visit of 2:1 with Paul's impending visit of 12:14 and 13:1 (thus 2:1, "I am determined that my next [= second] visit to you should be a pleasant one [as was my first]," White, "Visits" 89) is that this construes πάλιν with ἐλθεῖν in 2:1, overlooks the correspondence between τὸ μὴ . . . ἐλθεῖν (2:1) and οὐκέτι ἦλθον ("I refrained from coming," 1:23), presupposes κέκρικα, not ἔκρινα, in 2:1, and fails to do justice to τρίτον τοῦτο in 12:14 and 13:1 (see the Introduction, B.1.a.[2.a-b]).

abandonment of a plan — see on 1:23). But after considering his options, he decided (ἔκρινα) to spare the Corinthians (φειδόμενος ὑμῶν, 1:23) and avoid a δευτέρα λύπη, a second occasion for sorrow.

2:2 εἰ γὰρ ἐγὼ λυπῶ ὑμᾶς, καὶ τίς ὁ εὐφραίνων με εἰ μὴ ὁ λυπούμενος ἐξ ἐμοῦ; "For if I cause you pain, who then is there to cheer me except the very people who are being pained by me?" Paul is here explaining (γάρ) further why he decided not to revisit Corinth personally. He affirms that this decision had been partially determined (cf. 1:23; 2:1) by his reflection that to inflict pain on the Corinthians at that time would have effectively dried up the very source of his own happiness — the Corinthians themselves! His joy was inextricably bound up with theirs (1:24; 2:3; cf. Rom. 12:15). To cause them pain would be to experience pain himself, a pain that could be relieved and then converted into gladness only by their repentance (cf. 7:8-10).

εἰ . . . ἐγὼ λυπῶ ὑμᾶς. The emphatic ἐγώ points to Paul as the one who cooperates with the Corinthians in securing and maintaining their joy (1:24). This whole protasis alludes to the projected visit to Corinth that was canceled because it would have created λύπη (2:1). It appears that when he wrote the "severe letter," which was a substitute for the visit, Paul did not expect to cause pain (note the element of surprise in 7:8 when he describes the actual outcome of the letter, and the confidence expressed in 2:3b). But even if this protasis alludes to a specific occasion when Paul might have caused pain, the present tense λυπῶ, along with the rhetorical singular τίς and the generic articular present participles, ὁ εὐφραίνων and ὁ λυπούμενος, suggest that a general timeless truth about Paul's relations with those in his pastoral case is being stated. If this protasis referred to the letter of v. 4 and its cause and outcome, and ὁ λυπούμενος described the offender whose action triggered the "sorrowful letter," as Martin believes,[30] we would expect Paul to have written εἰ . . . ἐγὼ ἐλύπησα (or λελύπηκα) ὑμᾶς . . . εἰ μὴ ὁ λυπηθεὶς ἐξ ἐμοῦ;

καὶ τίς ὁ εὐφραίνων με εἰ μὴ ὁ λυπούμενος ἐξ ἐμοῦ; Standing at the head of this apodosis, καί means "then" and stresses the inevitability of the consequences if the protasis is fulfilled.[31] Given the plural ὑμᾶς in the protasis and the plurals in v. 3 (ἀφ᾽ ὧν . . . ὑμᾶς . . . ὑμῶν), the successive singulars τίς, ὁ εὐφραίνων, and ὁ λυπούμενος indicate that the Corinthians as a community are in view in the apodosis, so that εἰ μὴ ὁ λυπούμενος has the sense "except (you,) the people who are pained."[32] That Paul wrote ἐξ ἐμοῦ and not ὑπ᾽ ἐμοῦ is prob-

30. Martin (35), who renders ὁ λυπούμενος by "the person who *made me* sorrowful" (italics added; but cf. 30, "the person who is made sorrowful").

31. See the detailed discussion in Thrall (166-67), who carefully distinguishes (unlike BDF §442[8] and BAGD 392d, under I.2.h) the use of καί to introduce (normally independent) questions that often express surprise or ill-will, etc., and its use in conditional sentences with apodotic force, "emphasizing the logic of what is said" (167). Mark 10:26 (καὶ τίς δύναται σωθῆναι;) is an example of the former usage, 2 Cor. 2:2 of the latter.

32. Cf. Moffatt, JB; Plummer 30. If the singular is retained in translation, "the person who is pained," the reference will be to "the representative Corinthian" (Barrett 86).

ably insignificant, since in Hellenistic Greek ἐκ overlaps in meaning with ὑπό[33] and may denote "effective cause" ("by, because of"; BAGD 235b). But if ἐκ is here to be distinguished from ὑπό, it will denote the source or occasion of the pain.[34]

Finding this meaning of the verse "somewhat obscure," Héring places a question mark after με and renders the verse, "For if I make you sad, who then will make me glad? Certainly not (εἰ μή) the one who has been plunged into sorrow by me!"[35] In spite of its *prima facie* attractiveness, this proposal labors under two difficulties. First, εἰ μή cannot mean "certainly not." In oaths and asseverations, it is the simple εἰ (= Hebrew *'im*), not εἰ μή, that means "certainly not!"[36] And 7:8-9, 13, 16 show that it was precisely the Corinthians' grief, caused by Paul's "severe letter," that produced their repentance and thus Paul's joy.

2:3 καὶ ἔγραψα τοῦτο αὐτὸ ἵνα μὴ ἐλθὼν λύπην σχῶ. "In addition, I wrote as I did so that I would not have to come and be pained." Paul here states an additional (καί) purpose in writing the "severe letter": He wished to shield not only the Corinthians (1:23; 2:1-2) but also himself from further pain. As in Gal. 6:11 and Phlm. 19, ἔγραψα could be an epistolary aorist ("I write/am writing"),[37] but the majority of commentators and EVV (rightly) regard it as a preterit aorist ("I wrote").[38] This conclusion is supported by three considerations. (1) ἔγραψα is parallel to ἔκρινα (v. 1), "I decided [not to visit, but write]," with the intervening present tense λυπῶ being virtually gnomic and therefore no support for an epistolary ἔγραψα. (2) The four instances of ἔγραψα in 2:3, 4, 9 and 7:12 can be distinguished only with difficulty, given the similar descriptions in each place of the purpose or circumstances of the writing. But since 7:7-11, 15 describes the effect of the letter, all these cases of ἔγραψα must be preterit aorists. (3) 7:8 refers to ἡ ἐπιστολὴ ἐκείνη, "that letter," not ἡ ἐπιστολὴ αὕτη, "this letter."

τοῦτο αὐτὸ ἵνα κτλ. has been understood in two main ways. (1) τοῦτο αὐτό is an accusative of respect (or an adverbial accusative), meaning "for this very reason,"[39] with ἵνα considered either epexegetic ("namely that") or telic ("in order that"): "So the very reason I wrote was that . . ." (Moffatt).[40] The difficulty with this proposal is that elsewhere in the Pauline corpus when ἵνα or ὅπως follows (αὐτὸ) τοῦτο, εἰς is always found with this phrase — as in 2:9, εἰς τοῦτο

---

33. Zerwick §§87, 90; Zerwick and Grosvenor 537.
34. BAGD 481d; Barrett 87, possibly "sorrow that arises from me, on my account, sorrow that is occasioned rather than caused by my presence" (although he renders ἐξ ἐμοῦ with "by me" [86]).
35. Héring 14, followed by Martin 30.
36. See Mark 8:12; Heb. 3:11; 4:3, 5 (cited in BDF §372[4]).
37. Thus Barclay; Olshausen 284-85; Porter 399.
38. So also Robertson 846; BDR §334.
39. BAGD 123a; BDF §290(4).
40. Similarly Conybeare in Conybeare and Howson 443; Carrez 63, 65.

γὰρ καὶ ἔγραψα ἵνα κτλ.[41] Also, the adverbial τοῦτο αὐτό appears only with intransitive verbs (such as "come") or with transitive verbs that already have an object expressed (as in 2 Pet. 1:5).[42] The following alternative is therefore to be preferred. (2) τοῦτο αὐτό is the direct object of ἔγραψα, referring to either (a) some specific item in the letter ("this very thing") or (b) the letter as a whole ("this very letter"/"as I did"). Representative translations are (a): "I wrote this very thing, so that (telic ἵνα) . . .";[43] "This is precisely the point I made in the letter: I did not want, I said, . . . (epexegetic ἵνα)"; (NEB, REB; similarly Cassirer) or (b): "I wrote as I did to make sure that (telic ἵνα) . . ." (JB);[44] "I wrote to just this effect that I might not come (telic ἵνα) . . ." (Barrett 82, 87).

If the aorist participle ἐλθών is translated as "at my coming"[45] or "by coming" (Plummer 31, 50), there is no implication concerning the time or actuality of the coming: the visit referred to may be past or future, actual or hypothetical. With a past tense following (ἔδει), the coming can scarcely be future; with the word order ἵνα μὴ ἐλθών, not ἵνα ἐλθὼν μὴ λύπην σχῶ, the coming is probably presumed to be hypothetical rather than actual — "if I had come"[46] or "when I had come" rather than "when I do come"[47] or "when I did come."[48] Paul is describing the expected outcome of the projected visit that he has chosen to cancel: "so that I might not come and experience sorrow" (Thrall 163), or "so that I would not have to come and be grieved" (Furnish 153).

ἀφ' ὧν ἔδει με χαίρειν, "At the hands of those who ought to have made me rejoice." ἀφ' ὧν is elliptical, standing for ἀπὸ ἐκείνων ἀφ' ὧν ("by those by whom")[49] or possibly ἀπὸ ἐκείνων ἐφ' οἷς ("by those over whom"). If ἀπό does not express agency ("by"[50]), it should perhaps be rendered "at the hands of." με χαίρειν is the accusative and infinitive construction that normally follows the impersonal verb δεῖ. Some regard the imperfect ἔδει as here expressing an "unrealized present obligation,"[51] "(those who) ought to make me rejoice/ought to

---

41. Rom. 9:17; 14:9; Eph. 6:22; Col. 4:8. In Rom. 13:6; 2 Cor. 5:5; 1 Thess. 3:3; 1 Tim. 4:10 εἰς (αὐτὸ) τοῦτο is defined by what precedes.

42. Bultmann 46 (apparently following Windisch [80]).

43. Furnish 153 (who refers [160] τοῦτο αὐτό to the canceled visit of 2:1-2); similarly Lietzmann (104-5), who argues that since Paul wrote τοῦτο αὐτό and not ταῦτα (as in 13:10) it is most probable that he is quoting from the letter, the citation being possibly 2:3a (epexegetic ἵνα), 2:2, οὐ βούλομαι πάλιν ἐν λύπῃ πρὸς ὑμᾶς ἐλθεῖν (2:1), or φειδόμενος ὑμῶν οὐκέτι ἔρχομαι εἰς Κόρινθον (1:23).

44. Similarly TCNT, NIV, NJB; Bultmann 46; Martin 30; Klauck 28.

45. Lietzmann 104; Wendland 172.

46. TCNT; similarly Wolff 38-39.

47. Wand, Barclay; NAB[1], "when I come."

48. Williams; or "when I came" (RSV, NIV, NAB[2], NRSV).

49. If ἀφ' ὧν stands for ἀπὸ ἐκείνων οἷς ("at the hands of those regarding whom"), it is a matter of the attraction of the relative (οἷς) into the case of the omitted demonstrative antecedent (ἐκείνων; cf. BDF §294[4]).

50. BAGD 482a.

51. Robertson, *Pictures* 215; according to McKay ("Time" 218), ἔδει is "an excluded potential": *"(those from) whom I ought to have joy* (which I do not at present have)."

give me joy." Rather, since Paul is depicting the consequences *had* he visited Corinth, ἔδει will express an unfulfilled past obligation, "(those who) ought to have made me rejoice."[52] It is totally legitimate for Christian workers to expect that those whom they serve will afford them a constant source of pleasure. Paul certainly anticipated that he would derive joy from his converts at the parousia (1:14; 1 Thess. 2:19).

πεποιθὼς ἐπὶ πάντας ὑμᾶς ὅτι ἡ ἐμὴ χαρὰ πάντων ὑμῶν ἐστιν. "I am confident with regard to all of you that my joy means the joy of you all." Although πεποιθώς is a perfect with a present meaning,[53] this participle here relates to past time (ἔγραψα) "I felt sure of all of you" (Bultmann 37), "I had sufficient confidence in you . . ." (REB), although the implication of a present confidence cannot be excluded ("I was confident, and remain confident").[54] πεποιθώς is followed here by a dual construction: ὅτι defines the content of the confidence, and ἐπὶ πάντας ὑμᾶς denotes those in (ἐπί) whom the confidence was felt. ἐστιν could reproduce the present tense ("my joy is . . .") of that past confidence[55] (thus, "my joy was yours too," NJB), but it is more probably a gnomic or timeless present, indicating Paul's invariable attitude concerning the relationship between his joy and that of the Corinthians — "if I have joy, it is shared by you all." Paul is not affirming that the Corinthians' joy is dependent on his[56] but rather that his joy belongs to them all (ὑμῶν is a possessive genitive) or that his joy is so inextricably bound up with theirs that his joy and theirs amount to one and the same thing ("my joy means the joy of you all," supplying a second χαρά before πάντων). "The solidarity of brotherly love requires sharing the same feelings" (Spicq 3.76 n. 60).

How could Paul have expressed confidence in the Corinthians at the time he wrote the severe letter? Perhaps we should distinguish between the circumstances surrounding the writing of the letter and his anticipation of its outcome. 2:4 leaves no room for doubt that Paul was distressed and anxious when he wrote the severe letter, grieved at what had caused it. But 2:3 indicates that at the same time he had an unshakable confidence that the Corinthians would react positively to the letter, a buoyant assurance that whatever made him glad — such as their positive response — would give all of them pleasure too, for they were all one in joy, as in sorrow.

2:4 ἐκ γὰρ πολλῆς θλίψεως καὶ συνοχῆς καρδίας ἔγραψα ὑμῖν διὰ πολλῶν δακρύων. "For it was out of deep distress and anguish of heart and with many tears that I wrote to you." γάρ is not strongly causal here; it simply introduces a restatement of the fact that Paul avoided a painful visit by writing a let-

---

52. BAGD 172b, c: "The impf. ἔδει is used to denote . . . that someth(ing) that did not take place really should have happened: *should have, ought to have,*" citing 2 Cor. 2:3. Similarly RSV; Plummer 50; Zerwick and Grosvenor 537; Thrall 163, 168.

53. BDF §341; Robertson 881.

54. Cf. BAGD 639c.

55. See BDF §324 for this construction.

56. *Pace* Windisch 81.

ter (2:3). ἐκ describes the origin[57] and διά the circumstances[58] of the painful letter. It was born of deep-seated anguish and heartfelt distress and was produced amid many tears. συνοχή, formed from συνέχω ("hold together, oppress") and used only here and in Luke 21:25, means "oppression" or "compression,"[59] and in the NT "dismay" or "anguish." πολλῆς and καρδίας both qualify θλίψεως and συνοχῆς. Since 7:8-11 refers to the same letter as a whole as causing λύπη to the Corinthians, it is likely that 2:4 also is speaking of the entire "severe letter," not of various isolated parts.[60] By stating positively what personal emotions prompted this letter and accompanied its writing, Paul is excluding other explanations such as a desire for vindication or retaliation.

οὐχ ἵνα λυπηθῆτε ἀλλὰ τὴν ἀγάπην ἵνα γνῶτε ἣν ἔχω περισσοτέρως εἰς ὑμᾶς. "My aim was not to cause you pain but to let you know the love, the very intense love, I have for you." Later Paul celebrates a λύπη that corresponds to God's intention (κατὰ θεόν) and produces repentance (εἰς μετάνοιαν, 7:9-10). Here, then, he must be repudiating λύπη as an end in itself, but not λύπη as a God-appointed means of repentance. Alternatively, if οὐ(κ) . . . ἀλλά signifies "not so much X as Y" (cf. 2:5), Paul is affirming that his *principal* aim in writing the sorrowful letter was not to inflict the Corinthians with λύπη that he hoped would lead them to a change of heart, but to reassure them that his heart was brimming over with love for them. ἀγάπη and the infliction of λύπη are not incompatible. Pain inflicted by love can be a tool God uses to produce "a repentance that leads to salvation and leaves no regrets" (7:10).[61]

Not only the absolute οὐ(κ) . . . ἀλλά but also the irregular and therefore emphatic position of τὴν ἀγάπην before ἵνα draw attention to the fact of Paul's love, just as the adverb περισσοτέρως highlights the quality of that love. περισσότατα, the superlative of περισσῶς, was obsolescent in Hellenistic Greek, so the comparative περισσοτέρως was used for this elative superlative[62] and means "very intensely," "extremely abundantly," or simply "especially," "all the more." If this adverb qualifies ἀγάπην, the sense will be "the very intense love," "the extraordinary affection" (Goodspeed). If, on the other hand, it modifies εἰς ὑμᾶς and retains a comparative sense, the meaning is "especially for you," "my special love for you" (Moffatt).[63]

So, then, 2:4b states a second purpose that lay behind the tearful letter.

57. Robertson 598; but BAGD (235d) classifies ἐκ in 2:4 as denoting "circumstances which accompany an action without necessarily being the source of it."

58. BDF §223(3); BAGD 180c; Moule 57.

59. MM 611 cites P. Lond. 354 line 24 (ca. 10 B.C.), where the word apparently means "imprisonment."

60. See, *per contra,* Bernard 14.

61. "Charity desires the conversion of the guilty, and though it grieves over the ills of others and rejoices at their good (v. 3; 1 Cor. 13:6-7), it does not hesitate to cause them pain if the salvation of their souls is in question (2 Cor. 12:15)" (Spicq, *Agape* 184).

62. On this phenomenon of the comparative standing for the superlative, see BDF §§60(1), 244; Zerwick §147.

63. Similarly F. Hauck, *TDNT* 6.62.

It was not merely designed to avoid a second painful visit (2:1, 3). Although it arose from spiritual anguish and actually proved painful to its recipients (7:8), its aim was not vindictive or even vindicative. On the contrary, it sought to convince the Corinthians of the intensity of Paul's affectionate concern for them.

Bibliography

Batey, "Interactions" • H. Binder, *Der Glaube bei Paulus* (Berlin: Evangelische Verlagsanstalt, 1968) 57 • F. Buri, "'Nicht, dass wir Herren über euren Glauben wären' (2 Kor 1,24)," *Schweizerische Theologische Umschau* 35 (1965) 82-90 • Deissmann, *Light* 304 • G. Friedrich, "Glaube und Verkündigung bei Paulus," in *Glaube im Neuen Testament, H. Binder FS,* ed. F. Hahn and H. Klein (Neukirchener-Vluyn: Neukirchener, 1982) 93-113 • Hahn • Ljungman • Murphy-O'Connor 23-27 • Spicq, *Agape* 2.183-85 • Stählin, "Gebrauch"

4. Forgiveness for the Offender (2:5-11)

In this paragraph the focus of the apostle's attention continues to be the explanation and defense of his recent conduct (1:12–2:13), especially the circumstances that gave rise to the "severe letter." As in 1:23–2:4, so here also, Paul speaks about the matter of feeling pain, causing pain, and avoiding further pain and about his purposes in writing that painful letter. What is new is his reference to the individual at Corinth (τις or ὁ τοιοῦτος) whose irresponsible action had implicated the whole congregation and prompted the "severe letter." Now that this person had experienced λύπη (ἡ) κατὰ θεόν, the sorrow that accords with God's will and produces repentance (cf. 7:10), the Corinthians needed to discontinue their ἐπιτιμία and reaffirm their love for this repentant individual. If they failed to do this, the man's λύπη would consume him and Satan would triumph.

Particularly apparent here is Paul's sensitivity as a pastor: He avoids naming the culprit (vv. 5-8), he recognizes that Christian discipline is not simply retributive but also remedial (vv. 6-7), he understands the feelings and psychological needs of the penitent wrongdoer (vv. 6-8), he indirectly appeals to his own conduct as an example for the Corinthians to follow (v. 10), and he is fully aware of the divisive intention and operation of Satan within the Christian community (v. 11).

5But if anyone has caused pain, he has pained not me but to some extent — not to exaggerate — all of you. 6For this person the particular punishment imposed by the majority is sufficient. 7So, taking the opposite course, you should forgive and encourage him instead,[a] lest perhaps this person be overwhelmed by excessive pain. 8This is why I urge you to ratify your love for him. 9For my aim in writing[b] was also to ascertain whether^c you would pass the test of being obedient in all respects. 10*And the person whom you forgive for anything, I too forgive. For indeed, what I for my part have forgiven — if I have forgiven anything — I have forgiven for your sake in the sight of Christ,* 11*so that Satan may not gain the advantage over us, for we know well his schemes.*

TEXTUAL NOTES

a. The reading μᾶλλον ὑμᾶς enjoys strong and geographically diversified support: proto-Alexandrian (p⁴⁶ ℵ), later Alexandrian (C Ψ 0243 81 104 326 1739), Western (it^ar, dem, f, m, r1, x, z Tertullian), and Byzantine (K *Byz Lect*). Also, with μᾶλλον ("rather," "instead") being apparently tautologous after τοὐναντίον ("on the contrary"), this reading is more difficult than either ὑμᾶς (A B syr^p eth Jerome Augustine) or μᾶλλον (1881). The variant word order, ὑμᾶς μᾶλλον (D G 33 it^d, e, g goth Theodoret), lacks the breadth of support that favors μᾶλλον ὑμᾶς and may have arisen as a scribal effort partially to relieve the apparent tautology of τοὐναντίον μᾶλλον. Metzger proposes that the μᾶλλον of an original μᾶλλον ὑμᾶς was accidentally omitted in a few manuscripts and later added after ὑμᾶς ([1971] 576).

b. A superfluous ὑμῖν is added by (F G) 81 104 629 *pc* b vg^s.

c. The awkwardness of a double construction after ἵνα γνῶ, viz. a direct object τὴν δοκιμήν and an εἰ clause ("to see whether . . ."), may have prompted some scribes to substitute ἧ ("by/in which," referring back to τὴν δοκιμήν; A B 33) or ὡς ("namely that"; 460 1836 cop^sa?). The omission of εἰ by p⁴⁶ 436 2495 would have occurred accidentally, as a result of the juxtaposition of εἰ and εἰς.

2:5 εἰ δέ τις λελύπηκεν, οὐκ ἐμὲ λελύπηκεν. "But if anyone has caused pain, he has not pained me." As Paul proceeds to identify the cause of the earlier friction between himself and the Corinthians, he avoids naming the offender and plays down the severity of the λύπη he himself experienced. "In the hypothetical εἰ, as in the indefinite τις, there lies a delicate, tender forbearance."[1] But εἰ . . . τις is conditional only in form; in sense it is equivalent to ὅς, "the person who" (cf. εἴ τι in 7:14). The two cases of the perfect (λελύπηκεν) may imply that the pain is still felt (Windisch 84), but they should not be regarded as timeless ("if anyone causes any grief, he does not cause grief to me").[2] οὐκ ἐμέ ought not to be pressed so as to the exclude Paul from any personal experience of pain. On occasion he uses the negative, not with an absolute meaning ("not at all"), but in a relative sense "not so much," or "not primarily," or "not only" (cf. 1 Cor. 1:17; 2 Cor. 7:12).[3] It is therefore no argument against the sense "he has not so much

1. Meyer 444. Burton (§240, citing 2:5) observes that the occurrence of an indefinite pronoun in the protasis does not require that the supposition is general and not particular.
2. As Porter (268-69) argues.
3. Cf. Zerwick §445: "In disjunctive propositions, it is a Semitic peculiarity to express one member negatively so as to lay more stress on the other, saying 'not A but B' where the sense is 'not so much A as B' or 'B rather than A'" (citing Matt. 10:20; Mark 9:37; Luke 10:20; John 7:16; 12:44; 1 Cor. 1:17). Similarly BDF §448(1). This sense is recognized in 2:5 by Weymouth; Moffatt; Goodspeed; Wand; NAB¹; Bruce 185; Wolff 42; Thrall 171.

grieved me (as he has grieved all of you)" (NIV) to observe, as Meyer does (444), that "Paul does not say οὐ μόνον, ἀλλὰ καί."

ἀλλὰ ἀπὸ μέρους, ἵνα μὴ ἐπιβαρῶ, πάντας ὑμᾶς. "But to some extent — not to exaggerate — (he has pained) all of you." ἀπὸ μέρους, "in part" (as in 1:14; MM 399a), "in some degree" (BAGD 506b), "to some extent" (Barrett 89), may limit the number of persons affected by the λύπη: "not quite all of you were scandalized by the wrongdoer's action."[4] This would seem to imply a minority who did not share the λύπη felt by οἱ πλείονες (2:6) and so did not support the ἐπιτιμία imposed by the majority. But "partially all of you" is a strange way of saying "almost all of you." Alternatively, and preferably, this prepositional phrase may limit the extent to which the λύπη was felt by all the Corinthians: "all of you, to some extent."[5] We suggest that the λύπη inflicted on Paul was the offense itself (see below regarding its nature) and that the λύπη experienced by the Corinthians was their profound grief in the aftermath of the offense, a grief that produced in them the reactions listed in 7:7, 11.

Elsewhere in Paul the verb ἐπιβαρέω ("burden," "weigh down") is used transitively (1 Thess. 2:9; 2 Thess. 3:8). But here, in the absence of an expressed direct object (such as αὐτόν or τινὰ ὑμῶν), the verb probably bears an intransitive sense, "in order not to heap up a burden of words," "not to put it too severely" (NIV), "not to labour the point" (NEB), "not to exaggerate" (NJB).[6] This whole clause, ἵνα μὴ ἐπιβαρῶ, is not a second qualification of the following πάντας ὑμᾶς, but is an explanation for the insertion of ἀπὸ μέρους as an advance qualification of πάντας ὑμᾶς. It was not true that the unnamed offender grieved all the Corinthians equally, but it was true that all of them in some measure were pained by his action. It was to avoid the exaggeration ἀλλὰ πάντας ὑμᾶς that Paul added ἀπὸ μέρους.[7]

At this point, three questions must be considered. (1) Who was the offender? (2) What was the nature of his wrongdoing? (3) When did the offense occur?

(1) Because the offense occurred at Corinth and some type of penalty was imposed on the offender by the Corinthian church (2:6), it is almost universally assumed that ὁ ἀδικήσας (7:12) was a member of that church and therefore presumably a native Corinthian. But Barrett has argued that the offender was a visitor to Corinth, one of the pseudo-apostles, an anti-Pauline in-

---

4. Similarly Plummer 52, 56; Bultmann 48.

5. Similarly Barrett 89; Thrall 172.

6. Cf. Moffatt ("for I am not going to overstate the case"); JB ("not to overstate it"); Lietzmann 106 ("in order not to say too much").

7. Three alternative, but improbable, ways of construing ἀλλὰ κτλ. may be mentioned (for a full discussion, see Thrall 172-73): (1) πάντας is taken with ἐπιβαρῶ within the parenthesis, "that I may not burden all" (so Olshausen 286) (but this leaves ὑμᾶς strangely isolated). (2) A punctuation mark is placed after ἀπὸ μέρους, as in the KJV, "But if any have caused grief, he hath not grieved me, but in part: that I may not overcharge you all" (but it is doubtful whether ἀλλά may stand for εἰ μή, "except"). (3) οὐκ ἐμὲ λελύπηκεν is construed as a question expecting the answer "Yes," with ἀλλά introducing a qualification that incorporates v. 6.

truder.[8] If the offender were a native Corinthian whose action had been tolerated by a majority of the Corinthians so that they were implicated in his guilt,
how could Paul affirm, Barrett asks, that the Corinthians had proved themselves (to Titus) to be innocent (ἀγνοί) in every respect (ἐν παντί) as far as the
affair was concerned (τῷ πράγματι) (7:11)? And how could they have punished the person in question if they shared his guilt?

In response to Barrett's view, we may ask whether Paul could have or
would have demanded the punishment of a visitor to Corinth, especially if at least
some of the Corinthians regarded him as an "apostle of Christ" (cf. 10:7; 11:13)
accredited by letters from Judea (cf. 3:1). Moreover, would Paul have called for
ἐπιτιμία — be it "reproof" or "punishment" (see on 2:6) — and not rather expulsion? Would a mere visitor to Corinth submit to church discipline at Corinth?
Finally, it is doubtful, on this hypothesis, that Paul would have encouraged the reaffirmation of love for this repentant man, for this probably implied his readmis-
sion to fellowship. As for 7:11, Paul may be saying nothing more than that the
Corinthians, by their κατὰ θεὸν λύπη, had now shown themselves to be totally in
the right after their earlier complicity in the affair. In our view, the traditional understanding that the offender was a native Corinthian is eminently defensible.

(2) An inductive study of the relevant passages in 2 Corinthians suggests
that there are at least four characteristics of the offense that must be accommodated by any proposal concerning its specific nature.[9] (a) Basically, the offense involved two individuals — ὁ ἀδικήσας (7:12) = τις (2:5) = ὁ τοιοῦτος (2:6-7) =
αὐτός (2:8) = ὅς (2:10) and ὁ ἀδικηθείς (7:12). (b) The ἀδικία involved interpersonal relations, not a doctrinal dispute. (c) The action taken by ὁ ἀδικήσας caused
λύπη to all (or the majority) of the Corinthian congregation (2:5), to Paul (2:5,
where οὐ = οὐ πρῶτον), and to the offender himself after his repentance (2:7).
(d) The offense was so serious in nature that church discipline was required (2:6)
and forgiveness was needed after the offender's repentance (2:7, 10).

The time-honored identification of the offense sees it as the incest of
1 Cor. 5:1-13. But, with good reason, most modern writers reject this identification of ὁ τοιοῦτος of 2 Cor. 2:6-7 with ὁ τοιοῦτος of 1 Cor. 5:5, which usually
presupposes that 1 Corinthians is the "severe letter." (See the detailed discussion in the Introduction, A.2.c.[1].) The prevailing view in more recent times
identifies the ἀδικία as a verbal attack on Paul, involving an insult to his person
and a rejection of his authority. Two representative statements of this view may
be mentioned. Moffatt proposed that the person who insulted Paul was a "Corinthian who took umbrage at Paul's domineering methods of discipline" (Introduction 122 n. 2). More recently, F. Watson describes the issue at stake as
Paul's authority to punish: "A member of the congregation (perhaps the leader

---

8. 7, 86-90, 92-93, 212-13; "2 Cor. 7:12" 152-56. Murphy-O'Connor believes that the offender was a spokesman for a delegation from the church of Antioch that had been sent to exercise
that church's rights over congregations Paul had established in its name (*Paul* 293-94).

9. See the longer list in Allo 55.

of a group of dissidents) claims that *Paul's failure to carry out his threat* [of punishment, made in 1 Cor. 4:18-21] *is due to the fact that he does not have the power to do so, and that he is therefore no true apostle*" (343; cf. 344-45).

An interesting effort to combine these two identifications has been made by Kruse. He argues that the incestuous man of 1 Corinthians 5, not intimidated by Paul's demand for disciplinary action against him and still unrepentant, spearheaded an attack on Paul during Paul's "painful visit" by calling into question his credentials and authority. But the man repented of both offenses after the Corinthians imposed the discipline of excommunication (1 Cor. 5:3-5, 13) in response to Paul's "severe letter."[10] However, this proposal requires that the man offended twice, first by committing incest and then by openly rejecting Paul's authority. Yet 7:12 presupposes a single offense, with ὁ ἀδικήσας meaning "the person who did the wrong," which is also an unlikely way of describing an incestuous relationship that persisted from the time of 1 Corinthians (note ἔχειν, 1 Cor. 5:1) until the "severe letter," that is, for twelve months or more. And it is difficult to imagine that Paul would have expressed himself so benignly in 2:5-11 if the offender had so blatantly and persistently ignored Paul's censure of 1 Corinthians 5.

One further attempt to identify the offense should be noted. Thrall suggests that the ἀδικία was the misappropriation of collection funds intended for Jerusalem. A member of the Corinthian church stole from Paul money for the collection that had been entrusted to the apostle by another church member for temporary safekeeping. The thief was ὁ ἀδικήσας, and the original depositor was ὁ ἀδικηθείς.[11] For all its ingenuity and valiant effort to accommodate many items of evidence found in 2 Corinthians 2 and 7, this proposal cannot be deemed more than a highly suggestive, detailed hypothesis.

(3) As to the time of the offense, the majority of scholars place it during Paul's "painful visit."[12] But it seems easier to believe that Paul had already left Corinth when the personal effrontery occurred than that he ignominiously retreated to Ephesus, an insulted and broken man, only later to accomplish by a letter and the intervention of his delegate Titus what he had earlier failed to achieve in person.[13] Such a retreat would have made the subsequent veiled threat of 13:10 sound completely hollow: "I am writing this while absent from you so that when I come I may not have to deal with you severely in the exercise of that authority which the Lord has given me for building you up, not for

10. Kruse 42-45; "Offender" 129-39.
11. Thrall 68-69, 171, 495; "Offender" 74-76. Betz also links the ἀδικία with the collection. It was a formal charge by a Corinthian that Paul had initiated the collection for his own financial gain (97).
12. E.g., Kümmel, *Introduction* 283; Barrett 7, 89, 213; Barnett 372; Thrall 171, although earlier she surmised that the offense occurred after Paul's departure: "He attempted to reassert his authority by letter. . . . He would not have done this if he had had the opportunity of dealing with the offender in person on the spot" (*First Letter* 119-20).
13. Thus Mackintosh, "Visit" 226. This view is also defended by Allo ix, xii, 55, 62, 76.

tearing you down."[14] What is more, how could Paul have put Titus's mind to rest concerning the probable Corinthian reaction to the "severe letter" (7:13-15) if he himself had recently withdrawn from Corinth in frustration after the offense had been committed and the Corinthians had failed to rally to his defense?

We conclude, therefore, that the ἀδικία was a verbal assault on Paul's person and authority carried out by a member of the Corinthian church at some indefinite time between the "painful visit" and the "severe letter." With considerably less confidence we may conjecture that the offender was a spokesman for an anti-Pauline clique (see on 2:6), that he objected in particular to Paul's disciplinary methods such as those outlined in 1 Corinthians 5, and that he may have insulted Paul in the context of resisting the authority of one of Paul's representatives, such as Timothy, who would have reported the incident to Paul.

2:6 ἱκανὸν τῷ τοιούτῳ ἡ ἐπιτιμία αὕτη ἡ ὑπὸ τῶν πλειόνων. "For this person the particular punishment imposed by the majority is sufficient." The correlative adjective τοιοῦτος is used fifty-seven times in the NT, but rarely correlatively. Although it often means "such a person" (e.g., in 11:13),[15] when it is articular it can function (as here) as a less definite term for οὗτος,[16] simply "this person" or "this man" or "the man to whom I refer" (TCNT). Clearly the reference is to the unnamed individual (τις) of 2:5 who caused pain to Paul and the Corinthians.

Noting the general NT use of the cognate verb ἐπιτιμᾶν to denote a rebuke, Barrett argues that the NT *hapax legomenon* ἐπιτιμία means "reproof" (the Vulgate uses *obiurgatio* here).[17] But the more general meaning of "punishment" or "penalty" is to be preferred;[18] LSJ cites Wis. 3:10 and *OGIS* 669.43 (a papyrus from first-century-A.D. Egypt) in support of this rendering (667). Moreover, Paul uses ἐκδίκησις ("punishment") in 7:11 in reference to this same disciplinary act.[19] In this case ἐπιτιμία will bear the same sense as the classical term ἐπιτίμιον (usually in the plural), "penalty," rather than ἐπιτίμησις, "censure." αὕτη ("this") refers to the particular punishment of which Paul and his readers were aware ("the punishment in question").

The penalty was inflicted by οἱ πλείονες. Three proposals have been made regarding the meaning of this term here. (1) If it simply means "many" (Turner 30), the reference is simply to the plurality of participants. However, one would

14. Cf. Schmithals 104.

15. BAGD 821c; Thrall 163: "this sort of person . . . such a person" (on 2:6-7).

16. BDF §304; Turner 46. Both cite 1 Cor. 5:5; 2 Cor. 2:6-7; 12:2-3, 5 as instances of this usage. Similarly *EDNT* 3.364d.

17. Barrett 90; similarly Goodspeed, Berkeley; E. Stauffer, *TDNT* 2.627; Martin 30, 37 ("censure"); Young and Ford 263 ("rebuke"); Carrez 66 ("blâme").

18. So also MM 248d; NEB, REB, and most English versions; Plummer 52, 57; Lietzmann 106; Furnish 153, 155; Thrall 163, 173-74.

19. See BAGD 238d; Meurer 135-36.

not normally expect the article with πλείονες in this case. (2) If the expression represents the Hebrew *hārabbîm* ("the many"), especially as regularly used at Qumran,[20] Paul is describing the action of the whole community, "the main body" or "the general meeting" (NEB, REB) or "the full assembly," in which case "it is not a matter of a majority decision, but of a unanimous vote."[21] Against this is the fact that οἱ πολλοί (as in Rom. 12:5; 1 Cor. 10:17), not οἱ πλείονες, is the usual and natural Greek equivalent of *hārabbîm*. (3) οἱ πλείονες refers to "the majority,"[22] that is, "the greater number," as in 1 Cor. 10:5; 15:16; 2 Cor. 9:2, and Acts 19:32; 27:12. On this view, which is to be preferred, it is difficult not to envisage, especially with the use of the technical legal terms ἐπιτιμία ("penalty") and κυρόω ("ratify," 2:8) in the immediate context, some formal gathering of the whole Corinthian church where a deliberative decision was made that was approved and carried out by the majority but opposed by a minority. At any rate, Paul recognized that the exercise of church discipline was a function of the local church, not of an apostle, who belonged to the universal church. And to be effective, discipline in the local church must be agreed upon and implemented by the majority or the whole body, not imposed by the few.

The neuter ἱκανόν is not a case of incongruence in gender, grammatical discord between subject (ἡ ἐπιτιμία) and predicate, as Turner (311) alleges. Rather, ἱκανόν is a substantival use of the neuter adjective,[23] as in Matt. 6:34 (ἀρκετόν) and Luke 12:23 (πλεῖον). On the basis of Titus's report about the Corinthian response to the "severe letter" (7:7-11), Paul formed the opinion that the punishment already suffered by the offender was sufficient, since apparently it had achieved its purpose of engendering a "godly sorrow" that produced repentance (cf. 7:10). Since in 2:7 Paul recommends an end (cf. τοὐναντίον μᾶλλον) to the ἐπιτιμία, not a change of punishment, the sufficiency must relate to time rather than degree.[24]

What constituted the penalty cannot be known for sure. It may have been the forfeiting of church privileges such as participation in the Lord's Supper, exclusion from all social relations with other church members (cf. 1 Cor. 5:11, τῷ τοιούτῳ μηδὲ συνεσθίειν; 2 Thess. 3:14), or excommunication (cf. 1 Cor. 5:3-5, 13).[25] Whatever the actual penalty, 2:7 makes it clear that it was not irreversible: If the ἐπιτιμία led to λύπη and μετάνοια, the penalty could be discontinued.[26]

20. See J. Jeremias, *TDNT* 6.538-39.
21. G. Nebe, *EDNT* 3.102. Similarly Barrett 91; Meeks 130.
22. BAGD 689b (under II.2.a.α); 843b; Furnish 153, 155; Thrall 163, 175.
23. Winer 517; BDF §131(2). But Hughes contends that ἱκανόν is "a simple latinism (= *satis*)," citing Luke 22:38; Mark 15:15 (66 n. 11).
24. But cf. BAGD 374c ("the punishment is severe enough"); Conybeare in Conybeare and Howson 443 ("the punishment . . . is sufficient without increasing it").
25. Against the view that the punishment was a severe reprimand delivered in public is the consideration that in 2:7 Paul counsels the discontinuance of the penalty.
26. With this compare the distinction at Qumran between defaming or complaining against the whole congregation ("the many"), which led to permanent exclusion, and defaming or com-

If οἱ πλείονες implies a dissenting minority, what was their view — that the penalty was too severe or that it was too lenient? Since v. 7 begins with τοὐναντίον μᾶλλον ("on the contrary, . . . instead") and counsels the termination of the punishment, this minority view was more probably that of a pro-Pauline clique (cf. ἐγώ εἰμι Παύλου, 1 Cor. 1:12) which advocated the continuance or exacerbation of the ἐπιτιμία[27] than that of an anti-Pauline group which regarded the punishment as inappropriate or excessive.[28]

2:7 ὥστε τοὐναντίον μᾶλλον ὑμᾶς χαρίσασθαι καὶ παρακαλέσαι. "So, taking the opposite course, you should forgive and encourage him instead." ἱκανόν in v. 6 is to be construed with both τῷ τοιούτῳ (2:6) and ὥστε κτλ.: The penalty imposed by the majority was sufficient for the offender, given the nature of his offense and the fact of his repentance, but it was also so adequate that the Corinthians now needed to replace punishment with forgiveness and warm acceptance. The accusative and infinitive construction that follows ὥστε could be either ὑμᾶς χαρίσασθαι καὶ παρακαλέσαι, "sufficient, consequently, for you rather to forgive and comfort instead"[29] or ὑμᾶς [δεῖν] χαρίσασθαι κτλ., "so that, on the other hand, you should rather forgive and console him."[30] τοὐναντίον (= τὸ ἐναντίον, by crasis [Robertson 208]) means "on the contrary": "so far from inflicting severer punishment" (Barclay), the Corinthians should now pursue an opposite course, counsels Paul.[31] Their forgiveness of the offender would serve to assure him that God had also, in fact, forgiven him. In this way the community would in effect be remitting or loosing his sins (cf. Matt. 18:18; John 20:23) by declaring and confirming to him the reality of divine forgiveness. παρακαλέω here probably bears its common meaning of "encourage," "console" but its narrower sense, "try to conciliate," would not be inappropriate.

μή πως τῇ περισσοτέρᾳ λύπῃ καταποθῇ ὁ τοιοῦτος. "Lest perhaps this person be overwhelmed by excessive pain." μή πως, "lest perhaps," "lest it happen that," reflects either a fear ("perhaps he will be overwhelmed") or a wish ("may he not be overwhelmed").[32] The comparative περισσότερος functions as an elative superlative, so that τῇ περισσοτέρᾳ λύπῃ means "by excessive sorrow" (RSV, NRSV) or "by excess of grief" (Barclay).[33] It is not sorrow or pain after punishment from which Paul is shielding the wrongdoer, but an extreme

---

plaining against another member of the community, which incurred only temporary punishment (1QS 7.17-20).

27. Thus Zahn 1.333-35, 347 n. 6; Kennedy 101-9; Plummer 58; (CGT) 46-47, 117-18; Lake 170-72, 174; Manson 217 n. 2.

28. Thus Bernard 22-23, 48; Kümmel, *Introduction* 213; Hughes 68-69; South 92.

29. Thrall 163; cf. 176-77. Burton (§371) classifies ὥστε in 2:7 as denoting "tendency or conceived result thought of as such."

30. Martin 30, 37. Moule notes (144) an occasional tendency to ellipsis in the use of ὥστε, citing 2:7 and ὥστε [δύνασθαι] in 1 Cor. 13:2; Heb. 13:6. Windisch observes (87) that ὥστε depends on ἱκανόν and implies an ἀνάγκη or πρέπον.

31. Cf. the REB paraphrase: "Something very different is called for now."

32. Cf. Moulton 193, who speaks of the latent prohibitive force of μή.

33. The dative is causal ("by reason of"), instrumental ("by," "through"), or local ("in").

sorrow or excessive pain that would cause him to be overwhelmed. If the punishment were to be continued or increased now that this man (ὁ τοιοῦτος)[34] was repentant, he would suffer περισσοτέρα λύπη and consequently a καταποθῆναι, consuming despair, including a despair of ever being accepted back into the Corinthian assembly. When repentance is present after wrongdoing, there is always the danger of excessive punishment that leads to excessive sorrow and then despair.

2:8 διὸ παρακαλῶ ὑμᾶς κυρῶσαι εἰς αὐτὸν ἀγάπην. "This is why I urge you to ratify your love for him." διό looks back to μή πως κτλ. To protect the offender from immoderate grief and possibly from loss of faith (? = the κατάποσις), Paul now pleads for an affirmation or reaffirmation of love toward him, instead of any prolonging of his punishment. The repetition of the verb παρακαλεῖν in 2:6-7 is noteworthy. Paul pleads (παρακαλῶ) with the Corinthians to encourage (παρακαλέσαι) the wrongdoer.[35] The precise nature of their παράκλησις is unclear, but it included a κυρῶσαι, a formal and full reinstatement of the offender in the Corinthians' love, probably, by formal action. This colorful verb κυρόω, from (τὸ) κῦρος, "authority," means "act so as to make something effectual,"[36] and was used extensively as a technical term to denote the validation of legal actions.[37] In Gal. 3:15, the only other NT use of this verb, κυρόω refers to the ratification of a will (κεκυρωμένην διαθήκην), just as two verses later (Gal. 3:17) its opposite, ἀκυρόω, is used of the annulment of a covenant. Spicq renders our verse, "For this reason I exhort you to take an official stand of love toward him."[38] If the previous ἐπιτιμία had been a formal act, imposing punishment, this κύρωσις was also a formal act, imposing love. It was important for all the congregation to be as aware of this κύρωσις as they had been of the earlier ἐπιτιμία. The word order, with ἀγάπην standing last, highlights the oxymoron: the Corinthians were to give formal recognition, not to a decision or a document or a will — but to love.

2:9 εἰς τοῦτο γὰρ καὶ ἔγραψα ἵνα γνῶ τὴν δοκιμὴν ὑμῶν, εἰ εἰς πάντα ὑπήκοοί ἐστε. "For my aim in writing was also to ascertain whether you would pass the test of being obedient in all respects." εἰς τοῦτο anticipates the epexegetic ἵνα, "for this (purpose, namely) that,"[39] and introduces the third pur-

---

34. It is certainly possible that ὁ τοιοῦτος here looks beyond the present offender to "a person in his situation," "such a person."

35. See Bjerkelund 154.

36. Zerwick, *Analysis* 394. Cf. Burton, *Galatians* 179.

37. See MM 366; J. Behm, *TDNT* 3.1098-99; Spicq, *Agape* 185-87 ("In the papyri, *kuroō* ordinarily refers to a confirmation of some transaction with the government; it almost never appears in private contracts. The officials mentioned as responsible for the decision or pledge of execution are the prefect, the general, the royal scribe, the council, or even the divinity. Their positions gave juridical formality or at least a certain public character to the act of ratification [*kyrōsis*], whether it was applied to a debt, a rental of property, or simply a tax" [186]).

38. Spicq, *Agape* 185, 187.

39. BAGD 377b; cf. 229d. Comparable uses of this εἰς τοῦτο . . . ἵνα construction are found in John 18:37; Acts 9:21; Rom. 14:9, 1 Pet. 3:9; 4:6; 1 John 3:8.

pose of the "severe letter," which was to test the Corinthians' obedience.[40] Paul has already delineated two purposes: to avoid a second painful visit (2:3) and to reassure the Corinthians of his intense love for them (2:4).[41]

δοκιμή is a back-formation from δοκιμάζω, "put to the test" (BDF §110 [2]), and so can mean "testing," "test," or "ordeal" (as in 8:2). But it can also describe "the quality of the person who is δόκιμος" or "approved worth known by testing"[42] (as in 9:13; Phil. 2:22). Either sense is appropriate in this context: "to put you to the test"[43] or "to know your proven character" (NAB²). Whichever sense is preferred, the indirect question that follows, with εἰ = "whether,"[44] should be understood as an explication of the δοκιμή rather than as a second, distinct purpose of Paul's writing.[45] The Corinthians would give evidence of having passed the test (or of their proven character) by their total obedience.[46] But as Paul writes the present letter, he knows that these believers have in fact been successful in the test, for Titus has reported to him the ὑπακοή of them all (7:15).

To whom or what had the Corinthians been obedient? It is true that Paul envisages Christian obedience as being given to God (Rom. 6:16, 22) or to the gospel and its implications (Rom. 6:17; 10:16), but he would probably not have distinguished between obedience to the gospel of Christ and obedience to himself as an ambassador and apostle of Christ. It is also true that where he elsewhere refers to the obedience of his converts (2 Cor. 7:15; 10:6; Phil. 2:12; 2 Thess. 3:14; Phlm. 21), no object of that obedience is specified, but in each case the context seems to indicate that he himself, as the representative of Christ, is the one to be obeyed. This certainly must be the case when obedience is linked with "what I/we say" (τῷ λόγῳ ἡμῶν, 2 Thess. 3:14; ἃ λέγω, Phlm. 21). In considering this matter we should ignore neither 1:24 nor 2:9: Paul is not only the Corinthians' servant, working to achieve joy; he is also their father, requiring their filial obedience.[47] In the present case, the NEB and REB leave no room for ambiguity: "I wrote, I may say, to see how you stood the test, whether you fully accepted my authority."

2:10 ᾧ δέ τι χαρίζεσθε, κἀγώ. "And the person whom you forgive for anything, I too forgive." In full this elliptical sentence would read ἐκείνῳ δὲ ᾧ χαρίζεσθέ τι καὶ ἐγὼ χαρίζομαι αὐτό (Moule 130). In its predominant NT usage, χαρίζομαι means "graciously confer," "give freely as a favor," but in Paul, when that conferred favor is the remission of sins, the verb means "pardon,"

---

40. Cf. TCNT: "I had this further object, also, in what I wrote." But Furnish (153) renders καί by "indeed," and Thrall (163) by "actually."

41. For other purposes, see the Introduction, A.2.a.

42. Zerwick, *Analysis* 394. Similarly Spicq 1.360.

43. Wendland 173. So also BAGD 202d.

44. BDF §454(1); Robertson 1045.

45. *Pace* Furnish 153: "to know whether you would stand the test and whether you are in all respects obedient."

46. Cf. G. Schunack, *EDNT* 1.343: "The Church indicates its δοκιμή in 2 Cor. 2:9, when it is obedient to the apostle."

47. On this theme, see Holmberg 77-86.

"forgive,"[48] and is used with the accusative of the thing forgiven (here τι) and the dative of the person forgiven (ᾧ). The Corinthians had concurred with Paul's decision that the guilty man be punished; now he offers to concur with their decision that this repentant person be forgiven (Tasker 54-55). "Anyone who has your forgiveness has mine too" (NEB, REB). In 2:7 Paul has said, in essence, "You *should* forgive this man." Now he says, in effect, "*When* you do so, rest assured that my forgiveness is included in yours." But even if Paul here assumes their forgiveness — he does not say "*if* you forgive anyone" — the responsibility for deciding on a verdict of forgiveness rests with the Corinthians, a decision he trusts they will make after receiving the present letter.

καὶ γὰρ ἐγὼ ὃ κεχάρισμαι, εἴ τι κεχάρισμαι, δι' ὑμᾶς ἐν προσώπῳ Χριστοῦ. "For indeed, what I for my part have forgiven — if I have forgiven anything — I have forgiven for your sake in the sight of Christ." Having assured the Corinthians that their verdict of forgiveness would be his also, Paul hastens to add (καὶ γάρ, "for indeed") that he had already forgiven the man, if in fact there was anything to forgive. ὅ should not be treated as equivalent to ὅ τι (ἄν), "whatever."[49] There was no imprecision in Paul's mind regarding the need for forgiveness or exactly what had been forgiven. It is only in the following parenthetical εἴ τι κεχάρισμαι, where the fact of forgiveness is stated as a hypothesis, that indefiniteness and dismissiveness born of pastoral tact come to expression.

The two prepositional phrases with which the verse ends define the circumstances or motivation of Paul's forgiveness. δι' ὑμᾶς clearly implies that, in Paul's eyes, the primary motivation for his ready forgiveness of the offender — and, we may assume, his earlier demand for the offender's punishment contained in his "severe letter" — was the well-being of the Corinthian community. Doubtless, if only his own reputation or personal feelings had been at stake in this whole matter, he would have been willing to suffer wrong (cf. 1 Cor. 6:7), but since, as also in the case of the man guilty of incest (1 Corinthians 5), the common good was jeopardized and there was the imminent danger that the whole lump would be infected by a small piece of leaven (cf. 1 Cor. 5:6), and in this case the Corinthian loyalty to Paul and the gospel was at issue, neither the offense nor the need for forgiveness could be overlooked. Apparently Paul felt no need to offer forgiveness to the Corinthians themselves, although he had been deeply disappointed at their failure to defend him against the wrongdoer. But he had already pardoned the offender for their sake — to preserve their unity by bringing closure to the whole episode, and to relieve them of their patent embarrassment (cf. ὀδυρμός, 7:7; φόβος, 7:11) at not having acted against the offender before Paul wrote to them.

ἐν προσώπῳ Χριστοῦ. If πρόσωπον ("face") stands for "person" by synecdoche, "in the person of Christ" will mean "as the representative of Christ" (NEB, REB), "acting in Christ's place." But ἐν προσώπῳ is more proba-

---

48. 2 Cor. 2:7; 12:13; Eph. 4:32; Col. 2:13; 3:13.
49. But cf. Furnish 153: "and whatever I . . . have forgiven."

232

bly a Semitism representing Hebrew *lipnē,* "in the presence of."[50] In this case Christ either witnesses to the sincerity of Paul's forgiveness[51] or looks on approvingly.[52] Zerwick incorporates both senses in his paraphrase, "with Christ looking on attentively and giving his approval."[53] Jesus taught that willingness to forgive one's brother or sister was a precondition for the receipt of divine forgiveness (Matt. 5:12, 14-15; 18:23-35).

V. 10 affords perhaps the clearest evidence that the offense (cf. 2:5, 11) was basically a personal act of effrontery against Paul or possibly his acknowledged or delegated representative. There was need for Paul's personal forgiveness, although, in deference to the penitent offender's feelings, he discounts the personal pain he himself experienced (v. 5) and deliberately understates the seriousness of the offense (v. 10) lest anyone imagine that he considered himself virtuous in granting forgiveness so readily. All this would be inappropriate if he were describing a sin of incest (1 Corinthians 5).

2:11 ἵνα μὴ πλεονεκτηθῶμεν ὑπὸ τοῦ Σατανᾶ, οὐ γὰρ αὐτοῦ τὰ νοήματα ἀγνοοῦμεν. "So that Satan may not gain the advantage over us, for we know well his schemes." Here Paul states a second reason why forgiveness should be granted the offender. Not only would it rescue him from inordinate sorrow (2:7), it would also frustrate Satan's design of outwitting and defrauding Paul and the Corinthians. ἵνα μή looks back to the three uses of χαρίζομαι in v. 10: κεχάρισμαι (twice), of Paul's actual forgiveness, and χαρίζεσθε (and ultimately ὥστε . . . ὑμᾶς [δεῖν] χαρίσασθαι, v. 7), of the Corinthians' anticipated forgiveness. Paul had forgiven the offender and was encouraging the Corinthians to do the same, so that Satan might be deprived of any further advantage.

πλεονεκτέω, from πλέον ἔχειν ("[crave] to have more"), is an exclusively Pauline word, with four of his five uses in 2 Corinthians and this the only use of the passive.[54] The verb means "defraud," "outwit," "take advantage of (by deceit)." ὁ Σατανᾶς (also found in 11:14; 12:7) represents the Hebrew *śāṭān,* "adversary," "accuser" and is one of four designations of the devil found in 2 Corinthians; the others are ὁ θεὸς τοῦ αἰῶνος τούτου (4:4), Βελιάρ (6:15), and ὁ ὄφις (11:3). The proximity of Χριστός and Σατανᾶς in this one Greek sentence suggests that Paul sees two persons as having vested interests in Corinth: Christ, who approves of Paul's pardoning of the offender, and Satan, who hopes that the Corinthians will deny forgiveness to the man. As a master strategist who is consumed by πλεονεξία ("acquisitiveness"), Satan was bent on creating discord within the church at Corinth, either between the church at large and a dissident minority or between the repentant wrongdoer and his fellow Chris-

---

50. See Hughes 70-71 n. 18; Moule 184.

51. E. Lohse, *TDNT* 6.777; similarly Lietzmann 107.

52. BAGD 721b: *"before the face of Christ* that looks down with approval."

53. Zerwick, *Analysis* 394. There seems to be little reason to take ἐν προσώπῳ Χριστοῦ as an abbreviated oath, equivalent to ἐνώπιον τοῦ Χριστοῦ οὐ ψεύδομαι (cf. Gal. 1:20).

54. 2 Cor. 2:11; 7:2; 12:17-18; 1 Thess. 4:6. On the word group see G. Delling, *TDNT* 6.266-74; G. Finkenrath, *NIDNTT* 1.137-39.

tians. If the Corinthians withheld forgiveness now that the man was repentant, they would be playing into the hands of Satan, who already had gained one advantage when the man sinned. There is a point at which punishment can become purely vindictive (cf. v. 6) and suffering a penalty can drive one to despair (v. 7; Col. 3:21). Christian discipline certainly includes punishment administered in love, but it is not simply retributive or punitive; it is also remedial or reformatory (cf. 1 Cor. 5:5; 11:32; 2 Cor. 7:9, 10; 13:10). It aims at reinstatement after repentance, through forgiveness and reconciliation.

νόημα is also an exclusively Pauline word, denoting the function of the intellect (νοῦς), thus "thought," "mind" (as in 3:14; 4:4; 11:3; Phil. 4:7). But here νοήματα has the pejorative sense of "schemes," "designs," "plots," "stratagems" (= μεθοδεῖαι, Eph. 6:11; cf. πᾶν νόημα, 10:5). The combination οὐκ ἀγνοέω means not simply "I am not unaware," but, by litotes, "I know well," "I am fully aware."[55] The implication of v. 11 is that one of the Christian's defenses against the devil's stratagems is prior awareness of his purposes and methods, particularly his wish to turn good (the man's repentance) into evil (his downfall through excessive grief). To withhold forgiveness from a repentant person is to give the devil a τόπος (cf. Eph. 4:27), an opportunity to exert his influence and wreak havoc in the Christian community.

From 2 Cor. 2:5-11 as a whole we may identify six stages in successful church discipline.

1. ἀδικία (wrongdoing), which implies ὁ ἀδικήσας (the offending party, 7:12) and sometimes ὁ ἀδικηθείς (the offended party, 7:12),
2. ἐπιτιμία (punishment) (2:6), which is inflicted by οἱ πλείονες (the majority/the full assembly),
3. λύπη (pain, sorrow) (2:5, 7), which is suffered by the wrongdoer (2:7) and, in a different sense, by the congregation (2:5),
4. μετάνοια (repentance, implied in 2:6), which is the outcome of ἡ κατὰ θεὸν λύπη (godly sorrow; cf. 7:9-10, of the Corinthians),
5. ἄφεσις (forgiveness, 2:7, 10, χαρίζομαι), which is granted by the congregation as well as by ὁ ἀδικηθείς,
6. κύρωσις (affirmation) (2:8), involving restoration to full fellowship within the congregation.

For offenses serious enough to warrant corporate church discipline, stages 2.-5. are not only necessary but must occur in that fixed order. That is, it is inappropriate to move directly from 1. to 4. and 5. Moreover, 4. must precede 5. (cf. Luke 17:3).[56] And it should be observed that the aim of 2. and 3. is not vengeance but repentance.

---

55. Cf. BAGD 11b, 590b; Turner 282. As a parallel to 2:11, MM (4d) cites P. Tebt. II.314 line 3 (second century A.D.): πιστεύω σε μὴ ἀγνοεῖν, which could be rendered "I believe you are fully aware."

56. On these issues, see chapter 5 in R. Swineburne, *Responsibility and Atonement* (Oxford: Clarendon, 1989).

Bibliography (2:5-11)

Bibliography: Barrett, "2 Cor. 7:12" • Batey, "Interaction" • S. Cox, "That Wicked Person," *Exp,* 1st series, 3 (1875) 355-68 • Hainz 132-41 • Hall • Hanson, *Ministry* 66 • Kruse, "Offender" • Lampe 353-54 • F. O. Lindemann, "Latin cognitus and Greek ἀγνοέω," *SO* 38 (1963) 69-75 • Meeks 130-31 • Mullins, "Petition" • Murphy-O'Connor 23-27 • Schweizer, *Order* 721 • South 89-110 • Therrien 115-16, 254 • Thrall, "Offender."

5. Restlessness at Troas (2:12-13)

This is the final section in Paul's explanation of his recent conduct (1:12–2:13), and once again it focuses on his travel movements (cf. 1:8, 15-16, 23; 2:1). If 1:8-11 presupposes Paul's journey from Ephesus to Troas,[1] 2:12-13 actually refers to this journey.[2] The restlessness of spirit that Paul experienced in Troas was occasioned, at least in large measure, by his failure to meet Titus there — Titus who would bring news of the situation at Corinth in the wake of the "severe letter." This restlessness, in turn, caused Paul to curtail his preaching in Troas. By sketching this dramatic sequence of events — no Titus, no peace, no preaching — Paul was affording the Corinthians concrete proof of his deep affection for them of which he had spoken in 2:4. Or 2:12-13 could look back to 2:9. "There was a time, not too long ago, when I was at Troas eagerly awaiting news of you all and began to wonder whether you were in fact obedient to me in every regard." Alternatively, 2:11 could have triggered 2:12-15. If Paul could trace anything that prevented evangelistic or pastoral activity to the machinations of Satan (1 Thess. 3:18), perhaps he discerned one of Satan's stratagems (2:11) in the circumstances that forced him to cut short his missionary work in Troas.

12*Now I arrived in Troas to preach the gospel of Christ, but although a door stood open for me in the Lord's providence,* 13*I could get no peace of mind because I did not find my brother Titus there. So instead I said farewell to them and left for Macedonia.*

2:12 Ἐλθὼν δὲ εἰς τὴν Τρῳάδα εἰς τὸ εὐαγγέλιον τοῦ Χριστοῦ. "Now I arrived in Troas to preach the gospel of Christ." This describes Paul's journey (alone — note the singular ἐλθών) from Ephesus to Troas, roughly 260 miles (Burdick

---

1. See the commentary on 1:8 and the excursus after 1:11.

2. Cf. Georgi (193 n. 65): "The entire passage from 1:8 to 2:13 is written with an itinerary from Ephesus to Macedonia in mind. Paul has to explain this to the Corinthians in 1:12–2:11. 2 Cor. 1:10-11 draws the conclusion from 1:8-9 and has the stylistic function of rounding up the proemium. Hence, 2:12-13 actually constitutes the follow-up of 1:8-9."

41), probably in the spring of A.D. 56.[3] Perhaps one or two months earlier Titus had been dispatched to Corinth with the "severe letter" while Paul continued work in and around Ephesus,[4] to which he had returned after his brief "painful visit" to Corinth (although Murphy-O'Connor [*Paul* 296] and others argue that Paul went from Corinth to Macedonia). Paul's departure for Troas was probably precipitated by the Demetrius riot (Acts 19:23-41), but evidently he had already planned to leave Ephesus, for when earlier he sent Titus to Corinth, he arranged to meet him at Troas (see 2:13; by a specified date?), or, failing that, probably at Philippi (see 7:5).[5] So, then, unwelcome in Ephesus, Paul traveled north to Troas, possibly by a coasting vessel (cf. Acts 20:13-15 for a comparable voyage), in accordance with the plan outlined in 1 Cor. 16:5 and now readopted.[6]

There is debate whether ἡ Τρῳάς refers to the city of Troas, or to "the Troad," the region in the northwest corner of Asia Minor that included Troas.[7] It is true that the article is usually omitted with place names, and as Thrall points out (192), Paul always omits the article when he refers to towns or cities, but the term Τρῳάς seems to fall into a distinct category because: (1) its full name was Ἀλεξάνδρεια (ἡ) Τρῳάς, "the Trojan Alexandria," to distinguish it from other cities called Alexandria, so that Τρῳάς is adjectival in function and therefore technically subject to an article;[8] (2) of the six NT uses of Τρῳάς, four are anarthrous (Acts 16:8, 11; 20:5; 2 Tim. 4:13) and two articular (Acts 20:6; 2 Cor. 2:12). In these latter two cases, the article may be anaphoric, εἰς τὴν Τρῳάδα in Acts 20:6 referring back to ἐν Τρῳάδι in 20:5, and εἰς τὴν Τρῳάδα here in 2 Cor. 2:12 referring back to the mutually assumed knowledge of where Paul and Titus would meet.[9] Another reason that ἡ Τρῳάς here is probably the city of Troas is that Paul would be likely to arrange to meet Titus in a city, not a region.[10] Moreover, when Paul left the area, he said goodbye "to them" (αὐτοῖς), presumably people in a single location. As "a port of transshipment

---

3. See the Introduction, C.15.

4. Cf. Acts 19:22: "He stayed in Asia a little longer."

5. If the dispatch of Titus to Corinth with the "severe letter" was roughly contemporaneous with the sending of Timothy and Erastus to Macedonia (Acts 19:22), Paul's decision to leave Ephesus was made before the riot (Acts 19:23-41) since he hoped to meet Titus at Troas (2 Cor. 2:13; W. L. Knox, *Jerusalem* 340 n. 18; cf. 340 n. 22). The sudden outbreak of opposition at the time of the riot, which might reflect a sudden accession of numerous converts in Ephesus (cf. 1 Cor. 16:8), may have precipitated the withdrawal from Ephesus that Paul had in fact already contemplated (cf. W. L. Knox, *Jerusalem* 341 n. 22, 342 n. 30).

6. See the commentary on 1:15-16.

7. This latter (minority) view is held by BAGD 829a; TCNT ("the district round Troas"); Weymouth; A. P. Stanley 2.44 ("perhaps"); Manson 216 n. 1; Bruce, *Paraphrase* 129 n. 5; Robinson, *Redating* 49; Thrall 182-83.

8. Cf. Turner 171.

9. Cf. BDF §261 (1).

10. Plummer 64. Thrall's response to this argument (183), that Paul names the actual meeting place equally vaguely ("Macedonia" 7:5), seems to overlook the difference between a precise advance plan (2:12) and a subsequent general description (7:5).

both for goods and for travellers to any part of the Mediterranean" (Leaf 234), Troas was a strategic center for missionary activity.[11] "Here was a Roman and cosmopolitan population, reinforced by temporary sojourners suffering enforced delays far from their homes in many parts of the Roman world. A Christian community in such a place would have wide influence."[12]

That Paul intended to preach at Troas is clear from the expression εἰς τὸ εὐαγγέλιον τοῦ Χριστοῦ, where εἰς indicates purpose,[13] "for the purpose of bringing."[14] That he actually did proclaim the good news in Troas[15] is a fair inference from the following reference to an "open door," for this "door" would be recognized to be "open" only after he had grasped the opportunities for preaching initially afforded ἐν κυρίῳ. In the expression "the gospel of Christ," τοῦ Χριστοῦ is an objective genitive, the gospel "whose content is Christ" or "concerning Christ." But it is not impossible that it is simultaneously a subjective genitive, "the gospel brought by Christ."[16]

καὶ θύρας μοι ἀνεῳγμένης ἐν κυρίῳ. "But although a door stood open for me in the Lord's providence. . . ." As a metaphor, the opening of a door signifies the availability or presence of distinctive opportunities (cf. 1 Cor. 16:9; Col. 4:3; Rev. 3:8). Paul is probably referring to an actual, warm reception of his message, including provision of hospitality and general support, rather than simply to a promising prospect for evangelism. But as well as indicating fresh or unique opportunities for evangelism, this "opening of the door" in Troas signified the lifting of the previous prohibition to preach in Asia (Acts 16:6).[17] Following ἐλθών, the genitive absolute καὶ θύρας μοι ἀνεῳγμένης might mean either "when I came . . . and when a door was opened unto me" (RV) or "although I came (to Troas with a view to proclaiming the gospel of Christ) and although a door stood open for me" = "I arrived . . . but although. . . ."[18] As a perfect participle, ἀνεῳγμένης probably means not "was opened" (as if it were a narrative or aoristic perfect) but "stood open." Paul did not leave Troas because

11. Murphy-O'Connor is more specific. One reason Paul chose to work in Troas was its strategic location as a transit point for trade between Asia and Europe, and a Christian community there could serve as a link between the churches of those two areas (*Paul* 300).

12. Hemer, "Troas" 103. See also Burdick 31-65; E. M. Yamauchi, *ABD* 6.666-67.

13. Winer 347; Robertson 595.

14. BAGD 318a. Similarly Cassirer; Barrett 83.

15. So, e.g., Kümmel, *Introduction* 286; Manson 220 n. 2; 222 n. 1; Murphy-O'Connor 27; *Paul* 300.

16. Thus Zerwick §37 (who adds a third sense, "the good news preached by the apostle ἐν Χριστῷ i.e. by Christ's commission and with Christ's presence and assistance working in preacher and audience alike"); Spicq 2.89 and n. 35 (who labels this use a "comprehensive" genitive, where Christ is both object and author).

17. Consonant with Ramsay's observation that Troas was an ideal center and base for missionary activity (*HDB* 5.389, 400) is his suggestion that the "open door" of 2:12 implies either unimpeded opportunity for preaching in Troas or the strategic situation of Troas as a starting point for evangelization (*HDB* 4.814; cf. W. L. Knox, *Jerusalem* 333, 342 n. 31).

18. This genitive absolute is regarded as concessive by, among others, Plummer 53, 64; Barrett 83; TCNT, Weymouth, Moffatt; cf. Burton §452.

the opportunity for preaching there had ceased or been exhausted; on the contrary, that "door" remained open down to the time of writing — as Acts 20:6-12 would confirm. ἐν κυρίῳ may mean "by the Lord (Jesus)" or "in the Lord's providence" (Weymouth), so that Christ is portrayed in this verse as both the content of the gospel (τοῦ Χριστοῦ) and the one who provided opportunities to present the gospel message (ἐν κυρίῳ). In this case ἐν κυρίῳ makes explicit what was implied by the "theological passive" ἀνεῳγμένης. Or the phrase could signify "in the Lord's service," that is, "for serving the Lord" (REB).

2:13 οὐκ ἔσχηκα ἄνεσιν τῷ πνεύματί μου. "I could get no peace of mind." Because 7:5 continues the travel narrative broken off here at 2:13 and begins with similar wording, it is both appropriate and necessary to consider the verses together.[19]

2:13 οὐκ   ἔσχηκα ἄνεσιν τῷ πνεύματί μου
7:5b οὐδεμίαν ἔσχηκεν ἄνεσιν ἡ σάρξ   ἡμῶν

In 7:5 the grammatical subject has changed from "I" to "our flesh (= body)," and the singular (μου) has become the plural (ἡμῶν). The perfect tense of ἔχω is common to both verses and is probably aoristic in each case,[20] for by the time of writing Paul had in fact gained relief in mind and body (7:6, 13, 16),[21] so that ἔσχηκα cannot produce the sense, "having got no relief, I still have none."[22] Also, we might note that ἔσχηκα is structurally opposed to the aorist ἐξῆλθον. Since Paul so often uses the terms σάρξ and πνεῦμα antithetically, it is surprising to see them used here apparently synonymously. But if each term refers here to Paul's whole person viewed from a particular perspective, we may propose that πνεῦμα denotes the inward or psychical, and σάρξ the outward or physical, aspects of the restlessness (= absence of ἄνεσις, "relief from pressure").[23] In this way an aspectival distinction between σάρξ and πνεῦμα may be preserved, the former word denoting the seat of physical suffering, the latter the seat of spiritual sensibility. See further the Introduction, A.3.b. and the commentary at 7:5.

τῷ μὴ εὑρεῖν με Τίτον τὸν ἀδελφόν μου. "Because I did not find my

19. See also the Introduction, A.3.b.(2).

20. So also BDF §343 (2) for 2:13 only; Burton §80; Moulton 145, 238; Moule 14; Turner 70.

21. Compare ἐσχήκαμεν in 1:9 (see the comments there).

22. Robertson regards the three perfects of ἔχω in 2 Corinthians (1:9; 2:13; 7:5) as instances of "vivid dramatic recital" (*Pictures* 217; cf. 211, 239) where "an action completed in the past is conceived in terms of the present time for the sake of vividness" (*Grammar* 896; cf. 897 and 900-901, where he is less certain about 2:13 but still classifies it as a "[historical dramatic] present perfect").

23. Cf. Burton, *Spirit* 179, 185; Schauf 9-10; E. Schweizer, *TDNT* 6.435; 7.125. For the view that πνεῦμα here designates "the apportioned divine spirit," see Jewett 192-94. But the parallelism between 2:13 and 7:5 shows that both σάρξ and πνεῦμα allude to the believer's "natural feelings experienced in life" (Percy 11).

brother Titus there." This is the only NT instance of an articular infinitive in the dative case without a preposition. The sense is causal.[24] On Titus's movements during the period represented by 2 Corinthians, see the Introduction, C. His description as "my brother" testifies to the truth of Paul's affirmation in Gal. 3:28 (cf. Col. 3:11) that in Christ "all distinctions between Jew and Greek . . . have vanished" (TCNT), for Titus was a Greek (Gal. 2:3), a Gentile believer.

In this verse Paul traces his continual uneasiness of mind while staying at Troas to a single cause — his failure to meet Titus there. The non-arrival of Titus, the bearer of the "letter of tears" to Corinth, intensified Paul's uncertainty and fears (7:5) concerning the Corinthians.[25] Paul rightly sensed the gravity of the situation. Not only was the future of one of his potentially most influential young churches at stake, and with it perhaps the success of his "collection for the saints" as the climax of his Aegean ministry (cf. 9:1-5); his own status and freedom as apostle to the Gentiles were the ultimate questions raised by the test case of Corinth.[26] When the Corinthians heard of Paul's intense anxiety about their spiritual welfare, they would have specific evidence of his profound love for them.[27] Apart from the non-arrival of Titus, there may have been other secondary causes of Paul's unrelieved anxiety in Troas. He may well have been concerned about Titus's safety in travel; the repeated ἐν τῇ παρουσίᾳ (Τίτου) in 7:6-7 points to this. Also, he was doubtless dispirited by the opposition at Ephesus which had caused his premature departure from that city.[28] And, if at Troas he experienced a debilitating relapse of his recurrent malady,[29] this may have deepened his restlessness, even if he knew that God's grace was sufficient to match his need (2 Cor. 12:9).[30]

ἀλλὰ ἀποταξάμενος αὐτοῖς ἐξῆλθον εἰς Μακεδονίαν. "So instead I said farewell to them and left for Macedonia." ἀλλά sets up a contrast with θύρας μοι ἀνεῳγμένης (2:12): Instead of taking full advantage of the divinely provided opportunities for ministry at Troas, Paul set off for Macedonia. The special mention of the formal farewell (ἀποτάσσομαι is a Pauline *hapax legomenon*) perhaps reflects Paul's embarrassment at his premature departure from Troas (so soon after a premature departure from Ephesus!). One may gauge the

---

24. BAGD 516c; Winer 328; Burton §396; Robertson 532; Moule 44; Turner 142, 242.

25. But Barrett downplays Paul's anxiety about the church at Corinth and, drawing out the implications of 2 Cor. 7:6-7 (Paul's relief at the safe arrival of Titus), highlights his anxiety about Titus's safety while he brought back the Corinthian contribution to the collection for Jerusalem, a task that would expose him to robbers (cf. 2 Cor. 11:26; Barrett 20, 94; "Titus" 13 n. 33). But there is no evidence that Titus was the Corinthian delegate to Jerusalem or the actual bearer of Corinthian funds, and Acts 20:2-4 suggests that Corinth itself was the meeting point of the delegates, so that there would be no reason to have collection funds leave Corinth. Cf. Thrall 187.

26. For further details about Paul's circumstances at this time, see the excursus after 1:11 (C).

27. Cf. Rissi 16.

28. Ramsay (283-84) mentions this and also depression owing to ill health (2 Cor. 4:7-8).

29. See the excursus after 1:11.

30. Similarly Conybeare in Conybeare and Howson 437-38.

uniqueness of this situation by comparing 1 Cor. 16:8-9 with 2 Cor. 2:12-13. About eighteen months before writing 2 Corinthians, Paul had prolonged (ἐπιμενῶ) his stay in Ephesus because of (γάρ) unique opportunities and in spite of (adversative καί) outward opposition (1 Cor. 16:8-9). But in Troas he curtailed a visit in spite of unique opportunities and because of inward apprehension. αὐτοῖς implies that there were now some believers in Troas (cf. Acts 20:6-12), but whether they had come to faith through Paul, and, if so, whether it was during his earlier visit (Acts 16:8-10) or during the present abbreviated visit, cannot be known. Paul "departed for Macedonia" because he was now once again following the itinerary of 1 Cor. 16:5 and because if he had proceeded from Troas to Corinth without hearing of the state of affairs in the Corinthian church he would have been risking a second visit ἐν λύπῃ (which he had resolved to avoid, 2 Cor. 2:1) and contravening his arrangement to meet Titus in Troas or otherwise in Macedonia (in Philippi?). This departure for Macedonia from Troas is to be correlated with Paul's departure for Macedonia from Ephesus (Acts 20:1).[31]

Bibliography

Barrett, "Titus" • Burdick, "Troad" 50-65 • Crafton 158 • Fee, *Presence* 296 • Hemer, "Troas" • W. L. Knox 144 n. 2 • W. L. Knox, *Jerusalem* 340-42 nn. 18, 22, 30 • Kreitzer 25-28 • Leaf 141-44, 233-40 • Murphy-O'Connor 23-27 • Rissi 15-16 • Robinson, *Redating* 47-52, 54-55

C. Major Digression — The Apostolic Ministry Described (2:14–7:4)

At 2:14 there begins "the great digression" (2:14–7:4), as it is sometimes called. Although 7:5 naturally follows 2:13 in that it resumes the narrative of Paul's movements after leaving Ephesus, the conclusion is by no means inevitable that 2:14–7:4 (with or without 6:14–7:1) forms a distinct letter; indeed, the recapitulative character of 7:5 (καὶ γὰρ ἐλθόντων ἡμῶν εἰς Μακεδονίαν refers back to ἐξῆλθον εἰς Μακεδονίαν, 2:13) suggests that what intervenes between 2:13 and 7:5 was recognized by Paul as a digression.[1] Mention of his reunion with Titus in Macedonia (2:13) evokes a brief doxology (2:14), for in the favorable Corinthian reaction to the "letter of tears" reported by Titus Paul saw a vindication by God of his apostleship, not merely in Corinth but ἐν παντὶ τόπῳ. Thus Paul begins his description of the apostolic ministry (2:14–7:4), in which he lays bare successively its grandeur and superiority (2:14–4:6), its suffering

31. So also Bruce, *Acts* 422; Robinson, *Redating* 49.
1. Cf. Lietzmann 131. The internal unity and integrity within chs. 1–7 of 2:14–7:4 are discussed in the Introduction, A.3.b.

and glory (4:7–5:10), and its essence and exercise (5:11–6:10) before he returns by way of exhortation and ethical injunction (6:11–7:4) to the travel narrative (7:5-16). It is clear that while formally or schematically 2:14–7:4 is a digression, materially it is the essence of chs. 1–7, clothing with flesh the skeleton of the geographic notices concerning Paul's journey from Ephesus to Macedonia (1:8-11: Ephesus to Troas,[2] 2:12-13: to Troas and on to Macedonia, 7:5-16: to and in Macedonia).

1. The Grandeur and Superiority of the Apostolic Ministry (2:14–4:6)

For detailed structural analyses of 2:14–4:6, see the works of Theobald (1982),[3] Lambrecht (1983; cf. Garland 137-38),[4] Kleinknecht (1984),[5] and Rolland (1990).[6]

a. The Privilege of Apostolic Service (2:14-17)

As Paul launches into his lengthy depiction (2:14–7:4) of the ministry that God had entrusted to the apostles, it is fitting for him to stress at the outset the incomparable privilege of being a participant in God's triumphal procession, an agent in spreading the fragrant knowledge of Christ and the aroma of Christ that brings God pleasure. Not surprisingly, Paul then asks, "Who could possibly be qualified or adequate for such roles?" His answer? — only those who retain and preach the gospel in its pristine form and who are aware of their divine commission and accountability.

14*But thanks be to God, who in Christ is always leading us in his triumphal procession, and through us diffuses in every place the sweet odor of the knowledge of Christ.* 15*For we are the sweet fragrance of Christ[a] ascending to God, among both those who are being saved and those who are perishing.* 16*To the latter group it is a deadly[b] stench that leads to death; but to the former, it is a vitalizing[b] fragrance that leads to life. Now who is adequate for such ministry?* 17*For, unlike most people,[c] we are not in the habit of huckstering the word of God. On the contrary, we act from pure motives and, as persons sent from God, speak in the sight[d] of God and in the name of Christ.*

---

2. For the suggestion that ἐν τῇ Ἀσίᾳ (1:8) refers to Troas, see the commentary there and the excursus after 1:11.

3. Theobald 167-239.

4. Lambrecht, "Structure" 334-80, and his subsequent remarks (1994) on reactions to his proposals and on alternative proposals (Bieringer and Lambrecht 293-94).

5. Kleinknecht 242-304.

6. Rolland 73-84.

TEXTUAL NOTES

a. Clement of Alexandria reads κυρίου in the place of Χριστοῦ.

b. Although ἐκ is omitted before θανάτου and ζωῆς by some witnesses (D F G Ψ 𝔐 latt syr Ir^lat), the readings ἐκ θανάτου and ἐκ ζωῆς are to be preferred on the basis of: strong proto-Alexandrian (p⁴⁶ ℵ B 1739) and later Alexandrian (A C 0243 33 81 104 1175 Clement) support and the principle of *lectio difficilior potior,* since the repeated ἐκ . . . εἰς combination is exegetically baffling, whereas a simple θανάτου or ζωῆς may be adjectival ("deadly" and "life-giving" — thus Martin 44).

c. With strong Alexandrian MS support (proto-Alexandrian: ℵ B 1739, later Alexandrian: A C Ψ 0243 33 1881) and wide geographical representation (𝔐 lat cop Irenaeus Ambrosiaster Didymus), the reading πολλοί has a slight edge over λοιποί (p⁴⁶ D F G L 6 326 614ˢ 630 945 2495 *al* syr) with regard to external evidence. Given the similarity of the two words, either could have given rise to the other. However, it seems somewhat improbable that Paul would have charged that "the rest" (οἱ λοιποί = *all* others in a particular category) were peddlers or hucksters of God's word.

d. In place of the more general preposition κατέναντι, "in the sight of" (p⁴⁶ ℵ* A B C [P] 0243 33 81 [365] 630 1175 1739 1881 2464 *pc*), some scribe wrote κατενώπιον, "in the presence of" (ℵ² D F G Ψ 𝔐), a word reserved in early Christian literature for describing a relation to God (BAGD 421c).

2:14 τῷ δὲ θεῷ χάρις τῷ πάντοτε θριαμβεύοντι ἡμᾶς ἐν τῷ Χριστῷ. "But thanks be to God, who in Christ is always leading us in his triumphal procession." No one doubts that the transition from 2:13 to 2:14 is abrupt. Clearly Paul is moving from the specific (Titus, believers at Troas, Macedonia) to the general ("always . . . in every place"), but what triggered the transition? It seems to have been the word Μακεδονία, not as the province where there were especially faithful believers[7] or where there had been both eager acceptance of the gospel and fierce opposition to it (cf. 2:14-17),[8] but as the place where Paul gained relief from his unnerving restlessness through the safe arrival of Titus and his report of the further triumph of the gospel in the lives of the Corinthians (7:5-7). It is true that, on this view, Paul's mind has leaped forward past the further frustrating delay in receiving news about Corinth (7:5) to the arrival of Titus; but pleasant memories do easily displace unpleasant ones. Also, when the Corinthians heard the present letter read, they would have already known the positive nature of Titus's report and would therefore readily comprehend the movement of Paul's thought. In her detailed discussion of five explanations of the connection between 2:12-13 and 2:14-17, Thrall critiques the present proposal by noting that when Paul finally comes to describe his feelings on the receipt of news from Corinth (7:6-16), he employs the vocabulary of comfort and consolation, concepts that are entirely lacking in 2:14-17.[9] But could not an in-

---

7. Allo 45.

8. Murphy-O'Connor, "Macedonia" 100-102, citing (in particular) 1 Thess. 1:6-8; Phil. 2:14-16.

9. Thrall, "Thanksgiving" 103-4.

stance of divine power displayed in the midst of human weakness (Paul's recent success at Corinth through Titus) be viewed by Paul simultaneously as a divine triumph (2:14) and as a source of human comfort (7:6-7)?[10]

If 1:3 is not technically a thanksgiving but a doxology,[11] this is the first thanksgiving period in 2 Corinthians.[12] As in 1 Cor. 15:57, the distinctive word order (not χάρις [δὲ] τῷ θεῷ, as in 2 Cor. 8:16; 9:15) throws special emphasis on God as the one whose action has elicited the thanksgiving. That action is twofold, θριαμβεύοντι . . . καὶ . . . φανεροῦντι, and also is constant, for these participles are present tense, with the first, if not both, qualified by πάντοτε, "at all times, continuously."[13]

The verb θριαμβεύω is from the noun θρίαμβος, which was a hymn sung to Dionysus (Bacchus) during festal processions, a title of Dionysus, and also a rendering of the Latin term *triumphus*.[14] Linguistically θριαμβεύειν corresponds to the Latin verb *triumphare,* "to celebrate a triumph" (intransitive) or "to lead in triumph" (transitive). The Roman triumph was a victory procession celebrated by Roman generals on their return to Rome after a successful foreign campaign, although during the empire the privilege of celebrating a triumph became the prerogative of the emperor.[15] There are some who deny that the Roman triumph is the conceptual background to 2:14,[16] but, given the linguistic data mentioned above and the fact that about 350 triumphs are recorded in Greco-Roman literature,[17] it seems antecedently probable that Paul is alluding to this ceremony and its ritual when he uses θριαμβεύω here and in Col. 2:15, the only other NT use.

Some significant features of this ostentatious pageant may be briefly sketched.[18] At the head of the procession came the magistrates and the senate, followed by trumpeters and some spoils of wars such as vessels of gold or beaks of ships. Then came the flute players, ahead of white oxen destined to be sacrificed in the temples, along with some representative captives from the conquered territory, including such dignitaries as the king, driven in chains in front

10. Perriman discovers a "logical continuity" between 2:13 and 2:14. The adversative δέ of 2:14 highlights the consistency between 2:14-17 and 2:12-13; there is the triumph of God in spite of Paul's own uncertainty and restlessness (39-40).

11. See the commentary on 1:3.

12. But see Thrall, who regards 2:14-17 as a second thanksgiving period which introduces the section 2:14–7:4, a section which is integral to 1:1–7:16 ("Thanksgiving" 101-24).

13. πάντοτε is usually found with the present tense (Porter 187).

14. See LSJ 806.

15. The standard treatment of the triumph is by H. S. Versnel, *Triumphus: An Inquiry into the Origin, Development and Meaning of the Roman Triumph* (Leiden: Brill, 1970).

16. So, e.g., Field, 181; and Egan (34-62), who rightly observes that parallels are lacking in literature before Paul for metaphorical use of the concept of the Roman triumph (38 and n. 15); accordingly, Marshall ("Metaphor" 317) proposes that we may trace the existence of the Greek metaphor to "Paul's creative handiwork."

17. Marshall, "Metaphor" 304.

18. See, in particular, the descriptions found in Plutarch, *Aemilius Paulus* 32.1–36.6; Dio Cassius 6.23; and Josephus, *War* 7.153-55. Cf. Versnel 95.

of the ornate chariot of the general, the *triumphator* ("the one honored by the triumph"), who wore the garb of Jupiter *(ornatus Iovis)* and carried a scepter in his left hand. A slave held a crown over his head. The victorious soldiers followed, shouting *"Io triumphe!"* ("Hail, triumphant one!"). As the procession ascended the Capitoline Hill, some of the leading captives (usually royal figures or the tallest and strongest of the conquered warriors) were taken aside into the adjoining prison and executed. Sacrifices were offered upon arrival at the temple of Jupiter Capitolinus. Livy informs us of the two purposes of a triumph: to thank the gods who had guaranteed the victory and to glorify the valor of the *triumphator.*[19]

If, then, Paul has the picture of a Roman triumph in his mind as he dictates 2:14, with whom does he identify himself and his fellow apostles (ἡμᾶς)[20] — the soldiers who followed the general's chariot in jubilation or the captives who preceded it in ignominy? To answer this question we must consider more closely the meaning of θριαμβεύω in 2:14. No fewer than ten different senses have been proposed.[21] In Greek literature it sometimes means "exhibit (in a public procession)," "put on display," or "divulge" (see Egan 34-62), but more often it means "triumph over" and is followed by one of three prepositions (ἀπό, κατά, or ἐπί) or is used with a cognate accusative (θρίαμβον, νίκην).[22] The meaning "win a victory over" is not likely here, where neither a preposition nor a cognate accusative but a direct personal object is found (ἡμᾶς); in any case, if God's "triumph over" Paul referred to his Damascus conversion, the present participle and πάντοτε would have been inappropriate. Such evidence as we have that would shed light on first-century

19. Livy 45.39.10.

20. On the use of ἡμεῖς in Paul, see the introduction to 1:3-7.

21. See Hafemann, *Spirit* 21; *Defense* 18-19; Webb 75-76 n. 6. Scott alleges that by using θριαμβεύειν Paul evoked the image of the victorious Roman general riding in his triumphal chariot, which was a *quadriga,* a two-wheeled chariot drawn by four horses, and thereby the image of God in his throne-chariot *(merkabah),* which in Jewish tradition was often seen as a four-horse chariot drawn by the four living creatures of Ezekiel 1 ("Triumph" 262-68). In 2:14 Paul "exults in his Moses-like encounter" with this throne-chariot and so begins his typological comparison between Moses' ministry and his own ("Triumph" 271). In 2:14-16a he states "*in effect* that he has had a Merkabah encounter with God like that which Moses experienced on Sinai, that he has a unique role as revelatory mediator similar to that of Moses, and, furthermore, that his ministry is a matter of life and death just as Moses' was" ("Triumph" 274; italics added). In addition, Scott claims that 12:2-4 and 2:14, with Ps. 68(67):18-19 lying behind them, are "mutually interpretive as describing Paul's Merkabah experience" ("Triumph" 280) and then makes the sweeping assertion that these two passages in 2 Corinthians "make it clear that Paul's ascent to the Merkabah is as foundational to his own apostolic ministry as the *sessio ad dexteram* (Ps 110.1) is foundational to the Christology of the early church" ("Triumph" 281). Whatever is said about 12:2-4 (see the commentary there), Scott's proposal about 2:14 seems to be burdening the verb θριαμβεύειν with a metaphorical load it was not designed to bear. Was the *quadriga* so central in the imagery of the *triumphus* that it could form the bridge in Paul's thought from the Roman *currus triumphalis* to the Jewish *merkabah?*

22. LSJ 806.

use of this verb indicates that when it is followed by an accusative other than the cognate, that grammatical case refers to the thing or person that has been conquered, never the person triumphing or celebrating a victory.[23] That is, θριαμβεύω τινά means "lead someone (as a captive) in a triumphal procession." On this understanding, Paul sees himself not as the partner but as the prisoner of the *triumphator,* not as an exultant soldier but as a willing and privileged captive, a trophy of the general's victory, a one-time enemy who has been conquered.[24] His implied prior "defeat" will be his Damascus encounter when he surrendered to God or Christ.[25] In a similar way, Col. 2:15 says that God first disarmed (ἀπεκδυσάμενος) the powers and authorities and then boldly displayed them in public (ἐδειγμάτισεν ἐν παρρησίᾳ) by leading them, as already defeated enemies, in triumphal procession (θριαμβεύσας) through Christ (ἐν αὐτῷ). They were driven, as it were, before the victor's chariot as silent testimony to the superior might of their conqueror. While θριαμβεύω has the same meaning in 2 Cor. 2:14 and Col. 2:15 ("lead in triumphal procession"), the two objects differ (Paul and his fellow-apostles, hostile powers and authorities), and in one case they are (paradoxically) willing, joyful captives and vocal witnesses to the general's victory (cf. 2:14b), while in the other they are involuntary, sullen captives and silent witnesses to the commander's conquest.[26]

There is, of course, danger in pressing the metaphor. It is one thing to recognize that θριαμβεύω τινά means "lead someone (as a captive) in a triumphal procession," so that Paul regards himself as a defeated enemy, an αἰχμάλωτος, "a prisoner of war."[27] It is quite another to infer, as Hafemann does,[28] that these prisoners of war were "slaves" (δοῦλοι), a term Paul uses of himself (e.g., Rom.

---

23. Williamson 318-22; Breytenbach 269; Hafemann, *Spirit* 33-39; *Defense* 31-34. Although verbs in -εύω may have a causative sense (cf. μαθητεύω, "make a disciple of"; BDF §§148[1]; 309[1]), there is no lexical support for this sense ("cause to triumph") for θριαμβεύω, although it is preferred, *inter alios,* by Kinsey (282); Dupont (40); Louw and Nida (§39.60).

24. But some see τῷ . . . θριαμβεύοντι ἡμᾶς as an allusion to the Roman general who led his soldiers as partners in his triumph. In this case, "the apostles are joyful participants in their commander's triumphal procession" (Bruce 187 [cf. his *Paraphrase* 129]; similarly Goodspeed; JB; NJB; LSJ 806; Héring 18 and n. 12; Barrett 98 ["notwithstanding the lack of supporting lexical evidence"]). Marshall argues that θριαμβεύειν in 2:14 is a metaphor of shame by which Paul portrayed himself as a socially shameful figure (cf. 1 Cor. 4:9) ("Metaphor" 313-17).

25. Cf. Phil. 3:12, "Christ Jesus has made me his own"; Gale 149.

26. But, referring ἐν αὐτῷ in Col. 2:15 to the cross (cf. τῷ σταυρῷ, Col. 2:14) rather than to Christ, Williamson translates the verse: "Having stripped the powers and authorities he made a public example of them, exposing them to ridicule [θριαμβεύσας] on the cross" (326).

27. Paul uses συναιχμάλωτος, "fellow-prisoner," in Rom. 16:7; Col. 4:10; Phlm. 23.

28. Hafemann, *Spirit* 33-39; *Defense* 31-34; "Comfort" 334; "Weakness" 145 n. 24. Hafemann sees 2:14 as the "centre-piece" of his thesis that in 1 Cor. 4:6-16; 2 Cor. 1:3-11, 2:14-17; 4:7-12, 6:3-10; 12:1-10 "Paul portrays his apostolic suffering as the revelatory vehicle through which the knowledge of God as made manifest in the cross of Christ and in the power of the Spirit is being disclosed" ("Weakness" 136; also 145 n. 23; *Spirit, passim; Defense, passim;* and his commentary 107-10).

1:1),[29] and that since these enemies were slain during or after the procession, Paul envisaged God as leading him "as a slave to death." On this inference we may make two observations. First, εἰς θάνατον ("to death") in 2:16 refers to those *not* being saved (οἱ ἀπολλύμενοι), certainly not the category in which Paul saw himself. Second, not all the captives exhibited in the procession were executed. Indeed, Augustus prides himself on his clemency toward those prisoners (*Res Gestae* 1.4), and at an earlier time (61 B.C.) Pompey had refrained from such executions during his third triumph (Appian, *Mithridatic Wars* 12.117). Hafemann himself acknowledges this point: "at least a representative sample" of the prisoners were slaughtered, the rest being sold into slavery (108-9).

Who is the *triumphator* in this victory parade? With θριαμβεύοντι referring to τῷ θεῷ, it seems more appropriate to regard the triumph as God's, with ἐν τῷ Χριστῷ meaning "through (our union with) Christ" or "in the cause of Christ," than to take ἐν τῷ Χριστῷ as equivalent to ἐν τῷ θριάμβῳ τοῦ Χριστοῦ, "in Christ's triumphal procession" (NEB, REB).[30]

καὶ τὴν ὀσμὴν τῆς γνώσεως αὐτοῦ φανεροῦντι δι᾽ ἡμῶν ἐν παντὶ τόπῳ. "And through us (God) diffuses in every place the sweet odor of the knowledge of Christ." Since φανεροῦντι is coordinate with θριαμβεύοντι, both being present participles describing God's continuous action, it is fair to assume that τὴν ὀσμὴν κτλ. (v. 14b) should be understood against the same background as v. 14a, the Roman triumph.[31] Such an assumption seems justified by the presence of ὀσμή ("odor," "fragrance"), for included in the victory procession — at least on occasion — were those who burned incense along the triumphal route, others who carried and displayed spices brought from the conquered regions, and yet others who scattered garlands of flowers and sprinkled perfume along the streets.[32] As a result, pleasant fragrances filled the air and were widely diffused along the processional route.

With regard to the two genitives that follow τὴν ὀσμήν, the first (τῆς γνώσεως) could be subjective ("the fragrance that comes from knowing him,"

29. In his brief *TDNT* article on θριαμβεύω, G. Delling makes the same transfer. "In 2 C. 2:14 Paul describes himself as one of these prisoners [in God's triumphal procession]. But he regards it as a grace that in his fetters he can accompany God always and everywhere . . . in the divine triumphant march through the world, even though it be only as the δοῦλος Χριστοῦ" (*TDNT* 3.160). Similarly Williamson 324.

30. Two English translations actually see the triumph as Paul's: "Wherever I go, thank God, he makes my life a constant pageant of triumph in Christ" (Moffatt); "But to God be the thanks who in Christ ever heads our triumphal procession" (Weymouth).

31. But Hafemann (*Spirit* 43-51; *Defense,* 37-45; cf. Thrall 198-99, 207) finds at 2:14b a transition to the cultic language of OT sacrifice.

32. Horace, *Odes* 4.2.50-51; Suetonius, *Nero* 25.2; Appian, *Punica* 66. But Duff (168-69) finds the background of ὀσμή in the use of aromatic substances in epiphany processions in the Greco-Roman world to announce to the spectators the approach of the deity. "Hence, the apostle, the 'pleasing fragrance (εὐωδία) of Christ,' depicts himself as the harbinger of the deity's presence because it is through him that 'the knowledge of God' [cf. 4:6] is made known" (169). Duff finds other allusions to such processions in 4:10 (περιφέροντες) (169-70), 6:13 (πλατύνθητε) and 7:2 (χωρήσατε) (171-75). See further Duff, "Transformation" 233-43; "Metaphor" 79-92.

NRSV) but is most likely epexegetic ("that sweet incense, the knowledge of him," Weymouth). The second genitive (αὐτοῦ) is clearly objective ("the knowledge of him," "knowing him") but could refer to God[33] or to Christ.[34] According to Paul elsewhere, Christians have a knowledge of God (e.g., Gal. 4:9) and of Christ (e.g., Phil. 3:8, 10), but in favor of a reference to Christ is the following expression, Χριστοῦ εὐωδία ("the sweet fragrance of Christ," v. 15a), and the fact that in v. 14 Χριστῷ is a nearer antecedent than θεῷ. Perhaps Paul wrote αὐτοῦ to avoid a repetitious Χριστῷ . . . Χριστοῦ . . . Χριστοῦ.

The move from ἡμᾶς (v. 14a) to δι' ἡμῶν (v. 14b) is interesting. Paul the passive captive is also the active evangelist.[35] God's agent is none other than God's prisoner. These two motifs are united in Paul's picturesque self-description, "I am an ambassador in chains" (πρεσβεύω ἐν ἁλύσει, Eph. 6:20). Such paradoxes had an irresistible appeal to Paul, and 2 Corinthians is replete with them.[36] Since Paul's introductory thanksgivings regularly encapsulate themes that are developed subsequently,[37] it is no surprise that 2:14 illustrates a theme that is ubiquitous throughout the letter: divine power displayed in the midst of human weakness (cf. 12:9). If the time of that display is "always" (πάντοτε), its extent is "everywhere" (ἐν παντὶ τόπῳ),[38] that is, wherever people live.[39] When he says "in every place," Paul would be thinking in particular of Illyricum (Rom. 15:19), which he had visited shortly before writing 2 Corinthians. Such a visit would be included within Luke's summary statement in Acts 20:2, διελθὼν δὲ τὰ μέρη ἐκεῖνα, "When he had gone through those regions," that is, Macedonia (Acts 20:1) and its environs.[40]

In this frontispiece to Paul's apologetic description of the apostolic ministry (2:14–7:4), three main emphases are discernible.

1. Paul recognized the apostolic ministry to be God's ministry through the apostles. From first to last, always and everywhere, it is God who acts, leading his willing captives (ἡμᾶς) in his victory pageant and disseminat-

---

33. Thus "the knowledge of himself" (BAGD 852d; NEB, REB; Barrett 98; Scott, "Triumph" 273; cf. BAGD 586a; and Collange (31) and Hafemann (*Spirit* 44-45; *Defense* 38-39), both of whom follow Manson ("Suggestions" 157-62) who proposes that as the replacement of the Torah, Christ is "the fragrance of the knowledge of God." In Hellenistic Greek αὐτοῦ could function as a reflexive, equivalent to ἑαυτοῦ (or possibly αὑτοῦ; see Moulton and Howard 180-81; MM 94).

34. Thus Meyer 452; Plummer 70; Dupont 41 n. 2; Hughes 79; Denis 428.

35. Cf. Friesen 26.

36. See, e.g., 2 Cor. 1:4; 4:7-12, 16; 6:8-10; 7:4, 8; 8:2, 9, 15; 10:3; 12:9-10, 15; 13:4, 8.

37. Cf. O'Brien 263.

38. In spite of the position of πάντοτε between πῶ and θριαμβεύοντι, both of these adverbial expressions belong (at least logically) to each participle: the present participle φανεροῦντι (v. 14b) implies πάντοτε, and πάντοτε (v. 14a) implies ἐν παντὶ τόπῳ (God's triumphal procession goes everywhere).

39. Cf. BAGD 822b. Manson (208-9) argues that here and in 1 Cor. 1:2; 1 Thess. 1:8; and 1 Tim. 2:8 τόπος possibly refers to Christian places of worship.

40. For a discussion of the issues surrounding this mission in Illyricum, see the Introduction, p. 66.

ing the fragrant knowledge of Christ through those same triumphant captives (δι' ἡμῶν).

2. The focal point of this divine operation is Christ. The privilege of participating in God's triumph is accorded in and through Christ (ἐν τῷ Χριστῷ), and it is the knowledge of Christ (αὐτοῦ), a sweet aroma, that is diffused during that triumphal procession.

3. God's activity, focused in Christ, is ongoing (τῳ πάντοτε θριαμβεύοντι . . . καὶ . . . φανεροῦντι) and universal (ἐν παντὶ τόπῳ), without temporal or national boundaries. God's θρίαμβος is always and everywhere.

2:15 ὅτι Χριστοῦ εὐωδία ἐσμὲν τῷ θεῷ ἐν τοῖς σῳζομένοις καὶ ἐν τοῖς ἀπολλυμένοις. "For we are the sweet fragrance of Christ ascending to God, among both those who are being saved and those who are perishing." ὅ τι should be associated with δι' ἡμῶν rather than with χάρις or τὴν ὀσμήν in v. 14. The apostles were God's commissioned agents in the universal diffusion of the fragrant knowledge of Christ because they themselves, in person and in work, actually constituted the sweet-smelling fragrance of Christ. Whereas ὀσμή may refer to either a pleasant odor ("fragrance," e.g., John 12:3) or an unpleasant odor ("stench," e.g., Tobit 8:3), εὐωδία always denotes a pleasant smell. The combination ὀσμὴ εὐωδίας,[41] representing Hebrew rēᵃḥ nîḥôᵃḥ ("pleasing odor"), appears some forty-six times in the LXX, usually in reference to the sweet smell of the burnt offering (e.g., Gen. 8:21; Exod. 29:18; Lev. 1:9). So closely was this technical expression associated with sacrifice that each term on its own could retain sacrificial connotations,[42] as in Sir. 24:15, "Like cinnamon and aspalathus I have given forth a fragrance (δέδωκα ὀσμήν), and like choice myrrh I spread abroad an aroma (διέδωκα εὐωδίαν)." We suggest, therefore, that in 2:15a Paul's thought moves from the ὀσμή associated with the Roman triumph (v. 14) to the εὐωδία associated with OT sacrifice.[43]

If Χριστοῦ is a subjective genitive, the sense will be "We are indeed the incense offered by Christ to God" (NEB).[44] More probably, however, the genitive is possessive: "We are Christ's sweet fragrance that ascends to God." That is, as God's agents for the widespread diffusion of the gospel (2:14), as proclaimers of God's word (2:17), the apostles became the aroma of Christ that

41. In Phil. 4:18 this expression describes the generous gifts of the Philippians; in Eph. 5:2, the sacrificial self-giving of Christ.

42. Hafemann, *Spirit* 48-49; *Defense* 42-43.

43. Some have linked the term εὐωδία (and ὀσμή) with Jewish descriptions of wisdom (e.g., Sir. 24:12-15; 39:13-14), others with the concept of fragrance as a sign of the divine presence and life, an idea that was widespread in antiquity (Bultmann 63-67), and yet others with the title Χριστός (cf. 2:14) (from χρίω, "anoint") and the reference to anointing (χρίσας) in 1:21 (cf. Prümm 1.83-84) or with the Servant of Yahweh's triumphal procession (Webb 79-84).

44. Similarly Barrett (99), who translates "for we are the sweet savour of sacrifice that rises from Christ to God," commenting that for Paul "the apostles are the smoke that arises from the sacrifice of Christ to God, diffusing as it ascends the knowledge of God that is communicated in the cross."

was sensed by God. To the extent that they diffused the fragrance of Christ by life and word, they were the fragrance of Christ. On either view, τῷ θεῷ is locative, paralleling the dative (τῷ) κυρίῳ that often accompanies the technical expression ὀσμὴ εὐωδίας in LXX usage. But it could also be classified as a dative of advantage, "for God's sake" (NAB[1]), "to/for God's glory."[45] Whereas in v. 14 it is the gospel that is the sweet fragrance, in v. 15 it is the apostles as they embody and proclaim that gospel.

Because of the repeated ἐν τοῖς it is clear that two distinct categories are depicted by the phrase ἐν τοῖς σῳζομένοις καὶ ἐν τοῖς ἀπολλυμένοις (cf. 1 Cor. 1:18). Before the preposition ἐν ("among," "in the case of"), we must understand some phrase such as "and that role of being the aroma of Christ is discharged (among) . . . ." To translate these present participles as "those on the road to salvation/ruin"[46] or "those who are destined for salvation/destruction" (Barclay) is to treat them as futuristic presents (cf. Luke 13:23) or as substitutes for the rare future participle, for both translations envisage the salvation and destruction as future experiences (cf. Rom. 5:9; 13:11), not present realities. Paul viewed "salvation" (σωτηρία, σῴζομαι) as lying in the present as well as in the past and future,[47] so there can be no a priori objection to understanding οἱ σῳζόμενοι as "those who are being saved," which in fact is the rendering of the majority of English translations.[48] Since οἱ ἀπολλύμενοι is parallel, it may be rendered "those who are perishing,"[49] the implication being that ἀπώλεια, in the sense of being spiritually dead (Eph. 2:1) and under God's wrath (Rom. 1:18), is as much the present experience of οἱ ἀπολλύμενοι as σωτηρία, the enjoyment of God's approval and redemptive blessings, is the ongoing privilege of οἱ σῳζόμενοι.

What is remarkable about this twofold classification of human beings (cf. Rom. 2:6-11; 1 Pet. 2:7-8) is that for Paul it represented a radical readjustment

45. Cf. BAGD 329d ("for God"). Moffatt construes τῷ θεῷ with ἐσμέν, "I live for God (as the fragrance of Christ)."

46. Martin 44, 48; similarly NEB; REB; Barrett 95-96; Carrez 72; Thrall 190. Perhaps the intended sense is "on the way to *final* salvation."

47. E.g., of the past Rom. 8:24; 11:11; Eph. 2:5, 8, of the present 1 Cor. 1:18; 15:2; 2 Cor. 2:15; 6:2, of the future Rom. 5:9; 13:11; cf. Phil. 3:20. On the three-tiered tense structure of salvation in the NT, see Caird 118-35.

48. (RV), Moffatt, Goodspeed, RSV, NASB, GNB, JB, NIV, NJB, NAB[2], NRSV. Weymouth has "those whom He [God] is saving." Burton's discussion of this participle (§125) is somewhat confusing, for he seems both to allow and to disallow the rendering "those that are being saved" ("a Progressive Present of Simultaneous Action"), although he prefers to take the participle as "a General Present," "those that are [i.e., become] saved."

49. (RV), Moffatt, Goodspeed, RSV, NASB, NIV, NAB[2], NRSV. Interestingly, some translations appear to distinguish between the two participles. For instance, TCNT: "both among those who are in the path *of* Salvation and among those who are in the path *to* Ruin" (italics added; similarly NAB[1], NJB, Cassirer). Moulton comments (114-15): "In οἱ ἀπολλύμενοι, 1 Co 1[18] *al*, strongly durative though the verb is, we see perfectivity [ἀπο-] in the fact that the goal is *ideally* reached: a complete transformation of its subjects is required to bring them out of the ruin implicit in their state." This would seem to support the rendering given in BAGD 95b: "those who are lost."

of his thinking (cf. 2 Cor. 5:16-17). No longer was his outlook principally governed by the inherited distinction between Ἰουδαῖοι and Ἕλληνες or ἔθνη, between περιτομή and ἀκροβυστία, although he still employs that classification.[50] Now a person's relationship to Jesus the Messiah is the factor that determines Paul's principal and ultimate grouping of human beings. There are both Jews and Gentiles in both groups (Rom. 3:9, 22-23; 10:12-13). What distinguishes οἱ σωζόμενοι from οἱ ἀπολλύμενοι is "love for the truth (of the gospel)" (2 Thess. 2:10).

In 2:15 Paul is saying that as faithful preachers and followers of Christ, the apostles formed a sweet savor of Christ, an "unmistakable 'scent' of Christ" (Phillips), that rose up to God as a pleasing aroma (cf. Num. 15:7). Irrespective of the human response to the gospel, its proclamation delights God's heart, because it centers on the Son whom he loves.

2:16 οἷς μὲν ὀσμὴ ἐκ θανάτου εἰς θάνατον, οἷς δὲ ὀσμὴ ἐκ ζωῆς εἰς ζωήν. "To the latter group it is a deadly stench that leads to death, but to the former it is a vitalizing fragrance that leads to life." Several literary features are apparent in this verse: parallelism (οἷς . . . ὀσμή/οἷς ὀσμή and ἐκ . . . εἰς/ἐκ . . . εἰς), repetition (θανάτου/θάνατον and ζωῆς/ζωήν), contrast (μὲν . . . δέ and θάνατος/ζωή), and, in relation to v. 15, chiasmus:

A	τοῖς σωζομένοις	B	τοῖς ἀπολλυμένοις
B′	οἷς . . . εἰς θάνατον	A′	οἷς . . . εἰς ζωήν

That is, οἱ σωζόμενοι (A) will experience eternal life (A′), and οἱ ἀπολλύμενοι (B) will suffer eternal death (B′).

If one were to discern here not chiasmus (as do almost all commentators) but simple parallelism (A B A′ B′), "those who are being saved" (A) would be those who "have discovered the death of Christ [ἐκ θανάτου] and carry its fragrance [εἰς θάνατον]" (A′, while "those who are perishing" (B) would be "those who are affected by the fragrance of [Christ's risen] life [ἐκ ζωῆς] which leads to life [in the risen Christ] [εἰς ζωήν]" (B′).[51] In that case, the Χριστοῦ εὐωδία (2:15) is designed and beneficial for all, "saved" or "lost," but its effect on the two groups is different.[52] This novel reinterpretation is not without difficulties, however. How could Paul say that for οἱ ἀπολλύμενοι *as a group* the preaching of the cross, the aroma of Christ, was foolish (1 Cor. 1:18) or obscure (2 Cor. 4:3) and yet life-changing (εἰς ζωήν)? This interpretation seems to imply that all "the lost" would become "the saved." Again, without any explicit qualification, the terms ζωή and θάνατος are more naturally referred to the life and the death of the immediately preceding οἱ σωζόμενοι and οἱ ἀπολλύμενοι than to the life

---

50. E.g., Rom. 3:29; 9:24; 1 Cor. 1:24; 10:32; 12:13; Gal. 3:28; Col. 3:11.

51. Carrez, "Odeur" 135; cf. 139-40, 142, and his commentary 72, 79-80; "ΙΚΑΝΟΤΗΣ" 82-84.

52. Carrez, "Odeur" 138.

and death of Christ (with Χριστοῦ implied from Χριστοῦ εὐωδία?). To indicate the presence of chiasmus and remove ambiguity, οἷς . . . οἷς should be rendered "to the latter (group) . . . to the former (group)," rather than simply "to the one . . . to the other."[53]

In the repeated ἐκ . . . εἰς phrases, the two prepositions may be considered as together forming a single idiomatic sense unit or as expressing two separate ideas. If ἐκ and εἰς are construed together, the phrases may express:

exclusiveness, "the elimination of other possibilities," so that ὀσμὴ ἐκ θανάτου εἰς θάνατον means "a stench which is completely a matter of death," and ὀσμὴ ἐκ ζωῆς εἰς ζωήν, "a fragrance which is completely a matter of life" (Louw and Nida),[54]

continuous progression or succession, "from bad to worse, and from good to better, with death or life as the final outcome" (Zerwick).[55] Plummer (71) adduces the English expressions "from day to day" and "from strength to strength" as comparable usages, or

rhetorical emphasis, with εἰς κτλ. intensifying the effect of ἐκ. Perhaps Goodspeed's translation reflects this interpretation: "a deathly, deadly odor . . . a vital, live-giving one."[56]

Such ways of interpreting ἐκ . . . εἰς would be more apposite if these phrases modified verbs, but they qualify nouns, so that it is preferable to exegete the prepositions separately.[57] There seems to be general unanimity among commentators who take this approach that εἰς in each case expresses a result or effect: "leading to/resulting in (death or life)." ἐκ, on the other hand, could denote source ("arising from," "issuing from") or, consequently, nature ("characterized by" death or life, simply "of death," "of life,"[58] or "deadly," "life-giving").[59] If, then, we treat the prepositions separately and give the neutral term ὀσμή ("smell," "odor") a sense appropriate to the context, we may translate thus: "a deadly stench that leads to death . . . a vitalizing fragrance that leads to life."[60]

But who or what is the ὀσμή in this verse? Since ἐσμέν in v. 15 identifies

53. ὅς functions here as a demonstrative pronoun, "this (one)," an alternative to the less common ὁ μὲν . . . ὁ δέ, not as a relative pronoun (BAGD 585b; BDF §250; Turner 36).

54. Louw and Nida §78.48, who render the comparable ἐκ πίστεως εἰς πίστιν (Rom. 1:17) by "as exclusively a matter of faith" or "as a matter of faith from beginning to end."

55. Zerwick, *Analysis* 395.

56. Cf. BAGD 236c: "ἐκ — εἰς w[ith] the same word repeated gives it special emphasis"; 340d: "from life to life" = "ever more deeply into the divine life."

57. Cf. Thrall 204.

58. Cf. Winer 610: "an odor of death which, from its nature, can bring nothing else than death, etc."

59. It is certainly more difficult to regard ἐκ as denoting source than nature (see the options discussed by Thrall 204-7).

60. Cf. Plummer's paraphrase (53): "a savour exhaled from death and breathing death, . . . a savour exhaled from life and breathing life."

the aroma of Christ with the apostles as proclaimers of the fragrant knowledge of Christ (v. 14), the ὀσμή is either the gospel as proclaimed by the apostles or the apostles themselves as proclaimers. Either way, the messengers and the message are indistinguishable. So, then, Paul is envisaging a single message or group of messengers as creating, inevitably, a dual effect: the possession of eternal life as the final outcome of present σωτηρία and the experience of eternal perdition as the outcome of the present ἀπώλεια. "Life" results from a positive response to the apostolic preaching, "death" from a negative response (cf. Luke 2:34; John 3:36). One aspect of the potency of the cross of Christ (cf. 1 Cor. 1:17) is its power to attract and convert those who repent and to repulse and harden those who are unrepentant. To the former group the cross is a ground for boasting (Gal. 6:14), to the latter it is an occasion for offense (1 Cor. 1:23).[61] If, as we have suggested, 2:15 marks a transition in Paul's thought from the ὀσμή of the Roman triumph to the εὐωδία of OT sacrifice, there is no need, here in v. 16, to associate οἱ σῳζόμενοι with the victorious soldiers and οἱ ἀπολλύμενοι with the defeated captives of the *triumphus*,[62] although it is undoubtedly true that the fragrant smells associated with the triumph would have been a joyous token of life (ἐκ ζωῆς εἰς ζωήν) for the soldiers and an ominous sign of imminent death (ἐκ θανάτου εἰς θάνατον) for some of the captives. Nor need we posit any direct relation between the rabbinic concept of the Torah as simultaneously life-giving and death-dealing and Paul's depiction of the antithetical effects of the preaching of the gospel.[63]

καὶ πρὸς ταῦτα τίς ἱκανός; "Now who is adequate for such ministry?" Having spoken of the elevated calling and awesome responsibilities of the apostles (vv. 14-16a),[64] Paul poses an urgent question: "Who is equal to this task of dispensing and being the fragrance of Christ, a task that has eternal consequences?" The stimulus for the question, apart from the immediate literary context, may have been twofold: (1) Paul's recent missionary experience and (2) the probable claim of his opponents at Corinth. (1) His evangelistic experiences in recent years — at Thessalonica (Acts 17:1-9), Corinth (Acts 18:1-18),

---

61. Cf. 1 Pet. 2:6-8, where one and the same stone (= Jesus Christ) is a foundation stone (λίθος ἀκρογωνιαῖος) and a stumbling stone (λίθος προσκόμματος).

62. As, e.g., Bruce 188; Kent 173.

63. But that there is a general similarity is undeniable. "As the bee reserves her honey for her owner and her sting for others, so the words of the Torah are life-giving medicine *(sam ḥayyîm)* for Israel and a deadly poison *(sam hamāwet)* to the nations of the world" (*Deuteronomy Rabbah* 1.5). See the discussion in G. F. Moore, "Savour" 329-30; Manson, "Suggestions" 155-62. Just as the Torah had a beneficial effect on those who received and obeyed it and a lethal effect on those who rejected it, so the gospel or the proclaimers of Christ are a "life-giving medicine" to those who believe the gospel and so are being saved and at the same time a "deadly poison" to those who repudiate it and so are perishing. The difficulties with finding any close parallel is that Hebrew *sam* means "medicine" or "drug" but not "odor," and that neither ὀσμή nor εὐωδία ever means "medicine."

64. The word order, with πρὸς ταῦτα (literally, "to accomplish these things") standing first, emphasizes the dignity and gravity of the apostolic vocation.

and Ephesus (Acts 19:8-10) — provoked vigorous opposition from local Jews and raised for Paul in an acute form the question of his adequacy to be the aroma of Christ among his Jewish compatriots. "How could it [his ministry] have been from God if God's own people rejected it?" (Provence 56). (2) The immediate negative reference in v. 17 to "the many" who were marketing the word of God for profit suggests that they were boasting to the Corinthians of their credentials to declare God's message. In their own right, they apparently claimed, they were superbly qualified to be apostles and servants of Christ (cf. 3:5a; 11:13, 23).[65]

How did Paul expect his question to be answered? Both a positive and a negative response accord with the wider context. If the answer is "We apostles are qualified, for we are not cheap retailers of God's word," appeal for support may be made to 3:1, "Are we beginning to commend ourselves again?" On the other hand, if the implied answer is "No people are qualified if they depend on their own resources" (cf. 1 Cor. 15:9-10), support is found in 3:4-6, where self-reliance is seen to be a disqualification for ministry. Although most τίς questions elsewhere in Paul seem to imply a negative answer,[66] perhaps the consideration that ultimately favors an affirmative answer is the logical γάρ in v. 17a: "We are qualified, because. . . ."[67]

2:17 οὐ γάρ ἐσμεν ὡς οἱ πολλοὶ καπηλεύοντες τὸν λόγον τοῦ θεοῦ. "For, unlike most people, we are not in the habit of huckstering the word of God." Structurally, this whole verse enunciates one negative reason (οὐ γάρ) and four positive reasons (v. 17b) why Paul regarded himself as qualified for the apostolic vocation of being the aroma of Christ (vv. 15-16).

The verb καπηλεύω is a biblical *hapax legomenon,* but the cognate noun κάπηλος is found twice in the LXX (Isa. 1:22; Sir. 26:29). The verb was used in basically two senses, one neutral and one pejorative. Since a κάπηλος is a "retailer," καπηλεύω can mean simply "engage in retail trade (καπηλεία)," or "ply a petty trade." But because the κάπηλος was the "middle man" between the wholesaler (ἔμπορος) and the general public, he gained a reputation for manipulating prices or tampering with goods for the sake of profit. So καπηλεύω gained the sense "sell at illegitimate profit" or "adulterate," while the adjectives κάπηλος/καπηλικός meant "cheating" or "deceitful" and the adverb καπηλικῶς "in a mercenary spirit."[68] Closely associated with the verb, then, were ideas of

65. Georgi rightly recognizes that the question of ἱκανότης ("qualification," "competence") was central in Paul's dispute with his opponents (*Opponents* 231-34). The ἱκανο- root reappears in 3:5-6. There is no reason to think that Paul's use of ἱκανός was prompted by its use in Joel 2:11 (LXX καὶ τίς ἔσται ἱκανὸς αὐτῇ;, in reference to divine judgment; but see Georgi, *Opponents* 232-33) or in Exod. 4:10 (LXX οὐχ ἱκανός εἰμι, in reference to the call of Moses; but see Jones 40-41; Scott, "Triumph" 274).

66. Thrall 208 and n. 136.

67. See the discussion in Hafemann, *Spirit* 90-95; *Defense* 85-90; Grässer 13-14. Some English translations actually include an affirmative answer in their renderings: "I am" (Goodspeed, Moffatt), "Are not we?" (Berkeley). Cf. Héring 18.

68. See LSJ 875-76; H. Windisch, *TDNT* 3.603; Spicq 2.254-57.

trickery and greed, or — since the κάπηλος was often a wine merchant — adulteration and financial profit. In the philosophical realm, the word was used of the efforts of itinerant sophists to peddle their teaching for monetary gain. Thus we read in Lucian (*Hermotimus* 59): "Philosophers sell their knowledge like the wine merchants (κάπηλοι) do their wine — the majority of them (οἱ πολλοί) mixing it with water and adulterating it (δολώσαντες)[69] and giving a short measure." Since Paul is using the verb metaphorically, the neutral, literal sense obviously does not apply, so that pejorative overtones are inevitable, especially since he is castigating (by implication) the activity of some opponents. He is chiding οἱ πολλοί as fraudulent hucksters who adulterate God's word for profit. That is, as Windisch sums up the matter, they not only offer God's word for money but also falsify that word by making additions.[70] Paul is impugning both their motive (financial gain) and their technique (adulteration). ἐσμὲν . . . καπηλεύοντες is a periphrastic present; if, as is often the case with periphrastic tenses, linear action is being emphasized, the sense is, "we are not in the habit of making profit (out of God's message)."[71]

When πολλοί is articular, it may mean either "the many" or "the majority."[72] If, as here, the context suggests disapproval, "most people" or "the crowd" is an appropriate translation.[73] Certainly Paul is not disparaging all other Christian evangelists and teachers, as though he alone preached an unadulterated gospel. But he probably is referring, without statistical precision, to some indeterminate but sizable number of teachers who had visited Corinth, were known to the Corinthians, or were still resident in Corinth, who were profiting from preaching and corrupting the gospel (= "the word of God"; cf. 4:2-3; 1 Thess. 2:13).[74] On the assumption of the letter's unity, we may see οἱ πολλοί as referring in particular to the ψευδαπόστολοι who masqueraded as ἀπόστολοι Χριστοῦ (11:13) and introduced another Jesus, a different spirit, and a different gospel (11:4), that is, Paul's Judaizing opponents at Corinth.[75]

ἀλλ᾽ ὡς ἐξ εἰλικρινείας, ἀλλ᾽ ὡς ἐκ θεοῦ κατέναντι θεοῦ ἐν Χριστῷ λαλοῦμεν. "On the contrary, we act from pure motives, and, as persons sent from God, we speak in the sight of God and in the name of Christ." Here Paul

69. Note the use of δολοῦντες in 4:2.

70. H. Windisch, *TDNT* 3.604-5. But Hafemann argues that καπηλεύειν ("to sell" as a retail dealer sells his wares in the market) simply casts doubt on the genuineness of the ministry of οἱ πολλοί and criticizes their motives for seeking financial support, so that Paul does not contradict his own teaching about the basic legitimacy of deriving one's living from the gospel (1 Cor. 9:7-14; *Spirit* 106-26, 158-63, 172-74; *Defense* 101-26, 160-65, 174-76).

71. RV and Furnish (173) construe ἐσμέν closely with ὡς οἱ πολλοί, making καπηλεύοντες adjectival: "For we are not like so many, huckstering the word of God" (Furnish).

72. Since the Greek expression οἱ πολλοί is so common, there is no reason to follow Daniel in finding here a reference to *hārabbîm*, "the many," that is, members of the Qumran congregation, who with their distinctive interpretations "diluted the word of God" (553-67).

73. BAGD 688c. Young and Ford (264) have "like most of them."

74. On Paul's habit of not naming his opponents, see the Introduction, n. 171.

75. See the Introduction, B.4. ("Paul's Opponents in 2 Corinthians").

states four positive reasons that establish his competence and adequacy for his role as an ambassador of Christ. οὐ(κ) . . . ἀλλά is a favorite Pauline antithesis. The repetition of ἀλλ' ὡς suggests that the first item (ἐξ εἰλικρινείας) may belong to a separate category, Paul's conduct in general, while the last three prepositional phrases may relate primarily to Paul's speech (λαλοῦμεν).[76]

1. ὡς ἐξ εἰλικρινείας

Here ὡς is not hypothetical in sense ("as if"), but introduces an actual, characteristic quality (BAGD 898a). There is an ellipse of either an article or an articular participle,[77] ὡς (οἱ) ἐξ εἰλικρινείας or ὡς (οἱ) ἐξ εἰλικρινείας (ὄντες): "as those whose conduct is characterized by pure motives" or "as persons of sincerity" (NRSV).[78] If the κάπηλοι of v. 17a were acting with impure and deceitful motives as they dispensed the word of God, the opposite was true of Paul. He did not convert preaching into a means of personal gain.

2. ὡς ἐκ θεοῦ

If the previous phrase relates to the motives for Paul's conduct, this phrase portrays the origin of his proclamation. He declares the word of God as one "commissioned by God" (RSV), with the result that his message is unadulterated. Paul's affirmation in 1 Thess. 2:4, δεδοκιμάσμεθα ὑπὸ τοῦ θεοῦ πιστευθῆναι τὸ εὐαγγέλιον ("we have been approved by God to be entrusted with the gospel"), is simply an expansion of ἐκ θεοῦ . . . λαλοῦμεν here. This divine commissioning explains the potent effects — death or life, v. 16 — of Paul's preaching. His adequacy was derived exclusively ἐκ τοῦ θεοῦ (3:5), not from himself.

3. κατέναντι θεοῦ

God was not only the source of Paul's commission; he was also the witness and assessor of his work. Although Paul discharged his God-given commission among fellow humans, he was ultimately accountable not to any human court (cf. 1 Cor. 4:3; 2 Cor. 10:12) but to a heavenly judge. Consequently, he spoke "before God," "in the sight of God" (BAGD 421b).[79]

4. ἐν Χριστῷ λαλοῦμεν

While λαλεῖν certainly refers mainly to the announcement of the good news, it may stand, by synecdoche, for Paul's whole life as a servant of Christ (cf. 12:19).[80] ἐν Χριστῷ is almost a christological "blank check" to

---

76. But if ἀλλ' ὡς ἐξ εἰλικρινείας is associated directly with what follows, all four items could relate to speech: "On the contrary, our speech comes from sincere motives . . ." (Thrall 190).

77. Cf. Turner 158 n. 1.

78. For this sense of οἱ ἐκ . . . , see BAGD 235a (under 3.d.).

79. Since κατέναντι should be more closely associated with the idea of God's omniscience than with his omnipresence, "in God's sight" is a more appropriate rendering than "in God's presence"; see, however, Renwick 61-94.

80. Cf. Schütz 210-12.

be filled in with an amount appropriate in each context. Its principal senses, however, are "in the [body of] Christ," the corporate or collective sense, and "in [personal union with the risen] Christ," the individual sense. Here, with λαλεῖν, the meaning may be "as taught by Christ," which would be parallel to λαλοῦμεν . . . ἐν [λόγοις] διδακτοῖς πνεύματος ("we speak . . . in words taught by the Spirit," 1 Cor. 2:13; cf. 1 Cor. 12:3), or "in the name of Christ." Christ was the source of the authority and power of both his message and his ministry.

In an initial answer to his own question, "Who is adequate to fulfill such a calling?" (v. 16b), Paul thus enunciates several reasons for his "confidence before God" (3:5) with regard to his fitness to serve. "Unlike most people," he shunned preaching merely for profit and he rejected any diluting of the message; he operated with transparent motives; and his preaching and his ministry were carried out by divine commission, with a sense of accountability to God, and with the powerful authority of Christ.[81]

Bibliography

Baird, "Letters" • G. Barth • G. Bertram, "ἱκανός in den griechischen Übersetzungen des A.T. als Wiedergabe von Schaddaj," *ZAW* 70 (1958) 20-31 • Breytenbach, "Proclamation" • Carrez, "Odeur" • Carrez, "ΙΚΑΝΟΤΗΣ" • Collange 21-41 • Daniel • Denis • de Oliveira • Duff • Dupont 40-41 • Egan • Fallon, "Sufficiency" • Fee, *Presence* 298-99 • Friesen 25-30 • Gale 148-52 • Georgi, *Opponents* 229-46 • Grässer • Hafemann, *Spirit* 10-176 • Hafemann, *Defense* 7-179 • Hanson, *Paradox* 108-15 • Hanson, *Ministry* 49-50 • Heiny • Jones • Käsemann • Kent • Kinsey • W. L. Knox 129-31 • Koperski • Kreitzer 95-99 • Lambrecht, "Structure" • Lührmann 45-66, 159-61 • Luz, "Bund" • Manson, "Suggestions" • Marshall, "Metaphor" • McDonald • O. Michel, *Paulus und seine Bibel* (Gütersloh: Bertelsmann, 1929; reprinted Darmstadt: Wissenschaftliche Buchgesellschaft, 1972) 174-78 • G. F. Moore, "Savour" • Murphy-O'Connor 29-33 • Murphy-O'Connor, "Macedonia" • Murphy-O'Connor, "Judaizers" • Ollrog 33-37 • Oostendorp 31-51 • Patte • Perriman • Pope • Prat, "Triomphe" • Provence • Prümm, "Offenbarung" • Renwick 47-50, 94 • Schröter • Scott, "Triumph" • Stalder 150-51 • Theobald 167-239 • Thrall, "Thanksgiving" • Versnel • G. Wagner, "Alliance de la lettre, alliance de l'Esprit. Essai d'analyse de 2 Corinthiens 2:14 à 3:18," *ETR* 60 (1985) 55-65 • Williamson • Witherington, *Jesus* 109-11 • R. Yates, "Col. 2:15: Christ Triumphant," *NTS* 37 (1991) 573-91

---

81. In a manner strangely parallel to the proposal that three expressions in Heb. 2:17(!) (ἐλεήμων . . . ἀρχιερεύς, πιστὸς ἀρχιερεύς, and τὸ ἱλάσκεσθαι) anticipate the content of Heb. 4:14–5:10; 3:1-6a; and 8:1–10:18 respectively, Prümm (1.95-96) and Theobald (177) have suggested that ἐκ θεοῦ, κατέναντι θεοῦ, and ἐν Χριστῷ provide suitable headings for some subsequent sections of the letter (see Thrall [216] for details and analysis of these proposals).

b. The Results of the Ministry (3:1-3)

In 2:14-17, Paul has not only painted a graphic picture of the high privileges and forbidding responsibilities of an apostle; he has also implied that, by divine enablement, he is qualified and equipped to meet those challenges. This prompts him to anticipate the charge that he was writing his own testimonial (3:1a), which in turn reminds him of the testimonials that the Corinthians were receiving and writing (3:1b). He discounts any need for such commendatory letters for himself, on the ground that there already existed at Corinth and in his own heart a letter that commended him and could be read by anyone — the transformed lives of the Corinthians themselves.

1Are we once again beginning to commend ourselves? Or^a do we need, as some do, commendatory letters to you or from you?^b Surely not! 2You yourselves are our letter, written on our^c hearts, recognized and read by everybody. 3You are shown to be a letter that Christ wrote and we transcribed, written^d not with ink but by the Spirit of the living God, not on tablets of stone but on tablets that are hearts of flesh.^e

TEXTUAL NOTES

a. A Ψ 𝔐 read εἰ instead of ἤ through itacism (cf. Moulton and Howard 71-72).

b. After ὑμῶν, some witnesses add συστατικῶν (D[*] 𝔐 b[syr]) and others συστατικῶν ἐπιστολῶν (F G), possibly to create balance, but the majority of witnesses lack any addition (p⁴⁶ ℵ A B C Ψ 0243 6 33 81 365 630 1175 1739 1881 2464 *pc* f* vg).

c. A few witnesses (ℵ 33 88 436 1175 1881 *pc* eth^ro) read ὑμῶν, but the vast majority (p⁴⁶ A B C D G K P Ψ 614 1739 *Byz Lect* it vg syr^{p, h} cop^{sa, bo} goth arm) read ἡμῶν. The second person pronoun is preferred by several commentators (Héring 21 and n. 2; Barrett 96 and n. 3, 108; Bultmann 71; Martin 44 and note c, 51; Thrall 223-24) and some translations (RSV [but not NRSV], NAB¹ [but not NAB²]; also Bruce, *Paraphrase* 131), but most prefer ἡμῶν, whether it be rendered "our" (e.g., RV, NEB, REB) or "my" (e.g., Moffatt). Any appeal to Paul's argument in the immediate context is inconclusive, witness the fact that Martin clams that ὑμῶν "seems required by the context" (44), whereas Metzger (reflecting the UBS Committee in all four editions) maintains that ἡμῶν "seems to be demanded by the context" (509)! Equally inconclusive is an appeal to the presence of ἡμῶν in v. 2a and v. 3a or to 7:3 (ἐν ταῖς καρδίαις ἡμῶν), since ἡμῶν in 3:2 could be seen as scribal assimilation to 7:3, or the phrase in 7:3 (where the text is certain) could be claimed as a parallel supporting the originality of ἡμῶν in 3:2. I believe this is an instance where, with internal evidence almost evenly balanced, the consideration of external evidence, which favors ἡμῶν, should be determinative, although it would appear also that ἡμῶν is the more difficult reading (*pace* Murphy-O'Connor, "Ministry" 123-24). If the Corinthian letter was written on Paul's heart (ἡμῶν), it would come to be "known and read by all" only if he himself spoke of their faith everywhere (cf. 1 Thess. 1:7-8).

d. The asyndetic ἐγγεγραμμένη is more closely attached to the preceding statement by the insertion of καί in some witnesses (𝔓⁴⁶ B 0243 630 1175 1739 1881 *pc* f vg).

e. Instead of πλαξὶν καρδίαις σαρκίναις ("(on) tablets that are hearts of flesh"), which is the reading of most witnesses, some Greek mss (0243 630 1739) read πλαξὶν σαρκίναις ("fleshy tablets"), and a variety of witnesses (F Ψ 629 945 1505 *al* latt (syrᵖ) Irenaeusˡᵃᵗ Eusebius) read πλαξὶν καρδίας σαρκίναις ("fleshy tablets of the heart"), both variations being the result of scribal efforts to ameliorate the awkward apposition of καρδίαις σαρκίναις to πλαξίν. Westcott and Hort (so also Bultmann 74) conjecture that the original was simply καρδίαις σαρκίναις ("hearts of flesh"), which would create balanced parallelism ("not on tablets of stone, but on hearts of flesh"): "Πλαξίν [is] probably a primitive interpolation" (WH 1.578). "It is not unlikely that the second πλαξίν was a primitive clerical error suggested by the line above, and immediately discovered and cancelled by dots which escaped notice at the next transcription" (WH 2 Appendix.119). This proposal remains a conjecture; the text as it stands, while awkward, is not impossible.

3:1 Ἀρχόμεθα πάλιν ἑαυτοὺς συνιστάνειν; "Are we once again beginning to commend ourselves?" It is possible to regard this as an "open question" with no formal indication of the answer anticipated and only the context making it clear what answer is expected.[1] However, because the second question in this verse begins with ἤ ("or") and expects a negative response (μή), there are both formal and contextual reasons for expecting a "No."[2]

συνιστάνω is a late form of συνίστημι, illustrating the gradual decline of -μι verbs (absent in modern Greek) and the preference for the -ω conjugation in Hellenistic Greek.[3] Originally this verb meant "place together," "combine," but it came to mean "bring together as friends," "introduce/recommend someone to someone else" (τινά τινι; LSJ 1718 s.v.). Accordingly, the cognate adjective συστατικός means "for bringing together," "introductory," "commendatory," (LSJ 1735 s.v.), so that συστατικαὶ ἐπιστολαί (v. 2) refers to "letters of introduction/commendation" designed to bring together persons previously unknown to one another.

In posing this question Paul is probably anticipating a charge that could be leveled against him by someone at Corinth. His appeal to his "godly holiness and sincerity" (1:12) and his mention of the distinctive role of the apostles (2:14-16) and his own divine commission and authority (2:17) could well have prompted some Corinthian ill-disposed to Paul to say "once again you are beginning to indulge in your notorious habit of self-commendation." Whether it be taken with ἀρχόμεθα or with συνιστάνειν, πάλιν might well allude to earlier

1. Thus Moule 158.
2. BAGD 342b: "ἤ oft[en] occurs in interrog[ative] sentences . . . to introduce a question which is parallel to a preceding one or supplements it" (2 Cor. 3:1 is cited). Hafemann regards the second question in v. 1 as simply an explication or restatement of the first, so that the two questions constitute a single response to an anticipated objection that 2:17 was a case of "self-recommendation" (*Defense* 182-86).
3. Cf. BDF §§92-93; Robertson 315-16.

statements Paul had made to the Corinthians that could have been construed as self-advertisement,[4] to statements in 1 Corinthians[5] or in the "severe letter," or to comments made during the "painful visit."

If Paul expects (or hopes for) a resounding "No!" in answer to his question, how can he later engage, by his own confession, in comparable self-commendation (4:2; 6:4)? In reference to 3:1 some argue that συνιστάνειν does not mean "to commend" but "to introduce": Paul wants to avoid giving the impression that the Corinthians know nothing about him, so he rejects any idea that by speaking of himself as he has in 2:14-17 he is repeating the self-introduction he gave when he first arrived in Corinth.[6] This view would be more convincing if Paul had written χρῄζομεν πάλιν ἑαυτοὺς συνιστάνειν; ("Do we need to introduce ourselves again?" cf. v. 1b). In any case, 2:14-17 does not read like a convincing initial self-introduction that might have prompted Paul's question. On the wider issue of self-commendation in 2 Corinthians, it is preferable to distinguish two types of statement, a distinction suggested by Paul's own precise usage. When he uses the phrase ἑαυτὸν συνιστάνειν (3:1; 5:12; 10:12, 18), the sense is pejorative, of self-commendation that lacks the necessary supporting evidence and glorifies the self (ἑαυτόν is emphatic by position). But when he uses συνιστάνειν ἑαυτόν (4:2; 6:4; cf. 7:11),[7] the meaning is positive, of self-commendation or "boasting in the Lord" (cf. 10:13-18) that substantiates a God-given role by appealing to Christ's work in and through his servant and that enhances God's glory.[8] This latter type of self-commendation that leads to the praise of God, not to the praise of self,[9] is legitimate when circumstances render it necessary (cf. 12:11) — for instance, when the continuation of God's work is at stake or the integrity of God's servant has been called into question, both circumstances that obtained at Corinth.

ἦ μὴ χρῄζομεν ὥς τινες συστατικῶν ἐπιστολῶν πρὸς ὑμᾶς ἢ ἐξ ὑμῶν; "Or do we need, as some do, commendatory letters to you or from you? Surely not!" On the form of this question and the meaning of συστατικός, see above on v. 1a. "Letters of (re)commendation" συστατικαὶ ἐπιστολαί (or συστατικὰ

---

4. πάλιν is written "from the outlook of [Paul's] opponents" (Zerwick, *Analysis* 395).

5. E.g., 1 Cor. 4:15; 9:1, 15-22; 14:18; 15:10.

6. Tasker 59; Thrall 218.

7. Textual variants involving συνιστάνω, συνίστημι, and συνιστάω (each of which may mean "commend") are found in 4:2; 6:4; 10:18 (see the discussions there).

8. Cf. Bernard (52) who draws attention to the linguistic distinction. Belleville argues that there are two distinctive features in Paul's self-commendation in 2 Cor. 1–7: he writes from the standpoint not of his person but of his apostolic office, his credentials being ministerial and derivative, and he speaks in the plural as a representative of Christ's accredited ministers, rather than in the singular, with the block of material in 2:14–6:12 (apart from a conventional ἐλπίζω in 5:11) cast entirely in the first person plural ("Letter" 160-63).

9. If a careful distinction is drawn between self-commendation and self-praise, perhaps Marshall's criticism of the traditional view (265-68) loses its potency. He sees Paul's use of self-recommendation as a social rather than a moral issue, since recommendation either by a third party or by one's self was a common way to initiate a relationship of trust (268-77).

γράμματα) were given to travelers or emissaries to introduce them to persons in another town or country who could provide them with hospitality and meet their particular needs. Since the person recommended was in good standing with the recommender and the recipient was a friend or patron of the recommender, the "letter of commendation" virtually committed the recipient to comply with the request expressed in the letter. As well as third-party recommendation, there was self-recommendation in which individuals committed themselves to a reciprocal relationship based on mutual trust.[10]

Paul is not rejecting the use of letters of commendation here. Their use had already become established within the Christian world (see Acts 15:25-27; 18:27), and Paul himself had sought epistolary credentials from the high priest at Jerusalem before setting out for the synagogues of Damascus (Acts 9:2; 22:5). Also, he himself wrote what amounted to commendatory letters for Phoebe (Rom. 16:1-2), Timothy (1 Cor. 16:10-11), Titus and his companions (2 Cor. 8:22-23), Tychicus (Eph. 6:21-22; Col. 4:7-8), Mark (Col. 4:10), and Onesimus (Phlm. 10-12, 17-19). What he is contesting is any need for him, the spiritual father of the Corinthians (1 Cor. 4:14-15), to produce such endorsement of his person and work.

Given the proximity of 3:1 to 2:17, it is natural to assume that the τινές ("some") are οἱ πολλοί ("the many").[11] The "need" (cf. χρῄζομεν) for commendatory letters was probably felt by the Corinthians as well as by Paul's rivals at Corinth. Their deep appreciation of Apollos as a teacher who had come to Corinth with warm written commendation from the Ephesian Christians (Acts 18:27) meant that they were not averse to receiving epistolary credentials from the τινές on their arrival in Corinth (πρὸς ὑμᾶς). It is not impossible that these visitors came to Corinth with letters of their own that set out their credentials and introduced them (cf. 10:12). But συστατικῶν ἐπιστολῶν [τῶν] πρὸς ὑμᾶς is more likely to mean "commendatory letters that are addressed to you" by a third-party recommender than "commendatory letters that are brought to you" by persons who write their own testimonials, for all of the earliest Christian "letters of commendation" of which we have knowledge (see above) involve three parties, not merely two.

Who wrote the letters carried by the τινές? This raises the wider question of the relation between Paul's opponents in Corinth and the church of Jerusalem. In our discussion of this issue in the Introduction (B.4.c.) it is proposed that these letters of commendation emanated not from the three Jerusalem "pillars" (Gal. 2:9) or the Twelve but from one of "the churches of Christ in Judea" (Gal. 1:22) or from the Pharisaic wing of the Jerusalem church, those Judaizers who insisted on the scrupulous observance of the Mosaic Law as essential for salvation (Acts 15:5) and were unable to distinguish between the Law-abiding conduct of the Twelve and legalistic teaching.

10. See Keyes 28-44; C. H. Kim, *passim;* Marshall 91-129, especially 92; Spicq 3.342-43.
11. There is no need to assume that the "some" are "few" in number.

(ἐπιστολῶν) . . . ἐξ ὑμῶν is not evidence that Paul's opponents had already left Corinth,[12] for in conducting brief missionary forays from Corinth they may well have sought a Corinthian imprimatur on their work that would complement their letters from Judea or Jerusalem. On the other hand, Paul may be simply anticipating that the Corinthians would receive a request from his rivals for such testimonials.

If there was a specific charge against Paul that gave rise to this second question in v. 1, it might have run like this:

> Since Jerusalem is the fount of Christianity, those working outside Jerusalem must be able to give proof of their commission by letters of recommendation. We brought you Corinthians commendatory letters from Jerusalem and you yourselves have supplied us with such when we have visited other places. Why should you regard Paul as an exception? Does not his unconcern about letters of recommendation prove he is an intruder and imposter?

3:2 ἡ ἐπιστολὴ ἡμῶν ὑμεῖς ἐστε, ἐγγεγραμμένη ἐν ταῖς καρδίαις ἡμῶν, γινωσκομένη καὶ ἀναγινωσκομένη ὑπὸ πάντων ἀνθρώπων. "You yourselves are our letter, written on our hearts, recognized and read by everybody." The latter of the two questions posed in v. 1 Paul now answers explicitly. He implies that for him to carry commendatory letters to Corinth would be completely superfluous. The most complimentary letter he could possibly possess had already been written and was already in Corinth. Their very lives as men and women "in Christ," the result of the grace of Christ operative in Paul's ministry, were an eloquent letter that he could never forget and that everybody could read. To bring another letter would amount to a personal insult to the Corinthians; it certainly would ignore the past and present work of Christ in their hearts, of which they were constantly aware. They themselves were Paul's testimonial, guaranteeing his apostolic status and authority.

Stylistically, the first clause in this verse is notable for its asyndeton and the dramatic juxtaposition of ἡμῶν and ὑμεῖς. The word ἐπιστολή, which bore a literal sense in v. 1, is now used metaphorically[13] of the transformed lives of the Corinthians, which corporately composed a letter that was readable. The singular ἐπιστολή is not distributive ("you are individually our letters") but functions like a collective singular: the Corinthian Christians as a whole constituted a living letter that belonged to Paul (ἡμῶν), a letter that he helped to write and now could carry about with him, so to speak.[14] What made the letter noticeable was

---

12. As F. Watson (343) claims. Marshall contends that "it is entirely possible that *pros hymas* and *ex hymon* refer to an interchange of correspondence between the hybrists and the rival apostles prior to the latters' arrival in which they were invited by the hybrists to Corinth" (276).

13. Cf. BDF §488 (1[c]), citing a parallel movement from literal to figurative with τύπτειν in Acts 23:3. On Paul's ecclesiological use of the "letter" metaphor in 3:2-3, see further Scholtissek 183-205.

14. It is not possible to associate Paul's statement "You yourselves are our letter," with either πρὸς ὑμᾶς or ἐξ ὑμῶν, for that letter was written neither to the Corinthians nor by them.

its newness, as the Corinthians reflected in their characters "the new order" (τὰ καινά, 5:17) that came about through their conversion. So Paul is saying, "Your changed lives authenticate my ministry. You yourselves are my credentials as an apostle." He expresses a similar sentiment in 1 Cor. 9:2: "You yourselves are the seal (σφραγίς) that authenticates my apostleship in the Lord." Here was indisputable living testimony, not contestable written testimony.

The verb ἐγγράφω denotes the action of inscribing in a list, entering in a document, enrolling in a group, or engraving an inscription.[15] Paul may have in mind Jer. 38:33 (LXX; 31:33 MT) in reference to the new covenant (cf. 2 Cor. 3:6): ἐπὶ καρδίας αὐτῶν γράψω αὐτούς (viz. νόμους μου), "I will write [my laws] on their hearts," or possibly Prov. 3:3 (A): γράψον αὐτὰς ἐπὶ πλάτος [= πλακὸς] καρδίας σου, "Write [mercy and faithfulness] on the tablet of your heart," but in neither case is ἐγγράφω used.[16] Reasons for preferring the reading ἡμῶν over ὑμῶν are given in Textual Note c above. The "heart" (καρδία) is the seat of the emotions and affections, the center of the personality. The Corinthians were not merely frequently in Paul's thoughts or always in the back of his mind; they had been indelibly engraved (ἐγγεγραμμένη), perfect passive) on his heart, and so were in his heart (ἐν ταῖς καρδίαις ἡμῶν ἐστε, 7:3).

At first sight, the word order γινωσκομένη καὶ ἀναγινωσκομένη ("known and read") is strange, for a letter must be read before its contents can be known. Lexical explanations suggest that γινωσκομένη refers to an inspection or perusal that precedes actual reading. Logical explanations point out that a letter must be recognized as a letter before it is read or that handwriting (at least the signature; cf. 2 Thess. 3:17) be recognized before actual reading begins. Stylistic explanations account for the word order by observing that the simplex would naturally be used before the compound or that in cases of paronomasia the compound simply intensifies the preceding simplex form. Whichever explanation is preferred, this whole phrase, "recognized and read by everybody,"[17] should be construed with both preceding phrases. The "letter" was permanently open to examination (note two present participles) not only at Corinth where the Corinthians themselves lived out their newness of life in Christ. It was also available for universal inspection wherever Paul went with this heart-engraving and spoke of the faith and spiritual life of the Corinthians (cf. 7:14; 9:2-3; 1 Thess. 1:8).[18] In both "places" — at Corinth and through Paul — the letter could be read by one and all.

15. See G. Schrenk, *TDNT* 1.769.

16. Stockhausen (52-53, 80-81) appeals to the term ἐγγεγραμμένα in Exod. 36:21 (B) as an explanation of Paul's use of ἐγγράφω and argues that the ἐπιστολή of 2 Cor. 3:2 is parallel to the breastplate worn by Aaron, which was engraved with the names of the twelve tribes of Israel. "Paul carries the Corinthians themselves before the Lord in his heart as his 'letter,' not just the letters of their names on a stone tablet. A second deliberate use of ἐγγράφω in verse 3 reinforces this reinterpretation" (81). But see Hughes (91-92) on this possible allusion to Aaron's breastplate.

17. The nearest way English can reproduce the play on words is by assonance: "recognized and read."

18. Cf. Hays (127): "Paul carries around with him in his own heart the attestation that the Corinthians seek, because he bears *them* in heart and memory."

3:3 φανερούμενοι ὅτι ἐστὲ ἐπιστολὴ Χριστοῦ διακονηθεῖσα ὑφ' ἡμῶν.
"You are shown to be a letter that Christ wrote and we transcribed." The present
participle φανερούμενοι, which looks back to ὑμεῖς (3:2), may be middle, "you
show that you are,"[19] but since the previous phrase mentions those who read the
"letter," the participle is more probably passive, "you are shown to be."[20] It
could also be causal: ". . . recognized and read by everybody, *for* you are shown
to be. . . ."[21] To construe Χριστοῦ as an objective genitive ("a letter about
Christ") or a possessive genitive ("a letter belonging to Christ") is inappropriate
in a context that places no emphasis on the content of the letter or ambiguity
about its possession (cf. ἡμῶν, 3:2). Rather, Paul wishes to avoid giving the impression in v. 2 that either he or the Corinthians actually authored the letter: the
letter was "from Christ" (genitive of source or subjective genitive).[22]

Then Paul defines his own role, which was secondary: he could never
claim that the Corinthians were ἐπιστολὴ γεγραμμένη ὑφ' ἡμῶν, only ἐπιστολὴ
διακονηθεῖσα ὑφ' ἡμῶν. Christ was the author of the letter, Paul simply the
amanuensis. In bringing the ἐπιστολή into existence — in his pioneer evangelism in Corinth — he was merely Christ's agent (cf. 1 Cor. 3:6-7). It may have
been Paul's immediate circumstances — dictating to an amanuensis — that
suggested the whole metaphor of letter-writing which Paul seems to develop
here. Now it is true that διακονηθεῖσα ὑφ' ἡμῶν may not specify the nature of
Paul's secondary role, meaning simply "prepared by us" (NRSV) or "the result
of our ministry" (NIV). But since it is true in general that "Paul's rivers of imagery flood their banks" (Danker 52), it is not unlikely that Paul envisages himself here as the person who transcribes Christ's letter.[23] On the other hand, if the
phrase is rendered "delivered by us" (TNCT, Berkeley, RSV[24]), Paul can be
seen as the courier[25] only in relation to the founding of the Corinthian congregation, since the participle is aorist, not present. Certainly the occurrence of
this verb διακονέω at this point is significant, for it anticipates the coming
theme (note διάκονος in v. 6 and διακονία in vv. 7-9) of ἡ διακονία τοῦ
πνεύματος (v. 7) in the new covenant.

19. Goodspeed, Williams, Berkeley, RSV, NIV, NRSV; similarly Héring 21; Furnish 173,
180-81; Martin 44-51.
20. Cf. 1 John 2:19 (BDF §397 [4]).
21. So also Montgomery; Hafemann 117; *Defense* 205; Barrett 96 ("because it is manifest
that . . .").
22. Thus most commentators. So also Conybeare in Conybeare and Howson 445; TCNT;
GNB; Bruce, *Paraphrase* 131; Cassirer; Murphy-O'Connor, "Ministry" 125.
23. So, e.g., Weymouth, Moffatt, Montgomery; Wand; Bruce, *Paraphrase* 131; Stanley 74;
Meyer 461; Kümmel 199.
24. Similarly NEB, GNB, REB. Barrett has "supplied by us" (96).
25. So, e.g., Lietzmann 110; Baird, "Letters" 169-70 (who seems, appropriately, to derive
the idea of an ongoing courier role only from 3:2; on Baird's whole view, see Hafemann, *Defense*
200-205); Richard 347 and n. 32; Hays 127. Josephus, *Antiquities* 6.298 (cited in BAGD 184a) is
certainly a parallel for the notion of a delivery of a message; Acts 23:33 uses ἀναδίδωμι (a NT
hapax legomenon), not διακονέω, of the delivery of a letter.

ἐγγεγραμμένη οὐ μέλανι ἀλλὰ πνεύματι θεοῦ ζῶντος, οὐκ ἐν πλαξὶν λιθίναις ἀλλ᾽ ἐν πλαξὶν καρδίαις σαρκίναις. "Written not with ink but by the Spirit of the living God, not on tablets of stone but on tablets that are hearts of flesh." This is the second use of the perfect passive participle of ἐγγράφω in this paragraph, and again it modifies the term ἐπιστολή: "our letter . . . written in our hearts . . . Christ's letter . . . written . . . on tablets." Since in the second clause the writing is on tablets, ἐγγεγραμμένη could be rendered "inscribed" in both cases.[26] μέλανι and πνεύματι are both instrumental datives, but the transition from the inanimate ("not with ink") to the animate ("but by the Spirit") is unexpected and therefore dramatic. As for the final contrast, in the light of Paul's use of the imagery of "the letter written on the heart" thus far, we might have expected οὐκ ἐν χάρτῃ (or μεμβράναις) ἀλλ᾽ ἐν καρδίαις, "not on papyrus (or parchments) but on hearts," which would amount to a consistent, if unexciting, conclusion. But with his desire to compare the Mosaic and Christian ministries through a comparison of the old and new covenants, Paul "substitutes" "tablets of stone" for "papyrus" and "tablets that are human hearts" for the simple "hearts," a substitution that permits a contrast between "of stone," "stony" (λίθινος) and "of flesh," "human" (σάρκινος).

In the first of Paul's two οὐ(κ) . . . ἀλλά antitheses, "ink" is contrasted with "the Spirit." The term τὸ μέλαν ("ink") is derived from the adjective μέλας ("black"), for in Paul's time it was made of a mixture of carbon and gum. The writing utensil was a reed pen (κάλαμος) and the writing material was papyrus (χάρτης; cf. 2 John 12; 3 John 13). This is the only place in Scripture where we find the full expression πνεῦμα θεοῦ ζῶντος, "the Spirit of the living God," although the description of God as "the living God," common in both Testaments,[27] is found in Paul,[28] as is the expression "the Spirit of God."[29] Whereas ink was erasable (cf. Col. 2:13), the Spirit of God is ever-living, having an inexhaustible supply of creative energy. Human writers use ink that is perishable. The divine penman, Christ, writes his letters by means of the Spirit, whose person and work are imperishable. Paul is alluding to Exod. 31:18 (LXX), where it is said that when the Lord had finished speaking to Moses on Mount Sinai he gave him the two tablets (πλάκας) of the Testimony, which are further defined as "the tablets of stone inscribed by the finger of God" (πλάκας λιθίνας γεγραμμένας τῷ δακτύλῳ τοῦ θεοῦ; cf. Deut. 9:10). Paul's next phrase, οὐκ ἐν πλαξὶν λιθίναις, makes it clear that the γεγραμμένας of Exod. 31:18 has become

26. So Furnish 173; similarly Hafemann, *Defense* 198 and n. 48. Danker proposes the neutral term "record" as the most appropriate rendering of ἐγγράφω in vv. 2-3, since it covers writing by pen or by engraving tool (52).

27. E.g., Josh. 3:10; 1 Sam. 17:26; Isa. 37:4; Acts 14:15; Heb. 10:31; Rev. 7:2.

28. Rom. 9:26 (citing Hos. 2:1 [LXX 1:10]); 1 Thess. 1:9; 2 Cor. 6:16; 1 Tim. 3:15; 4:10.

29. E.g., Rom. 8:9, 14; 1 Cor. 2:11; 6:11; Phil. 3:3. That πνεύματι and θεοῦ are anarthrous does not in any way diminish the definiteness of the expression. "The canon of Apollonius" states that nouns in *regimen* generally either both have the article or both lack it (see Harris, *Jesus* 305-7). Compare ἐν τῷ πνεύματι τοῦ θεοῦ in 1 Cor. 6:11 with ἐν πνεύματι θεου in 1 Cor. 12:3.

γεγραμμένη here in 3:3, and τῷ δακτύλῳ τοῦ θεοῦ has become πνεύματι θεοῦ ζῶντος.[30]

If Jer. 38:33 (LXX) lies behind Paul's expression "written on our hearts" (v. 2) and Exod. 31:18 behind "written . . . by the Spirit of the living God" (v. 3a), two passages in Ezekiel are reflected in the final phrase in v. 3, "on tablets that are human hearts," 11:19 and 36:26-27a:[31]

> And I will give them a different heart (καρδίαν ἑτέραν) and will put a new spirit in them; I will remove from them their heart of stone (τὴν καρδίαν τὴν λιθίνην) and will give them a heart of flesh (καρδίαν σαρκίνην).

> And I will give you a new heart (καρδίαν καινήν) and will put a new spirit in you; I will remove from you your heart of stone (τὴν καρδίαν τὴν λιθινήν) and will give you a heart of flesh (καρδίαν σαρκίνην). And I will put my Spirit in you.

In these two passages the contrast is between two types of heart — one that is insensitive (λίθινος "stony") and one that is responsive (σάρκινος, "fleshy").[32] In reference to πλάκες ("tablets"), the adjective λίθινος had a neutral sense ("made of stone") (Exod. 31:18), but as applied to καρδίαι ("hearts"), it gains a pejorative sense ("stony"). Consequently, with λίθινος as the link word, Paul associates the καρδίαι λίθιναι of Ezekiel with the πλάκες λίθιναι of Exodus, "hearts of stone" with "tablets of stone," "stony hearts" with Moses and the old covenant.[33] And, by implication, καρδίαι σάρκιναι, sensitive human hearts, are linked with the work of God's Spirit under the new covenant (Jeremiah).[34]

In 3:2-3, then, Paul develops the imagery of the letter in several directions under the stimulus of passages drawn from Jeremiah, Exodus, and Ezekiel. The letter is the Corinthian church as a whole as transformed by the gospel in fulfillment of Jeremiah 31 (38 in the LXX) and Ezekiel 11 and 36. Christ, working through the Spirit, is the author of the letter, and Paul is the amanuensis. From one point of view, the letter is written on Paul's heart; from another, it is inscribed on the Corinthians' own hearts. So Paul delivers a powerful rebuttal to

---

30. Cf. Collange 51.

31. Similarly Richard 340-49.

32. "Pro-paroxytone adjectives in ινος almost without exception denote the material of which a thing is made" (Winer [98], citing σάρκινος, "fleshy," λίθινος, "of stone," and others; cf. Moulton and Howard, 378). Hickling (388) observes that in these two passages in Ezekiel "the *heart* of stone . . . clearly stands for obduracy in the face of God's will."

33. This is an illustration of the hermeneutical principle, *gezerah shawah* (verbal analogy from one verse to another), one of Hillel's seven *middoth* (on which see Ellis 41). Seifrid (110 and n. 57) may have overlooked the operation of this principle in 3:3 when he rejects Ezek. 36:26 and proposes Jer. 17:1 as the OT background to the expression καρδίαις σαρκίναις (which he renders by "fleshly hearts"). "The passage in Ezekiel does not use the metaphor of 'tablets' to describe the heart, or speak of inscription upon the heart" (110 n. 57).

34. Baird argues (unconvincingly) that the καρδίαι of 3:3, like the καρδίαι of 3:2, refers to *Paul's* heart ("Letters" 171-72).

his opponents. His commendatory letter was written before theirs; it was indelible; it was widely circulated, not confidential or unpublished; its author was Christ, not a partisan group from Judea or within the Jerusalem church. Proof of his genuineness as an apostle of Christ was to be found not in written characters but in human characters.[35]

Bibliography

Baird, "Letters" • G. Barth • Carrez, *Souffrance* 33-44, 81-82 • Denis • A. de Oliveira, "'Ihr seid ein Brief Christi' (2 Kor 3,3). Ein paulinischer Beitrag zur Ekklesiologie des Wortes Gottes," in R. Kampling and T. Söding (eds.), *Ekklesiologie des Neuen Testaments. FS für K. Kertelge* (Freiburg: Herder, 1966) 356-77 • de Surgy • Fee, *Presence* 302-4 • Friesen 30-37 • Goppelt 2.59, 121 • Hafemann, *Spirit* 180-225 • Hafemann, "Legitimacy" • Hanson, "Midrash" • Hanson, *Ministry* 50, 66-67 • Hays 122-53 • Hickling • Käsemann • Keyes • C. H. Kim • W. L. Knox 129-31 • Kreitzer 56-70 • Lane • Lührmann • Marshall 91-129, 259-77, 346-48 • Murphy-O'Connor, "Ministry" • Oostendorp 31-51 • Provence • Richard • Rissi 19-22 • Scholtissek • Seifrid 109-14 • Stockhausen 33-86 • Stockhausen, "2 Corinthians 3"

c. Competence for Service (3:4-6)

Paul has prepared the way for this discussion of competence to serve under the new covenant in two regards. First, he has asked "Who is qualified to serve as God's willing captive and as Christ's fragrance?" (2:14-16) and has given an abbreviated, apologetic answer (2:17). Now he expands on the statement "we speak as persons sent from God" (2:17b). Second, although 3:1-3 does not explicitly refer to the new covenant, the allusion to Jer. 31:33 (LXX 38:33) in the phrase "written in our hearts" (3:2) and the contrast between "tablets of stone" and "hearts of flesh" (3:3) are reminders of the institution of the old covenant and the promise of a new covenant.

4*Such is the confidence that we have through Christ toward God.* 5*Not that we are qualified in ourselves to claim*[a] *anything*[b] *as originating from ourselves.*[c] *Rather, our qualification comes from God,* 6*who indeed has qualified us as agents of a new covenant, one characterized not by written law but by the Spirit. Now the written law brings death,*[d] *but the Spirit imparts life.*

TEXTUAL NOTES

a. C D F G 629 *pc* read the present infinitive λογίζεσθαι.

b. 𝔓46 B omit τι, perhaps through homoioteleuton.

35. Cf. Hays: "Paul's intertextual trope hints . . . that in the new covenant incarnation eclipses inscription. By incarnation I mean . . . the enfleshment of the message of Jesus Christ in the community of Paul's brothers and sisters at Corinth" (129).

c. B F G *pc* read αὐτῶν, a not uncommon contraction of ἑαυτῶν.

d. Some witnesses (p⁴⁶* A C D 1881 𝔐) read αποκτενει, which may be a future (ἀποκτενεῖ) or a variant spelling of the present (ἀποκτένει). Cf. BAGD 93d.

3:4 πεποίθησιν δὲ τοιαύτην ἔχομεν διὰ τοῦ Χριστοῦ πρὸς τὸν θεόν. "Such is the confidence that we have through Christ toward God." πεποίθησις ("confidence," "trust") is a Pauline word not found elsewhere in the NT. Four of Paul's six uses are in 2 Corinthians (1:15; 3:4; 8:22; 10:2 and Eph. 3:12; Phil. 3:4). Bultmann observes that there is "no material difference" between this πεποίθησις and the παρρησία of 3:12 or the καύχησις of Rom. 15:17.[1] While Paul's "confidence" was a subjective conviction, it was based on objective facts. In this regard, τοιαύτην is retrospective (not prospective, as if πεποίθησις were defined by vv. 5b-6), alluding to at least two reasons for confidence. There was the character of Paul's apostolic ministry: he was God's agent in disseminating in every place the knowledge of Christ in an unadulterated form (2:14-17). The second demonstrable fact was the effectiveness of his service — that is, the very existence of a Christian church in Corinth demonstrated the reality of his apostleship (3:1-3). But beyond his being God's agent everywhere and Christ's amanuensis at Corinth, Paul's confidence was secure because it was διὰ τοῦ Χριστοῦ, that is, it resulted from his union with Christ, or, more specifically, it came as a gift from Christ. It could never be said that the πεποίθησις was δι' ἡμῶν; it was not the product of a pious wish or imagination. The prepositional phrase πρὸς τὸν θεόν should not be construed directly with πεποίθησιν ("confidence in God," GNB, NAB¹). There is not only the distance between the two expressions;[2] the usual prepositions with πεποίθησις are either εἰς (as in 8:22) or ἐν (as in Phil. 3:4).[3] The phrase may mean "toward God,"[4] "before God,"[5] or "in regard to God" (TCNT). All of Christian existence is "in relation to" God "through" Christ.[6]

3:5 οὐχ ὅτι ἀφ' ἑαυτῶν ἱκανοί ἐσμεν λογίσασθαί τι ὡς ἐξ ἑαυτῶν, ἀλλ' ἡ ἱκανότης ἡμῶν ἐκ τοῦ θεοῦ. "Not that we are qualified in ourselves to claim anything as originating from ourselves." As in the case of οὐχ ὅτι in 1:24, Paul is correcting a possible misinterpretation of his previous statement *(epanorthosis)*[7]: his confidence before God should not be taken to imply self-competence, far less any independence of God. In this further rejection of fallacious self-commendation (cf. 3:1a), Paul first speaks negatively (v. 5a), then

1. R. Bultmann, *TDNT* 6.8.

2. Contrast Rom. 5:1, εἰρήνην ἔχομεν πρὸς τὸν θεόν.

3. Cf. also ἐπί with the dative (1:9) or the accusative (2:3) after the cognate verb πείθω.

4. BAGD 643c, 710c; NAB².

5. Barrett 110; Furnish 173; Wolff 60. "In the presence of God" (Williams; Martin 44) is simply an expansion of "before God" (cf. 2:17; 4:2).

6. In Eph. 2:18 (cf. Rom. 5:1) we find this same combination of prepositions — πρός with God the Father, διά with Christ — when Paul is discussing access to God.

7. See the commentary on 1:24. Winer (555) observes that οὐχ ὅτι here should not be treated as equivalent to ὅτι οὐχ (ἱκανοί ἐσμεν), "for we are not competent."

positively (vv. 5b-6). [ἔστιν] οὐχ ὅτι means "it is not the case that," "it is not as if." ἀφ' ἑαυτῶν ("of/in/by ourselves")[8] may be paraphrased "depending on our own power/wisdom" or "on our own authority," and, standing with ἱκανοί ἐσμεν, it anticipates ἡ ἱκανότης ἡμῶν ἐκ τοῦ θεοῦ rather than ἐξ ἑαυτῶν. Some regard ἐξ ἑαυτῶν as simply repeating or redefining ἀφ' ἑαυτῶν,[9] but this overlooks the fact that ὡς ἐξ ἑαυτῶν qualifies λογίσασθαί τι, not ἱκανοί ἐσμεν. The phrase means "as originating/proceeding from ourselves" or "as belonging to ourselves" = "as our own."

There are three main ways of understanding the whole phrase λογίσασθαί τι ὡς ἐξ ἑαυτῶν:[10]

(1) Paul is rejecting any fitness for wise thinking that is independent of God. "It is not as though we were fit in our own wisdom to conceive a single thought on our own initiative."[11] "He has in view the whole work of thought within the framework of apostolic activity, i.e., thinking, judging, planning and resolving."[12]

(2) Paul is disclaiming any ability to form an accurate assessment of the results of his ministry (cf. 10:2). Plummer paraphrases the idea thus: "It is not a confidence that of ourselves we are competent to form any estimate of results."[13] A variation of this view links λογίσασθαί τι with an accurate analysis of the methods that ought to be employed in the discharge of the apostolic mission (Bernard 53) or a proper assessment of a preacher's potential (Georgi, *Opponents* 232).

(3) Paul is disowning any qualification to claim credit for himself for any aspect of his ministry. "It is not that we are adequate in ourselves to reckon anything to our credit" (Martin 44).

This third view, which is preferable, enjoys the support of many translations[14] and commentators.[15] It sees 3:5 as a commentary on 1 Cor. 15:9-10: all that Paul was as an apostle, along with all that he did as an apostle, unfit though he was for the role (οὐκ εἰμὶ ἱκανὸς καλεῖσθαι ἀπόστολος), was by the grace of

8. In the appropriate case and number, the reflexive pronoun ἑαυτοῦ may be used of all three persons (apart from the first person singular; see BAGD 211d, 212a-c).

9. E.g., TCNT: "by ourselves, as if on our own authority." Lietzmann (111) sees ἐξ ἑαυτῶν as a repetition caused by the circumstances of dictation.

10. The aorist infinitive λογίσασθαι is complementary and probably epexegetic after ἱκανοί: "qualified to reckon." But it may be consecutive/ecbatic: "adequate, so that we evaluate" (Furnish, 173, 183).

11. Bruce, *Paraphrase* 131. Cf. Bengel 3.364; BAGD 476b. This interpretation has sometimes been associated with the denial of free will or the doctrine of "total depravity," but such an association is certainly not necessary.

12. H. W. Heidland, *TDNT* 4.288; cf. Bultmann 75.

13. Plummer 83; but cf. 84. Similarly Barclay ("to reckon up the effect of anything that we have done"). Some translations take λογίσασθαί τι to mean something like "to form any estimate"; e.g., "to reach any conclusion" (Conybeare in Conybeare and Howson 445 n. 6; Montgomery); "to form any judgment" (TCNT, Moffatt).

14. RV, Goodspeed, RSV, NEB, JB, NAB[1], NIV, NAB[2], REB, NRSV, Cassirer.

15. E.g., Allo 83; Barrett 109; Furnish 173; Thrall 230; also Spicq 2.221.

God (1 Cor. 15:10). So claiming anything as his own or seeking credit for his work was inappropriate. Since God alone guarantees adequacy for Christian ministry (v. 5c), credit must go to God alone when it is carried out successfully. The Christian worker is ineligible to claim honor for success.

ἀλλ᾽ ἡ ἱκανότης ἡμῶν ἐκ τοῦ θεοῦ. "Rather, our qualification comes from God." This is the only use of ἱκανότης in the Greek Bible. However it is translated — the options are "fitness," "adequacy," "competence," "sufficiency," "qualification," and "capability" — an effort should be made to render the ἱκαν-root consistently in vv. 5-6: ἱκανοί and ἱκανότης (v. 5), ἱκάνωσεν (v. 6). It is unnecessary to restrict the noun here to some specific qualification, such as a God-given ability to think or judge aright (cf. λογίσασθαι) with regard to the ministry. As in 2:17, the ἱκανότης is general. The qualification that God gave Paul and his apostolic colleagues was the giftedness and motivation to fulfill their apostolic mission, to serve as God's agents under the new covenant (v. 6). ἐκ τοῦ θεοῦ matches the ἐκ θεοῦ of 2:17 and is the antithesis of both ἀφ᾽ ἑαυτῶν and ἐξ ἑαυτῶν.

In the LXX (ὁ) ἱκανός sometimes represents the Hebrew name *(El) Shaddai*[16] (by a suspect etymological derivation) and so became a divine title, "the (All-)Sufficient One," the one who is not only sufficient in himself but also able to provide others with total sufficiency.[17] Since Philo, too, sometimes speaks of God as "sufficient to himself" (ἱκανὸς ἑαυτῷ),[18] this Hellenistic Jewish way of conceiving of God may well have been familiar to Paul. If so, Paul could be saying in 3:5, "Our sufficiency derives from the All-Sufficient One." Just as his confidence came through Christ, his competence came from God, and he affirms this probably against the background of his opponents' claim to be self-sufficient.

Perhaps Paul is introducing here the prophetic motif of "sufficiency in spite of insufficiency." Hafemann finds v. 5 to be evocative of the prophetic call of Moses (Exod. 4:10; cf. 3:1–4:17), Gideon (Judg. 6:11-24), Isaiah (Isa. 6:1-8), Jeremiah (Jer. 1:4-10), and Ezekiel (Ezek. 1:1–3:11). "The prophet is not sufficient (competent) in himself (because of an obstacle to be overcome), but is nevertheless made sufficient by God's grace" (127; cf. *Moses* 39-62).

3:6 ὃς καὶ ἱκάνωσεν ἡμᾶς διακόνους καινῆς διαθήκης. "Who indeed has qualified us as agents of a new covenant." Against the πολλοί of 2:17 who claimed to be διάκονοι Χριστοῦ (11:23) and were preoccupied with qualifications (cf. 5:12; 11:18, 21b-23), Paul here defines the role for which he had God-given adequacy (v. 5). This relative clause is pivotal in the argument of ch. 3, for it brings together three crucial terms. ἱκάνωσεν looks back to ἱκανός

---

16. Ruth 1:20-21; Job 21:15; 31:2; 40:2; Ezek. 1:24 (A).

17. Cf. K. H. Rengstorf, *TDNT* 3.294 and n. 3; G. Kittel, *TDNT* 1.467. See further G. Bertram, "ΙΚΑΝΟΣ in den griechischen Übersetzungen des AT als Wiedergabe von *schaddaj*," *ZAW* 70 (1958) 20-31.

18. *Legum Allegoriae* 1.44; *De Cherubim* 46; *De Mutatione Nominum* 27, 46 (cited by Furnish 196).

(2:16) and ἱκανότης (3:5); διακόνους picks up διακονηθεῖσα (3:3) and anticipates the four uses of διακονία in 3:7-9; and διαθήκης prepares the way for the
comparison of the old and new covenants and their ministries that is found in
3:7-18.

καί may strengthen the relative ὅς ("it is he who . . . ," NEB, REB), emphasize the verb ἱκάνωσεν ("who has indeed qualified us," NAB[2]), or even point
to a further divine qualification ("who also . . . ," RV[19]; cf. 2:16-17). The aorist
ἱκάνωσεν refers to Paul's Damascus encounter with the risen Christ when he
was named a "chosen instrument" (σκεῦος ἐκλογῆς) of God and filled with the
Spirit (Acts 9:15, 17-19).[20] Paul discerned his God-given adequacy or qualification in his commission to bear witness to Christ (Acts 22:15; 26:16) and to suffer for Christ (Acts 9:16) and also in the divine provision of grace and power to
carry out that commission (1 Cor. 15:10; Col. 1:29). When followed by two accusatives (here ἡμᾶς διακόνους), ἱκανόω means "qualify someone for something" (BAGD 374d) in the sense of equipping him to fulfill a particular role.
διάκονος does not refer here to a church official ("deacon"; cf. Phil. 1:1; 1 Tim.
3:8) or to a "helper" or "servant" in the broad sense (as in Eph. 6:21) but to an
intermediary or agent.[21] As one entrusted with the gospel (1 Thess. 2:4), Paul
was God's "go-between" or agent in bringing people to faith (1 Cor. 3:5,
διάκονοι δι' ὧν ἐπιστεύσατε). Here, in 3:6, he is God's appointed agent in dispensing the new covenant,[22] that is, in declaring God's will as contained in the
gospel of Christ. Paul's role as a διάκονος of the new covenant presupposes
Christ's role as the μεσίτης of the new covenant (Heb. 9:15). In relation to the
καινὴ διαθήκη, Christ was the inaugurator and Paul an administrator.

In Hellenistic times, διαθήκη was the customary term for one's "last will
and testament," but in the LXX it regularly (some 270 times) renders the Hebrew
b*rît ("covenant"), so that the broad connotations of b*rît became attached to
διαθήκη.[23] In reference to God, a διαθήκη was the declaration of his "will" in
making an agreement with another party on conditions that he alone specified,
an agreement that was operative apart from the death of the testator. Although
the term συνθήκη ("treaty," "contract") is used thirteen times in the LXX (but not
rendering b*rît[24]), it is never found in the NT, presumably because it generally
denoted an agreement between equals that was arrived at by discussion and
sometimes compromise. Paul derived the expression (ἡ) καινὴ διαθήκη from the

19. Similarly Moffatt; Scharlemann 116 (ὅς καί = Latin *qui idem,* "yes, he also").
20. Cf. Acts 22:14-15; 26:15-18; 1 Cor. 15:8; Gal. 1:15-16.
21. On the meaning of διάκονος outside and within the NT, see Collins, *DIAKONIA, passim,*
especially 338-39; "Role" 34-44. His main thesis is that in Christian literature διακονία refers principally to "ministry under God," not benevolent social action. See also Cranfield, *Bible* 69-87.
22. In 3:6 καινῆς διαθήκης is an objective genitive, although the meaning would not be altered if this phrase were classified as a general genitive or a genitive of relation (e.g., "in the interests of a new agreement," Goodspeed).
23. See M. Weinfeld, *TDOT* 2.253-79; G. Quell, *TDNT* 2.106-24; J. Behm, *TDNT* 2.124-34.
24. Except for 4 Kgdms. 17:15 (A) (J. Behm, *TDNT* 2.126).

Last Supper tradition (1 Cor. 11:25), in which the cup signified the ratification of the new covenant by the shedding of Christ's blood (Luke 22:20; cf. Matt. 26:28; Mark 14:24), although ultimately the expression comes from Jer. 38:31 (LXX).

Since the adjectives καινός and νέος, both of which mean "new," share considerable semantic territory in NT usage,[25] it would be unwise to insist that in speaking of the "new" covenant Paul was emphasizing its newness in nature or quality (καινός) as opposed to its newness in time or origin (νέος). When Paul was writing, the inauguration of the new covenant through the death of Jesus was relatively recent, but he does not speak of a διαθήκη νέα (an expression found in Heb. 12:24). From the repeated (πολλῷ) μᾶλλον in 3:8-9, 11 it is clear that he is stressing the superiority of the new covenant over the old, and "καινός always implies superiority to that which is not καινός, whereas what is νέος may be either better or worse than what is not νέος" (Plummer 85; see below on 3:14). As for Jeremiah, so also for Paul, the main reason the new covenant could be called "new" was probably because in the new economy God's law would be written inwardly on the hearts of his people, not outwardly on tablets of stone (cf. 3:7), and God would do the writing himself (Jer. 31:33).[26] A καινὴ διαθήκη implies a παλαιὰ διαθήκη (3:14), and the new replaces the old not because the earlier διαθήκη has been fulfilled or renewed but because the later διαθήκη is inherently superior.

οὐ γράμματος ἀλλὰ πνεύματος· τὸ γὰρ γράμμα ἀποκτέννει, τὸ δὲ πνεῦμα ζῳοποιεῖ. "(A new covenant,) one characterized not by written law but by the Spirit. Now the written law brings death, but the Spirit imparts life." Here Paul contrasts the old and new covenants with reference to their dominant characteristic (γράμμα or πνεῦμα) and their inevitable outcome (ἀποκτέννει or ζῳοποιεῖ). It is not impossible, in the light of vv. 7-8 (ἡ διακονία τοῦ θανάτου . . . ἡ διακονία τοῦ πνεύματος), that the two genitives γράμματος and πνεύματος depend on διακόνους,[27] but it seems preferable to construe them with their immediate antecedent καινῆς διαθήκης.[28] In this case, the genitives are adjectival:[29]

25. See J. Behm, *TDNT* 3.447-54; 4.896-901; and Harrisville, *Newness, passim,* and his earlier article, "The Concept of Newness in the New Testament," *JBL* 74 (1955) 69-79.

26. Although Shead finds elements of both continuity and discontinuity in Jeremiah 30–31 (the "Little Book of Consolation"), he argues that the expression "a new covenant" signifies there not a renewed covenant but a radically new and different covenant and points to "a profound newness which leaves nothing untouched" (35-42; quotation from p. 41).

27. Thus Winer 191; Meyer 465; Plummer 88. However, the concept of serving or administering the Spirit is without parallel in the Pauline corpus. Even if τοῦ πνεύματος is seen, not as an objective but as an adjectival genitive, a difficulty remains, for then two different types of genitive (διαθήκης, objective; γράμματος and πνεύματος, adjectival) would depend on a single noun (διακόνους).

28. Murphy-O'Connor agrees, but believes that Paul is distinguishing two forms of the new covenant, one characterized by Letter and the other by Spirit. The contrast is between "letter-ministers" (represented by Paul's opponents) and "spirit-ministers" (33 n. 24; "Ministry" 116-17, borrowing expressions of Plummer 88).

29. This is suggested by their anarthrous state. However, sometimes the genitives are taken to be subjective (Bruce, *Paraphrase* 131: "a covenant which is constituted by the Spirit, not by a

the main and distinguishing feature of the new covenant is not γράμμα but πνεῦμα. Regarding this antithesis, several observations may be made.[30]

First, in spite of a long and influential tradition from the earliest times, the antithesis is not to be viewed as a hermeneutical axiom — that an allegorical or spiritual interpretation of the OT is to be preferred over the literal meaning (see the historical overview by W.-S. Chau). In a modern hermeneutical guise this γράμμα–πνεῦμα antithesis is taken to mean that in the exegesis of a text its underlying principles take precedence over the bare letter or its real intent over its actual words. Whatever sense is given to Paul's antithesis, in the final analysis that sense must be shown to be relevant to the immediate context, where Paul is giving an interpretation of Exod. 34:29-35. But in 3:7-11 he *is* concerned with actual words in this OT passage and with more than underlying principles (see the discussion in the introduction to 3:7-11 on his use of the LXX). And, given his attention in 3:7, 13 to the literal sense of Exodus 34, we cannot properly regard 3:6 as a theoretical justification for a purely "spiritual" interpretation of this OT text.

Second, although γράμμα means basically "letter (of the alphabet)" and so "what is written (using letters)," "a written document," in 3:6 it refers not to writing in general but to the Mosaic Law (especially the Decalogue) in particular. It is "written law" (Berkeley; cf. NAB[1]), a synonym for νόμος,[31] and more specifically "the law with its commands and regulations" (ὁ νόμος τῶν ἐντολῶν ἐν δόγμασιν, Eph. 2:15).[32] Instead of using a plural, such as δόγματα ("ordinances") or ἱερὰ γράμματα ("the sacred writings"; cf. 2 Tim. 3:15), Paul chose the singular, probably under the influence of the conjoined singular πνεῦμα.[33] Since 3:7 refers to a code engraved in letters (ἐν γράμμασιν) on stone, γράμμα was a convenient metonym for "the old covenant" (Tasker 62) which is not explicitly mentioned until 3:14 or for the old διακονία ("ministry/dispensation"; Luz 146), which is characterized in 3:7-11.

Third, Cranfield distinguishes γράμμα from νόμος as such, arguing that

---

written code"), objective (NEB: "a covenant expressed not in a written document, but in a spiritual bond"), or even epexegetic (TCNT: "a New Covenant, of which the substance is, not a written Law, but a Spirit").

30. For a history of the interpretation of the letter-spirit antithesis from Origen to Luther, see W.-S. Chau, *The Letter and the Spirit,* American University Studies, Series VII: Theology and Religion 167 (New York: Lang, 1995); and Schneider, "Antithesis" 164-87. The five most common views of the antithesis are briefly discussed by Gleason 70-76 (the literal and spiritual senses; the text as written and the Spirit as interpreter; legalistic misuse of the Law versus the Holy Spirit; outward conformity versus inward obedience to the Mosaic Law; the old covenant and the new covenant — the view that Gleason himself defends, 76-79). If one may speak of a "traditional" approach to 3:6 and 3:6-18 in modern times, it would be that Paul is here contrasting Law and Gospel, either as two eras in the history of salvation or as two ways of relating to God (see, e.g., Hofius, "Gesetz" 75-120; Osten-Sacken, *Heiligkeit* 87-115; Grindheim 97-115).

31. So also G. Schrenk, *TDNT* 1.766-67; Dunn, "Lord" 310 n. 2; Schneider 188-207.

32. Cf. Hofius, "Gesetz" 82; Fee, *Presence* 305-6.

33. Cf. Käsemann, *Perspectives* 143.

the "letter" is a distortion and misuse of the law, evidenced by a failure to recognize its true goal (τέλος, Rom. 10:4), which is to lead people to faith in Christ. γράμμα is νόμος "denatured," the letter of the law apart from the Spirit's invigoration, the law used legalistically as an imagined ground for righteousness.[34] But it is difficult to assign a negative connotation to the two uses of γράμμα in 3:6 (quite apart from the verb ἀποκτέννει) when in 3:7 Paul refers positively (ἐγενήθη ἐν δόξῃ) to the giving of the law, engraved ἐν γράμμασιν on stone tablets.[35] What is more, the matter of improper attitudes toward the Law is not dealt with until 3:14-15.

Fourth, πνεῦμα refers to the Holy Spirit, "the Spirit of the living God" (3:3), not the human spirit. "In St. Paul's writings πνεῦμα, when used for the human spirit, is contrasted with σῶμα (1 Cor. v.3), σάρξ (2 Cor. vii.1) and νοῦς (1 Cor. xiv.14), but *never* with γράμμα."[36] That Paul could contrast a thing (the written Law) with a person (the Spirit) is clear from 3:3, where μέλαν ("ink") is opposed to πνεῦμα.

Having indicated that the written Law was the hallmark of the old covenant, as the Spirit was of the new, Paul focuses on the outcome of the two covenants, again by a contrast: "Now the written Law always brings death, whereas (δέ) the Spirit always imparts life." While Paul viewed the Law as holy and spiritual (ἅγιος and πνευματικός, Rom. 7:12, 14), since it was a revelation of the will of God, he nevertheless recognized not only its impotence to impart life (Gal. 3:21) but also its ability to bring death: "The very commandment that was designed to bring me life (ἡ ἐντολὴ ἡ εἰς ζωήν), in fact brought me death" (Rom. 7:10). When the Law's demand for perfect obedience (Gal. 3:10) is unfulfilled, it pronounces the sentence of death, both spiritual death and physical death. The Law in its character or function as ἐντολή is simply an instrument of death, since it addresses sinful human nature (σάρξ), which cannot please God (Rom. 8:3, 8). For Paul, the elements in the trio Law, sin, and death are inseparable. Both the Law and sin can be said to bring death (Rom. 7:9-10 and 5:12, 21 respectively), although ultimate responsibility for the advent of physical and spiritual death was attributable to sin, which, "seizing the opportunity afforded by the commandment, deceived me, and used the commandment to kill me" (Rom. 7:11; cf. 7:8).[37]

Like ἀποκτέννει, the verb ζῳοποιεῖ is a gnomic present, depicting what is always and everywhere the case. When Paul observes here that the Spirit "imparts life" or when he describes the Spirit as "life-giving" (τῆς ζωῆς, Rom. 8:2; cf. Gal. 5:25), he is affirming that one characteristic — perhaps the principal characteristic — of the Spirit is that he perpetually grants the physical and spiritual life of

---

34. Cranfield 1.339-40; "Law" 152-53, 158-60. Similarly Käsemann, *Perspectives* 146-47, 154 (the "letter" is "the actual, ruling perversion of the documented will of God").

35. Cf. Thrall 235.

36. Bernard 54. For the view that the γράμμα–πνεῦμα contrast is simply the outward–inward antithesis, with πνεῦμα not referring to the Holy Spirit (cf. Rom. 2:28-29), see Hughes 96-101. Cf. Berkeley ("not of written law, but of a spiritual nature"), NEB.

37. Cf. Dodd, "Problems" 111-12.

which he is the source. In Pauline thought there are three stages in this vivifying work of the Spirit: regeneration, sanctification, and resurrection. The process of salvation began through "the washing of regeneration," which is equated with "the renewal (ἀνακαίνωσις) of the Holy Spirit" (Tit. 3:5). The second stage of renewal is the progressive transformation of believers into the image of Christ as they gaze on and then reflect the glory of the Lord, this whole process being the work of the Spirit (2 Cor. 3:18). This is a renewal of the mind (Rom. 12:2) or the attitude of the mind (Eph. 4:23) and corresponds to the strengthening (Eph. 3:16) or renewal (2 Cor. 4:16) of the inner person by the Spirit. Stage three occurs when the process of being conformed to the image of Christ reaches completion in a resurrection transformation effected and sustained by the Spirit (Rom. 8:11, 29) and in the receipt of eternal life from the Spirit (Gal. 6:8). In each stage of this vivification the Spirit works inwardly on the character or the body,[38] and this emphasis on inwardness is precisely the point in 3:6, as also in the other two passages where Paul uses the γράμμα–πνεῦμα antithesis (Rom. 2:28-29; 7:4-6).[39] Inward inscription on persons, not outward writing on stones, is the mark of the new covenant (cf. 3:7). That is to say, the new covenant is marked preeminently by inward divine enablement to carry out God's will.[40] For Paul, the law of Christ (Gal. 6:2), engraved on the hearts of believers by the life-giving Spirit, was the fulfillment of Jeremiah's prophecy that under the new covenant God would write his law on the hearts of his people (Jer. 31:33).[41]

38. Even the resurrection is said to be accomplished "through God's Spirit who dwells in you" (Rom. 8:11).

39. Note the ἐν τῷ φανερῷ–ἐν τῷ κρυπτῷ ("outwardly–inwardly") antithesis in Rom. 2:28-29. In Rom. 7:6 παλαιότης γράμματος ("the old bondage of the letter," "the old written regulations") is contrasted with καινότης πνεύματος ("the new life/conditions brought by the Spirit").

40. Cf. Gleason 69, 77-79.

41. But some scholars find continuity as well as discontinuity in the γράμμα–πνεῦμα antithesis, with the Mosaic Law given at Sinai being the common element. Hughes describes the contrast as being "between the law as *externally* written at Sinai on tablets of stone and the *same* law as written *internally* in the heart of the Christian believer" (100). More recently, Hafemann discovers the key to the meaning of the contrast in the immediate context, viz. 3:3, which alludes to Ezek. 11:19 and 36:26-27 with its reference to the Spirit's work, and Jer. 31:31-34 with its reference to the new obedience to the Law. Accordingly, γράμμα is "the Law itself without the Spirit" as experienced by the majority of Israelites under the Sinai covenant (cf. 3:14-15), the Law as acknowledged to be God's will but not kept, while πνεῦμα denotes "the Law with the Spirit" as experienced by believers under the new covenant in Christ, the law as obeyed from the heart by the power of the Spirit. "It is neither the Law nor the gospel itself that kills or makes alive, but the absence or presence of the Spirit (3:6c)" (131-33; quotations from pp. 133 and 146; see also his *Moses* 119-84, especially 171-73, developing the view of Provence 77). But is Paul concerned in 3:6 (which forms a prelude to 3:7-18) to indicate a new and positive role for the Law (cf. 132-33; *Moses* 146 n. 170, 441)? True, Paul's antithesis is highly abbreviated and pregnant with meaning, but one wonders how πνεῦμα can be brachylogy for "the Law with the Spirit"; if γράμμα in fact stood for the Law without the Spirit, one might expect the antithetical πνεῦμα to signify the Spirit without the Law. Yet Hafemann later insists that "far from being a 'freedom from the Law,' the freedom of v. 17b is . . . a freedom from the veil in order to create a freedom *'for the Law!'*" (*Moses* 405). A similar criticism of Hafemann's view is expressed by Seifrid. After noting that in 3:6 Paul speaks of the Law's right-

We conclude, therefore, that in 3:6 γράμμα denotes the Law regarded as external commandments that are not enshrined in the heart and that pronounce a death sentence. πνεῦμα, on the other hand, is the Spirit of God who indwells the hearts of believers and effects their revitalization both in the present age and in the age to come. Whereas the γράμμα is ἄψυχον ("lifeless"), the πνεῦμα is ζωοποιοῦν ("life-giving").[42]

Bibliography

G. Barth • G. B. Caird, "Everything to Everyone: The Theology of the Corinthian Epistles," *Int* 13 (1959) 387-99 • Carmignac • Carrez, *Souffrance* 36-37 • W.-S. Chau, *The Letter and the Spirit: A History of Interpretation from Origen to Luther* (New York: Lang, 1995) • Cohen • Denis • Dodd, "Problems" 110-12 • Ellis 25-27 • Friesen 33-47 • Gleason • P. J. Gräbe, *Der neue Bund in der frühchristlichen Literatur. Unter Berücksichtigung der alttestamentlich-jüdischen Voraussetzungen* (Würzburg: Echter, 2001) • Hafemann, *Moses* 1-35, 92-186, 437-49 • Hanson, *Ministry* 50, 67-68 • Hays 122-53 • Hickling • Hofius 75-120 • Hooker, "Scripture" • Kamlah, "Buchstabe" • Käsemann, *Perspectives* 138-66 • Kim 5-13, 128-29 • J. Kremer, "Neuere Methoden der Exegese dargestellt an 2 Kor 3,6b," *TPQ* 128 (1980) 24-29 • Lane • Lührmann • Luz, "Bund" • O. Michel, *Paulus und seine Bibel* (Gütersloh: Bertelsmann, 1929) 174-78 • Murphy-O'Connor 32-33 • Murphy-O'Connor, "Ministry" • Newman 229-35, 243 • Oostendorp 31-51 • Provence • P. Richardson • Rissi 22-25 • Scharlemann • Schneider, "Antithesis" • T. R. Schreiner 129-33, 141-42 • J. Schröter, "Schriftauslegung und Hermeneutik in 2 Korinther 3. Ein Beitrag zur Frage der Schriftbenutzung des Paulus," *NovT* 40 (1998) 231-75 • Shead • Stegemann • A. Stimpfle, "Buchstabe und Geist. Zur Geschichte eines Missverständnisses von 2 Kor 3,6," *BZ* 39 (1995) 181-202 • Stockhausen 33-86 • Stockhausen, "2 Corinthians 3" • W. C. van Unnik, "ἡ καινὴ διαθήκη, A Problem in the Early History of the Canon," *TU* 79 (1961) 212-27 • von der Osten-Sacken, "Geist" • S. Westerholm, "Letter and Spirit: The Foundation of Pauline Ethics," *NTS* 30 (1984) 229-48 • Witherington, *Jesus* 109-11

d. The Surpassing Glory of the New Covenant (3:7-11)

Thus far in ch. 3, Paul's thought has progressed from the idea of commendatory letters written on hearts by Christ to reflection on the new covenant under which the law would be written by God himself on responsive human hearts (Jer. 31:33; Ezek. 36:26). Against the backdrop of challenges to his apostolic qualifications, Paul then affirms his God-given commission to be an agent of this new covenant, whose hallmark is the inward work of God's life-giving

---

ful power to condemn and kill, and not simply its weakness (112), Seifrid observes that Hafemann (*Moses* 156-84) treats 3:7-11 "as a discussion of the ineffectual nature of the law apart from the Spirit — as if Paul anywhere speaks of an effectual law through the Spirit!" (112 n. 67).

42. Paul is not denying that the Spirit was operative under the old covenant. But, as Denney (747) comments, Paul is here characterizing the two covenants by their differences, not their similarities. "They differ as law differs from life, as compulsion from inspiration."

Spirit. It may have been Paul's dramatic statement that "the written Law kills" in 3:6b that prompted him to remind the Corinthians that the old covenant was itself attended by divine glory. But even in rejecting any supposition that the old dispensation totally lacked splendor, he now makes the point that the glory of the new covenant is so superior that the glory of the old fades into insignificance by comparison.

In 3:7-18 the primary OT stimulus for Paul's thought ceases to be Jeremiah and Ezekiel and becomes Exod. 34:29-35, the account of the interaction between Moses and the people of Israel after his receipt of the two tablets of the Law on Mount Sinai for the second time.[1] The text falls into two clearly defined parts: vv. 7-11 are a commentary on Exod. 34:29-30, with δόξα/δοξάζω the crucial terms,[2] and vv. 12-18 are a commentary on Exod. 34:33-35, with παρρησία and κάλυμμα the pivotal terms.[3]

At this point it will be helpful to provide a translation of the LXX of Exod. 34:29-35, indicating the Greek words or phrases that recur or are important in Paul's argument.

29As Moses was coming down from the mountain, he had the two tablets (πλάκες) in his hands. While he was descending he did not realize that the skin of his face had become radiant (δεδόξασται)[4] in appearance because he had been speaking[5] with the Lord. 30And when Aaron and all the elders of Israel saw Moses, the skin of his face was radiant (ἦν δεδοξασμένη)[6] in appearance, and they were afraid to approach him. 31But Moses called to them, and Aaron and all the leaders of the congregation returned to him, and Moses spoke with them. 32After this all the people of Israel (οἱ υἱοὶ Ἰσραήλ) came to him, and he delivered to them all the commandments that the Lord (κύριος) had given him on Mount Sinai. 33When Moses had finished speaking with them, he put (ἐπέθηκεν) a veil (κάλυμμα) over his face. 34But whenever Moses entered the Lord's presence (ἡνίκα δ' ἂν εἰσεπορεύετο Μωϋσῆς ἔναντι κυρίου) to speak with him, he would take off his veil (περιῃρεῖτο τὸ κάλυμμα)

1. In the context of Exodus 32–34, this section (34:29-35) serves to reestablish Moses as Yahweh's authoritative messenger in the eyes of the Israelites. After they had overcome their initial fear of approaching Moses because of his radiant face (34:30), they came close to him and "he made them responsible for everything Yahweh had told him on Mount Sinai" (34:32). This marked the recommitment of the people to their covenant relationship with Yahweh, which had been broken by the golden calf episode (32:2-35), and the reinstatement of Moses as Yahweh's intermediary after their earlier dismissal of Moses from any such role (32:1). Cf. Durham 465-67.

2. δόξα occurs eight times and δοξάζω twice in 3:7-11.

3. παρρησία ("openness," "boldness") occurs only once in 3:12-18, but that is in the opening verse (3:12), and this idea of freedom recurs in the last two verses (ἐλευθερία, 3:17; ἀνακεκαλυμμένῳ, 3:18). κάλυμμα occurs four times and the cognate ἀνακεκαλυμμένῳ once.

4. Or "the skin of his face shone" (see LEH 1.119 s.v. δοξάζω; Hofius, "Gesetz" 88) or "the appearance of his countenance had been endowed with splendor" (Furnish 205).

5. Or "while he had been speaking" (ἐν τῷ λαλεῖν αὐτόν).

6. Or "the skin of his face was shining" (see LEH 1.119 s.v. δοξάζω) or "(Moses' face) had been endowed with splendor" (Furnish 205).

until he went out. After he had gone out, he would tell (ἐλάλει) all the people of Israel (τοῖς υἱοῖς 'Ισραήλ) whatever the Lord (κύριος) had commanded him. 35The people of Israel (οἱ υἱοὶ 'Ισραήλ) saw that the face of Moses was radiant (δεδόξασται),[7] and so (καί) Moses placed (περιέθηκεν) a veil (κά-λυμμα) over his face until he went in to converse with the Lord.

Apart from the general consideration that when Paul cites the OT he usually uses the LXX, there is specific evidence in this case that he is dependent on the LXX: despite all the differences between Exod. 34:34 and 2 Cor. 3:16, the word order is retained in Paul's citation; the combination ἡνίκα δὲ ἐάν/δ' ἄν is a Pauline (and NT) *hapax legomenon;* Paul's δεδόξασται (3:10) reflects the two uses of that precise form in Exod. 34:29, 35; τὸ δεδοξασμένον (3:10) picks up ἦν δεδοξα-σμένη (Exod. 34:30); the iterative imperfect ἐτίθει (3:13) is reminiscent of the three iterative imperfects in the verse Paul cites (Exod. 34:34: εἰσεπορεύετο . . . περιῃρεῖτο . . . ἐλάλει). As points of interest, it is also worth noting that τὸ πρόσωπον (with a possessive genitive) occurs five times, οἱ υἱοὶ 'Ισραήλ three times, (τὸ) κάλυμμα three times, and the anarthrous κύριος three times.

A comparison of 2 Cor. 3:7-18 with Exod. 34:29-35 indicates several ways in which the OT passage differs from Paul's commentary. The Exodus narrative makes no mention of Moses' purpose in veiling his face, the fading splendor of his face, or the inability of the Israelites to gaze at his face because of its brightness. Aware of these differences, some scholars speak of 2 Cor. 3:7-18 as a "midrash" on Exodus 34,[8] some prefer the designation "pesher"[9] or "midrash pesher,"[10] while others appeal to the category of allegory.[11] Given the fact that specific reference to the Exodus story is found only in vv. 7, 13, and 16 of 2 Corinthians 3, it may be wiser to follow Hays's lead and describe 3:7-18 as "an allusive homily based on biblical incidents."[12]

7. Or "the face of Moses shone" (see n. 4).

8. E.g., Theobald 177-90; Hanson, "Midrash," *passim,* especially 21-22; Schmithals 287-88.

9. E.g., Stockhausen 123-53; "2 Corinthians 3" 143-64. Against such an approach, see Hafemann, *Moses* 398-99 n. 200, 457-58.

10. E.g., Hooker, "Scripture" 297; Martin 59-60.

11. E.g., Strachan 87. For further bibliographical data relating to these three categories, see Belleville, *Reflections* 172-73.

12. Hays 132, citing 1 Cor. 10:1-13 as another example. Vanhoye is right in observing that Paul's purpose in 3:7-11 is not to exegete Exodus 34 but to affirm the glory of the old ministry and to attribute superior glory to the apostolic ministry (159-80). Koch associates 3:7-18 with 11:22-23 (assuming that the same opponents are referred to in both passages; 305-24). The latter passage shows that Paul's adversaries viewed themselves as "servants of Christ" (11:23), which is a synthe-sizing self-description (310). Being themselves "the seed of Abraham" (11:22), who was the father of all nations and archetype of the proselyte, they believed they could integrate Gentiles into Abra-ham's "seed." In 3:7-18, with its contrast between the ministry of Moses (not the figure of Abra-ham) and Paul's ministry as a "servant of Christ" (cf. 11:23), we have the apostle's response, by way of an "implicit dialogue" (324), to his opponents' self-understanding. Paul does not put for-ward a superior view of Abraham but rather proposes "an alternative model" (316).

As to the origin of 3:7-18, some writers propose that it was an independent midrashic text created by Paul's opponents and that Paul sought to correct their erroneous views about Moses and the old covenant by various modifications and additions.[13] But this hypothesis creates as many problems as it solves. True, there is a high incidence of Pauline *hapax legomena* (11) in these twelve verses[14] and there are prima facie inconsistencies regarding (for example) Moses' motives for veiling his face (3:7, 13, ἀτενίσαι).[15] But alongside such apparent difficulties must be set the fact that the passage pulsates with typically Pauline antitheses[16] (see below). In addition, it would have been risky as well as tactless for Paul to include in his letter a document that was held in high regard by his opponents and also *(ex hypothesi)* by his readers when he had made what would appear to them to be arbitrary, high-handed changes to the text.[17] Furthermore, parallels are lacking in the literature of Paul's time for this putative technique of interacting with an alternative position by modifying a document used by one's opponents.[18] It is possible, of course, that 3:7-18 may originally have been the essence of a synagogue sermon preached by Paul, which might account for its unusual stylistic features and for the use of a scriptural passage (Exodus 34) as the basis for his comments and application.[19] But, equally, no objection can be raised against the view of Hickling that 3:7-18 forms "an extended, and itself rapidly burgeoning, exegesis of the phrase διακόνους καινῆς διαθήκης [3:6]."[20]

With regard to Paul's general stance in this passage, some regard him as polemical, attacking (for example) wandering Jewish-Christian preachers who promulgated a "heretical" Moses tradition and regarded themselves as θεῖοι ἄνδρες,[21] or Judaizers of Palestinian origin who saw no tension but only consonance between the Mosaic Law and the Spirit.[22] Yet others view Paul's purpose as basically apologetic, as (for example) he seeks vindication of his role as a διάκονος of the new covenant and so of his entitlement to appropriate respect,[23] or as he defends himself against the charges of non-Christian Jews in Corinth that he was vastly inferior to Moses.[24]

---

13. E.g., Schulz 1-30; Georgi, *Opponents* 264-71; Theobald 204-8. For a brief history of modern research on 3:7-18, see Hafemann, *Moses* 255-63.

14. But Thrall notes (296) that there are thirteen Pauline *hapax legomena* in 9:1-12.

15. See the apparent inconsistencies noted by Belleville ("Tradition" 167 n. 9) and her response ("Tradition" 168 and n. 12).

16. See Prümm, "Vergleich" 27-72; "2 Cor. 3" 164-203.

17. Cf. Collange 68.

18. Belleville, "Tradition" 186 n. 49.

19. Martin 59, developing a suggestion of Moule, *Birth* 54 n. 1.

20. Hickling 384; cf. 387.

21. Georgi, *Opponents* 229-83.

22. Oostendorp 31-51.

23. Hickling 381, 384.

24. Thrall 239, 246-48, 297. Thrall believes that in this way Paul was also responding to the needs of Jewish members of the Corinthian congregation whose minds were being unsettled by non-Christian Jews who were raising questions about Paul and his gospel.

Attention may now be given to the structure of 3:7-11. Half of the paragraph is taken up with a long, complex question (vv. 7-8), which is followed by three short sentences, each marked by γάρ (vv. 9-11). The most notable feature is the series of three carefully structured contrasts, perhaps prompted by the antithesis in 3:6b.

vv. 7-8	εἰ δὲ . . .	πῶς οὐχὶ μᾶλλον
v. 9	εἰ γὰρ . . .	πολλῷ μᾶλλον
v. 11	εἰ γὰρ . . .	πολλῷ μᾶλλον

This literary technique ("if X . . . , how much more Y") was one of the rabbinical exegetical "rules" (qal wāḥômer, "the light and the heavy"),[25] a technique also known as a minore (or minori) ad maius, "from the lesser to the greater." In such contrasts, the movement of thought is from "what is true" to "what is even more certainly true." This seems to be the case in vv. 7-8: "If the dispensation that brought death . . . was attended by glory . . . , even more certainly will the dispensation of the Spirit be accompanied by glory." V. 9, however, where περισσεύει intensifies πολλῷ μᾶλλον, makes a quantitative addition to the basic qal wāḥômer argument: ". . . , how much more surpassingly glorious is the dispensation that brings righteousness." While the third contrast (v. 11) has only πολλῷ μᾶλλον, it probably also involves a quantitative comparison because it follows v. 9, where the augment in quantity is explicit. So in vv. 7-11 Paul seems to be saying that if the Mosaic dispensation was glorious (a point readily conceded by his opponents), the new dispensation is not only even more certainly glorious (v. 8) but also incomparably more glorious (vv. 9, 11). This distinction between the first contrast and the second and third contrasts is supported by v. 10, where the glory of the old order is said to be totally eclipsed by comparison with the surpassing glory of the new order.[26]

These three qal wāḥômer contrasts are related to some ten antitheses found in vv. 3-11.

v. 3	μέλανι	πνεύματι
	πλαξὶν λιθίναις	πλαξὶν καρδίαις σαρκίναις
v. 6	τῆς παλαιᾶς διαθήκης (v. 14)	καινῆς διαθήκης
	γράμματος	πνεύματος

---

25. See SB 3.223-26; Bonsirven 83-85, 316-17.

26. See the discussion of these issues in Thrall (239-40), who believes that "basically . . . Paul is arguing that if Moses's ministry was glorious, so must his be," although in 3:9 "there may be a tendency to quantitative comparison" (240; cf. 249: in 3:9 a "quantitative plus" is added to the "logical plus"). She translates μᾶλλον in v. 8 by "yet more certainly," and πολλῷ μᾶλλον in vv. 9 and 11 by "much more certainly" (237). See further C. Maurer, "Der Schluss 'a minore ad majus' als Element paulinischen Theologie," TLZ 85 (1960) 149-52; H. Müller, "Der rabbinische Qal-Wachomer-Schluss in paulinischer Typologie," ZNW 58 (1967) 73-92; Theobald 177-83; Stockhausen 109-10, 113-22.

	γράμμα	πνεῦμα
	ἀποκτέννει	ζῳοποιεῖ
v. 7	ἡ διακονία τοῦ θανάτου	ἡ διακονία τοῦ πνεύματος (v. 8)
	τὴν δόξαν . . . τὴν καταργουμένην	τῆς ὑπερβαλλούσης δόξης (v. 10)
v. 9	τῇ διακονίᾳ τῆς κατακρίσεως	ἡ διακονία τῆς δικαιοσύνης
v. 11	τὸ καταργούμενον	τὸ μένον

It is sometimes claimed that in 2 Corinthians 3 Paul is contrasting two dispensations or ministries, not two covenants.[27] Such a distinction is difficult to sustain given the above set of antitheses, where one may justifiably equate "the old covenant" with "the ministry/dispensation of death" and "the ministry/dispensation of condemnation," and "the new covenant" with "the ministry/dispensation of the Spirit" and "the ministry/dispensation of righteousness." Moreover, in 3:6 Paul describes himself as a διάκονος καινῆς διαθήκης, where the two root ideas in question are brought together. Finally, the neuter τὸ μένον ("what is permanent," "the order destined to last forever") in v. 11 seems to subsume the three expressions καινὴ διαθήκη (v. 6), ἡ διακονία τοῦ πνεύματος (v. 8), and ἡ διακονία τῆς δικαιοσύνης (v. 9). We agree that the focus of Paul's attention is on the two disparate ministries or dispensations, for the elements of the διακονία contrasts are side-by-side (vv. 7-9) whereas the expressions παλαιὰ διαθήκη (v. 14) and καινὴ διαθήκη (v. 6) are not juxtaposed. But διακονία is inseparable from διαθήκη, since it is a "covenant" that is "administered" (cf. 3:6).

7Yet the dispensation that brought death, which was engraved in letters[a] on[b] stone, was attended by glory, so that the people of Israel were unable to gaze steadily at the face of Moses because of its glory, which in fact faded away. 8Will not, then, the dispensation of the Spirit even more certainly be accompanied by glory? 9For if there was glory in the dispensation[c] that brought condemnation, how much more surpassingly glorious[d] is the dispensation that brings righteousness. 10Indeed, in this respect, what once was glorious has lost its claim to glory, on account of the glory that surpasses it. 11For if what was destined to fade away came with glory, far greater will be the glory that accompanies what is destined to remain.

TEXTUAL NOTES

a. Under the influence of singular γράμματος in 3:6, some witnesses (B D*.c F G *pc* syr^p) read γράμματι in place of γράμμασιν.

b. ℵ² D¹ Ψ 1881 𝔐 lat Ambrosiaster add ἐν before λίθοις, perhaps because the locative dative is rare in the NT, its place being taken by prepositional phrases (Turner 242-43). Paul probably chose the simple λίθοις (read by p⁴⁶ ℵ* A B C D* F G P 0243 6 33 81 630 1739 *pc* Origen Epiphanius) to avoid four successive uses of ἐν(-).

27. E.g., Cranfield 855; "Law" 160; similarly Hafemann, "Argument" 291; *Moses* 449.

c. The external evidence supporting the dative τῇ διακονίᾳ (preferred by NA[26, 27] and UBS[3, 4]) is early and varied (p[46] ℵ A C D* F G Ψ 0243 33 104 326 630 1175 1739 pc[b] syr sa Ambrosiaster Pelagius) and stronger than the support for ἡ διακονία (B D[2] 1881 M a f vg bo), the reading preferred by NA[25] and UBS[1, 2] (with a "C" rating) or διακονία (81 629* 1505 2464 pc). Moreover, it is arguable that the dative is the more difficult reading, since it breaks the sequence of nominatives (ἡ διακονία) in vv. 7-9, and the dative of possession or the locative dative (however the dative here be construed) is uncommon in the NT. If τῇ διακονίᾳ be taken as original, the nominative may be explained as an assimilation to the preceding and following διακονία (Metzger 509). Whether the dative or the nominative be preferred, the sense is basically the same: "if the ministry/dispensation that brought condemnation was glorious. . . ."

d. Since the preposition ἐν is found with δόξῃ in vv. 7 and 8 (and 11), some scribe(s) added it to δόξῃ in v. 9 (ℵ[2] D F G Ψ 1881[c] M latt), but the simple δόξῃ, as a dative of respect or a locative dative after περισσεύω, is undoubtedly the original reading (as in p[46] ℵ* A B C 0243 33 81 326 1739 1881* pc).

3:7 Εἰ δὲ ἡ διακονία τοῦ θανάτου ἐν γράμμασιν ἐντετυπωμένη λίθοις ἐγενήθη ἐν δόξῃ. "Yet the dispensation that brought death, which was engraved in letters on stone, was attended by glory." This translation breaks up this long conditional sentence (vv. 7-8) into its constituent parts. In essence the sentence is εἰ δὲ ἡ διακονία τοῦ θανάτου . . . ἐγενήθη ἐν δόξῃ . . . πῶς οὐχὶ μᾶλλον ἡ διακονία τοῦ πνεύματος ἔσται ἐν δόξῃ; The intervening ὥστε clause serves to highlight the awesome character of the δόξα that belonged to the old covenant and therefore the (at least comparable) grandeur of the new covenant.

δέ points to a contrast with 3:6: although the written law (γράμμα) kills, the ministry that embodied that γράμμα was glorious (cf. NEB). εἰ introduces a protasis (εἰ . . . ἐγενήθη) assumed to be true. διακονία is a key word in 2 Corinthians, where twelve of Paul's twenty-two uses of the term are found. Its range of meaning is well illustrated by the RSV renderings within 2 Corinthians: "dispensation" (3:7-9), "ministry" (4:1; 5:18; 6:3), and, in reference to the collection, "relief" (8:4), "offering" (9:1), and "service" (9:12-13; cf. 11:8). Other translations proposed include "agency,"[28] "system of religion" (TCNT, in 3:7), "religion" (TCNT, in 3:8-9), and "administration" (Moffatt). Whether we prefer "ministry" or "dispensation" in 3:7-11, διακονία denotes the whole system of the Mosaic Law, along with its agents; personal and impersonal elements are blended in one. These five verses are notable for their lack of personal pronouns. Paul clearly has his own ministry in mind (cf. 3:6, 12; 4:1), but perhaps to deflect any further accusations of boasting he deals with the two dispensations and covenants with almost clinical abstraction. The genitive τοῦ θανάτου may be objective ("that brings death," Weymouth; "that brought death," NIV) or adjectival ("that is marked by death" or "that deals in death" [Furnish 202]). Just as γράμμα is picked up by διακονία, so ἀποκτέννει (3:6) is by τοῦ θανάτου. As we saw on 3:6, law stimulates sin (Rom. 7:8-9, 11; 1 Cor. 15:56b), and sin

---

28. Thrall 237 (for each use of διακονία in 3:7-11).

leads to death (Rom. 6:23; 1 Cor. 15:56a). Consequently, with the intermediate element of sin presupposed, Paul can say that the ministry of the old covenant, the dispensation of the written Law, is death-dealing. This, in sharp contrast with the Jewish view of the Law as life-giving.[29]

ἐν γράμμασιν refers to letters of the alphabet, written characters that make up words,[30] although the phrase could be a metonym for "writing" (thus Weymouth, NAB[1]). The perfect passive participle ἐντετυπωμένη ("engraved," "carved," "chiseled"[31]) qualifies διακονία and prompts the question: How could a ministry be "engraved"? True, Paul could have written, with greater clarity, ἡ διακονία τοῦ γράμματος ἐντετυπωμένου ἐν λίθοις (so Winer 635), but, as Winer observes, "Moses' *ministry* of death was in so far itself ἐν λίθοις ἐντετυπωμένη, as it consisted in communicating laws threatening and inflicting death, and in administering them among the people."[32] λίθοις, a locative dative, may refer to the two tablets of stone on which the Decalogue was inscribed (Exod. 31:18; 34:28-29), the πλάκες λίθιναι of 3:3; or, if it is a generalizing plural, it may mean simply "on stone" (RSV, NAB[1, 2]). Either way, the whole phrase, "engraved in letters on stone," is reminiscent of the contrast in 3:3 between tablets of stone and the tablets which are responsive human hearts and hints at the inferiority of the old covenant with its focus on externals.

If ἐγενήθη (= ἐγένετο) has the distinctive sense of γίνομαι, viz. "come to be," "come into existence," it will mean "was inaugurated" (NEB, REB) or "was ushered in" (Goodspeed). But since (1) γίνομαι sometimes serves as a substitute for εἰμί (BAGD 160b, c), (2) the apodosis of this conditional sentence reads ἔσται ἐν δόξῃ (v. 8), and (3) a form of εἰμί such as ἔσται must be understood with ἐν δόξῃ in v. 11, it is more probable that ἐγενήθη ἐν δόξῃ means "was attended by glory" or "was invested with glory" (Moffatt), referring to more than the inauguration of the Sinai covenant; on any view, ἐν denotes attendant circumstances. In the OT δόξα (= Hebrew *kābôd*) refers principally to the visible manifestation of God's nature, presence, and power.[33] The reference in 3:7 is not only to the glorious Sinai theophany but also to the glory on Moses' face. Paul's point is that, although the old covenant with its regulations pronounced doom on the disobedient, its inauguration and administration were marked by glorious phenomena, beginning with the awe-inspiring outward manifestations of God's presence at Sinai (Exod. 19:16-22) and continuing with the reflected

29. See SB 3.502, citing *Exodus Rabbah* 41.4.

30. BAGD 165b; G. Schrenk, *TDNT* 1.767, citing Exod. 36:39 (LXX). However, if ἐν γράμμασιν is construed with ἡ διακονία, the sense of 3:7a could be "if the system of religion which involved Death, embodied in a written Law and engraved on stones . . ." (TCNT).

31. The first pair of tablets are explicitly said to have been "inscribed by the finger of God" (Exod. 31:18; cf. 32:16). But in Exod. 34:28 it is unclear whether God or Moses inscribed the Decalogue on the second pair of tablets.

32. Winer 635. Cf. Meyer 467: "The Decalogue engraven on the two tablets was actually the ministerial document of Moses, as it were the registration of his office."

33. See M. Weinfeld, *TDOT* 7.22-37; G. von Rad, *TDNT* 2.238-42; G. Kittel, *TDNT* 2.242-45.

glory of Yahweh on Moses' face after his second period of communing with God on the mountain (Exod. 34:28-35).[34]

ὥστε μὴ δύνασθαι ἀτενίσαι τοὺς υἱοὺς Ἰσραὴλ εἰς τὸ πρόσωπον Μωϋσέως διὰ τὴν δόξαν τοῦ προσώπου αὐτοῦ τὴν καταργουμένην. "So that the people of Israel were unable to gaze steadily at the face of Moses because of its glory, which in fact faded away." ὥστε μή modifies ἐν δόξῃ and introduces a negative result.[35] The verb ἀτενίζω derives from the adjective ἀτενής ("stretched," "strained") and denotes prolonged, attentive observation, "keep one's eyes fixed on," "gaze intently at."[36] The aorist ἀτενίσαι is constative, viewing as a single conceptual unit the repeated inability of the Israelites to keep their gaze focused on the shining brilliance (δόξα) of Moses' face whenever he emerged from "the tent of meeting" (Exod. 33:7-11; 34:34-35).[37] It was probably from the juxtaposition of two statements in the LXX — "the skin of his face was radiant in appearance" and "they were afraid to approach him," Exod. 34:30 — that Paul inferred that the Israelites could not bear to look unflinchingly at Moses. Philo reflects a similar exegetical tradition when he states that "their eyes could not continue to stand the gleaming brightness that flashed from his countenance like the rays of the sun" (*Life of Moses* 2.70).

It is of interest that in Exodus 34 the MT says that the skin of Moses' face "emitted horn-like rays" (*qāran*, vv. 29-30, 35).[38] Given the relation of *qāran* to *qeren* ("horn"), the Vulgate rendered these three uses of the verb by the adjective *cornuta* [*facies sua*], "his face was horned." This explains the artistic representations of Moses with horns on his head such as Michelangelo's famous statue.

καταργέω is a favorite Pauline word; his use accounts for all but two of the twenty-seven NT occurrences. It is a compound of ἀργέω, "be inactive," which in turn is derived from the adjective ἀργός (a contraction from ἀ-εγρός), "not working (the ground)" and thus "inactive," "ineffective." The prefix κατά

34. "Just as in Romans vii the Law is both the *agent provocateur* leading men to sin, and yet in principle 'holy and just and good,' so the Mosaic mediation through which it was given, as described in II Corinthians iii, is a ministry of condemnation and death, and yet one which did after all once enjoy the bestowal of the divine glory" (Hickling 388).

35. BAGD 516a. These two facts make it legitimate to translate "with such glory that . . ." (similarly Goodspeed; Cassirer; Furnish 201) although such a rendering tends to downplay Paul's principal assertion — that there *was* glory attached to the old dispensation.

36. Cf. Spicq 1.227-28.

37. The Hebrew verbs in Exod. 34:34-35 that relate to Moses' action are imperfect in tense, indicating repeated, customary action: Moses' mediatorial role was continuous (Moberly 107; cf. Childs, *Exodus* 617). His face shone not only after his second descent from Mount Sinai but also whenever he came out of "the tent of meeting."

38. In Ps. 69:32 (MT) this verb *qāran* (in the hiphil) means "having horns" (in reference to a bull). Durham (467) suggests that the narrator in Exodus chose *qāran* rather than *hēʾîr* ("shine," "give light") to indicate that the light or shining was something external to Moses, "an appendage-light," a sign from Yahweh of Moses' authority.

seems here to have a causative sense: if the simplex ἀργέω is intransitive, "be out of action," the compound καταργέω is transitive in the active voice, "make/leave idle," "cause (something) to be out of action," "put out of action," "make ineffective," "render inoperative," "nullify," "abolish."[39] In the passive it is intransitive and means "cease," "pass away."[40]

Since καταργουμένην is articular in 3:7, qualifying τὴν δόξαν, it is adjectival (not adverbial) and therefore its tense (present) is only indirectly, not directly, related to the principal verb ἐγενήθη, which is aorist. If ὥστε μὴ δύνασθαι ἀτενίσαι κτλ. refers to repeated action in the past (see above), τὴν δόξαν . . . τὴν καταργουμένην, which occurs in the same clause, will mean "the glory . . . which in fact faded away [after each encounter with Yahweh]," or, "the glory . . . (even though it was a fading glory)" (NAB[1]). Several observations should be made about these renderings. (1) "In fact" seeks to represent the emphatic position of the participle, which alerts the reader either to the theme of evanescence that becomes so crucial in Paul's argument[41] (cf. τὸ καταργούμενον, 3:11, 13). (2) A concessive sense for the participle is legitimate[42] in light of Paul's paradoxical juxtaposition of two ideas — the reflection of divine glory in human features and the transience of this reflected glory. (3) Some writers object to the rendering of καταργέομαι by "fade."[43] But cannot "glory" that is emblazoned on a human countenance and yet is in process of "passing away" be said to be "fading"? Many English translations and commentators use "fade."[44] (4) Whatever symbolism is involved in Paul's use of δόξα, if there is a primary reference to the splendor seen on Moses' face, it is difficult to give a passive sense to the participle, "(glory) which was

39. Cf. LSJ 908 s.v.; Moulton and Howard 316.
40. BAGD 417c. Cf. 1 Cor. 13:8, where καταργηθήσεται is parallel to παύσονται ("will cease").
41. Scharlemann 116.
42. Such a sense is reflected in several translations: TCNT, NEB, GNB, JB, NAB[1], NIV, NJB, REB; also Conybeare in Conybeare and Howson 445; Martin 57.
43. E.g., Hanson, "Midrash" 14; Hafemann ("Glory" 37-40; see also his commentary 147-48; "Argument" 288, 294; *Moses* 301-9), who contends that the fourteen passive uses of this verb in Paul have the meaning "be rendered inoperative in regard to effects"; Baker (3, 9, 15), who prefers to render καταργέομαι by "hinder" or "block"; and Hays (133-35), who believes that the radiance on Moses' face symbolized the glory of the old covenant and its ministry and that τὴν καταργουμένην is not a narrative description of a fading glow on Moses' face but a "retrospective theological judgment" regarding "a glory that is now, through God's act in Christ, being nullified" (134). In a similar way, Hays renders τὸ καταργούμενον (3:11) by "that which is being nullified" (135). The difficulty with seeing the participle in 3:7 as "a theological afterthought" (135) is its tense. If the perspective is Paul's time of writing (cf. 219 n. 43), the aorist (τὴν καταργηθεῖσαν) rather than the present would be expected: Would Paul, writing in the mid-50s, say that the old covenant "*is being* nullified"? Hays's own paraphrase of 3:7 points up the problem: ". . . (a glory now nullified in Christ)" (135).
44. Moffatt, Montgomery, Williams, Berkeley, RSV, NEB, NASB, GNB, JB, Barclay, NAB[1], NIV, NAB[2], REB, Cassirer. Cf. Carrez 88 ("passagère de son visage") and the common German rendering "vergänglich" (Lietzmann 110; Wendland 178; Lang 271; Wolff 63), which could mean either "transient" or "fading" in reference to δόξα.

being abolished/nullified," "(glory) which was in process of abolition."[45] (5) τὴν καταργουμένην may be classified as an attributive participle expressing repeated action in the past.[46] (6) It might also be noted at this point that since the verb καταργέομαι appears as a neuter substantival participle in vv. 11 and 13 in reference to the era and order of the old covenant, it is relatively insignificant that Paul attaches the participle καταργουμένη to δόξα, not διακονία. The glory on Moses' face symbolizes the whole Mosaic dispensation, including its διαθήκη and its διακονία.

What was the source of Paul's view that the radiance of Moses' countenance "kept fading away"? Most Jewish texts that discuss the matter of the permanence of Moses' δόξα affirm either that it continued "forever"[47] or that it lasted until the day of his death (at 120 years of age).[48] But in pseudo-Philo's first-century-A.D. *Liber Antiquitatum Biblicarum (Book of Biblical Antiquities)* 19:16 it is said that at Moses' death "his countenance became glorious and he died in glory,"[49] which would imply that the initial δόξα was impermanent.[50] So Paul may have known a tradition that viewed Moses' δόξα as temporary. Alternatively, he may have inferred the diminution of the radiance from the OT text itself. If Moses was radiant whenever he emerged from "the tent of meeting" after an encounter with Yahweh (Exod. 34:35a) and his veil then prevented any prolonged sight of his face (Exod. 34:35b), it is natural to deduce that each encounter with Yahweh brought about a "recharging" with glory, which in turn implies a loss or fading of glory.[51] Taking a different approach to the OT data, Childs points out that apart from Exodus 34 no mention is ever made of Moses' shining face and that Exod. 40:35 indicates that Moses could not enter the tent of meeting because God's glory filled it. Midrashic exegesis could have deduced from these two texts, taken together, that the brilliance of Moses' face was not permanent (Childs 621).

3:8 πῶς οὐχὶ μᾶλλον ἡ διακονία τοῦ πνεύματος ἔσται ἐν δόξῃ; "Will not, then, the dispensation of the Spirit even more certainly be accompanied by glory?" This rhetorical question forms the apodosis of the long conditional sen-

---

45. Barrett 109, 116; *Adam* 51; cf. Thrall 237 ("radiance which was in process of effacement") and note her comments on 244 (the use of καταργέομαι was appropriate to the thing symbolized by the δόξα).

46. Some renderings take the participle as a futuristic present: KJV ("which glory was to be done away"); Barclay ("doomed to fade"); Zerwick and Grosvenor 539 ("destined to fade away").

47. E.g., *Seder Eliyahu Rabbah* 18: "lest you suppose that after Moses died the radiance vanished, it entered with him into his eternal abode and remains with him forever" (cited by Belleville, *Reflections* 67; cf. "Tradition" 179-80).

48. E.g., *Targum Onkelos* on Deut. 34:7 (SB 3.515, 575; McNamara 174). See further Belleville, *Reflections* 26-79; "Tradition" 169-86.

49. *Mutata est effigies eius in gloria et mortuus est in gloria.*

50. See McNamara 174; Belleville, *Reflections* 41; "Tradition" 173-74. Cf. *Zohar* 3.58a, which speaks of the "remnant" of the brightness on Moses' face (see Belleville, *Reflections* 75; "Tradition" 183-84).

51. Cf. Bruce 191; Hooker, "Scripture" 300.

tence that began with εἰ δέ in v. 7: "If the dispensation that brought death . . . was attended by glory, will not, then, . . . ?" It is the second element in the first of three *qal wāḥômer* (or *a minore ad maius*) arguments in 3:7-11 (see the introduction to this section): "if X is true, even more certainly is Y true." In rhetorical questions introduced by πῶς with a negative, "how [could/will] not?" the sense is "most surely" or "most certainly."[52] In the present case, the μᾶλλον of the *qal wāḥômer* argument converts this "most certainly" into "even more certainly." For the meaning of διακονία, see 3:7.

The genitive τοῦ πνεύματος is more probably adjectival ("the dispensation marked by the [gift and work of the] Spirit") than objective ("service rendered to the Spirit" [Isaacs] or "the ministry that imparts the Spirit") or subjective ("the dispensation instituted by the Spirit"[53]). Certainly the parallelism with ἡ διακονία τοῦ θανάτου (v. 7a) shows that Spirit is being seen as the Spirit of life (cf. Rom. 8:2). It is possible that ἔσται is a purely temporal future, referring to the glory of the future age[54] or the glory to be displayed at the parousia, although Bengel refers the glory to the present age as seen from the standpoint of the OT (3.365). But if the glory were wholly future in relation to the time of writing, some qualification of δόξῃ might have been expected such as ἐν δόξῃ τῇ μελλούσῃ ἀποκαλυφθῆναι (cf. Rom. 8:18; 1 Pet. 5:1). Since the δόξα described in 3:9 and 3:18 (cf. 4:17) was a present reality when Paul wrote, it is preferable to treat ἔσται as a logical future (Bultmann 81), although some commentators envisage this future as both logical and chronological.[55] ἐν δόξῃ specifies an attendant circumstance: "will be with glory = will be accompanied by glory."[56]

3:9 εἰ γὰρ τῇ διακονίᾳ τῆς κατακρίσεως δόξα, πολλῷ μᾶλλον περισσεύει ἡ διακονία τῆς δικαιοσύνης δόξῃ. "For if there was glory in the dispensation that brought condemnation, how much more surpassingly glorious is the dispensation that brings righteousness." Basically, this verse is a restatement of the essence of vv. 7-8, but as with any restatement there are differences alongside the basic similarity. These become clear when the verses are set out side-by-side.

---

52. BAGD 732c (cf. 489c), citing the present verse and also Rom. 8:32 ("He who did not spare his own Son, but gave him up for us all, how will he not [πῶς οὐχί; = he most certainly will] also, along with him, freely give us all things?").

53. But Zerwick (*Analysis* 396) proposes multiple senses for this genitive (cf. his *Biblical Greek* §38): "the ministry which has the Spirit as its beginning [subjective], its content [epexegetic], and its fruit [objective] (the gen[itive] limiting in a general sense)." The Latin runs: *ministerium quod Spiritum habet ut principium, argumentum, fructum (gen. generaliter determinans).*

54. So Meyer 468, citing 3:12 where δόξα is the object of ἐλπίς (cf. 3:11; Rom. 5:2). Similarly Winer 280; Belleville 99, 106 (citing Rom. 8:18, 23); Renwick 113-21, who finds an allusion to Hag. 2:9 (LXX), where ἔσται occurs.

55. E.g., Collange 77-78; Furnish 227-28.

56. BAGD (225b), however, classifies 3:8 under εἰμὶ ἔν τινι denoting "states of being," citing also Luke 11:21 (ἐν εἰρήνῃ); 23:12 (ἐν ἔχθρᾳ); and 23:40 (ἐν κρίματι).

7a εἰ δὲ   ἡ διακονία τοῦ θανάτου . . . ἐγενήθη   ἐν δόξῃ,
9a εἰ γὰρ τῇ διακονίᾳ τῆς κατακρίσεως   δόξα,
8   πῶς οὐχὶ μᾶλλον   ἡ διακονία τοῦ πνεύματος ἔσται ἐν δόξῃ;
9b πολλῷ   μᾶλλον περισσεύει ἡ διακονία τῆς δικαιοσύνης   δόξῃ.

Both *a minore ad maius* arguments compare two types of διακονία with regard to δόξα[57] and emphasize δόξα by placing it at the end of the clause. But there are several differences. (1) In the comparison of the two dispensations (v. 9), a τῆς κατακρίσεως–τῆς δικαιοσύνης antithesis replaces a τοῦ θανάτου–τοῦ πνεύματος contrast and τῇ διακονίᾳ replaces ἡ διακονία. (2) In the *a minore* argument there is not only a "logical plus" ("even more certainly"), as in vv. 7-8, but also a quantitative increment (περισσεύει, "much more surpassingly [glorious]").[58] (3) V. 9 is a statement, not a rhetorical question, and lacks a verb in the protasis.

τῇ διακονίᾳ (see Textual Note c.) may be classified as a dative of possession,[59] a locative dative,[60] or a dative of respect. κατάκρισις (3:9; 7:3) refers to the act of condemning, while κατάκριμα (Rom. 5:16, 18; 8:1) denotes the result of condemnation, that is, the punishment that is inflicted after the sentence of condemnation, thus "punishment," "doom," "penal servitude."[61] κατακρίσεως is probably an objective genitive, "(a dispensation) which leads to condemnation,"[62] "that brought condemnation." The dispensation of the Law pronounced a curse on people who failed to carry out the Law's regulations (Deut. 27:26), yet that era or ministry was "glorious" since that Law and those regulations expressed the sovereign will of God. πολλῷ is dative of the degree of difference: "(more) by much" (BAGD 688d). "The dispensation that brings/offers righteousness" (τῆς δικαιοσύνης, objective genitive)[63] is to be identified with "the dispensation of the Spirit" (3:8) and "the ministry of reconciliation" (5:18). δικαιοσύνη here is a relational rather than an ethical term, denoting a right standing before God, given by God (as in Rom. 1:17; 3:21-22; 10:3; Phil. 3:9), the status of being "in the right" before the court of heaven.[64] God's approval,

---

57. Provence rightly observes (72-73) that Paul does not contrast the function of the two διακονίαι (death-dealing versus life-giving) although one might have expected τῆς ζωῆς to be the contrast to τοῦ θανάτου (v. 7a).

58. Similarly Thrall 249.

59. "If glory belongs to the agency of condemnation" (Thrall 237; cf. 249 n. 399).

60. "In the administration" (Moffatt; Berkeley; Zerwick and Grosvenor 539).

61. Cf. BAGD 412a, b; Deissmann 264-65. On the difference between the -σις (act of) and -μα (result of) noun suffixes, see Moulton and Howard (355), who also note that in Hellenistic Greek -σις nouns sometimes express result.

62. Zerwick, *Analysis* 396.

63. Like κατακρίσεως, this genitive could be adjectival: "marked by condemnation . . . marked by righteousness." But Reumann (50) construes τῆς δικαιοσύνης as subjective ("that proceeds from righteousness").

64. Cf. G. Schrenk, *TDNT* 2.204. It is not surprising that some translations render δικαιοσύνη here by "justification" (e.g., JB, NRSV). But the notion of "acquittal" should be re-

not his condemnation, rests on those who are "in Christ." This being so, the new covenant and its administration must even more certainly than was the case under the old covenant be characterized by divine splendor, and also must abound (περισσεύει) far more in that splendor (δόξῃ).[65] What was a distinctive and positive feature of the old order must also characterize the new economy, but in greater measure. The new covenant has surpassing glory inasmuch as it is a more adequate revelation of God's character.

3:10 καὶ γὰρ οὐ δεδόξασται τὸ δεδοξασμένον ἐν τούτῳ τῷ μέρει εἵνεκεν τῆς ὑπερβαλλούσης δόξης. "Indeed, in this respect, what once was glorious has lost its claim to glory on account of the glory that surpasses it." Paul's comparison between the two economies or dispensations now advances one step further. The new dispensation or covenant is not merely characterized by greater glory. So dramatic is the difference between the two economies that what once was rightly considered resplendent now appears to lack any resplendence at all. The old economy suffers immeasurably from a comparison with the new.

Although this may represent the general drift of Paul's meaning, there are several exegetical issues of significance in this verse. With καὶ γὰρ ("indeed") Paul introduces a confirmation and development of his assertion in v. 9 that the ministry that provides righteousness is surpassingly glorious. The articular neuter participle τὸ δεδοξασμένον functions as an abstract substantive.[66] In the passive δοξάζω means "be glorified," "be endowed with splendor," "be glorious," so this perfect participle will mean "what has been glorified" (Thrall 237, 251), "what was endowed with glory" (NAB²), or, to bring out the sense of the perfect in relation to the aorist ἐγενήθη of v. 7, "what once was glorious." Since the perfect passive of δοξάζω is used three times in Exodus 34 in reference to Moses' face,[67] τὸ δεδοξασμένον in 2 Cor. 3:10 probably alludes to Moses' countenance, but the principal referent will be (as the neuter shows) to a more general idea, namely the Mosaic economy as a whole, its διαθήκη and its διακονία.[68] The combination οὐ δεδόξασται τὸ δεδοξασμένον creates a stunning oxymoron: "what has had splendor has not had splendor" (Furnish 204), "what was once considered glorious has lost all claim to glory" (NJB). After ἐγενήθη ἐν δόξῃ in v. 7, the perfect οὐ δεδόξασται describes a glory that no longer exists,

---

jected (*pace* Moffatt; Wand; NEB; REB; Barrett 116; Thrall 249), for, so far from being "declared innocent" (= acquitted) sinners are "pronounced guilty" as charged (Rom. 3:9, 19; 11:32) before acquiring, on the basis of the redemption achieved by Christ, a new, right, and permanent standing before God (= justification; Rom. 3:24).

65. BAGD (651a) renders περισσεύειν δόξῃ "be extremely rich in glory." δόξῃ is a dative of respect or reference, indicating the sphere in which the abundance is found. Standing without a preposition (cf. vv. 7-8), it matches δόξα in v. 9a.

66. Robertson 1109; Turner 151.

67. δεδόξασται (Exod. 34:29, 35), ἣν δεδοξασμένη (Exod. 34:30). See the introduction to 3:7-11 above.

68. Cf. Hafemann: "Paul's reference is to the ministry of the old covenant *as a whole*, especially its theological purpose (v. 9a) and results (v. 7)" ("Argument" 291).

having been superseded.[69] Such disparagement of the era of the old covenant, although relative (v. 7; cf. Rom. 7:12), indicates how thoroughly new Paul considered the new covenant (καινὴ διαθήκη, 3:6), the new creation (καινὴ κτίσις, 5:17), and the new order ([τὰ] καινά, 5:17).[70]

If ἐν τούτῳ τῷ μέρει is construed with τὸ δεδοξασμένον, the whole phrase will mean "that which has been partially glorified" (Héring 22) or "that which had partial glory" (Martin 57), with the limitation pointing to the transient and restricted character of the old administration.[71] But although μέρος can mean "part," it is ἀπὸ μέρους (1:14; 2:5) or ἐκ μέρους (1 Cor. 13:9, 12) that means "partially" or "in part." Also, on this view, τούτῳ would be superfluous and τό would normally be repeated before the qualifying prepositional phrase. Rather, ἐν τούτῳ τῷ μέρει means "in this matter" (as in 9:3; BAGD 506b), or "in this connection,"[72] and relates to οὐ δεδόξασται, referring back to περισσεύει in v. 9, that is, the superiority or the glory of the new dispensation,[73] or possibly forward to εἵνεκεν κτλ., the surpassing glory of the new covenant.[74] The final phrase in the verse affords the reason for the bold, absolute statement οὐ δεδόξασται: "on account of[75] [the comparison with] the surpassing[76] glory [of the new order that totally outshines the old]." That is, the old covenant has been "eclipsed" by the new, the Law by the gospel. But, as in astronomy, the light that has been eclipsed has not been extinguished but has been surpassed in splendor.

This verse, with its daring affirmation of the transcendent glory of the new age, has prompted some memorable analogies or summary statements. "If the sun is up, the brightness of the moon is no longer bright."[77] "The greater light obscures the less."[78] "Christ as the Sun of Righteousness has thrown Mo-

69. Moule 15. For a critique of the view that by adding οὐ and making other changes Paul has radically recast an inherited text, see Thrall 251-52.

70. Cf. John 1:17; Heb. 7:18-19; 8:6-7.

71. E. Hill (299-301) views v. 10 as an explanatory aside (with καὶ γάρ = "though in fact") which answers an unstated objection, namely that the new covenant lacks anything comparable to the radiant glory of Moses' face. Paul replies in effect: "the thing glorified in this latter (τούτῳ) case (v. 9b) — the glory of the new creation — has not yet been fully glorified (that awaits the consummation, 5:1, 4) because its glory is so overwhelming." Against this: τούτῳ may refer to what is uppermost in Paul's mind (the glory or superiority of the new order); τὸ δεδοξασμένον naturally looks back to v. 9a, repeating the "old-new" parallelism of vv. 7-9; οὐ should not be treated as equivalent to οὔπω ("not yet"); and the evident allusion to Exodus 34 in the two perfect passives in v. 10 is lost on this view.

72. J. Schneider, TDNT 4.596.

73. But Oostendorp (37) takes "in this respect" to refer back to v. 9 and "the power to confer righteousness and life."

74. Plummer 91-92; Barrett 117.

75. εἵνεκεν = Attic ἕνεκα (Moulton and Howard 67-68).

76. The ὑπερβαλλ- word group, a Pauline phenomenon within the NT, is common in 2 Corinthians: ὑπερβολή (1:8; 4:7, 17 twice; 12:7; other uses, Rom. 7:13; 1 Cor. 12:31; Gal. 1:13), ὑπερβάλλω as an attributive participle (3:10; 9:14; other uses, Eph. 1:19; 2:7; 3:19), ὑπερβαλλόντως (11:23).

77. Zerwick, Analysis 396.

78. Bengel 3.365-66.

ses in the shade."[79] "The glory of the law in the face of Moses has faded before the glory of the Gospel in the face of Jesus Christ."[80]

3:11 εἰ γὰρ τὸ καταργούμενον διὰ δόξης, πολλῷ μᾶλλον τὸ μένον ἐν δόξῃ. "For if what was destined to fade away came with glory, far greater will be the glory that accompanies what is destined to remain." This verse further explains ἡ ὑπερβάλλουσα δόξα (v. 10b) and summarizes vv. 7-10. It is the third *a minore ad maius* (or *qal wāḥômer*) argument in this paragraph.[81] V. 10 stated the implication of the second argument (v. 9), which itself was a restatement of the first (vv. 7-8). Although v. 11 lacks any explicit indication of a "quantitative plus" in addition to a "logical plus," such a quantitative plus is probable, since this verse follows v. 9 with its περισσεύει and v. 10 with its ὑπερβαλλούσης, so that πολλῷ μᾶλλον . . . ἐν δόξῃ will refer to a far greater quantity of glory as well as to a more certain presence of glory.[82]

Because the two substantival participles are antithetical, and the second (τὸ μένον) almost certainly refers to the new covenant (cf. 3:6) and its ministry, it is likely that τὸ καταργούμενον signifies the old covenant and its ministry,[83] although, being an abstract substantive, it could refer to the old economy in general or "the whole religious system based on the law."[84] It is not illegitimate to treat both these participles as timeless ("the transient . . . the permanent," Wand),[85] but while τὸ μένον clearly means "what lasts" indefinitely or forever, "what is destined to remain," τὸ καταργούμενον would seem to demand some indication of the time of the annulment or abolition or fading. Thrall renders the participle "what is being abolished," arguing that for Paul "in some sense" the Mosaic ministry and covenant remained in existence (3:14-15) while the preaching of the gospel and the conversion of Jews meant the old covenant was in the process of abolition.[86] But perhaps this line of reasoning proves too much — as long as Judaism continued, the process of abolition would continue, with-

79. Robertson, *Pictures* 221. But we need not endorse Hickling's surmise that between the use of Exod. 32:1-6 in 1 Cor. 10:1-11 and the use of Exod. 34:29-35 in 2 Cor. 3:7-18 there may have been a shift in Paul's evaluation of Moses. "He came to regard Moses himself as flawed in his mediatorial capacity, and to judge the whole dispensation of which he was the central figure as similarly, and fatally, flawed" ("Exodus" 374).

80. Vincent 816.

81. See the discussion of this form of argumentation in the introduction to 3:7-11.

82. *Pace* Thrall 237, 252 n. 421.

83. Similarly Bultmann 84; Furnish 205; Thrall 252. Hafemann believes that the expressions τὸ καταργούμενον and τὸ μένον are Paul's restatement of the "two age" concept that was common to the OT and early Judaism ("Argument" 297; *Moses* 333).

84. Barrett, *Adam,* 52 n. 1. Cranfield restricts the sense of τὸ καταργούμενον to the service that Moses rendered at the giving of the Law, a ministry that belonged to the time of expectation as opposed to the time of fulfillment ("Law" 160).

85. BAGD 417c renders τὸ καταργούμενον by "what is transitory"; similarly G. Delling, *TDNT* 1.454 ("transitory" = deprived of original value); F. Hauck, *TDNT* 4.575; H. Hübner, *EDNT* 2.268.

86. Thrall 237, 252-53; similarly Barrett 109, 118; Young and Ford 264; von der Osten-Sacken, "Geist" 230-31.

out the old covenant ever being finally abolished. Would Paul not have regarded the Mosaic covenant as terminated in effect when the new covenant was inaugurated by Christ's death? The alternative is to relate τὸ καταργούμενον to the time indicated by the constative aorist ἐγενήθη in 3:7: "what was destined to fade away."[87] Such a rendering preserves the verbal link with τὴν καταργουμένην in 3:7 ("which in fact faded away"), although there in 3:7 the allusion to the Mosaic order is secondary, whereas here in 3:11 the Mosaic economy is the focus, with Moses' face alluded to by the phrase διὰ δόξης.

Paul's stark contrast between τὸ καταργούμενον and τὸ μένον, between "what faded" and "what lasts" (Moffatt), epitomizes his view of religious history in the light of the cross of Christ. The old covenant and its ministry belonged to a vanishing order, an economy that began to fade immediately after its inception, as was typified by the divine glory reflected on Moses' face — a glory that began to fade as soon as he left the divine presence.[88] On the other hand, the new covenant and its ministry began in splendor and will always be invested with glory (τὸ μένον ἐν δόξῃ [ἔσται/ἐστίν]), for it constitutes God's final word to humankind. In the period between the two advents of Jesus, there is only one divine ordinance, the gospel, an eternal gospel (Rev. 14:6) of an eternal covenant (Heb. 13:20). It remains until the parousia, when its implications for all creation, animate and inanimate, will be fully realized (Rom. 8:18-23). The era of the gospel is permanent, never to be superseded, for it marks the end of the ages (1 Cor. 10:11), the culmination of God's redemptive purposes for the world (Gal. 4:4-5).

In the protasis ἐγενήθη or ἐγένετο may be understood; in the apodosis, ἐστί or ἔσται (as a logical future[89]). Some scholars distinguish διὰ δόξης from ἐν δόξῃ. "To the old dispensation glory was a phase, *through* which it passed; to the new it is a sphere *in* which it abides."[90] But such a distinction is unlikely: ἐν δόξῃ is applied to both covenants in 3:7-8, and Paul is not averse to stylistic variation with no difference in meaning (cf. διά–ἐν [as here] in Rom. 5:10; ἐκ–διά in Rom. 3:30; Gal. 2:16).[91] Both phrases describe attendant circumstances: "came with glory . . . will be accompanied by glory."[92]

This treatment of 3:7-11 may suitably conclude with a summary of Paul's comparisons between the two covenants that will highlight the theme of this section, which is the surpassing glory of the new covenant.

87. The rendering "fade (away)" for καταργέομαι in 3:11 is found in Moffatt, Goodspeed, Montgomery, RSV, NEB, NASB, NIV, NAB² ("what was going to fade"), REB ("what was to fade away"), Cassirer; Young and Ford 264.

88. The writer of Hebrews (8:13) says that God (the implied subject of πεπαλαίωκεν, as of μεμφόμενος in 8:8) assigned the old covenant to obsolescence when through Jeremiah (31:31-34) he spoke of the new covenant. "And what has become obsolete [BAGD 606a] and grown old will shortly disappear."

89. So, apparently, TCNT, Moffatt, NAB²; Barrett 109, 118; Carrez 88.

90. Plummer (CGT) 62; similarly Bernard 56; Hughes 105-6; Prümm 1.128 and n. 1.

91. But this is not to endorse Newman's assertion (233) that ἐν δόξῃ and διὰ δόξης throughout 2 Cor. 3:7-11 should be understood as expressing means.

92. So also Barrett 118.

Old Covenant	New Covenant
engraved on stone tablets (3:3, 7)	written on hearts-of-flesh tablets (3:3)
a death-dealing written code (3:6)	a life-giving Spirit (3:6)
dispensation of death (3:7)	dispensation of the Spirit (3:8)
dispensation of condemnation (3:9)	dispensation of righteousness (3:9)
glorious (3:7, 9-11)	glorious (3:8)
	far more glorious (3:9-11)
fading (3:7, 11)	permanent (3:11)

Bibliography

Baker • Balch • E. Bammel, "Paulus, der Moses des neuen Bundes," *Theologia* 54 (1983) 399-408 • Barrett, *Adam* 50-60 • Belleville, *Reflections* • Belleville, "Tradition" • E. F. F. Bishop, "Qumran and the Preserved Tablet(s)," *RevQ* 5 (1965) 253-56 • Carrez, *Souffrance* 33-44 • M.-A. Chevallier, *Esprit de Dieu, paroles d'hommes* (Neuchâtel: Delachaux et Niestlé, 1966) 91-99 • J. W. Doeve, *Jewish Hermeneutics in the Synoptic Gospels and Acts* (Assen: Gorcum, 1954) • Dumbrell • F. Dumermuth, "Moses strahlendes Gesicht," *TZ* 17 (1961) 241-48 • Ellis 25-27 • E. E. Ellis, "How the New Testament Uses the Old," in *New Testament Interpretation,* ed. I. H. Marshall (Exeter: Paternoster/Grand Rapids: Eerdmans, 1977) 199-219 • Fee, *Presence* 304-7 • Fitzmyer, "Glory" • Friedrich, "Gegner" • Friesen 47-53 • Göttsberger • Hafemann, *Moses* 265-334 • Hanson, "Midrash" • Hanson, *Ministry* 50, 68 • Hays 122-53 • Hickling • Hickling, "Exodus" • E. Hill • Jervell • Jones • Kim 5-13, 128-29 • Koch • Le Déaut • McNamara • McNamara, *Paraphrases* • Meeks, *Prophet-King* • Meeks, "Moses" • Moberly 106-9 • Murphy-O'Connor, "Judaizers" • Newman 229-35, 243 • Oostendorp 31-51 • D. Patte, *Early Jewish Hermeneutic in Palestine* (Missoula: Scholars, 1975) • Provence • Prümm, "Vergleich" • Prümm, "2 Kor. 3" • Renwick 52-54, 95-121 • Richard • Rissi 25-28 • T. R. Schreiner 81-83, 129-33, 141-42 • J. Schröter, "Schriftauslegung und Hermeneutik in 2 Korinther 3. Ein Beitrag zur Frage der Schriftbenutzung des Paulus," *NovT* 40 (1998) 231-75 • S. Schulz, "Die Decke des Moses. Untersuchungen zu einer vorpaulinischen Überlieferung in II Cor 3:7-18," *ZNW* 49 (1958) 1-30 • Shead • Stockhausen 87-153, 175-77 • Stockhausen, "2 Corinthians 3" • Theissen, *Aspects* 117-75 • Theobald 177-90 • Thielman 100-13 • Ulonska • Vanhoye • von der Osten-Sacken, *Heiligkeit* 87-115 • Witherington, *Jesus* 109-11 • E. Wong

e. Veiling and Unveiling (3:12-18)

In our introduction to 3:7-11, we observed that 3:12-18 is a commentary on Exod. 34:33-35, with παρρησία and κάλυμμα the crucial terms, that Paul is dependent primarily on the LXX, not the Hebrew text, of Exod. 34:29-35, and that in his "allusive homily" based on Exodus 34 Paul mentions three items not explicitly found in the Exodus narrative: the Israelites' inability to look intently at Moses' face (3:7; see the commentary there), the diminishing brightness of Moses' face (3:7; see the commentary there), and Moses' motivation in veiling his face (3:13).

Paul had been accused of underhanded ways and unscrupulous cunning (cf. 4:2). He needed therefore to show his transparent openness, his παρρησία (3:12). This he does by continuing his comparison of the two covenants, now focusing on the freedom and openness of the new dispensation as opposed to the obstruction of physical and spiritual vision under the old dispensation. Set over against the veiled face of Moses and the veiled hearts of Jews are the unveiled faces of all Christians, who experience the emancipation and transformation produced by the Spirit of the Lord. Christian παρρησία (3:12) and ἐλευθερία (3:17) are contrasted with Jewish "veiledness" (μὴ ἀνακαλυπτόμενον, 3:14b), Christian μεταμόρφωσις (cf. 3:18) with Jewish πώρωσις (cf. 3:14a). On the suggested origins of 3:7-18, see the introduction to 3:7-11.

Three main approaches have been taken regarding the structure of 3:12-18.

Chiastic (J. Lambrecht):[1]
A. 12-13a (13b)   — We (apostles)
  B. 14a
    C. 14b
      D. 14c   — They (Israelites)
    C'. 15
  B'. 16 (17)
A'. 18   — We (Christians)[2]

Syntactical (M. Theobald):[3]
I. 12: connecting verse
II. 13-18: Contrast between Moses and "we all"
  A. Negative: Moses' role (13-17)
    1. Moses' action
      (a) μή: objective aspect (13)
      (b) ἀλλά: subjective aspect (14a)
    2. Paul's explanation
      (a) μή: objective aspect (14b, c)
      (b) ἀλλά: subjective aspect (15-16)
    3. Transition (17)
    Two small units (17a, b)
  B. Positive: confessional statement (18)[4]

---

1. Lambrecht, "Structure" 357, 361-62, 364 (= Bieringer and Lambrecht 270, 274-75, 277).

2. This chiastic structure is adopted and simplified by Thrall, 189: A 3:12-13, we (ministers); B 3:14-17, they (Israelites); A' 3:18, we (Christians). For a critique of Lambrecht's proposal see Belleville, *Reflections* 176.

3. Theobald 190-95; cf. 195-211.

4. For a critique of Theobald, see Lambrecht, "Structure" 377-79 (= Bieringer and Lambrecht 290-92) and Belleville, *Reflections* 177.

Haggadic (L. L. Belleville):[5]

   I. 12: opening statement
  II. 13-14a (Exod. 34:33): text
 III. 14b-15: commentary
 IV. 16 (Exod. 34:34): text
  V. 17: commentary
 VI. 18 (Exod. 34:35): text and commentary combined

Our approach is a modification of Belleville's outline:

    12   thematic statement
    13   OT text: Exod. 34:33b, 35
   14-15 commentary
    16   OT text: Exod. 34:34a
   17-18 commentary

12*Since, then, we have such a hope, we act with great forthright openness.* 13*We do not act as Moses did: his habit was to put a veil over his*[a] *face to prevent the people of Israel from gazing steadily until the end*[b] *of what was fading away.* 14*But their minds were hardened. Indeed, right up to the present day,*[c] *when the old covenant is read, that same veil remains there, still unlifted, because only in Christ is it abolished.* 15*Yes, to this very day, whenever*[d] *Moses is read, a veil lies over their hearts.* 16*But whenever someone turns to the Lord, that veil is removed.* 17*Now this "Lord" is the Spirit, and where the Spirit of the Lord*[e] *is, there is*[f] *freedom.* 18*And all*[g] *of us, with unveiled faces, looking at the glory of the Lord as in a mirror,*[h] *are being transformed*[i] *into the same image, from one degree of glory to another. Appropriately, this transformation*[j] *comes from the Lord, who is the Spirit.*

TEXTUAL NOTES

a. ℵ D 𝔐 read ἑαυτοῦ in place of αὐτοῦ.

b. Under the influence of ἀτενίσαι . . . εἰς τὸ πρόσωπον in v. 7, A *pc* b f* vg (bo^mss) read πρόσωπον instead of τέλος.

c. Ψ 𝔐 syr^p read ἄχρι γὰρ τῆς σήμερον, omitting ἡμέρας, probably under the influence of ἕως σήμερον in v. 15.

d. By haplography several witnesses (D F G 0243 1739 1881 𝔐) omit ἄν, and, because ἡνίκα (without ἄν) would normally be followed by the indicative (see LSJ 775 s.v.), all these witnesses except D change ἀναγινώσκηται to ἀναγινώσκεται.

e. L reads τὸ ἅγιον instead of κυρίου, while 323 omits κυρίου.

f. To balance οὗ ("where"), numerous witnesses insert ἐκεῖ before ἐλευθερία (ℵ

---

5. Belleville, *Reflections* 177; cf. 178-91. In her (later) commentary (103), vv. 12-13a form the opening statement while vv. 13b-14a form section II. According to Belleville, in 3:12-18 Paul is answering "two different but related criticisms." In vv. 12-13, 18 he addresses the charge of "professional arrogance"; in vv. 14-17, the charge that he had lacked evangelistic success among his fellow Jews (102).

D[b, c] F G K L P Ψ 1881 𝔐 it[d, g] vg syr[h] cop[sa] goth arm eth Epiphanius). But the shorter reading, which has wide geographical support, is preferable (p[46] ℵ* A B C D* 0243 6 33 81 424[c] 1175 1739 1912 pc it[r] syr[p] cop[bo]); "furthermore, the use of ἐκεῖ to balance οὗ is apparently not in Paul's style (cf. Ro 4.15; 5.20)" (Metzger 509).

g. p[46] vg[ms] Speculum (Ps-Augustine) omit πάντες.

h. 33 reads κατοπτριζόμεθα.

i. p[46] reads κατοπτριζόμεθα οἱ . . . μεταμορφούμενοι, which reverses participle and finite verb (on this, see Wright 146 n. 26), while A and 614 make both verbs participial, just as 33 makes both verbs finite (see h).

j. B reads καθώσπερ (cf. Heb. 5:4; BAGD 391c).

3:12 Ἔχοντες οὖν τοιαύτην ἐλπίδα πολλῇ παρρησίᾳ χρώμεθα. "Since, then, we have such a hope, we act with great forthright openness." If οὖν looks back to 3:7-11 in general, τοιαύτην ἐλπίδα alludes to 3:11 in particular. As participants in the ministry of the new covenant, Paul and his fellow apostles and all proclaimers of the gospel had a confident expectation (ἐλπίς) that this new covenant was permanent and irrevocable (τὸ μένον, 3:11b), never to be superseded or surpassed in splendor.[6] Since they possessed (causal ἔχοντες) such a hope, their conduct was marked by the utmost freedom and boldness. Although χρώμεθα could be a hortatory subjunctive ("let us act"), the parallel in 4:1 (ἔχοντες τὴν διακονίαν ταύτην . . . οὐκ ἐγκακοῦμεν) shows that Paul is making an affirmation, not giving an exhortation. χράομαι often means "make use of," but in its three uses in 2 Corinthians (1:17; 3:12; 13:10) the verb bears the sense "act," "proceed," with the dative defining the characteristic shown.[7]

The colorful term παρρησία (from πᾶν + ῥῆσις, "speaking") referred originally to the freedom to speak all one's mind, then it came to denote frankness and openness in speech, and finally, with no necessary reference to speech, "boldness," "fearlessness," "forthrightness," "complete unreservedness." In Pauline usage παρρησία may be exhibited toward God and toward other people and in the proclamation of the gospel.[8] With the same phrase πολλὴ παρρησία occurring in 7:4, where the "confident frankness"[9] is directed πρὸς ὑμᾶς (cf. Phlm. 8), it is likely that Paul's relation to other people is principally in mind, whether the Corinthians as representative of all his converts, his opponents at Corinth and elsewhere, or those to whom he proclaimed the gospel. It was not only his speech but his whole way of life that was characterized by "forthright openness." He had nothing to conceal, but every reason for "fearless candor" (cf. 4:2).

6. This ἐλπίς differs from the πεποίθησις of 3:4a (which is a close verbal parallel to 3:12a) in that it relates to the future, not to the present (cf. Job 11:18, LXX). Hafemann regards the ἐλπίς as Paul's certain confidence that his ministry mediated the glory of God (*Moses* 338).

7. BAGD 884d.

8. See Marrow 444-46; D. E. Fredrickson, "Παρρησία in the Pauline Epistles," in J. T. Fitzgerald (ed.), *Friendship, Flattery, and Frankness of Speech: Studies on Friendship in the New Testament World* (Leiden: Brill, 1996) 163-83; Hafemann, *Moses* 338-47.

9. This is Thrall's rendering (237) of παρρησία in 3:12 (cf. 7:4, "I am very candid with you" [472]).

3:13 καὶ οὐ καθάπερ Μωϋσῆς ἐτίθει κάλυμμα ἐπὶ τὸ πρόσωπον αὐτοῦ. "We do not act as Moses did: his habit was to put a veil over his face." 3:7-11 was commentary on Exod. 34:29-30 (LXX), with δοξάζω the key term in the OT passage and δόξα the central motif in the NT commentary. Now, in vv. 13-18, after introducing the themes of freedom and openness (παρρησία, v. 12) that will also conclude the paragraph (ἐλευθερία, v. 17; ἀνακεκαλυμμένῳ προσώπῳ, v. 18), Paul continues his selective commentary on the Moses narrative, focusing on Exod. 34:33-35 LXX, where κάλυμμα (= Hebrew *masweh*, "covering," "veil") is central.[10] With the comparison οὐ καθάπερ there is an ellipsis — perhaps οὐ [χρώμεθα, from v. 12] καθάπερ, "we do not act as. . . ."[11] The contrast Paul draws between himself (and his associates) and Moses is not that of boldness (παρρησία) as opposed to timidity (Moses' "meekness" [Num. 12:3] should not be equated with fainthearted diffidence),[12] nor straightforward honesty in contrast with devious deceit, but rather openness as opposed to concealment,[13] with no necessary implication of duplicity in that concealment. But this paragraph ends with an implied similarity between Moses and all Christian believers (3:18) — transformation as a result of seeing God's glory.

ἐτίθει is an iterative imperfect: "it was Moses' custom to put a veil on his face." This allusion requires a careful examination of the sequence of events in Exod. 34:33-35 (LXX). 34:33 indicates that on the occasion of his (second) descent from Sinai, after he had finished speaking to the people, he put (ἐπέθηκεν) a veil over his face, the aorist depicting a single action. But in 34:34 three iterative imperfects appear: "Whenever Moses entered (εἰσεπορεύετο) the Lord's presence to speak with him, he used to take off (περιῃρεῖτο) his veil until he went out. After he had gone out, he would tell (ἐλάλει) all the people of Israel whatever the Lord had commanded him." Finally, in 34:35, where Moses' customary action is still being described, we read that "the people of Israel saw (εἶδον) that the face of Moses was radiant and so Moses placed (περιέθηκεν) a veil over his face until he went in to converse with the Lord." These two constative aorists depict repeated action unitarily. All this validates Paul's use of ἐτίθει. After his second descent from Sinai and initial speaking with the people and the veiling of his face (v. 33), the pattern of Moses' behavior was as follows:

10. There is no need to follow van Unnik in his complex explanation of Paul's movement of thought from παρρησία in v. 12 to κάλυμμα in v. 13, which is that, thinking in Aramaic but writing in Greek, Paul associated the idea of freedom with a covering since the Aramaic idiom "to uncover the face, or head" *(galleh 'appîn, rē'š)* signifies confidence and freedom, and the expression "with uncovered head" (cf. 3:18) means "in freedom" ("Face" 161, 169; cf. McNamara 176-77). See the critique of this view in Belleville, *Reflections* 215-17.

11. Cf. BDF §482. But Meyer (471; cf. Robertson 394) proposes supplying after οὐ the words τίθεμεν κάλυμμα ἐπὶ τὸ πρόσωπον ἡμῶν.

12. But see Childs, *Exodus* 623.

13. Cf. J. Jeremias, *TDNT* 4.869.

1. removal of the veil from his face (v. 34a),
2. conversing with Yahweh with unveiled face (v. 34a),
3. speaking to the people about the divine commandments with unveiled face (v. 34b), and
4. replacement of the veil on his face (v. 35b; ἐτίθει, 2 Cor. 3:13).

At stage 3 the people would have been dazzled by the brilliance of Moses' face (3:7) and would probably have noticed some fading of the brilliance even as Moses addressed them (this seems implied by the expression "gaze right to the end of what was fading" — see below). But it would seem that the periods when Moses was unveiled before the people were brief, whereas the times when he wore a veil were prolonged.

The Exodus narrative gives no explicit reason for Moses' recurrent veiling of his face, but many commentators assume that it was to avoid frightening the people or to protect them from prolonged exposure to the divine radiance and to mark clearly the difference between his official role as Yahweh's intermediary, regularly declaring Yahweh's words to Israel (the unveiled face), and his status as a private citizen, speaking his own words (the veiled face). But Exod. 34:35 contains a hint of Moses' purpose, if the καί that joins the two parts of the verse is rendered "and so":[14] "The people of Israel saw (εἶδον) that the face of Moses was radiant, and so (καί) Moses placed a veil over his face." That is, he wanted to prevent the people from being preoccupied with what they saw, from gazing in amazement, as opposed to giving attention to what they had heard. It is this idea, we suggest, that prompted Paul's statement in 3:13b.

πρὸς τὸ μὴ ἀτενίσαι τοὺς υἱοὺς Ἰσραὴλ εἰς τὸ τέλος τοῦ καταργουμένου. "To prevent the people of Israel from gazing steadily until the end of what was fading away." πρός with the articular infinitive expresses purpose.[15] A variety of proposals have been made regarding Paul's understanding of the reason for Moses' veiling of his face:[16]

> to prevent the Israelites from seeing that the splendor of his face was fading[17] and thus to preclude their disappointment[18] or their disparagement of his importance,[19]

14. For this use of καί, see BAGD 392c: "to introduce a result, which comes fr(om) what precedes," citing Matt. 5:15; 23:32; 2 Cor. 11:9; Heb. 3:19; 1 John 3:19.
15. Burton §414; Robertson 1075; Turner 144. It is doubtful whether πρὸς τό ever expresses result (Moulton 218; Robertson 1003), although occasionally it may mean "with reference to." But for a consecutive sense in 3:13, see Rissi 31.
16. For a summary of a partially different set of proposals, see Thrall 259-61. There is a well-documented treatment of the issues in Belleville, *Reflections* 206-8.
17. Oepke, *TDNT* 3.560; E. Lohse, *TDNT* 6.776.
18. Martin 68, 73.
19. Barrett 119.

to conceal from the Israelites the temporary nature of the whole Mosaic system[20] or the goal of the fading old covenant,[21]

to show the people, through an acted parable, that their sins had made them unable and unworthy to view even temporary glory without interruption,[22]

to prevent the glory of God from achieving its intended result, namely the judgment of the "stiff-necked" Israelites,[23]

to prevent the Israelites from continuing to gaze in amazement until his face had totally lost the brilliance of the reflected glory and to demonstrate that the glory of the Sinai covenant would be eclipsed.

Certain exegetical considerations support the feasibility of this last view. ἀτενίζω occurs fourteen times in the NT, twelve times in Luke-Acts, and twice

20. Dunn, "Lord" 311; Thrall 258 (Moses' action was educational, yet not without "some degree of intentional deception").

21. Provence 75-76.

22. Hughes 108-10; cf. Hickling 391 ("the end — like the beginning — of the period of transfiguration was too sacred for human gaze").

23. Hafemann, "Glory" 41; *Moses* 310-13, 354; "Comfort" 339; "Argument" 288-90; "Old Testament" 247-48; cf. Oostendorp 39-40. Hafemann argues (*Moses* 263-429; "Glory" 31-49; "Comfort" 339) that when 3:7-18 is read against the background of Exodus 32–34 it becomes clear that Paul has not deviated from the original meaning of the OT narrative in its canonical form but is providing a sober contextual interpretation. The Israelites could not gaze at the glory of the Lord reflected on Moses' face because they were a "stiff-necked people" (Exod. 32:9; 33:3, 5; 34:9), or, as Paul expresses it (3:14), "their minds were hardened." The veil was a symbol for the hard heart, yet also an expression of God's mercy, for without the veil the people would have been judged and destroyed by the reflected presence of God in the person of Moses (cf. Exod. 33:3, 5). Israel's sin prevented her from continually seeing God's glory. Hafemann renders 3:7b thus: the ministry of death came in glory "so that as a result, the sons of Israel were not able to gaze into the face of Moses because of the glory of his face, which was being rendered inoperative as to its effects" (namely divine judgment because of sin; "Glory" 40). 3:13 makes the same point with explicit reference to the purpose of the veil: Moses continually veiled himself "in order that . . . the sons of Israel might not look into the *telos* (gaze into the outcome or result) of that which was being rendered inoperative as to its effects" ("Glory" 40-41, 42). The veil pointed to sinfulness, but also prevented judgment. "In 2 Corinthians 3:7, 11, and 13 Paul's point is that the glory of Moses' face was rendered ineffective by the veil in that it stopped the destruction of the people that would otherwise have resulted" ("Comfort" 339).

One applauds Hafemann's concern to interpret Exod. 34:29-35 against its wider setting in chs. 32–34 and therefore to associate the themes of God's glory and Israel's sin (see also Dumbrell 180-85). But his interpretation creates some difficulties. (1) If the sight of God's glory brings judgment on sinners, how can one account for the regular, if brief, encounters between the Israelites and God's glory on the face of Moses (cf. Exod. 34:35)? (2) 2 Cor. 3:7 does not mention Moses' veil. Yet on Hafemann's view, such a reference is essential for the proper understanding of τὴν δόξαν . . . τὴν καταργουμένην. (3) If τὸ καταργούμενον in 3:11 has the same meaning as in 3:13 (as Hafemann assumes), how could "glory" come with glory (διὰ δόξης)? (4) The ideas of "gazing into an outcome" (*Moses* 365) and of "glory rendered inoperative in its effects" are unusual and awkward, if not impossible, notions. (5) Elsewhere in NT usage, ἀτενίζω always denotes physical sight, never mental recognition (see below). (6) On Hafemann's objection to the sense "fade" for καταργέομαι, see on 3:7.

in 2 Corinthians (3:7, 13). Outside the present verse, it always depicts physical sight, never mental recognition: "look intently at (something or someone)," never "perceive," "understand." In NT usage, ἀτενίζω describes an activity of the eyes, not of the mind. So it is highly improbable that 3:13b means "so that the people of Israel could not perceive the ultimate significance of that which was to be abolished."[24] Then the question arises whether anyone could be said to "look intently" (in a physical sense) at a "goal" (τέλος) or even to "gaze *steadily*" at the "end" (τέλος) of something.[25] Whereas in 3:7 ἀτενίζω εἰς means "gaze at," with τὸ πρόσωπον indicating the object, in 3:13 εἰς belongs with τὸ τέλος alone, meaning "until the end," "right to the end,"[26] with εἰς τὸ πρόσωπον αὐτοῦ understood from 3:7 as the object of ἀτενίσαι:[27] "to prevent the people of Israel from gazing steadily until the end of what was fading away." Also, an analysis of the NT use of ἀτενίζω shows that while the verb always denotes a fixed and prolonged gaze,[28] sometimes the context adds the connotation of expectation (Luke 4:20), terror (Acts 10:4), close inspection (Luke 22:56; Acts 11:6), or amazement (Acts 1:10; 3:12; 6:15). The idea of gazing in terror accords with the Israelites' reaction to the initial appearance of glory on Moses' face (Exod. 34:30); in fact they were unable to gaze steadily at his face on that occasion (2 Cor. 3:7). But with the repeated appearance of Moses before the people with a radiant face (Exod. 34:35), their initial fear would have turned to continual amazement, which may have prompted Moses to veil his face, lest they become preoccupied by his appearance as a divine "reflector" as opposed to his words as a divine spokesman.

But there may have been a second, closely related purpose in the veiling, as Paul understood it, implied in the substantival participle τοῦ καταργουμένου, "(until the end) of what was fading away." This neuter refers in the first

24. As Héring suggests (24). Cf. the awkward paraphrase of Martin (57): "to prevent the Israelites from fixing their eyes [to see] the significance of what was about to be done away."

25. Authorities who take τέλος in 3:13 in a teleological sense ("goal," "purpose," "significance") include Oostendorp 40 and n. 35; Rissi 32-33; Friesen 56-57; Badenas 75; Renwick 55, 135-45; Hafemann 155 n. 11; "Glory" 41; and especially Hays 136-40. Those who give τέλος a temporal meaning ("end," "termination," "cessation") include BAGD 811b; Collange 96; Furnish 201, 207, 232 ("extinction"); Schreiner 133; and especially Belleville, *Reflections* 201-2; Hofius, "Gesetz" 102-3, 110-11.

26. εἰς τέλος can mean "in the end" (Luke 18:5) but also "until the end" (Matt. 10:22; 24:13; Mark 13:13; BAGD 812a, citing also Epictetus 1.7.17; Josephus, *Antiquities* 19.96). τέλος is articular in 3:13 in accordance with "the canon of Apollonius," τοῦ καταργουμένου being naturally articular as a substantival participle. For the meaning "until" for εἰς in 3:13, see Bruce, *Paraphrase* 131; NEB; Cassirer; Hughes 109 n. 6 ("right on to the end"); Belleville 104 ("right down to the last glimmer"); *Reflections* 224 n. 1 ("right down to the end").

27. It is of interest that A *pc* b f* vg (bo^mss) read εἰς τὸ πρόσωπον in place of εἰς τὸ τέλος in 3:13. But this inferior reading necessitates taking τοῦ καταργουμένου as masculine, not neuter (as in 3:11).

28. On the general meaning of this verb, C. Mugber notes that it denotes "attentive and prolonged visual observation of an object" (*Dictionnaire historique de la terminologie optique des Grecs. Douze siècles de dialogues avec la lumière* [Paris: 1964] 63, cited by Spicq 1.227).

place to the δόξα of Moses' face[29] but also to the old covenant and its ministry (ἡ παλαιὰ διαθήκη in v. 14, ἡ διακονία τοῦ θανάτου/τῆς κατακρίσεως in vv. 7 and 9) of which the δόξα was a symbol.[30] Even at the time of Moses all three — glory, covenant, and ministry — had begun to "pass away" or "fade away."[31] The δόξα of Moses was therefore a symbol of both the splendor (3:7-8) and the impermanence (3:10, 13) of the old covenant. So each time Moses veiled his face (cf. ἐτίθει), he was dramatizing the impermanence of the newly established order.[32] Time after time his veil effected an eclipse of glory, an acted parable for the spiritually perceptive of the coming eclipse of the glory of the Sinai covenant.

On this view the purpose of Moses' veil was to prevent preoccupation with outward δόξα (cf. 5:14) and to point to the temporary character of the whole Mosaic system of covenant and law.[33] The first purpose is explicit (πρὸς τὸ κτλ.); the second is implicit in the neuter substantive τοῦ καταργουμένου.

3:14 ἀλλὰ ἐπωρώθη τὰ νοήματα αὐτῶν. ἄχρι γὰρ τῆς σήμερον ἡμέρας τὸ αὐτὸ κάλυμμα ἐπὶ τῇ ἀναγνώσει τῆς παλαιᾶς διαθήκης μένει. "But their minds were hardened. Indeed, right up to the present day, when the old covenant is read, that same veil remains there." Vv. 14 and 15 form Paul's commentary on Exod. 34:33b, 35, which he alluded to in v. 13 with "he [Moses] used to put a veil over his face." As in Romans 9–11, Paul here addresses the problem of Jewish unbelief regarding the Christian gospel. Perhaps some of Paul's opponents — possibly Jewish unbelievers in Corinth[34] — were suggesting to the Corinthian Christians that the general lack of response on the part of Jews to the Christian message was evidence that Jesus was not after all the Messiah and that Paul's gospel was not "good news." If Jesus so clearly fulfilled OT promises and if Paul's gospel was actually the new covenant prophesied by Jeremiah, why were the Jewish people not responding in greater numbers? If the background to 3:14-15 is some such Jewish reaction to Paul's ministry, we have

29. Cf. BAGD 811b, "the end of the fading (splendor)"; Zerwick, *Analysis* 396: τοῦ καταργουμένου refers to "the splendor on his [Moses'] face, whose fading showed the transitory nature of the Mosaic ministry (of Law)."

30. In 3:7 and 3:13 the reference to Moses' face (after ἀτενίσαι) is primary, and the allusion to the passing ministry and covenant secondary. In 3:11, on the other hand, the allusion to Moses' face comes with διὰ δόξης, not with τὸ καταργούμενον, which refers to the whole Mosaic economy.

31. For a defense of the rendering "fade away" for καταργέομαι in 3:13, see Belleville, *Reflections* 204-6.

32. If it be objected that the Israelites could learn the same lesson — the transient character of the old economy — by simply watching the splendor fade, one may observe that any degree of divine splendor — great or small, constant or fading — on a human face would so dazzle that it would be virtually impossible to perceive the significance of gradual fading — especially if the splendor was "recharged." A veiling, on the other hand, was a sudden eclipse of splendor.

33. It is possible for Paul to attribute a commendable motivation to Moses while contrasting his openness with Moses' concealment. But for the view that Moses' intent was to deceive the Israelites by concealing from them the transitory character of his glory (this being a type of the attitude of Paul's opponents), see Ulonska 378-88, especially 386.

34. Cf. Thrall 297; "Conversion" 197.

an adequate explanation of the transition from external veiling (v. 13) to internal veiling (vv. 14-15), from the Israelites of Sinai and the desert wanderings (v. 13) to the Jews of Paul's day (vv. 14-15).

ἀλλά ("but," "notwithstanding") points up a contrast with Moses' laudable attempt to have the Israelites realize the impermanence of the Sinaitic economy. Instead of recognizing the significance of the fading glory and Moses' veil, they became deadened in their powers of spiritual perception.[35] νόημα refers here to the faculty of thought and understanding. πωρόω comes from the noun πῶρος, a kind of marble used in building, and also any bony formation found on the joints, thus a "callus" that unites two parts of a fractured bone. The verb therefore had the medical sense "cause a callus to form," in the passive "become hard or thickened," and metaphorically "become insensitive or blind," intellectually or morally. πώρωσις, accordingly, means "petrifaction," "hardness," the "dulling" of perception.[36] ἐπωρώθη ("were hardened") may be a "theological passive" with God as the implied agent (cf. Deut. 29:4),[37] but an element of human agency need not be excluded.[38] Paul's point is that, unlike the Corinthians, whose hearts had become sensitive (καρδίαις σαρκίναις) due to the Spirit's softening work (3:3), the Israelites of Moses' day had calloused hearts that were insensitive to spiritual stimuli. The aorist ἐπωρώθη may be constative (of their continuous past state), or, as van Unnik suggests,[39] ingressive ("became hardened"). If Paul is already thinking of his Jewish contemporaries (in the αὐτῶν) as well as Jews of earlier times, the aorist may be gnomic ("are hardened"). The thought of hardened minds may have been prompted by recollection of Isa. 29:10 (the covering of the seers' heads) which is associated in Rom. 11:7-8 with divine hardening (cf. Isa. 6:9-10; Deut. 29:4),[40] but it is perhaps just as easy to find the link between vv. 13 and 14 in the repeated statement in Exodus 32–34 that the nation of Israel was "stiff-necked" (32:9; 33:3, 5; 34:9), unresponsive to the divine yoke.

γάρ is confirmatory ("indeed," NRSV).[41] ἄχρι . . . τῆς σήμερον ἡμέρας is clearly reminiscent of Deut. 29:3 LXX, ἕως τῆς ἡμέρας ταύτης, where Moses declares to the Israelites that "until the present day" Yahweh had not given them a heart (καρδίαν; cf. 2 Cor. 3:15) to understand, eyes to see, or ears to hear. In v. 13 Paul has spoken of a literal veil covering Moses' face. Now in vv. 14 and 15 he speaks of a figurative veil covering the hearts of Moses' descendants. He can call it the "same" veil in that it had the same effect of obscuring

---

35. There is little justification for the view of Collange (88-100) and Dalton (88-94) that in 3:14-16 Paul is responding to his Christian adversaries.

36. Cf. LSJ 1561 s.v.

37. Cf. Tasker 65, citing Rom. 11:7 and John 12:40.

38. Cf. Friesen 62-64, citing Exod. 7:13 (Pharaoh's heart was hardened) and 8:32 (Pharaoh hardened his heart). On this NT theme of πώρωσις or τύφλωσις ("blindness") see Lindars 159-67.

39. Van Unnik, "Face" 162.

40. Van Unnik, "Face" 162-63.

41. Thrall proposes, however, that γάρ here means "I say this because" (263 n. 510).

vision or hindering perception.[42] Paul likens the dulled minds of his Jewish contemporaries and their predecessors to hearts that have an obscuring veil permanently drawn across them: they fail to recognize the real purpose of "the old covenant" when it is publicly read in the synagogue on the Sabbath. ἐπὶ τῇ ἀναγνώσει means "at the public reading" (TCNT), "when (the old covenant) is read."[43] If ἐπί is rendered "upon (the reading),"[44] the implication is that three veils are mentioned in this paragraph — a literal one over Moses' face (v. 13), a metaphorical one over the old covenant (= Scripture) when it is read (v. 14), and a metaphorical one over the hearts of Paul's Jewish contemporaries (v. 15). But we should not overlook the distinction Paul draws between the veil that remains "at (the time of) the reading" (ἐπί + dative) and the veil that lies "over their hearts" (ἐπί + accusative). It is therefore preferable to see only two veils mentioned in vv. 13-15: one over Moses' face and another over Jewish hearts.[45]

The expression ἡ παλαιὰ διαθήκη, "the old covenant," may well be a Pauline coinage[46] as a natural deduction from Jeremiah's διαθήκη καινή (38:31, LXX) and from the eucharistic tradition of the cup as ἡ καινὴ διαθήκη ratified by Christ's blood (1 Cor. 11:25).[47] Here the phrase does not denote the OT as a whole[48] but the Sinaitic covenant in its written form, the Pentateuch, what v. 15 simply terms Μωϋσῆς.[49] Whereas the adjective ἀρχαῖος ("old") has the predominant sense of "ancient" or "venerable," παλαιός more often means "old" in the sense of "antiquated" or "dated." In the light of Paul's argument in 2:14–4:6 for the grandeur and superiority of the apostolic ministry, it is fair to observe that he has carefully chosen the adjectives he uses to qualify διαθήκη. The "old" covenant does not simply belong to former times (ἀρχαῖος); it is dated

---

42. Similarly Zerwick, *Analysis* 396. A. Oepke speaks of "an allegorical identity of type and antitype" (*TDNT* 3.560). Belleville prefers to see a similarity of function: "It is the 'same' veil because it serves to veil the covenantal glory down even to Paul's time" (*Reflections* 230-31).

43. BAGD 401a (cf. 503d, "at the reading"); similarly RSV, NEB, REB, NRSV. "At" = "at the time of," Plummer 93, 99; Barrett 110, 120; Furnish 202, 208.

44. E.g., Lietzmann 112; Friesen 61; Bultmann 86, 89; Thrall 237, 263.

45. *Pace* Fitzmyer ("Glory" 637), who finds four "uses" of the veil motif in 3:7-15.

46. So H. Seesemann, *TDNT* 5.720 n. 13.

47. While Hebrews refers to διαθήκη καινή (9:15; cf. 8:8) and διαθήκη νέα (12:24), it prefers the expression ἡ πρώτη διαθήκη (9:15; cf. 8:13) over Paul's ἡ παλαιὰ διαθήκη.

48. Carmignac (384-86) renders καινὴ διαθήκη in 3:6 by "New Testament" and ἡ παλαιὰ διαθήκη in 3:14 by "Old Testament," proposing that between A.D. 54 and 57 (the possible dates for 2 Corinthians) Paul could speak of a "New Testament," a collection that probably included 1 and 2 Thessalonians and 1 Corinthians, perhaps Galatians and even Philippians, along with Mark and possibly Matthew. Against this whole proposal, see Grelot 135-44; Furnish 184, 208-9. The most that can be said about the expression "at the reading of the old covenant" (3:14) is that Paul has unwittingly created for a later generation a useful distinction between the Scriptures of the old covenant and (potentially) any writings that would come to be associated with the new covenant. Cf. Richardson 230.

49. Dumbrell suggests that the reference is to "the Exod 19–34 selection [from the Torah]" (188).

(παλαιός). The "new" covenant does not simply belong to recent times (νέος); it is superior (καινός).

There are four main ways of construing the participle ἀνακαλυπτόμενον (see the commentary on 3:6).

> "The same veil remaineth unlifted; which *veil* is done away in Christ" (RV). Here ὅτι is construed as the neuter singular (ὅ τι) of the relative pronoun ὅστις. But in the only other uses of ὅ τι in Paul, the pronoun is indefinite, being followed by the indefinite particle ἐάν and the subjunctive (1 Cor. 16:2; Col. 3:17).[50]
>
> "The same veil *(voile)* . . . remains; [it] not being unveiled *(dévoilé)* to them that it [the old covenant] vanishes in Christ" (Allo).[51] In this case the participle is regarded as an accusative (or nominative) absolute and ὅτι becomes declarative ("that").[52] But given the use of ἀνακαλύπτω in v. 18 in reference to the removal of the veil, a general allusion to disclosure or revelation in this verse would lead us to expect ἀποκαλυπτόμενον.[53]
>
> "That same veil remains unlifted, because only through Christ is it taken away" (RSV).[54] On this view, the participle is predicative and ὅτι causal. But this understanding unduly minimizes the emphatic μένει, treating it as though it were simply ἐστί: "right up to the present day" the veil continues to stay (μένει) over the hearts of the Jews.
>
> "The same veil remains . . . , unlifted because (only) in Christ is it abolished" (Thrall).[55] This interpretation avoids the difficulties facing the other three options. The one difficulty of substance that attaches to this view is that elsewhere in the context (vv. 7, 11, 13) the verb καταργέομαι refers to what the veil covers, not to the veil itself, and in v. 16 the verb περιαιρέομαι is used to describe the removal of the veil. But, as Thrall suggests,[56] perhaps Paul has chosen a verb that aptly portrays the complete withdrawal, the final removal, of the veil, in contrast with Moses' veil, which was repeatedly removed and then put back on.

50. Thrall, "Conversion" 199 n. 7.

51. Allo 91, 93. This way of construing the participle is also advocated by A. P. Stanley 63; Moffatt; Montgomery; Hanson, *Ministry* 70; Prümm 1.142; Collange 99; Spicq 2.248. The last two authors take ἀνακαλυπτόμενον to be causal, "because it is not unveiled that. . . ."

52. The accusative absolute is rare in the NT (Robertson 490-91); the nominative absolute is more frequent (Robertson 459-60).

53. Cf. Bultmann 87.

54. Similarly NASB; BAGD 55c, 503d; Barrett 110, 120. Note also Field (182): "the same mystery [κάλυμμα standing for the thing veiled] . . . remaineth unrevealed, *namely* [ὅτι], that it [the old covenant] is done away in Christ."

55. Thrall 237, 265-66. Similarly Berkeley, NEB, JB, NJB, REB; A. Oepke, *TDNT* 3.561; Windisch 122; Furnish 202, 209; Wolff 69; Thielman 115-16.

56. Thrall 266; "Conversion" 200.

ὅτι ἐν Χριστῷ καταργεῖται. "Because only in Christ is it abolished." On the meaning of ὅτι and the reason for Paul's choice of the verb καταργέομαι, see the comments immediately above. Although μόνον ("only") does not stand before ἐν Χριστῷ, it is legitimate to supply it in translation on the basis of the unqualified absoluteness of "in Christ." This latter phrase may be expanded to mean "in union with Christ" (TCNT), "through union with Christ" (Goodspeed), "within the Christian community" (Thrall),[57] or "by being in Christ" (cf. ἐν Χριστῷ 'Ιησοῦ in Gal. 3:28).[58]

How καταργεῖται is translated depends in part on its implied subject. If the subject is taken to be the glory of the Mosaic covenant (cf. vv. 7, 13), then the verb will mean "is in the process of fading."[59] If the subject is the old covenant, the sense will be "is abrogated" (NEB), "is abolished" (Spicq 2.248), "is being annulled,"[60] or "is set aside" (Lietzmann, Schlatter).[61] Alternatively, if we take κάλυμμα as the subject, the verb may mean "is set aside" (NRSV), "is . . . abolished" (Thrall),[62] or "is . . . removed" (Goodspeed, Berkeley). The principal reason for preferring κάλυμμα as the subject is that, after τὸ αὐτὸ κάλυμμα . . . μένει, and then the neuter μὴ ἀνακαλυπτόμενον which naturally refers back to κάλυμμα, the reader would be hard pressed to envisage a change of subject with καταργεῖται.[63] It is certainly possible to see present tense καταργεῖται as denoting a process that was ongoing at the time of writing, but it is better, especially if κάλυμμα is the implied subject, to take it as a gnomic present, expressing a general truth, or as an iterative present, of the removal of the veil from a succession of hearts (cf. v. 15) when persons turn to the Lord (v. 16). If the old covenant were, in fact, the subject of καταργεῖται, we would have expected Paul to write κατήργηται ("has been annulled," "is void") or κατηργήθη ("was abrogated").

3:15 ἀλλ' ἕως σήμερον ἡνίκα ἂν ἀναγινώσκηται Μωϋσῆς κάλυμμα ἐπὶ τὴν καρδίαν αὐτῶν κεῖται. "Yes, to this very day, whenever Moses is read, a veil lies over their hearts." It is instructive to note the relationship between vv. 14 and 15:

v. 14	v. 15
1. τὰ νοήματα αὐτῶν	ἐπὶ τὴν καρδίαν αὐτῶν
2. ἄχρι . . . τῆς σήμερον ἡμέρας	ἕως σήμερον

57. Thrall 264; "Conversion" 210. Cf. Kümmel 200 ("in fellowship with Christ, in the Body of Christ").

58. Cf. Harris, "Prepositions" 1192.

59. Belleville 236; similarly Moffatt; Dunn, "Lord" 311 ("the old dispensation with its fading splendour").

60. Furnish 202, 210 (where he summarizes the arguments for taking "the old covenant" or "the veil" as the subject of καταργεῖται).

61. Lietzmann 112-13; Schlatter 516 (both have "beseitigt wird"). On this issue Friesen claims that "what is done away is the false idea of its [the old covenant's] finality and its independent authority apart from the gospel" (62).

62. Thrall 237, 266; "Conversion" 200.

63. Cf. Kümmel 200; Wolff 73-74.

3. τὸ αὐτὸ κάλυμμα   κάλυμμα
4. ἐπὶ τῇ ἀναγνώσει   ἡνίκα ἂν αςναγινώσκηται
5. τῆς παλαιᾶς διαθήκης   Μωϋσῆς
6. μένει   κεῖται

V. 15 is basically a restatement of v. 14 with some minor changes; ἀλλά, there-fore, means "Yes" (Moffatt, RSV, JB) or "Indeed" (NRSV).[64] Comments may now be made about each of the six points of comparison:

1. Like νόημα, καρδία may refer to the faculty of understanding, but here it probably has the wider connotation of a person's whole inner life, emotion and will as well as intellect. "Turning to the Lord" (v. 16), the appropriate re-sponse to the God of the new covenant, involves not merely the mind (the ap-prehension of the truth) but also the heart (the apprehension of the truth, the af-fection of the emotions, and the surrender of the will). καρδία is a distributive singular, "their hearts" (Turner 23).

2. No substantive distinction may be drawn between these two preposi-tional phrases. Both basically mean "until now" (= ἄχρι τοῦ νῦν, Rom. 8:22; or ἕως ἄρτι, 1 Cor. 15:6).

3. The fact that κάλυμμα is anarthrous in v. 15 is no indication that Paul is contemplating a different veil.[65] In his restatement of v. 14 he is simply reaf-firming that there is a veil which lies over Jewish hearts, referring to their in-ability to realize that the Mosaic order was temporary and their failure to recog-nize the glory of the new covenant. The veil was their blindness to truth, a τύφλωσις (cf. 4:4) that resulted from their πώρωσις (cf. 3:14).

4. There is precise parallelism here if ἐπί means "at the time of," "when." ἡνίκα ἄν, like ἡνίκα . . . ἐάν in v. 16, introduces an indefinite temporal clause, "whenever" (BAGD 348b); thus, "every time that Moses is read aloud" (BAGD 49a). Both the noun ἀνάγνωσις and the verb ἀναγινώσκω here refer to reading aloud in public (BAGD 49a, 51d, 52d), in this case, in the synagogue.[66]

5. Μωϋσῆς is here a metonym for the writings of Moses = "the old cove-nant" = the Pentateuch. That the prophets as well as "Moses" (Acts 15:21) were included in synagogue readings on the Sabbath is evident from Luke 4:16-17; Acts 13:27.

6. The two present tenses move the emphasis from the wilderness genera-tion (v. 14a) to the Jews of Paul's day. The resistance of the Jewish nation to Paul's gospel was foreshadowed in their obduracy during the time of Moses; there was scriptural precedent for a lack of response among Jews, so that Jew-

64. If v. 14 is taken to refer to a veil that is "upon (ἐπί) the reading of the old covenant," ἀλλά in v. 15 will be seen as intensifying ("what is more," Thrall 237, 266 n. 535) and so introduc-ing the new point that the veil does not really lie on the Scriptures themselves but on the hearts of those who hear them read. On the other hand, if ἀλλά bears its usual adversative sense, the contrast will be with the last clause in v. 14: "the veil is abolished in Christ, yet a veil remains."

65. *Pace* Belleville, *Reflections* 238.

66. See SB 4.154-65.

ish opposition to the gospel afforded no proof of Paul's apostolic illegitimacy, as some of his Jewish adversaries may have been alleging. The fault lay with the hearers of the message, not with the message or the messenger.

3:16 ἡνίκα δὲ ἐὰν ἐπιστρέψῃ πρὸς κύριον, περιαιρεῖται τὸ κάλυμμα. "But whenever someone turns to the Lord, that veil is removed." Paul has spoken of the hardened minds of Moses' generation (v. 14) and the veiled hearts of his own Jewish contemporaries (v. 15), just as he will soon speak of their blinded minds (4:4). He is clearly preoccupied with the reasons for Jewish unbelief. But, though he was deeply grieved by the general unresponsiveness of his compatriots to the gospel he proclaimed (Rom. 9:1-3), he realized that "the day of salvation" was still present (6:2), that the veil of ignorance concerning the new covenant and its glory could still be lifted from anyone's heart provided there was "conversion to the Lord."

Once again it will be useful to provide a visual comparison, this time between Paul's probable source and his use of it.

Exod. 34:34a	2 Cor. 3:16
1. ἡνίκα δ' ἂν	ἡνίκα δὲ ἐὰν
2. εἰσεπορεύετο	ἐπιστρέψῃ
3. Μωϋσῆς	
4. ἔναντι κυρίου	πρὸς κύριον
5. λαλεῖν αὐτῷ	
6. περιῃρεῖτο	περιαιρεῖται
7. τὸ κάλυμμα	τὸ κάλυμμα
8. ἕως τοῦ ἐκπορεύεσθαι	

Since so few words are identical between the two columns (only ἡνίκα and τὸ κάλυμμα), it is not surprising that some have denied that Paul is actually citing Exod. 34:34.[67] He does not quote precisely, but it is reasonable to suppose that he alludes primarily to that verse, or, to put the point another way, it was the principal OT basis for Paul's statement here;[68] ἡνίκα does not occur in the NT outside this verse and the preceding; the conjunction of περιαιρέομαι and τὸ κάλυμμα is found only in Exod. 34:34 and 2 Cor. 3:16 in the Greek Bible; the verb περιαιρέω is a *hapax legomenon* in Paul; Paul has been commenting on Exod. 34:29-35 in vv. 7-15, with ἐτίθει (v. 13) presupposing the iterative imperfects of Exod. 34:34 (LXX) that are not found elsewhere in this OT passage, so it comes as no surprise when he climaxes his use of Exodus 34 by referring to the removal of a veil; finally, adequate reasons may be given for the various changes Paul makes to the OT text:

1. No distinction can be drawn between ἡνίκα ἄν and ἡνίκα ἐάν, for ἐάν

67. E.g., Hermann 38; Wong 48 n. 1, 49-59.
68. Whether 3:16 should be classified as a citation with significant modifications, an allusive quotation, or a Pauline creation on the basis of Exod. 34:34 is therefore a moot question.

frequently stands for the indefinite particle ἄν, especially after relatives.[69] Both expressions may mean "whenever" = "every time that,"[70] a sense required with the iterative imperfect εἰσεπορεύετο in Exod. 34:34 and the present subjunctive ἀναγινώσκηται in 2 Cor. 3:15, and a meaning appropriate with the aorist subjunctive ἐπιστρέψῃ in 3:16.[71] Any sense of conditionality in 3:16 arises not from the particle ἐάν (as if it functioned here as a conditional conjunction, "if"),[72] but from the idea of indefiniteness that attaches to the frequentative use of ἡνίκα ἄν/ἐάν: "whenever" implies "if ever."[73]

2. Whereas the imperfect εἰσεπορεύετο depicts repeated entry (into "the tent of meeting") in the past on the part of a one person (Moses), the aorist ἐπιστρέψῃ signifies a single turning to the Lord in the future on the part of many persons. The change from εἰσπορεύεσθαι to ἐπιστρέφειν πρός was doubtless prompted by Paul's desire to express spiritual rather than physical movement, and possibly by his recollection of the use of ἐπιστρέφειν πρός in the same context (Exod. 34:31, of literal returning) and especially elsewhere in reference to a spiritual "turning to the Lord" (or, to God) in heartfelt repentance (e.g., 1 Kgdms. 7:3; Hos. 5:4; 6:1; Amos 4:6).[74] The closest NT parallel to 2 Cor. 3:16 is 1 Thess. 1:9, ". . . how you turned to God (ἐπεστρέψατε πρὸς τὸν θεόν) from idols," although the expression ἐπιστρέφειν ἐπὶ τὸν κύριον/ἐπὶ (τὸν) θεόν occurs several times in Acts.[75]

What is the implied subject of ἐπιστρέψῃ? Since αὐτῶν is the nearest antecedent, some propose that the subject is "any Jew" (cf. Rom. 11:14)[76] or "Israel"

69. BDF §107; BAGD 211d; Robertson 72, 80, 83, 181, 190-91. The reading ἡνίκα δ' ἄν in 3:16 (found in ℵᶜ B D *al;* WH margin) probably arose from assimilation to ἡνίκα ἄν in 3:15, which is a more literary form than ἡνίκα ἐάν. Cf. Plummer 102. On the elision of δέ, see Moulton and Howard 61.

70. Cf. LSJ 775 s.v. ἡνίκα; BAGD 348b, where a distinction is drawn between ἡνίκα ἄν with the present subjunctive (3:15), "whenever," and ἡνίκα ἐάν with the aorist subjunctive (3:16), "(at the time) when," "every time that."

71. "Whenever" is the rendering of ἡνίκα ἐάν in 3:16 found in TCNT, Weymouth, Moffatt, Goodspeed, Williams, Berkeley, NEB, NASB, GNB, Barclay, NAB¹, NIV, NAB², REB; and among the commentators, Barrett 110; Furnish 202; Martin 57; Thrall 237. Similarly Turner 113, citing Exod. 1:10 (LXX), καὶ ἡνίκα ἄν συμβῇ ἡμῖν πόλεμος ("and each time war breaks out for us").

72. *Pace* Wong 52-53.

73. Cf. ὅστις ἄν χέλῃ ("whoever wishes") = ἐάν τις θέλῃ ("if anyone wishes"), cited by BDF §377(1) in a different connection.

74. It is not impossible, although incapable of proof, that Paul was dependent on a Greek text of Exodus that read ἐπέστρεψεν (suggested by A. Oepke, *TDNT* 3.560; Bultmann 89) or ἐπέστρεφεν (suggested by Windisch 123). Le Déaut seeks to explain Paul's modification of Exod. 34:34 on the basis of his use of a "haggadic gloss" found in *Targum Pseudo-Jonathan* Exod. 33:7b, "everyone who used to return and show repentance with a perfect heart in the presence of Yahweh would go out to the tent . . ." (46). Similarly McNamara (180-81), who sees Paul in 2 Corinthians 3 as "merely christianizing a midrash already formed within Judaism" (*Paraphrases* 112). But Hickling points out that the only precise point of contact is between ἐπιστρέψῃ and *dhdr* ("who used to return"; 394 n. 1).

75. Acts 9:35; 11:21; 14:15; 15:19; 26:20; cf. 1 Pet. 2:25.

76. E.g., Belleville, *Reflections* 249-50.

as a nation (cf. Rom. 11:25-26).[77] Others appeal to the preceding expression ἐπὶ τὴν καρδίαν αὐτῶν and therefore suggest "their heart(s)"[78] or simply "the heart."[79] Other alternatives include Moses as a type of the Christian convert,[80] or an indefinite τις, "anyone," whether Jew or Gentile.[81] The very generality of this latter proposal makes it attractive,[82] for it accommodates the principal subjects of the preceding verses (Jews) yet does justice to the aphoristic nature of the verse, which would point to the inclusion of Gentiles, particularly since Paul's thought is probably already moving toward the climactic statement in v. 18, ἡμεῖς πάντες, "we, all of us," apostles and non-apostles, Jews and non-Jews.

3., 5., and 8. In order to universalize the Exodus passage and make it applicable to Christian conversion, Paul was compelled to omit the references to Moses, the purpose of Moses' encounter with Yahweh, and Moses' ensuing departure from Yahweh's presence and the implied replacement of the veil on his face.

4. Here the change is from entering the Lord's presence or being before the Lord (ἔναντι κυρίου) in "the tent of meeting," to turning to the Lord (πρὸς κύριον) in conversion. Although many scholars identify the κύριος in Paul's statement as Christ,[83] it is preferable to maintain an identity of referent from Exodus 34 to 2 Corinthians 3, namely Yahweh.[84] In Exod. 34:34 κύριος is undoubtedly Yahweh.[85] This is especially so since in each case κύριος is anarthrous, and in Pauline usage κύριος is usually Yahweh and ὁ κύριος is normally the Lord Jesus,[86] so that if κύριος in 3:16 referred to Jesus, we would expect

77. E.g., Windisch 123 ("in accordance with the analogy of Jer. 4:1": ἐὰν ἐπιστραφῇ Ἰσραήλ, λέγει κύριος, πρός με ἐπιστραφήσεται); Zerwick, *Analysis* 396 (Paul considers Moses' action of turning to the Lord a type of the future conversion of the people of Israel to the Lord); Wendland 181-82; Dumbrell 188.

78. E.g., Allo 92; Montgomery; cf. Weymouth: "whenever the heart of the nation shall have returned to the Lord." Dunn sees a designed ambiguity in the unspecified subject: both Moses and the Jews ("Lord" 313 n. 1).

79. E.g., Barrett 110, 122; Stockhausen 89 and n. 9.

80. E.g., Thrall 271.

81. "Anyone" (Furnish 202, 210-11, 234; similarly Wong 54); "anybody" (Williams); "a person" (NAB²); "one" (Berkeley, NRSV); "a man" (TCNT, RSV).

82. Some go one step further and make ἐπιστρέψῃ impersonal: "whenever there is a turning to the Lord" (Martin 57, 70; similarly Carrez 94; Wolff 69).

83. BAGD 460a; Meyer 477; Plummer 102 ("Κύριον here clearly means Christ, for it balances ἐν Χριστῷ, and Jews had no need to turn to Jehovah"); Windisch 123; Prat 2.437-38; Ulonska 387; Hermann 39-43; Rissi 36; Friesen 65; Capes 156-57. Kim argues that in 3:16-18 Paul alludes to the Damascus christophany: Paul regarded his own conversion as a paradigm for Christian conversion in that it involved two elements, "turning to the Lord [Jesus, 12 n. 6] and seeing the perfect revelation of God in Christ" (231).

84. Göttsberger 14; Schildenberger 457-58; Dunn, "Lord" 317; Collange 111, 125; Moule, "2 Cor. 3:18b" 234-35; Furnish 211-12, 234; Belleville, *Reflections* 255; Thrall 272-73, 278-82; "Conversion" 208-9, 214-15; Hafemann 160; *Moses* 392.

85. But Hanson ("Midrash" 1-22) argues that Paul understood Moses to have seen and conversed with the preexistent Christ in the sanctuary. So also R. P. C. Hanson 40; Oostendorp 42.

86. Cf. Zerwick §169; Turner 174; *Insights* 127.

Paul to have obviated ambiguity by writing either πρὸς τὸν κύριον or πρὸς κύριον Ἰησοῦν. There is also the consideration[87] that if turning to "the Lord" brings about the removal of the veil and thereby the new recognition that Jesus as Messiah is at the heart of the new covenant, then the turning must be toward Yahweh, not Jesus.

6. Although Paul employs the same verb (περιαιρέομαι) as Exod. 34:34,[88] he substitutes the present for the imperfect, to correspond to the indefinite future implied in ἡνίκα . . . ἐὰν ἐπιστρέψῃ ("whenever someone turns") and possibly to suggest the immediacy of the removal of the veil after the "conversion."[89] It is certainly possible that περιαιρεῖται, like περιῃρεῖτο, should be construed as middle ("he removes [the veil]") with either the believer[90] or the Lord[91] as the subject. But if the removal of the veil produces illumination to hardened or darkened minds (cf. 3:14; 4:4), divine agency seems more probable ("the veil is removed," passive), especially in the light of 3:18 and 4:6. The implied agent would then be "the Lord" (= Yahweh or Christ, depending on the identification of κύριος in v. 16a), or conceivably the Spirit (in anticipation of v. 17a).

7. If the κάλυμμα of Exod. 34:34 was the dark veil over Moses' face concealing the fading divine radiance, the κάλυμμα of 3:16 is the veil of darkness over the hearts of Jews and others that conceals the truth about the new covenant and Christ (3:14-15). With v. 16 alluding to vv. 14-15, the article with κάλυμμα is anaphoric: "that veil."

Paul was not discouraged as he contemplated his ministry, for he knew that although blindness of heart had to some degree befallen Israel (Rom. 11:25) so that even when the books of Moses were read, his Jewish contemporaries were largely unresponsive to the truth, yet any Jew, or for that matter any Gentile, who turned to the Lord God in repentance and faith, would have the veil of darkness permanently removed from his or her heart, just as in his own case "something like scales" had fallen from his eyes at his conversion (Acts 9:18). The gospel never will lose its potency as God's instrument to bring salvation to all who believe in it (Mark 1:15; Rom. 1:16).

3:17 ὁ δὲ κύριος τὸ πνεῦμά ἐστιν. οὗ δὲ τὸ πνεῦμα κυρίου, ἐλευθερία. "Now this 'Lord' is the Spirit, and where the Spirit of the Lord is, there is freedom." Few sentences in the New Testament have prompted more debate than

---

87. Cf. Belleville, *Reflections* 255.

88. If the prefix περι- retains any distinctive sense in this verb, it is not "(remove) from around" (*pace* Robertson 617-18; *Pictures* 222-23) but "(remove) completely" (intensive περι-; see Moulton and Howard 321).

89. Cf. Wand: "The moment they turn to the Lord that veil will be taken away." Hafemann takes ἡνίκα (ἐ)άν ("whenever") in v. 15 to mean "as often as," and in v. 16 "as soon as" (*Moses* 388).

90. "As in Exod., the verb is probably middle, not passive; 'but whenever one turns, he *ipso facto* takes away the veil: his own act of conversion removes it'" (Plummer [CGT] 65).

91. Barrett 110, 122; *Paul* 134; Richard 357.

this linguistically simple statement. Yet there is virtually a scholarly consensus regarding four related issues:[92]

Verse 17a must be interpreted in light of v. 16; both passages refer to a κύριος, presumably one and the same κύριος.

Word order and the use of κύριος in v. 16 make it probable that ὁ κύριος, not τὸ πνεῦμα, is the subject in v. 17a.[93]

Because good sense may be made of v. 17b as it stands, there is no need to resort to textual emendation.[94]

Because plausible connections of thought can be discerned between vv. 17-18 and vv. 7-16, there is no reason to classify vv. 17 and 18b as a Gnostic marginal gloss incorporated into the text.[95]

Assuming, then, that v. 17a relates in the first place to v. 16 and that ὁ κύριος is the subject in v. 17a, we may sketch the two main interpretations of the statement ὁ δὲ κύριος τὸ πνεῦμά ἐστιν. The still dominant view identifies the κύριος of vv. 16 and 17a as the risen Lord Jesus.[96] Proponents of this view must immediately address the questions: Does τὸ πνεῦμα refer to the Holy Spirit? If so, does ἐστίν serve to identify the risen Christ as the Holy Spirit? Almost all those who see here a reference to the Spirit carefully distinguish between functional equivalence or dynamic unity or "economic" identity on the one hand, and personal identification on the other,[97] for the phrase τὸ πνεῦμα κυρίου that

92. For a history of the interpretation of this verse, see B. Schneider 35-36; Prümm, "Auslegung" 316-45, 459-82; and the references in Belleville, *Reflections* 258 n. 2.

93. If τὸ πνεῦμα were the subject, Paul would probably have written either κύριος δὲ τὸ πνεῦμά ἐστιν (cf. John 1:1c; 4:24) or τὸ δὲ πνεῦμα ὁ κύριός ἐστιν (cf. John 6:63; 1 John 3:4). 3:17-18 figured prominently in early church discussions about the deity of the Holy Spirit, with the Greek Fathers often appealing to 3:17a and 3:18b to show that the Spirit "is called Lord" (κυριολογεῖται), that is, he is "God"; but, significantly, κύριος is always anarthrous in their restatement of Paul. For example, "Oecumenius well sums up the usual exegesis of the Greeks when he says . . . : Μὴ φοβοῦ, καὶ πρὸς τὸ Πνεῦμα ἐπιστρέφων πρὸς Κύριον ἐπιστρέφεις. Κύριος γὰρ τὸ Πνεῦμα καὶ ὁμοπροσκύνητον καὶ ὁμοούσιον Πατρὶ καὶ Υἱῷ" (Prat 2.436, emphasis added), "Do not fear, when you turn to the Spirit, you are turning to the Lord [God]. For the Spirit is the Lord and is adored in the same way as the Father and the Son and is of the same essence as the Father and the Son."

94. At least six different emendations have been proposed. (1) In place of ὁ: οὗ (J. Le Clerc, followed by Giglioli 263-76), "Now where the Lord (= Christ) is, the Spirit is in place." (2) In place of οὗ: (a) οὐ (Turner, *Insights* 128, "very tentatively"), "But the Spirit is not independent of the Lord" (= Yahweh); (b) a repeated οὗ: οὗ δὲ ὁ κύριος, τὸ πνεῦμά ἐστιν· οὗ δὲ τὸ πνεῦμα, κυρίου ἐλευθερία (Héring 25-27), "For where the Lord is, there is the Spirit (or spirit); and where the Spirit (or spirit) is, there is the liberty of the Lord." (3) In place of κυρίου: (a) κυριεύει (Michelsen, cited by Windisch 126; cf. MM 365a), "Where the Spirit rules, there is freedom"; (b) κύριον (Hort in WH 2. Appendix 119), "Where the Spirit is ruling, there is freedom"); (c) κύριος (Dobschütz, cited by Hughes 116 n. 16), "Where the spirit/Spirit is the Lord, there is liberty."

95. This view is defended by Schmithals 315-25. For a critique, see Thrall 278.

96. E.g., Hermann 39; Larsson 277; Friesen 67-68; Wolff 76.

97. E.g., Griffiths 82; Hill 278-79.

immediately follows in v. 17b prohibits any such equation of persons, as does Paul's regular differentiation between Christ and the Spirit.[98] The two are functionally or dynamically or experientially equivalent in that the Spirit mediates to believers the presence and power of the absent and exalted Lord, applying the benefits of Christ's redemption. Others regard τὸ πνεῦμα as the life-giving Spirit or spirit (cf. πνεῦμα ζῳοποιοῦν, 1 Cor. 15:45) of the new era, so that Christ is here described as the source of spiritual life and blessing.[99] Some equate τὸ πνεῦμα with the heavenly mode of existence or sphere or "substance."[100] Yet others identify τὸ πνεῦμα in 3:17a with τὸ πνεῦμα in 3:6: the Lord Christ is the inner, true meaning of Scripture, "the spiritual and prophetic sense hidden under the letter."[101]

The second main interpretation views v. 17a as a clarifying "update" on v. 16. "The 'Lord' (= Yahweh) of Exod. 34:34 is, in the present era, the Spirit mentioned in 3:3, 6, 8." In this case the article with κύριος is anaphoric:[102] "Now the Lord of whom this passage speaks is the Spirit" (NEB, REB), "Now what is signified by 'Lord' here is the Spirit" (Cassirer). Whereas in the old dispensation Moses was in the habit of removing the veil from his face whenever he entered "the tent of meeting" to converse with Yahweh, in the new order, when a person turns to the Spirit, the veil over the heart is forever removed. Support for this general understanding of v. 17a has been gaining momentum since Dunn's influential defense of the position in 1970.[103]

This view has two advantages: it ties v. 17a more closely to the immediate context than do competing interpretations, and it affords a more satisfying explanation of the use of the article with κύριος in vv. 16-18: the four anarthrous uses of κύριος refer to Yahweh, as does the one articular (= anaphoric) use in v. 17a. But it also prompts two questions. First, would Paul have "updated" Exodus 34 in such a bold manner? Comparable contemporizing of the biblical text is found at Qumran ("pesher" exegesis) and in Philo ("allegorizing" exegesis).[104] And

98. E.g., Rom. 1:4; 8:9; 1 Cor. 12:3; 2 Cor. 13:13; Gal. 4:6; Phil. 1:19. On this whole issue see Fatehi.

99. E.g., Stevens 443 ("the life-giving Spirit"); Hughes 115-16 ("life-giving spirit").

100. E.g., Jervell 268-69. Cf. Schweizer, *TDNT* 6.419: "πνεῦμα is defined as the mode of existence of the κύριος . . . and this means the power in which He encounters His community."

101. E.g., Prat 2.440; Göttsberger 14; Allo 93-96, 107-10.

102. Zerwick §169; *Analysis* 397 (in both places this is noted as a possibility); Turner, *Insights* 127. If, as Belleville proposes (*Reflections* 267), v. 17a should be translated "Now *the term* 'Lord' refers to the Spirit" (italics added), we would have expected τὸ δὲ κύριος (cf. Gal. 4:25, τὸ δὲ Ἁγάρ; Eph. 4:9).

103. Dunn, "Lord" 309-20, especially 313, 317; *Baptism* 136; Moule, "2 Cor 3:18b" 235; Collange 111; Scharlemann 116; Furnish 202, 212, 236; Martin 57, 70-71; Kruse 99; Talbert 145; Wright 144; Stockhausen 10, 130; Belleville 110; *Reflections* 261-62, 267; Watson 36; Thrall 274, 281; "Conversion" 213, 216; Fee, *Presence* 311-12; Hafemann 160; *Moses* 397-400. Earlier proponents of this general position include Bernard 57-58; Grech 421-22; Kümmel 200; Schildenberger 457-58; McNamara 183, 187-88 (a reference to Christ is also implied); *Paraphrases* 112.

104. See Belleville (*Reflections* 263-67) for documentation.

Paul himself elsewhere engages in similar contemporization by way of an exegetical gloss in, for example, Gal. 3:16; 4:25 (τὸ δὲ Ἁγὰρ Σινᾶ ὄρος ἐστὶν ἐν τῇ Ἀραβίᾳ); Rom. 10:6; 1 Cor. 15:56. Within 2 Corinthians we find the repeated ἰδοὺ νῦν of 6:2 contemporizing Isa. 49:8. Second, are there biblical parallels for the idea of "conversion to the Spirit"? In both Testaments an individual's "turning" in repentance is normally "to God."[105] But if human beings may rebel against the Spirit of God (Ps. 106:33), resist him (Acts 7:51), grieve him (Isa. 63:10; Eph. 4:30), and insult him (Heb. 10:29), presumably they may also "turn" to him in the sense of responding to his gracious overtures and in particular his gentle urging of the claims of the Messiah. When a person turns to the Spirit, he (the Spirit) immediately removes the veil of ignorance concerning Christ. Dunn proposes that turning to the Spirit simply means receiving the Spirit.[106]

Having supplied his brief exegetical gloss (δέ, "now") in v. 17a, Paul adds (δέ, "and") that the Spirit to whom people turn in the new dispensation brings them freedom. Wherever the Spirit of the Lord (God) is present and active, liberty is enjoyed and compulsion is absent. Although we might expect οὗ ("where") to be followed by ἐκεῖ ("there") (as in Matt. 18:20; Rom. 9:26), this is not always the case in Paul (see Rom. 4:15; 5:20). Because the expression πνεῦμα (τοῦ) κυρίου is so common in the LXX, in reference to the Spirit of Yahweh,[107] and is never used by Paul,[108] it is probable that κύριος here refers not to the Lord Jesus but to Yahweh. In the light of the canon of Apollonius, the anarthrous κυρίου may appear irregular, but since κύριος, like θεός, has virtually become a proper noun in the NT, the imprecision of articular usage that attaches to proper names has affected κύριος also.[109]

What is the nature of the ἐλευθερία that the Spirit mediates? First of all, it is doubtful that it includes hermeneutical freedom, as Hays argues — freedom from reading Scripture "slavishly according to the *gramma*," a freedom that involves "a transformed capacity to perceive the *telos* of Scripture" through Spirit-inspired reading.[110] It is significant that ἐλευθερία is unqualified, which suggests that Paul would not wish to exclude any type of freedom that is implied in the context, such as the freedom to speak and act openly (= παρρησία, v. 12);[111] freedom from the veil (vv. 14-16),[112] whether the veil of spiritual ignorance concerning truths of the new covenant[113] or the veil of hardheartedness

---

105. E.g., Deut. 30:10; Ps. 51:13; Isa. 55:7; Acts 14:15; 20:21; 1 Thess. 1:9.

106. Dunn, *Baptism* 136, following Lietzmann 113.

107. E.g., Judg. 6:34; 11:29; 1 Kgdms. 16:13-14; Isa. 11:2.

108. The expression is found only in Luke 4:18 (citing Isa. 61:1); Acts 5:9; 8:39.

109. Cf. Moule 115; Turner 174; Harris, *Jesus* 305-7, especially 306 n. 29.

110. Hays 149-53 (quoting 149, 151). Cf. Richardson 122: "What Paul is saying is that the Spirit (of Christ) is Lord of the Scriptures, and where the Spirit reigns there is full liberty of interpretation; we are no longer fettered by 'the letter' (cf. 3.6), i.e. the literalism which deadens."

111. Thielman 116; cf. van Unnik 165-66.

112. Wong 59, 63-64, 70.

113. Belleville, *Reflections* 270.

(vv. 13, 14);[114] freedom from the old covenant (v. 14)[115] or from the law and its effects (v. 6);[116] freedom to behold God's glory uninterruptedly (v. 18) or to conform to Christ (v. 18);[117] or freedom of access into the divine presence without fear.[118]

3:18 ἡμεῖς δὲ πάντες ἀνακεκαλυμμένῳ προσώπῳ τὴν δόξαν κυρίου κατοπτριζόμενοι. "And all of us, with unveiled faces, looking at the glory of the Lord as in a mirror." As he now develops (δέ, "and") the concept of freedom (ἐλευθερία, v. 17), especially the notions of freedom from veiling and freedom of access to God, Paul explicitly extends his thought to all Christian believers (ἡμεῖς . . . πάντες), whether or not they are Jews or apostles or gospel ministers.[119] With regard to access to God, πάντες eliminates all distinction between God's messengers and those to whom they are sent (cf. 1:21-22; 5:10). The one and the many of Exodus 34 (Moses and the Israelites) have become the "all" of 2 Corinthians 3. It was the privilege of Moses alone to glimpse Yahweh's glory when he saw his "form" (Num. 12:8) and his "back" (Exod. 33:23),[120] but now all Christians without distinction are privileged to witness that glory. Moreover, although Moses' face was unveiled when he was conversing with God and was reporting God's words to the congregation, it was thereafter veiled until he returned to the Lord's presence (Exod. 34:33-35). Christians, however, see the divine glory with permanently uncovered faces. The perfect participle ἀνακεκαλυμμένῳ stresses the permanence and irreversibility of their unveiled state. προσώπῳ is a distributive singular[121] and refers figuratively (by metonymy) to recognition and understanding so that the whole phrase ἀνακεκαλυμμένῳ προσώπῳ ("with unveiled faces"), which expresses accompanying circumstances[122] or manner[123] in relation to κατοπτριζόμενοι,[124] refers to the unimpeded vision of Christians in contrast to the impeded vision of Jews (vv. 14-15). An unremoved veil prevents recognition of the glory of the new covenant. A re-

114. Hafemann 160; "Comfort" 341; "Glory" 43.

115. Provence 81.

116. Barrett 123-24; cf. Hofius, "Gesetz" 120 (freedom from the Law's indictment and sentence of death). But Cranfield ("Law" 60) believes the ἐλευθερία to be freedom to obey the Law.

117. Davies, *Studies* 105.

118. Robertson, *Pictures* 223; Bruce, *Paul* 121; Scharlemann 117; Baker 14-15 ("freedom to come close to God, to live in his glory without harm").

119. But Belleville restricts ἡμεῖς πάντες to "all true gospel ministers without exception" (*Reflections* 276; cf. 275-76, 296).

120. Although Moses spoke to God "face to face" (Exod. 33:11), he did not see his "face," "for no one may see me and live" (33:20; cf. 33:23). Similarly, in the burning bush incident God appeared to Moses (Exod. 3:2, 4, 16) but his face was not seen, for Moses "was afraid to look at God" (3:6; cf. W. Michaelis, *TDNT* 5.331-33). See also Thrall 295; "Conversion" 228-29.

121. Cf. Turner 23.

122. Thrall 282 n. 654; "Conversion" 219.

123. Robertson 530; *Pictures* 223; Zerwick and Grosvenor 540. NEB and REB construe the phrase as causal: "because for us there is no veil over the face."

124. But Goodspeed ("reflecting . . . in our unveiled faces") and Spicq 1.419 ("reflecting on unveiled faces"; but cf. 2.248) take the dative to be locative.

moved veil not only guarantees recognition of that glory but also enables participation in that glory.[125]

In the active voice, the verb κατοπτρίζω (from κάτοπτρον = ἔσοπτρον [1 Cor. 13:12], "mirror") means "produce a reflection in a mirror"; in the middle, the sense is "look at oneself/something in the mirror."[126] In Hellenistic Greek both the active and the passive sense encroach on the domain of the middle, so that κατοπτρίζομαι as a middle could on occasion mean "reflect."[127] On the other hand, the ancient versions usually render this verb (which does not occur elsewhere in the Greek Bible) by "behold," "observe,"[128] and the notion of transformation by vision (κατοπτριζόμενοι . . . μεταμορφούμεθα) is more readily comprehensible than that of transformation by reflection, given a passage such as 1 John 3:2 (. . . ὅμοιοι αὐτῷ ἐσόμεθα, ὅτι ὀψόμεθα αὐτὸν καθώς ἐστιν). It is possible that the original reference to a mirror (κάτοπτρον) has been lost and that the verb simply means "look at" or "contemplate"[129] and is therefore almost equivalent to ἀτενίζω (vv. 7, 13).[130] But the real options are: "reflect like a mirror/as in a mirror"[131] or "behold/see as in a mirror."[132] This latter alternative is to be preferred. Some find both ideas in the verb ("see and then reflect"),[133] but the idea of reflection is rather contained by implication in the subsequent word εἰκών, which is a visible representation (or reflection) of some reality.

What Christians observe as though (reflected) in a mirror is "the glory of the Lord" (τὴν δόξαν κυρίου).[134] As in the parallel expression τὸ πνεῦμα κυρίου in v. 17, κύριος probably refers to Yahweh, not Jesus. In LXX usage (ἡ) δόξα κυρίου frequently refers to the glory of Yahweh, including, significantly, pas-

125. Cf. Friesen 59.
126. Cf. BAGD 424d; G. Kittel, *TDNT* 2.696. Robertson (810) classifies κατοπτριζόμενοι as an indirect middle: "beholding for ourselves in a mirror"; similarly Winer 254.
127. See Belleville (*Reflections* 280) for examples.
128. G. Kittel, *TDNT* 2.697.
129. Hugedé 54, 63; Hanson, "Midrash" 21.
130. Cf. Bultmann 94-95.
131. τὰ κατοπτρικά are "reflected images" and κατοπτρικῶς means "by reflection" (LSJ 929d). Among the English translations, "reflect" is found in RV, Weymouth, Moffatt ("mirror"), Goodspeed, Montgomery, Williams, NEB, GNB, JB, NIV. Among the commentators, Plummer 105-6 (but cf. 93); Schlatter 519-20; Allo 96-97; Dupont 119-20; "Chrétien" 400; Héring 25, 27; van Unnik, "Face" 167; Prümm 1.166, 175-79; de Boor 80; Spicq 2.248; Hooker, "Scripture" 301; Carrez 94, 101; Young and Ford 265; Stockhausen 89, 90 n. 11, 151; Belleville, *Reflections* 278-82.
132. English versions that have "behold" or "see" include TCNT, Berkeley, RSV, NASB, Barclay, NAB[1, 2], REB, NRSV. Among the commentators, Lietzmann 112-13; Göttsberger 15; Wendland 181; Kümmel 200; Barrett 110; Lambrecht, "Transformation" 296, 298-301; Furnish 202, 214; Martin 57, 71; Lang 273, 275-76; Wolff 69, 77-78; Thrall 238, 282, 290-92; Fee, *Presence* 316-17.
133. E.g., Bruce 193; *Paraphrase* 133 ("we reflect the glory upon which we look"); Kim 13 n. 2, 232, 237 (but, following Jervell [184-85], he regards "see as in a mirror" as the primary significance).
134. On the anarthrous state of κυρίου, see above on the phrase τὸ πνεῦμα κυρίου (3:17).

sages that refer to Sinai (Exod. 24:17) and the "tent of meeting" (Exod. 40:34-35; Lev. 9:5-6, 23; Num. 14:10; 16:19). Also, in 4:6 Paul refers to ἡ δόξα τοῦ θεοῦ ἐν προσώπῳ Ἰησοῦ Χριστοῦ, a composite statement which shows how ἡ δόξα τοῦ θεοῦ is related to Christ as [ἡ] εἰκὼν τοῦ θεοῦ (4:4). "The glory of the Lord" is God's glory as it is revealed in his image, Christ. If we must identify the "mirror" in which God's glory is seen, it is more likely to be Christ as present in the gospel[135] or the gospel, the essence of which is Christ,[136] or the gospel along with the Christian life as lived in the Spirit,[137] than gospel ministers[138] or Christians in general.[139]

A. L. Connolly has noted that in Classical writers mirror imagery commonly symbolized three ideas: purity (associated with a mirror's clean surface),[140] self-knowledge (as also in Jas. 1:23), or indirect knowledge (as also in 1 Cor. 13:12; 2 Cor. 3:18).[141] All "mirrored" knowledge is of necessity indirect knowledge, but indirect knowledge is not necessarily imprecise or inaccurate knowledge; a "mirror image" is indirect but may be perfectly clear. Significantly, there is here no ἐν αἰνίγματι ("dimly," "with blurring") as in 1 Cor. 13:12. The vision of God's glory accorded Christians is indirect, for it is mediated through the gospel, but it is clear, for the Christ who is proclaimed through the gospel is the exact representation (εἰκών) of God (4:4).

τὴν αὐτὴν εἰκόνα μεταμορφούμεθα ἀπὸ δόξης εἰς δόξαν. "We are being transformed into the same image, from one degree of glory to another." In the active voice the verb μεταμορφόω is followed by two accusatives, τινά τι, "transform someone into something"; in the passive, the accusative of the thing is retained — here τὴν αὐτὴν εἰκόνα.[142] αὐτήν has no explicit antecedent, but means "the same image as we see mirrored,"[143] that is, Christ as God's glory or God in Christ, rather than "the same image as each other,"[144] pointing to the family likeness of Christians. Although it is now the whole person rather than the face alone that reflects God's glory, Paul must be thinking principally of the transformation of "the inner person" (4:16b), the whole person as a "new cre-

---

135. Thrall, "Conversion" 217; cf. her commentary 283-85.
136. Vincent 818.
137. Lambrecht, "Transformation" 302-3, 307.
138. Belleville, *Reflections* 281 n. 1.
139. Wright 145-49.
140. It is inappropriate for commentators to observe (as is sometimes done) that since in Paul's time most mirrors were made of polished metal their image was imperfect, so that Paul is here implying the defective character of the mirrored image (as he actually does in 1 Cor. 13:12, δι' ἐσόπτρου ἐν αἰνίγματι . . . ἐκ μέρους).
141. A. L. Connolly in Horsley 4.150. Cf. Dupont 121-35.
142. Cf. BDF §159(4); Robertson 486. There is therefore no need to supply κατά (as Héring 27, but cf. his n. 22) or εἰς with τὴν αὐτὴν εἰκόνα.
143. Cf. JB, NJB: "the image that we reflect."
144. Wright 147; Belleville, *Reflections* 290 ("so to speak — carbon copies of one another"), 296 ("mirror images of each other"). Cf. Dumbrell 189 (the goal of the transformation is the same: recovery of the divine image, Gen. 1:26).

ation" (5:17) and as a participant in the life of the age to come, for he observes that "the outer person," the whole person as a mortal creature, is being worn down (4:16a), not transformed. When Jesus was transfigured, the change was outwardly visible (Matt. 17:2), but when Christians are transformed, the change is essentially inward, the renewing of the mind (Rom. 12:2), and becomes visible only in their Christ-like behavior.[145] The present participle κατοπτριζόμενοι defines the means of the ongoing transformation (μεταμορφούμεθα, present): it is by "seeing as in a mirror" that "change" is effected.[146] For Christians, both now and in the hereafter, there is "transformation by vision."[147] But whereas the present transformation is continuous and progressive and the vision is of an image (Christ as εἰκὼν θεοῦ), the future transformation is instantaneous and complete and the vision is direct (1 Cor. 13:12; 15:49; 1 John 3:2).[148]

The progressive nature of this present μεταμόρφωσις is expressed by the phrase ἀπὸ δόξης εἰς δόξαν. If ἀπό denotes source and εἰς result, this beginning and this end must both relate to believers' transformation and δόξα, for the whole phrase qualifies μεταμορφούμεθα. Therefore the meaning is less likely to be "from the Jewish vision of Yahweh's glory to the Christian vision of the glory of the new dispensation"[149] or *from* the splendor of the Lord *to* the splendor of the believer[150] than *from* initial glory already received through regeneration *to* final glory to be gained at the parousia[151] or *from* glory beheld *to* glory reflected.[152] Alternatively, and preferably, ἀπὸ δόξης and εἰς δόξαν should be considered together as expressing the nature or direction of the transformation: "with ever-increasing glory" (NIV, REB) or "from one degree of glory to another" (RSV, NRSV).[153] In stark contrast with the radiance on Moses' face that faded (3:7, 13), the glory of the Lord that is reflected in believers' lives gradually increases.[154] Justified at regeneration, believers are progressively sanctified

145. Thrall argues that if δόξα in the OT was God's power made manifest, then the powerful display of the resurrection life of Jesus in the midst of apostolic suffering (4:7-12) would show that in some sense the Christian δόξα may be perceived outwardly, though not as visible radiance ("Conversion" 218, 230). See also Richardson 67.

146. A modal sense for the participle ("by looking . . . as in a mirror") implies both a temporal ("as we look") and a causal ("because we look") meaning.

147. On the possible sources of Paul's motif of transformation by vision, see Thrall, 294-95; "Conversion" 223-26. For Qumran parallels to the motif of divine illumination of the face or the heart, see Fitzmyer, "Glory" 639-44.

148. In 1 Cor. 15:49 and 1 John 3:2 the futures are durative, with punctiliar action presupposed: φορέσομεν (see Metzger 502 for this reading) means "we shall (acquire and thereafter) bear (the image of the heavenly man)" (1 Cor. 15:49); ἐσόμεθα has the sense "we shall (become and thereafter) be (like him)" (1 John 3:2).

149. Turner, *Insights* 127.

150. Göttsberger 15.

151. Hickling 394.

152. R. P. C. Hanson 41; cf. Conybeare in Conybeare and Howson 446 and n. 7.

153. So also Martin 57, 72; Thrall 238; similarly Weymouth; Goodspeed; Plummer 93.

154. Hooker rightly observes that in 3:18 Paul has returned to his earlier theme (3:7-11) of the contrast between two kinds of glory ("Scripture" 301).

until their final glorification at the consummation (Rom. 8:29-30; 12:2; Eph. 4:23; Col. 3:10).[155] Christian transformation is neither instant deification nor mystical divinization. The ultimate δόξα, the last in the series ἀπὸ δόξης εἰς δόξαν, will be the believer's acquisition as the result of a final μετασχη-ματισμός, of τὸ σῶμα τῆς δόξης (Phil. 3:21; cf. Col. 3:4), a body suffused with the divine glory and perfectly adapted to the ecology of heaven (1 Cor. 15:43-44). Resurrection, according to Paul, was the acceleration and climax of the process of "Christification."[156] Through daily spiritual renewal (4:16) that leads to resurrection (5:4), believers regain the divine image, which was and still is defaced by sin (cf. 1 Cor. 15:49; Gal. 4:19).[157]

καθάπερ ἀπὸ κυρίου πνεύματος. "Appropriately, this transformation comes from the Lord, who is the Spirit." καθάπερ ("just as") signifies apt correspondence: "in keeping with,"[158] " — and that fittingly enough" (Cassirer), "as happens (in transformation by)."[159] ἀπό may denote agency ("by")[160] or cause ("because of"), but probably here specifies the origin of the transformation[161] or of the glory[162] (cf. 1 Pet. 4:14, "the Spirit of glory"). Many authorities regard κυρίου πνεύματος as a case of inverse dependence, "the Spirit of the Lord,"[163] with πνεύματος standing second for emphasis.[164] But there appear to be no NT exceptions to the rule that "if a prep[osition] is followed by two anarthrous substantives, both in the genitive case, it always qualifies the former."[165] It is therefore better to assume that πνεύματος is dependent on κυρίου, which leads to the following main translational options:[166]

155. Commenting on Rom. 8:30, Bruce notes: "Sanctification is glory begun; glory is sanctification completed" (*Romans* 178). For Paul "transformation," like salvation, was past (Gal. 2:20; 3:27), present (Rom. 12:2), and future (1 Cor. 15:51; Phil. 3:21). It is not possible, as Buck and Taylor allege (13-15), to trace development in Paul's thought regarding transformation — from a future hope realized at the parousia (1 Cor. 15:51) to a long-term process (2 Cor. 3:18; 4:16) to a present reality (Col. 3:1, 3-4).

156. See further Harris 105-7, 129-30, 224-25.

157. Cf. Jervell 174-75.

158. Moule, "2 Cor. 3:18b" 236.

159. Thrall 238.

160. Robertson 820; Spicq 1.419.

161. Young and Ford 265.

162. Moule, "2 Cor. 3:18b" 236.

163. Thus KJV; Vulgate *(tamquam a Domini Spiritu)*; BDF §474(4); Robertson, *Pictures* 223; Zerwick, *Analysis* 397 (but cf. Zerwick and Grosvenor 541); Héring 25, 28; Prümm 1.166, 195-98; Collange 123-24; Thrall 238 (but cf. her earlier "Conversion" 218, 232). RV mg. ("the Spirit *which* is the Lord") reflects inverse apposition, which is probably an unparalleled NT construction.

164. Collange 124.

165. Harris, "Prepositions" 1178; cf. Bultmann 343. But see BDF §474(4); Turner 218 and n. 2. In Matt. 24:31 μετὰ σάλπιγγος φωνῆς μεγάλης (B *f¹³* 33 𝔐 sa [syr^h**]) is the inferior reading (Metzger 51), and in any case the phrase may mean "with a trumpet-blast that sounds loud." In Heb. 6:2 βαπτισμῶν διδαχῆς (p⁴⁶ B it^d read διδαχήν), "teaching about baptism(s)," is not governed by a preposition.

166. To treat κυρίου as an adjective (thus "a Spirit exercising lordship" [Hort in WH 2. Appendix 119], "a sovereign Spirit") is unwarranted.

"the Lord of the Spirit"[167] = the Lord who sends or distributes the Spirit (πνεύματος, objective genitive), or,

with πνεύματος in epexegetic apposition to κυρίου,

"the Lord who is spirit"[168] (cf. John 4:24, of God; 1 Cor. 15:45, of Christ),

"the Lord who is Spirit" (JB, NEB),[169]

"the Lord, the Spirit" (TCNT, Montgomery, NASB, NRSV; cf. RV), or

"the Lord who is the Spirit" (Goodspeed, RSV, Barclay, NAB[1, 2], NJB, REB; cf. NIV).

If our interpretation of v. 17a is correct — "Now this 'Lord' (= "Yahweh" in Exod. 34:34) is in the present era experienced as the Holy Spirit" — v. 18c may be seen as an abbreviated restatement of this: "the LORD (= Yahweh), who is (now experienced as) the Spirit."[170] On this view, vv. 16-18 are pneumatological in emphasis.[171] The new era is the era of the Spirit, for as a result of conversion to the Spirit (vv. 16, 17a), there is liberation through the Spirit (v. 17b), including the lifting of the veil of spiritual ignorance and hard-heartedness, and also transformation by the Spirit (v. 18). The Spirit, his person and his work, is the hallmark of the new covenant.

3:12-18 incorporates contrasts between two ministries, two covenants, and two religions. It ends (in v. 18) with contrasts that are partly explicit and partly implicit, between two sets of persons, Moses and the Jews on the one hand, and Paul and Christians on the other. Under the new covenant, not one man alone, but all Christians behold and then reflect[172] the glory of the Lord.[173] Moreover, unlike the Jews, who still read the Law with veiled hearts, Christians, with unveiled faces, see in the mirror of the gospel the glory of Yahweh, which is Christ. Again, the glory is displayed not outwardly on the face but inwardly in the character. Finally, so far from waxing and waning, the glory expe-

167. BAGD 676c; Windisch 129-30.

168. Jervell 179; Spicq 1.419.

169. "Yahweh who is now being experienced as Spirit" (Dumbrell 189; also Moule, "2 Cor. 3:18b" 237).

170. Similarly Dunn, "Lord" 318; Moule, "2 Cor. 3:18b" 236-37. But both authors, in rendering 3:18c, have "who . . . is Spirit," whereas in relation to 3:17a they have "the Spirit" (Dunn, "Lord" 317-18; Moule, "2 Cor. 3:18b" 235).

171. Similarly Wong 70-72; Fee, *Presence* 311, 320.

172. As observed earlier, the idea of reflection is suggested by the phrase τὴν αὐτὴν εἰκόνα μεταμορφούμεθα, not by the verb κατοπτριζόμενοι.

173. For Paul, Moses was evidently not only a symbol of the old covenant but also, in a sense, a symbol of the new, for Moses, like Christians, enjoyed direct access to God's presence and saw God's glory with unveiled face. Cf. Hays 144-45 (Moses is both a foil and a paradigm), and Hafemann ("Comfort" 340-41; cf. "Glory" 43) who believes that Moses' experience in the tent of meeting was not qualitatively different from that of Christians under the new covenant. On the theme "Paul, the new/second Moses" see Jones 13-109, 256-316; "Moses" 219-41; Stockhausen 169-75.

rienced under the new covenant progressively increases until the Christian finally acquires a "glorious body" like that of the risen Christ.[174] All this constitutes further evidence of the grandeur and superiority of the apostolic ministry, which is the theme of 2:14–4:6.

Bibliography

Baker • Balch • Barrett, *Adam* 50-60 • Belleville, *Reflections* 172-301 • Belleville, "Tradition" • Braun 2.171 • Capes 155-57 • Carmignac • Carrez, *Souffrance* 33-44, 71-77, 81-87 • L. Cerfaux, "Kyrios dans les citations pauliniennes de l'Ancien Testament," in *Recueil Lucien Cerfaux* (Gembloux: Duculot, 1954) 1.173-88 • M. A. Chevallier, *Esprit de Dieu, paroles d'hommes* (Neuchâtel: Delachaux et Niestlé, 1966) 91-94, 97-98 • Dalton • Dumbrell • Dunn, "Lord" • Dupont, "Chrétien" • E. E. Ellis, "How the New Testament Uses the Old," in *New Testament Interpretation,* ed. I. H. Marshall (Exeter: Paternoster/Grand Rapids: Eerdmans, 1977) 199-219 • Fatehi • Fee, *Presence* 309-20 • Feuillet 113-61 • Fitzmyer, "Glory" • Friedrich, "Gegner" • Friesen 53-139 • Galletto • Giglioli • Göttsberger • Goppelt 2.120-22 • Grech • Greenwood • Grelot • Griffiths • Hafemann, *Moses* 335-436 • Hafemann, "Comfort" • Hafemann, "Glory" • Hanson 139-42 • Hanson, "Midrash" • Hanson, *Ministry* 68-72 • Hays 122-53 • Hermann 38-56 • Hickling • Hickling, "Exodus" • Hooker, "Scripture" • Hugedé 7-36 • Jervell 182-84 • Jones, "Moses" • Kim 5-13, 128-29 • Koch • Lambrecht, "Transformation" • Lambrecht, "Structure" • Lane • Larsson 284-87 • J. Lebourlier, "L'Ancien Testament, miroir de la gloire du Seigneur Jésus. Une lecture du chapitre 3 de la deuxième Épître aux Corinthiens," *BLE* 97 (1996) 321-29 • Le Déaut • Lindars 162-63 • U. Luck, "Historische Fragen zum Verhältnis von Kyrios und Pneuma bei Paulus," *TLZ* 85 (1960) 845-48 • S. Lyonnet, "S. Cyrille d'Alexandrie et 2 Co 3,17," *Bib* 32 (1951) 25-31 • McNamara 177-78 • McNamara, *Paraphrases* • Meeks, *Prophet-King* 100-285 • Moberly 106-9 • Moule, "2 Cor. 3:18b" • Murphy-O'Connor 34-40 • J. Murphy-O'Connor, "The New Covenant in the Letters of Paul and the Essene Documents," in M. P. Horgan and P. J. Kobelski (eds.), *To Touch the Text: Biblical and Related Studies in Honor of Joseph A. Fitzmyer, S.J.* (New York: Crossroad, 1989) 194-204 • Newman 227, 229-35, 243 • Oostendorp 31-51 • D. Patte, *Early Jewish Hermeneutic in Palestine* (Missoula: Scholars, 1975) • Provence • Renwick 123-60 • Richard • Rissi 28-41 • Schildenberger • Schmithals 315-25 • T. R. Schreiner 81-83, 129-33, 141-42 • J. Schröter, "Schriftauslegung und Hermeneutik in 2 Korinther 3. Ein Beitrag zur Frage der Schriftbenutzung des Paulus," *NovT* 40 (1998) 231-75 • Schulz • Shead • R. B. Sloan, "2 Corinthians 2:14–4:6 and 'New Covenant Hermeneutics' — A Response to Richard Hays," *BBR* 5 (1995) 129-54 • Stalder 50-56 • D. M. Stanley 131-34 •

---

174. If there is polemic in 3:7-18, it may be directed against the view (possibly held by Jews in Corinth who were adversely affecting some of the Corinthian Christians; cf. Thrall 297) that the Mosaic economy was of permanent validity (cf. καταργέομαι in 3:7, 11, 13) and was vastly superior in glory to the imagined glory of the Christian era. Hofius contends that those who contested Paul's apostleship maintained the relevance of the Sinaitic Torah in salvation through their attempted synthesis of Law and gospel ("Gesetz" 107 n. 203). For a rebuttal of the views of Georgi regarding Paul's opponents and his response to them in 3:7-18, see Thrall 246-48, 251-52, 258-59, 266-68, 273, 276, 288-89; Furnish 243-45.

Stegemann • Stockhausen 87-153, 175-77 • Stockhausen, "2 Corinthians 3" • Theissen, *Aspects* 117-75 • Theobald 190-211 • Thielman 113-18 • Thrall, "Conversion" • Ulonska • Vanhoye • van Unnik, "Face" • Vollenweider • von der Osten-Sacken, *Heiligkeit* 87-115 • W. S. Vorster, "2 Kor. 3:17. Eksegese en Toeligting," *Neot* 3 (1969) 37-44 • Wainwright 225-27 • J. Winandy, "L'énigme de 2 Co 3,17. Une bévue de scribe?" *RB* 107 (2000) 72-80 • Witherington, *Jesus* 109-11 • B. Witherington III, *Jesus the Sage: The Pilgrimage of Wisdom* (Edinburgh: Clark, 1994) 314-19 • E. Wong • Wright

f. The Light Brought by the Gospel (4:1-6)

These six verses have clear verbal and conceptual links with two preceding passages:

A. 4:1-6	2:14-17
v. 2 δολοῦντες τὸν λόγον τοῦ θεοῦ	v. 17 καπηλεύοντες τὸν λόγον τοῦ θεοῦ
v. 2 τῇ φανερώσει	v. 14 φανεροῦντι
v. 2 ἐνώπιον τοῦ θεοῦ	v. 17 κατέναντι θεοῦ
v. 3 ἐν τοῖς ἀπολλυμένοις	v. 15 ἐν τοῖς ἀπολλυμένοις
v. 5 κηρύσσομεν	v. 17 λαλοῦμεν
v. 6 τῆς γνώσεως τῆς δόξης τοῦ θεοῦ	v. 14 τῆς γνώσεως αὐτοῦ

These similarities would indicate that, like 2:14-17, 4:1-6 is dealing with the effects of the proclamation of the gospel against the backdrop of the activity of Paul's adversaries. Both passages are primarily apologetic and only secondarily polemical, but, as Plummer remarks (110), it is difficult to be sure in ch. 3 and 4:1-6 whether Paul is answering his opponents' charges or bringing charges of his own against them. Certainly the threefold use of οὐ(κ)/μή . . . ἀλλά (vv. 1b-2a, 2b, 5) points to an apologetic thrust:[1] Paul has not grown lax in the discharge of his commission (v. 1), has renounced (as always) secretive practices (2), does not adopt crafty techniques (v. 2), does not tamper with God's word (v. 2), and does not proclaim his own person (v. 5).

B. 4:1-6	3:7-18
v. 1 τὴν διακονίαν ταύτην	v. 8 ἡ διακονία τοῦ πνεύματος
v. 3 κεκαλυμμένον (twice)	v. 9 ἡ διακονία τῆς δικαιοσύνης
	vv. 13-16 κάλυμμα
	v. 18 ἀνακεκαλυμμένῳ
v. 4 ἐτύφλωσεν τὰ νοήματα τῶν ἀπίστων	v. 14 ἐπωρώθη τὰ νοήματα αὐτῶν
v. 4 τὸ μὴ αὐγάσαι	v. 7 μὴ δύνασθαι ἀτενίσαι
	v. 13 τὸ μὴ ἀτενίσαι
vv. 4, 6 φωτισμόν	v. 18 κατοπτριζόμενοι
vv. 4, 6 τῆς δόξης	vv. 7-11, 18 δόξα

1. On the significance of the οὐ(κ) . . . ἀλλά antithesis, see the Introduction, B.4.a.

Such an overlap of terms and concepts shows that several key themes of 3:7-18 are continued in 4:1-6: the glory of the Christian ministry, veiling, unresponsiveness of mind, and seeing and not seeing.[2]

Verses 1-6 fall neatly into three couplets:

vv. 1-2 The glory of the ministry prompts perseverance and openness.
vv. 3-4 The glory of the gospel is veiled to minds blinded by Satan.
vv. 5-6 The glory of God is known in the gospel of Jesus Christ as Lord.[3]

1*For this reason, and since we are entrusted with this ministry as recipients of mercy, we do not lose heart[a]. 2As it is, we have repudiated underhand and disgraceful ways: we refuse to act with unscrupulous cunning or to tamper with God's word. On the contrary, by setting forth the truth openly, we seek to commend[b] ourselves to the conscience of each and every person in the sight of God. 3Yet if in fact our gospel is "veiled," it is veiled only to those who are perishing; 4in their case, the god of this age has blinded the minds of those unbelievers, to prevent them from seeing[c, d] the light of the gospel that displays the glory of Christ, who is the image of God. 5For we do not proclaim ourselves; no, we proclaim Jesus Christ[e] as Lord, and ourselves as your slaves for Jesus' sake[f]. 6Because it is the God who[g] said "Light shall shine[h] out of darkness" who[i] has shone in our hearts to illuminate them with the knowledge of God's[j] glory[k] shining in the face of Christ[l].*

TEXTUAL NOTES

a. In place of ἐγκακοῦμεν, which has strong and diversified support (p⁴⁶ ℵ A B D* F G 33 81 326 1175 2464 *pc* cop), some witnesses (C D² Ψ 0243 1739 1881 𝔐) read ἐκκακοῦμεν, which also means "we lose heart." In the six NT uses of ἐγκακέω, TR reads ἐκκακέω.

b. Three passages in 2 Corinthians (4:2; 6:4; and 10:18) have textual variants relating to three verbs that can all mean "commend," συνίστημι, συνιστάνω, and συνιστάω (see BAGD 790 c, d). In 4:2, p⁴⁶ B P 0243 630 1175 1505 1739 1881 *pc* read συνιστάνοντες (from συνιστάνω), *lectio potior*, while ℵ C D* F G 33 81 326 *pc* have συνιστάντες (from συνίστημι), probably the result of parablepsis, the copyist's eye passing from the second to the third N of συνιστάνοντες (cf. Thrall 300 n. 765), and D² Ψ 𝔐 read συνιστῶντες (from συνιστάω), clearly an inferior reading.

c. There are two inferior variants for the uncompounded form αὐγάσαι: καταυγάσαι, "illuminate" (C D H 365 1175 *pc* Epiphanius) and διαυγάσαι, "dawn" (A 33 104 326 2464 *pc*)

d. Several witnesses (D² Ψ 0209 𝔐 vg^cl syr Speculum) add αὐτοῖς ("on them") after αὐγάσαι to complete the sense when that verb was understood to mean "shine."

2. But cf. Lambrecht, "Structure" 347-49, 364, who gives 2:14–4:6 a threefold division: A 2:14–3:6, B 3:7-18, A' 4:1-6.

3. Lambrecht also divides 4:1-6 concentrically: A 4:1-2: We (ministers), B 4:3-4: They (Israelites), A' 4:5-6: We (ministers) ("Structure" 363-64).

e. Although NA[25] preferred the less common Pauline order Χριστὸν Ἰησοῦν (read by B H Ψ 0186 0209 0243 33 1739 1881 𝔐 it[a, b] syr[p] Marcion *apud* Epiphanius Pelagius), NA[26, 27] rightly prefer Ἰησοῦν Χριστόν (read by p[46] ℵ A C D [F G P] 81 326 629 1505 *pc* lat syr[h] Ambrosiaster).

f. On external evidence the two readings διὰ Ἰησοῦ ("through Jesus[' power"]) and διὰ Ἰησοῦν ("for Jesus' sake") are rather evenly matched, each having proto-Alexandrian (Ἰησοῦ in p[46] ℵ* 1739; Ἰησοῦν in B) and later Alexandrian (Ἰησοῦ in C 0243 33 1881; Ἰησοῦν in A*[vid] H Ψ) support, although Ἰησοῦν has the stronger Western support (D F G). Also, since διὰ Ἰησοῦν recurs in 4:11, this reading is preferable here (so also Metzger 509-10; "B" rating in UBS[4] = "almost certain"). The readings that add or substitute the term Χριστός are clearly secondary.

g. 1311 *pc* omit ὁ before εἰπών.

h. λάμψει, "shall shine" (of a divine edict) is to be preferred over λάμψαι (either aorist infinitive "to shine" or aorist optative "let . . . shine," read by ℵ[2] C D[2] F G H Ψ 0209 33 1881 𝔐 latt) since it has superior external evidence (p[46] ℵ* A B D*0243 6 1739 2464 pc Clement of Alexandria Epiphanius) and is the more difficult reading, being unlike Gen. 1:3 (γενηθήτω φῶς, LXX).

i. D* F G 81 it vg[mss] Marcion *apud* Tertullian Ambrosiaster omit ὅς, a secondary reading that smooths the construction by avoiding the need to supply ἐστιν.

j. p[46] C* D* F G it[b, r] substitute αὐτοῦ for τοῦ θεοῦ to avoid unnecessary repetition — an obvious stylistic improvement and therefore a secondary reading.

k. 33 *pc* vg[ms] omit τῆς δόξης.

l. The shorter reading Χριστοῦ, which enjoys considerable external support (A B 33 1739* cop[sa] arm[mss] Marcion Tertullian Origen Ephraem Athanasius Chrysostom *al*) is to be preferred (as in NA[25] and UBS[1, 2], with no textual apparatus in the UBS editions) over Ἰησοῦ Χριστοῦ (p[46] ℵ C H K L P 049 056 075 0142 0209 most minuscules syr[p, h] cop[bo] goth arm *al*) or Χριστοῦ Ἰησοῦ (D F G 6 206 630 1739 1758 1881 1898 it[d, g] vg *al*), since it would be difficult to account for the omission of an original Ἰησοῦ (so Metzger and Wikgren in a minority opinion expressed in Metzger 510).

4:1 Διὰ τοῦτο, ἔχοντες τὴν διακονίαν ταύτην καθὼς ἠλεήθημεν, οὐκ ἐγκακοῦμεν. "For this reason, and since we are entrusted with this ministry as recipients of mercy, we do not lose heart." As we have seen, 4:1-6 resumes themes found in 2:14-17 and 3:7-18, so that διὰ τοῦτο looks back to these passages in general[4] and to 3:18 in particular. It was because Paul (and his fellow ministers) were God's honored agents in spreading the knowledge of God and in calling people to turn to the Lord of the glorious new covenant, and in particular because of the Spirit's liberating and transforming work, that Paul refused to waver in the discharge of his divine commission (οὐκ ἐγκακοῦμεν; cf. 4:16). The causal phrase ἔχοντες τὴν διακονίαν ταύτην narrows τοῦτο by referring to "this ministry," that is, the glorious ministry of the Spirit that provides righteousness (3:8-11), and this in effect supplies a second ground for Paul's deter-

---

4. Although the three expressions share virtually the same semantic territory, διὰ τοῦτο may be rendered "for this reason," διό (e.g., 4:16), "accordingly," and οὖν (e.g., 5:6), "therefore." διὰ τοῦτο is retrospective not prospective in reference, unless it is followed by ἵνα (e.g., 1 Tim. 1:16).

mination to be undaunted.[5] ἔχειν here has the sense of "be under something" or "have something over one,"[6] which suggests a rendering such as "since we are entrusted with this ministry" (cf. Weymouth and NRSV, "engaged in").

καθὼς ἠλεήθημεν ("as recipients of mercy") should be construed with what precedes.[7] Paul was a privileged participant in the ministry of the new covenant purely on account of God's gratuitous favor (ἔλεος). This phrase is scarcely distinguishable in sense from τῷ ἡμετέρῳ ἐλέει (cf. Rom. 11:31), "because of the mercy shown to us." ἠλεήθημεν is a theological passive, "we were shown mercy (by God)" (cf. 1 Cor. 7:25)[8] and alludes to Paul's conversion/call when he received mercy (ἠλεήθην) and was appointed to Christ's service (1 Tim. 1:12-13, 16; cf. Acts 9:15; 1 Cor. 15:9-10).[9] Paul was profoundly aware that neither his appointment as an agent of the new covenant nor his adequacy to serve in this role arose from human initiative or resources. They were, from first to last, ἐκ θεοῦ (cf. 2:17; 3:5) and διὰ τοῦ Χριστοῦ (cf. 3:4), never ἐξ ἑαυτῶν (cf. 3:5).

Found only in Koine Greek, the verb ἐγκακέω basically means "behave badly," especially in a cowardly (κακός) fashion or in reference to a culpable omission.[10] It is a small step to the two NT meanings: "become weary" (Luke 18:1; Gal. 6:9; 2 Thess. 3:13), "lose heart" (2 Cor. 4:1, 16; Eph. 3:13).[11] That is, weariness and despair that lead to slackening of effort or neglect of duty are ways of "conducting oneself remissly." Paul was determined that no opposition, no failure, would cause him to relax his efforts to fulfill his God-given calling. Firing that determination was his constant awareness of the inestimable glory of the Christian ministry (διὰ τοῦτο, ἔχοντες κτλ.). He had no reason to lose heart, for God in his mercy had granted him a privilege exceeding that of Moses: he had been called not to communicate the Law but to proclaim grace and truth (cf. 4:2; John 1:17). A minister of the gospel has a higher calling than even the mediator of the Law. Paul regarded this divine commission to serve under the new covenant as more than compensating for all the trials he endured for being true to his calling (4:8-12, 17; cf. Rom. 8:18).

4:2 ἀλλὰ ἀπειπάμεθα τὰ κρυπτὰ τῆς αἰσχύνης, μὴ περιπατοῦντες ἐν πανουργίᾳ μηδὲ δολοῦντες τὸν λόγον τοῦ θεοῦ. "As it is, we have repudiated underhand and disgraceful ways: we refuse to act with unscrupulous cunning or to tamper with God's word." As opposed to (ἀλλὰ) becoming disheartened

---

5. Cf. Barrett (136): "For this reason, and since. . . ."

6. BAGD 333a. Note the use of ἔχοντες in 3:12; 4:1, 13 and of ἔχομεν in 3:4; 4:7 (cf. Klauck, "Erleuchtung" 268-69).

7. *Pace* Bruce, *Paraphrase* 133: "and by God's mercy we do not lose heart" (similarly Weymouth).

8. ἐλεέω τινά means "show mercy on someone." The accusative in the active voice becomes the subject in the passive, "be shown mercy" (cf. BAGD 249d).

9. See Kim, 11 26.

10. Cf. LSJ 469 s.v.

11. See H. Grundmann, *TNDT* 3.486; Spicq 1.398-99; and especially Baumert 318-46.

(a thought to which he will return in 4:16), Paul had aggressively renounced practices which by their nature were totally foreign to the Christian minister's conduct. He is either defending himself against the malicious charges of some Corinthian opponents (cf. 7:2; 12:16) or attacking those whose ways of acting were secretive and shameful — or perhaps he is on defense and attack simultaneously.[12] The aorist ἀπειπάμεθα (from ἀπολέγομαί τι, "decline something offered to one or presented as an option") is timeless:[13] there was no time when it was not true that he had refused to adopt tactics unworthy of his calling.[14]

The colorful phrase τὰ κρυπτὰ τῆς αἰσχύνης has been translated in a myriad of different ways. τὰ κρυπτά may mean "secrets,"[15] "secrecy"[16]/concealment (concrete for the abstract), "acts of deceit,"[17] "secret dealings,"[18] "secretive practices,"[19] or "underhanded ways" (RSV). αἰσχύνη may mean either "a shameful thing," "a disgraceful deed," "a disgrace," or "a sense of shame."[20] Finally, the genitive τῆς αἰσχύνης may be epexegetic ("the secrecy which means shame," Weymouth, as revised by J. A. Robertson), possessive ("the secretive practices of disgraceful conduct," Thrall 297;[21] "the secrecy which marks a feeling of shame," Weymouth), subjective ("the secrecy prompted by shame," TNCT; "those practices which very shame conceals from view," Moffatt; "the behavior that shame hides," Barrett 127),[22] referential ("the shameful things that one hides," NRSV; "shameful practices devised in secret," Martin 74; "intrigues contrived in secret," Carrez 105), or adjectival ("disgraceful, underhanded ways," RSV; "hidden and shameful methods," Barclay; "secret ways of acting of which one ought to be ashamed," Zerwick).[23] Each of these renderings is defensible in the context; we have opted for an adjectival understanding of the genitive: "underhand and disgraceful ways."

The two participles that follow define the modes of conduct that Paul has

---

12. So, e.g., Collange 128.

13. Robertson classifies this form as an indirect middle (810; *Pictures* 224). With regard to a first aorist termination (-άμεθα) on a second aorist stem, see Zerwick §4 89, and especially Hort in WH 2. Appendix 164-65.

14. It is impossible to know whether Paul would have classified some of the techniques he used in persecuting Christians before his conversion as τὰ κρυπτὰ τῆς αἰσχύνης. Luke, at least, speaks of his "uttering murderous threats against the disciples of the Lord" (Acts 9:1), and Paul himself describes his misguided persecution as being violent (καθ' ὑπερβολήν, Gal. 1:13; cf. περισσῶς ἐμμαινόμενος, Acts 26:11).

15. Young and Ford 265.

16. TNCT, Weymouth.

17. Cf. Spicq 1.74.

18. Conybeare in Conybeare and Howson 446.

19. Thrall 297.

20. BAGD 25b, c distinguishes these two meanings as "an experience which comes to someone" and "a feeling that one has."

21. Thrall classifies this use as a genitive of relationship (303).

22. Similarly NEB, REB; BAGD, 83b, 454b.

23. Zerwick, *Analysis* 397.

renounced: "we refuse (μὴ . . . μηδέ . . .) to act . . . or to tamper. . . ."[24] It is possible that περιπατοῦντες κτλ. explains τὰ κρυπτά and that δολοῦντες κτλ. defines τῆς αἰσχύνης; at least, both participial phrases are examples of τὰ κρυπτὰ τῆς αἰσχύνης. Paul regularly uses περιπατέω of human conduct, especially in the moral domain.[25] The manner of one's conduct may be marked by the dative (12:18; Gal. 5:16), κατά (Rom. 8:4; 14:15), or, as here (cf. Rom. 6:4), by ἐν.[26] πανουργία, from πανοῦργος ("ready to do anything," especially anything bad), means "craftiness," "trickery," "knavery," or "unscrupulous cunning" (cf. Luke 20:23; 2 Cor. 11:3). In contrast to adversaries who may have been ready to use any tactics to achieve their goals, Paul completely rejected any shrewd underhandedness in his dealings with others, however laudable the end in view.

Behind the verb δολόω stands the noun δόλος, properly "bait" for fish, then "any cunning contrivance for deceiving," and finally "any trick" or (abstractly) "cunning" (LSJ 443 s.v.). So the verb means "ensnare" or "beguile" and on the other hand "falsify" or "adulterate" in reference to incense or wine or gold. Clearly 4:2 is closely related to 2:17: here δολοῦντες, there καπηλεύοντες, is followed by τὸν λόγον τοῦ θεοῦ. Both verbs may mean "adulterate," but, whereas καπηλεύω denotes falsification for financial gain, δολόω has no relation to monetary profit.[27] "The word of God" is here either the Christian message, the gospel, or the OT Scriptures. Paul may have been accused of twisting the OT to accommodate his "works-free" gospel or of adulterating the gospel by not insisting on Gentile compliance with the Mosaic Law. Whether or not there had been an accusation of falsification, Paul repudiates any suggestion that he had toned down or tampered with God's word by dishonest manipulation. His techniques as an evangelist and pastor have always been free of deceit and duplicity.

ἀλλὰ τῇ φανερώσει τῆς ἀληθείας συνιστάνοντες ἑαυτοὺς πρὸς πᾶσαν συνείδησιν ἀνθρώπων ἐνώπιον τοῦ θεοῦ. "On the contrary, by setting forth the truth openly, we seek to commend ourselves to the conscience of each and every person in the sight of God." τῇ φανερώσει (instrumental dative) stands in stark contrast (ἀλλά) to three preceding expressions, τὰ κρυπτά, ἐν πανουργίᾳ, and δολοῦντες. As vigorously as he repudiated secrecy, craftiness, and manipulation, Paul declared the truth in all circumstances, in particular the truth of the gospel, which focused on Jesus Christ as Lord (v. 5). φανέρωσις is "open proclamation" (BAGD 853b), a clear, candid, and full disclosure. It was by such an open declaration of the truth as he knew it, not by an appeal directed to partisan spirit or to human prejudices, that Paul sought to commend himself and his cause to everyone's conscience. συνιστάνοντες may be conative ("we seek to

---

24. But Plummer (111) regards μὴ περιπατοῦντες ἐν πανουργίᾳ as the result of the ἀπειπεῖν.
25. See H. Seesemann, *TDNT* 5.944-45; Banks, "Walking" 303-13.
26. G. Kittel, *TDNT* 2.374.
27. See on 2:17, especially the citation of Lucian, *Hermotimus* 59.

commend")²⁸ and either stands for συνιστάνομεν or specifies action concurrent with the (timeless) aorist ἀπειπάμεθα. ἑαυτούς stands for ἡμᾶς αὐτούς (cf. 3:1).

In the unique phrase πρὸς πᾶσαν συνείδησιν ἀνθρώπων, literally, "to every conscience of humankind," πᾶσαν is brought forward for emphasis, "each and every conscience of humankind" = "the conscience of each and every person," or "each and every human conscience."²⁹ The sense is not "to everyone's good conscience" (GNB) or "to every human being with a conscience" (JB, NJB) but "to every possible variety of the human conscience" (Bernard 59), Corinthian and non-Corinthian, Christian and non-Christian.³⁰ This necessary and permissible self-commendation (see on 3:1) was undertaken with God as onlooker and ultimate judge (ἐνώπιον τοῦ θεοῦ). Human consciences sometimes give fallible judgments (cf. 1 Cor. 4:4), but the divine verdict is infallible and therefore all-important.

4:3 εἰ δὲ καὶ ἔστιν κεκαλυμμένον τὸ εὐαγγέλιον ἡμῶν, ἐν τοῖς ἀπολλυμένοις ἐστὶν κεκαλυμμένον. "Yet if in fact our gospel is 'veiled,' it is veiled only to those who are perishing." The apostle was constantly reminded by the opposition to his message that not every human conscience perceived and embraced the truth that he proclaimed so openly and clearly (cf. 4:2). The veil had not been lifted from every heart (cf. 3:14-15); nor had every person turned to the Lord (cf. 3:16). Where there still were veiled hearts which failed to understand the meaning of the good news he proclaimed (τὸ εὐαγγέλιον ἡμῶν), they were the hearts of those who were perishing, those who were spiritually dead and already standing under God's wrath and whose judgment was therefore suspect (see on 2:15). On this view, εἰ δὲ καί means "yet if in fact,"³¹ with δέ adversative after τῇ φανερώσει and πᾶσαν and καί emphasizing the whole protasis.³² An alternative view takes εἰ . . . καί to mean "even if" (RSV, NASB, NRSV)³³ or "even though" (NAB²),³⁴ as in 4:16; 5:16; 7:8; 11:6; 12:11. In this case Paul is conceding, with the qualifications of vv. 3b-4, a real or a possible objection, namely that for some people the meaning and significance

28. If this participle is conative, there is no suggestion that Paul's self-commendation was or would be everywhere successful. It was his hope and intent that through the φανέρωσις all might espouse the truth and recognize the authenticity of his commission and the integrity of his conduct; but the facts proved otherwise.

29. Furnish 202. "To every human conscience" (Weymouth; BAGD 710d, 790d; Spicq 1.74; Thrall 297) perhaps renders the emphatic πᾶσαν too weakly.

30. Thrall usefully defines Paul's concept of συνείδησις as "a neutral inward faculty of judgment, possessed by all humanity, which evaluates conduct in an objective way in accordance with given and recognized norms" (132; cf. 301). See on 1:12.

31. Cf. Barclay, "But if in fact" (also de Boor 92); Weymouth ("If, indeed"); and Goodspeed ("If . . . at all").

32. Similarly Thrall 303 n. 792 (καί emphasizes what follows; note the repeated ἐστὶν κεκαλυμμένον); *Particles* 79-81 (δέ is "a balancing adversative which suggests a divergent possibility," 81).

33. So also BAGD 220a; Hughes 125 n. 28; Furnish 202, 219; Martin 78 (but cf. 74, "Yet if even our gospel preaching is veiled").

34. So also Plummer 113.

of his gospel was "veiled," hidden from their understanding. So the sense is "Even if — as I am willing to concede — my message is not everywhere understood and accepted, it is rejected only[35] by those who are perishing.[36]

On either view, the expression ἐστὶν κεκαλυμμένον, which focuses on the condition of "veiledness,"[37] alludes to the use of κάλυμμα in 3:14-16. But whereas in that passage the veil lay over the hearts of the Jews when the writings of Moses were read, here the veil remains upon the minds of unbelievers (v. 4) when the gospel of Paul is heard. As in 1 Thess. 1:5; 2 Thess. 2:14, τὸ εὐαγγέλιον ἡμῶν means "the gospel (of Christ) which we proclaim" (cf. Gal. 1:11; 2:2),[38] not "my particular understanding of the gospel."[39] Also, as in 2:15; 1 Cor. 1:18, τοῖς ἀπολλυμένοις refers to unbelieving Jews and Gentiles,[40] not to Judaistic Christians[41] and not (as a neuter) to "things that perish."[42] ἐν could be rendered "among"[43] (as in 2:15), but is better regarded either as a pleonastic substitute for the simple dative[44] or as meaning "in the case of."[45]

4:4 ἐν οἷς ὁ θεὸς τοῦ αἰῶνος τούτου ἐτύφλωσεν τὰ νοήματα τῶν ἀπίστων. "In their case, the god of this age has blinded the minds of those unbelievers." Here Paul makes it clear that the reason for the "veiledness" of the gospel in the case of those who are perishing (v. 3) is not the gospel itself (it brings enlightenment, v. 4b), nor himself as its agent, but the activity of Satan in blinding their minds to the truth of the gospel.

ἐν οἷς refers back to ἐν τοῖς ἀπολλυμένοις and may be epexegetic ("to those who are perishing . . . that is, to those . . .")[46] or resumptive ("in whose case," "In their case," Goodspeed, RSV, NRSV).[47] ὁ θεὸς τοῦ αἰῶνος is a unique

---

35. "Only" is supplied, on the basis of the flow of the argument, in the translations of Goodspeed, Williams; Martin 74; also Lietzmann 114; Wendland 185; Lang 276.

36. One need not follow A. Oepke (*TDNT* 3.557) in his claim that after ironically accepting the charge that his gospel was "covered," Paul "makes a humorous application. His gospel is certainly hidden for unbelievers who are on the way to destruction."

37. The periphrastic perfect ἐστὶν κεκαλυμμένον is virtually adjectival in sense ("is veiled"), "perfect in form more than in meaning" (Moule 18; but cf. Weymouth, "has been veiled"), yet may emphasize an "existing state" (Burton §84) without implying (*pace* Fanning 319) any occurrence that produced the condition.

38. ἡμῶν is a subjective, rather than a possessive, genitive (cf. BAGD 318b).

39. Cf. Schütz 71-78, against Fridrichsen, "Apostle" 1-23.

40. So also Hanson, *Ministry* 72-73. Thrall suggests that οἱ ἀπολλύμενοι may refer chiefly to the unbelieving Jews of Corinth (cf. Acts 18:4-6).

41. Menzies 28.

42. Bain 380 ("the transient elements in the older dispensation . . . [and] all these things which are seen and transient (4¹⁸)"); S. Davies 27 ("the things that . . . have perished . . . the entire furniture and ceremonial of the Mosaic economy"). Höpfl (428) notes that Erasmus understood (ἐν) τοῖς ἀπολλυμένοις to refer to "worldly passions" (*mundanis cupiditatibus*).

43. Robertson 587; Héring 29.

44. Thus Turner 264; cf. BDF §220(1).

45. Plummer 114.

46. Similarly Martin 74.

47. Similarly BAGD 85d; Plummer 94, 116; Zerwick and Grosvenor 541. ἐν οἷς = ὅτι ἐν τούτοις (Meyer 489), "for in the case of these people."

biblical expression and refers not to God the Father (as [ὁ] θεός generally does in the NT[48]), but to Satan.[49]

As a Christian rabbi, Paul divided time into two ages or aeons: "this age" (ὁ αἰὼν οὗτος, *ha'ôlām hazzeh*) and "the age to come" (ὁ αἰὼν ὁ μέλλων/ ἐρχόμενος, *ha'ôlām habbā';* cf. Eph. 1:21).[50] "This age," which Paul also describes as "this present evil age" (Gal. 1:4), will end with the arrival of the Day of the Lord (1 Thess. 5:2; 2 Thess. 2:2), which is "the coming of our Lord Jesus Christ" (2 Thess. 2:1; cf. 1 Cor. 1:8; 2 Cor. 1:14; Phil. 1:6). "The age to come" will see the consummation of the kingdom of God (1 Cor. 15:23-28; Eph. 5:5; 1 Thess. 2:12; 2 Tim. 4:1), which involves the eradication of evil and the transformation of God's children (Rom. 8:19-23). Such dualism as is found in Paul is temporal and ethical, not material or metaphysical.[51]

The genitive τοῦ αἰῶνος τούτου[52] may be classified as (1) epexegetic: "their god, which is this age" (cf. Phil 3:19),[53] (2) relational: "the god who operates during this age," (3) objective: "the god who rules over this age" (cf. ὁ ἄρχων τοῦ κόσμου, John 12:31),[54] or (4) possessive: "the one whom the unbelievers of this age (= οἱ ἄπιστοι) have as their god."[55] In the case of (1), ὁ θεός = "this age," the whole world-system as opposed to God (= the Johannine ὁ κόσμος); in the case of (2)-(4), ὁ θεός = Satan. The use of ἄρχων ("ruler") in reference to Satan in both Paul (Eph. 2:2) and John (John 12:31; 14:30; 16:11) supports option (3).

In a metaphorical sense τυφλόω means "deprive of (spiritual) sight," "prevent from understanding." In conjunction with this metaphor of "blinding," νοήματα is more appropriately rendered by "minds" than by "thoughts," but either way it is the understanding of the truth and the attractiveness of the gospel that are effectively blocked by the devil. 4:4 is closely related to 3:14a. There, the νοήματα of Jews are hardened by God (by implication); here, Satan blinds the νοήματα of all unbelievers, Jews or Gentiles. Both of the verbs used are causative and negative: πωρόω, "cause not to be responsive" (= "harden"),

48. See Harris, *Jesus* 29-47.
49. Thus BAGD 358b; A. Oepke, *TDNT* 3.557, and almost all modern commentators (but for an exception, see Young and Ford 115-17). The Judeo-Christian God is "king of the ages" (ὁ βασιλεὺς τῶν αἰώνων, 1 Tim. 1:17), not simply the "God of this (present) age."
50. See H. Sasse, *TDNT* 1.204-7. These ideas were probably current throughout the first century A.D., although the earliest clear rabbinic use of the two expressions together is about A.D. 50 (*Genesis Rabbah* 14; see SB 4/2, 815-16).
51. See further Furnish 220. For similarities between 4:4 and 1QS 3.13–4.26 in the idea of opposition between two powers and the concept of predestination, see Dautzenberg, "Überlegungen" 337-41.
52. It is assumed that this phrase is dependent on θεός; to construe it with τῶν ἀπίστων is a tortuous expedient (see the discussion of this option by Thrall 307).
53. Collange 133.
54. Cf. Luke 4:6; John 14:30; 16:11; Eph. 2:2; 6:12; 1 John 5:19. See W. Foerster, *TDNT* 2.79.
55. Cf. Louw and Nida §12.24; Rostron (181 n. 1), "He whom this age has elevated to the position of their God"; Cassirer, "the god whom the world worships."

τυφλόω, "cause not to understand" (= "blind"). The metaphors of πώρωσις and τύφλωσις are complementary, both denoting insensitivity to truth. Since Paul elsewhere speaks of God as blinding human eyes (Rom. 11:8, "God gave them . . . eyes that would not see"; cf. Rom 11:10), he must have understood this blinding of the understanding either as a divine judgment administered by Satan or, as seems preferable, as an accommodation within the divine will.[56] Even Satan's acts lie within God's sovereign control.

Syntactically, τῶν ἀπίστων is awkward. If ἀπίστων were adjectival modifying τὰ νοήματα ("unbelieving minds"[57]), we would have expected τὰ νοήματα τὰ ἄπιστα. Again, if τῶν ἀπίστων were in apposition to ἐν οἷς ("in their case . . . namely, that of believers"), ἐν τοῖς ἀπίστοις . . . τὰ νοήματα αὐτῶν would have been appropriate. It is probably wisest to attribute this grammatical irregularity to the circumstances of dictation (Windisch 135) or to Paul's wish to complement his statement about Satan's action by referring to human responsibility.[58] The connection between ἐν οἷς and τῶν ἀπίστων may be shown in translation by "in their case . . . of these unbelievers." As elsewhere in Paul, οἱ ἄπιστοι are unbelievers,[59] not Paul's Christian adversaries.[60] Moreover, since Paul regarded humans as by nature (φύσει) doomed to God's wrath (Eph. 2:3), which comes on "the sons of disobedience" (οἱ υἱοὶ τῆς ἀπειθείας, Eph. 5:6), the ἄπιστοι are not simply "those without faith," but rather "those rejecting faith" (= "the sons of disobedience"), "those refusing to believe."[61] But how is this unbelief related to Satan's act of blinding? The relationship is not made explicit and need not be one of cause and effect. But that the ἀπιστία *precedes* the τύφλωσις seems indicated by Paul's statement that Satan "blinded the minds of the(se) unbelievers,"that is, those who already were unbelievers, not, "so that they became unbelievers" or "who are now unbelievers."[62] Although οἱ ἄπιστοι as a category is coextensive with οἱ ἀπολλύμενοι, there was no fixity to the composition of that group of ἄπιστοι. By embracing the gospel, some ἄπιστοι receive the φωτισμός that emanates from that gospel and so take their place among οἱ σῳζόμενοι (cf. 2:15; Acts 2:47).

εἰς τὸ μὴ αὐγάσαι τὸν φωτισμὸν τοῦ εὐαγγελίου τῆς δόξης τοῦ Χριστοῦ, ὅς ἐστιν εἰκὼν τοῦ θεοῦ. "To prevent them from seeing the light of the gospel that displays the glory of Christ, who is the image of God." In Hellenistic Greek the

56. In illustration of this general point, compare Exod. 7:3 with Exod. 7:13 (nine times in Exodus the hardening of the pharaoh's heart is attributed to God, nine times to the pharaoh himself), and 2 Sam. 24:1 with 1 Chron. 21:1 (the census of Israel and Judah).

57. This is the rendering of BAGD 85d; E. Stauffer, *TDNT* 2.430; Conybeare in Conybeare and Howson 446-47; Bruce, *Paraphrase* 133.

58. Cf. Barrett 131.

59. In the singular (ὁ/ἡ) ἄπιστος (1 Cor. 7:12-13, 14 [twice], 15; 14:24; 2 Cor. 6:14; Tit. 1:15); in the plural (οἱ) ἄπιστοι (1 Cor. 6:6; 10:27; 14:22 twice, 23; 2 Cor. 6:15; 1 Tim. 5:8).

60. As Collange 134; Martin 78-79.

61. Cf. 2 Thess. 1:8; 2:10, 12.

62. "It was because they refused to believe that Satan had power to blind them" (Plummer 116; similarly Robertson, *Pictures* 225).

distinction between purpose and result had become imprecise, so that articular constructions involving εἰς can often be telic or consecutive.[63] And, from the perspective of logic, these two categories are closely related, for a purpose is an anticipated result and a result is an achieved purpose. Here, the final sense probably predominates.[64] Used intransitively, αὐγάζω, a NT *hapax legomenon* formed from the noun αὐγή ("radiance"; "dawn," Acts 20:11), means either "shine forth" or "dawn"; transitively, it means "see (distinctly)." If it is intransitive here, its subject (in the accusative) is τὸν φωτισμόν: "that the light . . . should not dawn *upon them*" (RV);[65] "so the splendor . . . does not shine on them."[66] But these renderings presuppose αὐτοῖς ("on them"), a reading without strong support (see Textual Note d.). On the other hand, if αὐγάσαι is transitive, the unexpressed but natural subject (to be supplied from τῶν ἀπίστων) is αὐτούς, and τὸν φωτισμόν is the object: "to keep them from seeing the light" (RSV, NRSV), "so that they cannot see the light" (NIV).[67] This interpretation accords better with the immediate and wider context. Note ἐτύφλωσεν, κατοπτριζόμενοι (3:18), and the parallel construction πρὸς τὸ μὴ ἀτενίσαι (3:13): believers "see" the divine glory, but unbelievers do not "see" it because Satan has "caused their minds not to see."

As an astronomical term, φωτισμός refers to refracted luminosity, the radiance of the moon as a reflection of the sun's light.[68] More generally, the term means "illumination," "light," "enlightenment." τοῦ εὐαγγελίου is genitive of source or origin:[69] "the light that comes from the gospel" and dispels the darkness of unbelief. τῆς δόξης is unlikely to be adjectival in import ("the glorious gospel," KJV; "the glorious Christ," Goodspeed), and could be epexegetic of τὸν φωτισμόν ("the revealed splendor of the Gospel, that is the glory of Christ," Martin 75), but is more probably a genitive of content[70] ("the gospel that contains the glory"), or an objective genitive[71] ("the gospel that displays the glory"). Plummer, in fact, combines the two: the gospel "which contains and proclaims the glory of the Messiah" (117). The final genitive in this typically Pauline concatenation of genitives, τοῦ Χριστοῦ, is possessive. It is Christ's own glory that is proclaimed in the gospel, and it is the gospel that creates illumination.

When Paul affirms that Christ is εἰκὼν τοῦ θεοῦ, he is not saying only that Christ "subsists in the form of God" (ἐν μορφῇ θεοῦ ὑπάρχων, Phil. 2:6), having the nature and attributes of God, or only that he is the "glory of God" (cf. τῆς

---

63. Cf. Zerwick §352; Moule 143 n. 2.

64. Carrez (105) has "His aim: that they may not perceive . . . ."

65. Similarly Goodspeed, NEB, REB; Robertson, *Pictures* 225; Bruce, *Paraphrase* 133.

66. Klauck 43; "Erleuchtung" 281-83; similarly Prümm 1.217-18.

67. Most translations and commentators have "see" for αὐγάζω in 4:4.

68. See Spicq 3.490 and n. 90.

69. Thus BDF §168(2); Turner 218; Zerwick and Grosvenor 541; Jervell 195.

70. Thus BDF §168(2). This classification is scarcely distinguishable from the epexegetic or appositive genitive ("the gospel that consists of the glory"); see BDF §167.

71. Thus BAGD 318a; Zerwick §47; Dautzenberg, "Überlegungen" 341; NAB[1], "the gospel showing forth the glory."

δόξης τοῦ θεοῦ ἐν προσώπῳ Χριστοῦ, 4:6; Acts 7:55), being the outshining of deity.[72] As God's εἰκών, Christ both shares and expresses God's nature.[73] He is the precise and visible representation of the invisible God (Col. 1:15, where τοῦ ἀοράτου is added to εἰκὼν τοῦ θεοῦ).[74] An εἰκών is a "likeness" (German *Bild*) or a "visible expression" *(Abbild)*. The degree of resemblance between the original and the copy must be assessed by the word's context, but it could vary from a partial or superficial resemblance to a complete or essential likeness. Given passages such as Phil. 2:6; Col. 1:19; 2:9, we may safely assume that for Paul εἰκών here, as in Col. 1:15, signifies that Christ is an exact representation *(Ebenbild)*[75] as well as a visible expression of God.[76] ἐστιν is a timeless present, indicating that Christ is eternally the perfect reflection of God or at least that in his glorified corporeality Christ remains forever God's visible expression.

4:5 οὐ γὰρ ἑαυτοὺς κηρύσσομεν ἀλλὰ 'Ιησοῦν Χριστὸν κύριον, ἑαυτοὺς δὲ δούλους ὑμῶν διὰ 'Ιησοῦν. "For we do not proclaim ourselves; no, we proclaim Jesus Christ as Lord, and ourselves as your slaves for Jesus' sake." What has Paul said that might have given rise to v. 5a (cf. γάρ, "for")? He may wish to prevent anyone from concluding that "our gospel" (v. 3) meant "the gospel about us." But far more probably his train of thought is this: "If the gospel proclaims the glory of Christ (v. 4b) and we preach the gospel (v. 3), that means we proclaim the glory of Christ, that is, Jesus Christ as Lord, Jesus Christ as risen and glorified."[77] Or he may be observing that though he sought to commend himself to every person's conscience (v. 2; cf. 1:12; 6:4), he never advertised or heralded himself, never pressed personal claims.

The word order ('Ιησοῦν Χριστὸν κύριον, not κύριον 'Ιησοῦν Χριστόν) and the parallel expression that follows (ἑαυτοὺς . . . δούλους, which can only mean

72. On the semantic overlap between μορφή, εἰκών, and δόξα in the LXX, see Martin, *Carmen* 102-19.

73. Similarly, in Johannine theology Jesus Christ as the λόγος both inherently participates in deity (John 1:1) and reveals the Father's person (John 1:14-18). See further Harris, *Jesus* 54-71. Cf. Feuillet ("Christ-Image" 1409-14), who argues that "if interpreted in the light of *Wisdom* 7:25-26, the title 'image of God' appears to be practically equivalent to the Johannine *Logos*" (1413; cf. Feuillet 150-58).

74. For an analysis and assessment of four of the possible origins of Paul's concept of Christ as εἰκὼν τοῦ θεοῦ (the early church's liturgical tradition, a Gnostic eikon concept, Wisdom-speculation in Hellenistic Judaism [e.g., Wisd. 7:26], a christological application of the rabbinic view of the brilliance of Adam's face), see Thrall 309-11. If an experiential trigger be sought for Paul's view, there is much to commend Kim's thesis that Paul obtained his conception at the Damascus christophany (223-33). Kim regards 2 Cor. 3:1–4:6 as the most convincing evidence supporting his proposal.

75. De Boor (92) and Wolff (83) have *Bild;* Lietzmann (114) and Wendland (185), *Abbild;* and Lang (276), *Ebenbild.*

76. τοῦ θεοῦ may be classified broadly as a genitive of relationship (cf. BDF §162; Turner 212) or more narrowly as a genitive of possession ("the image of God" is the image God has), but it could also be viewed as an objective genitive (that is, Jesus "images" God).

77. Of course, as elsewhere in 3:7–4:6, it is possible that Paul is attacking his opponents (who may have "preached themselves") or answering charges which had been leveled against him or which he anticipates; see Thrall (312-13) for a discussion of the various proposals.

"ourselves *as* slaves") show that κύριον is predicative, "Jesus Christ as Lord."[78] The two earliest christological confessions were ὁ Χριστὸς Ἰησοῦς, "Jesus is the Messiah" (Acts 18:5, 28; cf. 2:36; 9:22; 17:3), and κύριος Ἰησοῦς, "Jesus is Lord" (Rom. 10:9; 1 Cor. 12:3; cf. Phil. 2:11).[79] That Paul here encapsulates the gospel as focusing on Jesus Christ as κύριος, that is, as risen from the dead and exalted to universal dominion (Phil. 2:9-11),[80] does not mean, of course, that he had repudiated his earlier commitment to preaching "Christ crucified" (1 Cor. 1:23; 2:2; Gal. 3:1). It was only after and because of Christ's obedience to the point of death by crucifixion that God highly exalted him (Phil. 2:8-9). The death, resurrection, and exaltation of Jesus were always at the heart of the kerygma (Rom. 8:34; 1 Cor. 15:3-4).

Whenever worshiping Christians repeat the church's confession "Jesus is Lord," they are

1. implying that the Christ of faith was none other than the Jesus of history (Acts 2:34-36),
2. acknowledging the deity of Christ (John 20:28; Phil. 2:6, 9-11),
3. admitting the Lord's personal rights to absolute supremacy in the universe, the church, and individual lives (Acts 10:36; Rom. 10:12; 14:8; 1 Cor. 8:6; Jas. 4:15),
4. affirming the triumph of Christ over death and hostile cosmic powers when God raised him from the dead (Rom. 10:9; 14:9; Eph. 1:20-22; Col. 2:10, 15) and therefore also the Christian's hope of resurrection (1 Cor. 6:14; 2 Cor. 4:14),
5. epitomizing the Christian message (κήρυγμα; cf. Rom. 10:8-9; 2 Cor. 4:5) and defining the basis of Christian teaching (διδαχή; cf. Col. 2:6-7),
6. declaring everyone's accountability to the Lord, the righteous judge (1 Cor. 4:5; 2 Tim. 4:1, 8),
7. making a personal and public declaration of faith (Rom. 10:9), which testifies to their being led by the Holy Spirit (1 Cor. 12:3), and
8. repudiating their former allegiance to many pagan "lords" and reaffirming their loyalty to one Lord through and in whom they exist (1 Cor. 8:5-6; 1 Tim. 6:15).[81]

It is tempting to regard δέ here as meaning "and therefore," not simply "and."[82] Certainly the parallelism between "Jesus Christ as Lord" and "our-

---

78. So BAGD 431c; Spicq 2.350; Kramer 50 n. 110, 200, and all commentators.

79. In Col. 2:6 these two confessions seem to be combined: (παρελάβετε) τὸν Χριστὸν Ἰησοῦν τὸν κύριον, "(you received) the Messiah, namely Jesus the Lord."

80. Harris in *ISBE*², 3.158.

81. On the lordship (κυριότης) of Jesus as implying his resurrection and exaltation, see Harris 79-86.

82. There is certainly no contrast between v. 5a and v. 5b. δέ forms a link with Ἰησοῦν Χριστὸν κύριον, not with οὐ . . . ἑαυτοὺς κηρύσσομεν as though Paul were saying "we do not pro-

selves as your slaves," and the natural sequence of thought from lordship to slavery (κύριον . . . δούλους) suggest that acknowledgment of the lordship of Jesus leads naturally and inevitably to lowly service to one's fellow believers. To confess that "Jesus is Lord" is to say to other Christians "I am your slave"; slavery to Christ is exhibited in slavery to Christians.[83] Paul describes himself elsewhere as "a slave of (Jesus) Christ" (Rom. 1:1; Gal. 1:10; Phil. 1:1, along with Timothy) and implies that not only his fellow workers (σύνδουλος, of Epaphras [Col. 1:7; 4:12, δοῦλος] and Tychicus [Col. 4:7]) but all Christians are the slaves of Christ (1 Cor. 7:22b-23) or of God (Rom. 6:16-22).[84] But this is the only place where he speaks of himself and his fellow workers as the "slaves" of other believers, in the sense that "they are unconditionally obligated to serve them" (BAGD 205d). Paul would most gladly "spend and be utterly spent" for the sake of the Corinthians (12:15). He envisaged his relationship to Christ and his relationship to fellow Christians as one of slavery, that is, as unquestioning service for the benefit of the other, as the result of the unconditional but voluntary surrender of all personal rights.[85] In this lowly service to others, Paul was following in the footsteps of his Lord, who himself had adopted the status and role of a δοῦλος (Phil. 2:7; cf. John 13:2-5).[86] There was, however, one important difference between these two relationships: the Corinthians were not his κύριος any more than he was theirs (cf. 1:24). His service to them was διὰ Ἰησοῦν, "for Jesus' sake" — only Jesus Christ was κύριος.[87]

4:6 ὅτι ὁ θεὸς ὁ εἰπών, Ἐκ σκότους φῶς λάμψει, ὃς ἔλαμψεν ἐν ταῖς καρδίαις ἡμῶν. "Because it is the God who said 'Light shall shine out of darkness' who has shone in our hearts." Here Paul states the reason (ὅτι)[88] that he preached Christ and was devoted to the Corinthians (v. 5). It was because God had dispelled his darkness by illuminating his heart and had given him a knowl-

---

claim ourselves (as Lord) but as your slaves." With ἑαυτοὺς κτλ., the implied κηρύσσομεν will bear a general sense such as "we present," or this may be a case of zeugma, or (as Lietzmann [115] proposes) λογιζόμεθα ("we consider") should be supplied.

83. A similar correlation between commitment to the Lord and commitment to his people is evident in 8:5 in reference to the Macedonians.

84. In the history of the English Bible there has been a curious but inappropriate reluctance to translate δοῦλος by "slave," except where the context demands it (e.g., 1 Cor. 7:22-23; Col. 3:22; 4:1). "Servant" is the preferred rendering in most translations outside explicit contexts of slavery. This in spite of the fact that at least four other NT Greek words may appropriately be translated "servant": διάκονος, παῖς, ὑπηρέτης, οἰκέτης (not to mention μίσθιος and μισθωτός). Remarkably, the only use of "slave(s)" in the KJV is Rev. 18:13, where it renders σώματα. See further Harris, *Slave* 177-91, and more briefly Spicq 1.380-86; 3.1-3, 398-402; Goodspeed, *Problems* 139-41.

85. On the significance of the concept of slavery to Christ in Paul's life and theology, see Harris, *Slave, passim.*

86. For a review of the various interpretations of the phrase μορφὴν δούλου λαβών in Phil. 2:7 see O'Brien, *Philippians* 218-24.

87. For a telling application of 2 Cor. 4:5-7 to the preaching and pastoral tasks, see Cranfield, "Minister" 163-67.

88. But both BAGD (589d) and BDF (§456[1]) classify this use of ὅτι as a case for "loose subordination" (to be translated as "for").

edge of Christ he wished to share.[89] The spiritual principle is this: the person who has light (v. 5) is responsible to share that light (v. 4).

There is no need to regard this verse as anacoluthic,[90] for ἐστιν may be supplied before either ὁ θεός ("For it is the God who said . . . who has shone . . . ," RSV, NRSV) or ὃς ἔλαμψεν ("For God, who said . . . is the One who has shone . . . ," NASB). ὁ εἰπών is equivalent to a relative clause ὃς εἶπεν.[91] The translation "Light shall shine out of darkness" construes the future λάμψει as a "categorical imperative," as in ἀγαπήσεις τὸν πλησίον σου (Lev. 19:18; Matt. 5:43), "You shall love your neighbor."[92] Given this not infrequent use of the future tense in biblical Greek, it is unnecessary — although perfectly permissible — to translate λάμψει as though it were λαμψάτω (cf. Matt. 5:16), "Let (light) shine."[93] Whichever way φῶς λάμψει is rendered, the future is punctiliar, with consequent linear action assumed: "Light shall blaze forth and thereafter continue to shine."[94]

Although there is no direct quotation of an OT text, Paul seems to be alluding to Gen. 1:3-4 as modified by the expression φῶς λάμψει in Isa. 9:1.[95] These two texts read as follows in the LXX (points of contact are italicized).[96]

Gen. 1:3-4   καὶ *εἶπεν ὁ θεός*, Γενηθήτω *φῶς*. καὶ ἐγένετο *φῶς*. . . . καὶ διεχώρισεν ὁ θεὸς ἀνὰ μέσον τοῦ φωτὸς καὶ ἀνὰ μέσον *τοῦ σκότους*.

Isa. 9:1   ὁ λαὸς ὁ πορευόμενος ἐν *σκότει*, ἴδετε *φῶς* μέγα, οἱ κατοικοῦντες ἐν χώρᾳ καὶ σκιᾷ θανάτου, *φῶς λάμψει* ἐφ᾽ ὑμᾶς.

Because λάμψει is incontestably intransitive in meaning, it is probable that the adjacent ἔλαμψεν is also intransitive;[97] some, however, construe

---

89. Cf. Barclay: "This we must do because . . . ."

90. Several versions appear to treat ὅς as anacoluthic and so translate ὁ θεὸς ὁ εἰπών . . . ἔλαμψεν, "For God, who said . . . , has shone . . ." (NAB[1]; similarly Moffatt, Goodspeed, NEB, NIV, REB; also Furnish 202, 224). Also see note i. under Textual Notes. Héring 31 quite unnecessarily emends ὅς to ὅ (which then refers back to φῶς). Dautzenberg regards ὅς as functioning as a demonstrative introducing a new clause ("Überlegungen" 328).

91. Cf. Robertson 764; cf. 859.

92. See BDF §362; Zerwick §280.

93. This rendering is found in Goodspeed, NAB[1, 2], NIV, NJB, Cassirer.

94. Cf. JB, "Let there be light shining out of darkness."

95. Similarly Stockhausen 160-62 ("a composite quotation, a mutual interpretation of Genesis creation and Isaianic recreation," 160 n. 21); Hays 153 ("Paul's words . . . fuse Israel's confession of God as creator with Israel's hope of a messianic deliverer").

96. Other OT passages sometimes thought to have influenced Paul in 4:6 include (in the LXX): 2 Kgdms. 22:29 (καὶ κύριος ἐκλάμψει μοι τὸ σκότος μου); Pss. 17:29 (ὁ θεός μου, φωτιεῖς τὸ σκότος μου); 111:4 (ἐξανέτειλεν ἐν σκότει φῶς); Job 12:22 (ἐκ σκότους . . . εἰς φῶς); 37:15 (φῶς ποιήσας ἐκ σκότους); Isa. 42:6-7 (εἰς φῶς ἐθνῶν . . . καθημένους ἐν σκότει); 42:16 (ποιήσω αὐτοῖς τὸ σκότος εἰς φῶς); 49:6 (εἰς φῶς ἐθνῶν); 58:10 (τότε ἀνατελεῖ ἐν τῷ σκότει τὸ φῶς σου); 60:1-2. See, e.g., Oostendorp 48; Collange 139; Murphy-O'Connor 43.

97. Stanley suggests that the repetition of the verb λάμπω in the application (λάμψει . . . ἔλαμψεν) may indicate that Paul knew a form of Gen. 1:3 that contained this verb (216 n. 123).

ἔλαμψεν as causative, with φῶς as the implied direct object: "God . . . has caused a light to shine in our hearts."[98] But the transitive use of λάμπω is rare.[99] Since ἐν ταῖς καρδίαις ἡμῶν is parallel to the preceding ἐκ σκότους, Paul is not only depicting the heart as by nature dark through sin but also implying that conversion is the replacement of that darkness by light, a theme frequently expressed in the NT.[100] The καρδία denotes the whole person, with special reference to inward relations and religious experience.[101] ἐν may stand for εἰς and denote the goal of the divine illumination,[102] but more probably it is "pregnant" or proleptic, that is, it signifies "(into and thus) in," as when Paul says that God has called believers ἐν εἰρήνῃ (1 Cor. 7:15), into a state of peace *in* which they should now live.[103] Conversion is the flooding of the darkened human heart by divine light. Whereas "the god of this age" blinds the mind (v. 4), the God of the ages shines in the heart. Paul's thought moves from the physical creation (λάμψει) to the spiritual re-creation (ἔλαμψεν), from nature to grace. The God of redemption is none other than the God of creation.[104] "It is the same God who said . . . who has shone. . . ."[105] But not only is the agent the same; the result of the action is the same — the creation and diffusion of light and consequently the dispersing and dispelling of darkness.

πρὸς φωτισμὸν τῆς γνώσεως τῆς δόξης τοῦ θεοῦ ἐν προσώπῳ Χριστοῦ. "To illuminate them [our hearts] with the knowledge of God's glory shining in the face of Christ." For the term φωτισμός, see 4:4. The parallelism between τῆς γνώσεως here and τοῦ εὐαγγελίου in 4:4, both after τὸν φωτισμόν, suggests that τῆς γνώσεως also is genitive of source (or subjective genitive)[106] and that the knowledge that produces illumination is nothing other than knowledge of the gospel. But it is not impossible that τῆς γνώσεως is epexegetic ("illumination

---

98. Furnish 202; so also NEB, REB; Meyer 492-93; Dupont 37; Zerwick, *Analysis* 398 (the φῶς is the light of faith).

99. A. Oepke, *TDNT* 4.16.

100. E.g., Acts 26:18; Eph. 5:8; Col. 1:12-13; 1 Thess. 5:4-5; 1 Pet. 2:9.

101. But BAGD 403d and JB render καρδίαι here by "minds."

102. Thus A. Oepke, *TDNT* 4.25.

103. Cf. Col 3:15, ἡ εἰρήνη . . . εἰς ἣν καὶ ἐκλήθητε.

104. The christological hymn, Col. 1:15-20, makes the same point with regard to Christ. Note also the movement from the song of creation in Revelation 4 (vv. 10-11) to the song of redemption in Revelation 5 (vv. 9-10).

105. Noting the similarities and significant differences between 4:4 and 4:6, MacRae proposes that after boldly describing Satan as "the god of this world" — a designation that could be taken by a proto-gnostic to refer to the inferior demiurge-God of the Jews as opposed to the supreme God — Paul carefully forestalls any possible Gnostic-dualist misunderstanding or misuse of the description by insisting in 4:6 on the identity between the Creator God of Genesis and the God of enlightenment (420-31). This proposal accords with Paul's custom of forestalling misunderstanding of his previous statements (by epidiorthosis; see on 1:24), but although MacRae distinguishes developed Gnosticism from first-century "proto-gnosis" (430), there is no evidence for the existence of a first-century view of an inferior demiurge who might be described as "the god of this age."

106. A. Oepke, *TDNT* 4.26; Plummer 94, 120-21; Windisch 140; Héring 31 ("illuminating knowledge"); Furnish 224.

that consists in the knowledge," Barrett)[107] or even objective ("to reveal the knowledge," Zerwick).[108] Certainly, of the two genitives that follow, the first (τῆς δόξης) is objective, and the second (τοῦ θεοῦ) possessive. Seen as Paul's final comment on the Exodus 34 narrative, which formed the backdrop to 3:7-18, ἐν προσώπῳ Χριστοῦ must be rendered "(shining) on the face of Christ" (cf. 3:7),[109] and not "(embodied) in the person of Christ" (with πρόσωπον, "face," standing for "person" by synecdoche).

Two issues remain. First, is Paul alluding to his own conversion experience in 4:6? In itself the aorist ἔλαμψεν is ambiguous, for while it could refer to the Damascus christophany, it might equally well describe "a second act of cosmic creation"[110] or numerous conversion experiences. In each of these three cases ἔλαμψεν would be constative aorist. But it could also be gnomic, referring to God's perpetual illuminating. What makes an allusion to Paul's Damascus encounter with the risen Christ likely are the many similarities in thought and diction between 2 Cor. 4:6 and the three Lukan accounts of Paul's conversion in Acts. In both sets of data there are inward and outward aspects to the conversion, but while Paul emphasizes here the inward, the Acts accounts stress the outward phenomena.

2 Cor. 4:6	*Acts*
ἔλαμψεν	περιήστραψεν (9:3)
	περιαστράψαι (22:6)
	τὴν λαμπρότητα (26:13)
	περιλάμψαν (26:13)
ἐν ταῖς καρδίαις	hearing (9:4; 22:7, 14-15; 26:14)
	"seeing" (9:17, 27; 22:14-15; 26:13, 16 [twice], 19)
φωτισμός	φῶς (9:3; 22:6, 9, 11; 26:13)
τῆς δόξης	τῆς δόξης τοῦ φωτὸς ἐκείνου (22:11)
	ὑπὲρ τὴν λαμπρότητα τοῦ ἡλίου (26:13)
ἐν προσώπῳ Χριστοῦ	ἰδεῖν τὸν δίκαιον (22:14)[111]

The plural ἐν ταῖς καρδίαις (ἡμῶν) may seem a difficulty for the view that 4:6 refers primarily to Paul's Damascus experience since in 6:11 the singular ἡ καρδία (ἡμῶν) refers to Paul alone. It may be, however, that this plural is a hint

---

107. Barrett 127, 134; so also REB; Young and Ford 265.

108. Zerwick, *Analysis* 398; Louw and Nida §28.36; Sandnes 143, in the course of arguing that φωτισμός in 4:6 refers to the enlightenment that came to Paul himself in his Damascus "throne vision" (137-38) and that Paul viewed his apostolic commission in prophetic terms (145).

109. ἐν may justifiably be filled out with "shining in" (GNB; Louw and Nida §28.36; cf. NAB¹; Spicq 1.369; 3.484, "shining on"), "reflected in" (Bruce, *Paraphrase* 133), "which is radiant on" (Weymouth), or "seen in" (TCNT; Martin 75).

110. A. Oepke, *TDNT* 4.25.

111. In Acts 22:14 ἀκοῦσαι φωνὴν ἐκ τοῦ στόματος αὐτοῦ would seem to imply that the preceding statement ἰδεῖν τὸν δίκαιον includes the seeing of Christ's face.

that Paul viewed his own conversion experience, seen as the advent of light and the dispelling of darkness (not as involving a christophany), as a paradigm for all Christian conversion.[112]

Second, does φωτισμός refer to God's work in the human heart or to Paul's activity in preaching the gospel? An appeal is sometimes made to Acts 26:16-18 ("I have appeared to you for this purpose, to appoint you to serve and bear witness to the revelation of me you have already had . . . that they [the Gentiles] may turn from darkness to light") to support the view that while ἔλαμψεν alludes to Paul's conversion, πρὸς φωτισμόν depicts the purpose of his conversion, namely his dissemination of the gospel.[113] Now the πρός phrase certainly indicates the purpose of the λάμψις (BAGD 710a). But there is no reason to change the referent from ἔλαμψεν to φωτισμός,[114] especially since 4:4 indicates that the source of φωτισμός is the gospel (not Paul) and the cognate verb φωτίζω usually has a divine agent expressed[115] or implied.[116] In 4:6 Paul is affirming that God's act of shining in human hearts aims at his illumination of those hearts, an illumination that arises from knowing God's glory as it comes into clear focus on Christ's countenance.

Bibliography

Bain 380 • Baumert 114-17, 318-46 • Benoit 289-90 • Cranfield, "Minister" • Dautzenberg, "Überlegungen" • S. Davies • Dupont 36-39 • Eckstein 179-98 • Fitzmyer, "Glory" • Fowl 104-7 • S. R. Garrett, "The God of This World and the Affliction of Paul: 2 Cor. 4:1-12," in *Greeks, Romans, and Christians: Essays in Honor of Abraham J. Malherbe*, ed. D. L. Balch, et al. (Minneapolis: Fortress, 1990) 99-117 • Hanson, *Ministry* 72-75 • Hays 152-53 • Höpfl • K. Kertelge, "Jesus Christus verkündigen als den Herrn (2 Kor 4,5)," in K. Kertelge, et al. (eds.), *Christus bezeugen. FS W. Trilling* (Leipzig: St. Benno, 1989) 227-36 • Kim 5-13, 128-29, 137-268 • Klauck, "Erleuchtung" • Larsson 279-89 • Lindars 162-63 • MacRae • D. E. Marietta, "Conscience in Greek Stoicism," *Numen* 17 (1970) 176-87 • Muellensiefen • Murphy-O'Connor 42-44 • Newman 220-25, 229-35 • Oostendorp 47-49 • Sandnes 131-45 • Savage 111-29 • Stanley 215-16 • Stockhausen 154-77 • Thrall, "ΣΥΝΕΙΔΗΣΙΣ" • M. Uddin, "Paul, the Devil and 'Unbelief' in Israel (with Particular Reference to 2 Corinthians 3–4 and Romans 9–11," *TynB* 50 (1999) 265-80 • Zorrell

---

112. Similarly Theissen, *Aspects* 123 n. 16 (followed by Klauck, "Erleuchtung" 294); MacRae 423; Kim 6. Others who recognize an allusion to Paul's conversion in 4:6 include K. H. Rengstorf, *TDNT* 1.437; Newman 221-22; Thrall 317-18; Sandnes 134-38; Dautzenberg 326-33.

113. E.g., Plummer 121; similarly Bultmann 108; Oostendorp 48; Kim 9. Cf. Conybeare in Conybeare and Howson ("that [upon others also] might shine forth the knowledge . . . ," 447); Moffatt ("God . . . has shone within my heart to illuminate men with the knowledge . . .").

114. So, rightly, Thrall 318.

115. John 1:9; 1 Cor. 4:5; 2 Tim. 1:10; Rev. 21:23; 22:5.

116. Eph. 1:18; Heb. 6:4; 10:32. Eph. 3:9 is the one place where φωτίζω describes human (Paul's) action.

2. *The Suffering and Glory of the Apostolic Ministry (4:7–5:10)*

a. The Trials and Results of Apostolic Service (4:7-15)

In 2:14–4:6 Paul has described the consummate privilege of being a minister of the new covenant, whose glory far exceeds that of the Mosaic economy. Now he proceeds to show that the exercise of this glorious ministry of communicating the good news takes place, paradoxically, in circumstances that are anything but glorious. He faces incessant trials (4:8-9) and has repeated confrontations with death (4:10-12).[1] But in spite of these sufferings, silence is impossible, because faith in the gospel and Christian hope of resurrection necessitate fearless proclamation (4:13-14). Moreover, this frailty of the gospel's messengers (4:7a) has two beneficial effects: the power of the gospel to transform lives and his strength to endure suffering are seen to come from God, not from himself (4:7b); God, not man, is glorified, as God's grace spreads and thanksgiving to him is increased (4:15).[2] There are three main themes in 4:7-15: power in the midst of weakness (vv. 7-9), life in the midst of death (vv. 10-12), and faith leading to speech (vv. 13-14).

7*This treasure entrusted to us is contained in earthenware jars to make it clear that the extraordinary power is God's and is not derived from us.* 8*We are hard-pressed at every turn but not cornered, bewildered but not totally desperate,* 9*persecuted but not abandoned, struck down but not destroyed.* 10*We always carry around in our body the dying of Jesus, so that the life of Jesus may also be displayed in our body.*[a] 11*For we — who are alive — are continually*[b] *being handed over to death for Jesus' sake, so that the life of Jesus may also be displayed in our mortal flesh.* 12*So then, death is operative in us, but life in you.* 13*But since we have the same spirit of faith that is described in the scriptural text, "I believed and therefore I*[c] *spoke," we also believe and therefore we too speak.* 14*For we know that he who raised Jesus*[d] *will raise us with Jesus*[e] *in our turn and will bring us into his presence along with you.* 15*Yes, all this is for your benefit, so that when grace has widened its scope through more and more people, it may increase thanksgiving, to the glory of God.*

TEXTUAL NOTES

a. Perhaps wishing to make the thought explicitly universal, some scribe(s) substituted the plural τοῖς σώμασιν (א 0243 326 1739 1881 pc it[r, t] vg syr[p] bo[pt] Origen) for the singular.

b. In the place of ἀεί some witnesses (p[46] F G it[a, b] syr[p] Irenaeus[lat] Tertullian Am-

---

1. Cf. Bultmann 110: "The φανέρωσις of ἀλήθεια (4:2), or the φωτισμός of γνῶσις (4:6) occurs in the νέκρωσις of the ἔξω ἄνθρωπος (v. 16)."

2. Lambrecht ("Nekrosis" 315-17) defends a threefold structure for 4:7-15: vv. 7-12, vv. 13-14, and v. 15.

brosiaster) read εἰ: "For if we who are alive are being handed over to death for Jesus' sake, it is [supplying ἐστιν] so that the life of Jesus. . . ." But this destroys the parallelism with v. 10 (v. 11a explicates v. 10a), and the A of AEI could easily have been accidentally omitted.

c. After διό some witnesses (ℵ F G 0186 1175 syr) add καί under the influence of the following statement, διὸ καὶ λαλοῦμεν. Cf. Stanley 216.

d. Although there is early and diverse support for the longer reading τὸν κύριον Ἰησοῦν (ℵ C D F G Ψ 1881 𝔐 itᵃ, ᵇ syr bo, preferred by NA²⁷ and UBS⁴ with a {B} = "almost certain" rating; Metzger 510), the shorter text τὸν Ἰησοῦν is to be preferred (in spite of possible assimilation to Rom. 8:11a) on the basis of strong Alexandrian (p⁴⁶ B [1739] — proto-Alexandrian, [0243 33] 1175* — later Alexandrian) and considerable Western (itʳ vg Tertullian) support, the scribal tendency to add divine names (see the textual variants in 4:6), and the frequent occurrence of the simple title Ἰησοῦς in the context (4:10a, b, 11a, b, 14b; so Kramer 25 and n. 32, 211 n. 738, supporting the shorter reading; Metzger himself dissents from the majority UBS⁴ committee view).

e. To some scribe(s) the expression ἡμᾶς σὺν Ἰησοῦ ἐγερεῖ apparently seemed an exegetical conundrum and altered σὺν Ἰησοῦ (read by p⁴⁶ ℵ* B C D* F G P 0243 6 33 81 104 365 1175 1739 1881 2464 pc latt cop Tertullian) to the inoffensive διὰ Ἰησοῦ (ℵ² D¹ Ψ 𝔐 syr).

4:7 Ἔχομεν δὲ τὸν θησαυρὸν τοῦτον ἐν ὀστρακίνοις σκεύεσιν. "This treasure entrusted to us is contained in earthenware jars." δέ may set up a contrast between ἡ δόξα τοῦ θεοῦ (v. 6) and human beings as ὀστράκινα σκεύη ("clay pots"), but more probably it serves here as a simple transitional participle ("now," "then"; BAGD 171c) that may be left untranslated. As in 4:1, the verb ἔχω denotes possession not in the sense of personal ownership (as though Paul owned the "treasure" and hid it in a container for safekeeping) but in the sense of privileged guardianship.[3] "We are trustees of this treasure."

A θησαυρός was a storehouse or strong room for precious things or any receptacle for valuables; hence it referred to anything precious, "treasure." The word is found only here and in Col. 2:3 in the Pauline corpus. This treasure must be something explicitly mentioned in the context because of τοῦτον, whether it be the illumination that comes from the knowledge of God's glory (v. 6) or from the gospel (v. 4),[4] the gospel and its glory[5] or the gospel itself (vv. 3-4),[6] or the ministry of the gospel (v. 1).[7] Common to all these proposals is a reference to the gospel.

3. Cf. BAGD 333a (citing 4:1, but not 4:7), "have = have someth[ing] over one, be under someth[ing]."

4. E.g., Plummer 126; Bruce 197.

5. E.g., Lietzmann 115. To identify the treasure as "apostolic glory" (Cerfaux, *Christian* 339) is too restrictive.

6. E.g., Barrett 138.

7. E.g., Rissi 45; cf. Bultmann 112 ("the θησαυρός is Paul's διακονία as a διακονία τῆς δόξης"); Gräbe 148 (the treasure is "the ministry in the New Covenant, with everything pertaining to it: the proclamation of the gospel, the knowledge of the glory of God, the being changed, the enlightenment of the heart"); Savage 164 (the treasure is "the ministry of the gospel of the glory of God").

The adjective ὀστράκινος, from ὄστρακον ("baked clay," "earthen vessel," "potsherd"), means "made of clay," or more generally denotes breakableness.[8] In general, ὀστράκινα σκεύη may be "utensils of clay" or even "perishable earthenware," but in conjunction with the preposition ἐν the phrase must refer to jars or vases or pots made of clay; thus "earthenware containers" or "clay pots." Such vessels were regarded as fragile[9] and as expendable because they were cheap and often unattractive.[10] So the paradox Paul is expressing is that although the container is relatively worthless (cf. σκεύη . . . ὀστράκινα in 2 Tim. 2:20), the contents are priceless. Although the gospel treasure is indescribably valuable, the gospel's ministers are of little value in comparison. In describing those to whom the gospel is entrusted (1 Thess. 2:4) as "earthenware vessels," Paul is not disparaging the human body or implying that the body is merely the receptacle of the soul (as in many Hellenistic texts).[11] For him the σκεῦος ("object," "vessel," "jar") was no more the container in which was placed the "treasure" of the ψυχή than the "outer person" was a detachable outer garment clothing "the inner person" (cf. 4:16). σκεύη refers to whole persons, who, although insignificant and weak in themselves, become God's powerful instruments in communicating the treasure of the gospel.

ἵνα ἡ ὑπερβολὴ τῆς δυνάμεως ᾖ τοῦ θεοῦ καὶ μὴ ἐξ ἡμῶν. "To make it clear that the extraordinary power is God's and not derived from us." This defines the purpose — also an achieved result — of the stated paradox. It is precisely because the proclaimers of the gospel are in themselves frail and fragile (witness vv. 8-9!), relatively insignificant and unattractive, that people clearly recognize that the transforming power (δύναμις) of the gospel is God's alone and that the strength (δύναμις) of its ministers to endure hardship comes from God alone.[12] This emphasis on the divine source of power and enablement is reminiscent of 1:1-10, 21-22; 2:17; 3:4-6; 4:1 and anticipates 12:9; 13:4.

Since ἵνα here marks a divine purpose, not an aim devised by Paul, it carries with it the implication that the purpose is achieved. If ἵνα . . . ᾖ referred to an aim that might or might not be realized, Paul could be suggesting that under different circumstances — if, for instance, the treasure had been lodged in a superior vessel — the transcendent power would proceed from a human source.[13]

---

8. BAGD 587c. On adjectives of material ending in -ινος, see Moulton and Howard 359.

9. In Ps. 30:13 (LXX) the psalmist laments that he has become "like a shattered pot" (ὡσεὶ σκεῦος ἀπολωλός).

10. Lev. 11:33 (LXX) stipulates that if an unclean animal falls into a σκεῦος ὀστράκινον ("clay pot"), everything in the pot will be unclean, and the pot must be smashed (συντριβήσεται). Similarly, a σκεῦος ὀστράκινον touched by a person with a discharge must be broken (συντριβήσεται) (Lev. 15:12). See further SB 1.861; 3.516; and Lambrecht, "Nekrosis" 314 n. 19. Manson finds in ὀστράκινα σκεύη an allusion to the small, cheap, and fragile pottery lamps sold in Corinth ("Suggestions" 156); cf. Savage 165-66.

11. For example, commentators often cite Philo (Quod Deterius Potiori Insidiari Solet 170): τὸ ψυχῆς ἀγγεῖον τὸ σῶμα, "the vessel that contains the soul, namely, the body"; cf. De Somniis 1.26.

12. Thrall (324-25) rightly recognizes this double significance of δύναμις in 4:7.

13. Similarly Thrall 324 n. 923.

Rather, the sense of ᾗ is "may be seen to be": "in order that the surpassing greatness of the power may be seen to belong to God" (Weymouth), "to show the preeminent power as God's" (Martin 82),[14] "so that it may be made clear that this extraordinary power belongs to God" (NRSV).[15] On the other hand, if ἵνα is actually consecutive rather than merely telic, ᾗ will mean "is": "so that the immensity of the power is God's" (NJB). If the abstract noun ὑπερβολή ("excess," "extraordinary character," "exceeding greatness," "preeminence," "immensity") is rendered adjectivally, several appropriate words could qualify "power": "transcendent," "extraordinary," "overwhelming," "preeminent," "incomparable." In parallelism with ἐξ ὑμῶν, which unambiguously denotes derivation ("[not]^[16] proceeding from/originating in us"), τοῦ θεοῦ could convey the idea of origin, "may be seen to come from God" (TCNT),[17] but the construction of εἶναί or γίνεσθαί τινος regularly denotes possession, as in 10:7 (Χριστοῦ εἶναι, "to belong to Christ") and 1 Cor. 6:19 (οὐκ ἐστὲ ἑαυτῶν, "you do not belong to yourselves"), and this sense is to be maintained here.[18] Because the gospel treasure has been entrusted to frail mortals who lack inherent power, the δύναμις displayed through preaching and in suffering is demonstrably divine and not human.

4:8-9   In these verses we have a list of trials (περιστάσεις) Paul experienced in the course of his ministry. Similar catalogues of hardships are found in Rom. 8:35-39; 1 Cor. 4:9-13; 2 Cor. 6:4-10; 11:23-28; 12:10; Phil. 4:11-12. The literary background for Paul's use of this device has been found in the Cynic-Stoic diatribe (Bultmann, 1910),[19] Jewish apocalyptic literature (Schrage, 1974),[20] the OT and Jewish concept of "the afflictions of the righteous" (Kleinknecht, 1984),[21] or the Greco-Roman depiction of the Stoic sage (Fitzgerald, 1988).[22] With regard to 4:8-9, some have derived the actual imagery from wrestling[23] (a possibility for v. 9b), others from the manhunt[24] (this pro-

14. Similarly Plummer 127; Furnish 252; Thrall 320.

15. Similarly TCNT, Moffatt, Goodspeed, Williams, Berkeley, RSV, NEB, GNB, JB, Barclay, NAB¹, NIV, REB. Cf. Lietzmann 114; Spicq, "Image" 229.

16. When a ἵνα clause is continued by μή, μή alone is repeated (Robertson 1413).

17. Thus BAGD 225d; Robertson 514 (but cf. 497); *Pictures* 226.

18. Cf. Winer 195.

19. Through his 1910 dissertation, *Der Stil der paulinischen Predigt und die kynisch-stoische Diatribe* (19), R. Bultmann popularized the German term *Peristasenkataloge* for these "catalogues of hardships" or "recitals of hazards."

20. W. Schrage, "Leid, Kreuz und Eschaton: Die Peristasenkataloge als Merkmale paulinischer theologia crucis und Eschatologie," *EvT* 34 (1974) 141-75.

21. K. T. Kleinknecht, *Der leidende Gerechtfertigte: Die alttestamentlich-jüdische Tradition vom "Leidenden Gerechten" und ihre Rezeption bei Paulus* (Tübingen: Mohr, 1984) 365.

22. J. T. Fitzgerald, *Cracks in an Earthen Vessel: An Examination of the Catalogues of Hardships in the Corinthian Correspondence* (Atlanta: Scholars, 1988) 30, 49-50. Two more recent studies, both of which appeared in 1991, are by M. S. Ferrari and M. Ebner (see the bibliography under 4:7-15).

23. E.g., Spicq, "Image" 214-28, followed by Murphy-O'Connor 45.

24. E.g., Allo 113-14.

posal fits best with v. 9a), and yet others from military combat[25] (which may accord with v. 9b).

There are four balanced antitheses:

ἐν παντὶ θλιβόμενοι	ἀλλ' οὐ στενοχωρούμενοι,
ἀπορούμενοι	ἀλλ' οὐκ ἐξαπορούμενοι,
διωκόμενοι	ἀλλ' οὐκ ἐγκαταλειπόμενοι,
καταβαλλόμενοι	ἀλλ' οὐκ ἀπολλύμενοι.

These eight participles, along with περιφέροντες in v. 10, may all depend on ἔχομεν (v. 7), indicating the circumstances attendant on the apostolic vocation, but it is better to view them as syntactically absolute, standing for the indicative. Such a grammatical usage seems to be typical of 2 Corinthians.[26] Nonetheless, the antitheses document what Paul has said in v. 7: the first element in each antithesis illustrates human weakness, the second illustrates divine power. The antitheses are stated as generalities, but behind each there stand numerous experiences that validate the general statement, as we shall see from Acts.

The negated second element does not indicate a mere mitigation of the hardship; rather, it points to an actual divine deliverance (cf. 1:8-9); not simply a change of outlook on Paul's part, but God's intervention. In each case, the second element is an intense or extreme form of the first (Tannehill 84), even when the two verbs seem to be synonymous.[27] This intensification is most clearly seen in the paronomastic ἀπορούμενοι . . . ἐξαπορούμενοι (v. 8b).

Whether ἐν παντὶ is rendered locally ("on every side," "in every way") or temporally ("at all times"),[28] the phrase belongs with all four antitheses.[29] Windisch (143) aptly cites Theophylact: ἐν παντὶ καιρῷ καὶ τόπῳ καὶ πράγματι ("at all times and in every place and circumstance"). The constant nature of the afflictions is also reflected in the temporal adverbs πάντοτε (v. 10) and ἀεί (v. 11). Paul regarded suffering as intrinsic, not extrinsic, to his ministry (cf. 1:4-6; Gal. 6:17; Col. 1:24; Acts 9:16). So far from being an anomaly or a proof of the illegitimacy of his claim to apostleship (as some of his Corinthian opponents seemed to believe), his afflictions and hardships were the badge of his apostolicity, evidence that the power of God rested upon him.[30]

Although participles are generally negated by μή in NT Greek, here four occurrences of οὐ are found. This apparent irregularity may be explained in two ways: οὐ is negating a single concept,[31] and examples of οὐ with a participle in

25. E.g., Plummer 129 (as a possibility).
26. So also Hughes 141 n. 10 (citing 5:12; 7:5; 8:19-20, 24; 9:11, 13; 10:5, 15; 11:6).
27. As in the case of the first pair, since their noun equivalents, θλῖψις and στενοχωρία, are conjoined (not opposed) in 6:4 and Rom. 2:9; 8:35 (Furnish 254).
28. Barrett combines both ideas: "At all times and in every way" (136, 138).
29. So, e.g., Plummer 128, Bultmann 113.
30. Cf. Kraftchick 630-31.
31. BDF §430[3]; BAGD 590b.

the papyri reflect "the lingering consciousness that the proper negative for a statement of a downright fact is οὐ."[32] This irregular, emphatic use of οὐ justifies those translations that render this particle by "never" in vv. 8-9.[33]

4:8 ἐν παντὶ θλιβόμενοι ἀλλ᾽ οὐ στενοχωρούμενοι, ἀπορούμενοι ἀλλ᾽ οὐκ ἐξαπορούμενοι. "We are hard-pressed at every turn but not cornered, bewildered but not totally desperate." The verb θλίβω, like its cognate noun θλῖψις, can refer to physical, psychological, or spiritual pressure or affliction. Perhaps it occurs first in the list precisely because it is the most comprehensive term available to denote any type of distress or tribulation. Although troubles pressed on Paul from every quarter, he never found himself crushed or cornered. στενοχωρέω refers to confinement in a restricted space in either a literal or a metaphorical sense. Because the power of God was active in preserving his life and his spirit, Paul never found himself in a plight from which there was no escape (cf. 1 Cor. 10:13). Hampered on all sides — yes, but without room to breathe — no. Everywhere and at all times afflicted, but never at the end of his tether. Through divine intervention, he was always able to retain his buoyancy of spirit. Acts 18:12-17 illustrates this general truth. When the Corinthian Jews made a concerted attack on Paul and brought him before Gallio's tribunal, he was not left without room to operate, for the proconsul dismissed the charge of religious sedition made against Paul, thus enabling him to continue his work in Corinth for "many days longer" (Acts 18:18 RSV) and his missionary endeavors in the eastern Mediterranean for the next decade (A.D. 52-62) "with the assurance of the benevolent neutrality of the imperial authorities."[34]

ἀπορούμενοι and ἐξαπορούμενοι are middles used as intransitive actives.[35] If ἀπορέω means "be at a loss," in the case of ἐξαπορέω (see 1:8 for this verb) the "perfective ἐξ shows the ἀπορία in its final result of despair,"[36] "be totally at a loss." Paul was frequently "perplexed, but not driven to despair" (RSV, NRSV), "bewildered, but never at our wits' end" (REB), "near-desperate but not wholly desperate" (Thrall 320), "at a loss but not completely baffled" (Barrett 136). It is difficult to reproduce Paul's play on words. Denney suggests "put to it, but not utterly put out" (757). Hughes has "confused, but not confounded" (138 n. 7). We propose "at a loss, but not lost." The instance from Paul's life that readily comes to mind as an illustration of this claim is his traumatic experience in Asia (2 Cor. 1:8-10), for he himself admits that at that time he "despaired even of life" (ἐξαπορηθῆναι . . . καὶ τοῦ ζῆν, 1:8), using the verb which here he negates! We may account for this apparent contradiction by observing that Paul's Asian encounter with death, when he *did* despair, taught him

---

32. Moulton 232; similarly Robertson 1137-38.

33. TCNT (4 instances), Weymouth (4), Goodspeed (1), Williams (3), NEB (3), GNB (2), JB (4), Barclay (2), NAB[1] (3), NJB (3), REB (4), Cassirer (4).

34. Bruce, *History* 317; cf. his *Paul* 254-55.

35. Cf. Turner 56.

36. Moulton 237. On the perfective function of ἐκ/ἐξ in compound verbs, see Moulton and Howard 308-11; Robertson 596-97.

that there was no need ever again to despair with regard to any circumstance, for "the God who raises the dead" (1:9) was well able to deliver his servant from even extreme peril, if he so chose. On this view, 4:8b states aphoristically the lesson Paul learned from the experience recorded in 1:8-10.

4:9 διωκόμενοι ἀλλ᾽ οὐκ ἐγκαταλειπόμενοι, καταβαλλόμενοι ἀλλ᾽ οὐκ ἀπολλύμενοι. "Persecuted, but not abandoned; struck down, but not destroyed." In secular Greek διώκω regularly means "chase," denoting the pursuit of an animal in a hunt or of the enemy in battle. Its meaning was naturally extended to refer to persecution, a sense it often bears in Paul's letters (e.g., 1 Cor. 4:12; 15:9; Gal. 1:13, 23; Phil. 3:6). The doubly compounded verb ἐγ-κατα-λείπω denotes the complete (κατά) desertion (λείπω, "leave") of someone who is in (ἐν) a situation where aid is urgently needed.[37] It is used in Jesus' cry of dereliction (Matt. 27:46; Mark 15:34, citing Ps. 21:2 LXX) and also of Paul's experience of being "left in the lurch" by Demas (2 Tim. 4:10) and by his potential supporters at his final trial (2 Tim. 4:16). Here the verb is reminiscent of God's repeated promise never to abandon his own people (e.g., LXX Gen 28:15; Deut. 31:6, 8; Ps. 36:25, 28). So Paul's statement means "we are persecuted by men, but never abandoned by God" (Barclay).[38] Acts 16:16-40 is a vivid example of the truth of Paul's statement. At Philippi, after being hounded for many days by a slave girl who was possessed by a spirit of divination, Paul exorcised the spirit, but he and Silas were then seized by the girl's owners, dragged into the agora, and charged before the local magistrates with creating a breach of the peace. There followed a beating and imprisonment. But so far from abandoning them to their fate, God miraculously intervened on their behalf through an earthquake at midnight, which led to the conversion of the jailer and his household, the release of Paul and Silas, and the public apology of the magistrates.

καταβάλλω was a technical term in wrestling ("throw down"), in boxing ("knock down"),[39] and in battle ("strike down").[40] Thus Barclay renders the antithesis, "We are knocked down, but not knocked out," and Plummer paraphrases, "beaten to the earth, yet not killed outright" (123). But this verb, along with ἀπόλλυμι ("destroy"), has such a wide range of applications that it is unwise to restrict either term or both terms to a particular type of adversity. So the preferable translation is "struck down, but not destroyed" (RSV, NRSV), or in Wand's paraphrase, "beaten to my knees, but not finished off," or, we may propose, "knocked to the ground, but not permanently 'grounded.'" The obvious

---

37. "καταλείπω *abandon* (perfective) is supplemented with ἐν, pointing to the plight *in* which the victim is left" (Moulton and Howard 305).

38. If the background of the metaphor is taken to be a foot race, the meaning will be "pursued, but not overtaken" (Héring 31); if the manhunt, "hunted, but not caught up with" (Allo 113, 115, "pourchassés mais non dépassés"); if battle, "chased from the field, yet not left to the mercy of the foe" (Plummer 123).

39. See Windisch 144; Spicq, "Image" 226.

40. Plummer 129: "struck down, either ἐν ρομφαίᾳ (2 Kings xix.7), or ἐν μαχαίρᾳ (Jer. xix.7), or any other weapon (Hdt. iv.64)."

illustration of this aphorism is Paul's stoning at Lystra (Acts 14:19-20), when he was (literally!) struck down by a barrage of stones, dragged out of the city, and left for dead. On this occasion the divine aid came to Paul (at least in part) through the eager assistance of his converts in Lystra (Acts 14:20), so that (miraculously?) he was able to set out for Derbe the following day!

When these four pairs of antitheses are read, as they might be, as illustrations of the thematic statement in v. 7, it is clear that in Paul's estimation, this "hardship catalogue" demonstrates, not his virtuous character or his buoyant self-sufficiency or his steadfast courage amid adversity (as in the case, for example, of the Stoic sage), but his utter dependence as a frail human being on the superlative excellence (ὑπερβολή) of God's power.[41] Also, it was not a case of divine power revealing itself as weakness or transcending and replacing human weakness, but of divine power being experienced in the midst of human weakness.

4:10 πάντοτε τὴν νέκρωσιν τοῦ Ἰησοῦ ἐν τῷ σώματι περιφέροντες, ἵνα καὶ ἡ ζωὴ τοῦ Ἰησοῦ ἐν τῷ σώματι ἡμῶν φανερωθῇ. "We always carry around in our body the dying of Jesus, so that the life of Jesus may also be displayed in our body." Vv. 10 and 11 form a theological interpretation of the antitheses of vv. 8-9, so that the phrases ἡ νέκρωσις τοῦ Ἰησοῦ (v. 10a) and εἰς θάνατον παραδιδόμεθα διὰ Ἰησοῦν (v. 11a) sum up and explain the experience of being "hard pressed," "bewildered," "persecuted," and "struck down," and ἡ ζωὴ τοῦ Ἰησου (vv. 10b, 11b) accounts for Paul's preservation from being "cornered," "totally desperate," "abandoned," and "destroyed."

νέκρωσις occurs only here and in Rom. 4:19 in the Greek Bible. It may refer to the act or process of "putting to death" (thus "killing," "slaying"),[42] the process of "dying" or of "being put to death," "death,"[43] or the state of "deadness" (as in Rom. 4:19, of the "deadness" of Sarah's womb[44]).[45] The first meaning is active (= θανάτωσις),[46] the second and third, passive (= τὸ ἀποθνήσκειν and θάνατος, respectively). In favor of the second meaning is the fact that physicians used the term to describe the "withering or mortification of the body or of a sick member."[47] If νέκρωσις were merely a stylistic variant of θάνατος (as proponents of "death" as the meaning here tend to assume), one would have expected Paul to use his customary word for "death," θάνατος, in v. 10, then νέκρωσις in v. 11. Perhaps Paul uses νέκρωσις in v. 10 to portray not a single

---

41. "While the message about justification and that about the cross focus on the *iustitia aliena* and *sapienta [sic] aliena* (Rm. 1:16-17; 1 Cor. 1:18–2:5), in the context of Paul's sufferings the emphasis falls on the *vis aliena,* the *virtus aliena,* the *vita aliena*" (Gräbe 153).

42. This meaning is defended by BAGD 535d; Meyer 495-96; Windisch 145; Barrett 139-40; cf. de Boor (102, "die Tötung").

43. So, e.g., R. Bultmann, *TDNT* 4.895; Lambrecht, "Nekrosis" 309.

44. Some witnesses (D it syr^sin) read νέκρωσις for πώρωσις ("hardening") in Mark 3:5.

45. So, e.g., Güttgemanns 114-17; Collange 154-55; Thrall 331-32.

46. Thucydides 5.9.7.

47. R. Bultmann, *TDNT* 4.895, citing Galenus 18.1. And Plummer (130) cites Epictetus, *Dissertationes* 1.5.4, where ἀπονέκρωσις denotes the process of mortification.

event (the death of Jesus), but a prolonged process, the course of events leading up to Jesus' death (Meyer 496) or the daily trials and hardships that befell Jesus as an itinerant preacher,[48] either of which could be portrayed as his "being put to death" or "being given up to death" (cf. v. 11a) and would aptly foreshadow Paul's constant apostolic afflictions. That νέκρωσις depicts a process rather than an event also seems indicated by the precise parallelism between vv. 10 and 11,[49] so that v. 11a restates v. 10a: the νέκρωσις is nothing other than the ἀεὶ ... εἰς θάνατον παραδίδοσθαι (present tense). Paul faced perilous hazards every hour and death every day, as he says in 1 Cor. 15:30-31: "Why are we in jeopardy every hour? Death is my daily companion!" (cf. Rom. 8:36).[50] But if the νέκρωσις is seen as a constant "being delivered up to death," it is not merely the constant *danger* of death or "the daily liability to a violent death"[51] which is envisaged, but the actual experience of "deadly" trials, any one of which could deal the final blow of physical death.[52]

On this view of νέκρωσις, τοῦ Ἰησοῦ is a possessive genitive, "the dying experienced by Jesus." But for those who see in νέκρωσις a reference to the Christian's once-for-all baptismal identification with Christ in his death (Rom. 6:3-5),[53] the daily mortification of the sinful nature (Gal. 5:24; cf. Luke 9:23), or the gradual weakening of physical powers as a result of serving Christ (4:12, 16a), the genitive τοῦ Ἰησοῦ is "general" or relational, simply indicating the appurtenance of the believer's νέκρωσις to the earthly or risen Jesus.

περιφέρω is certainly an appropriate term for the peregrinations of an itinerant missionary such as Paul, but there is no allusion here to his missionary journeys; περι- simply means "here and there, wherever we go." Like the participles in vv. 8-9, περιφέροντες should be treated as syntactically independent, functioning as an indicative, especially since it supports a subordinate ἵνα clause (v. 10b). τῷ σώματι in v. 10a and v. 10b is a distributive singular ("our bodies") (Turner 24).

In v. 10b, whether καί ("also") is taken with the telic ἵνα or with ἡ ζωή, it points to the simultaneity of the περιφέρειν and the φανερωθῆναι. Just as the two elements in the four antitheses of vv. 8-9 are simultaneous, so also the νέκρωσις τοῦ Ἰησοῦ (v. 10a) and the ζωὴ τοῦ Ἰησοῦ (v. 10b) are coincident in the experience of Paul and his fellow workers. ἡ ζωὴ τοῦ Ἰησοῦ refers to the im-

48. Belleville, "Gospel" 142.
49. See below on v. 11.
50. Gal. 6:17 (ἐγὼ γὰρ τὰ στίγματα τοῦ Ἰησοῦ ἐν τῷ σώματί μου βαστάζω) is similar in thought to 2 Cor. 4:10, but narrower in reference. The στίγματα were only one instance of the νέκρωσις.
51. Vincent 820; similarly Louw and Nida (§23.99): "Paul was constantly in danger of dying in the same manner in which Jesus died, that is to say, by violence."
52. But this is not to deny that for Paul "behind the physical suffering lay a 'dying with Christ' which gave it meaning" (Barrett 140). Proudfoot has rightly observed that "Paul knows suffering as a *participatio Christi* and not as an *imitatio Christi* only" (160).
53. For a discussion of this view, see Thrall 332-34. She herself sees the significance of the περιφέρειν of the νέκρωσις τοῦ Ἰησοῦ as "primarily revelational" (334).

mortal life of the risen Jesus, not the earthly life of the historical Jesus. It is both the life that belongs to Jesus (possessive genitive) by virtue of his resurrection (Rom. 6:9-10) and the life that is imparted by Jesus (subjective genitive) through his Spirit (3:6; Rom. 8:2). This life of Jesus is intimately related to the power of God (v. 7), for both were operative in the preservation of Paul's body and spirit (vv. 8-9). Perhaps Paul regarded God's power as being exhibited (ᾗ, v. 7) through Jesus' risen life, which in turn was displayed (φανερωθῇ, vv. 10-11) "in" Paul's body, that is, by the recurring deliverances from despair and death he experienced. Now it is true that the final display of Jesus' resurrection life will occur when, as the deliverer (σωτήρ), he will transform the lowly bodies of believers by giving them the appearance and character of his own glorious body (Phil. 3:20-21). But any allusion to the resurrection here is decidedly secondary,[54] because νέκρωσις and ζωή are primarily concurrent present realities, and resurrection will be a μετασχηματισμός (cf. Phil. 3:21) of the body rather than a φανέρωσις in the body.

In this verse, then, Paul is making two important affirmations regarding Christian experience. First, the resurrection life of Jesus is evident at precisely the same time as there is a "carrying around" of his dying. Indeed, the very purpose of the believer's identification with Jesus in his sufferings is to provide an opportunity for the display of Jesus' risen life. Second, one and the same physical body is the place where the sufferings of Jesus are repeated and where his risen power is manifested.[55]

4:11 ἀεὶ γὰρ ἡμεῖς οἱ ζῶντες εἰς θάνατον παραδιδόμεθα διὰ Ἰησοῦν, ἵνα καὶ ἡ ζωὴ τοῦ Ἰησοῦ φανερωθῇ ἐν τῇ θνητῇ σαρκὶ ἡμῶν. "For we — who are alive — are continually being handed over to death for Jesus' sake, so that the life of Jesus may also be displayed in our mortal flesh." Basically this is a restatement of v. 10 (cf. γάρ), with certain changes or additions that clarify or expand the previous verse:

(1) Both ἀεί and πάντοτε (v. 10) mean "always," but ἀεί may stress duration: "continually," or even "continuously" (= without interruption).

(2) οἱ ζῶντες qualifies ἡμεῖς, "we who are alive" (NIV);[56] or better, "we — who are alive — (are continually being handed over to death)," which highlights the life-death paradox which is at the heart of vv. 10-11: we are "the living dead" or "the dying living"! A similar emphasis, in reverse, is found in 6:9: "as dying — but see, we live." It is also possible that ζῶντες bears an adverbial sense: "while we live" (RSV, NRSV)[57] or "although we are

54. *Pace* Lietzmann 115-16; Guntermann 65; Barrett 140. But v. 14 leads Hodge (95) to believe that a reference to the resurrection is included in v. 10.

55. It is possible, but unlikely, that ἐν in vv. 10b, 11b is instrumental ("through") rather than locative ("in").

56. Or "we, the living" (Carrez 111; de Boor 102). If Paul had meant "we who expect to live until the parousia" (cf. Barrett 140), he would probably have added a phrase such as (οἱ περιλειπόμενοι) εἰς τὴν παρουσίαν τοῦ κυρίου after ἡμεῖς οἱ ζῶντες (as in 1 Thess. 4:15).

57. Cf. BAGD 336a, "we during our (earthly) life."

alive,"[58] which comports with the paradox Paul is expressing, although this would normally be expressed by ἡμεῖς ζῶντες. Given the pronounced emphasis on physical suffering in vv. 8-10a, the ζωή here alluded to will probably be physical life, which also suits the reference to physical death in v. 11a (εἰς θάνατον). But, conceivably, ἡμεῖς οἱ ζῶντες could mean "we who live (for God's glory)," or "we who have the life of Jesus" (cf. v. 10b).[59]

(3) εἰς θάνατον παραδιδόμεθα explains "we carry around in our body the dying of Jesus" (v. 10a). The verb παραδίδωμι is used in Jesus' predictions of his "handing over" to the Jewish and Roman authorities (e.g., Mark 9:31; 10:33; cf. 1 Cor. 11:23). This "handing over" was recognized by the early Christians to be, in an ultimate sense, the work of God, who "gave him up (παρέδωκεν αὐτόν) for us all" (Rom. 8:32; cf. 4:25). Accordingly, passive παραδιδόμεθα,[60] describing Paul's incessant "delivery to death," undoubtedly implies divine agency. It was none other than God who was surrendering Paul into the hands of death (εἰς θάνατον).[61] In a similar context Paul expresses his conviction (δοκῶ) that "God has exhibited us apostles at the very end of the procession, like the men condemned to die in the arena (ὡς ἐπιθανατίους)" (1 Cor. 4:9, Goodspeed). What Paul is envisaging in 4:11a is not merely constant exposure to the threat of death,[62] where death is merely possible or imminent, but actual "encounters" with death (cf. v. 12a), which led to physical debilitation (v. 16a) or scarring (cf. Gal. 6:17).

(4) διὰ Ἰησοῦν should not be taken as an elucidation of τοῦ Ἰησοῦ in v. 10a (see the commentary there). It means "on Jesus' account" or "for Jesus' sake" (RSV, NRSV) (= "because of Jesus").[63] Paul's suffering was on account of his loyal preaching of the gospel of Jesus.

(5) ἵνα καὶ ἡ ζωὴ τοῦ Ἰησοῦ φανερωθῇ is found both in v. 11b and in v. 10b, in each case emphasizing that the death and the life of Jesus were simultaneously (cf. καί, "also") evident in Paul's experience (cf. 1:4a, 5). It was not a matter of "life" after "death" or even life through death, but of life in the midst of death.[64] Paul's repeated deliverances from death and his refusal to despair in the face of persistent opposition (vv. 8-9, 10a, 11a; cf. 1:9-10) formed an open display (φανερωθῇ) to the Corinthians and his converts in general of the resur-

58. Klauck 46; similarly Moffatt.

59. See Baumert 78-81.

60. But Weymouth construes this verb as a reflexive middle: "we, alive though we are, are continually surrendering ourselves to death"; so also Fitzgerald 180.

61. One wonders whether Paul is here personifying death (cf. Rom. 5:14, 17; 6:9; 1 Cor. 15:26, 55). Collange (158) draws attention to the paradox: God hands Paul over to the "anti-God" death.

62. *Pace* BAGD 351b (on 4:11-12).

63. "For Jesus' sake" (as in many English translations) need not mean "for Jesus' benefit" (*pace* Furnish 257), for the English expression "for X's sake" may signify "because of X" (as in "persecution for opinion's sake") as well as "in the interest of/for the benefit of X."

64. In his treatment of 4:7-15 (on pp. 94-126) Güttgemanns goes one step further, arguing that "the νέκρωσις is . . . the paradoxical epiphany of ζωή" (123).

rection life of Jesus.[65] Through Jesus he kept on winning overwhelming victories (ὑπερνικῶμεν) in the face of daunting hardships (Rom. 8:35-37). The power of Jesus' resurrection was seen in patient endurance of suffering (Phil. 3:10), not in miraculous signs or ecstatic phenomena.

In the Epistles and Revelation, the proper name Ἰησοῦς is generally anarthrous,[66] but here it is articular in the phrase τὴν νέκρωσιν τοῦ Ἰησοῦ (v. 10a) and the repeated expression ἡ ζωὴ τοῦ Ἰησοῦ (vv. 10b, 11b). In the latter case the article could be anaphoric ("the life of this same Jesus whose dying I am carrying about," v. 10b; "the life of this same Jesus on account of whom I am constantly handed over to death," v. 11b), but in all three instances the canon of Apollonius would account for the presence of the article.

(6) Replacing the simple ἐν τῷ σώματι ἡμῶν of v. 10b is the expanded and emphatic (by position) ἐν τῇ θνητῇ σαρκὶ ἡμῶν, "in our mortal flesh." The addition of θνητός and the substitution of σάρξ for σῶμα have the effect of emphasizing the transitory, creaturely, and weak nature of the body that, paradoxically, is the very place where Jesus' powerful risen life is on display.[67]

Paul evidently saw a parallelism between Jesus' life of suffering and his own. This would account for three distinctive features of vv. 10-11: his use of νέκρωσις ("dying") rather than θάνατος ("death," v. 10a), his choice of the evocative verb παραδίδωμι, and the four uses of the simple name Ἰησοῦς (cf. the further two uses in v. 14), a phenomenon that draws attention to the earthly life of Christ. At the same time, however, the single word that he uses in v. 12 to encapsulate his apostolic experience is not παθήματα (cf. 1:5-7) but θάνατος, so that his identification with Christ was not only with the sufferings of Christ but also with the death of Christ, which was the climax of his suffering. This link between suffering with Christ and dying with Christ is explicit in Phil. 3:10: participation in Christ's sufferings (κοινωνίαν παθημάτων αὐτοῦ) is indistinguishable from conformity to his death (συμμορφιζόμενος τῷ θανάτῳ αὐτοῦ). To suffer for and with Christ is to die with Christ. For the Christian suffering is not a sign of divine disappointment but an opportunity to divine engagement.

4:12 ὥστε ὁ θάνατος ἐν ἡμῖν ἐνεργεῖται, ἡ δὲ ζωὴ ἐν ὑμῖν. "So then, death is operative in us, but life in you." V. 12a summarizes vv. 8-9, 10a, and 11a. ὥστε is an inferential conjunction here (= ὥς τε), marking a strong conclusion.[68] ὁ θάνατος refers not merely to circumstances that brought Paul

---

65. If φανερωθῇ is seen as a constative aorist in vv. 10-11, in each case summing up unitarily repeated or constant displays, there would be an appropriate correspondence to the two presents, περιφέροντες (v. 10) and παραδιδόμεθα (v. 11). Bultmann comments (110) on the influential φανέρωσις concept in 2:14; 4:2, 6, 10-11.

66. Blass 152; Turner 167.

67. But Barrett (141) takes σάρξ here in its dominant Pauline sense of "our present self-centred, man-centred, existence."

68. Cf. LSJ 2041a s.v.; Moule 144. That is, ὥστε here is retrospective rather than prospective (as Baumert 81-83).

within death's shadow (cf. μέχρι θανάτου ἐγγίζειν, "to be at death's door," Phil. 2:30) but also to experiences that left him with death's "visiting cards" (so to speak), namely, τὰ στίγματα τοῦ Ἰησοῦ (Gal. 6:17) and the διαφθείρεσθαι of the ἔξω ἄνθρωπος (4:16a).[69] A few commentators construe ἐνεργεῖται as passive, which would yield the meaning "death is made active in us," with God or God's incomparable power (v. 7b) the implied agent.[70] But the majority of translations rightly take the verb as middle, "is at work," "is active," "operates" (with θάνατος as the subject).[71] ἐν ἡμῖν means "in us," in the sense of "in our body" or "in our life" or "in our case." This phrase picks up ἐν ὀστρακίνοις σκεύεσιν (v. 7), ἐν τῷ σώματι ἡμῶν (v. 10), and ἐν τῇ θνητῇ σαρκὶ ἡμῶν (v. 11).

Although δέ is not preceded by μέν in v. 12a,[72] the antithesis is dramatic, for ἡ ζωή is the opposite of ὁ θάνατος and the ἐν ἡμῖν we would have expected in v. 12b in the light of vv. 10b and 11b is "replaced" by ἐν ὑμῖν. This unexpected substitution introduces a new thought, namely that there is some correlation between Paul's incessant νέκρωσις and the Corinthians' enjoyment of spiritual well-being and vitality "in Christ" (cf. Rom. 6:4, 11).[73] Paul is not implying that without his θάνατος the Corinthians would never experience ζωή, any more than he is denying that he himself ever experienced ζωή (which would contradict vv. 10b and 11b). Rather, the relation between v. 12a and v. 12b is both causal and proportional. Because he was experiencing "death," they were experiencing "life."[74] Expressed in the terminology of 1:3-7, his was the θλῖψις, theirs the παράκλησις; his the παθήματα, theirs the σωτηρία. In that earlier passage, he said "I suffer for Christ; God comforts me; I comfort you during your suffering." Here his thought seems to be, "I suffer 'death' for your sakes (cf. v. 15a); you enjoy more of the risen life of Christ as a consequence." He apparently saw not only a causal but also a proportional relation between his "death" and the "life" of the Corinthian believers.[75] The deeper his experience of the trials and sufferings of the apostolic life, the richer their experience of the joys and privileges of Christian existence (cf. Col. 1:24; 2 Tim. 2:10). The "middle term" between his experience and theirs was the divine comfort that, having received, he could then dispense (cf. 1:4). This rich theology of

69. But it is 5:1 (and probably 4:14), rather than 4:12, that indicates Paul's expectation of a pre-parousia death.

70. Furnish 252, 257, 285, following Baumert 72-73, 267-83 ("der *Tod* wird in uns energisch vollzogen," 41, 72). See also Clark, "ἐνεργέω" 93-101.

71. So also BAGD 265b, c (in the NT ἐνεργέω in the middle voice is intransitive and always has an impersonal subject).

72. K L syr[h] actually read μέν . . . δέ.

73. But not all relate ἡ ζωή to the Corinthians. Cf. Isaacs, "the life which is restored to us, is a life of vigorous work among you"; and Plummer (123), "So then it is His death that takes effect in us while it is His life which, through its power in us, takes effect in you."

74. Cf. Conybeare in Conybeare and Howson (447): "So then death working in me, works life in you."

75. This notion of proportionality is clear in 4:17 and seems implied in 4:12 and 4:16.

suffering was forged on the anvil of his own experience of "the sufferings of Christ."

4:13 ἔχοντες δὲ τὸ αὐτὸ πνεῦμα τῆς πίστεως κατὰ τὸ γεγραμμένον, Ἐπίστευσα, διὸ ἐλάλησα, καὶ ἡμεῖς πιστεύομεν, διὸ καὶ λαλοῦμεν. "But since we have the same spirit of faith that is described in the scriptural text, 'I believed and therefore I spoke,' we also believe and therefore we too speak." δέ is adversative ("but"): although suffering is part and parcel of the apostolic ministry, faith in God and in the gospel cannot but lead to the proclamation of the good news, the open declaration of the truth (v. 2b). That is, δέ looks back to vv. 8-12a and forward to ἡμεῖς πιστεύομεν, διὸ καὶ λαλοῦμεν. The causal participle ἔχοντες also anticipates πιστεύομεν κτλ., with which it should be construed.[76] If πνεῦμα refers to the Holy Spirit, τῆς πίστεως will be an objective genitive, "the same Spirit, who prompts faith."[77] If, on the other hand, πνεῦμα here means "disposition" (as in 1 Cor. 4:21; Gal. 6:1; Eph. 4:23; 1 Pet. 3:4),[78] genitive πῆς πίστεως may be either objective, "the spirit imbuing our faith" (Cassirer), or more probably adjectival, "the same spirit of faith"[79] (= "the same spirit that is marked by faith," "the same disposition that believes").[80] τὸ αὐτὸ πνεῦμα clearly implies a comparison, so the question arises, With whom does Paul share this "spirit of faith"? Some argue that since in v. 12 Paul has emphatically distinguished his experience from that of the Corinthians, he now wishes to stress their common faith.[81] But the preceding context contains no reference to the πίστις of the Corinthians, and it is arbitrary to equate πίστις with ζωή (v. 12b). It is more natural to see τὸ αὐτό as anticipating the formula κατὰ τὸ γεγραμμένον, "(that is) in accordance with what stands written (in Scripture),"[82] so that Paul views himself as sharing "the same spirit of faith" as was expressed by the psalmist when he said "I believed, and therefore I spoke."[83]

In Psalm 116 the psalmist recounts and rejoices in a divine deliverance from some dire peril, and in the presence of the congregation assembled in the

---

76. Winer 351; Plummer 133.

77. Similarly Barrett 142.

78. See BAGD 675d for this meaning of πνεῦμα.

79. RSV, NEB, JB, NJB, REB, NRSV. Similarly Hughes 147 and n. 15.

80. Vincent (820) proposes a blending of these two senses of πνεῦμα: the human faculty of faith as a gift of the Spirit.

81. E.g., Strachan 96; Schmithals 162 (4:13-14 is aimed at preventing a misunderstanding of 4:12, namely that Paul was without signs of ζωή, such as πίστις); Baumert 83-84.

82. This introductory formula is unparalleled in Paul, who prefers καθὼς γέγραπται (8:15, 9:9; see Ellis 22-25). τὸ γεγραμμένον ("that which stands written," Lietzmann 116; Wendland 188; "the written text," Thrall 321) here denotes "S/scripture" (JB, NJB, NEB, REB, NRSV) or "the Scriptural text."

83. So also, e.g., Meyer 499; Allo 116; Windisch 148; Thrall 339. But some identify the other figure in Paul's comparison as the Messiah, of whom the psalmist, in Paul's view, was speaking, that is, Jesus Christ (Goudge 42; Hanson, *Ministry* 78; *Paradox* 53; Hays, "Use" 128-29). Then Ps. 116:3-4 is sometimes thought to portray Gethsemane, and vv. 5-9 Easter (e.g., Goudge 42).

temple courts he renders thanks to Yahweh and pours out a libation of wine before the altar as a thank offering in fulfillment of vows made during his profound distress. The precise nature of this affliction is unknown, but it involved danger to life (vv. 3, 8, 15), perhaps through illness or persecution, and human fickleness and unreliability (v. 11). From vv. 10-11 we learn that in the extreme circumstances that prompted his alarm, the psalmist declared "I am suffering terribly" (v. 10b) and "every human being is unreliable" (in meeting obligations; v. 11b), yet even at this time he retained his faith in the only One who keeps faith and is true to his covenant love and his promises (vv. 5-6). The Hebrew of v. 10a *(he' emantî, kî ꜥᵃdabbēr)* may be translated "I kept my faith, even when I said ('I am greatly afflicted')" (RSV, NRSV; similarly NAB[1]) or "I believed; therefore I said ('I am greatly afflicted')" (NIV).[84] This latter understanding is reflected in the LXX (115:1, ἐπίστευσα, διὸ ἐλάλησα)[85] and the Vulgate *(credidi, propter quod locutus sum).*[86]

In following the LXX text and omitting the psalmist's actual cry of affliction (ἐγὼ δὲ ἐταπεινώθην σφόδρα, "I have been greatly abased"), Paul is clearly focusing on the principle "faith leads to speech" or "believing is the ground (cf. διό) for speaking."[87] As the principle applies to his case, Paul is affirming that in spite of the inroads of θάνατος in his life (v. 12a), his unswerving belief in God and in the gospel as God's powerful instrument to bring salvation to everyone who has faith (cf. Rom. 1:16) made it natural and necessary for him to declare (λαλεῖν) the good news (cf. 1 Thess. 2:2). As he has already said to the Corinthians: "Woe to me if I do not preach the gospel!" (1 Cor. 9:16). And so the correspondence between Paul and the psalmist regarding faith and speech is complete: the psalmist believed, and so did Paul (καὶ ἡμεῖς, "we also"); as a result of belief the psalmist spoke, and so did Paul (διὸ καί, "therefore [we] too").

4:14 εἰδότες ὅτι ὁ ἐγείρας τὸν κύριον Ἰησοῦν καὶ ἡμᾶς σὺν Ἰησοῦ ἐγερεῖ καὶ παραστήσει σὺν ὑμῖν. "For we know that he who raised Jesus will raise us with Jesus in our turn and will bring us into his presence along with you." In this verse the apostle continues to explain what enabled him to discharge his ministry of preaching Christ faithfully and boldly (3:6; 4:1, 5), even though it involved hardship and affliction and encounters with death (4:8-12a). It was not

84. Vocalizing the verb as ꜥᵃdubbār (= puꜥal of *dibbēr*, "drive away," "pursue," "persecute"), Dahood proposes the translation "I remained faithful though I was pursued" (by the emissaries of Sheol) (144, 148; cf. "Quotations" 23-24).

85. Allen (113) raises the possibility that διό ("therefore") in the LXX may be a corruption of an original διότι ("because" = Hebrew *kî*; cf. the corruption of διότι in Isa. 3:8; Jer. 20:4).

86. Given the ambiguity of the MT, it is not surprising that one scholar (Hanson, *Ministry* 76 and n. 1) will say that the LXX misunderstands the Hebrew, while another (Ellis 152) will claim that Paul is in agreement with both the LXX and the MT (as also in 6:2 [citing Isa. 49:8] and 9:9 [Ps. 111:9]). On Paul's use of the Psalms, see Harman 1-23.

87. The Hebrew text of Psalm 116 is split into two separate psalms (114 and 115) in the LXX, so that v. 10 in the MT has become v. 1 of the LXX's Psalm 115. If Paul knew the Greek text in this form, the three words he quotes stand thematically at the head of a psalm.

only his sharing the psalmist's conviction that faith cannot remain silent (v. 13), but also his Christian conviction that Christ's resurrection was a pledge of the resurrection of believers (v. 14). If persecution or toil should precipitate his actual death, he knew that a resurrection comparable to Christ's was his destiny as a believer.

εἰδότες is causal ("for we know,"[88] "with the knowledge that"), specifying the second reason (cf. ἔχοντες, v. 13) that "we believe, and therefore we speak."[89] "God who raises the dead" (1:9) is here described as "he who raised Jesus." God's raising of Jesus was a particular instance — the most dramatic! — of his characteristic role (ὁ ἐγείρων, 1:9) as one who raises the dead (cf. Rom. 4:17). But the raising of Jesus was not simply the most celebrated illustration of God's revivifying power. For Paul, Christ's resurrection formed the guarantee of believers' resurrection, which is the probable significance of the phrase σὺν Ἰησοῦ.

It is clear that σύν here cannot signify "at the same time with" or "in conjunction with," for Jesus' resurrection lies in the past, not the future. If this preposition meant "in the company of," referring to the final state of permanent fellowship with Christ,[90] we would have expected εἶναι σὺν Ἰησοῦ (cf. 1 Thess. 4:17; Phil. 1:23). It is not impossible that the sense is "*in union with* him, and by virtue of that union,"[91] but this is precisely what Paul means by his common ἐν Χριστῷ formula. σὺν Ἰησοῦ may be paraphrased "in the wake of Jesus' resurrection," "to share Jesus' resurrection,"[92] or "in virtue of his resurrection."[93] There is a comparable use of σύν in 1 Thess. 4:14: "For since we believe that Jesus died and rose again, even so, through the power of Jesus (διὰ τοῦ Ἰησοῦ[94]) God will bring (= raise) with him (σὺν αὐτῷ) those who have fallen asleep." In this case σὺν αὐτῷ has the meaning "as pledged by the resurrection of Jesus." Support for this general understanding of σύν in the context of believers' future resurrection comes from Paul's notion of Christ or the resurrection of Christ as the ἀπαρχή ("firstfruits") of believers' resurrection (1 Cor. 15:20, 23). The two resurrections are essentially one, for the total harvest is representatively and potentially present in the firstfruits. As surely as the harvest follows the firstfruits, the resurrection of the members of the body will follow the resurrection of the Head. In Christ's resurrection from the dead as the firstfruits of the Easter har-

---

88. NEB, REB; similarly NIV, NRSV.

89. On this view both ἔχοντες and εἰδότες relate to the whole clause ἡμεῖς πιστεύομεν, διὸ καὶ λαλοῦμεν.

90. Thus, e.g., Héring 33. Thrall translates (321) ". . . will raise us also (to be) with Jesus," which is explained as "to join Jesus in the resurrection existence" (343). σύν can hardly be instrumental (= "through Jesus"), as Plevnik (91) alleges.

91. Plummer (CGT) 79; cf. Tasker (75), "in virtue of our union with Jesus."

92. Bruce, *Paraphrase* 135.

93. Plummer 123; cf. 134.

94. It is of interest that some scribe(s), sensing the difficulty of σὺν Ἰησοῦ in 2 Cor. 4:14, substituted διὰ Ἰησοῦν (see Textual Note e.). On the parallelism in content between 4:14 and 1 Thess. 4:14, see Plevnik 84-86.

vest, believers have the pledge of the full ingathering. This is how the fifth-century Antiochian commentator Theodoret understood 1 Cor. 15:20. "In the resurrection of our Savior we have a guarantee (ἐχέγγυον)of our resurrection" (*Comm.,* ad loc.).[95]

καὶ ὑμᾶς, "us also" (RSV, NRSV), "us . . . in our turn" (JB, NJB), could refer to Paul and other apostles or colleagues, but coming after v. 12a, which probably refers to Paul alone, ἡμᾶς in v. 14 should also be restricted to Paul himself. If so, there is a contrast, comparable to the ἐν ἡμῖν–ἐν ὑμῖν antithesis in v. 12, between καὶ ἡμᾶς and σὺν ὑμῖν. But whereas in v. 12 the contrast was simply between Paul and the Corinthians, here he himself represents believers who will die before the parousia and therefore be "raised with Jesus," while the Corinthians are assumed to be among, and representatives of, believers who will survive until the parousia and who therefore will be transformed, but not "raised," prior to the joint presentation of both parties before the presence of God. Several aspects of this reconstruction need elucidation or justification.

The excursus above on Paul's affliction in Asia (1:8-11) argued that at the time of 2 Corinthians (or at least of chs. 1–9) Paul seems to be assuming for the first time (to judge from his extant letters) that he will die before the parousia. If this is correct, it should occasion no surprise that here he speaks of his own resurrection, at the same time tactfully assuming his readers' survival until the parousia. So the ἡμεῖς-ὑμεῖς antithesis does not distinguish "we as Israelites" from "you as Gentiles," as Oostendorp (65-66) alleges, but "I, Paul" as a Christian who expects to die before the parousia from "you Corinthians," who may well be alive at the time of the second advent. 1 Corinthians 15 indicates that in Paul's thought both the living and the dead will be "transformed" on the last day (v. 50), but only the dead will be "raised" — vv. 51-52 clearly contrast two groups, "the dead" who "will be raised" and those (= "we who remain until the coming of the Lord," 1 Thess. 4:15) who "will be changed" but not resurrected. "Resurrection" implies prior death.[96]

If, as is necessary, ἡμᾶς is supplied with παραστήσει, the action denoted by this verb follows the resurrection (ἡμᾶς . . . ἐγερεῖ). Although παρίστημι has a wide range of meaning, here it refers to God's presentation of believers to

---

95. See further on this whole topic, Harris 108-14.

96. Baumert (89-93) takes ἐγερεῖ to refer, not principally to a future resurrection from the dead, but (figuratively) to Paul's repeated restoration to vitality in the midst of suffering. This future tense is taken to be "modal" (citing [90], *inter alios,* Zerwick §279): "he who raised the Lord Jesus (must) also raise us (again and again renewed) with Jesus" (435). But the parallelism between ὁ ἐγείρας (v. 14a) and ἐγερεῖ (v. 14b), together with the καί before ἡμᾶς, makes it likely that v. 14b refers to a future bodily resurrection. Furthermore, in spite of 1:9b, Paul uses ῥύομαι (twice), not ἐγείρω, in 1:10 when referring to divine intervention amid affliction. See further Murphy-O'Connor ("Faith," 543-50), who, like Baumert and Holleman (191-94), sees the "resurrection" of 4:14 as existential; and the response by Romaniuk ("Résurrection" 248-52; cf. Plevnik 92-93), who argues for the eschatological interpretation, citing Rom. 8:11 and 1 Cor. 6:14 as other Pauline passages that use the same pre-Pauline catechetical material.

himself (with ἑαυτῷ understood; cf. Eph. 5:27)[97] or to Christ as bridegroom (cf. 11:2)[98] on the last day, or his bringing of believers safely into his presence[99] or "before his face,"[100] or his presentation of the redeemed before the judgment seat of Christ (5:10; cf. Rom. 14:10).[101] [ἡμᾶς] σὺν ὑμῖν emphasizes the identical destiny of all believers. Whether or not believers pass through death, there will be a joint presentation of the living and the dead before God or Christ (cf. 1 Thess. 4:16-17, ἅμα σὺν αὐτοῖς).[102]

4:15 τὰ γὰρ πάντα δι' ὑμᾶς, ἵνα ἡ χάρις πλεονάσασα διὰ τῶν πλειόνων τὴν εὐχαριστίαν περισσεύσῃ εἰς τὴν δόξαν τοῦ θεοῦ. "Yes, all this is for your benefit, so that when grace has widened its scope through more and more people, it may increase thanksgiving, to the glory of God." Four syntactic questions face us immediately. First, is πλεονάσασα transitive ("having increased the thanksgiving"),[103] or intransitive ("having increased")? πλεονάζω is transitive only once in the NT (1 Thess. 3:12), but intransitive six times.[104] Word order also supports taking the verb intransitively in this verse.

Second, does διά govern τῶν πλειόνων or τὴν εὐχαριστίαν?[105] If the latter ("because of the thanksgiving of increasing numbers of people"), the normal word order would have been either διὰ τὴν τῶν πλειόνων εὐχαριστίαν or διὰ τὴν εὐχαριστίαν τῶν πλειόνων, so it is better to take διά with τῶν πλειόνων.

Third, is διὰ τῶν πλειόνων to be construed with πλεονάσασα or with τὴν εὐχαριστίαν?[106] In the latter case, the neat balance of πλεονάσασα διὰ τῶν πλειόνων and τὴν εὐχαριστίαν περισσεύσῃ is lost, and περισσεύσῃ is overloaded with two qualifiers while πλεονάσασα stands alone. Also, if there is no conceptual break after πλειόνων, the effect of the alliteration πλεονάσασα . . . πλειόνων is greatly reduced.

Fourth, is περισσεύῃ transitive ("cause (thanksgiving) to abound"), or intransitive ("abound")?[107] In favor of the former option is the natural association of augmented thanksgiving with the glory of God. And since περισσεύω can take a direct object, the fact that τὴν εὐχαριστίαν is adjacent to περισσεύσῃ sup-

---

97. Martin 90; cf. NJB, "bring us to himself."

98. Plummer (CGT) 79.

99. Cf. RSV, NEB, NIV, REB, NRSV; Thrall 344; Plevnik 92.

100. Klauck 47; Lang 282.

101. Meyer 500. In keeping with his view of ἐγερεῖ (see n. 96), Baumert takes παρίστημι here to mean "present openly" or "bring into the light" (cf. φανερωθῇ, 4:10-11) before other people (41, 94-95, 297-99, 435).

102. Cf. Bruce, *Thessalonians* 99: God "will . . . present us (who have been raised) with you (who will still be alive)."

103. E.g., Baumert 41, 105, 435; Theobald 222-24.

104. Rom. 5:20; 6:1; 2 Cor. 8:15; Phil. 4:17; 2 Thess. 1:3; 2 Pet. 1:8. See BAGD 667b.

105. Baumert (104, 109) mentions Erasmus, Luther, Calvin, and Bengel as holding this latter position. Similarly Weymouth, Montgomery.

106. This latter view is held, *inter alios,* by G. Delling, *TDNT* 6.265 n. 8; Lietzmann 116; Wendland 188; Allo 117-18; Lang 282.

107. In favor of the intransitive meaning is Baumert 41, 105, 300-310 (citing Rom. 3:7 as a close parallel), 435; Theobald 222-24.

ports this view. Many commentators[108] and English translations[109] support this understanding of the four syntactic points considered, although there is wide variation in the renderings given.

τὰ πάντα ("all this"[110]) refers to all that Paul does and that happens to him, but in particular his preaching (vv. 2-3, 5, 7) and his suffering (vv. 8-12). A verb in the present tense, such as ἐστιν or γίνεται ("happens"), needs to be supplied with δι᾿ ὑμᾶς, "for your benefit" (JB, NIV, NJB). The apostle reminds his converts that all aspects of his life promote not his own good but theirs — a sentiment already expressed in 1:6, 24; 4:5, 12 (cf. 5:13) and a potent illustration of the principle that "in the lives of those who love God, everything continually works together for good" (Rom. 8:28). The ἵνα clause that follows indicates basically that even this "all for you" principle serves a higher purpose, an increase in the volume of thanksgiving offered to God, which enhances his glory. It is possible that χάρις here refers to "the grace of apostleship" (χάριν καὶ ἀποστολήν, Rom. 1:5) granted to Paul, or to God's lavish provision for the spiritual welfare of his people, especially Paul himself, but in the light of the phrase that follows, with its reference to the multiplication of God's grace in the lives of ever-increasing numbers of people, this "grace" probably signifies "the work of grace in conversion" (BAGD 878a).

πλεονάσασα is a temporal aorist participle ("having widened its scope," Cassirer; "once it [grace] has spread"),[111] although several translations treat it as a present participle ("as it extends," NRSV),[112] probably on the assumption that thanksgiving accompanies, rather than merely follows, the spread of the gospel.[113] In 2:6 and 9:2 οἱ πλείονες means "the majority," but here Paul does not seem to have in mind a comparison between a majority at Corinth who would be responsive to grace and a minority who would resist that grace.[114] Rather, οἱ πλείονες means "the increasing numbers,"[115] "more and more people" (NASB, GNB, NIV, NAB², NRSV), or simply "many" (Turner 30) or "others," "even more" (BDF §244[3]). These would be new converts. διά is not spatial ("throughout") but modal ("through [the conversion of]").[116]

---

108. Plummer 123, 134-35; Windisch 150-51; Hughes 152; de Boor 102; Barrett 136, 144-45; Furnish 252, 260-61; Martin 82, 90-91; Wolff 88, 96; Thrall 321, 346-47.

109. RV, TCNT, Goodspeed, RSV, NEB, NASB, GNB, JB, NIV, NAB², REB, NRSV, Cassirer.

110. BAGD 633b ("as a summation of what precedes").

111. Similarly Barrett 136; Thrall 321. Louw and Nida (§59.67) explain the meaning of πλεονάζω as follows: "to increase considerably the extent of an activity or state, with the implication of the result being an abundance."

112. Also GNB, NJB, REB.

113. It is tempting to treat πλεονάσασα as a modal aorist participle ("by extending," "by enlarging its scope"), but such participles generally follow the finite verb (e.g., ἑαυτὸν ἐκένωσεν . . . λαβών, Phil. 2:7).

114. But see Barrett 144-45.

115. Moule 108. Similarly Goodspeed; Lietzmann 116; Wendland 188; Lang 282.

116. Referring τῶν πλειόνων to the Corinthians, Bernard takes διά to mean "through the [prayers of the] greater number of you" (63).

If πλεονάσασα points to an increase that results in abundance, περισσεύσῃ conveys the idea of an abundance that overflows. Bengel aptly observes that "πλεονάζω has the force of a positive; περισσεύω, of a comparative, Rom. v.20" (3.373). Paul is envisaging that, with the expansion of God's grace by means of the conversion of an ever-growing multitude of people, the volume of thanksgiving to God for the receipt of illumination (cf. 4:6) would be greatly augmented and therefore God's greater glory would be achieved.[117]

Bibliography

Bauer 107-15 • Baumert • P. Bonnard, "Mourir et vivre avec Jésus Christ selon St. Paul," *RHPR* 36 (1956) 101-12 • Bosenius 45-96 • M. Bouttier, "La souffrance de l'apôtre. 2 Co 4,7-18," in Lorenzi (ed.), *Diakonia* 29-49 • Bultmann, *Stil* • C. Chavasse, "Studies in Texts — 2 Cor. 4:7," *Th* 54 (1951) 99-100 • Crafton 87-93 • Dahood, "Quotations" • G. Delling, "Der Tod Jesu in der Verkündigung des Paulus," in *Haenchen FS* 85-96 • de Lorenzi (ed.), *Diakonia* • P. Duff, "Apostolic Suffering and the Language of Processions in 2 Corinthians 4:7-10," *BTB* 21 (1991) 158-65 • Ebner 196-242 • Fee, *Presence* 321-24 • M. S. Ferrari, *Die Sprache des Leids in den paulinschen Peristasenkataloge* (Stuttgart: Katholisches Bibelwerk, 1991) • Fitzgerald • S. R. Garrett, "The God of This World and the Affliction of Paul: 2 Cor. 4:1-12," in *Greeks, Romans, and Christians,* ed. D. L. Balch, et al. (Minneapolis: Fortress, 1990) 99-117 • P. J. Gräbe, *The Power of God in Paul's Letters* (Tübingen: Mohr, 2000) • E. Grässer, "Der Schatz in irdenen Gefässen (2 Kor 4,7). Existentiale Interpretation im 2. Korintherbrief," *ZTK* 97 (2000) 300-316 • Güttgemanns 199-281 • Hafemann, *Defense* 62-72 • Hafemann, *Spirit* 65-76 • Hanson, *Ministry* 75-79 • Hanson, *Paradox* 39-54 • Harman • Heckel 246-61 • Hodgson • P. Joüon, "Reconnaissance et action de grâce dans le NT," *RSR* 29 (1939) 112-14 • Kamlah, "Paulus" • Kleinknecht • Lambrecht, "Nekrosis" • Lambrecht, "Outlook" • Meeks 180-83 • Murphy-O'Connor 44-49 • Murphy-O'Connor, "Faith" • Noack, "Note" • Oostendorp 59-66 • Pate 77-106 • Perrin, "Passion" • Pickett 129-42 • Plevnik • Popkes 150-51 • Proudfoot • Rissi 42-64 • Savage 164-82 • Schrage • A. Schulz, "Leidentheologie und Vorbildethik in den paulinischen Hauptbriefen," in *Schmid FS* 265-69 • Schweizer, "Dying" • J. N. Sevenster, *Paul and Seneca* (Leiden: Brill, 1961) 230-36 • C. Spicq, "Image" • Stanley 216 • D. M. Stanley 134-38 • Tannehill 84-90 • Theobald 212-25, 233-39 • Witherington, *Jesus* 202-8 • C. Wolff, "Niedrigkeit und Verzicht in Wort und Weg Jesu und in der apostolischen Existenz des Paulus," *NTS* 34 (1988) 183-96

b. Glory through Suffering (4:16-18)

This passage is transitional. If 4:7-15 deals with "life" in the midst of "death" and 5:1-10 focuses on life after death, 4:16-18 incorporates those two themes in vv. 16 and 18 respectively, while v. 17 adverts to the theme of life through

---

117. BAGD (204a) translates εἰς τὴν δόξαν τοῦ θεοῦ (cf. Rom. 15:7; 1 Cor. 10:31; Phil. 1:11; 2:11) by "to the praise of God," noting the expressions δόξαν διδόναι τῷ θεῷ (e.g., Luke 17:18) = "praise God," and δὸς δόξαν τῷ θεῷ (John 9:24) = "give God the praise."

death, expressed in terms of future glory produced through present suffering. Paul's love of antithesis continues to be evident. The motif of θάνατος (in the broad sense of v. 12a) is present in vv. 16a, 17a and in the term τὰ βλεπόμενα (v. 18, twice) and looks back to vv. 8-9, 10a, 11a, and 12a and forward to 5:1a (καταλυθῇ). The motif of ζωή (cf. v. 12b) is found in vv. 16b, 17b and in the expression τὰ μὴ βλεπόμενα (v. 18, twice), picks up the same idea in vv. 8-9, 10b, 11b, and 12b, and anticipates 5:4b (ὑπὸ τῆς ζωῆς).

16*That is why we do not lose heart*[a]. *Rather, although our outward self is decaying, yet our inward*[b] *self is being renewed day after day.* 17*For this momentary*[c] *and light affliction of ours*[d] *is producing for us to an utterly incomparable degree an eternal load of glory* 18*because our eyes are fixed not on what can be seen but on what cannot be seen; for what can be seen is transient, but what cannot be seen is eternal.*

TEXTUAL NOTES

a. In place of ἐγκακοῦμεν, which has strong attestation (p⁴⁶ ℵ B D* F G 6 81 326 2464 *pc* cop), some witnesses (C D² Ψ 0243 33 1739 1881 𝔐) read ἐκκακοῦμεν. Thrall (347, 348 n. 1090) translates the latter verb "lose heart," "become weary," and the former "grow lax," although BAGD (215c, 240c) gives the meaning "lose heart" for both.

b. In the context there is no difference in meaning whether we read ἔσω ἡμῶν (the majority of witnesses), ἔσωθεν ἡμῶν (D² Ψ 1505 *pc*), ἔσωθεν (K L 629 1241 *pm*), or ἔσω (P 323 945 *pc*), but the first variant is to be preferred on the basis of the superior attestation and the Pauline parallels for ὁ ἔσω (ἄνθρωπος) in Rom. 7:22; Eph. 3:16.

c. Several witnesses (D* F G [latt syr] Tertullian) add πρόσκαιρον καί before ἐλαφρόν, an insertion that doubtless arose from a comparable πρόσκαιρος–αἰώνιος contrast in v. 18b.

d. ἡμῶν should be read after τῆς θλίψεως because of its strong and diversified support (ℵ Cᵛⁱᵈ D F G Ψ 0243 33 1739 1881 𝔐 latt syrʰ Origen), although two proto-Alexandrian manuscripts (p⁴⁶ B) along with syrᵖ omit ἡμῶν (the reading preferred in NA²⁵), probably to avoid a threefold repetition of ἡμῶν in vv. 16-17.

4:16 Διὸ οὐκ ἐγκακοῦμεν. "That is why we do not lose heart." διό looks back to vv. 14-15, and οὐκ ἐγκακοῦμεν to the same phrase in v. 1. Paul has now supplied several reasons for his refusal to grow discouraged in spite of seemingly overwhelming odds: his divine commission as a minister of a new and superior covenant (v. 1), the prospect of sharing Christ's triumphant resurrection from the dead (v. 14), and his immediate task of promoting the Corinthians' spiritual welfare and the glory of God (v. 15). On the meaning of ἐγκακέω, see 4:1.

ἀλλ' εἰ καὶ ὁ ἔξω ἡμῶν ἄνθρωπος διαφθείρεται, ἀλλ' ὁ ἔσω ἡμῶν ἀνακαινοῦται ἡμέρᾳ καὶ ἡμέρᾳ. "Rather, although our outward self is decaying, yet our inward self is being renewed day after day." Instead of (ἀλλά, "rather") losing courage and growing lax in the performance of his God-given duties, Paul was being renewed by God in his spiritual vitality from day to day for the carrying out of his ministry. And this in spite of the constant depletion of his physical powers by his toil, hardship, and suffering "on account of Jesus" (cf. 4:5, 11). The very simultaneity of these processes of διαφθορά and ἀνακαίνωσις suggests their proportionality. It was as though the more Paul expended himself physically for the gospel's sake (cf. 12:15), the greater his resilience spiritually. To Michelangelo is attributed the dictum: "The more the marble wastes, the more the statue grows."[1]

εἰ καί means "even though," "although,"[2] introducing a concessive clause that describes an actual circumstance. In the apodosis of such a clause, ἀλλά means "yet," "certainly," "at least" (BAGD §448 [5]) and "introduces *with emphasis* the opposite compensating relation" (Meyer 502). The two verbs διαφθείρεται and ἀνακαινοῦται depict incessant and therefore simultaneous processes.[3] The former may be translated as a passive ("is being destroyed," NAB¹; "is in process of destruction," Thrall 347) or intransitively ("is wasting away," RSV, NRSV; "is decaying," RV). Either way, what brought about the destruction or debilitation was the combined effect of Paul's circumstances. On the other hand, the implied agent behind the passive ἀνακαινοῦται ("is being renewed," RSV, NRSV) is the Spirit, as 3:18 and Eph. 3:16 make clear.

The phrase ἡμέρᾳ καὶ ἡμέρᾳ is unique in the Greek Bible, and although it is often described as a Semitism[4] it is more probably a colloquial use of the temporal dative, with the repeated ἡμέρᾳ denoting repetition,[5] "day after day," or, as in the colloquial English expression, "day in and day out." It is conceivable that the weakening and strengthening is progressive, that is, from one day to another or from one degree to another, but these twin processes are more probably to be seen as repeated "day after day."[6] If this is so, this process of renewal is unlike the process of transformation into the image of Christ, which is "from one degree of glory to another (more radiant degree)" (3:18).

In the balanced pair of expressions ὁ ἔξω ἡμῶν ἄνθρωπος and ὁ ἔσω ἡμῶν [ἄνθρωπος], the adverbs ἔξω–ἔσω, here used adjectively, may be rendered "outer–inner" or "outward–inward," while ἄνθρωπος has been variously translated — "man" (RV), "person" (Martin 82), "self" (Barclay, NAB²), "nature" (NRSV), "human nature" (NJB), "being" (GNB), "humanity" (NEB, REB in v. 16a) — and some versions render the complete phrases adverbially, "outwardly" and "inwardly" (TCNT, NIV). Because Paul's anthropology is

---

1. Cited by Vincent 821.

2. BAGD 220a; Burton §284; and almost all translations.

3. Cf. NAB¹: "our inner being is renewed each day even though our body is being destroyed at the same time."

4. E.g., BDF §200(1); BAGD 347a; Turner 243. The difficulty with seeing this phrase as a Hebraism or Semitism is that in the LXX Hebrew *yôm yôm*, "daily" (e.g., Ps. 68:20 [19]) is rendered ἡμέραν καθ᾽ ἡμέραν and *yôm wāyôm*, "day after day" (Esth. 3:4) by καθ᾽ ἑκάστην ἡμέραν (cf. Heb. 3:13), not by ἡμέρᾳ καὶ ἡμέρᾳ.

5. Cf. Robertson, *Pictures* 227. Winer (463) calls the expression a circumlocution for "daily" (= NT [τὸ] καθ᾽ ἡμέραν).

6. So also Furnish 262, 290.

aspectival not partitive, and synthetic not analytic,[7] when he speaks of "our out-ward self" and "our inward self" he is not thinking of two distinct entities, "the body" (σῶμα) and "the soul" (ψυχή), with the former as the receptacle for the latter.[8] He is, rather, contemplating his total existence from two contrasting viewpoints.[9] The "outer self" is the whole person from the standpoint of one's "creaturely mortality,"[10] the physical aspect of the person. ὁ ἔξω ἄνθρωπος is therefore indistinguishable from τὸ σῶμα (4:10), ἡ θνητὴ σάρξ (4:11),[11] and τὸ σῶμα τῆς ταπεινώσεως (Phil. 3:21).

The "inner self" is not to be equated with the νοῦς (as in Rom. 7:22), with "that which survives death," or even with the corporate new humanity in Christ. Rather it is the whole person as a "new creation" (5:17) or a "new person" (Col. 3:9-10), "the renewed being of the Christian,"[12] the spiritual aspect of the be-liever.[13] But if ὁ ἔξω ἄνθρωπος — not to be confused with ὁ παλαιὸς ἄνθρωπος (Eph. 4:22; Col. 3:9) — is virtually identical with τὸ ψυχικὸν σῶμα (cf. 1 Cor. 15:44), the physical body, it is obvious that ὁ ἔσω ἄνθρωπος cannot be equated with τὸ πνευματικὸν σῶμα (cf. 1 Cor. 15:44), the spiritual body, for the former is a present reality while the latter is a future acquisition. For Paul, the spiritual body was not simply the state of the renewed "inner self" at the time of the be-liever's death, but it seems a priori likely that he saw a relationship between the two, that he regarded resurrection not as a *creatio ex nihilo,* a sudden divine op-eration unrelated to the past, but as the fulfillment of a spiritual process begun at regeneration. The daily renewal of the "inward person" (4:16) contributed to-ward the progressive transformation of the believer into the image of Christ (3:18) in a process that would be accelerated and completed by resurrection. Paul does not explicitly say that his ἔσω ἄνθρωπος is the embryo of the spiritual body or bears its undeveloped image,[14] but the natural transition of his thought from 4:16 to 5:1-4 shows that this sentiment would have been congenial to him. As a result of the final convulsion of resurrection, the butterfly of the spiritual body will emerge from the chrysalis of the renewed "inner person."

7. Cf. Stacey 211-14.

8. But Grosheide (264) regards the ἔξω ἄνθρωπος as the ὀστράκινον σκεῦος (cf. 4:7) of the ἔσω ἄνθρωπος.

9. See the discussion of the issue in Thrall 348-51.

10. J. Behm, *TDNT* 2.699.

11. Thus Brandenburger 172 n. 5.

12. Kümmel, *Man* 43.

13. Louw and Nida render ὁ ἔξω ἡμῶν ἄνθρωπος by "our physical being" (§§23.146; 26.1), "the physical nature or aspect of a person" (§8.3), and ὁ ἔσω ἡμῶν [ἄνθρωπος] as "our spiritual be-ing" (§13.67), "the psychological faculty, including intellectual, emotional, and spiritual aspects" (§26.1). BAGD (68d) speaks of "the two sides of human nature . . . man in his material, transitory, and sinful aspects . . . and . . . man in his spiritual, immortal aspects, striving toward God." See also Grayston 55; Gundry 135-37 (who argues that "we cannot evade anthropological duality in II Cor. 4:16," 137); Rissi 65-73.

14. Héring boldly identifies the "inward man" with the new Adam concealed within each Christian, which bears the invisible and undeveloped image of the future resurrection body (28, 34; *Royaume* 204, 221). Cf. Pate 108-11.

4:17 τὸ γὰρ παραυτίκα ἐλαφρὸν τῆς θλίψεως ἡμῶν καθ᾽ ὑπερβολὴν εἰς ὑπερβολὴν αἰώνιον βάρος δόξης κατεργάζεται ἡμῖν. "For this momentary and light affliction of ours is producing for us to an utterly incomparable degree an eternal load of glory." γάρ may look back to v. 16a, affording another reason for the οὐκ ἐγκακοῦμεν (so Bultmann 127), or it may offer an explanation (note the anaphoric τό, "this") for the paradox of v. 16 ("even though . . . yet"). τὸ . . . ἐλαφρόν is an instance of the articular neuter singular adjective used as an abstract substantive,[15] "the lightness," "the insignificant character/amount." This construction has the effect of highlighting the idea of the adjective,[16] probably in contrast with the following word βάρος ("weight"). The adverb παραυτίκα ("immediately," "for the present") is here used as an adjective meaning "present" or, in contrast with αἰώνιος ("eternal," v. 17b) and as a virtual synonym for πρόσκαιρος ("transient," v. 18b), "temporary," "momentary."

The repetition of ὑπερβολή in the remarkable expression καθ᾽ ὑπερβολὴν εἰς ὑπερβολήν could merely point to intensification, "beyond all measure" (NRSV), "out of all proportion" (Martin 82), but it is preferable to represent clearly both emphatic elements, καθ᾽ ὑπερβολήν, "beyond measure," "utterly," and εἰς ὑπερβολήν, "to excess," by renderings such as "beyond all measure and proportion" (BAGD 840c), "beyond all comparison and estimate" (Isaacs), "to a degree immeasurable, to a degree exceeding all bounds" (Cassirer), "to an utterly extraordinary degree" (Thrall 347). The expression should be construed with κατεργάζεται,[17] not with βάρος[18] or δόξης;[19] that is, the degree of production, rather than the weight or the glory, surpasses all measure or bounds.

αἰώνιον βάρος δόξης means "an eternal weight of glory," or "a tremendous and eternal glory" (GNB, taking the noun βάρος adjectivally[20]); or, if the adjective αἰώνιον has been transposed for emphasis, "a weight of imperishable glory" (TCNT; similarly JB), "a load of eternal glory" (Cassirer), "a solid and eternal glory" (Williams). Derived from the noun αἰών ("age," "eternity"), the adjective αἰώνιος has two corresponding senses: "lasting for a (particular)age," "age-long," "aeonial,"[21] and "eternal" when used of the future age that was universally considered to be of endless duration. It is sometimes claimed that the

---

15. Cf. τὸ τῆς ὑμετέρας ἀγάπης γνήσιον (8:8), "the genuineness of your love"; Rom 2:4; 1 Cor. 1:25; Phil. 3:8. See BDF §263(2); Robertson 654, 793; Turner 14.

16. The alternative would be to say simply ἡ ἐλαφρὰ θλῖψις, "the light affliction." Some supply βάρος (from the context, or from v. 17b) with τὸ . . . ἐλαφρόν; thus "our present light burden of affliction" (Bernard 64; similarly Weymouth, NJB; Barrett 136).

17. So RV, TCNT, Barclay, Cassirer; Lietzmann 116; Plummer 123, 138; Wendland 191; de Boor 109; Barrett 137; Klauck 48; Lang 283; Martin 82; Young and Ford 266; Wolff 97; Thrall 347.

18. So Weymouth, Berkeley ("weight . . . that exceeds all calculations"), NJB; Bultmann 110, 128; Baumert 42, 131, 435; Furnish 252; Carrez 120.

19. Thus Moffatt, Goodspeed ("an eternal blessedness beyond all comparison"), Williams, GNB; also those versions that render βάρος verbally, REB ("an eternal glory which far outweighs them [our troubles]"), NEB, NIV.

20. So also Louw and Nida §78.23 ("tremendous glory").

21. Baumert renders αἰώνιος by "äonisch" in 4:17-18; 5:1 (42, 435; cf. 139-42).

adjective is fundamentally qualitative in meaning ("having the characteristics of the age" in question) and that the quantitative or temporal sense is secondary. Such a thesis would be difficult to sustain either from secular Greek literature or from the LXX, where temporal considerations predominate.[22] BAGD 28 has a threefold *temporal* classification of the NT meanings of αἰώνιος: "without beginning" (Rom. 16:25; 2 Tim. 1:9; Tit, 1:2), "without beginning or end" (Rom. 16:26; Heb. 9.14), and "without end" (e.g., Luke 16:9; 2 Pet. 1:11; Rev. 14:6). In 2 Cor. 4:17-18 and 5:1 this adjective describes that which has a beginning but no end (= the third category).

It may have been Hebrew *kābôd,* which can mean both "weight" and "glory," that prompted the Pauline coinage βάρος δόξης, "weight of glory."[23] Just as the nominative-plus-genitive construction τὸ . . . ἐλαφρὸν τῆς θλίψεως probably means "this [or "the"] light affliction," so βάρος δόξης could mean "(weighty =) tremendous glory" (GNB) or "solid glory" (Moffatt), but more probably it refers to the enormous weight or fullness[24] or utter substantiality that is a property of the glory (possessive genitive). The "weight" is "eternal" in the sense that it will remain undiminished and be unaffected by time. δόξα here is Pauline shorthand for all the blessings of the age to come, experienced proleptically in the present age. But one aspect of the δόξα that was reserved for the end of the present age is a resurrection characterized by δόξα (1 Cor. 15:43; Phil. 3:21). Paul could reify and therefore quantify δόξα, just as he could ἐλπίς (Col. 1:5; cf. κληρονομία in 1 Pet. 1:4).

The grammatical subject of κατεργάζεται is τὸ . . . ἐλαφρόν. But if this substantive is rendered adjectively, ἡ θλῖψις becomes the subject in effect. In the divine economy, affliction actually generates glory. This δόξα is not presented as a reward for suffering, as if suffering of itself were meritorious.[25] But δόξα is the God-ordained outcome of θλῖψις;[26] where there is suffering διὰ Ἰησοῦν (4:11), there is glory κατὰ χάριν (cf. Rom. 4:4). While there is a correspondence between the θλῖψις and the δόξα,[27] there is no precise proportionality, for the production of the glory operates "to an utterly incomparable degree." But, with that said, there must be some *unequal* correspondence, so that not only does affliction produce glory, but also, the greater the affliction, the greater the glory.

So then, Paul's point in v. 17 is this: when compared with the glory that was accumulating "beyond all measure and proportion," the suffering he was undergoing in the service of Christ appeared both insignificant and momentary.

22. See H. Sasse, *TDNT* 1.197-209.
23. Cf. Collange 177.
24. Thus Lietzmann 116; Wendland 191; Baumert 42, 435; cf. Furnish 252 ("abundance").
25. But NJB renders κατεργάζεται ἡμῖν by "is earning us"; similarly NAB[1].
26. Cf. REB: "Our troubles are slight and short-lived, and their outcome is an eternal glory . . ." (similarly NEB).
27. The four matching pairs in 4:17 should be noted: παραυτίκα–αἰώνιον, ἐλαφρόν–βάρος, θλίψεως–δόξης, ἡμῶν–ἡμῖν.

The suffering was real, not imaginary (cf. vv. 8-11), and if it were viewed κατὰ σάρκα, with a purely human assessment, it would seem burdensome and prolonged, but when viewed *sub specie aeternitatis,* in the light of eternity, the suffering took on the opposite hue — it seemed slight and temporary. The eye of faith creates a new perspective.[28]

4:18 μὴ σκοπούντων ἡμῶν τὰ βλεπόμενα ἀλλὰ τὰ μὴ βλεπόμενα· τὰ γὰρ βλεπόμενα πρόσκαιρα, τὰ δὲ μὴ βλεπόμενα αἰώνια. "Because our eyes are fixed not on what can be seen, but on what cannot be seen; for what can be seen is transient, but what cannot be seen is eternal." V. 18a explains why Paul's relentless suffering seemed light and transitory (v. 17a):[29] he had this paradoxical attitude toward affliction because his spiritual sights were set on the δόξα that could not be seen but was continuing to be produced (v. 17b). Heb. 11:25-27 records that Moses endured ill-treatment and abuse resolutely, "as one who saw him who is invisible." Paul, too, endured resolutely and viewed his present afflictions as minimal because his gaze was constantly fixed on invisible realities, realities that are worthy of focused attention because they are eternal, not transient.

σκοπέω, "focus one's attention on," is scarcely distinguishable in meaning from φρονέω (Rom. 8:5; Col. 3:2). Just as the English verb "look out for" can be used positively and negatively, so too with σκοπέω. Paul exhorts the Christians in Rome to "look out for" (= avoid) those who cause divisions (Rom. 16:17) and the Philippian believers to "look out for" (= care for) the interests of others (Phil. 2:4). Here the verb denotes fixity of gaze and attention, as opposed to a fleeting or casual glance. μὴ σκοπούντων ἡμῶν is an irregular genitive absolute since ἡμῶν refers to the same person(s) as the preceding ἡμῖν.[30] Strict grammar would require . . . ἡμῖν, μὴ σκοποῦσι τὰ βλεπόμενα, but Paul's choice of construction makes the participial clause more independent of the preceding statement and therefore more forceful.[31] This genitive absolute may express a condition ("provided our eyes are fixed . . . ," REB), a result ("So we fix our eyes . . . ," NIV), an attendant circumstance ("Meanwhile our eyes are fixed . . . ," NEB), or a reason ("because we look . . . ," NRSV). Of these four options, the third and fourth best suit the context; we have opted for the causal sense.[32] In translation the negative μή is most naturally separated from the verb σκοπούντων, as in the majority of translations: "because our eyes are fixed not on. . . ."

τὰ βλεπόμενα are "things perceived by the eyes,"[33] "what presents itself

---

28. Although the ἡμῶν–ἡμῖν of this verse has primary reference to Paul or to Paul and his fellow apostles or colleagues, the similar sentiment in Rom. 8:18 indicates that the truth of 2 Cor. 4:16 is applicable to all Christians.

29. Cf. Windisch 156.

30. D* F G read μὴ σκοποῦντες, which is an anacoluthic "hanging nominative" or a participle standing for a finite verb.

31. Cf. Winer 208; Buttmann 316; Zerwick §49.

32. Similarly Goodspeed, Williams, RSV; Lietzmann 116; Wendland 191.

33. Zerwick, *Analysis* 398.

to the eye,"[34] both the physical eye and the κατὰ σάρκα eye. Thus the sense is not simply "what is seen" (TCNT) (= τὰ ὁρατά), but "what can be seen" (NRSV[35]). Correspondingly, τὰ μὴ βλεπόμενα denotes not merely "what is unseen" (TCNT) (τὰ ἀόρατα; cf. Col. 1:16), but "what cannot be seen" (NRSV), "what escapes present perception."[36] The contrast between τὰ βλεπόμενα and τὰ μὴ βλεπόμενα is not a philosophical distinction between the visible and the invisible or the Platonic antithesis between the phenomenal which appears to be real and the noumenal which actually is real. It is, rather, a contrast between what is now seen by mortals and what is as yet hidden from mortal gaze because of human mortality and temporality. On this view, the antithesis reflects the Pauline tension between the "already" and the "not yet" (cf. Rom. 8:24-25; 1 Cor. 13:12) and so may be called temporal and eschatological rather than essential and philosophical.[37] When Paul says μὴ σκοπούντων ἡμῶν τὰ βλεπόμενα, he is not repudiating any interest in the material universe, any more than τὰ ἄνω φρονεῖτε, μὴ τὰ ἐπὶ τῆς γῆς (Col. 3:2) implies a rejection of the physical world and earthly relationships (cf. Col. 3:18–4:1). As noted on 2:5, Paul's οὐ/μὴ . . . ἀλλά antithesis is sometimes to be understood not absolutely ("not at all") but relatively ("not primarily"). Paul had not fixed his gaze exclusively on τὰ μὴ βλεπόμενα. Rather, he is affirming that his affections were set on "the realm above" (τὰ ἄνω, Col. 3:1-2), on lasting realities — some future, but others already present although still to be fully realized.

Paul's final statement, τὰ γὰρ κτλ., expressed as an axiom, gives his justification (γάρ) for his σκοπεῖν.[38] "For what can be seen is transient, but what cannot be seen is eternal." The adjective πρόσκαιρος means both "rooted in the time" (= "temporal") and "lasting only for a short time" (= "transitory," "transient").[39] On αἰώνιος, see v. 17. This adjective, found in three successive verses (4:17-18; 5:1), depicts permanent durability ("without end," "destined to last forever") rather than timelessness, so the πρόσκαιρος–αἰώνιος contrast here in v. 18 should not be seen as a time–eternity antithesis.

Since this verse comes at the end of a section (4:7-18) that deals with the trials of apostolic service and the glory that is generated by suffering, it would be strange if Paul's reference to τὰ βλεπόμενα and τὰ μὴ βλεπόμενα were unrelated to these themes. Indeed, his use of παραυτίκα in connection with θλῖψις (v. 17a) and his use of its virtual synonym πρόσκαιρος in connection with τὰ βλεπόμενα

---

34. E. Fuchs, *TDNT* 7.415.

35. So also BAGD 143c, 756d. Savage notes (184) the high incidence in 2:14–4:18 of words with visual connotations, "words which doubtless were chosen for their usefulness in correcting the display-conscious perspective of the Corinthian church."

36. W. Michaelis, *TDNT* 3.349.

37. Plummer aptly paraphrases v. 18 thus: "And we are sure of this, because we direct our gaze, not towards the fleeting things which we now see around us, but towards the lasting realities which to us are at present unseen" (124).

38. Carrez (120) renders γάρ by "indeed," "in reality" *(en effet)*.

39. G. Delling, *TDNT* 3.464.

(v. 18b) suggest that he includes his θλῖψις within τὰ βλεπόμενα. Probably also to be included within this category are the earthenware vessel, the dying of Jesus, the body, death on account of Jesus, the mortal flesh, and the outward self. Similarly, τὰ μὴ βλεπόμενα probably incorporates God's power, the resurrection and presentation of believers, the inward self, and the eternal weight of glory (see 4:7-17).[40] But all these are simply examples of Paul's twofold category.

Christians should be characterized by a fixation on invisible, eternal realities. Paradoxically, their eyes are riveted on what cannot be seen. The world of sense does not determine their outlook and action.

Bibliography

Baumert 114-42 • Carrez, *Souffrance* 119-20 • Cobb • Kim 324-26 • Lincoln 59-60 • Murphy-O'Connor 49-51 • Oostendorp 66-67 • Pate 107-36 • Rey, "Homme" • Rissi 65-73 • Robinson 75-78 • Savage 182-85 • Siber 67-76 • Theobald 225-32

c. Confidence in the Face of Death (5:1-10)

What Paul says in 5:1-10 is directly related to 4:7-18. There he pointed out that even in the midst of affliction, perplexity, and persecution, there was, through divine consolation, the hope of glory (4:8-9, 13-14, 17). Even in the presence of the ravages of mortality and death there was, through divine intervention, the operation of life (4:10-12, 16; cf. 6:9). This twofold theme — life in the midst of death, glory through and after suffering — is continued in 5:1-10. While several scholars would relate vv. 6-10 as well as vv. 1-5 to the parousia of Christ rather than to the death of the believer,[1] most commentators find it impossible to deny that Paul is here reckoning with either the possibility or probability of his own pre-parousia decease and is recounting the sources of divine comfort afforded the believer who stands within the shadow of death.[2] They reach this conclusion in the light of such factors as Paul's strange preoccupation in chs. 1–7 with his own deteriorating physical condition, explicit references in 4:7-15 to his constant exposure to suffering and death, the contrast between daily decay and daily renewal in 4:16-18, which forms the preface to 5:1-10, the opening conditional clause in 5:1 (in essence, "if I die before the parousia"), and the allusion to death in the phrase ἐκδημῆσαι ἐκ τοῦ σώματος in 5:8.

Paul mentions three sources of divine comfort: assurance that he would be-

40. Cf. W. Michaelis, *TDNT* 3.349; Klauck 48; and especially Theobald 238 (chart).

1. See, e.g., Lietzmann 117-19, 121; Hoffmann 267-85, especially 281, 284-85, 321.

2. Apparently for the first time in his apostolic career Paul now reckons seriously with the possibility — now a probability — of his death before the return of Christ. Previously, to judge by 1 Thess. 4:15, 17 and 1 Cor. 15:51, he had expected to be among those Christians living when Christ returned. But now, as a result of his recent devastating encounter with death in Asia (1:8-11), he realized that he was likely to die before the parousia, though he always entertained the hope of survival until the advent. See the discussion of these issues above in the excursus after 1:11.

come a possessor of a superior form of habitation (v. 1), an awareness that in giving the Spirit as the pledge of transformation God had committed himself to complete the good work of renewal he had begun (v. 5), and knowledge that death involves departure to Christ and leads to "walking in the realm of sight" (vv. 7-8). The tone of 5:1-10 is not one of cringing fear arising from human uncertainties but of buoyant assurance born of divine certainties. It is therefore consonant with the dominant mood of chs. 1–7 (χαίρειν δεῖ). The passage witnesses not to the confusion, but to the profusion, of Paul's thought when he was faced with the probability of his not surviving to witness the second advent in person.[3] With its recital of the compensations or rewards afforded an apostle enduring incessant suffering and facing probable death, 5:1-10 both contributes to Paul's *apologia* for the apostolic office (2:14–7:4) and illustrates the main theme (παράκλησις ἐν θλίψει) of chs. 1–7.[4] Yet since the acquisition of a spiritual body (v. 1), longing for inheritance (v. 2), tent-dwelling (v. 4), receipt of the Spirit (v. 5), walking in the realm of faith (v. 7), dwelling with Christ (v. 8), and accountability to Christ (v. 10) were not exclusively Pauline experiences or prerogatives, the whole passage is clearly applicable to Christians in general (cf. 2 Tim. 4:8).

With regard to the structure of 5:1-10 two points are noteworthy. First, there is significant *repetition* of terms or roots: οἰκία (v. 1, twice), στενάζομεν (vv. 2, 4), ἐπενδύσασθαι (vv. 2, 4), -δύεσθαι (vv. 2, 3, 4 twice), θαρρεῖν (vv. 6, 8), -δημεῖν (vv. 6 twice, 8 twice, 9 twice). Clearly the "housing" and "clothing" metaphors are crucial, and "confidence" counterbalances "groaning." Second, the *connective issue* has the effect of making 5:1-10 a closely knit paragraph:

γάρ ("for," v. 1) refers back to 4:18b ("what cannot be seen is eternal") and also through 4:16a (διό) to 4:14 (that is, the assured hope of resurrection in the event of death).

καὶ γάρ in v. 2 is confirmatory and evidential ("for also," "moreover"), while in v. 4 this phrase is resumptive and explanatory ("for indeed," "for it is a fact that").

εἴ γε καί (v. 3) introduces a parenthetical assumption ("assuming, that is"), correcting a possible misinterpretation of v. 2, namely that ἐνδύσασθαι ἀθανασίαν (1 Cor. 15:53), understood as the assumption of disembodied immortality, is the Christian ideal.

δέ (v. 5) is transitional ("now"), leading on to εἰς αὐτὸ τοῦτο ("for this very destiny," that is, "the transformation of the mortal body and the receipt of the spiritual body," vv. 1-4).

---

3. But compare the contention of C. A. A. Scott (140) that "the confusion of thought in this passage, which is undeniable, is a measure of the disturbance of mind caused by the necessity of [Paul's] adjusting himself to this new possibility" (of a pre-parousia death). For the history of the interpretation of this passage see F. G. Lang 9-161 (up to 1972); and more briefly Hoffmann 254-67 (up to 1966); Pate 1-31 (up to 1991).

4. But Barrett (51) sees 5:1-10 as "A digression illustrating further the relative unimportance of the earthenware container."

οὖν ("therefore," v. 6) grounds the confidence expressed in vv. 6, 8 (θαρροῦντες . . . θαρροῦμεν) on vv. 1-5, especially v. 5.

δέ (v. 8) is resumptive ("I repeat"), indicating that v. 7 is parenthetical and explanatory (γάρ, "for"), correcting a possible misinterpretation of v. 6, namely that present fellowship with Christ is illusory and that embodiment is a hindrance to spirituality.

διὸ καί ("that is why," v. 9) grounds Paul's aim to please Christ on his destiny of being with Christ (v. 8b).

γάρ ("for," v. 10) introduces a second reason for this aim of v. 9, Paul's accountability to Christ, which prompts (οὖν, "therefore," v. 11) his "fear of the Lord" (v. 11).

Two further observations are in order. First, in a remarkable way, the structure of vv. 6-8 corresponds to that of vv. 2-4. Vv. 4 and 8 are resumptive (καὶ γάρ, v. 4; δέ, v. 8), repeating (στενάζομεν, v. 4; θαρροῦμεν, v. 8) the principal verbs of vv. 2 and 6 (στενάζομεν, v. 2; θαρροῦντες, v. 6) after parentheses (vv. 3 and 7). Vv. 4 and 8 are also explicative, expanding (οἱ ὄντες and βαρούμενοι, v. 4) the earlier assertion (ἐν [τῷ σκήνει] τούτῳ στενάζομεν, v. 2) or complementing (ἐφ' ᾧ οὐ θέλομεν ἐκδύσασθαι ἀλλ' ἐπενδύσασθαι, v. 4; εὐδοκοῦμεν μᾶλλον ἐκδημῆσαι ἐκ τοῦ σώματος καὶ ἐνδημῆσαι πρὸς τὸν κύριον, v. 8) the preceding statements (ἐπενδύσασθαι ἐπιποθοῦντες, v. 2; εἰδότες ὅτι ἐνδημοῦντες ἐν τῷ σώματι ἐκδημοῦμεν ἀπὸ τοῦ κυρίου, v. 6). Structurally, therefore, v. 5 is pivotal since it forms the link between two units of thought (vv. 2-4 and vv. 6-8): δέ provides the general link and εἰς αὐτὸ τοῦτο the specific link with the preceding verses (vv. 1-4), while οὖν in v. 6, referring primarily to v. 5, grounds Paul's confidence in every circumstance (vv. 6, 8) on his possession of the pledge of the Spirit as a gift from God. And, it might be added, since within v. 5 the ὁ δούς clause specifies the mode of the κατεργάσασθαι, the ἀρραβών concept is central in the whole pericope. Second, that Paul is writing *currente calamo* or dictating *currente lingua* in 5:1-10 is apparent from the anacoluthon in v. 6 and the parenthetical character of vv. 3 and 7. The markedly antithetical features of the whole passage, and particularly of vv. 6 and 8, therefore bear eloquent testimony to the essentially antithetical nature of Pauline thought.

1*For we know that if our earthly tent-house is destroyed, we have a building from God, a permanent heavenly house not built by human hands. 2In this tent, moreover, we sigh, because we yearn to put on as an overgarment that heavenly dwelling of ours — 3assuming^a, that is, that when we have put it on^b, we shall not find ourselves disembodied. 4For indeed, as tent-dwellers^c, we sigh with a sense of oppression^d because, not wishing to become disembodied, we desire to put on our heavenly dwelling as an overgarment, so that what is mortal may be swallowed up by life. 5Now it is God who has prepared^e us for this very destiny and^f has given us the Spirit as a down payment and pledge. 6Therefore we are always confident, and because we know that we are absent^g from the Lord as long as we are living^h in this body — 7for* *we walk in the realm of faith, not of sight — 8we are confident, I repeat, and prefer to depart from this body and take up residence with the Lord. 9That is why we aim to be pleasing to him, whether resident in this body or absent from it. 10For all of us must appear before Christ's tribunal so that each may be duly recompensed for actionsᴶ,whether good or badᵏ, performed throughˡ the body.*

TEXTUAL NOTES

a. Although εἴπερ is read by several important witnesses (p⁴⁶ B D F G 33 1175 *pc*), εἴ γε, the reading found in the majority of witnesses (including ℵ C K L P), is to be preferred. Since the combination εἴπερ καί is much more common in Classical and Koine Greek than εἴ γε καί, Atticizing scribes are more likely to have altered an original εἴ γε καί to match predominant usage than to have changed an original εἴπερ καί to a rare combination of particles, especially since εἴ γε καί may have been thought to introduce an element of doubt that was foreign to the context (note οἴδαμεν, v. 1; θαρροῦντες, v. 6; θαρροῦμεν, v. 8). For a detailed defense of the originality of εἴ γε καί, see Thrall, "2 Corinthians 5:3" 223-29.

b. UBS¹, ² read ἐνδυσάμενοι (p⁴⁶ ℵ B C D² Ψ 0243 33 1739 1881 𝔐 lat syr cop Clement) without giving the textual variants ἐκδυσάμενοι (D*·ᶜ itᵃ, ᶠᶜ Marcion Tertullian Speculum) and ἐκλυσάμενοι (F G; = a scribal confusion of ΕΚΔ- and ΕΚΛ-). But UBS³ with a "D" rating (= "a very high degree of doubt") and UBS⁴ with a "C" rating (= uncertain) prefer ἐκδυσάμενοι (as also NA²⁶, ²⁷), rendering this verse, "inasmuch as we, though unclothed, shall not be found naked" (Metzger 511, though Metzger himself registers his support for ἐνδυσάμενοι). It is scarcely legitimate, however, to ignore the weighty external support for ἐνδυσάμενοι simply on the ground that the reading ἐκδυσάμενοι "suddenly lets in light where before darkness prevailed" (Vos 196-97; similarly Holleman 72-73). The verse is perfectly intelligible with ἐνδυσάμενοι as a parenthetical correction of a possible misinterpretation of v. 2 (see the commentary). Transcriptional probability also favors ἐνδυσάμενοι. ἐκδυσάμενοι is to be rejected as being the easier reading, an evident amendment to avoid the *prima facie* tautology of ἐνδυσάμενοι οὐ γυμνοί, "clothed, not naked." It is more probable that a scribe would alter ἐνδυσάμενοι to ἐκδυσάμενοι to create an antithesis with ἐπενδύσασθαι (corresponding, in reversed order, to that in v. 4) than that he should remove such an antithesis and produce apparent pleonasm by the reverse change. See further (also in defense of ἐνδυσάμενοι), Thrall, "2 Corinthians 5:3" 229-37, and K. Hanhart, "Hope in the Face of Death: Preserving the Original Text of 2 Cor 5:3," *Neot* 31 (1997) 77-86.

c. Rightly recognizing that ἐν τῷ σκήνει alludes to τοῦ σκήνους (v. 1) and ἐν τούτῳ (v. 2), some scribe(s) added τούτῳ after σκήνει (D F G 81 [104] 1505 *pc* it vgᶜˡ syr Tertullian Ambrosiaster Speculum).

d. Some witnesses (D*·ᶜ F G 1505 *pc*) read βαρυνόμενοι in place of βαρούμενοι. Both verbs, βαρύνω and βαρέω, mean "weigh down," "burden."

e. A few witnesses (D F G lat Ambrosiaster) read the present participle κατεργαζόμενος (cf. κατεργάζεται in 4:17).

f. Perhaps reflecting Paul's practice elsewhere (e.g., 1:22: ὁ καὶ σφραγισάμενος; Col. 1:8: ὁ καὶ δηλώσας), some witnesses read ὁ καὶ δούς (ℵ² D¹ [33] 𝔐 syrʰ Irenaeusᵛ·ˡ· Ambrosiaster) instead of ὁ δούς (p⁴⁶ ℵ* B C D* F G P Ψ 0243 6 630 1175 1739 1881 2464 *pc* lat syrᵖ cop Irenaeus Origen).

g. D (F G) read ἀποδημοῦμεν.

h. D* (F G) read ἐπιδημοῦντες.

i. Instead of θαρροῦμεν, several witnesses read θαρροῦντες (cf. v. 6) (‭א‬ 0243 6 33 81 630 1739 1881 2464 pc Tertullian).

j. In place of τὰ διὰ τοῦ σώματος πρὸς ἃ ἔπραξεν (read by the great majority of witnesses), D* F G read ἃ διὰ τοῦ σώματος ἔπραξεν, which, being both simpler and smoother, is a secondary reading.

k. There is strong external support for κακόν (p⁴⁶ B D F G Ψ 𝔐 Clement), but because ἀγαθόν–κακόν is the usual Pauline antithesis (Rom. 2:9-10; 3:8; 7:19; 12:21; 13:3; 16:19; cf. 7:21), with the ἀγαθόν–φαῦλον contrast occurring only once elsewhere (Rom. 9:11), it is probable that φαῦλον (read by ‭א‬ C 048 0243 33 81 326 365 630 1739 [1881] pc) is original.

l. p⁴⁶ 365 pc lat Cyprian read τὰ ἴδια τοῦ σώματος, "one's own actions that relate to the body."

5:1 Οἴδαμεν γὰρ ὅτι ἐὰν ἡ ἐπίγειος ἡμῶν οἰκία τοῦ σκήνους καταλυθῇ. "For we know that if our earthly tent-house is destroyed." γάρ looks back to 4:18b: "the earthly tent-house" (v. 1a) is one of the transient βλεπόμενα, and "the building from God" (v. 1b) is one of the eternal μὴ βλεπόμενα. So 5:1 as a whole is an illustration of the truth affirmed in 4:18b, with τοῦ σκήνους (v. 1a) looking back to πρόσκαιρα, and αἰώνιον (v. 1b) back to αἰώνια. More remotely, γάρ alludes to οὐκ ἐγκακοῦμεν (4:16a) and therefore reinforces 4:14. One reason for Paul's refusal to become discouraged, for his buoyancy of spirit, was his assured hope (εἰδότες, 4:14; οἴδαμεν, 5:1) of being resurrected as Christ was (4:14), his confident assurance of receiving "a building from God." In itself, οἴδαμεν is no proof that Paul was appealing to what was common knowledge among early Christians. If it is an epistolary plural, he may be pointing to a new revelation (cf. 1 Cor. 15:51; 1 Thess. 4:15; Job 19:25). If he includes the Corinthians (and therefore potentially all Christians) in this οἴδαμεν, he may be enunciating a truth he expects them to accept as apostolic teaching (cf. 1 Cor. 14:37-38).

It is highly unlikely that ἐὰν . . . καταλυθῇ is equivalent to εἰ καὶ . . . κατελύθη, ἀλλά . . . ("even if . . . should be destroyed, yet . . . "; cf. 4:16 for the construction) or κἂν . . . καταλυθῇ, since a concessive use of ἐάν (without other particles) seems to be lacking in Paul and in the NT in general. Furthermore, far from there being any indication in the context that Paul is merely envisaging his death as a remote and almost hypothetical possibility, 4:10-12, 14, 16 point to the apostle's awareness that at any time in the near future the ἐνέργεια τοῦ θανάτου (v. 12) could reach its climax in his actual death. Alternatively, ἐάν may here approximate to ὅταν ("when[ever]") in meaning. This temporal sense of ἐάν followed by the aorist subjunctive is found in the LXX, the Pauline epistles, and the rest of the NT.⁵ Such a meaning would not compromise the condi-

5. E.g., Isa. 24:13; Amos 7:2; Matt. 9:21; John 12:32; 1 Cor. 16:10; 2 Cor. 9:4; 13:2; Heb. 3:7; 1 John 2:28 (𝔐 reads ὅταν). Cf. BAGD 211b; Fanning 224 n. 46.

tionality of the protasis, for it was "when," but only when, the tent that formed his earthly house had been dismantled that Paul was to become a possessor of the οἰκοδομὴ ἐκ θεοῦ. He did not write ὅταν . . . καταλυθῇ because only the actual arrival of death would frustrate his natural desire to be alive to witness the parousia. But there is no reason not to give ἐάν its regular conditional sense, provided we qualify ἐάν . . . καταλυθῇ by an expression such as πρὸ τῆς παρουσίας τοῦ κυρίου ("before the coming of the Lord"): "if our earthly tent-house is destroyed" = "if I die" could not stand unqualified, since Paul believed in the universality of death (Rom. 5:12; 1 Cor. 15:22). With the aorist subjunctive ἐάν means "in the specific case that ever," with the context determining the degree of probability attaching to the "open" condition.[6] Here the context indicates that ἐάν means "if, as is probable."[7]

ἡ ἐπίγειος ἡμῶν οἰκία τοῦ σκήνους means "our earthly tent-dwelling" or "the tent which forms our earthly house," τοῦ σκήνους being an epexegetic genitive defining more closely the nature of the οἰκία.[8] οἰκία, like σκεῦος (4:7), is a metaphor describing the σῶμα. Less certain, however, is the precise connotation of σκῆνος,[9] which, on the lips of the apostle Paul, is a particularly allusive term.[10] To a Cilician σκηνοποιός ("leather worker" or "tentmaker"), it would readily evoke notions of travel and transitoriness, nomadic existence and pilgrimage. For a Jew, σκῆνος would be naturally associated with the desert wanderings of the Israelites after the exodus and the "festival of booths"[11] celebrated for seven days during the seventh month of each year. And to a Christian, the term would allude to the tabernacle (miškān, σκηνή, or σκήνωμα) as the locus of God's presence among his people during the wilderness wanderings (e.g., Exod. 40:34-38) and then to the indwelling of the Spirit of Christ as

6. G. van W. Kruger, "Conditionals in the New Testament: A Study in Their Rationale" (unpublished Ph.D. dissertation, University of Cambridge, 1967) 67, 98.

7. For Paul's preoccupation with death at the time of 2 Corinthians, see the excursus above after 1:11. Burton (§250; similarly Zerwick §320; *Analysis* 399; Turner 319) believes that a protasis that has ἐάν with the subjunctive (present or aorist) "states a supposition which refers to the future, suggesting some probability of its fulfilment."

8. Bachmann 215-17; Robertson 399, 498; Turner 214, 218.

9. See W. Michaelis, *TDNT* 7.381, who observes that in secular Greek σκῆνος normally means "body." Cf. Thrall 356 ("our earthly bodily dwelling"); cf. 357-58. Spörlein argues (136-37) that Paul no longer thought of σκῆνος as a metaphor for the body, so that the term simply means "body."

10. In light of the fact that σκῆνος does not appear in the Greek Bible outside Wis. 9:15 and 2 Cor. 5:1, 4, it is decidedly more probable that Paul derived the term from pseudo-Solomon than that he was dependent on Pythagorean or Platonic philosophy or commonplace Hellenistic religious terminology. But in spite of this one verbal coincidence (σκῆνος) and the two verbal similarities (γεώδης–ἐπίγειος, βαρύνω–βαρέω) between the two passages, the significant differences exclude the possibility of Pauline dependence with regard to content.

11. Yet the LXX never renders sukkâ by σκῆνος, but regularly by σκηνή (a word Paul never uses). Lowrie (56-57) proposes that Paul used σκῆνος rather than σκηνή because he wished to allude to the *ad interim* tent of meeting (Exod. 33:7-11) which was intended for provisional use until the tabernacle (LXX σκηνή) was constructed.

the mode of God's presence in believers during their pilgrimage of faith to the Promised Land of Christ's immediate presence.[12] Since this concept remains in or near the foreground of Paul's thought throughout the passage (vv. 2, 4, 6-7), it would seem likely that the καταλυθῆναι of v. 1 signifies the dismantling of a tent[13] rather than simply the demolition of a building. If, however, ἐὰν . . . καταλυθῇ refers generally both to the metaphors οἰκία and σκῆνος and to the σῶμα as the object signified, the κατάλυσις would merely denote "destruction" — whether of house, tent, or body. At any rate, the event is viewed as a specific single occurrence lying in the future.[14]

The close verbal similarity between 2 Cor. 5:1 and Mark 14:58 (in which, among other resemblances, καταλυθῇ corresponds to καταλύσω) might well reveal Paul's awareness that his own death, like his Lord's, could be sudden and violent (cf. Acts 21:13). However that be, the immediate background of the καταλυθῆναι must be sought in 2 Cor. 4:7-18. Paul envisages the dismantling of his earthly tent in death as the logical outcome of his repeated encounters with death or his protracted death for the gospel's sake (ἀεὶ . . . εἰς θάνατον παραδίδοσθαι διὰ Ἰησοῦν = ἡ νέκρωσις [= τὸ νεκροῦσθαι] τοῦ Ἰησοῦ, 4:10-11). Death as κατάλυσις[15] is the final stage of the process of διαφθορά, the termination of a lifetime of σπείρειν ἐν φθορᾷ (1 Cor. 15:42; cf. Sir. 14:17).[16] A διαφθείρεσθαι inevitably issues in a καταλυθῆναι. Still more is implied by this κατάλυσις. The οἰκία that is destroyed by death is described as ἐπίγειος. Death involves the loss not only of physical corporeality but also of earthly corporateness. These two losses are, of course, interrelated, for since death deprives a person of the σῶμα ψυχικόν, the organ of a person's relationship with others, it also involves the forfeiture of all earthly ties. But although at death Christians cease to be ἐν σαρκί, they do not cease to be ἐν Χριστῷ. There is no evidence in the Pauline corpus that death removes believers from their ἐν Χριστῷ incorporation: this persists at and after death, as the expression οἱ νεκροὶ ἐν Χριστῷ (1 Thess. 4:16) would indicate (cf. also Rom. 8:38-39; 14:8).

οἰκοδομὴν ἐκ θεοῦ ἔχομεν, οἰκίαν ἀχειροποίητον αἰώνιον ἐν τοῖς οὐρανοῖς. "We have a building from God, a permanent heavenly house not built by human hands." Some scholars have identified this οἰκοδομή with the church as the body of Christ or as the New Temple;[17] others equate it with celestial be-

---

12. Note the discussion of Wagner 384-85, 393.

13. Cf. Polybius 6.40.2; Job 4:21 (MT). This sense is reflected in Berkeley, JB; and Wand.

14. Cf. Turner 114-15.

15. Cf. Josephus, *War* 2.594.

16. For the view that Paul regarded physical death or death through Christ (1 Thess. 4:14) or in Christ (1 Cor. 15:18) as the consummation of believers' baptismal death with Christ and to sin (Rom. 6:1-11) — which makes effective their death with Christ realized in principle at Calvary (2 Cor. 5:14) — and the climax of daily and progressive mortification of the σάρξ (Gal. 5:24), see Feuillet, "Mort" 481-513.

17. Robinson 75-80; Ellis, *Interpreters* 41-42; Oostendorp 68-69 (the οἰκοδομή is the new Israel, the messianic people). Cf. F. G. Lang 125-30.

atitude,[18] with the heavenly temple,[19] with a celestial dwelling place (cf. John 14:2),[20] with a vestment of celestial glory,[21] with the heavenly mode of existence,[22] or with the glory and vastness of the age to come.[23] The principal objection to all such identifications lies in the fact that, in view of 4:16a, it seems incontestable that the ἐπίγειος οἰκία of 5:1a alludes primarily, if not solely, to the physical body and that therefore it would destroy the parallelism and opposition of the two parts of 5:1 if the second, antithetical οἰκία referred to anything other than some form of embodiment.[24] Moreover, the correspondence between Paul's delineation of the "building" in 5:1 and his description of the spiritual body in 1 Corinthians 15 also points unmistakably to the identification of the οἰκοδομή with the σῶμα πνευματικόν.[25] Both are of divine origin (ἐκ θεοῦ; cf. 1 Cor. 15:38), spiritual (ἀχειροποίητον; cf. 1 Cor. 15:44, 46), permanent and indestructible (αἰώνιον; cf. 1 Cor. 15:42, 52-54), and heavenly (ἐν τοῖς οὐρανοῖς; cf. 1 Cor. 15:40, 48-49).[26] If, on the other hand, as Feuillet argues, the heavenly dwelling is the resurrection body of Christ as the firstfruits of the new creation and so as virtually inclusive of the resurrection bodies of all Christians,[27] there is the difficulty of the idea that believers in any sense "possess" or will "possess" (ἔχομεν) Christ's heavenly body. Had Paul actually meant "we have a share" (= participate) in the body of Christ, would not μετέχειν have been used?

18. Calvin (67) believed that the postmortem blissful state of the soul is the beginning of the οἰκοδομή, the completion of which will be the glory of the final resurrection.

19. Wagner 380-84 (there is "a certain indefiniteness" in Paul's thought; the heavenly Temple is not unrelated to the glorious body of the believer); Hanhart 73, 167-72; "Hope" 453-54.

20. Tasker 78, 80; Martin 104.

21. Prat 2.367.

22. Grosheide 264-65, 269. The οἰκοδομή, already enjoyed imperfectly on earth (cf. ἐνδυσάμενοι, 5:3), will be fully possessed at death (ἐπενδύσασθαι, 5:2, 4) (271, 274, 281, 287). A not dissimilar view is held by Baumert (42-43, 144-67) for whom "the building from God" is the whole earthly person as a participant in salvation both now and after death.

23. Furnish 294-95 (the God-given οἰκοδομή includes the new Temple and the new Jerusalem itself and is a further description of the "absolutely incomparable, eternal abundance of glory," 4:17).

24. This argument assumes that οἰκίαν κτλ. is in apposition to οἰκοδομήν.

25. This identification is made by Meyer 507-8; Lietzmann 117; Plummer 143-44; Windisch 159-60; Allo 121, 138-39; Vielhauer 106; Bietenhard 226; Hughes 163-65; E. Schweizer TDNT 7.1061; Hoffmann 268-69; Prümm 1.271; McKelvey 144-47; Bruce 202; Lincoln 61; Kitzberger 118; Thrall 363-70.

26. The latter objection may also be leveled against the view of Whiteley that the "house not made by hands" is "a temporary phase of the eternal body of the deceased, just as the physical body is a temporary phase of the eternal body of the survivors [until the parousia]" (260). Against the related notion of the οἰκοδομή as an "interim body," see Allo 152-53; Feuillet, "Demeure" 168-71.

27. Feuillet, "Demeure" 360-78; also Collange 191. In a similar way, K. Smyth discovers the background to 5:1-5 and all the passages in which Paul speaks of "putting on" Christ or "the new man" in the concept of Christ as a heavenly garment, and ultimately in "the representation of the Heavenly Man as the true place of the redeemed soul" (225).

ἐκ θεοῦ is to be construed with οἰκοδομήν, not with ἔχομεν. God is related to the οἰκοδομή as its source (if, as would appear likely, οἰκοδομή signifies a "completed building"), "a building from (= given by) God," or possibly (if ἀχειροποίητον explicates τοῦ θεοῦ) its agent, "a building made by God" (cf. Heb. 11:10). ἐκ θεοῦ corresponds to ἐξ οὐρανοῦ in v. 2 and ὁ δὲ θεὸς δίδωσιν αὐτῷ σῶμα καθὼς ἠθέλησεν in 1 Cor. 15:38, although the latter passage refers in the first place to the γυμνὸς κόκκος of the previous verse.

οἰκίαν is in epexegetic apposition to οἰκοδομή. To judge by the other two NT uses of ἀχειροποίητος (Mark 14:58; Col. 2:11), the οἰκοδομή, as an οἰκία ἀχειροποίητος, is a spiritual or supernatural building "erected" purely by divine agency and belonging to the new creation (cf. Heb. 9:11). It is therefore an apt picture of the σῶμα πνευματικόν, a body that is animated and guided by the πνεῦμα — either the Spirit of God or the human spirit as revitalized by the divine Spirit. The resurrection body is a spiritual temple (cf. 1 Cor. 6:19, of the earthly body) constructed ἄνευ χειρῶν (cf. Dan. 2:34, 45; Mark 13:2).

In this verse αἰώνιος derives its precise significance (see the commentary on 4:18) from its implied contrast with ἐπίγειος and σκήνους on the one hand, and καταλυθῇ on the other. Compared with the earthly and therefore transient character of the σῶμα ψυχικόν, the σῶμα πνευματικόν is permanent,[28] transcending all the effects of time.[29] Compared with earthly corporeality, with its irreversible tendency to decay, which finally issues in death, the heavenly embodiment provided by God is indestructible, incapable of any deterioration or dissolution. These two characteristics of the spiritual body — permanence and indestructibility — are highlighted in 1 Corinthians 15: "the sowing is characterized by corruption, the rising[30] by incorruption" (ἐν ἀφθαρσίᾳ, v. 42); "the dead will be raised in a state of incorruption" (ἄφθαρτοι, v. 52); "for this corruptible body must put on immortality" (ἀφθαρσίαν, v. 53; cf. v. 54).

The prepositional phrase ἐν τοῖς οὐρανοῖς may be locative ("in heaven"), specifying the site of the inhabited οἰκία. But more probably it is a qualitative ("heavenly" = ἐπουράνιον).[31] Just as in 1 Cor. 15:40 the glory of terrestrial bodies (σώματα ἐπίγεια) is contrasted with the glory of celestial bodies (σώματα ἐπουράνια) and in 1 Cor. 15:48-49 the bodies and image (εἰκών) of earthly people (οἱ χοϊκοί) are compared with the bodies and image of heavenly people (οἱ ἐπουράνιοι), so in 2 Cor. 5:1 two σώματα and two phases or orders of human

28. αἰώνιος bears a similar meaning in 4:17 (in contrast to παραυτίκα, "momentary") and 4:18 (in contrast to πρόσκαιρος, "transient").

29. If the temporal significance of αἰώνιος in 4:17-18; 5:1 is pressed, the epithet then describes not that which is without beginning or end but that which has a beginning but no end (cf. αἰώνιος κληρονομία, Heb. 9:15). Certainly it could not be applied to an interim body or heavenly shelter designed to house the deceased Christian simply between death and resurrection.

30. On σπείρεται–ἐγείρεται, see Allo, *Première Épître* 423.

31. That the meaning of ἐν τοῖς οὐρανοῖς and οὐράνοις overlaps is seen by comparing Matt. 6:9 (πάτερ ἡμῶν ὁ ἐν τοῖς οὐρανοῖς; cf. Matt. 6:1) and Matt. 6:14, 26, 32 (ὁ πατὴρ ὑμῶν ὁ οὐράνιος).

existence are opposed in an "earthly-heavenly" (ἐπίγειος³²–ἐν τοῖς οὐρανοῖς) antithesis to which there also corresponds the ψυχικός–πνευματικός contrast of 1 Cor. 15:44, 46. ἐν τοῖς οὐρανοῖς therefore may well allude to the glorious nature of the heavenly εἰκών to be borne by οἱ χοϊκοί.³³

That Paul is alluding in v. 1 to the dominical saying recorded in Mark 14:58 is highly probable because of the remarkable verbal correspondence between the two passages (καταλύσω–καταλυθῇ, ἀχειροποίητον–ἀχειροποίητον, οἰκοδομήσω–οἰκοδομήν), which is perhaps highlighted by Paul's juxtaposition of καταλυθῇ and οἰκοδομήν. If, as Mark 14:57, 59 implies, Mark 14:58 preserves a malicious misrepresentation of a genuine saying of Jesus, the pristine form of the saying might well be found in John 2:19: "Destroy [λύσατε = ἐὰν λύσητε; cf. 2 Cor. 5:1] this temple, and in three days I will raise it up." However that may be, it appears certain that the original statement had several meanings, which were clarified after Christ's resurrection (cf. John 2:22). ναός ("temple") in John 2:21 ("But the temple he had spoken of was his body," NIV) seems to refer in the first place to the earthly body of Jesus as the locus of God's revelatory presence (cf. John 4:21-26), the true σκηνή (cf. John 1:14), and to his resurrection body as the true temple, and only secondarily to the new temple of the church. It seems, then, that in v. 1 the basis for Paul's assurance (οἴδαμεν) of heavenly embodiment was the raising of Christ, a basis he had already established in 1 Cor. 15:20-23.

Few verbal forms in the Pauline corpus have occasioned more discussion than the simple form ἔχομεν. In spite of Denney's stricture that "'we have it' means 'it is ours'; any more precise definition must be justified on grounds extraneous to the text,"³⁴ a definition more precise than his paraphrase must in fact be sought. Does "it is ours" denote a present possession or a future acquisition? In the NT the tense of the verb in the apodosis of a conditional sentence introduced by ἐάν and the aorist subjunctive is most frequently the future³⁵ and sometimes the present³⁶ (or perfect³⁷) or the aorist,³⁸ and indicative (although the imperative³⁹ or subjunctive⁴⁰ mood also occurs). Consequently, the reason for the present tense demands special consideration, as does the possibility that ἔχομεν here bears the sense of ἕξομεν or σχήσομεν. Before detailed discussion is undertaken, it may be helpful to provide an overview of the major interpreta-

---

32. ἐπίγειος is to be differentiated from χοϊκός ("made of earth"), γήϊνος ("earthy"), and ὀστράκινος ("earthen"). It is the equivalent of ἐπὶ γῆς ("on earth"), not ἐκ γῆς (as though opposed to ἐκ θεοῦ — *pace* Olshausen 313).

33. On the equivalence of the "image" (εἰκών) of the heavenly Man and the resurrection body, see Jervell 270 n. 346; Martin, *Carmen* 114-15.

34. Denney 760.

35. E.g., Matt. 5:13; 28:14; 1 Cor. 14:23.

36. E.g., 1 Cor. 7:39-40.

37. E.g., Rom. 7:2; 14:23.

38. E.g., 1 Cor. 7:28.

39. E.g., 1 Cor. 7:11.

40. E.g., John 8:51-52.

tions of ἔχομεν, on the assumption that the "God-given building" is the "spiritual body" of 1 Cor. 15:44. (Other identifications of the οἰκοδομή have been discussed above.)

A. Present possession of the spiritual body
   1. in heaven
   2. on earth, in embryonic form
B. Future acquisition of the spiritual body
   1. at death
      a. in reality
      b. as an ideal possession actualized at the parousia
   2. at the parousia

A.1. *Present possession of the spiritual body in heaven.* On this interpretation, the spiritual body of the believer already exists, in some sense, in heaven, "perhaps created from eternity."[41] It may be presently possessed because it already exists; yet this possession becomes actualized only through the future ἐπενδύσασθαι. The preparation of the glorified body ἐν τοῖς οὐρανοῖς (v. 1) at baptism is followed by its reception ἐξ οὐρανοῦ (v. 2) at the parousia. It must be admitted that the figurative language Paul employs in 5:1-4, where the resurrection body is conceived of as a building and as a garment, offers prima facie evidence that the σῶμα πνευματικόν actually preexists,[42] especially if ἐν τοῖς οὐρανοῖς is construed with ἔχομεν. A building could not be entered unless it were already built, nor a garment put on unless it were already made. Before the dwelling could be received ἐξ οὐρανοῦ it must exist ἐν τοῖς οὐρανοῖς.

Yet the fact that Paul chose to maintain a distinction between the two metaphors — the building is in fact not "entered" but "put on" (vv. 2-4), while the resurrection body is not explicitly described as a garment — indicates that the difference between the metaphors used and the realities signified must not be overlooked. The preexistence of the σῶμα πνευματικόν is a deduction from the imagery employed, not a necessary inference from the argument, where the emphasis falls rather on the contrast between two *successive* forms of embodiment than on any antithesis between two *coexistent* σώματα. Second, ἐξ οὐρανοῦ in v. 2 is patently the equivalent of ἐκ θεοῦ in v. 1, while ἐν τοῖς

41. Bousset 161; cf. 164; *Kyrios* 104. For the view that the spiritual body already exists ideally in the counsels of God, see Swete 29; cf. B. Weiss 2.57 n. 4; 61. Hunt (167) discovers a dual meaning in ἐν τοῖς οὐρανοῖς: (1) Each Christian, even on earth, possesses the σῶμα πνευματικόν "because he has already risen from the dead by incorporation into Christ's body, the Church." (2) The ἰδέα of the σῶμα πνευματικόν, in which all particular σώματα πνευματικά participate and which makes them what they are, exists now in the eternal world. Cf. Käsemann, *Leib* 165 (the οἰκοδομή is the εἰκών of the believer).

42. That Paul conceived of the existence of heavenly garments or σώματα πνευματικά prior to their being "put on," is postulated, in one form or another, by Lietzmann 117-18; Windisch 160-61, 164; W. L. Knox 137; *Jerusalem* 142; Brun 216, 218, 226, 228; Vielhauer 109. The parallels cited in support of this view include *Ascension of Isaiah* 7:22; 8:26; 9:2, 9, 17, 24; 11:40.

οὐρανοῖς is not to be construed directly with ἔχομεν, but (perhaps adjectivally, as if equivalent to ἐπουράνιον) with οἰκίαν.[43] Just as the οἰκητήριον is not ἐξ οὐρανοῦ until the ἐπένδυσις[44] of the οἰκία ἀχειροποίητος, so the οἰκοδομή is not ἐν τοῖς οὐρανοῖς until the κατάλυσις of the ἐπίγειος οἰκία.[45] Third, that the spiritual body is described as αἰώνιος (v. 1) need not imply that there was no time when it did not exist. As in 2 Cor. 4:17-18, the epithet looks toward the future, not the past, signifying not eternal preexistence but the future durability of the οἰκία ἀχειροποίητος.[46] Fourth, in his description of the relation between the σῶμα ψυχικόν and the σῶμα πνευματικόν Paul seems to use the notion of "change" (cf. 1 Cor. 15:51-54; 2 Cor. 5:2-4) as frequently as that of "exchange" (cf. 1 Cor. 15:44; 2 Cor. 5:1, 8). These two concepts, if pressed literally, respectively exclude and imply the existence of the heavenly body prior to its reception by the believer. Therefore they should not be regarded as mutually exclusive but as complementary, both emphasizing the radical difference between two forms of embodied existence. Finally, an inanimate or impersonal σῶμα would, in Pauline anthropology, amount to a contradiction in terms.

A.2. *Present possession of the spiritual body on earth, in embryonic form.* Reitzenstein isolates three coverings or garments in 2 Corinthians 4–5:[47] the earthly body, the inner man (ἔσωθεν ἄνθρωπος as he calls it), and the heavenly body. The first is discarded at death; the second, worn as a hidden undergarment under the earthly body, is the necessary presupposition for the receipt at the parousia of the overgarment of the body from heaven. Thus, even if stripped[48] of the physical body by death, the believer is not without a garment, but has the οἰκοδομή of the "inner man," the spiritual body in embryo.

It may be doubted, however, whether the equation of the οἰκοδομή with the ἔσω ἄνθρωπος (which presupposes that Paul is envisaging three, and not simply two, garments, the second of which forms an "interim body" preventing nakedness between death and the parousia) does justice to the antithesis in 5:1 between the perpetually deteriorating ἐπίγειος οἰκία and the stable permanency of the οἰκοδομή. Moreover, in v. 2 Paul yearns to "put on" his heavenly dwelling; but that building is portrayed as something new and external.

Both of these views (A.1. and A.2.) labor under a further difficulty. Any interpretation which sees ἔχομεν as indicating a present possession has the effect of converting a conditional sentence into a concessive sentence: "If and

---

43. Similarly Spörlein 141 n. 4. In his discussion of the question of the preexistence of the resurrection body (181-83) Guntermann (182) correctly observes that the phrases ἐκ θεοῦ, ἐξ οὐρανοῦ, and ἐν τοῖς οὐρανοῖς in no way indicate preexistence but "merely characterize the resurrection body with regard to its heavenly quality." There is, therefore, no need to supply ἀποκειμένην (Col. 1:5) or τετηρημένην (1 Pet. 1:4) with ἐν τοῖς οὐρανοῖς (as Windisch [160] suggests).

44. Although this noun is not attested, it may be conveniently used as the substantival equivalent of ἐπενδύσασθαι (2 Cor. 5:2, 4).

45. Cf. Alford 622.

46. Cf. Schlatter 545.

47. Reitzenstein 451-52.

48. Reitzenstein reads ἐκδυσάμενοι = εἰ καὶ ἐξεδυσάμεθα (451-52).

when I die, I acquire a spiritual body" becomes "Even if I die, I nevertheless still possess an οἰκοδομὴ ἐκ θεοῦ." As it is, the apodosis would become true if and only if, or when and only when, the protasis was fulfilled. Not before or until the κατάλυσις of the ἐπίγειος οἰκία has occurred can the receipt of the ἀχειροποίητος οἰκία take place. Just as καταλυθῇ specifies the future act of dying, so ἔχομεν refers to (or at least implies) a future act of acquisition. Furthermore, unless the "building from God" be distinguished from the "habitation from heaven" of v. 2, the possession of this building is a future experience, an object of earnest hope (ἐπενδύσασθαι ἐπιποθοῦντες, v. 2), not a present reality.

B.1.a. *Future acquisition of the spiritual body at death, in reality.* ἔχομεν "defines the moment of the acquisition: as soon as the καταλύεσθαι has set in, the deceased person has the body that comes from God in the place of the destroyed body."[49] On this view, ἔχομεν is present tense for two reasons. First, after ἐὰν . . . καταλυθῇ, which points to a single, specific occurrence in the future, a punctiliar future might have been expected in an apodosis whose realization was dependent on the prior or simultaneous fulfillment of the condition. And the successive aorists in vv. 2-4 (ἐπενδύσασθαι twice, ἐνδυσάμενοι, καταποθῇ) which are used to denote the future reception of the spiritual body would point in the same direction. But in Hellenistic Greek, the punctiliar future of ἔχειν (σχήσω, "I shall acquire") is scarcely ever found. And, at least in Pauline usage, ἕξω never expresses (although it always presupposes) punctiliar action.[50] Consequently ἔχομεν may stand for σχήσομεν in specifying a future acquisition.[51] And, it might be observed, the certainty of this future acquisition is expressed solely by οἴδαμεν — not by the tense of ἔχομεν. Second, alongside this linguistic and negative explanation of Paul's use of ἔχομεν should be set a theological and positive motive, the principal reason for the usage. He may have wished to indicate that between the destruction of the ἐπίγειος οἰκία and the receipt of the οἰκοδομὴ ἐκ θεοῦ there was no interval of homelessness. The moment one residence was destroyed, another was received. ἔχομεν would then point to an immediate succession between two forms of embodiment without implying a long-standing or even momentary coexistence of two bodies. "As soon as our earthly tent-dwelling is taken down, we are the recipients of a building from God."

The objections that can be raised against this position relate not to the exegesis of 2 Cor. 5:1 considered on its own but to wider exegetical and theological issues. First, there is the unambiguous statement in 1 Cor. 15:22-23 that those

49. Heinrici 172. For a list of other proponents of this view, see Harris 255 n. 2; cf. F. G. Lang 64-92. Among the most recent are Thrall (368-70, 391, but see her further suggestion on 392) and Goulder, *Mission* 259.

50. In eight of the twelve uses (excluding Mark 16:18 and including Rev. 2:10 [א 046 vg syr]) of ἕξω in the NT including the three Pauline occurrences, its linear significance is clear (Matt. 12:11; Luke 11:5; John 8:12; Rom. 13:3; 1 Cor. 7:28; Gal. 6:4; 2 Tim. 2:17; Rev. 2:10), while in Matt. 1:23 and possibly Mark 10:21 (= Matt. 19:21; Luke 18:22) ἕξω denotes punctiliar action.

51. That ἔχειν might be used in a punctiliar sense is apparent from Rom. 6:22 and 1 Cor. 9:17.

who belong to Christ will be "made alive" (ζωοποιηθήσονται = ἐγερθήσονται in 15:52) at his coming (ἐν τῇ παρουσίᾳ αὐτοῦ, 15:23). On the one hand, attempts to find in 1 Corinthians 15 inchoate adumbrations of the view that the loss of the σῶμα ψυχικόν was to be immediately followed by the reception of the σῶμα πνευματικόν are less than convincing.[52] On the other hand, many proposals have been made that seem to reconcile the apparently disparate views of resurrection at the parousia and resurrection at death.[53] Assessment of these proposed reconciliations is largely determined by the view taken of the possibility of development in Paul's eschatological thought[54] and of the presence of paradox in Jewish and Christian thought.[55] Second, since 2 Cor. 5:1-10 is prefaced by οἴδαμεν γάρ and Paul gives no indication that he has altered his view, it should be assumed that the doctrinal content of these verses will accord with Paul's previous teaching.[56] Third, to place the resurrection of the body at death is to rob the parousia of its temporal significance, do less than justice to the corporate emphases of Pauline eschatology, and remove the tension between the "already" and the "not yet" that characterizes the entire period between the two advents of Christ.[57] Fourth, non-Pauline parallels to the idea of transformation at death seem to be lacking.[58] Fifth, this view is said not to accord with the Pauline conception of the "substantial" identity between the earthly and heavenly bodies.[59]

B.1.b. *Future acquisition of the spiritual body at death as an ideal possession actualized at the parousia.* "He who has died *has,* from the moment of the state of death having set in, instead of the destroyed body, the body proceeding from God, not yet indeed as a *real* possession, but as an *ideal* possession, un-

---

52. First, Paul's use of the analogy of the seed cannot be taken to prove or even to suggest an immediate continuity between successive forms of embodiment (*pace* Charles 450, 453, 459). Second, in the statement "the dead will be raised imperishable" in 1 Cor. 15:52, becoming ἄφθαρτος need not precede the ἔγερσις which occurs at the parousia. Paul probably regarded the two events as concurrent (cf. Vos 213), not separated by the interval between the Christian's death and Christ's parousia. In the third place, that 1 Cor. 15:35 reads "With what kind of body do they come (ἔρχονται)?" and not "What kind of body do they receive [at the parousia]?" can scarcely be deemed significant (but cf. Hettlinger 188). Since this verse embodies Paul's version of his objector's questions (be the objector imaginary or real) and not his own queries (which might reflect his own thought), it is inadmissible to supply a phrase such as "with Christ at his coming" with the verb ἔρχονται and assume that Paul implies that the receipt of the spiritual body antedates the believer's emergence from the grave or coming with Christ.

53. Some ten such attempts are sketched in Harris 100-101. Of the proposed harmonizations the most attractive is the view that in the consciousness of the departed believer, who no longer inhabits the world of temporal sequences, the moment of death will also be the moment of resurrection. See, e.g., Bruce 204; *Paul* 312 and n. 40; Caird 272-73. The difficulty with this view, however, is that 5:8 seems to depict a conscious fellowship with Christ during the interval between death and resurrection.

54. See in particular Charles 437-63.

55. See, especially, Lowe 140-41; Moule, "Influence" 1-15; Caird, *Language* 247-48.

56. Guntermann 307-8; Allo 151, 156, 158; Feuillet, "Demeure" 175-76, 360.

57. Cf. Cullmann, *Retour* 20; *Immortality* 48-52; *Salvation* 267-68; *Time* 231, 237.

58. Cf. Hoffmann 255.

59. Cf. Guntermann 306-7; cf. 183-91.

doubtedly *to be realized* at the (near) Parousia."[60] Due weight is given here to the element of futurity in the apodosis of v. 1 and to the need to relate this apodosis to the time of death. Also, this view accords with 1 Corinthians 15 (resurrection at the parousia) and so avoids the need to explain why Paul's belief about the time of the receipt of the σῶμα πνευματικόν changed during the relatively brief period (six to eighteen months on any reckoning) between the writing of 1 Corinthians 15 and 2 Corinthians 5. But would a distinction between ideal and real possession have been congenial to Pauline thought? An affirmative answer is suggested when we consider his view of eternal life. Unlike John, for whom eternal life was both a future blessing and a present possession (e.g., John 5:24; 6:27), Paul apparently regarded "eternal life" (ζωὴ αἰώνιος) as a future acquisition,[61] presumably because it involved, like immortality, immunity from spiritual *and* physical death. Yet being in Christ brought newness of "life" (ζωή, Rom. 6:4; 2 Cor. 2:16; Col. 3:3-4). If Paul could speak of "life" that was both present and future (ζωῆς τῆς νῦν καὶ τῆς μελλούσης, 1 Tim. 4:8), might he not have conceived of "eternal life" as an ideal possession in the present that would become a real possession in the future? In a similar way, we may affirm of an heir that he *has* a certain inheritance even before the death of the testator. Further, it could be objected that Paul would have dated any ideal possession of the spiritual body from the time of the believer's election or regeneration, not simply from the time of death.[62] There could not, however, be "possession" of a spiritual body — whether real or ideal — as long as a believer possessed a physical body.

B.2. *Future acquisition of the spiritual body at the parousia.* "For we know that if we die before the parousia, we have (= shall assuredly possess) at the parousia a building from God." What is in fact to be a future acquisition has become, to faith, an assured possession of the present[63] — ἔχομεν is a futuristic present with a durative sense ("we [shall acquire and then] possess").[64] So assured was Paul of possessing the οἰκοδομή after the parousia that he could speak of it as though it were a present possession. This sure conviction arose from the apostle's knowledge of the character of God whose word was his deed, and in particular from the pledge of the resurrection–transformation that God had already given in the Spirit (v. 5).

Attractive though this view is, it is not without difficulties. Why did Paul not use the durative future ἕξομεν, which would have preserved the notion of

60. Meyer 508, followed by Alford 657.

61. Rom. 2:7; 5:21; 6:22-23; Gal. 6:8; 1 Tim. 1:16; 6:12; Tit. 1:2; 3:7; cf. Acts 13:46, 48.

62. Beyschlag (2.270) registers a similar objection.

63. This, in general terms, is the view held by Olshausen 314; Bachmann 219-20; Plummer 144; Deissner 57; Sickenberger 96; Vos 188; Filson 326; *Recompense* 121; Guntermann 66, 182; Robertson 1019; Allo 121, 139, 149; Hughes 163 n. 19; Hoffmann 270; Barrett 151; Gundry 150 (who notes the futuristic presents in 1 Cor. 15:12, 15-16, 29, 32, 35 [twice], 42, 43 [twice]; Lincoln 64. Other scholars (e.g., de Wette 213) believe that in using ἔχομεν Paul has simply overlooked the interval between death and resurrection.

64. Robertson 881-82; cf. Fanning 221-25, especially 224-25.

futurity after ἐὰν . . . καταλυθῇ without forfeiting the sense of certainty already expressed in οἴδαμεν? Again, what consolation would be offered Paul in the event of his *death* (ἐὰν . . . καταλυθῇ) by the knowledge that at the *parousia* he would receive a spiritual body? The moment when the consolation is needed must be the moment when the consolation is given; and the consolation received at death cannot simply be identical with that assurance of the future acquisition of the resurrection body, which is already possessed during life. Since the receipt of the σῶμα πνευματικόν *at the parousia* was (on this view) guaranteed whether or not death had occurred previously, any notion of conditionality in 5:1 is virtually obliterated.

Of the five basic views of ἔχομεν that have been outlined above, the most common are "resurrection at death" (B.1.a.) and "resurrection at the parousia" (B.2.). Those that have least difficulty attaching to them are "resurrection at the parousia" (B.2.) and "ideal possession of the spiritual body at death with real possession at the parousia" (B.1.b.). Of these two, the latter is to be preferred, as best doing justice to ἔχομεν while preserving resurrection for the parousia in accordance with 1 Corinthians 15.[65]

5:2 καὶ γὰρ ἐν τούτῳ στενάζομεν, τὸ οἰκητήριον ἡμῶν τὸ ἐξ οὐρανοῦ ἐπενδύσασθαι ἐπιποθοῦντες. "In this tent, moreover, we sigh, because we yearn to put on as an overgarment that heavenly dwelling of ours." The similarities between vv. 2 and 4 indicate that v. 4 repeats and amplifies the thought of v. 2:

V. 2	V. 4
καὶ γάρ	καὶ γάρ
ἐν τούτῳ	οἱ ὄντες ἐν τῷ σκήνει
στενάζομεν	στενάζομεν
ἐπενδύσασθαι ἐπιποθοῦντες	θέλομεν . . . ἐπενδύσασθαι

καὶ γάρ introduces a confirmatory or additional reason ("for also," "moreover"[66]) for Paul's assurance of his future acquisition of a spiritual body. If the raising up of the temple of Christ's body (John 2:19, 21; Mark 14:58) created Paul's certainty of his inheritance, that certainty was both evidenced and increased by the experience of Spirit-inspired στενάζειν. It matters little whether τῷ σώματι (cf. 4:10 twice; 5:6) ("in this present body," NEB) or τῷ σκήνει ("in this tent," NRSV) is supplied with ἐν τούτῳ, although the latter is more probable in the light of τοῦ σκήνους in v. 1 and ἐν τῷ σκήνει in v. 4.[67] On this understand-

---

65. I defended the "resurrection at death" view in 1971 (Harris, "Watershed"), but only "inclined" to it in 1983 (*Raised Immortal* 100), while preferring to leave open the two possibilities of resurrection at death or resurrection at the parousia (e.g., 196). For treatments of 2 Cor. 5:1-10 that discuss and reject the "resurrection at death" view, see Osei-Bonsu 81-101; Yates, "State" 310-22.

66. For this meaning of καὶ γάρ, see BAGD 151d; J. D. Denniston, *The Greek Particles* (Oxford: Clarendon, 1954²) 109 ("yes and," "and further"). Baumert (43, 350-80, 435) opts for "also indeed."

67. Some take ἐν τούτῳ as causal and retrospective, "because of the knowledge we have about 'a building from God' (v. 1)" (Furnish 266), "for this reason" (Bultmann 133; Carrez 124). But

ing, ἐν τούτῳ indicates the sphere and the time of the στενάζειν ("during earthly embodiment"), with the reason for the sighing or groaning specified by ἐπιποθοῦντες, "we sigh, because we long" (Weymouth).[68] A discussion of the nature of the sighing must be left until v. 4. Allo accurately summarizes Paul's use of ἐπιποθέω when he observes that in his writings this verb "always or almost always connotes intense regret at being distant or absent."[69] What Paul ardently longs for is expressed by the complementary infinitive ἐπενδύσασθαι and its object, τὸ οἰκητήριον ἡμῶν τὸ ἐξ οὐρανοῦ: "to put on as an overgarment that heavenly dwelling of ours." It comes as no surprise when a writer who makes rapid transitions from one metaphor to another (e.g., 1 Cor. 3:6-9a, 9b-17; 9:7) occasionally mixes his metaphors, as Paul does here ("putting on a dwelling"). Such a blending of figures (cf. 1 Cor. 15:23; Col. 2:7) would occur naturally, if not unconsciously, to a tentmaker from Cilicia, for Cilician haircloth was used to make both clothes and tents (but also see Ps. 103:1-2 LXX).

Whatever differences of meaning may lie behind οἰκοδομή, οἰκία (v. 1), and οἰκητήριον (v. 2), these three terms must designate one and the same reality, the resurrection body. Of these terms, only οἰκοδομή may denote the building process (οἰκοδόμησις, 1 Cor. 3:9) as well as its culmination in a completed edifice (οἰκοδόμημα); only οἰκία is applied to both earthly (v. 1a) and heavenly (v. 1b) corporeality; only οἰκητήριον, as the place where the activity of "dwelling" is carried out,[70] implies an οἰκητήρ ("inhabitant"). It is unlikely, however, that the progression οἰκοδομή–οἰκία–οἰκητήριον ("building–house–dwelling") represents three stages in the building process[71] and therefore three degrees of permanence or three different types of building. While each of the prepositional phrases in οἰκοδομὴ ἐκ θεοῦ, οἰκία ἐν τοῖς οὐρανοῖς (v. 1), and οἰκητήριον ἐξ οὐρανοῦ (v. 2) indicates the character of the spiritual body — it is supernatural and heavenly — ἐκ θεοῦ and ἐξ οὐρανοῦ specify the origin which gives rise to its nature, and ἐν τοῖς οὐρανοῖς describes its natural sphere. Since Paul does not maintain a distinction between οὐρανός and οὐρανοί,[72] there is no need to press the difference between the plural ἐν τοῖς οὐρανοῖς ("in heaven") and the singular ἐξ οὐρανοῦ (as if "from the sky"),[73] and then find in the latter phrase a possible allusion to the parousia[74] or to the concept of the angelic retinue of the Mes-

---

Meyer observes (510) that this meaning would presuppose ἐπὶ τούτῳ or ἐπὶ τοῦτο. Others treat it adverbially, "meanwhile" (NIV; Hughes 167 n. 27) or give it a general reference, "in this present state" (JB; similarly NJB).

68. So also Meyer 510; Alford 623; Plummer 145, 148; Windisch 161; Mundle 99; J. Schneider, *TDNT* 7.601 n. 4.

69. Allo 124.

70. Cf. BDF §109 (9).

71. Cf. Turner: "the sudden assumption of the *oikētērion* is but one stage in the process of *oikodomē*," which is "the whole process of transformation into the icon of Christ" (*Insights* 131).

72. See, e.g., ἐκ τῶν οὐρανῶν (1 Thess. 1:10) and ἀπ' οὐρανοῦ (1 Thess. 4:16) in reference to the parousia.

73. As Turner, *Insights* 139-30.

74. As Feuillet, "Demeure" 375 and n. 21.

siah bearing heavenly garments.[75] ἐξ οὐρανοῦ is either a circumlocution for ἐκ θεοῦ (v. 1),[76] "that comes from heaven," or is equivalent to οὐράνιον,[77] "heavenly" (Goodspeed, NEB, REB).

Any exegesis of vv. 2 and 4 must postulate a reason for Paul's use of the doubly compounded verb ἐπενδύειν, since in 1 Corinthians 15, in a similar context, the form ἐνδύειν is employed (1 Cor. 15:53 twice, 54 twice). It has become almost traditional to posit an essential distinction between these two verbs: the one (ἐνδύειν), it is claimed, is used of the resurrection of the dead, the other (ἐπενδύειν) Paul reserves as a distinctive term denoting the special experience of Christians who survive until the parousia. Those who have been temporarily stripped of their corporeality by death are *reclothed* at the resurrection by the spiritual body, while those who survive to witness the parousia are *overclothed* by the resurrection body: as T. S. Evans has aptly expressed it, "the naked indue, the not-naked superindue."[78]

On purely linguistic grounds, however, the validity of this alleged distinction, as it applies to 2 Corinthians 5, must be questioned. On the one hand, Hellenistic Greek is characterized not only by a preference for compound in place of simple forms but also by a tendency to reinforce compound forms (such as ἐνδύειν) by the addition of a further preposition (as in ἐπ-εν-δύειν).[79] That is, ἐπενδύειν may simply mean the same as ἐνδύειν.[80] On the other hand, Moulton cites ἐνδυσάμενοι in 5:3[81] as an example of the "survival in NT Greek of a classical idiom by which the preposition in a compound is omitted, without weakening the sense, when the verb is repeated." In such cases, claims Moulton, the simplex may be treated as fully equivalent to the compound, although he adds "but of course in any given case it may be otherwise explicable."[82] That is, perhaps ἐνδύειν (v. 3) = ἐπενδύειν (vv. 2, 4). What is more, the fourfold use of ἐνδύειν in 1 Cor. 15:53-54 with reference to the transformation (cf. ἀλλαγησόμεθα in vv. 51-52) which must be experienced by any corruptible mortals (τὸ φθαρτὸν τοῦτο, τὸ θνητὸν τοῦτο) before they can inherit incorruptibility

---

75. See Windisch 161, who later comments, however, that ἐξ οὐρανοῦ is "to be understood simply from the standpoint of the person on earth who is about to die, or as a synonym for ἐκ θεοῦ."

76. Hanhart, "Hope" 453; similarly H. Traub, *TDNT* 5.532 n. 289. On "heaven" as a substitute for "God," see Bietenhard 80-82.

77. Rosenmüller 304. In Luke 11:13, p[45] (579) 1424 (pc) it[e] vg[s] read ὁ οὐράνιος in place of ὁ ἐξ οὐρανοῦ.

78. T. S. Evans 174. This general approach to vv. 2-4 is taken by Meyer 511, 516; H. A. A. Kennedy 266; Deissner 60-62, 67, 86-87; Sickenberger 96; Guntermann 67-71; Sevenster 207; Berry 60, 63, 66; Hughes 168-69, 172; Menoud 66-67; Prümm 1.276; Barrett 153; Martin 105; Holleman 72.

79. Zerwick §484.

80. Thus Schmiedel 237-38; Bultmann, *Probleme* 11-12 (on the basis of the ἐκδύσασθαι–ἐπενδύσασθαι antithesis in v. 4 and the fact that the experience of ἐπενδύσασθαι cannot be restricted to survivors until the parousia); similarly in his commentary, 134.

81. On the textual problem involving ἐνδυσάμενοι, see Textual Note b.

82. Moulton 115.

and immortality shows that the verb is not used exclusively of the resurrection of the dead.[83] So then, the use of ἐπενδύειν need not mark a difference between the transformation of the living and the resurrection of the dead.[84]

Corroboration of the view that in vv. 2-4 Paul is envisaging the experience of all believers comes from the flow of argument in vv. 2-5, considered in reverse. The Spirit is the pledge (ἀρραβών, v. 5b) given to all believers of the accomplishment of "this very thing" (αὐτὸ τοῦτο, v. 5a), namely the swallowing up (καταποθῇ) of mortality by life (v. 4c), the receipt of a spiritual body. But this privilege of all Christians is the purpose or outcome (ἵνα) of the ἐπενδύσασθαι (v. 4b), an experience which therefore cannot be restricted to those who remain alive until the parousia.

If ἐπενδύειν = ἐνδύειν in vv. 2 and 4, the meaning of these two verbs will be simply "put on." But if ἐνδύειν = ἐπενδύειν in v. 3, the verbs will mean either "put on" or (better) "put on over"/"put on as an overgarment." In this latter case, where the ἐπι- carries special significance, that over[85] which the overgarment (ἐπενδύτης[86]) of the heavenly dwelling is placed may be the earthly body or human mortality (τὸ θνητόν, 1 Cor. 15:53-54; 2 Cor. 5:4), whether or not there is a period of disembodiment before the ἐπένδυσις.[87] Alternatively, Paul may have considered the "undergarment" (χιτών or ὑποδύτης) to be the "inner person" (4:16b).[88] One reason for Paul's use of ἐπενδύειν could conceivably have been to assert, against certain Corinthian "proto-gnostics" (cf. 1 Cor. 15:12) who might have maliciously understood the ἐνδύσασθαι ἀθανασίαν of 1 Cor.

83. That is, in 1 Cor. 15:53-54 ἐνδύειν is applied to the living (only) or to both the dead and the living, but not to the dead only.

84. There are a few scholars (e.g., A. Oepke, *TDNT* 2.320-21) and several translations (RV, NEB, GNB, NAB[1], NIV, NRSV) which give the middle (ἐπ)ενδύομαι a passive sense, "be clothed (upon)." Some versions and commentators lack consistency in this matter: e.g., RSV, "to put on" (v. 2), "by putting it on" (v. 3), "be further clothed" (v. 4); Plummer 145-47. BAGD (264b) prefers a passive sense for ἐνδύομαι in 1 Cor. 15:53-54, but not for ἐνδύομαι (264a) or ἐπενδύομαι (284d, 285a) in 2 Cor. 5:2-4. Bultmann makes the general observation (53) that the passive sense of the aorist middle is "extremely rare." T. S. Evans's remark (170) is appropriate: "The subjective Middle [ἐπενδύσασθαι, ἐνδυσάμενοι] expressive of action from within must not be ousted and replaced by the objective Passive [ἐπενδυθῆναι, ἐνδεδυμένοι] expressive of action from without."

85. There is no basis for treating the ἐπ(ι) — as intensive ("to put on in increasing measure" or "to be completely clothed") as though there were stages of incorporation into the body of Christ (as Hettlinger maintains, 189, 190 n. 5, 192, 193 n. 4) or degrees of investiture with the spiritual body. Moulton and Howard (313; also BAGD 284d) classify ἐπί in ἐπενδύειν as meaning "*in addition*, a natural development of *upon*"; but see Robertson 600.

86. ἐπενδύτης is used in John 21:7 of Peter's "outer garment," a fisherman's coat.

87. Scholars who refer v. 1 to resurrection at the moment of death contend that Paul chose ἐπενδύειν in preference to ἐνδύειν in order to indicate the continuity between the successive forms of corporeality — the σῶμα ψυχικόν and the σῶμα πνευματικόν — was such that the ἔνδυσις presupposed no ἔκδυσις and was therefore more accurately an ἐπένδυσις. He viewed himself as donning the resurrection body without having first doffed the earthly body — it was to be a case of addition without prior subtraction, a case not of investiture succeeding divestiture but of "superinvestiture" without any divestiture. Cf. Windisch 161.

88. Thus Wagner 389.

15:53-54 to imply that disembodied immortality formed the content of the Christian hope, that the house from heaven was put on *over, and therefore replaced,* the earthly house: it was not a case of simply assuming (ἐνδύειν) (a disembodied) immortality.[89]

5:3 εἴ γε καὶ ἐνδυσάμενοι οὐ γυμνοὶ εὑρεθησόμεθα. "Assuming, that is, that when we have put it on, we shall not find ourselves disembodied." The two important textual variants in this verse (εἴπερ and ἐκδυσάμενοι) have been considered under Textual Notes a. and b. In Pauline usage εἴ γε introduces a statement that makes explicit an assumption that lay behind some preceding assertion (Rom. 5:6, if the true reading; Gal. 3:4; Col. 1:23; Eph. 3:2; 4:21) and may thus also guard against a possible misinterpretation (Gal. 3:4; Col. 1:23). In the four or five NT (= Pauline) instances of εἴ γε outside 2 Cor. 5:3, only in Gal. 3:4 can a note of uncertainty be detected in the assumption thus introduced. In three cases (Rom. 5:6; Eph. 3:2; 4:21) Paul seems to have been quite assured or fully certain that the assumption made was correct. Thrall's detailed study of εἴ γε in Paul led her to conclude that these particles express assurance, not doubt:[90] "on the certain condition that."[91] As Heinrici puts it: εἴ γε "expresses in the form of a condition what in itself is a fact."[92] καί may then be rendered "assuming, that is," "presupposing, of course."[93]

If ἐνδυσάμενοι has the sense of the double compound ἐπενδυσάμενοι,[94] it is likely to have the same object as ἐπενδύσασθαι in v. 2, namely "our heavenly dwelling," the resurrection body. Those who supply "Christ" (cf. Gal. 3:27) or "the new man" (cf. Col. 3:9-10) as the object of ἐνδύσαμενοι[95] tend to minimize the significance of two facts: that the same root appears in three successive verses, the first of which (v. 2) should be seen as regulative, and that, in view of the use of ἐνδύομαι in 1 Cor. 15:53-54 in a similar context, it must remain improbable that a baptismal reference should be preferred to an eschatological one in 2 Cor. 5:3. In relation to εὑρεθησόμεθα, the aorist participle ἐνδυσάμενοι may denote either prior or coincident action. If coincident, it probably is modal, "by putting it on" (RSV);[96] if prior, it may be conditional ("if we have put it on"),[97] causal ("being thus clothed," NEB, REB), or temporal ("when we have put it on," TCNT).[98] Only if ἐνδυσάμενοι is treated as the equivalent of (οἱ)

---

89. On these issues, see further below under vv. 3-4.

90. Thrall, *Particles* 82-97.

91. Thrall 356.

92. Heinrici 176.

93. Cf. Plummer 147 ("Of course, on the supposition that"); Vincent (822); and F. G. Lang (195), "assuming [that]"; E. Schweizer, *TDNT* 7.1061 n. 380 ("presupposing at least"); Furnish 252 ("presupposing, of course"). Similarly Baumert 43, 380-86, 435. Several versions have "if indeed" (Weymouth, Barclay, NJB, NAB², NRSV).

94. See above on v. 2, where Moulton (115) is cited.

95. E.g., Wagner 389; Furnish 298.

96. So also Young and Ford 266; similarly GNB.

97. Bruce, *Paraphrase* 135; similarly Goodspeed.

98. So also Barrett 149; similarly Moffatt, NIV, Cassirer; Furnish 252-53; Thrall 356. Those

ἐνδεδυμένοι can this participle be conjoined with (οὐ) γυμνοί as predicative after εὑρεθησόμεθα: "('super-investiture' will occur only) on the supposition that we shall be found (at the coming of the Lord still) clothed, (and) not naked."[99] In this case ἐνδυσάμενοι would advert to physical embodiment ("clad in this earthly body" = "alive")[100] or to spiritual acceptability ("clothed in righteousness").[101] There are three difficulties facing such an interpretation: it is highly questionable whether the aorist middle participle of ἐνδύειν can denote a state rather than an action; there would appear to be no other instances in Paul's writings where a participle and an adjective are related asyndetically;[102] and that Paul would have regarded birth as the ἔνδυσις of a body of flesh may be doubted.

If εὑρεθησόμεθα is a "theological passive," it refers to God's or Christ's "discovery" of human beings at the parousia or the end (cf. 4:14; 5:10).[103] But in NT Greek passives not infrequently have a reflexive or intransitive sense,[104] so that in v. 3 the passive of εὑρίσκειν may mean "find oneself,"[105] "prove to be,"[106] or "be found to be" (French *se trouver*).[107]

Probably the most notorious crux of 5:1-10 is the meaning of γυμνοί. Bewildering though the variety of interpretations is, there seem to be three principal interpretations, which may be described as contextual, ethical, and anthropological, according to which this epithet means "homeless," "garmentless," or "bodiless" (respectively).

The strength of the first view lies in its consonance with the architectural imagery throughout vv. 1-9. Just as the ἐν- or ἐκ-δημεῖν metaphor of vv. 6-9 has an οἰκία (whether it be the earthly house, the heavenly home, or [by implication] the resurrection body) as its point of reference, so in vv. 1-4 the object of the ἐπένδυσις is an οἰκοδομή, οἰκία, or οἰκητήριον. If οἰκοδομὴν ἐκ θεοῦ is supplied with ἐνδυσάμενοι, γυμνοί may naturally allude to homelessness.[108]

Behind the "ethical" or "eschatological" interpretation of γυμνός there lies, it seems, the imagery employed in the Matthean parable of the wedding

---

who read ἐκδυσάμενοι treat this participle as temporal (NAB[2], NRSV; Bultmann 135) or concessive (Metzger [511], citing a majority textual view).

99. Similarly Conybeare in Conybeare and Howson 448 and n. 3; JB, NAB[1], NJB; Carrez 124, 131. See Bachmann's defense (224-29) of this general line of interpretation.

100. Thus Bengel 375; Meyer 511-12; Belser 161, 164, 171; Prat 2.367-68; Robinson 77; Hughes 170.

101. E.g., Olshausen 315-17; Grosheide 280-81.

102. Rom. 2:29; 1 Cor. 3:2; 1 Thess. 2:17 are not precise parallels, for they involve two substantives related asyndetically.

103. Thus Grayston 56; Wolff 109. Wenham ("Last Day" 478) finds in εὑρεθησόμεθα an allusion to Jesus' eschatological parables that refer to the returning Lord as "finding" his servants on the last day (e.g., Matt. 24:46). For a forensic sense for εὑρίσκεσθαι, see F. G. Lang 188.

104. Buttmann 52.

105. Goodspeed, NEB, REB, Cassirer; Zerwick and Grosvenor 543. Cf. Acts 5:39.

106. Thrall 356.

107. Weymouth; similarly Barrett 149. Cf. BAGD 325d.

108. See, e.g., Hodge 118; Tasker 79.

garment (Matt. 22:11-14). That person is γυμνός who is garmentless (οὐκ ἐνδεδυμένον ἔνδυμα γάμου, Matt. 22:11), lacking either faith (= "Christless") or works (= "fruitless"). Before God, the unbeliever will appear in the shameful nakedness (γυμνός = ἀσχημονῶν) of his wicked works, destitute of the baptismal robe of righteousness or the eschatological robe of immortality. Not having "put on Christ," the "natural" person will be found on the day of judgment simply ἐν Ἀδάμ, in the polluted garments of sin. Since the time of Irenaeus, this explanation of γυμνός in terms of αἰσχύνη[109] before God at the parousia — that is, primarily in terms of Hebraic thought — has commanded a following among exegetes.[110]

Traditionally, γυμνότης ("nakedness") has been regarded as the Pauline description of the Christian's state of incompleteness[111] after death and before resurrection. To be γυμνός is to be temporarily bodiless, without either physical or spiritual embodiment.[112] Alternatively, the γυμνότης of 5:3 has been understood as describing the fate of unbelievers, who are to be permanently without a spiritual body,[113] or the ideal of those pseudo-believers or unbelievers who long for the permanent disembodiment they imagine is brought by death.

A choice between these alternatives must await the discussion of v. 4, for clearly ἐκδύσασθαι there will shed light on the meaning of γυμνοί here. There I will defend the view that in v. 3 Paul is expressing, not fear of temporary physical disembodiment[114] or permanent spiritual disembodiment, but assurance of spiritual embodiment and rejection of any idealization of disembodiment that may have been advocated by certain gnosticizing Corinthians.

5:4 καὶ γὰρ οἱ ὄντες ἐν τῷ σκήνει στενάζομεν βαρούμενοι, ἐφ' ᾧ οὐ θέλομεν ἐκδύσασθαι ἀλλ' ἐπενδύσασθαι. "For indeed, as tent-dwellers, we sigh with a sense of oppression because, not wishing to become disembodied, we desire to put on our heavenly dwelling as an overgarment." Here Paul resumes (καὶ γάρ, "for indeed," "for it is a fact that") and expands the thought of v. 2 after the parenthetical aside of v. 3. οἱ ὄντες is generic and the article in ἐν τῷ σκήνει is anaphoric, "we who are in this tent," that is, "as tent-dwellers," although the parallelism with v. 6a suggests temporal overtones, "as long as we live in this tent,"[115] the implication then being that the cessation of tent-dwelling meant the cessation of the sighing (στενάζομεν). It was while, not because, Paul was embodied in the earthly body that he experienced a στενάζειν.

109. See, in particular, Ellis, *Interpreters* 44-45.

110. E.g., Calvin 67; Grosheide 270; Sickenberger 96; Wagner 392. Cf. F. G. Lang 140-44.

111. See Cullmann, *Time* 240-41; *Immortality* 52-57.

112. Cf. Deissner 97-100, 110, 118-19; Guntermann 145, 282, 310.

113. Thus Beyschlag 2.270; Charles 452; Mundle 101-2; Bietenhard 226; Menoud 67 n. 3.

114. See the arguments of Brandenburger (177 n. 1) against interpreting 5:3 as evidence of Paul's fear of a postmortem nakedness. Cf. Hoffmann 259, 275-76; Danker, "Consolation" 555 ("It would be unlikely that the apostle, who exhorted others not to despair in the face of death's reality, should himself reflect anxiety over temporary disembodiment").

115. Similarly Lietzmann 120; Lang 284.

Whether it denotes physical oppression ("burdened with affliction") or mental anguish ("oppressed by anxiety"), the circumstantial participle βαρούμενοι indicates the degree of intensity with which Paul sighed ἐν τῷ σκήνει, "we sigh with a sense of oppression." There is therefore no need to postulate a cause for the βαρεῖσθαι.

We have seen that in v. 2 ἐπενδύσασθαι ἐπιποθοῦντες defines the cause of the στενάζειν: "we sigh because we yearn . . . ." This makes it antecedently probable that in the resumptive v. 4 ἐφ' ᾧ . . . [θέλομεν] ἐπενδύσασθαι also specifies the reason for the sighing, "we sigh . . . because we desire to put on [our heavenly dwelling] as an overgarment." That ἐφ' ᾧ is causal ("inasmuch as," "because"), equivalent to ἐπὶ τούτῳ ὅτι, "for this reason, namely that," is recognized by the grammatical authorities.[116] While parallels for the translation of ἐφ' ᾧ by "on the condition that"[117] may be found in Classical and Hellenistic Greek, including the papyri, grave difficulties attach to that rendering here.[118] The reason for the apparently strange position of the negative (ἐφ' ᾧ οὐ, not οὐκ ἐφ' ᾧ, the text sometimes translated[119]) is that in this typically compressed clause, two assertions, antithetical in form, are expressed: "we do not desire to strip off," a negative statement, containing the rejected ground for the burdensome sighing, and "we desire to put on [our heavenly dwelling] as an overgarment,"[120] a positive declaration, affirming the real ground for the sighing. If Paul had written οὐκ ἐφ' ᾧ, there would have been a negative mold for what was essentially a positive assertion; a real reason, in this case positive in form, naturally takes precedence over a rejected reason in determining the nature of the conflation of the two statements. In vv. 2 and 4, then, there is a single positive reason for Paul's στενάζειν: not a Hellenistic depreciation of corporeality but an intense longing for investiture with a heavenly body, a body completely respon-

116. BAGD 287c, 585a; Robertson 604, 722, 963; BDF §235(2); Zerwick §127; *Analysis* 399; Moule 132; "Dualism" 118 n. 1; Turner 272, 319; *Insights* 131; cf. Moulton 107 ("in view of the fact that"). In each of the four instances of ἐφ' ᾧ in Paul (Rom. 5:12; 2 Cor. 5:4; Phil. 3:12; 4:10), the conjunction is probably causal (thus Thackeray 33-34; Freundorfer 130, 236-38). For the equation ἐφ' ᾧ = ἐπὶ τούτῳ ᾧ, see Baumert 195, 386-401.

117. H. C. G. Moule 37 and n. 3; Danker, "Consolation" 552-56 (Paul is willing to undergo death on the condition that he receives at the parousia after a period of temporary disembodiment the heavenly covering); cf. "Romans 5:12," 433 (ἐφ' ᾧ = "in view of the terms on which"). Thrall defended this rendering in 1962 (*Particles* 93-94), but opted for "because" in 1994 (356, 380-81).

118. (1) The future tense normally required after ἐφ' ᾧ or ἐφ' ᾧτε, when they mean "on condition that," is scarcely compensated for in 5:4 by the futuristic connotations of a verb of wishing (θέλομεν). (2) For the relation between στενάζομεν and the ἐφ' ᾧ clause to be intelligible (on this view), a parenthesis of some complexity must be supplied before ἐφ' ᾧ. "[But such sighing is permissible only] on condition that. . . ." (3) This interpretation overlooks the parallelism between v. 2 (where ἐπιποθοῦντες is causal) and v. 4.

119. E.g., KJV, RV, Moffatt, RSV (but cf. NRSV).

120. But Hanhart ("Hope" 455; cf. his *Intermediate State* 173-74) discovers in ἐπενδύσασθαι a reference to the Christian's receipt at death of the full measure of the life of the Spirit already partially received before death at baptism and in daily renewal (= ἐνδυσάμενοι, v. 3).

sive to the will of the Spirit and perfectly suited to the environment of heaven.[121]

But the nature of the sighing or groaning is nowhere specified in the passage. A comparison with a parallel use of this verb in Rom. 8:23 seems to indicate that this is Paul's term to describe the Christian's reaction to living "between the times" — between the two advents of Christ or between receiving the pledge of inheritance and the actual possession of the inheritance (Eph. 1:13-14). It describes not so much the tension that Christians might feel because of their simultaneous participation in the realities of two ages as the frustration they feel (but do not necessarily articulate; cf. Rom. 8:26) with the old age.[122] In particular it expresses their profound dissatisfaction or frustration with the limitations and disabilities of bodily existence on earth when compared with the glories of the new age, which include a body fashioned like Christ's own resplendent body (Phil. 3:21).

In the context, the aorist middle infinitive ἐκδύσασθαι means either "to put off [the garment of the mortal body],"[123] or "to divest ourselves,"[124] or "to have the old body stripped off" (NEB, REB).[125] Any one of these three meanings could produce the sense "to become disembodied." It seems clear that γυμνοί in v. 3 and ἐκδύσαθαι in v. 4 are intimately related in meaning. First, both terms are negative in sense and are applicable to some form of nakedness, γυμνός referring to the state itself and ἐκδύσασθαι to entrance upon that state. Second, a negative is directly or indirectly associated with each word (οὐ γυμνοὶ εὑρεθησόμεθα and οὐ θέλομεν ἐκδύσασθαι). And third, both words are juxtaposed to opposing terms (ἐνδυσάμενοι, ἐπενδύσασθαι).

In Paul's writings, in particular the Corinthian correspondence, an οὐ(κ) . . . ἀλλά antithesis (such as that in v. 4) often contains an explicit or implicit reference to a person or group (e.g., 2:17; 5:12; 10:18) or well-known conception (e.g., 1:24; 4:5) of which he expresses disapproval, ranging from mild disagreement (e.g., 1 Cor. 4:19) to uncompromising repudiation (e.g., 1 Cor. 6:13; 2 Cor. 10:4). On the basis, then, of this Pauline use of the οὐ(κ) . . . ἀλλά contrast, the similarity between vv. 3 and 4, and Paul's use of an εἴ γε clause to introduce a corrective to a possible misinterpretation of an immediately preceding statement,[126] we may propose that γυμνοί and ἐκδύσασθαι together form an allusion to some aberrant view of which Paul disapproves.[127] With ἐφ' ᾧ οὐ

121. θέλειν, rather than ἐπιποθεῖν, is used in v. 4 as the more appropriate, neutral term to stand with both the real and the rejected ground of the στενάζειν.

122. "Only in the moment when the mortal is swallowed up by life [5:4b] will the sighing which is a mark of all creatures in this age cease" (J. Schneider, *TDNT* 7.601).

123. Similarly JB; Conybeare in Conybeare and Howson 448; Thrall 356.

124. Cassirer; similarly BAGD 239a; Zerwick and Grosvenor 543; Furnish 253.

125. On the LXX usage of ἐνδύειν and ἐκδύειν, see Helbing 45-46.

126. See above on v. 3.

127. That both these terms are polemical is recognized by Bultmann 134-35, 137-38; *Probleme* 4; Schmithals 263-65; Hoffmann 272, 276-78, 285; and in reference to γυμνοί, E. Schweizer, *TNDT* 7.1061 and n. 380; Thrall 377, 379, 392 (cf. her *Particles* [94] regarding v. 4).

θέλομεν ἐκδύσασθαι Paul may be repudiating the view of the hereafter held by the precursors of Gnosticism at Corinth (1 Cor. 15:12), who appear to have taught, as a corollary of baptismal resurrection, that the Christian hope consisted primarily of emancipation from corporeal defilement. Similarly, v. 3 may be Paul's rebuttal of the fallacious deduction made by these Corinthian "protognostics" that the expression ἐνδύσασθαι ἀθανασίαν ("to put on immortality") used in 1 Cor. 15:53-54 implied that the believer's final destiny was disembodied immortality — "assuming, that is, that when we have put in on, we shall find ourselves to be not[128] disembodied [but permanently embodied]."[129]

ἵνα καταποθῇ τὸ θνητὸν ὑπὸ τῆς ζωῆς. "So that what is mortal may be swallowed up by life." Although ἵνα may sometimes introduce a result, more probably it here introduces the divine purpose (and therefore certain effect) of the "super-investiture." If καταπίνω means "swallow up," "w[ith] total extinction as a result,"[130] then τὸ θνητόν bears an abstract sense, "mortality"[131] or even "death,"[132] and v. 4b will closely parallel 1 Cor. 15:54b (citing Isa. 25:8), "death has been swallowed up (κατεπόθη) in victory."[133] On the other hand, if καταπίνω implies absorption[134] or transformation rather than annihilation, τὸ θνητόν, as a case of "abstract for concrete," will be indistinguishable from τὸ θνητὸν τοῦτο (1 Cor. 15:53-54), referring to "this mortal body,"[135] which is destined to be transformed through resurrection (1 Cor. 15:51-54; Phil. 3:21). The rendering "what is mortal" (RSV, NRSV) retains the abstract form but permits a specific reference to the earthly body.

If, then, the κατάποσις alludes to transformation,[136] an interesting pattern emerges with regard to the relation of 5:1-5 to 4:12-18:

128. It is surprising, in view of the considerable attention given by commentators to the position of the negative in v. 4 (ἐφ' ᾧ οὐ θέλομεν), that οὐ γυμνοὶ εὑρεθησόμεθα in v. 3 has not provoked more comment. Since "the negative stands as a rule before that which is negated" (BDF §433), might it not be that Paul here is intentionally isolating a term which his opponents had borrowed from his arsenal and converted to their own use in order to show that in no sense was the postmortem and final state of the Christian one of γυμνότης? "My assumption, to be sure, is that once the ἔνδυσις has taken place, we shall not ever find ourselves γυμνοί — as ἐν ὑμῖν τινες would have it" (cf. Goodspeed: ". . . I shall never find myself disembodied"; similarly Williams). Once the polemical background of the verse is recognized, the apparent tautology of ἐνδυσάμενοι οὐ γυμνοί is removed.

129. This proposal is discussed in more detail in the Introduction (B.4.e).

130. BAGD 416c.

131. Furnish 253; Thrall 356; Weymouth and REB ("our mortality").

132. Louw and Nida §13.43. The difficulty with a straight equation τὸ θνητόν = ὁ θάνατος is that the verbal adjective θνητός means "liable to die," "mortal," rather than "dead" (νεκρός), so that the abstract substantive τὸ θνητόν would mean "propensity to death," "mortality" (θνητότης), rather than "death."

133. Cf. Dupont, Union 138; Lambrecht, "Vie" 353-54, 361.

134. The word "absorbed" renders καταποθῇ in Goodspeed, NEB, REB, Cassirer.

135. On this view, the article in τὸ θνητόν will be anaphoric, referring back to σκῆνος (vv. 1, 4) = ἐπίγειος οἰκία (v. 1).

136. κατάποσις, like ἐπένδυσις, alludes to the transformation of the σῶμα ψυχικόν or ἔσω ἄνθρωπος into the σῶμα πνευματικόν, κατάποσις viewing the change from the side of the σῶμα

ἡ νέκρωσις (4:10a) → εἰς θάνατον παραδίδοσθαι (4:11a) → ἡ ἐνέργεια τοῦ θανάτου (4:12a) → διαφθορά (4:16a) → κατάλυσις (5:1a)

ἡ ζωή (4:10b, 11b) → ἀνακαίνωσις (4:16b) → κατάποσις (5:4b).

4:16 speaks of two concurrent processes which Paul knew to be operative in his life (cf. 4:10-11). One was the steady irreversible process of physical deterioration, the other was the daily inward process of spiritual renewal. The outcome of the former process is the destruction of the earthly tent-dwelling (5:1). The climax of the latter process, we suggest, is the swallowing up of the mortal body by immortal life, of mortality by immortality (5:4). But it is a distinctive climax. The believer's present lowly body can never in this life resemble Christ's resplendent body. Nor is complete conformity to the image of Christ (Rom. 8:29; 1 Cor. 15:49) ever attainable here and now. In describing the outcome of the process of renewal begun on earth, "swallowing up" must therefore imply the acceleration of the process of "Christification," that is, becoming like Christ.

There are several reasons for discerning in the term ἡ ζωή (v. 4) an allusion to immortality. First, in Pauline diction "life" can be an abbreviation for "eternal life," the positive aspect of immortality.[137] Second, in the parallel passage (1 Cor. 15:53-54) "this mortal body" puts on immortality. Third, "(eternal) life" and "immortality" are juxtaposed as virtually synonymous in Rom. 2:7 and 2 Tim. 1:10. And fourth, the antithesis to "what is mortal" that one would expect after "swallowed up" is "what is immortal" or "immortality." It is not necessary to see "(immortal) life" here as a personal agent, for the preposition ὑπό may be used of inanimate agencies (e.g., Col. 2:18) or personified forces (e.g., Luke 7:24) as well as personal agents. Yet, given Paul's doctrine of the resurrected Christ as "a life-giving spirit" (1 Cor. 15:45) and his belief in the revivifying activity of the Spirit (Rom. 8:2, 11; 2 Cor. 3:6), it is natural to find the source of this "life" in Christ or in the Spirit who indwells the believer. If this is so, we need not regard the "life" as some external force suddenly operating on Paul's mortality. Rather, we should see it as a power already working in Paul's life, and the "swallowing up" as a climax of that action.

It has been argued above that γυμνοί in v. 3 and ἐκδύσασθαι in v. 4 are both direct allusions to the view of certain Corinthian proto-gnostics for whom ἀθανασία, as disembodied γυμνότης, represented the *summum bonum* and the object of eager longing,[138] and that εἴ γε states the assumption *(siquidem)* on

---

ψυχικόν, ἐπένδυσις from the side of the σῶμα πνευματικόν. That καταποθῇ adverts to transformation has been observed by Kabisch 308; Bultmann, *Probleme* 10; L. Goppelt, *TDNT* 6.159.

137. E.g., Rom. 5:10; Phil. 4:3; 1 Tim. 6:19 compared with 6:12; 2 Tim. 1:1.

138. If this vocal sector of the Corinthian congregation had appealed to the Pauline use of the ambiguous term ἀθανασία in 1 Cor. 15:53-54 (δεῖ . . . τὸ θνητὸν τοῦτο ἐνδύσασθαι ἀθανασίαν, v. 53) in support of their views, at least a partial explanation is supplied for: Paul's substitution of ζωή for ἀθανασία in 5:4; the appearance of ἐπενδύειν in place of the simple ἐνδύειν; the assurance of 5:3 that the ἔνδυσις did not issue in γυμνότης; the repudiation in v. 4 of the aberrant notion (ἐκδύσασθαι [= ἐνδύσασθαι ἀθανασίαν or γυμνοὶ εὑρεθῆναι] ἐπιποθοῦμεν) which had given rise to the willful misrepresentation of the Pauline view of resurrection.

which Paul's argument proceeds, not a condition *(si tamen)* on the fulfillment of which the validity of the argument depends. In effect Paul is saying in vv. 2-4, "The ground of my στέναζειν is not a desire for divestiture followed by nakedness but a longing for a 'superinvestiture' followed by permanent embodiment. The object of my ἐπιπόθησις is not γυμνότης but an ἐπένδυσις. My assumption in speaking of an ἐπένδυσις is that once we have donned our house from heaven we shall not discover ourselves to be in a 'disembodied state.'" If v. 3 defines the outcome of the ἐπένδυσις negatively — it is not disembodied immortality — v. 4 defines it positively: it is the transformation of the mortal body by immortal life.

5:5 ὁ δὲ κατεργασάμενος ἡμᾶς εἰς αὐτὸ τοῦτο θεός. "Now it is God who has prepared us for this very destiny." The verb κατεργάζομαι has three basic meanings in the NT, depending on the construction found with it: with τι, "accomplish" something (Rom. 1:27, 2:9; 1 Cor. 5:3; Eph. 6:13); with τινί τι, "produce" or "bring about" something for someone (4:17; 7:11; 9:11); and with τινα εἴς τι, "prepare" or "equip" someone for something (the present verse).[139] Since no ὅπως or ἵνα clause follows εἰς αὐτὸ τοῦτο by way of definition, this phrase, which means (literally) "for this thing itself" = "for this very purpose/ experience/destiny," must refer back to some implied or explicit antecedent. There are two main options.[140]

Survival until the parousia.[141] That Paul believed that God had actually prepared or fashioned any or all believers for the receipt of an immortal body without the intervention of death, for "superinvestiture" rather that simply investiture, seems decidedly unlikely, since, however 2 Cor. 4:12 may be understood, Paul himself, who is certainly to be included among the ἡμᾶς of 5:5a, was not at this time expecting to be alive at Christ's advent (see 2 Cor. 4:14; 5:1),[142] and the possession of the Spirit, the heritage of all Christians without exception (Rom. 8:9), would in itself afford no guarantee of exemption from a pre-parousia death,[143] although the presence and activity of the Spirit in the believer might provoke or stimulate a desire to be among οἱ περιλειπόμενοι εἰς τὴν παρουσίαν τοῦ κυρίου (1 Thess. 4:15). While this interpretation might be consistent with the traditional distinction between ἐνδύειν and ἐπενδύειν (see above), it fails to distinguish between the universality of the Christian possession of the Spirit and the particularity of the experience of living to see the ad-

139. Cf. BAGD 421 c, d. For examples of this meaning ("prepare," "equip") in the LXX, see G. Bertram, *TDNT* 3.634.

140. Less likely alternatives include: (1) the body of Christ (= οἰκοδομὴ ἐκ θεοῦ) (Robinson 78), (2) the Christian overcoming of the dread of death or disembodied nakedness (Cullmann, *Time* 239, apparently), (3) the process of exchanging the transitory for the permanent (Moule, "Influence" 12; "Dualism" 118), and (4) the groaning of vv. 2, 4 (Bengel 3.375; Berry 65; Baumert 45, 200-202, 216-17, 435).

141. See, e.g., Kühl 15, 17-18, 37. Filson (*Recompense* 121), MacRory (343), and Zerwick (*Analysis* 399) relate εἰς αὐτὸ τοῦτο to the *desire* for transformation without death.

142. See the excursus above at 1:11.

143. Similarly Schmiedel 239; Mundle 105.

vent (cf. 1 Cor. 15:51) and does not reckon with Paul's admitted uncertainty concerning the time of the advent (1 Thess. 5:1-2).

The receipt and possession of the spiritual body,[144] which vv. 1-4 describe in various ways: as the acquisition (ἔχειν) of the οἰκοδομὴ ἐκ θεοῦ, the ἐπένδυσις of τὸ οἰκητήριον τὸ ἐξ οὐρανοῦ, and the κατάποσις of τὸ θνητόν. Inasmuch as ἵνα καταποθῇ τὸ θνητὸν ὑπὸ τῆς ζωῆς immediately precedes αὐτὸ τοῦτο, it may be presumed that the primary reference is to the action denoted by καταποθῇ.[145] Support for this general view is found in v. 5b, where the Spirit is described as the ἀρραβών, the Christian's pledge of future inheritance (Eph. 1:14) which includes the transformation of the weak, earthly body into a resplendent body like Christ's (Phil. 3:21). That is, the antecedent of the αὐτὸ τοῦτο corresponds to one part of the content of the ἀρραβών. Moffatt's rendering reflects such an understanding: "I am prepared for this change by God, who has given me the Spirit as its pledge and instalment."

As in 1:21, the position of θεός in its clause indicates that the word is to be emphasized. The omission of the article before θεός (although ℵ* has ὁ θεός) probably serves to isolate the predicate and stress the qualities or attributes (rather than the particular identity) of deity:[146] "Now he who has prepared us for this very destiny is none other than the God who is the creator and consummator of all things" (cf. 1 Cor. 8:6; Rom. 11:36). The κατεργάσασθαι denotes a characteristically or exclusively divine operation. The divine initiative is frequently stressed throughout 2 Corinthians 1-7.[147]

ὁ δοὺς ἡμῖν τὸν ἀρραβῶνα τοῦ πνεύματος. "Who gave/and has given us the Spirit as a down payment and pledge." When this whole verse is compared with 1:22, several important exegetical points emerge.

1:22 (θεός,) ὁ καὶ σφραγισάμενος ἡμᾶς

5:5   ὁ δὲ κατεργασάμενος ἡμᾶς εἰς αὐτὸ τοῦτο θεός

1:22 καὶ δοὺς   τὸν ἀρραβῶνα τοῦ πνεύματος ἐν ταῖς καρδίαις ἡμῶν

5:5 ὁ   δοὺς ἡμῖν τὸν ἀρραβῶνα τοῦ πνεύματος

In both verses τοῦ πνεύματος is an epexegetic genitive:[148] "the down payment and pledge consisting of the Spirit," or "the Spirit as a down payment and pledge."[149]

When God "gives" the Spirit to believers, he places him in their hearts.

144. E.g., Bachmann 232; Guntermann 72; G. Bertram, *TDNT* 3.635; Bruce 204.

145. So also Belser 162, 164; Plummer (CGT) 87; Wendland 195; Thrall 383-85.

146. Cf. Moulton 82-83; Burton, *Galatians* 228, 230.

147. Cf. 1:4, 9-10, 21-22; 2:14; 3:5-6; 4:6-7; 5:1, 5; 7:6.

148. Winer 531; Robertson 498; E. Schweizer, *TDNT* 6.422 n. 595; Hermann 33; Turner 214.

149. On the meaning of ἀρραβών, see 1:22. Here in 5:5, as in 1:22, some translations reflect the dual meaning of ἀρραβών: "pledge and foretaste" (Weymouth), "pledge and installment" (Moffatt), "deposit, guaranteeing what is to come" (NIV). See further Erlemann 202-23.

In each case the "giving" is intimately related to the action denoted by the articular aorist participle. In 1:22 the anarthrous δούς, joined to ὁ καὶ σφραγισάμενος ἡμᾶς by καί, is explicative: "(God it was) who also sealed us by giving us the pledge of his Spirit in our hearts." Similarly, in 5:5, although grammatically ὁ δούς = ὃς ἔδωκεν and although Paul did not write ὁ δὲ θεὸς κατειργάσατο ἡμᾶς εἰς αὐτὸ τοῦτο δοὺς κτλ., it may be proposed that ὁ δούς indicates the means by which God effected the κατεργάσασθαι and functions in the same way as an aorist participle of identical action which particularizes the action of the main verb (here ὁ κατεργασάμενος) by specifying its mode. "Now[150] God himself has prepared us for this very destiny by giving[151] us the down payment and pledge of the Spirit."

Just as the "sealing" occurred at the time of regeneration (cf. Eph. 1:13), so too did the "fashioning" or "preparation." If so, there seems to be a strong *prima facie* case for equating the articular participles which precede the phrase (ὁ) δοὺς (ἡμῖν) τὸν ἀρραβῶνα τοῦ πνεύματος and are defined by it with respect to their mode: God's preparation of believers εἰς αὐτὸ τοῦτο (= εἰς ἀπολύτρωσιν τοῦ σώματος, "for the redemption of the body"; cf. Eph. 1:14; Rom. 8:23) would, in this case, be indistinguishable from his sealing of them εἰς ἡμέραν ἀπολυτρώσεως, "for the day of redemption" (cf. Eph. 4:30).

The nature of the κατεργάσασθαι on this view may be summarized as follows. Effected by God at regeneration, the κατεργάσασθαι is God's sealing of believers by giving them the Spirit as a pledge of the acquisition of an immortal body (vv. 1-2) through the transformation of the mortal body at the parousia (v. 4).[152]

All this raises a further question. How did Paul discern in the presence and activity of the Spirit within his life a guarantee of the receipt of a resurrection body? In the first place, since the Spirit represented the "inbreaking" of the powers of the new eon (cf. Heb. 6:5),[153] his present activity was a token of the continuity of God's redemptive action in the present age and the age to come. The continuity between the two ages was for Paul pneumatological or christological

---

150. If the antecedent of αὐτὸ τοῦτο is vv. 1-4 in general, and καταποθῇ in particular, δέ is more probably continuative in function (thus Heinrici 183; Belser 162) than adversative (as Moule, "Dualism" 118 n. 1).

151. So also Gräbe 149; similarly Cassirer; Baumert 45, 217, 435 (". . . inasmuch as he gave . . .").

152. On this view, κατεργασάμενος is a constative aorist, but it would be possible to regard it as gnomic (cf. REB, "God himself has been shaping us") or inceptive ("the one who began our production," Thrall 356; cf. 384 and n. 1361).

153. Cf. Hill 273: "the gift of the Spirit here and now is, in fact, the substance of Paul's 'inaugurated eschatology.'"

rather than anthropological; it resided in the possession and activity of the Spirit (or union with Christ[154]), not in the persistence of an immortal *ego*.[155] Secondly, the Spirit *was* a pledge of inheritance because he *brought* its firstfruits — the spirit of sonship (Rom. 8:14-16), to be consummated in adoptive sonship (υἱοθεσία, Rom. 8:23; cf. Rev. 21:7), and the progressive renewal of the "inner person" (2 Cor. 3:18; 4:16; Eph. 3:16), to be consummated in their transformation (2 Cor. 5:4). Thirdly, the Spirit who empowered the daily re-creation of believers would also effect their resurrection transformation (Rom. 8:11; cf. 1 Cor. 6:14; Gal. 6:8b) and sustain their resurrection life (Rom. 1:4[156]).[157]

5:6 Θαρροῦντες οὖν πάντοτε καὶ εἰδότες ὅτι ἐνδημοῦντες ἐν τῷ σώματι ἐκδημοῦμεν ἀπὸ τοῦ κυρίου. "Therefore we are always confident, and because we know that we are absent from the Lord as long as we are living in this body. . . ." οὖν points back to vv. 1-5 and v. 5 in particular. With the assured hope of acquiring a glorified body as permanent housing (v. 1) and having a guarantee of that future transformation (vv. 2, 4) in the presence and activity of the Spirit within him (v. 5), Paul was full of confidence in any and every circumstance (πάντοτε), including the exigencies of apostolic service (4:8-11) and especially the approach of death (5:1). But inasmuch as θαρροῦντες is the positive equivalent of οὐκ ἐγκακοῦμεν (4:16), οὖν could also resume the thought of 4:16, especially since 4:16a looks back (διό) to the resurrection hope expressed in 4:14, just as οὖν in 5:6 alludes to the assurance of a resurrection transformation found in 5:1-5.[158] As is common in 2 Corinthians, a participle, θαρροῦντες, is equivalent to a finite verb, θαρροῦμεν.[159] V. 6 is anacoluthic because θαρροῦμεν δὲ καί (v. 8a) interrupts the grammatical connection of εἰδότες ὅτι κτλ. (v. 6) and εὐδοκοῦμεν μᾶλλον (v. 8).[160] Paul probably intended to say "So we are invariably confident; but because we realize that we are absent from the Lord's presence as long as this body forms our residence, it is our chosen preference . . . to take up residence with the Lord."[161] On this understanding, Paul grounds his εὐδοκεῖν μᾶλλον on an εἰδέναι: knowl-

---

154. The close relation between the indwelling Spirit as the pledge of inheritance (2 Cor. 1:22; 5:5; Eph. 1:13-14) and the indwelling Christ as the hope of Glory (Col. 1:27) is obvious.

155. Cf. Hermann 119 and n. 40.

156. Rom. 1:3-4 (cf. 2 Cor. 13:4a) refers to two successive stages or modes of Christ's existence. Before the resurrection, the flesh (κατὰ σάρκα) was the medium of his existence; after the resurrection, the Spirit of holiness (κατὰ πνεῦμα ἁγιωσύνης). What was true of Christ's postresurrection state may be presumed to be true of the Christian's (cf. Phil. 3:21); in any case, the concept of the σῶμα πνευματικόν indicates that in the resurrection body, the πνεῦμα (or Πνεῦμα?) forms the governing and vital principle. Cf. Vos 155-56, 165-70 ("the Spirit is both the instrumental cause of the resurrection-act and the permanent substratum of the resurrection-life," 169).

157. On these issues, see further Harris 143-49.

158. Cf. Kühl 19; Bultmann 140; *Probleme* 4.

159. This usage also occurs in 5:12; 6:3; 7:5; 8:19-20; 9:11, 13; 10:4b-6, 15; 11:6.

160. Heinrici 184; Schmiedel 238.

161. Others suggest that Paul intended to construe θαρροῦντες with εὐδοκοῦμεν (e.g., Winer 573) or with φιλοτιμούμεθα (v. 9) (Furnish 302, following Demke 599).

edge of being absent prompts a choice to be present; καί is adversative;[162] and as frequently in Paul, εἰδότες is causal.[163]

The antithetical pair of words, ἐνδημέω–ἐκδημέω, used in vv. 6, 8, and 9 are not found elsewhere in the Greek Bible. When the adjective ἔνδημος ("native") is used as a substantive, it refers to a person living at home or among his own people (δῆμος); it could even mean "a stay-at-home" (= ἀναποδήμητος). The corresponding adjective ἔκδημος ("abroad") could denote a person living away from home, living abroad, or living in exile. So ἐνδημέω means "be/live at home," "be in one's own country" (δῆμος), or more generally "dwell," while ἐκδημέω (= ἀποδημέω) means "be away from home," "be/live abroad," "be in exile," or as Louw and Nida express it, "be absent from a place where one rightfully or normally belongs."[164]

In the expression ἐνδημοῦντες ἐν τῷ σώματι, "'while/as long as we are living in this body,' the participle is temporal, and the article anaphoric,"[165] referring back to the ἐπίγειος οἰκία of v. 1 and the σκῆνος of v. 4, so that ἐν τῷ σώματι means more than "on earth."[166] With it we should understand (from 4:11b; 5:4b) τῷ θνητῷ "in this (mortal) body,"[167] not τῆς ἁμαρτίας (cf. Rom. 6:6), "in this (sinful) body."[168] Paul has in mind the physical body as the locus of human existence on earth, the frail and mortal σῶμα ψυχικόν. His thought here is neither dualistic ("the ghost in the machine")[169] nor derogatory ("this cursed body").[170] He is affirming that to be living on earth in a physical body inevitably means distance — indeed exile — from the risen Lord, who lives in heaven in a spiritual body (1 Cor. 15:44, 48-49; Phil. 3:20; 1 Thess. 4:16). To be ἐν Χριστῷ does not yet mean to be σὺν Χριστῷ (Phil. 1:23). Unlike Christ, Paul had his residence on earth, not heaven, but he recognized that his true home, his ultimate residence, was πρὸς τὸν κύριον (v. 8); in this sense he was an exile, ab-

162. Cf. καί in 1 Cor. 5:2; 16:12; 2 Cor. 6:8, 9 (three times); 11:33a. But some regard καί as concessive (= καίπερ) (Guntermann 72-73; and probably NAB², NRSV) or explicative (Wolff 97 and n. 242), and many as simply conjunctive (e.g., Furnish 253, 272).

163. E.g., 1:7; 4:14; 5:11.

164. Louw and Nida §85.21. See further W. Grundmann, TDNT 2.63-64; Spicq 1.453-54.

165. Cf. Carrez 133: "residence in this body means exile far from the Lord."

166. Louw and Nida (§23.91) render ἐνδημεῖν ἐν τῷ σώματι by "be alive here on earth."

167. Cf. Bultmann 140.

168. Pace Baumert 223-24.

169. But Jewett (275-77) sees Paul in vv. 6 and 8 borrowing the dualistic terminology of the gnosticizing members of the Corinthian congregation "in order to include and correct their conception within the traditional framework of future eschatology" (275). The use of σῶμα in these verses is based on the dualistic belief that only when the human spirit ecstatically transcends the body does it find its true pneumatic homeland with the Lord.

170. According to Murphy-O'Connor ("2 Cor. 5:6b" 214-21), the words "being at home in the body we are in exile from the Lord" are either a Corinthian slogan of the *pneumatikoi* of 1 Corinthians, cited here by Paul, or Paul's own formulation of what he thought would be the Corinthian misinterpretation of 5:1-5, namely that he devalued bodily existence. But the presence of an introductory εἰδότες ὅτι (cf. οἴδαμεν ὅτι in 1 Cor. 8:1, 4 introducing slogans) is an insufficient pointer to a slogan, when εἰδότες is linked to θαρροῦντες οὖν πάντοτε by καί (contrast 1 Cor. 8:1, 4).

sent from his home with the Lord (cf. NEB, REB: "we are exiles from the Lord").[171] And if an exile, also a pilgrim (cf. περιπατοῦμεν, v. 7).[172] But as well as regarding his separation from Christ as "spatial," Paul may have viewed it as "somatic." It is not simply a case of Christ's being "there" and Christians' being "here"; until Christians have doffed their earthly bodies and donned their heavenly, they are separated from their Lord by the difference between two modes of being, the σῶμα ψυχικόν and the σῶμα πνευματικόν.

5:7 διὰ πίστεως γὰρ περιπατοῦμεν οὐ διὰ εἴδους. "For we walk in the realm of faith, not of sight." This verse may be termed a parenthesis (in the technical sense[173]), since it is complete in itself, is connected with the preceding statement by way of explanation (γάρ), and obstructs the grammatical flow of v. 6. This is confirmed by the repetition of θαρρεῖν and the insertion of a resumptive δέ in v. 8, measures which prevent the parenthesis from obscuring the flow of thought. But before the function of this parenthesis can be profitably considered, two prior questions must be answered. Does εἶδος signify "external appearance" or "the act of seeing," "sight"? Does διά denote means ("by")[174] or attendant circumstances ("in," "in the realm of")?[175]

In each of the other (four) uses of εἶδος in the NT, the word has a passive, objective meaning, approximating to σχῆμα or possibly μορφή in sense and denoting the external appearance of something.[176] But it is perhaps easier to suppose that Paul has used εἶδος in an unusual sense (= ὄψις, "seeing," "sight"), which is possibly paralleled by Num. 12:8,[177] than that an objective notion (διὰ εἴδους) has been directly contrasted with a subjective (διὰ πίστεως). If the active, subjective significance of εἶδος is accepted,[178] Paul is here contrasting seeing with believing,

171. The εἰδότες clause of v. 6 may well supply (albeit indirectly) the negative and ultimate reason for Paul's "groaning" (στενάζειν), namely "spatial" absence from the Lord, the positive and explicit ground for the "sighing" being his longing for investiture with the σῶμα πνευματικόν. On the NT concept of the "foreignness" of Christians in the world, see G. Stählin, TDNT 5.29-31; cf. Hoffmann, 282-83.

172. Cf. Phil. 3:20; Heb. 11:13-16; 13:14; 1 Pet 1:17; 2:11.

173. See Winer 561-62, 565. Note the parentheses around this verse in KJV and Moffatt.

174. Most translations have "by faith, not by sight" (RV, Berkeley, RSV, NASB, NAB[1], NIV, NAB[2], NRSV; also BAGD 221b; Martin 96). Others also render διά as "by" (TCNT, Weymouth, Goodspeed, Montgomery, JB, Barclay, NJB, Cassirer; also Barrett 149 "on the basis of"). It is difficult clearly to distinguish "means" from "manner" ("with"; cf. A. Oepke, TDNT 2.66; Turner 267; Windisch 167; Bultmann 140); διὰ λόγου (Acts 15:27) could mean "by word (of mouth)" or "orally."

175. Similarly Moffatt; G. Kittel, TDNT 2.374; H. Seesemann, TDNT 5.945; Hatch 62 n. 4; Dupont 154; Zerwick §114; Analysis 399; Wolff 98; Thrall 357.

176. Luke 3:22; 9:29; John 5:37; 1 Thess. 5:22 (but perhaps "from every kind of evil"; cf. MM 182c, d).

177. Here Yahweh says of Moses: στόμα κατὰ στόμα λαλήσω αὐτῷ, ἐν εἴδει (MT mar'eh) καὶ οὐ δι' αἰνιγμάτων (cf. 1 Cor. 13:12).

178. This is the position of BAGD 221b; Rosenmüller 307; Lietzmann 120-21; Schlatter 552; Wendland 193, 195; Hansen 102-4; Kümmel 203; Hoffmann 283; Rissi 95. Note Theodoret's comment on vv. 6-8: "At present we do not see him [the Lord] with our physical eyes, but then indeed we shall, and we shall be with him" (Opera III.314 in J. A. Noesselt's 1771 edition: νῦν αὐτὸν

in much the same way as John 20:29 and 1 Pet. 1:8 contrast ὁρᾶν and πιστεύειν. It is faith, not sight, that determines and guides Christian conduct (περιπατεῖν). But whether εἶδος be active or passive in sense, it is possible that the verse is not simply a Christian maxim but has particular reference to "the Lord" in vv. 6 and 8: "our life is a matter of trusting him, without seeing him"; or "we live our lives in the sphere of faith, not in the presence of his visible form."[179]

The difficulty concerning διά is occasioned by the fact that while, in Pauline usage, διὰ πίστεως ("through faith") specifies the means by which the benefits of salvation are received,[180] περιπατεῖν is usually followed by κατά,[181] ἐν,[182] the simple dative,[183] or an adverb or adverbial phrase[184] when the manner, means, or time of the περιπατεῖν is designated. Because this περιπατεῖν διά combination is unique in Paul, διὰ πίστεως need not necessarily bear its customary sense of "by means of faith," especially since no object is expressed. It is preferable to conclude that both prepositional phrases in this verse describe accompanying circumstances ("we walk in the realm of faith, not of sight").[185]

Within 5:1-10, vv. 3 and 7 perform similar functions. While v. 3 sought to repudiate a misconstruction which had already arisen and might again arise from the term ἐνδύειν, v. 7 seeks to anticipate and rectify misinterpretations which might be prompted by the assertion that as long as Christians dwell in an earthly body they are absent from the Lord (v. 6). If "we are absent from the Lord" was interpreted by any of Paul's readers in an absolute sense, present fellowship with Christ would appear illusory. The separation, Paul answers, is relative not absolute: though absent from sight, the Lord is present to faith, yet it is not until he is

---

τοῖς τοῦ σώματος ὀφθαλμοῖς οὐχ ὁρῶμεν, τότε δὲ καὶ ὀψόμεθα, καὶ συνεσόμεθα; cited by Lietzmann 121). The passive sense of εἶδος ("outward appearance," F. G. Lang 195; "visible from," Baumert 435; "what is visible," Carrez 133) is also supported by Heinrici 185; Bachmann 234; Hatch 62 n. 4; Prat 2.376 n. 2; Dupont 109 n. 2.

179. Thrall 357; cf. 388-89; cf. Plummer 152. Far less likely is the proposal that the εἶδος is the resurrected form of the believer (thus G. Kittel, *TDNT* 2.374-75; cf. Jervell 270 and n. 346). Holloway (89-93), on the other hand, finds in v. 7 a contrast between two *present* modes of existence. Paul's point in vv. 6-10 is that the Corinthians, who looked at things κατὰ πρόσωπον (10:7), should intentionally orient their lives toward "the things not seen" (4:18), toward the life of faith (πίστις) rather than toward "the things seen" (4:18), toward outward appearance (εἶδος). "What is important is not where one resides — one's 'Aufenthaltsort,' but one's true home, the orientation of one's life — one's 'Heimatort'" (90, referring to F. G. Lang [191]).

180. E.g., Rom. 3:22, 25; Gal. 2:16; Eph. 2:8; also διὰ τῆς πίστεως in Rom. 3:30; Gal. 3:14; Eph. 3:12.

181. Rom. 8:4; 14:15; 1 Cor. 3:3; 2 Cor. 10:2; Eph. 2:2.

182. Rom. 6:4; 2 Cor. 4:2; 10:3; Eph. 2:2, 10; 4:17; 5:2; Col. 2:6; 3:7; 4:5.

183. 2 Cor. 12:18; Gal. 5:16.

184. Rom. 13:13; Eph. 4:1; Col. 1:10; 1 Thess. 2:12; 4:12; 2 Thess. 3:6, 11. Cf. also περιπατεῖν ὡς in Eph. 5:8; cf. Rom. 13:13; 1 Cor. 7:17, and περιπατεῖν καθώς in Eph. 4:17; Phil. 3:17.

185. In the one other NT use of περιπατεῖν διά (Rev. 21:24), the preposition probably also denotes attendant circumstances. Closely associated with this use of διά is the locative: for Schmiedel (238), Bachmann (234), and Deissner (76) διά denotes the area through which the περιπατεῖν occurs (or does not occur).

present also to sight that Christian existence will reach its true goal of consummated fellowship with him. Residence in the earthly σκῆνος implies not the absence or unreality of communion with Christ, but simply its imperfection during the course of the Christian's earthly life. While, as an explanatory parenthesis (γάρ) qualifying an apparently inaccurate statement in v. 6b, v. 7 was probably added quite naturally as Paul dictated, it is possible, at the same time, that he was prompted to make the spontaneous interpolation because he was aware that his innocent assertion in v. 6 as a whole, in the hands of his opponents (the τινές of 1 Cor. 15:12), could easily be misconstrued to imply that corporeality as such was an impediment to true spirituality: because it was simply earthly embodiment which caused "separation" from Christ, the body was an encumbrance that was best discarded. A second reason, therefore, for the insertion of this parenthesis may have been to forestall any such deduction.[186]

As well as implying that present fellowship with Christ is not illusory and that mortal embodiment is not a hindrance to spirituality, v. 7 emphasizes the "not yet" of Christian expectation, the fact that the end has not yet arrived. This accords with the themes of pilgrimage and hope that run through vv. 1-10: σκῆνος (vv. 1, 4) suggests travel and pilgrimage; στενάζειν (vv. 2, 4) points to the frustrating imperfection of mortal existence; ἐπιποθεῖν (v. 2) and θέλειν (v. 4) betoken intense desire for future blessings; an ἀρραβών (v. 5) is an installment that pledges the full inheritance; πίστις (v. 7) is a characteristic of pilgrims (cf. Heb. 11:8-9, 13);[187] although περιπατεῖν (v. 7) does not in itself imply pilgrimage,[188] it is not incompatible with this idea; ἐκδημῆσαι (v. 8) signifies itinerancy; ἐνδημεῖν πρὸς τὸν κύριον (v. 8) describes the believer's Promised Land; and at Christ's tribunal (v. 10) rewards will be received. V. 7 contributes to these themes by witnessing to the suspense and tension of earthly existence as a period of incompleteness.

In this respect v. 7 is closely related in meaning to three other Pauline passages, 2 Cor. 4:18; 1 Cor. 13:12. First, to walk in faith (περιπατεῖν διὰ πίστεως) is to keep the eye focused on things not yet visible (σκοπεῖν τὰ μὴ βλεπόμενα, 2 Cor. 4:18; cf. Heb. 11:1) and not to have the gaze fixed on things already present to sight (σκοπεῖν τὰ βλεπόμενα, 2 Cor. 4:18). Among τὰ μὴ βλεπόμενα — which include the αἰώνιον βάρος δόξης of 4:17 — must be reckoned the οἰκοδομὴ ἐκ θεοῦ of 5:1. But not until the objects of faith become real-

---

186. On this latter point, cf. Bultmann 141-42; *Probleme* 11; Schmithals 270-71; Hoffmann 280 and n. 126, 285.

187. Wagner argues that Paul draws a parallel between an apostle's wandering life and that of Abraham and of the Hebrew people in the desert (388).

188. In Paul περιπατεῖν is always the equivalent of ἀναστρέφειν, "behave," "conduct oneself," "live." NT use of περιπατεῖν has been well summarized by Burton (*Galatians* 298): "Occurring in the synoptic gospels exclusively, and in the Gospel of John, Revelation, and Acts almost exclusively, in the literal sense [the exceptions are John 8:12; 12:35; Acts 21:21; Rev. 21:24 (and Mark 7:5)], it appears in Paul and the epistles of John exclusively in the figurative sense, with the meaning 'to live,' 'to conduct one's self.'"

ities that are seen will the temporary accommodation of tent nomadism be re-placed by permanent residence in a heavenly dwelling.

Second, to lead a life of faith is to see only baffling, mirrored reflections of reality[189] and to have incomplete knowledge (1 Cor. 13:12[190]). In both 1 Cor. 13:12 and 2 Cor. 5:7, the contrast is between the ἄρτι of πίστις and the τότε of εἶδος.[191] The relation of διὰ πίστεως περπατεῖν to διὰ εἴδους περιπατεῖν is paral-lel to the relation of βλέπειν δι᾽ ἐσόπτρου ἐν αἰνίγματι to βλέπειν πρόσωπον πρὸς πρόσωπον, of γινώσκειν το ἐπιγνώσκειν.[192] Therefore it may be presumed that seeing Christ face-to-face, without the confused and distorted vision which is inevitable when looking δι᾽ ἐσόπτρου, along with "a complete mutuality of knowledge,"[193] form the content of the believer's ἐνδημεῖν πρὸς τὸν κύριον (= διὰ εἴδους περιπατεῖν).

Third, living in the realm of faith is indistinguishable from hoping for what is still unseen (Rom. 8:25). The Christian's salvation was born in hope (Rom. 8:24) and will be complete only when hope is realized: πίστις and ἐλπίς are coincident. περιπατεῖν διὰ πίστεως is the corollary of εἶναι ἐν πνεύματι (Rom. 8:9) or περιπατεῖν κατὰ πνεῦμα (Rom. 8:9; cf. Gal. 5:16), just as ἐν πίστει ζῆν (Gal. 2:20) is the corollary of ζῆν πνεύματι (Gal. 5:25), because, as the pledge of hope's realization (Rom. 5:5), the Spirit stimulates within the Christian a desire for τὰ μὴ βλεπόμενα, for the fulfillment of God's promises. *Ubi Spiritus, ibi exspectatio,* "Where the Spirit is, there is expectation." As long as Paul was required to "walk in the realm of faith," he was distant from the Lord and yet possessed of the pledge of the Spirit that a "walking in the realm of sight" was to follow.

5:8 θαρροῦμεν δὲ καὶ εὐδοκοῦμεν μᾶλλον ἐκδημῆσαι ἐκ τοῦ σώματος καὶ ἐνδημῆσαι πρὸς τὸν κύριον. "We are confident, I repeat, and prefer to depart from this body and take up residence with the Lord." After the parenthesis of v. 7, θαρροῦμεν picks up the θαρροῦντες of v. 6a, so that δέ is resumptive:[194] "we are confident, I say" (NIV), "Yes, we do have confidence" (NRSV). The verb εὐ-δοκέω may derive from εὖ + δέχομαι[195] ("I receive warmly") or from εὖ + δοκεῖ[196] ("it seems very good to me"). It means "I am well pleased." When followed by the

189. Goudge (48) quotes G. Estius: faith is "an imperfect and enigmatic vision."

190. On this verse see Dupont 105-48; Hugedé 151-90.

191. Faith is not essentially inferior to sight, but is merely temporally prior (cf. Hansen 104-5). When the object of faith is seen, its exercise becomes superfluous, just as the need for hope ceases when the hope is realized (Rom. 8:24). But if 1 Cor. 13:13 implies that πίστις as such is des-tined to survive the parousia (see Meyer 308-9, 519; Robertson and Plummer 299-300), this simply indicates that the idea of progress and successive goals was included within Paul's concept of the hereafter (cf. Baillie 228-37).

192. Cf. Mundle 27. Windisch (167) terms 2 Cor. 5:7 "an abridgement and elucidation" of 1 Cor. 13:12.

193. An expression of Barrett, *1 Corinthians* 307.

194. Winer 352; Robertson 1135.

195. Thus Zerwick, *Analysis* 399.

196. Thus Moulton and Howard 292.

infinitive (as here) it implies a definite choice;[197] with μᾶλλον, it expresses a clear choice of something as better, a "settled preference."[198] "We are willing rather" (Barclay) is too weak a rendering of εὐδοκοῦμεν μᾶλλον, while "we are resolved instead" (Furnish)[199] is too strong. "We would rather" (NAB[2], NRSV; cf. RSV, NEB) or "we prefer" (Williams, Berkeley, NIV) are preferable renderings.

Structurally, v. 8b is in antithetic parallelism with v. 6:

v. 6 ἐνδημοῦντες ἐν τῷ σώματι   ἐκδημοῦμεν ἀπὸ τοῦ κυρίου
v. 8 ἐκδημῆσαι   ἐκ τοῦ σώματος καὶ ἐνδημῆσαι   πρὸς τὸν κύριον

The basic contrast is not between two modes of human existence (ἐν τῷ σώματι and ἐκ τοῦ σώματος, signifying embodiment and disembodiment) or two possible relationships with ὁ κύριος (ἀπὸ τοῦ κυρίου and πρὸς τὸν κύριον), but between successive spheres of Christian residence (ἐν τῷ σώματι and πρὸς τὸν κύριον), residence in the body (v. 6a) and residence with the Lord (v. 8b). Since the verb ἐκδημεῖν may have a punctiliar sense ("go abroad," "emigrate") as well as a stative ("be away from home"), aorist ἐκδημῆσαι ("be exiled," JB, NJB, REB; "leave," NEB) need not be classified as ingressive, whereas ἐνδημεῖν is purely stative ("be/stay at home") so that ἐνδημῆσαι is a true ingressive aorist, here denoting entrance upon the state of dwelling (ἐνδημεῖν) with the Lord — thus "make our home" (TCNT, JB, REB), or "take up residence."

Against those exegetes who refer vv. 6-10 to the parousia,[200] it must be asserted that a temporal distinction can hardly be drawn between the destruction of the earthly house (v. 1) and departure from the mortal body (v. 8), referring the former to the time of death but the latter to the advent. The ἐκδημία of v. 8, like the κατάλυσις of v. 1, transpires at death. Moreover, there is no reason to suppose that an interval of time separates the ἐκδημῆσαι ἐκ τοῦ σώματος from the ἐνδημῆσαι πρὸς τὸν κύριον. Two contextual observations confirm that dwelling in the Lord's presence is the believer's experience immediately after death.[201] First, v. 6 states that residence in a physical body is contemporaneous with absence from the immediate presence of the Lord, clearly implying that

197. G. Schrenk, *TDNT* 2.741.

198. Bruce, *Paraphrase* 135.

199. Furnish 253, 273; similarly F. G. Lang 192-93, 195; Baumert 46, 233-36, 435.

200. E.g., Lietzmann 117-19, 121; Schweitzer 131, 135; Mundle, 97-98, 100, 106-9; Brun 209, 216-17, 221-23; Hoffmann 267-85, especially 281, 284-85, 321. On this view, it would seem, Paul is expressing in 5:8 his desire for transformation and the attainment of heavenly glory without death in preference to remaining in the body (5:6) — a singularly banal sentiment for Paul to express, as Allo (140; *Première Épître* 450 n. 2) appropriately observes.

201. But some commentators refer v. 8 not to death but to Christian experience before death. On this understanding, the verse depicts the Christian life as a constant transition, begun at baptism, from sin's dominion (signified by σῶμα) to the dominion of the Lord (Collange 235-37), or the Christian's deliberate choice to abandon more and more any preoccupation with the visible realm and to deepen one's relationship to the Lord (Baumert 46, 222), or a realignment of loyalties (Furnish 303). For a critique of these "ethical" interpretations of v. 8, see Thrall 390-91.

when the former ceases, so also does the latter. What v. 6 implies, v. 8 states positively. Second, in v. 7 walking διὰ πίστεως and διὰ εἴδους are presented as opposites, with no interval posited between the end of the one and the beginning of the other. To cease walking in the realm of faith is to commence life in the realm of sight, which v. 8b defines as an ἐνδημεῖν πρὸς τὸν κύριον and Phil. 1:23 as a σὺν Χριστῷ εἶναι.

Once it is recognized that the ingressive aorist ἐνδημῆσαι ("take up residence") has in itself no implication of movement or direction, the temptation of suggesting[202] that πρός denotes both linear motion and punctiliar rest on arrival loses its attractiveness — a claim which, in any case, overlooks the fact that in Hellenistic Greek the distinction between motion and rest has become obscured so that the preposition πρός with the accusative, when used to indicate a relationship between persons, may mean simply "with," "in the presence of."[203] πρὸς τόν κύριον may merely be the equivalent of ἔμπροσθεν τοῦ κυρίου, or better, παρὰ τῷ κυρίῳ. Moreover, when denoting a relationship between living persons (πρός τινα εἶναι [= εἶναι σύν τινι]), πρός itself contains no idea of reciprocity of action. But with this said, it seems inadequate to conclude that believers' dwelling with the Lord implies no more than their incorporation in Christ, or their impassive "spatial" juxtaposition to Christ, or a state of semiconscious subsistence or suspended animation. When Paul describes the future state of the believer as one of dwelling (ἐνδημεῖν) in the company of (πρός) the Lord, he must be referring to some heightened form of interpersonal communion, particularly since the eternal destiny of Christians[204] would scarcely be depicted as qualitatively inferior to their experience of fellowship with Christ on earth while walking διὰ πίστεως. Just as οἰκεῖν ἐν (used of the Spirit in the believer) "denotes a settled permanent penetrative influence,"[205] so ἐνδημεῖν πρός (used of the believer with the Lord) suggests a settled permanent mutual fellowship.

Scholars who interpret v. 1 as indicating that the spiritual body is received at the moment of death usually argue that the contrast between the two forms of embodiment (earthly and heavenly) found in vv. 1-4 does not recede from the apostle's gaze but remains basic to his thought in vv. 6-8, so that in v. 8b it must be assumed that the fellowship with the Lord is mediated through a heavenly body.[206] Just as in vv. 1-4 the -δημεῖν metaphor of vv. 6, 8 is implicit, so in vv. 6, 8 the -δύειν motif of vv. 2-4 is implicit. In v. 8, then, Paul does not imply that ἐνδημῆσαι πρὸς τὸν κύριον involves incorporeality.

But if ἐκδημῆσαι ἐκ τοῦ σώματος refers to death, and if Paul still believes

202. See, e.g., Hughes 178 n. 53.
203. See BDF §239(1); Regard 552, 556, 579; Moulton and Howard 467; Robertson 625; Moule 52-53; Turner 254, 274; B. Reicke, *TDNT* 6.722.
204. But Sevenster (207) distinguishes between a preliminary σὺν Χριστῷ εἶναι in a disembodied state immediately after death and the final σὺν κυρίῳ εἶναι (1 Thess. 4:17) in an embodied state after the parousia.
205. Sanday and Headlam 196.
206. E.g., Masson 259.

that the resurrection body is acquired at the parousia (1 Cor. 15:23, 42-44, 52),[207] it is difficult not to conclude that he regarded the interval between the individual's death and the parousia as one of disembodiment. Although Paul did not share the Orphic sentiment σῶμα σῆμα ("the body is a tomb") and although he never envisaged the Christian *summum bonum* as emancipation from corporeality,[208] apparently he could conceive of temporary disembodiment (cf. 12:2-3) as the lot of believers who die before the second advent. In this regard he may have viewed Christ's experience as paradigmatic. Just as Jesus experienced an interval of disembodiment between his death and his resurrection, so too will the Christian who dies before the parousia. Also, just as Paul must have believed in the preservation of the spirit of Jesus during his period of disembodiment, so also he taught the safekeeping of believers as, in a bodiless state, they await the resurrection:[209] they are in active communion with Christ in his immediate presence (v. 8b).[210] The difference between "the dead in Christ" and living Christians is not in their status (τὸ εἶναι ἐν Χριστῷ; cf. 2 Cor. 5:17; 1 Thess. 4:16), but in their somatic state (disembodied vs. embodied) and in the quality of their fellowship with Christ and the degree of their proximity to Christ (τὸ εἶναι σὺν Χριστῷ; cf. Phil. 1:23; 2 Cor. 5:8).

In 5:1-8 we find the essential ingredients of the Christian view of physical death:

1. Negatively, death means destruction (κατάλυσις, v. 1) and departure (ἐκδημία, v. 8).[211] When Christians die, their earthly house is demolished (v. 1), and they depart from mortal embodiment and the securities of earthly existence (v. 8). But their departure implies a destination as well as an evacuation, a "to" as well as a "from." Positively, death brings a change in the location of believers' residence. Absent from their bodily home on earth, they are at home with the Lord (v. 8). Death marks the termination of their temporary exile from the Lord (cf. v. 6) and the end of the pilgrimage of faith (cf. v. 7) and inaugurates a deeper communion with the risen Lord in heaven, an ἐνδημεῖν πρὸς τὸν κύριον (v. 8), a περιπατεῖν διὰ εἴδους (v. 7). If death removes the Christian from one

207. On this point, see above on ἔχομεν (v. 1).

208. The expression ἡ ἀπολύτρωσις τοῦ σώματος ἡμῶν in Rom. 8:23 cannot be pressed into service to support a contrary view. The genitive τοῦ σώματος is less probably a genitive of separation with τῆς ἁμαρτίας or τῆς ταπεινώσεως to be supplied than an objective genitive indicating that the glorious liberty of the children of God consists not of deliverance from embodiment but of the emancipation of the σῶμα from mortality (through its transformation).

209. This general position may be termed "holistic dualism," the view that Paul (and Scripture in general) teaches both the functional integration of human life and a disembodied intermediate state. See further Cooper; Osei-Bonsu, "Dualism" 571-90; "State" 169-94.

210. There is no justification for the view that nearness to or fellowship with Christ after death is a special privilege reserved for the Christian martyr (*pace* Tertullian, *De Resurrectione* 43.4; Schweitzer 135-37; Rex 75-78).

211. Mention might be made here of some interesting correspondences: κατάλυσις (2 Cor. 5:1) = τὸ σπένδεσθαι (2 Tim. 4:6) = τὸ ἀποθανεῖν (Phil. 1:21) = ἀπόθεσις (2 Pet. 1:14); ἐκδημία (2 Cor. 5:8) = ἀνάλυσις (2 Tim. 4:6; Phil. 1:23) = ἔξοδος (2 Pet. 1:15).

form of corporeity, the physical, it augments another, since to the ἐν Χριστῷ corporeity, which remains intact through death, is added a personal σὺν Χριστῷ εἶναι dimension.

2. Paul's personal attitude toward dying seems to have been ambivalent (cf. Phil. 1:21-25). Since death deprived human beings of their "psychical" corporeality (cf. 1 Cor. 15:44, 46) and corporateness, removing totally and finally the securities of earthly existence, and since physical death as a biological necessity was one manifestation of God's curse on humankind for their sin (Rom. 5:12; 6:23; 1 Cor. 15:56), Paul could never joyfully embrace the experience. On the other hand, since death's sting had been drawn by Christ's triumph over the grave (1 Cor. 15:55-57; 1 Thess. 4:14) and since death meant enriched communion with the Lord, the arrival of death was not to be dreaded (cf. Heb. 2:14-15). Death was neither welcomed nor feared.

3. The Christian view of death is inseparable from the Christian view of the resurrection. In this connection, four basic concepts appear in 5:1-8: κατάλυσις (v. 1), ἐκδημία (v. 8), ἐπένδυσις (vv. 2, 4), and κατάποσις (v. 4). These two pairs reflect two distinct but complementary ways of viewing Christian resurrection–metamorphosis (ἐπένδυσις, κατάποσις) and exchange (κατάλυσις, ἐκδημία). The σῶμα ψυχικόν may be said to be transformed into or replaced by the σῶμα πνευματικόν.[212]

4. Paul never despised mortal embodiment or longed for freedom from corporeality; after all, it is to the apostle that Christian theology owes the concept of the σῶμα πνευματικόν, the οἰκοδομὴ ἐκ θεοῦ. He did, however, eagerly anticipate the termination of the imperfection of life on earth (cf. Rom. 7:24). Inasmuch as death brings a most significant part of the Christian's inheritance — deepened fellowship with Christ — it terminates the στενάζειν which is the hallmark of heirs, of those who possess God's ἀρραβών.

5:9 διὸ καὶ φιλοτιμούμεθα, εἴτε ἐνδημοῦντες εἴτε ἐκδημοῦντες, εὐάρεστοι αὐτῷ εἶναι. "That is why we aim to be pleasing to him, whether resident in the body or absent from it." This verse is related to vv. 1-8 in much the same way as an ethical imperative frequently follows a doctrinal indicative in Paul's letters. After the recitation of soteriological facts there follows an enunciation of the consequences for behavior (cf. 1 Cor. 15:58 at the end of 1 Corinthians 15). But because Paul is recounting his own reaction to certain doctrinal truths rather than exhorting his readers to a particular course of action, the principal verb in v. 9 (φιλοτιμούμεθα) is in the indicative, not the imperative or subjunctive mood. διὸ καί either specifies a result[213] ("that is why"[214]) or states an inference which is

---

212. But Moule discerns a change in Paul's view of matter when 1 Corinthians 15 is compared with 2 Corinthians 4–5: The luxurious hope of having the heavenly body added to the earthly, which is thereby conserved in a "superimposed immortality" (1 Corinthians 15), gives place to the realistic acceptance of the need for the material body to be used up and exchanged for the heavenly (2 Corinthians 4–5; "Dualism" 107, 116-20, 123). Against this view see Gillman 439-54.

213. Cf. BDF §442(12), citing Luke 1:35; 11:49.

214. Cf. Didier 104-5.

self-evident ("therefore . . . also").[215] Paul's constant ambition to know Christ's approval (v. 9) was the direct consequence or obvious corollary of his awareness that death would terminate his absence from Christ and inaugurate a περιπατεῖν διὰ εἴδους πρὸς τὸν κύριον (vv. 6-8). To entertain the hope of person-to-person communion with Christ after death (v. 8b) inevitably and naturally prompted the aspiration of gaining acceptance in his eyes before and after death.

The verb φιλοτιμέομαι is formed from the adjective φιλότιμος (φίλος + τιμή), "loving honor," and therefore "ambitious," especially in a bad sense. Accordingly, in Classical Greek the verb meant "seek after honor," "act from love of honor," "be ambitious." Positively, it could mean "show patriotic zeal for"; negatively, "contend in rivalry."[216] But in the later Hellenistic period it came to bear the attenuated sense "strive eagerly,"[217] "aspire," "have as one's ambition" (cf. Rom. 15:20; 1 Thess. 4:11).[218] εὐάρεστοι αὐτῷ εἶναι, "to be pleasing to him [= ὁ κύριος, v. 8b]," "(constantly) to win his approval," cannot refer *merely* to the gaining of commendation at Christ's "tribunal" (v. 10), as is shown by the present tense of the infinitive (εἶναι, not γενέσθαι) and by two closely parallel passages (Col. 1:10; 1 Thess. 4:1) where the pleasing of God or Christ by a certain way of life (περιπατεῖν) is depicted as a present possibility. This phrase specifies a goal (= ἀγαθὸν πράσσειν, v. 10) that was attainable throughout life and that, whenever achieved, anticipated a favorable verdict at the judgment seat of Christ (v. 10); the one who would act as Paul's assessor at the judgment was also the one whom he sought to please while on earth.

The point of orientation with respect to the participles ἐνδημοῦντες . . . ἐκδημοῦντες may be either home (literally understood), the Lord, or the body. The first alternative — "whether we are at home or away from home" — ignores the distinctive use of the ἐνδημεῖν-ἐκδημεῖν motif in the immediate context. Against the second proposal[219] — "whether at home with the Lord (εἴτε ἐνδημοῦντες [πρὸς τὸν κύριον, cf. v. 8]) or absent from his presence (εἴτε ἐκδημοῦντες [ἀπὸ τοῦ κυρίου, cf. v. 6])" — it may be argued that in this case the alternative word order εἴτε ἐκδημοῦντες εἴτε ἐνδημοῦντες would have been expected,[220] since to mention a future state before a present condition would scarcely be congruous. The third solution, "whether resident in the body or absent from it,"[221] is to be preferred, since (1) it preserves the natural order of the present condition (ἐνδημοῦντες [ἐν τῷ σώματι, cf. v. 6]) — future state

---

215. BAGD 198d.
216. See LSJ 1941b.
217. MM 672b. Cf. Field 165.
218. BAGD 861c.
219. Thus Allo 132-33, 149; Héring 37 (cf. 39 n. 11).
220. This word order is found, in fact, in it^f g syr^p (Plummer 155).
221. This solution is advocated by Schmiedel 238; Plummer 154-55; Lietzmann 121; Belser 167; Windisch 169; Dupont 153-54; Feuillet 163, 397, 399; Jervell 270; Bultmann 143. Furnish suggests that Paul intended to leave the participles unqualified, with the result that the matter of "residency" is thoroughly relativized and shown to be irrelevant (304).

(ἐκδημοῦντες[222] [ἐκ τοῦ σώματος, cf. v. 8]); (2) it brings the specified alternatives into relation with those mentioned in Rom. 14:8 (ἐάν τε οὖν ζῶμεν ἐάν τε ἀποθνῄσκωμεν . . .) and Phil. 1:20 (. . . εἴτε διὰ ζωῆς εἴτε διὰ θανάτου), and (3) it anticipates the phrase διὰ τοῦ σώματος in v. 10. If, then, these two participles have the earthly body as their point of orientation, they designate two successive states, the states during and after earthly existence,[223] not the two classes of Christians (alive and dead) at the parousia.[224]

There is always a danger in pressing the undoubtedly rhetorical statement εἴτε ἐνδημοῦντες εἴτε ἐκδημοῦντες too stringently. No implication may be drawn from v. 9, for example, regarding the possibility of performing actions in the intermediate state that may be pleasing to Christ.[225] Not the participles, but φιλοτιμούμεθα . . . εὐάρεστοι αὐτῷ εἶναι bears the emphasis in the verse. Whatever his lot, Paul was always (πάντοτε) possessed of confidence in God as the fulfiller of his promises (v. 6) and always (εἴτε ἐνδημοῦντες εἴτε ἐκδημοῦντες; cf. NEB, "wherever we are, here or there") desirous of pleasing Christ (v. 9).

5:10 τοὺς γὰρ πάντας ἡμᾶς φανερωθῆναι δεῖ ἔμπροσθεν τοῦ βήματος τοῦ Χριστοῦ. "For all of us must appear before Christ's tribunal." Vv. 8-10 well illustrate the interrelatedness of eschatology and ethics. Paul's constant ambition to gain Christ's approval (v. 9) was prompted by two facts relating to the future — his destiny of dwelling with the Lord (v. 8) and his coming accountability to Christ (v. 10). That is, v. 9 looks back to v. 8 (". . . to take up residence with the Lord [v. 8] . . . *that is why* [διὸ καί] we make it our aim to gain his approval," v. 9) and forward to v. 10 ("we always aim to win his approval . . . *for* [γάρ] we must all appear before Christ's judicial bench," v. 10).

In conjunction with ἔμπροσθεν τοῦ βήματος and δεῖ, φανερωθῆναι must bear judicial overtones and refer to a compulsory appearance in the court of heaven before Christ's tribunal. But ὁ κύριος . . . φανερώσει τὰς βουλὰς τῶν καρδιῶν in 1 Cor. 4:5 suggests that to construe φανερωθῆναι in this middle sense ("appear") here in v. 10, as though it meant simply παραστῆναι (Rom. 14:10; cf. 2 Cor. 4:14), may be to ignore both the agency of Christ in the φανερωθῆναι and the fact that not merely an appearance or self-revelation, but, more significantly, a divine scrutiny and disclosure, is the necessary prelude to the receiving of appropriate recompense. Thus the alternatives seem to be that φανερωθῆναι means "to be made manifest" (RV; similarly Spörlein 151),[226] the

222. "The present tense is used instead of ἐκδημήσαντες, for the sake of rhetorical antithesis" (Bultmann 143). In view of the reference in v. 10 to a κομίσασθαι based exclusively on action performed διὰ τοῦ σώματος, and the fact that a φανερωθῆναι could not take place before an ἐκδημῆσαι ἐκ τοῦ σώματος had occurred, ἐκδημοῦντες in v. 9 probably alludes primarily to the judgment. Cf. the paraphrase of Delatte 433: "whether today in life or in the hour of judgement."

223. So also Sickenberger 97.

224. So Meyer 521; Hughes 178.

225. The basis for Christ's assessment of the believer's life and therefore for his approval is to be "actions carried out through the earthly body" (v. 10) and therefore during life.

226. If, as Bonsirven believes (281; cf. Yinger 40-41, 269), 5:10 is a "reminiscent citation" of the concluding verse of Ecclesiastes (LXX ὅτι σὺν πᾶν [σύμπαν, B] τὸ ποίημα ὁ θεὸς ἄξει ἐν

"appearance" being clearly presupposed, or "to appear" (NRSV), with the divine examination being tacitly assumed. The parallel with 1 Cor. 4:5 and the twofold use of φανεροῦσθαι in 2 Cor. 5:11 favor the former rendering; the judicial context and the parallel passage in Rom. 14:12 (ἄρα οὖν ἕκαστος ἡμῶν περὶ ἑαυτοῦ λόγον δώσει τῷ θεῷ) support the latter. This judicial appearance will take place before Christ's "judicial bench" or "tribunal" (βῆμα). Derived from the root of ἔβην ("I went"), βῆμα originally referred to a "step," the distance covered by a step of the foot (Acts 7:5); then it referred to a "step" in the sense of any raised place, thus "seat," "platform" (Acts 12:21); finally it denoted a speaker's platform, or the "seat" or "tribunal" of a magistrate. In this latter sense, an official may be said to "sit on" his judgment seat (Matt. 27:19; John 19:13; Acts 12:21; 25:6, 17) or a person may be said to appear or stand "before" a tribunal (Acts 25:10; Rom. 14:10; 2 Cor. 5:10). The use of the term in 5:10 would have been particularly evocative for Paul and the Corinthians since it was before Gallio's tribunal in Corinth that Paul had stood some four years previously (in A.D. 52) when the proconsul dismissed the charge that Paul had contravened Roman law (Acts 18:12-17). Archaeologists have identified this Corinthian βῆμα which stands on the south side of the *agora*.[227]

With the presence of a τοὺς πάντας before ἡμᾶς, it is beyond question that other persons besides Paul (Timothy and Silvanus, 1:1, 19) are embraced by the divine decree (δεῖ) which would compel attendance before the judgment seat of Christ. But is this assize to be restricted to believers? Scholarly opinion is divided on the point.[228] Nothing in the context excludes the application of τοὺς πάντας ἡμᾶς to all people, while ἕκαστος simply refers to every individual without exception within the specified group but does not define the extent of "the sum total of us."[229] There is one consideration, however, that favors the restriction of the expression to all Christians. Where Paul applies the principle of recompense according to works to all people (Rom. 2:6), there is found a description of two mutually exclusive categories of people (Rom. 2:7-10), not a delineation of two types of action (cf. εἴτε ἀγαθὸν εἴτε φαῦλον, 2 Cor. 5:10) which may be predicated of all people.

ἵνα κομίσηται ἕκαστος τὰ διὰ τοῦ σώματος πρὸς ἃ ἔπραξεν, εἴτε ἀγαθὸν εἴτε φαῦλον. "So that each may be duly recompensed for actions, whether good or bad, performed through the body." Here Paul states the purpose (ἵνα), and by

---

κρίσει, ἐν παντὶ παρεωραμένῳ, ἐὰν ἀγαθὸν καὶ ἐὰν πονηρόν), then φανερωθῆναι emphasizes the bringing into the light of judgment of everything previously hidden by ignorance or darkness (cf. 1 Cor. 4:5, on which see Turner, *Insights* 131-32).

227. See Murphy-O'Connor, *Corinth* 24-25, 28-29; Dinkler 118-33.

228. That 5:10 refers to the general judgment is maintained by, among others, Sickenberger 97; MacRory 349; F. Büchsel, *TDNT* 3.938; Spörlein 155; Yinger 260, 266-69. On the other hand, οἱ πάντες ἡμεῖς has often been taken to include simply all Christians: H. A. A. Kennedy 203; Plummer 155, 160; Filson, *Recompense* 88 and n. 3, 108, 118 (the verse applies "chiefly if not entirely" to Christians); Weiss, *Christianity* 2.560; Héring 39-40; *Royaume* 252; Cerfaux, *Christian* 207, 214; Whiteley 209, 272; Mattern 155, 157.

229. The rendering of Turner 201; cf. Robertson 773 ("we the whole number of us").

implication, the outcome, of the divine illumination of what previously had been hidden in darkness (1 Cor. 4:5). ἕκαστος, "each person," indicates that τοὺς πάντας ἡμᾶς does not imply judgment *en masse*.[230] Accountability and assessment are individual (cf. ἕκαστος ἡμῶν after πάντες in Rom. 14:10-12). In the middle voice, κομίζω ("bring") means "get for oneself," "get back," "receive back" what one owns or is owed or deserves. τά in the phrase διὰ τοῦ σώματος [πραχθέντα[231]] is not simply metonymy for "the consequences of," as though the κομίσασθαι were merely the outcome of some immanental process by which the reaping of consequences followed inexorably on the sowing of actions, for in this case the reference to an appearance and examination before the βῆμα would be rendered superfluous. The recompense received comes from Christ, for it is his tribunal. A comparison of Col. 3:25 with Col. 3:24 (cf. Eph. 6:8) suggests that in 2 Cor. 5:10 "so that each may receive back the things (performed through the body)" means "so that each may receive recompense[232] from the Lord for things (performed through the body)." διά is probably instrumental ("through"),[233] although a temporal sense is possible, "during (one's bodily life on earth)."[234] But the former implies the latter.[235] πρὸς ἃ ἔπραξεν, "in accordance with[236] the things[237] which (= what) he has done," or "in proportion to[238] his deeds," points to the exactitude and impartiality (cf. Eph. 6:9; Col. 3:25) of the recompense meted out by the divine assessor. ἀγαθόν and φαῦλον should be construed with their immediate antecedent ἃ ἔπραξεν, not with the more remote κομίσηται . . . τά. If so, these adjectives do not represent two possible verdicts (commendation-condemnation) or two types of recompense (reward-punishment),[239] but two kinds of action (good-bad). The change from the plural ἃ to the singular ἀγαθὸν . . . φαῦλον, "deeds . . . whether[240] they be good or bad"[241] may therefore be inconsequential. But if Plummer is right in

---

230. Cf. the function of ἕκαστος δέ after ἕν εἰσιν in 1 Cor. 3:8.

231. πραχθέντα or πεπραγμένα (or even εἰργασμένα), rather than merely γενόμενα or ὄντα, should be supplied with τά.

232. The expression "receive recompense" is found in NRSV; Plummer 124; Barrett 149; Martin 96; Thrall 357; cf. TCNT, "reap the results." See further Yinger 262-63.

233. Thus Robertson 582; Heinrici 190; Plummer 158; Sickenberger 97; Windisch 172.

234. Similarly GNB, NIV; BAGD 443a; Louw and Nida §90.92; Kühl 28-29 (who maintains that a temporal antithesis governs the whole passage); Yinger 264-65.

235. Cf. Bachmann 242-43.

236. Thus Winer 405; BDF §239(8); Zerwick, *Analysis* 399; Turner 274.

237. πρός belongs to an omitted demonstrative pronoun (BAGD 583, b, c) such as ἐκεῖνα.

238. So Allo 133; Moule 53; Louw and Nida §90.92. Barrett (150) and Thrall (357) prefer "in relation to."

239. The RSV rendering, "so that each one may receive good or evil, according to what he has done in the body" (similarly Goodspeed) has been (appropriately) changed in the NRSV to "so that each may receive recompense for what has been done in the body, whether good or evil."

240. As in v. 9, the correlatives εἴτε . . . εἴτε are probably copulative in function (approximating to καί . . . καί; cf. BDF §454 [3]) rather than merely disjunctive. ᾖ rather than ἐστιν should probably be supplied (cf. Turner 302).

241. While φαῦλος can mean "worthless" (see MM 665), it is doubtful whether the term is

proposing that the change in number is significant, so that Paul is implying that conduct will be judged as a whole, that "it is character rather than separate acts that will be rewarded or punished,"[242] we must insist that it is character as evidenced in separate acts, if not specific actions as reflective of character.

The personal character of the retributive process and the fact that recompense might be received for good as well as for bad actions prove that, in Paul's thought, the notions of recompense and reward are not incompatible.[243] Reward may be recompense for good; the "suffering of loss" (ζημιωθήσεται, 1 Cor. 3:15), the forfeiture of reward or privilege, may be part of the requital for evil.[244] Whatever else may be involved in the Christian's μισθός,[245] an essential element in it is God's ἔπαινος (1 Cor. 4:5; cf. εὐάρεστοι, 2 Cor. 5:9; τιμή, Rom. 2:10) and δόξα (2 Cor. 4:17; Rom. 8:17-18), which may be given or withheld, and given in varying measure. If, in 1 Cor. 4:5, Christ is the assessor of evidence and God the executor of judgment, in 2 Cor. 5:10 both roles are fulfilled by Christ. In Pauline thought it is sometimes Christ,[246] sometimes God,[247] and sometimes God through Christ[248] who exercises judgment upon humans.[249]

Since, then, the tribunal of Christ is concerned with the assessment of

related to ἀγαθός in 5:10 in the same way that καλάμη is related to χρυσός in 1 Cor. 3:12, the one word denoting superior quality, the other inferior (but see Héring 40). See further Textual Note k. If φαῦλον is to be distinguished from κακόν, it refers to what is morally evil from the point of view of its negative worthlessness, its "good-for-nothingness."

242. Plummer 158. But if it were action regarded in its totality that Paul had in mind, he probably would have written εἴτε τὸ ἀγαθόν εἴτε τὸ φαῦλον (cf. Rom. 13:3-4). Given the plural πρὸς ἅ, it is strange that H. Preisker can claim (TDNT 4.721 n. 107) that "for Paul judgment is by ἔργον (1 C. 3:13ff.; Gl. 6:4; Phil. 1:6; Col. 1:10; 1 Th. 1:3), not ἔργα."

243. For a detailed defense of this view, see Filson 83-135.

244. If it be objected that Christians could not be recompensed for sins that have been forgiven, one must recall that even in this life Christians who sin may receive recompense for "deeds performed through the body" (cf. 1 Cor. 5:4-5; 11:29-30). In 1 Cor. 3:10-15, observes Filson (Recompense 91-92; cf. 108), "it seems suggested that the sin of those who are admitted to the Kingdom will be punished by assignment of inferior privileges or a lower place in the future kingdom."

245. See the discussions of Guntermann 222-27; H. Preisker and E. Würthwein, TDNT 4.695-728. In his examination of "The New Testament Conception of Reward," Reicke ("Reward" 195-206) isolates three tenses of Christian reward in (1) the Christian servant's initial engagement for service to and communion with God (e.g., Eph. 1:5f.; Col. 1:12ff.), (2) the Christian's continuing service in communion with God (e.g., 1 Cor. 9:18; Phil. 1:21f.), and (3) the Christian's "promotion to more or less elevated stages of heavenly service" (e.g., Eph. 1:12; Phil. 2:10f.) and "a highly ameliorated communion with God" (201). "What the servant receives in reward is nothing but communion with God — but as the service of God is just a form of communion with God, there is an intimate relation, if not identity, between this service and this reward" (196; cf. 205).

246. 1 Cor. 4:4; 2 Cor. 5:10; 2 Thess. 1:8; and cf. the frequent references to the day of the Lord (Jesus Christ) — 1 Cor. 1:8; 5:5; 2 Cor. 1:14; Phil. 1:6, 10; 2:16; 1 Thess. 5:2.

247. Rom. 2:3, 5, 11; 3:6; 14:10.

248. Rom. 2:16; 1 Cor. 4:5; cf. Acts 17:31.

249. See further Guntermann (204-8), who rightly repudiates (citing 1 Thess. 3:13; 2 Thess. 1:8; 1 Cor. 4:5 in support) as untenable the view that Paul taught two judgments — one of humankind at large conducted by God (e.g., Rom. 2:5, 12) and one of believers conducted by Christ (e.g., 2 Cor. 5:10) (208).

works, not the determination of destiny,[250] it will be apparent that the Pauline concepts of justification on the basis of faith and recompense in accordance with works may be complementary.[251] Not status but reward is determined ἔμπροσθεν τοῦ βήματος τοῦ Χριστοῦ, for justification as the acquisition of a right standing before God anticipates the verdict of the Last Judgment. But, already delivered from ἔργα νόμου (Rom. 3:28) by justifying faith, the Christian is presently committed to τὸ ἔργον τῆς πίστεως (1 Thess. 1:3), "action stemming from faith," which will be assessed and rewarded at Christ's tribunal.

When would the φανερωθῆναι occur? By some it has been referred to a so-called "particular judgment" occurring after the death of each individual;[252] by others, to a judgment which takes place at or after the parousia.[253] V. 10 clearly implies that the requital is made immediately after the φανερωθῆναι, but Paul does not specifically relate this φανερωθῆναι to the time of the receipt of the spiritual body (v. 1), to the time of the εὑρεθήσεσθαι (v. 3), or to the moment of departure from earthly existence (v. 8). While ἔκαστος means "each individually," it need not imply "each in his turn, at death" as opposed to "each, separately, at the parousia." Nor does Paul's desire to gain Christ's approval when ἐκδημῶν [ἐκ τοῦ σώματος] (v. 9), that is, at the βῆμα τοῦ Χριστοῦ, necessarily associate the φανερωθῆναι with the ἐκδημῆσαι ἐκ τοῦ σώματος (v. 8) which occurs at death. The issue, it seems, cannot be finally decided. But in comparison with the supreme and sobering fact of his accountability to Christ, the precise time of the φανερωθῆναι would have been a matter of relative insignificance to Paul.

In summary, for Paul this φανερωθῆναι involved the appearance and examination before Christ's tribunal of every Christian without exception for the purpose of receiving an exact and impartial recompense (including the receipt or deprivation of commendation) which would be based on deeds, both good and bad, performed through the earthly body. The fear inspired by this expectation (v. 11) doubtless intensified Paul's ambition that his life should meet with Christ's approval both during life and at the βῆμα (v. 9).[254]

---

250. Cf. Wagner 391; Hughes 181-82. If the judgment in 5:10 is restricted to Christians, φαῦλον πράσσειν must involve displeasing Christ (cf. 5:9) and therefore the forfeiture of his commendation, but not the passing of a sentence of condemnation. Cf. Mattern 156-57.

251. "The doctrine of judgment by works is the constant presupposition of the doctrine of justification by faith. Without it, the latter loses its seriousness and depth" (F. Büchsel, *TDNT* 3.938 n. 68; similarly, G. Schrenk, *TDNT* 2.208). But Weiss (*Christianity* 2.560) was "disposed to think of this [2 Cor. 5:10] as a lapse into the Jewish legalistic mode of thought, as a loss of the enthusiastic point of view of one who has been redeemed from retribution."

252. Thus Schmiedel 240; Beyschlag 267-68; Allo xxv, 133, 159; *Première Epître* 66-67; Feuillet, "Demeure" 397-401; Mattern 161.

253. Thus Kühl 28, 38; Lietzmann 122; Deissner 81-85; Guntermann 75, 301-2; Prümm II/1. 419, cf. II/2. 698-99.

254. It might be observed here that the nearest Pauline parallel to 2 Cor. 4:16–5:10 as a whole is Rom. 8:18-25; outside the Pauline epistles, Heb. 11:13-16 and 1 John 3:2-3 provide the closest resemblance. Of single verses, 5:1 is similar to Mark 14:58 and John 2:19; vv. 2-4 to 1 Cor. 15:53-54, v. 5 to 2 Cor. 1:22; v. 7 to 1 Cor. 13:12; v. 8 to Phil. 1:23; v. 10 to Rom. 14:10 and 1 Cor. 4:5.

2 Cor. 5:1-10 affords no evidence of a complete or even partial Hellenization of Paul's anthropology or eschatology.[255]

(1) In calling the body a σκῆνος (v. 1) Paul is alluding to the destructibility and relative impermanence of mortal embodiment and perhaps to the imperfection of Christian existence upon earth. There is no implication that the σκῆνος (or the σκεῦος of 4:7) is the container of which the ψυχή is the contents (οἰκία ψυχῆς σῶμα), that the physical body is a detachable, worthless, or despicable outer garment which oppresses the soul and hampers its free expression.

(2) The origin of Paul's στενάζειν (vv. 2, 4), his sense of frustration under the conditions of mortality, his profound dissatisfaction with the limitations of a σάρξ-dominated σῶμα, is not to be located in a Hellenistic depreciation of corporeality, but in his yearning for an ἐπένδυσις (vv. 2, 4), for investiture with the heavenly body, and in his absence from the Promised Land, from the immediate presence of the Lord (v. 6). And if Paul "sighed" in physical corporeality because he longed for spiritual corporeality, that longing arose because God had given him the Spirit as the pledge of the receipt of the σῶμα πνευματικόν and as the agent in its creation. That is, if the ground of the στενάζειν was the ἐπιποθεῖν ἐπενδύσασθαι, the source of the ἐπιπόθησις was the presence and activity of the Spirit as an ἀρραβών.

(3) Whatever the source of the term θαρρεῖν (vv. 6, 8), Paul's confidence in the face of death was not grounded in the imperishability of the soul but in his present possession of the Spirit as the divine pledge of his future acquisition of immortality. The object of Paul's hope for the future was not emancipation from all corporeality but the replacement of a lower by a higher corporeality, of the σῶμα ψυχικόν by a σῶμα πνευματικόν which would perfectly mediate consciousness of the presence of the Lord. For Paul immortality was not a natural attribute of the human soul which guaranteed its survival through and after death, but a gift from God which the Christian gained at the parousia by means of the resurrection.

(4) While ἐκδημῆσαι alludes to an alteration of location or shift of residence, it need not imply that the period prior to the μετοίκησις was an exile. Paul did not regard the soul as exiled from its true abode in heaven because of its association with materiality. Redemption was not a progressive deliverance of the soul from materiality, consummated at death, but a progressive sanctification of the whole person issuing in a transformation at the parousia.

Bibliography

Baumert 142-262 • Bauer 116-27 • Berry • Best, *Body* 219 • Borse • Bruce, "Immortality" • Brun • Cassidy • Cooper 155-63 • S. Cox, "The Earnest of the Spirit," *Exp* 2/7 (1884) 416-26 • Crafton 87-93 • Craig • Cranford • Danker, "Consolation" • Davies •

255. But Walter discovers in 2 Cor. 5:1-10 a synthesis of biblical and Hellenistic eschatology that results from Paul's deliberate "Hellenizing" (53-64).

Demke • Dodd 83-128 • Dupont, *Union* • Ellis, "Eschatology" • Erlemann • Fee, *Presence* 324-27 • Feuillet, "Demeure" • Feuillet, "Mort" • Gillman • F. Glasson, "2 Corinthians v. 1-10 versus Platonism," *SJT* 43 (1990) 145-55 • Goulder, *Mission* 254-59 • Gundry 149-54 • Hanhart 149-79 • Hanhart, "Hope" • K. Hanhart, "Hope in the Face of Death: Preserving the Original Text of 2 Cor 5:3," *Neot* 31 (1997) 77-86 • Hanson, *Ministry* 50, 79 • Haulotte • Hettlinger • Hoffmann 253-85 • Holleman 72-75 • Holloway 83-93 • Hunzinger • Jeremias • Kitzberger 117-22 • Kreitzer, *Jesus* 107-12 • Lambrecht, "Vie" • F. G. Lang • Lillie • Lincoln 55-71 • Lowrie • Luz 359-69 • Mattern • Mitton • Moule, "Dualism" • Mundle • J. Murphy-O'Connor 49-55 • Murphy-O'Connor, "2 Cor 5:6b" • Oostendorp 68-74 • Osei-Bonsu • Osei-Bonsu, "Dualism," *SJT* 40 (1987) 571-90 • Osei-Bonsu, "State" • Pate 1-31, 107-36 • Rissi 73-98 • Roetzel • U. Schnelle, *Wandlungen im paulinischen Denken* (Stuttgart: Katholisches Bibelwerk, 1989) 42-45 • Sevenster • Sevenster, "Bemerkungen" • Spörlein 129-60 • Thrall, *Particles* 82-95 • Thrall, "2 Corinthians 5:3" • Vos • Wagner • Walter • N. M. Watson, "2 Cor. 5:1-10 in Recent Research," *ABR* 23 (1975) 33-36 • Wenham, "Last Day" • Witherington *Jesus* 167-68, 202-8 • Wonneberger 315-17 • Yates, "State" • Yinger 260-70 • Zorn

3. The Essence and Exercise of the Apostolic Ministry (5:11–6:10)

a. Motivation for Service (5:11-15)

As Paul continues to describe his apostolic ministry (2:14–7:14), he defines what motivates his unremitting devotion to the task (5:11-15), what constitutes the essence of his message (5:16–6:2), and what characterizes the performance of his ministry (6:3-10).[1]

11*Since, then, we know the fear of the Lord, we try to persuade[a] people, but what we are is plain to God — and I hope it is also plain to your consciences. 12We[b] are not trying to commend ourselves to you again; rather, we are giving you cause to boast about us[c] so that you may have a reply to those who boast about appearance and not[d] character. 13For if we are out of our mind, it is for God's glory; if we are in our right mind, it is for your benefit. 14For Christ's love controls us, because we reached this conviction, that[e] one died for all, which means that all died. 15And he died for all so that those who live should no longer live for themselves but for the one who died and rose again for them.*

TEXTUAL NOTES

a. Some witness have the (hortatory) subjunctive πείθωμεν (p[46] P Ψ 629 2464 *pc* vg[ms]), "let us persuade."

b. The conjunction γάρ is added by some witnesses (D[2] 048 33 𝔐 sa).

c. There is strong testimony (p[46] ℵ B 33 *pc* it[g] vg[ms]) supporting ὑμῶν ("opportu-

---

1. Lambrecht finds a concentric structure in 5:11–6:10: 5:11-13, self-defense; 5:14-21, emissary of Christ; 6:1-10, self-defense ("Reading" 162-63).

nity to boast about yourselves"), but this may well be a case where the canon *lectio difficilior potior* ("the more difficult reading is to be preferred") is inapplicable (*pace* Collange 248), since sometimes the more difficult reading is so difficult as to be highly improbable or virtually impossible. Would Paul ever provide his converts with an opportunity to boast about themselves — as opposed to boasting in the Lord (1 Cor. 1:31) or in God's work in other believers (2 Cor. 1:14)? In addition, as Barrett (162 n. 1) observes, "about yourselves" would normally be expressed by ὑπὲρ ὑμῶν αὐτῶν or ὑπὲρ ἑαυτῶν. The reading ὑπὲρ ἡμῶν should be preferred.

d. Instead of μὴ ἐν καρδίᾳ some witnesses read οὐκ ἐν καρδίᾳ (D* F G) or simply οὐ καρδίᾳ (C D² Ψ 𝔐) (a locatival dative). The particle μή negates participles (καυχωμένους is understood with μὴ ἐν καρδίᾳ) and οὐ negates single words or phrases (BDF §426). Enjoying both proto-Alexandrian (p⁴⁶ ℵ B 1739) and later Alexandrian (0243 33 81 104 1881) support, the reading μὴ ἐν καρδίᾳ is preferable, although the meaning is the same with all three variants.

e. To anticipate the inferential ἄρα, many witnesses read ὅτι εἰ εἷς ("that if one . . .") (ℵ² C* 048 0243 81 104 365 629ᶜ 630 1175 1739 1249 *pm* itᶠ vg sa boᵐˢ), but this is clearly a scribal amelioration and therefore secondary.

5:11 Εἰδότες οὖν τὸν φόβον τοῦ κυρίου ἀνθρώπους θείθομεν, θεῷ δὲ πεφανερώμεθα· ἐλπίζω δὲ καὶ ἐν ταῖς συνειδήσεσιν ὑμῶν πεφανερῶσθαι. "Since, then, we know the fear of the Lord, we try to persuade people, but what we are is plain to God — and I hope it is also plain to your consciences." οὖν may refer back to 5:1-10 as a whole, but more probably it alludes to v. 10 alone, viz. the fact of the inescapable accountability to Christ as judge, which Paul now defines subjectively as "the fear of the Lord." Not a few commentators perceive in 5:1-10 an expression of Paul's fear of the process of dying or of temporary or permanent disembodiment. But the only φόβος that Paul explicitly acknowledges as his own is this fear before "the Lord both of the dead and of the living" (Rom. 14:9), who would scrutinize his life and render an exact and impartial recompense (v. 10). On this understanding, ὁ φόβος τοῦ κυρίου means not "fear [concerning the coming condemnation of unbelievers, cf. Rom. 2:2-3, 5, 8-9] inspired by the Lord" (= subjective genitive),[2] far less "the terrifying nature (= τὸ φοβερόν; cf. Heb. 10:31; 12:21) of the Lord" (= possessive genitive),[3] but "reverential awe directed to the Lord" (= objective genitive[4]). Given the close connection (through οὖν) between vv. 10 and 11, ὁ κύριος will be Christ (cf. Eph. 5:21), not God.[5] Corresponding to this positive sense of φόβος ("reverential awe") with the risen Christ as the object is the negative connotation of fear

2. τοῦ κυρίου is taken as a subjective genitive by TCNT; Zerwick and Grosvenor 544, although Zerwick (*Analysis* 399) simply lists the options: "φόβος either active: what incites fear, a judgement by which God causes fear; or passive: fear with which we reverence God."

3. Thus many older commentators, following Chrysostom.

4. So also Robertson 500; Turner, *Words* 383-84; this usage is common in the LXX (see Thrall 401 n. 1465).

5. *Pace* Furnish 306. Nor could the whole expression mean "the fear [of Christ] inspired by the Lord" (= God the Father).

(= dread) of displeasing Christ (cf. v. 9) and of having one's works assessed as being φαῦλος (v. 10). εἰδότες is causal, "because we know," and, being followed by the accusative, not a ὅτι clause (as in 4:14; 5:6), it denotes not merely intellectual apprehension but conviction that influences conduct.[6] It was Paul's "consciousness of his responsibility" (Bultmann 147), his "sense of accountability" (Furnish 306), that prompted his incessant endeavor to win people to faith. Along with 5:8-9, this verse illustrates the fact that Paul's actions were guided and his ambitions molded by doctrinal convictions.

There is no need to find in the expression ἀνθρώπους πείθομεν an allusion to the rhetorical techniques of the orators of Paul's day[7] or a slogan of Paul's opponents (cf. 1 Cor. 2:4; Gal. 1:10) which he cites and counters by claiming that *his* "persuasion" arises from awareness of his responsibility before Christ (v. 10) and involves openness before God (v. 11b; cf. 4:2).[8] πείθομεν is probably a conative present[9] ("we try to persuade"), referring not to action begun but either interrupted or unsuccessful, but to action that is incomplete, not yet fully accomplished.[10] This verb bears a comparable conative sense in Acts 18:4 (ἔπειθεν); 19:8 (πείθων); 28:23 (πείθων).[11] Of what did Paul try to convince people? First, of the truth of the gospel, especially the messiahship (Acts 17:2-3) and lordship (1 Cor. 12:3; 2 Cor. 4:5) of Jesus; in this case ἀνθρώπους would denote people in general, both Jews and Greeks (cf. Rom. 1:16). Second, in the present letter he was attempting to persuade the Corinthians of the truth concerning himself, namely that his apostolic credentials and conduct were sound (cf. 3:1-6; 4:1-6) and that his motives were pure and sincere (cf. 1:12).[12] The general reference to all people would explain why Paul did not write simply ὑμᾶς πείθομεν. In Paul's judgment the aim of seeking to win Christ's approval (v. 9) apparently did not exclude the goal of seeking human acceptance (cf. 6:13), provided that acceptance was sought for the benefit of the gospel. If Paul had been rejected by the Corinthians *en masse,* the progress of the gospel in Corinth and elsewhere would have been hindered. On the other hand, if his sphere of influence among the Corinthians became enlarged through their recognition and defense of his apostolic credentials, they could form a base for the expansion of the gospel beyond Corinth (cf. 10:15-16; Rom. 15:24).

6. Some translations try to catch this sense: "It is with this knowledge of what the fear of the Lord means" (Goodspeed), "We know what it means to fear the Lord" (GNB).

7. As Betz, *Galatians* 54 n. 103, commenting on Gal. 1:10.

8. As Bultmann 147; cf. Pate 138-39, 155 n. 29.

9. So also TCNT, Weymouth, Barclay, NIV, NRSV; Robertson 880; *Pictures* 229; Zerwick and Grosvenor 544; Turner 63; Spicq 3.75; Bruce 206; Martin 121. The conative present is a variation of the present tense as action in progress (cf. Burton §11).

10. This distinction obviates the difficulty Lambrecht ("Reading" 165-66) finds in treating πείθομεν as a conative present.

11. So also Spicq 3.75 n. 52; but, given the use of the verb in Acts 12:20; 13:43; 14:19, it is improbable (*pace* Spicq 3.75 and n. 53) that the verb when transitive (in the present, imperfect, and aorist tenses) has gained a technical meaning in the language of Luke: "try to convince."

12. Cf. Collange 245.

But whether or not the persons to whom Paul addressed his appeal recognized his claims about the gospel or about himself, God recognized him for what he was: "But what we are is plain to God." Although no μέν precedes δέ, this conjunction is strongly adversative. ἄνθρωποι might entertain prejudices against Paul and his gospel, they could misunderstand his message or malign his character, but to God who was devoid of both prejudice and partiality, Paul's character and motives were permanently exposed and perfectly known. Here Paul is resuming the theme of openness that was found in 3:12, 18; 4:2. The change from the aorist of φανερόω (v. 10) to the perfect (v. 11, twice) is significant. In v. 10 the constative aorist φανερωθῆναι depicts the appearance before Christ's tribunal as a simple occurrence, portraying its bare facticity. Whether it be a single appearance involving all Christians or a succession of appearances involving individual Christians, the occurrence is conceived of unitarily. But the two perfects πεφανερώμεθα and πεφανερῶσθαι (v. 11) are stative, denoting an existing condition that results from an implied earlier occurrence, "be in a revealed state."[13] Thus θεῷ . . . πεφανερώμεθα will mean "we are well known to God" (BAGD 853a), that is, "what we are is known to God" (RSV) or "our motives are plain to God" (TCNT), or "To God our lives lie open" (NEB, REB). Similarly ἐλπίζω . . . πεφανερῶσθαι[14] means "I hope that we are . . . well known" (NRSV), or "I hope it [what we are] is known" (RSV), or "I hope that . . . they [our motives] are plain" (TCNT). Paul was eagerly desirous (ἐλπίζω)[15] that the Corinthians would all come to share (δὲ καί, "and, in addition," "indeed . . . as well") the divine assessment of his person and ministry and motives. But this was not a foregone conclusion, which may explain the change from the plural to the singular (πεφανερώμεθα . . . ἐλπίζω), a change that has the effect of intensifying the potency of Paul's appeal. Only here in the Greek Bible is συνείδησις found in the plural; the sense may be "each and every conscience" (cf. 4:2, πρὸς πᾶσαν συνείδησιν).[16]

5:12 οὐ πάλιν ἑαυτοὺς συνιστάνομεν ὑμῖν, ἀλλὰ ἀφορμὴν διδόντες ὑμῖν καυχήματος ὑπὲρ ἡμῶν. "We are not trying to commend ourselves to you again; rather, we are giving you cause to boast about us." Having spoken of his transparency before God and the Corinthians (v. 11b), Paul anticipates and corrects an inaccurate impression that may be gained from these assertions (prodiorthosis): "No, we are *not* trying to commend ourselves[17] to you all over again."

13. Cf. Fanning 115, 396; Porter 393.
14. Elsewhere in the NT, the aroist infinitive (not the perfect) follows ἐλπίζω (e.g., 1 Cor. 16:7; Phil. 2:19, 23).
15. There is no reason to dilute the meaning of ἐλπίζω from "hope" to something approximating "think" (as in BDF §350).
16. Cf. Plummer 169. On the meaning of συνείδησις, see 1:12. Thrall argues convincingly that in Pauline usage συνείδησις "denotes a neutral inward faculty of judgement, possessed by all humanity, which evaluates conduct in an objective way in accordance with given and recognized norms" (132). See further her article "ΣΥΝΕΙΔΗΣΙΣ" 118-25.
17. In the appropriate case, ἑαυτοῦ may be used of all three persons (see BAGD 211d, 212a-c; Zerwick §209).

οὐ is emphatic by position, and συνιστάνομεν may be conative ("we are not try-ing to commend") or even inceptive ("we are not beginning to commend"; cf. 3:1, ἀρχόμεθα . . . συνιστάνειν;). On "self-commendation" in 2 Corinthians, see on 3:1. On the contrary (ἀλλά), Paul was affording his addresses with an oppor-tunity to boast about him, giving them an incentive or a suitable basis for rally-ing to his defense. Being coordinate with the finite verb συνιστάνομεν, the par-ticiple διδόντες functions as an indicative (δίδομεν)[18] ("we are not commending . . . but giving . . ."), although some would supply γράφομεν ταῦτα, "[we are writing this] in order to give. . . ."[19] ἀφορμή[20] was used of a base of operations for an expedition, especially an offensive in war, and also of the resources needed to launch the expedition.[21] Its range of meanings includes "starting point," "cause," "occasion," "instigation," "incentive," "opportunity," and it is found only in Paul (Rom. 7:8, 11; 2 Cor. 5:12; 11:12; Gal. 5:13; 1 Tim. 5:14). Here καύχημα denotes not the content or object of boasting, what one is proud of, but the act of boasting, pride; not *materies gloriandi*, but *gloriatio*.[22] That is, καύχημα here seems indistinguishable from καύχησις;[23] contrast with this 1:12, 14 where both terms denote the content of boasting. Thus "cause for pride in us" (TCNT) or "an incentive to be proud of me" (Moffatt). Although ὑπὲρ ἡμῶν may bear its common meaning of "on our behalf," "for our benefit" (= "to achieve our vindication") (Hodge 130), more probably ὑπέρ has the sense of περί, "about," "concerning,"[24] as in 7:14; 8:23; 9:2; 12:5 (twice) where καυχάομαι is also found (except for 8:23).

What was this basis for pride in him that Paul was supplying to his con-verts at Corinth? It was their firsthand knowledge of his life and ministry, em-bedded in their consciousness and consciences (v. 11b) — knowledge of his missionary and pastoral endeavor and accomplishments, and memory of his ap-ostolic suffering for the cause of Christ. It was communicated to them by all that Paul was writing, especially in 2:14 onward.

ἵνα ἔχητε πρὸς τοὺς ἐν προσώπῳ καυχωμένους καὶ μὴ ἐν καρδίᾳ. "So that you may have a reply to those who boast about appearance and not character." Paul's provision of a basis for pride in him had a particular purpose. It was so that (ἵνα) the Corinthians might have ample ammunition with which to defend his apostleship against his opponents who were in the habit of priding them-selves on position and privilege rather than on the state of the heart.

18. BDF §468(1); Zerwick §374; Turner, *Style* 89.

19. Blass 284; cf. Winer 352; Buttmann 393; Robertson 439.

20. Etymologically, ἀφορμή denotes a place from which (ἀπό) an assault or onrush (ὁρμή) arises.

21. LSJ 292 s.v.; G. Bertram, *TDNT* 5.472. MM notes that in the papyri ἀφορμή means "in-citement" but more often "opportunity" (98d, 99a).

22. So Plummer 170, against Meyer 524.

23. Zerwick, *Analysis* 400; Bultmann 148; Spicq 2.302. Elsewhere in 2 Corinthians καύχημα signifies the content of boasting (1:14; 9:3).

24. BAGD 839a; BDF §231(1); Zerwick §96.

With ἔχητε we could supply καύχημα ("reason for boasting"), ἀφορμήν[25] ("basis," "opportunity"), or ἀφορμὴν καυχήματος ὑπὲρ ἡμῶν;[26] or, better still, a colorless τι ("something"), or τι λέγειν, in which case ἔχητε would be transitive, "have something to say" (Williams, NEB, NAB[1, 2], REB), or λέγειν τι, where ἔχητε would be intransitive, "be in a position to say something."[27] πρός here means "against" (as in Acts 6:1; 1 Cor. 6:1; Col. 2:23; 3:13), in the sense of "in defense against," "in response to"; the whole phrase ἵνα ἔχητε πρός will then mean, "so that you may have a reply ready for . . ." (Weymouth). οἱ καυχώμενοι are Paul's adversaries at Corinth,[28] including not only the church members who were disenchanted with Paul but also the visitors from outside who were bent on usurping Paul's sphere of influence in Corinth. Their pride was constantly focused (τοὺς . . . καυχωμένους) on what was external, what caught the eye, what was clearly demonstrable, not on what was inward, what was not outwardly evident or fully provable. The ἐν προσώπῳ . . . ἐν καρδίᾳ antithesis does not describe manner, "openly . . . secretly," but the object, and by implication the ground, of the καυχᾶσθαι,[29] "those who boast in outward appearance and not in the heart" (NRSV) (cf. Rom. 2:28-29). Because πρόσωπον usually denotes the "face" or "outward appearance," it has been suggested that ἐν προσώπῳ refers to what may be expressed on the face,[30] such as piety or zeal, especially during religious ecstasy (cf. ἐξέστημεν, v. 13). But it is preferable to take πρόσωπον as a metonym for "what is outward," "externals," and καρδία as standing for "what is inward," the "character." On this understanding, πρόσωπον corresponds to τὰ βλεπόμενα (4:18) and κατὰ σάρκα (5:16; 11:18),[31] while καρδία matches τὰ μὴ βλεπόμενα (4:18) and κατὰ κύριον (11:17). The contrast is between "externals" and "inward reality" (Moffatt).[32] Apparently Paul's rivals at Corinth were making superficial claims to superiority over him — such as their relation to the Jesus of history (5:16) and to Palestinian orthodoxy (11:22) or their greater number of visions and revelations (cf. 12:1-7). Paul was content to take his stand on what was "in the heart" — transparency before God and people and the testimony of the conscience (v. 11b). For the

25. Plummer 170.
26. Meyer 525.
27. Bultmann 148, citing John 8:6; Acts 4:14; 25:26; Tit. 2:8 for this meaning of ἔχειν. Héring paraphrases ἀφορμὴν διδόναι as "to put in the position" (41).
28. But Thrall identifies οἱ καυχώμενοι as non-Christian Jews, who compared Paul unfavorably with Moses whose face was transfigured. "They boast, Paul would be saying, of the glorified *face* of Moses as attesting the splendour of the old covenant, and refuse to see the actualisation of the promised new covenant in the *hearts* (3.3) of those who have responded to the gospel" (405).
29. Noting that in NT usage ἐν with καυχᾶσθαι always denotes the object (525), Meyer observes that "the object is conceived as that in which the καυχᾶσθαι is causally based" (525 n. 2).
30. "They wear a look of apostolic virtue which they do not possess" (Plummer 171).
31. Cf. Collange 249.
32. Similarly BAGD 403c, "externals and inner attitude of heart." Cf. 1 Kgdms. 16:7: ἄνθρωπος ὄψεται εἰς πρόσωπον, ὁ δὲ θεὸς ὄψεται εἰς καρδίαν. Bieringer proposes that the contrast is between insincerity and honesty (290-98, as cited by Lambrecht, "Reading" 170).

Christian superficial appearances count for nothing, the state of the heart is everything.

5:13 εἴτε γὰρ ἐξέστημεν, θεῷ· εἴτε σωφρονοῦμεν ὑμῖν. "For if we are out of our mind, it is for God's glory; if we are in our right mind, it is for your benefit." Whatever the background to this difficult verse, its general import seems clear. Paul disowns self-interest as a motive for any of his action; whether his actions be judged irrational or rational, all is for God's glory and the benefit of others (1 Cor. 10:31; 2 Cor. 4:5, 15). Of this the Corinthians can be justly proud (v. 12). This interpretation accords well with his following appeal (v. 14) to Christ as "the man for others" and his definition of the purpose of Christ's death (v. 15) — that believers should lead a life that is not centered on self but on Christ.

In 5:9-10 εἴτε . . . εἴτε means "whether . . . or," but here, standing with finite verbs, these particles mean "if . . . if." The second aorist active form ἐξέστημεν (from ἐξίστημι, "drive one out of one's mind," "amaze"[33]) is intransitive in meaning, either "we were out of our senses"[34] (constative aorist) or "we are beside ourselves" (RSV, NRSV) (timeless aorist).[35] In the former case, the reference will be either to a single specific occasion when Paul was (thought to be) "beside himself," or to habitual or intermittent conduct in the past viewed as a unit. θεῷ and ὑμῖν are probably datives of "advantage,"[36] indicating the person(s) whose interests are positively affected by the verbal notion although they could be more general datives of reference,[37] or even datives that indicate the addressee.[38] With these datives there is an ellipsis of ἐστιν: "it is for God's glory . . . it is for your benefit."[39]

Verse 13a has been explained in three main ways: (1) Paul's critics had accused him of religious mania, of being "out of his mind" (cf. Mark 3:21; John 10:20),[40] perhaps because of his allegedly esoteric teaching (cf. Acts 26:24)[41] or his indefatigable zeal and tireless work (cf. 6:4-5; 11:23-28). To this charge

33. On this verb, see A. Oepke, *TDNT* 2.459-60; Spicq 2.24-29.

34. BAGD 276c. ἐξέστημεν is taken to be preterite also by TCNT, Goodspeed, JB ("If we seemed out of our senses . . . if we are being reasonable now . . ."), Barclay, NJB; BDF §342(1) ("we yielded to ecstasy"); Wendland 200; Lambrecht, "Reading" 172; Klauck 53; Carrez 141; Thrall 400.

35. So also Burton §47; Porter 228; cf. Moulton 134 (on the parallel ἐξέστη in Mark 3:21).

36. BAGD 357d; BDF §188(2); Robertson 539; Bultmann 149; Wolff 116.

37. Turner 238.

38. Cf. REB, "If these are mad words, take them as addressed to God; if sound sense, as addressed to you."

39. Those who take ἐξέστημεν as preterite would supply ἦν with θεῷ (e.g., Goodspeed, JB). But BDF §479(1) takes the ellipses to be ἐξέστημεν and σωφρονοῦμεν, and Lambrecht would supply (apparently) ἐφανερώθημεν and πεφανερώμεθα (cf. v. 11) ("Reading" 172-73, following Bieringer 313-14).

40. Thus Hughes 191. Mark 3:21 records that "people were saying" (ἔλεγον) of Jesus "he has lost his senses" (ἐξέστη).

41. Acts 26:24 notes that after Paul had recounted his conversion, the Roman procurator Festus "exclaimed with a loud voice, 'Paul, you are out of your mind (μαίνῃ); your great learning is driving you insane (εἰς μανίαν).'" To this Paul replies, "I am not out of my mind, most noble Festus, but I am speaking words of sober truth (ἀληθείας καὶ σωφροσύνης ῥήματα)."

he replies, "That is for God to judge." (2) Paul is referring to his experience of religious ecstasy,[42] such as glossolalia (cf. 1 Cor. 14:2, 18) or visions (cf. Acts 22:17-21; 2 Cor. 12:1-7), when to some he seemed "beside himself." "It is a matter between God and me alone," he answers. (3) Paul is acknowledging previous exaggerated behavior, but is assuring the Corinthians that God knew that his exaggerations were well intentioned; "we were open to God."[43] The corresponding contrasts in v. 13 would be: (1) religious "madness" vs. a sane, balanced approach to ministry; (2) ecstatic experience vs. rational speech (?= tongues vs. prophecy); (3) exaggerated behavior vs. sobriety of conduct. Of the three explanations,[44] the first seems the most apt. The link with v. 12 would then be as follows: "We are certainly not promoting ourselves [v. 12a], for (γάρ) whether our words and conduct be thought irrational [v. 13a] or rational [v. 13b], God and you are the ones for whom I speak and work, just as my life is an open book to God and you [v. 11b]."[45]

5:14 ἡ γὰρ ἀγάπη τοῦ Χριστοῦ συνέχει ἡμᾶς. "For Christ's love controls us." Here Paul explains why (cf. γάρ, "for") he was devoted to the service of God and the Corinthians (v. 13), why a life of self-pleasing was impossible for him. Very few commentators take τοῦ Χριστοῦ as an objective genitive ("love of Christ," "our love for Christ"),[46] the vast majority regarding it as a subjective genitive ("Christ's love," "the love Christ showed"; cf. Gal. 2:20).[47] Support for this latter view may be found in: (a) Pauline usage, in which a personal genitive after ἀγάπη always denotes the person having or showing love, not the one receiving it,[48] and in which Christ is never the object of believers' ἀγάπη; and (b) the immediate context, where the focus is on Christ's death (ἀπέθανεν . . .

---

42. Thus Bultmann 149-50; Wolff 120; Thrall 406-7 ("if we were in ecstasy, it was God's concern," 400); Fee, *Presence* 329; Barnett 39 n. 152, 284-85 (who interprets 5:13 in the light of 12:1-5).

43. Thus Lambrecht, "Reading" 172-73, following Collange 250 and Bieringer 309-13. Lambrecht renders ἐξέστημεν, "we have exaggerated" (in Bieringer and Lambrecht 412; cf. 374-75).

44. Four further explanations of v. 13a may be mentioned. (4) Paul had been criticized for his self-commendation (cf. v. 12a), which appeared to be sheer lunacy. "It is a defense of God's cause," Paul replies. (5) In Jewish eyes, Paul's conversion was evidence of his madness, but in Paul's judgment it simply promoted God's glory. (6) Paul is defending himself against the charge of "a supposedly 'eccentric' assertion of apostolic authority" (A. Oepke, *TDNT* 2.460). (7) The verbs ἐξίστημι and σωφρονέω were used in the rhetorical handbooks in reference to proper rhetorical style. In v. 13 Paul is seeking to explain his unpolished oratory (cf. 10:10; 11:6; 12:19; 13:3) to those whose rhetorical tastes were more refined. The verse may be paraphrased thus: "If, as some of you complain, my speech was unpolished and excessive [on my first visit], credit that to God's account; if I am presently [in my writing] reasonable and lucid, credit that to yours" (Hubbard 39-64; quotation from p. 61).

45. Sumney identifies a connection between v. 13 and v. 12b. "Judgements about apostolic legitimacy [cf. v. 13] cannot be made on the basis of appearance" (144).

46. As, e.g., Héring 41-42.

47. So BAGD 6a; Robertson 499; *Pictures* 230; Wendland 177; Thüsing 102; Furnish 305, 309; Thrall 400, 408 n. 1512.

48. Rom. 5:5; 8:35, 39; 15:30; 2 Cor. 8:24; 13:13; Eph. 2:4; 3:19; Phil. 1:9; Col. 1:8, 13; 1 Thess. 3:6; 2 Thess. 1:3; 3:5; Phlm. 5, 7.

ἀπέθανεν . . . τῷ . . . ἀποθανόντι, vv. 14-15) as an evidence of his self-sacrificial love. But several scholars believe that both senses were intended by Paul.[49] Commenting on this phrase, Zerwick (§36) maintains that "in interpreting the sacred text . . . we must beware lest we sacrifice to clarity of meaning part of the fulness of the meaning." No one doubts that believers' love for Christ motivates their actions, but here Paul is concentrating on an earlier stage of motivation, namely the love shown by Christ in dying for humankind.

In its basic sense, συνέχω means "hold (something) together" to prevent its falling apart.[50] From this sense of "hold fast/tight" there naturally developed the positive idea of constraint or compulsion, and the negative notion of restraint, as when the banks of a river "hem in" the flow of water or the walls of a narrow lane "confine" travel. Most suggested renderings of συνέχει in this verse fall under the category of constraint: "constrains,"[51] "impels,"[52] "compels,"[53] "urges (us) on,"[54] "overmasters,"[55] "completely dominates,"[56] "overwhelms."[57] One of the few versions reflecting the idea of restraint is the NEB ("For the love of Christ leaves us no choice"), while Plummer paraphrases Paul's thought by "restrains us from self-seeking" (173)[58] and "keeps me from selfish motives" (165). The rendering that best captures this dual notion of constraint and restraint is "controls (us)."[59] Christ's love is a compulsive force in the life of believers, a dominating power that effectively eradicates choice in that it leaves them no option but to live for God (cf. θεῷ, v. 13a) and Christ (τῷ . . . ἀποθανόντι καὶ ἐγερθέντι, v. 15b).

κρίναντας τοῦτο, ὅτι εἷς ὑπὲρ πάντων ἀπέθανεν· ἄρα οἱ πάντες ἀπέθανον. "Because we have reached this conviction, that one died for all, which means that all died." The aorist participle κρίναντας, which modifies ἡμᾶς, is probably causal and preterite ("because we reached this conviction"), although it could be causal and perfective ("because we are convinced," RSV, NIV, NRSV), or temporal and perfective ("once we have reached the conclusion," REB).[60] In it-

49. E.g., Bengel 3.382; Lietzmann 124; Allo 165; Zerwick §36; *Analysis* 400; Spicq 3.341 n. 16; *Agape* 2.186; Turner 210, but cf. 211; Allmen 33-34; Romaniuk 18-19; Collange 253 n. 2.

50. On the range of meaning of this verb, see H. Koester, *TDNT* 7.877-85; Spicq 3.337-41; *Agape* 2.190-93.

51. RV, Williams; Young and Ford 266.

52. Berkeley, NAB[1, 2].

53. TCNT, NIV; A. Kretzer, *EDNT* 3.306; Martin 117; Belleville, "Discipleship" 130.

54. BAGD 789b; NRSV; Lietzmann 124; Windisch 181; Thüsing 102; Romaniuk 19; Klauck 53; Lang 293.

55. Weymouth, Montgomery.

56. H. Koester, *TDNT* 7.883; similarly J. P. Lewis in Lewis (ed.) 129; E. Stauffer, *TDNT* 1.49 ("holds us captive"). Cf. the use of συνέχομαι in Luke 12:50 ("I am wholly governed") and συνείχετο in Acts 18:5 ("he began to devote himself totally [to preaching]").

57. JB, NJB.

58. Cf. J. P. Lewis in Lewis (ed.) 39.

59. Goodspeed, RSV, NASB, Barclay, REB; Louw and Nida §37.17; Barrett 162 ("controls our actions"); Bultmann 152; Thrall 400.

60. κρίναντας is unlikely to be a timeless aorist, since before his conversion Paul had not

self κρίνω could indicate a decision,[61] a conclusion,[62] or a conviction.[63] Given the content[64] of the κρίμα, viz. the recognition that the death of Christ means the death of "all," the idea of a decision made seems less apposite than the concept of a conclusion or conviction reached.

εἷς ὑπὲρ πάντων ἀπέθανεν is reminiscent of the formula Χριστὸς ὑπὲρ ἡμῶν ἀπέθανεν (Rom. 5:8; cf. 1 Cor. 15:3), with εἷς substituted for Χριστός and πάντων for ἡμῶν. This modification — the introduction of the εἷς-πάντες motif (cf. Rom 5:15-19) — suggests that Paul has the Adam-Christ or First Adam–Second Adam antithesis in mind.[65] But how extensive is the category indicated by πάντες? The issue cannot be settled apart from considering the three uses of πάντες in vv. 14-15a and the expression οἱ ζῶντες in v. 15: ὑπὲρ πάντων . . . οἱ πάντες . . . ὑπὲρ πάντων . . . οἱ ζῶντες. Three options present themselves.

(1) All four expressions refer to Christ's people, believers in Christ,[66] with the threefold πάντες synonymous with the second πολλοί in Rom. 5:15, 19,[67] viz. the "many" who are recipients of God's grace and gift and who are constituted righteous.

(2) All four expressions refer to the whole of humankind,[68] with πάντες meaning "all without exception."

(3) The three uses of πάντες denote all people, with οἱ ζῶντες describing those "in Christ."[69]

In evaluating these options, several considerations should be borne in mind. First, each view rightly recognizes that the three successive uses of πάντες must have the same referent, since οἱ before πάντες is anaphoric, pointing to the πάντες just mentioned, thus "they all";[70] and, whether καί in v. 15a is

---

shared the view that the death of Christ was beneficial (cf. ὑπέρ). Also, if Paul had been expressing a circumstance concurrent with the συνέχει (cf. TCNT, "when we reflect that . . ."), he would have used the present participle κρίνοντας.

61. E.g., Furnish 305, 310.

62. E.g., Weymouth, Berkeley, NEB, NASB, Barclay, REB.

63. E.g., Moffatt, Goodspeed, Williams, RSV, NIV, NAB[1, 2], Cassirer.

64. ὅτι . . . ἀπέθανεν, along with the ἄρα clause, defines the τοῦτο (cf. τοῦτο . . . ὅτι in Rom. 2:3; 6:6; 2 Cor. 10:7, 11).

65. Cf. Lambrecht, "Reading" 179-80; Pate 139-40. Goulder finds Adam-Christ theology in 5:14-15 but takes εἷς and the subject of ἀπέθανεν (both instances) to be Adam. "One man, Adam, died as agent for all, and so all humankind died; 'and he [Adam] died as agent for all [humankind] in order that [in the providence of God] those who are alive [today] might no longer live to themselves, but to him who died and rose for them [Christ]'" (Mission 265). It is, however, unconvincing to take ὑπέρ in vv. 14 and 15a as merely a "rhetorical parallel" to ὑπέρ in v. 15b.

66. E.g., Martin 131, 143.

67. Bruce 207.

68. E.g., Lambrecht, "Reading" 175-76.

69. E.g., Meyer 528-30; Dunn, "Death" 130-31.

70. BDF §275(7); Thrall 400.

epexegetic[71] or conjunctive,[72] the phrase εἰς ὑπὲρ πάντων ἀπέθανεν must bear an identical sense in vv. 14 and 15. Second, an unqualified οἱ ζῶντες would be a strange way of referring to all human beings[73] but a natural way of describing those who enjoy new life (cf. Rom. 6:4) in Christ after their "death" (ἀπέθανον, v. 14). This consideration would exclude the second option. Third, it seems illegitimate to argue on the basis of the (correct) equation οἱ ζῶντες = Christians, that the preceding οἱ πάντες must also be a narrower group than the whole human race.[74] The very addition of the expression οἱ ζῶντες suggests that a new, distinct category is being introduced; while all persons "died" when Christ died, not all rose to new life when he rose from the dead. If "those who live" referred to the same group as the "all" of vv. 14-15, we would have expected Paul to write simply καὶ ὑπὲρ πάντων ἀπέθανεν ἵνα μηκέτι ἑαυτοῖς ζῶσιν κτλ., or . . . ἵνα ζῶντες μηκέτι κτλ. This consideration weights the balances against option one and in favor of the third alternative.

Paul's threefold use of ὑπέρ in vv. 14-15 does not throw decisive light on these issues, for both in the NT and in Hellenistic Greek in general this preposition may denote either representation ("on behalf of," "for the sake of") or substitution ("in the place of").[75] When Christ died, he was acting both on behalf of and in the place of[76] all human beings. He represented them by becoming their substitute. Such an understanding suits the repeated phrase ὑπὲρ πάντων (vv. 14, 15a), but in the case of ὑπὲρ αὐτῶν (v. 15b) mere representation must be in mind if this phrase qualifies both τῷ . . . ἀποθανόντι and [τῷ] ἐγερθέντι, since Paul never portrays the resurrection of Jesus as being "in the place of" believers.

ἄρα οἱ πάντες ἀπέθανον states the consequence of Christ's death, the inferential ἄρα[77] introducing a virtual apodosis: "[if/since] one died for all, then. . . ."[78] This resultative sense can be well represented in translation by "which means that (all died)."[79] Given the fact that ἀπέθανον is aorist, there is no reason to distinguish this death from the time of the death indicated by the earlier aorist ἀπέθανεν, the time of Christ's crucifixion. When Christ died, all died; what is more, his death involved their death. Those who identify the three

71. Hahn, "Tag" 248; BDF §442(a).
72. That is, v. 15 could be the second element of Paul's conviction (κρίναντας).
73. But cf. NEB ("men, while still in life . . ."); Cassirer; Plummer 175; Thrall 412.
74. *Pace* J. Murray 81.
75. It is sometimes suggested that in Pauline thought Christ died on behalf of the entire human race but in the place of only believers. But Paul never uses ἀντί in relation to the benefits of the death of Christ. See further Harris, "Prepositions" 1196-97. That ὑπέρ denotes substitution in the phrase ὑπὲρ πάντων is recognized by, among others, Robertson 631; *Pictures* 230; Denney, *Death* 101-3; Hughes 193; Bultmann 151; H. Riesenfeld, *TDNT* 8.513.
76. This dual sense of ὑπέρ is proposed by Windisch 182; Collange 254; Martin 130-31.
77. On the position of ἄρα, see Thrall, *Particles* 36.
78. Similarly TCNT, Moffatt, Williams, JB, NAB[1], NJB. Many witnesses in fact add εἰ before εἰς (see Textual Note e. above).
79. Cf. Barrett 162; GNB; Barclay, ". . . and that the inevitable conclusion is that all died."

πάντες of vv. 14-15 as believers find in ἀπέθανον a reference to Christians' "mystical" death with Christ (cf. Rom. 6:3-4)[80] or their potential death to sin, self, and the world (cf. Rom. 6:2, 6, 10-11; 15:1-3; Gal. 2:20; 6:14; Col. 2:20).[81] But if, as we have argued, πάντες is universal in scope in vv. 14-15, this death may be the death deservedly theirs because of sin,[82] or an objective "ethical" death that must be appropriated subjectively by individual faith,[83] or a collective participation in the event of Christ's death by which sin's power was destroyed.[84] It is certainly more appropriate to see this ἀποθανεῖν of the πάντες as an actual "death" than as a potential "death."[85]

5:15 καὶ ὑπὲρ πάντων ἀπέθανεν, ἵνα οἱ ζῶντες μηκέτι ἑαυτοῖς ζῶσιν ἀλλὰ τῷ ὑπὲρ αὐτῶν ἀποθανόντι καὶ ἐγερθέντι. "And he died for all so that those who live should no longer live for themselves but for the one who died and rose again for them." From the time of his conversion, or shortly thereafter, Paul had two convictions (κρίναντας) about the death of Christ. The first related to the consequence (ἄρα) of his death, viz. the "death" of the whole human race (v. 14b). The second involved the purpose (ἵνα) of his death, viz. that those enjoying new life "in Christ" (οἱ ζῶντες) should also live "for Christ" (v. 15). Replacing the slavery to self that is the hallmark of the unregenerate state should be an exclusive devotion to the crucified and resurrected Messiah. The intended result of the death of Christ was the Christian's renunciation of self-seeking and self-pleasing and the pursuit of a Christ-centered life filled with action for the benefit of others, as was Christ's life (cf. ὑπέρ, vv. 14-15, three times). This, it seems, is the essential thrust of v. 15.

Because vv. 14 and 15 are so closely related (with the repetition of ὑπὲρ πάντων ἀπέθανεν),[86] several exegetical issues found in v. 15 were mentioned or discussed in v. 14. (1) καί may be either epexegetic ("that is to say"), with what follows being an expansion or particularization;[87] or (better) simply conjunctive, standing for καὶ ὅτι (after κρίναντας).[88] (2) ὑπέρ with πάντων probably signifies both representation and substitution, but with αὐτῶν merely representation. (3) πάντων refers to the whole human race, "all humanity" (NJB). (4) οἱ

---

80. Tannehill 66.

81. Cf. J. P. Lewis in Lewis (ed.) 40, 52, 133-34.

82. Tasker 86 (although there is ambiguity in his argument); Wolff, "Knowledge" 86, following F. Froitzheim, *Christologie und Eschatologie bei Paulus* (Würzburg: Echter, 1979) 41, 43.

83. Meyer 529; cf. Alford 663.

84. Thrall 411.

85. But see Otis 559-60, 563, who argues vigorously (but misguidedly) that ἵνα μηκέτι κτλ. in v. 15 shows that ἀπέθανον in v. 14 refers to a potential physical death, a readiness to die for Christ's sake: "all who have experienced the benefit of his death should die, if need be, to bring to others the knowledge of that death" (563).

86. But v. 15 differs from v. 14 in focusing on: (1) the intended purpose (ἵνα) rather than the actual result (ἄρα) of Christ's death, and therefore on the future rather than the past; and (2) a "death-life" rather than a "one-many" antithesis.

87. Cf. BAGD §442(9).

88. Cf. Meyer 530.

ζῶντες introduces a new category of persons, distinct from and narrower than (οἱ) πάντες, and refers to those who are "alive to God in Christ Jesus" (Rom. 6:11; cf. 2 Cor. 4:10b, 11b).[89] While all persons died, in one sense, when the Man who represented them died, not all were raised to new life when he rose. Paul is not suggesting that irrespective of their response and attitude, all people have new life in Christ or experience selfless living. There is universalism in the scope of redemption, since no person is excluded from God's offer of salvation; but there is a particularity in the application of redemption, since not everyone appropriates the benefits afforded by this universally offered salvation.

ἵνα introduces an intended result, not an automatic outcome; but when believers do make Christ the focal point of their thinking and acting, that is, when they do "live for" him, one divine purpose of Christ's death is achieved. μηκέτι ("no longer," "not any more," NJB) implies that prior to conversion, self-pleasing is the driving force behind human behavior. After conversion, the motivation for all of life should be the desire to please Christ (cf. 5:9; Eph. 5:10; Col. 1:10), who, as κύριος, has proprietary rights over his willing δοῦλοι (cf. 1 Cor. 7:22-23). The datives with ζῶσιν, viz. ἑαυτοῖς and τῷ . . . ἀποθανόντι καὶ ἐγερθέντι, are datives of advantage, "for the benefit of."[90] Whether believers live or die, they do so as servants who are the property of, and responsible to, the Lord (Rom. 14:8; cf. Rom. 7:4; 1 Cor. 6:19-20). Furnish aptly comments that "for Paul, freedom means transfer from one dominion to another: from law to grace (Rom. 6:14), from sin to righteousness (Rom. 6:18), from death to life (Rom. 6:21-23), from flesh to Spirit (Rom. 8:4ff.); or, as he puts it here, from self to Christ" (328).

The position of ὑπὲρ αὐτῶν between τῷ and ἀποθανόντι might suggest that this prepositional phrase qualifies only "for the one who died," but since ἀποθανόντι and ἐγερθέντι are both modified by a single article and Paul believed that Christians benefited (cf. ὑπέρ) from the resurrection of Christ (Rom. 4:25; 6:4), ὑπὲρ αὐτῶν may be construed with both participles, "for him who died and rose again on their behalf" (NASB).[91] The passive voice of ἐγείρω may bear an intransitive sense, so that ἠγέρθη may, like ἀνέστη, mean "he rose."[92] Accordingly ἐγερθέντι may mean "rose (again)" or "was raised (to life)." To translate this participle intransitively does not, of course, invalidate the frequent NT assertions of the Father's role in raising Jesus;[93] it simply coheres with one NT tradition that ascribes the resurrection to Jesus' own power (cf. John 2:19-22; 10:18).

Within vv. 9-15 Paul specifies five motives for Christian service: the de-

89. Defenders of the equation "οἱ ζῶντες = believers" include Windisch 183; Thüsing 103; Dinkler, "Verkündigung" 172; Furnish 311; Carrez 146; Martin 132; Wolff 116, 121.

90. BDF §188(2); Robertson 539.

91. So also TCNT, Moffatt, Montgomery, GNB, JB, NRSV.

92. Cf. BDF §78; Zerwick §231; Turner 57.

93. E.g., (with ἐγείρω) Acts 3:15; Rom. 10:9; 1 Pet. 1:21; (with ἀνίστημι) Acts 2:24, 32; 13:34.

sire to please Christ in all circumstances (v. 9); awareness of ultimate accountability to Christ = "the fear of the Lord" (vv. 10, 11a); his preoccupation with God's glory and his converts' well-being (v. 13); the example of Christ's love (v. 14a); and living for Christ as a response to his death and resurrection (v. 15). Here, then, is clear evidence of the Christocentric focus of Pauline ethics.[94] Christian conduct is motivated and determined by Christ.

Bibliography

Best, *Body* 54-55, 61-63 • Breytenbach, *Versöhnung* 125-29 • Crafton 94-97 • Denney, *Death* 100-103 • Dunn, "Death" • M. S. Enslin, "The Constraint of Christ," *CrQ* 11 (1934) 315-22 • Fee, *Presence* 327-30 • Fürst • Furnish, *Theology* 167 • Goulder, *Mission* 260-67 • G. S. Hendry, "ἡ γὰρ ἀγάπη τοῦ Χριστοῦ συνέχει: 2 Cor 5:14," *ExpT* 59 (1947-48) 82 • M. Hubbard, "Was Paul Out of His Mind? Re-Reading 2 Corinthians 5.13," *JSNT* 70 (1998) 39-64 • Kim, "Reconciliation" • Kraftchick • Lambrecht, "Reading" • Lewis • Murphy-O'Connor 55-63 • Oostendorp 52-58 • Otis • Pate 137-57 • Rebell 11-30 • Romaniuk, "Origine" • K. Romaniuk, "La crainte de Dieu à Qumrân et dans le Nouveau Testament," *RevQ* 13 (1963) 29-38 • C. Spicq, "L'étreinte de la charité," *ST* 8 (1955) 123-32 • Spicq, *Agape* 187-94 • D. M. Stanley 138-44 • Tannehill 65-69 • Thrall, "ΣΥΝΕΙΔΗΣΙΣ" • Thüsing 101-5 • Wolff, "Knowledge"

b. The Message of Reconciliation (5:16–6:2)

For Paul the essence of the apostolic ministry was the proclamation of God's act of reconciling sinful humanity to himself through the death of the sinless Christ (vv. 18-21), a gracious act which inaugurated "the era of salvation" (6:2). When the benefits of that reconciliation are personally appropriated, the believer enters a new order of reality "in Christ" (v. 17) where there are altered attitudes toward Christ and other people (v. 16), the forgiveness of sins (v. 19), and a permanently right relationship with God (v. 21).

Paul's role as Christ's ambassador and God's mouthpiece (v. 20a) was twofold, evangelistic and pastoral: it involved, first, the universal proclamation of reconciliation in Christ (vv. 18b, 19b) and the invitation to respond, "Be reconciled to God!" (v. 20b); second, the appeal to those already reconciled to God to persevere in grace, not to fail to profit from God's grace that is perpetually offered during the gospel era (6:1-2).

It is sometimes argued (1) that vv. 18-21 are a fragment of a pre-Pauline hymn;[1] or (2) that these verses contain previously formulated tradition regarding reconciliation to which Paul has added two interpretative glosses (v. 19b, "not reckoning against them their trespasses"; v. 20c, "we beg [you] on Christ's

---

94. It is interesting that in the catalogue of domestic duties in Col. 3:18–4:1, whenever motivation for behavior is explicitly stated (3:18, 20, 22; 4:1), it is invariably christological, κύριος always being the point of reference.

1. Käsemann, "Reconciliation" 52-57.

behalf, 'Be reconciled to God' ");[2] or (3) that v. 19ab (ὡς ὅτι . . . αὐτῶν) is pre-Pauline tradition.[3] These three proposals have been subjected to penetrating criticism by Thrall,[4] who concludes that "the theory of Paul's quotation of tradition [in 5:18-21] is by no means compelling, and should probably be rejected."[5] Certainly Paul should not be denied the luxury of linguistic and conceptual *hapax* or *dis legomena* such as may be found within vv. 18-21.

Although Paul is speaking in this paragraph primarily of his own apostolic vocation, the use of first person plurals will generally include his apostolic and evangelistic colleagues, and by implication all believers. Certainly ἡμᾶς in v. 18a and ἡμεῖς in v. 21b refer directly to all Christians, while ἡμῶν in v. 21a will include all people (as does οἱ πάντες in vv. 14-15). But in 6:1 the plurals refer to Paul (and possibly Timothy) alone, as ὑμᾶς indicates.

16*So then, from now on we regard no one from a worldly perspective. Even though[a] we once viewed Christ from a worldly perspective, yet now we no longer do so.* 17*So if anyone is in Christ, there is a new creation: the old order has passed away; see, a new order[b] has begun.* 18*Now all this comes from God, who reconciled us to himself through Christ and gave us the ministry of reconciliation,* 19*to the effect that God was in Christ, reconciling the world to himself, not holding people's transgressions against them. And he entrusted to us this message[c] of reconciliation[d].* 20*We are therefore[e] ambassadors for Christ, since God does in fact make his appeal through us. On Christ's behalf we make this entreaty: "Get reconciled to God!"* 21*For God caused Christ, who knew nothing of sin, to be sin for our sake, so that by being in him we might become the righteousness of God.* 6:1*So then, as God's co-workers, we indeed appeal[f] to you not to receive God's grace in vain,* 2*For God says, "At the time of my favor, I listened to you, and on the day of salvation, I came to your aid. Listen! Now is the time of God's good favor[g]. Listen! Now is the day of salvation!"*

TEXTUAL NOTES

a. Most early or reliable witnesses read εἰ καί (p[46] ℵ* B D* 0225 0243 33 326 1739 1881 1249 *pc* Eusebius), "even if," "although" (cf. 4:16; 7:8; 12:11). Perhaps to make the concession unambiguous (εἰ καί could mean "if indeed"), F G read καὶ εἰ. Because they "improve" the text by making the link with v. 16a explicit, the readings εἰ δὲ καί (ℵ[2] C[2] D[2] Ψ 𝔐 syr[h]) and εἰ δέ (K) are clearly secondary.

b. καινά, "new things," "a new order," is read by p[46] ℵ B C D* F G 048 0243 365

2. Martin 138-41; *Reconciliation* 94-95.
3. Stuhlmacher 77 n. 2.
4. Thrall 445-49 ("Excursus VII").
5. Thrall 449. See also Bieringer in Bieringer and Lambrecht 445-56 ("2 Kor 5,19a und die Tradition"), who reaches the same conclusion regarding 5:19a. Thrall sees 5:18-21 as Paul's response to Jewish claims that the Mosaic covenant is entirely sufficient for accomplishing atonement and restoring one's relation to God (438-39). For a defense of the chiastic structure of these verses (A=v. 18b, B=18c, A=19a, b, B=19c, B=20, A=21), see Hofius, "2 Kor 5,19" 3-10.

629 1175 1739 1249 *pc* vgst cop Clement) and is the preferred reading. The alternative readings — τὰ πάντα καινά (6 33 81 614 630 1241 1505 1881 *pm* vg$^{a, b}$ vg^{cl} (Ambrosiaster) and καινὰ τὰ πάντα (D^2 K L P Ψ 104 326 945 2464 *pm* syr^h) — are secondary as (i) longer readings, (ii) having inferior textual support, and (iii) probably arising to balance τὰ ἀρχαῖα and under the influence (by dittography) of the following τὰ δὲ πάντα. Cf. Metzger 511.

c. In the place of τὸν λόγον (p^{34} ℵ B C D^2 048 33 1739 1881 𝔐 vg syr), p^{46} reads τὸ εὐαγγέλιον ("the gospel") while D* (adding τοῦ) F G (vg^a) have the conflated reading εὐαγγελίου τὸν λόγον ("the message of the gospel").

d. After τῆς καταλλαγῆς, D* F G add ὅν "with respect to which," viz. τὸν λόγον), perhaps to establish a close connection between vv. 19 and 20, and therefore in v. 20a omit οὖν (as also do p^{46} Ψ vg^b). For an alternative explanation, see Thrall 436 n. 1721.

e. The conjunctive οὖν should be retained, as in p^{34} ℵ B C D^2 048 33 1739 1881 𝔐 vg syr.

f. Because some scribe(s) construed καί as conjunctive, παρακαλοῦντες (p^{46} D F G 2495 *pc* a b) naturally followed the previous participle, συνεργοῦντες.

g. Instead of εὐπρόσδεκτος F G read the uncompounded form δεκτός, probably to align Paul's comment with the previous quotation from Isa. 49:8 (LXX), καιρῷ δεκτῷ.

5:16 Ὥστε ἡμεῖς ἀπὸ τοῦ νῦν οὐδένα οἴδαμεν κατὰ σάρκα. "So then, from now on we regard no one from a worldly perspective." In v. 16 and in v. 17 the conjunction ὥστε ("for this reason," "therefore," "so then") introduces a consequence[6] of what is affirmed in vv. 14-15 concerning the death and resurrection of Jesus[7] or concerning the controlling power of Christ's love in Paul's life and his living for Christ.[8] V. 16 states a negative consequence, and v. 17 a positive.[9] Thus v. 16 should be seen as neither traditional nor parenthetical. ἡμεῖς ("For ourselves,"[10] TCNT; "with us," NEB, REB) refers principally to Paul but also reflects a distinctive Christian outlook (cf. τις in 5:17). In v. 16b, on the other hand, the first person plurals (ἐγνώκαμεν . . . γινώσκομεν) probably refer to Paul alone. The expression ἀπὸ τοῦ νῦν, common in the papyri (Deissmann 253), means "from now on," "henceforward," "for the future," with the point of orientation (implied in ἀπό) being not the time of writing or even the time when Paul reached the conclusion of vv. 14-15 (cf. κρίναντας, v. 14),[11] but the time of salvation that was inaugurated with the death and resurrection of Christ (cf. the repeated νῦν in 6:2)[12], that is, the new age, and more particularly the time of Paul's own conversion.[13]

---

6. Cf. Barrett's translation: "(16) The consequence of this is . . . (17) A further consequence is that . . ." (162); Thrall 400: "Consequently, . . . Consequently, . . ."; cf. Moule 144.

7. D. M. Stanley 140; Thrall 420, 424.

8. Thüsing 105.

9. Stanton 91.

10. Cf. ἐγώ, "for myself," in 1:23.

11. As Moffatt, "Once convinced of this"; Plummer 165, 176.

12. Thus Cambier, "Connaissance" 80; Tannehill 67; Martyn 273; cf. 274 ("the turn of the ages"), 285-86.

13. Thus Kim 13-14; Thrall 414-15.

Verse 16 uses two verbs of "knowing," οἶδα and γινώσκω (twice). In Classical Greek the verbs are usually distinguishable in meaning, οἶδα signifying the possession of knowledge, "know (of/about)", and γινώσκω denoting the acquisition of knowledge, "come to know," "ascertain"; or, more generally, οἶδα pointing to knowledge that comes by insight or intuition without intermediate means, and γινώσκω portraying knowledge that is gained by instruction or observation or experience. But such distinctions cannot be consistently maintained for Hellenistic Greek[14] or the NT in particular[15]. Here in 5:16, the change from οἴδαμεν to ἐγνώκαμεν is determined by the absence of a perfect of εἰδέναι, the form οἶδα being itself perfect with a present meaning. Then, when another present is required (in v. 16c), it is natural for Paul to move from ἐγνώκαμεν to γινώσκομεν rather than reverting to οἴδαμεν (Plummer [CGT] 94). Clearly, in this verse γινώσκομεν [κατὰ σάρκα] is synonymous with the earlier οἴδαμεν κατὰ σάρκα, both verbs meaning not "know about," but "view," "regard," "appraise," "value" (cf. 1 Thess. 5:12). In the present context the common Pauline expression κατὰ σάρκα could mean: (1) "from a human point of view" (RSV, NRSV), "in a merely human fashion,"[16] "at the human level,"[17] "simply as a man" (Weymouth)[18]; (2) "from a worldly point of view" (NIV), "by the standards of the flesh" (JB); or (3) "on the basis of externals" (cf. ἐν προσώπῳ, 5:12), "by what is external" (Moffatt), "according to external distinctions."[19] Paul is affirming that with the advent of the era of salvation in Christ, and ever since his own conversion to Christ, he has ceased making superficial, mechanical judgments about other people on the basis of outward appearances — such as national origin, social status, intellectual capability, physical attributes, or even charismatic endowment and pneumatic displays (cf. 1 Cor. 1:5, 7). Perhaps he is hinting that the Corinthians too should not make superficial assessments of others — such as Paul, their spiritual father — on the basis of such inappropriate criteria.

εἰ καὶ ἐγνώκαμεν κατὰ σάρκα Χριστόν, ἀλλὰ νῦν οὐκέτι γινώσκομεν (5:16 b, c). "Even though we once viewed Christ from a worldly perspective, yet now we no longer do so." "V. 16a is anthropological, v. 16bc Christological. V. 16a is the main enunciation, v. 16bc its exemplary confirmation."[20] εἰ καί is sometimes taken to introduce a hypothetical condition that expresses a real possibility but with no indication of actuality (cf. Gal. 5:11):[21] "Supposing we have

14. H. Seesemann, *TDNT* 5.116.

15. According to Burdick's analysis of the use of οἶδα and γινώσκω in Paul, in 18 instances (out of the 153 uses of the two verbs) the words seem interchangeable (344-56). But note also the comments of Silva 184-207; Porter 282-87 (who proposes that γινώσκω, the broader term, is used of knowledge possessed by means of acquisition or without it, and οἶδα of knowledge without any reference to acquisition, 285).

16. Thrall 400.

17. Young and Ford 267.

18. Cf. BAGD (408a), "simply as a physical being" (noted as one option).

19. Plummer 176; cf. 165.

20. Lambrecht, "Reading" 177.

21. Lietzmann calls this a "hypothetical, real condition" (125). A hypothetically unreal con-

known Christ according to the flesh, despite that fact we know him thus no longer" (Bultmann 156). On this view, v. 16b is seen as an "extreme instance" of v. 16a: if it is inappropriate to view Christ κατὰ σάρκα, how much more improper is it to regard anyone else κατὰ σάρκα (v. 16a). "Even with respect to Christ it is true that οὐδένα οἴδαμεν κατὰ σάρκα."[22] But it is unclear how an appeal to an inappropriate estimation of Christ automatically invalidates an improper view of people in general. It seems better to treat εἰ καί as introducing a real condition, depicting an actual situation of the past: "Even though[23] we once regarded Christ from a human point of view, we regard him thus no longer" (RSV).

If κατὰ σάρκα is construed with the noun Χριστόν, it is adjectival in import:[24] "Christ in the flesh" (JB[25]), "Christ as a man" (Weymouth). But if the phrase is taken with the verb ἐγνώκαμεν, it is adverbial:[26] "from a human point of view," "as far as externals are concerned."[27] Several considerations favor the adverbial sense.[28]

1. Although Paul elsewhere uses κατὰ σάρκα as a modifier of both nouns and verbs, when the expression qualifies a noun, it always follows the noun (Rom. 1:3; 4:1; 9:3; 9:5, with τό; 1 Cor. 1:26; 10:18),[29] whereas when it qualifies a verb it either precedes (e.g., 2 Cor. 10:3) or follows (e.g., 2 Cor. 11:18).

2. In v. 16a κατὰ σάρκα is separated from οὐδένα and follows the verb οἴδαμεν, so that in the parallel v. 16b, where κατὰ σάρκα stands after ἐγνώκαμεν, we would expect the phrase to qualify the verb.

3. If κατὰ σάρκα belongs with Χριστόν, it would be the only case in Paul where this phrase has a negative connotation when associated with a noun.[30]

4. It is doubtful whether κατὰ σάρκα is equivalent to ἐν (τῇ) σαρκί or ὡς ἄνθρωπος.

When it introduces the apodosis of a conditional sentence, ἀλλά means "yet," "certainly," or "at least" (BAGD 38d). The absence of an explicit object (αὐτόν = Χριστόν) is evidence that the emphasis falls on the "knowing."[31] Also,

---

dition (εἰ καὶ ἔγνωμεν) would be rendered "Supposing/Even if we had known." But, surprisingly, BAGD (161a) suggests that this is a possible rendering of the text as it stands.

22. Bultmann 155; cf. Furnish 330.

23. Cf. BDF §§374, 457. It is just possible that καί is to be separated from εἰ and construed with the whole protasis, "If, indeed, ..."

24. Thus, e.g., Georgi, *Opponents* 276-77; Dinkler, "Verkundigung" 174 n. 14.

25. The note in the Standard Edition of the JB reads: "Paul seems to be protesting against the restriction of the apostolic privilege to those who had known Jesus in his earthly life."

26. Thus, e.g., Cambier, "Connaissance" 82; Martyn 274; Fraser, "Knowledge" 298; W. Grundmann, *TDNT* 9.546 n. 343.

27. BAGD 744a (but see also 407d, 408a).

28. Both Windisch (185) and Bultmann (154; *Theology* 1.239) argue that the sense is not materially altered whether κατὰ σάρκα is treated as adjectival or adverbial.

29. In Rom. 8:5 οἱ . . . κατὰ σάρκα ὄντες = οἱ ὄντες οἱ κατὰ σάρκα, and in Eph. 6:5/Col. 3:22 τοῖς κατὰ σάρκα κυρίοις = τοῖς κυρίοις τοῖς κατὰ σάρκα.

30. E. Schweizer, *TDNT* 7.131 n. 259; Wolff, "Knowledge" 89.

31. F. W. Danker in Lewis (ed.) 115.

428

κατὰ σάρκα must be supplied after γινώσκομεν (a reading actually found in D E G), for the absolute statement "now we no longer know Christ" would be impossible.

The overall meaning of this historically important verse may now be discussed. Basically, two negative statements are made, one associated with οὐδένα and one with οὐκέτι. First, Paul is rejecting (in v. 16a) any assessment of human beings that is based on the human or worldly preoccupation with externals. It was now his custom to view people, not primarily in terms of nationality but in terms of spiritual status. The Jew-Gentile division was less important for him than the believer-unbeliever distinction,[32] which was based (he implies) on a κατὰ πνεῦμα or κατὰ σταυρόν attitude.[33] Both people and events were seen in the light of the new creation. We may trace this alteration of attitude to the time of Paul's conversion and, in particular, to the role of Ananias. When Ananias addressed Saul as Σαοὺλ ἀδελφέ (Acts 9:17; 22:13), "Brother Saul," it was not only a case of one Jew greeting another, but also, and more importantly, one Christian welcoming another into the community of the Messiah. For Paul ἀδελφός thereafter signified not only "fellow Israelite"[34] but also "fellow believer" (Jew or Gentile) in Jesus of Nazareth,[35] now the exalted Lord. Second, Paul is repudiating (in v. 16b, c) as totally erroneous his sincere yet superficial preconversion estimate of Jesus[36] as a misguided messianic pretender, a crucified heretic,[37] whose followers must be extirpated (Acts 9:1-2; 26:9-11), for he had come to recognize the Nazarene as the divinely appointed Messiah whose death under the divine curse (Gal. 3:13; cf. Deut. 21:23) in fact brought life (vv. 14-15). So then, two basic and profound changes had been brought about in Paul's attitude as a result of his Damascus encounter with the risen Lord: he now recognized and proclaimed Jesus as Messiah and Lord (Acts 9:22; 17:3; Rom. 10:9); he now viewed Gentile believers as Abraham's offspring, fellow citizens, brothers and sisters in Christ (Gal. 3:26-29; Eph. 2:11-19) while Jewish unbelievers were in need of salvation in Christ (Rom. 10:1-4). And these

---

32. See, e.g., Rom. 2:28-29; 10:12-13; 1 Cor. 5:12-13; Gal. 3:28; 6:10; Eph. 2:11-22; Col. 3:11.

33. Cf. Martyn 285: "The essential failure of the Corinthians consists in their inflexible determination to live either *before* the cross (the super-apostles of 2 Corinthians) or *after* the cross (the Gnostics of 1 Corinthians) rather than *in* the cross."

34. See Acts 22:1; 23:1, 6; 28:17.

35. E.g., 1 Cor. 1:1, 10, 26; 2:1; 2 Cor. 1:1, 8. Note also Rom. 10:1 where ἀδελφοί is distinguished from αὐτῶν (= Israelites).

36. The cry Ἀνάθεμα Ἰησοῦς, "Jesus be cursed!" (1 Cor. 12:3) may have epitomized Paul's own attitude — based on κατὰ σάρκα knowledge — toward Jesus during his persecution of the infant church.

37. Similarly, Fraser, "Knowledge" 301, 310; O. Betz 172-75, 179; W. Grundmann, *TDNT* 9.546 n. 343; Kim 14-15; Wolff, "Knowledge" 88. It is more probable that Χριστόν refers to a particular person, Jesus the Messiah, than to the messianic office or to a messianic ideal (as Zerwick, *Analysis* 400), for the parallel term οὐδένα ("no one") in v. 16a clearly alludes to real people, not a function or concept (cf. Allo 168).

two changes were not unrelated. A new attitude toward Jesus Christ prompts a new outlook on those for whom Christ died (cf. 1 Cor. 8:11). When we come to share God's view of Christ (cf. 1 Pet. 2:6-7), we also gain his view of people in general.

If these conclusions are correct, it follows that in 5:16 Paul is *not* (1) disclaiming interest in the historical Jesus;[38] (2) declaring knowledge about the historical Jesus irrelevant[39] or relatively unimportant;[40] (3) testifying to a post-conversion change of view from a particularist to a universalist view of Jesus and his message;[41] (4) primarily concerned with rebutting his opponents' aberrant views;[42] or (5) alluding to a personal encounter with Jesus during his early life.[43] Nor is the verse a marginal gloss that was created by a dualistic Gnostic (possibly a former member of the church in Corinth) as a conclusion based on v. 17, but included in the text by a scribe as v. 16.[44]

5:17 ὥστε εἴ τις ἐν Χριστῷ, καινὴ κτίσις· τὰ ἀρχαῖα παρῆλθεν, ἰδοὺ γέγονεν καινά· "So if anyone is in Christ, there is a new creation: the old order has passed away; see, a new order has begun." The Vulgate, taking τις with κτίσις, reflects an alternative punctuation: "So if any new creature is in Christ, old things have passed away: look! everything has become new."[45] Héring, too, would place a comma after κτίσις and a period after παρῆλθεν. "If anyone is a new creature in Christ, then — for him — the old order has passed and a new world has arisen" (43). But this punctuation (1) converts a pungent aphorism into a trite truism; (2) destroys the symmetry of the four balanced elements; and (3) ill accords with the position of ἐν Χριστῷ.[46]

Of the four units that comprise the verse, the first two are elliptical. We could supply (italics supplied):

(1) γίνεται . . . ἔστιν, "So, if anyone *comes to be* in Christ, *there is* a new creation" (Martin 135; similarly Moffatt);

38. E.g., Klausner 436-37, who argues that the Jesus of the Damascus vision, the spiritual Jesus, was for Paul the essential Jesus. On Paul's knowledge and use of Jesus traditions, see Fraser, *Jesus and Paul, passim;* and more recently, Wenham, *Paul: Follower of Jesus or Founder of Christianity, passim.*

39. Schoeps 57, 108.

40. W. L. Knox (149; *Gentiles* 181) regards 5:16 as an "incautious outburst," uttered "in the heat of controversy," declaring that knowledge of the earthly ministry of Jesus was of "comparatively small importance."

41. If ἀπὸ τοῦ νῦν refers to the new age or to the time of Paul's conversion, such an attitudinal "second conversion" is excluded.

42. E.g., Dupont 182-86; D. M. Stanley 140; Georgi, *Opponents* 253, 298-99 n. 167. For a review of the distinctive views of Georgi and Martyn on 5:16, see Fraser 54-59; "Knowledge" 305-10.

43. Thus Schmithals 302-15, especially 313-14; similarly Güttgemanns, 288-98.

44. E.g., Weiss, *Paul* 40-48.

45. *Si qua ergo in Christo nova creatura, vetera transierunt: ecce facta sunt omnia.*

46. It is also significant that in the only other Pauline use of καινὴ κτίσις (Gal. 6:15), this expression stands independently.

(2) ἐστιν . . . ἔστω, "Therefore if any man *be* in Christ, *let him be* a new creature" (KJV mg);

(3) ἐστιν . . . ἐστιν, "So, if anyone *is* in Christ, *there is* a new creation" (Furnish 306);

(4) ἐστιν . . . ἐστιν, "Therefore, if any one *is* in Christ, *he is* a new creation"
(RSV, NIV).

Regarding (1), it is awkward to supply two different verbs, although the verb
γίνομαι does occur in v. 17b; to supply γίνεται . . . γίνεται ("comes to be . . .
comes into existence") or even γέγονεν . . . γέγονεν ("has come to be . . . has
come into existence") would be easier. Against (2) is the observation that an exhortation is out of place in the midst of a series of Christian verities (vv. 14-19).
Most translations and commentators supply ἐστιν . . . ἐστιν.

ὥστε states a second consequence of vv. 14-15,[47] although some relate the
consequence to v. 14 alone,[48] or to vv. 15-16,[49] or to v. 16.[50] One result of
Christ's death and resurrection (vv. 14-15) is the possibility (cf. εἰ) of a καινὴ
κτίσις. εἴ τις, "if anyone," standing without qualification, must be all-
embracing, excluding no one. It is equivalent to ὅστις ("whoever")[51] or πᾶς . . .
ὃς ἄν, "everyone who" (cf. Rom. 10:12-13) and points to the eradication of any
distinction between Jew and Gentile with regard to receiving God's mercy and
salvation. In status before God through Christ, and in accessibility to all the
spiritual benefits that flow from that status, "there is neither Jew nor Greek"
(Gal. 3:28; cf. Eph. 2:11-22; Col. 3:11). "The dividing wall that formed a bar-
rier (τὸ μεσότοιχον τοῦ φραγμοῦ)" separating Jew and Gentile has been demolished in the person and work of Christ (Eph. 2:14).

The phrase ἐν Χριστῷ is so ubiquitous in Paul's writings (over 160 uses[52])
and the person of Christ so central that, not surprisingly, some scholars regard
this as the central or unifying motif in Pauline theology.[53] Of the main interpretations of the phrase — the local or "mystical," the ecclesiological, the eschatological, the soteriological, the representative, and the personal[54] — the approaches that accommodate the largest number of uses seem to be the personal
and the ecclesiological. That is, "in Christ" often means "in personal union
with the risen Christ" or "in the body of Christ" (= the church). Neither the indi-

47. So Barrett 173; Furnish 332; Wolff, "Knowledge" 91; Thrall 424.
48. E.g., J. P. Lewis in Lewis 41.
49. Plummer (CGT) 94; but cf. (ICC) 179.
50. Windisch 189; Collange 263-64.
51. In Mark 8:34 A C² θ 𝔐 syr^h read ὅστις, while the preferred text, εἴ τις, is read by ℵ B C*
D *al.*
52. This number includes instances where ἐν αὐτῷ or ἐν ᾧ refers to Christ (e.g., Col. 1:14,
17).
53. Schweitzer (in his *Mysticism*), for instance, saw the quintessence of Pauline teaching as
"mystical" redemption through "being-in-Christ."
54. For sketches of the history of interpretation, see Longenecker 160-70; Wedderburn
351-56; "Observations," 83-97.

vidual nor the corporate dimension of the phrase should be ignored. In addition, we should not overlook the fact that the preposition ἐν in this phrase expresses (in different contexts) a wide range of ideas or relationships — incorporation ("in the person or body of Christ"), union ("in fellowship with/united to Christ"), sphere of reference ("in Christ" = "Christian"), agency ("through the work of Christ"), cause ("as a result of solidarity with Christ"), mode ("by being in Christ"), location ("centered/concentrated in Christ"), or basis ("on the authority of Christ").[55] In 5:17 ἐν Χριστῷ may be paraphrased "united in faith to the risen Christ."

Were it not for the conditional and individual cast of the sentence ("if anyone"), we might readily find in the phrase καινὴ κτίσις a reference to a cosmic and ontological reality brought into existence by the Christ-event.[56] As it is, the εἰ and the τις combine to give καινὴ κτίσις a personal reference relating to an individual's faith-union with Christ. It would make no sense to render εἴ τις by "since anyone"; then "since everyone" would be εἰ πᾶς/πάντες. So the existence of the καινὴ κτίσις is conditional upon a person's coming to be "in Christ."[57] Whether κτίσις here means "act of creating" or "creature"[58] (= κτίσμα)/"being," the focus is on divine agency (cf. v. 18a), be it the agency of Christ[59] or (as is more probable) of God. Already in this letter Paul has depicted conversion as a creatorial act of God, comparable to the initial creation of light (4:6). Now, with the adjective καινή, he emphasizes the altered nature of the converted person or the newness of God's creatorial action. The rendering "there is a new creation" (REB) reproduces the ambiguity of the Greek, which could mean "there is a newly-created being" (Thrall 400)/"he or she is a newly-created person"[60] or "there is a new act of creation" (Barrett 162). Like the Johannine γεννηθῆναι ἄνωθεν (John 3:7) and the Petrine ἀναγεννηθῆναι ("to be born anew/again," cf. 1 Pet. 1:3, 23), the Pauline καινὴ κτίσις refers to individual rebirth or regeneration (παλιγγενεσία, Tit. 3:5) as God's sovereign and creatorial act. Yet it is true that the renewal of the individual in conversion prefigures the renewal of the cosmos at the end (cf. ἐν τῇ παλιγγενεσίᾳ, Matt. 19:28; also Rom. 8:19-23) (Harris 166-71). If, then, the emphasis in v. 17a is anthropological and personal, not cosmological and eschatological, we may perhaps discover the background for Paul's use here of καινὴ κτίσις, not in the

55. For examples of these uses, see Harris, "Prepositions" 1192.
56. Cf. Stuhlmacher, "Erwägungen" 1-35.
57. Similarly Thrall, 427. On the other hand, when Paul says in Gal. 6:15 (where the only other NT use of καινὴ κτίσις occurs; see Adams 235-36) that "neither circumcision nor uncircumcision amounts to anything; all that counts is the new creation," he is thinking more abstractly, so that καινὴ κτίσις may mean "the new humanity" (= ὁ καινὸς ἄνθρωπος, Eph. 4:24; see also Eph. 2:15; Col. 3:10; cf. Chilton 312, citing the analogous bᵉrîyyāh in later rabbinic Hebrew; m. 'Aboth 1:12; 4:1; 6:1) or "incorporation into a new system of reality" (Vos 49).
58. Thus RV, Weymouth, NASB; BAGD 394b, 455d (but cf. 489b, "creation"); Reumann 51 and n. 65; Carrez 144; Wolff 116. On the linguistic background of κτίσις, see Adams 77-80.
59. On Christ as the creator of "the new man," see Jervell 268-69.
60. Cf. TCNT, "he is a new being"; Cassirer, "he has in fact been created anew."

Isaianic passages that describe the restoration of Israel[61] and cosmic renewal when the new age dawns,[62] but in the Jewish apocalyptic and rabbinic description of the sinner who repents or the Gentile who converts to Judaism as a "new creature" *(bᵉriyyâ ḥadāšâ)*.[63]

The theology of the NT — or indeed Pauline theology — could be written around this theocentric concept of "newness" (καινότης, Rom. 6:4; 7:6), which is summed up in the statement, ἰδού καινὰ ποιῶ πάντα (Rev. 21:5; cf. Isa. 43:19, LXX), "See! I make everything new!"[64] In the new era brought by Christ, there is the new wine of the new age (Mark 2:22; Luke 5:37-38), the new covenant (Luke 22:20; 1 Cor. 11:25; 2 Cor. 3:6; Heb. 8:8, 13; 9:15; 12:24), the new creation/creature (2 Cor. 5:17; Gal. 6:15), the new man/humanity (Eph. 2:15; 4:24; Col. 3:10), the new song of redemption (Rev. 5:9; 14:3), the new name for believers (Rev. 2:17; 3:12), and the new commandment of love (John 13:34; 1 John 2:8). In the consummated kingdom there will be the new wine of the heavenly banquet (Mark 14:25), a new heaven and a new earth (Rev. 21:1; cf. 2 Pet. 3:13), and a new Jerusalem (Rev. 3:12; 21:2).

Verse 17b, which is reminiscent of Isa. 44:18-19 in terminology (but not content),[65] explains καινὴ κτίσις first negatively (τὰ ἀρχαῖα παρῆλθεν), then positively (ἰδοὺ γέγονεν καινά). Many translations indicate this relationship of v. 17b to v. 17a by placing a colon after "new creation/creature/being." The change from the articular τὰ ἀρχαῖα to the anarthrous καινά may be represented in translation by "the old order" and "a new order" (NEB, REB), or, taking τά as possessive (cf. τις), "his old life" and "a new life" (NEB mg, REB, mg). The rendering "the old . . . the new" (NIV) presupposes τὰ καινά.[66] τὰ ἀρχαῖα, "things of the past,"[67] cannot refer to the cosmos, for its renovation or annihilation (or re-creation by purification) lies in the future (Rom. 8:21; cf. 2 Pet. 3:7, 10-13) and παρῆλθεν could not be a proleptic aorist. Rather, it refers to the whole set of conditions and relationships that marked believers in their unregenerate state when they behaved κατὰ σάρκα, that is, they were governed in thought and action by the desires of the σάρξ (cf. Rom. 8:2, 4; Eph. 2:3) and so were under the dominion of sin and death (cf. Rom. 8:2), and when they made value judgments κατὰ σάρκα (cf. 5:16), that is, assessed others by external and

---

61. Isa. 42:9; 43:18-19; 45:17; 48:6; 65:18.

62. Isa. 65:17; 66:22.

63. SB 2.421-23; 3.519; G. F. Moore 1.533; and especially Sjöberg 57-59.

64. On this general topic, see Harrisville, *Newness;* Mell, *Neue Schöpfung;* Hubbard, *New Creation;* and more popularly, Hoch, *All Things New.*

65. Isa. 43:18-19 (LXX): 18Μὴ μνημονεύετε τὰ πρῶτα καὶ τὰ ἀρχαῖα μὴ συλλογίζεσθε. 19ἰδοὺ ποιῶ καινὰ ἃ νῦν ἀνατελεῖ, καὶ γνώσεσθε αὐτά.

66. See Textual Note b.

67. Zerwick and Grosvenor 545. Both ἀρχαῖος and παλαιός mean "old," and both may be contrasted with καινός (cf. παλαιότης–καινότης in Rom. 7:6). If the two adjectives differ in emphasis, ἀρχαῖος signifies "ancient," "original," "belonging to former times," and therefore "venerable," whereas παλαιός means "in existence for a long time" and therefore "obsolete" or "antiquated." But even in the papyri this distinction "is naturally worn thin on occasion" (MM 81b).

worldly standards. In parallelism with τὰ ἀρχαῖα, although placed last for emphasis, καινά is the subject of γέγονεν, not a predicate adjective with either τὰ ἀρχαῖα[68] or τὰ πάντα understood.[69] If καινά picks up the phrase καινὴ κτίσις, then εἴ τις ἐν Χριστῷ may be understood before ἰδοὺ γέγονεν καινά. That is, καινά, as well as εἴ τις and καινὴ κτίσις, refers principally to individual experience rather than to corporate or cosmic realities. When a person becomes a Christian,[70] he or she experiences a total restructuring of life that alters its whole fabric — thinking, feeling, willing, and acting. Anyone who is "in Christ" is "Under New Management" and has "Altered Priorities Ahead," to use the wording sometimes found in shop windows and (in Britain) on roads. And the particle ἰδού ("behold!" "see!") functions like such a sign, stimulating attention; but here it conveys also a sense of excitement and triumph. Nor should we overlook the difference between the aorist παρῆλθεν and the perfect γέγονεν: one set of conditions and relationships has come to an end or passed out of existence; another brand new set has already begun or has come to stay. Here Paul is clearly emphasizing the radical discontinuity between the pre- and post-conversion states, but in other contexts he implies the coexistence or interpenetration of the present age and the age to come (e.g., 1 Cor. 10:11; Gal. 1:4)[71] and speaks of the ongoing renewal of the believer (Rom. 12:2; 2 Cor. 3:18; Col. 3:10). Nor could he ever forget that all of humankind was currently subject to the ravages of decay and death and that release from our bondage to mortality would come only with the resurrection (cf. Rom. 7:24; 8:19-23; 1 Cor. 15:42-44, 53-54; Phil. 3:20-21).

The relation of v. 17 to what precedes is significant. Christian conversion, that is, coming to be in Christ (v. 17a), produces dramatic change (v. 17b): life is no longer lived κατὰ σάρκα, but κατὰ πνεῦμα. Paul implies that a change of attitude toward Christ (v. 16b) brings about a change of attitude toward other people (v. 16a) and a change of conduct from self-pleasing to Christ-pleasing (vv. 9, 15), from egocentricity to theocentricity.

5:18 τὰ δὲ πάντα ἐκ τοῦ θεοῦ τοῦ καταλλάξαντος ἡμᾶς ἑαυτῷ διὰ Χριστοῦ καὶ δόντος ἡμῖν τὴν διακονίαν τῆς καταλλαγῆς. "Now all this comes from God, who reconciled us to himself through Christ and gave us the ministry of reconciliation."

Verses 18-21 deal with two clearly defined topics: (A) God's act of reconciling the world through the work of Christ, and (B) the ministry and message

---

68. As RV: "the old things are passed away; behold, they are become new." Cf. Martin 135: "the old order has gone, to be replaced by the new"; also note the comment of Hughes (203), "the old things became and continue to be new."

69. As NRSV: "everything old has passed away; see, everything has become new!"

70. Not inappropriately, Meyer renders ἐν Χριστῷ in v. 17a as "a Christian" (534).

71. For Paul the two ages were not successive epochs (as in Jewish apocalyptic) but concurrent orders which not only coexisted (thus Goguel 329) but also interpenetrated, producing the "already–not yet" dialectic epitomized in Paul's maximum ὡς μή ("as if not") (cf. Barrett, *Adam* 104-15).

of reconciliation entrusted by God to Christ's ambassadors. Vv. 18 and 19 each treat both topics, in the order A, B. V. 20 is concerned with B, and v. 21 with A.[72]

Although τὰ πάντα can mean "the universe" (e.g., Phil. 3:21; Col. 1:16-17), there is nothing in the immediate context to suggest that Paul is here affirming the divine origin of the cosmos.[73] Rather, "all this" (RSV, REB, NRSV), "all these consequences" (Barrett 162),[74] looks back to the new attitudes of v. 16 and the new creation of v. 17, that is, the new order (καινά, v. 17), all the benefits of the Christ-event; Paul declares that "from first to last this has been the work of God" (NEB). δέ is probably transitional ("now"), but Paul may possibly be anticipating a failure on the part of some (thus adversative δέ, "but") to recognize that all the dramatic changes of vv. 16-17 were God's doing. In vv. 18-21 Paul proceeds to explain how this newness came about.

The word group that relates to "reconciliation" is exclusively Pauline within the NT: καταλλάσσω occurs six times,[75] ἀποκαταλλάσσω three times,[76] and καταλλαγή four times.[77] Only one of these thirteen is not theological in import.[78] It is little wonder, therefore, that some scholars regard reconciliation as the "leading theme" or "center" of Paul's thought and ministry.[79] Basically, καταλλαγή means "exchange," especially of money or merchandise.[80] In the papyri it is used most often of the changing of money from one currency into another (Spicq 2.263). Metaphorically it denoted the exchange or substitution of

72. See I. H. Marshall 122.

73. But Héring sees Paul's statement in v. 18a, which he renders "the author of all the worlds is God" (42), as a counter to the type of Gnosticism that attributed creation to the initiative of a demiurge (43). Cf. Güttgemanns (313-17), who suggests that Paul is opposing a Gnostic doctrine of creation's self-redemption.

74. That τὰ πάντα can have a general reference (as well as meaning "the universe") is clear from 4:15; 12:19 (cf. BAGD 632d, 633a).

75. Rom. 5:10 twice; 1 Cor. 7:11; 2 Cor. 5:18-20. The basic meaning of ἀλλάσσω is "make other than it is" (from ἄλλος, "other"), "change."

76. Col. 1:20, 22; Eph. 2:16. By etymology ἀποκαταλλάσσω signifies "effect a thorough (-κατα-) change (-αλλάσσω) back (ἀπο-)" (cf. Moulton and Howard 298). See also Porter, Καταλλάσσω 183-85). Both F. Büchsel (TDNT 1.258) and Porter see this verb as a coinage by Paul.

77. Rom. 5:11; 11:15; 2 Cor. 5:18-19.

78. 1 Cor. 7:11, of a woman being reconciled to her husband.

79. See, e.g., Martin, Reconciliation, especially 3-6, 46-47, who refers to J. Weiss, T. W. Manson, H. Ridderbos, and P. Stuhlmacher as his predecessors in holding this view. For a review of proposals concerning the origin of Paul's concept of reconciliation, see Kim, "Reconciliation" 363-66. Kim himself traces the origin to Paul's theological reflection on his Damascus experience (20; "Reconciliation" 360-84). "On the Damascus road Paul himself experienced God's reconciling him, a hostile enemy, to himself, forgiving his sins and making him a new creature by his grace" ("Reconciliation" 383). Kim perceives allusions in 2 Cor. 5:13-19 to Paul's Damascus encounter with Christ in ἐξέστημεν (v. 13), συνέχει and κρίναντας (v. 14), vv. 16-17 as a whole, and the three aorist participles of vv. 18-19 (καταλλάξαντος . . . δόντος . . . θέμενος; "Reconciliation" 368-71).

80. For discussions of this word group, see F. Büchsel (TDNT 1.251-59; Dupont, Réconciliation, passim; Spicq, 2.262-66; I. H. Marshall 119-21, 127; Porter, Καταλλάσσω 23-116; Breytenbach 40-83, 104.

peace for war, of love for anger, or of friendship for enmity. As a Pauline theological term depicting the relationship of God with humans, "reconciliation" denotes a transformation of relations, not in the sense that original friendly relations are restored (humans are by nature at enmity with God, Rom. 5:10; Eph. 2:1-3) but in the sense that friendly relations now replace former hostility.[81] Reconciliation restores humans to a proper relationship with God (the vertical aspect) and with fellow human beings (the horizontal aspect), just as sin produces in humans a twofold alienation, from God and from other human beings. Reconciliation comes about "by making peace" (ἀποκαταλλάξαι εἰρηνοποιήσας, Col. 1:20; cf. Eph. 2:15) and results in the slaying of animosity or the termination of hostility (ἵνα . . . ἀποκαταλλάξῃ . . . ἀποκτείνας τὴν ἔχθραν, Eph. 2:15-16). The need for reconciliation is the absence of harmony and presence of hostility between God and humans that is caused by human sin. Being ἁμαρτωλοί (Rom. 5:8), humans are ἐχθροί (Rom. 5:10), ἀσεβεῖς and ἀσθενεῖς (Rom. 5:6). This same link between sin and enmity with God is expressed in another reconciliation passage — "although you were at one time estranged from God and enemies in your minds because of your evil deeds, you also he has now reconciled" (Col. 1:21-22). In 2 Corinthians 5 the need for the creation of harmonious relations with God is implied by the reference to self-pleasing (v. 15), παραπτώματα (v. 19), and ἁμαρτία (v. 21).

Apart from not explicitly linking human sin with the need for reconciliation, v. 18 expresses the four essential ingredients in the apostle's concept of καταλλαγή.

1. *God (the Father) is both the initiator and goal of reconciliation.* Reconciliation stems from God and ends with God. τοῦ καταλλάξαντος qualifies τοῦ θεοῦ and is equivalent to ὃς κατήλλαξεν, "who reconciled."[82] Building on the preliminary formulations and findings of I. H. Marshall, Porter has shown that Paul's use of καταλλάσσω is unprecedented in earlier Greek. "Paul uses καταλλάσσω in the active voice with the offended and hence angered party in a relationship (i.e. God) as (grammatical) subject taking the initiative in effecting reconciliation between himself and the offending party."[83] Or, as Marshall had

81. On the question as to whether the hostility between God and humans is mutual and whether the subsequent change of attitude is mutual, see Morris 193-98, 219-23, who concludes "that there is a very real hostility on the part of God to all that is evil, and that this hostility is not incompatible with a deep love of God for sinners" (198), and "that reconciliation includes what we must call a change on the part of God as well as on the part of man, since the wrath of God is no longer directed towards man" (223). Cf. Denney 769-70. Similarly, citing the three parallels in Luke 15 that describe "God's joy over one sinner reclaimed" (103), Stagg comments that "estrangement is personal and affects all persons involved. Likewise, reconciliation is personal and affects all persons involved" (103-4).

82. This articular participle is descriptive and nonrestrictive, "God, who reconciled" (see on these points, Burton §§295, 426; Robertson 764, 859).

83. Porter, *Καταλλάσσω* 16. On the use of καταλλαγή-terminology in Hellenistic Judaism, see Breytenbach 69-78; and, more briefly, F. Büchsel, *TDNT* 1.254, 258; I. H. Marshall 120-21, 129-30.

earlier expressed the point, "whereas in popular usage 'to reconcile Y to one-self' means 'to remove Y's grounds for being offended,' Paul uses the phrase to mean 'to remove Y's offense.'"[84] For Paul, reconciliation does not occur apart from God or in spite of God, but because of God. Once God has taken the initiative in removing the obstacle to fellowship, there is no need for humans to try to assuage God's anger. God's initiative in reconciling is also expressed in 5:19; Col. 1:20[85] and 1:22,[86] but in Eph. 2:16 Christ is the one who reconciles Jews and Gentiles to God. The personal goal of reconciliation is expressed in vv. 18 and 19 by ἑαυτῷ, "to himself"; in v. 20 and Rom. 5:10; Eph. 2:16 by τῷ θεῷ; in Col. 1:20 by εἰς αὐτόν/αὑτόν, "to himself."[87] Other goals of reconciliation are the presentation of believers before God as holy and without blemish and re-proach (Col. 1:22), and, by implication, deliverance from God's wrath (Rom. 5:9-10). Romans 5 also shows that reconciliation stems from God's love, for while v. 8 affirms that Christ's death is an evidence of God's love, v. 10 says that Christ's death achieved reconciliation.

2. *Christ was God's agent in achieving reconciliation.* To bring about reconciliation, God acted διὰ Χριστοῦ, "by means of Christ," a sentiment that is expressed in Col. 1:20 by δι' αὐτοῦ . . . δι' αὐτοῦ "through him . . . through him alone"; in Rom. 5:10 by διὰ τοῦ θανάτου τοῦ υἱοῦ αὐτοῦ; in Col. 1:22 by ἐν τῷ σώματι τῆς σαρκὸς αὐτοῦ διὰ τοῦ θανάτου, "through Christ's death in his physical body"; and in Eph. 2:16 by διὰ τοῦ σταυροῦ, "through the cross." Thus "the message of reconciliation" (v. 19) is "the message of the cross" (1 Cor. 1:18).

3. *Human beings and the whole created universe are the objects and principal beneficiaries of God's reconciling action.* God is never the object of the verb (ἀπο)καταλλάσσω in the active voice, and never the subject in the passive. Others do not "reconcile" God, nor is he ever said to "be reconciled."[88] In v. 18 ἡμᾶς has been taken to refer to: (i) Paul alone, although not in an exclusive sense;[89] (ii) Paul and his addressees;[90] (iii) all believers,[91] or (iv) all humanity.[92] In the light of v. 19 where the object of reconciliation is κόσμον, the "world" of human beings (as the following αὐτοῖς and αὐτῶν would indicate; cf. καταλλαγὴ κόσμου, Rom. 11:15), ἡμᾶς probably refers to the entire human race. In Col. 1:21 the object is ὑμᾶς, "you (Colossians)"; in Eph. 2:16, τοὺς ἀμφοτέρους, "(us) both," namely Jews and Gentiles. In Col. 1:20, however, the object of ἀπο-καταλλάξαι is τὰ πάντα, "the universe (in its entirety)," embracing, it would

---

84. I. H. Marshall 130; cf. 127, "X removes the cause of his own anger against Y, namely, Y's sin."

85. This assumes that πᾶν τὸ πλήρωμα means "God in all his fullness."

86. *Pace* Porter, Καταλλάσσω 177, 183, 189.

87. See Harris, *Colossians* 50-51.

88. Cf. Ladd 492-93.

89. Lambrecht, "Reading" 183; Wolff, "Knowledge" 93 (on the basis of the parallelism between καταλλάξαντος ἡμᾶς and δόντος ἡμῖν).

90. Bieringer in Bieringer and Lambrecht 425.

91. Furnish 317.

92. Allo 171.

seem, inanimate nature (cf. Col. 1:20c; Rom. 8:19-21), the world of humankind (cf. Col. 1:20c, 21-22) and those angelic powers that were opposed to God (cf. Col. 1:16, 20c). Col. 1:21-23, and especially the conditional clause in Col. 1:23a, "make it clear that while the whole universe has now been restored to its God-ordained destiny [= reconciled], viz. its proper relation to Christ, in an objectively real reconciliation, still the benefits of this reconciliation are not experienced by individual human beings automatically, apart from their faith."[93]

4. *Reconciliation is an accomplished fact on God's side, yet it must be embraced on the human side.* That reconciliation has been achieved is evident from the aorist (καταλλάξαντος; see also Rom. 5:10; Col. 1:20, 22; Eph. 2:14-16) in v. 18, the imperfect ἦν . . . καταλλάσσων in v. 19, and the fact that it occurred "through [the death of] Christ" (v. 18; cf. Rom. 5:10; Eph. 2:16; Col. 1:22). From one point of view, it is a *fait accompli,* standing complete quite apart from any human response. God has, on one occasion and decisively, dealt with the cause of enmity and removed the obstacle to fellowship, namely human sin (see v. 21). Yet to the description of God as τοῦ καταλλάξαντος ἡμᾶς Paul adds καὶ δόντος ἡμῖν τὴν διακονίαν τῆς καταλλαγῆς, "and gave us the ministry of reconciliation." This addition is paralleled in v. 19 by the statement θέμενος ἐν ἡμῖν τὸν λόγον τῆς καταλλαγῆς, "he entrusted to us this message of reconciliation," which indicates that the gift (δόντος) is a trust (θέμενος) and that the ministry (διακονίαν) is essentially a proclamation (λόγον). Reconciliation is a fact, but it must be offered in proclamation and received by the hearer (cf. v. 20, "Become reconciled to God" and τὴν καταλλαγὴν λαμβάνειν in Rom. 5:11). Since these latter two stages — proclamation and receipt — must take place before the two alienated parties, God and human beings, begin to enjoy friendly relations, there is a sense in which reconciliation is an incomplete, ongoing process.[94] Not all humans are rightly related to God; some still stand under his wrath (Rom. 1:18). So the task of soliciting human acceptance of God's offer of reconciliation (= τὴν διακονίαν τῆς καταλλαγῆς) was committed by God to Paul and his colleagues (τοῦ θεοῦ . . . δόντος ἡμῖν). The parallelism between ἡ διακονία τῆς καταλλαγῆς and the expressions ἡ διακονία τοῦ πνεύματος (3:8) and ἡ διακονία τῆς δικαιοσύνης (3:9) suggests that ἡμῖν is narrower than the whole Christian community and yet wider than Paul alone,[95] either Paul and the other apostles, or Paul and all his colleagues in ministry, apostles and others (as in vv. 19c, 20). With both καταλλάξαντος and δόντος

---

93. Harris, *Colossians* 51. "Christ's death is seen as *sufficient* for all, but only *efficient* for those who respond to the offer of salvation" (Witherington, *Narrative Thought* 165).

94. Fitzmyer ("Reconciliation" 176) argues that Paul sees himself as "extending" the ministry of reconciliation — there is the Christ-event, then his announcing its effect, and his striving to have people appropriate the benefits of reconciliation. Cf. I. H. Marshall 128.

95. If ἡμῖν refers to Paul alone (thus Bieringer in Bieringer and Lambrecht 425-26), δόντος could allude to Paul's conversion (cf. Acts 9:15; 26:17-18), although Hanson (*Ministry* 81) insists that the two aorist participles (καταλλάξαντος . . . δόντος) must refer to simultaneous actions. Furnish (317, 336) takes ἡμῖν to include all believers.

governed by a single article (τοῦ), the close association between God's work of reconciliation and the apostolic ministry of proclamation (cf. v. 19) is intimated.[96] The divine act of reconciliation is necessarily complemented by the human ministry of reconciliation.[97] διακονία here refers not to an office but to the function of serving,[98] the role of presenting for acceptance God's offer of reconciliation. The genitive τῆς καταλλαγῆς could be qualitative ("that is characterized by reconciliation," "reconciling"), epexegetic ("that consists in [announcing] reconciliation," "whose content/essence is reconciliation"), or even a genitive of respect ("with reference to/that relates to reconciliation"), but more probably it is objective ("that proclaims/presents reconciliation").

Paul never speaks of "the ministry of justification," only of the διακονία "of the Spirit" (3:8), "of righteousness" (3:9), and "of reconciliation" (5:18). That justification and reconciliation are closely related is clear from the parallelism of Rom. 5:1 and 5:11, and 5:9 and 5:10. But the terms are not synonymous, as Cerfaux contends (140-41). Some subordinate reconciliation to justification (e.g., Käsemann, who coins the expression *justificatio inimicorum,* "the justification of enemies");[99] others find justification to be subsidiary to reconciliation.[100] Rom. 5:1 (δικαιωθέντες . . . εἰρήνην ἔχομεν) would suggest that justification is the "logical foundation" (Fung 255) for reconciliation, that it is a case of reconciliation by means of justification. Reconciliation is neither central nor peripheral in Pauline theology, yet it is integral to his central theme of God the Father's salvation through Christ. By that salvation sinners are justified and thereby reconciled and adopted as God's sons and daughters.

5:19 ὡς ὅτι θεὸς ἦν ἐν Χριστῷ κόσμον καταλλάσσων ἑαυτῷ. "To the effect that God was in Christ, reconciling the world to himself." The combination ὡς ὅτι has been understood in three basic ways:

(1) as comparative: "as (it is indeed certain), that . . ."[101] with ὅτι sometimes thought to introduce a quotation;[102]
(2) as causal, with ὡς ὅτι equivalent to ὅτι: "because";[103]

---

96. See Hofius ("Erwägungen" 196-99) for the possible background of this conjunction in Isa. 52:13–53:12 (the Servant's role) and Isa. 52:6-10 (the proclaimer's role).

97. Cf. G. Bornkamm, *TDNT* 6.682.

98. But see Bieringer in Bieringer and Lambrecht 426-27. On the term διακονία, see Bieringer in Bierenger and Lambrecht 413-21.

99. Käsemann, "Reconciliation" 49-64, especially 52.

100. E.g., Fitzmyer, "Reconciliation" 172-73, 184-85 n. 44; F. Büchsel, *TDNT* 1.257-58.

101. Wolff 161; similarly Thrall 400, 432.

102. Collange 270; Furnish 306, 317-18 ("As it is said:"). Accepting Furnish's rendering, although not his suggestion that v. 19a, b is a citation of a traditional formulation (Furnish 334), Thrall paraphrases ὡς ὅτι by "Similarly (so one might put it)" (432).

103. Lang 294, 301; cf. Robertson 963-64 (but cf. his *Pictures* 232, "how that"); Meyer 536 ("because, indeed," "as it is the case, because"). The Vulgate has *quoniam quidem,* "since indeed." See also Esth. 4:14. Kim regards 5:19a, b (ὡς . . . αὐτῶν) as a Pauline parenthesis that states the ground (ὡς ὅτι) for v. 18 ("Reconciliation" 367).

(3) as epexegetic: "namely, that" (NASB; similarly Bultmann 161 n. 167), "that" (NIV), "that is" (RSV, NRSV),[104] "how" (Goodspeed), "to the effect that" (Turner 137), "What I mean is, that" (NEB).[105]

In Paul's other two uses of ὡς ὅτι (11:21; 2 Thess. 2:2), the particle ὡς could express the falsity of the following assertion (Vulgate *quasi,* "as though"), but this is certainly not the case in 5:19a and in these three instances ὡς ὅτι probably means either "that" (11:21) or "to the effect that" (5:19; 2 Thess. 2:2). Nor is it clear that the expression is elliptical or the pointer to a citation. And, given the similarities between v. 19 and v. 18 it is simplest to take ὡς ὅτι as restating, rather than grounding, the thought of v. 18. Thus option (3) is to be preferred.

Since it would be awkward, if not illogical, to translate θεὸς ἦν ἐν Χριστῷ κόσμον καταλλάσσων ἑαυτῷ by "God was reconciling to himself the world that is in Christ" (which, in any case, would require (τὸν) κόσμον τὸν ἐν Χριστῷ or τὸν ἐν Χριστῷ κόσμον),[106] there remain three viable translational alternatives:[107]

(1) "It was God who in Christ was reconciling the world to himself" (Barrett),[108] or "God was near at hand, to reconcile the world to himself in Christ."[109] It does not follow that because θεός is anarthrous, it must be predicative;[110] it is probably anarthrous because it is emphatic — "God and no other" (cf. v. 18a), "even God," "Yes, God" (Cassirer), or "God as he is in himself."[111] Moreover, since θεὸς ἦν could naturally be construed with either ἐν Χριστῷ or καταλλάσσων, it is unlikely that θεὸς ἦν is independent. And θεὸς ἦν ὁ . . . καταλλάσσων would be the normal Greek behind these two translations.[112]

(2) "In Christ God was reconciling the world to himself,"[113] or "God, through Christ, was reconciling the world to Himself."[114] These renderings take

104. Cf. Bieringer in Bieringer and Lambrecht 457 ("das heist"), 433-37.

105. In later Greek ὡς ὅτι = ὅτι, "that" (Moulton 212; MM 463d, 703b; cf. BDF §396).

106. This interpretation would require not only a different word order but also νῦν before ἐν Χριστῷ.

107. For a review of the exegesis of 5:19a, see Bieringer in Bieringer and Lambrecht 437-45 (with a chart on 437).

108. Barrett 162, 177; similarly BAGD 589b; Prümm II/1.316, 342.

109. Bieringer in Bieringer and Lambrecht 457; similarly Lietzmann 126; Dinkler, "Verkündigung" 177; Klauck 55.

110. *Pace* E. Stauffer, *TDNT* 3.103 n. 253.

111. Phil. 2:13 is the only other clear NT instance of an anarthrous θεός as subject with εἶναι expressed; in Rom. 8:33b and 1 Thess. 2:5, εἶναι is unexpressed (see Harris, *Jesus* 32, 34).

112. Cf. Hofius, "2 Kor 5,19" 7 n. 19.

113. Thus RSV mg.; NRSV; Martin 135; similarly TCNT, Weymouth, Moffatt, JB, NAB[1,2], NIV; Plummer 183 (but cf. 165); Wendland 201; Furnish, 306; Young and Ford 267; Breytenbach 111; Thrall 400, 433, who takes ἐν Χριστῷ to mean "in the personal destiny of Christ as representative *man*" (434).

114. Barclay; similarly Goodspeed, Williams, GNB, Cassirer.

ἦν . . . καταλλάσσων as a periphrastic imperfect "marking the process of reconciliation"[115] or its incompleteness, or standing for an aorist[116] (κατήλλαξεν), and ἐν Χριστῷ as either locatival ("in Christ") or instrumental ("through Christ").

(3) "God was in Christ, reconciling the world to himself,"[117] or "God was in Christ reconciling the world to himself" (RSV).[118] Here there is no periphrastic construction, ἐν Χριστῷ is an adverbial predicate, and καταλλάσσων is temporally undefined, being less verbal than adjectival in import (almost = "as a reconciler").

Nothing in the immediate context, it would appear, demands that any of the renderings under (2) and (3) be excluded as inappropriate, and each embodies a typically Pauline sentiment, that is, either that it was in or through Christ that God effected reconciliation (Rom. 5:10-11; 2 Cor. 5:18; Col. 1:19-20, 22) or that God was present in Christ (e.g., Col. 1:19; 2:9) and reconciled humans or the universe (e.g., Eph. 2:16; Col. 1:20).

But there are some five considerations that weight the scales in favor of the first translation given under (3). First, the periphrastic imperfect construction is infrequent in the Pauline corpus (only three instances — Gal. 1:22-23; Phil. 2:26)[119] and no words (other than the inconsequential δέ in Gal. 1:22) intervene between the copula and the participle. Second, with regard to non-Pauline uses of the periphrastic imperfect, where words are found between the copula and participle (5 instances),[120] (a) in only one case (Acts 19:14) does the participle govern a direct object (cf. κόσμον in 2 Cor. 5:19), and then it is the colorless τοῦτο; and (b) the intervening words should be construed with the copula when they can be (as in Acts 11:5; 19:14[121]); θεὸς ἦν ἐν Χριστῷ as a

115. Vincent 824, who adds that "God was engaged in reconciling the world from the beginning, and that in Christ."

116. Collange 271 and n. 2, followed by Thrall 434. Rebell actually translates ἦν . . . καταλλάσσων by "hat . . . versöhnt" (73, 97).

117. Similarly KJV; Windisch 193; Hughes 208; de Boor 130; Carrez 152; Lang 294; Hofius, "Erwägungen" 187; "2 Kor 5,19" 19 and n. 19.

118. Also RV, NEB, NJB, REB, NRSV mg.; similarly Weymouth, Montgomery, Berkeley, NASB; Conybeare in Conybeare and Howson 449-50. It is impossible to know whether these translations have sought to create an ambiguity in meaning by omitting a comma after "Christ"; all the translators would have known of the KJV comma. But at least in the case of the RSV, NEB, and REB, where the alternative marginal rendering gives the opposite view ("in Christ God was reconciling" in RSV, "God was reconciling the world to himself by Christ" in NEB and REB), one may assume that the translation in the text should be read in the KJV sense; but conceivably, some of these translations may be trying to reproduce an ambiguity they believe Paul intended.

119. In Tit. 3:3 the present participles πλανώμενοι, δουλεύοντες, διάγοντες, and μισοῦντες clearly function as adjectives in conjunction with ἀνόητοι, ἀπειθεῖς, and στυγητοί, all of which are dependent on ἦμεν.

120. Acts 2:5; 10:30; 11:5; 16:12; 19:14.

121. Cf. Weymouth: "While I was (ἐγὼ ἤμην) in the town of Jaffa, offering prayer

thought-unit is certainly not incomprehensible.[122] Third, elsewhere when Paul uses the verb καταλλάσσειν and specifies Christ as God's agent in effecting reconciliation, the διά phrase employed to express the latter idea either precedes (as in Col. 1:20; cf. Rom. 5:11) or follows (as in Rom. 5:10; 2 Cor. 5:18; cf. Col. 1:22) the fixed order: verb (καταλλάσσειν) — object(s) of reconciliation — goal of reconciliation. This might lead us to expect, if ἐν Χριστῷ in v. 19 specified or implied agency and ἦν . . . καταλλάσσων were a periphrastic imperfect, that ἐν Χριστῷ would precede θεός or follow ἑαυτῷ (although, on any view, κόσμον is not in its normal position). That is, ἐν Χριστῷ would be likely to be placed outside the verbal unit ἦν . . . καταλλάσσων. Fourth, it would be repetitious to have the notion of agency expressed twice (if ἐν Χριστῷ is merely a stylistic variant of διὰ Χριστοῦ[123]) within one sentence (in Greek), although if ἐν Χριστῷ = "in and through Christ"[124] this difficulty is partially relieved. Fifth, so far from being an impossible sentiment,[125] the idea of God's being present and active in Christ through whom he (God) effected reconciliation accords with Paul's conviction of the essential link between the person and the work of Christ.[126]

On this view θεὸς ἦν ἐν Χριστῷ does not refer to the incarnation[127] — ἦν is not to be equated with ἐσκήνωσεν, "took up residence" — but refers either to the entire life of Christ on earth, or (less probably) to that particular time when reconciliation was being achieved,[128] without implying that God is not "in Christ" presently (cf. John 17:21) or that God was not present and active in Christ before the passion.[129] Perhaps ἦν and καταλλάσσων are related as expressing something akin to cause and effect: it was only because God in all his fullness had chosen to dwell in Christ (Col. 1:19), only because there dwelt embodied in Christ the total plenitude of deity (Col. 2:9), that reconciliation was

---

(προσευχόμενος)" (Acts 11:5); "there were (ἦσαν) seven sons of one Sceva, a Jew of high priestly family, who were doing (ποιοῦντες) this" (Acts 19:14).

122. These first two arguments are refinements of one part of my view expressed in "Prepositions" 1192-93, which was critiqued by Porter, Καταλλάσσω 133-35.

123. As BAGD 414a; Lietzmann 126; Dinkler, "Verkündigung" 177; Porter, Καταλλάσσω 135.

124. Cf. Romaniuk 257; Bieringer in Bieringer and Lambrecht 457.

125. "For Paul . . . the εἶναι of God ἐν Χριστῷ is an inconceivable idea" (Bultmann 161).

126. Collange (271) argues that the symmetry between the three participles, καταλλάσσων, λογιζόμενος, and θέμενος supports view (3), but this argument is weak, for the second and third could very suitably define what was involved in the process of reconciliation (see Porter, Καταλλάσσω 135).

127. Cf. Bruce 209: "Paul is not here combining with his statement about reconciliation a statement about the incarnation."

128. For the latter view, see de Boor 140-41; Lang 301-2.

129. To treat ἦν as an independent verb avoids any need to explain the change from the aorist participle (καταλλάξαντος) in v. 18 to the (ex hypothesi) periphrastic imperfect in v. 19 in describing the identical act of reconciliation. Note, for example, Bruce's somewhat strained explanation (209): "The periphrastic construction emphasizes the imperfect or continuous aspect of the verb; only with the response of faith can the aorist tense be used as in verse 18."

accomplished. A functional christology presupposes, and finds its ultimate basis in, an ontological christology.[130] Not only was Christ God's agent in effecting reconciliation (Rom. 5:10-11; 2 Cor. 5:18; Col. 1:19-22); he also mediated the divine presence, thus giving validity to his reconciliatory sacrifice. God was in Christ and therefore acted through Christ (cf. John 14:10b, "the Father who dwells in me does his works"). Paul here alludes to Christ as the focus of divine revelation ("God was in Christ") and therefore as the means of divine redemption ("reconciling the world to himself"; cf. v. 18).[131] In the expression "God was in Christ" there is also implied an identity between the redemptive action of Christ and that of God. *Ubi Christus, ibi Deus,* "where Christ is (active), there God is (active)."

If κόσμος here refers to the totality of creation (e.g., Rom. 1:20; 1 Cor. 3:22), it is equivalent to τὰ πάντα in Col. 1:20, which also is the object of the verb καταλλάσσειν. "All things in heaven and on earth," which were created by Christ (Col. 1:16), were also reconciled through him (Col. 1:20), including the rebellious ἀρχαὶ καὶ ἐξουσίαι ("powers and authorities" — cf. Col. 1:16; 2:15). But Paul can also use κόσμος of the world of human beings (e.g., 1:12; Rom. 3:6; 5:12-13),[132] a sense that seems demanded here[133] by the αὐτοῖς and αὐτῶν that follow (in a *constructio ad sensum*) and by the reference to παραπτώματα.[134] The movement from ἡμᾶς (v. 18) to κόσμον (v. 19) with regard to the objects of reconciliation is not a movement from the anthropological to the cosmological,[135] but from the narrower to the wider anthropological focus.

μὴ λογιζόμενος αὐτοῖς τὰ παραπτώματα αὐτῶν, καὶ θέμενος ἐν ἡμῖν τὸν λόγον τῆς καταλλαγῆς. "Not holding people's transgressions against them. And he entrusted to us this message of reconciliation." The two participles (λογιζόμενος and θέμενος) are probably not periphrastic, with ἦν implied from v. 19a (as Bernard 72), for that would tend to make the achieving of reconcilia-

---

130. Cf. Col. 2:9-10, where there is a similar movement from ontological to functional christology. It is only because the total plenitude of deity resides in Christ (Col. 2:9) that the Colossians (and all believers) have their completeness in and through him (Col. 2:10). But against such an understanding of 5:19a, see Bieringer in Bieringer and Lambrecht 439-40.

131. Such an understanding of v. 19a does not convert a soteriological statement into a revelatory one (as Martin 154 alleges). The whole context is undoubtedly focused on soteriology, but if an explicit connection between the person and work of Christ is made in v. 19a, this does not compromise the soteriological focus.

132. Gal. 6:14 is a parallel for an anarthrous but definite use of κόσμος. On the use of κόσμος in Greek literature (including the LXX), see Adams 42-77.

133. So also I. H. Marshall 123; Adams 235; and especially Hofius, "2 Kor 5,19" 8 n. 23; and Bieringer in Bieringer and Lambrecht 447-51, 457.

134. According to Martin (140, 150, 153; *Reconciliation* 93-97, 106-7, 109-10), the *Vorlage* of 5:18-21, "a carefully prepared piece of soteriological credo" (*Reconciliation* 94), spoke of cosmic restoration, but Paul applied it to the Corinthian situation by adding v. 19b (μὴ λογιζόμενος αὐτοῖς τὰ παραπτώματα αὐτῶν), which locates reconciliation in forgiveness and in interpersonal relations, and v. 20c (δεόμεθα ὑπὲρ Χριστοῦ, καταλλάγητε τῷ θεῷ), which is a pastoral plea for the Corinthians to accept his God-given authority.

135. As Fitzmyer, "Reconciliation" 169, 185 n. 48.

tion by the death of Christ and the granting of forgiveness based on that death contemporaneous actions (ἦν with two present participles) and the entrusting of the message of reconciliation an illogical antecedent action (ἦν with the aorist participle, "and he had entrusted").[136] Rather, these two participles state two implications or consequences of reconciliation,[137] the first (forgiveness) being related to humans in general (αὐτοῖς . . . αὐτῶν = κόσμον, v. 19a), the second (proclamation) being related to Paul and his colleagues in particular (ἐν ἡμῖν).

λογίζομαι τί τινι, an accountant's expression meaning "put something down on someone's account," came to be used in a pejorative sense, "count/hold something against someone." παράπτωμα, originally a falling beside (from παρά and πίπτω) or away, a slip or lapse, also denotes a stepping across or beyond (παρά) some limit or boundary; hence a trespass and then a transgression or sin. παραπτώματα in v. 19 and ἁμαρτία in v. 21 refer to the same entities.[138] As a result of the reconciliation achieved by Christ's "becoming sin" (v. 21), God no longer[139] debits believers' accounts with a listing of their trespasses. This non-imputation of sin ("not holding people's transgressions against[140] them") is perhaps the closest Paul or any NT writer comes to defining forgiveness.[141] Certainly forgiveness does not mean that "when God forgives, he forgets," as is so often asserted, for however this divine "forgetting" is defined, it compromises his omniscience. Rather, when God forgives our sins, he chooses not to reckon them against us. When God forgives, he does not forget, but chooses not to "remember." One of the distinctive features of the new covenant of Jeremiah 31 is the divine promise, "I will forgive their wickedness and will remember their sins no more" (Jer. 31:34; cf. Heb. 8:12-13), where the synonymous parallelism indicates that God's forgiving is his "no-longer-remembering." As well as having this new covenant passage in Jeremiah in mind, Paul undoubtedly was thinking of Ps. 31:2 (LXX), μακάριος ἀνήρ, οὗ οὐ μὴ λογίσηται κύριος ἁμαρτίαν, "Happy is the man to whom the Lord does not reckon sin," a passage he cites and comments on (using λογίζομαι as his verbal link) in Rom. 4:3-8.

136. Luke 23:19 would seem to be the only clear NT use of ἦν with the aorist participle (see Burton §20; but Turner 89 allows ἦν θέμενος in our passage).

137. Plummer (165, 184) regards these two participles as modal: "by not reckoning . . . , and by having deposited . . ." (184). But it is more satisfactory to regard the participles as expressing two distinct results of reconciliation, and (with Hofius, "2 Kor 5, 19" 7 and many EVV) to treat the aorist participle θέμενος as equivalent to the finite verb ἔθετο, "he entrusted."

138. See Bultmann 162 and M. Wolter, *EDNT* 3.33-34 on the relation between παράπτωμα and ἁμαρτία.

139. It is probable that μή implies μηκέτι ("no longer," thus NEB, REB), as in 1:9, for there was a time, before their conversion, when God did reckon the trespasses of people against them (Rom. 3:19, 23). Note also οὐ μὴ . . . ἔτι, "no more" in a similar context in Heb. 8:12 (citing Jer. 38:34, LXX).

140. αὐτοῖς is a "dative of disadvantage." It is not simply the case that "he [God] did not keep their sins in mind" (Louw and Nida §29.4; similarly GNB).

141. "In its content, the μὴ λογιζόμενος αὐτοῖς τὰ παραπτώματα αὐτῶν corresponds to the ἀφιέναι τὰς ἁμαρτίας" (Bultmann 162).

θέμενος ἐν ἡμῖν is probably a stylistic variant of δόντος ἡμῖν (v. 18), thus "he entrusted to us," with θέμενος the equivalent of a finite verb (ἔθετο) and ἐν ἡμῖν = εἰς ἡμᾶς = ἡμῖν. Alternatively, the phrase may mean "he placed in our hands/care/mouth/heart,"[142] or even "he has established among us" (Furnish 306). Several translations link the phrase with ὡς ὅτι, which results in the sense, "I mean that God . . . , and that he has entrusted . . ." (NAB).[143] τὸν λόγον τῆς καταλλαγῆς is clearly parallel to διακονίαν τῆς καταλλαγῆς (v. 18). The ministry is the proclamation of the message. Whether God is said to "give the ministry of reconciliation" (v. 18) or "to entrust the message of reconciliation" (v. 19) to Paul and others,[144] the emphasis is on the privilege and obligation of the task of proclaiming that reconciliation. "λόγος is the message which the διάκονος (minister) proclaims by word but no less by his whole existence."[145] The genitive τῆς καταλλαγῆς may be classified in the same ways as in v. 18 (see above). Here, too, it is probably an objective genitive: "(the ministry) that proclaims reconciliation."

This verse, then, identifies Christ as the person in whom God is revealed (v. 19a) and through whom God effects reconciliation (v. 19b), a reconciliation that results in the forgiveness of sins (v. 19c) and the preaching of the cross (v. 19d).

5:20 ὑπὲρ Χριστοῦ οὖν πρεσβεύομεν ὡς τοῦ θεοῦ παρακαλοῦντος δι᾽ ἡμῶν· "We are therefore ambassadors for Christ, since God does in fact make his appeal through us." πρεσβεύειν means "to be/work as an ambassador," or more broadly, "to function as a representative of a ruling authority" (Louw and Nida §37.88). It was used of the emperor's legates[146] and of embassies between towns.[147] The corresponding NT noun, πρεσβεία, refers to an "embassy" or "delegation"; or, as an abstract for a concrete noun, "ambassador(s)" (Luke 14:32; 19:14).[148] To be an ambassador in the ancient world (Greek, Roman, or Jewish), as in modern times, involved three things: (1) a commissioning for a special assignment; (2) representing the sender; and (3) exercising the authority of the sender. It was universally expected that an ambassador, whatever his message and however delicate or risky his mission, would be treated with respect and dignity, accorded appropriate hospitality, and guaranteed a safe exit. There was what Philo calls a "law with regard to ambassadors" (*De Vita Mosis*

---

142. Wolff, "Knowledge" 94: "the message entrusted to him has grasped his entire inward being."

143. Similarly TCNT, Weymouth, Montgomery, NEB.

144. The primary reference in ἡμῖν is probably to Paul and his colleagues, but Wolff ("Knowledge" 94) restricts it to Paul himself, while Windisch (194) and Hanson (*Ministry* 80-81) relate it to all believers.

145. Lambrecht, "Reading" 185.

146. Deissmann, *Light* 378-79.

147. MM 534d.

148. The expression πρεσβεύειν πρεσβείαν means "to travel as an ambassador." Ignatius affirms that it is appropriate for the church in Philadelphia to appoint a deacon to travel to the church in Syrian Antioch "as God's ambassador" (θεοῦ πρεσβείαν; *Philippians* 10.1).

1.25), for the envoy represented the messenger and acted on his behalf and in his place, thus embodying his authority. To disregard or insult the envoy was to disregard or insult the sender.[149]

In saying ὑπὲρ Χριστοῦ . . . πρεσβεύομεν Paul is asserting more than the simple fact that he is "Christ's ambassador" (which would be Χριστοῦ πρεσβεία/πρεσβευτής ἐσμεν). As an ambassador he worked both "on behalf of Christ" and "in the place of Christ." That is, there is no need here to choose between the notions of representation and substitution for ὑπέρ; both concepts are present,[150] given the use of ὑπέρ in v. 14 (see above) and its association here with πρεσβεύειν.[151] Not only in the words he spoke but also in his whole life Paul was acting in Christ's name and place. His status was not dependent on the Corinthians to whom he had been sent but on Christ who had sent him (cf. 1:1). This intimate link between agent and principal is encapsulated in the aphorism of Rabbinic Judaism, "the one who is sent is as the one who sent him," "a man's agent is as the man himself."[152] Paul's ambassadorial role was grounded (οὖν) on the divine act of reconciliation (v. 18a) and the institution of the ministry of reconciliation (vv. 18b, 19c). But Furnish (338) sees οὖν as also linking the section 2:14–5:19 with 5:20–9:15. In acting as an ambassador for Christ Paul believed that he was simultaneously God's mouthpiece: "in the conviction that (ὡς) God does in fact make his appeal through us." When ὡς is followed by the genitive absolute construction, it expresses "subjective motivation" (BDF §425[3]), and, depending on the context, may refer either to mere supposition ("as though," "on the pretext that")[153] or to actual fact ("since," "in the conviction that").[154] In the present case Paul is speaking of an undeniable fact, not an inaccurate assumption. So the sense is not "God, as it were, appealing to you through us" (TCNT),[155] but "with the confidence that God himself makes his appeal through us."[156] 1 Thess. 2:13 expresses a similar sentiment. The Thessalonians had accepted the word of God as spoken by Paul "not as the word of mere human beings but as what it really is (καθώς ἐστιν ἀληθῶς) — the

149. See further Mitchell 644-51 and Garland 295-98.

150. So also Winer, "in his name and behalf (consequently, in his stead)" (384).

151. The substitutionary sense of ὑπέρ here is recognized by Prümm 1.345; Zerwick §91; *Analysis* 400; Klauck 56; Carrez 153 (among others). But in Eph. 6:20, where Paul says he is an ambassador in chains (πρεσβεύω ἐν ἁλύσει) "for the sake of" the gospel, ὑπέρ denotes representation, clearly not substitution.

152. *m. Berakoth* 5.5. See further SB 3.2; K. H. Rengstorf, *TDNT* 1.414-16.

153. E.g., 1 Cor. 4:18; 1 Pet. 4:12; cf. Acts 27:30 (προφάσει ὡς).

154. E.g., 2 Pet. 1:3.

155. But the concessive sense ("as though," "as if," "as it were") need not involve pure supposition. For example, Robertson supports a concessive meaning (1140) but later notes that "Paul endorses the notion that he is an ambassador of God and ὡς is not to be interpreted as mere pretence" (1141); similarly, Lambrecht 99 (but cf. his earlier "Reading" 185 ["since"]).

156. Similarly, Martin, *Reconciliation* 107; Collange 274; Wolff, "Knowledge" 95; Thrall 437 ("certain that"). Some interpreters move beyond "subjective motivation" to causation: "seeing that" (Plummer 185; Spicq 1.193 n. 25; Goodspeed), "since" (NRSV).

word of God." δι' ἡμῶν, "through us" (= by our mouth/words), certainly includes Paul and his fellow apostles but probably also all proclaimers of reconciliation. Whoever declares "the message of reconciliation" (v. 19) is both a delegated representative of Christ and an actual spokesperson for God. But for all their exalted status, such persons are not plenipotentiaries; they have not been invested with the full power of independent action, for they deliver rather than create the message and lack any authority to alter that message.

δεόμεθα ὑπὲρ Χριστοῦ, καταλλάγητε τῷ θεῷ. "On Christ's behalf we make this entreaty: 'Get reconciled to God!'" There may be no distinction between the two verbs of entreaty found in v. 20 (see 8:4), but if Paul intends any distinction, παρακαλέω may be seen as more personal and δέομαι more formal.[157] But here neither verb denotes a dispassionate and detached request but rather an impassioned and urgent entreaty. The second use of ὑπὲρ Χριστοῦ links the δέησις with the ambassadorship: whether performing the general role of envoys (πρεσβεύομεν) or issuing a specific entreaty (δεόμεθα), Paul and his colleagues were acting ὑπὲρ Χριστοῦ, "for Christ," on his behalf and in his stead. Moreover, this repeated prepositional phrase suggests that the principal role of Christ's ambassadors is issuing the evangelistic treaty to be reconciled to God. Nor should we distinguish the παράκλησις from the δέησις; God's pleading through Paul may be identified with Paul's entreaty on behalf of Christ. The aorist imperative passive form καταλλάγητε is unlikely to be a reflexive passive, "reconcile yourselves (to God),"[158] whatever allowance be made for synergism (cf. 6:1-2), because whenever this verb is applied to the atonement, God, and only God, is the reconciler (see above on v. 18).[159] While it is possible that this passive is permissive, "let yourselves be reconciled (to God),"[160] it is more probably a true passive, "be reconciled,"[161] or, to bring out the ingressive sense of this aorist, "get reconciled," with God as the implied agent. But a pressing question remains: To whom is this imperative addressed? Three answers have been given.

1. *Unbelievers* within, or at least associated with, the Corinthian church. 1 Cor. 14:23-24 makes it clear that "unbelieving outsiders" (ἰδιῶται ἢ ἄπιστοι) sometimes attended the Corinthian assembly. But Paul gives no indication that he is directing the entreaty of v. 20b to a minority at Corinth (such as the τινες of 10:2).

2. *Corinthian believers* in general, or at least those Corinthians who were still antagonistic to Paul. According to Martin, Paul "has taken language more germane to a call to unbelievers and has applied it to the strained relationships

---

157. See Mullins, "Petition" 46-54; "Formulas" 380-90; MM.

158. As Carrez (153-54) and Lambrecht (100, 106; "Reading" 188-89) propose.

159. It is this point that invalidates Lambrecht's appeal (100) to the passive forms of καταλλάσσω in Matt. 5:24 and 1 Cor. 7:11.

160. Thus Lietzmann 126; Zerwick, *Analysis,* 400; Dinkler, "Verkündigung" 179; Wolff 116.

161. So also Thrall, "Salvation" 231 n. 12.

with the church by calling on them to accept his God-given authority implicit in his apostolic office (2 Cor. 10:8; 13:10-11) and to return to his side as children to a grieved father."[162] Martin regards this imperative as a fresh application and adaptation of the apostolic kerygma that focuses on reconciliation (150-51, 155-56). Against this general view, which has been espoused by several recent commentators,[163] we may make the following observations: (a) There is no ὑμῶν with δεόμεθα (compare 6:1, παρακαλοῦμεν . . . ὑμᾶς).[164] (b) If δι' ἡμῶν includes other persons in addition to Paul, the following plural (δεόμεθα) can hardly be restricted to Paul and his particular pastoral situation. (c) At Corinth reconciliation to God and reconciliation to Paul might have been inseparable, as Martin alleges, but the two ideas are distinct, being related as cause and effect. (d) To paraphrase "Be reconciled to God" as "Let your reconciliation be effectual"[165] or "Live as reconciled people"[166] is to confuse the vertical and horizontal aspects of Christian reconciliation. Certainly there is no reason to imagine that Paul could envisage any believers experiencing a second or renewed reconciliation *to God* comparable in significance and effect to the first that they had experienced at conversion.

3. *Any evangelistic audience* that Paul and others might address in their capacity as ambassadors of Christ.[167] On this view, which is to be preferred, καταλλάγητε τῷ θεῷ (v. 20d) defines the preceding δέησις ἡ ὑπὲρ Χριστοῦ (v. 20c), is the essence of God's παράκλησις (v. 20b), and summarizes ὁ λόγος τῆς καταλλαγῆς (v. 19d). Support for this interpretation is as follows.

(a) It construes καταλλάσσω in its distinctive soteriological sense in Paul, so that the imperative "Get reconciled to God" encapsulates the kerygma itself rather than being an application or extension of the kerygma.

(b) It accords well with the context. This apostolic command defines the apostolic entreaty (v. 20c) and forms a natural transition to v. 21 with its description of the divine action that provided the ground for reconciliation.

(c) There is no ὑμῶν with δεόμεθα nor ὑμᾶς with παρακαλοῦντος. Only at 6:1 does Paul direct his entreaty explicitly to the Corinthians (see also 6:11, 13); in vv. 14-21 we find no form of ὑμεῖς.

(d) 5:11 forms a close parallel to v. 20d. "We try to persuade people (ἀνθρώπους)," principally of the truth of the gospel, or "to be reconciled to God."

---

162. *Reconciliation* 109.

163. Lambrecht 100 (the appeal of v. 20 is the center and focus of vv. 14-21); Barnett 310 n. 44, 311-12; Garland 298-300. Also Beale (556-57), although he allows that "Paul may well be exhorting believers to live according to their calling of reconciliation and for unbelievers to accept this calling" (557 n. 1).

164. Also in 10:2 δέομαι is found without an expressed object but there the implied ὑμῶν could refer only to the Corinthians.

165. Barrett (under "Discussions") in Lambrecht, "Reading" 209.

166. This is the import of Hanson's view (*Ministry* 82-83).

167. καταλλάγητε τῷ θεῷ "is the apostle's summons to the as yet unconverted world" (Windisch 196); similarly Meyer 539; Köstenberger 328-31.

If the main task of Christ's envoys is to implore people to become reconciled to God,[168] there must be a sense in which reconciliation is an ongoing process, just as vv. 18-19 present reconciliation as an accomplished fact.[169] In the divine economy, the declaration of "the message of reconciliation" (v. 19), or, in other words, the preaching of the cross of Christ (1 Cor. 1:18, 23) with the attendant entreaty to be reconciled to God, is the link between the objective work of reconciliation accomplished by Christ and the subjective appropriation of its benefits by the sinner. Paul saw himself and everyone who proclaims reconciliation in Christ as trustees of a message (v. 19), ambassadors for Christ, and mouthpieces for God (v. 20). As such they enjoy incomparable dignity, yet their task is the lowly one of παράκλησις and δέησις. This simultaneous conjunction of dignity and humility forms an exquisite paradox first exemplified in the person and ministry of Christ.

5:21 τὸν μὴ γνόντα ἁμαρτίαν ὑπὲρ ἡμῶν ἁμαρτίαν ἐποίησεν. "For God caused Christ, who knew nothing of sin, to be sin for our sake."[170] The two ways of viewing the structure of the whole verse may be set out diagrammatically as follows:

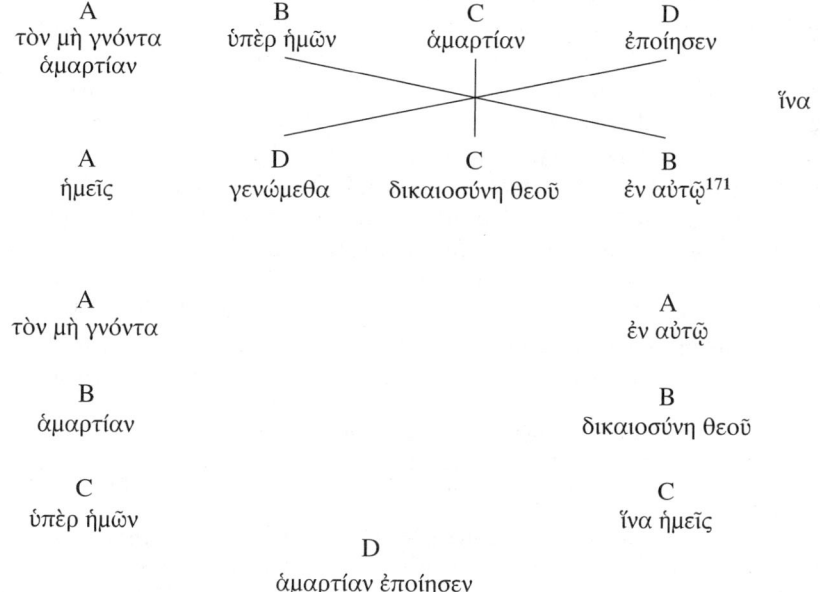

168. Thüsing (106-7) makes a series of interesting equations: living for Christ (v. 15) = being governed and compelled by Christ's love (v. 14) = carrying out the work of directing people back to God (v. 20) = living for God (Rom. 6:11).

169. Cf. Schütz (181): "The gospel is the extension of the Christ-event."

170. For the history of the interpretation of this verse, see Gloer 95-107; Sabourin in Lyonnet and Sabourin 185-289, especially 250-53; and for a comprehensive classification of views on the meaning of ἁμαρτίαν ἐποίησεν, Bieringer in Bieringer and Lambrecht 473-95 (chart on p. 495).

171. Cf. Barrett 179.

In the former case, the chiasm is imperfect ABCD/ADCB; in the latter, it is complete, ABCDCBA, and the focal point is ἁμαρτίαν ἐποίησεν.

The absence of a connective particle (= asyndeton) (contrast the verses that precede and follow) adds solemnity to the words of v. 21 and draws attention to their significance. Several statements in the immediate context may have prompted v. 21: the repeated affirmation that Christ "died for all" (ὑπὲρ πάντων ἀπέθανεν, vv. 14b, 15a; similarly v. 15b) led Paul to explain how humans benefited (cf. ὑπὲρ ἡμῶν, v. 21a) from Christ's death; v. 21 expands on "all this comes from God" and "through Christ" in v. 18; the reference to God's non-imputation of trespasses to believers (v. 19) naturally reminded Paul of God's "imputation" of human sin to Christ (v. 21a); the evangelistic watch cry, "Be reconciled to God" (v. 20), led the apostle to specify the basis (v. 21a) and the result (v. 21b) of reconciliation. Whether we focus on one or on all of these preceding statements, there can be little doubt that v. 21 arises naturally from the context and coheres with it.

Behind the Greek verb γινώσκειν here lies the Hebrew verb *yāda'*, "have personal acquaintance or experience with." The close parallel in Rom. 7:7 (γνῶναι ἁμαρτίαν) also suggests that where γινώσκειν is followed by ἁμαρτία as a direct object, it denotes knowledge gained by personal participation, as generally in Classical Greek usage (see on 5:16).[172] Although Christ was aware of the reality of sin and observed sin in others (cf. Heb. 12:3), he himself, Paul affirms, never had personal involvement in sin. The expression ὁ μὴ γνοὺς ἁμαρτίαν means "he who never knew sin" (TCNT), "the sinless one" (JB), with μὴ signifying "not (ever)" = "never,"[173] and the articular aorist participle being timeless[174] so that one cannot exclude either the pre-existence or the earthly life of Jesus from the "time" of the sinlessness.[175] Yet Paul's main focus is on Christ's freedom from sin as a human being during his whole earthly life, rather than on his pre-incarnate sinlessness. Neither outwardly in act nor inwardly in attitude did Christ sin, and at no time was his conscience stained by sin. This is

172. In this verse the use of γινώσκειν rather than εἰδέναι is in itself insignificant, since ᾔδειν (pluperfect with imperfect meaning) is the only past tense of οἶδα.

173. It is sometimes asserted that μή points to a subjective appraisal on the part of God (as the implied subject of ἐποίησεν). "The sinlessness of Jesus was present to the consciousness *of God,* when He made Him to be sin" (Meyer 539; similarly Bernard 73). "The μὴ γν. carries us back to the conception of him [God] who makes him ἁμαρτία; τὸν οὐ γνόντα would be objective and equivalent to τὸν ἀγνοοῦντα" (Winer 484). But this is to overlook the fact that μή is the usual particle that negates participles in Hellenistic Greek, so that the Classical Greek distinction between οὐ and μή (with the latter signifying a subjective assessment) should not be pressed. That is, τὸν μὴ γνόντα simply states the bald fact that Jesus was a complete stranger to sin. What Meyer says is doubtless true, but its truth does not rest on the use of μή. In any case, γνόντα is participial only in form; with the article it functions as a substantive.

174. It is the articular state of γνόντα that makes it inappropriate to attach the idea of causation ("since he did not know sin") or of concession ("though . . .") to this participle.

175. For the view that τὸν μὴ γνόντα ἁμαρτίαν refers only to Christ's preexistence, see Branick 246-62. For the view that it means that "Christ gave no recognition to the power of sin," see Grayston 62.

Paul's only explicit affirmation of Christ's sinlessness, although if the "obedience" of Christ mentioned in Rom. 5:19 and Phil. 2:8 refers to "Christ's perfect fulfillment of God's righteous requirements,"[176] then these two verses imply that Christ was without sin. In its testimony to the sinlessness of Jesus, the NT is uniform.[177]

With the next phrase, "he [God] made himself [Christ] to be sin," we penetrate to the center of the atonement and stand in awe before one of the most profound mysteries in the universe. All the interpretations of the phrase have in common the idea of identification, the understanding that God caused Christ to be identified in some way with what was foreign to his experience, namely human sin. ἐποίησεν is here used with a double accusative, one a direct object (τὸν μὴ γνόντα), the other a predicate (ἁμαρτίαν). Although ποιεῖν τι can mean "make something into something (else),"[178] the meaning here is not "God made the sinless one into sin" (JB[179]), but "God *caused* the sinless one *to be* sin," where ποιεῖν denotes causation or appointment[180] and points to the divine initiative. But we should not forget that matching the Father's set purpose to deliver Christ up to deal with sin (Acts 2:23; Rom. 8:32) was Christ's own firm resolution to go to Jerusalem to suffer (Mark 8:31; Luke 9:51). Jesus was not an unwilling or surprised participant in God's action.

But when did this identification of Christ with sin take place? There are two options — the incarnation (sometimes including the whole earthly life of Jesus) and the crucifixion.[181] In either case ἐποίησεν points to an action that was specific and limited in time. On the incarnational view, God identified Christ with sin when Christ assumed a human nature that was subject to the consequences of sin, viz. suffering and death; in other words, when he gained at the incarnation "a body characterized by death" (Rom. 7:24). This approach is probably reflected in NEB ("God made him one with the sinfulness of man") and GNB ("God made him share our sin"),[182] and is not without its defenders.[183] Support for this position is often found in Rom. 8:3, which NEB renders: "By sending his own Son in a form like that of our own sinful nature, and as a sacrifice for sin, he [God] has passed judgement against sin within that very na-

---

176. Cranfield 290 (on Rom. 5:19).

177. John 7:18; 8:46; Acts 3:14; Heb. 4:15; 7:26; 1 Pet. 1:19; 2:22; 3:18; 1 John 3:5.

178. E.g., ποιήσετε αὐτὴν [σεμίδαλιν] δώδεκα ἄρτους, "you shall make it [fine flour] into twelve loaves" (Lev. 24:5).

179. So also Young and Ford 267; Dunn, *Theology* 222.

180. Cf. Homer, *Odyssey* 1.387 (ποιεῖν τινα βασιλῆα); Gen. 27:37 (εἰ κύριον αὐτὸν πεποίηκά σου . . .). See LSJ s.v. ποιέω A.III.

181. Sometimes these two options are combined (e.g., Windisch 196-98).

182. On this latter rendering, see Ellingworth, "2 Cor. 5:21" 237-41.

183. E.g., Whiteley 137; Käsemann, *Perspectives* 43 (following Kertelge 211); and, more cautiously, Hooker, 349-61 (who warns against "driving a wedge between incarnation and crucifixion," 353); "Suffering" 70. Grayston understands ἁμαρτίαν ἐποίησεν to mean that God made Christ "a victim of the power of Sin in that all his goodness was so turned as to destroy himself and to create unbelief among those who were most zealous for God" (62).

ture." But we must observe that Paul does not say that Christ was sent "in sinful flesh" (ἐν σαρκὶ ἁμαρτίας), only "in the likeness of sinful flesh" (ἐν ὁμοιώματι σαρκὸς ἁμαρτίας). By using the term ὁμοίωμα, which here points to similarity, not identity, he avoids suggesting that by the incarnation Christ assumed "sinful flesh" or a "sinful nature." Paul might have said simply ἐν σαρκί (cf. John 1:14; 1 John 4:2; 2 John 7), but not ἐν σαρκὶ ἁμαρτίας. Christ's participation in human nature did not constitute a sin or make him a sinner, nor is it to be equated with his "becoming sin."[184]

It is true that v. 21 makes no explicit reference to the death or the cross of Christ, but this is no objection to the cultic or sacrificial view that localizes the ποίησις in the crucifixion, since the death of Jesus is mentioned three times in vv. 14-15 and διὰ Χριστοῦ (v. 18) is clearly equivalent to διὰ τοῦ θανάτου τοῦ υἱοῦ αὐτου [= τοῦ θεοῦ] (Rom. 5:10). According to a long and distinguished tradition, the second ἁμαρτία in v. 21 refers to a "sin offering."[185] It is pointed out that two Hebrew sacrificial terms, ḥaṭṭā'ṯ and 'āšām, can mean both "sin" and "sin offering," so that in v. 21 ἁμαρτία could mean first "sin," then "sin offering" (= περὶ ἁμαρτίας θυσία; cf. Heb 10:26). Appeal is made to Paul's statements in Rom. 8:3 (God sent his Son περὶ ἁμαρτίας, "as a sin offering," NRSV mg.);[186] and in Gal. 3:13 ("Christ has redeemed us from the curse that the law pronounces, by becoming a curse for us"). The OT background for this interpretation may be found in Leviticus 4 with its instruction concerning the sin offering; or in Isaiah 53 which speaks of Yahweh's making his servant's life a sin offering 'āšām; LXX, ἐὰν δῶτε περὶ ἁμαρτίας (v. 10), and affirms that "Yahweh laid on him [his servant] the iniquity of us all" (LXX, καὶ κύριος παρέδωκεν αὐτὸν ταῖς ἁμαρτίαις ἡμῶν) (v. 6); or in the Day of Atonement drama of Leviticus 16:5-10, 20-22, where the scapegoat is driven into the desert, carrying on its head "all the wickedness and rebellion of the Israelites — all their sins" (v. 21).[187]

Some of the objections to this view are insubstantial and may be answered:[188] the absolute ἁμαρτία means "sin offering" in Exod. 29:14; Lev.

---

184. Moreover, it is illegitimate to argue that Christ received the "sin principle" (ἁμαρτία) at the incarnation (= "God caused him to be sin"), but was free of any transgression (ἁμαρτία = παράπτωμα; cf. 5:19).

185. Recent proponents of this view include Sabourin in Lyonnet and Sabourin 251-53; Prümm 1.346-60; Bruce 210; Stuhlmacher, *Reconciliation* 59; Martin 135, 157 (he sees 5:21 as non-Pauline); Talbert 167-68. Versions that reflect this view include NEB mg., NIV mg. (1984), NJB ("a victim for sin"), NLT.

186. Although the LXX usually translates ḥaṭṭā'ṯ (when it means "sacrifice for sin") by περὶ ἁμαρτίας (= τὸ δῶρον/τὸ ζῷον περὶ ἁμαρτίας; e.g., Lev. 16:5; cf. Heb. 10:6, 8), this phrase may mean "to deal with sin" in Rom. 8:3.

187. For this latter view, see Bernard 73; Héring 45; Dunn, *Theology* 220; "Death" 133. On the scapegoat as a "type" of Christ in the history of doctrine, see Sabourin in Lyonnet and Sabourin 269-89.

188. The classic statement of objections is found in Bachmann 272; and for a systematic response, see Sabourin in Lyonnet and Sabourin 414-24.

4:24; Num. 18:9;[189] ἁμαρτία is found in 5:21, rather than the expected περὶ ἁμαρτίας, because of the literary contrast between ἁμαρτία and δικαιοσύνη θεοῦ;[190] on any view, ἁμαρτία does not carry precisely the same meaning in its two occurrences in 5:21.[191] But it remains true that (i) ἁμαρτία does not bear the meaning "sin offering" anywhere else in Paul or the NT; (ii) Paul here probably construes ἁμαρτία in a more personal, interrelational sense than is represented by "sacrifice for sin" or "victim for sin"; (iii) one might have expected a verb such as προέθετο (cf. Rom. 3:25) or ἔδωκεν or ἔθηκεν if ἁμαρτία signified "sin offering"; and (iv) if ἁμαρτία is parallel to δικαιοσύνη θεοῦ, it is more likely to bear a judicial or forensic sense than a sacrificial or cultic meaning.

There are three other possibilities regarding the meaning of ἁμαρτία:

1. *Sinner* (ἁμαρτία being abstract for concrete). God treated Christ as if he were a sinner[192] or as a sinner.[193] As Meyer expresses it: "ἐποίησε expresses the *setting up of the state,* in which Christ was actually exhibited by God as the *concretum* of ἁμαρτία, as ἁμαρτωλός, in being subjected by Him to suffer the punishment of death" (539).

2. *Sin bearer* (again, abstract for concrete).[194] On the cross Christ bore the penalty of sin or the divine wrath against human sin.

3. *Sin.* God treated Christ as if he were sin;[195] or, in a pregnant mysterious sense, God actually caused Christ to be sin,[196] that is, to be the very personification of sin. "Christ is made one with the reality of sin and its consequences."[197] Christ "came to stand in that relation with God which normally is the result of sin, estranged from God and the object of his wrath."[198] V. 21a stands in stark contrast to v. 19b. Because of God's transference of sinners' sin on to the sinless one, because sin was reckoned to Christ's account, it is not now reckoned to the believer's account. This total identification of the sinless one with sinners at the cross, in assuming the full penalty and guilt of their sin, leaves no doubt that substitution as well as representation was involved.[200] Jesus died a death under the divine wrath that was deserved by sinners. The divine action specified by ἐποίησεν was ὑπὲρ ἡμῶν, "for us," that is, both "on our behalf" and "in our place" (cf. Gal. 3:13, Χριστὸς . . . γενόμενος ὑπὲρ ἡμῶν κατάρα). In Rom. 5:8,

189. For further examples, see Sabourin in Lyonnet and Sabourin 252-53, 253 n. 27.
190. Sabourin in Lyonnet and Sabourin 251-52.
191. Sabourin 421.
192. Garland 302.
193. Bultmann 165; *Theology* 1.277; Guthrie 466; CEV.
194. Bernard 73; H. Riesenfeld, *TDNT* 8.510.
195. Zerwick and Grosvenor 545.
196. Robertson, *Pictures* 233 ("God 'treated as sin' the one 'who knew no sin'").
197. Bieringer, "Sünde" 508.
198. Barrett 180.
199. Cf. Denney (*Death* 160): "In His death everything was made His that sin had made ours — everything in sin except its sinfulness" (cited by Bruce, *Galatians* 166).
200. *Pace* Hooker 349-61; Dunn, "Death" 125-41 (on both of which, see Kim 276-77 n. 3).

which also refers to the death of Christ ὑπὲρ ἡμῶν, no reference is made to Christ's sinlessness, only to human sinfulness (ἁμαρτωλῶν ὄντων ἡμῶν), but ὁ δίκαιος could legitimately be added to Χριστός (cf. 1 Pet. 3:18, δίκαιος ὑπὲρ ἀδίκων). Here in v. 21, reference is made to Christ's sinlessness but not to human sinfulness, but ὄντων ἁμαρτωλῶν (cf. Rom. 5:8) or ὄντων ἐχθρῶν (cf. Rom. 5:10) or ὄντων νεκρῶν τοῖς παραπτώμασιν (cf. Eph. 2:5) could appropriately be added to ἡμῶν. The referent in this ἡμῶν will be humans in general.

We conclude that in v. 21a Paul is not saying that at the crucifixion the sinless Christ became in some sense a sinner, yet he is affirming more than that Christ became a sin offering or even a sin bearer. In a sense beyond human comprehension, God treated Christ as "sin," aligning him so totally with sin and its dire consequences that from God's viewpoint he became indistinguishable from sin itself.

ἵνα ἡμεῖς γενώμεθα δικαιοσύνη θεοῦ ἐν αὐτῷ. "So that, by being in him, we might become the righteousness of God." The conjunction ἵνα here denotes a purpose, and, by implication, a result: "so that we might become, as indeed we have. . . ." This desired result and achieved outcome was future to Christ's being "made sin," being true either of believers' present state or of their eternal destiny. But since there is no ground for equating "the righteousness of God" with "the crown of righteousness" that God will award to believers at the parousia (2 Tim. 4:8) or with God's immortality (1 Tim. 6:15-16) that will be acquired by believers by means of resurrection (1 Cor. 15:52-54), the content of this ἵνα clause must relate to the present state of believers.

Perhaps the key to this difficult clause lies with the verb γίνομαι. Commentators and translators have construed it in three basic ways.

1. *Participation:* ". . . in order that in union with him we might share the righteousness of God" (GNB).[201] On this view θεοῦ is a possessive genitive, "that God has." Even if a distinction is drawn between participating in God's uprightness and intrinsically possessing that uprightness, the problem remains that while γίνομαι regularly may mean "come to be," it is difficult to justify lexicographically the meaning "come to share." One would have expected σχῶμεν ("that we might have") or μετασχῶμεν ("that we might share") to be found instead of γενώμεθα.

2. *Action:* "So that we, linked with him, might do what God considers right" (Danker).[202] In this case θεοῦ probably is an objective genitive, "(what is right) in the eyes of God." There is no question that δικαιοσύνη can occasionally

---

201. Perhaps the NEB reflects this interpretation: ". . . so that in him we might be made one with the goodness [REB "righteousness"] of God himself." Similarly Plummer 187: "It is by union of Christ with man that Christ is identified with human sin, and it is by union of man with Christ that man is identified with Divine righteousness." For the view that γενέσθαι δικαιοσύνη θεοῦ refers to believers' experience of the saving power of God, see Stuhlmacher 74-77; Wolff 133; "Knowledge" 96.

202. In Lewis 105; similarly in his commentary, p. 84. For Thüsing 108 "being God's righteousness" may be equated with "living for God" (Rom. 6:10-11).

have the sense "what is right," but "*doing* what is right" would be ποιεῖν (τὴν) δικαιοσύνην (as in 1 John 2:29; 3:7, 10; Rev. 22:11) or ἐργάζεσθαι δικαιοσύνην (as in Acts 10:35) or πράσσειν (τὴν) δικαιοσύνην, as in *2 Clement* 19:3).

3. *Change*: ". . . so that in him we might become the righteousness of God" (RSV, NRSV). Here the genitive θεοῦ could be possessive ("that God has") or subjective ("that God provides") or objective ("in relation to God," "before God"). δικαιοσύνη is an "abstract for concrete," being used in parallelism to ἁμαρτία (second use) in v. 21a. So it is possible that it stands for δίκαιοι ("righteous") or οἱ δίκαιοι ("[God's] righteous people"). "We must become righteous people, i.e. righteous with God's righteousness" (Lambrecht 101). But Ladd aptly observes (487) that δικαιοσύνη "in this context [5:21] is not an ethical subjective righteousness any more than the "sinfulness" of Christ is ethical subjective sinfulness." Rather, δικαιοσύνη stands for δικαιωθέντες (BAGD 197a) or δίκαιοι (in a forensic rather than ethical sense). On this view, the ἵνα clause could mean "so that in him we might be justified before God" (cf. δικαιωθῆναι ἐν Χριστῷ, Gal. 2:17),[203] or "so that in him we might become righteous through God's action." Either way, ἐν αὐτῷ probably bears a local sense,[204] "by being in him" [Christ] who is our righteousness (1 Cor. 1:30).[205]

So γίνομαι may be given its most common meaning ("become," "be") and points to the change of status that accrues to believers who are "in Christ" and that is the ground of the "new creation" (v. 17). "To become the righteousness of God" is to gain a right standing before God that God himself bestows (cf. Rom. 5:17; Phil. 3:9). It is to be "constituted righteous" in the divine court, so that γενέσθαι δικαιοσύνη θεοῦ = κατασταθῆναι δίκαιοι (Rom. 5:19). Although the term λογίζομαι is not used in v. 21 (but cf. v. 19), it is not inappropriate to perceive in this verse a double imputation: sin was reckoned to Christ's account (v. 21a), so that righteousness is reckoned to our account (v. 21b). Certainly the literary symmetry of the juxtaposed opposites, ἁμαρτία and δικαιοσύνη,[206] supports such an inference. As a result of God's imputing to Christ something that was extrinsic to him, namely sin, believers have something imputed to them that was extrinsic to them, namely righteousness.[207]

---

203. Similarly Fung 255-56.

204. Thus forensic (δικαιοσύνη) and "mystical" (ἐν αὐτῷ/ = ἐν Χριστῷ) motifs are linked. Some, however, take ἐν αὐτῷ in an instrumental sense (e.g., Dinkler, "Verkündigung" 181), as parallel to διὰ Χριστοῦ in v. 18 and, on some views, to ἐν Χριστῷ in v. 19.

205. Balancing the "Christ-for-us" motif in v. 21a is the "we-in-him" concept in v. 21b.

206. Cf. a similar juxtaposition of opposites in Gal. 3:13-14: κατάρα ("curse") — εὐλογία ("blessing").

207. But one cannot say on the basis of v. 21 that the righteousness *of Christ* is imputed to believers, for it is here δικαιοσύνη *θεοῦ* (righteousness "before God," or "bestowed by God") that is imputed, on the basis of Christ being believers' righteousness (= ἐν αὐτῷ). While the expression "the righteousness of Christ" (δικαιοσύνη Χριστοῦ), which occurs frequently in Reformed theology, is not a NT phrase, it expresses a NT truth, namely that through Christ's "act of righteousness" (δικαίωμα) there comes justification that leads to life (Rom. 5:18).

According to Wright ("Righteousness" 208; cf. also Ziesler 159-61), δικαιοσύνη θεοῦ in

That Isaiah 53 was in Paul's mind when he penned 5:21 seems indicated by the three elements of the verse that reflect statements made in that chapter concerning Yahweh's servant.[208]

(1) Christ as sinless (v. 21a) —
". . . he had done no violence, and there was no deceit in his mouth" (Isa. 53:9).
(2) Christ as "made sin" (v. 21a) —
"When you [Yahweh] make his life an offering for sin . . ." (Isa. 53:10).
(3) The resulting benefit (v. 21b) —
"The righteous one, my servant,
shall make many righteous" (Isa. 53:11, NRSV).

In a manner unparalleled in the NT, this verse invites us to tread on sacred ground. We should never overlook the wonder and mystery of the fact that it was the all-holy God himself who caused Christ, his spotless Son, to become sin and therefore the object of his wrath. Paul had had no hesitation to say, "God was in Christ" (5:19). Could it have been his acute awareness of this awe-inspiring mystery that prevented his saying boldly, "God caused Christ, the sinless one, to be sin," and prompted him to avoid actually naming God and Christ although the referents are unambiguous?[209]

6:1 Συνεργοῦντες δὲ καὶ παρακαλοῦμεν μὴ εἰς κενὸν τὴν χάριν τοῦ θεοῦ δέξασθαι ὑμᾶς. "So then, as God's co-workers, we indeed appeal to you not to receive God's grace in vain." The first two verses of ch. 6 belong together, v. 2 affording the scriptural justification (γάρ) for the appeal of v. 1, and they form the practical conclusion (δέ, "so then"; cf. RSV, NAB²) to Paul's explanation of how the new order (καινά, 5:17) came into existence (5:18-21). As so often in Paul's letters, it is the case of an ethical imperative — here in the form of an apostolic plea, παρακαλοῦμεν κτλ. — following a doctrinal indicative (5:16-21). καί is not to be taken with δέ but with παρακαλοῦμεν, "we indeed appeal."[210] Whereas in

---

5:21 refers to God's covenant faithfulness that was evident through Paul's own ministry, so that Paul himself is "a revelation in person of the covenant faithfulness of God." But such a view destroys the parallelism between ἁμαρτία and δικαιοσύνη (ἁμαρτία would become "covenant disloyalty" — Thrall 444), restricts the ἡμεῖς arbitrarily to Paul and his ministry, and robs the characteristically Pauline phrase ἐν Χριστῷ of its potency.

208. This is pointed out by Hoad 254. Citing seven references in Isaiah 53 to the Servant as sin-bearer (vv. 4-6, 8, 10-12), Barnett concludes that "God made him . . . sin" is "an apt summary of the entire chapter" (313 n. 61), which is Paul's "major intellectual quarry for this verse" (314 n. 67). See further Hofius, "Erwägungen" 196-99.

209. It is interesting to recall that in the closest parallel to 2 Cor. 5:21, namely Gal. 3:13 ("Christ . . . became a curse [κατάρα] for us, for it is written 'cursed [ἐπικατάρατος] is everyone who is hanged on a tree'"), Paul omits the ὑπὸ θεοῦ of Deut. 21:23 (LXX) to avoid the suggestion that Christ was cursed "by God."

210. Other suggested renderings of καί here are "also" (Thrall 451), "actually" (Lambrecht in Bieringer and Lambrecht 500; but "also" in his later commentary, p. 108), and "once again" (JB).

5:20 the παράκλησις was God's, but issued by Paul, in 6:1 it was Paul's (and perhaps also that of Timothy, 1:1),[211] but we may assume that here too he was acting as God's mouthpiece. This verbal link between παρακαλοῦμεν in 6:1 and παρακαλοῦντος in 5:20, along with the explicit reference to θεοῦ in 5:21, makes it likely that the person with whom Paul was cooperating in ministry (συνεργοῦντες) was God,[212] although, given 5:20 ("we are ambassadors for Christ . . . on Christ's behalf, we make this entreaty") and ἐν αὐτῷ at the end of 5:21, a case could be made for Christ as Paul's fellow worker.[213] But whether we supply (τῷ) θεῷ/ or (τῷ/) Χριστῷ with συνεργοῦντες, Paul regarded his entitlement to issue this exhortation to the Corinthians as coming from his partnership with a divine figure. That is, the participle συνεργοῦντες may be circumstantial ("As God's fellow workers," NIV; "Sharing in God's work," NEB, REB) or causal ("Since we are at work with God," Carrez 156). As for the precise nature of the cooperative enterprise, the preceding context suggests several options. But any suggestion must be consonant with Paul's following exhortation not to let God's grace come to nothing. The cooperation could be in the effort to persuade people of the truth of the gospel (5:11) or in the general exercise of "the ministry of reconciliation" (5:18) or in the proclamation of the specific "message of reconciliation" (5:19), namely, "Get reconciled to God!" (5:20).

Three questions must be asked about Paul's παράκλησις. To whom is it addressed? What is its content? Why did he need to make the appeal?

The word ὑμᾶς, that is, "(all of) you Corinthians" would seem to settle the matter of Paul's addressees. But at least two commentators propose that Paul's exhortation is directed to unbelievers, whether people in general (so Hodge 154) or "some at Corinth who, while they may have heard the apostolic gospel, had not received it in such a way that it became a regenerating influence in their lives" (Tasker 91). But either way, one would then have expected ἀνθρώπους (cf. 5:11) or ἐν ὑμῖν τινας (cf. 1 Cor. 15:12) instead of the unqualified ὑμᾶς, and τὴν χάριν τοῦ θεοῦ δέξασθαι in the place of μὴ εἰς κενὸν τὴν χάριν τοῦ θεοῦ δέξασθαι.

Paul's urgent appeal to the Corinthians is "not to receive God's grace in vain." In the Pauline corpus ἡ χάρις τοῦ θεοῦ is often simply the apostle's short-

---

211. The following catalogue of hardships (vv. 4-10) is so specific that they must be principally Paul's adversities. If so, the prefixed appeal of v. 1 will probably be primarily Paul's. Both Moffatt and Goodspeed render παρακαλοῦμεν by "I appeal."

212. Thus most commentators (e.g., Windisch 199; Barrett 183; Collange 285; also Ellis, "Co-Workers" 440), often citing 1 Cor. 3:9, θεοῦ γάρ ἐσμεν συνεργοί, which, in light of the following two uses of θεοῦ as a possessive genitive, probably means "we are *God's* fellow workers" rather than "we are coworkers *for* God." Cf. 1 Thess. 3:2. Some translations make the reference to God explicit (TCNT, NEB, GNB, NIV, REB, CEV, NLT).

213. Thus Meyer 544-45. Isaacs paraphrases thus: "Officially we are Christ's ambassadors, personally we are His fellow-workers." The strong support from the immediate context for "God" or "Christ" as the implied referent of συν- renders it improbable that ὑμῖν should be supplied with συνεργοῦντες, as in NAB[1], "As your fellow workers"; also Allo 173; Prümm 1.361 (citing 1:24, συνεργοί ἐσμεν τῆς χαρᾶς ὑμῶν, "we work with you for your joy").

hand for all the benefits of the gospel that are secured by Christ and mediated by the Spirit.[214] In this context (5:16-21) those blessings are in particular the arrival of the new order with its new attitudes and new life (5:16-17), the receipt of reconciliation with God through the forgiveness of sins (5:18-19), and the acquisition of a right standing before God (5:21). All of this is included in what Paul calls σωτηρία in 6:2. But within the wider context of the letter, "the grace of God" will also refer to the present opportunity that the Corinthians have to become fully reconciled to Paul.[215] From this perspective 6:1 is in part a preparation for Paul's entreaty in vv. 11-13 for the Corinthians to throw their hearts wide open to him. With this said, it remains unlikely that he is equating his own ministry at Corinth with "the grace of God,"[216] for τὴν χάριν τοῦ θεοῦ stands unqualified (contrast the same expression in 8:1); that is, he did not write τὴν χάριν τοῦ θεοῦ τὴν εἰς ὑμᾶς δι' ἡμῶν, "God's grace shown to you by us."

It is certainly possible that the aorist infinitive δέξασθαι has a preterite sense, referring to the time of the Corinthians' conversion: "we urge you not *to have received . . .*" (Barclay; italics mine).[217] Elsewhere in Paul this verb in the aorist tense describes the initial receipt of the gospel.[218] On the other hand, as an aorist infinitive δέξασθαι expresses simply the act or acts of receiving without any reference to time,[219] and here it probably envisages multiple future acts of receiving,[220] conceived of as a unit. Had Paul used the present infinitive, (μὴ εἰς κενὸν . . .) δέχεσθαι, he could be understood as implying that the Corinthians were currently receiving God's grace but failing to profit by it. Moreover, in Paul the aorist infinitive is not uncommon with παρακαλέω.[221] To be preferred, therefore, is the rendering "we appeal to you not *to receive* the grace of God in vain" (NAB[2]; italics mine);[222] that is, "do not now or ever receive. . . ." The assumption is that God's grace is a stream that is constantly flowing and so always available for refreshment.

When the adjective κενός is used figuratively, of things, it means either "empty" (i.e. without content) or, as here, "vain" (i.e., without purpose or result).[223] To receive God's grace "in vain" (εἰς κενόν) is not to "reject" it (as NLT) or even to "neglect" it (as JB),[224] but to receive it without profit, without

---

214. For the wide range of use of the term χάρις in 2 Corinthians 8–9, see the note at 8:1.

215. So also Lambrecht in Bieringer and Lambrecht 520-21.

216. But see Beale 562-63.

217. Similarly Collange 281, 286; Carrez 156; NEB, GNB, NJB, REB.

218. 2 Cor. 11:4; 1 Thess. 1:6; 2:13; 2 Thess. 2:10.

219. Cf. Thrall 451 n. 1825; Winer 332; Burton §113, 236.

220. *Contra* Lambrecht 108 and in Bieringer and Lambrecht 526.

221. Rom. 12:1; 15:30; 2 Cor. 2:8; Eph. 4:1; 1 Tim. 1:3. The present infinitive is used with παρακαλέω in Rom. 16:17; Phil. 4:2; 1 Thess. 4:10; 1 Tim. 2:1; Tit. 2:6.

222. Similarly Wendland 201; Barrett 182; Furnish 338, 341; Young and Ford 267; Thrall 449, 451; TCNT, Goodspeed, Williams, Berkeley, RSV, NASB, NAB[1], NIV, NRSV.

223. So Paul can speak of "running" in vain (Gal. 2:2; Phil. 2:16a) or laboring in vain (Phil. 2:16b; 1 Thess. 3:5).

224. Both of these renderings imply non-receipt.

the intended effect being achieved. The grace is accepted, but it never attains its goal; it comes to nothing.

If, then, εἰς κενὸν . . . δέξασθαι connotes fruitless reception, not outright repudiation, Paul is exhorting his Corinthian converts not to fail to profit from the proffered divine grace, or, expressed positively, to give God's grace an effective welcome, to capitalize on opportunities for spiritual growth.[225] But the question remains: How might the Corinthians let God's grace come to nothing? Answers are necessarily speculative, but they would probably include the following. In general, God's grace would be ineffective if the Corinthians squandered God-given opportunities for bringing spiritual benefit to themselves and to unbelievers (cf. Col. 4:5b, "making the most of opportunity"), and if they failed to exercise the ministry of reconciliation (5:18) and to fulfill their role as Christ's ambassadors (5:19); more specifically, if they accommodated the false apostles (11:13-15), or embraced a "different gospel" (11:4), or failed to repudiate paganism (6:14-18) and personal sin (7:1; 12:20-21), or spurned Paul's overtures of reconciliation (6:13; 7:2).[226] On this latter point, the Corinthians would have realized that if God's grace to them was currently being expressed (in part) by Paul's invitation to warm, open, reciprocal relations, a failure to be fully reconciled to Paul would amount to a receipt of God's grace in vain.[227]

But what if at any point the Corinthians did receive God's grace yet failed to benefit from it? Would they forfeit their place in God's salvation? The text does not address this issue. Certainly, if God's grace flows continuously, a single failure to benefit from it would not stem the flow. What would be compromised, however, would be the receipt of commendatory recompense at Christ's tribunal (5:10).[228]

6:2 λέγει γάρ, Καιρῷ δεκτῷ ἐπήκουσά σου καὶ ἐν ἡμέρᾳ σωτηρίας ἐβοήθησά σοι. "For God says, 'At the time of my favor, I listened to you, and on the day of salvation, I came to your aid.'" Technically, this verse forms a parenthesis,[229] for the participles of v. 3 resume the construction of v. 1.[230] Citing the LXX version of Isa. 49:8, which accurately renders the Hebrew text, Paul explains why (γάρ) his addressees should not let God's grace, whenever received, prove ineffective in their experience. The subject to be supplied with λέγει

225. Cf. CEV: "We beg you to make good use of God's kindness to you."

226. Gundry Volf argues that "the suggestion that receiving the grace of God in vain has to do with resistance to the apostle" enjoys the strongest contextual support (277-79; quotation from p. 279).

227. Cf. Fitzgerald 184; Belleville 164.

228. See the treatment of these issues in D. A. Carson, "Reflections on Christian Assurance," *WTJ* 54 (1992) 1-29; and for a different approach, I. H. Marshall, *Power;* Oropeza.

229. The first two editions of the UBS Greek text enclose the verse within dashes. Meyer calls the verse "a parenthetic urgent *inducement* for complying with this exhortation [of v. 1] without delay" (545). Barnett (46-47, 318, 377 n. 24), however, regards 6:2, with its quotation of a text from a section of Isaiah (chs. 40–55) on which Paul was greatly dependent for much of his thinking in this letter, as arguably the key verse not only in 2:14–7:4 but also in the entire letter (chs. 1–13).

230. Robertson 440. However, the two participles in v. 3 probably stand for finite verbs.

could be ἡ γραφή (cf. Rom. 4:3) but is more probably ὁ θεός (from 5:20 and 6:1; cf. 6:16) or ὁ κύριος (from the introductory formula οὕτως λέγει κύριος in Isa. 49:8).[231]

Isa. 49:1-13 is the second of the four so-called "Servant Songs"[232] in which the circumference of the term "Israel" expands and contracts, sometimes being a corporate reference to the whole nation or to the faithful remnant within the nation, and sometimes being an individual reference to the Messiah as ideal Israel. In Isaiah 49 Yahweh's servant cannot be the nation as a whole, for "my servant, Israel" (v. 3) has the task of restoring Israel (vv. 5-6, 8). In its original context v. 8a contains Yahweh's promise to his servant (σου . . . σοι) of answered prayer and personal support "in the time of my favor" or "in the day of salvation," that is, at the time of the nation's return from their Babylonian exile. In spite of being "despised and abhorred" by the nation (v. 7), the servant would receive ready help (v. 8a) and divine vindication (vv. 7, 8b). He would ultimately be rewarded (v. 4b) by spiritual offspring (cf. 53:10) of both Jews and Gentiles (vv. 5-6).

There are three aspects of Paul's ministry that correspond to Isa. 49:1-6.

Isa. 49

1. his call, as one set apart before his birth (Gal. 1:15-16)	v. 1	"Before I was born the LORD called me"
	v. 5	"He who formed me in the womb to be his servant"
2. his twofold mission (Acts 9:15; 22:15; 26:17):	v. 5	"to bring Jacob back
to Israel		. . . and gather Israel" (cf. v. 6)
to Gentiles	v. 6	"I will also make you a light for the Gentiles"
3. certain misgivings about the result of his mission (Gal. 2:2; 4:11; Phil. 2:16; 1 Thess. 3:5)	v. 4	"I have labored in vain, I have spent my strength for nothing and to no purpose"

To judge from these correlations and from other citations of and allusions to the "Servant Songs" in the Pauline epistles[233] and in sections of Acts that relate to Paul,[234] Paul envisaged his ministry as a continuation of the role of the Servant of Yahweh.

231. On introductory formulas in Paul, see Ellis 22-25, 48-49; Koch 25-32.
232. The others are Isa. 42:1-9 (or perhaps 1-4 or 1-7); 50:4-9 (or perhaps 4-11); and 52:13–53:12.
233. E.g., Isa. 52:15 in Rom. 15:21; Isa. 53:1 in Rom. 10:16.
234. E.g., Isa. 42:7 in Acts 26:18; Isa. 49:6 in Acts 13:47.

It is, however, a giant step to move from this inference to the suggestion of Lane that "Paul found in [the] recital of the call, disparagement, and vindication of the servant in Isaiah 49 a paradigm for his relationship with the Corinthians,"[235] so that 6:2 should be interpreted of Paul's own experience. God had listened to his cry as one "despised and abhorred" by the Gentiles, whose apostolic toil at Corinth seemed to have been "for nothing." The day of his vindication had arrived, for "the time of God's tolerance of insubordination" to Paul was past (Lane 20). In a similar fashion Beale interprets v. 2a to mean that God himself will aid Paul, whose ministry is in danger of being received "in vain" (εἰς κενόν; cf. Isa. 49:4), in order to reaffirm his calling as the official divine spokesman of the message of reconciliation.[236]

Now it is one thing to recognize that Isaiah 49 influenced Paul's understanding of his self-identity (see the correlations set out above) and to discover certain similarities between the situation of the Isaianic servant and Paul's predicament at Corinth. But it is quite another matter to see Isaiah 49 as paradigmatic for Paul's relation to the Corinthian church. That chapter certainly speaks of the disparagement (v. 7a), discouragement (v. 4a), and vindication (vv. 4b, 7b, 8b, 13) of Yahweh's servant — items paralleled in Paul's experience with the Corinthians — but (i) the part of v. 8 that he cites describes divine succor, not humiliation or vindication; (ii) both verbs in 2 Cor. 6:2 (ἐπήκουσα, ἐβοήθησα) are aorist indicatives, pointing to divine assistance already received, not aid that Paul hoped would be given him to cope with the Corinthian discontent;[237] (iii) although the phrase εἰς κενόν (6:1) is verbally comparable to κενῶς, εἰς μάταιον, and εἰς οὐδέν in Isa. 49:4,[238] it is the Corinthians, not Paul, who are facing the danger of a certain ineffectiveness; (iv) Paul's primary focus in the quotation is on the nouns (καιρός, ἡμέρα σωτηρίας), not the verbs, as is shown by v. 2b; (v) the natural antecedent of σου and σοι in 6:2 (here construed as collective singulars) is the immediately preceding ὑμᾶς (viz. the Corinthians), which stands at the end of the verse not only for emphasis but also as a further link (in addition to γάρ) with v. 2.

We conclude, then, that when Paul cites Isa. 49:8 he is thinking primarily of the Corinthians' experience, not his own.[239] In their case, "the time of God's

---

235. Lane 19, who believes that in 5:20–6:2 Paul is exercising the role of a messenger of the covenant lawsuit, appealing to the Corinthians for reconciliation to God and to himself (18-19).

236. Beale 561-64, in the course of arguing that "in 2 Cor. 5,17–7,4 Paul's understanding of reconciliation is a result of his meditation on the Isaianic restoration context [Isaiah 40–66]" (563).

237. The LXX renders the two Hebrew prophetic perfects ("I will answer you . . . I will help you," JB, NIV, NRSV) by the aorist, which in the indicative only rarely as a proleptic aorist bears a future sense.

238. Isa. 49:4 (LXX): "I have labored to no purpose (κενῶς); I have spent my strength in vain (εἰς μάταιον) and for nothing (εἰς οὐδέν). Therefore my cause is with the Lord and my labor is before my God."

239. So also Lambrecht 108-9, 111 in Bieringer and Lambrecht 525-26. Hughes (219) discerns three applications of the quotation: to the Corinthians; to Paul, who experienced God's help in evangelism; and to Christ as Yahweh's Servant.

favor" was the time of their conversion when God graciously heard and answered (ἐπήκουσά σου)[240] their cry for help, "the day of (their) salvation" when God deigned to come to their aid (ἐβοήθησά σοι).[241] ἐν ἡμέρᾳ σωτηρίας stands in synonymous parallelism to καιρῷ δεκτῷ, so that "the day that brings salvation"[242] is none other than "the time when God's favor is shown."[243]

ἰδοὺ νῦν καιρὸς εὐπρόσδεκτος, ἰδοὺ νῦν ἡμέρα σωτηρίας. "Listen! Now is the time of God's good favor. Listen! Now is the day of salvation!" In *pesher* style, Paul now applies the OT text to the contemporary situation.[244] Having exhorted the Corinthians about the future (v. 1) and having reminded them of the past (v. 2a), he now focuses on the present (νῦν . . . νῦν). The "now" referred to is not simply or primarily the time of the appeal in v. 1 (cf. σήμερον in Heb. 3:7), but the new era inaugurated by the death and resurrection of the Messiah, Jesus Christ, the period between the two comings of Christ.[245] Paul's main point is not that "today" is the only day of grace that is available for decision,[246] but that believers are now always in the dispensation of God's good favor,[247] a unique time in the history of God's saving acts, so that a response to God's grace (v. 1) is perpetually appropriate. So we may say that the repeated ἰδοὺ νῦν emphasizes the "presentness," availability, and privilege of salvation, and, by implication, the danger and culpability of procrastination.

Verse 2 states two reasons why the Corinthians should not let the grace of God be ineffective in their lives. First, they have already benefited from God's grace in his answering of their prayer and his coming to their aid; that is, they have been recipients of the grace of salvation. Second, they are privileged to

240. Both in Classical Greek and in inscriptions and papyri ἐπακούω ("hear," "pay attention") often means "hear and answer" with regard to prayer. See Spicq 1.443-44 for examples. In the LXX the verb usually refers to God's hearing a request with favor and therefore answering or responding (e.g., Prov. 15:29, "God . . . hears the prayer of the righteous").

241. In Isa. 49:8 ἡμέρα σωτηρίας refers to "the day of deliverance," the return from exile; in 2 Cor. 6:2a to "the day of salvation," the time of conversion; in 6:2b, to "the period of salvation," the gospel era.

242. The attributive/adjectival/Semitic genitive is common with ἡμέρα, e.g., Luke 1:80; Rom. 2:5; 1 Pet. 2:12.

243. The Hebrew phrase *bᵉʿēt rāṣôn* could mean "in the time of my favor" (NIV, REB, NRSV) or "in an acceptable time" (RV). Correspondingly, καιρῷ δεκτῷ may be rendered "in the time of my favor" (NIV; similarly NEB, REB) or "at the acceptable time" (RSV). In the latter case, δεκτῷ will mean "acceptable (to God)" (cf. Phil. 4:18).

244. Cf. Ellis 143, who, however, sees all of v. 2 as a quotation from early Christian tradition.

245. Just as καιρός can mean "period of time" as well as "point of time," so too ἡμέρα can mean "era" (e.g., John 8:56) as well as "(point of) time" (e.g., Mark 2:20b).

246. Cf. GNB: "Listen! This is the hour to receive God's favor; today is the day to be saved!"

247. Cf. NJB: "Well, now is the real time of favor, now the day of salvation is here." εὐπρόσδεκτος may simply be a stylistic variant for δεκτός, but with καιρός it probably carries an intensive or superlative sense, either "the *truly* favorable time," "a *very* acceptable time," or (reflecting the Hebrew term *rāṣôn,* "favor"), "the time of God's *good* favor."

live in the great "Now" of the gospel era when there is opportunity to profit from God's grace.

Bibliography

Adams 42-80, 234-47 • Beale • Bieringer, "Sünde" • Bieringer, "Versöhnung" • Bieringer, "Diakonia" • R. Bieringer, "Traditionsgeschichtlicher Ursprung und theologische Bedeutung der ΥΠΕΡ-Aussagen im Neuen Testament," in F. Van Segbroeck et al. (eds.), *The Four Gospels 1992: FS for F. Neirynck* (Leuven: Leuven University/Peeters, 1992) 1.219-48 • Brauch, "Perspectives" • Breytenbach 107-43 • Breytenbach, "Bemerkungen" • Burdick • Cambier, "Connaissance" • C. B. Cousar, "2 Corinthians 5:17-21," *Int* 35 (1981) 180-83 • Denney, *Death* 103-7 • de Oliveira 290-95, 396-409 • Dunn, "Death" • Dupont 180-86 • Dupont, *Réconciliation* • Ellingworth, "2 Cor. 5:21" • Ellis 143, 152 • R. J. Erickson, "Oida and Ginōskō and Verbal Aspect in Pauline Usage," *WTJ* 44 (1982) 110-22 • Fee, *Presence* 330-32 • H. J. Findeis, *Versöhnung — Apostolat — Kirche: Eine exegetisch-theologische und rezeptionsgeschichtliche Studie zu den Versöhnungsaussagen des Neuen Testaments (2 Kor, Röm, Kol, Eph)* (Würzburg: Echter, 1983) • G. Fitzer, "Der Ort der Versöhnung nach Paulus. Zu der Frage des 'Sühnopfers Jesu,'" *TZ* 22 (1966) 161-83 • J. A. Fitzmyer, "Reconciliation in Pauline Theology," in *To Advance the Gospel: New Testament Studies* (New York: Crossroad, 1981) 162-85 (originally published in *McKenzie FS* 155-77) • Fraser, "Knowledge" • Friedrich 24-56 • Furnish, *Theology* 148-49 • Furnish, "Reconciliation" • Gloer • Goppelt 2.42-43, 136-39 • Goppelt, *Christologie* 147-64 • Hahn, "Tag" • Hainz 272-80 • Hanson, *Ministry* 50-51, 80-84 • Hanson, *Paradox* 55-78 • Hoad • Hoch • Hofius, "Erwägungen" • Hofius, "2 Kor 5,19" • Hooker • A. N. Jannaris, "Misreadings and Misrenderings in the New Testament. III," *Exp* 5/10 (1899) 142-53 • E. Käsemann, "The Saving Significance of the Death of Jesus in Paul," in his *Perspectives* 32-59 • Käsemann, "Reconciliation" • E. Käsemann, "'The Righteousness of God in Paul,'" in his *Questions* 168-82 • Kertelge 99-107 • Kim 13-20, 311-15 • Koperski • Kreitzer 105-17 • Lambrecht, "Reading" • G. W. H. Lampe, "The New Testament Doctrine of ΚΤΙΣΙΣ," *SJT* 17 (1964) 449-62 • Lane • Lewis • Lohse, "Amt" • Lyonnet and Sabourin 245-53 • J. I. H. McDonald, "Paul and the Preaching Ministry," *JSNT* 17 (1983) 35-50 • I. H. Marshall • Martin, *Reconciliation* 90-110 • Martyn • Michel • Mitchell, "Envoys" 644-51 • Murphy-O'Connor 58-65 • M. Neary, "Creation and Pauline Soteriology," *ITQ* 50 (1983-84) 1-34 • J. Y. Noh, "An Exegesis of 2 Corinthians 5:16-21, and Its Contribution to Pauline Theology" (unpublished Ph.D. dissertation, Trinity Evangelical Divinity School, 1997) • A. Nygren, *Die Versöhnung als ottestat* (Gütersloh: Bertelsmann, 1932) • Oropeza • Pate 140-47 • Rebell 31-97 • Reumann 33-34, 51-52 • Rey 35-43 • Rey, "Homme" • Romaniuk 16-25, 216-92 • Sabourin • Schütz 175-78 • Souček • D. M. Stanley 138-44 • Stanton 88-93 • Stöger • Stuhlmacher 74-77 • Stuhlmacher, "Erwägungen" • Tannehill 68-69 • V. Taylor, *Forgiveness and Reconciliation: A Study in New Testament Theology* (London: Macmillan, 1948²) 70-108 • Thrall, "Salvation" • Thüsing, "Christologie" • D. L. Turner, "Paul and the Ministry of Reconciliation in 2 Cor. 5:11–6:2," *CTR* 4 (1989) 77-95 • von Allmen • D. Wenham, *Paul: Follower of Jesus or Founder of Christianity?* (Grand Rapids: Eerdmans, 1995) 400-402 • Wright, "Righteousness" • Ziesler 158-65

c. The Hardships and Triumphs of Apostolic Service (6:3-10)

At first glance, there appears to be an abrupt transition at v. 3. Paul moves from an appeal to his converts not to receive God's grace without benefit — an appeal validated by the citation of Isa. 49:8 — to an assertion of the probity of his conduct (vv. 3-4a) and a recitation of his apostolic hardships (vv. 4b-10). But this transition is less awkward if we recognize that the overall theme of this section (5:11–6:10) is the essence and exercise of the apostolic ministry. After describing what is the essential nature of that ministry, viz. the plea to unbelievers to accept God's reconciliation (5:20) and the challenge to believers to profit from God's grace (6:1-2), both of which are motivated by Christ's love (5:14), Paul explains what is involved in the exercise of that ministry (6:3-10). His purpose in sketching the characteristics of his "style of ministry" is not only to provide ammunition so that the Corinthians can defend him against the charges of his detractors (cf. 5:12), but also, and principally, to validate his credentials as an ambassador of Christ (5:20), as a suffering and therefore true apostle. As well as the Corinthians themselves being his "letter of recommendation" (cf. 3:2-3), his sufferings also fell into that category. He regarded his sufferings not as the arbitrary strokes of fate but as a divinely appointed "credentialing" of his apostleship. But 6:3-10 also serves as a fitting prelude to Paul's passionate request to the Corinthians for openness and reciprocity of relations (6:11-13). How could they, in their relative comfort, not be profoundly moved by his catalogue of afflictions — moved to deeper affection for their spiritual father?

Within 2 Corinthians there are four "catalogues of hardships," 4:8-9; 6:4b-10; 11:23b-29; 12:10.[1] The "tribulation list" in 6:4b-10 may be analyzed by structure or by content (see p. 465). This analysis shows that the catalogue is sophisticated from the viewpoint of structure and style. Two of the common meanings of ἐν and of διά with the genitive are employed (as it happens, in a chiastic arrangement, ABBA, circumstances — means — means — circumstances). There are breaks in the repetition to avoid monotony: the qualification of the four nouns in the second set (b) of 1; the absence of a matching or antithetical phrase in 2(a); the presence of ἰδού and μή in the second element in 3(a); the isolation of the final ὡς ... καί antithesis and the presence of matching accusatives. Then there are the literary flourishes of anaphora (ἐν, 19x; διά, 3x; ὡς, 7x), homoioteleuton (-[ι]αις in 1[a], -ιας in 2[b], -μενοι in 3[a], assonance and paronomasia (δυσφημίας–εὐφημίας in 2[b]; ἔχοντες–κατέχοντες in 3[c]), and chiasmus (δόξης–ἀτιμίας–δυσφημίας–εὐφημίας in 2[b]).

Paul's elevated style in this section should not be taken as an indication that he is using some preexistent text, whether of his own composition or bor-

---

1. Cf. Rom. 8:35b; 1 Cor. 4:10-13; Phil. 4:12. In the Hellenistic period περίστασις (literally "a standing around") meant, in a neutral sense, "circumstance(s)," or, in a negative sense, "unfavorable/adverse circumstance(s)," "difficulty," "hardship," or "crisis." Correspondingly, there were "catalogues of vicissitudes" and "catalogues of hardships." For more detail, see Fitzgerald 33-46.

Analysis of 6:4b-10[2] by Construction

1. ἐν + dative

   (a) plural (9x) (vv. 4b-5): "in (the midst of)"   CIRCUMSTANCES
ἐν θλίψεσιν	ἐν πληγαῖς	ἐν κόποις
ἐν ἀνάγκαις	ἐν φυλακαῖς	ἐν ἀγρυπνίαις
ἐν στενοχωρίαις	ἐν ἀκαταστασίαις	ἐν νηστείαις

   (b) Singular (8x) (vv. 6-7a): "by (means of)"   MEANS
ἐν ἁγνότητι	ἐν πνεύματι	ἁγίῳ
ἐν γνώσει	ἐν ἀγάπῃ	ἀνυποκρίτῳ
ἐν μακροθυμίᾳ	ἐν λόγῳ	ἀληθείας
ἐν χρηστότητι	ἐν δυνάμει	θεοῦ

2. διά + genitive

   (a) plural (1x) (v. 7b): "by (means of)"   MEANS

   διὰ τῶν ὅπλων τῆς δικαιοσύνης
       τῶν δεξιῶν καὶ ἀριστερῶν

   (b) singular (4x) (v. 8a): "in (the midst of)"   CIRCUMSTANCES[3]
διὰ	δόξης	καὶ ἀτιμίας
διὰ	δυσφημίας	καὶ εὐφημίας

3. ὡς + nominative   ASSESSMENTS

   (a) . . . καί (4x) (vv. 8b-9)
ὡς πλάνοι	καὶ	ἀληθεῖς
ὡς ἀγνοούμενοι	καὶ	ἐπιγινωσκόμενοι
ὡς ἀποθνῄσκοντες	καὶ ἰδοὺ	ζῶμεν
ὡς παιδευόμενοι	καὶ μὴ	θανατούμενοι

   (b) . . . δέ (2x) (v. 10a-b)
ὡς λυπούμενοι	ἀεὶ	δὲ χαίροντες
ὡς πτωχοὶ	πολλοὺς	δὲ πλουτίζοντες

   (c) . . . καί (1x) (v. 10c)

   ὡς μηδὲν ἔχοντες   καὶ πάντα κατέχοντες[4]

---

2. It is assumed that ἐν ὑπομονῇ πολλῇ ("with great endurance") is a general heading for vv. 4b-5 (or even vv. 4b-10). See on v. 4.

3. This attempt to distinguish between the meanings of ἐν and διά does not invalidate Moule's observation (196) that "II Cor. vi.4-10 is an impassioned and almost lyrical passage, where precision in the interpretation of the prepositions is probably impossible because the 'catalogue' has lured the writer into repeating a preposition in some instances where in sober prose it might have been unnatural." It would be improper, however, to translate successive identical prepositions within a group in different ways, as is done (for example) in the Berkeley version of v. 6b: "through [ἐν] kindness by [ἐν] the Holy Spirit in [ἐν] unpretended love."

4. Barré observes (524) that the list is progressive in arrangement: "the number of words in each member increases from two to six, and the list moves from an impersonal perspective (the *en*-section, which begins with abstract nouns) to a personal perspective (the *hōs* section)."

rowed (with modifications and additions) from some Stoic source.[5] He was not incapable of lofty diction, witness 1 Cor. 13:1-13 or Rom. 8:28-39 or Col. 1:15-20. Certainly, the autobiographical touches are so particularistic in v. 5 and the polemical note so pronounced in vv. 8-10 that we may safely assume that if Paul has incorporated some existing text into his argument at this point, he himself was its composer.

It is evident that vv. 4b-10 is no simple "catalogue of *hardships*," for Paul mentions positive "means" (vv. 6-7) as well as negative "circumstances" (vv. 4b-5, 8-10), and in his antitheses (vv. 8-10), one element is positive.

Analysis of 6:3-10 by Content

1. Commendation vs. Offense (vv. 3-4a)

3We are trying to put no obstacle whatsoever in anyone's way, so that our ministry[a] may not be discredited. 4On the contrary, as God's servants, we try to commend[b] ourselves in every way by our steadfast endurance:

2. Catalogue of Hardships and Triumphs (vv. 4b-10)

a. Outward Circumstances (vv. 4b-5)

in afflictions
in calamities
in dire straits
sin beatings
in imprisonments
in riots
in hard labor
in sleepless nights
in hunger;

5. For the latter view, see Höistad 22-27; Collange 290-91. Hodgson (59-80) has demonstrated that the "tribulation list" was a widespread literary convention of the first century, evidenced not only in Stoicism (see Bultmann, *Stil* 71-72) and Jewish apocalyptic (see Schrage 141-75), but also in Josephus, Plutarch, Arrian, the Pharisaic Judaism of the Mishnah, and incipient Gnosticism. It should also be noted that *2 Enoch* 66:6, a frequently cited parallel to 2 Cor. 6:4-10 (see, e.g., Windisch 206), is "no longer seen as a pre-Christian, Jewish parallel to Paul's catalogues, but as an echo of the latter, esp. 2 Cor 6:4ff." (Fitzgerald 17 n. 56), since the passage is found only in a later medieval Christian recension of *2 Enoch* (recension A) (Fitzgerald 16-17 n. 56).

b. Qualities of Character (v. 6)

6*by purity*
by understanding
by patience
by kindness
by the gifts of the Holy Spirit
by sincere love;

c. Spiritual Equipment (v. 7)

7*by declaring the truth*
by the power of God
by the weapons of righteousness
for the right hand and the left;

d. Vicissitudes of Ministry (vv. 8-10)

8*in honor and dishonor*
in ill repute and good repute;
as deceivers and yet truthful
9*as unknown and yet well known*
as facing death, and yet, see, we live on
as punished^c and yet not killed
10*as sorrowful but always rejoicing*
as poor but enriching many
as having nothing and yet possessing everything.

TEXTUAL NOTES

a. Sensing that Paul is discussing his own ministry, some witnesses (D F G 629 1505 *pc* it vg^ww syr cop Ambrosiaster) add ἡμῶν, in order to remove ambiguity.

b. As in 4:2 and 10:18, this verse exhibits variants from three verbs, all of which may mean "commend" (see BAGD 790c, d). The form συνιστῶντες (from συνιστάω), read by ℵ² D² Ψ 048 1881ᶜ 𝔐, is secondary, lacking any firm Pauline parallels (so Thrall 300 n. 765). The reading συνιστάντες (p⁴⁶ ℵ* C D* F G 0225 0243 33 81 1739 1881*ᵛⁱᵈ *pc* Clement of Alexandria) (from συνίστημι), though having strong proto-Alexandrian and Western support and preferred by NA²⁷, is probably inferior to συνιστάνοντες (B P 104 1175 1505 *pc*) (from συνιστάνω), since the former reading may have arisen by parablepsis (see on 4:2).

c. In the place of παιδευόμενοι ("being punished"), supported by the majority of witnesses, D* F G it Ambrosiaster (Western witnesses) read πειραζόμενοι ("being tested"), probably because to some scribe the idea of Paul's suffering corrective discipline was offensive.

467

6:3 μηδεμίαν ἐν μηδενὶ διδόντες προσκοπήν. "We are trying to put no obstacle whatsoever in anyone's way." We have dealt with the apparent abruptness of the transition from v. 2 to v. 3 in the introduction to this section. The intimate link between the message and the messenger — they stand together — also explains this transition. Any "credentialing" of the messenger, such as we find in vv. 3-10, serves to reinforce or even validate the authority of the message (5:16–6:2).[6] Certainly, once the asyndetic transition has been made, Paul moves forward with stylistic vigor in "a stream of diction swelling onward with ever increasing grandeur" (Meyer 544).

It is tempting to explain διδόντες in v. 3 and συνιστάνοντες in v. 4 as dependent (along with συνεργοῦντες in v. 1) on παρακαλοῦμεν[7] after the parenthetical v. 2, indicating circumstances attendant on Paul's exhortation. But given the frequency with which participles stand for finite verbs in 2 Corinthians,[8] it is better (as in 5:12) to construe διδόντες as equivalent to δίδομεν.[9] The present tense is durative (Turner 343) and probably also conative (cf. Plummer 166): "We are trying to put no obstacle. . . ." That is, the effort to avoid offense had been Paul's constant *modus operandi*. προσκοπή (from προσκόπτω, "take/give offense") means "an occasion for taking offense" (BAGD 716b) and is indistinguishable in meaning from the more common πρόσκομμα, "obstacle, hindrance." The word order, with μηδεμίαν standing first and separated from προσκοπήν, emphasizes the negative: "no offence at all" (cf. BAGD 518a), "no obstacle whatsoever." ἐν μηδενί may be neuter ("in no way") or masculine ("in no one's way"), although with the alliterative double negative (μηδεμίαν ἐν μηδενί), the sense would be either "in any way" (or "in anything [we do]") or "in anyone's way." Although ἐν μηδενί is balanced by ἐν παντί ("in every way") in v. 4, it need not be taken as neuter, for the notion of an obstacle (προσκοπή) implies a person who may stumble. The expression προσκοπὴν διδόναι means "put an obstacle in (someone's) way" (BAGD 193a), not simply "give cause for offense." So we may follow the NRSV: "We are putting no obstacle in anyone's way."[10] This "anyone" may be a believer or an unbeliever, for 1 Cor. 10:32 shows that the principle of avoiding any προσκοπή applies both within and outside the church: "Give no offense (ἀπρόσκοποι . . . γίνεσθε) to Jews or to Greeks or to the church of God" (cf. Rom. 14:13).[11]

ἵνα μὴ μωμηθῇ ἡ διακονία, "so that our ministry may not be discredited."

---

6. On Windisch's proposal (202) that 6:14–7:1 may have originally followed 6:2, see Bultmann 168; Furnish 353.

7. Thus Bernard 74; Allo 173-74; Lambrecht 109.

8. See 5:12; 7:5; 8:19-20; 9:11, 13; 10:4, 15; 11:6.

9. So also Zerwick §374, but cf. his *Analysis* 401; BDF §468(2). Technically, because διδόντες and συνιστάνοντες resume a participial form in v. 1 (συνεργοῦντες), v. 3 is not an anacoluthon. If these two participles in vv. 3-4 function as finite verbs, there is no need to mark v. 2 with dashes as parenthetical (see UBS[3, 4], as opposed to UBS[1, 2] which show dashes).

10. Similarly TCNT, RSV, NIV, NJB; Carrez 158.

11. Cf. G. Stählin, *TDNT* 6.753-54.

Here Paul states the purpose behind his constant avoidance of offense. The verb μωμάομαι, "find fault with," used here and in 8:20 but nowhere else in the NT, is formed from the name Μῶμος, a figure in Greek literature (probably not mythological) who personifies fault-finding and ridicule. In these two NT uses the censure involved is expressed by humans, not God, so there is no allusion to the judgment seat of God (Rom. 14:10) or of Christ (2 Cor. 5:10). ἡ διακονία may refer to "the" apostolic ministry in general (Barrett 182 n. 1), or to "this ministry" (of reconciliation, 5:18; anaphoric article) (Furnish 343), or to "our ministry" (possessive use of the article). Paul's preoccupation in the context is with the "credentialing" of his own ministry, so that the last interpretation, which is supported by most translations,[12] is to be preferred.

We are now in a position to seek to identify the nature of προσκοπή that Paul tries to avoid. In the narrower sense, on the basis of the ἵνα μή clause, we may identify the "obstacle" or "cause for offense" as any action that brought Paul's service into disrepute or caused it to be ridiculed or laid it open to censure. On a wider front, it would be any action that prevented the Corinthians from experiencing full reconciliation with Paul or harmony with one another, or that prevented the advancement of the gospel (cf. 1 Cor. 9:12b)[13] and the proclamation of the truth (4:2; 5:11).[14]

The initiative in this effort to avoid offense lay with Paul (διδόντες = δίδομεν), but in itself Paul's effort was no guarantee that there would be no offense given or censure received. He is thinking of unnecessary offense and unjustified censure. After all, many accusations had apparently been leveled against Paul by the Palestinian interlopers and also by the Corinthians themselves,[15] and he was always aware that his preaching of Christ crucified was "a stumbling block (σκάνδαλον) to Jews and folly to Gentiles" (1 Cor. 1:23; cf. Gal. 5:11). But where he was able to avoid putting an obstacle in anyone's path, he professed to be scrupulously careful. The issue at stake was not his reputation but the progress of the gospel.

The principle enunciated in v. 3 is timeless and universally relevant. Christian ministry is discredited when the Christian gives offense by un-Christian conduct. For the believer, who is called to embody as well as declare the good news, a lifestyle that is inconsistent with the message proclaimed undermines or at least jeopardizes the credibility of the gospel. Since the message and the messenger belong so closely together, inappropriate behavior by the messenger reflects adversely on the message. Expressed positively, the upright life of the messenger demonstrates and enhances the power of the message. It is always true that the life of the Christian is the most eloquent advertisement for the gospel.

12. TCNT, Weymouth, RSV, NEB, GNB, JB, NIV, NJB, REB, NRSV.
13. "We endure anything to avoid hindering in any way (ἵνα μή τινα ἐγκοπὴν δῶμεν) the progress of the gospel of Christ."
14. In the Pastoral Epistles concern is expressed that the word of God not be discredited (Tit. 2:5) and that the name of God and Christian teaching not be defamed (1 Tim. 6:1).
15. See the Introduction, B.4.

6:4 ἀλλ' ἐν παντὶ συνιστάνοντες ἑαυτοὺς ὡς θεοῦ διάκονοι ἐν ὑπομονῇ πολλῇ. "On the contrary, as God's servants, we try to commend ourselves in every way by our steadfast endurance." The conjunction ἀλλά signals a contrast ("on the contrary," NAB[1, 2]) between the (implied) giving of offense (v. 3) and the supplying of commendation (v. 4).[16] "In every way" or "in all circumstances" (adverbial ἐν παντί[17] as in 7:11; 11:9) Paul sought to commend himself and the Christian cause to "the conscience of each and every person" (4:2). If, like διδόντες in v. 1, συνιστάνοντες stands for a finite verb (συνιστάνομεν; cf. 4:2) and is both durative and conative ("we are trying to commend ourselves," TCNT[18]), Paul is presenting here in vv. 3-4a an apostolic ideal, just as in vv. 4b-10 we are introduced to apostolic realities. One must distinguish between Paul's laudable goal of avoiding all offense and of engaging in compelling self-commendation, and what he actually achieved in these two areas. A similar situation confronts us in 1 Cor. 10:33 where he claims κἀγὼ πάντα πᾶσιν ἀρέσκω, which must mean "I, also, try to please everybody in everything" (TCNT) or "For my part I always try to be considerate to everyone" (REB),[19] not, "I myself (actually) please everyone in everything I do."

The references to ἡ διακονία (v. 3) and θεοῦ διάκονοι (v. 4) allude to ἡ διακονία τῆς καταλλαγῆς (5:18) and ultimately to διάκονοι καινῆς διαθήκης (3:6). Taking συνιστάνω or συνίστημι[20] in the sense "cause to know," "show," or "give proof of," some versions take ὡς θεοῦ διάκονοι as providing the complement to ἑαυτούς, as if Paul had written ὡς θεοῦ διακόνους.[21] But the nominative διάκονοι should be rendered, "as God's servants, we try to commend ourselves. . . ."[22] That is, those in God's service should commend themselves in a manner appropriate to their vocation.[23]

Here again, as at 3:1; 4:2; 5:12, we confront the issue of self-commendation.[24] At 3:1 we suggested, on the basis of the data in 2 Corinthians, that two types of self-commendation should be delineated, one type that glorifies the self (= "self-praise") and is illegitimate, another type that leads to the praise of God (= "boasting in the Lord") and is legitimate. In the latter case the focus is on a God-given role that is exercised amid human weakness, in God's power and for God's glory.[25] Such a distinction between justifiable and unjusti-

---

16. A similar contrast is found in 1 Cor. 10:32-33: "Give no offense . . . just as I for my part try to please everyone in everything I do."

17. A temporal sense ("on every occasion") is possible but less likely.

18. The conative sense is also reflected in the renderings of Weymouth, NEB, REB; cf. Plummer 166.

19. Similarly RSV, NEB, NAB[1, 2], NIV.

20. See Textual Note b.

21. E.g., NJB: "In everything we prove ourselves authentic servants of God." Similarly Louw and Nida §§28.49; 88.29.

22. Cf. Robertson 454, 481.

23. Cf. Thrall 455 n. 1857.

24. On this issue in 2 Corinthians, see Hafemann, "Legitimacy" 66-88.

25. In Greek and Roman rhetorical theory a distinction was drawn between offensive and

fiable self-commendation would not have been lost on Paul's readers. Indeed, Danker (91) suggests that "Paul's Greco-Roman-oriented addressees . . . could be expected to condone the apostle's self-adulation, since a person of Paul's distinction as God's envoy would be expected to refute the charges of detractors through a recital of virtues."

That ἐν ὑπομονῇ πολλῇ is a general heading for vv. 4b-5 seems indicated by several facts. (a) Within vv. 4b-5, ὑπομονῇ is the only noun in the singular and the only qualified noun (πολλῇ). (b) Without this phrase, vv. 4b-5 contains a triad of three sets of nouns (see foregoing "Analysis"), a clearly intentional arrangement. (c) This phrase is separate from what follows, referring not to a trial but to behavior (Bultmann 170). (d) A similar phrase (ἐν πάσῃ ὑπομονῇ) occurs in 12:12 as a general covering comment. Very appropriately, in some EVV a colon is placed after the rendering of ἐν ὑπομονῇ πολλῇ, with a new sentence in v. 6 that repeats part of v. 4a (so NEB, JB, REB).

Among the virtues most cherished by both Greeks and Romans was "patient endurance" (ὑπομονή, *patientia*), the ability to stand up under the pressure of adversity and to endure suffering. But such endurance, especially as fortitude under persecution and unremitting adherence to the faith, also became a principal Christian virtue.[26] Here it prefaces Paul's "blizzard of troubles" (Chrysostom) listed in vv. 4b-5, indicating how he faced adversity. In *1 Clement* the writer maintains that "Paul showed the way to the prize for patient endurance (ὑπομονῆς βραβεῖον)" (5:5) and became "the greatest example of patient endurance (ὑπομονῆς . . . μέγιστος ὑπογραμμός)" (5:7).

ἐν θλίψεσιν, ἐν ἀνάγκαις, ἐν στενοχωρίαις. "In afflictions, in calamities, in dire straits." Here follows Paul's catalogue of hardships and triumphs (vv. 4b-10; see the "Analysis" above). The present triad is the first of three triads that deal with Paul's "outward circumstances" (vv. 4b-5). The plurals in the nine items under this heading may be classified as generalizing (thus "in affliction, in hardship, in distress," etc.) but more probably refer to multiple instances of each trial (thus Thrall 450: "in situations of affliction, calamity, and trouble, on occasions of . . ."; cf. BDF §142; Turner 28). θλῖψις (literally "pressing," "pressure") is a general, all-encompassing term, meaning "affliction" or "tribulation." In keeping with the theme of παράκλησις ἐν θλίψει that dominates chs. 1–7, the word appears frequently in the letter.[27] Undoubtedly the most dramatic θλῖψις Paul ever encountered in his career had occurred relatively recently (see 1:8-11) and significantly affected his outlook on life and death (see the Excursus after 1:11). ἀνάγκη also can mean "pressure" of any type (cf. 9:7, ἐξ ἀνάγκης, "under pressure"), thus "necessity," "obligation," but here in the

---

inoffensive self-praise. See Danker 87-91 and especially Fitzgerald 107-14. "Proper self-praise acknowledges a debt outside itself and aims at a benefit beyond itself" (Fitzgerald 114; cf. 205). For instance, the self-praise of the Stoic sage was deemed inoffensive if the ὑπομονή or μακροθυμία to which he laid claim benefited others or could be attributed to divine power.

26. See, e.g., Mark 13:13; Luke 8:15; 21:19; Rom. 5:3-4; 15:4-5; Col. 1:11; Heb. 10:36; 12:1.

27. 2 Cor. 1:4, 8; 2:4; 4:17; 6:4; 7:4; 8:2, 13.

plural it refers to "calamities" (BAGD 52d; BDF §142). In a literal sense στενοχωρία refers to confinement in a narrow space and so "restriction," "restraint." Our expressions "tight corners/spots" or "dire straits" (NEB) catch the sense suitably. When, in 4:8, Paul affirms that although he was hard-pressed at every turn, he was "not cornered" (οὐ στενοχωρούμενοι), he means that through God's gracious intervention he was never without "a way out" (ἔκβασις, 1 Cor. 10:13). It is this earlier statement of Paul that makes it unlikely (*pace* Plummer 194) that there is a progression in this triad from what is avoidable ("afflictions"), to what is unavoidable ("calamities"), to situations where no escape is possible ("dire straits"). On the other hand, we need not follow Wolff (139) in viewing the three items of the triad as synonymous, referring to exceedingly difficult circumstances ("adversities"), with the threefold repetition emphasizing that extraordinary difficulty.[28]

6:5 ἐν πληγαῖς, ἐν φυλακαῖς, ἐν ἀκαταστασίαις. "In beatings, in imprisonments, in riots." These three items form the second of the three triplets specifying the external conditions of Paul's ministry. πληγή (from πλήσσω, "strike") refers to "a blow," especially one inflicted by the lash, thus "stroke," and then "stripe," "wound." In 11:24-25 Paul refers to receiving such beatings from the Jews ("the 40 strokes minus one") and the Romans ("beaten with rods"; as in Philippi, Acts 16:23, 37). But the blows could also have been inflicted by the fist (cf. κολαφιζόμεθα, literally, "we are struck with the fist," 1 Cor. 4:11). φυλακή, "prison," here means "imprisonment" (the concrete for the abstract). We know for sure of only one imprisonment that Paul had suffered — that at Philippi, Acts 16:23-40 — before the time of writing 2 Corinthians (represented by Acts 20:2a), which well illustrates the necessarily selective nature of Luke's historiography in the book of Acts. In 11:23, where the phrases ἐν πληγαῖς and ἐν φυλακαῖς recur (in reversed order), the "beatings" are said to be "far worse" (ὑπερβαλλόντως) and the imprisonments "far more" (περισσοτέρως) than any suffering experienced by Paul's opponents at Corinth. Although ἀκαταστασίαι can refer to "disorder" (12:20) or "unruliness" (1 Cor. 14:33, singular), here it denotes "riots" (NRSV) or "tumults" (RSV), such as Paul had already encountered at Pisidian Antioch (Acts 13:50), Iconium (Acts 14:5), Lystra (Acts 14:19), Philippi (Acts 16:22), Thessalonica (Acts 17:5-7), Berea (Acts 17:13), Corinth (Acts 18:12-17), and Ephesus (Acts 19:23–20:1). As Paul uses the term here, it indicates specific cases of social disorder ranging from minor disturbances to actual lynchings, but always involving mob action.

ἐν κόποις, ἐν ἀγρυπνίαις, ἐν νηστείαις, "In hard labor, in sleepless nights, in hunger." If the second triad (v. 5a) in Paul's "outward circumstances" (vv. 4b-5) depicts sufferings directly inflicted by others, this third triad describes

---

28. But he helpfully points out (139 n. 481) the close association of θλῖψις and στενοχωρία (Deut. 28:53, 55, 57; Esth. 1:1g; Ps. 118:143; Isa. 8:22; 30:6; Rom. 2:9; 8:35) and of θλῖψις and ἀνάγκη (Job 15:24; Ps. 118:143; Zeph. 1:15; 1 Thess. 3:7). Also, ἀνάγκη and στενοχωρία are linked in 2 Cor. 12:10.

self-imposed hardships (similarly Plummer 194-95). Each of the three items could refer to the circumstances that Paul faced in pursuing his craft as a tentmaker or leather worker (Acts 18:3), or to conditions of life that arose from the fulfillment of his itinerant missionary role. κόπος is laborious toil that leads to fatigue. Paul worked assiduously at his trade so that he could maintain his financial independence from those to whom he was currently ministering (1 Cor. 4:12; 9:15; 2 Cor. 11:7, 9-10, 12). But ἐν κόποις is also an apt description of his energetic but tiring work as an evangelist and pastor (κόπος refers to missionary labor in 10:15; 11:23).[29] We should not find in the phrase ἀγρυπνίαις an allusion to a medical condition of recurrent insomnia. ἀγρυπνία, "sleeplessness," "watchfulness" (in a negative or a positive sense),[30] denotes any interference with normal sleep, whatever the cause. Twice Paul mentions his manual "toil" (κόπος) and "labor" (μόχθος) as work carried out "night and day" (νυκτὸς καὶ ἡμέρας) (1 Thess. 2:9; 2 Thess. 3:8). In addition, however, he can speak of his spiritual instruction and counseling (νουθετῶν) as being given "night and day" (νύκτα καὶ ἡμέραν) (Acts 20:31). So whether the loss of sleep arose from the pressing need for self-support or from the prolonged hours spent preaching and teaching (cf. Acts 20:7, 11),[31] the "sleepless nights" (ἀγρυπνίαι) (TCNT, NRSV) were the result of Paul's choice. In itself νηστεία can refer to "fasting" that is voluntary or involuntary. Accordingly, some interpret ἐν νηστείαις as a reference to "hunger brought about by necessity" (BAGD 538a) or involuntary abstinence from food (Bernard 76).[32] On the other hand, 11:27 seems to distinguish λιμός ("hunger" due to lack of food; cf. πεινῶμεν in 1 Cor. 4:11) from νηστείαι, which would suggest that the latter term signifies voluntary fasts (cf. Acts 13:2-3; 14:23). Moreover, in the NT the term νηστεία never describes compulsory fasting (Meyer 547). So then, items two and three in this triplet refer (respectively) to a voluntary abstention from sleep and from food.

6:6 ἐν ἁγνότητι, ἐν γνώσει, ἐν μακροθυμίᾳ, ἐν χρηστότητι. "By purity, by understanding, by patience, by kindness." As Paul's catalogue continues, he now moves on from the "outward circumstances" (vv. 4b-5) that serve to commend himself and his ministry to the Corinthians, to a listing of six God-given qualities of character (v. 6) or inward graces that further constitute that commendation. After nine cases of "local" ἐν ("in") in three triads (vv. 4b-5), we have eight instances of "instrumental" ἐν ("by") in a pair of tetrads (vv. 6-7a)

29. There is no reason to render ἐν κόποις as "overworked" (presumably on the basis of the plural), as NEB, REB, and Louw and Nida §23.73 ("overwork").

30. The cognate verb ἀγρυπνέω means (literally), "I am not asleep," and so "I am/lie awake," "I pass sleepless nights" (cf. ἠγρύπνησα, Ps. 101:8), "I am watchful" (cf. ἠγρύπνεις, "you kept yourself awake," 2 Sam. 12:21).

31. It is far less likely that ἐν ἀγρυπνίαις adverts to "vigils" (NAB[2]), although ἀγρυπνοῦντες in Eph. 6:18 denotes alertness for prayer (cf. Acts 16:25). Bishop (29-31) suggests that the background of Paul's "sleepless nights" was the Near Eastern institution of *sahrah,* the practice of sitting up at night to talk.

32. Similarly Bultmann 171: "Compulsory deprivation due to lack of money or time for meals"; Wolff, "Humility" 145 ("shortages of food").

(see the "Analysis"), indicating the means by which Paul endured his trials[33] and further commended himself.[34] The ἁγνότης that Paul seeks to exhibit is "purity" both of morals and of intention (cf. the use of ἁγιότης, "holiness," in 1:12). Such probity of life or innocence of behavior was the corollary of his renunciation of dishonesty and refusal to adopt crafty ways (4:2). In 11:3 ἁγνότης is linked with ἁπλότης ("sincerity") (but see the textual question) in describing "a sincere and pure devotion to Christ" (RSV) that the Corinthians were in danger of forfeiting because of their flirting with another gospel (11:4).

Because ἐν γνώσει is not qualified by an objective genitive such as θεοῦ (cf. 10:5) or ἀληθείας (cf. 1 Tim. 2:4) and the context affords no indication of the content of the γνῶσις, it is probably wise to give the word a broad rather than a narrow meaning, rendering it as "understanding" (NIV) or "discernment" (Cassirer) rather than seeing it as shorthand for λόγος γνώσεως ("the utterance of wisdom"), one of the Holy Spirit's gifts (1 Cor. 12:8) or as a polemical thrust against false or esoteric wisdom. Nowhere is the apostle's insight and tact more apparent than in his dealings with the Corinthians by visit and by letter, so that his readers should have readily recognized γνῶσις as one of the legitimate grounds for his self-commendation (cf. 11:6).[35] μακροθυμία is cognate with μακροθυμέω, "I defer my anger" and thus "I am long-tempered." This "patience" or "longsuffering" is linked, as here, with χρηστότης ("kindness") in Rom. 2:4; Gal. 5:22; Col. 3:12; cf. 1 Cor. 13:4 where the verbal forms are conjoined and patience is mentioned first among the qualities of love (ἡ ἀγάπη μακροθυμεῖ, χρηστεύεται). "While ὑπομονή is the courageous fortitude which endures adversity without murmuring or losing heart, μακροθυμία is the forbearance which endures injuries and evil deeds without being provoked to anger (Jas. i.19) or vengeance (Rom. xii.19)" (Plummer 196).[36] Corresponding to this distinction is the fact that it is μακροθυμία, not ὑπομονή, that is described in the NT as a divine virtue.[37] χρηστότης ("kindness"), too, is both a divine attribute (Rom. 2:4; 11:22; Eph. 2:7; Tit. 3:4) and a human virtue, a fruit of the Spirit (Gal. 5:22) to be displayed by all believers (Col. 3:12; cf. Eph. 4:32). Paul's treatment of ὁ ἀδικήσας (7:12) in 2:6-8 is a superlative example of that blend of "patience" and "kindness" that should characterize all Christians.

ἐν πνεύματι ἁγίῳ, ἐν ἀγάπῃ ἀνυποκρίτῳ, "By the gifts of the Holy Spirit, by sincere love." At this point Paul begins the second of his two tetrads (vv. 6-7a). These four items (vv. 6b-7a) are composed of "two-word" qualities, the

---

33. Or possibly the manner ("with") in which Paul faced adversity.

34. NEB and REB begin a new sentence at v. 6 and supply συνιστάνοντες (or συνιστάντες) ἑαυτούς from v. 4a: "We recommend ourselves by . . ." Bruce (*Paraphrase* 139) supplies "We seek to be characterized by . . ." and NAB[1], "conducting ourselves with . . ."

35. Commenting on the juxtaposition of ἁγνότης and γνῶσις, Garland wisely observes (308) that "moral integrity without knowledge can create almost as much havoc as a lack of integrity."

36. On the distinction between these two words, see further Turner, *Words* 315-19.

37. Of God, Rom. 2:4; 9:22; 1 Pet. 3:20; of Christ, 1 Tim. 1:16; 2 Pet. 3:15. In 2 Thess. 3:5 τοῦ Χριστοῦ is a subjective genitive, and in Rev. 3:10 μου qualifies τὸν λόγον, not τῆς ὑπομονῆς.

second word in the first pair being in the dative case (ἁγίῳ, . . . ἀνυποκρίτῳ), with the second word in the second pair being in the genitive (ἀληθείας . . . θεοῦ).

What is initially striking about the phrase ἐν πνεύματι ἁγίῳ is the presence of an apparent reference to the Holy Spirit in a list of Christian virtues, and what is more, the reference does not stand at the beginning or end of the list (as one might expect) to indicate its distinctiveness or to point to the Spirit as the source of Christian graces (cf. Gal. 5:22-23). This has prompted some to argue that πνεῦμα here is the human spirit, so that the whole phrase means "in a holy spirit" (NAB[2]) or "by a spirit of holiness" (JB) or "by . . . holiness of spirit" (NRSV; similarly Goodspeed).[38] Now it is true, as Barrett (187) observes, that elsewhere in Paul's letters πνεῦμα may refer to the human spirit (e.g., 1 Cor. 2:11; 2 Cor. 7:1, 13), but the fact remains that whenever Paul applies the adjective ἅγιος to the term πνεῦμα, the referent is invariably the Holy Spirit.[39] The difficulty of having a mention of the third person of the Trinity in the midst of an enumeration of moral qualities is lessened if we recognize in the phrase ἐν πνεύματι ἁγίῳ a case of metonymy, with "the Holy Spirit" standing for "gifts of the Holy Spirit" (NEB, REB)[40] or "the grace of the Holy Spirit."[41] A similar case where πνεῦμα may signify the gifts of the Spirit is Gal. 3:5: "He who supplies you with the Spirit (τὸ πνεῦμα)[42] and works miracles among you — does he do this because you observe the law, or because you believe what you heard?"[43] Perhaps Paul was prompted to include this reference to the Holy Spirit when he recalled that the purity, understanding, patience, and kindness he had just mentioned (v. 6a) were actually gifts or fruit of the Spirit (cf. 1 Cor. 12:8, γνῶσις; Gal. 5:22, where μακροθυμία and χρηστότης occur in the same order; 5:23, ἐγκράτεια).

Just as in Attic Greek the term ὑποκριτής referred to "one who plays a part" on the stage, especially the comedian, so too the derived negative adjective ἀν-υπόκριτος originally meant "not good at acting on the stage," and then metaphorically, "without hypocrisy," "free from pretense."[44] So ἐν ἀγάπῃ ἀνυποκρίτῳ will mean "by a love free from affectation" (JB), "by sincere love" (cf. Rom. 12:9). In such unhypocritical love "the manifestations of affection match the sincerity of the attachment: one does not play-act . . ." (Spicq 1.135).

38. Among the commentators this view is espoused by Plummer (166, "in a spirit that is holy"; 196-97) and Barrett ("in a holy spirit," 186-87). But in his earlier (1903) CGT commentary, Plummer was inclined to see ἐν πνεύματι ἁγίῳ as a reference to the Holy Spirit (100).

39. Rom. 5:15; 9:1; 14:17; 15:13, 16, 19; 1 Cor. 6:19; 12:3; 2 Cor. 13:13; Eph. 1:13; 4:30; 1 Thess. 1:5, 6; 4:8; 2 Tim. 1:14; Tit. 3:5; cf. Rom. 1:4.

40. So also Allo 176.

41. Bruce, *Paraphrase* 139. Cassirer renders the phrase, "by being imbued with the Holy Spirit" (332).

42. The anarthrous state of πνεῦμα in the phrase ἐν πνεύματι ἁγίῳ is in itself no indication of indefiniteness ("in a spirit that is holy"); all the nouns in vv. 4b-7a are anarthrous, as is common in prepositional phrases (BDF §§255, 257[2]) and in lists (cf. 11:23, 26-27).

43. πνεύματα stands for "manifestations of the Spirit" (RSV) in 1 Cor. 14:12, and for "spiritual gifts" in 1 Cor. 14:32.

44. See Spicq 1.134 n. 2.

If Paul believed that he commended himself and his ministry (v. 4) by the qualities mentioned in v. 6, then we may fairly assume that he also believed that the Christian ministry is discredited (cf. v. 3) if its representatives were characterized by impurity, insensitivity, short-temperedness, unkindness, or hypocritical love.[45]

6:7 ἐν λόγῳ ἀληθείας, ἐν δυνάμει θεοῦ. "By declaring the truth, by the power of God." Here Paul completes his second tetrad of "two-word" characteristics (vv. 6b-7a). Three times Paul uses the expression ὁ λόγος τῆς ἀληθείας (Eph. 1:13; Col. 1:5; 2 Tim. 2:15), once defining it as "the gospel" (τὸ εὐαγγέλιον, epexegetic apposition, Eph. 1:13) and once defining the ἀληθεία as "the gospel" (τοῦ εὐαγγελίου, epexegetic genitive, Col. 1:5). The anarthrous expression ἐν λόγῳ ἀληθείας is not to be distinguished in meaning from the articular ἐν τῷ λόγῳ τῆς ἀληθείας, given the canon of Apollonius.[46] In the present context ἀληθείας could be an attributive genitive, giving to the whole phrase the meaning "the message characterized by truth," "the true message," or "truthful speech,"[47] but in light of the close parallel in 4:2 (τῇ φανερώσει τῆς ἀληθείας, "by setting forth the truth openly"), λόγος should be given a verbal sense, with ἀληθείας construed as an objective genitive, "by declaring the truth" (NEB, REB).[48] As in Col. 1:5; 2 Thess. 2:12 the "truth" is to be identified with the gospel.

One of the dominant themes of 2 Corinthians is δύναμις θεοῦ, "the power of God," or more precisely, δύναμις θεοῦ ἡ ἐν ἀσθενείαις, "the power of God displayed in the midst of weakness." ἐν δυνάμει θεοῦ means "by the power that God supplies" (θεοῦ is a subjective genitive) and is precisely equivalent to the Petrine expression, ἐξ ἰσχύος ἧς χορηγεῖ ὁ θεός (1 Pet. 4:11). Already Paul has indicated his total reliance, in the wake of his devastating experience in Asia, on God's power that can even raise the dead (1:9). This utter dependence on God's power in all aspects of his life and ministry forms a stark contrast to the self-sufficiency and vigorous independence of the ideal Stoic sage who in his own person was "unconquered and unconquerable."[49] In the present context the operation of God's power is associated indirectly with the Holy Spirit (ἐν πνεύματι ἁγίῳ, v. 6) and directly with the task of preaching (ἐν λόγῳ ἀληθείας).[50] The same three items are linked in 1 Cor. 2:4 where Paul affirms that his message and preaching were accompanied by a demonstration of the Spirit's power.[51]

Plummer has suggested "a possible arrangement" of Paul's list thus far (CGT 100): "(1) ὑπομονή, exhibited ἐν θλίψεσιν, κτλ., (2) ἁγνότης, (3) γνῶσις,

45. Cf. Garland 310.

46. This is the grammatical principle that nouns in regimen generally either both have the article or both lack it (see further Harris, *Jesus* 305-7).

47. For the latter meaning, see BAGD 35d; Weymouth, RSV, NIV, NRSV.

48. So also Plummer 197; Thrall 460-61.

49. *Stoicorum Veterum Fragmenta* 1.53.1-2 (§216), cited by Fitzgerald 139.

50. Cf. Bruce's paraphrase of v. 7a: "while we proclaim the truth in the power of God" (*Paraphrase* 139).

51. ὁ λόγος μου καὶ τὸ κήρυγμά μου . . . ἐν ἀποδείξει πνεύματος καὶ δυνάμεως.

(4) μακροθυμία, (5) χρηστότης, all of which spring from Πνεῦμα Ἅγιον, exhibited ἐν ἀγάπῃ κτλ., and from δύναμις θεοῦ."

διὰ τῶν ὅπλων τῆς δικαιοσύνης τῶν δεξιῶν καὶ ἀριστερῶν. "By the weapons of righteousness for the right hand and the left." Paul's use of military metaphors is no indication of a special interest in the art of warfare, for such terminology was common coin in the ancient world.[52] Yet he conceives of the Christian ministry and the Christian life in general, from one viewpoint, as being a battle (cf. 10:3-5). The parties involved in this ceaseless warfare are not reason and passion, as in later Stoicism,[53] but the flesh and the Spirit (Gal. 5:17), the law of sin and the law of God (Rom. 7:22-25; cf. 8:2), and in an ultimate sense, Satan and his minions and God and his people (Eph. 6:11-17).

To relieve the tedium of further cases of ἐν, Paul changes his repeated preposition to διά, with the first instance bearing an instrumental sense ("by"), the second and third (in v. 8a) denoting accompanying circumstances ("in," "with").[54] There are four possible ways of understanding the genitive τῆς δικαιοσύνης that qualifies τῶν ὅπλων:

(1) qualitative: "weapons characterized by righteousness," "righteous weapons";
(2) objective: "weapons for defending righteousness," "weapons with which to fight for righteousness" (Zerwick and Grosvenor 546);
(3) epexegetic: "weapons consisting of righteousness" (Thrall 461-62), "we have righteousness as our weapon" (GNB; Louw and Nida §6.29);[55]
(4) subjective: "weapons supplied by righteousness,"[56] "weapons that (the God of) righteousness provides." In this case righteousness is either the righteousness that comes by faith (so Meyer 548), or, better, a metonym for God (cf. Eph. 6:11, 13).

Support for view (4) may be found in the close parallel in Eph. 6:11 (cf. 6:13), ἐνδύσασθε τὴν πανοπλίαν τοῦ θεου, "Put on the full armour provided by God" (REB; similarly NEB), and the parallelism with the preceding phrase ἐν δυνάμει θεοῦ, "by the power that God provides." But what are these weapons provided by God? It is unlikely that they are to be identified as virtues already mentioned in v. 6a or as any or all of the items in the tetrad of vv. 6b-7a.[57] Prob-

---

52. See Barth 2.787-93.

53. See, e.g., Seneca, *Ep.* 97.

54. In defense of this view, Collange notes (296) that vv. 7b and 8a are not formally identical and that v. 7b belongs to v. 7a (cf. the same δύναμις–ὅπλον link in 10:4; Eph. 6:10-11) and v. 8a to vv. 9-10.

55. Cf. Bruce, *Paraphrase* 139: "Righteousness is our armour"; Phillips, "Our sole defence, our only weapon, is a life of integrity." The equation, δικαιοσύνη = moral integrity, is typical of view (3).

56. So Turner 207; G. Schrenk, *TDNT* 2.210; Reumann 52.

57. But see U. Wilckens, *TDNT* 8.570.

ably the answer is to be found in the phrase that qualifies τῶν ὅπλων, namely τῶν δεξιῶν καὶ ἀριστερῶν. A ὅπλον δεξιόν is a weapon used in the right hand and a ὅπλον ἀριστερόν is a weapon used in the left, so that τὰ ὅπλα τὰ δεξιὰ καὶ ἀριστερά will refer to weapons, presumably two in number,[58] one for the right hand, another for the left. The sword in the right hand (cf. Eph. 6:17) is used for offense, the shield in the left (cf. Eph. 6:16) for defense.[59] We should not, however, take the next step and identify the sword as ἡ μάχαιρα τοῦ πνεύματος and the shield as ὁ θυρεὸς τῆς πίστεως as in Ephesians 6, for that degree of specificity lies beyond the time of 2 Corinthians. But some commentators find in the qualification τῶν δεξιῶν καὶ ἀριστερῶν simply a reference to Paul's readiness to repel an attack from any quarter (Hughes 231) or "the completeness of the equipment provided by God" (Barrett 188).[60]

Thus far in his catalogue of hardships and triumphs (vv. 4b-10) Paul has sought to commend his ministry not only by enumerating his unquestionable trials (vv. 4b-5) and patent virtues (v. 6) but also by pointing to the gifts and empowering of the Spirit (ἐν πνεύματι ἁγίῳ . . . ἐν δυνάμει θεοῦ),[61] his proclamation of a gospel that embodied truth, and his wielding of divinely provided weapons of attack and defense. Now the focus shifts from spiritual equipment for ministry (v. 7) to a recitation of the vicissitudes involved in the fulfillment of his calling (vv. 8-10).

6:8 διὰ δόξης καὶ ἀτιμίας, διὰ δυσφημίας καὶ εὐφημίας. "In honor and dishonor, in ill repute and good repute." As we have seen (at v. 7), these two cases of διά denote attendant circumstances:[62] "amid honour and disrepute, amid slander and praise" (TCNT). With regard to content (positive and negative senses), we have here a chiastic arrangement, ABBA.[63] Although δόξα generally means "splendor" or "glory" in Paul's letters, here it bears the sense "good reputation" or "renown," in contrast with ἀτιμία, "bad reputation" or "disrepute."[64] After the healing of the lame man at Lystra, Paul and Barnabas were honored (improperly!) by being called Hermes and Zeus (Acts 14:8-12). On the other hand, appropriate honor was given to Paul when the Galatian believers re-

58. Note the anarthrous ἀριστερῶν ("weapons . . . for the right and left [hands]"). The plurals τῶν δεξιῶν καὶ ἀριστερῶν are determined by the plural τῶν ὅπλων.

59. Some translations actually render δεξιῶν by "for attack/offense," and ἀριστερῶν by "for defense" (thus Berkeley, NJB; also BAGD 106d [citing Plutarch, *Moralia* 201D; Polyaenus 8.16.4]; 575d; cf. 174d; Louw and Nida §6.29; Lambrecht 112).

60. "The arms form a panoply; neither side is unarmed or unprotected" (Plummer [CGT] 101). It seems highly improbable (but see Garland 311) that the reference to "right" and "left" reflects the ancient view that associated good fortune with the right side and bad fortune with the left, so that δεξιῶν here signifies prosperity and ἀριστερῶν adversity.

61. Cf. Fee, *Presence* 333.

62. So also Zerwick §114; Thrall 461.

63. Other cases of chiasmus in 2 Corinthians are found at 2:15-16; 5:21; 7:14; 9:6; 10:11; 12:9; 13:3.

64. In the δόξα–ἀτιμία antithesis in 1 Cor. 11:14-15, δόξα has the sense "(justifiable) pride," and in 1 Cor. 15:43 "splendor" or "glory."

fused to scorn or despise him because of his bodily ailment but instead received him as if he had been "an angel of God — or Christ Jesus himself!" (Gal. 4:14). As for ἀτιμία, Paul seems to have been regularly slighted or defamed by his adversaries at Corinth and elsewhere (cf. 1 Cor. 4:10, ἡμεῖς . . . ἄτιμοι). For example, he had been castigated for fickleness (1:17), suspected of acting from worldly motives (10:2), and treated with contempt for his personal appearance and his speaking ability (10:10).

In a play on words (δυσ-φημία, "ill repute"; εὐ-φημία, "good repute") Paul restates and thus emphasizes the contrast between good and bad reputations. But whereas the former pair (δόξα — ἀτιμία) refers to non-verbal reactions to Paul as well as to statements made about him, the present pair probably describes a twofold verbal reaction (φημία, from φήμη, "report," "repute"), now praise or acclaim, now defamation or slander (cf. Rom. 3:8; 1 Cor. 4:13). The implication of both pairs is that irrespective of the ways in which Paul was treated, he maintained his spiritual equilibrium and contentment (cf. Phil. 4:11-12; 1 Tim. 6:6).

At this point the syntactical construction changes and we have a further seven antitheses, all introduced by ὡς ("as"),[65] with the second element prefaced by adversative καί ("and yet," BAGD 392d) five times and adversative δέ ("but") twice. It will be useful to set out the antitheses in two columns so that we can ascertain if there is any conceptual element common to each column.

A			B	
1. as deceivers	and	yet	truthful	
2. as unknown	and	yet	well known	
3. as facing death	and	yet, see,	we live on	
4. as punished	and	yet not	killed	
5. as sorrowful		but always	rejoicing	
6. as poor		but	enriching	many
7. as having nothing	and	yet	possessing	everything

Several possibilities emerge.

(a) Items under A portray an ill report (δυσφημία), those under B a good report (εὐφημία, v. 8a). But 5A, 6A, and 7A do not readily fit this scheme.

(b) The first item in each contrast depicts external appearance, how things appear to be, while the second refers to internal reality, how things actually are; the antithesis is between "seeing and being" (Meyer 548). But 3B and 4B are both externally verifiable.

(c) The first element represents a κατὰ σάρκα outlook, a worldly assess-

65. "As vv. 9-10 shows, ὡς does not mean 'as if,' of the outward appearance, but 'as,' of the actual state" (Lietzmann 128); but see Barnett 331 and n. 2.

ment, the second a κατὰ πνεῦμα perspective or a divine viewpoint.[66] But again, 3B and 4B are not exclusively spiritual or divine perspectives.

(d) It seems preferable, therefore, to see all seven antitheses as expressing two concurrent and paradoxical realities of Paul's apostolic life.[67] Behind each antithesis there may lie some allegation or unflattering observation made by Paul's calumniators, so that vv. 8b-10 may not merely be self-commendatory (cf. v. 4) and afford a model of exemplary attitudes but may also serve an apologetic or even polemical purpose.[68] On a wider literary front these antitheses illustrate two themes that are central in this letter — life in the midst of death (note the third antithesis; cf. 4:10-12); and, more directly, the all-surpassing power of God evident in the midst of human weakness (cf. 4:7; 12:9-10) as Paul not only patiently endures hardships (cf. 6:4) but finds in them occasions for the display of God's strength so that he wins glorious victories (cf. ὑπερνικῶμεν, Rom. 8:37) over his trials. As James expresses it (1:2), he was finding supreme joy when surrounded by various trials (cf. 1 Pet. 1:6; 4:12-14).[69]

ὡς πλάνοι καὶ ἀληθεῖς. "As deceivers and yet truthful." The term πλάνος, from πλανάω, "lead/go astray," "deceive," is used as an adjective in 1 Tim. 4:1 (πνεύματα πλάνα, "deceitful spirits") but here is used substantivally, "deceiver" or "imposter." Obviously Paul did not regard himself as a deceiver, so the sense must be "considered impostors" (BAGD 666a) or "treated as impostors" (RSV, NRSV). During his ministry Jesus had been accused of leading the people astray (πλανᾷ, John 7:12), and after his death he had been called "that imposter" (ἐκεῖνος ὁ πλάνος, Matt. 27:63). It was now a case of "like master, like slave" (cf. Matt. 10:25), as Paul in turn was deemed a deceiver, perhaps in connection with his altered travel plans (1:15–2:1), perhaps because his pastoral techniques or financial dealings were seen as manipulative (cf. πλεονεκτέω in 7:2; 12:17), or perhaps those of his compatriots who saw Jesus as a messianic pretender viewed Paul as a champion of a false Messiah and therefore a deceiver. Whatever the reason or reasons for this charge against Paul, he rebuts it in the only way he can — by affirming his truthfulness (ἀληθεῖς). His divine call and mission are genuine (cf. Gal. 1:1, 15-16), his message is true (4:2; 6:7), and he does not lie (cf. οὐ ψεύδομαι in 11:31; Rom. 9:1; Gal. 1:20; 1 Tim. 2:7). What Paul signifies by ἀληθεῖς ("truthful," "honest," "genuine") is partly summed up in 2:17, "we act from pure motives, and, as persons sent from God, we speak in the sight of God and at Christ's direction."

---

66. Similarly Bruce 212. JB in vv. 8b-10 has "taken for imposters . . . said to be dying . . . rumoured to be executed . . . thought most miserable . . . taken for paupers . . . for people having nothing. . . ." Wand achieves the same effect by the use of quotation marks: "I am an 'imposter' . . . 'unknown' . . . 'defunct' . . . 'beaten' . . . 'gloomy' . . . 'poverty-stricken' . . . 'penniless.' . . ."

67. For an overview of "paradoxicality" in Paul, see Hotze 72-138.

68. But Fitzgerald sees all of 6:3-10 as primarily paraenetic in function, providing the "character basis" on which Paul's exhortation rests (184-201, 204).

69. For an illuminating set of parallels between 6:4-10 and various Synoptic beatitudes, see Hanson, *Paradox* 69.

6:9 ὡς ἀγνοούμενοι καὶ ἐπιγινωσκόμενοι. "As unknown, and yet well known." As elsewhere in these antitheses, the ὡς clause states one assessment of some aspect of Paul's life or ministry, while καί (or δέ in the first two contrasts in v. 10) introduces another, totally different estimation.[70]

(1) Here the contrast may be between views of Paul held outside and within the church. The sense is not exactly "obscure yet famous" (JB) or "as nobodies to these, and celebrities to those" (Plummer 166), but rather that non-believers would or did view him as an insignificant non-entity, someone uncelebrated for wisdom or scholarship or oratorical skills (cf. Windisch 208), whereas believers in general acknowledged his apostolic calling and recognized his distinctive gifts. Thrall comments (465) that "since this section as a whole (vv. 3-10) is primarily concerned with the apostle in relation to his fellow-men and to external circumstances it is probable that ἐπιγινωσκόμενοι does refer to human recognition."

(2) It is, however, equally possible that a human perspective is being contrasted with a divine viewpoint that is shared by some humans. Apparently Paul's rivals at Corinth and some of the Corinthians influenced by them regarded him as non-credentialed as an apostle or at least as lacking the proper apostolic credentials (cf. 3:1; 5:12; 10:10; 11:6; 1 Cor. 9:1). In contrast, Paul's genuine apostolicity was known to God (1:1; Gal. 1:1) and recognized by the "pillars" of the Jerusalem church (Gal. 2:7, 9), and Paul still hoped it would be recognized by the Corinthians themselves (5:12) (Barrett 189). Support for this second view may be found in 1 Cor. 13:12 where the same verb, ἐπιγινώσκω, is used in the passive (as here) with God as the implied agent ("then I shall know in full even as I have been fully known [ἐπεγνώσθην]").[71]

ὡς ἀποθνήσκοντες καὶ ἰδοὺ ζῶμεν. "As facing death, and yet, see, we live on." "Death-life" terminology is common in Paul's letters, especially 2 Corinthians. It is possible but unlikely that Paul is speaking here of death to sin and self (Rom. 6:1-14) through being crucified with Christ (Gal. 2:20), for this is a wholly positive spiritual concept for Paul whereas the antithetical καί presupposes that the preceding concept is in some sense negative in import. At best ἀποθνήσκοντες could refer to both physical death and spiritual mortification (thus Martin 181-82). Another option is to relate ἀποθνήσκοντες purely to physical debilitation and ζῶμεν to spiritual rejuvenation, which would make this antithesis precisely parallel to 4:16 (εἰ καὶ ὁ ἔξω ἡμῶν ἄνθρωπος διαφθείρεται, ἀλλ᾽ ὁ ἔσω ἡμῶν ἀνακαινοῦται ἡμέρᾳ καὶ ἡμέρᾳ). To be preferred, however, is the view that sees in ἀποθνήσκοντες a reference to continual exposure to physical death or encounters with death, and in ζῶμεν a reference to on-going physical life: "as ever at death's door, and yet behold! we live on"

---

70. Citing v. 9 BAGD (392d) observes that καί "emphasiz(es) a fact as surprising or unexpected or noteworthy."

71. On either view, the prefix ἐπι- is intensive (BAGD 291a): "well known" (view 1) or "fully known" (view 2).

(Plummer 166); "we are constantly exposed to death, and yet (as you see) we continue to live."[72] Two points support this interpretation. (1) Paul has already mentioned such exposure (4:10-11) and such encounters (1:9-10; 4:12) as he did earlier in 1 Cor. 15:30-31 ("Why do we face danger every hour? Not a day passes without my being at death's door") and will later in 11:23 (ἐν θανάτοις πολλάκις). (2) The whole phrase alludes to Ps. 117:17 (LXX): "I shall not die (οὐκ ἀποθανοῦμαι), but I shall live (ζήσομαι) and recount what the Lord has done." (The next phrase is based directly on the following verse in this psalm — see below.) Since the psalm is a song of thanksgiving for victory in battle, the reference to escape from death and to the celebration of divine deliverance by the living must apply to physical life and death. (3) As well as meaning "I am dying," the present tense of ἀποθνῄσκω can mean "I stand in danger of death."[73]

ἰδού marks a surprise, introducing something contrary to all appearance or expectation. The change from participles to finite verb (ζῶμεν)[74] — and further participles follow — also indicates the intensity of Paul's relief at deliverance from death: "As dying, and yet here we are — alive!" The classic instances of such an experience for Paul occurred at Lystra when, after being pelted with stones and left for dead, he simply stood up (ἀναστάς), perhaps in answer to prayer offered by the recent converts from Lystra who had formed a circle around him (Acts 14:19-20); and "in Asia" when, after being utterly and unbearably crushed so that he despaired of life, he was delivered by the God who raises the dead (1:8-10).

ὡς παιδευόμενοι καὶ μὴ θανατούμενοι. "As punished and yet not killed." Both participles are in the passive voice. But who is the implied agent or agents? If Paul has in mind purely human action, the sense could be either "rumoured to be (= ὡς) executed before we are sentenced [to death]" (JB), or "scourged but not executed" (NJB). In the former case the point is the patent miscarriage of justice; in the latter, the avoidance of the death penalty. Neither interpretation can be ruled out as impossible, but both must be deemed improbable because although a life setting could be envisaged for both views, they overlook the unambiguous OT background of the statement.

With regard to agency, the choice is not between human action and divine action, but between human action and divine action lying behind human action. Those who carry out the punishment and yet do not kill Paul are humans, but their actions fulfill a divine purpose. This becomes clear when we consider the OT passage which lies behind our phrase. "The Lord punished me severely (παιδεύων ἐπαίδευσεν) and yet (καί) he did not give me over to death (τῷ θανάτῳ)" (Ps. 117:18, LXX). Psalm 118 (in the MT and EVV) is the last song

---

72. Bruce, *Paraphrase* 139.

73. Cf. BAGD 91d, citing *inter alios* Phalaris, *Epistle* 52 ("ἀποθνῄσκοντες = be in danger of death").

74. Sometimes Paul follows a finite verb with coordinate participles (5:12; 7:5; 8:19; 9:11, 13; 10:4, 15 [twice]; 11:6) (Zerwick §374), while at other times (as here in 6:9; cf. 1 Cor. 7:37), a participle is followed by καί and a finite verb (Zerwick §375).

and the climax of the "Egyptian Hallel" (Psalms 113–18) that was sung at the great Jewish religious festivals and is frequently cited or alluded to in the NT. It is a processional thanksgiving liturgy, celebrating a God-given military victory. In the presence of the congregation the king testifies to Yahweh's powerful intervention in answer to prayer when he and his army were confronted in war by a confederacy of nations (possibly 2 Chron. 20:1-30). "Yahweh's right hand has done mighty things! Yahweh's right hand is lifted high; Yahweh's right hand has done mighty things!" (Ps. 118:15b-16). In spite of being brought face to face with death, the king was spared: "I did not die, but survived[75] to proclaim what Yahweh has done" (v. 17). Paul has alluded to this verse in the previous phrase (ὡς ἀποθνῄσκοντες καὶ ἰδοὺ ζῶμεν). Then the king continues: "Yahweh punished me severely, but he did not give me over to death" (v. 18). That is, the king interprets the machinations of his enemies that led to the endangerment of his life as evidence of Yahweh's drastic but beneficial discipline. So too, we suggest, Paul perceives the disciplinary hand of God behind the punishing hand of man.[76] Paul had endured physical punishment for the gospel's sake (e.g., Acts 16:22-23; cf. 2 Cor. 11:23, "with innumerable beatings"), but the outcome had not been death but the benefits of παιδεία κυρίου, whose "fruit is seen in the peacefulness of a righteous life" (Heb. 12:11, TCNT). Trials and hardships are not proof of God's displeasure but are evidence of his painful but loving discipline (cf. Prov. 3:11-12; Heb. 12:4-11) that seeks the refinement of our faith (cf. 1 Pet. 1:6-7). "In Rev 3:19 the basic principle of παιδεία κυρίου is adopted: ὅσους ἐὰν φιλῶ, ἐλέγχω καὶ παιδεύω, God Himself intervenes with educative punishments in the life of men because He loves them and can in this way kindle zeal for repentance."[77]

6:10 ὡς λυπούμενοι ἀεὶ δὲ χαίροντες. "As sorrowful but always rejoicing." The noun λύπη ("pain," "sorrow") and the cognate verb λυπέω ("cause pain/sorrow") are common in this epistle, being used six times and twelve times (respectively), out of twenty-four total Pauline uses. Sometimes Paul's sorrow was personal, as when he was grieved by slander or groundless accusation (2:5; see the commentary there) or when he was acutely disappointed by the behavior of his converts (2:4). But at other times his sorrow was vicarious, as when he sympathized with others in pain (cf. 1 Cor. 12:26). But perhaps his deepest sorrow was occasioned by the unbelief of his fellow Jews (Rom. 9:1-3); this caused him "great grief" (λύπη . . . μεγάλη) and "constant anguish" (ἀδιάλειπτος ὀδύνη) (Rom. 9:2). Yet whatever the reason for his sorrow, his joy was inextinguishable. This joy is "in the Lord" (cf. Phil. 3:1; 4:4) in the sense that he is its object (cf. Rom. 5:11; Ps. 32:11; 64:10) and it is prompted by having or remembering all the spiritual benefits afforded those

---

75. That these two MT verbs are preterits seems indicated by the conceptual parallelism with v. 18. The LXX, however, construes them as futures (ἀποθανοῦμαι . . . ζήσομαι).

76. Cf. 12:7-9 where Paul's σκόλοψ τῇ σαρκί is ἄγγελος Σατανᾶ and yet was given by God (ἐδόθη, 12:7).

77. G. Bertram, *TDNT* 5.623.

"in Christ." Because those benefits are unchanging, the joy can be constant (cf. πάντοτε with χαίρετε in Phil. 4:4; 1 Thess. 5:16), as Jesus promised (John 16:22), and it can be experienced in the midst of suffering (Rom. 5:3-5; cf. Jas. 1:2-4; 1 Pet. 4:13).

ὡς πτωχοὶ πολλοὺς δὲ πλουτίζοντες. "As poor but enriching many." It is unlikely that both πτωχοί and πλουτίζοντες are to be taken literally, for Paul would scarcely credit himself with enriching the poor in the Jerusalem church by the monetary gifts of Gentile believers (Rom. 15:25-27); moreover, that collection was still in progress at the time of writing (8:1–9:15). Nor are both terms likely to be figurative,[78] for, unlike Matt. 5:3 (μακάριοι οἱ πτωχοὶ τῷ πνεύματι), the word πτωχοί is unqualified here, so the assumption must be that Paul is envisaging material poverty. So we conclude that πτωχοί is to be understood literally and πλουτίζοντες figuratively.[79]

Paul elsewhere attests to his material poverty. "To the present time we are hungry and thirsty, we are poorly clothed . . . and homeless" (1 Cor. 4:11; cf. Rom. 8:35; 2 Cor. 11:9, 27; Phil. 4:11-12). Apparently his manual labor in tentmaking (Acts 18:3), what he calls "working with our own hands" (1 Cor. 4:12; cf. 1 Thess. 2:9; 2 Thess. 3:7-8), served simply to meet the basic necessities of life (Acts 20:34);[80] he never accumulated any money or possessions beyond what was essential for the sustaining of his life and ministry.[81] The few gifts that he did accept from certain Macedonian churches (11:8-9; Phil. 4:15-18) would have fallen within this category. His poverty was a matter of choice, not circumstance. He wished to avoid ever giving the impression that the gospel was not free of charge or that monetary gain was his motivation for preaching (11:7-12; 1 Cor. 9:12, 15, 18). Also, he chose never to become in any sense a burden to his converts (11:9; 12:13, 16).

As in 9:11 and 1 Cor. 1:5, the only other NT uses of πλουτίζω, the verb carries a figurative sense and relates to present not eschatological enrichment.[82] Through Paul the Corinthians had been enriched in Christ in every way (1 Cor. 1:5). In this pattern of "poverty–enrichment of others" Paul was following the example of Jesus (8:9).[83] The paradoxical reality the apostle expresses in this antithesis may be usefully compared with the sentiments of Prov. 13:7: "Some pretend to be rich, yet have nothing; others pretend to be poor, yet have great wealth" (NRSV). Paul did not pretend to be poor but actu-

---

78. But see Martin 184, following Collange 299.

79. So also, among others, Furnish 359; Barnett 333.

80. Accordingly, ὑστερηθείς (11:9) probably refers to the lack of such basic necessities.

81. Acts 24:26, which speaks of Felix's hope of receiving a bribe from Paul, is no proof that Paul was not materially impoverished. In his defense before Felix Paul had mentioned that he had come to Jerusalem with "alms and offerings" (Acts 24:17). Presumably Felix therefore assumed that Paul had access to finances that could be tapped for a bribe that would secure his release. Or Felix may have thought that Paul's friends (Acts 24:23) might provide funds.

82. E. Bammel, *TDNT* 6.910 and n. 226, who notes that the present antithesis "is the only one to transcend the sphere of the personal" (cf. πολλούς) (*TDNT* 6.910).

83. Cf. F. Hauck and W. Kasch, *TDNT* 6.329.

ally was impoverished, and as opposed to having great wealth himself, he specialized in imparting to others "the incalculable riches of Christ" (Eph. 3:8) or "the superlative worth of knowing Christ" (Phil. 3:8; cf. Rom. 10:12; 11:12; Col. 1:25-27).

ὡς μηδὲν ἔχοντες καὶ πάντα κατέχοντες. "As having nothing and yet possessing everything." To express the contrast Paul reverts to καί ("and yet") after using δέ ("but") in the two preceding antitheses. Regarding the ten participles in vv. 9-10, Robertson comments, "When Paul's heart was all ablaze with passion, as in 2 Corinthians, he did pile up participles like boulders on the mountainside, a sort of volcanic eruption" (1136). The difference between the two verbs involved in the wordplay (ἔχοντες–κατέχοντες; see also 1:13; 3:2; 4:8) is that between simple and secure possession[84] or possibly temporary and permanent possession, with ἔχω here meaning "have as one's own" (BAGD 332a), and κατέχω, "keep in one's possession" (BAGD 423a).[85] Clearly μηδέν and πάντα cannot be interpreted literally; both terms are relative, being rhetorical hyperbole.[86] μηδὲν ἔχοντες will mean either "thought of as having nothing" (Spicq 2.290), "taken . . . for people having nothing" (JB), or, if this is Paul's own appraisal of his situation, "with little more than life's necessities — food, clothing, and shelter[87] — and often without even these" (cf. 1 Cor. 4:11; 11:27).[88] In modern Western terms, he lived well below "the poverty line."[89] But in spite of being poor, even by ancient standards, Paul saw himself as securely possessing everything that was real and worthwhile, everything of eternal value (cf. 4:18). He regarded "everything" (πάντα) — all his past privileges and sources of confidence — as "loss" (ζημία) in view of the incomparable value of knowing Christ (Phil. 3:7-8) at the same time as viewing "everything" (πάντα) as his own because he belonged exclusively to Christ (cf. 1 Cor. 3:21-23) and therefore was destined to share, along with all believers, the unfading glory of God's own life (Rom. 8:17, κληρονόμοι . . . θεοῦ).

On this supremely high but beautifully simple note Paul concludes his

84. Cf. Bruce, *Paraphrase* 139: "We are destitute, and yet secure in our possession of everything."

85. On the range of meaning of κατέχω in the NT, see Spicq 2.285-91. The present antithesis is paraphrased in *Ep. Diog.* 5:13 as πάντων ὑστεροῦνται, καὶ ἐν πᾶσι περισσεύουσιν, "they lack everything, and yet have everything in abundance," in reference to early Christians. *Epistle to Diognetus* 5:12-14 is clearly dependent on 2 Cor. 6:8-10.

86. This statement was a rhetorical commonplace, especially in the Stoic and Cynic traditions; see Furnish 348; Mealand 277-79, who cites (278) pseudo-Crates, *Epistle* 7 ἔχοντες μηδὲν πάντ' ἔχομεν ("although we have nothing, we possess everything").

87. 2 Tim. 4:13 mentions Paul's βιβλία ("books," probably the Scriptures) and μεμβράναι ("parchments" may refer to personal papers, possibly including copies of letters he had sent to churches and letters he had received from churches).

88. Paul's "having nothing" should not be seen as the result of the surrender of possessions or money to achieve a state of poverty.

89. But Paul can hardly be called a "pauper" (a rendering of πτωχός in the sixth antithesis, found in Moffatt and JB [but not NJB]), if this term bears its usual meaning of "a person without the means of livelihood."

recitation of his apostolic hardships and triumphs. His aim throughout has been to commend himself and his ministry to the Corinthians "in every way" (ἐν παντί) (v. 4a) — by sketching his external circumstances (vv. 4b-5), by describing his spiritual characteristics (v. 6) and equipment (v. 7), and by outlining the paradoxes of apostolic life (vv. 8-10).

Bibliography

Bash • Bultmann, *Stil* • Ebner 243-330 • Fee, *Presence* 332-35 • A. M. Festugière, "ΥΠΟΜΟΝΗ dans la tradition grecque," *RevScRel* 21 (1931) 477-86 • Fitzgerald • Fridrichsen, "Stilparallele" • Friedrich • Furnish, "Reconciliation" • P. J. Grabe, *The Power of God in Paul's Letters* (WUNT 123; Tübingen: Mohr, 2000) • Güttgemanns • Hafemann, *Defense* 72-79 • Hafemann, *Spirit* 76-83 • Hahn, "Tag" • Hanson, *Ministry* 84-85 • Hanson, *Paradox* 55-78, 120-23 • Hodgson • Höistad • Kamlah • Kleinknecht • Lambrecht, "Time" • C. U. Manus, "Apostolic Suffering (2 Cor 6:4-10): The Sign of Christian Existence and Identity," *Asia Journal of Theology* 1 (1987) 41-54 • Mealand • Murphy-O'Connor 63-65 • Neumann • L. A. Rood, "Le Christ comme δύναμις θεοῦ," *RechBib* 5 (1960) 93-108 • Schrage • W. C. van Unnik, "Die Rücksicht auf die Reaktion der Nicht-Christen als Motiv in der altchristlichen Paränese," in *Judentum–Urchristentum–Kirche* (Festschrift for J. Jeremias), ed. W. Eltester (Berlin, 1960) 221-34 • A. von Harnack, "κόπος (κοπιᾶν, οἱ κοπιῶντες) im frühchristlichen Sprachgebrauch," *ZNW* 27 (1928) 1-10 • Wibbing

4. The Openness and Consolation of the Apostolic Ministry (6:11–7:4)

Paul's depiction of the apostolic ministry now takes a decidedly pastoral turn as he focuses in detail on his present relationship with his converts at Corinth. It is no coincidence that immediately after vividly portraying what he has endured as one of God's servants, he launches into what may be described as the most intensely personal and emotionally charged portion of his letter (6:11–7:4). This is unquestionably the "psychological moment" for his series of paternal pleas (πλατύνθητε, 6:13; καθαρίσωμεν . . . ἐπιτελοῦντες, 7:1; χωρήσατε, 7:2) and apostolic directives (μὴ γίνεσθε, 6:14; ἐξέλθατε . . . ἀφορίσθητε . . . μὴ ἅπτεσθε, 6:17). When he says that he has πολλὴ παρρησία in relation to the Corinthians (7:14), the three main meanings of παρρησία (see BAGD 630c, d) all seem to be relevant: he speaks very candidly with them, concealing nothing and passing over nothing ("frankness"); he is transparently honest with them ("openness"); he bluntly exposes sensitive issues and confronts the Corinthians directly with what they need to do ("boldness"). As he addresses them with this total freedom of speech, he calls them to reciprocal affection (6:11-13; 7:2-3) and holiness of life (6:14–7:1) before expressing his confidence, pride, and joy in them (7:4).

a. A Plea for Generous Affection (6:11-13)

In this section Paul is acting as a "minister of reconciliation" in a different sense than that expressed in 5:18-19. "The message of reconciliation" (5:19) is concerned with divine-human relations, but once humans are reconciled to God, they are obliged and equipped to become reconciled to one another; that is, they become agents of reconciliation in the horizontal dimension. Here Paul is seeking to convert the Corinthians' partial reconciliation with himself into full reconciliation, to restore cordial, reciprocal relations, such as he seems to have enjoyed with the Philippian believers. He expressed a similar thought in 1:13b-14a, contrasting the Corinthians' partial understanding and appreciation of him (ἐπέγνωτε ἡμᾶς ἀπὸ μέρους, v. 14a) with the full understanding and appreciation he hoped to gain (ἐλπίζω δὲ ὅτι ἕως τέλους ἐπιγνώσεσθε, v. 13b). So then, Paul is both an agent of reconciliation in that he initiates the movement toward harmony, and a participant in the process of reconciliation in that he is one of the parties involved in that process. In that sense he is reflecting God's role as both agent and participant in divine-human reconciliation.

11*Corinthians, we are speaking frankly to you; our^a heart is wide open to you.*
12*There is no restriction in our affection for you, but there is in yours for us.*
13*Now as a comparable recompense — I am speaking as to my children — open wide your hearts also.*

TEXTUAL NOTES

a. Although the proto-Alexandrian MSS ℵ and B (along with 0243 1881 2464 *pc*) read ὑμῶν, this reading is to be rejected as impossible in the context (literally, "your heart is wide open [to us]"). It probably arose through the scribal error of itacism.

6:11 Τὸ στόμα ἡμῶν ἀνέῳγεν πρὸς ὑμᾶς, Κορίνθιοι, ἡ καρδία ἡμῶν πεπλάτυνται· "Corinthians, we are speaking frankly to you; our heart is wide open to you." It is only when his emotions are deeply stirred in the course of dictating a letter that Paul addresses the recipients directly. Ὦ ἀνόητοι Γαλάται, ("O foolish Galatians," Gal. 3:1) shows Paul's chagrin at the Galatians' senselessness in failing to see that the Judaizers had cast a spell on them. Then in Phil. 4:15 he addresses the Philippians directly (Φιλιππήσιοι) as he expresses his warm appreciation for their initiative in entering into a financial partnership with him.[1] In 6:11-13 Paul indicates his deep emotion and tender affection by the use of direct address (Κορίνθιοι, v. 11) and the paternal appeal to his children in the faith (τέκνοις, v. 13). Although the term Κορίνθιοι is narrower than the addressees mentioned in 1:1 ("the church of God that is in Corinth, together with all God's people who are in the whole of Achaia"), we may regard it as

---

1. The only other cases of direct address are 1 Tim. 1:18; 6:20, where (τέκνον) Τιμόθεε indicates Paul's warm paternal affection (cf. Gal. 4:19).

shorthand for the whole group. There is no reason to believe that Paul is now addressing only one sector of the Corinthian church.

The opening of the mouth may be a circumlocution for "speaking" or "beginning to speak," so that ἐν ἀνοίξει τοῦ στόματός μου (Eph. 6:19) may mean "when I speak" (NRSV) or "when I begin to speak" (TCNT).[2] Clearly, neither of these meanings is applicable here in v. 11; it is obvious that Paul is "speaking" to the Corinthians. Moreover, the parallel statement in v. 11b (note the asyndeton) speaks of the wide openness of Paul's heart, not simply the expression of his heart. The reference is to uninhibited, frank speech. Τὸ στόμα ἀνοίγειν πρός τινα means "to be completely open with someone" (Louw and Nida §§33, 252).[3] ἀνέῳγεν is an (intransitive) perfect with a present stative meaning,[4] "is open" (also 1 Cor. 16:9). So the literal rendering of our phrase is "our mouth is open toward you,"[5] but the sense is "we are speaking frankly to you."[6] Whether Paul is referring back to 6:3-10[7] or to the whole letter up to this point,[8] it is impossible to say, but it would be unwise to exclude a prospective glance as well, since 6:11–7:4 in particular is marked by an open frankness.

The verb πλατύνω, "enlarge," "broaden" (from πλατύς, "broad"), (pass.) "be wide open," is found only three times in the NT — here and in v. 13 figuratively, and in Matt. 23:5 literally, of the Pharisees' phylacteries. In the present case the perfect tense (πεπλάτυνται) does imply a previous action, but as generally with the perfect, the emphasis is on the resulting present state, "is open wide" (BAGD 667a), "stands wide open" (Zerwick and Grosvenor 546). So we move from "is open" (ἀνέῳγα, v. 11a) to "is wide open" (πεπλάτυνται, v. 11b)[9] and from τὸ στόμα to ἡ καρδία. The mouth expresses what is in the heart (Matt. 12:34): Paul's frank talking to the Corinthians testified to his unrestricted love for them (πρὸς ὑμᾶς is to be supplied from v. 11a).[10] He is "ready to receive them with all their worries and suspicions, their complaints and accusations."[11]

2. But in Ezek. 29:21; 33:22 "the open(ed) mouth" refers to the removal of muteness; in Ezek. 16:63, to self-justification (cf. Rom. 3.19).

3. Surprisingly, BAGD 710c classifies πρός here as expressing a "hostile relationship," "against."

4. Fanning 299 (who notes that this type of perfect has "no implication of a prior action which produced the state"); Robertson 895 (a durative perfect).

5. BAGD 71c; similarly RSV.

6. Cf. Montgomery: "I am unsealing my lips to you." NEB and REB translate "we have spoken very frankly [NRSV, frankly] to you," but it would seem appropriate to catch the present implications of ἀνέῳγεν. Barrett renders the idiom differently, "I have let my tongue run away with me" (191), but Paul's complete freedom of speech is still the import.

7. Thus Meyer 551; Martin 185.

8. Thus Thrall 468.

9. But Bieringer ("Liebe" 193-213), noting the στενοχωρέω–πλατύνω contrast in vv. 11b-12a, finds the central notion in v. 11 to be that of breadth rather than openness.

10. Plummer (203) cites Bengel: Ab ore ad cor concludere debebant ("They ought to have made a deduction from the mouth to the heart").

11. G. Bertram, TDNT 7.608, citing Bengel: Sat spatii habet cor nostrum ad vos capiendos ("Our heart has enough room to contain you").

We cannot know when Paul's heart for his converts at Corinth became "enlarged," but they could find evidence of that "enlargement" and "wide-openness" in his decision to visit them after the limited success of 1 Corinthians, in his decision to spare them a second painful visit (2:1) and to write a letter instead so that they might see the intensity of his love for them (2:4), and in his writing the present letter with its pastoral concern for "the wrongdoer" and the church (2:5-11).[12]

6:12 οὐ στενοχωρεῖσθε ἐν ἡμῖν, στενοχωρεῖσθε δὲ ἐν τοῖς σπλάγχνοις ὑμῶν. "There is no restriction in our affection for you, but there is in yours for us." It was undoubtedly the idea of enlargement in v. 11b (πεπλάτυνται) that triggered the opposite notion of narrowing or restriction that is expressed in v. 12. στενοχωρέω (from στενός, "narrow," and χῶρος, "place," "space") means "restrain," "cramp," "press upon," "confine" (see 4:8). In translating this verb here, some EVV use the idea of restraint,[13] others constraint[14] or pressure,[15] or lack of space.[16] ἐν ἡμῖν is sometimes taken in an instrumental sense ("by us"),[17] but the two uses of ἐν in this verse more probably describe the sphere in which (local ἐν) the restraint or restriction operates (v. 12b) or does not operate (v. 12a). "In us" means "in our heart"[18] (cf. 7:3, ἐν ταῖς καρδίαις ἡμῶν ἐστε) or, better, "in our affection" (cf. v. 12b, ἐν τοῖς σπλάγχνοις ὑμῶν). "You are not short of space in our affection (for you)" is litotes for "you enjoy full space in our affection" or "I love you with an expansive heart."[19] Paul is reassuring the Corinthians of the breadth and depth of his love for them, perhaps against the backdrop of a charge that he had little love for them (cf. 11:11) or that there was insufficient room for them in his heart. Moffatt's rendering graphically reflects such an understanding of v. 12: "'Restraint'? — that lies with you, not me."

12. If a particular OT passage is in Paul's mind as he writes v. 11, it may be Ps. 118:32 (LXX): "I ran in the path shown in your commands, when you enlarged my heart (ὅταν ἐπλάτυνας τὴν καρδίαν μου)," where the "widened heart" denotes increased understanding and responsiveness. The only other place in the LXX where καρδία and πλατύνω are used together is Deut. 11:6 (apart from a variant reading in Deut. 6:12): "Take heed, lest your heart become inflated (μὴ πλατυνθῇ ἡ καρδία σου) and you transgress and serve other gods and worship them." (On this verse as a possible background to 6:11 and 6:16, see Thrall, "Problem" 146; and especially Murphy-O'Connor, "Context" 273-75.) Beale, on the other hand (followed now by Thrall, 469-70), sees in 6:11b (ἡ καρδία ἡμῶν πεπλάτυνται) a reference to Isa. 60:5 and the "restoration from exile" motif that appears in 6:16-18 (576-77); so also Webb 151-54, 175.

13. E.g., NRSV: "There is no restriction in our affections, but only in yours"; similarly RSV, NASB.

14. E.g., NEB: "On our part there is no constraint; any constraint there may be is in yourselves"; similarly JB, NAB[2].

15. Young and Ford 267: ". . . there's no pressure on you from us, but you are pressurized by your own feelings."

16. E.g., NAB[1]: "There is no lack of room for you in us; the narrowness is in you"; similarly TCNT, Weymouth, Goodspeed, Berkeley; Barrett 191; Furnish 359; Thrall 450.

17. Thus RSV, NASB, NAB[2]; Furnish 359.

18. Bultmann 176; BAGD 766c, "in the open heart of the apostle."

19. Cf. Zerwick, *Analysis* 401.

Paul's basic point in vv. 11b and 12a is that his "heart" for the Corinthians is wide open, not constricted. In medical terms, an enlarged heart is a dangerous liability; in spiritual terms, an enlarged heart is a productive asset.

τὰ σπλάγχνα are "the inward parts," the upper or nobler viscera, including the heart, lungs, liver, kidneys, and spleen, as distinguished from τὰ ἔντερα, the lower viscera, bowels, intestines.[20] Metaphorically, σπλάγχνα refers to the seat of the emotions, thus "feelings" or "affections," especially those of pity and love. Often, as here, it is synonymous with καρδία (cf. 7:15; Col. 3:12). In fact, BAGD (763a, 766c) render ἐν τοῖς σπλάγχνοις ὑμῶν by "in your own hearts." In using the second person (στενοχωρεῖσθε) in v. 12b as well as in v. 12a, Paul skillfully focuses attention on the Corinthians' attitude; to have written στενοχωρούμεθα δὲ ἡμεῖς κτλ. would have emphasized Paul's deprivation, not their shortcomings.[21] Certainly, v. 12b is a serious charge that Paul levels against his converts in Corinth, and it is as direct as it is serious. "You have too narrow a space for me in your heart; you do not give me love comparable to mine for you."[22]

6:13 τὴν δὲ αὐτὴν ἀντιμισθίαν, ὡς τέκνοις λέγω, πλατύνθητε καὶ ὑμεῖς. "Now as a comparable recompense — I am speaking as to my children — open wide your hearts also." Thus far in this brief paragraph (vv. 11-13) Paul has given the Corinthians an assurance of his total openness with them in both speech and feeling (v. 11), indicating his desire for complete harmony with them. Then he states directly and unequivocally that whatever restricts deep mutual affection lies on their side, not his (v. 12). Now in v. 13 he challenges them to match his initiative by opening their hearts wide to him. Plummer aptly summarizes the central point of vv. 11-13: "Let me have some return for my affectionate frankness" (202). The whole paragraph relates to unreciprocated affection.

ἀντιμισθία is "that which is given in return (ἀντί) as a recompense."[23] That is, in return for giving the Corinthians his "wide-open" heart, Paul is requesting that they give him their "wide-open" hearts as a recompense. This recompense will thus match (cf. τὴν αὐτήν) his initiating gift; it will be "a recompense in like kind" (RV), "the equivalent recompense" (Thrall 450), "a comparable recompense." τὴν αὐτήν points to similarity or equivalence ("the

---

20. For this distinction see Aeschylus, *Agamemnon* 1221.

21. Both instances of στενοχωρεῖσθε in this verse are to be taken as passive in both form and meaning ("you are restricted/constricted/cramped"); it is unlikely that the second instance is a reflexive middle (as Barnett 336 n. 8, apparently) ("you cramp yourselves") since such reflexives are rare in the NT.

22. Zerwick, *Analysis* 401.

23. Zerwick, *Analysis* 401. Héring (49) defines it as "a service rendered in exchange for some other service." In its only other NT use (Rom. 1:27) ἀντιμισθία refers negatively to punishment, thus "due penalty" or "penal recompense." It may be a Pauline coinage from ἀντίμισθος ("as a reward," "paying back") (a suggestion of Robertson, *Pictures* 236). In *2 Clement* 1:3, 5; 9:7; 15:2 the term expresses the grateful response to God appropriate for humans.

same," "of the same kind"), rather than fairness;[24] Paul is asking for repayment in the same coin, namely complete candor and warm love.

Several explanations have been given of the unusual grammatical construction. τὴν αὐτὴν ἀντιμισθίαν could be classified as an accusative of respect ("with regard to an equivalent recompense"), or as an accusative absolute[25] ("as a recompense of like kind"), or as an accusative with a verb such as δότε or ἀποδιδόντες unexpected due to the parenthesis ὡς τέκνοις λέγω.[26] Or perhaps we should follow Rückert and regard Paul's statement as an abbreviation for ὡσαύτως δὲ καὶ ὑμεῖς πλατύνθητε, ἥτις ἔσται ἡ ἐμὴ ἀντιμισθία,[27] "Now you too in the same way open wide your hearts — this will be my recompense!" Such is Paul's meaning.

Once Paul has mentioned "a recompense of like kind," he injects a parenthesis (ὡς τέκνοις λέγω) to remind the Corinthians that the reciprocity he expects (πλατύνθητε καὶ ὑμεῖς) is between parent and child.[28] Paul could mean "I speak just as any father would to his own children," but given the fact that the Corinthians actually were his children "in the faith" (cf. 1 Tim. 1:2) or "in the Lord" (cf. 1 Cor. 4:17), it is far more probable that he means "I am speaking as (ὡς) to my children," that is, "inasmuch as you are my children."[29] τέκνον is a more intimate term than υἱός and is a common way Paul refers to his converts.[30] By appealing to his distinctive spiritual relationship to the Corinthians (cf. Gal. 4:19) Paul prepares the way for his climactic entreaty, "you must open wide your hearts also,"[31] where πλατύνθητε (literally "be enlarged") picks up πεπλάτυνται in v. 11b. Love given should be matched by love returned, especially in family relationships. "Children should love a loving father" (Isaacs). As a spiritual father Paul was naturally distressed whenever his children failed to reciprocate his ex-

---

24. But cf. NEB, REB ("in fair exchange"); NIV ("as a fair exchange").

25. Thus Meyer 553; Bernard 77.

26. Cf. Plummer 204; Windisch 211.

27. L. J. Rückert, *Der zweite Brief Pauli an die Korinther* (Leipzig: Deichert, 1837) 204, cited by Bultmann 177. Other explanations of the construction are: adverbial accusative ("by way of recompense in kind"; cf. Moule 34); accusative in apposition to the rest of the sentence (minus the parenthesis) ("You also, do enlarge your hearts — the equivalent recompense," Thrall 471; cf. Moule 35-36); "abbreviation combined with apposition," τὸ δὲ αὐτό, ὅ ἐστιν ἀντιμισθία (Winer 530, 620); apposition to an omitted cognate accusative, thus τὸν αὐτὸν πλατυσμὸν ὡς ἀντιμισθίαν (Lietzmann 129; Windisch 211; cf. BDF §154; Turner 245); a combination of τὸ δὲ αὐτό "in the same way," and κατ' ἀντιμισθίαν, "by way of recompense" (a proposal of Moule 160).

28. Plummer suggests (204) that by inserting this parenthesis Paul softens the severity of στενοχωρεῖσθε (v. 12b).

29. On this view ὡς introduces an actual characteristic quality (BAGD 898a, citing this verse).

30. E.g., of Timothy, 1 Cor. 4:17; 1 Tim. 1:2, 18; 2 Tim. 1:2; 2:1; of Titus, Tit. 1:4; of Onesimus, Phlm. 10. There is no reason to see in the use of τέκνοις here an allusion to the Corinthians' immaturity (cf. 1 Cor. 3:1-3), for then νηπίοις might have been expected (cf. 1 Cor. 3:1).

31. BDF §465(2) cite this parenthesis as (apparently) an instance of prodiorthosis (cf. §495[3]), an anticipatory correction of or apology for an expression that could be offensive — here πλατύνθητε καὶ ὑμεῖς (see also 11:1, 16, 21, 23).

pressions of love. Here was the Corinthians' chance to re-establish proper reciprocity (cf. Héring 49). "See to it that you too (καί) become expansive and wide-hearted in your love for me." In effect, the appeal is "Be fully reconciled to me as an appropriate expression of your reconciliation to God" (cf. 5:20). What was involved in that total reconciliation is indicated in the paragraph that follows (6:14–7:1), namely withdrawal from all compromising liaisons with the world.

Bibliography

Beale 576-77 • Bieringer, "Liebe" • Crafton 100-101 • Murphy-O'Connor 67-68 • Murphy-O'Connor, "Context" • Thrall, "Problem" 146

b. Minor Digression — Call to Holiness (6:14–7:1)

The issue of the authenticity and integrity of this passage is dealt with in detail in the Introduction (A.3.c.), where it is argued that the paragraph is genuinely Pauline, perhaps composed by Paul previously and now used to encourage the Corinthians to sever all ties with any form of idolatry and thus become "wide-hearted" (cf. 6:13) in their affection for him.

There is no stylistic analysis of the passage better than that offered by Lambrecht, which is reproduced here.[1]

A	6:14a		μὴ γίνεσθε ἑτεροζυγοῦντες ἀπίστοις·
B	14b	a	τίς γὰρ μετοχὴ δικαιοσύνῃ καὶ ἀνομίᾳ;
	14c	b	ἢ τίς κοινωνία φωτὶ πρὸς σκότος;
	15a	a′	τίς δὲ συμφώνησις Χριστοῦ πρὸς Βελιάρ,
	15b	b′	ἢ τίς μερὶς πιστῷ μετὰ ἀπίστου;
	16a	c	τίς δὲ συγκατάθεσις ναῷ θεοῦ μετὰ εἰδώλων;
C	16b		ἡμεῖς γὰρ ναὸς θεοῦ ἐσμεν ζῶντος·
	16c	-	καθὼς εἶπεν ὁ θεὸς ὅτι
	16d	a 1	ἐνοικήσω ἐν αὐτοῖς καὶ ἐμπεριπατήσω,

1. Lambrecht, "Fragment" 148, and (in English translation) in his commentary 123-24. For a similar analysis, see J. M. Scott, *Adoption* 193; "Scripture" 97, who argues that vv. 16c-18c are introduced as a single quotation, "a citation and combination" (D.-A. Koch) like Rom. 3:10-18, of three parts of three lines each, the central part being

διὸ ἐξέλθατε ἐκ μέσου αὐτῶν
καὶ ἀφορίσθητε, λέγει κύριος,
καὶ ἀκαθάρτου μὴ ἅπτεσθε

("Scripture" 77, 82-85). "Thus God's promises of a reciprocal relationship between himself and his people expressed in the first person singular [vv. 16d-f, 17d-18b] bracket a center of parenesis which gives the practical implications of this relationship to God" ("Scripture" 77). See also Betz, *Galatians* 329-30.

16e	2	καὶ ἔσομαι αὐτῶν θεός,
16f	3	καὶ αὐτοὶ ἔσονταί μου λαός.
17a	b	διὸ ἐξέλθατε ἐκ μέσου αὐτῶν καὶ ἀφορίσθητε,
17b	-	λέγει κύριος,
17c	b′	καὶ ἀκαθάρτου μὴ ἅπτεσθε·
17d	a′	1′ κἀγὼ εἰσδέξομαι ὑμᾶς
18a		2′ καὶ ἔσομαι ὑμῖν εἰς πατέρα,
18b		3′ καὶ ὑμεῖς ἔσεσθέ μοι εἰς υἱοὺς καὶ θυγατέρας,
18c	-	λέγει κύριος παντοκράτωρ.

D	7:1a	a	ταύτας οὖν ἔχοντες τὰς ἐπαγγελίας, ἀγαπητοί,
	1b	b	καθαρίσωμεν ἑαυτοὺς ἀπὸ παντὸς μολυσμοῦ σαρκὸς καὶ πνεύματος,
	1c	c	ἐπιτελοῦντες ἁγιωσύνην ἐν φόβῳ θεοῦ.

Several structural features are worthy of note.

1. Each of the five rhetorical questions under section B begins with the interrogative adjective τίς and expects the answer, "None at all!"
2. The first four questions form two pairs and an a b a′ b′ pattern, while the fifth question concludes the series and, with the expression ναῷ θεοῦ, announces a dominant theme (v. 16b) in section C.
3. In section C there are three OT quotations (v. 16d, e, f; v. 17a, c; vv. 17d, 18a, b). We find the three quotation formulae placed symmetrically: at the beginning (v. 16c) and at the end (v. 18c) of the unit, and at the center (v. 17b) of the middle quotation.[2] The similarity of thought between v. 16e, f in the first citation and v. 18a, b in the third is also noteworthy.

With regard to content, the passage contains six imperatives (three of which belong together), and seven promises that fall into two groups (v. 16 and vv. 17-18). These exhortations and promises are related by means of conjunctions.

Exhortations		*Essence of Exhortation*
1. μὴ γίνεσθε ἑτεροζυγοῦντες	(6:14)	Avoid mismatched unions
2. ἐξέλθατε		
3. ἀφορίσθητε	(6:17)	Be separate from all that is unclean
4. μὴ ἅπτεσθε		
5. καθαρίσωμεν	(7:1a)	Be separate from all that defiles
6. ἐπιτελοῦντες	(7:1b)[3]	Pursue holiness

2. Lambrecht, "Fragment" 150.
3. For the imperatival import of this participle, see on 7:1.

Since the first four imperatives are second person plural, we may assume that they apply primarily and distinctively to the Corinthians, whereas the last two (first person plural) are applicable equally to Paul and to the Corinthians (and, by implication, to all believers). Although only the first and fourth exhortations are negative in form, all but the sixth are negative in import, calling for separation from evil in any form; the sixth, however, is positive, with its call for the pursuit of holiness.

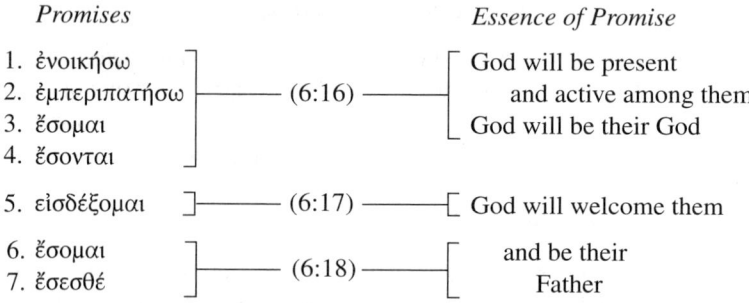

Relation of Exhortations and Promises

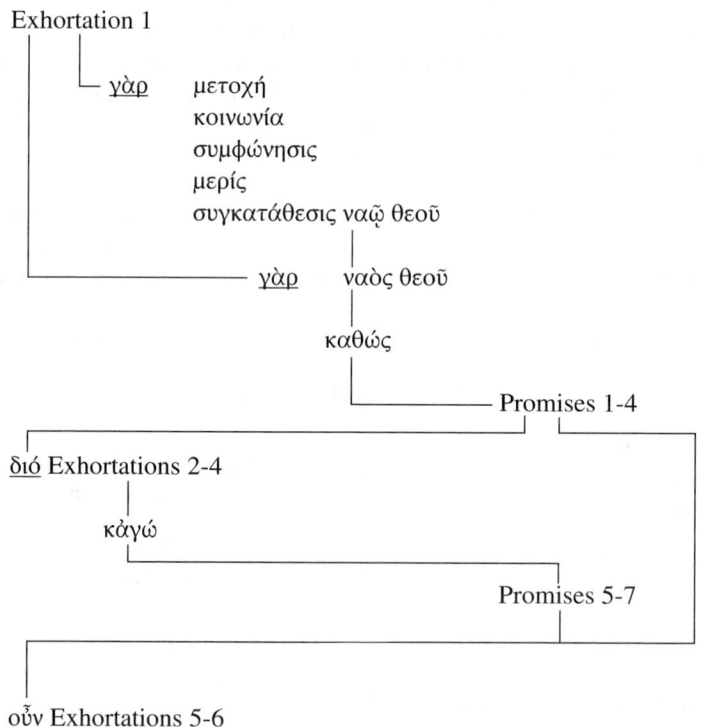

The two instances of γάρ introduce the bases for the exhortation, "Do not be harnessed in an alien yoke," while the second γάρ also justifies the statement that the temple of God is incompatible with idols. καθὼς κτλ. prefaces the OT proof that Christians constitute God's temple (promises 1-4). These promises then form the basis (διό) for the three imperatives of v. 17 (ἐξέλθατε . . . ἀφορίσθητε . . . μὴ ἅπτεσθε). καί (in κἀγώ) introduces the result ("then," "in that case") if those three commands are obeyed, that is, promises 5-7 will be true. Finally, οὖν looks back to all seven promises as the ground for the double exhortation of 7:1 (καθαρίσωμεν . . . ἐπιτελοῦντες).

Verses 16-18 form a catena of OT quotations, drawn from the Law and the Prophets (both "former" and "latter") of the Hebrew canon.

Verse	Quotation Formulas	Phrase	OT Source (LXX)
16	καθὼς εἶπεν ὁ θεὸς ὅτι	ἐνοικήσω ἐν αὐτοῖς	Lev. 26:11 καὶ θήσω σκήνην μου ἐν ὑμῖν . . .
		καὶ ἐμπεριπατήσω,	Lev. 26:12 καὶ ἐμπεριπατήσω ἐν ὑμῖν
		καὶ ἔσομαι αὐτῶν θεός,	καὶ ἔσομαι ὑμῶν θεός,
		καὶ αὐτοὶ ἔσονταί	καὶ ὑμεῖς ἔσεσθέ
		μου λαός.	μου λαός.
			Ezek. 37:27 καὶ ἔσται ἡ κατασκήνωσίς μου ἐν αὐτοῖς, καὶ ἔσομαι αὐτοῖς θεός, καὶ αὐτοί μου ἔσονται λαός.
17	διὸ		Isa. 52:11 ἀπόστητε ἀπόστητε ἐξέλθατε ἐκεῖθεν καὶ ἀκαθάρτου μή ἅπτεσθε,
		ἐξέλθατε ἐκ	ἐξέλθατε ἐκ
		μέσου αὐτῶν καὶ	μέσου αὐτῆς
	λέγει κύριος	ἀφορίσθητε καὶ ἀκαθάρτου μὴ ἅπτεσθε	ἀφορίσθητε
			Ezek. 20:34 καὶ ἐξάξω ὑμᾶς ἐκ τῶν λαῶν
		καγὼ εἰσδέξομαι ὑμᾶς,	καὶ εἰσδέξομαι ὑμᾶς ἐκ τῶν χωρῶν οὗ διεσκορπίσθητε ἐν αὐταῖς
18		καὶ ἔσομαι ὑμῖν εἰς πατέρα	2 Kgdms. 7:14 ἐγὼ ἔσομαι αὐτῷ εἰς πατέρα,

Quotation Formulas	Phrase	OT Source (LXX)
	καὶ ὑμεῖς ἔσεσθέ εἰς υἱοὺς	καὶ αὐτὸς ἔσται μοι εἰς υἱόν.
		Isa. 43:6 ἄγε τοὺς υἱούς μου ἀπὸ γῆς πόρρωθεν
	καὶ θυγατέρας,	καὶ τὰς θυγατέρας μου ἀπ' ἄκρων τῆς γῆς.
		2 Kgdms. 7:8 καὶ νῦν τάδε ἐρεῖς τῷ δούλῳ μου Δαυιδ Τάδε
λέγει κύριος παντοκράτωρ		λέγει κύριος παντοκράτωρ

14*Do not be harnessed in an alien yoke with unbelievers. For what kinship is there between righteousness and lawlessness? Or what fellowship is there between light and darkness?* 15*And what concord does Christ*[a] *have with Beliar*[b]*? Or what does a believer*[c] *have in common with an unbeliever?* 16*And what agreement has the temple of God with idols? For we*[d] *are the temple of the living God, as God said: "I will live in their midst and move among them, and I will be their God, and they shall be my*[e] *people."* 17*"Therefore, come out from among them and separate yourselves, says the Lord, and do not touch what is unclean. Then I will welcome you* 18*and will be a father to you, and you shall be sons and daughters to me, says the all-sovereign Lord."* 7:1*So then, dear friends, since these great promises are ours, let us cleanse ourselves of everything that may defile body or spirit*[f] *and complete our consecration by our reverence*[g] *for God.*

TEXTUAL NOTES

a. In the place of Χριστοῦ (p⁴⁶ ℵ B C P 0243 33 81 326 1175 1739 1881 *pc* lat Clement Ambrosiaster), which is undoubtedly the true reading, D (F G) Ψ 𝔐 syr read Χριστῷ, an obvious assimilation to the datives of the preceding antitheses.

b. Clearly there was uncertainty about the Greek form of the Hebrew term *bᵉlîyaʿal*, "worthlessness." Instead of Βελιάρ, the preferable reading, some witnesses have Βελιάν (D K Ψ 6 *pc* [b] vg^ms) or Βελιάβ (F G d) or Βελιάλ (*pc* lat Tertullian). The interchange of the two liquid consonants λ and ρ by dissimilation was a not uncommon phenomenon in spelling (see Moulton and Howard 2.103).

c. B 33 *pc* read πιστοῦ under the influence of the preceding Χριστοῦ, which also follows a nominative singular.

d. There are three variants:
  (1) ἡμεῖς γὰρ ναὸς θεοῦ ἐσμεν (B D* L P 6 33 81 [104] 326 365 1175 1881 2464 *pc* cop Origen)
  (2) ὑμεῖς γὰρ ναὸς θεοῦ ἐστε (p⁴⁶ [ℵ²] C D² F G Ψ [0209] 𝔐 lat syr Tertullian)
  (3) ἡμεῖς γὰρ ναοὶ θεοῦ ἐσμεν (ℵ* 0243 1739 *pc* Clement Augustine).

Although the third variant has proto-Alexandrian (א* 1739) and later Alexandrian (0243) support, it is secondary, "correcting" the singular ναός. The first two variants both have Alexandrian and Western witnesses, but the second arose, as Metzger suggests (512), because of the parallel in 1 Cor. 3:16 (οὐκ οἴδατε ὅτι ναὸς θεοῦ ἐστε) and the second plurals in vv. 14 and 17.

e. There is no reason to prefer μοι (D F G Ψ 0209 1881 𝔐 latt syr cop Tertullian Eusebius Epiphanius) over μου with its strong external support (p⁴⁶ א B C Iᵛⁱᵈ P 0243 33 81 1175 1739 pc Clement Origen). μου λαός is nicely parallel to the preceding αὐτῶν θεός, and μοι may have arisen from v. 18.

f. p⁴⁶ has the locatival dative πνεύματι. Marcion's text read αἵματος, not πνεύματος, thus creating the stereotyped phrase σὰρξ καὶ αἷμα (cf. 1 Cor. 15:50) and avoiding the idea (abhorrent to dualistic anthropology) that the spirit could be defiled (Héring 52 n. 2).

g. Instead of φόβῳ θεοῦ, p⁴⁶ has ἀγάπῃ θεοῦ, probably a scribal error (cf. Jude 21, ἑαυτοὺς ἐν ἀγάπῃ θεοῦ τηρήσατε) or perhaps prompted by the notion that the love of God, not the fear of God, was the motivation for holiness. The reading of p⁴⁶ is defended — unsuccessfully, I believe — by Ker (195-96).

6:14 There is no question that the transition from 6:13 to 6:14 (as also from 7:1 to 7:2) is abrupt. But several considerations lessen this sense of awkwardness.[4] (1) In 6:14–7:1 Paul is indicating why the Corinthians are restricted in their affections for him (6:12) and how they can enlarge their hearts toward him (6:13). They are continuing to flirt with paganism, but now must fully comply with his earlier injunctions to shun idolatry in any form (φεύγετε ἀπὸ τῆς εἰδωλολατρίας, 1 Cor. 10:14) and to shun all immorality (φεύγετε τὴν πορνείαν, 1 Cor. 6:18). Openheartedness to Paul and full reconciliation with him would be achieved only when they made a total break with paganism. Such a break would demonstrate their reconciliation to God (5:20) and their ongoing receipt of God's grace with benefit (cf. 6:1).[5] (2) Abrupt transitions (e.g., 2:13-14) and digressions (e.g., 1 Corinthians 13 between 1 Cor. 12:31 and 14:1) are natural and typical when writing is by dictation. (3) There may have been a dictation break at 6:13, and, on resuming, Paul decided to address the persistent Corinthian problem of idolatrous relationships that accounted for their embarrassed reserve toward him (6:12-13). (4) Perhaps Paul has incorporated here, without modification or adjustment to the immediate context, an ethical homily of his own composition that calls for holiness of conduct.[6]

Μὴ γίνεσθε ἑτεροζυγοῦντες ἀπίστοις. "Do not be harnessed in an alien yoke with unbelievers." In this periphrastic present, γίνομαι replaces εἰμι (γίνεσθε for

4. In the Introduction (A.3.c[1]) it is suggested that the presence of overlapping literary techniques (namely *inclusio* and chiasmus) in 6:11–7:4 points to the integration of 6:14–7:1 with its context.

5. But Isaacs proposes a link between 6:14 and 6:12-13 that is not specifically related to the Corinthian situation: "I do not ask you to be indiscriminate in your sympathies. Do not associate with unbelievers" (15).

6. See the Introduction, n. 56.

the obsolescent ἔστε).[7] There is therefore no need to give γίνεσθε an inceptive sense,[8] "do not get harnessed . . ." The negated present imperative prohibits either the continuation of an action ("cease to," "stop") or a course of action that must always by avoided ("keep from," "don't ever"). So, correspondingly, the sense may be "Stop forming intimate and inconsistent relations with unbelievers" (Williams);[9] or, "Do not be mismatched with unbelievers" (NRSV), "Do not be yoked together" (NIV). Neither interpretation can be excluded: the Corinthians may well have been guilty of such relations, and Paul could be issuing a general prohibition that was applicable to both the present and the future.

The verb ἑτεροζυγέω is not found elsewhere in biblical Greek nor in Greek literature before the Christian era. Literally it means "pull the yoke [ζυγός] in a different [ἕτερος] direction than one's fellow," and figuratively, "make a mismatched covenant," "mismate" (Spicq 2.80).[10] In this periphrastic construction, then, it means "be yoked in unequal partnership" (LSJ 701 s.v.), with the second element (-ζυγέω) "governing" the first (ἑτερο-) (BDF §119[1]). When the cognate adjective ἑτερόζυγος, "unevenly yoked," "yoked to a stronger," is used substantively (as in Lev. 19:19), it refers to an animal of a different kind. This OT passage prohibits the cross-breeding of animals. "You shall not mate different kinds of animals" (Lev. 19:19),[11] which the LXX renders "You shall not breed your cattle with an animal that uses another yoke (ἑτερο-ζύγῳ . . ."[12] Similarly, Deut. 22:9-11 prohibits a mixing of diverse elements: two different kinds of animals in ploughing ("Do not plough with an ox and a donkey yoked together," 22:10 [LXX has simply ἐπὶ τὸ αὐτό, "together"]),[13] two different kinds of seeds in sowing (22:9),[14] and two different kinds of yarn in making textiles (22:11). In alluding to Lev. 19:19 and Deut. 22:10 by the use of the verb ἑτεροζυγέω, Paul is saying that just as the yoking together of animals of two disparate species to form a team will result in an incongruous mismatch, so close attachments and intimate association between believers and un-

---

7. Cf. Moulton and Howard 203; and Mark 9:3; Col. 1:18; Heb. 5:12; Rev. 3:2 (γίνου γρηγορῶν); 16:10.

8. But BDF §354 regards γίνομαι with the present participle as denoting here the beginning of a state, "do not lend yourselves to. . . ." Similarly Barclay; Cassirer 332 ("Take care that you do not become unevenly matched").

9. Similarly Zerwick, *Analysis* 402; Conybeare in Conybeare and Howson 450 ("Cease to yoke yourselves unequally . . .").

10. It is the opposite of συζυγέω, "be yokefellows" (not found in the NT). The adjectival form σύζυγος, "yokefellow," occurs in Phil. 4:3.

11. The MT could also be rendered "You shall not make your animals fall down with an unequal yoke."

12. Commenting on the parallel passage, Deut. 22:9-11, Philo observes that "the lawgiver . . . commands breeders not to breed from animals of different species (ἑτεροζύγοις)" (*De Specialibus Legibus* 4.203).

13. Further instances of such illegitimate "mixing" of animals is given in one of the tractates of the Mishnah, "Diverse Kinds" (*Kilaim* 8.2-4).

14. The purpose of these two prohibitions (Deut. 22:9-10) was to ensure the preservation of diversity in the created order by disallowing the contamination of a species.

believers will produce an ill-matched union and total dissonance. "Keep out of all incongruous ties with unbelievers" (Moffatt). Winer acutely remarks that Paul means "μὴ γίν[εσθε] ἑτερ[οζυγοῦντες] καὶ οὕτως ὁμοζυγοῦντες (σύ-ζυγ.)ἀπίστοις 'do not put yourselves into an unsuitable yoke,' that is, 'be not united in the same yoke with unbelievers'" (221).[15]

But are the ἄπιστοι in fact "unbelievers"? According to one view that has had several recent defenders,[16] the ἄπιστοι are Paul's opponents, the "false apostles" (ψευδαπόστολοι) of 11:13 who are competitors with Paul for the affection of the Corinthians (cf. 6:13; 7:2). Now it is true that *later* in the letter the false apostles are portrayed as Satan's minions and as people masquerading as agents of light and righteousness (11:13-15), descriptions reminiscent of 6:14-15, but Paul's readers could not yet be expected to make those associations, especially since the term ἄπιστοι has already been used unambiguously in 4:4 to refer to unbelievers whose minds have been blinded to the light of the gospel by Satan, "the god of the present age." Furthermore, in 1 Corinthians the term is used eleven times, either substantivally or adjectivally, in reference to non-Christians.[17] So the other major view, reflected in most English versions, takes ἄπιστοι to mean "unbelievers," either in the sense of those outside the faith[18] or outside the church, those whom Paul in a later letter refers to as οἱ ἔξω, "those outside" (Col. 4:5),[19] or in the sense of those who do not believe in Christ.

What is the unequal yoke or mismatched union signified by ἑτερο-ζυγοῦντες? Webb has identified some eight different proposals, six of which are related to issues mentioned in 1 Corinthians,[20] while two suggestions arise from

15. ἀπίστοις may be explained as a dative of respect/reference, or as brachylogy for σὺν ἀπίστοις (cf. σύζυγος τινί). BDF §193(3) and Robertson 529 classify this dative as "associative" (or comitative). But Meyer (554) rejects the rendering "with unbelievers" for ἀπίστοις, proposing "do not draw for *unbelievers* a strange yoke," with the yoke being one drawn by unbelievers. This "ethical" dative "denotes a fellowship, in which the unbelieving partner *forms the standard which determines* the mode of thought and action of the Christian partner."

16. Collange 305-6, 316-17; Dahl, "Fragment" 62-69; Rensberger 25-49; Patte 45 and n. 59; deSilva 17-19, 105-6; "Decision" 3-16; Scott 152-53, 163. On this view, see further n. 68 below and Webb 194.

17. 1 Cor. 6:6; 7:12-13, 14 (twice), 15; 10:27; 14:22 (twice), 23-24.

18. Cf. TCNT, "those who reject the Faith"; Cassirer 332, "those who do not share your faith." If ἄπιστοι here has any connotation beyond "unbelievers," it is that of evildoing (BAGD 85d), in light of the following contrast, δικαιοσύνη–ἀνομία.

19. So also Webb 198-99, who also provides a detailed critique of the "ἄπιστοι = false apostles" view (189-98) and discusses (184-88) the proposals of Derrett, 231-50 (ἄπιστοι = "untrustworthy persons"), Betz, "Fragment" 89-90, 100 (ἄπιστοι = gentile Christians who do not keep the Torah), and Newton 112-13 (and others, now including Goulder 53-57) (ἄπιστοι = immoral Christians). For the view that the ἄπιστοι are unfaithful, apostate Christians, see Young and Ford 33-34. Murphy-O'Connor sees 6:14a as an appeal to the πνευματκοί of 1 Corinthians, who had welcomed the Judaizers and whose comportment was, at least in part, that of unbelievers, "to eradicate the 'unbelieving' side of their personalities. . . . 'Do not blend belief and unbelief'" ("Philo" 142; also his *Theology* 68-69).

20. Namely, taking grievances before pagan courts (1 Cor. 6:1-11); sexual immorality/visiting (temple) prostitutes (1 Cor. 6:12-20); mixed marriages (1 Cor. 7:12-15, 39); eating meat offered

the local context at Corinth.[21] Webb himself concludes (1) that Paul is calling for selective, not complete, separation from pagans;[22] (2) that the action Paul disallows is linked with literal idolatry (6:16);[23] and (3) that the most probable identifications of the "unequal yoke" are engaging in sexual acts with temple prostitutes and participation with pagans in temple feasts.[24]

Webb's first two conclusions are clearly defensible. If we assume Pauline authorship of the paragraph (so that there are not two differing levels of meaning — a pre-Pauline and a Pauline), his instruction in v. 14a must be assumed to be compatible with his directions regarding social relations with unbelievers given to the same church some eighteen months earlier. First, in 1 Cor. 5:9-11 he corrects a misinterpretation of his instruction to the Corinthians in the "previous letter" to stop associating with immoral people (1 Cor. 5:9). He did not mean, he explains, that all social intercourse with those outside the church should be cut off, for such drastic action would necessitate leaving human society altogether (1 Cor. 5:10). Rather, his intent was that the Corinthians should repudiate all social intercourse with a professed believer who was guilty of immorality or greed or was an idolater, reviler, drunkard, or robber (1 Cor. 5:11). Second, he encourages Christians who find themselves in mixed marriages (presumably as a result of their conversion to Christ) not to seek divorce from the unbelieving spouse who consents to maintain the marriage (1 Cor. 7:12-14). Third, he assumes that believers will receive and accept invitations to meals with unbelievers in their homes (1 Cor. 10:27).[25]

Since one of the five antitheses in vv. 14-16 refers to "idols" ("What agreement has the temple of God with idols?" v. 16), we must assume that what Paul disallows in v. 14a is somehow associated with "idolatry." But does the term εἴδωλα ("idols") refer to literal idol-worship, or is it a metonym for any form of association with idol-worship, or is it a metaphor for immorality in general? Now Paul can equate "acquisitiveness" (πλεονεξία) with idolatry (Col. 3:5, cf. Eph. 5:5), but in the Corinthian context where literal idolatry was rife and where the issue of "food offered to (actual) idols" (εἰδωλόθυτα) presented a crucial spiritual dilemma to Christians (1 Corinthians 8–10), it is *a priori* likely that a reference to εἴδωλα is not metaphorical but literal or metonymical.[26] And generally in Pauline diction the εἰδωλ- root refers to literal

---

to idols at pagan temples (1 Cor. 8:10; 10:14-22); eating meat offered to idols at a pagan's home (1 Cor. 10:27-28); speaking in tongues when unbelievers are present at the service (1 Cor. 14:22-25) (Webb 203-12, where the views are summarized and critiqued).

21. Namely, business partnerships with unbelievers; maintaining membership in a pagan cult (Webb 212-13).

22. Webb 202, 213.

23. Webb 193-94, 202-3.

24. Webb 204, 209-11, 214.

25. Also, any evangelistic endeavor undertaken by the Corinthians ideally presupposed not only incidental verbal contact but also ongoing personal involvement.

26. So also Webb 202-3.

idolatry,[27] most notably where there is a contrast, as in 6:16, between "the living God" and "(lifeless) idols" (cf. 1 Thess. 1:9).

Regarding identifications of the "mismatched union," we must remain uncertain.[28] Paul may be calling the Corinthian believers to withdraw from "the cultic life of the city" in general,[29] or, more specifically, from any participation in pagan religious practices or ceremonies associated with local temples or cults.[30] Either way, he would be demanding withdrawal from (at least) membership in local pagan cults and attendance at the lavish banquets held in temples under the auspices of a god.[31] But the entreaty may be broader. The Corinthians were to avoid any public or private relationship with unbelievers that was incompatible with or would compromise Christian standards, Christian adherence to monotheism, and Christian witness.[32]

τίς γὰρ μετοχὴ δικαιοσύνη καὶ ἀνομία; ἢ τίς κοινωνία φωτὶ πρὸς σκότος; "For what kinship is there between righteousness and lawlessness? Or what fellowship is there between light and darkness?" These are the first two of five rhetorical questions, each of which expects the answer "None whatsoever!" and illustrates (γάρ) the radical incompatibility of Christian and pagan values, the total incongruity of permanent intimate fellowship between believers and unbelievers. Since these antitheses follow and illustrate an injunction involving persons (γίνεσθε . . . ἀπίστοις, v. 14), each antithesis should perhaps be seen as a contrast between two sets of people (as in the fourth, "believer . . . unbeliever"), the first two antitheses referring to groups on the basis of the principle of "abstract for concrete," the third and fifth, by metonymy.

1. those who do right	those who do wrong
2. those who live in the light	those who live in darkness[33]
3. followers of Christ[34]	followers of Beliar/Satan
4. believers	unbelievers
5. worshipers of God	worshipers of idols

27. E.g., εἰδωλεῖον (1 Cor. 8:10); εἰδωλόθυτος (1 Cor. 8:7); εἰδωλολάτρης (1 Cor. 10:7); εἰδωλολατρία (1 Cor. 10:14); εἴδωλον (1 Cor. 12:2).

28. Given his uncertainty about Pauline authorship of 6:14–7:1, Furnish prefers to avoid any specific identification, suggesting a general sense comparable to James's admonition (Jas. 1:26) "to keep oneself unstained from the world" (372).

29. Barnett 345.

30. Fee restricts the application to sharing (cf. μερίς, 6:15) in cultic feasts in the temples of demonic spirits ("Food" 158-60; cf. 1 Cor. 10:14-22), but the second element in the five antitheses of 6:14-16 (viz. lawlessness, darkness, Beliar, unbelievers, idols) suggests a wider application.

31. For details about cults in Corinth, see Savage 49-51, who notes (49 n. 207) that he found references in the archaeological and literary sources to some thirty-four deities in Corinth.

32. Examples would include the contracting of mixed marriages (cf. Deut. 7:1-4; 1 Cor. 7:39) and initiating litigation before unbelievers in cases involving believers (1 Cor. 6:1-8).

33. Number 2 is the rendering of Louw and Nida §34.7. Fitzmyer regards the light-darkness contrast as simply another way of saying "sons of light" and "sons of darkness" ("Qumran" 208-9).

34. (ὁ) Χριστός signifies "the body of Christ," "Christians" in 1 Cor. 12:12.

Μετοχή refers to a partnership, a sharing of common goals or activities. Standing in contrast with ἀνομία, "lawlessness," "wickedness" (cf. Rom. 6:19), δικαιοσύνη bears an ethical not a forensic sense, denoting uprightness of conduct. The two datives are possessive: "What sharing in common belongs to righteousness and iniquity?"[35]

In the second antithesis, if κοινωνία is to be distinguished in meaning from μετοχή, it refers to active fellowship in pursuing common interests.[36] Again, the dative (φωτί) is possessive. "What consort can light possibly have with (πρός replacing the dative) darkness?" This light-darkness antithesis, so common in the Dead Sea Scrolls,[37] particularly in the form "sons of light" and "sons of darkness,"[38] is found elsewhere in Paul.[39]

6:15 τίς δὲ συμφώνησις Χριστοῦ πρὸς Βελιάρ; "And what concord does Christ have with Beliar?" In this verse Paul continues to emphasize the radical difference between Christianity and heathendom; they stand diametrically opposed to each other, lacking the common ground that would permit any association. A συμφώνησις is an agreement, the outcome of a joint decision, often of a group.[40] Louw and Nida (§31.15) bring out Paul's meaning vividly: "Do Christ and Beliar agree on anything?" The term Βελιάρ (for this form, see Textual Note b.) is found only here in the NT. Paul's usual word for the devil is (ὁ) Σατανᾶς (10 uses; e.g., 2:11; 11:14; 12:7), but 4:4 (ὁ θεὸς τοῦ αἰῶνος τούτου) shows that his usage is not rigid. Βελιάρ or the variant spelling Βελιάλ represents the Hebrew term b^eliya'al, which means "worthlessness" or "destruction."[41] It is probably never a proper name for Satan in the OT, although it personified the forces of evil and chaos, so that the expression b^enê b^eliya'al ("sons of worthlessness" = "wicked men") is used of the homosexuals at Gibeah (Judg. 19:22; 20:13) and the wicked men who seduced people to worship other gods (Deut. 13:14; EVV, 13:13). In the Qumran texts b^eliya'al is the angel of enmity whose domain is darkness and who counsels evil and superintends angels of destruction, "the lot of Belial," who fight against the sons of light, "the lot of God."[42] "In the Pseud-

---

35. Thrall 474 n. 2010; cf. BDF §189(1) who observe that in the NT "the classical distinction, whereby the genitive [of possession] is used when the acquisition is recent or the emphasis is on the possessor (e.g. R[om.] 14:8) and the dative [of possession] when the object possessed is to be stressed, is customarily preserved." This would support the rendering "For what do righteousness and wickedness have in common?" (NIV). ἐστι must be supplied in each of the antitheses.

36. This is because πρός after κοινωνία points to a "living relationship, intimate converse . . . personal intercourse" (Robertson 625).

37. E.g., 1QS 3:3, 20-21, 25; 1QM 1:11; 13:5, 15.

38. E.g., 1QS 1:9-10; 1QM 1:1.

39. Rom. 13:12; 2 Cor. 4:6; Eph. 5:8; 1 Thess. 5:5.

40. The word is followed by the τινὸς πρός τινα construction, "(agreement) of someone with someone" (BAGD 781a).

41. On possible derivations of the Hebrew term, see B. Otzen, *TDOT* 2.131-33, and more briefly Hughes 248-49 n. 12.

42. E.g., 1QM 1:1; 13:2, 4-5, 11-12; 17:5-6; 1QS 2:2, 5. See further Huppenbauer; von der Osten-Sacken.

epigrapha (esp. in the Martyrdom of Isa. and XII P. [*Testaments of the Twelve Patriarchs*]), Beliar is primarily the tempter who lures man into sin by his spirits and rules over sinful man."[43] Although Beliar is sometimes identified with the Antichrist in the Pseudepigrapha,[44] there is no reason to assume that the antithesis in 6:15 is between Christ and Antichrist.[45] Rather, as the embodiment of righteousness Christ is set over against Beliar as the embodiment of iniquity; Christ, the ruler in the kingdom of light, is contrasted with Satan, the ruler of the domain of darkness (cf. the two preceding antitheses, and Col. 1:12-13). As in the *Testaments of the Twelve Patriarchs* (e.g., *Testament of Levi* 18:12), Βελιάρ is here the name of the devil, the enemy of God.[46]

ἢ τίς μερὶς πιστῷ μετὰ ἀπίστου; "Or what does a believer have in common with an unbeliever?" Having spoken of Christ in the third antithesis, Paul now contrasts those who believe in Christ with those who do not,[47] again to emphasize their essential incompatibility. Although Paul uses the word ἄπιστος as both an adjective ("unbelieving"; e.g., 1 Cor. 7:12-14) and a noun ("unbeliever"; e.g., 1 Cor. 6:6; 10:27), elsewhere he uses πιστός as an adjective in both a passive sense ("faithful," "dependable")[48] and an active ("trusting," "exercising faith")[49] sense, but apart from the later Pastoral Epistles, not as a noun.[50] But it was a natural development, on the analogy of ἄπιστος, for πιστός to come to be used, as here, substantively of someone who believes in Christ. πιστῷ is a dative of possession after μερίς, "share." "What shared commitments belong to the believer along with the unbeliever?" This absence of μερίς between believer and unbeliever refers to characteristics and interests peculiar to believers, such as concern for the will and glory of God,[51] not to necessities of life shared by all humans, such as food, clothing, and shelter. In our discussion of 6:14a we saw that Paul was not rigorously separatist, calling for believers' total separation from unbelievers. Correspondingly, he is not here denying the common humanity of believers as citizens of the present cosmos, saying that the Christian and the non-Christian have nothing in common. But there are radical differences in behavior and motivation between these two classes of people.

43. B. Otzen, *TDOT* 2.136.

44. E.g., *Testament of Dan* 5:1, 10; *Ascension of Isaiah* 4:2-13; *Sibylline Oracles* 2:167-70; 3:63-74.

45. *Pace* Lietzmann 129.

46. A close parallel to the second and third antitheses is found in *Testament of Levi* 19:1, "Choose for yourselves light or darkness, the law of the Lord or the works of Beliar."

47. But TCNT takes the referent implied by πιστῷ and ἀπίστου to be the Christian faith rather than Christ: "those who accept the Faith . . . those who reject it."

48. E.g., 1 Cor. 1:9; 10:13.

49. E.g., Gal. 3:9; cf. John 20:27.

50. In 1 Tim. 4:10, 12; 5:16; 6:2b (ὁ) πιστός means "believer."

51. "The unbeliever's life is centred on self, the believer's on Christ; the treasure of the one is here on earth, of the other in heaven; the values of the one are those of this world, of the other those of the world to come; the believer seeks the glory of God, the unbeliever the glory of men" (Hughes 251).

503

6:16 This verse forms a bridge within 6:14-18 since it contains the last of the five rhetorical questions and the first of the four scriptural citations. These contrasts and quotations provide the twofold basis for the injunction, "Do not be yoked together with unbelievers."[52]

τίς δὲ συγκατάθεσις ναῷ θεοῦ μετὰ εἰδώλων; "And what agreement has the temple of God with idols?" It will now be clear that all five antitheses (vv. 14b-16a): (1) are rhetorical questions that expect the answer "None at all!"; (2) express contrasts between mutually exclusive entities, righteousness, light, Christ, believer, and the temple of God as opposed to lawlessness, darkness, Beliar, unbeliever, and idols;[53] (3) begin with (ἤ) τίς, used here as an interrogative adjective; (4) have ἐστι understood — "What X *is there/can there be* between Y and Z?" where X basically expresses the idea of commonality.[54] After the two preceding pairs of rhetorical questions, this final question forms a climax, being (as Thrall [475] points out) the only antithesis that mentions a specific danger (namely idolatry) that might arise from association with unbelievers. But this final antithesis, with its reference to the ναὸς θεοῦ, is also the genesis of the "temple of God" motif that is central to the remainder of this paragraph. The contrast here is not between the temple of God and temples that contain idols, for there is no ναοῦ before εἰδώλων, but "between God's sanctuary,[55] in which not even an image of Himself might be put up, and images of false gods" (Plummer 208). Idolatry and its associated immoral practices such as temple prostitution were a detestable abomination to Jews.[56] In his missionary preaching Paul implored his Gentile audiences "to turn to God from idols, to serve a living and true God" (1 Thess. 1:9; cf. Acts 14:15). So Paul's point in this antithesis is that simultaneous involvement in the worship of the living God (= "the temple of God") and the practices associated with the worship of lifeless images (= "idols") is an impossibility.

ἡμεῖς γὰρ ναὸς θεοῦ ἐσμεν ζῶντος. "For we are the temple of the living God." This remarkable claim explains (γάρ) the previous reference to "the temple of God" and, more remotely, gives further justification for the exhortation of 6:14a (see the earlier diagram, "Relation of Exhortations and Prom-

---

52. Note the presence of γάρ in 6:14 and 6:16; both instances refer back to 6:14a, although the main function of γάρ in 6:16 is to explain the preceding reference to the temple of God.

53. The first element in the antitheses is a dative of possession in the case of δικαιοσύνη, φωτί, πιστῷ, and ναῷ, with one instance of a genitive of possession (Χριστοῦ), while the construction in the second element is a dative of possession (ἀνομίᾳ), πρός with the accusative (πρὸς σκότος, πρὸς Βελιάρ), or μετά with the genitive (μετὰ ἀπίστου, μετὰ εἰδώλων).

54. All five terms that stand with τίς have the general connotation of commonality. (Robertson remarks [1184] that δέ in vv. 15-16 marks "a succession of steps in the same direction.") In fact, in three cases (μετοχή, κοινωνία, μερίς) BAGD propose the rendering "What does Y *have in common* with Z?" (514c, 439a, 505c, respectively), and O. Betz regards συμφώνησις, μετοχή, and κοινωνία as bearing the same sense (*TDNT* 9.308 n. 16).

55. On the difference between ναός and ἱερόν, see below.

56. But if εἰδώλων is here a metonym, it will refer to the worship or the worshipers of idols rather than to iniquity.

504

ises"). Two words, the first and the last, are particularly emphatic, ἡμεῖς by its presence and ζῶντος by its position. "It is we — yes, we Christians — who form the dwelling place of God[57] who, unlike idols, is living." Lest his readers should imagine that in the previous contrast he was thinking of a particular literal temple in which God dwelt, Paul hastens to assure them that he was speaking metaphorically, and in so doing makes the theological affirmation that triggers the following OT citations. Both instances of the anarthrous combination ναὸς θεοῦ in this verse may be rendered "*the* temple of God" on the basis of the canon of Apollonius.[58] Whereas ἱερόν denotes the whole temple complex (at Jerusalem), including adjacent buildings and the various courts, ναός refers more specifically to the sanctuary itself.[59] It comes as no surprise, then, that when the NT applies the temple motif to the universal church (Eph. 2:21) or a particular church (1 Cor. 3:16-17) as a community, or to individual believers (1 Cor. 6:19), ναός, not ἱερόν, is used. ἡμεῖς is to be taken in its broadest sense — Paul, the Corinthians, and all believers. Corporately the Christian community is the new divine sanctuary, the place where the living God most fully expresses his presence. He is called "the living God," not only in contrast with the lifeless idols in pagan temples but also in the sense that his indwelling of his people is no static presence among them but active involvement in stimulating and maintaining their life (note the following ἐμπεριπατήσω [ἐν αὐτοῖς]).

καθὼς εἶπεν ὁ θεὸς ὅτι Ἐνοικήσω ἐν αὐτοῖς καὶ ἐμπεριπατήσω καὶ ἔσομαι αὐτῶν θεός, καὶ αὐτοὶ ἔσονταί μου λαός. "As God said: 'I will live in their midst and move among them, and I will be their God, and they shall be my people.'" This particular introductory formula καθὼς εἶπεν ὁ θεὸς ὅτι is unique in the NT and is well rendered by TCNT, "This is what God meant when he said . . ." (ὅτι is recitative). In this first OT citation Paul is basically following the LXX of Lev. 26:11-12 (see the preceding chart) but changes the second person plural pronouns to the third person plural on the basis of Ezek. 37:27 and omits the irrelevant phrase "and my soul shall abhor you" from Lev. 26:11b.[60] The difficulty with Paul's phrase ἐνοικήσω ἐν αὐτοῖς is that in the LXX ἐνοικεῖν is never used with God as the subject (Windisch 216 n. 3), so that "I will live in their midst" could be explained as an inference that Paul draws from ἐμπεριπατήσω [ἐν αὐτοῖς] or, better, as his paraphrase of "I shall set my tabernacle (σκήνην

57. Cf. the similar emphasis in 1 Cor. 3:17 ("God's temple . . . and that is precisely what you are," οἵτινές ἐστε ὑμεῖς).

58. There is no justification for translating ἡμεῖς . . . ναὸς θεοῦ ἐσμεν ζῶντος as "we (individually) are temples of the living God." The case is otherwise in 1 Cor. 6:19 where the subject is the distributive singular τὸ σῶμα (ὑμῶν) (Turner 23): "your bodies are temples (ναός) of the Holy Spirit who is in (each of) you."

59. But on occasion the terms are synonymous; note, for example, the use of ναός in Matt. 27:5 and John 2:20.

60. For detailed discussion of Paul's changes and their significance, see Webb 33-40 (who argues for the dominant influence of the Ezekiel text; also Cerfaux 286 n. 1); Stanley 217-21 (who sees Lev. 26:11-12 as dominant; also McKelvey 94-95).

μου)⁶¹ in your midst" (Lev. 26:11a)⁶² in the light of the Spirit's indwelling of the church (1 Cor. 3:16-17) in fulfillment of God's promise (Ezek. 37:14). "God no longer dwells *with* his people in a sanctuary which they make for him [cf. Exod. 25:8]; he dwells *in* them, and *they* are his temple."⁶³ Paul's ἐν αὐτοῖς should probably be taken in a corporate sense ("in their midst") to correspond to his earlier affirmation "We (as a body) form the temple of the living God," although he would not deny that an individual sense ("within them") was also true (Rom. 8:11; 2 Tim. 1:14). However, when we supply (as we must) ἐν αὐτοῖς with ἐμπεριπατήσω, this prepositional phrase will mean "among them": God promises not only to live in the midst of his people but also to "move among them," a living God actively promoting and protecting the welfare of his people.

Both Lev. 26:12 and Ezek. 37:27 contain the covenant formula that Paul cites: "I will be their/your God, and they/you shall be my people."⁶⁴ In the former case, it was associated with the constitution of the nation of Israel as Yahweh's people after their deliverance from Egypt in the first exodus (see Lev. 26:13). In the latter case the twofold covenant formula was associated with the reconstitution of the nation as Yahweh's people after their restoration from exile in a second exodus (see Ezek. 37:11-14, 21).⁶⁵ Paul saw that with the death and resurrection of Christ not only had the new age dawned (6:2) but also God's people had been reconstituted for a final time. It was now God the Father of the Lord Jesus Christ who was "their God," that is, the God whom they worshiped; it was now the Christian community of both Jews and Gentiles who were God's people (μου λαός) and God's temple (ναὸς θεοῦ).

In 1:20 Paul affirmed that God's promises, however many they may be, find their answering "Yes" in Christ. Here in 6:16 are four divine promises — ἐνοικήσω, ἐμπεριπατήσω, ἔσομαι, ἔσονται⁶⁶ — which have had Christ's "Yes" pronounced upon them.

6:17 διὸ ἐξέλθατε ἐκ μέσου αὐτῶν καὶ ἀφορίσθητε, λέγει κύριος, καὶ

---

61. Following Stanley 218-19, who prefers the Göttingen LXX reading (σκήνην) over Rahlfs' reading (διαθήκην).

62. It should be noted that the use of recitative ὅτι (after a quotation formula) does not necessarily point to a *verbatim* reproduction of an OT text.

63. McKelvey 95. In the OT God dwells with and among his people rather than in them, so that Israel is never identified with God's temple (cf. Furnish 363).

64. On the formula, "Yahweh the God of Israel, Israel the people of Yahweh" as central to Israelite religion, see R. Smend, *Die Mitte des Alten Testaments* (Zürich: EVZ-Verlag, 1970) 49, 55, reviving J. Wellhausen's thesis.

65. On this, see further Scott, "Scripture" 78-82 (also *Adoption* 195-201), who concludes that "the conflation of Lev. 26.11-12 and Ezek. 37.27 in our passage presents the promise of the New Covenant in conscious continuity with the Sinai Covenant" (82).

66. These four futures are durative, not punctiliar. On the motif of "promise" as central to the OT, see W. C. Kaiser, Jr., *Toward an Old Testament Theology* (Grand Rapids: Zondervan, 1978) 1-69, and more briefly, "The Centre of Old Testament Theology: the Promise," *Them* 10 (1974) 1-10.

ἀκαθάρτου μὴ ἅπτεσθε· κἀγὼ εἰσδέξομαι ὑμᾶς. "Therefore, come out from among them and separate yourselves, says the Lord, and do not touch what is unclean. Then I will welcome you." On the basis of (cf. διό, "therefore") the assurance that the Christian church forms the new temple (v. 16a) and the evidence of that fact found in the promises of v. 16b, Paul now issues a threefold call for separation, and then gives the assurance of divine acceptance if that call is heeded (note καί [in κἀγώ], "then"). The conjunction διό introduces natural consequences of the distinctive and privileged relationship between God and his reconstituted people. Being God's temple incurs obligations of purity. It is not that obedience to the call for separation creates that relationship, but once that relationship has been created it demands separation from all that is unholy (cf. 1 Cor. 3:16-17). At the heart of Pauline ethics (and NT ethics in general) stands this relation between theological proclamation and moral exhortation, between affirmation and appeal, between the indicative and the imperative. Christians corporately form God's temple (6:16); they therefore must keep that temple pure (6:17). The indicative is prior to and the basis of the imperative.

After inserting διό Paul cites a modified form of Isa. 52:11 (LXX) (see the earlier chart) which reads: "Depart, depart, come out from there and do not touch what is unclean. Come out from her [Babylon], be separate, you who carry the vessels of the LORD." The twice-repeated "Depart, depart" is the last of four such repetitions[67] which are God's responses to the human appeal to him, "Awake, awake! Clothe yourself with strength, O arm of the LORD" (51:9). In Isaiah 52 God addresses the exiles in Babylon, announcing to them the "good news" of their return to Jerusalem from exile, that is, their "redemption" (52:3, 9). ἐξέλθατε occurs twice in 52:11, once followed by ἐκεῖθεν ("from there") and once by ἐκ μέσου αὐτῆς [= Βαβυλῶνος; cf. Isa. 48:20]. Paul opted for the second ἐξέλθατε where the more specific αὐτῆς could be appropriately adapted to the Corinthian situation by being changed to αὐτῶν (= the ἄπιστοι of 6:14; cf. ἀπίστου, 6:15).[68] Also, by reproducing the second ἐξέλθατε he could place the intervening phrase καὶ ἀκαθάρτου μὴ ἅπτεσθε that related to things ([τὸ] ἀκαθάρτου) after the two imperatives that related to people (αὐτῶν).[69] In its orig-

---

67. The others are "I, I am he" (Isa. 51:12), "Rouse yourself, rouse yourself" (51:17), "Awake, awake" (52:1).

68. But some take αὐτῶν (as well as ἀπίστοις· in v. 14) to refer to Paul's opponents (e.g., Scott 156), while TCNT renders αὐτῶν by "the nations," and Webb (214) equates αὐτῶν with "the idol-gods of the temple cults." If αὐτῶν denotes Paul's adversaries, the command "come out from among them" sounds decidedly odd. Unless these rivals outnumbered the members of the Corinthian congregation — which is impossible — Paul would have addressed the Corinthians *ex hypothesi* with words such as those used in 1 Cor. 5:13 with regard to the incestuous man, ἐξάρατε τούτους ἐξ ὑμῶν αὐτῶν, "Drive these people out from among you," rather than "come out from among them." That is, a minority "comes out" from the majority, not a majority from a minority. In the present case, the Corinthian Christians form the minority, and their pagan contemporaries the majority.

69. For full details of Paul's changes and possible reasons for them, see Webb 40-41; Stanley 221-27. Webb suggests that Paul may have adopted the distinctive new exodus proclamation

inal context Isa. 52:11 was addressed to the nation of Israel as represented by the priests and Levites, "you who carry the vessels of the LORD" that had been taken to Babylon (Ezra 1:7-11; 2 Chron. 36:10). By omitting the phrase οἱ φέροντες τὰ σκεύη κυρίου Paul makes the three imperatives applicable to Christians.

ἐξέλθατε, a variant form of ἐξέλθετε,[70] could mean "go out" (cf. Isa. 52:11, NRSV) or "come out." The latter rendering is preferable in light of the subsequent word of welcome, εἰσδέξομαι ὑμᾶς. The use of the phrase ἐκ μέσου αὐτῶν, rather than simply ἐξ αὐτῶν, emphasizes the totality of the separation.[71] "Come away from among them" (BAGD 275a).[72] In the context we must supply ἐκ μέσου αὐτῶν or ἀπ' αὐτῶν with ἀφορίσθητε. This passive imperative may be translated "be separate" (RSV, NRSV), "be separated" (Young and Ford 268), or, construing the passive as reflexive,[73] "separate yourselves" (NEB, GNB, REB). Both aorists, ἐξέλθατε and ἀφορίσθητε, here express single, unrepeated action, with the second reinforcing the first and both reiterating the injunction of 6:14a. In form, the two imperatives of 6:17 are positive while the imperative in 6:14 is negated, but in content they all call for an identical separation — albeit a partial separation — from unbelievers.

Like the negated present imperative in v. 14a (see above), μὴ ἅπτεσθε could be enjoining an end to an action ("Stop touching," Williams)[74] or the perpetual avoidance of an action ("Do not touch what is unclean" = "touch nothing unclean" [many EVV] = "touch no unclean thing," NIV). In Isa. 52:11 [τοῦ] ἀκαθάρτου, "what is unclean" (BAGD 29a), stands in contrast to τὰ σκεύη κυρίου, "the (sacred) vessels of the LORD" and therefore probably refers to pagan religious objects associated with the idolatry of Babylon (cf. Gen. 31:19; 35:2; Josh. 24:23). In 2 Cor. 6:17, where the term stands alone, it bears a moral sense and refers to any association with paganism, and idolatry in particular, that might compromise Christian adherence to righteousness (cf. 6:14). As in the phrase παντὸς μολυσμοῦ in 7:1, the reference is non-specific, and while the whole injunction, "touch nothing unclean," would include the shunning of idolatry (1 Cor. 10:14), it is closer to 1 Thess. 5:22, "Shun every form of evil." Just as the priests and Levites and the Israelites in general were to leave behind in Babylon anything that might compromise their purity, so the Corinthians were to repudiate Gentile uncleanness of any type.[75] This apostolic command, then, looks back to 6:14a and forward to 7:1.

"Come out from" because of his close identification with the mission and message of the Servant of Yahweh (128-31, 158, 182).

70. See Moulton and Howard 208; Zerwick §489.

71. On the anarthrous state of μέσου, see BDF §264(4). In Rev. 18:4 ἐξέλθατε ὁ λαός μου ἐξ αὐτῆς (= Βαβυλῶνος) refers to the withdrawal of the church ("my people") from the allurement and judgment of the world (= "Babylon the Great," Rev. 18:2).

72. NEB and REB bring out the sense of ἐκ μέσου αὐτῶν by "(come away) and leave them."

73. Thus Zerwick and Grosvenor 547.

74. Cf. Robertson 853.

75. Cf. McKelvey 96.

It will be clear that 6:17 affords no ground for so-called "secondary separation," where one group of Christians dissociates itself from or repudiates another. Paul is here dealing with believer-unbeliever relations; he is not describing relations among believers. Yet elsewhere he does state certain specific circumstances that justify separation — even if temporary — among believers.[76]

κἀγὼ εἰσδέξομαι ὑμᾶς derives from Ezek. 20:34 (LXX)[77] and is the first of three divine promises that presuppose compliance with the preceding three imperatives (καί, "then," expressing a result; cf. BAGD 392 s.v. καί I.2.f.). If κἀγώ (= καὶ ἐγώ by crasis) results from the union of the καί of Ezek. 20:34b and the ἐγώ of 2 Kgdms. 7:14a,[78] Paul has neatly coalesced the two passages. As was the case with Isa. 52:11, this phrase, "then I will welcome you,"[79] occurs in a context where Yahweh promises to rescue his people from exile. "I will bring you out from the nations, and I will gather you (καὶ εἰσδέξομαι ὑμᾶς) from the countries where you were scattered, with a mighty hand, with an outstretched arm, and with outpoured wrath" (Ezek. 20:34, LXX). Significantly, the emphasis on the wrath of God as effecting the judgment and purification of his redeemed people that is so pronounced in Ezek. 20:34-38 is noticeably absent from the Pauline passage, where the emphasis rests on the warm welcome that God promises to give those who have separated themselves from pagan ways. God's approval of his people is dependent on their obedience to his commands. Separation from the world (6:14, 17a-c) leads to fellowship with God (6:17d-18) (cf. Jas. 4:4).

6:18 καὶ ἔσομαι ὑμῖν εἰς πατέρα, καὶ ὑμεῖς ἔσεσθέ μοι εἰς υἱοὺς καὶ θυγατέρας, λέγει κύριος παντοκράτωρ. "And I will be a father to you, and you shall be sons and daughters to me, says the all-sovereign Lord." These two promises complete the trilogy of divine promises that express the result of obedience to the threefold exhortation of 6:17, and they also complete the third quotation in vv. 16-18 (see the earlier chart). Paul's main source for v. 18 is the LXX text of 2 Sam. (2 Kgdms.) 7:14, "I will be a father to him, and he will be a son to me." Paul has changed αὐτῷ . . . αὐτός to the second person plural ὑμῖν . . . ὑμεῖς, and the singular υἱόν to the plural υἱούς.[80] The construction εἶναι εἰς with the accusative, found twice in this verse, is used in place of a predicate nominative.[81] The usage is not "un-Greek,"[82] but it does betray some Semitic

---

76. Namely, when a person "who bears the name of brother or sister" (1 Cor. 5:11, NRSV) continues unrepentantly in overt immorality (1 Cor. 5:1, 13); when someone actively propagates false doctrine (Rom. 16:17); and when a person creates dissension in the congregation (Tit. 3:10-11).

77. On this and other possibilities (especially Ezek. 11:17; Zeph. 3:20), see Webb 43-52.

78. This is suggested by Scott, "Scripture" 85-86; Webb 46 n. 4.

79. εἰσδέχομαι means "accept/receive" with friendliness and therefore into fellowship (see W. Grundmann, *TDNT* 2.57).

80. On Paul's sources for 6:18, see Webb 52-58; Stanley 227-30.

81. Robertson 458, 595; Moulton and Howard 462-63; Turner 253. The futures ἔσομαι and ἔσεσθε are durative ("will/shall be"), not punctiliar ("become," Goodspeed).

82. See Moulton 71-72.

influence.[83] ὑμῖν may be taken as a dative of possession and therefore equivalent to ὑμῶν (similarly, μοι, as equivalent to μου) (cf. αὐτῶν θεός and μου λαός in 6:16) (thus JB, NRSV, "your father . . . my sons and daughters"), but the Greek word order, although reflecting the Hebrew text, suggests that these two datives are emphatic, ". . . a father to you . . . sons and daughters to me."[84]

In 2 Sam. 7:11-16, the heart of the so-called "Nathan oracle," God promises to David a royal dynasty that will last forever, including a special father-son relationship to Solomon and successive Davidic kings (2 Sam. 7:14). This unique divine-human relationship, first promised to David's offspring and later extended to include the whole nation (Jer. 31:9, "I am Israel's father, and Ephraim is my firstborn son"), now finds its fulfillment, Paul asserts, in the filial relationship of the Christian community to God as Father.[85] There is still only one Father, but now there are many sons. Then to show that women and girls have parity of status in God's family with men and boys (cf. Gal. 3:28), Paul adds "and daughters" to the phrase "you will be sons to me."[86] καὶ θυγατέρας probably stems from Isa. 43:6 (LXX),[87] which reads, "Bring my sons from a distant land and my daughters from the ends of the earth." This verse and the previous one refer to the second exodus, so that this addition to the quotation from 2 Sam. 7:14 has the effect of linking the Davidic promise with the "restoration" theology of Ezek. 20:34.[88]

If we compare v. 18 with v. 16, we see that Paul has moved from the temple motif to the image of the family. θεός has become πατήρ. By combining Ezek. 30:24 with 2 Sam. 7:14 in a single quotation Paul indicates that the welcome (cf. εἰσδέξομαι, v. 17) accorded those who depart from paganism in all its forms is that of a Father to his sons and daughters. Also, the corporate terms ναός and λαός have become individualized as υἱοί and θυγατέρες. Christians are not only God's temple and God's people but they are also individual members of his family.[89] To put it another way: in v. 16 God is the θεός of the new Israel, and the new Israel is the λαός of God (cf. Jer. 31:33); in v. 18 God is the πατήρ of the new Israel, and the new Israel are the υἱοί and θυγατέρες of God.

Paul concludes his final quotation with the formula λέγει κύριος παντοκράτωρ, the expression used in 2 Sam. (Kgdms.) 7:8 at the beginning of

---

83. BDF §145.

84. Thus RV, Williams (". . . to you . . . of mine"), NASB, NJB, NAB², Cassirer; among the commentators, Barrett 193; Furnish 360; Carrez 163-64; Young and Ford 268. Some EVV have ". . . to you . . . my sons and daughters" (e.g., NEB, NAB¹, REB).

85. This promise, "I will be a father to him, and he will be a son to me," is applied to Christ in Heb. 1:5, and to the Christian who conquers in Rev. 21:7 (where "God" replaces "father").

86. This addition must have special significance since the word θυγάτηρ occurs nowhere else in the Pauline letters where the term υἱοί regularly embraces both male and female believers.

87. But Olley (208-12) argues for Deut. 32:19 as the principal source.

88. Cf. Scott 157; Webb 58.

89. Fee finds implicit Spirit language in vv. 16-18: it is by God's Spirit that the church becomes "the temple of the living God," that God "dwells among them," that God "has become a father for you" (*Presence* 337-38).

the Nathan oracle: "This is what (τάδε) the LORD Almighty says." παντο-κράτωρ is formed from πάντα and κρατῶν, "laying hold of all things" or "exercising power over all things" (cf. BDF §119[1])[90] so that it is virtually equivalent to ὁ παντοδύναμος (cf. Wisd. 7:23), "the One who is able to do all things," "the all-powerful One." That κύριος here refers to God the Father (not Christ) is evident from the two uses of θεός in v. 16 and the reference to fatherhood in v. 18 (Capes 114).

The three quotations in vv. 16-18, two of them being composite citations,[91] well illustrate Paul's *pesher* hermeneutical technique, in which he cites an OT passage or combination of passages, and interprets it from the viewpoint of the messianic age (cf. 6:2) and with some alteration to the wording,[92] in order to show its contemporary application and relevance.[93] For instance, "God's command to Israel concerning Babylon (αὐτῆς) is now applied to the relation of Christians with unbelievers (αὐτῶν); the promise given to Israel 'personified' in Solomon (αὐτῷ . . . αὐτός) is fulfilled in true Israel, the members of Christ's body (ὑμῖν . . . ὑμεῖς)" (Ellis 144).

7:1 ταύτας οὖν ἔχοντες τὰς ἐπαγγελίας, ἀγαπητοί, καθαρίσωμεν ἑαυτοὺς ἀπὸ παντὸς μολυσμοῦ σαρκὸς καὶ πνεύματος, ἐπιτελοῦντες ἁγιωσύνην ἐν φόβῳ θεοῦ. "So then, dear friends, since these great promises are ours, let us cleanse ourselves of everything that may defile body or spirit." Glimpses of the apostle's emotions at this point in the dictation of his letter have already been provided by his direct address, Κορίνθιοι, in 6:11 and his reference in 6:13 to his converts as his τέκνα. Those indications of stirred emotions and pastoral affection are now reinforced by another direct address, ἀγαπητοί, "dear friends" (BAGD 16c; NIV) or "dear brothers" (JB) (cf. 12:19). The inferential οὖν ("so then") is explicated by the causal participle ἔχοντες ("since we have"). Even if Paul had written simply καθαρίσωμεν οὖν ἑαυτούς, the overall sense would not be materially different. Both the hortatory subjunctive καθαρίσωμεν and the virtual imperative ἐπιτελοῦντες find their justification and basis (οὖν ἔχοντες) in the Christian possession of "these promises" (cf. 1:20), that is, the seven promises mentioned in 6:16-18 (see the preceding chart). ταύτας is emphatic by position and is therefore virtually equivalent to τηλικαύτας (ἐπαγγελίας) "so great (promises)."[94]

"Let us cleanse ourselves" cannot refer to literal ceremonial washing (as

---

90. Of the ten NT uses of this title, nine are found in Revelation (1:8; 4:8; 11:17; 15:3; 16:7, 14; 19:6, 15; 21:22).

91. Namely, Lev. 26:11-12 and Ezek. 37:27 in v. 16, and Ezek. 20:34, 2 Kgdms. 7:14, and Isa. 43:6 in vv. 17-18.

92. On adaptation of the source text in the writings of Paul and his contemporaries, see Stanley 342-60, who notes that "the percentage of adapted citations identified in Paul's letters (60 percent) places him at the high end of the spectrum among the authors surveyed" (348).

93. On this technique in Paul, see Ellis 139-49.

94. Cf. Moffatt, "As these great promises are ours"; Plummer's paraphrase, "Seeing then that the promises which we have are no less than these" (202).

in Num. 8:6-7) since the cleansing involves "spirit" as well as "body"; the reference is to figurative purification or purity (as in 1 Cor. 7:34). As used here, the expression καθαρίζω ἀπό ("cleanse from") is elliptical, with ἀπό denoting separation.[95] The sense is "Let us cleanse ourselves[96] [by keeping clear of . . .]." There is no necessary implication that Paul and the Corinthians were already defiled in body or spirit and so needed cleansing, just as "let us throw off the deeds of darkness" (Rom. 13:12) need not imply that Paul and the Roman believers were clothed in evil. The constant need to repudiate any possible defilement (παντὸς μολυσμοῦ) is Paul's point.[97] The aorist καθαρίσωμεν does not point to a single decisive act but to repeated action conceived of unitarily. μολυσμός, "defilement," "pollution," a NT *hapax legomenon,* denotes something that makes a person ceremonially or morally unclean and therefore unfit for worship. In each of its three LXX uses it is linked with the defilement of idolatry (Jer. 23:15; 1 Esdr. 8:80 [EVV, 8:83]; 2 Macc. 5:27; cf. the cognate verb μολύνω, "defile," in 1 Cor. 8:7).

Some have argued that since Paul often sets the terms σάρξ and πνεῦμα in opposition (e.g., Gal. 5:16-17) and would never call for the cleansing of the σάρξ, only its crucifixion (cf. Gal. 5:19-21, 24), the expression μολυσμὸς σαρκὸς καὶ πνεύματος, where σάρξ and πνεῦμα are conjoined, cannot be Pauline.[98] But there is evidence in Paul's letters of a non-pejorative use of σάρξ where it is synonymous with σῶμα[99] and of a popular, non-theological use of σάρξ and πνεῦμα where they refer, in a complementary not antithetical way, to the outward and inward aspects of the person.[100] So we propose that σαρκός and πνεύματος are objective genitives after μολυσμοῦ[101] and refer to the whole person viewed physically and spiritually, outwardly and inwardly.[102] Paul is indicating that both body and spirit are defiled by pagan practices. 1 Cor. 6:15-17 expresses a similar sentiment: to defile one's body in immorality is also to defile one's spirit.[103]

This urgent call to avoid both physical and spiritual defilement restates the earlier entreaties to repudiate unholy alliances (6:14) and to reject the pagan

---

95. Accordingly, it is better to follow CEV ("We should stay away from everything that keeps our bodies and spirits from being clean") than Bratcher 73 ("Let us make ourselves pure by getting rid of everything that makes our bodies and our souls impure").

96. ἑαυτούς = ἡμᾶς αὐτούς. In Hellenistic Greek the third person reflexive ἑαυτοῦ is regularly used (in the appropriate case and number) of all three persons.

97. BAGD 631c classifies this use of πᾶς with an anarthrous noun in the singular under the heading "including everything belonging, in kind, to the class designated by the noun, *every kind of, all sorts of,* for the words παντοδαπός and παντοῖος."

98. E.g., Schmiedel 253-54 (cited by Thrall 30 n. 189).

99. E.g., 4:11; 10:3; Gal. 2:20.

100. E.g., 2:13 compared with 7:5; Col. 2:5.

101. It is possible, but unlikely, that σαρκός is a subjective genitive and πνεύματος an objective genitive ("[defilement] that stems from the flesh or that invades the spirit").

102. "Without and within" (Bruce, *Paraphrase* 141).

103. Cf. Schlatter 579.

way of life (6:17, three imperatives). In all these cases Paul seems to have up-permost in his mind the danger that the Corinthian believers constantly faced of idolatrous associations that would jeopardize their devotion to Christ (cf. 11:3). In 7:1, however, he includes himself in the exhortation and expands it to incor-porate the rejection of every possible form of defilement, idolatry or otherwise, that might harm the believer.

ἐπιτελοῦντες ἁγιωσύνην ἐν φόβῳ θεοῦ. "(And let us) complete our conse-cration by our reverence for God." Unlike Hebrew, Greek is a language that pre-fers subordination over coordination in its grammatical constructions. Instead of completing v. 1 with the coordinated καὶ ἐπιτελέσωμεν ("and let us com-plete"), Paul adds the subordinate participle ἐπιτελοῦντες. But such participles often assume the mood of the finite verb on which they depend (here καθαρίσωμεν). So it is entirely appropriate, and preferable, to render ἐπιτελοῦντες by "(and) let us complete . . ."[104] or "(Let us cleanse ourselves . . . and) complete,"[105] which indicates that this participle is in effect imperatival and expresses an additional exhortation.[106] Although ἁγιωσύνην ("sanctifica-tion," "holiness," "consecration"; cf. Rom. 1:4; 1 Thess. 3:13, the only other NT uses) is anarthrous, it is legitimate to supply the possessive "our," given the context (καθαρίσωμεν ἑαυτούς).[107]

Whether we render ἐπιτελοῦντες by "complete" or "bring to completion" or "make perfect,"[108] a process of sanctification (ἁγιωσύνη) is involved (note the present tense of the participle), not the acquisition of perfect holiness.[109] The same person who affirmed that he had "not yet reached perfection" and that his calling was perpetually to "press forward" (Phil. 3:12-14) would hardly envisage a permanent arrival at holiness in the present age. From 1 Thess. 3:13 it is clear that believers are "unblameable in holiness" or "faultlessly pure" (Goodspeed) only at the second advent. But how is this maturing in holiness re-lated to the self-purification mentioned earlier in the verse? If in fact they are separate ongoing processes and not related as cause and effect, then we may say that they are complementary obligations resting on all believers.

104. Similarly Moffatt, GNB, Barclay, REB, Cassirer, NLT; also Carrez 164.

105. Similarly TCNT, Weymouth, Goodspeed, Berkeley, RSV, NEB, NAB, NIV; also Lang 308; Wolff 144.

106. But it is possible that ἐπιτελοῦντες expresses an "attendant consequence" (Barnett 356), "thus completing . . . ," which would make the perfecting of holiness the outcome of the self-purification (also Martin 210). JB, on the other hand, construes ἐπιτελοῦντες as telic, "(let us wash off . . .), to reach perfection of holiness," and de Boor (157) regards it as circumstantial, "while *(indem)* we bring holiness to completion."

107. Thus NEB, NAB[1], NJB, REB.

108. Moulton and Howard classify ἐπιτελέω among those verbs in which the prepositional prefix (ἐπι-) has a directive force, "indicating the concentration of the verb's action upon some ob-ject" (312).

109. *Pace* BAGD 10c: "Of Christians ἐπιτελεῖν ἁγιωσύνην *to perfect holiness* = become per-fectly holy," citing 2 Cor. 7:1. But elsewhere (BAGD 302c) this phrase is rendered "bring about sanctification."

In the phrase ἐν φόβῳ θεοῦ, the genitive is clearly objective, but the preposition may be taken in three ways:

(1) causal: "because we fear God" (NLT), "out of reverence for God" (NIV) (cf. Eph. 5:21);[110]
(2) circumstantial: "all the while reverencing God," "in an atmosphere of reverential fear for God"; or
(3) instrumental: "by reverence for God" (Goodspeed); "by living in awe of God" (GNB).

A preference may be expressed for the third option. One would expect that in speaking of so crucial an issue as the perfecting of holiness, Paul would indicate the means by which it could be achieved. And certainly a reverential awe and holy dread (φόβος) before God[111] would promote the pursuit of holiness in thought and action, particularly if the expression φόβος θεοῦ alludes to the final judgment and human accountability to God (note the phrase φόβος κυρίου [= Christ] in 5:11 after 5:10, and the title κύριος παντοκράτωρ in 6:18).

As we look back on 6:14–7:1 as a whole, several observations are appropriate. First, the temple motif is central throughout the paragraph and forms the ultimate basis for Paul's appeal for holiness.[112] After introducing this motif in the final and climatic antithesis ("What agreement has the temple of God with idols?" 6:16), Paul immediately makes the crucial affirmation, "It is we [Christians] who constitute the [new] temple of the living God" (6:16). This is then explained (καθώς) by three scriptural citations, one of which (Lev. 26:11-12 with influence from Ezek. 37:27) indicates how believers are God's temple (6:16), while the next (Isa. 52:11) states the necessary consequences (διό) of being God's temple (6:17), and the last (Ezek. 20:34 and 2 Sam. 7:14 with influence from Isa. 43:6) declares the results of obedience to God's call to maintain the purity of that temple (6:17-18). The final verse (7:1) restates the repeated pleas for separation from evil, linking this separation with the advance in holiness that comes through the fear of God.

Second, the paragraph affords several examples of the indicative–imperative dialectic that is so characteristic of Pauline ethics: "You are; therefore be!" All six of his exhortations are securely grounded (γάρ . . . γάρ . . . διό . . . οὖν) on statements of theological truth (the seven promises) or on self-evident facts (the five antitheses) (see the preceding chart).

Third, in Paul's thought the Christian life is in essence an advance in holi-

110. See BAGD 261, III.3.a. for this use of ἐν.
111. φόβος θεοῦ occurs only in 7:1 and Rom. 3:18 (citing Ps. 35:2, LXX [EVV 36:1]). Paul uses the common LXX phrase φόβος κυρίου in 5:11 in reference to Christ (cf. 5:10) and replaces κυρίου by Χριστοῦ in Eph. 5:21. His expression μετὰ φόβου καὶ τρόμου (1 Cor. 2:3; 2 Cor. 7:15; Eph. 6:5; Phil. 2:12) may have "God (the Judge)" as the implied object (see O'Brien, *Philippians* 282-84). See further on this theme, Barth 662-68; H. Balz and G. Wanke, *TDNT* 9.189-219.
112. So also McKelvey 97; Newton 111, 113.

ness, an ἐπιτελεῖν ἁγιωσύνην (7:1), a bringing to maturation of our consecration to God. This process of sanctification involves first and foremost a sense of awe and dread before the omnipotent Lord (ἐν φόβῳ θεοῦ, 7:1) but also a repudiation of evil in every form (ἀκαθάρτου μὴ ἅπτεσθε [6:17] and ἀπὸ παντὸς μολυσμοῦ [7:1]), especially the avoidance of close, permanent alliances with unbelievers (6:14, 17).

Bibliography

A. J. Adewuya, *Holiness and Community in 2 Cor. 6:14–7:1: Paul's View of Communal Holiness in the Corinthian Correspondence* (New York: Lang, 2001) • Beale • Belleville, *Reflections* 94-103 • Betz, "Fragment" • Bieringer, "Kontext" • Braun 1.201-3; 2.165-80 • Capes 111-15 • Dahl, "Fragment" • Daniel • Derrett • deSilva, "Decision" • S. J. DeVries, "Note Concerning the Fear of God in the Qumran Scrolls," *RevQ* 5 (1964-66) 233-37 • Duff • Ellis 48-49, 90-92, 144 • Fee, "Food" • Fee, *Presence* 336-38 • Fitzmyer, "Qumran" • B. Gärtner, *The Temple and the Community in Qumran and the New Testament* (Cambridge: Cambridge University Press, 1965) 49-56 • Gnilka • Goulder • Gunther 308-13 • Huppenbauer • Kamlah 28-30 • Ker • C. R. Koester 127-29 • Kreitzer 30-35 • Kuhn • Lambrecht, "Fragment" • Lane 23-25 • McKelvey 93-98 • Moffatt, "Corinthians" • Murphy-O'Connor 67-70 • Murphy-O'Connor, "Context" • Murphy-O'Connor, "Philo" • Newton 110-14 • Olley • Patte • Rensberger • Sass, "Waffen" • Schütz 165-86 • Scott, *Adoption* 187-220 • Scott, "Scripture" • Skeat • Stachowiak • Stanley 217-30 • Thrall, "Problem" • von der Osten-Sacken • Walker • Walker, "Structure" • Webb • Webb, "Unbelievers" • Webb, "Yoke" • Zeilinger

c. Paul's Pride and Joy (7:2-4)

Viewed as a unit, these three verses occupy a pivotal place in the structure of 2 Corinthians. In the immediate context, after the digressive plea for separation from idolatry and for purity of life (6:14–7:1), they resume the theme of the need for warm reciprocal relations between Paul and the Corinthians that was expressed in 6:11-13.

6:11-13	7:2-4
We are speaking frankly to you (6:11a)	I am perfectly frank with you (7:4a)
Our heart is wide open to you. There is no restriction in our affection for you (6:11b-12a)	Your place in our hearts is secure (7:3b, REB)
Open wide your hearts also (6:13b)	Make room for us in your hearts (7:2a)

But the verses look forward as well as backward. With its buoyant optimism, v. 4 anticipates 7:5-16, which records Paul's consummate relief at the positive news brought by Titus regarding the Corinthian response to the "severe letter." Thus καύχησις (v. 4) prepares the way for κεκαύχημαι . . . ἡ καύχησις ἡμῶν (v. 14); τῇ παρακλήσει (v. 4) anticipates ὁ παρακαλῶν . . . παρεκάλεσεν (v. 6), ἐν τῇ παρακλήσει ᾗ παρεκλήθη (v. 7), and παρακεκλήμεθα . . . Ἐπὶ δὲ τῇ παρακλήσει ἡμῶν (v. 13); τῇ χαρᾷ (v. 4) looks forward to χαρῆναι (v. 7), χαίρω (v. 9), ἐχάρημεν ἐπὶ τῇ χαρᾷ (v. 13), and χαίρω (v. 16); and τῇ θλίψει (v. 4) is picked up by θλιβόμενοι (v. 5).[1] So it is that the whole section 7:2-16 lays the psychological groundwork for Paul's admonitions regarding the completion of the collection (chs. 8–9) and his remonstrance with the Corinthians regarding his opponents (chs. 10–13) which are the necessary preparation for his imminent visit (12:14; 13:1). Finally, on a broader front, 7:2-4 concludes the major digression (2:14–7:4), Paul's description and defense of his apostolic ministry, that forms the heart not only of chs. 1–7 but also of the whole letter. At 7:5 Paul resumes the travel narrative that was broken off at 2:13.

2*Make room for us in your hearts. We have wronged no one, corrupted no one, defrauded no one.* 3*I do not say this to condemn you, for I have already told you that you have such a place in our heart that we are one with you in death and in life.* 4*I am totally frank with you, I freely boast about you. In all our affliction I am filled with comfort and overflowing with[a] joy.*

TEXTUAL NOTES

a. B adds ἐν before τῇ χαρᾷ, perhaps on the model of (the simplex) περισσεύω ἐν ("abound with") in Rom. 15:13.

7:2 Χωρήσατε ἡμᾶς· οὐδένα ἠδικήσαμεν, οὐδένα ἐφθείραμεν, οὐδένα ἐπλεονεκτήσαμεν. "Make room for us in your hearts. We have wronged no one, corrupted no one, defrauded no one." With the plea that the Corinthians should open their hearts sufficiently wide to accommodate him, Paul reiterates the request made in 6:13b, πλατύνθητε καὶ ὑμεῖς, "you also, open wide your hearts," now making explicit that it is for him (ἡμᾶς) that the Corinthians need to make space in their affections. By this repetition the apostle tacitly acknowledges that he has digressed in 6:14–7:1. Justification for supplying ἐν ταῖς καρδίαις ὑμῶν with χωήσατε ἡμᾶς[2] may be found in 6:11-12 and 7:3. We may perhaps account for the sudden transition after this plea for space by suggesting that with the threefold protestation of innocence Paul is insisting that there is no reason for the Corinthians not to open their hearts to him, no reason for them to remain restricted in their affections (cf. 6:12): "I am innocent of any wrongdoing; no one of you

1. Cf. Lietzmann 131. These verbal links argue for the unity of 7:5-16 with (at least) 2:14–7:4 and against the supposition that 2:14–7:4 (with or without 6:14–7:1) forms a separate letter (see the Introduction, A.3.a.).

2. Most translations supply "in your hearts" or the equivalent (also BAGD 890a). But Allo (188, followed by Héring 53) takes χωρέω here to mean "understand," citing Matt. 19:11-12.

has ever suffered at my hands." We might have expected a γάρ after the first οὐδένα, but by this asyndeton Paul perhaps betrays his quickening pace of dictation and his eagerness for full reconciliation.[3] Notable too is the repeated οὐδένα and the successive aorists which could point to a single occasion or to three separate occasions, but, seen as constative aorists, probably have reference to no particular occasion, but view Paul's past relations with the Corinthians summarily; thus "on no occasion did I wrong, corrupt, or defraud anyone." Paul could be defending himself against charges of a general or a specific nature. If general, the three verbs could be almost synonymous, describing Paul's scrupulous respect of the Corinthians' proper rights.[4] On the other hand, if Paul is responding to particular accusations, οὐδένα ἠδικήσαμεν could allude to a charge that he had been too stern in dealing with the incestuous man of 1 Cor. 5:1-13 or with the offender mentioned in 2 Cor. 2:5-11; 7:12 (where the same verb is used, τοῦ ἀδικήσαντος). φθείρω here will mean either "ruin financially"[5] or "corrupt" in the matter of doctrine or morals. Correspondingly, behind οὐδένα ἐφθείραμεν may lie the charge that Paul had brought economic ruin on some believers at Corinth by insisting that certain business associations or practices were incompatible with Christian standards (cf. 1 Cor. 6:7; 15:33) or that Paul's teaching on freedom in Christ had led some down the road of libertinism (cf. 1 Cor. 6:12-20). As for the third denial, οὐδένα ἐπλεονεκτήσαμεν, the twofold use of the same verb (πλεονεκτέω, "take advantage of," "exploit," "defraud") in 12:17-18 in connection with accusations of financial exploitation, strongly suggests that the underlying charge may have been one of financial manipulation, perhaps in relation to the collection for the Jerusalem church (cf. 8:20-21).[6]

Paul knew of nothing in his past conduct or teaching that lent any substance to the charges that had been leveled against him. But he is not merely insisting that the charges are groundless (cf. 6:3). Being innocent of wrongdoing, he is worthy of more than the Corinthians' toleration; he deserves their full openheartedness — "Grant me space in your hearts!" The Corinthians were already in Paul's heart (3:2, reading ἡμῶν; 7:3); now he must be in their hearts.[7] In 6:11–7:2 he is calling for a realignment of "heart boundaries." On one side, the Corinthians need to expand their affections and embrace Paul (6:11-13; 7:2a), yet on the other side they must curb their affections and exclude idolatrous associations (6:14–7:1).[8]

7:3 πρὸς κατάκρισιν οὐ λέγω, προείρηκα γὰρ ὅτι ἐν ταῖς καρδίαις ἡμῶν

---

3. The only connective in 7:2-4 occurs in v. 3 (γάρ).

4. Thus Héring 53. Cf. Isaacs' paraphrase (15-16): "I have outraged no man's rights, have tampered with no man's integrity, have exploited no man's weakness."

5. See BAGD 857b for this possible meaning; also G. Harder, *TDNT* 9.102, who adds, however, "in the light of exaggerated criticism it is meant ironically and not in a moral or religious sense."

6. Similarly Thrall 482; G. Delling, *TDNT* 6.273.

7. Cf. Patte 48.

8. Cf. Garland 343.

ἐστε εἰς τὸ συναποθανεῖν καὶ συζῆν. "I do not say this to condemn you,[9] for I have already told you that you have such a place in our heart that we are one with you in death and in life." Paul, ever sensitive to possible misinterpretation of his innocent statements, now seeks to avoid any misunderstanding of the vigorous rebuttal he has just issued (v. 2b).[10] "I am not putting you in the wrong when I say this." The mention of the charges did not imply that the Corinthians really believed them.[11] Or Paul may mean that his effort to defend himself and clear his name did not amount to laying blame at their door. "My words are no reflection on you" (REB).

Now, with the only connective found in these three verses Paul gives the reason (γάρ) why he could never censure the Corinthians without cause: they had always been firmly planted in his affections.[12] A spirit of censure is incompatible with a spirit of love. It was not that Paul's love for them had just begun or that they were unaware of it. He had told them of his deep affection "already" (or "previously") (προ-), possibly on an earlier visit but more probably in the present letter at 3:2 ("You yourselves are our letter, written on our hearts") or 6:11b-12a ("Our heart is wide open to you. There is no restriction in our affection for you").[13] To indicate what secure placement in the heart involved, Paul adds εἰς τὸ συναποθανεῖν καὶ συζῆν.

εἰς with the articular infinitive may express purpose or result (BDF §402[2]). In the present case it expresses the result ("so that") of Paul's having the Corinthians in his heart, which then justifies the rendering ". . . such a place that. . . ." The unexpressed subject of the two infinitives will be ἡμᾶς, understood as a reference to Paul (with the repeated συ(ν) — meaning "with [you Corinthians]") or to Paul and the Corinthians (with συ(ν) — meaning "together" or "with one another"). There are three basic ways of understanding the references to death and life.

Death	Life
1. Past and present spiritual death with Christ to sin (cf. Rom. 6:6, 8, 10-11; 2 Cor. 5:14; Col. 2:12-13)	Present spiritual life with Christ (cf. 2 Tim. 2:11; 2 Cor. 5:15)
2. Future physical death in Christ (Phil. 1:23)	Future eternal life in Christ (1 Thess. 4:17)
3. Future physical death	Present physical life

9. πρός here indicates a goal aimed at, "for the purpose of" (BAGD 710a; also 412b). ὑμῶν (objective genitive) is to be understood with (τὴν) κατάκρισιν.

10. This is a case of epidiorthosis (as also in 12:11) (see BDF §494[3]).

11. The source of the accusations is not known. They may have arisen from the intruders from Palestine with whom certain Corinthian "proto-gnostics" had closed ranks (see the Introduction, B.4.).

12. εἶναι ἐν means "have a place in" (BAGD 404b) and the present tense ἐστε suggests "you have a *secure* place." Even if the plurals καρδίαις and ἡμῶν are pressed, with allusions to Timothy (1:1) and/or Titus (7:15), Paul is clearly the principal referent (cf. 6:11-12).

13. Thrall suggests (484) that ἐν ταῖς καρδίαις ἡμῶν is an expansion of ἐν ἡμῖν (6:12).

518

These three views may perhaps be described as the christological,[14] the eschatological,[15] and the anthropological.[16] The first view reflects Pauline teaching about death and resurrection with Christ and has the support of the close parallel in 2 Tim. 2:11. However, the absence of an explicit mention of Christ that would make an allusion to the baptismal death-resurrection formula ambiguous is the Achilles' heel of this interpretation.[17] The difficulty with the second view is that it is unlikely that ζῆν would refer to eternal life when it lacks a clarifying qualification such as εἰς τοὺς αἰῶνας or ἐν ἀφθαρσίᾳ. On the third view the reference is simply to the two possible anthropological states — life and death — and is a traditional way of expressing permanent friendship or loyalty or love (cf. Mark. 14:31; John 11:16): "if you live, I live; if you die, I die."[18] Paul is declaring that his destiny, now and always, will be interwoven with that of the Corinthians. Neither the arrival of death nor the vicissitudes of life could divorce them from his affection (cf. Meyer 563). The surprising word order "death-life" is no impediment for this view, since parallels for this word order exist,[19] and more importantly, in this letter Paul is particularly aware of his mortality (4:10-12, 16; 6:9; 11:23) and assumes that he will probably die before the parousia of Christ (4:14; 5:1).[20]

7:4 πολλή μοι παρρησία πρὸς ὑμᾶς, πολλή μοι καύχησις ὑπὲρ ὑμῶν· "I am totally frank with you, I freely boast about you." Having declared his undying love for the Corinthians (v. 3), Paul now states two consequences of that love, frankness of speech and freedom in boasting. παρρησία has a wide range of meaning, from openness in speaking all one's mind to fearlessness in general (see on 3:12). Some prefer the meaning "confidence" here (e.g., RSV, "I have great confidence in you"), perhaps under the influence of 7:16 ("I rejoice that I have complete confidence [ἐν παντὶ θαρρῶ] in you").[21] But 6:11a and the re-

---

14. This general position is represented by Stählin 503-21; Tannehill 93-94; and (apparently) Carrez 170, who cites Rom. 14:7-8.

15. Thus Lambrecht 125-27; "2 Cor. 7:3" 571-87.

16. This view is endorsed by most commentators (e.g., Barrett, 204, "you are in our hearts, bound up with us in death and in life," taking ὑμᾶς as the unexpressed subject of the infinitives; Wolff 153-54; Thrall 483-84), and, unambiguously, by those translations that use the idiom "come death, come life" (thus NEB, REB).

17. In 2 Tim. 2:11 (εἰ γὰρ συναπεθάνομεν, καὶ συζήσομεν) there is an explicit reference to Christ in the preceding verse and a repeated ἐκεῖνος in vv. 12-13 (which is part of the same "sure saying").

18. Horace, *Odes* 3.9.24, is frequently cited: tecum vivere amem, tecum obeam libens ("with you I would love to live, with you I would gladly die"). On the use of this traditional formula of fidelity in a military context, see Spicq 3.330 and especially Olivier 104-113.

19. E.g., 2 Kgdms. 15:21 (LXX); Euripides, *Orestes* 307 (cited by Bultmann 178). Some EVV (TCNT, Goodspeed, GNB, JB, NIV, NJB) unnecessarily alter the word order to conform to the more common "live-die" sequence.

20. Murphy-O'Connor maintains that Paul "typically adapts" the traditional formula by inverting the word order "so that it becomes a subtle invitation to die to Sin and to live for Christ (5:15)" (70).

21. Cf. 1:15; 2:3; 1 Tim. 3:13 (πολλὴν παρρησίαν); Heb. 10:19.

markable candidness apparent in 6:14–7:1 strongly support the sense "freedom of speech," "frankness to address them openly, to speak to them candidly, and to exhort them boldly" (Marrow 445).[22] καύχησις refers to the act of boasting, although (like καύχημα) it sometimes signifies the object of boasting, one's pride. Both senses accord with the context, so, not surprisingly, some translations prefer a rendering such as "I have great pride in you" (RSV, NRSV) (cf. 1 Cor. 15:31),[23] while others take καύχησις in the sense of "boasting" (e.g., NASB) (cf. 8:24). Either way, ὑπέρ means "concerning" (= περί[24]) or the equivalent, rather than "on behalf of" (so also in 7:14).

There is clear parallelism between these two phrases, with the emphasis in each case falling on the extent (πολλή . . . πολλή . . .) of the frankness and the boasting: "I am totally frank. . . . I freely boast."[25] But there is also a contrast between the two phrases. The παρρησία is directed to the Corinthians, the καύχησις to others about the Corinthians. Isaacs catches the contrast well (16): "To you I speak boldly of your faults: to others I speak no less boldly of your merits."

πεπλήρωμαι τῇ παρακλήσει, ὑπερπερισσεύομαι τῇ χαρᾷ ἐπὶ πάσῃ τῇ θλίψει ἡμῶν. "In all our affliction I am filled with comfort and overflowing with joy." At this point Paul's thought is already in process of returning to his travel narrative that he left at 2:13 and of recalling his excited relief at Titus's arrival in Macedonia. This is shown by three terms that are used here but also are central ideas in vv. 5-16, verses that describe that arrival: παρακλήσει (see vv. 6, 7, 13), χαρᾷ (see vv. 7, 9, 13, 16), and θλίψει (see v. 5). Moreover, when Paul says τῇ παρακλήσει and τῇ χαρᾷ he is thinking of a particular time (or specific occasions) when he experienced παράκλησις and χαρά, the "comfort" that was needed and the "joy" that was appropriate in the circumstances (cf. Prümm 1.385 n. 1).[26]

So complete is Paul's comfort as he writes and as he reflects on the recent past[27] that he does not say simply παρακαλούμεθα ("we are comforted") as in 1:4, 6, or παρακεκλήμεθα ("we have been comforted") as in 7:13, but πεπλήρωμαι τῇ παρακλήσει, "I am filled with comfort."[28] The perfect tense points to a present state (note the present ὑπερπερισσεύομαι that follows) that

22. πρὸς ὑμᾶς here means "in relation to you," "with you."

23. So also Olson, "Confidence" 283, but one need not follow him in his argument that Paul, like other Hellenistic writers, uses such expressions of confidence "to undergird" the purpose of his letter, by increasing the likelihood of a favorable hearing (295), "whether or not the confidence is actually warranted by the situation" (282).

24. On this overlap of meaning between ὑπέρ and περί, see Zerwick §96.

25. Some versions reproduce the emphatic word-order: "Great is . . . , great is" (RV, Montgomery, NASB; also Carrez 169; Lang 306.

26. This reflects the grammatical principle that an articular abstract noun often refers to a "concrete application" of the noun (see Zerwick §§176, 179; Turner 176-77).

27. See numbers 19-20 in the "Chronology" (Introduction C.).

28. The perfect passive of πληρόω is followed by either the genitive (Rom. 15:14) or the dative (Rom. 1:29) of the thing that fills (BAGD 671a).

arose from an implied past action ("I was filled with comfort"), namely the receipt of comfort when Titus arrived with good news about the Corinthian situation (vv. 6-7). In the compound verb ὑπερπερισσεύω the prefix is well represented by the English "over": "I am overflowing with joy" (BAGD 841d), "I am overjoyed" (RSV, NRSV), "I am overcome with joy" (Furnish 384), "I bubble over with joy."[29] Like his friend Barnabas who rejoiced (ἐχάρη) when he saw evidence of God's gracious activity among the believers in Antioch (Acts 11:23), Paul experienced exquisite delight as he recalled the positive Corinthian response to Titus's mission (7:5-16; note the verb χαίρω in 7:9, 13, 16) and also remembered the successful resolution of the problem of the wrongdoer (2:5-11; 7:12). Various problems certainly remained in the Corinthian church (witness chs. 8–13), but Paul kept fresh in his memory the triumphs of God's grace that he had already witnessed or experienced — a salutary lesson for all pastors.

It is probable that the expression ἐπὶ πάσῃ τῇ θλίψει ἡμῶν belongs to both of the previous phrases,[30] since the next three verses refer explicitly to Paul's "joy" (v. 7) and especially his "comfort" (v. 6) in the midst of his affliction (cf. ἐν παντὶ θλιβόμενοι, v. 5). It is not impossible that ἐπί (with the dative) is causal ("because of all our affliction," NAB[2]) or expresses the basis or ground of the joy (and comfort) ("at all our affliction"[31]); 1:4-6 could be appealed to in support of such renderings. More probably, ἐπί is here temporal ("during") or locatival ("in," "in the midst of," "amid"; cf. 1:4a).[32] At first sight the plural ἡμῶν seems surprising, given the two preceding singular verbs and the repeated μοι. But rapid oscillation from singular to plural (as here) or from plural to singular (as in 1:13) is not uncommon in Paul's letters.

With its two pairs of balanced phrases, with its remarkable asyndeton that produces a staccato effect of heightened emotion, and with its expression of the principal theme of chs. 1–7, παράκλησις ἐν θλίψει, v. 4 forms a fitting climax to Paul's extended description of the apostolic ministry (2:14–7:4).

Bibliography

Carrez, "Le 'Nous'" • J. Dupont, "Ad commoriendum et ad convivendum (2 Cor 7,3)," in *Teologia-Liturgia-Storia* (Festschrift for C. Manziana) (Brescia, 1977) 19-28 • J. Lambrecht, "2 Cor. 7:3" • Marrow • Olivier • Olson, "Confidence" • Stählin • Tannehill 90-98 • Theobald 275-76.

29. Bruce, *Paraphrase* 141. This verb represents an advance on πεπλήρωμαι: "my cup is full of comfort; indeed, it overflows with joy" (cf. NEB, REB). τῇ χαρᾷ is an instrumental dative; Classical Greek would normally have used the genitive (BDF §195[2]).

30. Thus NJB; Plummer (CGT) 112.

31. Zerwick and Grosvenor 547, citing Zerwick §126.

32. Thus, "in all our affliction" (RV, NASB, NRSV; Furnish 193; Thrall 472; similarly BAGD 631d).

D. Paul's Joy at the Corinthians' Repentance (7:5-16)

These verses mark Paul's return to the travel narrative that was suspended at 2:13 for a "major digression" (2:14–7:4). 1:8-11 presupposed Paul's journey from Ephesus to "Asia" (= Troas[1]) (spring 56; cf. Acts 20:1); 2:12-13 actually recounts this journey to Troas and mentions Paul's departure for Macedonia; now 7:5-16 describes his arrival in Macedonia and recounts events that took place there (spring-summer 56).[2]

But what were the historical circumstances that brought Paul to Macedonia? After his second visit to Corinth, which turned out to be painful (2:1; cf. 12:21; 13:2), he returned to Ephesus (summer or fall 55). When he heard of the troubling action of "the wrongdoer," which directly involved him, he seems at first to have planned to pay the church another personal visit to try to rectify the situation, but on reflection he came to the decision (ἔκρινα . . . ἐμαυτῷ, 2:1) to spare the Corinthians a further "painful visit" (1:23; 2:1-2) and instead to pay them a visit by means of a stern letter (= the "severe letter"; 2:3-4) that called on the congregation to punish the wrongdoer (cf. 2:6, 9). Titus was dispatched with this letter, probably with the task of explaining and reinforcing Paul's directives expressed in the letter.[3] Apparently Paul asked Titus to meet him in Troas, or, if circumstances at Corinth or travel arrangements delayed him, they were to meet in Macedonia (2:13), which probably meant Philippi.[4] In the event, the pair met each other in Macedonia, not Troas, but even that meeting did not take place as soon as Paul had hoped and expected (7:5).

Verses 5-16 recount (1) the consummate relief and deep joy felt by Paul when he learned from Titus that the Corinthians had responded positively to the "severe letter" (vv. 5-7, 9, 13, 16); (2) the Corinthians' response to this letter (vv. 8-11); (3) Paul's purposes in sending the letter (v. 12); and (4) Titus's reaction to his encounter with the Corinthians (vv. 13b-15). Thus Paul concludes his discussion, begun in 2:1-11, about the "severe letter."[5] Earlier his concern had been with the circumstances surrounding the writing of that letter (2:1-4) and the treatment of the offender after his repentance (2:5-11). Here in ch. 7 the focus falls on Titus as Paul's emissary and intermediary (7:6-7, 13b-15) and on the church's reaction to the letter (7:8-12). There can

---

1. On this point see the commentary at 1:8 and the Excursus after 1:11.

2. For these suggested dates, see the Introduction, C.

3. There were three ways in which Paul could make his presence and apostolic authority felt in his churches — by a personal visit, by an emissary, and by a letter (Funk, "Parousia" 258). But Mitchell (641-62) has rightly challenged Funk's proposal that visits by envoy or letter were seen by Paul as inadequate substitutes for his physical presence.

4. See n. 251 in the Introduction.

5. It is interesting to note that the λυπ- word group is found eight times in 2:1-11 and eight times in 7:5-13a.

be little doubt that the placement of this glowing report about Corinthian attitudes and Titus's role immediately before chs. 8–9 was designed to prepare the Corinthians psychologically for Titus's next visit to them when he would have a different but equally delicate mission — to facilitate the completion of the collection.

We have seen that with its reference to boasting, comfort, joy, and affliction, v. 4 anticipates vocabulary and themes in vv. 5-16 (see the commentary on 7:4). Indeed, the idea of "comfort in the midst of affliction" is one of the central themes in chs. 1–7. Also noticeable within vv. 5-16 is the contrasting pair, sorrow and joy. "Godly sorrow" (ἡ . . . κατὰ θεὸν λύπη, v. 10), that is, "sorrow in accordance with God's will" (cf. ἐλυπήθητε . . . κατὰ θεόν, v. 9; τὸ κατὰ θεὸν λυπηθῆναι, v. 11), produces genuine repentance that leads to salvation (v. 10) and is evidenced in altered attitudes and behavior (v. 11). But joy is also a prominent theme, being referred to in each of the three sections of vv. 5-16 (note also ὑπερπερισσεύομαι τῇ χαρᾷ in v. 4 and χαίρω in v. 16):[6]

vv. 5-7	ὥστε με μᾶλλον χαρῆναι ("so that I rejoiced all the more," v. 7): joy at Titus's safe arrival and encouraging report
vv. 8-13a	νῦν χαίρω ("now I rejoice," v. 9): joy over the Corinthians' godly sorrow that led to their repentance
vv. 13b-15	περισσοτέρως μᾶλλον ἐχάρημεν ἐπὶ τῇ χαρᾷ Τίτου ("we rejoiced more than ever at the joy of Titus," v. 13b): joy because of Titus's joy.

To help us trace the elements of Paul's thought in vv. 5-16, it may prove useful to set out in chronological order the various events and experiences referred to or implied in this passage.

1. Paul writes the "severe letter" (vv. 8, 12) in Ephesus.
2. He boasts to Titus about the Corinthians (v. 14).
3. Titus is sent to Corinth with the letter (cf. v. 6).
4. The Corinthians welcome Titus "with fear and trembling" (v. 15).
5. When they hear the letter, the Corinthians feel sorrow (vv. 8-9).
6. They repent of their inaction about the wrongdoer, rectify the situation, and show eager concern for Paul (vv. 7, 9, 11-12).
7. From their response Titus derives refreshment and joy (v. 13b).
8. Paul (now in Macedonia) is downhearted owing to a combination of circumstances (vv. 5-6).
9. Paul and Titus meet somewhere in Macedonia (vv. 5-7).
10. Titus reports on the Corinthians' sorrow (vv. 8-11), repentance (vv. 7, 9),

6. Barnett 366. For a detailed stylistic analysis of 7:5-16, see Theobald 273.

and obedience (v. 15), and feels his own affection for the Corinthians deepen as he gives his report (v. 15).

11. Hearing of the Corinthians' sorrow and grief, Paul at first regrets having written the letter (v. 8b), but his regret is short-lived (v. 8a) as he learns of their repentance.

12. Paul feels relief, comfort, and joy at the Corinthians' response to his letter (vv. 6-7, 9, 13, 16).

13. His joy is increased as he observes Titus's joy (v. 13b).

14. Paul feels relieved and grateful that his boasting to Titus about the Corinthians proved justified (v. 14).

15. Paul assures the Corinthians that they are now blameless with regard to the whole affair (v. 11) and that he now has complete confidence in them (v. 16).

1. Comfort in Macedonia (7:5-7)

Here Paul resumes his travel narrative by indicating that his emotional and physical restlessness, experienced in Troas (2:13), continued even after his arrival in Macedonia and that relief and joy came only when Titus arrived safely and brought the reassuring news that the Corinthians had repented and acted resolutely in the matter of the wrongdoer (cf. 2:6).

7:5 is closely parallel to 2:13.

2:13a	οὐκ	ἔσχηκα	ἄνεσιν	τῷ πνεύματί	μου
7:5b	οὐδεμίαν	ἔσχηκεν	ἄνεσιν	ἡ σὰρξ	ἡμῶν
2:13b	ἀλλὰ . . .	ἐξῆλθον		εἰς Μακεδονίαν	
7:5a	καὶ γὰρ	ἐλθόντων ἡμῶν		εἰς Μακεδονίαν	

The relevance of this parallelism for the question of the integrity of the letter is discussed in the Introduction, A.3.b.(2).

These three verses are remarkable for their use of both plural and singular first person pronouns. So we have ἡμῶν (v. 5), ἡμᾶς (v. 6), and ἡμῖν . . . ἐμοῦ . . . με (v. 7). The occurrence of both singular and plural within one Greek sentence (v. 7), along with the parallelism between 7:5 and 2:13 (partially set out above) where the μου . . . με . . . μου and the singular verbs ἔσχηκα and ἐξῆλθον of 2:13 are replaced by the plurals ἐλθόντων ἡμῶν . . . ἡμῶν in 7:5, shows that Paul is speaking of his own experience alone.[7] In addition, it is unlikely that he would refer to others' inward fears (v. 5) that contributed to his and their despondency (τοὺς ταπεινούς, v. 6).

7. So also Barrett 206; but for an opposite view, see Furnish 385-86.

5*Indeed, even after we came into Macedonia, this body of ours had[a] no relief. On the contrary, we were harassed in every way — outwardly there were conflicts, and inwardly fears.[b] 6But God, the Comforter of the depressed, comforted us by the coming of Titus, 7and not only by his coming but also by the comfort he had received at your hands. For he reported to us your longing, your penitence, your eagerness to take my side, so that I rejoiced all the more."*

TEXTUAL NOTES

a. The more difficult reading here is certainly the perfect ἔσχηκεν (read by ℵ C D Ψ 0243 33 1739 1881 𝔐). The change to the aorist ἔσχεν (read by p⁴⁶ B F G K) was probably occasioned by scribal concern for grammatical correctness or by the accidental omission of the letters — ηκ-.

b. In the place of the plural φόβοι, some witnesses (p⁴⁶ pc syrᵖ Tertullian) read the singular φόβος, a scribe perhaps believing that it is possible only to have one fear at a time or that it was unbecoming for Paul to confess to multiple fears. Clearly, φόβοι balances μάχαι in typically Pauline fashion.

7:5 Καὶ γὰρ ἐλθόντων ἡμῶν εἰς Μακεδονίαν οὐδεμίαν ἔσχηκεν ἄνεσιν ἡ σὰρξ ἡμῶν. "Indeed, even after we came into Macedonia, this body of ours had no relief." Καὶ γάρ could mean "for indeed," looking back to v. 4b and explaining (in vv. 5-7) how joy came to Paul in the midst of his affliction. Alternatively, as Paul resumes the account of his movements from 2:13, γάρ could function as a connective ("indeed") and καί could mean "even," being linked with the following temporal genitive absolute construction; thus, "even after we came" (similarly RSV, JB, NRSV).[8] On this latter view, which is preferable, Paul is stressing that even his arrival in Macedonia did not bring him relief (ἄνεσις) from the disquiet that had unsettled him in Troas and had caused his early departure from that city (2:13; see the commentary there). From the fact that Paul ultimately met Titus in Macedonia (7:5-6), and not in Troas as he had expected (2:13), we may deduce that when he sent Titus off from Ephesus as his envoy to Corinth with the "severe letter," the arrangement was that they should meet in Troas or, failing that, in Macedonia (probably Philippi).[9]

ἔσχηκεν is the third case in 2 Corinthians of the perfect tense of ἔχω. Here and in 2:13 (ἔσχηκα) the perfect is probably aoristic, since at the time of writing Paul already had gained relief (7:5-6, 13) so that no thought of a continuing state was in Paul's mind.[10] On the other hand, in 1:9 ἐσχήκαμεν is probably per-

---

8. Cf. Carrez 171: "En effet lorsque nous sommes arrivé."

9. Any arrangement for a reunion had to be provisional, for there were unpredictable factors such as the time needed for the Corinthians' deliberation over the contents of the letter and their possible punishment of the wrongdoer (cf. 2:6; 7:12), and the availability (assuming that Titus planned to travel by sea) of a ship from Corinth to Troas, or from Corinth to Neapolis (the port of Philippi) should Titus be delayed in Corinth.

10. So also Moulton 145 ("with great hesitation," 238); Burton §80; Moule 14; Turner 70

fective, since Paul still was very conscious of "the verdict of death" at the time of writing.[11]

In the introduction to the present section we saw the close verbal parallelism between 2:13 and 7:5. "Relief" (ἄνεσις) was denied him both in Troas (2:13) and (initially) in Macedonia (7:5), but whereas in 2:13 he identifies his πνεῦμα as the location of his restlessness, in 7:5 he refers to his σάρξ. If we regard these two terms here as virtually synonymous and as denoting the whole person, we should retain an aspectival distinction, with πνεῦμα referring to an emotional or spiritual agitation, and σάρξ describing physical restiveness and emphasizing the frailty and vulnerability of the human condition (cf. NEB, "this poor body of ours").[12] But it is also possible that σάρξ functions in 7:5 as a broader term, incorporating both inward and outward conditions, since it is followed by ἐν παντὶ θλιβόμενοι — ἔξωθεν . . . ἔσωθεν. . . .[13]

ἀλλ᾽ ἐν παντὶ θλιβόμενοι — ἔξωθεν μάχαι, ἔσωθεν φόβοι. "On the contrary, we were harassed in every way — outwardly there were conflicts, and inwardly fears." So far from gaining release from his anxiety and restiveness by meeting Titus on his arrival in Macedonia, Paul suffered hardship on all sides. Following ἡ σὰρξ ἡμῶν, the participle θλιβόμενοι could be explained in several ways:

1. as an anacoluthon, "as if Paul had written in the previous part of the sentence οὐδεμίαν ἄνεσιν ἐσχήκαμεν τῇ σαρκὶ ἡμῶν" (Winer 352, given as one alternative);
2. as a "construction according to sense," following ἡμῶν;
3. as the participle in a periphrastic construction, with ἦμεν/ἤμεθα or (the historic present) ἐσμέν supplied on the basis of ἡ σὰρξ ἡμῶν;
4. as an absolute use of the participle, with the sense of an imperfect indicative[14] (following ἔσχηκεν) (cf. the participle in 5:12; 8:4; 9:11, 13; 11:6).

What Paul meant by ἐν παντί ("in every way," "at every turn," "on all sides") is defined by ἔξωθεν . . . ἔσωθεν, a contrast which has as its point of ref-

---

("narrative perfects"). All except Moule also treat ἐσχήκαμεν in 1:9 as aoristic. But BDF §343(2) takes the perfects in 1:9 and 7:5 as genuine perfects.

11. See the discussion at 1:9 and 2:13.

12. In 7:5 "σάρξ is used in the neutral sense of the 'I' in its corporeality" (Bultmann 52). But Gundry (144) argues that in 2:13 and 7:5 (and 7:13) "Paul carefully chooses his terms after the pattern of an anthropological duality of flesh as body and spirit as the incorporeal part of man."

13. σάρξ here is "the seat of sensations and the emotions" (Spicq 3.237, citing 7:5). "According to 2 C. 7:5 ἡ σὰρξ ἡμῶν = ἡμεῖς, and it expressly embraces inner anxieties too, though external affliction is primary here (but not in 2:13)" (E. Schweizer, TDNT 7.125).

14. Thus Zerwick and Grosvenor 548; similarly Zerwick §374; Moulton 235; Moule 179; Turner 343.

erence Paul's own person, not the church. That is, the afflictions were around (ἔξωθεν, "outwardly") and within (ἔσωθεν, "inwardly") him, not outside and inside the church, among unbelievers and believers. So rightly Moffatt, "all around me . . . in my own mind." The matching plurals μάχαι and φόβοι (with ἦσαν or εἰσίν understood) may refer to "cases of" conflict and fear (cf. Turner 28) but probably denote multiple conflicts and fears.[15] In secular usage μάχη ("fighting," "battle") applied to strife ranging from marital discord to legal controversy. In NT usage (7:5; 2 Tim. 2:23; Tit. 3:9; Jas. 4:1) the word is always plural and always figurative, meaning "quarrels" or "disputes," or, as a generalizing plural, "wrangling" or "controversy." Precisely what these conflicts were in Paul's case and where they originated, we have no way of knowing. But we may speak with more confidence about Paul's φόβοι. Since his fears were allayed and replaced by joy (7:7, 9, 13) and comfort 7:6, 13) as a result of the safe arrival of Titus with good news about Corinth, we may fairly assume that these fears were various: a haunting uncertainty about Titus's reception at Corinth (cf. 7:13, 15); a persistent apprehension about the Corinthian reaction to the "letter of tears" delivered by Titus (cf. 7:11-12), especially given Titus's failure to meet Paul in Troas (2:13) and initially in Macedonia (7:5); anxiety that he had caused the Corinthians unnecessary pain by his "severe letter" (cf. 7:8) with its call for disciplinary action against the wrongdoer; concern that his boasting to Titus about the Corinthians might prove unfounded and therefore acutely embarrassing (cf. 7:14); anxiety about the safety of Titus in travel (note the repeated ἐν τῇ παρουσίᾳ Τίτου/αὐτοῦ in 7:6-7); fear concerning the influence of his opponents on the Corinthian congregation (cf. 11:3); apprehension that on his forthcoming visit to Corinth he might find some members indulging in unchristian conduct (12:20-21). It was multiple and disconcerting fears such as these that led to Paul's self-confessed state of depression (cf. τοὺς ταπεινούς, 7:6).

While no one in the ancient world could outmatch Paul in showing fortitude in adversity,[16] it is of particular interest that in this verse he openly admits to being in emotional turmoil and having persistent fears. So far from being imperturbable or being a model of inner tranquility,[17] he was deeply affected by his circumstances, especially his pastoral circumstances (cf. 11:28-29), although he was certainly not emotionally fragile.

7:6 ἀλλ' ὁ παρακαλῶν τοὺς ταπεινοὺς παρεκάλεσεν ἡμᾶς ὁ θεὸς ἐν τῇ

---

15. But BAGD 863d renders φόβοι by "feelings of anxiety." Windisch (226) suggests that ἔξωθεν μάχαι, ἔσωθεν φόβοι could be a play on Deut. 32:25 (LXX), ἔξωθεν . . . μάχαιρα . . . ἐκ τῶν ταμιείων φόβος ("outwardly . . . the sword . . . out of the innermost parts, fear").

16. Cf. ὑπομονῇ πολλῇ ("by our steadfast endurance"; cf. 12:12) in 6:4, which stands as a general heading for the afflictions listed in 6:4-5.

17. In the case of the ideal sage of the ancient world, "the catalogues [of hardships] depict and celebrate the greatness of his invincible virtue, the power and tranquility of his philosophically informed mind" (Fitzgerald 115).

παρουσία Τίτου. "But God, the Comforter of the depressed, comforted us by the coming of Titus." In the midst of Paul's traumatic circumstances (cf. ἀλλά), God intervened to bring him παράκλησις, including ἄνεσις, both to his πνεῦμα (cf. 2:13) and to his σάρξ (7:5). The articular present participle ὁ παρακαλῶν expresses a timeless truth about God — he is the One who is always ready to comfort and console. There are several such timeless affirmations about God in 2 Corinthians:

1:3	ὁ πατὴρ τῶν οἰκτιρμῶν καὶ θεὸς πάσης παρακλήσεως
1:4	(ὁ . . . θεὸς . . .) ὁ παρακαλῶν ἡμᾶς
1:9	ὁ θεὸς ὁ ἐγείρων τοὺς νεκρούς
7:6	ὁ παρακαλῶν τοὺς ταπεινοὺς . . . ὁ θεός
13:11	ὁ θεὸς τῆς ἀγάπης καὶ εἰρήνης

What is distinctive about 7:6 is the emphatic word order, with ὁ θεός standing in epexegetic apposition after the description of him; literally, "the One who comforts the downcast . . . , namely God." This portrayal of God alludes to Isa. 49:13 (LXX), "God has shown mercy to his people and has comforted the afflicted ones among his people" (ὁ θεὸς . . . τοὺς ταπεινοὺς τοῦ λαοῦ αὐτοῦ παρεκάλεσεν).[18] In 6:2 Paul has already cited a passage from this chapter of Isaiah which deals with the role of the Servant of Yahweh (49:1-7) and the promised restoration of Israel from exile (49:8-26).

In secular Greek ταπεινός refers to what is "low" in topography ("low-lying"), in status (in a bad sense, "poor"; in a good sense, "lowly"), in circumstances ("humbled"), or in spirit ("downcast") (see LSJ s.v.). In the present context τοὺς ταπεινούς is less likely to have a moral sense, "the lowly" (RV, Barclay), than a psychological, "the downcast" (RSV, NRSV), "the down-hearted" (GNB), "the dejected" (Moffatt), "the depressed" (Weymouth, NASB).[19] While Paul does not explicitly say that he was dejected at this time, this is a legitimate assumption, given the parallelism between ὁ παρακαλῶν τοὺς ταπεινούς and παρεκάλεσεν ἡμᾶς. The main cause of his despondency was doubtless his various anxieties or fears (φόβοι, 7:5), but a contributing factor may have been the aftereffects of his putative illness in Troas.[20] Since Paul was

---

18. The same theme of divine comfort is expressed in Isa. 40:1; 51:3, 12; 52:9; 61:2; 66:13.

19. But it is possible that the meaning of τοὺς ταπεινούς in Isa. 49:13, namely "those who have been brought low" or "the afflicted ones," also applies in 7:6.

20. On this latter point, see on 2:13 and the Excursus after 1:11. Conybeare sees Paul's dejection as not so much "occasioned by an increase of the chronic malady under which St. Paul suffered" as augmented by that cause (in Conybeare and Howson 437). "The real cause of his grief was the danger which now threatened the souls of his converts, not in Corinth only, or in Galatia, but everywhere throughout the Empire" (in Conybeare and Howson 438). Cf. Findlay 96: "Never had he [Paul] felt himself so helpless, so beaten down and discomfited, as on that melancholy journey from Ephesus to Macedonia, and while he lay upon his sick-bed (perhaps at Philippi), knowing not whether Titus or the messenger of death would reach him first."

feeling afflicted or harassed (θλιβόμενοι, 7:5) at the time when God "comforted" (RSV) or "consoled" (NRSV) or "encouraged" (GNB) him (παρεκάλεσεν), this verse, like 7:4, illustrates one of the central themes of chs. 1–7, ἡ παράκλησις ἡ ἐν θλίψει, "comfort in affliction." παρεκάλεσεν is a constative aorist, depicting unitarily the divine comfort given over a period of time that incorporated Titus's arrival and the subsequent detailed report regarding the situation at Corinth.

In the phrase ἐν τῇ παρουσίᾳ Τίτου, the preposition could be temporal in sense, "when/as soon as Titus came," but is more probably instrumental, "by the coming of Titus." παρουσία here signifies not merely Titus's actual arrival in Macedonia but also his presence (cf. 10:10 for this meaning) with Paul after arrival; thus Plummer paraphrases (216), "by the arrival and company of Titus." This long-awaited coming, which is merely assumed in 2:13-14, prompted Paul's thanksgiving (χάρις, 2:14), his comfort (παράκλησις, 7:4-6, 13), and his joy (χαρά, 7:4, 7, 9, 13).

This verse is a beautiful portrayal of Paul's theocentric worldview. The relief from ἄνεσις of πνεῦμα and σάρξ and the deliverance from despondency that he so urgently needed had in fact come to him through the arrival of Titus with his welcome news about Corinth. But in these specific historical circumstances Paul was able to discern gracious divine intervention. "It was the Comforter of the dejected, even God, who comforted us — comforted us by the coming of Titus."

7:7 οὐ μόνον δὲ ἐν τῇ παρουσίᾳ αὐτοῦ ἀλλὰ καὶ ἐν τῇ παρακλήσει ᾗ παρεκλήθη ἐφ' ὑμῖν. "And not only by his coming but also by the comfort he had received at your hands." Sometime before Paul was comforted, his emissary Titus had himself been comforted by the positive reception he was given by the Corinthians. Here Paul is affirming that his own sense of being consoled and encouraged (7:6) was deepened as a result of hearing Titus's review of recent events in Corinth.[21] The Corinthians themselves already knew the effect of the "severe letter." What they would now learn from the present letter was "Titus' interpretation of what he had found at Corinth and Paul's response to that" (Furnish 391). Titus represents the Corinthians to Paul just as he had represented Paul to the Corinthians; he is a "two-way envoy" (Mitchell, "Envoys" 654). Both instances of ἐν are instrumental, as also is ᾗ (literally, "the comfort *by which* he had been comforted"). ἐν τῇ παρακλήσει must mean "by [his report of] the comfort . . ." (cf. GNB). ἐφ' ὑμῖν may be rendered "among you" (BAGD 287a), "about you" (NEB, NRSV, REB), "on your account" (Weymouth), or "at your hands" (Young and Ford 268). Very sensitively, Paul is focusing on the Corinthian congregation's laudable reaction to

---

21. For comparable "comfort amid affliction" derived from good news about a church, see 1 Thess. 3:6-7 regarding Timothy's arrival in Corinth (cf. Acts 18:5) with news of the Thessalonian church.

Titus as Paul's envoy rather than on the role or achievement of Titus. As Lietzmann observes (131), Paul does not say "by the comfort he [Titus] brought me concerning you" but "by the comfort he had received at your hands."

ἀναγγέλλων ἡμῖν τὴν ὑμῶν ἐπιπόθησιν, τὸν ὑμῶν ὀδυρμόν, τὸν ὑμῶν ζῆλον ὑπὲρ ἐμοῦ ὥστε με μᾶλλον χαρῆναι. "For he reported to us your longing, your penitence, your eagerness to take my side, so that I rejoiced all the more." The use of the verb ἀναγγέλλω ("carry back news of," "report") here is very appropriate,[22] for in secular sources it is often used of a report given by an envoy who had returned from a mission (see LSJ 100 s.v.). In the place of the form ἀναγγέλλων, which is anacoluthic, we might have expected either a genitive absolute construction, ἀναγγέλλοντος αὐτοῦ, or a participle, ἀναγγέλλοντος, that agreed with the preceding αὐτοῦ. This may be a case of "construction according to sense" with the participle ἀναγγέλλων adverting to the subject of παρεκλήθη (i.e., Titus), or, better, an instance of the nominative absolute (nominativus pendens) (so Lietzmann 131), here used in a causal sense (= ἀνήγγειλεν γάρ), "for he reported."[23]

Titus's report focused on three aspects of the Corinthian response to the "severe letter," each expressed by a single noun. We have no option but to fill out the content of each noun on the basis of the wider context of Paul's recent relationship with the Corinthian congregation, but that relation was so complex that we must remain uncertain about the specific content of each word. (The same applies to the seven corresponding nouns in v. 11, two of which [ἐπιπόθησις and ζῆλος] also occur here.) ἐπιπόθησις ("ardent desire") may refer to the Corinthians' longing to see Paul himself (cf. 2:1 and ἐπιποθοῦντες ἡμᾶς ἰδεῖν, 1 Thess. 3:6) or to be reconciled to him or to do what was right by him. Their ὀδυρμός was their "mourning" or "grieving" over recent events that had distressed Paul, perhaps in particular their disloyal behavior or their failure to act against the wrongdoer before the "severe letter" arrived. When Titus told Paul of their ζῆλος, the reference may have been to their "eagerness" or "enthusiasm" to put themselves in the right and to make amends for the past, particularly by complying with Paul's disciplinary directives expressed in the "severe letter." The prepositional phrase ὑπὲρ ἐμοῦ, which qualifies τὸν ὑμῶν ζῆλον and therefore might normally be expected to be prefaced by τόν (BDF §272), means "on my behalf" or "to take my side" (NEB, REB). If the phrase were given the

---

22. The only other use in Paul is in Rom. 15:21, citing Isa. 52:15 (LXX).

23. Cf. Williams, "because he kept telling me." Meyer (565-66), however, takes ἀναγγέλλων in a temporal sense ("while he announced"), arguing that Titus's own comfort was renewed in the act of communicating to Paul what he had experienced at Corinth. But this view may overlook the fact that the aorist παρεκλήθη expresses a past action antecedent to another past action, viz. παρεκάλεσεν (7:6), and so should be rendered (literally), "he had been comforted" (cf. Zerwick and Grosvenor 548, citing Zerwick §290). Imperfect παρεκαλεῖτο would better accord with Meyer's interpretation.

sense "with respect to me" = "for me"), it could be construed with each of the three preceding nouns (as Furnish [386-87] proposes). With the repeated ὑμῶν and its delicate placement each time between article and noun,[24] we have a hint of a splendid new complementarity: what previously had been true of Paul in his dealings with the Corinthians — longing, mourning, enthusiasm — had now become true of the Corinthians themselves in their relation to their spiritual father.[25]

ὥστε με . . . χαρῆναι points to an actual result, "as a consequence, I rejoiced." μᾶλλον is a comparative (of the adverb μάλα, "very"), used here absolutely, that is, without the object of comparison expressed.

(1) If μᾶλλον here means "rather" (Thrall 486, 489 and n. 26), there is a contrast between Paul's previous affliction (7:5) and dejection (7:6) and his present joy. "Rather" than continuing in depression, he experienced joy as a result of Titus's report (similarly Windisch 228-29).[26]

(2) If μᾶλλον means "still more" (BDF §244[2]; RSV, NRSV; Theobald 273 n. 86), two stages of Paul's joy are being described. It is implied that he rejoiced when Titus returned from Corinth (note τῇ χαρᾷ in 7:4), but on hearing Titus's favorable report that joy was increased; he now rejoiced "to a greater degree" than before, or "now more than ever" (BAGD 489a, citing 7:7).[27]

Both interpretations accord with the context, but the second is to be preferred because the implied contrast is simpler (viz. "joy–joy" as opposed to "joy–sorrow").

No OT verse better sums up Paul's feelings as expressed in 7:5-7 than Ps. 94:19: "When anxiety was great within me, your consolation brought joy to my soul" (NIV).

Bibliography

C. K. Barrett, "2 Cor. 7:12" • Barrett, "Titus" • Carrez, "Le 'Nous'" • Crafton 153-61 • Ellis, "Co-workers" • Kantzer • Lightfoot, *Biblical Essays* 273-84 • Mitchell, "Envoys" • Murphy-O'Connor 70-74 • Ollrog 33-37 • Theobald 272-74 • Welborn 95-131.

---

24. Namely, τὴν ὑμῶν ἐπιπόθησιν, τὸν ὑμῶν ὀδυρμόν, τὸν ὑμῶν ζῆλον.

25. Cf. Denney 778-79.

26. Cf. Conybeare's rendering, "so that my sorrow has been turned into joy" (in Conybeare and Howson 452).

27. Cf. NEB, REB: "and that has made me happier still."

2. The Severe Letter and Its Effects (7:8-13a)

Paul's emotional state — whether one of dejection, regret, relief, or joy — at this stage of his apostolic career was closely connected with the circumstances leading to and resulting from his writing and sending of a "severe letter" to the Corinthians.[1] (This same letter is sometimes called the painful letter, the sorrowful letter, the intermediate/interim letter, or the letter of tears.) These six verses are an account of the effects of this letter on its recipients, as reported by Titus to Paul in Macedonia, and also the effect of that report on Paul himself.

But we may well ask: Why does Paul recount recent events that were already so well known to the Corinthians? First, he wishes to congratulate them for their positive reaction to his pastoral letter, a reaction that seemed to surpass even his fondest hopes, and to tell them of his own enthusiastic delight at their response to the letter (7:9, 11a, 13a). Second, he wants to assure them that from his point of view they are now completely in the right or blameless with respect to the whole matter of the wrongdoer and his punishment (7:11). Third, he aims to establish or confirm in the eyes of the Corinthians the skill and reliability of Titus as an envoy and intermediary who accurately represents both parties (Paul and the Corinthians) (7:13b-15), in preparation for Titus's next role at Corinth, which was to facilitate the completion of the collection (chs. 8 and 9).

Theologically, the passage is significant for its portrayal of the salutary effects of enduring sorrow or grief "in accordance with God's will" or "in the way God intended" (κατὰ θεόν, three uses in 7:9-11): protection from possible psychological or spiritual damage (7:9); experiencing a repentance that will issue in salvation and so leaves no regrets (7:10); behavior that is in keeping with that repentance (7:11).

8*For even though I caused you sorrow by my letter,[a] I do not regret it. Although[b] I did regret it (for I see[c] that my letter caused you sorrow, even if only temporarily),* 9*now I rejoice, not because you were caused sorrow but because your sorrow led to your repentance. For you experienced sorrow in accordance with God's will and so you suffered no harm at our hands.* 10*Godly sorrow, you see, brings about[d] a repentance that leads to salvation and is never regretted, but worldly sorrow produces death.* 11*Just consider what this actual experience of godly sorrow[e] has produced in you[f]: what earnestness, what concern to clear yourselves, what indignation, what alarm, what yearning[g], what zeal, what resolve! At every point you have shown yourselves to be blameless in[h] this matter.* 12*So then, although I did write to you, it was not on account of the wrongdoer nor[i] on account of the person who was wronged but so that your[j] devotion to us[j] might be made clear to you in the sight of God.* 13a*Because of this we have been comforted.*

---

1. On the identification of this "severe letter," see the Introduction, A.2.c.

TEXTUAL NOTES

a. The addition of προτέρᾳ before ἐπιστολῇ (1505 pc syr^h) is an obvious second-ary clarification ("my former letter"), as is the addition of μου after ἐπιστολῇ (D* F G). The article τῇ with ἐπιστολῇ is sufficient to indicate possession.

b. B adds an adversative δέ after εἰ, probably to indicate that εἰ καὶ κτλ. is to be taken with what follows.

c. There are three variants:

(1) βλέπων p^{46*} vg
(2) βλέπω p^{46c} B D* it sa Ambrosiaster
(3) βλέπω γάρ ℵ C D^1 F G Ψ 0243 33 1739 1881 𝔐 vg^{mss} syr bo

Although the first reading has slender support, it is defended as original by Hort (in WH 2. Appendix 120; also Hughes 269 n. 6; Moffatt, "when I discovered"; Goodspeed, NEB, and GNB, "when I saw"; cf. REB), who suggests that the abbreviation ω̄ (for ων) was read as ω, producing the second reading, and that γάρ was added to ease the awk-ward construction. The second reading enjoys strong proto-Alexandrian (B) and West-ern (D*) support and is the most difficult reading, being anacoluthic. If it is original, the other two readings could have arisen as natural scribal efforts to remove the awk-ward syntax (by adding ν to βλέπω or by inserting γάρ). This reading is defended by Barrett (210) and was the preference of NA^{25} and of UBS$^{1, 2}$ with a "C" rating (= con-siderable doubt). Printing βλέπω (411), WH regards it as "probably a primitive error for βλέπων" (578). βλέπω γάρ is a reading with wide and strong geographic distribution, being represented in the Alexandrian, Western, and Byzantine families. As for the rise of the other two variants, "copyists rightly sensed that a new portion of the discourse begins with εἰ καὶ μετεμελόμην . . . , and therefore the main clause was taken to begin either at βλέπω, with the consequent omission of γάρ, or at νῦν χαίρω, with the substi-tution of the participial form βλέπων as a gloss for βλέπω γάρ" (Metzger 512). This reading is found in NA^{27} and UBS$^{3, 4}$ (with γάρ bracketed), in UBS^3 with a "D" rating (= a very high degree of doubt) and in UBS^4 with a "C" rating (= uncertain). It is here assumed to be original.

d. The reading ἐργάζεται (p^{46} ℵ* B C D P 81 1175 pc [33:$h.t.$] Clement) is to be preferred over κατεργάζεται (ℵ^2 F G Ψ 0243 0296 1739 1881 𝔐 Eusebius Didymus) not only because of its superior external testimony but also because the simplex form is a more difficult reading than the common compound form, which will have arisen under the influence of the following κατεργάζεται.

e. Some witnesses add ὑμᾶς after λυπηθῆναι (ℵ^2 D Ψ 𝔐 a f vg Clement Pelagius) to make the subject of the infinitive unambiguous, but the reading is secondary to the original text (p^{46} ℵ* B C F G 0243 33 81 630 1739 1881 2464* pc b r p Ambrosiaster).

f. As a dative of respect (or of advantage) ὑμῖν, read by (p^{46}) ℵ* B D K L Ψ 0243 6 33 81 630 1175 1241 1739 1881 pm (b) r p Clement, needs no preposition, but ἐν is added by ℵ^2 C F G P 104 326 365 629 1505 2464 pm a vg syr Ambrosiaster Pelagius.

g. In place of ἐπιπόθησιν (cf. 7:7), p^{46} ℵ* 1505 pc read ἐπιποθίαν ("desire," "longing"), a noun found only in Rom. 15:23.

h. As it stands, τῷ πράγματι (ℵ B C D* F G 0243 33 81 1175 1739 1881 2464 pc lat Clement Ambrosiaster) is a perfectly legitimate dative of respect, but scribal ped-antry added ἐν (D^1 Ψ 𝔐 d syr).

i. The addition of ἀλλ' before οὐδὲ ἕνεκεν (so ℵ^2 B 365 1175 pc Ambrosiaster) may have been prompted by the multiple cases of ἀλλά in v. 11 or by the following phrase ἀλλ᾿ ἕνεκεν.

j. Itacism accounts for the frequent textual variants involving ἡμεῖς and ὑμεῖς and derived forms. Following τὴν σπουδήν there are four variants, the first two of which are so difficult as to be scarcely tolerable (especially the second):

> ὑμῶν τὴν ὑπὲρ ὑμῶν ℵ D*·c F 0243 629 *pc*
> ἡμῶν τὴν ὑπὲρ ἡμῶν D¹ G d vgᵐˢ
> ἡμῶν τὴν ὑπὲρ ὑμῶν 323 945 *pc* lat Ambrosiaster
> ὑμῶν τὴν ὑπὲρ ἡμῶν the rest of the witnesses

While 2:4 supports the third reading, 2:9 (τὴν δοκιμὴν ὑμῶν), 7:7 (τὸν ὑμῶν ζῆλον ὑπὲρ ἐμοῦ) and especially 7:11 (σπουδήν, in reference to the Corinthians) support the fourth reading, which is clearly original (Bultmann 59).

7:8 ὅτι εἰ καὶ ἐλύπησα ὑμᾶς ἐν τῇ ἐπιστολῇ, οὐ μεταμέλομαι· εἰ καὶ μετεμελόμην (βλέπω γὰρ ὅτι ἡ ἐπιστολὴ ἐκείνη εἰ καὶ πρὸς ὥραν ἐλύπησεν ὑμᾶς), ₉νῦν χαίρω. . . . "For even though I caused you sorrow by my letter, I do not regret it. Although I did regret it (for I see that my letter caused you sorrow, even if only temporarily), ₉now I rejoice. . . ." Allied to the textual issues in this verse (discussed above under Textual Notes) is the question of punctuation. There are basically two options.

1. If a period is placed after εἰ καὶ μετεμελόμην, this phrase is construed with the concessive (or conditional) sentence that precedes (εἰ καὶ . . . οὐ μεταμέλομαι) and forms a second protasis (". . . although I did regret it").[2] In this case βλέπω or βλέπω γάρ begins a new sentence. Thrall supports this option[3] but points out two difficulties: a complex conditional sentence results; νῦν χαίρω lacks explicit connection with what precedes (491). Also, if the βλέπω or βλέπω γάρ clause looks back to ἐλύπησα, a certain tautology would result.[4]

2. If εἰ καὶ μετεμελόμην begins a second concessive (or conditional) sentence, the apodosis is νῦν χαίρω κτλ. (7:9). In this case the clause βλέπω . . . ὑμᾶς forms a parenthesis that may be marked off by brackets[5] or by dashes.[6] The translation given above reflects this second main interpretation.

---

2. On the relation between concessive and conditional sentences, see Burton §278 and Robertson 1026.

3. So also Weymouth and Barnett 371-72 n. 1; cf. RV, Barclay.

4. This may explain why the NRSV makes εἰ καὶ μετεμελόμην . . . ὑμᾶς a parenthesis.

5. So UBS¹⁺ ²⁺ ³ (UBS³ corrected, ⁴ and NA²⁷ have commas); and NAB¹⁺ ², Cassirer; Conybeare in Conybeare and Howson 452; Furnish 384.

6. So TCNT, NASB, NIV, NJB; Martin 212; Carrez 171. Some versions, reading βλέπων, do not treat εἰ καὶ μετεμελόμην as a protasis nor νῦν χαίρω κτλ. as an apodosis; so NEB, "I may have been sorry for it when I saw (βλέπων) that the letter had caused you pain, even if only for a time; but now I am happy . . ."; similarly Moffatt, Goodspeed, GNB.

Paul now candidly concedes a fact[7] that had become clear from Titus's report — the Corinthians had been pained by his recent "severe letter,"[8] a letter that he himself had written "out of deep distress and anguish of heart and with many tears" (2:4). But despite their pain, he now had no regrets (οὐ μεταμέλομαι)[9] about writing and sending the letter that caused the pain, because, as v. 9 will indicate, their pain and sorrow had prompted their repentance. εἰ καί occurs three times in this verse, in each case introducing a concession that is factual,[10] "even if[11] (as is the case)" or "though[12] (as is true)."

But the absolute οὐ μεταμέλομαι could be taken by his addressees as an indication of heartless insensitivity. So Paul hastens to assure them that he had at one time felt regret about the letter and the sorrow it had caused, although now he was joyful, not regretful. The imperfect μετεμελόμην points to some period in the past, of indefinite length, when Paul felt regret — actual regret,[13] rather than merely an inclination to regret.[14] When was this regret felt? It could have been in Ephesus, after Paul had sent the letter, or in Troas (cf. 2:12-13) and then Macedonia (cf. 7:5-6) before Titus arrived, but more probably it was in Macedonia as Paul listened to Titus's report and for some indefinite time thereafter, but before 2 Corinthians was written. Certainly we must carefully distinguish the sorrow he felt as he dictated this "letter of tears" (cf. 2 Cor. 2:4) from the regret he felt when and after he heard of its dramatic effect on the Corinthians.

The reason Paul had regrets is given in the parenthetical clause introduced by βλέπω γάρ. It was the clear recognition (that he still has — note the present βλέπω, not simply ἔβλεψα or ἔβλεπον) that his letter had caused sorrow, even though it was only for a time (εἰ καὶ πρὸς ὥραν)[15] and not permanent.[16]

---

7. ὅτι here serves as a loose connective, "for" (BAGD 589d), "in fact" (Moffatt), or "the truth is."

8. For extrabiblical examples of grief as a result of reading a letter containing bad news, see Spicq 2.420 n. 15.

9. The two uses of μεταμέλομαι in this verse refer to a feeling of anxiety about a past action that one wishes could be undone.

10. Cf. Burton §284.

11. So Moule 167; Young and Ford 268.

12. So RV, NASB. Sometimes these renderings are mixed: "though . . . even if . . . though" (TCNT); "even if . . . though . . . though" (RSV, NRSV); cf. "although . . . although, albeit" (Thrall 486).

13. Cf. Robertson (*Pictures* 240): "I was in a regretful mood."

14. Some give μετεμελόμην a "conative" sense: "I was inclined to regret" (Danker 109; similarly Furnish 387). But we must reject the TCNT rendering, "Even if I were inclined to regret it. . . ."

15. This period may have been the time between the Corinthians' hearing of the letter and their longing for Paul (ἐπιπόθησιν [7:7, 11]) (so Barnett 374 n. 9).

16. If εἰ καί is construed with ἐλύπησεν (rather than with πρὸς ὥραν alone), a verb is lacking after ὑμᾶς (so Zerwick, *Analysis* 403) and must be supplied. Weymouth, for example, has "I see that that letter, even though for a time it gave you pain, *had a salutary effect*" (italics mine), citing (487 n. 4) similar instances of *aposiopesis* (a sudden breaking off of what is being said, usually owing to its remarkable nature) in Exod. 32:32; Mark 7:11 (KJV); Luke 19:42; John 6:62; Acts 23:9. Others

ἐλύπησεν, like the earlier ἐλύπησα, is a constative aorist, envisaging the Corinthians' experience of distress, however prolonged, as a unit.[17]

7:9 νῦν χαίρω, οὐχ ὅτι ἐλυπήθητε, ἀλλ᾽ ὅτι ἐλυπήθητε εἰς μετάνοιαν. ". . . now I rejoice, not because you were caused sorrow but because your sorrow led to your repentance." With νῦν χαίρω we reach the apodosis of the concessive clause that began with εἰ καὶ μετεμελόμην, "Although I did regret it . . . now I rejoice." By the time of writing, Paul's temporary regret about sending a letter that had caused anguish had given place to overflowing joy (cf. 7:4). But the apostle was always aware of those who were inclined to misunderstand his actions or misrepresent his motives, and who might in the present situation charge him with deriving joy from the pain and sorrow he had caused his converts at Corinth. So, having mentioned his present joy, he proceeds to rebuff any such misunderstanding by declaring that he gained no pleasure from having caused the Corinthians to feel deep sorrow (οὐχ ὅτι ἐλυπήθητε[18]). This absolute negation of one reason[19] for his joy — Corinthian sorrow — is followed by the actual reason for his present delight, which happens to be a qualification of the repudiated reason (ἐλυπήθητε εἰς μετάνοιαν):[20] the Corinthians had come to repentance as a result of their painful sorrow. εἰς is resultative (BAGD 229c, 512d); their pain brought their repentance, "your pain induced you to repent" (Moffatt).[21] The salutary outcome of the letter more than compensated for the grief it caused.

The noun μετάνοια ("repentance") occurs comparatively rarely in the Pauline corpus (Rom. 2:4; 2 Cor. 7:9-10; 2 Tim. 2:25), the verb μετανοέω ("repent") only once (2 Cor. 12:21). Cranfield accounts for this rarity by suggesting that Paul regarded repentance as "an integral element of πίστις. He may well also have felt that the word itself had been devalued by the tendency in Judaism to understand it legalistically" (144-45 n. 2).[22] Paul has used a related verb, μεταμέλομαι ("regret," "be remorseful"), twice in 7:8 (KJV renders it there by "repent"). Etymologically, μετανοέω denotes an altered (μετα-) view or attitude (νοῦς), and μεταμέλομαι an altered (μετα-) mood or interest (μελεῖ, "it is an object of concern"). The distinction between these verbs and between the corresponding nouns, μετάνοια ("a change of mind") and μεταμέλεια ("remorse") (a word not found in the NT), is preserved in Classical Greek, but Hellenistic us-

---

believe that in 7:8-9 Paul is condensing several thoughts (see Danker 109, and Barrett 209-10 who renders what he believes Paul "*meant* to say").

17. This verb λυπέω refers here to the causing of distress, not simply the hurting of feelings (as Goodspeed in vv. 8-9; Moncure 477) or even the wounding of feelings (NEB on v. 9).

18. The form ἐλυπήθητε appears three times in 7:9. Some grammarians take these to be ingressive aorists, "became grieved" (Robertson 834; Turner 72; Fanning 262 citing the first two occurrences), but there is no reason not to regard all three as the more common constative aorist.

19. The sense is not materially altered whether the two instances of ὅτι in the verse are rendered "because" (so, e.g., RSV, NRSV) or "that" (so, e.g., NASB, NEB).

20. Cf. Winer 496 and n. 2.

21. For the contrast between the immediate pain caused by discipline and the ultimate spiritual benefit, see Heb. 12:11 and Spicq 1.437 n. 60.

22. Similarly J. Behm, *TDNT* 4.1005.

age often blurs the distinction.[23] In the present context there is a clear difference between the two concepts. Paul's "regret" arose instinctively when he was confronted with the effect of his "severe letter" on the Corinthians. The Corinthians' "repentance," on the other hand, was a radical change of outlook that produced "grieving" (ὀδυρμός, 7:7) over their recent action and inaction and a radical change of behavior (7:11). It would seem, therefore, that sorrow, whether in the form of λύπη or ὀδυρμός, can precede or follow μετάνοια, but cannot be identified with that change of mind or heart.

ἐλυπήθητε γὰρ κατὰ θεόν, ἵνα ἐν μηδενὶ ζημιωθῆτε ἐξ ἡμῶν. "For you experienced sorrow in accordance with God's will and so you suffered no harm at our hands." Paul now explains (γάρ) how the Corinthian experience of pain or sorrow led to their repentance. It was because λύπη that is εἰς μετάνοιαν (v. 9a) is nothing other than λύπη that is κατὰ θεόν ("in accordance with God's will," v. 9b), the inference being that God himself uses sorrow or grief to bring about repentance. The phrase κατὰ θεόν occurs three times in vv. 9-11, in each case qualifying the λυπ- root: ἐλυπήθητε . . . κατὰ θεόν (v. 9), ἡ . . . κατὰ θεὸν λύπη (v. 10), τὸ κατὰ θεὸν λυπηθῆναι (v. 11). Although the phrase need not be translated the same way in each verse,[24] it always depicts the λύπη as being in conformity to God's will and purpose, and so is equivalent, as Bultmann notes (55), to κατὰ τὸ θέλημα τοῦ θεοῦ (Gal. 1:4; cf. Rom. 8:27). It may therefore be rendered "in accordance with the will of God" (Lang 313; Thrall 486), "in a godly way" (Moule 59; Turner 268), or "in God's way" (Zerwick and Grosvenor 548).

Because the Corinthian sorrow was "as God intended" (NIV) and so produced repentance, Paul's letter that had caused temporary pain did not cause any harm. ἵνα may be given a final sense ("in order that"),[25] but a consecutive sense ("so that")[26] seems more appropriate in the context: the result of the Corinthian λύπη ἡ κατὰ θεόν was their total preservation (cf. ἐν μηδενί, "in no way") from any adverse effect that Paul's letter could possibly have caused.[27] The "severe letter," which Paul alludes to by ἐξ ἡμῶν ("because of us"[28] or "at our hands"[29]), was not only totally successful in bringing the Corinthians to

23. See O. Michel, *TDNT* 4.626-29, who cites (4.627) as an example of this blurring Jer. 4:28 (οὐ μετανοήσω) in comparison with Jer. 20:16 (οὐ μετεμελήθη), both passages in reference to Yahweh. See also Trench 255-61.

24. Goodspeed, for example, renders the phrase by "as God meant you to do" (v. 9), "that God approves" (v. 10), and "God-given" (v. 11).

25. So TCNT; Meyer 569; Barrett 205.

26. So RSV, NRSV; Lietzmann 132.

27. The categories of purpose and result tended to become blurred in Hellenistic Greek so that ἵνα was sometimes ecbatic and ὥστε sometimes telic (see Zerwick §§351-53). This partial blurring is not surprising when one remembers that a purpose is an intended result and a result is an achieved purpose. In the present case, Bultmann (56) suggests that ἵνα, though "probably intended as consecutive," is also final, "since the result complies with the divine intention."

28. Thus Robertson 599; Turner 260.

29. Thus TCNT; Thrall 486. If there is a wider allusion in ἐξ ἡμῶν than to the "severe letter," the phrase will mean "from what we did" (REB).

their senses but also providentially prevented the alienation of the Corinthians from God and from Paul.[30]

Verses 8 and 9 prompt several observations.

(1) "Regret" and "repentance" are not theological synonyms. People may be regretful or remorseful about their conduct yet not have a change of heart and behavior, as shown by Judas (Matt. 27:3-5) and Esau (Heb. 12:16-17).[31]

(2) Sorrow, pain, or grief that results in repentance is in accord with the divine will and has a place in the post-conversion experience of the Christian (cf. 12:21).

(3) When pain is inflicted or sorrow is experienced "in a godly way" or "as God intends" (κατὰ θεόν), spiritual benefit results.

7:10 ἡ γὰρ κατὰ θεὸν λύπη μετάνοιαν εἰς σωτηρίαν ἀμεταμέλητον ἐργάζεται. "Godly sorrow, you see (γάρ), brings about a repentance that leads to salvation and is never regretted." This sentence is an explanatory commentary on two expressions in 7:9, ἐλυπήθητε εἰς μετάνοιαν and ἐλυπήθητε . . . κατὰ θεόν. Paul is moving from the specific instance (v. 9) to the general principle (v. 10). λύπη refers to sorrow, grief, or pain such as the Corinthians experienced as a result of Titus's visit with the "letter of tears." As before, κατὰ θεόν is shorthand for "according to God's will" and so may appropriately be rendered by the English shorthand "godly," although more specific nuances such as "(Pain) borne in God's way" (REB) or "(sorrow) that God uses" (Carrez 171) or even "(sorrow) that relates the sorrower to God" (Berkeley) or "(Grief) that submits itself to God" (Wand) can be justified from the context. In discussing 7:9 we saw that for Paul, as for other NT writers, μετάνοια denotes a positive change of mind or attitude that is expressed in altered, improved behavior. So the general principle that Paul enunciates on the basis of v. 9 is this: When λύπη is borne κατὰ θεόν, it "brings about" or "gives rise to" (ἐργάζεται, BAGD 307b) genuine repentance.[32]

The two new elements in v. 10a are the prepositional phrase εἰς σωτηρίαν and the adjective ἀμεταμέλητον. When Paul speaks of μετάνοιαν εἰς σωτηρίαν, he is relating repentance to salvation not as cause and effect but as antecedent and result, "a repentance that leads to (εἰς) salvation,"[33] a repentance "whose

---

30. Some take ζημιόω here to mean "suffer loss" (so BAGD 338c; RSV), with the "loss" being Paul's decision not to return to Corinth (Héring 55), the forfeiture of future reward but not salvation (cf. 1 Cor. 3:14-15) (Hughes 270), or the forfeiture of rewards and "salvation" (cf. 7:10) (Garland 355).

31. "Sorrow for wrong-doing, which leaves God out of account, is merely remorse, that melancholy compound of self-pity and self-disgust" (Tasker 105).

32. On λύπη producing repentance, cf. Plutarch, *Moralia* 476F.

33. Only if εἰς is taken to mean "with respect to" or "in connection with" can μετάνοιαν εἰς σωτηρίαν mean "salutary repentance," as Zerwick and Grosvenor (548) propose.

fruit is salvation" (Plummer 216). σωτηρία probably refers to both present spiritual vitality and future eternal life.[34] ἀμεταμέλητον (a two-termination adjective) may qualify either σωτηρίαν or μετάνοιαν.[35] Word order might suggest the former option,[36] but to say that salvation is "not to be regretted" is so self-evident as to be otiose. There are several exits from this dilemma. One is to follow the Vulgate (which reads *paenitentiam in salutem stabilem operatur*)[37] and take ἀμεταμέλητον to mean "secure" or "immutable" *(stabilis),* but this presupposes ἀμετάβλητον ("unchangeable"). Another is to propose that ἀμεταμέλητον "expresses by way of litotes the eternal satisfaction of the σωτηρία, and is selected with a glance back to what was said in ver. 8 [οὐ μεταμέλομαι . . . μετεμελόμην]" (Meyer 569). Yet another solution is to take σωτηρία in the specific but unusual sense of "release," presumably referring to release from grief or sorrow.[38]

In spite of the difficulty of the word order — which is merely apparent[39] — it is preferable to take ἀμεταμέλητον with μετάνοιαν,[40] which creates an oxymoron by means of *paronomasia* (μετά), "repentance not to be repented of" (Bruce 218), "a repentance not to be regretted" (BAGD 45c).[41] An alternative approach is to relate ἀμεταμέλητον to the whole phrase μετάνοιαν εἰς σωτηρίαν; thus "repentance — unto — salvation which is not to be regretted"[42] or "salvation — producing repentance that brings no regret."[43]

ἡ δὲ τοῦ κόσμου λύπη θάνατον κατεργάζεται. "But worldly sorrow produces death." Whereas the preceding statement of general principle (v. 10a)

---

34. But Thrall sees σωτηρία here as "final deliverance from divine wrath and final restoration to divine glory" (492).

35. If ἀμεταμέλητον is construed as a neuter accusative singular, it could qualify the whole expression ἡ . . . κατὰ θεὸν λύπη; thus apparently REB, "Pain borne in God's way brings no regrets but a change of heart leading to salvation." Moncure takes ἀμεταμέλητον as a parenthetical adverbial neuter accusative: "For the hurting of your feelings in accord with God's will produces repentance unto salvation — that's why I don't regret it — . . ." (cf. 7:8) (476-77).

36. E.g., Berkeley ("a repentance that leads to salvation such as is never regretted"); Schlatter 587.

37. *Stabilem,* too, could modify *paenitentiam* or *salutem.*

38. Cf. Bruce, *Paraphrase* 141: "Grief which comes from God leads to repentance and brings about a release over which no one need repent."

39. Paul's phrase μετάνοιαν εἰς σωτηρίαν ἀμεταμέλητον is simply elliptical for μετανοίαν τὴν εἰς σωτηρίαν καὶ ἀμεταμέλητον. The repentance is "never regretted" *because* it leads to salvation; this would explain the word order. The point is lost in Thrall's rendering, "For godly grief effects a repentance not to be regretted and leading to salvation" (486). But see her later comment (492): "It is a grief which is productive of a repentance resulting in salvation, and thus not to be regretted."

40. Thus most EVV; also Windisch 232 ("Paul wants to say that μετάνοια creates a permanent situation and excludes a relapse, another change of mind"); O. Michel, *TDNT* 4.629 ("What is of God causes no remorse").

41. It is true that ἀμετανόητον ("requiring no second repentance") would have been a more precise *paronomasia,* but there is at least a conceptual oxymoron.

42. Hughes 271-72 n. 11; also Barrett 205, 211; Louw and Nida §25.271.

43. Bultmann (56) and Lang (314) propose that τοῦ κόσμου = κατὰ σάρκα.

was triggered by Paul's reflection on recent events in Corinth, this statement arose as a contrast (adversative δέ) to that earlier affirmation.

ἡ . . . κατὰ θεὸν   λύπη μετάνοιαν εἰς   σωτηρίαν . . . ἐργάζεται (v. 10a)
ἡ . . . τοῦ κόσμου λύπη   θάνατον   κατεργάζεται (v. 10b)

We might have expected κατὰ τὸν κόσμον to match κατὰ θεόν,[44] but the change may be merely stylistic so that the contrast is between λύπη "borne in God's way" and λύπη "borne in the world's way" (NEB, REB), or, as Wand proposes, between "grief that submits itself to God" and "grief that ignores God." In these cases τοῦ κόσμου is an adjectival genitive, "worldly," "characterized by the world's attitudes,"[45] or an instance of "abstract for concrete," ἡ τοῦ κόσμου λύπη signifying "sorrow as those of the world experience it."

As an example of "worldly grief," Garland (355) refers to the grief-stricken merchants and slave traders of Rev. 18:11-13 who mourn the loss of their heartless profits, and as an instance of "godly grief" that produced repentance he points to John Newton's confession of wretchedness and blindness in the hymn "Amazing Grace." Barnett, on the other hand, suggests (377 n. 20) that Paul may have been thinking of David's deep sorrow over his sin (Ps. 51:1-11) in contrast with Esau's shallow remorse (Gen. 27:38, 41; cf. Heb. 12:16-17).

Sorrow that is marked by the world's godless attitudes and is borne in a bitter, resentful way, "produces death." κατεργάζεται may be taken as a stylistic variant of ἐργάζεται (thus Barnett 377) so that both verbs may be rendered "brings" (NIV), "brings about" (Furnish 384), "effects" (Barrett 205), or "produces" (RSV, NRSV). But if we give the prefix κατά its perfective force (see Moulton and Howard 316), there will be an emphasis on "the result rather than the process of the action" (MM 335d), so that we could translate ἐργάζεται by "brings about" and κατεργάζεται by "produces."[46] The result produced by worldly sorrow is death (θάνατος). We should not restrict the meaning of θάνατος here to either moral ruin or eternal death. "Just as σωτηρία is spiritual soundness tending to eternal life, so θάνατος means spiritual deadness tending to eternal death" (Plummer [CGT] 115).[47] "The world's grief is deadly in its effect" (Bruce, *Paraphrase* 141), producing resentment, bitterness, and hardness

44. If κατὰ θεόν has the sense "ordained by God," τοῦ κόσμου could mean "produced by the world" (subjective genitive; cf. Williams), i.e., arising from worldly pursuits or a worldly outlook.

45. Cf. Winer 402 n. 1.

46. Cf. Hughes (272 n. 12) who suggests two pairs of renderings, one of which is "produces" and "produces its fulfilment in," with the intensive compound "designed to emphasize the inevitability of the outworking in death of the sorrow of the world." But Vincent suggests that the difference between the simplex and compound verbs is that "between contributing to a result and achieving it" (828), perhaps "promotes" and "produces" (respectively).

47. Barnett relates both σωτηρία and θάνατος in 7:10 to the Corinthian situation: repentance toward Paul and therefore toward God "confirmed the Corinthians in their salvation" (378); continued unrepentance could have ultimately led to their spiritual death (377; cf. 372).

of heart. What makes affliction beneficial is not the actual experience of suffering but the reaction to it; a "godly" or positive reaction brings spiritual benefit, both now and in the hereafter, whereas a "worldly" or negative reaction causes irreparable harm.

7:11 ἰδοὺ γὰρ αὐτὸ τοῦτο τὸ κατὰ θεὸν λυπηθῆναι πόσην κατειργάσατο ὑμῖν σπουδήν, ἀλλὰ ἀπολογίαν, ἀλλὰ ἀγανάκτησιν, ἀλλὰ φόβον, ἀλλὰ ἐπιπόθησιν, ἀλλὰ ζῆλον, ἀλλὰ ἐκδίκησιν. "Just consider what this actual experience of godly sorrow has produced in you: what earnestness, what concern to clear yourselves, what indignation, what alarm, what yearning, what zeal, what resolve!" The apostle now illustrates (ἰδού, "consider!"[48]) the beneficial outcome of godly sorrow by referring in detail to the Corinthians' response to the pain and sorrow created by his "severe letter." If they had not received Titus "with fear and trembling" (7:15) and had not reacted positively to the letter he carried by showing a humble willingness to follow God's will, opposition to Paul would have increased and they would have become illustrations of the deadly effect of sorrow "borne in the world's way." As it was, they were participants in σωτηρία, not θάνατος (cf. 7:10).

γάρ functions here as a loose connective, comparable to δέ:[49] "*Just* look at" (JB, NAB¹, NJB), "Mark well, *then*" (Cassirer) (italics mine). αὐτὸ τοῦτο (literally, "this very thing") is nominative after ἰδού but may be translated as though it were a direct object.[50] Standing in apposition to τοῦτο is the substantival infinitive τὸ . . . λυπηθῆναι (BDF §399[1]; Robertson 1078), which is qualified by κατὰ θεόν (cf. 2:1) and, with τοῦτο, forms the subject of κατειργάσατο, a constative aorist:[51] "Just consider what this actual experience of godly sorrow has produced in you."[52] V. 10 specifies repentance as the outcome of ἡ κατὰ θεὸν λύπη, so that the list here in v. 11 of seven attitudes or qualities exhibited by the Corinthians during Titus's visit as a result of their "godly sorrow" may be seen as "fruit (= conduct) that is consistent with repentance" (Luke 3:8).

Instead of repeating the exclamatory πόσος (BAGD 694b) with each of the seven nouns in his list, Paul follows up the initial πόσην . . . σπουδήν with six instances of ἀλλά.[53] This conjunction is here not adversative but copulative, forming a series of emphatic additions, "not only this, but also" (BDF §448 [6]).[54] Originally, σπουδή meant "haste," "speed" (cf. Mark 6:25, μετὰ

---

48. ἰδού here is "a call to closer consideration and contemplation" (BAGD 371a).

49. Cf. BAGD s.v. γάρ 4.

50. "Ἴδε with nom. as object is explained by the fact that, like ἰδού, ἴδε has become a stereotyped particle of exclamation" (Turner 231). On the nominative with ἰδού, see Robertson 460, 1193.

51. On the meaning of κατὰ θεόν, see 7:9, and of κατεργάζομαι, see 7:10.

52. ὑμῖν is locatival (BAGD 694b; Robertson 523) rather than a "dative of advantage" ("for you") (BAGD 421d).

53. Some EVV render the πόσην . . . ἀλλά sequence by "what . . . what . . . !" (e.g., RSV, NRSV), others by "how . . . how . . . !" (e.g., Goodspeed).

54. While this affords a case of polysyndeton (Theobald 273), it is not obvious that the series is "rhetorically ascensive" (BAGD 38d); for example, both σπουδή and ζῆλος can mean "eagerness" or "zeal."

σπουδῆς, "in a hurry"), then "earnestness" or "zeal," especially in religious matters. Evidently the Corinthians had shown seriousness of purpose and an eagerness to obey Paul's directives (cf. 2:9) and resolve the matter of ὁ ἀδικήσας (7:12) quickly, aware as they were of their earlier indifference and negligence. Clearly ἀπολογία does not denote here, as it regularly does (e.g., 2 Tim. 4:16), a formal judicial defense,[55] but rather refers to the Corinthians' readiness or eagerness to defend themselves (cf. BAGD 96a; NAB[1]) and thus clear themselves from blame (cf. RSV, NRSV). There is the implication that Paul had laid some charge against them, either in his letter or orally through Titus, to which they had responded with vigor. Possibly the accusation was that they had failed to act on their own initiative out of respect for Paul and take his side against the wrongdoer; but we can only speculate on the nature of the charge. Their "indignation" (ἀγανάκτησις) was probably twofold — at the wrongdoer, for his action, which they now saw as a brazen challenge to Paul's authority; and at themselves, for their failure to defend their spiritual father after he had been denigrated in their hearing. The reason for their "apprehension" or "alarm" (φόβος) may have been uncertainty about the effect of their disloyalty on Paul and on their own future as a small, struggling Christian congregation, or deep concern that unless they repented Paul would be forced to visit them "with a rod" (1 Cor. 4:21).

Another outcome of the Corinthians' repentance was a renewed affection for Paul and therefore a "yearning" (ἐπιπόθησις) to see him in person (cf. 7:7; 1 Thess. 3:6) and be assured of restoration to his trust. As in v. 7, ζῆλος may refer to their "eagerness" or "zeal" to comply with Paul's wishes as expressed in his letter and explained by Titus, and so be reconciled to Paul. The final item in Paul's list of the "fruit of repentance" is ἐκδίκησις, which need not signify "a desire for vengeance" (Barrett 205) but rather a nobler (see Rom. 12:19) "readiness to see justice done" (NIV) or "determination to punish the wrongdoer."[56] Alternatively, the term may refer simply to the "infliction of punishment" (Thrall 486), stressing through the implied πόσην the severity of the penalty. It was the Corinthian indignant zeal to punish, expressed by the terms ἀγανάκτησις, ζῆλος, and ἐκδίκησις, that prompted their over-energetic discipline of the offender that is implied in 2:6-7.[57]

ἐν παντὶ συνεστήσατε ἑαυτοὺς ἁγνοὺς εἶναι τῷ πράγματι. "At every point

55. Because Paul uses certain legal terms in this verse — ἀπολογία, ἐκδίκησις ἁγνός, συνιστάναι ("prove"), πρᾶγμα ("suit") — we need not conclude (with Bultmann 57-58) that Paul conceives of his relationship to the Corinthian congregation as legal, not personal. Legal terminology used to describe a temporary situation is not incompatible with the regular familial terms that Paul uses to describe that relationship, terms such as τέκνα (6:13) and ἀγαπητοί (7:1; cf. 1 Cor. 4:14, τέκνα μου ἀγαπητά).

56. Bruce, Paraphrase 141. Barrett makes the interesting observation that Paul's list moves from the Corinthians' defense against some Pauline charge (ἀπολογία) to a virtual counter-charge against the offender (ἐκδίκησις) (211-12).

57. Cf. Bruce 165.

you have shown yourselves to be blameless in this matter." This crowning affirmation has been understood in two ways. According to Barrett, the aorist συνεστήσατε refers to the time of Titus's visit to Corinth with the "severe letter" when to his satisfaction — and now Paul's — the Corinthians had proved that they were and always had been completely innocent (ἁγνοί) of any complicity in the wrongdoing of ὁ ἀδικήσας. His rendering reads: "In every respect you showed that you *were* innocent in the matter" (212; italics mine). The Corinthian punishment of the offender would hardly have been an appropriate act if they had shared his guilt.[58] On the other view (reflected in the translation above), Paul is saying that by their repentance (7:9) and subsequent conduct (7:11a) as reported by Titus, the Corinthians have demonstrated that they are *now* completely in the right. Their previous complicity in the offense by failing to punish the wrongdoer had now been reversed; they had vigorously exacted his punishment (2:6; 7:11, ἐκδίκησις).

Several points may be brought forward in the support of the latter interpretation. First, we must distinguish the guilt of the offender from the guilt of the Corinthians. That man (ὁ τοιοῦτος, 2:6) was guilty because of his act of defiance. The Corinthians were guilty because of their initial failure to reprove the man and support Paul; their silence had, in effect, given consent. Consequently, they could be innocent of the man's offense, whether he was an insider or (as Barrett argues[59]) an outsider, and yet guilty of culpable inaction, an offense that made their repentance (7:9) necessary. That is, they had not always been innocent (ἁγνοί) in the affair, but their recent actions had now put them in the clear in Paul's estimation. So then, the Corinthians could simultaneously punish the offender (2:6; 7:11) and repent of their own offense (7:9). Second, Paul's summary of the Corinthian reactions to his letter contains two terms that point to or at least hint at their awareness of their own guilt — ὀδυρμός ("mourning," 7:7) and φόβος ("fear," 7:11).[60] Third, the use of εἶναι[61] as opposed to γενέσθαι supports the view that Paul is affirming "you are [now] blameless," not "you were [always] blameless."[62] In making this affirmation Paul is undoubtedly assuming that the congregation will now follow his further directions given in 2:6-8 regarding the full reinstatement of the wrongdoer within the church as a loved member.

The verb συνίστημι/συνιστάνω generally has the sense "commend" in

58. Barrett 212; "2 Cor. 7:12" 153-54. Thrall, too, believes that Paul is declaring that the Corinthians were totally innocent of complicity in the offense, but for her the ἀδικία was the misappropriation of funds for Paul's collection (see n. 75 below).

59. Barrett 7, 86-90, 92-93, 212-13; "2 Cor. 7:12" 152-56. For a critique of this view, see on 2:5.

60. Identifying this φόβος as "the fear of Paul's indignation, or of his breaking off relations with the community," Bultmann comments that "the term φόβος makes clear that they have a bad conscience" (57).

61. εἶναι serves as a copula before the predicate accusative ἁγνούς.

62. Cf. Bachmann 304; Allo 198-99.

2 Corinthians[63] (but here the constative aorist συνεστήσατε means "you have demonstrated" (BDF §406[1]) and is followed, irregularly, by the accusative and infinitive construction (BAGD 790d).[64] When used of women, ἁγνός means "chaste" (cf. 11:2); here it bears a forensic sense, "free of guilt," "innocent," "blameless." In the designedly colorless phrase, τῷ πράγματι ("in this matter"), the article is anaphoric, "that well-known matter under discussion,"[65] and the dative is a dative of respect.[66]

7:12 ἄρα εἰ καὶ ἔγραψα ὑμῖν, οὐχ ἕνεκεν τοῦ ἀδικήσαντος, οὐδὲ ἕνεκεν τοῦ ἀδικηθέντος, ἀλλ᾽ ἕνεκεν τοῦ φανερωθῆναι τὴν σπουδὴν ὑμῶν τὴν ὑπὲρ ἡμῶν πρὸς ὑμᾶς ἐνώπιον τοῦ θεοῦ. "So then, although I did write to you, it was not on account of the wrongdoer nor on account of the person who was wronged but so that your devotion to us might be made clear to you in the sight of God." Here we have the last reference in 2 Corinthians to the "severe letter": it is called ἡ ἐπιστολή and ἡ ἐπιστολὴ ἐκείνη in 7:8, and on four occasions Paul refers to it by ἔγραψα (2:3, 4, 9 and here in 7:12).[67] It is interesting that whenever ἔγραψα is used, it is followed by a statement of purpose (ἵνα, 2:3, 4, 9; ἕνεκεν, 7:12 [third instance]). Clearly Paul was aware that his motivation for sending such a powerful missive, with its potential for causing sorrow and grief (cf. 2:4; 7:8-11) and even harm (cf. 7:9b), would come under scrutiny at Corinth and could easily be misinterpreted.

When ἄρα occurs at the beginning of a sentence in Paul's letter, it is always connective, expressing consequence,[68] "so then." But this creates a logical anomaly, for Paul's purpose in writing is here stated as the consequence of the outcome of the letter (namely v. 11). We have to suppose that the letter's purpose is being viewed retrospectively in light of its effects (Thrall 495). At least Paul's positive statement of his aim in writing (v. 12b) was influenced by his knowledge of the letter's outcome. This is hardly surprising since at the time that letter was written he was full of uncertainty as to how the Corinthians would react to it, so much so that he was exceedingly restless (2:13; 7:5) and fearful (7:5) as he awaited news from Corinth. οὐχ ἕνεκεν . . . οὐδὲ ἕνεκεν expresses two negated reasons why Paul wrote (ἔγραψα) his "severe letter" (causal ἕνεκεν, "on account of"). But the third use of ἕνεκεν in this verse (ἀλλ᾽ ἕνεκεν) is final, "in order that," expressing a positive purpose of that letter.[69] But in reality what we find here is not two rejected causes and one acknowledged purpose, but a comparison of three purposes. Two observations will establish

---

63. 3:1; 4:2; 5:12; 6:4; 10:12, 18; 12:11 (see further on 3:1).

64. ἑαυτούς = ὑμᾶς αὐτούς (see Zerwick 209).

65. Zerwick, *Analysis* 403.

66. BDF §197; Zerwick §53.

67. Paul refers to the present letter by τὸ γράφειν (9:1) and γράφω (13:10); γράφομεν (1:13) refers to his previous correspondence with the Corinthians, as does (αἱ) ἐπιστολαί in 10:9-11.

68. Thrall, *Particles* 10-11; cf. BAGD 104a ("so," "as a result," "consequently").

69. So also REB, NRSV; Barrett 205; Carrez 171. For the final sense of the third ἕνεκεν, see BAGD 264d; Moule 83, 140. But Robertson (1073) takes all three uses of ἕνεκεν as causal.

the point. (1) A stated cause can imply a purpose. So, "on account of the wrong-doer" (ὁ ἀδικήσας) implies "in order to secure the punishment of the wrong-doer"; "on account of the person wronged" (ὁ ἀδικηθείς) implies "in order to seek redress for the one wronged." (2) Paul sometimes reflects the Semitic idiom by which the comparison "not so much X, as Y" or "not primarily X, but Y" is expressed as a stark contrast, "not X, but Y." Thus "I desire mercy, not sacrifice" (Hos. 6:6, cited in Matt. 9:13; 12:7) means "My desire is principally for mercy rather than sacrifice."[70] Precise parallels to 7:12 (with the order οὐ(κ) . . . ἀλλά)[71] are found in 2:5, οὐκ ἐμὲ λελύπηκεν, ἀλλὰ . . . πάντας ὑμᾶς, and 1 Cor. 1:17, οὐ . . . ἀπέστειλέν με Χριστὸς βαπτίζειν ἀλλὰ εὐαγγελίζεσθαι. So then, in 7:12 Paul is comparing two secondary purposes with his primary object that he recognized clearly in retrospect.[72]

One subsidiary objective was the punishment of ὁ ἀδικήσας, "the offender," the same person who was referred to in ch. 2 as ὁ λελυπηκώς (2:5) and ὁ τοιοῦτος (2:6). We have argued above (in the Introduction [B.1.c.] and in the commentary on 2:5) that the ἀδικία this man committed (sometime after Paul's "painful visit" but before his "severe letter") was a serious personal insult that was directed against Paul or possibly his representative and that amounted to an open act of defiance.[73] The other secondary purpose was to secure vindication for ὁ ἀδικηθείς, "the person offended," "the injured party." On the view just summarized, this person was Paul himself[74] or perhaps his representative (such as Timothy).[75] That Paul could objectify his own experience and speak of himself in the third person is clear from 12:2-10.

With the benefit of hindsight Paul identifies his main objective in writing the "severe letter"[76] as being to make clear to the Corinthians the reality of their

70. Some LXX manuscripts (B L P) have the interpretive rendering ἤ ("more than") rather than the literal καὶ οὐ ("and not"). Cf. περισσότερον in Mark 12:33.

71. 7:9 is not parallel, for οὐχ ὅτι ἐλυπήθητε is an absolute negation.

72. "He is in effect using the common Semitic idiom which states as a contrast what in reality is a comparison" (Tasker 107); cf. Plummer 224; Bruce 218, "not so much . . . as." But see *per contra* Meyer 571-72.

73. Barnett proposes that the act of injustice was opposition to Paul's attempt at discipline during the "painful visit" (29, 372, 380-81).

74. *Pace* Kümmel (206) and especially Windisch 237-39.

75. On Thrall's "hypothetical reconstruction of events" ("Offender" 71) surrounding the ἀδικία, a Corinthian church member had entrusted Paul (on his "interim" or "painful visit") with some monies destined for the Jerusalem relief fund, for temporary safekeeping. It was stolen (the ἀδικία) by another person in the church (ὁ ἀδικήσας). The congregation failed to act against this offender when he protested his innocence, but the "severe letter" prompted their further investigation of the matter and ultimately the thief's confession and punishment. On this reconstruction, ὁ ἀδικηθείς was the original depositor who had been wronged by the theft (68-69, 171, 495; "Offender" 74-75). Those who equate 2 Cor. 2:5-11 and 7:12 with 1 Cor. 5:1-13 usually identify ὁ ἀδικηθείς as the father of the man who was guilty of incest with his stepmother. On the difficulty of this identification, see the Introduction, A.2.c.(1).

76. ἔγραψα must be supplied with the first negative (thus οὐκ ἔγραψα ἕνεκεν κτλ.) and possibly also before the third ἕνεκεν (thus ἀλλ' ἔγραψα ἕνεκεν κτλ.).

devotion to him. τὴν σπουδὴν ὑμῶν τὴν ὑπὲρ ἡμῶν, literally, "your devotion which (you have) for us," is the subject of the articular (genitive after ἕνεκεν) infinitive φανερωθῆναι. In 7:11; 8:7-8 σπουδή means "earnestness" or "eagerness," but here, followed by ὑπέρ, it signifies "devotion" (BAGD 763d) or "earnest care" (TCNT). Evidently Paul construed the Corinthian reaction to his demand (in the "severe letter") for the punishment of the wrongdoer as a gauge of their loyalty to him and their zealous concern for himself (cf. 2:9; 7:15). ἐνώπιον τοῦ θεοῦ is emphatic by position and belongs with φανερωθῆναι (Lietzmann 133) rather than with the remote ἔγραψα (as Plummer 216, 225-26). It was only "in the sight of God" that the Corinthians came, and would come, to a realization of their deep-seated devotion to their father in Christ (cf. 1 Cor. 4:15). As in 4:2, the phrase ἐνώπιον τοῦ θεοῦ draws attention to God's awareness of the reality of a situation and his knowledge of people's hearts (cf. καρδιογνώστης, Acts 1:24; 15:8), in spite of actions or events that might give a different impression of a situation (cf. 8:21, and κατέναντι θεοῦ in 2:17; 12:19).

7:13a διὰ τοῦτο παρακεκλήμεθα. "Because of this we have been comforted." As he concludes his discussion of the "severe letter" and its effects (vv. 8-13a), Paul returns to his overriding theme of comfort (see vv. 4, 6). Although v. 7 speaks of the comfort of Titus, the plural verb παρακεκλήμεθα will refer to Paul alone (cf. πεπλήρωμαι τῇ παρακλήσει, v. 4), being triggered by ὑπὲρ ἡμῶν in v. 12. As in v. 4, the perfect tense focuses attention on the present reality of the comfort, with the past receipt of this comfort (παρεκάλεσεν ἡμᾶς ὁ θεός, v. 6) presupposed. The referent of τοῦτο need not be restricted to the σπουδή of vv. 11-12 but incorporates all the content of vv. 5-12, namely relief from depression and fear (vv. 5-6), the safe arrival of Titus with good news about Corinth (vv. 6-7), and the salutary benefits of the Corinthians' repentance (vv. 8-12).

Bibliography

Barrett, "2 Cor. 7.12" • Barrett, "Titus" • Bosenius 7-43 • Carrez, "Le 'Nous'" • Crafton 143-44, 153-61 • Ellis, "Co-Workers" • Kantzer • Lampe • Lightfoot 273-84 • Moncure • Murphy-O'Connor 70-74 • E. G. Thomson, "Μετανοέω and μεταμέλει in Greek Literature until 100 A.D.," in *Historical and Linguistic Studies in Literature Related to the New Testament,* second series, vol. 1 (Chicago: University of Chicago, 1909) 358-64 • Trench 255-61

3. The Joy and Affection of Titus (7:13b-16)

In this section Paul concludes his account, begun in 2:1-11, of the circumstances surrounding the "severe letter" he had sent to the Corinthians. His focus in 7:5-13a was on his own reaction to Titus's report (7:5-9, 13a) and on the Corinthian response to that letter (7:9-12). Now he turns his attention to the experience of Titus himself, the delegate whom he had entrusted with delivering the letter, explaining its contents to the recipients, and applying its instructions. There can be little doubt that this description of Titus's indebtedness to the Corinthians and his deep affection for them was designed by Paul to pave the way for Titus's further delicate mission to Corinth, which is discussed in chs. 8 and 9 (see especially 8:16-17, 23; 9:5).

13b*But^a in addition to our own comfort, we rejoiced more than ever at the joy of Titus, because his spirit has been refreshed by all of you. 14For if I have indulged in some boasting about you to him, I was not made to look foolish. On the contrary, just as everything^b we said to you was true, so our^c boasting before^d Titus turned out to be the truth as well. 15And his heart goes out to you all the more as he recalls the obedience of all of you — how you received him with fear and trembling. 16I rejoice that in every respect I have confidence in you.*

TEXTUAL NOTES

a. The omission of δέ (p^46 81 104 365 629 630 1175 *al*) would mean that ἐπὶ τῇ παρακλήσει ἡμῶν κτλ. could be construed with the preceding verb παρακεκλήμεθα.

b. In the place of the direct object, πάντα, some witnesses read πάντοτε (C F G 81 105 *pc* syr^h cop), and 326 reads πάντων (a scribal error).

c. The reading of B F (ὑμῶν) makes little sense unless it is regarded as an irregular objective genitive after ἡ καύχησις.

d. A strong case can be made for the originality of the reading ἐπὶ Τίτου (no ἡ before ἐπί), which was preferred by NA^25; it has primary (א* B) and secondary (81 326 1881) Alexandrian support, and the article may have been added to conform to classical standards. On the other hand, ἡ ἐπὶ Τίτου (NA^27) is probably the more difficult reading and has the support of the Majority Text (𝔐) as well as primary (p^46 1739) and secondary (C 0243 33) Alexandrian witnesses. This latter reading is to be preferred. The other reading ἡ πρὸς Τίτου (D F G P Ψ 365 614 1175 *pc* latt) reflects a scribal preference for the more usual πρός ("boasting to Titus") over the less common ἐπί ("boasting before/in the presence of Titus").

7:13b Ἐπὶ δὲ τῇ παρακλήσει ὑμῶν περισσοτέρως μᾶλλον ἐχάρημεν ἐπὶ τῇ χαρᾷ Τίτου, ὅτι ἀναπέπαυται τὸ πνεῦμα αὐτοῦ ἀπὸ πάντων ὑμῶν. "But in addition to our own comfort, we rejoiced more than ever at the joy of Titus, because his spirit has been refreshed by all of you." Paul has already expressed his joy at the comfort he himself had received at the hands of Titus as God's agent (vv. 4, 6-7).[1] Now, "over and above" or "in addition to" (ἐπί; cf. Col. 3:14) this comfort, he expresses his exquisite pleasure at Titus's own joy. Just as in vv. 6-7 Titus's comfort is one reason for Paul's comfort, so here Titus's joy[2] is one reason

---

1. Note, in particular, ὑπερπερισσεύομαι τῇ χαρᾷ (7:4), παρεκάλεσεν ἡμᾶς ὁ θεός (7:6), ὥστε με μᾶλλον χαρῆναι (7:7).

2. It makes little difference whether the genitive Τίτου is classified as possessive ("which Titus has") or as subjective ("which Titus experienced"; so BAGD 875c, citing also 1:24; 8:2).

for Paul's joy. ἐπὶ τῇ χαρᾷ defines the object ("at," NRSV) or cause ("because," Thrall 497) or basis[3] of Paul's delight. The intensity or heightening of the apostle's joy is portrayed by the double comparative περισσοτέρως μᾶλλον, "even much more" (BAGD 651d), "more than ever," "even more greatly" (Louw and Nida §78.31). It is a case of the comparative of the adverb περισσῶς strengthened by μᾶλλον, although some regard μᾶλλον as pleonastic.[4]

Although the ὅτι clause could define the content of Paul's joy (ἐχάρημεν), "we rejoiced . . . that . . . ," more probably it denotes the reason (causal ὅτι) for Titus's joy. It is difficult to decide which sense of ἀναπαύω ("set at rest," "refresh") is intended in this verse, for both of these principal meanings of the verb suit the context. Like Timothy before him (cf. 1 Cor. 16:10), Titus doubtless had some misgivings and trepidation about the kind of reception he would receive at Corinth, given the divisiveness, excitability, and immaturity of the converts there.[5] So their united and mature reaction to the letter that Titus brought to them would have given him not inconsiderable relief, would have set his mind at rest (cf. NRSV). But in the wake of that emotional relief, and partly as a result of it, he would have been refreshed in spirit (cf. NIV).[6] So both ideas — refreshment and repose — are probably implied (Plummer 217). Through the use of the perfect tense ἀναπέπαυται Paul is indicating that Titus had experienced spiritual relief and renewal not only in Corinth but also in Macedonia up to the time of writing, just as the perfects in 7:4 (πεπλήρωμαι τῇ παρακλήσει) and 7:13a (παρακεκλήμεθα) point to Paul's enjoyment of comfort even as he wrote the present letter. τὸ πνεῦμα refers to the inward aspects of the self, although Bultmann renders ἀναπέπαυται τὸ πνεῦμα αὐτοῦ simply by "he was refreshed" (60).

This rejuvenation had come to Titus ἀπὸ πάντων ὑμῶν, "by all of you," or, as JB paraphrases the whole thought, "thanks to you all,[7] he has no more worries." As also in the case of the comparable phrase in 7:15, τὴν πάντων ὑμῶν ὑπακοήν, the difficulty revolves around the word πάντων. How can Paul claim that *all* the Corinthians had refreshed Titus (7:13) and had been obedient (7:15)

3. Robertson, *Pictures* 241.

4. Robertson 1205; Zerwick, *Analysis* 403.

5. It would appear that after the ἀδικία that prompted Paul's "severe letter," Titus replaced Timothy as the apostle's agent in Corinth (see n. 247 in the Introduction). Perhaps Timothy had been unsuccessful in an effort to encourage the Corinthians to act on Paul's injunctions in 1 Cor. 5:2, 4-5, 13 regarding the man guilty of incest. He may even be the person referred to as ὁ ἀδικηθείς (see on 7:12).

6. A comparable refreshment of πνεῦμα is mentioned in 1 Cor. 16:18 in reference to Paul himself, and of σπλάγχνα ("heart") in Phlm. 7 in reference to the Colossian believers and in Phlm. 20 in reference to Paul. On the use of ἀναπαύω in Greek literary and non-literary sources, see Clarke 278-86, who also examines these four Pauline uses of the phrase "refresh the heart" (287-96). "There was no religious precedent for the concept of the refreshment of the lives of fellow adherents in pagan Corinthian or other Graeco-Roman religions" (299).

7. After a passive verb ἀπό sometimes denotes agency (= ὑπό) (BDF §210[2]; Zerwick §90; Turner 258). See, e.g., Luke 7:35; Acts 4:36; 15:4; Jas. 1:13.

during Titus's recent visit, when he still needs to remonstrate with at least some of these believers (e.g., 6:12-18; 12:20-21) and answer criticisms leveled against him (e.g., 1:17; 4:2; 6:3; 7:2; 12:16), and when he anticipates the possibility of needing to exercise severe discipline on his forthcoming visit (10:2; 13:2, 10)? Had Titus misread the situation at Corinth? Are Titus and Paul both guilty of an unwarranted optimism or of exaggeration for effect?

An adequate answer to these questions lies in several observations. First, there can be no denying that even when ch. 7 was written, problems remained in the Corinthian congregation. They needed to make a clean break with idolatrous associations (6:14–7:1) and to bring their stalled collection to a satisfactory completion (chs. 8–9), while some of their number needed to repent of the sexual immorality that had been evident on Paul's second visit (12:21; 13:2). It was *after* 2 Corinthians 1–9 had been written that the situation at Corinth worsened and the smoldering unrest that is reflected in the criticism of Paul was fanned into flame by the insidious influence of the false apostles (10:2, 10, 12; 11:4, 13-15, 18-23). But in these first nine chapters there is no evidence of open revolt against Paul.[8] Second, in our discussion of 2:6 we saw that the term οἱ πλείονες probably means "the majority" and points to a dissident minority who were ultra-Paulinists, not anti-Paulinists. All the congregation had supported the punishment of the wrongdoer, but a pro-Pauline group had argued that the punishment should continue or increase. So 2:6 is no indication that the ὑπακοή of 7:15 was not given by all the Corinthians. Third, there is no reason to discount the possibility that all members of the congregation, although perhaps with different degrees of enthusiasm, had contributed to the soothing and refreshment of Titus's spirit (7:13) and had submitted to the instructions of Paul and Titus regarding the discipline of the wrongdoer (7:15).

7:14 ὅτι εἴ τι αὐτῷ ὑπὲρ ὑμῶν κεκαύχημαι, οὐ κατῃσχύνθην. "For if I have indulged in some boasting about you to him, I was not made to look foolish." Paul's purpose in this verse is to congratulate the Corinthians for so responding to his "severe letter" and Titus's visit that his earlier boasting to Titus about them proved justified and not an embarrassment. This in turn would encourage them to ensure a further vindication of his boasting when Titus and his two associates arrived to facilitate the completion of the collection (8:24, "Give them proof . . . of the truth of the boast about you that we made to them"; cf. 9:3).

With ὅτι Paul furnishes a further reason for his joy (ἐχάρημεν, v. 13):[9] the Corinthians had not disappointed him.[10] Apparently, before he sent Titus off with the "severe letter" he felt it necessary to reassure Titus of the Corinthians'

---

8. This presupposes that there is an interval between the writing of chs. 1–9 and chs. 10–13 of sufficient length to allow for this deterioration to take place. See the Introduction, 30–31.

9. BDF §456(1) cites this use of ὅτι (also 4:6; 7:8) as an instance of loose subordination.

10. ὑφ' ὑμῶν ("by you") is understood with οὐ κατῃσχύνθην. Cf. TCNT: "you did not put me to shame."

ζῆλος, their basic "enthusiasm" or "zeal," that he hoped, under God, would guarantee their receiving Titus gladly and responding to him willingly.[11] After the event, he twice mentions this ζῆλος as characterizing their response (7:7, 11; cf. 9:2). Titus may have needed some such reassurance because he knew of Timothy's earlier experience with the Corinthians (cf. Acts 18:5; 1 Cor. 4:17; 16:10-11)[12] or because he himself had already visited Corinth to initiate the collection.[13] Yet Paul's boasting seems to have been somewhat tentative or at least not unqualified — τι . . . κεκαύχημαι means "I have been boasting a little" (TCNT) or "I have been somewhat boastful" (NRSV).[14] It is uncertain whether κεκαύχημαι is an aoristic perfect[15] ("I boasted") or indicates some loose connection between the past and the present; this latter view is preferable, since Paul continues to boast about the Corinthians (cf. 7:4) although not only to Titus (cf. 9:2).

ἀλλ' ὡς πάντα ἐν ἀληθείᾳ ἐλαλήσαμεν ὑμῖν, οὕτως καὶ ἡ καύχησις ἡμῶν ἡ ἐπὶ Τίτου ἀλήθεια ἐγενήθη. "On the contrary, just as everything we said to you was true, so our boasting before Titus turned out to be the truth as well." So far from being let down and embarrassed by a failure of the Corinthians to live up to his generous assurances to Titus about them, Paul felt totally justified to have boasted as he did, because of their ready compliance to his directions during Titus's recent visit. ἀλλά introduces a strong contrast ("on the contrary") to οὐ κατησχύνθην, a contrast that takes the form of a comparison (ὡς . . . οὕτως καί) between all his verbal communication (ἐλαλήσαμεν) with the Corinthians on the one hand, and his boasting before Titus on the other. Both were true (ἐν ἀληθείᾳ . . . ἀλήθεια), but only the boasting needed to be shown to be true by subsequent events (ἐγενήθη[16]). πάντα ἐν ἀληθείᾳ ἐλαλήσαμεν ὑμῖν, literally, "we spoke everything to you in truth," will refer to Paul's initial proclamation of the good news at Corinth (1:18-19), all his pastoral instruction given during the two previous visits, and the three letters he had sent since his founding visit (namely the "previous letter," 1 Corinthians, and the "severe letter").[17] In all of these communications he had invariably spoken truthfully. So too, recent events at Corinth had shown that his boasting "in the presence of" Titus (ἐπί[18]) was spoken truthfully. What he had said *about* them, like what he had said *to* them, was true.

11. But Barnett argues that Paul's confidence was not in the Corinthians themselves, "but in God who was so evidently at work in their lives through his Spirit" (385, citing 1:18-22; 3:2-3, 18; 6:1; 13:5).

12. On this see the Introduction, n. 247.

13. On this see the Introduction, n. 249 and the commentary on 8:6.

14. Paul's assertion in 7:4 πολλή μοι καύχησις ὑπὲρ ὑμῶν ("I freely boast about you") relates more to 9:2 than to 7:14.

15. On this phenomenon, see Turner 68-71, 81; Fanning 299-303.

16. ἐγενήθη = ἐγένετο (see Zerwick §§229-30).

17. It is unlikely that ἐλαλήσαμεν is an epistolary aorist, referring to the present letter, since it stands in parallelism to the preterit aorist ἐγενήθη.

18. For this sense of ἐπί, see BAGD 286b, 426b; Robertson 603.

7:15 καὶ τὰ σπλάγχνα αὐτοῦ περισσοτέρως εἰς ὑμᾶς ἐστιν ἀναμιμνῃσκομένου τὴν πάντων ὑμῶν ὑπακοήν. "And his heart goes out to you all the more as he recalls the obedience of all of you." V. 13 spoke of Titus's joy in experiencing the relief and refreshment afforded him by the Corinthians on his recent visit. Now Paul assures them of Titus's love, which grows stronger even as he recalls their humble responsiveness. They had brought Titus joy; he reciprocates with love. As in 6:12, τὰ σπλάγχνα ("the inward parts") is a synonym for ἡ καρδία as the seat of the emotions, especially love. So the term may be rendered "heart" (RSV, NRSV) or "affection" (NASB, NIV) or "love" (GNB). The issue in 6:12 was the constriction of affection; here it is the generous outflowing of affection. εἰς ὑμᾶς ἐστιν should be seen as a dynamic not a static notion: not "(his heart) is inclined toward you" (BAGD 225a), but "(his heart) goes out to you" (BAGD 763a). It is unlikely that περισσοτέρως is a true comparative, "even more," "far more," suggesting that Titus's love was now much stronger than on his first visit. Rather, this comparative adverb bears an elative sense, "all the more," "very intensely," or "exceedingly" (= ὑπερβαλλόντως; thus BDF §60[3]).[19] ἀναμιμνῃσκομένου agrees with the previous αὐτοῦ and is a genitive absolute with a temporal sense, indicating action contemporaneous with ἐστιν. It was in the process of recalling ("as he recalls") the Corinthians' obedience to both Paul and himself that Titus's tender feelings of love for them grew stronger.[20] The significance of πάντων ὑμῶν (here a subjective genitive) was discussed at 7:13, where the same expression occurs.

ὡς μετὰ φόβου καὶ τρόμου ἐδέξασθε αὐτόν. ". . . — how you received him with fear and trembling." The aorist ἐδέξασθε is constative, referring not only to the Corinthians' ready welcome to Titus on his arrival (so NEB, REB) but also to their general receptiveness and responsiveness throughout his visit. Accordingly, ὡς should be seen not as temporal ("when," NAB[1, 2]) or causal ("because," Héring 57) but as epexegetic ("how [that]," Muraoka 61;[21] "in that"): ". . . as he remembers the obedience of you all — how you received him with fear and trembling" (Thrall 486). On this showing, what Titus recalled was not two distinct items — their obedience and their welcome or receptiveness (so RSV, NRSV) — but their obedience as shown by their general receptivity.[22] The expression μετὰ φόβου καὶ τρόμου, found only in Paul (here and in Eph. 6:5; Phil. 2:12; cf. 1 Cor. 2:3), is often taken to describe "a nervous anxiety to do [one's] duty" (Plummer 228). While this sense suits all four Pauline uses, it

19. See the discussions of περισσοτέρως at 1:12 and 2:4.
20. The ὑπακοή should not be restricted to "obedience" shown to Titus (as NEB, REB); Titus was Paul's delegate, and the letter he delivered and explained must have contained (on any view) directives that Paul expected to be obeyed. Cf. BAGD 837a.
21. Muraoka cites (61-62) several NT and LXX instances of this use of ὡς "to add an explanatory extension" (an expression from Grimm-Thayer's *Lexicon*) and argues that this distinctive biblical Greek idiom is largely due to the influence of the Hebrew ᵃšer, which is basically "a mark of relation" (62).
22. So also Weymouth, NASB, Barclay, NIV.

ignores the distinctive LXX use of the conjoined terms φόβος and τρόμος to denote a Godward rather than a humanward reaction. "Trembling and fear" or "fear and trembling" describes the human reaction to God's power in protecting his people (Exod. 15:16; Deut. 2:25; 11:25; Isa. 19:16) or the appropriate human attitude before the divine majesty (Ps. 2:11). If, then, the phrase "with fear and trembling" is likely to have a Godward orientation, it will depict in its four Pauline occurrences an overwhelming sense of responsibility to God for one's action in a particular situation.[23] The Corinthians were aware of what was at stake in the way they treated Titus, who was Paul's envoy and so God's representative as well. They knew they would have to give account to God for their conduct — hence their warm receptiveness. The full circle had been turned. On his first visit to the Corinthians Paul had come "in much fear and trembling" (1 Cor. 2:3); now these same Corinthians had received Paul's emissary with the same "fear and trembling."

7:16 χαίρω ὅτι ἐν παντὶ θαρρῶ ἐν ὑμῖν. "I rejoice that in every respect I have confidence in you." Paul now returns to the dominant motif, in vv. 4-16, namely joy: τῇ χαρᾷ (v. 4), χαρῆναι (v. 7), χαίρω (v. 9), ἐχάρημεν (v. 13), τῇ χαρᾷ Τίτου (v. 13), χαίρω (v. 16). His ἄνεσις (v. 5) had now been replaced by χαρά. Although there is no νῦν with χαίρω in v. 16 (cf. v. 9), the emphasis still falls on the complete restoration of Paul's confidence in the Corinthians. They had obeyed his instructions (v. 15) and had vindicated his boasting about them (v. 14); they had assuaged Titus's anxious spirit and had brought him joy (v. 13); and they had shown "eagerness" (σπουδή, vv. 11-12) and "zeal" (ζῆλος, vv. 7, 11) for right relations with Paul. ὅτι may introduce either the ground ("because," RSV, NRSV) or the content ("that," NJB; Barrett 206) of Paul's joy. When θαρρέω is followed by ἐν, it means "have confidence in" or "rely on"; when followed by εἰς (as at 10:1), it has the sense "be bold against/toward." But here Paul is not merely "able to depend" (BAGD 352a) on the Corinthians; he actually does have complete (ἐν παντί, "in every respect") confidence in them. Their behavior in the recent past gave him a resilient optimism about the imminent future. He expected that they would rise to the occasion and bring their collection for the poor in the Jerusalem church to a worthy conclusion by excelling in the grace of giving (8:7), and also make the necessary adjustments to their attitudes and behavior before his own arrival in the near future (12:14, 20-21; 13:1-2, 5, 10).[24] He believed that a further personal visit was now not only possible but would be a happy reunion quite unlike his "painful visit" (cf.

---

23. Cf. O'Brien, *Philippians* 282-84, who argues that the phrase "has to do with an attitude of due reverence and awe in the presence of God, a godly fear of the believer in view of the final day" (283).

24. Hughes (282) regards 7:16 as "the delicate pin around which the whole of the epistle pivots," since here Paul looks back and is encouraged by the Corinthian response to Titus's visit with the "severe letter," and looks forward with confidence in a positive Corinthian reaction to his appeal in chs. 8 and 9 for sacrificial giving and to his denunciation of the false apostles in chs. 10–13.

2:1, 3), for Titus had reassured him of the Corinthians' yearning (ἐπιπόθησις, vv. 7, 11) to see him. Yet his "resilient optimism" did not prevent his later expressing real fears about the church (12:20-21; 13:2, 10), fears that reflected the deteriorating situation at Corinth that had developed after his writing of chs. 1–9.

Bibliography

Barrett, "2 Cor. 7.12" • Clarke • Crafton 153-61 • Kantzer • Lightfoot 273-84 • Ollrog 33-37

II. PAUL'S SUMMONS TO COMPLETE THE COLLECTION (2 CORINTHIANS 8–9)

At 2 Corinthians 8 Paul reaches the second major section of his letter. In chs. 1–7 (Part I) the principal subject he treats is his apostleship, as he explains his conduct and apostolic ministry and thus defends his apostolic status. In chs. 8–9 (Part II) the main theme is the collection, as he exhorts the Corinthians to complete their contribution toward the collection for the poor in the Jerusalem church in advance of his arrival. In chs. 10–13 (Part III) his chief concern is with his adversaries, as he seeks to vindicate his own apostolic authority against the claims of his opponents to genuine apostolicity. These three parts of the letter are closely interrelated, since it was Paul's opponents, in league with a minority anti-Pauline clique of malcontents in the Corinthian church, who were challenging his apostleship, and it was these same adversaries, interlopers from Judea, who were inhibiting the progress of the collection, apparently by taking up a Corinthian offer of financial support and thus becoming a financial burden on the church.[1]

Paul's collection for the poor is discussed in detail in the Introduction (B.5). It is important to reiterate here that the genesis of this collection is not to be found in a decision of the Jerusalem leaders to impose an obligation on Gentile churches that would illustrate the supremacy of the mother-church, but in a convergence of Paul's own concerns such as his wish to fulfill a promise of financial aid, to express in a tangible way the interdependence of the members of the body of Christ, to have Gentile believers dramatize in material terms their spiritual indebtedness to the church in Jerusalem, to symbolize the unity of Jew and Gentile in Christ, and to win over those Jewish Christians who entertained suspicions about his Gentile mission.

Paul refers to the whole project in a wide variety of ways that reflects its paramount significance in his estimation.

---

1. All of these points are developed in the Introduction, B.4.

Phrases

[ἡ] κοινωνία . . . εἰς τοὺς πτωχοὺς τῶν ἁγίων τῶν ἐν Ἰερουσαλήμ. (Rom. 15:26)	"[the] contribution . . . for the poor among God's people in Jerusalem"
ἡ διακονία ἡ εἰς τοὺς ἁγίους (2 Cor. 8:4; 9:1)	"the charitable gift/relief aid/service for God's people"
ἡ λογεία ἡ εἰς τοὺς ἁγίους (1 Cor. 16:1)	"the collection/contribution for God's people"
ἡ διακονία μου ἡ εἰς Ἰερουσαλήμ (Rom. 15:31)	"my service for Jerusalem"
ἡ χάρις ὑμῶν εἰς Ἰερουσαλήμ (1 Cor. 16:3)	"your gift for Jerusalem"
[τὸ] τῶν πτωχῶν μνημονεύειν (Gal. 2:10)	"remembering the poor"

Words

λογεία (1 Cor. 16:1-2)	"collection," "contribution"
εὐλογία (2 Cor. 9:5, twice)	"generous/willing gift," "gift of blessing"
χάρις (2 Cor. 8:1, 9; 9:8, 14) (2 Cor. 8:4) (2 Cor. 8:6) (2 Cor. 8:7) (2 Cor. 8:19)[2]	"grace" "privilege," "favor" "act of grace," "charitable act" "work of grace," "gift of charity" "offering," "charitable work," "work of grace"
κοινωνία (2 Cor. 8:4; 9:12-13)	"sharing," "taking part," "partnership"
διακονία (2 Cor. 8:4; 9:1, 12-13)	"charitable gift," "relief aid," "service"
λειτουργία (2 Cor. 9:12)	"(public) service"

There is also a cluster of phrases or terms used in 2 Corinthians 8–9 that are associated with the collection but are not descriptions of it.[3]

---

2. In 2 Cor. 8:16; 9:15 χάρις means "thanks."
3. Cf. Dahl 37-38; Betz 196 n. 1.

τὸ πλοῦτος τῆς ἁπλότητος (2 Cor. 8:2)	"rich generosity"
ἡ ἔνδειξις τῆς ἀγάπης (2 Cor. 8:24)	"the evidence/proof of love"
τὰ γενήματα τῆς δικαιοσύνης (2 Cor. 9:10)	"the fruits/harvest of righteousness"
ἡ διακονία τῆς λειτουργίας ταύτης (2 Cor. 9:12)	"the charitable gift/act of this service"
ἡ δοκιμὴ τῆς διακονίας ταύτης (2 Cor. 9:13)	"the evidence of this charitable gift," "the proof afforded by this service"
ἡ ἁπλότης τῆς κοινωνίας (2 Cor. 9:13)	"generosity in sharing," "the generosity of the partnership"
ἁπλότης (2 Cor. 8:2; 9:11, 13)	"generosity," "liberality"
ἀγάπη (2 Cor. 8:7-8, 24)	"love"
σπουδή (2 Cor. 8:7-8)	"earnestness," "zeal"
προθυμία (2 Cor. 8:11-12, 19; 9:2)	"eagerness," "readiness"
περίσσευμα (2 Cor. 8:14, twice)	"abundance," "plenty"
ἁδρότης (2 Cor. 8:20)	"liberal gift," "lavish generosity"
ἔργον ἀγαθόν (2 Cor. 9:8)	"good work"
σπόρος (2 Cor. 9:10)	"seed," "store of seed," "resources"

If περὶ δέ ("now concerning") in 1 Cor. 16:1 introduces a topic mentioned or discussed in the Corinthians' putative letter to Paul, it is clear that they already knew of Paul's projected collection and it is probable that they had already indicated their willingness to contribute. Also, the abrupt way in which the apostle introduces the theme of "the collection for God's people" at 1 Cor. 16:1, with no reference to the collection's destination (but see 1 Cor. 16:3) and purpose or to any motivation for contributing, presupposes the Corinthians' acquaintance with the project. We cannot be sure when they first heard of the venture, but it may have been in Paul's "previous letter" (cf. 1 Cor. 5:9, 11), written perhaps in A.D. 53, or by news from the Galatian churches referred to in 1 Cor. 16:1. The apostle's directions regarding the collection (1 Cor. 16:2) repeat what he had already told the Galatians to do (1 Cor. 16:1): Every Sunday each believer was privately to set aside and store up some money in proportion to the gains of the previous week, so that special collections would not be needed after Paul arrived (and, one may surmise, so that a more substantial sum would be collected than was likely without systematic giving).

Whether the Corinthians acted on these instructions, we do not know. There are reasons for believing that Titus's first visit to Corinth (before his visit with the "severe letter") may have been to help to initiate the collection.[4] However that be, by the time of 2 Corinthians progress on the collection had evidently been stalled,[5] owing especially to (1) the disturbing events that occurred during Paul's "painful visit"; (2) the baneful action of "the wrongdoer" mentioned in 2:5-11; 7:12 which adversely affected Corinthian attitudes to Paul; and (3) the negative influence of the interlopers from Judea, who at least for a period seem to have been a financial burden on the Corinthians (cf. 11:7-12, 20; 12:13-16). If, on his second visit to Corinth, Titus tried to revive the flagging collection once he saw that the church had responded favorably to the "severe letter," no significant progress was made, although there had been some giving (8:10b). The essence of Paul's call in 2 Corinthians 8–9 is νυνὶ δὲ καὶ τὸ ποιῆσαι ἐπιτελέσατε, "Now then, complete the work" (8:11).

It is possible that each of Paul's five post-conversion visits to Jerusalem mentioned in Acts may have been directly or indirectly connected to the collection.

1. A.D. 35 (Acts 9:26-30; Gal. 1:18-24)
   Paul witnesses or at least hears about the nature and extent of the material poverty within the Jerusalem church.
2. A.D. 46 (Acts 11:30; 12:25; Gal. 2:1-3, 6-10)
   Paul and Barnabas deliver the relief fund from the church of Antioch, and Paul is exhorted (and agrees) to continue remembering the poor (Gal. 2:10).
3. A.D. 49 (Acts 15:4-29; Gal. 2:4-5)
   As Jewish-Gentile relations are discussed, Paul perceives that a collection project that involved Gentile gifts for the poor within the Jerusalem church that were delivered by Gentile believers would not only relieve need but also symbolize and strengthen Jew-Gentile unity in Christ.
4. A.D. 52 (Acts 18:22)
   Whatever Paul's other reasons for this visit,[6] if he shortly thereafter trav-

---

4. See on 8:6 and n. 249 in the Introduction.

5. Paul must have learned of the halting of the collection at Corinth from Titus, but he makes no reference to the source of his knowledge, probably for diplomatic reasons (Barnett 387).

6. According to the Western text of Acts 18:21 Paul was anxious to reach Jerusalem in time to celebrate one of the Jewish feasts.

els "through the Galatian region" (Acts 18:23) and gives the Galatian churches instructions about the collection (cf. 1 Cor. 16:1),[7] one purpose for this brief visit to Jerusalem may have been to indicate to the Jerusalem leaders his intention to initiate this collection in fulfillment of their expressed wish (cf. Gal. 2:10).

5. A.D. 57 (Acts 21:17–23:30)
Along with the delegates from the Gentile churches (Acts 20:4), Paul delivers the collection.

What do we know about the success of the collection in Corinth and in Jerusalem? About five months after he wrote 2 Corinthians, Paul wrote to the Christians in Rome (early A.D. 57) while visiting Corinth in accordance with his stated plans (2 Cor. 12:14; 13:1-2; cf. Acts 20:2-3; Rom. 16:23; 1 Cor. 1:14) on what was to be his third and final visit to the city. In Rom. 15:26-27a he states that "Macedonia and Achaia have been pleased (εὐδόκησαν) to make some contribution for the poor among God's people in Jerusalem. Yes, they were pleased to do so (εὐδόκησαν γάρ)." "Achaia" here refers to the people in the churches of Achaia, including the Corinthians (cf. 2 Cor. 9:2).[8] Clearly, then, the believers at Corinth had heeded Paul's appeal and brought their collection to completion. As for the collection's success in Jerusalem, we have argued above[9] that it was the Jerusalem leaders who "warmly welcomed" or "eagerly received" (ἀσμένως ἀπεδέξαντο) the Gentile delegation who delivered the offering (Acts 21:17).

A. The Need for Generosity (8:1-15)

Not a few scholars regard 2 Corinthians 8 or 2 Corinthians 9 or both chapters as originally separate letters, and either divorced from the rest of the Corinthian correspondence or attached to some part of the canonical 2 Corinthians. The arguments of these scholars are considered in the Introduction (A.3.d), where it is concluded that chs. 8 and 9 belong together and belong to chs. 1–7.

There can be little doubt that 7:4-16 forms an ideal psychological platform from which to launch an appeal for the completion of the collection project. With the encouraging report about the Christians in Corinth brought by Ti-

---

7. Thus Bruce, *Paul* 319.

8. Even if we give κοινωνία its more common meaning of "fellowship," and follow Peterman in rendering Rom. 15:26 by "Macedonia and Achaia were pleased to establish fellowship with the poor" ("Contribution" 457, citing BAGD 439a [paragraph 1]) (cf. NRSV "to share their resources"), the reference is still to the collection. Peterman regards τινά in the phrase κοινωνίαν τινά as denoting "a particular kind of fellowship . . . an exchange of material goods for spiritual goods" (cf. Rom. 15:27) ("Contribution" 463). Certainly Paul's use of τινά ("some/a particular contribution") should not be regarded as a disparaging comment on the size of the contribution (see n. 225 in the Introduction).

9. See the Introduction, B.5.e.

tus, Paul's deep-seated fears about their future and his own are allayed (7:5-6), his joy knows no bounds (7:4b), his confidence in the Corinthians is complete (7:16), and he can be "totally frank" with them (7:4a).[10] As far as content is concerned, the principal link between chs. 8 and 9 and what precedes is Titus and his missions to Corinth. Paul's report of Titus's eminently successful recent visit with the "severe letter," when the Corinthians received him "with fear and trembling" and complied with his requests (7:15), refreshed his spirit (7:13b), and deepened his affection for them (7:15), is an ideal prelude to the announcement in 8:6, 16-17 of Titus's imminent return visit that he would undertake "with much enthusiasm and on his own initiative" (8:17). Specific conceptual and verbal links between chs. 7 and 8[11] include the idea of "zeal," "earnestness," or "enthusiasm," which is expressed by use of the σπουδ- root some seven times in these two chapters, three times in reference to the Corinthians (7:11-12; 8:7) and twice with regard to Titus (8:16-17), and the notion of Paul's boasting (καύχησις) about the Corinthians (7:14; 8:24).

1. The Generosity of the Macedonians (8:1-6)

Paul's aim in 2 Corinthians 8–9 is not simply to have the Christians in Corinth finalize their collection (8:6, 11), and do so before he arrives (9:4-5), but also to have them contribute generously. Of the three sections in chs. 8–9 (namely 8:1-15; 8:16–9:5; 9:6-15), the first and third focus on this "generosity" (ἁπλότης, 8:2; 9:11, 13) — the need for it (8:1-15), and its results (9:6-15).[12] So Paul begins with an appeal to the example of the Macedonians, whose "extreme poverty welled up in rich generosity" (8:2, NIV). It is not surprising that he should think of these Macedonian believers since he was writing from Macedonia (cf. 7:5) and was currently visiting churches in that province (cf. 9:2, καυχῶμαι Μακεδόσιν).

8:1Now we must tell you, brothers and sisters, about the grace of God that has been granted to the churches of Macedonia, 2how, amid a severe test caused by affliction, their exuberant joy and extremeᵃ poverty combined to overflow in lavishᵇ generosity. 3For they gave according to their means, as I can affirm, and even beyondᶜ their means, of their own accord. 4They begged us most urgently for the favor of participation in this service for God's people.ᵈ 5And their giving was not what we expected. Instead, they dedicated themselves first of all to the Lord,ᵉ

---

10. In his outline Furnish (384; cf. 433) includes the "preliminary assurances of confidence" in 7:4-16 as the first section of "the collection for Jerusalem" (7:4–9:15).

11. Cf. Talbert 182.

12. This suggests an ABA structure for these two chapters. Talbert (181-88) also proposes an ABA pattern: A. Why the Corinthians need to complete their collection (8:1-15); B. A commendation of the representatives (8:16–9:5); A¹. Why the Corinthians need to give generously (9:6-14). On the isolation of units within chs. 8 and 9, see O'Mahony 96-103.

and also to us, in keeping with God's will. 6As a result, we appealed to Titus that just as he had previously made a beginning,ᶠ so he should also complete among you this work of grace as well.

TEXTUAL NOTES

a. The accusative βάθος (read by 𝔭⁴⁶ D* *pc* bo) in place of the genitive βάθους after κατά does not substantially alter the meaning of the phrase, since κατὰ βάθους (lit. "down to the depth") and κατὰ βάθος ("from depth to depth"; distributive κατά) both mean "extreme (poverty)."

b. In place of the preferred reading τὸ πλοῦτος (𝔭⁴⁶ ℵ* B C P 0243 6 33 81 104 1175 1739 2464 *pc*), a variety of witnesses (ℵ² D F G Ψ 1881 𝔐) read τὸν πλοῦτον. In Paul πλοῦτος is neuter (in the nominative and accusative) eight times and masculine (in the nominative, accusative, and genitive) five times (Moulton and Howard 127).

c. Perhaps under the influence of ὑπὲρ δύναμιν in 1:8 ("beyond one's strength [to bear]"), Ψ 𝔐 read ὑπέρ instead of παρά (ℵ B C D F G 0243 6 33 81 1175 1739 1881 2464 *pc*). Either way, the meaning is the same: "beyond (their) ability/means/resources."

d. After τοὺς ἁγίους a number of minuscule manuscripts (6 945 *al*) add the awkward gloss δέξασθαι ἡμᾶς (see Metzger, *Text* 194), "begging us (ἡμῶν) that we (ἡμᾶς) would accept their gift and participation."

e. 𝔭⁴⁶ *pc* a f r vgᵐˢ Ambrosiaster read θεῷ (reflected in JB), perhaps through assimilation to the following διὰ θελήματος θεοῦ.

f. B *pc* read ἐνήρξατο, perhaps under the influence of Gal. 3:3; Phil 1:6 where ἐνάρχομαι and ἐπιτελέω occur together (see Plummer, 237).

8:1 Γνωρίζομεν δὲ ὑμῖν, ἀδελφοί, τὴν χάριν τοῦ θεοῦ τὴν δεδομένην ἐν ταῖς ἐκκλησίαις τῆς Μακεδονίας. "Now we must tell you, brothers and sisters, about the grace of God that has been granted to the churches of Macedonia." In Paul the combination of δέ ("now") and ἀδελφοί marks a transition to a new topic[13] or to a new aspect of a topic.[14] In the present case, it is a new topic, his collection "for the poor among the saints at Jerusalem" (Rom. 15:26), although nowhere in these two chapters (2 Corinthians 8–9) does he mention the destination of the offering (8:4 refers simply to "the saints"). With γνωρίζομεν ὑμῖν Paul introduces information worthy of special attention (cf. 1 Cor. 12:3; 15:1; Gal. 1:11): "We would like to inform you, brothers and sisters, about . . ." (Furnish 398).

χάρις is the key term in 2 Corinthians 8–9,[15] occurring ten times in six different senses.

1. "Grace," referring either to God's unconditional kindness lavishly displayed (8:9) or to God's enablement, especially his enablement to participate worthily in the collection (8:1; 9:8, 14).

13. E.g., 1 Cor. 1:10; 12:1; 15:1; 16:15.
14. E.g., 1 Cor. 4:6; 7:29; 14:6.
15. For general observations regarding the use of χάρις in connection with the collection, see Nickle 109-10; Panikulam 38-40; Prümm II/2.37-40.

2. "Privilege" or "favor," used of the honor or opportunity of participating in the offering (8:4).
3. "Act of grace," denoting the collection itself as a charitable and generous act (8:6).
4. "Grace of giving," referring to the virtuous act of sharing or of affording help (8:7).
5. "Offering" or "charitable work," describing the collection as an expression and proof of goodwill (8:19).
6. "Thanks," the verbal expression of gratitude for an act of benevolence (8:16; 9:15).

It cannot be coincidental that χάρις is found at the beginning (8:1) and at the end (9:14-15) of these two chapters, to form an *inclusio*, just as the term occurs at or near the beginning and the end of each of Paul's letters,[16] forming the opening chord and dying refrain of every Pauline symphony.

In the phrase τὴν χάριν τοῦ θεοῦ, the accusative is a direct object after γνωρίζομεν, not an accusative of respect; and τοῦ θεοῦ is a subjective genitive or genitive of source, not a possessive genitive. That is, the reference is not to God's character of generous benevolence, but to God's granting the Macedonian believers the desire and ability to contribute worthily to the collection. The result of that χάρις is indicated in v. 2, namely joyful and generous giving.[17] ἡ χάρις τοῦ θεοῦ, God's gift of enablement to his people, cradles Paul's whole discussion, for this phrase occurs in 8:1 in reference to the Macedonians, and in 9:14 in reference to the Corinthians, although in the latter passage it is qualified by the adjective ὑπερβάλλουσα ("unbounded," "extraordinary"). Paul recognized that apart from "God's grace" the whole venture would falter, but that if that grace operated unhindered among the Corinthians, as it had among the Macedonians, the project would prove successful.

As a "theological passive" δεδομένην has "God" as the implied agent, which confirms that the preceding τοῦ θεοῦ is rightly seen as a subjective genitive. Quite appropriately, therefore, some versions (e.g., REB; Carrez 177) render the whole phrase, "the grace that God has given." As a perfect participle δεδομένην points to the fact that God's grace was not only once given to the churches of Macedonia but also continued to operate among them at the time of writing (Plummer 233).[18] That is, the warm generosity of the Macedonian believers (8:2-3) was generated and sustained by God's grace — not by psychological manipulation or pastoral acumen. ταῖς ἐκκλησίαις τῆς Μακε-

---

16. Rom. 1:7; 16:20; 1 Cor. 1:3; 16:23; 2 Cor. 1:2; 13:13; Gal. 1:3; 6:18; Eph. 1:2; 6:24; Phil. 1:2; 4:23; Col. 1:2; 4:18; 1 Thess. 1:1; 5:28; 2 Thess. 1:2; 3:18; 1 Tim. 1:2; 6:21; 2 Tim. 1:2; 4:22; Tit. 1:4; 3:15.

17. Lietzmann (133) and NEB, however, take generosity to be the χάρις.

18. It makes no significant difference to the meaning whether ἐν is construed as equivalent to εἰς (cf. Moule 76) or to the simple dative (BDF §220[1]), or is rendered by "among" (Robertson 587; Young and Ford 269).

δονίας refers to the Christians in all the congregations throughout the Roman province of Macedonia, including the churches of Philippi, Thessalonica, and Berea.[19]

8:2 ὅτι ἐν πολλῇ δοκιμῇ θλίψεως ἡ περισσεία τῆς χαρᾶς αὐτῶν καὶ ἡ κατὰ βάθους πτωχεία αὐτῶν ἐπερίσσευσεν εἰς τὸ πλοῦτος τῆς ἁπλότητος αὐτῶν. "(We must tell you . . .) how, amid a severe test caused by affliction, their exuberant joy and extreme poverty combined to overflow in lavish generosity." Paul now specifies how the grace of God (v. 1) was exhibited in the lives of the Macedonian Christians — in joy amid affliction and generosity in spite of poverty. ὅτι is dependent on γνωρίζομεν: "We want you to know about the grace of God, how (ὅτι). . . ."[20] If we render ἐν πολλῇ δοκιμῇ θλίψεως by "amid a severe test caused by affliction," we are making several exegetical decisions.

1. ἐν points to accompanying circumstances: "in the midst of," "while passing through," "under."
2. πολλῇ describes the degree of the δοκιμή, "severe" (Moffatt, Barclay), although used with a noun in the singular πολύς may also indicate quantity (see BAGD 687d, 688a), thus "much (testing)" (Martin 248), "continual (ordeals)" (NJB).
3. Although the word δοκιμή, a coinage of the Hellenistic age, may mean "approvedness" (the quality of being approved) or character (as in Rom. 5:4), here, in conjunction with πολλή, it means "test" or "ordeal" (BAGD 202d).[21] That is, it does not indicate the result of testing, that is, proven faith, but the testing itself. What was being tested is not stated, but it could have been their faith (Barclay; cf. 1 Pet. 1:7) or their courage and constancy.[22]
4. θλίψεως is a subjective genitive, "brought about by affliction,"[23] rather than an epexegetic genitive, "consisting of affliction,"[24] where the δοκιμή is the θλῖψις. This particular θλῖψις need not be related to Paul's own θλῖψις experienced in Macedonia (7:5), but, given the fact that the persecution of the Macedonian believers is well documented,[25] their "affliction" may well have been persecution.

The structure of the remainder of this verse may be most clearly seen in diagrammatic form.

19. On the history and the churches of Macedonia, see F. F. Bruce, *ABD* 4.454-57. Macedonia was a senatorial province from 27 B.C.–A.D. 15, and again after A.D. 44.

20. Similarly RV, TCNT, Weymouth, Cassirer; Allo 211; Barrett 216; Martin 248. But it is also possible to regard ὅτι as causal (so Furnish 398; Betz 37).

21. For a defense of the meaning "verification," see Meyer 578.

22. *Virtus* (so Zerwick, *Analysis* 404).

23. Similarly NEB, GNB, JB; Barrett 216; Martin 248.

24. Similarly Zerwick and Grosvenor 549; Bruce, *Paraphrase* 143.

25. Acts 17:5-8; Phil. 1:28-30; 1 Thess. 1:6; 2:14; 3:3-4; 2 Thess. 1:4-7.

	ἡ	περισσεία	τῆς χαρᾶς	αὐτῶν
καὶ	ἡ κατὰ βάθους	πτωχεία		αὐτῶν
ἐπερίσσευσεν	εἰς	τὸ πλοῦτος	τῆς ἁπλότητος	αὐτῶν

This diagram highlights the presence of alliteration (π = three times) and repetition (αὐτῶν three times); the twofold subject περισσεία, πτωχεία) followed by a singular verb (ἐπερίσσευσεν); and the central importance of the two genitives (χαρᾶς and ἁπλότητος), both of which are dependent on quantitative nouns (περισσεία, πλοῦτος) that are the equivalent of adjectives, producing the sense "exuberant joy" and "lavish generosity."[26]

The theme of "joy in the midst of affliction," a common early Christian motif,[27] was sounded in 7:4 in reference to Paul himself. Now the Macedonians are seen to exhibit the same quality (θλίψεως . . . τῆς χαρᾶς), as an evidence of God's grace (v. 1) at work within them. When Paul speaks of "the abundance (περισσεία) of their joy" rather than simply "their abundant joy," he is drawing attention to the boundlessness and effervescence of their joy.[28]

Another paradox expressed in this verse is, "generosity in the midst of poverty."[29] In itself πτωχεία signifies "great poverty." But to emphasize that the Macedonians had reached "the very depths of destitution" (Barclay), Paul adds the remarkable qualification κατὰ βάθους, literally "down to the depth," referring not to "ever-deeper poverty," but "poverty at the deepest," "rock-bottom poverty" (Barrett 216), "extreme/profound poverty."[30] Betz observes that "ancient sources indicate that poverty was a way of life in Macedonia generally."[31] But the dire poverty of the believers there was undoubtedly linked with their θλῖψις: in their case persecution created or at least aggravated their destitution. Also, we cannot doubt that the radical poverty of the Macedonian Christians gave them a special empathy with "the poor" (οἱ πτωχοί) in the Jerusalem church (Rom. 15:26), just as their experience of suffering gave them a particular affinity with the churches of Judea which also had suffered at the hands of their own people (1 Thess. 2:14).

But in spite of their profound destitution, these Macedonians had "shown themselves lavishly open-handed" (NEB, REB) in giving. ἁπλότης is an exclusively Pauline word (seven uses). On three occasions it refers to "sincerity" or "simplicity" of mind (2 Cor. 11:3) or heart (Eph. 6:5; Col. 3:22), a simple-

26. After τὸ πλοῦτος, τῆς ἁπλότητος (αὐτῶν) may be construed as a genitive of relation/reference, "lavishness in relation to their generosity" = "their lavish generosity." Similarly τῆς χαρᾶς (αὐτῶν) after ἡ περισσεία: "the exuberance in relation to their joy" = "their exuberant joy.")

27. See, e.g., Matt. 5:10-12; Acts 5:41; 1 Thess. 1:6; Jas. 1:2; 1 Pet. 1:6. See further Prümm II/2.29-31. For an ABCC^{1}B^{1}A^1 pattern in 2 Corinthians 8–9, see Rolland 76-77.

28. The περισσ- word group occurs frequently in 2 Corinthians 8–9: περισσεύειν (8:2, 7 [twice]; 9:8, 12), περισσεία (8:2), περίσσευμα (8:14, twice), and περισσός (9:1).

29. Cf. the paradox in 8:9, "enrichment through (someone else's) poverty."

30. So also BDF §225; Robertson 607.

31. Betz 43; cf. 50 and n. 87.

heartedness that prompts action that is full of integrity and not duplicitous.[32] But in Rom. 12:8; 2 Cor. 8:2; 9:11, 13 it is used in contexts that deal with giving and denotes open-hearted liberality, that is, "generosity."[33] The development from the meaning "singleness" or "sincerity" to the sense "open-heartedness" or "generosity" is well illustrated by two texts:[34]

> *Testament of Issachar* 3:8 (second century B.C.): "For out of the generosity of my heart (ἐν ἁπλότητι καρδίας μου) I provided everything from my earthly goods for the poor and the oppressed"; and
>
> Josephus, *Antiquities* 7.332 (late first century A.D.): Ornan the Jebusite offers to provide King David, free of charge, his threshing floor for the building of an altar, and with plows and oxen for a burnt offering. "But the king answered that he warmly appreciated his generosity (τῆς ἁπλότητος) and magnanimity," but wished him to accept the full price.

When Paul uses the noun τὸ πλοῦτος[35] ("the riches/wealth") rather than the adjective πλούσιος ("rich") to describe the nature of the Macedonians' generosity, he is emphasizing the lavishness and liberality of that generosity. Given their poverty, the term πλοῦτος is clearly figurative,[36] denoting not the actual size of their contribution to the collection, but the open-hearted and open-handed attitude they showed in their giving.

This was not the first time that the Macedonian believers had acted with warm generosity. Their record, as far as we can ascertain it, can be set out in four stages.

1. In about A.D. 50 the Christians in Philippi entered into a financial partnership with Paul sometime after his first visit (Phil. 1:5; 4:15), and even before he had left Macedonia they sent him a gift "more than once" (Phil. 4:16).

---

32. In 1 Chr. 29:17 (LXX); Wis. 1:1; *Testament of Reuben* 4:1; *Testament of Simeon* 4:5 ἁπλότης is qualified by καρδίας (as in Eph. 6:5; Col. 3:22) and means "integrity/sincerity (of heart)," while in 2 Kgdms. 15:11; 1 Macc. 2:37, 60 it has the sense "innocence" or "guilelessness."

33. Cf. BAGD 86a; Betz 44 n. 35 and the literature cited there.

34. These two references are cited by Bauernfeind, *TDNT* 1.387, who also defends the meaning "generosity." For a contrary view, see Nickle 104-5; Amstutz 103-11, who defends the rendering "sincerity" in 8:2; 9:11, 13. In 8:2 Barrett translates ἁπλότης by "simple-hearted goodness" (216), while Young and Ford have "single-minded commitment" (269).

35. In Paul πλοῦτος is neuter eight times (in the nominative and accusative cases), and masculine six times (including 1 Tim. 6:17) (nominative, accusative, and genitive) (Moulton and Howard 127). The πλου- word group is found four times in 2 Corinthians 8–9: πλοῦτος (8:2), πλούσιος (8:9), πλουτέω (8:9), πλουτίζω (9:11). On the πτωχεία–πλοῦτος pair, see Prümm II/2.23-29.

36. Usually πλοῦτος denotes moral or spiritual riches or wealth in Paul's letters. When this term and the cognate adjective πλούσιος are used of material riches or earthly possessions, the words are qualified (1 Tim. 6:17, τοῖς πλουσίοις ἐν τῷ νῦν αἰῶνι . . . ἐπὶ πλούτου ἀδηλότητι).

2. Late in 50 Silas and Timothy brought financial aid from the Macedonians to Paul in Corinth (Acts 18:5; 2 Cor. 11:9).
3. Before the fall of 56 the Macedonians had contributed generously to Paul's collection for Jerusalem (2 Cor. 8:1-4; cf. Rom. 15:26).
4. In 60 or 61 the Philippians sent Epaphroditus to Rome to bring Paul relief supplies (Phil. 2:25; 4:18).

As already indicated, we have a case in this verse of a twofold subject followed by a singular verb: ἡ περισσεία . . . καὶ ἡ . . . πτωχεία . . . ἐπερίσσευσεν. There is no need to overcome this difficulty by supplying ἐστι (to correspond to δεδομένην) (so Meyer 578 and n. 1) or ἦν or ἐγένετο with ἡ περισσεία.[37] When a singular verb follows a twofold subject, the verb may be said to agree with the nearer subject (here ἡ . . . πτωχεία) or the more important subject,[38] or with the two subjects considered as a unit of thought. The evident wordplay, ἡ περισσεία . . . ἐπερίσσευσεν (literally, "the overflowing . . . overflowed" or "the abundance . . . was present in abundance") that links the two subjects together, supports this latter interpretation. Thus, "their exuberant joy and extreme poverty combined to overflow in lavish generosity." Both ἐπερίσσευσεν (v. 2) and ἔδωκαν (v. 5) are constative aorists, referring to successive acts of giving that are viewed comprehensively. In 9:2 Paul indicates that only "the majority" (οἱ πλείονες) of the Macedonians had contributed to the collection. Perhaps a minority still planned to do so and the majority were themselves continuing to give in the manner described in 1 Cor. 16:2.[39]

Our verse, then, presents us with two stunning paradoxes — joy in the midst of testing and affliction, and generosity in spite of affliction and poverty.[40] Both the joy and the generosity were attributable to the operation of divine grace (v. 1) (Therrien 97). Significantly, the presence and activity of God's grace did not relieve the Macedonians' affliction and poverty but it did prompt their open-hearted and open-handed generosity. Just as "material wealth . . . may cloak spiritual poverty," as in the case of the Laodiceans,[41] so also material poverty may cloak spiritual wealth, as in the case of the Macedonians, for they were prime exhibits of God's grace (cf. Rev. 2:9).

8:3 ὅτι κατὰ δύναμιν, μαρτυρῶ, καὶ παρὰ δύναμιν αὐθαίρετοι. "For they gave according to their means, as I can affirm, and even beyond their means, of their own accord." Having mentioned the Macedonians' single-minded generosity in attitude and action (v. 2b), the apostle proceeds to give fourfold evidence of their liberality. (1) They contributed to the collection far more generously than their impecunious state really permitted them (v. 3a). (2) They

---

37. As, e.g., Betz 37: "the abundance of their joy [occurred] in a terrible ordeal of distress."
38. See Smyth §966c for Classical Greek usage.
39. See the commentary on 9:2.
40. This assumes that ἐν πολλῇ δοκιμῇ θλίψεως qualifies ἡ κατὰ βάθους πτωχεία κτλ. as well as ἡ περισσεία κτλ.
41. Garland 367, citing Rev. 3:14-22.

contributed without anyone's prompting or pressure (v. 3b). (3) With great insistence they begged to be able to contribute (v. 4). (4) They did not limit their contribution to financial aid (v. 5).

Some commentators (e.g., Allo 213) regard ὅτι in v. 3, like ὅτι in v. 2, as dependent on γνωρίζομεν (v. 1), but it is preferable to treat it as causal ("for"), introducing the evidence in vv. 3-5 for the Macedonian generous liberality. However we construe the participle δεόμενοι in v. 4, some finite verb must be supplied in v. 3, and it seems more appropriate to understand ἔδωκαν ("they gave")[42] from v. 5 than to supply a different verb such as ἐποίησαν ("they acted"[43]). In the matching pair κατὰ δύναμιν . . . παρὰ δύναμιν, the two prepositions do not express a stark antithesis, "according to . . . contrary to," as in Rom. 11:24,[44] but a mild contrast, "according to . . . beyond," as in Josephus, *Antiquities* 3.102, 104.[45] δύναμιν refers to "resources/means" or "ability/capability."[46] "For they gave to the limit of their resources . . . and even (ascensive καί) beyond that limit" (cf. NEB, REB). With the parenthetical μαρτυρῶ (note the singular; cf. 8:8, 10), Paul registers his personal testimony[47] that the Macedonians had given not simply what they could afford but beyond what their very slender means really allowed. He is not suggesting that their judgment was unbalanced or reckless but is affirming that their generosity surpassed any natural expectation (cf. v. 5a).

A second evidence of the Macedonians' munificence was their volunteering to participate in the collection. The adjective αὐθαίρετος is not found in the LXX and occurs only here and in v. 17 (in reference to Titus) in the NT. Formed from αὐτός and αἱρέομαι ("choose"), it means "of one's own choice," "by free choice."[48] When Paul says that the Macedonian believers gave αὐθαίρετοι, he probably is affirming two facts: they gave on their own initiative, quite apart from any suggestion from Paul (who was undoubtedly hesitant to propose any Macedonian involvement in the collection, given their radical poverty), and "of their own free will," without any coercion on his part (cf. the repeated εὐδόκησαν in Rom. 15:26-27).[49] But if in this context the term excludes human

42. Thus RSV, GNB, JB, Barclay, NIV, NRSV; Héring 58; Martin 253; Wolff 166.

43. Thus Barrett 220; Betz 37.

44. κατὰ φύσιν . . . παρὰ φύσιν, "according to/by nature . . . contrary to nature," "naturally . . . unnaturally" (cf. Rom. 1:26).

45. Cf. ὑπὲρ δύναμιν in 1:8, "beyond our ability (to endure)."

46. MM note (171d) that the phrase κατὰ δύναμιν ("according to one's means") is very common in contemporary marriage contracts.

47. Furnish's rendering "I swear" (400) is too strong. For the use of the verb μαρτυρέω in the papyri to confirm a signature (cf. the English "witness"), see MM389b.

48. In 2 Macc. 6:19; 3 Macc. 6:6; 7:10 the adverb αὐθαιρέτως refers to action undertaken of one's own accord.

49. This assumes that αὐθαίρετοι stands independently (so also RV, TCNT, Weymouth, RSV, NASB, JB, Barclay, NAB², NRSV, NLT; Furnish 400; Martin 248; Wolff 166. Some, however, connect αὐθαίρετοι with δεόμενοι: "Entirely on their own, they . . . pleaded," NIV; similarly Moffatt, Goodspeed, NEB, GNB, REB; Barrett 216; Betz 37. WH, NA²⁷, and all four UBS editions print a comma before αὐθαίρετοι and none after. But the notion of "pleading of one's own accord" or "begging on one's own initiative" is a strange and awkward idea.

pressure, it does not exclude divine influence (Meyer 580), for their freewill action resulted from divine grace (v. 1) and accorded with the divine will (v. 5). 9:2 does not contradict this understanding of αὐθαίρετοι. If in 8:3 Paul is claiming that the overall Macedonian participation was not the result of his prompting or pressure, he could still affirm (in 9:2) that his boasting to the Macedonians about the Achaean initial zealous commitment to the project had "stimulated" them in their giving.

8:4 μετὰ πολλῆς παρακλήσεως δεόμενοι ἡμῶν τὴν χάριν καὶ τὴν κοινωνίαν τῆς διακονίας τῆς εἰς τοὺς ἁγίους. "They begged us most urgently for the favor of participation in this service for God's people." Here we find a third indication (see on v. 3) of the Macedonians' magnanimous spirit — their urgent pleading to be involved in the collection. Neither Paul nor anyone else had urged or pressured them to participate (v. 3). In fact, their involvement had resulted from *their* urging Paul to grant their earnest request to be permitted to participate.

It is unsatisfactory to construe the participle δεόμενοι as dependent on an implied ἔδωκαν (in v. 2) (so Barnett 395 n. 30), or on the actual verb ἔδωκαν in v. 5 (so Furnish 401) (since καί intervenes). We should rather take the participle as standing for a finite verb (as in 5:12; 7:5; 9:11, 13)[50] such as ἐδεήθησαν or ἐδέοντο (Windisch 245) which would comport with the following καί . . . ἔδωκαν of v. 5.[51] This pleading or begging was undertaken "with great insistence" (Martin 248) or "with the utmost urgency" (Wand 63) or "with earnest entreaty" (Weymouth). This colorful qualification of δεόμενοι, along with the repeated εὐδόκησαν ("they were delighted") in Rom. 15:26-27, witnesses to the enthusiasm shown by the Macedonians in supporting the collection.[52] In v. 1 χάρις denoted an enablement given by God; here χάρις refers to a favor sought from Paul,[53] "the favor of being allowed to participate" in his relief project. It makes little difference whether τὴν χάριν καὶ τὴν κοινωνίαν is taken to mean "a favor, namely (epexegetic καί), participation,"[54] or "the favor of participation," which would be a case of hendiadys (thus most EVV).[55] In Paul's letters κοινωνία always implies an active sharing rather than a passive partnership; the Macedonians were craving the privilege of active involvement in the collection, not only by contributing money, but also, as v. 5 indicates, by making personnel available

50. As in 5:12; 7:5; 9:11, 13 (so Moule 179).

51. Such an understanding obviates the need to have a dash after ἁγίους (as in UBS[1, 2, 3]), presumably to indicate an anacoluthon. UBS[3] (corrected), UBS[4], and NA[27] print a comma after ἁγίους.

52. Cf. Nickle 106.

53. After δέομαι, the construction is τινός τι "beg someone for something," here ἡμῶν . . . τὴν χάριν. For χάρις = "favor," see Acts 24:27; 25:3, 9.

54. As Plummer (CGT) 124: "the grace, *viz.* the fellowship"; so also Wolff 166.

55. Hendiadys ("one by means of two") is the expression of a single idea through two separate words coordinated by καί. Technically, whereas epexegetic καί indicates an exact equation of two elements (ἡ χάρις = ἡ κοινωνία), the καί used in hendiadys points to a relation, not to a precise identity ("a favor involving participation").

as needed. While the term κοινωνία does not refer to the collection itself (as being an "act of fellowship"), it is used three times in connection with the collection, meaning "participation" (8:4) or "contribution" (9:13; Rom. 15:26).[56]

Betz suggests (46, 90) that the next phrase was the official name for Paul's collection for Jerusalem — ἡ διακονία ἡ εἰς τοὺς ἁγίους, "the charitable collection for the saints," "the service/relief aid for God's people." However that be, διακονία seems to have become a technical term in the early church for charitable financial relief within congregations (Acts 6:1) and between them (Acts 11:29; 12:25; Rom. 15:31).[57] In the present verse τῆς διακονίας is an objective genitive after τὴν κοινωνίαν, and the article is anaphoric, "this relief work," "this (act of) service." εἰς may express goal ("destined for," "designed for the help of" [Barclay]) or benefit ("for the benefit of").[58] As in 1 Cor. 16:1; 2 Cor. 9:1, εἰς τοὺς ἁγίους is an abbreviation of εἰς τοὺς πτωχοὺς τῶν ἁγίων τῶν ἐν Ἰερουσαλήμ (Rom. 15:26), "for the poor among the saints in Jerusalem," but it was not the case that Paul reserved the title οἱ ἅγιοι for believers in Jerusalem (see on 1:1). Also, there is no significance in the fact that Jerusalem is unnamed in 2 Corinthians 8–9 (cf. Rom. 15:25-26; 1 Cor. 16:3).

The Macedonian request for the pleasure of sharing in this relief project was perhaps conveyed by the Macedonians Gaius and Aristarchus, whom Luke describes as Paul's "companions in travel" (Acts 19:29). When the request was made is uncertain, but because 1 Cor. 16:1 refers only to "the churches of Galatia," and not also to the Macedonian churches, and because 1 Cor. 16:5 that mentions Paul's intended visit to Macedonia makes no reference to the collection, it is fair to assume that Macedonian involvement in the offering began after the spring of A.D. 55, the probable date of 1 Corinthians (falling between vv. 20 and 21 of Acts 19 in the Lukan narrative). It is therefore possible that one reason why Paul sent Timothy and Erastus into Macedonia (Acts 19:22) was to commence the collection project there. Whatever the chronology of the Macedonians' participation, it is clear that Paul readily granted their very urgent request!

8:5 καὶ οὐ καθὼς ἠλπίσαμεν ἀλλ᾽ ἑαυτοὺς ἔδωκαν πρῶτον τῷ κυρίῳ καὶ ἡμῖν διὰ θελήματος θεοῦ. "And their giving was not what we expected. Instead, they dedicated themselves first of all to the Lord, and also to us, in keeping with God's will." With this statement Paul gives yet another (the fourth) sign of the open-handed liberality of the Macedonians (see on v. 3):[59] their lavish

---

56. On the significance of the term κοινωνία in reference to the collection, see Nickle 105-6, 122-25; Prümm II/2.45-48. For the rabbinical practice of showing fellowship through an offering, see SB 3.316.

57. On the term διακονία as it relates to the collection, see Nickle 106-9; Panikulam 40-42; Prümm II/2.43-44.

58. Cf. Deissmann 117-18, 194-95.

59. Cf. Meyer (579), who argues that vv. 3-5 contain four "modal definitions" attached to ἔδωκαν. But some regard ἑαυτοὺς ἔδωκαν πρῶτον τῷ κυρίῳ καὶ ἡμῖν as the *explanation* for the surpassing of Paul's hopes (Héring 59) or for the Macedonians' extraordinary generosity (Bruce 221; *Paraphrase* 143).

giving was not restricted to financial relief but included the giving of their very selves.

In two regards the giving of the Macedonians exceeded Paul's expectations (ἐλπίζειν here = προσδοκᾶν, Windisch 247): he had expected a smaller amount of money to be given by them than in fact they contributed (after all, they were not only under persecution but were desperately poor); he had expected them to make only monetary gifts, whereas they surrendered themselves to the Lord and to Paul himself for the promotion of the collection. With regard to both the size of their gift and the extent of their giving they surprised Paul and surpassed his expectations.

After καί, which is here merely conjunctive, we must supply ἔδωκαν from the following clause. Literally, "And [they gave] not as we expected." ἀλλά ("instead") contrasts the Macedonians' actions with Paul's expectations. Instead of conforming to Paul's expectations — which were born of reality — the actions of the Macedonians outstripped what he had been expecting. Their giving involved their persons (ἑαυτούς is emphatic by position) as well as their possessions. ἑαυτοὺς ἔδωκαν . . . τῷ κυρίῳ cannot refer to their conversion experience because of the καὶ ἡμῖν that follows. It must have been a rededication of their lives to the Lord Jesus[60] for a specific task that involved Paul, namely the facilitating of the collection among the churches in Macedonia. In reference to the κύριος, the "giving" was self-surrender,[61] devotion to his service, as at conversion. In reference to Paul, the "giving" was the offer and promise of personal assistance with the collection in any way he might choose ("they put themselves at my disposal," Moffatt).[62] The adverb πρῶτον does not mean simply "before (they made their gift)," but points to a priority in both importance and time.[63] "First and foremost" or "primarily," they dedicated themselves to the Lord and his work, but in addition that self-dedication occurred "before" they made themselves available to Paul. Perhaps the rendering "first of all" retains the ambiguity. If it were simply a matter of temporal priority — "first to the Lord, then to us" — we would have expected ἔπειτα (as in 1 Cor. 15:46) or εἶτα (as in 1 Tim. 3:10) to follow πρῶτον. As it is, a simple καὶ ἡμῖν, "and also to us," follows πρῶτον τῷ κυρίῳ. The phrase διὰ θελήματος θεοῦ, a favorite Pauline expression, especially in salutations,[64] belongs with the whole preced-

---

60. τῷ κυρίῳ refers to Christ (so Barrett 221; Martin 255) rather than to God (as Héring 59; Betz 48), for the articular κύριος generally refers to the Lord Jesus in Paul (cf. Zerwick §169).

61. The phrase ἑαυτὸν (παρα)διδόναι is used by Paul to describe Christ's voluntary self-surrender to death (Gal. 2:20; Eph. 5:25; 1 Tim. 2:6; Tit. 2:14). But Héring takes the expression "they gave themselves to the Lord" to refer to approaching God in prayer, with his reply being to urge them to give themselves to Paul (59).

62. Perhaps the Macedonians were also committing themselves to Christian service in general. Among Paul's co-workers were several Macedonians — Gaius and Aristarchus (Acts 19:29), Jason (Acts 17:6-9), Epaphroditus (Phil. 2:25-30), Sopater and Secundus (Acts 20:4) (cf. Bernard 85).

63. So also Hughes 292.

64. 1 Cor. 1:1; 2 Cor. 1:1; Eph. 1:1; Col. 1:1; 2 Tim. 1:1.

ing clause and not simply καὶ ἡμῖν.[65] Devotion to Christ was as much "in keeping with God's will" as was commitment to Paul, Christ's ambassador.

With v. 5 Paul's appeal to the example of the Macedonian believers comes to an end. In particular he has drawn attention to their joy and generosity in giving (v. 2), their sacrificial and voluntary giving (v. 3), their unexpected initiative (v. 4), and their recognition that giving was an act of devotion to Christ and his representatives (v. 5). The implications of Paul's appeal would not have been lost on the Corinthians. If they permitted the same divine grace (8:1; cf. 9:14) to be operative in their lives,[66] they would exhibit the same praiseworthy qualities as marked the Macedonians and so bring their own languishing collection to a satisfactory conclusion. Paul is not promoting a contest between the Macedonians and the Corinthians to see who would be first in generosity (*pace* Betz 49), but although his aim in appealing to the Macedonian example may not have been to embarrass the Corinthians, that would probably have been its partial effect. For example, he was about to implore them to finish their collection (vv. 7, 11); the Macedonians had implored him to let them begin theirs (v. 4)!

Three important principles emerge from v. 5. First, self-surrender to Christ takes precedence over availability and loyalty to any of his servants. Second, dedication to Christ involves dedication to his servants, so that dedication to them is in reality service to Christ. Third, the giving of one's self should precede and accompany the giving of one's possessions. Paul enunciates this principle in typically antithetical form in 12:14 when he says to the Corinthians, "I desire not your possessions but yourselves (οὐ . . . ζητῶ τὰ ὑμῶν ἀλλὰ ὑμᾶς)."

8:6 εἰς τὸ παρακαλέσαι ἡμᾶς Τίτον ἵνα καθὼς προενήρξατο οὕτως καὶ ἐπιτελέσῃ εἰς ὑμᾶς καὶ τὴν χάριν ταύτην. "As a result, we appealed to Titus that just as he had previously made a beginning, so he should also complete among you this work of grace as well." Although the Greek sentence that begins in v. 3 continues to the end of v. 6, there is a break in thought at the end of v. 5 as Paul moves from describing the actions of the Macedonians to drawing a conclusion from their example. On the basis of his rehearsal in vv. 1-5 of the outstanding spiritual qualities of the Macedonians, Paul proceeds to press in vv. 6-12 for generous giving and a prompt completion of the Corinthian offering for Jerusalem.

It was mainly the unexpected and enthusiastic involvement of the Macedonians in the collection that led Paul (resultative/ecbatic εἰς[67]) to request and

65. Given the difficulty of relating ἑαυτοὺς ἔδωκαν to ἡμῖν, Wand makes διὰ θελήματος θεοῦ a qualification of καὶ ἡμῖν: ". . . and also to me (so far, of course, as is consistent with the will of God)" (63).
66. Paul had already reminded the Corinthians that they had been enriched by the grace of God in speech and knowledge (1 Cor. 1:4-5; cf. 2 Cor. 8:7).
67. Robertson 1003, 1072; Moule 141. In this context it seems inappropriate to expand "so that (we urged Titus)" into "in such a manner that" (so BDF §402[2]) or "to such a degree that" (so Turner 143). But Meyer (581) seeks to defend a final sense for εἰς here.

encourage Titus to pay another visit to Corinth.[68] But that motivation was doubtless reinforced as Paul remembered Titus's recent diplomatic success in Corinth (cf. 7:5-16). Who better to dispatch to Corinth than someone who had initiated the collection there (see below), who was the most recent member of the Pauline circle to visit the Corinthian church, and who enjoyed the confidence and respect of the Corinthians (7:13b, 15)? V. 17 indicates that Titus responded to Paul's request enthusiastically.

The context of Paul's hortatory appeal is defined by the ἵνα clause; that is, ἵνα is epexegetic rather than telic.[69] Titus was being urged by Paul to "complete" (ἐπιτελέσῃ) a particular "work of grace," just as he had "already made a beginning" (προενήρξατο). The verb προενάρχομαι, "make a beginning beforehand," is found only here and in v. 10 in the NT and never in pre-Christian Greek (including the LXX). Here προ- signifies "before the time of writing," and specifically, "during the previous year" (ἀπὸ πέρυσι, v. 10). Ascough is right in observing that the verb ἐπιτελέω ("complete"), which occurs in vv. 6 and 11 (twice), is pivotal in vv. 1-15 (586). The essence of Paul's appeal to the Corinthians in these verses is "Complete (ἐπιτελέσατε, v. 11a) what you have begun!" But it is doubtful whether this verb needs to be given a specialized connotation, whether from the realm of governmental administration (Betz 54, 65)[70] or public obligation and benefaction (Danker 122, 127) or religious duty (Ascough 598-99).[71] In its three uses in ch. 8 it simply carries its basic and general sense of the successful completion of a task[72] and is contrasted with προενάρχομαι.[73]

There is an interesting correspondence between v. 6 and vv. 10-11 with regard to the use of these verbs: in the former case, Titus is the subject; in the latter instance, the Corinthians.

---

68. Both τὸ παρακαλέσαι in 8:6 and τὴν . . . παράκλησιν in 8:17 denote an appeal that is hortatory. In the light of [Τίτος] τὴν . . . παράκλησιν ἐδέξατο ("[Titus] welcomed our appeal") (8:17), τὸ παρακαλέσαι (8:6) is unlikely to be an epistolary aorist (as Bernard [85] proposes).

69. For the construction παρακαλέω followed by the accusative of the person and ἵνα, see 1 Cor. 1:10; 16:12; 1 Thess. 4:1.

70. Betz stresses the legal and official nature of ch. 8: "it is an official letter sent by an individual writing in an official capacity to a corporate body, the church at Corinth, along with officially appointed envoys" (134). Consequently he sees the language that Paul employs as technical terms drawn from the realm of official Graeco-Roman law and administration (see the comments of O'Mahony 172-74). For example, παρακαλεῖν (8:6) is a term used of "the appointment of legal or political representatives" (54); thus, "we have appointed Titus" (37). ἐπιτελεῖν (8:6, 11) refers to the completion of an administrative act (65). Or again, πρόσωπον (8:24) has the legal sense of *persona*, so that "the two brothers were the legal and political *persona* of the churches they represented" (86).

71. Ascough surveys (590-97) the inscriptional uses of ἐπιτελέω in religious contexts, especially the carrying out of ritual duty, sacred festivals and funerary rites, the fulfillment of oaths, and religious benefaction.

72. On the biblical use of ἐπιτελέω, see Ascough 588-90.

73. For the association of ἐνάρχομαι and ἐπιτελέω, see Gal. 3:3; Phil. 1:6.

Titus	Corinthians
προενήρξατο (8:6)[74]	προενήρξασθε (8:10)
ἐπιτελέσῃ (8:6)	ἐπιτελέσατε (8:11)

From this correspondence we may make two significant deductions.[75] First, since in vv. 10-11 these two verbs refer unambiguously to the Corinthian collection, in v. 6 τὴν χάριν ταύτην, the direct object of ἐπιτελέσῃ, will also denote the Corinthian offering, and this phrase may be supplied as the direct object of προενήρξατο.[76] In any case, the correlatives καθὼς . . . οὕτως and the first καί ("also," which belongs with ἐπιτελέσῃ rather than οὕτως) suggest an identity of object for these two verbs in v. 6. Second, if both Titus and the Corinthians may be said to have "made a beginning" on the same collection at Corinth, and both are being called on to complete it, clearly the Corinthians are the principal actors (it is their collection, not Titus's) and Titus has a secondary role — that of facilitator. He was to help them to complete the offering, just as he had helped them begin it.[77]

It is highly unlikely that Titus was instrumental in starting the collection at Corinth during his visit with the "severe letter;"[78] his mission at that time was too delicate and important to be jeopardized by money matters (although Paul may have encouraged Titus to try to revive the collection project if his principal goal was achieved). This leads us to conclude that Titus "began" the collection during the year before 2 Corinthians was written (see v. 10 on ἀπὸ πέρυσι), probably after 1 Corinthians had been received.[79] On this view, Titus was Paul's envoy to Corinth on three occasions:[80]

1. After the receipt of 1 Corinthians at Corinth, to help to start the relief fund (8:6a; 12:18) (see Watson 333-35).
2. After Paul's "painful visit," to deliver the "severe letter" (7:6-15).
3. At some indefinite time after he had been reunited with Paul in Macedo-

74. After the aorist τὸ παρακαλέσαι, this aorist has a pluperfect sense, "had previously made a beginning" (see Zerwick §290).

75. Barrett, however, distinguishes the time of the Corinthians' "beginning" from that of Titus ("Titus" 10-11). But 1 Cor. 16:1-4 need not imply that the Corinthians had already begun their collection.

76. Cf. Martin 248, "as he had previously begun this gracious service." But he refers this to Titus's work on the collection in Macedonia, contrasting εἰς ὑμᾶς ("for you") with an implied εἰς αὐτούς ("for them") (248, 255). Others take προενήρξατο as a reference to Titus's recent "mission of reconciliation" as one manifestation of God's grace (e.g., Bruce 221).

77. Some EVV reflect this understanding of Titus's role; see Conybeare in Conybeare and Howson 453; GNB, REB.

78. *Pace* Barrett, "Titus" 10.

79. But Hughes (293-94) and Barnett (401 n. 53) believe that Titus began the collection at Corinth before 1 Corinthians was written, possibly when he was the bearer of the "previous letter" (1 Cor. 5:9).

80. Similarly Vielhauer, *Geschichte* 145; F. Watson 335.

nia (7:6), to deliver 2 Corinthians and to help to complete the collection (8:6b, 16-17).

The significance of the second καί in v. 6 should not be overlooked. Paul was urging Titus to complete among[81] the Corinthians "this work of grace as well" (καὶ τὴν χάριν ταύτην), or, as Weymouth renders it, "this act of beneficence also." By this adjunctive use of καί Paul is alluding to a previous occasion on which Titus had performed a χάρις, a gracious act of service, among the Corinthians.[82] The allusion must be to Titus's dramatic success on his second visit as he delivered and reinforced the effect of Paul's "severe letter."[83]

Bibliography

Ascough • Berger, "Almosen" • Bieringer, "Teilungshypothesen" 98-104 • Bruce, "Jerusalem" • Buck • Cerfaux, *Church* 130-41 • Dahl 37-38 • Dockx • Georgi 75-92 • Hainz, *Koinonia* 104-5, 134-41, 151-61 • Holmberg 35-57 • Joubert • Joubert, "Rhetoric" • Keck • Keck, "Christianity" • J. G. Lodge, "The Apostle's Appeal and Readers' Response: 2 Corinthians 8 and 9," *ChicStud* 30 (1991) 59-75 • Lüdemann 77-100 • McDermott • Morrice 111-33 • Munck 288-92, 295-97 • Murphy-O'Connor 78-81 • Nickle • O'Mahony • Panikulam 31-57 • Theobald 279-82 • Therrien 96-97, 254 • Verbrugge

2. A Plea for Liberal Giving (8:7-12)

In 8:1-6 Paul has described the enthusiastic and sacrificial involvement of the Macedonian Christians in his relief fund (vv. 1-5) and has indicated his own response to their generous participation (v. 6). At v. 7 he turns from an emotive description of the Macedonians to an intense urging of the Corinthians in an exhortation that weaves a narrow path between repeated commands and outright cajoling. In vv. 7-12 he is merely giving advice (v. 10), but advice that he certainly expects to be accepted and acted upon! The Corinthians should capitalize on the promising start they made in deciding to contribute, by completing their offering with a liberal contribution (cf. 9:5). Although this collection project was Paul's own service for Jerusalem (ἡ διακονία μου ἡ εἰς Ἰερουσαλήμ, Rom. 15:31) in the sense that it began and was completed at his initiative, here in 2 Corinthians 8–9

---

81. If εἰς ὑμᾶς is construed with ἐπιτελέσῃ, it will mean "among you" (Goodspeed, JB) or "for your benefit" (Betz 37); if with τὴν χάριν ταύτην, "on your part" (NIV).

82. This allusion explains why it is preferable to translate τὴν χάριν ταύτην by a neutral expression such as "work of grace" or "act of benevolence," rather than by a phrase that refers only to the collection, such as "this charitable collection" (Betz 37).

83. Cf. Martin 255. But some see the allusion as being to the Corinthians, not to Titus: "in addition to the graces of repentance and goodwill" (Bernard 86), or "in addition to whatever else [God] has yet to complete among you" (Vincent 829).

he clearly wishes the Corinthians, like the Macedonians, to claim ownership of the undertaking and contribute with promptness and generosity.

8:7*Now then, just as you excel in everything else — in faith and speech and knowledge, in total earnestness, and in the love that we inspired in you[a] — excel in this gracious undertaking as well. 8I am not saying this as an order, but by mentioning the eagerness shown by others I am seeking to verify[b] the reality of your own love as well. 9For you know the grace that was shown by our Lord Jesus Christ[c], that though he was rich he became poor for your[d] sake, so that by his[e] poverty you might become rich.*

10So then, I am simply giving you my advice in this matter. For this is fitting in your case, seeing that you led the way[f] last year not only in taking action but also in desiring to do so. 11But now complete your action as well, so that your eager desire may be matched by your completion of the project, as your resources permit. 12For if this eager desire to give is present, the gift is fully acceptable according to whatever one has, not according to what one does not have.

TEXTUAL NOTES

a. Apart from two readings that are poorly attested (viz. ὑμῶν ἐν ὑμῖν, 326 629 2464 *pc*, and ἡμῶν ἐν ἡμῖν, 263), there are two variants: (1) ὑμῶν ἐν ἡμῖν, supported by ℵ C D F G Ψ (33) 𝔐 lat syr[h], and (2) ἡμῶν ἐν ὑμῖν, read by p[46] B 0243 6 104 630 1175 1739 1881 *pc* r syr[p] cop Ambrosiaster. In its context (τῇ ἐξ . . . ἀγάπῃ) the first reading will mean "your love for us"; and the second, "our love for you" or "the love that you have received from us" (Carrez 181) or "the love we inspired in you" (NASB). There is probably no textual problem in 2 Corinthians where commentators and EVV are so evenly divided. For instance, reading (1) is reflected in RV, Moffatt, RSV, NEB, GNB, Barclay, NIV, NJB, REB, Cassirer, NLT, and reading (2) in TCNT, Weymouth, Goodspeed, Williams, NASB, JB, NAB[1, 2], NRSV. It is incontestable that reading (1), "your love for us," suits the context where Corinthian gifts or graces are being mentioned, and has wide geographical support, with Alexandrian, Western, and Byzantine families well represented. But reading (2) has proto-Alexandrian (p[46] B 1739) and later Alexandrian (0243 104 1175 1881) Greek manuscript support and is the more difficult reading, even with the alternative translations. Significantly, this second reading is preferred in UBS[1, 2, 3] with a "D" rating (= a very high degree of doubt), in UBS[4] with a "C" rating (= uncertain), and in NA[27]; also WH 1.412 and Metzger 512-13. It is the reading we adopt.

b. D* F G read δοκιμάζω to match the preceding λέγω, but the participle δοκιμάζων is to be preferred as the more difficult reading. For a coordinate participle after a finite verb in Paul, see BDF §468 (1); Zerwick §374.

c. B sa omit Χριστοῦ.

d. C K 6 323 614 *al* Eusebius Didymus[pt] substitute the inclusive ἡμᾶς (= "for both us and you," i.e., for all believers) for ὑμᾶς.

e. The more common αὐτοῦ is substituted for ἐκείνου in D F G syr[p] Didymus without altering the sense.

f. In place of the doubly compounded form προενήρξασθε (see 8:6), D* F G 629* have the less difficult ἐνήρξασθε.

8:7 ἀλλ' ὥσπερ ἐν παντὶ περισσεύετε, πίστει καὶ λόγῳ καὶ γνώσει καὶ πάσῃ σπουδῇ καὶ τῇ ἐξ ἡμῶν ἐν ὑμῖν ἀγάπῃ, ἵνα καὶ ἐν ταύτῃ τῇ χάριτι περισσεύητε. "Now then, just as you excel in everything else — in faith and speech and knowledge, in total earnestness, and in the love that we inspired in you — excel in this gracious undertaking as well." If ἀλλά expresses a contrast, it may that between the Corinthians and Titus (cf. 8:6) (so Winer 451), or that between two incentives — what God had enabled the Macedonians to do and what God had done for the Corinthians (Plummer 237-38). But more probably it is transitional (Lietzmann 134), introducing an exhortation with emphasis,[1] "Now then" (Moffatt), "Come now." ὥσπερ stands in the protasis of a comparison, with οὕτως understood before ἵνα. After affirming that the Corinthians "overflow" or "excel" (περισσεύετε) in every spiritual endowment (ἐν παντί), Paul supplies five specific examples of such giftedness in what effectively forms a parenthesis (πίστει . . . ἀγάπῃ). To avoid a monotonous repetition of ἐν, he uses the simple dative in each of the five nouns,[2] resuming ἐν in the [οὕτως] ἵνα καί clause. πίστις may possibly refer to personal trust in Christ (Eph. 1:15), but in the present context it probably refers to the faith to work miracles (1 Cor. 12:9-10; 13:2), that is, wonder-working faith rather than saving faith.[3] λόγος, eloquence in declaring the truth, and γνῶσις, spiritual perceptiveness, are similarly conjoined in 1 Cor. 1:5, 7 as χαρίσματα. When πᾶς is used with an articular singular noun, it may mean "every," "every kind of," or "full/greatest/all" (denoting the highest degree) (BAGD 631b, c), so that πάσῃ σπουδῇ may mean "(in) every kind of zeal" (Barrett 216; Betz 37) or "in complete earnestness" (NIV), "whole-hearted enthusiasm" (Young and Ford 269). The difficult textual issue in the fifth element of Paul's list is discussed above under "Textual Notes" (a.), where a preference is expressed for the reading τῇ ἐξ ἡμῶν ἐν ὑμῖν ἀγάπῃ. Since ἀγάπη is qualified, it is articular. ἐξ denotes source and ἐν location: "the love that was derived from us and now resides in you," "the affection that we have awakened in you" (TCNT), "the love that is in you, implanted by us" (Weymouth). Paul is here referring to the Corinthians' love for Christ and for fellow believers that his proclamation of the gospel had generated in them.[4] On the basis of their superlative spiritual enrichment in Christ (cf. 1 Cor. 1:5) in these five spheres, Paul launches his appeal for an equivalent lavishness in the grace of giving; the movement from περισσεύετε to ἵνα . . . περισσεύητε is the movement from the indicative to the imperative: "Just as you overflow . . . , [so] overflow. . . ." But not all agree that this absolute use of ἵνα with the subjunctive is imperatival.

1. Thus Zerwick, *Analysis* 404.

2. These five datives may be explained as datives of respect/reference or as datives with an implied ἐν.

3. Cf. Spicq, *Agape* 210.

4. It is true that in 6:12-13 Paul has spoken of the restrictedness of the Corinthians' affection for him. This fact simply shows that in 8:6 he is not thinking of their love for himself. We are unpersuaded by Murphy-O'Connor's view that in 8:7a Paul is speaking with "his tongue in his cheek" (81).

There are three basic ways of construing ἵνα in this verse.

1. A verb may be supplied before ἵνα, which then will define content:

(a) βλέπετε, "see that . . ." (RSV, NIV; Barrett 216).
(b) παρακαλῶ, "I urge you to . . ." (Barclay; Plummer 238; cf. MM 305b).
(c) θέλομεν, "we want you to . . ." (GNB, NRSV).[5]
(d) αἰτοῦμαι, "I ask you to . . ." (TCNT).

2. Standing absolutely, ἵνα expresses a wish: ". . . may you (abound) . . ." (Lambrecht 135, 137; Zerwick and Grosvenor 550).[6]

3. Standing absolutely, ἵνα expresses a command: "excel (also in this gracious work)" (Salom 134).[7] This understanding of ἵνα . . . περισσεύητε is shared by most grammarians.[8] Sometimes this imperatival sense is expressed in translation in terms of obligation[9] or necessity.[10]

So then, Paul uses a relatively uncommon construction[11] as a substitute for the imperative[12] as he entreats the Corinthians to match their rich giftedness with lavish giving. καί ("also," "as well") points to this hoped-for correspondence and justifies Goodspeed's insertion of the word "else" after "in everything": "Just as you excel in everything else . . . you must excel in this generous undertaking too." The phrase ἐν ταύτῃ τῇ χάριτι illustrates the versatility of the term χάρις in Paul's thought, which is reflected in the rich diversity of renderings of this word here — "act of generosity" (Barclay), "gift of charity" (Betz 37), "service of love" (GNB), "privilege of liberality" (Isaacs), "gracious enterprise" (Moffatt), "generous service" (NEB, REB). Paul's point is that the receipt of χάρις should lead to the giving of χάρις; grace received should prompt grace given.

8:8 Οὐ κατ' ἐπιταγὴν λέγω, ἀλλὰ διὰ τῆς ἑτέρων σπουδῆς καὶ τὸ τῆς ὑμετέρας ἀγάπης γνήσιον δοκιμάζων. "I am not saying this as an order, but by mentioning the eagerness shown by others I am seeking to verify the reality of your own love as well." With λέγω we should probably supply τοῦτο (cf. 1 Cor. 7:6) and find a retrospective reference to v. 7b with its mild imperative rather

---

5. This view is defended at length by Verbrugge 247-51, who takes Paul's assertion in 8:8a literally.

6. But cf. Zerwick §415 and his *Analysis* 404, where wish and command are subsumed under the imperative. Cf. Robertson 933.

7. Similarly Morrice "ἵνα" 328; Furnish 399. After his examination of possible NT examples of imperatival ἵνα in the light of general Hellenistic usage, Salom concludes that "it is found in both second and third persons and is used for commands, entreaties, and requests" (138).

8. Winer 451; Moulton 178-79; BDF §387 (3); Robertson 994; Moule 144 ("do please abound"); Turner 95; *Insights* 147. Also BAGD 378b; 899c.

9. E.g., NEB; Betz 37 but cf. 58 and n. 145; Wolff 169; Spicq, *Agape* 210, 212.

10. E.g., Goodspeed; Allo 215.

11. See the discussions of Salom and Morrice, "ἵνα," and the literature cited there.

12. BDF §387 (3) rightly observes that περισσεύετε would have been ambiguous (as imperative or indicative).

than a prospective allusion to the direct imperative ἐπιτελέσατε of v. 11.[13] οὐ κατ᾽ ἐπιταγήν has been understood in two ways: Paul is declaring either that he has no specific command from God or Christ regarding the collection to which he can appeal,[14] or that he is not issuing an apostolic directive that he will enforce.[15] Plummer rightly distinguishes the use of οὐ κατ᾽ ἐπιταγήν here and in 1 Cor. 7:6 from the expression κατ᾽ ἐπιταγὴν (τοῦ) θεοῦ in Rom. 16:26; 1 Tim. 1:1; Tit. 1:3 (239). The former negated phrase denotes Paul's refraining from dictatorial tactics (cf. 1:24) or from an assertion of his apostolic authority (cf. Phlm. 8-9). The latter qualified expression refers to the divine will or decree regarding salvation or Paul's apostleship. If in fact Paul was acknowledging in v. 8a the absence of any definitive command of the Lord regarding the collection, we would have expected ἐπιταγή to be qualified by κυρίου, as in 1 Cor. 7:25 (περὶ δὲ τῶν παρθένων ἐπιταγὴν κυρίου οὐχ ἔχω, γνώμην δὲ δίδωμι; cf. 1 Cor. 7:10; 2 Cor. 8:10a). As it is, Paul is not giving his instructions about the collection "by way of command" (de Boor 178; Barrett 216) or "in the spirit of a command" (Williams). He realized that if he resorted to issuing a series of commands that could be obeyed mechanically, his stress on the voluntary nature of Christian giving (see 8:3; 9:5, 7) would be compromised, he could lay himself open to the charge of domineering (cf. 1:24), and both his motivation for promoting the collection and the gift itself might become suspect in the eyes of the Corinthians and the recipients in Jerusalem.

Rather than (note ἀλλά) acting like a dictator and removing the elements of free choice and warm spontaneity from contributors to the collection, Paul preferred to use "friendly emulation" (Bruce 222) as a means of arousing the Corinthians to action and assessing the genuineness of their love. The verb δοκιμάζω means "put to the proof," "approve by testing," "discover to be suitable through examination," and differs from πειράζω ("test") in that it implies an expectation that the testing will produce a positive outcome. The participle δοκιμάζων stands for a finite verb δοκιμάζω (read by D* F G; see Textual Note b.),[16] and the same construction, negative + finite verb + ἀλλά + present participle, is found in 5:12; 7:5. It may bear a telic sense ("in order to prove," Carrez 181; Plummer 239) or a conative ("I am simply trying to test," Williams; similarly GNB). Originally the adjective γνήσιος ("born in wedlock") denoted the natural or legitimate son as opposed to the adopted or illegitimate. Thus, in a figurative sense, it came to mean "regular," "genuine."[17] τὸ τῆς ὑμετέρας ἀγάπης γνήσιον, where the articular neuter singular adjective creates an ab-

---

13. But Verbrugge (280 n. 24) proposes that by omitting τοῦτο Paul is qualifying what follows as well as what precedes: "I am not speaking by way of command [in this matter]."

14. So Carrez 182; Barnett 405-6; Hafemann 336-37, 343-44; cf. Horsley 2.86 (§49).

15. For the use of λέγω referring to a written communication, cf. 1 Cor. 6:5; 7:6; 15:51; 2 Cor. 6:13 (BAGD 469d).

16. But it could be thought of as depending on an implied λέγω (after ἀλλά) (thus Meyer 584).

17. F. Büchsel 1.727.

stract substantive, means "what is genuine with respect to your love" (BDF §263[2]; Turner 14), "the reality/genuineness of your love."[18]

The way Paul sought to verify the reality of the Corinthians' love was "by mentioning the eagerness shown by others." In this phrase διὰ τῆς ἑτέρων σπουδῆς, διά is instrumental,[19] ἑτέρων is a subjective genitive and refers to the Macedonians (cf. 8:1-5),[20] and σπουδῆς bears its customary sense in 2 Corinthians 7–8 of "eagerness," "earnestness," or "enthusiasm."[21] Paul is making use of the example of the Macedonians' enthusiastic generosity as a convenient benchmark or measuring rod that would afford the Corinthians an opportunity of proving to him, to the Jerusalem believers, and to everyone how genuine was their love for fellow believers. The Macedonians had already given such proof (cf. 8:2-5); now was the Corinthians' chance to do the same. This contrast is reflected in the ἑτέρων–ὑμετέρας antithesis and by καί ("[your own love] as well"). In this appeal to the generosity of the Macedonians as a touchstone, the apostle is not promoting a contest among rivals (*pace* Betz 48-49) but encouraging friendly imitation among equals. It was the spectacular success of the collection in Macedonia, contrary to all expectations (8:2-3), that prompted Paul to work toward comparable success in Corinth where the Christians found themselves in much more favorable circumstances. Unlike the Macedonians, they were not facing persecution or experiencing desperate poverty (cf. 8:2).

8:9 γινώσκετε γὰρ τὴν χάριν τοῦ κυρίου ἡμῶν Ἰησοῦ Χριστοῦ. "For you know the grace that was shown by our Lord Jesus Christ." In his effort to prompt the Corinthians to complete their contribution to the collection (v. 6), Paul has appealed thus far to the precedent of the sacrificial and spontaneous generosity of the Macedonians (vv. 1-5), along with their enthusiasm in participating (v. 8), to the Corinthians' own auspicious initial involvement (v. 6), and to their reputation for spiritual excellence (v. 7). Now he appeals to the ultimate incentive for wholehearted participation, the supreme and purest motivation. γάρ introduces the reason why the Corinthians should excel in the grace of giving

18. But, taking γνήσιος in its derived sense of "regular," "in accord with the rule," Spicq argues that Paul is suggesting that generous almsgiving is the "normal" expression of true Christian love. "Generosity is love's way of being 'true'" (*Agape* 197-98; citation from p. 198).

19. It is possible to take διά in this context to mean "in comparison with" (Young and Ford 269; similarly NIV) or "against" (JB, NAB[1], NJB, NRSV), but a simple reference to the conveying of information is adequate, "by mentioning" (Furnish 399; similarly Carrez 181, "je vous cite"), "by telling you" (NEB, REB), "I am merely calling your attention to" (Plummer's paraphrase, 238-39).

20. On ἕτερος = ἄλλος, see Zerwick §153, who discusses NT indications of "the obsolescence in Hellenistic Greek of the category of duality." The difficulty with taking ἑτέρων as an objective genitive ("your eagerness to help others," Spicq, *Agape* 197; also Therrien 98, following the tentative suggestion of Allo 216-17) is that ὑμῶν would have been expected after σπουδῆς to remove ambiguity, and the allusion to the Macedonians in the adjunctive καί ("also," "as well") is obscured.

21. In 8:7 both σπουδή and ἀγάπη are Corinthian qualities, but in 8:8 σπουδή relates to the Macedonians and ἀγάπη to the Corinthians.

(v. 7b)²² or why Paul refrains from reliance on commands to give (v. 8a) (Plummer 240), namely the knowledge that Christ himself gave voluntarily and sacrificially for the benefit of others and so is the supreme model to be followed in giving. This knowledge was held in common by the Corinthians (γινώσκετε)²³ and all believers, who had come to apprehend and encounter the generous kindness of Christ. Both cognitive and experiential knowledge is involved. ἡ χάρις here is the personal quality of benevolence displayed in the gracious action of "becoming poor." Since χάρις here is both an attribute and an act, "benevolence-in-action,"²⁴ the genitive that follows τοῦ κυρίου . . . Ἰησοῦ Χριστοῦ should be regarded as subjective rather than merely possessive. The combination of γινώσκειν and the full title ὁ κύριος Ἰησοῦς Χριστός qualified by the inclusive ἡμῶν suggests that this whole verse may have been a confessional and liturgical affirmation that Paul applies to the Corinthians ("you know").²⁵

ὅτι δι᾽ ὑμᾶς ἐπτώχευσεν πλούσιος ὤν, ἵνα ὑμεῖς τῇ ἐκείνου πτωχείᾳ πλουτήσητε. "That though he was rich he became poor for your sake, so that by his poverty you might become rich." This whole statement defines (ὅτι, "namely that") the nature of Christ's χάρις. The parallelism between ἡ χάρις τοῦ θεοῦ in v. 1 and ἡ χάρις τοῦ κυρίου ἡμῶν Ἰησοῦ Χριστοῦ is evident. Just as the grace of God was displayed in the Macedonians' generous giving (v. 2) and self-giving (v. 4), so also the grace of Christ was shown in this generous self-giving. Within v. 9b also, there is clear parallelism.

ὅτι	δι᾽	ὑμας		ἐπτώχευσεν	πλούσιος ὤν,
ἵνα		ὑμεῖς τῇ ἐκείνου	πτωχείᾳ		πλουτήσητε

If δι᾽ ὑμας is emphatic by position, ὑμεῖς is emphatic by nature: "all for your sake . . . you, yes you" (Plummer 239). With regard to the other two pairs, there are two principal issues: What was the nature of Christ's wealth and poverty? Do ἐπτώχευσεν and τῇ ἐκείνου πτωχείᾳ refer to precisely the same phenomenon?

There is no question that πλουτήσητε, an ingressive aorist ("become rich/ be enriched"), refers to believers' spiritual enrichment, not their economic wealth or security. It denotes their participation, now and in the future, in the benefits of the salvation secured by Christ, including such benefits as forgiveness (5:19), restoration to right relations with God (5:18), and receipt of the

---

22. Thus Thrall, *Particles* 93.

23. That γινώσκετε is indicative, not imperative, is shown by the presence of γάρ, not οὖν, and because knowledge of Christ's self-giving can be assumed to be general Christian property.

24. This meaning of χάρις also suits the Pauline opening salutations where, except for Col. 1:2; 1 Thess. 1:1, Christ is referred to (jointly with God the Father) as the source of χάρις, and the Pauline closing benedictions where sometimes Christ is mentioned (as the possessor and giver of χάρις) (Rom. 16:20; 1 Cor. 16:23; 2 Cor. 13:13 [EVV 13:14]; Gal. 6:18; Phil. 4:23; 1 Thess. 5:28; 2 Thess. 3:18; Phlm. 25) and sometimes χάρις stands alone (Eph. 6:24; Col. 4:18; 1 Tim. 6:21; 2 Tim. 4:22; Tit. 1:4).

25. Cf. Martin 263, citing Kramer §66b.

Spirit (1:22; 5:5). If πλουτήσητε refers to spiritual wealth, it is *a priori* probable that the cognate and parallel term πλούσιος also describes spiritual rather than economic richness.[26] Dunn argues that πλούσιος refers to the spiritual wealth of communion with God and consciousness of sonship (Mark 14:36) enjoyed by Jesus during his earthly life, while ἐπτώχευσεν points to the withdrawal of that communion and his sense of spiritual abandonment on the cross, expressed in the cry of desolation (Mark 15:34).[27] The weakness of this view is its depiction of the riches-poverty contrast merely in terms of the human consciousness of Jesus. This may explain why Dunn later expanded the allusion in "he became poor" to "the tremendous personal cost of Jesus' ministry and particularly the willing sacrifice of his death."[28] But this in turn raises questions about the nature of the richness that preceded the self-impoverishment. More straightforward and more consonant with the temporal riches-poverty sequence is the traditional and prevailing view that πλούσιος describes the glory of heavenly existence and ἐπτώχευσεν points to the relative lowliness and destitution of earthly existence.[29] Christ himself chose[30] to exchange his royal status as an eternal inhabitant of heaven for a slave's status as a temporary resident on earth.[31] If ὤν denotes Christ's real and personal preexistence, ἐπτώχευσεν depicts his preincarnate choice. He surrendered all the insignia of divine majesty and assumed all the frailty and vicissitudes of the human condition.

Our second question involves the relationship between the two cognate words ἐπτώχευσεν and τῇ πτωχείᾳ. Generally the aorist of a stative verb (here πτωχεύω "be extremely poor")[32] denotes entrance upon that state, thus "became poor." Grammarians regularly cite ἐπτώχευσεν as an instance of this ingressive

---

26. But Buchanan has conjectured (202-9) that Jesus was a building contractor and businessman who had given his wealth to some sect and had chosen the role of poverty.

27. *Christology* 121-22; cf. *Theology* 291, where he seems to allow an allusion to Jesus' relative material poverty (cf. Mark 10:28-39; Matt. 8:20/Luke 9:58) in ἐπτώχευσεν, although the principal reference is to Christ's obedience to the point of death on the cross. Murphy-O'Connor adopts a similar view (83), although he finds the thought underlying 8:9 in 5:21 (which suggests that "rich" includes sinlessness and "becoming poor" includes "becoming sin").

28. *Theology* 292.

29. See, e.g., Georgi 83; Craddock 166-68, who includes in Christ's self-impoverishment his subjection to "the elemental powers of the universe."

30. Some translations reflect this point: "he made himself poor" (GNB, NAB[1]; also Spicq 2.310), "he impoverished himself" (Cassirer).

31. With this notion of exchange — poverty instead of riches — 8:9 is unlike Phil. 2:6-7, where it is not the case that the preexistent Christ exchanged "the form of God" for "the form of a slave," but rather "displayed the nature or form of God in the nature or form of a slave" (O'Brien, *Philippians* 224, citing F. F. Bruce, *Philippians* [San Francisco: Harper, 1983] 46). Dunn objects to the traditional interpretation of 8:9 on the ground that Paul would then be speaking — in atypical fashion — of "a one-stage act of abasement" and of Christ's grace *without relating these concepts to the cross and the resurrection* (*Theology* 291). But Paul should not be denied the luxury of conceptual *hapax legomena*.

32. Used literally, πτωχεύω means not merely "I am a poor person (πένης)" but "I am a beggar" or "I am desperately poor," and πτωχεία, "beggarliness," "beggary," or "destitution." Used figuratively, both terms denote extreme deprivation or destitution.

aorist.[33] If this is so, and the reference is to the actual incarnation (= Christ's "becoming flesh" at his conception) and τῇ . . . πτωχείᾳ, an instrumental dative, describes the same event, Paul is affirming that believers' spiritual enrichment (= their salvation) comes "by means of" the incarnation. But such an assertion would compromise his repeated insistence that salvation comes by the death-resurrection of Jesus.[34] There are three possible exits from this dilemma, each of which is satisfactory, although the third is to be preferred.

1. πτωχείᾳ can be given a wider reference than ἐπτώχευσεν, namely the incarnation, life, and death-resurrection of Jesus.
2. The dative τῇ . . . πτωχείᾳ can be taken to mean "as a result of His poverty" (Wand) (dative of cause),[35] with a distinction being drawn between the act of incarnation and its soteriological consequences.
3. ἐπτώχευσεν can be interpreted as a constative aorist,[36] comprehending Christ's incarnation, life, and death-resurrection in a single glance as "becoming poor," as self-impoverishment, with πτωχείᾳ referring to that same sequence of events as "poverty."[37]

On this last view, which we adopt, ἐπτώχευσεν is wider than the Johannine σὰρξ ἐγένετο (John 1:14), which refers to the incarnation itself, and also broader than the Pauline ἑαυτὸν ἐκένωσεν, which is defined modally as μορφὴν δούλου λαβών and ἐν ὁμοιώματι ἀνθρώπων γενόμενος (Phil. 2:7), and so denotes the incarnation and life of Christ.

In this verse, then, Paul is reminding the Corinthians how gracious the Lord Jesus Christ was, for although (ὤν)[38] he was rich beyond telling in the glory of his preexistent life in heaven, he became desperately poor in comparison with that richness, by assuming the relative poverty of his whole life on earth, a poverty that paradoxically brought believers spiritual enrichment. In appealing to Christ's example, Paul is not calling on the Corinthians to contribute to the collection in such a way that they become impoverished and the poor in Jerusalem become rich.[39] Vv. 13-15 address that misunderstanding. Nor is he

33. Burton §§37, 41; Robertson 834; Moule 11; Turner 71-72; *Insights* 150; Fanning 262.
34. E.g., Rom. 5:10; Gal. 6:14.
35. On the dative of cause, see BDF §196; Turner 242. BAGD 674a notes that τῇ . . . πτωχείᾳ may be dative of instrument or of cause.
36. That the aorist of stative verbs can be constative is incontestable (see Fanning 262).
37. Craddock (165-67) takes a similar view, although he retains the term "incarnation" for the whole Christ-event, noting (167) that "by his death, Christ's becoming poor was made complete."
38. "A concessive participle refers to a fact which is unfavorable to the occurrence of the event denoted by the principal verb" (Burton §438, citing 2 Cor. 8:9; 1 Cor. 4:12; Gal. 2:3). Even if ὤν is regarded as temporal, "(at a time) when he was rich" (so Meyer 584), the meaning of the verse is not affected.
39. *Pace* Nickle 18 n. 23, we need not find in the reference to Christ becoming poor Paul's response to a putative excuse of the Corinthians for not contributing to the collection, namely that a substantial contribution would make them economically vulnerable.

issuing a call to abject poverty or to asceticism. But he is seeking to stimulate generous, sacrificial giving. If the Corinthian believers contributed in this way, they would be emulating the Macedonians (vv. 2-5), following Christ's example (v. 9), and exhibiting God's grace (v. 1). The Macedonians gave when they were desperately poor; Christ gave when he was incalculably rich. In their present economic circumstances the Corinthians fitted somewhere between these two extremes.

8:10 καὶ γνώμην ἐν τούτῳ δίδωμι· τοῦτο γὰρ ὑμῖν συμφέρει, οἵτινες οὐ μόνον τὸ ποιῆσαι ἀλλὰ καὶ τὸ θέλειν προενήρξασθε ἀπὸ πέρυσι. "So then, I am simply giving you my advice in this matter. For this is fitting in your case, seeing that you led the way last year not only in taking action but also in desiring to do so." In v. 8 Paul has stated what is not his approach in dealing with the Corinthians in the matter of the collection — he has no intention of resorting to apostolic commands. Here in v. 10 he informs them of his chosen approach "in this matter" — giving them his "considered opinion" (γνώμη, NEB, NJB) about what they should do, that is, his "advice" (NIV, REB; Barrett 216). However, this link between v. 10a and v. 8a does not imply that v. 9 is parenthetical; on the contrary, v. 9 is a motivational climax that shows why commands are unnecessary.

γάρ introduces the reason for this chosen approach. τοῦτο may refer in general to participation in the collection (Windisch 254; Barrett 216), but more probably it summarizes what immediately precedes, namely "my giving you my advice" (Lietzmann 134; Héring 60).[40] Advising rather than commanding was the proper course for Paul to follow in dealing with the Corinthian believers, for it was they who had already led the way in both action and intention. So τοῦτο γὰρ ὑμῖν συμφέρει means "For this is fitting in your case" rather than "for this is to your advantage" (NASB). The expediency implied by συμφέρει ("it is expedient/advantageous/fitting") did not involve some benefit that would accrue to the Corinthians if they completed their collection, but rather was appropriate or advantageous action that Paul himself was taking in the case of the Corinthians (ὑμῖν, "in your case"). What made their case distinctive was the fact that they enjoyed a special place in the history of the collection project: they had made a beginning (προενήρξασθε) before other contributors in two respects, being the first to start contributing (τὸ ποιῆσαι), and even before that, the first to decide to contribute (τὸ θέλειν). That beginning was made as far back as "last year" (ἀπὸ πέρυσι).

Several aspects of this understanding of the verse merit more attention. Although in Biblical Greek the distinction between ὅς and ὅστις is not regularly maintained, sometimes the context supports a distinction, with ὅστις bearing a

---

40. The RSV, however, seems to take τοῦτο as prospective, looking forward to νυνὶ . . . ἐπιτελέσατε in v. 11, so that vv. 10b-11a define Paul's advice. "And in this matter I give my advice: it is best for you now to complete what a year ago you began not only to do but to desire." But this overlooks δὲ καί and the repetition of τὸ ποιῆσαι and weakens οἵτινες and the one imperative, ἐπιτελέσατε) in 2 Corinthians 8–9.

qualitative sense ("being of such a character as to . . .") or a causal meaning ("inasmuch as").[41] Here, either sense is suitable. The Corinthians were distinctive either as "people who . . ." or "seeing that you. . . ." The two articular infinitives, τὸ ποιῆσαι and τὸ θέλειν, are direct objects of προενήρξασθε[42] and are anaphoric in import, pointing to well-known facts.[43] The difference in tense between the two infinitives (ποιῆσαι — θέλειν) is significant. The Corinthians' active participation in the collection had been interrupted before the time of writing but their desire or will to contribute remained steady.[44] But why does Paul mention action before intent in a construction (οὐ μόνον . . . ἀλλὰ καί)[45] that suggests that the second element is even more important than the first? The unexpected order reflects Paul's emphasis throughout 2 Corinthians 8–9 on attitude and motivation rather than on the material result.[46] If intent remains present and with it motivation, from one viewpoint acting on one's intent may be assumed to follow. On the other hand, if desire and motivation lapse, action becomes unlikely. By inverting the natural order, Paul is highlighting the priority of motivation in both time and importance[47] and also complimenting the Corinthians for their unswerving desire to participate in the project. We may explain the προ- in προενήρξασθε (literally, "you began earlier") as "before other contributors" or "before the Macedonians" (who are not mentioned in 1 Cor. 16:1-4), or (BAGD 705b) as anticipating ἀπὸ πέρυσι. The same verb occurred in 8:6 (προενήρξατο) in reference to Titus's role in helping to initiate contributions to the collection in Corinth. Here the verb refers to that same general time ("last year") but focuses on the Corinthians' own dual role in "beginning" the collection — their desire and decision to participate and their actual initial participation.[48]

ἀπὸ πέρυσι qualifies προενήρξασθε rather than τὸ θέλειν alone. This phrase means "last year" (MM 510d), that is, "in/during the past year," but it is uncertain which calendar Paul was following — one in which the new year began on January 1 (the Roman year), in the spring (the Jewish ecclesiastical year), in midsummer (Athenian Olympiads), or in the fall (the Jewish civil and Macedonian year).[49] However, it seems likely that Paul, a Roman citizen, writing to a

41. See the discussion in Moule 123-24; Zerwick §§215-20; BAGD 587a, b.

42. But Betz (37) takes the infinitives as accusative of respect ("in regard . . . to").

43. Cf. BDF §399 (1), which notes in general that "without this anaphoric reference, an infinitive as subject or object is usually anarthrous."

44. Cf. Zerwick, *Analysis* 404. There is no suggestion in τὸ θέλειν of Corinthian initiative (*pace* NJB: "You were the first . . . even to conceive the project"; Héring 61).

45. Cf. 7:7; 8:19, 21; 9:12.

46. Nickle 18 n. 24, 126 and n. 213.

47. Betz suggests that Paul "regarded pure activism as easier to accomplish than sincere motivation" (64).

48. Even if a considerable time elapsed between the "desiring" and the "doing," we have no way of determining the length of the interval. Certainly the Corinthians may have agreed to participate long before they began to do so, just as they may have heard of the relief fund long before they decided to contribute.

49. See Allo 218; Windisch 255.

Roman colony (Corinth) probably from Philippi, a Roman colony, would be using the Roman calendar. If so, and if 2 Corinthians 1–9 was written during the summer of 56,[50] "last year" will refer to any time during 55. More specifically, it will denote the time when the Corinthians received Paul's response (in 1 Cor. 16:1-4) to their questions about the collection and acted on his instructions, around spring 55, about fifteen months before 2 Corinthians 1–9 was written.[51]

8:11 νυνὶ δὲ καὶ τὸ ποιῆσαι ἐπιτελέσατε. "But now complete your action as well." Having given the Corinthians a compliment in v. 10 ("You led the way . . ."), he now issues them with a challenge which is essentially, "Finish what you started!" They had demonstrated a considerable time ago ("last year," v. 10) their desire to be involved in the collection project and had actually begun to participate, so that what was now required in their case was simply an exhortation to finish, not a command to begin. The GNB rendering catches the point graphically: "On with it, then, and finish the job!"

νυνὶ δέ ("But now") looks back to ἀπὸ πέρυσι (v. 10), while καί alludes to τὸ θέλειν. They were to complete their action (τὸ ποιῆσαι) on the project as the complement (καί, "as well") of their ongoing desire to participate. ἐπιτελέσατε is the only unambiguous imperative in 2 Corinthians 8–9, although ἵνα . . . περισσεύητε in 8:7 is probably imperatival, "a gentle substitute for the direct imperative" (Plummer 238) (see above on that verse).[52] It is significant that Paul indulges in this "mild injunction" (Martin 265) only after he has mentioned various motives that should impel them to further action (vv. 1-9) and has commended them for their primacy in intent and action (v. 10). This absence of multiple imperatives (cf. 8:8a, "This is not meant as an order," NEB, REB) is no indication that Paul had forfeited much of his authority at Corinth owing especially to the influence of the intruders, but is testimony to his pastoral tact; recourse to commands is out of place where voluntary giving is concerned. ἐπιτελέω was regularly used in connection with the performance of religious rites,[53] but in general use it meant simply "carry a task through to completion" (perfective ἐπι-, Robertson 600). In the Corinthians' case this "completion" probably involved the resumption of the practice of setting aside

---

50. See the Introduction C, number 19.

51. A similar conclusion (about sixteen months) was reached by Lüdemann 97-98. If the RSV rendering of ἀπὸ πέρυσι is followed ("a year ago"), the summer of 55 would (on our analysis) be referred to.

52. Verbrugge (25-94, 145-293) distinguishes what he calls the "commanding letter," represented by 1 Cor. 16:1-2 where Paul assumes the Corinthian acceptance of his authority to issue commands (διέταξα . . . ποιήσατε . . . τιθέτω), from "letters of request," represented by 2 Corinthians 8–9 where Paul merely asks for the Corinthians' compliance, using "a more sophisticated, rhetorical approach" (271). But quite apart from the question whether Verbrugge has been successful in isolating a particular type of ancient letter that may be termed the "commanding letter," one may doubt whether Paul has changed his tactics or leadership style between 1 and 2 Corinthians (252-53, 259-60, 271), given ἐπιτελέσατε (8:11) and ἵνα . . . περισσεύητε (8:7), although Paul sees himself as giving advice (8:10), not as speaking "by way of command" (κατ᾽ ἐπιταγήν, 8:8).

53. See G. Delling, *TDNT* 8.61, and notes on 8:6.

weekly installments (1 Cor. 16:2), so that by the time Paul arrived, the whole project at Corinth would be complete (9:3-5).[54]

ὅπως καθάπερ ἡ προθυμία τοῦ θέλειν οὕτως καὶ τὸ ἐπιτελέσαι ἐκ τοῦ ἔχειν. "So that your eager desire may be matched by your completion of the project, as your resources permit." The purpose of Paul's call for completion (v. 11a) is here stated: a correspondence (καθάπερ . . . οὕτως καί, "just as . . . so also") between the Corinthians' carrying through of the collection project and their original enthusiasm in desiring to participate in it.

The subjunctive ᾖ or γένηται must be supplied after ὅπως (or οὕτως καί), "so that [there may be]." ἡ προθυμία τοῦ θέλειν may be rendered in a variety of ways, depending on whether προθυμία is translated as "readiness," "willingness," or "eagerness," and whether θέλειν is here taken to denote "desire," "will," or "purpose": "readiness of desire" (Cassirer), "willing readiness" (TCNT),[55] "eager willingness" (NIV, NAB²), "willing purpose" (Young and Ford 270), "eagerness of desire" = "eager desire." One might have expected ἡ προθυμία τοῦ θέλειν to be balanced by ἡ προθυμία τοῦ ἐπιτελέσαι, "eagerness in completing [the project]."[56] But while Paul is doubtless concerned that "eagerness" or "willingness" (προθυμία) should continue to be shown, his main concern is for actual completion; hence the simple τὸ ἐπιτελέσαι, "your completion [of the project]."[57] By means of the addendum ἐκ τοῦ ἔχειν (literally, "out of the having") he reassures the Corinthians that he is not expecting them to give "beyond their means" (παρὰ δύναμιν, 8:3) as the Macedonians did. While their giving was to be generous and sacrificial, it was nevertheless to be "in proportion to what you possess" (Betz 37), "according to your means" (Barclay), "so far as your resources permit" (NJB). This phrase, ἐκ τοῦ ἔχειν, is virtually indistinguishable in contextual meaning from κατὰ δύναμιν (8:3) and is similar to the expression καθὸ ἐὰν ἔχῃ ("according to whatever one has") in 8:12.

8:12 εἰ γὰρ ἡ προθυμία πρόκειται, καθὸ ἐὰν ἔχῃ εὐπρόσδεκτος, οὐ καθὸ οὐκ ἔχει. "For if this eager desire to give is present, the gift is fully acceptable according to whatever one has, not according to what one does not have." Paul now explains (γάρ) and reinforces the brief phrase found at the end of v. 11, ἐκ τοῦ ἔχειν, "according to your means." He seems to be anticipating and correcting a possible misunderstanding (= prodiorthosis) of his earlier references or allusions to the Macedonians as a model of Christian giving (8:1-5, 8, 10). "I am not suggesting that you should give 'beyond your means,' as they did, only 'ac-

---

54. But Bruce suggests that Paul is simply requesting "a final, specially liberal, addition" to accumulated installments (221).

55. When "readiness" is used to translate προθυμία, it will signify "(eager) willingness," not "a state of preparedness" (as in the expression "all is in readiness").

56. The NEB and REB rendering in fact reflects such an understanding: "be as eager to complete the scheme as you were to adopt it" (similarly GNB; NLT).

57. Remarkably, there are six uses in vv. 10-11 of the substantival articular infinitive: τὸ ποιῆσαι (twice), τὸ θέλειν, τοῦ θέλειν, τὸ ἐπιτελέσαι, τοῦ ἔχειν.

cording to your means'" (cf. 8:3). V. 12, then, justifies Paul's stance, against the background of v. 3.

In form the verse is aphoristic, which explains why there is no τινί with πρόκειται and no τις with ἔχῃ. εἰ introduces an open condition ("if"), but since the protasis states a condition that must be fulfilled before the protasis is true, εἰ could also be rendered "provided that" (NEB) or "as long as" (JB, NJB). If ἡ προθυμία refers back to ἡ προθυμία τοῦ θέλειν (v. 11), the article may be regarded as anaphoric and the word rendered not simply "eagerness," but "this eager desire" (just mentioned). The προ- in πρόκειται does not denote temporal priority but location, so that the verb should be rendered not "comes first,"[58] but ("lies before one" =) "is present," "is forthcoming" (Cassirer), "already exists" (Barclay).

A distinction should probably be drawn between δεκτός and εὐπρόσδεκτος (see on 6:2), with the latter term having an intensive force, "fully/very acceptable." It is found only five times in the NT, four uses being in Paul.[59] Since we find a deep concern expressed throughout Scripture about God's acceptance or rejection of human offerings or gifts,[60] it is proper to understand (τῷ) θεῷ with εὐπρόσδεκτος.[61] What was acceptable to God was the issue, not what was pleasing to Paul or the Jerusalem believers or what was "appropriate" in the matter of giving. As to the subject of εὐπρόσδεκτος (ἐστιν), there are two options.[62]

1. ἡ προθυμία, taken as a personified abstraction (Meyer 588; Furnish 406). It is difficult to see how "eagerness (to give)" or "willingness (to give)" in itself could be acceptable to God "according to one's possessions." But the difficulty is overcome if the subject of εὐπρόσδεκτος (ἐστιν) is taken to be "eagerness/willingness" as expressed in the act of giving.
2. The gift that is given by the person who has "eager desire" or "willingness." We can reach this conclusion by supplying τινί with πρόκειται or τις with ἔχῃ[63] (hence the -ος termination in εὐπρόσδεκτος)[64] and then ar-

---

58. Cf. Young and Ford 270: "For if that purpose comes first, . . ."; also KJV ("For if there be first . . .").

59. In 2 Cor. 6:2 it means "(the time) of God's good favor" (interpreting Isa. 49:8). Spicq (2.137) proposes that in Rom. 15:16 the sense is "very acceptable [to God]," and in Rom. 15:31 "much appreciated." In 1 Pet. 2:5 sacrifices that are offered through Jesus Christ are said to be "fully acceptable to God" (εὐπροσδέκτους θεῷ) because they are spiritual.

60. E.g., Gen. 4:3-5 (cf. Heb. 11:4); 8:20-21; Lev. 9:22-24; Phil. 4:18; Heb. 13:16.

61. So, explicitly, NEB, GNB, REB. For explicit reference to God in connection with pleasing "sacrifices," see Rom. 12:1 (θυσίαν . . . εὐάρεστον τῷ θεῷ); Phil. 4:18 (θυσίαν δεκτήν, εὐάρεστον τῷ θεῷ); Heb. 13:16 (τοιαύταις . . . θυσίαις εὐαρεστεῖται ὁ θεός).

62. An impersonal subject ("it is acceptable") would require εὐπρόσδεκτον.

63. C² L add τις after ἔχῃ, while D F G add it after ἔχει. Goodspeed has "If a man is willing to give. . . ."

64. The gender of εὐπρόσδεκτος (masculine or feminine) must be accounted for. It is arbitrary — even if convenient — to supply ἡ δωρεά.

guing that by metonymy "a person" here stands for "a person's gift,"[65] "the gift[66] (in question)." This explanation of the subject of εὐπρόσδεκτος (ἐστιν) is preferable.

If προθυμία is one basis on which God judges the acceptability of a gift, giving in accordance with one's resources is another. καθὸ ἐὰν ἔχῃ means "according to whatever one has," where (1) καθό = καθ' ὅ, "according to what," "in proportion to what," "by its comparison with what" (TCNT), (2) ἐάν = ἄν, (3) [ὅ] ἐάν means "whatever," and (4) ἔχω means "have for disposal."[67] We should carefully differentiate ἐὰν ἔχῃ (subjunctive) from ἔχει (indicative) in the following phrase, οὐ καθὸ οὐκ ἔχει ("not according to what one does not have"). In the former case, the amount possessed is indefinite; in the latter, the non-possession is a definite fact. It is the difference between whatever a person may happen to have and what a person actually does not have.[68] Paul's point is that in evaluating a gift God takes fully into consideration an individual's particular economic circumstances. As 1 Cor. 16:2 had expressed it, the Corinthians were each to put aside and save some money, "however one has prospered." God does not expect people to do the impossible and give what they do not possess at the time, what is unavailable for disposal.

Several significant principles of Christian stewardship emerge from this verse.

1. All giving is conducted under God's omniscient gaze. Whatever is the motivation of the giver of a gift and whatever is the reaction of its recipient, God is the final adjudicator of the gift's value.

2. There are two criteria by which God assesses the acceptability of a gift. First, the gift must be an expression of an "eager desire to give" (ἡ προθυμία [12] = ἡ προθυμία τοῦ θέλειν [11]). In vv. 11-12 προθυμία is not merely a willingness or eagerness to give, but an enthusiastic willingness to give that results in actual giving.[69] The corollary of this criterion is that if gifts are reluctantly or grudgingly given (cf. 9:7), they do not receive the divine approval. Second, the gift should be in proportion to one's re-

---

65. Cf. TCNT, "a man's gift." JB has "a man is acceptable. . . ."

66. So Conybeare in Conybeare and Howson 454; Weymouth, Berkeley, NIV, NRSV; Zerwick and Grosvenor 550; Betz 37, 66.

67. For the last point, see Lietzmann 134; Cassirer, "proportionate to whatever means may be at a person's disposal." But Hughes (305 n. 30) argues strongly that ἔχειν here means "to be able": "readiness, when it is present, is acceptable in accordance with the measure of its ability, not in accordance with what is impossible" (305, taking ἡ προθυμία as the subject of ἔχῃ and ἔχει).

68. So Winer 307; Plummer 244; Zerwick, *Analysis* 404-5.

69. Cf. *EDNT* 3.156 and K. H. Rengstorf (*TDNT* 6.699) who observes that Paul's "concern is for an attitude which will be more than a ready agreement with his project, which will be characterized by action as well as willingness, and which will thus rest on a consciously accepted obligation that is nevertheless free and not grounded in command or law." Rengstorf suggests the rendering "cheerful resolution" for the four uses of προθυμία in 2 Corinthians 8–9.

sources.[70] On this principle no person can claim an exemption from the obligation to give; no one is too poor to give — witness the case of the desperately poor Macedonians (8:2). In enunciating this principle of giving ἐκ τοῦ ἔχειν (8:11) or καθὸ ἐὰν ἔχῃ (8:12), Paul is advocating prudence and the avoidance of recklessness in giving. However, occasional disproportionate giving, that is, giving beyond one's actual resources (παρὰ δύναμιν, 8:3), is a tribute and testimony to God's grace (8:1-2). Yet if such disproportionate giving were the norm, resources for giving would be rapidly depleted (9:10 not withstanding).

3. If Paul had advocated the practice of tithing, this would have been an appropriate place for him to mention or defend it. But so far from championing the practice of giving by percentage, he argues for proportional giving.

Bibliography

P. Angstenberger, *Der reiche und der arme Christus. Die Rezeptionsgeschichte von 2 Kor 8,9 zwischen dem zweiten und dem sechsten Jahrhundert* (Hereditas 12) (Bonn: Borengässer, 1997) • Ascough • Barrett, "Titus" • J. M. Bassler, *God and Mammon: Asking for Money in the New Testament* (Nashville: Abingdon, 1991) • R. Brändle, "Geld und Gnade (zu II Kor 8,9)," *TZ* 41 (1985) 264-71 • Craddock • F. B. Craddock, *The Pre-Existence of Christ in the New Testament* (Nashville: Abingdon, 1968) 99-106 • W. P. de Boer, *The Imitation of Paul* (Kampen: Kok, 1962) 61-62 • Dunn, *Christology* 121-23 • Dunn, *Theology* 291-92 • Dupont, "Christ" • Fee, *Presence* 339 • A. Feuillet, "L'homme-Dieu considéré dans sa condition terrestre," *RB* 51 (1942) 70-73 • Feuillet, *Christologie* • Georgi 82-84 • J. Habermann, *Präexistenzaussagen im Neuen Testament* (Europäische Hochschulschriften, Series XXIII, vol. 362; Frankfurt am Main: Lang, 1990) • Hamerton-Kelly • Larsson • Murphy-O'Connor 81-85 • Nickle 18, 126 • Panikulam 51-53 • Ross • Salom • W. Schrage, *Die konkreten Einzelgebote in der paulinischen Paränese* (Gütersloh: Mohn, 1961) • D. M. Stanley 144-45 • Theobald 281-83 • Therrien 97-100, 253 • Verbrugge 247-54

3. The Aim of Equality (8:13-15)

In the first twelve verses of 2 Corinthians 8 Paul has pointed the Corinthians to the sterling example of the Macedonians as worthy of emulation. References to these other contributors to the collection are explicit in vv. 1-5, 8 and implicit in vv. 10-12. Now, in vv. 13-15, he begins to discuss the relationship between the Corinthians and the recipients of this charitable gift, "the poor among the saints in Jerusalem" (Rom. 15:26), who are referred to explicitly by the word ἐκείνων

---

70. In Tob. 4:8 almsgiving is to be "according to your wealth (κατὰ τὸ πλῆθος)" or "according to the little you have (κατὰ τὸ ὀλίγον)." See also Philo, *Quis Rerum Divinarum Heres Sit* 145; and, for this principle of proportionate giving in Judaism, SB 3.523.

(v. 14, twice) and implicitly by the word ἄλλοις (v. 13) and the expression ὁ τὸ ὀλίγον [ἔχων] (v. 15). The focus in these three verses is on one of the purposes of the collection project — the achievement of "equality" (ἐξ ἰσότητος, v. 13; ὅπως γένηται ἰσότης, v. 14) between the relatively prosperous Corinthians and the poor within the Jerusalem church. He shows that this is a divinely sanctioned goal by citing an incident during the wilderness journey of God's people when God himself created comparable equality by miraculously equalizing the quantities of manna that each person had gathered (v. 15).

13*Certainly our intention is not that others should have relief and^a you hardship; rather, it is a question of equality.* 14*At the present moment your surplus can meet their deficiency, so that some day their surplus can^b in turn meet your deficiency, in order that there may be equality —* 15*as it is written, "The person who had much did not have too much, and the one who had little did not have too little."*

TEXTUAL NOTES

a. The insertion of δέ after ὑμῖν (ℵ² D F G Ψ 𝔐 lat syr^h Clement Ambrosiaster) relieves the asyndeton and makes explicit the contrast between ἄλλοις ἄνεσις and ὑμῖν θλῖψις, but this reading is clearly a stylistic amelioration and therefore inferior. The reading without δέ (ℵ* B C 048 0243 33 81 323 1739 1881 *pc* d p Cyprian) is to be preferred.

b. To avoid two successive cases of γένηται and to create precise parallelism with the preceding clause, some witnesses (p^46 0243 630 1175 1739 1881 *pc*) omit the γένηται before εἰς τὸ ὑμῶν ὑστέρημα.

8:13 οὐ γὰρ ἵνα ἄλλοις ἄνεσις, ὑμῖν θλῖψις, ἀλλ' ἐξ ἰσότητος. "Certainly our intention is not that others should have relief and you hardship; rather, it is a question of equality." We cannot be sure what prompted this typical Pauline οὐ . . . ἀλλά contrast. He could be giving the reason (γάρ, "for") he was advocating proportional giving (in vv. 11-12), "not so that . . . but out of a concern for equality." But it is better to relate this verse to the wider context and see it as affirming (γάρ, "certainly")[1] one of Paul's aims in prosecuting this whole collection project,[2] against the backdrop of an actual or possible Corinthian objection to the scheme:[3] "he wants to burden us so that others can take their ease," or "If

1. For this sense of γάρ, see BAGD 152 s.v. 3. Most EVV leave γάρ untranslated.
2. Cf. Betz's rendering "For the purpose [of the collection] is . . ." (37).
3. Alternatively, but less probably, he may have been concerned lest any of his addressees should imagine that he was expecting them to follow Christ's example (8:9) slavishly, for Christ had exchanged "riches" for "poverty" in order to "enrich" others. Barnett considers 8:8-15 under the heading "Possible Misunderstandings Anticipated" (404) and identifies three possible misunderstandings to which Paul is responding (388, 404-5): he is giving "advice," not a "command" (8:8-11); he is not calling the Corinthians to give more than they have (8:11-12); the Jerusalemites' relief is not at the expense of Corinthian impoverishment (8:13-15).

we give sacrificially, the Jerusalem poor will be financially comfortable, and we economically depressed."

There is no need to regard οὐ . . . ἵνα as imperatival, "Let there not be . . ." or to supply θέλω or (τοῦτο) λέγω before ἵνα. The phrase expresses content, "It is not that," "There is no question (of relieving others)" (NEB, REB), or purpose, "Our intention is not that." After ἵνα we must supply ᾖ (Robertson 395) or γένηται (cf. v. 14; 1 Cor. 1:31) (BAGD 378c): "our aim is not that there should be relief for others and hardship for you." Both ἄλλοις and ὑμῖν are datives of respect (or of "advantage" and "disadvantage," respectively), with ἄλλοις referring principally to the Jerusalem poor[4] and ὑμῖν referring to the Corinthians as representative of all contributors to the collection. While θλῖψις is a common Paul word, especially in 2 Corinthians,[5] ἄνεσις is rare, with 2 Thess. 1:7 the only Pauline instance outside 2 Corinthians (2:13; 7:5; 8:13). The contrast between this pair of words (cf. 2 Thess. 1:6-7), which is heightened by asyndeton, is that between economic hardship (θλῖψις) and relief from economic drought (ἄνεσις). Paul is repudiating any suggestion that his purpose in conducting this relief operation was to create luxury in Jerusalem but privation in Corinth and elsewhere. The rich were not being called to embrace poverty so that the poor might become rich; that would simply perpetuate inequality. Rather (ἀλλά), it was a matter of pursuing equality. He was calling on those believers who enjoyed a greater share of material benefits to ensure that their fellow believers who were economically destitute should not continue in destitution but have sufficient resources to afford the necessities of life.

Following the rejected aim (οὐ . . . ἵνα) comes the positive statement, ἐξ ἰσότητος, "it is a question of establishing equality" (Carrez 184). There is an issue of punctuation at this point. Some Greek texts (WH, UBS¹⁻³), EVV (e.g., Weymouth, RSV, NRSV), and commentators (e.g., Lietzmann 134; Barrett 226) place some stop after θλῖψις and construe ἐξ ἰσότητος with ἐν τῷ νῦν καιρῷ κτλ., giving a sense such as "I do not mean that . . . , but that as a matter of equality . . ." (RSV; cf. BAGD 381b). Such a construction certainly makes good sense; however, in Paul's use of the οὐ(κ) . . . ἀλλά contrast, the positive element is usually found in the same sentence as the negative element,[6] and this punctuation produces an awkward repetition within one sentence (namely, ἐξ ἰσότητος . . . ἵνα γένηται ἰσότης). So it is preferable to place a stop after ἰσότητος[7] and begin a new sentence with v. 14. In the phrase ἐξ ἰσότητος the preposition specifies the underlying principle ("[it is, ἐστι] on the basis of

---

4. ἑτέροις (cf. ἑτέρων, 8:8) would have referred exclusively to the Jerusalemites (cf. Meyer 589).

5. Of the 45 NT uses of θλῖψις, 24 are found in Paul, of which 9 are in 2 Corinthians (1:4 [twice], 8; 2:4; 4:17; 6:4; 7:4; 8:2, 13; cf. θλίβω, 1:6; 4:8; 7:5).

6. 1:12, 13, 19; 2:4, 17; 4:5; 5:4; 10:13; 12:14 (10:12 is not a true exception).

7. Thus NA²⁷, UBS⁴; and, e.g., NEB, NASB, JB, NIV, NJB, REB; Lang 319; Wolff 170. On this view, the phrase balancing οὐ . . . ἵνα is simply ἀλλ' ἐξ ἰσότητος. Admittedly, this makes v. 14 asyndetic. (Some versions begin v. 14 with ἀλλ', e.g., NEB, REB.)

equality" [BAGD 235d]) or the effective cause ("because of [the need for] equality" (de Boor 178)).[8]

ἰσότης ("equality," "fair dealing") was an important concept in mathematics, law, philosophy, and political theory. "The high regard of the Greeks for ἰσότης is reflected in its personification in Euripides (*Phoen.* 536) and in its evaluation by Aristotle as a means of fostering unity and solidarity in the state."[9] It was also seen as a key element in interpersonal relations, so that true friends were ἴσοι καὶ ὅμοιοι, equal in value, like-minded, and committed to each other.[10] So when Paul appeals to the need for equality, he presupposes the Corinthians' commitment to the well-known principle of equality and fair dealing (cf. Col. 4:1) and in particular their awareness of the commonality, friendship, and solidarity in Christ that bound Gentile and Jewish Christians together.

8:14 ἐν τῷ νῦν καιρῷ τὸ ὑμῶν περίσσευμα εἰς τὸ ἐκείνων ὑστέρημα. "At the present moment your surplus can meet their deficiency." Paul now explains how the equality (ἰσότης) he has just mentioned will be achieved between the Corinthian and Jerusalemite believers at the present time (v. 14a) and in the indefinite future (v. 14b). In the phrase ὁ νῦν καιρός, the temporal adverb νῦν functions as an adjective (cf. τὸ νῦν, 5:16). Although the phrase in Romans (Rom. 3:26; 8:18; 11:5) refers to the present Christian dispensation, and not simply to "the present circumstances," there is no justification (*pace* Martin 267-70) for finding here in v. 14 a contrast between "the present time (= age)" and "the age to come" when God's final purposes for the world will be fulfilled.[11] Corresponding to "at the present time" is an implied indefinite time such as "later on" (Weymouth) or "some day" (Barclay) or "at some future date."

Whether we render τὸ περίσσευμα as "abundance" or "surplus," the reference is to the relative wealth of the Corinthians in comparison with οἱ πτωχοί in the Jerusalem church (Rom. 15:26).[12] Paul knew — probably from personal experience and observation — that the majority, if not all, of the Corinthians had some disposal income, some money available to them on a regular basis (cf. 1 Cor. 16:2) that was over and above what they needed for essentials.[13] It was this "surplus," accumulated in weekly installments (1 Cor. 16:2), that would

8. But Georgi (87-89) takes ἐκ as meaning "out of" or "from" (with ἐξ ἰσότητος as "practically interchangeable with ἐκ θεοῦ," 89), so that the divine principle of ἰσότης is "the actual source of giving and receiving" (89).

9. G. Stählin, *TDNT* 3.346; cf. Iori 425-38. On Philo's treatise on ἰσότης (*Quis Rerum Divinarum Heres Sit* 141-206) and its possible relation to Paul's thought in 8:13-15, see Georgi 85-91, 138-40.

10. Cf. G. Stählin, *TDNT* 3.346-47.

11. The difficulty with this view is that the purpose of the reciprocal giving mentioned in v. 14 is said to be "equality" (ὅπως γένηται ἰσότης), which most naturally refers to the same type of "equality" as in v. 13b, viz. economic parity.

12. Cf. the use of ἐπτώχευσεν and τῇ πτωχείᾳ in 8:9 in reference to relative poverty.

13. Cf. Murphy-O'Connor 77, who also observes that since the Corinthians were to save in order to contribute, they must not have had a sizeable surplus.

meet the "deficiency" or "shortage" or "shortfall" (τὸ ὑστέρημα; cf. 9:12)[14] of those in Jerusalem (ἐκείνων).[15] With εἰς we must supply ἔσται or γίνεται (cf. γένηται εἰς in the parallel phrase in v. 14b); thus "(your surplus) will make up for/can supply (their deficiency)."[16]

Reasons for the poverty among some members of the Jerusalem church are discussed in the Introduction (B.5.a). Some have suggested that in organizing the collection Paul was responding to a specific need in Jerusalem, such as the failure of the harvest in the fall of A.D. 54, a sabbatical year.[17] But the lengthy period involved in arranging for this relief fund — about five years, A.D. 53-57 — suggests, rather, that Paul was addressing a long-standing need. Then there is the request of the three "pillars" in the Jerusalem church in A.D. 46 that Paul and Barnabas should "go on remembering the poor" (τῶν πτωχῶν ἵνα μνημονεύωμεν, Gal. 2:10). Two separate monetary collections for the church in Jerusalem were made, one prompted by famine in Judea (Acts 11:28), organized by the believers in Syrian Antioch, and delivered by Paul and Barnabas in A.D. 46 (Acts 11:29-30; Gal. 2:1-3, 6-10), which was the prototype for the second, "the great collection," organized by Paul and delivered by him and delegates from the Gentile churches in A.D. 57 (Acts 20:4; 21:17; Rom. 15:25-31; 1 Cor. 16:1-4; 2 Corinthians 8–9).

ἵνα καὶ τὸ ἐκείνων περίσσευμα γένηται εἰς τὸ ὑμῶν ὑστέρημα, ὅπως γένηται ἰσότης. "So that some day their surplus can in turn meet your deficiency, in order that there may be equality." At first sight it might appear that ἵνα points to a motive that could impel the Corinthians to meet the "deficiency" at Jerusalem from their "surplus" (v. 14a). That is, provided they contributed at the present time, they could rest assured that on some future occasion, in a reversal of circumstances and roles, those at Jerusalem would relieve their need. Such motivation, however, would fly in the face of Jesus' call to do good, "expecting nothing in return" (Luke 6:35). It is therefore preferable to treat ἵνα as introducing a divinely ordered purpose,[18] or (better) as ecbatic in import, stating a consequence. On this latter view, the outcome of Corinthian giving according to their present resources would be reciprocity (cf. καί, "in turn") if there were a change of economic circumstances in Corinth and Jerusalem. Cer-

---

14. On the περίσσευμα–ὑστέρημα pair, see Prümm II.2.31-33.

15. Twice in this verse ἐκείνων is opposed to ὑμῶν (in an ABBA pattern), denoting "persons in their absence deictically" (Turner 45; cf. 46).

16. The difficulty with taking τὸ ὑμῶν περίσσευμα to mean "a larger contribution from you," and τὸ ἐκείνων ὑστέρημα, "a small contribution from others" (the paraphrase of Isaacs) is that Paul has ἐκείνων, not ἑτέρων (cf. 8:8), referring to the poor in Jerusalem, not "others" (= other contributors).

17. So Jeremias, *Abba* 237-38.

18. Doubting whether 8:14 is in fact a concession to Greek thinking (i.e., *do ut des,* "I give so that you may give [in return]"), G. Stählin asks, "May it not be that the ἰσότης commended by Paul is an application of the Golden Rule of Lk. 6:31, especially if we do not link the ἵνα of v. 14 too closely with what precedes, but see in it the indication of a divinely given objective rather than of human purposes, as in the concluding ὅπως clause?" (*TDNT* 3.348).

tainly Paul is not predicting economic dearth in Corinth and prosperity in Jerusalem; indeed, the chronic poverty in Jerusalem and the long-standing prosperity of Corinth rendered it unlikely that there would ever be such an economic reversal. But it is the principle of reciprocal sharing that Paul is defending.

But not all scholars understand the second περίσσευμα and ὑστέρημα in v. 14 as references to a financial surplus and shortfall. As a result of receiving financial aid from their Gentile brothers and sisters, Jerusalem believers would continue to supply them with their "surplus," the spiritual blessings of the gospel (cf. Rom. 15:27),[19] including advice, example, and prayers. Such an interpretation is certainly admissible, but it has several disadvantages: (1) it compromises the parallelism between the two parts of v. 14 which is highlighted by καί, "in turn"; (2) it dilutes the implicit "now–then" contrast in v. 14 that points to a purely future Jerusalem "surplus"; and (3) it does not cohere naturally with the OT allusion in v. 15 that describes purely material equality.

Such reciprocity in sharing material resources had the purpose (cf. ὅπως) of establishing "equality." Vv. 13 and 14 both end with a reference to ἰσότης, which is "the criterion (ἐξ ἰσότητος) and goal (ὅπως γένηται ἰσότης) of action" (G. Stählin, *TDNT* 3.348). Although equality in this context does not refer to the absence of distinction and the parity of status between Jew and Gentile in Christ (Rom. 10:12; Gal. 3:28), it is certainly a natural expression of the parity and unity that exist among all believers. Here ἰσότης involves (negatively) the equalization of economic burdens and (positively) the equal supply of the necessities of life. It is achieved by giving that is proportionate to the resources available at any given time (vv. 11-12).

8:15 καθὼς γέγραπται, Ὁ τὸ πολὺ οὐκ ἐπλεόνασεν, καὶ ὁ τὸ ὀλίγον οὐκ ἠλαττόνησεν. " — as it is written, 'The person who had much did not have too much, and the one who had little did not have too little.'" The equalization of provision that v. 14 has spoken of is now illustrated from the experience of God's people in the wilderness (Exod. 16:11-36).[20] In response to the grumbling of the Israelites about the food available in the wilderness, God provided them with quail in the evening and "thin flakes like frost" (= manna) in the morning (Exod. 16:13-14). There were three requirements regarding this manna. People were to gather an omer each (= about 2 quarts or 2.3 liters, by dry measure) (Exod. 16:16, 18); it was to be eaten on the day it was gathered, otherwise it became wormy and vile-smelling (Exod. 16:19-20); it was to be gathered before it melted (Exod. 16:21). Probably because of differences in age and vigor, some people gathered a lot and some a little (Exod. 16:17). But in the process of measuring the manna after it had been collected, there was a miracu-

19. So, e.g., Allo 220-21; Zerwick, *Analysis* 405; U. Wilckens, *TDNT* 8.598; Nickle 120-21, 121 n. 179. Barnett combines both exegetical options regarding περίσσευμα and ὑστέρημα in 8:14b. The Corinthians would definitely benefit from the Jerusalemites' "loving and prayerful fellowship," and would relieve the Corinthians' shortfall "if reversed economic circumstances arose" (414).

20. For the association of the term ἰσότης with Exod. 16:18, see Philo, *Quis Rerum Divinarum Heres Sit* 191.

lous equalizing of supply to one omer apiece, so that "the one who gathered a lot had nothing over, and the one who gathered a little had no shortage" (Exod. 16:18). It has been suggested that the shortfall of some was relieved by the generous and voluntary giving of those who had gathered more than they needed,[21] but the account is silent about any such sharing, and the phrase "when they measured it [the collected manna] by the omer" in v. 18 points to God's miraculous intervention at that time, comparable to his ensuring that there was no putrefaction on the Sabbath of the double measure of manna gathered on the sixth day (Exod. 16:20-24).[22]

This is the fourth of the five places in 2 Corinthians where the OT is cited.[23] καθὼς γέγραπται (cf. 9:9) is Paul's favorite introductory formula.[24] The term γέγραπται, common in the papyri in reference to the authoritative character of a document,[25] points to the permanence of the scriptural text as well as its authority ("it stands written").

Paul's citation is drawn from the LXX but differs from it in three respects.

LXX	Paul
καὶ μετρήσαντες τῷ γομὸρ	
οὐκ ἐπλεόνασεν ὁ τὸ πολύ,	ὁ τὸ πολὺ οὐκ ἐπλεόνασεν,
καὶ ὁ τὸ	καὶ ὁ τὸ
ἔλαττον	ὀλίγον
οὐκ ἠλαττόνησεν	οὐκ ἠλαττόνησεν

1. Paul omits "and when they measured it by the omer" because this is not relevant to his central point of the equality of divine provision in spite of initial differences.
2. He moves ὁ τὸ πολύ to the beginning of the sentence to create precise parallelism between the two parts.
3. He replaces ἔλαττον ("less") by ὀλίγον to emphasize the deep poverty of the Jerusalem poor.[26]

Although Paul does not explicitly apply the citation to the matter under discussion, clearly he regards ὁ τὸ πολύ as descriptive of the Corinthians and ὁ τὸ ὀλίγον as referring to the Jerusalem poor. With ὁ we must supply in each case the participle ἔχων,[27] "the person who had," although some prefer, on the

21. So Spicq 2.230-31. Hughes suggests that there was a pooling of all the manna collected, followed by an equitable distribution to each person (307).
22. Cf. B. J. Malina, *The Palestinian Manna Tradition* (Leiden: Brill, 1968) 17.
23. The others are found at 4:13; 6:2, 16-18; 9:9. On the use of the OT in 2 Corinthians, see Hafemann, "Argument" 282-87; "Old Testament" 246-57.
24. See Ellis 22-25, 48-49.
25. Deissmann 113-14, 249-50; MM 133a.
26. For alternative explanations of the differences from the LXX, see Stanley 231-33.
27. Thus, e.g., Winer 589; Lietzmann 135; Robertson 1202; Georgi 198 n. 20.

basis of references to "gathering" in Exod. 16:16-17 (cf. Exod. 16:21-22, 26-27), to supply συλλέξας,[28] "the person who gathered." It is preferable to supply ἔχων, given the three uses of ἔχειν in 8:11-12 and the fact that the Corinthians are to "scatter" rather than "gather" (cf. 9:9). Paul's reference to this OT incident is so brief and so lacking in detail that we must assume that his addressees were familiar with the story; he is counting on shared knowledge.

Both ἐπλεόνασεν and ἠλαττόνησεν are constative aorists that view repeated states in a summary fashion. Each time manna was collected and then measured, the person who had gathered more than was necessary or permitted found that he had nothing over the one omer limit, while the person who had gathered only a small amount discovered that he did not fall short of the limit. ἐλαττονέω, "have less" (cf. ἐλάσσων, "less"), "go short," "possess too little of something," is a NT *hapax* and rare in the papyri.[29] The articular neuter singular adjectives τὸ πολύ and τὸ ὀλίγον refer to a particular definite entity (BDF §263 [1]), "a large amount" and "a small amount."

By his appeal to the story of the manna Paul is not simply illustrating the principle of equity between the "haves" and the "have-nots." This Exodus incident affords divine sanction for the principle, for God not only provided the Israelites with the food necessary for maintaining life but also acted equitably, so that inequalities were eliminated. Nevertheless, there is an implicit contrast between Israelite and Christian experience.[30] The equality that the people of God of old experienced in the wilderness was the result of a divine miracle and was enforced and inescapable. The equality to be experienced by the new people of God, on the other hand, would be the result of human initiative and would be voluntary and so not automatic.[31]

Bibliography

Ascough • Barrett, "Titus" • Dupont, "Christ" • Georgi 84-92 • Hanson 174-77 • Hays 87-91 • Iori • Koch, *Schrift* 258-60 • Nickle • Stanley 231-33 • Theobald 284-89

B. The Mission of Titus and His Companions (8:16–9:5)

2 Corinthians 8–9 is basically Paul's summons to the Corinthians to fulfill their intent (8:11; 9:2) and their promise (9:5) to contribute to his collection for destitute believers in Jerusalem (9:12; Rom. 15:26). At the beginning and end of

---

28. Thus, e.g., BDF §481; Zerwick, *Analysis* 405; Furnish 408.

29. Spicq (1.469) cites three examples from the papyri.

30. In his discussion of Paul's use of Exod. 16:18, Hays speaks of "the full range of resonant significations evoked by Paul's metaleptic use of quotation . . . here in 2 Cor. 8:15 his pithy quotation, without even mentioning Moses or manna or Israel, rings like a tuning fork struck and balanced on a sounding surface. Little is said, much suggested" (90-91).

31. Cf. Windisch 259.

these two chapters he focuses on the motives that should impel them to prompt action, describing first the need for generosity in giving (8:1-15), then the results of such generosity (9:6-15). Nestled between these two sections that deal with motivation for action is a passage (8:16–9:5) in which Paul indicates how he plans to facilitate the fulfillment of their intent and promise. He is about to dispatch a three-man delegation to Corinth (8:16-24), who, in advance of his own arrival, will assist the progress of the collection and oversee its completion, so that pressured giving can be avoided once he arrives (9:3-5).

1. The Delegates and Their Credentials (8:16-24)

We have argued in the Introduction (A.4) that Paul's main purpose in writing this letter was to prepare the way so that his imminent visit to Corinth would be enjoyable. One crucial aspect of that preparation was the dispatch to Corinth of Titus, his personal delegate, and two Christian brothers, appointees of the Macedonian churches, to facilitate arrangements for the completion of the collection. Now, finally, after more than seven chapters, Paul formally introduces and commends these three men who themselves will have delivered to the Corinthians for public reading this letter that announces that imminent visit. 8:16-23 forms Paul's own "letter of commendation" (ἐπιστολὴ συστατική; cf. 3:1-3; 3 John 12), with a direct appeal to the Corinthians attached (8:24). Following traditional procedures for the commissioning of an emissary or delegate,[1] Paul mentions three items regarding each of the delegates — identification, relationship to the sender(s), and credentials for the intended role.

There are three notable characteristics of Paul's "letter of accreditation" for these emissaries. First, the authorization is markedly *personal*. Titus shares Paul's own zeal (τὴν αὐτὴν σπουδήν) for the Corinthians (8:16) and is his partner (κοινωνὸς ἐμός) and comrade in toil (συνεργός) (8:23). Both the unnamed brothers are being sent by Paul (συνεπέμψαμεν, 8:18, 22) and are his brothers in Christ (τὸν ἀδελφὸν ἡμῶν, 8:22; ἀδελφοὶ ἡμῶν, 8:23). The first brother was appointed by the churches to be Paul's traveling companion (συνέκδημος ἡμῶν, 8:19) in dealing with the collection, while Paul himself had verified the earnestness of the second brother in many ways and often (ἐδοκιμάσαμεν, 8:22). Second, the accreditation is not only personal but also *ecclesial*. Although Titus was going to Corinth as Paul's personal envoy and as leader of the delegation (see on 8:16), the two associates who were accompanying him were delegates of the (Macedonian) churches (ἀπόστολοι ἐκκλησιῶν, 8:23), with the first brother highly respected throughout all the (Macedonian) churches (διὰ πασῶν τῶν ἐκκλησιῶν, 8:18) for his services to the gospel and duly appointed by them (χειροτονηθεὶς ὑπὸ τῶν ἐκκλησιῶν, 8:19) to act as Paul's traveling companion.

---

1. See Betz 40-41, 70-82, 137-39. But one need not follow Betz in regarding the rhetoric of 8:16-23 as "administrative, or juridical" (139), and 8:24 as the *peroratio* of a judicial speech.

Third, the authorization of the two brothers is *christological*. They were δόξα Χριστοῦ (8:23), men whose character and conduct were a credit to Christ and brought him honor. Moreover, we may fairly assume that, along with Paul about whom this is said, they were involved in the relief operation "to promote the honor of the Lord himself" (πρὸς τὴν αὐτοῦ τοῦ κυρίου δόξαν, 8:19). Already being men in whom Christ was glorified, they were aiming to honor him still further.

But in 8:16-23 Paul is not simply declaring the credentials of the three delegates. He is also writing defensively, countering actual or possible allegations about the sincerity and transparency of his motives (8:19-21; cf. 1:17; 2:17; 4:2; 5:12; 6:3; 10:2), particularly regarding money matters (cf. 7:2; 12:16-18). He is engaged in a delicate balancing act, wanting to avoid any suggestion that the collection was merely a tool for his self-aggrandizement (cf. 8:19, "for the glory of the Lord *himself*"), yet unable to deny that the whole enterprise was his own and that he was ultimately its administrator (. . . τῇ διακονουμένῃ ὑφ᾽ ἡμῶν, 8:19-20), even if he was working with and through colleagues. The net result of his own accreditation and dispatch of the three men on their mission to Corinth was to distance himself from the detailed organization of the relief operation. He was aiming to do what was right in the eyes of the Corinthians (8:21), which involved the avoidance of any direct contact with the funds being collected and the provision of independent witnesses and collaborators to ensure the integrity of the scheme.

8:16*Thanks be to God, who has put[a] in the heart of Titus the same zeal for you as I have.* 17*For, to be sure, he welcomed our appeal, but being extremely zealous he is setting off to visit you on his own accord.* 18*With him we are sending the brother[b] who is praised throughout all the churches for his work for the gospel.* 19*In addition to this, he has also been appointed by the churches to be our traveling companion in connection with[c] this work of grace that we are administering in order to honor the Lord himself[d] and to show our goodwill.* 20*We are putting this precaution in place lest anyone should discredit us over this lavish gift that we are administering.* 21*Indeed, we are giving forethought[e] to what is honorable, not only in the Lord's[f] eyes but also in human eyes.* 22*In addition, we are sending with them our brother whose eagerness we have often tested and proved in many ways and[g] who is now all the more eager because of[h] his profound confidence in you.* 23*If there is any question about Titus, he is my colleague and fellow worker in your service; if our brothers are in question, they are envoys of the churches and an honor to Christ.* 24*So give these men public proof[i] of your love and of the truth of our boasting about you, so that the churches can see it.*

TEXTUAL NOTES

a. With strong Alexandrian and Western support, the aorist participle δόντι (the reading preferred by UBS[1-4] and NA[27]) has slightly more impressive external support

596

than does the present participle διδόντι with its Alexandrian and Byzantine witnesses. Both readings accord with the context, but the aorist may refer back to Titus's positive experience at Corinth on his most recent visit (7:7, 13b, 15). On the other hand, the aorist itself could possibly be gnomic ("God, who puts . . ."). The EVV are divided in their preference.

b. ℵ* P *pc* have the inferior word order τὸν ἀδελφὸν μετ᾽ αὐτοῦ, instead of μετ᾽ αὐτοῦ τὸν ἀδελφόν.

c. The external evidence is rather evenly divided between σύν (p⁴⁶ ℵ D G K Ψ 614 𝔐 it^{d, g, 61} syr^h goth) and ἐν (B C P 0225 0243 6 33 81 104 365 630 1175 1739 1881 2464 *al* f vg syr^p cop^{sa, bo} arm eth Ambrosiaster). But it is easier to believe that copyists substituted ἐν for σύν to avoid the unusual use of σύν with an impersonal object (τῇ χάριτι) than that σύν was substituted for ἐν to conform with the preceding συνέκδημος (cf. Metzger [1971] 581-82). WH reads ἐν, while UBS¹⁻⁴ and NA²⁷ read σύν.

d. In the place of αὐτοῦ, read by ℵ D¹ Ψ 1881* 𝔐 syr (p⁴⁶ 33: *h.t.*) and placed in square brackets by NA²⁷ and UBS⁴ (with a "C" rating), several witnesses have αὐτήν (P 0243 630 1739 1881^c *pc* vg^ms), while others omit either word (B C D* F G L 81 104 326 365 629 1175 2464 *al* lat cop Ambrosiaster). This omission produces an easier reading which is therefore probably secondary. The reading αὐτήν, which agrees with τὴν . . . δόξαν (giving the awkward sense "the same glory"), may have arisen to avoid the unusual expression αὐτὸς ὁ κύριος, "the Lord himself" (but see 1 Thess. 4:16). Barrett raises the possibility that Paul wrote αὐτοῦ, then added τοῦ κυρίου to avoid ambiguity: "his glory — I mean, the Lord's" (217 n. 2).

e. Proto-Alexandrian (p⁴⁶ ℵ B 1739) and Western (D F G latt) witnesses have the unexceptional reading προνοοῦμεν γάρ, but there is a secondary participial reading προνοούμενοι (further explaining στελλόμενοι [v. 20]), either with γάρ (C 0225 33 81 326 365 1505 *pc* Clement) or without γάρ (Ψ 𝔐).

f. Instead of κυρίου (which reflects Prov. 3:4), a few witnesses read τοῦ κυρίου (1845 *pc*) or τοῦ θεοῦ (p⁴⁶ [*pc*] lat syr^p Ambrosiaster).

g. P^{46vid} *pc* omit δέ.

h. B adds δέ after πεποιθήσει, which has the effect of making πεποιθήσει πολλῇ τῇ εἰς ὑμᾶς a separate statement.

i. Since the imperatival use of the participle is not a common NT idiom (see on 8:24), a scribal change from the participle ἐνδεικνύμενοι (read by B D* E F G 33 *pc* b p vg^ms) to an imperatival form ἐνδείξασθε (ℵ C D^{b, c} K L P Ψ 0225 0243 1739 1881 𝔐 lat) is readily explicable, but a change in the opposite direction is highly improbable. So although the external evidence, considered alone, is inconclusive, transcriptional probabilities favor ἐνδεικνύμενοι as the original reading (so UBS¹⁻⁴, NA²⁷; but WH opts for the imperative).

8:16 Χάρις δὲ τῷ θεῷ τῷ δόντι τὴν αὐτὴν σπουδὴν ὑπὲρ ὑμῶν ἐν τῇ καρδίᾳ Τίτου. "Thanks be to God who has put in the heart of Titus the same zeal for you as I have." Although this verse begins a new section, we may perhaps discern a conceptual link between v. 15 and v. 16. The same God who gave the Israelites manna in the wilderness gave Titus a zealous devotion for the Corinthians; Titus's σπουδή, like the Israelites' manna, was supernaturally supplied. Three times in 2 Corinthians Paul bursts out in thanksgiving to God for his gracious intervention — in bringing him spectacular relief from restless anxiety concerning the Corinthian situation (τῷ δὲ θεῷ χάρις, 2:14; cf. 7:5-7); in providing the unspeakably precious gift of his Son (χάρις τῷ θεῷ, 9:15); and here in inspiring Titus with an eager desire for the Corinthians' welfare (χάρις δὲ τῷ θεῷ, 8:16).[2] Also the phrase (ὁ) θεὸς ὁ δούς occurs three times in this epistle.

1:21-22	θεός, ὁ . . . δοὺς	τὸν ἀρραβῶνα τοῦ πνεύματος	ἐν ταῖς καρδίαις ἡμῶν
5:5	θεός, ὁ δοὺς	ἡμῖν τὸν ἀρραβῶνα τοῦ πνεύματος	
8:16	τῷ θεῷ τῷ δόντι	τὴν αὐτὴν σπουδὴν ὑπὲρ ὑμῶν	ἐν τῇ καρδίᾳ Τίτου

A comparison of the first two passages shows that διδόναι τι ἐν τῇ καρδίᾳ is comparable to saying διδόναι τινί τι, so that in 8:16 ἐν τῇ καρδίᾳ Τίτου is equivalent to (τῷ) Τίτῳ, except that "in the heart of Titus" points to the inwardness of the gift. ἐν could be taken to stand for εἰς (cf. Rev. 17:17; BDF §218) but is better explained, as in 1:22, as a pregnant use (Robertson 585; Zerwick, *Analysis* 405) with the notion of direction (εἰς) presupposed and the emphasis falling on the final location of the gift.[3] In Paul's thought God not only knows the heart (1 Cor. 14:25; cf. Acts 1:24; 15:8) but also acts on the heart, enlightening it (Eph. 1:18), encouraging it (Col. 2:2), and, as here, inspiring it with enthusiasm (σπουδή). Paul does not state when God kindled this zeal in Titus, but it may well have been during one of his two previous visits (see on 8:6) or at least as a result of them (cf. 7:13b-15).

Although both the Corinthians (in 7:11-12; 8:7) and the Macedonians (in 8:8) are said to have σπουδή, the presence of ὑπὲρ ὑμῶν ("for you," "for your welfare") after τὴν αὐτὴν σπουδήν shows that αὐτήν must refer to the "same" zeal as Paul himself has for the Corinthians. Throughout this letter Paul is concerned to establish the identity of outlook and action between himself and Titus, who was now Paul's principal representative in dealings with the church in Corinth. Paul saw him as an ideal emissary, for he shared Paul's own commitment to strive for the Corinthians' highest spiritual good. This emphasis on identity of dedication to the Corinthians' welfare is also a feature of the apologetic rhetorical questions regarding Titus in 12:18 (τῷ αὐτῷ πνεύματι . . . τοῖς αὐτοῖς ἴχνεσιν). It would have been reassuring to the believers in Corinth to know that Titus's eager desire — and, by implication, Paul's — was not for their money but for their well-being (ὑπὲρ ὑμῶν; cf. 12:14, "What I want is not your possessions but you") and that this affectionate concern for them that was shared by Titus and Paul was in itself a reflection of God's own affection for them.

8:17 ὅτι τὴν μὲν παράκλησιν ἐδέξατο, σπουδαιότερος δὲ ὑπάρχων αὐθαίρετος ἐξῆλθεν πρὸς ὑμᾶς. "For, to be sure, he welcomed our appeal, but being extremely zealous he is setting off to visit you on his own accord." In this

---

2. The ἔστω is to be understood with each phrase (cf. Robertson 396; BDF §128[6]).
3. Cf. Ezek. 36:27: τὸ πνεῦμά μου δώσω ἐν ὑμῖν.

verse Paul presents twofold evidence (ὅτι, "for")[4] that Titus shared his own zeal (σπουδή, 8:16) for the Corinthians. First, he welcomed Paul's request or appeal (παράκλησις, BAGD 618a) that he should return to Corinth to help to finalize the collection. παράκλησιν looks back to τὸ παρακαλέσαι in 8:6, where Paul's appeal to Titus was the upshot of the enthusiastic response of the Macedonians to the relief project (8:1-5). Héring suggests two reasons for Paul's delaying of his own return visit to Corinth and thus his request to Titus: his ongoing work in Macedonia; and his wish to have as little personal involvement in the collection as possible, in order to avoid malicious charges (cf. 8:20) (61-62). It was fitting for Paul to issue Titus with an "appeal," for it was not his way of operating to give orders to his colleagues (cf. 1:24), and in any case Titus had only relatively recently returned from Corinth. So Titus's ready and warm acceptance (ἐδέξατο) of Paul's request witnesses to his graciousness and his being a genuine κοινωνός and συνεργός (8:23).

The second evidence of Titus's σπουδή was his eager decision to return to Corinth, made without any pressure from Paul. σπουδαιότερος δὲ ὑπάρχων qualifies what follows rather than (as REB) what precedes,[5] as is shown by the μὲν . . . δέ contrast. The comparative adjective σπουδαιότερος could be taken as a simple positive ("eager," "zealous")[6] or as a true comparative ("more concerned than ever," JB), but more probably it is an elative comparative ("very zealous," BDF §244 [2]; Turner 30). ὑπάρχων may point to an essential quality ("in his characteristic earnestness," Plummer 247), or simply be equivalent to ὤν, with causal overtones (cf. BAGD 838a). αὐθαίρετος links Titus with the Macedonians, who contributed to the relief fund "of their own accord" (see on 8:3); the implicit suggestion is that the Corinthians too should act of their own free will. If we wonder how it could be simultaneously true that Titus acceded to Paul's request and acted "on his own accord," we should note, first of all, the μὲν . . . δέ contrast ("to be sure . . . but . . ."; cf. BAGD 502a),[7] which suggests that Paul was aware of the paradox. Perhaps he is saying that his request turned out to be superfluous, for Titus was already eager to go to Corinth (Barrett 228), or he may be simply emphasizing Titus's enthusiastic response to his appeal (Nickle 18 n. 25). However that be, the Corinthians needed to know two facts, which accounts for the two parts of the verse: Titus was coming to Corinth "of his own unprompted choice" (Plummer 246), yet he was also coming in response to Paul's suggestion and therefore with the apostle's full support.

4. For this use of ὅτι with the sense "as is proved by the fact that," see Zerwick §§420-22; cf. Barclay.

5. But NIV and Martin 271 ("with all eagerness and on his own initiative") take σπουδαιότερος . . . ὑπάρχων and αὐθαίρετος as coordinate.

6. Cf. Cassirer, "being the eager man that he is." Some EVV relate σπουδαιότερος and αὐθαίρετος as though they denoted cause and effect or as if Paul had written οὕτως δὲ σπουδαῖος (e.g., Goodspeed, ". . . he goes to you really of his own accord, he is so devoted to you").

7. Several EVV (e.g., NASB, Barclay, NIV), however, treat μὲν . . . δέ as though it were indistinguishable from οὐ μόνον . . . ἀλλὰ (καί).

ἐξῆλθεν, like three other verbs in chs. 8 and 9, is an epistolary aorist,[8] "he is set-ting off" or "he is about to depart" (Betz 38).[9]

8:18 συνεπέμψαμεν δὲ μετ᾽ αὐτοῦ τὸν ἀδελφὸν οὗ ὁ ἔπαινος ἐν τῷ εὐαγγελίῳ διὰ πασῶν τῶν ἐκκλησιῶν. "With him we are sending the brother who is praised throughout all the churches for his work for the gospel." In order to safeguard the integrity of the collection project in Corinth (cf. 8:20-21), Paul knew that he would need to send to Corinth more than his personal assistant, Titus (8:23). In vv. 18-19 we find his commendation of the first of the two extra envoys who would act as observers and thus as guarantors of the whole collection. πέμπω is Paul's usual term for the dispatch of an envoy to a church.[10] The prefix συν- im-plies "togetherness," in the sense of both accompaniment and comradeship; Paul was sending this additional emissary as Titus's companion in travel and also as his colleague. As in v. 22, συνεπέμψαμεν is an epistolary aorist[11] and an epistolary plural (as throughout vv. 16-24, except for v. 23a), but in v. 22 no μετά follows the συν-.[12] ἀδελφός here signifies not only a fellow Christian but also a colleague in Christian work.[13] The article τόν does not here denote possession ("his brother," Goodspeed)[14] but either points to "the well-known brother" (Williams) or has a forward reference ("that brother who . . . ," Furnish 420; cf. BDF §258[1]).

8. So also συνεπέμψαμεν (8:18, 22) and ἔπεμψα (9:3). Others (Moule 12; Fanning 282) would add ἡγησάμην (9:5), and Plummer even includes ἐδέξατο (8:17). But Allo (222-23, 227, 229, 231) regards all these verbs as preterit aorists, denoting past time. According to him, 8:16-24 and 12:14-18 formed commendation for Titus and his two colleagues (who had left Paul for Corinth af-ter ch. 7 had been written) when Paul's motives concerning the collection had been impugned as a result of the activity of these three men in Corinth (222-23, 329).

9. The epistolary aorist involves action that is contemporaneous or future at the time of writ-ing but will be past when the letter is read; such action is courteously portrayed from the perspec-tive of the reader. The difficulties with the proposal of McKay ("Observations" 154-58) that the aorists ἐξῆλθεν (8:17) and συνεπέμψαμεν (8:18) are historic but συνεπέμψαμεν (8:22) epistolary, are twofold (as he himself acknowledges, 157 and n. 8): συνεπέμψαμεν αὐτοῖς in 8:22 must be taken to mean, "we are sending *to be* with them"; exactly the same form of the same verb (συνπέμπω) must be understood in different senses.

10. E.g., 1 Cor. 4:17; 16:3; 2 Cor. 9:3.

11. Fanning (281-82) notes that the form ἔπεμψα or ἐπέμψαμεν is the most common episto-lary aorist in the NT.

12. For μετά following a συν- compound, see Acts 1:26; Gal. 2:12 (see further Robertson 560-62; Moule 92).

13. On the use of ἀδελφός for a colleague in Christian ministry or an "associate-in-mission," see Ellis, "Co-workers" 445-51 (but see the critique of Ollrog 78 n. 93). Since ἀδελφός occurs "in the honorary declarations commonly made by Hellenistic rulers" (72), Betz proposes that Paul con-sidered the two "brothers" of 8:18-23 as "church–political allies" (73) as well as fellow Christians (72-73). This is in keeping with Betz's general thesis that in 2 Corinthians 8 Paul is influenced by contemporary administrative language (see on 8:6).

14. Taking this view and also arguing that the first unnamed brother is Luke, Souter con-cludes that Titus and Luke were brothers (285) and surmises that these two brothers were the repre-sentatives (though unnamed in Acts 20:4) of the Philippian church in the collection delegation ("Relationship" 335). But it would surely have precipitated, not avoided, criticism (cf. 8:20-21) if Paul had sent members of the same family to ensure the probity of the management of the collec-tion. Moreover, τὸν ἀδελφὸν τὸν κατὰ σάρκα would have put the blood relationship beyond doubt.

Paul mentions two particular qualifications of this "brother" for the task he was entrusting to him — he was highly respected "throughout all the churches" (v. 18b), and he had been appointed "by the churches" (v. 19). ἔπαινος speaks of his high renown or splendid reputation. In a similar way Luke speaks of the youthful Timothy as "well spoken of" (ἐμαρτυρεῖτο) by the Christians at Lystra and Iconium (Acts 16:2). Praise from fellow believers anticipates praise (ἔπαινος) from God (1 Cor. 4:5) and is perhaps the best indication available this side of God's judgment seat (Rom. 14:10-12) of the Lord's opinion of his servants. In the phrase ἐν τῷ εὐαγγελίῳ the preposition may mean "in the sphere of" or "in the matter of" or "in connection with," and it is unclear what aspect of τὸ εὐαγγέλιον generated the praise, whether the "preaching" of the gospel,[15] or, more generally, the "spreading" of the gospel (JB, Cassirer), or still less specifically, "service(s)" for the gospel (NEB, NIV, REB; Kümmel in Lietzmann 207).[16] Support for this latter very general sense may be found in three Pauline passages where the notions of service (λατρεύω, Rom. 1:9), labor (συνήθλησαν, Phil. 4:3) and work (συνεργόν, 1 Thess. 4:2) are linked with the phrase ἐν τῷ εὐαγγελίῳ. We must supply a verb such as ἀγγέλλεται (BAGD 179d) or ἐξελήλυθεν (cf. 1 Thess. 1:8) with the expression διὰ πασῶν τῶν ἐκκλησιῶν, which means "throughout all the churches," not "by all the churches" (as Moffatt, NIV; cf. ὑπὸ τῶν ἐκκλησιῶν, v. 19). We could restrict πασῶν to mean "all the Macedonian churches" (cf. 8:1), but there is no reason not to include all the churches of the Pauline mission (the same expression is found in 11:28; 1 Cor. 7:17)[17] or even all Christian churches in general (Wolff 177).

But why are this "brother" and the "brother" mentioned in v. 22 not named, especially since they are so warmly commended by Paul? Some have suggested that these two men subsequently lost their good name at Corinth, so that their names were deleted from Paul's letter.[18] But rather than appealing to some putative deletion of the names by the Corinthian church or by the collector of the Pauline corpus, we should entertain the possibility that Paul himself chose to omit the names.[19] Betz proposes that by the omission Paul was defending the primacy of Titus in the delegation and ensuring the limited role of the two "brothers" who, as attendants (ἀκόλουθοι = Latin *legatorum comites*), lacked any authority to negotiate apart from Titus (73-74). There can be little doubt that Titus was the leader of the delegation (see on 8:23), but it is less clear that the churches, as opposed to Paul, took the initiative in the appointment of the two delegates (as Betz [73] suggests). Perhaps we can best account for the anonymity of the two brothers by submitting that although the Corinthians had

15. So Thrall (548), pointing to the five other Pauline examples of ἐν τῷ εὐαγγελίῳ (Rom. 1:9; 1 Cor. 9:18; 2 Cor. 10:14; 1 Thess. 3:2; cf. Phil. 4:3). Also RSV, GNB, NJB, NRSV; Wolff 174.

16. Since οὗ ὁ ἔπαινος is equivalent to ὃς ἐπαινεῖται, it is better to render the phrase "who is praised/renowned" rather than "whose [services] are praised."

17. Morgan-Wynne 172-73.

18. So, e.g., Lietzmann 137; Héring 62-63.

19. So also Thrall 559.

heard about (at least) one of the brothers, they had not met either of the two, but since all three delegates were the bearers of the present letter, the two ἀδελφοί would be introduced to the church by Titus.[20] Numerous efforts have been made to identify the "brother" of v. 18, but the very diversity of the suggestions indicates that certainty is impossible.[21]

8:19 οὐ μόνον δὲ ἀλλὰ καὶ χειροτονηθεὶς ὑπὸ τῶν ἐκκλησιῶν συνέκδημος ἡμῶν σὺν τῇ χάριτι ταύτῃ. "In addition to this, he has also been appointed by the churches to be our traveling companion in connection with this work of grace." Paul now states a second, even greater qualification of "the well-known brother."[22] Not only was he highly esteemed throughout the Christian world for his distinctive service for the gospel (v. 18). He was also (καί) an appointee of the churches. Whether or not v. 19 is regarded as a parenthesis,[23] χειροτονηθείς must be regarded as an absolute participle that is coordinate with a finite verb (συνεπέμψαμεν, v. 18) and stands for a finite verb,[24] in this case in the indicative (ἐχειροτονήθη). Because χειροτονηθείς . . . συνέκδημος (nominative) refers back to τὸν ἀδελφόν (accusative), v. 19 is anacoluthic. Four stages may be traced in the meaning and use of the verb χειροτονέω. Originally it meant simply "stretch out (τείνω) the hand (χείρ)";[25] then it came to mean "elect by raising the hand/by show of hands," as in democratic elections that took place in an "assembly" (ἐκκλησία) in Greek cities; then, without reference to the mode of election, it meant "appoint" (as in the only other NT use of the verb, Acts 14:23[26]); finally, in post-NT ecclesiastical usage it assumed the sense "ordain by the laying on of hands." In the present case, as in Acts 14:23, the sense is "appoint," without any

---

20. Cf. Plummer 248; Barrett 228.

21. The suggestions include Luke (Hughes 313) (an identification reflected in the Collect for St. Luke's Day in the Book of Common Prayer), Barnabas, Apollos (Martin 275), Mark, Erastus, Silas, and from the list of the collection delegates in Acts 20:4, Sopater, Aristarchus, Secundus, Gaius, Timothy, Tychicus, and Trophimus. See the discussion in Allo 224-26; Thrall 561-62. The term εὐαγγέλιον was not applied to a written document before the second century, so that the phrase ἐν τῷ εὐαγγελίῳ cannot be used to identify the "brother" as Mark or Luke or any other author of a "gospel" (cf. Luke 1:1). Murphy-O'Connor suggests (86; *Paul* 315) that the unnamed brother was a Corinthian who was in Macedonia as an evangelist, so that the Corinthians, hearing Paul's eulogy of the man, would have felt both flattered and relieved.

22. After οὐ μόνον δέ (literally, "And not only [is this the case]"), ἀλλὰ καί ("but also") introduces an even more significant credential. BAGD (528a) calls this whole expression "ellipsis w[ith] supplementation of what immediately precedes," citing this passage and Rom. 5:3, 11; 8:23; 9:10 (also BAGD 38a).

23. Verse 19 is printed as a parenthesis in WH and UBS[1-3] but not UBS[3(corrected), 4]; also Robertson 439; Meyer 542. This allows στελλόμενοι (v. 20) to be treated as dependent on συνεπέμψαμεν (v. 18).

24. Other instances of the phenomenon in 2 Corinthians are found in 5:12; 6:3; 7:5; 9:11, 13; 10:4, 15; 11:6; cf. BDF §468(1); Zerwick §374; Turner 343.

25. Although the verb does not occur in the LXX, the substantive χειροτονία occurs in Isa. 58:9 in reference to "the pointed finger," a gesture of accusation or contempt.

26. "And after they (Paul and Barnabas) had appointed elders for them (the believers in the South Galatian churches) in each church, with prayer and fasting they committed them to the Lord in whom they had put their trust."

implication about the mode of the appointment[27] but with the implication that some authority was acting in making the appointment. But unlike Acts 14:23 where there was appointment to an office (eldership) (cf. *Didache* 15:1), here it was a case of selection and commissioning for a specific task, namely acting as Paul's traveling companion and assistant (συνέκδημος)[28] in conveying the collection to Jerusalem. Since Paul was sending the three-man delegation to Corinth in advance of his own arrival (9:3-5), this "brother" of vv. 18-19 would be accompanying Paul not to Corinth but from Corinth onward (cf. Acts 20:3-4). There is clearly a link between the high reputation of this "brother" (v. 18) and his appointment as Paul's traveling colleague (v. 19). His choice by "the churches" reflected their lofty estimate of his distinguished contribution to the gospel. A similar link is found in Acts 16:2-3 with regard to Timothy: "He was well spoken of by the believers in Lystra and Iconium. Paul wanted Timothy to accompany him" (σὺν αὐτῷ ἐξελθεῖν; cf. συνέκδημος).

The number and the identity of the churches involved in this appointment are not known. It is not likely that we should supply τῆς Ἰουδαίας (cf. Gal. 1:22) or τῶν οὐσῶν ἐν τῇ Ἰουδαίᾳ (cf. 1 Thess. 2:14) with τῶν ἐκκλησιῶν.[29] Acts 20:4 makes no reference to delegates or assistants from Judea who were part of Paul's entourage with the collection, although it is undeniable that appointees from the churches of Judea would be suitable witnesses and guarantors of the probity of all matters concerning the collection as well as being a visible evidence of the unity of Jewish and Gentile churches. Moreover, if Paul was uncertain (as Rom. 15:30-31 suggests) whether his "service for Jerusalem" would be acceptable to the believers there, it is unlikely that they themselves had appointed supervisory delegates (cf. Thrall 559). While it is possible that the appointing churches were Asian (thus Hughes 316), more probably they were Macedonian (so Lietzmann 137),[30] given three facts: Paul was writing the present letter from Macedonia; he was currently visiting the Macedonian churches (9:2, καυχῶμαι Μακεδόσιν); they had recently completed their relief offering in exemplary fashion (8:1-5) so that their appointees, assuming that the second "brother" was also appointed by the same churches (cf. 8:23, ἀδελφοὶ ἡμῶν, ἀπόστολοι ἐκκλησιῶν), would be ideally equipped to help Titus supervise the revival and completion of the Corinthian collection as well as travel with Paul to Jerusalem.[31]

---

27. But Georgi (73) speaks of this appointee as "elected by democratic vote."

28. More is implied in the term συνέκδημος (as used here, and in Acts 19:29 of Gaius and Aristarchus) than mere accompaniment in travel and yet less than formal collegiality (so Young and Ford [270], "as our fellow missionary"). NEB and REB have "to travel with us and help (in this beneficent work)."

29. But see Hainz 149-57 and Nickle 18-22 for a defense of this view. Nickle, further, argues (20-22) that the "brother" of vv. 18-19 is Judas, and the "brother" of v. 22 is Silas (cf. Acts 15:22, 27, 32).

30. Thrall adequately responds (560) to Nickle's objections (19-20) to this view.

31. Georgi entertains the possibility that the appointing church was Ephesus or some con-

This appointee was to travel "with" (συν-έκδημος) Paul and "with" (σύν = "in connection with," "in dealing with") the collection, which is here termed ἡ χάρις αὕτη, "this work of grace" (Cassirer; Carrez 186), "this service of love" (GNB), "this act of charity" (Barclay), "this benevolence" (Furnish 420). Paul refers to the collection itself as χάρις also in 8:6-7 and 1 Cor. 16:3.

(τῇ χάριτι ταύτῃ) τῇ διακονουμένῃ ὑφ᾽ ἡμῶν πρὸς τὴν αὐτοῦ τοῦ κυρίου δόξαν καὶ προθυμίαν ἡμῶν. "(. . . this work of grace) that we are administering in order to honor the Lord himself and to show our goodwill." As a διάκονος καινῆς διαθήκης (cf. 3:6) and a διάκονος τοῦ εὐαγγελίου (cf. Col. 1:23), Paul saw himself as in the process of organizing or administering (διακονουμένῃ, present participle) a διακονία ἡ εἰς τοὺς ἁγίους (8:4; 9:1; cf. 9:12-13; Rom. 15:31). He recognized that while others were or were to be his traveling companions and assistants in the project (cf. Acts 20:4), he himself was, in the final analysis, its sole administrator (ὑφ᾽ ἡμῶν[32]), responsible for its genesis, its organization, its completion, and its safe delivery to Jerusalem. The same phrase occurs in the next verse.

Paul's twofold purpose in organizing the collection is now stated:[33] it was "for" (= "to promote,"[34] πρός) the glory of the Lord himself, and "for" (= "to show";[35] πρός also qualifies προθυμίαν) Paul's goodwill. That is, with both τὴν . . . δόξαν and [τὴν] προθυμίαν, the preposition πρός is telic ("for the purpose of"), although the nature of the purpose differs slightly, "to promote/enhance . . . to show/give evidence of."[36] One of Paul's motives — undoubtedly the dominant one — in prosecuting this relief fund was to enhance the glory of the Lord God, probably because the success of the project would prompt people to praise God (9:11-13). As in 3:18, ἡ δόξα (τοῦ) κυρίου probably refers to the glory of God rather than the glory of Christ, a verdict supported by the use of κύριος in v. 21. The emphatic αὐτοῦ ("himself"), occurring between two instances of ἡμῶν, draws attention to the fact that his motivation was not self-

gregation in Galatia in which case the Macedonian churches would have confirmed the appointment (73; Georgi is speaking only of the first delegate, but he appears to assume [74-75] that the second unnamed person was appointed by the same congregations).

32. This is an epistolary plural (cf. the same phrase in 3:3, ἐστὲ ἐπιστολὴ Χριστοῦ διακονηθεῖσα ὑφ᾽ ἡμῶν), in spite of the fact that Timothy is co-sender of the present letter (1:1) and is named in Acts 20:4 as one of Paul's companions traveling with the collection.

33. Several commentators (e.g., Windisch 264; Kümmel in Lietzmann 207; Hughes 316) construe πρὸς τὴν κτλ. with χειροτονηθείς rather than (as we prefer) with διακονουμένῃ ὑφ᾽ ἡμῶν. The problem with that construal is the distance between χειροτονηθείς and πρὸς τὴν κτλ., and the unlikelihood that a delegate's appointment by certain churches would show or increase Paul's own προθυμία. Moreover, to take πρὸς τὴν κτλ. with the immediately preceding phrase ("is being administered by us") makes perfectly good sense, especially with the ὑφ᾽ ἡμῶν . . . ἡμῶν link.

34. So also Barclay; Plummer 246; Isaacs.

35. So also many EVV, including RSV, NEB, NRSV, REB.

36. But Lietzmann takes πρός . . . προθυμίαν ἡμῶν to mean "in accordance with our desire" (136; cf. Moffatt, "His appointment has my full consent"), and Windisch, "to the heightening of our joy" (264), while Thrall renders πρός in each case by "resulting in" (543; cf. 549-50, citing BAGD s.v. III.3.b.).

centered; it was a desire for the Lord's own glory that impelled his action. The second, and subsidiary, motive Paul mentions is his wish to demonstrate for all to see his "goodwill" (προθυμία, RSV, NRSV) toward the mother-church of Christendom.[37] Such a purpose is wholly understandable, given the suspicions that many Jerusalemites had about Paul's Gentile mission, not to speak of their vivid memory of his earlier violent persecution of their church (cf. Acts 9:1-2; 22:4-5; 26:9-11). These two purposes are closely related in Paul's thought, as the single preposition and article would indicate (cf. 9:13; Zerwick §184), although the ultimate purpose was much broader and much more significant than the subsidiary aim. When Paul's "goodwill" toward fellow believers in the Jerusalem church became apparent to all with the completion and delivery of the offering, God's honor would be enhanced. A similar twofold pattern is found in 9:12 (on which see below): "The carrying out of this act of service is not only supplying the needs of God's people [at Jerusalem], but is also overflowing in many expressions of thanks to God."

8:20 στελλόμενοι τοῦτο μή τις ἡμᾶς μωμήσηται ἐν τῇ ἁδρότητι ταύτῃ τῇ διακονουμένῃ ὑφ' ἡμῶν. "We are putting this precaution in place lest anyone should discredit us over this lavish gift that we are administering." Not without cause, Paul was very aware of the need for great circumspection with regard to money matters, especially at Corinth where he had his detractors (cf. 2:17; 7:2; 11:7-9; 12:14-18). As a vigorous defender of his own financial independence of the Corinthians (1 Cor. 9:12b, 15, 18; 2 Cor. 11:9-12), he was particularly susceptible to a malicious charge of embezzlement with respect to the collection — that, like Ananias before him, he was "keeping back" (cf. ἐνοσφίσατο, Acts 5:2) part of the fund for his private use, or, in modern terms, he was siphoning off a percentage of the proceeds. It is against this background that we should understand this verse.[38]

στελλόμενοι is best regarded as an absolute participle, standing for a finite verb (στελλόμεθα) in a construction that is anacoluthic since this participle does not accord with χειροτονηθεὶς . . . συνέκδημος (cf. BDF §468[1]; Robertson 431, 1039).[39] "Paul would not let himself be caught in a net of mere grammatical niceties" (Robertson 1136). The verb στέλλω bears a bewildering variety of meanings in Greek literature.[40] Its basic meaning of "set," "place" was ex-

---

37. Even if προθυμία is rendered "eagerness/readiness to help/serve" (cf. Goodspeed, NEB, NIV, REB), the reference is to the church of Jerusalem. By using the same term (προθυμία) of himself that he uses (in 8:11-12; 9:2) of the Corinthians, Paul underlines his oneness with them in the project (K. H. Rengstorf, *TDNT* 6.700).

38. Betz believes that the charge of corruption was "one of the principal arguments of Corinthian anti-Paulinism" (143-44).

39. But some commentators (e.g., Meyer 592-93) relate στελλόμενοι to συνεπέμψαμεν (v. 18), taking v. 19 as parenthetical. Meyer takes the participle to be causal: "inasmuch as we thereby avoid this, that no one . . ." (593). It is highly unlikely that στελλόμενοι is a case of *constructio ad sensum*, referring to the members of the churches who appointed the "brother" (v. 19).

40. See K. H. Rengstorf, *TDNT* 7.588-89.

tended to "put something in (its right) place" = "make ready," used of sails (Homer, *Odyssey* 3.11) or troops (Herodotus 3.141), and "restrain." In the LXX and NT it is used only in the middle voice, and, when followed by ἀπό, it means "draw back from" something (Mal. 2:5) or someone (2 Thess. 3:6, the only other NT use of the verb). Here in 8:20, where no ἀπό follows, the sense of στελλόμενοι τοῦτο seems to be "we are putting this [precaution] in place,"[41] with the direct object τοῦτο pointing back to vv. 18-19,[42] namely the dispatch in the company of Titus of a well-known, highly respected Christian brother who had been appointed by the churches.[43] This understanding of στελλόμενοι τοῦτο is supported by the explanatory προνοοῦμεν γάρ in v. 21, "For we are taking into consideration," "For we are taking forethought."

What Paul was taking steps to avoid was that anyone should have an excuse to find fault with the way he handled the munificent fund he was organizing. After a verb expressing caution and forethought (στελλόμενοι), the clause introduced by the conjunction μή (see BAGD 517b) defines what Paul wished to avoid, namely an accusation of improper financial conduct. μωμάομαι ("find fault with," "discredit") is found only in 6:3 and here in the NT. In 6:3 it was Paul's apostolic ministry in general or the ministry of reconciliation in particular that was a possible target of censure. Here it is Paul's integrity in managing a sizeable relief fund. The noun ἁδρότης, cognate with the adjective ἁδρός ("stout," "dense," "full-grown"), means "abundance," "plentifulness" and could refer to stoutness or vigor of body, density of vegetation, or ripeness of fruit. In reference to money (as here), it signifies "lavishness" or "lavish generosity," and thus (as abstract for concrete) "lavish gift" (NAB²), "large sum" (NJB), or "large fund" (JB). Clearly Paul was expecting that the Corinthians would give generously, just as the Macedonians had (8:2).[44] He could have repeated τῇ χάριτι ταύτῃ from v. 19 (cf. v. 7), just as he repeats τῇ διακονουμένῃ ὑφ᾽ ἡμῶν,[45] but he chose instead to use a picturesque term that denotes profuseness and mu-

---

41. Rengstorf opts for the sense "inasmuch as I see to it, or take steps (lest . . .)" (*TDNT* 7.590). It is unnecessary to find in the term στέλλομαι a nautical metaphor relating to the furling or shortening of sails when coming ashore or avoiding danger (as Hughes 318 n. 46), although the resulting sense of taking precautionary measures is appropriate. Nor do we need to follow Barnett (423 n. 42), who, noting that στέλλομαι is cognate with ἀπόστολοι (8:23) and congruent with συμπέμπω (8:18, 22), proposes the meaning "send."

42. If τοῦτο is prospective, not retrospective, it is defined by μή τις κτλ. Cf. Lambrecht 135: "This we want to avoid: that one might blame us. . . ."

43. But in the wider context τοῦτο may refer to Paul's dispatch of all three emissaries.

44. Although the term ἁδρότης refers to the collection fund as a whole, in reference to the Corinthians the word is (as Hughes 318-19 n. 47 observes) both a compliment and an incitement " — a compliment because it implies that their character is such as to cause Paul to expect that they will give generously, and an incitement to them in consequence not to disappoint this expectation."

45. As in v. 19, this phrase underlines Paul's ultimate responsibility for this whole relief operation; he might have assistants and overseers but he was the "project manager." But some EVV link the thought of τῇ διακονουμένῃ ὑφ᾽ ἡμῶν with μωμήσηται ἐν: "What we are specially guarding against is that any fault should be found with us in regard to our administration of this charitable fund" (similarly Moffatt, NEB, GNB, Barclay, REB).

nificence. He knew that the larger the sum of money collected, the greater the possibility that he would be suspected of embezzlement. But he also saw that if he took steps to make others responsible for the actual handling of the funds, whatever their size, any ground for suspicion "in connection with (= over) this lavish gift" would be removed.

8:21 προνοοῦμεν γὰρ καλὰ οὐ μόνον ἐνώπιον κυρίου ἀλλὰ καὶ ἐνώπιον ἀνθρώπων. "Indeed, we are giving forethought to what is honorable, not only in the Lord's eyes but also in human eyes." Still speaking of the precautionary measure of sending to Corinth an accredited delegate of the churches (vv. 18-20), Paul now restates positively what is couched in negative terms in v. 20. His careful forethought is aimed at doing what is seen to be right and honorable as well as avoiding censure. Without using any introductory formula, he is clearly alluding to, if not citing, the LXX text of Prov. 3:4.[46]

Prov. 3:4	2 Cor. 8:21
προνοοῦ	προνοοῦμεν γὰρ
καλὰ	καλὰ οὐ μόνον
ἐνώπιον κυρίου	ἐνώπιον κυρίου ἀλλὰ
καὶ	καὶ ἐνώπιον
ἀνθρώπων	ἀνθρώπων

Paul's adaptation of the LXX is significant. He is not giving an exhortation or stating a general principle, but justifying his own conduct (προνοοῦμεν γάρ). The addition of the ascensive οὐ μόνον . . . ἀλλὰ καί (BAGD 38a) and the repetition of ἐνώπιον serve to highlight the second element ("in human eyes"). Paul certainly believed that the human appraisal of conduct was less significant than the divine evaluation (10:18; 1 Cor. 4:3-5), but he also realized that a reputation for dishonesty of any sort impeded the progress of the gospel (cf. 6:3) and, positively, that a clear conscience before other people enhanced the gospel or at least removed a potential stumbling block to the success of the gospel (cf. Acts 24:16; 1 Tim. 3:7; Tit. 2:9-10).

προνοέω, used only here and in Rom. 12:17; 1 Tim. 5:8, denotes advance (προ-) thinking or planning (cf. πρόνοια in Acts 24:2), and more generally, making provision for or taking into consideration or being solicitous for; perhaps "we

46. It is of special interest that this same passage, Prov. 3:4, is cited in the tractate of the Mishnah that deals with "Shekel Dues" *(Shekalim)* as scriptural justification for the extraordinary precautions that were taken to ensure that the man responsible for making an appropriation from the Temple treasury should give no occasion for a charge of pilfering. "He who entered (the shekel-chamber) to make the appropriation did not wear a sleeved cloak or shoes or sandals or phylacteries or an amulet, lest if he became poor people might say that he became poor because of a sin against the shekel-chamber, or if he became rich they might say that he became rich from the appropriation taken from the shekel-chamber; for a man must be blameless before people as before God, for it is written, 'And be guiltless towards the Lord and towards Israel' [Num. 32:22]. And again it says, 'So you will find favor and good understanding in the sight of God and people' [Prov. 3:4]" *(m. Shekalim 3:2).* See further SB 1.766.

are giving forethought to" catches the sense here.[47] It is followed by the genitive (as in 1 Tim. 5:8; Polycarp, *Philippians* 6:1[48]) or the accusative (Rom. 12:17 and here). καλά is an anarthrous substantivized adjective (BDF §264[2]), and as a generalizing plural is scarcely distinguishable from (τὸ) καλόν; thus "what is honorable" (RSV), in the sense of being above reproach (cf. v. 20), or "what is right" (NIV) in the sense of being morally praiseworthy. ἐνώπιον κυρίου ("before/in the presence of the Lord") means "in the Lord's eyes/sight" or "in the opinion of the Lord" (cf. BAGD 270d), with κύριος here signifying (as in Prov. 3:4, where the MT has *ʾelōhîm*) the Lord God, not the Lord Christ. It was appropriate for Paul to give special consideration to doing what was honorable in the Lord's estimation since he was conducting the whole project "for the Lord's glory" (8:19). But his precautionary measures were also taken to ensure that his handling of the relief fund was seen to be honest "in human eyes" (ἐνώπιον ἀνθρώπων).[49]

This same OT text is alluded to in Rom. 12:17, προνοούμενοι καλὰ ἐνώπιον πάντων ἀνθρώπων, "Give forethought to what is honorable in the eyes of everyone." What Rom. 12:17 and 2 Cor. 8:21 have in common is that doing what is good in the judgment of Christians and non-Christians alike (Rom. 12:17)[50] and doing what is honorable in the sight of God and humans (2 Cor. 8:21) are in each case to be brought about by careful consideration and advance planning (προνοέω). However, καλά in 2 Cor. 8:21 has a more specific reference than in Rom. 12:17, adverting to honest and honorable action in financial matters rather than simply the performance of praiseworthy acts.

8:22 συνεπέμψαμεν δὲ αὐτοῖς τὸν ἀδελφὸν ἡμῶν ὃν ἐδοκιμάσαμεν ἐν πολλοῖς πολλάκις σπουδαῖον ὄντα. "In addition, we are sending with them our brother whose eagerness we have often tested and proved in many ways." The second anonymous representative of the churches (v. 23) is now introduced and his credentials given. As in v. 18 συνεπέμψαμεν is an epistolary aorist, but in this case no μετά follows the συν-. αὐτοῖς refers to Titus (vv. 16-17) and the unnamed brother of vv. 18-19. When Paul calls this third member of the trio "our brother," he is not identifying him as his relative (whether brother or cousin) but as a fellow believer and also (as the following description indicates) as a colleague in Christian ministry (see v. 18). Like the first delegate who would accompany Titus to Corinth, he remains nameless, probably because both would be personally introduced by Titus when the present letter was read aloud at Corinth (see further on v. 18).

Only the context determines whether δοκιμάζω refers to testing ("put to the test," "examine") or to the outcome of testing ("prove by testing," "approve

---

47. TCNT gives προνοοῦμεν a conative sense ("we are trying to make arrangements [which shall be right]").

48. προνοοῦντες ἀεὶ τοῦ καλοῦ ἐνώπιον θεοῦ καὶ ἀνθρώπων.

49. Cf. Cicero, *De Officiis* 2.21.75: "The most important part of all administration of state affairs and public service is the avoidance of even the slightest suspicion of self-seeking."

50. In Rom. 12:17 it is improbable that ἐνώπιον has the sense of the dative ("to all people") or that ἐνώπιον πάντων ἀνθρώπων qualifies προνοούμενοι, not καλά.

after testing"). Since Paul is here stating a person's qualification for specialized service, the reference is not simply to testing but to this person's emergence from testing with proven character. Here the construction with δοκιμάζω, a verb of cognition, is the accusative (ὅν) followed by a "supplementary participle" (BDF §416[2]), ὄντα. Both ἐν πολλοῖς and πολλάκις qualify ἐδοκιμάσαμεν: Paul had had opportunity to test and verify this man's keenness and devotion (σπουδαῖον) on repeated occasions (πολλάκις) and in many ways or areas (ἐν πολλοῖς), presumably some or many of them related to finances.[51] ἐδοκι-μάσαμεν is a summary or constative aorist, comprehending all the occasions and ways in a single glance (cf. Fanning 173-74, 258-59). It is not explicitly said that the man had been chosen and appointed by the churches, as was the case with the first unnamed delegate (v. 19), but it is a plausible assumption, for both men are called "delegates of the churches" (v. 23).[52] If so, Paul is again following his practice, first stated in 1 Cor. 16:3 (οὓς ἐὰν δοκιμάσητε . . . τούτους πέμψω), of sending delegates who had been chosen by churches. But this concurrence with the decision of local churches was apparently not seen by Paul as a threat to or contradiction of his apostolic authority.

νυνὶ δὲ πολὺ σπουδαιότερον πεποιθήσει πολλῇ τῇ εἰς ὑμας. "(Our brother . . .) who is now all the more eager because of his profound confidence in you." In the past this brother had shown himself to be diligent and enthusiastic in various circumstances. At the time Paul was writing, however (νυνὶ δέ), that diligence and enthusiasm, now directed to the Corinthians themselves, had become all the more intense by reason of the total confidence he had in them. πολύ, the (accusative singular) neuter of the adjective πολύς, is used as an adverbial accusative equivalent in meaning to πολλῷ, "much," heightening the comparative σπουδαιότερον (referring back to ὅν); thus "much more zealous," "all the more eager." πεποιθήσει πολλῇ is a dative of cause (see BDF §196), with πολλῇ denoting degree (BAGD 688b), "deep/absolute confidence."[53] Perhaps on the basis of 7:16 (ἐν παντὶ θαρρῶ ἐν ὑμῖν), the KJV takes this πεποίθησις to be Paul's, but as Martin notes (277), Paul's confidence is unlikely to have reinforced this delegate's enthusiasm. In any case, if the reference were to Paul we would have expected an expression such as τῇ πολλῇ πεποιθήσει ἡμῶν, to remove ambiguity. The source of this delegate's profound confidence is not known, but it may have resulted from an earlier visit to Corinth (with Ti-

---

51. Harrison (43-44) has pointed out the similarity between Paul's procedures regarding finances and those in contemporary cultic associations: the management of funds must be carried out by men of integrity.

52. Betz argues that the two brothers were "co-opted" by Paul as members of the mission when he assumed final responsibility for the delegation (40, 73; but cf. 78). Also, he proposes that Paul's acceptance of these two envoys of the churches indicates his endorsement of their appointment by democratic election (χειροτονηθείς, 8:19) and that this endorsement is "an undeniable instance in which Paul's thinking underwent a process of Hellenization" (75). But we saw above (on 8:19) that this verb in itself gives no conclusive evidence of the mode of the appointment.

53. This verse is notable for its alliteration and assonance: . . . πολλοῖς πολλάκις . . . πολὺ . . . πεποιθήσει πολλῇ. . . .

tus?) or from conversations with Titus (cf. 7:7, 11, 13b-15) or with Paul who had recently been boasting (καυχῶμαι) to the Macedonians about the Corinthians' "readiness" of intent and their eagerness to contribute to the collection (9:2). Whatever the source, this envoy felt sure that the forthcoming mission to Corinth would be successful and that the believers there would give liberally to the relief fund. Not only was Titus eager to visit and assist the Corinthians (τὴν ... σπουδὴν ὑπὲρ ὑμῶν ... σπουδαιότερος, 8:16-17); this delegate, too, already known for his eager zeal (σπουδαῖον ὄντα), was keen to visit them (πολὺ σπουδαιότερον). Paul is hinting that the Corinthians had no reason to fear the delegates but every reason to show them warm love (cf. 8:24).

8:23 εἴτε ὑπὲρ Τίτου, κοινωνὸς ἐμὸς καὶ εἰς ὑμᾶς συνεργός. "If there is any question about Titus, he is my colleague and fellow worker in your service." In this elliptical verse, which is asyndetic and verbless, Paul gives a summary recommendation of all three delegates. When the correlatives εἴτε ... εἴτε ("whether ... or," "if ... if") are not followed by a finite verb, there is an ellipsis (BDF §§446, 454[3]); here, "if [someone asks]" or "if [there is any question]." Once again (cf. vv. 20-21) Paul is exercising forethought and taking a precautionary measure, anticipating issues that may arise when the delegation reaches Corinth. As often in 2 Corinthians, ὑπέρ has the sense "about" or "concerning."[54] That Titus was the leader of the delegation seems indicated by several facts: he is mentioned first in vv. 16-22 and also in this summary in v. 23; he alone is explicitly Paul's appointee (vv. 16-17, 23a), the other two being sent by Paul (vv. 18, 22) but appointed by the churches (vv. 19, 23); only he is named in this "letter of commendation" (vv. 16-23); the contrast between ἐμός and ἡμῶν in v. 23, along with the εἴτε ... εἴτε differentiation, suggests a distinction between Titus and his two fellow envoys. [ἐστιν] κοινωνὸς ἐμός, "my associate/partner/colleague" or my "friend-in-work" (Ollrog 77), points to shared commitments in the whole gospel enterprise as well as in the relief aid for Jerusalem.[55] The phrase εἰς ὑμᾶς συνεργός denotes collaboration between Titus and Paul in "the work of the Lord"[56] at Corinth. Titus was Paul's co-worker or fellow laborer "in relation to" (εἰς) the Corinthians, where that relation was one of service, although they had not served at Corinth at the same time.[57] Less proba-

---

54. 2 Cor. 1:7, 8; 5:12; 7:4, 14; 8:23, 24; 9:3; 12:5 (twice), 8. Most of these instances occur with the καυχ- root (καυχάομαι, καύχημα, καύχησις) (cf. BAGD 839a). But in 8:23 Betz gives ὑπέρ a technical sense: "On behalf of Titus: my partner representing me, and a fellow worker assigned to you" (38). Paul is authorizing Titus to be "his legal and administrative representative" (79). The absence of this ὑπέρ formula in reference to the two "brothers" (v. 23a) shows that they were not authorized to represent Paul as Titus did (80). But on this view, see the comments of Thrall 553.

55. For a very useful chart listing Paul's colleagues in the Christian mission and the terms used to describe them, see Ellis, "Co-Workers" 438.

56. Cf. 1 Cor. 16:10 in reference to Timothy: τὸ ... ἔργον κυρίου ἐργάζεται ὡς κἀγώ (cf. Rom. 16:21).

57. On the significance of the term συνεργός in Paul, see Ollrog 66-72. εἰς ὑμᾶς need not be taken to limit Titus's work in association with Paul to ministry in Corinth (pace Schlatter 603, who compares the unqualified description of Timothy as ὁ συνεργός μου in Rom. 16:21).

bly, συν- indicates cooperation with God (cf. 6:1) or with the Corinthians (cf. 1:24) (so Ollrog 70).[58]

εἴτε ἀδελφοὶ ἡμῶν, ἀπόστολοι ἐκκλησιῶν, δόξα Χριστοῦ. "If our brothers are in question, they are envoys of the churches and an honor to Christ." The balance between v. 23a and b is clear: in each case there is an identification followed by a double description. We might have expected ὑπὲρ ἀδελφῶν ἡμῶν to match ὑπὲρ Τίτου, but the construction is broken in dictating (Plummer 251), with the nominative ἀδελφοί resuming κοινωνός and συνεργός. Since εἰσίν must be supplied with ἀπόστολοι, this word is predicative and accordingly anarthrous, so that there can be no objection to rendering ἀπόστολοι ἐκκλησιῶν as "the emissaries of the churches" (NJB) or "the delegates of the congregations" (Martin 271), also bearing in mind the canon of Apollonius. By using the term ἀπόστολος of these two Christian brothers, Paul is not suggesting that they shared his status as ἀπόστολος Χριστοῦ Ἰησοῦ (1:1), someone who, like the Twelve (Matt. 10:2; 1 Cor. 15:5, 7), had seen the risen Lord (1 Cor. 9:1) and had been commissioned directly by Christ to exercise a distinctive leadership role within the church (1 Cor. 15:9-11; Gal. 1:1). Rather than being ἀπόστολοι Χριστοῦ (11:13; cf. 1 Thess. 2:7; Jude 17), these men were ἀπόστολοι ἐκκλησιῶν "envoys belonging to, sent by, and representing the churches."[59] In our discussion at 1:1 we distinguished three uses of the term ἀπόστολος in Paul — in reference to the Twelve and himself; of a limited number of church leaders who had a permanent but specific commission from Christ or the local church; and of those with a temporary and humanly approved commission, such as Epaphroditus, the envoy of the Philippian church (Phil. 2:25), and these two emissaries of 2 Cor. 8:23.[60] Which congregations appointed these two delegates is not known for sure,[61] but although the churches of Judea have been proposed (see on v. 19), it was more probably the Macedonian churches (cf. 8:1, 19, 24). Significantly, it was the Christians from Macedonia who had offered Paul their services in connection with the collection project (8:5).

The second summary description of the two ἀδελφοί was that they were δόξα Χριστοῦ. Occasionally this phrase is referred to its immediate antecedent ἐκκλησιῶν, so that it is the sending churches that form "the glory of Christ" in the

---

58. Hainz expands 8:23a thus: "(with regard to the preaching of the gospel) my partner, with regard to you (in the establishment and strengthening of the church) a co-worker (with me and with God)" (*Koinonia* 106).

59. This expression ἀπόστολοι ἐκκλησιῶν is a notable instance where one hesitates to opt for a single use of the genitive (cf. the phrase [ὁ] δέσμιος [τοῦ] Χριστοῦ Ἰησοῦ [Eph. 3:1; Phlm. 1, 9]); possessive, subjective, and objective nuances all seem to be implied.

60. Richardson suggests that in the Lukan expression οἱ ἀπόστολοι βαρναβᾶς καὶ Παῦλος (Acts 14:14), two distinct senses of ἀπόστολος are coalesced. Paul is an "apostle of Christ," but Barnabas is an "apostle" or emissary commissioned by the church of Antioch (Acts 13:3) (320). But Barnabas probably belongs to the second of the three categories we have distinguished (see on 1:1).

61. Moffatt and Barclay seem to give ἀπόστολοι a technical sense and to construe ἐκκλησιῶν as a generalizing plural referring to the church in general: "apostles of the Church/church" (Barclay and Moffatt respectively).

sense that they shine "like lights in the world" (Phil. 2:15) and so glorify Christ.[62] But this is unlikely, given the parallelism between v. 23a and b, and the infelicitous syntax involved. The delegates are said to be "the glory of Christ" in that they were "an honor to Christ" (TCNT) or "a credit to Christ" (Goodspeed) either by their exemplary lives and service or because they were trophies of Christ's saving grace; or in that they were an embodiment or worthy reflection of Christ's glory;[63] or in that they were "men in whom Christ is glorified" (Weymouth); or in that they promoted Christ's glory (cf. 3:18; 8:19) (Thrall 555). But for a link between "the glory of Christ" in 8:18, 23, the ministry of the new covenant, and the prophecies of Isaiah 60–62, see Carrez 188; "Souffrance" 90-91.

8:24 τὴν οὖν ἔνδειξιν τῆς ἀγάπης ὑμῶν καὶ ἡμῶν καυχήσεως ὑπὲρ ὑμῶν εἰς αὐτοὺς ἐνδεικνύμενοι εἰς πρόσωπον τῶν ἐκκλησιῶν. "So give these men public proof of your love and of the truth of our boasting about you, so that the churches can see it." This concluding appeal is based on (cf. οὖν) the whole preceding "letter of commendation" (vv. 16-23) but particularly on the summary of the delegates' credentials in v. 23. τὴν . . . ἔνδειξιν . . . ἐνδεικνύμενοι[64] is clearly a play on words, but while paronomasia involves the repetition of words similar in sound, they need not be similar or identical in meaning, even when (as here) they are related etymologically. But the common suggestion that the present case may be represented in English — although unidiomatically — by "demonstrate the demonstration" or "exhibit what is to be exhibited" overlooks the fact that there is a certain distinction of meaning between ἔνδειξις and ἐνδείκνυμι, apart from the obvious difference between a noun and a verb. ἔνδειξις is the act or means of making something known or obvious or visible, thus "demonstration," "proof," "indication." While ἐνδείκνυμι (only found in the middle voice in the NT) may mean "demonstrate" or "prove," the public nature of the demonstration is emphasized. "The noun describes a demonstration properly speaking, a means of proving something hidden; the verb refers to a manifestation of the proof by its being brought to the attention of others."[65] Thus, "give public proof. . . ." Others place the emphasis on the clarity of the proof, "clear proof" (Cassirer), "conspicuous proof" (Plummer 246), "unanswerable proof" (Barclay), or on the proof being by action.[66]

---

62. Barnett 427 and n. 67 (where Barrett [230] is wrongly cited as supporting this view; the RSV [and NRSV] is ambiguous).

63. "'They are Christ's own reflection' — that is, they are the very representatives of the heavenly splendor of Christ!" (Georgi 75), but that is not to say that Paul is ascribing "much higher rank and more prestige" to these two envoys than to Titus (as Georgi 75 asserts). While Titus was not ἀπόστολος ἐκκλησιῶν, Paul would hardly have denied him the title δόξα Χριστοῦ in another context.

64. For a defense of this reading over the imperative ἐνδείξασθε (preferred by WH; Plummer 251), see the Textual Note i.

65. Spicq, *Agape* 214, who renders 8:24, "Give publicly, therefore, for all the congregations to see, the demonstration of your love and of my right to boast of you."

66. Zerwick, *Analysis* 405, who defines ἔνδειξις as "comprobatio (quae factis fit)" ("proof [that is shown by actions]") and ἐνδείκνυμι/ἐνδείκνυμαι as "factis comprobo" ("I prove by actions").

Several explanations have been given of the participial form ἐνδει-κνύμενοι.[67]

1. Meyer (596) takes the participle in a temporal sense and supplies ἐνδείκνυσθε after it. "When you accordingly show . . . , you do it. . . ." He claims that "we have here an *indirect* exhortation, which puts the matter as a point of honor, and so touches the readers more effectively, without directly making a demand on them" (596; italics his). But a direct imperative is certainly not out of place (cf. 8:11, ἐπιτελέσατε) as the climax of a brief commendatory letter (vv. 16-23).
2. Turner regards the participle as elliptical, with ἔστε (imperative) to be understood: "You must be showing . . ." (*Insights* 166 and n.), although he allows for the possibility of an imperatival participle here.[68]
3. Daube prefers the imperative reading ἐνδείξασθε but suggests that if the participle be read, "it is best explained as loosely connected with the ὑμᾶς of verse 22" (481),[69] a verdict followed tentatively by Barrett in the absence of a better solution (230-31). But, given the distance between ὑμᾶς and ἐνδεικνύμενοι, any connection seems doubtful.
4. According to Verbrugge ἐνδεικνύμενοι originally stood at the end of an independent letter (ch. 8) with a conventional epistolary conclusion such as ἔρρωσθε ("Farewell!") or ἀσπάσασθε ("Greet . . .") which the redactor of the letter omitted (257). But an appeal to the putative work of such a redactor is unconvincing. Moreover, it is unlikely that a letter would end with its final, crucial thrust committed to a "dangling participle" in an otherwise verbless sentence.
5. The most satisfactory solution is to treat ἐνδεικνύμενοι as an instance of an imperatival participle[70] that occurs outside a parenetic context and apart from an adjacent finite verb.

There were two elements in this open demonstration that Paul was calling on the Corinthians to give. First, they were to afford proof of their love. τῆς

---

67. It is inadequate to account for this participle: as being an absolute use, standing for the indicative; as being an anacoluthon, on the principle that all participles which cannot be grammatically related to a finite verb are anacoluthic; or as simply a case of stylistic infelicity.

68. See his *Syntax* 303; *Style* 89. (He accents the imperative as ἐστέ.) Turner acknowledges that ἔστε never occurs in the NT (or the LXX — see Moulton and Howard 203) but believes that it "is frequently to be understood" (*Insights* 166 n.).

69. In his "Appended Note: Participle and Imperative in 1 Peter" (467-88 in Selwyn) Daube argues that examples of the imperatival participle in the NT (in Romans, Ephesians, Colossians, Hebrews, and 1 Peter) may be due to Hebrew influence, reflecting imperatival participles in Tannaitic rules (but see the comments of Turner, *Insights* 167-68). Daube appears to disallow 8:24 as an imperatival participle (481) on the ground that such NT participles are found only in general rules and not in commands addressed to specific people on specific occasions (470).

70. Thus, e.g., Moulton 181; Moule, "Peculiarities" 158; Martin 272, 279; Thrall 555; Spicq, *Agape* 214; and most EVV.

ἀγάπης ὑμῶν means simply "the love you have" (ὑμῶν, possessive genitive), "the love that is in you" (Cassirer). The recipients of their Christian love are not specified, but even if the primary focus is on the three delegates (and, by implication, the churches that two of them represent), there is no reason to exclude love for Paul, for Christ, and for the indigent members of the Jerusalem church (cf. Wolff 179). Second, the Corinthians were to give outward evidence of the truth of Paul's boasting about them (ἡμῶν καυχήσεως ὑπὲρ ὑμῶν). Apparently Paul had been boasting about the Corinthians' love[71] and perhaps also their commitment to the collection project shown in their readiness of intent (9:2; cf. 8:10-11). But it is also possible that ἡμῶν καυχήσεως means "our right to boast"[72] or "our pride in you" (NEB, REB) or "the reason for our pride in you" (NIV).

But to whom was this proof to be given? Whether we construe εἰς αὐτούς with καυχήσεως or with ἐνδεικνύμενοι (as seems more probable), the αὐτοί are most naturally taken to be the three delegates who would soon be in Corinth interacting with the believers there. To take εἰς αὐτούς with καυχήσεως and as referring to boasting "to believers in other churches [than Corinth]"[73] is an awkward application of "construction according to sense." We may fairly assume that the Corinthians would be providing this tangible proof of their genuine love and Paul's accurate boasting by receiving the delegates warmly, offering them hospitality, cooperating with their suggestions regarding the collection, and, above all, by actually bringing the collection to a successful conclusion.

εἰς πρόσωπον τῶν ἐκκλησιῶν, literally "in the face of the churches," means "before/in the presence of the churches,"[74] presumably the Macedonian churches from which the delegates probably came, but it is not impossible that ἐκκλησίαι here includes all Christian congregations of the time, but notably the mother-church in Jerusalem. Paul is reminding the Corinthians that since the delegates will be reporting back to their sending churches the outcome of their visit to Corinth, they need to conduct themselves during the visit as if they were in full view of those churches. The Corinthians would have been fully aware that envoys were to be treated as one would treat the principal,[75] so that what-

---

71. The single article with ἀγάπης and καυχήσεως points to the close relationship between the love and the boasting (cf. Zerwick §184; *Analysis* 405).

72. Allo 229; Spicq, *Agape* 214.

73. Zerwick, *Analysis* 405.

74. Hughes believes that εἰς πρόσωπον is probably a Semitism representing *lipnê*, "in the presence" (321 n.50). This is possible, but where this Hebrew expression means "under the eye and regard of," it is usually rendered in the LXX by ἐναντίον (e.g., Gen. 17:18) or ἐνώπιον (e.g., Ps. 61:8). In the view of Betz (85-86), πρόσωπον here reflects the Roman legal concept of *persona*, so that "the two brothers were the legal and political *persona* of the churches they represented" (86). He renders v. 24 by "Therefore show to them, as to the person of the churches, the evidence of your love and our boast about you" (38). Moule draws attention (159-60) to two "Peculiarities in the Language of II Corinthians": "the almost obsessive frequency" (159) of the word πρόσωπον in 2 Corinthians (12 uses out of 23 in the Pauline corpus) and the high incidence in 2 Corinthians 8 of sentences (10 or 11) without a "main" (or finite) verb.

75. Cf. the article by Mitchell on "New Testament Envoys."

ever "demonstration" (ἔνδειξις) was given to the delegates as representatives of certain churches or of Paul (in the case of Titus) was also a "demonstration" to their principals.[76] The Corinthians were now the actors, and other churches the witnesses.

Bibliography

Barrett, "Titus" • Barrett, *Signs* 45 • Barrett, "Shaliaḥ" • Carrez, *Souffrance* 90-91 • Ellis, "Co-Workers" • Hainz 147-57 • Lambrecht, "Boasting" • McKay, "Observations" • Meeks 65-67 • Mitchell, "Envoys" 644-51 • Morgan-Wynne • Moule, "Peculiarities" • Murphy-O'Connor 85-88 • Nickle 18-22 • Ollrog 33-37, 52-58 • E. Percy, *Die Probleme der Kolosser und Epheserbriefe* (Lund: Gleerup, 1946) 337-39 • Souter • Souter, "Relationship" • Stowers • Therrien 95-96, 256 • Verbrugge 254-60

2. The Need for Readiness (9:1-5)

In our discussion of the integrity of chs. 8 and 9 (Introduction, A.3.d.), we sought to establish that these two chapters belong together and that ch. 9 continues and elaborates the themes of ch. 8. On this view 9:1-5 belongs with 8:16-24 in dealing with one and the same "Mission of Titus and His Companions" (8:16–9:5). But what is the function of 9:1-5 in relation to 8:16-24?

In 8:21 Paul applies the general principle of Prov. 3:4 to his own conduct in organizing the collection: "We are giving forethought to what is honorable, not only in the Lord's eyes but also in human eyes." He planned to implement this principle in two ways. He was sending a three-man delegation to Corinth to oversee the finalization of the collection there and to guarantee the integrity of the process (8:16-24); and he was dispatching this delegation in advance of his own visit to Corinth (9:5), so that when he finally arrived contributions to the relief fund would not need to be made — the collection would be "ready" (9:3) — and so that he himself could avoid all personal contact with the money involved. Again, in 8:24, in the course of encouraging the Corinthians to show love to the three delegates, Paul had referred to his boasting to these men about the Corinthians, presumably about their eager willingness and settled intent to contribute to the fund (cf. 8:10-11; 9:2). Now he expresses his nagging unease that if other Macedonians came to Corinth with him (perhaps bearing the completed Macedonian collection), and the Corinthian collection was discovered on their arrival to be still incomplete, Paul and the Corinthians would feel humiliated and ashamed because of his inappropriate boasting and improper confidence

---

76. Wolff goes so far as to render εἰς αὐτοὺς . . . εἰς πρόσωπον τῶν ἐκκλησιῶν by "with respect to them, (that is) with respect to the churches!" (175). This reflects the repetition of εἰς but overlooks πρόσωπον. Georgi has ". . . to them (as well as) in the presence of the congregations" (75).

615

(9:2-4).[1] So, then, the emphasis in 9:1-5 is on a twofold need. First, the Corinthian need for "readiness" of completion before Paul's arrival, that is, the completion of their contribution to the relief fund with a willingly given and generous gift. Second, the need shared by Paul and the Corinthians to avoid the shame of having his boast about their "readiness" of intent proved empty.[2]

9:1*For concerning this service for God's people, there is no need[a] for me to continue writing to you like this. 2For I know your eager willingness which I am boasting about on your behalf to the Macedonians, telling them that Achaia has been ready since last year, and it was your[b] zeal[c] that has been a stimulus to most of them. 3But I am sending the brothers so that our boasting about you may not be proved empty in this matter, and so that you may be ready (just as I kept telling them you would be), 4lest if some Macedonians come with me and find you are not ready, we perhaps be put to shame — to say[d] nothing of yourselves — with regard to this undertaking.[e] 5So I have thought it necessary to urge the brothers to go on to[f] you ahead of me and to organize in advance your gift of blessing, previously promised, so that it may thus be ready as indeed a gift of blessing and[g] not as a gift that reflects avarice.*

TEXTUAL NOTES

a. p[46] g read the comparative περισσότερον ("rather superfluous"), perhaps a scribal correction to soften the blunt περισσόν ("superfluous").

b. ἐξ is added before ὑμῶν in D F G Ψ 0209 ℵ vg[ms] syr[h], probably to make it unambiguous that the meaning is "the zeal shown by you" (ὑμῶν, subjective genitive), not "their zeal for you" (ὑμῶν, objective genitive, as in 11:8). The simple ὑμῶν (p[46] ℵ B C P 0243 6 33 81 326 630 1175 1739 1881 *pc* lat syr[p] cop Ambrosiaster) is the preferred reading.

c. In Classical Greek ζῆλος is masculine, but in Hellenistic Greek it is either masculine or neuter. Since ζῆλος is usually masculine in the NT (John 2:17; Acts 5:17; 13:45; Rom. 10:2; 2 Cor. 7:7, 11; Jas. 3:14), with Phil. 3:6 (cf. Acts 5:17 B*) the only unambiguous instance of the neuter (7 NT uses of ζῆλος are ambiguous), a scribal change from τό (read by p[46] ℵ B 33 1175 *pc*) to ὁ (C D F G Ψ 0243 1739 1881 𝔐) is more probable than a change in the opposite direction.

d. Although the reading λέγωμεν has early and geographically diversified support (ℵ B C[2] Ψ 0209 0243 33 1739 1881 𝔐 f vg syr sa[mss] bo) and is preferred by WH, the singular λέγω, read by p[46] C* D F G 048 a p vg[mss] sa[ms] Ambrosiaster, is preferable on two grounds (thus Metzger 514): λέγωμεν may be explained as a scribal assimilation to the immediately preceding καταισχυνθῶμεν ἡμεῖς; the first person singular predominates in the context (vv. 1-3, 5).

---

1. Lambrecht argues that the lengthy addition to ch. 8, which is ch. 9, is probably prompted by the rather unexpected mention of boasting in 8:24 which forced Paul to explain the content and implications of that boasting ("Boasting" 359, 365, 367-68).

2. For this distinction between readiness of intent and readiness of completion, see the commentary on 9:2.

e. After ἐν τῇ ὑποστάσει ταύτῃ, the qualification τῆς καυχήσεως is added by ‭א‬²
D² (Ψ) 0209 𝔐 syr⁽ᵖ⁾ under the influence of a similar phrase in 11:17; it is a secondary
scribal clarification. The best Alexandrian (𝔭⁴⁶ ‭א‬* B 1739) and Western (D* F G) witnesses read simply ἐν τῇ ὑποστάσει ταύτῃ.

f. In the place of εἰς ὑμᾶς several witnesses (B D F G 365 1175 1505 pc) have the
secondary reading πρὸς ὑμᾶς, probably because when literal movement is expressed, εἰς
is generally used with impersonal objects and πρός with personal (Harris, "Prepositions" 1184).

g. καί is omitted by 𝔭⁴⁶ ᵛⁱᵈ ‭א‬* F G latt syrᵖ, probably to heighten the stark contrast
between ὡς εὐλογίαν and μὴ ὡς πλεονεξίαν.

9:1 Περὶ μὲν γὰρ τῆς διακονίας τῆς εἰς τοὺς ἁγίους περισσόν μοί ἐστιν τὸ
γράφειν ὑμῖν. "For concerning this service for God's people, there is no need for
me to continue writing to you like this." Although a number of scholars regard
ch. 9 as originally an independent letter,[3] we would argue that ch. 9 is closely
bound to ch. 8 by various contextual and grammatical links, especially here in
v. 1.

1. While the phrase περὶ δέ regularly introduces a new topic,[4] there is no evidence in extant Greek literature that the phrase περὶ μὲν γὰρ ever has an
   introductory function.[5] On the contrary, it always expresses a close relationship to what precedes.[6] In 9:1 μέν looks forward to δέ in v. 3 ("although . . . yet"), but γάρ looks back to 8:24, so that 9:1-4 (vv. 3-4 are one
   sentence) gives an explanation why the Corinthians should give the three
   delegates proof of the rightness of Paul's boasting about them (8:24), that
   is, he had in fact been boasting about the Corinthians' "readiness" and
   was sending the three brothers to ensure that this boasting would not turn
   out to be unwarranted. Alternatively, the sequence of thought that called
   for an explanatory γάρ may have been as follows. "I have been speaking
   about the three delegates and your need to welcome them warmly, for
   there is not need for me to write any further about the collection itself."[7]
2. The reference to ἡ διακονία ἡ εἰς τοὺς ἁγίους (9:1) repeats the identical
   phrase in 8:4 (see the commentary there) so that the article τῆς with
   διακονίας is naturally regarded as anaphoric, "this service (for God's peo-

3. For a classification and discussion of these views, see the Introduction, A.3.d.
4. E.g., 1 Cor. 7:1; 8:1; 12:1; 16:1.
5. See the detailed analysis of the issue in Stowers 340-48. In the only other NT instance of
this phrase (Acts 28:22, where μέν is *solitarium*), it provides the reason ("for with regard to this
sect, we know that it is denounced on all sides") why the local leaders of the Jews expressed a desire to have Paul himself state his views.
6. Stowers 345.
7. Cf. Wendland's rendering (222) of 9:1: "For I certainly do not need to write to you further
about the service (itself) which is destined for the saints." It is far less likely that γάρ is merely transitional ("now," Cassirer) or emphatic ("indeed," TCNT; "really," JB, NJB), or supports an unexpressed thought (so BAGD 152a, apparently), or is a redactional addition (Verbrugge 100-101;
Thrall 42, 564). On the other hand, γάρ could be inferential in 9:1 ("so," Furnish 421).

ple)"[8] which Paul has been discussing in ch. 8, especially if there had been a dictation break at the end of that chapter.

3. As in Phil. 3:1, the present infinitive γράφειν probably indicates action in progress, "to be writing."[9] As with τῆς διακονίας, the article with γράφειν will be anaphoric; thus "to go on with this writing," or "to be writing to you [as I have done]" (Martin 282-83), or "to go on writing to you like this" (Barrett 233).[10]

4. The introduction in 9:3 of a reference to sending "the brothers" (ἔπεμψα δὲ τοὺς ἀδελφούς), without any indication of their identity or their number, is strange unless "the brothers" are the three spoken of in 8:16-24 where the term ἀδελφός is used three times and a compound of πέμψω twice (8:18, 22).

When Paul comments "It is superfluous[11] for me to write any further to you about this act of service that is intended for (εἰς) God's people," yet proceeds to speak further (in 9:2-15) about this charitable project, he is employing the rhetorical device known as *paraleipsis*.[12] In this "figure of thought" (σχῆμα διανοίας) a speaker or writer professes to pass over a certain matter only to mention or expound it. Heb. 11:32-38 is the most celebrated NT example.

9:2 οἶδα γὰρ τὴν προθυμίαν ὑμῶν ἣν ὑπὲρ ὑμῶν καυχῶμαι Μακεδόσιν ὅτι Ἀχαΐα παρεσκεύασται ἀπὸ πέρυσι. "For I know your eager willingness which I am boasting about on your behalf to the Macedonians, telling them that Achaia has been ready since last year." In this verse Paul explains why (cf. γάρ) it was unnecessary for him to dwell further on issues related to the collection (v. 1). It was because he was well aware how willing and eager the Corinthians were to participate in the project; in fact, he had been constantly boasting about their eager willingness to contribute as he continued his ministry in Macedonia.

As in 8:19, προθυμία may here mean "goodwill" (Furnish 420-21) or "eagerness to help" (NIV; cf. NEB, REB), although, given the fact that προθυμία

---

8. This point, or the suggestion of Plummer (252 n.) that εἰς τοὺς ἁγίους replaces the ταύτης one might have expected with τῆς διακονίας, partially answers the objection of Thrall (39, 42, 564 n. 7) regarding the omission of ταύτης. But she rightly observes (39) that apart from 8:4 and 9:1 each reference to the collection itself in chs. 8 and 9 is qualified by the demonstrative pronoun (8:6-7, 19-20; 9:5, 12-13).

9. In Phil. 3:1 τὰ αὐτὰ γράφειν ὑμῖν, "to be writing the same things to you," probably refers to Paul's treatment in Phil. 3:2-11 of matters that he had earlier communicated orally to the Philippians (thus O'Brien 352). The only other uses of this γράφειν in the Pauline corpus are in 1 Thess. 4:8; 5:1, where the present infinitive is timeless.

10. On this view, τὸ γράφειν in 9:1 points backward, and the anarthrous γράφειν in Phil. 3:1 points forward (see previous note). There is a remarkable parallel to 9:1 in P. Oxy. 7.1070[17] (cited in MM 277b): τὸ μὲν οὖν γράφειν σοι περὶ τῶν πραγμάτων ἡμῶν . . . περιττὸν νῦν ἡγησάμην. "So I now regard it as superfluous . . . to write to you further about our business" (my translation).

11. Technically, τὸ γράφειν ("this [continuance in] writing") is the subject of ἐστιν, but it is not inappropriate to translate the verse as though ἐστιν were impersonal.

12. Gk. παράλειψις, "a passing over" (= Latin *praeteritio* or *praetermissio*), sometimes transliterated as *paralepsis* or *paralipsis* (as BDF §495[1]).

may mean "willingness," "readiness," "eagerness," or "goodwill" (cf. BAGD 706c), the word may have the sense of "goodwill" in 8:19 and "eager willingness" here (cf. NRSV).[13] In Classical Greek a variety of cases and constructions follows the verb καυχάομαι (often εἴς τι), but when it is used transitively in the NT the full following construction (as here and in 7:14) is τί τινι ὑπέρ τινος, "say someth[ing] boastingly (or in pride) to someone concerning someone" (BAGD 426a). Accordingly, ἥν, which refers to τὴν προθυμίαν ὑμῶν, should be seen as a direct object (cf. 7:14; 10:8; 11:30), not an accusative of respect. After τὴν προθυμίαν ὑμῶν the phrase ὑπὲρ ὑμῶν ("concerning you") seems somewhat redundant and suggests that here it may bear the sense "in your honor"[14] or "on your behalf,"[15] which would hint that Paul was concerned with enhancing the Corinthians' reputation among other believers, an interesting backdrop to 9:4.

If the Corinthians' eager willingness to participate in the collection was the content of Paul's boasting, that content is more closely defined by the clause ὅτι Ἀχαΐα παρεσκεύασται ἀπὸ πέρυσι. With ὅτι we must understand λέγων ("telling them that . . ."), although ὅτι could be taken as recitative: "'Achaia,' I tell them, 'has been ready since last year!'"[16] Because Paul refers to Achaia, and not to the Corinthians, some have found in this fact evidence that ch. 9 is a separate circular letter to Christians of Achaia outside of Corinth (e.g., Betz 91-93, 139-40). But there are other adequate explanations of this fact. "Achaia" may refer to all the Christians in the Roman province of Achaia, including the Corinthian believers (cf. Rom. 15:26),[17] with Paul choosing to speak of "Achaia" either perhaps to avoid exaggeration about "readiness" (since the Corinthians had done comparatively little about the collection) (Plummer 254) or because he is reproducing his actual boast to the Macedonians (Meyer 601). Alternatively, "Achaia" may in fact refer simply to Corinth, that is, the believers in Corinth. In this case, Ἀχαΐα stands instead of Κόρινθος either because Paul has just mentioned the believers in another Roman province (Macedonia) or because he "flatters the Corinthians by this virtual identification of the province with their own city" (Tasker 123). In favor of this second option is the fact that if the content of Paul's boasting is the Corinthians' eager willingness (προθυμία) as further defined by the ὅτι clause, then Ἀχαΐα will

13. Also, we have proposed that when ἡ προθυμία is qualified by τοῦ θέλειν (as in 8:11 explicitly and in 8:12 implicitly), the resulting sense is "eagerness of desire" = "eager desire." In the only other NT use (in addition to 8:11-12, 19; 9:2) of προθυμία, it means "eagerness" (Acts 17:11).

14. Zerwick, Analysis 406.

15. Cf. BAGD 839a, which notes that when ὑπέρ is "about equivalent to περί [τινος]," it often at the same time means "in the interest of" or "in behalf of."

16. Bruce, Paraphrase 145, 147; similarly Carrez 188; Wolff 180.

17. However understood, the term Ἀχαΐα is a case of a country signifying its inhabitants, in this instance its Christian inhabitants (cf. BAGD 128a). Both TCNT and Weymouth render Ἀχαΐα by "you in Greece." Although we know of no churches in Achaia apart from Corinth and Cenchreae (Rom. 16:1), the two qualifiers in 2 Cor. 1:1 ("together with all [πᾶσιν] God's people who are in the whole [ὅλῃ] of Achaia") point to a considerable number of believers living outside of Corinth or Cenchreae.

naturally refer back to the ὑμῶν in the phrase τὴν προθυμίαν ὑμῶν and the ὑμῖν of v. 1, that is, the Corinthians (on the assumption of the unity of chs. 8 and 9). Note also the following τὸ ὑμῶν ζῆλος.

In the middle voice παρασκευάζω means "prepare (oneself)" or "make preparations," and in the perfect tense "be ready" (cf. BAGD 622b), so that with the following qualification ("since last year") Ἀχαΐα παρεσκεύασται will mean "Achaia has been ready." But vv. 3-5 clearly imply that the Corinthians were not yet "ready" (note the same root, παρεσκευασμένοι, in v. 3 and ἀπαρασκευάστους in v. 4). How is this apparent discrepancy to be explained?[18] Did Paul exaggerate the extent of the Corinthians' "readiness" in order to encourage the Macedonians to contribute quickly and generously?[19] Perhaps the solution lies in a distinction between two types of preparedness or readiness, what Hughes (324) calls a "preparedness of intention" and a "preparedness of completion." In 8:10-11 Paul indicates that the Corinthians had led the way during the previous year not only in taking action regarding the collection but also in desiring (τὸ θέλειν) to do so, but now needed to complete (ἐπιτελέσατε . . . τὸ ἐπιτελέσαι) their action as well. What Paul had been boasting to the Macedonians about was the Corinthians' preparedness or "readiness" of desire or intention (τὸ θέλειν)[20] that was the prerequisite for any "readiness" of completion (τὸ ἐπιτελέσαι). He had been saying that they were "ready to give" (NIV) or "ready to undertake this service" (Phillips), not that they "had everything ready" (NEB, REB) in the sense of having all the money for the relief fund collected, "ready" for transfer to Jerusalem. It is the sequence τὴν προθυμίαν ὑμῶν ἣν . . . καυχῶμαι . . . ὅτι . . . παρεσκεύασται that suggests that the "readiness" actually was the "eager willingness" to contribute to the charitable offering. Moreover, 8:10-11 speaks of ἡ προθυμία τοῦ θέλειν, "eagerness of desire" or "eager desire," that was evident in the Corinthians "last year," an eager desire about which Paul had boasted to the three delegates (8:24) as well as to the Macedonians. Also, it was the zeal (ζῆλος) shown by the Corinthians, not the successful completion of their offering, that spurred the Macedonians on to action (v. 2b). On this interpretation of παρεσκεύασται, Paul was being completely truthful, neither going "somewhat" beyond the facts (as Plummer [254] suggests) nor "perhaps" being overly optimistic (as Barrett [234] submits).

18. Thrall discusses three proposed solutions (but not the one espoused below in the text) and finds each inadequate (565-66). Her own suggestion is that Paul boasts to the Macedonians about the situation he found in Corinth after arriving on the "interim (= second) visit," when "preparations for the Corinthian contribution appeared to be well in hand" (566). But this overlooks the updated, negative information that Titus must have brought to Paul in Macedonia on his return from delivering the "severe letter," information that prompted Paul to write chs. 8 and 9.

19. Martin, who regards ch. 9 as "a separate composition but written in swift succession to chap. 8" and as having a wider audience than ch. 8 (namely, all the Christians in the city of Corinth and beyond in the province of Achaia) (250), nevertheless believes that in 9:2 "Achaia" refers to Achaean Christians, not Corinthian believers, so that Paul is speaking "the sober truth" when he says that "Achaia has been prepared since last year."

20. The term "readiness" here means not simple "willingness" (= προθυμία) but the state of being prepared (contrast n. 55 in the section 8:7-12).

In 8:10 ἀπὸ πέρυσι means "last year," referring to the time at which something occurred, namely the commencement of the collection in Corinth. Here it means "since last year," denoting the time from which something is measured, viz. Corinthian "readiness." The Corinthians had been "ready to give" ever since Titus had helped them initiate their collection (8:6, 10) (spring 55), or even before that, when they requested information from Paul about procedures to follow in arranging their contributions (cf. 1 Cor. 16:1) (early 55).

The present tense καυχῶμαι is significant. It not only indicates that Paul is in Macedonia as he writes and that the boasting is constant. It also is further evidence that 2 Corinthians was not written immediately after he had arrived in Macedonia (see the commentary on 7:8). At the same time this letter was being composed he was boasting to the Macedonians, whether the Philippians, the Thessalonians, the Bereans, or other Christians in the province, presumably while he was engaged in evangelistic and pastoral work in at least some of these churches.[21] Further, καυχῶμαι Μακεδόσιν suggests that the Macedonian collection was not yet complete, in spite of the aorists in 8:2 (ἐπερίσσευσεν), 8:5 (ἔδωκαν), and 8:2 (ἠρέθισεν). For why would Paul bother to boast to the Macedonians about the Corinthian readiness in order to stir them to action if their collection was already *complete*?

καὶ τὸ ὑμῶν ζῆλος ἠρέθισεν τοὺς πλείονας. "And it was your zeal that has been a stimulus to most of them." Here Paul states the result of his incessant boasting. ζῆλος, "zeal," "enthusiasm," is simply a more intense form of προθυμία, "eager willingness"; indeed, προθυμίαν ἔχειν means "have zeal." Evidently Paul was boasting about both of these Corinthian qualities as they related to the collection, just as he had applauded Titus's "zeal" (σπουδή, 8:16; σπουδαῖος, 8:17) and that of the second unnamed brother (σπουδαῖος, 8:22 twice) in the same regard. In the expression τὸ ὑμῶν ζῆλος the personal pronoun is emphatic, being in the attributive position (cf. 1:6; 12:19; 13:9):[22] "and it was really your zeal that stimulated most of them" (TCNT). ἐρεθίζω, which has a negative sense in Col. 3:21 ("Do not rouse your children to anger"), the only other NT use of the verb, here bears a positive meaning, "stir up," "stimulate," "spur on." τοὺς πλείονας may be an elative comparative (cf. Turner 30), "very many" or "a great number," but more probably it has the same sense as in 2:6, "the majority" or "most," referring to the Macedonians, although Carrez (188, 191) sees a reference to all the churches contributing to the fund for the Jerusalem church. Those who were spurred on by Paul's account of the enthusiasm of the Corinthians were roused not to compete with them (as Betz 93) and not so much to emulate them (Barrett 234) as simply to follow the example of their keenness, which led these Macedonians to give sacrificially and generously (8:2). If the expression οἱ πλείονες implies a minority (cf. 2:6) who were not spurred on by the Corinthian example, we have no way of knowing the reasons

---

21. See the suggested "Chronology" (Introduction, C.), items 17-19.
22. Turner 190; also BDF §284 (2).

for their inaction.[23] Perhaps they were among those Macedonian believers who had already supported Paul financially (11:8-9) and felt they were unable to do more (Thrall 567). Perhaps they were so poverty-stricken (cf. 8:2) that they were not able to contribute at the time but planned to do so as soon as their circumstances changed.

The relation between the Corinthian and Macedonian examples in chs. 8 and 9 may now be summarized.

1. The Corinthians showed an "eager desire" (ἡ προθυμία τοῦ θέλειν, 8:11) and an "eager willingness" (προθυμία, 9:2) to take part in the collection, which led them to begin the project (8:10) with Titus's help (8:6).
2. Paul appealed to this Corinthian preparedness or "readiness" of intent and also to their zeal (ζῆλος) when encouraging the Macedonians to continue with their own collection. His appeal proved successful, for the majority of Macedonians were spurred on to imitate the Corinthians' enthusiasm (9:2) as they brought their offering nearer to completion.
3. By the time Paul wrote 2 Corinthians the Macedonian collection was well advanced, so that he could inform the Corinthians that the Macedonian believers had given willingly and generously in spite of their destitute state and arduous trials (8:2-5).
4. Because the Corinthian offering was languishing, Paul appealed to the Macedonian example of liberal giving (8:1-5, 8) to encourage the Corinthians to bring to completion (8:6-7, 10-11) the generous gift they had promised to contribute (9:5).
5. So then, just as the Corinthian ζῆλος had been an actual stimulus to the Macedonians (9:2), the Macedonian σπουδή became a potential stimulus to the Corinthians (8:8).

9:3 ἔπεμψα δὲ τοὺς ἀδελφούς, ἵνα μὴ τὸ καύχημα ἡμῶν τὸ ὑπὲρ ὑμῶν κενωθῇ ἐν τῷ μέρει τούτῳ, ἵνα καθὼς ἔλεγον παρεσκευασμένοι ἦτε. "But I am sending the brothers so that our boasting about you may not be proved empty in this matter, and so that you may be ready (just as I kept telling them you would be)." Vv. 3 and 4 are one sentence that contains four purpose clauses, the first three being dependent on ἔπεμψα and the last on καταισχυνθῶμεν ἡμεῖς.

v. 1		μὲν . . .				
v. 3	ἔπεμψα	δὲ τοὺς ἀδελφούς,	ἵνα	μὴ . . .	κενωθῇ	
			ἵνα	. . .	παρεσκευασμένοι	ἦτε
v. 4				μή πως . . .	καταισχυνθῶμεν	ἡμεῖς
			ἵνα	μὴ	λέγω	ὑμεῖς

---

23. Betz (93 n. 30) wonders whether the Bereans became contributors only at the end (cf. Acts 20:4, "Sopater of Berea").

Through these first three purpose clauses Paul gives three reasons — two negative and one positive — for his sending of the three brothers to Corinth:

(a) to prevent his boasting to the brothers about the Corinthians (8:24) from turning out to be unjustified (v. 3a);
(b) to make sure that the Corinthians were in a state of full readiness with regard to their collection when he arrived (v. 3b);
(c) to avoid humiliation in the event that some Macedonians should come with him and find the Corinthians unprepared (v. 4).

The conjunction δέ looks back to μέν in v. 1: "Although (μέν) it is superfluous for me to write any further . . . , yet (δέ) I am sending the brothers." If, however, the correlatives μὲν . . . δέ do not point to a contrast, at least they specify successive points, "in the first place . . . in the second place" (Plummer 246-47, 253-54). As was the case with συνεπέμψαμεν in 8:18, 22, ἔπεμψα is probably an epistolary aorist (Fanning 282), but when ch. 9 is regarded as a separate, later composition (so Martin 250) this aorist is naturally taken as preterit and not epistolary (Martin 284). There is good reason for believing that τοὺς ἀδελφούς refers to all three delegates whose credentials are given in 8:16-23: the article could be anaphoric ("the brothers mentioned earlier"); they are introduced here without any qualification that gives their identity or their number; the two unnamed men of ch. 8 are each called an ἀδελφός (8:18, 22) and together are called ἀδελφοί (8:23), while Titus is referred to as Paul's ἀδελφός in 2:13; it would be strange for Titus to be excluded from this reference to "the brothers" when the two ἀδελφοί of 8:23 were traveling with him (8:18, 22) and he was leading the delegation. (Paul's "sending" [ἔπεμψα] of Titus is not incompatible with Titus's going to Corinth "on his own accord" [αὐθαίρετος, 8:17].)

One of Paul's purposes in dispatching the brothers was to avoid (ἵνα μή) having his boasting come to nothing. The normal distinction between καύχημα and καύχησις is that the former denotes the content or object of boasting, the latter the act of boasting. Here, then, καύχημα is what was said by Paul as he boasted,[24] namely that the Corinthians were "ready" in the sense of having an eager willingness (προθυμία) and zeal (ζῆλος) concerning the relief project (v. 2). But since the distinction is not uniform (e.g., in 1:12 καύχησις means "what we boast about"), it is possible that καύχημα here signifies the act of boasting.[25] The plural ἡμῶν reflects the similar expression ἡμῶν καυχήσεως in 8:24; apart from this ἡμῶν and καταισχυνθῶμεν ἡμεῖς in 9:4, only the singular is found in 9:1-5. The articular phrase τὸ ὑπὲρ ὑμῶν serves to avoid misunderstanding (BDF §269[2]) by preventing ὑπὲρ ὑμῶν from being construed with κενωθῇ. As well as meaning "empty" in a literal or figurative sense, the verb

24. So BAGD 426a; Bultmann, *TDNT* 3.649 n. 35.
25. Thus Zerwick, *Analysis* 406.

κενόω may carry the meaning "render void," so that the passive means "be made void" or "come to nothing." If κενωθῇ is classified as an effective or resultative aorist, the emphasis will fall on the existing result, captured by the English "be proved empty."[26] The boasting would prove hollow if, through the lack of the necessary organization, the Corinthians failed to translate their enthusiasm for the project into action. ἐν τῷ μέρει τούτῳ, "in this particular matter" (Barclay),[27] refers to the relief fund in general or to the actual completion of the collection in particular, and thereby limits the area where Paul's boasting about the Corinthians might turn out to be invalid.

Paul's second aim — this time a positive one — in sending the three-man delegation to Corinth ahead of him was to ensure that the Corinthians were fully ready by the time he arrived, just as he had been reassuring the men that they would be. παρεσκευασμένοι ἦτε is a rare periphrastic perfect subjunctive after ἵνα (see 1:9 for another), here formed by the perfect participle middle[28] with the subjunctive of εἰμί. The literal sense is "(so that) you may be in a state of having prepared yourselves," thus "(so that) you may be ready." With the perfect, the emphasis is on a continuous, settled state of readiness. Perhaps it is to bring out this connotation or the implied contrast with παρεσκεύασται ἀπὸ πέρυσι in v. 2 that some versions add "really" or "truly" with the word "ready."[29] It would seem clear that whereas in v. 2 the "readiness" was a matter of preparedness of intent (cf. 8:10-11, τὸ θέλειν), here it is a case of preparedness of completion (cf. 8:11, τὸ ἐπιτελέσαι) (cf. Hughes 324).[30] That Paul was expecting that the funds would all be collected by the time he arrived (and, by implication, that his boasting would not prove empty), is clear from καθὼς ἔλεγον, "just as I kept telling them you would be."[31] The imperfect is iterative, and the persons to whom Paul gave these repeated reassurances were the ἀδελφοί who are explicitly mentioned in the same verse, not the Macedonians (as Plummer 254) who are but one party of addressees (cf. 8:24) implied by the phrase τὸ καύχημα ἡμῶν.

9:4 μή πως ἐὰν ἔλθωσιν σὺν ἐμοὶ Μακεδόνες καὶ εὕρωσιν ὑμᾶς ἀπαρασκευάστους καταισχυνθῶμεν ἡμεῖς, ἵνα μὴ λέγω ὑμεῖς, ἐν τῇ ὑποστάσει ταύτῃ. "Lest if some Macedonians come with me and find you are not ready, we perhaps be put to shame — to say nothing of yourselves — with regard to this undertaking." For an analysis of the structure of vv. 3-4, see on v. 3. Here in

---

26. Barclay; Barrett 231; similarly NEB, REB, ". . . to ensure that what we have said about you in this matter should not prove to be an empty boast." BAGD 428b suggests the rendering "lose its justification," and A. Oepke, "come to nothing" (*TDNT* 3.661).

27. For μέρος meaning "matter," "affair," see BAGD 506b; MM 399a (4).

28. Not passive (as Robertson 375; *Pictures* 247); see BAGD 622b.

29. JB, "really are ready"; Lang 322, "tatsächlich"; Wendland (222), de Boor (188), and Wolff 180 all have "wirklich" in brackets; Carrez (189), "réellement"; Conybeare in Conybeare and Howson 455, "truly." Both Moffatt and Goodspeed have "all ready."

30. NLT paraphrases v. 2 "ready to send an offering," and v. 4 "really are ready . . . with your money all collected."

31. Cf. RSV, NIV, NRSV: "as I said you would be"; similarly Moffatt; Martin 280.

v. 4 Paul states a second negative reason for his dispatch of the three emissaries to Corinth — his concern about mutual humiliation if the Corinthians should be discovered to be still unprepared when he arrived. The word order μή πως ἐάν (not μὴ ἐάν πως) indicates that the uncertainty expressed by the enclitic particle πώς ("somehow," "perhaps") relates to καταισχυνθῶμεν and not ἔλθωσιν, or εὕρωσιν:[32] "lest[33] if . . . , we perhaps be put to shame." Since Μακεδόνες is anarthrous, it is unlikely to refer to the two unnamed brothers of 8:18-23 who were probably Macedonian, but will refer to an indefinite number of persons from Macedonia ("some Macedonians"), probably the bearers of the Macedonian collection, who would probably accompany Paul on his next visit to Corinth.[34] Significantly, it was the Macedonian believers who had put themselves at Paul's disposal to assist him in any way he wished with regard to the collection (8:5). ἐάν qualifies both ἔλθωσιν and εὕρωσιν and should be rendered "if," but with ἔλθωσιν the sense is "if, as is probable,"[35] while with εὕρωσιν the meaning is "if, as is possible." That is, Paul was expecting to have an escort as he came to Corinth[36] but believed that his fear that the Corinthians would not have completed their offering by the time he arrived would not be realized. If, however, his fear was realized and the Corinthians were discovered by the Macedonians (εὕρωσιν) to be "not ready" (ἀπαρασκευάστους[37]), he would be not merely acutely embarrassed but actually shamed or disgraced (καταισχυνθῶμεν ἡμεῖς); everyone would see that his insistence (cf. ἔλεγον, v. 3) that they would in fact be fully prepared was a groundless boast. Paul really wishes to say μή πως . . . καταισχυνθῆτε ("lest . . . you perhaps be humiliated"), but to avoid offending his readers (note πώς, "perhaps") or in an appeal to their reputation he applies the point primarily to himself (ἡμεῖς) but then adds a parenthetical application to the Corinthians (ἵνα μὴ λέγω ὑμεῖς, "not to say, 'you'"[38]) ostensibly as an afterthought, but in effect this seeming afterthought is all the more potent for being parenthical.[39] Paul is not trying to cajole the Corinthians into compliance by fostering rivalry between the Achaians in the south and the Macedo-

32. But cf. NJB: "if by chance some of the Macedonians came."

33. If, in translation, a new sentence is begun with v. 4, μή could be rendered by "Otherwise" (TCNT, Cassirer; cf. NRSV) or by "Or else" (Betz 87).

34. Nickle, who denies that the two delegates of 8:18-23 were Macedonians (19-20), believes that these "Macedonians" are the delegates from Macedonia chosen to accompany Paul to Jerusalem with the collection (cf. 1 Cor. 16:4; Acts 20:4) (22 n. 38).

35. Cf. the similar sense of ἐάν with the aorist subjunctive in 5:1. But JB takes ἐάν with ἔλθωσιν as expressive of certainty (also Tasker 124): "If some of the Macedonians who are coming with me. . . ."

36. An escort, "after the fashion of the ancient church," comments Meyer (602), citing Acts 17:14-15; Rom. 15:24; 1 Cor. 16:6; 2 Cor. 1:16.

37. The adjective ἀπαρασκεύαστος ("unprepared," "not ready") is a *hapax* in Biblical Greek, standing for the more common ἀπαράσκευος.

38. De Boor 188; similarly Wendland 222; Lang 322. Alternatively: "not to mention you" (Martin 281; Betz 87), "to say nothing of yourselves" (Furnish 421), "not to speak of your shame" (Louw and Nida §31.84).

39. Cf. BDF §495(1); Robertson 1199; *Pictures* 247.

nians in the north, but he *is* appealing to their reputation and so their desire to avoid "shame."[40] As also was the case with his plan to send a three-man delegation to Corinth, Paul wished to exert legitimate psychological pressure on the Corinthians, knowing as he did the erratic progress of the collection at Corinth thus far.[41]

In the final phrase of this long and somewhat awkward sentence (vv. 3-4), ἐν τῇ ὑποστάσει ταύτῃ, the preposition may mean "in (regard to)" or "because of," but there has been a wide variety of renderings of ὑπόστασις[42] which may be grouped into three categories.

1. By far the most common rendering in EVV is "confidence"[43] or the equivalent.[44] Spicq argues for "assurance,"[45] and the use of ὑπόστασις in Ruth 1:12, Ezek. 19:5, and Ps. 38:8 (where it stands in parallelism to ὑπομονή, "hope," "expectation" [see Ps. 9:19]) shows that the meaning "expectation" or "hope" is not impossible.

2. "Situation," "condition": thus "in this situation, i.e., on the basis of overhasty praise."[46]

3. "Project,"[47] "undertaking,"[48] "plan"; "enterprise" or "venture."[49]

The two main options seem to be: "because of this confidence of ours [in boasting about your readiness]" (9:3b), that is, "for having expressed such confidence" (Goodspeed); or, "with regard to this project/undertaking [of boasting]" (cf. 11:17). If linguistic considerations favor the latter alternative, the context seems to favor the former, "in view of the typical correspondence of expectation and being ashamed" (as Bultmann expresses it).[50]

9:5 ἀναγκαῖον οὖν ἡγησάμην παρακαλέσαι τοὺς ἀδελφοὺς ἵνα προ-

---

40. On "social shame" in the ancient world and on θριαμβεύειν in 2:14 as a metaphor of social shame, see Marshall, "Metaphor" 302-17.

41. "Given the Corinthian unhappiness that Paul had declined to receive their patronage, but that the Macedonians had sent him money to support his ministry serving the Corinthians (see . . . 11:8-9), his present challenge that the Corinthians not lose face in the presence of poor Macedonians is very pointed" (Barnett 433 n. 34).

42. Plummer notes (255) that in the LXX it renders some fifteen Hebrew words.

43. RV, TCNT, Weymouth, Goodspeed, Williams, NEB, NASB, NJB, REB, Cassirer. Among the commentators Lietzmann 136-37; Plummer 247, 255; Barrett 234.

44. Moffatt, RSV, GNB, JB, NAB¹, NIV, NAB².

45. Spicq 3.422; also Carrez 189 (". . . cette belle assurance!"); Young and Ford 271.

46. H. Dörrie, Ὑπόστασις. *Wort- und Bedeutungsgeschichte* (Nachrichten der Akademie der Wissenschaften in Göttingen. I. Philologisch-historische Klasse, 3) (Göttingen, 1955) 39, as cited by Koester, *TDNT* 8.584 n. 119. Also (apparently) BAGD 847a, adding the meaning "frame of mind"; cf. Martin 281 ("because of this eventuality").

47. Koester, *TDNT* 8.584-85 ("plan" or "project"); Danker 136 and BAGD³ 1040d; Betz 87, 95; Thrall 568-70 (a detailed defense of Koester's view).

48. Furnish 427-28; Danker 136; Lambrecht 144; NRSV (but "confidence" in 11:17).

49. G. Harder, *NIDNTT* 1.712.

50. R. Bultmann, *TDNT* 1.190.

ἔλθωσιν εἰς ὑμᾶς καὶ προκαταρτίσωσιν τὴν προεπηγγελμένην εὐλογίαν ὑμῶν. "So I have thought it necessary to urge the brothers to go on to you ahead of me and to organize in advance your gift of blessing, previously promised." οὖν may look back to the three reasons given in vv. 3-4 for the sending of the envoys but more probably only v. 4 is in view, namely, Paul's desire to avoid mutual humiliation. As Plummer paraphrases the connection: "To avoid this possible discredit I thought it absolutely necessary . . ." (247). As in the closely parallel Phil. 2:25,[51] ἡγησάμην should be taken as an epistolary aorist,[52] but understandably most EVV render it as a past ("I thought") since the "urging" of the brothers had already taken place at the time of writing and they acceded to Paul's request. "I have thought it necessary" (NEB, REB) catches the sense, as also in 2 Macc. 9:21. ἀναγκαῖον is indirectly opposed to περισσόν (v. 1; cf. μὲν . . . δέ, vv. 1, 3). In ch. 8 Paul is said to have "urged" or "requested" Titus (8:6) and to be "sending" the two unnamed brothers (8:18, 22); in ch. 9 he "sends" Titus as well as the other two delegates (9:3) and "urges" or "requests" the other two as well as Titus (9:5).[53] So, then, all three men were "sent" ([συν-]πέμπω) by Paul after responding to his "urging" or "requesting" (παρακαλέω). This threesome not only delivered and explained the present letter (the canonical 2 Corinthians, in our view) but also stayed on in Corinth to facilitate the completion of the collection there.

ἵνα προέλθωσιν . . . καὶ προκαταρτίσωσιν defines not the purpose but the content of the παράκλησις, and is equivalent to an infinitive expressing the object after a verb of asking such as παρακαλέω,[54] as if Paul had written . . . παρακαλέσαι τοὺς ἀδελφοὺς προελθεῖν . . . καὶ προκαταρτίσαι. Paul requested the three to form an advance party to Corinth with regard to the collection, to go on ahead (προέλθωσιν) of him and to make arrangements in advance (προκαταρτίσωσιν) of his own arrival. The emphasis, and the new element in comparison with the use of (συμ-)πέμπω in 8:18, 22; 9:3, is found in the repeated prefix προ-, "in advance" or "ahead of me." Clearly Paul was not expecting to stay in Macedonia indefinitely but to follow the "advance party" relatively soon. That interval would not only allow the Corinthians adequate time to complete their contribution under the direction of the three but would also permit the Macedonians to finalize arrangements for their own offering, including perhaps the election of delegates (the Μακεδόνες of 9:4). The verb προκαταρτίζω may bear a neutral sense, "get things ready in advance" (Betz 87) or "make arrangements in advance" (Thrall 563), but given the fact that the simplex καταρτίζω means "put in order" (cf. 13:11, καταρτίζεσθε, "mend your ways," BAGD 417d) and that the Corinthians had a propensity for disorderliness (cf. 1 Cor. 14:33, 40), this verb

51. Ἀναγκαῖον δὲ ἡγησάμην Ἐπαφρόδιτον . . . πέμψαι πρὸς ὑμᾶς.

52. Robertson, Pictures 248; Moule 12; Fanning 282. For the use of ἀναγκαῖον ἡγεῖσθαι in the papyri, see MM 31c, 277b.

53. As in 8:6, Betz regards παρακαλεῖν in 9:5 as having a technical administrative sense, "appoint" (87, 88) or "commission" (95).

54. Cf. Zerwick §§406-7.

627

may here mean "make things straight in advance" (cf. Cassirer) or "rectify things ahead (of my arrival)." Apparently, what the Corinthians lacked was organizational skills,[55] a need perhaps reflected in their own earlier request for directions concerning the collection (cf. 1 Cor. 16:1-2).

In 1 Cor. 16:1 Paul had called the offering for the Jerusalem poor a λογεία. Now he twice refers to it as a εὐλογία ("blessing"),[56] his regular word for a benefit bestowed by God (e.g., Eph. 1:3; cf. Gen. 29:25). In the NT the εὐλογ- word group usually describes the God-man relationship, in either direction, but on occasion εὐλογέω describes human interrelationships (e.g., Rom. 12:14; 1 Cor. 4:12), just as in the LXX εὐλογία sometimes denotes a gift that is bestowed by one person on another, as a "blessing."[57] It is this latter usage that supports the view that in 9:5 εὐλογία means "gift of blessing,"[58] referring to the collection as the love-gift of the Corinthians that would be a blessing to the destitute believers in Jerusalem (9:12), that would prompt the Jerusalemites to bless God (9:11-13), and that would lead to God's gracious blessing on their own lives (9:8-10).[59] On a broader plane, Paul saw the collection as a Gentile εὐλογία directed toward the Jerusalem church, a material "blessing" given in gratitude for spiritual blessings (cf. the τὰ πνευματικά–τὰ σαρκικά antithesis in Rom. 15:27; 1 Cor. 9:11).

This "gift of blessing," says Paul, had been "already promised" or "previously pledged" (προεπηγγελμένην), not by him to those in Jerusalem, but by the Corinthians to him. While he did not view his collection in mercenary terms — it was not a tax on Gentile churches levied by the mother-church — he regarded any voluntary, verbal commitments to contribute as serious obligations that must be honored. The perfect participle προεπηγγελμένην implies that the pledge or promise retained its validity; it had not been nullified and was still an obligation awaiting fulfillment. In the two previous προ- compounds in this verse (προέλθωσιν and προκαταρτίσωσιν), the point of orientation was his next visit to Corinth; in this third instance, it is the time of writing. Presumably the Corinthians had pledged their support in the letter they sent him (? early in 55) that requested advice about the collection (cf. 1 Cor. 16:1).

ταύτην ἑτοίμην εἶναι οὕτως ὡς εὐλογίαν καὶ μὴ ὡς πλεονεξίαν. "So that it [your gift] may thus be ready as indeed a gift of blessing and not as a gift that reflects avarice." If vv. 3-4 gave three reasons for Paul's dispatch of the delega-

---

55. Similarly Hughes 327 n. 58; Betz 93.

56. It is possible that Paul has engaged in a play on words: he hopes the Corinthian offering will be a "really fine" (εὐ-) (Hughes 327 n. 59) or "first-rate" or "bountiful" collection (λογεία, sometimes spelled λογία).

57. E.g., Gen. 33:11; 1 Kgdms. 25:27; 4 Kgdms. 5:15.

58. So Lietzmann 138; Wendland 222; de Boor 188; Lang 322; Betz 87, 99; Wolff 180. Also SB 3.524, who define "a gift of blessing" as "a gift which is accompanied by a desire for [the recipient's] blessing."

59. But the Corinthians' gift as a εὐλογία remained a purely human action (*pace* Theobald 290-91), although human εὐλογία is an imitation of divine εὐλογία (Prümm II/2.36).

tion to Corinth, this concluding statement in v. 5 supplies the reason why he was dispatching them in advance of his own arrival (v. 5a) — to ensure that their contribution was ready as a generous gift that brought blessing and not as a miserly gift that stemmed from covetousness. From one perspective Paul has now reached the climax of chs. 8 and 9 with this reference to the completion of the Corinthians' action (cf. 8:11, τὸ ποιῆσαι ἐπιτελέσατε); the remainder of ch. 9 simply reviews the results of their anticipated generous giving.

The accusative ταύτην, which refers back to εὐλογίαν, is the subject of the telic infinitive εἶναι,[60] "so that it may be ready." But to take εἶναι as consecutive also makes good sense in the context, "then it will be ready."[61] Previously the notion of "readiness" had been expressed by the verb παρασκευάζομαι (vv. 2-3); now the adjective ἕτοιμος is used, to express readiness of completion, as v. 3 does. Paul wants the collection money to be all in hand before his arrival, ready for immediate transmission to Jerusalem. Used with ἕτοιμος, the verb οὕτως ("in this way," "thus") will be retrospective and carry the sense "when I arrive" (GNB) or "with the help of the delegates."

Perhaps no word in 2 Corinthians has been given a wider variety of meanings than πλεονεξία in 9:5. Etymologically it means "(a craving) to have more" (πλεὸν ἔχειν), and thus refers to self-seeking acquisitiveness or ruthless greed.[62] We may arrive at the likely meaning of this term in the present verse by a series of steps.

1. μὴ ὡς πλεονεξίαν clearly stands in parallelism to ὡς εὐλογίαν and in contrast (μή).
2. In the absence of strong indications to the contrary, one may assume that the second use of εὐλογία in this verse carries the same basic meaning as the first, namely "blessing" or "gift of blessing."[63]
3. Given the parallelism mentioned above, the agent involved in the hypothetical πλεονεξία is likely to be the same as with εὐλογία, that is, the Corinthians.[64]
4. Verse 6 is relevant to the interpretation of πλεονεξία since it begins with τοῦτο δέ, "What I mean is this," or "My point is this," which looks back to v. 5 as well as forward.

60. So also Robertson, *Pictures* 248; Zerwick and Grosvenor 552.
61. Moule (141) leaves open both options.
62. See E. Klaar, "Πλεονεξία, -έκτης, -εκτεῖν," *TZ* 10 (1954) 395-97.
63. BAGD (323a) expresses a slight preference for "blessing" in v. 5a and "generous gift" or "bounty" in v. 5b. Some EVV have slightly different renderings for the two uses of εὐλογία: e.g., "gift . . . willing gift" (RSV), "bounty . . . genuine bounty" (REB), "bountiful gift . . . voluntary gift" (NRSV).
64. But some EVV and commentators see the putative πλεονεξία as that of Paul. Thus RV, ". . . ready, as a matter of bounty, and not of extortion" (similarly Furnish 421); RSV, "not as an exaction"; Martin 281, "not as money wrung out of you" (similarly Barrett 235, who notes that 12:17-18 seems to indicate that Paul had been accused of extorting money from the Corinthians through the collection).

5. In v. 6 there is a contrast between φειδομένως ("sparingly," "sparsely") and ἐπ᾽ εὐλογίαις ("generously," "bountifully") where the latter phrase corresponds verbally to εὐλογία in v. 5, and the former word corresponds conceptually to πλεονεξίαν. If so, εὐλογία will allude to a gift that is generous and bountiful,[65] and πλεονεξία to a gift that is scanty and stingy.[66]

6. On this view, then, ἑτοίμην . . . ὡς εὐλογίαν will mean "ready as indeed[67] a gift of blessing," that is, a bountiful gift given enthusiastically, while καὶ μὴ ὡς πλεονεξίαν will mean "and not as a gift of avarice,"[68] that is, "a gift that reflects avarice,"[69] a scanty contribution given grudgingly. Paul is contrasting two attitudes toward giving — generosity and stinginess, not two ways of securing a gift (by voluntary act or by extortion). Whereas eighteen months previously Paul had said that each of the Corinthians should regularly put aside some money in keeping with their income and save it up, "so that collections need not be taken when I come" (1 Cor. 16:2), here in 9:5 he is saying in effect, "I am sending these three delegates in advance of my own visit to help you organize your offerings, so that collections need not be taken when I come." The work of the delegates at Corinth would be a protection against "last-minute" giving that would tend to result in a minimal gift parted with reluctantly.

Bibliography

Bornkamm, "History" • H. Dörrie, Ὑπόστασις. Wort- und Bedeutungsgeschichte (Nachrichten der Akademie der Wissenschaften in Göttingen. I. Philologisch-historische Klasse 3; Göttingen, 1955) 35-92 • Funk • Georgi 75-79, 93-94 • F. Horst, "Segen und Segenhandlungen in der Bibel," EvT 52 (1947) 223-37 • E. Klaar, "Πλεονεξία, -έκτης, -εκτεῖν," TZ 10 (1954) 395-97 • Lambrecht, "Boasting" • Meeks 65-67 • Mitchell, "Envoys" • Murphy-O'Connor 88-89 • Nickle • Stowers • Theobald 290-91

65. It is significant that in compounds (such as εὐανδρία, "abundance of men") εὐ- implies abundance (LSJ s.v. VI).

66. "Some offerings exhibit covetousness on the part of the giver by their very niggardliness" (Robertson, Pictures 248).

67. A word such as "indeed" (so also Betz 87; similarly Lietzmann 138) highlights the repetition of εὐλογία and also the following contrast.

68. So also Lietzmann 138; Wendland 222; Lang 322; similarly Betz 87. Lietzmann observes that because of the parallelism πλεονεξία has a pregnant meaning: "a gift that is accompanied by the sentiment of avarice, instead of the sentiment that attaches to a gift of blessing" (137-38).

69. Cf. BAGD 667d, "a gift that is grudgingly granted by avarice"; Zerwick, Analysis 406, "a gift so small that it expresses the avarice of the giver." Delling sees the πλεονεξία as involving a calculating and close scrutiny of the gift so as to gain some personal advantage (TDNT 6.273). Thrall renders the relevant phrase, "and not a reflection of (your own) covetousness" (563), and interprets πλεονεξίαν in the light of the use of the cognate verb πλεονάζω in 8:15, ὁ τὸ πολὺ οὐκ ἐπλεόνασεν. Just as "the desire of some Israelites to have more than they needed was frustrated by the divine miracle of equalization" (573), so the Corinthians were not to entertain a "desire to have more" (= πλεονεξία) than their fellow believers in Jerusalem, but were to give bountifully, not sparingly (573).

C. The Resources and Results of Generosity (9:6-15)

If the heart of 8:1-15 is found in the actual entreaty, "Finish the project!" (τὸ ποιῆσαι ἐπιτελέσατε, 8:11), the essence of ch. 9 could be summed up in the plea, "Be ready before I arrive!" that is, "Prior to my upcoming visit, have all the collection funds in hand, ready for transmission to Jerusalem." Such a plea is implicit in vv. 3 and 5, ἔπεμψα . . . τοὺς ἀδελφοὺς . . . ἵνα . . . παρεσκευασμένοι ἦτε (v. 3), . . . ἵνα . . . προκαταρτίσωσιν τὴν . . . εὐλογίαν ὑμῶν, ταύτην ἑτοίμην εἶναι (v. 5). With this indirect exhortation in 9:3, 5 the climax of chs. 8 and 9 is reached. The rest of ch. 9 reverts to considerations of motivation for giving, such as we find in 8:1-15. So then, in 9:6-15 Paul sketches the results of generosity, the benefits of generous giving. These benefits of lavish sowing are basically two: first, in vv. 6-11, God's spiritual and material enrichment of the giver, enabling further generous giving (ἐν παντὶ πλουτιζόμενοι εἰς πᾶσαν ἁπλότητα, 9:11); second, in vv. 12-15, the offering up to God of prayers of thanksgiving (πολλῶν εὐχαριστιῶν τῷ θεῷ, 9:12) and of intercession (αὐτῶν δεήσει ὑπὲρ ὑμῶν, 9:14). The term ἁπλότης, "generosity," is the key common factor in these two sections, being found in v. 11 and v. 13.

1. God's Enrichment of the Giver (9:6-11)

What is noteworthy about this paragraph is Paul's extended use of agricultural imagery. The Christian who gives is viewed as both a sower and a reaper, what is given is the seed, and the outcome of the giving is the harvest. It is not an oversimplification to say that the whole paragraph shows how applicable and true in the realm of Christian giving is the general agricultural principle, stated in v. 6, that scanty sowing results in a meager harvest, while plentiful sowing produces a bountiful harvest — provided we always remember what Paul affirms elsewhere, that ultimately it is only God who produces the harvest (cf. 1 Cor. 3:7). The emphasis on God as the primary actor is unmistakable in vv. 8 and 10.

9:6*What I mean is this: The one who sows sparingly will also reap sparingly, and the one who sows generously will also reap generously. 7Each person should give as much as he has decided[a] in his heart to give, not with regret or under compulsion, for it is the cheerful giver that God loves. 8Indeed, God has the power[b] to provide you with every kind of blessing in abundance, so that in every circumstance you may always have everything you need and still have ample resources for every kind of good work. 9As it stands written:*

He scatters abroad, he gives to the needy;
his righteousness remains forever.[c]

10*Now he who supplies "seed[d] for sowing and bread for eating" will supply[e] and multiply[e] your store of seed and also enlarge[e] the harvest from your righteous-*

ness. 11*You will be enriched in every way in order to show generosity of every kind, and through us such generosity^f will produce thanksgiving to God.*^g

TEXTUAL NOTES

a. In the place of the perfect προήρηται (read by ‭א‬ B C F G P 0243 6 33 104 365 1175 1739 1881 *pc* lat cop Cyprian), some witnesses (D Ψ 048 𝔐) read the present προαιρεῖται, which converts a reference to a specific, past decision made by each Corinthian into a general timeless principle of giving. Alternatively, the present tense reading, which is clearly secondary, may have arisen through itacism.

b. Because the verb δυνατέω ("have power," "be able") is rare (only here and in 13:3; Rom. 14:4 in the NT and never in the LXX), some witnesses replace the reading δυνατεῖ (p⁴⁶ ‭א‬ B C* D* F G 104 t vg Ambrosiaster) by the common adjective δυνατός ("powerful," "able") (twelve uses in Paul, including 10:4; 12:10; 13:9) (C² D² Ψ 048 0243 1739 1881 𝔐 b) or by δύναται (33 *pc* f g p vgᵐˢ), a very common verb.

c. The only difference between Paul's citation of Ps. 111:9 in 9:9 and the LXX version is his omission of τοῦ αἰῶνος after εἰς τὸν αἰῶνα. Not surprisingly, therefore, some witnesses (F G K 0243 6 326 629 630 1241 1739 1881 *al* a vgᶜˡ boᵐˢˢ) add this τοῦ αἰῶνος in what is clearly an easier, and therefore secondary, reading.

d. In favor of σπέρμα (read by ‭א‬ C D¹ Ψ 048 0209 0243 33 1739 1881 𝔐, and preferred by WH, UBS¹, ², and NA²⁵) two considerations may be urged: (1) this reading is found in the LXX text (i.e., Isa. 55:10) that Paul is here alluding to; and (2) it can claim to be the harder reading because it destroys the σπόρον . . . σπόρον parallelism in the verse. But against these data we may set compelling arguments for the originality of σπόρον (read by UBS³, ⁴ and NA²⁷): (1) it is read by the best Western uncials (D* F G) as well as by strong proto-Alexandrian witnesses (p⁴⁶ B); (2) it preserves the parallelism between ἐπιχορηγῶν σπόρον and χορηγήσει . . . τὸν σπόρον ὑμῶν; and (3) it deviates from the LXX text of Isa. 55:10 (σπέρμα τῷ σπείροντι) and can therefore lay claim to being the harder reading.

e. In the context, where the emphasis falls on the power of God to supply all the Corinthians' needs (v. 8), expressions of calm confidence by means of the future indicative (χορηγήσει . . . πληθυνεῖ . . . αὐξήσει, "[God] will supply . . . multiply . . . enlarge") (‭א‬* B C D* P 33 81 326 1175 2464 *pc* latt) are more appropriate than expressions of prayerful desire by means of the aorist optative (χορηγήσαι . . . πληθύναι . . . αὐξήσαι, "May he [God] supply . . . multiply . . . enlarge") (‭א‬² D² Ψ 0209 0243 1739 1881 𝔐). Scribes may have altered the original indicatives to the optative to avoid having Paul suggest that God would invariably act in a particular way. Some witnesses mix the two moods: F G read χορηγήσαι . . . πληθύναι . . . αὐξήσει, while p⁴⁶ 104 have χορηγήσει . . . πληθυνεῖ . . . αὐξήσαι (which BDF §471[4] claims could be the original reading).

f. Instead of ἥτις, a few witnesses (p⁴⁶ D* 326 b Ambrosiaster) read εἴ τις, clearly a scribal error, perhaps caused by itacism.

g. D* has an anarthrous θεῷ, and B an anarthrous θεοῦ; both readings are probably scribal errors.

9:6 τοῦτο δέ, ὁ σπείρων φειδομένως φειδομένως καὶ θερίσει, καὶ ὁ σπείρων ἐπ᾽ εὐλογίαις ἐπ᾽ εὐλογίαις καὶ θερίσει. "What I mean is this: the one who sows sparingly will also reap sparingly, and the one who sows generously will also reap generously." τοῦτο δέ not only looks forward ("And remember this," Cassirer; "Now this *I say*," NASB) but also backward, with the "sparingly–generously" contrast restating the εὐλογίαν–πλεονεξίαν antithesis of v. 5 in reverse order, and the repeated ἐπ᾿ εὐλογίαις reflecting the repeated εὐλογίαν also in v. 5. So τοῦτο δέ is appropriately rendered "What I mean is this":[1] or "The point is this" (RSV, NRSV). Given the use of the full expression τοῦτο δέ φημι in 1 Cor. 7:29; 15:50, it is safe to assume that here φημί or λέγω can be supplied,[2] that τοῦτο is both prospective and retrospective,[3] and that δέ is transitional, not adversative.

What follows τοῦτο δέ is an agricultural axiom, stated aphoristically without consideration of differing circumstances or exceptions. "'scanty sowing, scanty harvest; plentiful sowing, plentiful harvest'"[4] (TCNT). The proverb is expressed in the form of two juxtaposed chiasms (ABBA). It is assumed that the person who sows (ὁ σπείρων, generic article) is also the person who reaps (καὶ θερίσει, adjunctive καί[5] and a gnomic future).[6] φειδομένως, a *hapax* in Biblical Greek, is an adverb formed from the present participle (φειδόμενος) of φείδομαι, "spare," thus "sparingly" or "meagerly" or "with a niggardly hand" (Weymouth). Matching this adverb of manner is the prepositional phrase ἐπ᾿ εὐλογίαις, literally "on the basis of blessings,"[7] that is, in the hope of receiving the blessing of a bountiful harvest (cf. 1 Cor. 9:10), and so, as the opposite of φειδομένως, "bountifully," "generously," "liberally."[8] The reference back to εὐλογία in v. 5 is clear, whether we translate that word there as "gift of blessing" or "generous gift," referring to a liberal gift that is freely given and that blesses the recipient. If Paul is stating a general principle of farming in this verse, θερίσει is unlikely to refer to a single harvest such as the harvest at the end of the age (*pace* Plummer 258), although that is the application in Gal. 6:7-8 where the harvests to be reaped are φθορά and ζωὴ αἰώνιος. But as the general principle of v. 6b is applied to the Corinthian situation in vv. 8-14, the harvest to be reaped from lavish and joyful sowing is declared to be God's material and spiritual prospering to make further liberal giving possible (vv. 8-11), the relief of need (v. 12a), and

1. Bruce, *Paraphrase* 147. In his paraphrase Phillips ends the paragraph with v. 6.

2. But Meyer (604) construes τοῦτο as an accusative absolute, "Now as concerns this [viz. ὡς εὐλογίαν κτλ.], it is the case that. . . ."

3. Similarly Thrall 573 nn. 61, 62.

4. On the agricultural metaphor of sowing and reaping in Paul, see Betz 98-100; Williams 38-40.

5. But καί could be seen as emphatic, "indeed," "certainly."

6. Contrast with this John 4:36-38, which illustrates the saying, "One sows and another reaps" (John 4:37).

7. Cassirer has "by a rule of bountifulness"; Isaacs, "on generous lines . . . on lines no less generous"; Winer (392), "*with* blessings, so that blessings attend."

8. Young and Ford express this contrast colorfully: "with a closed fist . . . with an open hand" (271). The two adverbial ideas could be rendered by direct objects, as in GNB: "the person who sows few seeds will have a small crop; the one who sows many seeds will have a large crop."

prayers of thanksgiving and intercession on the part of the beneficiaries of the sowing (vv. 12b-14).

Paul's point is the correspondence between the quantity of seed sown and the quantity of the harvest.[9] He is implying that a meager contribution from the Corinthians would produce some harvest, but his desire and aim was for a sizable gift that would produce a correspondingly substantial harvest of benefits for both givers and recipients. Paul would have been fully aware, of course, that on occasion there could be poor harvests even after extensive sowing (cf. Hag. 1:6), for other circumstances such as the climate or the condition of the soil could affect the nature of the harvest. One could even, metaphorically speaking, sow wheat but reap thorns (Jer. 12:13) or sow the wind and reap the whirlwind (Hos. 8:7). But such exceptions apart, Paul knew that it was true in the realm of financial stewardship as also in farming that generous sowing meant a generous harvest.

This reference to the quantitative aspect of giving did not mean that Paul had surrendered his primary interest in the qualitative. He has already hinted that attitude is more important than the actual amount given (8:11-12): in God's eyes an eager desire to give that is translated into actual giving is one of the criteria that determines the acceptability of a gift; the other criterion is that the size of the gift should accord with one's resources, however meager or substantial they may be. Now in ch. 9 he stresses that sowing that is truly generous or giving that is truly lavish will not be marked by a desire to manipulate the situation for one's own advantage (μὴ ὡς πλεονεξίαν, v. 5), nor by regret (μὴ ἐκ λύπης, v. 7), nor by surrender to pressure (μὴ . . . ἐξ ἀνάγκης, v. 7). Rather, the person who gives should take delight in giving, should be a cheerful giver (ἱλαρὸς δότης, v. 7).

Paul presents v. 6 as a self-evident truth with which his readers will concur. No precise parallel is known to us; indeed, the φειδομένως–ἐπ᾽ εὐλογίαις antithesis is probably a Pauline creation. But the general thought, "As you have sown, so you shall reap" (Cicero, *De Oratore* 2.65 [261]), was a commonplace in contemporary morality,[10] as also in the Jewish wisdom tradition (e.g., Job 4:8; Sir. 7:3), with the closest parallel being in the Greek *Apocalypse of Baruch* (= *3 Baruch*), possibly a product of Syrian Judaism in the second century A.D., "Those who have sown well, also reap well" (*3 Baruch* 15:2, Greek). But what prompted Paul to cite this axiom? Gale suggests (163) that it may have been Prov. 22:8 (LXX), ὁ σπείρων φαῦλα θερίσει κακά ("the one who sows evil will reap trouble"), since Paul immediately goes on (in v. 7) to allude to the next sentence in Proverbs, ἄνδρα ἱλαρὸν καὶ δότην εὐλογεῖ ὁ θεός (Prov. 22:8a, LXX) (on which see below).

9:7 ἕκαστος καθὼς προῄρηται τῇ καρδίᾳ, μὴ ἐκ λύπης ἢ ἐξ ἀνάγκης·

---

9. Furnish rightly observes that in Gal. 6:7-8 the issue is the content of the sowing ("to his own flesh . . . to the Spirit"), here the quantity of the sowing (447).

10. See the references cited in Georgi 200 n. 7.

"Each person should give as much as he has decided in his heart to give, not with regret or under compulsion." Here is supplementary advice about sowing generously. Being both asyndetic and elliptical, this statement is correspondingly forceful. With ἕκαστος we may supply the aorist optative δῴη (Lietzmann 138), "May each give," or some imperative such as δότω (Winer 587) or διδότω (Robertson, *Pictures* 248), "Let each give," or ποιείτω (Robertson, *Pictures* 248), "Let each act," "Let each do this [sow generously, v. 6]." The omission of a verb serves to emphasize motivation for action (cf. καρδία, λύπη, ἀνάγκη) as opposed to the act of giving itself.[11] As in 1 Cor. 16:2 and Acts 11:29, both passages that describe financial giving, the use of ἕκαστος highlights individual responsibility to contribute to an offering that would in fact be sent as a single corporate gift.[12] If the meaning of καθώς ("as," "just as") is expanded, it will carry the sense "what/as much as (he has decided)." As the perfect of προαιρέομαι, "choose (for oneself)," "decide," προῄρηται points to a settled decision to contribute a certain amount to the collection, whether on a regular basis (as in 1 Cor. 16:2) or in a single gift.[13] The decision was to be private (τῇ καρδίᾳ, locative dative), not public, and the giving was to be purposeful, not impulsive.[14]

ἐκ λύπης and ἐξ ἀνάγκης are not exactly "different ways of stating the same fact,"[15] although the two ideas are closely related, but are two different subjective states that may accompany (ἐκ λύπης)[16] or give rise to (ἐξ ἀνάγκης) the action of giving: inward sorrow at losing what is given, and outward compulsion that forces one to give, giving that is reluctant and giving that is pressured. To give regretfully or under constraint is to sow sparingly (v. 6), to act with an unwilling heart (cf. v. 7a), and to give joylessly (cf. v. 7b). Paul knew that spontaneity and warmth would be absent from the Corinthians' giving if coercion were present, whether the pressure to give came from him or from any of his representatives. The contemporary analogy for this Jerusalem collection

11. Verbrugge finds in the omission of an imperative such as διδότω a softening of Paul's tone, a view that reflects his overall thesis that in 2 Corinthians 8–9 "Paul displays extreme hesitancy to tell the Corinthians to get on with the project of the collection for Jerusalem" (259).

12. Acts 11:29-30 refers to relief aid for Judean Christians sent from the Antiochian believers by the hand of Barnabas and Saul — a collection that was a forerunner of Paul's "great collection."

13. A similar emphasis on giving in accordance with the promptings of the heart is found in the accounts of the monetary or material offerings made for the construction of the tabernacle (e.g., Exod. 25:2, "You are to receive the offering for me from all whose hearts prompt them to give"; Exod. 35:21, "all who were willing and whose hearts moved them came and brought an offering to the Lord to be used for the Tent of Meeting"). But in 2 Cor. 9:7 a decision about the amount to be given is involved.

14. The repeated εὐδόκησαν in Rom. 15:26-27 also makes it clear that the decision to contribute to the collection rested wholly with the donors.

15. Plummer 259, who explains "The man who gives ἐξ ἀνάγκης gives ἐκ λύπης."

16. ἐκ may on occasion denote "circumstances which accompany an action without necessarily being the source of it" (BAGD 235 s.v. 3.g.γ., citing 2 Cor. 2:4: ἐκ πολλῆς θλίψεως; cf. 482a, where ἐκ λύπης is rendered "reluctantly").

was not the obligatory annual Temple tax that was levied on all adult male Jews,[17] but the voluntary offerings that Jews, proselytes, and even Gentiles made in Jerusalem.[18] More remotely, the closest OT analogy is the "freewill offerings" of money and materials given by the Israelites for the construction of the tabernacle (Exod. 25:1-9; 35:4-9, 20-29; 36:2-7).

ἱλαρὸν γὰρ δότην ἀγαπᾷ ὁ θεός. "For it is the cheerful giver that God loves." Here Paul supplies a scriptural motive for avoiding giving that is reluctant or pressured. Prov. 22:8a (LXX) reads ἄνδρα ἱλαρὸν καὶ δότην εὐλογεῖ ὁ θεός, "God blesses the man who is cheerful and a giver" = "a cheerful and generous man." Paul's text differs in two respects.

1. ἱλαρὸν qualifies δότην, and ἄνδρα and καὶ are omitted.
2. ἀγαπᾷ replaces εὐλογεῖ.

These differences may be accounted for by saying that Paul is quoting from memory,[19] is following a Greek text or form of the LXX not known to us,[20] or has made deliberate changes. Given Paul's propensity for slightly modifying texts to suit their new context[21] and the general similarity between the two texts, it is not inappropriate to assume his dependence on Prov. 22:8a and to seek reasons for his changes. The first change removes the awkward conjunction of adjective (ἱλαρόν) and noun (δότην), both qualifying ἄνδρα, and makes the aphorism applicable to both women and men. Various reasons have been suggested for the change from εὐλογεῖ to ἀγαπᾷ (both are gnomic presents, expressing timeless truths): to avoid emphasizing "the material or supernatural rewards of generosity";[22] to appeal to a higher motive for cheerful and willing giving than the hope of reward, namely a desire for God's love;[23] or Paul may have been influenced by a later verse (v. 11) in Prov. 22, ἀγαπᾷ κύριος ὁσίας καρδίας, "the Lord loves holy hearts."[24] Whatever the reason for the change, with the word ἀγαπᾷ Paul is affirming that God has a special love for those who are cheerful as they give,[25] in that he showers them with special blessings[26] or takes special pleasure in the type of giving — cheerful giving — that reflects his own manner of giving (cf. Heb. 13:16).

---

17. See SB 1.760-70; Nickle 74-93.
18. So G. Kittel, *TDNT* 4.283; E. Bammel, *TDNT* 6.909.
19. So Plummer 259.
20. Cf. Hughes 331 n. 65.
21. See, most recently, Stanley, *Paul and the Language of Scripture*.
22. Spicq, *Agape* 31.
23. Windisch 277, citing John 14:21, 23; Heb. 13:16.
24. A view mentioned by Betz (107), who himself proposes that "Paul attempted to quote a scriptural proverb from memory" (107).
25. Both ἱλαρόν and ὁ θεός are emphatic by position: "It is the cheerful giver who is loved by God."
26. Cf. Deut. 15:10, "Give generously to him [a poor fellow countryman], and do so without a grudging heart, for because of this the LORD your God will bless you in all that you do and in all that you undertake."

As to attitude, giving should be cheerful, not reluctant;[27] as to motivation, giving should result from a desire to gain God's favor, not from external constraint. From this perspective ἱλαρόν matches ἐκ λύπης, and ἀγαπᾷ answers to ἐξ ἀνάγκης.

9:8 δυνατεῖ δὲ ὁ θεὸς πᾶσαν χάριν περισσεῦσαι εἰς ὑμᾶς. "Indeed, God has the power to provide you with every kind of blessing in abundance." Vv. 8-14 form a commentary on the notion of "reaping bountifully" (v. 6b), indicating the benefits that accrue to the giver if the principles of giving stated in vv. 6b-7 are followed.[28] δέ is emphatic ("indeed") rather than merely continuative ("and"). περισσεύω here is transitive, "cause to abound," "give in abundant measure," "provide richly," and, along with πᾶσαν ("every kind of," BAGD 631c), points to the bounty of God's provision. Once again the key word of 2 Corinthians 8–9 (χάρις) appears, this time having the connotation of εὐλογία so that πᾶσαν χάριν means "every kind of blessing" or "every benefit" (Furnish 441). Some restrict χάρις here to earthly blessings or temporal benefits or material prosperity,[29] but since the Macedonians' generosity of spirit is attributed to the operation of God's χάρις in their lives (8:1-4) and the use of πᾶσαν does not encourage any restriction of sense, it is preferable to regard χάρις as encompassing both material and spiritual blessings or benefits. Paul does not see this rich divine provision as a reward for generosity, as though some prior bargain had been struck between the giver and God, but it is the God-ordained outcome of generous and cheerful giving. It is God who grants the harvest, not humans who earn or deserve it. And if God's blessing results from generous giving, as Deut. 15:10 so emphatically asserts,[30] it is also true that it is God who implants in humans the χάρις of προθυμία, the "grace" of "the willingness to give" (cf. 8:11-12).

ἵνα ἐν παντὶ πάντοτε πᾶσαν αὐτάρκειαν ἔχοντες περισσεύητε εἰς πᾶν ἔργον ἀγαθόν. "So that in every circumstance you may always have everything you need and still have ample resources for every kind of good work." The provision of πᾶσα χάρις was designed to promote, not passive ease, but active benevolence, as well as supplying adequately all personal needs. ἵνα is probably final ("so that . . . you may have," REB) but may be consecutive ("thus you will have," NEB). Especially noteworthy in this verse is the alliteration involving the initial π, the four uses of πᾶς (cf. πάντοτε; BDF §488[1a]), and the two in-

---

27. On the link between giving and cheerfulness, see, e.g., Sir. 35:11; and for rabbinical teaching, SB 3.524.

28. Some commentators, however, link v. 8 principally with v. 7 and believe that in v. 8 Paul is discussing the resources of grace that God makes available for cheerful generosity rather than the recompense that follows bountiful sowing (see, e.g., Thrall 578).

29. E.g., Meyer 605; Hodge 220.

30. See n. 26 and the emphatic "for because of this" (in Deut. 15:10), namely the act of giving freely and ungrudgingly. The twofold biblical principle is "bless others, because you have been blessed by God" (cf. Deut. 15:14); "bless others, in order to be blessed by God" (e.g., Deut. 14:28-29; 15:10, 18; Prov. 22:9; cf. 1 Pet. 3:9).

stances of περισσεύω. These last two features stress the totality and profusion of God's provision.

αὐτάρκεια was an important term in Greek philosophy, especially among the Stoics and Cynics, denoting the self-sufficiency and contentment of the person who was self-supporting and independent of other people and of circumstances.[31] In comparison with that viewpoint, the present passage has two distinguishing features. First, for Paul αὐτάρκεια is not "self-sufficiency" but "God-sufficiency," not reliance on one's own inner resources apart from any outside help, but a total dependence on God's unlimited ability to create the desire to give and to supply the resources to give. When Paul uses the cognate adjective αὐτάρκης in Phil. 4:11, he is describing the state of contentedness he had reached, whatever his circumstances, whether he was facing plenty or hunger, bounty or need (Phil. 4:12). But his ability to cope contentedly with affluence or poverty was dependent on the empowering of Christ (Phil. 4:13); this is a "Christ-sufficiency." Second, for Paul αὐτάρκεια involves not "self-sufficiency" but sufficiency for self and ample resources for others. The only other NT use of αὐτάρκεια is in 1 Tim. 6:6. "Godliness (εὐσέβεια) with contentment (αὐτάρκεια) is great gain." That is, the practice of the Christian faith yields high dividends when it is accompanied by "contentment" with one's possessions and lot in life. Such αὐτάρκεια means being free from πλεονεξία, "the desire to have more," "acquisitiveness," and the attendant disregard of the needs and rights of others. In 9:8, then, πᾶσαν αὐτάρκειαν ἔχοντες refers to one's own contented possession of the necessities of life, both material and spiritual, as a result of God's gracious provision.[32] But this contented possession was not an end in itself, for "everything you need" (πᾶσαν αὐτάρκειαν) is linked with having "ample means" (BAGD 651a) available for doing "every kind of good work,"[33] that is, a surplus from which the needs of others can be met.[34] "The Christian αὐτός cannot be considered in isolation. His αὐτ-άρκεια arises only when the ἄλλος has a share in it" (G. Kittel, *TDNT* 1.467). In v. 8a περισσεῦσαι is transitive ("cause to abound," "supply richly") and a timeless aorist, whereas in v. 8b περισσεύητε is intransitive ("abound," "have in excess of what is necessary") and present tense, of an ongoing surplus.

31. On the relation of Paul's concept of αὐτάρκεια to Greek philosophy, see further Betz 110-11.

32. It is significant that the only use of the cognate verb αὐταρκέω ("supply with necessaries," "maintain") in the LXX occurs in Deut. 32:10 in reference to God's providential care of Israel in the wilderness by providing not only food but also instruction (ἐπαίδευσεν αὐτόν) and careful protection (διεφύλαξεν αὐτόν).

33. That link, implied by the participle ἔχοντες, is probably temporal ("while you have"), but may be causal ("because you have") or even modal ("by having," Betz 87; cf. 110). If ἔχοντες is rendered as a finite verb ("so that you may have"), the temporal significance of ἔχοντες can be brought out by translating περισσεύητε as "and still have ample resources."

34. The contrast between Corinthian need and that of others is well reflected in Moffatt's rendering: ". . . so that you may always have quite enough for any emergency of your own and ample besides for any kind act to others."

In the adverbial expression ἐν παντί and πάντοτε, as also in the final phrase εἰς πᾶν ἔργον ἀγαθόν,[35] Paul looks beyond the pressing matter in hand — the finalizing of the collection project at Corinth — to a lifestyle of cheerful giving that will be resourced by God. The addition of καὶ εἰς πάντας at the end of v. 13 points in the same direction — Paul is saying in effect, "Give generously now, and you will find that God maintains your desire to give and increases your resources for further giving."

9:9 καθὼς γέγραπται, Ἐσκόρπισεν, ἔδωκεν τοῖς πένησιν, ἡ δικαιοσύνη αὐτοῦ μένει εἰς τὸν αἰῶνα. "As it stands written: "He scatters abroad, he gives to the needy; his righteousness remains forever." Both of the OT quotations in chs. 8 and 9 are introduced by the formulaic καθὼς γέγραπται, "as it stands written" (see on 8:15). Here in 9:9 Paul applies the general expression, "every kind of good work," to the issue of the "good work" of the collection[36] by citing the LXX text of the first two lines of Ps. 111:9, with only one insignificant difference.[37]

Psalm 112 (LXX, 111) develops the last verse of Ps. 111 (v. 10), "The fear of Yahweh is the beginning of wisdom; all who follow his precepts have good success." It depicts the conduct and character of "the person who fears Yahweh, who finds great delight in his commands" (Ps. 112:1), illustrating the general truth that prosperity and blessedness are the reward of reverence and obedience. Such a person is prosperous (vv. 2-3), generous (vv. 4-5), and stable (vv. 6-8). The psalm concludes with a summarizing contrast between the godly person who lavishes his gifts on the poor, whose righteousness stands firm forever, and whose dignity is exalted (v. 9), and, on the other hand, the wicked person who is vexed, evanescent, and frustrated (v. 10).

One may wonder why Paul did not choose to cite Prov. 22:9 (LXX) ("The one who has pity on the poor will himself be continually sustained, for he has given to the poor from his own resources"),[38] given the fact that he has cited Prov. 22:8a in 9:7 and perhaps alluded to Prov. 22:8 in 9:6. It was probably because Ps. 111:9 (LXX) refers to the scattering of seed (ἐσκόρπισεν), to giving to the poor (ἔδωκεν τοῖς πένησιν), and to the handsome dividends that come from such giving (ἡ δικαιοσύνη αὐτοῦ μένει εἰς τὸν αἰῶνα), and so was even more suitable in the context.

ἐσκόρπισεν and ἔδωκεν are gnomic aorists and together may form a hendiadys; thus "(as the Scripture says,) He scatters his gifts" (Goodspeed). But, alternatively, ἔδωκεν may define the nature of the scattering, so that the

---

35. This expression, πᾶν ἔργον ἀγαθόν, is common in the Pastorals (1 Tim. 5:10; 2 Tim. 2:21; 3:17; Tit. 1:16; 3:1; also Col. 1:10; 2 Thess. 2:17).

36. There is no reason to follow Bernard in regarding vv. 9-10 as parenthetical, "containing an illustrative quotation and its application" (93).

37. Paul omits τοῦ αἰῶνος after εἰς τὸν αἰῶνα; it is simply the difference between "forever" and "forever and ever." Stanley notes that elsewhere in the Psalms there is considerable textual variety with expressions such as εἰς τὸν αἰῶνα τοῦ αἰῶνος (233 and n. 173).

38. Prov. 22:9 (LXX): ὁ ἐλεῶν πτωχὸν αὐτὸς διατραφήσεται· τῶν γὰρ ἑαυτοῦ ἄρτων ἔδωκεν τῷ πτωχῷ.

two verbs could be rendered separately. Moreover, when σκορπίζω is used of seed (or the like), it means "scatter abroad (or widely)";[39] thus (in hendiadys) "He lavishes his gifts" (REB) or "He gives generously" (GNB). To "scatter far and wide" is the opposite of giving grudgingly and sowing sparingly, and the same as sowing generously (vv. 5-6). πένης differs from πτωχός in intensity. Whereas ὁ πτωχός is the person who is destitute or abjectly poor, ὁ πένης (a NT *hapax*) is the man who seeks to earn a living by occasional labor, the day-laborer, and thus "the poor man."[40] Perhaps the difference can be preserved by rendering τοῖς πένησιν as "the needy" (NEB, GNB, REB). But this is not to imply that as Ps. 111:9 is applied to the present situation, "the poor" (οἱ πτωχοί, Rom. 15:26) in the Jerusalem church were merely unemployed; they were completely destitute, totally dependent on others for livelihood.

Some argue that the implied subject of these two aorists is God.[41] After all, ὁ θεός is the explicit subject in the previous verse (v. 8) and the unambiguous although implicit subject in the following verse (v. 10), and in Ps. 110:3 the same phrase that occurs in Ps. 111:9 (viz. ἡ δικαιοσύνη αὐτοῦ μένει εἰς τὸν αἰῶνα τοῦ αἰῶνος) is applied to Yahweh (cf. κύριε, Ps. 110:1, LXX). But there are compelling reasons for believing that the implied subject of these two verbs in Paul's use of this quotation is "the representative Corinthian contributor" (Thrall 583). (1) Apart from the final verse, the subject of Psalm 112 (LXX, 111), including v. 9, is "the person who fears Yahweh" (Ps. 112:1). (2) 2 Cor. 9:9 has several links with the immediate context: (a) the subject of the immediately preceding subordinate clause is "you (Corinthians)" (ἵνα . . . περισσεύητε, v. 8), so that an individualizing of the second person plural by a third person singular is not surprising; (b) ἐσκόρπισεν looks back to ὁ σπείρων (v. 6, twice); (c) ἔδωκεν picks up the implied verb δότω (or διδότω) from v. 7; (d) τοῖς πένησιν refers to τοὺς ἁγίους (v. 1), who are οἱ πτωχοὶ τῶν ἁγίων τῶν ἐν Ἰερουσαλήμ (Rom. 15:26). (3) the individualized ἡ δικαιοσύνη αὐτοῦ becomes the corporate τῆς δικαιοσύνης ὑμῶν in v. 10.

If God is the implied subject in the first line of the citation, ἡ δικαιοσύνη αὐτοῦ will naturally refer to his covenantal faithfulness to his people.[42] But if the God-fearer or the generous Corinthian giver is the subject, as we have argued, then δικαιοσύνη will refer either to specific acts of charity (cf. πᾶν ἔργον ἀγαθόν, v. 8),[43] including almsgiving (ἐλεημοσύνη; cf. Matt. 6:1-2),[44] or,

---

39. In P. Lond. 131 recto[421] (A.D. 78-79) the verb is used of the spreading of fertilizer all over tilled fields (see MM 579 s.v.).

40. The cognate verb πένομαι, when used intransitively, means "seek a living by physical toil," "be needy."

41. E.g., Georgi 98; Betz 111-12; Barnett 439-40; also BAGD 757a. For the view that the subject is primarily Christ, who is active in the giving of the Corinthians, see Hanson 179-80.

42. So Barnett 440, following Furnish 448-49 (who espouses this view tentatively, 442). Hanson (180) sees δικαιοσύνη as Christ's righteousness displayed in Christians.

43. Cf. Williams, "his deeds of charity"; JB, "his good deeds."

44. Similarly Hughes 333. In Matt. 6:1 many witnesses (L W Z Θ *f*[13] 33 𝔐 f k syr[p, h] mae)

more generally, to "benevolence" (φιλανθρωπία) (NEB, REB) or "upright-ness" (NJB).[45]

Again, in reference to God, (ἡ δικαιοσύνη αὐτοῦ) μένει εἰς αἰῶνα will mean that his righteousness "remains into eternity" (Betz 87) or "endures for-ever." If, on the other hand, αὐτοῦ has a human referent, the psalmist and Paul will be affirming that both in the present life and in the life to come the benevo-lence of the person who gives generously to the needy will be remembered and rewarded by God (Plummer 257, 262); or that "his uprightness will never be forgotten" (Goodspeed);[46] or that the effect and reward of his acts of piety will endure forever (Bruce 227); or that "his benevolence stands fast for ever" (NEB),[47] in the sense that his generosity to the poor will remain a way of life, not an isolated or irregular action, because God constantly supplies him with the resources to give (vv. 8, 10). Of these four alternatives that understand αὐτοῦ to be the pious person who contributes generously to the support of the needy, the last seems most plausible with its close link to the preceding and fol-lowing verses.

9:10 ὁ δὲ ἐπιχορηγῶν σπόρον τῷ σπείροντι καὶ ἄρτον εἰς βρῶσιν χορηγήσει καὶ πληθυνεῖ τὸν σπόρον ὑμῶν. "Now he who supplies 'seed for sow-ing and bread for eating' will supply and multiply your store of seed." V. 10 reit-erates and expands v. 8, now using the farming imagery of v. 6 that is resumed by ἐσκόρπισεν in v. 9. The conceptual parallelism may be shown thus.[48]

v. 8	v. 10
δυνατεῖ . . . ὁ θεὸς	ὁ . . . ἐπιχορηγῶν
πᾶσαν χάριν περισσεῦσαι πᾶσαν αὐτάρκειαν ἔχοντες }	χορηγήσει . . . τὸν σπόρον ὑμῶν
περισσεύητε	πληθυνεῖ τὸν σπόρον ὑμῶν
εἰς πᾶν ἔργον ἀγαθόν	αὐξήσει τὰ γενήματα τῆς δικαιοσύνης ὑμῶν

What the two verses have in common is the ringing assurance of God's bounti-ful provision that makes possible generous actions of every sort.

If the compound verb ἐπιχορηγέω implies an abundant supply (note ἐπι-),

---

read ἐλεημοσύνην in the place of δικαιοσύνην. On the rabbinical interpretation of Ps. 112:9 in refer-ence to almsgiving, see SB 3.525.

45. In 2 Cor. 9:9 and 9:10 G. Schrenk takes δικαιοσύνη to mean "right conduct worked out in acts of love" (*TDNT* 2.210). Barrett believes that it is "not impossible" that δικαιοσύνη in 9:9 has its characteristically Pauline forensic sense: the man who obeys God's will by caring for the poor "maintains his justified relation with God" (238).

46. This interpretation is supported by Ps. 111:6 (LXX), εἰς μνημόσυνον αἰώνιον ἔσται δίκαιος, "the righteous person will be in everlasting remembrance" (= will be remembered forever); cf. Prov. 10:7.

47. Similarly Moffatt, Williams, REB; A. P. Stanley, "and yet his beneficence remains inex-haustible for all time" (179); Thrall 582.

48. Cf. Barnett 441.

the simplex χορηγέω that follows will have the same connotation.⁴⁹ ὁ ἐπιχορηγῶν describes a divine trait: when God provides, he does so lavishly. For other stylistically comparable phrases in 2 Corinthians that describe God's characteristics, see 1:4; 7:6 (ὁ παρακαλῶν); 1:9 (ὁ ἐγείρων); 1:21 (ὁ βεβαιῶν . . . καὶ χρίσας); 1:22 (ὁ σφραγισάμενος . . . καὶ δούς); 2:14 (ὁ θριαμβεύων); 5:5 (ὁ κατεργασάμενος . . . ὁ δούς); 8:16 (ὁ δούς).

What God bountifully supplies is σπόρον τῷ σπείροντι καὶ ἄρτον εἰς βρῶσιν. Since this very phrase occurs in Isa. 55:10 (LXX) (with σπέρμα instead of σπόρον), there can be little doubt that Paul is quoting this passage (see NA²⁷); no introductory formula occurs since the citation is fragmentary. Yahweh's declaration in Isa. 55:10-11 is that his word, his decree (cf. Isa. 45:23; 55:12-13), is as invariably effective as the rain and snow when they slowly and silently water and transform the earth. After precipitation falls, the earth buds and flourishes and yields "seed for the sower and bread for eating." What this text says the earth does, Paul affirms God himself does. εἰς βρῶσιν is parallel to τῷ σπείροντι, and βρῶσις refers to "the act of eating," not to "food" (βρῶμα, as NAB²). This suggests that τῷ σπείροντι (literally, "for the sower") may be a case of "concrete for abstract," meaning "for sowing."⁵⁰ There is no reason to construe ἄρτον εἰς βρῶσιν with χορηγήσει, given the conjunction of these two words (σπόρον, βρῶσιν) in Isaiah as the joint objects of a single verb (δῷ [LXX], "yields").

Since Paul knew that the God of nature is also the God of salvation, his thought naturally moves from God's characteristically bountiful provision in supplying seed for people to sow and thus bread for them to eat, to his certain provision — and multiplication! — of full resources that will enable the Corinthians to "sow generously." This movement is marked by a change from a participle (ὁ ἐπιχορηγῶν) to three future indicatives (χορηγήσει . . . πληθυνεῖ . . . αὐξήσει) (see Textual Note e.). In this verse the first use of σπόρος is literal ("seed"), while the second is figurative ("store of seed," BAGD 763c; NIV; or "seed for sowing," NJB, NRSV) and refers to the Corinthians' "resources" (RSV) that could be used to contribute to relief aid, or as BAGD (763c) expresses it, "your store of things to distribute to the needy." This store of seed, says Paul, is "yours" (ὑμῶν) in the sense "for you to sow" (cf. εἰς ὑμᾶς in v. 8) — not "for you to hoard." God's supply of resources is designed to bring about equality through the sharing of burdens (cf. 8:13-14). The addition of καὶ πληθυνεῖ after χορηγήσει points, on a literal plane, to the creation of a surplus of seed sufficient for next year's sowing as well as this year's, and metaphorically, to the rich bounty of God's provision of resources for giving. That is, πληθυνεῖ simply augments χορηγήσει: "(God) will provide you with ample

---

49. See Moulton 115 for this idiom (cf. ἐπενδύσασθαι . . . ἐνδυσάμενοι in 5:2-3). Originally χορηγέω meant "lead the chorus (χορός)" in a Greek drama, then "defray the expenses of training and supplying a chorus," and generally "furnish abundantly with supplies" (see LSJ 1998 s.v.).

50. NAB¹ reverses the process: "seed for the sower and bread for the eater" ("abstract for concrete").

store of seed for sowing" (NJB). But the verb also illustrates the proverb, "Some give freely, yet gain even more" (Prov. 11:24), indicating, however, that at least in the present case the reason for the multiplication of resources is God's generous provision. Murphy-O'Connor observes that in speaking with such certitude about God's provision, Paul is assuming that believers are authentic, that God's gifts are given through humans, and that each local church is not only itself a genuine community but also united in love to other congregations (93).

καὶ αὐξήσει τὰ γενήματα τῆς δικαιοσύνης ὑμῶν. "And (he will) also enlarge the harvest from your righteousness." If v. 8a contains an unmistakable citation of a portion of Isa. 55:10 (LXX), v. 8b includes a clear allusion to a phrase found in Hos. 10:12 (LXX). "Sow for yourselves righteousness, reap the fruit of life . . . seek Yahweh until the harvest of righteousness (γενήματα δικαιοσύνης) comes to you" (MT, "until he comes and waters you with righteousness").[51] Within Hos. 10:11-14a, which is Yahweh's indictment of Israel after the announcement of her punishment (vv. 9-10), there is found v. 12, an exhortation that serves to remind Israel of both lost opportunities and future possibilities. Paul was drawn to this verse probably because of its use of four crop farming terms (σπείρω, τρυγάω, καρπός, γένημα)[52] as well as by the actual phrase γενήματα δικαιοσύνης ("the harvest of righteousness") that encapsulates the theme of vv. 6-11 (the results of generosity) and repeats the key word δικαιοσύνη ("righteousness" = deeds of piety) that occurred in the quotation of Ps. 111:10 (LXX) in v. 9.[53] γένημα, from γίνομαι, refers to vegetable produce, thus "fruit" or "crop," and is to be distinguished from γέννημα,[54] which is cognate with γεννάω and is used only of living creatures, thus "child" or "offspring."[55] Used figuratively (as here), γενήματα denotes "fruits" or "results," or, as a generalizing plural, the "yield" or "harvest." τῆς δικαιοσύνης is a subjective genitive, "produced by/springing (up) from righteousness," and ὑμῶν is emphatic, not by position but by the implied comparison with the "be-

---

51. σπείρατε ἑαυτοῖς εἰς δικαιοσύνην, τρυγήσατε εἰς καρπὸν ζωῆς . . . ἐκζητήσατε τὸν κύριον ἕως τοῦ ἐλθεῖν γενήματα δικαιοσύνης ὑμῖν. The εἰς with δικαιοσύνην and καρπόν represents *lamedh* in each case, which here in effect marks the direct object (cf. Jer. 40:2).

52. Betz rejects any allusion to Hos. 10:12 (LXX). "Rather, the notion [of 'the fruits of righteousness'] belongs to a complex of agrarian metaphors popular both in Jewish circles and in Hellenistic morality" (114-15). On the other hand, Cassirer and Wendland (223) indicate both Isa. 55:10 and Hos. 10:12 as quotations in their translations, as also WH in their Greek text.

53. But some give δικαιοσύνη a different meaning in vv. 9 and 10. Barnett, e.g., writes: "God's covenantal 'righteousness' (as in v. 9) has bestowed his forensic righteousness upon his people in Christ (5:21; cf. 3:9), which in turn is to be expressed in the righteousness of generosity" (441-42) (cf. Murphy-O'Connor 92). For an eschatological interpretation of the expression γενήματα δικαιοσύνης in v. 10, see Nickle 137; Martin 292.

54. In spite of the spelling γέννημα found everywhere in the Textus Receptus (except in Luke 12:18).

55. See Deissmann 109-10, 184.

nevolence" or "acts of charity" (δικαιοσύνη) of the pious man of Ps. 111:10 (LXX) (see v. 9).[56]

Paul's point is that in addition to providing plentiful resources for the Corinthians' giving, God would also increase (καὶ αὐξήσει[57]) the material and spiritual benefits that would accrue to them and to the poor in Jerusalem as a result of their generous benevolence. Two agents are involved in the production of this "harvest." If it springs up from the Corinthians' δικαιοσύνη, it is enlarged by God's direct action (αὐξήσει; cf. 1 Cor. 3:7).[58] So then, from this verse we may identify four stages in the movement from seed to full harvest.

1. God supplies and multiplies the Corinthians' store of seed intended for sowing (τὸν σπόρον ὑμῶν).
2. The Corinthians sow this seed by giving generously (= δικαιοσύνη = σπείρειν ἐπ᾽ εὐλογίαις, v. 6).
3. A rich harvest (γενήματα = θερίζειν ἐπ᾽ εὐλογίαις, v. 6) results from their δικαιοσύνη.
4. God swells (αὐξήσει) that harvest, enlarging its proportions.

9:11 ἐν παντὶ πλουτιζόμενοι εἰς πᾶσαν ἁπλότητα, ἥτις κατεργάζεται δι᾽ ἡμῶν εὐχαριστίαν τῷ θεῷ. "You will be enriched in every way in order to show generosity of every kind, and through us such generosity will produce thanksgiving to God." This verse is transitional. The first part summarizes v. 8, with πλουτιζόμενοι, a theological passive, matching δυνατεῖ . . . ὁ θεὸς πᾶσαν χάριν περισσεῦσαι εἰς ὑμᾶς, with ἐν παντί repeated, and with εἰς πᾶσαν ἁπλότητα corresponding to ἵνα . . . περισσεύητε εἰς πᾶν ἔργον ἀγαθόν. The second part of this verse announces the main theme of vv. 12-15, the offering of thanksgiving to God that would be occasioned by the generosity of the Corinthians. Both parts indicate the result of v. 10.

The nominative participle πλουτιζόμενοι has been explained in three ways.

1. As being in apposition to ἔχοντες (v. 8), with vv. 9 and 10 forming a parenthesis (Bernard 93; WH; KJV). But this is a long grammatical parenthesis and vv. 9-10 naturally develop v. 8 (see on vv. 9-10).

2. As anacoluthic (Meyer 608), with the nominative derived from the preceding genitive ὑμῶν with which it ought grammatically to agree (Plummer 264). In the exigencies of dictation "Paul has forgotten how the sentence is going" (Barrett 239).

3. As standing for a finite verb (Zerwick, *Analysis* 407; Moule 179; Allo 235), that is, as being a participle used absolutely (Lietzmann 138; Robertson,

---

56. For the rendering "almsgiving" for δικαιοσύνη in both v. 9 and v. 10, see Weymouth, Montgomery; Lietzmann 138.

57. αὐξάνω here is used transitively, "cause to grow," "increase," as in 1 Cor. 3:6-7 (BAGD 121d).

58. Cf. Gal. 6:8, where the source of the harvest of eternal life is the Spirit.

Pictures 249). Within this category one must decide on the person and mood of the finite verb or independent participle. Betz translates "we are wealthy," seeing a reference to God's abundant care for humankind in general (115). But if v. 11 sums up v. 8 and in a more general sense vv. 6-10 (so Furnish 450), it is improbable that πλουτιζόμενοι has a wider referent than the Corinthians (thus second person plural, "you"). As for mood, there are three possibilities:

(a) imperative (Moulton 181-82, but see 181 n. 3; BDF §468(2), apparently; Turner, *Insights* 166; *Style* 89 [supplying ἔστε]; Zerwick and Grosvenor 553);

(b) optative: "May you be abundantly enriched" (Weymouth, who, however, takes the preceding three verbs as futures, not optatives; see Textual Note e.);

(c) indicative, either the present ("you are enriched")[59] or the future ("you will be enriched").[60]

To take πλουτιζόμενοι as standing for a future indicative seems preferable, given the three preceding futures. As in 6:10 the verb πλουτίζω is figurative, but whereas in 6:10 it is used in the active voice ("cause to become rich"), here it is passive ("be made rich," "be enriched").

ἐν παντί indicates the extent of the enrichment — "in every respect." Just as πᾶσαν χάριν in v. 8 should not be restricted to material bounty, so too ἐν παντί incorporates both economic and spiritual blessings. The purpose of the divine enrichment is signified by εἰς πᾶσαν ἁπλότητα, "in order to show generosity of every kind." But πᾶσαν could denote degree rather than diversification; thus "for the greatest generosity" (Furnish 443), or, "so that . . . you can show perfect liberality" (Goodspeed). This phrase parallels εἰς πᾶν ἔργον ἀγαθόν in v. 8, the crucial point in each case being that the divine beneficence is designed not to facilitate the accumulation of wealth but to make possible all kinds of liberality. We receive in order to give, not in order to hoard. In v. 8 the progression is from πᾶσαν χάριν to πᾶν ἔργον ἀγαθόν; here it is from ἐν παντὶ πλουτιζόμενοι to πᾶσαν ἁπλότητα. Enrichment of every kind leads to, or leaves the way open for, generosity of every kind (παντὶ . . . πᾶσαν). Being qualified by πᾶσα, the term ἁπλότης will here (cf. its use in 8:2; 9:13) have the concrete sense "act of generosity" or "generous gift." Once again, as in v. 8b, Paul seems to be thinking momentarily beyond the immediate occasion for generosity — the chance to contribute toward relief for Jerusalem — to future opportunities to share with others the resources provided by God. But his immediate concern always remains paramount, as the next phrase makes clear.

Paul believed that the Corinthian generosity was of such a nature that it

---

59. Thus Barrett 232; Furnish 443; Young and Ford 271; Barnett 438 n. 21; Thrall 563.

60. Thus the majority of EVV (e.g., RSV, NEB, NRSV, REB); Martin 287; Lambrecht 145. Also, Carrez 194; Lietzmann 138; Wendland 223; de Boor 191; Lang 324.

would produce thanksgiving to God. If the antecedent of the relative pronoun ὅστις is determinate (as in the present case [ἁπλότητα]), it means "which is of such a nature that," "such that."[61] Paul hoped and expected that the Corinthians would imitate the Macedonians (cf. 8:1-5) in giving sacrificially and enthusiastically and that they would acknowledge that God was the ultimate source of the gifts given (cf. 9:8, 10). Such ἁπλότης would prompt prayers of thanksgiving to be offered by the recipients of those gifts. The present tense κατεργάζεται may point to Paul's confidence about the success of the collection at Corinth (a present expressing certainty), or may be taken as a futuristic present ("will produce"[62]). τῷ θεῷ ("toward God," BAGD 328c) belongs with εὐχαριστίαν (not κατεργάζεται) (Windisch 281), following the model of the dative with εὐχαριστέω (e.g., 1 Cor. 1:4) (BDF §187[8]). On the principle that "every generous act of giving . . . is from above" (Jas. 1:17, NRSV), the Jerusalem poor could be expected to render thanks to God for the generosity of the Corinthians and others. These recipients would be told that it was God who had instilled the desire to give (cf. 8:10-11) and had provided the resources to give (cf. 9:8, 10). The thanksgiving is given to the ultimate benefactor, God, not to the intermediaries, the Corinthians, although v. 14 indicates that intercessory prayer (δεήσει ὑπὲρ ὑμῶν) would be offered on the Corinthians' behalf. δι' ἡμῶν ("through us," literary plural) means "through our action in administrating this fund" and looks back to the repeated expression τῇ διακονουμένῃ ὑφ' ἡμῶν ("that we are administering") that qualifies "this work of grace" (8:19) and "this lavish gift" (8:20).

We saw in vv. 8 and 10 Paul's emphasis on the supreme role of God in Christian stewardship. He is both the first and the last item in the progress from sowing to harvest; he provides the seed and swells the harvest. V. 11 encapsulates this emphasis on the priority and finality of God that mark the paragraph, 9:6-11. God enriches the Corinthians, who then give generously so that the beneficiaries give thanks to God. As Paul expresses it in another context, ἐξ αὐτοῦ . . . καὶ εἰς αὐτὸν τὰ πάντα (Rom. 11:36).

Bibliography

Davies, *Gospel* 200-203 • Gale 162-63 • Georgi 75-79, 93-102 • Hainz, *Koinonia* 141-44 • Hanson 177-81 • Morrice 46-47 • Murphy-O'Connor 89-94 • Nickle 104-5 • Seifrid 87-88 • Stanley 233-34 • Theobald 291-98 • Verbrugge 258-60 • H. J. Wicks, "St. Paul's Teaching as to the Rewards of Liberality," *ExpT* 29 (1917-18) 424-25 • D. J. Williams 38-40 • Ziesler 162

---

61. Zerwick §215; *Analysis* 407.
62. Similarly TCNT, Moffatt, Goodspeed, NEB, REB; Plummer 257; Martin 287.

2. The Offering of Prayer to God (9:12-15)

2 Cor. 9:6-15 describes two outcomes or benefits of generous giving. In vv. 6-11 the benefit is ongoing enrichment by God in both the material and the spiritual realm, an enrichment that aims to promote ongoing generosity. The second result of liberality, sketched in vv. 12-15, relates to the recipients of the Corinthians' gift, the Jerusalem poor in particular and the whole Jerusalem church in general. They would offer many prayers of gratitude to God for his superlative grace in the lives of the Corinthians that was shown in their generosity, and they would intercede for their fellow believers in Corinth in prayers that expressed their affectionate longing for them. Appropriately, Paul concludes with an expression of thanks to God for his gift that exhausts all description, the gift of the Messiah.

Garland (400) has pointed out the verbal correspondence between the beginning of ch. 8 and the end of ch. 9 that forms a kind of *inclusio* and supports the unity of these two chapters.

ἡ χάρις τοῦ θεοῦ	8:1; 9:14
δοκιμή	8:2; 9:13
περισσεύω	8:2; 9:12 (also 8:7, twice; 9:8, twice)
ἁπλότης	8:2; 9:13 (also 9:11)
διακονία	8:4; 9:12-13 (also 9:1)

9:12*For the carrying out of this act of service is not only supplying the needs of God's people but is also overflowing in many expressions of thanks[a] to God.* 13*Because of[b] the evidence that this service provides, people will give glory to God for the obedience that is prompted by your confession of the gospel of Christ, and for the generosity of your sharing with them and with everyone.* 14*And as they pray for you[c] they will yearn for you, because of the surpassing grace of God that rests on you.* 15*Thanks be to God for his gift that is indescribable!*

TEXTUAL NOTES

a. In the place of the genitive plural εὐχαριστιῶν (read by ℵ B C D G K P Ψ 81 614 1739 𝔐 it vg syr[p, h] cop[sa, bo] goth), a few witnesses have the accusative singular εὐχαριστίαν (p⁴⁶ [d g r] [eth] Cyprian Ambrosiaster Augustine) or accusative plural εὐχαριστίας (arm) under the influence of the construction in 9:11 (δι᾽ ἡμῶν εὐχαριστίαν τῷ θεῷ) (see Metzger 582-83).

b. To avoid asyndeton B sa add καί before διά.

c. The reading (ἡμῶν) found in ℵ * B 1881 *pc* vg[ms] does not accord with the context, where the recipients' reaction to the Corinthians' gift (thus ὑμῶν) is the matter being discussed and ὑμᾶς follows. ἡμῶν may have arisen under the influence of δι᾽ ἡμῶν in 9:11: prayer "for us" as a result of "our work as agents."

9:12 ὅτι ἡ διακονία τῆς λειτουργίας ταύτης οὐ μόνον ἐστὶν προσαναπληροῦσα τὰ ὑστερήματα τῶν ἁγίων, ἀλλὰ καὶ περισσεύουσα διὰ πολλῶν εὐχαριστιῶν τῷ θεῷ. "For the carrying out of this act of service is not only supplying the needs of God's people but is also overflowing in many expressions of thanks to God." V. 11 ends with a summary statement of the second result of generosity, the offering of prayers of thanksgiving and petition to God. This is the theme of vv. 12-15 (note the initial ὅτι in v. 12). But v. 12a also briefly revisits the idea of relieving need through the sharing of resources that finds its classic expression in 8:14-15. In some editions of the Greek text[1] v. 12 is marked off by dashes as parenthetical, doubtless to relieve the grammatical tension created by the participle δοξάζοντες in v. 13, which would then be in apposition to πλουτιζόμενοι in v. 11. But there is no reason to understand δοξάζοντες this way (see on v. 13), particularly since the subject of these two participles is, in all probability, different. UBS[4] and NA[27] treat v. 12 as contributing to the argument in its own right.[2]

The phrase ἡ διακονία τῆς λειτουργίας ταύτης may be construed in two basic ways.

1. "The charitable act of this public service" (Betz 87; cf. 117), where διακονία signifies an act of charitable service, or, more specifically, a "kind contribution" (BAGD 184c),[3] and τῆς λειτουργίας is an epexegetic genitive,[4] defining more precisely the nature of the "service."
2. "The execution of this act of public service" (Barrett 239), where διακονία is distinguished from λειτουργία (both terms may mean "service") by referring to an "enactment" (Georgi 103) or "carrying out" or "performance" of an act of service[5] and τῆς λειτουργίας is an objective genitive. Since the emphasis falls on the λειτουργία rather than the διακονία, this interpretation may be happily rendered "this service that you perform" (NIV; similarly GNB; Martin 287) or "this act of service, when carried out, . . ."

In Classical usage λειτουργία denoted "public service" carried out by private citizens at their own expense, such as financing the choruses in dramas, but also any public service, including the service of the gods (LSJ s.v. 1036). The etymology of the word, λήϊτος ("relating to the people," "public"; cf. λαός) and ἔργον, "work," "service," highlights its two essential ingredients. In LXX usage it became a technical term for priestly service in the Temple (e.g., 2 Chron. 35:16 LXX). It comes as no surprise, then, to discover that translators and commentators take λειτουργία in our verse in one of three senses — "public service"[6] performed for the benefit of the community, be it the community at large

1. WH; UBS[1, 2, 3]; also taken as parenthetical by Robertson 434-35, 439.
2. UBS[4] prints τῷ θεῷ· . . . τῷ θεῷ·, and NA[27] τῷ θεῷ· . . . τῷ θεῷ.
3. In Rom. 15:31, too, διακονία may mean "contribution" (BAGD 184c).
4. So Plummer 265; Spicq 2.382 n. 13; Hainz, *Koinonia* 142.
5. In Acts 12:25 διακονία may refer to the task of delivering relief aid.
6. E.g., TCNT, NAB[2]; Barrett 239; Betz 87.

or the Christian community; religious or priestly or "holy service";[7] or "service"[8] in a nontechnical, popular sense.[9] One hesitates to exclude any one of these connotations, for Paul uses the term in a religious sense in Phil. 2:17 (where θυσία also occurs) (cf. λειτουργός in Rom. 15:16) and in a popular sense in Phil. 2:30 (cf. λειτουργός in Rom. 13:6), while the collection was aimed at promoting the welfare of the Christian community in Jerusalem.[10] "The rendering of this act of service" refers to the collection project as a whole but with special reference to the role of the Corinthians and other contributors rather than to the distinctive role of Paul (cf. v. 12) or of the Corinthians alone.

By means of the οὐ μόνον . . . ἀλλὰ καί pairing Paul specifies the twofold harvest of the Corinthian δικαιοσύνη (cf. v. 10), relief for fellow believers and praise to God. When he uses the verb προσαναπληρόω ("fill up," "supply") (found only here and in 11:9 in the NT), he is not suggesting that the Corinthian monetary contribution on its own would meet the economic needs of the poor in the Jerusalem church, but he is affirming that their contribution would help to fill up or relieve their needs; other churches were also contributing (cf. προσ-, "in addition").[11] ἐστὶν προσαναπληροῦσα is a periphrastic present ("is supplying," or "is to supply" if the present is futuristic), a construction not nearly as common in the NT as the periphrastic imperfect. The plural ὑστερήματα (cf. the singular in 8:14; 11:9) points to "the varying needs of numerous people."[12] What Paul himself had experienced — the supply of need (9:12) — he was now seeking to provide for others. As in 8:4; 9:1; Rom. 15:25 οἱ ἅγιοι refers to οἱ πτωχοὶ τῶν ἁγίων τῶν ἐν Ἰερουσαλήμ (Rom. 15:26).

The second aspect (cf. 9:6-11) of the harvest resulting from the Corinthian service of giving was a widespread outpouring of gratitude to God. (ἐστὶν) περισσεύουσα continues the quantitative imagery of προσαναπληροῦσα: "this act of service" would not end, in its results, with the "filling up" of needs but would also "overflow" in a flood of thanksgiving to God. In the phrase διὰ πολλῶν εὐχαριστιῶν τῷ θεῷ, (1) διά is probably local ("in") but could, alternatively, denote mode ("in the form of"[13]) or attendant circumstances ("with," "in the midst of") or agency ("through"); (2) πολλῶν is an adjective in the attributive position, not a substantive ("of many people"), for in that case we would have expected πολλῶν to follow εὐχαριστιῶν; (3) the plural εὐχαριστιῶν (cf. 1 Tim. 2:1) refers to acts or prayers of thanksgiving (cf. BAGD 328d) or "ex-

7. E.g., JB; Spicq 2.382; cf. Furnish 451; Georgi 103, 203 n. 40.
8. E.g., Weymouth, GNB; Martin 287.
9. Thus H. Strathmann, *TDNT* 4.227; cf. 217-18.
10. On λειτουργία in connection with the collection, see Panikulam 42-43; Prümm II/ 2.48-49.
11. Weymouth has "helps to relieve"; Plummer proposes "[is] filling up in addition," "[is] helping to fill" (265). Etymologically, προσαναπληρόω means "add something (προσ-) so as to bring up (-ανα-) to a state of fullness (-πληροῦν)" (Hughes 337 n. 72).
12. Zerwick, *Analysis* 407.
13. Zerwick and Grosvenor 553.

pressions of thanks" (NIV); and (4) τῷ θεῷ (see on v. 11) refers to thanksgiving prayers that are "offered to God" or "directed to God," rather than to an undefined "abundance" (cf. περισσεύουσα) that is "for God" (dative of advantage)[14] or "to the glory of God" (in which case εἰς τὴν δόξαν τοῦ θεοῦ [4:15] or εἰς δόξαν θεοῦ [Phil. 2:11] might have been expected).[15]

But Paul did not place these two purposes of the collection — human relief and divine praise — on an equal footing. οὐ μόνον . . . ἀλλὰ καί here is ascensive,[16] with the first, historical purpose subsidiary to the second, theological aim. The act of kindness, though important, is less important than the act of praising God; φιλανθρωπία takes second place to δοξολογία. It would have been unthinkable for Paul to reverse the order, since for him the praise and glory of God always was the highest good and ultimate goal (Rom. 15:7; 1 Cor. 10:31; Eph. 1:12, 14; Phil. 2:11), and God (τῷ θεῷ) vastly more significant than humans (τῶν ἁγίων).

With this giving of thanks to God by the grateful recipients of the collection,[17] the full circle is complete. God blesses the Corinthians with his extraordinary grace (v. 14) in richly providing for their own material and spiritual needs (vv. 8-11a). This enables them to sow generously and cheerfully (vv. 6-7) by giving "a gift of blessing" (εὐλογία, v. 5) by which the physical needs of others are met (v. 12a). In gratitude for the generosity of God's people, those who receive this "gift of blessing" acknowledge God as the ultimate source of the gift and so bless him with prayers of thanksgiving (vv. 11b, 12b). To define this circle in terms of χάρις, God gives his "grace" to his people (8:1; 9:14), who then give a "gift of grace" (8:7) which prompts the giving of "thanks" (εὐ-χαρισ-τία, 9:11b-13) to God. As in v. 10, God is both first and last.

The dual purpose (or result) of the collection expressed here invites comparison with the twofold aim stated in 8:19.

8:19	9:12
πρὸς τὴν αὐτοῦ τοῦ κυρίου δόξαν	(διὰ) πολλῶν εὐχαριστιῶν τῷ θεῷ
(πρὸς) προθυμίαν ἡμῶν	ἐστὶν προσαναπληροῦσα τὰ ὑστερήματα τῶν ἁγίων

From this comparison we may infer two things: that a crucial ingredient in the enhancement of the glory of the Lord that would be brought about by the col-

14. Thus Barclay: "the ministration of this act of voluntary service . . . also does something special for God through the many thanksgivings it produces"; similarly Plummer 257; but cf. 267.

15. Cf. Georgi 103 ("the abundance is an increase of the δόξα θεοῦ"), who acknowledges his dependence on the discussion of this passage in G. H. Boobyer, *"Thanksgiving" and the "Glory of God" in Paul* (Borna-Leipzig: Noske, 1929) 2-3, 70, 78-80.

16. BAGD 38a; cf. BDF §448(6).

17. Others, too, may be implied by the adjective πολλῶν ("*many* expressions of thanks"), such as the Corinthians and other donors, and Paul himself. But the subject of δοξάζοντες in 9:13 is probably only Christians in Jerusalem and others who may hear about the collection.

lection was the offering of widespread thanksgiving to him;[18] and that the supply of the physical needs of the poor in the Jerusalem church was an evidence of Paul's "goodwill" (προθυμία) toward his fellow believers in Jerusalem.

9:13 The syntactical relationships in this complex verse (the sentence ends in v. 14) may be illustrated by a diagram.

$$
\begin{array}{llll}
\text{διὰ τῆς} & \text{δοκιμῆς} & \text{τῆς} & \text{διακονίας} \quad \text{ταύτης} \\
& & & \qquad\qquad \text{δοξάζοντες τὸν θεόν} \\
\text{ἐπὶ τῇ} & \text{ὑποταγῇ} & \text{τῆς} & \text{ὁμολογίας} \quad \text{ὑμῶν} \\
& & & \qquad \text{εἰς τὸ εὐαγγέλιον τοῦ Χριστοῦ} \\
\text{καὶ [ἐπὶ]} & \text{ἁπλότητι} & \text{τῆς} & \text{κοινωνίας} \\
& & & \qquad \text{εἰς αὐτοὺς} \\
& & & \qquad \text{καὶ εἰς πάντας}
\end{array}
$$

διὰ τῆς δοκιμῆς τῆς διακονίας ταύτης δοξάζοντες τὸν θεόν. "Because of the evidence that this service provides, people will give glory to God." Just as v. 12 is a commentary on v. 11b, so too v. 13, with its further reference to the praise of God, is an elucidation of v. 12. What is new in v. 13 is Paul's explanation of the reason for (διά) and the basis or content of (ἐπί) that praise. Generally, διά with the genitive denotes agency or instrumentality, but occasionally, as here, this construction is indistinguishable from διά with accusative denoting cause (BAGD 181a, "because of"; Lietzmann 139).[19] As in 13:3, δοκιμή has the sense of "proof" or "evidence,"[20] and the genitive that follows (τῆς διακονίας ταύτης) will be subjective: "(the evidence) provided by this service" = "that this service provides,"[21] where the διακονία refers to the Corinthians' participation in the collection, their provision of relief aid.[22] But the question remains: Of what will the Corinthians' charitable offering afford evidence? Some find the evidence in the obedience (Barrett 232) or the obedience and sincerity/generosity[23] that Paul goes on to mention in the verse, but while that identification is certainly possible, it seems better to identify the "evidence" or "proof" in

18. This assumes that ὁ κύριος in 8:19 refers to the Lord God (see the discussion there).

19. Others take διά here to mean "occasioned by" (Hodge 225; cf. Winer 381) or "induced by" (Georgi 202 n. 31).

20. δοκιμή is a rare word, not found before Paul. Although "proof" is not given as a meaning in BAGD 202d (where "approved character" is the suggested meaning in 9:13), Danker himself (145) understands it in this sense here, and LSJ 442 s.v. lists "proof" as a meaning. W. Grundmann gives the meanings as "testing" (as in NRSV at 9:13) or "certifying" (TDNT 2.255), and on 9:13 comments that "the Corinthians can give proof of themselves in the collection" (TDNT 2.259).

21. Similarly TCNT, Weymouth, NEB, REB; Furnish 440; Thrall 563. This meaning is sometimes said to reflect a genitive of apposition (Hughes 338 n. 74) or an epexegetic genitive (Thrall 588 n. 177).

22. But Georgi gives διακονία here a specialized sense — the actual transfer of the collection to Jerusalem (103, 105, 202 n. 31), translating 9:13a as "Occasioned by this transfer (the διακονία), a successful (completion of a) test, they glorify God" (103).

23. So Bruce, *Paraphrase* 147; Barnett 445-46.

a more comprehensive way as the Corinthians' genuine brotherly love (cf. 8:8, 24; Rom. 12:9-10), or the genuineness and robustness of their faith, or (following Plummer 257) their Christian character.[24]

The unexpected nominative participle δοξάζοντες has been explained in the same three basic ways as πλουτιζόμενοι in v. 11.

1. As being in apposition to πλουτιζόμενοι, which itself is seen to be in apposition to ἔχοντες (v. 8) and as dependent on περισσεύητε (v. 8). In WH vv. 9-10 are marked off with brackets as a parenthesis, and v. 12 is marked as parenthetical by commas and dashes (, — . . . , —).
2. As anacoluthic, "as if ὅτι πολλοὶ εὐχαριστοῦσιν had preceded" (Winer 572). "If a sentence is continued by means of participles, these, when at a distance from the governing verb, not infrequently assume an abnormal case" (Winer 572, citing 9:11, 13).
3. As standing for a finite verb (Zerwick, *Analysis* 407; Moule 179; Thrall 588),[25] that is, as being an absolute participle (Lietzmann 139; Robertson, *Pictures* 250). Most who understand δοξάζοντες this way take the participle as a substitute for the indicative, sometimes the present,[26] but usually the future,[27] although occasionally this participle is construed as imperatival.[28]

But is the implied subject of δοξάζοντες second person, "you (Corinthians),"[29] or third person, "they[30]/people"?[31] Against seeing the Corinthians as the referent is the change of focus marked by the phrase εὐχαριστίαν τῷ θεῷ in v. 11b. In vv. 6-11a the center of attention is the Corinthians and God's provision for their generous giving, but thereafter (vv. 11b-14) the emphasis falls on the recipients of that giving and the cause and content of their praise of God. Moreover, it would be arbitrary to postulate two different subjects, one for the thanksgiving (the beneficiaries in Jerusalem) and another for the

---

24. "Affliction tested the reality of the Macedonians' Christianity (viii.2), benevolence will be a proof in the case of the Corinthians" (Plummer 266).

25. For this usage, cf. 5:12; 6:3; 7:5; 8:19-20; 9:11; 10:4, 15 (twice); 11:6; see BDF §468 (1); Zerwick §374; Turner 343.

26. E.g., RV, NAB[1, 2], NRSV; Furnish 440.

27. Thus most EVV and commentators: e.g., NEB, REB; Carrez 194.

28. Moulton 181; Turner, *Insights* 166 (and the note, "Supply, 'they ought to be' before 'praising God'"); *Style* 89.

29. Thus RSV, NAB[2], NRSV; Barnett 445 and n. 49; Lambrecht 148, 151; "Boasting" 366. TCNT makes "you" the subject but takes δοξάζω in a causative sense, "you cause men to praise God"; cf. Weymouth, "you cause God to be extolled."

30. Thus most EVV and commentators: e.g., RV, NASB; Thrall 563.

31. NIV (1995); cf. "men" (Moffatt, NIV [1973], Cassirer). NEB supplies "many" as the subject of δοξάζοντες, reflecting the πολλῶν at the end of v. 12 (whether adjective or substantive). Martin, who seems to prefer this option (cf. 1:11; 2:6), discerns a reference to "the Corinthians who remained loyal to Paul's cause, and who now welcome the action of the entire church as expressed in the raising of the offering" (294).

glorifying (the Corinthians). The εὐχαριστία is part of the δοξολογία, and the same party is responsible for both actions, viz. "the poor among God's people in Jerusalem" (Rom. 15:26) who are the immediate recipients of the collection,[32] and, more generally the whole Jerusalem church and other believers who learned of the collection, such as "the churches of Christ in Judea" (Gal. 1:22). The rendering "people will give glory to God" adequately represents this broad implied subject and the future sense of the present participle that is suggested by the context. It is very significant that in Acts 21:17-20 Luke indicates that after the collection had been received at Jerusalem and the church's leaders had heard Paul describe in detail all that God had done among the Gentiles through his ministry, "they began glorifying God" (ἐδόξα-ζον τὸν θεόν, Acts 21:20).[33]

The object of δοξάζω is not always God, for in Paul this verb can on occasion denote the honor one person does to another (1 Cor. 12:26) or God's own act of sharing his δόξα with humans (Rom. 8:30). But in an ultimate sense δόξα belongs exclusively to God (Rom. 11:36; 16:27). "Giving glory" to God (δοξο-λογία) is a broader concept than "giving thanks" to God (εὐχαριστία),[34] for it includes not only praise (cf. Luke 2:20; Acts 4:21) but also an adoring recognition and acknowledgment that God is clothed in splendor and is the source of all that is good and holy. However, thanksgiving addressed to God is a primary way in which the glory of God is increased.

ἐπὶ τῇ ὑποταγῇ τῆς ὁμολογίας ὑμῶν εἰς τὸ εὐαγγέλιον τοῦ Χριστοῦ καὶ ἁπλότητι τῆς κοινωνίας εἰς αὐτοὺς καὶ εἰς πάντας. "(. . . people will give glory to God) for the obedience that is prompted by your confession of the gospel of Christ, and for the generosity of your sharing with them and with everyone." Here Paul states the basis and content of the δοξάζοντες, with ἐπί introducing "that upon which . . . an action . . . is based" (BAGD 287c). But a basis for praise and worship naturally becomes the content of that worshipful praise.[35] This same ἐπί ("for") is to be understood before ἁπλότητι. So then, within this verse, διά denotes the cause, and ἐπί the basis and content, of the δοξολογία,[36] and, by implication, of the εὐχαριστία (vv. 11b, 12b).

Just as the verb ὑποτάσσω means "subject" and in the passive "obey," so the cognate noun ὑποταγή means both "subjection" and "obedience." The genitive τῆς ὁμολογίας ("confession," "profession") is probably either epexegetic ("the obedience *consisting of* your confession")[37] or subjective ("the obedience

---

32. REB makes this explicit: "those who receive it [this aid] will give honour to God."

33. See further in the Introduction, B.5.e.

34. In Rom. 1:21 giving thanks to God is mentioned as one aspect of glorifying God.

35. Zerwick regards ἐπί as introducing "the object of praise" (*Analysis* 407). For the construction δοξάζω ἐπί, where the preposition specifies basis and content, see Luke 2:20; Acts 4:21; Polybius 6.53.10.

36. Winer, however, takes διά to denote the occasion, and ἐπί the cause ("on account of") (381); so also Georgi 105. RSV and NRSV render διά with "by" (of means).

37. Thus Georgi 105, 204 n. 43; Thrall 563, 589-90; RSV, "obedience in acknowledging."

prompted by your confession"),[38] although some have suggested it is objective ("obedience *to* your confession")[39] or adjectival ("your *professed* obedience").[40] On each view, except the last, εἰς τὸ εὐαγγέλιον τοῦ Χριστοῦ is construed with the immediately preceding noun ὁμολογίας, "your confession of the gospel of Christ," where "confession" denotes "acceptance of its claim and [an] expression of commitment" (O. Michel, *TDNT* 5.125), and referential εἰς ("with reference to") points to what is confessed or professed.[41] Betz, however, argues that ὁμολογία here bears a legal meaning, "contractual agreement," so that in the estimation of the Jerusalem Christians the donation by the Achaians would have signified their "obligatory submission" (ὑποταγή) to the Jerusalem church (= "the gospel of Christ") (25, 122-24). But it is difficult to imagine that any such contract existed in documentary form, as Betz proposes, or even as a verbal agreement, so that Paul could call it *"your* contractual agreement" (significantly Betz does not translate ὑμῶν in his renderings of the whole expression ἡ ὑποταγὴ τῆς ὁμολογίας ὑμῶν on pp. 87, 123). For further comments on Betz's view, see Thrall 589-90 and O'Mahony 172-74. That this is not a necessary interpretation, even if ὁμολογία is given a technical meaning, may be seen from the fact that Danker, who also takes ὁμολογία as a reference to a contractual obligation, concludes that "Paul images the Corinthians as having contracted for participation in the task of proclaiming Christ" (145). And, on a more general plane, Berger argues that so far from expressing the supremacy of the Jerusalem church and the dependence of the Pauline communities, the collection was a recognition of fellowship and independence ("Almosen" 198-99). Christ is certainly the content of the εὐαγγέλιον ("the gospel concerning Christ," τοῦ Χριστοῦ an objective genitive); he may also be seen as its source ("the gospel brought by Christ," subjective genitive) (cf. 2:12, 10:14).[42]

We assume that τῆς ὁμολογίας is a subjective genitive: a confessional adherence to the gospel produces obedience. But obedience to what? Perhaps to God (as NEB, REB), but more probably to the dictates of the gospel of Christ, a gospel that demands that believers should help to relieve need both inside and outside the family of believers (Rom. 12:13; Gal. 6:9-10; cf. Luke 6:38; 1 Tim. 6:18; Heb. 13:16). BAGD aptly sums up the sense: "your confessing the gospel finds expression in obedient subjection to its requirements" (568d).

As he anticipates the response of the Jerusalem church to the collection,

---

38. Similarly BAGD 568d; Barnett 445 n. 51. Cf. ὑπακοὴ πίστεως ("the obedience prompted by faith") in Rom. 1:5; 16:26.

39. NRSV; Hughes 339 n. 75 (citing a similar expression in 10:5, ὑπακοὴ τοῦ Χριστοῦ, "obedience to Christ"); Lambrecht 145. NAB² sees the genitive as denoting relation, ("obedience in relation to your confession" =) "your obedient confession."

40. Bruce, *Paraphrase* 147; KJV, "your professed subjection."

41. For the combination ὁμολογία εἰς Plummer cites (266) the parallel in Justin, *Dialogue with Trypho* 47, τὴν εἰς τὸν Χριστὸν τοῦ θεοῦ ὁμολογίαν.

42. So also Spicq 2.89, who speaks (n. 35) of a "'comprehensive' genitive" (both subjective and objective); cf. Zerwick (§37).

Paul foresees another item for which those believers will praise and worship God — (δοξάζοντες τὸν θεὸν . . . καὶ) [ἐπὶ] ἁπλότητι τῆς κοινωνίας [ὑμῶν] εἰς αὐτοὺς καὶ ἐπὶ πάντας. At 8:2 we discussed the meaning of ἁπλότης and saw that although in Pauline usage it sometimes means "sincerity" or "simplicity," in Rom. 12:8 and the three occurrences in 2 Corinthians 8–9 (8:2; 9:11, 13) it has the sense of "generosity."[43] It would be a generosity "displayed in sharing" (τῆς κοινωνίας)[44] material resources with the poor in the Jerusalem church (εἰς αὐτούς) and also "with everyone" (ἐπὶ πάντας). Some, however, give κοινωνία a more specific sense arising from the present context, "(the generosity of) your contribution" (RSV, NAB²).[45] While support for this sense may be found in the expression κοινωνίαν τινά ("some contribution") in Rom. 15:26 in connection with the same collection, the difficulty in the present case is that Paul adds καὶ ἐπὶ πάντας, which seems to imply a wider circle that will, on other occasions, benefit from the Corinthians' κοινωνία.[46] It is better, therefore, to give this term a broader sense such as "sharing" or "fellowship" or "partnership" or even (cf. BAGD 439b) "altruism."

On occasion the πάντας in καὶ ἐπὶ πάντας is restricted to fellow Christians (Barnett 446) or to other churches (Bernard 94; Georgi 106), or is taken to mean that when relief is given to the mother church all Christians benefit indirectly,[47] presumably by the example of Christian fellowship thus afforded or by the cementing of Jew-Gentile relations. But such a restriction seems unwarranted. V. 8 has already envisaged a situation of benevolence beyond the charitable offering for Jerusalem, when God would provide the Corinthians with "every kind of blessing in abundance" so that they would have "ample resources for every kind of good work" (εἰς πᾶν ἔργον ἀγαθόν). So πάντας would appear to refer to "everyone else in need," whether believer or unbeliever.[48] Such an interpretation finds support in the close parallel in Gal. 6:10, "As we have opportunity, let us do good to all people (πρὸς πάντας), especially to those who belong to the family of faith (πρὸς τοὺς οἰκείους τῆς πίστεως)." In both verses πάντας is all-embracing.

In v. 13, then, Paul anticipates that after the collection has been com-

43. Taking ἁπλότης in 9:13 to refer to "single-minded generosity" (340), Hughes refers to the term's "proper force" as being "singleness of purpose leading to liberality in giving to others" (340 n. 76). Georgi (105-6) and Wolff (183) opt for the rendering "simple goodness," while Windisch (285) and Bruce (*Paraphrase* 147) propose "the sincerity (of your fellowship)."

44. Similarly GNB, NAB¹, NRSV. On this view τῆς κοινωνίας is a genitive of reference or relation.

45. Also Zerwick and Grosvenor 553; similarly Plummer 257, 266. However κοινωνίας is rendered, ὑμῶν is probably to be supplied with it, on the basis of the parallelism between τῆς ὁμολογίας ὑμῶν εἰς . . . and τῆς κοινωνίας εἰς. . . .

46. Cf. Campbell 373.

47. Cf. Plummer 257, 267 (citing 1 Cor. 12:26); Zerwick, *Analysis* 407, "because [the collection] helps the mother church, it helps all."

48. Weymouth has "all who are in need," while NEB and REB render εἰς πάντας by "to the general good."

pleted at Corinth and the whole collection delivered to Jerusalem, the believers there, along with others, would give glory to God because of (διά) the evidence of genuine faith and love in the Corinthians as demonstrated by their service of generous giving, and for (ἐπί) three items — for the Corinthians' confession of faith in the gospel of Christ (= their conversion), for their consequent obedience to the gospel's requirement that they contribute to the needs of others, and for the proof of that obedience in their generous sharing with the needy both in Jerusalem and elsewhere. From this summary of the content of this complex verse, several points emerge.

1. Gratitude for the monetary gift itself was secondary to gratitude for the conversion of the Gentile Corinthians and for their Christian character as reflected in the gift. If some Jewish believers in Jerusalem needed proof or reassurance of the reality of Gentile faith (especially in light of reported irregularities in the Corinthian church), and of the success of the Pauline mission, here was evidence that should satisfy even the most skeptical.

2. The close connection between the cause (διά) and the content (ἐπί) of the δοξολογία is evident.

3. If the sequence is conversion — obedience to the implications of the gospel — sharing resources with those in need, clearly the second and third items in the sequence are closely associated.[49] This may explain why ἐπί is not repeated before ἁπλότητι and why this noun is anarthrous.[50]

9:14 καὶ αὐτῶν δεήσει ὑπὲρ ὑμῶν ἐπιποθούντων ὑμᾶς διὰ τὴν ὑπερβάλλουσαν χάριν τοῦ θεοῦ ἐφ᾿ ὑμῖν. "And as they pray for you they will yearn for you, because of the surpassing grace of God that rests on you." Thus far in the paragraph (vv. 12-15) Paul's focus has been on the response of the recipients of the collection in relation to God (τῷ θεῷ [v. 12] . . . τὸν θεόν [v. 13]) — they will offer him thanks (v. 12) and give him glory (v. 13). Now, in v. 14, the center of interest is the response of the believers in Jerusalem as beneficiaries to the believers in Corinth as donors — they will pray for them and yearn after them.

The expression αὐτῶν δεήσει poses a syntactical problem.

1. It may be dependent on δοξάζοντες (v. 13),

(a) with ἐπί (τῇ) understood before δεήσει, so that "and for their prayer" is a third "object of praise" (after ὑποταγῇ and ἁπλότητι);[51] or

(b) with δεήσει construed as an instrumental dative ("they glorify God

---

49. Wolff (183) actually takes the καί before ἁπλότητι to be epexegetic ("namely").

50. The nonrepetition of the article before the second of two coordinated nouns points to a conceptual unity between them (and sometimes to their identity).

51. Zerwick, *Analysis* 407.

for . . . , and for . . . ; And by their prayer for you," KJV) and ἐπιποθούντων taken in apposition to αὐτῶν ("while/for they long for you").[52]

(a) is difficult, because whoever is the subject of δοξάζοντες ("they" or "you"; see on v. 13), in the putative threefold object of praise there is a move from ὑμῶν to αὐτῶν. (b) involves an awkward change from ἐπί (once explicitly and once implicitly) in v. 13 to an instrumental dative in v. 14, and an unnatural position for αὐτῶν.

2. It may be part of a genitive absolute clause, καὶ αὐτῶν δεήσει ὑπὲρ ὑμῶν ἐπιποθούντων ὑμᾶς,[53] in which the present participle ἐπιποθούντων replaces a future tense finite verb ("they will yearn"), and δεήσει is a dative expressing

(a) means: "by praying,"[54] or
(b) location: "in their prayer,"[55] or
(c) attendant circumstances: "as they pray."[56]

Some take καί to be adjunctive ("also"), in the sense that Paul joins the Jerusalemites in prayer and longing for the Corinthians (Barnett 447 n. 61), or as indicating reciprocity ("in turn"), in the sense that the Jerusalem believers were now reciprocating the Corinthians' sincere fellowship (Meyer 612). Either view is possible, but καί may be simply conjunctive ("and"), as Paul moves to a fresh aspect of the Jerusalemite response to the collection.

Our preference is for 2(c). "And as they pray for you they will yearn for you." As an earnest petition for particular needs, δέησις ("petition," "entreaty") is a specific form of προσευχή ("prayer"), although προσευχή, like αἴτημα ("request"), may also refer to specific petitionary prayer (e.g., Phil. 4:6; 1 Tim. 2:1). The basic meaning of ἐπιποθέω is "eagerly desire," but when the verb depicts interpersonal relations it gains the sense of "have deep affection for."[57] Either meaning is suitable in the present context, and both are represented in the EVV: "they feel a yearning for you" (Berkeley); "their hearts will go out to you" (NEB, REB). Weymouth combines both elements, "they themselves . . . pour out their longing love towards you." But since this verb often signifies a longing to see someone,[58] we incline toward the sense, "they will yearn for

52. Cf. Bruce, *Paraphrase* 147.
53. This is recognized, *inter alios,* by Windisch 285; Allo 237.
54. Cf. Georgi 106: "In prayer for you they prove their yearning for you."
55. Barrett 232; Lambrecht 145, 148; Thrall 563. NIV and Martin 287 take δεήσει as a generic singular: "in their prayers."
56. Wolff 183 and n. 140; similarly NEB, REB; Furnish 440, 445.
57. Cf. Spicq 2.58-60; "Ἐπιποθεῖν" 184-95.
58. Cf. ἐπιποθεῖν ἰδεῖν in Rom. 1:11; 1 Thess. 3:6; 2 Tim. 1:4; cf. Phil. 2:26, and note ἐπιπόθησις in 2 Cor. 7:7, 11 and ἐπιποθία in Rom. 15:23. Allo observes that in Paul ἐπιποθέω "al-

you." The recipient of a gift naturally longs to meet the donor, express gratitude in person, and forge a personal relationship. After receiving the gift from Gentile believers, Christians in Jerusalem would long to thank them in person and to verify and applaud in person the evidence of God's grace in their lives.

The reason (διά + accusative) for this prayerful longing is now given. It was "on account of your having God's grace resting upon you in a degree above all measure" (Cassirer). With this reference to ἡ χάρις τοῦ θεοῦ an *inclusio* is formed with 8:1 (see O'Mahony 94). What had been true of the Macedonians would also be true of the Corinthians; they would be recipients of God's grace that prompted and enabled giving. Here the χάρις is given or shown by God (τοῦ θεοῦ, subjective genitive),[59] is "extraordinary" or "surpassing" (ὑπερβάλλουσαν; cf. 3:10) in that it is given in unbounded measure, and "rests on"[60] the Corinthians (ἐφ᾽ ὑμῖν) in that it is not simply "granted to" them (cf. τὴν δεδομένην ἐν, 8:1) but is poured out "on" them (ἐφ᾽ ὑμῶν qualifies ὑπερβάλλουσαν). As to the precise nature of the χάρις in this context, it is probably God's gracious action in inspiring generous giving (cf. vv. 6-8) and in supplying the resources to give (vv. 8-11), or, less probably, his favor in including Gentiles, as represented by the Corinthians, in his plan of salvation.[61]

There is no ambiguity in Paul's description of the projected response in Jerusalem to the delivery of the monetary gift from the Gentile churches (vv. 11b-14). Jewish believers there would respond positively by offering prayers of gratitude and intercession. But the question arises: How could Paul speak so confidently of these outcomes when three or four months later he issues to the church in Rome a particularly urgent call for prayer that his "service for Jerusalem may prove acceptable to God's people" (Rom. 15:31)?[62] For several reasons this confidence cannot be dismissed as misguided. First, Paul is trusting in God's ability (cf. δυνατεῖ δὲ ὁ θεός, 9:8) to produce the positive outcome he envisages. Second, by assuming that the Corinthians will contribute generously he is actually encouraging their enthusiastic participation in the project, and by stating his aims and hopes as though they had already been achieved he is contributing to their actual fulfillment. Third, the concern reflected in Rom. 15:31 may have arisen as a result of news received after the present letter had been sent (Bruce 228). Perhaps the two areas of concern mentioned in Rom. 15:31 were closely connected; opposition to Paul from "the unbelievers in

---

ways or almost always" expresses intense regret at being distant or absent (124). This would be true even in 2 Cor. 5:2.

59. So also (explicitly) Moffatt, Goodspeed, NEB, GNB, JB, NAB[1], NIV, NJB, REB, NRSV.

60. Similarly Weymouth, Cassirer; cf. NAB[2].

61. For the latter view see Lambrecht 151.

62. The urgency of Paul's entreaty may be seen in the authority to which he appeals ("the Lord Jesus Christ") and the ground of his appeal ("the love that the Spirit inspires"), and also in his request that the Roman Christians should join him in earnest and persistent prayer (συναγωνίσασθαί μοι ἐν ταῖς προσευχαῖς) (Rom. 15:30).

Judea" may have adversely affected the attitude of some within the Jerusalem church. Fourth, in the event, Paul's anxiety about his reception among believers in Jerusalem proved to be unfounded and his confidence proved to be legitimate. From Acts 21:17-20 we learn that the Jerusalem leaders (as representatives of the whole church) "warmly welcomed" (ἀσμένως ἀπεδέξαντο, Acts 21:17) Paul and the delegates on their arrival in Jerusalem with the offering, and "glorified God" (Acts 21:20) on receiving a detailed account of Paul's διακονία (Acts 21:19; cf. the use of the same word in reference to the collection in Rom. 15:31; 2 Cor. 8:4; 9:1, 13).[63] Luke's ἐδόξαζον τὸν θεόν (Acts 21:20), written in retrospect, answers to Paul's δοξάζοντες τὸν θεόν (2 Cor. 9:13), written in prospect.[64]

9:15 χάρις τῷ θεῷ ἐπὶ τῇ ἀνεκδιηγήτῳ αὐτοῦ δωρεᾷ. "Thanks be to God for his gift that is indescribable!" The link with the previous sentence (vv. 13-14) is both conceptual and verbal. Having spoken of praising God for generous giving between humans, Paul now says in effect, "Let us all give thanks to God for *his* supremely generous gift to us!" αὐτοῦ is emphatic in this attributive position.[65] χάρις, such a central term in these two chapters (8:1, 4, 6-7, 9, 16, 19; 9:8, 14-15), provides the verbal link. But whereas in v. 14 it refers to the goodwill and kind acts of a benefactor, here in v. 15 it denotes the gratitude of beneficiaries, expressed verbally. It is a case of transition by way of paronomasia (Georgi 107). There are three instances in 2 Corinthians of the combination χάρις and τῷ θεῷ (with ἔστω understood, BDF §128[6]).

2:14   τῷ δὲ θεῷ χάρις τῷ . . . θριαμβεύοντι . . .
8:16   χάρις δὲ τῷ θεῷ τῷ δόντι . . . (cf. 1 Cor. 15:57)
9:15   χαρὶς τῷ θεῷ ἐπὶ τῇ . . . αὐτοῦ δωρεᾷ.

In each case, God is the one who acts and gives and to whom thanks is directed; recognition of this action or giving prompts the gratitude; and the reason for the thanksgiving is always stated. In the first instance an articular present participle qualifies τῷ θεῷ, denoting repeated action, while in the second and third instances a single, unrepeated act of giving is envisaged (τῷ δόντι and τῷ . . . δωρεᾷ).

Several identifications of the δωρεά have been proposed.[66]

---

63. See further on Acts 21 in the Introduction, B.5.e.

64. But the subject of Luke's ἐδόξαζον (the Jerusalem leaders) is narrower than the subject of Paul's δοξάζοντες (the whole church of Jerusalem, and perhaps believers elsewhere in Judea).

65. Cf. BDF §284 (3).

66. It seems unlikely that the δωρεά is the collection itself viewed with all its wide-ranging implications (Menzies 68, acknowledging, however, that Paul may also be thinking of God's gift of Christ from which all giving flows). Dunn raises the possibility that the δωρεά may be the Holy Spirit (169; *Theology* 710).

1. God's gracious action that prompted the Macedonians to give (8:1) and would also be operative among the Corinthians (9:14) (Furnish 452).
2. The "precious boon" of brotherly love and unity between Gentile and Jewish Christians (Plummer 257, 267-68). This doxology is "based on hope rather than on fact" (Plummer 268).
3. "The whole salvation event" (Lambrecht 148), "the whole . . . work of redemption" (Meyer 612), or God's "universal Gospel announced in Paul's message and ministry" (Martin 295).
4. Christ himself. This is the majority view among the commentators.[67]

The immediate context certainly lends support to options 1-2, but a wider reference for δωρεά (options 3-4) seems appropriate in this concluding doxology. In the parallel uses of the χάρις τῷ θεῷ formula in Paul, the reason for the expression of thanks, where stated, is unambiguous,[68] but here the stated occasion or reason (ἐπί)[69] for gratitude is ambiguous, for this is the only use of δωρεά in 2 Corinthians 8–9 (or in the whole letter). It would hardly be surprising if Paul ends his prolonged appeal to the Corinthians for prompt and unselfish giving by reverting to the principal motivation for such action, God's giving of the person of Christ, who impoverished himself for the benefit of others (8:9; cf. Rom. 8:32). Another reason for preferring options 3 or 4 is the colorful adjective ἀνεκδιήγητος, "not (ἀν-) able to be described (cf. διηγέομαι, 'describe') exhaustively (-ἐκ-)," "inexpressible," "indescribable,"[70] which is an apt description of Christ or of God's salvation but less appropriate if applied to a specific divine act (option 1) or to Jewish-Gentile brotherhood (option 2). Human words are inadequate to express the worth and the magnificence of the person of Christ or of divine redemption. But, paradoxically, such a δωρεά should elicit χάρις, the expression of gratitude in human words. So, we suggest, δωρεά in this verse refers to Christ and the salvation he brings.

Bibliography

Boobyer 2-3, 79 • Georgi 75-79, 102-9 • Hainz, *Koinonia* 142-44 • Murphy-O'Connor 94-95 • Nickle 104-10 • O'Brien, "Structure" 60-62 • Spicq, "Ἐπιποθεῖν" 184-95 • Theobald 298-302 • Therrien 97-100, 253, 296 • Wiles 248-53

67. E.g., Strachan 145; Tasker 130; Hughes 342; Carrez 195; Witherington 428; Scott 189; Garland 415.

68. Namely, Rom. 6:17; 1 Cor. 15:57; 2 Cor. 2:14; 8:16. In Rom. 7:25 no reason for the χάρις is mentioned.

69. Cf. BAGD 878c and εὐχαριστέω ἐπί τινι in 1 Cor. 1:4; 1 Thess. 3:9.

70. This word is a *hapax* in the LXX and NT. It occurs as a variant (in B L) (ἀνεκδιήγητον) in the expression θαυμασμὸν ἀδιήγητον, "a wonder beyond description," in *Aristeas* 99. In *1 Clement* 49:4 it is applied to (metaphorical) heights, in 61:1 to God's might, and in 20:5 ἀνεκδιήγητα κρίματα, "indescribable judgments (or, punishments) (of the underworld)," is set in parallelism to ἀνεξιχνίαστα, "the incomprehensible depths (of the abysses)."

III. PAUL'S DEFENSE OF HIS APOSTOLIC AUTHORITY
(2 CORINTHIANS 10–13)

After the warmhearted appeals of chs. 8 and 9, the change of tone at 10:1-2 to vigorous and sustained self-defense, self-assertion, and polemic comes as "a bolt from the blue."[1] This difference in tone and technique between chs. 1–9 and chs. 10–13 may be easily overdrawn, for there are elements of remonstrance in the earlier chapters (e.g., 2:17; 5:12; 6:14) and reassurances of warm affection in the last four chapters (e.g., 11:2; 12:14b-15a). Nevertheless, the suddenness of the change at 10:1 calls for some explanation. No special explanation is required, of course, for those who argue that 2 Corinthians 10–13 is part of the earlier "severe letter" (the "Hausrath hypothesis") or "part perhaps nearly the whole" (Furnish 459) of a letter later than 2 Corinthians 1–9 (the "Semler hypothesis"), for in those cases a totally different occasion and purpose is postulated for these four chapters. It is those who defend the integrity of 2 Corinthians who must suggest adequate reasons for the change of tone and style. Nine such explanations are mentioned in the Introduction (p. 30 above). It is my contention (see above, pp. 30-31, 50-51, 104-5) that chs. 1–9 were written in stages over a considerable period and that after Paul had written these chapters, he received distressing news of further problems at Corinth that prompted him to write chs. 10–13 and then send off all thirteen chapters as a single letter.[2] What this news might have been can only be conjectured. We may suppose that the intruders from Judea had become more open and aggressive in their effort to discredit Paul and that the Corinthians in general had become more receptive to their teaching and more open to their influence. On this view 2 Corinthians 10–13 is Paul's response to more intense opposition at Corinth.[3]

---

1. On the issues raised in this whole paragraph, see the more detailed treatment in the Introduction, pp. 29-51.

2. Barnett voices an objection to this view with the question, "But would Paul have sent a letter the first part of which would now be redundant? (23; but cf. 450 n. 1; similarly Martin xlvi; Murphy-O'Connor, *Paul* 254; cf. Trobisch 37). It would seem, however, that 2 Corinthians 1–9 as it stands would still have been eminently relevant if the last four chapters were written in light of new adverse developments at Corinth. Believers there would still have needed to hear of Paul's recent miraculous deliverance from a deadly peril (1:3-11), of his answer to criticisms of his recent conduct (1:12–2:13), and of his joy at their reaction to the "painful letter" (7:5-16), not to mention his timeless description of the apostolic ministry (2:14–7:4), his clarion call to holiness (6:14–7:1), and his ringing challenge to bring their collection to fruition (8:1–9:15). Had Paul wished to rewrite any part of 2 Corinthians 1–9, perhaps his references to his opponents would have become more frequent and more specific.

3. Those who regard 2 Corinthians 10–13 as a separate letter written after 2 Corinthians 1–9 (or 1–8) regularly speak of a fresh "crisis" at Corinth (e.g., Martin xxxvi, who attributes this to "the arrival and influence of the anti-Pauline teachers of 11:4-18" [298]; Kruse 169-70, whose "analysis" of 2 Corinthians has two parts, "Paul's Response to a Crisis Resolved (1:1–9:15)" and Paul Responds to a New Crisis (10:1–13:14)" [54-55]; cf. his *Paul* 151, 156; similarly Murphy-O'Connor, *Paul* 30, 301; Sampley 10, 13-15, 18).

With chs. 10–13 we reach the third major division of the letter. After explaining his recent conduct and describing his exercise of the apostolic ministry (chs. 1–7) and summoning the Corinthians to complete their collection (chs. 8–9), Paul proceeds to defend his apostolic authority (chs. 10–13). Each of these three sections contributes directly to the overall purpose of the letter, viz. preparation for an imminent visit that Paul undoubtedly hopes will bring him pleasure, not pain (see pp. 52-53 above). But with their repeated references or allusions to a forthcoming visit, these last four chapters see Paul particularly focus on that preparation: (1) by defending his apostolic authority against the rival claims to apostleship made by his Judaizing adversaries in Corinth; (2) by giving the Corinthians alternative criteria for evaluating these rival claims; and (3) by warning them that he stood ready to exercise discipline should that prove necessary.[4]

Some believe that 10:1 marks not only a change of tone but also a change of audience. Wikenhauser, for example, suggests that chs. 1–9 are addressed to the whole congregation, whereas chs. 10–13 deal with Paul's rivals and the section of the Corinthian church that was giving them a hearing (397-98). But not only is there no indication of a change in the persons addressed and no appeal to the example of the supposed penitent majority. The data clearly indicate that the second person plural continues to refer to the initial addressees, viz. the Corinthian church as a whole along with all the believers elsewhere in Achaia (1:1) — as when Paul speaks of being present with or among them (10:1; 11:9; 12:12, 14, 20), of coming to them with the gospel (10:14; 11:7), of his paternal jealousy for them (11:2) and devotion to them (12:15), or of their corporate obedience (10:6), upbuilding (10:8; 12:19; 13:10) and restoration (13:9, 11). Also, the reference to "other churches" in 11:8 suggests that the whole Corinthian church is being addressed.

But alongside these ubiquitous second person plural references there is frequent mention of certain nameless individuals in the third person, both singular and plural. These terms are listed, along with the probable referent, in the table on page 663.

A. The Exercise of Apostolic Authority (10:1-18)

Twice in 2 Corinthians 10–13 Paul affirms that his apostolic authority is derived from the risen Lord (10:8; 13:10). In both places he also states that that gift of ἐξουσία was designed to be exercised for building up, not for tearing down (εἰς οἰκοδομὴν καὶ οὐκ εἰς καθαίρεσιν). Yet from 13:10a it is clear that if circumstances warranted he would use that same authority in drastic or severe action (ἀποτόμως χρῆσθαι [ὑμῖν]) against some of the Corinthians, a sentiment

---

4. Sampley (35; cf. 7, 19) gives 2 Corinthians 10–13 the heading "Paul's Preparation for a Showdown Visit."

10:2	τινάς	B and C
		(and possibly A)
7	τις	A
10	φησίν	B and A
11	ὁ τοιοῦτος	B and A
12	τισὶν . . . αὐτοί	A
15	ἀλλοτρίοις	D
16	ἀλλοτρίῳ	D
17	ὁ . . . καυχώμενος	E and A
18	ὁ . . . συνιστάνων . . . ἐκεῖνος	E and A
11:4	ὁ ἐρχόμενος	A
5	τῶν ὑπερλίαν ἀποστόλων	D
12	τῶν θελόντων	A
13	οἱ . . . τοιοῦτοι	A
	ψευδαπόστολοι	A
	ἐργάται δόλιοι	A
	ἀποστόλους Χριστοῦ	A
15	οἱ διάκονοι αὐτοῦ	A
	διάκονοι δικαιοσύνης	A
18	πολλοί	A
20	τις (five uses)	A
21	τις	A
22	Ἑβραῖοι . . . Ἰσραηλῖται . . . σπέρμα Ἀβραάμ	A
23	διάκονοι Χριστοῦ	A
29	τίς (twice)	E
11:16	τις	E
12:6	τις	E
11	τῶν ὑπερλίαν ἀποστόλων	D
21	πολλούς	C
13:2	τοῖς προημαρτηκόσιν	C

A — the Palestinian intruders or their ringleader
B — those Corinthians who (at least in part) supported the intruders and felt estranged from Paul
C — certain unrepentant Corinthians[5]
D — the Jerusalem Twelve[6]
E — any believer, especially any Corinthian believer

5. In the Introduction I have argued that at the time of 2 Corinthians Paul was facing two sets of opponents at Corinth, one from outside the Corinthian congregation (Judaizers from Judea), the other from within (Corinthian proto-gnostics, including both libertines and ascetics). These two groups (A and C in the classification), I suggested, formed an "alliance of convenience" in their common opposition to various aspects of Paul's teaching and to Paul himself (pp. 80-87 above). Other Corinthians, it seems, were inclined to side with the intruders against Paul (group B in the suggested classification).

6. I am assuming that the expression οἱ ὑπερλίαν ἀπόστολοι (11:5; 12:11) is Paul's ironical description of the view of the Twelve held by οἱ ψευδαπόστολοι (11:13) (see above, pp. 74-76).

equally clear in 10:2.[7] Being potent, that authority was effective when exercised and would bring about submissive obedience to Christ (and his agent, Paul) (10:3-6). Moreover, his apostolic authority was legitimately exercised in Corinth, for this city was included within the assignment given to him by God (10:12-16).

Throughout the section 10:1–11:15 there is a strong undercurrent of direct or indirect charges against Paul's rivals. They are not submissive to Christ; they lack authority from the Lord; they have no God-assigned sphere of operation in Corinth yet boast of their success there; they promulgate a different gospel; they are a financial burden on the Corinthians; and so far from being apostles of Christ and agents of righteousness, they are in reality Satan's deputies and deceitful operators.

1. The Potency of Apostolic Authority (10:1-11)

In this section Paul is responding to an impression about him that had gained currency at Corinth, namely, that he had two radically different *personae* — "Paul the bold" and "Paul the timid." Safely distant from Corinth, he was a man of bold authoritarianism as he wrote his letters, but face to face he was a pathetically weak creature (10:1, 9-10). He corrects this caricature and serves notice on the Corinthians by assuring them that he is fully prepared, if necessary, to display confident boldness when he next visits (10:2, 11). In a series of metaphors drawn from military warfare (10:3-5), the justice system (10:6), and architecture (10:8), he affirms both his authority to act boldly and the overwhelming potency of such action.

10:1*I, then, Paul myself, appeal to you by the meekness and forbearance of Christ — I, who face to face with you am "timid" but when absent am "bold" in dealing with you. 2Yes, I implore you not to force me when present to act boldly with the confidence that I reckon I will dare to use against certain people who reckon that we conduct our lives according to worldly principles. 3For though we live in the world, we do not wage war with human resources. 4For the weapons of our warfare[a] are not the weapons of the world but are powerful for God in demolishing strongholds. We demolish sophistries 5and every proud obstacle that sets itself up against the knowledge of God; we take every device captive for obedience to Christ; 6and we stand ready to punish any trace of disobedience once your own obedience is complete.*

7Look at what is staring you in the face. If anyone is confident[b] in his own mind that he belongs[c] to Christ, let him go on to consider by[d] himself that just as he belongs[e] to Christ, so also do we. 8For if[f] I do boast[g] a little too much about our authority, which the Lord gave me[h] for building you up and not for pulling you

---

7. Whether that severe action constituted καθαίρεσις will be discussed at 10:8.

down, I shall not be ashamed of it. 9*I say this so that I may not seem as if I am trying to terrify you with my letters.* 10*For some are saying,*[i] *"His letters*[j] *are tyrannical and aggressive; his personal presence, on the other hand, is weak and his eloquence is contemptible."* 11*Such a person should reckon with this — that when we are present we will be in our actions exactly the same that we are in word through our letters when absent.*

TEXTUAL NOTES

a. Some witnesses (D² K L 1175 1241 1881 *al*) read στρατιᾶς, from στρατιά, "army," which occasionally bears the sense of στρατεία, "campaign" (BAGD 770d). Other manuscripts have στρατείας (B² [F G στρατῖας] Ψ 33 81 104 365 630 1505 1739 *pm*), the reading preferred by UBS[1, 2, 3, 4] and NA²⁷. The witnesses that have the unaccented στρατιας (p⁴⁶ ℵ B* C D* P 2464) probably support the reading στρατείας, for by itacism στρατία = στρατεία (Deissmann 181-82).

b. B reads δοκεῖ πεποιθέναι, "(if anyone) seems to be convinced/certain," probably a scribal alteration to avoid having Paul make what seemed too generous a concession to his adversaries.

c. After Χριστοῦ several witnesses (D* F G a vg^mss Ambrosiaster) read δοῦλος, "(that he is) Christ's slave" (cf. Gal. 1:10), which is a scribal effort to make explicit what is implied by the possessive genitive Χριστοῦ.

d. In place of ἐφ' ἑαυτοῦ (read by the strong proto-Alexandrian combination p⁴⁶ ℵ B as well as by L 1175 1505 *pc*), some witnesses read ἀφ' ἑαυτοῦ (C D F G H Ψ 0209 0243 33 1739 1881 𝔐 syr). Both expressions may mean "by himself" = "on his own initiative." The secondary variant ἀφ' ἑαυτοῦ may have arisen because of the similarity in sound between ἐφ- and ἀφ-.

e. p⁴⁶ contains the scribal error ὁ Χριστός in the place of (the second) Χριστοῦ.

f. External evidence supporting the inclusion of τέ before γάρ (ℵ C D Ψ [0209] 𝔐 f [r] vg syr Ambrosiaster) is almost as strong as the evidence for its omission (p⁴⁶ B F G H 0243 6 33 365 630 1175 1739 1881 *pc* it vg^mss). But internal evidence tips the scales in favor of τέ, for the combination τὲ γάρ, without a subsequent τέ or καί, in the sense of γάρ or καὶ γάρ (an Aristotelian use), is not common (only here and in Rom. 7:7; 14:8 in the NT) (Thrall 623 n. 209; *Particles* 96-97, in both places citing J. D. Denniston, *The Greek Particles* [Oxford: Clarendon, 1954²] 536; cf. BDF §443[3]). Turner observes (339, citing Rom. 7:7; 2 Cor. 10:8) that "at times τέ before γάρ appears to be a superfluous affectation." UBS[1, 2, 3, 4] and NA²⁷ place τέ in brackets.

g. Grammatical considerations (ἐάν with the subjunctive) support the reading καυχήσωμαι (B C D F G Ψ 1739 1881^c 𝔐), although many witnesses have the indicative καυχήσομαι (ℵ L P 0209 0243 6 104 326 1175 1241 1505 1881* *al* [g]), a scribal error, while p⁴⁶ harmonizes the two readings by conflation (καυχήσωμαι, καυχήσομαι), "if I do boast . . . , I will boast . . ." (cf. the following future indicative αἰσχυνθήσομαι).

h. Under the influence of the parallel in 13:10 (where μοι occurs) and the preceding ἡμῶν, some witnesses insert ἡμῖν either after ὁ κύριος (ℵ² D² F G [0209] 𝔐 syr^h) or before ὁ κύριος (P Ψ 629 1505 1881 *pc* it). But the strongest textual testimony omits ἡμῖν (p⁴⁶ ℵ* B C D* H 0243 33 81 365 630 1175 1739 2464 *pc* b vgst).

i. The singular φησίν is read by the majority of witnesses (cf. τις in v. 7 and ὁ τοιοῦτος in v. 11) and is the preferred reading, but the plural φασίν is found in B lat syr, while some witnesses omit a verb (p⁴⁶ vid 1881 b boᵐˢˢ Ambrosiaster). This singular is probably generic in sense; thus "some are saying."

j. Because μέν usually stands as the second word in the first element of a μὲν . . . δέ contrast, some witnesses (א² D F G I Ψ 0209 0243 33 1739 1881 𝔐 syrʰ) have "corrected" the more difficult and probably original reading αἱ ἐπιστολαὶ μέν (read by p⁴⁶ vid א* B H 326 1175 *pc*) to αἱ μὲν ἐπιστολαί.

10:1 Αὐτὸς δὲ ἐγὼ Παῦλος παρακαλῶ ὑμᾶς διὰ τῆς πραΰτητος καὶ ἐπιεικείας τοῦ Χριστοῦ. "I, then, Paul myself, appeal to you by the meekness and forbearance of Christ." On Paul's return to Macedonia after missionary work in Illyricum (Rom. 15:19)[8] he doubtless continued his pastoral ministry there (cf. διελθών in Acts 20:2, of a "preaching tour") and probably at this time received disturbing news of the worsening situation at Corinth and so began to write 2 Corinthians 10–13. Those who maintain that these four chapters form a separate letter must assume that the redactor has omitted an opening greeting and any other introductory material such as a thanksgiving (e.g., Thrall 599, who also sees δέ as a redactional addition [10]). Defenders of the epistle's integrity on the other hand, sometimes find evidence of the continuity between chs. 9 and 10 in the use of παρακαλῶ in 10:1, for statements introduced by παρακαλέω are sometimes preceded by thanksgivings or doxologies — here 9:12-15.[9] This argument does not pretend to be conclusive; indeed, 1 Cor. 1:10 shows that παρακαλῶ may introduce the body of a letter. Nor need δέ be adversative, with Paul contrasted sharply with the "brothers" mentioned in 8:6, 16-19, 22, 24; 9:3-5 (so Wolff 195).[10] As so often in Paul, δέ may be loosely resumptive, "then."

Αὐτὸς ἐγὼ Παῦλος, a *hapax legomenon,* combines two Pauline expressions: αὐτὸς ἐγώ, "I myself" (e.g., 12:13; Rom. 7:24) and ἐγὼ Παῦλος (e.g., Gal. 5:2; Phlm. 19). As well as anticipating v. 1b ("The very Paul who . . . , this same Paul appeals to you"; cf. Plummer 271-72), this expression stresses the intensely personal nature of his appeal, reflects his recognition of the great significance of the issues to be discussed, and alludes to his apostolic authority. Perhaps Paul is also now distinguishing himself from his co-author or co-sender Timothy (1:1) (Jülicher 102; Black 133) or from the three delegates who, like Paul, will soon be visiting Corinth (9:3-5). "He is defending *his* authority, explaining the theological significance of *his* weakness, and warning of *his* power and willingness to discipline the disobedient vigorously when *he* comes" (Garland 426). Some scholars have alleged that these last four chapters were written in Paul's own hand (cf. Gal. 6:11),[11] but in the absence of an ex-

---

8. Both of these regions, Macedonia and Illyricum, could be subsumed under Luke's general expression τὰ μέρη ἐκεῖνα ("those districts") in Acts 20:2; cf. Bruce, *Acts* 423.

9. Cf. 1 Thess. 4:1 after 1 Thess. 3:11-13, or Rom. 12:1 after Rom. 11:33-36 — so Bjerkelund 149-55, followed by Witherington 432; Garland 425 n. 24.

10. Other German commentators who render δέ in 10:1 by "aber" ("but") include Lietzmann (138), Wendland (226), de Boor (196), and Lang (328).

11. E.g., Bahr 37; Bates 67 ("perhaps"); Belleville 32-33.

pression such as τῇ ἐμῇ χειρὶ (Παύλου)[12] or ἔγραψα/γράφω ὑμῖν,[13] this seems improbable.

Paul's appeal to all the Corinthians (παρακαλῶ ὑμᾶς) is issued "by" (διά) the meekness and forbearance of Christ, where διά signifies "by means of (the example of)" = "on the basis of" (cf. Rom. 12:1; BAGD 180c), or "in the name of" (cf. Rom. 15:30; 1 Cor. 1:10).[14] This verse differs from 1 Cor. 1:10 in that there the appeal is made to the ὄνομα or overall known character of Christ, whereas here the ground of the appeal is two particular aspects of Christ's character. Both πραΰτης and ἐπιείκεια can mean "gentleness" (see BAGD 292c, 699a) and refer to a calm, gracious disposition that is not given to retaliation or malice, so that it is not surprising to find πραΰτης closely associated with μακροθυμία, "tolerance," "forbearance" (Gal. 5:22-23; Col. 3:12) and ταπεινοφροσύνη, "humility," "lowliness" (Eph. 4:2; Col. 3:12; cf. Matt. 11:29). Although the two words share some semantic territory, they are not synonyms.[15] πραΰτης may be rendered "meekness," or as Bruce suggests (229), "considerateness," "unassumingness." Positively, the person who is πραΰς shows patient submissiveness; negatively, he or she is free from contentiousness and aggression.[16] ἐπιείκεια occurs only here and in Acts 24:4, where it refers to "(customary) graciousness" (BAGD 292c). An astonishing variety of renderings of this word is found in EVV and in commentaries in English: "kindness," "considerateness," "magnanimity," "reasonableness," "fairness," "forbearance," "yieldingness," "moderation," "gentleness," "clemency," "consideration," "patience," "self-forgetfulness," "great-heartedness," "selflessness." Etymologically, ἐπιείκεια refers to the virtue of pursuing "what is equitable" (ὃ ἔοικεν = τὸ εἰκός) (Zerwick, *Analysis* 407), but the sense of "fairness" or "reasonableness"[17] is less apposite when this term is applied to Christ than the notion of "forbearance," for in the LXX the word

12. Cf. 1 Cor. 16:21; Gal. 6:11; 2 Thess. 3:17; Col. 4:18; Phlm. 19.

13. Cf. 1 Tim. 3:14; Phlm. 21.

14. In the only other Pauline use of διά with the genitive after παρακαλέω — namely, 2 Cor. 5:20, ὡς τοῦ θεοῦ παρακαλοῦντος δι' ἡμῶν — the preposition expresses simple instrumentality ("through us"). It is just possible that the use of διά τινος in Rom. 12:1; 15:30; 2 Cor. 10:1 is a Latinism, reflecting requests or oaths made "by the gods" *(per deos),* and expressed by πρός τινος in Attic Greek (see LSJ 1497 s.v. πρός, A.I.4). Cf. A. Oepke, *TDNT* 2.68; Leivestad 156; Bjerklund 164-67.

15. The terms are conjoined in Plutarch, *Pericles* 39; Philo, *De Opificio Mundi* 103; *Diognetus* 7.4; cf. Tit. 3:2. Louw and Nida include πραΰτης and ἐπιείκεια within the semantic domain of "gentleness, mildness," defining πραΰτης as "gentleness of attitude and behavior, in contrast with harshness in one's dealings with others" (§88.59), and ἐπιείκεια as "the quality of gracious forbearing" (§88.62).

16. See further F. Hauck and S. Schulz, *TDNT* 6.645-51.

17. Cf. Plummer's paraphrase (270), "unfailing fairness." "While πραότης [an earlier form of πραΰτης] may be wholly passive, ἐπιείκεια involves action; it rectifies the errors of strict justice and makes allowances for particular cases" (Plummer [CGT] 145, citing Aristotle, *Ethica Nicomachea* 5.10.6). "The person characterized by *epieikeia* is reasonable, a respecter of social norms" (Spicq 2.36), is willing to be accommodating, and has a predilection toward friendliness (Spicq 2.37-38).

group ἐπιείκεια–ἐπιεικής–ἐπιεικῶς describes God's character of gracious forbearance.[18] Given the semantic overlap between πραΰτης and ἐπιείκεια and the anarthrous state of ἐπιεικείας in 10:1, there is good reason to treat the whole phrase as a hendiadys, with the second element qualifying the first, thus "forbearing meekness," or possibly the first qualifying the second, thus "meek forbearance."[19]

The genitive τοῦ Χριστοῦ may be simply possessive ("belonging to Christ"), but more probably it is subjective ("shown by Christ"). But the question is: When did Christ exhibit this "meekness and forbearance" or "forbearing meekness"? The reference may be to: (1) his condescension in the incarnation when he became "a poor and lowly human being" (cf. 8:9, ἐπτώχευσεν πλούσιος ὤν)[20]; (2) his gentle demeanor throughout his earthly life (cf. Matt. 11:29, πραΰς εἰμι καὶ ταπεινὸς τῇ καρδίᾳ)[21]; (3) his nonretaliation during his passion (cf. 1 Pet. 2:23, ὃς λοιδορούμενος οὐκ ἀντελοιδόρει, πάσχων οὐκ ἠπείλει); or (4) his mercy and "clemency" as heavenly judge (cf. 1 Cor. 7:25).[22] The difficulty with view (1) is that the reference to the kenosis of the preexistent Christ is simply assumed to be the expression of the πραΰτης and ἐπιείκεια, which in themselves are character traits and not actions. On view (4) ἐπιείκεια, as "clemency," would presumably refer to the mercy of Christ in forgiving all those who call on his name for salvation (Rom. 10:11-13). But how would such "clemency" relate to his "meekness" when he is now the reigning and conquering κύριος (1 Cor. 15:25; 2 Thess. 1:7-10; 2:8)? A combination of views (2) and (3) seems the best interpretation. Paul is appealing to the "unassumingness" and "yieldingness" (Bruce 229) displayed by Christ during his incarnate life, and in particular during his final hours. Such a description of the observed demeanor of Christ is entirely appropriate when we recall (with Plummer 273) that it had been foretold that the messianic king would be πραΰς (Zech. 9:9), that Jesus had declared himself to be πραΰς (Matt. 11:29), and that he had affirmed the blessedness of οἱ πραεῖς (Matt. 5:5).[23] Moreover, there are numerous episodes recorded in the Gospels in which Jesus was seen to be "meek" and "forbearing,"[24] some of which must have been known to Paul,[25]

18. E.g., 1 Kgdms. 12:22; Ps. 85:5; Dan. 3:42; 4:27; 2 Macc. 10:4.

19. Young and Ford render the hendiadys by "gentle restraint" (271). Isaacs identifies πραΰτης καὶ ἐπιείκεια as Christ's "gentle readiness to respond to any personal appeal" such as Paul is now making.

20. Leivestad 161; cf. 163-64, who is followed by Furnish 460; Holland 252; Peterson 78, among others.

21. Plummer 273; Allo 242; Kümmel 208; Stanton 108; Belleville, "Gospel" 141.

22. Thrall 597, 601-2.

23. Plummer accounts for the use of Χριστοῦ instead of the expected Ἰησοῦ (cf. 4:10-11; Rom. 8:11; 1 Thess. 4:14) when referring to the earthly life of Christ by noting that some Corinthians claimed to belong to Christ in a special sense (ἐγὼ δὲ Χριστοῦ, 1 Cor. 1:12).

24. E.g., Matt. 20:20-28; Mark 9:35-40; 10:13-16; 14:55-61; 15:16-19; Luke 23:34; John 13:2-17.

25. On the issue of Paul's awareness of Jesus traditions, see, e.g., M. B. Thompson, *Clothed*

and through him to the Corinthians, particularly if his description of love (1 Cor. 13:4-7) was recognized by them to be a summary of Christ's exhibited character.

This first part of 10:1 stands as a rubric for chs. 10–13. Evidently Paul regarded what he was about to write as an appeal (παρακαλέω) or urgent request (δέομαι, 10:2) that was based on his own character and authority as known to the Corinthians (αὐτὸς ἐγὼ Παῦλος) and the universally recognized character and bearing of Christ. He was not about to issue a series of rebukes (ἐπιτιμάω) or commands (ἐπιτάσσω, διατάσσομαι, παραγγέλλω), all verbs used elsewhere in the Pauline corpus.

(Αὐτὸς . . . ἐγὼ Παῦλος . . .) ὃς κατὰ πρόσωπον μὲν ταπεινὸς ἐν ὑμῖν, ἀπὼν δὲ θαρρῶ εἰς ὑμᾶς. "(I, Paul myself . . .) — I, who face to face with you am 'timid' but when absent am 'bold' in dealing with you." Although the immediate antecedent of ὅς is τοῦ Χριστοῦ, this relative pronoun refers back to Παῦλος, as the following θαρρῶ makes clear (Betz, *Paulus* 46).[26] The apostle is here reproducing the gist of an accusation leveled against him by certain Corinthians (NEB, NAB and REB add "you say" in parenthesis[27]) and doubtless endorsed by the Palestinian interlopers. The full "text" of the accusation is found in v. 10, introduced by the generic singular φησίν ("some are saying"): "His letters are weighty and vigorous, but when he appears in person he is weak and his eloquence amounts to nothing." Already in v. 1b Paul has this charge in mind but probably only the terms ταπεινός and θαρρεῖν were actually part of the charge;[28] hence the quotation marks around "timid" and "bold" (as in NIV).[29] His response to the accusation begins in v. 2.[30]

According to his critics, Paul was bold and courageous at a distance but cowardly and weak when personally present. He wore two faces. The terms or expressions in vv. 1-11 that belong to each "face" may be set out as follows.

---

with Christ: The Example and Teaching of Jesus in Romans 12:1–15:31 (JSNTSS 59; Sheffield: Sheffield Academic, 1991).

26. It can scarcely be the case that ὅς is intentionally ambiguous, suggesting "even if only briefly and indirectly" that Jesus too was ταπεινός (Peterson 81; cf. Güttgemanns 139-40).

27. Wolff adds in parenthesis "according to your opinion" (194). Cf. Cassirer, "I, the man supposed to be. . . ."

28. But according to Betz (45-57), in 10:1 Paul is not simply anticipating the accusation of v. 10 but already responding to it, so that the ταπεινός–θαρρεῖν antithesis is introduced by Paul himself. In applying the term ταπεινός to himself Paul aligns himself with the Cynic tradition in which the genuine philosopher had, like Socrates, an unimpressive external appearance (σχῆμα). The terms θαρρεῖν (10:1) and τολμᾶν (10:2), and probably the expression θαρρεῖν τῇ πεποιθήσει, are drawn from the vocabulary of contemporary rhetoric (52 and n. 59, 67-68).

29. TCNT, however, includes all of v. 1b in the accusation (along with "show my boldness" in v. 2): "I who, 'in your presence, am humble in my bearing towards you but, when absent, am bold in my language to you'"; similarly Moffatt, Williams.

30. Harada observes (124) the parallelism between vv. 1-2 and vv. 8-11: (1) the christological endorsement of Paul's stance (vv. 1 and 8); (2) the opponents' accusation (vv. 1b and 10; in v. 1 Paul reverses the "weightiness–weakness" antithesis); (3) Paul's defense against the alleged accusation (vv. 2 and 11).

Paul the Timid	Paul the Bold
Παῦλος ὁ ταπεινός	Παῦλος ὁ θαρρῶν
παρών (2)	ἀπών (1)
κατὰ πρόσωπον (1)	
ταπεινὸς ἐν ὑμῖν (1)	θαρρῶ εἰς ὑμᾶς (1)
	ἐκφοβεῖν . . . διὰ τῶν
	ἐπιστολῶν (9)
ἡ . . . παρουσία τοῦ σώματος	αἱ ἐπιστολαί . . .
ἀσθενὴς καὶ ὁ λόγος	βαρεῖαι καὶ ἰσχυραί (10)
ἐξουθενημένος (10)	οἷοί ἐσμεν τῷ λόγῳ
τοιοῦτοι καὶ παρόντες τῷ ἔργῳ (11)	δι' ἐπιστολῶν ἀπόντες (11)

For Paul's opponents, what determined the change in his *modus operandi* or his character was the purely external factor of his location — whether he was present with them (παρών, v. 2) or absent from them (ἀπών, v. 1). Brave talk in letters came readily when he was out of sight; he was fearlessly outspoken and even audacious, they said, when he was at a safe distance. But once he appeared in person, boldness gave place to timidity; he became a pathetically weak figure, they claimed, humbly subservient and deferential. On this showing, ταπεινός does not bear its positive NT sense of "humble,"[31] but carries a pejorative meaning,[32] "timid" (NIV, REB), "feeble" (NEB),[33] "condescending" (Williams), "obsequious,"[34] or "servile,"[35] although the English adjective "humble" (RSV) may itself have a disparaging sense,[36] which would be appropriate if Paul is using ταπεινός ironically.[37] θαρρῶ bears a meaning diametrically opposed to τα-

31. In Greek thought ταπεινός generally signified a shameful subjection, but in Jewish thought an appropriate submission to God and his will (see W. Grundmann, *TDNT* 8.1-15).

32. The noun ταπεινοφροσύνη ("humility") also may, exceptionally, bear a negative sense: in Col. 2:18, 23 it refers to "false humility" or "flaunted humility."

33. In his paraphrase Wand identifies (66-71) five charges leveled against Paul: feebleness (10:1-18), refusal of hospitality (11:1-15), defective authority (11:16-33), lack of spiritual experience (12:1-13), and the question of support (12:14-21).

34. Cf. Cassirer, "I, the man supposed to be a groveller"; Plummer 270, "I, whom you accuse of grovelling."

35. "Paul in Corinth is accused of a petty disposition and servile appearance" because of his refusal of support (11:7) (W. Grundmann, *TDNT* 8.17). "Beseeching and admonishing are regarded by them [his critics] as the expression of a mean and servile mind. Outer appearance and inner attitude combine in the judgment that Paul is ταπεινός" (Grundmann, *TDNT* 8.19 n. 55). Taking ταπεινός as virtually synonymous with ἀσθενής (10:10), Marshall regards both terms as referring to the "base posture or servile status" that Paul was charged with adopting while at Corinth (323), a posture of the objectionable flatterer whose conduct was characterized by inconstancy (324-25).

36. But Lambrecht (153) renders v. 1b by "I who admittedly (am) humble when face to face among you," claiming that Paul admits the data that prompted the accusation yet rejects his opponents' interpretation of those data.

37. Cf. the renderings of Moffatt ("humble enough . . . outspoken enough") and Goodspeed ("so humble . . . so bold").

670

πεινός,[38] signifying haughtiness (Martin 297, 303), outspokenness (Weymouth, Moffatt), or audacity (Wolff 194). An additional contrast is represented by ἐν ὑμῖν . . . εἰς ὑμᾶς. Standing on its own the former phrase would mean "among you" or "in your midst," but the whole expression κατὰ πρόσωπον . . . ἐν ὑμῖν yields the sense "in your presence" (ASV) or "when personally present with you" (cf. BAGD 406b) or "when face to face with you."[39] θαρρῶ εἰς ὑμᾶς means not simply "[I am] bold in my language to you" (TCNT), but "bold in dealing with you."

What particular circumstances may have contributed to the rise of these two charges? Perhaps Paul's call for the corporate discipline of the man guilty of incest (1 Cor. 5:1-13) and, more recently (in the "severe letter," 2 Cor. 2:3-4; 7:8), his insistence on the corporate punishment of "the wrongdoer" (cf. 2 Cor. 2:6; 7:12), may have helped to prompt the accusation of "boldness at a distance." Similarly, a contributing factor to the charge of "weakness in person" may have been his inability during his recent "painful visit" (2 Cor. 2:1) to discipline those guilty of immorality and bring them to repentance (2 Cor. 12:21; 13:2), an inability he himself calls a "humiliation" ([φοβοῦμαι] μὴ πάλιν . . . ταπεινώσῃ με ὁ θεός μου πρὸς ὑμᾶς, 2 Cor. 12:21).[40]

Whatever the origin of the charges, already in v. 1 Paul has hinted that one of them — "bold when absent" — is false, for here he is, away from the Corinthians, not issuing a bold command but making an impassioned appeal (παρακαλῶ).

10:2 δέομαι δὲ τὸ μὴ παρὼν θαρρῆσαι τῇ πεποιθήσει ᾗ λογίζομαι τολμῆσαι. "Yes, I implore you not to force me when present to act boldly with the confidence that I reckon I will dare to use." Here in v. 2a Paul begins to respond to the twofold charge of v. 1b that he was bold when absent but weak when present: when he is next with them, he will, if necessary, be bold (θαρρῆσαι), not timid or feeble (ταπεινός, v. 1), but he implores them to spare him that necessity. Then in v. 2b he refers to a further, more general accusation which prompts the response of vv. 3-8, while in vv. 9-11 he returns to the charge mentioned in v. 1b.

Many EVV seem to regard δέ as a loose connective and so do not represent it in translation. But this conjunction could here be adversative,[41] with παρὼν θαρρῆσαι standing in opposition to ἀπὼν . . . θαρρῶ in v. 1b, but more probably is resumptive ("*Yes,* I implore you"[42]), indicating that δέομαι κτλ. is picking up παρακαλῶ (v. 1) and specifying the content of Paul's appeal.[43] If

---

38. Note μέν . . . δέ, with μέν standing, exceptionally, in the fourth (not second) place in its clause. A comparable ταπεινός — θαρρέω contrast is found in Philo, *Quis Rerum Divinarum Heres Sit* 29.

39. So RSV, NASB, NIV, NAB², REB, NRSV.

40. Similarly Barnett 461, 464-65.

41. So KJV; de Boor 196; Wolff 194.

42. Similarly RV, NJB.

43. Cf. the same παρακαλέω–δέομαι sequence in 5:20. But Lambrecht rejects the view that δέομαι takes up the idea of παρακαλῶ, arguing that after παρακαλῶ Paul intended to give a moral exhortation regarding the implications of "obedience to Christ" (10:5) such as is actually found in 12:19–13:11, so that 10:2 continues the digression or excursus that began in 10:1b and runs to 13:10 (or 12:18), an excursus "somewhat analogous to 2:14–7:4 ("Appeal" 407-8, 410-11,

these two verbs are related in this way, the addressee of the entreaty (δέομαι, "beg," "implore") will be the Corinthians, with ὑμῶν supplied after δέομαι in parallelism with παρακαλῶ ὑμᾶς. Although the substantive δέησις always refers to prayer addressed to God, this is not the case with the cognate verb, as 8:4 indicates.[44] The negated articular infinitive τὸ μὴ . . . θαρρῆσαι could be construed as an accusative of respect or reference after δέομαι, "I implore you with regard to my not being bold" = "I implore you to ensure that I am not bold," but more probably[45] it is the direct object, reflecting the δέομαι τί τινος ("request something from someone") construction and defining the content of the entreaty. Literally, "I implore the-not-being-bold"[46] = "I ask that . . . I need not show boldness" (BAGD 175b) or "I ask you not to force me to be bold."[47]

The adverbial participle παρών ("when present") is nominative, as opposed to the accusative that one expects for the "subject" of an infinitive, because it agrees with the subject of δέομαι (Robertson 1037-38, 1083; BDF §409[5])). Paul is referring to a possible display of boldness, not simply whenever he may chance to visit Corinth again but when he visits in the near future (9:4-5; 12:14, 20-21; 13:1-2, 10). If it proves necessary at that time, he will display that boldness (literally) "with the confidence with which I reckon to dare," that is, "with the confidence that I reckon I will dare to use." Both datives, τῇ πεποιθήσει and ᾗ, are instrumental (Windisch 294). The combination θαρρῆσαι τῇ πεποιθήσει could be rendered as a unit — either "bold confidence" (Conybeare in Conybeare and Howson 457) or "confident boldness" (Barrett 243). This confidence was a "self-assurance" (REB) born of his conviction that as a divinely appointed apostle he had a God-given right to exercise discipline within his churches if the need arose (cf. 10:8; 13:10). λογίζομαι points to Paul's intention or expectation regarding his forthcoming visit, should his earnest plea to the Corinthians fall on deaf ears. This assumes that λογίζομαι is

414-16). But in another contribution published the same year (1996), Lambrecht suggests that 10:7–12:13 with its discussion of boasting is the digression ("Self-Commendation" 328-31). In his most recent article on chs. 10–13, he proposes that there are "three unequal rings which loosely surround" the fool's speech (11:22–12:10), each with its own theme: (1) 10:1 and 13:11 form a slender frame of moral exhortation; (2) 10:2-18 and 13:1-10 (see his chart of comparisons, "Context" 315 n. 19) are a double defense of his apostolic authority; (3) 11:5-12 and 12:11b-18 (see the chart of comparisons, "Context" 318 n. 23) are denials of his inferiority in spite of his outward appearance and his refusal of support ("Context" 305-24; quotation from p. 323). But having isolated these concentric features, Lambrecht is careful not to present chs. 10–13 as a rigid or formal ring composition ("Context" 320).

44. But Prümm (1.568-69), Schlatter (614), and others would supply τοῦ θεοῦ after δέομαι. Cf. Barclay, "It is my prayer that. . . ."

45. So Robertson 490, 519, 1083.

46. BDF §399(3) notes that here τὸ μή is equivalent to a ἵνα μή clause.

47. The notion of necessity or of being forced or compelled is implicit in the negative request made to the Corinthians. Paul wishes to avoid (cf. μή) having to act in a certain way. Most EVV supply words such as "compel," "force," "drive," "have to." REB has "Spare me when I come, I beg you, the need for. . . ."

middle. If it were a passive ("the confidence with which *I am reckoned* to show boldness"),[48] (1) we might have expected to find ἀπών with τολμῆσαι since the idea of "boldness when absent" (v. 1b) is the essential point in the criticism of Paul, and (2) the parallelism between λογίζομαι and τοὺς λογιζομένους would be destroyed (Meyer 618). If τολμῆσαι is taken to be synonymous with the earlier θαρρῆσαι,[49] the change perhaps being prompted by a desire for stylistic variation, then λογίζομαι τολμῆσαι will mean "I reckon to show boldness." But if τολμῆσαι is related to the preceding πεποίθησις, then this phrase may be rendered "(with the confidence that) I reckon I will dare to use." In this latter case, which is preferable, an infinitive such as χρᾶσθαι ("to use") must be supplied as the complement of τολμῆσαι.[50]

In v. 2a, then, Paul is pleading with the Corinthians to avoid forcing him to act boldly (= "severely," ἀποτόμως, 13:10) in a display of his confidence as an apostle having the Lord's authority (10:8). In effect he is saying, "Don't mistake the timidity that some people credit me with (ταπεινός, v. 1b) for weakness and the inability or unwillingness to act with authority and dispatch."[51]

(τῇ πεποιθήσει ᾗ λογίζομαι τολμῆσαι) ἐπί τινας τοὺς λογιζομένους ἡμᾶς ὡς κατὰ σάρκα περιπατοῦντας. "(. . . with the confidence that I reckon I will dare to use) against certain people who reckon that we conduct our lives according to worldly principles." The thinly veiled threat of v. 2a was not directed against the whole Corinthian church (ὑμᾶς, v. 1) — they were the addressees of the appeal (παρακαλῶ, v. 1) and the entreaty (δέομαι, v. 2a) — but only against "certain persons" (τινας) who are not addressed directly. Although Paul does not say ἐπί τινας ὑμῶν ("some of you"; cf. ἐν ὑμῖν τινες in Cor. 15:12), he is probably referring to a segment of the Corinthian church that sided with the intruders from Judea and were infected with their negative attitudes toward Paul. It is possible that the intruders themselves are included within the τινας, but the primary reference is probably to the Corinthian anti-Paulinists.[52]

What these opponents were alleging about Paul is introduced by τοὺς λογιζομένους, which clearly looks back to λογίζομαι in a wordplay that involves two contrasting "reckonings." Paul "reckons" that he will dare to act with πεποίθησις on his forthcoming visit if the situation demands it, and his adver-

48. The Vulgate has *existimor audere*. If λογίζομαι is passive, ἐπί τινας qualifies θαρρῆσαι.

49. So Windisch 294. He believes that τολμῆσαι is here used in an absolute sense (also BAGD 822a). Cf. Lambrecht 152: "(the confidence with which I intend) to show daring"; similarly Weymouth; NAB²; Furnish 454, "to summon up courage."

50. Similarly NAB¹; Barrett 243; Thrall 597. For this construction of τολμάω followed by a complementary infinitive, see Rom. 5:7; Phil. 1:14. But in 2 Cor. 11:21 τολμάω is twice used absolutely. In philosophical contexts this verb is used positively of the philosopher who courageously speaks the truth, and negatively in polemic against sophists (Betz, *Paulus* 67-68).

51. The misunderstanding of Paul's ταπεινότης also assumes that he cannot be κατὰ πρόσωπον θαρρῶν" (Bultmann 183).

52. Furnish (461, 464) takes the τινες to be the rival apostles; Barnett sees them as members of the congregation (461 and n. 27); while Lambrecht allows a reference to both groups (154; "Appeal" 399).

saries "reckon" that he acts κατὰ σάρκα. While the wordplay may be suitably represented by the translation "reckon" in both places (so Weymouth, Barclay, NJB), in one case (λογίζομαι) the "reckoning" involves intention or expectation, and in the other (τοὺς λογιζομένους) it is a matter of having an opinion or making a claim.[53] This articular participle is equivalent to a relative clause (οἳ λογίζονται), and the present tense may point to the ongoing nature of the opinion or claim: "some who have been arguing that . . ." (Wand). In any discussion about Paul's opponents it is important to bear in mind Lüdemann's caveat that "not everyone assailed by Paul had previously launched an attack on the apostle" (*Opposition* 64; cf. 31-32), but in the present case we may fairly assume that his opponents were actively propagating their views, so that the charge here mentioned, whether expressed in Paul's words or theirs, would have been well known to the Corinthians. The ὡς before the actual charge (namely, κατὰ σάρκα περιπατεῖν) could be explained as "almost pleonastic" before the predicate accusative περιπατοῦντας,[54] but in the present context where the charge is repudiated, ὡς is better seen as indicating a "subjective and false opinion" (Lambrecht 154) or a quality wrongly attributed.[55]

Two general considerations help us in our effort to determine the nature of the allegation against Paul. (1) In Pauline use περιπατέω usually refers to human conduct in its broadest sense, with an accompanying preposition designating the sphere (ἐν) or the norm (κατά) of that conduct.[56] So the charge is likely to relate not merely to Paul's speech or to his actions or to his attitudes, but to his whole life. (2) Given the centrality of the σάρξ–πνεῦμα contrast in Paul's letters, and presumably also in his preaching, we may assume that his opponents' accusation focused on his relation to the Spirit. If this is so, he may have been charged with living his life apart from the Spirit's direction, or without the Spirit's power, or devoid of the Spirit's gifts. For Paul's critics, a κατὰ πνεῦμα περιπατεῖν existence may have meant living under the Spirit's direction, or exercising his power, or exhibiting his gifts. Perhaps the charge that Paul conducted his life "according to worldly principles"[57] was a "catch-all" designation, sufficiently broad to encompass any behavioral characteristic that might mark a person who lacked the life of the Spirit.[58]

53. Thus (for τοὺς λογιζομένους) "entertain the notion" (Berkeley), "think" (JB), "reason" (Furnish 454); or "accuse" (NAB[1]), "charge" (NEB).

54. One option mentioned by BAGD 898b, citing 1 Cor. 4:1 (οὕτως ἡμᾶς λογιζέσθω ἄνθρωπος ὡς ὑπηρέτας Χριστοῦ) as well as 2 Cor. 10:2.

55. Both BAGD (898b, c) and Zerwick (*Analysis* 407-8) mention these two ways of understanding ὡς ("almost pleonastic" or introducing a false claim).

56. See R. Bergmeier, *EDNT* 3.75.

57. A wide variety of renderings of κατὰ σάρκα in this verse has been offered (in addition to "according to the flesh"): "(acting) from worldly motives" (Goodspeed), "in worldly fashion" (RSV), "according to worldly standards" (Martin 297), "by worldly principles" (Weymouth), "in a merely human fashion" (Thrall 597), "(behavior . . .) dictated by human weakness" (REB), "on the physical level" (BAGD 649c).

58. According to E. Schweizer, κατὰ σάρκα περιπατεῖν refers to a life on earth where the ori-

The gist of vv. 1b-2 may be stated as follows. "Some say I am timid and servile when present with you but full of courage and boldness in my letters when at a safe distance. Let me state my intent (though I plead with you to ensure that it never comes to this[59]): I shall be bold and confident, when I see you shortly, against certain persons of your number — those who persist in thinking and claiming that my outlook and behavior lack the signs of the Spirit's presence."[60]

10:3 ἐν σαρκὶ γὰρ περιπατοῦντες οὐ κατὰ σάρκα στρατευόμεθα. "For though we live in the world, we do not wage war with human resources." Having stated or summarized the charge against him that was circulating at Corinth (v. 2b), Paul now vigorously repudiates the charge. Plummer rightly observes that γάρ implies a contradiction: "That charge is false, *for* . . ." (275). At the same time Paul is hinting at his ability to deal with opposition. In responding to the allegation he picks up each element of the charge but indulges in a wordplay on σάρξ[61] and when negating κατὰ σάρκα he substitutes the verb στρατεύομαι for περιπατέω.

Two opposing uses of σάρξ are juxtaposed. In the phrase ἐν σαρκί it refers to life on earth in its totality, the universal human condition shared by believer and non-believer alike.[62] Every human, by definition, lives "in the flesh," that is, "in the world."[63] The phrase κατὰ σάρκα, on the other hand, means "by human methods" (NJB) or "with human resources,"[64] and points forward to the next verses which describe the divine resources and methods of warfare. The negative affirmation in v. 3b is asyndetic, but its juxtaposition with a positive statement in v. 3a shows that the two statements are antithetical and περιπατοῦντες is concessive ("though we live").[65]

Rather than baldly stating οὐ κατὰ σάρκα περιπατοῦμεν in response to his

---

entation of thought is to the σάρξ, a life which regards σάρξ as its norm (*TDNT* 7.130 and n. 257). Thrall summarizes and evaluates seven different interpretations of the charge against Paul (605-7).

59. It was in the Corinthians' hands to determine whether or not Paul would act with πραΰτης and ἐπιείκεια (Bultmann 183).

60. The possible nature of Paul's proposed discipline will be discussed at 10:6.

61. Martin has commented (300) that in this passage Paul "re-mints" derogatory statements, giving them a "novel twist," either by fresh application, so that λογίζομαι (v. 2b) is taken up by λογιζομένους (v. 2c), λογισμούς (v. 4), and λογιζέσθω (v. 7); or by a play on words, so that κατὰ σάρκα (v. 2) becomes ἐν σαρκί (v. 3), with a change of meaning.

62. ἐν σαρκὶ περιπατεῖν is materially equivalent to (τὸ) ζῆν ἐν σαρκί (Gal. 2:20; Phil. 1:22). On the other hand, ἐν (τῇ) σαρκὶ εἶναι (Rom. 7:5; 8:8-9) means "be in an unregenerate (and sinful) state" (BAGD 744c).

63. Cf. 1:12, ἀνεστράφημεν ἐν τῷ κόσμῳ, and *Barnabas* 10:11, ὁ δίκαιος . . . ἐν τούτῳ τῷ κόσμῳ περιπατεῖ.

64. Paul's distinction between ἐν σαρκί and κατὰ σάρκα is reproduced in *Diognetus* 5:8, "Their [Christians'] lot is cast 'in the flesh,' but they do not live 'after the flesh.'" But Bultmann maintains that in both parts of v. 3 "the σάρξ- concept is the same. σάρξ is the worldly and empirical" (184).

65. That περιπατοῦντες is concessive is recognized (among others) by Moule 102; Turner 157; Zerwick and Grosvenor 554; and by most EVV.

critics, Paul substitutes the verb στρατευόμεθα, "we wage war," "we do battle," "we conduct our campaign." It is not that Paul was averse to affirming that his life was not guided by human or worldly principles (see Rom. 8:4); he believed that while ἐν σαρκί existence was inevitable, κατὰ σάρκα existence was reprehensible. Rather, this change to a verb denoting warfare not only gives the lie to the accusation that he is timid and weak (ταπεινός, v. 1b) but also enables him to move from a defensive to an offensive posture in the following verses.

The depiction of the Christian life as a military operation (στρατεία, v. 4) is a common theme in Paul.[66] What is distinctive about 10:3-6 is (1) that the struggle is not simply "against the spiritual forces of evil in the heavenly realms" (Eph. 6:12) but in particular against his rivals at Corinth, and (2) that the military metaphor is sustained, using technical vocabulary drawn from siege warfare.[67] On this latter point, the following expressions *may* carry a specialized meaning within this sustained metaphor.

1. ὅπλα (v. 4): "siege engines" (Bruce 230)
2. καθαίρεσις (v. 4): demolition
3. ὀχυρώματα (v. 4): "strongholds," "fortresses," "fortified vantage points" (Martin 301)
4. λογισμοί (v. 4): "bastions of argumentation" (Wand)
5. ὕψωμα (v. 5): "rampart" (Moffatt), "battlement" (Young and Ford 271)
6. ὕψωμα ἐπαιρόμενον (v. 5): "raised rampart" (Malherbe 144)
7. αἰχμαλωτίζω (v. 5): "take prisoner" (Moffatt), "carry off into captivity" (Weymouth)
8. νόημα (v. 5): "battle-plan," "project" (Moffatt), "device" (Plummer 277), "opposing design" (Plummer 277)
9. ὑπακοή (v. 5): "subjection" (Weymouth), "submission" (Moffatt)
10. ἐν ἑτοίμῳ ἔχω (v. 6): "be at the ready" ("like a soldier on standby," Williams 217)
11. παρακοή (v. 6): "insubordination."

That Paul is using military terminology in vv. 3-6 is clear, even if it is not as extensive as the possibilities set out above. But there is no scholarly unanimity about the specific background to his use. Several suggestions have been made.

1. Windisch (297) proposes that Paul saw himself as falling heir to the calling and power of the wise man (σοφός) of Prov. 21:22 who "attacks fortified cities and demolishes the fortress in which the ungodly trusted."

---

66. Rom. 13:12; 1 Cor. 9:7; 2 Cor. 6:7; Eph. 6:11-17; Phil. 2:25; 1 Thess. 5:8; 1 Tim. 1:18; 6:12; 2 Tim. 2:3-4; 4:7; Phlm. 2. See further Barth 787-803.

67. See Williams 216 and nn. 51-56 (pp. 231-32) for a summary of procedures in laying siege to a city.

2. Witherington (438) alleges that Paul is portraying himself as the poor sage of Eccl. 9:14-16 who saved his city by his wisdom when it was surrounded and threatened by huge siege works and yet his wisdom was despised. So now Paul "must deliver his besieged converts from the lofty walls the opponents have built against them."

3. Scott (201) discerns the background of 10:3-6 in the "law of envoys": mistreating an ambassador, such as Paul considered himself (5:20), constituted an act of war.

4. For Lane, Paul's language reflects the formulations of the covenant lawsuit of the ancient Near East, echoing "the threat of an angered suzerain to his faithless vassals: he will overthrow his vassal's towers and lead his people captive; he will destroy his boastful arguments and punish his disobedience." Vested with the authority of the Great King, Paul knows that his suzerain will support him in administering covenant discipline (26).

5. Malherbe has argued (143-73) that in 10:3-6 Paul uses two military images that were popular in the first century and that were derived from the Greek philosopher Antisthenes (c. 455-360 B.C.), who applied the imagery of a fortified city to the sage's rational faculties with which he fortifies himself, and applied the imagery of a soldier's personal armor to the garb of Odysseus, the proto-Cynic. Paul "describes his own weapons in terms approximating the self-description of the rigoristic Cynic and describes his opponents' fortifications in terms strongly reminiscent of the Stoic sage" (166).

6. 10:3-6 may allude to the circumstances of the Third Mithridatic War against Rome when over a hundred rock fortresses along the Cilician coast were demolished by the Romans with the aid of a siege-train in their raids on the Cilician pirates, and more than ten thousand insurgents were taken into captivity (Appian, *Roman History* 12.14.96).[68] These events would certainly have been known to a native of Cilicia such as Paul of Tarsus.

Of these various proposals the last has much to commend it, but in fact there is no need to identify a single source for Paul's use of military terminology in 10:3-6. The imagery of Greco-Roman siegecraft was in common use by the first century A.D., especially among Stoics.[69]

10:4a τὰ γὰρ ὅπλα τῆς στρατείας ἡμῶν οὐ σαρκικὰ ἀλλὰ δυνατὰ τῷ θεῷ πρὸς καθαίρεσιν ὀχυρωμάτων. "For the weapons of our warfare are not the weapons of the world but are powerful for God in demolishing strongholds." Proof that Paul was not waging his war with merely human resources (v. 3b) is now given (note γάρ). The weapons he uses to fight with are not forged by human hands but have divine potency. What is open to question is whether or not

---

68. See M. Cary, *A History of Rome* (New York: Macmillan, 1954²) 348-50.
69. See Malherbe 143-56 and the literature cited there.

this portion of the verse (τὰ . . . ὀχυρωμάτων) forms a parenthesis. In the KJV and RV it is marked off with brackets and a semicolon, in WH and UBS[1, 2, 3] with dashes. Although v. 4a is verbless and three present participles in vv. 4b-6 (namely, καθαιροῦντες . . . αἰχμαλωτίζοντες . . . ἔχοντες) could be taken as dependent on στρατευόμεθα (v. 3) — factors that might suggest a parenthesis — it is better to mark off τὰ . . . ὀχυρωμάτων simply with commas (so NA[27], UBS[4]) and regard the participles as nominative absolutes, standing for finite verbs. Vv. 4b-5 follow on directly from v. 4a, with καθαιροῦντες looking back to πρὸς καθαίρεσιν, not to στρατευόμεθα.[70] On the structure of vv. 3-6, see further at the beginning of the commentary of vv. 4b-5.

ὅπλα are instruments of war, both offensive and defensive weapons. In siegecraft they are "siege engines" (Bruce 230). The expression τὰ ὅπλα τῆς στρατείας ἡμῶν invites comparison with Paul's later expression ἡ πανοπλία τοῦ θεοῦ (Eph. 6:11, 13). The two phrases are complementary, for "the weapons we use in our warfare" (τῆς στρατείας, possessive genitive) are supplied by God, while "all the armor supplied by God" (τοῦ θεοῦ, subjective genitive) is for use in Christian warfare. In 6:7 τὰ ὅπλα τῆς δικαιοσύνης τῶν δεξιῶν καὶ ἀριστερῶν ("the weapons supplied by righteousness for the right hand and the left") may be the sword for offense and the shield for defense, but here in 10:4 the weapon that is powerful in achieving God's purposes (θεῷ) of promoting the knowledge of God (cf. v. 5) and producing obedience to Christ (v. 5) is probably the gospel of Christ. Although the "military campaign" (στρατεία) in which Paul was engaged at present was against opposition in Corinth, it was merely part of his wider mission and ministry of discharging his commission to preach and defend the gospel, so that vv. 3-5 (but not v. 6) should not be interpreted narrowly as having relevance only to the Corinthian situation.

Paul insists that the weapons used in his campaign were not the ordinary ones of this world (σαρκικά).[71] This is his fourth use in vv. 2-4 of the σάρξ concept (κατὰ σάρκα, vv. 2-3; ἐν σαρκί, v. 3; σαρκικά, v. 4), whose root idea may be rendered in each case by "flesh(ly)"[72] or "human"[73] or "world(ly)."[74] This term σαρκικά corresponds to the earlier phrase κατὰ σάρκα (v. 3) and is set in opposition (ἀλλά) to both of the following words, δυνατά and τῷ θεῷ, for the adjective σαρκικός points to both humanness and weakness. Because we might

70. But Barclay places v. 4a in parenthesis and begins v. 5 with "Our campaign is such that. . . ."

71. In adjectives, the -ικός termination signifies "with the characteristics of" (Moulton and Howard 378), so that σαρκικός means "having the marks of the σάρξ," just as πνευματικός means "characterized by the (human) spirit/(divine) Spirit."

72. E.g., Lambrecht 152 ("according to the flesh" [twice], "in the flesh," "fleshly").

73. E.g., Thrall 597 ("in a merely human fashion"/"in merely human ways," "in the human world," "merely human").

74. E.g., Martin 297 ("according to worldly standards"/"as the world does," "in this world," "worldly").

have expected Paul to say πνευματικά (in contrast to σαρκικά), δυνατά is all the more emphatic; Furnish 454 suggests "mightily effective."

Explanations of the dative τῷ θεῷ are various (listed here in ascending order of probability).

1. A dative of possession: "God's (powerful weapons)" (GNB; Louw and Nida §§7.21; 20.54; similarly NLT). But the word order is against this; Paul did not write τῷ θεῷ (καὶ) δυνατὰ πρὸς κτλ. Moreover, this dative tends to put the emphasis on the object possessed rather than the possessor (cf. BDF §189), which is inappropriate in the present case.

2. An instrumental dative: "through God" (KJV; Lang 328; Wolff 194, 198; cf. also Barclay, Carrez 197). But ἐν normally precedes this dative when the reference is to a personal agent (cf. BDF §219[1]).

3. A circumlocution for the elative superlative, modeled on the Hebrew idiom in which lēlōhîm expresses this superlative: "very (mighty)" (Turner, Style 91);[75] "enormously (powerful)" (NAB²), "divinely (potent)" (NEB; similarly Moffatt, Goodspeed, NASB; Hughes 351 and n. 6).[76] Jonah 3:3 LXX (πόλις μεγάλη τῷ θεῷ, "an exceedingly large city") is an example of this usage, and in the NT possibly Acts 7:20 (ἀστεῖος τῷ θεῷ, "very beautiful," GNB). But this rare Septuagintalism would scarcely have been recognized by the Corinthians.

4. An ethic(al) dative[77]: "(wielded) in the sight of God" (Cassirer); "(powerful) in God's eyes/estimation," "before God" (RV). Comparable uses may be found in Acts 7:20 (ἀστεῖος τῷ θεῷ); 23:1 (πεπολίτευμαι τῷ θεῷ); Barnabas 4:11 (ναὸς τέλειος τῷ θεῷ); 8:4 (μεγάλοι τῷ θεῷ). This same thought is expressed in 4:2; 7:12 by ἐνώπιον τοῦ θεοῦ.

5. A dative of advantage: "for God" (Weymouth),[78] "in God's cause" (JB, NJB), "for God's sake" (cf. θεῷ in 5:13). That is, Paul's weapons were powerful in achieving God's purposes, in God's service.[79] This dative, designating the person whose interest is affected (BDF §188[2]); cf. §192), is more common with verbs than with adjectives (here δυνατά) but is the preferred explanation of τῷ θεῷ. Paul sees himself as a military commander and strategist in God's service, not his own, who uses spiri-

---

75. But earlier (*Grammar* 238) he took it as a "dative of advantage" (see #5. below).

76. Modern Greek reflects this idiom in adjectives with a θεο- prefix meaning "extremely," "utterly"; e.g., θεοσκότεινος, "pitch-dark"; θεόγυμνος, "stark naked."

77. Sometimes called the "sympathetic dative" or the "dative of feeling." In Classical Greek it usually involved the first or second person of the personal pronoun, denoting special interest in some action or statement (Smyth §1486).

78. So also Moulton and Howard 443; Lietzmann 140; Wendland 226; de Boor 196; Barrett 251; Bultmann 185; Furnish 454; Thrall 597, 610.

79. Sometimes this meaning is extended — illegitimately, it would seem — to refer to God's enabling power: "with God's help" (Berkeley, REB), "in the strength of God" (Conybeare in Conybeare and Howson 457), "as God empowers [us]" (Martin 297).

tual weapons that are potent in carrying out the purposes of the Supreme Commander.

While God's ultimate purpose was to promote the true knowledge of himself (v. 5a) and total obedience to Christ (v. 5b), this would be achieved only after the destruction of opposition. In the prosecution of God's cause, Paul's weapons were "powerful for the demolition of strongholds." δυνατὸς πρός τι means "powerful enough for something" (BAGD 208d; cf. TCNT, REB), with πρός introducing the purpose and result (cf. Turner 274). What are destroyed or overthrown or torn down (cf. καθαίρεσις) are not the enemies themselves, as in an actual στρατεία, but the actions of enemies, the "fortresses" they have built in opposition to the gospel. ὀχύρωμα, a "fortified place," is cognate with ὀχυρόω ("fortify") and ὀχυρός ("firm," from ἔχω, "hold firm"). In the LXX the word usually bears a literal sense, referring to a "fortress" or "stronghold" or sometimes a "prison" (e.g., Gen. 39:20), but occasionally it is figurative (e.g., Prov. 10:29, "The fear of the LORD is the stronghold [ὀχύρωμα] of his holy one"). Paul is possibly referring to Prov. 21:22:

πόλεις ὀχυρὰς ἐπέβη σοφὸς   A wise man attacks fortified cities
καὶ καθεῖλεν τὸ ὀχύρωμα,   and demolishes the fortress
ἐφ' ᾧ ἐπεποίθεισαν οἱ ἀσεβεῖς   in which the ungodly trusted

The three slender verbal links with Paul are καθεῖλεν–καθαίρεσιν (v. 4), ὀχύρωμα–ὀχυρωμάτων (v. 4), and perhaps ἐπεποίθεισαν–τῇ πεποιθήσει (v. 2).[80] But the concept of demolishing a fortress was so commonplace that it is unnecessary to trace a specific source.

10:4b-5 λογισμοὺς καθαιροῦντες καὶ πᾶν ὕψωμα ἐπαιρόμενον κατὰ τῆς γνώσεως τοῦ θεοῦ, καὶ αἰχμαλωτίζοντες πᾶν νόημα εἰς τὴν ὑπακοὴν τοῦ Χριστοῦ. "We demolish sophistries and every proud obstacle that sets itself up against the knowledge of God; we take every device captive for obedience to Christ." Vv. 3-6 form one sentence in Greek, and it is important to determine the relationship of the parts. There is only one finite verb, στρατευόμεθα (v. 3), which is preceded by a concessive participle (περιπατοῦντες, v. 3) and followed by three coordinated participles (καθαιροῦντες . . . καὶ αἰχμαλωτίζοντες [v. 5] . . . καὶ . . . ἔχοντες [v. 6]) and then one subordinate clause (ὅταν κτλ., v. 6). Although it is possible to construe these three coordinated participles as dependent on στρατευόμεθα, defining the means of the warfare (so Malherbe 166

80. Gale maintains the possible influence of Prov. 21:22 on two grounds: a similar picture of a siege is found in that verse; and in 9:6 Paul borrows from "an adjacent passage" (viz. Prov. 22:8) (*Analogy* 164). For the suggestion that the phrase δυνατὰ . . . πρὸς καθαίρεσιν ὀχυρωμάτων may be an echo of Zech. 9:12 (LXX), see Hanson, *Paradox* 100-101. Heidland believes it is possible that Paul is alluding to the tower of Babel (Gen. 11:4) (*TDNT* 5.591). For similarities and differences between Paul's imagery and a comparable passage in Philo (*De Confusione Linguarum* 128-31), see Malherbe 145-47.

n. 130), so that v. 4 is parenthetical (so WH, UBS[1, 2, 3]), it is preferable to treat them as equivalent to finite verbs,[81] since they are all masculine nominative plurals and therefore not in agreement with the preceding neuter ὅπλα[82] and since the first participle καθαιροῦντες is conceptually and linguistically related to the word καθαίρεσιν that immediately precedes. The first καί in v. 5 links λογισμούς and ὕψωμα as joint objects of καθαιροῦντες. But how are these two objects related to ὀχυρωμάτων? There are three alternatives:

1. λογισμούς explains ὀχυρωμάτων, and πᾶν ὕψωμα defines these two terms after an epexegetic καί (". . . that is, every obstacle");
2. ὀχυρώματα and πᾶν ὕψωμα constitute the λογισμοί (Malherbe 147; Williams 216);
3. ὀχυρωμάτων is defined by both λογισμούς and πᾶν ὕψωμα, the two coordinated objects of καθαιροῦντες. This third option is to be preferred, given the word order (which is against the second option above) and the naturalness of taking καί as conjunctive ("and") when it is between two nouns that are dependent on a single verb (καθαιροῦντες).

So with regard to the structure of vv. 3-6 which form one sentence in Greek, we conclude: that v. 4 is not parenthetical; that it affords the evidence that Paul was not conducting his campaign using worldly resources (v. 3b); that λογισμοί and πᾶν ὕψωμα are illustrations of ὀχυρώματα; that each of the three instances of καί in vv. 5-6 is conjunctive; that the three plural participles in vv. 4b-6 are nominative absolutes serving as finite verbs; that the printed Greek text of vv. 3-6 should therefore have commas after the following words: στρατευόμεθα (v. 3), ὀχυρωμάτων (v. 4), θεοῦ (v. 5), Χριστοῦ (v. 5), and παρακοήν (v. 6), as in UBS[4] and NA[27].

λογισμούς alludes to τοὺς λογιζομένους (v. 2) and clearly has a pejorative sense — not "reasonings" or "calculations" in a neutral sense,[83] but "false arguments" (Louw and Nida §7.21), "plausible fallacies" (Barclay), "sophistries,"[84] or, in this military context, "citadels of argumentation." Paul has in mind the specious arguments of his opponents in the alliance of Judaizing intruders and disaffected Corinthians,[85] in particular the specific criticism of him mentioned in v. 2b. But a more general reference to the thoughts and sentiments of a self-vaunting reason should not be excluded.[86]

Paul's second example of his "demolition of strongholds" is his overthrow

81. So also Hughes 354 n. 10; Furnish 454, 458-59; Lambrecht 155, among others. Participles function in a similar way in 5:12; 6:3; 7:5; 8:19-20; 9:11, 13; 10:15 (twice); 11:6 (cf. Turner 343).

82. Meyer relates these three participles to ἡμῶν in v. 4a as the logical subject (619-20).

83. In connection with taxes, λογισμός can mean "computation" (MM 378d).

84. BAGD 386d; 477a; NEB, REB; Cassirer has "vain human sophistries."

85. See the Introduction, B.4.d.

86. Cf. Heidland, TDNT 4.287.

of "every proud obstacle that sets itself up against the knowledge of God." In an abstract sense ὕψωμα means "height" (Rom. 8:39) or "exaltation" (Job 24:24; Jdt. 10:8). Applied to physical military defenses, it refers to "what is lofty," a "fortress with high towers" (G. Bertram, *TDNT* 8.614), or a "rampart" (Moffatt). Related to such usage is the metaphorical sense of "arrogant attitude" (Thrall 597), "towering conceit" (Isaacs), "presumptuous notion" (NJB), "proud obstacle" (RSV, NRSV). Reinforcing the notion of literal or figurative "elevation" that is intrinsic to ὕψωμα is the present participle ἐπαιρόμενον (from ἐπαίρω, "raise up"), which is not middle but passive, whether it means "(that is) raised up"/"erected" or "that rises up/raises itself up."[87] This ὕψωμα is no neutral "lofty thing"; it is set up or sets itself up "against" or "in defiance of" (κατά) the authentic knowledge of God. Standing between λογισμούς and γνώσεως, the expression πᾶν ὕψωμα is likely to refer to every type (πᾶν) of idea or argument that is capable of preventing people from arriving at true and emancipating knowledge, the knowledge of God (τοῦ θεοῦ, objective genitive) through the gospel of Christ.[88] There is a contrast between certain λογισμοί which must be overthrown and ἡ γνῶσις τοῦ θεοῦ which must be promoted, between impersonal argumentation and personal knowledge, and between false and true knowledge. Paul's campaign strategy was not to ignore, dismiss, or ridicule his opponents' ideas and arguments, but to "demolish" (καθαιρέω) them by exposing their fallacies. For him such demolition was indistinguishable from God's "thwarting" of "the cleverness of the clever" (1 Cor. 1:19, citing Isa. 29:14). In speaking of his καθαίρεσις of λογισμοί and πᾶν ὕψωμα, Paul is certainly not denigrating rational thought and logical argumentation. His own letters are replete with careful and convincing argument. It is not "reasoning" as such that is attacked here but fallacious reasoning and conceited argument.[89]

If one aspect of Paul's ongoing spiritual campaign (στρατεία) was demolition (καθαίρεσις) (v. 4), another was the taking of captives. In this context of military terminology αἰχμαλωτίζω means "take captive," "lead into captivity,"[90] although in another context it may mean "carry off into error" = "deceive" or "ensnare" (as in 2 Tim. 3:6). Here in 10:5 the picture is of "prisoners of war bound hand and foot and turned over to a new authority" (Spicq 1.451). Just as

87. BAGD 282a does not recognize a middle use of ἐπαίρω in the NT, citing both 10:5 and 11:20 as figurative passive uses, and giving the meanings "rise up," "offer resistance," "be in opposition" for 10:5 and "be presumptuous," "put on airs" for 11:20. Plummer, however, sees ἐπαίρεται in 11:20 as definitely middle, and ἐπαιρόμενον in 10:5 as probably so (277).

88. But Martin (306) suggests that at 10:5 there is perhaps a change of metaphor, so that Paul is referring to a wall of rivalry that his opponents have erected between himself and his Corinthian converts, a wall that must be torn down to guarantee their access to the truth of the gospel.

89. Heidland comments: "Far from repudiating λογίζεσθαι altogether, he [Paul] demands its renewal" (*TDNT* 4.288, citing 1 Cor. 4:1; 2 Cor. 10:7, 11; 12:6).

90. Etymologically, this verb derives from αἰχμή ("war") and ἁλωτός ("captured"), a verbal adjective from ἁλίσκομαι ("be captured"). So, like αἰχμαλωτεύω, the verb αἰμαλωτίζω means "take captive (in war)." Cf. the similar verb συλαγωγέω, which means not only "carry off (ἄγω) as booty (σύλημα)" but also "carry off into (the slavery of) error" (Col. 2:8).

in v. 4 it was not people but their "false reasonings" that were overthrown (λογισμοὺς καθαιροῦντες), so here it is not people but their "every device" or "every design" (πᾶν νόημα) that is carried off into captivity. Now it is true, of course, that people reason and formulate designs, but Paul would never have described his mission as aimed at "destroying" people or "leading them into captivity" against their will. He attacks "sophistries" (λογισμοί) and "every scheme" (πᾶν νόημα) that seek to evade the truth and compelling force of the gospel, but he does not assail those who present those arguments or devices.[91]

There are at least three reasons why νόημα probably has a negative sense in 10:5. (1) In 2:11 νοήματα is used of the "wiles" or nefarious "designs" or "maneuvers" of Satan. BAGD (540d) cites 2:11 and 10:5 as the two instances in Paul where νόημα means "purpose" in the bad sense of "design." (2) When we consider the three actions spoken of in 10:4b-6, which are expressed by or associated with the three nominative plural participles (namely καθαιροῦντες, αἰχμαλωτίζοντες, ἐν ἑτοίμῳ ἔχοντες ἐκδικῆσαι πᾶσαν παρακοήν), the first and third actions are negative in sense, so that the intervening action is also likely to have a pejorative meaning, especially since the verb αἰχμαλωτίζω in itself refers in a depreciatory sense to the carrying off of prisoners of war into captivity or slavery. (3) The other three uses of νόημα in this letter (apart from 2:11; 10:5) are connected negatively with the "hardening" (3:14) or the "blinding" (4:4) or the "corrupting" (11:3) of the mind or outlook. We suggest, then, that in the present context πᾶν νόημα refers to every kind of "device," "design," "scheme" or "thought" that had the effect of preventing people from knowing God.[92] If the military imagery is pressed, the reference may be to hostile plans of battle engineered by Paul's rivals at Corinth to undermine the loyalty of the Corinthians to him. But we should also recognize a general reference to the faulty patterns of thought that Paul knew from personal experience to be characteristic of unbelievers and that hindered their response to the gospel of Christ.

Whoever entertained these faulty or rebellious "thoughts" — whether unbeliever or rival — the aim of Paul in taking these νοήματα captive was to lead them to ἡ ὑπακοὴ τοῦ Χριστοῦ. The thought is not "every scheme that is opposed to obedience to Christ," which would be πᾶν νόημα τὸ κατὰ τῆς ὑπακοῆς τοῦ Χριστοῦ. Rather, εἰς introduces the purpose ("for obedience") and perhaps also the direction ("into subjection") of the capture.[93] τοῦ Χριστοῦ is unquestionably an objective genitive;[94] any reference to the obedience shown by Christ

91. However, if πᾶν νόημα is taken to be equivalent to πάντα νοῦν ("every mind"), νόημα could by synecdoche refer to the whole person. In that case Paul would be speaking of his commission to capture "every person" for voluntary allegiance to Christ (cf. Col. 1:28-29).

92. For the view that Paul is referring to the rhetorical devices used by his rivals to influence the Corinthian church, see DiCicco 169.

93. Since Paul did not write τῇ ὑπακοῇ τοῦ Χριστοῦ or simply τῷ Χριστῷ, Meyer believes that "obedience to Christ is here conceived of as a locality into (εἰς) which captives are led" (621).

94. Robertson 500; BAGD 837a. Bultmann (186) takes εἰς τὴν ὑπακοὴν τοῦ Χριστοῦ as equivalent to εἰς τὸ ὑπακούειν τῷ Χριστῷ.

(subjective genitive, as in Rom. 5:19) would be out of place in the context. But does ὑπακοή denote the voluntary obedience to Christ given by believers or the involuntary submission to Christ experienced by the "schemings" (and their owners) that have been reduced to captivity? If πᾶν νόημα has negative connotations (see above), then the latter will be the case: Paul envisages every rebellious thought or scheme as not only being captured but also being reduced to servitude to Christ or being forced to render allegiance to Christ, the victorious and reigning Lord. So all-encompassing was Paul's view of the lordship of Christ that he foresaw the day when all sentient beings, whatever their location (whether above, on, or below the earth), would acknowledge the universal supremacy of Christ (Phil. 2:9-11). Here in 10:5, even impersonal opposing schemes, and by implication their perpetrators, would be forced into submissive obedience to Christ the victor.[95] If, on the other hand, νόημα is understood in a more personal sense — "After the city's defenses have been demolished, the defenders themselves are taken prisoner" (Furnish 462-63) — the reference will be to unbelievers who are conquered by the gospel and so are won over "for obedience to Christ," which is "faith's obedience" (Rom. 1:5) or the obedience to the gospel (Rom. 10:16) (Furnish 463).[96]

10:6 καὶ ἐν ἑτοίμῳ ἔχοντες ἐκδικῆσαι πᾶσαν παρακοήν, ὅταν πληρωθῇ ὑμῶν ἡ ὑπακοή. "And we stand ready to punish any trace of disobedience once your own obedience is complete." As the long Greek sentence that runs from verses 3 to 6 concludes, we find the third (ἔχοντες) of the coordinated nominative plural participles that function as finite verbs. Each of these present participles indicates an action that Paul constantly undertakes with the powerful weapons he uses in God's service (v. 4a):[97] he destroys (καθαιροῦντες) false argumentation and every proud obstacle that inhibits the knowledge of God (vv. 4b-5a); he carries off in captivity (αἰχμαλωτίζοντες) for obedience to Christ every opposing design (v. 5b); and he holds himself (ἔχοντες) in readiness to punish every expression of disobedience (v. 6a). That is, in wielding his effective weaponry he is engaged in destruction, capture, and punishment. The repeated πᾶς in vv. 5-6 (πᾶν ὕψωμα . . . πᾶν νόημα . . . πᾶσαν παρακοήν) points to the completeness of the rout and victory. No foe remained; all were either destroyed or captured or punished.

The expression ἐν ἑτοίμῳ ἔχω, "stand at the ready," may be a Latinism (namely, *in promptu habeo*) and indistinguishable in meaning from ἑτοίμως ἔχω (12:14).[98] "Like a soldier on standby" (Williams 217), Paul was fully prepared to use his authority "with severity" (ἀποτόμως, 13:10). He would not hesitate to carry out his intent to act boldly (λογίζομαι τολμῆσαι, 10:2), if the situation at

95. Cf. Cassirer's rendering: "And we take captive every human device to secure its submission to Christ"; similarly Plummer 271, 277; Bruce, *Paraphrase* 149.

96. But Thrall (614, 616) is inclined to relate v. 5b to the Corinthians themselves.

97. Note the threefold repetition of "with them" (= "the weapons I use for fighting") in Bruce's paraphrase of vv. 4-6 (*Paraphrase* 149).

98. Cf. Polybius 2.34.2; Philo, *Legatio ad Gaium* 259.

Corinth did not change. As in 12:14 and 13:1 Paul is stressing the nearness of his visit. In seeking to combat opposition at Corinth, he was clearly at a decided disadvantage in being absent. Perhaps these repeated intimations of the imminence of his visit partly compensated for this disadvantage.

As a constative or summary aorist, ἐκδικῆσαι, "to exercise justice on," "to visit condign punishment on" (Cassirer), need not refer to a single act but does view the punishment, whatever its nature or duration, as a unit of thought. πᾶσαν παρακοήν could refer to "any act of disloyalty" (GNB) or "every act of rebellion" (TCNT), or even "any trace of disobedience" (Goodspeed), but the expression could be personalized, if the abstract παρακοή stands for the concrete οἱ παρακούοντες and means "any who refuse to obey" or "all who may be disobedient" (Conybeare in Conybeare and Howson 457). There may possibly be an allusion in the whole phrase ἐκδικῆσαι πᾶσαν παρακοήν to the Roman military practice of completely subjugating a region where rebellion was persistent,[99] but Moffatt has pressed the imagery too far (and anachronistically) with his rendering: "I am prepared to court-martial anyone who remains insubordinate."

But who were these people who were liable to incur Paul's punishment? There is clearly a contrast (and wordplay) between παρακοή and ὑπακοή within v. 6.[100] The "obedience" is that of the Corinthians (ὑμῶν) and emphatically so ("your own obedience"), as the word order shows. If the "disobedience" also was theirs, we might well ask, Why would Paul plan to punish the Corinthians for their disobedience only after (ὅταν, "when") their obedience had reached completion (πληρωθῇ)? That would be the time for remitting punishment (Barrett 253). One solution would be to relate the παρακοή to a Corinthian minority and the ὑπακοή to the majority.[101] But in the absence of a ὑμεῖς–τινές distinction such as is found in 10:1-2, it is better to assume that the disobedience is shown by persons other than the Corinthians, persons from outside the Corinthian congregation. If Paul has in mind the agreement of Gal. 2:7-10, then the action of these intruders (the "false apostles" of 11:13) that calls for punishment would be "breach of contract," the invasion of Paul's legitimate mission field in contravention of the division of apostolic labor agreed to by the Jerusalem "pillars" and Paul (Gal. 2:9) (Barrett 253-54; "Opponents" 239). But even if the principal referents are the Palestinian intruders, we should not exclude a secondary reference to the Corinthian dissidents who were persisting in their divisiveness and immorality (12:20-21), for in 13:2 Paul explicitly warns them that on his imminent visit he will not spare them (οὐ φείσομαι) their deserved punishment. But one is reluctant to broaden the "disobedience" still further (*pace* Windisch 299) to include any opposition Paul might encounter in prose-

---

99. Williams maintains that the image is of "the pacification of a region — the aftermath of breaching its strongholds" (217).

100. Note also the two sets of alliteration in v. 6a.

101. "The disobedient [among the Corinthians] include those who think that Paul walks according to the flesh, are guilty of sexual immorality, continue in the association with idolatry (12:21; 13:2), and promote false apostles" (Garland 438).

cuting his apostolic mission elsewhere, for the punishment that Paul threatens is related directly to the Corinthians' obedience. It was only after (cf. ὅταν) their own obedience had been brought to completion that Paul would be able to dispense justice. The verb πληρόω, "bring to completion" (BAGD 671b), implies the concluding of a process already under way. Recently, "all" the Corinthians had "obeyed" Titus and by implication Paul himself with regard to the disciplining of the wrongdoer during Titus's visit with the "severe letter" (7:14; cf. 2:9).[102] Now that obedience needed to be put beyond all question.[103] Such necessary preliminary submissiveness would be achieved, we may assume, when the Corinthians ceased to support the interlopers in any way (11:4, 19-20), gave Paul their unqualified recognition and love (6:11-13; 10:7, 15; 12:11, 15; 13:6), and made a decisive break with all idolatrous associations (6:14–7:1). There were therefore two stages in Paul's projected action: first, the πλήρωσις ("completion") of the Corinthians' ὑπακοή; then the ἐκδίκησις of παρακοή, wherever that disobedience was found at Corinth. Paul recognized that unless any disciplinary action he might take was supported by the Corinthians as a whole, it would remain largely ineffective; for maximum success it would need corporate reinforcement.

What form the punishment would take is not stated. The mere expulsion of the intruders from the Corinthian congregation would scarcely amount to a penalty of τὸ ἐκδικῆσαι, "retributive justice." Perhaps we should think of a formal "handing over" to Satan that would precipitate physical illness and suffering (cf. 1 Cor. 5:4-5) or some miraculous use of apostolic power (cf. Acts 5:1-10; 13:8-11).[104]

10:7 Τὰ κατὰ πρόσωπον βλέπετε. "Look at what is staring you in the face." In relation to its object, βλέπετε has been understood in three ways:

1. As an indicative, expressing a question. "Do you look to what can be seen outwardly (Bultmann 187)?[105] Whether the clause is rendered this way, or, as Isaacs proposes in his paraphrase, "Have you regard only for that which meets the eye?" the implied reproof may allude to 5:12 with its reference to those who pride themselves on appearances and externals.
2. As an indicative, making a statement. "You are looking at the outward appearance of things" (GNB),[106] again with a possible allusion to 5:12. The

---

102. On the implication of the expression πάντων ὑμῶν in 7:15, see the commentary at 7:13 where the same phrase occurs.

103. No objective genitive follows ὑμῶν ἡ ὑπακοή to indicate who is obeyed. But whether we supply τοῦ εὐαγγελίου τοῦ Χριστοῦ (cf. 9:13) or τοῦ Χριστοῦ (cf. 10:5) or εἰς ἐμέ (cf. 2:9; 7:15; Phil. 2:12; Phlm. 21), the overall sense would not be altered because in Paul's view obedience to Christ and his gospel involved obedience to him as Christ's apostle (1:1) and ambassador (5:20).

104. Cf. Meyer 622; Thrall 615-16.

105. Similarly KJV; Weymouth; Conybeare in Conybeare and Howson 457; Meyer 623.

106. Similarly RV, TCNT, NIV; Plummer 279; Forbes 28 n. 26; Pickett 196 n. 109, following Robinson 26 ("You see only the end of your nose").

Corinthians' failure was that they had restricted vision, seeing only externals; they needed to look below the surface and see deeper realities. Their preoccupation with the confident claims of the Judaizing interlopers regarding their commendation from Jerusalem (cf. 3:1), their status as servants of Christ and of righteousness (11:15, 23), and their pure pedigree (11:22), needed to be replaced by sane judgment based on more adequate criteria for determining genuine apostleship. This interpretation accords with the wider context but has one drawback. If Paul were contrasting how the Corinthians were viewing matters (v. 7a) with how they ought to be (v. 7b), an adversative such as ἀλλά might have been expected in v. 7b (cf. Héring 71).

3. As an imperative. "Look at what is before your eyes" (RSV, NRSV) or "Look facts in the face" (NEB, REB).[107] Strong support for this view comes from the fact that the verbal form βλέπετε is always imperatival in Paul. Elsewhere it stands first in its clause,[108] but we may account for the unusual word order here by assuming that Paul wishes to emphasize the stark reality of the evidence confronting the Corinthians. This imperative may mean "Look at!" "Notice!" (BAGD 143d), or "Be alert to" (Furnish 465).[109]

κατὰ πρόσωπον qualifies τά, not βλέπετε,[110] so that this articular prepositional phrase (literally, "the things according to the face") will refer either to "outward appearances" (Louw and Nida §31.31), "what is superficial" (JB mg.) or "what lies in front of you" (Barclay), "what is obvious" (BAGD 406b).[111] So we may render the whole expression "Face plain facts" (JB) or "Look at the obvious facts" (NIV mg.) or "Look at what is staring you in the face." Although τά could be a generalizing plural (thus "this obvious fact," Moffatt), it more probably points to several facts that the Corinthians were to consider carefully — in the immediate context, that Paul "belonged to Christ" as much as any other person did (v. 7b), that he derived his apostolic authority directly from the Lord and exercised it for the upbuilding of his converts (v. 8), and that his actions matched his words (v. 11);[112] in the wider context, that the Corinthians' very existence in

107. Similarly JB, Barclay; Lietzmann 140; Windisch 300; Barrett 254, 256; Carrez 201; Thrall 597, 618-19.

108. 1 Cor. 1:26 (?); 8:9; 10:18; 16:10; Gal. 5:15; Eph. 5:15; Phil. 3:2 (three uses); Col. 2:8; (4:17, βλέπε).

109. Bultmann notes (187 n. 6) that K. Grobel (in a letter) gives βλέπετε a negative connotation. He construes τὰ κατὰ πρόσωπον in the light of κατὰ πρόσωπον ("face to face") in v. 1. "As touching my presence in person, take care!" or "Beware of eye to eye!" Paul would then be warning, "Do not suppose that personal encounter will be to your advantage!"

110. As NAB[1], "You view things superficially."

111. Danker seems to take κατά in a distributive sense: the addressees were to look at one another, "face by face, one by one, on down the line," recognizing that each one belonged to Christ (153).

112. The τά of v. 7a is picked up by the expression τοῦτο λογιζέσθω ... ὅτι in vv. 7b and 11.

Christ as a result of his preaching (1:19) validated his apostleship (3:1-5), and that his pioneer evangelism in Corinth established their city as his legitimate and distinctive field of pastoral activity (10:13-15).

εἴ τις πέποιθεν ἑαυτῷ Χριστοῦ εἶναι, τοῦτο λογιζέσθω πάλιν ἐφ' ἑαυτοῦ ὅτι καθὼς αὐτὸς Χριστοῦ οὕτως καὶ ἡμεις. "If anyone is confident in his own mind that he belongs to Christ, let him go on to consider by himself that just as he belongs to Christ, so also do we." The apostle now specifies one of the "obvious facts" that the addressees must reckon with. He moves from the second person plural (βλέπετε) to the third person singular (τις). This could indicate that this "someone" or "anyone" represented the Corinthian congregation as a whole or a group within it,[113] but, given this person's claim to belong to Christ in a distinctive way (see below), it seems more likely that τις points to a particular individual, the ringleader of the Judaizing intruders who expressed the viewpoint of them all.

The dative with πέποιθα (a second perfect with a present meaning, "be confident, convinced") is rare in Hellenistic prose (MM 501a). If ἑαυτῷ is a dative of respect ("with regard to himself," Barrett 256), the word has no negative connotation. But if this dative is locatival ("in his own mind," BAGD 639d; or, "in himself," Lambrecht 153), the subjective character of the confidence is stressed, "with connotations of presumption" (Spicq 3.76 n. 58).[114] The self-confident claim was inappropriate. Paul is stating the person's claim for the sake of argument but is not affirming the truth of the claim (cf. Windisch 302).

That "belonging to Christ" (Χριστοῦ εἶναι) was the essence of the claim and that this was a slogan of Paul's opponents is generally affirmed (e.g., Wendland 229). It is also usually (and rightly) assumed that Χριστοῦ is a possessive genitive[115] rather than a genitive of source (= to have one's credentials "from Christ"). But the precise meaning of Χριστοῦ εἶναι in the present context is hotly debated. Paul's rivals have been understood as claiming:

1. that they were, unlike Paul, really "Christ's property," that is, Christians.[116] In Paul's own usage "belonging to Christ" was synonymous with "being in Christ" or being a Christian (cf. Rom 8:9; 14:8; 1 Cor. 3:23; 15:23; Gal. 3:29; 5:24);

2. that they were companions and disciples of the earthly Jesus and were thus "in a dominical succession";[117]

3. that they belonged to the "Christ party" of 1 Cor. 1:12;[118]

---

113. Cf. Conybeare in Conybeare and Howson 457, "If there be any among you . . ."; NRSV, "If you are confident . . . ."

114. Allo speaks of Paul's "disdainful irony" in the expression πέποιθεν ἑαυτῷ (246-47).

115. See BAGD 225 s.v. εἰμί IV.2. Also, Χριστοῦ is a predicate genitive in an accusative and infinitive construction of indirect speech where the accusative (ἑαυτόν) is unexpressed (cf. Rom. 5:19).

116. E.g., Oostendorp 18-19; but see Kümmel 208.

117. E.g., Hughes 356; cf. the expression ὅτι Χριστοῦ ἐστε ("because you belong to Christ") in Mark 9:41 (on which see Theissen 46-47 and the comments of Thrall 622).

4. that they were commissioned directly by the earthly Jesus or some of his original disciples,[119] or were inspired directly by the risen Christ;[120]
5. that they were, in a distinctive sense, Christ's servants, being his genuine apostles.[121]

It seems unlikely that, in competition with Paul, his rivals would make such a commonplace claim as "we are (true) Christians," an assertion that lacks any distinctiveness (view 1). Since Paul had no personal knowledge of Jesus of Nazareth and yet claims (in v. 7b) to "belong to Christ," the second interpretation presupposes two different senses for Χριστοῦ εἶναι, which is not impossible but is more difficult than assuming an identity of meaning for Paul and his rivals. With regard to view 3, the silence of 2 Corinthians regarding any of the four groups mentioned in 1 Cor. 1:12 suggests that they were now inoperative,[122] especially since 2 Cor. 12:20 refers in general to ongoing "quarreling" (ἔρις) and "disputes" (ἐριθείαι) within the church; and, having repudiated all such factionalism in 1 Cor. 1:11-13, Paul would scarcely have identified himself (οὕτως καὶ ἡμεῖς, 2 Cor. 10:7b) with any group (cf. Plummer 280). However, the present supercilious claim to a certain spiritual exclusiveness and superiority is comparable to the spirit reflected in the earlier watchcry of the "Christ party," "I belong to Christ" (1 Cor. 1:12) (cf. Plummer xxxvii).[123] As for the fourth proposal, there is no clear indication elsewhere in 2 Corinthians that Paul's detractors claimed a special, direct association with the historical Jesus or the exalted Christ. This points to the strength of view 5, for there is specific evidence in this letter that they laid claim to being "servants of Christ" (διάκονοι Χριστοῦ, 11:23), and indirect evidence that they also professed to be "apostles," since Paul calls them "false apostles" (ψευδαπόστολοι) and accuses them of masquerading as Christ's apostles (11:13). That a special relationship to Christ is implied by Χριστοῦ εἶναι in this context seems indicated by v. 8, where Paul explains (γάρ) his own belonging to Christ (cf. οὕτως καὶ ἡμεῖς, v. 7c) in terms of his having distinctive and incontestable (οὐκ αἰσχυνθήσομαι)

118. E.g., Conybeare in Conybeare and Howson 457 n. 4; Allo 246, 272-74.
119. E.g., Murphy-O'Connor 103; similarly Furnish 476 and Menzies 72 (the earthly Jesus).
120. Héring 72.
121. Similarly Windisch 301-2; Barrett 257; Thrall 621-22; but each with slight modifications. Windisch allows that the claim may have included reference to the external advantages of a personal knowledge of the earthly Jesus and personal discipleship, or to an association with the primitive Palestinian church. Barrett agrees with Käsemann (36) that the ultimate issue was whether or not Paul was a Christian, while Thrall suggests that for Paul's rivals Χριστοῦ εἶναι may have been a claim to be Christ's agents in the sense of being missionaries in Christ's family who were dependent on others for the supply of material needs (cf. Mark 9:41) whereas for Paul himself the expression was shorthand for being Christ's apostle.
122. But Allo argues that the "Christ party" may have been perpetuated or reconstituted as a result of the activity of the intruders (272-74).
123. Cf. Weymouth's rendering: "that he specially belongs to Christ." The addition of δοῦλος after Χριστοῦ in 10:7 in D* F G a vg^mss Ambrosiaster (see Textual Note c. above) reflects this sense of distinctiveness.

authority as an apostle who serves by building up the Christian community. The issue at stake was not Paul's status as a genuine Christian but his position as a true apostle with authority. Yet the one ultimately involved the other, for a false apostle hardly belonged to Christ.[124]

The expression τοῦτο λογιζέσθω . . . ὅτι, where the τοῦτο looks forward to ὅτι (literally, "this . . . namely that"),[125] appears again in v. 11. In each case Paul may well be alluding to the use of the same verb in v. 2, ἐπί τινας τοὺς λογιζομένους: "Let those who are given to 'reckoning' or making assessments take these further points into consideration." If πάλιν is construed with the prepositional phrase ἐφ' ἑαυτοῦ that follows, the sense will be "again by himself" (Barrett 256, "probably"; Lambrecht 156) or "(in himself) . . . again within himself" (NASB). On this understanding ἐφ' ἑαυτοῦ would have no negative connotations such as the earlier ἑαυτῷ may have had (see above), since Paul is now stating what he believes to be a fact (namely, οὕτως καὶ ἡμεῖς). Alternatively, if we construe πάλιν with λογιζέσθω, the phrase will mean "let him go on to consider" (Zerwick and Grosvenor 554) and the following ἐφ' ἑαυτοῦ may be rendered "relying on himself" or "of his own accord" (Zerwick, *Analysis* 408). Again, if one relates πάλιν to the whole phrase τοῦτο λογιζέσθω . . . ἐφ' ἑαυτοῦ, this adverb could mean "on the other hand" (BAGD 607a; Bultmann 188) or "conversely" (Thrall 623). Of these three exegetical options, the second is to be preferred; Paul is encouraging those who claim a special relation to Christ to follow their own initiative of thought and progress to a further stage of reflection. The new thought that ought to dawn on these people is that Paul himself has just as strong a claim to a special relation to Christ as (καθὼς . . . οὕτως) they claim to have.[126] ἡμεῖς matches αὐτός, which refers back to τις, the implied subject of λογιζέσθω. καί may be simply adjunctive ("also") but could be considered emphatic ("most certainly," Wand), being a case of "litotes that is full of irony" (Allo 247).

In this verse, then, Paul is citing the assured opinion of an individual (τις) who was the spokesperson for the outlook of Paul's rivals at Corinth, and he seems to be arguing by way of concession.[127] He acknowledges his competitors' claim to belong to Christ in a distinctive way, although with ἑαυτῷ ("in his own mind") he emphasizes the subjective nature of the confident assessment and thereby hints at its presumptuousness. While not endorsing the truth of their claim, he uses it as a springboard to assert his own distinctive relation to Christ, presumably as a slave and apostle of Christ (cf. Rom. 1:1) and one who

---

124. Cf. Käsemann 11-12, 34-36.

125. But Barclay takes ὅτι in a causal, not an epexegetic, sense: ". . . let him examine his own case again, because, just as he belongs to Christ, so do we also."

126. According to Peterson (93; cf. 87-93, 105-32), 10:7-11 forms the *propositio* where Paul lays out in order the three main topics he will discuss in the *probatio* (11:1–12:18): (1) 10:7 ("Paul too belongs to Christ") is taken up in 11:1-15; (2) 10:8-10 ("Paul is able to boast of his authority without shame") is developed in 11:16–12:13; and (3) 10:11 ("Paul will act with consistency when he arrives in Corinth") is enlarged on in 12:14-18.

127. Similarly Scott 196. That Paul sometimes argues *e concessis* is clear from 1 Cor. 15:29.

wields authority (note ἐξουσία in v. 8), a status that corresponds to their claim — implied in v. 7 — of special servanthood (11:23) and apostleship (cf. 11:13). It is only when Paul reaches 11:13-15 that he expresses his own view of his opponents' status — they are in reality false, not true, apostles (11:13) and Satan's, not Christ's, servants (11:15).

10:8 ἐάν τε γὰρ περισσότερόν τι καυχήσωμαι περὶ τῆς ἐξουσίας ἡμῶν ἧς ἔδωκεν ὁ κύριος εἰς οἰκοδομὴν καὶ οὐκ εἰς καθαίρεσιν ὑμῶν, οὐκ αἰσχυνθήσομαι. "For if I do boast a little too much about our authority, which the Lord gave me for building you up and not for pulling you down, I shall not be ashamed of it." The apostle now provides evidence (γάρ) of his belonging to Christ in a special way (v. 7) — from the Lord he had received apostolic authority about which he could justifiably boast.[128] The enclitic particle τέ should be retained in the text, but with regard to sense it is probably a "superfluous affectation" (Turner 339), with the combination τὲ γάρ (without a subsequent τέ or καί[129]) being equivalent to a simple γάρ (see Textual Note f.), although some regard τέ as reinforcing the new thought (Windisch 303 n. 1) or as strengthening ἐάν to produce the sense "even if."[130] When ἐάν is followed by the subjunctive in a conditional sentence, the expectation of fulfillment ranges from slight possibility to virtual certainty, depending on the context.[131] In the present case (ἐάν . . . καυχήσωμαι), Paul certainly goes on to boast regarding his authority (see, for example, vv. 13-16), so that in this protasis he must be expressing his expectation in a guarded fashion[132] that reflects his unease at being forced to boast at all (cf. 11:16-18, 21, 30; 12:1, 11). This is the first use in 2 Corinthians 10–13 of the verb καυχάομαι, a key term in these chapters.[133]

Formed from the adjective περισσός ("abundant," "over and above"), the comparative περισσότερον may here be either *adjectival,* agreeing with τι, or *adverbial,* with τι serving to moderate the idea ("somewhat," "rather").[134]

(a) *Adjectival*

In this case περισσότερόν τι is the direct object of καυχήσωμαι[135] and means "something more" (Meyer 624), "(if I make) a further boast"

---

128. But γάρ could be confirmatory ("Indeed," NEB, REB) or merely transitional ("Now," NRSV).

129. But in Rom. 14:8 τέ is copulative, so that ἐάν τε γάρ . . . ἐάν τε means "for just as when . . . so also when," and ἐάν τε . . . ἐάν τε means "not only if . . . but also if" (BAGD 807c).

130. Thus RSV, NAB[2], NRSV; Furnish 466; Carrez 201. This is possible, but "even if" is more often expressed by εἰ καί in Paul (e.g., 7:8 [twice]).

131. Cf. the use of ἐάν γάρ with the present subjunctive in 1 Cor. 4:15; 9:16; 14:14, and with the aorist subjunctive in 1 Cor. 8:10; 2 Cor. 12:6.

132. This is true whatever sense is given to the qualifying phrase περισσότερόν τι.

133. See also 10:13, 15-17; 11:12, 16, 18, 30; 12:1, 5-6, 9. On this theme in Paul, see R. Bultmann, *TDNT* 3.648-52; Fahy, "Boasting"; P. Genths, "Der Begriff des καύχημα bei Paulus," *NKZ* 38 (1927) 501-21; Lambrecht, "Boasting"; Prümm, II/2.78-80, 340-55; Travis, "Boasting"; Wong 121-30; and especially Zmijewski, *Narrenrede,* and Bosch, *"Gloriarse."*

134. For the use of τις, see LSJ 1797 s.v. τις A.II.11.c.

(Barrett 258), "(if I should boast) in some further respect" (Thrall 597; cf. 624 n. 21), with the implied earlier boasting found either in vv. 3-6 or in v. 7.

(b) *Adverbial*

(i) The comparative may stand for the positive (cf. Turner 30-31); thus περισσότερόν τι will mean "rather much" (Zerwick and Grosvenor 554; Lambrecht 156) or "somewhat freely" (Moffatt, NIV), "somewhat extravagantly" (Cassirer)

(ii) περισσότερον may be a true comparative, although the comparison is not explicitly stated; thus (with τι) "somewhat more" (Hughes 359 n. 14),[136] "a little more" (Furnish 466).[137]

(iii) The comparative may denote excess ("too much");[138] thus (with τι) "a little too much" (Goodspeed, RSV, NAB[2], NRSV; Carrez 201), "rather too much" (JB, NJB).

All of these options are grammatically and contextually defensible, but a preference may be expressed for this last exegetical option (b.iii). Paul is intending to boast — "in the Lord," 10:17 — about his authority as it will be displayed on his next visit (10:11; 12:20; 13:2-3, 10) and as it will now be seen in his vigorous defense of his allotted task in Corinth (10:13-16). But perhaps to deflect any adverse reaction to this boasting, he apologizes in advance (by the figure known as prodiorthosis) by gently chiding himself: "If I do boast a little too much . . ."[139] or "If I am somewhat over-boastful . . ." (NEB). In a similar way he later will plead in advance with the Corinthians to show patience with his foolish boasting (11:1, 16).

Of central importance in 2 Corinthians 10–13 is Paul's twice-repeated reference to his authority which the Lord had given him for the purpose of building up, not tearing down.

10:8 . . . περὶ τῆς ἐξουσίας ἡμῶν ἧς[140] ἔδωκεν ὁ κύριος

13:10 . . . κατὰ τὴν ἐξουσίαν ἣν ὁ κύριος ἔδωκεν μοι,

10:8 εἰς οἰκοδομὴν καὶ οὐκ εἰς καθαίρεσιν ὑμῶν

13:10 εἰς οἰκοδομὴν καὶ οὐκ εἰς καθαίρεσιν

---

135. The construction καυχάομαί τι περί τινος means "say something (τι) boastingly concerning something" (cf. BAGD 426a), "make a boast about something."

136. Hughes completes the comparison thus: "a bit more than I should ordinarily regard as fitting or have done previously" (359 n. 14).

137. BAGD (651 s.v. περισσός 3.) notes that the comparative of περισσός may be a colloquial substitute for μᾶλλον; cf. BAGD 651 s.v. περισσότερος 3.

138. For this use of the comparative in Classical Greek, see Smyth §1082c.

139. It is less likely that Paul himself is reacting to an accusation of "boasting too much" made by his opponents.

140. This genitive is an instance of the attraction of the relative (ἥν) into the case of its antecedent (ἐξουσίας) (cf. BDF §294).

A comparison of these two passages shows that the authority was vested in Paul personally (μοι) and not simply in the apostles as a group (ἡμῶν is probably an epistolary plural; cf. the two singulars καυχήσωμαι . . . αἰσχυνθήσομαι in the same verse). Since it lacks any ὑμῶν, 13:10 enunciates the general principle, while 10:8 with ὑμῶν applies it explicitly to the Corinthians.[141] Whether or not the relative clause ἧς . . . ὑμῶν in v. 8 is marked off as parenthetical,[142] it is a crucial affirmation that the principal purpose (εἰς) of Paul's receipt and exercise of his authority was positive, not negative, and was for the upbuilding of the Corinthian congregation, and by implication (cf. 13:10), other Christian churches for which he was responsible.

In the present context the aorist ἔδωκεν points to a single event — Christ's appointment of Paul as an authoritative apostle at the time of his conversion.[143] Although God was also actively involved in Paul's call into apostleship and service (1 Cor. 1:1; Gal. 1:1, 15-16; 2 Tim. 1:1), it is more probable that ὁ κύριος here is the Lord Jesus, since, as Thrall observes (624), the authority referred to in v. 8 is that of one who claims to belong to Christ (v. 7). As the opposite of καθαίρεσις, the act or process of destroying, οἰκοδομή here denotes the act or process of building (= οἰκοδόμησις),[144] not the result of construction, that is, a building (= οἰκοδόμημα) (as at 5:1). In its active, metaphorical sense in Paul, this term describes spiritual consolidation and strengthening, whether of the church viewed corporately (e.g., 1 Cor. 14:12) or of believers considered individually (e.g., Rom. 14:19).[145] In each case Paul's aim was to produce maturity (τελειότης) (Eph. 4:12-13, of the church; Col. 1:28, of individual believers) and to achieve the common good (cf. 1 Cor. 12:7, where πρὸς τὸ συμφέρον parallels εἰς οἰκοδομήν in 2 Cor. 10:8).[146] In the present instance the οἰκοδομή of the Corinthians (12:19) would be accomplished by their complete obedience to Christ and to Paul (10:6; cf. 11:3), by their repudiation of Paul's adversaries, and, more generally, by their "restoration" (κατάρτισις, 13:9; cf. καταρτίζεσθε, 13:11).

---

141. In 10:8 ὑμῶν should be regarded as qualifying both καθαίρεσιν and οἰκοδομήν (thus almost all translations), as is commonly the case when a single possessive pronoun stands after the second of two coordinated anarthrous nouns. But Thrall renders the relevant phrases, "for constructive purposes and not for your destruction" (597).

142. As in the ASV, TCNT, Moffatt, NEB, REB.

143. Acts 9:15; 22:15; 26:15-16; 1 Cor. 9:1; Gal. 1:1; 1 Tim. 1:12; 2:7; 2 Tim. 1:11.

144. As also in Rom. 14:19; 15:2; 1 Cor. 14:3, 12, 26; 2 Cor. 12:19.

145. But Kitzberger (127) refers οἰκοδομή in 10:8 to the founding of churches, noting (127 n. 326) that Vielhauer (73) believes that the emphasis rests on the furtherance and preservation of the church.

146. On the innovative character of Paul's concept of οἰκοδομή, Judge comments that "the notion of the gifts of the Spirit opens to everyone, however limited in genetic endowment or social opportunity, the promise of being able to contribute to the upbuilding of a new structure of human relations. Such a mode of tackling the problems of oppression in human culture and society is an historical innovation of the first order. It may perhaps be called the first structural approach to human relations" ("Conformity" 24).

Why Paul added the phrase καὶ οὐκ εἰς καθαίρεσιν ὑμῶν to the positive statement εἰς οἰκοδομήν is not immediately clear. It is unlikely that he is simply making the allusion to Jeremiah (whether 1:10 or 24:6) unambiguous, so that the addition is without relevance to Paul's situation. Nor is the reference to καθαίρεσις simply a foil to highlight the positive content of οἰκοδομή. It could be Paul's blunt rebuttal of a charge that had gained circulation at Corinth to the effect that his pastoral techniques were high-handed and heavy-handed (cf. 1:24). Such a charge may have arisen as a result of his handling of the case of the man guilty of incest (1 Cor. 5:1-13). But more probably there were two quite different purposes behind the antithesis. One aim of Paul may have been to contrast the friction and division within the Corinthian congregation caused by his rivals (cf. 11:2-4; 12:20) who used domineering and injurious tactics (11:20), with his own commitment to promoting harmony and unity within the church (cf. 1 Cor. 1:10-13; 3:4-9, 21-23; 11:17-22, 27-34) and his exclusive dedication to their spiritual strengthening, their "edification" (οἰκοδομή, 12:19[147]). Paul's other purpose in adding the phrase "and not for pulling you down" may have been to reassure the Corinthians that the ultimate goal in the exercise of his divinely given authority was invariably the positive one of building them up, not the negative one of destroying them and their faith. Only in the case of obstacles to the knowledge of God was καθαίρεσις his ultimate goal (10:4-5, καθαίρεσιν . . . καθαιροῦντες). But Paul is not rejecting "destruction" as a legitimate, intermediate technique that may be used in the shaping of his converts' conduct. After all, the OT is replete with examples of God's devastating, judgmental action against his people that was brought about because of their disobedience (e.g., Deut. 28:15-68; Jer. 25:4-11), but God's aim was always their ultimate restoration to obedience and right relations with him (e.g., Jer. 30:3-22; Hos. 6:1-2).[148] As in literal construction work, "demolition" may sometimes be a necessary prelude to the actual building process. That Paul contemplated the possibility of "tearing down" or reproving or punishing some of the Corinthians is clear from 13:10 where he warns that unless they respond to his admonitions, it may prove necessary for him to take severe action (ἀποτόμως χρᾶσθαι = καθαίρεσις). But, as in 1 Cor. 5:5, the ultimate aim was their salvation on the Day of the Lord. Even if καθαίρεσις was sometimes a prerequisite for οἰκοδομή, it could never be the ultimate goal of Paul's pastoral ministry; ultimacy always belonged to upbuilding.[149]

For a comparable contrast between ultimate and immediate purpose, stated in terms of a stark antithesis, we may appeal to a passage such as Ezek.

147. There are only four uses of οἰκοδομή in 2 Corinthians: 5:1 (of the believer's spiritual body); 10:8 and 13:10 (the verses under consideration); and 12:19.

148. Cf. Vielhauer 11-12.

149. For the idea of rebuilding after destruction, see Ezek. 36:26 and Jer. 31:28 ("'Just as I watched over them [the houses of Israel and Judah] to pluck up and tear down, and to overthrow, destroy and inflict disaster, so I will watch over them to build and to plant,' says the LORD").

36:22: "It is not for your sake, O house of Israel, that I [the sovereign LORD] am about to do these things ["restore them to the promised land and give them prosperity there], but for the sake of my holy name, which you have profaned among the nations to which you came" (cf. Ezek. 36:32).

Paul's "build–destroy" imagery is reminiscent of two passages in Jeremiah although there is no precise verbal overlap. At Jeremiah's commissioning Yahweh says, "See, today I give you authority over nations and kingdoms, to pluck up and to tear down, to destroy (LXX, ἀπολλύειν) and to overthrow, to build (LXX, ἀνοικοδομεῖν) and to plant" (Jer. 1:10). Then, in promising that the exiles from Judah will return from Babylon, Yahweh informs Jeremiah, "I will set my eyes upon them for their good, and I will bring them back to this land. I will build them up (ἀνοικοδομήσω αὐτούς) and not tear them down (καὶ οὐ μὴ καθελῶ); I will plant them and not pluck them up" (Jer. 24:6). Conceptually, the latter passage, with its "build up . . . and not tear down" contrast, is closer to Paul's statement, but when we recall the probable influence of the call narrative of Jer. 1:4-5 (along with Isa. 49:1-6) on Paul's own sense of mission (Gal. 1:15-16), it may well be that he intended to draw a contrast between his mission and that of Jeremiah as it is described in Jer. 1:10. Both men were given divine authority to act (Jer. 1:9-10; 2 Cor. 10:8; 13:10) and were to be engaged in the tasks of building up and pulling down (Jer. 1:10; 2 Cor. 10:4, 8; 13:10), but whereas Jeremiah's commission as a prophet of the old covenant had been principally for "tearing down,"[150] Paul's commission as a minister of the new covenant (3:6) was principally for "building up."[151]

Our verse ends with the apostle's strong declaration by means of litotes that when he engages in his projected boasting concerning his apostolic authority, he will certainly not be put to shame (οὐκ αἰσχυνθήσομαι). This may mean that he will not be shown up before Christ's judgment seat (cf. 5:10) as having acted inappropriately in his boasting. But rather it points to his assurance that his boasting is justified because it is based on the truth and is within assigned limits (cf. 10:13-15), so that neither on his forthcoming visit to Corinth nor at any time in the future will he be embarrassingly exposed as an imposter.

10:9 ἵνα μὴ δόξω ὡς ἂν ἐκφοβεῖν ὑμᾶς διὰ τῶν ἐπιστολῶν. "I say this so that I may not seem as if I am trying to terrify you with my letters." Before we consider how this statement relates syntactically to what precedes or follows (which is the main exegetical issue), it will be helpful to make some exegetical comments on individual words and phrases. The verb δοκέω here bears an intransitive sense, "seem" or "have/give the appearance of," with an implied dative of the person involved, namely ὑμῖν, the Corinthians.[152] ἐκφοβεῖν is a NT

150. This seems to be indicated by Jer. 1:10 where four of the six verbs are negative in import ("pluck up . . . tear down . . . destroy . . . overthrow") and only the final two are positive ("build . . . plant").

151. A not dissimilar point is made by Hafemann (398).

152. Thus "lest I should seem [to you]" may also be rendered "lest you should imagine" (as Conybeare in Conybeare and Howson 457).

hapax legomenon although it is not uncommon in the LXX (fourteen uses) where on six occasions it is found in the stylized phrase οὐκ ἔσται ὁ ἐκφοβῶν, "no one will terrify you."[153] The prefix ἐκ- may have a causative force (Robertson 597), "cause to be afraid," "frighten," but more probably it is intensive, "terrify" or "frighten to distraction" (Hughes 361 n. 17), "scare to death" (Furnish 468). In this case the rendering "overawe" (TCNT, Moffatt, Cassirer) or "intimidate" (NAB[1]; Thrall 597) is perhaps too mild. ὡς ἄν, sometimes written ὡσάν, may be translated in any one of three ways: "as if," where ἄν probably = ἐάν (Robertson 959), "as it were" (Moulton 167), or "so to speak" (Thrall 597). The expression should be construed with ἐκφοβεῖν ὑμᾶς, toning down the effect of that strong verb, "to be trying to scare you to death,[154] so to speak," rather than with δόξω, "give the appearance as it were."[155] Finally, the article with ἐπιστολῶν denotes possession, "my letters," and may also point to certain well-known letters (the anaphoric use of the article). It is possible that the term ἐπιστολῶν is a case of "concrete for abstract" (thus "correspondence," Thrall 597), and that the plural is generalizing (thus "by letter," JB, NJB); on the other hand, διὰ τῶν ἐπιστολῶν probably means simply "by/with/by means of my letters."

The awkward syntax of the verse has given rise to conflicting proposals, here listed in ascending order of probability.

1. Paul has indulged in a "colloquial turn of speech: '. . . as though all that we can do is scare people through letters'" (Danker 155; similarly McCant 108). But this hardly does justice to ἵνα μὴ δόξω.
2. ἵνα μὴ δόξω κτλ. follows directly on οὐκ αἰσχυνθήσομαι: ". . . I am not going to be shamed into letting you think that I can put fear into you only[156] by letter" (NJB), or ". . . I will not be shamed into seeming not to terrify you with my letters" (Young and Ford 272).[157] But did Paul actually intend to put fear into the Corinthians by his personal presence on his next visit or by his very letters?
3. If ἵνα μὴ δόξω κτλ. is regarded as a protasis, v. 11 may be the apodosis, with the intervening v. 10 being an explanatory parenthesis. "Lest I should seem to be relying on letters to frighten you into obedience (for

153. Lev. 26:6; Deut. 28:26; Ezek. 34:28; 39:26; Mic. 4:4; Zech. 3:13; cf. Judg. 16:25; Nah. 2:11; 1 Macc. 14:12.

154. This translation assumes that the present infinitive ἐκφοβεῖν is both durative and conative — so also TCNT, GNB, NIV, NRSV.

155. So Hughes 361 n. 18, who gives the sense thus: Paul "has no intention of terrifying them out of their wits by the letters he writes, as though putting on a show of authority from a safe distance" (361).

156. The supplying of μόνον before ἐκφοβεῖν is also supported by Héring 72; Wolff 200, 202 and n. 66.

157. Similarly Bultmann 189, who also suggests (among other options) supplying "but I will know how to use my ἐξουσία" before ἵνα μὴ δόξω κτλ. Bultmann's further suggestion that ἵνα may here be resultative (cf. Héring 72) certainly eases the difficulty of attaching v. 9 to v. 8.

this is what they are accusing me of), let anyone who thinks this take note of the fact that what I say in my letters I carry out in practice" (Harvey 96 n. 13).[158] But the asyndetic ἵνα clause is a difficulty for this view; a connective such as δέ or καί would have been expected (Héring 72).[159]

4. Furnish (465, 467-68) proposes that βούλωμαι be supplied with ὡς ἄν: " — lest I should seem as if I wanted to be scaring you with my letters."[160] Against this Thrall notes that when δοκέω means "seem," an infinitive, not a subjunctive clause, normally follows (627 n. 227, citing BAGD 202 s.v. δοκέω 2.a.), while ὡς ἄν or ὡς ἐάν with the subjunctive means "when" or "as soon as," not "as if" (627 n. 227, citing BAGD 898 s.v. ὡς IV.1.c.).

5. ἵνα could be imperatival.[161] "May I not seem as one frightening you through letters" (NAB²); "So you must not think of me as one who . . ." (NEB, REB; similarly Cassirer).

6. ἵνα μὴ δόξω is elliptical. When one appeals to the possibility of an ellipsis as an explanation of an exegetical difficulty, the simpler the suggested necessary addition and the more innocuous its meaning, the more convincing the explanation.[162] These considerations favor supplying before ἵνα either θέλω, with a transposition of the negative, which would give the sense, "I do not want (to seem . . .)"[163] or τοῦτο λέγω (cf. 1 Cor. 7:6; Col. 2:4), "I say this. . . ."[164] In the former case, however, we might have expected Paul to write οὐ θέλω δοκεῖν ὡς ἄν ἐκφοβεῖν κτλ. (cf. 1 Cor. 16:7; 2 Thess. 3:10).

My suggested translation is "I say this so that I may not seem as if I am trying to terrify you with my letters." The word "this" would refer back to Paul's statement in v. 8 that his authority was not given so that he could destroy the Corinthians. In vv. 8-9 he is saying in effect, "My divinely given commission is to build you up, not to scare you to death and destroy you through overpowering letters." On this view, ἐκφοβεῖν is related to καθαίρεσιν in v. 8 and also, through ὅτι (v. 10), to the terms βαρεῖαι ("tyrannical") and ἰσχυραί ("ag-

---

158. Similarly Martin 310 (but see 298); Garland 445 n. 103.

159. δέ is actually read by H vg *al.* (see BDF §483).

160. This suggestion was prompted by Moule's parenthetical comment in a discussion of the interchange of ἐάν and ἄν (152) that ἵνα μὴ δόξω ὡς ἄν ἐκφοβεῖν ὑμᾶς appears to be a conflation of ἵνα μὴ δόξω ἐκφοβεῖν ὑμᾶς ("lest I should seem to terrify you") and ἵνα μὴ δόξω ὡς ἐὰν ἐκφοβεῖν ὑμᾶς βούλωμαι ("lest I should seem as though I wanted to terrify you"). But Moule's own solution regarding v. 9 seems to be to supply a verb of wishing *before* ἵνα μὴ δόξω (145).

161. On this construction, see above on 8:7.

162. More complex and therefore less convincing completions of the ellipsis include the following: "I will not say more than that" (Plummer's paraphrase [279]); "I forbear to do this [namely bring my authority into play]" (Barrett 259).

163. Thus Goodspeed, Williams, NIV, NRSV; Carrez 201; Lambrecht 153; similarly NASB, JB, GNB, NAB¹.

164. Thus Conybeare in Conybeare and Howson 457; TCNT; Thrall 597.

gressive") in v. 10. To try to scare the Corinthians into submission by what some regarded as tyrannical letters (v. 10) would be to destroy them. The letters referred to in vv. 9 and 10 could include the "previous letter" of 1 Cor. 5:9, 11 and 1 Corinthians itself, but the main allusion will be to the "severe letter" mentioned in 2 Cor. 2:3-4; 7:12 with its apparent demand for the summary punishment of the offending church member.[165]

10:10 ὅτι, Αἱ ἐπιστολαὶ μέν, φησίν, βαρεῖαι καὶ ἰσχυραί, ἡ δὲ παρουσία τοῦ σώματος ἀσθενὴς καὶ ὁ λόγος ἐξουθενημένος. "For some are saying, 'His letters are tyrannical and aggressive; his personal presence, on the other hand, is weak and his eloquence is contemptible.'" The singular verb (φησίν) could point to the allegation of an imaginary objector, in the tradition of the "diatribe";[166] thus "Someone will say" (GNB). Paul is certainly capable of creating a lengthy and detailed theological objection to be answered (see, e.g., Rom. 3:7), but it seems inconceivable that he would provide such a convenient tool of self-disparagement for his antagonists to use against him, when he normally avoids citing the criticism of his detractors *verbatim,* lest the very repetition of a charge should actually reinforce it. Rather, φησίν may bear an impersonal sense, "it is said" (NEB, REB; Furnish 468) like the German "sagt man" (Wendland 229; de Boor 202) or the French "dit-on" (Carrez 201), or refer to Paul's critics in general, both Corinthians and intruders, as represented by a particular spokesman (B reads φασίν; see Textual Note i.); thus "to quote my opponents" (Barclay) or "some are saying."

The accusation clearly falls into two parts, marked by the correlatives μὲν . . . δέ, one relating to writing while absent, the other relating to action while present (cf. vv. 1, 11).[167] But is the first part complimentary to Paul (even if it forms a grudging concession) and the second disdainful, or are both parts contemptuous? Two considerations support the latter option. First, it seems *a priori* unlikely that a slogan of Paul's opponents would encapsulate a compliment to Paul, even if that compliment served to highlight the contrasted disdain. Second, the introductory ὅτι does not simply explain why reference is made to letters in v. 9 (as Thrall suggests [629]) but actually affords proof that at least to some people Paul's letters seemed thoroughly terrifying (cf. ἐκφοβεῖν, v. 9).[168] If this is so, the two adjectives βαρεῖαι and ἰσχυραί will here not mean "weighty and strong" (RSV, NRSV) or "impressive and telling" (Goodspeed)[169] — com-

---

165. But scholars who regard 2 Corinthians 10–13 as part or the whole of the "severe letter" tend to look to passages in 1 Corinthians to fulfill this reference to terrifying letters. Plummer (282), for example, refers to 1 Cor. 5:3-5, 9, while F. Watson (343-44) mentions 1 Cor. 4:18-21.

166. Thus BDF §130(3), citing Bultmann, *Stil* 10, 67.

167. This reverses the order of the contrast found in v. 1 (also expressed by μὲν . . . δέ): timid when present — bold when absent (v. 1); audacious when absent — weak when present (v. 10).

168. But Hughes (361 n. 17) views ἐκφοβεῖν as "an ironically exaggerated echo of the calumny of Paul's opponents."

169. Other proposed renderings of ἰσχυραί include "vigorous" (TCNT), "forceful" (NAB²), and "effective" (BAGD 383b).

plimentary statements — but "tyrannical[170] and aggressive" or "severe[171] and forcible[172]" or "burdensome[173] and violent[174]." Such a view of Paul's letters with their repeated directives could easily have prompted the charge that by his letters he was trying to scare his converts out of their wits (ἐκφοβεῖν).[175]

In contrast with Paul's bold, authoritarian style when at a safe distance — so the allegation ran — his personal presence was feeble and his powers of speech amounted to nothing. παρουσία ("presence") may refer simply to "being present," with τοῦ σώματος emphasizing the actual or personal nature of the presence and ἀσθενής meaning "weak" in the sense of "feeble" or "puny." Thus, "when he is actually present he is weak" (Furnish 465) or "when he appears in person he is seen to be but a feeble man" (Cassirer).[176] ἀσθενής would then be almost synonymous with ταπεινός in v. 1. Alternatively, παρουσία may bear a broader meaning that includes the ideas of appearance and demeanor (cf. the English word "presence"). In this case, as an adjectival or Semitic genitive, τοῦ σώματος will mean "bodily," "personal" or "physical"[177] and ἀσθενής "insignificant" or "unimpressive." Thus, "his personal appearance is insignificant" (TCNT, Goodspeed) or "his personal presence is unimpressive" (Weymouth, NASB).[178] If this whole phrase relates to one of the accepted qualifications for oratorical prowess (see below),[179] this second, alternative view is to be preferred.

However we understand ὁ λόγος in this context, the epithet ἐξουθενη-μένος, the perfect passive participle of ἐξουθενέω, "ignore," "despise," describes either what is unworthy of attention, "of no account," "negligible," or what is worthy of disdain, "contemptible." If λόγος refers to content ("word," "what is spoken"), it could scarcely advert to the message he preached; no rival

---

170. Spicq 2.416 n. 8. Plummer mentions "tyrannical and violent" as a possible rendering of this pair of epithets if the statement is not complimentary (282).

171. BAGD 134b (but "weighty" is proposed at 301a and 383b); GNB, NAB².

172. Weymouth, Montgomery.

173. βαρύς is used of onerous burdens (Matt. 23:4) and of burdensome commandments (1 John 5:3). Cf. Furnish (468), "demanding."

174. In Matt. 14:30 ἰσχυρός describes a wind that is "ferocious."

175. If αἱ ἐπιστολαί refers to the "previous letter," to 1 Corinthians, and to the "severe letter" (see on v. 9), there is reason to believe that Paul's authoritarian instructions in his letters — if that is how they were regarded — may have seemed to become progressively more strident.

176. JB expresses the thought colloquially: "when he is with you you see only half a man."

177. Gundry (48) sees τοῦ σώματος as referring to "outward physicality."

178. Cf. Moffatt, "his personality is weak." With the word παρουσία before τοῦ σώματος, it is unlikely that ἀσθενής refers either to physical sickliness (cf. 1 Cor. 11:30) or to Paul's social lowliness as an artisan (as Hock 60).

179. On the importance of the public speaker's physical appearance for effective communication, see Epictetus 3.22.86-89. But we need not assume that the rather unflattering apocryphal description of Paul's appearance that has survived in *The Acts of Paul and Thecla 3* is accurate, or if it is, that it would have disqualified him from due recognition as an orator (see the discussion in Garland 448-49). That ancient text, dating from the end of the second century A.D., reads as follows. "And he [Onesiphorus] saw Paul coming, a man of short stature, bald, bowlegged, in good health, with eyebrows meeting and nose somewhat hooked, full of charm."

of Paul could make the assertion at Corinth that Paul's preaching amounted to nothing or was ineffective, for the very existence of the Corinthian congregation, the product of Paul's preaching (1:19; 3:2-3), would give the lie to such a claim. It could, however, refer in general to what Paul said, as in Bruce's paraphrase: "no one pays any attention to what he says" (149). It is better, though, to interpret λόγος here, as most EVV do, as "speech," in the sense of "power of speech" (Cassirer), "eloquence" (Weymouth), or even "rhetoric" (Martin 298). Paul's critics were affirming that his speaking ability, including his ability in extempore speech,[180] was wholly without merit.[181]

In the ancient rhetorical handbooks ὑπόκρισις denoted an orator's "delivery," which included not only his verbal and elocutionary skills but also his bodily "presence," the impression made by his physical appearance, his dress, and his general demeanor.[182] The dual allegation of Paul's adversaries reflects these two aspects of ὑπόκρισις.[183]

Savage offers a different understanding of v. 10b. He argues that when the Corinthians allege that Paul's bodily demeanor is "weak," they are faulting him for his failure to assert himself aggressively in punishment and discipline, as his rivals did (11:20) (64-69). When they allege that his speech is "contemptible," they are faulting him for his refusal to indulge in the abusive and arrogant rhetoric that was so popular in first-century Corinth (69-80; cf. 46-47). These comments are made in the context of Savage's identification (12) of four areas in which Paul is faulted by the Corinthians — his refusal to boast (54-64), his weak physical presence, his unskilled speech, and his refusal to accept financial support (80-99). This disagreement between Paul and his converts reflected a conflict between the secular outlook of the Corinthians and Paul's Christ-centered viewpoint, a "radical disjunction" that prompted Paul's paradoxical description of the Christian ministry as being essentially power through weakness (99).

10:11 τοῦτο λογιζέσθω ὁ τοιοῦτος, ὅτι οἷοί ἐσμεν τῷ λόγῳ δι' ἐπιστολῶν ἀπόντες, τοιοῦτοι καὶ παρόντες τῷ ἔργῳ. "Such a person should reckon with

---

180. Winter believes that 10:10 "reflects a continuing debate among the sophists over written versus extempore oratory."

181. It is probable that this contempt for Paul's λόγος included scorn for his diction. His oriental pronunciation of Greek was probably offensive to the cultured Corinthians.

182. See further Winter, *Philo* 208-13, and, more briefly, "Paul" 28-29, 32-33.

183. Winter has argued that some Corinthians were angered by Paul's critique of the sophistic tradition (in 1 Corinthians 1–4 and 9), and, along with other anti-Paulinists, persuaded the Corinthian congregation as a whole to request the return of the rhetorically accomplished Apollos, an invitation he rejected for the present (1 Cor. 16:12). As a result, certain Jewish Christian itinerant teachers, trained in rhetoric, were recruited to teach the congregation. These are the ones who now, borrowing certain rhetorical categories from Paul's critique, mockingly note that at a distance he himself writes impressive and persuasive letters that show rhetorical skill yet he shows himself to be an unpresentable and inarticulate orator (10:10) (*Philo* 145-46, 203-8). But Barnett (476-77) identifies the primary criticisms leveled against Paul in v. 10b as his unimpressive attempts at discipline on his most recent visit (cf. 10:1-2; 12:21; 13:2) and his sending, instead, of a letter (the "severe letter") in the place of a return visit (cf. 1:15–2:3).

this — that when we are present we will be in our actions exactly the same that we are in word through our letters when absent." The section 10:1-11 ends as it began, with an allusion to a description of Paul that was circulating in the Corinthian congregation. According to some, there were two Pauls, or at least two faces of the one Paul, apparent in his dealings with his converts at Corinth. There was the man who was bold and terrifying when he wrote letters while absent from the church, and there was the man who was timid and weak when he appeared in person.[184] The contrasts were four in number: with regard to Paul's location, absence and presence are contrasted; with respect to his mode of communication, letter and visit; concerning his action, word and deed are contrasted;[185] and regarding his attitude, boldness and timidity.

ὁ τοιοῦτος means either "this individual" (Lambrecht 153) or "such a person" (BAGD 821c), although for the sake of consistency those who render φησίν as a plural ("they say" or "some say") sometimes translate ὁ τοιοῦτος the same way ("Such people," Goodspeed, NIV). The person or persons referred to are those who say or think that Paul was despotic by letter when absent but unimpressive in both demeanor and speech when present (vv. 9-10). Paul now insists that people with this viewpoint, many of whom were already given to "reckoning" or making assessments (τινὰς τοὺς λογιζομένους, v. 2), needed to make a further assessment (λογιζέσθω) — that on his next visit to Corinth he would be as resolute in deed as he had been in word. As in v. 7, τοῦτο points forward to ὅτι ("this, namely that . . ."). But the subjects in vv. 7 and 11 are probably different, τις (v. 7) being the ringleader of the interlopers from Judea, and ὁ τοιοῦτος (v. 11), along with the implied subject of φησίν (v. 10), referring representatively or generically to both the Corinthian anti-Paulinists and the intruders.

οἷοι . . . τοιοῦτοι are correlatives, literally "of what sort . . . of such a sort," thus "as . . . so." The pair point to correspondence in quality, and that correspondence is evident in Paul's character (οἷοι . . . τοιοῦτοι, not simply ὅ . . . τοιοῦτο, "what . . . such") as well as in what he does (τῷ λόγῳ . . . τῷ ἔργῳ, "in word . . . in deed/our actions," both datives of respect). What was true of Paul in the letters he wrote would equally be true of him in his actions; there would be a precise correspondence (note the καί with τοιοῦτοι; cf. 1 Cor. 15:48). "We will be in our actions exactly the same as we are in word through our letters."[186] In saying οἷοί ἐσμεν . . . δι᾽ ἐπιστολῶν Paul is not necessarily concurring with

---

184. This is a composite picture, drawn from 10:1 and 10:9-11.

185. For this contrast regarding action, cf. Col. 3:17, πᾶν ὅτι ἐὰν ποιῆτε ἐν λόγῳ ἢ ἐν ἔργῳ . . . , "Whatever you are doing, whether in word or in deed . . . ." On the λόγος–ἔργον word-pair in 2 Corinthians 10–13, see H. W. Merritt, *In Word and Deed: Moral Integrity in Paul* (New York: Lang, 1993) 111-52; and in the Greco-Roman world, Danker 156.

186. δι᾽ ἐπιστολῶν may be instrumental ("through our letters") or may indicate the manner of acting ("by letters" [Lambrecht 153]); or, if ἐπιστολῶν is a generalizing plural, "by letter" [BAGD 180b], "by correspondence" [Thrall 597; cf. Zerwick §114]). Some link δι᾽ ἐπιστολῶν closely with ἐν λόγῳ — thus "in our written word" (Zerwick and Grosvenor 555), "in the words of our letters" (Furnish 469).

his adversaries' claim in v. 10a about the nature or effect of his letters, however v. 10a is understood. If, as we have argued above, that claim alleged that his letters were vigorously authoritarian, he would certainly not have agreed! On the contrary, he wanted to prevent his converts from imagining that he was aiming to terrorize them and stun them into compliance whenever he wrote to them (v. 9). Against the backdrop of the earlier charge that he showed indecision and vacillation in his travel plans (1:17) and the present charge that he was bold when absent but timid when present (10:1, 9-10), Paul affirms here in v. 11 in a rhetorically charged statement[187] both his constancy of character and his consistency in conduct.[188]

But the verse is more than an affirmation of the precise correspondence between two modes of Paul's "presence," the epistolary and the personal;[189] it also contains a thinly disguised threat. To match the ἐσμέν with οἷοι,[190] some translations and commentators supply or understand an ἐσμέν with τοιοῦτοι καί.[191] But there are persuasive reasons for supplying the future ἐσόμεθα.[192] (1) If ἀπόντες has a specific reference, relating to particular letters Paul had written to Corinth, the parallel word παρόντες is also likely to be specific, referring to his forthcoming visit (12:14; 13:1-2). In a similar "absent–present" antithesis[193] in 13:10, παρών relates specifically to this visit as a time when

187. Note the chiastic antitheses τῷ λόγῳ . . . ἀπόντες . . . παρόντες τῷ ἔργῳ.

188. As well as having the phrase τοῦτο λογιζέσθω . . . ὅτι in common, vv. 7 and 11 both relate to consistency. If v. 7 is a call for consistency in assessment, v. 11 is an assertion of consistency in action.

189. For a discussion of the relation between the personally present "I" (the visit) and the epistolary "I" (the letter), two different but complementary ways by which Paul fulfills his apostolic vocation, see Bosenius, especially 7-43, 97-167. Funk has shown (249-68) that Paul's apostolic "presence" with his congregations was possible in three different but related ways — a letter, an envoy, and his own presence, and in that order with regard to effectiveness in mediating his apostolic authority. Letter and envoy were substitutes for his personal presence, "less effective perhaps, but sometimes necessary" (258).

190. The change from the singulars in vv. 8-9 to the plural in v. 11 is probably another case of Paul's (unconscious?) stylistic oscillation between singular and plural; ἐσμέν, like ἡμῶν (v. 8), is an epistolary plural.

191. Thus RV, Weymouth, NASB, Barclay, NAB², Cassirer; Plummer 279, 284; Allo 248; Zerwick and Grosvenor 555; Wolff 200.

192. As also KJV, TCNT, Moffatt, Goodspeed, NEB, GNB, JB, NAB¹, NIV, NJB, REB, NRSV; Héring 72; de Boor 202; Barrett 255; Carrez 201; Lang 330, 331-32; Martin 298, 313; Young and Ford 272; Barnett 478; Lambrecht 158; Thrall 597, 634 n. 284.

193. This antithesis is common in chs. 10–13:

ἀπών	—	κατὰ πρόσωπον (10:1)
ἐπιστολαί	—	ἡ παρουσία τοῦ σώματος (10:10)
ἀπόντες	—	παρόντες (10:11)
ἀπὼν νῦν	—	ὡς παρών (13:2)
ἀπών	—	παρών (13:10)

Cf.   1 Cor. 5:3, ἀπὼν τῷ σώματι — παρὼν δὲ τῷ πνεύματι
Phil. 1:27, εἴτε ἐλθὼν καὶ ἰδὼν ὑμᾶς — εἴτε ἀπών
Col. 2:5,   εἰ γὰρ καὶ τῇ σαρκὶ ἄπειμι — ἀλλὰ τῷ πνεύματι σὺν ὑμῖν εἰμι.

Paul hopes to avoid having to exercise his authority severely. So παρόντες in v. 11 is appropriately rendered "when I come" (NEB, REB) or "when I arrive" (Moffatt, Goodspeed). (2) Embroiled as he is in dealing with the current crisis in Corinth, Paul is unlikely to be simply stating a timeless general truth (ἐσμέν) that is not specifically related to the present situation (". . . such as we are in speech . . . , that very thing we are in deed," Barclay). Rather, he is issuing a warning to the Corinthians that when he arrives they will see for themselves that there is no discrepancy between his words and his deeds. (3) The preceding future οὐκ αἰσχυνθήσομαι (v. 8) points to Paul's next visit as well as to the future in general. (4) This view of v. 11 is consonant with his explicit threats of decisive action on his coming visit against opponents (10:2, 6) or those recalcitrant Corinthians who persist in sexual immorality (12:20-21; 13:2; cf. 13:10).

So then, confronted by a persistent rumor (vv. 1, 10) that had the effect of creating two Pauls, one an absent despot and the other a weakling when present, Paul assures his converts at Corinth that he is no schizophrenic. The same qualities, resolve, and authority that were evident in his letters would be demonstrated unambiguously on his imminent visit.

Bibliography

Bahr • Barrett, "Christianity" • Bauer 127-28 • Betz, *Paulus* 44-69 • Bosenius 7-43, 97-167 • Carrez, "Le 'Nous'" • Carson • Chevallier • Crafton 103-36 • A. J. Dewey, "A Matter of Honor: A Social-Historical Analysis of 2 Corinthians 10," *HTR* 78 (1985) 209-17 • DiCicco • Dupont 39-40 • Fee, *Presence* 340-42 • J. T. Fitzgerald, "Paul, the Ancient Epistolary Theorists, and 2 Corinthians 10–13," in D. L. Balch, et al. (eds.), *Greeks, Romans, and Christians. Festschrift for A. J. Malherbe* (Minneapolis: Fortress, 1990) 190-200 • Forbes • Güttgemanns 135-41 • Hanson, *Paradox* 99-108 • Harada • Heckel • Holland • Horrell 220-29, 296-312 • Judge • Käsemann • Kleinknecht • Kolenkow • Lambrecht, "Appeal" • Lambrecht, "Self-Commendation" • Leivestad • Lohse, *Verteidigung* • Loubser 507-21 • Malherbe, "Paul" • Marshall • Marshall, "Hybrists" • Marshall, "Invective" • H. W. Merritt, *In Word and Deed: Moral Integrity in Paul* (New York: Lang, 1993) 111-52 • Murphy-O'Connor 99-103 • Murphy-O'Connor, "Date" • Oostendorp 17-30 • Peterson 75-93, 148-51 • Sampley, "Opponents" • Savage 64-80 • Schmithals 176-79 • Schütz • Spencer, "Irony" • Strecker • Sumney 149-79 • Sumney, *Servants* 102-33 • Travis • Vielhauer 72-78 • F. Watson • V. Weber, "Erklärung von 2 Kor. 10,1-6," *BZ* 1 (1903) 64-78 • Welborn 77-94 • Welborn, "Identification" • Wilckens 46-47

2. Legitimate Spheres of Activity and Boasting (10:12-18)

There are two noteworthy features in this paragraph. One is the high number of repeated words or phrases, repetitions that point to the central issues at stake in Paul's contest with his opponents. The other feature is the frequent use of the

703

negative οὐ, from which we may deduce the activities of Paul's rivals that he categorically rejects.

Repetition

οὐ . . . ἀλλά (13)	οὐ . . . ἀλλά (18)
συγκρῖναι ἑαυτούς (12)	συγκρίνοντες ἑαυτούς (12)
τῶν ἑαυτοὺς συνιστανόντων (12)	ὁ ἑαυτὸν συνιστάνων (18)
οὐκ εἰς τὰ ἄμετρα καυχησόμεθα (13)	οὐκ εἰς τὰ ἄμετρα καυχώμενοι (15)
κατὰ τὸ μέτρον τοῦ κανόνος οὗ	κατὰ τὸν κανόνα ἡμῶν (15)
ἐμέρισεν ἡμῖν ὁ θεὸς μέτρου (13)	
ἐφικέσθαι ἄχρι καὶ ὑμῶν (13)	(ὡς μὴ) ἐφικνούμενοι εἰς ὑμᾶς (14)
ἄχρι καὶ ὑμῶν (13)	ἄχρι . . . καὶ ὑμῶν (14)
ἐν ἀλλοτρίοις κόποις (15)	ἐν ἀλλοτρίῳ κανόνι (16)

Negative (οὐ[1])

In reference to Paul	In reference to Paul's rivals
οὐ . . . τολμῶμεν (12)	οὐ συνιᾶσιν (12)
οὐκ . . . καυχησόμεθα (13)	οὐ . . . ὁ ἑαυτὸν συνιστάνων (18)
οὐ . . . ὑπερεκτείνομεν ἑαυτούς (14)	
οὐκ . . . καυχώμενοι (15)	
οὐκ ἐν ἀλλοτρίῳ κανόνι καυχήσασθαι (16)	

When combined, these two stylistic features suggest that the essence of the paragraph is as follows. Certain persons had invaded Paul's legitimate jurisdiction or sphere of activity in Corinth and were commending themselves on the basis of work that he had done in Corinth and were therefore boasting outside proper limits. In repudiating their invasion of territory that was foreign to them but "home" to him, Paul rejects: comparison with those who indulge in self-promotion (v. 12); boasting beyond proper limits (vv. 13, 15); overreaching God-appointed limits (v. 14); boasting of work done in another's sphere of activity (v. 16); self-commendation (v. 18; cf. v. 12). Although Paul refers explicitly — but still anonymously — to these intruders only in v. 13 (τισὶν κτλ.), they are principally in his mind as he seeks to supply the Corinthians with reliable criteria for determining who has legitimate authority within their congregation. Having reassured his converts of the reality and potency of his apostolic authority in general (10:1-11), Paul now proceeds to establish, against the counterclaim of his rivals, that this authority of his is legitimately exercised in Corinth, since Corinth was his area of work and influence, his assignment allotted to him by God, and God had confirmed this assignment by prospering his pioneer preaching in the city. The undeniably awkward syntax of parts of this paragraph (vv. 13, 15-16) is testimony to Paul's emotional intensity as he vigorously defends the territory that he regarded as "home soil."

---

1. In v. 14 the negated participle (μὴ ἐφικνούμενοι) is qualified by ὡς ("as if").

10:12*True, we lack the boldness to classify or compare ourselves with any of those who commend themselves. But when they measure themselves against one another and compare themselves with one another, they lack understanding.*[a] 13*We, however, will not boast*[b] *beyond proper limits but will take as a limit for our boasting the assignment that God has allocated to us as a limit, an assignment that certainly reaches as far as you.* 14*For we are not*[c] *overreaching our limit, as if it does not reach to you, for we were the first to come even as far as you with the gospel of Christ.* 15*We do not boast beyond proper limits in the labors of others. But we do have the hope that as your faith goes on increasing, with your aid our work may be enlarged — in accordance with our assignment — until it overflows.* 16*That is, we hope to preach the gospel in areas beyond you, without boasting about work already done in someone else's assigned area.* 17*Rather, "Let the one who boasts, boast in the Lord."* 18*For it is not the person who commends*[d] *himself who is approved, but the person whom the Lord commends.*

TEXTUAL NOTES

a. There are two main readings: (1) a longer reading, οὐ συνιᾶσιν. ἡμεῖς δέ ("... they lack understanding. But we ..."), supported by both proto-Alexandrian (p[46] B 1739) and later Alexandrian (H[vid] 0243 33 81 104 1175 1881) witnesses and preferred by NA[27], UBS[1, 2, 3] with a "C" rating (= considerable doubt), and UBS[4] with a "B" rating (= almost certain) and most translations and commentators; and (2) a shorter reading that omits these four Greek words and is supported by mainly Western witnesses (D* F G it[ar, b, d, f, g, o] vg[ms] Ps-Cyprian Ambrosiaster Varimadum) and is preferred by some commentators (e.g., Windisch 309; Käsemann 56-57; Héring 73; Bultmann 192-93; *Probleme* 21; also Moffatt; BDF §416[2]). The sense of the Western text will be (reading the participles μετροῦντες and συγκρίνοντες in v. 12b as first person, referring to Paul): "When/Though we measure ourselves against ourselves and compare ourselves with ourselves (i.e., in relation to our God-given commission; cf. v. 13), we will not be boasting beyond proper limits. . . ." Apart from the weaker external support for this shorter, Western reading (the reading ἡμεῖς δέ [it[s] vg Pelagius] "appears to be an imperfect restoration of the shortened text," Metzger 514), it presents several difficulties: (i) the notion of valid self-assessment using standards of one's own making is strange, and it is not likely that ἐν ἑαυτοῖς could carry the sense "by the standard God has given us"; (ii) as a strong adversative, ἀλλά coheres better with a dramatic "we–they" contrast than with a contrast between types of comparison, one that Paul rejects (v. 12a) and one that he undertakes (v. 12b).

There are two further variants, both derived from the longer, Alexandrian reading. ℵ* 88 read συνίσασιν (from σύνοιδα, "be aware of") in place of συνιᾶσιν (from συνίημι, "understand"); thus "they are unaware [that they do so]." This is clearly a transcriptional error; in any case, such a concession on Paul's part would be out of keeping with his aggressive stance toward his opponents. The other variation of the Alexandrian reading is συνιοῦσιν (instead of συνιᾶσιν) (D[2] Ψ 075 0150 0209[vid] 6 256 263 365 424 436 459 1241 1319 1573 1852 [1912] 2127 2200 *Byz* [K L P] *Lect* Chrysostom Augustine), simply an alternative spelling. (It is extremely unlikely that συνιουσιν should be read as a dative plural (συνίουσιν), "but we . . . unwise as we are [in their estimation]" — see Plummer 285).

Versional evidence (it^r vg^{mss} syr$^{p, h}$ cop$^{sa, bo}$ arm geo slav) could support either συνίουσιν or συνιᾶσιν. The omission of οὐ before συνίουσιν. ἡμεῖς δέ in 1603 is obviously accidental.

The longer reading is to be preferred since (i) it has stronger external support; (ii) there are contextual difficulties with the shorter reading (see above); (iii) the longer reading more easily accounts for the rise of all the variants than does the shorter reading (which itself probably arose either as a transcriptional accident when a copyist's eye passed from οὐ to οὐκ and the intervening words were omitted [thus Metzger 514] or as an effort to remove the harsh οὐ συνιᾶσιν. See further the discussions of Wong 97-103 and especially Thrall 636-39, both of whom opt for the longer reading).

b. F G a read καυχώμενοι in place of καυχησόμεθα, under the influence of v. 15 where the same phrase (οὐκ εἰς τὰ ἄμετρα) as in v. 13 precedes the verb. D* omits any verb.

c. We may account for the reading in B (ὡς γάρ) by supposing that a scribe omitted οὐ from the phrase οὐ γὰρ ὡς μὴ ἐφικνούμενοι to avoid an apparent double negative (οὐ . . . μή) and then transposed γάρ into its usual second place. The sentence would then be a question: "For are we overreaching ourselves . . . ?"

d. Instead of συνιστάνων (read by p^{46} ℵ B D* F G H I^{vid} P 021 0243 6 33 81 104 365 1175 1505 1739 2464 al), D^2 Ψ 1881 𝔐 read συνιστῶν, the participle of a less common form (συνιστάω) of the verb συνιστάνω (see BAGD 790c and comparable variants at 4:2; 6:4).

10:12 Οὐ γὰρ τολμῶμεν ἐγκρῖναι ἢ συγκρῖναι ἑαυτούς τισιν τῶν ἑαυτοὺς συνιστανόντων. "True, we lack the boldness to classify or compare ourselves with any of those who commend themselves." Of the three main themes in 10:12-18 — commendation, boasting, and territoriality — vv. 12 and 18 mention the first theme (τῶν ἑαυτοὺς συνιστανόντων . . . ὁ ἑαυτὸν συνιστάνων . . . συνίστησιν) and enclose the section (vv. 13-17) that deals with illegitimate and legitimate boasting and with territorial rights at Corinth. γάρ may be simply transitional ("Now," "Well"), equivalent to δέ (so BAGD 152c; Zerwick §473), but in the context it is more probably affirmative ("No doubt," Cassirer; "indeed," Goodspeed; "True"). Paul is conceding (cf. Wong 79-83, 112) that there is one respect in which his accusers are right when they consider him "timid" (ταπεινός, v. 1): He lacks the audacity (οὐ . . . τολμῶμεν) to include himself in the same class (ἐγκρῖναι) as certain self-promoters or even (ἢ) to compare (συγκρῖναι) himself with them. In Paul the verb τολμάω ranges in meaning from acting with impropriety ("presume"; e.g., 1 Cor. 6:1) to having the courage to act ("be bold"; e.g., Phil. 1:14). This latter sense is appropriate here where, with exquisite irony, Paul draws back from taking that same audacious action (τολμῆσαι) that he had promised to show (10:2) and later does show (11:21).[2] Yet along with the irony of feigned timidity, Paul is presenting himself as a man of moderation and restraint — those essential Greek virtues — who avoids immoderate boasting or inordinate claims (cf. οὐκ εἰς τὰ ἄμετρα . . . ἀλλὰ κατὰ τὸ μέτρον . . . , v. 13).[3] Both ἐγκρίνω and συγκρίνω are followed by the τινά τινι

2. On irony in Paul, see Reumann, "Irony"; and n. 32 in the section 11:16-21a.
3. Cf. Marshall 200-201, 366-69.

("someone with something") construction; here ἑαυτούς[4] τισιν. ῎Εγκρῖναι is to adjudge as being *within* [ἐν] the class of, and thus as being on an equality with, someone or something else. Συγκρῖναι is to judge in company *with* [σύν] someone or something else, and thus to compare for purposes of classification" (Hughes 364 n. 21).[5] In Paul's day "comparison" (σύγκρισις) was an accepted convention in Greek education, in public dialogue, and in historiography.[6] Sophists, for example, in their eagerness to attract students or lure them away from rival teachers, would not hesitate to engage in σύγκρισις.[7] Presumably Paul's opponents had been making some comparisons between themselves and him.[8] Paul withdraws from any such contest, knowing that comparison with those he considered inferior in certain regards was as foolish as comparison with those who might be superior. It would only be "as a fool" (ἐν ἀφροσύνῃ, 11:17, 21) that he would stoop to engage in comparisons (11:21b–12:11).

With the expression τισὶν τῶν ἑαυτοὺς συνιστανόντων Paul refers for the fifth time in this chapter (cf. vv. 2, 7, 10-11) to the beliefs or actions of certain nameless individuals at Corinth.[9] As in v. 7, the reference is probably only to the intruders, not also to those disaffected Corinthians who made up the other segment in the anti-Pauline alliance. If the genitive is possessive, the sense will be "certain people who belong to the class of self-commenders" (cf. Moffatt; Meyer 627); if epexegetic, "those who rate themselves so highly" (GNB); if partitive, "some of those who commend themselves" (Martin 314), or "any of those who put forward their own claims" (NEB). By τῶν ἑαυτοὺς συνιστανόντων Paul is likely to be referring to any members of a specific group at Corinth, not to self-commenders in general, nor to all his opponents as self-commenders, nor to a clearly defined subset of self-praisers. Paul knows of two types of "self-commendation," one positive and one negative (see on v. 18), and here he is alluding to illegitimate self-praise that aims at impressing others by exalting one's self, one's pedigree, abilities, and achievements (cf. 11:13, 18, 21-23). In the an-

4. For this use of ἑαυτούς in reference to the first person plural (= ἡμᾶς αὐτούς), see Turner 42; Zerwick §209.

5. Various efforts have been made to reproduce the wordplay (on κρίνω) in translation: "pair or compare" (Plummer 285), "compete or compare" (Hughes 364 n. 21, noting that ἐγκρίνω was also used of admitting athletes as competitors), *aequiparare aut comparare* (cf. Zerwick, *Analysis* 408), and "zuzurechnen oder gleichzurechnen" (de Boor 205).

6. See Betz, *Paulus* 119-20; Marshall 53-55, 348-53; Forbes 2-8.

7. Forbes (7) cites a first-century letter written by a student to his father in which he complains that his teacher, one Didymus, who used to be a mere provincial teacher, "sees fit to enter into comparison (εἰς σύγκρισιν)" with more able teachers (P. Oxy. 2190, lines 23-28).

8. According to Forbes (15-16), the anti-Pauline polemic of the "united front" of Judaizing interlopers and Corinthian anti-Paulinists included the charge that Paul was inconsistent (cf. 10:1, 7-11) and hence a flatterer (κόλαξ), and possibly also insincere and hence a dissimulator (εἴρων), someone who pretends to be less than he is. This polemic "also took the form of studied mutual comparisons among the leaders of the alliance, most probably in terms of friendly rivalry and mutual esteem, while the real cutting edge of the comparisons was directed against Paul" (15, citing [28 n. 74] 10:12-13).

9. On the rhetorical technique of not naming one's adversaries, see Marshall 341-48.

cient world, however, self-praise was regarded as justified not only if one needed to defend one's reputation or answer accusations but also if the self-adulation afforded a model for people to follow, thus stimulating excellence.[10]

ἀλλὰ αὐτοὶ ἐν ἑαυτοῖς ἑαυτοὺς μετροῦντες καὶ συγκρίνοντες ἑαυτοὺς ἑαυτοῖς οὐ συνιᾶσιν. "But when they measure themselves against one another and compare themselves with one another, they lack understanding." The thrust of Paul's charge seems to be this. One aspect of his rivals' self-praise (τῶν ἑαυτοὺς συνιστανόντων, v. 12a) involved making measurements (μετροῦντες) and comparisons (συγκρίνοντες) within their own limited circle of like-minded people (ἐν ἑαυτοῖς . . . ἑαυτοῖς) as a means of validating their ministry at Corinth in the eyes of the Corinthians. But to be valid, any measurement or comparison of abilities or achievements requires some external criteria as a basis for evaluation. It is a senseless undertaking (οὐ συνιᾶσιν) to act as your own appraiser or write your own testimonial and then congratulate yourself on the splendid appraisal or the glowing reference.

The strong contrast signified by ἀλλά is that between Paul's rejection of comparisons (v. 12a) and his opponents' approval of them (v. 12b); the verb συγκρίνω is the element common to both parts of the verse.[11] There is no need to render αὐτοί by "(they) themselves" since this use may reflect the strengthening of the reflexive by αὐτός that is common in Attic Greek (BDF §283[4], citing 10:12). Ἐν ἑαυτοῖς . . . ἑαυτοῖς could be translated "by themselves . . . with themselves" (RV, NIV), but these may be instances where the reflexive pronoun (ἑαυτοῖς) is used for the reciprocal pronoun (ἀλλήλοις);[12] thus "by one another . . . with one another" (RSV, NRSV). Either way, ἐν is instrumental, indicating the standard of measurement used. It makes little difference to the sense whether we understand the two coordinated participles (μετροῦντες καὶ συγκρίνοντες) as temporal ("when they measure . . ."; e.g., RSV), or modal ("by/in measuring . . ."; e.g., Carrez 204), or even causal ("because they measure . . ."; e.g., Wong 109), but the temporal sense is preferable (as, e.g., in NIV; Lambrecht 163).[13] With the expression μετρέω ἐν ("measure by the standard of") Paul introduces a central issue in this paragraph: What is an appropriate standard of measurement for determining ministry rights at Corinth? This motif of measurement recurs in the phrase εἰς τὰ ἄμετρα (vv. 13, 15) and in the two uses of μέτρον in v. 13. οὐ συνιᾶσιν, "they lack understanding," may be litotes for "they are fools"

10. See the ancient literature cited by Fitzgerald 109 nn. 176-77, Forbes 8-10, and Heckel 145-59, especially Plutarch's *On Inoffensive Self-Praise* (on which see Marshall 353-54 and Betz, *Paulus* 75-79; "De Laude" 367-93).

11. On the Western text that relates both parts of v. 12 to Paul, see Textual Note a. above.

12. For this usage see BDF §287; Robertson 690; Moule 120; Turner 43-44. Col. 3:13 is a classic instance (ἀνεχόμενοι ἀλλήλων καὶ χαριζόμενοι ἑαυτοῖς).

13. But Turner construes these participles as predicative: "they do not realize that they are measuring themselves by their own standards . . ." (160). The word order counts against this construal; the contrast (ἀλλά) between Paul and his rivals is blunted; and it is unlikely that they would be unaware of engaging in σύγκρισις. Moreover, there is no difficulty with an absolute use of συνίημι (see, e.g., Mark 7:14; 8:17, 21; Rom. 3:11; 15:21).

or "How stupid they are!" (GNB).[14] However that be, the contrast between οὐ συνιᾶσιν and the earlier οὐ . . . τολμῶμεν is stark. Paul showed merely lack of "courage"; his rivals show lack of sense. Better to be without audacity than to be without rationality! But a further implication may be present. If the Corinthians tried to assess Paul's credentials against the artificial and subjective criteria used by his detractors,[15] they too would be guilty of sheer folly.

This verse contains two rhetorical flourishes: the repetition of the prefix σύν (συγκρῖναι — συνιστανόντων . . . συγκρίνοντες . . . συνιᾶσιν) and an ABCC′B′A′ chiasm (ἑαυτοῖς ἑαυτοὺς μετροῦντες . . . συγκρίνοντες ἑαυτοὺς ἑαυτοῖς). By such skill with words Paul prompts the imagination to consider what he will do with comparable action, given his assurance in the previous verse (v. 11) that his actions will correspond to his words (cf. Danker 158).

10:13 ἡμεῖς δὲ οὐκ εἰς τὰ ἄμετρα καυχησόμεθα, ἀλλὰ κατὰ τὸ μέτρον τοῦ κανόνος οὗ ἐμέρισεν ἡμῖν ὁ θεὸς μέτρου, ἐφικέσθαι ἄχρι καὶ ὑμῶν. "We, however, will not boast beyond proper limits but will take as a limit for our boasting the assignment that God has allocated to us as a limit, an assignment that certainly reaches as far as you." If the link between the two parts of v. 12 was the verb συγκρίνω, the bond between v. 12 and v. 13 is the idea of measurement. Paul's antagonists were measuring (μετροῦντες) themselves against a false standard of measurement — "themselves," (ἐν) ἑαυτοῖς, v. 12 — and were boasting "beyond proper limits" (εἰς τὰ ἄμετρα). Paul, however (ἡμεῖς δέ, "But we," "As for us, however" [GNB] is contrasted with αὐτοί), restricted his boasting to a limit (κατὰ τὸ μέτρον . . . μέτρου) fixed by God's assignment of his distinctive sphere of service. V. 12b implies that to reject external criteria for evaluating authenticity is to think irrationally. By way of contrast, Paul now presents an external, rational criterion, namely God's meting out to him a particular assignment for his ministry, a field that included Corinth.

In the adjective ἄμετρος the alpha privative need not be pressed to give the meaning "not able to be measured," "immeasurable." The sense can also be "not keeping to a particular or due limit (μέτρον)." Accordingly, the prepositional phrase εἰς τὰ ἄμετρα need not mean "to a limitless degree," but rather "immoderately" (Marshall 368), or "beyond limits" (BAGD 45c; NRSV), that is, beyond particular or appropriate limits ("due limits," Weymouth, Cassirer; "proper limits," NIV; Martin 314). If Paul is saying "I shall avoid excessive or immoderate boasting," there may be a further allusion (cf. οὐ . . . τολμῶμεν, v. 12) to his being a man of moderation, one who adhered to the celebrated maxim μηδὲν ἄγαν (Pindar, *Fragment* 216) (Latin *ne quid nimis*), "nothing too much," that is to say, "everything in moderation."[16] But Paul's main point here is not his adherence to a Greek ideal but the confinement of his boasting to appropriate limits. He would be transgressing such limits if he boasted about another person's work (ἐν

14. On the possible backgrounds to this use of συνίημι, see Wong 110-12, 113.
15. What these criteria might have been is discussed by Thrall 641-42.
16. Cf. Betz, *Paulus* 130-31.

ἀλλοτρίοις κόποις, v. 15) or invaded another person's territorial assignment (ἐν ἀλλοτρίῳ κανόνι, v. 16). Positively, he would be keeping to due limits if his boasting was restricted to what God had apportioned as his lot (v. 13b). We propose, then, that the meaning of εἰς τὰ ἄμετρα should be determined by the immediate context, although Paul would probably not be averse to being seen as a person of moderation (cf. Phil. 4:5), provided moderation was not regarded as incompatible with passionate devotion to Christ. When the apostle affirms that he will not exceed due limits in his boasting, he implies that some boasting is legitimate, but it is not until v. 17 that he states what makes boasting permissible — it must be "in the Lord" (ἐν κυρίῳ), that is, about the character and actions of the Lord, including his achievements in and through the lives of his servants.[17] That Paul's rivals were boasting is explicitly stated in 11:12, 18. But here in ch. 10 Paul implies that their boasting was beyond due limit since it was centered on themselves (v. 12a), not the Lord (cf. vv. 17-18), it lacked a divine standard and divine authorization (v. 13), and it concerned work accomplished by others (Paul) (v. 15) in foreign territory (Paul's) (v. 16).

As opposed to boasting beyond appropriate limits, Paul was adhering to a limit in his boasting, which he now proceeds to discuss. After ἀλλά we must supply either the present tense καυχώμεθα, or from v. 13a the future καυχησόμεθα (as Wolff 204).[18] The appropriate limit is boasting that is κατὰ τὸ μέτρον.[19] Basically the term μέτρον refers to the "measure" or standard by which something is measured, or, by metonymy, what is measured by that measure or standard, "the measured part." The meaning "limit" (see LSJ 1123 s.v. 3.b.) arises naturally, because sometimes the standard of measurement or what is measured forms a boundary (in a literal or figurative sense) beyond which it is not permissible or legitimate to go.[20] To translate μέτρον here by "limit"[21] or "limits"[22] seems very appropriate, for it reflects the verbal link with the preceding expression εἰς τὰ ἄμετρα, which we have rendered "beyond proper limits." But the crucial question is: How are the two terms μέτρον and κανών in the

---

17. See further on v. 17. Paul saw that his indulging in "foolish boasting" (11:16–12:10) did not follow the Christian way of boasting (οὐ κατὰ κύριον) (11:16-17) but was a regrettable necessity (12:11), given the practice of his rivals of engaging in self-praise and the propensity of the Corinthians to be dazzled by their verbal bravado.

18. Barrett (265, followed by Furnish 471) gives ἀλλά the sense "but only" on the basis of the usage ἀλλά = εἰ μή ("except") (see, e.g., BDF §448[8]) or ἀλλά = ἀλλ' ἤ ("except") (LSJ 68 s.v. ἀλλά I.3). But the presence of εἰς τὰ ἄμετρα in v. 13a makes the sense "except" difficult, although "but only" is suitable.

19. But Héring (73; similarly NJB, but cf. JB) converts κατὰ τὸ μέτρον into a verbal concept: "we shall measure."

20. The expression ἐμαυτὸν μετρῶ (Ignatius, Trallians 4:1), (literally) "I take the measure of myself," means "I keep myself within bounds" (BAGD 514d).

21. Berkeley, Cassirer.

22. TCNT, Weymouth, Moffatt, Montgomery, Williams, GNB; Plummer 285. Sometimes "limits" is used to render the whole expression τὸ μέτρον τοῦ κανόνος (Goodspeed, RSV, NAB²; cf. BAGD 515b).

phrase τὸ μέτρον τοῦ κανόνος related, when each of them can mean "rule" or "limit"? We must therefore discuss the meaning of κανών and the function of the genitive τοῦ κανόνος.

The word κανών, which is closely related to the Hebrew *qāneh* ("reed," "rod"), basically refers to a straight rod or rule used as a measure or as a test of straightness.[23] It occurs only three times in the LXX, in reference to a philosophical rule or principle (4 Macc. 7:21), the rail of a bed or the bedpost (Judg. 13:6), or a rigid rule by which someone acts (Mic. 7:4). In the NT it is an exclusively Pauline word, found in Gal. 6:16 of the "rule" or norm or principle of newness in Christ (Gal. 6:15) that is to regulate Christian conduct, and the other three times are in vv. 13, 15 and 16 of 2 Corinthians 10. The wide variety of proposed meanings for the term in 10:13 (apart from "rule" or "standard") may be grouped under five categories with regard to conceptual background. Many translations have variations in vv. 15 and 16.

1. Carpentry:
   yardstick (JB)
   Massstab ("yardstick," "measuring rod") (Lietzmann 142; Schatter 624; Lang 332)
   Richtschnur ("plumb line," "guiding principle") (Wendland 231; de Boor 205)
2. Surveying:
   "measuring line" (Vincent 835).[24]
3. Athletics:
   "lane" (Hughes 366-67).[25]
4. Territory:
   "sphere" (TCNT, Weymouth, NEB(?), NASB, Barclay, REB(?), Cassirer[26]
   "province" (RV; LSJ 875 s.v. II.5.b;[27] Metzger, *Canon* 290; Barrett 265, 268; Wong 134-35)
   "limit" (BAGD 504d, 515b; cf. 403a; Spicq 2.301 n. 24).

---

23. In the second century κανών came to refer to the "rule of faith" (revealed truth), and in the fourth century, a normative list of books recognized as authoritative for Christians ("canon"). On the history of the term, see Metzger, *Canon,* Appendix I (289-93).

24. "The image is that of surveying a district, so as to assign to different persons their different parcels of ground" (Vincent 834; similarly Lightfoot, *Galatians* 224).

25. Hughes believes κανών refers to the lane that was measured out and marked for each runner. In support he cites a phrase in the second-century-A.D. grammarian Julius Pollux, *Onomasticon* 3.15 (LSJ 875 gives the reference as 3.151), τὸ μέτρον τοῦ πηδήματος κανών, which we might render "a lane is the width of a leap." Hughes finds an athletic metaphor also in the terms ἐγκρῖναι ("compete," v. 12) (364 n. 21) and μεγαλυνθῆναι ("enlargement" of the track [τὸν κανόνα], v. 15) (368-69 n. 28).

26. All of these translations use the word "sphere" in vv. 13, 15, and 16. NRSV has "sphere of action" in vv. 15-16 (RSV has "field" in these two verses).

27. "Sphere of action" is also given as a meaning.

5. Administration:
   "jurisdiction" (Furnish 471; Witherington 440 n. 46; Scott 198)
   "competence" (Lambrecht 165)
   "specifications" (Carrez 204, 206, *cahier des charges*)
   "schedule of services" (Strange)
   "territorial schedule" (Thrall 635, 647)[28]
   "assignment" (BAGD 507-8 [2000 edition])

The strongest candidates for consideration are found in the last two categories, territory and administration. There are several indicators in vv. 13-16 of location and movement which would support territorial overtones in the word κανών: ἐφικέσθαι ἄχρι καὶ ὑμῶν (v. 13), ἐφικνούμενοι εἰς ὑμᾶς . . . ἄχρι γὰρ καὶ ὑμῶν ἐφθάσαμεν (v. 14), εἰς τὰ ὑπερέκεινα ὑμῶν . . . ἐν ἀλλοτρίῳ κανόνι (v. 16). There is also the likelihood that as he writes vv. 13-16 Paul has in mind the "missionary concordat" of Gal. 2:7-9.[29] Although, technically, this accord referred to an ethnic not a geographical distinction (ἡμεῖς εἰς τὰ ἔθνη, αὐτοὶ δὲ εἰς τὴν περιτομήν, Gal. 2:9), it was probably understood by Paul as reflecting a mainly geographical division of missionary labor.[30] He doubtless realized that there were ambiguities in the accord — there were Gentiles in Palestine and Jews in the Diaspora — but if he saw the agreement, sealed with handshakes of friendship and partnership (Gal. 2:9), as ratifying principal emphases in missionary endeavor, he could well have regarded the arrival and activity in Corinth of missionaries from Judea as a breach of the intent of the agreement. After all, Corinth was a predominantly Gentile city and had now been evangelized in accordance with the letter of the Jerusalem concordat. Moreover, these missionaries were not in Corinth to support Paul (as Apollos had been, 1 Cor. 3:5-6) but to supplant him. All of this suggests that investing κανών with a territorial or geographical sense — whether "sphere" or "province" or "limit" — is permissible in the present context.

28. In v. 15 Thrall renders κανών by "schedule," in v. 16 by "scheduled area."

29. Numbers of scholars see this concordat as being in the background of Paul's discussion in 10:12-18. E.g., Barrett 265; "Opponents" 65; "Christianity" 294; Bruce 234; Martin 317, 325; "Theology" 67-68, 79; Barnett 485; "Opposition" 13-14; Thrall 646. Furnish's two objections to this view (472) — that the term κανών is not found in Gal. 2:1-10 and that nothing in 2 Corinthians 10 requires that Paul has this missionary concordat in mind — fall short of being conclusive. A stronger but still not compelling objection is expressed by Hafemann when he claims that "the two passages are not dealing with the same issue: Galatians 2:7-10 concerns respective spheres of ministry, whereas 2 Corinthians 10:13-16 concerns apostolic authority in a particular local church" (419).

30. See Bruce, *History* 270; *Galatians* 125; *Paul* 154-55. Evidence for this lies in at least three directions. (1) At the time of his conversion Paul sensed a call to both Gentiles *and* Jews (Acts 9:15; 22:15, 21; 26:17). (2) He sought to evangelize both groups (cf. Rom. 1:12), his policy being to use the synagogue as a base for his evangelistic efforts in Gentile cities (e.g., Acts 18:1-11). (3) When he speaks in Romans 15 of fulfilling his divinely given commission, he declares that he no longer has any scope for pioneer evangelism in the regions "from Jerusalem all the way around to Illyricum" (Rom. 15:19, 23) and states his intent to move on to Spain via Rome (Rom. 15:24, 28). Throughout his missionary career Paul's strategic planning was geographical in orientation.

Strong support for an administrative sense comes from a first-century-A.D. bilingual (Latin and Greek) inscription from Pisidia in which κανών signifies an official "schedule" in regard to regional responsibilities for providing billeting and transport services for officials of the empire (Horsley 1.36-45). In his comment on the inscription Judge observes that "the κανών in itself is not a geographical concept but the services it formulates are in this case geographically partitioned." As Paul uses the term, it refers to the territorial commitment that God had measured out for him ("κανών" 45). On the basis of the same inscription Strange concludes that in 2 Corinthians 10 κανών signifies a schedule of services (preaching the gospel in Paul's case) to be performed within a designated territory (168), and the 2000 edition of BAGD classifies the three uses of κανών in 2 Corinthians 10 under the heading "set of directions or formulation for an activity" (507-8), gives the meanings as "assignment" and "formulation," and asserts that in 2 Corinthians κανών denotes "the mission assignment given to Paul, which included directions about geographical area" (508, citing Strange 167-68 and de Oliveira 141-42 n. 306).

We propose that the word "domain" is an apt rendering of κανών in all three verses (vv. 13, 15, 16) where it appears in 2 Corinthians 10, but that "assignment" is an even better choice, although in v. 16 "assigned area" is probably a necessary variation.[31]

In the phrase κατὰ τὸ μέτρον τοῦ κανόνος, the genitive can be construed in two ways.[32]

1. As *epexegetic:* "taking for our measure the yardstick . . ." (JB), "according to the limit, namely the assignment. . . ."[33] Probably to be included here are those translations that render the expression τὸ μέτρον τοῦ κανόνος by a single word — such as "limits" (Goodspeed, RSV, NAB²), "field" (NIV, NRSV), "bounds" (NAB¹), or "criterion" (Young and Ford 272).
2. As *subjective:* "the measure given by the drawn measuring-line" (Meyer 630), "the limit determined by our specifications *(cahier des charges)*" (Carrez 204).[34]

Before we can make a decision on this point we must consider other grammatical issues in this verse.

31. Witherington believes that "the translation 'jurisdiction' best conveys both the idea of geographical limits and the idea of an area of service" (440 n. 46). But just as the rendering "specification" has strong mathematical associations, and "schedule" has timetabling connotations (as least in the U.S.A.), so "jurisdiction" has inapplicable legal overtones.

32. In a translation such as "according to the measure of the province" (RV), it is unclear whether the genitive τοῦ κανόνος has been seen as possessive, subjective, or epexegetic.

33. Similarly Lambrecht 166.

34. Also taking τοῦ κανόνος as a subjective genitive are H. W. Beyer, *TDNT* 3.599 n. 12; Vincent 835; Schlatter 624; Bultmann 194; Hafemann 403.

First, the antecedent of οὗ is more probably κανόνος,[35] the nearer noun, than μέτρον, the more distant noun. It is easier to imagine that ὅν (referring to κανόνος) has been attracted into the case of its immediate antecedent (τοῦ κανόνος) than that ὅ (referring to μέτρον) has been attracted into the case of a word (τοῦ κανόνος) that is not its actual antecedent.

Second, μέτρου stands in apposition to οὗ (Hughes 367 n. 26). This simple explanation of the case of μέτρου seems preferable to the suggestion that μέτρου is attracted (? from μέτρον) into the case of the relative (Robertson 719) or that "οὗ is probably attracted from ὅ (referring to μέτρον) to κανόνος and then μέτρου repeated, lest οὗ be referred to κανόνος" (BDF §294[5]).[36] If, then, μέτρου is appositive and οὗ refers to κανόνος, Paul is equating μέτρον and κανών, so that the genitive in the phrase τὸ μέτρον τοῦ κανόνος will be epexegetic (option #1 above).

Third, the repetition of μετροῦ simply establishes the point that the limit Paul carefully adheres to (cf. κατά) in his boasting is precisely the same limit as God set when he allocated to Paul his "assignment."

In the present context the aorist ἐμέρισεν points to a specific time when God allocated to Paul a distinctive share (μερίς) in his distribution of responsibilities within the church.[37] This divine allotment to Paul occurred at the time of his conversion when he was commissioned to preach Christ among the Gentiles (Gal. 1:16; cf. 2:7-8),[38] but this commissioning was subsequently recognized and endorsed by the "pillars" of the Jerusalem church (James, Cephas, and John) in the accord of Gal. 2:9.[39] We may therefore define Paul's distinctive "assignment" (κανών) as the preaching of Christ throughout the Gentile world,[40] provided that (1) we understand that preaching broadly as "fulfilling the gospel of Christ" (Rom. 15:19) by initial evangelizing and the subsequent nurture of converts and establishment of churches;[41] and (2) we recognize that the evangelization of his fellow Jews was not outside his "assignment," even if it formed a subsidiary aspect (see n. 30).[42]

---

35. So Zerwick, *Analysis* 409 and, it would seem, most EVV.

36. The same reasoning is found in Zerwick and Grosvenor 555; so also Turner 324; Barrett 266; Furnish 472; Wolff 204 and n. 75. NAB[1] cuts the Gordian knot by rendering ὁ θεὸς μέτρου, "the God of moderation" (cf. NIV mg. "the God of measures"), an altogether improbable solution.

37. For the construction μερίζω τινί τι, "apportion something (here, ὅν attracted to become οὗ) to someone (here, ἡμῖν)," cf. Rom. 12:3; 1 Cor. 7:17; Heb. 7:2.

38. See Kim 56-66.

39. So also Allo 251; Barnett 485.

40. For a parallel to this idea of an allotted κανών, see *1 Clement* 41:1 where each believer is encouraged "not to overstep the appointed assignment/domain of his/her ministry (μὴ παρεκβαίνων τὸν ὡρισμένον τῆς λειτουργίας αὐτοῦ κανόνα)." In *1 Clement* 1:3 (ἐν τῷ κανόνι τῆς ὑποταγῆς) κανών may bear the sense "assignment" (as BAGD [2000 edition] 507) or "rule."

41. Cf. O'Brien, *Mission* 38-43.

42. According to J. Guhrt and H.-G. Link, κανών in 2 Corinthians 10 "stands for the rule that Paul is active wherever the gospel has not yet been proclaimed (cf. Rom. 15:20f.)" (*NIDNTT* 3.400). Similarly, Marshall believes that the "calling to which he [Paul] limits himself [in 2 Cor. 10:16] is to found and build up churches in areas where other apostles have not been" (370).

The distinctive nature of Paul's assignment is reflected in the juxtaposition of ὑμῖν and ὁ θεός. The apostle is not comparing two separate but complementary assignments, his own and that of his opponents. Nothing is said of their κανών. In fact, 11:13-15 suggests that he would have emphatically denied that they, as purveyors of a false gospel (11:4; cf. 2:17), had a legitimate sphere of activity among any Christian congregations. As opposed to his adversaries who were using one another as the standard of measurement for determining authenticity (10:12), "a human and self-determined standard" (Lietzmann 143), Paul could appeal to an external criterion that was determined by God, the "assignment" that God had allotted him. The irony of the situation was that the person (Paul) who was judged to be living and behaving on a purely natural level (κατὰ σάρκα, 10:2) in fact was living within God's limits (μέτρον), while those who commended themselves in fact were boasting on a purely natural level (κατὰ σάρκα, 11:18).[43]

Some commentators regard the infinitive ἐφικέσθαι as telic ("so that we might reach [as far as you]");[44] others view it as consecutive ("with the result that we reached").[45] In each case this aorist infinitive is probably loosely attached to ἐμέρισεν, another aorist. But if the concept of κανών is the central feature of v. 13, it is preferable to see ἐφικέσθαι as epexegetic,[46] simultaneously illustrating and restricting the term κανών.[47] In the concluding phrase ἄχρι καὶ ὑμῶν, the adverb ἄχρι has an inclusive sense, "up to and including," "as far as" (BAGD 128d), "all the way to," while καί is emphatic, "indeed," "certainly." Paul is observing that his assignment "certainly reaches as far as" the Corinthians. At present they may represent the extreme limit, geographically speaking, in the outworking of his assignment, but they assuredly fell within the boundaries of his κανών.[48] "Paul's reasoning moves from a general (i.e., the gentiles

---

43. Cf. Harada 151.

44. E.g., Barrett 255; Thrall 647 n. 370. Cf. BDF §390.

45. E.g., Windisch 310; Bultmann 194; Wolff 204 and n. 76. It is no difficulty for this view that there is no ὥστε before ἐφικέσθαι (cf. BDF §391[4]).

46. That ἐφικέσθαι is epexegetic is recognized by Robertson 1078; Zerwick and Grosvenor 555; Lambrecht 166. That it is epexegetic of κανών seems to be reflected in several EVV: Weymouth, Moffatt ("That sphere [κανών] stretches to include yourselves"), Bruce (*Paraphrase* 149), GNB, JB, Barclay, Cassirer. Cf. Hafemann 403: the κανών (which he takes to be the "standard of judgment" that determined Paul's apostolic authority in Corinth) is the fact that Paul founded the Corinthian church. In his paraphrase of 10:13, Danker links κανόνος closely with ἐφικέσθαι: "In this way we shall keep our boast in line with the direct route *(kanon)* that God has measured out for us, namely, one that proceeds without deviation right to you at Corinth" (158).

47. Robertson notes that the appositional infinitive (used with nouns) is sometimes distinguished from the epexegetic infinitive (used with verbs), although the two are basically the same, both being limitative. "With nouns the appositional inf. restricts or describes it" (1078, citing 2 Cor. 10:13).

48. A different approach is represented by Scott (7-10, 198-99; *Paul* 149-62). In his view Paul's argumentation in 10:12-18 reflects his "fundamentally Jewish perspective on world geography and ethnography" (8) that may be traced back to the "Table of Nations" in the genealogy of Genesis 10. According to this "Table" the sons of Japheth were assigned the area (including Asia

as a whole) to a more specific sense (i.e., the Corinthians in particular)" (Wong 139).

We see, then, that 10:13 states two criteria by which the Corinthians could properly assess the legitimacy of Paul's missionary activity in Corinth, including his exercise of apostolic authority. First, there was his God-given assignment at the time of his conversion to be a bearer of the good news to the Gentile world, an assignment that was later recognized and reaffirmed by the Jerusalem church. Second, there was the evidence of that divine commissioning in the establishment of a Christian congregation in Corinth. And Paul believed that pioneer evangelism in an area brought the right and privilege of pastoral ministry in that area, although others who shared his commitment to the true gospel could be involved in watering what he had planted (1 Cor. 3:5-10).

10:14 οὐ γὰρ ὡς μὴ ἐφικνούμενοι εἰς ὑμᾶς ὑπερεκτείνομεν ἑαυτούς, ἄχρι γὰρ καὶ ὑμῶν ἐφθάσαμεν ἐν τῷ εὐαγγελίῳ τοῦ Χριστοῦ. "For we are not overreaching our limit, as if it does not reach to you, for we were the first to come even as far as you with the gospel of Christ." Vv. 14-16 form a conceptual unit,[49] and syntactical interrelationships can be conveniently shown as follows. Indentation signifies conceptual dependence or grammatical subordination.

οὐ . . . ὑπερεκτείνομεν ἑαυτούς
    ὡς μὴ ἐφικνούμενοι εἰς ὑμᾶς (ἄχρι . . . Χριστοῦ) (v. 14)
οὐκ . . . καυχώμενοι
ἐλπίδα δὲ ἔχοντες
    μεγαλυνθῆναι (v. 15)
    εὐαγγελίσασθαι
        οὐκ . . . καυχήσασθαι (v. 16)

With its two negative statements (οὐ and μή), the first part of v. 14 restates as an elucidation (γάρ) what is said positively in v. 13. "We are not overreaching ourselves" corresponds to "[we will boast] in accordance with our limit" (v. 13b), while "as if we do not reach you" matches "(an assignment) that certainly reaches as far as you" (v. 13c). Because v. 14 is explanatory (γάρ) and the expression οὐκ εἰς τὰ ἄμετρα καυχησόμεθα (v. 13) is repeated in v. 15 (with οὐκ . . . καυχώμενοι), some treat v. 14 as parenthetical.[50] This is possible, but the

Minor and Europe) to the north and west of Palestine (Gen. 10:2-5), the sons of Ham the area to the south of Palestine (Egypt and North Africa) (Gen. 10:6-20), and the sons of Shem the region to the east of Palestine (Mesopotamia and Arabia) (Gen. 10:21-31), with Palestine itself at the point of intersection of these three spheres. As a result of the allocation of territory in the "apostolic council" of Gal. 2:7-9, Paul's mission encompassed the territory of the Japhethites, namely Asia Minor and Europe from Cilicia to Spain, so that Corinth fell within his divinely allotted territorial jurisdiction. In 2 Cor. 10:12-18, as apostle to the nations (Rom. 11:13), Paul is defending his claim to this jurisdiction over the Corinthian church.

49. KJV and RV have a colon at the end of v. 14 and a semicolon (KJV) or comma (RV) after v. 15, while NASB has a semicolon after v. 14 and a comma after v. 15.

50. As, e.g., WH and Meyer 632.

link between v. 14b and v. 15a suggests otherwise: Paul's reaching Corinth with the gospel shows that his boasting about Corinth is not beyond proper limits and in someone else's labors.

In verbs compounded with ὑπέρ (there are fourteen in the NT), the prefix may be intensive (e.g., ὑπερπλεονάζω, "abound exceedingly," 1 Tim. 1:14) or may indicate excess, as in ὑπερεκτείνω here, "stretch out (ἐκτείνω) beyond (ὑπέρ) [the measure assigned]."[51] This notion of excess is regularly rendered in English by the prefix "over," so that ὑπερεκτείνω may be translated "overstretch," "overextend," or "overreach." Paul does not specify the limit that he refuses to overstep, but ἑαυτούς could refer to "our claims" (Young and Ford 272) or "the limits of my authority" (Montgomery)[52] or his apostolic prerogative (Scott 199) or "the limits of our province" (Plummer 285) or "our commission" (NEB, REB) or "the limits set by God" (BAGD 840d), which on our view would refer to Paul's "assignment" (κανών) to be "an apostle to the Gentiles" (ἐθνῶν ἀπόστολος, Rom. 11:13). Since the verb ὑπερεκτείνω is a NT *hapax legomenon,* it could be a term used by Paul's opponents in charging him with an improper use of authority, a charge he here denies. But since, to judge by 11:20, they themselves were given to using high-handed tactics, it is more likely that this verb, perhaps a Pauline coinage, implicitly expresses Paul's accusation that his rivals were guilty of encroaching on his domain in Corinth.[53]

Whereas οὐ negates ὑπερεκτείνομεν ἑαυτούς as a matter of fact, μή negates the participial phrase ἐφικνούμενοι εἰς ὑμᾶς to produce a supposition that is contrary to fact,[54] with ὡς simply reinforcing that supposition; literally, "as if not reaching you." We should take seriously the present tense of the participle,[55] particularly since the aorist ἐφθάσαμεν follows and the aorist ἐφικέσθαι precedes. Perhaps ἐφικνούμενοι suggests that Corinth remains within Paul's appointed sphere of influence, is still part of his divinely ordained assignment. Or the present tense may point to Paul's ongoing pastoral care (cf. 11:28).[56] If we were to convert Paul's negative statement, "as if our remit does not include you," into a positive affirmation, the sense would be, "since you are within those limits [of the work which God has set for us, v. 13]" (GNB).

In a statement that may well be parenthetical (so Bultmann 194-95), Paul now provides the proof (γάρ) that he is not overstepping proper limits when he

51. Cf. Moulton and Howard 326.
52. Cf. Weymouth: "For there is no undue stretch of authority on our part, as though it did not extend to you."
53. But there need be no suggestion that his rivals are "little men" given to overstretching (as Allo 252 suggests).
54. Cf. Winer 474; Turner 285.
55. It would seem to be unwise, if not illegitimate, to treat ἐφικνούμενοι as equivalent to ἐφικόμενοι and render the whole expression, "(We are not overstretching our commission,) as we would be if we had never come to you" (REB; similarly NIV, Cassirer).
56. But Thrall suggests (648) that the participle may be "simply attracted" into the tense of the main verb ὑπερεκτείνομεν. Her own rendering is, "as though not yet reaching you" (635).

claims (v. 13) that his "assignment" includes the Corinthians: "We were the first to come even as far as you with the gospel of Christ."

In Hellenistic Greek φθάνω generally means simply "come," "arrive," as in Matt. 12:28//Luke 11:20; Rom. 9:31; Phil. 3:16; 1 Thess. 2:16. Accordingly, some take ἐφθάσαμεν to mean "we arrived."[57] But in Classical Greek the verb often means "come before/first" or "precede,"[58] so that, for example, ὁ φθάσας means "the firstcomer" and τὸ φθάνον means "previous time," while in 1 Thess. 4:15 οὐ μὴ φθάσωμεν τοὺς κοιμηθέντας must mean "we shall not *precede* those who have fallen asleep." If this were the sense in 10:14, we might have expected an object such as ἐκείνους ("them," i.e., Paul's rivals), matching τοὺς κοιμηθέντας in 1 Thess. 4:15 (so Meyer 632), but the absolute use of the verb with the meaning "come first" has parallels in Classical Greek.[59] It is the context that supports seeing a sense of priority in ἐφθάσαμεν. Since Paul's opponents had also "reached" Corinth, it would be significant to establish his distinctiveness; he was the first to arrive (Thrall 648). Again, although the change from ἐφικνέομαι to φθάνω could be explained as prompted by stylistic variety (Furnish 472), it may be that Paul wishes to make an additional point. Not only did his "assignment" (κανών) reach all the way to Corinth (v. 13); he was the pioneer evangelist in Corinth, the first to come there with the good news, so that the Corinthian church formed a natural "home base" for launching a westward extension of his ministry (v. 15).[60] Moreover, with the following two verses (vv. 15-16) alluding to pioneer evangelism, a reference in v. 14 to priority of arrival would be entirely appropriate. Then there is the important point (mentioned by Wong 146) that in a letter written some five or six years earlier, Paul had used φθάνω in the sense "come before" or "precede" (1 Thess. 4:15). So we concur with those EVV and commentators that take ἐφθάσαμεν to mean "we were the first to come" or the like.[61]

It was as an ambassador (5:20) "bringing the Good News about Christ" (GNB) that Paul arrived in Corinth before the interlopers. As in v. 13, ἄχρι . . . καὶ ὑμῶν ("even as far as you") suggests that Paul regarded Corinth as being at that time (cf. v. 16) the most distant outpost of the gospel in the arc from Jerusalem to Illyricum (Rom. 15:19). ἐν τῷ εὐαγγελίῳ means "with the gospel," where ἐν denotes attendant circumstances or has the "sociative" sense of "bringing."[62] τοῦ Χριστοῦ is an objective genitive ("about Christ," BAGD 318b) and possibly also a subjective genitive ("brought by Christ"); cf. 2:12; 9:13 and references there.

10:15 οὐκ εἰς τὰ ἄμετρα καυχώμενοι ἐν ἀλλοτρίοις κόποις. "We do not

---

57. Thus BAGD 857a; G. Fitzer, *TDNT* 9.90; GNB, JB, NAB[1], NIV, Cassirer; Meyer 632; Bultmann 195; Furnish 472.

58. See LSJ 1926 s.v. φθάνω.

59. See LSJ 1927 s.v. φθάνω II.

60. Cf. Martin 322; Wong 146-47.

61. TCNT, Weymouth, Moffatt, Goodspeed, RSV, NEB, NASB, Barclay, NJB, NAB[2], REB; Allo 252; Héring 73-74; Hughes 366 n. 24; Bruce 233; Barrett 266-67; Martin 322; Lambrecht 166; Wong 145-47; Thrall 648-49 (but cf. 635).

62. Cf. BAGD 259b; Zerwick §§116-17.

boast beyond proper limits in the labors of others." This is a repetition of v. 13a with two differences — the substitution of the present participle καυχώμενοι for the future, finite verb καυχησόμεθα, and the addition of ἐν ἀλλοτρίοις κόποις. While εἰς τὰ ἄμετρα has the same sense as before, "beyond proper limits" (see v. 13), now, after v. 13b, τὸ μέτρον signifies Paul's allocated "assignment." It is possible that καυχώμενοι is dependent on ὑπερεκτείνομεν ("we are not overreaching our limit . . . , that is, we are not boasting beyond proper limits"), with v. 14b a parenthesis (cf. Bultmann 194-95),[63] but the syntax is smoother if both καυχώμενοι and (the later) ἔχοντες are taken as absolute participles, standing for finite verbs,[64] a relatively common phenomenon in 2 Corinthians (see on 9:13). In the NT, as in Hellenistic Greek generally, μή normally negates the participle. Here the use of οὐ(κ) with καυχώμενοι indicates an emphatic, decisive negation (cf. 4:8-9).[65] Neither in the future (οὐ(κ) . . . καυχησόμεθα, v. 13)[66] nor at the present (οὐ(κ) . . . καυχώμενοι) would Paul boast beyond legitimate limits, as would be the case if he took credit for "the labors of others." For Paul, boasting was outside proper limits if it was concerning work others had done or it went beyond one's God-given assignment (v. 13b). In the phrase ἐν ἀλλοτρίοις κόποις, the preposition may be instrumental[67] ("by" = "on the basis of," Wand) or may indicate the content[68] ("about") of the boasting. κόπος refers to arduous toil (see on 6:5; 11:23) with the plural pointing to individual acts (BAGD 443d), but in the present context it signifies the results of that strenuous work, the fruits not simply of missionary endeavor in general but of pioneer evangelism in particular. The whole phrase explains in specific terms what εἰς τὰ ἄμετρα boasting may involve.

There is no need to assume that Paul here is answering an accusation made by his adversaries to the effect that he was trying to take credit for work done by Cephas at Corinth (cf. 1 Cor. 1:12; 3:22; 9:5; 15:5).[69] Rather, as in vv. 13a, 16b where we also find a prefaced οὐ(κ), Paul himself is indirectly leveling a charge against his boastful rivals. Their offense, in his view, was not merely that they were trying to reap what he had sown — that in itself was sometimes both inevitable and proper (cf. John 4:37-38) — but that they were bent on harvesting a crop in someone else's field (Paul's).[70]

63. Meyer (632), seeing all of v. 14 as parenthetical, regards καυχώμενοι as dependent on the καυχησόμεθα to be supplied after ἀλλά in v. 13. But this leaves the following participle ἔχοντες inadequately accounted for grammatically.

64. So, e.g., Lietzmann 143; Plummer 289; Zerwick and Grosvenor 555; Lambrecht 166 ("perhaps").

65. Cf. Moulton 231-32; Robertson 1137-38.

66. However, καυχησόμεθα could be a gnomic future, equivalent to a present.

67. Thus Zerwick, *Analysis* 409.

68. Bultmann, *TDNT* 3.648 n. 35, citing other examples in Rom. 5:3; 1 Cor. 3:21; 2 Cor. 12:9.

69. Cf. Martin 323. That there was a synagogue at Corinth at this time — a possible base for Jewish Christian missionaries — is clear from Acts 18:4-8 (see further Barrett, "Cephas" 35-36).

70. It is of interest that in his *Art of Rhetoric* (*Rhet.* 1384a.7) Aristotle notes that one mark of the ἀλαζών, the pretentious and boastful imposter, is taking credit for what someone else has done.

ἐλπίδα δὲ ἔχοντες αὐξανομένης τῆς πίστεως ὑμῶν ἐν ὑμῖν μεγαλυνθῆναι κατὰ τὸν κανόνα ἡμῶν εἰς περισσείαν. "But we do have the hope that as your faith goes on increasing, with your aid our work may be enlarged — in accordance with our assignment — until it overflows." If, negatively, Paul repudiated illegitimate boasting (οὐκ . . . καυχώμενοι), positively he embraced a hope for a grand-scale enlargement of his ministry. Like καυχώμενοι, the participle ἔχοντες is used absolutely, equivalent to a finite verb (see above). The infinitive μεγαλυνθῆναι defines the content or object of the ἐλπίς, in the same construction that can be used with the cognate verb ἐλπίζω (cf. 1 Cor. 16:7). Paul's ἐλπίς was no vague longing or optimistic self-confidence but a confident assurance born of trust in God's enablement to fulfill his commission. If μεγαλυνθῆναι be regarded as a true passive, it will mean "be praised," the implied subject ("we" = Paul) being "we in our labors" and so "our work," and the ones praising being the Corinthians (ἐν ὑμῖν = "among you") (Furnish 473). Paul's bold statement in Rom. 11:13 ("I magnify [δοξάζω] my ministry") is certainly a relevant parallel (Furnish 473), and Paul would naturally hope that his work would "be held in high esteem" (cf. Acts 5:13) by the Corinthians, but since v. 16 speaks of a geographical expansion of his ministry, it is better to recognize here an intransitive sense of the passive of μεγαλύνω: "grow" or "increase" (thus BAGD 497a).[71] Although grammatically Paul himself, as the subject of ἐλπίδα ἔχοντες, is the one who "increases," in reality by metonymy the growth or expansion belongs to his "sphere of action" (NRSV), his "field of activity" (Weymouth), his "apostolic achievement" (Thrall 650), or more simply his "influence" (Goodspeed) or "position" (Cassirer), or more broadly his "work" (GNB). Clearly Paul's work would expand by stages (note the plural τὰ . . . [μέρη] in v. 16); the aorist μεγαλυνθῆναι envisages those successive stages as a single whole. This "expansion" is the central concept in this verse, but there are four qualifiers of μεγαλυνθῆναι, two before this verb and two after.

1. αὐξανομένης τῆς πίστεως ὑμῶν is a genitive absolute clause that probably has a temporal sense, "as your faith goes on increasing" (αὐξανομένης, present participle), but not "after your faith has increased" (which would require an aorist participle). It is not impossible that πίστις here refers to the Corinthians' "faithfulness" to Paul himself (cf. ὑμῶν ἡ ὑπακοή, 10:6) or to his mission assignment, but it seems wiser to give πίστις its predominant Pauline meaning of a confident trust in Christ or God that is expressed in good works (Gal. 5:6; 1 Thess. 1:3). In the present case this increase in faith would doubtless be shown in Corinthian support of Paul's westward evangelistic endeavors (v. 16), certainly by prayer (cf. 1:11) and possibly also by the provision of supplies (cf. the use of προπέμπω in 1:16). If ἐν ὑμῖν means "with your aid" (see 2. below), this interpretation is strength-

71. LXX examples of these meanings include 1 Kgdms. 2:21; 3:19; 3 Kgdms. 10:23; 2 Chron. 9:22; 2 Esdr. 9:6; Mic. 5:4; Lam. 4:6; Ezra 16:7; Dan. (θ) 8:9-10.

ened. Paul assumes that the Corinthians' faith will continue to become stronger,[72] and he may be hinting that the relation between this strengthening of their faith and the expansion of his work is more than mere concomitance. To be sure, their growing faith will not cause or guarantee that expansion, but Paul probably saw their growth in faith as facilitating this particular advance of the gospel.[73] An increase of faith at Corinth would facilitate and enhance his ministry expansion beyond Corinth.[74]

2. ἐν ὑμῖν may be construed with αὐξανομένης τῆς πίστεως ὑμῶν (so Bultmann 196), but the result would be a tautology (ὑμῶν . . . ἐν ὑμῖν); as Plummer puts it, "if their faith increases, it must increase in them and among them" (289). But if the phrase is taken with μεγαλυνθῆναι (so most EVV and commentators), the ἐν could be local ("among you"; or "in your estimation," Barrett 267; Lambrecht 167), or instrumental ("by your aid," Bruce, *Paraphrase* 151), or may indicate attendant circumstances ("with your help"). In the first case Paul may be envisaging two stages in the enlargement of his ministry — to begin with, among his converts at Corinth, then in regions beyond them (v. 16).[75] In the last two cases, ἐν ὑμῖν μεγαλυνθῆναι may be defined by v. 16a, that is, by Paul's evangelization westward.

3. κατὰ τὸν κανόνα ἡμῶν functions as an assurance that in the anticipated expansion of his work, Paul would not be flouting his κανών, would not be overreaching his limits (cf. v. 14a), but would be adhering closely to his God-given "assignment" (v. 13).[76] The expression is an abbreviation of κατὰ τὸ μέτρον τοῦ κανόνος οὗ ἐμέρισεν ἡμῖν ὁ θεὸς μέτρου (v. 13), Paul's regulative principle for expansion, as also for boasting.

4. εἰς περισσείαν is poised between μεγαλυνθῆναι, which it clearly modifies after the intervening parenthetical κατά phrase,[77] and the explanatory εἰς . . . εὐαγγελίσασθαι. It is not merely an afterthought[78] but rather is an intensification of μεγαλυνθῆναι, literally, "to (the point of) abundance,"[79] and so, "(. . . our work may be enlarged . . .) until it overflows." The phrase is expressive of Paul's hope in God, not simply his confidence in the Corinthians.

72. Louw and Nida comment (§78.5) that since πίστις expresses a state (of trust), αὐξάνομαι is more likely to express intensity of degree than quantity.

73. But Schlatter goes a stage further. "The prerequisite for the extension of his effectiveness is that the faith of the Corinthians increases." Paul could not evangelize elsewhere if the Corinthian congregation was disintegrating (625).

74. Cf. Moffatt: ". . . my hope rather is that the growth of your faith will allow me to enlarge the range of my appointed sphere."

75. Héring, however, takes ἐν ὑμῖν to mean "among you Greeks," or "in Greece," with no reference to Paul's work in Corinth (75 n. 19).

76. Cf. Cassirer: ". . . while still keeping within our sphere"; similarly NEB, REB.

77. Both Plummer (285) and Furnish (465) mark off this κατά phrase as parenthetical.

78. As Barrett ("Christianity" 293-94) proposes.

79. The phrase has been rendered in a variety of ways, ranging from "greatly" (BAGD 650c; RSV, NRSV) or "more and more" (Zerwick, *Analysis* 409), to "to a vast extent" (Zerwick and Grosvenor 555) or "to the highest degree" (Lietzmann 143).

10:16 εἰς τὰ ὑπερέκεινα ὑμῶν εὐαγγελίσασθαι, οὐκ ἐν ἀλλοτρίῳ κανόνι εἰς τὰ ἕτοιμα καυχήσασθαι. "That is, we hope to preach the gospel in areas beyond you, without boasting about work already done in someone else's assigned area." While it is clear that the first of the three aorist infinitives (viz. μεγαλυνθῆναι) in the Greek sentence that includes vv. 15 and 16 is dependent on ἐλπίδα ἔχοντες ("we do have the hope that . . . our work may be enlarged"), there is no unanimity concerning the syntactical function of the second and third infinitives, εὐαγγελίσασθαι and καυχήσασθαι, within the sentence. εὐαγγελίσασθαι could be regarded as dependent on ἐλπίδα ἔχοντες,[80] or on μεγαλυνθῆναι,[81] or on εἰς περισσείαν,[82] and as stating a purpose (telic)[83] or a result (consecutive or ecbatic)[84] or an explanation (epexegetic).[85] For its part καυχήσασθαι could be seen as telic[86] or ecbatic,[87] and as dependent on ἐλπίδα ἔχοντες[88] or on μεγαλυνθῆναι[89] or on the whole preceding clause. These syntactical ambiguities arise in part from the fact that both clauses in v. 16 are asyndetic. Our proposed solution, reflected in the translation given above, may be set out diagrammatically as follows.

ἐλπίδα ἔχοντες (= ἔχομεν) (v. 15)
  μεγαλυνθῆναι (v. 15)   : content of Paul's ἐλπίς (1)
  εὐαγγελίσασθαι (v. 16a): content of Paul's ἐλπίς (2)
              : epexegetic of μεγαλυνθῆναι
    οὐκ . . . καυχήσασθαι (v. 16b): result of εὐαγγελίσασθαι

On this understanding, Paul's hope is single — that his sphere of work may be enlarged. But what this hoped-for expansion of his ministry would involve is defined as the evangelization of the regions beyond Corinth. And if he engaged in pioneer evangelism beyond the present westward limit of his work but still in accord with his assignment (v. 15), he would be able to avoid priding himself (as his adversaries did) on ready-made achievements in someone else's assigned territory.

We may explain the εἰς with εὐαγγελίσασθαι (1) by finding here a case of εἰς = ἐν (see Turner 254-55; Zerwick §§99-111) ("preach *in* areas . . ."), or (2) by translating the verb as "carry/bear good news *to* areas . . ." (cf. NEB, JB,

---

80. Thus Furnish 465, 473; Carrez 204; Wong 164; Lambrecht 163; also Weymouth, Goodspeed, NAB[1], Bruce, *Paraphrase* 151.

81. Bultmann 196-197; Conybeare in Conybeare and Howson 458.

82. Barrett 255.

83. Meyer 633-34; Wolff 204; also RV, TCNT, RSV, NASB, NIV, NAB[2], NRSV.

84. Martin 315; Thrall 651 and n. 399; also NEB, GNB, NJB, REB, Cassirer.

85. Lietzmann 142; Plummer 285; also JB; Bruce, *Paraphrase* 151.

86. Wolff 204; NASB.

87. Thrall 652 n. 402; GNB.

88. Lietzmann 144; Wong 164-65; Lambrecht 166; Young and Ford 272.

89. This would seem to be the case for those who take both εὐαγγελίσασθαι and καυχήσασθαι as telic (Wolff 204; NASB) or as ecbatic (Thrall 651 and n. 399; 652 n. 402; GNB).

REB), or (3) by treating τὰ [μέρη], "the areas" as signifying, by metonymy, "the people of the areas."[90] ὑπερέκεινα, a NT *hapax legomenon,* is a compound adverb (ὑπέρ + ἐκεῖνα) used here as an improper preposition with the genitive (ὑμῶν).[91] With τά we must supply μέρη; thus "the areas/regions beyond you." Paul is referring to places where Christ's name was not yet known (cf. Rom. 15:20), and in particular Spain (Rom. 15:24, 28).[92] Given the first-century setting of Paul's statement, it is inappropriate to press the expression "beyond you" geographically and to conclude that Paul must be writing from Ephesus, since a Macedonian provenance would suggest that "beyond you" meant North Africa. Paul is thinking strategically, not geographically, with his point of orientation probably not the place of writing but the region where Christianity began, as in Rom. 15:19 ("from Jerusalem all the way around to Illyricum").[93] In vv. 15-16a he seems to be viewing Corinth as a base for missionary expansion to the west, and although here he does not use the technical term προπέμπω (see on 1:16), he may well be hoping, especially if ἐν ὑμῖν (v. 15) means "by/with your help," that the Corinthians will send him on his way westward with the necessary supplies such as money, food, or even traveling companions.[94]

With the verb καυχάομαι the object of boasting or pride could be expressed by εἰς or by ἐν, both of which may mean "with reference to" or "about." In the present instance, since ἐν is regularly locative and εἰς is regularly referential, it is better to translate ἐν ἀλλοτρίῳ κανόνι as "*in* someone else's assigned area," and εἰς τὰ ἕτοιμα as "*about* work already done."[95] After ἐν the word κανών will not mean "assignment" (as in vv. 13, 15) but "assigned area" or "allotted territory." We take τὰ ἕτοιμα, literally "things ready/prepared," to mean "what has been accomplished" (BAGD 316c), "work already done" (NEB, REB) or "ready-made achievements" (Barrett 255), referring in this context to evangelistic and pastoral service already and successfully carried out by others.[96]

90. Cf. BAGD 228c; but cf. 317d. For this use of metonymy, see Bullinger 574, citing Isa. 41:1 ("Be silent before me, you islands!").

91. Cf. Moule 86. Meyer (634) cites the verdict of Thomas Magister (a grammarian of the 13th and 14th century A.D.): "rhetoricians say ἐπέκεινα [cf. Acts 7:43] . . . but only the rabble say ὑπερέκεινα."

92. If pioneer evangelism is in mind, the allusion will not include Rome, where a church was already established, although Italy in general could be included; nor will it include Illyricum (Rom. 15:19), which Paul may have recently visited.

93. On the possible relevance of 10:16 to the question of the provenance of 2 Corinthians 1–13 or 10–13, see the Introduction, A.3.e.(2).

94. That the church in Rome could also be viewed as a launching pad for westward expansion (see Rom. 15:24) does not invalidate this possibility.

95. For this understanding of καυχάομαι εἰς in 10:16, see BAGD 425d; Meyer 634, citing Aristotle, *Politica* 5.10.

96. It is less likely that τὰ ἕτοιμα means "what is already settled [for someone by God]" (cf. Kümmel 209; Héring 75), referring to the distinctive assignment that God has given to some person.

In this second part of v. 16 Paul is principally repudiating[97] any boasting on his part that glories in the accomplishments of others carried out in their own assigned area.[98] But, as elsewhere in this paragraph, he is indirectly accusing his opponents, charging them with illegitimate boasting, that is, with taking pride in work actually done by him in Corinth, his ordained and therefore legitimate field of endeavor. So far from pursuing pioneer evangelism as Paul did, his rivals were content to invade someone else's allotted territory — Paul's — and arrogate to themselves credit for his success there.[99]

10:17 Ὁ δὲ καυχώμενος ἐν κυρίῳ καυχάσθω. "Rather, let the one who boasts, boast in the Lord." After speaking in vv. 13-16 of inappropriate boasting, Paul now enunciates the one principle that determines whether or not boasting is legitimate. Although he uses no introductory formula such as καθὼς γέγραπται (cf. 1 Cor. 1:31) to indicate that a scriptural citation follows, he is clearly quoting a line from the LXX of Jer. 9:23 (EVV, 9:24),[100] which runs as follows:

ἀλλ' ἢ ἐν τούτῳ καυχάσθω ὁ καυχώμενος, συνίεν καὶ γινώσκειν ὅτι ἐγώ εἰμι κύριος ποιῶν ἔλεος καὶ κρίμα καὶ δικαιοσύνην ἐπὶ τῆς γῆς, ὅτι ἐν τούτοις τὸ θέλημά μου, λέγει κύριος.

In adapting the LXX text Paul has omitted the initial ἀλλ' ἢ ("but rather"), has advanced ὁ καυχώμενος, and has substituted ἐν κυρίῳ for ἐν τούτῳ.[101] The result of the changes is a maxim that is capable of being applied to different contexts. Paul's only other citation of the aphorism is in 1 Cor. 1:31, where it serves to counteract prideful boasting in human wisdom, power, pedigree, and strength (1 Cor. 1:26-29). Here in 10:17 its function is to counteract prideful boasting

---

97. οὐ(κ), rather than the expected μή, is found with the infinitive καυχήσασθαι, since ἐν ἀλλοτρίῳ κανόνι stands in contrast to εἰς τὰ ὑπερέκεινα ὑμῶν (cf. Meyer 634; BDF §426). It is unnecessary to follow Windisch's proposal (314) that θέλοντες be supplied after οὐκ or before καυχήσασθαι (cf. Lang 332; NIV).

98. *1 Clement* 41:1 also speaks of the need to avoid transgression of an appointed sphere (τὸν ὡρισμένον . . . κανόνα), in this case by being pleasing (reading εὐαριστείτω with C L S) to God "in one's own rank" (ἐν τῷ ἰδίῳ τάγματι) (? = not in another person's area of ministry).

99. It seems highly improbable that the term ἀλλοτρίῳ in the expression ἐν ἀλλοτρίῳ κανόνι is an indirect reference to Peter, as though Paul is rejecting the idea that Corinth fell within Peter's assigned field. While it is possible that Peter visited Corinth between A.D. 52 (the founding of the church there) and A.D. 55 (the writing of 1 Corinthians) (see 1 Cor. 1:12; 3:22; 9:5), there is no evidence that Paul's rivals were claiming that they had fallen heir to Peter's role in Corinth (but see Barrett, "Cephas" 1-12). According to Lang, however, Paul's opponents were wandering Jewish-Christian missionaries who came to Corinth, perhaps as self-styled envoys of Peter's mission, in order to oppose Paul as an illegitimate apostle (358-59). See also Thrall 940.

100. The LXX expansion of the Hebrew text in 1 Kgdms. 2:10b is very similar to the LXX of Jer. 9:23 (ἀλλ' ἢ . . . ἐπὶ τῆς γῆς) and is probably dependent on it. See further Schreiner 541-42; Wong 174-76.

101. See Stanley 187-88 for a discussion of possible reasons for the changes; also Heckel 162-82, 191-94.

about someone else's successful ministry carried out in someone else's God-assigned sphere of activity.

To decide what Paul signifies by ἐν κυρίῳ, we must examine what ἐν τούτῳ refers to in the original context. The contrast in Jer. 9:22-23 (LXX) (EVV, 9:23-24) is between improper and proper boasting, between boasting of one's wisdom, strength, and riches as though these gifts were derived from oneself, and boasting "about this: understanding and knowing that I am the LORD who exercises mercy, judgment and righteousness on the earth, for my pleasure[102] resides in these." That is to say, boasting is legitimate if it focuses on who Yahweh is ("I am the LORD . . . my pleasure") and what he does ("who exercises mercy, judgment and righteousness"). "Glorying in God" is at the heart of OT religion,[103] so that pride in human qualities or achievements or advantages is seen as a usurpation of God's glory and a rejection of dependence on him.[104] Similar sentiments mark NT religion.[105] If, then, we understand ἐν κυρίῳ against its OT background, the expression may be regarded as shorthand for the character and deeds of the Lord. And grammatically, the preposition ἐν will specify the object of the boasting: "No, let him who boasts make the Lord the object of his boast" (Cassirer).

But the question arises: Who is the κύριος in Paul's modified citation of Jer. 9:22 (LXX)? Is it God[106] or is it Christ?[107] While it is true that in Paul's usage the anarthrous κύριος usually refers to God[108] and the article with κύριος in v. 18 could be anaphoric, there are compelling reasons for believing that κύριος in v. 17 refers to Christ.

1. In 1 Cor. 1:30-31 the same OT statement is probably applied to Christ. "Boasting in the Lord" (1 Cor. 1:31) is taking pride in the salvific work of "righteousness, sanctification, and redemption" that Christ accomplished as believers' true wisdom (1 Cor. 1:30).
2. The concept of "boasting in Christ" is found in Phil. 3:3: "We are the true circumcision . . . priding ourselves only on Christ Jesus" (καυχώμενοι ἐν Χριστῷ Ἰησοῦ) (Goodspeed). Cf. Rom. 15:17-18; 1 Cor. 15:31; Gal. 6:14; Phil. 1:26).
3. The prepositional phrase ἐν κυρίῳ regularly refers to Christ in Paul's letters.[109]

---

102. For θέλημα meaning "pleasure," see Eccl. 5:3 (LXX).

103. E.g., 1 Chron. 16:10, 28-29; Pss. 34:2-3; 44:8; 66:2.

104. E.g., Ps. 10:3-4; Isa. 2:11-12; Jer. 13:15-16.

105. Cf. Luke 12:16-20; Rom. 3:27; 5:11; 1 Cor. 1:29-31; 3:21; Gal. 6:14; Eph. 2:8-9; Phil. 3:3; Jas. 4:16. It is interesting that D. M. Stanley's treatment of "the phenomenon of prayer in Saint Paul" has as its main title, *Boasting in the Lord* (New York: Paulist, 1973).

106. Thus, e.g., Meyer 634; Lambrecht 167; and especially Wong 176-82; "Lord" 243-53.

107. Thus, e.g., Furnish 474; Capes 135-36; Thrall 652-53.

108. Cf. Zerwick §169; *Analysis* 397.

109. ἐν κυρίῳ Ἰησοῦ is found in Rom. 14:14; Phil. 2:19, and ἐν κυρίῳ refers to Christ in Rom. 16:2, 8, 11-13, 22; 1 Cor. 16:19; Gal. 5:10; Eph. 4:17; 5:8; 6:1, 10, 21; Phil. 2:24; 3:1; 4:1, 2, 4, 10; Col. 3:18, 20; 4:7; 1 Thess. 3:8; 5:12; 2 Thess. 3:4, 12; Phlm. 16, 20.

4. Paul sometimes applies to Christ OT passages that refer to Yahweh (e.g., Isa. 28:16 in Rom. 9:33; 10:11; Isa. 45:23 in Phil. 2:10-11; Joel 2:32 in Rom. 10:12-13; Ps. 68:18 in Eph. 4:8).[110]

Linking the OT background of v. 17 with the identification of κύριος as Christ, we may conclude that the verse has the sense "Let the person who boasts,[111] boast about who Christ is or what he has done."[112] This latter sentiment is expressed in Rom. 15:17-18, where Paul's "glorying in Christ (τὴν καύχησιν ἐν Χριστῷ 'Ιησοῦ) about matters pertaining to God" (τὰ πρὸς τὸν θεόν, 15:17), namely his priestly service to the Gentiles (15:15b-16), is defined as pride in what Christ had accomplished through him in bringing the Gentiles to obedience (15:18). His pride in his service was legitimate because the conversion of the Gentiles was in reality not his achievement but Christ's work, with him merely as Christ's instrument.

In Paul's view, then, for boasting to be legitimate, it must have two characteristics — it must not be boasting about personal status or accomplishments but only about who the Lord is or what he has accomplished; it must be confined to the Lord's accomplishments within one's divinely allotted assignment or sphere of activity. Judged by these criteria, Paul's boasting — implied throughout 10:12-18 — was appropriate or "within proper limits" (cf. εἰς τὰ ἄμετρα, vv. 13, 15), for he attributed the success of the gospel at Corinth (1:19, 21-22; cf. 1 Cor. 3:9) to God's power working through him (3:5; 4:7; 5:17-18; 10:4-5; cf. 1 Cor. 3:6-7), and his God-given assignment (10:13) was evangelism focused on the Gentiles (Gal. 2:7-9; cf. Rom. 15:15-16), a field of activity that included Corinth (10:13-14), where, as a result of his preaching, a Christian community had been established that constituted his validating letter of commendation (3:2-3).

Given the importance of καυχάομαι and the maxim of 10:17 in chs. 10–12,[113] it will be helpful to classify according to construction the uses of this verb in the whole letter. In some cases (e.g., 7:14) more than one construction is used.

1. Transitive (accusative): 7:14; 9:2; 10:8; 11:16, 30b (cf. BDF §148[2]) ("boast about," "say something boastingly," BAGD 426a).
2. Intransitive

110. See further Capes, *passim.*

111. If ὁ καυχώμενος is given a conditional sense, "If anyone would boast" (REB; similarly NEB; Barrett 255), it could be classed as a Semitism (see Barrett, *1 Corinthians* 61).

112. Cf. GNB: "Whoever wants to boast must boast about what the Lord has done."

113. See Heckel 172-214. Of the 37 NT uses of καυχάομαι, 35 are in Paul (the other two are Jas. 1:9; 4:16), and of these, 20 are in 2 Corinthians and 17 are in 2 Corinthians 10–12 (6 in ch. 10, 6 in ch. 11, and 5 in ch. 12; the other three instances occur in 5:12; 7:14; 9:2). As for the cognate substantives, καύχησις occurs six times in 2 Corinthians, five times in reference to the act of boasting (7:4, 14; 8:24; 11:10, 17) and once of the content of boasting (1:12), while καύχημα is found three times, twice of the content of boasting (1:14; 9:3) and once of the act of boasting (5:12).

A. Absolute: 10:17a; 11:18b, 30a; 12:1, 6.
B. With the dative (7:14; 9:2) ("before," BDF §187[4]; or simply "to," BAGD 426a)
C. With prepositions
   (i) εἰς (10:16) ("with reference to," "about")[114]
   (ii) κατά (11:18a) (literally "according to [the flesh]")
   (iii) ὑπέρ (7:14; 9:2) (= περί, "concerning," "about"; cf. BDF §231 [1]) (12:5a, b) ("on behalf of" or "about")
   (iv) περί (10:8) ("concerning," "about")
   (v) ἐν (5:12 [twice]; 10:15, 17b; 11:12; 12:5, 9) ("in," "about")

10:18 οὐ γὰρ ὁ ἑαυτὸν συνιστάνων, ἐκεῖνός ἐστιν δόκιμος, ἀλλὰ ὃν ὁ κύριος συνίστησιν. "For it is not the person who commends himself who is approved, but the person whom the Lord commends." With its mention of self-commendation this verse looks back to v. 12 by way of an *inclusio*, τῶν ἑαυτοὺς συνιστανόντων . . . ὁ ἑαυτὸν συνιστάνων. But whereas there the reference was to particular unnamed individuals (τινές) who were engaging in self-promotion, here the reference is generic, adverting to the "self-praiser." The link with v. 17 is also close. It is appropriate for the person who wants to boast or must boast to make the Lord the object of his boast (v. 17), since (γάρ) priding oneself on the Lord and his achievements bring the Lord's commendation and approval (v. 18).

ὁ ἑαυτὸν συνιστάνω is not merely someone who "thinks well of himself" (GNB) but someone who actively engages in self-promotion, using both words and deeds. Such self-glorification is the opposite of "boasting about the Lord" and disqualifies a person from divine approbation. Apparently Paul did not regard self-commendation as improper in itself, for he himself indulges in it (4:2; 6:4), so we are forced to conclude that there are two types of "self-commendation" (see on 3:1). One type, expressed by the phrase ἑαυτὸν συνιστάνω (3:1; 5:12; 10:12, 18), consists of self-praise, boasting of one's pedigree and accomplishments, and is driven by ruthless ambition. The other type, expressed by the phrase συνιστάνω ἑαυτόν (4:2; 6:4), is based on a divine commission that is carried out in God's power and for God's glory. Whereas the former type of commendation is engaged in readily whenever an opportunity for self-advancement presents itself, the latter is carried on reluctantly when God's work is in danger of being discredited (4:2; 6:4). Perhaps we may distinguish the two types by calling the negative form "self-praise," and the positive form "commendation of the self." It will immediately be recognized that there is a close correlation between "self-praise" and illegitimate boasting, for improper boasting is prideful, based on self-trust, and is self-centered, focusing on who one is or what one has accomplished. Similarly, "commendation of the self" is

---

114. In 10:13, 15 εἰς is to be construed with τὰ ἄμετρα (literally "to limitless things," thus "beyond limits," BAGD 45c), not with καυχάομαι.

closely connected to legitimate boasting, for permissible boasting is humble, based on dependence on God, and is Christ-centered, focusing on who he is or what he has done.[115]

But the main point of the verse is not to indicate that Paul's opponents are disqualified from the Lord's approval. The apostle presupposes that, unlike his rivals, he is one whom the Lord commends and of whom he approves. And why? He has adhered to his divinely given assignment in his work at Corinth (v. 13) and in his planned expansion beyond Corinth (vv. 15-16); he has experienced God's validation of his ministry in Corinth by the establishment of a church there (v. 14; cf. 3:1-3; 1 Cor. 3:6-7); and he is careful to boast only about the Lord (v. 17).

The phrase ἐκεῖνός ἐστιν δόκιμος is the pivot on which the verse turns. ἐκεῖνος is emphatic, "he and he alone" (NEB). δόκιμος, from δοκιμάζω, "approve by testing," means "approved as genuine after testing," and with this adjective we must understood an expression such as παρὰ τῷ κυρίῳ or κατέναντι/ ἐνώπιον κυρίου ("in the sight of the Lord") on the basis of the following ὁ κύριος. To bring out the positive import of the verse one could translate it this way: "For a person has the Lord's approval, not when he commends himself but when the Lord commends him." The only approval that finally counted for Paul was that of Christ at his tribunal (cf. 5:10; 1 Cor. 4:4-5a);[116] it was this that he made it his ambition to secure (5:9). We could legitimately treat (ὁ κύριος) συνίστησιν[117] and δόκιμος (παρὰ τῷ κυρίῳ) as virtually synonymous expressions,[118] but δόκιμος is probably the broader term, implying an evaluation or testing of an individual that leads to his or her full acceptance as a person worthy of praise and reward.

Bibliography

Capes 135-36 • G. Delling, "Zum steigernden Gebrauch von Komposita mit ὑπέρ bei Paulus," *NovT* 11 (1969) 129-53 • Fahy • Forbes • Forbes, "Paul" • M. D. Goulder, *Early Christian Conflict in Corinth: Paul and the Followers of Peter* (Peabody: Hendrickson, 2001) • Hafemann, "Legitimacy" • Heckel 13-20, 144-214, 295-96 • J. Henning, "The

---

115. Lambrecht has argued that while "boasting in the Lord" — boasting of what God has accomplished — is legitimate, it is nonetheless always dangerous, for it may descend into sinful self-commendation, and in one sense it is always foolish, for it may easily be misunderstood. However, it may be useful for rightful self-defense ("Self-Commendation" 327-46).

116. This assumes that ὁ κύριος has the same referent as in v. 17 (the article may be anaphoric). Barnett, however, refers κυρίῳ (v. 17) to Yahweh and ὁ κύριος (v. 18) to Christ (492 n. 61; 493 n. 68).

117. There is no difference in meaning between συνίστημι in v. 18b and συνιστάνω in vv. 12, 18a, the latter verb being simply a late form of συνίστημι; both mean "commend." In Biblical Greek verbs in -μι or -νυμι are less common than in Classical Greek and are often replaced by thematic forms in -ω (cf. Zerwick §493).

118. Goodspeed renders the two words by "approves" and "approved."

Measure of Man: A Study of 2 Cor. 10:12," *CBQ* 8 (1946) 332-43 • Holmberg 45-48, 76-79 • Judge • Lambrecht, "Self-Commendation" 327-35 • Lüdemann, *Opposition* 92-93 • Marshall • Metzger, *Canon* 289-93 • Murphy-O'Connor 104-6 • Oostendorp 17-30 • Peterson 93-104 • Schmithals 184-87 • Schütz 165-86 • Schreiner • Scott, *Nations* 149-62 • Stanley 186-88 • Strange • Theobald 253-58 • Therrien 109-12 • Wong • Wong, "Lord"

B. Boasting "as a Fool" (11:1–12:13)

1. A Plea for Tolerance (11:1-6)

At the end of ch. 10 (10:12-18) Paul chided his opponents for their self-praise and their pointless comparisons and identified the difference between illegitimate and legitimate boasting. To speak pridefully of oneself is improper; to speak proudly about the Lord is commendable. One might therefore expect that if Paul were to boast, his boasting would be of the legitimate variety. But in 11:21b–12:13 (or 12:10), the so-called "Fool's Speech," he will in fact be boasting illegitimately, "in an unspiritual fashion" or "as the world does" (κατὰ σάρκα, 11:18), engaging in unadulterated self-eulogizing, speaking of his own pedigree, achievements, and privileges in comparison with the lineage and accomplishments of the rival missionaries at Corinth. Such an unexpected about-face demands an explanation (not given until 11:18; 12:11) and a plea for patient understanding, which is found in 11:1-6 (as also in 11:16-21a). Three reasons are given, each introduced by γάρ, why the Corinthians ought to be willing to tolerate his foolish boasting:[1] (1) he is intensely jealous for their highest spiritual good, especially when their corporate purity is endangered (v. 2); (2) they are already tolerant toward theologically deviant visitors to Corinth (v. 4; cf. 11:19-20); (3) he is not inferior to the "superlative apostles" to whom his rivals were apparently appealing (v. 5).

Some light on the dilemma Paul faced — "To boast or not to boast? That is the question" — may be found in a well-known passage in Prov. 26:4-5 where there is a dramatic juxtaposition of two apparently contradictory proverbs that give advice to the wise man regarding fools.

> 4Do not answer a fool in terms of his folly,
>   lest you become like him yourself.
> 5Answer a fool in terms of his folly,
>   lest he imagines himself to be wise.

---

1. Cf. Bultmann 199-201, 203 (although his understanding of v. 5 is different); Barrett 277-78; Garland 417, 558; Thrall 656, 664, 671. Some take γάρ in v. 5 as connective or as affirmative (see the commentary there).

The purpose of the juxtaposition is not merely to show that proverbs cannot be absolutized. Rather, it indicates that the truth lies in both proverbs considered together. The sage is obliged to teach the fool for fear that the fool should deem himself wise (v. 5), but such instruction or dialogue could prove perilous to the sage's sanity (v. 4; cf. Prov. 10:14, 21). That is, both ignoring the fool and trying to answer the fool are procedures fraught with danger. If Paul refused to adopt the tactics of his adversaries and refrained from foolish boasting, he would risk losing the Corinthians to a false gospel (11:4), but if he chose to indulge in a temporary foray into foolish boasting he risked being misunderstood by the Corinthians and playing into the hands of his rivals. Because the former risk was the greater, he chose the way of "a little bit of foolishness" (11:1), "a little boasting" (11:16). Paul is not aiming to answer the "fools" (11:19) themselves; he does not expect to win over his opponents. But he is seeking to alert the Corinthians to the folly of these intruders who engage in self-praise and internal comparisons, without being aware of their foolishness (10:12). Paul, however, is totally aware of the folly of his ironic self-eulogizing (11:1, 16-18, 21b; 12:11) but judges that no other technique will be as effective in bringing the Corinthians to their senses, foolish as they themselves are in submitting to the intruders' demands (11:20-21). Paul is saying in effect, "For the benefit of you fools I shall become a fool, in order to win fools" (cf. 1 Cor. 9:19-23).

11:1*If only you would put up with me in a little bit[a] of foolishness[b]! Yes, do put up with me!* 2*For I am jealous for you with a jealousy such as God has, because I betrothed you to one husband in order to present you as a pure maiden to Christ himself.* 3*But I am afraid that[c] just as the snake deceived Eve by his cunning, your minds may somehow be corrupted[d] and lured away from your single-mindedness and your purity[e] in relation to Christ[f].* 4*For in fact you put up with it[g] well enough if some interloper preaches another Jesus than the Jesus we preached, or if you receive a different Spirit from the Spirit you received or a different gospel from the gospel you embraced.* 5*For[h] I reckon I am not at all inferior to those superlative apostles.* 6*Even if I lack skill in oratory, I certainly do not in knowledge. On the contrary, in our dealings with you we have made this clear[i] in every way and in all circumstances.*

TEXTUAL NOTES

a. Although there is wide geographical support (F G H 𝔐 it Lucifer Ambrosiaster) for the omission of τι in the phrase μικρόν τι ("a little bit"), there is superior attestation for its inclusion (p⁴⁶ ℵ B D Ψ 0121 0243 6 33 365 1739 1881 *al* f t vg syr[h]). The omission was undoubtedly prompted by the belief that τι was otiose; μικρὸν ἀφροσύνης conveys the same sense.

b. Some witnesses (F G 6 81 630 1175 *pc*) add the article τῆς before ἀφροσύνης, others have the dative (of reference) τῇ ἀφροσύνῃ (H 𝔐), perhaps to relieve the apparent difficulty of having two genitives dependent on ἀνείχεσθε, but the most reliable set of witnesses has the anarthrous ἀφροσύνης (p⁴⁶ ᵛⁱᵈ ℵ B D P Ψ 0243 33 1739 1881 *pc*).

c. Instead of μή πως ("lest perhaps," "[I am afraid] that . . . somehow"), some witnesses have clearly secondary readings, μήποτε ("lest at any time") (thus F G 630 1505 1739 1881 *pc* vg^ms) or μή ("lest") (D* lat Julius Cassianus^Cl), while 0243 has the impossible μήτε.

d. In some witnesses (D¹ Ψ 0121 0243 0278 1739 1881 𝔐 lat syr Ambrosiaster), οὕτως or οὕτω is read before φθαρῇ as the correlative of ὡς, but being the easier reading it should be rejected and the simple φθαρῇ preferred (as in 𝔭⁴⁶ ℵ B D* F G H P 33 81 1175 *pc* r Julius Cassianus^Cl Clement Lucifer).

e. A choice must be made between the two main readings:

(1) ἀπο τῆς ἁπλότητος   𝔭⁴⁶ ℵ* B D^(2) F G 33 81 104 (326)
καὶ τῆς ἁγνότητος   *pc* a r syr^h** cop Pelagius
(2) ἀπὸ τῆς ἁπλότητος   ℵ² H Ψ 0121 0243 1739 1881 𝔐
(b) f* vg syr^p Julius Cassianus^Cl

A lack of substantial external support makes either of the other two variants unlikely original readings: ἀπὸ τῆς ἁγνότητος (Lucifer Ambrose Augustine Vigilius) and ἀπὸ τῆς ἁγνότητος καὶ τῆς ἁπλότητος (D*vid it^d Epiphanius). Reading (1), which is found in WH, UBS^1, 2, 3, 4 (in each case with a "C" rating), and NA²⁷ inside square brackets, is to be preferred on several grounds: (a) the combination of proto-Alexandrian (𝔭⁴⁶ ℵ* B) and Western (F G) witnesses is formidable support; (b) reading (2) may be accounted for by haplography due to homoeoteleuton (-ότητος), while the reading D*vid it^d Epiphanius "may be the result of mere inattention on the part of the copyists" (Metzger 515); (c) the longer reading coheres with the context (Thrall 663), with ἁπλότητος corresponding to ἑνὶ ἀνδρί, and ἁγνότητος to παρθένον ἁγνήν. See further Metzger 514-15.

f. The sense is not altered whether we read εἰς Χριστόν (with ℵ F G 0121 0243 365 630 1175 1505 1739 1881 *al*) or, better (cf. τῷ Χριστῷ, v. 2), εἰς τὸν Χριστόν (𝔭⁴⁶ B D H Ψ 33 𝔐 Julius Cassianus^Cl Clement Epiphanius).

g. The external evidence supporting ἀνείχεσθε (imperfect) (𝔭³⁴ ℵ D² F G H (Ψ *al*: ἠνείχεσθε) 0121 0243 0278 1739 1881 𝔐 lat syr) is comparable in quality to that supporting ἀνέχεσθε (present) (𝔭⁴⁶ B D* 33 *pc* r sah). Now it is true that the imperfect is the more difficult reading following the two presents (κηρύσσει . . . λαμβάνετε) and the other reading (ἀνέχεσθε) could have arisen from that same form in v. 20 (so Zmijewski 93); however, the present tense reading is more probably original since (a) an unequivocal and ironical statement, "you put up with it/him well enough," better accords with Paul's directness in the context (cf. vv. 6, 8, 10, 13-15), than does a hypothetical (with ἄν understood) and more gentle statement, "if someone comes and preaches . . . you would tolerate him well enough"; (b) ἀνέχεσθε harmonizes with the two uses of that present indicative in vv. 19-20 (ἀνέχεσθε in v. 1 is probably an imperative); (c) the variant ἀνείχεσθε may have been prompted by its use in v. 1; and (d) the imperfect "would detract from the force of v. 4 as giving grounds both for the fear of v. 3 and for Paul's plea in v. 1" (Thrall 666). Against reading ἀνείχεσθε as ἄν εἴχεσθε, see Bultmann 202.

h. B reads δέ in the place of γάρ, perhaps to effect a μέν (v. 4) — δέ correlation.

i. Probably because one would expect (as in 2:14) an object to be expressed with an active participle such as φανερώσαντες (read by ℵ* B F G 33 *pc*), some witnesses supply ἑαυτούς ("we have made ourselves clear") (thus 0121 0243 630 1738 1881 *pc*) and others have a passive participle (φανερωθέντες, 𝔭³⁴ ℵ² D² Ψ 0278 𝔐 r [vg^cl]; or φανερωθείς [agreeing with ἰδιώτης in number], D* [lat Ambrosiaster]). 𝔭⁴⁶ omits all of v. 6b (ἀλλ' . . . ὑμᾶς), no doubt because of a transcriptional error.

731

11:1 Ὄφελον ἀνείχεσθέ μου μικρόν τι ἀφροσύνης· ἀλλὰ καὶ ἀνέχεσθέ μου. "If only you would put up with me in a little bit of foolishness! Yes, do put up with me!" Before Paul actually begins (at 11:21b) his "foolish boasting," he ironically craves the Corinthians' indulgence in this unpleasant but necessary project, first by means of an ardent wish, then with a direct request. ὄφελον should not be seen as the first person singular second aorist of ὀφείλω ("owe") (ὤφελον) without the augment, although historically this may be the origin of the form (Moulton and Howard 191).[2] Rather, it is the aorist participle with ἐστίν to be supplied (BDF §67[2]), signifying "that which ought to be if one only had one's wish — 'would that'" (Louw and Nida §71.28). In the NT this uninflected particle, which means "Would that," "O that," "If only," introduces either an unattainable wish, with the imperfect expressing present time (ἀνείχεσθε here, and Rev. 3:15) and the aorist indicative past time (1 Cor. 4:8) (BDF §359[1]),[3] or an attainable wish (with the future indicative) that is not seriously entertained (Gal. 5:12) (Zerwick §355).[4] In each of these four NT uses of ὄφελον there is a clearly ironical flavor to the wish expressed. While it is possible to construe μου with ἀφροσύνης and regard μικρόν τι as the object of ἀνείχεσθε ("I hope you will put up with a little of my foolishness," NIV),[5] the position of μου favors taking it with ἀνείχεσθε[6] and μικρόν τι as an accusative of respect or "general reference" ("I should like you to bear with me in a little foolishness," REB).[7] In addition, this understanding is supported by the following ἀνέχεσθέ μου (v. 1b), where μου is the object, whether the verb be indicative or imperative.[8] In the present context of playful irony, μικρόν τι, "a little bit," could be rendered "(a) little display" (Martin 327) or "a small sample" (Héring 77).[9]

ἀφροσύνης, which may be classed as a partitive genitive (Zerwick and Grosvenor 556), could refer to the foolish talk or, more specifically, to the foolish boasting that was forced on Paul by circumstances at Corinth (cf. 12:11). ἀφροσύνη should not be seen as a synonym for μωρία.[10] In Paul's usage μωρία

2. Some inferior witnesses (D³ F G K L) actually read ὤφελον (the text preferred by Héring 77). Outside the NT εἰ γάρ or εἴθε is sometimes used with ὤφελον to express past unattained wishes (LSJ 480 s.v. εἰ A.2.c.).

3. But Burton (§27) relates 1 Cor. 4:8 to present time.

4. Similarly Moulton 200, 201 n. 1; Robertson 923, 1004; Moule 137.

5. So also Bultmann 199; Martin 327, 331; Thrall 658.

6. Thus Meyer 638 (who rightly observes that if μου belonged with ἀφροσύνης, its position standing apart and prefixed would be "emphatic," an emphasis not suited to this enclitic form); Windisch 317-18; Wong 186-87.

7. Thus Plummer 293; Robertson 486; *Pictures* 257.

8. It is unnecessary to follow Böttrich (138-39) in supplying ἀφροσύνης with ἀνέχεσθε in v. 1b, or Thrall (658 n. 22) in assuming that v. 1b is an abbreviation of v. 1a (which she renders [656] "Would that you tolerated a little foolishness on my part!").

9. But it is possible that μικρόν is used adverbially "(some foolishness) for a little (while/ time)" (Bruce, *Paraphrase* 151; Winer 302).

10. In the LXX ἀφροσύνη occurs 36 times, μωρία only twice (Sir. 20:31; 41:15), while in the NT ἀφροσύνη is found four times (three in 2 Corinthians 11 [11:1, 17, 21]) and μωρία five times (all in 1 Corinthians 1-3 [1:18, 21, 23; 2:14; 3:19]).

has distinctly theological overtones, denoting a perceived lack of understanding of certain ideas, usually as the result of a worldly outlook, whereas ἀφροσύνη refers to an act of deliberate folly in pursuing a particular course of action in order to achieve commendable ends, and therefore is neither ignorant stupidity nor crass foolhardiness. In his program of boasting Paul is "foolish," not because he lacks knowledge (he rejects such a supposition in v. 6), but because he imitates his adversaries by engaging in self-praise and comparisons (cf. 10:12) and by boasting of outward appearances (cf. 5:12).[11] The opposite of this foolishness (= foolish boasting, 11:16-17) is boasting about the Lord (10:17), the kind of boasting of which the Lord approves (10:18).[12]

Having expressed an impassioned wish in v. 1a, Paul promptly replaces or corrects it with an unambiguous request, "Yes, do put up with me!" What he had stated as an unattainable wish (ὄφελον with the imperfect indicative) was, in fact, capable of fulfillment. Both commentators and EVV are divided between taking ἀνέχεσθε as an indicative[13] and rendering it as an imperative.[14] In the former case ἀλλά will bear an adversative sense, and καί will reinforce the facticity of the statement, "but indeed you are bearing with me" (NASB), and Paul will be expressing either his "hopeful expectation" (Bultmann 200) or his awareness that the Corinthians had already been humoring a little of his foolishness (possibly in 6:3-10 or 10:13-16). In the latter case ἀλλά will introduce an emphatic addition, "yes" or "indeed" (Turner 330), and καί will strengthen the imperative: "yes, do put up with me" (Barrett 270). The main reason for preferring this latter alternative is that "the following verses more logically give reasons why the Corinthians should listen to Paul than why they are in fact listening to him" (Peterson 105). Also, when Paul resumes the ἀφροσύνη theme in 11:16-19, he issues a request for acceptance of his foolish boasting (. . . ὡς ἄφρονα δέξασθέ με, 11:16).

The apostle is clearly uneasy about his foray into "foolishness"; he does

11. Of 11:1 Forbes says, "Now begins the 'foolishness' . . . or ironic parody of the self-praise and comparisons of his opponents." Hafemann argues that "Paul's 'foolishness' in 11:1–12:13 consists *only* in his being forced to boast in his 'strength' [423]. . . . The boasting in 11:21b-23a and 12:1-4 is foolish because it focuses on Paul's human distinctives and private spiritual experiences instead of calling attention to the Lord as the giver of all things in Christ (cf. 1 Cor. 1:26-31)" (424). Boasting in weakness is legitimate because it reveals Christ's power (424 and nn. 3, 4).

12. Suggested reasons why Paul calls his boasting "foolish" are numerous. Wong identifies seven (imitational, polemical, psychological, sociological, rhetorical, Judaic, theological) and classifies some 43 scholars according to these seven categories (7-39; see the chart on p. 39). He himself prefers the "imitational" (Paul's boasting imitates the foolish boasting of his opponents), the "Judaic" (in the OT boasting and foolishness are closely linked conceptually and linguistically), and the "theological" (boasting contradicts Christian principles), but finds the last reason the most satisfying (37-38, 189-93).

13. E.g., JB, Barclay, NIV, NJB, Cassirer; Windisch 318; Zmijewski 77-79; Böttrich 138; Barnett 498.

14. E.g., Weymouth, NEB, GNB, NAB², NRSV; Allo 275; Wong 50, 184; Lambrecht 172; Thrall 659.

not relish the prospect of entering the forbidden territory of self-promotion and invidious comparisons. This would account for two facts: his "boasting as a fool" is marked off by prodiorthosis in 11:1 and 11:16 and epidiorthosis in 12:11, that is, by an apology given (respectively) in advance and in retrospect;[15] and his furnishing of three reasons (in vv. 2-5) for this necessary but distasteful foray.

11:2 ζηλῶ γὰρ ὑμᾶς θεοῦ ζήλῳ, ἡρμοσάμην γὰρ ὑμᾶς ἑνὶ ἀνδρὶ παρθένον ἁγνὴν παραστῆσαι τῷ Χριστῷ. "For I am jealous for you with a jealousy such as God has, because I betrothed you to one husband in order to present you as a pure maiden to Christ himself." Structurally, there are three elements in this verse, marked by γάρ . . . γάρ . . . παραστῆσαι: (1) one reason (γάρ) for the Corinthians' requested tolerance (v. 1b) — Paul's godly jealousy; (2) the reason (γάρ) for his jealousy — his betrothal of the Corinthians; (3) the purpose (παραστῆσαι) of the betrothal — his presentation of them to Christ.

We have seen that in vv. 2-5 Paul gives three substantial reasons for his appeal for tolerance (ἀνέχεσθέ, v. 1b), thereby indicating his considerable unease in embarking on this journey of boasting and his clear realization of the considerable danger in imitating the worldly tactics of his opponents. His first reason is his jealous concern for his converts. ζηλῶ here could mean simply "I am deeply concerned about you" (cf. BAGD 338a) or "I care deeply for you" (Furnish 484), but the following reference to the need for pre-nuptial purity (παρθένον ἁγνήν) suggests that the more intensive and specialized meaning, "I am jealous" (= ζηλοτυπέω, Meyer 639) or "I am jealously concerned" (Thrall 656), is intended in the context, particularly since the character of Paul's ζῆλος is described as being θεοῦ. In the phrase θεοῦ ζήλῳ, the dative expresses manner (sometimes called the "associative dative") and the construction ζηλῶ . . . ζήλῳ imitates the Hebrew absolute infinitive,[16] although there is some precedent for the construction in Classical Greek.[17] For its part the genitive θεοῦ has been seen as subjective ("with a jealousy God inspires [in me]"[18]), qualitative ("a divine jealousy"[19]), or possessive ("God's own jealousy,"[20] or "a jealousy which God has"[21]). However, Paul is not simply indicating the source of his ζῆλος although God is undoubtedly its ultimate origin, nor is he merely affirming that it is supernaturally strong (one possible sense of "divine"). He is claiming to have a jealousy such as God himself has, or a jealousy that has the characteristics of God's jealousy (a "godly" or "divine" jealousy). The OT depicts Yahweh not simply as a jealous God (Deut. 4:24), one consumed with holy zeal for his name, but as a God whose very name is Jealous (Exod. 34:14). His jeal-

---

15. Cf. BDF §495(3); Robertson 1199. We may compare the function of 1 Cor. 4:6-7 and 4:14-15 in relation to Paul's indictment of boasting in 1 Cor. 4:8-13.

16. See BDF §198(6); Zerwick §60; Moulton and Howard 443-44.

17. See Smyth §1577.

18. Martin 327; also Lietzmann 144; Wolff 211 n. 114.

19. Moffatt, RSV, NEB, NRSV, NIV ("godly jealousy"); Thrall 656.

20. Weymouth, JB, NJB, NAB[1] ("of God himself"); Barrett 270.

ous anger burns against sin (Exod. 20:5; Ezek. 23:25), especially idolatry (Deut. 6:15; Josh. 24:19-20; Nah. 1:2), yet his jealous care protects his people (Ps. 17:7-8; Prov. 18:10; Isa. 41:10). As the verse goes on to show, Paul's godly jealousy for his spiritual daughter (the Corinthian congregation) is evidenced in his passionate concern to protect her purity from being violated by potential paramours in the period between her betrothal and her wedding day. No rivals to her one husband, Christ, would be tolerated.[22] If she were caused to fall, he would burn with jealous anger (cf. 11:29).

The second element in this verse is the reason for Paul's ongoing jealousy: When the Corinthians responded to his preaching of the good news, he betrothed them as a bride to a heavenly bridegroom, Jesus Christ, and thereby committed himself to guarding her virginity — her undivided loyalty to Christ — until the consummation of her marriage at Christ's appearance from heaven.

Formed from the noun ἁρμός ("a joining," "a joint"), ἁρμόζω has the basic meaning of "join," "fit together," but in reference to marriage it means in the active voice, "give in marriage," "promise (someone) for marriage"; in the middle, "take as wife," "betroth oneself (to someone)"; and in the passive, "be married (to someone)." In Classical Greek, therefore, ἡρμοσάμην σε would mean "I took you as my wife" or "I betrothed myself to you," but there is general consensus that in 11:2 the middle ἡρμοσάμην ὑμᾶς has the force of the active[23] and so is equivalent to ἥρμοσα ὑμᾶς, meaning either "I gave you in marriage" or "I betrothed you." Because Paul assumes that the betrothal (ἡρμοσάμην) will inevitably lead to the presentation (παραστῆσαι) of the bride to the bridegroom, and that there will be a considerable interval between these two events, with the betrothal lying in the past and the consummation of the marriage lying in the future, he must have in mind Jewish, not Greek or Roman, marriage procedures.[24]

In the OT and in NT times betrothal was a formal marriage contract in which the young woman passed from her father's authority to the authority of her husband. The couple were legally "husband" and "wife" (Deut. 22:23-24; Matt. 1:18-19, 24) so that a betrothed woman was a "widow" if her fiancé died (m. Yebamot 4:10; 6:4; m. Ketubbot 1:2) and a betrothal could be dissolved only through death or by a formal divorce (Matt. 1:19; m. Gittin 6:2; m. Ketubot 4:2;

21. Meyer 639.
22. See John 447-48.
23. See, e.g., LSJ 243 s.v. ἁρμόζω I.2; BDF §316(1); BAGD 107d; cf. Zerwick §235. But Robertson (Pictures 257) seems to prefer the Classical sense of the middle when he comments that "Paul treats the Corinthians as his bride." On this view ἑνὶ ἀνδρί must be construed with παραστῆσαι.
24. On the Greek side a formal betrothal (ἐγγύησις), which may have involved a legal marriage contract, was followed either immediately or after an interval by the escorting of the bride to her husband's home. Among the Romans, before a marriage took place there was usually but not necessarily a betrothal ceremony (sponsalia) that involved negotiations between the intending bridegroom or his father and the father of the potential bride, along with the exchange of gifts, but marriage did not inevitably follow, for either party could dissolve any marriage arrangement by a repudium.

m. Yebamot 2:6). About a year after the betrothal, as the climax of the wedding festivities, the woman left her parents' house to live with her husband (*m. Ketubot* 5:2; *m. Nedarim* 10:5). In Matt. 1:18 συνέρχομαι ("come together") refers to the commencement of both domestic and sexual relations between an espoused couple, while in Matt. 1:20, 24 παραλαμβάνω ("take into one's home") denotes the husband's act of taking his betrothed wife into his own home and thereby converting betrothal into "marriage."

But how does Paul see his role in the betrothal of the Corinthian congregation to Christ? Four suggestions have been made.

1. *The friend of the groom or the groomsman.*[25]
   That is, Paul is ὁ φίλος τοῦ νυμφίου (John 3:29) or ὁ παρανύμφιος, the bridegroom's "best man," who has wooed the bride, who protects her virginity, and who conducts her to the bridegroom at the wedding.[26] Bruce (234) notes the possibility that Paul was acquainted with the Jewish tradition that Moses was the παρανύμφιος who presented Israel to Yahweh as his covenant bride, although the literary expression of this tradition dates from later times.[27]

2. *The friend of the bride (ἡ παρανύμφος).*
   According to M. Barth, of the two special assistants at a Jewish wedding — the "friend of the bridegroom" and the "friend of the bride" — it was the role of the latter to present the bride to the bridegroom.[28]

3. *The Father's agent.*
   "Paul assumes the role of a father's agent, commissioned to betroth the Father's Son."[29]

4. *The father of the bride.*[30]
   This understanding of Paul's function is to be preferred: because elsewhere in the Corinthian correspondence he views himself as the parent of his converts at Corinth (1 Cor. 4:15; 2 Cor. 6:13; 12:14); because his paramount desire to present the church to her heavenly bridegroom as a παρθένος ἁγνή corresponds to the obligation of the bride's father to protect the virginity of his daughter between betrothal and marriage (cf. Deut. 22:13-21); and because if Paul could refer to a colleague as his

25. So Bernard 100; Martin 207, 332; Witherington 445 and n. 18; Wolff 211.
26. J. Jeremias, *TDNT* 4.1101, 1104, citing (1101 n. 19) SB 1.45-46, 500-504.
27. Namely, *Mekilta* on Exod. 19:17; *Exodus Rabbah* 41.1 on Exod. 34:1; *Numbers Rabbah* 12:8.
28. *Ephesians* 678-79, 679 n. 277; Similarly D. J. Williams 54.
29. Batey, "Image" 176; also his *Nuptial Imagery* 12, 16, but on p. 63 "the friend of the bridegroom."
30. Thus Allo 276; Héring 78; Furnish 499; Peterson, "Conquest" 263; Thrall 661. Also Plummer 293-94; although earlier (1903) he saw Paul as "best man": At the second advent of Christ, Paul would be the παρανύμφιος, just as John the Baptist had been at Christ's first advent (John 3:29) ([CGT] 160). Schlatter (629) and Crafton (113 n. 1, 125) speak in more general terms of Paul as a marriage broker; cf. JB, "I arranged for you to marry Christ."

child "in the Lord" (1 Cor. 4:17)[31] and his converts as his children (1 Cor. 4:14), there is no difficulty in thinking he could regard a whole congregation collectively (ὑμᾶς) as his daughter "in the Lord."

In the OT the husband-wife and bridegroom-bride metaphors regularly describe the relation of Yahweh to his people, Israel.[32] The nation is Yahweh's spouse, so that turning away from him is spiritual adultery.[33] In the NT the same two metaphors are used to depict the relation of Christ to his people, the church.[34] But whereas in the case of Yahweh and Israel, there are only two parties and Yahweh the husband is jealous, here in 11:2 there are three parties — Christ, the Corinthian church, and Paul — and the jealousy that is "God's own jealousy" is not Christ's (the bridegroom) but Paul's (the father of the bride).[35]

The juxtaposition of the plural ὑμᾶς and the singulars ἡρμοσάμην, ἑνὶ ἀνδρί and παρθένον ἁγνήν is dramatic. It was the entire Corinthian church, regarded corporately and as representative of all believers (cf. Eph. 5:32), which was the betrothed bride of Christ. In contemporary texts, individual sacred virgins in various cults could be described as the ἱερὰ παρθένος of a particular god, but "we have no analogy to a group of people being regarded collectively as a παρθένος" (Horsley 1.71). Matching the one bride is the "one husband" (or "one man," Cassirer; Barrett 270),[36] with ἑνί expressing the exclusivity of the relationship. Just as there are not multiple brides of Christ, so too there is one bridegroom, and only one; this bride has and needs no husband in addition to Christ.

The third element in this verse expresses the purpose of Paul's action in betrothing the church to Christ[37] — to present her in virgin purity to her husband at his appearance. παραστῆσαι defines the aim of the betrothal (ἡρμοσάμην) and is used with a τινά τινι ("someone to someone") construction: "in order to present you as a pure maiden to Christ himself."[38] This verb points

31. Cf. 1 Tim. 1:2; 2 Tim. 1:2; 2:1; Tit. 1:4.
32. E.g., Isa. 54:5-6; 62:5; Jer. 3:14; Hos. 2:19-20. See further Ortlund, *passim;* N. Stienstra, *YHWH Is the Husband of His People: Analysis of a Biblical Metaphor with Special Reference to Translation* (Kampen: Kok Pharos, 1993).
33. Jer. 3:1-21; Hos. 2:2; 4:12.
34. Matt. 9:15; 25:1-10; Mark 2:19-20; Luke 5:34-35; John 3:29; Eph. 5:27, 32; Rev. 19:7; 21:2, 9; 22:17. See further Windisch 320-22.
35. Cf. Gale 165.
36. There can be no objection to translating ἀνδρί by "husband," for the man legally became the husband at the time of betrothal and not simply on the wedding day (unlike the modern Western distinction between engagement and marriage) (see above).
37. It is unnecessary as well as impossible to determine precisely when betrothal took place; ἡρμοσάμην points simply to the bare facticity of Paul's past action. Certainly the Corinthians were not betrothed one by one.
38. The word order, with ἑνὶ ἀνδρί intervening between ὑμᾶς and παρθένον ἁγνήν, makes it unlikely that ἑνὶ ἀνδρί should be construed with παραστῆσαι, as NEB, REB: "I betrothed you to Christ, thinking to present you as a chaste virgin to her true and one husband" (similarly Louw and Nida §57.81).

to a solemn or formal presentation, as when the infant Jesus was "presented" to the Lord by his parents in the Temple (Luke 2:22).[39] Since the same verb is used in 4:14 of God's "presentation" of believers to himself or to Christ or before Christ's tribunal after the resurrection (ἐγερεῖ καὶ παραστήσει), we may safely conclude that Paul's "presentation" of the Corinthians to Christ would also occur on the last Day.[40] Confirmation of this may be found in the use of παρίστημι in Eph. 5:27; Col. 1:22 in reference to the church's being presented before God or Christ in unblemished purity at the parousia. παρθένον ἁγνήν stands in apposition to an implied ὑμᾶς, the direct object of παραστῆσαι (cf. Wolff 209). Perhaps sensing that the adjective ἁγνήν is pleonastic with παρθένον ("chaste virgin") and that wedding symbolism is dominant, some render this phrase "pure bride" (Goodspeed, RSV; Furnish 484) or "faithful bride" (Weymouth). But the pleonasm is not stark, for on occasion παρθένος could denote an unmarried woman who was not a virgin.[41] Clearly, παρθένον ἁγνήν emphasizes undefiled virginity. τῷ Χριστῷ is emphatic by position and should not be construed with ἡρμοσάμην (so RSV, NEB, REB); the sense is ". . . to one husband . . . I refer, of course, to Christ."

For Paul, the church stands in the interval between betrothal and wedding day. His nuptial metaphor reflects the ubiquitous NT tension between the "already" and the "not yet." The bride has already been betrothed to the groom, but the marriage has not yet been consummated.[42] At the parousia, that is, on the day that wedding festivities begin (cf. Rev. 19:7), the παρθένος ἁγνή will enter her bridegroom's home, not in the sense that their marriage is then inaugurated but in the sense that it will then be consummated. With the preaching of the good news at Corinth, Paul's evangelistic role was fulfilled and the church that had been created there was betrothed to Christ. But his pastoral role always remained incomplete, for he aimed to preserve the virginity of the infant church right up to her wedding day (v. 2), to maintain her exclusive devotion to Christ (cf. v. 3), and to counter the efforts of foreign lovers (such as his rivals at Corinth) to entice her away from her one and only husband (cf. v. 4). This jealousy for the church's purity was prompted by Paul's paternal affection and expressed the very jealousy of God.

11:3 φοβοῦμαι δὲ μή πως, ὡς ὁ ὄφις ἐξηπάτησεν Εὕαν ἐν τῇ πανουργίᾳ αὐτοῦ, φθαρῇ τὰ νοήματα ὑμῶν ἀπὸ τῆς ἁπλότητος καὶ τῆς ἁγνότητος τῆς εἰς

---

39. Sometimes παρίστημι has been given the technical sense of "give away," describing parents' role in giving their daughter to her husband. "I engaged you to one man, to give you away to Christ as a pure virgin" (Young and Ford 272; similarly JB; NJB has "a virgin pure for presentation to Christ"). But such "modernizing" is inappropriate.

40. Although we endorse the view that in 11:2 Paul sees himself as the bride's father, it must be admitted that παραστῆσαι well suits the role of the bridegroom's or the bride's "friend," if ancient Jewish marriage procedures are pressed (see above). However, Paul can use παρίστημι of his own presentation of persons before God at the parousia (Col. 1:28).

41. See LSJ 1339 s.v. παρθένος I.2.

42. See Batey, "Image" 180-82.

τὸν Χριστόν. "But I am afraid that just as the snake deceived Eve by his cunning, your minds may somehow be corrupted and lured away from your single-mindedness and your purity in relation to Christ." In v. 2 Paul has expressed his aim and hope in betrothing the Corinthian church to Christ. He wished to conduct her safely to her bridegroom's heavenly home and present her to him in virgin purity. Now in v. 3 he qualifies (δέ, "but") his hope by admitting a fear that his goal may somehow (πώς) not be achieved. His fear is twofold — the corruption of his converts' minds (φθαρῇ τὰ νοήματα ὑμῶν) and the loss of their initial single-mindedness and purity (ἀπὸ τῆς ἁπλότητος καὶ τῆς ἁγνότητος). The construction φοβοῦμαι μή πως with the subjunctive is found only twice in the NT,[43] here and in 12:20 where Paul states his fear about Corinthian conduct.

νοήματα here refers to "thinking processes" and "attitudes," as in 3:14; 4:4, not to "stratagems" (as in 2:11) or (in the singular) to a "design" (10:5). Paul saw that the principal danger confronting the Corinthian church at the time of writing was intellectual deception, not moral corruption, but a deception that could lead to spiritual apostasy (6:1). It was their adulterous flirting with a false gospel (v. 4), their countenancing of a different Jesus and an alien Spirit (v. 4), that constituted the main hazard. If they embraced the alternative Jesus, Spirit, and gospel being offered by the intruders, their thoughts would be "corrupted"[44] or "led astray."[45]

If this intellectual deception took place, the casualty would be their single-mindedness and purity. The combination of φθαρῇ and ἀπό is pregnant,[46] so that ". . . be corrupted from" means ". . . be corrupted and thus lured away from," with ἀπό expressing separation, alienation (BDF §211) or diversion. Thrall combines the two notions (". . . your minds might be corruptly diverted from . . . ," 656), while NEB, REB separate them[47] (". . . your thoughts may be corrupted and you may lose . . ."). The Corinthians were in danger of losing two distinct Christian virtues, ἡ ἁπλότης and ἡ ἁγνότης ἡ εἰς τὸν Χριστόν.[48] EVV often coalesce these two notions and supply an appropriate common idea such as "devotion" or "commitment" that coheres with εἰς τὸν Χριστόν; thus "a sincere and pure devotion to Christ" (RSV, NRSV) or "a total and pure commitment to Christ" (Furnish 484). But we should not overlook the article before ἁγνότητος, remembering that with two coordinated nouns the repetition of the article distinguishes the two nouns,[49] especially when the number and gender of the two are the same. If ἁπλότητος and ἁγνότητος were virtual synonyms (cf.

---

43. The same phrase is followed by the (perfect) indicative in Gal. 5:11; elsewhere in the NT φοβέομαι μή is found only in Acts 5:26; 23:10; 27:17, 29; Heb. 4:1.

44. JB, "your ideas may get corrupted."

45. BAGD 273a, 540d, 857c; Weymouth, Goodspeed, RSV, NIV, NJB, NRSV.

46. Lietzmann (145) suggests that this combination is analogous to πλανᾶσθαι ἀπό ("be led astray from"; cf. Jas. 5:19).

47. Similarly BAGD 86d; GNB, JB, NAB¹, Cassirer.

48. This assumes that τῆς ἁγνότητος is part of the original text (see Textual Note e.).

49. Cf. Zerwick §184; Turner 181-82.

Zmijewski 87) or formed a single conceptual unit, we would expect ἁγνότητος to be anarthrous.[50]

As in Eph. 6:5; Col. 3:22, ἁπλότης has the sense of "sincerity" or "single-mindedness" or "simplicity," that singleness of mind and purpose that finds expression for Christians in an exclusive preoccupation with pleasing Christ (5:9).[51] The person who is characterized by ἁπλότης has no divided loyalties and is not duplicitous but shows unswerving commitment to a person or cause. ἁγνότητος is a clear verbal link with (παρθένον) ἁγνήν in v. 2. When the Corinthian church was betrothed to Christ, she was a "pure maiden," adhering to pure doctrine. Paul's fear now is that her original purity or virginity might be forfeited through the enticements of paramours. If she adhered to the false doctrine of the intruders (v. 4), she would lose the pristine purity that she had "in relation to Christ" (εἰς τὸν Χριστόν),[52] her heavenly bridegroom and one husband.[53] As purveyors of a false gospel (v. 4), Paul's rivals were those who (unwittingly) were defiling a betrothed maiden.

With the expression "just as the snake deceived Eve by his cunning" Paul states a precedent that informs his fear. It would appear that he intends his hearers to recognize three parallels between the record of Eve's temptation by the snake in Gen. 3:1-13 and the situation he himself faced in Corinth.

First, just as Eve was deceived in her thinking (Gen. 3:1-6) and so lost her innocence (Gen. 3:7),[54] so too the Corinthian church was at risk of being deluded in thought (φθαρῇ τὰ νοήματα ὑμῶν) and so losing her virginity (ἀπὸ . . . τῆς ἁγνότητος). In response to God's inquiry, "What is this you have done?" Eve declares, "The snake deceived me (ὁ ὄφις ἠπάτησέν με, LXX)" (Gen. 3:13). As in 1 Tim. 2:14, Paul uses the compound verb ἐξηπάτησεν, where the prefix ἐκ- points to "successful deceit" (Moulton and Howard 311) or, more probably, to complete deception. With the movement from παρθένον ἁγνήν (v. 1) to ἁγιότητος (v. 2) Paul is clearly developing the betrothal-marriage analogy further (see above), but he may also be introducing a new analogy, that of "the church as in some sense the last Eve, related to Christ in the same way that

50. Recognition of this grammatical point is reflected in the renderings of RV, Weymouth ("their single-heartedness and their fidelity to Christ"), Barclay; also Lambrecht 172. It is true that both genitives (ἁπλότητος and ἁγνότητος) are dependent on the one preposition ἀπό, but this fact does not lessen the significance of the second τῆς. The singular τῆς (εἰς τὸν Χριστόν) is also significant in this regard since it refers only to ἁγνότητος; cf. RV, "the simplicity and the purity that is toward Christ."

51. On this theme see Harris, *Slave* 97-98, 143. In 8:2; 9:11, 13 and Rom. 12:8, ἁπλότης means "generosity" (see the discussion at 8:2). All seven NT uses of this word are Pauline. See further Amstutz; Spicq 1.169-73.

52. It is improbable that this phrase should be rendered "(purity) due from you to the Christ" (TCNT).

53. It is significant that vv. 2 and 3 both end with a reference to ὁ Χριστός; he is the exclusive point of orientation for his bride, and she owes him constant faithfulness.

54. For Jewish traditions about the deception of Eve, see *1 Enoch* 69:6; *Apocalypse of Abraham* 23; *Life of Adam and Eve* 44:2-5; *Jubilees* 3:17-35; and Thackeray 50-55.

Eve was related to Adam — derived from him, existing for his sake, and for him only."[55] It is sometimes alleged (e.g., by Batey, "Image" 177) that Paul is alluding here to the rabbinical tradition that the serpent seduced Eve to sexual immorality.[56] Now although the verb ἐξαπατάω, "I turn (someone) away from the right road by deceit" (Zerwick, *Analysis* 409), could be rendered "entice" or "lure," it need not refer to sexual seduction. For Paul, the means of the deceit was not lust, but cunning (ἐν τῇ πανουργίᾳ αὐτοῦ), and the word νοήματα, not σώματα, is the subject of φθαρῇ. We need not go outside Genesis 3 to explain the expression ὁ ὄφις ἐξηπάτησεν Εὔαν.

Second, just as Eve's deception was carried out by the snake (= the devil),[57] so too the cause of any enticement toward disloyalty among the Corinthians was Satan. Although no agent is expressed with the passive φθαρῇ (τὰ νοήματα ὑμῶν), the parallelism in the verse and the explicit reference to ὁ Σατανᾶς in v. 4 indicate that we should take Satan to be the one who corrupts the thinking of the Corinthians. If Satan, as "the god of this (present) age," is capable of blinding the minds (νοήματα) of unbelievers (4:4), it is not unjustified to assume that he could also pervert the thoughts of believers. Moreover, he has the ability to gain the advantage over believers by means of his stratagems (2:11) and to trick them by masquerading as an angel of light (11:14). In each case the sphere of his most virulent attack is the mind. But in the case of the Corinthians it was through his deputies that Satan would accomplish his purposes of deceiving the mind (cf. 11:13-15).

Third, just as Satan operated by craftiness (ἐν τῇ πανουργίᾳ αὐτοῦ)[58] in beguiling Eve, so too his agents were using cunning in beguiling the Corinthians. Genesis 3 begins with the assertion that "the snake was more crafty (LXX, φρονιμώτατος, 'most shrewd') than all the wild animals the LORD God had made" (Gen. 3:1). This craftiness was evident in his casting doubt on God's intent (Gen. 3:1, "Did God really say, 'You must not eat from any of the trees in the garden'?"[59]), on God's threat (Gen. 3:4, "You will not 'certainly die'" [cf.

---

55. Barrett, "Opponents" 239; cf. Minear 55; Ellis 129; Ortlund 151-52; Batey 12 ("Just as Eve had aspired to be like God, knowing good and evil [Gen. 3:5-6], and had revealed only her nakedness, so the Corinthians were in danger of being seduced by false promises of *gnosis*").

56. *b. Yebamot* 103b; *b. 'Abodah Zarah* 22b; *b. Shabbat* 146a (cited by Lietzmann 145). Earlier testimony to this tradition is found in 4 Macc. 18:7-8 (perhaps first century A.D.). The mother of the seven noble sons who were martyred under Antiochus Epiphanes says of herself, "I was a pure virgin (παρθένος ἁγνή). . . . No seducer of the desert nor deceiver in the field defiled me; nor did the deceitful serpent despoil me of the purity of my virginity."

57. In Jewish thought the snake, as the archetypal unclean animal, symbolized opposition to God and so naturally came to be identified with the epitome of such opposition, namely, the devil or Satan. But Rev. 12:9 and 20:2 are the only explicit biblical identifications of the Edenic snake with the devil or Satan. (See also, however, Luke 10:18-19 and Rom. 16:20, which may allude to Gen. 3:15.) On this tradition see W. Foerster, *TDNT* 5.577-78.

58. On the use of the word πανουργία as a term of abuse directed against the sophists, see Betz, *Paulus* 104-5.

59. This question involved a blatant distortion of God's actual permission (Gen. 2:16).

2:17]), and on God's motivation (Gen. 3:5, "For God knows that when you eat
of it [the tree of the knowledge of good and evil, 2:17], your eyes will be
opened, and you will become like God, knowing good and evil"). As for the
cunning of the interlopers from Judea, they had mastered the art of masquerading already perfected by their principal (11:13-15, where μετασχηματίζω,
"masquerade," "disguise," occurs three times), and, like the Edenic snake, they
would deceive by means of cunning words (cf. Rom. 16:18). "Paul sees *words*
— erroneous in content but smooth of delivery — as Satan's instrument to se-
duce the church from her loyalty to Christ" (Barnett 502).

11:4 εἰ μὲν γὰρ ὁ ἐρχόμενος ἄλλον Ἰησοῦν κηρύσσει ὃν οὐκ ἐκηρύξαμεν,
ἢ πνεῦμα ἕτερον λαμβάνετε ὃ οὐκ ἐλάβετε, ἢ εὐαγγέλιον ἕτερον ὃ οὐκ ἐδέξασθε,
καλῶς ἀνέχεσθε. "For in fact (μὲν γάρ) you put up with it well enough if some
interloper preaches another Jesus than the Jesus we preached, or if you receive
a different Spirit from the Spirit you received or a different gospel from the gospel you embraced." γάρ introduces a second reason justifying Paul's request for
tolerance (ἀνέχεσθέ μου, v. 1). "You Corinthians cheerfully put up with someone who comes along with a message totally different from the message that we
preached and you yourselves espoused. So you should put up with me — no intruder! — in a bit of foolishness." Perhaps Paul is simultaneously justifying his
fear expressed in v. 3.[60] "I am anxious about your spiritual welfare because you
readily tolerate a newcomer who proclaims a new message."

In the conditional sentence εἰ ὁ ἐρχόμενος . . . κηρύσσει . . . , καλῶς
ἀνέχεσθε, the protasis states a present reality ("if, as is the case"), not some hypothetical possibility ("if it were the case that" = εἰ . . . ἐκήρυσσεν) (as Munck
176-78). The condition is assumed to be true (cf. Zerwick §311); a certain type
of proclamation was actually being made at Corinth at the time Paul was writing (note κηρύσσει, not ἐκήρυξεν). In other contexts ὁ ἐρχόμενος ("he who
comes") is a title of the Messiah,[61] but here it means "your visitor"[62] (anaphoric
article) or "some interloper"[63] (generic article), the implication being that this
person comes from outside Corinth. He comes on the scene at Corinth as an intruder.[64] Simply because the singular is used we need not assume that an isolated individual is in mind. He may be the ringleader or spokesman of the visitors, or the reference may be generic.[65] This latter possibility is to be preferred
in light of the use of ὁ τοιοῦτος (10:11), φησίν (10:10), and τις (10:7, 12; 11:20,

60. So also Barrett 274; Thrall 664, 666. There is no *a priori* reason why a conjunction
should not fulfill a double role, provided it is given the same sense in each case.

61. E.g., Matt. 11:3; 21:9; 23:39; Luke 7:19-20; John 11:27; Heb. 10:37.

62. Barrett 270; Thrall 656.

63. Moffatt; cf. Lambrecht 172 ("a newcomer").

64. ἔρχομαι is used of false teachers who "appear" (BAGD 311b) or "come on the scene";
e.g., 2 Pet. 3:3; 1 John 2:18. There is no reason to follow Schlatter (631-32, 635) in seeing ὁ
ἐρχόμενος as a theological adjudicator from Jerusalem.

65. Cf. ὁ ταράσσων (Gal. 5:10); ὁ συλαγωγῶν (Col. 2:8) (Bultmann 202). On Paul's practice
of not naming his opponents, see Marshall 341-48; "Invective" 366-67.

five times) in the immediate context, alongside the plurals οἱ τοιοῦτοι (11:13), πολλοί (11:18), and εἰσίν (11:22-23, four times). This substantival participle ὁ ἐρχόμενος is equivalent to a substantival adjective with a generic sense (ὁ δίκαιος = οἱ δίκαιοι).[66]

There is a distinct pattern in Paul's description of the intruders' message and its relation to his own message.

some intruder preaches	Jesus	*we* preach*ed*
you receive	Spirit	*you* receiv*ed*
[*you* receive]	gospel	*you* embrac*ed*

Although it is not explicitly stated, the pattern suggests that both the intruder(s) and Paul preached "Spirit" and "gospel" as well as "Jesus," and that the Corinthians received or embraced "Jesus" as well as "Spirit" and "gospel." Also, we may assume that λαμβάνετε ("you receive") is to be supplied in the third phrase on the basis of the second, and that the three aorists in the ἄλλον/ἕτερον . . . ὃν/ὃ οὐκ construction, viz. ἐκηρύξαμεν, ἐλάβετε, ἐδέξασθε, refer to the time of the Corinthians' conversion (1:19). ἐδέξασθε is probably a synonym for ἐλάβετε, with the distinction being not in the verb used but in what is received, the gift of the Spirit or the teaching contained in the gospel. Similarly, ἕτερος should here be probably considered synonymous with ἄλλος,[67] used for stylistic variety,[68] although one would not want to disallow a distinction between the two words in Gal. 1:6-7.[69]

Some translations and commentators take πνεῦμα ἕτερον to mean "a different spirit."[70] This "spirit" could be either a worldly spirit (1 Cor. 2:12) such as a spirit of bondage (Rom. 8:15; Gal. 2:4; 4:24) or of fear (Rom. 8:15) or of timidity (2 Tim. 1:7) that was the opposite of the spirit of freedom (3:18; Gal. 2:4; 5:1) or of joy (Rom. 14:17; Gal. 5:22; 1 Thess. 1:6) or of power (Col. 1:11; 2 Tim. 1:7) proclaimed by Paul,[71] or an "attitude to living" that contradicts Paul's "strength-as-weakness (ἀσθένεια) teaching and practice."[72] Against tak-

---

66. Cf. BDF §§263(b); 264(6).

67. So, e.g., Windisch 327. Zerwick (§153) sees in the use of ἕτερος for ἄλλος an instance of "the obsolescence in Hellenistic Greek of the category of duality"; cf. Acts 4:12; 1 Cor. 12:9-10. But Vincent posits a distinction: "*Another* denies the identity; *a different* denies the *similarity of nature*" (836).

68. BDF §306(4); BAGD 315b; Turner 197. Note also the variety in word order — ἄλλον Ἰησοῦν but πνεῦμα ἕτερον.

69. Cf. Robertson 747 (Paul "admits ἕτερον, but refuses ἄλλο"); Burton 22-24, 420-22 ("For Paul ἕτερος suggested difference of kind more distinctly than did ἄλλος and . . . the latter, in contrast with ἕτερος, signified simply numerical non-identity," 422). For a different view, see BDF §306(4).

70. E.g., JB, Barclay, NJB, Cassirer; BAGD 678a ("a different [*kind of*] spirit"); Lambrecht 174.

71. So Plummer 297; Hughes 377-78.

72. Martin 336, citing Black 132-38; "Weakness" 77-93.

ing πνεῦμα as a reference to a spirit or attitude, Fee argues[73] (convincingly in our view) that coming between "Jesus" and "gospel," the word πνεῦμα is likely to be related to these two terms, as the "Spirit" is in fact, and so intimately; and that the verb λαμβάνω, which Paul elsewhere uses with reference to the receipt of the Holy Spirit,[74] ill accords with any other sense of πνεῦμα.

Jesus-Spirit-gospel is an apt summary of Christianity (cf. Windisch 327), and what Paul himself signified by these key terms is unambiguous. His κήρυγμα centered on Jesus Christ crucified and risen,[75] on the gift of the Spirit of God or of Christ as the fulfillment of promise and the pledge of inheritance,[76] and on the good news of forgiveness and reconciliation in Christ as the instrument of God's saving power.[77] He knew that these three elements stood or fell together, for "another Jesus" would inevitably mean both a "different Spirit," since the Spirit is the Spirit of Jesus Christ (Rom. 8:9; Phil. 1:19), and a "different gospel," since the gospel is about Jesus Christ (2 Cor. 2:12; 9:13; 10:14). His opponents apparently used the same three terms, but their content was so different that the message they were proclaiming amounted to a perversion of the gospel, indeed a false gospel, no gospel at all. The threefold antithesis expressed by ἄλλον/ἕτερον . . . ὃν/ὃ οὐκ underlines this radical divergence between the two messages to which the Corinthians had been exposed. But it is a hazardous — indeed, an impossible — undertaking to try to specify the precise content of the opponents' message. Proposals are not in short supply[78] and are comparably divergent. To illustrate this latter point from two recent commentators, according to Barnett (505) Paul uses the name "Jesus" (cf. "Christ" in vv. 2-3) because his "historic Jewish persona was being emphasized at the expense of his risen Lordship." Thrall, on the other hand, believes that the "another Jesus" proclaimed by Paul's rivals was "a splendid figure of post-resurrection glory by contrast with the Pauline gospel of the crucified Christ" (940; cf. 669-70).[79] Certainly Paul's concern is not with the details of the "different gospel" being propounded — he offers no rebuttal — but with the Corinthians' response to the rival message and to his own ("you receive . . . you received . . . [you receive] . . . you embraced") and with the consequences of a total Corinthian capitula-

73. Fee, *Presence* 344; "Gospel" 121-22.
74. Rom. 8:15; 1 Cor. 2:12; Gal. 3:2; cf. John 20:22; Acts 8:15; 10:47; 19:2.
75. E.g., 1 Cor. 1:23; 15:1, 3-4; 1 Thess. 4:14; 2 Tim. 2:8.
76. E.g., Rom. 8:9; 2 Cor. 1:22; 5:5; Eph. 1:13-14.
77. E.g., Rom. 1:16; 2 Cor. 5:19.
78. Convenient summaries are found in Furnish 500-502; and especially in the excursus in Thrall 667-70, who classifies the various proposals under three headings: "the opponents preach a Judaizing gospel; they propound a Christology different from Paul's own; the attack on his apostleship implies the advocacy of an alien gospel" (667).
79. Similarly Murphy-O'Connor, "Jesus" 238-51 ("Paul uses it [the name 'Jesus'] to counteract the propaganda of those whose distaste for a crucified Christ led them to invent 'another Jesus'" [238], whose earthly life as a miracle-worker was authenticated by his resurrection as "the Lord of glory").

tion to this alien gospel (11:3).[80] It was not merely the presence of rivals at Corinth that aroused Paul's anger, the fact that they had invaded foreign territory (10:13-16), but their arrival in Corinth as purported agents of Christ (11:13, 23) declaring a gospel that he knew to be not only different in emphasis from the gospel that he had preached and to which the Corinthians had responded, but so different in content that it could be described only as a "totally other," that is, a false gospel (cf. Gal. 1:6-7).

The apodosis of the conditional sentence, καλῶς ἀνέχεσθε, "you put up with it well enough" (BAGD 401c), "you are marvellously tolerant" (TCNT), is harsh but ironical (cf. καλῶς in Mark 7:9).[81] But behind the irony is profound disquiet — distress that the Corinthians so readily accepted novelty and elevated form over content, manner over matter. The implied object of ἀνέχεσθε is τοῦτο, "this" or "it," that is, the appearance of intruders with a false gospel, although the object supplied from the context could be αὐτοῦ,[82] that is, the intruder (ὁ ἐρχόμενος). As in vv. 1, 19-20 ἀνέχομαι refers simply to toleration of a person's actions or ideas. There is no justification for linking λαμβάνετε and ἀνέχεσθε and finding an allusion to actual hospitality, provided by Jewish households within the Corinthian church (as Barnett 38, 506 proposes).

11:5 λογίζομαι γὰρ μηδὲν ὑστερηκέναι τῶν ὑπερλίαν ἀποστόλων. "For I reckon I am not at all inferior to those superlative apostles." On any view the transition from v. 4 to v. 5 seems abrupt, which may explain why γάρ has been understood in different ways — as adversative ("but"),[83] as copulative ("and"),[84] or as causal ("for").[85] The latter rendering is to be preferred if, as we have argued, this verse provides a third reason why Paul believes the Corinthians should accommodate him in his excursion into foolish boasting (v. 1).[86] His reasoning seems to be as follows. "You Corinthians put up with my rivals' appeals to the 'superlative apostles' in Jerusalem and their comparisons between those apostles and me. Then you should tolerate me as well, since I consider myself to rank on a par with those apostles." But such an understanding presupposes an answer to the crucial exegetical question to be

---

80. "Paul's antagonists were to him a snake [cf. 11:3] under the flower of a different gospel — enticing but deadly" (Batey; "Image" 177).

81. Although not endorsing the idea, Plummer (297-98) mentions the possibility that καλῶς is not ironical and the whole sentence is interrogative. "'If people come and behave in this way, is it seemly [καλῶς] that you should tolerate them?'" (298). But the undoubted irony of ἡδέως . . . ἀνέχεσθε τῶν ἀφρόνων ("you gladly tolerate fools") in v. 19 discounts this proposal.

82. Lambrecht (174) supplies "that person." ἀνέχομαι is generally followed by the accusative of the thing or the genitive of the person.

83. NIV; Lambrecht 174; similarly Wendland 235; Lang 336.

84. Lietzmann 146; cf. NJB ("Now,"), Barclay ("Well,"), Weymouth and Cassirer ("Why,"). For γάρ = δέ, see BAGD 152c and Zerwick §473, both citing this verse and 1:12; 10:12. Several translations (TCNT, RSV, NAB[1], REB, NRSV) have no rendering for γάρ, as also GNB and Furnish 489 who have a new paragraph beginning at this verse.

85. RV, Goodspeed, NASB, NAB[2]; Barrett 277-78.

86. So also Barrett 277-78; Thrall 671.

considered below: Who are οἱ ὑπερλίαν ἀπόστολοι who are mentioned here and in 12:5?

There are no grammatical ambiguities in the verse. ὑστερηκέναι is a complementary infinitive after λογίζομαι, with the subject of the infinitive identical with that of the governing verb.[87] "The perfect marks not only a past (xii.11, ὑστέρησα) or present inferiority (Rom. iii.23, ὑστεροῦνται), but an abiding one."[88] μηδέν is an accusative of respect,[89] literally "with respect to nothing," that is, "in no way at all," "not in any degree." τῶν ὑπερλίαν ἀποστόλων is a genitive of comparison, since that idea is implied when the verb ὑστερέω means "be inferior to." ὑπερλίαν is a compound adverb (ὑπέρ, "beyond," + λίαν, "exceedingly," "overmuch") meaning "beyond measure" or "exceedingly,"[90] here used adjectivally, while τῶν is anaphoric, pointing to a well-known entity, "these/those," "those . . . of yours." An amazing array of renderings for ὑπερλίαν is found among the commentators and translations — "superlative," "superlatively great," "famous," "highest ranking," "very special," "(apostles) par excellence," "arch-(apostles)," "top," "ultra," "super-extra," "exalted," "eminent," "super-(apostles)," "superfine," "extra-super," "surpassingly superior," "extra-special," "pre-eminent."

Since the issue of the identity of οἱ ὑπερλίαν ἀπόστολοι has been discussed in the Introduction (B.4.d.), here we shall merely set out the options and restate the principal arguments for the general position we espouse (#2 below).

1. If οἱ ὑπερλίαν ἀπόστολοι are (οἱ) ψευδαπόστολοι (11:13), that is, Paul's rivals at Corinth, then the expression "the superlative apostles" is *either* the self-description of "the false apostles" *or* the Corinthians' appraisal of "the false apostles" *or* Paul's sarcastic/ironical description of "the false apostles" or of their own opinion of themselves.

2. If οἱ ὑπερλίαν ἀπόστολοι are not (οἱ) ψευδαπόστολοι, then the expression "the superlative apostles" is *either* "the false apostles'" description of the Twelve or the so-called three "pillars" (στῦλοι, Gal. 2:9, namely James, Cephas, and John) in the church of Jerusalem *or* Paul's own commendatory or derogatory description of the Twelve or the Three *or* his parodying of the Corinthian view of "the false apostles" *or* his own ironical description of the exalted view of the Twelve held by "the false apostles."[91]

---

87. Cf. BDF §§392(1)(a); 397(2).

88. Plummer (CGT) 164; cf. Zmijewski 115-16; Fanning 396-97.

89. BAGD 518b calls it an accusative of the inner object.

90. Héring (77 n. 1) claims that ὑπερλίαν "= 'beyond all measure' should not simply indicate a higher grade, but something which defies any comparison." But this adverb also means "exceedingly" (LSJ 1866 s.v., who translate οἱ ὑπερλίαν ἀπόστολοι as the '*super*-Apostles'") or "excessively" (Marshall 372, who notes [372 n. 109] that when used pejoratively λίαν connotes excess).

91. That Paul himself may have coined the expression οἱ ὑπερλίαν ἀπόστολοι is recognized by (among others) Plummer (299); and Furnish (490), both of whom note Paul's fondness for com-

In the Introduction I have endeavored to defend this last position. The most compelling arguments in favor of drawing a distinction between "the superlative apostles" and "the false apostles" (#2 above) are these. First, it is difficult to imagine that Paul would refer to himself as "in no way inferior" to false teachers whom he describes as "deceitful workmen" (11:13) and servants of Satan (11:15). It would be very appropriate for him to claim equality with the Twelve or the Three, but wholly incongruous to claim to be not a whit behind "false apostles." Second, when Paul compares himself with the "false apostles" he speaks boldly and positively and claims superiority (". . . so am I [11:22, three times] . . . I am more . . . much harder . . . more frequently . . . more severely," 11:23 [NIV]), but when he compares himself with "the superlative apostles" he speaks mildly and negatively and implies equality ("I am not at all inferior," 11:5; 12:11). Third, the apostles who are "false" provoke Paul's forthright and direct denunciation (11:13, 15), even if he takes their allegations and claims seriously, whereas he treats the apostles who are "superlative" indirectly (11:5; 12:11) and with a gentle irony that is comparable to his depiction of the Three as "those who were reputed (οἱ δοκοῦντες) to be pillars" (Gal. 2:9; cf. Gal. 2:6).[92] Fourth, whatever the source of the expression οἱ ὑπερλίαν ἀπόστολοι, would Paul himself have applied the term ἀπόστολοι, however understood, to those he describes as ψευδαπόστολοι?[93] This phrase, "by whomsoever used, could not well be applied to men of lower apostolic status than theirs," namely "the Jerusalem apostles, including James" (Bruce 236-37).

In 10:12 Paul disavows comparison between himself and his rivals, although he engages in such in 11:22-29 as part of his κατὰ σάρκα boasting (11:18). Here in 11:5, on our view, he resorts to comparison between himself and the Jerusalem leaders, claiming that he is "in no respect" (μηδέν) inferior to them. μηδέν is surprising, since Paul was not a Judean Jew, was not a member of the mother church in Jerusalem, and was without a personal acquaintance with Jesus. But a rigorist understanding of μηδέν is inappropriate in the context. μηδὲν ὑστερηκέναι, "to be in no way inferior," is litotes for εἶναι ἴσα ἐν παντί (cf. Phil. 2:6), "to be equal in every way," and Paul has in mind his parity of status as an apostle (as in 1 Cor. 9:1; 15:5, 8-11) (note τῶν . . . ἀποστόλων) and as a person competent in knowledge of the faith (γνῶσις, 11:6). This assertion of equality is a response to unfavorable comparisons between Paul and the original apostles being made by his rivals who were illegitimately invoking the au-

---

pounds of ὑπέρ in 2 Corinthians: ὑπεραίρομαι (12:7, twice), ὑπερβαλλόντως (11:23), ὑπερβάλλω (3:10; 9:14), ὑπερβολή (1:8; 4:7, 17; 12:7), ὑπερέκεινα (10:16), ὑπερεκτείνω (10:14), ὑπερπερισσεύω (7:4). For satirical terms comparable to Paul's ironical expression, see Betz, *Paulus* 121 n. 570.

92. Cf. Käsemann 45. On the four uses of δοκέω in Galatians 2, see Barrett, " 'Pillar' Apostles" 1-4.

93. In 11:13 he speaks of them as *masquerading* "as apostles of Christ" (εἰς ἀποστόλους Χριστοῦ), while διάκονοι Χριστοῦ (11:23) is another of their self-descriptions (εἰσίν; has the sense, "Do they claim to be?").

thority of the Twelve (and James) in support of their own Judaizing program at Corinth. Paul's overall point in v. 5 is that if the Corinthians tolerated intruders who brought a counterfeit gospel (v. 4) and made inflated claims concerning the Jerusalem leadership (cf. v. 5), they ought also to bear with him in his "bit of foolishness" (v. 1).

11:6 εἰ δὲ καὶ ἰδιώτης τῷ λόγῳ, ἀλλ' οὐ τῇ γνώσει, ἀλλ' ἐν παντὶ φανερώσαντες ἐν πᾶσιν εἰς ὑμᾶς. "Even if I lack skill in oratory, I certainly do not in knowledge. On the contrary, in our dealings with you we have made this clear in every way and in all circumstances." In examining 10:10 we saw that some persons at Corinth, perhaps the coalition of anti-Pauline Corinthians and the intruders from Judea, were contending that Paul's ability in public speaking was contemptible. In addition, these intruders were evidently comparing him adversely with the twelve apostles and James, saying among other things that he was inferior (cf. ὑστερηκέναι, 11:5) to them in knowledge, perhaps knowledge of the historical Jesus and knowledge of Christian truth. Here in v. 6 Paul responds to these two criticisms,[94] conceding his amateur status in oratory but claiming not to be amateurish in knowledge.

Since δέ is here a loose connective (BAGD 220a suggests "and"), it is left untranslated in most EVV. εἰ . . . καὶ ἰδιώτης [εἰμι][95] is an actual concession, corresponding to the protasis in a "first class" conditional sentence where the condition is assumed to be a reality.[96] Thus "Even if (as is true) I am unskilled . . . ," or "Granted that I lack skill" (Cassirer).[97] Originally, an ἰδιώτης was a person whose interests and concerns were restricted to his own affairs (τὰ ἴδια) and who took no active part in public life.[98] Then it came to be applied to someone without formal rank (such as a private as opposed to an officer, or a layman as opposed to a priest) or someone without specialized training (the amateur as opposed to the professional). But although technically a "non-professional," an ἰδιώτης could be knowledgeable in a particular field. The term "does not rule out the individual's informal acquaintance with a subject or practice in it."[99] So then, when Paul concedes that he is ἰδιώτης τῷ λόγῳ (dative of respect) he is not deny-

94. If in fact "the superlative apostles" (11:5) are the "false apostles" (11:13), Paul's rivals in Corinth, he may be responding in 11:6 to their claim to be superior to him in oratorical skill (see Barnett 34 n. 139, 508 n. 8, 509) and in knowledge.

95. D* E actually read εἰμί here.

96. "The event referred to in the concessive clause [of this type] is in general not contingent, but conceived of as actual" (Burton §284, citing in Paul's letters 2 Cor. 4:16; 7:12; 11:6; 12:11; Phil. 2:17; Col. 2:5).

97. But Thrall (656) construes καί with ἰδιώτης: "But if in respect of oratory I am indeed a layman. . . ." It is possible that when Paul says he is "a layman in speech," he is conceding a point for the sake of argument (cf. Moffatt, "I am no speaker, perhaps") or even speaking ironically with deliberate rhetorical affectation (as Judge 37, who, along with Danker [165], refers to Dio Chrysostom, *Orations* 42:3, for comparable self-depreciation in the midst of evidence of rhetorical sophistication).

98. On this word, see H. Schlier, *TDNT* 3.215-17; Spicq 2.212-14.

99. Kennedy, *Interpretation* 95.

ing that he has any knowledge of rhetoric. As Judge observes, there is no unambiguous evidence that Paul had mastered the arts of rhetoric through tertiary-level training under a recognized sophist, but even if he was not formally trained in rhetoric, he must have been familiar with the rhetorical fashions of his time and area, that is, the more florid "Asianic" type of rhetoric.[100] If, as we have suggested, ὁ λόγος in 10:10 refers to Paul's speaking ability, including adroitness in extempore speech, it is likely that τῷ λόγῳ has a similar reference, "public speaking" (NJB), "rhetoric" (Berkeley) or "oratory" (Thrall 656).[101]

While agreeing with his opponents that he was an amateur in public speaking, Paul repudiates their view that he was unskilled in knowledge, inferior to the Twelve with regard to knowledge. ἀλλ' οὐ[κ ἰδιώτης], "certainly not [unskilled/an amateur]," expresses the repudiation baldly, with the implied double negative "not unskilled" being litotes for "very skilled" or "well trained." τῇ γνώσει, like the preceding τῷ λόγῳ, is a dative of respect (on which see BDF §197). But what is this γνῶσις in which Paul excels? Whether we regard it as knowledge of God through Christ (cf. 2:14; 4:6; 10:5),[102] as the mystery of Christ (Eph. 3:4-5; cf. 1 Cor. 2:6-11),[103] or simply as the gospel,[104] it is essentially his insight into revealed divine truth. Given the distinctly Christian nature of γνῶσις in Paul,[105] it is improbable that Paul is saying "I am not an orator but I am a philosopher,"[106] or that he is contrasting his capacity as an orator with his knowledge of rhetoric.[107]

If the first ἀλλά may be rendered "certainly,"[108] the second has the sense of "on the contrary." So far from being inexpert in knowledge, Paul had made plain the fact that he was not deficient in knowledge of God's truth. The partici-

---

100. Judge 40-41; "Conformity" 12-13.

101. If 10:10 is closely parallel to 11:6, it is unlikely that ὁ λόγος in 11:6 refers to ecstatic speech (as Käsemann 35; Friedrich, "Gegner" 182-83) or to gnostic speculations (as Bultmann 204, citing 1 Cor. 2:4). Linking 10:10 and 11:6, Savage argues that Paul's opponents criticize him "for refusing to indulge in the imposing and abusive rhetoric" that characterized first-century-A.D. orators (71; cf. 30-31, 46-47).

102. Savage 79.

103. Tasker 150.

104. Hafemann 431; *Defense* 146 and n. 124.

105. See the classic work by Dupont, *Gnosis: La connaissance religieuse dans les épîtres de Saint Paul* (Paris: Gabalda, 1949).

106. But Betz (59-60, 66) argues that in saying he is "a novice in speech but not in knowledge," Paul aligns himself with Cynic philosophers who, in their dispute with the sophists, gave priority to content (γνῶσις) over form (λόγος).

107. Thus Winter 216-17. According to Winter, Paul "manifested" (φανερώσαντες) his knowledge of rhetoric by his readiness to defend himself before Gallio (Acts 18:14) and by his use of rhetorical devices and forms in his letters, although he felt compelled to repudiate the deceit that often accompanied spoken rhetoric. His educational status was that of a person "trained in rhetoric but not living the professional life of a public orator and teacher, even though he engaged in public proclamation and private instruction" (218; cf. Isocrates, *Antidosis* 201, 204).

108. Cf. BDF §448(5); BAGD 38d (both observe that in the apodosis of a conditional sentence, ἀλλά means "yet," "certainly," "at least."

ple φανερώσαντες functions as a finite verb (= ἐφανερώσαμεν)[109] and is clearly an epistolary plural. Some object needs to be supplied with this verb. Suggestions include "my meaning"[110] (which corresponds to the textual addition ἑαυτούς — see Textual Note i.), "God's truth,"[111] or even "the mystery of knowledge/of the faith."[112] It is better to supply from the immediate context either αὐτήν (= τὴν γνῶσιν,[113] "our knowledge" [Thrall 656] or knowledge of the gospel) or τοῦτο, "this,"[114] that is, the fact that Paul was not unskilled in spiritual insight. εἰς ὑμᾶς, "in our relations with you" (Cassirer), "in my dealings with you" (Goodspeed), is scarcely distinguishable from "to you" (ὑμῖν), but given the emphatic position of the phrase and the fact that φανερόω is normally followed by the dative of the person, we should probably translate by "in our dealings with you." The *prima facie* tautology of ἐν παντὶ . . . ἐν πᾶσιν[115] might suggest that this is merely an emphatic way of saying "in every conceivable way" (NAB[1]), but the two phrases are separated by φανερώσαντες and should be distinguished, with ἐν παντί indicating means ("in every way") and ἐν πᾶσιν extent ("in all circumstances" or "in all matters" [Young and Ford 272]). Some EVV, however, take (ἐν) πᾶσιν as masculine rather than neuter, which produces the meaning "among all men" (RV, Montgomery),[116] "before everyone" (NJB), or "in the sight of all men" (BAGD 852d), that is, openly not secretly. On our view ("in every way and in all circumstances"), Paul is emphasizing the comprehensiveness of his demonstration in his dealings with the Corinthians that he was no layman with regard to true γνῶσις, that he was very competent in understanding and communicating the divine truth that was enshrined in the gospel.

From this verse we learn that for Paul matter was more significant than manner. An accurate knowledge of the gospel (cf. v. 4) was more important than eloquence in preaching it.

Bibliography

E. Baasland, "Christus und das Verlorene Paradies," in *Text and Theology: Festschrift for Magne Saebø*, ed. A. Tångberg (Oslo: Verbum, 1994) 67-94 • Barrett, *Signs* 36-38,

---

109. Thus, e.g., Zerwick §374; Turner 343; Wolff 216, 219 n. 171. Cf. the participles in 5:12; 6:3; 7:5; 8:19-20; 9:11, 13; 10:4b-6, 15.

110. Cf. Moffatt, "I never failed to make myself intelligible to you"; Wand, "I always managed to convey my full meaning to you."

111. Martin 327; cf. NEB, REB.

112. Lietzmann 147, citing 2:14.

113. BAGD 852d; Plummer 300.

114. E.g., TCNT, NASB, NAB[1, 2].

115. It is unnecessary to assume a primitive textual error here and assert that Paul wrote or meant to write ἐν παντὶ πάντα φανερώσαντες ἐν πᾶσιν καὶ εἰς ὑμᾶς (cf. 9:8, 11; 1 Cor. 9:22; 10:33; 12:6) (a suggestion reported by Plummer 300).

116. "The ἐν παντί (in every respect) and ἐν πᾶσιν (among all) fits well. Paul has offered γνῶσις neither partially nor only to a favored few" (Bultmann 204-5).

46 • Barrett, "Opponents" • Batey 12-17 • Batey, "Image" • Bieringer, "Jealousy" 246-53 • C. Böttrich, "2 Kor 11,1 als Programmwort der 'Narrenrede,'" *Bib* 88 (1997) 135-39 • E. Brandenburger, *Adam und Christus* (Neukirchen-Vluyn: Neukirchener, 1962) 45-50 • Crafton 103-27 • Ellis 61-63, 86, 129 • Fee, *Presence* 342-46 • Fee, "Gospel" 111-33 • Gale 164-67 • Hock 50, 62-65 • Holsten • R. Infante, "Immagine nuziale e tensione escatologica nel Nuovo Testamento. Note a 2 Cor. 11,2 e Eph. 5,25-27," *RivB* 33 (1985) 45-61 • John • Kee • Marshall • McClelland • Meeks 71-72 • Mitchell, "Perspective" • Murphy-O'Connor, "Jesus" • Oostendorp 17-30 • Ortlund 147-52 • Peterson 105-9 • Peterson, "Conquest" • J. P. Sampley, *"And the Two Shall Become One Flesh": A Study of Traditions in Ephesians 5:21-33* (Cambridge: Cambridge University Press, 1971) 81-85 • E. P. Sanders, "Paul on the Law, His Opponents, and the Jewish People in Philippians 3 and 2 Corinthians 11," in P. Richardson and D. Granskou (eds.), *Anti-Judaism in Early Christianity, I: Paul and the Gospels* (Waterloo: Wilfrid Laurier University, 1986) 75-90 • Savage 70-80 • Sumney 149-79 • Sumney, *Servants* 102-33 • Thrall, "Super-Apostles" • Winter 213-18 • Wong 50-53, 182-93 • Zmijewski

2. Financial Dependence and Independence (11:7-12)

Money matters have already been alluded to in this letter, in each case in a negative context. Paul was not in the habit of making profit from the word of God (2:17); he had "exploited" no one (7:2; cf. 12:17-18, where the same verb, πλεονεκτέω, is used); and he had repudiated underhand and disgraceful ways (4:2). But some eighteen months earlier he had dealt explicitly and at some length with the issue of his financial relationship to the Corinthian community (1 Cor. 9:3-18). There he is at pains to defend himself — both his apostolic authority (cf. 1 Cor. 9:1-2) and his financial conduct — against those who were in the process of investigating him or trying to examine him (1 Cor. 9:3; cf. 1 Cor. 4:3).[1] He establishes two basic principles — his right as an apostle to receive support from those who benefited from the spiritual seed he had sown (1 Cor. 9:4-12a, 13-14), and his right to forgo that support if there were practical or theological reasons for doing so (1 Cor. 9:12b, 15-18).

We cannot be sure what prompted the Corinthians to criticize Paul's decision not to accept their offer of support (1 Cor. 9:12b, 15). Perhaps they felt that his manual labor (Acts 18:3; 1 Cor. 4:12) was inconsistent with his apostolic status. Or they may have thought that he had breached the conventions of patronage according to which a visiting teacher would be fully supported by wealthy patrons.[2] Marshall argues that certain wealthy people that formed one

---

1. The present participle τοῖς . . . ἀνακρίνουσιν (1 Cor. 9:3) could be either linear or conative.

2. Patronage was ubiquitous in Greco-Roman society. See Chow 30-82, and especially his identification of seven features of the patron-client relation — reciprocating, asymmetrical, particularistic and informal, supra-legal, binding and long-range, voluntary, and vertical (31-33). Chow's purpose, in his work on *Patronage and Power,* is to show "the relationship between many of the problems in 1 Corinthians and the activity of some powerful patrons in the Corinthian church" (189).

of the Corinthian factions offered money to Paul as a gesture of friendship, not as the payment of wages, and that his rejection of this offer amounted to a declaration of "enmity,"[3] so that thereafter "Paul was engaged in ritual enmity with certain Corinthians and their associates."[4] But one wonders whether in personal relationships, even against a first-century backdrop of the reciprocity of benefactions, there are not more than two possible options, friendship or enmity.[5] Paul does not accuse any of the Corinthians of active enmity, but he does chide them for their lack of overt love for him, for their constricted affections (6:12-13; 12:15; cf. 8:7-8, 24). It was a matter of intensity of love. "If I love you the more, am I loved [by you] the less?" (12:15). We should not equate the absence of strong love or of expressions of love with the presence of virulent animosity. As for himself, Paul is anxious to reassure the Corinthians of his paternal love for them (2:4; 6:6, 11-13; 7:3; 11:11; 12:15). Cf. Savage 90.

A more probable reason for the Corinthian discontent over Paul's stance regarding finances was his acceptance of aid from Macedonian believers while he was resident in Corinth and still refusing their own offer of help (11:9). It would have seemed that Paul was operating on a double standard (cf. 1:17) and showing partiality to special friends in the north.

A further complication was the apparent willingness of Paul's rivals to accept financial support from at least some of the Corinthians. These rivals were evidently among the οἱ πολλοί who were making a petty trade out of preaching (2:17). They were "devouring" (κατεσθίει, 11:20) the Corinthians in the sense of eating them "out of house and home" (Barrett 291). Also, in 12:13 Paul states emphatically (αὐτὸς ἐγώ) that he himself (ἐγώ) for his part (αὐτός) had not been a burden on them, implying that others had been. See also the commentary on 11:12. This receipt of support from a local Christian commu-

---

3. Marshall 218-33, 257, 397; similarly Forbes 14-15. But the crucial question is whether, in the case of persons who professed oneness in Christ, Paul's assumed rejection of this proffered friendship would have been viewed as an assertion of animosity. Both Marshall and Forbes have been influenced by the views of Judge, who has drawn attention to two socio-cultural expectations that the Corinthians had of Paul which he deliberately rejects, "two fault-lines that run through the Corinthian correspondence, and throw up repeated shocks in his relations with his own converts at Corinth" ("Conformity" 12): his rejection of the arts of platform rhetoric; his refusal of monetary support (11:7-12). In one case, his amateurish speech (11:6) would have deeply disappointed the Corinthians; in the other case, his refusal of their offer of friendship would have been seen by them as a declaration of enmity ("Conformity" 12-15). Judge makes these observations while arguing that with regard to societal structures Paul accepted rank but repudiated the established system of status. See further his earlier essay *Rank and Status in the World of the Caesars and St. Paul* (Christchurch: University of Canterbury Publications, 1982).

4. Marshall, "Invective" 362 n. 18. According to Marshall, enmity and invective had two aims — to win over one's hearers and to shame and humiliate one's opponents ("Invective" 362, 373).

5. But in relation to ancient patron-client relations, Horsley asserts that "once relationship is established between two people it can only be one of friendship or enmity. Friendship cannot simply dissipate into nothing, but has to be actively withdrawn and this creates a relationship of enmity" (1.136).

nity was probably regarded by the intruders (and possibly by the Corinthians) as evidence of their apostolic legitimacy.

As he resumes his ἀπολογία from 1 Cor. 9:3, Paul does not restate his right to support (although this is implied in 11:9) but focuses on his reasons for financial independence of the Corinthians — to preach the gospel to them "free of charge" (11:7) and to avoid being a financial burden on them (11:9) — and his unwavering determination to remain independent (11:9-10, 12).

11:7*Or did I commit a sin in lowering myself[a] so that you might be elevated, by preaching the gospel of God to you without payment? 8I robbed other churches by taking wages from them so as to serve you. 9And when I was with you and became needy, I did not burden anyone, for the brothers came from Macedonia and supplied my need. In every way I have kept myself from being a burden to you, and I will continue to do so. 10As Christ's truth is in me, as far as I am concerned this boasting of mine will not be silenced throughout the districts of Achaia. 11Why? Because I do not love you? God knows I do! 12But what I am doing I shall also continue to do, in order to cut off the opportunity of those who want an opportunity to be regarded as on par with us in what they boast about.*

TEXTUAL NOTES

a. Probably as the result of a scribal omission of a single letter (M), some manuscripts (D F G K* L P 365 *pc*) read ἑαυτόν in place of ἐμαυτόν (read by p[34, 46] ℵ B Ψ 0121 0278 33 1739 1881 𝔐 syr). In the appropriate case, the reflexive pronoun ἑαυτοῦ may be used of all three persons, apart from the first person singular (see BAGD 211-12 s.v. ἑαυτοῦ).

11:7 Ἦ ἁμαρτίαν ἐποίησα ἐμαυτὸν ταπεινῶν ἵνα ὑμεῖς ὑψωθῆτε, ὅτι δωρεὰν τὸ τοῦ θεοῦ εὐαγγέλιον εὐηγγελισάμην ὑμῖν; "Or did I commit a sin in lowering myself so that you might be elevated, by preaching the gospel of God to you without payment?" It is possible to regard vv. 7-15 as a lengthy parenthesis between the imperative ἀνέχεσθέ μου of v. 1 that is followed by the threefold grounding (γάρ) of vv. 2-6, and the comparable δέξασθέ με of v. 16 (cf. πάλιν λέγω). Seen in this light, vv. 7-15 contrast Paul's financial independence of the Corinthians with the (implied) financial dependence of the "false apostles." But it is better to view vv. 7-12 and vv. 13-15 as separate but related units of thought, with the link between v. 6 and vv. 7-12 being Paul's successive responses to two accusations, namely that he was inferior to "the superlative apostles" in knowledge (v. 6), and that he had offended the Corinthians by his unwillingness to accept their offer of financial support (vv. 7-12).[6]

The particle ἤ here introduces a rhetorical question (BAGD 342b) that

6. According to Hafemann, however, the link between vv. 6 and 7 is that the genuine nature of Paul's knowledge (= the gospel) (v. 6) was evidenced by his ministry that aimed at exalting the Corinthians (*Suffering* 149-50).

Paul himself would have answered negatively (cf. Rom. 3:29), although some Corinthians would have given a positive answer were it not for the way in which Paul poses the question (". . . so that you might be elevated . . ."). "How could I be offending you when you benefited from my action?" Along with 12:13, where Paul mockingly asks for the Corinthians' forgiveness for an "injustice" (ἀδικία), this verse represents the most acute form of his stinging irony.[7] "Did I, the apostle who brought you the message of reconciliation through the forgiveness of sin (5:18-19), myself commit a sin against you when I brought about your elevation to riches in Christ?" Given Paul's frequent use of irony throughout 2 Corinthians 10–13, there is no reason to think that he refers to an actual sin, such as disobedience to the Lord's command (διέταξεν) "that those who preach the gospel should receive their living from the gospel" (1 Cor. 9:14), or is using ἁμαρτία in the diluted sense of "mistake."[8] After the constative aorist ἐποίησα that encompasses the total time of Paul's residence in Corinth, ἐμαυτὸν ταπεινῶν defines the mode of the putative sin ("in/by humbling myself"), while ὅτι introduces either its cause ("because")[9] or its content ("in that" or "by"),[10] although the sense differs little whichever of these alternatives is preferred.[11]

In 12:21 the verb ταπεινόω has the sense "humiliate," but here it means "humble" or "demean" or, in contrast with the verb ὑψόω ("exalt," "elevate") that follows, "lower."[12] This self-humbling of Paul probably involved three elements — his renouncing of the apostolic right to support (cf. 1 Cor. 9:6, 11-12a, 14); his support of himself by manual labor (Acts 20:34; 1 Thess. 2:9; 2 Thess. 3:8; 1 Cor. 4:12); and his contentment (cf. Phil. 4:11-12) with the Spartan lifestyle and scant means of the first-century artisan (cf. Hock 34-35). A philosopher or teacher of the Hellenistic age could gain his financial support in five ways:[13] by begging; by charging fees for his instruction; by becoming a resident in a patron's household where he received regular wages for teaching the patron's sons; by accepting voluntary contributions from followers; and by his own physical labor. Apparently Paul's normal means of support was to engage in his trade of making tents and other leather goods (cf. σκηνοποιός, Acts 18:3[14]) as he

---

7. Apart from 5:21 and 11:7 Paul never uses the expression "commit (a) sin" (ἁμαρτίαν ποιέω).

8. As Zerwick and Grosvenor 557; Witherington 448.

9. Thus NRSV, "by humbling myself . . . , because I proclaimed . . ." (similarly RV, RSV, Barclay; cf. Zmijewski 122-23).

10. Thus Lambrecht 172, "in humbling myself . . . , in that I preached . . ." (similarly Zerwick and Grosvenor 557) and Barrett 270, "in humbling myself . . . , by preaching . . .").

11. It is possible but unlikely that the ὅτι clause is a modal or causal definition of ἐμαυτὸν ταπεινῶν: "by humbling myself . . . , that is, by preaching . . ."; or, "in humbling myself . . . — I mean because I told you God's Good News . . ." (TCNT; similarly Moffatt).

12. The rendering "degrade" (Goodspeed; BAGD 804d) is appropriate only in the sense "reduce to a lower rank."

13. Cf. Hock 52-59; Marshall 226-30, 296-98.

14. See Hock 20-21; "Workshop" 441 n. 8.

pursued his evangelistic and pastoral work, but on occasion he accepted aid from fellow believers (Phil. 4:15-16; 2 Cor. 11:8-9).[15] The first three possible ways of gaining a livelihood were totally foreign to Paul's *modus operandi*.[16]

If we are left to infer the precise nature of Paul's self-abasement, this is not the case with its purpose. He "lowered" himself in order that (ἵνα) the Corinthians might be "elevated" (cf. NIV). Paul is not speaking of elevation to a place of social eminence or material prosperity or enhanced honor,[17] or of exemption from the burden of supporting Paul,[18] or even of the Christian's future elevation to share God's glory (Rom. 5:2) or Christ's glory (Rom. 8:17).[19] The "exaltation" was a present reality for the Corinthian believers. It was their being lifted up from the futility of their pre-Christian existence and "from the degradation of idolatry" (Plummer 301), to the privileged status of membership in the family of the one true God (cf. 1 Thess. 1:9), of becoming sons and daughters of the almighty Lord (6:18), of spiritual enrichment (cf. 9:11).[20] This new status had come about by Paul's preaching of the gospel of God (11:7b), by the Corinthian response to it, and above all by God's granting them all the benefits of salvation.

In this "lowered–elevated" contrast and the implied "poverty–riches" antithesis, a link with two previous verses (6:10 and 8:9) may be intended.

6:10	8:9	11:7
ὡς πτωχοὶ	ἐπτώχευσεν	ἐμαυτὸν ταπεινῶν
πολλοὺς (δὲ)	. . . (ἵνα) ὑμεῖς	(ἵνα) ὑμεῖς
πλουτίζοντες	. . . πλουτήσητε	ὑψωθῆτε

In 6:10 it is Paul himself, who, though poor materially, enriches many spiritually, whereas in 11:7 it is by self-humbling and only indirectly that Paul elevates (= enriches) the Corinthians.[21] But both verses represent significant variations on the theme "Those who humble themselves will be exalted" (Matt.

15. But it is doubtful whether Paul's acceptance of gifts as well as his support from tentmaking should be included in what he regarded as "demeaning," as Hock alleges ("Tentmaking" 561). The thrust of Hock's article is that "by working at a slavish and demeaning (cf. 2 Cor. 11:7) trade Paul sensed a considerable loss of status, a loss that makes sense only if he were from a relatively high social class" (564; cf. 562).

16. But for the suggestion that Paul sought the patronage of some wealthy Corinthians, see Marshall 144-47, 168.

17. It is unclear what is intended by the GNB rendering: "I humble myself in order to make you important."

18. "Just as the ταπεινῶν consists in a refusal of support, so the ὑψωθῆτε is explained by the ἀβαρῆ in verse 9" (Bultmann 205).

19. Cf. Lietzmann 147.

20. Cf. Wolff ("Humility" 155): "from the depths of alienation from God into saving eschatological fellowship with God."

21. Several EVV, however, render ὑψωθῆτε with the active voice. E.g., REB has "humbling myself in order to exalt you" (cf. NEB, "lowering myself to help in raising you").

23:12), for others derive the benefit of enrichment, either in spite of Paul's poverty (6:10) or through his self-lowering (11:7). The parallel between 11:7 and 8:9 suggests the presence of the "imitation of Christ" motif in 11:7. The Corinthians had been enriched primarily by the "poverty" of Christ (8:9) but also, in a secondary and indirect sense, by the self-abasement of Paul as a true apostle of Christ.[22]

The nature or content (ὅτι) of the supposed "sin" was the fact that Paul had preached the gospel of God to the Corinthians without payment. The verb εὐαγγελίζομαι is usually followed by the accusative of the thing proclaimed (here the cognate accusative τὸ εὐαγγέλιον) and the dative of the person who receives the message (ὑμῖν) (cf. 1 Cor. 15:1). We may account for the singular εὐηγγελισάμην, in contrast with ἐκηρύξαμεν (11:4) and the explicit reference in 1:19 to Silvanus and Timothy as fellow evangelists at Corinth, by assuming that the present charge of fiscal insensitivity was directed at Paul alone or at Paul in particular. In its position τοῦ θεοῦ is emphatic; elsewhere we always find τὸ εὐαγγέλιον τοῦ θεοῦ when articles are used.[23] The implication is that the rival missionaries are not preaching *God's* gospel (cf. 11:4) and are accepting payment (cf. δωρεάν) for preaching even their *own* gospel! Whether τὸ εὐαγγέλιον is qualified by τοῦ θεοῦ (only here in 2 Corinthians) or by τοῦ Χριστοῦ (2:12; 9:13; 10:14[24]), the genitive is probably both subjective ("from God/Christ") and objective ("concerning God/Christ").

What made it totally appropriate for Paul to proclaim the good news δωρεάν (the accusative of δωρεά, used adverbially), "free of charge," "without fee or reward," was the fact that this gospel of God is essentially the offer of a gift (δωρεά), the gift of righteousness (ἡ δωρεὰ τῆς δικαιοσύνης, Rom. 5:17). The repetition and the juxtaposition of εὐ(αγγέλιον) and εὐ(ηγγελισάμην) draw attention to the goodness and value of God's good news, which nonetheless Paul preaches at no charge to the hearer.[25] This correlation between the gospel offered as a gift and its being proclaimed "free of charge" (δωρεάν = ἀδάπανον, 1 Cor. 9:18) doubtless appealed to Paul's sense of theological congruity, so much so that he viewed payment for declaring the good news as putting "an obstacle in the way of the gospel of Christ" (1 Cor. 9:12b). But there were also practical reasons for his settled determination never to become a burden on his converts. Such a practice effectively distinguished him from the peripatetic lecturers, some of them notorious for their rapacity, who charged fees for their instruction.[26] Again, to remain financially independent meant freedom from any

22. Cf. Zmijewski 127.

23. Rom. 15:16; 1 Thess. 2:2, 8-9; cf. εὐαγγέλιον θεοῦ (Rom. 1:1), the only other Pauline use of the phrase.

24. The other Pauline instances of τὸ εὐαγγέλιον τοῦ Χριστοῦ are Rom. 15:19; 1 Cor. 9:12; Gal. 1:7; Phil. 1:27; 1 Thess. 3:2.

25. Paul's implied claim, δωρεὰν εὐαγγελίζομαι, corresponds to Jesus' injunction at his commissioning of the Twelve, δωρεὰν δότε, "give without pay" (Matt. 10:8; cf. Rev. 21:6; 22:17).

26. See Barnett 517 n. 32 for evidence.

assumed special obligation to donors (cf. 1 Thess. 4:11-12) and from the temptation and danger of showing partiality to one segment of the church in return for their generosity.[27] Finally, "such disinterestedness enhanced his credibility, because it showed that he preached out of utter conviction; necessity was laid upon him and he had no choice (1 Cor. 9:16)" (Murphy-O'Connor 111).

11:8 ἄλλας ἐκκλησίας ἐσύλησα λαβὼν ὀψώνιον πρὸς τὴν ὑμῶν διακονίαν. "I robbed other churches by taking wages from them so as to serve you." As is sometimes the case with asyndetic sentences such as this, a contrast with what precedes is implied (cf. 7:2). "Rather than accepting payment from you for my preaching (cf. v. 7b), I plundered other churches. . . ." συλάω, found only here and (in the LXX) in *Epistle of Jeremiah* 17 (EVV, 18), means "strip off," "plunder," "carry off as booty" (in the latter sense it means the same as συλαγωγέω [Col. 2:8], another NT *hapax*), and was frequently used in Classical Greek of the despoiling of the enemy, in particular the act of stripping off armor from a slain enemy.[28] In the papyri it denotes the theft of tools and the pillaging of the contents of a house (MM 596d).[29] When the apostle "confesses" to having despoiled or robbed churches, the expression is clearly figurative (as the following two words, λαβὼν ὀψώνιον, show), hyperbolic, ironical, and certainly surprising, given his earlier defense (7:2) against the charge of exploitation.[30] He is probably not repeating a Corinthian charge.[31]

Who are the "other churches" that Paul despoiled? From Phil. 4:15 we learn that in the early days of the Philippians' acquaintance with the gospel (ἐν ἀρχῇ τοῦ εὐαγγελίου), when Paul had left Macedonia, no church entered into partnership with him as far as giving and receiving were concerned, with the one exception of the Philippians (εἰ μὴ ὑμεῖς μόνοι). If here in 11:8 Paul is referring to the Philippian church alone, the plural ἐκκλησίας may be generalizing or rhetorical,[32] or could refer to house congregations in Philippi.[33] Alternatively, we could take ἄλλας ἐκκλησίας to mean "*believers* in churches other than Corinth" (the whole for the part), or interpret Phil. 4:15 as indicating that although it was only the Philippian church that entered into a semi-formal "partnership

---

27. Cf. Murphy-O'Connor 306-7; Thrall 701-6; Peterman 168-71.

28. See LSJ 1671 s.v. συλάω.

29. Spicq (3.315-16) discerns the legal sense of συλάω in 11:8. "By using and abusing the Macedonians' accommodating attitude toward him, he exercised the right of seizure/reprisal (*sulai* [σῦλαι]) against the compatriots of his debtors [the Corinthians]" (3.316). From the Macedonians he had taken the minimum salary (ὀψώνιον) due him from the Corinthians (3.316).

30. According to Gale (167), Paul's imagery suggests that "as a soldier took from a defeated foe that for which no service had been rendered in return, so also the apostle has received from 'other churches' a contribution for which no corresponding service had been given. (The service has been to the Corinthians instead.)" Gale also notes (168) three ways in which the imagery is inapplicable — the contributing churches were not an opposed and defeated enemy; no force was used; Paul was not guilty of improper conduct.

31. As Sampley [*Partnership* 84] alleges.

32. A possibility mentioned by Plummer (CGT) 167.

33. So Peterman 146 n. 134.

in the gospel" (Phil. 1:5) with regard to giving and receiving, other churches such as those at Thessalonica and Berea, or individuals in those churches, may have contributed money or supplies to Paul on occasion. Since Paul came to Corinth from Macedonia via Athens (Acts 17:13-15; 18:1), we may assume that when he left Macedonia for Achaia, the believers in Philippi and perhaps Thessalonica and Berea sent him on his way with the necessary provisions for his evangelistic effort in the south. Since 11:9 begins with καὶ παρὼν πρὸς ὑμᾶς, "and when I was present with you," where καί means "moreover" or "in addition" rather than "that is" or "so that," a separate, additional gift from Macedonia is being referred to in v. 9 (*pace* Pratscher 289).

λαβὼν ὀψώνιον specifies the mode of the "robbery": "I robbed other churches by accepting support from them" (RSV, NRSV). The acceptance of support was the plundering — a fine oxymoron. The word ὀψώνιον is the cognate of the verb ὀψωνέω, "buy fish," "purchase provisions," which itself is a compound of ὄψον ("cooked fish," "food") and ὠνέομαι ("buy," "purchase"). "When the compound ὀψώνιον was formed, the emphasis was shifted from 'fish' to the element of 'purchase.' Thus the new word came to mean 'buying of provisions' and 'provisions bought.' "[34] In the papyri, as well as meaning "provisions" or "victuals," the term denotes a soldier's "ration-money" or "allowance," a bank clerk's "salary," a policeman's "pay," a music student's "scholarship," a laborer's "wages," and even a magician's "fee."[35] Now it is certainly possible that Paul, perhaps speaking facetiously, is saying that he accepted monetary payments from "other churches" as the "wages"[36] or "pay"[37] rightly due to him for his services, but more probably he is referring to general "provisions"[38] for travel to Achaia and accommodation there, that is, "support,"[39] that was given him by the churches of Macedonia on his departure from that province. On this view the constative aorist ἐσύλησα refers to a single action.

If the plundering was carried out, paradoxically, by means of receiving, the purpose of the robbery was scarcely less paradoxical. There was robbery in

---

34. Caragounis 48, who argues that the four NT uses of ὀψώνιον (Luke 3:14; Rom. 6:23; 1 Cor. 9:7; 2 Cor. 11:8) are best rendered by "shoppings" *(sic)* or "provisions," the word's original and longest-attested meaning (49-57). He believes that the sense of "wages" is the connotation rather than the denotation of the term (49).

35. See LSJ 1283 s.v. ὀψώνιον; MM 471-72; Spicq 2.600-603, who contends that the commonest meaning of the word in the papyri and elsewhere is that of "remuneration for a given task" (2.602); Horsley 2.93. The word (in the plural) occurs only three times in the LXX, meaning "wages" (1 Esdr. 4:56; 1 Macc. 3:28) or "provisions" (1 Macc. 14:32).

36. Thus RV, NASB, NJB. MM (472) cite P. Oxy. IV.744[7] from the first century B.C. as parallel to 2 Cor. 11:8: "as soon as we receive wages (ὀψώνιον λάβωμεν) I will send them to you."

37. Thus TCNT, Weymouth, Moffatt, Barclay; Wolff 216; Thrall 656.

38. Caragounis 53 ("provisions" such as foodstuffs and perhaps clothes, "though the possibility that some money also was included can not be ruled out"); similarly Spicq 2.603. Cassirer has "maintenance" and Martin (327) "expenses," while Carrez (213; cf. also Héring 79) renders ὀψώνιον by *de quoi vivre,* "the means of livelihood."

39. Thus RSV, NEB, NAB[1], NIV, REB, NRSV; BAGD 602c; Lambrecht 172.

Macedonia in order for there to be service in Corinth (πρὸς τὴν ὑμῶν διακονίαν)! πρός has the sense "with a view to" or "for the purpose of," and the objective genitive ὑμῶν ("service to you") is emphatic by position (cf. Turner 189). A contrast between Paul and his rivals is implicit; they exploit the Corinthians (11:20), Paul serves them and aids in their elevation. He recognized that the essence of his relation to his converts was one of service (cf. 1 Cor. 16:15) — a model for Christian pastors of every age. Also, ὑμῶν corresponds to the earlier ἄλλας. The Macedonian believers gave freely (cf. 8:1-2) to support Paul, with the result that he was able to declare the good news to the Corinthians free of charge;[40] in this way these Macedonians indirectly contributed to the Corinthians' elevation.[41]

11:9 καὶ παρὼν πρὸς ὑμᾶς καὶ ὑστερηθεὶς οὐ κατενάρκησα οὐθενός· τὸ γὰρ ὑστέρημά μου προσανεπλήρωσαν οἱ ἀδελφοὶ ἐλθόντες ἀπὸ Μακεδονίας. "And when I was with you and became needy, I did not burden anyone, for the brothers came from Macedonia and supplied my need." If v. 8 dealt with an event that occurred before Paul's arrival in Corinth on his first visit, v. 9 describes events that took place during that visit (probably fall 50–spring 52[42]). In addition (καί) to despoiling other churches in order to render service to the Corinthians (v. 8), Paul refrained from becoming a financial encumbrance on any of them even when he was actually giving that service and his resources dried up. But relief had come with the arrival of Christian friends from Macedonia who brought gifts.

The temporal relation between the linear present participle παρών, the ingressive aorist participle ὑστερηθείς,[43] and the constative aorist (οὐ) κατενάρκησα may be set out diagrammatically as follows.

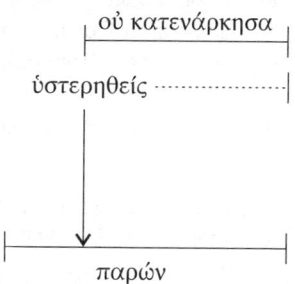

40. Just as ἀπ' αὐτῶν is implied after ὀψώνιον, so δωρεάν (from 11:7) is to be supplied after διακονίαν.

41. Cf. Meyer 647.

42. See the Introduction, C.

43. Both of these participles bear a temporal sense: "while I was with you, and when my resources failed. . . ." But NEB (and REB) gives ὑστερηθείς a conditional and frequentative sense, "if I ran short."

44. This rendering (found in Moffatt, Berkeley, NEB, REB) well catches the ingressive sense of the aorist ὑστερέω, (passive) "be lacking," "go short." Cf. Barrett (270), "fell into want."

45. Cf. this same expression in Gal. 4:18, 20.

46. Moule 53; cf. Moulton and Howard 467.

That is, while resident in Corinth, Paul "ran short"[44] of funds to supply the necessities of life, but even during the resulting period of need, he never squeezed charity from anyone. πάρειμι πρός τινα means "be present with someone" (BAGD 624b, 711a),[45] where πρός denotes position, not motion or direction.[46]

One of the most expressive words in 2 Corinthians is καταναρκάω, a verb found only three times in the Greek Bible, here and in 12:13-14. The simplex form ναρκάω, "grow stiff/numb," occurs five times in the LXX,[47] while the cognate noun νάρκη denotes the "numbness" caused (for example) by palsy or by fright, but also refers to the "torpedo" or electric ray that benumbs anyone who touches it, so that the Egyptian eel that numbed its victims by an electric ray was called νάρκη ποταμία.[48] As a medical term, the compound form καταναρκάω (in the passive) means "grow numb," "be anaesthetized."[49] In Paul's three uses of this verb it is in the active voice and is used figuratively, meaning "be a burden to"[50] or "encumber," so that κατενάρκησα will not differ in meaning from κατεβάρησα (12:16) or ἐβάρυνα (cf. ἐβαρής in 11:9).[51] According to Jerome, this figurative use of καταναρκάω was a Cilician idiom for the Latin *gravare*, "weigh down, burden."[52] In the present context the "burden" that Paul refrained from imposing on the Corinthians was financial or economic,[53] but if he was aware of the medical use of the verb his intended meaning may be "I benumbed no one by becoming a financial parasite."[54] οὐθείς, from οὔτε εἷς, is a variant form of οὐδείς. The two negatives οὐ . . . οὐθενός strengthen each other,[55] "no one at all," "not a soul." Paul "burdened no one" at Corinth in that he neither asked anyone for monetary support nor accepted gifts from anyone.

The policy of financial independence of the Corinthians that Paul maintained in principle, he had no occasion at Corinth to be tempted to abandon in practice, for (γάρ) his needs were met by fellow believers from Macedonia. τὸ

47. Gen. 32:26, 33 (twice) (EVV 32:25, 32), of the numbing of the sinew of Jacob's hip; Job 33:19; Dan. 11:6 (LXX).

48. LSJ 1160 s.v. ναρκάω.

49. Cf. LSJ 902 s.v. καταναρκάομαι. Spicq (2.267 n. 2) cites Hippocrates (*Epidemiae* 6.7.3): "It is necessary through change to stir up timid, benumbed (κατανεναρκωμένους) individuals to the things that they are neglecting."

50. BAGD 415a. "It is indeed possible that from the meaning 'be numb and dull' there was a transition to 'be inactive, burdensome'" (Spicq 2.267-68).

51. Then οὐ κατενάρκησα οὐθενός would be equivalent to ἀβαρῆ ἐμαυτὸν . . . ἐτήρησα (11:9).

52. *Epistle* 121.10.4, cited by BAGD 415a. See the significant comment on this point in Hughes 387 n. 51.

53. But a less specific sense is possible: Paul's "presence at Corinth was not taxing for the community" (Spicq 2.268), or "I never became an encumbrance on any of you" (Wand). See also Garland 479-82.

54. Cf. Plummer (CGT) 168: "Here the 'numbness' is caused by *pressure;* 'paralyzing a man by squeezing money out of him.'" One thinks of the slang expression "to sting someone," meaning "to swindle, overcharge, cripple with expenses."

55. BAGD 590d; Robertson 1165.

. . . ὑστέρημά μου, "my deficiency," "what I lacked," refers to the needs that arose after his own financial resources (through tentmaking and the support from "other churches" [v. 8]) had failed (ὑστερηθείς). On the verb προσαναπληρόω, found only twice in the NT (9:12; 11:9), see on 9:12. Since one of the tendencies of Hellenistic and Biblical Greek was a preference for compound forms, which often bear the sense of the "simple" form (here ἀναπληρόω, "fill up") (see Zerwick §484), προσαναπληρόω may mean simply "fill up," "supply,"[56] but as in 9:12 the prefix προσ- probably has special significance (see Moulton and Howard 324; MM 546a), so that προσανεπλήρωσαν will mean either "(they) fully supplied" (Weymouth, Cassirer) or "(they) supplied [in addition]," that is, in addition to the ὀψώνιον (v. 8), which also was from Macedonia in all probability.

"The brothers" may be unnamed because they were known to the Corinthians (anaphoric article, οἱ) and were merely, in this case, bearers of a corporate gift or gifts. Being anarthrous, ἐλθόντες is probably not adjectival,[57] so that we should render the whole clause "the brothers came from Macedonia and supplied . . . ," or "when the brothers came from Macedonia, they supplied . . . ," although this differs little in meaning from "the brothers *who* came from Macedonia supplied. . . ." Possible further light on this incident comes from two quarters. To the Philippians Paul says καὶ ἐν Θεσσαλονίκῃ καὶ ἅπαξ καὶ δὶς εἰς τὴν χρείαν μοι ἐπέμψατε (Phil. 4:16), which may be rendered "both [when I was] in Thessalonica, and more than once [when I was in other places] you sent me gifts to relieve my need."[58] If Corinth was one of those "other places," Paul may be alluding to a gift from Philippi (= "Macedonia" in 11:9) that reached him in Corinth at the hands of "the brothers"; in that case, τὴν χρείαν μοι (Phil. 4:16) would match τὸ . . . ὑστέρημά μου (11:9). More important is Acts 18:5.[59] From the outset of his first visit to Corinth Paul had supported himself by plying his trade as a tentmaker (Acts 18:3), but Luke notes that after Silas (= Silvanus) and Timothy arrived from Macedonia, Paul "'was wholly absorbed in preaching' [συνείχετο τῷ λόγῳ, Acts 18:5] . . . in contrast to the activity cited in vs. 3" (BAGD 789b). Whether the imperfect συνείχετο is linear in sense (as in the BAGD rendering) or is inceptive ("[Paul] began to devote himself entirely [to preaching]"), it is a fair inference that (1) the arrival of these two "brothers" "from Macedonia" (cf. 11:9) brought about the change in Paul's routines, and (2) the change was prompted, in particular, by the monetary gifts they brought from Philippi (cf. Phil. 4:15-16) and perhaps Thessalonica and Berea also. On this interpretation of the evidence, the ἀδελφοί are Silvanus and Timothy, who, significantly, are the co-authors or co-senders of the two Thessalonian letters (1 Thess. 1:1; 2 Thess. 1:1), which were written from Cor-

56. See LSJ 1501 s.v.; BAGD 711d.
57. Cf. Robertson 778.
58. See L. Morris, "ΚΑΙ ΑΠΑΞ ΚΑΙ ΔΙΣ," *NovT* 1 (1956) 205-8 for this interpretation of Phil. 4:16.
59. Similarly Allo 283; Bruce, *Paul* 252.

inth (both probably in A.D. 50). Whether this Macedonian gift was providentially timed to meet Paul's need, or was given in response to a known need, we do not know. But it affords further evidence of Macedonian generosity in spite of poverty (8:2).

We are now in a position to reconstruct the possible stages of Paul's means of support during his first visit to Corinth (fall 50–spring 52; 18 months, Acts 18:11).

1. When Paul arrived in Corinth he had with him some "provisions" (ὀψώνιον), perhaps money, clothing, and food, that had been given by a Macedonian church (Philippi; Phil. 4:16) or churches (11:8).
2. He immediately began work as a tentmaker in the company of Aquila and Priscilla (Acts 18:2-3; cf. 1 Cor. 4:11-12). Normally this manual labor provided adequately for Paul's own maintenance (we may be sure at minimum levels!) and even the needs of his colleagues (Acts 20:34).
3. Shortly after, the supplies from Macedonia were exhausted and he found himself in need (ὑστερηθείς, 11:9). Perhaps his tentmaking business had taken time to become established and he was devoting as much time as possible to evangelism. But even when his resources failed he did not impose on the Corinthians for aid (11:9).
4. Relief came with the arrival of Silas and Timothy from Macedonia, bearing gifts from believers in that province (11:9; Acts 18:5; and probably Phil. 4:16).[60]
5. These gifts enabled Paul to devote his whole attention to the task of preaching and teaching (cf. Acts 18:5). How long this respite from tentmaking lasted cannot be known.

καὶ ἐν παντὶ ἀβαρῆ ἐμαυτὸν ὑμῖν ἐτήρησα καὶ τηρήσω. "In every way I have kept myself from being a burden to you, and I will continue to do so." Paul's previous affirmation of financial independence from the Corinthians related to a particular time during his first visit (ὑστερηθεὶς οὐ κατενάρκησα οὐθενός). Now he states the general principle behind his past practice and confirms its applicability in the future. ἐτήρησα is a constative (= summary or complexive) aorist, encompassing all of Paul's previous relations with the Corinthian believers. τηρήσω is a linear future, expressing a continuous attitude from the present time forward: "I will go on doing so" (Barclay), that is, avoiding being a burden. ἀβαρής, a *hapax legomenon* in Biblical Greek, is formed from the negating α- privative + βαρύς, "heavy," "weighty," thus "bringing no weight," "not burdensome." In the context the burden referred to is pecuniary (cf. ἐπιβαρῆσαι in 1 Thess. 2:9). ἐν παντί qualifies both ἐτήρησα and τηρήσω. "In

---

60. On Bruce's chronology (*Acts* 93) the two Thessalonian letters, in which Silas and Timothy were named as co-authors or co-senders, were written in late 50, so the interval between Paul's arrival in Corinth (fall 50) and the arrival of the gifts that brought relief was relatively brief.

every regard" Paul had made a point of refusing to live at the Corinthians' expense, and "in every regard" — whatever the circumstances — he would maintain this policy. Nothing had caused him to deviate from this policy, and nothing would. "As in the past, so in the future: I will never be a burden to you!" (GNB).

The three tenses of Paul's policy come to expression several times in chs. 11 and 12.

Past	Present	Future
ἐτήρησα (11:9)		τηρήσω (11:9)
		οὐ φραγήσεται (11:10)
	ποιῶ (11:12)	ποιήσω (11:12)
οὐ κατενάρκησα (12:13)		
		οὐ καταναρκήσω (12:14)
οὐ κατεβάρησα (12:16)		

Such a demonstration of Paul's consistency of action was significant when we remember that he had been accused of vacillating indecision (1:17). We discuss the precise nature of this policy and Paul's reasons for adopting it in our commentary on 11:10.

11:10 ἔστιν ἀλήθεια Χριστοῦ ἐν ἐμοὶ ὅτι ἡ καύχησις αὕτη οὐ φραγήσεται εἰς ἐμὲ ἐν τοῖς κλίμασιν τῆς Ἀχαΐας. "As Christ's truth is in me, as far as I am concerned this boasting of mine will not be silenced throughout the districts of Achaia." This is an expansion and confirmation of ἐν παντὶ ἀβαρῆ ἐμαυτὸν ὑμῖν . . . τηρήσω (v. 9), with the future φραγήσεται corresponding to τηρήσω. If we define a biblical "oath of confirmation" broadly as a direct or indirect appeal to the deity as the guarantor of the truth of a statement, especially one that the readers cannot verify for themselves, this verse constitutes an oath (cf. 1:18, 23; 11:11, 31; 12:2-3),[61] "By Christ's truth in me" (GNB). But on a narrower definition of an "oath of confirmation" which would require an introductory verb of swearing (cf. ὤμοσεν ἐν . . . ὅτι, Rev. 10:6) or a direct invocation (cf. μάρτυρα τὸν θεὸν ἐπικαλοῦμαι, 1:23), this verse is simply a solemn declaration.[62] Either way, the affirmation is even stronger than κατέναντι θεοῦ ἐν Χριστῷ λαλοῦμεν (2:17; 12:19), and may be rendered "As surely as the truth of Christ is in me" (NEB, REB). That is, "the truth of Christ dwells in me and will testify to and guarantee my truthfulness when I say that. . . ." Paul's appeal is not to "truth about Christ" (objective genitive) that is communicated in his preaching but to divine "truth given by Christ" (subjective genitive) that he has personally appropriated and is therefore in him (cf. 13:3) in the same way that the mind of Christ (1 Cor. 2:16) and the Spirit of Christ (Rom. 8:9) dwell in him.[63]

61. So also Spicq 2.302; Robertson 1034; Bultmann 206; Furnish 493.
62. Both Bernard (102) and Hughes (389) speak of v. 10a as an "asseveration."
63. It is improbable that Χριστοῦ is an adjectival/Semitic genitive ("Christian [truth]," so Moule 112) or has intensive force, "the most unquestionable truth" (a view cited by Winer 248).

ὅτι introduces the content of the oath. As in 7:4, 14; 8:24; 11:17, καύχησις denotes the act of boasting, so that ἡ καύχησις αὕτη will mean either "this boasting" or "this boasting of mine" (from "this my boasting," possessive article). From the context we may infer that Paul was "boasting" about his financial independence of the Corinthians, his not being a burden on the church, or the related issues of his choice not to exercise his apostolic right to support and his proclamation of the gospel free of charge. Whatever the exact content of the claim, it was an act of boasting because it related to the future (οὐ φραγήσεται; cf. vv. 9, 12) as well as the present (v. 12) and the past (v. 9). Also, this boasting was "in the Lord" (10:17) because a choice to be independent of Corinthian support meant that the progress of the gospel of free grace in Christ was unhindered (1 Cor. 9:12b).

In Classical Greek φράσσω generally means "fence in," but in the NT the verb denotes closure or blockage, and either of these senses is appropriate in the present context. Meaning "close," "stop," it refers to the closing of the mouth, either of lions (Heb. 11:33) or of humans in God's presence (Rom. 3:19). Accordingly, Windisch views καύχησις as a pregnant expression for τὸ στόμα μου καυχώμενον, "my mouth in its boasting," so that Paul means "my mouth will not be closed regarding the announcement of this boast" (337). Even without an allusion to the mouth, a similar sense results: "this boasting will never be stifled in me" (Lambrecht 172) or "this boast will not be silenced" (Barclay). But φράσσω may also mean "block," "bar," and describe a path that is obstructed by thornbushes (Hos. 2:8; EVV 2:6) or a door that is blocked up with bricks (MM 675c). In that case Paul will mean "this boast shall not be barred to me" (Thrall 656) or "I will not allow myself to be blocked from such boasting" (Zerwick, Analysis 411). Whichever sense of φράσσω is preferred, the general import of οὐ φραγήσεται is the same. If an agent in the closure or blockage is implied, it may be indefinite ("by anything/anyone") or more specific ("by my opponents"). Paul's opponents would stand to gain by the silencing of his boasting, for apparently they wanted him to alter his policy so that they could claim parity with him regarding finances (11:12).

The position of εἰς ἐμέ ("with respect to me") and the absence of an article (ἡ εἰς ἐμέ) suggest that this phrase should be construed with οὐ φραγήσεται, not with ἡ καύχησις αὕτη. If so, the sense will not be "this boast of mine" (RSV, GNB, NRSV) or "this boasting of mine" (Furnish 484; Martin 327), where "of mine" renders εἰς ἐμέ,[64] but "this boast shall not be barred to me" (Thrall 656) or "this boasting will never be stifled in me" (Lambrecht 172), or "as far as I am concerned this boasting of mine[65] will not be silenced."[66] Perhaps this phrase

---

64. To interpret εἰς ἐμέ as "(this pride which you [Achaian believers] have) toward me" (Zmijewski 139) is to ignore: the word order and the absence of ἡ; the usual sense of καύχησις in 2 Corinthians, viz. "(act of) boasting"; the fact that in 2 Corinthians 10–12 it is Paul or his opponents who are involved in καύχησις.

65. We have seen above that ἡ καύχησις αὕτη could be rendered "this boasting of mine."

66. Cf. Barrett 270: "I shall not be silenced in this boasting."

implies that others might try to mute Paul's boasting, by suggesting (for example) that it stemmed from lovelessness (cf. v. 11). ἐν τοῖς κλίμασιν τῆς Ἀχαΐας, "throughout the districts[67] of Achaia," is not designed to imply that in other places Paul might restrict or reverse his policy, but simply mentions the general region that corresponds to the destination of the letter, the Corinthian church along with believers throughout Achaia (1:2), in places such as Cenchreae and Athens.

How may we summarize Paul's policy regarding his financial relationship with his churches? Was it consistent?[68] His conduct seems to have been governed by two principles.

1. Paul always refused financial aid for himself from those to whom he was currently ministering. He himself gives three reasons for this stance. First, he wished to avoid being a financial encumbrance, an economic parasite, on his converts (11:9; 12:13-14, 16; 1 Thess. 2:9). He probably saw this as an evidence of his love (cf. 11:11; 12:15). Second, by offering the "price-less" good news totally free of charge, he was dramatizing in his own conduct the very appeal of the gospel as the good news of God's free grace (cf. 11:7; 1 Cor. 9:12b, 18). Third, he wanted to maintain an advantage over any rivals who accepted payment for their services (11:12). No one could accuse Paul of preaching for profit. We may speculate on further reasons for his vigorous independence. Fourth, he may have wished to avoid entering a relationship that could be construed as a patron-client contract which placed him under certain social obligations to a restricted segment of a church (cf. 1 Thess. 4:11-12).[69] Fifth, with respect to the Corinthians, Savage proposes that Paul was aiming at weaning them away from their eagerness to boast about their generosity in giving (96, 98). Sixth, financial independence may have appealed to a natural desire for self-sufficiency. H. W. Heidland comments (*TDNT* 5.592): "Not claiming the ὀψώνιον is an act of freedom on the apostle's part in relation to the churches and also a venture of faith, which refuses any assured basis of subsistence." Closely related to Paul's motivation for being financially independent of his converts were his motives for choosing to support himself by manual labor[70] — his wish to provide his converts with a model of self-support by hard work (2 Thess. 3:6-9; cf. 1 Thess. 4:11) and of earning money in order to give to the needy (Eph. 4:28; cf. Acts 20:35), and his desire to be distinguished from fee-charging traveling lecturers.

2. Paul sometimes accepted gifts from distant fellow believers (11:8-9; Phil. 4:16) or as he was leaving a region (1:16; Rom. 15:24; 1 Cor. 16:6), in

67. If τὰ κλίματα is a generalizing plural, it will refer to "'the region of Achaia,' the province in its entirety" (BAGD 436b); thus Barrett 270, "in the whole province of Achaea," or Goodspeed, "anywhere in Greece."

68. See the discussions in Pratscher 284-98; Horrell 210-16; Peterman 163-67; Thrall 706-8.

69. Cf. Garland 481-82; Murphy-O'Connor, *Paul* 306.

70. Cf. Barnett 517-18 n. 32; "Tentmaking' in *DPL* 926-27.

each case to enable him to pursue new evangelistic or pastoral opportunities, not as payment for services already rendered. We have seen (at 1:16) that the verb προπέμπω means not only "accompany," "escort,"[71] but also "help forward," "send on one's way" (BAGD 709 s.v.), in reference to equipping a person with provisions for a journey,[72] such as food and money and possibly also transport, traveling companions, and letters of introduction. According to his stated plans Paul hoped to receive such gifts when he set out from Corinth (1 Cor. 16:6; 2 Cor. 1:16) and Rome (Rom. 15:24).[73] Whether his hopes were realized, we do not know, but these texts in which προπέμπω is used witness to his expectation of receiving provisions for travel and further service. But the question then arises: How can he say to the Corinthians, in reference to the past, ἐν παντὶ ἀβαρῆ ἐμαυτὸν ὑμῖν ἐτήρησα (11:9), and with regard to the future, ἡ καύχησις αὕτη οὐ φραγήσεται εἰς ἐμέ? Perhaps the answer lies in distinguishing carefully between the two principles outlined above. In 11:9-10, 12; 12:14 Paul says that he *will* not[74] accept financial support from the Corinthians, that is, while he is present with them; οὐ φραγήσεται and the other futures have special but not exclusive reference to the upcoming third visit. In 11:9; 12:13, 16 he affirms that he *was* not a financial burden while with them, that is, during his first and second visits. But when he writes οὐ φραγήσεται (11:10) or οὐ καταναρκήσω (12:14; see also 11:9, 12) he is not excluding the future possibility of accepting aid from the Corinthians, if it were offered, for service outside Corinth. Nor did his *financial* independence mean he refused to accept the gift of hospitality from anyone at Corinth. On the contrary, he stayed with Aquila and Priscilla during his first visit (Acts 18:3), and on his third visit he was a guest in the home of Gaius (Rom. 16:23, written from Corinth).

11:11 διὰ τί; ὅτι οὐκ ἀγαπῶ ὑμᾶς; ὁ θεὸς οἶδεν. "Why? Because I do not love you? God knows I do!" It appears that some at Corinth — whether native Corinthians or intruders, or both — had maliciously suggested that the reason for Paul's adamant refusal to accept support was his lack of love for his supposed friends. Why else would he not reciprocate their overtures of friendship? If this verse were not a reply to a charge, we would expect Paul to have answered his own question (διὰ τί;) by ὅτι ἀγαπῶ ὑμᾶς ὡς ὁ θεὸς οἶδεν. He himself would never make the suggestion that he was loveless. See, to the contrary,

---

71. As in Acts 20:38; 21:5.

72. This latter point is clear from Tit. 3:13: "Make every effort to send Zenas the lawyer and Apollos on their way (σπουδαίως πρόπεμψον); see that they are not short of anything (ἵνα μηδὲν αὐτοῖς λείπῃ)." Note also the use of ὑπολαμβάνειν ("support") in 2 John 8 after προπέμψας in 2 John 6.

73. Other uses of προπέμπω in this sense are Acts 15:3 (in reference to Paul, Barnabas, and others as delegates of the church at Antioch), 1 Cor. 16:11 (Timothy), Tit. 3:13 (Zenas and Apollos), and 2 John 6 (itinerant Christian workers).

74. JB and Lambrecht (172) render the οὐ before φραγήσεται by "never," perhaps partly under the influence of the introductory oath formula. But Furnish does not regard the οὐ as absolute: "at least in the foreseeable future Paul intends that the congregation shall not be burdened with responsibility for his maintenance" (509).

6:11-13; 7:3; 12:15. As in Rom. 9:32, ὅτι following the interrogative διὰ τί; means "because" rather than "that."[75]

Faced with such a hurtful accusation and aware that any further attempt to justify his motives would be fruitless, the apostle invokes the omniscience of God to testify to the reality and depth of his love for the Corinthians, just as in the previous verse he had appealed to "the truth of Christ" as the guarantee of the truthfulness of his boast. In both verses he is employing oath formulas, as also in 1:18, 23; 11:31; 12:2-3. A fuller form of the abbreviated formula ὁ θεὸς οἶδεν is found in 11:31, ὁ θεὸς καὶ πατὴρ τοῦ κυρίου Ἰησοῦ οἶδεν . . . ὅτι οὐ ψεύδομαι, although in 11:11 the content of the divine knowledge ("God knows") is not "that I do not lie," but may be assumed to be "that I do love you," or possibly "the truth about that" (Barrett 270) or "whether that is true or not" (Plummer 301).[76] Such an appeal to God's all-knowingness presupposes a belief that God is καρδιογνώστης (Acts 15:8), "the One who knows people's hearts."[77] God read Paul's heart and knew the intensity of his love as well as the motives for his actions that he had outlined in vv. 7-10. We may sense the ardor of Paul's agitated emotions here by the successive oaths in vv. 10-11 and the extraordinary brevity of the two questions and one affirmation in v. 11.

11:12 ὃ δὲ ποιῶ καὶ ποιήσω, ἵνα ἐκκόψω τὴν ἀφορμὴν τῶν θελόντων ἀφορμήν, ἵνα ἐν ᾧ καυχῶνται εὑρεθῶσιν καθὼς καὶ ἡμεῖς. "But what I am doing I shall also continue to do, in order to cut off the opportunity of those who want an opportunity to be regarded as on a par with us in what they boast about." Because this verse refers to certain persons who entertain a particular desire (τῶν θελόντων), persons who then (οἱ . . . τοιοῦτοι) are described as to origin, conduct, and destiny (vv. 13-15), many Greek editions, translations, and commentators make v. 12 the beginning of a new paragraph (vv. 12-15).[78] But the links between v. 12 and vv. 7-11 are even stronger: the antecedent of ὃ is found in v. 9 (not being burdensome); the future ποιήσω corresponds to φραγήσεται (v. 10) and τηρήσω (v. 9); and the double use of ποιέω looks back to ἐποίησα (v. 7). So it seems more appropriate to regard v. 12 as the end rather than the beginning of a paragraph (vv. 7-12[79] or vv. 5-12[80]).

As well as comparing themselves with one another (10:12), Paul's opponents were apparently comparing themselves with Paul himself with regard to their respective financial relations with the Corinthians; they accepted support (see the introduction to this section), but Paul did not. In all probability they re-

---

75. Cf. NEB, "Is it that I do not love you?" REB has "Because. . . ."

76. Spicq (*Agape* 32) comments: "The great-souled Apostle cannot lower himself to answer reproaches which border on insolence. He is answerable only to God; God knows whether I love you and he knows the reasons for my conduct."

77. In Acts 1:24 this noun is applied to the risen Jesus; cf. 1 Cor. 4:4-5.

78. E.g., UBS[1-4], NA[27]; NEB, GNB, REB; Carrez 215; Lang 336-37. Some see the unit of thought as vv. 1-15 (Barrett 270-71), vv. 5-15 (Wolff 215-16), or vv. 7-15 (Thrall 656).

79. E.g., NIV.

80. E.g., Lambrecht 172.

garded themselves as on a par with Paul or superior to him (cf. 10:7, 10; 11:6, 22-23) in every area except one acutely embarrassing respect — he was financially independent of the Corinthians and not a burden on them. His resolute stance on financial support effectively deprived them of the opportunity to be known as those who were working at Corinth on precisely the same terms as he was. Recognizing their desire for parity of status, Paul simply reaffirms here in v. 12 his choice of independence and thus frustrates their longing for equality.

δέ is probably adversative ("but").[81] After rejecting one alleged reason for his ongoing policy of financial independence (v. 11), Paul now supplies a positive reason in answer to the question διὰ τί;. Basically, it was to deprive his adversaries of the desired parity. In the expression ὃ ποιῶ καὶ ποιήσω, the crucial issue is the meaning of καί. If it is conjunctive ("and"), the whole clause forms the subject, "What I am doing and will do," and before the statement of purpose (ἵνα) one must supply a word such as γίνεται ("happens," "is done"[82]), or ἐστιν,[83] or διὰ τοῦτο ποιῶ[84] ("I do for this purpose, that . . ."). While this makes ποιῶ καὶ ποιήσω parallel to ἐτήρησα καὶ τηρήσω (v. 9) (Allo 284), we can avoid the need to supply a word or phrase before ἵνα by taking καί as adjunctive ("also") and making ὃ ποιῶ the full extent of the relative clause, "What I am doing, I shall (also) continue to do."[85] In this case, in accordance with v. 10, ἵνα κτλ. specifies "the aim inducing the future continuance of his conduct" (Meyer 649).

That aim was to "cut off the opportunity of those who want an opportunity." Elsewhere in the NT ἐκκόπτω ("cut off," "cut down") is used of limbs that are amputated from a body, or of branches that are removed from a tree, or of a tree that is felled. Here, in reference to ἀφορμή ("occasion," "opportunity"; see on 5:12), the verb means "do away with," "put an end to," "eliminate."[86] But what was this "opportunity" or "occasion" that Paul sought to remove? Some look to the general context and speak of "occasion for calumny"[87] or "an opportunity to boast about support received, as if about apostolic privilege."[88] But if we regard the second ἵνα clause (ἵνα . . . εὑρεθῶσιν . . .) as dependent on the second ἀφορμήν, Paul himself defines the nature of the "opportunity" he aimed to eliminate by his continued refusal of support. It was the opportunity, sought by his rivals, to be "recognized" (NRSV) or "considered" (NIV) by the Corinthians as working on the same terms as Paul or as Paul's equals (καθὼς καὶ ἡμεῖς).

81. So Weymouth; Barclay; Barrett 270; Wolff 216.
82. Thrall 656 (cf. 690 n. 247).
83. Cf. Allo 285. But in his commentary he seems to prefer supplying a phrase such as τοῦτο ποιῶ.
84. Windisch (339) suggests this or γίνεται as suitable words to be supplied.
85. So most EVV and commentators.
86. ἵνα ἐκκόψω τὴν ἀφορμήν could be rendered "in order to chop away the base" (Young and Ford 273), or even "to cut the ground from under" (NEB, REB; similarly Goodspeed), since ἀφορμή regularly referred to a "base of operations."
87. G. Bertram, *TDNT* 5.473. Similarly TCNT, "some ground for attacking me."
88. Zerwick, *Analysis* 411.

εὑρεθῶσιν ("be discovered to be," "be regarded") is not to be equated with a simple ὦσιν or γένωνται. What was all-important for Paul's opponents was the Corinthian perception of them; they wished to be recognized as equal with Paul in the matter about which they boasted.

But not all regard the second ἵνα clause as defining ἀφορμήν and therefore as indicative of the desire of Paul's rivals. Meyer, for example, regards the second ἵνα clause as the aim of ἐκκόψω . . . ἀφορμήν and thus the second and final aim of ὃ δὲ ποιῶ καὶ ποιήσω. Paul not only wished to deprive his adversaries of their desired opportunity to slander him as selfish and greedy; he also wished to force them to become financially independent of the Corinthians and so prove the unselfishness about which they had been boasting (649-51).[89] But such an altruistic motive on Paul's part in dealing with his opponents is hard to reconcile with the next three verses. Shaming his opponents out of their selfishness toward his own selfless stance on finances is out of keeping with Paul's approach. And success in one such minor skirmish would not substantially contribute to winning the war. It is more satisfactory to take the second ἵνα clause as pointing to the desire of Paul's adversaries to bring him "down" to their level of financial dependence than the desire of Paul to bring them "up" to his level of financial independence.[90]

In the phrase ἐν ᾧ καυχῶνται, the preposition ἐν that governs the relative pronoun ᾧ belongs also with the demonstrative pronoun that is concealed within the relative pronoun; thus "in that in which" (BAGD 583b, c), "in what they boast about."[91] Given the cryptic nature of this expression, it is not surprising that many different identifications of the rivals' area of boasting have been proposed.

1. Their "mission" (RSV, NAB[2]) or "ministry" (NAB[1]).
2. Their claimed apostleship (Moffatt, Goodspeed, NEB, REB).
3. The legitimacy of their Corinthian ministry, Corinth as their legitimate field of operation (cf. 10:15-16) (Martin 348-49).
4. "The apostolic right to support by the churches" (G. Bertram, *TDNT* 5.473).
5. "The dignity of being Apostolic missionaries" (Plummer 307).
6. Their superiority to Paul in authority and message (Plummer [CGT] 170).
7. Financial support from the Corinthians as proof of their being recognized as genuine "apostles of Christ" (cf. 11:13).[92]

89. Cf. Hock 101 n. 118.

90. Mozley (212-14) has revived the view of Chrysostom and Calvin that Paul's opponents boasted of refusing support, so that his own refusal of support meant that they would be found to be as he was and therefore at no advantage over him. However, 11:20 seems to fly in the face of the assumption that his rivals refused support.

91. It is possible that ἐν ᾧ bears a temporal sense, "while they boast" = "in their boasting" (Barrett 271).

92. Similarly Hughes 391-92.

Each of these proposals arises from the wider context; nos. 4 and 7 (my prefer-ence) have the advantage of reference to finances, the issue under consideration in vv. 7-12.

To summarize our view of v. 12, Paul's opponents were in receipt of sup-port from the Corinthians, and, pointing to the "apostolic" right to support, they viewed this support as evidence of their genuine apostleship. Nevertheless they also recognized this support as a distinct disadvantage when their stance on fi-nances was compared by the Corinthians with Paul's. So they wanted to goad him to alter his policy and accept support so that the embarrassing difference between them could be eradicated.[93] Paul, however, resolved not to surrender his advantage over his rivals, namely that no one could ever charge him with preaching for a fee or for profit or with burdening his converts. Rather, he planned to continue his present policy in order to undercut his rivals' desire to be on a par with him with regard to financial support.[94]

Bibliography

Betz, *Paulus* 57-66 • Caragounis • D. L. Dungan, *The Sayings of Jesus in the Churches of Paul: The Use of the Synoptic Tradition in the Regulation of Early Church Life* (Ox-ford: Blackwell, 1971) 27-40, 76-77 • Hafemann, *Defense* 145-54 • Hock • Holsten • Judge • Judge, "Conformity" • Käsemann • Marshall 165-258 • Mozley • Murphy-O'Connor 110-13 • Oostendorp 75-79 • Peterman • Pratscher • Savage 80-93 • Theissen 27-67 • Zmijewski

3. False Apostles (11:13-15)

In 10:7, for the sake of argument, Paul reports the self-confident claim (τις πέποιθεν ἑαυτῷ) of the spokesman for the Judaizing interlopers to "belong to Christ" (Χριστοῦ εἶναι). That is, these rival missionaries professed to be, in a distinctive sense, Christ's agents (cf. 11:23), his genuine apostles. Here in 11:13-15 Paul strips off their disguise and reveals their true identity — they in fact belong to Satan (οἱ διάκονοι αὐτοῦ, v. 15), not to Christ; they are part of Sa-tan's nefarious task force (ἐργάται δόλιοι, v. 13), not agents of righteousness (διάκονοι δικαιοσύνης, v. 15); and they are false apostles (ψευδαπόστολοι, v. 13), not apostles of Christ (ἀποστόλους Χριστοῦ, v. 13). The explicit or im-

---

93. On this understanding Paul might have been expected to write ἵνα . . . εὑρεθῶμεν καθὼς καὶ αὐτοί (or ἵνα ἐν ᾧ καυχῶνται αὐτοί, κἀγὼ εὑρεθῶ [Bultmann 207]), "so that . . . we may be re-garded as they are," i.e., in receipt of support from the church. The reason, however, for the present wording may be the apostle's wish to focus on how his rivals wanted to be regarded by the Corinthi-ans. This seems an adequate response to the one substantial objection (cf. Thrall 691) that has been raised to the view espoused.

94. A similar view has been expressed by Lietzmann 148; Plummer 307-8; Allo 285; Hughes 390-92; Kruse 189-90.

plied antitheses between their claims (cf. μετασχηματίζομαι in vv. 13, 15) and the real situation may be set out as follows.[1]

Claim	Reality
v. 13 ἀπόστολοι Χριστοῦ	ψευδαπόστολοι
v. 13 [ἐργάται ἀληθεῖς]	ἐργάται δόλιοι
v. 15 διάκονοι δικαιοσύνης	οἱ διάκονοι αὐτοῦ [= Σατανᾶ]
(cf. v. 23, διάκονοι Χριστοῦ)	

11:13*For such people are false apostles, deceitful workers, disguising themselves as "apostles of Christ." 14And no wonder[a]! For Satan himself disguises himself as an angel of light. 15So it is not a great surprise if his servants also disguise themselves as servants of righteousness. But their fate will accord with their works.*

TEXTUAL NOTES

a. Some witnesses (D[1] Ψ 0121 𝔐) read θαυμαστόν ("remarkable thing"), but θαῦμα, read by 𝔭[46] ℵ B D* F G P 098 0243 0278 6 33 81 326 365 630 1175 1739 1881 2464 *pc* Origen, is to be preferred, not only because of superior external attestation (which includes the proto-Alexandrian and the best Western witnesses) but also because it is the more difficult reading (there are 43 uses of θαυμαστός in the LXX, and six in the NT, but only two uses of θαῦμα in the LXX and two in the NT [here and in Rev. 17:6]).

11:13 Οἱ γὰρ τοιοῦτοι ψευδαπόστολοι, ἐργάται δόλιοι, μετασχηματιζόμενοι εἰς ἀποστόλους Χριστοῦ. "For such people are false apostles, deceitful workers, disguising themselves as 'apostles of Christ.'" If, with Martin (327), we render γάρ by "on the contrary," Paul is contrasting his rivals' desire for parity with him (v. 12) with the reality of their identity. Better, he is simply explaining ("for") why any notion of equality between himself and his opponents is completely unwarranted. It is possible that οἱ τοιοῦτοι could mean "people such as these" (as in 1 Cor. 7:28), referring to a class of persons who had certain characteristics in common, in this case those given to boasting (v. 12). But the apostle is not reflecting abstractly on the traits or identity of boasters. Nor is he issuing a warning to his rivals that unless they cease their activities in Corinth they will become "false apostles." With οἱ τοιοῦτοι, "such men/people," he is referring explicitly to his adversaries, "they" (= people with these characteristics).[2] "These people" (JB, NJB) (= οὗτοι) or "Those men" (GNB) (= ἐκεῖνοι) is perhaps too weak a rendering. The subject of the implied εἰσίν is not οἱ τοιοῦτοι

---

1. On the stylistic features of 11:13-15, see Zmijewski 166-67. On the use of πάθος in 11:1-15, see Thrall 698-99 (with references to DiCicco 170-73, 182-83).

2. A similar use of ὁ τοιοῦτος referring to a specific individual or individuals is found in 2:6-7; 10:11; 12:2, 5; and cf. οἱ τοιοῦτοι in Rom. 16:18. But in 1 Cor. 16:16 οἱ τοιοῦτοι seems to mean "these people and others like them."

ψευδαπόστολοι ("such false apostles"), but οἱ τοιοῦτοι alone, with ψευδ-απόστολοι being the anarthrous predicate.

That Paul's opponents claimed to be genuine ἀπόστολοι is evident from the latter part of this verse. He bluntly rejects their claim by calling them ψευδαπόστολοι, "false apostles,"[3] a NT *hapax legomenon* and probably also a Pauline coinage.[4] In Paul's view they were "false" because: they lacked the authorization of Christ (cf. 1:1); they preached a "different gospel" (11:4); they were trespassing on foreign territory, Paul's own domain in Corinth (cf. 10:15-16); they used cunning, deceptive techniques (cf. δόλιοι, 11:13) to achieve their goals (cf. 4:2); they assumed disguises (μετασχηματίζομαι, 11:13, 15); they excelled in domination (11:20), not service (cf. 11:8), and so failed to reflect the character of Christ (cf. 10:1; 13:4).

We have argued above that these ψευδαπόστολοι should not be equated with οἱ ὑπερλίαν ἀπόστολοι of 11:5; 12:11.[5] One reason for maintaining a distinction between them is apparent in the present passage. Whereas Paul adopts a defensive posture of non-inferiority when he speaks ironically of the "superlative apostles," he ruthlessly attacks the "counterfeit apostles," the Judaizing missionaries from Judea. With respect to the former group he is remarkably restrained; with regard to the latter group he unhesitatingly passes sentence (11:15).

Paul's next two descriptions of his antagonists develop the idea of falsehood (ψευδ-). In the early church ἐργάτης ("worker") was a technical term denoting a person engaged in Christian service,[6] particularly missionary activity.[7] No doubt Paul's rivals saw themselves as ἐργάται in this sense, but for him they were "workers" only in the rudimentary sense that they were "at work" within the Corinthian church. Because this ἔργον was marked by deceit, treachery, and cunning, they are called ἐργάται δόλιοι, "deceitful workers," "dishonest workmen" (BAGD 203b; Goodspeed), "crooked in all their practices" (NEB).[8] Isaacs' rendering, "industrious schemers," neatly highlights (by inversion) the significant word in the expression. Just as certain agitators in Rome did not serve the Lord Christ but were slaves to their own appetites and deceived (ἐξαπατῶσιν) the hearts of innocent people with their smooth and flattering words (Rom. 16:17-18), so at about the same time (the mid-50's) these "work-

3. Other renderings of ψευδο- include "counterfeit," "sham," "bogus," "fake." Other Pauline compounds using this prefix are ψευδομάρτυρες (1 Cor. 15:15) and ψευδάδελφοι (2 Cor. 11:26; Gal. 2:4). Paul does not use ψευδοδιδάσκαλος (2 Pet. 2:1), ψευδοπροφήτης (e.g., 1 John 4:1), or ψευδόχριστος (Matt. 24:24; Mark 13:22).

4. So, among others, Kümmel 211.

5. See the Introduction, B.4.d, and the commentary at 11:5.

6. Matt. 10:10//Luke 10:7; 1 Tim. 5:18; 2 Tim. 2:15. Compare the use of ἔργον in 1 Cor. 3:13-15; 16:10.

7. Matt. 9:37-38//Luke 10:2. See Georgi, *Opponents* 40.

8. REB has "confidence tricksters (masquerading as apostles of Christ)." The cognate verb δολιόω has the connotation "deceive by using trickery and falsehood" (Louw and Nida §88.154).

ers" in Corinth were similarly self-serving, deceiving the minds of the Corinthians (cf. 11:3), diverting their affections from Christ (cf. 11:3), and seeking to reduce them to subservience (11:20).

Falsehood was also evident in their manner of operating — pretending to be what they were not. Vv. 13-15 are bound together by the threefold use of μετασχηματίζω, where this verb (in the middle) "has the negative sense[9] of *pretend to be someone/hypocritically act as someone/masquerade as someone,* with the assumed role indicated by εἰς or ὡς."[10] The guise they habitually assumed (μετασχηματιζόμενοι) was that of ἀπόστολοι Χριστοῦ, an expression which, like ἐργάται, was undoubtedly a self-designation.[11] There was an alteration of their outward appearance (σχῆμα), but their real identity as ψευδαπόστολοι remained unchanged (Bernard 103). This notion of pretense makes v. 13 closely parallel to Rev. 2:2 where the Ephesian believers are applauded because they "have tested those who call themselves 'apostles,' but are not, and found them to be false."

11:14 καὶ οὐ θαῦμα, αὐτὸς γὰρ ὁ Σατανᾶς μετασχηματίζεται εἰς ἄγγελον φωτός. "And no wonder! For Satan himself disguises himself as an angel of light." The deceptive masquerading of the "false apostles" (v. 13) should occasion no surprise, Paul says, because the arch-deceiver Satan (cf. John 8:44), also regularly uses a disguise, although a different one, for he makes himself out to be a shining angel sent by God. ἐστίν is frequently omitted in exclamations ("And no wonder!" REB).[12] θαῦμα, from θάομαι, "I gaze at in wonder," refers to what prompts amazement, so that τὰ θαύματα is used of jugglers' tricks. The presence of αὐτός with ὁ Σατανᾶς, "Satan himself," "even Satan" (RSV, NRSV),[13] hints at what becomes explicit in v. 15, namely that Satan is a principal whose agents follow his example. Even if the present tense μετασχηματίζεται points to Satan's habitual conduct, a reference to his current masquerading at Corinth should not be excluded; if so, Weymouth's "can disguise himself" is misleading.

ἄγγελον φωτός could be rendered in four ways (here listed in ascending order of probability).

---

9. In Phil. 3:21 μετασχηματίζω bears a positive sense, referring to Christ's future transformation of believers' bodies by giving them the character of his own glorious, resurrection body. In the only other NT use of the verb (1 Cor. 4:6), it probably means "apply allusively" (see Thiselton 348-51). The only LXX use is in 4 Macc. 9:22 in reference to the apparent transformation of a martyr into immortality by fire (ὥσπερ ἐν πυρὶ μετασχηματιζόμενος εἰς ἀφθαρσίαν).

10. J. M. Nützel, *EDNT* 2.419. But Zerwick (*Analysis* 411) believes that in v. 15 ὡς means "as if (they were)."

11. So Georgi, *Opponents* 32, 40. Appropriately, Moffatt places "apostles of Christ" in quotation marks.

12. BDF §127(4). On the ellipse of the copula ἐστι in Paul, see Turner 299-303. Windisch notes (341-42) that καὶ οὐ θαῦμα (or similar phrases) is a transitional formula that belongs to the diatribe.

13. For αὐτός meaning "even," see BAGD 123 s.v. 1.h.

1. "A messenger from God" (cf. Schlatter 647), where φῶς is metonymy for "God" and the genitive is subjective.
2. "A messenger of [the world of] light" (cf. BAGD 871d, 513c), where φωτός is either a possessive genitive ("belonging to") or a genitive of source ("from").
3. "A shining angel" (Goodspeed), where φωτός is an adjectival or Semitic genitive, equivalent to φωτεινόν ("shining") (cf. Moule 175, "perhaps").
4. "An angel of light" (most EVV) or "a messenger of light" (Martin 327), where the genitive is adjectival ("characterized by light") or possibly objective ("bringing light").

Paul's point is that Satan habitually tries to achieve his villainous aims within the church by craftily assuming the guise of a heavenly emissary who embodies all that is upright and true. But while appearing to represent the realm of light (= purity and truth), in reality he represents the domain of darkness (= impurity and falsehood), which is his natural habitat (cf. 4:4; Acts 26:18; Eph. 6:12; Col. 1:13).

What is the source of this description of one of Satan's techniques?[14] Neither Gen. 3:1-5 nor Job 1:6-12 nor 1 Kgs. 22:19-23 offers a precise parallel.[15] It is in the pseudepigrapha that we find the closest conceptual parallels. For the idea of Satan or the devil adopting a disguise, we find in the *Testament of Job* (first century B.C. or A.D.) no fewer than four different disguises mentioned — as a beggar (6:4), as the king of the Persians (17:2), as a great whirlwind (20:5), and as a bread seller (23:1).[16] The notion of an angelic disguise is found in two places (first century A.D.). In the *Life of Adam and Eve (Vita)* 9:1 Satan transforms himself "into the brightness of angels" before beguiling Eve for a second time. In the Greek text of the *Life,* the *Apocalypse of Moses,* Satan comes to Eve over the walls of Paradise "in the form of an angel (ἐν εἴδει ἀγγέλου)" (*Apocalypse of Moses* 17:1) and tempts her to disobey God's command (cf. Gen. 3:3). But we need not posit Paul's reliance on these Jewish traditions for the expression ἄγγελος φωτός.[17] It could be a Pauline coinage, prompted on the one hand by the common association of Satan with darkness (6:14-15) and deception (4:4) and of God or Christ with light and illumination (4:6; Rom. 13:12,

14. See the extended note in Windisch 342-43.
15. Bernard suggests that such passages may perhaps sufficiently account for the image, although he believes "some Rabbinical tradition" is a more likely source (103). The accounts of the temptation of Jesus depict Satan as appealing to the text of Scripture (Ps. 91:11-12; the quotation is from the LXX, Ps. 90:11-12) — albeit with a crucial omission, "in all your ways" — to justify his proposal that Jesus should throw himself down from the pinnacle of the Temple (Matt. 4:5-6; Luke 4:9-11), but there is no reason to think that Paul had this episode in mind.
16. In *Testament of Reuben* 5:6 (second century B.C.) the guardian angels disguise themselves in male form (μετεσχηματίζοντο εἰς ἄνδρα) before cohabiting with human females (cf. Gen. 6:1-4).
17. In the DSS the archangel Michael is described as the "Prince of Lights" (1QM 13:10; 1QS 3:20; cf. 1QM 17:6), but we need not infer (*pace* M. D. Johnson, *OTP* 2.260 n. 9) that Paul may have believed that Satan disguised himself as Michael.

14; Eph. 5:11-14), and on the other hand by his own experience and observation of Satan's various stratagems (2:11).

11:15 οὐ μέγα οὖν εἰ καὶ οἱ διάκονοι αὐτοῦ μετασχηματίζονται ὡς διάκονοι δικαιοσύνης, ὧν τὸ τέλος ἔσται κατὰ τὰ ἔργα αὐτῶν. "So it is not a great surprise if his servants also disguise themselves as servants of righteousness. But their fate will accord with their works." The presence of οὖν and the adjunctive use of καί ("also")[18] indicate a close logical relation between v. 14 and v. 15. Arguing *a maiori ad minus* ("from the greater to the lesser"),[19] Paul concludes that if the principal adopts a disguise (v. 14), we should expect — or not be surprised, οὐ μέγα [θαῦμα] — that his agents do the same. Like κύριος, like δοῦλοι or διάκονοι (cf. Matt. 10:25). There may be a second element in the correspondence suggested by καί. Not only do both parties (Satan and his deputies) engage in a masquerade; the nature of the disguise is essentially the same, so that those who masquerade as "servants of righteousness" act as "angels of light" (cf. v. 14).

As with οὐ θαῦμα in v. 14, ἐστι is to be supplied with οὐ μέγα, which is litotes for "a simple thing" (NEB) or "easy enough" (REB). οἱ διάκονοι αὐτοῦ means "the servants who belong to him" (αὐτοῦ a possessive genitive), where Satan is the κύριος and the ψευδαπόστολοι are his δοῦλοι, or simply "those who serve him" (αὐτοῦ an objective genitive). διάκονοι is scarcely distinguishable from ἐργάται ("workers") in meaning,[20] but in the context the term gains the sense of "agents" or "deputies." Paul regarded his rivals not simply as "false apostles" (v. 14), as serious as that charge was, but also as Satan's minions. Human opposition to his ministry was prompted and directed by the devil, the archenemy of God, of the gospel, and of the church.[21] For the Corinthians the warning was clear: "If you follow these intruders, you are siding with Satan against God."

In the Corinthian congregation Satan's agents posed as "servants of righteousness." The genitive δικαιοσύνης could be adjectival "righteous" or "upright," but more probably is objective, "men in the service of righteousness" (Cassirer). Clearly δικαιοσύνη does not carry its distinctive Pauline sense of a right standing before God that is graciously given by God and received by faith. Nor will it refer to a righteousness that depends on works[22] or Torah observance,[23] not only because it lacks a qualification such as τῆς ἐξ ἔργων or τῆς ἐκ

---

18. Robertson 1180. Burton (§282) and Turner (321) observe that εἰ καί here is not concessive ("even though"); εἰ is conditional and καί adjunctive ("if . . . also").

19. So Meyer 652; Wolff 224.

20. Cf. Ellis, "Co-Workers" 441.

21. At a later time (about A.D. 170), Dionysius, bishop of Corinth, claimed (according to Eusebius, *Hist. Eccl.* 4.23.12) that his own epistles had been tampered with or "filled with tares" by certain "messengers of the devil" (οἱ τοῦ διαβόλου ἀπόστολοι).

22. As Tasker 154.

23. As Barnett 527, who observes that in Phil. 3:2, 6 Paul seems to connect "evil workmen" (τοὺς κακοὺς ἐργάτας) with "righteousness under the Law" (δικαιοσύνην τὴν ἐν νόμῳ) (527 n. 19).

νόμου[24] but also because "Judaizers" advocating this position would not be in disguise.[25] Probably the term here has a broad and general sense, "(agents) of good" (NEB, REB) or "(servants) of uprightness" (Goodspeed, NJB). Since διάκονοι δικαιοσύνης is reminiscent of the earlier phrase ἡ διακονία τῆς δικαιοσύνης (3:9) that describes Paul's ministry,[26] there may be here in v. 15 an implicit contrast between Paul's rivals who are self-styled "servants of righteousness" working under disguise as agents of Satan, and Paul himself, a true servant of righteousness working openly under a commission from God (10:13; cf. 3:5; 4:7) as a true apostle of Christ (1:1).

Having outlined the charges against his opponents (vv. 13-15a), Paul concludes with an oblique indication of their sentence (v. 15b).[27] Three comparable statements from later Pauline letters shed light on his meaning.

Rom. 3:8   ὧν τὸ κρίμα ἔνδικόν ἐστιν ("Their condemnation is just") (concerning his slanderers).

Phil. 3:19   ὧν τὸ τέλος ἀπώλεια ("Their end is destruction") (concerning the enemies of the cross of Christ).

2 Tim. 4:14   ἀποδώσει αὐτῷ ὁ κύριος κατὰ τὰ ἔργα αὐτοῦ ("The Lord will repay him according to his deeds") (concerning Alexander the coppersmith).

From a comparison of these passages with 11:15b it becomes clear that at the future Great Unmasking of disguises it is the Lord Jesus himself (cf. 1 Cor. 4:5; 1 Thess. 4:6; 2 Thess. 1:8) who will preside and pass a sentence that determines the "end" or "final destiny" (τέλος) of Satan's agents. That sentence will involve their "destruction" just as they themselves were destroying the temple of God at Corinth (cf. 1 Cor. 3:16-17), and it will be "just" since the recompense meted out will accord with actual deeds performed (cf. 5:10),[28] not with false external appearances (cf. μετασχηματίζομαι in vv. 13, 15).

Bibliography

Barrett, "Opponents" • Barrett, "2 Cor. 11:13" • Barrett, Signs 36-37, 46 • Carrez, Souffrance 75-76 • Georgi, Opponents 32-40 • Käsemann • Kleinknecht 292-93 • McClelland • Oostendorp • Sumney 149-79 • Sumney, Servants 102-33 • Thrall, "Super-Apostles" • Yinger 271-72 • Zmijewski

24. Cf. Bultmann 209.

25. Cf. Windisch 343.

26. It is interesting that Barnett (19) points to this verbal link as one evidence of the unity of chs. 1–9 and 10–13, whereas Thrall, who argues (5-20) that chs. 1–8 form a letter that precedes chs. 10–13, proposes that Paul's rivals are taking up his own expression and applying it to themselves (697).

27. Cf. Yinger 271, with reference to Zmijewski 167 n. 419.

28. κατὰ τὰ ἔργα αὐτῶν corresponds to ἐργάται δόλιοι (v. 13).

4. Justification for Foolish Boasting (11:16-21a)

In 10:12-18 Paul identified two types of boasting, the improper (about oneself) and the proper (about the Lord), represented by his rivals and himself (respectively). At 11:1 the notion of foolishness (ἀφροσύνη), that is, foolish boasting,[1] was introduced. This is boasting which, while improper in that it relates to one's own status and achievements, is necessary, given certain circumstances. After registering (11:1) and justifying (11:2, 4-5) a plea for the Corinthians' tolerance as he embarks on such boasting, Paul digresses to defend his resolute stance on financial independence (11:7-12) and to bare his soul regarding his estimate of his opponents (11:13-15). Now in 11:16-21a he revisits (πάλιν λέγω, v. 16) this theme of foolish boasting and offers a further reason why his converts ought to accommodate him as he plays the fool. Already they have happily tolerated not merely fools but overlords who are bent on dominating and exploiting them (vv. 19-20), a role Paul had never played (v. 21a). How much more should they put up with him in a bit of foolish boasting! He is ready, finally, to begin his actual boasting in what has come to be called the "Fool's Speech" *(Narrenrede)* (11:21b–12:13).[2]

Although the apostle decides, for the sake of his converts at Corinth, to play his opponents' "game" of boasting and to follow their "rules," he does so very reluctantly (cf. Zmijewski 217). His embarrassed displeasure is shown by his three efforts actually to begin boasting (see 10:8; 11:1, 16) and by his repeated apologetic explanations. His confident boasting as a fool is not at the Lord's direction (11:17), is conducted in a worldly fashion (11:18), is not really profitable (12:1), and is forced on him by the Corinthians themselves (12:11).[3] Paul's wearing of a fool's mask was the result, not of disinterested experimentation on his part, but of the Corinthians' immaturity in being dazzled by the barefaced bragging of the intruders. In a sense, his converts rather than his rivals had dictated his *modus operandi*. It was not that his adversaries had chosen the path of boasting about pedigree and accomplishments and that Paul had imi-

---

1. Although the ideas of "foolishness" and "boasting" are first brought together in 11:16, it is clear that in 11:1 ἀφροσύνη alludes to *foolish* boasting, as the parallelism between μικρόν τι ἀφροσύνης (11:1) and ἵνα κἀγὼ μικρόν τι καυχήσωμαι (11:16) indicates.

2. Some call 11:1–12:13 the "Fool's Speech" and divide it into an introduction (11:1-21a), the actual speech (11:21b–12:10), and an epilogue (12:11-13) (e.g., Barnett 494). McCant proposes a similar analysis: (1) *prodiorthosis* (advance justification, 11:1-21a), (2) body of the "Fool's Speech" or Foolish Discourse (11:21b–12:10), and (3) *epidiorthosis* (subsequent justification, 12:11-18) (114-16; "Thorn" 557-58). On the stylistic character of 11:16–12:11, see Martin 357-60, who usefully summarizes scholarship on this issue from J. Weiss down to P. Marshall, to which may be added A. B. Spencer's *Paul's Literary Style: A Stylistic and Historical Comparison of II Corinthians 11:16–12:13, Romans 8:9-39 and Philippians 3:2–4:13* (Jackson: Evangelical Theological Society, 1984) and her article on irony in Paul (*NovT* 23 [1981] 349-60).

3. In a similar vein, Furnish remarks that the prologue (11:1-21a) to the Fool's Speech could have been restricted to 11:16, and the "epilogue" (12:11-13) to 12:11. "But in both cases Paul's uneasiness about this whole *business of boasting* (11:17) leads him into a nervous prolixity" (498).

tated their style. They had used boasting as their chosen technique to win over the Corinthians who were then bewitched by their boasting, so that Paul had no choice but to adopt an approach that had already proved successful with the Corinthians if he was to win back their wholehearted support and affection. This "foolish boasting," then, is a classic example of Paul's pastoral adaptability (cf. 1 Cor. 9:22).

11:16*I say again: let no one think me a fool. But if you think otherwise, at least accept me as a fool, so that I too may boast a little.* 17*What I am saying, I am not saying at the Lord's^a direction, but as it were in my own foolishness as I undertake this boasting.* 18*Since many are boasting as the world^b does, I also will boast that way.* 19*For you gladly tolerate fools, being so sensible yourselves!* 20*Indeed, you tolerate it if someone enslaves you, if someone exploits you, if someone ensnares you, if someone puts on airs, if someone strikes you in the face.* 21a*To my shame I confess that we have been weak^c in comparison.*

TEXTUAL NOTES

a. A few inferior witnesses read θεόν (a f r t vg^cl Ambrosiaster Pelagius) in place of κύριον, perhaps under the influence of κατὰ θεόν in 7:10-11; cf. also Rom. 8:27; Eph. 4:24. One minuscule (69) reads κατὰ ἄνθρωπον, an expression found three times in 1 Corinthians (1 Cor. 3:3; 9:8; 15:32).

b. κατὰ σάρκα is a common Pauline expression (20 uses, six in 2 Corinthians), so that the inclusion of the article (κατὰ τὴν σάρκα) in ℵ² B D¹ Ψ 0121 1739^c 1881^c 𝔐, though a more difficult reading, is to be rejected in favor of Paul's invariable usage (found in 𝔭⁴⁶ ℵ* D* F G H 098 0278 33 81 104 365 629 1175 1505 1739* 1881* *al*).

c. In place of ἢ σθενήκαμεν (𝔭⁴⁶ ℵ B H 0243 0278 33 81 1178 1739* 1881 *pc*), many witnesses read ἠσθενήσαμεν (D F G I^vid Ψ 0121 1739^c 𝔐).(UBS⁴ provides fuller textual data.) Since the perfect has the stronger external support and is the more difficult reading, it is to be preferred. The change from the perfect to the aorist may be the result of a simple transcriptional error (σ for κ). On the other hand, some scribe(s) may have been troubled by Paul's confession, ἡμεῖς ἠσθενήκαμεν, and, to avoid any suggestion that he was currently "weak," substituted the aorist. It is of interest that in the main Western witness (D) ἐν τούτῳ τῷ μέρει, "in this matter," is added at the end of the sentence, thus "limiting the idea of 'weakness' to the contrast with his [Paul's] opponents' violence [11:20]" (Plummer 318).

11:16 Πάλιν λέγω, μή τίς με δόξῃ ἄφρονα εἶναι· εἰ δὲ μή γε, κἂν ὡς ἄφρονα δέξασθέ με, ἵνα κἀγὼ μικρόν τι καυχήσωμαι. "I say again: let no one think me a fool. But if you think otherwise, at least accept me as a fool, so that I too may boast a little." With the resumptive πάλιν λέγω ("I repeat"), the reader is directed back to v. 1 where there is a similar request for Corinthian tolerance of some ἀφροσύνη on Paul's part. Yet there are significant differences between the two verses. In v. 16 ἄφρων ("foolish") replaces ἀφροσύνη ("foolishness") and δέξασθέ με replaces ἀνέχεσθέ μου. A plea for toleration of Paul

778

in a little folly (v. 1) becomes a plea for acceptance of him in a little foolish boasting along with a prefaced injunction not to deem him a fool (v. 16). In light of the similar thrust of the two verses, some regard vv. 2-15 as a digression,[4] but although v. 16 is clearly resumptive of v. 1, vv. 2-6 contain reasons that justify v. 1's call for toleration, so that it is perhaps better to view vv. 7-15 as the digression.

μή with the aorist subjunctive and a second person subject commonly expresses a prohibition. Here, however, with a third person subject (τις [ὑμῶν]), the same construction expresses an intense wish (a hortatory subjunctive[5]); the tone is less peremptory than is the case with a second person command or prohibition.[6] μή . . . δόξῃ forbids a future action and is ingressive, "let no one get the idea" (BDF §336[3]). It is implied that none of Paul's readers (or hearers) had that idea,[7] but he was aware that some might easily misunderstand his wearing of a fool's mask. δοκέω is followed by the accusative and infinitive (here με . . . εἶναι) when its subject (τις) is not identical with that of the infinitive (BAGD 202a). Acutely embarrassed at the role he is being forced to play (cf. 12:11), Paul is saying, "When I assume my disguise as a fool [at v. 22], let none of you come to the conclusion that I am actually foolish (ἄφρων)." But he recognizes that this is in fact a distinct possibility, given the Corinthian propensity to believe the allegations of his rivals (cf. 5:13), so he immediately adds εἰ δὲ μή γε, (literally) "but if not," "but otherwise" = "but if (you think) otherwise"[8] = "but if you do think me a fool."[9] His request is that if they must regard him as a fool, then at least they should give him the favorable reception that they would accord a fool. κἄν, formed by crasis from καὶ ἐάν, here means "at least,"[10] although some regard it as elliptical so that κἄν ὡς ἄφρονα δέξασθέ με stands for δέξασθέ με, καὶ ἐὰν ὡς ἄφρονα δέξησθέ με,[11] "Accept me, even if you accept me as a fool." In the text as it stands, δέξασθε precedes με for emphasis (BDF §473[1]). The "acceptance" Paul sought was the Corinthian willingness to give him a fair hearing.[12] He needed that acceptance so that he could boast just as his rivals did. ἵνα is telic rather than imperatival.[13] κἀγώ, "I too," "I for my part," "I in turn," implies that others

---

4. E.g., Kruse 191; Peterson 112 n. 206. But Martin argues that vv. 1-15 form a digression (328-29).

5. Moule 22. Identical constructions are found in 1 Cor. 16:11; 2 Thess. 2:3.

6. Cf. Moulton 178.

7. Robertson 853.

8. With this phrase εἰ δὲ μή γε there is an ellipsis of a verb after εἰ (cf. BDF §§376, 439[1]) that is to be supplied from the context. γε strengthens and emphasizes the negative particle μή (see Thrall, *Particles* 9-10).

9. Cf. Cassirer: "Or if you cannot but regard me as one [a fool]. . . ."

10. BAGD 153a, 402c; Wolff 225; Lambrecht 188.

11. Meyer 654; so also Robertson 1023, 1025. But Moule (151) proposes δέξασθέ με, καὶ ἐὰν ᾖ μόνον ὡς ἄφρονα, "receive me, even if it be only as a fool."

12. Cf. Goodspeed: "show me at least the patience you would show a fool."

13. Cf. Martin 356 ("let me in turn have a little boast").

were already boasting; Paul could not be accused of initiating this business of self-promotion. μικρόν τι, "a little"[14] is the direct object of καυχήσωμαι.[15] Using the figure known as litotes (understatement for effect), Paul plays down the extent of his imminent boasting — although the "fool's speech" runs from 11:21b to 12:13 — in order to draw attention to the unbridled boasting of his opponents (cf. 10:13).

We may indicate the thrust of this verse in an expanded paraphrase. "Once again I appeal to you: let none of you get the idea that I am a fool when I indulge in some foolish boasting. However, if you do see it that way, at least show me the tolerance and patience you would show to a fool, so that I may do a little boasting of my own, just as others do."

11:17 ὃ λαλῶ οὐ κατὰ κύριον λαλῶ, ἀλλ᾽ ὡς ἐν ἀφροσύνῃ, ἐν ταύτῃ τῇ ὑποστάσει τῆς καυχήσεως. "What I am saying, I am not saying at the Lord's direction, but as it were in my own foolishness as I undertake this boasting." As in v. 16, Paul is here anticipating a possible misinterpretation of the boasting he will shortly undertake. There the misconception that might arise was that he was actually foolish; here, that he was boasting at the Lord's direction or on his authority. In both verses his recognition that boasting is essentially foolish finds unambiguous expression. ὃ λαλῶ refers specifically to what Paul is about to utter in his foolish boasting, not to whatever he says at any time; Paul did not write ὅ τι ἂν λέγω and the present tense λαλῶ is futuristic, not gnomic. Although λαλῶ is repeated, the emphasis is on the content of what Paul says (ὃ λαλῶ), not on the fact of his speaking.

The abbreviated phrase κατὰ κύριον ("according to the Lord [Jesus]") has been understood in several ways:

1. "after the Lord" (RV), "as the Lord would" (NASB, NIV), "following the Lord's way" (NJB), which probably means "in accordance with the character or example of Christ,"[16] or marked by the meekness and gentleness of Christ (10:1).
2. "as a Christian" (NEB; Héring 81), "in a Christian way" (Thrall 713). Support for this view may be found in the occasional NT use of prepositional phrases with κύριος or Χριστός as substitutes for the adjective or noun Χριστιανός ("Christian").[17]
3. "inspired by the Lord" (Moffatt, Barclay). This sense is possible, provided we do not conclude that Paul is "uninspired" in his boasting in the sense that it is παρὰ κύριον, "contrary to the Lord('s will)."

14. Literally, "a little something" = "a little (bit)," where τι is substantival (Robertson 743). It is possible that μικρόν τι means "for a little while" (Barrett 288) (accusative of extent of time).

15. For constructions with καυχάομαι, see the commentary at 10:17.

16. Sanday and Headlam 396 (commenting on the phrase κατὰ Χριστὸν Ἰησοῦν in Rom. 15:5), cited by Hughes 398, who espouses this view.

17. See, e.g., ἐν κυρίῳ (Col. 3:18), ἐν Χριστῷ (2 Cor. 12:2). Furnish (485) renders κατὰ κύριον by "as one in the Lord."

4. "with the Lord's authority" (RSV, NRSV).
5. "prompted by the Lord" (JB), "at the Lord's direction."[18]

There is not a great difference between these options. Boasting ὡς ἐν ἀφροσύνῃ (v. 17) or κατὰ σάρκα (v. 18), with self-promotion and invidious comparisons, could never be said to accord with Christ's example, to be the Christian way, to be inspired by the Lord, or to be with his authority or at his direction. But #5 is perhaps to be preferred. Paul's use of boasting as a manner of argumentation against those who employed this technique (v. 18) was the result of his own choice and not at the specific prompting or direction of the Lord Jesus. We find a comparable situation in 1 Corinthians 7. Confronted with pressing pastoral problems where he knew of no definitive word of Christ that would settle the issue, Paul simply confesses, "I say, not the Lord" (λέγω ἐγὼ οὐχ ὁ κύριος, 1 Cor. 7:12) or "I have no command of the Lord, but I give my opinion" (ἐπιταγὴν κυρίου οὐκ ἔχω, γνώμην δὲ δίδωμι, 1 Cor. 7:25), while still retaining his awareness of having the Spirit of God enlighten his mind (1 Cor. 7:40).[19] Similarly here in 11:17 he freely admits that in employing his rivals' worldly tactics he is not following some specific dominical direction; but we may assume he would equally confidently say, "I think I have the Spirit of Christ."

If his boasting was not κατὰ κύριον, it was ὡς ἐν ἀφροσύνῃ, "as it were in my own foolishness." ὡς softens the following expression (Zerwick, *Analysis* 411) and testifies to Paul's discomfort in finding himself, by his own decision, in a state of folly or playing the part of a fool. His folly is taken on,[20] not actual (cf. v. 16a).[21] He wishes the Corinthians to recognize the distinction between a temporary playing of the role of a fool and actually being a fool. And for him the ἄφρων is not the fool of Greek drama, far less the court jester or clown, but rather the person who thinks or acts improperly and without due measure.

As in 9:4, there is a disagreement about the meaning of ὑπόστασις, and a similar range of translations has been proposed.[22] We follow Danker in preferring "undertaking" in both passages.[23] In that case ἐν ταύτῃ τῇ ὑποστάσει τῆς καυχήσεως will mean (literally) "in this undertaking of boasting," that is, "as I undertake this boasting," where (1) ἐν is temporal, (2) the genitive is epexegetic, and (3) the demonstrative adjective ταύτῃ becomes attached in sense to τῆς καυχήσεως.[24]

18. Cf. Barrett 290 ("at his command and with his authority").
19. Cf. Meyer 654.
20. Cf. 12:11 γέγονα ἄφρων, "I have been making a fool of myself" (Goodspeed).
21. BAGD (898 b, c) classifies this ὡς as introducing "a quality wrongly claimed, in any case objectively false."
22. "Confidence" (e.g., RSV, NASB, Barclay, NRSV), "assurance" (Spicq 3.422 and n. 5), "ground" (Martin 362-63), "business" (Moffatt; Furnish 485), "venture/enterprise" (G. Harder, *NIDNTT* 1.712), "topic" (Wolff 225), "project" (BAGD³ 1041a; Thrall 714; cf. H. Koester, *TDNT* 8.585).
23. Danker 136 ("project" or "undertaking"), 176.
24. ἐν could also be causal ("because of") or mean "in respect of" (Thrall 709), "with regard

11:18 ἐπεὶ πολλοὶ καυχῶνται κατὰ σάρκα, κἀγὼ καυχήσομαι. "Since many are boasting as the world does, I also will boast that way." This verse looks back to δέξασθέ με in v. 16 (Bultmann 211) and supplies one reason for Paul's request that the Corinthians accept him in his boasting. If πολλοί refers only to Paul's rivals, it is a derogatory "overstatement," but more probably it focuses attention on them within a wider group of boasters (including some Corinthians) who sought human adulation through self-praise. κατὰ σάρκα stands in contrast to κατὰ κύριον (v. 17) and in parallelism to ἐν ἀφροσύνῃ (v. 17).[25] As with οἱ καυχώμενοι mentioned in 5:12, who boasted "about appearance and not character" (ἐν προσώπῳ καὶ μὴ ἐν καρδίᾳ), these boasters evaluated themselves and others from a purely human and worldly viewpoint, without due regard for the divine perspective, and so prided themselves on outward and natural advantages of ancestry and privilege (cf. v. 22). κατὰ σάρκα, then, describes both the type of boasting (foolish, worldly) and its content (outward appearances, human advantages).

When Paul affirms κἀγὼ καυχήσομαι, he is not simply indicating that he, like his opponents, would engage in boasting. He is giving notice that, like them, he will be boasting κατὰ σάρκα — as extraordinary as that sounds. "I also will boast that way." Such boasting may be unprofitable, but it was necessary (12:1) and inevitable (12:11) without being sinful, although for Paul the phrase κατὰ σάρκα often has connotations of sinfulness (e.g., Rom. 8:4-8, 10, 12-13). But why would Paul have omitted this crucial qualifying phrase? Perhaps he could not bring himself to say he was acting κατὰ σάρκα when some had accused him of making plans κατὰ σάρκα (1:17); the Corinthians were not adept at making fine distinctions. Whatever the reason, Paul realized that if he was to boast "as the world does," he could not simultaneously claim to be speaking "at the Lord's direction" (v. 17): κατὰ σάρκα καυχᾶσθαι and κατὰ κύριον λαλεῖν were mutually exclusive.[26] But such carefully calculated adaptability (cf. 1 Cor. 9:19-23) in making temporary use of his opponents' worldly techniques seemed justified to Paul, not simply because "many others" were bragging (v. 18) but also because this appeared to be the most effective way, given the spiritual immaturity and the gullibility of the Corinthians, to bring them to their senses and thus prevent their spiritual defilement (11:2-3). "My rivals make a practice of boasting in the way people of the world do, and you are dazzled into meek compliance with them (11:20), so I in turn will employ the

---

to" (Lambrecht 187). If τῆς καυχήσεως is an adjectival genitive, the sense would be "in this boastful confidence" (e.g., Barrett 288); if it is a "general" or "relational" genitive, "in this confident boasting" (Bruce, *Paraphrase* 153; similarly NAB[1], NIV).

25. Being virtually an abstract, σάρξ is anarthrous (Turner 177). The textual variant (κατὰ τὴν σάρκα; see Textual Note b.) means "from their human viewpoint" (cf. John 8:15). See Winer 117; Meyer 655 and n. 2.

26. Cf. Peterson 115: "The boasting that Paul will do first will be κατὰ σάρκα (v. 18), which is always ἐν ἀφροσύνῃ (v. 17). This boasting, at least at first, will not be κατὰ κύριον, not the boasting ἐν κυρίῳ of 10:17. Paul will, eventually, come to that; but not yet."

same techniques to bring about your restoration (κατάρτισις, 13:9) and edification (οἰκοδομή, 12:19)." An additional justification for Paul's "foolish boasting" is given at 12:11 (see the commentary there).

11:19 ἡδέως γὰρ ἀνέχεσθε τῶν ἀφρόνων φρόνιμοι ὄντες. "For you gladly tolerate fools, being so sensible yourselves!" This γάρ introduces a reason that justifies not only Paul's plea for acceptance as a fool (v. 16) but also his prospective venture into foolish boasting (vv. 17-18).[27] ἡδέως . . . ἀνέχεσθε is closely parallel to καλῶς ἀνέχεσθε (11:4); the Corinthians displayed their tolerance "gladly" as well as "splendidly." Those described as οἱ ἄφρονες ("the foolish," "fools") are indistinguishable from the πολλοί who brag in the manner of worldlings (v. 18), in particular Paul's rivals, the Judaizing intruders. In the phrase φρόνιμοι ὄντες, the participle could be concessive ("Although you are so wise," Montgomery; "For all your cleverness," TCNT), but it is more likely to be causal ("Since you are so wise").[28] Paul could well have followed "You gladly tolerate fools" by saying "since you too are foolish," but with exquisite irony he concludes, "being so sensible yourselves!"[29] That is, in their "wisdom" they accommodate fools with pleasure. Both ἀνέχεσθε and φρόνιμοι (cf. 1 Cor. 4:10) are ironical;[30] Paul is not praising their tolerance and their wisdom but is highlighting their misdirected tolerance and their false wisdom, as the next verse makes clear. As a juxtaposition of opposites, τῶν ἀφρόνων φρόνιμοι is dramatic, especially since the two words share the same root (φρον-).[31]

In 2 Corinthians 10–13 irony is a frequently used weapon in Paul's arsenal.[32] BDF §495(2) finds in 11:19-20 irony "of the sharpest kind." Unlike σαρκασμός ("mockery," "sarcasm"), irony does not tear the σάρξ. It delivers a jolt to the system and aims to correct attitudes and prompt remedial action. In the present verse Paul is seeking to jolt the Corinthians into realizing how fool-

27. But if ἀνέχεσθε (v. 19) looks back directly to δέξασθε (v. 16), the two intervening verses (vv. 17-18) could be regarded as a parenthesis (as Moffatt, RSV [but not NRSV]; Furnish 484-85, 496; Thrall 715, following Zmijewski 205).

28. So also Plummer 315.

29. Danker (177) speaks of "an arresting bit of satirical wordplay: 'You brainy people *(phronimoi)* are delighted to put up with the brainless *(aphrones).*'"

30. But Holland demurs. "When the Corinthians 'suffer fools gladly' they are in fact exhibiting what was widely recognized as the behavior of the wise person in the face of the tribulation caused by fools" (257). But is accommodating fools the same as tolerating them *gladly?*

31. Efforts to reproduce this wordplay in English have not been totally successful: "senseless–sensible" (Plummer 315), "brainless–brainy" (Danker 177), "irrational–rational."

32. On irony in these chapters, see Loubser 507-21; Holland 250-64, who defines irony as "the pretense that what is said 'hides' from the reader the true state of affairs while in fact revealing it" (250); and Spencer 133-279; "Irony" 349-60, who concludes that Paul's tone in 11:16–12:13 is sardonic ("bitterly ironical"), not sarcastic ("sneering, caustic, cutting, or taunting") (351). Spencer's findings contrast with Murphy-O'Connor's view that in chs. 10–13 "free rein" is given to Paul's emotions so that "the rigid control he normally imposed on his passionate nature dissolves in the heat of his anger" (*Paul* 320), and also to "his capacity for sarcasm and irony" (*Paul* 319). More generally, see Reumann, "Irony"; and on "paradoxical irony" in Paul with special reference to 1 Cor. 4:9-13, see Plank, *Paul and the Irony of Affliction.*

ish they are in submitting so willingly to the abusive exploitation of the intruders (v. 20).[33] And with regard to his own situation he is arguing that if the Corinthians gladly put up with real fools, they should certainly tolerate him in his assumed and moderate foolishness.

11:20 ἀνέχεσθε γὰρ εἴ τις ὑμᾶς καταδουλοῖ, εἴ τις κατεσθίει, εἴ τις λαμβάνει, εἴ τις ἐπαίρεται, εἴ τις εἰς πρόσωπον ὑμᾶς δέρει. "Indeed, you tolerate it if someone enslaves you, if someone exploits you, if someone ensnares you, if someone puts on airs, if someone strikes you in the face." Repeating ἀνέχεσθε from v. 19, Paul gives specific evidence (γάρ, "indeed," "in fact") of the Corinthians' cheerful toleration of fools.[34] Once again (as in vv. 4, 19) ἀνέχεσθε does not applaud their tolerance (but cf. 1 Cor. 4:12) but is sharply ironical: "In your 'wisdom' (φρόνιμοι, v. 19) you actually go on putting up with[35] aggressive authoritarianism!" As Fitzgerald (206) comments, endurance of abuse is ironically portrayed as wisdom.

In the five examples of this abuse that Paul proceeds to document, the reader or hearer is struck by the fivefold repetition of εἴ τις ("if someone") (cf. 1 Tim. 5:10). This has the effect of letting each item stand on its own, thus increasing the paradox step by step and hammering home the message, "You are in the habit of tolerating anything from anyone."[36] But in spite of this unexpected repetition, the focus of the verse is not on the abusers[37] with their arrogance and systematic exploitation but on the Corinthians (ἀνέχεσθε) with their naivety and shocking tolerance. As in 11:4, the present indicative after εἰ (five instances) points to an actual current situation, not a hypothetical future possibility; nor are these indicatives conative, "if someone tries to. . . ."

1. *Domination* (καταδουλοῖ) The uncompounded (or simplex) form δουλόω also means "enslave" (e.g., 1 Cor. 9:19), so that in the compounded form καταδουλόω the prefix κατα- may be "perfective" (thus Robertson 606) in the sense that the servitude was total, "reduce to abject slavery" (Plummer 316; Barclay), but the point cannot be pressed, given the general preference in Hellenistic Greek for compound forms.[38] Although Paul does not use the middle voice, it is implied that Paul's rivals were making the Corinthians slaves *to*

---

33. Hughes sees 11:19 as intended "not as a gibe but as a goad" (399).

34. But it is possible that γάρ functions in the same way as γάρ in v. 19 (see the commentary there); thus BAGD 152a cites 11:19-20 as an instance where a repeated γάρ introduces successive arguments for the same assertion.

35. In v. 1 ἀνέχεσθε is probably imperative, not indicative, but in vv. 4, 19-20 the same form is clearly indicative, not imperative.

36. This repetition is usually called anaphoric (e.g., Windisch 347), although some would restrict anaphora to the repetition of a single word, usually at the beginning of successive sentences (as, e.g., πίστει in Heb. 11:3-31, eighteen times) (see Bullinger 199-205).

37. As in 10:7 and 11:21, τις is probably generic, referring to the interlopers, as does τινές in 3:1; 10:12. This non-naming of Paul's opponents prevents any enhancement of their status (cf. Marshall 341-48).

38. See Zerwick §484; cf. Moulton 115.

themselves. In the only other NT use of this verb (Gal. 2:4), the intruders in Galatia are said to have infiltrated the ranks of Paul and his party in order to spy out their freedom in Christ and bring them into bondage or make them slaves (ἡμᾶς καταδουλώσουσιν), not to themselves but to the Mosaic law.[39] But apart from this difference, the two verses are identical in being in the active voice with a direct object. What was involved in the despotism of these κύριοι at Corinth and the subjection of their δοῦλοι is not indicated, but we may surmise that the intruders assumed control of the Corinthians' souls (cf. Moffatt) or ordered them about (cf. GNB). In effect the Corinthians had forfeited their freedom.

2. *Exploitation* (κατεσθίει) Once again, the prefix κατα- may have a "perfective" sense; thus "eat something till it is finished,"[40] "eat up." Paul's only other use of this verb is in Gal. 5:15 in reference to the in-fighting and party strife of the Galatians. "If you persist in biting one another and tearing one another to pieces (κατεσθίετε), watch out that you are not annihilated by one another." Jesus denounced the scribes as "those who devour (οἱ κατεσθίοντες) widows' houses" (Mark 12:40), referring to illegal appropriation of property (BAGD 422b). When Paul uses this verb of his rivals' actions, he is probably not referring to their creating or fostering party strife, but to their parasitical attachment to the Corinthians, their living "on" or "off" them (cf. Goodspeed), that is, at the Corinthians' expense (cf. Weymouth), demanding and receiving payment for "services rendered," eating them "out of house and home."[41] Against the background of 11:7-12, it is hard not to discern in κατεσθίει an allusion to the intruders' financial dependence on believers at Corinth.

3. *Entrapment* (λαμβάνει) One of the meanings of λαμβάνω in Classical Greek was "take by violence, carry off as prize *or* booty."[42] Consequently Lattey suggests the sense, "if anyone lays hands upon you," with the implication of violence leading to the climactic "strikes you in the face" (148). But there is no reason to think that physical violence is in mind, far less sexual violation. The ὑμᾶς found with καταδουλοῖ is to be understood with both κατεσθίει and λαμβάνει, so that ὀψώνιον ("provisions," "wages") need not be supplied as an object on the basis of the earlier expression λαβὼν ὀψώνιον (v. 8). Rather, the exegetical key is found in 12:16, where Paul states a charge leveled against him: δόλῳ ὑμᾶς ἔλαβον, "I entrapped you by trickery." In 11:20, then, λαμβάνω de-

---

39. The inferior variant καταδουλώσωνται (middle) does suggest subjection "to themselves" (Bruce, *Galatians* 113).

40. Moulton 111. As illustrating the perfective force of this verb, MM cites P. Ryl. II.152[13] (A.D. 42), which refers to the destruction of pastureland by sheep: they "overran, cropped (κατέφαγαν), and utterly destroyed it" (336b). Louw and Nida render κατεσθίω by "exploit completely," "take complete advantage of" (§88.145).

41. For this latter rendering, see Bruce, *Paraphrase* 153; Barrett 288.

42. See LSJ 1026 s.v. I.1.b.

notes bringing someone under one's sway by craftiness — not simply getting someone in one's clutches (cf. NEB, REB) or power (cf. TCNT; Barrett 288), but "taking someone in" (BAGD 464c; Goodspeed), trapping (cf. GNB) or ensnaring someone (Barclay). Support for this interpretation may be found in the use of λαμβάνω in connection with hunting or fishing (e.g., Luke 5:5).

4. *Haughtiness* (ἐπαίρεται)   Of the 19 NT uses of ἐπαίρω ("lift up"), only in 10:5 and 11:20 is the verb used figuratively.[43] Here the passive is reflexive, "if someone exalts himself,"[44] that is, "gives himself airs,"[45] "puts on airs."[46] But the intruders not only had an attitude of superciliousness; they exalted themselves *over* the Corinthians, so that ἐπαίρεται takes on the connotation of arrogant behavior toward the Corinthians (cf. Barclay; Héring 82).[47]

5. *Insult* (εἰς πρόσωπον ὑμᾶς δέρει)   In this expression πρόσωπον probably refers to the cheek (σιαγών),[48] for among the Jews — and the intruders were Jews (11:20) — a slap or blow on the cheek, especially the right cheek (with the back of the hand),[49] was a way to humiliate a person (cf. Job 16:10; Lam. 3:30). Now it is possible that the expression is figurative, referring to outrageous verbal attacks, but a literal sense cannot be deemed unlikely when we remember that (1) religious authorities sometimes expressed their strong disapproval of what seemed to them to be flagrant verbal disrespect by striking the offender or ordering him struck (John 18:22; Acts 23:2), perhaps, as Zerwick (*Analysis* 411) suggests, to reduce him to silence; (2) religious leaders were prone to be tempted to assert their authority by bullying their subordinates (note the use of μὴ πλήκτην, "not violent," "not/nor given to blows" [Weymouth] in the qualifications for overseers, 1 Tim. 3:3; Tit. 1:7). But if we adopt a literal interpretation, there is no need to suppose that all the Corinthians were subject to such indignities or that there were many such incidents. All that we must assume is that those who were insulted this way meekly tolerated the indignity (ἀνέχεσθε).

Looking back over these five indictments, we notice, first of all, their similarity — all represent actions or attitudes of domineering, callous κύριοι (cf. καταδουλοῖ), bent on having their own way, with this end justifying any means used. Indeed, the last four indictments could be regarded as elucidations of the first (Barrett 291). Someone who has been reduced to slavery (καταδουλοῖ)

---

43. Vincent 838.
44. Cf. NJB, "sets himself above you"; Young and Ford 273, "sets himself up (in your way)."
45. Weymouth, Moffatt, Cassirer.
46. Goodspeed, RSV, NEB, NAB², REB, NRSV.
47. Cf. Louw and Nida §88.212, "behaves haughtily toward you."
48. The εἰς before πρόσωπον points to a part of the body to or on which an act is done (Turner 256).
49. Cf. Matt. 5:39; *m. Baba Qamma* 8:6.

would expect to be exploited (κατεσθίει), taken advantage of (λαμβάνει), treated arrogantly (ἐπαίρεται), and physically abused (δέρει). Second, the conduct of the intruders is the antithesis of pastoral service; it was not πρὸς τὴν ὑμῶν διακονίαν (11:8). Paul doubtless hoped that his converts would make the obvious comparison between his way of operating and that of the rival missionaries. He was their δοῦλος, not their κύριος (4:5); he had remained financially independent (11:7-12); he had refused to act with unscrupulous cunning (4:2); he did not lord it over them and their faith (1:24); he was committed to protecting them from spiritual violation (11:2).

11:21a κατὰ ἀτιμίαν λέγω ὡς ὅτι ἡμεῖς ἠσθενήκαμεν. "To my shame I confess that we have been weak in comparison." After recounting the misguided tolerance that the Corinthians in their "wisdom" (v. 19) had shown toward the imperious interlopers (v. 20), Paul makes an ironical contrast between his own conduct toward the Corinthians and the behavior of his rivals.

Sometimes the ἀτιμία is thought to be the shame of the Corinthians. They ought to feel ashamed that they so readily tolerated the despotism and exploitation of the intruders,[50] or ashamed that Paul had shown such weakness in comparison.[51] In the former case the shame is defined by v. 20; in the latter, the shame explained by ὡς κτλ., and the statement is intensely ironical. But if Paul was referring to the Corinthians' shame, we would expect κατὰ τὴν ἀτιμίαν ὑμῶν or κατὰ τὴν ἀτιμίαν or ὑμῖν λέγω (cf. 1 Cor. 6:5; 15:34).[52] With ἀτιμία or λέγω unqualified in one of these ways, it is more natural to relate κατὰ ἀτιμίαν to Paul's own "shame."[53]

The combination ὡς ὅτι has been translated in four basic ways, here listed in ascending order of probability.

1. "Because," with ὡς pleonastic and λέγω retrospective to v. 20. "To (my) shame I say (it), because *we* are weak (in comparison with that)" (Wolff 225, who comments [228 n. 225] that as in 5:19 ὡς ὅτι has substantiating significance).[54]

2. "As though," with ὅτι redundant and λέγω probably retrospective. "I speak by way of disparagement, as though we had been weak" (RV).[55] This makes ὡς ὅτι ἡμεῖς ἠσθενήκαμεν equivalent in meaning to ὡς ἡμῶν ἀσθενησάντων (a genitive absolute clause) (cf. Moulton 212).

50. Cf. NJB, "I say it to your shame; perhaps we have been too weak."
51. Cf. JB, "I hope you are ashamed of us for being weak with you instead!"
52. Word order counts against Conybeare's proposal (460 and n. 4 in Conybeare and Howson) to construe κατὰ ἀτιμίαν with v. 20: "Nay, you bear with men . . . though they smite you on the face, to degrade you. I say that I was weak." In that case κατὰ ἀτιμίαν would naturally be found after εἴ τις.
53. So, e.g., Meyer 657; Plummer 312, 317; Allo 290. κατὰ here denotes purpose ("to my shame") (BAGD 407a), although Winer would allow both purpose and result ("as a reproach," "by way of reproach") (402-3).
54. Similarly Barclay; Windisch 348. In Esth. 4:14 too ὡς ὅτι is causal.
55. Similarly Weymouth; Robertson, *Pictures* 260; Héring 83 (but cf. 82).

3. "As [you say:]," with λέγετε (or λέγουσιν[56]) supplied after ὡς, ὅτι taken as recitative ("that" or :), and λέγω pointing either backward or forward. "I say this to my shame. As you say: we have been weak" (Thrall 709; also 719-20).[57]

4. "That" or :, with ὡς redundant, λέγω prospective, and ὅτι ἡμεῖς ἠσθενήκαμεν defining the content of the confession. "To my shame I must confess: We were indeed too weak for that" (Lang 340), or "I admit, to my shame, that we have been weak" (TCNT).[58]

This fourth alternative is to be preferred since (1) it is natural to take ὅτι as explicative after λέγω; (2) there is justification for treating ὡς ὅτι as equivalent to ὅτι;[59] and (3) on this view there is no need to supply a(nother!) verb of saying after ὡς.

ἠσθενήκαμεν may be treated as an aoristic perfect (so Turner 70), "we were weak";[60] or as a "perfect of resulting state" (so Fanning 291-92), with the emphasis on the present condition rather than on the implied anterior action, "we are weak";[61] or, preferably, as a perfect that encompasses both past and present, with the emphasis in the context falling on the past, "we have been weak."[62] That is, from his first contact with the Corinthians right up to the time of writing, Paul had shown himself to be "weak,"[63] not merely in the sense of being "timid" (cf. ταπεινός, 10:1) or having an "unimpressive" (ἀσθενής) personal "presence" (10:10) but mainly in the sense that he had been too "weak" to dominate and exploit the Corinthians as his rivals had been doing (11:20). The contrast with his rivals is made clear by the emphatic ἡμεῖς. Accordingly, ἠσθενήκαμεν will mean "we have been too weak (for that)" (Lambrecht 187)[64] or "we seem to have been weaklings in comparison"

56. So Lietzmann 149 ("perhaps").

57. Similarly NEB, REB. Without supplying λέγετε, Zerwick comments that "ὡς suggests that the following assertion (ὅτι) comes from the viewpoint of someone else" (*Analysis* 411); cf. Plummer 317; Barnett 533 and n. 23. Thrall argues that ἡμεῖς ἠσθενήκαμεν reflects the Corinthian view which resulted from an accusation against Paul made by a rival missionary who was in Corinth at the time of Paul's interim visit, in advance of the full contingent of rival missionaries (720-21; cf. 629-30).

58. Similarly Moffatt, Goodspeed, NASB, GNB, NAB[1], NIV, NAB[2], Cassirer; Meyer 656; Barrett 292; Bultmann 212; Zerwick and Grosvenor 558; Lambrecht 187. RSV and NRSV treat λέγω as parenthetical: "To my shame, I must say, we were too weak for that!"

59. BDF §396 ("apparently," in 5:19; 11:21; 2 Thess. 2:2); MM 463d, 703b. If this equation ὡς ὅτι = ὅτι (that appears in later Greek) is anticipated in Paul's usage, then this phrase will mean "to the effect that" (5:19; 2 Thess. 2:2) (cf. Turner 137), or "that" when it is preceded by λέγω (11:21).

60. Similarly, e.g., RSV, GNB, NIV, NRSV; Lietzmann 148.

61. Barclay; Wolff 225.

62. On the textual variant ἠσθενήσαμεν, see Textual Note c.

63. This reflexive sense of ἠσθενήκαμεν is suggested by BAGD 589b ("we have conducted ourselves as weaklings"); similarly Windisch 348; Zerwick, *Analysis* 411.

64. Cf. Danker's colloquial paraphrase of this verse. "I hate to say it. We've lacked the spunk for that" ("Debt" 274).

(Furnish 485). This stinging irony[65] is made all the more potent by the stark brevity of ἠσθενήκαμεν.[66]

Bibliography

Becker 231-39 • Betz, *Paulus* 78-84 • Heckel 194-202 • Holland • Judge • Lattey • Loubser • Marshall 352, 373 • Peterson 112-14 • Plank • Reumann, "Irony" • Spencer 133-279 • Spencer, "Irony" • A. Vitti, "Signa apostolatus Pauli. Animadversiones in 2 Cor. 11,19–12,9," *VD* 8 (1928) 75-80, 106-10, 176-84 • Zmijewski

5. Paul's Heritage and Trials (11:21b-29)

Although Paul has censured his rivals for indulging in pointless comparison with one another (10:12) and in unbridled boasting (10:13, 15-16, by implication), he now proceeds to engage in comparisons and boasting himself, but only in the disguise of a fool, as he begins the "Fool's Speech" (11:21b–12:13). We have already noted his reluctance actually to begin this "foolish" comparison and boasting (see 10:8; 11:1, 16). Further evidence of his gnawing discomfort, even as he begins, is that he injects two reminders of his folly: ἐν ἀφροσύνῃ λέγω (11:21b) and παραφρονῶν λαλῶ (11:23).

Analysis of 11:21b-29 by Construction

1. Repetition of τολμάω (v. 21b)

| ἐν ᾧ δ' ἄν τις | τολμᾷ, . . . | | BOLD |
| | τολμῶ | κἀγώ. | CLAIMS |

2. Four questions (εἰσίν; vv. 22-23a)

Ἑβραῖοί	εἰσιν;	κἀγώ.	PEDIGREE
Ἰσραηλῖταί	εἰσιν;	κἀγώ.	
σπέρμα Ἀβραάμ	εἰσιν;	κἀγώ.	
διάκονοι Χριστοῦ	εἰσιν;	ὑπὲρ ἐγώ.	

3. ἐν + dative plural + adverb (v. 23b)

ἐν	κόποις	περισσοτέρως,	GENERAL
ἐν	φυλακαῖς	περισσοτέρως,	SUFFERING
ἐν	πληγαῖς	ὑπερβαλλόντως,	
ἐν	θανάτοις	πολλάκις·	

4. Numeral adverb + aorist (vv. 24-25), illustrating ἐν θανάτοις πολλάκις (v. 23b)

| ὑπὸ Ἰουδαίων | πεντάκις . . . | ἔλαβον, | REPEATED |
| | τρὶς | ἐραβδίσθην, | EXPOSURE |

---

65. This seems a more appropriate description than "acidic sarcasm" (McCant 131).

66. Zmijewski (230) claims to have found a crescendo of irony in 11:19-21a, from witty satire (v. 19), to grotesque parody (v. 20), to parodic self-caricature (v. 21a).

ἅπαξ	ἐλιθάσθην,	TO
τρὶς	ἐναυάγησα,	DEATH
[ἅπαξ] . . .	πεποίηκα· (perfect)	

5. Κινδύνοις ("dangers"), illustrating ὁδοιπορίαις πολλάκις (v. 26)
   (a) followed by genitive plural (source)
   κινδύνοις ποταμῶν,
   κινδύνοις λῃστῶν,   SPECIFIC
   (b) followed by ἐκ (source)   DANGERS
   κινδύνοις ἐκ γένους,   associated
   κινδύνοις ἐξ ἐθνῶν,   with
   (c) followed by ἐν (location)   TRAVEL
   κινδύνοις ἐν πόλει,
   κινδύνοις ἐν ἐρημίᾳ
   κινδύνοις ἐν θαλάσσῃ,
   κινδύνοις ἐν ψευδαδέλφοις,

6. Pairs of dative singular, separated by ἐν + dative plural + adverb
   (v. 27; cf. v. 23b)
   κόπῳ καὶ μόχθῳ,
           ἐν ἀγρυπνίαις   πολλάκις,   TOIL
   ἐν λιμῷ καὶ δίψει,   and
           ἐν νηστείαις   πολλάκις,   DEPRIVATION
   ἐν ψύχει καὶ γυμνότητι·

7. Two substantival phrases in epexegetic apposition (v. 28)
   . . . ἡ ἐπίστασίς μοι   ἡ καθ' ἡμέραν,   ANXIOUS
       ἡ μέριμνα   πασῶν τῶν ἐκκλησιῶν.   CONCERN
                                  for churches

8. Two rhetorical questions (τίς . . . καὶ οὐκ . . .) (v. 29)
   τίς ἀσθενεῖ,   καὶ   οὐκ   ἀσθενῶ;   ANXIOUS
   τίς σκανδαλίζεται, καὶ   οὐκ ἐγὼ πυροῦμαι;   CONCERN
                                      for individuals

Analysis of 11:21b-29 by Content

In this whole section there is an extended comparison between Paul and his rivals at Corinth. The two key expressions are κἀγώ ("I too"; four uses in vv. 21b-22) and ὑπὲρ ἐγώ ("I more"; v. 23a), the former pointing to his equality with his rivals in certain limited respects, the latter to his vast superiority.[1]

1. Equating Paul's opponents with οἱ ὑπερλίαν ἀπόστολοι, Heckel (49) sees in the litotes of 11:5 ("I reckon I am not at all inferior to those superlative apostles") the principal thesis of the "Fool's Speech," repeated at 12:11 as part of the conclusion (12:11-13) of that speech. 11:6-15 develops the negative idea of inferiority found in 11:5, while 11:21b–12:10 (the "Fool's Speech" proper) develops the two positive ideas of Paul's equality with his rivals (κἀγώ) (11:21b-22) and his superiority (ὑπὲρ ἐγώ) (11:23a–12:10) over them. Martin describes 11:21–12:18 as Paul's

From this perspective we may divide 11:21b-29 into three sections of unequal length.

1. Equality in bold boasting (v. 21b)

21b*Yet in whatever way any of them is bold — I speak in pure folly — I am just as bold myself.*

2. Equality in nationality and heritage (v. 22)

22*Are they Hebrews?*   *So am I.*
Are they Israelites?   *So am I.*
Are they descendants of Abraham?
So am I.

3. Superiority in service and suffering (vv. 23-29)

23*Are they "servants of Christ"? I am out of my mind when I speak this way — but I am a better servant:*

with far more labors,
with far more imprisonments,
with far worse floggings[a],
often at death's door;

24*five times*	*I received from the Jews the "forty lashes minus one,"*
25*three times*	*I was beaten with rods,*
once	*I was pelted with stones,*
three times	*I was shipwrecked,*
a night and a day	*I have spent adrift at sea;*

26*on frequent journeys, exposed to*
dangers	*from rivers,*
dangers	*from bandits,*
dangers	*from my people,*
dangers	*from Gentiles,*
dangers	*in the city,*
dangers	*in the desert,*
dangers	*on the sea,*
dangers	*among false brothers;*

27*with[b]* *labor* *and toil,*
        with   *frequent sleepless nights,*
in   *hunger* *and thirst,*
          frequently going without food,
    cold *and virtually naked.*

"'kerygmatic autobiography,' his *apologia pro vita sua,* which is also *pro evangelio suo*" (xxxvii).

28*Not to mention other things, there is what presses^c on me^d every day — my anxiety for all the churches.*

29*Who is weak,*	*and I am not weak?*
Who is led astray into sin,	*and I am not ablaze with anger?*

TEXTUAL NOTES

a. In these last two phrases, there are five variations in word order:

(1) ἐν φυλακαῖς περισσοτέρως, ἐν πληγαῖς ὑπερβαλλόντως (p⁴⁶ B D*·² [0243] 33 629 630 [1739 1881] *pc* lat Ambrosiaster)

(2) ἐν πληγαῖς περισσοτέρως, ἐν φυλακαῖς ὑπερβαλλόντως (‫א‬* F G Origen)

(3) ἐν φυλακαῖς ὑπερβαλλόντως, ἐν πληγαῖς περισσοτέρως (P)

(4) ἐν πληγαῖς ὑπερβαλλόντως, ἐν φυλακαῖς περισσοτέρως (‫א‬² D¹ H Ψ 0121 𝔐 syr⁽ᵖ⁾)

(5) ἐν πληγαῖς ὑπερβαλλόντως (Clement)

On the basis of their very weak (readings [3] and [5]) or comparatively weak (reading [4]) external support, these three readings can be regarded as secondary. Readings (1) and (2) both have strong proto-Alexandrian and Western support, but (1) seems to be original since (2) represents a *prima facie* natural gradation of severity of suffering (labors–floggings–imprisonments–brushes with death). Both περισσοτέρως and ὑπερβαλλόντως may mean "to a much greater degree" (BAGD 651d, 840b).

b. Under the influence of the following four cases of ἐν, some witnesses (‫א‬² H 0121 33 1881 𝔐 lat Ambrosiaster) read ἐν κόπῳ. The reading without ἐν (as in p⁴⁶ ‫א‬* B D F G Ψ 0243 1739 *pc*) is to be preferred as *lectio difficilior* and as having superior attestation.

c. External evidence supports ἐπίστασις (p⁴⁶ ‫א‬ B D F G H* 0243 0278 33 81 326 1175 1739 1881 *pc*) over ἐπισύστασις (Hᶜ Iᵛⁱᵈ Ψ 0121 𝔐). On the possible meanings of ἐπίστασις, see the commentary at 11:28. Etymologically, ἐπισύστασις is "a being gathered (-στασις) together (-συ(ν)-) against (ἐπι-)," thus "disturbance," "insurrection." In Acts 24:12 it also appears as a variant (supported by 𝔐) of ἐπίστασις in the phrase ἐπίστασιν ποιοῦντα ὄχλου, "provoking a collecting of a crowd" = "stirring up a crowd" (RSV, NRSV). It is difficult to make any sense of ἐπισύστασις in 11:28 (unless it refers to the combined opposition of Paul's adversaries — see Field 185); it may have arisen by dittography of the first σ in ἐπίστασις and a subsequent correction by the insertion of υ.

d. If, following ‫א‬² D Ψ 0121 0243 1739 1881 𝔐 lat Ambrosiaster, we read ἡ ἐπίστασις *μου*, the reference will be to the "oversight" or "attention" given by Paul (subjective genitive); but μοι has stronger attestation (p⁴⁶ ‫א‬* B F G H 0278 33 81 1175 *pc* b d) and produces the meaning "the pressure on me," "what presses on me," where μοι naturally follows an ἐπί compound.

11:21b ἐν ᾧ δ' ἄν τις τολμᾷ, ἐν ἀφροσύνῃ λέγω, τολμῶ κἀγώ. "Yet in whatever way any of them is bold — I speak in pure folly — I am just as bold myself." After ironically apologizing for failing to match the conduct of his adversaries in dominating the Corinthians (v. 21a, with reference to v. 20), Paul proceeds to indicate his ability and willingness — indeed, his determination — to match them in their proud boasts. He is about to play his rivals at their own game, judging that only this technique will jolt his converts at Corinth (cf. 12:11) into recognizing the character of true apostleship, namely, the "weakness" of suffering service in imitation of the suffering ministry of Christ.[2]

δέ is adversative. In both parts of v. 21 there is a comparison between Paul and his opponents. In v. 21a he ironically acknowledges his inferiority to them in despotism, while in v. 21b he claims complete parity with them in bold boasting. Since there is no indication of a change of referent for τις between v. 20 to v. 21, we must assume that this indefinite pronoun continues to refer to Paul's rivals (τις a generic singular, as in 10:7);[3] thus "any of them."[4] But because τις looks forward to κἀγώ ("I too"), the rendering "anyone else"[5] is also appropriate, provided it is not taken to refer to someone other than Paul's rivals.[6] As in 11:12, ἐν ᾧ means "in that in which,"[7] with the difference that ἄν here adds the notion of indefiniteness: "in whatever way/respect/sphere."[8] In the light of what follows in vv. 22-29, the particular "ways" in mind relate to ancestry and service.[9] That same wider context shows that the two absolute uses of τολμάω ("dare," "be bold") in this verse depict boldness in boasting or in making claims. "But whatever anyone dares to boast of" (RSV, NRSV), or "Whatever bold claims anyone makes" (NJB).[10] We may account for the change from καυχάομαι in vv. 16 and 18 to τολμάω here by observing that Paul has already said (in v. 18), "they boast and I will too," and now wishes to emphasize the identical spheres of boasting and the brazenness of his opponents' vaunts.

κἀγώ (= καὶ ἐγώ by crasis) occurs six times in vv. 16-22. In each case Paul is establishing his parity with his rivals. Here the parity is not simply boldness in boasting but boldness in boasting about the same matters as his rivals.[11] But before he expresses this equality (by τολμῶ κἀγώ), he inserts a parenthesis[12] that apologizes in advance for his bold claim:[13] "I speak in pure folly."[14] What made

2. For the sequence Servant of Yahweh–Christ–Paul with regard to suffering, see Kamlah 217-32.

3. BAGD 820a cites 2:5; 10:7; 11:21 as instances where τις refers to a definite person.

4. Bruce, *Paraphrase* 153.

5. So BAGD 822a; Goodspeed, NIV.

6. Barrett believes that with τις Paul's thought has moved to his rivals' principals in Jerusalem, whose authority they seem to have claimed (292).

7. See the discussion at 11:12.

8. Cf. "on whatever score" (Zerwick and Grosvenor 558); "whatever the subject on which (others are not afraid to boast)" (TCNT); "no matter in what respect" (Cassirer).

9. Cf. Héring 82: "But whatever qualification may be advanced . . . I can advance it also."

10. NEB and REB seek to reflect the indefiniteness of τις and ἄν and the absolute use of τολμάω: "But if there is to be bravado"; cf. also Plummer 312, "wherever real courage is exhibited."

11. JB separates these two items. "But if anyone wants some brazen speaking . . . then I can be as brazen as any of them, and about the same things"; cf. BAGD 822a.

12. So BAGD 469b and many EVV (e.g., TCNT, RSV, NIV).

13. On prodiorthosis (an anticipatory correction), see BDF §495(3); Robertson 1199.

14. Some EVV add "still" to their rendering of ἐν ἀφροσύνῃ λέγω (e.g., JB, REB), others "now" (e.g., NAB[1], NJB). Note also the resonant assonance of λέγω τολμῶ κἀγώ.

Paul's statement "I am just as bold myself" "absolutely foolish" was that it involved inane comparison (for which he had castigated his rivals, 10:12) and was boasting "as the world does" (κατὰ σάρκα, 11:18). That is, he was doing what his foolish rivals (10:12; 11:19) were accustomed to doing.

11:22 Ἑβραῖοί εἰσιν; κἀγώ. Ἰσραηλῖταί εἰσιν; κἀγώ. σπέρμα Ἀβραάμ εἰσιν; κἀγώ. "Are they Hebrews? So am I. Are they Israelites? So am I. Are they descendants of Abraham? So am I." Since vv. 22-23a are a set of comparisons between Paul and his rivals, it is fair to assume that Paul's repeated claim (κἀγώ) is in fact a counterclaim; he can match their claims at every point. If so, εἰσιν; has the sense "Are they, in their claims, . . . ?" His opponents would have known that they could not deny that Paul was Jewish by birth[15] and spoke both Hebrew and Aramaic,[16] but, if we may hypothesize about their claims concerning themselves and their observations regarding Paul, they may have pointed to their own "pure" Jewish descent and to Paul's less than pure lineage as a Diaspora "Hellenist" — he was not born in Israel, but outside the borders of the "holy land"; he was not normally resident in Judea, and so more affected by Hellenistic influences; he had not been a companion or early disciple of Jesus, and so had been denied the benefits of firsthand acquaintance with Jesus.[17] That is, they may have defined "pure" lineage in reference to birth and residence in Israel and personal knowledge of the earthly Jesus.

Ἑβραῖοι. This term is found only here and in Phil. 3:5 (twice) and Acts 6:1.[18] In the latter passage it is contrasted with Ἑλληνισταί ("Hellenists," "Grecian Jews") and therefore probably points to both linguistic and cultural distinctiveness, referring to Aramaic-speaking Jews of the Jerusalem church who attended synagogues where Hebrew was used and yet could converse in Greek. Both by inclination and by training their affinities lay with Palestinian orthodoxy. The Hellenists, on the other hand, spoke only Greek and attended a separate synagogue where Greek was used (such as "the Synagogue of the Freedmen," Acts 6:9).[19] Their intellectual and cultural roots lay in the Diaspora.[20] In

---

15. According to Epiphanius (*Adversus Haereses* 30.16), the Ebionites believed that Paul was a Gentile by birth who had been circumcised so that he could marry the high priest's daughter (cited by Plummer 320).

16. That Paul spoke Aramaic is clear from Acts 21:40; 22:2; cf. 9:4; 26:14, and, judging from his use of the OT (see Ellis 12-14), he knew Hebrew also.

17. On this latter point, cf. Kümmel 211.

18. On this term, see W. Gutbrod, *TDNT* 3.389-90; Windisch 350-51; Georgi, *Opponents* 41-46; Thrall 723-27, 730, 941.

19. Similarly Bruce (*Paul* 42), who notes that "we know from inscriptions in Rome [*CIG* iv.9909] and Corinth [B. Powell, 'Greek Inscriptions from Corinth,' *AJA* series 2, 7 (1903) 60-61, no. 40] that each of these cities contained a 'synagogue of (the) Hebrews': such a designation may point to a meeting-place for Palestinian (and probably Aramaic-speaking) Jews, over against others used by Greek-speaking Jews."

20. But the differences between Palestinian and Diaspora Judaism must not be exaggerated — see I. H. Marshall, "Palestinian and Hellenistic Christianity: Some Critical Comments," *NTS* 19 (1972-73) 271-87; M. Hengel, *Judaism and Hellenism: Studies in Their Encounter in Palestine*

Phil. 3:5 there is no explicit contrast between Ἑβραῖος and Ἑλληνιστής so that the linguistic associations of the term Ἑβραῖος are not to the fore. When Paul asserts he is "a Hebrew with Hebrew parents" (Ἑβραῖος ἐξ Ἑβραίων), he "is claiming, not merely Jewish nationality, but descent from a Palestinian family. This factor, along with the Pharisaic orientation of the family (Ac. 22:3), is the reason why Aramaic is his mother tongue; it is not because he speaks Aramaic that he calls himself Ἑβραῖος ἐξ Ἑβραίων."[21] Similarly, in 11:22 κἀγώ [εἰμι Ἑβραῖος] should be given a geographical sense. Paul is affirming his status as "a Jew of Palestinian descent."[22] But not only were Paul's family roots in Palestine. According to Acts 22:3 he had spent his formative years in Jerusalem, receiving both his elementary and his higher education there.[23] He begins his address to the Jerusalem Jews with the words, "I am a Jew, born at Tarsus in Cilicia, but brought up in this city [= Jerusalem], educated under the teaching of Gamaliel according to the strict interpretation of our ancestral law."

Ἰσραηλῖται. Like Ἑβραῖοι, this is an archaizing term with a nuance of special solemnity. It denotes those who belong to Israel, the chosen, covenant people of Yahweh.[24] Israelites are citizens of "the commonwealth of Israel" (Eph. 2:12). "Israel" was the name God gave to Jacob that was also applied to his descendants (Gen. 32:28, 32). As opposed to the more general term for Jews, namely Ἰουδαῖος (195 NT uses, including v. 24 in the present context),[25] Ἰσραηλίτης is used rarely in the NT (nine uses), of which three are in Paul (Rom. 9:4; 11:1; 2 Cor. 11:22) and in two of these (Rom. 11:1; 2 Cor. 11:22) this term is associated with the expression σπέρμα Ἀβραάμ.[26]

σπέρμα Ἀβραάμ (literally "seed of Abraham").[27] Elsewhere Paul applies this concept to Jesus as the promised Messiah (Gal. 3:16, 19), but as used here in v. 22 it refers to Jews as heirs of the promises that God made to Abraham — the promise of an everlasting covenant in which he would be Abraham's God and the God of his descendants (Gen. 17:7), and the promise of blessing to all nations through his descendants (Gen. 22:18). There is no reason to think that

---

during the Early Hellenistic Period, 2 vols. (Philadelphia: Fortress, 1974); M. Hengel, *The "Hellenization" of Judaea in the First Century after Christ* (Philadelphia: Trinity Press International, 1989).

21. W. Gutbrod, *TDNT* 3.390.

22. W. Gutbrod, *TDNT* 3.390. According to Jerome (*De Viris Illustribus* 5; *Commentary on Philemon* 23) and Photius (*Quaestiones ad Amphiochium* 116), Paul's family was from Gischala in Galilee, but we have no way to assess the reliability of these traditions.

23. See W. C. van Unnik, *Tarsus or Jerusalem? The City of Paul's Youth* (London: SCM, 1962) (reprinted in Unnik 1.259-327); and for a contrary view, Turner, *Insights* 83-85.

24. Note the juxtaposition of τὸν λαὸν αὐτοῦ (= τοῦ θεοῦ) and Ἰσραηλίτης in Rom. 11:1.

25. As used by Gentiles, the term Ἰουδαῖος tended to be derogatory, signifying those who adhered to Jewish ancestral customs or whose lives were lived ἐν τῷ Ἰουδαϊσμῷ (Gal. 1:13-14).

26. H. Kuhli regards the terms Ἰουδαῖος and Ἰσραηλίτης not as synonyms but as homoionyms, "since they are 'interchangeable insofar as they refer to a single concept, but not in their nuances and evocative power'" (*EDNT* 2.205, quoting S. Ullmann, *Grundzüge der Semantik* [1972] 102).

27. On this expression see Windisch 351-52; Georgi, *Opponents* 49-60; Thrall 727-29.

Paul's adversaries were using this expression in a distinctly Christian sense to refer to those who belong to Christ as "Abraham's seed" (Gal. 3:29)[28] or were impressing on the Corinthians Paul's point that "not all of Abraham's children are his true descendants" (Rom. 9:7, NRSV). In all three designations in 11:22, genuine Jewishness is the point under consideration in the mind of Paul's rivals and of Paul himself.

Even if we allow, with Lietzmann (150), that we have in v. 22 "three descriptions of the same idea of 'full-blooded Jew,'" we need not agree with Bultmann that "any differentiation is scarcely intended" (214). There seems to be a progression of privilege,[29] whether we express this as a movement of thought from nationality to theocracy to messianic privilege (so Meyer 658), or from racial to religious/salvation-historical to theological categories (so Lambrecht 190, 197), or from descent to citizenship to heritage.[30]

11:23 διάκονοι Χριστοῦ εἰσιν; παραφρονῶν λαλῶ, ὑπὲρ ἐγώ. "Are they 'servants of Christ'? I am out of my mind when I speak this way — but I am a better servant." To judge from vv. 22-23a, there seem to have been two bases for the claim of Paul's adversaries to superiority over him: the purity of their Jewishness (cf. v. 22), and their status as "servants of Christ" (cf. v. 23a). To the former claim Paul responds in effect, "I am just as 'pure' as they are!" (cf. κἀγώ). To the latter claim he replies, "I am a vastly better servant of Christ (cf. ὑπὲρ ἐγώ), as is shown by my record of unparalleled suffering in Christ's service" (cf. vv. 23b-29).

If διάκονοι Χριστοῦ (cf. Col. 1:7; 1 Tim. 4:6) was one of the self-designations of Paul's rivals, it is unlikely that the expression means simply "Christian workers" (Goodspeed). Whether we render the phrase "agents of Christ" (Thrall 722) or "Christ's envoys/personal representatives" (cf. Georgi, *Opponents* 32)[31] or "servants/ministers of Christ" (so most EVV), it reflects a claim made by Paul's adversaries (hence the quotation marks in my translation above), and is not an incontestable fact that Paul was obliged to accept, such as his opponents' status as "Hebrews," "Israelites," and "descendants of Abraham." Just as his rivals passed themselves off as "Christ's apostles" (v. 13), so also they claimed to be "Christ's servants" (v. 23). From Paul's perspective, in each case it was an assumed disguise. This parallelism between ἀπόστολοι Χριστοῦ in v. 13 and διάκονοι Χριστοῦ in v. 23 removes Thrall's objection[32] that all four questions in vv. 22-23a are parallel in pointing to what Paul himself does not deny. Also, it is difficult to imagine, if not inconceivable, that he

28. But for the opposite view see Zmijewski 239-40.
29. W. Gutbrod speaks of "a progressive loftiness of designation" (*TDNT* 3.390).
30. But Héring (83) distinguishes the trilogy as referring to language, religion, and race.
31. For a critique of Georgi's proposal, see J. N. Collins, "Envoys" 88-96. Collins's own understanding of the διακον- word group is set out in his monograph *DIAKONIA: Reinterpreting the Ancient Sources* (New York: Oxford University Press, 1990), and more briefly in his article, "The Mediatorial Aspect of Paul's Role as *Diakonos*," *ABR* 40 (1992) 34-44.
32. Thrall 731; "Super-Apostles" 51.

would simultaneously regard these rivals as "servants of Satan" (v. 15) in an unqualified sense and "servants of Christ" (v. 23) in an unqualified sense, as
though they were capable of serving two radically different masters at the same
time (cf. Luke 16:13). To explain this apparent anomaly, Thrall suggests the
analogy of Peter's dual role in Matt. 16:16-23, acting now as God's agent and
now as Satan's agent (731-32). But that duality of role is explicitly related to
two isolated and vastly different statements that Peter makes (namely a confession of Jesus' messiahship and a rebuke of Jesus' intent to suffer). In 2 Corinthians 11 it is a matter of simultaneous service, not successive declarations.

If κἀγώ (v. 22) expressed Paul's claim to equality with his rivals with regard to nationality and heritage, ὑπὲρ ἐγώ states his claim to superiority with respect to service and suffering, as vv. 23b-29 will show. ὑπέρ is here used adverbially (see Moulton and Howard 326), "more," reflecting the fact that
prepositions were originally adjuncts to verbs, "ad-verbs."[33] "I more," "I, to a
higher degree" (cf. BDF §230) (= ἐγὼ μᾶλλον; cf. Phil. 3:4) is an abbreviated
form of "I am so even more (than they)" (BAGD 839c), or "I am/have been a
better servant of Christ than they claim to have been."[34] For the sake of the comparison that follows, Paul is allowing his rivals' estimate of themselves as
διάκονοι Χριστοῦ and claiming to be vastly superior to them in that role.[35]

παραφρονῶν λαλῶ (literally, "I speak as one beside himself") is an advance on ἐν ἀφροσύνῃ λέγω (v. 21); it was folly to say τολμῶ κἀγώ with regard
to making bold claims (v. 21), but it is utter insanity to say ὑπὲρ ἐγώ with respect to service for Christ. Any boasting about service for Christ, and certainly
any comparisons, are not only foolish but totally preposterous. παραφρονῶν
anticipates ὑπὲρ ἐγώ (by prodiorthosis; BDF §495[3]) rather than looking back
to the preceding question, as though Paul were declaring their claim to be sheer
madness. Although he did not write ὡς παραφρονῶν, "as if a madman," it is not
inappropriate to render παραφρονῶν λαλῶ by "I am speaking like an insane
person" (Louw and Nida §30.24) or "I am talking as if I were beside myself"
(BAGD 623c), since he is not confessing to actual insanity; thus we may translate, "I am out of my mind when I speak this way."

ἐν κόποις περισσοτέρως, ἐν φυλακαῖς περισσοτέρως, ἐν πληγαῖς
ὑπερβαλλόντως, ἐν θανάτοις πολλάκις. "(. . . I am a better servant:) with far
more labors, with far more imprisonments, with far worse floggings, often at
death's door." At this point Paul begins the third and longest of his four lists of

---

33. See Harris, "Prepositions" 1172. To indicate this distinctive use of ὑπέρ, it is sometimes
accented ὕπερ (WH 1.416; Robertson 244; Moulton and Howard 326).

34. Cf. Phillips: "I have more claim to this title than they." Certainly Paul is not saying "I am
more than a διάκονος Χριστοῦ," as if being an ἀπόστολος Χριστοῦ (cf. 1:1) or a δοῦλος Χριστοῦ (cf.
Rom. 1:1) were a more exalted status.

35. Plummer, however, believes that "for the sake of argument he [Paul] is willing to assume
that *in some sense* they are what they claim to be" (321, italics mine). More apposite is his footnote:
"We may compare the action of Christ, who does not challenge the confident statement of either the
rich man (Mk. x.20) or the sons of Zebedee ([Mk.] x.39), but answers as if it were true" (321 n.).

sufferings found in 2 Corinthians.[36] Whereas in 6:4b-5, 8-10 the sufferings be-
fall him as θεοῦ διάκονος (cf. 6:4b), in 11:23b-29 they come to him as διάκονος
Χριστοῦ (cf. 11:23a).[37] That no distinction is intended is clear from the fact that
five items are common to the two lists: ἐν κόποις, ἐν φυλακαῖς, ἐν πληγαῖς
(11:22 and 6:5), ἐν ἀγρυπνίαις, ἐν νηστείαις (11:27 and 6:5). Vv. 23b-29 are an
avalanche of hardships that sweeps the reader along in dazed disbelief. Yet
Paul's focus is not on any stoical indifference to suffering or even patient endurance of affliction but on Christ's grace in upholding him in the midst of his
weakness (11:30; 12:9-10; cf. 1 Cor. 15:10), or, as he has expressed it earlier,
on God's power in leading him in triumphal procession through his union with
Christ (2:14). What must have surprised the Corinthians was that Paul seeks to
establish his superiority in Christ's service by tabulating his adversities rather
than by appealing to his success in founding congregations in strategically important centers around the Aegean, or by referring to the number of converts
won, or by citing miracles performed. Rather, appeal is made to evidence of his
shame and dishonor. "What he has endured is the seal of his Apostleship"
(Plummer 322). "He . . . does not view his suffering as an apostle as a tedious
detour; it is rather the main highway" (Garland 307).

This paradox does not make necessary the conclusion that Paul is here
parodying the pretentious claims of his rivals[38] or the contemporary standards
of greatness as epitomized in the *res gestae* of Augustus.[39] He is simply "out-
boasting the boasters" (McCant 131), showing that he outranks his opponents
as a servant of the Lord (cf. 3:6; 6:4),[40] and, paradoxically, taking pride in his
weaknesses (11:30) — all in order to win his converts back to their former affections (cf. 6:11-13; 11:3).

Each of the twenty-six items in the catalogue contributes to the evidence
for Paul's "superiority," so the meaning is not substantially altered whether we
render the four instances of ἐν by "in (the midst of)" (local ἐν; cf. 6:4b-5; 11:26),
"with" (circumstantial or causal), "with respect to" (referential), or "because of"
(causal). κόπος ("toil," "labor") was the tradesman's term for the strenuous exer-
tions of those engaged in manual labor and the word may refer to this in 6:5 (see
the commentary there), but here too it probably also describes Paul's evangelistic and pastoral work (cf. its use in 10:15),[41] with the same connotation of rigor-

36. The others are 4:8-9; 6:4b-5, 8-10; 12:10; cf. Rom. 8:35; 1 Cor. 4:9-13. On these "catalogues of hardships," see the introduction to 6:3-10.

37. Cf. Collange 294.

38. As Forbes (18), who argues that in 2 Corinthians 10–12 Paul's "boasting" should be
seen as a parody of Greco-Roman conventions of rhetorical self-advertisement involving comparison, self-praise, and irony (2-22).

39. As Witherington 450-52, and, less confidently, Ebner 131. On the issue of parody in
2 Corinthians 10–12, see Travis 529-31, and the general evaluation of Thrall 757-58.

40. Danker 180, who also suggests that Paul is assuming the role of the Greco-Roman "endangered benefactor" (180-81, citing Demosthenes' *De Corona* 173, 249).

41. Cf. the use of the cognate verb κοπιάω in 1 Cor. 15:10; Gal. 4:11; Phil. 2:16. But Barnett
(541), and with some hesitance, Furnish (536), relate κόποις to Paul's manual labor as a crafts-

ous and exhausting toil, toil that could prove a burden (11:28), even if it was prompted by love (1 Thess. 1:3).[42] The plural κόποις may be generalizing ("labor") or may refer to individual acts (BAGD 443d). The adverb περισσοτέρως is the comparative of περισσῶς ("exceedingly"). After ὑπὲρ ἐγώ ("I more"), it probably retains a comparative force, with the sense "far more (labors),"[43] just as in the following phrase it seems to mean "far more (imprisonments)."[44] Now it is true that we have no knowledge that Paul's rivals had ever been imprisoned (or flogged or shipwrecked!), so that the comparison cannot involve numeration.[45] Moreover, the next two adverbs, ὑπερβαλλόντως and πολλάκις, need not involve a comparison. But that is not to say that any notion of comparison after ὑπὲρ ἐγώ is irrelevant or that the comparison is simply with the majority of Christ's servants. The implications of ὑπὲρ ἐγώ must be taken seriously even if we acknowledge that Paul is not engaged in specific comparisons but is establishing his general credentials as a διάκονος Χριστοῦ over against the groundless claim to that title made by his opponents. A title beneath the picture of Paul's hardships found in vv. 23b-29 would read διάκονος Χριστοῦ γέγονα.[46]

φυλακή can mean "guard," "(the act of) guarding," or "the place of guarding," "prison." Here "prison" signifies "imprisonment" (concrete for abstract), with the plural referring to various imprisonments ("spells of imprisonment," Thrall 722), although BAGD 867d relates the plural to several (different) prisons. From Acts we know of only one imprisonment of Paul before the present letter was written (the time represented by Acts 20:2a) — his imprisonment, along with Silas, in Philippi (Acts 16:23-40) — but Luke's history is patently selective.[47] 1 Clement 5:6 mentions some seven imprisonments (ἑπτάκις δεσμὰ

---

man. Barnett suggests that "had Paul accepted the patronage of the members of the churches — protection, payment, and gifts — many of the sufferings now listed would not have occurred" (541).

42. Cf. F. Hauck, *TDNT* 3.829. For the thesis that "the mythological labors of Heracles, as they were understood in the first century by Plutarch and Arrian, is a history of religions background which illumines Paul's trial list at 2 Cor 11:23-29 as effectively as Stoic and apocalyptic parallels, and perhaps even more," see Hodgson 59-80 (quotation from p. 61).

43. BAGD 651d gives three possible meanings for περισσοτέρως in 11:23: "to a much greater degree, far more, far greater (than Paul's opponents)."

44. But given the tendency in Hellenistic Greek for superlative forms to disappear, Hughes proposes (405-6 n. 71) that the repeated περισσοτέρως has a superlative force ("very abundantly"); "Paul is saying that as a minister of Christ he surpasses the pseudo-apostles altogether, he is beyond their range" (405 n. 71).

45. There is no reason to assume with Fitzgerald that the letters of recommendation brought by Paul's opponents contained their own list of hardships (Fitzgerald 25 and n. 95, following O. Wischmeyer, *Der höchste Weg* [Gütersloh: Mohn, 1981] 85-86, especially nn. 218-20). Indeed, Barnett remarks that Paul's adversaries probably regarded his tribulations as signs of his inferiority and incompetence (534).

46. Bultmann (215-16) maintains that διάκονος Χριστοῦ ἐγενόμην should be supplied with v. 23b. Since Paul continues to be Christ's servant, γέγονα (or εἰμί) seems more appropriate than ἐγενόμην (or ἦν).

47. Duncan argued that during Paul's Asian ministry (Acts 19:1–20:1) he suffered three "imprisonments," which Duncan (at first) defined as protective custody under police supervision. For details, see the Excursus after 1:11, B.3.

φορέσας, literally "having worn fetters seven times"). It was Paul's experience of actual imprisonment that probably prompted his self-description (ὁ δέσμιος (τοῦ) Χριστοῦ 'Ιησοῦ, "the prisoner of Christ Jesus,"[48] although this expression refers to more than his frequent incarcerations.[49]

πληγή denotes a "blow" inflicted by any implement of punishment (including the fist) and the resulting "wound." Here the reference is to occasions when he was given "blows"; thus "beatings" or "floggings." These he describes as ὑπερβαλλόντως,[50] which may mean "beyond measure," thus "with countless floggings" (Lambrecht 187) or "with excessive floggings" (Berkeley); or if this adverb here continues an explicit comparison, "to a much greater degree,"[51] thus "with . . . far worse beatings" (Furnish 512) or "scourged more severely" (NEB, REB). "The marks (στίγματα) of Jesus" that Paul carried in his body (Gal. 6:17) may have resulted not only from his stoning at Lystra (Acts 14:19; 2 Cor. 11:25) but also from his "countless beatings." The competitor in boxing (ἀγωνιστής) boasted of injuries inflicted on his opponent; Paul, of wounds received in his own body.

The fourth instance in v. 23 of ἐν + dative plural + adverb is ἐν θανάτοις πολλάκις, literally "often in deaths," where the plural points to "encounters with death" (Bruce, *Paraphrase* 153), "mortal dangers" (Thrall 722), or the different types of death encountered. The whole phrase may be rendered "many a time face to face with death" (NEB, REB), or "often at death's door" (TCNT). One such brush with death has already been described in 1:8-10, while 4:11 speaks of Paul's being constantly handed over to death and 6:9 depicts his continual exposure to physical death. A similar sentiment is expressed in 1 Cor. 15:31: "Not a day but I am at death's door (καθ' ἡμέραν ἀποθνῄσκω)" (Moffatt). Cf. Rom. 8:36. Death was Paul's daily companion, constantly at his side.

It is possible that the apostle has mentioned these four general categories of hardship in a progression of increasing severity of suffering: toil–imprisonment–beatings–encounters with death. But if so, the categories are not mutually exclusive, for a beating could be linked with an imprisonment (as at Philippi, Acts 16:22-23), and exposure to death could be the result of a beating (see on vv. 24-25). With more confidence we may argue that the phrase ἐν θανάτοις πολλάκις is illustrated in vv. 24-25, just as ὁδοιπορίαις πολλάκις (v. 26a) is illustrated in the remainder of v. 26.[52] See above, "Analysis of 11:21b-29 by Construction."

---

48. Eph. 3:1; Phlm. 1, 9; cf. τὸν δέσμιον αὐτοῦ, 2 Tim. 1:8.

49. See Harris, *Slave* 117-18.

50. This adverb is formed from the present participle of ὑπερβάλλω ("surpass"), a verb used in reference to δόξα (3:10) and χάρις (9:14).

51. Cf. BAGD 840b.

52. So Plummer 327. But Ellingworth goes one stage further. He views ἐν θανάτοις πολλάκις, "many times near death," as beginning a new stage of Paul's argument in which he stresses the number of times he has suffered this or that affliction (245-46). For their part, Zmijewski (248) and Barnett (541) regard the four phrases in v. 23b as headings or summaries for what follows.

11:24 ὑπὸ Ἰουδαίων πεντάκις τεσσεράκοντα παρὰ μίαν ἔλαβον. "Five times I received from the Jews the 'forty lashes minus one.'" Now the illustrations begin of the statement "often near death": πολλάκις is followed by πεντάκις (v. 24) . . . τρὶς . . . ἅπαξ . . . τρίς (v. 25).[53] "The thirty-nine stripes" was the official punishment of the synagogue, alluded to by Jesus when he warned his disciples that some of them would be handed over to local Jewish councils (συνέδρια) and scourged "in their synagogues" (ἐν ταῖς συναγωγαῖς αὐτῶν, Matt. 10:17; cf. 23:34). This punishment has its origin in the regulations of Deut. 25:2-3 concerning the penalty to be meted out to the guilty person who deserved a flogging. The number of lashes was to correspond to the gravity of the offense, but in no case was it to exceed forty lest the offender should suffer gross public humiliation. We may explain the change from forty to thirty-nine strokes as the maximum permissible penalty as resulting from (1) a concern to avoid a miscount that would infringe a commandment; or (2) the fact that the instrument of punishment had three straps, so that thirteen strokes was the maximum permitted; or (3) an interpretation of the juxtaposed words *bᵉmispār 'arbā'îm* (LXX, ἀριθμῷ τεσσαράκοντα), literally, "by number forty," in Deut. 25:2-3 to mean "a number near to forty" (*m. Makkot* 3:10). Josephus also refers to the "forty stripes minus one" (*Antiquities* 4:238, 248); clearly the later comparable reference in the Mishnaic tractate *Makkot* ("Stripes") reflects practice that dates back at least to the first century A.D.[54]

In the expression τεσσεράκοντα παρὰ μίαν, we note that the preposition παρά has the unusual sense of "less" (BDF §236[4]) or "minus"; that πληγάς ("strokes") must be supplied (as in Luke 12:47) with τεσσεράκοντα, or πληγήν with μίαν; that τεσσεράκοντα was more often spelled τεσσαράκοντα until the Byzantine period.[55]

The construction λαμβάνειν τι ὑπό τινος means "be given something by someone" (BAGD 465c). ὑπὸ Ἰουδαίων, "at the hands of the Jews," does not amount to a general indictment of the Jewish people,[56] but it does strike a note of pathos after Paul's defense of his Jewishness in v. 22. ἔλαβον is the first of four successive constative aorists,[57] where action, whether single, protracted, or repeated, is viewed as constituting a single fact: ἔλαβον (v. 24), ἐρραβδίσθην, ἐλιθάσθην, ἐναυάγησα (v. 25). In the case of ἔλαβον, five separate incidents are comprehended in a single glance — "I received beatings from the Jews (five times, actually)."

None of the floggings is mentioned in Acts, and where and when they oc-

---

53. Hughes, however, links ὁδοιπορίαις πολλάκις (v. 26) closely with ἐν θανάτοις πολλάκις (v. 23) on structural grounds, and so regards vv. 24-25 as "a parenthesis of particularity" (408).

54. For discussions of *m. Makkot* 3:1-16, see SB 3.527-30.

55. Moulton and Howard 66 and n. 3; cf. BDF §29(1).

56. This point does not need to be attached to the anarthrous state of Ἰουδαίων (as Danker 181, comparing ὑπὸ τῶν Ἰουδαίων in 1 Thess. 2:14); nouns in lists tend to be anarthrous (cf. vv. 26-27).

57. The constative aorist is also called "complexive" or "summary," or "historical" (Burton §38) or "global" (Zerwick §253).

curred is unknown.[58] Nor can we know precisely why Paul was given these synagogal punishments;[59] but possible reasons are not difficult to find, such as disregard of food laws by eating unclean food (cf. *m. Makkot* 3:2) and encouraging other Jews to do so (cf. 1 Cor. 10:25, 27),[60] or the rejection of the need for circumcision by male Gentiles as a sign of inclusion within the people of God (cf. Gal. 5:11). But an even more probable reason would have been a charge of blasphemy, understood either as "defiant sin,"[61] which could involve the two offenses already mentioned, or as the dishonoring of God and his people by promulgating a messianism that focused on a crucified Jesus of Nazareth and affirmed his deity.[62] The punishment for blasphemy was removal from the community (Num. 15:30-31, and at a later period *m. Keritot* 1:1), but from the Mishnah we learn that scourging could be a substitute for "extirpation" (*m. Makkot* 3:15). If this was true also in the first century, Paul's "blasphemy" that merited permanent removal from the synagogue could have been punished instead by flogging.[63] Nor should we forget that he may have been punished for more than one reason on each of the five occasions. We may gauge the seriousness with which Paul's offense was viewed on each occasion from the fact that he incurred the maximum penalty each time.

Paul's testimony regarding his five beatings is significant in several ways.

1. There is irony in the fact that as a Christian Paul repeatedly received the very punishment — synagogal floggings — that he, as a ruthless persecutor of Christians, had repeatedly caused to be meted out to them or himself had inflicted on them (Acts 22:19; 26:11).

2. Paul must have been robust to survive all five floggings and resilient to face the last four. In *m. Makkot* 3.14 the possibility of a person's dying during or after the thirty-nine strokes is envisaged, and the judgment is made that "the scourger is not culpable." Josephus calls this punishment "most ignominious" (αἰσχίστη) for a free man (*Antiquities* 4:238).

3. This testimony affords further evidence of Paul's Jewishness (cf. v. 22).

---

58. Allo (296) speculates that they might have taken place at Damascus (Acts 9:23), Jerusalem (Acts 9:29), Pisidian Antioch (Acts 13:50), Iconium (Acts 14:2, 5), and early in his Ephesian ministry (Acts 19:9; cf. 1 Cor. 15:32).

59. That these punishments were all given by officials connected with the synagogue is clear from the fact that they are described as the "forty lashes minus one," the synagogue's official and maximum corporal punishment.

60. See Harvey, "Aspects" 79-86. Harvey (119) believes that the floggings were the result of Paul's determination "to enjoy access to the synagogue even though continuing to show contempt for certain 'observances of the law.'"

61. Num. 15:30 reads "Anyone who sins defiantly, whether native-born or alien, blasphemes the LORD and must be cut off from among their people."

62. The technical understanding of blasphemy as the use of the divine name (*m. Sanhedrin* 7:5) was not established until after the first century.

63. Punishment in the synagogue is associated with blasphemy in Acts 26:11, but that blasphemy was presumably a cursing of Christ (cf. Ἀνάθεμα Ἰησοῦς, 1 Cor. 12:3).

Not only by lineage but also in practice he was a Jew, attending the synagogue[64] and being subject to its discipline.

4. His ongoing submission to the authority of the synagogue was doubtless prompted by his desire to maintain an open door for evangelism among his fellow Jews (cf. Rom. 9:1-3; 10:1) as well among the Gentiles who attended synagogue services.

11:25 τρὶς ἐρραβδίσθην, ἅπαξ ἐλιθάσθην, τρὶς ἐναυάγησα, νυχθήμερον ἐν τῷ βυθῷ πεποίηκα. "Three times I was beaten with rods, once I was pelted with stones, three times I was shipwrecked, a night and a day I have spent adrift at sea." Further illustrations are given of being "exposed to death" (v. 23b). If the thirty-nine stripes, a Jewish punishment, was one example of πληγαί (v. 23), being beaten with rods, a Roman punishment, was another. ῥαβδίζω (Latin *virgis caedere*) means "beat with a rod (ῥάβδος) (or rods)." ῥαβδοῦχοι (Latin *lictores*), literally "rod-carriers" (EVV "lictors"), were officials who attended Roman magistrates and carried as symbols of authority bundles of rods (Latin *fasces*) of elm or birch wood with an axe (Latin *securis*) inserted among them, signifying magistrates' right to inflict either corporal or capital punishment. One of the three times Paul was beaten with the lictors' rods was at Philippi in about A.D. 50 (Acts 16:19-24). After Paul had exorcised a divining spirit from a certain slave girl there, the girl's owners brought Paul and Silas before the two local magistrates (ἄρχοντες) or "praetors" (στρατηγοί), who summarily stripped them and ordered the lictors "to beat them with rods" (ῥαβδίζειν, Acts 16:22). Nothing is known from Acts of the other two comparable beatings; Paul's catalogue of trials provides significant biographical data that complement and supplement the information found in Acts.

Generally a Roman citizen such as Paul[65] was exempt from this punishment, but this right was not always upheld in the provinces,[66] and the local magistrates involved in the three cases in question might have considered Paul's behavior to be a minor offense, in which case a public flogging was not illegal.[67] With this said, the question remains why, at least in the case at Philippi, Paul did not inform the authorities of his Roman citizenship before he was flogged. Perhaps he wished to be identified with Christ in his suffering (cf. 1:5; 4:7-11; Phil. 3:10; Col. 1:24). Perhaps he wanted to provide his converts who would face persecution with an example of patient suffering (cf. 2 Tim. 3:10-11); at least he would not want to be seen to be using a convenient

---

64. Cf., e.g., Acts 9:20; 17:2; 18:4.

65. See Acts 16:37-38; 22:25-29, and note Paul's appeal to Caesar (Acts 25:12), a right exercised only by Roman citizens.

66. For instance, Cicero accuses Verres, governor of Sicily, of having Roman citizens beaten (*In Verrem* 2.5.139-40), and Josephus reports that Gessius Florus, procurator of Judea, had scourged (and crucified) Jews of equestrian rank (*War* 2.305-8). For an indication that a savage scourging could lead to death, see Cicero, *In Verrem* 2.5.142 (regarding Gaius Servilius).

67. See Sherwin-White 71-74.

escape-hatch that was unavailable to some or most of his converts.[68] And is it possible that at Philippi, caught up in a rapid succession of events (Acts 16:18-22), Paul and Silas judged that it would be to the advantage of the infant church if they remained silent about their Roman citizenship until the incident was over, so that the praetors, obliged to give an official apology yet fearing a complaint to Rome about their conduct (cf. Acts 16:38-39), would be less willing to persecute the new converts?[69]

The single instance of stoning referred to by ἅπαξ ἐλιθάσθην occurred at Lystra (Acts 14:19-20).[70] That this stoning was not a carefully calculated penalty for alleged blasphemy (cf. Lev. 24:16) inflicted by the Jews of Antioch and Iconium but rather a spontaneous action of an incited crowd (Acts 14:19) seems clear from: (1) the rapid reversal of the Lystrans' attitude to Paul and Barnabas, from adoration (Acts 14:11-13) to animosity; and (2) the fact that Paul survived the pelting with stones (Acts 14:20), which would not have been the case if it were a judicial penalty (cf. Lev. 24:16).[71]

Acts makes no mention of the three shipwrecks Paul refers to. The shipwreck described in Acts 27:39-44 occurred after 2 Corinthians was written (that is, at the time represented by Acts 20:2a). Hughes (411) lists some nine sea voyages mentioned in Acts that Paul undertook before Acts 20, to which we may add the return journey of Ephesus–Corinth–Ephesus that is called the "painful visit" (see on 1:16; 2:1), and probably a coastal voyage from Troas to Neapolis (2:13; 7:5), journeys not recorded in Acts.[72] The sailing vessels Paul traveled in were probably not renowned for their seaworthiness, being wooden, leaky, and without life rafts. In the ancient world all sea voyages, including coastal journeys, were viewed with trepidation and as potentially life-threatening.[73] Inscriptions and votive tablets that are addressed to various deities (e.g., "to Pan of the Successful Journey," Πανὶ Εὐόδῳ), thanking them for deliverance from the dangers of the sea, bear eloquent testimony to this fear and to the relief felt upon reaching harbor safely.[74]

---

68. Cf. Thrall 742. See her Excursus (XIII) on "11.25: Paul's punishment and Roman law" (739-42).

69. The magistrates' concern about their illegal action is clearly shown by their apology to Paul and Silas and their respectful request that they should leave the city (Acts 16:39).

70. ἅπαξ supports the view that the intent of the people of Iconium to stone Paul and Barnabas (Acts 14:5) was not fulfilled (Bruce, *Acts* 325).

71. νομίζοντες αὐτὸν τεθνηκέναι ("supposing that he was dead") (Acts 14:19) does not invalidate this point. If the execution had been official, there would need to be more than an impression or supposition (νομίζοντες) that Paul was dead.

72. Osborne proposes (61, 63) that these three shipwrecks took place during Paul's "silent years" (? A.D. 35-45).

73. On the dates when sea travel was considered (relatively) safe, see the Introduction, n. 257. It is easy to overlook the extensive nature of Paul's sea voyages (see the estimates in E. Haenchen, *The Acts of the Apostles* [Philadelphia: Westminster, 1971] 702-3). With good reason Ramsay entitled his work *St. Paul the Traveller and Roman Citizen* (London: Hodder & Stoughton, 1896).

74. See A. L. Connolly in Horsley 4.113-17, and more generally, Murphy-O'Connor, "Road" 38-47; L. Casson, *Travel in the Ancient World* (London: Allen & Unwin, 1974).

The night and day Paul spent adrift at sea may have been during yet another shipwreck, but more probably it occurred in the course of one of the three shipwrecks already mentioned. νυχθήμερον has been understood in various ways.

1. As an adverb: "by night and day" (Moulton in Moulton and Howard 269 and n. 2).
2. As an adverbial accusative of the adjective νυχθήμερος, "lasting a night and a day" (cf. BAGD 547a; Moulton and Howard 283).
3. As a neuter noun (LSJ 1186 s.v. II.) and the direct object of πεποίηκα (Hughes 412 n. 77; cf. BDF §121).
4. As a neuter noun and an accusative of extent of time with ποιέω, "spend," "stay" (BAGD 682c).[75]

This last explanation is to be preferred although the sense is not materially altered however the form is explained. ἐν τῷ βυθῷ means "on the open sea," "in the deep," or (so BAGD 148c) "adrift at sea." That is, the terrifying twenty-four hours was spent at the mercy of the waves, presumably clinging to some of the ship's wreckage (cf. Acts 27:44) but always in danger of drowning. Quite often πεποίηκα is treated as an aoristic perfect equivalent to ἐποίησα,[76] but following four aorists in vv. 24-25 this perfect is unlikely to be merely a stylistic change. Rather, in his mind's eye Paul is vividly recalling a harrowing (and possibly recent) experience of prolonged exposure to imminent death[77]: "a night and a day I have spent adrift at sea."

11:26 ὁδοιπορίαις πολλάκις, κινδύνοις ποταπῶν, κινδύνοις λῃστῶν, κινδύνοις ἐκ γένους, κινδύνοις ἐξ ἐθνῶν, κινδύνοις ἐν πόλει, κινδύνοις ἐν ἐρημίᾳ, κινδύνοις ἐν θαλάσσῃ, κινδύνοις ἐν ψευδαδέλφοις. "On frequent journeys, exposed to dangers from rivers, dangers from bandits, dangers from my people, dangers from Gentiles, dangers in the city, dangers in the desert, dangers on the sea, dangers among false brothers." After speaking of his general suffering (v. 23b) and his repeated exposure to death (vv. 24-25), with special reference to shipwreck (v. 25b), Paul moves on to name other specific dangers associated with travel. Just as ἐν θανάτοις πολλάκις (v. 23b) formed a heading for vv. 24-25, so now ὁδοιπορίαις πολλάκις is a rubric for the rest of v. 26. Some EVV reflect this link between the "journeys" and the "dangers" in translation. For example, "During my frequent journeys I have been exposed to dangers . . ." (Martin 367). Others (e.g., Wolff 228) place a colon after "journeys." At first sight the eight dangers seem to be arranged neatly in four pairs: rivers–robbers,

---

75. Cf. the use of ποιέω with χρόνον (Acts 15:33; 18:23), with μῆνας τρεῖς (Acts 20:3), and with ἐνιαυτόν (Jas. 4:13) (cited by BAGD 682c).

76. So, e.g., among the grammarians Winer 272; BDF §343(2); Burton §§80, 88; Turner 70.

77. Similarly Moulton 144; Robertson 897; *Pictures* 262 ("The memory of it survives like a nightmare"); Zerwick, *Analysis* 412.

Jews–Gentiles, city–wilderness, sea–false brothers.[78] The second and third pairs form natural contrasts, and the two items in the first pair would be naturally associated in Paul's mind as he recalled the perils of crossing the Taurus mountain range between Perga and Pisidian Antioch (Acts 13:14; 14:24), a journey notorious for cascading torrents and hidden bandits. Because the last pair (sea–false brothers) seem oddly matched, some have suggested an alternative arrangement of the eight pairs. Windisch envisages that ἐν ψευδαδέλφοις has been accidentally displaced, so that the original order was rivers–robbers, Jews–Gentiles–false brothers, city–wilderness–sea (= the whole world); that is, one pair and two triplets (358). More satisfactory is Thrall's proposed arrangement: two pairs (rivers–bandits, Jews–Gentiles), a triplet (city–desert–sea), and a climactic "amongst pseudo-Christians" (722, 742-43).[79]

ὁδοιπορία, "journey(ing)," refers to travel on land, usually on foot. NEB and REB render ὁδοιπορίαις πολλάκις by "I have constantly been on the road." Since, in ancient times, any major journey by sea or by land was a hazardous undertaking, the transition from "journeys" to "dangers" is a natural one. The eight dangers listed are each introduced by κινδύνοις, which, like ὁδοιπορίαις, is probably a dative expressing attendant circumstances ("with"),[80] comparable to the fourfold ἐν + dative in v. 23b and v. 27, although the dative could be instrumental ("by means of," "through")[81] or locatival ("in"[82] or "amid"[83]). The plural κινδύνοις may refer to multiple dangers; or it could be generalizing ("danger," e.g., RSV, NRSV; Lang 342).

Both ποταμῶν and λῃστῶν are genitives of source: "(dangers) from rivers . . . from bandits."[84] These "dangers from rivers" are those encountered while trying to cross rivers (bridges being uncommon in remote areas) or while seek-

---

78. See above, "Analysis of 11:21b-29 by Construction."

79. Barré's explanation of the odd final pair is strained. He discovers an alternation of words denoting "people" and "places": places (rivers)–people (robbers)–people (Jews–Gentiles)/places (city–wilderness)–places (sea)–people (false brothers) (504-5). Moreover, he finds a correspondence between "rivers" and "sea" (both water) and between "robbers" and "false brothers" (both enemies) (504-5).

80. English idiom, however, suggests "*on* frequent journeys" and "*exposed to* dangers." BDF §198 classifies this use of the dative as "associative," designating "accompanying circumstances and manner."

81. So Bultmann 216, noting that "the διάκονος Χριστοῦ ἐγενόμην [cf. v. 23a] is always in view."

82. So most translations — e.g., NASB, JB; Wolff 228; Lambrecht 187.

83. Weymouth, Cassirer ("amidst").

84. BDF §166; Spicq 2.394. Unnecessarily, Turner classifies these as genitives "of place" (212). (The other example he cites, αἵματος σταυροῦ, "blood shed on the cross" [Col. 1:20], is simply a genitive of reference or relation.) Robertson calls these two examples objective genitives (500-501), a broad category for Robertson that embraces "genitives of 'looser relation'" (500). We should remember that as the adnominal case the genitive basically limits the application of a noun with regard to kind, by indicating the class or category (Latin *genus*) to which it belongs, just as the accusative limits the application of a verb with regard to extent. Thus basically, "dangers in relation to rivers" = "dangers arising from rivers."

ing to avoid being swept away by the sudden flooding of rivers.[85] Plummer notes (326) that Frederick I (Barbarossa) was drowned in the river Calycadnus in Cilicia, not far from Tarsus, in 1190 during the Third Crusade. λῃσταί (from λῃίζομαι, "seize as booty") are "bandits," "brigands," or even "pirates,"[86] not light-fingered thieves but strong-arm thugs. Although the *Pax Romana* greatly reduced brigandage, "in Asia Minor, brigandage was never eliminated; not only were the mountainous regions particularly conducive to it, but its coastline provided choice sites for piracy, 'brigandage at sea.'"[87]

Acts is replete with examples of the dangers Paul faced from his fellow countrymen (ἐκ γένους, "at the hands of the people/my countrymen" = Jews; cf. BAGD 156c).[88] Even after his initial preaching in the synagogues of Damascus following his conversion (Acts 9:20-22), "the Jews conspired to kill him" (Acts 9:23). Such persecution, although not always murderous in intent, was to become the pattern of his ministry.[89] It was not only his message of a crucified and exalted Messiah who fulfilled OT promises that provoked intense opposition from his fellow Jews. There was also his "success" in luring away from Judaism to "the Nazarene sect" (Acts 24:7) many Gentile "God-fearers" (e.g., Acts 13:26; 14:16; 17:4), who, attracted by the monotheism of the Jewish faith and its rigorous ethical demands, regularly attended the synagogue. Such converts formed the nucleus of Paul's churches. But opposition to Paul was not restricted to his fellow countrymen; there were perils "at the hands of Gentiles" (ἐξ ἐθνῶν). Acts records two notable examples, the disturbance at Philippi that led to his flogging and imprisonment (along with Silas) (Acts 16:16-24) and the Demetrius riot at Ephesus that prompted his departure from that city (Acts 19:23–20:1). On one occasion, in Iconium, Jews and Gentiles acted in unison in endangering Paul's life (Acts 14:5). That Paul did not court persecution is clear from his action on this occasion, for as soon as he and Barnabas heard of the plot to mistreat them and stone them, "they made their escape" (κατέφυγον, Acts 14:6).[90]

The next three perils belong together, as places where Paul met danger. Just as "Jews" and "Gentiles" encompass all people, so "city," "desert," and "sea" incorporate every area on earth. Paul was unsafe wherever he went. The contrast between ἐν πόλει and ἐν ἐρημίᾳ is that between inhabited and largely uninhabited regions, between "the crowded city" and "the lonely desert" (A. P. Stanley), between city streets and the open country. "Dangers on the sea" is not simply a repetition of v. 25b. "There are other κίνδυνοι ἐν θαλάσσῃ besides

---

85. Sometimes ποταμῶν is rendered "floods" (Wand; NAB[1]; Spicq 2.394).

86. In his paraphrase A. P. Stanley has "robbers and pirates" (253).

87. Spicq 2.393, with supporting references in n. 14.

88. On the reasons for the Jewish persecution of Paul, see Kruse, "Persecution" 260-72; and more briefly in *DPL* 19.

89. See Acts 9:29; 13:45, 50; 14:2, 19; 17:5, 13; 18:6, 12; 19:9; 21:27-36; 23:12-13.

90. Similarly, on his third and final visit to Corinth he altered his travel plans when he discovered a Jewish plot against him (Acts 20:2-3).

shipwreck and exposure in the sea, such as bodily injury, fire, loss of property" (Plummer [CGT] 182).

"Dangers among false brothers" stands alone at the end of Paul's list (see Thrall's structural analysis [742-43] mentioned above), probably because he viewed it as the most hurtful and insidious peril of all. External dangers that threatened his own life were one thing; treacherous opposition that undermined his work was quite another thing. He could cope with life-threatening hazards from without more easily than with work-undermining perils from within. ψευδάδελφοι are "false brothers," "counterfeit Christians," "people masquerading as brothers" (NJB). The only other use of the term is in Gal. 2:4 in reference to Judaizers who had been "smuggled in" (παρεισάκτους) and then had "infiltrated" (παρεισῆλθον) into Paul's company "in order to spy out" (κατασκοπῆσαι) the freedom Paul and others enjoyed "in the fellowship of Christ Jesus." Their ultimate aim was to impose on Gentile converts the obligation to observe the Mosaic Law, and in particular, the rite of circumcision. Apparently, connotations of furtive action and treachery attached to the term ψευδάδελφος in Paul's mind. Héring suggests that these "false brothers" may have been traitors who denounced Paul before civic or religious authorities (86). By writing ἐν ψευδαδέλφοις, not ἐκ ψευδαδέλφων (which would be parallel to ἐκ γένους and ἐξ ἐθνῶν), Paul may be indicating that while other perils came and went, the danger of having his ministry compromised by the machinations of false Christians was ever present. Since he terms his rivals at Corinth ψευδαπόστολοι (11:13), he may include them within these ψευδάδελφοι, but the latter has a wider reference in this context.

11:27 κόπῳ καὶ μόχθῳ, ἐν ἀγρυπνίαις πολλάκις, ἐν λιμῷ καὶ δίψει, ἐν νηστείαις πολλάκις, ἐν ψύχει καὶ γυμνότητι. "With labor and toil, with frequent sleepless nights, in hunger and thirst, frequently going without food, cold and virtually naked." V. 26 has specified eight dangers Paul encountered on his "frequent travels." Now he mentions six hardships or deprivations that result from the "labor and toil" he expends in his missionary endeavors. In this general sense κόπῳ καὶ μόχθῳ stands as a heading for what follows (Peterson 120). Whereas κόπος occurs eighteen times in the NT (eleven in Paul), μόχθος is found only three times, always in conjunction with κόπος and always standing second (11:27; 1 Thess. 2:9; 2 Thess. 3:8). Both words can mean "exertion" or "effort," referring to arduous toil, but only κόπος can also denote the "weariness" or "exhaustion" that results from this profound strenuous labor.[91] But if it were Paul's intent to allude to this "exhaustion" in his three uses of this phrase, we would expect the order μόχθος καὶ κόπος. So we should assume that the words are used here as virtual synonyms,[92] signifying the "labor and toil" that

---

91. See the discussions of κόπος in Spicq 2.322-29, especially 329; F. Hauck, *TDNT* 3.827-30; and of μόχθος in Spicq 2.526-27. Paul uses κόπος to describe both missionary labor (1 Cor. 3:8; 2 Cor. 10:15; 1 Thess. 3:5) and Christian activity in general (1 Cor. 15:58; 1 Thess. 1:3).

92. Cf. Spicq 2.526 ("In an ordinary figure of speech of this sort, it is not possible to distinguish precisely the meanings of the components [of the phrase]"). NEB and REB render the whole phrase, "I have toiled and drudged."

Paul expended in supporting himself by plying his trade and in fulfilling his missionary vocation (see the comments on κόπος at 6:5; 11:23). The assonance of o–ῳ may be reproduced in the archaic English phrase "toil and moil" (Plummer 327). The two datives denote accompanying circumstances ("with"), as in the case of ὁδοιπορίαις and κινδύνοις in v. 26.[93]

On the expression ἐν ἀγρυπνίαις, see 6:5, where the same phrase occurs. I argued there that these "sleepless nights" (ἀγρυπνίαι; BAGD 14b) were voluntary,[94] as Paul pursued his missionary tasks and engaged in manual labor to support himself. The tasks that led to "many a sleepless night" (TCNT) may have included prayer vigils as well as preaching engagements (cf. Acts 20:7, 9, 11, 31). All the instances of ἐν in this verse should be seen as circumstantial ("with") or locative ("in," "in conditions of"), comparable to the significance of the two datives κόπῳ and μόχθῳ.

It is improbable that ἐν λιμῷ καὶ δίψει means "in famine and drought,"[95] for while λιμός often means "famine," there is no evidence that δίψος can bear the sense of "drought." Given the hundreds of miles that Paul traveled on foot, often across uninhabited terrain, it is not surprising to learn of the unavailability of food and water at least on some occasions, if not frequently.[96] Also, his unwillingness to accept payment for spiritual "services rendered" could have sometimes led to "hunger and thirst" when his own resources dried up (cf. ὑστερηθείς, 11:9).

Although the phrase ἐν νηστείαις πολλάκις is often taken to refer to lack of food,[97] reasons for understanding it of voluntary abstention from food ("often fasting," Barrett 288; "frequently going without food")[98] are not lacking. First, ἐν λιμῷ has just referred to involuntary "fasting," and a repetition of this thought is therefore unlikely. Second, self-imposed hardships (cf. ἐν ἀγρυπνίαις above) should not be deemed inappropriate in a list of trials if those hardships were imposed in fulfillment of one's mission; going without sleep and food in order to support or further one's ministry would certainly fit that category. Third, structurally the two phrases ἐν ἀγρυπνίαις πολλάκις and ἐν νηστείαις πολλάκις are identical. If the former describes voluntary sleeplessness (see above), the latter may depict voluntary "fasting." Fourth, νηστείαι need not re-

93. Others take the datives as locative, "in" or "in the midst of" (Barrett 288). See Textual Note b.

94. But Louw and Nida (§23.73) believe that in 6:5; 11:27 the ἀγρυπνία ("sleeplessness," "failure to sleep") "was evidently the result of external circumstances which prevented normal sleep." Certainly the "wakefulness" of Paul and Silas after their beating in Philippi (Acts 16:24-25) would fit into this category.

95. As Bishop 169 suggests.

96. Cf. 1 Cor. 4:11, ἄχρι τῆς ἄρτι ὥρας καὶ πεινῶμεν καὶ διψῶμεν, "Up to the present moment we go hungry and thirsty."

97. E.g., Moffatt ("starving many a time"); Martin 367 ("often deprived of food"); similarly BAGD 538a; TCNT, Goodspeed.

98. So also Weymouth, Wand, NEB, NAB[1, 2]; Meyer 661; Plummer 312, 328; Hughes 413; Barrett 300; Thrall 722, 747.

fer to formal religious rites associated with self-discipline or prayer, but may here denote merely going without meals[99] in order to achieve a particular goal, such as earning sufficient money to enable financial independence (cf. 1 Cor. 9:12b, 18; 2 Cor. 11:7-12) or engaging in conversation about the gospel or preparing for special ministry opportunities.[100]

ἐν ψύχει καὶ γυμνότητι, literally, "with/in cold and nakedness," "cold and virtually naked," refers to conditions Paul faced as a craftsman,[101] or, more probably, as a regular traveler and occasional prisoner. As Paul dictated this phrase, memories of being drenched in rivers or at sea, of being assailed by bandits, or of languishing in freezing prisons may have arisen in his mind. It is possible that the phrase is a case of hendiadys, "frozen from want of clothing" (Wand), "cold because of near-nakedness." Also, γυμνότης may stand for "destitution" (Martin 367) or "exposure" (NEB, REB) by metonymy.

11:28 χωρὶς τῶν παρεκτὸς ἡ ἐπίστασίς μοι ἡ καθ᾽ ἡμέραν, ἡ μέριμνα πασῶν τῶν ἐκκλησιῶν. "Not to mention other things, there is what presses on me every day — my anxiety for all the churches." There are five main exegetical issues in this verse and each issue may be conveniently raised by means of a question.

How is this verse related to what precedes? That is, does χωρὶς τῶν παρεκτός mean "Apart from what is external" or "Apart from what I leave unmentioned"?[102] As an improper preposition παρεκτός means "besides," "apart from," "except for."[103] But here it is an adverb meaning "besides," "outside" (BAGD 625a) and is used adjectivally with the article. If Paul had wanted to speak of "things outside," "external matters,"[104] we might have expected him to write χωρὶς τῶν ἔξω or χωρὶς τῶν ἔξωθεν.[105] We follow those exegetes and EVV that take τῶν παρεκτός to mean "things besides," that is, "other things, which I pass over" (Weymouth), "what I leave unmentioned" (Bultmann 217, supplying

---

99. Hughes 413. Robertson (408) notes that the plural of abstract substantives lays stress on the separate acts; cf. BDF §142 and the use of κόποις in 6:5; 10:15; 11:23. Some EVV render the plural (ἐν) νηστείαις by "fastings" (Weymouth, NAB[1, 2]; Plummer 312), others by "fasting" (e.g., Thrall 722), presumably treating the plural as generalizing.

100. There is only a fine line distinguishing such voluntary fasting from "compulsory deprivation due to lack of money or time for meals" (Bultmann 171, commenting on ἐν νηστείαις in 6:5).

101. See Hock 84 n. 94.

102. These two possibilities are given by BAGD 625a. It is rightly assumed that τῶν is neuter, not masculine. But it is inappropriate to construe χωρὶς τῶν παρεκτός with what precedes, as Moffatt does (". . . cold and ill-clad, and all the rest of it"). While this might seem a suitable conclusion to vv. 23b-27, it makes ἡ ἐπίστασις κτλ. asyndetic, and this prepositional phrase forms an appropriate transition to the climax of vv. 28-29.

103. LSJ 1334 s.v. παρεκτός I; BAGD 625 s.v. 2. The two NT instances are παρεκτὸς λόγου πορνείας (Matt. 5:32), "except on the ground of immorality," and παρεκτὸς τῶν δεσμῶν τούτων (Acts 26:29), "except for these chains."

104. This, basically, is how τῶν παρεκτός is understood by LSJ 1334 s.v. παρεκτός II; RV, NEB, NJB, REB; Robertson 547; Barrett 288.

105. Cf. the use of οἱ ἔξω in 1 Cor. 5:12-13; Col. 4:5; 1 Thess. 4:12 and οἱ ἔξωθεν in 1 Tim. 3:7. See Plummer 329.

γινομένων),[106] or simply "other things"[107] or "other matters."[108] On this under-standing, "the things omitted" (τὰ παραλειφθέντα, Chrysostom) would refer to additional examples of suffering,[109] while the "other things" could be either fur-ther instances of suffering or (as Thrall 749) things other than the pressure of anxiety. If, then, Paul has chosen not to mention any more trials, we may infer that he saw vv. 23b-27 as an illustrative and not an exhaustive list of his apos-tolic afflictions. As we move from vv. 23b-27 to vv. 28-29 we are not merely progressing from external to internal hardships but from various intermittent physical hardships that lay in the past to a single constant spiritual burden of the present.

Does ἡ ἐπίστασίς μοι refer to the "pressure" that Paul feels, or to the "re-sponsibility" that weighs on him? We should note, first of all, that ἐστίν ("there is") is understood before ἡ ἐπίστασις (so most EVV); that the dative μοι "is de-pendent on the verb [ἐφίστασθαί τινι] implicit in ἐπίστασις" (Bultmann 217); and that the qualifying prepositional phrase ἡ καθ' ἡμέραν stands in the em-phatic predicate position, with κατά being distributive (BAGD 406d), "every day," "from day to day," "day in and day out." A bewildering variety of render-ings for ἐπίστασις has been proposed, each with proponents and lexicographi-cal support.[110] They include: attention/care/preoccupation, supervision/over-sight, onset/concourse, interruption/delay/hindrance(s), caballing/conspiring against, pressure. BAGD 300b and the majority of commentators (rightly) pre-fer "pressure."[111] The NEB and REB opt for "responsibility," probably because this term embraces the ideas in the first two sets of proposals.

How is ἡ μέριμνα related to ἡ ἐπίστασις? Since both terms can mean "care," they could be virtual synonyms, although μέριμνα denotes "anxious care." Alternatively, they could be related as cause (ἡ μέριμνα κτλ.) and effect (ἡ ἐπίστασις): "the daily pressure upon me imposed by my anxious care for all the churches" (Thrall 722; similarly NRSV).[112] But such a relation would be more normally expressed by the subjective genitive; in this case, τῆς μερίμνης. It seems preferable to regard ἡ μέριμνα as standing in epexegetic apposition:[113]

---

106. Similarly NEB mg., GNB; Plummer 312, 329; Windisch 360; Allo 298; Hughes 415 n. 78; Furnish 512; Wolff 228, 235; Lambrecht 192. If ἡ ἐπίστασις κτλ. is regarded as explaining χωρὶς τῶν παρεκτός, this could be an example of paralipsis (see BDF §495) (so Zmijewski 269), but such an apposition would be both strained and strange; as Winer (533) comments, "such a solecism is not to be credited to Paul."

107. RSV, NRSV; Thrall 722.

108. Louw and Nida §58.38.

109. Cf. NAB[1], "Leaving other sufferings unmentioned."

110. See the discussion in BAGD 300b; Hughes 415-16 n. 79.

111. E.g., Plummer 329-30; Hughes 415 n. 79; Bultmann 218; Martin 367, 381; Thrall 749.

112. But on p. 749 and n. 671 Thrall expresses a preference for construing ἡ μέριμνα κτλ. as appositional and explicative. Barnett suggests an opposite relation. Paul's "sense of 'anxiety' was fed by the daily 'assault' *(epistasis)* of the reports about those churches [churches established by his apostolic mission] that came to him, whether by letter or by personal contact" (548).

113. So almost all EVV.

"what presses on me every day — my anxiety for all the churches" (τῶν ἐκκλησιῶν is an objective genitive). Paul's anxious concern for all his congregations and all of the individuals within them (v. 29) was shown in his intense jealousy (cf. ζῆλῶ) for their constant purity (11:2) and his fear (cf. φοβοῦμαι) that they might lose their original single-mindedness and pure devotion to Christ (11:3) and be characterized by discord and factiousness (12:20). If μέριμνα defines ἐπίστασις, we may assume that Paul's anxiety or anxious care was "day in and day out," like the pressure. What the psalmist said of the Lord, "he daily bears our burdens" (Ps. 68:19), Paul's converts could say of their spiritual father — if they realized it![114]

Does Paul's confession to having μέριμνα fly in the face of Jesus' admonitions about avoiding μέριμνα in Matt. 6:25-34?[115] Whether Paul knew of this teaching of Jesus, we cannot ascertain. But even if he did, he would not have sensed any discrepancy between his conduct and Jesus' instructions. His anxious concern arose from his single-minded pursuit of the kingdom of God (cf. Matt. 6:33). On a daily basis he was grappling with present problems involving others, not with future uncertainties concerning himself (cf. Matt. 6:25, 31, 34). Finally, his anxiety related to the lasting and substantial matters of the spirit, not to the fleeting and relatively insignificant issues of food and clothing (cf. 11:27; Matt. 6:25, 28, 31).

Does πασῶν τῶν ἐκκλησιῶν refer only to the churches Paul founded (so Wolff 236)?[116] It is possible that the article is possessive, so that the sense is "all our congregations" (NEB). 1 Cor. 7:17 might seem to support this view: οὕτως ἐν ταῖς ἐκκλησίαις πάσαις διατάσσομαι. But there it is clearly a matter of Paul's own pastoral rule (διατάσσομαι) and therefore his own churches. Certainly Paul's primary concern was always with his own congregations — their unity, their adherence to the apostolic gospel, their Christian behavior — and he was preoccupied with pioneer evangelism (Rom. 15:20), not with visiting various churches. But his deep pastoral concern for churches other than those he had personally founded seems undeniable. He wrote letters to such churches (Colossae, Laodicea [Col. 4:16], Rome); he reports that he "struggled earnestly" (perhaps principally through intercessory prayer) for believers whom he did not know personally (Col. 2:1-2); he arranged for the exchange of his pastoral letters between Colossae and Laodicea (Col. 4:16); he visited the Jeru-

---

114. It is of interest that never in the NT is μέριμνα ("anxiety," "worry," "care," BAGD 504 s.v.) (six uses) or the cognate verb μεριμνάω (19 uses) used of God; he is never anxious or worried. When 1 Pet. 5:7 says, "Cast all your anxiety (μέριμναν) on him [God]," the text continues "for your welfare is his concern" (ὅτι αὐτῷ μέλει περὶ ὑμῶν), not, "for he is anxious (μεριμνᾷ) about you" (although μεριμνάω can have the non-pejorative sense of "be concerned for," "care for"; see BAGD 505 s.v.).

115. There are six uses of μεριμνάω in this passage, five of them calling for the avoidance of worry (Matt. 6:25, 27-28, 31, 34).

116. But in 8:18 Wolff takes διὰ πασῶν τῶν ἐκκλησιῶν to refer to all Christian churches in general (177).

salem church several times after his conversion,[117] sometimes visiting other Christian groups on his way (e.g., Acts 15:3); among his own churches he organized a collection to relieve need among destitute believers in the Jerusalem church (Rom. 15:25-26). Also, it would be an anomaly if Paul had "great sorrow and unceasing anguish" (λύπη . . . μεγάλη καὶ ἀδιάλειπτος ὀδύνη) for all his fellow Jews, his kindred by race (Rom. 9:1-3), but lacked μέριμνα for all his fellow believers in Christ, his kindred by faith, wherever they were found. Knowledge of the situation of believers outside his immediate orbit would reach him through Christian travelers.[118] We conclude that although the primary reference in πασῶν τῶν ἐκκλησιῶν is to churches in which Paul exercised pastoral care, a wider reference to other Christian congregations should not be excluded.[119]

11:29 τίς ἀσθενεῖ, καὶ οὐκ ἀσθενῶ; τίς σκανδαλίζεται, καὶ οὐκ ἐγὼ πυροῦμαι; "Who is weak, and I am not weak? Who is led astray into sin, and I am not ablaze with anger?" Paul's anxious concern (μέριμνα, v. 28) was not only for "all the churches" but also for individuals within those churches. He is not responding to a charge that he was aloof from his converts or was unfeeling, but is merely giving two illustrations of his μέριμνα for needy individual fellow believers. It seems highly improbable that this verse contains two explicit contrasts between Paul and his rivals (τις).[120] Throughout vv. 23b-28 there has been an implicit contrast between the two, but the contrast that began explicitly in v. 23a with ὑπὲρ ἐγώ and continued throughout v. 23b then recedes more and more into the background as the foreground is taken up simply with Paul's "boasting" in his sufferings as a superlative "servant of Christ." The interrogative τις of v. 29 need not be identified as having the same referent as the distant indefinite τις of v. 21b or the even more distant indefinite τις of v. 20. It is unlikely that those who apparently exercised authority with conspicuous highhandedness and drama (v. 20) should at the same time project themselves as "weak" and "offended."[121] Rather, τις refers to any of Paul's fellow believers and introduces a question to which the answer "nobody" is expected.[122]

There is certainly no unanimity among commentators and others concerning the meaning of the three verbs in this verse. ἀσθενεῖ could be given a physical sense, describing the weakness that results from illness (cf. Phil.

---

117. See Acts 9:26; 11:30; 15:2-4; 18:22; 21:17-19.

118. Cf. ἐδηλώθη . . . μοι, 1 Cor. 1:11; ἀκούεται, 1 Cor. 5:1.

119. Cf. Plummer 330: "Every Christian centre had claims on his thought and sympathy, those most of all of which he had intimate knowledge."

120. As Barré (508-9, 518) and Holland (259-60) allege.

121. Barré understands ἀσθενεῖ and σκανδαλίζεται in a different sense. He paraphrases v. 29 thus. "If anyone [of my opponents can boast that he] is being tripped up [by the agents of Satan in the eschatological struggle that characterizes true apostolic ministry], I [can boast that I] am being tripped up too! If anyone [of my opponents can boast that he] is being ensnared [by the agents of Satan in the eschatological struggle that characterizes true apostolic ministry], *I* [can go one better and boast that I] am being tried in the fires of the eschatological ordeal!" (518; cf. 508). For a critique of Barré's view, see Thrall 753.

122. For this latter point see BAGD 819a.

2:26-27) or from persecution. If it is given a moral or psychological meaning, it could depict a person who was faint-hearted and fearful (BAGD 115c) or burdened down with the "anxieties of the world" (αἱ μέριμναι τοῦ αἰῶνος, Mark 4:19; cf. 1 Cor. 7:33). Some find sociological overtones in the verb, a reference to those who lack power and status.[123] Again, if ἀσθενεῖ bears a religious sense, it may mean "weak in conscience" (so Bruce 244) or "weak in faith or life" (Plummer 313). σκανδαλίζεται has been taken to mean "is offended" (Barrett 288), "is tripped up" (Martin 367), "(Whose conscience) is hurt" (Goodspeed), or "is led into sin" (Thrall 722). Finally, we may find in πυροῦμαι (literally, "I am on fire") an allusion to burning with shame (Barclay) that Christ was dishonored or as if the sin were one's own, or with distress (GNB, Cassirer) at the fall of a fellow believer, or with a longing to restore the person whose faith has been "upset" (Phillips), or with anger (REB) or indignation (TCNT, Weymouth, Moffatt, RSV, NEB, NAB[1,2], NRSV) at the person who caused another to sin.

How are we to find our way through this maze of options? One clue to the meaning of ἀσθενεῖ and σκανδαλίζεται is found in 1 Cor. 8:7-13, where the two notions are juxtaposed and the only other Pauline uses of the verb σκανδαλίζω occur.[124] There Paul is encouraging certain "knowledgeable" Corinthians to avoid exercising their Christian liberty regarding the eating of "food sacrificed to idols" in such a way that the weak conscience of fellow believers was wounded (by their disregarding the dictates of their conscience) and they be thus caused to fall into sin. The apostle concludes, "Therefore, if what I eat (βρῶμα) causes my fellow believer to sin (σκανδαλίζει), I will never eat meat again, so that I may not cause them to sin (σκανδαλίσω)" (1 Cor. 8:13). But since in 2 Cor. 11:29 ἀσθενεῖ stands unqualified, it would be unwise to restrict its application to weakness in conscience or faith (cf. Rom. 14:1), although Paul may particularly have in mind immaturity in understanding the implications of Christian freedom. His emphasis in v. 29a is on his empathetic identification with his fellow believers in their weakness, whatever its precise nature — physical, psychological, social, or spiritual.[125]

Against the backdrop of 1 Cor. 8:7-13, τις σκανδαλίζεται; is more likely to mean "Who is led into sin?" than "Who is offended?" especially if "offend" is given a psychological sense of "cause resentment" or "make angry."[126] The

123. Forbes 19-20; Andrews 270-71, 276. For an analysis of Andrews' view that in 11:23b-29 Paul is placing himself in "the role of populist leader or demagogue" (276) and that in 11:29 he is presenting himself as one "weak" and "burnt up" who can therefore identify with those who are "weak" and "entrapped" (276), see Lambrecht, "Strength" 285-90; Thrall 753-54.

124. There are five uses of the ἀσθεν- root in 1 Cor. 8:7-13: ἀσθενής (v. 7), τοῖς ἀσθενέσιν (v. 9), ἀσθενοῦς (v. 10), ὁ ἀσθενῶν (v. 11), ἀσθενοῦσαν (v. 12). σκανδαλίζω is found twice in v. 13. On the textual question involving σκανδαλίζεται in Rom. 14:21, see Metzger 469.

125. A similarly comprehensive view of ἀσθενεῖ is taken by Meyer 663; Windisch 361; Thrall 751-52; Lambrecht 192.

126. "Offend" can, of course, have the legal sense of "transgress" or the religious sense of "stumble morally" or "do wrong."

idea of one person's causing another to sin is most dramatically presented in Matt. 18:6-7 (ὃς . . . ἂν σκανδαλίσῃ ἕνα . . . οὐαὶ τῷ ἀνθρώπῳ δι' οὗ τὸ σκάνδαλον ἔρχεται).

Although Barré alleges that in the NT πυρόω always occurs in an eschatological context (as in Dan. 11:35; 12:10, Θ) and never refers to burning with emotion (512, 518), his effort in an earlier article[127] to exclude the meaning "burn with passion" for πυρόω in 1 Cor. 7:9 is less than convincing.[128] BAGD (731 s.v.) cites three passages in 2 Maccabees (namely, 4:38; 10:35; 14:45) where πυρόω refers to being inflamed with anger.[129] The emotions that consumed Paul when he saw or heard that a fellow Christian had been led into sin were distress at that person's fall and anger at those responsible for the "ruining" of a brother or sister for whom Christ died (cf. 1 Cor. 8:11). To give πυροῦμαι a muted sense such as "sympathetic sorrow"[130] or "sympathy and a desire to help"[131] does less than justice to the intensity of emotion expressed by this verb when it is used figuratively.[132]

Verse 29 flows on naturally from v. 28. The pastoral care that involved the "pressure" of "anxiety" for the welfare of churches (v. 28) also involved empathetic identification with individuals in their weakness, whatever its nature (v. 29a), and intense and jealous protection of their spiritual welfare (v. 29b).

Bibliography

Andrews • Barré • Becker 170-78, 231-39 • Bishop, "Famine" • Bishop, "Nights" • Bultmann, *Stil* 71-80 • Collins, "Envoys" • Ebner 93-172, 387-97 • Ellingworth, "Grammar" • M. S. Ferrari, *Die Sprache des Leids in den paulinischen Peristasenkatalogen* (Stuttgart: Katholisches Bibelwerk, 1991) 237-59 • Fitzgerald • Fridrichsen • Fridrichsen, "Nachtrag" • S. Gallas, "'Fünfmal vierzig weniger einen. . . .' Die an Paulus vollzogenen Synagogalstrafen nach 2 Kor 11,24," *ZNW* 81 (1990) 178-91 • Georgi, *Opponents* 27-32, 41-60, 252, 279-80, 294 n. 122 • Harding, "Historicity" • Harvey, "Aspects" • Hodgson • Judge, "Conflict" • Kamlah, "Paulus" • Kim 34-39 • Kleinknecht • Koch • Kruse, "Persecution" • Lambrecht, "Strength" • MacDonald 49-50 • R. MacMullen, *Enemies of the Roman Order: Treason, Unrest and Alienation in the Empire* (Cambridge: Harvard University, 1966) 255-68 • Marshall • Murphy-O'Connor 115-17 • Murphy-O'Connor, "Road" • Oostendorp 7-16 • Osborne • Peterson 115-22 • V. C.

127. "To Marry or to Burn: *pyrousthai* in 1 Cor. 7:9," *CBQ* 36 (1974) 193-202.

128. See the discussion in Thiselton 516-19, who himself translates 1 Cor. 7:9 thus: "But if they do not have power over their passions, let them get married; for it is better to marry than for their passions to burn" (514).

129. Cf. also Philo, *De Vita Mosis* 2.280.

130. Lang 345; *TDNT* 6.950.

131. Windisch 361; cf. BAGD 731b.

132. The insertion of ἐγώ in the second question perhaps marks a heightening of emotion and also serves to contrast Paul's response to the "stumbling" ("I, for my part") with the implied role of the person causing another to sin (*pace* Turner 38: "the sudden insertion of ἐγώ is gratuitous and meaningless").

Pfitzner, *Paul and the Agon Motif: Traditional Athletic Imagery in the Pauline Letters* (Leiden: Brill, 1967) • E. P. Sanders, "Paul on the Law, His Opponents, and the Jewish People in Philippians 3 and 2 Corinthians 11," in *Anti-Judaism in Early Christianity. Vol. 1: Paul and the Gospels,* ed. P. Richardson (Waterloo: Wilfrid Laurier University, 1986) 75-90 • Schmithals 163-64, 207-8 • Schrage • Spencer • Thiessen 121-43 • Travis

6. Escape from Damascus (11:30-33)

These four verses begin a new section.[1] Vv. 21b-29 contain a list of hardships that Paul patiently endured as a servant of Christ who was in a different league from his rivals (11:23a). That bold boasting in a worldly fashion (11:18, 21b) is now over, and although his reluctant boasting continues, its focus has changed. "If there has to be still more boasting, my choice is to boast now about things that show up my weakness" (a paraphrase of 11:30).[2] V. 29 serves a transitional function with its references to ἀσθένεια: after mentioning the weakness of other believers which he shares (v. 29), Paul proceeds to cite (in 11:32–12:10), with a prefaced oath as to his truthfulness (v. 31), two prime instances of his own weakness (v. 30) — his humiliating escape from Damascus (11:32-33), and his permanent receipt of a debilitating "thorn in the flesh" (12:1-10). In vv. 30-31 there are three clear links with 12:1-10:[3] καυχᾶσθαι δεῖ (11:30; 12:1); the association of the future καυχήσομαι with "weaknesses" (11:30; 12:5, 9); and the correspondence of οὐ ψεύδομαι (11:31) to ἀλήθειαν γὰρ ἐρῶ (12:6).

11:30*If boasting is necessary, I will boast about examples of my*[a] *weakness.* 31*The God*[b] *and Father of the Lord Jesus, who is blessed to all eternity, knows that I am not lying.* 32*In Damascus the ethnarch under King Aretas was guarding the city of the Damascenes in order to*[c] *arrest me,* 33*but I was let down in a basket through a window in the wall and so escaped out of his hands.*

TEXTUAL NOTES

a. The omission of μου after τῆς ἀσθενείας (in 𝔭46 vid B H 1175) may have arisen when a scribe, taking τῆς to be possessive ("my weakness"), regarded μου as otiose.

b. Under the influence of LXX usage, D* adds τοῦ Ἰσραήλ after ὁ θεός, an addi-

---

1. In UBS[1-4] v. 30 begins a new paragraph, but not in WH, NA[27].

2. It is difficult to believe that Paul viewed his hardships (11:21b-29) as illustrations of his weakness (*pace* Windisch 362; Bultmann 217-18; Black 144-46), when he undertook the recital of his trials in an attitude of boasting "in the way the world does" (κατὰ σάρκα, 11:18) and with a view to establishing his superiority over his rivals as a servant of Christ (11:23a). His survival of encounters with death (ἐν θανάτοις πολλάκις, 11:23b-25) and with the dangers associated with travel (ὁδοιπορίαις πολλάκις, 11:26) would, if anything, point to his physical stamina and resilience.

3. Thrall 759 (following Zmijewski 276), who, however, regards vv. 30-31 as transitional (758-61), being both retrospective and prospective (as also Plummer 331-32).

tion that emphasizes the continuity between the old and the new covenant; "the God of Israel" is none other than "the Father of the Lord Jesus."

c. In the phrase πιάσαι με (the reading of B D* it[ar, b, d, f, o] vg syr[p] cop[sa] arm Eusebius Ambrosiaster Pelagius), "in order to arrest me," the infinitive is telic, but to "improve" the style the participle θέλων was added, either before πιάσαι (F G [1739 με πιάσαι] it[g] syr[h] cop[bo] eth) or after με (ℵ D² H Ψ 075 0121 0150 0243 33 81 104 1175 1881 Byz [K L P] Lect geo slav Chrysostom), so that πιάσαι became a (smoother?) complementary infinitive, "wishing to arrest me." The change also anticipated the fact, made explicit in the next verse, that the ethnarch's plan to apprehend Paul was unfulfilled. For these reasons the addition of θέλων is clearly secondary. In UBS[1, 2, 3] πιάσαι με is the preferred text, with a "C" rating (= considerable doubt); in UBS[4], with a "B" rating (= almost certain).

11:30 Εἰ καυχᾶσθαι δεῖ, τὰ τῆς ἀσθενείας μου καυχήσομαι. "If boasting is necessary, I will boast about examples of my weakness." BAGD (172b) classify this use of δεῖ as denoting "an inner necessity, growing out of a given situation." In the present case the "given situation" that necessitated Paul's use of boasting was not merely the Corinthians' ready acceptance of boasters (cf. 10:12-18; 11:12, 18), but in particular his recognition that they would regain their original undivided allegiance to Christ (cf. 11:3) only by his own skilled use of his rivals' successful but worldly technique of boasting. So strong was the Corinthians' own penchant for boasting (1 Cor. 1:26-29; 4:6-7)[4] that καυχᾶσθαι δεῖ, "boasting is a necessity," may have been one of their watchwords.[5] εἰ points to an assumption ("if, as is the case"), not a mere possibility, so that it bears the sense of ἐπεί, "since." In the context the present tense of καυχᾶσθαι and the future tense of καυχήσομαι are probably of special significance, as indicating durative and punctiliar action (respectively): "If I must go on boasting, then I shall change tack and boast no longer of my hardships (11:21b-29) but of my weakness."[6] Boasting κατὰ σάρκα (11:18) gives place to boasting κατὰ πνεῦμα, so to speak, for boasting about one's weakness amounts to "boasting in the Lord" (10:17) since acknowledged human weakness is the scene of Christ's power (12:9).[7]

When, as here, καυχάομαι is used transitively (with the accusative), it means "boast about/of";[8] Classical Greek would normally use εἰς (cf. 10:16). Whereas in 12:5, 9 καυχήσομαι is followed by ἐν ταῖς ἀσθενείαις (μου), "in my weaknesses," here it is preceded by τὰ τῆς ἀσθενείας μου, which means not "my weakness" or "my own feebleness" (JB), but (literally) "the things of

4. See Savage 22-23, 41, 54-62.
5. A suggestion made by Barrett 302, 306.
6. Plummer, however, finds in καυχήσομαι Paul's "general intention and guiding principle; it covers the whole of this foolish glorying" (331; similarly Tasker 167; Zmijewski 278-79; Forbes 20).
7. Cf. Savage 63-64. Black comments that the obverse of "boasting in weakness" is "glorying in God's power" (144).
8. See the analysis of constructions with καυχάομαι at 10:17.

(= relating to) my weakness," that is, "the things that show up my weakness" (NEB, REB), "examples of my weakness," where the "general genitive" points to a relationship defined by the context. The instances he will cite are his escape from Damascus (11:32-33) and his receipt of a σκόλοψ (12:7-9).

11:31 ὁ θεὸς καὶ πατὴρ τοῦ κυρίου Ἰησοῦ οἶδεν, ὁ ὢν εὐλογητὸς εἰς τοὺς αἰῶνας, ὅτι οὐ ψεύδομαι. "The God and Father of the Lord Jesus, who is blessed to all eternity, knows that I am not lying." Here we have a traditional oath formula combined with a traditional doxological formula. Given this formal combination, it is not altogether adequate to explain this oath as "an example of *horkou schema* [ὅρκου σχῆμα] or *figura iusiurandi,* a recognized rhetorical ornament" (Judge 47). At 11:10 we defined a biblical "oath of confirmation" in broad terms as "a direct or indirect appeal to the deity as the guarantor of the truth of a statement, especially one that the readers cannot verify for themselves." Here, as opposed to 1:23 (Ἐγὼ . . . μάρτυρα τὸν θεὸν ἐπικαλοῦμαι), the appeal is indirect; here, as opposed to 11:11, the fuller form of the abbreviated formula, ὁ θεὸς οἶδεν, is found. "God . . . knows that I am not lying" is equivalent to "God . . . is witness to the truth of what I say" (Wand). The negative and positive are combined in Rom. 9:1 (Ἀλήθειαν λέγω ἐν Χριστῷ, οὐ ψεύδομαι) and 1 Tim. 2:7 (ἀλήθειαν λέγω οὐ ψεύδομαι). What is it that Paul has said or will say that has divine validation as to its truthfulness? Some refer the oath to Paul's litany of trials (11:23b-29),[9] others to the preceding verse (11:30) with its paradoxical claim that he will boast only about his weaknesses,[10] while yet others discover a forward reference to 11:32-33.[11] Hughes is probably right in applying the oath both to v. 30 and to the instances of Paul's weakness cited in 11:32-33 (his escape from Damascus) and 12:7-8 (his "thorn in the flesh") (419-20).[12] To Paul, an oath seemed demanded because of the extraordinary circumstances that gave rise to these two incidents (the animosity of King Aretas and the ascent into paradise) and because the trustworthiness of his word had been impugned (cf. 1:17-18). This solemn appeal to God's knowledge of his truthfulness (cf. 11:11) was not, of course, a repudiation of Christ's ban on unnecessary or frivolous oath-taking (cf. Matt. 5:33-37; cf. Jas. 5:12).

The expression ὁ θεὸς καὶ πατὴρ τοῦ κυρίου Ἰησοῦ also occurs in 1:3 (with the addition of ἡμῶν and Χριστοῦ). As coordinated personal nouns standing under the nexus of a single article, θεός and πατήρ have a single referent; "God" is none other than "the Father of the Lord Jesus." This identity of person is also made clear by the phrase ἀπὸ θεοῦ πατρὸς ἡμῶν in 1:2 where πατρός stands in epexegetic apposition to θεοῦ, "from God (who is) our Father." If, then, θεός and πατήρ are linked together by a single article yet separated by καί, the probability is that the dependent genitive τοῦ κυρίου Ἰησοῦ is related as

9. E.g., Windisch 362; Bultmann 218.
10. E.g., Martin 384; Thrall 762-63.
11. E.g., Bruce 244; *Paraphrase* 155; Witherington 458.
12. Furnish sees a primary reference to v. 30 and a secondary reference to vv. 32-33 (540).

much to θεός as to πατήρ. That is, God is not only the Father of the Lord Jesus but also the God of the Lord Jesus.[13] So it is preferable to render the whole expression by "the God and Father of the Lord Jesus,"[14] rather than by "God, the Father of the Lord Jesus."[15] To express this latter sense we would expect ὁ θεὸς ὁ πατὴρ κτλ. or ὁ θεὸς πατὴρ κτλ.[16] It is true that the unambiguous statement "the God of our Lord Jesus Christ" (ὁ θεὸς τοῦ κυρίου ἡμῶν Ἰησοῦ Χριστοῦ) is found only in Eph. 1:17, but for the grammatical reason given above we may legitimately infer from the expression ὁ θεὸς καὶ πατὴρ τοῦ κυρίου (ἡμῶν) Ἰησοῦ (Χριστοῦ) found in Rom. 15:6; 2 Cor. 1:3; 11:31; Eph. 1:3 (also 1 Pet. 1:3) that the Father is the "God of Jesus."[17]

The doxology has two parallels in Romans.

2 Cor. 11:31 ὁ θεὸς . . . ,   ὁ ὢν   εὐλογητὸς εἰς τοὺς αἰῶνας, . . .
Rom. 1:25   . . . τὸν κτίσαντα, ὅς ἐστιν εὐλογητὸς εἰς τοὺς αἰῶνας, ἀμήν.
Rom. 9:5   . . . ὁ Χριστὸς . . . , ὁ ὢν . . . εὐλογητὸς εἰς τοὺς αἰῶνας, ἀμήν.[18]

In our verse, it is natural to find the antecedent of ὁ ὢν in ὁ θεὸς καὶ πατήρ, since both expressions are nominative; if the articular participle referred to τοῦ κυρίου Ἰησοῦ we would expect τοῦ ὄντος.[19] The parallel in Rom. 1:25 shows that ὁ ὢν is probably relatival (= ὅς ἐστιν, "who is"). Such a relatival use of the articular participle is not uncommon in NT Greek (see BDF §412), and there are eight other NT uses of ὁ ὢν (or οἱ ὄντες) in this sense.[20] But it is also possible that ὁ ὢν is substantival, in apposition to ὁ θεὸς καὶ πατήρ: "The God and Father . . . , he who is blessed forever, . . ." (RSV).[21] This articular participle should be seen as introducing a descriptive, not a volitive, doxology;[22] it means "(he) who is," not "(blessed) be he" (NRSV[23]). εὐλογητός, "blessed," has the

13. So also Thrall 102, 762.
14. All 18 EVV consulted translate the expression this way. So also most commentators; e.g., Lietzmann 150; Wolff 229; Lambrecht 187.
15. So Furnish 513; Carrez 224; Lang 342.
16. Cf. the text and variants in Col. 1:3. The preferred text reads Εὐχαριστοῦμεν τῷ θεῷ πατρὶ τοῦ κυρίου ἡμῶν Ἰησοῦ Χριστοῦ πάντοτε ("We always give thanks to God, the Father of our Lord Jesus Christ"), where D* G 2005 Chrysostom read τῷ θεῷ πατρί. The other variant τῷ θεῷ καὶ πατρί (ℵ A C² Dᶜ I K P Ψ 33 81 614 *Byz Lect*) would produce the sense "the God and Father. . . ."
17. Note also those passages in which Jesus speaks of "my God" (Matt. 27:46//Mark 15:34; John 20:17; cf. Rev. 3:2, 12), and those in which reference is made to "his God and Father" (Rev. 1:6) or "your God" (Heb. 1:9), where "his" and "your" refer to Jesus.
18. On the punctuation and exegetical problems of Rom. 9:5, see Harris, *Jesus* 143-72.
19. Any possible reference to Jesus is excluded in the REB rendering ("He who is blessed for ever, the God and Father . .") and in Young and Ford (274) ("The God and Father . . . , God who is blessed for ever, . . .").
20. John 1:18; 11:31; 12:17; Acts 11:1; Rom. 9:5; 2 Cor. 5:4; Eph. 2:13; Col. 4:11 (see also John 3:13 v. l.).
21. Similarly RV, Cassirer; Barrett 289; Martin 367; Lambrecht 187.
22. For this distinction, see 1:3.
23. Similarly NEB, NAB¹.

sense "worthy and entitled to receive worship and praise from every sentient being, whether angelic, human, or demonic."[24] Being an epithet that is applied only to God or Christ, it may (with the article) stand as a periphrasis for the divine name (Mark 14:61). It scarcely does justice to the phrase εἰς τοὺς αἰῶνας to render it "ever(-blessed)" (Martin 367), for it is an abbreviation of εἰς τοὺς αἰῶνας τῶν αἰώνων (Gal. 1:5; Phil. 4:20; 1 Tim. 1:17; 2 Tim. 4:18) and may be rendered "to all eternity" (BAGD 27c; cf. BDF §141[1]).[25] As H. Sasse observes (TDNT 1.199), this plural use of αἰών in doxologies "is simply designed to emphasize the idea of eternity which is contained but often blurred in the sing[ular] αἰών." Paul has inserted this doxology in the middle of the sentence (thus no ἀμήν; cf. Rom. 1:25; 9:5) perhaps because he is about to appeal boldly and once more (cf. 11:11) to the divine omniscience (οἶδεν). Some EVV reflect this unusual position of the doxology between subject and verb by making it a parenthesis, using either brackets or dashes.[26]

11:32 ἐν Δαμασκῷ ὁ ἐθνάρχης Ἀρέτα τοῦ βασιλέως ἐφρούρει τὴν πόλιν Δαμασκηνῶν πιάσαι με. "In Damascus the ethnarch under King Aretas was guarding the city of the Damascenes in order to arrest me." Sometimes the account of Paul's escape from the clutches of Aretas (in vv. 32-33) is seen as being "out of context, out of style, quite out of connexion."[27] But if the position of this pericope is so inappropriate, it is difficult to imagine what prompted Paul's amanuensis or a scribe to insert the story at this point. It is decidedly more satisfactory to regard this pericope as an instance of Paul's weakness and humiliation (v. 30),[28] and as a demonstration of God's intervention (through Paul's friends in Damascus) to preserve his chosen instrument (cf. Acts 9:15) from danger, that is, as an evidence of God's or Christ's power operating in the midst of human weakness (4:7; 12:9-10). Paul may have had additional reasons for including this episode. Because it was probably the first attempt on his life, it had been indelibly impressed on his memory. Also, his detractors may have pointed to it as unassailable proof of his cowardice (cf. 10:1, 10). Whatever the reasons for its inclusion at this point, the episode, narrated here with remarkable economy of language, forms a striking literary backdrop for what follows:

24. For this threefold division, see Phil. 2:10 (ἐπουρανίων καὶ ἐπιγείων καὶ καταχθονίων).

25. Cf. Carrez 224, "pour l'éternité"; and most German commentators render εἰς τοὺς αἰῶνας by "in Ewigkeit" (not, "auf Ewig," "for ever") — e.g., Lietzmann 150; Wendland 240; Lang 342; Wolff 229.

26. So TCNT, Weymouth, NEB, JB, NAB[1], NJB, NRSV.

27. So Bishop (189), who proposes that the gloss that has crept into 2 Corinthians 11 (namely vv. 32-33) rightly belongs between Gal. 1:17 and 1:18. Betz, following Windisch (363-66), regards vv. 32-33 as a later interpolation (73 n. 201).

28. So also Hughes 422; Barrett 303; Furnish 541-42. Martin proposes that the OT passage which in 10:4-5 Paul applies to himself as a "wise man" (Prov. 21:22, "A wise man scales the cities of the mighty and brings down the stronghold in which the godless trust," LXX [Martin's translation]), he has reapplied in v. 33 to his opponents or to the Corinthians as "the wise." If they scaled the city walls of the mighty, he could manage only to be let down in a fish basket (384-85). But Paul's readers could scarcely be expected to recognize such a reapplication.

first, an embarrassing descent to escape the hands of men, then an exhilarating ascent into the presence of God (12:2-4).

The Ἀρέτας ὁ βασιλεύς that Paul refers to is Aretas IV who ruled the desert kingdom of Nabataea (= the "Arabia" of Gal. 1:17) from 9 B.C. to A.D. 40.[29] His daughter was married to Herod Antipas, tetrarch of Galilee and Perea, but about A.D. 27 Antipas divorced her in favor of Herodias, formerly the wife of one of his brothers, Herod Philip (Matt. 14:3-4). Aretas's revenge for his daughter's ill-treatment came in A.D. 36 when he contested a boundary with Antipas, defeating Antipas's army. The emperor Tiberius sent Vitellius, legate of Syria, to punish Aretas, but the death of the emperor in A.D. 37 ended the expedition (Josephus, *Antiquities* 18.109-26).

There are three main ways of understanding the historical background to v. 32, and they correspond to the three possible meanings of ἐθνάρχης.

1. *Tribal chief.* On this view the "ethnarch" was a Bedouin sheikh of some Nabatean tribe, lying in wait outside the walls of Damascus to arrest Paul when he exited.[30] But there are two difficulties: Paul's escape down the city wall (v. 32) implies that the danger lay within the city, not outside; at this stage in their history the Nabateans were no longer nomadic (Riesner 85).

2. *Governor* (many EVV) or *viceroy* (Ogg 19, 22) or *prefect* (Meyer 666). In this case the assumption is that the whole city of Damascus was under Nabatean rule at the time and that the ethnarch was Aretas's representative in that city.[31] In support of this view it is argued (1) that ἐφρούρει τὴν πόλιν suggests that the ethnarch exercised authority over the entire city, with ἐφρούρει meaning "kept (the city of the Damascenes) with a garrison" (KJV);[32] (2) that the absence of Roman coins in Damascus dating from A.D. 34-62 (including the reigns of Caligula [Gaius] and Claudius, A.D. 37-41 and A.D. 41-54 respectively) indicates non-Roman rule in Damascus during those years;[33] and (3) that Damascus may have been handed over to Nabatean sovereignty by Caligula between A.D. 37 and A.D. 40 to placate Aretas after the abortive campaign of Tiberius against Aretas.[34]

Regarding these three points: (1) ἐφρούρει τὴν πόλιν need mean nothing more than "kept the city under observation" (NEB, REB) or "was keeping a close watch on the city" (NAB[1]) or "had patrols out in the city" (Moffatt). But

---

29. For a history of Nabatea, see Lawlor, *The Nabataeans,* Negev in *ANRW* II/8.549-635, Bowersock, *Roman Arabia,* and, more briefly, Starcky, *BA* 18 (1955) 84-106. On Aretas IV, see Steinmann, *Aretas IV* and *BZ* 7 (1909) 174-84, 312-41, and, more briefly, D. F. Graf in *ABD* 1.374-75.

30. This basic position is held by Lenski 1289; Lang 345. For other proponents see Riesner 84 n. 66, 85 n. 67.

31. So, e.g., Allo 301-2; Ogg 19-22; Bowersock 68-69; Taylor 719-28; Welborn 52-71; Thrall 769-70.

32. Welborn, "Tirocinium" 52, 54-55, 59, 70.

33. E.g., E. Schürer, *The History of the Jewish People in the Age of Jesus Christ,* vol. 1, rev. and ed. G. Vermes, F. Millar, and M. Black (Edinburgh: Clark, 1973) 582.

34. Cf. Ogg 22.

the Lukan parallel passage (Acts 9:24, "they were watching the gates") suggests that Paul's meaning may be "kept guards at the city gates" (NLT).[35] In any case, Paul did not say τὴν πᾶσαν πόλιν, and if the ethnarch controlled the city one wonders why an immediate arrest was not possible once Paul was found, without garrisoning the whole city. (2) The gap in the numismatic record is negative, and therefore indecisive, evidence. Moreover, Roman coins from Damascus are extremely rare even under Augustus, Tiberius, and Nero.[36] (3) If Damascus was in Nabatean hands at the time of Paul's escape, it is uncertain how and when it ceased to be under Roman control.[37]

3. *Head of an ethnic community* (cf. ἔθνος, "race," "people" + ἄρχων, "ruler"). On this interpretation, the ethnarch was the head of a colony of Nabateans in Damascus, and in this capacity the representative of King Aretas in that city.[38] Several considerations support this view.

(a) The Jewish ἐθνάρχης in Alexandria performed a similar role, representing Jewish interests there (Josephus, *Antiquities* 14.117; Strabo 17.798).

(b) Nabatean governors bore the title στρατηγός, not ἐθνάρχης (Knauf 146 n. 6).

(c) Archaeology and topography have established the existence of a Nabatean quarter in the northeast sector of Damascus before the first century A.D.[39]

(d) Gal. 1:17 speaks of Paul's return to Damascus from Arabia, which indicates that at least either at the time of his return (c. A.D. 35) or at the time of writing (c. A.D. 48 if early, c. A.D. 55 if late) Damascus was not under Nabatean control.[40]

(e) Just as ἐφρούρει need not indicate a formal garrisoning of the whole city of Damascus (see above under [2]), πιάσαι need not point to a formal arrest by a military commander, as if ἐθνάρχης were equivalent to

---

35. Even Field, who believes the ethnarch was in possession of the whole city, says, "We must understand that he placed a watch at the gates" (187, citing in support Dionysius of Halicarnassus, *Antiquitates Romanae* 5.57). While οἱ φρουροῦντες can mean "the guardians" (see LSJ [1957] s.v. I.), ἐφρούρει τὴν πόλιν could scarcely mean "was guardian of the city" (Bowersock 68-69), since Paul continues πιάσαι με ("to arrest me").

36. See Riesner 80-82.

37. This is acknowledged by Welborn ("Tirocinium" 67 n. 117), citing three possibilities suggested by Steinmann (26-38).

38. Thus Burton 57; Bruce 245; *Paul* 81; *Galatians* 96; Knauf 146-47; Klauck 90-91; Riesner 85-86. The NEB and REB rendering ("the commissioner of King Aretas") would fit views (2) and (3), if we take a "commissioner" to be the representative of a supreme authority in a region. Knauf argues that the ἐθνάρχης was "the head of the Nabataean trade colony in Damascus, who at the same time probably represented the interests of the Nabataean state, and so was a kind of consul" (147).

39. See the evidence cited by Riesner 86-87.

40. Otherwise this would be equivalent to saying that someone returned to Chicago from Illinois or to London from England.

στρατηγός. It may refer to a simple "seizing" by those guarding the city exits.[41]

If, with many EVV,[42] we translate the genitive Ἀρέτα τοῦ βασιλέως by "under King Aretas," "under" may have the sense "at the time of" or "appointed by" (Wand). But probably more is implied: the ethnarch was "acting for" Aretas (Isaacs) or even "acting by King Aretas' order" (Phillips).[43] However that be, some reason must be given for the virulent opposition of Aretas or his ethnarch. It could have been prompted by Paul's evangelistic activity in Damascus itself, but it seems more likely, in the light of Paul's argument in Galatians 1, that his visit to Arabia (Gal. 1:17) was undertaken to begin fulfilling his commission to "preach him [the Son of God] among the Gentiles" (Gal. 1:16). Commenting on Gal. 1:16-17, Lake observes that "the antithesis is not between conferring with flesh and blood in Jerusalem, and conferring with God in the desert, but between obeying immediately the commission of God to preach to the Gentiles, and going to some human source in Jerusalem in order to obtain authority or additional instruction. St. Paul's argument seems to me to require the sense 'As soon as I received my divine commission, I acted upon it at once, without consulting any one, and began to preach in Arabia'" (320-21).[44]

11:33 καὶ διὰ θυρίδος ἐν σαργάνῃ ἐχαλάσθην διὰ τοῦ τείχους καὶ ἐξέφυγον τὰς χεῖρας αὐτοῦ. "But I was let down in a basket through a window in the wall and so [consecutive καί] escaped out of his hands." In spite of the ongoing precautions (ἐφρούρει, linear imperfect) taken by the ethnarch, his desire to have Paul seized (v. 32) was frustrated by a stratagem carried out by Paul's supporters in Damascus. The escape was made διὰ θυρίδος . . . διὰ τοῦ τείχους. To reflect these two uses of διά + genitive, the phrases are sometimes rendered "through a window . . . through the wall" (Thrall 722). Clearly Paul escaped by passing "through" both the window and the wall, but English idiom prefers to say "through a window in the wall" (RSV, NRSV). "Along the wall" (BDF §223[5]) is a dubious rendering of διὰ τοῦ τείχους in 11:33, however one translates the same phrase in Acts 9:25 (where there is no διὰ θυρίδος).[45] This θυρίς should not be thought of as a rectangular opening enclosed with glass or shutters but as a narrow vertical opening in the wall to admit light and air and to

---

41. Cf. Riesner 88. He also notes that the expression πόλις Δαμασκηνῶν is attested on coins as a designation of this Roman free city (87). If this phrase was regarded as a title of honor, Δαμασκηνῶν (the genitive denoting the inhabitants of the city — BAGD 685c) should not be regarded as redundant after ἐν Δαμασκῷ ("When I was in Damascus").

42. E.g., RSV, GNB, NAB², NRSV.

43. Such an assumption answers Meyer's objection (given in defense of view [2]) "that Paul would have had no reason for adding Ἀρέτα *(sic)* τοῦ βασιλέως, if at the very time of the flight the Roman city had not been exceptionally (and temporarily) subject to Aretas" (666).

44. Similarly Bruce, *Galatians* 96; *Paul* 81-82; and for Paul's preaching in Arabia, Masson, "Note" 165-66.

45. RSV has "over the wall" in Acts 9:25.

enable people to see out (= the technical term "loophole," used by Moffatt and Wand).[46]

The agents implied by the passive ἐχαλάσθην ("I was let down") must have been at least sympathizers of Paul who were concerned for his safety. Luke's parallel account calls them "his disciples" (οἱ μαθηταὶ αὐτοῦ, Acts 9:25), which perhaps means simply "his converts" (NEB). Evidently his Damascene preaching of Jesus as the Son of God and the Messiah (Acts 9:20, 22) had proved fruitful. If, then, Paul left Damascus with the help of his Christian friends, and perhaps at their urging, his departure can scarcely be deemed a desertion of the infant Damascus church[47] or the action of a "runaway."[48]

It has become commonplace for commentators to mention the novel suggestion of Judge that in recounting his humiliating descent down the Damascene wall Paul is parodying the Roman award — the *corona muralis,* the "wall crown" — given to the first soldier to scale a fortified city wall under enemy attack. So far from being "first up," Paul was "first down."[49] Now there can be little doubt that the residents of Roman Corinth — Paul's addressees — would have known of this military award (στέφανος τείχικος in Greek), but it is less than certain that they would have recognized an allusion to this in the phrase ἐχαλάσθην διὰ τοῦ τείχους, for in the supposed reversal of imagery the crucial element of "firstness" is missing.

The final issue to be considered is the relation between Paul's account of his escape and Luke's narrative in Acts 9:23-25. For ease of comparison the two accounts may be reproduced, with information peculiar to each italicized.

Acts 9:23-25

23(Ὡς δὲ ἐπληροῦντο ἡμέραι ἱκαναί), συνεβουλεύσαντο οἱ Ἰουδαῖοι ἀνελεῖν αὐτόν· 24ἐγνώσθη δὲ τῷ Σαύλῳ ἡ ἐπιβουλὴ αὐτῶν. παρετηροῦντο δὲ καὶ τὰς πύλας ἡμέρας τε καὶ νυκτὸς ὅπως αὐτὸν ἀνέλωσιν· 25λαβόντες δὲ οἱ μαθηταὶ αὐτοῦ νυκτὸς διὰ τοῦ τείχους καθῆκαν αὐτὸν χαλάσαντες ἐν σπυρίδι.

2 Cor. 11:32-33

32ἐν Δαμασκῷ ὁ ἐθνάρχης Ἀρέτα τοῦ βασιλέως ἐφρούρει τὴν πόλιν Δαμασκηνῶν πιάσαι με, 33καὶ διὰ θυρίδος ἐν σαργάνῃ ἐχαλάσθην διὰ τοῦ τείχους καὶ ἐξέφυγον τὰς χεῖρας αὐτοῦ.

46. Cf. ἐπὶ τῆς θυρίδος in Acts 20:9 (of Eutychus seated "in the window" = "on the window ledge," NEB); διὰ τῆς θυρίδος in 1 Kgdms. 19:12 (LXX) (of David's escape "through the window").

47. But see Trocmé 475-79.

48. But see Welborn, "Runaway."

49. Judge, "Conflict" 44-45. On this award, see Polybius 6.39.5; Livy 6.20.8; 10.46.3; 26.48.5; Aulus Gellius, *Noctes Atticae* 5.6.16. For a picture of this "wall crown" adorning the head of the Greek goddess Τύχη, see Plate VIII in Furnish (between pp. 314 and 315).

Differences between these two accounts

	Acts	2 Corinthians
(1) Opposition	οἱ Ἰουδαῖοι	ὁ ἐθνάρχης Ἀρέτα τοῦ βασιλέως
(2) Aim	(συνεβουλεύσαντο . . .) ἀνελεῖν αὐτὸν [Σαῦλον] . . . ὅπως αὐτὸν ἀνέλωσιν	(ἐφρούρει . . .) πιάσαι με
(3) Action Taken	παρετηροῦντο . . . τὰς πύλας	ἐφρούρει τὴν πόλιν Δαμασκηνῶν
(4) Mode of Escape	ἐν σπυρίδι	ἐν σαργάνῃ

Are these four apparent discrepancies irreconcilable?

(1) Is it not possible that there was a coalition in Damascus among those opposed to Paul, although the motives for their animosity differed? The Nabatean ethnarch may have been acting at the direction of Aretas, who sought reprisal for Paul's sowing of religious discord in Nabatea through his preaching of a Jewish Messiah. The Jews, on the other hand, must have resented Paul's evangelistic success in their Damascene synagogues (cf. Acts 9:20-22) in preaching what to them was an aberrant form of their faith and so may have eagerly cooperated with the ethnarch.[50] Alternatively, the initiative in opposition may have come from the Jews, who capitalized on official Nabatean hostility toward Paul and enlisted the ethnarch's support to capture him.[51]

(2) Even if the Nabatean ethnarch and the Damascene Jews were united in their desire to silence Paul, they may have differed in the intensity of their antagonism and in the intended way of silencing him. The Jews plotted to kill (ἀνελεῖν) him, the ethnarch wanted to apprehend him or take him into custody (πιάσαι), perhaps with a view to questioning him or sending him for trial in Nabatea itself.

(3) In discussing v. 32 we saw that Paul's expression ἐφρούρει τὴν πόλιν probably means "kept guards at the city gates" (NLT) or "had the gates of the city guarded," which matches Luke's "they kept watch on the gates."

50. That there were numerous Jews in Damascus at that time is clear from Josephus, *Bellum Judaicum* 2.559-61; 7.368.

51. Some scholars, however, prefer Paul's testimony over Luke's. Masson, for instance, argues that in Acts 9:23-25 Luke shows a literary dependence on 2 Cor. 11:32-33 but refers to opposition from Jews rather than from the ethnarch (as a result of Paul's preaching in Arabia) in order to preserve Peter's role, described in Acts 10–11 (the Cornelius episode), as the first missionary to the Gentiles ("Note" 164-66). Or again, Harding doubts Luke's reliability in referring to Jewish antagonism to Paul in Damascus, alleging a Lukan propensity to heighten the guilt of the Jews both in his gospel and in Acts (528-29). It is unlikely (*pace* Hughes [424], who entertains this possibility) that the ethnarch was himself a Jew, so that the guard he appointed was composed entirely of Jews.

(4) Whereas English has the one comprehensive term "basket," NT Greek has three words[52]: κόφινος was a stiff wicker basket, generally used for agricultural purposes (Hort 567-68); σπυρίς (sometimes spelled σφυρίς) was a flexible mat-basket, made of materials such as rushes and often used for carrying fish or edibles generally (Hort 567); σαργάνη also was a flexible woven basket, sometimes sufficiently large to carry sizable shields (Hort 571).[53] Both a σπυρίς and a σαργάνη could be large and sturdy enough to hold a person.

As we relate Acts 9 to 2 Corinthians 11 and Galatians 1, Paul's movements may be summarized as follows.

(a) Conversion outside Damascus (Acts 9:1-8)
(b) Residence in Damascus (Acts 9:9-24)
(c) Preaching in Damascene synagogues (Acts 9:20-22)
(d) In Arabia (= the Nabatean kingdom) (Gal. 1:17)
(e) Return to Damascus (Gal. 1:17)
(f) Escape from Damascus (Acts 9:25; 2 Cor. 11:32-33)
(g) First post-conversion visit to Jerusalem (Acts 9:26-29; Gal. 1:18-24).

What made Paul's escape from Damascus so memorable was that it took place at night, not in daylight; he exited through a window and down the city wall, not via the city gates; he left in a basket, not on foot or horseback. It is highly ironical that the man who had set his face toward Damascus in a daylight advance against his foes (Acts 9:1-2; 22:6) now turned his back on Damascus in a nocturnal retreat from his foes (note also the contrasting warrior image in 10:3-6).

Bibliography

Becker 231-39 • Bishop • Bonnard • Bowersock • Fahy • Harding, "Historicity" • Hort • Jewett, *Chronology* 30-33 • Judge • Knauf • Lake 320-23 • J. I. Lawlor, *The Nabataeans in Historical Perspective* (Grand Rapids: Baker, 1973) • Masson, "Note" • A. Negev, "The Nabataeans and the Provincia Arabia," *ANRW* II/8, 549-635 • Ogg • Osborne • Riesner 75-89 • E. Schürer, "Der Ethnarch des Königs Aretas, 2 Kor. 11,32," *TSK* 72 (1899) 95-99 • B. Schwank, "Neue Funde in Nabatäerstädten und ihre Bedeutung für die neutestamentliche Exegese," *NTS* 29 (1983) 429-35 • Starcky • Steinmann • A. Steinmann, "Aretas IV, König der Nabatäer," *BZ* 7 (1909) 174-84, 312-41 • Taylor • Travis • Trocmé • Welborn, "Tirocinium" • Welborn, "Runaway"

52. For the four Hebrew terms for "basket," see Spicq 3.229 n. 1.
53. See further Spicq 3.229-30, who also regards σπυρίς and σαργάνη as almost synonymous and as being of various sizes and shapes.

7. A Vision and Its Aftermath (12:1-10)

We have seen that 11:30-33 begins a new section, with three specific links with 12:1-10.[1] These ten verses fall into three sections: (1) v. 1 introduces the theme of "visions and revelations"; (2) vv. 2-6 describe Paul's ascent into paradise; (3) vv. 7-10 recount his subsequent receipt of a "thorn in the flesh" and the outcome.[2] Sections (1) and (3) are linked by the words ἀποκαλύψεις (v. 1) and τῶν ἀποκαλύψεων (v. 7); sections (2) and (3) by the phrase καυχήσομαι ἐν ταῖς ἀσθενείαις (μου) (vv. 5, 9). As Paul continues to boast (v. 1) of things that demonstrate his weakness (11:30), he cites a second celebrated instance. There was not only his ignominious nocturnal escape from Damascene plotters (11:32-33), but also his painful and incapacitating physical malady, his "thorn in the flesh," that was his constant companion (12:7). But to explain why he was given this σκόλοψ he needed to recount, in outline form, his privileged journey to paradise some fourteen years earlier (12:2-4). That necessity afforded him a suitable opportunity (in 12:5-6) to address an issue that his opponents' claims to special "visions and revelations" (cf. 12:1) had raised among the Corinthians — the relevance of such spiritual experiences in assessing claims to apostolic authority.

Verses 2-10 depict a fascinating sequence of events: a heavenly ascent (vv. 2-4), immediate(?) receipt of the σκόλοψ (v. 7), immediate(?) and repeated prayer for its removal (v. 8), denial of the petition (implied by the adversative καί) after the third request but Christ's assurance of his gracious power to endure the σκόλοψ (v. 9a), Paul's consequent ability (οὖν, v. 9b; διό, v. 10) to boast about (v. 9b) and take pleasure in (v. 10) his weaknesses. Clearly, then, vv. 9-10 form the climax of 12:1-10, just as 12:1-10 is the acme of the whole "Fool's Speech" (11:21b–12:13).

According to Betz, 12:1-10 is a parody of accounts of ecstatic rapture (vv. 2-4) and healing miracles (vv. 7b-10), both being contemporary forms of religious propaganda. In the former case, Paul recounts a vision but denies being able to communicate what he has heard; in the latter case, he imitates a Hellenistic narrative of a healing miracle but the expected divine oracle provides no cure.[3] Certainly a revelatory experience that produces no revelation and a healing narrative without an actual physical healing could be understood as parodic, but could not these ironical features arise from the actual events themselves rather than be a literary construct, even if based on a historical nucleus? That is, the ῥήματα were, paradoxically, ἄρρητα (v. 4), because they were in fact incapable of being communicated in human language, while the divine response to Paul's thrice-repeated petition was a denial of the physical healing requested (v. 8) but the provision of spiritual healing (v. 9). Moreover, although the two

1. See the introduction to 11:30-33.

2. Some, however, divide 12:1-10 into five structural units: v. 1, introduction; vv. 2-4, rapture into paradise; vv. 5-7a, character and grounds for boasting; vv. 7b-9a, the σκόλοψ and its persistence; vv. 9b-10, strength in weakness (Spittler 262 n. 17).

3. Betz, *Paulus* 72-73, 84-100; "Christus-Aretalogie" 288-305.

putative parodies appear in the "Fool's Speech," Paul's style in 12:1-10 is formal and elevated, not in any sense satirical or jocular, with multiple references to God's knowledge (vv. 2-3) and action (ἐδόθη [v. 7] is a "theological passive"), and to the person of Christ (vv. 1-2, 8-9).[4]

12:1*It is necessary[a] to boast[b]. Although[c] boasting is not beneficial[d], I will come to visions and revelations granted by the Lord. 2I know a man in Christ who, fourteen years ago — whether in the body, I do not know, or out of the body, I do not know (God knows) — was caught up to the third heaven. 3Indeed, I know that such a man — whether in the body or apart from[e] the body, I do not know[f] (God knows) — 4was caught up into paradise and heard inexpressible words that a human is not permitted to utter. 5I will boast about such a man, but about myself I will not boast[g], except of my[h] weaknesses. 6But if I do wish to boast[i], I shall not turn out to be foolish, for I shall be speaking the truth; but I refrain, lest anyone should esteem me beyond what he sees in me or hears from me in any respect[j]. 7And because of the extraordinary nature of the revelations, therefore[k], so that I might not become over-elated, there was given me a thorn in the flesh, a messenger of Satan[l] sent to pommel me, so that I might not become over-elated[m]. 8About this I implored the Lord three times that it should leave me. 9But he has said to me, "My grace is sufficient for you; for my power[n] reaches perfection[o] in weakness." Very gladly, therefore, I will rather boast of my[p] weaknesses, in order that the power of Christ may rest upon me. 10That is why I take pleasure in weaknesses, in insults, in[q] calamities, in persecutions and[r] difficulties, endured for Christ. For when I am weak, then I am strong.*

TEXTUAL NOTES

a. In the place of δεῖ (p⁴⁶ B D² F G H L P 0243 0278 6 33 81 104 365 629 630 1175 1241 1739 1881 2464 *pm* latt syr sa bo^ms), some witnesses have δέ (ℵ D* Ψ bo [Ambrosiaster]), which is an easier (and therefore probably secondary) reading that avoids asyndeton, while other inferior witnesses read δή (K 0121 945 1505 *pm*), an uncommon NT particle meaning "indeed," "therefore" and used only once by Paul (1 Cor. 6:20) (but see Hughes 428 n. 97). For conjectural emendations on this verse, see Windisch 367.

b. Those witnesses that read εἰ before καυχᾶσθαι δεῖ (ℵ² H 81 326 1175 *pc* a f vg sa Ambrosiaster) have been influenced by the wording of 11:30.

c. The best array of witnesses (proto-Alexandrian — p⁴⁶ ℵ 1739; later Alexandrian — H 0243 33 81 1175; Western — F G) reads δέ after ἐλεύσομαι, answering to the earlier μέν, although B has the stronger δὲ καί ("yet indeed"), and D Ψ 1881 𝔐 syr have γάρ, which leaves μέν without its customary δέ.

d. As the most difficult reading, and with superior attestation (p⁴⁶ ℵ B F G (P: -ρει) 0243 0278 33 1175 1739 *pc* [f vg] cop), συμφέρον μέν is to be preferred over συμφέρει (D* 81) and συμφέρει μοι (D¹ H Ψ 1881 𝔐 it vg^ms syr^h Ambrosiaster Pelagius), where συμφέρει simply matches the following finite verb ἐλεύσομαι in the δέ- clause.

---

4. Cf. Thrall 777; "Journey" 350. See further on Betz's view, Zmijewski 379; Wolff 241.

e. Under the influence of the corresponding phrase in v. 2, some witnesses (א D²
F G H Ψ 0121 0243 0278 33 1739 1881 𝔐 latt) read ἐκτός in place of χωρίς (p⁴⁶ B D*
Methodius[acc. to Epiphanius]), which is the more difficult reading and probably original.

f. Perhaps to avoid an unnecessary repetition of the same phrase found in the parallel statement in v. 2, some witnesses (B sa Irenaeus[lat]) omit οὐκ οἶδα. It is less likely
that the phrase was added in v. 3 under the influence of v. 2.

g. Instead of οὐ, a few witnesses (p⁴⁶ lat) read the stronger οὐδέν ("in no respect").

h. In the phrase ἐν ταῖς ἀσθενείαις (read by p⁴⁶ B D* 0243 0278 6 33 1175 1739 *pc*
syr cop) the article is clearly possessive in the light of the preceding ἐμαυτοῦ ("my
weaknesses"), but many witnesses (א D² F G Ψ 0121 1881 𝔐 lat Ambrosiaster) add μου
after ἀσθενείαις to remove any ambiguity.

i. p⁴⁶ alone has the reading (ἐὰν . . .) θέλω, καυχήσομαι ("[if] I choose, I shall
boast"), which may have arisen (as Thrall 799 n. 213 suggests) through two independent
scribal errors — "the accidental omission of the ΗΣ of θελήσω and the assimilation of
καυχήσασθαι to the previous καυχήσομαι of v. 5b."

j. External attestation is strong both for the shorter reading, ἀκούει (א* B D² F G
I 6 33 81 1175 1739 *pc* a b vg[st] cop) (preferred by WH) and for the longer reading,
ἀκούει τι (p⁴⁶ א² D* Ψ 0243 0278 1881 𝔐 f vg[cl] syr[h] Ambrosiaster). Clearly the latter
reading is the more difficult, and copyists may have dropped τι as being superfluous and
disruptive to the syntax (as Metzger 516 notes). All four editions of the UBS text and
NA²⁷ include τι in their text but within square brackets (indicating a disputed reading).
In its present position after ἀκούει, τι is certainly awkward (if it had preceded ἀκούει or
followed λογίσηται, it would have been readily intelligible), so it could be a case where
the principle *lectio difficilior potior* ("the more difficult reading is to be preferred") is inapplicable. But this difficult reading should not be considered impossible and dismissed
as a scribal error, for τι may be construed as an accusative of respect ("in any respect")
that is parallel to the preceding με, which is probably also such an accusative ("with respect to me" = "in me"). Thrall tentatively proposes (801 n. 228) that τι was displaced
from an original position after λογίσηται.

k. διό is omitted by many witnesses (p⁴⁶ D Ψ 1881 𝔐 lat sa Irenaeus[lat]) but should
be retained as the probable original reading (preferred by WH, NA²⁷, and UBS[1, 2, 3] with
a {D} rating [= very high degree of doubt], and by UBS⁴ with a {C} rating [= uncertain])
on the basis of (i) strong external attestation (א A B F G 0243 33 81 1175 1739 *pc* syr[h]
bo); (ii) its being the more difficult reading (assuming that v. 7a begins a new sentence
— see the commentary there); (iii) the frequency of διό in Paul (27 of 53 NT uses, of
which nine are in 2 Corinthians, including this instance).

l. In place of the form Σατανᾶ, read by p⁴⁶ א* A* B D* F G 0243 1739 *pc,* some
witnesses read the indeclinable form Σατάν (א² Aᶜ D¹ Ψ 33 1881 𝔐 syr[h]). Σατάν transliterates the Hebrew *śāṭān* while Σατανᾶς represents the Aramaic *sāṭānāʾ*.

m. The second occurrence of the phrase ἵνα μὴ ὑπεραίρωμαι in v. 7 is omitted by א*
A D F G 33 629* *pc* lat Irenaeus[lat], doubtless because the phrase is repetitive and seems
otiose. But its originality is defensible on the ground of external support (p⁴⁶ א² B I[vid] Ψ
0243 0278 1739 [1881] 𝔐 a syr cop Cyprian Ambrosiaster) and internal consistency (Paul
is emphasizing the paradoxical spiritual benefit of God's giving of the σκόλοψ). UBS⁴
gives this reading a {B} rating (= almost certain), although UBS¹ accorded it a {D} rating
(= very high degree of doubt), and UBS[2, 3] a {C} (= considerable doubt). (Note that the significance of the ratings differs somewhat between UBS[1, 2, 3] and UBS⁴. WH alleges that
"somewhere" in v. 7 there is a primitive corruption of the text (2. Appendix 120.)

n. Perhaps sensing that ἡ . . . δύναμις ἐν ἀσθενείᾳ τελεῖται is not simply an aphorism unrelated to the context, some copyist(s) added μου after δύναμις, a reading found in ℵ² Aᶜ D¹ Ψ 0243 0278 33 1739 1881 𝔐 syr boᵖᵗ Irenaeusᵃʳᵐ. Superior witnesses, however, do not include μου (p⁴⁶ ᵛⁱᵈ ℵ* A* B D* F G latt sa boᵖᵗ Irenaeusˡᵃᵗ). But the article with δύναμις may be treated as possessive.

o. Because of its stronger external support (ℵ* A B D* F G 623), the reading τελεῖται (from τελέω) is to be preferred over τελειοῦται (from τελειόω) (ℵ² D¹ Ψ 0243 0278 33 1739 1881 𝔐), although both verbs would here have the same meaning ("reach perfection").

p. As in 12:5, some witnesses add μου after ἐν ταῖς ἀσθενείαις, while others do not. Here, however, there is slightly stronger support for its inclusion (ℵ A D F G Ψ 0278 33 1881 𝔐 latt syrᵖ sa) than for its omission (B 6 81 1175 1739 pc syrʰ bo Irenaeus). It is the preferred reading in UBS¹, ², ³, ⁴ and NA²⁷, but not in WH. μου may have been omitted under the influence of ἐν ταῖς ἀσθενείαις in 12:5.

q. p⁴⁶ ℵ* read καί before ἀνάγκαις instead of ἐν. This appears to be a stylistic improvement for it creates a pattern of two coordinate phrases after the general expression ἐν ἀσθενείαις (so also Thrall 829 n. 450).

r. καὶ (p⁴⁶ ℵ* B 104 326 1175 pc) is to be preferred over either καὶ ἐν (0243 0278 630 1739 1881 pc) or ἐν (ℵ² A D F G Ψ 33 𝔐 latt syr Tertullian) since it has strong Alexandrian support and is the more difficult reading, ἐν simply continuing the preceding pattern and καὶ ἐν being a secondary conflation.

12:1 Καυχᾶσθαι δεῖ, οὐ συμφέρον μέν, ἐλεύσομαι δὲ εἰς ὀπτασίας καὶ ἀποκαλύψεις κυρίου. "It is necessary to boast. Although boasting is not beneficial, I will come to visions and revelations granted by the Lord." If we regard καυχᾶσθαι δεῖ as a general statement,⁵ even a Corinthian watchword (Barrett 306) that Paul reproduces as being relevant to his present situation, the sense will be "It is necessary to boast" or "I must boast" (in the latter case with με understood as the subject of the infinitive). Alternatively, the present infinitive may bear a linear sense: "There must be further boasting" (Lambrecht 199) or "I must go on boasting" (NAB¹). Either way, καυχάομαι is used absolutely,⁶ referring to boasting as such, not specifically to boasting in weakness (as in 11:30b) or boasting about "visions and revelations" (12:1b). "Boasting" has already figured prominently in chs. 10 and 11, and this motif continues unabated in ch. 12.⁷ What gave rise to this necessity to boast? Apparently the Corinthians not only readily accommodated boasters (10:12-18) but also had been responding favorably to the κατὰ σάρκα boasting of Paul's rivals (cf. 11:12, 18) so that Paul sensed he must employ the same tactics if their influence on the Corinthians was to be eclipsed. "It is not expedient to boast, but it might be even more inexpedient not to boast" (Barrett 306).

5. Sometimes this phrase is treated as a question; e.g., JB; Carrez 226 ("Must one boast? That is totally useless!").
6. As also in 10:17a; 11:18b, 30a; 12:1, 6 (see the commentary at 10:17).
7. See 10:8, 13, 15-17; 11:10, 12, 16-18, 30; 12:1, 5-6, 9. Of the 59 NT uses of the καυχ-root (καυχάομαι, καύχημα, καύχησις), 55 are found in the Pauline corpus, with 29 of these being in 2 Corinthians.

The participle συμφέρον could be considered an accusative absolute (Robertson 1130), but it is better to supply ἐστίν (so Turner 88; BAGD 780b), since the omission of ἐστίν (see BDF §127, especially [2]) is a much more common phenomenon than the accusative absolute construction (see BDF §424). In that case, οὐ συμφέρον ἐστίν is equivalent to οὐ συμφέρει, the reading of numerous witnesses (see Textual Note d.), meaning "there is nothing to be gained by it" (BAGD 780b) or "it is not beneficial [to boast]."[8] οὐ, rather than the expected μή (see BDF §426), is used with the participle, either because οὐ would be the normal negative with the periphrastic construction συμφέρον ἐστίν, or because the single idea of inexpediency is being negated.[9] The conceptual combination "necessary, (but) not expedient" is reminiscent of 1 Cor. 6:12, ἔξεστιν ἀλλ' οὐ . . . συμφέρει, "(it is) allowable but not profitable." Paul saw boasting as necessary in the Corinthian setting and yet as serving no good purpose in and of itself. οὐ συμφέρον is a fresh apology for his "foolish boasting" (cf. 11:1, 16) which caused him such embarrassment (11:17-18, 21b). The expression cannot be pressed as if it were an absolute statement, "boasting is never beneficial," for he endorses "boasting in the Lord" (10:17) and boasting in weaknesses (11:30; 12:5, 9).

In spite of recognizing that boasting was generally disadvantageous (οὐ συμφέρον), Paul moves on to the theme of "visions and revelations." μὲν . . . δέ, "although . . . (yet)," highlights this contrast. ἐλεύσομαι . . . εἰς, where εἰς = πρός (Zerwick §97), marks a transition to a new topic (Windisch 369), "I shall move on to" (Furnish 513) or "I am going to deal with" (cf. BAGD 311c). ὀπτασίαι and ἀποκαλύψεις should not be regarded as virtually synonymous[10] nor as forming a hendiadys ("visionary revelations," or "revelatory visions"). Of the two terms, "revelation" is the broader. A vision is always seen, whereas a revelation may be seen or may be received in some other way; all visions are also revelations, but not all revelations come through visions. A vision, however, is a common way of receiving a revelation.[11] The fact that the term ἀποκαλύψεις stands alone in v. 7 (τῇ ὑπερβολῇ τῶν ἀποκαλύψεων) suggests that "revelations," not "visions," are the principal focus in vv. 2-4. This is borne out by the verbs ἤκουσεν and λαλῆσαι in v. 4, although a visual recognition of the third heaven and paradise is obviously implied (vv. 2, 4). It might seem strange that although Paul cites only a single ascent to heaven in vv. 2-4,[12] he speaks in the plural of "visions" (v. 1) and of "revelations" (vv. 1, 7). Michaelis suggests that Paul has simply adduced a "selected example" (*TDNT* 5.353), while Lincoln

8. Expressed in full, the Greek would be οὐ συμφέρον ἐστὶν καυχᾶσθαι.

9. Cf. BDF §430(3). See the commentary at 4:8.

10. W. Michaelis argues (*TDNT* 5.353) that because in 12:7 only ἀποκαλύψεις is mentioned, ὀπτασίαι and ἀποκαλύψεις in 12:1 "seem to be interchangeable (perhaps relating to the subjective and objective aspects of the same thing. In any case ἀποκαλύψεις is the chief concept ('ὀπτασίαι and other ἀποκαλύψεις')."

11. Cf. Meyer 672, citing Dan. 9:23; 10:1, 16; Luke 1:22; Acts 26:19.

12. On the relation between v. 2 and vv. 3-4, see on v. 3.

opines that Paul originally intended to relate several visionary experiences but decided to refrain (72, 76). It is certainly inappropriate to deduce that Paul is here referring to "his *many* 'visions and revelations'" (Tabor 21, 36; italics his), although the book of Acts mentions numerous visions Paul had.[13] The plurals may be generalizing or categorical (see Zerwick §7), a view supported by the anarthrous state of these two nouns in v. 1. Paul is proceeding to discuss the topic, "visions and revelations granted by the Lord," not moving on to treat "the various visions and revelations granted to me by the Lord."[14] Paul's discussion of this topic was probably prompted by his opponents' claims to spiritual experiences of this type in response to a Corinthian "insistence on 'spiritual' and ecstatic phenomena as the marks of apostleship."[15]

Standing after two conjoined nouns that are dependent on a single preposition (εἰς), κυρίου will qualify both ὀπτασίας and ἀποκαλύψεις. The referent may be God,[16] since the anarthrous κύριος is usually Yahweh in Paul[17]; however, the anarthrous state of the dependent genitive κυρίου is determined by the preceding anarthrous nouns (the canon of Apollonius), so that particular argument is here inconclusive. More probably, κύριος refers to the Lord Jesus,[18] as in v. 8 (see the discussion there). The translation "visions and revelations of the Lord" (as, e.g., RV, RSV, NRSV) leaves open the question whether κυρίου is an objective or a subjective genitive, although the English phrase "of the Lord" here more probably refers to the content or object of the "visions and revelations" than to their giver or source. Some who regard κυρίου as an objective genitive support their view by appealing to the fact that Paul saw the risen Lord at the time of his conversion and call (1 Cor. 9:1; 15:8; Gal. 1:16; cf. 2 Cor. 4:6) (Lambrecht 200), and this was the basis of his apostolic commission (Scott 222). But elsewhere Paul speaks of his Damascus encounter with the exalted Lord — called an ὀπτασία in Acts 26:19 — as *sui generis,* quite distinct from other ὀπτασίαι.[19] Paul's gospel came to him δι' ἀποκαλύψεως Ἰησοῦ Χριστοῦ (Gal. 1:12; cf. Eph. 3:3), "through a revelation of Jesus Christ," that is, when God saw fit to reveal (ἀποκαλύψαι) his Son to and in Paul (Gal. 1:15-16). His subsequent "visions and revelations," as recorded in Acts, did not communicate the gospel to him as his initial ἀποκάλυψις had done. His encounter with the

13. Acts 9:11-12; 16:9-10; 18:9-10; 22:17-21; and at a time later than 2 Corinthians, Acts 23:11; 27:23-24.

14. Similarly Bultmann 219; Georgi, *Opponents* 281.

15. Barrett 312; cf. "Opponents" 251. Similarly Lincoln 74-75; Thrall 773. At a later time Paul's opponents at Colossae also presumed to parade their visionary experiences (Col. 2:18; on which see my *Colossians* 121-22). On Paul and "mysticism," see Bruce, "Mystic" 66-75; Penna 235-73 ("Problems and Nature of Pauline Mysticism").

16. So, e.g., Strachan 30 ("probably").

17. Cf. Zerwick §169.

18. So BAGD 460a; Plummer 336.

19. W. Michaelis argues vigorously that "Paul does not reckon the Damascus experience among ὀπτασίαι and ἀποκαλύψεις κυρίου." When Paul does speak of seeing the Lord, the reference is always to the Damascus road encounter (*TDNT* 5.357).

risen Christ near Damascus was foundational for his gospel and unrepeatable. This same point lessens the potency of Thrall's observation (again in defense of seeing κυρίου as an objective genitive) that in Pauline usage elsewhere, when ἀποκάλυψις is followed by the genitive (Rom. 2:5; 8:19; 1 Cor. 1:7; Gal. 1:12), that genitive denotes the content of the revelation.[20] It is better to take κυρίου as a subjective genitive, "granted by the Lord"[21] or simply "from the Lord."[22] In the following verses that describe Paul's ascent to paradise as one instance of "visions and revelations," there is no reference to his actually seeing the risen Christ although v. 4 would have afforded an ideal opportunity to recount such an experience.[23]

Such an understanding of κυρίου accords with the emphasis throughout the paragraph on the divine initiative.

κυρίου (v. 1)	granted by the Lord
ἁρπαγέντα (v. 2)	was caught up
ἡρπάγη . . . καὶ ἤκουσεν (v. 4)	was caught up . . . and heard
ἐδόθη (v. 7)	was given
[ὁ κύριος] εἴρηκεν μοι (v. 9)	[the Lord] has said to me

Paul's own initiative came into play only after the vision and revelation had been given and the thorn in the flesh received, when he implored the Lord three times (v. 8).

12:2 οἶδα ἄνθρωπον ἐν Χριστῷ πρὸ ἐτῶν δεκατεσσάρων — εἴτε ἐν σώματι οὐκ οἶδα, εἴτε ἐκτὸς τοῦ σώματος οὐκ οἶδα, ὁ θεὸς οἶδεν — ἁρπαγέντα τὸν τοιοῦτον ἕως τρίτου οὐρανοῦ. "I know a man in Christ who, fourteen years ago — whether in the body, I do not know, or out of the body, I do not know (God knows) — was caught up to the third heaven." To show the Corinthians that he was not at all deficient in ecstatic experiences, as some imagined, Paul now begins to describe an ascent to heaven that occurred many years previously. First, he identifies the person who ascended, then successively the time, the circumstances, and the destination of the ascent.

The form οἶδα occurs five times in vv. 2-3. Three times it is negated and follows εἴτε (v. 2) or εἴτε . . . εἴτε (v. 3) and has the sense "I am unaware." Twice

---

20. Thrall 775; "Journey" 359.

21. NEB, REB, Cassirer; Furnish 513; similarly TCNT, Weymouth, Goodspeed, GNB, Barclay.

22. JB, NIV, NJB. Most commentators, too, construe κυρίου as a subjective genitive (e.g., Meyer 671; Bernard 109; Plummer 336, 338; Bruce 246; Martin 397; Barnett 558). Some prefer the nomenclature genitive of "origin" (e.g., Zmijewski 328) or genitive of "author" (e.g., Windisch 368; J. Jeremias, *TDNT* 5.770; Schäfer 21).

23. It is possible but unlikely that with κυρίου Paul intended to convey both objective and subjective senses (so Garland 508 n. 359); unlikely, especially if it is suggested that each sense was relevant to a particular party — the objective sense to Paul's opponents, and the subjective to Paul himself (as Zmijewski 330-31).

it is followed by an accusative and has the sense "I am acquainted with" (v. 2)
or "I am aware of the fact that" (v. 4).

| οἶδα | ἄνθρωπον . . . | ἁρπαγέντα (v. 2) |
| οἶδα τὸν τοιοῦτον | ἄνθρωπον . . . | ὅτι ἡρπάγη (vv. 3-4) |

But "I know" and "I do not know" are perfectly adequate renderings and have
the advantage of consistency of translation. ἁρπαγέντα is a "supplementary
participle" after a verb denoting cognition (οἶδα) (BDF §416 [2]) and is used
instead of the more common ὅτι clause (cf. v. 4) or infinitive.[24]

ἐν Χριστῷ should be construed with the preceding word ἄνθρωπον rather
than with οἶδα or with the distant ἁρπαγέντα ("caught up in/by Christ's
power"), although one would normally have expected ἄνθρωπον τὸν ἐν
Χριστῷ,[25] "a man *who is* in Christ." We need not assume that in the present context ἄνθρωπον ἐν Χριστῷ means "a man who was in ecstasy with Christ"
(Plummer 336). The whole phrase may be a periphrasis for "a Christian,"[26] or
the prepositional phrase may be the equivalent of an adjective, thus "a Christian
man."[27] Because Paul is speaking of himself (see below), there is no need to
translate ἄνθρωπος by "person" (Lambrecht 199) or "someone" (NAB[2]). In the
end we need not shy away from the straightforward rendering, "a man in
Christ," where ἐν Χριστῷ is an abbreviation for "in union with the risen Christ
and therefore in the body of Christ."[28] As for the identity of this person, we may
safely disregard the suggestion that he is Apollos[29] or a fellow Christian known
to Paul,[30] for there are compelling reasons that point to Paul himself as the referent. (1) He knew the exact time in the distant past when the vision and revelation took place ("fourteen years ago," v. 2). (2) He knew that the person had
heard "things which cannot be put into words" (v. 4, GNB). (3) He knew that
this ἄνθρωπος was uncertain of his bodily state during the vision (vv. 2-3).
(4) The giving and receiving of the "thorn" followed as a direct consequence
(διό, v. 7) of the revelatory vision described in vv. 2-4, and that "thorn" was
given, says Paul, "to me" (μοι, v. 7), to pommel him and to prevent his becoming overly inflated (v. 7). (5) It would have been irrelevant to the Corinthian situation for Paul to have related an extraordinary experience that happened to
some Christian unknown to them but known to him.

24. Cf. BAGD 555d-556a; Robertson 1035, 1041.
25. Cf. Turner 221.
26. BAGD 556a; Héring 89.
27. Weymouth, NEB, REB; cf. BAGD 260a.
28. Cf. Cassirer's rendering, "a certain man, one united to Christ." Allo proposes "a man
(who lives) in Christ" (304). Pate believes that "man in Christ" refers to Paul's Adam-Christ
typology (*Glory* 129-30). *A Man in Christ* is the title of an influential book on Pauline theology by
J. S. Stewart (London: Hodder, 1935).
29. So L. Herrmann, "Apollos," *RSR* 50 (1976) 330-36.
30. So M. Goulder, "Vision and Knowledge," *JSNT* 56 (1994) 53-71. For a critique of
Goulder's view, see Thrall 778-79.

But why does the apostle objectify his experience and speak in the third person in vv. 2-4, even distinguishing between himself and "the man involved" (ὁ τοιοῦτος) in v. 5? It is more than a rhetorical ploy, a conventional avoidance of boasting about oneself.[31] Nor is it merely a desire to avoid egocentricity[32] by following the rabbinic practice of using "this man" as a periphrasis for "I" (see SB 3.530-31). Rather, he was embarrassed at needing to engage in fruitless boasting (v. 1) and found in this objectifying of his experience[33] a convenient way of distancing himself from this necessary but futile boasting that in itself did not contribute to the common good (cf. 12:19; 1 Cor. 12:7). Again, this literary technique enabled him to avoid suggesting that he was in any sense a special kind of Christian. The vision and revelation had been given to him as "a man in Christ," not as an apostle of Christ or persecuted believer who merited a reward for service rendered or suffering endured. From first to last the initiative lay with God. Finally, although Paul recognized the honor involved in being the recipient of a vision ("I will boast about such a man," v. 5), he wanted to dispel any idea that it added something to his status as an apostle or was relevant for the assessment of his apostleship. As Murphy-O'Connor observes, the episode "did not change him [Paul] in any way, and did not provide him with any information he could use. The criticism of his opponents is all the more effective for being unstated. If their experience was the same as Paul's, it contributed nothing to their ministry. If it was something about which they could talk, it was less ineffable than his!" (*Paul* 320).

There is general agreement that πρὸ ἐτῶν δεκατεσσάρων means "fourteen years ago,"[34] but this is an uncommon meaning of πρό[35] (which usually means "before," of place or time) and an unusual use of the genitive. John 12:1 affords a close parallel, since πρὸ ἓξ ἡμερῶν τοῦ πάσχα means "properly '6 days ago, reckoned from the passover'" (BDF §213), that is, "six days before the passover." In the present instance we might have expected the accusative, expressing extent of time, πρὸ δεκατέσσαρα ἔτη, "before [the present time] by fourteen years," "fourteen years ago." Moule suggests that this genitive may "define quantity simply, comparable to a genitive of price, with the 'linear' idea of extent scarcely visible" (74).

If the vision occurred fourteen years before the time of writing (A.D. 56), it took place about A.D. 43 by inclusive reckoning. None of Paul's other visions or revelations that we know of from his epistles or from Acts can be identified with this ὀπτασία, as the chart on pp. 836-37 seeks to indicate.

---

31. But see Betz 75-77, 95; Lincoln 75.

32. As Héring 89 n. 1.

33. Cf. Lambrecht 200: "In an ecstatic experience a kind of retreat of the ego, with the consequent possibility of objectification, is supposed to occur."

34. BAGD 317a; Moule 74; most EVV. Moulton's rendering, "fourteen years before" (101), is awkward, when there is no indication of the point from which measurement is made.

35. MM 536c cites as a parallel usage πρὸ ἡ]μερῶν τριῶν, "three days beforehand" (P. Fay. 122[23], c. A.D. 100).

Possible Identification	*Difficulty with the proposal*
1. Gal. 2:2 (instruction given to Paul κατὰ ἀποκάλυψιν to go up to Jerusalem)[36]	Date too late: either c. A.D. 46 (if Galatians 2 = Acts 11:30) or c. A.D. 49 (if Galatians 2 = Acts 15)[37] Content of the ἀποκάλυψις divulged (Gal. 2:1-2) yet the content of Paul's revelation beyond words (2 Cor. 12:4)
2. Acts 9:3-19; 22:6-10; 26:12-18 (Paul's conversion encounter with the risen Jesus)[38]	Date too early: c. A.D. 33 Content of the encounter divulged (Acts 22:7-8; 26:14-18) The experience was "in the body" (Acts 9:4; 22:7; 26:14; but cf. 2 Cor. 12:2-3)
3. Acts 11:25-26 (a vision during Paul's year in Antioch, possibly in connection with his commissioning to missionary service as apostle to the Gentiles, Acts 13:1-3)[39]	Date probably too late: c. A.D. 45-46 Luke's account gives no hint of a vision or a rapture
4. Acts 16:9-10 (Paul's vision of the man of Macedonia)	Date too late: c. A.D. 49 Not a heavenly vision (cf. 2 Cor. 12:2) Content of the vision divulged (Acts 16:9)
5. Acts 18:9-10 (the Lord's reassurance to Paul in a vision at Corinth)	Date too late: c. A.D. 51 Content of the vision divulged

36. So Belser 346 (as cited by Thrall 784 and n. 87).

37. These dates and those below are drawn from or consonant with dates suggested by Bruce, *Acts* 92-93.

38. Buck and Taylor 222-24. In 1936 ("'Fourteen Years Later': A Note on the Pauline Chronology," *JR* 16 [1936] 346-47) and again in 1939 ("The Pauline Chronology," *JBL* 58 [1939] 15-17), J. Knox defended the view that the intervals of fourteen years mentioned in Gal. 2:1 and 2 Cor. 12:2 have a common *terminus a quo*, namely Paul's conversion near Damascus in c. A.D. 37. However, in 1950, in his book *Chapters* (78 n. 3) he expressed the opinion that "the two intervals of fourteen years are probably a mere coincidence." For the differences between 12:1-5 and Gal. 1:11-17, see Baird 651-62. Paul's refusal to divulge the content of the ῥήματα heard in paradise (12:4) stands in stark contrast to his public "placarding" of the gospel he received through the Christophany at Damascus (Gal. 1:12, 15-16; 3:1). His conversion was more akin to a prophetic call where the vision prompts the message (e.g., Isa. 1:1; 6:1-13), than to a mystical encounter where the vision is an end in itself, simply an experience to be enjoyed.

39. Cf., e.g., Allo 307.

6. Acts 22:17-21 (Paul's trance [ἔκστασις] in the temple in Jerusalem)[40]

Date too early: c. A.D. 35, during Paul's first post-conversion visit to Jerusalem (Acts 9:26-30; Gal. 1:18) Content of the vision divulged (Acts 22:18, 21)

We must therefore conclude that the only information we have concerning Paul's ascent to heaven is contained in 2 Cor. 12:2-4. If it occurred about A.D. 43, it was during the decade of Paul's life about which nothing is known other than that some or all of it was spent in Syria-Cilicia (Gal. 1:21), the period between his first post-conversion visit to Jerusalem (Gal. 1:18-20 = Acts 9:26-30), c. A.D. 35, and his arrival in Antioch from Tarsus (Acts 11:25-26), c. A.D. 45.[41]

But why did Paul bother to date his ecstatic experience? Certainly the dating of the ascent to paradise as "fourteen years ago" would have had the effect of confirming the factuality of the event, but Paul's purpose may have been to draw attention to his prolonged silence about the episode; it was only the present contest with his rivals, brought on by the Corinthians' disloyalty to him, that had forced him (cf. 12:1, 11) to break that silence and reluctantly mention his privileged ascent to heaven. Even if the Corinthians already knew of Paul's rapture — although that is far from certain — they were learning for the first time some details of the experience. Was he hinting that ecstatic experiences, as private encounters with God (cf. 5:13), were not to be publicized unnecessarily, and, as God-given privileges, added nothing to a person's standing or role in the church?[42] Another reason Paul dated this episode may have been to indicate how long he had been grappling with his painful and frustrating "thorn in the flesh," for clearly the σκόλοψ was given to him promptly after this "marvelous revelation," in order to curb any inordinate pride (v. 7). The weakness in which he had learned to take pleasure (v. 10) had been a present reality throughout all his Corinthian ministry and for several years before. This point would become apparent, of course, only after the Corinthians had heard this whole paragraph.

ἁρπαγέντα is a "theological passive" with a phrase such as ὑπὸ τοῦ θεοῦ understood. Paul's ascent was not the result of a self-induced trance or any other form of psychological preparation. This verb ἁρπάζω ("snatch away," "catch up") points to a sudden rapture, as when believers who are alive at the parousia will be "caught up" (ἁρπαγησόμεθα) in the clouds (1 Thess. 4:17) or "the Spirit of the Lord snatched Philip away (ἥρπασεν)" (Acts 8:39). The suddenness of Paul's ascent into heaven stands in contrast to the slow departure of Jesus into heaven at his ascension that is suggested by the imperfect ἀνεφέρετο in Luke 24:51 and the expressive statement in Acts 1:10, ἀτενίζοντες ἦσαν εἰς τὸν οὐρανὸν πορευομένου αὐτοῦ ("they were gazing intently into the sky while He was departing," NASB).

40. See, e.g., Morray-Jones 265-92.
41. Similarly Bruce 246; *Paul* 134.
42. For a defense of the view that Paul highly valued ecstatic experiences, see Saake 404-10.

With regard to the purpose or outcome of heavenly journeys described in antiquity,[43] Tabor identifies four generally distinct types of ascent (57-111): (1) ascent as an invasion of heaven by an earthly mortal; (2) ascent as a visit into the divine realm to receive revelation; (3) a permanent ascent to the heavenly realms to obtain immortality; and (4) ascent as a foretaste of a later final ascent. The first, second, and fourth types involve a "round-trip" journey from earth to heaven and back again, whereas the third is a "one-way" ascent.[44] Tabor regards the first two categories as relatively rare (77) and places 2 Cor. 12:1-10 in the fourth category (81, 124). "Generally speaking, the first two categories are more characteristic of the ANE [Ancient Near East] or archaic period, which would include most texts of the Hebrew Bible (OT). The latter two categories are more typical of the Hellenistic period, which reflects the perspective of the NT."[45] He finds (118) the best parallel to Paul's language in the *Life of Adam and Eve* 25:3, where Adam says to his son Seth, "I was carried off into the Paradise of righteousness, and I saw the Lord sitting and his appearance was unbearable flaming fire. And many thousands of angels were at the right and at the left of the chariot."[46]

Twice in this verse the conditional conjunction εἴτε ("whether") is used before οὐκ οἶδα to introduce an indirect question[47] in which there is an ellipsis of a finite verb (ἦν, "he was").[48] That εἴτε . . . ὁ θεὸς οἶδεν is parenthetical[49] is indicated by the resumptive τὸν τοιοῦτον ("such a man"; see on v. 3) that looks

43. On ascent to heaven in Judaism, Christianity, Gnosticism, and other sources, see the monograph by Himmelfarb, the articles by B. H. Young ("Ascension Motif") and D. L. Halperin ("Heavenly Ascension"), and, with special attention to Merkabah mysticism, J. W. Bowker ("'Merkabah' Visions") and P. Schäfer ("Hekhalot Literature").

44. Spittler notes (262 n. 20) that R. Meyer distinguishes a *Himmelfahrt* (a permanent ascent to heaven) from a *Himmelreise* (a journey to heaven and back).

45. J. D. Tabor, "Heaven, Ascent to," *ABD* 3.91.

46. Translation of M. D. Johnson in Charlesworth 2.266, 268. According to Scott (64, 221, 237; cf. "Triumph" 279-81), 12:2-4 (and 10:4) relates to Paul's heavenly encounter with the *merkābâ* (the divine "throne-chariot" of Ezekiel 1 and 10), also alluded to in 2:14 (61-64, 224).

The main reasons why some scholars interpret Paul's ascent as a *merkabah* vision are: (1) a contemporary of Paul, Johanan ben Zakkai, taught *merkabah* contemplation to some of his pupils (Bowker 157) and such contemplation may have formed part of Paul's Pharisaical training (Bowker 158-59, 172); (2) direct descent from Abraham, such as Paul claims in 11:22, was seen as a prerequisite for *merkabah* contemplation (Bowker 158); (3) references to being "caught up" (cf. ἁρπαγέντα, 12:2; ἡρπάγη, 12:4), the "third heaven" (τρίτου οὐρανοῦ, 12:2), and "paradise" (τὸν παράδεισον, 12:4) are also found in *merkabah* mystical texts. But such grounds are too slender a basis for the conclusion drawn. Paul shows no interest in certain distinctives of *merkabah* texts such as an emphasis on the extreme danger of *merkabah* contemplation, techniques for inducing trances or the ecstatic state, contemplation of the "chariot" chapters of Ezekiel as the means of "seeing again" the vision described there, or descriptions of the throne-chariot and its occupant. See further Schäfer 32-35.

47. BAGD 556b; Robertson 1045. Sometimes (e.g., NJB; Héring 89; Carrez 226) εἴτε in vv. 2 and 3 is thought to introduce direct questions. In the NT, as opposed to classical usage, εἰ sometimes introduces direct questions (Robertson 916; Turner 333), but it is doubtful whether εἴτε serves this purpose.

48. Cf. BDF §§446; 454(3).

49. This is recognized by most EVV and commentators, with the parenthesis marked by dashes (e.g., NASB; Heckel 53, 301) or brackets (e.g., GNB; Furnish 513).

back to ἄνθρωπον ἐν Χριστῷ. If there had been no parenthesis, τὸν τοιοῦτον would not have been needed. On occasion translations faithfully reproduce the awkwardness of this repetition of the referent,[50] but most versions smooth over the infelicity by inserting a relative pronoun: "I know a man in Christ who fourteen years ago was caught up to the third heaven" (RSV).

It is purely coincidental that the "proper" preposition ἐν here modifies an anarthrous noun (ἐν σώματι), while the "improper" preposition ἐκτός is followed by an articular noun (ἐκτὸς τοῦ σώματος), as also χωρίς in v. 3,[51] for "proper" prepositions often govern articular nouns and "improper" prepositions can be used with anarthrous nouns. ἐν σώματι is anarthous (but cf. 5:6) since it is a colloquialism.[52] In both prepositional phrases it is the present physical body that is being spoken of in a generic sense: "in the body" (not, "in his body") and "out of the body" (not, "out of his body"), that is, "in an embodied state" and "in a disembodied state." Although Paul was certain that he was transported to heaven, he professed ignorance whether his body was actually carried up or whether his spirit was wafted to the heavenly realm while his body remained on earth (? in a comatose state). Given his certainty that "something" was caught up to heaven, and the possibility that he was "out of the body," it seems inadequate to paraphrase εἴτε ἐν σώματι . . . εἴτε ἐκτὸς τοῦ σώματος by "whether he was literally carried up, or whether heaven was disclosed to him" (Stanley 253) or "whether this actually happened or whether he had a vision" (GNB). In each of these paraphrases the second alternative could have occurred ἐν σώματι. Certainly these two references to the σῶμα should not be treated as basic building blocks for a reconstruction of Paul's anthropology, but he does seem in this passage to envisage the possibility of sentient and rational experience in a disembodied state, albeit temporarily. That is, he can conceive of temporary disembodiment in exceptional circumstances created by God, and yet insist that the final state of believers is one of embodiment (5:1). Over against his own unawareness of his bodily state during his revelatory vision, Paul sets divine knowledge (ὁ θεὸς οἶδεν;[53] cf. 11:11) — knowledge that he is not lying (cf. 11:31) in claiming ignorance, or, more probably, knowledge of his actual somatic state during the whole experience. Why in vv. 2 and 3 he so emphatically denies knowledge of his physical circumstances during the episode remains uncertain.[54] Perhaps he is

---

50. E.g., Barrett 305: "I know a man in Christ, fourteen years ago (whether he was in the body, or out of the body, I do not know — God knows), I know that a man like that was caught up as far as the third heaven." Even here the second "I know" has been supplied. See also Thrall's rendering (772). Apparently Paul considered it necessary to restate (by τὸν τοιοῦτον) the object of οἶδα because of the lengthy parenthesis, εἴτε . . . ὁ θεὸς οἶδεν.

51. "Proper" prepositions are those that can be compounded with verbs; "improper," those that are not so used.

52. Cf. BDF §255; Robertson 791-92.

53. MM notes that οἶδεν γὰρ (ὁ) θεός is a "common asseveration in the Christian papyri" (439d).

54. Bultmann proposes that "the parenthesis is intended to describe the strangeness of the event, for which not Paul but God alone is answerable" (221).

emphasizing that direct encounter with the realities of the heavenly realm is so overwhelming and awe-inspiring that consciousness of the physical world is totally eclipsed. And, at least indirectly, he is affirming that embodiment is no impediment to spiritual experience (cf. 5:6-7 and commentary there).

Although Paul was unaware of his bodily state while and after being "caught up," he was fully aware of his location — "the third heaven." In Judaism, when a plurality of heavens is mentioned, the number varies from two to ten, although seven came to be the usual number,[55] as in *Ascension of Isaiah* 6:13; 7:13–9:18; *2 Enoch* (A-text) 3–22. It is unlikely that Paul was operating with a cosmological scheme of seven heavens, for if he could claim to have ascended only to the third of seven heavens, his opponents could easily depreciate the significance of his ascent, especially if they were able to claim ascent to a higher heaven.[56] On the basis of the formula "heaven and the heaven of heavens" in 1 Kgs. 8:27,[57] the rabbis deduced that there were three heavens, so that the third heaven was the highest heaven (SB 3.531). It is probable that this was Paul's cosmology,[58] so that when he says ἕως τρίτου οὐρανοῦ, "right up to the third heaven,"[59] he means "into the immediate presence of God." We cannot be sure that he regarded the first heaven as the clouds and atmosphere, and the second heaven as the sun and stars, for it is possible that Calvin is correct in affirming that here "the number three is used as a perfect number to indicated what is highest and most complete" (156).

12:3-4 The relationship of vv. 3-4 to v. 2 is most clearly seen in tabular form. Differences are indicated by italics.

First Description (v. 2)	*Second Description* (vv. 3-4)
οἶδα	καὶ οἶδα
ἄνθρωπον ἐν Χριστῷ	τὸν τοιοῦτον ἄνθρωπον —
πρὸ ἐτῶν δεκατεσσάρων —	
εἴτε ἐν σώματι	εἴτε ἐν σώματι
οὐκ οἶδα,	
εἴτε ἐκτὸς τοῦ σώματος	εἴτε χωρὶς τοῦ σώματος
οὐκ οἶδα,	οὐκ οἶδα,
ὁ θεὸς οἶδεν —	ὁ θεὸς οἶδεν —
ἁρπαγέντα τὸν τοιοῦτον	ὅτι ἡρπάγη
ἕως τρίτου οὐρανοῦ.	εἰς τὸν παράδεισον
	καὶ ἤκουσεν ἄρρητα ῥήματα ἃ οὐκ ἐξὸν
	ἀνθρώπῳ λαλῆσαι.

55. H. Traub, *TDNT* 5.511.
56. Cf. Heckel 61-62.
57. The expression is also found in Deut. 10:14; 2 Chron. 2:6; 6:18; Neh. 9:6.
58. So also, e.g., Hughes 433; Klauck, "Himmelfahrt" 155; Thrall 789-90.
59. The use of ἕως, "as far as" (BAGD 335a; NEB, REB), "all the way to" (Cassirer), is no proof that Paul regarded the third heaven as the highest (*pace* Barnett 562 n. 28), for the preposition ἕως need denote only the final extent of the ascent.

3"Indeed, I know that such a man — whether in the body or apart from the body, I do not know (God knows) — 4was caught up into paradise and heard inexpressible words that a human is not permitted to utter." Because there are both similarities and differences between the two descriptions, it is not surprising that varying conclusions have been drawn concerning the relation of vv. 3-4 to v. 2. Focusing on the differences, some have argued that Paul is recounting two distinct experiences,[60] or two successive stages of a single experience.[61] Others, drawing attention to the similarities, believe that only one ascent is being described.[62] Of these three views, the first has few modern proponents, so we shall focus on the second and third.

Tabor accounts for the parallel structure in vv. 2-4 by arguing that Paul is describing a two-stage journey to paradise (115-21). The first stage involved receiving revelations of heavenly secrets in the "third heaven" (of seven heavens); the second stage transported him to paradise, to God's very throne in the highest (seventh) heaven, where he heard "things unutterable."[63] Tabor's main argument in favor of a two-stage ascent seems to be that Paul's mention of the "third heaven" would be strange if he thought it was the highest; the expression hints at other levels beyond (119). He also points to the apparent redundancy if "Paul says the same thing two times using the same language almost word for word" (115).

On the former point, the only indication of Paul's belief in a multiplicity of heavens is the phrase ἕως τρίτου οὐρανοῦ.[64] That he believed in seven heavens is an inference from τρίτου along with the assumption that there were seven as opposed to, say, five or ten heavens in his cosmology.[65] It would be no less justifiable to assume that for Paul the third heaven was the highest of the three, particularly since the NT never uses the expression "the highest heaven" (= ὁ οὐρανὸς τοῦ οὐρανοῦ, Deut. 10:14). On Tabor's latter point, the repetition is by no means precise (see the underlined words in the table above). Along with the repetition, which may reflect his reluctance to speak of his privileged ascent, his awe at the exceptional character of the event, and his emphasis on the divine initiative in the whole occurrence, we find significant details added, namely his arrival in paradise and the reference to the revelation received (v. 4). The movement from v. 2 to vv. 3-4 is not unlike the movement from the first to the second element in the synthetic parallelism of Hebrew poetry, where the second element repeats, adds, and intensifies.[66]

60. E.g., Plummer 344; Schlatter 663; Wendland 246; Saake 406 n. 11.
61. E.g., Meyer 676; Betz 91; Rowland 381-82; Tabor 115-21. Plummer notes that Clement of Alexandria and Erasmus held this view (344).
62. E.g., Lincoln 77; Schäfer 22; Thrall 790-92; "Journey" 356-58.
63. Tabor compares the two-stage journey of Menippus to see Zeus (as reported by Lucian, *Icaromenippus* 22), first to the moon, then onward to the highest heaven (115).
64. The NT use of the plural οὐρανοί imitates the plural (of "spatial extension"?) of the Hebrew term "heaven" (*šāmayim*).
65. On the various Jewish cosmological schemes, see H. Traub, *TDNT* 5.511-12; Lincoln 78-79.
66. Cf. Zmijewski 335.

We may mention two further points against this view. In the case of a two-stage rapture one would expect an indication that the second stage was a continuation of the journey, but a phrase such as μετὰ ταῦτα, ἐκεῖθεν is lacking (Windisch 371). Again, why would Paul mention the third heaven if nothing of consequence happened there? It is inadequate to claim that "the ἕως τρίτου οὐρανοῦ was a break, as it were, a resting-point of the *raptus*" (Winer 676). On the other hand, a mention would be relevant if the third heaven was regarded as the location of paradise (Thrall, "Journey" 357).

The arguments against a two-stage ascent outlined above also afford positive support for the "single experience" view. We may observe, further, that a single — and precise — date is given (in v. 2), not the two that we would expect if two ascents were involved. Correspondingly, there is only one reference to the content of the revelation (v. 4), whereas one would expect some vision or revelation to be associated with the third heaven (v. 3) also. As for the καί before οἶδα, it may be simply conjunctive ("and"), with no implication as to whether the ascent had two stages or one; or it may be adversative ("[I do not know . . .] I do know, however, that . . . ," JB), adjunctive ("And I also know," Cassirer), or emphatic/ascensive ("Indeed," Furnish 526). The latter three meanings suit a one-stage rapture.

Literally rendered, οἶδα τὸν τοιοῦτον ἄνθρωπον . . . ὅτι ἡρπάγη means "I know such a man . . . *that* he was caught up," that is, "I know *that* such a man . . . was caught up."[67] As Meyer notes (676), the construction imitates the idiom οἶδα σε τίς εἶ (Mark 1:24), literally, "I know you who you are," that is, "I know who you are." In the present case, the expression "such a man," which should be the subject of the subordinate clause "that he was caught up," is brought forward into the main clause and becomes the object.[68] An alternative explanation of this strange accusative would be to regard it as an accusative of respect: "And I also know, with regard to this man, that he . . ." (Cassirer). The combination ὁ τοιοῦτος (ἄνθρωπος) occurs in vv. 2, 3, and 5 (also in 2:6-7; 10:11; 11:13), where it may be a less definite term for οὗτος,[69] but still referring to a definite individual: "this man" (RSV, vv. 3, 5), "this person" (NAB², vv. 3, 5), "this same man" (NEB, REB, v. 3), "the man in question" (Heckel 301). But it is perfectly legitimate to retain the distinctive sense of τοιοῦτος, provided the notion of definiteness is not lost: "such a man," "a man like that" (Barrett 305, vv. 2, 3, 5). The disjunctive correlatives εἴτε . . . εἴτε ("whether . . . or") introduce an indirect question in which a finite verb (ἦν) is understood[70] (see on v. 2, where εἴτε . . . εἴτε are not correlatives).

---

67. Field raises the possibility (187) that here and in 1 Cor. 1:16 οἶδα may mean "I remember," a usage known in Classical Greek.

68. This usage is a case of hyperbaton (or transposition), the placing of words out of their natural and usual grammatical order.

69. Thus BDF §304; Turner 46.

70. Cf. Turner 333.

On the parenthesis εἴτε . . . ὁ θεὸς οἶδεν, which is almost identical to the parenthesis in v. 2,[71] see the commentary on v. 2.

The second part of v. 4, καὶ ἤκουσεν ἄρρητα ῥήματα ἃ οὐκ ἐξὸν ἀνθρώπῳ λαλῆσαι, contains four exegetical ambiguities. First, ῥήματα may bear its usual sense of "words," or, under the influence of its Hebrew equivalent (deḇārîm) which may mean "words" or "things"/"matters," it may mean "things."[72] Second, like the English adjective "ineffable," ἄρρητος can mean either "that cannot be expressed" or "that must not be expressed" (see BAGD 109 s.v.). That is, it may refer to either impossibility or impermissibility, or, as Spittler (264) expresses it, the term may describe what is "inexpressible by nature" or what is "inexpressible by prohibition."[73] Third, the relative clause introduced by ἃ may define what is meant by ἄρρητα ῥήματα, or it may give a second characterization of the ῥήματα (in addition to ἄρρητα). Fourth, ἐξόν, the participle of ἔξεστι, is used only twice in the NT, both times in the nominative (Robertson 491), once with ἦν (Matt. 12:4) and here with ἐστίν understood.[74] Like ἔξεστι, ἐξόν [ἐστιν] may mean "it is permitted" or (less commonly) "it is possible."

These ambiguities give rise, of course, to a variety of possible meanings. Three representative categories of translation may be mentioned.

1. Referring both ἄρρητα and οὐκ ἐξόν to impermissibility, with ἃ κτλ. virtually epexegetic.
   - "things that must not be divulged, which it is forbidden a human being to repeat" (Furnish 513).[75]
   - "things that are not to be told, that no mortal is permitted to repeat" (NRSV).
2. Referring ἄρρητα to impermissibility and οὐκ ἐξόν to impossibility.
   - "things which must not and cannot be put into human language" (JB).
3. Referring ἄρρητα to impossibility and οὐκ ἐξόν to impermissibility.[76]

---

71. There are two insignificant differences between the two parentheses: οὐκ οἶδα occurs only once in v. 3, after the disjunctives εἴτε . . . εἴτε; χωρίς ("apart from") (v. 3) replaces ἐκτός ("out of") (v. 2).

72. Cf. the use of ῥῆμα in 13:1; Matt. 18:16 (both citing Deut. 19:15); Luke 1:37; 2:15, 19; Acts 5:32; 13:42.

73. Thrall labels the pair of meanings, "impossible to express" and "forbidden to express" (794).

74. Robertson 881; Turner 88; cf. BDF §127(2). Since ἐξόν ἐστιν would be a periphrastic construction, the negative particle οὐ (rather than the expected μή with a participle) is permitted with ἐξόν (cf. οὐ συμφέρον in v. 1).

75. Similarly Spittler 264; Lincoln 82; Thrall 794, who allows the possibility that the connotation "impossible to express" may be "hovering" in the background (of ἄρρητα) as well.

76. If one were to follow Windisch (377-78) in finding the background of ἄρρητα ῥήματα in the terminology of the mystery religions where religious rites and secret truths were not to be divulged to the uninitiated, Moffatt's translation would be apt: "sacred secrets which no human lips can repeat."

- "things which cannot be put into words, things that human lips may not speak" (GNB).[77]
- "words said that cannot and may not be spoken by any human being" (NJB).[78]
- "inexpressible[79] words that a human is not permitted to utter."[80]

There is an advantage in retaining "words" for ῥήματα, since Paul probably intended ἄρρητα ῥήματα to be oxymoronic, "unutterable utterances" (Young and Ford 274) or "utterances unutterable" (Cassirer), that is, divine words that cannot be expressed in human language. The relative clause ἃ κτλ. adds a second characteristic of the ῥήματα. They were not only beyond the reaches of human language; God does not, in any case, permit human beings to clothe these transcendent heavenly utterances in the puny garb of earthly language.[81] Paul gives no indication of the content of these "unutterable utterances" that he was privileged to hear. Tentative proposals include angelic praise,[82] perhaps expressed in "the tongues of angels" (1 Cor. 13:1), the mysteries of God's person (1 Cor. 2:10-11),[83] unutterable divine names,[84] and disclosures about the end of the world,[85] including the blessings of the Age to Come. But in the final analysis, we must be content with Theodoret's conclusion: "the person [Paul] who has seen these things — he knows."[86]

Two further issues arise in v. 4. What is the relation of "paradise" to the "third heaven" (v. 3)? Did Paul see Christ in paradise?

Pairi-daēza is an old Persian word referring to a walled "enclosure,"

---

77. Similarly NAB[1], NIV; Young and Ford 274. It is impossible to determine the intent of translations that render ἄρρητα by "ineffable" or "unspeakable" and οὐκ ἐξόν by "cannot."

78. This rendering construes ἀνθρώπῳ (in sense) with both ἄρρητα and οὐκ ἐξόν.

79. Unlike the word "ineffable," the adjective "inexpressible" means only "that cannot be expressed in words," not also "that must not be expressed."

80. Cf. Bruce 247: "things which it was impossible as well as impermissible to describe"; similarly *Paul* 134.

81. Such an interpretation answers the objection, "How can the disclosure of a revelation be forbidden unless it is possible?" (cf. Thrall 794 n. 169). Cf. Hughes 439: the revelation Paul received "was an ineffable communication intended for him alone, which also, *even if it were possible,* it was not lawful for him to repeat" (439; italics mine).

82. Bietenhard 167. W. Foerster translates ἃ κτλ. by "which it is not possible for a man to utter" and comments, "We are to think of the praise of angels which in its supraterrestrial glory surpasses every possibility of human expression" (*TDNT* 2.561 n. 1).

83. Morray-Jones 281.

84. Thrall, "Journey" 361.

85. Meyer 677 n. 2.

86. αὐτὸς οἶδεν ὁ ταῦτα τεθεαμένος (cited by Meyer 677, without reference). Paul's "failure" to disclose the content of the ῥήματα was remedied (!) by a second-century Coptic *Apocalypse of Paul* (Nag Hammadi Gnostic Codices V.2), on which see Klauck, "Himmelfahrt" 151-90; and a fourth-century Latin *Apocalypse of Paul* (found in Hennecke and Schneemelcher 755-98), on which see Young 95-103. In the latter work the author overcomes the difficulty of the ἄρρητα ῥήματα by distinguishing (in ch. 21) between what Paul was permitted to relate and what he could not disclose.

whether a garden or a park. The term was borrowed by Hebrew *(pardēs)*, Aramaic *(pardêsā')*, and Greek (παράδεισος[87]). Thirteen times in Genesis 2–3 παράδεισος refers to the "garden" *(gan)* of Eden.[88] In the NT παράδεισος occurs only three times — here and in Luke 23:43 and Rev. 2:7. In the later Judaism of the NT period three aspects or stages of paradise were distinguished: the first paradise, the garden of Eden; the hidden or intervening paradise of the present, the abode of the righteous departed, located either in various places on earth or in heaven; and the paradise of the age to come, located on earth or in the new Jerusalem.[89] In the NT it is the concept of "the tree of life" that links the first paradise and the last (Gen. 2:9; Rev. 2:7; 22:2, 14, 19), while the hidden paradise and the eschatological paradise are linked by the motif of residence and association with Christ. So, in the "paradise of God," the heavenly garden of God, the Eden above, it is Christ who will grant God's immortality to victorious believers (Rev. 2:7). Also, it was Jesus who promised the penitent malefactor residence with him in (the hidden, heavenly) paradise after death (Luke 23:43). 12:4, too, seems to refer to this same heavenly paradise where departed believers are already with Christ (cf. 5:8; Phil. 1:23).

As for the relation of παράδεισος and τρίτος οὐρανός, there are three possibilities. For those who discern two stages in Paul's ascent to paradise, the two expressions are, of course, distinct.[90] But we have argued above (under v. 3) in favor of seeing a single event in vv. 2-4. Accordingly, paradise may be seen as a synonym for the third (highest) heaven,[91] or, as in *2 Enoch* (A) 8:1; *Apocalypse of Moses* 40:1 and probably 37:5, it can be regarded as within the third heaven.[92] Perhaps the different prepositions used in vv. 2 and 4 support this latter option, "as far as (ἕως) the third heaven," indicating the "height" of Paul's rapture, and "into (εἰς) paradise," specifying its "depth."[93] We conclude, then, that in 12:4 Paul refers to his visit to the "hidden" paradise, the dwelling place of the righteous dead, which is located within the third (= the highest) heaven, the abode of God.

If this conclusion is right, it might seem inevitable that on his visit to paradise Paul saw the exalted Christ, for he believed that the righteous dead were "with the Lord" (5:8) or "with Christ" (Phil. 1:23), and that Christ was now at God's right hand in heaven (Rom. 8:34; Col. 3:1).[94] The difficulty, however, is that Paul refers only to what he heard (ἤκουσεν), not to anything he saw. True,

---

87. "A garden of fruit-trees (protected presumably by a wall) is the general idea of it as seen in the papyri where it is very common" (MM 482a).

88. Gen. 2:8-10, 15-16; 3:1-3, 8 (twice), 10, 23-24. In three passages (Neh. 2:8 [= 2 Esdr. 12:8]; Eccl. 2:5; Cant. 4:13) παράδεισος renders the Hebrew *pardēs*.

89. For details see J. Jeremias, *TDNT* 5.766-68.

90. E.g., Meyer 676; Tabor 118-19.

91. Strachan 31; Barrett 310; Scott 64, 224.

92. Lincoln 79; Schäfer 22; Thrall 791. But both *2 Enoch* and the *Apocalypse of Moses* have mixed traditions about the location of paradise (Tabor 116-17).

93. Thus Hughes 437. On this matter of dimension, see Sylvia 462-72.

94. Those who argue that Paul actually saw the risen Lord include Tabor 124; Morray-Jones 277-78, 283; Thrall 797; "Journey" 359, 362.

he must have seen something that indicated he was in paradise, unless this too was announced to him. But it would be extraordinary if he had actually seen Christ at this time and yet not have mentioned the fact (cf. 1 Cor. 9:1; 15:8), for such an experience would have been unique for him. At Damascus he had been confronted by the risen Christ who spoke from heaven (Acts 9:3-6; 22:6-8, 10; 26:13-18), while Paul himself was on earth. In the present case he would have seen the exalted Lord while he too was in heaven, an experience that anticipated the final destiny of believers (1 Thess. 4:17).[95] In view of Paul's silence about what he saw during his time in paradise,[96] and his silence about the identity of the speaker of the ῥήματα, it is not inappropriate to assume that he heard the sound of words which he understood but did not see the form of the speaker or speakers (cf. Deut. 4:12). But this is not to suggest that the experience had a minimal impact on him. On the contrary, after his conversion encounter with the living Christ, probably no event had a greater influence in strengthening his motivation for serving and pleasing Christ (5:9, 15) and his fortitude for enduring suffering (cf. Acts 9:16; Rom. 8:18).

12:5 ὑπὲρ τοῦ τοιούτου καυχήσομαι, ὑπὲρ δὲ ἐμαυτοῦ οὐ καυχήσομαι εἰ μὴ ἐν ταῖς ἀσθενείαις. "I will boast about such a man, but about myself I will not boast, except of my weaknesses." In v. 2a Paul made a technical distinction between himself (οἶδα) and another person (ἄνθρωπον ἐν Χριστῷ), with this man then being described as τὸν τοιοῦτον (v. 2) and τὸν τοιοῦτον ἄνθρωπον (v. 3). Here in v. 5 the distinction is maintained (τοῦ τοιούτου . . . ἐμαυτοῦ), but now Paul explicitly associates himself with both parties by the use of the repeated καυχήσομαι. The reality that the two parties are actually one becomes increasingly clear in vv. 6-7 with the personal pronouns ἐμὲ . . . με . . . ἐμοῦ (v. 6) . . . μοι (v. 7) and with the disappearance of any reference to ὁ τοιοῦτος, so that τούτου in v. 8 refers not to "this man" but to σκόλοψ or ἄγγελος. We discussed in v. 2 possible reasons why Paul created this distinction. What he distinguishes by the τοῦ τοιούτου–ἐμαυτοῦ antithesis (adversative δέ) is not two selves, an "ecstatic" self and a non-"ecstatic" self, or a "visionary" Paul and a non-"visionary" Paul, or "Paul the apocalyptist" (ὁ τοιοῦτος) and "Paul the man and apostle" (ἐγὼ αὐτός) (Lietzmann 155). Rather, the distinction is between someone who was the privileged recipient of a vision and a revelation, and someone who was simply one person among many who were "in Christ" (v. 2).

95. For a defense of the view that Paul regarded his mystical ascent to heaven as a proleptic experience of the parousia and of the restoration of the paradise that Adam forfeited, see Pate 107-42.

96. "In paradise, Paul should have viewed the final abode of the souls of the righteous (2 Esdr 8:51-52; Luke 23:43); and in the highest heaven, he should have seen cosmic paraphernalia, angelic beings, and the radiant throne of God (2 Enoch 20:1-4; T. Levi 3:1-8; 3 Apoc. Bar. 11:1-9)" (Baird 655, citing [n. 19] M. E. Stone, "Lists of Revealed Things in the Apocalyptic Literature," in *Magnalia Dei: The Mighty Acts of God: Essays . . . in Memory of G. E. Wright* [ed. F. M. Cross, W. E. Lemke, and P. D. Miller; Garden City: Doubleday, 1976] 414-52).

The apostle was willing to boast about ὁ τοιοῦτος because no credit would come to him personally if he boasted about "another person" and about an event that was wholly God's doing; it was, as Bultmann says (222), "a mere happening" for which Paul was not responsible. In addition, such foolish boasting (11:1, 16-17) had become necessary (12:1, 11) in the prevailing climate at Corinth (11:18). On the other hand, he was not prepared to boast about himself, about the "extraordinary revelations" given him (11:7), because that would detract from the Lord's preeminence and would suggest his own distinctiveness and eminence as a Christian or as an apostle. He would boast only about his weaknesses, "his humiliations and sufferings" (Forbes 21), those experiences that enabled Christ's power to be fully evident in his life (12:9). He hoped that such carefully circumscribed boasting would reap two benefits — it would draw attention to the Lord and his generous provision of power in the midst of Paul's weakness, and also it would help the Corinthians recognize how foolish the intruders were in boasting of their strengths (cf. 11:18, 20-21) and as a consequence would reignite the flame of the Corinthians' undivided loyalty to Christ (11:2-3) and to Paul himself (6:13; 10:6; 12:15). Indeed, it was these two elements that determined what was legitimate boasting. It must be ἐν κυρίῳ (10:17), about the person and work of the Lord; and it must be πρὸς τὸ συμφέρον (cf. 1 Cor. 12:7), "for the common good" of upbuilding the church (10:8; 12:19; 13:10).

Both instances of ὑπέρ could be rendered "on behalf of" (= "in the interest of"),[97] but more probably ὑπέρ here has the sense of περί, "about," "concerning."[98] As in v. 2 (cf. v. 3), ὁ τοιοῦτος may mean "this man," "the man involved," or "such a man." While it is possible that τοῦ τοιούτου is neuter ("Of such an experience," Wand; "Of such an instance," Berkeley), it is highly unlikely since τὸν τοιοῦτον (ἄνθρωπον) is masculine in vv. 2 and 3, and here in v. 5 ἐμαυτοῦ is parallel to τοῦ τοιούτου. With his rendering, "I am prepared to boast," Moffatt catches well the sense of the two gnomic futures, καυχήσομαι ... καυχήσομαι.[99] οὐ ... εἰ μή, "not ... except," may also be rendered by "only," as in Barrett's translation: "on my own behalf I will boast only in my weaknesses" (305). After καυχάομαι, the preposition ἐν introduces the object of the boasting, "about," "of," in which case it is synonymous with the two preceding cases of ὑπέρ (= περί).[100] In the expression ταῖς ἀσθενείαις the article is possessive, "my weaknesses" (so most EVV; see Textual Note h.), and the plural may

---

97. E.g., Barrett 305; Thrall 772.

98. E.g., Zerwick §96; Bultmann 222; *TDNT* 3.649 n. 35; cf. BDF §231(1) and BAGD 839a (noting that when ὑπέρ is "about equivalent" to περί, it often simultaneously bears the sense "in the interest of" or "in behalf of" — see BAGD 425d).

99. On this usage see BDF §349(1). Similarly, in Rom. 5:7 τις ἀποθανεῖται means "one is willing to die" (cf. Turner 86).

100. So, e.g., Zerwick and Grosvenor 560; Lambrecht 199. But H. A. A. Kennedy takes ἐν here and in v. 9 as causal (cited by Moulton and Howard 463). For constructions after καυχάομαι, see on 10:17.

be generalizing ("weakness," Lang 346; cf. v. 9a) or may refer to "times of weakness" (cf. BAGD 115b) or simply "weaknesses" (as in vv. 9b, 10), that is, "the things that show how weak I am" (GNB). The Damascus escape was one such instance (11:32-33); the debilitating "thorn" (vv. 7-8) was another. Black regards καυχᾶσθαι ἐν ἀσθενείαις as the general theme of chs. 10–13, with δύναμις ἐν ἀσθενείᾳ (12:9) forming the specific theme (147).

12:6 ἐὰν γὰρ θελήσω καυχήσασθαι, οὐκ ἔσομαι ἄφρων, ἀλήθειαν γὰρ ἐρῶ· φείδομαι δέ, μή τις εἰς ἐμὲ λογίσηται ὑπὲρ ὃ βλέπει με ἢ ἀκούει τι ἐξ ἐμοῦ. "But if I do wish to boast, I shall not turn out to be foolish, for I shall be speaking the truth; but I refrain, lest anyone should esteem me beyond what he sees in me or hears from me in any respect." Lest the Corinthians should imagine that Paul had nothing to boast about in addition to his weaknesses (cf. v. 5), he now disabuses them of that possible misunderstanding. If in fact he chose to boast about himself and his "strengths" — all his visions and revelations, his status and accomplishments — he would not be shown up as someone who foolishly was trafficking in fancy, for he would be declaring irrefutable facts. He had good reason to boast if that was his wish. But he repudiates that option of self-promotion so that the Corinthians should form an accurate estimate of him and his ministry — not an opinion based on his boasting but an assessment that relied on their own observation of his conduct and their own evaluation of his teaching. In the context of vv. 1-5 Paul is implying that esoteric visions or revelations do not afford a legitimate basis for evaluating apostolic authority. It is the "weakness" of humble, suffering service for the corporate good — what Paul means by διακονία (cf. 11:8) — not private ecstatic experience, that forms the proper credentials of ministry and the true sign of apostleship.

Since ἐάν is only rarely followed by the future indicative,[101] θελήσω should be construed as aorist subjunctive,[102] with the combination expressing a condition that is capable of being fulfilled, although the context (φείδομαι δέ) shows that this possibility will not become a reality. So ἐὰν γάρ should not be rendered "Even if" (= κἄν) (NIV; Martin 408), but either "For if" (Thrall 772) where γάρ explains why the choice of the theme of weakness (v. 5) was not forced on Paul by lack of other material (Barrett 312), or "But if" (Lambrecht 202) where γάρ introduces a statement that is antithetical to "about myself I will not boast."[103] The verb θέλω here expresses a simple desire ("wish") or a "deliberate preference" ("choose," so Barrett 312). With the complementary infinitive καυχήσασθαι, we need to supply an object from the context — "about myself" (v. 5), "of the revelations" (v. 7) (Heckel 301), "of the excellence of

---

101. There are textual issues with each of the actual or possible NT instances: Luke 19:40 (ἐὰν οὗτοι σιωπήσουσιν, read by ℵ A B L N W Δ 579 *al*, and preferred in NA²⁷); Acts 8:31 (ἐὰν μή τις ὁδηγήσει με, read by p⁵⁰ ℵ [B*] C E L 6 614 1175 *al*, and preferred in NA²⁷); Matt. 18:19; Rev. 2:22. See the grammatical discussion in Robertson 1009-10.

102. On the relation between the aorist subjunctive and the future indicative, see Robertson 924-25.

103. For the adversative sense of γάρ, see BAGD 152 s.v. 4.

these revelations" (v. 7) (Spicq 2.300 n. 21), or "of other visions and revelations" (v. 1). οὐκ ἔσομαι ἄφρων does not mean "I shall not be playing the fool," but "I shall not turn out to be foolish" or "(If I should decide to boast,) I should not be made to look foolish" (JB), where ἄφρων does not allude to the foolishness of boasting (cf. 11:17, 21b, 23a; 12:11) but to the folly of speaking untruths; a fool does not speak the truth but lies (cf. 11:31). ἀλήθειαν γὰρ ἐρῶ supplies the reason Paul would not be caught out as a foolish liar if he decided to boast about himself and his ecstatic experiences or pastoral achievements: he would be speaking the sober truth and not rehearsing claims that lacked substance. This emphasis on truthtelling could be a hint that Paul's opponents were laying claim to spiritual experiences they had never had,[104] but, as Wolff observes (245 n. 342), in that case we would have expected an emphatic ἐγώ with ἔσομαι.

Barrett takes φείδομαι as conative and would supply ὑμῶν (cf. 1:23): "I am trying to spare you" (312). But with no personal object expressed or needed, it is better to treat this use of φείδομαι as absolute ("I refrain")[105] and supply τοῦ καυχᾶσθαι[106] ὑπὲρ ἐμαυτοῦ or the like. "But [adversative δέ] I refrain [from boasting about myself]."[107] In the clause μὴ . . . λογίσηται, μή is not a negative particle but a conjunction introducing a negative purpose clause.[108] Clearly the clause expresses a deep concern on Paul's part, if not a fear (as though φοβούμενος stood before μή; cf. 11:3; 12:20-21).[109]

λογίζομαι τινί τι is a commercial expression meaning "set something down to someone's account,"[110] "to credit something to someone." But in the present instance there is no dative or accusative with λογίσηται. We could treat εἰς ἐμέ as equivalent to ἐμοί (cf. Turner 253) and ὑπὲρ κτλ. as the direct object of λογίσηται. This would produce a sense such as "lest anyone should credit me with a reputation that exceeds what he sees me to be or anything that he hears from me."[111] But if we surrender the possible commercial sense of λογίζομαι and give this verb the intransitive of meaning of "make an evaluation," "form a judgment," render εἰς ἐμέ by "with respect to me,"[112] and perhaps supply τό before ὑπὲρ κτλ., a rendering such as Barclay's would result: "I forbear to boast in

104. Cf. Barrett 312; "Opponents" 245; Lincoln 75.
105. So also Bultmann 223, giving φείδομαι the sense "I do without it," "I forego it."
106. So BAGD 854d; Meyer 679; also Zerwick, *Analysis* 413.
107. It is possible that φείδομαι is a futuristic present, indicating present intent, "I will avoid boasting" (Louw and Nida §13.152).
108. Cf. BAGD 517b, citing Mark 13:36 and Acts 27:42 as parallel uses of μή with the aorist subjunctive; Robertson 988.
109. Cf. Héring 89: ". . . for fear of arousing an impression. . . ."
110. Cf. LSJ 1055 s.v. λογίζομαι I.3.a. 2 Cor. 5:19 affords an example of this construction: μὴ λογιζόμενος αὐτοῖς τὰ παραπτώματα αὐτῶν.
111. Thrall 772. She retains τι ("anything") as original but suggests that it may be displaced (801 n. 228). A commercial sense is given to λογίζομαι here by RV, TCNT, NASB; BAGD 476a; BDF §145(2) ("perhaps").
112. For this sense of εἰς, see BAGD 230 s.v. 5.

case anyone forms a judgment about me beyond what he sees in me and hears from me."[113] Either way, ὑπέρ means "beyond" or "in excess of," and points to a crediting or an evaluation that outstrips what is warranted by the evidence.[114]

In the clause ὑπὲρ ὃ βλέπει με, the relative pronoun ὅ means "that which" = "what," the subject of βλέπει is the preceding τις now individualized, and με is probably an accusative of respect ("with respect to me" = "in me"[115]), although some supply ποιοῦντα after με ("what one may see me doing"[116]) while others supply "to be" after με, which makes ὅ predicative ("what he sees me to be"[117]). As for the final clause in the verse, ἢ [ὑπὲρ ὃ] ἀκούει τι ἐξ ἐμοῦ, "or [beyond what] he hears from me in any respect," the difficult indefinite pronoun τι (assuming its originality — see Textual Note j.), could — with difficulty — be assumed to be displaced and so translated as if it followed λογίσηται[118] or preceded ἀκούει,[119] but it is easier to render it "perhaps"[120] or "possibly,"[121] or, best of all, construe it as an accusative of respect and therefore parallel to με, "in any respect."[122]

βλέπω and ἀκούω form a natural pair although the reverse order ("hear"– "see") is also found.[123] Seeing and hearing encompass the two primary ways in which an evaluation of a person can be undertaken — by observing conduct and by listening to what is said. In Paul's case the reference would be to all his behavior as a person and as a missionary-pastor, and to all his preaching and teaching, that is, to his διδασκαλία ("teaching") and ἀγωγή ("conduct"),[124] which are the first two characteristics of Paul's life that he says Timothy has observed (2 Tim. 3:10). Paul's fear was that his converts might gain an impression of him that went beyond the evidence of their own eyes and ears and did not correspond

113. EVV that give a similar, noncommercial sense to λογίζομαι here include Weymouth, Moffatt, Goodspeed, RSV, NEB, GNB, JB, NAB¹, NIV, NJB, NAB², REB, NRSV.

114. For this sense of ὑπέρ, see BAGD 839 s.v. 2.

115. This is the rendering of BAGD 143c; Barrett 313; Wolff 239. Phil. 4:9 is a close parallel, ἃ . . . εἴδετε ἐν ἐμοί.

116. Furnish 513, 528, following Zmijewski 360.

117. Thrall 772, 801-2; Zerwick and Grosvenor 560.

118. Furnish 513: "so that no one can credit me with *something* beyond what one may see me doing or hear from me" (italics mine).

119. Thrall 772 (cf. 801 n. 228): "lest anyone should credit me with a reputation that exceeds what he sees me to be or *anything* that he hears from me" (italics mine).

120. Wolff 239.

121. Meyer 679, who regards τι as a "condensed expression" for *si quid quando audit* ("if he ever hears anything").

122. Cf. Heckel 301.

123. For the βλέπω–ἀκούω pairing, see Mark 8:18; Rom. 11:8. For the reverse order ἀκούω –βλέπω, see Matt. 11:4; 13:14; Acts 8:6; 28:26. A pairing of ὁράω and ἀκούω is found in Matt. 13:15; Acts 28:27; Rom. 15:21; 1 Cor. 2:9; Phil. 4:9.

124. Barnett identifies what Paul's converts "see" and "hear" as his "weaknesses" and his preaching of Christ (respectively) (565). For Cambier, the couplet βλέπειν–ἀκούειν refers not to Paul's deeds and words but to the lowliness and external weakness that marked his ministry and that shows his acceptance of his role as a faithful servant of Christ ("Critère" 498-505). But such an interpretation coheres better with ὃ βλέπει με than with ἀκούει (τι) ἐξ ἐμοῦ.

to reality, an impression that could easily be created if he dwelt on the details of any spectacular visions or revelations he had experienced. What authenticated his apostleship and his ministry was not some written record of unverifiable otherworldly encounters but the living record of his converts' changed lives (3:2-3) and their careful estimation of his conduct and teaching.[125]

12:7 καὶ τῇ ὑπερβολῇ τῶν ἀποκαλύψεων, διό, ἵνα μὴ ὑπεραίρωμαι, ἐδόθη μοι σκόλοψ τῇ σαρκί, ἄγγελος Σατανᾶ ἵνα με κολαφίζῃ, ἵνα μὴ ὑπεραίρωμαι. "And because of the extraordinary nature of the revelations, therefore, so that I might not become over-elated, there was given me a thorn in the flesh, a messenger of Satan sent to pommel me, so that I might not become over-elated." Both in 11:30 and in 12:5 Paul indicated his (reluctant) willingness to boast about his weaknesses. His first dramatic example was his humiliating exit from Damascus (11:32-33); the second is his permanent receipt of a debilitating "thorn." The exit was a single episode that nevertheless was emblazoned on his memory because of its ignominy. The "thorn," on the other hand, was a recurrent trial that could incapacitate and humiliate him at any time. Being both past and present, "weakness" was integral to Paul's experience.

καὶ τῇ ὑπερβολῇ τῶν ἀποκαλύψεων may be construed as the conclusion of v. 6 or as the beginning of v. 7. Perhaps the best way to clarify the relevant exegetical issues is to consider representative translations. Any italics are mine.

1. Verse 7a as the conclusion of v. 6
  (a) "But I refrain, *lest* any one should credit me . . . , *and because* of the marvellous character of the revelations. It was for this reason . . ." (TCNT). On this interpretation two reasons are given for the φείδομαι, one negative (μή τις κτλ.) and one positive (τῇ ὑπερβολῇ, causal dative), with a conjunctive καί linking them. διό begins a new sentence, as often in Paul (see Textual Note k.).
  (b) "But I am declining to do this, so that no one can credit me with something beyond what one may see me doing or hear from me, *specifically, because of* the extraordinary character of the revelations" (Furnish 513). Here καί is epexegetic and introduces a second explanatory phrase (τῇ ὑπερβολῇ, causal dative) dependent on φείδομαι (Furnish 528). Others render καί, when considered to be epexegetic, by "namely."[126] NRSV appears to give καί an ascensive sense, ". . . even considering the exceptional character of the revelations." Or again, Young and Ford (274) seem to treat καί as emphatic: "but I refrain, in case anyone should reach an estimate of me *based on* more than he sees of me or hears from me, *indeed on the basis of* extraordinary revelations." These diverse interpretations

---

125. Since 12:6 directly addresses the matter of the proper criteria for the assessment of Paul, a central concern in chs. 10–13, it seems inappropriate to read this verse as a parenthesis (so Moffatt and Wand). On this possibility, see the comments of Cambier, "Critère" 504.

126. Zmijewski 355; "Kontextbezug" 271 and n. 42; Wolff 239, 246; Heckel 69, 301.

of καί highlight what are the main difficulties with this view of vv. 6-7a
— the presence of καί and the stylistically awkward position of the
phrase that follows. On this understanding we would have expected Paul
to write φείδομαι δέ, μή τις τῇ ὑπερβολῇ τῶν ἀποκαλύψεων εἰς ἐμὲ
λογίσηται κτλ., which, interestingly, is the sense reflected in Goodspeed's
translation (see below).

(c) "But I will refrain from it, for I do not want anyone *to be influenced by*
the wonderful character of these revelations *to think* more of me than is
justified by my words or conduct" (Goodspeed).[127]

The strongest argument in favor of this understanding of v. 7a is the resulting
position of διό as the first word in the sentence, a position this conjunction regularly holds in Paul.[128] Other arguments sometimes adduced in support[129] are
either unconvincing or inconclusive. For example, it is claimed that if v. 7a concludes v. 6, we have (i) two parallel triads that are antithetical, and (ii) the neat
repetition of ἵνα μὴ ὑπεραίρωμαι as a framework for the intervening statement
ἐδόθην . . . κολαφίζῃ. Or again, it is argued that if v. 7a is linked with v. 7b, a
cumbersome multiplication of datives results, ἐδόθη is distant from τῇ
ὑπερβολῇ, and διό stands awkwardly between a causal dative (τῇ ὑπερβολῇ) and
a telic ἵνα.[130]

2. Verse 7a as linked with v. 7b

(a) "*As to* the extraordinary revelations, in order that I might not become
conceited I was given a thorn in the flesh" (NAB[1]). Here τῇ ὑπερβολῇ is a
dative of respect, ἵνα μὴ ὑπεραίρωμαι is linked with ἐδόθη, and καί is untranslated.

(b) "And to keep me from being too elated *by* the abundance of revelations, a
thorn was given me in the flesh" (RSV).[131] In this case τῇ ὑπερβολῇ is
seen as an instrumental dative construed with ἵνα μὴ ὑπεραίρωμαι, while
διό is either rejected as a secondary reading or left untranslated. The difficulty with this rendering, apart from the reasons for retaining διό (see
Textual Note k.), is the word order. Paul did not write (διὸ) ἵνα μὴ τῇ
ὑπερβολῇ τῶν ἀποκαλύψεων ὑπεραίρωμαι, ἐδόθη κτλ.

(c) "And *because of* the surpassing greatness of the revelations, *for this reason,* to keep me from exalting myself, there was given me a thorn in the
flesh" (NASB).[132] On this view the dative τῇ ὑπερβολῇ is causal and διό

127. NJB and NAB[2] also ignore καί in their rendering of v. 7a.
128. As in 1:20; 2:8; 4:16; 5:9; 6:17; 12:10.
129. Notably by Zmijewski 354-55; "Kontextbezug" 268-71.
130. WH prints διὸ ἵνα μὴ ὑπεραίρωμαι κτλ. but suspects that "some primitive error [is]
probable" in vv. 6-7 (1.578; similarly Hort in WH 2. Appendix 120).
131. Similarly GNB, JB, NIV, REB; Héring 89; Lang 346.
132. Similarly Hughes 449 n. 138; Thrall 772, and the RV, which treats the initial phrase τῇ
ὑπερβολῇ τῶν ἀποκαλύψεων as anacoluthic (so also Zerwick, *Analysis* 413; Prümm 1.656).

looks back to the preceding phrase. This understanding of the construction is preferable. True, διό is pleonastic, "an emphatic redundancy" (Hughes 449 n. 138), but it does serve as a bridge between the cause of the ἐδόθη (viz. τῇ ὑπερβολῇ τῶν ἀποκαλύψεων) and its purpose (viz. ἵνα μὴ ὑπεραίρωμαι).[133] A more natural sense results if we relate τῇ ὑπερβολῇ τῶν ἀποκαλύψεων forward to the giving of the thorn, as denoting its cause, than if we refer this phrase retrospectively to Paul's refraining from boasting (1[a] above) or to the danger of an inflated opinion of him (1[b] and [c] above).

If we render τῇ ὑπερβολῇ as an abstract noun, the sense will be "the exceptional greatness" (NJB), "the stupendous grandeur" (Weymouth), or "the extraordinary nature," but it is not inappropriate to render it adjectivally, "the extraordinary revelations" (BAGD 840b). But we need not (*pace* Scott 227) see the expression as hyperbole and as expressing the extraordinary number as well as the extraordinary quality of the revelations. The plural τῶν ἀποκαλύψεων (possessive genitive) may be generalizing ("the revelation granted to me," Barclay) or may refer to other extraordinary revelations Paul had received in addition to the unique event described in vv. 2-4 (Thrall 806). But it seems best to account for this plural in the light of the multiple ῥήματα he had heard (v. 4); the "words" conveyed "revelations."[134]

If the reason for God's giving of the σκόλοψ was "the extraordinary nature of the revelations" Paul had received, the purpose of God's action was to prevent Paul's becoming overly elated, ἵνα μὴ ὑπεραίρωμαι. A unique privilege could easily generate a sense of spiritual superiority or even presumptive arrogance. Whether we render ὑπεραίρομαι by "(be) unduly elated" (NEB, REB) or "become over-elated" (Cassirer) or "become conceited" (Martin 388),[135] the prefix ὑπερ- signifies "excess" (Robertson 629). This negative purpose clause precedes the main verb (ἐδόθη) for added emphasis (Turner, *Style* 94).

ἐδόθη μοι σκόλοψ τῇ σαρκί, ἄγγελος Σατανᾶ. The word order indicates that σκόλοψ, not ἄγγελος, is the subject of ἐδόθη;[136] it would be strange (if ἄγγελος were the subject) for an appositional phrase, σκόλοψ τῇ σαρκί, to precede the subject. The noun σκόλοψ is cognate with the verb σκάλλω, "hoe," "hack," "stir up," and signifies "something pointed," whether a sharp stake (σκόλοπες refers to a defensive "palisade"), a javelin, the point of a fishing hook, a splinter, or a thorn.[137] Classical Greek usage might suggest "stake" as Paul's meaning, but

---

133. Some translations (e.g., NEB; Lambrecht 199) bring διό forward — illegitimately it would seem — to the beginning of the sentence, making it refer (presumably) to v. 6b.

134. So also Price 35.

135. So also NAB[1]; Louw and Nida §20.27 (cf. §88.211, "be puffed up with pride").

136. But cf. Weymouth: "lest I should be over-elated there has been sent to me, like the agony of impalement, Satan's angel."

137. See LSJ 1613 s.v.; G. Delling, *TDNT* 7.409-13 (who prefers "thorn" or "splinter," 412); Park 179-83 (who prefers "stake," 183).

Septuagintal usage should here be regarded as regulative. In its four LXX uses σκόλοψ never means "stake." In Num. 33:55 a warning is given to the Israelites that if they fail to destroy all the inhabitants of Canaan, those who are left will be "thorns in your eyes (σκόλοπες ἐν τοῖς ὀφθαλμοῖς ὑμῶν) and arrows in your sides (βολίδες ἐν ταῖς πλευραῖς ὑμῶν)." Similarly, in Ezek. 28:24 opponents of the Israelites who dishonored them are compared to "a bitter thorn (σκόλοψ πικρίας) and a painful briar (ἄκανθα ὀδύνης)." Then in Hos. 2:8 God warns his unfaithful wife Israel that he will hedge up her chosen path with thorns (ἐγὼ φράσσω τὴν ὁδὸν αὐτῆς ἐν σκόλοψιν)." Finally, in Sir. 43:19 wintry icicles are compared to "pointed thorns (σκολόπων ἄκρα)." The meaning "thorn" is appropriate in all four of these LXX uses of σκόλοψ. Two further illustrations of the meaning "thorn" or "splinter" may be given. Field (187) cites a passage from a second-century-A.D. writer of fables, Valerius Babrius (*Fab.* 122). A donkey stepped on a σκόλοψ and became lame. Meeting a wolf, he appealed to him to pull out the thorn (τὴν ἄκανθαν) from his foot. MM refers (578) to a third-century-A.D. papyrus in which a mother speaks of her son's sore foot "because of a splinter (ἀπὸ σκολάπου [= σκόλοπος])" (*BGU* 2.380[9]). We concur with Bernard's judgment that "St. Paul's trial is compared to the vexatious irritation of a thorn rather than to the agonizing and fatal torture of impalement on a stake" (111).[138]

Although τῇ σαρκί qualifies σκόλοψ (not ἐδόθη),[139] just as μοι belongs with ἐδόθη, τῇ σαρκί more closely defines the indirect object μοι. If σάρξ here refers to the corrupt human nature, τῇ σαρκί will be a dative of disadvantage, "for the (inconvenience of the) flesh," that is, to curb evil desires, to prevent "the lower nature" from becoming aggressive.[140] But more probably this dative is locative[141] and σάρξ denotes the physical body, "in the flesh," that is, "(a thorn) lodged in the flesh." But even if τῇ σαρκί is rendered "for the flesh," the reference may be to the physical body,[142] presumably then with the dative being classified as a dative of disadvantage[143] or of respect. In addition, the article with σαρκί may be possessive: "in my flesh" (NIV, REB) or "to pierce my flesh" (TCNT). The commonest rendering, "a thorn in the flesh," may be safely followed.[144]

138. Most EVV and commentators prefer the meaning "thorn" in 12:7, some opt for "stake" (Barclay; A. P. Stanley 254; Schlatter 666; Hughes 447; Alexander 470 ["no trifling prickle, but a ghastly stake"]; Park 183), while Bruce (*Galatians* 208; *Paul* 135, 227) prefers "splinter." There is no reason to follow Schlatter when he claims that σκόλοψ means "beam" and is here a synonym for σταυρός (666 and n. 1). Some EVV "translate" the metaphor of σκόλοψ τῇ σαρκί: "a bitter physical affliction" (Goodspeed), "a sharp physical pain" (NEB), "a painful physical ailment" (GNB).

139. But RSB and NRSV have "a thorn was given me in the flesh." Cf. Allo: "μοι and τῇ σαρκί are two complements of ἐδόθη, the second explaining the first" (310).

140. Thus, e.g., Tasker 174-75.

141. Robertson (528) recognizes this as a possibility (see also Scott 240). On the locatival dative, see Moule 44, 46-47; Turner 242-43.

142. So Plummer 348; Thrall 772, 807.

143. So Hughes 447 n. 133, 448; McCant, "Thorn" 567.

144. Thus BAGD 756c; RV, Moffatt, NASB, JB, NAB[1], NJB, NAB[2]; similarly RSV, NRSV.

854

Since ἄγγελος Σατανᾶ stands in apposition to σκόλοψ τῇ σαρκί, there must be some sense in which the thorn was Satan's own agent or deputy, whether we translate the phrase as "an angel of Satan" or "a messenger of Satan."[145] It is not simply a case of Satanic inspiration behind some human adversary of Paul, but of Satan's use of Paul's σκόλοψ by means of one of his demonic deputies (see further below, on ἐδόθη). The genitive Σατανᾶ[146] may be possessive ("belonging to Satan"), or better, subjective ("sent by Satan").

The aorist passive ἐδόθη prompts two questions. When was the "thorn" given, and by whom? Even if καί, the first word in v. 7, is a simple connective ("and") and not consecutive ("and so"),[147] this conjunction suggests a specific link between the experience recorded in vv. 3-4 and Paul's receiving of the "thorn." Indeed, if the σκόλοψ was given "because of the extraordinary character of the revelations" conveyed to Paul during his time in paradise, it is a fair assumption that he received the "thorn" shortly, if not immediately, after his ascent into the third heaven, that is, some fourteen years prior to the time of writing (v. 2).[148]

As for the agent behind the "giving," there are obviously two possibilities — either Satan (or his ἄγγελος) or God (or Christ). If Satan was seen by Paul as sometimes a source of human illness (cf. 1 Cor. 5:5) and the σκόλοψ was some physical malady, it is conceivable that the passive voice of ἐδόθη conceals a reference to Satan. However, because a positive spiritual purpose of the δοῦναι — to prevent over-elation or conceitedness — is stated in advance of the verb ἐδόθη, it is unlikely that Paul's readers would assume Satanic agency in the giving of the "thorn."[149] Also, as Plummer observes (348), if Paul had intended to imply that Satan was the agent, δίδωμι, a word often used of the bestowal of divine favors,[150] would probably have been replaced by a more apposite term such as ἐπιτίθημι (Luke 10:30; 23:26; Acts 16:23), or βάλλω (Rev. 2:24), or ἐπιβάλλω (1 Cor. 7:35). Far more probably, ἐδόθη is a "theological passive,"

---

145. For the notion of the ἄγγελοι of the devil or Satan, see Matt. 25:41; Rev. 12:7, 9.

146. This is a "Doric genitive" (also 2:11) (see Robertson 254-55). All of the 36 NT uses of Σατανᾶς are articular (as at 2:11; 11:14) except for Mark 3:23 (two uses); 8:33 (vocative); Luke 22:3; and the present verse where the canon of Apollonius accounts for the anarthrous state.

147. For this latter usage, see BAGD 392 s.v. I.2.f.

148. In his provocative article, "Punished in Paradise (An Exegetical Theory on II Corinthians 12:1-10)," R. M. Price argues that the thorn was literally a demon or malevolent angel sent to punish Paul in the heavenly throne-room itself for his pride in his enviable privilege as a recipient of ineffable revelations. Three times Paul appeals to the exalted Lord for relief (12:8), who finally declares, "My grace is sufficient for you, for my power is made perfect in weakness" (12:9) (36-37). Against this improbable theory, see Furnish 550; Thrall 817. Appealing, as Price also does (36-37), to Jewish "throne-mysticism" texts that depict angels or demons as attacking visionaries who were deemed unworthy of ascending to heaven, Scott develops the possibility that the ἄγγελος Σατανᾶ tormented Paul during his journey to reach the divine throne-room (228).

149. Pace Danker (193): "The humor in Paul's reference to Satan lies in the fact that Satan, who is known in Jewish tradition as God's arch-rival, with a colossal ego, would cross the rhetorical stage as a competitor who sends Paul an antidote to possible pride and arrogance."

150. E.g., 1:22; 8:1; 10:8; Gal. 3:21; Eph. 3:8.

with God as the implied agent, as is the case with the earlier passives, ἁρπαγέντα (v. 2) and ἡρπάγη (v. 4). Moreover, the giving of the "thorn" was designed to achieve a beneficial and therefore a divine purpose (ἵνα μὴ ὑπεραίρωμαι, twice in v. 7).

Here, then, we are confronted with a paradox. One and the same σκόλοψ was simultaneously given by God and used by Satan; a δῶρον θεοῦ is also an ἄγγελος Σατανᾶ. It is not that God is here working through Satan,[151] or that there is dual agency, divine and demonic,[152] but that Satan is active at the same time as God and by his permission. As Paul experienced his σκόλοψ, he discovered it to be both a gift from God and a tool of Satan — in the first case, because it deflated pride (ἵνα μὴ ὑπεραίρωμαι); in the second case, because it inflicted suffering (ἵνα με κολαφίζῃ). The deflation of pride is God's distinctive work (Prov. 16:5; Isa. 13:11; Matt. 23:12; Luke 1:51), while the infliction of suffering is Satan's distinctive work (Job 1:8-19; 2:3-7; Luke 13:16; 1 Cor. 5:5). Also, if the σκόλοψ was a recurrent physical ailment (see below), it may have sometimes constituted a hindrance to the propagation of the gospel, either by exciting the contempt of Paul's hearers (cf. Gal. 4:13-14) or by so incapacitating him that travel plans were frustrated.

The verse ends with two ἵνα clauses, one positive in form but negative in content (ἵνα με κολαφίζῃ), the other negative in form but positive in content (ἵνα μὴ ὑπεραίρωμαι). This second telic clause is an exact and therefore emphatic repetition[153] of the earlier stated purpose of the bestowal of the σκόλοψ — to curb the spiritual elation that might constantly arise from Paul's remembrance of his unique privilege as one who had experienced an ascent into paradise and had received revelations there. The verb κολαφίζω, in the first telic clause, means "strike with the fist" (a κόλαφος is a "blow with the fist" or "a box on the ear"), or, more generally, "maltreat violently," "batter," "knock about."[154] Because the sense is metaphorical, the subject of κολαφίζῃ could be either ἄγγελος or (possibly) a personified σκόλοψ. The present tense points to continual or recurrent buffeting, just as ὑπεραίρωμαι indicates the constant danger of conceitedness or improper elation that Paul faced.

Some EVV refer both purpose clauses to ἄγγελος Σατανᾶς: "an angel of Satan to beat me and keep me from getting proud" (NAB¹).[155] This has the effect of applying the second instance of ἵνα μὴ ὑπεραίρωμαι to Satanic purpose,

151. As Thornton (151-52) proposes. In her treatment of 12:7-10 in the light of "the Job model of affliction" where Satan attacks God's righteous servants, Garrett emphasizes that "*God has granted Satan the authority to harass Paul.* . . . God permits Satan's intervention because it will keep Paul humble. . . . The devil sometimes *serves* God's aims, but he does not *sympathize* with them" (90-91).

152. As Thrall (808) suggests. Meyer speaks of Satan as "only the *mediate* giver" (680).

153. On the textual issue here, see Textual Note m.

154. "Christ, too, was κολαφιζόμενος [cf. Matt. 26:67//Mark 14:65]; His κολαφίζοντες were those who crucified Him but finally Satan and his minions" (K. L. Schmidt, *TDNT* 3.821).

155. Similarly Moffatt, GNB, JB.

but this seems less likely than explaining the repetition of this statement as emphatic, to safeguard the overarching purpose of God in the midst of the machinations of Satan. Through their punctuation, other EVV leave open the possibility that both purpose clauses could qualify σκόλοψ or ἄγγελος Σατανᾶ: "a thorn was given me in the flesh, a messenger of Satan, to harass me, to keep me from being too elated" (RSV).[156] The best alternative is to relate ἵνα με κολαφίζῃ exclusively to ἄγγελος Σατανᾶ and to regard ἵνα μὴ ὑπεραίρωμαι as an emphatic repetition: "I was given a thorn in my flesh, a messenger of Satan sent to buffet me; this was to save me from being unduly elated" (REB).[157]

From vv. 7-10 we may deduce that this σκόλοψ had certain characteristics.[158]

(1) It was given to Paul as a direct consequence of the revelations he received in paradise (καὶ τῇ ὑπερβολῇ τῶν ἀποκαλύψεων . . . ἐδόθη μοι σκόλοψ, v. 7).

(2) It caused him acute pain (σκόλοψ), either physically or psychologically (τῇ σαρκί), which prompted him to seek its removal (vv. 7-8).

(3) He regarded it as simultaneously a gift from God and an instrument of Satan (v. 7).

(4) It was a permanent condition (implied by the two presents, ὑπεραίρωμαι and κολαφίζῃ [v. 7], and by the negative divine response to his three requests for its removal [vv. 8-9]), yet its exacerbations were intermittent (implied by τρίς, v. 8).

(5) It was humbling, for it was designed to curb or prevent spiritual arrogance (ἵνα μὴ ὑπεραίρωμαι) over the extraordinary nature of the revelations received (v. 7).

(6) It was humiliating, comparable to receiving vicious blows about the face (ἵνα με κολαφίζῃ, v. 7).

(7) It caused Paul to feel weak (vv. 9-10), yet the weakness it caused was an object of boasting (v. 9; cf. v. 5) and a source of pleasure (v. 10).

Although Paul has not identified the "thorn," commentators have not been slow to attempt the impossible. Paucity of data and the ambiguity of Paul's lan-

---

156. Similarly Goodspeed, NAB².

157. Similarly RV, NASB, Barclay, NRSV, Cassirer; among the commentators, Héring 89; Barrett 305; Furnish 513; Carrez 226; Lambrecht 199. Robertson cites ἵνα με κολαφίζῃ as an instance where a relative pronoun might have been used in place of ἵνα (960), and this is reflected in the renderings of Wendland (243) and Lang (346).

158. The following list anticipates the exegesis of vv. 8-10. Lightfoot's description of the characteristics of the σκόλοψ (Galatians 189-90) presupposes that the phrase δι' ἀσθένειαν τῆς σαρκός in Gal. 4:13 alludes to the same phenomenon as 2 Cor. 12:7 (Galatians 186, 190), a presupposition shared by Bruce (Galatians 208; Paul 136), Heckel ("Dorn" 65-92), and Hafemann, "Weakness" 133-36, but contested by Mullins 300-301 and McCant 145-46; "Thorn" 564. The expression διὰ τὴν ἀσθένειαν τῆς σαρκός in Rom. 6:19 refers to the limitations of understanding imposed by a fleshly outlook.

guage have frustrated — and will always frustrate — all efforts to reach finality in this enigmatic question. We may parallel the similarly inconclusive attempts made by historians to diagnose the complaint of the emperor Claudius.[159] If, in fact, Paul had identified his σκόλοψ, Christians of subsequent generations who lacked his particular affliction would have tended to regard his experience, as summarized in vv. 8-10, as largely irrelevant to their situation. As it is, multitudes of believers, with a variety of "thorns," have been challenged and consoled as they have made Paul's experience their own. Of course, Paul's silence about the precise nature of his σκόλοψ was not prompted by the need of successive generations; his readers were doubtless already aware of its nature.

The proposed identifications, legion in number, may be classified under three main headings.[160] Some representative proponents will be listed under each category.

A. Spiritual or psychological anxiety
   (1) pangs of conscience about his earlier misdeeds in Jerusalem as a persecutor, which gave him a sense of unworthiness (Schlatter 667)
   (2) anguish over Israel's stubborn disbelief (Menoud, "Thorn" 24-26)
B. Opposition to Paul
   (1) Opponents in general (Andriessen 462-68; Barré, "Qumran" 225-27; Woods 50-51; Murphy-O'Connor 119; *Paul* 321-22; Barnett 570 ("the rise of the Judaizing, anti-Paul movement")
   (2) A single opponent (Mullins 301-2; Forbes 21; NAB² 513, note on 12:7b)
   (3) Opposition at Corinth
       • the opposition and insults of the "false apostles" (11:14) (Bieder 332; Binder 10-11)
       • the accusation of Paul's detractors at Corinth that he was an ἄγγελος Σατανᾶ, having been a persecutor of the church (Thierry 309)
       • the rejection of the legitimacy of Paul's apostolate by a minority in the "sick" Corinthian church (McCant 149-50; "Thorn" 550-72)
C. Physical malady
   (1) Unspecified as to its nature (BAGD 441b, 743b, 756c; K. L. Schmidt, *TDNT* 3.820; Dodd 68; Bruce, *Paraphrase* 155; *History* 245; Bultmann 116, 224; Black 146; Fee, *Presence* 352-53; Thomas 45-47)
   (2) Specified
       • Fever: (a) malarial (Ramsay 94-97; Allo 311, 320-21; Prumm 1.664-65)

---

159. See M. Grant, *The Roman Emperors* (New York: Scribner's, 1975) 33.
160. Surveys of the interpretation of Paul's σκόλοψ are found in Lightfoot, *Galatians* 186-91; Plummer (CGT) 239-45; Allo 313-21; Hughes 442-46; Thrall 809-18.

(b) Malta (Alexander 547-48)
- Defective vision (Nisbet 126; Leary 520-22)
- Migraine headaches (Uhle-Wettler[161]; Heckel, "Dorn" 76; Thrall 818).

The present writer believes that some kind of physical ailment most easily accommodates the seven characteristics of the σκόλοψ outlined above.

12:8 ὑπὲρ τούτου τρὶς τὸν κύριον παρεκάλεσα ἵνα ἀποστῇ ἀπ᾽ ἐμοῦ. "About this I implored the Lord three times that it should leave me." Naturally enough, Paul seems to have been repelled by the suffering that the "thorn" caused him (cf. ἵνα με κολαφίζῃ, v. 7) and to have been unaware of the spiritual benefit that it had brought him or could bring him (cf. ἵνα μὴ ὑπεραίρωμαι, v. 7), for he prayed fervently for its removal. Since the focus in v. 7 was on the grammatical subject of the sentence, the σκόλοψ τῇ σαρκί, and not on the appositive ἄγγελος Σατανᾶ, it is appropriate to find the antecedent of τούτου (which may be masculine or neuter) in the σκόλοψ (masculine) or "in the matter of the σκόλοψ" (neuter). In the latter case ὑπὲρ τούτου will mean "regarding this matter" (Carrez 226), "Concerning this thing" (RV), or simply "about this" (RSV, Barclay, NRSV).[162] This last rendering has the advantage of (potentially) reproducing the ambiguity of the Greek. But some commentators, pointing to the fact that ἀφίστημι always has a personal subject in its NT uses,[163] contend that ἄγγελος Σατανᾶ must be the referent of both τούτου and ἀποστῇ.[164] If so, ὑπὲρ τούτου means "Concerning this angel" (Barrett 305), "About this one" (Lambrecht 199), or "concerning him" (Cassirer). In response we may observe that in v. 7 ἄγγελος need not be a *personal* emissary of Satan; that the implied subject of ἀποστῇ in v. 8 may be a personified σκόλοψ; and that, in any event, examples of an impersonal subject of the intransitive use of ἀφίστημι (+ ἀπό) are not unknown.[165] However ὑπὲρ τούτου is rendered, the preposition carries the sense of περί, "about," "concerning,"[166] as frequently in 2 Corinthians (see on 1:7-8).

In secular Greek παρακαλέω is a common word for invoking a deity for aid.[167] In the Gospels it is regularly used to describe requests made to Jesus for his help, whether in healing (e.g., Matt. 8:5; Mark 8:22) or in granting a favor (e.g., Mark 5:17-18). The boon Paul sought in his urgent entreaty was the departure of the "thorn," the ἵνα clause indicating the content, not the purpose, of

---

161. As cited by Spicq 3.236 n. 28.

162. So also, e.g., Thrall 722, 818 n. 371.

163. E.g., Luke 4:13; Acts 12:10; 22:29; 1 Tim. 4:1; 2 Tim. 2:19; Heb. 3:12.

164. Plummer 353; Hughes 441 n. 120; 449 n. 139; Lambrecht 203.

165. E.g., θλῖψις (Hermas, *Similitudes* 7.7), ζωή (Hermas, *Similitudes* 8.6.4), σύνεσις (Hermas, *Similitudes* 9.22.2), πονηρία (Hermas, *Vision* 3.6.1) — cited by BAGD 127 s.v. ἀφίστημι 2.c.

166. Moule 65; Zerwick §96. But BDF §231(1) suggests "because of that."

167. See O. Schmitz, *TDNT* 5.775.

the παράκλησις:[168] "that it should once and for all go away from me," "that it should leave me" (ἵνα ἀποστῇ ἀπ' ἐμοῦ).[169]

It is scarcely open to question that the person addressed in Paul's plea for relief from the battering of the ἄγγελος Σατανᾶ was the Lord Jesus. (1) ὁ κύριος from v. 8 is the implicit subject of εἴρηκεν in v. 9, so that μου in the expression ἡ χάρις μου must also refer to "the Lord." But the closely related δύναμις in v. 9a (note γάρ and the possessive article ἡ[170]) is defined in v. 9b as ἡ δύναμις τοῦ Χριστοῦ. (2) The articular κύριος normally refers to Christ in Paul.[171] (3) In 13:7 prayer addressed to God the Father is expressed by εὐχόμεθα . . . πρὸς τὸν θεόν. Now it is clear that in the early church prayers both of thanksgiving and of petition were normally directed to God the Father (e.g., Phil. 1:3; 4:6). Eph. 2:18 expresses the norm: Christians, both Jews and Gentiles, enjoy access to the Father, through Christ, in one Spirit (πρός–διά–ἐν). But on occasion an individual believer (Acts 7:59-60; 9:10-17; 22:16, 19; 2 Cor. 12:8) or a group of believers (Acts 1:24; 9:21; 1 Cor. 1:2; 16:22; Rev. 22:20) seems to have invoked the Lord Jesus directly.[172] Such a practice occasions no surprise, given the early Christian belief in the deity of Christ.[173] Paul addressed his earnest request to the risen Lord, not merely because Christ is the chief antagonist of Satan and his agents (cf. 1 Cor. 15:24; Eph. 6:10, 12; Col. 2:15) such as the ἄγγελος Σατανᾶ,[174] or because, as the early Jesus, he was the healer of illness, but perhaps also because the extraordinary revelations that occasioned the giving of the σκόλοψ (v. 7) emanated from the Lord Jesus (v. 1).

But what is the significance of the adverb τρίς ("three times") that stands, in an emphatic position,[175] before the phrase τὸν κύριον παρεκάλεσα? If Paul had wished to indicate simply that his request to the Lord was made "often,"[176] one wonders why πολλάκις (8:22; 11:23, 26-27) was not used (Plummer 353). If τρίς was intended to emphasize the intensity of Paul's desire,[177] would not that emphasis have been expressed by a word such as πολλά (Mark 5:10, 23) or

---

168. For a similar use of ἵνα in reference to prayer, see 1 Cor. 14:13; Col. 1:9; cf. Matt. 24:20; 1 Cor. 1:10.

169. The second or strong aorist forms of ἀφίστημι are intransitive in meaning. Acts 5:37 contains the only transitive (causal) use of this verb in the NT (ἀπέστησεν). See BAGD 126-27 s.v. Without compromising this grammatical point, some EVV render ἵνα ἀποστῇ ἀπ' ἐμοῦ using a transitive verb: "to rid me of him" (Weymouth), "to relieve me of it" (Moffatt), "to take it away from me" (NIV).

170. NIV, "my power." See also Textual Note n.

171. Cf. Zerwick §169.

172. On Paul's practice, see D. M. Stanley, Boasting 52-53, 81-83, 104, 109-10, 182. But it is not clear simply on the basis of 1 Thess. 3:11-12; 2 Thess. 2:16-17; 3:5, 16; 2 Cor. 1:20; Eph. 5:19 that Paul "frequently . . . turned in prayer to Christ while praying to God" (Boasting 104).

173. See Harris, Jesus, passim, especially 315-17.

174. Cf. Windisch 388.

175. See Turner 227.

176. So Calvin 160.

177. G. Delling, TDNT 8.222.

σπουδαίως (Luke 7:5) with παρεκάλεσα?[178] Again, it seems improbable that the threefold request was prompted by Paul's awareness of Christ's threefold petition in Gethsemane (Matt. 26:44; Mark 14:41),[179] or that τρίς signifies the completed nature of the entreaty[180] or means "three times in succession on one occasion" as though only a prayer offered three times was effective.[181] There is no compelling reason to resist the natural sense of τρίς, "Three different times" (NLT). If so, this adverb could point either to repeated requests soon after the first onset of the σκόλοψ (Bruce 249) or to three separate occasions when a particularly severe attack of the σκόλοψ prompted an especially fervent request for its removal.[182] On the basis of this latter view we may cautiously proceed to use other data in 2 Corinthians (1:8-11; 2:12-13; 12:2) and Acts (13:13-14) to try to identify these three occasions — an effort tentatively made in section B.5. of an Excursus after 1:11 on "Paul's Affliction in Asia (2 Corinthians 1:8-11): Paul's Personal Background to 2 Corinthians."

We may see τρὶς . . . παρεκάλεσα, then, as precisely parallel to τρὶς ἐραβδίσθην (11:25). In both cases three separate events are in mind and a constative aorist views these events in their similarity or identity as constituting a unified whole. It is not the tense of the verbs but the accompanying adverb that indicates the repetition of the action; the constative aorist can also depict single or protracted action. Similarly, in the case of τρὶς . . . παρεκάλεσα it is not the tense but the context (vv. 9-10) that shows that additional requests of the same kind are not contemplated (cf. Turner 72).

12:9 καὶ εἴρηκέν μοι· ἀρκεῖ σοι ἡ χάρις μού, ἡ γὰρ δύναμις ἐν ἀσθενείᾳ τελεῖται. "But he has said to me, 'My grace is sufficient for you; for my power reaches perfection in weakness.'" Although Paul's request for the removal of his "thorn" had been earnest (παρεκάλεσα, "I implored") and repeated (τρίς) (v. 8), it was denied. However (adversative καί[183]), a much greater boon was received — the assurance of the risen Christ's grace and power to cope with weakness, especially the weakness occasioned by onslaughts of the σκόλοψ.

Whereas Paul's request was reported in indirect speech (v. 8), Christ's response is given in direct speech. Also, καὶ εἴρηκεν (perfect) stands in stark contrast to τρὶς τὸν κύριον παρεκάλεσα (aorist): "Three times I made an urgent appeal to the Lord. . . . But his answer has been. . . ." The petition had been made three times, but now, with an explicit answer received, the act of petitioning the Lord lay totally in the past and would not be repeated. On the other

---

178. Cf. O. Schmitz, *TDNT* 5.794.

179. As Tasker (178) seems to suggest. McCant ("Thorn" 571) outlines some eight possible parallels between Jesus and Paul in what McCant calls "this parodic healing story" (= 12:7-10).

180. G. Delling (*TDNT* 8.222) deals with 12:8 under the general rubric, "Threefold performance of an action or the threefold occurrence of an event shows that it is complete, finished, definitive."

181. Cf. Windisch 389.

182. Similarly Hughes 449.

183. This is recognized by many EVV (Moffatt, RSV, NEB, JB, NJB, REB, NRSV).

hand, the Lord's reply, although given only once (after the third petition), was permanently valid,[184] a point also made by the two timeless or durative presents, ἀρκεῖ and τελεῖται, that form part of that reply. For Paul, his urgent requests were a memory of the past, but Christ's reassuring answer was a reality of the present. Another contrast between v. 9 and what has preceded relates to the ἄρρητα ῥήματα of v. 4. Whereas the things Paul heard in paradise were both impossible and impermissible to express in human language, Christ's reply to Paul's plea was both possible and permissible to describe. How Christ communicated his response is not stated. It may have been in a vision (cf. Acts 18:9), or when Paul had fallen into a trance during prayer (cf. Acts 22:17-18, 21), or through the testimony of the Spirit (cf. Acts 20:23), or simply during meditation on the crucifixion and resurrection of Christ, events which epitomize the three central concepts in Christ's message to Paul (v. 9a) — grace, weakness, and power.

Of the two affirmations that comprise Christ's word to Paul, the first is in effect a promise and the second is an explanatory justification (γάρ) of that promise. Christ assures Paul that the supply of his grace (cf. 13:13) for the carrying out of Paul's ministry, and in particular for the bearing of the pain and buffeting of the σκόλοψ, would never run dry. He needed nothing more than Christ's grace. Having that, he had the strength to endure all things (cf. 1 Cor. 13:7) and to do all things to the glory of God (cf. 1 Cor. 10:31). In Phil. 4:13 he later encapsulates his own response to this promise of complete sufficiency: "I am strong enough to meet all circumstances through my union with him who strengthens me."[185]

That the second element of Christ's word is inseparably related to the first is shown by the explanatory γάρ and by the chiastic structure of the two elements (A B C C′ B′ A′) to which O'Collins (534) has drawn attention.

A ἀρκεῖ	C′ ἡ δύναμις
B σοι	B′ ἐν ἀσθενείᾳ
C ἡ χάρις μου	A′ τελεῖται

This structure makes it improbable that the second statement (C′ B′ A′) is merely aphoristic, expressing a universally valid principle that is applicable to believer and unbeliever alike. Similarly, this chiastic or concentric structure makes it probable that the second statement relates principally to Christ's δύναμις and Paul's ἀσθένεια. Now it is true that at first sight the second affirmation seems to be an aphorism, given its brevity, the anarthrous ἀσθενείᾳ, and

---

184. Usually the perfect indicative presupposes a past act or event but emphasizes the present results. "The perfect combines in itself, so to speak, the present and the aorist in that it denotes the *continuance* of *completed action*" (BDF §340). For example, the famous ἐγήγερται of 1 Corinthians 15 (seven uses) implies the past event of Christ's resurrection (ἠγέρθη) but highlights the present consequences of that event — "he is alive" (cf. 2 Cor. 13:4, ζῇ, "he lives").

185. πάντα ἰσχύω ἐν τῷ ἐνδυναμοῦντί με.

present tense of τελεῖται.[186] But we should not overlook (1) the (possessive) article with δύναμις[187] which matches ἡ χάρις (μου), (2) the subsequent ἡ δύναμις τοῦ Χριστοῦ (v. 9b), and (3) Paul's restatement of ἐν ἀσθενείᾳ by the phrase ἐν ταῖς ἀσθενείαις μου (v. 9b). As Paul heard and now recounts this second affirmation of Christ, his primary thought would have been of Christ's power reaching its zenith in his own weakness.

In the present context it seems impossible to posit a precise distinction between δύναμις and χάρις; here they are essentially synonymous.[188] Both denote divine gifts of enablement, the power for Paul to fulfill his apostolic calling of service and suffering (4:7; 6:7; 13:4; 1 Cor. 15:10). What is more, both are renewable endowments, not once-for-all acquisitions; the constancy of the supply of χάρις and δύναμις is implied by the presents ἀρκεῖ and τελεῖται. The basic meaning of τελέω is "bring something to its τέλος," whether that "end" be a termination or a goal. There is a colorful array of possible renderings or paraphrases for the passive τελεῖται:[189] "finds its consummation" (BAGD 811a), "attains its perfection" (TCNT), "is most fully seen" (REB), "is at full stretch" (NJB), "is made fully present" (Furnish 513), "realizes its full potential" (Carrez 226), "is truly efficacious" (G. Delling, TDNT 8.59), "has unhindered scope" (Meyer 684), "reaches its zenith." If this second dominical statement in v. 9a is not a general maxim (see above), ἀσθένεια here will not refer to generic human weakness. First and foremost it will refer to the weakness Paul felt during and after an assault of his σκόλοψ, then more generally to his weakness as "a slave of Christ Jesus" (Rom. 1:1) who, in obedience to his apostolic calling, suffered as a slave would, being "hardpressed at every turn" (4:8), an object of dishonor and scorn (6:8; 1 Cor. 4:9-10), economically poor (6:10; 1 Cor. 4:11), and constantly exposed to death (6:9; 11:23; 1 Cor. 15:30-31).[190] But we should probably find a still broader reference in ἀσθένεια, a reference to attitudinal weakness, the acknowledgment of one's creatureliness and of one's impotence to render effective service to God without his empowering.

To consider the meaning of the preposition ἐν before ἀσθένεια is to investigate how δύναμις is related to ἀσθένεια. Grammatically, it is possible that ἐν is instrumental: "it is only by means of conscious weakness that perfect power is

---

186. Cf., e.g., 1 Pet. 4:8, ἀγάπη καλύπτει πλῆθος ἁμαρτιῶν.

187. EVV that render ἡ δύναμις by "my power" include RSV, GNB, JB, NIV; TCNT ("my strength"); also O'Collins 534; Carrez 226; Barnett 573 n. 30. Only if ὁ κύριος in v. 8 referred to God could δύναμις in v. 9a refer to God's power.

188. So also Bultmann 226. In general, however, χάρις is the broader term in Paul's thought, referring to the divine beneficence and all the benefits that come to humans because of that undeserved kindness, especially the blessings of salvation.

189. G. Delling (TDNT 8.59 n. 8) seems to distinguish between middle and passive meanings of τελέω, but BAGD 810-11 s.v. lists no distinctive middle senses. What appear to be middle senses in English are perhaps simply translational variants for the passive.

190. "'Weakness' is the condition of being subject to 'insults, hardships, persecutions, difficulties' (12:10)" (Murphy-O'Connor 119-20).

developed" (Williams).[191] However, it is improbable that the acknowledgment of weakness itself triggers the operation of "perfect power." Where this rendering is helpful is in its recognition that ἀσθένεια does not refer to weakness as such (whatever its nature) but to "conscious" or acknowledged weakness, and that there is a pre-condition (note "only") to be met before the statement becomes true. It is better to give ἐν a local sense, "in the midst of weakness" (TCNT; Gräbe 153) or "in (the presence of) weakness" (BAGD 811a). δύναμις and ἀσθένεια are related not only by succession — first weakness, then power, as in the case of the resurrection of Christ (13:4)[192] and of believers (1 Cor. 15:43)[193] — but also by simultaneity (cf. 4:10-11). It is "in the midst of weakness" that Christ's power reaches its plenitude; "weakness" is the sphere where his power is revealed. It is precisely when or whenever (ὅταν) Paul is weak that he experiences Christ's power (v. 10b).[194] We conclude that ἀσθένεια is both a prerequisite[195] and a concomitant of Christ's power. His enabling strength cannot operate without a prior confession of weakness and need. If self-sufficiency is claimed, his power will be neither sought nor experienced.[196] But if weakness is recognized, his power will be sought and granted. Then it will operate at the same time as the weakness and find unhindered scope in the presence of that weakness.[197] "My risen power finds its full scope and potency in your acknowledged weakness."

ἥδιστα οὖν μᾶλλον καυχήσομαι ἐν ταῖς ἀσθενείαις μου, ἵνα ἐπισκηνώσῃ ἐπ᾽ ἐμὲ ἡ δύναμις τοῦ Χριστοῦ. "Very gladly, therefore, I will rather boast of my weaknesses, in order that the power of Christ may rest upon me." Here in v. 9b Paul states an outcome (οὖν) of the Lord's response (v. 9a) to Paul's request (v. 8). If "weakness" is the place where Christ's power realizes its full potential (v. 9a), then Paul will not hesitate to boast of his many "weaknesses." The move from the singular to the plural of ἀσθένεια is significant. As in v. 10, ἀσθένειαι are particular experiences of infirmity that are evidence of the underlying ἀσθένεια. ἥδιστα, the superlative of ἡδέως, has an elative sense,[198] "very

191. The title of Savage's recent book on "Paul's understanding of the Christian ministry in 2 Corinthians," *Power through Weakness,* might suggest that God's or Christ's power comes by means of weakness, but his intended sense is rather "power manifested through weakness" (187; cf. 190). He equates this "weakness" with "human self-negation" (168-69), "the humility of faith" (186), "cross-shaped humility" (189), the opposite of the aggressiveness and self-boasting of Paul's opponents (187).

192. καὶ γὰρ ἐσταυρώθη ἐξ ἀσθενείας, ἀλλὰ ζῇ ἐν δυνάμεως θεοῦ (2 Cor. 13:4).

193. σπείρεται ἐν ἀσθενείᾳ, ἐγείρεται ἐν δυνάμει (1 Cor. 15:43).

194. Stressing this simultaneity, O'Collins refers to 1 Cor. 2:3-4. "When he [Paul] was with the Corinthians 'in weakness and in much fear and trembling' his 'message' was characterized by 'the Spirit and power'" (536).

195. So Lietzmann 156; Windisch 392; Black 147.

196. Savage illustrates from the OT the principle that "where there is pride and arrogance there cannot, by definition, be divine power" (167).

197. It may also be that τελεῖται implies proportionality (cf. Black 159), "the greater the acknowledged weakness, the more evident Christ's power" (cf. Eph. 3:16; Phil. 4:13).

198. BDF §60(2); Robertson 670; Moulton and Howard 165.

gladly" (Furnish 513), "all the more gladly" (BAGD 344a; RSV, NRSV), or "with the greatest gladness" (Barclay). μᾶλλον does not intensify ἥδιστα (cf. BDF §246) but implies a comparison. Paul would boast of his infirmities[199] rather than complaining of them (Weymouth), or, as is more appropriate in the context, rather than praying for their removal (cf. v. 8),[200] or rather than boasting of anything else (Cassirer) such as his ascent into paradise (Barnett 575) or his strength (Barrett 317), although the position of μᾶλλον is a difficulty for this latter alternative.

If we give ἵνα its normal telic sense of "in order to" (GNB) or "so that" (Barclay), we might seem forced to conclude that boasting of weaknesses was a prerequisite for experiencing Christ's power. Sensing that difficulty, some EVV regard ἵνα as consecutive, "and then the power of Christ will come and rest upon me" (NEB; similarly Moffatt), or even causal, "because then the power of Christ will rest upon me" (REB).[201] Alternatively, ἵνα could be related not to καυχήσομαι but to ταῖς ἀσθενείαις μου, "my weaknesses whose divine purpose is that Christ's power should rest upon me"[202] or "my weaknesses whose consequence is to allow the power of Christ to rest upon me."[203] Others argue that it must be the visibility of Christ's power that is in Paul's thought: "that the power of Christ may be seen to reside with me."[204] Perhaps the problem can be alleviated if we assume here the same thought that must be implied in the phrase ἡ . . . δύναμις ἐν ἀσθενείᾳ τελεῖται (v. 9a), namely that the acknowledgment of "weakness" is a precondition for the exercise of Christ's power. The sense would then be: "I will very gladly boast of my weaknesses — weaknesses I gladly confess to having — in order that the power of Christ may rest upon me."[205]

ἐπισκηνόω, a rare word never found in Biblical Greek apart from this use, means "raise a tent (σκηνή) [over]," "be quartered in" (LSJ 656 s.v.), "take up residence in a tent or dwelling" (W. Michaelis, TDNT 7.386). If the aorist ἐπισκηνώσῃ is ingressive, it will mean "come to rest"[206] or "take up its abode";[207] if constative, "rest," "dwell," or "reside." Some find an allusion in this verb to the Shekinah (šᵉḵînâ), the glorious "Presence" of the Lord, noting that in the LXX σκηνή represents both the Tent of Meeting and the overshadowing divine glory.[208] However that be, it is appropriate to find tent imagery in the

199. With καυχάομαι, ἐν here means "about," "concerning" (see on 10:17 and Moule 79), rather than "because of" (Moulton and Howard 463; Black 156) or "in the midst of."

200. Zerwick, *Analysis* 413; Black 156; Heckel 101-2; Lambrecht, "Self-Commendation" 337 n. 26.

201. On "causal ἵνα," see Zerwick §§413-14, 414 n. 7; Turner 102-3.

202. A proposal reflecting an editorial comment of C. E. B. Cranfield made to Thrall (827).

203. A possible understanding mentioned by Thrall (827).

204. Cf. Furnish 531, and the extended discussion of Thrall (827-28), who favors this general view. Both translate ἵνα in a telic sense (Furnish 513; Thrall 772).

205. Cf. Calvin 161.

206. Zerwick and Grosvenor 560; Lambrecht 200, 204.

207. Bruce, *Paraphrase* 155.

208. For details see Hughes 452-53 n. 141.

verb,[209] especially since Paul has used such imagery in reference to the body in 5:1 (ἡ ἐπίγειος ἡμῶν οἰκία τοῦ σκήνους, "our earthly tent-dwelling"). When the power of Christ pitched its tent over Paul, there was not only divine empowering for life and service but also divine protection, as a tent protects its inhabitants.[210] We could treat ἐπί as equivalent to ἐν, "that the power of Christ may dwell in me" (BAGD 298d),[211] but there is no reason to disallow the sense "over" or "upon"[212] — either "that the power of Christ may be pitched like a tent over me" (Young and Ford 274), or "that the power of Christ may rest upon me" (BAGD 289a).[213] Finally, we should note the emphatic position of ἡ δύναμις τοῦ Χριστοῦ, "that Christ's power — yes, his very power — may rest upon me." The permanent enabling and protection of the power of Christ more than compensated for the intermittent buffeting of "the messenger of Satan" (v. 7). Paul could now very gladly boast of his weaknesses.

12:10 διὸ εὐδοκῶ ἐν ἀσθενείαις, ἐν ὕβρεσιν, ἐν ἀνάγκαις, ἐν διωγμοῖς καὶ στενοχωρίαις, ὑπὲρ Χριστοῦ. ὅταν γὰρ ἀσθενῶ, τότε δυνατός εἰμι. "That is why I take pleasure in weaknesses, in insults, in calamities, in persecutions and difficulties, endured for Christ. For when I am weak, then I am strong." It was precisely because (διό, "that is why") Paul's weaknesses provided him with the opportunity to experience Christ's power (v. 9b) that he could even take pleasure in them. It may seem appropriate, since οὐκ εὐδοκέω ἐν can mean "reject" (Hab. 2:4 cited in Heb. 10:38), to give εὐδοκέω ἐν the sense "accept"[214] or "consent to"[215] or "be well content with/in,"[216] but a more overtly positive sense is preferable, "take pleasure in" or "delight in," when we consider a parallel use in 2 Thess. 2:12, εὐδοκήσαντες τῇ ἀδικίᾳ, in reference to those who "have delighted in wickedness."[217] Paul not only boasted of his weaknesses (v. 9b) but also "delighted" in them, not in the sense that he morbidly reveled in them but in the sense that he joyfully used them as occasions to know and prove the res-

209. E.g., Barclay, "so that the power of Christ may pitch its tent upon me."

210. Cf. GNB, "in order to feel the protection of Christ's power over me"; similarly Goodspeed ("may shelter me"), Plummer 337 ("may spread a sheltering cover over me").

211. Cf. Polybius's use of ἐπισκηνόω in reference to soldiers taking up residence "in" quarters (4.18.8, ἐπὶ τὰς οἰκείας; 4.72.1, ταῖς οἰκείαις). Paul could mean "that Christ's power may take up quarters within me."

212. But W. Michaelis alleges that ἐπί here points to entry into, not descent upon, with the verb being "horizontally orientated rather than vertically" (*TDNT* 7.387).

213. Cf. 1 Pet. 4:14 ("the Spirit of glory and of God rests on you," ἐφ' ὑμᾶς ἀναπαύεται); Luke 1:35 ("the power of the Most High will overshadow you," δύναμις ὑψίστου ἐπισκιάσει σοι). Some EVV treat ἐπισκηνόω as synonymous with ἐπισκιάζω, "overshadow" — see TCNT, Weymouth.

214. Barnett 575-76.

215. Spicq 2.103 n. 23.

216. NEB; Barrett 306.

217. Cf. εὐδόκησας ἐν αὐτοῖς ("you took pleasure in them") in Ps. 43:4 (LXX). G. Schrenk (*TDNT* 2.741) observes that "εὐδοκῶ ἐν ἀσθενείαις implies that the warring aspects of the apostolic life can be a source of gratification because everything takes place ὑπὲρ Χριστοῦ." Similarly BAGD 319b.

urrection power of Christ (cf. Phil. 3:10). ἐν ἀσθενείαις stands as a general rubric[218] before four instances of weakness: "in weaknesses such as. . . ." All five plurals may be generalizing and so translated by the singular,[219] or the plurals may refer to "cases of weakness. . . ."[220] ἐν ὕβρεσιν could refer to "insults" of a verbal kind, that is, what is said in slander or the act of being slandered, or to "insults" of a physical kind, that is, insolent mistreatment.[221] ἀνάγκαι denotes "calamities" (BAGD 52d) or "catastrophes" (see on 6:4), διωγμός is the general word for persecution of any nature, while στενοχωρίαι are "grievous difficulties" (Weymouth) or "dire straits" (see on 6:4).[222] The position of ὑπὲρ Χριστοῦ suggests that it should be construed with the list of hardships just enumerated; thus, ". . . and distresses, endured on behalf of Christ" (Barrett 306).[223] But it is not impossible to take the phrase with εὐδοκῶ; thus, "That is why, for Christ's sake, I delight in . . ." (NIV).[224] If we prefer the former option, ὑπὲρ Χριστοῦ gives a second reason why Paul can delight in his weaknesses. Not only do those ἀσθένειαι provide occasions when Christ's power can rest upon him (v. 9b); they are borne as a consequence of serving Christ and for his glory.

ὅταν (γὰρ[225]) ἀσθενῶ, τότε δυνατός εἰμι has aptly been called Paul's "personal motto" (Spittler 266). This paradoxical principle, which lay at the center of Paul's life and ministry, is an explicitly and intensely personal application of v. 9b, "power reaches perfection in weakness." There the explicit contrast was between δύναμις and ἀσθένεια, although there was an implicit contrast between *Christ's* power and *Paul's* weakness (see on v. 9). Here, however, the explicit antithesis is between two concurrent states of Paul himself, with no explicit reference to Christ, although such a reference is clearly implicit. When Paul acknowledged his weakness and expressed his dependence on Christ, he became simultaneously "powerful" with Christ's resurrection power.[226]

Behind ἀσθενῶ we should probably see an allusion to the physical debility brought about by assaults of Paul's σκόλοψ τῇ σαρκί, but also to the external afflictions encountered during his service for Christ, circumstances such as "insults, calamities, persecutions and difficulties" (cf. v. 10a) that prompted a sense of helplessness and drove him to turn to Christ in prayer. The Paul who was ταπεινός (10:1) and ἀσθενής (10:10) was the true Paul; lowliness and

218. Cf. the role of ἐν ὑπομονῇ πολλῇ in 6:4, and of ὁδοιπορίαις πολλάκις in 11:26.

219. So NEB. REB has "a life of weakness, insult, hardship, persecution, and distress."

220. Turner 28.

221. See Louw and Nida §§20.19; 33.391; 88.131.

222. Zerwick defines στενοχωρία as "so severe an affliction that a person does not know how to avoid it or where to turn" (*Analysis* 413).

223. Similarly REB, NRSV.

224. Similarly RSV, NEB.

225. The reason why (γάρ) experiencing affliction could, paradoxically, produce pleasure (v. 10a) was that acknowledged "weakness," leading to dependence on Christ, released his strength (v. 10b).

226. To render δυνατός by "powerful" (Furnish 513; Martin 389; Young and Ford 274) reflects the verbal link with δύναμις, "power."

weakness were the hallmarks of his ministry. Yet it was precisely this ἀσθένεια, whether physical, psychological, or spiritual, that caused him to rely wholly on Christ and so occasioned his strength. Behind δυνατός εἰμι we should see an allusion, not to Paul's own ability to cope with adversity by harnessing all his personal resources, but to his experience of Christ's power, sometimes in delivering him from adversity, sometimes in granting him strength to endure hardship, but always in equipping him for effective service. There is grammatical justification for translating ὅταν with the present subjunctive[227] by "whenever"[228] rather than by "when," but the rendering "whenever I am weak, then I am strong" (NRSV)[229] could suggest that there were only isolated occasions when Paul felt "weak" and so was "strong" through Christ. Isaacs's paraphrase illustrates the point: "for my moments of weakness are the moments of my greatest power." If, however, "weakness" was Paul's conscious attitude of humble dependence on Christ in all circumstances but especially in adverse situations, then correspondingly the experience of having Christ's power resting on him would be a constant reality. "When I am weak, then I am strong" (RSV)[230] leaves open this interpretation.

Bibliography

Andriessen • Baird • Barré, "Qumran" • Bauer 128-30 • Becker 231-39 • E. Beecher, "Dispensation of Divine Providence toward the Apostle Paul," *BSac* 12 (1855) 499-527 • E. Benz, *Paulus als Visionär* (Wiesbaden: Steiner, 1952) • Best, *Body* 219-20 • Betz, *Paulus* 92-100 • Betz, "Christus-Aretalogie" • Binder • Black 145-72, 222-53 • Bonnard • Bowker • Bruce, "Mystic" • Cambier, "Critère" • Cambier, "Lecture" • Carpus, "The Strength of Weakness," *Exp* 1/3 (1876) 161-84 • Clavier • Fee, *Presence* 346-54 • H. Foschiani, "'Datus est mihi stimulus' (2 Cor. 12,7)," *VD* 5 (1925) 26-29 • Garland, "Authority" • Garrett • M. D. Goulder, "Vision and Knowledge," *JSNT* 56 (1994) 53-71 • Güttgemanns • Hafemann, "Weakness" • Halperin • Heckel 52-121, 202-15, 272-88, 296-325 • Heckel, "Dorn" • L. Herrmann, "Apollos," *RevScRel* 50 (1976) 330-36 • Himmelfarb • M. Himmelfarb, "The Practice of Ascent in the Ancient Mediterranean World," in *Death, Ecstasy, and Other Worldly Journeys,* ed. J. J. Collins and M. Fishbane (Albany: SUNY, 1995) 123-37 • V. Jegher-Bucher, "Der Pfahl im Fleisch. Überlegungen zu II Kor 12,7-10 im Zusammenhang von 12,1-13," *TZ* 52 (1996) 32-41 • Käsemann • Klauck, "Himmelfahrt" • Kreitzer 121-27 • Leary • J. A. L. Lee, *A Lexical*

---

227. ἀσθενῶ is almost certainly present subjunctive although the present indicative after ὅταν is not unknown (see Robertson 972-73).

228. See BAGD 588a; Turner 112.

229. So also Barclay; Thrall 772; Lambrecht 200, who also notes that the paradox of v. 10b follows the distinction between Paul's weakness and Christ's power in vv. 9-10a and "is not absolute. Weakness is not strength. . . . So we can paraphrase verse 10b: 'For whenever as creature and sinner I am weak, then the strength of Christ is strong in me'" ("Self-Commendation" 339, referring to his article "Nekrosis" 131).

230. So also Weymouth, NEB, NASB, GNB, NIV, NAB², REB; similarly RV, TCNT, Moffatt, Goodspeed, JB, NAB¹, NJB; Barrett 306; Furnish 513; Martin 389.

Study of the Septuagint Version of the Pentateuch (Chico: Scholars, 1983) 53-56 • Lincoln 71-86 (virtually identical with Lincoln, "Paul") • E. Lombard, "Les extases et les souffrances de l'apôtre Paul. Essai d'une interprétation de II Cor 12:1-10," *RTP* 36 (1903) 450-500 • W. H. Mare, "The New Testament Concept regarding the Regions of Heaven with Emphasis on 2 Corinthians 12:1-4," *GTJ* 11 (1970) 3-12 • Marguerat • McCant, "Thorn" • Menoud, "Thorn" • Morray-Jones • Mullins • Murphy-O'Connor 119-21 • Nielsen • Nisbet • O'Collins • Park • Pate, *Glory* 107-42 • Penna 235-73 • R. M. Price • Rowland • J.-P. Ruiz, "Hearing and Seeing but Not Saying: A Look at Revelation 10:4 and 2 Corinthians 12:4," *SBL 1994 Seminar Papers,* ed. E. H. Lovering, Jr. (Atlanta: Scholars, 1994) 182-202 • R. Russell, "Redemptive Suffering and Paul's Thorn in the Flesh," *JETS* 39 (1996) 559-70 • Saake • Schäfer • Schmithals 209-18 • Scholem 14-19 • Segal • Segal, "Ascent" • Segal, "Ecstasy" • A. F. Segal, "Paul and the Beginning of Jewish Mysticism," in *Death, Ecstasy, and Other Worldly Journeys,* ed. J. J. Collins and M. Fishbane (Albany: SUNY, 1995) 95-122 • M. Smith, "Ascent to the Heavens and the Beginning of Christianity," *Eranos Jahrbuch* 50 (1981) 147-222, 403-30 • Spittler • D. M. Stanley, *Boasting* 44-59 • Sumney, "Weakness" • Sylvia • Tabor 32-34, 36-37, 44-45, 57-127 • Tannehill 98-100 • Theobald 244-53 • Thierry • Thomas • Thornton • Thrall, "Journey" • D. Trakatellis, "Power in Weakness — Exegesis of 2 Cor 12,1-13," in E. Lohse (ed.), *Verteidigung und Begründung des apostolischen Amtes (2 Kor 10–13)* (Benedictina 11; Rome: Abbazia San Paolo fuori le mura, 1992) 65-86 • C. S. Ward, "2 Cor. 12:9 in the Revised Version," *ExpT* 23 (1911-12) 39 • L. Woods, "Opposition to a Man and His Message: Paul's 'Thorn in the Flesh' (2 Cor 12:7)," *ABR* 39 (1991) 44-53 • B. H. Young • Zmijewski • Zmijewski, "Kontextbezug"

8. Proof of Apostleship (12:11-13)

These three verses form the conclusion to the "Fool's Speech" (11:1–12:13)[1] although some regard them as an epilogue to that speech seen as running from 11:1 to 12:10.[2] Paul chides the Corinthians for failing to champion him against the intruders from Palestine and for forcing him thereby to use the disagreeable tactic of foolish boasting in remonstrating with the Corinthians (v. 11a). Once again (cf. 11:5) he asserts his equality with the "superlative apostles" in Jerusalem (v. 11b), an equality shown by his patiently exhibiting at Corinth the marks of true apostleship by means of signs, wonders, and miracles (v. 12). He reminds them also that he remained financially independent of them at that time — an "injury" for which he playfully asks forgiveness (v. 13). This last verse serves as a transition to vv. 14-18 where he promises not to be a financial burden on them during his forthcoming visit.

---

1. The two brief asyndetic statements, γέγονα ἄφρων· ὑμεῖς με ἠναγκάσατε, point to the closure of the speech. Peterson notes three aspects of 12:11-13 that recall the beginning of the "Fool's Speech": ἄφρων (12:11) looks back to ἀφροσύνη (11:1); 12:11 and 11:5 both contain Paul's claim not to be inferior to οἱ ὑπερλίαν ἀπόστολοι; and ἀδικίαν (12:13) matches ἁμαρτίαν (11:7) as ironic descriptions of Paul's refusal to be a financial burden on the Corinthians (128).

2. See, e.g., Furnish 552, 554; Wolff 250-51.

Behind these verses there probably lie three charges against Paul made by his adversaries at Corinth, whether the intruders or some native Corinthians:

(1) that he was inferior to the Twelve, "the superlative apostles" (v. 11), and in fact was "nothing" or "a nobody" (οὐδέν) (v. 11);
(2) that he had not exhibited "the characteristics of a true apostle" (v. 12);
(3) that, as a result of his ministry, the Corinthians were "worse off" than other Christian churches (v. 13).

12:11*I have been a fool.ᵃ You are the ones who forced me to it. For it is I who ought to have been commended by you. For in no wayᵇ have I proved inferior to those superlative apostles, even though I am "nothing."* 12*At least, the signs of an apostle were produced in your midst with the utmost endurance, throughᶜ signs and marvels and through powerful deeds.* 13*In what way, then, were you worse offᵈ than the other churches, except that I myself did not burden you? Forgive me for this offense!*

TEXTUAL NOTES

a. After ἄφρων some witnesses (Ψ 0243 1881 𝔐 b syr⁽ᵖ⁾) read καυχώμενος ("by boasting"), which, although true to the context, is clearly secondary, lacking strong external support.

b. Two important proto-Alexandrian witnesses (p⁴⁶ B) read τί ("in anything") after γάρ, which seems otiose after οὐδέν ("in no way," "not at all"). But that could have been the reason for its omission.

c. Instead of σημείοις τε (read by p⁴⁶ ℵ* B [F G] 0243 0278 33 81 326 630 1175 1739 1881 2464 pc g), some witnesses omit the enclitic particle τέ (A D* pc lat Ambrosiaster Pelagius), perhaps viewing it as superfluous with καί or as spoiling the καὶ . . . καί pattern, while other authorities (ℵ² D² Ψ [1505] 𝔐 vg^cl) have ἐν σημείοις, a secondary reading possibly prompted by a desire to clarify the relation between σημεῖα and σημείοις.

d. In the place of ἡσσώθητε (from ἑσσόομαι), F G read ἐλαττώθητε (from ἐλαττόω). Both verbs mean "be worse off" (see BAGD 248b, 313c).

12:11 Γέγονα ἄφρων· ὑμεῖς με ἠναγκάσατε· ἐγὼ γὰρ ὤφειλον ὑφ᾽ ὑμῶν συνίστασθαι. οὐδὲν γὰρ ὑστέρησα τῶν ὑπερλίαν ἀποστόλων, εἰ καὶ οὐδέν εἰμι. "I have been a fool. You are the ones who forced me to it. For it is I who ought to have been commended by you. For in no way have I proved inferior to those superlative apostles, even though I am 'nothing.'" As Paul reflects on what he has dictated to his amanuensis, beginning at 11:1, or (possibly) as he has the amanuensis read back to him what he has dictated, he makes an admission but immediately qualifies it. The admission — not a question — is γέγονα ἄφρων, "I have been 'playing the fool'" (TCNT), not "I have become (irreversibly!) a fool." By writing as he had, by engaging in "foolish boasting" (cf. 11:1, 16-18, 21b, 30; 12:1), by indulging in comparisons with his opponents (11:22-29;

12:1-5), by boasting "as the world does" (11:18), he had been "foolish" (ἄφρων). Not everything in the "Fool's Speech" (11:1–12:10) had been foolish or boasting, but he recognized the principal thrust of that "speech." Yes, he had worn a fool's mask, but he was no fool (11:16; 12:6) and the mask had now been removed (note the perfect γέγονα). The qualification, stated abruptly (asyndetically), is ὑμεῖς με ἠναγκάσατε. "Temporarily a fool — but you it was (ὑμεῖς) who forced my hand." Paul has already given several reasons for his καυχᾶσθαι κατὰ σάρκα (11:16-21a). Now a further justification is given: Corinthian attitudes left him no option but to indulge in foolish boasting. γάρ introduces the explanation for that "compulsion" (ἠναγκάσατε). "For it is I (ἐγώ) who ought to have been commended by you."[3] Because the Corinthians had failed to "commend" him, to rally to his defense and act as his vindicators, he had been forced to boast himself. Had they commended him as they should have, he would not have been compelled to "play the fool" and engage in self-praise.[4] At the heart of the issue were interpersonal relationships, as is shown by the emphatic phrases ὑμεῖς με . . . ἐγώ . . . ὑφ' ὑμῶν. Although the Corinthians had every reason to champion their spiritual father, since they themselves were his commendatory letter (3:2), they had failed him at precisely that point of commendation, apparently preferring rather to commend his intruding rivals. As a justification for previous boasting, the first half of v. 11 is a case of *epidiorthosis,* an explanation, apology, or correction added (ἐπι-) in retrospect.[5]

As in Classical Greek the imperfect (without ἄν) in expressions of necessity or obligation denotes action that is or was necessary or required but that does not or did not take place (BDF §358[1]). Accordingly, the imperfect ὤφειλον with the present infinitive συνίστασθαι may mean either "I ought to be commended"[6] or "I ought to have been commended."[7] Since Paul is here rehearsing the past,[8] the latter translation is the more appropriate.

With a second γάρ Paul gives the reason why his Corinthian converts should have given him loyal support and vocal approval (συνίστασθαι): he was not in the least inferior to "the superlative apostles." It is certainly possible that with the present tense εἰμί that follows (εἰ καὶ οὐδέν εἰμι), the aorist ὑστέρησα

3. If there is an ellipsis after ἠναγκάσατε, it may be "(you forced me) into self-commendation." But Lambrecht suggests "I would not have done it by myself, for . . ." (211). He represents γάρ by "In fact" (also Young and Ford 275). Weymouth has "Why," and NRSV, "Indeed."

4. In his commentary Talbert gives chs. 10–13 the heading, "The Sorry Necessity of Self-Praise" (vii, 109). Marshall usefully summarizes (353-54) the various circumstances that Plutarch in his essay "On Praising Oneself Inoffensively" mentions as justifying self-praise. How Paul's practice relates to these guidelines is discussed by Betz 75-79; see also Marshall 354-55.

5. See BDF §495(3).

6. Barrett 318; Martin 425; Lambrecht 210; cf. Robertson, Pictures 266 ("an unfulfilled obligation about the present").

7. Winer 282; Bultmann 230; RSV; similarly BAGD 599a; Furnish 552; Thrall 842.

8. Note γέγονα and the following constative aorists ὑστέρησα (v. 11) and κατειργάσθη (v. 12).

may be gnomic ("in no way am I inferior," Martin 425),[9] but more probably, like the next three aorists, it is constative, referring to the sum total of Paul's Christian service at Corinth and elsewhere. "For in no way (οὐδέν[10]) have I proved inferior to those superlative apostles." Reasons for identifying οἱ ὑπερλίαν ἀπόστολοι as the Twelve in Jerusalem are given in the Introduction (B.4.d.) and are summarized at 11:5. Paul's thought moves from the Corinthian failure to support him to a comparison with the Twelve because his rivals were comparing him unfavorably with those original apostles.[11] His response is that if he is on a par with the Twelve (cf. 1 Cor. 15:8-11) with respect to his service, he is certainly worthy of the Corinthians' wholehearted endorsement.[12] For the wide variety of renderings for ὑπερλίαν in the expression οἱ ὑπερλίαν ἀπόστολοι, see the commentary at 11:5. On my view this expression is a Pauline coinage, his ironical description of the false apostles' exalted view of the Twelve. The delicacy of his position with regard to those who were apostles before him (Gal. 1:17) should not be overlooked. He could never dissociate himself from Jerusalem as the birthplace of Christianity (cf. Rom. 15:19) nor from the Twelve as the first proclaimers of the good news. Yet he must dissociate himself from the inflated view of the Twelve and the distorted view of apostleship being promulgated by his adversaries at Corinth.

If Paul had been dismissed by some at Corinth as being οὐδέν, "nothing," "a non-entity," "a nobody" (cf. 6:9), the expression εἰ καὶ οὐδέν εἰμι[13] could be an ironical reference to that taunt.[14] "If, as some of you say (cf. 10:10, φησίν, . . . ὁ λόγος ἐξουθενημένος), I amount to nothing, then those whom you regard so highly and who are my equals, must also be nobodies, not worthy of consideration!" Given the fact that other derogatory terms such as ἔκτρωμα (1 Cor. 15:8)

9. In a similar passage where Paul compares himself with "the superlative apostles" (11:5), we find λογίζομαι . . . μηδὲν ὑστερηκέναι where the perfect has a present sense, "I reckon I am not at all inferior."

10. This οὐδέν is an accusative of respect (see BDF §160), whereas the next οὐδέν is a nominative complement: "in nothing inferior . . . even though I am nothing."

11. Cf. Bruce 249-50: "Even if he was but a cipher [εἰ καὶ οὐδέν εἰμι], as his opponents alleged, yet the record of his service compared favourably with that of the superlative apostles to whom his critics appealed. . . . Similarly in 1 C.15.8ff. he maintains that even if he be, as his opponents alleged, a mere *ektrōma* compared with the original apostles, yet his commission as a witness to the risen Christ is as valid as theirs, and his achievement, by God's grace, superior to theirs."

12. Barrett restricts the reference in ὑστέρησα to "the substance of Paul's dealings with Corinth" and suggests that Paul's point is this: "If he is equal to the super-apostles he is not inferior to the intruders" (320). In a similar vein Martin contends that Paul's reference here to "the 'super'-apostles is intended as an indirect polemic against the false apostles. If the false apostles . . . claimed that they were patterned after the super-apostles, this would account for the reference. Then if Paul was at least equal to the super-apostles, how could he be an inferior apostle?" (433).

13. If this phrase were construed with v. 12, one would expect μέντοι ("nevertheless") rather than μέν *solitarium* after τά.

14. Similarly Murphy-O'Connor 122. For the view that the Socratic notion of "nothingness" (οὐδενία) forms the background to Paul's use of the phrase οὐδέν εἰμι (cf. 1 Cor. 3:7; 13:2), see Betz, *Paulus* 122-128 and the comments of Thrall 836-37.

or ταπεινός (10:1) seem to have been used of Paul at Corinth, and that he could use such a term for his own purposes (see 1 Cor. 15:8-9), this understanding of οὐδέν is perfectly legitimate. On the other hand, in saying "even though I am nothing," Paul may be intensely serious. In spite of being not one whit inferior to the Twelve with respect to faith and service, he was, in his own estimation, "nothing," the least important of the apostles and not worthy to bear the title "apostle" because he once persecuted God's church (1 Cor. 15:9).[15] Whatever he was in relation to the Twelve and whatever had been accomplished at Corinth were due solely to God's grace that was with him (1 Cor. 15:10; cf. 2 Cor. 3:5; 4:7). Perhaps we need not choose between the "ironical"/"serious" alternatives. Even if Paul's primary intent was irony, he would gladly have acknowledged the truth that apart from God's prospering of his service he amounted to nothing (1 Cor. 3:6-7).[16]

12:12 τὰ μὲν σημεῖα τοῦ ἀποστόλου κατειργάσθη ἐν ὑμῖν ἐν πάσῃ ὑπομονῇ, σημείοις τε καὶ τέρασιν καὶ δυνάμεσιν. "At least, the signs of an apostle were produced in your midst with the utmost endurance, through signs and marvels and through powerful deeds." Here Paul reminds his converts of certain distinguishing features of his work at Corinth that showed he was a genuine apostle who was in no way inferior to the Twelve and therefore was worthy of their full endorsement (cf. v. 11). He appeals to what his converts had themselves seen and heard during his founding visit (σημεῖα . . . κατειργάσθη ἐν ὑμῖν). He wanted their opinion of him and their assessment of his apostleship to correspond to reality as they had experienced it and not outstrip the evidence of their physical and spiritual senses (12:6).

When the particle μέν is not followed by the customary δέ (μέν *solitarium*), it may be concessive or restrictive (Robertson 1151), giving the sense "at least,"[17] or it may still point to a contrast which in this case must be supplied from the context — the signs were produced, "but you paid no attention" (BAGD 503a).[18] Either way, v. 12 supplies the evidence for Paul's being "in no way inferior" to the superlative apostles (v. 11b) and the reason why the Corinthians should have been rallying to support him (v. 11a). Although σημεῖον is used twice in this verse, it bears a different meaning in each case, as is shown by the qualification that follows each use.[19] τοῦ ἀποστόλου, "of an apostle" (where the article is generic[20]) or "of apostleship"[21] (where the concrete stands for the abstract), indicates that σημεῖα means "marks" or "characteristics,"[22] not

---

15. Similarly Hafemann 466; *Defense* 154 n. 141.

16. Similarly, for a dual sense, Barrett 320, and from a different perspective, Thrall 837.

17. So Conybeare in Conybeare and Howson 462; de Boor 237; Barrett 320.

18. Perhaps "indeed" (Meyer 686; Wolff 250) is an effort to catch this sense.

19. On the use of σημεῖον in Paul, see K. H. Rengstorf, *TDNT* 7.258-60; Spicq 3.249-54.

20. BAGD 550b; Robertson 408, 757.

21. Lietzmann 156; Wand.

22. For σημεῖον meaning "distinguishing mark," see Gen. 4:15; 2 Thess. 3:17. In 12:12a the σημεῖα are marks of authentication, not (as BAGD 621d proposes) "the signs by which an apostle demonstrates his authority."

"(miraculous) signs,"[23] while τε καὶ τέρασιν, "and wonders," shows that σημείοις means "(miraculous) signs," not "marks." τὰ σημεῖα τοῦ ἀποστόλου will therefore mean "the things that mark the true apostle" (JB) or "the marks that signify the genuine apostle" (Williams) or "the apostolic signs" (Furnish 552; Thrall 832).[24] The origin of the phrase is unknown. It could have been a catchphrase or slogan of Paul's opponents for whom miracle-working was the main sign of genuine apostleship,[25] or of the Corinthians themselves who required proof that Christ spoke in Paul (13:3).[26] On the other hand, we should not dismiss the possibility that the phrase was a Pauline coinage, prompted perhaps by his contest with his missionary rivals at Corinth regarding the credentials of true apostles.

κατειργάσθη is a case of a transitive deponent verb with a passive sense (Turner 58), "(the signs . . .) were performed/produced."[27] Meyer suggests that a reference to Paul's action is implied:[28] "The *I* . . . retreats modestly behind the passive expression" (687). But if the σημεῖα are identified with or closely related to the σημείοις, it is more probable that this is a "theological passive,"[29] with God or Christ or the Spirit as the implied agent, given the close parallel in Rom. 15:18-19. "I will venture to speak only of what Christ has accomplished (κατειργάσατο) through me to bring the Gentiles to obedience, by word and deed, through the power displayed in signs and wonders (ἐν δυνάμει σημείων καὶ τεράτων), and through the power of the Spirit of God." Plummer observes that in v. 12 Paul "does not say κατειργασάμην ['I produced'], because he himself is οὐδέν [v. 11]. *His* contribution to the result is expressed by ἐν πάσῃ ὑπομονῇ" (CGT 208), although Paul would also affirm that it is God who gives perseverance (Rom. 15:5, ὁ . . . θεὸς τῆς ὑπομονῆς). Paul had toiled at Corinth "with the utmost endurance," but it was God who had produced the evidence that authenticated his apostleship (cf. 1 Cor. 3:5-9), the proof that the Corinthians demanded that Christ was speaking through him (13:3).

In the phrase ἐν πάσῃ ὑπομονῇ, which is to be taken with what precedes,[30] ὑπομονή refers to Paul's "patient endurance" (see on 6:4) or "fortitude," ἐν denotes attendant circumstances ("with," "in," "amid"), and the anarthrous πᾶς expresses "the highest degree" (BAGD 631c) of that endurance ("constant," "utmost," "unfailing").[31] Although ὑπομονή is not an exclusively apostolic vir-

---

23. *Pace* Moffatt: "the miracles that mark an apostle"; similarly Louw and Nida §91.3.

24. Cf. K. H. Rengstorf, *TDNT* 7.258, "visible things which make an apostle discernible as such." τοῦ ἀποστόλου is a possessive genitive, and the wider context justifies the insertion of a word such as "true" or "genuine" before "apostle" (see BAGD 503a; RSV, NEB).

25. So Käsemann 35; Kümmel 213.

26. So Barrett 321; "Opponents" 245; Murphy-O'Connor 122.

27. Clearly κατεργάζομαι here bears a positive sense. For its pejorative use, see 7:10; Rom. 1:27; 2:9; 1 Cor. 5:3.

28. See also NEB, NAB[1], REB.

29. G. Bertram, *TDNT* 3.635 supplies διὰ θεοῦ.

30. UBS[1-4] and NA[27] print a comma after ὑπομονῇ. Héring (95) and Barrett (318, 321) construe this phrase with σημείοις κτλ. For the difficulties with that view, see Thrall 838.

31. It is possible, however, that ἐν is instrumental ("by means of"; cf. ἐν ὑπομονῇ πολλῇ in

tue (see its use in 1:6 in reference to the Corinthians), we need not deny that Paul here regards it as one of the distinguishing features (σημεῖα) of a true apostle (cf. ἐν ὑπομονῇ πολλῇ in 6:4),[32] and a crucial one that distinguished him from his rivals whose activity at Corinth occasioned no persecution and therefore no endurance of affliction. The opposition that Paul patiently endured at Corinth is outlined in Acts 18:6-10.

The expression σημεῖα καὶ τέρατα ("signs and marvels") is a common LXX phrase,[33] used especially of the miraculous events surrounding the Exodus.[34] It also often occurs in the NT,[35] particularly in the book of Acts.[36] On five occasions[37] we find these two plural terms associated with δύναμις or δυνάμεις, the usual word in the Synoptic Gospels for "miracle" or "deed of power" (cf. BAGD 208a). This trilogy, "signs and marvels and powerful deeds," probably does not refer to three distinct types of miracle but to miracles in general considered from three different aspects — their ability to authenticate ("signs"), to arouse awe ("marvels"), and to display divine power ("powerful deeds").[38] Since Luke does not mention any miracles performed in Corinth during Paul's initial visit of about eighteen months (Acts 18:1-18), we can only guess at their nature (cf. 1 Cor. 2:4). Perhaps they included healings,[39] exorcisms, and divinely orchestrated circumstances accompanying conversions.[40] Miracles were a concomitant of Paul's preaching in Galatia (Gal. 3:5; cf. Acts 14:3, 8-10), Macedonia (1 Thess. 1:5; cf. Acts 16:16-18), Corinth (1 Cor. 2:4; 2 Cor. 12:12), and Asia (Acts 19:11-12) and are highlighted more in Luke's record in Acts than by Paul himself in his letters. Clearly miracles occurred regularly during the founding of Paul's churches.

6:4) and that the anarthrous πᾶς means "every kind of" (see BAGD 846b and 631 s.v. 1.a.β. for this sense; cf. εἰς πᾶσαν ὑπομονήν in Col. 1:11).

32. So also Spicq 3.420. Such a view is reflected in the renderings of TCNT, NJB, and Cassirer. We should observe that the presence of the phrase ἐν πάσῃ ὑπομονῇ prevents any conflict between 12:12 and 12:9. The principle that Christ's power comes to perfection in the midst of Paul's weakness (12:9) is not invalidated by the fact that he was the divine instrument for the working of miracles, since those miracles were performed "amid unflagging endurance" of persecution and hardship. Fee regards "signs and wonders" as evidence of the "already" aspect of the "already–not yet" tension in Paul's understanding of the kingdom, and "endurance in affliction" as evidence of the "not yet" aspect, with the Spirit as the bridge between the two (*Presence* 357).

33. E.g., Isa. 8:18; 20:3.

34. E.g., Exod. 7:3; Deut. 6:22; 7:19; Jer. 39 (EVV 32):20-21.

35. E.g., Mark 13:22; John 4:48.

36. E.g., Acts 4:30; 5:12. The order τέρατα καὶ σημεῖα is found in Acts 6:8; 7:36.

37. Acts 2:22; Rom. 15:19; 2 Cor. 12:12; 2 Thess. 2:9; Heb. 2:4.

38. Cf. Calvin 164, followed by Tasker 180; Hughes 457. Joined by τε καί, the terms σημείοις and τέρασιν belong more closely to each other than to δυνάμεσιν.

39. For instances of healings and exorcisms performed through Paul, see Acts 13:11; 14:8-10; 16:18; 19:11-12; 28:3-6, 8.

40. Cf. Windisch 397; Héring 95. Paul would have wholeheartedly endorsed, as relevant also to his Corinthian ministry, what Luke says regarding his initial sojourn in Ephesus: "God did extraordinary miracles by the hands of Paul" (Acts 19:11).

The dative case in the phrase σημείοις τε καὶ τέρασιν καὶ δυνάμεσιν has been understood in four different ways, assuming that σημείοις is somehow related to σημεῖα.

1. As a *locatival* dative ("in"): "The signs that mark a true apostle were most patiently shown when I was among you, in signs, wonders, and marvels" (Goodspeed).[41]
2. As an *instrumental* dative ("by means of"): "The signs of a true apostle were performed among you with all perseverance, by signs and wonders and miracles" (NASB).[42]
3. As an *epexegetic* dative ("consisting of"): "The things that mark an apostle — signs, wonders and miracles — were done among you with great perseverance" (NIV).[43]
4. As a *sociative* dative ("accompanied by"): "The marks of a [true] apostle were displayed [by God] among you in all persistence, [along with] signs and wonders and mighty works" (Martin 425).[44]

It is difficult to decide between these four alternatives, each of which is defensible, although of these four uses of the dative, the first and the third are the least common, and the second the most common. There is no substantial difference between views (1), (2), and (3), for if "the marks of an apostle" were displayed *in* the miracles (#1) or *by means of* the miracles (#2), it is fair to assume that in some sense the miracles were the "marks" (#3). On the other hand, view (4) largely distinguishes the "marks" from the miracles, even if (as Hughes [457] believes) the latter together constitute one of those "marks."[45] But is it probable that Paul would leave undefined, or only partly defined, such a crucial concept as "the marks of an apostle" when the question of the legitimacy of his apostleship is at the heart of chs. 10–13? Our preference is for view (2).

In this verse, then, Paul is appealing to God's working of miracles during his ministry at Corinth as divine accreditation of his apostleship. By the "signs, marvels, and powerful deeds" that accompanied Paul's service, God was testifying to his authentic apostolicity.[46] In themselves these miracles were no evi-

41. Similarly Plummer 356; Wendland 250-51.

42. Similarly RV; Zerwick, *Analysis* 413; Bruce, *Paraphrase* 157; de Boor 237; Bultmann 231; Furnish 552-53; Wolff 250; Fee, *Presence* 354; Barnett 579, 581-82; Lambrecht 212; Thrall 832, 838 n. 514.

43. Similarly Moffatt, GNB, JB, NAB[1]; Lietzmann 156; K. H. Rengstorf, *TDNT* 7.258 (apparently). But if σημείοις was, in fact, epexegetic of σημεῖα κτλ, we would have expected Paul to use apposition, viz. σημεῖα τε καὶ τέρατα καὶ δυνάμεις.

44. Similarly Weymouth; Hughes 457; Peterson 129; Hafemann 467.

45. NEB equates the "marks" with Paul's work in Corinth which was accompanied by the "miracles." "The marks of a true apostle were there, in the work I did among you, which called for such constant fortitude, and was attended by signs, marvels, and miracles" (similarly REB).

46. Similar notions of divine attestation by miracles are expressed elsewhere in the NT. Acts 2:22 speaks of Jesus of Nazareth as accredited by God "by powerful deeds, marvels, and signs

dence of apostleship, for signs and wonders could be counterfeited[47] and the working of miracles was not a privilege reserved for apostles but a gift of the Spirit that might be given to anyone in the congregation (1 Cor. 12:10-11, 28-29). But for Paul miracles were not the sole basis for apostolic accreditation. He himself had already indicated — or at least implied — that there were additional bases: (1) what the Corinthians had observed in his conduct (ὅ [τις] βλέπει με, 12:6); (2) what they had heard from him in any respect ([ὅ τις] ἀκούει τι ἐξ ἐμοῦ, 12:6); and (3) his converts' own experience of spiritual renovation in Christ (3:2; 5:17; cf. 1 Cor. 9:1-2). Under the heading of his conduct we should place his miracles (12:12; possibly 6:7 and 1 Cor. 2:4), his endurance of persecution (4:8-9; 6:4-5, 8-9; 11:23-27; 12:12), his sincerity and holiness (1:12; 2:17; 6:6), and his openness (4:2; 5:11; 6:11). Under his teaching we should place his faithful preaching of Christ crucified and risen in adherence to the original apostolic gospel (cf. 11:4; 1 Cor. 1:23; 15:1, 3-4; 2 Tim. 2:8), preaching that had proved effective in the conversion of the Corinthians.

It is arbitrary to distinguish between these various criteria, designating some primary and others secondary.[48] All belong together, confirming one another.[49] On the other hand, these authenticating signs exhibited by someone who was already an apostle should not be confused with the two qualifications that had to be met in the case of someone who was to become an apostle, namely a visual encounter with the risen Lord (1 Cor. 9:1; 15:7-8), without necessarily having had personal knowledge of the earthly Jesus, and a commissioning to apostleship by the risen Christ (1:1; Rom. 1:1; Gal. 1:1).

12:13 τί γάρ ἐστιν ὃ ἡσσώθητε ὑπὲρ τὰς λοιπὰς ἐκκλησίας, εἰ μὴ ὅτι αὐτὸς ἐγὼ οὐ κατενάρκησα ὑμῶν; χαρίσασθέ μοι τὴν ἀδικίαν ταύτην. "In what way, then, were you worse off than the other churches, except that I myself did not burden you? Forgive me for this offense!" In this verse, as also in the previous two verses, Paul seems to be addressing a complaint made against him (see the introduction to this section). Here the grievance appears to have been that in comparison with "the other churches" the Corinthians had been disadvantaged by some action or actions of Paul. If, as Thrall maintains (841), Paul is now giv-

---

(δυνάμεσι καὶ τέρασι καὶ σημείοις)." In Acts 14:3 Luke notes that at Iconium the Lord confirmed the message spoken by Paul and Barnabas by allowing "signs and marvels" (σημεῖα καὶ τέρατα) to be performed by them (cf. Acts 4:29-30; 8:13; 15:12). Then in Heb. 2:4 God is said to have corroborated the testimony of the early disciples about Christian salvation "by signs and marvels and various miracles (σημείοις τε καὶ τέρασιν καὶ ποικίλαις δυνάμεσιν)." But for the view that in Paul's thought miracles accompany rather than validate the apostolic ministry, see Barrett, "Council" 14-32, especially p. 19.

47. Cf. 2 Thess. 2:9 and Mark 13:22.

48. As Martin does (438).

49. Without rating them, Lightfoot proposes two categories of signs: "moral and spiritual gifts — patience, self-denial, effective preaching"; and supernatural powers, "signs, wonders, and mighty deeds." But he adds that Paul himself does not make such a distinction between the signs, viewing them simply as different manifestations of "one and the same Spirit" (1 Cor. 12:11) (*Galatians* 99).

ing a further reason why the Corinthians should have commended him (cf. vv. 11-12), he is giving that reason in a very negative cast. Rather, he is questioning how they can feel slighted when they had witnessed miracles and other evidence of his apostolic status[50] and when he had patiently toiled for their benefit (cf. 12:19b) amid opposition (v. 12). Literally, "What is there, then (γάρ),[51] with respect to which (ὅ, accusative of respect[52]) you came off worse in comparison with (ὑπέρ)[53] the other churches . . . ?"[54]

ἡσσώθητε is from the verb ἐσσόομαι, "be inferior to," "be worse off" (+ ὑπέρ), the Ionic form of the Attic ἡττάομαι (BDF §34[1]; cf. 2 Pet. 2:19-20). The reason (or reasons) for the Corinthian feeling of inferiority must remain conjectural,[55] although it is clearly related to Paul in some way. His qualification of his question by εἰ μὴ κτλ. might suggest that his refusal to accept the Corinthians' offer of maintenance while accepting it from other churches was the point of dissatisfaction (see 11:7-12), but it would be strange for him to respond to such a charge by conceding it — unless the qualification simply means "at least you were not poorer!" The "other churches" with which the Corinthians compared themselves may have been those founded by Paul,[56] or, more generally, other Christian churches known to them or about which they had heard, whether those churches be Pauline or non-Pauline.

Although Paul questions the validity of the (unstated) reason or reasons for the Corinthians' belief that they had been devalued by him — he does not doubt the reality of their feelings[57] — he concedes that there *was* one area where they might have felt disadvantaged, depending on one's viewpoint. It was that he had refused to squeeze charity out of them (cf. Barclay), to cripple them with expenses (cf. Cassirer), to hang as a dead weight upon them (cf. Weymouth), to sponge upon them (cf. NEB; Plummer 356). These are some of the colorful renderings of κατενάρκησα ὑμῶν. Behind αὐτὸς ἐγώ, "I myself," "I alone" (BAGD 122d), lies an allusion to others who did not refrain from accepting remuneration from churches. The "others" could be the false apostles at Corinth (cf. 11:20) or even genuine apostles who had served in non-Pauline

50. Windisch (397) rightly recognizes that v. 13 alludes principally to ἐν ὑμῖν in v. 12.

51. For this use of γάρ in questions, see BAGD 313c and 152 s.v. 1.f. This latter BAGD reference corresponds to LSJ 338 s.v. I.4. (γάρ in abrupt questions) to which Barrett (322) appeals, although he believes that γάρ here cannot be translated.

52. Moule 131.

53. ὑπέρ ("beyond," "over and above") can bear the sense "in comparison with" or "than" when used with verbs that express a comparison (cf. Luke 16:8) (see BAGD 839b).

54. It is highly improbable that Paul himself would suggest to his converts that they were somehow worse off than other believers.

55. Georgi, e.g., suggests that they felt deprived of some of the spiritual gifts so that an aspect of their church life was missing (*Opponents* 292 n. 87; followed by Martin 345, 438).

56. According to Furnish, Paul's congregations in Macedonia are specifically in view, as in 11:8-9 (553, 556).

57. Paul's question focuses on the possible reason(s) for their feelings: "In what way, then, were you worse off . . . ?"

churches. Positively, Paul is reminding the Corinthians that although they had received all the benefits of a true apostolic ministry (v. 12), they had been charged nothing for his services! For treating them in such a dreadful way, he pleads for their forgiveness. "Forgive me for this offense!" ἀδικία, like ἁμαρτία in 11:7, does not refer to a sin against God,[58] the usual sense of these words, but to an imagined wrong against fellow humans, yet Paul's playful request does illustrate the principle that forgiveness is sought from the person offended. When χαρίζομαι means "give graciously as a favor" or "forgive," it is followed by the dative of the person (here μοι) and the accusative of the thing (τὴν ἀδικίαν ταύτην).[59] Evaluations of Paul's technique here range from acidic, mocking sarcasm (McCant 154-55) to affectionate irony (Hughes 459).[60] If irony can be the simulated adoption of a serious tone,[61] then Paul is ironical, and the words that immediately follow (vv. 14-15) testify to his deep affection. With its reference to Paul's not being a burden on his Corinthian converts, this verse forms a transition to the next section (vv. 14-18) where that notion is central.

Bibliography

Barrett, "Opponents" • Barrett, *Signs* 37-38, 46 • Becker 231-39 • A. C. Clark, "Apostleship: Evidence from the New Testament and Early Christian Literature," *VoxEv* 19 (1989) 49-82 • Fee, *Presence* 354-57 • Fuchs • Jervell, "Charismatiker" • J. Jervell, "The Signs of an Apostle: Paul's Miracles," in his *The Unknown God: Essays on Luke-Acts and Early Christian History* (Minneapolis: Augsburg, 1984) 77-95 (= ET of "Die Zeichen des Apostels. Die Wunder beim lukanischen und paulinischen Paulus," SNTU.A 4 [1979] 54-75) • Meeks 71-72 • Murphy-O'Connor 122-24 • Oostendorp 7-16, 75-79 • R. Schnackenburg, "Apostles before and during Paul's Time," in *Bruce FS* (1) 287-303

C. The Planned Third Visit (12:14–13:10)

In the Introduction we have shown that throughout 2 Corinthians there are many direct or indirect references to Paul's visits to Corinth — whether those visits be actual, planned but not carried out, or imminent — and that the unifying purpose of the whole letter is to prepare the Corinthians for his forthcoming visit so that it might prove mutually beneficial and enjoyable, not

---

58. That Paul is not referring to a sin that requires human and divine forgiveness is clear from the fact that his decision to refuse financial support *from the Corinthians* had been made on principle (11:7) and was unshakeable (11:9-10, 12; 12:14).

59. See BAGD 876 s.v. 1 and 2.

60. Cf. Plummer (360), who observes that in reality Paul's refusal of support was an advantage to the Corinthians, but "with playful irony he treats it as if it were an injury."

61. On irony (εἰρωνεία) and the "ironic person" or "self-depreciator" (εἴρων) in Greek thought, see Forbes 10-13.

painful.[1] Naturally, the nearer Paul comes to the end of his letter, the more often he refers to this next visit (see 12:14, 20-21; 13:1-2, 10).[2] From 12:14 to 13:10 we learn that some Corinthians needed to prepare by repentance (12:20-21; 13:2), and all by self-examination (13:1, 5, 11), so that Paul could avoid fulfilling his threat to exercise severe discipline (13:2, 10). For his part Paul would be preparing by praying for their restoration (κατάρτισις, 13:9) to total devotion to Christ (cf. 11:3) and to himself (cf. 6:12-13; 10:6b; 12:15), knowing that in that process of divine restoration the Corinthians themselves needed to cooperate (καταρτίζεσθε, 13:11).

1. A Promise Not to Be Burdensome (12:14-18)

As Paul announces his third visit (v. 14), he makes the Corinthians two promises. His practice of not being a financial encumbrance on them will not change (οὐ καταναρκήσω, v. 14) and he will very gladly spend his resources and all his energies (δαπανήσω καὶ ἐκδαπανηθήσομαι) for their spiritual benefit (v. 15). If vv. 14-15 relate to his future conduct, vv. 16-18 are concerned with his past conduct, as he responds (vv. 17-18) to the accusation that although he had been technically independent of the Corinthians in financial matters (οὐ κατεβάρησα ὑμᾶς, v. 16a), nevertheless he had operated clandestinely through his agents to defraud them financially (v. 16b). The essential points of vv. 14-18 may be set out as follows.

vv. 14-15a Paul's future conduct
   οὐ καταναρκήσω
               δαπανήσω καὶ ἐκδαπανηθήσομαι
vv. 16-18 Paul's past conduct
   οὐ κατεβάρησα ὑμᾶς
               μὴ . . . ἐπλεονέκτησα ὑμᾶς;

We should not overlook the intensely personal and highly emotive nature of these five verses, which makes them comparable to 6:11-13. First singular verbs occur thirteen times, ὑμᾶς eight times, and the emphatic ἐγώ twice. We find no fewer than five rhetorical questions that betray Paul's pained bewilderment, one introduced by an interrogative εἰ (v. 15), two by μή(τι) (vv. 17-18) expecting the answer "No!" and two by οὐ (v. 18) that assume a "Yes!" response. Also, Paul actually reproduces the potent charge that he was by nature an unscrupulous trickster (ὑπάρχων πανοῦργος) who had victimized the Corinthians with his cunning (δόλῳ ὑμᾶς ἔλαβον) (v. 16).

1. See the Introduction A.3.e.(3)(a).
2. Earlier references to his forthcoming visit are found in 9:3-5; 10:2, 11. There are allusions to the visit in 10:6 and 13:4, while on four occasions he indicates his intention not to be a financial burden on the Corinthians (11:9-10, 12; 12:14), presumably when he next stays in Corinth.

12:14*Look! This*[a] *is the third time I am ready to visit you, and I will not be a burden; for what I am wanting is not your possessions but you yourselves. For children ought not to save up for their parents,*[b] *but parents for their children.* 15*So for my part I will very gladly spend and be completely spent for your souls. If*[c] *I love*[d] *you the more, am I loved the less?* 16*Be that as it may, I was not a burden*[e] *on you. But, crafty schemer that I am, I took you in by a trick.* 17*Surely I did not exploit you through any of the men I have sent to you?* 18*I urged Titus to visit you, and with him I sent the brother whom you know. Surely Titus did not exploit you? Did we not conduct ourselves with the same spirit? Were our footsteps not the same?*

TEXTUAL NOTES

a. Some witnesses (K L P 614 629 945 1241 *pm* b) omit τοῦτο, which would produce a similar sense, "Look! For a third time. . . ."

b. In p⁴⁶ 0243 630 1739 1881 *pc* θησαυρίζειν precedes τοῖς γονεῦσιν, an inferior reading resulting (as in the case of note a. above) from a transcriptional error.

c. Supported by strong proto-Alexandrian (p⁴⁶ ℵ* B), later Alexandrian (A 33 81), and Western (F G) witnesses, the reading εἰ is to be preferred over εἰ καί (ℵ² D¹ Ψ 0243 1738 1881 𝔐 f vg syr) where καί strengthens the condition ("if indeed") or εἰ καί is concessive ("even if"). A few witnesses (D* a g r Ambrosiaster) have neither εἰ nor εἰ καί (see Metzger 517). The reading εἰ is preferred by WH, UBS¹, ², ³, ⁴, and NA²⁷.

d. On the basis of external evidence, a preference may be expressed for ἀγαπῶν (p⁴⁶ ℵ² B D F G Ψ 0243 1739 1881 𝔐 latt) over ἀγαπῶ (ℵ* A 33 104 1241 1505 *pc*) (preferred by UBS¹, ²), since the participial form has the support of strong Alexandrian witnesses (proto-Alexandrian, p⁴⁶ B 1739; later Alexandrian, 0243 1881) and the best Western uncials (D F G), and enjoys wider geographical distribution. In addition, on internal evidence ἀγαπῶν is the more difficult reading, since it requires the reader/listener either to supply the finite verb εἰμί (creating the periphrastic construction εἰμὶ ἀγαπῶν) or to take εἰ to be interrogative. However, with regard to the derivation of variants, neither reading is superior, for (as Metzger [517] observes) each may be explained on transcriptional grounds as arising from either adding or dropping ν before η (ΑΓΑΠΩ[Ν]ΗΣΣΟΝ). UBS³, ⁴ and NA²⁷ print ἀγαπῶ[ν], while WH, Lietzmann (158), and Windisch (401) prefer ἀγαπῶ, but we follow the majority of the UBS committee (see Metzger 517), and, among others, Thrall (848-49) in preferring ἀγαπῶν. On the punctuation issue in this verse, see the commentary.

e. The reading οὐ κατεβάρησα ὑμᾶς (A B D² Ψ 0243 33 1739 𝔐) is undoubtedly original, with p⁴⁶ D* reading the easier simplex form of the verb (οὐκ ἐβάρησα ὑμᾶς) (cf. 1:8; 5:4) and ℵ F G 81 104 326 629 1881 *pc* reading οὐ κατενάρκησα ὑμῶν (104 1881 *pc* have ὑμᾶς) under the influence of the same phrase in v. 13.

12:14 Ἰδοὺ τρίτον τοῦτο ἑτοίμως ἔχω ἐλθεῖν πρὸς ὑμᾶς, καὶ οὐ καταναρκήσω·. "Look! This is the third time I am ready to visit you and I will not be a burden." The demonstrative particle ἰδού[3] marks a transition, recaptures the

---

3. ἰδού is the second aorist imperative middle of ὁράω (i.e., ἰδοῦ), accented differently to show it is the particle (BAGD 370 s.v.).

readers' attention, and points to the importance of what follows.[4] Since τρίτον τοῦτο[5] precedes ἑτοίμως ἔχω,[6] it might seem that Paul is simply indicating a willingness, for a third time, to visit Corinth. But in fact he has coalesced two distinct thoughts into one: he is coming on a third visit, and he is now ready to come. That the reference is to a third coming, not a third willingness or readiness, is clear from 13:1 (τρίτον τοῦτο ἔρχομαι πρὸς ὑμᾶς) and from the next statement ("I will not be a burden"): Paul could be burdensome only on his arrival, not on his readiness to depart (Meyer 688). "What is 'thrice' resolved has no significance for the context" (Bultmann 233).[7] Paul is saying, "Note well! I have made the necessary preparations for a third visit to you."[8] His aim is not to incite fear, but to give "fair warning" (cf. 12:20-21; 13:1-2) and so encourage repentance.

Having announced his imminent visit, he immediately clarifies what his financial relationship to the Corinthians will be during the visit, "and I will not be a burden" (καὶ οὐ καταναρκήσω [ὑμῶν]).[9] He is reaffirming that he will not deviate from his established policy regarding Corinth of being financially independent, of refusing to enter a client-patron relationship, of waiving his apostolic right to support. After his unambiguous statements on the matter in 11:9-10, 12, it may seem strange that he now returns to the same topic, but this is evidence of the sensitivity and centrality of the issue in Paul's relations with the church and is an indication of the influence of his opponents' strategy of seeking to discredit him in the eyes of the Corinthians by pointing to his waiver of an apostolic right as proof of his counterfeit apostleship. However, in reaffirming his position of independence he gives two additional justifications for his stance that we must now consider.

οὐ γὰρ ζητῶ τὰ ὑμῶν ἀλλὰ ὑμᾶς, οὐ γὰρ ὀφείλει τὰ τέκνα τοῖς γονεῦσιν θησαυρίζειν, ἀλλὰ οἱ γονεῖς τοῖς τέκνοις. "For what I am wanting is not your possessions but you yourselves. For children ought not to save up for their parents, but parents for the children." The *first reason* (γάρ) for Paul's refusal to make himself a burden at Corinth was his total lack of interest in acquiring any

4. Cf. BAGD 307-71 s.v. 1.a., 1.b.ε. For the view that the conclusion of the letter begins at 12:14, not 13:11, see Schnider and Stenger 73, 75, and the critique by Thrall 904.

5. This phrase may mean either "now for the third time" or "this is the third time" (BAGD 826d; cf. Robertson 702).

6. The expression ἑτοίμως ἔχειν (also found in Acts 21:13; 1 Pet. 4:5) means "be in a condition of readiness"; ἔχω is used intransitively with a predicative adverb (ἑτοίμως, "readily") and an infinitive (ἐλθεῖν) that indicates what Paul was ready to do (see Burton §376). For the idiom, see Moule 161; Turner 226. For examples in the papyri, see MM 258c.

7. See further in the Introduction, B.1.a.

8. To avoid any ambiguity, many EVV explicitly relate τρίτον τοῦτο to ἐλθεῖν — e.g., "Now I am ready to visit you for the third time" (NIV; similarly Moffatt, NEB, JB, Barclay, NJB, NAB[2], REB, NRSV).

9. See the commentary at 11:9 for the meaning and use of the verb καταναρκάω and for a reconstruction of the possible stages in Paul's sources of support during his founding visit in Corinth, and at 11:10 for a summary of his financial policy in relation to his churches.

of his converts' possessions or money (cf. Phil. 4:17). οὐ ζητῶ is an absolute and timeless disavowal of the "desire to possess,"[10] while τὰ ὑμῶν ("what belongs to you," possessive genitive) refers to any property owned, including financial assets. What he *did* want to obtain, however, was the Corinthians themselves (ὑμᾶς), that is, their spiritual well-being, their "souls" (v. 15). "It is your salvation I want, not your money or your gifts."

There is, we suggest, a correspondence between the negative and the positive elements in the two οὐ γάρ . . . ἀλλά antitheses. The negative οὐ γάρ ὀφείλει τὰ τέκνα τοῖς γονεῦσιν θησαυρίζειν corresponds to οὐ . . . ζητῶ τὰ ὑμῶν. That is, it was because (cf. γάρ) children are under no obligation to support[11] their parents that Paul did not seek financial support from his Corinthian children in Christ (οὐ . . . ζητῶ τὰ ὑμῶν) and could promise not to make any financial demands on them during his forthcoming visit (οὐ καταναρκήσω). Here, then, we have the *second reason* for Paul's decision not to be a financial deadweight on the church in Corinth — children are not responsible for their parents' support.[12] But the two positive elements also match each other. [ὀφείλουσιν] οἱ γονεῖς τοῖς τέκνοις [θησαυρίζειν] corresponds to [ζητῶ] ὑμᾶς. That is, it was because parents are under an obligation to support their children that Paul was "looking out for" the Corinthians, seeking their highest spiritual good. What the apostle presupposes in using this parent-child imagery is his role of spiritual fatherhood and his role as the Corinthians' one and only father in Christ. They are his "dearly loved children" (τέκνα μου ἀγαπητά, 1 Cor. 4:14).[13] "For though you have countless tutors in Christ, you do not have multiple fathers. For I myself became your father in Christ Jesus, through preaching the gospel to you" (1 Cor. 4:15). His spiritual paternity (cf. 6:13; 11:2) gave him a distinctive right, which could not be claimed by his rivals, to care for his children's spiritual welfare, a right he was eager to exercise (ζητῶ).[14]

---

10. BAGD 339a classify ζητέω in this verse under the meanings "try to obtain, desire to possess τὶ someth[ing]."

11. θησαυρίζω here refers to "saving up" money or "laying up (money) in store," not in order to provide an inheritance but in order to have sufficient financial resources to render support. Appropriately, GNB renders the verb "provide for," and NEB, REB, and Cassirer have "make provision for."

12. οὐ . . . ὀφείλει τὰ τέκνα here stands in stark contrast with ἐγὼ . . . ὤφειλον ὑφ' ὑμῶν συνίστασθαι (12:11). Although the Corinthians had no obligation to support Paul (given his decision to waive his apostolic right to support), they did have an obligation to commend him but failed to do so.

13. Cf. Gal. 4:19; 1 Thess. 2:7, 11. For Paul's spiritual fatherhood of individual believers, see Phil. 2:22; 1 Tim. 1:2; 2 Tim. 1:2; Tit. 1:4; Phlm. 10.

14. On the theme of spiritual fatherhood in Paul, see P. Gutierrez, *La paternité spirituelle selon saint Paul* (Paris: Gabalda, 1968). For Jewish and Greco-Roman views on fatherhood in the first century, see E. M. Lassen, "The Use of the Father Image in Imperial Propaganda and 1 Corinthians 4:14-21," *TynB* 42 (1991) 127-36 (especially 128-33); A. A. Myrick, "'Father' Imagery in 2 Corinthians 1–9 and Jewish Paternal Tradition," *TynB* 47 (1996) 163-71 (especially 164-67); and Burke 59-80. On Paul's use of maternal imagery in reference to himself, see B. R. Gaventa, "The Maternity of Paul: An Exegetical Study of Galatians 4:19," in *The Conversation Continues: Studies*

In chs. 11 and 12, then, Paul justifies his inflexible policy of financial independence of the Corinthians on several grounds.[15]

(1) He wanted to dramatize the fact that the gospel he preached was free of charge (11:7), and, by doing so, to avoid any accusation that his preaching was motivated by monetary gain (cf. 6:3; 1 Cor. 9:12b).

(2) He wished never to be a financial "dead-weight"[16] on the Corinthians, a millstone around their necks (11:9; 12:13-14, 16).

(3) He was determined never to forfeit the advantage he enjoyed over the rival missionaries at Corinth who apparently (cf. 11:20) received remuneration from the church there (11:12).

(4) He had no designs on their possessions or money, only on the good of their persons (12:14a).

(5) Children are not expected to accumulate resources so that they can support their parents (12:14b).

But would Paul have regarded his statement that "children are not responsible to save up for their parents" as universally applicable and without exceptions? Certainly not! He must have viewed this as a general principle (note the gnomic present ὀφείλει and the plurals τέκνα and γονεῦσιν) with obvious exceptions and not as a rigid law that was everywhere applicable, for the following reasons.[17] (1) He himself received financial support from some of his spiritual children (11:8-9; Phil. 4:15-16). (2) In 1 Cor. 9:14 he appeals to a dominical provision (see Luke 10:7) that allows for the support of Christian evangelists, presumably (among others) by those who have responded to the preaching of the gospel. (3) He knows of another "natural law" — that of appropriate returns for labor expended (1 Cor. 9:3-9, 13) — that must stand alongside the "natural law" of 12:14b.[18] (4) In 1 Tim. 5:8 he requires believers to provide for the needs (προνοεῖ) of their own families, which would include, in certain circumstances (cf. Mark 7:9-13), the care of parents by children. So we conclude that, as is sometimes the case with Paul's οὐ(κ) . . . ἀλλά contrasts,[19] the antithesis in v. 14b is not absolute but relative: "it is not normally

in Paul in Honor of J. Louis Martyn, ed. R. Fortna and B. R. Gaventa (Nashville: Abingdon, 1990) 189-200.

15. For other grounds that may be inferred from Paul's situation, see the commentary on 11:10.

16. In 12:13-14 Weymouth renders καταναρκάω by "be/hang as a dead weight" (literally "a stupefying weight," 496 n. 3), possibly under the influence of a Latin equivalent *gravare,* "weigh down, burden" (see BAGD 415 s.v.).

17. Cf. Windisch 399-400; Bultmann 233.

18. Philo speaks of a "natural law" (νόμος φύσεως) according to which the property of parents may be inherited by their children, although parents themselves may not inherit their children's property (*De Vita Mosis* 2.245). For some expressions in antiquity of the mutual responsibilities of parents and children, see Peterson, "Conquest" 265-66.

19. See the discussion at 2:5.

(or principally) that children must provide for their parents, but parents for their children."[20]

12:15 ἐγὼ δὲ ἥδιστα δαπανήσω καὶ ἐκδαπανηθήσομαι ὑπὲρ τῶν ψυχῶν ὑμῶν. εἰ περισσοτέρως ὑμᾶς ἀγαπῶν, ἧσσον ἀγαπῶμαι;. "So for my part I will very gladly spend and be completely spent for your souls. If I love you the more, am I loved the less?" In the first part of this verse, as a dedicated father Paul promises his unceasing and self-sacrificing devotion to the spiritual well-being of his children in the faith at Corinth. In the second part, as a frustrated lover he expresses his disappointment at their failure to reciprocate his paternal love.

The double reference to parenthood (οἱ γονεῖς) in v. 14b makes it clear that when Paul speaks of his expenditure and his love and uses the emphatic ἐγώ in v. 15, he is thinking of his role as a spiritual father. His sense of fatherhood in relation to his converts originated in his role as the evangelist through whose preaching they had come to believe (cf. 1 Cor. 3:5; 4:15).[21] If δέ is adversative ("but"), he is contrasting his glad and lavish generosity in giving to his children with what might be expected of normal fathers; he outstrips ordinary expectations. "I promise to do even more than natural fathers" (Theodoret).[22] This is certainly possible, but it is better to see v. 15a as an explanation (δέ = "for") or as a consequence (δέ = "so") of the axiom expressed in v. 14b. θησαυρίζειν in v. 14 does not refer to hoarding resources but to saving them up *for use,* so that v. 15a affords an illustration (ἐγώ, "for my part," "as for me" [NEB])[23] of the exuberant (ἥδιστα, "very gladly"[24]) and liberal use of a father's resources.

In a literal sense δαπανάω refers to the spending of money or concrete resources. In Acts 21:24, for example, it is used of the paying of expenses, the defraying of the cost of sacrifices. Figuratively, as here, it denotes the exertion of great effort (Louw and Nida §42.27). καὶ ἐκδαπανηθήσομαι intensifies the idea of expenditure, with ἐκ- used in a "perfective" sense, "spend *out,* spend wholly."[25] "I will expend myself and be utterly expended for your sake." Both his energies and even his life[26] will be used up for the spiritual welfare of his

20. Cf. Plummer 362: "Very often one of two alternatives is in form negatived, not in order to exclude it absolutely, but to show its inferiority to the other alternative." As examples Plummer cites Mark 2:17; 6:4; 9:37; Luke 10:20; 14:12; 23:28; John 12:44; and Hos. 6:6.

21. It is therefore not surprising that paternal imagery is absent from Romans, since Paul had not founded the church in Rome.

22. ἐγὼ δὲ τῶν φύσει πατέρων καὶ πλέον τι ποιεῖν ἐπαγγέλλομαι (cited, with approval, by Meyer 689). Similarly Plummer 362; Allo 328.

23. ἐγώ could also allude to Paul's opponents who exhibited tyrannical, not genuinely paternal, characteristics (11:20).

24. As in 12:9, ἥδιστα is an elative comparative (BDF §60[2]).

25. Moulton and Howard 311; similarly Robertson 596. Others express ἐκ- by "to the uttermost" (Barclay) or "to the limit" (NEB, REB). Compare the effect of (οὐκ) ἐξαπορούμενοι following ἀπορούμενοι in 4:8.

26. BAGD (238b) takes the passive of ἐκδαπανάω here to mean "*be spent*[,] of the sacrifice of one's own life."

converts. Although it is possible that the simplex verb refers to money and concrete resources, and the compound verb to personal resources ("all I have and all I am," Goodspeed),[27] it is more likely that both verbs describe the willing sacrifice of personal resources such as physical and spiritual vigor. We could take ὑπὲρ τῶν ψυχῶν ὑμῶν to mean little more than ὑπὲρ ὑμῶν,[28] but the use of ψυχή indicates that the benefit (implied by ὑπέρ) to be felt by the Corinthians lay in the spiritual realm rather than in the physical or financial. Neither energy nor life itself would be spared by Paul as he worked for their salvation. He is not instituting a new policy that would take effect when he arrived on his third visit. Rather, he is reaffirming, with regard to that visit, what had always been true of his service to the Corinthians.

In 11:2 Paul presents himself as the protective father of the bride, the whole Corinthian congregation being his daughter "in the Lord." Here in 12:15a he presents himself as the devoted, self-giving father of his spiritual children at Corinth, bent on contributing energetically to their highest spiritual good. This shows that for Paul fatherhood involves a nurturing role, and not merely an educating and admonishing role (1 Cor. 4:14-15; 1 Thess. 2:11-12), a disciplinary role (1 Cor. 4:15, 21; cf. 2 Cor. 13:10), or a modeling role (1 Cor. 4:15-16). His aim was to bring each of his converts to maturity in faith and in the knowledge of God's will (Col. 1:9, 23, 28), and to achieve this goal he toiled and strove with the energy that Christ powerfully generated within him (Col. 1:29).

If we follow p[46] B F G and read εἰ περισσοτέρως ὑμᾶς ἀγαπῶν in v. 15b,[29] there are two ways of construing these words.

1. As the *protasis* of a conditional sentence in which v. 15a is the apodosis: "I will very gladly spend and be completely spent for your souls, if, loving you the more, I am loved the less."[30] Meyer takes this "if" (εἰ) to relate to a purely hypothetical situation — "in view of the possible case, that . . ." — with Paul showing "tender delicacy in the expression of a harsh thought" (689). But, as Thrall (849) notes, "the apostle's self-sacrifice for his spiritual children would hardly be *conditioned* by their *lack* of love for him."

2. As the first part of a *rhetorical question* that is separate from v. 15a. Although there are no other examples of the interrogative use of εἰ in Paul, instances are found elsewhere in the NT as well as in the LXX.[31] On this understanding of εἰ, three translations are possible:

27. Similarly Moffatt, Williams, GNB, NIV.

28. E. Schweizer, *TDNT* 9.648; NEB, NIV, REB, NRSV have "for you"; GNB, "in order to help you."

29. See Textual Notes c. and d.

30. This translates the Greek text found in WH's margin. Reading εἰ καὶ . . . ἀγαπῶν, Allo translates ". . . I shall completely expend myself for your souls . . . even if the more I love you, the less I am bound to be loved." "Paul affirms unconditionally his limitless devotion" (327).

31. See BAGD 219 s.v. εἰ V.1., citing Gen. 17:17; 44:19; Amos 3:3-6; 6:12; Matt. 12:10; 19:3; Mark 10:2; Luke 13:23; 22:49; Acts 1:6; 7:1; 19:2; 21:37; 22:25. Cf. BDF §440(3), who regard the usage as probably a Hebraism.

(a) "Because I love you more, must I be loved the less?" (JB, taking ἀγαπῶν as causal).[32]

(b) "Loving you the more, am I loved the less?" (Thrall 832).

(c) "If I love you the more, am I to be loved the less?" (NASB). The EVV or commentators who propose a rendering such as this[33] may be translating the indicative (εἰ . . .) ἀγαπῶ *or* may be giving the participle ἀγαπῶν a conditional sense (after an interrogative εἰ).

There is no significant difference between these three renderings, and almost all translations and commentators rightly take v. 15b as a rhetorical question.

If the comparative adverb περισσοτέρως (see 11:23) here means "far more" or "more intensely," Paul could be comparing the strength of his love with that of others,[34] whether other teachers or his opponents. But for such a contrast ἐγώ (αὐτός) would be required with ἀγαπῶ(ν) (Bultmann 234). Nor is it probable that he is comparing his love for the Corinthians with his love for his other churches or with the measure of love required of fathers. Rather, περισσοτέρως stands opposed to ἧσσον,[35] "less" (of degree) (BDF §61[1]), "to a lesser extent," so that this pair means "(the) more . . . (the) less" (BAGD 4c; 349a).[36]

In this cry from Paul's heart (cf. 11:11), which is simultaneously a gentle rebuke that solicits a change in the Corinthians' hearts, he is expressing his disappointment that his paternal love is not being reciprocated by his children (note the present tenses of ἀγαπῶν and ἀγαπῶμαι).[37] Whereas Aristotle believed that in the "unequal friendship" that obtains between parent and child, "the better of the two parties . . . should receive more affection than he bestows" (*Ethica Nicomachea* 8.7.2), Paul was seeking from his spiritual children a love comparable in intensity to his own, the rectification of the obvious disparity that was currently true (cf. 6:11-13). But he was concerned not only at the absence of reciprocation; he does not simply ask, "If I love you, why do you not love me in return?" He is distressed also that there seems to be an inverse proportion: the warmer his love, the cooler theirs! The stronger his determination to spare them the burden of supporting him — an expression of his love, as he saw it — the weaker their affection for him seemed to be, since, from their perspective, his continuing rejection of their offer of support diminished their love for him.

From this verse we may infer that Paul regarded his ministry as a joyful

32. Similarly Moffatt, Goodspeed, GNB, JB, NJB.

33. RV, Weymouth, RSV, NEB, Barclay, NAB¹, NIV, NAB², REB, NRSV; Lietzmann 158; Barrett 318; Furnish 557; Carrez 232; Lang 353; Lambrecht 210.

34. Moffatt has "more than others."

35. ἧσσον is the neuter of ἧσσων, "lesser," which serves as the comparative of ὀλίγος ("little").

36. But it is possible that περισσοτέρως is equivalent to ὑπερβαλλόντως (thus BDF §60[3]), "immeasurably," "exceedingly," "to excess" (Barclay), "excessively" (Berkeley).

37. Martin, however, relates v. 15b to the upcoming visit. In a "new campaign" of increased love Paul plans "to expend both his resources and his energy to the point of exhaustion," but he nevertheless entertains a fear: " 'Will my increased affection result in less love from the Corinthians?' " (444).

endeavor (ἥδιστα), as essentially self-giving (δαπανήσω), as requiring sacrifice (ἐκδαπανηθήσομαι), as aiming at promoting the spiritual welfare of others (ὑπὲρ τῶν ψυχῶν ὑμῶν), and as an expression of love (ὑμᾶς ἀγαπῶν).[38]

12:16 ἔστω δέ, ἐγὼ οὐ κατεβάρησα ὑμᾶς· ἀλλὰ ὑπάρχων πανοῦργος δόλῳ ὑμᾶς ἔλαβον. "Be that as it may, I was not a burden on you. But, crafty schemer that I am, I took you in by a trick." The focus now moves from Paul's future conduct (vv. 14-15a) to his past conduct (vv. 16-18). ἔστω (literally, "let it be") may be prospective, introducing a point that all parties would agree on, viz. that Paul had never imposed on the congregation financially. "Let it be assumed that I did not burden you" (NRSV).[39] But Robertson is probably right in observing that the unexpressed subject of ἔστω is the preceding sentence (v. 15b) (392). On this view ἔστω is retrospective, "Be that as it may" (Weymouth, NIV).[40] "Whatever is the answer to that question [v. 15b], the incontestable fact remains: I myself (ἐγώ) was not an imposition on you." What *was* contested was the significance of that fact: did it express love (as Paul believed) or lack of love (as the Corinthians seemed to think) (cf. v. 15b)? καταβαρέω means "put pressure or weight (βάρος) on," thus "burden (someone, τινά)," so that οὐ κατεβάρησα ὑμᾶς is indistinguishable in meaning from οὐ κατενάρκησα ὑμῶν (v. 13; cf. 11:9a, b).

Standing over against (cf. ἀλλά) that incontrovertible fact was the view that Paul in his craftiness had ensnared the Corinthians by a trick. ὑπάρχων πανοῦργος means "since I am crafty by nature," where the causal participle[41] refers to an inherent characteristic (ὑπάρχων = ὢν φύσει).[42] The adjective πανοῦργος is formed on the analogy of κακοῦργος (= κακόν + ἔργον, "carrying out an evil deed") and means, etymologically, "capable of all work" (πᾶν + ἔργον),[43] "ready to do anything,"[44] or, in a pejorative sense, "up to every conceivable trick." The dual sense of this word is represented in the LXX: positively, it means "prudent," "wise,"[45] and negatively, "crafty" (Job 5:12). In the NT, however, the word group πανουργία[46] and πανοῦργος (found only here)[47]

---

38. For a defense of the thesis that Paul's paternal role (as portrayed in 1 Thess. 2:11-12) involved both authority (cf. the Roman *paterfamilias*) and affection (cf. the Roman emperor as *pater patriae*), see Burke 59-80.

39. Similarly Goodspeed, RSV, NEB, GNB; Furnish 557; Martin 444.

40. Some take ἔστω δέ to be a Corinthian reaction. "But let that pass, you say" (Moffatt) or "'Ah!' you say, 'that is all very well'" (Cassirer). δέ is either transitional ("now") or adversative ("but"); if the former, it need not be represented in translation.

41. So Moule 103; Turner 157.

42. Similarly Plummer 363; Hughes 464 n. 150; Thrall 832. But BAGD 838a takes ὑπάρχων to be a substitute for ὤν.

43. O. Bauernfeind, *TDNT* 5.722.

44. LSJ 1299 s.v.; BAGD 608 s.v.

45. E.g., Prov. 12:16; 13:1, 16; 14:8, 24.

46. "Craftiness," "cunning" (5 NT uses: Luke 20:23; 1 Cor. 3:19; 2 Cor. 4:2; 11:3; Eph. 4:14).

47. On the use of πανοῦργος in anti-sophistic polemic, see Betz, *Paulus* 104-6 and the observations of Thrall 850-51.

always bears a negative sense. δόλῳ is an instrumental dative, "by cunning," "through a trick." As in 11:20, λαμβάνω introduces a metaphor drawn from fishing or hunting, where "take" means "catch" or "snare," although in reference to persons who are "duped" or deceived the sense will be "take in."

What was the origin of this view of Paul's past conduct? It is conceivable that he himself is anticipating a possible charge against him. "Paul imagines to himself a dialog with the Corinthians and expresses it succinctly in the first person."[48] Accordingly, some renderings of v. 16 add "(I suppose)" (Young and Ford 275) or "someone will say" (GNB). But while Paul might have imagined or anticipated an accusation that he had ensnared the Corinthians by a cunning trick, it is difficult to believe that he would have prefaced it with ὑπάρχων πανοῦργος, "unscrupulous trickster that I am." Rather, he seems to be reproducing an actual charge, or at least a persistent rumor,[49] that originated with his opponents (Weymouth adds "they say"; cf. φησίν in 10:10) or with the Corinthians themselves (RSV adds "you say"). Whichever group was responsible for the rumor or the charge, the other would have readily believed and perpetuated it.

Verses 17 and 18 give some substance to the charge. Paul's trickery involved the use of his associates, especially Titus and "the brother," as his agents in exploiting his converts. That the alleged deceit related to financial dealings is obvious from the context. The accusation seems to have run along these lines. "Although Paul has consistently refused to exercise the apostolic right to support and accept our offer of patronage, he has nevertheless gained access to our finances by surreptitious scheming. The collection he has been organizing is ostensibly to relieve the needs of the poor in the Jerusalem church, but in fact he has used his intermediaries to ensure that our contributions ended up in his own hands."

12:17 μή τινα ὧν ἀπέσταλκα πρὸς ὑμᾶς, δι' αὐτοῦ ἐπλεονέκτησα ὑμᾶς; "Surely I did not exploit you through any of the men I have sent to you?" V. 16b has stated in broad outline the charge that had been leveled against Paul. His rebuttal in v. 17, also couched in general terms, is in effect an invitation to the Corinthians to adduce any evidence of exploitation through any of his deputies. As also in v. 18, πλεονεκτέω refers to Paul's alleged exploitation of the Corinthians by taking advantage of their willingness to contribute to the collection, all the time siphoning off funds for himself through financial intermediaries. There can be little doubt that the charge Paul is answering was particularly painful to him. It related to his collection for Jerusalem that symbolized the climax of his Aegean ministry and was the "crown jewel" (Sampley 6) of his work. But even more distressing was the fact that the accusation involved his carefully chosen and trusted associates who had been dispatched by him to work on his behalf in

48. Danker 202, who paraphrases the verse this way: "Very well, 'You didn't freeload,' you will say to me. But in the same breath, 'Ah, but you were clever and took advantage of us in our naiveté.'" Cf. Lietzmann 159.

49. It seems unlikely that Paul would formally respond (even if it be by rhetorical questions, vv. 17-18) to an imagined accusation.

Corinth; the principal was naturally jealous of his agents' reputations as well as his own.

Two grammatical issues call for comment, namely ἀπέσταλκα and the expression τινὰ ὧν. Since the perfect ἀπέσταλκα occurs in the midst of aorists it may readily be explained as an aoristic perfect in narrative.[50] However, if this perfect depicts multiple, intermittent "sendings" whose influence remains, we have an instance of "the present perfect of broken continuity" (Robertson 896) that describes "iterative process" (Robertson 893).[51] Moulton renders ὧν ἀπέσταλκα by "of those whom (from time to time) I have sent" (144). In the phrase τινὰ ὧν, the relative pronoun stands for τούτων (or ἐκείνων) οὓς (ἀπέσταλκα),[52] "(which) of these/those whom (I sent)." Because τινά and (δι') αὐτοῦ refer to the same person, we may explain the whole sentence as an anacoluthon (possibly reflecting Semitic influence — Moule 176) in which Paul begins the sentence with one construction in mind but then alters that intended construction.[53] In this case τινά should be classified as a "pendent accusative,"[54] and the anacoluthon could be indicated by a dash: "Any of those whom I have sent to you — did I defraud you through him?" (Barrett 318).[55] But most EVV remove the anacoluthon in translation.

12:18 παρεκάλεσα Τίτον καὶ συναπέστειλα τὸν ἀδελφόν· μήτι ἐπλεονέκτησεν ὑμᾶς Τίτος; οὐ τῷ αὐτῷ πνεύματι περιεπατήσαμεν; οὐ τοῖς αὐτοῖς ἴχνεσιν; "I urged Titus to visit you, and with him I sent the brother whom you know. Surely Titus did not exploit you? Did we not conduct ourselves with the same spirit? Were our footsteps not the same?" As Paul continues his rebuttal of the charge of exploitation by entrapment (vv. 16-17), he repeats in specific terms the point made in general terms in v. 17, namely that no one of his envoys was ever guilty of exploiting the Corinthians. Now the focus is on Titus, his principal agent to Corinth in recent times, and on the visit or visits Titus made when financial exploitation was possible. V. 18a states the relationship between himself and Titus — that of principal and agent. V. 18b assumes that

---

50. Thus BDF §343(2); Turner 70; also Burton §88 ("probably," but without reference to narrative).

51. Such a use of the perfect differs from the iterative imperfect in that the results of the iteration are in mind.

52. BDF §466(1); Zerwick §29. Robertson explains the genitive ὧν as attracted from the accusative οὓς into the case of the unexpressed antecedent τούτων (*Pictures* 268).

53. Buttmann 381; Plummer 364, who suggests that Paul originally intended the question to read, "Have I ever sent anyone to you through whom you were defrauded?" Windisch proposes "Have I sent anyone through whom I exploited you?" (μή τινα ἀπέσταλκα δι' οὗ ἐπλεονέκτησα ὑμᾶς;) (403).

54. Thus Meyer 690; Zerwick and Grosvenor 561.

55. Zerwick, however, finds in τινά an instance of "inverse relative attraction," where the case of τινά (accusative) is determined by the accusative that is latent in ὧν (= ἐκείνων οὓς) (§29). But Robertson rejects this explanation, preferring to call the whole sentence anacoluthic (436, 717-18). If the accusative of respect were not rare in the NT and in Hellenistic Greek generally (see Zerwick §§53, 74), we might be tempted to explain τινά that way (as Hughes does, 466 n. 153).

the Corinthians knew of Titus's impeccable conduct (cf. 7:13b-15) and appeals to the principle that the agent is the *alter ego* of the principal: what the agent does or does not do, the principal does or does not do. If Titus was not guilty of defrauding or taking advantage of the Corinthians, neither was Paul. The conduct of both parties had been governed by the same outlook, and their course of action had been identical. Only one conclusion was therefore possible. The charge against Paul was completely unjustified; he was not a crafty embezzler of the Corinthian contributions to the Jerusalem fund.[56]

As in 8:6; 9:5 (cf. 8:17), it is difficult to know whether παρακαλέω refers to a simple request or to a request accompanied by strong encouragement (= "appeal to," "urge").[57] Perhaps Paul's requests were always urgings! With παρεκάλεσα we must supply a clause such as ἵνα ἔρχηται πρὸς ὑμᾶς ("to come to you") (Windisch 403). συναποστέλλω means "send off (ἀπό) in someone's company (σύν)," thus "send with." It implies that "the brother" played a role subordinate to Titus, which would explain why Titus and not "the brother" is referred to in the following three rhetorical questions.[58] The article with ἀδελφόν could be possessive ("his brother"[59] or "our brother") but is more probably anaphoric ("the well-known brother" or "the brother whom you know"); cf. 1:1.

Like μή (v. 17), μήτι shows that a negative response to the question is expected ("surely . . . not?"), just as the repeated οὐ anticipates a positive answer.[60] With these two interrogative particles, οὐ (or οὐχί) and μή (or μήτι), sometimes the expected answer may come after the hearer's or reader's careful evaluation of the question, but usually it would come immediately (as in vv. 17-18) after recognition that the information contained in the question was true or false.

The subject of περιεπατήσαμεν will be Paul and Titus; some EVV have "he and I" to remove the ambiguity of "we."[61] The same verb is implied in the final rhetorical question. All four aorists in this verse allude to a visit or visits that Titus made to Corinth during which he organized or handled contributions to Paul's collection for Jerusalem. The identity of this visit or these visits is discussed in detail in the Introduction (A.3.e.[2]), where it is concluded that 12:18 refers to (i) Titus's initiation of the collection mentioned in 8:6a, or (ii) his delivery of the "severe (or sorrowful) letter" when he endeavored to revive the

---

56. What particular circumstances involving Titus's conduct gave rise to the charge against Paul cannot be known. See the discussion in Thrall 855-57. For a first-century example of actual embezzlement of gifts that were destined for Jerusalem, see Josephus, *Antiquities* 18.81-84.

57. See the possible meanings of παρακαλέω given in BAGD 617 s.v. 2. and 3.

58. No reference is made to Timothy since there is no evidence that his visit referred to in 1 Cor. 16:10-11 (on which see the Introduction, n. 249) involved finances.

59. Either "his (physical) brother" (Robertson, *Pictures* 268, "probably"; cf. 8:18) or "his brother (in Christ)."

60. See BDF §§427(2), 440; Turner 282-83.

61. Weymouth, Goodspeed, GNB, JB, NJB.

flagging collection, or (iii) both of these visits. Regarding these two visits of Titus, see the Introduction (n. 249) and the commentary at 2:12-13; 7:7-15; and 8:6a.

Fee argues vigorously (357-59) that τῷ αὐτῷ πνεύματι should be rendered "in the same Spirit," an interpretation (we observe) that is reflected in several EVV.[62] Noting the comparable phrase πνεύματι περιπατεῖτε in Gal. 5:16, he suggests that "walking in/by the Spirit" is the basic form of Paul's ethical imperative" (358), so that without the second question (οὐ τοῖς αὐτοῖς ἴχνεσιν;) one would naturally understand πνεύματι as referring to the Holy Spirit. In fact, he argues, this second question is not an explanation of τῷ αὐτῷ πνεύματι but simply a development of the metaphor of "walking." He also points to the expression ἐν τῷ αὐτῷ πνεύματι in 1 Cor. 12:9 in a context that speaks of diversity of gifts yet the oneness of the giver (1 Cor. 12:11) (359). Although Gal. 5:16 and 1 Cor. 12:9 lend support to this view, the parallelism between τῷ αὐτῷ πνεύματι and τοῖς αὐτοῖς ἴχνεσιν[63] suggests that πνεύματι is being used anthropologically in reference to a "disposition of mind" (Zerwick, *Analysis* 414) or attitude.[64] In all three NT uses of ἴχνος ("footprint") (Rom. 4:12; 2 Cor. 12:18; 1 Pet. 2:21) the word is figurative in meaning. "Did we not walk (supplying περιεπατήσαμεν) in the same footsteps?" or "Were our footsteps not the same?" refers to the identity of course or track followed by Titus and Paul that was the corollary of their identity of outlook. Between the two there was perfect harmony in both inward attitude and outward action. If the Corinthians knew Titus to be innocent of financial chicanery, so too Paul was innocent.

Bibliography

Barrett, "Titus" • E. Best, *Paul and His Converts* (Edinburgh: Clark, 1986) • Burke • J. N. Court, "The Controversy with the Adversaries of Paul's Apostolate in the Context of His Relations to the Corinthian Congregation (2 Corinthians 12,14–13,13)," in E. Lohse (ed.), *Verteidigung und Begründung des apostolischen Amtes (2 Kor 10–13)* (Benedictina 11; Rome: Abbazia San Paolo fuori le mura, 1992) 87-105 • Fee, *Presence* 357-59 • Gale 170-72 • Gutierrez • Hafemann, *Defense* 154-60 • Kennedy 115-25 • Lightfoot 273-84 • Meeks 65-67 • Ollrog 33-37 • Oostendorp 75-79 • Peterson 130-32 • Peterson, "Conquest" • Spicq, *Agape* 2.33-35

---

62. RV, Weymouth, NEB, NJB, REB; also Meyer 690; Stanley 272; Windisch 404; Wand; Zerwick and Grosvenor 561 (but not Zerwick, *Analysis* 414).

63. But πνεύματι is the dative of attendant circumstances or manner (cf. BAGD 649c) ("with"), while ἴχνεσιν is a locatival dative ("in").

64. So also, e.g., Furnish 560; Martin 449; Thrall 855.

2. Fears about the Corinthians' State (12:19-21)

With his imminent visit uppermost in his mind, Paul repudiates any suggestion that his main object in writing to the Corinthians in preparation for his visit was to defend himself against charges that had been leveled against him. His overriding aim was not self-defense but their edification (v. 19). And their upbuilding was an urgent need, for he had a threefold fear[1] about what might happen on his arrival — that there might be mutual disappointment and embarrassment (v. 20a); that he might find evidence of factiousness and disharmony (v. 20b); and that he might be humiliated before his converts and find many still unrepentant about their immoral behavior (v. 21).

12:19*Have you been thinking all this time*[a] *that we are defending ourselves before you? Rather, it is in the sight of God*[b] *and in Christ*[c] *that we are speaking. Everything, dear friends, is for your upbuilding.* 20*For I fear that when I come I might perhaps find you not the kind of people I wish, and that I myself might be found to be in your view the kind of person you do not wish: I fear there might perhaps be discord,*[d] *jealousy,*[e] *angry outbursts, factiousness, slandering, gossiping, arrogance, disorder.* 21*I fear too that when I come*[f] *my God may again humble*[g] *me in my relations with you, and that I may grieve over many who have sinned previously and did not repent of the impurity and sexual immorality and debauchery in which they had indulged.*

TEXTUAL NOTES

a. πάλαι ("for a long time," "all this time") is to be preferred over πάλιν (read by ℵ² D Ψ 0278 𝔐 g vg^mss syr bo) because (i) it has superior attestation, with proto-Alexandrian (ℵ* B 1739), later Alexandrian (A 0243 33 81 1175 1881), and Western (F G) textual representatives; and (ii) it is the more difficult reading, since πάλιν ("again") is a very common adverb (28 uses in Paul) and may be explained as an assimilation to its use in 3:1 and 5:12 in a similar context, while πάλαι is found only here in Paul and does not bear its usual sense of "long ago." Probably under the influence of 12:18, p⁴⁶ reads οὐ πάλαι, which makes v. 19a a question that expects an affirmative answer.

b. In place of κατέναντι θεοῦ (cf. 2:17), which has very strong attestation (p⁴⁶ ℵ A B F G 0243 0278 6 33 81 365 630 1175 1739^txt 1881 2464 *pc*), some witnesses read κατενώπιον τοῦ θεοῦ (D [P* omits τοῦ] Ψ 𝔐) and 1739^mg Origen have the redundant ἐνώπιον τοῦ θεοῦ καὶ ἐναντίον τοῦ θεοῦ.

c. p⁴⁶ b d Ambrosiaster omit ἐν Χριστῷ.

d. The plural ἔρεις is read by B D F G Ψ 𝔐 latt syr^h sa bo? goth, but the singular ἔρις (p⁴⁶ ℵ A 0243 33 326 945 1505 1739 1881 *al* syr^p bo?) is to be preferred since the plural doubtless arose under the influence of the plurals that follow ζῆλος (so Metzger 518).

---

1. This threefold fear is expressed by φοβοῦμαι . . . μή πως . . . μή πως (v. 20) . . . μή . . . (v. 21) (see Kitzberger 130). Several EVV recognize this by repeating three times (twice in v. 20, once in v. 21) the verb "I am afraid" or "I fear" (thus TCNT, NEB, GNB, Barclay, Young and Ford 275, REB, NRSV).

e. As was the case with ἔρις (see d. above), the singular ζῆλος (p⁴⁶ A B D* F G 33 326 *pc* syrᵖ boᵐˢ) has been altered to the plural ζῆλοι in many witnesses (ℵ D¹ Ψ 0243 1739 1881 𝔐 latt syrʰ sa bo?) in order to conform with the six following plurals.

f. From the standpoint of grammatical correctness, ἐλθόντος μου (read by p⁴⁶ ℵ* A B D F G L P 6 33 81 104 326 365 1175 1241 2464 *pm*) breaks the "rule" that in a genitive absolute construction the noun or pronoun should be unrelated to other parts of the sentence (see, e.g., 2:12), for μου is picked up by με. Accordingly, some witnesses "correct" the text to read either ἐλθόντα με ταπεινώσῃ ὁ θεός μου πρὸς ὑμᾶς (ℵ² Ψ 0243 0278 33 1739 [1881] 𝔐 lat?) or ἐλθόντα με πρὸς ὑμᾶς ταπεινώσῃ με ὁ θεός μου (D⁽¹¹⁾ syrᵖ). It should be noted, however, that this "rule" is not regularly adhered to in the NT or in Hellenistic Greek in general (see BDF §423; Turner 4, 322-23).

g. If φοβοῦμαι (from v. 20) is to be supplied before μή, then the aorist subjunctive ταπεινώσῃ (ℵ* A K 326) will be the preferred reading. The future indicative ταπεινώσει (p⁴⁶ B D F G L P 6 33 81 104 365 1175 1241 2464 *pm*), which would naturally require a preceding οὐ, not μή, may have arisen through a transcriptional error caused by itacism (-ῃ and -ει sounded identical — see Robertson 193). This reading may have persisted because μή was understood as interrogative (cf. vv. 17-18): "When I come, surely my God will not again humiliate me . . . ?"

12:19 Πάλαι δοκεῖτε ὅτι ὑμῖν ἀπολογούμεθα; κατέναντι θεοῦ ἐν Χριστῷ λαλοῦμεν· τὰ δὲ πάντα, ἀγαπητοί, ὑπὲρ τῆς ὑμῶν οἰκοδομῆς. "Have you been thinking all this time that we are defending ourselves before you? Rather, it is in the sight of God and in Christ that we are speaking. Everything, dear friends, is for your upbuilding." Skilled pastor that he was, Paul was always anticipating his converts' reactions to what he was saying. He knew the Corinthians' predilection for criticism well enough to know that as they heard this long letter being read aloud, some would be thinking that he had been conducting a prolonged self-defense that was motivated by personal resentment at the charges that had been directed against him and by a desire for personal vindication. So he poses a probing question (v. 19a).[2] Without any introductory interrogative particle such as οὐ or μή(τι) (cf. vv. 17-18), the question is open and is not in itself accusatory. If the sentence is read as a statement,[3] there is a sharper, accusatory tone that is less compatible with the warmth and sensitive indirectness of Paul's approach here (note ἀγαπητοί and see below on v. 20).

When πάλαι ("long ago," "formerly") is used with the present tense (δοκεῖτε), it has the meaning "up to now," "for a long time now," or "all this time." The durative δοκεῖτε is "the present of past action still in progress" (Robertson 879), so that past and present time are united in one phrase (πάλαι δοκεῖτε) (Moulton 119).[4] English expresses this by the perfect tense ("Have you been thinking all this time . . . ?"), whereas some other languages reproduce the

2. Thus KJB, TCNT, RSV, NIV, NRSV; WH, UBS¹, ², ³; and, among the commentators, Plummer 367; Hughes 469 n. 156; Martin 450; Lambrecht 214; Thrall 859.
3. Thus RV, Weymouth, NEB, NASB, GNB, JB, Barclay, NJB, REB; UBS⁴, NA²⁷; Barrett 326; Furnish 557.
4. Cf. BAGD 605c; BDF §322; Turner 62; MM 475b.

Greek idiom and use the present.⁵ Similarly, ἀπολογούμεθα may also be a durative present ("we have been defending ourselves," RSV, NRSV) and possibly λαλοῦμεν as well ("we have been speaking," RSV, NJB), but it is not necessary to translate these two verbs this way. With the verb ἀπολογέομαι ("defend oneself"), used only here and in Rom. 2:15 in Paul, the dative (ὑμῖν) denotes the person before whom the defense is given (cf. Acts 19:33).⁶

The phrase κατέναντι θεοῦ ἐν Χριστῷ λαλοῦμεν also occurs in 2:17. In both places the prepositional phrases probably bear the same sense: "in the sight of God" presupposes God's "all-knowingness" and refers to his role as the witness and assessor of everything Paul said and did (cf. Rom. 14:10);⁷ "in Christ" may be shorthand for "in the name of Christ," referring to Paul's role as a person commissioned and empowered by Christ and representing him.⁸ But in 2:17 λαλοῦμεν primarily denotes Paul's proclamation of the good news, and perhaps also, by synecdoche, his whole apostolic life. Here in 12:19 λαλοῦμεν has a more specific sense, describing his self-defense throughout the present letter. It is therefore improbable that the first person plural is an instance of the apostolic "we," with Paul here associating Silvanus and Timothy (cf. 1:19) with himself, an apostle, in the apostolic task of proclaiming the gospel.⁹

κατέναντι θεοῦ, being asyndetic, stands in contrast with ὑμῖν. Paul had not been indulging in an ordinary, self-serving defense before the Corinthians as his jury (cf. 1 Cor. 4:3). Not so!¹⁰ As always, God was his real audience, the God whom he sought to please (1 Thess. 2:4; 4:1) and to whom he was ultimately accountable for all his words and actions. Yes, what he had been writing *was* a defense of his conduct, integrity, and authority, but it was not delivered before a Corinthian bar.

Another powerful contrast is that between ἀπολογούμεθα and ὑπὲρ τῆς ὑμῶν οἰκοδομῆς. At first hearing it might have appeared that Paul's "apology" was motivated by an egotistic and selfish desire for vindication and the pro-

---

5. E.g., Carrez renders πάλαι δοκεῖτε by "Depuis longtemps vous pensez" (235).

6. ἀπολογούμεθα could be conative: "we have been trying to defend ourselves" (GNB; similarly Wand; Phillips).

7. But Renwick argues (72-74) that κατέναντι θεοῦ ἐν Χριστῷ refers to Paul's standing literally "in God's presence," through Christ, and that he deliberately chose the word οἰκοδομή (in the phrase ὑπὲρ τῆς ὑμῶν οἰκοδομῆς) to describe the apostolic task (cf. 10:8; 13:10) as being "to *build a building* — the Temple, the church of God — in which one could live κατέναντι θεοῦ, in the presence of God" (74). Note also Cassirer's rendering of this phrase: "as men standing in God's very presence."

8. Louw and Nida combine these two prepositional phrases in sense: "we speak (as those who) in the sight of God (are) in Christ" (§90.20). Other renderings of ἐν Χριστῷ include "as Christian men" (NEB), "as Christians" (REB), "as those in Christ" (NIV), "as a follower of Christ" (Goodspeed), "in union with Christ" (TCNT; Wand), "as Christ would wish us to speak" (GNB).

9. As Carrez (235-36; "Le 'Nous'" 480) alleges.

10. The contrast is variously indicated in the EVV: "No" (TCNT, Moffatt, NEB, GNB, REB), "Far from it" (Cassirer), "But" (RV, JB), "In reality" (Weymouth), "Actually" (Phillips, NASB); cf. "You are wrong" (Barrett 328).

tection of his reputation, but in reality (δέ) this "apology" and all that he said and did (τὰ πάντα) was aimed at building up the Corinthians. In its attributive position, ὑμῶν is emphatic:[11] "*Your* edification, not *my* self-justification, is my primary aim." As Kitzberger expresses it, the antithesis and emphasis in v. 19 is "Not I, but you!" (129) (cf. 1 Cor. 10:33). Yet, in the circumstances that were prevalent in Corinth, that main aim of upbuilding was achieved in part by self-defense (cf. 12:11); when circumstances required it, self-defense was part of Paul's strategy, as 1 Cor. 9:3 makes clear. οἰκοδομή here refers to more than benefit (as JB) or help (as GNB). It denotes progress in the Christian life (Zerwick, *Analysis* 414), in particular the strengthening of individual and corporate faith (cf. 1 Cor. 14:12, 26; 16:13; 1 Thess. 3:2). ὑπέρ will here have a telic sense, "with a view to" (Weymouth) or "for the purpose of" (Barrett 326)[12] or simply "for," so that ὑπὲρ τῆς ὑμῶν οἰκοδομῆς is not materially different from εἰς οἰκοδομὴν . . . ὑμῶν (10:8; cf. 13:10). As in 7:1, the direct address ἀγαπητοί reassures his converts of his tender affection for them (cf. τέκνα in 6:13; 12:14), even if his love is not adequately reciprocated by them (cf. 6:12-13; 12:15). "Dear friends" is an adequate translation[13] although the archaic "beloved"[14] has the advantage of possibly including an allusion to God's love for them as well as a reference to Paul's. As suggested above, τὰ πάντα has primary reference to what Paul had written up to that point, but it also includes all his words and actions in relation to the Corinthians.[15] Since the sentence in which τὰ πάντα occurs is verbless, this expression should be taken as the subject, with ἐστίν supplied,[16] although it is not impossible that it is the object, with either λαλοῦμεν (from v. 19b)[17] or ποιοῦμεν[18] supplied.

12:20 φοβοῦμαι γὰρ μή πως ἐλθὼν οὐχ οἵους θέλω εὕρω ὑμᾶς, κἀγὼ εὑρεθῶ ὑμῖν οἷον οὐ θέλετε, μή πως ἔρις, ζῆλος, θυμοί, ἐριθεῖαι, καταλαλιαί, ψιθυρισμοί, φυσιώσεις, ἀκαταστασίαι. "For I fear that when I come I might perhaps find you not the kind of people I wish, and that I myself might be found to be in your view the kind of person you do not wish: I fear there might perhaps

---

11. Turner 190. Other examples of this emphatic ὑμῶν are 1:6 (twice); 7:7 (three times), 15; 8:14; 9:2; 13:9.

12. Cf. BAGD 838 s.v. 1.b.

13. BAGD 6c; TCNT, Weymouth, Goodspeed, GNB, NIB, NJB, REB.

14. Furnish 557; Martin 450; Lambrecht 211; Thrall 857.

15. That is, the wider reference could be to all Paul said by letter or by deputy when he himself was absent and all he did when present at Corinth (cf. 10:11). Kitzberger identifies τὰ πάντα as everything Paul did and said — past, present, and future — in the actual Corinthian situation (131, 133).

16. So RV. Some EVV leave the sentence verbless (e.g., RSV, NASB, NJB).

17. So Plummer 368; Thrall 861 (but see her translation, p. 857).

18. EVV that presuppose ποιοῦμεν generally invert the word order; thus "Everything we do . . . (is) . . ." (NIV, NRSV). NAB¹ apparently reads τὰ δὲ πάντα as τάδε πάντα ("all these things') and construes the expression with what precedes: "Before God I tell you, in Christ, I have done everything to build you up, my dear ones."

be discord, jealousy, angry outbursts, factiousness, slandering, gossiping, arrogance, disorder." If the main purpose of the canonical 2 Corinthians is to prepare the way for Paul's forthcoming visit to Corinth (12:14; 13:1), it is no surprise that he seeks to identify and remove the obstacles that would or might prevent that visit from being pleasant and mutually beneficial.[19] His first visit to the city had been both unnerving and exhilarating (Acts 18:1-11; 1 Cor. 2:1-5), while his second had been painful and humiliating (2:1; 12:20). Naturally he wanted his third to be enjoyable, not painful, and refreshing, not wearisome, both for himself and for his converts. Here in v. 20 he identifies one such obstacle — internal strife and factionalism.

Structurally, φοβοῦμαι is followed by two μή πως clauses that define the content of the fear.

φοβοῦμαι . . . μή πως . . . εὕρω . . . κἀγὼ εὑρεθῶ
[φοβοῦμαι]   μή πως . . . [γένωνται][20]

Although some EVV do not represent the enclitic particle πώς in translation,[21] perhaps assuming that it merely strengthens the sense of uncertainty implicit in φοβέομαι μή with the subjunctive,[22] it is important to see it as a qualification of Paul's fears and to render it by a word or phrase such as "somehow," "perhaps," or "in some way or other." While he entertained genuine fears that were based on information he had recently received and on his own knowledge of Corinthian proclivities, he still hoped that his fears would not materialize and that his friends at Corinth would set their house in order before his arrival.[23]

The other structural issue relates to the position of the negatives in v. 20a.

οὐχ οἵους θέλω εὕρω ὑμᾶς
κἀγὼ εὑρεθῶ ὑμῖν οἷον οὐ θέλετε

It is illegitimate to relate these negatives to εὕρω and εὑρεθῶ,[24] and it is unnecessary to relate the first negative to εὕρω.[25] If we take the word order as it stands (which produces a perfectly appropriate sense in the context), then (a) both uses of εὑρίσκω are positive, (b) οὐχ negates οἵους θέλω ("not the kind of people I

19. See further in the Introduction A.3.e.(3).
20. That is, "I fear there might perhaps be. . . ." Instead of γένωνται (BAGD 519d; Bultmann 237), we could supply εὑρεθῶσιν (from v. 20a) (Plummer 369) or ὦσιν (Furnish 561) or ᾖ (Turner 302).
21. E.g., KJV, JB, NAB[1, 2].
22. Cf. Turner 99.
23. "Paul hopes for the best, yet is prepared for the worst" (Martin 461).
24. As the NIV does: "For I am afraid that when I come I may not find you as I want you to be, and you may not find me as you want me to be." Also Martin 450-51.
25. As, e.g., Carrez 235; Lambrecht 211. Grammars often cite 12:20 as an example of οὐ negating the verb in a clause expressing apprehension and introduced by the conjunction μή (πως) — see BDF §428(6); Robertson 1159, 1174; Moule 157; Turner 283.

wish [you to be]"),[26] and (c) οὐ negates θέλετε[27] ("the kind of person you do not wish [me to be]").[28] οἵους = τοιούτους οἵους and οἷον = τοιοῦτον οἷον, "the kind of people/person such as. . . ." V. 20a sums up the remainder of the letter: vv. 20b-21 explicate οὐχ οἵους θέλω, and 13:1-10 develops οἷον οὐ θέλετε. What Paul wished for the Corinthians was the opposite of vv. 20b-21, namely their upbuilding (v. 19). What they would not wish would be for Paul to arrive "rod in hand" (ἐν ῥάβδῳ, 1 Cor. 4:21) with a view to καθαίρεσις (cf. 10:8; 13:10).

Before we leave v. 20a, some other points deserve mention. If γάρ is translated by "for" (as in many EVV), one must supply from the context the thought that is to be supported:[29] ("There is reason to take thought for this objective [of οἰκοδομή]), for . . ."[30]; or "([You] are still in great need of οἰκοδομή), for. . . ."[31] Some EVV have no rendering for γάρ,[32] which probably assumes that it functions here as a weak connective, equivalent to δέ.[33] Other suggested renderings — less apt in the context — are "in fact" (Carrez 235) and "of course" (Wolff 257).[34] After the passive εὑρεθῶ it is tempting to regard ὑμῖν as a dative of the agent ("by you"),[35] not a common NT usage,[36] but more probably it is a dative of reference or respect, either "in your view" (Thrall 857) or "in my dealings with you."[37] Note the instance of chiasmus (A B C C′ B′ A′) in θέλω εὕρω ὑμᾶς, κἀγὼ εὑρεθῶ . . . θέλετε, which has the effect of highlighting the essentially personal character of Paul's relationship to the Corinthian congregation. Finally, his tactfulness and gentleness are clearly evident in v. 20a,[38] as he expresses his own fear and avoids laying charges, as he adds the mollifying πώς, as he uses the two negatives (οὐχ . . . οὐ) and the generalizing οἵους . . . οἷον, and as he changes from the active to the passive voice (εὕρω . . . εὑρεθῶ).

What follows the second μή πως specifies the evils Paul fears he may find present among the Corinthians. φοβοῦμαι should be supplied before μή πως and γένωνται (ἐν ὑμῖν) after; thus "I fear there might perhaps be (among you). . . ."

26. Similarly BAGD 325b; Burton §475, who observes (more generally; cf. n. 25 above) that in clauses introduced by the conjunction μή ("lest"), the negative is οὐ.

27. Several EVV take the second οὐ with οἷον (Moffatt, RSV, NEB, NASB, GNB, Barclay, NAB², NRSV; also Barrett 326; Furnish 557), perhaps to create parallelism to οὐχ οἵους.

28. This general understanding of the role of the negatives in v. 20a is represented in the renderings of RV, TCNT, REB, NJB, and Thrall 857. For instance: "I am afraid that in one way or another, when I come, I may find you different from what I should like you to be, and you may find me what you would not like me to be" (NJB).

29. See BAGD 152 s.v. 1.e.

30. Barrett, "Opponents" 246.

31. Plummer 366, 368.

32. E.g., NEB, JB, NJB, REB.

33. See BAGD 152 s.v. 4.

34. Cf. BAGD 152 s.v. 3.

35. So Martin 451; Lambrecht 211; and those EVV that render εὑρεθῶ ὑμῖν by "you may find me" (Weymouth, Goodspeed, NEB, REB).

36. See BDF §191; Turner 240.

37. Cf. Robertson 534, 539.

38. Cf. Plummer 368.

ἔρις, "discord," "strife," or "quarreling," is found only in Paul's letters (9 instances) and is the opposite of εἰρήνη, "peace," "undisturbedness" (cf. Gal. 5:20, 22; 1 Tim. 2:2). One aspect of this "contentiousness" will have been disputes over the rival claims of Paul and his opponents. In 7:7, 11; 9:2 ζῆλος has a positive sense, "eagerness" or "zeal," but here its negative meaning is applicable, "jealousy" or "envy," so that it is synonymous with φθόνος. Given the rife factionalism at Corinth and the association of ζῆλος with ἔρις here and in Rom. 13:13; 1 Cor. 3:3; Gal. 5:20, ζῆλος could bear the sense, "party strife" (Wand), "rivalry," or "party-attachment" (BAGD 337d). Common to the good and bad senses of ζῆλος is the idea of strong emotion, which may be expressed positively in "emulation" (a Classical Greek meaning) or "enthusiasm," or negatively in "envy" or "resentment." The next six terms are plural, pointing to individual instances of the vice in question; thus "acts of . . ." or "expressions of."[39] Accordingly, θυμοί are "outbursts of anger" (BAGD 365c) or "angry outbursts" (Bruce, *Paraphrase* 157). If we render it "explosive tempers" (Furnish 557), the reference is to tempers that do explode rather than might explode. "As compared with ὀργή, θυμός denotes an outburst of passion, ὀργή a more settled indignation; in accordance with which distinction θυμός tends to be used of the reprehensible anger of men, ὀργή of the righteous wrath of God" (Burton, *Galatians* 307). Apart from two uses in Aristotle where it refers to "intrigue aimed at obtaining an official post by suspect means,"[40] the word ἐριθεία is unknown in the Greek language before NT times, but it occurs seven times in the NT,[41] twice in lists of vices (12:20; Gal. 5:20). In spite of the superficial similarity, it is etymologically unrelated to ἔρις; in any case, the meaning "strife" is unlikely since synonyms would be out of place in a brief list of sins. The term is derived from ἔριθος, "a hired worker," and ἐριθεύομαι, "work for daily hire" or "hire party agents," so that ἐριθεία came to denote a "party spirit" (Weymouth, Cassirer), "the factious spirit" (Barclay) or "factiousness" (Thrall 857), and thus "intrigues" (JB),[42] "personal rivalries" (NEB, REB).

The next pair of words refers to verbal sins; Lambrecht renders the pair "words of slander and gossip" (211). καταλαλία is "evil-speaking" or "slander," with the plural referring to instances of slander, thus "slandering." ψιθυρισμός, "whisper," is "an onomatopoetic word for the sibilant murmur of a snake charmer (Eccl. 10:11)."[43] The verb ψιθυρίζω means "speak in a low voice,"

39. The plural of abstract substantives emphasizes the separate acts (Robertson 408; cf. BDF §142).

40. Spicq 2.70 n. 5. The two occurrences in Aristotle are *Politica* 1302ᵇ4; 1303ᵃ14.

41. Rom. 2:8; 2 Cor. 12:20; Gal. 5:20; Phil. 1:17; 2:3; Jas. 3:14, 16.

42. LSJ 688 s.v. II. gives the meaning "intrigues," "party squabbles" for ἐριθεῖαι in Gal. 5:20. See further Burton, *Galatians* 308-9 ("self-seeking," "selfishness"), Spicq 2.70-71 (The "connotations of intrigue, disputation, and chicanery appear in all the NT texts," 70), and F. Büchsel, *TDNT* 2.660-61 ("base self-seeking" or "baseness"). For 12:20 and Gal. 5:20 BAGD 309c gives the meanings "disputes" or "outbreaks of selfishness."

43. Robertson, *Pictures* 269.

"mutter," "mumble," and the cognate noun ψιθυριστής (Rom. 1:29) refers to a person who conducts "secret attacks on a person's character as compared with κατάλαλος [Rom. 1:30], an open detractor" (MM 698b). ψιθυρισμός, then, is "the clandestine speech of the detractor,"[44] "whispered gossip" (Thrall 857), with the plural pointing to instances of gossip, "gossiping." Literally, φυσίωσις means "a puffing up" and so in medical usage referred to "inflation" or "swelling" (cf. our English word "puffiness"). To have an inflated view of one's importance was to be filled with φυσίωσις, "conceit," "pride" (= inflation of mind), so that φυσιώσεις could be rendered "cases of arrogance" (Furnish 557).[45] Finally, ἀκαταστασίαι are "disturbances" of the public order, manifestations of "disorder," or general unruliness.[46]

Some have suggested that these eight vices form a series of four pairs.[47] But although ἔρις and ζῆλος may be closely associated (as in Rom. 13:13; 1 Cor. 3:3; Gal. 5:20), quarreling as the result of jealousy, and καταλαλιαί could be linked to ψιθυρισμοί, both being sins of the tongue, a comparable link cannot be easily found for the second and fourth pairs.

Since 1 Corinthians shows that most if not all of the sins in this vice-catalogue were present in the congregation eighteen or so months previously,[48] there is no reason to assume that their presence at the time 2 Corinthians was written should be attributed to the adverse influence of Paul's rivals. However, the persistence and intensity of these congregational sins were doubtless the result of their influence.[49] There may have been rivalry not only between those Corinthians who championed Paul's adversaries and those who supported Paul himself,[50] but perhaps also within the anti-Pauline group as some sided with one of the Judaizing intruders and some with another.

12:21 μὴ πάλιν ἐλθόντος μου ταπεινώσῃ με ὁ θεός μου πρὸς ὑμᾶς, καὶ πενθήσω πολλοὺς τῶν προημαρτηκότων καὶ μὴ μετανοησάντων ἐπὶ τῇ ἀκαθαρσίᾳ καὶ πορνείᾳ καὶ ἀσελγείᾳ ᾗ ἔπραξαν. "I fear too that when I come my God may again humble me in my relations with you, and that I may grieve over many who have sinned previously and did not repent of the impurity and sexual immorality and debauchery in which they had indulged." The two fears ex-

---

44. Zerwick, *Analysis* 414.

45. The several references in 1 Corinthians to being "puffed up" (φυσιόω) (1 Cor. 4:6, 18-19; 5:2; 8:1; 13:4) illustrate the Corinthian tendency to pride.

46. Mitchell (*Paul* 173) believes that ἀκαταστασία here refers to "party strife" and not simply general confusion, but this would make it synonymous with ἐριθεία (or ζῆλος). It is of interest that some forty years after 2 Corinthians the church at Corinth was still plagued by discord and factionalism, as *1 Clement* (c. A.D. 96) indicates. The terms ζῆλος, ἔρις, and ἀκαταστασία appear in *1 Clement* 3:2, and ἔρεις and θυμοί in *1 Clement* 46:5.

47. E.g., Plummer 369; Windisch 408.

48. See 1 Cor. 1:10-13; 3:1-4, 17-18, 21; 4:6, 10, 18-19; 5:2, 6; 6:1, 6, 8; 8:1-2; 11:16, 18-19; 15:33-34.

49. Cf. Barrett 329-30, citing his "Opponents" 247.

50. That at least a few Corinthians identified themselves with Paul is a fair inference from 2:6 (see the commentary there).

pressed in v. 20 are introduced by μή πως, "(I fear) that . . . perhaps." This third fear (v. 21), with φοβοῦμαι to be supplied, is introduced by μή alone,[51] perhaps suggesting that Paul regarded the possibility of a humiliation at Corinth, leading to grief over unrepentant sinners, as even more real than the other two fears. If this further fear materialized, it would be after his arrival (ἐλθόντος μου, "when I come," a temporal use of the genitive absolute). Word order might suggest that πάλιν belongs to this phrase; thus "when I come again," "on my return."[52] But there are several compelling reasons for construing πάλιν with ταπεινώσῃ,[53] or with the whole statement ἐλθόντος . . . ὑμᾶς.[54] (1) By its position πάλιν is emphatic. Since v. 20 has already mentioned a "coming" (ἐλθών), the point emphasized is more likely to be the possibility of yet another humiliation. If πάλιν is taken with ἐλθόντος, it is superfluous, not emphatic.[55] (2) 2:1 speaks of the possibility of another painful visit (τὸ μὴ πάλιν ἐν λύπῃ πρὸς ὑμᾶς ἐλθεῖν). (3) Without an added πάλιν, ἔρχομαι can mean "come back," "return" (e.g., 1:15, 23; 2:3; 1 Cor. 4:18-19; 16:11) (4) As a genitive absolute ἐλθόντος μου is grammatically subordinate and therefore unlikely to be qualified by an emphatic πάλιν.[56]

Paul's third fear about his approaching visit has two ingredients — apprehension that God may permit him to suffer another humbling experience while at Corinth, and fear that he may have cause to grieve over certain unrepentant Corinthians. These two aspects must be considered in more detail.

First, the fear of fresh humiliation.[57] What constituted this potential humiliation is not stated, but there are three hints in the context. God would be its cause or at least would permit it to occur (ταπεινώσῃ με ὁ θεός μου);[58] it would directly involve the Corinthians (whether πρὸς ὑμᾶς means "in your presence"[59] or "in my relations with you"[60]) rather than the rival missionaries; it

51. It is possible but improbable that μή is interrogative: "Surely, when I come, my God will not again humiliate me . . . ?"

52. Thus RV, TCNT, Weymouth, Moffatt, Goodspeed, NEB, GNB ("the next time I come"), JB ("on my next visit"), NJB, NRSV, Cassirer; Lietzmann 158; Windisch 409.

53. Thus Conybeare in Conybeare and Howson 357 n. 1, 463; Barclay, REB; Plummer 369; Barrett 326; Furnish 562; Lang 354; Martin 465; Wolff 257, 260. The placement of "again" in several EVV (RSV, NASB, NAB[1], NIV, NAB[2]) leaves the issue potentially ambiguous.

54. Meyer 693; Winer 554 n. 1; Plummer (CGT) 217.

55. Plummer 369.

56. If this expression were not subordinate, we would expect a concordant participle, ἐλθόντα με (see Textual Note f.).

57. I am using the term "humiliation" in the (legitimate) sense of "being made humble," not of having one's dignity or self-respect injured. Most EVV and commentators render ταπεινώσῃ by "humiliate," but the unambiguous "humble" is preferred by RV, TCNT, Montgomery, RSV, NIV, NRSV, and Martin 451; Barnett 596.

58. There is no reason to follow Bultmann in his proposal that an οὐ has been omitted before ταπεινώσῃ (239; *Probleme* 30-31).

59. Weymouth, NEB, GNB, Barclay, REB. Others have "before you" (BAGD 804d; Moffatt, NASB, NAB[1, 2]) or "in front of you" (NJB).

60. Isaacs; similarly TCNT, Cassirer, Wand; Meyer 693; Plummer 370. It was "in reference to" (πρός) the Corinthians, not in relation to his opponents, that Paul would be humbled. That is, the

would entail Paul's discovery that the Corinthians were not in a spiritual state such as he would wish them to be (οὐχ οἵους θέλω εὕρω ὑμᾶς, v. 20), that they were beset by social and sexual sins such as those listed in v. 20b and v. 21b. Paul could attribute this "humbling" to God because God could turn Paul's painful discovery of those sins among his own converts[61] into spiritual benefit if Paul himself was thereby brought low before God and if his subsequent action of "not sparing" them punishment (13:2) brought about their repentance and thus their οἰκοδομή (v. 19; cf. 10:8; 13:10). The previous "humbling" alluded to by πάλιν may have been either the result of the offense against Paul committed by ὁ ἀδικήσας (2:6-8; 7:12) in the Corinthian congregation, or, more generally, the Corinthian failure to side with Paul decisively during the "painful visit."

Second, the fear of having to mourn. After the implied φοβοῦμαι before μή, πενθήσω is more probably aorist subjunctive ("I fear . . . that I may grieve") than future indicative ("and I shall grieve"[62]). In the former case, a second fear is specified. On either view the grieving may be the result of the humbling. After discovering that his converts were still entwined in obvious sin, Paul would naturally react by "mourning" over them,[63] as if they were spiritually dead, that is, unresponsive to God.[64] Such mourning was one aspect of his "anxious concern" (μέριμνα) for all the churches (11:28). Paul's only other use of πενθέω is in 1 Cor. 5:2 where, as here, the grief is over the believer who continues in sin without repentance, not over the excommunication that would result.

Those Paul would grieve over are described as πολλοὺς τῶν προημαρτηκότων καὶ μὴ μετανοησάντων κτλ. With regard to this difficult expression, we may make four observations.

(1) Paul is clearly not suggesting that there are some sinners who failed to repent over whom he would not mourn. This being so, τῶν προημαρτηκότων should be taken as an epexegetic genitive, "many who have sinned earlier/previously,"[65] not as a partitive genitive, "many of those

---

"humbling" was not the fact that his rivals would be able to claim that his gospel was powerless to reform conduct.

61. Conybeare renders πρὸς ὑμᾶς by the expression "by your faults" (in Conybeare and Howson 463); cf. "on your account" (JB). A similar link between Paul's humiliation and Corinthian sin is reflected in the comment of W. Grundmann (*TDNT* 8.17) that "this humiliation consists not only in the contempt which he suffers in the community but also in the threat to his crown and repute through a congregation which has fallen into sin." Bultmann (239, followed by Martin 465-66) argues that "the humiliation would consist in the apostle's having to use his ἐξουσία, given him for οἰκοδομή, for καθαίρεσις."

62. Similarly JB, NIV, NJB.

63. When πενθέω is used transitively, it is followed by the accusative of the person mourned over (BAGD 642d; cf. BDF §148[2]).

64. Barnett goes one step further. He believes that the humiliation is Paul's voluntary self-humbling before the Corinthians *by* his public mourning over the unrepentant (596 and n. 14).

65. Similarly TCNT, Weymouth, Moffatt, Goodspeed, GNB, NAB[1], NIV, REB, NRSV; Furnish 557; Martin 467; Lambrecht 215 ("Paul seems to mean: 'Among those who sinned before there are many who have not repented; I may have to grieve over those many'"). Some arrive at this sense

who have sinned before."[66] Cassirer renders "many of your number, sinners of long standing."

(2) Since a single article modifies both participles, those who sinned previously are not to be distinguished from those who did not repent.

(3) Because the two participles are juxtaposed, we should differentiate between the perfect tense and the aorist. τῶν προημαρτηκότων (cf. 13:2) refers to "those who have persisted in their former sins"[67] right up to the present time, whereas (τῶν . . .) μὴ μετανοησάντων are "those who did not repent" after Paul called them to repentance during his second visit (the "painful visit"), or after they had received the "severe letter."

(4) προ- in the participle προημαρτηκότων refers to some earlier period up to the time of writing, perhaps the period after their conversion (during Paul's first visit),[68] but certainly including the period during and after his "painful visit."

ἐπὶ τῇ ἀκαθαρσίᾳ κτλ. belongs with μετανοησάντων ("repent of," BAGD 512a), not with the more remote πενθήσω ("mourn . . . because of"). Now it is true that elsewhere in the NT, when μετανοέω is followed by a preposition, that preposition is ἀπό or ἐκ.[69] But this is the only use of μετανοέω in the epistles, and in the LXX μετανοέω ἐπί is not uncommon.[70] The sins of which "many" Corinthians refused to repent were three, all sexual sins, which would account for the single article that binds them together in a conceptual unity. All three are mentioned in Gal. 5:19 (in a different order), as the first three of the "deeds of the flesh." ἀκαθαρσία is "impurity," especially of a sexual nature (e.g., Rom. 1:24; Eph. 4:19). πορνεία, "immorality," "sexual vice," refers to illicit sexual activity of any sort, especially prostitution and fornication. The third term, ἀσέλγεια, describes sexual conduct that lacks any moral restraint, unbridled and shameless sexual activity comparable to that of animals, "licentiousness," "gross sensuality," "debauchery." Between them, the three terms depict impure, immoral, and dissolute sexual behavior[71] and testify to the rampant depravity in

---

by suggesting that πολλοὺς τῶν προημαρτηκότων is "imprecise wording" for πολλοὺς τοὺς προημαρτηκότας (Lietzmann 160; also BAGD 702d; Bultmann 239).

66. Similarly RV, RSV, NEB, NASB, NAB²; Wolff 257; Thrall 857, 868. Windisch (410, following E. Kühl and others) proposes that by the use of the partitive genitive Paul is intimating a modest hope that with the success of the present letter at least a few would come to repentance before his arrival.

67. Similarly Goodspeed; Furnish 557; Zerwick and Grosvenor 562.

68. But Georgi (*Opponents* 237, followed by Thrall 868-69) takes the two participles to refer to those Corinthians who had never forsaken their pagan ways and become believers in Jesus.

69. ἀπό (Acts 8:22; cf. μετανοίας ἀπό, Heb. 6:1); ἐκ (Rev. 2:21-22; 9:20-21; 16:11).

70. Joel 2:13; Amos 7:3, 6; Jonah 3:10; 4:2. These points are made by Plummer (CGT) 218.

71. In the final phrase of the verse, ᾗ ἔπραξαν ("in which they had indulged"), the relative pronoun, though singular (agreeing in number with its immediate antecedent), refers to all three (feminine gender) antecedents (cf. the effect of the single article), and is attracted from ἥν into the case of its antecedent (ἀσελγείᾳ).

the city of Corinth and the clinging pagan background of some of the Corinthian converts (cf. 1 Cor. 6:9-11).

A comparison of the list of sins in v. 20 with the three sins mentioned in v. 21 shows that each set is distinctive, with no common items. This might lead us to suppose that there were two distinct categories of Corinthians — those who, adversely influenced by the intruders from Palestine, were given to strife and factionalism, and those who were still pursuing the sexual vices of their pre-Christian days.[72] Our suggestion, however, is that no part of the Corinthian congregation was totally free of the sins mentioned in v. 20, while v. 21 is speaking of the libertine morals of a "proto-gnostic" wing of the church.[73] It was to this latter group in particular, but also to the whole church, that Paul directed his exhortations, "Keep away from immorality" (1 Cor. 6:18) and "Let us cleanse ourselves of everything that may defile body or spirit" (7:1).

Bibliography

Barrett, "Opponents" 246-48 • Bultmann, *Probleme* 30-31 • Güttgemanns 142-54 • Heckel 41-44, 50 • Kitzberger 129-33 • Murphy-O'Connor 128-31 • Renwick 72-74 • Roetzel • Vielhauer • Wibbing

3. Warning of Impending Discipline (13:1-4)

We have seen that what Paul hoped not to find at Corinth on his third visit is described in 12:20b-21, namely factionalism and immorality. What he surmised the Corinthians would not want him to be on that visit is stated in 13:1-4, namely someone who administers punishment. That is, 12:20b-21 explains the expression φοβοῦμαι . . . μή πως . . . οὐχ οἵους θέλω εὕρω ὑμᾶς (12:20a), while 13:1-4 explains φοβοῦμαι . . . μή πως . . . κἀγὼ εὑρεθῶ ὑμῖν οἷον οὐ θέλετε (12:20a). His purpose in expressing those fears about his forthcoming visit was to encourage a change of behavior prior to his arrival. But he sensed that the mere expression of his personal forebodings would not be sufficient to shake the Corinthians from their lethargy about their sins. So he repeats a warning that he had given as he departed from Corinth after his second visit: "On my return I will not spare you" (v. 2). This punitive action would give the Corinthians the proof they were demanding that he was Christ's spokesman and agent (v. 3a). He then develops a comparison be-

---

72. Barrett, e.g., distinguishes between "new sinners" (v. 20b) and "old sinners" (v. 21b) ("Opponents" 248). According to Barnett, the two groups within the Corinthian church are "(1) those who regarded Paul as unspiritual and fleshly [10:1-11], and (2) the persistently immoral [12:21; 13:2]." The first group were probably critical of Paul's handling (during his second visit) of the moral problems of the second group (453).

73. This latter point is developed in detail in the Introduction, B.4.d.

tween the two states of Christ (weakness–power) and his own dual approach in dealing with the Corinthians (vv. 3b-4).

If we wonder how Paul can so easily combine expressions of tender affection (11:11; 12:15, 19) with an ominous threat of discipline ("I will not spare you," 13:2), we need think only of his earlier question, posed by him as a father (ἐγὼ ὑμᾶς ἐγέννησα, 1 Cor. 4:15) to his dearly loved children (τέκνα μου ἀγαπητά, 1 Cor. 4:14), "Choose, then: am I to come to you with a rod in my hand, or with love and a gentle spirit?" (1 Cor. 4:21, REB).

13:1*This is the third time I am coming[a] to you. "On the testimony of two or three witnesses shall every issue be settled." 2Those who have continued in their former sins and all the rest I have already warned, and now, when absent[b], I am forewarning you just as when I was present on my second visit, that on my return[c] I will not spare you 3 — since[d] you demand proof that Christ speaks through me, Christ who is not weak in dealing with you but shows his power among you. 4For indeed[e] he was crucified because of his weakness, but he lives because of God's power. For we also are weak, in union with[f] him, but in our dealings with you[g] we shall be fully alive[h], along with[i] him, because of God's power.*

TEXTUAL NOTES

a. ἐτοίμως ἔχω ἐλθεῖν (A vg^ms) is a secondary reading prompted by 12:14.

b. After νῦν some witnesses (D¹ Ψ 𝔐 vg^ms syr sa [bo]) add γράφω, but the shorter reading (read by p⁴⁶ ℵ A B D* F G I 0243 6 33 630 1175 1739 1881 *pc* lat) is to be preferred, not only because of the superior external attestation but also because there is no reason an original γράφω (cf. 13:10) would be omitted. For the significance of the KJV rendering of the longer reading (νῦν γράφω), see Hughes 476 n. 169.

c. p⁴⁶ F G omit εἰς τό before πάλιν, probably under the influence of πάλιν ἐλθόντος μου in 12:21.

d. In the place of ἐπεί (read by the majority of witnesses) we find ἐπειδή (6 *pc*), εἰ (Epiphanius), and the same-sounding ἤ (a f vg Pelagius), all variants arising from scribal error (addition, omission, and itacism respectively). Some witnesses (F G 0278^vid b d r Ambrosiaster) read ὅτι instead of ἐπεί, which produces the same meaning. This variant may have arisen because of the preceding ὅτι (v. 2), although there ὅτι is recitative, whereas here in v. 3 it is causal.

e. The insertion of εἰ ("if") before ἐσταυρώθη (thus ℵ² A D¹ Ψ 1881 𝔐 lat syr Ambrosiaster) has the effect of subordinating the idea of weakness to that of power, and thus the crucifixion to the resurrection. The reading without εἰ has much stronger textual support (p⁴⁶ vid ℵ* B D* F G K P 0243 33 81 104 365 1241ˢ 1739 *al* cop Eusebius).

f. In some witnesses (ℵ A F G *pc* r syr^p bo) σὺν αὐτῷ is read in place of ἐν αὐτῷ (which has the even stronger support of B D Ψ 0243 0278 33 1739 1881 𝔐 a vg syr^h sa Ambrosiaster), doubtless under the influence of the later σὺν αὐτῷ (Metzger 518).

g. εἰς ὑμᾶς is omitted by B D² r, perhaps by error or perhaps (as Metzger [519] suggests) because it was seen as an "awkward addendum" that could be taken with either ζήσομεν or δυνάμεως θεοῦ.

h. In both Attic and Koine Greek two futures of ζάω are found: ζήσω (active) and ζήσομαι (middle) (see BDF §77). In 13:4 ζήσομεν (א A B D* F G 0243 0278^vid 33 81 104 365 630 1175 1241^s 1739 1881 2464 *al*) has much stronger textual attestation than ζησόμεθα (D² Ψ 𝔐). It is in quotations from the LXX that Paul uses the middle form (Zerwick §226). 𝔭⁴⁶ reads the present tense (ζῶμεν), under the influence of the preceding ζῇ (v. 4a).

i. Some witnesses (𝔭^46vid D*,c 33 326 *pc* [g] Pelagius^pt) read ἐν αὐτῷ in place of the stronger reading σὺν αὐτῷ, by assimilation to the preceding ἐν αὐτῷ (see note f. above).

13:1 Τρίτον τοῦτο ἔρχομαι πρὸς ὑμᾶς· ἐπὶ στόματος δύο μαρτύρων καὶ τριῶν σταθήσεται πᾶν ῥῆμα. "This is the third time I am coming to you. 'On the testimony of two or three witnesses shall every issue be settled.'" Once again Paul announces his imminent visit, this time omitting the notion of readiness (cf. 12:14, ἑτοίμως ἔχω ἐλθεῖν).[1] Since there is no evidence that the present letter was written en route to Corinth, ἔρχομαι must be a futuristic present ("I shall be coming," NAB¹; = "I am coming," NAB²), denoting a present intention regarding future action.[2] τρίτον, a neuter adjective, is used absolutely, without an accompanying substantive ("the third time").[3] The addition of τοῦτο produces the sense "this is the third time" or "now for the third time" (BAGD 826d). Implied are two previous visits — the founding visit (Acts 18:1-18) and the "painful visit" (cf. 2:1).[4]

Very abruptly, without any connecting particle and without any introductory formula (cf. 10:17) such as καθὼς γέγραπται (cf. 8:15; 9:9), Paul introduces a citation of Deut. 19:15. His thought has moved swiftly from his arrival in Corinth (ἔρχομαι πρὸς ὑμᾶς) to the urgent church business he may have to conduct there. Deut. 19:15-21 deals with the law regarding witnesses, which aimed to protect the person accused of a crime against inadequate witness (v. 15) and against malicious witness (vv. 16-21; cf. Exod. 20:16). The requirement (v. 15) of multiple witnesses — three, or at least two[5] — to establish the case against the accused was a distinctive of OT legal procedure and of rabbinic jurisprudence (see van Vliet *passim*);[6] neither Roman nor Greek law in the first century rejected the validity of the testimony of a single witness (van Vliet 11-25).

Paul's citation is essentially the same as the LXX of Deut. 19:15, the only differences being that the LXX repeats ἐπὶ στόματος between καί and τριῶν and

---

1. For a discussion of the implications of 12:14 and 13:1 for any reconstruction of Paul's relation to the church at Corinth, see the Introduction, B.1.a.

2. Cf. Fanning 223.

3. Robertson 674, who also entertains the possibility that τρίτον may here function as a cognate accusative (Robertson 478).

4. On the latter visit, see the Introduction, B.1.

5. If Deut. 19:15 establishes the principle of "a minimum of two witnesses" for an accusation to be upheld, the same principle can be stated as "more than one witness." Thus the death penalty for idolatry or for murder was to be imposed only on the testimony of more than one witness (Deut. 17:6 and Num. 35:30 respectively).

6. Cf. SB 1.790-91; Josephus, *Antiquities* 4.219; *Life* 256.

repeats μαρτύρων after τριῶν.[7] Several matters in the citation require clarification. ἐπί here means "on the basis of" or simply "on," while στόμα ("mouth"), by metonymy, refers to what the mouth utters, "testimony" (cf. Luke 19:22), so that ἐπὶ στόματος means "on the basis of the testimony" = "on the evidence" (BAGD 286c) or "on the testimony."[8] The καί that joins δύο (μαρτύρων) and τριῶν is equivalent to ἤ ("or"),[9] with "two or three" meaning "two or more" (no upper limit!) or "three, or at least two" (JB). σταθήσεται, "shall be established/decided/substantiated/settled," is an instance of the use of the future indicative in OT legal language to render a "categorical injunction" (BDF §362) and so is equivalent to an imperative. Generally ῥῆμα denotes a spoken word, but here it represents the Hebrew term *dābār* and refers to a subject spoken about (πρᾶγμα), thus "matter," "issue,"[10] or in a specifically legal sense, "case," "charge." As a phrase σταθήσεται πᾶν ῥῆμα may therefore be rendered in a variety of ways, such as:

Every matter must be established (NIV)
Every case is to be decided (Moffatt)
Any accusation must be upheld (GNB)
Every issue . . . shall be settled (Cassirer)

But who or what are the "two or three witnesses"? Three main answers have been given to this question.

(1) The witnesses cannot be identified, for Paul is speaking in general terms of the legal stringency that would apply during his formal inquiry into the charges made against him[11] or into the offenses (cf. 12:20-21) that required discipline.[12] Charges not substantiated by at least two witnesses would be ruled out of court.

Now it is true that Matt. 18:16 and 1 Tim. 5:19 refer to this OT stipulation in the context of church discipline, which would suggest that such an application of the OT principle was recognized and approved within the early church. Nevertheless, in the present case we may question whether a judicial investigation would be necessary to identify offenses that were already common knowledge among the Corinthians and whether Paul would initiate quasi-legal proceedings in which the Corinthians would bring or support charges against one another (cf. Plummer 372). The only form in which this view could be counte-

---

7. Paul's citation is even closer to Matt. 18:16, which has ἤ instead of Paul's καί, and (ἵνα . . .) σταθῇ in the place of σταθήσεται.

8. ἐπί alone bears this sense in the (partial) citations of Deut. 19:15 in 1 Tim. 5:19; Heb. 10:28.

9. Cf. Matt. 18:16b, 20. For this usage see BAGD 391; LSJ 857 s.v. καί VI. B.1., citing Thucydides 1.82, ἐτῶν δύο καὶ τριῶν ("two or three years").

10. Cf. BAGD 735d.

11. Tasker 186.

12. Meyer 700; Denney 806; Allo 335; Hafemann 489-90. "With regard to every offense he [Paul] will then ascertain by the statements of two or three witnesses what actually happened" (Schlatter 675).

nanced would be to suppose that in responding to accusations against himself Paul envisaged bringing forward multiple witnesses — such as Timothy and Titus[13] — who would be able to vouch for his personal integrity in any "issues" under consideration. But any form of this view has the not inconsiderable disadvantage of ignoring any association between τρίτον and τριῶν or between δύο (v. 1) and δεύτερον (v. 2), links which would seem to be the natural starting point for identifying the "witnesses."

It is preferable to identify the witnesses as warnings and/or visits.

(2) The two witnesses are the two warnings (προείρηκα καὶ προλέγω) in v. 2 that "attest Paul will make concrete his οὐ φείσομαι" ("I shall not spare"),[14] or the reference to "two or three witnesses" has a general import, reminding the Corinthians "You have had due warning, as prescribed; I am now about to take action."[15]

(3) The three witnesses are Paul's three visits to Corinth, two past (founding visit and "painful" visit) and one future.[16] Often these visits are linked with warnings. Klauck, for example, believes that the witnesses are the three visits and the two warnings (of v. 2) given on different occasions (100). But there may have been three warnings, the first being 1 Cor. 4:21.

So we conclude that if it is appropriate to identify the witnesses, they are both visits and warnings, or, rather, warnings that are associated with visits.[17] This does justice to the τρίτον–τριῶν and δύο–δεύτερον associations in vv. 1-2 and to the notion of warning that dominates v. 2. The visits and warnings were multiple even though only one person was doing the visiting and warning. Paul is applying the Deuteronomic legal principle in a way that was typical of contemporary Judaism — to forewarn those suspected of an offense that they were liable to punishment. Paul is saying in effect, "Sufficient and statutory warning has been given to you Corinthians; punitive action is imminent."

13:2 προείρηκα   καὶ   προλέγω
       ὡς παρὼν τὸ δεύτερον καὶ   ἀπὼν νῦν
                 τοῖς προημαρτηκόσιν καὶ
                 τοῖς λοιποῖς πᾶσιν
     ὅτι   ἐὰν ἔλθω εἰς τὸ πάλιν
         οὐ φείσομαι.

13. "Titus and Timothy, for example, and even God" (Garland 541). Hyldahl ("Einheit" 303-4) thinks of Titus and "the brother" (12:18). Scott suggests that the two (or three) witnesses may be Paul himself (cf. 1:12) and God (cf. 1:23) (and Christ) (250, citing John 8:12-20, especially vv. 17-18).

14. Bultmann 241, followed by Lang 356.

15. Barrett 333 (citing van Vliet 96 n. 8), followed by Martin 470.

16. Lietzmann 160; Plummer 372; Windisch 413; Bruce 252-53; Lambrecht 211; Thrall 874-76.

17. It would be straining at the metaphor to identify the three witnesses as two visits and one letter (as A. P. Stanley [265, 273] does).

"Those who have continued in their former sins and all the rest I have already warned, and now, when absent, I am forewarning you just as when I was present on my second visit, that on my return I will not spare you." In this complicated verse the differing tenses of the verb προλέγω (perfect and present) support a linking of προείρηκα with ὡς παρὼν τὸ δεύτερον and of προλέγω with ἀπὼν νῦν, but there is no reason, in spite of the three apparently parallel instances of καί, to relate τοῖς προημαρτηκόσιν only to προείρηκα, and τοῖς λοιποῖς πᾶσιν only to προλέγω.[18] That is to say, the warning introduced by ὅτι was spoken twice (προείρηκα and προλέγω), on each occasion to two groups, τοῖς προημαρτηκόσιν and τοῖς λοιποῖς πᾶσιν.

But what were those two occasions, and who were those two groups? In the phrase ὡς παρὼν τὸ δεύτερον, the conjunction ὡς is correlative with καί (= οὕτως), "as when present . . . so now when absent."[19] The definite article with δεύτερον, "the second time," not "a second time," shows that ὡς should not be rendered "as if" and joined closely to προλέγω, "(I do say beforehand,) as if I were present the second time, even though I am now absent" (RV margin). Such an understanding makes καὶ ἀπὼν νῦν redundant, gives καὶ ἀπών a concessive sense (as though Paul had written καίπερ rather than καί), and ignores the parallelism between παρών and ἀπών.[20] This "second time" (τὸ δεύτερον) was the "painful visit" implied by 2:1, and the other occasion when Paul issued the warning, "On my return I will not spare you," was in the present verse (προλέγω) in anticipation of his third visit.[21]

As for the two sets of people addressed in Paul's warning, there is general agreement that τοῖς προημαρτηκόσιν refers to the same unrepentant sinners who are mentioned in 12:21 (πολλοὺς τῶν προημαρτηκότων καὶ μὴ μετανοησάντων κτλ.).[22] As in 12:21, so in 13:2, the perfect tense of the participle indicates that their sinning persists to the time of writing; thus, "those who have continued in their former sins," people we have called "proto-gnostic libertines" (see on 12:21). There is, however, no unanimity about the identity of τοῖς λοιποῖς πᾶσιν, "all the others/rest." They have been seen as all those who had lapsed into sin since Paul's last (= second) visit and needed his warning (Plummer 366, 373); as "anyone else" at Corinth who may have been sinning by sexual immorality or by strife but was unknown to Paul (Martin 451, 455, 471); as those adversely affected by the false apostles and guilty of the sins

18. If in fact we associated "all the others" only with "I forewarn," then Paul's fresh warning, "I will not spare you," given in advance of his forthcoming visit, would not include the very ones who were still unrepentant.

19. For ὡς . . . καί as correlatives, see BAGD 897c, citing also Matt. 6:10; Acts 7:51; Gal. 1:9; Phil. 1:20.

20. Hyldahl's rendering, "as (already) present . . . and (yet actually) now absent" ("Einheit" 304) tries to avoid these difficulties.

21. So also Bultmann 241; Barrett, "Opponents" 248.

22. On the basis of the repetition of the articular participle οἱ προημαρτηκότες of 12:21 in 13:2, Windisch believes τοῖς προημαρτηκόσιν should be supplemented by καὶ μὴ μετανοήσασιν (from 12:21) (415).

listed in 12:20b (Barrett 333; "Opponents" 248); or as all the other members of the congregation, "the rest of you as well" (Moffatt), those not guilty of the particular sins committed by οἱ προημαρτηκότες (see 12:21b)[23] but who nevertheless needed a warning for the sake of deterrence.[24] On this last view, which is to be preferred, the two groups mentioned in 13:2 embrace the whole church, just as 12:20-21 does.[25] It is no difficulty that Paul did not write πᾶσιν ὑμῶν or ὑμῖν πᾶσιν after τοῖς λοιποῖς.

When the perfect tense of προλέγω, here προείρηκα, is contrasted with the present,[26] here προλέγω, it means "have said someth[ing] before or previously" and connotes warning (BAGD 704d). In certain contexts to say something in advance is to issue a warning, and since οὐ φείσομαι is obviously a warning it is appropriate to render προείρηκα by "I have already warned" and προλέγω by "I forewarn."[27] In the former case, προ- signifies before the time of writing; in the latter, before the forthcoming third visit. The content of the warning is introduced by a "declarative" ὅτι and indirect speech (Robertson 1035), although Paul may be reproducing the actual words (recitative ὅτι) he used on his departure after the "painful visit."[28] When he departed at that time, ἐάν may have expressed his uncertainty, not about the likelihood of a return, but about its timing: "whenever I return." But now, having announced his imminent return (12:14; 13:1), ἐάν must mean "when."[29] The forthcoming visit is certain, although its character remains uncertain, given Paul's deep fears (12:20-21). Perhaps we can reproduce this latent ambiguity of ἐάν by rendering ἐὰν ἔλθω εἰς τὸ πάλιν with "on my return" (NIV) or "the next time I come" (GNB). This assumes (rightly) that εἰς τὸ πάλιν = πάλιν[30] and that this phrase belongs with ἔλθω, not with οὐ φείσομαι.[31]

---

23. Similarly Windisch 415. Others who refer τοῖς λοιποῖς πᾶσιν to the rest of the congregation sometimes add a different qualification — e.g., those who have tacitly condoned immoral conduct within the congregation (Furnish 570, 576).

24. Similarly Meyer 702-3.

25. This is rightly recognized by Martin (471).

26. A comparable present–aorist juxtaposition is found in Gal. 5:21 (προλέγω ὑμῖν, καθὼς προεῖπον); cf. Gal. 1:9; 1 Thess. 4:6.

27. See also LSJ 1488 s.v. προλέγω II.3 for the meaning "caution," "warn."

28. Recitative ὅτι is indicated by quotation marks in Conybeare (in Conybeare and Howson) 464 and Allo 337, and by a colon (with no "that") in GNB, NIV; Lietzmann 160; Carrez 237; Wolff 257 (among others).

29. So Weymouth, NEB, JB, NJB, REB; and among the commentators Hughes 476 n. 170; Martin 451, 472; Lambrecht 221; Thrall 871, 877. On the temporal sense of ἐάν when it is followed by the aorist subjunctive, see BAGD 211b s.v. 1.d and the commentary at 5:1 and cf. 1 Cor. 16:10 (RSV).

30. Thus BAGD 228d, 606d; Moule 69 ("again," "for another visit").

31. So almost all EVV. Against Windisch (415) and Allo (337) who construe εἰς τὸ πάλιν with οὐ φείσομαι, we contend that it is far from evident that on the "painful visit" Paul showed no leniency toward the recalcitrant members of the Corinthian congregation. Rather, God humbled him in his relation to them (12:20). And it is decisive disciplinary action in person (cf. ἔλθω), rather than by letter (such as the "severe letter"), that is in mind.

Originally φείδομαι ("spare," "refrain") referred to refraining from killing (= sparing) a defeated enemy and thus could also mean "be merciful towards,"[32] meanings also found in the LXX.[33] Here in 13:2 it is used absolutely, and some EVV reflect this: "I shall have no mercy" (JB, NJB), "I shall not spare" (Thrall 871), "I will show no leniency" (NEB, REB, Cassirer). But it is perfectly legitimate to supply an object, such as οὐδενός ("anyone," BAGD 854d), αὐτῶν ("them"), or ὑμῶν ("you").[34] If the two groups mentioned in v. 2a incorporate the whole church, "I will not spare you" is the preferable translation.

The punishment Paul was threatening to inflict was obviously severe (cf. 13:10), which would seem to rule out public censure, or, as Barrett proposes (334), the declaration that those who were denying the gospel by their behavior had alienated themselves from God and fallen back into Satan's realm.[35] So the options would appear to be (1) removal from the church (cf. 1 Cor. 5:13), provided Paul had the support of the majority (cf. 2:6; 10:6) for such drastic action; or (2) handing the offenders over to Satan "for the destruction of the flesh" (1 Cor. 5:5; cf. 1 Tim. 1:20), a penalty which probably refers to the suffering of an illness that may lead to death (cf. 1 Cor. 11:30) unless there was repentance. Certainly Paul longed that the wrongdoers would repent, but in the absence of repentance no mercy would be shown. It would be a case of καθαίρεσις (10:8; 13:10) or ἀποτόμως χρᾶσθαι (13:10) or ἐν ῥάβδῳ ἐλθεῖν (1 Cor. 4:21).

13:3 ἐπεὶ δοκιμὴν ζητεῖτε τοῦ ἐν ἐμοὶ λαλοῦντος Χριστοῦ· ὃς εἰς ὑμᾶς οὐκ ἀσθενεῖ ἀλλὰ δυνατεῖ ἐν ὑμῖν. "— since you demand proof that Christ speaks through me, Christ who is not weak in dealing with you but shows his power among you." One reason Paul planned to exercise uncompromising discipline (οὐ φείσομαι, v. 2) on his next visit was the prolonged refusal of certain members of the congregation (οἱ προημαρτηκότες, 12:21; 13:2) to repent of their immorality. But he believed this disciplinary action would achieve a further purpose — it would satisfy the demand of some or all of the Corinthians for specific, visible proof that he was indeed Christ's spokesman, one of Christ's genuine apostles. Those who had issued this demand (cf. ζητεῖτε) for convincing evidence (δοκιμή) would not have expected their challenge to be met by painful punitive measures. Their expectation, perhaps, was for additional miraculous signs (cf. 12:12) or specialized ecstatic experiences (cf. 12:6) or aggressive authoritarianism (cf. 11:20) or polished rhetoric (cf. 10:10). Once more we see the radical difference between the criteria for determining genuine apostleship that the Corinthians were using and those espoused by Paul.

The causal ἐπεί looks back to οὐ φείσομαι, not to the remote προλέγω, and introduces a supplementary reason Paul would not be merciful toward any impenitent Corinthians. The δοκιμή is the οὐ φείσομαι. But proof of what? "(Of

32. See LSJ 1920 s.v. I.
33. E.g., 1 Kgdms. 15:3 ("spare"); Exod. 2:6 ("have mercy on").
34. NIV and Martin (451) rearrange the word order and treat τοῖς προημαρτηκόσιν καὶ τοῖς λοιποῖς πᾶσιν as the object of οὐ φείσομαι. A. P. Stanley (273) supplies an impersonal object, "my power."

the fact) that Christ speaks through me." This rendering assumes that (1) τοῦ ... Χριστοῦ is an objective genitive, indicating what was to be proved;[36] (2) τοῦ ... λαλοῦντος Χριστοῦ is equivalent to ὅτι ὁ Χριστὸς λαλεῖ;[37] and (3) ἐν is instrumental[38] rather than local in meaning ("through" rather than "in"). The question at issue was not whether Paul enjoyed personal communion with Christ or received messages directly from Christ ("that Christ speaks *in* me"), but whether he was, as he claimed to be (5:20), an ambassador who reliably represented the intent of Christ in his words and deeds,[39] whether the message he had delivered to the Corinthians by word and deed accurately reflected the mind of Christ. It was the validity of his apostleship that was being questioned.

The essence of the Corinthian demand is clear: "We want proof that you are Christ's mouthpiece." But since Paul follows the mention of this demand with a reference to Christ's power (δυνατεῖ ἐν ὑμῖν), it is probably fair to infer that their high-handed request included such a reference, perhaps in order to contrast Paul's "weakness" among them (as they saw it; cf. 10:1, 10) with Christ's power among them. If so, their demand may have been something like this: δοκιμὴν ζητοῦμεν τοῦ ἐν σοὶ λαλοῦντος Χριστοῦ, ὃς δυνατεῖ ἐν ἡμῖν. "We demand proof that Christ, who works powerfully among us, is using you as his spokesman." On this understanding Paul has added εἰς ὑμᾶς οὐκ ἀσθενεῖ ἀλλά as a foil for the reference to Christ's power and as a preparation for the weakness–power/strength antithesis (cf. 12:9-10) that is a crucial ingredient in v. 4.

εἰς ὑμᾶς (A) οὐκ ἀσθενεῖ (B) ἀλλὰ δυνατεῖ (B′) ἐν ὑμῖν (A′) forms a chiasmus that has the effect of highlighting items A and A′, that is, the personal relationship of Christ to the Corinthians, just as at the end of the next verse (v. 4) εἰς ὑμᾶς focuses attention on Paul's relation to them. The prepositions εἰς and ἐν, "toward" and "among," are themselves not antithetical; indeed, one could argue that ἐν ὑμῖν is simply a stylistic variant of εἰς ὑμᾶς, "in relation to you," "in dealing with you," since Paul concludes v. 4 with εἰς ὑμᾶς. Both ὑμᾶς and ὑμῖν will refer to the whole church, not to any particular section within it, and ὑμῖν will bear a corporate rather than an individual sense, "in your midst, "among you," rather than "within each of you." ἀσθενέω ("be weak") and δυνατέω ("be

35. A similar position is taken by Murphy-O'Connor 132-33. "If the community did not respond to his admonitions, the only alternative was for him to declare that the quality of their lives, both individually and collectively, did not conform to the gospel and that they were not in fact Christians" (132).

36. But Meyer (703-4) considers it a subjective genitive; the Corinthians want the Christ speaking in Paul to assert himself against those within the church who are disobedient and impenitent.

37. Even in its present position and its anarthrous state λαλοῦντος could be equivalent to a relative clause (see Turner 152). Cf. Furnish (568): ". . . proof of the Christ who speaks through me." On the other hand, τοῦ should not be construed with λαλοῦντος: ". . . proof that the one speaking in me is Christ" (Young and Ford 275).

38. So Wolff 257; Heckel 122, who draws attention to the "correlative" statements in 2:17 and 12:19, κατέναντι θεοῦ ἐν Χριστῷ λαλοῦμεν.

39. λαλοῦντος should be given a broad sense that relates to behavior in general, although with primary reference to words spoken. That is, ἐν ἐμοί connotes "through what I say and do."

strong")[40] are clearly antonyms, with οὐκ ἀσθενεῖ serving to emphasize its positive counterpart, δυνατεῖ. Both are gnomic presents, matching the preceding λαλοῦντος and referring to all the benefits of salvation, but in the immediate context where we find references to a future visit (ἔρχομαι, v. 1; ἐὰν ἔλθω, v. 2) and to future action (οὐ φείσομαι, v. 2), the particular time when Christ will be seen to be not weak but strong is Paul's imminent visit. "When I come, Christ's word to you through me will be powerful — and painful!" δυνατεῖ is not a calm reassurance but a forbidding promise.[41]

Let us summarize the thrust of this verse. When, on his third visit, Paul exercised discipline against those who persisted in sin, he would be providing proof — in a way the Corinthians were not expecting or wanting (cf. 12:20) — not only that Christ was using him as his agent (that is, was "speaking" through him) but also that Christ was powerfully active in their congregation. When they received punishment at Paul's hand, perhaps by being "consigned to Satan for the destruction of the flesh" (cf. 1 Cor. 5:5),[42] they would in fact be undergoing the Lord's discipline (cf. 1 Cor. 11:30, 32).

13:4 "For indeed he was crucified because of his weakness, but he lives because of God's power. For we also are weak, in union with him, but in our dealings with you we shall be fully alive, along with him, because of God's power." It will be useful to set out the Greek text (including v. 3b) in diagrammatic form (see p. 914) so as to highlight the repetitions and contrasts which will afford a basis for our exegesis of the verse.[43]

In these three sentences the common feature is the weakness–power motif: οὐκ ἀσθενεῖ–δυνατεῖ (v. 3b), ἐξ ἀσθενείας–ἐν δυνάμεως θεοῦ (v. 4a), ἀσθενοῦμεν–ἐκ δυνάμεως θεοῦ (v. 4b). V. 4 develops this motif of v. 3b by adding to it the death–life antithesis (ἐσταυρώθη–ζῇ, v. 4a) and the union with Christ theme (ἐν αὐτῷ–σὺν αὐτῷ, v. 4b).

1. *The repetition of καὶ γάρ.* For the sake of consistency it might seem preferable to translate both instances by "for indeed,"[44] with the first explaining or illustrating v. 3b and the second developing v. 3a. But since in v. 4b Paul is draw-

---

40. δυνατέω is a uniquely Pauline word (3 uses) that is twice followed by an aorist infinitive when it means "be able" (9:8; Rom. 14:4), while here it means "be strong" (BAGD 208c). It is a "back-formation" from the more common cognate verb ἀδυνατέω (cf. BDF §108[2]) and always refers to divine power.

41. That δυνατεῖ intimates powerful discipline is recognized by (among others) Meyer 704; Hafemann 490, 492. Hughes (477-78) and Scott (250, 252) see a parallel between Yahweh's vindication of Moses' authority during Korah's rebellion by the destruction of the rebels (Num. 16:28-32) and Christ's powerful vindication of Paul's authority when unrepentant Corinthians are punished. There are, however, no specific pointers in the text that would lead us to think this analog is in Paul's mind.

42. Thrall speaks of "the miraculous infliction of bodily suffering" (878), referring to Acts 5:3-5, 9-10 (878 n. 57).

43. Heckel arranges his diagram of vv. 3b-4 on the basis of past, present, and future tenses (139).

44. So Barrett 327; Thrall 871 (but see her discussion on p. 885).

Weakness	Power		Referent
3b ὃς . . . οὐκ ἀσθενεῖ εἰς ὑμᾶς	ἀλλὰ δυνατεῖ ἐν ὑμῖν.		Christ
4a καὶ γὰρ ἐσταυρώθη ἐξ ἀσθενείας	ἀλλὰ ζῇ ἐκ δυνάμεως θεοῦ.		
4b καὶ γὰρ ἡμεῖς ἀσθενοῦμεν ἐν αὐτῷ	ἀλλὰ ζήσομεν σὺν αὐτῷ ἐκ δυνάμεως θεοῦ εἰς ὑμᾶς.		Paul

ing a parallel between his ministry and the career of Christ outlined in v. 4a, there is sound reason to render the second καὶ γὰρ (ἡμεῖς) by "for we also."[45]

2. *The repetition of οὐκ/γάρ . . . ἀλλά.* In v. 3b οὐκ ἀσθενεῖ is basically a foil, highlighting its positive counterpart, ἀλλὰ δυνατεῖ. But in the case of the two γάρ . . . ἀλλά antitheses in v. 4, the first element is not merely a foil to the second, although the second (ζῇ κτλ. and ζήσομεν κτλ.) bears the emphasis.[46]

3. *The repetition of ἐκ (ἐξ).* If we assume that it is more likely that ἐκ bears the same sense in each part of v. 4a than a different sense,[47] it would be difficult to give ἐξ ἀσθενείας the meaning "from a position of weakness" (Spittler 262) or "out of a condition of weakness" (Hughes 478), because such senses do not suit the phrase ἐκ δυνάμεως θεοῦ. The most appropriate meaning for ἐκ in both cases is either "through" (RV) where that word means "under the conditions of" (Tasker 188) or "due to" (so, apparently, Thrall 871, 884), or, better, "because of" (NASB; Barrett 327),[48] "as a result of" (BAGD 115b). Christ was crucified "because of his weakness" and he now lives "because of God's power." We need not supply θεοῦ after ἀσθενείας on the basis of the parallelism and 1 Cor.

45. Similarly Conybeare in Conybeare and Howson 464 ("And so I, too"); Berkeley, GNB; and especially Lambrecht 224; "Self-Commendation" 344 n. 43; "Notes" 591-94, 596.

46. Lambrecht argues that both cases of the γάρ–ἀλλά construction in v. 4 are equivalent to the μὲν γάρ–δέ construction where "the μέν- clause has a concessive nuance, and the real reason is found in the δέ- clause" ("Self-Commendation" 344; cf. "Notes" 594-95). Accordingly, in both of these articles as also in his commentary (220), he renders the contrast by "although . . . certainly," with the second clause in v. 4a expressing the motivation for v. 3b, and the second clause in v. 4b the motivation for οὐ φείσομαι (v. 2) ("Self-Commendation" 344; "Notes" 595).

47. See Heckel 129 and n. 48. Some, however, render ἐξ ἀσθενείας by "in weakness" and ἐκ δυνάμεως θεοῦ by "by the power of God" (e.g., Barclay; Furnish 568; Lambrecht 220, but see his "Notes" 595).

48. A causal sense is given to ἐκ in the phrase ἐξ ἀσθενείας by BAGD 235c (ἐκ denoting "the reason which is a presupposition for someth[ing]"); Robertson 598 ("cause or occasion"); Turner 260; Carrez 238.

1:25; the "weakness" was Christ's. Some take that weakness to be his helplessness or defenselessness before unjust accusation or "the weakness essentially inherent in moral human existence,"[49] but if Paul is emphasizing that this ἀσθένεια was self-imposed, it would refer to the "weakness" of his obedience to God "all the way to death" (μέχρι θανάτου, Phil. 2:8 GNB),[50] or even to his non-retaliation or non-aggressiveness during his Passion (cf. Matt. 26:52, 67-68; 27:11-14, 27-31; 1 Pet. 2:23).

4. *The repetition of ἐν δυνάμεως θεοῦ.* It is significant that both uses of this phrase are directly related to ζωή. Christ's risen life (ζῇ, v. 4a) is sustained "because of God's power," and Paul would show himself to be very much alive (ζήσομεν, v. 4b) on his next visit "because of God's power." Divine δύναμις and every expression of ζωή are inseparably related. On the concept of δύναμις θεοῦ, see the commentary on 6:7. There, as here, θεοῦ is a subjective genitive. On the significance of ζῇ, see #6 below; for ζήσομεν, see #7.

5. *The repetition of εἰς ὑμᾶς.* Standing at the beginning and end of vv. 3b-4, this phrase forms a kind of *inclusio.* In its non-literal sense, it means, basically, "in reference to you," "with regard to you" (NJB), so that in the present context where the focus is on Paul's projected punitive measures against the Corinthians (οὐ φείσομαι, v. 2) the sense will be "in dealing with you"[51] or "in our dealings with you."[52] It is the parallel with εἰς ὑμᾶς οὐκ ἀσθενεῖ (v. 3b) that shows that εἰς ὑμᾶς in v. 4b belongs with ζήσομεν,[53] not with δυνάμεως θεοῦ.[54]

6. *The death–life antithesis* (v. 4a). The change of tense from aorist (ἐσταυρώθη) to present (ζῇ) intensifies the contrast already indicated by ἀλλά. Christ was crucified once, but his risen life continues.[55] This stark contrast[56] is a variation on a more common formula where καί, not ἀλλά, links two aorists; e.g., Ἰησοῦς ἀπέθανεν καὶ ἀνέστη ("Jesus died and rose again," 1 Thess. 4:14). ζῇ presupposes ἔζησεν ("came to life," Rom. 14:9) or ἠγέρθη ("was raised," "rose"), is equivalent to πάντοτε ζῶν (ἐστι) (Heb. 7:25), and implies ζῶν ἐστι εἰς τοὺς αἰῶνας τῶν αἰώνων (see Rev. 1:18 and cf. Rom. 5:10; 6:9).

49. Thrall 884, referring to Heckel 124-25; similarly Belleville, "Gospel" 155; cf. BAGD 115b, "his weak nature." Heckel discusses some five different ways of understanding the clause καὶ γὰρ (εἰ) ἐσταυρώθη ἐξ ἀσθενείας (124-30).

50. Meyer (704) and Black (162) both relate the ἀσθένεια to Christ's obedience to God by which he assumed weak human nature and submitted to the cross. Commenting on 1 Cor. 4:8-13, Fitzgerald suggests that the "weakness" of the apostles (1 Cor. 4:10) was "their failure to retaliate (1 Cor. 4:12b-13a), their failure, either aggressively or defensively, to abuse others (contrast Wis 2:10-11)" (139).

51. RSV, NRSV; Lambrecht 220.

52. BAGD 336c (second instance); Belleville, "Gospel" 156; Thrall 871. But Martin sees v. 4 as a transition to a more optimistic attitude about the Corinthians, so that the second εἰς ὑμᾶς is rendered "when serving you" (451, 456; cf. NIV, "to serve you").

53. So most EVV; Meyer 707; Hughes 479 n. 175.

54. ". . . the power of God *directed* toward you" (NASB); W. Grundmann, *TDNT* 2.315.

55. Cf. Heckel 130.

56. Cf. Acts 2:23-24; 4:10; 10:39-40.

7. *The weakness–life antithesis* (v. 4b). Following the singulars of vv. 1-3a, ἡμεῖς probably refers to Paul alone, so that ἀσθενοῦμεν will sum up the effect of his own hardships (4:8-12; 6:4-5, 8-10; 11:23b-27; 12:10), perhaps with special reference to his σκόλοψ (12:7). And in comparison with his rivals (cf. 11:20), he will have seemed to the Corinthians to be timid (10:1) and unimpressive (10:10).[57] Indeed, in 11:21 Paul's "weakness" (ἠσθενήκαμεν) was his perceived failure to assert his authority by oppressive tactics.

At first sight ζήσομεν σὺν αὐτῷ might appear to express the resurrection hope of living in Christ's presence, given (1) the use of ζάω in v. 4a to depict Christ's risen life; (2) the use of σὺν Ἰησοῦ in reference to believers' resurrection in 4:14;[58] (3) the description in 1 Thess. 4:17 of the Christian's destiny as "being with the Lord" (σὺν κυρίῳ ἐσόμεθα; cf. 1 Thess. 4:14; Phil. 1:23). But several obstacles confront this view. The εἰς ὑμᾶς that follows ζήσομεν suggests that the "living" occurs before Paul's death and involves others as well as Paul and Christ;[59] Paul's focus in the context is on solving the problem of unrepentant believers (12:21; 13:2), not on rejoicing in his final destiny; while ζάω sometimes is simply equivalent to βιόω, "pass one's life," it can also mean (in reference to things) "be in full vigor,"[60] and of people "be strong/efficient," with the participle ζῶν signifying "powerful," "efficacious," so that ζήσομεν may be paraphrased "we shall show ourselves alive and effective"[61] or "I shall be full of life and vigour" (Plummer 366). These considerations lead us to conclude that in the expression ζήσομεν σὺν αὐτῷ ἐκ δυνάμεως θεοῦ εἰς ὑμᾶς Paul is speaking of his imminent visit to Corinth when, in unison with Christ and with God's power, he would act decisively and vigorously against unrepentant evildoers within the congregation.[62] ζήσομεν corresponds to οὐ φείσομαι (v. 2).

8. *The Christ–Paul parallel* (ἐν αὐτῷ–σὺν αὐτῷ, v. 4b).[63] καὶ . . . ἡμεῖς,

---

57. Cf. Thrall 885.

58. But Murphy-O'Connor believes that in 4:14 Paul is depicting his planned visit to Corinth as a "resurrection" (48; "Faith" 543-50).

59. Espousing the eschatological interpretation, Barrett seeks to overcome this difficulty by positing anticipated resurrection life and power. "God will grant him [Paul] such a measure of resurrection life as will suffice to deal with the situation in Corinth" (337). Heckel, too, believes that an eschatological understanding of ζήσομεν is not incompatible with a reference to the Corinthian situation Paul would confront on his next visit (133 and n. 69, 138). Similarly Hafemann: "The surprising thing is that Paul declares that he is *already* experiencing the resurrection and will do so in a dramatic fashion when he returns to Corinth" (492).

60. See LSJ 758 s.v. ζάω II.

61. Similarly Zerwick, *Analysis* 415.

62. Similarly, among others, Meyer 705; Plummer 375; Hughes 479, 482; Bultmann 244; Lambrecht 221, 226; "Self-Commendation" 345 n. 44; Schütz 215; Murphy-O'Connor 133; "Faith" 548-49. Héring, however, discovers in the expression ζήσομεν σὺν αὐτῷ (v. 4) an allusion to the two aspects or stages of "resurrection" in Christ — new life on earth through the Spirit, then bodily resurrection at the End. But these two stages are intimately related in that the "inner man" (4:16) is the germ of the "resurrection man" that will be revealed at the parousia (Rom. 8:19) (100 n. 4).

63. On this see Heckel 131-38.

"we also" (v. 4b), points to a correspondence between the experience of Christ (v. 4a) and that of Paul (v. 4b), "as Christ, so we."[64] Both knew weakness, willingly accepted; both are "alive" because of God's power. But the correspondence was not superficial, for Paul's experience was a direct consequence of his union with Christ that is expressed by ἐν and σύν. As a result of being in Christ (ἐν αὐτῷ), Paul shared in the weakness of his crucified Master. As a result of his fellowship with Christ (σὺν αὐτῷ), he shared in the power of his risen Lord (vv. 3b, 4a), a power imparted by God (θεοῦ). But as well as a correspondence there is a contrast between Christ and Paul. Whereas Christ's states (death and resurrection) are successive, first ἐσταυρώθη then ζῇ, Paul's states (weakness and vitality) are, at least potentially, simultaneous, ἀσθενοῦμεν and ζήσομεν. This simultaneity of νέκρωσις and ζωή, of εἰς θάνατον παραδίδοσθαι and ζωή, has already been expressed in 4:10-11.

In v. 4, then, Paul is asserting that Christ's career is the pattern for his own ministry.[65] Just as Christ was crucified because of his "weakness" and now lives because of God's power, so Paul, as a result of his faith union with Christ, shares the "weakness" of Christ's passion and the effective power of God.[66]

Bibiography

Barrett, *Signs* 43-44 • P. Beasley-Murray, *Power for God's Sake: The Use and Abuse of Power in the Local Church* (Carlisle: Paternoster, 1998) • Black 160-72 • Fee, *Presence* 359-62 • P. J. Gräbe, *The Power of God in Paul's Letters* (Tübingen: Mohr, 2000) • Güttgemanns 142-54 • Heckel 121-43, 300 • B. S. Jackson, "'Two or Three Witnesses,'" in *Essays in Jewish and Christian Legal History* (Studies in Judaism in Late Antiquity 10; Leiden: Brill, 1975) 153-71 • Lambrecht, "Notes" • Oostendorp 17-30 • Schmithals 193-96 • Schütz 214-18 • Siber 168-77 • D. M. Stanley 145-47 • Tannehill 98-100 • Therrien 112-14, 252, 254 • van Vliet 34-48

4. A Plea for Self-Examination (13:5-10)

There are two distinct features in this paragraph. First, in vv. 5-7 the δοκιμ-root, a favorite Pauline word group, occurs five times.[1]

1. δοκιμάζω (v. 5), "test with a view to approving," "approve after testing," "prove." Seventeen of the twenty-one NT uses of this verb are found in Paul.

---

64. Lambrecht finds a chiasmus in the subjects of vv. 1-4: Paul (vv. 1-2) (A), Christ (v. 3) (B), Christ (v. 4a) (B'), Paul (v. 4b) (A').

65. Cf. W. Grundmann, *TDNT* 7.784.

66. Cf. Bruce 253; Black 163.

1. On the whole δοκιμ- word group, see W. Grundmann *TDNT* 2.255-60; Spicq 1.353-61; and the monograph by G. Therrien, *Le discernement dans les écrits pauliniens* (Paris: Gabalda, 1973).

2. δόκιμος (v. 7), "passing the test," "approved," "proven." All but one (Jas. 1:12) of the seven NT uses are Pauline.[2]
3. ἀδόκιμος (vv. 5-7), "failing the test," "unapproved," "counterfeit." All but one (Heb. 6:8) of the eight NT uses are Pauline.[3]

Paul's use of this word group in vv. 5-7 in reference to himself and the Corinthians was probably triggered by his earlier reference (in 13:3) to the Corinthian demand that he supply proof (δοκιμή) that Christ was speaking through him.[4]

Second, within this paragraph Paul's emotions seem to oscillate between hope and fear regarding his converts at Corinth. He hopes they will discover him to be "not unapproved" (οὐκ . . . ἀδόκιμοι, v. 6) and that on his forthcoming visit he can be "weak" (χαίρομεν . . . ὅταν ἡμεῖς ἀσθενῶμεν, v. 9a) by not having to deal with them severely, and he prays for their "restoration" (κατάρτισις) to spiritual wholeness (v. 9b). Yet, in keeping with his deep-seated apprehension about their ongoing divisive and immoral ways (12:20-21), he fears that after all he may have to act "with unrelenting severity" (ἀποτόμως) against any dissidents (v. 10). This ambivalence is explicit in v. 7 when he prays that the Corinthians may do no wrong (reflecting his fear) but rather may do what is right (reflecting his hope).

13:5*Test yourselves, to see if you are in the faith; examine yourselves. Surely you know this for sure about yourselves, that Jesus Christ[a] is[b] in you? — unless, of course, you fail the test. 6And I hope you will know for certain that we also do not fail the test. 7But we pray[c] to God that you may not do anything wrong, not so that we may appear as having passed the test, but so that you may do what is right — even if we may seem to have failed the test. 8For we cannot do anything to oppose the truth but only to support the truth. 9For we rejoice when we are weak but you are strong. Indeed, what we pray for is this, your restoration. 10The reason I am writing these things when I am absent is that when I am present I may not have to deal severely with you as I exercise the authority which the Lord gave me for building up and not for pulling down.*

TEXTUAL NOTES

a. There is strong support (‭א‬ A F G P 0243 326 629 630 1175 1241ˢ 1739 1881 2464 *al* b vg Clement Ambrosiaster) for the order Χριστὸς Ἰησοῦς, but the more common Pauline order Ἰησοῦς Χριστός (B D Ψ 33 𝔐 a vgᵐˢ syr) is perhaps to be preferred.

b. The smoother reading, with ἐστίν added after ἐν ὑμῖν (‭א‬ A D¹ F G Ψ 0243 1739 1881 𝔐), is probably secondary. The text without ἐστίν (𝔭⁴⁶ B D* 33 *pc* Clement), being elliptical, is more difficult and therefore probably original, although the copula ἐστίν is commonly omitted in NT usage (BDF §127).

---

2. Rom. 14:18; 16:10; 1 Cor. 11:19; 2 Cor. 10:18; 13:7; 2 Tim. 2:15.
3. Rom. 1:28; 1 Cor. 9:27; 2 Cor. 13:5-7; 2 Tim. 3:8; Tit. 1:16.
4. All seven NT uses of δοκιμή ("proof," "ordeal"; "approvedness," hence "character") are found in Paul (Rom. 5:4 [twice]; 2 Cor. 2:9; 8:2; 9:13; 13:3; Phil. 2:22).

c. Under the influence of the preceding first person singular verb ἐλπίζω (v. 6), some witnesses (D² Ψ 0243 1739 1881 𝔐 a b vg^{mss} syr^p sa^{ms} Ambrosiaster) read εὔχομαι in place of the first person plural εὐχόμεθα which is read by a superior set of witnesses (p^{46} ℵ A B D* F G K P 33 81 104 365 1175 1241^s 1505 2564 al lat syr^h co) and conforms to the following plurals.

13:5 Ἑαυτοὺς πειράζετε εἰ ἐστὲ ἐν τῇ πίστει, ἑαυτοὺς δοκιμάζετε·. "Test yourselves, to see if you are in the faith; examine yourselves." When challenged to supply proof (δοκιμή) of his being Christ's agent in Corinth (13:3), Paul had responded with a warning that on his next visit he would show no mercy (οὐ φείσομαι) to the recalcitrant members of the congregation (13:2). Now he offers his own challenge, clearly implying by the repeated ἑαυτούς,[5] which stands in the emphatic position,[6] that the Corinthians ought to examine their own status and conduct rather than his.[7] "It is your own selves — not me — that you must put to the test. . . . It is your own selves that you must examine." The challenge is issued to the whole congregation, not simply to a segment of it such as "those who have continued in their former sins" (οἱ προημαρτηκότες, 12:21; 13:2). Clearly πειράζω here bears a neutral sense, "put to the test," not its pejorative sense of "entice to evil," "tempt" (as in 1 Cor. 7:5; Gal. 6:1). πειράζω and δοκιμάζω could be treated as synonymous (Wolff 263) or as "virtually" so (Furnish 571), but perhaps there is a slight difference of emphasis, with πειράζω signifying "determine the nature of something by submitting it to testing" (cf. Louw and Nida §27.46), and δοκιμάζω, "test the genuineness of something with a view to approving it."

After πειράζετε, the interrogative particle εἰ could introduce a direct question[8]: "Examine yourselves: are you living the life of faith?" (NEB, REB). Bultmann believes the parallelism with ἑαυτοὺς δοκιμάζετε supports construing the εἰ clause separately (377). But most EVV rightly regard εἰ ("whether," "if") as introducing an indirect question[9] and supply a verb such as "to find out"[10] or simply "to see" (NIV) with εἰ. The precise significance of the combination εἶναι ἐν is uncertain. It may mean "adhere/conform to" or "continue/live in,"[11] or this construction could be a periphrasis for an adjective, so that ἐστὲ ἐν τῇ πίστει = ἐστὲ πιστοί, "you are believing/true believers."[12] ἡ πίστις may refer to the core of

5. The third person form of the reflexive pronoun (ἑαυτοῦ) may be used of all three persons (see Zerwick §209; Moule 120; and BAGD 211-12 s.v.).

6. See Turner 349.

7. The two presents, πειράζετε and δοκιμάζετε, need not be seen as iterative (as Barclay, "Keep testing . . . Keep proving"), for the present imperative may also express general directives that are less peremptory and more gentle than those expressed by the aorist imperative.

8. For this use of εἰ, see BDF §440(3); Turner 333.

9. So also BAGD 219d; Robertson 1045.

10. GNB; Spicq 1.356 n. 20.

11. Cf. the classical use of εἶναι ἐν in the sense "be engaged in" (LSJ 488 s.v. εἰμί C.IV.3.a.).

12. So BAGD 225b. A comparable example would be ἐν βάρει εἶναι (1 Thess. 2:7) = βαρεῖς εἶναι, "be burdensome." Cf. Bruce's paraphrase (159), "to see if you are true believers."

apostolic teaching as epitomized in the gospel (Gal. 1:23), the gospel that had been delivered to the Corinthians in its purity (1 Cor. 15:1-5) and was under attack in Corinth (11:4). On this view Paul is requesting self-examination regarding their adherence to an unadulterated form of the gospel.[13] "Put yourselves to the proof, to see whether you are holding to the Faith" (TCNT). Alternatively, ἡ πίστις may here denote personal trust in Christ as a *modus vivendi:* "whether you are living in faith" (GNB), "are you living the life of faith?" (NEB, REB), "whether you are controlled by faith" (Danker 210). But in a context that emphasizes the need for proper Christian action (12:20-21; 13:7, ἵνα ὑμεῖς τὸ καλὸν ποιῆτε) the most satisfactory option is to take ἡ πίστις in a broad sense as referring to Christian conduct that accords with Christian doctrine. That is, "being in the faith" means continuing true to the faith in conduct as well as in belief.[14] An emphasis on conduct is suggested by the following unqualified ἑαυτοὺς δοκιμάζετε when it is read in the light of Gal. 6:4, τὸ . . . ἔργον ἑαυτοῦ δοκιμαζέτω ἕκαστος. For the Corinthian believers the main "work" that would demonstrate their true πίστις was obedience (cf. ὑπακοὴ πίστεως, "the obedience that springs from faith," Rom. 1:5; 16:26), obedience to Paul and to the gospel he proclaimed (2:9; 10:6). So then, εἰ ἐστὲ ἐν τῇ πίστει in 13:5 should not be equated with τῇ . . . πίστει ἑστήκατε in 1:24 where there is a contrast between the Corinthians' firm standing in their own πίστις (= personal trust) and any domineering control of their faith that Paul might be thought to exercise.[15]

ἢ οὐκ ἐπιγινώσκετε ἑαυτοὺς ὅτι Ἰησοῦς Χριστὸς ἐν ὑμῖν; εἰ μήτι ἀδόκιμοί ἐστε. "Surely you know this for sure about yourselves, that Jesus Christ is in you? — unless, of course, you fail the test." As in 11:7 the particle ἢ introduces a rhetorical question, here a question that Paul expects will be answered affirmatively,[16] as is shown by the presence of οὐ(κ) (BDF §427[2]). After his twofold invitation to the Corinthians to scrutinize their conduct and attitudes (v. 5a), Paul now appeals with confidence to their theological self-awareness. ἐπιγινώσκετε need mean no more than "you realize/recognize" (γινώσκετε), but in a rhetorical question that expects the answer "Yes, indeed!" the intensifying prefix ἐπι- may well prompt the sense "you know for sure." ἑαυτούς is probably an accusative of respect, "about yourselves" (TCNT, NASB), "about your state" (Plummer 366), although it could be construed as a direct object with the ὅτι clause providing further definition.[17]

---

13. In 1 Cor. 16:13 γρηγορεῖτε ("keep alert") precedes στήκετε ἐν τῇ πίστει ("stand firm in the faith"), calling for alertness to the truth of the gospel and to the danger of its corruption.

14. Such an understanding is perhaps reflected in the renderings of NRSV ("Examine yourselves to see whether you are living in the faith") and Cassirer ("It is your own selves that you ought to be examining to make sure that you are true to the faith").

15. There is therefore no reason to deny (cf. Furnish 31) that 1:24 and 13:5 could stand in the same letter.

16. Several EVV begin v. 5b with "Surely . . ." (TCNT, NEB, GNB, REB, Cassirer).

17. Cf. Thrall 871: "Or do you not surely recognise yourselves — recognise that . . ."; similarly NJB.

What Paul assumed that his Corinthian converts knew for certain was the fact that (ὅτι) Jesus Christ was indwelling each of them (cf. Rom. 8:9-10) and was also active corporately in their congregation (ἐν ὑμῖν; cf. 13:3). Through his Spirit the risen Christ was both "within" and "among" (ἐν) the Corinthians.[18] But it was not only this bare fact that they needed to be reminded of, but in particular what that fact implied for their present Christian living,[19] namely their need to continue true to the faith (v. 5a) as it was embodied in Paul and his gospel, by turning from their divisive and immoral ways and altering their attitude to their spiritual father.

If Paul's rhetorical question ends with ἐν ὑμῖν,[20] the last four words of the verse form what might be called a parenthetical aside or hypothetical modification, " — unless, of course, you fail the test" (NAB²).[21] But there can be no objection to ending the question with ἐστέ.[22] Does Paul expect the Corinthians to fail the test and be proven counterfeit, through their concluding that Christ did not reside within and among them? Almost certainly not, for the following reasons. (1) ἢ οὐκ ἐπιγινώσκετε κτλ. expects an affirmative answer and εἰ μήτι introduces a hypothetical modification ("unless it were so," BDF §376) (as εἰ μήτι ἄν does in 1 Cor. 7:5 — BDF §376). (2) With their pride in their knowledge (cf. 1 Cor. 1:5; 4:6; 8:1, 10-12), the Corinthians would be unlikely to conclude that they were "unapproved" (ἀδόκιμοι) in any sense. (3) Only the assumption that the Corinthians would see themselves as δόκιμοι contributes to Paul's argument. If their Christian status is genuine, so too must be his status as Christ's apostle, since they came to faith through him. "In the logic of the argument, the greater the affirmation of the Corinthians' provenness, the more undeniable Paul's provenness" (Gundry Volf 219).[23] (4) If Paul had entertained real doubts about their status as true believers, he would hardly have addressed them as "the church of God" (1:1) or as his spiritual children (6:13; cf. 12:14; 1 Cor. 4:15) and claimed them as his validating credentials (3:1-3). We conclude that εἰ μήτι ἀδόκιμοί ἐστε is an ironical aside[24] in which Paul challenges his converts to doubt their own authentic

18. This dual sense of ἐν is recognized by Martin 478, 480; Thrall 871 and n. 1, 891 n. 159, 892.

19. Bultmann gives ὅτι the sense "what it means that" (245).

20. So WH, UBS¹⁻⁴, NA²⁷.

21. The same rendering of εἰ μήτι is found in NEB, NAB; Furnish 572. Cf. "Unless indeed," TCNT; Barrett 327; Burton §469; "unless, that is," NJB; Zerwick and Grosvenor 562; "unless perhaps," Carrez 240; Thrall 871. Some render εἰ μήτι by "If not"; so JB; Lang 355; Lambrecht 220.

22. Thus KJV, Weymouth, NASB, Barclay, NIV; Martin 451.

23. Gundry Volf takes ἀδόκιμοι in 13:5 to mean "rejected as nonconverts" (223, 225; cf. 217, 226).

24. The presence of irony here is recognized by Hughes 481 ("mildly ironical"); Martin 479; Barnett 608; Thrall 892; Gundry Volf 219; Brown 177 ("irony — bordering on sarcasm"). I. H. Marshall, however, rendering εἰ μήτι by "except if," maintains that Paul here momentarily admits the possibility that some Corinthian believers may prove failures in the test (*Power* 111-12, 119 n. 73).

Christian existence! Yet we must also allow, with Gundry Volf (218, 223-25), a possible allusion to some Corinthians who needed to be exposed as falsely professing Christians.

13:6 ἐλπίζω δὲ ὅτι γνώσεσθε ὅτι ἡμεῖς οὐκ ἐσμὲν ἀδόκιμοι. "And I hope you will know for certain that we also do not fail the test." δέ is simply conjunctive. Just as the Corinthians should engage in self-examination (v. 5a) and realize the truth about themselves (v. 5b), so too (δέ) Paul hopes they will become convinced of the truth about him — that he is not unauthorized but is a genuine "ambassador for Christ" (cf. 5:20). After the singular ἐλπίζω, the plural pronoun ἡμεῖς will refer to Paul alone rather than to his associates at Corinth, Silvanus and Timothy (1:19), as Furnish (578) proposes. We note the singulars in vv. 2-3, 6a, 10 and the plurals in vv. 4, 6b-9. The first ὅτι introduces the content of the ἐλπίς, the second the content of the γνῶσις. On the basis of the principle that when the simplex form of a verb (here γνώσεσθε) closely follows the compound form (here ἐπιγινώσκετε), the simplex may carry the sense of the compound,[25] we may suggest that γνώσεσθε means not simply "you will discover" but "you will know for certain." In the final phrase of the verse the emphatic ἡμεῖς may be rendered "we also" (Héring 100) or "we, in turn" (Thrall 871). We may explain the double negative οὐκ . . . ἀδόκιμοι ("not unapproved," "failing the test") as litotes for δόκιμοι ("approved," "passing the test"; cf. v. 6) or as reflecting an actual charge made against Paul, namely that he was "unaccredited."

As a whole the verse may be understood in two ways. "I expect that on my next visit you will come to see, if I need to exercise discipline, that I am not unapproved but that Christ is active in and through me."[26] The alternative view may be paraphrased thus. "I hope that as a result of your self-examination[27] you will realize that you pass the test and are approved, and so I too must pass the test and be approved since it was through me that you came to be in Christ and now have Christ within and among you (cf. v. 5b)." Almost all commentators hold some form of this latter view. If the Corinthian self-audit yielded a positive result — assurance that they were in Christ and Christ in them — they would also have to come to a positive evaluation of Paul as an apostle of Christ (1:1), as belonging to Christ (10:7), as a servant of Christ (11:23), and as Christ's spokesman (13:3). The Corinthians' genuine faith and Paul's genuine apostleship were inextricably related; they stood or fell together. If they were true believers, he was a true apostle, since they had come to faith through his preaching (1:19; 3:1-3; 11:2). On the other hand, if their faith was counterfeit, so too was his apostolicity. After v. 5 we might have expected Paul to say "I hope you

---

25. See Moulton 115; cf. ἐνδυσάμενοι after ἐπενδύσασθαι in 5:2-3.

26. This seems to be the view of Meyer (706), who comments that "the object of the hoping is not the *desert of punishment* on the part of the readers, but the δοκιμή of the apostolic authority *in the event* of their deserving punishment" (italics his).

27. Although holding this second view, Barnett (609) and Lambrecht (222) relate γνώσεσθε to Paul's upcoming third visit.

will discover that *you* pass the test," but he says "I hope you will know for certain that *we* also (ἡμεῖς) do not fail the test," for he assumes that the Corinthians will give themselves a "pass" on their self-audit and hopes that they will clearly perceive the indissoluble link between their "pass" and his "pass." The one discovery should lead to the other, and their recognition of Paul's accreditation would result from their own self-scrutiny and reflection, not from his punitive action on his next visit. Paul longed with intensity (ἐλπίζω) for this recognition, and just as the prayer reports in vv. 7 and 9 point to the main thrust of his letter (Wiles 241), this expression of hope in v. 6, as often in his letters (see Olson 595-96), betrays his purpose in writing and the point of his argument.

13:7

Paul's prayer	εὐχόμεθα δὲ πρὸς τὸν θεὸν			
content	μὴ ποιῆσαι	ὑμᾶς	κακὸν	μηδέν,
negative aim	οὐχ ἵνα	ἡμεῖς	δόκιμοι	φανῶμεν,
positive aim	ἀλλ' ἵνα	ὑμεῖς τὸ	καλὸν	ποιῆτε,
qualification		ἡμεῖς δὲ ὡς	ἀδόκιμοι	ὦμεν.

"But we pray to God that you may not do anything wrong, not so that we may appear as having passed the test, but so that you may do what is right — even if we may seem to have failed the test." V. 6 might have suggested to the Corinthians that Paul's preoccupation was with his own vindication, not their well-being. So he proceeds to correct that possible misunderstanding — through *epidiorthosis* (see BDF §495[3]) — by assuring them of the primacy of their welfare. δέ ("But") introduces this corrective. His primary concern, as shown by his prayer, was for the Corinthians' rejection of all wrongdoing (κακόν) and pursuit of right conduct (τὸ καλόν), rather than their recognition of his authenticity (οὐχ ἵνα ἡμεῖς δόκιμοι φανῶμεν).

Paul's prayer (παρεκάλεσα) in 12:8 was directed, exceptionally, to "the Lord [Jesus]." Here his prayer (εὐχόμεθα)[28] is addressed to "God" [the Father], in accordance with his general practice (cf. Eph. 2:18). The content of the prayer is expressed by the accusative and infinitive, (μὴ) ποιῆσαι ὑμᾶς, just as in v. 9 it is expressed by the simple accusative (τοῦτο) (BAGD 329c). On this understanding, ὑμᾶς is the subject of ποιῆσαι and κακὸν μηδέν its object: "we pray . . . that you may not do anything wrong," with the emphatic μηδέν signifying "anything (wrong)" (NIV, NRSV; Carrez 240).[29] Lietzmann, however, takes "God" to be the implied subject of ποιῆσαι so that ὑμᾶς is its object. "But we pray to God that he may do you no harm (160; cf. 161-62) [through my discipline]." But against this position we observe that (i) the clear parallelism between μὴ ποιῆσαι ὑμᾶς κακὸν μηδέν and ἵνα ὑμεῖς τὸ καλὸν ποιῆτε shows that ὑμᾶς is the subject of ποιῆσαι and that ποιῆσαι κακόν refers to wrongdoing, not

---

28. εὔχομαι (7 NT uses, of which 3 are in Paul: 13:7, 9; Rom. 9:3) is more literary than προσεύχομαι (86 NT uses).

29. Cf. BDF §431(2).

to pain or harm resulting from the administering of punishment;[30] and (ii) a second object after ποιεῖν κακόν would be expressed not by the accusative (ὑμᾶς, "do *you* harm") but by the dative (ὑμῖν; cf. Matt. 20:32; 21:40; Acts 9:13).[31]

It is not impossible that the repeated ἵνα continues to define the content of Paul's prayer,[32] but since the accusative and infinitive construction has already expressed this, it seems more probable that both ἵνα clauses should be seen as telic,[33] defining first negatively (οὐχ ἵνα), then positively (ἀλλ' ἵνα) the purpose of the prayer. But it is not a case of two purposes, one rejected and one accepted. As sometimes elsewhere (e.g., 2:5; 7:12), the οὐ(κ) . . . ἀλλά antithesis is not absolute ("not at all X, but only Y"), but relative ("not primarily X, but Y"). In the light of v. 6 Paul could scarcely deny an interest in being recognized as δόκιμος, but he could truthfully affirm that his aim in praying that the Corinthians "avoid the wrong course" or "not go wrong" (Moffatt) was principally to enable them to "take the honorable course" or "come right" (Moffatt). The two complementary phrases ποιεῖν κακόν and τὸ καλὸν ποιεῖν[34] might appear to be simply general expressions for "doing evil/wrong" (cf. Rom. 3:8; 13:10) and "doing good" (cf. Rom. 7:21; Gal. 6:9), or for disobeying or obeying God's will (cf. Rom. 12:2, 9, 21). But set in the midst of references to Paul as ἀδόκιμοι (vv. 6, 7d) or δόκιμοι (v. 7b), these phrases take on more specific connotations, we suggest. The Corinthians would be doing wrong or following the wrong path if they refused to repent of sin (cf. 6:14–7:1; 12:20-21; 13:2), if they continued to harbor Paul's rivals and their false gospel, or if they refused to recognize Paul as being δόκιμος, God's approved apostle to Corinth (cf. 10:13-14). On the other hand, they would be doing what was right or pursuing the right course if they once more (cf. 7:9) repented of wrongdoing, if they rejected the interlopers from Palestine, and if they fully embraced Paul and his gospel. When this happened, their "obedience" (ὑπακοή) to Paul would be brought to completion (10:6; cf. 2:9; 7:15).

To emphasize yet again the priority he gave to ensuring the Corinthians' well-being, Paul ends with a self-effacing concession. At all costs they must do what is right, even if that meant that from their standpoint he seemed to lack authenticating proof (δοκιμή, v. 3). Much better for them to repent of wrongdoing and revise their attitude toward him and his rivals and so not need the evidence of Paul's apostleship that would be given through stern discipline on his next

---

30. Cf. Allo 339; Thrall 894.

31. Kümmel 214; Bultmann 247. For the same two reasons it is improbable that the implied subject of ποιῆσαι is Paul (". . . that we [ἡμεῖς] may not do you any harm").

32. Cf. Ignatius, *Philadelphians* 6:3; Hermas, *Similitudes* 5.2.10; BDF §392(1)(c). The double ἵνα is taken this way by Wiles 245 (supplying εὔχομαι before ἵνα, 244); Thrall 895 (with some reserve).

33. So Winer 460; Meyer 707; Plummer 366, 377; GNB. But Zerwick (§415, giving the reference as 2 Cor. 13:17) takes the second ἵνα as imperatival, expressing an independent wish ("On the contrary, may you do what is right").

34. If there is an aspectual difference between (μὴ) ποιῆσαι and (ἵνα . . .) ποιῆτε, the aorist points to any specific future action or all future action viewed collectively, while the present alludes to linear or repeated action.

visit, than that they should remain unrepentant and unreformed and so incur discipline and thereby witness the authentication of his apostolic power. This seems to be the thrust of the words ἡμεῖς δὲ ὡς ἀδόκιμοι ὦμεν, whether we translate them "while (δέ) we for our part remain as it were (ὡς) without authentication," or "even if (δέ) we in turn may seem (ὡς) to have failed the test."[35] Three different types of "test" seem implied in vv. 5-7.[36] In v. 5 the test is the Corinthians' self-examination to determine whether they are continuing true to the faith, a test Paul expects them to pass. In v. 6 the test is their evaluation of the authenticity of Paul's apostleship, a test he hopes he will pass. Finally, in v. 7 the test is the proof of apostolic authority shown in his discipline of unrepentant sinners; this test he will gladly fail.

By disclosing the content and purpose of his prayer, Paul is indirectly exhorting his converts to mend their ways and so avoid the drastic punishment of which he had warned them in vv. 1-4.

13:8 οὐ γὰρ δυνάμεθά τι κατὰ τῆς ἀληθείας, ἀλλὰ ὑπὲρ τῆς ἀληθείας. "For we cannot do anything to oppose the truth but only to support the truth." If we took the first person plural in δυνάμεθα to refer to humans in general, this verse could be described as purely aphoristic and unrelated to a particular situation. "Truth is impregnable but thrives on validation." But like the expressions ποιεῖν κακόν and τὸ καλὸν ποιεῖν in v. 7, what at first sight seems to have a very general import takes on a more specific meaning in the context. We have seen that the sense of the final clause in v. 7 is "even if, because of your repentance and obedience, evidence of my apostolic authority through disciplinary action is not called for and so I may appear to have failed the test." Against that backdrop v. 8 explains (cf. γάρ) why disciplinary action would be inappropriate in such circumstances. When "truth" (= authentic Christian conduct[37]) prevails, when there is repentance and uprightness (= τὸ καλὸν ποιεῖν, v. 7), no discipline is required, but when "truth" is absent, when disobedience and impenitence are present, disciplinary action is demanded. "We could never act[38] against the truth, but only[39] in support of it." Paul was both able and willing, if necessary, to act decisively to reestablish "truth," that is, to work toward restoring the Corinthians to wholeness (κατάρτισις, v. 9) in attitude and behavior. Whatever Paul's *modus operandi* on his forthcoming visit to Corinth — whether wielding the rod or acting in gentleness, cf. 1 Cor. 4:21 — his actions would accord with

35. Cf. Barclay's paraphrase: ". . . even if that means that there will be no opportunity for us to prove our authority"; similarly Zerwick, *Analysis* 415; Hughes 482 and n. 178.

36. Cf. Martin 481-82.

37. Cf. Allo 340: ἀλήθεια here is "Christian purity of behavior."

38. With δυνάμεθα we should supply ποιεῖν (BAGD 207b, citing Mark 9:22, εἴ τι δύνῃ, "if you are able *to do* anything"). In the present context οὐ . . . δυνάμεθα describes not absence of power but inability by reason of choice.

39. Since the οὐ(κ) . . . ἀλλά antithesis here is absolute (but cf. v. 7 and the commentary there), it is appropriate to supply μόνον ("only") after ἀλλά, as also RSV, NEB, NIV, REB, NRSV; Héring 101; Barrett 339; Wolff 257.

the "truth." Admittedly this is not a usual sense of ἀλήθεια in Paul, but since this word stands opposed to ἀδικία in Rom. 1:18; 2:8; 1 Cor. 13:6; 2 Thess. 2:10, 12, clearly it shares considerable semantic territory with one meaning of δικαιοσύνη (the opposite of ἀδικία), namely right conduct (cf. 9:9-10).[40]

Alternatively, or in addition, we could treat ἀλήθεια as a synonym for the gospel.[41] In Eph. 1:13 ὁ λόγος τῆς ἀληθείας is defined as τὸ εὐαγγέλιον, while in 4:2; 6:7; Col. 1:5; 2 Thess. 2:12 ἡ ἀλήθεια is to be identified as the gospel. On this view Paul is tracing his preoccupation with the Corinthians' spiritual well-being and his relative unconcern about the possibility of seeming to be ἀδόκιμος (v. 7) to his commitment to serve the gospel. As an agent of Christ (cf. 5:20; 13:3) in whom the truth resides (11:10; cf. Eph. 4:21; John 14:6) he was unable to act in a way that compromised the gospel and he refused to alter its content (2:17; 4:2).[42] Positively, he was under compulsion to propagate it, for it had been entrusted to him as a precious deposit (1 Cor. 9:16-17; Gal. 2:7; 1 Thess. 2:4; 1 Tim. 1:11).

13:9 χαίρομεν γὰρ ὅταν ἡμεῖς ἀσθενῶμεν, ὑμεῖς δὲ δυνατοὶ ἦτε· τοῦτο καὶ εὐχόμεθα, τὴν ὑμῶν κατάρτισιν. "For we rejoice when we are weak but you are strong. Indeed, what we pray for is this, your restoration." Evidence of Paul's commitment to working for the "truth" (v. 8) was found in his pleasure when the Corinthian believers were "strong" in their faith. That is, v. 9 confirms (γάρ, "For" or "Indeed") v. 8.[43] The "weakness" Paul speaks of could be the devoted, self-effacing service that marked his whole apostolic ministry (cf. 12:9-10; 13:4),[44] but the context suggests a more specific *primary* sense. Paul is "weak" when he is seemingly "unapproved" (ἡμεῖς δὲ ὡς ἀδόκιμοι ὦμεν, v. 7), not needing to demonstrate his apostolic authority by exercising discipline.[45] He is not weak in himself but only in relation to the Corinthians and only if he can come to them without rod in hand (cf. 1 Cor. 4:21); εἰς ὑμᾶς should be understood with ἀσθενῶμεν, so that "when we are weak [in our dealings with you]" is the opposite of "we shall be alive . . . , because of God's power, in our dealings with you" (εἰς ὑμᾶς, 13:4). Just as Paul recoils from the prospect of having to act decisively against the recalcitrant offenders in Corinth (v. 10), so he rejoices at the prospect of arriving in Corinth and finding the believers repentant and reconciled to him. If a specific sense is preferred for ἀσθενῶμεν,

---

40. G. Schrenk takes δικαιοσύνη in 9:9-10 to signify "right conduct worked out in acts of love" (*TDNT* 2.210). For the close association of δικαιοσύνη with ἀλήθεια, see Eph. 4:24; 5:9; 6:14. For ἀλήθεια as virtually equivalent to δικαιοσύνη, see Jas. 3:14; 5:19.

41. So Meyer 708; Plummer 367; Bultmann 248; Furnish 573, 579; Thrall 896-97.

42. In v. 8a there could be a polemical thrust, as Martin (483) and Barnett (611) suggest, for Paul's opponents were "false apostles" (11:13) and "false brothers" (11:26) who tampered with the truth (2:17; cf. 4:2) and declared a different gospel (11:4).

43. So Meyer 708; Plummer 278. But Scott regards the γάρ in v. 8 and in v. 9 as introducing a reason that Paul was more concerned about the Corinthians' well-being than about his own reputation (255).

44. Similarly Thrall 897, giving ὅταν the sense "whenever."

45. Meyer 708; Zerwick, *Analysis* 415; Hughes 483.

the matching term δυνατοί will also bear a particular meaning, namely having robust spiritual health, strong in the faith (cf. v. 5), strong in the Lord (cf. Eph. 6:10), and therefore not needing rectifying discipline (cf. vv. 2, 10).

But how is Paul's weakness related to the Corinthians' strength? Clearly the two concepts are contrasted — a fact confirmed by the emphatic ἡμεῖς–ὑμεῖς antithesis and the adversative δέ — and the weakness and strength are experienced simultaneously,[46] although (unlike 12:10) ὅταν is not followed by τότε. But it is not the case that Paul's weakness produced their strength,[47] unless the "weakness" were taken to be his self-expenditure for the Corinthians' welfare (cf. 12:15). Rather, his weakness resulted from their strength, for if the Corinthians were strong in Christ, reformed in attitude and conduct, Paul would have no occasion to use his apostolic power ἀποτόμως or εἰς καθαίρεσιν (v. 10).

As in v. 7a, Paul now gives a prayer report, "tacitly suggesting to a divided congregation that unitedly they join in his prayers for themselves" (Wiles 247). Whether τοῦτο looks back to δυνατοὶ ἦτε, his correspondents' "moral and spiritual strength" (Thrall 898), or forward to τὴν ὑμῶν κατάρτισιν (BDF §290 [3]) ("this . . . namely . . ."),[48] this latter phrase stands in epexegetic apposition to τοῦτο. Even if τοῦτο is prospective (as we believe), the κατάρτισις is closely related to the preceding notions of spiritual well-being (v. 9a) and the avoidance of wrong and pursuit of what is right (v. 7).[49] With εὐχόμεθα we must understand πρὸς τὸν θεόν from v. 7; it is a prayer addressed to God, not a request made to the Corinthians.[50]

Since κατάρτισις is a rare word in Greek and a *hapax legomenon* in the Greek Bible, its meaning is to be determined from cognate terms. (1) The verb καταρτίζω means basically "make ἄρτιος" (= "complete," "perfect," "exactly fitting"), and thus "adjust," "put in order," "restore,"[51] especially of the restoration of something to its former or its proper condition,[52] although it can also mean "prepare," "train," "equip." As a medical term it is used of the setting of broken bones; as a political term, it refers to the reconciliation of warring factions. (2) In

---

46. Some (e.g., Barclay, Cassirer) render δέ by "while." Others give δέ a conditional sense: "if" (TCNT, Moffatt, Goodspeed) or "if only" (NEB, NJB, REB).

47. However, a cause-effect relation is evident in two closely parallel passages. In 1:3-7 Paul's affliction (θλῖψις) and sufferings (παθήματα) actually lead to the Corinthians' comfort (παράκλησις) and salvation (σωτηρία), while in 4:12 his "death" (θάνατος) actually promotes their "life" (ζωή).

48. So also Robertson 698, who notes the difference in gender between τοῦτο and κατάρτισις.

49. That is to say, the καί with τοῦτο should be rendered by "indeed" (NEB) or "actually" (Isaacs) or "then" (REB), rather than by "also" (Weymouth, GNB) or "too" (Barclay). Prayer for κατάρτισις was not separate from Paul's preoccupation with the Corinthians' spiritual health (vv. 7, 9a).

50. But cf. Moffatt: "mend your ways, that is all I beg of you"; similarly Héring 102.

51. See LSJ 910 s.v.; BAGD 417-18 s.v.

52. E.g., 2 Esdr. 4:12 (of city walls); Ps. 79:16 (of a vine); Matt. 4:21 and Mark 1:19 (of fishing nets).

927

Eph. 4:12 the noun καταρτισμός, a NT *hapax,* may mean "training" or "perfecting" or "equipping," but only the second of these meanings would be apposite in 2 Cor. 13:9. In Isa. 38:12 (Symmachus) it means "restoration" or "reconciliation" (LSJ 910 s.v.). (3) ὁ καταρτιστήρ, a term never used in the Greek Bible, refers to "one who restores order." From these cognate words we may deduce that κατάρτισις signifies a "return to order" (Allo 340), "repairing what is broken and restoring what is lost" (Tasker 190), and rectifying shortcomings (cf. 1 Thess. 3:10). The most appropriate renderings of the term are "perfecting" (RV, Weymouth, Goodspeed), in the sense of being made complete (cf. BAGD 418a),[53] or, better, "restoration."[54] In the present context the reference would be to a "return to uprightness" (Héring 102), or, more specifically, to being set right with God, with Paul, and with one another.[55] The Corinthians needed to be restored to undivided and pure devotion to Christ (cf. 11:3), to uninhibited love for Paul (6:12-13; 12:15), and to harmonious fellowship with one another (cf. 12:20; 13:11). This κατάρτισις was a crucial aspect of their οἰκοδομή (10:8; 12:19; 13:10). Finally, the emphatic position of ὑμῶν[56] shows that Paul's focus, his pastoral preoccupation, was on *their* restoration, not his own vindication (cf. v. 7).

13:10 διὰ τοῦτο ταῦτα ἀπὼν γράφω, ἵνα παρὼν μὴ ἀποτόμως χρήσωμαι κατὰ τὴν ἐξουσίαν ἣν ὁ κύριος ἔδωκέν μοι, εἰς οἰκοδομὴν καὶ οὐκ εἰς καθαίρεσιν. "The reason I am writing these things when I am absent is that when I am present I may not have to deal severely with you as I exercise the authority which the Lord gave me for building up and not for pulling down." If 13:1-4 is basically a warning about impending discipline, 13:5-10 is essentially an exhortation to avoid that discipline. By indicating in v. 10 the purpose of his writing, Paul shows the intensity of his desire that the Corinthians should make his punishment unnecessary through their repentance and restoration.

διὰ τοῦτο ("this is why") may look back to ὑμεῖς . . . δυνατοί and τὴν ὑμῶν κατάρτισιν in v. 9. In this case Paul is writing in order to bring about the spiritual health and restoration of his correspondents. But in the other two places in Paul where διὰ τοῦτο is followed by a ἵνα clause (Phlm. 15; 1 Tim. 1:16), this phrase is prospective, "for this reason, (namely) that," so this understanding is preferable here.[57] That is, his aim in writing[58] is to avoid having to exercise stern disci-

53. The "perfecting" would relate, not to character (so Weymouth, Goodspeed, and Plummer 367), but to relationships — toward God/Christ, Paul, and other believers. Given the common assumption that in reference to persons "perfection" signifies "faultlessness" and "perfect" means "faultless," it seems unwise to translate τὴν ὑμῶν κατάρτισιν by "your perfection" (NIV) or ". . . that you may become perfect" (TCNT, NRSV) or ". . . that you should be made perfect" (NJB), although the paraphrase ". . . that you should grow towards perfection" (Cassirer) overcomes this difficulty.
54. Thus LSJ 910 s.v. I; Barrett 327; Furnish 573; Martin 451; Carrez 240; Thrall 871.
55. Cf. NEB: "Indeed, my whole prayer is that all may be put right with you."
56. See the commentary on 12:19.
57. So BAGD in three places (181b under διά; 377b under ἵνα; 597a under οὗτος); also Barrett 327, 340; Bultmann 249.
58. When Paul refers to his present writing by the use of the verb γράφω, sometimes he uses

pline. It is undoubtedly true, however, that his prayer for the Corinthians' spiritual vitality and amendment (vv. 7, 9) also reflects his purpose in writing. Those who treat διὰ τοῦτο as retrospective usually relate ταῦτα to all of chs. 10–13.[59] But if διὰ τοῦτο is prospective, ταῦτα may refer to a more restricted section within chs. 10–13 such as 12:19–13:4 or 10:1-11 (so Bultmann 249), although a wider reference to the whole canonical letter is possible (so also Barnett 614), provided his desire to avoid another painful visit is seen as part of his overall purpose to pave the way for a mutually pleasant and profitable visit.[60]

When χράομαι is followed by an adverb, it means "act" or "deal." ἐχρήσαντο . . . παρανόμως (Job 34:20), for example, means "they acted unlawfully." The adverb ἀποτόμως ("sharply,"[61] "severely," "rigorously"; cf. Tit. 1:13) points to "unsparing severity" (Barrett 340), "thoroughgoing sternness" (Meyer 709), or "inflexibly sharp judgment" (H. Koester, *TDNT* 8.108), so that ἀποτόμως χρήσωμαι may be translated "deal . . . severely" (Cassirer) or "act drastically" (Young and Ford 276). It was summary punishment of this sort that Paul longed to avoid. He had no desire to exercise his divinely given ἐξουσία in drastic, punitive action, but if circumstances demanded such action he would not shrink from it (οὐ φείσομαι, 13:2). The choice lay with his converts and depended on their responsiveness to his injunctions.[62]

In Paul's eyes a disposition of meekness (cf. 10:1) and a display of strength (cf. 13:2, 10) were not incompatible. If, as the adage puts it, "meekness is not weakness but harnessed strength," the use of power when occasion warrants it is no contradiction of meekness. Paul would have known that Moses, described as the meekest man on the earth,[63] was nevertheless capable of great anger and a display of his God-given authority (Num. 16:15-33). And Danker notes that "from a Jewish perspective, the conjunction [of meekness and vehemence] is in harmony with God's own display of wrath and power while engaged in the salvation of Israel."[64]

If in fact Paul found it necessary to act harshly against the Corinthians, he

---

the epistolary aorist (Rom. 15:15; 1 Cor. 9:15; Gal. 6:11; Phlm. 19, 21; cf. Rom. 16:22), sometimes the present (1 Cor. 4:14; 14:37; 2 Cor. 1:13; [9:1]; 13:10; Gal. 1:20; [Phil. 3:1; 1 Thess. 4:9; 5:1]; 1 Tim. 3:14; cf. 2 Thess. 3:17).

59. E.g., Windisch 424-25; Martin 485; Thrall 899-900.

60. Furnish alleges (580; similarly Windisch 424-25) that while v. 10 is a suitable statement of the purpose of chs. 10–13, "it is ill-suited as a description of the purpose of chaps. 1-9." The arguments he adduces in support of this assertion are adequately answered by Garland (551-52).

61. Noting that ἀποτόμως and ἀποτομία ("severity," Rom. 11:22) are derived from τέμνω ("cut"), Héring believes that ἀποτόμως χράομαι should be rendered by "cut to the quick" (102).

62. Commenting on Paul's earlier rhetorical question to the Corinthians, "Am I to come to you rod in hand or with love and a gentle spirit" (1 Cor. 4:21), Barrett (*1 Corinthians* 119) observes, "The question is whether love is to be expressed in gentleness or violence, and this will depend not on Paul's mood but on the Corinthian response to his admonition (verse 14)."

63. πραῢς σφόδρα παρὰ πάντας τοὺς ἀνθρώπους τοὺς ὄντας ἐπὶ τῆς γῆς (Num. 12:3). Cf. Sir. 45:4; Philo, *De Vita Mosis* 2.279.

64. Danker (149), citing Wis. 11:20-26; 12:1-27; Hos. 11:8-9; Pss. Sol. 8:28-34; 13:6-8.

knew that such action would still be in keeping with his apostolic authority and its primary aim of οἰκοδομή. This assumes that κατὰ τὴν ἐξουσίαν κτλ. qualifies ἀποτόμως χρήσωμαι.[65] Here the apostle is repeating almost verbatim what he said in 10:8.[66] Our discussion of these two passages at 10:8 arrived at the following conclusions: the ἐξουσία is apostolic authority given to Paul personally at the time of his conversion; ὁ κύριος is the Lord Jesus; οἰκοδομή refers to the act or process of building, involving individuals as well as churches; and — a conclusion particularly relevant in the present context — καθαίρεσις sometimes necessarily precedes οἰκοδομή, so that "destruction" and "upbuilding" are not mutually exclusive categories. But Kitzberger is correct to infer from εἰς οἰκοδομήν that οἰκοδομή describes "the content and goal of apostolic activity" (137).

From 13:5-10, then, we sense that as Paul writes the present letter and anticipates his next visit to Corinth, he experiences the same two emotions he felt when he wrote the "severe letter," sent it off to Corinth with Titus, and anticipated Titus's report on the situation — hope for the Corinthians' repentance and restoration (cf. 7:9-11), yet fear that they would not respond favorably to his pleas for action (cf. 7:5, 14).

The reasons for believing that 2 Corinthians was a successful letter and that Paul's promised visit to Corinth was not unpleasant are rehearsed in the Introduction under "The Occasion, Purpose, and Outcome of 2 Corinthians" (A.4.).

Bibliography

Brown • D. A. Carson, "Reflections on Christian Assurance," *WTJ* 54 (1992) 1-29 • Gundry Volf 217-25, 283-87 • Güttgemanns 142-54 • Heckel 44-47 • Kitzberger 134-38 • I. H. Marshall, *Power* 111-12 • Olson • Oostendorp 17-30 • W. Rebell, *Gehorsam und Unabhängigkeit. Eine sozialpsychologische Studie zu Paulus* (Munich: Kaiser, 1986) 143-45 • Wiles 241-48

D. Conclusion (13:11-13)

The majority of scholars maintain either that 13:11-13 forms the conclusion to chs. 10–13 (regarded as a distinct letter) or that these three verses are the ending of our canonical 2 Corinthians (regarded as a single letter). For alternative theories see the Introduction (A.3.a), Martin (492), and Thrall (4, 901). Verbal links between v. 11 and what precedes that would support these majority views are twofold: χαίρετε looks back to χαίρομεν (v. 9); καταρτίζετε picks up τὴν ὑμῶν κατάρτισιν (v. 9). Certainly there is an abrupt change of tone between vv. 10

---

65. Thrall (900), however, relates κατὰ τὴν ἐξουσίαν κτλ. to the preceding μή: Paul's aim is *not* to act harshly, an object that accords with the authority that was given him for his converts' edification, not their destruction.

66. Lambrecht has identified eight similarities between chs. 10 and 13 (158-59).

and 11, but such changes are not uncommon in Paul (see, e.g., 1 Cor. 16:21-22; Phil. 3:1-2) so that Mackintosh's claim (337-38) that the transition from 13:2b, 10 to 13:11 forms "an absolute *non sequitur*" is scarcely justified.

Weima has pointed out (209) that all four of the customary elements in Paul's letter closings are found in vv. 11-13: (1) exhortation (v. 11a); (2) peace benediction (v. 11b); (3) greetings (v. 12; EVV vv. 12-13); (4) grace benediction (v. 13; EVV v. 14). He also notes (208-9) that the transition to the closing hortatory section that is (typically) marked by the phrase λοιπόν, ἀδελφοί (v. 11) is followed by five present imperatives (as in 1 Cor. 16:13-14), imperatives that "all deal in one way or another with the problem of division in the Corinthian church" (209). For a chart that compares the various elements in the letter endings of all NT epistles, see Schnider and Stenger 75.

13:11*Finally, brothers and sisters, rejoice, work at your restoration, heed my appeals, have a common mind, cultivate peace, and the God of love and peace shall be with you.* 12*Greet one another with a holy kiss. All God's people greet you.* 13*The grace of the Lord Jesus Christ,[a] and the love of God, and the fellowship of the Holy Spirit,[b] be with you all.[c, d]*

TEXTUAL NOTES

a. A few witnesses (B Ψ 323 1881 *pc*) omit Χριστοῦ, perhaps to make this benediction conform to the (abbreviated) benediction in 1 Cor. 16:23 where the preferred, shorter text reads ἡ χάρις τοῦ κυρίου Ἰησοῦ μεθ᾽ ὑμῶν (see Metzger 503-4). But Thrall (921) makes a strong case for the possible originality of the shorter text in 2 Cor. 13:13.

b. p[46] omits ἁγίου.

c. The omission of ἀμήν after ὑμῶν has the crucial support of p[46] ℵ* A B F G 0243 6 33 630 1175 1241ˢ 1739 1881 *pc* sa bo[ms] Ambrosiaster, although some witnesses (ℵ² D Ψ 𝔐 lat syr bo) add ἀμήν (cf. Rom. 16:27; Gal. 6:18) to conform to liturgical practice. On the liturgical use of ἀμήν, see Deichgräber 25-27; H. Schlier, *TDNT* 1.335-36.

d. The original "subscription" to 2 Corinthians reads πρὸς Κορινθίους β (p[46] ℵ* A B* 33 *pc*), but subsequent witnesses add "(it) was written from Philippi" (B[c] L P 642 *al*) or "(it) was written from Philippi in Macedonia through Titus and Luke [as scribes and/ or messengers]" (K *al* Euthalius[mss]), with other MSS adding the name of Barnabas (201 205 209 328 337). See Metzger 519; Thrall 922 and n. 385.

13:11 Λοιπόν, ἀδελφοί, χαίρετε, καταρτίζεσθε, παρακαλεῖσθε, τὸ αὐτὸ φρονεῖτε, εἰρηνεύετε καὶ ὁ θεὸς τῆς ἀγάπης καὶ εἰρήνης ἔσται μεθ᾽ ὑμῶν. "Finally, brothers and sisters, rejoice, work at your restoration, heed my appeals, have a common mind, cultivate peace, and the God of love and peace shall be with you." With the phrase λοιπόν, ἀδελφοί (cf. Phil. 4:8) Paul introduces his concluding exhortations (v. 11a), greetings (v. 12), and benedictions (vv. 11b, 13). The adverbial expression (τὸ) λοιπόν is an accusative of respect, "with respect to what remains," "as far as the rest is concerned," and has a variety of meanings.[1] Here it points to concluding comments and means "finally."[2] This is the third use of the vocative ἀδελφοί in 2 Corinthians (see 1:8; 8:1; 12:19). Paul uses the term here in addressing the whole Corinthian congregation in order to remind them of the unity that believers have in Christ (note also μετὰ πάντων ὑμῶν in v. 13) and of the parity of status between all the sons and daughters (cf. 6:18) within God's family. They are family, and Paul, an apostle, is also their ἀδελφός. Although he occasionally uses ἀδελφός of one's neighbor (1 Thess. 4:6) or of his own kindred by race (Rom. 9:3), the term usually refers to fellow Christians (e.g., 8:23; 11:9; Rom. 8:29), and its conjunction with ἀγαπητοι,[3] or an expression such as ἠγαπημένοι ὑπὸ τοῦ θεοῦ,[4] gives it overtones of family love or God's paternal love.

With regard to the translation of χαίρετε, it is interesting to observe that most EVV render this imperative by "farewell"[5] or "good-bye"[6] while most commentators prefer the rendering "rejoice."[7] Now it is incontestable that χαῖρε (singular) and χαίρετε (plural) are a form of greeting used at a time of leave taking as well as of meeting.[8] But this is probably an instance where the commentaries are to be preferred over the translations. Several considerations support the rendering "rejoice."

1. χαίρετε heads a list of imperatives addressed to the readers/hearers, so it is likely that this is also an injunction directed to them (rather than Paul's saying "I bid you farewell"), especially since in a similar place in another Pauline letter χαίρετε clearly means "rejoice," being qualified by πάντοτε (1 Thess. 5:16).
2. NT parallels for the use of χαίρετε (or χαῖρε) as a farewell greeting are lacking, whereas on six occasions these words are initial salutations.[9]
3. In three places χαίρειν ("greeting!") stands at the *beginning* of a letter (Acts 15:23; 23:26; Jas. 1:1),[10] and in one of these cases the letter ends with ἔρρωσθε ("farewell") (Acts 15:29).
4. In 13:9 the verb χαίρω means "rejoice."
5. If χαίρετε meant "good-bye," one would expect it to be placed at, rather than near, the end of the letter.

1. See BAGD 480 s.v. λοιπός 3.b.; Moule 161; Thrall 25-30.
2. But some EVV take λοιπόν to be purely transitional: "And now" (NEB, GNB, NAB[1], REB).
3. 1 Cor. 15:58; Phil. 4:1; cf. Eph. 6:21; Col. 4:7, 9; Phlm. 16.
4. 1 Thess. 1:4; cf. 2 Thess. 2:13.
5. KJV, RV, RSV, NEB, NRSV, REB; Cassirer; also Plummer 380; Lietzmann 160.
6. TCNT, Moffatt, Goodspeed, GNB, NIV; also Barrett 341.
7. Windisch 426; Wendland 259; Allo 343; Héring 102-3; Hughes 486; Prümm 1.728; de Boor 254; Bultmann 249; Furnish 581; Carrez 242; Lang 359; Martin 490 note a., 498; Wolff 266; Lambrecht 227; Thrall 904, 906; also BAGD 874a; Weymouth, NASB, NAB[2].
8. See LSJ 1970 s.v. III.1-2.
9. Matt. 26:49; 27:29; 28:9 (χαίρετε); Mark 15:18; Luke 1:28; John 19:3.
10. Note also the expression χαίρειν λέγειν in 2 John 10-11.

Although the content of the rejoicing or its reason is not stated, perhaps we should supply ἐν κυρίῳ (as in Phil. 3:1; 4:4a). Like boasting (10:17), rejoicing has its principal focus on who the Lord is and what he has accomplished. In spite of the Corinthians' need for restoration (13:9) and in spite of Paul's threat of discipline (13:2, 10), they can and must rejoice "in the Lord."

At 13:9 (where the noun κατάρτισις occurs) we saw that the basic sense of καταρτίζω is "put in order," "restore."[11] Accordingly, if καταρτίζεσθε is middle (with a reflexive sense) it will mean "set yourselves in order," "aim for restoration" (Martin 490, 498-99), "mend your ways,"[12] or "put things in order" (NRSV). On the other hand, if this form is passive, the sense will be "be restored [by God]," where the passive is permissive (Windisch 426; Furnish 585), "let yourselves be restored," "cooperate in your restoration" (Thrall 904).[13] Either way, the action of the Corinthians is being called for. Paul's prayer for their restoration (v. 9) would be answered in part by their work in setting right what was amiss.

A similar uncertainty regarding voice arises with παρακαλεῖσθε. The renderings "encourage one another"[14] and "exhort one another"[15] construe the verb as middle; this meaning is, however, expressed by παρακαλεῖτε ἀλλήλους in 1 Thess. 4:18; 5:11. So we prefer the passive sense, "be exhorted," that is, "heed my appeals,"[16] or "accept admonition."[17] What exhortations or appeals might Paul be thinking of? He had exhorted them (παρακαλῶ/παρακαλοῦμεν) to reaffirm their love to the penitent wrongdoer (2:8) and not to receive God's grace in vain (6:1). Also, they were to heed his call for a decisive break with all idolatrous associations (6:14–7:1), for a warm reception and generous hospitality to be shown to the three delegates (8:24), for an enthusiastic and prompt contribution to the Jerusalem relief fund (chs. 8 and 9), for altered attitudes toward himself (chs. 10–13), and in general for readiness for his imminent visit.

The fourth and fifth imperatives belong closely together. τὸ αὐτὸ φρονεῖτε, literally "think the same thing," is a summons to "agree in the Lord" (Phil. 4:2, where the same expression occurs; cf. Rom. 12:16; 1 Cor. 1:10), to "have the mind of Christ" (1 Cor. 2:16), to share an identical outlook and common action. Dissension and strife still plagued the Corinthian believers (12:20). But living in agreement with one another would pave the way for the fulfillment of the next imperative. εἰρηνεύετε, "cultivate peace," is an injunction to

11. See also Spicq 2.18-20, 271-74.
12. Moffatt, RSV, NEB, REB; Lambrecht 227.
13. Renderings that involve the word "perfection" (e.g., Weymouth, "secure perfection of character"; NIV, "aim for perfection") are open to misunderstanding (see the commentary on 13:9).
14. NJB; Héring 102; Martin 490.
15. Barrett 341, but see 342.
16. Similarly RSV, NEB, NIV, NRSV, REB, Cassirer; Furnish 581; Lambrecht 227.
17. Thrall 904. Allo (343) renders καταρτίζεσθε and παρακαλεῖσθε together by "accept correction and exhortation."

pursue peace as though it were a quarry (τὰ τῆς εἰρήνης διώκωμεν, Rom. 14:19),[18] not only in relations within the church (Mark 9:50; 1 Thess. 5:13) but also in dealings with nonbelievers (Rom. 12:18).

All five imperatives are in the present tense, suggesting that Paul saw these virtues or actions as ideal Christian characteristics that were to be constantly cultivated before his arrival: rejoicing in the Lord, working for restoration, responsiveness to exhortation, unity of outlook and action, and the cultivation of peace. Taken as a whole, they summarize the preparation Paul hoped the Corinthians would make for his visit.

Several exegetical comments must be made about the final statement in v. 11, "and the God of love and peace shall be with you."

1. As in v. 13 (ἡ ἀγάπη τοῦ θεοῦ) and in the NT in general,[19] ὁ θεός refers to the Father.
2. The two genitives that follow ὁ θεός, namely τῆς ἀγάπης καὶ εἰρήνης, are descriptive: God is characterized by love and peace in the sense that these are divine attributes and also divine gifts.[20] Such an understanding of these genitives is supported by 2 Thess. 3:16 "Now may the Lord of peace (τῆς εἰρήνης) himself give you peace (τὴν εἰρήνην) continually and in every way."
3. The expression ὁ θεὸς τῆς εἰρήνης is found four times elsewhere in Paul,[21] but the phrase ὁ θεὸς τῆς ἀγάπης is, surprisingly, unparalleled elsewhere in the NT or in the LXX, although comparable ideas are found in both Testaments.[22] Paul's peace benedictions usually refer to God as "the God of peace." The unique addition of τῆς ἀγάπης here and its position before τῆς εἰρήνης were perhaps prompted by Paul's awareness that ἀγάπη was the main virtue absent from Corinthian relationships (cf. 1 Cor. 8:1; 12:31b–13:7) and that ἀγάπη was needed if they were comply with his admonition to "have a common mind" (v. 11a).[23] Also, a conjunction of ἀγάπη and εἰρήνη was natural since both are the fruit of the Spirit (Gal. 5:22; cf. 2 Tim. 2:22; Jude 2),[24] and just as τῆς εἰρήνης recalls εἰρηνεύετε (v. 11a), so τῆς ἀγάπης anticipates ἡ ἀγάπη in v. 13.[25]
4. When εἶναι μετά ("be with") is used of God's or Christ's presence with humans, it signifies the divine favor and aid as supporting some human

18. Paul is calling not merely for the absence of bickering but also for initiatives and efforts toward the restoration of peace (Depasse-Livet 11).

19. See Harris, *Jesus* 40-47, 271, 274-75, 282.

20. Cf. BAGD 357d: these genitives depict "what God brings about, in accordance w[ith] his nature."

21. Rom. 15:33; 16:20; Phil. 4:9; 1 Thess. 5:23; cf. 1 Cor. 14:33; 2 Thess. 3:16; and *Testament of Dan* 5:2 (for the only Jewish example).

22. E.g., Deut. 7:9; Ps. 17:7; Rom. 5:8; 1 John 4:8, 16.

23. Cf. Weima 92-93, 212.

24. Spicq, *Agape* 215.

25. Cf. Martin 500.

934

endeavor[26] or intervening in some human situation.[27] The particular form that this divine help would take in the present case was the granting of love and peace.

5. There are two ways of understanding the relation of v. 11b to v. 11a. If καί is given the sense "and then" (Weymouth),[28] its clause will state the result of seeking to follow the five preceding injunctions. τοῦτο ποίει καὶ ζήσῃ ("Do this, and [then] you will live," Luke 10:28) would be structurally parallel, with an imperative + καί + a future indicative.[29] Phil. 4:9b affords a precise structural and verbal parallel: . . . ταῦτα πράσσετε· καὶ ὁ θεὸς τῆς εἰρήνης ἔσται μεθ᾽ ὑμῶν. In 13:11 Paul would be suggesting, not that the divine presence was conditional upon or a reward for obeying his admonitions, but that God's presence was a natural consequence of obedience. Alternatively, v. 11b may specify the divine resources of love and peace that will enable the Corinthians to follow Paul's injunctions given in v. 11a (Barrett 343; cf. 9:8-11). This view, which is to be preferred, has the advantage of relating the two descriptive genitives (τῆς ἀγάπης and τῆς εἰρήνης) directly to v. 11a. God is not only characterized by love and peace; he also actually imparts these virtues to empower believers to fulfill what is required of them (v. 11a). Since the verb in v. 11b is an indicative (ἔσται), not an optative (εἴη), the statement Paul makes is in effect a promise.[30]

13:12 ἀσπάσασθε ἀλλήλους ἐν ἁγίῳ φιλήματι. ἀσπάζονται ὑμᾶς οἱ ἅγιοι πάντες. "Greet one another with a holy kiss. All God's people greet you." From the papyri we learn that ἀσπάζομαι was the regular term in contemporary letters for conveying greetings (MM 85-86). On occasion the verb meant no more than "pay respects to," but as used at the end of Paul's letters it refers to hearty Christian greetings, whether or not it is qualified by ἐν κυρίῳ πολλά (as in 1 Cor. 16:19). We may be tempted to believe that the aorist ἀσπάσασθε is significant since it is preceded by five present imperatives (v. 11a) and followed by the present indicative ἀσπάζονται (v. 12b). But this change to the aorist is probably without special significance (so Turner 75) since a (complexive) aorist imperative is regularly used in prayers and greetings (BDF §337[4]). Because Paul is writing to Christian believers, ἀλλήλους does not have a universal reference (= "anyone you meet") but refers to "each one of God's people in Christ Jesus" (Phil. 4:21).

---

26. E.g., Matt. 28:20; John 3:2; Acts 10:38; 18:10.

27. E.g., Luke 1:28; John 16:32; Acts 7:9 (cf. Gen. 39:2, 21).

28. For this use of καί, see BAGD 392 s.v. I.2.f.

29. Similarly Matt. 4:19; 8:8; Mark 6:22; Jas. 4:7, 10.

30. With justification, then, Héring (102) and Depasse-Livet (11) speak of 13:11b as "a benediction in the form of a promise." It should be noted that the term "benediction" may be used to include "both affirmations regarding the grace and peace of God in which they [Paul's readers] already participate [cf. v. 11b] and (wish-) prayers that they may appreciate and experience these blessings more fully [cf. v. 13]" (P. T. O'Brien, *DPL* 68).

In the phrase ἐν ἁγίῳ φιλήματι, the preposition may be instrumental or may indicate accompanying circumstances; either way, the appropriate rendering is "with (a holy kiss)." In the other three Pauline uses of this phrase ἁγίῳ follows φιλήματι (Rom. 16:16; 1 Cor. 16:20; 1 Thess. 5:26).[31] This kiss is "holy" for at least three reasons. (1) It is an expression of ἀγάπη (commitment to another's highest welfare),[32] not of ἔρως (or ἔρος) (erotic desire); in 1 Pet. 5:14 it is actually called φίλημα ἀγάπης. (2) It is a sincere kiss that signifies genuine fellowship in Christ, not an insincere kiss of deceit, as Judas's kiss was (Luke 22:48). (3) It is a kiss exchanged between οἱ ἅγιοι; note the movement from ἁγίῳ to ἅγιοι in this verse.

As well as expressing love and unity,[33] the "holy kiss" signified reconciliation (cf. Gen. 33:4; 45:15; Luke 15:20) and forgiveness, and so naturally came to be associated in the post-NT period with the celebration of the Lord's Supper,[34] perhaps under the influence of Jesus' word in Matt. 5:23-24.[35] In addition, the "holy kiss" exhibited Christian liberty, the transcending of divisions based on gender, race, and status, for the kiss was exchanged by male and female, Jew and Greek, slave and free (cf. Gal. 3:28). The initiative in giving the kiss could, apparently, rest with the female or the male believer.[36] Paul "was certainly the first popular ethical teacher known to instruct members of a mixed social group to greet each other with a kiss."[37] Paul's injunction was particularly relevant in Corinth where quarreling needed to be replaced by reconciliation, factionalism by unity, and arrogance by love (cf. 12:20). As to the origin of the practice in Christian circles, perhaps it was the concept of the church as a brotherhood of believers or as the family of God that led to the transference of the kiss given among physical relatives to a kiss exchanged between spiritual relatives in the Christian community.

ἀσπάζονται ὑμᾶς οἱ ἅγιοι πάντες. In many EVV ch. 13 is divided into fourteen verses, so that this sentence is v. 13 and the final benediction is v. 14.[38] But in other EVV,[39] and in WH, NA[27], and UBS[1-4], following the versification

31. The other three uses of φίλημα in the NT are Luke 7:45; 22:48; 1 Pet. 5:14.

32. Perhaps this is why Héring (103) renders the phrase, "with the Christian kiss."

33. When the Ephesian elders said farewell to Paul at Miletus, believing that they would never see his face again (cf. Acts 20:25, 38), they threw their arms around his neck and "covered him with kisses" (Bruce's rendering [Acts 437] of κατεφίλουν; cf. κατεφίλει in Luke 7:38), a sign of their love and respect and their unity in Christ.

34. On post-NT developments relating to the φίλημα ἅγιον, see G. Stählin, TDNT 9.142-45, who himself finds a link between the kiss and the Eucharist in 1 Cor. 16:20-24 (TDNT 9.139-40).

35. Perhaps it was such considerations that prompted the NEB and REB to render ἅγιον φίλημα by "the kiss of peace" (a patristic expression — see, e.g., Tertullian, De Oratione 18) in all four Pauline uses.

36. There is no reliable evidence that at the outset the kiss was exchanged only between elders or males, or only when the letter that mentioned it was read in the church.

37. W. Klassen, ABD 4.92; cf. "Sacred Kiss" 130. On the kiss in ancient Judaism and in Greco-Roman society, see G. Stählin, TDNT 9.119-27; W. Klassen, ABD 4.90-91.

38. KJV, RV, TCNT, ASV, Weymouth, Moffatt, Goodspeed, RSV, NEB, NASB, NIV, Cassirer.

39. GNB, JB, NAB[1], NJB, NAB[2], NRSV.

of the Greek text in 1551 by Robert Estienne, there are only thirteen verses, so that this sentence is part of v. 12 and the final benediction is v. 13. The division of 2 Corinthians 13 into fourteen verses seems to have begun with the second folio edition of the "Bishops' Bible" (1572) (Furnish 583).

If "all the saints" refers to Christians who are actually with Paul when he completes the letter,[40] they are probably Philippian believers.[41] Alternatively, the reference could be to believers throughout Macedonia,[42] including those in Philippi, Thessalonica, and Berea. Or again, οἱ ἅγιοι πάντες may signify the church as a whole, with Rom. 16:16 ("All the churches of Christ greet you") being a parallel expression. In his capacity as "apostle to the Gentiles" (Rom. 11:13) Paul was not reluctant to speak about and on behalf of "all the churches" (cf. 8:18; 11:28; 1 Cor. 7:17; 14:33). His work in connection with "the collection for the poor" put him in touch with believers in Galatia (1 Cor. 16:1), Macedonia (8:1-5), and Asia (cf. Acts 20:4). So Paul is probably conveying to the Corinthians the hearty Christian greetings of the whole church as he knew it, thereby reminding them of a wider Christian community who had a vested interest in the healthiness of the church in Corinth. He was not alone in seeking their welfare, and there were others to whom they were accountable.[43]

13:13 Ἡ χάρις τοῦ κυρίου Ἰησοῦ Χριστοῦ καὶ ἡ ἀγάπη τοῦ θεοῦ καὶ ἡ κοινωνία τοῦ ἁγίου πνεύματος μετὰ πάντων ὑμῶν. "The grace of the Lord Jesus Christ, and the love of God, and the fellowship of the Holy Spirit, be with you all." Instead of concluding his letter with a generalized wish such as is found in contemporary letters (e.g., ἐρρῶσθαι ὑμᾶς εὔχομαι, "I pray you may fare well"), Paul closes with a benediction in the form of a wish.[44] Compared with his other closing benedictions, this verse contains two distinctives: (1) He refers not only to χάρις but also to ἀγάπη and κοινωνία; (2) he refers not only to the Lord Jesus Christ but also to God and the Holy Spirit.[45]

The genitive in the first element of the triad is clearly subjective. Salvation and all its associated blessings (χάρις) were brought (8:9) and are being brought (12:9) by Christ. But although in Pauline benedictions Christ is the sole source of χάρις, in Pauline salutations (including 1:2) God the Father and Christ are generally mentioned as the joint source of χάρις.[46] This illustrates the

---

40. Cf. similar references in 1 Cor. 16:20; Phil. 4:21.

41. For a discussion of the place of writing, see the Introduction B.3.b. and Textual Note d. above.

42. Cf. 1 Cor. 16:19, "The churches of Asia send greetings."

43. Cf. Weima 212-13.

44. 13:11b was a benediction in the form of a promise (see n. 30 above).

45. Contrast this with Rom. 16:20b; 1 Cor. 16:23; Gal. 6:18; Phil. 4:23; 1 Thess. 5:28; 2 Thess. 3:18; Phlm. 25. These passages and others that do not explicitly link χάρις with Christ are conveniently set out in chart form in "Table 1. *Grace Benedictions*" in Weima 80. For a general discussion of these "grace benedictions" in Paul, see Weima 78-87; Maleparampil 84-87.

46. Rom. 1:7; 1 Cor. 1:3; Gal. 1:3; Eph. 1:2; Phil. 1:2; 2 Thess. 1:2; 1 Tim. 1:2; 2 Tim. 1:2; Phlm. 3. The exceptions are Col. 1:2; 1 Thess. 1:1.

point that the χάρις, ἀγάπη, and κοινωνία that are attached to the three persons mentioned in this verse should not be thought of as exclusive characteristics. Other examples of this fact would include the phrases ἡ χάρις τοῦ θεοῦ (1 Cor. 1:4), ἡ ἀγάπη τοῦ Χριστοῦ (5:14; Rom. 8:35), ἡ ἀγάπη τοῦ πνεύματος (Rom. 15:30), and κοινωνία . . . Ἰησοῦ Χριστοῦ (1 Cor. 1:9). But why, in this embryonic trinitarian formulation, do we find the unexpected order, Christ-God-Spirit? Three reasons may be suggested for the "priority" of Christ in this triadic structure. (1) Paul began the benediction with his customary reference to "the grace of (our) Lord Jesus (Christ)" and then expanded it. (2) Christ's grace is the means by which God's love reaches the believer. As Paul expresses it in Rom. 8:39, nothing can separate believers "from the love of God that is revealed in [the grace of] Christ Jesus our Lord" (ἀπὸ τῆς ἀγάπης τοῦ θεοῦ τῆς ἐν Χριστῷ Ἰησοῦ τῷ κυρίῳ ἡμῶν). The third element of the triad also is dependent on the first. It was through the grace of Christ exhibited in the cross that God demonstrated his love (Rom. 5:8) *and* that believers came to participate in the Spirit's life and so form the community of the new Age. (3) The verse does not describe relationships within the Trinity but the chronological order (so to speak) of the believer's experience of God: we come to Christ and so encounter God and then receive his Spirit.

Without embarrassment Paul has conjoined the Lord Jesus Christ and the Holy Spirit with God in a benediction, just as God the Father and Christ are presented in 1:1 as forming a single source of divine grace and peace. In both cases parity of status between Christ and God is implied by the juxtaposition, for it would be blasphemous for a monotheistic Jew to associate a mere mortal with God in a formal, religious salutation or benediction. But these are not the only evidences in the Pauline epistles of a high christology. That Paul believed in the deity of Christ is also indicated by his description of Christ as sharing the divine nature (Rom. 9:5; Phil. 2:6; Tit. 2:13) and attributes (Eph. 4:10; Col. 1:19; 2:9), as being the object of saving faith (Rom. 10:8-13) and of human and angelic worship (Phil. 2:9-11), as being the addressee in petitionary prayer (1 Cor. 1:2; 16:22; 2 Cor. 12:8), and as exercising exclusively divine functions, such as creational agency (1 Cor. 8:6; Col. 1:16), the forgiveness of sins (Col. 3:13), and final judgment (1 Cor. 4:4-5; 2 Cor. 5:10; 2 Thess. 1:7-9).[47]

Although ἡ ἀγάπη τοῦ θεοῦ could mean "love for God" (objective genitive),[48] parallelism with the preceding phrase and the appropriateness of expressing a divine blessing in a benediction favor taking τοῦ θεοῦ as a subjective genitive. Paul is expressing his wish and prayer that the love God has already poured out (Rom. 5:5) and demonstrated (Rom. 5:8) may continue to fortify his readers. He realized that only by fresh infusions of divine love would they be able to heed his appeals (παρακαλεῖσθε, v. 11a). This wish,

47. See further Harris, *Jesus* 315-17.
48. Cf. ἡ . . . ἀγάπη τοῦ Χριστοῦ (5:14; see the discussion there).

therefore, functions in the same way as the assurance of the presence of ὁ θεὸς τῆς ἀγάπης does in v. 11b in relation to the injunctions of v. 11a; the one enables the other.[49] As elsewhere in Paul (and the NT) (ὁ) θεός signifies the Father.[50]

The most difficult exegetical problem in this verse arises from the phrase ἡ κοινωνία τοῦ ἁγίου πνεύματος. If the genitive is subjective, the sense will be "the fellowship with one another that is engendered by the Spirit" or "the participation granted by the Spirit in himself" or "the sense of community created by the Spirit." Arguments adduced in support of such an interpretation are as follows.

(1) Given the close parallelism between the three elements in the triad (viz. an articular abstract noun in the nominative followed by an articular personal noun in the genitive, with two cases of a conjunctive καί), it is antecedently probable that the third genitive will function in the same way as the first and second, that is, as a subjective genitive.[51]

(2) Such a view accords well with the context. If the Spirit fostered fellowship between the Corinthian believers, the harmony, reconciliation, and unity that Paul longed for (v. 11a) would be achieved. Moreover, the activity of the Spirit is highlighted throughout 2 Corinthians.[52]

(3) The concept of believers' personal communion *with* the Spirit is an unparalleled Pauline notion, whereas the idea of the Spirit's creating unity among believers finds a close parallel in Eph. 4:3, ". . . making every effort to maintain the unity engendered by the Spirit (τὴν ἑνότητα τοῦ πνεύματος) by binding peace on yourselves." Cf. also 1 Thess. 1:6, μετὰ χαρᾶς πνεύματος ἁγίου, "with joy inspired by the Holy Spirit" (RSV, NRSV).

On the other hand, if the genitive is objective[53] we could render the phrase "participation in the Holy Spirit" (Barrett 341; Furnish 581), or "communion with the Holy Spirit" (Thrall 904; cf. TCNT). How has this view been supported?

---

49. There is an interesting parallel to the movement from ὁ θεὸς τῆς ἀγάπης (v. 11) to ἡ ἀγάπη τοῦ θεοῦ (v. 13) — albeit in reverse order — in Philippians 4, where Paul speaks first of ἡ εἰρήνη τοῦ θεοῦ (Phil. 4:7), then of ὁ θεὸς τῆς εἰρήνης (Phil. 4:9).

50. The only exceptions in Paul are Rom. 9:5 (of Christ); 1 Cor. 8:5 (twice); 2 Cor. 4:4; Gal. 4:8b; Phil. 3:19; 2 Thess. 2:4a; Tit. 2:13 (of Christ). See further Harris, *Jesus* 45-46, 271, 275.

51. Those who argue this way include Plummer 383-84; Schlatter 682; Champion 131-32; Tasker 191-92; Hughes 489-90; Spicq, *Agape* 217; Bruce 255; Zerwick and Grosvenor 563; Schneider, "II Cor. 13:13" 440; Maleparampil 95. Others who support the subjective genitive sense include Héring 103; Ladd 588; Belleville, "Polemic" 289-90; Scott 265.

52. See Belleville, "Polemic" 281-304; Martin, "Spirit" 113-28.

53. Supporters of this view include Meyer 710-11, 711 n. 1; Lietzmann 162; Windisch 428; Seesemann 72-73, followed by Kümmel 214; F. Hauck, *TDNT* 3.807; Goodspeed, *Problems* 170; Moule 41; Hermann 136-37; Barrett 344-45; Furnish 584; Wolff 269; Martin, "Spirit" 127 (but cf. his earlier commentary 491 note i, 506); Thrall 904, 919. This view may be held without embracing Kramer's proposal that the third element of the triad is Paul's addition to a binitarian creed that involved two subjective genitives (20b).

(1) Although κοινωνία has a wide range of meanings in the NT,[54] when it is followed by a genitive, it is usually synonymous with μετοχή or μετάλημψις and means "participation (in)," "a partaking of," and the genitive specifies the object in which one partakes.[55] Thus κοινωνία . . . τοῦ αἵματος τοῦ Χριστοῦ . . . κοινωνία τοῦ σώματος τοῦ Χριστοῦ (1 Cor. 10:16), "participation in the blood of Christ . . . in the body of Christ."[56] Even when that "object" is personal, κοινωνία can still signify a "sharing in": ἐκλήθητε εἰς κοινωνίαν . . . Ἰησοῦ Χριστοῦ, "you were called to share in [the life of] . . . Jesus Christ" (cf. NEB, REB)/"to have fellowship with . . . Jesus Christ" (GNB) (1 Cor. 1:9).

(2) 1 Cor. 12:13 affords a close conceptual parallel to this phrase. After speaking of an outward "immersion in the Spirit," the verse speaks of an inward participation in the Spirit. "For in one Spirit we were all baptized into one body — Jews or Greeks, slaves or free — and we were all given one Spirit to drink."

(3) The closest verbal parallel to our phrase is in Phil. 2:1, εἴ τις κοινωνία πνεύματος, which in all probability means "if any participation in the Spirit."[57]

(4) This view, too, suits the context. Common participation in the one Spirit would promote harmony and dispel factionalism (cf. 12:20; 13:11), just as adherence to the one name of the Lord Jesus Christ prompted unity and banished dissensions (1 Cor. 1:10).

Some argue that both the subjective and objective senses are implied or intended.[58] In his *EDNT* article on the κοιν- root, which draws on his earlier monograph *(KOINONIA)*, J. Hainz argues for a unified structure in Pauline usage of the word group: "fellowship/partnership (with someone) through (common) participation (in something)" (*EDNT* 2.304).[59] ἡ κοινωνία τοῦ (ἁγίου) πνεύματος he renders by "the *partnership* [through common participation] of the (Holy) Spirit" (*EDNT* 2.305). But it is not clear that the notions of fraternal fellowship created by the Spirit and common participation in the Spirit could be

54. See BAGD 438-39 s.v. On the κοινων- root in the LXX and NT, see Schneider, "II Cor. 13:13" 423-27.

55. On possible constructions with κοινωνία in Greek, see F. Hauck, *TDNT* 3.798; J. Hainz, *EDNT* 2.303.

56. Cf. 2 Cor. 8:4; Phil. 3:10.

57. See O'Brien, *Philippians* 172-74; Martin, "Spirit" 115.

58. Thus Prümm 1.732; McDermott 223-24; Schneider, "II Cor. 13:13" 422, 440, 446; Panikulam 70, 75 (apparently); Barnett 618 (but cf. 618 n. 14); Maleparampil 95, 106, 111. It seems unnecessary to create a separate category of genitival usage to accommodate cases where both the objective and subjective senses could be implied or intended (as D. B. Wallace does ["Plenary Genitive"] in his *Greek Grammar Beyond the Basics: An Exegetical Syntax of the New Testament* [Grand Rapids: Zondervan, 1996] 119-21, although he does not cite 2 Cor. 13:13 as a possible example).

59. Cf. his *Koinonia* 54, 61 (as cited by Martin 491, 505).

simultaneously present in our phrase. Schweizer seems to be on safer ground when he opts for the subjective sense — "the 'Spirit's giving of a share (in Himself)' "[60] — but adds "which may well include brotherly fellowship too. Materially this amounts to the same thing as the exposition in terms of an obj[ective] gen[itive]" (*TDNT* 6.434).[61]

Clearly the evidence supporting the two main options[62] is rather evenly balanced, although I believe the arguments for the objective sense are slightly stronger. Paul is expressing a wish that the Corinthians should continue (cf. 1 Cor. 1:7; 12:13) in their common participation in the Spirit's life, power, and gifts (cf. 1 Cor. 12:7; 14:1). Yet this "participation in the Spirit" inevitably results in an ever-deepening fellowship among believers.

The presence of πάντων in the phrase μετὰ πάντων ὑμῶν (cf. 2 Thess. 3:18; Tit. 3:15) is significant. No sections of the Corinthian church — not even the rebellious elements — were excluded from Paul's benediction.[63] Does it also suggest that he expected a positive response to his letter, as earlier to his "severe letter" (cf. 7:14)? With this final phrase we should understand the optative εἴη[64] rather than the indicative ἐστίν or the imperative ἔστω.[65]

It is a singular paradox that a letter so full of indignation, remonstrance, and gyrating emotions should conclude with the most elevated trinitarian affirmation in the NT[66] couched in the form of a benediction addressed to all the members of a factious church.

---

60. Similarly Depasse-Livet 13; Spicq, *Agape* 217-18 (the Spirit gives himself to believers, infusing them with Christian virtues and communicating to them all the blessings of salvation).

61. "Practically the two meanings coincide" (Denney 809).

62. It is highly unlikely that τοῦ πνεύματος is an adjectival or attributive genitive, "spiritual fellowship" (as suggested by A. Souter, *A Pocket Lexicon to the Greek New Testament* [Oxford: Clarendon, 1916] 136; and P. C. Bori, *KOINΩNIA: L'idea della communione nell' ecclesiologia recente e nel Nuovo Testamento* [Brescia, 1972] 98 ["spiritual communion"], as cited by McDermott 227). Nor should κοινωνία πνεύματος be treated as equivalent to πνεῦμα κοινωνίας, as Di Marco 63-75. It is impossible to know whether an objective or a subjective sense is intended in the common English translation, "the fellowship of the Holy Spirit" (Weymouth, Moffatt, RSV, NASB, GNB, JB, Barclay, NAB¹, NIV, NJB, NAB², REB).

63. Cf. Weima 82.

64. The singular εἴη would agree with the nearest subject or with the three subjects regarded as a whole. The forms εἴησαν and εἶεν are not found in the NT.

65. See Weima 83-84. But Schneider takes the statement of v. 13 to be both affirmative and optative. The Corinthians had already received the grace of Christ, the love of God, and the fellowship of the Spirit; Paul is praying and wishing that they "open themselves ever more to Christ, to God, to each other" ("II Cor. 13:13" 440-41; quotation from p. 441). On the textual question involving ἀμήν, see Textual Note c.

66. Of course this affirmation is far removed from any formal doctrine of the Trinity, but here and elsewhere in the NT (e.g., Matt. 28:19; John 14:16-17; 1 Cor. 12:4-6; 2 Cor. 1:21-22; Gal. 4:6; Eph. 4:4-6; 1 Pet. 1:2; 1 John 4:2) we have the building materials that were incorporated into the final edifice. Historically, we may say that the doctrine was initially generated by the "overlapping binitarianisms" found in the NT (namely God and Christ, God and the Spirit, and Christ and the Spirit). See R. R. Williams, "Overlapping Binitarianisms in the New Testament," in *Studia Evangelica*, Vol. 5.2: *The New Testament Message*, ed. F. L. Cross (Berlin: Akademie, 1968) 30-36;

Bibliography

Belleville, "Polemic," especially 288-90 • Campbell • Champion 25-37, 128-32 • Cuming • Depasse-Livet • Di Marco • Doty 39-43 • Fee, "Gospel" 130-32 • Fee, *Presence* 362-65 • Goodspeed, *Problems* 169-70 • Hainz, *Koinonia* 47-54 • M. Hengel, "Das Bekenntnis zum dreieinigen Gott (2. Kor. 13,11-13)," *ThBeitr* 16 (1985) 195-200 • Hermann 135-38 • G. Jourdan, "ΚΟΙΝΩΝΙΑ in 1 Corinthians 10:16," *JBL* 67 (1948) 111-24 • Klassen • Maleparampil 79-112, 237-60 • Martin, "Spirit" • McDermott • T. Y. Mullins, "Benediction as a NT Form," *AUSS* 15 (1977) 59-64 • Panikulam 58-79 • Richards • H. Riesenfeld, "Was bedeutet 'Gemeinschaft des Heiligen Geistes'? Zu 2. Kor. 13,13; Phil. 2,1 und Röm. 8,18-30," in Y. Congar (ed.), *Communio Sanctorum* (Geneva: Labor et Fides, 1982) 106-13 • Ross • Schneider, "II Cor. 13,13" • Schnider and Stenger 76-167 • Seesemann • Spicq, *Agape* 2.215-18 • Thraede • W. C. van Unnik, "'Dominus Vobiscum': The Background of a Liturgical Formula," in A. J. B. Higgins (ed.), *New Testament Essays: Studies in Memory of T. W. Manson* (Manchester: Manchester University, 1959) 270-305 • von Dobschütz • Wainwright 241-42 • Weima 78-101, 208-15 • J. A. D. Weima, "The Pauline Letter Closings: Analysis and Hermeneutical Significance," *BBR* 5 (1995) 1-22

---

and Maleparampil 247-48. On triadic formulas in Paul, see Windisch 429-31 (and the comments of Bultmann 252 and Thrall 915-16); von Dobschütz 117-47; Wendland 260-61; Lang 360-62; and especially Maleparampil 237-60.

Expanded Paraphrase of 2 Corinthians

In preparing an expanded paraphrase of the Greek text that reflects the exegetical decisions arrived at in the commentary and that gives special attention to the connections of thought and transitions, I have benefited from the earlier work of this nature by A. P. Stanley (1855), A. Plummer (ICC) (1915), W. H. Isaacs (1921), J. W. C. Wand (1946), J. B. Phillips (1958), and F. F. Bruce (*Paraphrase,* 1965).

1This letter comes from Paul, a special envoy of Christ Jesus commissioned by the will of God, and from our Christian brother and colleague Timothy who is well known to you all, and is addressed to the church of God as it is found in Corinth, along with all of God's chosen and holy people who live anywhere in the province of Achaia.

2May you experience in ever-increasing measure the grace and peace that come jointly from God our heavenly Father and our Lord Jesus Christ.

3May the God and Father of our Lord Jesus Christ receive his due honor, love, and praise! As a Father his compassion is unparalleled, and as God he is the one source of true comfort and encouragement. 4For he it is who always comforts and encourages us in all our distressing experiences. He does so for this express purpose — that we may always be able to comfort and encourage those in any kind of distress by bringing them the same comfort that we ourselves constantly receive from the very hands of God. 5We can mediate the divine comfort in this way because the sufferings we endure as a result of our union with Christ and service for him are multiplied in our lives and through Christ our experience of God's comfort is correspondingly multiplied to the same extent. 6Either way you stand to gain: Our experience of affliction has in view your encouragement amid affliction and your spiritual well-being; similarly, our experience of God's comfort is designed to ensure your encouragement and comfort — your comfort which energizes you to endure patiently the same kind of sufferings as we also endure. 7So then, our confident expectation about your spiritual welfare remains unshaken, knowing as we do that when you share in Christ's sufferings you will assuredly also share in the divine comfort.

8Why am I telling you about God's comfort in the midst of affliction? This is why: As you know, we recently experienced a severe affliction in the province of Asia. I do not want you, my brothers and sisters, to remain unaware of its severity. So severe was this affliction, in fact, that we were excessively crushed and were driven beyond our power of endurance. 9The result was that we were forced to abandon even any hope of survival. Yes, in our own mind we ourselves felt we had already been sentenced to death, but this experience of coming to the end of our tether was intended to force us to quit relying on our own resources and rely solely on the God who restores the dead to life. 10For it was God who rescued us from these immense and distressing encounters with death by a veritable resurrection, and he will rescue us yet again; rather, I should say that we have fixed our hope on him for future deliverance, 11which will come about provided you, for your part, work together with us and for us by your intercession. If so, then thanksgiving that is offered by a multitude of persons will arise to God on our behalf — thanksgiving for God's gracious gift of deliverance and preservation granted to us in answer to the prayers of many people.

12Now this is what we are proud of and our only reason for boasting — the indisputable testimony given by our conscience that all our conduct before people in general and more particularly before you has been guided by that purity and sincerity that have their source in God. Our action has been dictated and marked not by ordinary human cleverness but by God's grace. 13aFor it has always been my habit to write only what you can immediately recognize as true when you read it; there is no hidden meaning lying below the surface. 13b-14At present, you have come to know and understand our motives and intentions only in part, but it is my eager hope that you will soon come to see with full clarity that it is as appropriate for you to be proud of us now as it is for us to be proud of you on the Day when the Lord Jesus comes.

15So confident was I of this mutual esteem that I had a plan in Ephesus to visit you first of all so that you might have the advantage of a double visit from me: 16One visit on my way to Macedonia and another when I returned to you from Macedonia and was helped forward by you as I traveled on to Judea. 17Now that you know that my plans changed, tell me this: When I made my plan to pay you a double visit, was I guilty of fickleness? Do I make my plans tongue in cheek and as the mood suits, so that my "Yes" means "No" and my "No" means "Yes"?

18God is my faithful witness — our words to you have never been inconsistent, an ambiguous blend of "Yes" and "No." 19The model I follow is the Son of this faithful God, namely Jesus Christ, who was proclaimed among you by the three of us, by me, Silvanus, and Timothy. With regard to his own promises, God did not vacillate between "Yes" and "No"; rather, his assured "Yes" has taken effect in Christ. 20For however many promises God may have made, they all find their corresponding "Yes" in Christ who fulfills them. This is why our "Yes" of concurrence and commitment, our answering "Amen," goes up to God through Christ and brings God glory through us. 21And it is none other than this God who causes us, along with you, to be firmly established in our relationship to Christ, the Anointed One, and who consecrated us all for his service. 22This same God sealed us as his own protected possession when he placed his Spirit in our hearts as the deposit and guarantee of our full inheritance.

23Now to return to my particular case, let me tell you precisely why I refrained from returning to Corinth as I had intended. I call as my witness this faithful, unchanging God of whom I have just spoken — and my life will be forfeit if I lie — that the reason for the cancellation of my visit was not fickleness or duplicity but to avoid causing further pain. 24I am not implying that in making these decisions that involve you I have control over you with regard to your faith, for you are established in your faith quite independently of any human. What I *do* imply is that I am committed to working with you to promote your joy. 2This being so, I resolved in my own mind not to put you or myself through the sorrow of another painful visit in person. 2For if I, the promoter of your joy, cause you pain, then who else is there to cheer my spirits except you — those very people who are pained by me? 3Moreover, I wrote as I did, instead of coming myself, precisely so that I could avoid a visit that would prove painful to me, the pain coming from those who ought to have been a constant source of joy to me. You will understand that I had, and have, sufficient confidence in you all to know that if I have joy, that joy is shared by all of you. 4Now the letter that I wrote you instead of another visit arose from intense affliction and anguish of heart, and I shed many tears while writing it. My purpose was certainly not to cause you pain. Rather, it was to make you aware of how profound is my concern and care for your welfare.

5If the behavior of a certain person has been a cause of pain, let it be said that he caused pain not so much to me, but to some extent — not to exaggerate or overstress the matter — he has injured all of you. 6The punishment which the majority of you imposed on the person in question is sufficient in the circumstances. 7So now, instead of adding to the penalty, you should do the opposite and turn and forgive and restore him to his place among you. If you fail to do this for him, a person in his situation runs the risk of being engulfed by excessive remorse. 8I therefore plead with you, not to censure him further but rather to reassure him plainly and formally of your loving acceptance of him. 9This too was exactly why I wrote to you instead of coming — to put you to the test and see whether you are obedient in all respects. 10Now rest assured that when you do forgive this man, I too do the same. Indeed, whatever forgiveness I for my part granted him, if such was necessary, was given for your sake and under Christ's watchful eye. 11I forgave him, and ask you to do the same, in order to avoid letting Satan gain any further advantage over us, for we are fully cognizant of his nefarious intentions and particular stratagems in these circumstances.

12There was a time, not too long ago, when I was anxious about your obedience to me. When I arrived at Troas, my aim was to proclaim the gospel of Christ; to be sure, remarkable opportunities for preaching were opened up by the Lord's overruling. 13But in spite of this, I experienced a deep restlessness of

945

spirit that prevented my grasping these opportunities, because I was disappointed not to find my brother Titus there — Titus, who was to bring news about you. So, instead of preaching there, I said farewell to the believers in Troas and set off across the Aegean for Macedonia to meet Titus as soon as possible.

14But thanks are due to God because, as always, through our union with Christ he honors us with a place in his triumphal procession as his willing prisoners, and wherever we go he uses us as his instruments to diffuse that sweet odor which is the personal knowledge of Christ. 15As those who proclaim Christ, we are an aroma of Christ that rises up to God in heaven like sweet-smelling incense, whether we are working among those who are enjoying the benefits of salvation or among those who are not and so are perishing. 16In the case of the latter group, this odor is experienced as a deadly stench and so leads to death for them, whereas for the former group, this odor has a life-giving fragrance and so produces life for them. 17To be a sweet fragrance of Christ is an awesome responsibility. Who could possibly be qualified or adequate for such a daunting task? Through God's grace, we are! For unlike most teachers, we are not fraudulent hucksters, making a profit out of proclaiming God's message and adulterating it at the same time. On the contrary, we act in a sincere and straightforward manner. When we deliver our message, it is as persons who have been commissioned by God, who remember that we are accountable to him, and who work under the supervision of Christ.

3Since I claim, by God's grace, to be qualified to proclaim a message that involves eternal issues of life and death, some of you may be thinking that I am flaunting my credentials all over again. Surely I do not need, as some people apparently do, letters of recommendation that are addressed to you or are written by you? 2Why, we need no such letters, for it is you yourselves who are our commendatory letter, a letter that is indelibly engraved on our very hearts and that is open for anyone anywhere to peruse and read. 3It is apparent to all that you are a letter composed by Christ and transcribed by us, written not with ink that can be erased but by the Spirit of the ever-living God whose work cannot be erased; and written not, as the Law was, on lifeless tablets of cold stone, but on the living tablets of sensitive human hearts.

4The confidence we have that we speak from God and that we had a part in the production of Christ's letter in Corinth is no illusion: It is a confidence that comes through Christ and that stands up before God. 5There is no question of our being confident that on our own authority we are qualified to claim credit for any results of our ministry. 6No, the only but adequate qualification we have to minister comes from God himself. He is the one who in reality has qualified us, by his commission and equipping of us, to serve as his agents in promulgating the new covenant spoken of by Jeremiah. This covenant has as its hallmark not some outward, lifeless written law but the Spirit of God living and active within his people. Indeed, that written law is simply an instrument of death as it prompts sin, whereas the Spirit infuses life into believers, both now and in the age to come.

7Now if the Law's dispensation that brought death, which was engraved in letters as a written code on tables of stone, was accompanied by such dazzling glory that the Israelites could not look unflinchingly at Moses' face because of its radiance, even though it was a fading glory, 8how much more certainly will the dispensation of the Spirit be attended by divine glory! 9For if the dispensation that pronounces condemnation on people was itself an expression of God's glory, surely the dispensation that puts people in the right before God will far exceed that earlier dispensation in glory. 10In fact, with regard to this matter of glory, the former order of things that once seemed so resplendent seems now to have no splendor at all when it is compared with the superlative and surpassing glory of the new order. 11For if an order that was doomed to fade away (like the glory on Moses' face) was inaugurated amid glory, how much more must the order that is destined to last forever be accompanied by divine, permanent glory!

12So, then, we have a confident expectation that the new covenant which is incomparably glorious will endure forever. This confidence gives us great openness and freedom in speech and action. 13We do not act the way Moses did, for he was in the habit of veiling his face in order to stop the Israelites from prolonging their amazed, intent gaze at his face until the very end of what was gradually but relentlessly fading away. 14But their ability to perceive the significance of the fading glory and the veiling was impaired. What is more, to this very day, whenever the Jews hear the old covenant read publicly in their synagogues, the same veil of ignorance concerning the temporary nature of that old covenant still lies over their minds. This impenetrable veil remains unlifted, because only when they come to be in the Messiah is the veil set aside. 15The fact is that down to this day whenever the Law of Moses is read in their hearing, a veil of ignorance and misapprehension lies over their hearts. 16However, just as Moses removed his veil whenever he entered the presence of the Lord, so now, whenever someone — Jew or Gentile — turns to the Lord, the veil that prevents their seeing the truth is removed from their heart. 17Now what is meant by "the Lord" in this scriptural passage is the Spirit of the new covenant, and where the Spirit of the Lord is present and active, there is not bondage but freedom, freedom from the veil of ignorance about Christ and freedom of access into God's presence without fear. 18All Christians have a glory like that of the unveiled Moses: Without a veil on our faces we all gaze at the glory of God in the person of Christ as in a mirror, and so we are progressively transformed into that self-same image of Christ in ever-increasing degrees of glory, and so we reflect his glory. This work of transformation comes from the Lord, that is, the Spirit.

4It is because of the Spirit's transforming work under the new covenant, and in particular because we have been entrusted with this glorious ministry (the result of God's mercy shown to us), that we do not slacken in our efforts to carry out our commission. 2On the contrary, from the very first we have repudiated all conduct that could be described as secretive or disgraceful — or, to put it another way, we have always refused to adopt crafty techniques and we have always refused to falsify God's word by dishonest manipulation. Rather, we state the truth candidly and boldly, as we seek to commend ourselves and our teaching to the conscience of every last person. And all of this takes place under God's all-discerning eye. ₃But if there still is a "veil" covering the meaning of the good news that we openly and boldly proclaim, the veil is found not everywhere and is not of our making; the veil lies over the hearts only of those who even now are perishing, ₄for in their case, another god, the god who rules over this present evil age, has effectively blinded their understanding, unbelievers as they are. His nefarious aim is this: To prevent them from gaining the illumination that comes from the gospel — the gospel which displays the glory of Christ, who himself is the visible and exact representation of God. ₅Indeed, the glory of Christ, because it is certainly not our own selves that we proclaim in the gospel; it is Jesus Christ as the risen and glorified Lord. As for us, we present ourselves to you as simply your slaves, in the service of Jesus who himself, as our example, adopted a slave's role. ₆This attitude of service is appropriate because it is the God of creation who said in the beginning, "Let light shine forth from the darkness," who has now, as the God of the new creation in Christ, flooded our hearts with light, the enlightenment that comes from knowing God's glory that is emblazoned on the face of Christ.

₇So, then, we have been entrusted with a priceless treasure, the glorious gospel of Christ. Yet this treasure is contained in earthenware jars that are fragile, unattractive, and relatively worthless. But this is to make it evident to all that the incomparable transforming and staying power of this gospel is God's and does not derive from us. ₈Troubles press on us from every quarter, but we are never hemmed in and crushed; often bewildered by circumstances, but never driven to utter despair. ₉We are relentlessly pursued or persecuted by others, but never abandoned by God; often knocked to the ground, but never permanently "grounded." ₁₀Wherever we go, we carry around in our body a "dying" such as Jesus experienced, so that, simultaneously, the resurrection life of Jesus may be put on display in this same body by the divine deliverance we experience and the fortitude we are enabled to show. ₁₁What I am saying is this: We, who are very much alive, are in fact being constantly delivered (by God) into the hands of death on Jesus' account, so that at the same time Jesus' powerful risen life may be displayed in this weak and transitory human frame. ₁₂And so it is that death is operative in our body, whereas life is at work in your experience.

₁₃There is a scriptural passage that says, "I believed, and therefore I spoke." We have the same spirit of faith as the psalmist did, and this explains why we also have a belief that leads to speech, a faith that cannot remain silent. ₁₄Another reason why we faithfully preach Christ is our sure knowledge that the God who raised Jesus from the dead will raise us in our turn by virtue of Jesus' resurrection and will safely bring us into his immediate presence, side by side with you. ₁₅Yes, all that we do (such as our preaching) and all that happens to us (such as our suffering) serves to promote your good, so that after grace has broadened its scope through the conversion of an ever-increasing number of people, it may cause thanksgiving to God to reach flood proportions, which will lead to his greater glory.

16So then, with this task of seeking your welfare and God's glory, it is no wonder that we do not become discouraged or grow lax in our ministry. Instead, although our body with its physical powers is progressively decaying, yet our inner person is being rejuvenated day after day. 17For our present afflictions might seem burdensome and prolonged, but they are in fact insignificant and momentary when compared with the undiminished load of glory that these afflictions are producing for us to a degree that is beyond all measure and proportion. 18Yes, they seem light and temporary afflictions because our gaze is focused not on those things that belong to the world of sense and can be perceived by the eye, but on realities that are at present unseen; for what can be seen belongs to the realm of time and is transient, but what cannot be seen is destined to last forever.

5For it is part of our Christian tradition that if this earthly body which we call a tent-house is destroyed by death, we have the assured hope of receiving a building that God supplies, a house that is not constructed by human hands, that is destined to last forever, and whose site is heaven. 2What is more, being housed in this tent we constantly sigh with longing because we yearn to put on over it, as someone would don an overgarment, our dwelling that is supplied from heaven. 3This presupposes, to be sure, that once we have put on this new dwelling, our spiritual body, we shall never experience disembodied nakedness. 4For it is a fact that as those who still live in this present temporary dwelling, we sigh under a burden of oppression because, so far from wishing to be divested of all embodiment, we desire to put on the overgarment of the heavenly body, so that our present body which is subject to death may be completely swallowed up by immortality. 5Now the one who has prepared us for this very experience of putting on immortality is none other than God himself, and his preparation was his giving us the Spirit as a pledge of this transformation.

6For this reason we never cease being confident in every circumstance; however, because we realize that as long as we are resident in this present body, we are absent from our home with the Lord — 7for we do indeed conduct our lives in the realm of faith, not yet in the realm of sight. 8We are always confident, I repeat, and it is our settled preference to leave our present home in this body and to take up our final residence in the immediate presence of the Lord. 9In accordance with this preference we make it our aim constantly to be approved by him, whether we are resident in this earthly body or absent from it and in his presence. 10For by God's decree, all of us without exception will stand before Christ's tribunal without any pretense, so that every last one of us may be duly requited for actions that we have carried out during our life on earth, whether those actions be good or worthless.

11We are fully aware, then, of our accountability to the Lord as our judge, and so we regard him with reverential awe. So we endeavor to persuade everyone of the truth of the gospel and of our integrity as messengers of the gospel. What we are and what our motives are have always been open to God's scrutiny; and I hope these things are abundantly clear to your consciences as well. 12No, it is not the case that we are trying, all over again, to commend ourselves to you and to justify ourselves before you. On the contrary, we are affording you with a solid and suitable basis for taking real pride in us and championing our cause, so that you may have ample ammunition against our opponents who constantly pride themselves on position and privilege rather than on the state of the heart. 13If, to some people, we have seemed insane, it was for God's glory. If, on the other hand, we are in full control of our senses, it is always for your good. Either way, selfishness is excluded, 14for the example of Christ's love controls our actions and leaves us no choice but to serve God and you. The conclusion we reached long ago was this: That one person died for all, and therefore in one sense all died — his death was their death. 15And the reason for his death for all? He died so that those who enjoy newness of life in him should quit living for themselves and live wholly for the one who himself both died and rose again for them.

16The death and resurrection of Christ have produced two further results. First, for the future, we refuse to estimate anyone by the external standards of the world. Indeed, even if before our conversion we thought of Christ from the standpoint of the world as a mere human being and as a messianic pretender, now we no longer view him that way. 17Second, whenever people are united in faith to the risen Christ, God performs a new act of creation and they are altogether new persons. In fact, the old state of affairs has entirely disappeared and a brand new order has come into existence for all to see.

18This new situation is wholly God's doing, for he is the one who restored us to his favor through the work of Christ and entrusted us with the task of announcing this reconciliation. 19Its essence is this: God was present in Christ and operative through him when he was reconciling humankind to himself, no longer debiting people's offenses to their account. And the obligation and privilege of declaring this message of reconciliation God has entrusted to our care. 20So we are acting on Christ's behalf and in his place as his special envoys. It is, in reality, God himself who issues his appeal through our words. As Christ's representatives, then, we make this entreaty when we preach: "Get reconciled to God!" 21How did that reconciliation come about? Christ was totally devoid of sin. Yet God caused him to be sin on our behalf and in our place, so that as a result of being united with Christ we might become righteous before God.

6As coworkers in God's service, we issue this appeal to you: Whenever you receive God's grace, do not let it be without profit. 2For in Scripture the Lord says this:

"At the time appointed by me to show you favor, I listened to your cry, and on the day appointed by me to bring you salvation, I came to your aid."

950

Listen carefully: The present age is the time when God's gracious favor is shown; the present era is the time when God brings salvation.

₃In all our work we are striving to avoid putting any obstacle in anyone's way, so that no one may have reason to discredit or ridicule our service for God. ₄Instead, as genuine servants of God, we are endeavoring so to live and work that in every regard our conduct may be commendable, as we show the utmost patience in situations of affliction, necessity, and distress; ₅or when we are beaten, imprisoned, and mobbed; or at those times when we are burdened with work, sleepless nights, and fasting. ₆Further, we commend ourselves by our innocent behavior and pure intentions, our knowledge of the truth, our endurance of wrongs, and our kindness of heart; also by exercising the gifts of the Holy Spirit, by showing unaffected love, ₇by declaring the message of truth, and by exhibiting God's power. The weapons we wield are those of righteousness for the right hand (attack) and for the left (defense), ₈all the while persevering amid honor and dishonor, ill repute and good repute. We are regarded as deceivers, though in reality we are true and speak the truth; ₉we are treated as "nobodies" who are ignored, yet what we are is well known; we are constantly at death's door, and yet (as is evident to all!) we are well and truly alive; we stand under God's discipline, but our lives are spared; ₁₀we are burdened with sorrow, but our joy is inextinguishable; we may be desperately poor ourselves, but we enrich many others; we may have next to nothing to call our own, and yet we have everything of significance secure in our possession.

₁₁My dear Corinthian friends, we have been speaking to you freely, not keeping anything back. We have thrown our heart wide open, hiding nothing from you. ₁₂If there is any restriction of affection between us, it lies on your side, not on our side. ₁₃I am looking only for an equivalent return on my investment (after all, I have the right to speak to you as my children): My heart is wide open; you must open wide your hearts too, and remove that restriction.

₁₄But there are limits to that wide-heartedness. Do not get harnessed in a mismatched union with unbelievers. Think about it! What possible partnership can exist between righteousness and unrighteousness? Or what do light and darkness have in common? Nothing! ₁₅What meeting of minds could there ever be between Christ and his followers and the devil and his? Or how can a believer become a partner with an unbeliever? ₁₆What accord can the temple of God ever have with lifeless idols? For he is a living God and we — yes, we — are his temple. This is what he meant when he said: "I will dwell in their midst, I will move among them; I will be their God, they shall be my people." ₁₇So come out from among the unbelievers and be totally separate from them and their evil ways (says the Lord). Have nothing to do with what is unclean. "If you obey these commands, I will receive you as my own ₁₈and be a father to you, and you shall be sons and daughters to me," says the all-sovereign Lord. 7So then, my dear friends, these momentous promises are ours. Therefore let us keep clear of everything that may defile either body or spirit, without or within, and let us bring to completion our consecration to God by having a reverential awe and holy dread before him.

2Let me repeat: Make room for me in your affections. (Remember, I have made room for you!) And why not? There is no one at all whom I have ever wronged or ruined or defrauded. 3I am not putting you in the wrong when I say this; I have already told you that you have an assured place in my heart — so much so that we are together, come death, come life. 4In what I am saying to you I am being perfectly frank, but know also that I boast about you to others no less frankly. So it is that even in the midst of all the affliction that I have to bear, I am comforted to the full and overflow with joy.

5For indeed, even after I had arrived in Macedonia, my body gained no relief at all from the troubles that beset me. Far from it; hardships confronted me on every side: Conflict raged around me and anxiety reigned within. 6But God, who always stands ready to bring comfort and encouragement to those who are downcast, comforted and encouraged me by the arrival and company of Titus. 7But it was not only the comfort of his presence that delighted me, but also hearing about the great encouragement he had received at your hands, for he brought a welcome report of how you longed to see me and be reconciled to me, how you were deeply sorry over your disloyal behavior, and how eagerly you made amends for the past. All this added to my delight.

8The truth is, although I realize that I caused you sorrow by my most recent letter, I do not now regret having written it. Even if at one stage I did regret it — I am aware that I did cause you real sorrow with that letter, though that sorrow was short-lived — 9now I am glad about the whole matter, not regretful. I am not glad because you were caused sorrow, but glad that your sorrow led to your repentance. For yours was the kind of sorrow that God approves of and sets a limit to. As a result you came to no harm because of my letter. 10For sorrow that is according to God's will and borne in God's way produces a repentance that leads to salvation and will never be viewed with regret. On the other hand, sorrow that is characterized by the world's attitudes and borne in the world's way produces deadly effects.

11Just look, for example, at your own experience, at the effect that sorrow has when it is according to God's will and borne in God's way! Look at the zealous concern it produced in your hearts, what eagerness to clear yourselves from blame, what indignation with the guilty party, what alarm over your behavior and its results, what longing to see me in person, what zeal in following my instructions, what resolve to see justice done through the punishment of the wrongdoer! In every one of these points you have put yourselves in the right with regard to this unpleasant matter. 12So then, although I decided to write to you in the strong terms that I did, it was not principally to get the wrongdoer punished or to secure redress for the wronged party. It was for your benefit — to make it perfectly clear to you all in the sight of God what a zealous concern you in fact have for us. 13It is this response of yours to my letter that has brought me such comfort and encouragement.

But in addition to the comfort that all this gave us, we found a further reason for special delight in witnessing Titus's joy; for he was greatly relieved and refreshed in spirit by the warm welcome you all gave him. 14I had, in fact, boasted a little to him about you, and I have had no reason to be embarrassed by that boasting. On the contrary, just as all that we have ever said to you has been the unvarnished truth, so too all that we said in praise of you in the hearing of Titus has proved to be nothing but the truth. 15So it is that his deep feelings of affection for you grow stronger and stronger as he recalls the ready obedience shown by all of you in the way you received him with fear and trembling, knowing that you were accountable to God for your conduct. 16I am full of joy that I can now be confident of you in every regard.

8Now, my dear brothers and sisters, I would like to draw your attention to God's grace that has been and still is being shown among the churches of Macedonia. 2They were undergoing a severe testing of their faith brought on by hardships. Nevertheless, even in these dire circumstances, their boundless joy, coupled (surprisingly!) with their rock-bottom poverty, has overflowed in magnificent liberality and generosity. 3The truth is, they contributed to the collection fund, as I can testify, not merely as far as their resources would allow but even beyond those resources, and what is more, they acted on their own initiative, without my prompting and without pressure from me. 4With urgent appeals they pleaded with us that they might be permitted, as a favor to them, to share in this task of bringing relief to God's people in Jerusalem. 5And the size and extent of their giving were not what we had expected. On the contrary, they gave themselves to the Lord first and foremost, and they also put themselves at our disposal; both of these acts were in obedience to God's will. 6The upshot of all this was that we have encouraged Titus to visit you again. Already he has made an auspicious start with you on the collection; now we want him to bring to a successful completion the present gracious work in addition to his previous service.

7Well now, my friends, you know that you are rich in spiritual blessings of every kind — in strong faith, eloquent speech, and deep knowledge, in wholehearted earnestness and enthusiasm, and above all in the rich love that was generated by our preaching and now is evident in you. You must now ensure that you are equally rich in the grace of generosity.

8In saying this I am not issuing a command or laying down a rule that you must obey. I am, however, seeking to elicit evidence of the genuineness of your own love as well, by appealing to the example of the eager cooperation shown by the Macedonian believers. 9Giving commands is out of place; you do not need to be reminded of the example given by our Lord Jesus Christ, who was immeasurably generous. Though he was rich in his heavenly, eternal glory, it was for your sake that he became extremely poor in his earthly, human state, in order that you, yes you, might become incalculably rich as a result of his poverty.

10On this matter of participation in the collection, I am giving you no command but only my considered opinion and advice, for this is the appropriate way to treat you. After all, it was you who led the way last year by giving the Macedonians an example to follow, not only by taking action in giving, but even before that, by wanting to do so. 11Now, however, I want you to finish carrying out the project as well. This will mean that the completion of the project, using the resources that you have, will match the eagerness of desire that you showed at the outset. 12Where there is such an eagerness to give, God accepts the gift and judges its value in relation to whatever people have at their disposal, not in relation to what someone does not have.

13Our aim in this whole enterprise is not that other people should get relief from their financial burdens at the cost of your financial hardship. No, our concern is for the equalizing of burdens. 14In the present circumstances of special need in Jerusalem, you have a considerable surplus of resources that can be applied to their deficiency of resources, so that on some future occasion their surplus will in turn serve to supply your deficiency. The purpose will be equality of provision, 15a point made in the scriptural account of the manna. "The person who had much did not have anything extra, and the person who had only a little did not have any shortage."

16I am very grateful to God for putting into the heart of Titus a zeal for your welfare as enthusiastic as my own. 17Evidence of his eager desire for you may be found in the fact that he readily consented to my appeal. What is more, because he is very eager to help, he is setting off to visit you on his own initiative. 18And we are sending as his colleague the well-known brother whose services in spreading the gospel are highly praised throughout all the churches of Macedonia. 19But not only does he have a fine reputation. These churches have formally appointed him to be our traveling companion and helper in connection with this benevolent gift that we are administering to promote the Lord's own glory and as a token of our own goodwill toward our fellow believers in Jerusalem and our eager readiness to help them. 20In acting this way we are trying to take every precaution to ensure that no one will have any reason to find fault with us in the way we handle this large sum of money that we are administering. 21For we are making careful arrangements to do what is right and honorable, not simply from God's perspective but also from the perspective of men and women.

22Moreover, along with Titus and the brother just mentioned we are sending another Christian brother of ours. He is someone whose diligence and earnest devotion we have been able to test and prove in many circumstances and on many occasions. In the present matter that diligence and that earnestness of his are all the stronger owing to the total confidence that he has in you. 23If questions are raised about the credentials of Titus, remember that he is a partner of mine who has shared in my labors regarding you. If questions are raised about the two brothers we are sending with Titus, know that they are delegates of the Macedonian churches and each of them is a trophy of Christ's grace. 24So then, give these men visible and clear proof that your Christian love is genuine and that my boasting about you was true, so that the churches they represent can see your fine Christian conduct.

9For, first of all, with regard to this charitable contribution that is designed to help the poor Christians in Jerusalem, it is superfluous for me to dwell further on this topic as I write to you. 2For I know full well how willing and eager you are to help with this relief aid. Indeed, I have been boasting about your eager willingness to the Macedonians here. I have been telling them with pride that you in Achaia have been standing ready since last year. As a result, the infectious example of your zeal has stirred the majority of them into action. 3But, second, I am sending Titus and the two church delegates just to ensure that my forthright boasting about your eagerness and readiness may not prove to be simply empty words in this matter of the collection, and also to ensure that you are in fact fully ready, just as I was assuring them you would be. 4Otherwise, if some Macedonian visitors were to come with me on my visit to you and find your collection not complete, we would perhaps be embarrassed and ashamed — to say nothing of your shame — because of our confident boasting about you. 5To avoid such a thing from happening I considered it necessary to urge these three brothers to visit you before I come and organize the completion of this generous gift before my arrival — a gift that you have already promised. I want it to be ready as a result of their visit, as a generous gift that brings blessing and not as a gift that reflects avarice and so is given grudgingly.

6What I am saying is summed up in the farming axiom: If you sow sparingly, you will also reap a meager harvest; but if you sow on generous principles, you will also reap a bountiful harvest. 7I want each of you to give just what you have already resolved in your mind to give. Don't give regretfully, as though giving involved a painful loss, nor under pressure, as though giving were compulsory. Such giving would be pointless, for God loves and prospers the person who gives cheerfully.

Indeed, God is fully able to shower you with every kind of blessing in plentiful measure, so that in all circumstances and at all times you may have total sufficiency for your own needs and at the same time abundant means to carry out good work of every kind to others. 9That is precisely what Scripture says about the generous person:

He scattered his gifts far and wide; he freely gave to the needy.
His deeds of piety will continue as long as he lives.

10God is the one who bountifully produces seed for people to sow and thus bread for them to eat, so he will certainly provide and multiply seed for you to sow and he also will increase the harvest produced by your deeds of piety. 11You will be enriched by God in every way, and this will enable you to show all kinds of generosity. Your generosity will be such that, when it is channeled through this relief fund I am administering, it will be sure to produce a harvest of much thanksgiving to God on the part of the recipients.

12For when you and other contributors perform this act of public service, you are not merely meeting the physical needs of the poor among God's people in Jerusalem. In addition, your giving will overflow in a flood of thanksgiving to God. Indeed, this service of giving will provide such unmistakable evidence of your love and the genuineness of your faith that people will glorify God, praising and worshiping him for two things — first, that you are obedient to the implications of the gospel of Christ as the result of confessing your faith in its truth, and second, that you are generous in sharing your material resources with them, and, as opportunity arises, with everyone in need. 14What is more, your fellow believers in Jerusalem and elsewhere will pray for you, and their hearts will be drawn to you in yearning love because God's grace rests on you in such marvelous measure. May God be praised for *his* gift of Christ and the salvation he brought, a gift that no words can adequately describe!

10Now it is I myself — Paul — who is making a personal appeal to you on the basis of the gentle meekness and unfailing forbearance of Christ — I, whom you imagine to be a timid creature when actually face to face with you but bold and supercilious at a safe distance. 2What I am begging of you is this: Don't force me, when I am present with you, to display that bold forthrightness and confidence that I have in mind to dare to use against certain members of your congregation who imagine that we think and act in a worldly and unspiritual manner. 3For though we lead ordinary human lives, the campaign in which we are engaged is not dependent on human resources. 4For the weapons we fight with are not the ordinary ones of this world. On the contrary, they are superbly effective in God's service for the demolition of the strongholds that oppose the gospel. With these divine weapons we demolish bastions of argumentation 5and every presumptuous idea that raises itself up to oppose the knowledge of God given in the gospel of Christ. What is more, with these weapons we take every rebellious thought and plan of action into captivity in order to achieve its total submission and obedience to Christ. 6Finally, with these weapons we are fully ready to punish any and every act of disobedience or disloyalty once your own total obedience and loyalty are evident.

7Squarely face what are plain facts. If there is someone who is quite sure in his own mind that he beyond everyone else belongs to Christ, let him think again on his own initiative and come to realize this fact: Just as surely as he belongs to Christ, so too do we belong to Christ as his apostle and slave. This is no flight of fancy, for if I seem to boast a little extravagantly about my apostolic authority which the Lord conferred on me — authority designed to build you up, not tear you down — I shall not be shamed by this projected boasting of mine. 9I mention this matter of not tearing you down lest I should appear to you to be attempting to strike terror into you, so to speak, by means of my correspondence. 10For, to quote my critics, "His letters are overwhelming and strongly worded; his physical presence, however, is altogether unimpressive and feeble, and his rhetorical skills are contemptible." 11People who say this kind of thing must reckon with this fact: There is no difference, only an exact correspondence, between what we are like in words through the letters we write when we are away from you, and what we will be like in our actions when we are present with you.

12Some of you accuse me of being "timid." Indeed, we are not sufficiently "bold" to pair or compare ourselves with certain individuals who indulge in self-commendation and self-justification in an effort to establish their own reputation. But they show how foolish they themselves are by measuring themselves against their own standards and by comparing themselves with one another within their own group. 13For our part, however, we shall not set up our own standard and boast outside our legitimate limits. Rather, in our boasting we shall adhere to our limit which is the mission assignment that God has meted out to us as a limit for our work — and that assignment certainly includes you at Corinth. 14For we are not exceeding the limits of our jurisdiction as though you are not included within my legitimate sphere of activity. Why, we were the first to reach all the way to you as bearers of the good news about Christ. 15As I have said, we do not boast outside our legitimate limits, infringing on territory assigned to others and taking credit for their work. We are hopeful, however, that as your faith continues to grow, we may experience, with your help, an enlargement of our work and influence — still in accord with our assigned sphere of activity, of course — an expansion on a grand scale. 16What I mean is: We hope to preach the good news in regions that lie beyond you in the west. So then we shall never need to boast outside our legitimate limits with regard to another person's assigned sphere and work already carried out there. 17Only one type of boasting is legitimate: "Let the person who boasts boast about the Lord's accomplishments." 18It is not the person who commends himself and so fails to honor the Lord who is approved of by the Lord. It is the person whom the Lord himself commends who gains real approval.

11I know it is foolish to boast, but I dearly wish that you would tolerate me when I engage in a little foolishness that I deem necessary at this time. Yes, please do try to tolerate me as I do this. 2And why should you put up with me? First, because I have a deep jealousy over you like God's own jealousy for his people: I betrothed you to one husband and one only, and my aim is to present you to him at the End in virgin purity — I refer, of course, to Christ. 3But in spite of that hope I have a real fear that somehow your thoughts and attitudes may be corrupted and you get to be enticed away from your original singleness of purpose and purity in relation to Christ, your heavenly bridegroom, in the same way that the serpent completely deceived Eve by his cunning half-truths. 4Second, you show exquisite toleration toward the newcomer who arrives on your scene preaching another Jesus than the Jesus I preached, or if you receive a different Spirit from the Spirit you actually did receive or a different gospel from the gospel you actually accepted. 5Third, you should be tolerant toward me, for I reckon that I am not in any way inferior to those "superlative" apostles you hear about. 6True, you may think I am an amateur in rhetorical skills, and I am, but in knowledge that is worth having — knowledge of divine truth — I am certainly no amateur. On the contrary, in all our relations with you we have made this perfectly clear in a wide variety of situations.

7Or was it a grievous wrong that I did when I took a humble place so that you might occupy an exalted place? I am referring to the fact that I proclaimed to you the good news from and about God — news beyond price — without accepting any payment or reward. 8This was possible only because I plundered churches other than yours, and so impoverished them, for I accepted their contributions to my traveling and living expenses so that I could serve you entirely free of charge. 9And when I was staying with you and found that my resources had dried up — even then I did not burden anybody. For all my needs were fully met, you remember, by those brothers when they arrived from Macedonia. Yes, right up to the present I have, in every respect, refused to become a burden on you, and I will continue to refuse to do so. 10I appeal to Christ's own truth that is in me when I assure you that as far as I am concerned no one anywhere throughout Achaia is going to silence this boast of mine that I preach without payment and remain financially independent. 11And why this inflexible stand? Is it because I do not love you, as some wrongly imagine? God knows how much I love you. 12The course I have been following of being financially independent of you, I shall continue to pursue, so that I can eliminate the opportunity that my rivals so dearly want of being considered by you as no different from myself in the matter of their much-vaunted apostleship, both of us receiving support from you.

13Equality with such people is out of the question, for they are counterfeit apostles, men who work cunningly and deceitfully by passing themselves off as Christ's true apostles. 14Their tactics are not at all surprising when we remember that Satan, that arch-deceiver, also regularly adopts the disguise of a shining angel sent by God. 15It is nothing extraordinary, then, if Satan's agents also wear a disguise, passing themselves off as agents promoting righteousness. But their disguise will be stripped away, for their final destiny will match their evil actions.

16Once again I appeal to you: Let none of you get the idea that I am a fool when I indulge in some foolish boasting. However, if you do see it that way, at least show me the tolerance and patience you would show a fool, so that I may do a little boasting of my own, just as others do. 17But in doing this I am not speaking with the Lord's specific authority and at his direction, but in this business of confident boasting I am playing the part of a fool. 18Since so many others are making a practice of boasting of their pedigree and accomplishments, I will do the same. 19You are so wise yourselves that you take pleasure in tolerating fools! 20That is obvious, for you even put up with whatever my rivals choose to do to you — with those who take complete control of you, those who eat up your resources, those who inveigle you into their power, those who treat you with arrogance, those who hit you in the face. 21aAs for our treatment of you, I am ashamed to confess that we must have seemed very weak in comparison with them!

21bI may have been "weak" in comparison with my rivals, but in whatever area any of them makes a bold claim, there I am bold too. (I say this as a fool, of course.) 22Consider nationality and heritage. Do they pride themselves on being Hebrews? I am one too. Israelites? So am I. Lineal descendants of Abraham? I am their equal there too. 23Consider service. Do they claim to be servants of Christ? Here I am speaking with extreme folly: I not only match them but far surpass them as a true servant of Christ, with my labors far surpassing theirs, with my imprisonments far more numerous, with beatings far surpassing theirs, and with frequent brushes with death. 24Consider these other sufferings. On five occasions I was given the regulation thirty-nine strokes of the lash at the hands of the Jews. 25Three times I was beaten with rods by the Romans. Once I was stoned. Three times I suffered shipwreck. I have spent a whole night and day adrift on the open sea. 26Again and again I have undertaken perilous journeys, my life imperiled while crossing rivers, in encounters with bandits, in attacks from my fellow countrymen and from the Gentiles. I have faced danger in crowded cities and in desolate country, danger on the sea, and danger among counterfeit brothers. 27I have served Christ in strenuous labor and exhausting toil, with sleepless nights beyond number amid hunger and thirst, many times undergoing fasts, and enduring cold and lack of clothing. 28Quite apart from many other bodily hardships which I pass over, there is a pressure that weighs heavily on me every day — I refer to my anxious concern for my fellow believers in all the churches. 29What brother or sister is weak in any way, and I do not share their weakness? What brother or sister is caused to stumble, and I do not burn with distress and with anger at the person who caused this?

30If there has to be still more boasting, my choice is to boast now about things that show up my weakness. 31The God and Father of the Lord Jesus — God who is entitled to eternal praise — knows that I am speaking the unadorned truth in saying that 32when I was in Damascus the representative of King Aretas kept guards at the gates of the city of the Damascenes so as to capture me. 33However, I escaped from his clutches through the action of some of my friends who lowered me in a basket through a narrow opening in the city wall.

12I must carry on boasting; you forced me to it. Such boasting brings no real benefits to me or to anybody else. Nevertheless I will move on to another subject — visions and revelations given to me by the Lord Jesus. 2Here is one such vision. I know a Christian man who, some fourteen years ago, was transported right up to the third heaven. Whether it was a physical experience or a spiritual encounter, I simply do not know; God alone knows. 3But what I do know is that this man I am speaking about — whether his experience was physical or spiritual, I do not know; God alone knows — 4was transported into Paradise, into God's presence. There he heard divine words that cannot be expressed in human language, divine words that human beings are not permitted to utter. 5I am willing to boast about a man like that, but I have decided not to boast of anything personal, except with regard to my weaknesses. 6Yes, I have decided not to boast about myself, but if I do choose to boast this way I shall certainly be seen to be no fool, for what I say will be the sober truth, solid fact. But in fact I do refrain from such boasting, because I want to be sure that no one forms a higher opinion of me than is warranted by what they see in my conduct or hear from my lips. 7The revelations God gave me were extraordinarily wonderful. So, to prevent me from becoming unduly elated about these, God gave me a painful physical ailment that was also a messenger from Satan sent to harass me, to prevent me from becoming unduly elated. 8On three different occasions I prayed to the Lord Jesus about this ailment, begging him to make it depart from me. 9But his answer to me has been this: "My grace is adequate for all your needs; in fact, my power is most potent in the midst of your weakness." So then, I now very gladly boast of my weaknesses rather than asking the Lord to remove them — weakness I gladly confess to having — so that the power of Christ may rest upon me and form its protective cover over me. 10That is why I take pleasure in my weaknesses, such as random insults, dire privations, persecutions, and desperate situations, endured for Christ's sake. For it is precisely when I experience and acknowledge my weakness that through Christ I am truly strong.

11I have been making a fool of myself in doing this boasting, but the fault is yours, not mine. You it was who forced me to do it. You have been harboring and endorsing my opponents when you should have been giving me your loyal support and vocal approval. You owed me this, for even though I am a nonentity I have not proved inferior to those superlative Jerusalem apostles in any respect. 12The signs of genuine apostleship were clearly evident as I was working among you with the greatest of patient endurance. You saw the signs and wonders as well as other displays of God's power that all authenticate my apostleship. 13How can you think I have treated you poorly? In what possible way have you come off worse than the other churches, unless it be that I did not make myself a financial burden on you? Please forgive me for injuring you in this way!

14Look here! I am all ready, for this third time, to pay you a visit, and when I see you my practice of not making myself a burden on you will not change at all. And why? Because it is not your resources I am after, but your well-being in Christ. Remember: You are my children in the Lord, and children are generally under no obligation to store up resources for their parents' well-being; it is parents who have that duty toward their children. 15So then, as your father in Christ, I will most gladly spend all I have and myself be totally spent for your spiritual benefit. If my love for you is so strong, will yours for me be proportionately weak? 16However that be, you admit that I myself was not a financial burden on you. But, some of you say, I showed my natural craftiness by taking you in with the trick of using emissaries to get your money. 17Of the people I have sent to visit you, did any one ever exploit you for my profit? Surely not! 18I urged Titus to visit you, and with him I sent along the brother whom you know. Titus did not exploit you, did he? Was our behavior not governed by the same outlook? Did we not follow exactly the same course of action?

19No doubt you have been thinking all along that I am writing all this as my defense before you, I suppose? No, it is before God and in the name of Christ that I am speaking this way. Let me assure you, too, that everything I am doing is to promote the strengthening of your faith, my dear friends. 20But I have several fears. I am afraid that when I arrive I may perhaps discover you to be not the sort of people I would want you to be, and that, as a result, you may discover me to be the sort of person you would not want me to be. That is, I am fearful that I may find among you evidence of quarreling, envying, anger, rivalry, slandering, gossiping, arrogance, and general unruliness. 21Also, I dread the possibility that after I arrive my God may once again, as he did before, cause me to be humbled in my dealings with you, and I would have reason to mourn over many who have persisted in their former sins and never repented of their impure, immoral, and dissolute behavior.

13I repeat, this is the third time I am coming to visit you. Remember what Scripture says about settling issues: "Every point must be established on the basis of the evidence provided by three, or at a minimum two, witnesses." 2When I was with you on my second visit I gave due forewarning to those who continue in their former sins, and to the rest of you as well, that I will not refrain from punishing you when I return. Now, while I am still absent, I repeat that forewarning — when I return I will not spare you. 3It is you, remember, who are eager to have proof that it is really Christ who is speaking when I speak — Christ, who is not weak in the way he deals with you but makes his great power felt in your midst. 4For, to be sure, he was crucified because of his "weakness" in obeying God and in not retaliating, but now he lives a resurrection life sustained by God's power. Yes indeed, we share in his weakness, but we also share in his resurrection life because of God's power, and that will be evident in the way we deal with you.

5It is your own selves — not me — that you must put to the test — to find out whether you are continuing true to the faith. It is your own selves you must examine. You must know, do you not, this truth about yourselves, that Jesus Christ is within you and in your midst — unless, of course, you have failed to stand the test. 6And I certainly hope that as a result of your own self-scrutiny you will come to know for sure that we too have not failed to pass the test. 7Our prayer to God is that you may be kept from doing anything wrong. That is our prayer — not in order that we should be seen to have passed the test, but so that you may take the right course in the present circumstances, even if that means we may seem to have failed the test in that we do not need to exercise discipline. 8Certainly, all our powers are dedicated to defending the truth of the gospel and true Christian living, not opposing them. 9When your Christian faith is strong and so I am "weak" in not needing to exercise my authority, I am pleased. That is precisely what I am praying for — I mean your restoration to strong faith. 10There is a reason for my writing like this while I am still away from you. It is so that when I am with you I may not have to act drastically and summarily in using the authority that the Lord Jesus entrusted to me for positive, constructive work, not for negative, destructive work.

11Finally, brothers and sisters, rejoice in the Lord. Work together to achieve your restoration, respond to my appeals, be united with one another in your outlook and action, and cultivate peace with everyone. And, to strengthen you for this, God, the source of love and peace, will be with you.

12When you meet, exchange a sacred kiss with one another. All of God's people — here and elsewhere — send you their greetings. 13May the grace that comes from our Lord Jesus Christ, and the love that comes from God our Father, and your common participation in the life and power of the Holy Spirit, be the constant portion of you all!

Index of Subjects

Index of Authors

This index includes only those authors cited in the text or footnotes, not all those listed in the bibliographies and not the authors of individual translations or paraphrases or articles in dictionaries.

Adams, A., 432, 443
Aejmelaeus, L., 34
Ahern, B. M., 145, 207
Alexander, W. M., 171, 854, 859
Alford, H., 58, 104, 171-72, 376, 379, 381, 422
Allen, L. C., 352
Allmen, D. von, 419
Allo, E. B., 17, 25, 37-39, 42, 50, 59, 67, 80, 85, 103, 152, 171, 188, 193, 225-26, 242, 268, 303, 308, 311, 314, 341, 344, 351-55, 372-73, 378-79, 381, 400, 404, 407, 409, 419, 429, 437, 457, 468, 475, 516, 543, 561, 565, 575, 577, 582, 592, 600, 602, 614, 640, 657, 668, 688-90, 702, 714, 718, 733, 736, 761, 768, 770, 787, 802, 811, 821, 834, 836, 854, 858, 886, 907, 910, 924-25, 928, 932, 933
Amador, J. D. H., 43
Amstutz, J., 183, 563, 740
Andrews, S. B., 814
Andriessen, P., 858
Appelbaum, S., 788
Arai, S., 77
Ascough, R. S., 570
Aus, R. D., 98

Bachmann, P., 42, 104, 169, 370, 379, 385, 392, 397, 407, 452, 543
Badenas, R., 299
Bahr, G. J., 42, 666
Baillie, J., 399

Bain, J. A., 372
Baird, W., 836, 846
Baird, W. R., 263, 265
Baker, W. R., 284, 313
Banks, R., 83, 133, 324
Barclay, J. M. G., 67
Barnett, A. E., 2-3
Barnett, P., xiii, 30, 42-43, 47, 49, 80, 86, 139, 153, 226, 418, 448, 456, 459, 479, 484, 490, 501, 513, 534-35, 540, 545, 550, 556, 566, 571, 576, 588, 592, 606, 612, 626, 640-41, 643, 645, 651-52, 654, 657, 661, 671, 673, 700, 702, 712, 714, 728-29, 733, 742, 744-45, 748, 756, 765, 775-77, 788, 798-800, 811, 833, 840, 850, 858, 863, 865-66, 876, 902, 904, 921-22, 929, 940
Barré, M. L., 465, 806, 813, 815, 858
Barrett, C. K., 18, 25, 34, 39, 74-75, 79-80, 84, 86, 94, 103, 129-30, 133, 136, 141-43, 145, 148, 155, 157, 162, 170, 180, 184, 186, 188, 193-94, 203, 205, 208, 215, 217-19, 224-28, 237, 239, 245, 247-49, 257, 263, 267-68, 285, 288-91, 297, 302-3, 307-9, 313-14, 323-24, 329, 336, 339, 342-43, 345-47, 349, 351, 356, 361, 366, 379, 382, 384-85, 396, 399, 407, 412, 419, 421, 426, 431-32, 434-35, 440, 448-49, 453, 457-58, 469, 475, 478, 481, 488-89, 510, 519, 524, 536-37, 539-40, 542-44, 552, 561-63,

970

Index of Greek Words Discussed

INDEX OF GREEK WORDS DISCUSSED

987